LIFE APPLICATION
New Testament Commentary

Life Application® New Testament Commentary

Bruce Barton, D.Min.
Philip Comfort, Ph.D.
Grant Osborne, Ph.D.
Linda K. Taylor
Dave Veerman, M.Div.

Tyndale House Publishers, Inc.
WHEATON, ILLINOIS

Edited by Philip W. Comfort and Dan Lins

Library of Congress Cataloging-in-Publication Data

Life application New Testament commentary / Bruce Barton . . . [et al.].
    p. cm.
  Includes bibliographical references (p.).
  ISBN 0-8423-7066-8 (hardbound)
  1. Bible. N.T.—Commentaries. I. Title: New Testament commentary. II. Barton, Bruce B.
BS2341.2.L54 2001
225.7—dc21   2 001023464

Printed in the United States of America

04   03
6   5   4   3

contents

introduction

This *Life Application New Testament Commentary* is designed as a helpful tool for anyone who desires to study God's word more deeply. Developed by the team that produced the best-selling *Life Application Bible,* this commentary seeks to help the reader not only understand Scripture, but also understand what it means in his or her life.

After developing the *Life Application Bible,* we desired to do a further and deeper exposition of every verse in the New Testament. Because of space limitations in any Bible, however, we decided to develop a series of commentaries on each New Testament book. This comprehensive commentary currently exists in the form of a set of seventeen books. These commentaries are comprehensive verse-by-verse studies of the entire New Testament. Each verse entry explains the text, ties the text to the overall themes of the Bible, and applies the verse to daily life through application notes written especially for the commentary. Charts, book introductions, and section introductions round out this readable series of commentaries.

We believe that many people would now benefit if that material were at their fingertips in one helpful volume. This is what you hold in your hands—a condensed version of the seventeen-volume Life Application Commentary series, giving you pertinent information on every verse in the New Testament. This volume also includes a harmony of the Gospels feature (page 1275). Through its unique and simple numbering system, you can read any Gospel account and view it in relation to the entire life of Christ. These numbers are in italics and are found at the end of the chapter subheadings.

So how is this commentary different from other New Testament commentaries? First, you will quickly discover its readability. It is written with you in mind.

- the reader who wants to understand God's word more deeply
- the teacher who wants that extra bit of application to help students take God's word with them during the rest of the week
- the small group leader who desires to have pertinent and interesting information to share with the group in the study
- the pastor who knows the vital importance of application in his or her sermons

Second, you will find that each entry is clear, easy to follow, and gives information that you can use. You will find material that you can remember and share with others, and you will learn information that reveals the dynamic power of God's word in people's lives today. Does God's word apply to you—your students, your small group members, your congregation—today? Of course! And this commentary helps guide you to see that application.

Why is application so important? God urges us to apply his word. Isaiah wrote, "Will not even one of you apply these lessons from the past?" (Isaiah 42:23), and Paul wrote, "We are confident in the Lord that you are practicing the things we commanded you, and that you always will" (2 Thessalonians 3:4). Applying God's word is a vital part of our relationship with Him; it is the evidence that we are obeying him.

Application is *not* just accumulating knowledge. Many other commentaries will do a good job giving facts and figures—*knowledge*. However, history is filled with people who knew lots of facts and figures from the Bible but did not know Jesus Christ personally. Those facts and figures did not change their lives. In addition, application is *not* just trying to make the passage relevant. Making the Bible relevant only helps us to see that the same lessons that were true in Bible times are true today; it does not show us how to implement God's word in the problems and pressures we face everyday.

Application begins by knowing the facts—understanding the timeless truths of God's word—and understanding the Bible's relevance. But application is more than that. Application focuses on the truth of God's word, shows us what to do about what is being read, and motivates us to respond to what God is teaching. Application is putting into practice what we learn. Application is deeply personal—unique for each individual. It makes a relevant truth a personal truth. Application involves developing a strategy and action plan to live our lives in harmony with the Bible. It is the biblical "how to" of life.

So enjoy your Bible. Enjoy the journey of discovering God's plan of salvation. Enjoy this *Life Application New Testament Commentary.* Use it to help you learn more; allow it to challenge you to change your life.

We especially want to thank Dr. Grant Osborne, Professor of New Testament at Trinity Evangelical Divinity School, for serving as General Editor of the commentary series. We also want to thank Dr. Philip Comfort who brought his Bible knowledge and expertise to this project. Special thanks also goes also to: David Veerman, Neil Wilson, Greg Asimakouopoulos, Dr. Mark Fackler, Jonathan Farrar, Christopher Hudson, Kent Keller, Dr. J. Richard Love, and Len Woods for their invaluable contributions to this project.

Dr. Bruce Barton
Linda K. Taylor

LIFE APPLICATION
New Testament Commentary

Jesus' earthly story begins in the town of Bethlehem in the Roman province of Judea (2:1). A threat to kill the infant king led Joseph to take his family to Egypt (2:14). When they returned God led them to settle in Nazareth in Galilee (2:22-23). At about age thirty, Jesus was baptized in the Jordan River and was tempted by Satan in the Judean wilderness (3:13; 4:1). Jesus set up his base of operations in Capernaum (4:12-13) and from there ministered throughout Israel, telling parables, teaching about the Kingdom, and healing the sick. He traveled to the region of the Gadarenes and healed two demon-possessed men (8:28ff); fed over five thousand people with five loaves and two fish on the shores of Galilee near Bethsaida (14:15ff); healed the sick in Gennesaret (14:34ff); ministered to the Gentiles in Tyre and Sidon (15:21ff); visited Caesarea Philippi, where Peter declared him as the Messiah (16:13ff); and taught in Perea, across the Jordan (19:1). As he set out on his last visit to Jerusalem, he told the disciples what would happen to him there (20:17ff). He spent some time in Jericho (20:29) and then stayed in Bethany at night as he went back and forth into Jerusalem during his last week (21:17ff). In Jerusalem he was crucified, but he rose again.

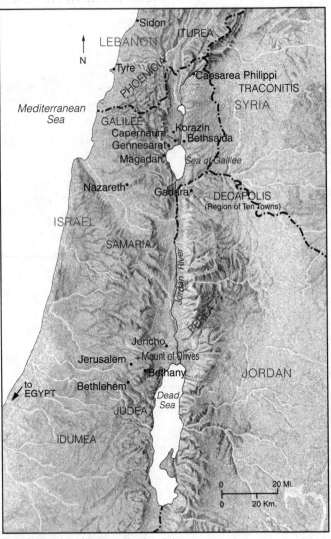

The broken lines (— · —·) indicate modern boundaries.

MATTHEW

INTRODUCTION

Predictions, projections, and best guesses—everyone likes to state what they think the future will hold. Meteorologists forecast the daily weather, sports journalists predict the outcome of a championship series, pollsters project the probable winner of an election, news commentators declare the direction of the nation, and futurists explain what the world will be like a few decades hence. In addition, our daily conversations are sprinkled with future talk: "Who do you think will win?" "What are your retirement plans?" "What will your son do after graduation?"

Often these amateur prophecies are not fulfilled exactly as stated: Partly sunny turns into a downpour, the underdog becomes an upset victor, a technological breakthrough changes the way we live, and an unexpected event alters our plans.

With biblical prophets, the story reads quite differently. Inspired by God, each of their predictions would come true, in exact detail.

The Gospel of Matthew provides amazing examples of the power and accuracy of God's prophets who had foretold the coming of the Messiah. From his humble birth by a virgin (see Isaiah 7:14) in Bethlehem (see Micah 5:2), to his crucifixion (see Psalm 22:14, 16-17) with criminals (see Isaiah 53:12), to his resurrection from the dead (see Psalm 16:10), Jesus did what the prophets had predicted—he fulfilled every prophecy and fit every description of the Jewish Savior.

As you read this Gospel, follow the dramatic story, predicted in detail centuries before, of Jesus, the Messiah, King of kings and Lord of lords . . . and *your* Savior too.

AUTHOR

Matthew (Levi): former tax collector and one of the original twelve disciples

Although the text of this Gospel names no author, the early church nearly unanimously ascribed authorship to Matthew the apostle. A hint of Matthew's authorship comes from the references to taxes. For example, 17:24-27 describes the incident when the Temple tax collectors asked Peter whether Jesus paid taxes. This incident is found only in Matthew, and it is the kind of story that a former tax collector would include.

The content of this Gospel certainly points to a Jewish author, thereby pointing to Matthew as a leading candidate. The following evidence indicates that this book was written by a Jew primarily to a Jewish audience.

The vocabulary and style of writing. The term "Kingdom of Heaven," a distinctly Jewish description, appears in no other Gospel. The phrase "Son of Man" refers to the prophecy in Daniel 7:13 and would have been understood and appreciated by Jewish readers. In addition, Jerusalem is called the "holy city" (27:53) and the "city of the great King" (5:35), and the Jewish people are called "God's lost sheep" (10:6; 15:24).

The highlighted topics. This book has much to say about the law, religious defilement, keeping the Sabbath, the Kingdom, Jerusalem, the Temple, David, the Messiah, fulfillment of Old Testament prophecies, and Moses. All of these would be pertinent topics for Jewish readers.

The genealogy. Jesus' ancestry is traced from a Jewish perspective, from Abraham (the father of the Jewish nation), through David (the greatest king of Israel), to Jesus.

Old Testament references. This Gospel is saturated with citations from the Old Testament Scriptures. Fifty-three of these references are quotations and seventy-six are allusions. Usually these references are used to prove a point, especially regarding Jesus as the Messiah who fulfills Old Testament prophecies.

Jewish customs. The book refers to a number of Jewish customs and leaves them unexplained—for example, the reference to ceremonial cleansing (15:2). The author knew that Jewish readers would understand these customs and need no explanations.

Emphasis on Peter. This Gospel tells much about Peter's calling, his interaction with Jesus, and his denial. Peter was known as the apostle to the Jews because that is where he concentrated his ministry.

Matthew makes few appearances in Scripture. We first meet him when Jesus calls him to be an apostle: "As Jesus was going down the road, he saw Matthew sitting at his tax-collection booth. 'Come, be my disciple,' Jesus said to him. So Matthew got up and followed him" (9:9). In the parallel accounts in Mark 2:14-17 and Luke 5:27-32, Matthew is called Levi.

As a "tax collector," Matthew worked for the hated Roman government, having paid Rome for the right to collect taxes from his own people; thus, he would have been seen as a collaborator with the enemy. In addition, to make their living tax collectors were allowed to add their commission to the taxes. Many were quite wealthy, having increased their personal worth at the expense of their countrymen. Thus, tax collectors were viewed as dishonest swindlers. Zacchaeus, another tax collector, came to Christ through a dramatic confrontation (Luke 19:1-9). Scholars surmise that Matthew may have collected tolls and customs from those crossing the Sea of Galilee at Capernaum. When Jesus called him, Matthew immediately left this lucrative tax-collection career and followed the Lord.

Soon after this dramatic calling, Matthew hosted a dinner for Jesus and the other disciples. The dinner guests also included "tax collectors and many other notorious sinners" (9:10). Evidently, Matthew wanted to introduce Jesus to his friends and associates. This disturbed the Pharisees and teachers of religious law (the religious establishment), who wondered why Jesus would associate with such undesirables. Jesus answered that he had come "to call sinners, not those who think they are already good enough" (9:13).

Matthew is next mentioned in the list of the twelve disciples, where he is called "Matthew (the tax collector)" (10:3; see also Mark 3:18 and Luke 6:15). The only other reference to Matthew is in another list of the disciples in Acts 1:13. After Jesus' ascension into heaven, the disciples gathered regularly with others for prayer. At one of these gatherings, they chose a man to take the place of Judas among the Twelve. After this incident, the Bible records nothing more about Matthew, and nothing is known for sure about him. Tradition holds that he preached the gospel for eight years throughout Judea and then traveled to Persia, Parthia, and Ethiopia, where he died as a martyr in about A.D. 62.

DATE AND SETTING
Probably written from Antioch (in Syria) in about A.D. 60

Jerusalem was totally destroyed in A.D. 70 by the Romans. That there is no mention in Matthew of this terrible event having already occurred (24:1-22 is a prediction by Jesus of this event) indicates that the Gospel must have been written before that time. However, it could not have been written much earlier if, as many scholars believe, Mark was the first Gospel to be written and Matthew and Luke relied on his writings and compared their records to his (see Luke 1:1-4). In this case, Mark would have written his account in approximately A.D. 55–60, with Matthew and Luke following soon thereafter in approximately A.D. 60.

The place of writing is also unknown. The Jewish orientation of this Gospel suggests that it was written in Palestine. However, many surmise that Matthew wrote from Antioch. For example, Ignatius chose Antioch, a Gentile city, over Palestine because Matthew wrote in Greek instead of Hebrew. Furthermore, many of the original disciples had migrated to Antioch (Acts 11:19-27), and the great concern in the book for Gentiles tends to confirm this as the city.

It is difficult to determine if the Gospel was originally written in Greek, or written in Aramaic and then translated into Greek. Some scholars point out that because the book contains several untranslated Aramaic terms, it is unlikely that it was originally written in Aramaic (otherwise those terms would have been translated or explained).

AUDIENCE
Greek-speaking Jews who believed in Jesus as Messiah

Matthew mentions no specific audience. It seems clear, however, that his primary audience was Jewish because, as stated above, the book has a distinctly Jewish flavor. Note especially the scores of references to words, statements, and stories in the Old Testament. Throughout the Gospel, Matthew carefully pointed to Old Testament prophecies that had found fulfillment in statements, circumstances, and actions surrounding Jesus.

It seems, however, that the Jews to whom this book was written were expected to understand Greek because Matthew may have written originally in Greek, the common language of commerce, and not in Hebrew or Aramaic. Matthew did not take time to explain Jewish customs (for example, ceremonial cleansing and Passover), for these would have been understood by a Jewish audience. But he did stop to interpret words like "Immanuel" (1:23), "Golgotha" (27:33), and Christ's prayer on the cross, which was in Aramaic (27:46). This also indicates that the primary language of these readers probably was Greek.

OCCASION AND PURPOSE
To prove that Jesus is the Messiah, the eternal King

Neither Matthew nor the other Gospels gives any indication of a special occasion or specific incident that motivated Matthew to write. Early church fathers, Irenaeus (fl. c. 175–195) and Origen (c. 185–251), said that Matthew had been written for converts from Judaism, Jews who had embraced Jesus as their Messiah. Actually, until the dramatic conversion of Cornelius through Peter (Acts 10) and the missionary journeys of Paul (Acts 13–28), nearly all of the converts to Christianity were Jews. These new believers needed confirmation that Jesus had indeed met the messianic requirements and had fulfilled the ancient prophecies. Matthew's Gospel gave that confirmation.

In addition to encouragement and assurance of Jesus' true identity, Matthew's account helped believers to refute unbelieving Jews who would argue against them and persecute them. Matthew showed how Christ's death and resurrection fulfilled the promises made to Abraham and David.

While Luke and John clearly gave their purpose for writing (see Luke 1:4 and John 20:31), Matthew has no such purpose statement. But the very first verse provides a strong hint of the focus of the content of this book: "This is a record of the ancestors of Jesus the Messiah, a descendant of King David and of Abraham." Jesus is immediately identified with the royal line of David and with Abraham, the father of all Jews. Matthew's Jewish readers would have immediately caught the significance of these references to their great and revered ancestors.

Matthew's style and method indicate his aim. Throughout his Gospel, he presents the various incidents in the life of Jesus as fulfillments of messianic prophecies, providing a cumulative demonstration that Jesus was the Messiah foretold in the Old Testament. Matthew, the Hebrew tax collector, knew how Jews thought and felt; he wrote for the Hebrew mind.

Matthew also wrote to explain Jesus' Kingdom program. The first-century believers who had left all to follow Christ must have wondered what would become of them and what would happen in the future. So Matthew explained how and why Jesus was rejected by Israel and God's program following that rejection.

MESSAGE
Matthew begins his account by giving Jesus' genealogy. He then tells of Jesus' birth and early years, including the family's escape to Egypt from the murderous Herod and their return to Nazareth. Following Jesus' baptism by John (3:16-17) and his defeat of Satan in the wilderness, Jesus begins his public ministry by calling his first disciples and giving the Sermon on the Mount (chapters 5–7). Matthew shows Christ's authority by reporting his miracles of healing the sick and the demon-possessed, and even raising the dead.

Despite opposition from the Pharisees and others in the religious establishment (chapters 12–15), Jesus continued to teach concerning the Kingdom of Heaven (chapters 16–20). During this time, Jesus spoke with his disciples about his imminent death and resurrection (16:21) and revealed his true identity to Peter, James, and John (17:1-5). Near the end of his ministry, Jesus entered Jerusalem in a triumphant procession (21:1-11). But soon opposition mounted, and

Jesus knew that his death was near. So he taught his disciples about the future—what they could expect before his return (chapter 24) and how to live until then (chapter 25).

In Matthew's finale (chapters 26–28), he focuses on Jesus' final days on earth—the Last Supper, his prayer in Gethsemane, the betrayal by Judas, the flight of the disciples, Peter's denial, the trials before Caiaphas and Pilate, Jesus' final words on the cross, and his burial in a borrowed tomb. But the story does not end there, for the Messiah rose from the dead—conquering death and then telling his followers to continue his work by making disciples in all nations.

The main themes in the Gospel of Matthew include: *Jesus Christ the King, The Messiah, Kingdom of God, Jesus' Teachings,* and *Resurrection.*

Jesus Christ the King (1:1–2:12; 8:1–10:42; 11:20–12:13; 14:13-36; 15:21-28, 32-39; 17:1-13; 21:12-17, 23-27; 27:37; 28:16-20). Jesus is revealed as the King of kings: He was conceived by the Holy Spirit and born of a virgin (1:18-25); as a baby, he received gifts and worship from the kings of the east (2:1-12); he was endorsed and affirmed by God the Father (3:16-17); he defeated Satan (4:1-11); he taught with authority (7:28-29); he demonstrated his power over sickness (8:1-13), death (9:23-26), nature (8:23-27), and demons (8:28-34); he triumphed over death (28:1-10). These dramatic and profound incidents show Jesus' true identity.

IMPORTANCE FOR TODAY. Jesus cannot be equated with any person or power. He is, above all, the supreme ruler of time and eternity, heaven and earth, humans and angels. He lives today, sitting at the right hand of the Father, and he will return as the Judge of all the earth (25:31-46). Too often we live as though Jesus were merely an impressive historical figure, or we treat him as just a traveling companion on our journey through life. Instead, we should give him his rightful place as king of our lives, our sovereign ruler to whom we give our total devotion and obedience.

Who sits on the throne of your life? Submit to your Lord and King.

The Messiah (2:14-15, 21-23; 3:1–4:11; 4:13-16; 12:15-21; 13:13-15; 16:1-4, 13-20; 20:29–21:11; 22:41-46; 24:1-35; 26:1; 27:66). Jesus fulfilled the inspired predictions of the prophets concerning the Messiah, the one for whom the Jews had been waiting for centuries. Yet tragically, they didn't recognize their Messiah when he came because they were expecting a conquering king, one who would deliver them from Roman oppression. If they had read deeper, they would have realized that the "Son of Man" must first suffer and die (17:22-23) as the "suffering Servant" (Isaiah 53) before returning in power and glory. They would have realized that the true purpose of God's anointed deliverer was to free people from sin's oppression, not merely to defeat the Romans and rule an earthly empire.

IMPORTANCE FOR TODAY. Because Jesus fulfilled the prophecies recorded in the Old Testament, we can see that the Bible is true and reliable. Because Jesus was sent by God, we can know that we can trust him with our lives. It is worth everything we have to acknowledge Jesus as Lord and give ourselves to him because he came to be our Messiah and our Savior. Jesus knows us totally and loves us perfectly. He became one of us to bring us to God. Now that's Good News!

Do you understand and feel Christ's love? He wants only the best for you. Trust him.

Kingdom of God (4:17, 23-25; 5:17-20; 9:35; 11:1-19; 12:22-37; 13:10-52; 16:24-27; 18:1-6; 19:13–20:16; 20:20-28; 21:28–22:14; 24:36–25:46). Jesus came to earth, as God in the flesh, the Messiah, to begin his Kingdom. This Kingdom, however, is not earthly, determined by geography, military might, political power, or financial influence. God's Kingdom is a kingdom of the heart, and his subjects include all who submit to him and acknowledge Christ as their sovereign Lord. Eventually, God's full Kingdom will be realized at Christ's return when he comes to annihilate the forces of evil and gather his loyal subjects to himself.

IMPORTANCE FOR TODAY. Because Christ's Kingdom is first a kingdom of the heart, we enter the Kingdom through heartfelt faith in Christ as God's Son and our Savior, trusting in him alone to save us from sin and to change our life. Once we belong to him, we must do the work of his Kingdom, living for him and spreading the Good News about Christ to others. And we must always be prepared for his return.

If Jesus were to return today, would you be ready? Live with the expectation that Christ might return at any moment.

Jesus' Teachings (5:1-9; 12:38-58; 15:1-20, 29-31; 16:5-12; 17:14-21, 24-27; 18:7-12; 21:18-22; 22:15-22, 34-40; 23:1-39; 28:20). Jesus was a master teacher, teaching with authority and reaching people at their point of need. Jesus taught the people through sermons, illustrations, parables, and personal example. Through these teachings, he revealed the true ingredients of faith, how to be fruitful, and how to guard against hypocrisy. Those who were listening and were open and ready understood Jesus and gladly received and responded to the truth.

IMPORTANCE FOR TODAY. We can know what God is like by looking at Jesus (see John 14:6-10). And we can know how God wants us to live by listening carefully to what Jesus taught. His teachings show us how to live for him right now and how to prepare for life in his eternal Kingdom. Jesus lived what he taught, providing the perfect example for us to follow.

Take a close look at Jesus and check out his teachings: "Anyone who is willing to hear should listen and understand!" (11:15).

Resurrection (16:21-23; 17:22-23; 20:17-19; 22:23-33; 28:1-15). When Jesus rose from the dead, conquering sin and death, he rose in power as the true King. With this incredible victory, the most important event in history, Jesus proved that he truly was the Son of God and that what he lived and taught was true. He also established his credentials as King with power and authority over evil. Jesus does not lie in a grave in Palestine. He is alive!

IMPORTANCE FOR TODAY. Christ's resurrection shows that not even death could stop God's plan of offering eternal life. Jesus is true and alive; we serve a risen Savior! The Resurrection also gives hope to all who believe in Jesus; we know that we will live with him and that one day we will experience a resurrection like his. No matter how bleak the outlook or difficult and painful our situation, we can hope in him. In the meantime, our role is to tell his story to all the earth so that everyone may share in his victory. This world is dying and passing away, but Jesus is alive and people can live forever.

What can you do to remember the Resurrection? To whom can you tell this glorious news?

OUTLINE OF MATTHEW

I. Birth and Preparation of Jesus, the King (1:1–4:11)
II. Message and Ministry of Jesus, the King (4:12–25:46)
    A. Jesus begins his ministry
    B. Jesus gives the Sermon on the Mount
    C. Jesus performs many miracles
    D. Jesus teaches about the Kingdom
    E. Jesus encounters differing reactions to his ministry
    F. Jesus faces conflict with the religious leaders
    G. Jesus teaches on the Mount of Olives
III. Death and Resurrection of Jesus, the King (26:1–28:20)

MATTHEW 1

THE RECORD OF JESUS' ANCESTORS / 1:1-17 / 3

More than 400 years had passed since the last Old Testament prophecies, and faithful Jews all over the world were still waiting for the Messiah (Luke 3:15). Under the inspiration of the Holy Spirit, Matthew wrote this book to Jews to present Jesus as King and Messiah, the promised descendant of David who would reign forever (Isaiah 11:1-5). The Gospel of Matthew links the Old and New Testaments, containing many references to show how Jesus fulfilled Old Testament prophecies. Jesus was a Jew, lived among the Jews, and followed their laws (insofar as they were truly God's laws), and he fulfilled the Old Testament Scriptures as he did so.

1:1 A record of the ancestors of Jesus the Messiah. The first seventeen verses of Matthew's Gospel present Jesus' ancestry. Because a person's family line proved his or her standing as one of God's chosen people, Matthew began by showing that Jesus was **a descendant of King David and of Abraham,** fulfilling Old Testament prophecies about the Messiah's line ("father of" can also mean "ancestor of"). Matthew traced the genealogy back to Abraham, through Joseph. Matthew's genealogy gives Jesus' legal (or royal) lineage through Joseph, a descendant of King David (see also 2 Samuel 7:16; Isaiah 9:6-7; Revelation 22:16).

1:2 Abraham was the father of Isaac. The phrase *was the father of* can also mean "was the ancestor of." Thus, there need not be a direct father-son relationship between all those listed in a genealogy. In ancient times, genealogies were often arranged to aid memorizing. Thus Matthew recorded his genealogy in three sets of fourteen generations (see 1:17). *Abraham* was called by God, received God's covenant promises, and

believed that God would keep his promises (Genesis 15:6). His story is told in Genesis 11–25. Abraham *was the father of Isaac.* Abraham and Sarah wondered if God would ever send them the promised son, but God always keeps his promises. See Genesis 21–22.

Isaac was the father of Jacob. These three men—Abraham, Isaac, and Jacob—are often named together as the "patriarchs," fathers of the nation and receivers of God's covenant (see Genesis 50:24; Exodus 3:16; 33:1; Numbers 32:11; Luke 13:28; Acts 3:13; 7:32).

Jacob was the father of Judah and his brothers. Jacob had twelve sons by his wives Rachel and Leah, who became the twelve tribes of Israel (see Genesis 49:1-28). Matthew, desiring to trace Jesus' royal lineage, made special note of *Judah* because the royal line was to continue through him (Genesis 49:10).

1:3 Perez and Zerah (their mother was Tamar). An interesting sidelight appears in this verse. One might expect a genealogy to avoid mention of less reputable ancestors, but Judah's sons were born by Tamar, who had prostituted herself to her father-in-law. The story of Judah and Tamar is told in Genesis 38. While Judah was the father of Perez and Zerah, he was not married to their mother *Tamar*. Perez and Zerah were twins (see also 1 Chronicles 2:4). The line tracing Perez to King David is also recorded in Ruth 4:12, 18-22.

Hezron . . . Ram. Not much is known about *Hezron* and *Ram*. Hezron is mentioned in Genesis 46:12 and 1 Chronicles 2:5. Ram (or Aram) is mentioned in 1 Chronicles 2:9.

1:4 Amminadab and **Nahshon** are mentioned in Exodus 6:23–Amminadab's daughter and Nahshon's sister, Elisheba, married Aaron who became Israel's high priest. See also Numbers 1:7; 2:3; 7:12-17. **Salmon** is mentioned again only in the genealogy in Ruth 4:18-21. These men are also listed in 1 Chronicles 2:10-11.

1:5 Boaz (his mother was Rahab) . . . Obed (his mother was Ruth) . . . Jesse. *Rahab* is the woman of Jericho who hid Israel's spies and eventually was saved by them when the Israelites destroyed Jericho. Rahab was a prostitute (Joshua 2:1) who came to believe in Israel's God. Rahab is included in the Hall of Faith in Hebrews 11. There is a chronological problem in making Rahab the actual mother of Boaz, however. As with the phrase "father of," those listed as mothers in a genealogy may be ancestors rather than actual mothers.

The book of Ruth tells the story of *Boaz* and a young woman named *Ruth*, who had come to Israel from the nearby nation of Moab. Boaz married Ruth, and they became the parents of *Obed* (Ruth 4:13-17). Obed later became the father of *Jesse* (Ruth 4:21-22). See also 1 Chronicles 2:12.

1:6 Jesse had several sons, one of whom had been anointed by the prophet Samuel to be the next king of Israel after King Saul (see 1 Samuel 16:5-13). The story of **King David** is told in 1 and 2 Samuel, with the transfer of his throne to his son Solomon recorded in 1 Kings 1.

Solomon (his mother was Bathsheba, the widow of Uriah). The story, recorded in 2 Samuel 11, describes how *Solomon* was born to David and *Bathsheba*, and how David had *Uriah* murdered. God was very displeased with David's evil actions, and the first child born to David and Bathsheba died (2 Samuel 11:27–12:23). The next child born was Solomon, who later ruled Israel during a reign that would later be described as the golden age of the nation. His God-given wisdom became known worldwide, and he wrote many of the proverbs in the book of Proverbs, as well as Ecclesiastes and Song of Songs. His story is told in 1 Kings 1–11 and 2 Chronicles 1–10.

1:7 Solomon's evil son **Rehoboam** split the kingdom because of a prideful and ill-advised decision (see 1 Kings 12:1-24). Two kingdoms emerged: the southern kingdom, called Judah, was ruled by Rehoboam; the northern kingdom, called Israel, was ruled by Jeroboam. Rehoboam's son, **Abijah** (also called Abijam), was also an evil king (1 Kings 15:3-4). **Asaph** is also called Asa, who was a godly king (1 Kings 15:11).

1:8 Good King Asaph (Asa) was the father of another good king, **Jehoshaphat** (1 Kings 22:43). However, Jehoshaphat's son **Jehoram** (also called Joram) was evil (2 Kings 8:18). Jehoram's son **Uzziah** (also called Azariah) provides an example of how this phrase did not always mean actual "father of." According to the same genealogy in 1 Chronicles 3:10-14, Matthew omitted three names between Jehoram and Uzziah: these three kings were Ahaziah, Joash, and Amaziah. Probably Matthew did not include these names in order to keep his pattern of three sets of fourteen generations in this genealogy.

1:9 Jotham walked steadfastly before the Lord (2 Chronicles 27:6), but his good influence did not extend to his son, for **Ahaz** was evil, to the point of sacrificing his son in the fire (2 Kings 16:3-4). Following the exceedingly evil reign of Ahaz came the prosperous reign of the good king **Hezekiah** (2 Kings 18:5).

1:10 Manasseh. Hezekiah obeyed God, but his son, *Manasseh*, was the most evil king who reigned over the southern kingdom (2 Chronicles 33:9). At the end of his life, however, Manasseh repented of his horrible sins (2 Chronicles 33:13). Unfortunately, Manasseh's son **Amos** (also called Amon) assumed too much of his father's character. Amos did evil, worshiping and offering sacrifices to idols (2 Chronicles 33:22-23). Once again, God had mercy on the nation and Amos's son, **Josiah,** attempted to undo all his father's evil deeds (2 Kings 23:25).

1:11 Jehoiachin and his brothers (born at the time of the exile to Babylon). Matthew omitted another name from the lineage. Josiah was actually the father of Jehoiakim who was deported to Babylon when he rebelled against Nebuchadnezzar. After Jehoiakim was taken away, his son *Jehoiachin* (also called Jeconiah) reigned in Jerusalem. Jehoiachin reigned for only three months before Nebuchadnezzar laid siege to Jerusalem, causing the city to surrender. The phrase *and his brothers* refers to Jehoiachin's brother Zedekiah whom Nebuchadnezzar placed on the throne of Jerusalem as a puppet ruler. Zedekiah made the grave mistake of also rebelling against Nebuchadnezzar, and this brought down the final wrath of Babylon. Nebuchadnezzar conquered Judah completely, destroying Jerusalem, including its beautiful Temple. The entire nation of Judah was taken into *exile to Babylon* (2 Kings 24:16–25:21). This occurred in 586 B.C.

1:12 After the Babylonian exile: Jehoiachin was the father of Shealtiel. In this final grouping, *Jehoiachin* is listed as *the father of Shealtiel,* agreeing with 1 Chronicles 3:17. In saying that **Shealtiel was the father of Zerubbabel,** Matthew departed from the genealogy in 1 Chronicles 3:19 which lists Pedaiah as Zerubbabel's father. However, Matthew agrees with several other scriptures that list Shealtiel as Zerubbabel's father (Ezra 3:2; 5:2; Nehemiah 12:1; Haggai 1:1; 2:2, 23. *Zerubbabel* figured prominently in Judah's history *after the exile.* When the people of Judah were finally allowed to return to their nation, Zerubbabel became their governor (Haggai 1:1) and began work on God's Temple (Ezra 5:2). God greatly blessed his servant Zerubbabel, reaffirming and guaranteeing his promise of a Messiah through David's line (Haggai 2:23).

1:13-15 Abiud . . . Eliakim . . . Azor . . . Zadok . . . Akim . . . Eliud . . . Eleazar . . . Matthan . . . Jacob. Nothing is known from Scripture about any of these men. In the Messiah's line ordinary people were included, who had never been listed in any genealogies and had never had their stories told throughout the generations.

1:16 The royal line continued through **Joseph** who, though he was not Jesus' father, was **the husband of Mary. Mary was the mother of Jesus, who is called the Messiah.** Matthew had completed his goal in listing this genealogy—showing, beyond any doubt, that Jesus was a descendant of David, thus fulfilling God's promises.

1:17 Fourteen generations from Abraham to King David, and fourteen from David's time to the Babylonian exile, and fourteen from the Babylonian exile to the Messiah. The Gospel breaks Israel's history into three sets of fourteen generations, but there were probably more generations than those listed here. Genealogies often compressed history, meaning that not every generation of ancestors was specifically listed.

A problem also seems to arise in comparing Matthew's genealogy with Luke's (recorded in Luke 3:23-37). Matthew's differences can be explained by his omitting names in order to achieve his symmetry of three sets of fourteen generations. Also, most likely Luke was tracing Jesus' natural human ancestry through Joseph, while Matthew was focusing on the legal and royal names to emphasize the succession of the throne of David and Jesus' arrival as the promised King. Matthew stressed Israelite history. Luke's longer genealogy traces Jesus' ancestry through David's son Nathan, not through Solomon, as Matthew did. Matthew also includes the names of four women, which Luke does not.

AN ANGEL APPEARS TO JOSEPH / 1:18-25 / 8
In this section, Matthew relates the story behind Jesus' birth. Although God's actions were beyond their comprehension, and although they may have faced misunderstanding and questioning looks from those around them, Mary and Joseph willingly followed God's · guidance. How willing are we to do what God wants, no matter what? Can we follow God's guidance without question?

1:18 Now this is how Jesus the Messiah was born. In 1:16, Matthew had stated that Mary was Jesus' mother, but he did not name Joseph as his father. This needed some explanation, for, taken at face value, it sounded immoral. Jesus' **mother, Mary, was engaged to be married to Joseph.** Modern readers need to understand the traditions involved in ancient Jewish marriages. First, the two families would agree to the union and negotiate the betrothal. Next, a public announcement would be made and the couple was "pledged." Though the couple was not officially married, their rela-

tionship could be broken only through death or divorce. Sexual relations were not yet permitted. This second step lasted for a year. During that time, the couple would live separately, with their parents. This waiting period would demonstrate the bride's purity. If she were found to be pregnant during that time, the marriage could be annulled.

Because Mary and Joseph were pledged to be married, they had not yet had sexual relations, **but while she was still a virgin, she became pregnant by the Holy Spirit.** Mary was pledged and pregnant, and Joseph knew that the child was not his own. Mary's apparent unfaithfulness carried a severe social stigma. According to Jewish civil law, Joseph had the right to divorce her. The law also explained that the penalty for unchastity was death by stoning (Deuteronomy 22:23-24), although this was rarely carried out at this time. Removing any doubt of Mary's purity, Matthew explained that Mary was pregnant **by the Holy Spirit.** During Old Testament times, the Spirit acted on God's initiative (for example, Genesis 1:2). Thus, the divine initiative in Jesus' conception was made clear. Luke 1:26-38 records this part of the story.

1:19 Joseph, her fiancé, being a just man, decided to break the engagement quietly, so as not to disgrace her publicly. Being a **just man,** Joseph did not want to go against God's laws. To marry Mary would have been an admission of guilt when he was not guilty. To have a public divorce would have disgraced Mary, and apparently Joseph's compassion would not allow him to do that. Therefore, he chose the option, also lawful, to have a private divorce before two witnesses (Numbers 5:11-31) and **break the engagement quietly.**

1:20 An angel of the Lord appeared to him in a dream. "Joseph, son of David," the angel said, **"do not be afraid to go ahead with your marriage to Mary. For the child within her has been conceived by the Holy Spirit."** As Joseph began to move forward on his decided course of action, God intervened. The conception of Jesus Christ was a supernatural event, so God sent angels to help certain people understand the significance of what was happening (see 2:13, 19; Luke 1:11, 26; 2:9). In this case, an angel **appeared to [Joseph] in a dream.** Dreams function in the Bible as a means to convey God's message to people.

Angels are spiritual beings, created by God, who help carry out his work on earth. They bring God's messages to people (Luke 1:26), protect God's people (Daniel 6:22), offer encouragement (Genesis 16:7), give guidance (Exodus 14:19), carry out punishment (2 Samuel 24:16), patrol the earth (Zechariah 1:9-14), and fight the forces of evil (2 Kings 6:16-18; Revelation 20:1-2). The angel who appeared to Joseph was one of God's messengers, sent to set Joseph straight in his dealings with Mary.

The angel called Joseph **son of David,** signifying that Joseph had a special role in a special event. The angel explained that Joseph was to take Mary as his wife, for the child was to be in the royal line of David. Joseph was not to **be afraid** to take Mary as his wife—no matter what the social repercussions might be. Mary had committed no sin. God himself had caused this

pregnancy, and the child would be very special—God's Son.

1:21 "And she will have a son, and you are to name him Jesus, for he will save his people from their sins." *Jesus* is the Greek form of "Joshua." The name means "the Lord saves." The baby Jesus would be born to **save his people from their sins.** From the very start, the book explains to its Jewish audience that Jesus would not save the people from Rome or from tyranny, nor would he set up an earthly kingdom. Instead, Jesus would save people from sin.

1:22-23 All of this happened to fulfill the Lord's message through his prophet. Throughout his Gospel, Matthew quoted or alluded to Old Testament Scripture to show how Jesus fulfilled it. Jesus was to be called **Immanuel (meaning, God is with us)** as predicted in Isaiah 7:14. Jesus was God in the flesh; thus God was literally "with us." The point was not that Jesus would ever bear the name "Immanuel," but rather this name described Jesus' role—to bring God's presence to people. Jesus Christ, who was himself God (John 1:1), brought God to earth in his human body—living, eating, teaching, healing, dying.

1:24 When Joseph woke up, he did what the angel of the Lord commanded. Although he knew that taking Mary as his wife might be humiliating, Joseph chose to obey the angel's command to marry her. He did not hesitate. The decision was no longer difficult, for he simply did what he knew God wanted him to do.

Apparently, Joseph broke with tradition and **brought Mary home to be his wife,** even though the customary one-year waiting period had not passed. However, Joseph did as God commanded and "completed" their marriage by taking Mary to live with him. No matter what the social stigma, no matter what the local gossips thought about this move, Joseph knew he was following God's command in marrying and caring for Mary during her pregnancy.

1:25 But she remained a virgin until her son was born. To end any doubts about the conception and birth of Jesus while Mary was still a virgin, Matthew explained that Mary remained a virgin **until her son was born.** These words also set aside the notion that Mary lived her whole life as a virgin; after Jesus' birth, Joseph and Mary consummated their marriage and Jesus had several half brothers (12:46). Two of Jesus' half brothers figured in the early church—James, leader of the church in Jerusalem, and Jude, writer of the book that bears his name.

Traditionally, baby boys were circumcised and named eight days after birth. Luke records that "eight days later, when the baby was circumcised, he was named Jesus" (Luke 2:21). Joseph did everything that God had told him through the angel (1:21), naming the baby his God-given name: **Jesus.**

MATTHEW 2

VISITORS ARRIVE FROM EASTERN LANDS / 2:1-12 / 12

Matthew did not record the details of Jesus' birth, as did Luke in the well-known chapter 2 of his Gospel. Only Matthew, however, records the visit of the wise men. These men traveled thousands of miles to see the king of the Jews. When they finally found him, they responded with joy, worship, and gifts. This is so different from the approach people often take today. Some expect God to come looking for us, to explain himself, prove who he is, and give us gifts. But the truly wise still seek and worship Jesus today for who he is, not for what they can get.

2:1 Jesus was born in the town of Bethlehem in Judea, during the reign of King Herod. The tiny **town of Bethlehem** is about five miles south of Jerusalem. The prophet Micah had prophesied that the Messiah would be born there (Micah 5:2). To distinguish this Bethlehem from other towns with the same name, Matthew added **in Judea.** The land of Israel was divided into four political districts and several lesser territories. Judea (also called Judah) was to the south, Samaria in the middle, Galilee to the north, and Idumea to the southeast. Jerusalem was also in Judea and was the seat of government for **King Herod.** While many Herods are mentioned in the Bible, this was Herod the Great, who ruled from 37 to 4 B.C.

About that time some wise men from eastern lands arrived in Jerusalem. Not much is known about these **wise men.** Also called Magi, they may have been from the priestly caste in Persia; they were not kings. Tradition says they were men of high position from Parthia, near the site of ancient Babylon (the book of Daniel refers to the wise men of Babylon; see Daniel 2:12, 18; 4:6, 18). The traditional view that there were three wise men comes from the three gifts presented to Jesus (2:11), but the Bible does not say how many wise men came.

2:2 "Where is the newborn king of the Jews? We have seen his star as it arose, and we have come to worship him." The wise men said they had seen Jesus' **star.** In the Old Testament, through a man named Balaam, God had referred to "a star" rising from Jacob (Numbers 24:17). How did these wise men know that the star represented the Messiah, the one who was **the newborn king of** the Jews? (1) They could have been Jews who remained in Babylon after the Exile and knew the Old Testament predictions of the Messiah's coming. (2) They may have been eastern astrologers who studied Old Testament manuscripts. Because of the Jewish exile centuries earlier, a large Jewish population still existed there, and they would have had copies of the Old Testament. (3) They may have had a special message from God directing them to the Messiah.

Matthew made a significant point in highlighting the **worship** of these wise men, which stood in contrast to the Jewish religious leaders who knew the Holy Scriptures and did not need to travel far to find their Messiah. The Jewish leaders directed the wise men to Bethlehem, but they did not go themselves (2:4-6).

2:3 Herod was deeply disturbed. The wise men's news **deeply disturbed** Herod because he knew that the Jewish people expected the Messiah to come soon (Luke 3:15). Most Jews expected the Messiah to be a great military and political deliverer, like Judas Maccabees or even Alexander the Great. Herod the Great was obviously disturbed for several reasons:

- Herod was not the rightful heir to the throne of David; he reigned by appointment from Rome. Many Jews hated Herod as a usurper. If this baby really was a rightful heir to the throne, Herod could face trouble from the Jews.
- Herod was ruthless, and because of his many enemies, he was suspicious that someone would try to overthrow him.

- Herod didn't want the Jews, a religious people, to unite around a religious figure.
- If these wise men were of Jewish descent and from Parthia (the most powerful region next to Rome), they would have welcomed a Jewish king who could swing the balance of power away from Rome.

That **all of Jerusalem** was troubled along with King Herod indicates that the leaders and lay-people also felt concern over word of a child born in the Jewish royal line, the line of David. Any who knew Herod's ruthlessness may have feared his aroused suspicions.

2:4 Herod needed some advice from the experts, so **he called a meeting of the leading priests and teachers of religious law.** The **leading priests** were mostly Sadducees, while the **teachers of religious law** (sometimes called "scribes") were mostly Pharisees. These two groups did not get along because of vast differences in their beliefs about the law. The Sadducees believed only the Pentateuch (the first five books of the Old Testament) to be God's word; the Pharisees and teachers of the law were the professional interpreters of the law, the legal specialists of Jesus' day. Among these men Herod hoped to find someone who could explain where **the Messiah would be born.**

2:5-6 The prophet Micah had given the exact location of the Messiah's birth seven centuries earlier (Micah 5:2). Matthew often quoted Old Testament prophets to show how perfectly Jesus fulfilled the prophecies about the Messiah. The Jewish religious leaders understood that the Messiah would be born in **Bethlehem of Judah.** This fact was well known to all Jews (John 7:41-42). Ironically, when Jesus was born, these same religious leaders became his greatest enemies. When the Messiah for whom they had been waiting finally came, they wouldn't recognize him.

2:7 Herod called the **wise men** back to him in order to answer their question (2:2). However, he also needed to know the age of this "king." Herod deduced that if he knew **the exact time when they first saw the star,** he would know the child's age. Since the star had appeared two years earlier, Herod soon ordered the killing of all boys two years old and under (see 2:16).

2:8 Herod sent the **wise men** to **Bethlehem** and said, **"Search carefully for the child. And when you find him, come back and tell me so that I can go and worship him, too!"** Herod would

not let rumor of a future king go unchecked. But Herod did not want to worship Jesus; he planned to kill him.

2:9 Having been told that the child was to be born in Bethlehem, **the wise men went their way. Once again the star appeared to them** as they traveled toward **Bethlehem.** Then, the star **stopped over the place where the child was.** Matthew does not tell us what the star looked like, how it moved, or how the wise men found the child from the movement and stopping of the star. But Matthew made his point that God had purposely sent this star to guide these men to his Son.

2:10 When they saw the star, they were filled with joy! The star's movement had been visible to these men who studied the sky and watched the stars. They had followed this star across thousands of miles. They had not found the child in the palace in Jerusalem as they had expected. So they had wearily continued on their way, only to once again follow the moving star. No wonder that when they saw that the star had stopped, they were **filled with joy.**

2:11 Jesus was probably one or two years old (a child) when the wise men found him. By this time, Mary and Joseph were living in a **house.** The wise men gave expensive gifts because these were worthy presents for a future king. **Gold** was a gift for a king (Psalm 72:15). **Frankincense,** a glittering, odorous gum obtained from the bark of certain trees, was a gift for deity (Isaiah 60:6). **Myrrh,** a valued spice and perfume (Psalm 45:8), also came from trees and was used in embalming; thus, it was a gift for a person who was going to die (Mark 15:23; John 19:39). These gifts certainly would have provided the financial resources for Joseph and Mary's trip to Egypt and back (2:13-23).

These wise men, astrologers from the east, **fell down** and **worshiped** the young king of the Jews, indicating a further fulfillment of prophecy (Psalm 72:10-19).

2:12 They went home another way, because God had warned them in a dream not to return to Herod. Going back through Jerusalem would make it impossible to avoid Herod; so the wise men went out of Bethlehem in another direction. In this story, God reveals his care for his Son as the hostile world already was attempting to take the young child's life. In the Gospel of Matthew, divine intervention is a major theme. Matthew shows how God superintended Jesus' life in order to accomplish the divine plan.

THE ESCAPE TO EGYPT / 2:13-18 / 13

Even before the tiny baby could speak, the worldly powers, led by Satan himself, were moving against him. Herod, a ruthless king who had killed three of his own sons to secure his power, was afraid of losing that power, so he embarked on a plan to kill the tiny child who had been born "king of the Jews." In his madness, Herod murdered innocent children, hoping to kill this one child. Herod stained his hands with blood, but he did not harm Jesus. No one can thwart God's plans.

2:13-15 An angel of the Lord appeared to Joseph in a dream. This was the second dream or vision that Joseph received from God (see 1:20-21). **An angel of the Lord** warned Joseph that **Herod is going to try to kill the child.** The angel told Joseph exactly what to do: **Get up and flee to Egypt with the child and his mother.** Joseph obeyed **that night,** taking Jesus and Mary on the seventy-five mile journey to Egypt, escaping from Bethlehem under cover of darkness. The angel instructed Joseph, **"Stay there until I tell you to return"** (see 2:20). Going to Egypt was not unusual. Egypt had been a place of refuge for Israelites during times of political upheaval (1 Kings 11:40; 2 Kings 25:26). There were colonies of Jews in several major Egyptian cities. Egypt was a Roman province, but outside Herod's jurisdiction. **They stayed there until Herod's death. This fulfilled what the Lord had spoken through the prophet: "I called my Son out of Egypt."** Joseph followed the angel's instructions and remained in Egypt until the death of Herod (see 2:19-20). Thus, Jesus was kept safe. Even more important, however, this event fulfilled the prophecy of Hosea 11:1.

2:16 Herod was furious when he learned that the wise men had outwitted him. When this king became infuriated, his anger knew no bounds.

History documents the terrible acts of this evil man. At this point, all Herod knew was that a future king, still a child, lived in Bethlehem. After the wise men explained that **the star first appeared to them about two years earlier** (2:7), Herod deduced that the child would not be more than two years old. So **he sent soldiers to kill all the boys in and around Bethlehem who were two years old and under.**

2:17-18 Matthew saw that the grieving of the mothers in Bethlehem **fulfilled the prophecy of Jeremiah** in Jeremiah 31:15. **Rachel** was one of the wives of Jacob, one of the great men of God in the Old Testament. From Jacob's twelve sons had come the twelve tribes of Israel. Rachel was the symbolic mother of the nation; she had been buried near Bethlehem (Genesis 35:19). The Jeremiah passage describes Rachel, the "mother" of the nation, **weeping and mourning unrestrained . . . refusing to be comforted** because her children had been taken away into captivity. **Ramah** was a staging point of deportation (Jeremiah 40:1). The mothers in Bethlehem also wept and mourned for the little boys killed by the soldiers. Matthew compared the grief of the mothers at the time of the Exile to the grief of the mothers of the slaughtered children.

THE RETURN TO NAZARETH / 2:19-23 / 14

God carefully protected his Son's life, guiding Joseph as he took the child away from Israel when he was in danger, and then as he returned to Israel when it was once again safe. God was working out his plan of salvation for our sakes. Believers ought to read this story with awe as they watch God working behind the scenes to protect the life of Jesus Christ on this earth.

2:19-21 The **angel of the Lord** had promised that Joseph would be told when it would be safe for him and his family to return to Israel (2:13). The angel instructed Joseph to **"get up and take the child and his mother back to the land of Israel, because those who were trying to kill the child are dead."** So Joseph returned immediately to Israel with Jesus and his mother. How long they had been in Egypt is unknown.

But when the angel commanded them to return to Israel, Joseph did not hesitate.

2:22 Herod had divided his kingdom into three parts, one for each son. **Archelaus** received Judea, Samaria, and Idumea, ruling over Judea. Archelaus, a violent man, began his reign by slaughtering three thousand influential people. He proved to be such a poor ruler that he was deposed in A.D. 6.

Joseph had heard about Archelaus and **was afraid to go back to Bethlehem**, which was in the district of Judea. Once again, God guided Joseph, warning him in a **dream** not to go into the region of this evil ruler, but **to go to Galilee.**

2:23 Joseph returned to his hometown of **Nazareth (Luke 2:4),** a town in southern Galilee near the crossroads of great caravan trade routes. The Roman garrison in charge of Galilee was housed there.

The Old Testament does not record the specific statement **He will be called a Nazarene.** Matthew may have been referring to Isaiah 11:1 where the Hebrew word for "branch" (*netser*) is similar to the word for "Nazarene." Others say he may have been referring to a prophecy unrecorded in the Bible or to a combination of prophecies. Matthew painted a picture of Jesus as the true Messiah announced by God through the prophets. Jesus, the Messiah, had unexpectedly humble beginnings and would be despised by those to whom he came, just as the Old Testament had predicted.

MATTHEW 3

JOHN THE BAPTIST PREPARES THE WAY FOR JESUS / 3:1-12 / 16

When John "began preaching" (3:1), the people were excited. They considered John to be a great prophet, and they were sure that the eagerly awaited age of the Messiah had come. John spoke like the prophets of old, saying that the people must turn from their sin to avoid punishment and turn to God to experience his mercy and approval. This is a message for all times and places, but John spoke it with particular urgency because he was preparing the people for the coming Messiah and for his Kingdom. How much urgency do you feel for those who still need to hear the message?

3:1 In those days John the Baptist began preaching in the Judean wilderness. In these few words, Matthew summed up the story that Luke would record in greater detail (see Luke 1:5-25, 39-45, 57-80). John **began preaching** a message of repentance. The word translated "preaching" comes from the Greek word meaning "to be a herald, to proclaim." Matthew described John as a herald proclaiming news of the coming King, the Messiah. The title **"the Baptist"** distinguished this John from many other men with the same name; baptism was an important part of his ministry (3:6).

John's mother, Elizabeth, was a cousin to Jesus' mother, Mary. Thus, Jesus and John the Baptist were distant cousins. It is likely that they knew of each other, but John probably did not know that Jesus was the Messiah until he baptized Jesus (see 3:16-17).

3:2 "Turn from your sins and turn to God, because the Kingdom of Heaven is near." John the Baptist's preaching focused specifically on one message—preparing hearts for the coming Messiah. Preparation could only occur through repentance. John called the people to repent—to **turn** away from sins and **turn to God.** To be truly repentant, people must do both. John preached that the people could not say they believed and then live any way they wanted (see 3:7-8). Sin is wrong, and people need to change both their attitude and their conduct.

Why did they need this radical repentance? **Because the Kingdom of Heaven was near.** The phrase indicates a present reality and a future hope. Today Jesus Christ reigns in the hearts of believers, but the Kingdom of Heaven will not be fully realized until all evil in the world is judged and removed. Christ came to earth first as a Suffering Servant; he will come again as King and Judge to rule victoriously over all the earth.

3:3 Isaiah had spoken of John when he said, **"He is a voice shouting in the wilderness: 'Prepare a pathway for the Lord's coming! Make a straight road for him!'"** Isaiah was one of the greatest prophets of the Old Testament and one of the most quoted in the New. Isaiah recorded God's promise to bring the exiles home from Babylon. He also wrote about the coming of the Messiah and the person who would announce his coming, John the Baptist (Isaiah 40:3). Like Isaiah, John was a prophet who urged people to confess their sins and live for God.

The word **prepare** refers to making something ready; the word **pathway** could also be translated "road." The picture could come from the ancient Middle Eastern custom of sending servants ahead of a king to level and clear the roads to make them passable for his journey. The people in Israel needed to prepare their minds to eagerly anticipate their King and Messiah.

3:4 John's clothes were woven from camel hair, and he wore a leather belt. John dressed much like the prophet Elijah (2 Kings 1:8), also considered a messenger preparing the way for God (see Malachi 3:1; 4:5). John's striking appearance reinforced his striking message, distinguishing him from the religious leaders, whose flowing robes reflected their great pride in their position (12:38-39). Having separated himself from the evil and hypocrisy of his day, John lived differently from other people to show that his message was new. His diet, **locusts and wild honey**, was common for survival in the desert regions.

3:5 People from Jerusalem and from every section of Judea and from all over the Jordan Valley went out to the wilderness to hear him preach. John attracted so many people because he was the first true prophet in four hundred years. His blasting of both Herod and the religious leaders was a daring act that fascinated common people. But John also had strong words for the others in his audience; they, too, were sinners and needed to repent. His message was powerful and true.

3:6 They confessed their sins. Confession is more than simply acknowledging one's own sinfulness; it is agreeing with God's verdict on sin and expressing the desire to get rid of sin and live for God. Confessing means more than verbal response, affirmation, or praise; it means agreeing to change to a life of obedience and service. After this, John **baptized them in the Jordan River.** When you wash dirty hands, the results are immediately visible. But repentance happens inside, with a cleansing that isn't seen right away. So John used a symbolic action that people could see: baptism. For baptism, John needed water, and he used the Jordan River.

3:7 John gladly baptized the many repentant people who came to him, confessing their sins

and desiring to live for God. But when John saw many **Pharisees and Sadducees**, he exploded in anger at the hypocrisy of these religious leaders. The **Pharisees** separated themselves from anything non-Jewish and carefully followed both the Old Testament laws and the oral traditions handed down through the centuries. The **Sadducees** believed the Pentateuch alone (Genesis–Deuteronomy) to be God's word. John **denounced them. "You brood of snakes!" he exclaimed.** John had criticized the Pharisees for being legalistic and hypocritical, for following the letter of the law while ignoring its true intent. He had criticized the Sadducees for using religion to advance their political position. He obviously doubted the genuineness of their desire **to be baptized**. John called them a **brood of snakes** (Jesus also used this term—see 12:34; 23:33), thereby conveying how dangerous and cunning they were and suggesting that they were offspring of Satan (see Genesis 3; John 8:44). His question stung with sarcasm, **"Who warned you to flee God's coming judgment?"** The religious leaders had always applied the **coming judgment** to judgment on the Gentiles; John applied it to the religious leaders. The reason for John's harshness is revealed in his words that follow.

3:8 True repentance is seen by the actions and character it produces. The Pharisees and Sadducees thought they had a corner on righteousness, but the way they lived revealed their true character. So John said, **"Prove by the way you live that you have really turned from your sins and turned to God."** John the Baptist called people to more than words or ritual; he told them to change their behavior. If we have really turned from our sins and turned to God, our words and religious activities must back up what we say. God judges our words by the actions that accompany them. Do your actions match your words?

3:9 John continued: **"Don't just say, 'We're safe—we're the descendants of Abraham.' That proves nothing."** Somewhere over the years, the Jews erroneously decided that the promise given to the patriarchs was guaranteed to all their descendants, no matter how they acted or what they believed. John explained to them, however, that relying on **Abraham** as their ancestor would not qualify them for God's Kingdom. John probably pointed at stones in the riverbed and said, **"God can change these stones here into children of Abraham."** The apostle Paul would later explain this to the Romans: "Not everyone born into a Jewish family is truly a Jew! Just the fact that they are descendants of Abraham doesn't make them truly

Abraham's children. . . . It is the children of the promise who are considered to be Abraham's children" (Romans 9:6-8).

3:10 "Even now the ax of God's judgment is poised, ready to sever your roots. Yes, every tree that does not produce good fruit will be chopped down and thrown into the fire." God's message hasn't changed since the Old Testament; people will be judged for their unproductive lives. Just as a fruit tree is expected to bear fruit, God's people should produce a crop of good deeds (3:8). John compared people who claim they believe God but do not live for him to unproductive trees that will be cut down. The ax is lying at the root of the trees, poised and ready to cut down those trees that do not bear good fruit. Not only will the trees be **chopped down**, but they will be **thrown into the fire**, signifying complete destruction. God has no use for people who call themselves Christians but do nothing about it.

3:11 "I baptize with water those who turn from their sins and turn to God." John explained that baptism demonstrated repentance. This was the beginning of a spiritual process. Baptism was an "outward" sign of commitment. To be effective, it had to be accompanied by an "inward" change of attitude leading to a changed life. John's baptism did not give salvation; it prepared a person to welcome the coming Messiah and receive *his* message and *his* baptism.

John knew that the Messiah would be coming after him. Although John was the first genuine prophet in four hundred years, Jesus the Messiah would be infinitely greater than he—"so much

greater that I am not even worthy to be his slave." John was pointing out how insignificant he was compared to the one who would come. John the Baptist said, "He must become greater and greater, and I must become less and less" (John 3:30). What John began, Jesus finished. What John prepared, Jesus fulfilled.

John's statement, **"He will baptize you with the Holy Spirit and with fire,"** revealed the identity of the one who is more powerful than John himself. All believers, those who would later come to Jesus Christ for salvation, would receive the baptism of the Holy Spirit and the fire of purification (one article precedes these words, indicating that they were not two separate baptisms but one and the same). The experience would not necessarily be like that recorded in Acts 2, but the outcome would be the same. This baptism would purify and refine each believer.

3:12 "He is ready to separate the chaff from the grain with his winnowing fork. Then he will clean up the threshing area, storing the grain in his barn but burning the chaff with never-ending fire." Threshing was the process of separating the grains of wheat from the useless outer shell called chaff. This was normally done in a large area called a threshing floor, often on a hill, where the wind could blow away the lighter chaff when the farmer tossed the beaten wheat into the air. A **winnowing fork** is a pitchfork used to toss wheat in the air in order to separate wheat from chaff. Wheat is gathered; chaff is burned. John spoke of repentance, but he also spoke of judgment upon those who refused to repent.

THE BAPTISM OF JESUS / 3:13-17 / 17
The beautiful story of Jesus' baptism by John in the waters of the Jordan River reveals a God of love, who came to earth as a human being to identify with human beings. If Jesus was going to offer salvation to sinners, he needed to identify with sinners. He did this by submitting to John's baptism for repentance and forgiveness of sins. God's Son came to earth to bring salvation to those who believe. Have you believed in Jesus and made him Lord of your life?

3:13 Galilee was the name of the northern region of Palestine. At this time, Jesus was probably about thirty years old (Luke 3:23). He traveled the long distance on foot to meet John the Baptist and **be baptized** by him.

3:14-15 But John didn't want to baptize him. "I am the one who needs to be baptized by you," he said, "so why are you coming to me?" John did not think that Jesus needed to be baptized for

repentance. But Jesus said, **"It must be done, because we must do everything that is right."** Jesus had come to be baptized because it would be the proper way for him to obey God in every aspect of life. Jesus didn't need to admit sin— he was sinless (John 8:46; 2 Corinthians 5:21; Hebrews 4:15; 1 John 3:5). Jesus was baptized: (1) to confess sin on behalf of the nation; (2) to accomplish God's mission and advance God's work in the world; (3) to inaugurate his public ministry to bring the message of salvation to all people; (4) to show support for John's ministry; (5) to identify with the penitent people of God, thus with humanness and sin; (6) to give us an example to follow. Jesus, the perfect man, accepted baptism in obedient service to the Father, and God showed his approval.

3:16 After his baptism, as Jesus came up out of the water, the heavens were opened and he saw the Spirit of God descending like a dove and settling on him. The opening of the **heavens** presented God's intervention into humanity via the human presence of God in Jesus Christ. It was as if the heavens rolled back to reveal the invisible throne of God (Isaiah 63:19–64:2). The action of the **Spirit of God descending like a dove** was a sign that Jesus was the Messiah and that the age of the Spirit predicted by the prophets was formally beginning (Isaiah 61:1). The descending of the Spirit signified God's workings in the world; therefore, the arrival of the Messiah would have been marked by the descending of the Spirit, in this case, in the form of a dove. This was his royal anointing (see Isaiah 11:2; 42:1).

3:17 And a voice from heaven said, "This is my beloved Son." While all believers would eventually be called "sons of God" (or "children of God"), Jesus Christ has a different, unique relationship with God; he is the one unique Son of God. The phrase, **"I am fully pleased with him,"** means that the Father takes great delight, pleasure, and satisfaction in the Son. This echoed two Old Testament passages (Psalm 2:7; Isaiah 42:1). The voice from the throne of heaven described Jesus' status both as the Servant who would suffer and die and as the King who would reign forever.

In 3:16-17, all three persons of the Trinity are present and active. The doctrine of the Trinity, which was developed much later in church history, teaches that God is three persons and yet one in essence. God the Father speaks; God the Son is baptized; God the Holy Spirit descends on Jesus. God is one, yet in three persons at the same time. This is one of God's incomprehensible mysteries. Other Bible references that speak of the Father, Son, and Holy Spirit are Matthew 28:19; John 15:26; 1 Corinthians 12:4-13; 2 Corinthians 13:14; Ephesians 2:18; 1 Thessalonians 1:2-5; and 1 Peter 1:2.

MATTHEW 4

SATAN TEMPTS JESUS IN THE WILDERNESS / 4:1-11 / 18

From Jesus' temptation we can learn that following our Lord can bring dangerous and intense spiritual battles. Our spiritual victories may not always be visible to the watching world. We must use the power of God to face temptation and not try to withstand it in our own strength.

4:1 The same Holy Spirit who had sent Jesus to be baptized led him **out into the wilderness . . . to be tempted there by the Devil.** Jesus took the offensive against the enemy, Satan, by going into the wilderness to face temptation. "Devil" in Greek means "accuser"; in Hebrew, the word "Satan" means the same (4:10). Satan is a fallen archangel. He is a real created being, not symbolic, and is constantly fighting against those who follow and obey God.

The word "tempted" means "to put to the test to see what good or evil, strengths or weaknesses, exist in a person." The Devil's temptations focused on three crucial areas: (1) physical needs and desires, (2) possessions and power, and (3) pride (see 1 John 2:15-16 for a similar list). This tempta-

tion by the Devil shows us that Jesus was human, and it gave Jesus the opportunity to reaffirm God's plan for his ministry. It also gives us an example to follow when we are tempted.

4:2 For forty days and forty nights he ate nothing and became very hungry. Fasting was used as a spiritual discipline for prayer and a time of preparation for great tasks that lay ahead. At the end of this forty-day fast, Jesus obviously was famished. His status as God's Son did not make this fast any easier; his physical body suffered the severe hunger and pain of going without sustenance. The three temptations recorded here occurred when Jesus was at his most physically weakened state.

4:3 The Devil phrased his temptation by saying, "If you are the Son of God." The word "if" did not imply doubt; both Jesus and Satan knew the truth. Instead, Satan tempted Jesus with his own power. Because Jesus was the Son of God, then he certainly could change **stones into loaves of bread** in order to satisfy his hunger. "God's Son has no reason to be hungry," Satan suggested. He wanted Jesus to use his power and position to meet his own needs.

4:4 But Jesus told him, "No! The Scriptures say, 'People need more than bread for their life; they must feed on every word of God.'" Jesus answered with words from Deuteronomy 8:3. In all three quotes from Deuteronomy (Matthew 4:4, 7, 10), the context shows that Israel failed each test each time. Jesus conveyed to Satan that while the test may have caused Israel to fail, it would not work with Jesus. To truly accomplish his mission, Jesus had to be completely humbled. Making himself bread would have shown that he had not quite set aside all his powers, had not humbled himself, and had not identified completely with the human race. But Jesus refused, showing that he would use his powers only in submission to God's plan.

4:5-6 The next temptation was set in **Jerusalem**, the religious and political seat of Palestine. The **Temple** was the religious center of the Jewish nation and the place where the people expected the Messiah to arrive (Malachi 3:1). The Temple was the tallest building in the area, and this **highest point** was probably the corner wall that jutted out of the hillside. This time, Satan used Scripture to try to convince Jesus to sin. Satan quoted words from Psalm 91:11-12: **"If you are the Son of God, jump off! For the Scriptures say, 'He orders his angels to protect you. And they will hold you with their hands to keep you from striking your foot on a stone.'"** Satan wanted Jesus to test his relationship with God to see if God's promise of protection would prove true. Satan was quoting Scripture out of context, making it sound as though God protects anyone, even if they attempt to defy natural law. In context, the psalm promises God's protection for those who, while being in his will and serving him, find themselves in danger. It does not promise protection for artificially created crises in which Christians call to God in order to test his love and care.

4:7 Jesus responded from Deuteronomy 6:16, "The Scriptures also say, 'Do not test the Lord your God.'" In this passage, Moses was referring to an incident during Israel's wilderness wanderings, recorded in Exodus 17:1-7. The people were thirsty and ready to mutiny against Moses and return to Egypt if he did not provide them with water. God supplied the water, but only after the people had "tested the LORD by saying, 'Is the LORD going to take care of us or not?'"

Jesus could have jumped from the Temple; God could have sent angels to bring him safely to the ground. But it would have been a ridiculous test of God's power, and it would have been out of God's will. Jesus knew that his Father could protect him; he also understood that all his actions were to be focused on fulfilling his Father's mission, even if it meant suffering and death (which, of course, it did).

4:8-9 Next the Devil took him to the peak of a very high mountain and showed him the nations of the world and all their glory. "I will give it all to you," he said, "if you will only kneel down and worship me." This experience was probably visionary. The **nations of the world** are under Satan's dominion (John 12:31). Satan knew that one day Jesus Christ would rule over the earth (see Philippians 2:9-11). His temptation was, "Why wait? I can give this to you now!" Satan tempted Jesus to take the world as an earthly kingdom right then, without carrying out his plan to save the world from sin. For Jesus, that meant obtaining his promised dominion over the world without experiencing the suffering and death of the cross. Satan offered a painless shortcut. But Satan didn't understand that suffering and death were a part of God's plan that Jesus had chosen to obey.

4:10 Jesus dismissed Satan with the words, **"Get out of here."** For Jesus to take a shortcut to the goal—ruling the world by worshiping Satan (4:9)—would be to break the first commandment, **"You must worship the Lord your God; serve only him"** (Deuteronomy 6:4-5). Jesus would take the path of submission to God. Only by doing so would he be able to accomplish his mission of bringing salvation to the world.

4:11 Since Jesus was superior to Satan, Satan had to do as Jesus commanded. So **the Devil went away.** This would only be the first of many encounters that Jesus would have with Satan's power. That **angels came and cared for Jesus** in no way lessens the intensity of the temptations that Jesus faced. They may have brought him food, but they also attended to his spiritual needs.

JESUS PREACHES IN GALILEE / 4:12-17 / 30

Jesus moved from Nazareth, his hometown, to Capernaum, on the northwest shore of the Sea of Galilee. This became Jesus' home base during his ministry in Galilee. Matthew explained how Jesus' move had been prophesied in Scripture. Jesus' actions, words, and movements showed his obedience to God's will and fulfilled the Scriptures about him. Matthew continued to assure his Jewish readers that Jesus' life fulfilled Scripture and that Jesus truly was the promised Messiah.

4:12-13 When Jesus heard that John had been arrested, he left Judea and returned to Galilee. But instead of going to Nazareth, he went to Capernaum, beside the Sea of Galilee. Matthew mentioned the arrest of John the Baptist as merely a signal for the ministry of Jesus into **Galilee,** his home region. He moved from **Nazareth** (where his family had settled, 2:23) to **Capernaum.** The region of Zebulun and Naphtali originally belonged to two of the twelve tribes of Israel. They had been allotted this territory and had settled it during the conquest of Canaan under Joshua (see Joshua 19:10-16, 32-39).

4:14-16 This fulfilled Isaiah's prophecy: "In the land of Zebulun and of Naphtali, beside the sea, beyond the Jordan River—in Galilee where so many Gentiles live—the people who sat in darkness have seen a great light. And for those who lived in the land where death casts its shadow, a light has shined." Matthew continued to show how all of Jesus' life, even his travel, followed God's plans and fulfilled Scripture. Some Jewish readers may have wondered why Jesus' ministry was not focused in Jerusalem and the Temple. However, Matthew explained that Jesus' move to the region of Galilee fulfilled Isaiah 9:1-2. Isaiah had prophesied that the Messiah would be a **light** to the land of **Zebulun** and **Naphtali.** These words foreshadow Jesus' mission: He came to preach salvation by grace to the entire world.

4:17 Jesus started his ministry with the same message that people had heard from John the Baptist: "Turn from your sins and turn to God." Becoming a follower of Christ begins with repentance, turning away from our self-centeredness and self-control. The next step is to turn the right way, to Christ.

The Old Testament prophets often spoke of the future Kingdom, ruled by a descendant of King David, that would be established on earth and exist for eternity. Thus, when Jesus said, **"The Kingdom of Heaven is near,"** the Jews understood him to mean that the Messiah had come to inaugurate his long-awaited earthly kingdom. This caused great excitement among the people. The problem arose, however, in misunderstanding the nature of this Kingdom and in timing its arrival. The Kingdom of Heaven began when God entered history as a human being. But the culmination of the Kingdom of Heaven will not be fully realized until all evil in the world has been judged and removed. Christ came to earth first as the Suffering Servant. When he returns, he will come as King and Judge to rule over all the earth. The Kingdom begun with Jesus' birth would not overthrow Roman oppression and usher in universal peace. The Kingdom of Heaven that began quietly in Palestine was God's rule in people's hearts. Thus, the Kingdom was as "near" as people's willingness to make Jesus King over their lives.

FOUR FISHERMEN FOLLOW JESUS / 4:18-22 / 33

One day as Jesus was walking beside the Sea of Galilee, he saw two sets of brothers who were fishing. Jesus told these men—Peter, Andrew, James, and John—to leave their fishing business and "fish for people"—to bring others to God. Jesus was calling them away from their financially productive trade to be productive spiritually. All of Christ's followers need to fish for souls.

4:18 Located 650 feet below sea level, the **Sea of Galilee** is a large lake—150 feet deep and surrounded by hills. Fishing was the main industry for the approximately thirty towns surrounding the Sea of Galilee during Jesus' day.

Jesus **saw two brothers—Simon, also called**

Peter, and Andrew. Jesus did not approach Simon (whom we know as Peter) and Andrew as strangers. We know from the Gospel of John (1:35-49) that they had had previous contact. Jesus was walking on the beach with a purpose—to find certain fishermen whom he wanted to call to follow him. Jesus found them **fishing with a net, for they were commercial fishermen.** Using nets was the most common method of fishing. A circular net (ten to fifteen feet in diameter) would be thrown into the sea. Then it would be drawn up, and the catch hoisted into the boat.

4:19 Jesus called out to them, **"Come, be my disciples, and I will show you how to fish for people!"** Jesus told Simon (Peter) and Andrew to leave their fishing business and to follow him. Jesus was asking these men to become his disciples and to begin fishing for people. These disciples were adept at catching fish, but they would need special training before they would be able to fish for people's souls. Jesus was calling them away from their trade to help others believe the Good News.

4:20 After their previous meeting with Jesus, Simon Peter and Andrew had returned to fishing. But when Jesus called them to follow him as disciples, **they left their nets at once and went with him.** These men already knew Jesus, so when Jesus called them, they were willing to follow him. When Jesus calls, people must be willing to realign previous plans and goals, sometimes leaving something important in order to follow Jesus.

4:21-22 Not far down the beach were **two other brothers, James and John.** Their father, **Zebedee,** owned a fishing business where they worked with Peter and Andrew (Luke 5:10). James and John were **sitting in a boat . . . mending their nets.** The weight of a good catch of fish and the constant strain on the nets meant that fishermen had to spend a lot of time keeping their nets repaired and in good shape.

John and Andrew had met Jesus previously (John 1:35-39). James probably knew about Jesus from his brother. When Jesus called them, **they immediately followed him, leaving the boat and their father behind.**

JESUS PREACHES THROUGHOUT GALILEE / 4:23-25 / 36

Jesus became well known very quickly. Certainly his acclaimed ability to heal diseases caused people to bring sick family and friends to him. Some simply followed him from place to place to hear him speak and see his miracles. Some who followed also came to believe in him, accepting the Good News about the Kingdom.

4:23 Jesus traveled throughout Galilee teaching in the synagogues, preaching everywhere the Good News about the Kingdom. And he healed people who had every kind of sickness and disease. Jesus was teaching, preaching, and healing—the three main aspects of his ministry. "Teaching" shows Jesus' concern that people learn; "preaching" shows his concern for commitment; and "healing" shows his concern for physical wholeness. Jesus' healing miracles authenticated his teaching and preaching; they proved that he truly was from God.

When Jesus arrived in a town, he first went to the synagogue. Most towns that had ten or more Jewish families had a synagogue. The building served as a religious gathering place on the Sabbath and as a school during the week. The leader of the synagogue was an administrator who often invited rabbis to teach and preach. Jesus had opportunity to share the Good News of the Kingdom to the Jews who came to the synagogues. The "Good News" was that the Kingdom of Heaven had arrived.

4:24 News about him spread far beyond the borders of Galilee. Those who heard him told family and friends, who told others, so that the news spread throughout all **Syria.** "Syria" may refer to the area to the north of Galilee, indicating that Jesus' fame had spread beyond the borders of Palestine. Jesus cured everyone—**whatever their illness and pain, or if they were possessed by demons, or were epileptics, or were paralyzed—he healed them all.** Why did Jesus perform physical healings? As Creator, Jesus wanted people to have health and wholeness rather than illness. The healings also showed Jesus' compassion for suffering people and revealed that the Kingdom had arrived in power and presence.

4:25 Large crowds followed him wherever he went—people from Galilee, the Ten Towns, Jerusalem, from all over Judea, and from east of the Jordan River. The **Ten Towns** refers to a league of ten Gentile cities east of the Sea of Galilee that had joined together for trade and mutual defense. The city of **Jerusalem** was in the region of **Judea.** The region **east of the Jordan River** most likely refers also to Gentile territory. The news about Jesus was out; Jews and Gentiles were coming long distances to hear him.

MATTHEW 5

JESUS GIVES THE BEATITUDES / 5:1-12 / 49

Matthew 5–7 is called the Sermon on the Mount because Jesus gave it on a hillside near Capernaum. This sermon probably covered several days of preaching, if not more. In it, Jesus revealed his attitude toward the law of Moses, explaining that he requires faithful and sincere obedience, not ceremonial religion. The Sermon on the Mount challenged the teachings of the proud and legalistic religious leaders of the day. It called people back to the messages of the Old Testament prophets who, like Jesus, had taught that God wants heartfelt obedience, not mere legalistic observance of laws and rituals.

The most well-known portion of the Sermon on the Mount is known as the Beatitudes (5:3-10). These are a series of blessings promised to those who exhibit the attributes of God's Kingdom. The Beatitudes

- present a code of ethics for the disciples and a standard of conduct for all believers,
- contrast Kingdom values (what is eternal) with worldly values (what is temporary),
- contrast the superficial "faith" of the Pharisees with the real faith that Christ wants, and
- show how the future Kingdom will fulfill Old Testament expectations.

5:1-2 Jesus often presented his teaching up on a **mountainside. His disciples** came to him, and he **sat down to teach them.** The **crowds were gathering,** seated on the slopes below him. Jesus most likely gave these teachings primarily to the twelve disciples, but the crowds were present and listening. Much of what Jesus said referred to the ideas that had been promoted by the religious leaders of the day. The disciples, the closest associates of this popular man, might easily have been tempted to feel important, proud, and possessive. However, Jesus told them that instead of fame and fortune, they could expect mourning, hunger, and persecution. Jesus also assured his disciples that they would receive rewards, but perhaps not in this life.

5:3 The Beatitudes describe how Christ's followers should live. Each beatitude tells how to be blessed. To be blessed means more than happiness; it means to be favored and approved by God. According to worldly standards, the types of people whom Jesus described don't seem to be particularly blessed by God. But God's way of living usually contradicts the world's. Jesus explained that **"God blesses those who realize their need for him, for the Kingdom of Heaven is given to them."** Only those who humbly depend on God are admitted into the Kingdom of Heaven. The final consummation of all these rewards, and of the Kingdom itself, lies in the future. However, believers can already share in the Kingdom (as far as it has been revealed) by living out Jesus' words.

5:4 In another seeming contradiction in terms, Jesus explained that **"God blesses those who mourn, for they will be comforted."** Tied with the beatitude in verse 3, this means that humility (realization of one's unworthiness before God) also requires sorrow for sins. Whether Jesus' followers mourn for sin or in suffering, God's promise is sure that they will be comforted. Only God can take away sorrow for sin; only God can forgive and erase it. Only God can give comfort to those who suffer for his sake because they know their reward in the Kingdom.

5:5 **"God blesses those who are gentle and lowly, for the whole earth will belong to them."** The words translated **gentle and lowly** convey humility and trust in God. Gentle and lowly people do not look down on themselves, but they do not think too highly of themselves either. Ironically, it will not be the arrogant and wealthy people who get everything. Instead, **the whole earth will belong to** the gentle. Jesus used "earth" to refer to the future inheritance of the Kingdom. According to Revelation 21–22, believers will enjoy a new heaven and a new earth. God will one day freely give his true disciples what they did not grasp for themselves on earth.

5:6 "God blesses those who are hungry and thirsty for justice, for they will receive it in full." The words **hungry and thirsty** picture intense longings that people desire to satisfy—necessities that they cannot live without. Those who have an intense longing for justice (righteousness) are blessed. Most likely, this refers to personal justice—being so filled with God that the person completely does God's will. Justice refers to total discipleship and complete obedience. It may also refer to justice for the entire world—an end to the sin and evil that fill it. In both cases, God's promise is sure; **they will receive it in full.** He will completely satisfy spiritual hunger and thirst.

5:7 "God blesses those who are merciful, for they will be shown mercy." Merciful people realize that, because they received mercy from God, they must extend mercy to others. **Mercy** implies generosity, forgiveness, and compassion, and a desire to remove the wrong as well as alleviate the suffering. This promise does not guarantee mercy from people. The believers' comfort comes in the knowledge that, no matter how the world treats them, God will show them mercy both now and when he returns.

5:8 "God blesses those whose hearts are pure, for they will see God." People characterized as pure in heart are morally pure, honest, and sincere. They are people of integrity and single-minded commitment to God. Because of their sincere devotion to Christ, **they will see God** here and now through the eyes of faith (Hebrews 11:27), and finally face-to-face (1 John 3:2).

5:9 "God blesses those who work for peace, for they will be called the children of God." God calls his children to be peacemakers. This involves action, not just passive compliance. Peacemakers actively **work for peace,** to cause reconciliation, to end bitterness and strife. This peace is not appease-ment but dealing with and solving problems to maintain peace. Arrogant, selfish people do not concern themselves with peacemaking. Peacemakers **will be called the children of God** because they reflect their Father's character.

5:10 "God blesses those who are persecuted because they live for God, for the Kingdom of Heaven is theirs." Persecution should not surprise Christians. People who put others before themselves will seldom receive applause and honors. Often, they will be **persecuted** instead. Because **they live for God,** they stand out from the world and become marks for enemy attacks. The world is under Satan's control, and believers belong to the opposing army. The reward for these believers will be **the Kingdom of Heaven.** God will make up for the suffering that his children have undergone because of their loyalty to him.

5:11 "God blesses you when you are mocked and persecuted and lied about because you are my followers." Jesus was telling his disciples that they shouldn't be surprised when people mock them, persecute them, and lie about them. Jesus would face such treatment. Later, he explained to his followers that they should expect nothing different (10:18; 24:9; John 15:20).

5:12 Jesus described the way the disciples should respond to persecution: **"Be happy about it! Be very glad!"** This refers to deep, spiritual joy that is unhindered and unchanged by what happens in this present life. A person with righteous character can rejoice and be glad because of the promise: **a great reward awaits you in heaven.** The persecution will pale in comparison to the great reward.

Besides that, the disciples had good company: **the ancient prophets were persecuted, too.** Jesus placed his disciples in a long line of God's followers who lived righteously and spoke truthfully—only to suffer for it. Jesus explained that to live and speak for God in the face of unjust persecution, as the ancient prophets did, would bring great reward in heaven.

JESUS TEACHES ABOUT SALT AND LIGHT / 5:13-16 / 50

In these verses, Jesus explained to his disciples the true nature of their calling. They would be salt in a dreary world, light in a dark and evil world. But they would do this only because of the one who came as "the light of the world." This handful of men brought salt that we can taste and light that we can see even today. We, in turn, must pass "salt" and "light" along to others.

5:13 Jesus' questions, **"But what good is salt if it has lost its flavor? Can you make it useful again?"** did not expect an answer, for once salt has deteriorated, it cannot be used as a preservative. As salt preserves and brings out the best flavor of food, so believers should be **the salt of the**

earth and affect others positively. Jesus told his disciples that if they wanted to make a difference in the world, they would have to be different from the world. God would hold them accountable to maintain their "saltiness" (that is, their usefulness). We must be different if we want to make a difference.

5:14 "You are the light of the world." As salt makes a difference in people's food, so light makes a difference in their surroundings. Jesus would later explain, "I am the light of the world. If you follow me, you won't be stumbling through darkness, but will have the light of life" (John 8:12). Christ's disciples must live for Christ, shining **like a city on a mountain, glowing in the night for all to see.** They are like lights in a dark world, showing clearly what Christ is like. Because Jesus is the light of the world, his followers must reflect his light.

5:15 "Don't hide your light under a basket! Instead, put it on a stand and let it shine for all." People place lights on stands for them to spread their warm glow. The disciples should continue to reflect the light of their Master, the light of the world. They must not try to conceal their light any more than they would light a lamp and then hide it. Being Christ's disciples means spreading the light to everyone with whom we have contact.

5:16 "In the same way" that a light shines from a stand, Christ's disciples must let their light shine before others by letting their **"good deeds shine out for all to see, so that everyone will praise your heavenly Father."** Jesus made it clear that there would be no mistaking the source of a believer's good works. The believer's light shines not for himself but to reflect the light back to the Father and so direct people to him.

JESUS TEACHES ABOUT THE LAW / 5:17-20 / 51

God gave moral and ceremonial laws to help people love him with all their hearts and minds. By Jesus' time, however, religious leaders had turned God's laws into a confusing mass of rules. When Jesus talked about a new way to understand the law, he was trying to bring people back to its original purpose. Jesus did not speak against the law itself but against the abuses and excesses to which it had been subjected.

5:17 Jesus did not come as a rabbi with a brand new teaching; he came as the promised Messiah with a message heard from the beginning of time. **"Don't misunderstand why I have come. I did not come to abolish the law of Moses or the writings of the prophets. No, I came to fulfill them."** Jesus completes and transcends the law. The Old Testament law is not rescinded but now must be reinterpreted and reapplied in light of Jesus. God does not change his mind. Jesus' coming had been part of God's plan from Creation (see Genesis 3:15).

5:18 Jesus used the words **"I assure you"** several times in his speaking. They signal that what he said next is of vital importance. In these words, Jesus ascribed the highest authority to God's law. Not only did Jesus fulfill the law, but **until heaven and earth disappear** (meaning until the end of the age) the law will not change. Not the **smallest detail**, not the least stroke of a pen, will be set aside from **God's law**. Jesus' statement certifies the absolute authority of every word and letter of Scripture. Everything prophesied in God's law **will remain until its purpose is achieved**. Everything will be accomplished.

5:19 Jesus will fulfill and accomplish the entire Law and the Prophets (5:17-18), so his followers

must also keep even **the smallest commandment** included in the Law and the Prophets. In addition, if teachers influence others to break even the smallest law, they will be called **least in the Kingdom of Heaven**. Because the Law and the Prophets point forward to Jesus and his teaching, **anyone who obeys God's laws and teaches them will be great in the Kingdom of Heaven.** Those who treated any part of the law as "small," and therefore breakable, would themselves be called "least" and, presumably, be excluded. Jesus explained to his disciples, the men who would be responsible to carry on his message, that they must live carefully and teach carefully, not taking God's word lightly. Jesus' followers must respect and obey God's word if they want to accomplish great things for him.

5:20 Jesus expected his followers to **obey God better than the teachers of religious law and the Pharisees**, a seemingly impossible task. The **teachers of religious law** were teachers and lawyers in Jewish courts. The **Pharisees** were exacting and scrupulous in their attempts to follow God's law, as well as hundreds of traditional laws. How could Jesus reasonably call his followers to a greater righteousness than theirs?

Jesus was not placing impossible demands on his followers in order for them to **enter the**

Kingdom of Heaven. Jesus was speaking about the attitude of the heart. The Pharisees were content to obey the laws outwardly without humbly looking to God to change their hearts (or attitudes). Jesus was saying, therefore, that the quality of our righteousness should exceed that of the teachers of the law and the Pharisees, who looked pious, but were far from the Kingdom of God. True followers of God know that they cannot do anything to become righteous enough to enter the Kingdom of Heaven, so they count on God to work his righteousness within them.

JESUS TEACHES ABOUT ANGER / 5:21-26 / 52

In the following verses, Jesus will say, six times, "You have heard . . . but I say." With these words Jesus showed the true intent of God's law. To keep the law as God intended, the people could not get by with lip service and with obeying the letter of the law alone. Jesus' teaching reached to the application of the law, into people's motives and attitudes.

5:21 "You have heard that the law of Moses says, 'Do not murder. If you commit murder, you are subject to judgment.'" Jesus was quoting from the Ten Commandments, called **the law of Moses.** The Pharisees were teaching that the command against murder, found in Exodus 20:13, referred just to taking another person's life. Murderers were **subject to judgment** (i.e., execution; see Exodus 21:12; Leviticus 24:17) through certain legal proceedings, also described in the law.

5:22 "But I say, if you are angry with someone, you are subject to judgment!" Jesus taught that his followers should not even become angry enough to murder, for then they would already have committed murder in their heart. "Anger," here, refers to a seething, brooding bitterness that always threatens to leap out of control, leading to violence, emotional hurt, increased mental stress, spiritual damage, and, yes, even murder. Anger keeps us from developing a spirit pleasing to God. Jesus added, **"If you say to your friend, 'You idiot,' you are in danger of being brought before the court."** To stoop to insulting or calling a fellow believer a derogatory name makes one liable to prosecution. Angry words and name-calling reveal a heart far from God. **"And if you curse someone, you are in danger of the fires of hell."**

In the Bible, three words are used in connection with eternal punishment: (1) *Sheol,* or "the grave," is used in the Old Testament to mean the place of the dead, generally thought to be under the earth. (See Job 24:19; Psalm 16:10; Isaiah 38:10.) (2) *Hades* is the Greek word for the underworld, the realm of the dead. It is the word used in the New Testament for Sheol. (See Matthew 16:18; Revelation 1:18; 20:13-14.) (3) *Gehenna,* or hell, was named after the Valley of Hinnom near Jerusalem where children had been sacrificed by fire to the pagan gods. (See 2 Kings 23:10; 2 Chronicles 28:3.)

5:23-24 "So if you are standing before the altar in the Temple, offering a sacrifice to God, and you suddenly remember that someone has something against you, leave your sacrifice there beside the altar. Go and be reconciled to that person. Then come and offer your sacrifice to God." At certain times of the year, Jews brought sacrifices to be offered at the **altar in the Temple** in Jerusalem. The Jews brought their gifts as a matter of course, as part of keeping God's law. But Jesus explained that those who come into God's presence to worship must come with pure hearts, not hindered by broken relationships that they had the power to mend. Jesus explained that if the worshiper remembered someone's anger against him or her, that person should leave the gift and go immediately to **be reconciled** to the offended brother or sister. Then he should come back to worship and offer his or her gift.

5:25-26 "Come to terms quickly with your enemy before it is too late and you are dragged into court, handed over to an officer, and thrown in jail. I assure you that you won't be free again until you have paid the last penny." In Jesus' day, a person who couldn't pay a debt would be thrown into prison. Debts were repaid by selling property or going into contract as an indentured servant. If a person had no way to earn money to pay back the debt, the debtor could very well die in prison. Jesus recommended that his followers take immediate action to settle matters before the angry person handed them over to the judge. Under Roman law, the plaintiff went with the defendant to court. On the way, they could settle matters however they wished. But once a legal verdict was reached, it could not be changed.

It is practical advice to resolve our differences with our enemies before their anger causes more trouble. In a broader sense, these verses advise us to get things right with our brothers and sisters before we have to stand before God.

JESUS TEACHES ABOUT LUST / 5:27-30 / 53

In his teaching about lust, Jesus literally got to the heart of the matter by explaining that sin begins in the heart. With strong language, Jesus described how his followers must rid themselves of sin. While we cannot be sinless until we finally are with Christ, we must keep a watch on our thoughts, motives, and temptations in the meantime. When we find a destructive habit or thought pattern, we need to get rid of it.

5:27-28 Again Jesus quoted one of the Ten Commandments, **"Do not commit adultery"** (Exodus 20:14). According to the Old Testament law, a person must not have sex with someone other than his or her spouse. Jesus said, **"But I say, anyone who even looks at a woman with lust in his eye has already committed adultery with her in his heart."** Even the desire to have sex with someone other than your spouse is mental adultery and thus is sin. Jesus emphasized that if the act is wrong, then so is the desire to do the act. The word **lust** denotes the desire for an illicit relationship. To be faithful to your spouse with your body but not your mind is to break the trust so vital to a strong marriage. Jesus was condemning the deliberate and repeated filling of one's mind with fantasies that would be evil, if acted out.

5:29-30 When Jesus said to get rid of your **eye** or your **hand**, he was speaking figuratively. He didn't mean literally to **gouge out** an eye, because even a blind person can lust. But if that were the only choice, it would be better to go into eternal life with one eye or hand than to go to hell physically intact. This strong language describes how Jesus' followers should renounce anything that would cause them to sin or turn away from the faith. Believers must get rid of any relationship, practice, or activity that leads to sin. The reason? Jesus explained that **"It is better for you to lose one part of your body than for your whole body to be thrown into hell."** This is radical discipleship. While none of us will ever be completely free from sin until we get a new glorified body, God wants an attitude that renounces sin instead of one that holds on to it.

JESUS TEACHES ABOUT DIVORCE / 5:31-32 / 54

Divorce is as hurtful and destructive today as in Jesus' day. God intends marriage to be a lifetime commitment (Genesis 2:24). People should never consider divorce an option for solving problems or a way out of a relationship that seems dead. In these verses, Jesus was also attacking those who purposefully abused the marriage contract, using divorce to satisfy their lustful desire to marry someone else. Make sure your actions today help your marriage grow stronger rather than tear it apart.

5:31 Jesus again pointed out a law from the Old Testament that his listeners knew well. **The law of Moses,** in Deuteronomy 24:1-4, said that **a man can divorce his wife by merely giving her a letter of divorce.** The subject of divorce was hotly debated among the Jews at this time. Some religious leaders took this to mean that a man could divorce his wife for almost any reason. In a culture where husbands viewed their wives as "property," divorce was fairly easy to obtain. However, other leaders said that divorce could be granted only in cases of adultery.

5:32 **"But I say that a man who divorces his wife, unless she has been unfaithful, causes her to commit adultery."** The religious leaders permitted easy divorce, as well as remarriage after divorce. But Jesus said that the sacred union of marriage should not be broken and that to

remarry after divorce was committing adultery. However, Jesus here gave one exception regarding divorce: "marital unfaithfulness." For a man to divorce his wife because **she has been unfaithful** was simply a recognition that his union with her had been ended by her sexual union with another. It would be possible, then, that adultery would be an exception to the prohibition against remarriage. This does not mean that divorce should automatically occur when a spouse commits adultery. The word translated "unfaithfulness" implies a sexually immoral lifestyle, not a confessed and repented act of adultery. Those who discover that their spouse has been unfaithful should first make every effort to forgive, reconcile, and restore their relationship.

However, Jesus would not stand for men tossing aside their wives. Marriage is so sanctified in God's eyes that **anyone who marries a divorced** woman commits adultery. Notice that while the divorced woman would become an adulteress, the man who divorced his wife would be at fault—he causes her to become an adulteress. Jesus will explain his strong words in 19:3-12 on the grounds that God originally intended marriage to be for life.

God created marriage to be a sacred and permanent union and partnership between a man and a woman. When the husband and wife both enter this union with that understanding and commitment, they can provide security for each other, a stable home for their children, and strength to weather life's storms and stresses.

JESUS TEACHES ABOUT VOWS / 5:33-37 / 55

In Jesus' day, people commonly made oaths, or vows. Although God's law took these vows very seriously, many of the religious leaders had invented legal maneuvers to get around keeping their vows. Jesus told his followers not to use vows—their word alone should be enough. Are you known as a person of your word?

5:33 "Again, you have heard that the law of Moses says, 'Do not break your vows; you must carry out the vows you have made to the Lord.'" Jesus did not refer to any specific commandment, but he summed up Old Testament teachings on the subject of vows (see Exodus 20:7; Leviticus 19:12; Numbers 30:2; Deuteronomy 5:11; 6:13; 23:21-23). When a person made a vow, it bound him or her to keep it, whether it was a vow to another person or a vow made to the Lord.

5:34-36 However, Jesus told his followers, "Don't make any vows!" The religious leaders had designed an elaborate system indicating how binding a vow was depending on how the vow had been made. The leaders said that if they swore by heaven or by the earth or by Jerusalem, they could get out of their vow without penalty because they did not make the vow in God's

name. Jesus explained that a vow is a vow. A promise is binding before God, no matter what words are used. Jesus added, "Don't even swear, 'By my head!' for you can't turn one hair white or black." Even the hairs on people's heads belong to God, so a person cannot get around a vow by swearing by his head. Jesus' followers ought to be so well known for their honesty and truthfulness that they do not need to make vows.

5:37 Jesus emphasized that his followers should just say a simple, "Yes, I will," or "No, I won't." When they say yes they mean yes, and when they say no they mean no. "Your word is enough." People need vows only when telling lies is a possibility. "To strengthen your promise with a vow shows that something is wrong." Keeping promises builds trust and makes committed human relationships possible.

JESUS TEACHES ABOUT REVENGE / 5:38-42 / 56

When people hurt us, often our first reaction is to get even. Instead, Jesus said we should do good to those who wrong us! Instead of keeping score, we should love and forgive. This is not natural; it is supernatural. Only God can give us the strength to love as he does.

5:38 "You have heard that the law of Moses says, 'If an eye is injured, injure the eye of the person who did it. If a tooth gets knocked out, knock out the tooth of the person who did it.'" This example came from God's law as recorded by Moses in Exodus 21:23-25; Leviticus 24:19-20; and Deuteronomy 19:21. While the law sounds severe to us, in its time it set guidelines against what may have been escalating personal vendettas among people. The principle of retribution gave judges a formula for dealing with crime. That is, "Make the punishment fit the crime." The law

limited vengeance and helped the court administer punishment that was neither too strict nor too lenient.

5:39 "But I say, don't resist an evil person!" Jesus focused on the attitudes of his followers when dealing with evil individuals. The world advocates getting even, looking out for oneself, and protecting one's "personal rights." Jesus' followers, however, were to hold loosely to their "rights," preferring to forgo those rights for the sake of bearing witness to the gospel and the Kingdom. Being willing to set aside one's personal rights, however, does not mean that believers have to sit passively while evil goes unhindered.

To be **slapped on the right cheek** was literally a blow from the back of someone's hand, an act that even today shows the greatest possible contempt. According to Jewish law, the one who slapped another faced punishment and a heavy fine. Thus, the law was on the side of the victim. Jesus said not to take the legal channels, however, but to offer the other cheek for a slap as well. Jesus did not ask his followers to do what he would never do; he received such treatment and did as he had commanded (26:67; see also Isaiah 50:6; 1 Peter 2:23). Jesus wanted his followers to have an unselfish attitude that willingly follows the way of the cross instead of the way of personal rights. They should entrust themselves to God who will one day set all things right.

To many Jews, these statements were offensive. Any Messiah who would turn the other cheek was not the military leader to revolt against Rome. Because the Jews were under Roman oppression, they wanted retaliation against their enemies, whom they hated. But Jesus suggested a new, radical response to injustice: Instead of demanding rights, give them up freely! According to Jesus, it is more important to give justice and mercy than to receive it.

5:40 "If you are ordered to court and your shirt is taken from you, give your coat, too." The **coat** (or cloak) was a valuable possession. Making clothing was difficult and time-consuming. As a result, coats were expensive, and most people owned only one. A coat could be used as a blanket, a sack to carry things in, a pad to sit on, a pledge for a debt, and, of course, clothing. The **shirt** was an inner garment worn next to the skin. Jesus said to let the person take both. Again Jesus focused on the attitude expected of his followers. They should hold their possessions very loosely.

5:41 "If a soldier demands that you carry his gear for a mile, carry it two miles." This alludes to the forced labor that soldiers could demand of ordinary citizens to carry their loads a certain distance (**a mile** was the term for one thousand paces). The Jews hated this law because it forced them to show their subjection to Rome. Yet Jesus said to take the load and **carry it two miles.** Jesus called for a serving attitude (as he himself exemplified throughout his life and especially at the cross). Jesus' words probably shocked his hearers. Most of the Jews, expecting a military Messiah, would never have expected to hear Jesus issue a command of nonretaliation and cooperation with the hated Roman Empire. By these words, Jesus was revealing that his followers belong to another Kingdom. They need not attempt to fight against Rome, which would not serve God's plan. Instead, they should work on behalf of God's Kingdom. If doing so meant walking an extra mile carrying a Roman soldier's load, then that was what they should do.

5:42 "Give to those who ask, and don't turn away from those who want to borrow." Jesus' followers should have a generous spirit. Because they loosely hold on to their personal rights and possessions, they can freely give when the need arises and won't turn away from the one who wants to borrow. Jesus' followers must willingly put others' needs before their own.

JESUS TEACHES ABOUT LOVING ENEMIES / 5:43-48 / 57

By telling us not to retaliate against personal injustices (5:38-42), Jesus keeps us from taking the law into our own hands. This also keeps our focus on him and not on our own rights. By loving and praying for our enemies, we prove our relationship to our Father, show his love in an unlovely world, and overcome evil with good.

5:43-44 "You have heard that the law of Moses says, 'Love your neighbor' and hate your enemy." The Pharisees interpreted Leviticus 19:18 as teaching that they should love only those who love in return. The **neighbor** refers to someone of the same nationality and faith. While no Bible verse explicitly says "hate your enemy," the Pharisees may have reinterpreted some of the Old Testament passages about hatred for God's enemies (see, for example, Psalm 139:19-22 and 140:9-11). But Jesus explained, **"But I say, love your enemies! Pray for those who persecute you!"** If you can do that, you truly show that Jesus is Lord of your life. Jesus explained to his disciples that they must live by a higher standard than what the world expects—a standard that is impossible to reach on mere human strength alone. People who have experienced God's love understand what it means to be loved undeservedly. Only with the help of God's Spirit can his people love and pray for those who seek to do them harm (see Romans 12:14-21).

5:45 "In that way you will be acting as true children of your Father in heaven." The Father in heaven shows undiscriminating love to all people, giving his sunlight to both the evil and the good, and sending rain on the just and on the unjust as well. Therefore, his **children** (those who believe in him) must reflect his character and show undiscriminating love for both friends and enemies. God's love reaches out to all people. God's people must do the same.

5:46-47 "If you love only those who love you, what good is that?" Jesus has been explaining the much higher standards that are expected of his followers, standards higher than what the world or even their religion accepted. Why the command to love enemies? Because that will mark Jesus' followers as different, with hearts and minds turned over to God alone, who can help them do just that. Anybody can love those who love them—that comes naturally, even for **corrupt tax collectors**. In

the same way, **"If you are kind only to your friends, how are you different from anyone else? Even pagans do that."** Those disciples who live for Christ and are radically different from the world will receive their reward.

5:48 "But you are to be perfect, even as your Father in heaven is perfect." The word translated **perfect** can also be translated "mature" or "full-grown." Jesus' followers can be perfect if their behavior is appropriate for their maturity level— perfect yet with much room to grow. The perfection Jesus required of his followers did not include strict and flawless obedience to minute laws. It called, instead, for an understanding of how the law pointed to the heavenly Father who is himself perfect. Those who loved God and desired to follow him would keep his law as he required. They did this, not because they were already perfect, but because they were striving to be perfect, to reflect their Father's character.

MATTHEW 6

JESUS TEACHES ABOUT GIVING TO THE NEEDY / 6:1-4 / 58
It's easier to do what is right when we gain recognition and praise. To be sure our motives are not selfish, we should do our good deeds quietly or in secret, with no thought of reward. Jesus says we should check our motives in generosity, prayer, and fasting. Check the motives behind your next good deed by asking, "Would I still do this if no one would ever know that I did it?"

6:1 "Don't do your good deeds publicly, to be admired." At first reading, these words seem to contradict what Jesus had just told his disciples in 5:14-16, "Let your good deeds shine out for all to see." In 5:16, however, Jesus gave his disciples the correct motive for their deeds: that people might praise God. Jesus warned that doing **good deeds just to be admired** means that **you will lose the reward from your Father in heaven.** God rewards good deeds done for his glory alone.

6:2 "When you give a gift to someone in need, don't shout about it as the hypocrites do." The first "good deed" Jesus used as an example was giving to the needy. The Jewish law commanded giving to those in need (Deuteronomy 15:10-11). Jesus expected his followers to do likewise, follow-

ing God's law. However, Jesus' followers were to have a different motive for their giving than did the **hypocrites**. "Hypocrite" was the Greek word for "actor," one who wore a mask and pretended to be someone he or she wasn't. The term, as used here, describes people who do good deeds for appearance only, to be praised by others—not out of compassion or other good motives. (Many of the religious leaders did just this; later Jesus calls the Pharisees hypocrites, see 23:13-29.) The phrase **blowing trumpets in the synagogues and streets** probably is not literal, but it pictures people calling attention to themselves. These empty acts and whatever human praise is received are **all the reward they will ever get**. God will reward those who are sincere in their faith and whose motive in all their good deeds is to glorify him.

6:3-4 The phrase **"don't tell your left hand what your right hand is doing"** teaches that motives for giving to God and to others must be pure. The hyperbole emphasizes the total lack of ostentation. No one should call attention to the act. It is easy to give with mixed motives, to do something for someone if it will benefit us in return.

Jesus advised, however, that giving must be done **in secret**. Jesus' words do not forbid record keeping, receipting, or reporting procedures used in good stewardship. But he condemned practices to impress others. Those who give in secret will receive a **reward** from the **Father**, a reward of greater value because it will be perfect and eternal.

JESUS TEACHES ABOUT PRAYER / 6:5-15 / 59

A second act of piety Jesus addressed was prayer. Some people, especially the religious leaders, wanted others to think they were very holy—and public prayer was one way to get attention. There is a place for public prayer, but to pray only where others will notice you indicates that your real intention is to please people, not God.

6:5 These praying **hypocrites** had motives other than piously observing the exact daily prayer times. When they prayed **publicly on street corners and in the synagogues where everyone** could see them, they were not praying at all. Jesus taught that we find the essence of prayer not in public but in private communication with God. For these hypocrites, people's praise **is all the reward they will ever get.**

6:6 The prayer life of Jesus' followers would be radically different from that of the hypocritical religious leaders. Jesus did not condemn public prayer. Jesus' point, however, was that people who prayed more in public than in private should consider their motives. If they really wanted to fellowship with God, Jesus suggested this: **"When you pray, go away by yourself, shut the door behind you, and pray to your Father secretly."** Private prayer enables believers to pour out their hearts to God, express their true feelings, and listen in the quietness for God's answer.

6:7-8 While Jesus encouraged persistent prayer (Luke 18:1-8) and soon would give a pattern for prayer (see 6:9-13), he condemned the shallow repetition of words by those who did not have a personal relationship with the Father. Jesus told his followers, **"Don't babble on and on as people of other religions do."** The believers did not pray to idols of wood or stone; they prayed to the one living and true God. God doesn't need our prayers; but he wants our prayers and knows that we need them. Prayer develops the trust that says, "Father, you know best."

6:9 Jesus said, **"Pray like this."** His pattern was: praise God (6:9), intercede for his work in the world (6:10), ask for provision of individual daily needs (6:11), and request help in daily struggles (6:12-13). This pattern helps believers understand

the nature and purpose of their personal prayers in their relationship with their Father.

The phrase **Our Father in heaven** indicates that God is majestic and holy; he transcends everything on earth. But he is also personal and loving. The first line of this model prayer is a statement of praise and a commitment to honor God's holy **name**. Christians, who bear the holy name of Christ, must be responsible to honor him in every aspect of their lives. When we pray for God's name to be **honored**, we pray that this world will honor his name, and we look forward to Christ's return when that will be a reality.

6:10 The desire that God's **Kingdom come soon** refers to God's spiritual reign, not Israel's freedom from Rome. God announced his Kingdom in the covenant with Abraham (8:11; Luke 13:28), and pious Jews were still waiting for it. Jesus' followers recognize that the Kingdom began with his coming to earth. Matthew's readers understood the Kingdom to be present in believers' hearts as Christ reigned there (Luke 17:21). To look forward to God's coming Kingdom is to pray that more and more people will enter it. This prayer also reaffirms belief that one day all evil will be destroyed, that God will establish the new heaven and earth, and that his glory will be known to all the nations (Psalm 110:1; Revelation 21:1).

Praying **may your will be done** does not imply resignation to fate; rather, it is a prayer that God's perfect purpose will be accomplished in this world (**on earth**) as it already is **in heaven.**

6:11 Verses 11 and 12 are requests for personal needs. We must trust God daily to provide what he knows we need. The word **today** suggests that we should not worry about what God already knows we need (6:8). Believers must trust God for provision and not worry. That God gives daily **food** does not negate people's responsibility to work. Instead, it acknowledges that God is Sustainer and Provider.

6:12 "Forgive us our sins, just as we have forgiven those who have sinned against us." A believer who understands the greatness of the forgiveness that he or she has received can willingly extend such forgiveness to others for their wrongs. The flip side of this thought reveals the selfishness of a person who seeks God's forgiveness yet willfully refuses to forgive others. Jesus expands on this in 6:14-15.

6:13 The Greek word translated **temptation** does not mean "enticement to do evil" but "testing." Sometimes God allows his people to be "tested" by temptation. But this testing is never without a purpose: God is always working to refine his people, teach them to depend on him, and strengthen their character to be more like him. How he does this differs in every person's life. The prayer, then, is that we not **yield to temptation.**

Jesus wanted his followers to place their trust in God during trying times and to pray for deliverance **from the evil one** and his deceit. All Christians struggle with temptation. Believers who pray these words realize their sinful nature and their need to depend on God in the face of temptation.

6:14-15 Jesus gave a startling warning about forgiveness: **"If you refuse to forgive others, your Father will not forgive your sins"** (see also 6:12). Living in relationship with God requires constant repentance of the sins that plague us. Because believers must come to God constantly for confession and forgiveness, refusing to forgive others reveals a lack of appreciation for the mercy received from God. All people are on common ground as sinners in need of God's forgiveness. If we don't forgive others, we are in fact denying and rejecting God's forgiveness of us (see Ephesians 4:32; Colossians 3:13). Later, Jesus told a parable depicting such a situation (18:23-35).

JESUS TEACHES ABOUT FASTING / 6:16-18 / 60
Jesus addresses the third act of piety—fasting. People fast (go without food) so that they can spend more time in prayer. This act is both noble and difficult. The purpose of fasting is to provide time for prayer, to teach self-discipline, to remind God's people that they can live with a lot less, and to help them appreciate what God has given.

6:16 Fasting was mandatory for the Jewish people once a year, on the Day of Atonement (Leviticus 23:32); however, people could **fast** individually or in groups while praying for certain requests (see, for example, Esther 4:16). Fasting could have great spiritual value, but some **hypocrites,** such as the Pharisees, had turned it into a way to gain public approval. During a fast, they made themselves **look pale and disheveled so people** would **admire them.** The Pharisees negated the purpose of their fasting by making sure others knew that

they were fasting. Public recognition would be their **only reward.**

6:17-18 When you fast, Jesus said, go about your normal daily routine; don't make a show of it. Then **no one** but God **will suspect you are fasting.** Jesus commended acts of self-sacrifice done quietly and sincerely. He wanted people to adopt spiritual disciplines for the right reasons, not from a selfish desire for praise. As with the other disciplines, the **reward** would come from God, not from people.

JESUS TEACHES ABOUT MONEY / 6:19-24 / 61
Jesus had been teaching about how his followers should live differently from those in the current religious establishment. The section about money focuses on true discipleship and how wealth is often the most common distraction from such discipleship. Our attitude toward money is often the pulse of the heart of our discipleship.

6:19 Jesus' followers do not concern themselves with amassing possessions and wealth; they refuse to **store up treasures here on earth.**

Those treasures by their very nature cannot be secure, and death would cause a person to lose them.

6:20-21 How does a person **store** his **treasures in heaven?** Storing treasures in heaven includes, but is not limited to, tithing our money. It is also accomplished through bringing others to Christ and all acts of obedience to God. That "treasure" is the eternal value of whatever we accomplish on earth. Acts of obedience to God, laid up in heaven, are not susceptible to decay, destruction, or theft. Nothing can affect or change them; they are eternal.

The final sentence points out the significance of Jesus' words: **"Wherever your treasure is, there your heart and thoughts will also be."** Wherever our focus lies, whatever occupies our thoughts and our time—that is our "treasure." Jesus contrasted heavenly values with earthly values when he explained that our first loyalty should be to those things that do not fade, cannot be stolen or used up, and never wear out. He calls for a decision that allows us to live contentedly with whatever we have because we have chosen what is eternal and lasting.

6:22-23 Jesus described the "spiritual vision" his disciples should have, requiring us to see clearly what God wants us to do and to see the world from his point of view. **Your eye is a lamp for your body** means that through the eyes the body receives light, allowing it to move. In the Old Testament, the "eye" denoted the direction of a person's life. **A pure eye** focuses on God and **lets sunshine into** a person's **soul,** so that he can serve God wholeheartedly. **An evil eye** represents materialism, greed, and covetousness. Such a person may think he has light; in reality, he **shuts out the light** and is in spiritual **darkness.** This could mean a sort of "double vision"—trying to focus on God and earthly possessions. It will lead to gloom in life and darkness in eternity. **How deep that darkness will be** for those who see the light but are not focused on God. In these words, Jesus was calling his followers to undivided loyalty—eyes fixed and focused on him.

6:24 Continuing the theme of his disciples having undivided loyalty, Jesus explained that **no one can serve two masters.** All human beings face the inescapable choice about whom they will serve. They can choose to serve themselves—to pursue **money** and selfish pleasures—or they can choose to serve **God.** Either we store our treasures with God (6:20-21), we focus our "eyes" on him (6:22-23), and we serve him alone—or else we do not serve him at all.

JESUS TEACHES ABOUT WORRY / 6:25-34 / 62

Jesus continued to highlight Kingdom priorities–the attitude toward life that his disciples should exemplify. They need not be overly concerned about food or clothing because they know that God will care for them. Worrying about food and clothing should never take priority over serving God. When we worry over lack of food or inadequate clothing, we immobilize ourselves and focus on the worry.

6:25 The command **don't worry about everyday life** does not imply complete lack of concern, nor does it call people to be unwilling to work and supply their own needs. **Food, drink, and clothes** are less important than the life and body that they supply. Because God sustains our lives and gives us our bodies, we can trust him to provide the food and clothing he knows we need. Worry immobilizes us, but trust in God moves us to action. We work for our money to supply food and clothing, but we must always remember that these ultimately come from God's hands. When the need arises, we need not worry, for we know that our God will supply.

6:26 The **birds** need food, and the heavenly Father knows it. They are dependent upon God's daily provision because they cannot **plant or harvest or put food in barns.** They work—they hunt for it and then bring it back to their families—but they don't worry. If God cares for the birds, making sure that the natural order of his creation supplies food for them, how much more will he care for a hungry human being? People are **far more valuable to him than** the birds. Jesus was teaching total dependence upon God as opposed to humanity's self-sufficiency. All that we have ultimately comes from God's hand. Jesus was not prohibiting his followers from sowing, reaping, and gathering food (that is, working for it); but he was prohibiting worrying about having enough food.

6:27 Many of us would do well to ask ourselves this question every morning: **"Can all your worries add a single moment to your life?"** Daily we face new challenges, concerns, problems, and choices. Will we worry, or will we pray? Will worrying be of any help whatsoever? Worry may damage our health, cause the object of our worry to consume our thoughts, disrupt our productivity, negatively affect the way we treat others, and reduce our ability to trust in God. Worry may, in reality, take time away from our span of life rather than adding to it. It accomplishes nothing.

6:28-30 Sitting on the grassy hillside, Jesus may have gestured to the **lilies**, probably referring generally to the bountiful flowers in Israel, and pointed out that those lovely flowers don't have to **work or make their clothing**. As in 6:26, Jesus was not condoning laziness while waiting for God to supply. Instead, he wanted his disciples to place their lives and needs in God's hands, refusing to worry over basic needs. To **worry about your clothes** shows little faith in God's ability to supply. God "clothes" the flowers and grass of the field that are **here today and gone tomorrow.** If his creation clothes the earth with beauty and color so rich that even King **Solomon in all his glory** could not match it, then he will **surely care for you.**

6:31-32 Because God provides food and clothing not only for birds and flowers but even more for his precious human creation, **don't worry.** Do not spend energy fretting over **having enough food or drink or clothing.** Worry has no place in the lives of Jesus' disciples because their **heavenly Father already knows all** their **needs.**

6:33 Jesus' followers must settle the question of priorities and **make the Kingdom of God** their **primary concern.** To do that, we must consistently honor and represent the Kingdom. Then the way we deal with family, friends, work, leisure, etc., will all be transformed. What is most important to you? People, objects, goals, money, pleasure, and other desires all compete for priority. Any of these can quickly bump God out of first place if you don't actively choose to give him first place in every area of life. Strangely enough, when you get your priorities right, Jesus promised that God **will give you all you need from day to day if you live for him.** When Jesus' followers seek his Kingdom first, God takes care of their needs.

6:34 Because God cares for his people's needs, Jesus says, **"Don't worry about tomorrow."** In an appeal to common sense, Jesus explained that what we worry about happening tomorrow may not happen, so we will have wasted time and energy worrying. We need to reserve that energy because **today's trouble is enough for today.** We only add to today's burdens when we worry about the future. All the anxieties about tomorrow will not change the outcome, for **tomorrow will bring its own worries.** The burdens of today are enough, so let God take care of them. We must trust God for today without worrying about tomorrow.

MATTHEW 7

JESUS TEACHES ABOUT JUDGING OTHERS / 7:1-6 / 63

Jesus' words about judging may be the most-often-misquoted text from the Bible. People frequently apply it as if it were a flat command against all moral judgment. In fact, people use it to judge what they consider a judgmental attitude on the part of another. Jesus, however, gave these words as one negative application of the Golden Rule. That is, we should not treat others as we do not want to be treated. We should seek to measure ourselves and others by the same standards.

7:1-2 The command **"Stop judging others"** does not refer to judging in a court of law, nor is it a blanket statement against critical thinking. Believers should be discerning and make certain judgments. For example, Jesus said to expose false teachers (7:15-23) and to admonish others in order to help them (18:15). Paul taught that we should exercise church discipline (1 Corinthians 5:1-5). But followers of Christ should not be

critical or condemning in their attitudes toward others. A judgmental, critical spirit differs radically from love. Believers' special position with Christ does not give them license to take God's place as judge. Those who judge in that manner will find themselves **judged** likewise by God. As God will have mercy on the merciful (5:7) and forgive those who forgive (6:14-15), he will condemn those who condemn: **"Whatever measure you use in judging** others, it will be used to measure how you are judged." Jesus said it was unacceptable to excuse personal sin while holding others accountable for similar behavior. When you perceive a fault in others, your first impulse may be to confront or reject that person. But ask yourself first if your awareness of the failure mirrors your own life. Your effort to help will be in vain if the person can point out the same fault in you. Practice your own remedy before you ask them to do it.

7:3-5 The word **speck** is also translated "splinter"; **log** is also translated "plank" or "beam." Many have taken this metaphor to mean that Christians should never correct anyone—one's personal sins before God are too great to even consider dealing with others' sins. However, Jesus' point was that while we all have sin in our lives (some as small as a speck; some as large as a log), we are responsible to both deal with our own sin and then help others. Jesus revealed incredible understanding of human nature. How easy it is for us to overlook our own sins yet easily spot sin in others. How

true that the sin we most clearly see in others is also present in us. Believers should first deal with their own sins, but they also must correct and guide erring brothers and sisters (see Galatians 6:1; James 5:19-20).

7:6 While believers were not to judge others (7:1-5), Jesus warned against a complete lack of discernment about people's attitudes toward the gospel—**what is holy.** These **unholy people** are those who, when presented with the gospel, treat it with scorn and contempt. The futility of teaching the gospel to people who do not want to listen is as futile as giving **pearls to swine.** Such people will only tear apart what we say. Pigs do not realize the value of pearls; all they know is that they cannot eat them, so they spit them out and then **trample** them into the mud. Contemptuous, evil people cannot grasp the value of the gospel, so they scornfully cast it away. We should not stop giving God's word to unbelievers, but we should be wise and discerning so as not to bring scorn to God's message.

JESUS TEACHES ABOUT ASKING, LOOKING, KNOCKING / 7:7-12 / 64

Beginning in chapter 5, the Sermon on the Mount has thus far explained to Jesus' followers the lifestyle and life attitudes that he expected from them. Some may have heard and thought the demands to be impossible. Here Jesus gave the answer to those thoughts and questions—ask, look, knock. The ability to live for God is only a prayer away.

7:7-8 Jesus' followers can **keep on asking, keep on looking,** and **keep on knocking,** indicating the importance of persistent, consistent prayer in their lives. Only through prayer can believers stay in contact with God, know what he wants them to do, and then have the strength to do God's will in all areas of life. God will answer believers who persistently ask, look, and knock. Believers, however, must not take Jesus' words as a blank check; prayer is not a magical way to obtain whatever we want. Jesus had already explained some conditions on this promise: His followers were to show mercy and forgiveness to others (5:7; 6:12), avoid praying in order to get attention (6:5-6), and be willing to persevere in prayer. Our requests must be in harmony with God's will ("your will be done," 6:10), accepting his will above our desires.

7:9-11 If **sinful people** would not think of giving a child a **stone** that looked like a **loaf of bread** or a dangerous **snake** instead of a **fish,** then **how much more** will a holy God acknowledge and answer our requests? In these words, Jesus

revealed the heart of God the Father. God is not selfish, begrudging, or stingy; his followers don't have to beg or grovel when they come with their requests. He is a loving Father who understands, cares, comforts, and willingly gives **good gifts to those who ask him.** If humans can be kind, imagine how kind God can be.

7:12 This is commonly known as the Golden Rule: **Do for others what you would like them to do for you.** Many religions teach a negative version of this statement. Confucius said, "What you do not want done to yourself, do not do to others." By stating this positively, Jesus made the statement even more significant. It may be easy to refrain from harming others, but it is much more difficult to take the initiative in doing something good for them. This is the key to the radical discipleship that Jesus wants. The Golden Rule is the foundation of active goodness and mercy—the kind of love God shows to us every day. This rule sums up **all that is taught in the law and the prophets.** When we follow the Golden Rule, we keep the rest of God's commands.

JESUS TEACHES ABOUT THE WAY TO HEAVEN / 7:13-14 / 65

In the closing verses of the Sermon on the Mount, four different contrasts represent four warnings that focus on future final judgment. Jesus was speaking about the Kingdom of Heaven and describing clearly that some will enter it and some will not. The basis for a person's final destination begins with that person's decisions about Jesus himself.

7:13-14 People are presented with two ways, represented by two gates—one gate is narrow, the other is wide. Jesus commanded his followers to **enter God's Kingdom only through the narrow gate. This gateway is small, and the road is narrow,** but it alone leads **to life**—eternal life. Through the wide gate, however, **the highway to hell is broad** and it is **the easy way.** There is plenty of room for **many** people to wander in and continue in whatever direction they wish. This road leads to hell.

The gateway leading to life is small not because it is difficult to become a Christian but because there is only one way and **only a few** decide to walk that road. Believing in Jesus is the only way to eternal life because he alone died for our sins and made us right before God.

JESUS TEACHES ABOUT FRUIT IN PEOPLE'S LIVES / 7:15-20 / 66

Jesus warned against false teachers. Many powerful speakers claim to have important ideas for Christians to hear. There are literally hundreds of cults vying to recruit new members. Add to the list those who present special angles on church doctrine coming from big and small denominations—there's a dazzling array of choices. Jesus wanted his followers to be able to separate the good (teaching that leads to Christ), the bad (off-center but benign ideas tacked on to the gospel), and the ugly (false teaching).

7:15 The Old Testament frequently mentions **false prophets** (see 2 Kings 3:13; Isaiah 44:25; Jeremiah 23:16; Ezekiel 13:2-3; Micah 3:5; Zechariah 13:2). False prophets claimed to receive messages from God, but they prophesied only what the king and the people wanted to hear. False teachers are just as common today. Jesus says to **beware of** those whose words sound religious but who are motivated by money, fame, or power. These false prophets will come in among the believers like **wolves** who are **disguised as harmless sheep.** Jesus warned his followers that false prophets would come (see also 24:11; Mark 13:22-23). Very shortly, these words began to come true. False teachers infiltrated the early churches just as the gospel message was spreading (see Acts 20:29; 2 Corinthians 11:11-15; 2 Timothy 2:14-19; 2 Peter 2:1-3, 17-22; 1 John 2:18, 22; 4:1-6). While Jesus did not elaborate on the form of their false teaching, it follows from the context that they would teach a way of salvation that did not include a narrow gate and a hard road (7:13-14). Indeed, many of the false teachers about whom Peter, John, and Paul later warned were teaching such a message. Jesus' followers would need the ability to discern true sheep from wolves in sheep's clothing. How could they do this? Jesus explained how in the following verses.

7:16-18 Fruit is a metaphor for both character and conduct. Jesus' followers would be able to **detect** false prophets **by the way they act.** In the Old Testament there were tests for a true prophet. The law found in Deuteronomy 13:1-5 required a prophet to be put to death if he promoted rebellion against God. Deuteronomy 18:14-22 taught the Jews to reject a prophet who contradicted previous revelations from God or whose message failed to come true. The evil character and conduct of these false teachers would reveal that they were no more than wolves in sheep's clothing. No matter what a person claims to be, his or her true character will eventually reveal itself. Fruit is **good** or **bad** depending on the health of the tree. **Healthy** trees bear good fruit, and **unhealthy** trees bear bad fruit. Jesus' followers would be able to discern false teachers because in their teaching they minimize Christ and glorify themselves. False prophets would not speak the truth; God's true prophets would not speak falsely. Jesus warned that prophets and teachers are like trees: Examine them and their "fruit" closely.

7:19 A person's mere profession of faith will be meaningless at the final judgment. Any who claim Christ's name but do **not produce good fruit** will be like worthless trees to be **chopped down and**

thrown into the fire. In fact, some will have professed faith, only to face judgment in the end (as explained in the following verses, 7:21-23).

7:20 Repeating from 7:16 the method of discerning false prophets, Jesus explained that **the way to identify a tree or a person is by the kind of fruit that is produced.** Good teachers consistently exhibit good behavior and high moral character as they attempt to live out the truths of Scripture. This does not mean we should throw out Sunday school teachers, pastors, and others who are less than perfect. Every one of us is subject to sin, and we must show the same mercy to others that we need for ourselves. When Jesus spoke about bad trees, he meant teachers who deliberately teach false doctrine. We must examine the teachers' motives, the direction they are taking, and the results they are seeking. Those who should not be teaching will be recognizable by their fruit.

JESUS TEACHES ABOUT BUILDING ON A SOLID FOUNDATION / 7:21-29 / 67

Jesus is more concerned about our "walk" than our "talk." He wants his followers to do right, not just say the right words. Your house (which represents your life) will withstand the storms of life only if you do what is right instead of just talking about it.

7:21 Jesus called himself **Lord** and referred to God as **my Father in heaven,** thereby thinly veiling his claim to be the Messiah. Jesus revealed his part in the coming final judgment in these words. Because people's "fruit" reveals who they really are (7:20), then it follows that simply calling Jesus "Lord" is not enough: **Not all people who sound religious are really godly.** It is much easier to *profess* Christianity than to *possess* it. Those who will **enter the Kingdom of Heaven** are only those who **obey.**

7:22-23 On judgment day only a person's relationship with Christ—acceptance of him as Savior and obedience to him—will matter. That day will be the final day of reckoning when God will settle all accounts, judging sin and rewarding faith. Notice that Jesus placed himself as judge—**many will tell me.**

Jesus exposed those people who sounded religious and did religious deeds but had no personal relationship with him. False prophets will be able to prophesy (referring not just to telling the future, but to teaching), cast out demons, and perform miracles. Claims to great power, invoking the name of Christ, and powerful deeds will be no guarantee for heaven. Jesus will send away those who do not know him personally. They may have done impressive deeds, but Jesus will say, **"I never knew you. Go away."** In other words, "I never had a personal relationship with you, and I never went with you to do these deeds you claim. You can have no part in my Kingdom."

7:24-25 Jesus' true followers not only hear his words, but act on them, allowing his message to make a difference in their lives. In this teaching, Jesus explained that a true follower, by acting on his words, is **like a person who builds a house on solid rock.** The one who builds "on rock" is a hearing, responding disciple, not a phony, superficial one. Practicing obedience builds on the solid foundation of Jesus' words to weather the storms of life: through **rain, floodwaters,** and **winds** their foundations on solid rock will be unaffected.

7:26-27 In contrast to the wise person (7:24), the **foolish** person **hears** Jesus' **teaching and ignores it.** While both people build houses, and while those houses may even look identical, only one house will stand the test. Only the person who hears and does God's word will receive God's reward. The house built **on sand** will collapse. When the storms came, the person turned away, life crumbled, and the end was **a mighty crash**—final judgment, destruction (7:13-14), and separation from God (7:22-23). As character is revealed by fruit (7:20), so faith is revealed by storms. The wise person, seeking to act upon God's word, builds to withstand anything. It will be the foundation, not the house, that will determine what happens on the day of judgment.

7:28-29 The words **after Jesus finished speaking** signal the end of Jesus' teaching on discipleship and a return to the narrative in Matthew. Jesus had completely **amazed** the **crowds** by his **teaching.** He was **unlike the teachers of religious law,** for they often quoted from well-known rabbis in order to give their words more authority. But Jesus didn't have that need. Because Jesus was the Son of God, he knew exactly what the Scriptures said and meant. He was the ultimate **authority.** He didn't need to quote anyone because he was the original Word (John 1:1). The people had never heard such teaching.

MATTHEW 8

JESUS HEALS A MAN WITH LEPROSY / 8:1-4 / 38

Matthew arranged the following accounts topically, not chronologically. Mark and Luke recorded some of the following events, but placed them in different locations, probably in the chronological sequence of events. The following section features a series of miracles that demonstrated the power of the Kingdom in action. This first miracle involved a man who had been estranged from the Jews because of a dreaded disease.

8:1 Whenever we see Jesus, we usually see **large crowds** following him. The people were astonished at Jesus' authority in his teaching (7:28-29), so they followed him to see and hear more.

8:2 Leprosy, like AIDS today, was a terrifying disease because there was no known cure. In Jesus' day, the Greek word for "leprosy" was used for a variety of similar skin diseases, and some forms were contagious. If a person contracted the contagious type, a priest declared him a leper and banished him from his home and city. This also excluded him from participating in any social or religious activities (according to the law in Leviticus 13–14). The leper went to live in a community with other lepers until he either got better or died. This was the only way the people knew to contain the spread of the contagious forms of leprosy.

This man took a great risk when he **approached Jesus.** His kneeling reveals his desperation, humility, and recognition of Jesus' authority. His words to Jesus reveal his faith. If his disease were to disappear, a priest could declare him well, but only Jesus could **make him well.** The words **"if you want to"** reveal the man's faith in Jesus' authority in this matter of healing; Jesus' ability was never in question. This man wanted to be clean—a huge request. The man wanted to become a person again, to be reunited with his family and community. He knew Jesus could do it.

8:3 Matthew revealed Jesus' heart of compassion. All people shunned lepers, but Jesus **touched** this man covered with a dreaded, contagious disease. That Jesus' touch precedes his pronouncement of healing indicates his sovereignty

over the Jewish law not to touch a leper (Leviticus 5:3; 13:1-46; Numbers 5:2). In touching the leper, Jesus became "unclean." He did not worry about becoming ritually unclean when there was a genuine need.

When Jesus answered the man, **"I want to,"** he showed his willingness and ability to meet this social outcast's most basic need. With the words **"Be healed"** the **leprosy** immediately disappeared. The words and the touch were simple but effective, thereby revealing Jesus' divine authority over sickness.

8:4 The law required a **priest** to **examine** a healed leper (Leviticus 14). Then the healed leper was to give an **offering** at the Temple. Jesus adhered to these laws by sending the man to the priest, thereby demonstrating high regard for **the law of Moses.** Jesus also told him, **"Don't talk to anyone along the way."** The warning was an earnest and forceful admonition. Jesus' mission was to preach the Good News of the Kingdom of God, and he did not want the crowds descending on him to see miracles or to benefit from his power. Such people would not be receptive to hear and to respond to the gospel.

Some think that the word **anyone** refers to the priests. Jesus would show the religious authorities that he was not anti-law, but the only one who could truly fulfill the law. If the priest declared that the healing had taken place but refused to accept the person and power of Christ who had done it, that priest would be condemned by the evidence. However, Jesus may have intended the testimony to be a positive one to the people who witnessed the healing. Mark records that the man disobeyed Jesus' warning (see Mark 1:45).

A ROMAN OFFICER DEMONSTRATES FAITH / 8:5-13 / 68

This event is also recorded in Luke 7:1-10. This miracle occurred to a person who, because of his race and occupation, was not close to the Jewish faith. In this story and the previous one (the healed leper), Jesus willingly dealt with people the Jews shunned.

8:5-6 Capernaum, located on the northwestern shore of the Sea of Galilee, was the largest of the many fishing towns surrounding the lake. Jesus had recently moved to Capernaum from Nazareth (4:12-13). Capernaum was a thriving town with great wealth as well as great sin and decadence. Near a major trade route, it housed a contingent of Roman soldiers. The city was filled with heathen influences from all over the Roman Empire. This was a needy place for Jesus to challenge both Jews and non-Jews with the gospel of God's Kingdom.

This **Roman officer** (also called a centurion) had control over one hundred soldiers. The Jews hated Roman soldiers for their oppression, control, and ridicule; the Jews considered them "unclean" because they were despised Gentiles. This Roman officer was apparently different from many other soldiers who despised the Jews. He may have been a "God-fearer" who worshiped the God of Israel but was not circumcised (see Acts 2:5; 10:2). He had apparently heard about Jesus' healing powers. He may have known about the healing of the Roman official's son (which probably occurred earlier, see John 4:46-54). While this soldier's concern about a **servant** may seem unusual, the Jewish historian Josephus wrote that Roman soldiers had many servants who actually trained and fought with them. So this servant may have been his personal attendant with whom he felt a close bond. This officer made an appeal on behalf of his servant who had become **paralyzed and racked with pain,** and was near death (Luke 7:2). The centurion, a military authority, addressed Jesus as **Lord,** showing respect for Jesus' authority in this area of healing (see also 8:2).

8:7 Jesus said, "I will come and heal him." Jews generally did not enter Gentile homes because it made them ceremonially "unclean." However, as Jesus had willingly touched a leper (which was against the law) to heal him, so Jesus would willingly enter a Gentile home if needed. For Jesus, doing good always transcended both Levitical regulations and Sabbath tradition.

8:8-9 The officer protested that he was **not worthy to have** Jesus come to his **home.** Luke 7:7 seems to show that he was thinking more of his own moral unworthiness. He saw that Jesus' authority was greater than his own and that Jesus need not personally visit his home. The officer understood that Jesus only needed to **say the word** to heal his servant. He understood the power of Jesus' words.

The officer carried a certain amount of **authority** and so was accustomed to being obeyed. He may have applied his understanding of military orders to Jesus—realizing that Jesus' power and authority came from God. When Jesus spoke, God spoke. Whatever he understood, the officer had absolutely no doubt that Jesus could merely speak the word and heal the servant.

8:10 This man's genuine faith **amazed** Jesus. He said to those gathered around him (the disciples, as well as other onlookers and followers) that he had not found **faith** such as that **in all the land of Israel.** In other words, this Gentile's faith put to shame the stagnant piety that had blinded many of the Jewish religious leaders. Without the benefit of growing up to memorize the Old Testament Scriptures and to learn from esteemed Jewish leaders, this Gentile had understood the need to depend totally on Jesus' power. He knew, without a doubt, that Jesus could do what seemed impossible. Such faith both astonished and pleased Jesus.

8:11-12 Most Jews looked forward to the day when the Jews that had been scattered all over the world would return to Jerusalem to enjoy the company of the Messiah and the patriarchs in a great banquet (Psalm 107:3; Isaiah 25:6; 43:5-6). It was predicted that some **Gentiles** would also return to witness this great event and to partake of it vicariously (Isaiah 2:2-3). But Jesus speaks of the Gentiles coming **from all over the world** to **sit down** at this **feast** with the patriarchs. A Jew who would sit at a table with a Gentile would become defiled; yet Jesus pictured **Abraham, Isaac, and Jacob** sitting down with Gentiles at this banquet of celebration in **the Kingdom of Heaven.** In addition, Jesus explained that while many Jews believed that their lineage in the Jewish race assured their reservations at the banquet, this simply was not the case (see also John the Baptist's words in 3:7-10). In fact, some Jews, instead of having assured seats at the banquet, would find themselves **cast into outer darkness.** The "darkness" is a place **where there will be weeping and gnashing of teeth**—a common biblical description of hell.

The Gospel of Matthew emphasizes this universal theme—Jesus' message is for everyone. The Old Testament prophets knew this (see Isaiah 56:3, 6-8; 66:12, 19; Malachi 1:11), but many New Testament Jewish leaders chose to ignore it. Each individual has to choose to accept or reject the gospel, and no one can become part of God's Kingdom on the basis of heritage or connections. Having a Christian family is a wonderful blessing, but it won't guarantee our eternal life. Each person must decide to believe in and follow Christ.

8:13 Jesus then told the **officer** to return home; Jesus would grant his request. When Jesus spoke the word, **the young servant was healed that same hour,** meaning immediately.

JESUS HEALS PETER'S MOTHER-IN-LAW AND MANY OTHERS / 8:14-17 / 35

Jesus' compassion reached out to a third category of people viewed as "second-class citizens"—women.

8:14-15 Peter's mother-in-law was in bed with a high fever. A malaria-type fever was common to this region because of marshes near the mouth of the Jordan River. We don't know for sure what this fever signified, but the Greek word for "fever" in the noun form is also the word for "fire"; thus, she was burning with a severe fever. Jesus went to the mother-in-law's bedside and **touched her hand.** For a rabbi to touch a woman who was not his spouse was against Pharisaic regulations; for him to touch a person with a fever was prohibited by Jewish law. Jesus did both in order to heal a sick person, as well as to show his authority. Jesus' touch on the woman's hand brought complete healing. In fact, **she got up and prepared a meal for him.** Matthew recorded this detail to show that her healing was instant and complete. She didn't need time to recuperate from her illness; she was immediately well enough to serve her guests.

8:16 The people came to Jesus on Saturday **evening** after sunset. According to Mark 1:21 and Luke 4:31, the day had been the Sabbath, the Jews' day of worship and rest, lasting from sunset Friday to sunset Saturday. Jewish law prohibited traveling and carrying burdens on the Sabbath, so they waited until evening, after the sun went down. When the Sabbath ended, the people searched for Jesus. A steady stream of sick and demon-possessed people were being carried to Jesus and he healed them all.

8:17 Matthew pointed to Jesus' fulfillment of prophecy, quoting from **Isaiah** 53:4. Jesus has authority over all evil powers and all earthly disease. He also has power and authority to conquer sin. Sickness is not always the punishment for sin. Rather, sickness can best be seen as a real and constant possibility of life in a fallen world. Physical healing in a fallen world is always temporary. In the future, when God removes all sin, there will be no more sickness and death. Jesus' healing miracles were a taste of what all believers will one day experience in God's Kingdom.

JESUS TEACHES ABOUT THE COST OF FOLLOWING HIM / 8:18-22 / 122

This crossing of the lake didn't actually occur after the events just recounted; the storm occurred after the second period in Capernaum according to Mark 4:35-41. The testing of the followers is recorded in Luke 9:57-62 as being after Peter's confession. Matthew grouped the events thematically to show Jesus' impact on people.

Following Jesus is not always easy or comfortable. Often it involves great cost and sacrifice, with no earthly rewards or security. Jesus did not have a place to call home. You may find that following Christ costs you popularity, friendships, leisure time, or treasured habits. While the cost of following Christ is high, the value of being Christ's disciple is even higher.

8:18 Jesus healed many people in Capernaum, and his ministry attracted a lot of attention. Crowds continued to gather around him, but Jesus had ministry to do in other places as well. So **he instructed his disciples to cross to the other side of the lake,** to the eastern shore.

8:19-20 This teacher of religious law addressed Jesus as **teacher** (or "rabbi") and explained that he wanted to **follow** Jesus wherever he went. A rabbi's disciples "followed" him by observing the rabbi in his daily tasks, as well as sitting under and living by his teachings.

Jesus' words to the scribe about having **no home** were more like a challenge than a rebuke or invitation. Jesus focused on the requirements of true discipleship. He wanted true followers who understood the cost of following him. To be Jesus' disciple, a person must willingly put aside worldly security. In the context of Jesus' present ministry, to follow him meant to be constantly on the move, bringing his message to people in many places.

Here, for the first time, Matthew recorded Jesus calling himself **Son of Man**. This was an Old Testament name for the Messiah and was Jesus' favorite designation for himself. The expression occurs eighty-one times in the Gospels, always said by Jesus (twice others said it, but they were quoting Jesus). Calling himself the Son of Man, Jesus was pointing to himself as the Messiah (see Daniel 7:13).

8:21-22 The teacher wanted to follow Jesus, but Jesus reminded him of the cost of discipleship (8:19-20) and tested his level of commitment. This man apparently wanted to follow Jesus, but he wanted to first return home to **bury** his father. In ancient cultures, this was a sacred responsibility. It is possible that this disciple was not asking permission to go to his father's funeral, but rather to put off following Jesus until after his father had died. Perhaps he was the firstborn son and wanted to be sure to claim his inheritance. Perhaps he did not want to face his father's wrath if he left the family business to follow an itinerant preacher. Whether his concern was fulfilling a duty, financial security, family approval, or something else, he did not want to commit himself to Jesus just yet. Jesus sensed this reluctance and challenged him to consider that his commitment had to be without reservation. Jesus was not advising that children disregard family responsibilities. Rather, Jesus was responding to this disciple's qualifying use of **first**. Jesus must always come "first," *then* all other human loyalties.

Jesus' response is part of the radical discipleship theme: **Let those who are spiritually dead care for their own dead.** In other words, let those who have not responded to the call to commitment stay home and handle responsibilities such as burying the dead. While to us this may sound heartless, it was not without precedent. A high priest and those who had taken the Nazirite vow were required by the law to avoid the corpse of even a parent (Leviticus 21:11; Numbers 6:6). A later Jewish precedent says that a student of the Torah should not stop his study to bury the dead. Jesus placed commitment to God even above these precedents. His direct challenge forces us to ask ourselves about our priorities in following him. We must not put off the decision to follow Jesus, even though other loyalties compete for our attention.

JESUS CALMS THE STORM / 8:23-27 / 87
This miracle shows Jesus' power over the natural world.

8:23-25 Jesus and the disciples **got into the boat** to cross to the other side of the Sea of Galilee, as had been planned (8:18). This boat probably was a fishing boat because many of Jesus' disciples were fishermen. Josephus, an ancient historian, wrote that there were usually more than three hundred fishing boats on the Sea of Galilee at one time. This boat was large enough to hold Jesus and his twelve disciples. Mark explained that it was evening when they finally set sail (Mark 4:35), which was not unusual because Peter was used to fishing at night (see John 21:3) when fishing was best.

The Sea of Galilee is an unusual body of water. It is relatively small (13 miles long, 7 miles wide), but it is 150 feet deep, and the shoreline is 680 feet below sea level. Storms can appear suddenly over the surrounding mountains, stirring the water into violent twenty-foot waves. Even though several of these men were expert fishermen and knew how to handle a boat, they had been caught without warning in this **terrible storm.**

While the **waves** swept over the boat, **Jesus was sleeping.** That Jesus could sleep during this storm indicates his complete exhaustion; it also depicts the realness of his human nature. The disciples **woke him up, shouting, "Lord, save us! We're going to drown!"**

8:26 Abruptly awakened from a deep sleep, Jesus arose and rebuked his frightened disciples. The disciples had seen Jesus do wonderful miracles, but they had not taken their knowledge of his power and applied it to every situation. So he asked them, **"Why are you afraid? You have so little faith!"** They wanted him to do something; he wanted them to trust him! Standing in the stern of the rocking ship, Jesus **stood up and rebuked the wind and waves, and suddenly all was calm.** The power of the Teacher to speak and control the waves shocked the disciples. The storm was out of control, their fears were out of control, but Jesus was never out of control.

8:27 The disciples still did not completely understand, as their question betrayed: **"Who is this?"** they asked. They should have known because this miracle clearly displayed Jesus' divine identity.

JESUS SENDS DEMONS INTO A HERD OF PIGS / 8:28-34 / 88

Matthew recorded the following miracle to show Jesus' power over the supernatural realm. This also shows the ultimate goal of Satan and his demons—utter destruction.

8:28 The **land of the Gadarenes** is located southeast of the Sea of Galilee, near the town of Gadara, one of the most important cities of the region. Gadara was a member of the Decapolis, or Ten Cities, which had independent governments and were largely inhabited by Gentiles. This was Gentile territory, revealing a new direction for Jesus' ministry.

As they landed, **two men who were possessed by demons** met them. They were bloody, out of control, and apparently strong and frightening (Mark 5:4-5). Demon-possessed people are controlled by one or more demons. Demons are fallen angels who joined Satan in his rebellion against God and are now evil spirits under Satan's control. They help Satan tempt people to sin and have great destructive powers. These men were clearly hopeless without Christ. Although we cannot be sure why demon possession occurs, we know that evil spirits can use the human body to distort and destroy a person's relationship with God. Demons had entered these men's bodies and were controlling them.

8:29 Though aware of who Jesus was and of his power over them, the demons still attempted to defend themselves by **screaming** and by calling Jesus by his divine name. The loud voice shows the demons' fierce and violent nature. The demons wanted Jesus to leave them alone, saying that Jesus had **no right to torture** them. The word for "torture" is graphic and correct. The Bible says that at the end of the world, the Devil and his demons will be thrown into the lake of fire (Revelation 20:10). The demons' question revealed that they knew their ultimate fate. The demons hoped that Jesus would not send them to their fate **before God's appointed time.**

8:30-31 The demons wanted a "home" and wanted to possess a living being. On the hillside were enough physical animal hosts for all these demons to inhabit. **Pigs** were unclean animals, so they provided a fitting habitation for the demons. So the demons asked to be sent into the herd. Why didn't Jesus just destroy these demons—or send them away? Because the time for such work had not yet come. Jesus healed many people of the destructive effects of demon possession, but he did not yet destroy demons. In this situation, Jesus wanted to show Satan's destructive power and intent. Many ask the same question today—why doesn't Jesus stop all the evil in the world? His time for that has not yet come. But it will come. The book of Revelation portrays the future victory of Jesus over Satan, his demons, and all evil.

8:32 In every case when confronted by Jesus, demons lost their power. Jesus' simple command, **"Go!"** showed the extent of his authority over the demons. He did not need to perform a lengthy exorcism. God limits what evil spirits can do; these demons could do nothing without Jesus' permission.

When the demons entered the pigs, **the whole herd plunged down the steep hillside into the lake and drowned in the water.** Jesus granted the demons' request to enter the pigs and destroy the herd, but he stopped their destructive work in people, particularly the men they had possessed. Jesus also taught a lesson by giving the demons permission to enter the pigs. He showed his disciples, the townspeople, and even us who read these words today the absolute goal of Satan and his demons. They want total and complete destruction of their hosts.

8:33-34 When Jesus performed this miracle, he again gained immediate publicity. **The herdsmen,** astonished and upset at what had happened, **fled** and told the amazing story. **The entire town came out to meet Jesus.** Among these would have been the owner of the herd who, doubtless, was not pleased at the loss of the livestock.

The people could have responded in several

ways. They could have been overjoyed to see Jesus on their own shore. They also could have responded with joy that Jesus had healed the demon-possessed men. They could have been thrilled to have seen a healing of such magnitude with their own eyes. Instead, **they begged him**

to go away and leave them alone. Unfortunately for them, Jesus did as they asked. And there is no biblical record that he ever returned. Sometimes the worst that can happen to us is for Jesus to answer one of our poorly considered requests.

MATTHEW 9

JESUS HEALS A PARALYZED MAN / 9:1-8 / *39*

The events in 8:28-34 had occurred on the other side of the Sea of Galilee (Jesus and the disciples had gotten there by boat, 8:18, 23). The events Matthew placed at the end of chapter 8 and the beginning of chapter 9 are not in chronological sequence (see the Harmony of the Gospels, pages 1275–1281).

9:1 Jesus climbed into a boat and went back across the lake to Capernaum. This city became Jesus' base of operations while he was in Galilee (see 8:5-6).

9:2 Some people, remembering that Jesus had healed many people in Capernaum on an earlier visit (8:14-17), **brought** a friend who needed Jesus' help. The friend was **paralyzed** and lying **on a mat, a stretcher that the men could carry. Jesus saw their faith** acted out in their determination. They knew that if they could just get near Jesus, Jesus could heal. Jesus said to the paralyzed man, **"Take heart, son! Your sins are forgiven."** Several verses in the Old Testament indicate that sickness and death result from humanity's sinful condition (see, for example, Psalms 41:3-4; 103:2-3; and James 5:13-18 for the New Testament parallel). So God works forgiveness and healing together. That does not mean that we can measure a person's spiritual health by looking at his or her physical health. But all sickness and death are the result of evil and sin. This man was paralyzed because of sin (in the world and in every human heart)—that was the root cause. Jesus spoke first to that condition. The man needed spiritual healing, so Jesus forgave his sins. Then Jesus healed the man.

9:3 These **teachers of religious law** were the legal specialists in Jesus' day. Jesus' teaching and popularity had prompted a special investigation by the powerful leaders of the Jewish faith. Jealous of Jesus' popularity and power, these men hoped to find something to criticize or even condemn in

Jesus' teaching. When they heard Jesus tell the paralyzed man that his sins were forgiven, they were shocked. Because only God can forgive sins, Jesus was claiming to be God. In Jewish law, this was **blasphemy,** which was punishable by death (Leviticus 24:16). In labeling Jesus' claim to forgive sins as blasphemous, the religious leaders showed that they did not understand that Jesus *was* God. Jesus had God's power and authority to heal bodies and forgive sins. Forgiveness of sins was a sign that the messianic age had come (Isaiah 40:2; Joel 2:32; Micah 7:18-19; Zechariah 13:1). Unfortunately, it did not occur to these Jewish leaders that perhaps this man was their Messiah.

9:4 When Jesus became human, he restrained the full use of his powers, yet he could still see each person's thoughts, intents, and motives. Jesus **knew** what these teachers **were thinking.** They could not hide their hostility at Jesus' words. Their thoughts of Jesus as a blasphemer were **evil.**

9:5 It would take someone of great power and authority to forgive sins. Yet making a statement concerning forgiveness of sins could be said without having to be verified. Healing the paralyzed man would be open to immediate public verification. Jesus was offering to do an **easier** task (healing the man) as public evidence that the more difficult, "secret" task (forgiving his sins) was also accomplished. Jesus wanted to show that he had the power to forgive sins by showing that he had the power to make a paralytic **get up and walk.**

9:6-7 Jesus' authority extended from spiritual healing to physical healing. The physical healings revealed this to the world. One who could heal a paralytic could also forgive sins. Jesus spoke to the doubtful Jewish teachers, **"I will prove that I, the Son of Man, have the authority on earth to forgive sins."** Jesus spoke with commanding authority, showing that he expected immediate obedience. He told the paralyzed man to **stand up, take his mat, and go on home.** The man did as Jesus said. The healing unmistakably revealed Jesus' power and authority. The teachers who questioned Jesus' ability to forgive sins (9:3) saw the formerly paralyzed man get up and walk. Jesus'

question in 9:5 forced their answer: Jesus had the power to make the paralyzed man walk; thus, he also had the authority to forgive his sins.

9:8 Jesus did this miracle in front of **the crowd** that had gathered in this home to hear Jesus speak (Mark 2:2). Their **fear** was appropriate in the presence of one who displayed **such great authority** (that is, authority to forgive sins). What was the result of this fear? The people **praised God.** While the religious leaders had previously called Jesus a blasphemer, the people recognized God's power and realized that Jesus had authority from God.

JESUS EATS WITH SINNERS AT MATTHEW'S HOUSE / 9:9-13 / 40

Matthew's radical obedience would cause a great change in his life. He was probably very wealthy—tax collecting was a lucrative occupation—so when Matthew walked away from his booth, he snubbed Rome and a lifetime of potentially great wealth. Several of the other disciples could always return to fishing, but Matthew could never turn back.

9:9 **Matthew** (the author of this Gospel) was a Jew who worked for the Romans (specifically for Herod Antipas) as the area's tax collector. (In Mark and Luke, he is called "Levi." Most people in this day had two or three names: a Jewish name, a Roman name, and possibly a Greek name. Levi was his Jewish name, Matthew his Roman name.) He collected custom duties from the citizens, as well as from merchants passing through town. (Capernaum was a customs post on the caravan route between Damascus to the northeast and the Mediterranean Sea to the west.) Tax collectors took a commission on the taxes they collected, so most of them overcharged and kept the profits. Thus, most Jews hated tax collectors because of their reputation for cheating, their support of Rome, and their constant contact with "unclean" Gentiles. A Jew who accepted such an office shamed his family and friends and was excommunicated from the synagogue.

The **tax-collection booth** was an elevated platform or bench. Everyone knew who Matthew was, and anyone passing through the city who had to pay taxes could find him easily. One day Jesus walked right up to Matthew's booth and said, **"Come, be my disciple."** That Jesus called such a notorious person into his circle of disciples certainly must have shocked the other disciples, as well as the trailing crowd. Matthew recognized that Jesus was not inviting him; Jesus was calling him. So **Matthew got up and followed him.**

9:10 **Matthew** called his friends together to meet Jesus too, inviting him to a **dinner** along with his

fellow tax collectors and **other notorious sinners.** At Matthew's house there gathered a crowd that Jesus could not reach in the synagogues. The tax collectors had been excommunicated. The term "sinners" referred not only to immoral and pagan people, but also to the common people who were not learned in the law and did not abide by the rigid standards of the Pharisees.

9:11 According to the **Pharisees**, contact with these **scum** made a Jew unclean; to sit and **eat** with such people was particularly heinous. The Pharisees would have nothing to do with such people. But not so with Jesus, who stooped to the level of the poor, unlearned, common people—even sinners! Thus, the Pharisees pulled his disciples aside and asked why Jesus did this. They fashioned their question as an accusation.

9:12-13 The Pharisees' question apparently made its way to Jesus' ears. The first part of Jesus' answer was from a common proverb. **Healthy people don't need a doctor;** the doctor's waiting room is filled with **sick people.** Jesus then told these self-righteous Pharisees to **go and learn,** implying that they did not understand their own Scriptures. The Pharisees thought they knew Scripture perfectly; Jesus told them to go back and study again the words of God spoken through the prophet Hosea, **"I want you to be merciful; I don't want your sacrifices"** (Hosea 6:6). God did not want the Israelites' rituals; he wanted their hearts. Jesus challenged the Pharisees to apply Hosea's words to themselves. God wants a heart attitude that includes a right relationship with him and with others, an attitude that reaches out to those in physical and spiritual need.

Jesus did not come to call **those who think they are already good enough** (like these Phari-sees), for the self-righteous do not recognize their sinfulness. But these **sinners** saw their need. Jesus, the Great Physician, healed people of physical ill-nesses, but he knew that all people are spiritually sick and in need of salvation.

RELIGIOUS LEADERS ASK JESUS ABOUT FASTING / 9:14-17 / 41

The Pharisees questioned Jesus about those with whom he had fellowship at meals. They also questioned why Jesus and his disciples feasted instead of fasting on the customary days. Jesus showed the need for joy because the Messiah had come.

9:14 The disciples of John the Baptist were a group that lasted into the second century (see Acts 19:1-9). These men and **the Pharisees** were fast-ing—going without food in order to spend time in prayer. The Old Testament Law set aside only one day a year as a required day of fasting for all Jews (Leviticus 16:29). The Pharisees, however, fasted on Mondays and Thursdays (see Luke 18:12) as an act of piety, and most likely they promoted this among the people.

The tense of the verb *fast* indicates that the feast at Matthew's house happened at the very time that these people were fasting, apparently on one of the weekly fasting days. John's disciples fasted as a sign of mourning for sin and to prepare themselves for the Messiah's coming. John the Baptist was in prison, and these disciples found themselves siding with the Pharisees on this issue. But they were fast-ing when they should have been feasting with Jesus.

9:15 While Jesus walked the earth, his presence was a cause for celebration—the Messiah had come! Jesus' presence was as joyous as the presence of the **groom** at a wedding feast. The picture of Jesus as a "groom" comes from the Old Testament description of the wedding feast that God will prepare for himself and his people (Isaiah 54:5-6; Hosea 2:16-20). **Wedding guests** do not mourn or fast; a wedding is a time of celebration and feast-ing. Likewise, Jesus' coming was a sign of celebra-tion. Jesus did not condemn fasting—he himself fasted (Luke 4:2). He emphasized that fasting must be done at the right time for the right reasons.

Jesus knew, however, that soon he would be **taken from them.** The Greek word translated "taken from" is in Isaiah 53:8, a verse prophesying the Messiah's violent death. The disciples would grieve for their crucified Master, and the world (the mass of people opposed to Jesus) would rejoice. But the disciples' grief would not last long; their sorrow would turn to joy when they saw their risen Lord.

9:16 Jesus' arrival on earth ushered in a new cove-nant between God and people. The new covenant called for a new way of expressing personal faith. The newness of the gospel could not be combined with the legalism of the Pharisees any more than a piece of **unshrunk cloth** should be used as a **patch** on **an old garment.** When the garment is washed, the patch will shrink, pull away from the old gar-ment, and leave a **bigger hole than before.** The par-ables of the cloth and the wineskins (9:17) apply to more than just fasting or to the Pharisees. They speak of Jesus' entire mission and the new era he inaugurated by his entrance into human history.

9:17 In Bible times, people stored wine in goat-skins sewn around the edges to form watertight bags (called **wineskins**). New wine expanded as it fermented, stretching its wineskin. After this wine had aged, old and brittle wineskins would burst if fresh wine was poured into them. **New wine,** therefore, would always be put into **new wineskins.** The new wine was the newness of the gospel as exemplified in the person of Jesus Christ (John 2:1-11). Like old wineskins, the Pharisees and indeed the entire religious system of Judaism had become too rigid to accept Jesus. They could not contain him or his message in their traditions or rules. Their understanding of faithfulness to the law had become unsuitable for the fresh, dynamic power of Christ's message. They were the self-appointed guardians of the "old garment" and the "old wineskins."

Jesus did not come to abolish or annul the Law and the Prophets but to fulfill them (5:17). But this fulfillment required new approaches and new structures. Jesus' words, **"That way both the wine and the wineskins are preserved,"** reveal that the new wine needed to be preserved in new forms. The new way of obedience to the law would be found in the authoritative teaching of Jesus. His purpose was to bring in something new, though God's prophets had told about it centuries before. This new message said that God's Son would come to earth to offer all people forgiveness of sins and reconciliation.

JESUS HEALS A BLEEDING WOMAN AND RESTORES A GIRL TO LIFE / 9:18-26 / 89

In this new Kingdom, joy predominates (9:15) and love in action takes the place of rigid law-keeping. Matthew followed the previous account of Jesus' response to the questioning Pharisees and disciples of John the Baptist with the account of Jesus reaching out to two more unclean people—a woman with a bleeding disorder and a dead child—healing one and raising the other to life.

9:18-19 Jesus was interrupted at his meal by a man who came with a need. Mark and Luke say this man's name was Jairus (Mark 5:22; Luke 8:41). He was **the leader of a synagogue,** the local center of worship. The synagogue leaders were responsible for supervising worship services, caring for the scrolls, running the daily school, keeping the congregation faithful to the law, distributing alms, administering the care of the building, and finding rabbis to teach on the Sabbath. The leader of the local synagogue exerted great influence in his community, yet Jairus **knelt** before Jesus, indicating homage and courtesy as he came with his urgent request. Matthew abbreviated this story by quoting the father as saying, "My daughter has just died."

9:20-21 In the crowd pressing on Jesus was another desperate person in need of divine help. A woman **had had a hemorrhage for twelve years.** This bleeding was painful and may have been a menstrual or uterine disorder. She had been to many doctors, had spent all her money, but had received no cure (Mark 5:26). The bleeding caused the woman to be in a constant condition of ceremonial uncleanness (see Leviticus 15:25-33). She could not worship in the synagogue and she could not have normal social relationships, for under Jewish law, anyone who touched her also became unclean. Thus, the woman had been treated almost as severely as a leper.

She worked her way through the crowd and **came up behind** Jesus. She believed that she only had to **touch his robe** (the **fringe**) and she would **be healed.** She may have feared that Jesus would not touch her if he knew her condition, that Jesus would not risk becoming unclean in order to heal her. Or she may have feared that if her condition became known to the crowd, the people who had touched her would be angry at having become unclean unknowingly. The woman knew she could receive healing, but she tried to do it as unobtrusively as possible.

9:22 Jesus healed the woman—her faith appropriated the healing, and Jesus perceived what had happened. He **turned** and spoke words of comfort to the woman, **"Your faith has made you well."** Jesus explained that it was not his clothing that had healed her; rather, her faith in reaching out to the one person who could heal her had allowed that healing to take place. Not only did she have faith, but she had also placed her faith in the right person. **At that moment,** she was delivered from her bleeding and her pain.

9:23-24 At Jairus's home, **the noisy crowds** and **funeral music** were part of the customary ritual of mourning. Jesus, however, spoke words of encouragement: **"The girl isn't dead; she's only asleep."** The girl was indeed dead, and everyone from the family to the mourners knew it. Jesus knew it too, but his words tested the faith of the crowd and revealed to Jairus the hope beyond all hope of what Jesus was about to do.

9:25-26 Jesus took the child's father and mother and the three disciples who had come and **went in** where the child was. Jesus did no incantations and spoke no magic words, as other healers of the day normally did. He simply went to the girl's bedside and **took** her **by the hand.** The fact that Jesus touched the girl's hand would have amazed the synagogue leader and the disciples. Touching a dead body meant to become unclean. Touching the dead girl confirmed once again that to Jesus, compassion was more important than the letter of the law. Jesus took the girl's hand in his, he issued a command (Mark 5:41), and the dead child **stood up.** Jesus had authority and power over humanity's greatest enemy—death. Mark explained that Jesus had commanded the parents not to advertise the miracle (Mark 5:43). However, despite Jesus' command to the contrary, **report of this miracle swept through the entire countryside.**

JESUS HEALS THE BLIND AND MUTE / 9:27-34 / 90

Matthew showed how Jesus was maligned by those who should have received him most gladly. While the Pharisees questioned, debated, and dissected Jesus, people were being healed and lives changed right in front of them. Their skepticism was based on jealousy of Jesus' popularity. The opposition to Jesus was intensifying; Jesus was far too powerful and popular for the Pharisees' comfort.

9:27 Two blind men cried out for **mercy**, which meant they wanted Jesus to help them. Isaiah had prophesied that a day would come when God would open the eyes of the blind (Isaiah 29:18; 35:5-6; 42:7). These men called Jesus **Son of David,** a popular way of addressing Jesus as the Messiah. It was known that the Messiah would be a descendant of David (Isaiah 9:7). This is the first time this title is used in Matthew.

9:28 Jesus didn't respond immediately to the blind men's pleas, but they persisted, following Jesus **right into the house** where he was staying. The focus of this story is the power of faith. Jesus asked these blind men first if they had faith (**Do you believe?**). These men answered Jesus' question about their belief, saying, **"Yes, Lord."** The use of the word "Lord" reveals their faith in Jesus' power and authority to heal them.

9:29-31 Because these men believed, Jesus **touched their eyes** and **suddenly they could see.** The words **because of your faith** do not mean "in proportion to," but "in response to." This healing was a powerful example that Jesus was the Messiah. Healing of the blind had never occurred in the Old Testament or in Judaism before Jesus.

Jesus told the men not to **tell anyone** because he was concerned for his ministry. Jesus did not want to be known as just a miracle worker; he wanted people to listen to his words that would heal their broken spiritual lives. Jesus' mission was to preach the Good News of the Kingdom of God. If crowds descended on him to see amazing healings and dead people raised, they would not be coming with the heart attitude needed to hear and respond to the gospel. Obviously the blind men would not be

able to hide their healing for long. What, exactly, did Jesus expect? Jesus simply wanted these men to keep the details to themselves and think about them. He wanted them to worship quietly and treasure in their hearts what Jesus had done. He wanted them to focus on the spiritual aspect. Above all, he did not want more advertisement of his healing power. But the men could not contain themselves; they told everyone in that area what Jesus had done.

9:32 Jesus could hardly come or go without someone in need coming to him! This time, as Jesus and his disciples were leaving, **a man who couldn't speak because he was possessed by a demon** was brought to Jesus. Such disabilities are not always the work of demons, because Jesus healed many people of illness and disability without casting out demons. Matthew wanted his readers to understand, however, that in this situation a demon was at work. While Jesus was on earth, demonic forces seemed especially active. Although we cannot always be sure why or how demon possession occurs, it causes both physical and mental problems. In this case, the demon made the man unable to talk.

9:33-34 After Jesus **cast out the demon,** the mute man was able to speak. Once again, the ever-present **crowds marveled.** They had never seen anything like this. The **Pharisees,** however, saw something entirely different: **"He can cast out demons because he is empowered by the prince of demons."** This chapter has the Pharisees accusing Jesus of four different sins: blasphemy, befriending outcasts, impiety, and serving Satan. They tried to explain Jesus away by saying that he was only imitating God but was really in league with Satan— and that's why the demons obeyed him.

JESUS URGES THE DISCIPLES TO PRAY FOR WORKERS / 9:35-38 / 92

From 9:35 through 10:42, Matthew recorded a second discourse of Jesus, focusing on mission. (The first discourse was the Sermon on the Mount, recorded in chapters 5–7.) Jesus continued to share the Good News of the Kingdom to all who would listen, and he exemplified the task and pattern his disciples would follow after his return to heaven.

9:35 Jesus **traveled through all the cities and villages of that area.** The **Good News about the Kingdom** was that the promised and long-awaited Messiah had finally come. His healing miracles were a sign that his teaching was true.

9:36 Wherever Jesus went, **crowds** gathered, and Jesus **felt great pity for** them. The word "pity" describes the deep mercy of God. The prophet Ezekiel compared Israel to **sheep without a shepherd** (Ezekiel 34:5-6; see also Numbers 27:17; 1 Kings 22:17); Jesus saw that the people **didn't**

know where to go for help. These words stress people's helplessness without God. Jesus came to be the Shepherd, the one who could show people how to avoid life's pitfalls (see John 10:14; 1 Peter 2:25).

9:37-38 Jesus looked at the crowds following him and referred to them as a field ripe for **harvest,** but **the workers** to bring in the harvest **are so few.** These "workers" were the disciples, then few in number. Jesus commanded his disciples to **pray to the Lord who is in charge of the harvest; ask**

him to send out more workers for his fields. These workers must warn people of coming judgment and call them to repentance. Many people are ready to give their lives to Christ if someone would show them how. We are to pray that people will respond to this need for workers. Often, when we pray for something, God answers our prayers by using *us.* Be prepared for God to use you to show another person the way to him. Chapter 10 will describe this mission and what it will involve in more detail.

MATTHEW 10

JESUS SENDS OUT THE TWELVE DISCIPLES / 10:1-16 / 93

This chapter continues Jesus' second discourse recorded by Matthew. This second discourse began at 9:35 and ends at 10:42. Matthew 10:1-16, closely parallel to Mark 3:13-19 and 6:7-13, describes Jesus' appointment of the Twelve for their first apostolic mission. Though this was the first time they went out on their own, they had been given authority from Jesus to carry on the work of preaching and healing.

10:1 Jesus had many **disciples** (learners), but he appointed **twelve** to whom he gave authority and special training. These men were his inner circle and received the most intense training. We see the impact of these men throughout the rest of the New Testament. They started the Christian church. The Gospels call these men the "disciples" or the "Twelve"; the book of Acts calls them "apostles."

The choice of twelve men is highly symbolic. The number twelve corresponds to the twelve tribes of Israel (19:28), showing the continuity between the old religious system and the new one based on Jesus' message. These men were the righteous remnant (the faithful believers throughout the Old Testament who never abandoned God or his law) who would carry on the work the twelve tribes were chosen to do—to build the community of God. The number was so important that when Judas Iscariot killed himself, the disciples chose another man to replace him (see Acts 1:15-26).

This records the first time Jesus sent these disciples out on their own. These twelve men had Jesus' **authority** over the forces of evil. Jesus empowered his disciples **to cast out evil spirits.** Jesus also gave these disciples power **to heal every kind of disease and illness.** It was important that they have these powers because Jesus was extending his mission

through them. Jesus directly confronted demons and sicknesses. The disciples carried on Jesus' purpose and his power.

10:2-4 In verse 1, these men are called "disciples"; here, the word **apostles** is used to stress their role as messengers, "sent-ones."

The first name recorded was **Simon** to whom Jesus had given the name **Peter** (see John 1:42). Peter had been a fisherman (4:18). He became one of three in Jesus' core group among the disciples. He also confessed that Jesus was the Messiah (16:16). Although, later, Peter would deny ever knowing Jesus, Peter eventually would become a leader in the Jerusalem church, write two letters that appear in the Bible (1 and 2 Peter), and be crucified for his faith.

Andrew was Peter's brother and also a fisherman (4:18). Andrew had been a disciple of John the Baptist and had accepted John the Baptist's testimony that Jesus was "the Lamb of God." He had left John to follow Jesus. Andrew and John were Jesus' first disciples (John 1:35-40); Andrew then had brought Peter to Jesus (John 1:41-42).

James and John had also been fishermen (4:21).

James would become the first apostle to be martyred (Acts 12:2). John would write the Gospel of John, the letters of 1, 2, and 3 John, and the book of Revelation. The brothers may have been related to Jesus (distant cousins); at one point, their mother requested special places for them in Christ's Kingdom (20:20-28).

Philip was the fourth to meet Jesus (John 1:43). Philip then brought **Bartholomew** (John 1:45). Philip probably knew Andrew and Peter because they were from the same town, Bethsaida (John 1:44). Scholars think that Bartholomew is the same person as Nathanael. Bartholomew was an honest man (John 1:47).

We often remember **Thomas** as "Doubting Thomas" because he doubted Jesus' resurrection (John 20:24-25). But he also loved the Lord and was a man of great courage (John 11:16). When Thomas saw and touched the living Christ, doubting Thomas became believing Thomas.

Matthew, author of this Gospel, described himself by his former profession, probably to show the change that Jesus had made in his life. Also known as Levi, he had been a **tax collector** (9:9). Thus, he had been a despised outcast, but he had abandoned that corrupt (though lucrative) way of life to follow Jesus.

James is designated as **son of Alphaeus** to differentiate him from the James in 10:2.

Thaddaeus is also called "Judas son of James" (see Luke 6:16; Acts 1:13).

Simon was probably not a member of the party of Zealots, for that political party did not appear until A.D. 68. Most likely the word *zealot* indicates zeal for God's honor and not extreme nationalism; it was an affectionate nickname.

Judas Iscariot. The name "Iscariot" is probably a compound word meaning "the man from Kerioth." Thus, Judas's hometown was Kerioth in southern Judea (see Joshua 15:25), making him the only one of the Twelve who was not from Galilee. It was Judas, son of Simon Iscariot (John 6:71), **who later betrayed** Jesus to his enemies and then committed suicide (27:3-5; Luke 22:47-48).

10:5-6 Jesus gave specific **instructions,** however, regarding the focus of their ministry: **"Don't go to the Gentiles or the Samaritans."** A "Gentile" was anyone who was not a Jew. The "Samaritans" were a race that resulted from intermarriage between Jews and Gentiles after the Old Testament captivities (see 2 Kings 17:24). This did not mean that Jesus opposed evangelizing Gentiles and Samaritans; in fact, Matthew had already described Jesus'

positive encounter with Gentiles (8:28-34), and John 4 recounts his conversation with a Samaritan woman. Jesus' command to go **only to the people of Israel** means that the disciples should spend their time among the Jews (see also 15:24). These words restricted the disciples' "short-term" mission. Jesus came not to the Jews only, but to the Jews "first" (Romans 1:16). God chose them to tell the rest of the world about him. Later, these disciples would receive the commission to "go and make disciples of all the nations" (28:19). Jewish disciples and apostles preached the gospel of the risen Christ all around the Roman Empire, and soon Gentiles were pouring into the church. The Bible clearly teaches that God's message of salvation is for all people, regardless of race, sex, or national origin (Genesis 12:3; Isaiah 25:6; 56:3-7; Malachi 1:11; Acts 10:34-35; Romans 3:29-30; Galatians 3:28).

10:7-8 Jesus sent his disciples out to **announce** that **the Kingdom of Heaven was near.** Jesus was talking about a spiritual kingdom. The Kingdom is still "near." Jesus, the Messiah, has already begun his Kingdom on earth in the hearts of his followers. One day the Kingdom will be fully realized.

The disciples were also to use the authority and power Jesus had given them (10:1). He gave the disciples a principle to guide their actions as they ministered to others: **Give as freely as you have received.** The disciples had received salvation and the Kingdom without cost; they should give their time under the same principle. Because God has showered us with his blessings, we should give generously to others of our time, love, and possessions.

10:9-10 These instructions seem, at first, to be contrary to normal travel plans, but they simply reveal the urgency of the task and its temporary nature. Jesus sent the disciples in pairs (Mark 6:7), expecting them to return with a full report. This was a training mission; they were to leave immediately and travel light, taking along only minimal supplies. They were to depend on God and on the people to whom they ministered (10:11). The disciples were to leave at once, without extensive preparation, trusting in God's care rather than in their own resources. Jesus said **those who work deserve to be fed,** meaning that those who minister are to receive care from those to whom they minister (see Luke 10:17; 1 Timothy 5:18). Jesus' instructions pertained only to this particular mission. Different times and situations would call for different measures, but Christian workers still can reveal the simplicity of Christ when they carry out ministry without excessive worldly entanglements.

10:11 Each pair of disciples would **enter a city or village** and **stay** in a **worthy** person's house (that is, the home of a believer who had invited them to lodge there during their ministry). The command to stay there until they left the city cautioned them never to offend their hosts by looking for "better" lodging in a home that was more comfortable or socially prominent. To remain in one home would not be a burden for the home owner because the disciples' stay in each community would be brief. The "worthy" were those who would respond to and believe the gospel message.

10:12-13 As the disciples entered **someone's home**, they were to give it a **blessing**. At this time, people believed that blessings could be given as well as taken back. **If it turns out to be a worthy home** (that is, had accepted them and their message), then the blessing of peace would **stand.** But if the household did not accept their message, then the disciples would **take back the blessing.** The peace returning from that house also indicated judgment to come (10:15). Those who would receive the disciples also would receive the Messiah. Those who cared for God's emissaries would receive blessing in return (10:40).

10:14 The disciples should also expect rejection, such as Jesus had faced in Decapolis (8:34). So Jesus further instructed that **if a village** did not **welcome** them (that is, take them in and offer hospitality) and refused even to **listen to** them, then they should **shake off the dust of that place from** their feet as they left.

Shaking off dust that accumulated on one's sandals showed extreme contempt for an area and its people, as well as the determination not

to have any further involvement with them. To shake the dust off one's feet was a gesture of total repudiation. Shaking off the dust of a place, Jesus said, would be a testimony against the people. Its implications were clear and had eternal consequences. Jesus was making it clear that the listeners were responsible for what they did with the gospel. As long as the disciples had faithfully and carefully presented the message, they were not to blame if the townspeople rejected it. Likewise, we are not responsible when others reject Christ's message of salvation, but we do have the responsibility to share the gospel clearly and faithfully.

10:15 God had destroyed **the wicked cities of Sodom and Gomorrah** by fire from heaven because of their wickedness (Genesis 19:24-25). To Jews, the judgment of these cities was a lesson not only in punishment of great evil, but also in the finality of divine judgment. Those who reject the gospel will be worse off **on the judgment day** than the wicked people of these destroyed cities who never had heard the gospel at all.

10:16 The disciples would go out with the message **as sheep among wolves** (the "wolves" were the enemies of the believers—in this context probably the Jewish religious leaders). The solution? **Be as wary as snakes and harmless as doves.** These words may have come from a local proverb. To be "wary as snakes" speaks of prudence or cleverness. To be "harmless as doves" is to be sincere and to have pure intentions. Jesus' followers would need both to be prepared for the battles that lay ahead. They would need to be unafraid of conflict but also able to deal with it in integrity.

JESUS PREPARES THE DISCIPLES FOR PERSECUTION / 10:17-42 / 94
The new movement of Christianity would eventually face great opposition—from Jews and Gentiles alike. While it may not have seemed possible as these disciples roamed the hillsides with this popular teacher, a day would come when some would have to choose between their faith and persecution (or death). Jesus warned that they would need to focus on their mission and turn their defense into a testimony for their faith.

10:17-18 The danger of arrest and persecution would come from without (**governors, kings**) and from within (**courts, synagogues**). These persecutions would provide **opportunity** for **witness to the world.** Later, the disciples experienced these hardships (Acts 5:40; 12:1-3; 22:19; 2 Corinthians 11:24).

10:19-20 Jesus told the disciples that **when** (not "if") they were **arrested**, they should not worry

about what to say in their defense. **You will be given the right words at the right time**—God's Spirit would speak through them. The phrase **Spirit of your Father** is Old Testament language and recalls the inspiration of the prophets. Jesus described the Holy Spirit as a defense lawyer coming to the disciples' aid. This promise of an infilling of the Holy Spirit was fulfilled in Acts 2, where the Spirit empowered the disciples to speak. Some mistakenly think this means believers do not have to prepare to present the gospel because God will take care of everything. Scripture teaches, however, that we are to make carefully prepared, thoughtful statements (Colossians 4:6). Jesus was telling his followers to prepare but not to worry. He promised special inspiration for times of great need.

10:21-22 Jesus detailed some aspects of the coming persecution. The Jews considered family denunciations and betrayals a sign of the end times. These words may allude to Micah 7:6. This passage speaks of internal corruption in Israel; Jesus said this was a sign of the last days. Not only will faith in Jesus tear families apart, but believers will also find that **everyone will hate** them. As Jesus' disciples share his authority, they will also share his sufferings. **Those who endure to the end** (meaning wholly, completely) will enter into Christ's Kingdom. Standing firm to the end is not a way to **be saved** but the evidence that a person is really committed to Jesus. Persistence is not a means to earn salvation; it is the by-product of a truly devoted life.

10:23 While Jesus told the disciples to expect persecution, he also warned them against foolhardiness. If they faced persecution in one town, they were to **flee to the next.** They ought not cast their pearls before swine (7:6), nor should they abort their ministry in fear. They were to leave and move on if the persecution became too great. Perhaps this is part of being "wary as snakes" (10:16).

"**I assure you that I, the Son of Man, will return before you have reached all the towns of Israel.**" This difficult sentence has received many interpretations. Following are five:

1. Some have understood this to focus on the immediate context of verses 5-16. The disciples would not have time to go through all the towns before Jesus would catch up with them. This interpretation is too simple, however, given the language in the text that refers to events after the resurrection of Christ. At the time of Matthew's writing, the disciples had completed the mission, so Jesus obviously was referring to something else.
2. Some suggest that the coming of the Son of Man refers to his coming judgment against the Jews, fulfilled in the destruction of Jerusalem in A.D. 70. But it is an unlikely interpretation to connect the destruction of Jerusalem with the return of the Son of Man.
3. Albert Schweitzer made this the key to his interpretation of Jesus' understanding of his ministry. Schweitzer explained that Jesus expected the end of time to happen before the

disciples finished this mission. When it did not happen, said Schweitzer, Jesus switched to a more active role and tried to force it to come through his crucifixion. This view misinterprets Jesus' words to apply only to the immediate context (as does number 1 above).
4. Still others explain that the "coming" refers to Jesus' appearance in triumph after his resurrection.
5. Because of the events of the book of Acts, it seems more likely that Jesus was referring to events after his resurrection. The meaning of his words would be that the task of the mission to the Jews would be so great and so difficult (for many would refuse to believe) that it would not be accomplished even by the time of his second coming.

10:24-25 Jesus used a common proverb stated two ways. A **student** or **servant** is not **greater than** the **teacher** or **master.** In Judaism, a student (disciple) shared the daily experiences of his teacher; in pagan cultures, a servant fought beside his master. Both receive the same treatment. The Pharisees had **called** Jesus **the prince of demons** when they accused Jesus of using Beelzebub's power to drive out demons (see 12:24). If Jesus, who is perfect, was called evil, **how much more will it happen to** Jesus' followers.

10:26 Jesus' followers can expect persecution, but they must never be **afraid.** The gospel mission must be accomplished. The truths entrusted to the disciples will be known no matter what the opposition.

10:27 The **darkness** is not a picture of sin but of privacy. What Jesus had told them privately they were to proclaim publicly. These phrases describe bold, public proclamation of the truths that Jesus had taught the disciples privately. The disciples had a mission and a responsibility to teach what they learned from Jesus.

10:28 People might be able to **kill the body,** but they would not be able to **touch the soul.** The only one worthy of our fear is God, **who can destroy both soul and body in hell.** The worst that people can do (kill the body) does not compare with the worst that God can do. We are not to be afraid of people, but we are to be afraid of (that is, be in awe of) God.

10:29-31 This awesome God whom we are to fear (10:28) is also the God who cares about the smallest **sparrow.** When we fear him, we have nothing to worry about because he loves us. Sparrows were the cheapest type of living food sold in the market; a **penny** was the smallest copper coin. Sparrows were not of high value in the world—a penny could buy two of them. Yet God is so concerned for them that not one falls to the ground without God's consent. That God knows the number of **the very hairs** on our heads shows his concern about the most trifling details about each of us. Because God is aware of everything that happens to sparrows, and because he knows every tiny detail about us, Jesus concludes that his followers need never **be afraid.** Sparrows will fall to the ground; God's people will die, sometimes by martyrdom. Yet we are so valuable that God sent Jesus, his only Son, to die for us (John 3:16). Because God places such value on us, we need never fear personal threats or difficult trials.

10:32-33 People have a clear choice. Everyone who **acknowledges** Jesus Christ (that is, publicly confesses faith in or declares allegiance to him) will be acknowledged by Christ before his **Father in heaven.** Jesus' followers would face earthly courts of law where they would have to publicly claim to belong to Jesus Christ, usually at their peril (10:17-25). But for the disciple to acknowledge Jesus means that Jesus will claim that disciple as his own before the Father in heaven.

However, the person who **denies** his relationship to Jesus Christ would in turn face denial by Jesus before the Father. These words refer to those whose true allegiance would be revealed under pressure. Jesus was making the astounding statement that each person's standing before God is based on his or her relationship to Jesus Christ. Jesus is the advocate whose intercession before God will depend on one's faithfulness in acknowledging him.

10:34 The Jews believed that when the Messiah came, he would usher in a time of world peace. Jesus' first arrival would not bring that universal peace. The very nature of Jesus' claims forces people to make a choice. They must choose to believe who he said he is, or they must choose to reject him. Jesus did not come to bring **peace** but a **sword** (that is, division) that separates families, friends, and nations. Conflict and disagreement will arise between those who choose to follow Christ and those who do not. In saying this, Jesus was not encouraging disobedience to parents or conflict at home. Rather, he was showing that his presence demands a decision.

10:35-36 Jesus was quoting from Micah 7:6 (already alluded to in 10:21). In Micah, these divisive conditions led to a yearning for the Messiah; in this context they were caused by the Messiah's coming. Jesus explained the response to his call—there will inevitably be conflict between those

who respond and those who do not. Sometimes the reaction is violent, and angry family members become like **enemies.** Jesus did not come to make such divisions happen; instead, his coming, his words, and his call inevitably will cause conflict between those who accept him and those who reject him.

10:37 Jesus did not force his followers to break family ties to follow him (as opposed to some present-day cults). Jesus was pointing out that his disciples must have singular loyalty to him. When discipleship conflicts with family loyalty, following Jesus must take the priority over natural **love** of family. If one must choose, one must take Jesus.

10:38 These words applied to the disciples and to all who want to be **worthy of** Jesus ("worthy" meaning willing to follow and serve, as in 10:11). To **take up your cross** was a vivid illustration of the humility and submission that Jesus asked of his followers. When Jesus used this picture of his followers taking up their crosses to follow him, the people knew what it meant. For some, taking up the cross might indeed mean death; for all, it means denying self. To **follow** Christ is a moment-by-moment decision, requiring denial of self. Following Jesus means taking the same road of sacrifice and service that he took. The blessing for us is that he walks with us along the way.

10:39 This verse is a positive and negative statement of the same truth: Clinging to this life may cause us to forfeit the best from Christ in this world and in the next. The Christian life is a paradox: To attempt to **find** (or save) your life means only to **lose** it. A person who "finds" his or her life to satisfy desires and goals apart from God ultimately "loses" life. Not only does that person lose the eternal life offered only to those who believe and accept Christ as Savior, but he or she loses the fullness of life promised to those who believe. By contrast, those who willingly "lose" their lives for the sake of Christ actually "find" them. They will receive great reward in God's Kingdom. To lose one's life for Christ's sake refers to a person refusing to renounce Christ, even if the punishment were death.

It would be easier to give one's life in battle or in martyrdom than what Christ actually asks of us. Not only does Christ demand loyalty over family, he also demands loyalty over every part of our life. The more we love this life's rewards (leisure, power, popularity, financial security), the more we will discover how empty they really are. The best way to "find" life, therefore, is to loosen our greedy grasp on earthly rewards so that we can be free to follow Christ. We must risk pain, discomfort, conflict, and stress. We must acknowledge Christ's claim over our destiny and our career. In doing so, we will inherit eternal life and begin at once to experience the benefits of following Christ.

10:40-42 In 10:11-14, Jesus described how the disciples should go about their ministry—staying in homes of worthy people. Those who would **welcome** the disciples would receive great reward. The word "welcomes" may refer both to hospitality (receiving the messenger) as well as conversion (receiving the message). Jesus' representatives carry all his authority. Those who welcome the disciples welcome Jesus; those who welcome Jesus

welcome **the Father who sent** Jesus. Again Jesus unmistakably claims his relationship to God. Jesus spoke these words to his twelve disciples, but then repeated the saying three more times using prophets, righteous people, and little ones. To give **a cup of cold water** was an important act of courtesy and hospitality. The disciples definitely were "little ones" who were insignificant and despised in the eyes of the world. Those who would welcome the disciples merely because they were disciples would not lose their reward. Because the disciples would come with God's authority, their acceptance by people would test the people's attitudes toward God. It is *that* attitude that leads either to reward or loss of reward.

MATTHEW 11

JESUS EASES JOHN'S DOUBT / 11:1-19 / 70

Opposition against Jesus began to grow, as Jesus had prophesied in chapter 10. Even John the Baptist had some misunderstanding. At first the opposition is implicit; later it will be explicit.

11:1 This verse forms a transition from chapter 10. Jesus **finished** instructing his twelve disciples (for the time being) and **went off teaching and preaching in towns throughout the country.**

11:2-3 King Herod, also known as Herod Antipas, had imprisoned **John the Baptist** (4:12). While John sat in **prison,** word came to him about **all the things the Messiah was doing.** John the Baptist had his own **disciples** who apparently remained close to him during his imprisonment. They brought news of Jesus' activities—most likely those deeds that reflected that he was the Messiah (such as those described in chapters 8 and 9). But Jesus' peaceful teaching and healing ministry may not have seemed to measure up to people's expectations for a militaristic Messiah. Perhaps John was wondering about the veiled terms in which Jesus was giving his teachings. This caused John to wonder, so he sent his disciples back to Jesus with a question, **"Are you really the Messiah we've been waiting for, or should we keep looking for someone else?"** John had baptized Jesus, had seen the heavens open, and had heard the voice of God (3:13-17), yet he was experiencing periods of doubt and questioning.

11:4-6 Jesus answered John's doubts by telling John's disciples to **go back to John and tell him**

about what they had **heard and seen.** Jesus pointed to his acts of healing and preaching. These words reflect Isaiah 35:5-6, Isaiah's prophecy of the final Kingdom. The Messiah's arrival was the first phase of this coming Kingdom, and Jesus fulfilled these words. That **the Good News is being preached to the poor** reflects Isaiah 61:1. "The poor" are the small group of faithful followers, the oppressed and afflicted, who respond to the Good News. **God blesses** them because they **are not offended** at Jesus, but willingly accept him as the promised Messiah.

11:7-8 As John's disciples left with Jesus' message, Jesus took the opportunity to address the crowds. He asked three questions and gave three answers. John the Baptist came preaching in the **wilderness,** and people went out to listen to him (3:1, 5). Jesus asked if the people had gone into the wilderness to see **a reed, moved by every breath of wind.** To compare a person to a reed was to say that the person was without moral fiber or courage, easily tossed about, never taking a stand on anything. Obviously, they did not go to see a "reed"—John's fiery preaching was anything but that. The people who went out to see him had been attracted by the opposite quality.

Second, Jesus asked if they had gone out to **see**

a man dressed in expensive clothes. Obviously, John's rough attire (3:4) hardly qualified. The people who went out to see John liked his prophetic power in contrast to the worldliness in the palaces and even in their own Temple.

11:9-10 In this third question, Jesus asked if the people had gone out into the wilderness to see **a prophet.** That was, in fact, true—they had. The people knew that John's appearance meant that something new was about to happen; many believed the age of the Messiah had come. They had seen, Jesus said, **more than a prophet.** Jesus described John as "more" because he had inaugurated the messianic age and had announced the coming Kingdom of God (see also 3:3). More than being a prophet, John also had been the subject of prophecy, fulfilling Malachi 3:1.

11:11 John the Baptist's role as forerunner of the Messiah put him in a position of great privilege, described as "more than a prophet" (11:9) with **none greater.** No man ever fulfilled his God-given purpose better than John. Yet in God's coming Kingdom, **the most insignificant person** will have a greater spiritual heritage than John because he will have seen and known Christ and his finished work on the cross. John would die before Jesus would die and rise again to inaugurate his Kingdom. Jesus' followers, because they will witness the Kingdom's reality, will have privilege and place **greater** than John's.

11:12 There are several views about the meaning of this verse. Most likely, this is a reference to Jesus' opponents. Jesus was explaining that as his **Kingdom** advanced, attacks against it by **violent people** would increase. He referred not to just one type of opposition, but to opposition in general. John the Baptist, as herald of the arrival of the Kingdom of Heaven, was already experiencing the attacks of evil men (Herod) against God's Kingdom. The conflict had begun.

11:13-15 All the teachings of the Scriptures had prophesied about the coming of God's Kingdom.

John fulfilled prophecy, for he himself was **Elijah, the one the prophets said would come** (Malachi 4:5). John was not a resurrected Elijah, but he took on Elijah's prophetic role—boldly confronting sin and pointing people to God (Malachi 3:1). Jesus understood how difficult it was for the people to grasp all that they were seeing and hearing. Indeed, many would be unwilling to believe. Only those who were **willing to hear** would be able to **listen and understand.** Only those with the desire of true disciples could truly understand Jesus' words.

11:16-19 Jesus condemned the attitude of his **generation.** No matter what he said or did, they took the opposite view. They were cynical and skeptical because he challenged their comfortable, secure, and self-centered lives. Jesus compared them to **children playing a game in the public square.** The thrust is that some of the children called out to others to join them, but their companions ignored their invitation and went on playing their own games. Jesus' generation, like the children in the square, was unresponsive to the calls issued by John the Baptist and by Jesus.

Jesus continued that **John the Baptist didn't drink wine and he often fasted,** yet that did not satisfy the Jews. They assumed that he was **demon possessed** (or was merely deranged). In contrast, Jesus (here he called himself **the Son of Man**) came eating and drinking, but that did not satisfy the Jews either. They labeled him as **a glutton and a drunkard** who hung out with the lowest sort of people. Many of the Jews in Jesus' generation, including most of the religious establishment, simply refused to listen and went about their own "games."

But God's **wisdom** is seen in Jesus' deeds. People could see the Kingdom's power through Jesus' miracles. These miracles showed that Jesus' teaching was **right.** People might reject both the miracles and the teaching, but that will not change the truth nor will it hinder the Kingdom's arrival.

JESUS PROMISES REST FOR THE SOUL / 11:20-30 / 71

Jesus' gracious invitation of rest and freedom extends to all. No one is omitted or neglected. All we must do is acknowledge our need and come to him. The "rest" that Jesus gives equals eternal life (Hebrews 4:9) and brings love, healing, and peace with God, not the cessation of work, effort, worship, or service.

11:20 The cities Jesus denounced were those **where he had done most of his miracles.** Because his words were vindicated by his deeds (11:19),

those people should have been eager to turn from their sins and believe. Instead, they rejected Jesus, the Messiah.

11:21-22 For their unbelief, the unrepentant cities would receive judgment and **horrors** (an expression of grief or regret). The people of **Korazin** and **Bethsaida** had seen Jesus firsthand (both cities were in Galilee); yet they stubbornly refused to repent of their sins and believe in him. **Tyre and Sidon** were ancient Phoenician cities with a long-standing reputation for wickedness (Isaiah 23; Ezekiel 27–28; Amos 1:9-10). God had destroyed those cities for their opposition to his people and for their wickedness as centers of Baal worship. Jesus said that if he had done miracles in those wicked cities, the people **would have sat in deep repentance. Sackcloth** and **ashes** were symbols of humiliation, grief for sin, and repentance. Because Korazin and Bethsaida had rejected Jesus, they would suffer even greater punishment than that of the wicked cities who had not seen Jesus. Those people had less opportunity to believe; therefore, they would be accountable for less. Similarly, nations and cities with churches on every corner and Bibles in every home will have no excuse on **judgment day** if they do not repent and believe.

11:23-24 Jesus singled out the city of **Capernaum** for special denunciation. Jesus had made his home in this city (4:12-13) and had performed countless miracles there (8:5-17; 9:2-8, 18-33; Mark 1:23-28). But would it **be exalted to heaven** for that reason? Instead of being "exalted," they would be **brought down to the place of the dead.** Instead of "heaven," they would experience "hades," the word for the grave, the abode of the dead. Here Jesus used the term in a general sense for God's judgment.

As in 11:21-22 above, Jesus was comparing a city that he personally had visited (in this case, had lived in) with one of the most evil cities in the Old Testament. Indeed, if the city of **Sodom** had seen Jesus' **miracles,** Sodom **would still** have existed in Jesus' day. (God had destroyed the cities of Sodom and Gomorrah for their extreme wickedness, see Genesis 18–19.) Jesus implied that the city would have repented of its sin and therefore would not have been destroyed by God. Capernaum itself would be worse off than the worst of the Old Testament cities, simply because it was the home of the Messiah. Its people had seen Jesus, and they had rejected him.

11:25-26 Jesus' response to this rejection, however, was to praise his Father. He praised God for hiding the significance of his words and miracles **from those who think themselves so wise and clever** and for revealing them **to the childlike** (those open to humbly receiving the truth of God's

word). That God had revealed himself in this way was not an accident; it **pleased** him. Spiritual understanding is not dependent on status, race, or education—it is God's gift. (See also Isaiah 29:14; 1 Corinthians 1:19-20; James 4:6.)

11:27 Jesus clearly stated his relationship to the Father of whom he spoke in 11:25. He made three unmistakable claims to having a special relationship with God:

1. **My Father has given me authority over everything.** These words explain shared knowledge. There are no secrets between Father and Son and never have been. Jesus is the only source of the revelation that is hidden or revealed (11:25-26).
2. **No one really knows the Son except the Father.** In the Old Testament, "know" means more than knowledge; it implies an intimate relationship. The communion between God the Father and God the Son is the core of their relationship. Those who make Jesus out to be nothing more than a great teacher have ignored such statements as this, statements that force us to a decision as to whether Jesus really is who he claimed to be.
3. **No one really knows the Father except the Son and those to whom the Son chooses to reveal him.** For anyone else to know God, God must reveal himself to that person, by the Son's choice. How fortunate we are that Jesus has clearly revealed to us God, his truth, and how we can know him. People can approach God only through Jesus—he truly is the only way (John 14:6).

11:28 While those wise and learned in their own eyes are blinded to the truth (11:25-26), Jesus invites those who **are weary and carry heavy burdens.** The "wise and learned" Pharisees had placed so many rules and regulations on the people that religion had become like "labor," and a life of devotion to the Law had become a burden to carry (see 23:1-4). But Jesus invited the "little ones," true disciples with eyes open to see the truth, to **come to** him and find **rest** from these labors. Jesus was clearly admonishing them to abandon Pharisaic legalism and join him. Those who follow Christ will find refreshment in their renewed relationship with him, freedom from guilt over sin, deliverance from fear and despair, and the promise of continued help and guidance from the Holy Spirit. (See Hebrews 3–4 for more on the New Testament view of rest.)

11:29-30 A **yoke** is a heavy wooden harness that fits over the shoulders of animals, such as oxen, that is attached to a piece of equipment that the animals are to pull. The law was a "yoke" that was considered hard to bear. Jesus used the familiar phrasing used of the law as an invitation to discipleship. "Take off the burdensome yoke of the Pharisee-styled law," Jesus said, and **"take my yoke upon you."** Following Jesus would not be a free ride; Jesus had already described the persecution and rejection his followers could expect (10:17-42). They were not free from all constraints; they would carry a yoke, but it would be **light.**

Again, this did not belittle the importance or difficulty of carrying out his mission; indeed, Jesus asked for *more* than mere obedience to the law. Discipleship requires extraordinary effort. These words focused on Jesus' care and concern for his followers, his promise of guidance and presence (28:20), and the ultimate future rewards.

Jesus said, **"Let me teach you."** Jesus, their leader and example, was also the ultimate servant, **humble and gentle.** His path of humble service is the pattern for us to follow.

MATTHEW 12

THE DISCIPLES PICK WHEAT ON THE SABBATH / 12:1-8 / 45
At this point, Matthew returned to an order of events matching Mark's Gospel. The sections included in 9:18–11:30 are out of order chronologically, but placed thematically according to Matthew's focus on Jesus' teachings.

12:1-2 Jesus and his disciples, still in Galilee, went out **walking through some grainfields.** The disciples **were hungry,** so they **began breaking off heads of wheat and eating the grain.** They were not stealing grain; God's law called for this kind of sharing among his people (Deuteronomy 23:25). But harvesting was forbidden **on the Sabbath** (Exodus 34:21). The disciples, however, were picking grain because they were hungry, not because they wanted to harvest the grain for a profit. Thus, they were not breaking God's law. According to the religious leaders, the disciples were technically "harvesting," because they were picking wheat and rubbing it in their hands. The Pharisees were determined to accuse Jesus of wrongdoing. They even followed him around on the Sabbath in order to do so!

12:3-4 Jesus' answer to the Pharisees (12:3-8) contains four arguments explaining why his disciples' actions were lawful to do on the Sabbath (12:2): (1) David's example (12:3-4), (2) the priests' example (12:5-6), (3) proof from the prophets (12:7), and (4) proof from who Jesus himself was (12:8).

First, Jesus reminded the Pharisees of an example from the life of **King David.** This story is recorded in 1 Samuel 21:1-6. Each week twelve loaves of **special bread** (the Bread of the Presence), representing the twelve tribes of Israel, were placed on a table in the Tabernacle. After its use, it was to be eaten only by **priests.** On one occasion, when

fleeing from Saul, David and his men had been given this consecrated bread to eat by Abiathar, the high priest. The loaves given to David were the old loaves that had just been replaced. God did not punish David because his need for food was more important than the priestly regulations. When Jesus compared himself and his disciples to David and his men, Jesus was saying, in effect, "If you condemn me, you must also condemn David." Jesus was not condoning disobedience to God's laws. Instead, he was emphasizing discernment and compassion in enforcing the ceremonial laws, something the self-righteous Pharisees did not comprehend.

12:5-6 Jesus responded to the Pharisees' accusation with a second answer, using an example from the **priests** who served in the **Temple.** Jesus again repeated the question, **"Haven't you ever read in the law of Moses?"** to show these self-righteous Pharisees that while they had the law memorized, they really didn't understand it. The Ten Commandments prohibit work on the Sabbath (Exodus 20:8-11). That was the "letter" of the law. But because the purpose of the Sabbath is to rest and to worship God, the priests had to perform sacrifices and conduct worship services—in short, they had to **work.** Their "Sabbath work" was serving and worshiping God, which God allowed. Thus, even though they technically broke the Sabbath, God held them guiltless.

Just as the priestly duties in the **Temple** surpass

Sabbath regulations about work, so Jesus' ministry transcends the Temple. The Pharisees were so concerned about religious rituals that they missed the whole purpose of the Temple—to bring people to God. Because Jesus Christ is **even greater** than the Temple, how much better can he bring people to God. Our love and worship of God are far more important than the created instruments of worship.

12:7 Jesus used a third proof from the Old Testament prophets to answer the Pharisees. Jesus repeated common Old Testament words (1 Samuel 15:22-23; Psalm 40:6-8; Isaiah 1:11-17; Jeremiah 7:21-23; Hosea 6:6). The statement **"I want you to be merciful; I don't want your sacrifices"** means that rituals and obedience to the law are valuable only if carried out with an attitude of love for God.

The Pharisees' rigid guidelines had caused them to be unable to see beyond the letter of the law. So in condemning Jesus and his disciples, they had **condemned those who aren't guilty.** The disciples were no more guilty of breaking the law than priests who did their duty on the Sabbath.

12:8 Jesus' fourth answer to the Pharisees' accusation (12:2) focused on who he was. When Jesus said that he (again, calling himself **the Son of Man**) was **master even of the Sabbath,** he was claiming to be greater than the law and above the law. To the Pharisees, this was heresy. They refused to believe that Jesus, the divine Son of God, had created the Sabbath. The Creator is always greater than the creation; thus, Jesus had the authority to overrule their traditions and regulations.

JESUS HEALS A MAN'S HAND ON THE SABBATH / 12:9-14 / 46

As if to illustrate that the commandment to love takes precedence over the law, Jesus went to the synagogue where he healed a man with a deformed hand.

12:9-10 It was the Sabbath (12:1), and according to his regular custom, Jesus went to the **synagogue.** There was **a man with a deformed hand.** Jesus' reputation for healing (even on the Sabbath, see Mark 1:21-26) had preceded him, but would he dare heal on the Sabbath with **Pharisees** watching? Healing, they argued, was practicing medicine, and they had a law that a person could not practice his profession on the Sabbath. As they pointed to the man with the deformed hand, the Pharisees tried to trick Jesus by asking him if it was **legal to work by healing on the Sabbath day.** Their motive, however, was not to gain information; they were **hoping he would say yes, so they could bring charges against him.** Sabbath rules said that people could be helped on the Sabbath only if their lives were in danger. If Jesus had waited until another day, he would have been submitting to the Pharisees' authority, showing that their petty rules were equal to God's law. If he healed the man on the Sabbath, the Pharisees could claim that because Jesus broke their rules, his power was not from God. But Jesus made it clear how ridiculous and petty their rules were. God is a God of people, not of rules. The best time to reach out to someone is when he or she needs help.

12:11-12 Instead of answering the Pharisees' question, Jesus responded with an illustration and a question of his own. A sheep that had fallen into a pit was in danger. If this occurred on the **Sabbath,** the sheep's owner was allowed to **pull it out,** even though this constituted work. If it is acceptable to do good to a sheep on the Sabbath, doesn't it also follow that people can **do good** for other people **on the Sabbath?**

12:13 Jesus refused to play by the Pharisees' rules. After pronouncing that it was lawful to do good on the Sabbath (12:12), Jesus did exactly that. He told the man to **reach out** his hand. The moment the man did so, **it became normal.** No particular action of Jesus is recorded; he told the man to move, and with that movement, healing arrived. Jesus did nothing that could be called "work," but the Pharisees would not be swayed from their purpose.

12:14 The **Pharisees** were outraged. In their fury, they determined to kill Jesus. Ironically, the Pharisees had accused Jesus of breaking their law about healing on the Sabbath, yet they were planning (on the Sabbath) to kill him. Their hatred drove them to plot murder—an act that was clearly against God's law.

LARGE CROWDS FOLLOW JESUS / 12:15-21 / 47

Jesus was not afraid of the religious leaders. Jesus had been aggressively confronting the Pharisees' hypocrisy, but here, however, he decided to withdraw from the synagogue before a major confrontation developed. Jesus did this because it was not time for him to die. He still had many lessons to teach his disciples and the people.

12:15-16 Despite his withdrawal, Jesus could not escape the crowds. **Many people** continued to follow him, and Jesus had compassion on those who were sick, and he **healed** them; however, he also **warned them not to say who he was.** Jesus did not want people coming to him for the wrong reasons.

12:17-21 In these verses, Matthew gets to the focus of this chapter—Jesus as the one who **fulfilled prophecy.** The people expected the Messiah to be a king. This quotation from **Isaiah** 42:1-4 showed that the Messiah was indeed a king, but it illustrated the kind of king he would be—a quiet, gentle ruler who brings justice to the nations.

RELIGIOUS LEADERS ACCUSE JESUS OF GETTING HIS POWER FROM SATAN / 12:22-37 / 74

Leaving the chronology in these verses, Matthew gives an example of the intensifying conflict between Jesus and the religious leaders. The religious leaders had already decided that they wanted to kill Jesus (12:14), so they began looking for any opportunity to accuse him.

12:22 A man who was **demon-possessed, blind,** and **unable to talk** was brought to Jesus for healing, and Jesus **healed** him.

12:23 The crowd was amazed when they saw the man healed. **"Could it be that Jesus is the Son of David, the Messiah?"** The Jews understood that the promised Messiah would be a son (descendant) of King David (see Isaiah 9:6-7; 11:1; Jeremiah 23:5-6). They were puzzled because, despite all his miracles, Jesus just did not seem to be the Messiah they were expecting.

12:24 Apparently another delegation of **Pharisees** had come from Jerusalem. The people were "amazed," but these leaders refused to believe that Jesus' power was from God. They could not deny the reality of Jesus' miracles and supernatural power, for he had indeed been casting out demons. So the Pharisees accused him of having **power from Satan.**

12:25-26 Jesus **knew their thoughts.** In the Incarnation, Jesus gave up the complete and unlimited use of his supernatural abilities, but he still had profound insight into human nature (see 9:4). Jesus responded to them in a parable—a simple example from life that would reveal the absurdity of their charge. Following the obvious conclusion of their accusation—that Satan was driving himself out of people—Jesus indicated that if that were true, it would then mean that there was civil war in the kingdom of evil. No king would throw his own soldiers out of his kingdom; neither would Satan throw his soldiers out because his kingdom would then be **divided against itself.** Such a kingdom would be **doomed.** Jesus implied that it would be impossible for Satan to cast out his demons.

12:27 Jesus was not the first person to exorcise demons. In the first century, exorcism was a thriving business. Exorcists would employ complex incantations, magical charms, and even visual effects. Jesus, however, needed only his authoritative word. His constant success, the ease with which he **cast out demons,** and the reactions of the demons made Jesus' exorcisms notable. Jesus was saying, "If it takes Satan's power to drive out demons, then those of your own group who claim to drive out demons must also be demon-possessed." The Pharisees who had cast out demons would **judge** these other Pharisees for implying that being able to exorcise demons meant being in league with Satan.

12:28 There is no question that it was **by the Spirit of God** that Jesus cast out demons. That **the Kingdom of God has arrived** shows that Jesus' exorcisms were specific evidence of the presence of Kingdom power. That Jesus was powerfully casting out demons and plundering Satan's kingdom revealed that the Kingdom of God had begun.

12:29 This picture reflects a situation in the ancient world where wealthy people's homes were virtual fortresses, and their servants could form a small army. Jesus called Satan **a strong man.** His **house** is the realm of evil where there is sickness, demon possession, and death. The only way he could be **robbed** would be for someone to first tie him up; the only way for the demons to be cast out is for someone to first overpower Satan. Jesus' advent into the world did just that (1 John 3:8). Although Satan still works in our world, God is in control. Jesus, as God, has "tied up" Satan in one sense; Satan's ultimate doom is sure.

12:30 It is impossible to know about Christ and remain neutral indefinitely. Anyone who is not actively **helping** him has chosen to oppose him. To refuse to follow Christ is to choose to follow Satan.

12:31 Jesus would no longer reason with his accusers; he was giving them a solemn warning. Jesus had just been accused of being in league with Satan and had soundly refuted those charges. Here he had a few words for these so-called teachers of the law, the Jewish leaders.

First, he made the reassuring promise: **Every sin or blasphemy can be forgiven.** Those who believe in Jesus will be forgiven of all sins (evil acts, good acts not done, evil thoughts, evil motives, etc.) and of all blasphemies (evil words said against God). When there is confession and repentance, no sin is beyond God's forgiveness.

But **blasphemy against the Holy Spirit** is a sin that **can never be forgiven.** This refers to an attitude. Those who defiantly deny Jesus' power and persistently refuse to believe that he is the Messiah are blaspheming the Holy Spirit. Jesus' words were addressed directly to the Pharisees. They had blasphemed the Spirit by attributing to Satan the power Christ had in performing miracles. This is the unforgivable sin—the deliberate refusal to acknowledge God's power in Christ. It indicates an irreversible hardness of heart. Forgiveness would not be possible because it never would be sought.

12:32 Blasphemy against the Holy Spirit—denying the power behind Jesus' ministry—**will never be forgiven.** The mighty works done by the Spirit were unmistakable announcements that the Kingdom had arrived. Those who dared to attribute these works to Satan were not ignorant; instead, they had made up their minds *not* to believe. Jesus said that those who slander the Holy Spirit will not be forgiven—not because their sin is worse than any other, but because they will never ask for forgiveness.

12:33 Just as a good **tree** bears **good** fruit and a diseased (or **bad**) tree bears inedible fruit, so the fruits of a person's life will show the quality of his or her character. **Fruit** is a comprehensive word, referring to teaching, character, and action. Our character is revealed by our conduct.

12:34-35 Jesus called the Pharisees a **brood of snakes** (see also 3:7; 23:33), rebuking them for their hypocritical accusation against him (12:24). Jesus called them **evil,** as seen by their words (their "fruit," 12:33). Because they were evil, how could they possibly **speak what is good and right?** The Pharisees could not hide their evil behind their status, robes, and position; their words betrayed their true character.

12:36-37 These verses are found only in Matthew. Jesus explained that words matter—each person will **give an account on judgment day of every idle word** he speaks. The word "idle" refers not to mindless small talk or carefree jokes, but to broken promises, unkept commitments, and unpaid vows. Such words are better indicators of a person's true character than his or her carefully planned and prepared statements and speeches. No word is insignificant to God because every spoken word reveals what is in the heart. Words will be a basis for judgment: **The words you say now reflect your fate then.**

RELIGIOUS LEADERS ASK JESUS FOR A MIRACULOUS SIGN / 12:38-45 / 75

The Pharisees (here joined by the teachers of religious law) wanted Jesus to authenticate by a sign the special relationship he claimed to have with God. In a separate incident recorded in 16:1-4, the Pharisees and Sadducees would ask Jesus for a miraculous sign. Jesus responded to both requests the same way.

12:38 Some **teachers of religious law** joined the **Pharisees** and asked Jesus for **a miraculous sign**—that is, some miracle proving that he was the Messiah. But they were not sincerely seeking to know Jesus. They had already seen enough miraculous proof to convince them that he was the Messiah, but they had already decided not to believe in him. More miracles would not change their minds.

12:39-40 Jesus refused to give the religious leaders a sign. Instead, he explained that a sign would come in *his* timing and that the sign would be unmistakable. The only sign they would get would be **the sign of the prophet Jonah.** Jonah was a prophet sent to the Assyrian city of Nineveh (see the book of Jonah). As Jonah was **three days and three nights** in the **belly of the great fish,** so Jesus would be **in the heart of the earth for three days and three nights.** Jesus' resurrection would prove that he is the Messiah. Three days after his death Jesus would come back to life, just as Jonah had been "brought back" to life after spending three days in the fish.

12:41 The people of Nineveh will **condemn** those of Jesus' generation **on judgment day.** The pagans **repented at the preaching of Jonah,** but the Jews and their religious leaders refused to repent at Jesus' preaching. **Someone greater than Jonah** refers to Jesus himself and his proclamation of the Kingdom's arrival (see also 12:6). Jesus was their promised Messiah. The religious leaders who knew prophecy should have been the first to proclaim Jesus as God's Son. Instead, they rejected him; thus, they will face condemnation for their refusal to believe.

12:42 The queen of Sheba had traveled from southern Arabia to see Solomon, king of Israel, and to learn about his great wisdom (1 Kings 10:1-10). This unbelieving Gentile recognized the truth about God when it was presented to her, unlike the Jewish religious leaders who refused the truth even though it was staring them in the face. That queen will **rise up against this genera-tion** and condemn those who refused to believe **someone greater than Solomon**—the Messiah himself.

12:43-45 To further describe how it will be with this evil generation (12:39, 45), Jesus told a para-ble focusing on the attitude of the nation of Israel and the religious leaders in particular. There is danger in attempting to be neutral about Jesus. Unfilled and complacent people are easy targets for Satan.

The **evil spirit** was not "cast out," but for some reason had left a person. The **desert** was believed to be the habitation of demons. Because demons need a place to live (**rest**), this demon returned to its **former home.** In its absence, the demon's "home" had been cleaned up, but it was still **empty.** Therein lay the problem and the crux of Jesus' teaching. The nation had been swept "clean" by the teaching and preaching of John the Baptist and of Jesus. Many had come to repent. But if the nation did not turn around, truly repenting from sin and turning to Jesus as their Messiah and Sav-ior, they would be no better off than a clean but empty house. Into that house comes worse evil than before. Jesus pictured the demon finding **seven other spirits** and returning to the clean house. The person, now filled with eight demons instead of one, is definitely **worse off than before.** God's people, **this evil generation,** privileged with prophecy and promises, would be faced with horrible judgment for rejecting their Messiah.

JESUS DESCRIBES HIS TRUE FAMILY / 12:46-50 / 76

In this section, Jesus was not denying his responsibility to his earthly family. He would provide for his mother's security as he hung on the cross (John 19:25-27). His mother and brothers would be present in the Upper Room at Pentecost (Acts 1:14). Instead, Jesus was pointing out that spiritual relationships are as binding as physical ones, and he was paving the way for a new community of believers to be formed. This family would be characterized by love.

12:46-47 Jesus' **mother** was Mary (Luke 1:30-31), and his **brothers** were probably the other children Mary and Joseph had after Jesus (see also Mark 6:3-4). Based on 13:55, these were Jesus' half brothers, Mary and Joseph's other children, because Jesus' father was God, not Joseph. Appar-ently Mary had gathered her family, and they had gone to find Jesus. Mark explained that Jesus' family thought he was "out of his mind" (Mark 3:21). Mary hoped to use her personal relationship with Jesus to influence him. She saw her son in a busy ministry that was taking its toll on him. Perhaps she hoped to get him to come home and rest. **As Jesus was speaking,** the message from his family was relayed to him. Jesus' family thought that because of their relationship with him, he would answer their request.

12:48 Instead of going outside to see what his family members wanted, Jesus looked at the crowd and asked an odd question, **"Who is my mother? Who are my brothers?"** Jesus knew why his family had come, yet he used their visit as a lesson in discipleship. A relationship with Jesus was not limited to those in his immediate family. Jesus opened this relationship to all people. His question could be rendered, "Who are the types of people who can have a family relationship with me?"

12:49-50 Jesus **pointed to his disciples** and answered his own question. The types of people who can have a relationship with him are those who do the **will** of the **Father in heaven.** They listen, learn, believe, and follow. Obedience is the key to discipleship. In these words, Jesus explained that in his spiritual family, the rela-tionships are ultimately more important and longer lasting than those formed in his physical family.

MATTHEW 13

JESUS TELLS THE PARABLE OF THE FOUR SOILS / 13:1-9 / 77

Jesus left the synagogue and began to teach outdoors. He left those opposed to him and reached out to the responsive people. Jesus had already made unmistakable claims about his true identity, and there was increasing division between those who accepted and those who rejected. The religious leaders had already decided that Jesus was not the Messiah.

Jesus began teaching a series of parables about the Kingdom of Heaven. These "parables" hid the truth from those who had their minds made up, having already chosen to reject Jesus. Those who truly wanted to know Jesus and listened carefully would understand his words.

13:1-2 Earlier **that same day,** Jesus had been accused of being under Satan's power (12:22-37), had turned down the religious leaders' request for a miracle (12:38-45), and had dealt with his family who had come to take him home (12:46-50). Then, **Jesus left the house and went down to the shore** of the Sea of Galilee and **sat and taught** from a **boat.**

13:3 Jesus used **many stories,** or parables, when teaching. Parables use familiar scenes and everyday objects and relationships to explain spiritual truths. They compel listeners to discover truth, while at the same time they conceal the truth from those too lazy or too stubborn to see it. This "Kingdom parable" gave a familiar picture to Jesus' audience—a **farmer** planting **seed,** with the resulting increase dependent on the condition of the soil. In ancient Israel, farmers sowed seed by hand, scattering (13:4) handfuls of seed onto the ground from a large bag slung across the shoulders. No matter how skillful, no farmer could keep some of his seed from falling on the path, being scattered among rocks and thorns, or from being carried off by the wind. So the farmer would throw the seed liberally, and enough would fall on good ground to ensure a good harvest.

13:4 Some of the seed **fell on a footpath.** The hard and compacted soil of the path made it impossible

for the seed to penetrate. So it sat on top, as tempting morsels for **birds.**

13:5-6 Some of that seed **fell on shallow soil with underlying rock.** Unlike the path, rocky ground had some soil to accept the seed, but not much. The seed **sprang up quickly,** but the **sun** took the moisture out so rapidly that the young plant **died.**

13:7 Some of the farmer's seed **fell among thorns.** Thorns rob the sprouts of nutrition, water, light, and space. Thus, when the thorns **shot up,** the good seed was **choked out** and could not grow.

13:8 However, some of the seed landed in **fertile soil** and yielded **thirty, sixty,** or even up to a **hundred times** the amount of seed sown. A farmer would be happy indeed to see his crop multiply even ten times. Thirty, sixty, or a hundred would be a marvelous yield.

13:9 Human ears **hear** many sounds, but there is a deeper kind of listening that results in spiritual understanding. Jesus was speaking of the response of the mind and heart necessary to **understand** spiritual truth. Some people in the crowd were only curious about Jesus; a few were looking for evidence to use against him; others truly wanted to learn and grow. Jesus' words were for the honest seekers. Those who honestly seek God will have spiritual hearing.

JESUS EXPLAINS THE PARABLE OF THE FOUR SOILS / 13:10-23 / 78

When speaking in parables, Jesus was not hiding truth from sincere seekers, because those who were receptive to spiritual truth understood the illustrations. To others, they were only stories without meaning. Jesus purposely spoke in parables to weed out the halfhearted and curiosity-seekers from the true seekers. His words, like the farmer's seed, fell on various types of hearts. Those who truly heard and understood would become his followers.

13:10 When Jesus got away from the crowd and was alone with his true followers (the twelve disciples and the larger group of believers), a more intimate question-and-answer period followed. His followers asked him why he told **stories** that seemed to confuse his listeners and obscure the message.

13:11 Jesus revealed that understanding the truth of the gospel comes as a gift of God to those he has chosen. The **you** to whom Jesus spoke was the group of his true followers. God had given this understanding of **the secrets of the Kingdom of Heaven** to the disciples as a permanent possession, a distinguishing mark of discipleship. They understood, though only partially, the "secret" that God's Kingdom had arrived among them in the person of Jesus. Those who **have not** been given this knowledge are those who willfully reject the gospel message.

13:12 To those who are open to Jesus' teaching, God will give more understanding and an abundance of knowledge. In contrast are those who are not listening—Jesus says that even what they have will be taken away from them. Those who "not listening" were the religious leaders and the vast majority of the Jews. They thought they were privileged and secure as God's chosen people, but they would lose that position. We are responsible to use well what we have. When people reject Jesus, their hardness of heart drives away or renders useless even the little understanding they had.

13:13 The parable of the farmer accurately pictured the people's reaction to all of Jesus' parables. Jesus would not explain the parables to all the people; rather, he would answer questions about his parables with other parables because, he said, **"People see what I do, but they don't really see. They hear what I say, but they don't really hear, and they don't understand."** The parables could not penetrate the hard soil of unbelief already characterizing unbelievers' hearts. These unbelievers had already rejected Jesus; no amount of explaining or talking would make any difference. The soil of their heart was hard; the seed of the word would not grow; the parables would be nothing more than strange stories to them. Jesus was not hiding truth from sincere seekers because those who were receptive to spiritual truth understood the illustrations.

13:14 The parables allowed Jesus to give spiritual food to those who hungered for it; but for the others, Isaiah's prophecy explained their situation. God told **Isaiah** that people would **hear** but

not understand and **see** but **not perceive its meaning** (Isaiah 6:9); Jesus witnessed the same reaction to his teaching. By quoting from the prophet Isaiah, Jesus was explaining to this inner group of followers that the crowd resembled the Israelites about whom Isaiah had written. God had told Isaiah that the people would listen but not learn from his message because their hearts had hardened beyond repentance. Yet God still sent Isaiah with the message because even though the nation itself would not repent and would reap judgment, some individuals *would* listen.

13:15 Neither Isaiah's nor Jesus' audiences were denied the opportunity to **turn** and receive healing (forgiveness). Instead, refusing to listen would mean that the people's **hearts** were **hardened.** No matter how much they saw of Jesus' miracles or heard of his teaching, they never would be able to understand because they had deliberately chosen to reject him.

13:16 The images of "seeing" and "hearing" refer to knowledge of God's revelation. The disciples were **blessed** above the people in the crowd because they could **see** and **hear** what the prophets had foretold. God gave them spiritual enlightenment to understand and accept the person and message of Jesus.

13:17 The Kingdom of God was a mystery to the **prophets** of the Old Testament because, though they wrote about it, they did not understand it (as Paul explains in Romans 16:25-26). The believers who knew Jesus personally received spiritual insight that illuminated the mystery. In these words, Jesus was explaining that *he* was the fulfillment of the prophecies (see 1 Peter 1:10-12).

13:18-19 Jesus explained the **story** about the **farmer sowing grain.** The farmer was Jesus (see also 13:37) and, by extension, anyone after him who would teach and preach **the Good News** (represented by the **seed**). Jesus was sowing the word among the crowd of followers. The parable revealed people's varying responses to the gospel message. The attitude or condition of their hearts would govern their response.

The word makes no impression on some people. For those who hear and **don't understand,** the seed lands on a hard heart. Then **the evil one** (Satan) **snatches** it away. Perhaps the person feels no need in his or her heart, no desire for anything other than this life, no guilt of sin or need of forgiveness.

13:20-21 The rocky soil represents people who joyfully receive the Good News of the gospel because of the promises offered. These people understand some of the basics but do not allow God's truth to work its way into their souls and make a difference in their lives. **Their roots don't go very deep,** and although they are **fine** at first, **they wilt as soon as they have problems or are persecuted.** Satan can always use sorrow, trouble, and persecution to draw such "shallow" people away from God.

13:22 **The thorny ground** is Satan's most subversive tactic of all. These people **hear and accept the Good News,** giving hope of a harvest. But thorns grow up and choke out the growing seed. **All too quickly the message is crowded out by the cares of this life and the lure of wealth.** Worldly worries, the false sense of security brought on by prosperity, and the desire for material things plagued first-century disciples as they do us today. Daily routines overcrowd and materialistic pursuits distract believers, choking out God's word so that **no crop is produced.**

13:23 But other people are like **good soil**— they hear the word and **accept** it. These are the true disciples—those who have accepted Jesus, believed his words, and allowed him to make a difference in their lives. These people **produce a huge harvest.** They tell the Good News to others who tell it to others and so on. The desire to evangelize the world should naturally follow from a life rebuilt around God's word.

JESUS TELLS THE PARABLE OF THE WEEDS / 13:24-30 / 80

While the Kingdom message is being sown, it faces a variety of different receptions. Some may have thought that the inauguration of the Messiah's Kingdom would be accompanied by cataclysmic events. That did not seem to be happening with Jesus. In the Jewish mind, the coming of the Messiah signaled the coming of God's promised Kingdom. Jesus stated that the Messiah had arrived with his Kingdom, but the fulfillment of the Messianic Kingdom would be delayed until he comes a second time. What, then, is the Kingdom of Heaven like? The parables in this chapter answer this question.

13:24-26 Jesus explained that the Kingdom grows quietly and abundantly, yet evil still exists in the world. The picture of weeds planted in the fields was a known practice in ancient warfare and feuds—destroy a nation's (or person's) agricultural base and his military power would also be destroyed. Because no one recognized the **weeds,** both **grew** at the same time.

13:27-28 The **servants** knew the master had sowed **good seed.** While the servants would expect a few weeds, instead the field was **full of weeds.** Who are these "weeds"? Jesus would soon explain that "the weeds are the people who belong to the evil one" (13:38). They may be people in the church who appear to be believers but who never truly believe. To interpret the meaning more broadly, the Kingdom of God is present and growing in a world full of sin and unbelief. The **enemy,** Satan (13:39), is always working to obstruct the growth of God's Kingdom. The enemy caused a problem, so the servants dutifully asked if they should **pull out the weeds.**

13:29-30 The owner decided that the wheat and weeds should **grow together until the harvest**— a common metaphor for the final judgment (Jeremiah 51:33; Hosea 6:11; see also Revelation 14:14-16). Jesus was making the point that while his coming signaled the arrival of the Kingdom, its consummation would be delayed. God will not eliminate all opposition until the end of the age. The children of God and children of Satan would grow together "until" the harvest; then, God would judge and **sort out** his children from Satan's children.

JESUS TELLS THE PARABLE OF THE MUSTARD SEED / 13:31-32 / 81

No one parable can completely describe God's Kingdom in all its aspects, so Jesus gave several. Through this parable, Jesus explained that his Kingdom would have a small beginning. Indeed, it began with Jesus alone and, upon his ascension, was left in the care of twelve apostles and just a few hundred other followers.

13:31-32 Jesus compared this beginning to the **mustard seed,** which was the **smallest** seed that a farmer used. The mustard seed was so small that it would take almost twenty thousand seeds to make one ounce. Modern critics have pointed out that the mustard seed is *not* the smallest seed that exists. But Jesus was not making a scientific statement.

Though the mustard seed is not the smallest seed in all of creation, it was used in rabbinic proverbs to designate the smallest of things. No other seed so small produced such a large plant. Jesus' point was that just as a tiny seed will grow into a large plant, so God's Kingdom will produce many people who truly believe.

JESUS TELLS THE PARABLE OF THE YEAST / 13:33-35 / 82

Like the parable of the mustard seed, this parable stresses small beginnings with great growth. Yeast permeates and transforms; thus, we see another aspect of the Kingdom.

13:33 In other Bible passages, **yeast** is used as a symbol of evil or uncleanness (see 16:6). Here it is a positive symbol of growth. Although yeast looks like a minor ingredient, it permeates **every part of the dough.** Although the Kingdom had small beginnings, it would grow to have a great impact on the world.

13:34-35 The first half of the quoted verse follows the first part of Psalm 78:2. The second half (**since the creation of the world**) seems to be an independent rendition of the end of Psalm 78:2. Psalm 78 reviews Israel's history from the time of slavery in Egypt to David's reign. This psalm was told over and over to each generation so they would not forget God and make the same mistakes as their ancestors. The **mysteries hidden** refers to God's mighty acts in redeeming his people despite their sin and unfaithfulness.

JESUS EXPLAINS THE PARABLE OF THE WEEDS / 13:36-43 / 83

The young weeds and the young blades of wheat look the same and can't be distinguished until they are grown and ready for harvest. Weeds (unbelievers) and wheat (believers) must live side by side in the world. God allows unbelievers to remain for a while, just as a farmer allows weeds to remain in his field so that the surrounding wheat won't be uprooted with them. At the harvest, however, the weeds will be thrown away.

13:36 In 13:1, Jesus had "left the house" to sit beside the sea. There he spoke publicly to the crowds. Jesus' movement back **into the house** signifies a movement away from the crowds and to private discussion with **his disciples.** Jesus' followers had the knowledge of the secrets of the Kingdom (13:11) and the ability to "see" and "hear" (13:16), but they still needed his help in understanding all his words.

13:37-39 Jesus described the identity of the important parts of the parable of the weeds recorded in 13:24-30. Jesus explained to his listening disciples that **the good seed represents the people of the Kingdom,** sown by **the Son of Man** in the **field** of the **world.** In this world also exist **people who belong to the evil one,** sown by him into this world. At **the end of the world,** the **angels** would come and the **harvest** would begin.

13:40-42 At this harvest, God will separate his people from Satan's people. As the harvesters collect **the weeds** into bundles to be destroyed, so Satan's works and Satan's people will be thrown **into the furnace**—a metaphor for final judgment (see Daniel 3:6). Jesus often used the term **weeping and gnashing of teeth** to refer to the coming judgment (see 8:12; 13:50; 22:13; 24:51; 25:30). The "weeping" indicates sorrow or remorse, and "gnashing of teeth" shows extreme anxiety or pain. Those who say they don't care what happens to them after they die don't realize what they are saying. God will punish them for living in selfishness and indifference to him. Jesus, who has already identified himself as **the Son of Man** (8:20; 9:6; 10:23; 11:19; 12:8, 32, 40), revealed that he will inaugurate the end of the age and the final judgment.

13:43 Reflecting words from Daniel 12:3, Jesus described the final glory of **the godly.** Those who receive God's favor stand in bright contrast to those who receive his judgment. Heaven will be a glorious place!

JESUS TELLS THE PARABLE OF THE HIDDEN TREASURE / 13:44 / 84
The parable of the hidden treasure and the parable of the pearl merchant (13:45-46) form a pair and belong together. They teach the inestimable value of the Kingdom.

13:44 To teach the inestimable value of the Kingdom of Heaven and of being part of that Kingdom, Jesus described it as a **treasure** found **hidden in a field.** The man who discovered the treasure in the field stumbled upon it by accident but knew its value when he found it. Some have wondered about the morality of a man obtaining a treasure in this way, but Jesus was not teaching a moral lesson. He was merely showing the value of this treasure that is worth every sacrifice and commitment to obtain. The Kingdom of Heaven is more valuable than anything else we can have, and a person must be willing to give up everything to obtain it.

JESUS TELLS THE PARABLE OF THE PEARL MERCHANT / 13:45-46 / 85
This parable and the previous parable of the hidden treasure (13:44) are a pair and should be studied together (as noted by the word "again" in verse 45).

13:45-46 In the previous parable, Jesus described a man stumbling upon a treasure. In this parable, Jesus pictured a wealthy **pearl merchant.** Pearls were especially valued in the Near East. **A pearl of great value** could obviously set up this merchant for life. Knowing pearls, this merchant searched earnestly for one of great value. When he found it, **he sold everything** he had to buy it. Some may discover the Kingdom (13:44); some may seek earnestly and finally obtain it. In both cases, the men recognized the value of what they had found and willingly invested everything to find it. The Kingdom of Heaven is so valuable that it calls for a total investment (radical discipleship) from those who find it.

JESUS TELLS THE PARABLE OF THE FISHING NET / 13:47-52 / 86
The parable of the fishing net deals with the dividing of people much as the parable of the wheat and weeds does.

13:47-48 This parable pictures a dragnet perhaps drawn between two boats and dragged in a wide semicircle. **Fish of every kind** are caught and the fishermen **drag** the net to the beach where they **sort** the fish. They put **good fish into crates and throw the bad ones away.**

13:49-50 While the parable of the wheat and weeds highlighted the length of time during which good and evil people must coexist before the judgment, this parable focuses on that final judgment. As the net catches all kinds of fish, the gospel message will go out to all kinds of people. **At the end of the world,** the **angels** will **separate the wicked people from the godly.** Like the fish that are thrown away, **the wicked** will be thrown **into the fire** (a metaphor for judgment, see 13:40-42).

13:51-52 Because the disciples now understood these parables, Jesus said, "Every teacher of religious law who has become a disciple in the Kingdom of Heaven is like a person who brings out of the storehouse the new teachings as well as the old." The disciples who understood Jesus' words were the "teachers of the law" in his Kingdom. In other words, the current teachers of religious law did not understand, so their teaching was invalid. The disciples understood God's real purpose in the law as revealed in the Old Testament; therefore, they had a real treasure. The disciples would bring this treasure "out of the storehouse" in that their responsibility would be to share what they had learned with others. The disciples had gained this treasure through Jesus' instruction, so they were able to understand and use the best of older wisdom, as well as the new insights that Jesus brought to them. True teachers see the value of both old and new.

The Old Testament points the way to Jesus, the Messiah. Jesus always upheld the authority and relevance of the Scriptures. Those who understand Jesus' teaching about the Kingdom of Heaven receive a double benefit. This was a new treasure that Jesus was revealing. Both the old and new teachings give practical guidelines for faith and for living in the world. The religious leaders, however, were trapped in the old and blind to the new. The religious leaders were looking for a physical and temporal kingdom (brought on by military strength and physical rule), but they were blind to the spiritual significance of the Kingdom that Christ had brought.

THE PEOPLE OF NAZARETH REFUSE TO BELIEVE / 13:53-58 / 91

Jesus had been born in Bethlehem, but he had been reared in Nazareth (Matthew 2:19-23; Luke 2:39-40). This was not the first time he had spoken and taught in Nazareth (Luke 4:14-30).

13:53-54 A previous visit to **Nazareth** by Jesus to teach had been given a less than positive response; in fact, the people had tried to kill him. This trip to Nazareth, therefore, is significant. The people of Nazareth were about to receive a second chance to believe; unfortunately, they again rejected the Lord.

The **synagogue** was the center of the town. This was really a key place for Jesus to meet the people. When he taught there, the people were **astonished** at his **wisdom** and his **miracles**. They knew Jesus' miracles were supernatural, but they wondered about their source (the options were either God or Satan—see 12:24) and how Jesus could do them.

13:55-56 Jesus was teaching effectively and wisely, but the people of his hometown saw him as only **a carpenter's son** (referring to Joseph) whose family they also knew well. Jesus had been almost thirty years old before he began his public teaching ministry, and he had never been formally trained as a rabbi. For the years before that, he had been at home, learning the trade of carpentry from his father. The listing of the brothers (see also 12:46-49) indicates that the people knew the family well—the mother, the brothers, the sisters. Apparently they were all ordinary people, and Jesus had experienced an ordinary childhood. The residents of Jesus' hometown could not bring themselves to believe Jesus' message. Jesus had come to them as a prophet who challenged them to respond to spiritual truth.

13:57 Jesus' claims caused the people in his hometown to be **deeply offended.** They stumbled over his words and could not accept them. He was one of their peers, and their preconceived notions about who he was made it impossible for them to accept his message. They also may have been jealous. Jesus had come to them as a prophet, but they saw only a hometown boy.

Jesus used a common proverb found in rabbinic literature. It is significant that Jesus applied the word **"prophet"** to himself, thus specifically claiming to be God's messenger. Jesus was not the first prophet to be rejected **in his own hometown** (see Jeremiah 12:5-6). Jesus also experienced rejection by members **among his own family** (John 7:5). Some of Jesus' family did believe in him after his resurrection (Acts 1:14).

13:58 Jesus could have done greater miracles in Nazareth, but he chose not to do so because of the people's unbelief. **Unbelief** blinds people to the truth and robs them of hope. These people missed the Messiah. When Jesus performed mighty works, his goal was to further the Kingdom of God, not to try to convince a group of stubborn people who had already thoroughly rejected him. To do miracles in Nazareth would be of no value because the people did not accept his message or believe that he was from God. Therefore, Jesus looked elsewhere, seeking those who would respond to his miracles and message. We need to proclaim the gospel. At times, however, we need to move on, to other towns and people.

MATTHEW 14

HEROD KILLS JOHN THE BAPTIST / 14:1-12 / 95

Matthew continued to record various responses to Jesus. The Pharisees had accused him of being under Satan's power (12:22-37). Other religious leaders had expressed their rejection

(12:38-45). Jesus' own family thought he had gone crazy (12:46-50). Finally, the people of Jesus' hometown had rejected him (13:53-58).

This chapter gives the story of a government leader's misunderstanding of Jesus' identity. Herod thought that Jesus was the resurrected John the Baptist, who had been arrested just prior to the beginning of Jesus' public ministry. Because John had ministered in Perea ("east of the Jordan River," John 1:28), he was under Herod's jurisdiction. The arrest marked the end of John's public ministry. He was imprisoned for some time prior to his death (see 11:2-6).

14:1-2 Herod Antipas ruled over the territories of Galilee and Perea. He was the son of Herod the Great, who had ordered the killing of the babies in Bethlehem (2:16). Eventually he would hear Jesus' case before the crucifixion (Luke 23:6-12). Herod's guilt over John's death led him to think that his worst nightmares had come true: **John the Baptist** had **come back to life again.** John had done no **miracles** (John 10:41); he had simply preached and prepared the way for Jesus. But Herod identified Jesus with John.

14:3-4 Herod's personal guilt was well placed, for he had ordered **John** to be **arrested and imprisoned.** Ironically, this "powerful" king did this in response to pressure from **Herodias (the former wife of Herod's brother Philip).** Philip was Herod's half brother. When Herod Antipas met Herodias, his brother's wife, he divorced his first wife and married Herodias. Herodias was the daughter of Aristobulus, another half brother. Thus, Herodias was a half niece to both Philip and Herod (and they, in turn, were her half uncles). She married her half uncle Philip and then divorced him to marry another half uncle, Herod. Thus, in marrying, Herodias and Herod had committed adultery, as well as a type of incest. John the Baptist condemned Herod and Herodias for living immorally. It was **illegal** for Herod to be married to her.

14:5 Rebuking a tyrannical Roman official who could imprison and execute him was extremely dangerous, yet that is what John had done. In addition, there was political tension over Herod's divorce of his first wife—the daughter of the king of a neighboring country. This was explosive enough without John bringing up the illegal marriage. John's public denunciation of the incest and adultery of Herod and Herodias was too much for them to bear, especially Herodias, whose anger turned to hatred. Mark's Gospel focuses on Herodias, who was both wicked and ruthless in her attempts to kill John the Baptist. While Matthew's account seems to say that **Herod would have executed John,** we can combine the accounts to see a wicked yet weak ruler who was not in a hurry to kill John because he

was **afraid** of the people, who **believed John was a prophet.** For Herod to put to death one of the Jews' prophets could have caused a huge revolt in his territory and certainly would have created great discontent.

14:6-7 That **Herod** had imprisoned John the Baptist was not enough for the angry Herodias. She continued to nurse her grudge against John for speaking publicly about her sins, biding her time until she would get her way and have John killed. Then on Herod's **birthday,** the opportunity arrived. Mark wrote that Herod gave a banquet for many notable men from governmental, military, and civil positions in Galilee (Mark 6:21). According to the Jewish historian Josephus, **Herodias's daughter** (by her marriage with Herod Philip) was Salome, a young woman in her middle teens. Herodias sent Salome into the banquet hall to **dance.** Afterwards, the king **promised with an oath to give her anything she wanted.**

14:8 Apparently, Salome had already been prompted by her mother, so she responded, **"I want the head of John the Baptist on a tray!"** Herod, faced by drunk and smirking officials who waited to see what he would do, was too weak to object. Herodias would have her way. Herod caved in under the social pressure and John's death was sealed.

14:9-10 Herod **was sorry** because he had put himself in this position **in front of his guests,** and yet he considered John a holy man whom he both respected and feared (Mark 6:20). Herod had made a promise and had sealed it with an **oath.** Such words were considered irrevocable. To back out on the promise would show his important guests that Herod was not a man of his word or that he was afraid of this "unimportant" prisoner in a dungeon. So, **John was beheaded.**

14:11 An executioner beheaded John and brought **his head** to the girl **on a tray.** Herod fulfilled his oath and saved face before his guests. But he had been manipulated by his wife and was left with great fear over what he had done in killing a holy man. Herod's guilt could not be assuaged. Thus, when Jesus came on the scene, Herod thought that John had come back to life (14:2).

14:12 John the Baptist apparently still had **disciples,** even though many had left him to follow

Jesus (which John was content for them to do, see John 1:35-37). When they heard that John had been beheaded, they came, took away his corpse, and gave it a proper burial. Then, they **told Jesus.** Matthew's mention of this report to Jesus shows the close link between John's and Jesus' ministries.

JESUS FEEDS FIVE THOUSAND / 14:13-21 / 96

Apart from Jesus' resurrection, this is the only miracle that appears in all four Gospels, showing its importance to Jesus' ministry and to the early church. While many people have tried to explain away the incident, it is clear that all the Gospel writers saw this as a wonderful miracle. In Matthew and Mark, this miracle follows the account of Herod's tragic feast where John the Baptist was killed. The placement of the event creates a stark contrast between Herod's grisly orgy and the miraculous feast that Jesus provided for the multitude. Like each of Jesus' miracles, the feeding of the five thousand demonstrated his control over creation and showed that God will provide when we are in need.

14:13-14 News of John's death resulted in Jesus' desire to pull away and be alone for a while with his disciples. Jesus and the disciples got into a **boat** and withdrew **to a remote area.** Luke says they went to Bethsaida (Luke 9:10). But the **crowds** would not let them get away, so they **followed by land.** As soon as Jesus landed, the rest was over because **a vast crowd** waited on the shore. Far from feeling impatience and frustration toward these needy people, Jesus **had compassion on them and healed their sick.** While Jesus had hoped to be alone with the disciples for a time of rest, he did not send away this needy crowd. He had compassion for the people and took it upon himself to meet their needs. Jesus knew that his time on earth was short, so he took advantage of every opportunity to teach the Good News of the Kingdom to those willing to listen.

14:15 Jesus had been teaching the people until **evening.** Sunset was approaching, and the disciples wondered what Jesus planned to do with this crowd that had come far from their homes to be with them in this **desolate place.** The disciples brought their suggestion to Jesus: **"Send the crowds away so they can go to the villages and buy food for themselves."**

14:16 The disciples were very concerned regarding the people's needs. After all, the people would need to reach a nearby town before sunset if they were going to obtain food. Jesus' answer both astounded and exasperated them: **"That isn't necessary—you feed them."** Jesus directly involved his disciples in the miracle so that it would make a lasting impression on them.

14:17-18 There was nothing in the crowd but **five loaves of bread and two fish**—common staples for the poor of Jesus' day. Apparently, in their hurry, no one else in the crowd had thought to bring along food to eat. A young boy offered his lunch to the disciples (John 6:8), but the disciples could see only the impossibility of the situation. Jesus had an entirely different approach, and he asked the disciples to **bring** the loaves and fish to him.

14:19 Jesus, acting as the host of the soon-to-be banquet, took the loaves and fish, looked up to heaven, **and asked God's blessing on the food.** As Jesus broke the loaves, the miracle occurred. He broke the loaves and gave them to his disciples to then give **to the people.** The disciples acted as waiters to the groups of hungry people seated on the grass, taking bread and fish, distributing it, and then returning to Jesus to get more. They continued to serve the crowd until everyone had had enough to eat.

14:20 The five loaves and two fish multiplied so that all the people could eat **as much as they wanted.** Even the **leftovers** were more than they had begun with.

14:21 The Greek word translated **men** is *andres,* meaning not "people" but "male individuals." Therefore, there were five thousand men, **in addition to** the women and children. The total number of people Jesus fed could have been over ten thousand. Jesus did what the disciples thought to be impossible. He multiplied five loaves and two fish to feed over **five thousand** people.

JESUS WALKS ON WATER / 14:22-33 / 97

The miracles of Jesus walking on the water and calming the storm (8:23-27) were a double demonstration of Jesus' power over nature. Matthew and Mark highlighted the effects of these miracles on those who witnessed them.

14:22 As soon as the crowd had been fed and the disciples had picked up the scraps, Jesus **immediately** got his disciples and the crowd moving. His sudden desire to dismiss the crowd and send the disciples off in their boat is explained in John's Gospel. Upon seeing (and participating in) the miracle of multiplied loaves and fish, the people wanted to take Jesus by force and make him king (John 6:15). Before the crowd could become an unruly mob, Jesus sent the disciples **back into the boat** and **sent the people home.**

14:23-24 Jesus went **up into the hills by himself to pray.** Jesus wanted time to communicate with his Father. During his ministry on earth, Jesus was in constant contact with the Father—he may have gone off alone to pray often, so his desire to do so may not have surprised the disciples, who departed in the boat as instructed. The disciples had left sometime before sunset, so by the time **night fell,** they were **far away from land.** They got into **trouble,** however, facing **strong wind** and **heavy waves.** At least the last time this had happened, Jesus had been in the boat with them (8:23-27). This time, Jesus was alone on the land, and the disciples were left to fend for themselves (or so they thought) against another raging storm.

14:25 From evening until **about three o'clock in the morning,** the disciples had been out on the sea, much of that time fighting a strong headwind and high waves. Jesus **came to them, walking on the water.** The Old Testament often describes God's control over the seas. Jesus' walking on the sea was an unmistakable picture of his divine identity and power (see Job 9:8; 38:16; Psalm 77:19; Isaiah 43:16).

14:26 The disciples were battling exhaustion even before they got into the boat to head back across the lake. Their anticipated rest in a solitary place had been interrupted by the crowds (14:13-14). They had been battling the buffeting waves for some time. Suddenly, in the predawn mist, Jesus came walking toward them on the water. They reacted in **terror,** imagining that they were seeing **a ghost.** Once again, Jesus was doing the unexpected and the impossible. Again the disciples were not ready to grasp what it meant.

14:27 Jesus called out to the disciples over the storm, telling them, **"Don't be afraid."** The literal reading for **"I am here"** is "I am"; it is the same as saying "the I AM is here" or "I, Yahweh, am here" (see Exodus 3:14; Isaiah 41:4; 43:10; 52:6). Jesus, the "I AM," came with unexpected help and encouragement during the disciples' time of desperate need. Their need was real; their fear was real. But in the presence of Jesus, fear can be dismissed.

14:28-29 Peter was not putting Jesus to the test, something we are told not to do (4:7). Instead, he was the only one in the boat who reacted in faith. His impulsive request to also walk **on water** led him to experience a rather unusual demonstration of God's power. Jesus' presence in the storm caused Peter to exercise a fearless faith. But notice that he did so only with Jesus' command to **come.** Notice also that he asked only to do what Jesus was doing; that is, he wanted to share in Jesus' power, some of which the disciples had already been experiencing (10:1).

14:30 Peter started to **sink** because he took his eyes off Jesus and focused on the **high waves** around him. His faith was strong enough to trust that he could walk on the water. But when he realized that he was in a terrifying storm, his faith wavered.

Although we start out with good intentions, sometimes our faith is weak. In Peter's faltering faith we can see the path of discipleship. We have to exercise faith to have the power, but often we stumble and fail to grasp it fully. When Peter's faith faltered, he reached out to Christ, the only one who could help. When you are apprehensive about the troubles around you and doubt Christ's presence or ability to help, remember to put your eyes on Jesus.

14:31 Jesus' immediate response showed Peter that divine undergirding and power are present in times of testing. Jesus **grabbed** Peter, saving him from drowning in the waves. Peter had taken his eyes off Christ and was focusing instead on his situation. Jesus' question focused on why Peter allowed the wind and waves to overwhelm his **faith.** He momentarily despaired and so began to sink. His **doubt** became his downfall.

14:32 Jesus and Peter then **climbed back into the boat** with the rest of the disciples. Then, as had occurred once before when the disciples had experienced another storm, **the wind stopped.** Jesus had revealed to them his complete mastery over nature.

14:33 The disciples' declaration, **"You really are the Son of God!"** indicates a progression in faith. While the disciples **worshiped him,** they still had much to learn about who Jesus was and what he had come to do.

JESUS HEALS ALL WHO TOUCH HIM / 14:34-36 / *98*
The storm had blown the disciples off course, so they did not land at Bethsaida as planned (14:22; see also Mark 6:45). They landed at Gennesaret, a small fertile plain located on the west side of the Sea of Galilee. The small town there had the same name. Capernaum sat at the northern edge of this plain.

14:34-36 Jesus was well-known in the region of Galilee, and his presence always created great excitement. Immediately upon getting out of the boat, people recognized Jesus, and a flurry of activity began. There still would be no rest for him. The **news** of Jesus' arrival **spread quickly** through the area. As Jesus moved through the region, people brought **all their sick to be healed.** Perhaps

the story had spread of the woman in Capernaum who had been healed by touching Jesus' robe, for at this time the people **begged him to let them touch even the fringe of his robe.** No one missed out on Jesus' loving compassion; **all who touched it were healed.** But as the woman in Capernaum learned, healing came from faith in Jesus, not from his garment (9:20-22).

MATTHEW 15

JESUS TEACHES ABOUT INNER PURITY / 15:1-20 / *102*
Another delegation came from Jerusalem to investigate this new rabbi who was causing such a stir throughout the country. Again the Pharisees and teachers of religious law, Jesus' main opponents, raised an issue with Jesus. They wanted to debate Jesus about his disciples' disregard of their oral traditions and rituals.

15:1-2 A delegation came **from Jerusalem,** the center of Jewish authority, and was made up of **Pharisees** (who advocated detailed obedience to the Jewish law and traditions) and **teachers of religious law** (professional interpreters of the law who especially emphasized the traditions). As these religious leaders scrutinized Jesus and his disciples, they noticed that some of his **disciples** were eating without first performing the **tradition of ceremonial hand washing.** This referred not to washing for cleanliness, but to a particular kind of washing that made a person "ceremonially clean" before eating. The Pharisees called this a "tradition," but they believed that it had the same authority as God's law. Their underlying question was, "If you are really a rabbi, as holy, righteous, and versed in the law as we are, then you should know that we don't eat without first ceremonially

washing our hands." Many religious traditions are good and can add richness and meaning to life. Traditions should help us understand God's laws better, not become laws themselves.

15:3-4 Jesus didn't answer their question until 15:10-11. Instead, he dealt with the issue of authority—**your traditions** versus **the direct commandments of God.** Jesus would show that the religious leaders, who had supposedly devoted their lives to protecting the law, had become so zealous for their traditions that they had missed the point of God's law entirely.

Jesus quoted one of the Ten Commandments: **honor your father and mother** (Exodus 20:12). The commandment did not apply just to young children but to anyone whose parents were living. "Honor" includes speaking respectfully and showing care and consideration. The same law is written negatively in Exodus 21:17, **anyone who speaks evil of father or mother must be put to death.** "Speaking evil" (also translated "cursing") means to criticize, ridicule, or abuse verbally. Such action carried a severe penalty.

15:5-6 Jesus then went on to explain how some of the Pharisees had found a way to completely side-step God's command to honor parents: **"But you say, 'You don't need to honor your parents by caring for their needs if you give the money to God instead.'"** Jesus was referring to the vow of "Corban" which allowed a person to dedicate money or property for God's exclusive use, but it could still be used by the donor. This vow was grossly misused. A man could use an article vowed to God indefinitely, but could not transfer it to anyone else. The Pharisees had allowed men to dedicate money to God's Temple that otherwise would have gone to support their parents. But some found a way to keep from doing so and still use their money or property as they chose. A man could simply take the vow of Corban, saying that all his money was dedicated to God. Although the action—dedicating money to God—seemed worthy and no doubt conferred prestige on the giver, these people were ignoring God's clear command to honor their parents. Even worse, this was an irrevocable vow. If a son were to later decide that he needed to help his parents, the Pharisees would not permit it. Jesus rightly said that the Pharisees nullified **the direct commandment of God** by allowing their **tradition** to violate the fifth commandment.

15:7-9 Jesus blasted these self-righteous leaders with one word; he called them **hypocrites.** Jesus then quoted the Scripture that they claimed to know so well. The great prophet **Isaiah** had described these religious leaders: they gave **honor** with their lips, but their **hearts** were **far away** (Isaiah 29:13). They had replaced **God's commands with their own man-made teachings.** Isaiah explained that **their worship is a farce.** Our actions and our attitudes must be sincere. If they are not, Isaiah's words also describe us. The Pharisees knew a lot about God, but they didn't know God.

15:10-11 The Pharisees thought that to eat with defiled hands meant to be defiled (15:1-2). Jesus explained that they were wrong in thinking they were acceptable to God just because they were "clean" on the outside. Defilement is not an external matter (keeping food laws, washing ceremonially, keeping Sabbath requirements), but an internal one. The phrase **"You are not defiled by what you eat"** refers directly to the Pharisees'

question about the disciples eating with "defiled" hands. A person does not become morally defiled by eating with hands that have not been ceremonially washed. Instead, **"you are defiled by what you say and do."** The condition of a person's heart will be revealed by his or her words and actions.

15:12 The concept that people were not defiled by "what goes into the mouth" was revolutionary to the Jews—and especially to the Pharisees, who had built a whole set of rules governing such matters. Mark added the parenthesis that by saying this Jesus had declared all foods clean (Mark 7:19). By so doing, he was establishing himself as the right interpreter of Scripture. Leviticus 11 contains many of the Jewish dietary laws, including a list of foods considered "clean" and "unclean." Over the years, however, the laws had become more important than the reasons for them and the meanings behind them. As the Jews interpreted the dietary laws, they believed that they could be clean before God because of what they had refused to eat. But Jesus explained that sin and defilement do not come from eating the forbidden foods. Rather, they come from the disobedience that begins in the heart. No wonder Jesus **offended the Pharisees!**

15:13-14 The Pharisees may have been offended, but Jesus would add more, explaining that they were being rejected as leaders of God's people. They claimed to be God's true people, but like a weed growing in a flowerbed, they would be **rooted up.** The Pharisees claimed to be leaders of the people (see Romans 2:19), but Jesus turned this around to show that they themselves were **blind guides leading the blind.** They were very proud of their wisdom and enlightenment, so Jesus' indictment would have stung. Their failure to understand God and his desires for people would prove to be disastrous for them and for those who followed them. **Both fall into a ditch** is probably a picture of judgment (see Isaiah 24:18; Jeremiah 48:44).

15:15 Peter often would act as spokesman for the disciples, so he asked Jesus to **explain** what he meant (15:10-11). Later, Peter would be faced with the issue of clean and unclean food (see Acts 10:9-15). Then he would learn that nothing should be a barrier to proclaiming the gospel to the Gentiles (non-Jews). Even more, he would learn that everything created by God is good.

15:16-17 Jesus explained that what goes into a person cannot make that person unclean. Thus, to eat food with hands that may have touched a "defiled" person or article did not mean that the person was ingesting defilement. Logically, as Jesus explained, food **passes through the stomach and then goes out of the body.** It has no effect whatever on the moral condition of the heart. Sin in a person's heart is what defiles that person, not the lack of ceremonial cleansing or the type of food eaten.

15:18-20 Defilement occurs because of sinful thoughts, attitudes, and actions. Sin begins in a person's heart, and **evil words come from an evil heart and defile the person who says them.** All evil acts begin in **the heart.** Jesus made it clear why people sin—it's a matter of the heart. Our hearts have been inclined toward sin from the time we were born. While many people work hard to keep their outward appearance attractive, what is in their hearts is even more important. When people become Christians, God makes them different on the inside, beginning with the heart.

JESUS SENDS A DEMON OUT OF A GIRL / 15:21-28 / 103

Jesus traveled about thirty miles to the region of Tyre and Sidon. These were port cities on the Mediterranean Sea north of Israel. Both cities had flourishing trade and were very wealthy. Jesus withdrew to Gentile territory to evade the opposition of the Pharisees.

15:21-22 Apparently, a woman had heard about Jesus' miracle-working power and how he could cast out demons, so she wasn't going to miss a chance to see him. The woman called Jesus **Lord, Son of David,** showing her acceptance of Jesus' identity as the Jewish Messiah. She may have been a Greek proselyte. Sometimes Gentiles would convert to Judaism, attracted by its strong moral qualities. This woman came to Jesus on behalf of her **daughter,** who was tormented by **a demon.**

15:23 The woman continued to follow after them, and she continued to shout. Finally, the **disciples** urged Jesus to **tell her to leave.** Jesus, always compassionate, would heal the woman's daughter, but not just to make her stop following them. He had a lesson about faith that he needed to teach this woman. In so doing, he would teach the disciples a lesson as well.

15:24 Jesus' words do not contradict the truth that God's message is for all kinds of people (Psalm 22:27; Isaiah 56:7; Matthew 28:19; Romans 15:9-12). After all, when Jesus said, **"I was sent only to help the people of Israel . . . not the Gentiles,"** he was in Gentile territory. He ministered to Gentiles on many other occasions (4:24-25; 8:5-13). Jesus was simply telling the woman that Jews were to have the first opportunity to accept him as the Messiah because God wanted them to present the message of salvation to the rest of the world (see Genesis 12:3). While on earth, Jesus restricted his mission to the people of Israel. He was doing his Father's will (11:27) and fulfilling the promise God made to Jews in the Old Testament. The restricted mission of Jesus and the disciples echoes the principle recorded in 10:5-6.

15:25-26 Undaunted by Jesus' apparent unwillingness to respond to her request, the woman **came and worshiped him,** pleading for help. Jesus' answer comes in the language of a parable; therefore, we must not press the details too far. The simple parable meant that the **children** at the table should be fed before the pets; it would not be right to take the children's food and **throw it to the dogs.** By these words, Jesus may have meant that his first priority was to spend time feeding his children (teaching his disciples), not to take food away from them and throw it to the pets (just anyone). Jesus was not insulting the woman; instead, he was saying that she must not demand what God had ordained for the Jews. She should wait until God's appointed time—when the Gentiles would receive the Good News of the gospel.

15:27 This Gentile woman understood Jesus' parable. Her answer was wise, for she explained to Jesus, by extending his parable, that children often drop morsels of food to their dogs. Not all the Jews accepted Jesus, while some Gentiles chose to follow him. Why couldn't she have some of those **crumbs** that the Jews didn't want? She adroitly pointed out that **even dogs** ate with (not after) the children. She did not ask for the entire meal; she was perfectly willing to take second place behind the Jews. All she wanted right then was a few crumbs—or one "crumb" in particular—one miracle of healing for her daughter.

15:28 Jesus was delighted by the faith of the woman. He granted her request because of her humility and persistence. She had made her request in faith that Jesus could perform the healing. She understood Christ's lordship, and she understood the priorities of his mission. No wonder Jesus exclaimed, **"Your faith is great."** On that basis, Jesus **healed** the woman's daughter.

JESUS HEALS MANY PEOPLE / 15:29-31 / *104*

Then Jesus left the vicinity of Tyre, and returned to the Sea of Galilee. He did not go into Jewish regions, however, but traveled to the northeastern shore of the lake instead, into a primarily Gentile area.

15:29-31 A **vast crowd** surrounded Jesus. They wanted to be healed, and **he healed them all.** The phrase **and they praised the God of Israel** indicates that this was a Gentile crowd. Matthew was showing his Jewish readers that the Gentiles would share with the Jews in the blessings of their Messiah. While Jesus came to the lost sheep of Israel (15:24), he did not restrict his ministry to the Jews alone.

JESUS FEEDS FOUR THOUSAND / 15:32-39 / *105*

Differences in details distinguish this miracle from the feeding of the five thousand described in chapter 14. At that time, those fed were mostly Jews. At this second miracle, Jesus ministered to a mixed crowd of Jews and Gentiles in a predominantly Gentile region.

15:32 This story sounds very much like the feeding of the five thousand recorded in 14:13-21, but it is a separate event. In this episode, the crowd had been following Jesus for **three days,** listening to his teaching and observing his miracles. Jesus took the initiative in his concern for their need for food, and he shared his concern with the disciples. The wording probably does not mean that the people hadn't eaten for three days. Instead, whatever supplies they had brought along were depleted; so most of them had nothing left to eat. Thus, Jesus was concerned not to **send them away hungry.**

15:33 Although the **disciples** had already seen Jesus feed over five thousand people, they had no idea what he would do in this situation, and wondered **where** they would **get enough food** for everyone. Perhaps they didn't expect Jesus to perform the same miracle when the crowd was Gentile and not Jewish (thus revealing their spiritual blindness). Jesus had already found the resources in a previous remote place for an even larger crowd, yet the disciples were completely perplexed as to how they should be expected to feed this crowd.

People often give up when faced with difficult situations. Like the disciples, we often forget God's provision for us in the past. When facing a difficult situation, remember what God has done for you and trust him to take care of you again.

15:34 In the Bible, the number **seven** often signifies perfection or completeness, as in the seven days of creation (Genesis 1) and offering forgiveness seven times (Matthew 18:21). Thus, in this passage some have seen the number seven to have symbolic significance. It may hint at the worldwide scope of Jesus' message.

15:35-36 Jesus **took the seven loaves and the fish** and **thanked God** for the provision he was about to give. Next Jesus **broke** apart the loaves and had the disciples pass them out as before.

15:37-38 As had happened before, each person in the crowd ate and was filled. No one went away hungry from this banquet. The seven loaves and few fish multiplied so that, again, even the leftovers were more than the food Jesus had started with. As before, the number of those who ate, **four thousand men,** meant that there were four thousand men **in addition to all the women and children** who were there.

15:39 Once Jesus knew the people had eaten their fill and would not faint from hunger on their journey home (15:32), he **sent the people home.** Jesus and the disciples **crossed over to the region of Magadan** (also called Dalmanutha), a town located on the western shore of the Sea of Galilee. Magadan was Mary Magdalene's hometown (Luke 8:2-3). This meant a return back to Jewish territory. There Jesus would face further conflict with the Pharisees and Sadducees (16:1-4).

MATTHEW **16**

LEADERS DEMAND A MIRACULOUS SIGN / 16:1-4 / *106*
Following the visit to Gentile territories where the Gentiles saw Jesus' miracles and reacted by praising the God of Israel (15:31), Jesus returned to Jewish territory, only to face a test from the unbelieving religious leaders. As recorded in 12:38-39, they had previously asked for a sign; here they resumed their challenge to Jesus' authority. Matthew pictured the striking contrast of responses to Jesus.

16:1 The religious leaders weren't going to give up in their relentless attempts to discredit Jesus before the crowds. So, upon Jesus' return, **the Pharisees and Sadducees came to test Jesus' claims.** The Pharisees and Sadducees were Jewish religious leaders of two different parties, and their views were diametrically opposed on many issues. The Pharisees carefully followed their religious rules and traditions, believing that this was the way to God. They also believed in the authority of all the books of Scripture that we now call the Old Testament and in the resurrection of the dead. The Sadducees accepted only the books of Moses as Scripture and did not believe in life after death. These two groups, however, had something in common: Jesus was their enemy.

They demanded that Jesus **show them a miraculous sign from heaven.** From their standpoint, this test would show that Jesus was a false prophet. A miraculous sign showed a prophet's reliability—if a prophet said something would happen and it came to pass, this would demonstrate that in all his prophecies he was telling the truth from God. A sign also authenticated the power and authority of the prophet. But Jesus would not give them the sign they demanded. He had in mind an even greater evidence of his power.

16:2-3 The Pharisees and Sadducees had tried to explain away Jesus' other miracles as sleight of hand, coincidence, or use of evil power, but they believed that only God could do a sign from heaven. This, they were sure, would be a feat beyond Jesus' power. Although Jesus could have easily impressed them, he refused. He knew that even a miracle in the sky would not convince them that he was the Messiah because they had already decided not to believe in him. So, instead, he spoke to them in a parable. Jesus' meaning was that while these leaders could discern the signs of the **weather** by watching the sky, they could not **read the obvious signs of the times.** They asked for a sign from heaven; they had the ultimate sign standing in front of them! They could not interpret the coming of God's Kingdom with the appearance of God's Messiah.

16:4 Jesus explained that a sign would come— in *his* timing—and that this sign would be unmistakable. By using **the sign of the prophet Jonah,** who had been inside a great fish for three days, Jesus was predicting his death and resurrection. Jesus' resurrection, of course, would be the most spectacular sign of all.

JESUS WARNS AGAINST WRONG TEACHING / 16:5-12 / *107*
The Jews were required to celebrate an annual period beginning with the Passover during which no yeast was to be found in their homes; all bread had to be made without yeast (Exodus 12:14-20). Yeast is a key ingredient in bread, for it causes the dough to rise. "Yeast" in this passage symbolizes evil.

16:5-6 Jesus had left his confrontation with the Pharisees abruptly, and the disciples had gone with him. Apparently, at some point out on the sea, they

realized that they **had forgotten to bring any food.** The disciples were worrying about bread, so Jesus used the opportunity to teach of the danger of the

yeast of the Pharisees and Sadducees. Jesus was teaching that just as only a small amount of yeast was needed to make a batch of bread rise, so the evil teachings and hypocrisy of the religious and political leaders could permeate and contaminate the entire society. The wrong teachings of the Pharisees were leading the entire nation astray.

16:7-8 After hearing Jesus' warning against wrong teaching, the disciples quietly talked among themselves. They didn't understand the warning. They interpreted Jesus so literally that they missed his point entirely. Jesus' rebuke, **"You have so little faith!"** refers both to their lack of faith in realizing that he could supply bread as needed (as he had already done miraculously two separate times) and to their lack of understanding regarding his teachings. These men, closest to Jesus, would carry a huge responsibility after he was gone. Jesus wanted to be sure that they were getting the message.

16:9-10 Jesus' question, **"Won't you ever understand?"** emphasized that, at this point in his

ministry, the disciples should have begun to understand and perceive who Jesus was. After all they had seen and heard, they should have understood. Jesus had shown compassion on people and had performed miracles to meet their needs. Thus, the disciples should have understood that Jesus would meet their needs as well—whether for bread or for spiritual insight regarding the religious leaders. Jesus wanted the disciples to think about what they had seen, especially in the two feeding miracles. If they considered what had happened, they would have to conclude that Jesus was their Messiah, the Son of God.

16:11-12 The disciples should have realized that Jesus was not **talking about food.** Instead, he wanted the disciples to **beware of the yeast of the Pharisees and Sadducees.** Jesus was severing the disciples from all links to their religious past and the authority of the religious leaders, and was attaching them exclusively to himself.

PETER SAYS JESUS IS THE MESSIAH / 16:13-20 / 109

A beautiful site on the northern shore of the Sea of Galilee, **Caesarea Philippi** was located about twenty-five miles north of Bethsaida, on the slopes of Mount Hermon. The city was primarily non-Jewish, known for its worship of Greek gods and its temples devoted to the ancient god Pan. Jesus spoke to the disciples about who they believed him to be.

16:13-14 As Jesus and the disciples walked toward the city, Jesus asked his disciples what they had heard from the people regarding his identity: **"Who do people say that the Son of Man is?"** The disciples answered Jesus' question with the common view that Jesus was one of the great prophets who had come back to life. This belief may have stemmed from Deuteronomy 18:18, where God said he would raise up a prophet from among the people. Herod had thought that Jesus was **John the Baptist** come back to life (14:1-2), so apparently this rumor was widespread. The people considered Jesus to be **Elijah** because Elijah had been a great prophet, and one like him was expected to come before the Messiah arrived (see Malachi 4:5). **Jeremiah** may have been considered because, according to Jewish legend, he was "immortal" (his death is not mentioned in Scripture)—thus, like Elijah, he did not die but was taken to heaven.

16:15-16 The people may have had various opinions and ideas about Jesus' identity, but Jesus was concerned about what his chosen twelve believed about him. So **he asked them, "Who do you say I am?"** Peter, often the one to speak up

when the others might be silent, declared what he had come to understand, **"You are the Messiah, the Son of the living God."** In his declaration, Peter proclaimed Jesus to be the promised King and Deliverer. This is the core of the gospel message.

The disciples, however, still needed further understanding. Although it certainly had already crossed all of their minds that Jesus might be the Messiah, they still needed to learn about their role as agents of the promised Messiah and their role in his Kingdom. They did not yet fully understand the *kind* of king Jesus would be. Peter, and indeed all Israel, expected the Messiah to be a conqueror-liberator who would free the nation from Rome. Jesus would be a totally different kind of liberator, for he would conquer sin and death and free people from sin's grasp.

16:17 All of the disciples may have had glimmers of understanding about who Jesus was, but Jesus perceived the depth of Peter's confession of faith. Thus Jesus called him **blessed,** meaning especially favored by God's gracious approval.

Peter is pictured as the focus of divine revelation. No **human being** had showed Peter the truth he had just spoken (16:16); instead, Jesus' **Father** in **heaven** had **revealed** it to him. Then, as now, true understanding of who Jesus is and the ability to confess that fact come not from our human nature or will, but from God alone.

16:18 The name **Peter** had already been given to Simon when Jesus first met him (John 1:42). Here Jesus gave the name new meaning. Jesus said, **"You are Peter** [*Greek petros*]**, and upon this rock** [*Greek petra*] **I will build my church."** While the wordplay is evident, what did this rock refer to? The "rock" on which Jesus would build his church has been identified in four main ways:

1. *Jesus himself* as the divine architect of our faith and that he himself is the chief cornerstone. But this truth does not seem to be what the language conveys here. The focus was on Peter.
2. *Peter as the supreme leader or first "bishop" of the church,* promoted by Roman Catholic scholars. It gives authority to the hierarchy of their church and regards Peter and each of his successors as the supreme pontiff of the church. There is no mention of succession in these verses, however, and while the early church expressed high regard for Peter, there is no evidence that they regarded him as final authority.
3. *The confession of faith that Peter gave and that all subsequent true believers give.* This view was promoted by Luther and the reformers as a reaction to view number two.
4. *Peter as the leader of the disciples.* Just as Peter had revealed the true identity of Christ, so Jesus revealed Peter's identity and role. While apostolic succession cannot be found in this context or in any of the epistles, Peter's role as a leader and spokesman of the church must not be discounted. Peter received the revelation of insight and faith concerning Christ's identity, and is the first who confessed Christ.

Though the word "church" (*ekklesia*) is found in the Gospels only in Matthew, the concept is found throughout all four Gospels. Jesus' words reveal that there would be a definite interim period between his death and second coming called the "church age." "Church" means "the called out people of God." Peter's individual authority became clear in the book of Acts as he became the spokesman for the disciples and for the Christian community. Later, Peter reminded Christians that they were the church built on the foundation of the apostles and prophets, with Jesus Christ as the cornerstone (1 Peter 2:4-8; see also 1 Corinthians 3:11). All believers are joined into this church by faith in Jesus Christ as Savior, the same faith that Peter expressed here (see also Ephesians 2:20-21;

Revelation 21:14). True believers like Peter regard their faith as a revelation from God and are willing to confess him publicly. Jesus praised Peter for his confession of faith. Faith like Peter's is the foundation of Christ's Kingdom.

The **powers of hell** represent Satan and all his minions. These words may be interpreted as the power of Satan on the offensive against the church. Christ promises that Satan will not defeat the church; instead, his sphere of operation will be defeated. In these words Jesus gave the promise of the indestructibility of the church and protection for all who believe in him and become part of his church.

16:19 The meaning of this verse has been a subject of debate for centuries. Some say **the keys of the Kingdom of Heaven** represents the authority to carry out church discipline, legislation, and administration (18:15-18); others say the keys give the authority to announce the forgiveness of sins (John 20:23). Most likely, the "keys" are the Kingdom authority given to the church, including the opportunity to bring people to the Kingdom of Heaven by presenting them with the message of salvation found in God's word (Acts 15:7-9). They are also the keys to prohibiting and allowing (18:18-20). Peter had been told about the foundation of a building that Christ would build and then was given the keys to that building. The "keys" suggest not that he was a "doorman," controlling who would enter the building; rather, they portray a "steward," who would administer the building.

Earth and **heaven** refer not to spatial relationships, but to the divine, heavenly authority behind the disciples' earthly actions. "Locking" and "opening" were a rabbinic concept that could have two meanings: to establish rules or to discipline. The disciples would be involved in a certain amount of rule making in building God's community (such as determining what kind of conduct would be worthy of its members), and they would have authority to discipline other members of the community. Thus, the words also refer to the disciples' inspiration as proclaimers of God's new revelation.

The religious leaders thought they held the keys of the Kingdom, and they tried to shut some people out. We cannot decide to open or close the Kingdom of Heaven for others, but God uses us to help others find the way inside. To all who believe in Christ and obey his words, the Kingdom doors are swung wide open.

16:20 Jesus **sternly warned** his disciples **not to tell anyone that he was the Messiah** because at this point they didn't fully understand the significance

of Peter's confession. Everyone still expected
the Messiah to come as a conquering king. But
even though Jesus was the Messiah, he still had
to suffer, be rejected by the leaders, be killed, and

rise from the dead. When the disciples saw all this
happen to Jesus, they would understand what the
Messiah had come to do. Only then would they
be equipped to share the gospel around the world.

JESUS PREDICTS HIS DEATH THE FIRST TIME / 16:21-28 / 110

From this point on, Jesus spoke plainly and directly to his disciples about his death and
resurrection. He began to prepare them for what was going to happen to him by telling
them three times that he would soon suffer and die and then be raised back to life (16:21-28;
17:22-23; 20:17-19).

16:21 The phrase **from then on** marks a turning
point. Jesus began teaching clearly and specifically
what they could expect so that they would not be
surprised when it happened. Contrary to what they
thought, Jesus had not come to set up an earthly
kingdom. He would not be the conquering Messiah because he first had to **suffer** and **be killed.**
For any human king, death would be the end. Not
so for Jesus. Death would only be the beginning,
for **he would be raised on the third day.**

Jesus knew from what quarters the rejection
would come: **the leaders and the leading priests
and the teachers of religious law.** These three
groups made up the Jewish council, the Jewish
supreme court that ultimately sentenced Jesus to
be killed (27:1). Notice that opposition came not
from the people at large, but from their leaders—
the very people who should have been the first to
recognize and rejoice in Messiah's arrival.

16:22 This was too much for **Peter.** Having just
confessed his heartfelt belief in Jesus, Peter certainly found it most unnerving that the king would
soon be put to death. So he took Jesus aside and
corrected him. Peter sought to protect Jesus from
the suffering he prophesied. But if Jesus hadn't
suffered and died, Peter would have died in his
sins. Great temptations can come from those
who love us and seek to protect us. Be cautious
of advice from a friend who says, "Surely God
doesn't want you to face this." Often our most
difficult temptations come from those who try
to protect us from discomfort.

16:23 In his wilderness temptations, Jesus had been
told that he could achieve greatness without dying
(4:8-9). **Peter,** in his rebuke of Jesus' words about
dying, was saying the same thing. Trying to circum-
vent God's plan had been one of Satan's tools; Peter
inadvertently used Satan's tool in trying to protect
his beloved Master. This would be a **dangerous
trap to** Jesus, so Jesus rebuked Peter. God's plan
included suffering and death for the Messiah. Jesus
would fulfill his mission exactly as planned.

16:24 Jesus invites every person to follow him;
they must have a willingness to **put aside selfish
ambition,** to **shoulder** their **cross,** and to **follow.**

To "put aside selfish ambition" means to surrender immediate material gratification in order
to discover and secure one's true self and God's
interests. It is a willingness to let go of selfish
desires and earthly security. This attitude turns
self-centeredness to God-centeredness. "Self" is
no longer in charge; God is.

To "shoulder the cross" was a vivid illustration
of the humility and submission that Jesus was
asking of his followers. Death on a cross was a
form of execution used by Rome for what they
considered dangerous criminals. A prisoner
carried his own cross to the place of execution,
signifying submission to Rome's power. Following Jesus, therefore, meant identifying with Jesus
and his followers, facing social and political
oppression and ostracism, and no turning back.
For some, taking up the cross might indeed mean
death. To "follow" Christ is also a moment-by-
moment decision, requiring compassion and
service. Following Jesus doesn't mean walking
behind him, but taking the same road of sacrifice
and service that he took.

16:25 The Christian life is a paradox: To attempt
to **keep your life** means only to **lose** it. A person
who "saves" his or her life in order to satisfy
desires and goals apart from God ultimately
"loses" life. Not only does that person lose eternal
life, but he or she also loses the fullness of earthly
life promised to those who believe.

By contrast, those who willingly **give up** their
lives for the sake of Christ actually **find true life.**
To be willing to put personal desires and life itself
into God's hands means to understand that nothing
that we can gain on our own in our earthly lives can
compare to what we gain with Christ. Jesus wants us
to choose to follow him rather than to lead a life of
sin and self-satisfaction. He wants us to stop trying
to control our own destiny and to let him direct us.

When we give our lives in service to Christ, however, we discover the real purpose of living.

16:26 To reinforce his words in 16:25, Jesus asked his listeners a rhetorical question. What good would it be for a person to **gain the whole world** (that is, to have power or financial control over the entire world system of which Satan is the head), but **lose** his or her **soul** (that is, to lose eternal life with God)? Every person will die, even those most powerful or most wealthy. If they have not taken care to "save" their lives for eternity with God, then they gain nothing and lose everything.

Many people spend all their energy seeking pleasure. Jesus said, however, that a world of pleasure centered on possessions, position, or power is ultimately worthless. Whatever a person has on earth is only temporary; it cannot be exchanged for his or her soul. Believers must be willing to make the pursuit of God more important than the selfish pursuit of pleasure. If we follow Jesus, we will know what it means to live abundantly now and to have eternal life as well.

16:27 Jesus, here again using the self-designation of **Son of Man,** said that he **will come** again, but at that time he will be in his exalted state as King and Judge. The judgment referred to here is positive, involving the Son of Man's loving acceptance of true disciples. While Jesus called his followers to deny themselves, take up their crosses, and follow, he also promised great reward. Their self-denial

and discipleship would not be wasted. Their repayment would come in the glorious future Kingdom of God.

16:28 When Jesus said some **will not die** before seeing the coming of the **Kingdom,** he may have been referring to

- Peter, James, and John, who would witness the Transfiguration a few days later;
- those who would witness the Resurrection and Ascension;
- the Holy Spirit's coming at Pentecost; and
- all who would take part in the spread of the church after Pentecost.

Some people reading this passage have assumed that Jesus was promising that the disciples would not die before he came back to set up his glorious Kingdom. Perhaps the disciples themselves at first thought that Jesus was referring to his glorious rule on earth. But the disciples have died, so this passage must be interpreted differently. Jesus' Transfiguration, which immediately follows (17:1-13), was a preview of that coming glory. At the Transfiguration, Peter, James, and John saw Jesus' glory, identity, and power as the Son of God. Thus, certain disciples were eyewitnesses to the power and glory of Christ's Kingdom. Jesus' point was that his listeners would not have to wait for another Messiah because the Kingdom was among them, and it would soon come in power.

MATTHEW 17

JESUS IS TRANSFIGURED ON THE MOUNTAIN / 17:1-13 / 111
The time frame of "six days later" ties into 16:28. If Jesus had been referring to his coming Transfiguration, then three of those with Jesus at the time (Peter, James, and John) did get a glimpse of the Kingdom during this significant event. These three disciples comprised the inner circle of the Twelve. Seeing Jesus transfigured was an unforgettable experience for Peter (see 2 Peter 1:16).

17:1-2 Jesus took the disciples **up a high mountain**—either Mount Hermon or Mount Tabor. A mountain was often associated with closeness to God and readiness to receive his words. God had appeared to both Moses (Exodus 24:12-18) and Elijah (1 Kings 19:8-18) on mountains. The Transfiguration was a glimpse of Jesus' true glory, a special revelation of his divinity to Peter, James, and John. This was God's affirmation of every-

thing Jesus had done and was about to do. The Transfiguration clearly revealed not only that they were correct in believing Jesus to be the Messiah (16:16), but that their commitment was well placed and their eternity was secure. Jesus was truly the Messiah, the divine Son of God.

The Greek word translated "transfigured" is *metamorphothe*, from which we get our word "metamorphosis." The verb refers to an outward change that comes from within. Jesus' change was not a change merely in **appearance**; it was a complete change into another form. On earth, Jesus appeared as a man, a poor carpenter from Nazareth turned itinerant preacher. But at the Transfiguration, Jesus' body was transformed into the glorious radiance that he had before coming to earth (John 17:5; Philippians 2:6) and that he will have when he returns in glory (Revelation 1:14-15).

17:3 Moses and Elijah were considered the two greatest prophets in the Old Testament. They were the primary figures associated with the Messiah (Moses was his predictor and Elijah was his precursor), and they both experienced theophanies—that is, special appearances of God (Exodus 24; 1 Kings 19). Moses represented the law, or the old covenant. He had written the Pentateuch and had predicted the coming of a great prophet (Deuteronomy 18:15-19). Elijah represented the prophets who had foretold the coming of the Messiah (Malachi 4:5-6). Moses' and Elijah's presence with Jesus confirmed Jesus' messianic mission to fulfill God's law and the words of God's prophets (5:17). Their appearance also removed any thought that Jesus was a reincarnation of Elijah or Moses.

17:4 Peter suggested making **three shrines**, one for each of them. He may have thought that God's Kingdom had come when he saw Jesus' glory. Perhaps Peter had overlooked Jesus' words that suffering and death would precede glory. He saw the fulfillment of Christ's glory for a moment and wanted the experience to continue. Regardless of his motives, he had mistakenly made all three men equal. He had missed Jesus' true identity as God himself.

17:5 Just as God's voice in the cloud over Mount Sinai gave authority to his law (Exodus 19:9), God's voice at the Transfiguration gave authority to Jesus' words. A **bright cloud** suddenly appeared and God's **voice** spoke from the cloud, singling out Jesus from Moses and Elijah as the long-awaited Messiah who possessed divine authority. As he had done at Jesus' baptism, the Father was identifying Jesus as his **beloved Son** and the promised Messiah.

17:6-8 When the disciples heard God's voice speaking directly to them as they were enveloped by the luminous cloud, they were **terrified.** Throughout Scripture, the visible glory of deity creates fear (see Daniel 10:7-9). But Jesus told them not to be afraid. Peter may have wanted to keep Jesus and Elijah and Moses there in shrines on the mountainside, but his desire was wrong. The event was merely a glimpse of what was to come. Thus, **when they looked** up, the cloud and the prophets were gone. The disciples had to look only to Jesus. He alone was qualified to be the Savior.

17:9 Jesus instructed Peter, James, and John not to tell anyone about what they had seen, presumably not even the other disciples because they would not fully understand it, until Jesus would be **raised from the dead.** This is the only injunction to silence given by Jesus with a time limit. It suggests that once the temporary time limit had expired, the three would not need to keep Jesus' identity secret anymore. Furthermore, after the Resurrection, these disciples would understand the Transfiguration and be able to correctly interpret and proclaim it.

17:10 The appearance of **Elijah** on the mountain caused a question in the disciples' minds. Based on Malachi 4:5-6, the Jewish teachers believed that Elijah had to **return before the Messiah** to usher in the messianic age. Elijah had appeared on the mountain, but he had not come in person to prepare the people for the Messiah's arrival (especially in the area of repentance). The disciples fully believed that Jesus was the Messiah, but they wondered about the prophecy regarding Elijah.

17:11-13 Jesus explained to the disciples that the Jewish teachers correctly understood that **Elijah** would come before the Messiah and bring spiritual renewal (see Malachi 4:5-6). Elijah was supposed to come first, but Jesus explained that, in fact, Elijah had **already come.** Jesus was referring to **John the Baptist,** not to a reincarnation of the Old Testament prophet Elijah. John the Baptist had taken on Elijah's prophetic role; he boldly confronted sin and pointed people to God.

JESUS HEALS A DEMON-POSSESSED BOY / 17:14-21 / *112*
Even though the disciples had been given much power (10:8), Matthew records the failure of the disciples throughout this section (14:16-21, 26-27, 28-31; 15:16, 23, 33; 16:5, 22; 17:4, 10-22). It serves to teach that the power to heal is God's and must be appropriated by faith.

17:14-15 Jesus, Peter, James, and John came down from the mountain and returned to the other nine disciples and **a huge crowd.** A man had asked for mercy on his son, who had **seizures** and was suffering terribly. Mark gives more detail, for the man explained that he had come looking for Jesus to heal his son who was possessed by an evil spirit, making him unable to utter any sound (also he could not hear, see Mark 9:25). This was not just a case of epilepsy; it was the work of an evil spirit. The demon's destructive intent is seen in that the boy would often fall into the **fire** or **water.**

17:16 Having heard of Jesus' power to cast out demons, the father had come to Jesus, hoping for a cure for his son. He **brought** his son to the **disciples** to drive out the spirit, an appropriate request since the disciples had been given this power (10:1). But the disciples could not drive out the demon.

17:17-18 Jesus cried out in exasperation, fed up with unbelief and lack of faith. His unusual words carry a biting rebuke. The disciples had been given the authority to do the healing, but they had not yet learned how to appropriate God's power. Jesus' frustration was with the **stubborn, faithless people,** including the crowd, the teachers of religious law, the man, and the nine disciples. His disciples merely reflected that attitude of unbelief so prevalent in the society.

Then Jesus **rebuked the demon,** and it came out of the boy.

17:19-21 The disciples had been unable to drive out this demon, and they asked Jesus why. They had cast out demons before; why hadn't this demon responded? Perhaps the disciples had tried to drive out the demon with their own ability rather than God's. If so, their hearts and minds were not in tune with God, so their words had no power.

Jesus pointed to the disciples' lack of **faith.** Jesus wasn't condemning the disciples for substandard faith; he was trying to show how important faith would be in their future ministry. It is the power of God, not our faith, that can move a **mountain,** but faith must be present to do so. As the **mustard seed** that grew into a large garden plant (13:31-32), even a small "seed" of faith is sufficient.

There is great power in even a little faith when God is with us. If we feel weak or powerless as Christians, we should examine our faith, making sure we are trusting not in our own abilities to produce results but in God's. If we are facing problems that seem as big and immovable as mountains, we must turn our eyes from the mountain and look to Christ for more faith. Then, as Jesus promised, **nothing** will be **impossible.**

Verse 21 does not appear in most modern translations because the best Greek manuscripts do not have it.

JESUS PREDICTS HIS DEATH THE SECOND TIME / 17:22-23 / 113

17:22-23 The disciples still resisted Jesus' predictions of his suffering and death. This was the second time he clearly told the disciples that he **(the Son of Man)** would suffer (see 16:21). Whereas Jesus had spoken before about being rejected, this time he added the element of betrayal. He again said that he would be **killed** and **be raised from the dead.** There was again the assurance of victory, although the disciples always seemed to miss this point.

PETER FINDS THE COIN IN THE FISH'S MOUTH / 17:24-27 / 114
This return to Capernaum would be Jesus' last visit prior to his death. Only Matthew records this incident—perhaps because he had been a tax collector himself.

17:24 All Jewish males (age twenty and older) had to pay a **Temple tax** every year (Exodus 30:11-16). The amount was equivalent to about two days' wages for the average worker. The money went for public sacrifices and then for the upkeep of the Temple. Tax collectors set up booths to collect these taxes. These **tax collectors** were probably the Temple commissioners who went through Palestine annually (these were not the same people

who collected the Roman tax, such as Matthew). These collectors **came to Peter.** He may have been seen as a leader in this band of Jesus' followers, or he may have been approached because he was "head of the household" and a homeowner in Capernaum. These men asked Peter if Jesus **(your teacher)** would be paying the Temple tax. To not pay the tax indicated a desire to separate from the religious community.

17:25-26 Peter answered a question without really knowing the answer, thereby putting Jesus and the disciples in an awkward position. Jesus used this situation, however, to emphasize his kingly role. Jesus' question generalized the issue from the Jewish tax to all taxes. **Kings** collected taxes from **foreigners**, but never from **their own people** (referring to their family). If the tax is the Temple tax, then it belongs to God, and as a royal child of the king, there would be no need for Jesus to pay tax to his Father. By these words, Jesus once again established his identity as the Son of God.

17:27 Just as kings pay no taxes and collect none from their family, Jesus, the King, owed no Temple tax because he and his "children" belonged to another Kingdom. But Jesus supplied the tax payment for both himself and Peter rather than **offend** those who didn't understand his kingship. Jesus taught his disciples that at times it would be important to submit for the sake of their witness. (See also Romans 13:1-7; 1 Timothy 2:1-3; Titus 3:1-3, 8; 1 Peter 2:13-17.)

MATTHEW 18

THE DISCIPLES ARGUE ABOUT WHO WOULD BE THE GREATEST / 18:1-6 / 115

All believers are presently part of the Kingdom, yet the consummation of that Kingdom is still in the future. In the meantime, we must learn to live together in a way that pleases God. In this chapter, Matthew included a fourth discourse that deals with life in the community of believers.

18:1 The opening phrase **about that time** ties this event to the previous teaching (17:24-27). The disciples wondered about this coming Kingdom of which Jesus would be the king. In addition, Jesus' talk of his coming death probably made them wonder how they were to run the Kingdom in his absence. The disciples were naturally curious about their position in the coming Kingdom. This question, **"Which of us is greatest?"** also may have been fueled by the special privileges given to Peter, James, and John at various times—most recently their trip with Jesus to the mountain and then their silence about what had happened there (17:1-9).

18:2-4 To answer the disciples' question, Jesus **called a small child over to him.** The disciples needed to **become as little children.** Jesus wanted them to change their attitude toward greatness. The disciples had become preoccupied with the organization of an earthly kingdom and were seeking positions of advantage. Jesus used a child to help his self-centered disciples get the point. They were to have servant attitudes, not being "childish" (arguing over petty issues) but "childlike," with **humble** and sincere hearts. God's people are called to humility and unconcern for social status. Those who persist in pride and "ladder climbing" for the sake of status in

this world **will never get into the Kingdom of Heaven.** By contrast, those who, in humility, realize their need of a Savior, accept him, and move into the world to serve, not only enter the Kingdom but will be **greatest in the Kingdom of Heaven.** True humility means to deny oneself, to accept a position of servanthood, and to completely follow the Master.

18:5 Jesus was also teaching the disciples to welcome children. This was a new approach in a society where children were usually treated as second-class citizens. Jesus equated the attitude of welcoming children with a willingness to receive him. An attitude that **welcomes a little child like this** readily welcomes and embraces believers of little worldly importance and low status. This shows an attitude that also welcomes the Savior, for he too was of little worldly importance and of low status. In God's Kingdom, greatness lies in acceptance of and dependence upon the Savior. Together in the church, believers are to welcome and love one another, encourage one another, allow everyone a place to shine according to their gifts, and appreciate one another.

18:6 As in 18:5, **these little ones** refers not just to children but to Jesus' "little ones"—the disciples. Jesus warned that anyone who turns people away from him will receive severe punishment. A **mill-**

stone was a heavy, flat stone used to grind grain. To have a millstone tied around one's **neck** and then be **thrown into the sea** meant certain death by drowning. Even the horror of such a death was minor compared to what this person would face in eternity.

JESUS WARNS AGAINST TEMPTATION / 18:7-9 / *117*
With strong language (not meant to promote self-mutilation), Jesus described how the disciples should renounce anything that would cause them to sin or turn away from the faith.

18:7 Jesus described two **terrible** situations in the verse. First, it **will be terrible for anyone who causes others to sin**. Second, **it will be** terrible **for the person who does the tempting.** Jesus' followers face constant temptations from the world to do evil. Yet this does not excuse those individuals who are the cause of stumbling. This responsibility to lead people correctly applies to individuals, churches, and institutions. No person or organization should lead people astray into sin.

18:8-9 The action of surgically cutting **sin** out of their lives should be prompt and complete in order to keep them from sin. All who desire to follow Jesus must remove any stumbling blocks that cause sin. Jesus did not mean to literally cut off a part of the body; he meant that any relationship, practice, or activity that leads to sin should be stopped. As a person would submit to losing a diseased appendage (**hands** or **feet**) or a sense (sight) in order to save his or her life, so believers should be just as willing to "cut off" any temptation, habit, or part of their nature that could lead them to hold on to this world and turn away from Christ and into sin. Just cutting off a limb that committed sin or gouging out an eye that looked lustfully would still not get rid of sin, for that must begin in the heart and mind. Jesus was saying that people need to take drastic action to keep from stumbling. The reason? Jesus explained that it would be better to have lost some worldly possession, attitude, or action than to keep it and **be thrown into hell.** This is true, radical discipleship. While no person will be completely sin-free until eternity, God wants an attitude that renounces sin instead of one that holds on to sin.

JESUS WARNS AGAINST LOOKING DOWN ON OTHERS / 18:10-14 / *118*
This verse is found only in Matthew and bridges from the concept of leading the little ones astray to seeking them when they do go astray (see also 18:6).

18:10-11 Little ones can refer to both children and disciples. The words **don't despise** pointed directly at the pious religious leaders who showed nothing but contempt for those below them on the "spiritual ladder" (see, for example, Luke 18:9-14 about the Pharisee and the tax collector). The reason the "little ones" should not be despised is because **in heaven their angels are always in the presence of my heavenly Father.** Some have seen in these verses the concept of guardian angels. These words neither prove nor condemn the concept. Being in God's presence means having access to God, so these angels are ministering angels (see Hebrews 1:14). The Old Testament does not speak about guardian angels assigned to God's people, but it does speak of angelic intercession and help (as in Psalm 91:11). Also, in Daniel 10:10-14, angels watch over nations. The meaning here is that God's people are constantly represented before the Father; therefore, each one of us has special importance (see Hebrews 1:14).

Verse 11 is not found in the earliest and best manuscripts; therefore, it is not included in most modern versions.

18:12 Jesus was addressing his disciples, reminding them that God's care extends to each of his "little ones" (here portrayed as **sheep**). If a sheep should go astray from the flock, God, like a protective **shepherd, will go out into the hills to search for the lost one.** God is concerned about every single believer and will actively go in search of those who have "gone astray" (meaning they have gotten out of a right relationship with him, are heading toward false teaching, are heading down a dangerous path in life, or are falling into sin).

18:13-14 The sheep went astray, but the shepherd sought after it. The Father does not want any of his flock to wander away. God so loves each of his followers that, should they go astray, he actively seeks and rejoices when they return to him. A sheep that is not "found" (that is, one that willingly refuses faith) will face a consequence—that sheep will **perish.** But God does not want that to happen. He will **rejoice over** a "lost" person who is "found!" And God wants faithful believers to be part of the rescue team. Our follow-through care of new Christians, our small group ministry, and our individual contact with fellow believers should demonstrate the Great Shepherd's care for his sheep.

JESUS TEACHES HOW TO TREAT A BELIEVER WHO SINS / 18:15-20 / *119*

The thrust of the parable in 18:12-14 leads naturally into the area of discipline. Note that the rigid use of excommunication (18:8-9) was muted by the law of love, which seeks to bring the straying believer back into the fold.

18:15 These are Jesus' guidelines for dealing with those who sin against us. These guidelines were meant for Christians and for discipline and conflict resolution in the context of the church. These steps are designed to reconcile church members who disagree, so that the church body can live in harmony.

Jesus explained that the person who has been offended must first **go privately and point out the fault.** A personal confrontation, carried out in love, will allow the sinning member the opportunity to correct himself. However, the person doing the confronting ought to be very certain of his accusation and that he is doing this out of true humility with a view to restoration of the other (see Galatians 6:1-4). Many misunderstandings and hurt feelings can be solved at this stage, but this is not a license for a frontal attack on every person who hurts or slights us. Personal action saves church leaders from getting involved in everyone's personal concerns. Personal confrontation also keeps believers from gossiping with one another. Instead, believers are to be mature enough to go directly to the source and deal with the problem at that level.

18:16 If the personal confrontation yields nothing, then the confronter is to proceed to step two. In this step, he takes **one or two others** along. This is backed up by Old Testament Law (see Deuteronomy 19:15). These "others" also ought to help in reconciliation at this second meeting, hoping to settle the matter privately. An erring person might be willing to listen to the wise counsel of these others. In addition, they serve as **witnesses** to this meeting.

18:17 If the additional witnesses can accomplish no reconciliation and the **person still refuses to listen,** then the third step is to **take** the **case to the church.** The objective at this point still is not disciplinary action but helping the sinning person to see his or her fault, repent, and be restored. But even the law of love has its limit.

The fourth and last step is to disassociate with that person. The goal, even through this difficult act, is to help the person see his or her sin and repent. Paul recommended such action to the church in Corinth (see 1 Corinthians 5:1-13; 2 Corinthians 2:5-11; 2 Thessalonians 3:14-15). The person should be treated **as a pagan or a corrupt tax collector.**

While all people in the church are "sinners saved by grace," and while no church will ever be free of members who commit sin, the person described here has a huge blind spot to sin, and many people can see it. Yet this person refuses to listen to those whom God sends to help. In the church, believers are to teach, challenge, encourage, admonish, help, and love each other. But there can be no true fellowship with a believer who commits sin and refuses the loving guidance of his or her fellow church members.

18:18 This verse parallels the similar authority given to Peter and the disciples in 16:19. Here the authority belongs to the church—the word **you** is plural. **What they prohibit** and what they **allow** refer to the decisions of the church in conflicts and discipline. Among believers, there is no court of appeals beyond the church. Ideally, the church's decisions should be God-guided and based on discernment of his word. Believers have the responsibility, therefore, to bring their problems to the church, and the church has the responsibility to use God's guidance in seeking to discipline members.

18:19-20 In context, the application of this verse applies to matters of church discipline. **Two** people **agree,** and God stands **among them** as they work through their disagreement. If the matter must go before the church, God is there helping those in agreement to deal with the sinning member as they ought. Indeed, God may be using the people to "chase down the lost sheep," so to speak, and bring him or her back "into the fold."

JESUS TELLS THE PARABLE OF THE UNFORGIVING DEBTOR / 18:21-35 / *120*
At this point, the perspective shifts to showing God's grace and how ridiculous it is for us to withhold forgiveness from those who sin against us.

18:21 Peter asked Jesus a question commonly discussed in rabbinic debates. The common answer was that it was considered sufficient to **forgive** three times. Peter may have chosen the number **seven** not only to indicate generosity, but also because the number seven is commonly used in the Bible to communicate completeness.

18:22 Jesus' answer did not mean his followers ought to keep count up to **seventy times seven;** rather, this statement means not to keep track of numbers at all. There ought to be no limit to a believer's willingness to forgive another believer (within the confines of the steps set out above in helping to restore straying believers, 18:15-20). All believers ought to willingly forgive, for all believers have already been forgiven far beyond their comprehension, as the following parable shows.

18:23-24 This parable is recorded only in Matthew and illustrates the need for unlimited forgiveness in the body of Christ. A **king** decided that he wanted to go over the books with his accountant. This first man found himself in debt for a huge sum of money.

18:25 The man **couldn't pay** the king the millions that he owed, so the king **ordered** that he, his family, and his possessions be sold **to pay the debt.** The sale of family as well as possessions to pay debts was common in ancient times.

18:26-27 The man humbly **fell down before the king and begged** for patience. The merciful king was **filled with pity, released him and forgave his debt.** This highly unlikely turn of events would have surprised Jesus' listeners. What an incredible load must have been taken from his shoulders! Unfortunately, the story doesn't end here.

18:28-31 The king had forgiven a debt of millions of dollars and had let his servant go free. But when that servant left, he went to a fellow servant who owed him a few thousand dollars. He grabbed him by the throat and demanded instant payment. The thousands he was owed was a significant amount, but compared to the millions, it was extremely small. The fellow servant also begged for patience but was refused, arrested, and jailed until the debt could be paid.

Compared to what the first servant had been forgiven, his refusal to forgive another was appalling. Apparently **other servants** (other court officials) thought his behavior was appalling as well, so they **went to the king and told him what had happened.**

18:32-33 For some reason, the first servant just didn't understand. After being forgiven millions of dollars, he threw into prison a fellow servant who owed him a few thousand. But before he continued too far on his merry way, he found himself summoned back to the **king.** The king, who had been so merciful, angrily reproved the servant for accepting forgiveness and then being unwilling to extend forgiveness to another. The servant should have had **mercy** on his fellow servant.

18:34 The **king** was so **angry** that he **sent the man to prison.** Because this man would not forgive another, the king decided not to forgive his debt either. Instead, the man would be imprisoned **until he had paid every penny.** This man effectively received a life sentence.

18:35 The king in the parable represents the **heavenly Father** and pictures his role as judge. In the context of interchurch discipline, the parable could underscore the corporate responsibility of the church to deal righteously with erring members. This includes harsh judgment on those who hurt the fellowship by refusing to forgive one another. But because God has forgiven all our sins, we should not withhold forgiveness from others. Realizing how completely Christ has forgiven us should produce a free and generous attitude of forgiveness toward others. When we don't forgive others, we are saying that we appreciate God's love and forgiveness but that we're unwilling to give it to anyone else.

MATTHEW 19

JESUS TEACHES ABOUT MARRIAGE AND DIVORCE / 19:1-12 / *173*

Both Matthew and Mark note the geographic shift in Jesus' ministry from Galilee to Judea and the area east of the Jordan River. John the Baptist had ministered there, and crowds had come to Jesus from the region earlier (see Mark 3:8). Jesus continued his ministry, but he was moving toward his death in Jerusalem.

19:1-3 The **Pharisees** hoped to trap Jesus by getting him to choose sides in a theological controversy regarding **divorce.** The debate focused on Moses' words about divorce in Deuteronomy 24:1-4. Some thought a man could divorce his wife for almost any reason. Others thought that a man could divorce his wife only if she had been unfaithful to him. If Jesus were to support divorce, he would be upholding the Pharisees' procedures; they doubted that Jesus would do that. If Jesus were to choose sides in the controversy, some members of the crowd would dislike his position, for some may have used the law to their advantage to divorce their wives. Or, if he were to speak against divorce altogether, he would appear to be speaking against Moses.

19:4-6 The Pharisees had quoted Moses' writings in Deuteronomy; Jesus also quoted from Moses' writings (Genesis 1:27; 2:24), but he went back to Genesis, **the beginning,** referring to the ideal state of creation and particularly of marriage. In creating **male and female,** God's plan was that in marriage the husband and wife **are united into one.** The wife is not property, but a person created in God's image. Jesus drew a distinction: God's creation of marriage and his absolute command that it be a permanent union versus the provisions written hundreds of years later that tolerated divorce because of people's utter sinfulness (19:8). The Pharisees regarded Deuteronomy 24:1 as a proof text for divorce. But Jesus focused on marriage rather than divorce. The Pharisees regarded divorce as a legal issue rather than a spiritual one; marriage and divorce were merely transactions similar to buying and selling land (with women being treated as property). But Jesus condemned this attitude, clarifying God's original intention; that marriage bring unity that **no one** should **separate.**

19:7-8 The Pharisees asked why Moses allowed divorce. They wondered if Jesus was saying that Moses had written laws contrary to God's commands. In reality, Moses had instituted divorce laws to help its victims. Under Jewish law, only a husband could initiate and carry out a divorce. The civil laws protected the women, who, in that culture, were quite vulnerable when living alone. Because of Moses' law, a man could no longer just throw his wife out—he had to write **an official letter of divorce** so she could remarry and reclaim her dowry. This was a major step toward civil rights for women, for it made a man think twice before sending his wife away. Moses' words gave protection to the wife and limited abuses of divorce.

In Moses' time, as well as in Jesus' day and today, the practice of marriage fell far short of God's intention. Jesus said that Moses **permitted divorce** only because of people's **hard-hearted wickedness,** referring to a stubborn, willful attitude. Many refused to follow through with their marriages as God had intended, so God allowed divorce as a concession to their sinfulness. Jesus turned the Pharisees' "test" question back on them by using it as an opportunity to review God's intended purpose for marriage and to expose their spiteful motives in testing Jesus.

19:9 Jesus had clearly explained that divorce dissolves a divinely formed union. Some men were divorcing in order to get remarried. The rabbis' interpretation of Moses' law permitted remarriage after divorce, but Jesus explained that marriage after divorce is **adultery.** However, he gave one exception: **unless** the **wife has been unfaithful** (see also 5:32). Scholars agree that Jesus' words refer to both husbands and wives; that is, the unfaithfulness of one could be grounds for divorce by the other (see Mark 10:12).

While the application of Jesus' words requires interpretation to specific situations, one truth is inescapable: God created marriage to be a sacred, permanent union and partnership between husband and wife. When both husband and wife enter this union with that understanding and commitment, they can provide security for each other, a stable home for their children, and strength to weather any of life's storms or stresses.

19:10 The **disciples** believed Jesus upheld such an impossible standard that it would be **better** for people **not to marry** than to enter into the covenant of marriage. It seemed better not to make the vow than to make the vow and not be able to keep it.

19:11-12 The high ideal of marriage was not for everyone, but **only those whom God helps.** Those given that responsibility are expected to adhere to it. There are some to whom this gift of marriage is *not* given. A "eunuch" is an emasculated male—a man with no testicles. Some **are born as eunuchs,** who perhaps had physical limitations that prevented their marrying. Others were **made that way by others,** such as those servants who, in ancient cultures, were castrated in order to serve the master without sexual distractions. **Some choose not to marry for the sake of the Kingdom of Heaven,** voluntarily remaining abstinent because, in their particular situation, they could serve God better as single people. Jesus himself would be in this category, as was the apostle Paul.

JESUS BLESSES THE CHILDREN / 19:13-15 / *174*
Jesus wanted little children to come to him because he loves them and because they have the kind of attitude needed to approach God. He didn't mean that heaven is only for children but that people need childlike attitudes of trust in God. The receptiveness of little children was a great contrast to the stubbornness of the religious leaders who let their education and sophistication stand in the way of the simple faith needed to believe in Jesus.

19:13-15 It was customary for people to bring their **children** to a rabbi for a blessing. Thus people were bringing children to Jesus so that he could **lay his hands on them and pray for them.** The disciples thought the children were unworthy of the Master's time. In the first century, Jewish households were patriarchal—men came first, followed by women and children. The disciples apparently viewed these parents and children as an intrusion and a drain of time and energy. So they **told** the people **not to bother** Jesus with their children.

Jesus told his disciples to **let the children come** because **the Kingdom of Heaven belongs to such as these.** The disciples must have forgotten what Jesus had said about children earlier (see 18:4-6). Anyone of any age who exhibits such faith and trust is promised access to Jesus and to the Kingdom.

JESUS SPEAKS TO THE RICH YOUNG MAN / 19:16-30 / *175*
While the children came readily to Jesus, a rich young man had difficulty. He wanted to get close, but he wanted to do so on his own terms. To this man seeking assurance of eternal life, Jesus pointed out that salvation does not come from good deeds but from submitting humbly to the lordship of Christ.

19:16 A man ran up to Jesus who wanted to be sure he would receive **eternal life.** He asked **what good things** he should **do** to get it. He viewed eternal life as something that one achieves.

19:17-19 At first, Jesus did not address the man's question but, instead, challenged him to think about God. Goodness is not measured by one's works; in fact, **only God is good.** Jesus wanted the man to turn his attention from himself and instead think about God's absolute goodness.

In response to the young man's question about how to have eternal life, Jesus told him to **keep the commandments,** and then he listed five of the Ten Commandments (numbers five through nine) and added Leviticus 19:18 (**love your neighbor as yourself**)—all referring to relationships with others.

19:20 The man sincerely believed that he had **obeyed all these commandments,** yet he felt that something was lacking. The powerful lesson here is that even *if* a person could keep all these commandments perfectly, which this man claimed to have done, there would still be a lack of assurance of salvation. The answer was that keeping the commandments perfectly could not save anyone—for obedience is not a matter of law keeping, it is a matter of the heart. This was a mind-bending revelation to this young man and to all of Jesus' listeners.

19:21 Jesus' words, **if you want to be perfect,** can be translated, "if you want to be mature or full-grown." The man said he had never once broken any of the laws Jesus mentioned, so he may have felt that he had attained a certain level of perfection. But the law was not the standard of perfection, God was. Jesus lovingly broke through the man's pride by pointing out that despite his self-proclaimed obedience, he still had a long way to go in understanding what God desired. Jesus told him, **"Sell all you have and give the money to the poor."** This challenge exposed the barrier that could keep this man out of the Kingdom: his love of money. Ironically, his attitude made him unable to keep the first commandment, one that Jesus did not quote: "Do not worship any other gods besides me" (Exodus 20:3). The young man did not love God with his whole heart as he had presumed. In reality, his many possessions were his god, his idol. If he could not give these up, he would be violating the first commandment.

The task of selling all his possessions would not, of itself, give the man eternal life. But such radical obedience would be the first step for this man to become a follower of Jesus. The man thought he needed to *do* more; Jesus explained that there was plenty more he could do, but not in order to obtain eternal life. Instead, he needed an attitude adjustment toward his wealth. By putting his **treasure in heaven** and following Jesus along the road of selflessness and service to others, the man could be assured of his eternal destiny.

19:22 This man's **many possessions** made his life comfortable and gave him power and prestige. When Jesus told him to sell everything he owned, Jesus was touching the very basis of the man's security and identity. He could not meet the one requirement that Jesus gave—to turn his whole heart and life over to God. The one assurance he wanted, eternal life, was unattainable because he deemed the price too high. The man came to Jesus wondering what he could do; he left seeing what he was unable to do. How tragic—to be possessed by possessions and miss the opportunity to be with Jesus.

19:23-24 Jesus looked at his disciples and taught them a lesson from this incident with the rich young man. Jesus explained that it was **very hard for a rich person to get into the Kingdom of Heaven** (not impossible, but hard). Jesus used a common Jewish proverb of a **camel** unable to **go through the eye of a needle** to describe the diffi-culty of the rich entering God's Kingdom. Wealth can be a stumbling block. The rich, with most of their basic physical needs met, often become self-reliant. When they feel empty, they can buy something new to dull the pain that was meant to drive them toward God. Their abundance and self-sufficiency become their deficiency. People who have everything on earth can still lack what is most important—eternal life.

19:25-26 The **disciples** wondered what Jesus meant. The Jews looked upon wealth as a blessing from God, a reward for being good, a sign of his special favor. If the rich—those who from the disciples' vantage point seemed to be first in line for salvation—cannot be saved, then **who in the world can be saved?**

In reality, it is not just the rich who have difficulty, for salvation is not possible for anyone from a human standpoint. No one can be saved by his or her wealth, achievements, talents, or good deeds: **Humanly speaking, it is impossible.** But the situation is not hopeless, for God has an entirely different plan: **With God everything is possible.** Salvation cannot be earned; God gives it to us as a gift.

19:27 Peter mentioned that the disciples had **given up everything to follow** Jesus. Peter's question, **"What will we get out of it?"** emphasizes that the disciples had done the ultimate in self-denial and had followed Jesus' call. While Peter's question seems somewhat selfish, he was merely thinking about rewards from the standpoint of his Jewish background. In the Old Testament, God rewarded his people according to his justice, and obedience often brought reward in this life (Deuteronomy 28). But Jesus explained to Peter that obedience and immediate reward are not always linked. If they were, good people would always be rich, and suffering would always be a sign of sin. The disciples' true reward (and ours) was God's presence and power through the Holy Spirit. The reward also includes the assurance of salvation and eternal life (an assurance that the rich young man lacked, 19:20). Later, in eternity, God will reward his people for faith and service (see 5:12).

19:28 Peter and the other disciples had paid a high price—leaving their homes and jobs—to follow Jesus. But Jesus reminded them that following him has its benefits as well as its sacrifices. The Jews looked forward to a restoration at the messianic age at the end of the world based on Old Testament prophecy (Isaiah 65:17; 66:22). They believed that a golden age similar to the days when David ruled the kingdom would be restored. This would occur when the **Son of Man** is seated on his **glorious throne in the Kingdom.** Jesus made it clear that this was an event still in the future. The disciples had been hoping that it would happen immediately, but Jesus' constant talk of his coming death made them wonder what would happen to them in this whole scenario and who would rule in Jesus' absence.

Jesus clarified that the time would come when he would rule. They, in turn, would **sit on twelve thrones, judging the twelve tribes of Israel.** This may refer to the apostles ruling the tribes of Israel at Christ's return. The exact time and nature of that role is not specified. But it may also picture the disciples overseeing the church, which will have a prominent place in God's plan.

19:29 Jesus assured the disciples that anyone who gave up something valuable for his sake would be repaid a hundred times over, although not necessarily in the same form. For example, someone may be rejected by his or her family for accepting Christ, but he or she will gain the larger family of believers with all the love it has to offer.

Here is the answer to the rich young ruler's question about how to obtain eternal life. Jesus explained that by submitting to his authority and rule, making him top priority over all else, and

giving up anything that hinders following him, each person can **have eternal life.** For the rich young man, that meant giving up money as his idol. For each person the sacrifice may be different, though no less difficult. We may have little or much, but are we willing to give it all up in order to have eternal life?

19:30 Jesus had already shown that the "greatest" are like "little children" (18:1-4). In the world to come, the values of this world will be reversed. Those who believe but who still seek **to be important** here on earth will **be the least** in heaven. Jesus may have been referring to the disciples' mixed-up motives. They had given up everything and hoped for rewards and for status in God's Kingdom. Jesus explained that yearning for position would cause them to lose any position they might have. Christ's disciples who have humbly served others are most qualified to be great in heaven. Rewards in heaven are not given on the basis of merit or "time served" or other earthly standards. What matters in heaven is a person's commitment to Christ. Radical discipleship is a willingness to follow totally and accept the consequences, a willingness to surrender everything to and for the service of Christ. It is the only path to reward.

MATTHEW 20

JESUS TELLS THE PARABLE OF THE VINEYARD WORKERS / 20:1-16 / 176

This parable further explains Jesus' words in 19:30 explaining the "first and last" saying by focusing on the landowner's generosity in welcoming everyone into his field. Jesus further clarified the membership rules of the Kingdom of Heaven—entrance is by God's grace alone.

20:1-7 In this parable, God is the **owner,** believers are the **workers,** and the **vineyard** is the **Kingdom of Heaven.** The landowner went out **early one morning** to find some workers to whom he **agreed to pay the normal daily wage.** Then the owner went out again **at nine o'clock in the morning** and **hired** more workers. They agreed to be paid **whatever was right at the end of the day.** He did the same thing **at noon** and again **at five o'clock that evening.** These last men were willing to work for that last hour, even though they would not earn much money.

20:8-10 At **evening** (referring to sunset), the **workers** were called to collect the day's wages. This was required by Jewish law so that the

poor would not go hungry (see Leviticus 19:13; Deuteronomy 24:14-15). The landowner paid **a full day's wage** even to **those hired at five o'clock.** When those who worked less time received a full day's wage, the laborers who had been **hired earlier** and had worked throughout the day **assumed they would receive more.**

20:11-15 Everyone who had been hired during the day received the same amount, no matter what time they started. This caused complaint from those who had worked all day in the hot sun. **"Those people worked only one hour, and yet you've paid them just as much,"** they protested. The owner explained, however, that he had not done wrong by the workers who had worked hard all day; he had paid them the amount they had agreed upon. Obviously, the landowner could pay whatever he chose as long as he cheated no one. Why should they be **angry** because he had been **kind?**

In this parable, Jesus pointed out that salvation is not earned, but given freely only because of God's great generosity, which goes far beyond our human ideas of what is fair. The message of the parable is that God's loving mercy accepts the lowest member of society on an equal footing with the elite. This parable may have been addressed in the presence of the religious leaders who "grumbled" because Jesus chose the "lowly" disciples and spent time with those considered unclean and sinful (Luke 15:1-2). Those who come to God—regardless of social strata, age, material wealth, or heritage, and

no matter when in life they come—will all be accepted by him on an equal footing. Such generosity, such grace, ought to cause all believers great joy.

20:16 The reversal noted in these words (and in 19:30) points out the differences between this life and life in the Kingdom. Many people we don't expect to see in the Kingdom will be there. The criminal who repented as he was dying (Luke 23:40-43) will be there, along with people who have believed and served God for many years. God offers his Kingdom to all kinds of people everywhere. God's grace accepts the world's outcasts. No one has a claim to position in the Kingdom; God will make the appointments—the **last** and **first** places cannot be earned, bought, or bargained for (see 20:20-23).

JESUS PREDICTS HIS DEATH THE THIRD TIME / 20:17-19 / 177
Jesus and the disciples continued toward Jerusalem. Jesus led the way, determined to go to the city where he knew he would die (see also Luke 9:51).

20:17-19 Jesus had just spoken to the disciples about facing persecution and had told them of his impending death twice before (see 16:21; 17:22, 23). However, this is the first mention of it occurring in **Jerusalem** itself, of the involvement of **Romans,** and that he would be **crucified.** Jesus clearly explained what would happen to him, but the disciples didn't really grasp what he was saying. Certainly they did not want to believe that he might die. Jesus said he was the Messiah, but they thought the Messiah would be a conquering king. Instead, Jesus clearly explained that he, the **Son of Man,** the human being who was

also the Messiah, God's Son, would be **betrayed** to the Jewish leaders.

Jesus added that **on the third day,** he would be **raised from the dead,** but the disciples heard only his words about death. Because Jesus often spoke in parables, the disciples may have thought that his words on death and resurrection were another parable they weren't astute enough to understand. The Gospel records of Jesus' predictions of his death and resurrection show that these events were God's plan from the beginning and not accidents (see, for example, Psalm 22:6-8; Isaiah 50:6; 52:13–53:12).

JESUS TEACHES ABOUT SERVING OTHERS / 20:20-28 / 178
Matthew created a dual contrast by including Jesus' comment on his impending death between the section on rewards and eternal life and the request from the mother of James and John. The consistent misunderstanding represents a pattern of response to Jesus. He shattered the expectations and interpretations of others. How often do our prayers evoke the same response from God? We hardly ever know what we're asking. Fortunately, God isn't bound by our requests. He lovingly edits our prayers. So, ask what you will today for yourself and for others, but remember that God will always do what is best.

20:20 As the disciples followed Jesus toward Jerusalem, they knew he believed he would die—he had told them three times. What was to become of his Kingdom? Who would be in charge after his death? Among themselves, the disciples were arguing about this issue. Then **the mother of James and John** came to ask a **favor** of Jesus. She was apparently among Jesus' regular followers who were not part of the Twelve. She was at the cross when Jesus was crucified (27:56). Some have suggested that she was the sister of Mary, the mother of Jesus. Thus, she and her sons may have hoped that their close family relationship would lend weight to their request. Also, James and John were brothers who, along with Peter, made up the inner circle of disciples (17:1).

20:21 In ancient royal courts, the persons chosen to **sit** at the **right** and **left** hands of the king were highly honored. James and John's mother wanted her sons to sit beside Christ in the most honored places in the Kingdom. They all understood that Jesus would have a Kingdom; however, until after the Resurrection, none of them fully understood that Jesus' Kingdom was not of this world; it was not centered in palaces and thrones, but in the hearts and lives of his followers.

20:22 Jesus responded that in making such a self-centered request, they did not know **what** they were **asking.** To request positions of highest honor meant also to request deep suffering, for they could not have one without the other. Jesus asked first if they were **able to drink from the bitter cup of sorrow** that he would drink. The "cup" to which Jesus referred is the same "cup" that he would mention in his prayer in Gethsemane (26:39). It is the cup of suffering that he would have to drink in order to accomplish salvation for sinners. Jesus' "cup" of suffering was unique and only he could drink the particular "cup" that would accomplish salvation. Jesus was asking James and John if they were ready to suffer for the sake of the Kingdom. James and John replied that they were **able** to drink the cup. Their answer may not have revealed bravado or pride as much as it showed their willingness to follow Jesus whatever the cost. However, their desertion of Jesus in the Garden of Gethsemane revealed how unready they really were for what this "cup" entailed (26:56).

20:23 Jesus said these two disciples would **indeed drink from** the cup of suffering. James died as a martyr (Acts 12:2); John lived through many years of persecution before being forced to live the last years of his life in exile (Revelation 1:9).

Although Jesus knew that these two disciples would face great suffering, this still did not mean that he would grant their request for great honor. Suffering is the price of greatness, but it is the price required to follow Christ at all. They would follow and they would suffer, but they would not thereby sit at his right and left in the Kingdom. Jesus would not make that decision; instead, his **Father has prepared those places for the ones he has chosen.** Although Jesus will distribute eternal rewards (2 Timothy 4:8), he will do so according to the Father's decisions. Jesus showed

by this statement that he was under the authority of the Father, who alone makes the decisions about leadership in heaven. Such rewards are not granted as favors. They are reserved for those whom God selects.

Jesus didn't ridicule James and John for asking, but he denied their request. We can feel free to ask God for anything, but our requests may be denied. God wants to give us what is best for us, not merely what we want.

20:24-25 The **ten other disciples** were **indignant** that James and John had tried to use their relationship with Jesus to grab the top positions. Why such anger? Probably because *all* the disciples desired honor in the Kingdom. Perhaps Peter, his temper getting the best of him, led the indignant ten disciples, for he had been the third with James and John in the group closest to Jesus. This probably seemed like a real slight to him. The disciples' attitudes degenerated into pure jealousy and rivalry.

Jesus immediately corrected their attitudes, for they would never accomplish the mission to which he had called them if they did not love and serve one another, working together for the sake of the Kingdom. So he patiently called his disciples together and explained to them the difference between the kingdoms they saw in the world and God's Kingdom, which they had not yet experienced.

The Gentile kingdoms (an obvious example being the Roman Empire) have leaders who **lord it over** people, exercising authority and demanding submission (see 1 Peter 5:1-3). In Gentile kingdoms, people's greatness depended on their social standing or family name. But Jesus explained that his Kingdom would be completely different.

20:26-28 In a sentence, Jesus taught the essence of true greatness: **Whoever wants to be a leader among you must be your servant.** Greatness is determined by servanthood. The true leader places his or her needs last, as Jesus exemplified in his life and in his death. Being a "servant" did not mean occupying a servile position; rather, it meant having an attitude of life that freely attended to others' needs without expecting or demanding anything in return. Servant leaders appreciate others' worth and realize that they're not above any job. Seeking honor, respect, and the attention of others runs contrary to Jesus' requirements for his servants. Jesus described leadership from a new perspective. Instead of using people, we are to serve them.

Jesus' mission was to serve others and to give his life away. A real leader has a servant's heart. The disciples must be willing to serve because their Master set the example. Jesus explained that he **came here not to be served but to serve others.** Jesus' mission was to serve—ultimately by giving his life in order to save sinful humanity. His life wasn't "taken"; he "gave" it by offering it

up as a sacrifice for people's sins. A **ransom** was the price paid to release a slave from bondage. Jesus paid a ransom for us, and the demanded price was his life. Jesus took our place; he died the death we deserved.

JESUS HEALS TWO BLIND BEGGARS / 20:29-34 / 179

Jesus and the disciples were on the way out of Jericho, continuing southward toward Jerusalem. The Old Testament city of Jericho had been destroyed by the Israelites (Joshua 6:20), but during Herod the Great's rule over Palestine, he had rebuilt the city (about a mile south of the original city) as a site for his winter palace. Jericho was a popular and wealthy resort city, not far from the Jordan River, about eighteen miles northeast of Jerusalem.

20:29-31 These **two blind men were sitting beside the road** begging. The blind men **heard** that Jesus was at the head of an approaching crowd. In order to be heard above the din, **they began shouting** for Jesus' attention. They had undoubtedly heard that Jesus had healed many (including blind people—see 9:29-31), and they hoped that Jesus would **have mercy** on them and heal their eyes. There were no healings of the blind in the Old Testament; the Jews believed that such a miracle would be a sign that the messianic age had begun (Isaiah 29:18; 35:5).

The crowd tried to get the men to **be quiet.** It was most natural for the people, even Jesus' disciples, to attempt to shield Jesus from being harassed by beggars. But this only caused the men to shout

louder. They kept on crying out in an attempt to gain Jesus' attention.

20:32-34 Although Jesus was concerned about the coming events in Jerusalem, he demonstrated what he had just told the disciples about service (20:26-28) by stopping to care for the blind men. Blindness was considered a curse from God for sin (John 9:2), but such an idea did not hinder Jesus. Because Jesus probably knew what the men wanted, his question was not to gain information, but to allow them to specify their need and, in the process, to declare their faith that Jesus could meet that need. The result of the blind men's request was that Jesus **touched their eyes** and **instantly they could see.**

MATTHEW 21

JESUS RIDES INTO JERUSALEM ON A DONKEY / 21:1-11 / 183

This was the first day of the week that Jesus would be crucified (commonly know now as Palm Sunday), and the great Passover festival was about to begin. Jews would come to Jerusalem from all over the Roman world during this week-long celebration to remember the great Exodus from Egypt (see Exodus 12:37-51). Matthew concentrated chapters 21 and 22 in the Temple area to show Jesus' authority and superiority over the Jewish leaders and their way of thinking.

21:1-5 The **Mount of Olives** is a ridge about two and a half miles long on the other side of the Kidron Valley east of Jerusalem. The Mount of Olives is important in the Old Testament as the place of God's final revelation and judgment (see Ezekiel 43:2-9; Zechariah 14:1-19).

Jesus was in **Bethphage** and sent two disciples

to a nearby village (probably Bethany) to get the **donkey** and her **colt** and bring them back. When Jesus entered Jerusalem on a donkey's colt, he affirmed his messianic royalty, as well as his humility. The people recognized that he was fulfilling **prophecy.** The first part comes from Isaiah 62:11, the rest from Zechariah 9:9.

21:6-8 The colt, never having been ridden (Mark 11:2), did not have a saddle, so the disciples **threw their garments over the colt** so that Jesus could sit on it. The action of placing the cloaks on the donkey and Jesus riding it connotes majesty (see 2 Kings 9:13). Crowds of people had already gathered on this stretch of road a mile outside of Jerusalem, going to the city for the festival. The crowd's spontaneous celebration honored Jesus as they **spread their coats on the road ahead of Jesus** and **cut branches from the trees.** Some were spread along Jesus' path; others were probably waved in the air (see Psalm 118:27). The branches, probably from olive or fig trees, were used to welcome a national liberator and symbolized victory. This verse is one of the few places where the Gospels record that Jesus' glory was recognized on earth. Today Christians celebrate this event on Palm Sunday.

21:9 The **crowds** chanted words from Psalm 118:25-26. "Long live the King" was the meaning behind their joyful shouts because they knew that Jesus was intentionally fulfilling prophecy. This was the crowd's acclamation that he was indeed the long-awaited Messiah. The people were sure their liberation from Rome was at hand. While the crowd correctly saw Jesus as the fulfillment of these prophecies, they did not understand where Jesus' kingship would lead him. They expected him to be a national leader who would restore their nation to its former glory; thus, they were deaf to the words of their prophets and blind to Jesus' real mission. When it became apparent that Jesus was not going to fulfill their hopes, many people would turn against him. Another crowd would cry out, "Crucify him!" when Jesus stood on trial only a few days later.

21:10-11 The people in Jerusalem were naturally very interested in who was causing the furor. When Jesus had been born and the wise men had come seeking him, the entire city had been "disturbed" (2:3). Once again, Jesus caused a great disturbance in this great city. To the question, **"Who is this?"** came the reply, **"It's Jesus, the prophet from Nazareth in Galilee."** But Jesus was not just another prophet; he was *the* prophet who was to come (Deuteronomy 18:15-18). No wonder the city was in an uproar!

JESUS CLEARS THE TEMPLE AGAIN / 21:12-17 / *184*

Jesus entered the great city and went to the Temple, entering its outer courts, as did many in the crowd. People came to the Temple in Jerusalem to offer sacrifices. God had originally instructed the people to bring sacrifices from their own flocks (Deuteronomy 12:5-7). However, the religious leadership had established four markets on the Mount of Olives where such animals could be purchased. This greatly angered Jesus.

21:12-13 The high priest had authorized a market with **merchants** and **money changers** to be set up right in the Court of the Gentiles, the huge outer court of the Temple. The Court of the Gentiles was the only place Gentile converts to Judaism could worship. But the market filled their worship space with merchants so that these foreigners, who had traveled long distances, found it impossible to worship. The chaos in that Court must have been tremendous. The money changers exchanged all international currency for the special Temple coins—the only money the merchants would accept. The money changers did big business during Passover with those who came from foreign countries. The inflated exchange rate often enriched the money changers, and the exorbitant prices of animals made the merchants wealthy.

Because both those who bought and those who sold were going against God's commands regarding the sacrifices, Jesus **began to drive** them **out.** This is the second time that Jesus cleared the Temple (see John 2:13-17). Jesus became angry because God's house of worship had become a place of extortion and a barrier to Gentiles who wanted to worship. Jesus quoted from Isaiah 56:7 and used it to explain that God's **Temple** was meant to be **a place of prayer,** but the merchants and money changers had **turned it into a den of thieves.**

21:14 It was significant that **the blind and the lame** came to Jesus in the Temple. Usually they were excluded from worship in the Temple based on laws stemming from 2 Samuel 5:8. With the coming of the Messiah, Jesus himself welcomed them and **healed them there in the Temple.** This was also an expected result of the messianic age (Isaiah 35:5).

21:15-16 Jesus' actions in the Temple provoked the anger of the religious leaders. The **children** who were in the Temple were crying out, **"Praise God for the Son of David,"** echoing the cries made by the crowd along the road to Jerusalem (21:9). The religious leaders' question indicated that they objected to the concept of Jesus as "the Son of David." But Jesus heard what the children were saying and did not stop them, for what they said was true.

21:17 With the religious leaders plotting to kill him, Jerusalem would hardly be a safe place for Jesus to spend the night. So when evening came, Jesus and the disciples left the city and returned to **Bethany.** Most pilgrims who traveled to Jerusalem for the great feasts found lodging outside the city.

JESUS SAYS THE DISCIPLES CAN PRAY FOR ANYTHING / 21:18-22 / 188

After their stay in Bethany overnight (21:17), Jesus and the disciples got up and headed back into Jerusalem. Bethany was about two miles outside of Jerusalem, making it a suburb of the city.

21:18-20 Fig trees were a popular source of inexpensive food in Israel. In March, the fig trees had small edible buds; in April came the large green leaves. Then in May, the buds would fall off and be replaced by the normal crop of figs. This incident occurred in April, and the green leaves should have indicated the presence of the edible buds that Jesus expected to find on the tree. This tree, however, though full of **leaves,** had no buds. The tree looked promising but offered no fruit.

Jesus did not curse this fig tree because he was angry at not getting any food from it. Instead, this was an acted-out parable intended to teach the disciples a lesson. By cursing the **fig tree,** Jesus was showing his anger at religion without substance. Jesus' harsh words to the fig tree could be applied to the nation of Israel and its beautiful Temple. Fruitful in appearance only, Israel was spiritually barren. Just as the fig tree looked good from a distance but was fruitless on close examination, so the Temple looked impressive at first glance, but its sacrifices and other activities were hollow because they were not done to worship God sincerely.

After Jesus spoke these words, **the fig tree withered up.** This parable of judgment on spiritually dead people revealed its severity. The early church later applied this parable to the total destruction of Jerusalem in A.D. 70.

21:21 Jesus did not explain why he cursed the fig tree, and we don't know whether the disciples understood Jesus' meaning. Yet his words to them could mean that they must have **faith** in God. Their faith should not rest in a kingdom they hoped Jesus would set up, in obeying the Jewish laws, or in their position as Jesus' disciples. Their faith should rest in God alone.

Jesus then taught them a lesson about answers to prayer. Jesus had cursed the fig tree; the fig tree had died; the disciples had expressed surprise. Jesus explained that they could ask anything of God and receive an answer. Jesus then used a **mountain** as a figure of speech to show that God could help in any situation. Jesus' point was that in their petitions to God they must believe and not **doubt.** The kind of prayer Jesus meant was not the arbitrary wish to move a mountain of dirt and stone; instead, he was referring to prayers that the disciples would need to faithfully pray as they faced mountains of opposition to their gospel message in the years to come. Their prayers for the advancement of God's Kingdom would always be answered positively—in God's timing.

21:22 This verse was not a guarantee that the disciples could get anything they wanted simply by asking Jesus and believing. God does not grant requests that will hurt people or that will violate his own nature or will. Jesus' statement was not a blank check to be filled in by believers, not a "name it and claim it" theology. To be fulfilled, requests made to God in **prayer** must be in harmony with the principles of God's Kingdom. They must be made in Jesus' name (John 14:13-14). The stronger our faith, the more likely our prayers will be in union with Christ and in line with God's will; then God will be happy to grant them. God can do anything, even what seems humanly impossible.

RELIGIOUS LEADERS CHALLENGE JESUS' AUTHORITY / 21:23-27 / 189

The basic theme of this whole section is that Jesus was taking on the religious leaders at their own game and defeating them with their own logic. Jesus was triumphant in his dealings with them, and this angered them even more.

21:23 Jesus and the disciples **returned to the Temple,** where Jesus had thrown out the merchants and money changers the day before. A delegation of **leading priests and other leaders**

came up to him. They asked for his credentials and demanded that he tell them who gave him the **authority** to **drive out the merchants from the Temple.**

If Jesus were to answer that his authority came from God, which would be tantamount to declaring himself as the Messiah, they would accuse him of blasphemy and bring him to trial (blasphemy carried the death penalty, Leviticus 24:10-23). If Jesus were to say that his authority was his own, the religious leaders could dismiss him as a fanatic and could trust that the crowds would soon return to those with true authority (themselves).

21:24-26 Jesus would not let himself be caught; turning the question on them, he exposed their motives and avoided their trap. Jesus' question seems totally unrelated to the situation at hand, but Jesus knew that the leaders' attitude about John the Baptist would reveal their true attitude toward him. In this question, Jesus implied that his authority came from the same source as John the Baptist's. So Jesus asked these religious leaders what they thought: **Did John's baptism come**

from heaven [thus, from God] **or was it merely human?**

The interchange recorded among these factions of the religious leaders revealed their true motives. They weren't interested in the truth; they simply hoped to trap him. If they answered that John's baptism had come from heaven (with God's authority), then they would incriminate themselves for not listening to John and believing his words.

21:27 The Pharisees couldn't win, so they hoped to save face by refusing to answer. Thus, Jesus was not obligated to answer their question. In reality, he had already answered it. His question about John the Baptist implied that both he and John received their authority from the same source. The religious leaders had already decided against Jesus, and nothing would stand in the way of their plan to kill him. They had already rejected both Jesus and John as God's messengers, carrying on a long tradition of the leaders of Israel rejecting God's prophets. This was the point that Jesus made in the following parable (21:28-32).

JESUS TELLS THE PARABLE OF THE TWO SONS / 21:28-32 / 190
Jesus continued his conversation with the religious leaders who had attempted to trip him up with a trick question (21:23-27). This parable was spoken directly to them, and it showed them their true position in the Kingdom of Heaven.

21:28-30 The **man** in this parable represents God, while the **two sons** represent, respectively, the "sinners" (or outcasts among the Jews) and conservative Jews.

The first son said he would not go to the **vineyard, but changed his mind and went anyway.** This son represents the "sinner" and outcast who rejected the call but "repented" and then obeyed.

The second son said he would go to the vineyard, but then **didn't go.** This son represents the Jewish leaders of the day who said "yes" to the Kingdom message (that is, they accepted the outward call to Jewish piety) but did not obey its intent. They rejected the call to true obedience. They said they wanted to do God's will, but they constantly disobeyed. They lacked insight into God's real meaning, and they were too stubborn to listen to Jesus.

21:31 Jesus directed his question to the religious leaders, and they gave the obviously correct

answer. The son who did what his father wanted was the son who eventually obeyed. Jesus explained that **corrupt tax collectors and prostitutes will get into the Kingdom of God before** the religious leaders. These were astounding words. The tax collectors and prostitutes were representative of the despised classes, those who were the most despicable to the self-righteous leaders. The pious religious leaders had said they would "go to the vineyard" but then had refused. The tax collectors and prostitutes had obviously strayed from God, but those who repented of their sin *would* enter the Kingdom of God.

21:32 The reaction to John the Baptist spelled out the reaction to the one John proclaimed—Jesus, the Messiah. Even when the religious leaders saw how sinful people repented and believed, these leaders still **refused to turn** and **believe.** Neither, then, would they believe Jesus.

JESUS TELLS THE PARABLE OF THE EVIL FARMERS / 21:33-46 / 191
In this parable, Jesus displayed his knowledge of the religious leaders' murderous plot (21:45).

21:33 The main elements in this parable are (1) the **landowner**—God, (2) the **vineyard**—Israel, (3) the **farmers**—the Jewish religious leaders, (4) the landowner's **servants**—the prophets and priests who remained faithful to God and preached to Israel, (5) the **son**—Jesus, and (6) the **others**—the Gentiles. In a vineyard such as this, the **lookout tower** would have been for guards who would protect the farm from thieves; the **wall** would have kept wild animals out.

21:34-36 The rent on the farm was paid by crops at harvesttime, a common practice in this culture. So, as expected, the landowner **sent his servants** to collect the rent in the form of a **share of the crop**. But **the farmers grabbed his servants**, beating, killing, and stoning them. More servants were sent, and they received the same treatment. These "servants" refer to the prophets who had been sent to Israel over the centuries. Some had been beaten (Jeremiah 26:7-11; 38:1-28), some had been killed (tradition says Isaiah was killed; John the Baptist had been killed, Matthew 14:1-12), some had been stoned (2 Chronicles 24:21). Jesus was reminding the religious leaders that God's prophets often had been ridiculed and persecuted by God's people.

21:37-39 The landowner then **sent his son**, thinking that surely the tenants would respect his son. The historical situation behind this section reflects the law that property would go to anyone in possession of it when the master died. So the tenants assumed that by killing the son and **heir** to the property, they would **get the estate**. So they **murdered** the son. With these words, Jesus was revealing to the religious leaders his knowledge of their desire to kill him.

21:40-41 Jesus' question forced the religious leaders to announce their own fate. These words allude to Isaiah 5:5 and continue the same imagery. In their answer to Jesus, the religious leaders announced themselves to be **wicked men** who deserved **a horrible death. Others** would take over what they thought they had (see 21:43).

21:42 The imagery of the **stone rejected by the builders** is taken from Psalm 118:22-23, referring to the deliverance of Israel from a situation when it seemed that their enemies had triumphed. Their deliverance could only be attributed to God's miraculous intervention. Although Jesus had been rejected by many of his people, he will become the **cornerstone** of his new building, the church (see Acts 4:11 and 1 Peter 2:6-7). It seemed that Jesus had been rejected and defeated by his own people, the Jews, but God would raise him from the dead and seat him at his own right hand.

21:43 A nation that will produce the proper fruit refers to the Gentiles who will be added to make up God's people (21:41). By their rejection of the prophets' message and finally of the Son himself, Israel showed that they were incapable of repentance and belief. So the Kingdom would **be taken away** from them and given to a unity of Jews and Gentiles, a foreshadowing of the church. The same presentation is given by Paul in Romans 11:11-24.

21:44 Jesus used this metaphor to show that one **stone** can affect people different ways, depending on how they relate to it (see Isaiah 8:14-15; 28:16; Daniel 2:34, 44-45). Ideally they will build on it; many, however, will stumble over it. At the Last Judgment, God's enemies will be crushed by it. At that time, Christ, the "building block," will become the "crushing stone." He offers mercy and forgiveness now, and he promises judgment later.

21:45-46 It seems that the religious leaders finally understood something, for here **they realized he was pointing at them**, that they were the "wicked men" who were plotting to kill the son and who would have the "vineyard" taken away from them. They must have become very angry, so much so that **they wanted to arrest him**. The Jewish leaders wouldn't do so because they feared the crowds. To arrest Jesus would have caused an uprising against them and an uproar that they couldn't afford with the Romans ready to come down on them. The crowds **considered Jesus to be a prophet**.

MATTHEW 22

JESUS TELLS THE PARABLE OF THE WEDDING DINNER / 22:1-14 / 192
Jesus had already told two parables focusing on rejection of him as God's Son and God's
resulting judgment. The parable of the two sons (21:28-32) showed how the rewards of the
sons were switched according to their ultimate service rendered. The parable of the wicked
tenants (21:33-46) explained that "others" would be given the vineyard. The following parable
of the wedding feast showed that those least expected would be invited to the feast.

22:1-3 In this parable, Jesus pictured the Kingdom
of Heaven being offered to those who might be least
expected to enter it. A **king** gives a **great wedding
feast for his son.** In this culture, two invitations
were expected when banquets were given. The first
asked the guests to attend; the second announced
that all was ready. When the king **sent his servants
to notify everyone that it was time to come,** this
referred to the second invitation. These invitees had
already accepted the first invitation. At this second
one, however, these guests **refused.** Like the son
who said he would go to the vineyard and didn't
(21:30) and the tenant farmers who refused to pay
the rent (21:34-39), these guests reneged on an earlier agreement.

22:4-6 The meal was ready, but these guests **ignored**
the announcement, placing a higher priority on
their farms and businesses. The seizing and killing
of these **messengers** stretches the imagination for
this story, but probably recalls the same meaning as
in the parable of the wicked tenants who killed the
servants—prophets whom God had sent to offer his
invitation.

22:7-8 The king's invitation had been refused and his
servants murdered, so he **became furious.** Sending
his army and destroying the city has been interpreted
as referring to the destruction of Jerusalem in A.D. 70.
More likely it refers to the final war between good
and evil, a very popular theme in passages about the
end times (Isaiah 25:6-8; Ezekiel 39:17-24; Revelation 19:17-21). The feast was ready and waiting, but
his guests were not **worthy of the honor.** This is similar to the giving of the vineyard to "others" in the
previous parable (21:41). The Kingdom will go to
those whom God has deemed "worthy."

22:9-10 The king still wanted to share his banquet,
so he ordered his servants to **go out to the street**

corners and invite everyone they found. They did
so, bringing both **good and bad** (meaning they
didn't discriminate about social standing, reputation, or moral character) for the feast. The metaphor
focuses on the outcasts and sinners (see also 21:31-
32) as well as righteous people. An unlikely scenario
in ancient times, this scene pictures God's gracious
invitation to all kinds of people—Jew and Gentile,
rich and poor, male and female, good and bad. As
the servants gathered all who would respond, so
God gives salvation to all who hear and respond.

22:11-12 **The proper clothes for a wedding** probably refers to clean, fresh clothing. It was unthinkable
to come to a wedding banquet in soiled clothes.
This would insult the host, who could only assume
that the guest was ignorant, had not truly been
invited, or was not prepared for the banquet. When
the king pointed this out, **the man had no reply,** so
the king declared him unprepared and unworthy.

The wedding clothes picture the righteousness
needed to enter God's Kingdom—the total acceptance in God's eyes that Christ provides for every
believer (Isaiah 61:10). Christ has provided this garment of righteousness for everyone, but each person
must put it on (accept Christ's gracious provision
of his life given for us) in order to enter the King's
banquet (eternal life). There is an open invitation,
but we must be ready. For more on the imagery of
clothes of righteousness and salvation, see Psalm
132:16; Zechariah 3:3-5; Revelation 3:4-5; 19:7-8.

22:13 In the final judgment, God's true people will
be revealed. Claiming to belong at the wedding feast
while refusing to wear the correct garments was like
the nation of Israel claiming to be God's people
but refusing to live for him. Like the wicked tenants
who deserved "a horrible death" (21:41), so this
impostor at the banquet found himself tied up and

thrown **into the outer darkness where there is weeping and gnashing of teeth**—a common biblical description of hell (see also 8:12; 13:42, 50).

22:14 Those who are **called** but reject God's invitation will be punished, as will those who seem to accept the call but fail to follow through. The use of the word "called" means "invited," not the irresistible call of God as Paul used it (see Romans

8:28-29). The invitation had gone out to all Israel, but only a few had accepted and followed Jesus. **Chosen** refers to the elect. Jesus was applying this teaching to the Jews, who believed that because they were descendants of Abraham, they would be sure to share in the blessings of God's Kingdom through the Messiah. But Jesus taught that not all those invited would actually be among the chosen of God.

RELIGIOUS LEADERS QUESTION JESUS ABOUT PAYING TAXES / 22:15-22 / 193

The Pharisees and Herodians who approached Jesus usually were parties in conflict, with one side against Rome and one side pro-Rome. They sent young men in the hope that Jesus would not suspect them of trickery.

22:15-16 The **Pharisees** were a religious group opposed to the Roman occupation of Palestine. The **supporters of Herod** were a political party that supported the Herods and the policies instituted by Rome. These antagonistic groups found a common enemy in Jesus. Pretending to be honest, they flattered Jesus before asking him their trick question, hoping to **trap** him.

22:17-19 The Jews hated to **pay taxes** to Rome because the money supported their oppressors and symbolized their subjection. Anyone who avoided paying taxes faced harsh penalties. Thus, this was a valid (and loaded) question, and the crowd around Jesus waited expectantly for his answer. Matthew, as a former tax collector, was certainly interested in Jesus' response to this question.

The Pharisees were against these taxes on religious grounds; the Herodians supported taxation on political grounds. Thus, either a yes or a no could get Jesus into trouble. If Jesus agreed that it was right to pay taxes to Caesar, the Pharisees would say he was opposed to God, and the people would turn against him. If Jesus said the taxes should not be paid, the Herodians could hand him over to Herod on the charge of rebellion.

Jesus saw through their flattering words to the underlying **evil motives**. He then asked his questioners to produce a **Roman coin used for the tax** so he could use it to make a point.

22:20-22 The coin had a **picture** of the reigning Caesar. The **title** referred to Caesar as divine and

as "chief priest." The Caesars were worshiped as gods by the pagans, so the claim to divinity on the coin itself repulsed the Jews.

Jesus said, **"Give to Caesar what belongs to him"**—that is, the coin bearing the emperor's image should be given to the emperor. In other words, having a coin meant being part of that country, so citizens should acknowledge the authority of Caesar and pay for the benefits accorded to them by his empire (for example, peace and an efficient road system). The Pharisees and Herodians tried to make it appear that it was incompatible to be a Jew and pay taxes to a pagan emperor who claimed to be divine. But Jesus explained that no such incompatibility existed because God was ultimately in control. They would lose much and gain little if they refused to pay Caesar's taxes (see Romans 13:1-7; 1 Timothy 2:1-6; 1 Peter 2:13-17).

Paying the taxes, however, did not have to mean submission to the divinity claimed by the emperor. The words on the coins were incorrect. Caesar had the right to claim their tax money, but he had no claim on their souls. The Jews knew that **everything that belongs to God must be given to God.** While they lived in the Roman world, the Jews had to face the dual reality of subjection to Rome and responsibility to God. Jesus explained that they could do both if they kept their priorities straight. The tax would be paid as long as Rome held sway over Judea, but God had rights on eternity and on their lives.

RELIGIOUS LEADERS QUESTION JESUS ABOUT THE RESURRECTION / 22:23-33 / 194

The combined group of religious leaders from the Council had failed with their first question (21:23-27); the paired antagonists of Pharisees and Herodians had failed with a political question (22:15-22); here the Sadducees, another group of religious leaders, smugly stepped in to try to trap Jesus with a theological question.

22:23 The **Sadducees** honored only the Pentateuch—Genesis through Deuteronomy—as Scripture, and they rejected most of the Pharisees' traditions, rules, and regulations. The Sadducees said **there is no resurrection** because they could find no mention of it in the Pentateuch. Apparently, the Pharisees had never been able to come up with a convincing argument from the Pentateuch for the resurrection, and the Sadducees thought they had trapped Jesus for sure.

22:24 Moses had written that **if a man dies without children,** his unmarried brother (or nearest male relative) **should marry the widow and have a child who will be the brother's heir.** The first son of this marriage was considered the heir of the dead man (Deuteronomy 25:5-6). The main purpose of the instruction was to produce an heir and guarantee that the family would not lose their land. The book of Ruth gives an example of this law in operation (Ruth 3:1–4:12; see also Genesis 38:1-26). This law, called "levirate" marriage, protected the widow (in that culture widows usually had no means to support themselves) and allowed the family line to continue.

22:25-28 The Sadducees used an example of a woman who had been married, one at a time, to **seven brothers.** When all eight of them were resurrected, **whose wife will she be?** This was a tongue-in-cheek question meant to prove that it was ridiculous to believe in a resurrection. The Sadducees erroneously assumed that if people were resurrected, they would assume physical bodies capable of procreation. Because they could not conceive of a resurrection life, they decided that God couldn't raise the dead. And since they thought that Moses hadn't written about it, they considered the case "closed."

22:29-30 Jesus wasted no time dealing with their hypothetical situation but went directly to their underlying assumption that resurrection of the dead was impossible. Jesus clearly stated that these Sadducees were wrong about the resurrection for two reasons: (1) They didn't **know the Scriptures** (if they did, they would believe in the resurrection because it is taught in Scripture), and (2) they didn't **know the power of God** (if they did, they would believe in the resurrection because God's power makes it possible). Igno-

rance on these two counts was inexcusable for these religious leaders.

Furthermore, resurrection will not be an extension of earthly life. Instead, life in heaven will be different. Believers **will be like the angels in heaven** regarding marriage. Those in heaven will no longer be governed by physical laws but will share the immortal and exalted nature of angels, living above physical needs.

Jesus was not teaching that people will not recognize their spouses in heaven. Jesus was not dissolving the eternal aspect of marriage, doing away with sexual differences, or teaching that we will be asexual beings after death. Jesus was not intending to give the final word on marriage in heaven. We cannot learn very much about sex and marriage in heaven from this one statement by Jesus. His point was simply that we must not think of heaven as an extension of life as we now know it. Our relationships in this life are limited by time and death. We don't know everything about our resurrection life, but Jesus was affirming that relationships will be different from what we are used to here and now. Jesus was showing that the Sadducees' question was completely irrelevant. But their assumption about the resurrection needed a definitive answer, and Jesus was just the one to give it.

22:31-32 The Sadducees' underlying comment regarded their view of the absurdity of resurrection. Their question to Jesus was intended to show him to be foolish. So Jesus cut right to the point: **as to whether there will be a resurrection of the dead,** Jesus answered them from the book of Exodus (3:6). God would not have said, **"I am the God of Abraham, the God of Isaac, and the God of Jacob,"** if Abraham, Isaac, and Jacob were dead (he would have said, "I *was* their God"). Thus, from God's perspective, they are alive. This evidence would have been acceptable in any rabbinic debate because it applied a grammatical argument. God had spoken of dead men as though they were still alive; thus, Jesus reasoned, the men were not **dead** but **living.** God would not have a relationship with dead beings. Although men and women have died on earth, God continues his relationship with them because they are resurrected to life with him in heaven. Therefore, the Sadducees were wrong in their mistaken assumption about the resurrection.

RELIGIOUS LEADERS QUESTION JESUS ABOUT THE GREATEST COMMANDMENT / 22:34-40 / 195

The questions leading up to the one recorded in this section were intended to trap Jesus rather than to find answers. Here, however, an expert in religious law asked Jesus to condense the Law to a single principle.

22:34-36 Next **an expert in religious law** stepped up to **trap** Jesus with another question, **"Which is the most important commandment in the law of Moses?"** The legal expert was referring to a popular debate about the "more important" and "less important" of the hundreds of laws that the Jews had accumulated. The Pharisees had classified over six hundred laws and would spend much time discussing which laws were weightier than others. Jesus' definitive answer about the resurrection caused this man to hope that Jesus might also have the final answer about all these laws.

22:37-38 Jesus referred to Deuteronomy 6:5 to show that a person's total being must be involved in loving God. Nothing must be held back because God holds nothing back: **You must love the Lord your God with all your heart, all your soul, and all your mind.** The word for "love" is *agapao*, totally unselfish love, a love of which human beings are capable only with the help of

the Holy Spirit. The **heart** is the center of desires and affections, the **soul** is a person's "being" and uniqueness, the **mind** is the center of a person's intellect. To love God in this way is to fulfill completely all the commandments regarding one's "vertical" relationship.

22:39-40 There is a **second** and **equally important** law that focuses on "horizontal" relationships— dealings with fellow human beings. Jesus quoted Leviticus 19:18: **"Love your neighbor as yourself."** The word "neighbor" refers to fellow human beings in general. The love a person has for himself or herself (in the sense of looking out for oneself, caring about one's best interests, etc.) should also be directed toward others.

In answer to the man's question, Jesus explained that **all the demands of the prophets are based on these two commandments.** By fulfilling these two commands to love God totally and love others as oneself, a person will keep all the other commands.

RELIGIOUS LEADERS CANNOT ANSWER JESUS' QUESTION / 22:41-46 / 196

This was still presumably Tuesday of Jesus' final week on earth. Jesus had answered questions from various groups of religious leaders: the Pharisees, Herodians, and Sadducees. Then Jesus turned the tables and asked the Pharisees a question that went right to the heart of the matter—what they thought about the Messiah's identity. The central issue of life for these ancient religious leaders (as well as for us) is Jesus' true identity.

22:41-42 The Pharisees expected a **Messiah**, but they erroneously thought he would be only a human ruler who would reign on King David's throne, deliver the Jews from Gentile domination by establishing God's rule on earth, and restore Israel's greatness as in the days of David and Solomon. They knew that the Messiah would be a **son** (descendant) **of David,** but they did not understand that he would be more than a human descendant—he would be God in the flesh.

22:43-46 Jesus quoted Psalm 110:1 to show that David, speaking under the influence of the Holy

Spirit, understood the Messiah to be his **Lord** (that is, one who had authority over him), not just his descendant. If the great King David himself called the coming Messiah his Lord, then how could the Messiah be merely David's son (meaning "descendant")? David himself didn't think the Messiah would be just a descendant; instead, David, under the inspiration of the Holy Spirit, had realized that the Messiah would be God in human form and would deserve due respect and honor.

The silence of Jesus' opponents shows their total defeat. This was Jesus' last controversy with the religious establishment.

MATTHEW 23

JESUS WARNS AGAINST THE RELIGIOUS LEADERS / 23:1-12 / *197*

Chapter 23 serves as a transition between the controversy narratives and the Olivet Discourse. Jesus made many scathing remarks to the religious leaders, but not *all* of them were evil (consider Nicodemus in John 3 and Joseph in Mark 15:43). Jesus attacked their legalism that had become a stumbling block for the Jews.

23:1-4 Jesus turned his attention **to the crowds and to his disciples,** as he spoke about the religious leaders whose pride and hypocrisy made them far from the type of followers God desires. To be **the official interpreters of the Scriptures** referred to their authority. Because of that authority, the people ought to **practice and obey whatever they say.** This seems strange at first because of Jesus' denouncement of much of their teaching (see 12:1-14; 15:1-20; 16:6-12; 19:3-9). Yet Jesus did not toss aside the religious leaders as worthless; he understood the need for their function when they taught correctly. But he did question their actions. For all their teaching, the leaders did not **practice what they** were teaching. Also the Pharisees were notorious for adding minute details and requirements to the law that made it **impossible** for the average person to keep the law. After giving the people all these impossible commands, the leaders would **never lift a finger to help ease the burden.** They offered the people no practical advice in working the law out in their lives or in building a relationship with the heavenly Father.

23:5-7 As they made their living keeping all their tiny laws, the teachers of the law and Pharisees were very aware of the attention they received from the people—and they loved it. **Everything** they did was **for show.** They did not keep the laws because they loved God, but because they loved human praise.

They wore **prayer boxes with Scripture verses inside.** Very religious people wore these boxes on their forehead (tied around the head by a strap) and on their arms so as to obey—literally—Deuteronomy 6:8 and Exodus 13:9, 16. But the prayer boxes had become more important for the status they gave than for the truth they contained. The **extra long tassels** on the robes were again simply to make them more noticeable. The **head table**

at banquets received special treatment during the meal. **The most prominent seats in the synagogue** faced the congregation and were reserved for the most important people. To be called **Rabbi** (meaning "teacher") was treasured for the status it gave a person as a leading teacher of the Torah. In short, the religious leaders had lost sight of their priority as teachers and were enjoying their position merely because of the "perks" it offered. Jesus condemned this attitude.

23:8-10 In these words, Jesus described true discipleship. **Don't ever let anyone call you "Rabbi,"** did not mean that Jesus refused anyone that title. Rather, this means that a learned teacher should not allow anyone to call him "rabbi" in the sense of "great one." Why? Because there is only one "Great One," **one teacher,** and all rabbis are under his authority. True disciples are united under one authority (**all of you are on the same level as brothers and sisters**) and do not establish a hierarchy of importance.

Don't address anyone here on earth as Father does not mean that we cannot use the word for a parent. Again, Jesus was speaking in the context of the rabbi and disciple relationship. Disciples would call their rabbi "father," and the relationship could be compared to that between a father and son. This command gives the flip side of the first one. While rabbis must not accept homage from disciples, the disciples were not to revere any rabbi or put him on a pedestal.

The third command repeats the first one, but adds the emphasis of **the Messiah.** All rabbis (all learned teachers) fall under the authority of **one master.** Jesus, of course, was referring to himself.

23:11-12 The heart of discipleship is not found in outward appearances or long tassels or places of honor. It comes from servanthood and humility. Jesus had explained in 20:26 that true greatness comes from being a servant. The true leader places his or her needs last, as Jesus exemplified in his life and in his death. Being a **servant** did not mean occupying a servile position; rather, it meant having an attitude of freely attending to others' needs without expecting or demanding anything in

return. Trying to **exalt** oneself runs contrary to Jesus' requirements for his servants. Only those who **humble themselves** will find true greatness in God's Kingdom. This completely opposed the attitudes and actions of the Jewish religious leaders.

JESUS CONDEMNS THE RELIGIOUS LEADERS / 23:13-36 / 198

Matthew included seven denunciations against the Jewish leaders whom Jesus unhesitatingly called "hypocrites." Being a religious leader in Jerusalem was very different from being a pastor in a secular society today. Israel's history, culture, and daily life revolved around its relationship with God. The religious leaders were the best known, most powerful, and most respected of all leaders. Jesus made these stinging accusations because the leaders' hunger for more power, money, and status had made them lose sight of God, and their blindness was spreading to the whole nation.

23:13-14 The **teachers of religious law** and **Pharisees** were **hypocrites.** Their rejection of Jesus and emphasis on their petty demands had the effect of locking people out of the **Kingdom** and keeping themselves out as well. Anyone who might have gotten in through a saving relationship with God was stopped by these Pharisees. They made God seem impossible to please, his commands impossible to obey, and thus the Kingdom an impossible goal. (Verse 14 is not present in the best ancient manuscripts.)

23:15 The **teachers of religious law** and **Pharisees** were guilty of perverting their own converts, who were attracted to status and rule keeping, not to God. By getting caught up in the details of the Pharisees' additional laws and regulations, they completely missed God, to whom the laws pointed. A religion of deeds pressures people to surpass others in what they know and do. Thus, a hypocritical teacher was likely to have students who were even more hypocritical. Making converts was laudable. But when the ones doing the converting are children **of hell,** then their converts will likely meet the same end.

23:16-19 Jesus pointed out the leaders' hypocrisy regarding the binding power of oaths made to God for dedication for service or for contributions of property. The leaders should have been guides for the blind but instead were **blind** themselves. Two examples were given of the ridiculous lengths to which the overly legalistic system had gone—swearing by the **Temple** or the **gold,** and swearing by the **altar** or the **gift.** In one case, the oath could not be broken; in the other case, it could. Jesus illustrated the minute (and ridiculous) distinctions.

23:20-22 Jesus had explained that his followers should not need to make any oaths at all, for

to do so would imply that their word could not be trusted (5:33-37). The leaders, by attempting to make distinctions in oaths, had lost sight of the fact that all oaths are made before God and should be equally binding. In other words, no oath should be made with a loophole.

23:23 The hypocrisy of the scribes and Pharisees lay in their careful obedience to the small details of the law (tithing **even the tiniest part of** their **income**) while they ignored larger issues that were far more important—such as dealing correctly with other people and building a relationship with God (**justice, mercy, and faith**).

It is possible to carefully obey certain details of God's laws but still be disobedient in our general behavior. For example, we could be very precise and faithful about giving ten percent of our money to the church but refuse to give one minute of our time in helping others. Tithing is important, but giving a **tithe** does not exempt us from fulfilling God's other directives. The last phrase sums up all the "woes." We also must not **leave undone the more important things.** Jesus was not negating faithfulness to God's law; rather, he was condemning a concern for minor details that replaced true piety and discipleship.

23:24 How **blind** these religious leaders were— **guides** who were leading the people astray! Jesus used a play on words here—the Aramaic words for "gnat" and "camel" are very similar. The Pharisees strained their **water** so they wouldn't **accidentally swallow a gnat**—an unclean insect according to the law. Meticulous about the details of ceremonial cleanliness, they nevertheless had lost their perspective on the matters of justice, mercy, and faithfulness (23:23), symbolized by the **camel.** The camel was not only the largest creature in the

Near East but was also unclean. As the Pharisees took great care of the smallest details in order to remain pure, they had become unclean in the most important areas. Ceremonially clean on the outside, they had corrupt hearts.

23:25-26 The Pharisees were so obsessed about having contact with only **clean** things that they not only washed the kitchen utensils but also made certain that the utensils were ceremonially clean. Staying ceremonially clean was the central focus of the Pharisees' lifestyle. Jesus pointed out that they had taken care of the **outside,** but neglected their own filth on the **inside,** for they were **full of greed and self-indulgence.** Jesus condemned the Pharisees and religious leaders for outwardly appearing saintly and holy but inwardly remaining full of corruption and greed.

23:27-28 Like **whitewashed tombs,** the religious leaders had put on a **beautiful** appearance, but inside they were full of **dead people's bones and all sorts of impurity.** They were supposed to be the holy men and instead were filled with **hypocrisy** (in their wrongful application of God's law and their attempts to make others live up to their standards) and **lawlessness** (in their evil deeds, such as those described in 15:5-6 and 23:14).

23:29-32 Continuing the imagery of the white-washed tombs, Jesus centered on the **tombs of the prophets** and the **graves of the godly people,** which were revered. This was ironic because these martyrs had, in most cases, been killed by the religious establishment of the day. For example, the prophet Zechariah was executed (2 Chronicles 24:20-22) and the prophet Uriah was killed (Jeremiah 26:20-23). While the current religious leaders said that they **never would have joined** their ancestors **in killing the prophets,** Jesus pointed

out that they were no different from their ancestors at all for they were plotting to kill another messenger from God—the Messiah himself.

23:33-34 By using the description of **snakes** and **vipers,** Jesus called the teachers and Pharisees contemptible and obnoxious creatures. Their punishment evokes the imagery of **hell** and its eternal fires. There will be no escape for these men, for they had already cast aside any hope of salvation.

The **prophets, wise men,** and **teachers of religious law** to whom Jesus referred were probably leaders in the early church who eventually were persecuted, scourged, and killed, just as Jesus predicted. The people of Jesus' generation said they would not act as their fathers did in killing the prophets whom God had sent to them (23:30), but they were about to kill the Messiah himself and his faithful followers. Thus, they would become guilty of all the righteous blood shed through the centuries.

23:35-36 Jesus gave two examples of Old Testament martyrdom. **Abel** was the first martyr (Genesis 4); **Zechariah** was the last mentioned in the Hebrew Bible, which ended with 2 Chronicles according to their canon. Zechariah is a classic example of a man of God who was killed by those who claimed to be God's people (see 2 Chronicles 24:20-21). In both cases, the call for vengeance is explicit (Genesis 4:10; 2 Chronicles 24:22). In 23:30, now **all the accumulated judgment of the centuries** would come **upon the heads of this very generation.** The current religious establishment would be guilty of all of their deaths, for they would be guilty of murdering the Messiah and would face judgment for that act. The destruction of Jerusalem in A.D. 70 was a partial fulfillment of Jesus' words.

JESUS GRIEVES OVER JERUSALEM AGAIN / 23:37-39 / 199

These verses bridge the gap between Jesus' denunciation of the Judaism of the religious leaders (that had become horribly corrupt) and his explicit prediction of the destruction of the Temple in chapter 24.

23:37 Jerusalem was the capital city of God's chosen people, the ancestral home of David, Israel's greatest king, and the location of the Temple, the earthly dwelling place of God. It was intended to be the center of worship of the true God and a symbol of justice to all people. But Jerusalem had become blind to God and insensitive to human need. Jerusalem here stands for all the Jewish people, but this prophecy specifically looks to the

city's destruction. The Jewish leaders had stoned and killed **the prophets** and others whom God had sent to the nation to bring them back to him. By their constant rejection of God's messengers, they had sealed their fate. Jesus **wanted to gather** the nation and bring it to repentance, but the people **wouldn't let** him. Here we see the depth of Jesus' feelings for lost people and for his beloved city that would soon be destroyed. Jesus took no pleasure in denouncing the religious establishment or in prophesying the coming destruction of the city and the people that rejected him. He had come to save, but they would not let him.

23:38-39 Jesus may have been alluding to Jeremiah 12:7. Jeremiah had prophesied the coming destruction of the Temple by the Babylonians. The nation's sin sealed their punishment, and God's presence left the Temple. When Jesus Christ came, God himself again stood in the Temple. But the people's refusal to accept him would have severe consequences, for he would again leave the Temple. The Temple stood for the people's relationship with God; an **empty and desolate** Temple meant separation from God.

MATTHEW 24

JESUS TELLS ABOUT THE FUTURE / 24:1-25 / 201

Chapter 24 contains a conversation between Jesus and his disciples as they left the Temple and began their walk back to Bethany where they were spending their nights. This may have been either Tuesday or Wednesday evening of the week before the Crucifixion. This was Jesus' last visit to the Temple area. He would do no more preaching or public teaching. A casual remark by a disciple led Jesus to make a startling prophetic statement about the fate of the magnificent Temple.

24:1 One of the disciples pointed out to Jesus **the various Temple buildings**, remarking on their incredible beauty (Mark 13:1). Although no one knows exactly what the Temple looked like, it must have been magnificent, for in its time it was considered one of the architectural wonders of the world. The Temple was impressive, covering about one-sixth of the land area of the ancient city of Jerusalem. It was not one building, but a majestic mixture of porches, colonnades, separate small edifices, and courts surrounding the Temple proper. The Jews were convinced of the permanence of this magnificent structure, not only because of the stability of construction, but also because it represented God's presence among them.

24:2 Jesus acknowledged the great buildings but then made a startling statement: This wonder of the world would be **completely demolished**. As in the days of the prophet Jeremiah, the destruction of the Jews' beloved Temple would be God's punishment for turning away from him. This would happen only a few years later when the Romans sacked Jerusalem in A.D. 70. The sovereign judgment of God was to fall upon his unbelieving people; and just as Jesus as Lord of the Temple had proclaimed its purification, here he predicted its destruction.

24:3 The **Mount of Olives** rises above Jerusalem to the east. As Jesus was leaving the city to return to Bethany for the night, he would have crossed the Kidron Valley, and then he would have headed up the slope of the Mount of Olives. From this slope, he and the disciples could look down into the city and see the Temple. The prophet Zechariah predicted that the Messiah would stand on that very mountain when he would return to set up his eternal Kingdom (Zechariah 14:1-4). This place evoked questions about the future, so it was natural for the disciples to ask Jesus when he would come in power and what they could expect at that time.

The disciples' question had two parts. They wanted to know **when** this would happen and what would be the **sign** that would **signal** Jesus' **return and the end of the world.** In the disciples' minds, one event would occur immediately after the other. They expected the Messiah to inaugurate his Kingdom soon, and they wanted to know the sign that it was about to arrive.

Jesus gave them a prophetic picture of that time, including events leading up to it. He also talked about far future events connected with the last days and his second coming when he would return to earth to judge all people. As many of the Old Testament prophets had done, Jesus predicted both near and distant events without putting them in chronological order. The coming destruction of Jerusalem and the Temple only foreshadowed a future destruction that would precede Christ's return. Some of the disciples lived to see the destruction of Jerusalem in A.D. 70, while some of the events Jesus spoke of have not yet—to this day—occurred. But the truth of Jesus' prediction regarding Jerusalem assured the disciples (and assures us) that everything else he predicted will also happen.

24:4-5 Jesus knew that if the disciples looked for signs, they would be susceptible to deception. There would be many false prophets (24:24) with counterfeit signs of spiritual power and authority. Jesus predicted that before his return, many believers would be misled by false teachers coming **in** his **name**—that is, claiming to be **the Messiah.** Throughout the first century, many such deceivers arose (see Acts 5:36-37; 8:9-11; 2 Timothy 3; 2 Peter 2; 1 John 2:18; 4:1-3).

24:6-8 As political situations worsen, as **wars** ravage the world, Jesus' followers should not be afraid that God has lost control or that his promises will not come true. Just as false messiahs and religious frauds come and go, so do political and natural crises. Even when the world seems to be in chaos, God is in control. **These things must come** as part of God's divine plan. However, the wars and rumors of wars do not signal **the end.** The disciples probably assumed that the Temple would only be destroyed at the end of the age as part of God establishing his new Kingdom. Jesus taught that horrible events would happen, **but the end won't follow immediately.** Instead, this will be but **the beginning of the horrors to come.** Jesus' words indicated to the eager disciples that there would be a span of time before the end of the age and the coming Kingdom—it would not come that week, or immediately upon Jesus' resurrection, or even right after the destruction of Jerusalem. First, much suffering would occur as a part of life on earth, while history would move toward a single, final, God-planned goal—the creation of a new earth and a new Kingdom (Revelation 21:1-3).

24:9 Jesus personalized his prophecy by explaining that the disciples themselves would face severe persecution; thus, they must be on their guard in order to stay true to the faith. As the early church began to grow, the disciples' **allegiance** to Jesus caused them to be **hated all over the world.** To believe in Jesus and stay strong to the end (24:13) will take perseverance because our faith will be challenged and opposed. Severe trials will sift true Christians from phony believers.

24:10 Jesus warned that such severe persecution may lead to the defection of some members. The fear and persecution will be so intense that people will **betray and hate each other** in order to keep themselves safe. It will be dangerous to be a Christian.

24:11-12 Not only will believers face defection and betrayal from within the body, but also **false prophets will appear** and their teachings will **lead many people astray.** The Old Testament frequently mentions false prophets (see 2 Kings 3:13; Isaiah 44:25; Jeremiah 23:16; Ezekiel 13:2-3; Micah 3:5; Zechariah 13:2). False prophets claimed to receive messages from God, but they said what the people wanted to hear, even when the nation was not following God. We have false prophets today, popular leaders who tell people what they want to hear—such as "God wants you to be rich," "Do whatever your desires tell you," or "There is no such thing as sin or hell." Jesus said false teachers would come, and he warned his disciples, as he warns us, not to listen to their dangerous words.

False teaching and loose morals bring a particularly destructive disease—the loss of true **love** for God and others. Love grows **cold** when sin turns our focus on ourselves and our desires.

24:13 Only Jesus' faithful followers will enter God's Kingdom. The stress in this verse is not on endurance, but on salvation; the verse offers both a promise and a warning. **The end** refers to the consummation of the Kingdom at Christ's return. This became a precious promise to believers who were struggling during intense persecution throughout the history of the church. Enduring to the end does not earn salvation for us; it marks us as already saved. The assurance of our salvation will keep us going through times of persecution. While some will suffer and some will die, none of Jesus' followers will suffer spiritual or eternal loss.

24:14 Jesus said that before his return, **the Good News about the Kingdom** (the message of salvation) would be **preached throughout the whole world.** Some have misconstrued Jesus' predictive prophecy; it does not necessarily mean that every last tribe must hear the gospel before Christ returns. But this was the disciples' mission—and it is ours. Jesus talked about the end times and final judgment to emphasize to his followers the urgency of spreading the Good News of salvation to everyone.

24:15-16 Jesus warned against seeking signs, but as a final part of his answer to the disciples' second question (24:3), he gave them the ultimate event that would signal coming destruction. The **sacrilegious object that causes desecration** refers to the desecration of the Temple by God's enemies. Matthew urged his readers to understand Jesus' words in light of the prophecy from the Old Testament prophet **Daniel** (see Daniel 9:27; 11:31; 12:11). The first fulfillment of Daniel's prophecy occurred in 168 B.C. by Antiochus Epiphanes when he sacrificed a pig to Zeus on the sacred Temple altar and made Judaism an outlaw religion, punishable by death. This incited the Maccabean wars.

The second fulfillment occurred when Jesus' prediction of the destruction of the Temple (24:2) came true. In just a few years (A.D. 70), the Roman army would destroy Jerusalem and desecrate the Temple.

Based on 24:21, the third fulfillment is yet to come. Jesus' words look forward to the end times and to the Antichrist. In the end times, the Antichrist will commit the ultimate sacrilege by setting up an image of himself in the Temple and ordering everyone to worship it (2 Thessalonians 2:4; Revelation 13:14-15).

Many of Jesus' followers would live during the time of the destruction of Jerusalem and the Temple in A.D. 70. Jesus warned his followers to get out of Jerusalem and **Judea** and to **flee to the hills** across the Jordan River when they saw the Temple being profaned. This proved to be their protection, for when the Roman army swept in, the nation and its capital city were destroyed.

24:17-20 There is undoubtedly a dual reference both to the historical present and to the distant future. First, this section prophesied the profaning of the Temple by the Roman armies. The **flight with haste** may focus on going to the mountains. Jesus told people to get away immediately, not worrying about their possessions. Jesus expressed sympathy and concern for those who would have difficulty fleeing because they were **pregnant** or had small children. Jesus told the disciples to pray that the crisis would not break in winter because that would make it difficult for everyone to get away. They should pray for nothing to hinder their flight. These people literally would be running for their lives.

The destruction of the Temple would also be a sign pointing to the final desecration that precedes the second coming of Christ (2 Thessalonians 2:4). They could be fleeing the judgment of God that would fall upon the land of Judea, or fleeing from the Antichrist.

24:21 Jesus gave this warning to get out quickly **for that will be a time of greater horror than anything the world has ever seen or will ever see again.** Great suffering is in store for God's people throughout the years ahead. The Jewish historian Josephus recorded that when the Romans sacked Jerusalem and devastated Judea, one hundred thousand Jews were taken prisoner and another 1.1 million died by slaughter and starvation. Jesus' words also point ultimately to the final period of tribulation at the end of the age because nothing like it had ever been

seen or would ever be seen again. Yet the great suffering is tempered by a great promise of hope for true believers.

24:22 Many interpreters conclude that Jesus, talking about the end times, was telescoping near-future and far-future events, as the Old Testament prophets had done. Many of these persecutions have already occurred; more are yet to come. While a certain amount of persecution happened in the destruction of Jerusalem, Jesus may also have envisioned the persecution (tribulation) of believers throughout the subsequent years. The persecution will be so severe that those days had to be **shortened**—that is, if they did not have a specific ending time, **the entire human race** would be **destroyed.** This refers to physical survival (as opposed to 24:13, which speaks of spiritual survival). The time would be cut short **for the sake of God's chosen ones** so that the destruction will not wipe out God's people and thus their mission. God is ultimately in charge of history and will not allow evil to exceed the bounds he has set.

Who are the "chosen ones"? In the Old Testament, this refers to Israel, particularly those who are faithful to God (see 1 Chronicles 16:13; Psalm 105:43; Isaiah 65:9, 15; Daniel 12:1). In the New Testament, this refers to the church—all believers (Romans 8:33; Colossians 3:12; 2 Timothy 2:10; 1 Peter 1:1-2). Some believe that these verses mean that before the beginning of the world, God chose certain people to receive his gift of salvation. Others believe that God foreknew those who would respond to him and therefore he predestined them. What is clear is that God's purpose for people was not an afterthought; it was settled before the foundation of the world.

There are three main views regarding the identity of God's chosen ones and the coming time of tribulation. Each view interprets this verse differently:

Pretribulationists believe that the chosen ones are the Jews who will have returned to the Lord and will join the believers (taken to heaven before the Tribulation) at the end of three and a half years.

Midtribulationists believe that the chosen ones are the church (all true Christians, both Jews and Gentiles). Jesus will return in the middle of the Tribulation and take them with him.

Posttribulationists believe that the chosen ones are the church (all true Christians, both Jews and Gentiles) who will persevere throughout the Tribulation period, which will be ended by God for their sakes.

When the time of suffering comes, the important point for the disciples and all believers to remember is that God is in control. Persecution will occur, but God knows about it and controls how long it will take place. The main thrust of Jesus' teaching is to show God's mercy toward the faithful and to show that God is loving and sovereign. He will not forget his people.

24:23-25 These **false messiahs and false prophets will rise up** and be able to **perform great** miraculous signs and wonders designed to convince people that their claims are true. But their "power" will be by trickery or from Satan, not from God. Yet they will be so convincing that they might even **deceive God's chosen ones.** If we are prepared, Jesus says, we can remain faithful. With the Holy Spirit's help, the elect will not give in and will be able to discern that what the deceivers say is false.

JESUS TELLS ABOUT HIS RETURN / 24:26-35 / 202

In times of persecution even strong believers will find it difficult to be loyal. They will so much want the Messiah to come that they will grasp any rumor that he has arrived. But if believers have to be told that the Messiah has come, then he hasn't. Christ's coming will be obvious to everyone.

24:26-27 Jesus had already warned his followers that false messiahs and false prophets will come and attempt to lead many astray (24:23-25). Others will think they have found the Messiah and will try to convince people by saying that he can be found in a certain place. The **desert** refers to prophetic expectation regarding an Elijah-prophet, similar to John the Baptist, who would come (Isaiah 40:3; Malachi 4:5). Jesus explained that, by contrast, his coming would be as obvious and unmistakable as a flash of **lightning** bursting across **the entire sky.** Lightning may flash in one part of the sky and be seen just as clearly in another part; **so it will be when the Son of Man comes.**

24:28 This verse, probably quoting a well-known proverb of the culture, looks to the Second Coming as a time of judgment. Jesus was telling his audience that, just as you know a **carcass** must be nearby if you see **vultures** circling overhead, so his coming will be unmistakenly marked by various signs.

24:29 After the time of tribulation, nature itself would experience changes intended to contrast with the pseudo signs of the false messiahs. There will be a variety of changes—the **sun** going dark, the **moon** not being seen, **stars** falling, heavenly bodies being **shaken** (see also Revelation 6:12-14).

   Coming persecutions and natural disasters will cause great sorrow in the world. But when believers see these events happening, they should realize that the return of their Messiah is near and that they can look forward to his reign of justice and peace. Rather than being terrified by what is happening in our world, we should confidently await Christ's return to bring justice and to restore his people.

24:30 The **Son of Man will appear in the heavens** just as he would leave. His second coming will have universal impact. **There will be deep mourning among all the nations of the earth** because unbelievers will suddenly realize that they have chosen the wrong side. Everything they have scoffed about will be happening, and it will be too late for them. After the cosmic events recorded in 24:29, all the people on earth **will see the Son of Man arrive on the clouds of heaven with power and great glory.** Jesus' return will be unmistakable; no one will wonder about his identity. The "clouds" are pictured as the Son of Man's royal chariot, bringing him from heaven to earth as the powerful, glorious, and divine Son of Man.

24:31 Upon his return to earth, Jesus will **send forth his angels** to **gather together his chosen ones from the farthest ends of the earth and heaven.** This gathering of the chosen ones signifies the triumphant enthronement of the Son of Man, who will be revealed in all his power and glory. Jesus' second coming marks the core of the Christian hope. **The sound of a mighty trumpet blast** will signal the gathering of God's people. When he comes, the whole world will know that Jesus is Lord.

   As in 24:22, three main views of the Tribulation interpret this verse in different ways:

Pretribulationists would say that this "gathering" refers to the gathering of Jewish saints (also as in 24:22), not the church. The "rapture" (taking believers to heaven) occurred before the Tribulation and concerned only the church.

Midtribulationists would say that this verse refers to the rapture and that it identifies both the church and the Jewish saints. This event will occur in the middle of the Tribulation, with the outpouring of God's wrath on the world occurring in the last half of that period.

Posttribulationists would say that the rapture and revelation are a single event, and this pictures the only return of Christ at the end of the Tribulation. There, as here, he will come to gather his saints and to judge unbelievers.

24:32-33 Using a parable, Jesus answered the disciples' question regarding when the events he spoke about would happen (24:3). The disciples, like anyone living in Palestine, knew when summer would come by observing a **fig tree.** The dry, brittle twigs getting tender with rising sap and the leaves coming out were certain signs that **summer was near.** Inherent in this process is patient waiting. There is no hurrying the natural cycle of the fig tree. So all believers must patiently await the Second Coming.

This verse means that the second coming of Jesus is both certain and near. The fulfillment of Jesus' prophecy would assure the disciples that the other prophecies he had given regarding the end times would also come true.

24:34 There are three views of the meaning of the words: **this generation will not pass from the scene before all these things take place.** (1) It refers only to those alive at the time Jesus spoke who still would be alive at the destruction of Jerusalem; (2) it refers to the end times only; (3) it refers both to the destruction of Jerusalem and the end times—the destruction of Jerusalem containing within itself the elements of the final end times.

"This generation" could refer both to those living at a given time as well as to race or lineage (therefore, he would be speaking of the Jewish race). That makes the third view above most likely. The events of 24:1-28 would occur initially within the lifetime of Jesus' contemporaries. Not that all the problems would stop at the end of their lifetimes, but that *all these things* would be under way, verifying what Jesus had said. Jesus explained that many of those alive at that time would witness the destruction of Jerusalem. In addition, the Jewish nation would be preserved and remain on earth, so Jews also would witness the end-time events (see also 16:28).

24:35 There could be no doubt in the disciples' minds about the certainty of these prophecies. While **heaven and earth** would eventually come to an end, Jesus' **words** (including all his teachings during his time on earth) would **remain forever.**

JESUS TELLS ABOUT REMAINING WATCHFUL / 24:36-51 / *203*
While Jesus had given general "signs" to watch for regarding the coming of the end, he clearly explained to the disciples that the exact day or hour was not known by the angels or the Son (Jesus himself). It is good that we don't know exactly when Christ will return. If we knew the precise date, we might be tempted to be lazy in our work for Christ. Worse yet, we might plan to keep sinning and then turn to God right at the end.

24:36 When Jesus said that even he did not know the time of the end, he was affirming his limitations as a human (see Philippians 2:5-8). Of course, God the Father knows the time, and Jesus and the Father are one. But when Jesus became a man, he voluntarily gave up the unlimited use of his divine attributes. On earth, Jesus laid aside his divine prerogatives and submitted to the Father's will. Thus, **only the Father** knows exactly when Jesus will return. The emphasis of this verse is not on Jesus' lack of knowledge, but rather on the fact that **no one knows.** It is God the Father's secret to be revealed when he wills. No one can predict by Scripture or science the exact day of the Second Coming. Jesus was teaching that preparation, not calculation, was needed.

24:37-39 The first outpouring of God's judgment upon sinful people **in Noah's day** has a natural connection with the final outpouring at the Lord's return. People will be going about their daily business, just as they were in Noah's time (Genesis 7:17-24). Just as the flood caught them unawares (and after it was too late) and swept them away in judgment, so it will be **when the Son of Man comes** (see also 1 Peter 3:20-21).

24:40-42 To further illustrate the suddenness of his return, Jesus pictured "business as usual" in Palestine—the men out working in the field; the women doing domestic chores such as grinding grain. The Second Coming will happen so suddenly that in the blink of an eye, one of those people may be **taken** and the other **left.** The reason? One was ready and one was not. Believers must be on guard and alert, constantly ready for him to come at any time. Christ's second coming will be swift and sudden. There will be no time for last-minute repenting or bargaining. The choice that people have already made will determine their eternal destiny.

24:43-44 Jesus again pointed out the need for constant vigilance. A **homeowner** cannot know when a **burglar** might come to break into his home, so he must **stay alert.** So it will be with the return of Christ. He will come **when least expected.**

24:45-47 In ancient times it was a common practice for masters to put one servant in charge of all the household business. The **servant,** described as **faithful** and **sensible,** parallels the disciples, who were given unprecedented **responsibility** by Jesus. Yet it also describes those appointed to positions of leadership in the church who should be found faithfully carrying out their duties when Jesus (**the master**) returns. These servants will be given great rewards.

24:48-51 Some servants, however, might decide to take advantage of their leadership positions, bullying others and indulging themselves. The servant may have thought his master would be gone a long time, but one day, **the master will return unannounced and unexpectedly.** It will be sudden and without warning, and the evil servant will be "caught in the act." The master's judgment against his wicked servant will be extremely severe. Even worse than that horrible punishment will be the servant's eternal destiny. He will be assigned to a place of **weeping and gnashing of teeth** (referring to hell). God's coming judgment is as certain as Jesus' return to earth.

MATTHEW 25

JESUS TELLS THE PARABLE OF THE TEN BRIDESMAIDS / 25:1-13 / 204
Jesus told the following parables to clarify further what it means to be ready for his return and how to live until he comes. The ten bridesmaids (25:1-13) teach that every person is responsible for his or her own spiritual condition. Some will be included while others will not. No parable by itself completely describes our preparation. Instead, each presents one part of the whole picture.

25:1 All weddings in Israel at this time included the processional of the bridegroom to the bride's family home. These **ten bridesmaids** were going out to **meet the bridegroom,** who was coming to the bride's home to join the procession back to his house for the ceremony and the wedding banquet. This happened after dark, and in villages and towns without streetlights; so their **lamps** lit the way. Everyone was required to carry his or her own lamp.

25:2-7 The **foolish** bridesmaids were unprepared; they **took no oil for their lamps.** If their lamps burned out, they would be unable to light them again. The **wise** bridesmaids had brought along **extra oil.** Finally **at midnight,** the bridegroom arrived. Everyone **got up and prepared their lamps** in anticipation of the procession.

25:8-9 The **foolish** bridesmaids realized that their lamps were **going out,** but the wise bridesmaids explained that they didn't **have enough** to share. This was not selfishness, but rather the realization that if they shared their little oil, then *all* the torches would burn low and there would not be enough light for the wedding procession. Jesus' focus was on the foolish people's unprepared-

ness. When Jesus returns to take his people to heaven, we must be ready. Spiritual preparation cannot be bought or borrowed at the last minute. No one can rely on anyone else. Our relationship with God must be our own.

25:10-12 While the foolish bridesmaids were off trying to buy oil, the bridegroom came and everyone proceeded on to the wedding banquet. The central focus of the parable lies in the words **and the door was locked.** Jesus' point, again, is that to not be ready at the right time means to miss out completely. There is a finality to the shutting of that door. Those outside will not have another chance to be let in.

25:13 Jesus concluded with the application that his true followers must **stay awake and be prepared** because he will return when they will least expect it. God may delay his return longer than we might prefer or expect. We must be prepared for such a delay—counting the cost of discipleship and persevering faithfully until he returns. Those who are unfaithful must realize that neglecting Christ's invitation may lead to irreversible consequences and the time of opportunity to believe may pass.

JESUS TELLS THE PARABLE OF THE LOANED MONEY / 25:14-30 / *205*

The following parable explains *how* Jesus' followers are to remain prepared during their wait for his return. While the previous parable about the wise and foolish bridesmaids stressed readiness, this parable focused on using the waiting time well.

25:14-15 The **man going on a trip** was wealthy enough to have **servants** and to have an amount of money that he wanted invested and multiplied while he was gone. He divided the **money** among his three servants. Each received different amounts **in proportion to** his **abilities.** The different sums of money point out how God recognizes each person as a unique individual with varied circumstances and personality. What he "gives" to each person is exactly what that person can handle. If any of these servants failed in the assignment, his excuse could not be that he was overwhelmed. The money represents any kind of resource that believers are given. God gives us time, abilities, and other resources according to our abilities, and he expects us to invest them wisely until he returns.

25:16-18 The first two servants **doubled** the money the master had given them. But the third servant **dug a hole in the ground and hid the master's money.** This would not have seemed unusual to Jesus' listeners, for in the ancient world, it was not an uncommon way to safeguard one's valuables (see 13:44). We do not know why he did it; he could have been lazy or afraid.

25:19-23 The first servant brought the **doubled** money, and his master was pleased with his efforts and with the profit. The reward for the servant's faithfulness is even greater responsibility. The second servant had also faithfully fulfilled his responsibility. He had been given less money, but he had done everything he could and brought a **doubled** return to the master. Because he had faithfully discharged his responsibility, even though he had less than the first servant, he received the same reward, commendation, and privileges.

We are responsible to use well what God has given us. The issue is not how much we have but how well we use what we have. Each believer should faithfully carry out the duties entrusted to him or her by God and multiply his or her God-given gifts for the sake of the Kingdom.

25:24-25 The third **servant** made excuses instead of realizing that, from the start, his responsibility was to serve his master to the best of his ability. To refuse to serve reveals a lack of love and little desire to accomplish anything for the master. He hoped to play it safe and protect himself from his hard master, but he had accomplished nothing for him. His words to the master reveal a self-centered character. He accused his master of being **hard.** His accusation was an attempt to cover up his own irresponsibility.

We must not make excuses to avoid doing what God calls us to do. God truly is our Master, so we must obey him. Our time, abilities, and money aren't really ours; we are caretakers, not owners. When we ignore, squander, or abuse what we have been given, we are rebellious and deserve to be punished.

25:26-27 Using the servant's own words, the master pointed out that he had every right to require that his servants fulfill their responsibilities. He had not expected much of this servant in the first place; that's why the servant received so little. So even putting the money in the **bank** to earn **interest** would have been enough. Yet the **wicked and lazy servant** had not even done that.

25:28-29 The master severed his relationship with this servant, took away the money, and gave it to the one who had earned the most. Jesus had already taught the concept: **to those who use well what they are given, even more will be given** (13:12). This parable describes the consequences of two attitudes regarding Christ's return. The person who diligently prepares for it by investing his or her time and talent to serve God will be rewarded. The person who has no heart for the work of the Kingdom will be punished. God rewards faithfulness. Those who bear no fruit for God's Kingdom cannot expect to be treated the same as those who are faithful.

25:30 To fail to do good with what God has entrusted to us, to fail to use it to increase his Kingdom, is a grievous sin that will receive severe punishment—for it means that one never knew or loved the Master. The **outer darkness** and **weeping and gnashing of teeth** picture the anguish of hell (see 8:12; 13:42, 50; 22:13; 24:51).

Watching and waiting for the Kingdom means being prepared. Being prepared means making ready for it by increasing the glory of God in this world through good deeds. Good deeds are best performed through the talents God has given us and should be done to the best of our ability.

JESUS TELLS ABOUT THE FINAL JUDGMENT / 25:31-46 / 206
This parable of the sheep and goats builds Jesus' message of judgment and salvation. Those who believe will naturally serve others in need.

25:31-33 This verse pictures Jesus when he will return, not as the humble carpenter from Nazareth but **in his glory.** The sight will be spectacular when the **angels** accompany the Son and we see him **upon his glorious throne** (see also 16:27-28; 24:30-31; Zechariah 14:5). He will come as Judge, for **all the nations will be gathered in his presence** (see Psalm 110:1; 2 Corinthians 5:10).

Jesus used **sheep** and **goats** to picture the division between believers and unbelievers. Jesus, the Judge, **will separate them.** While all "nations" are before him, he will separate individuals, for each individual is responsible for his or her own salvation (as seen in the parable of the bridesmaids, 25:1-13). This "separation" became a picture for the Last Judgment.

25:34-39 The "sheep" are at his **right** hand, and are identified as God's chosen people who **inherit the Kingdom prepared for** them. This Kingdom, existing from the beginning of time, is sure and unchangeable. Believers need never doubt its existence. The reason they are ushered into the Kingdom is that they gave to those who had need. This list describes acts of mercy people can do every day. These acts do not depend on wealth, ability, or intelligence; they are simple acts freely given and freely received. Jesus demands our personal involvement in caring for others' needs (Isaiah 58:7). That this list is repeated four times in this parable indicates its importance as a guide for practical discipleship. The list is not exhaustive; instead, it represents all types of good deeds. This parable is not teaching salvation by good deeds, but evidence of salvation through good deeds.

The **righteous** are surprised at the King's words. He commends them for their acts of kindness to him, but they realize that they did not have opportunity to do such kindnesses to him directly.

25:40 The basis of reward rests on the acts of kindness each individual believer did for other believers, for in so doing, they did those kindnesses for the **King** himself. Through the Holy Spirit, Jesus is present in even the most humble or "insignificant" follower of Christ. How we treat lowly and needy fellow Christians determines how truly we love Jesus. If Christians who have resources would help needy fellow Christians, non-Christians would be totally persuaded of the validity of Christian love. Such love for others glorifies God by reflecting our love for him.

25:41 For the goats (**those on his left**), however, the story is different. These "goats," mingling every day as they did with the sheep, may have thought that they could get by unnoticed. But God would separate them, and their judgment would be severe. There will be no middle ground at the final judgment—either a person is a "sheep" or a "goat." And the result will be either the Kingdom (25:34) or **eternal fire prepared for the Devil and his demons** (referring to hell) and separation from God forever (indicated by the words **"away with you"**). For more on hell, see 5:22.

25:42-43 The sin noted by the King was not active evildoing but failure to do good. As in 25:35-36, the list is not comprehensive, but it represents good deeds that people often fail to do. Doing wrong in ignorance may be excusable (see Acts 3:17; 1 Timothy 1:13), but when believers neglect to help those in need, they disobey Christ. These actions do not take special talents, gifts, or lifestyles. One need not be rich to carry these out. Failure to do them then shows a lack of love for Christian brothers and, by extension, for the Lord himself.

25:44-45 The evildoers, also, were surprised at the King's words. How could he say that they had neglected to do acts of kindness to him personally when, in reality, that would seem to be an impossibility? So he explained that in neglecting to do these kindnesses to even **the least** of the Christian brothers and sisters, they had neglected to do so for him. By that neglect, they had shown no true salvation, for their salvation had not manifested itself in good deeds as it would naturally do. Their failures were not acts of wickedness, but refusals to do good and to show compassion.

25:46 God will separate his obedient followers from pretenders and unbelievers, and their destinies will be vastly different. The real evidence of our belief is the way we act. To treat all persons we encounter as if they are Jesus is not easy. What we do for others demonstrates what we really think about Jesus' words to us—feed the hungry, give the homeless a place to stay, look after the sick. How well do your actions separate you from pretenders and unbelievers? Will you be sent away to **eternal punishment** or **eternal life?**

MATTHEW 26

RELIGIOUS LEADERS PLOT TO KILL JESUS / 26:1-5 / 207
Starting in this chapter and through the end of the book, we find the climax of Jesus' ministry. Matthew recorded little teaching (as opposed to John who recorded lengthy teaching at the Last Supper) and instead focused on Jesus' completion of the work that he had come to do. Jesus moved into the final days of his earthly ministry and to the act that he ultimately came to accomplish—death for sins. This was never a surprise to Jesus; in fact, he had already told his disciples on three different occasions that he would suffer and die (see 16:21-28; 17:22-23; 20:17-19). As if echoing these warnings, Jesus reminded his disciples that the time had come for these things to be fulfilled.

26:1-2 That Jesus would **be betrayed and crucified** during **Passover** was deeply significant with respect to Jewish history. The "Passover" commemorated the night the Israelites were freed from Egypt (Exodus 12)—when God "passed over" homes marked by the blood of a lamb. This was the last great plague on Egypt when, in unmarked homes, the firstborn sons died. After this horrible disaster, Pharaoh allowed the Israelites to leave. Annually, Hebrew families would celebrate the Passover meal, a feast with the main course of lamb. The sacrifice of a lamb and the spilling of its blood commemorated Israel's escape from Egypt, when the blood of a lamb painted on their doorposts had saved their firstborn sons from death. This event foreshadowed Jesus' work on the cross. As the spotless Lamb of God, his blood would be spilled in order to save his people from the penalty of death brought by sin.

26:3-5 The Jewish leaders plotted **secretly** to kill Jesus. They met **at the residence of Caiaphas,** the ruling **high priest.** Caiaphas was the leader of the religious group called the Sadducees. Caiaphas served for eighteen years, longer than most high priests, suggesting that he was gifted at cooperating with the Romans.

They did not want to attempt to arrest Jesus **during the Passover** because they realized that to do so could cause a **riot** on his behalf. During this holiday, Jerusalem, a town of about 50,000, would swell to 250,000 people. The leaders feared that an uprising might bring the wrath of Rome. They may have planned to arrest Jesus after the Feast when the vast crowds were gone. Perhaps Judas's unexpected offer (26:14-16) caused them to move sooner than they had planned, but, as this passage implies, all was proceeding according to God's timetable.

A WOMAN ANOINTS JESUS WITH PERFUME / 26:6-13 / 182
Matthew sandwiched this beautiful event between two sections dealing with the plot to eliminate Jesus. Most likely, John's Gospel placed this event in its chronological position. This act of devotion by Mary, who is a true heroine in this narrative, contrasts with the treachery of the villains—the religious leaders and Judas.

26:6-7 **Bethany** was located on the eastern slope of the Mount of Olives (Jerusalem is on the western side). This town was the home of Jesus' friends Lazarus, Mary, and Martha. Jesus had been returning to Bethany from Jerusalem each night during this final week, probably staying with these dear friends (21:17).

One night, a dinner had been prepared with

Jesus as the honored guest. The host, **Simon,** did not have **leprosy** at this time, for lepers were forced to live separately from people. Jesus may have healed Simon of his leprosy, but he had the nickname as a former leper.

The **woman** who **came in** was probably Mary, the sister of Martha and Lazarus. She had **a beautiful jar of expensive perfume** which she **poured** on Jesus'

head. Such an anointing, using expensive oil, pictured a royal anointing appropriate for the Messiah.

26:8-9 Mary's gift to Jesus was worth a year's wages. The disciples concluded that the expensive ointment had been wasted on Jesus, and they rebuked Mary for such an act because the perfume could have been **given** to the **poor.** Where Matthew says **the disciples,** John specifically mentions Judas (John 12:4-5). Judas's indignation over Mary's act of worship would not have been based on concern for the poor, but on greed. Because Judas was the treasurer of Jesus' ministry and had embezzled funds (John 12:6), he no doubt wanted the perfume sold so that the proceeds could be put into his care.

26:10-11 Jesus reprimanded the disciples for their lack of insight. Their words criticized Mary's actions, but Jesus' words comforted her. The expensive perfume poured on Jesus had been **a good thing**—a beautiful act of love and sacrifice—and Jesus declared it to be so. This was a unique act for a specific occasion—an anointing that anticipated Jesus' burial and publicly declared faith in him as Messiah. In saying **you will always have the poor among you,** Jesus was not saying that we should neglect the poor, nor was he justifying indifference to them. Believers should show kindness to the poor, and opportunities to do so would continue until the end of time. There would always be poor people who would need help.

The phrase **I will not be here with you much longer** meant that Jesus would soon be gone from them physically. Jesus' purpose in these words was to explain that the opportunity to show him such devotion and to anoint him with oil (in preparation for burial) would soon pass. Jesus was affirming Mary's unselfish act of worship and highlighting the special sacrifice that Mary had made for him. The essence of worshiping Christ is to regard him with utmost love, respect, and devotion, as well as to be willing to sacrifice to him what is most precious.

26:12-13 Mary may not have set out to anoint Jesus **for burial;** she was merely showing great respect for the Teacher she so loved and respected. She may not have understood Jesus' approaching death any more than the disciples, although she was known for truly listening to Jesus (Luke 10:39). She may have realized something was going to happen to Jesus, for all knew he was in great danger, and thus she sympathized with him and honored him with the greatest gift she could give.

Mary's unselfish act would be **preached throughout the world** along with **the Good News.** This has come true because we read about it today. While the disciples misunderstood Jesus' mission and constantly argued about places in the Kingdom, and while the religious leaders stubbornly refused to believe in Jesus and plotted his death, this one quiet woman so loved Jesus and was so devoted to him that she considered no sacrifice too great for her beloved Master. She is an example to us all of unselfish devotion to our Savior.

JUDAS AGREES TO BETRAY JESUS / 26:14-16 / 208

26:14-16 Why would one of Jesus' twelve disciples, **Judas Iscariot,** want to betray Jesus? The Bible does not reveal Judas's motives other than gaining money. Judas knew that the **leading priests** had it in for Jesus, and he knew they would have the power to arrest Jesus. So that was where he went. Judas's greedy desire for money could not be fulfilled if he followed Jesus, so he betrayed him in exchange for **pay** from the religious leaders. To have discovered a traitor among Jesus' followers greatly pleased the religious leaders. They had been having difficulty figuring out how to arrest Jesus (26:3-5), so when an offer of help came from this unexpected corner, they took advantage of it.

Matthew alone has the exact amount of money Judas accepted to betray Jesus—**thirty pieces of silver,** the price of a slave (Exodus 21:32). This fulfilled Zechariah 11:12-13 (see also Jeremiah 18:1-4; 19:1-13; 32:6-15).

DISCIPLES PREPARE FOR THE PASSOVER / 26:17-19 / 209

The Passover took place on one night and at one meal, but the Festival of Unleavened Bread, which was celebrated with it, would continue for a week. The chronology of the events of Jesus' final week is as follows:

Thursday—Lambs were slain in the afternoon, Passover began at 6:00 P.M., Last Supper, Gethsemane, arrest

Friday—Official trial, Crucifixion, burial by sundown, Feast of Unleavened Bread and Sabbath began at 6:00 P.M.

Saturday—Jesus' body was in the tomb

Sunday—Early morning Resurrection

26:17-19 Jesus' disciples asked him, **"Where do you want us to prepare the Passover supper?"** Peter and John were sent to make preparations (Luke 22:8)—buying and preparing the unleavened bread, herbs, wine, and other ceremonial food. Jesus told the two disciples that as they entered Jerusalem, they would meet a **certain man.** In Mark, Jesus explained that this man would be carrying a jar of water (Mark 14:13). Ordinarily women, not men, would go to the well and bring home the water. So this man would have stood out in the crowd. This may have been a prearranged signal, or Jesus may have supernaturally known that this man would be there and would lead them to the right house. This private location kept the plans secret and security tight. Tradition says that this may have been Mark's home (the writer of the Gospel). If this speculation is true, the owner of the house would have been Mark's father and one of Jesus' followers. He knew exactly who **the Teacher** was and probably knew the disciples by sight. The disciples did as Jesus directed and made preparations for the others.

JESUS AND THE DISCIPLES SHARE THE LAST SUPPER / 26:20-30 / 211

On that evening, Jesus and the disciples arrived in Jerusalem. The Passover meal was supposed to be eaten in Jerusalem after sunset and before midnight. The disciples and Jesus took their places on the couches around the table.

26:20-22 While they were eating, Jesus said, "The truth is, one of you will betray me." His words caused quite a stir among the disciples. Jesus had told them three different times that he would soon die, but news that one of them was a traitor saddened them greatly. Although the other disciples were confused, Judas was not. Apparently, Judas was not obvious as the betrayer, so each disciple asked Jesus for assurance.

26:23-24 Jesus would be betrayed and would die as he had already told his disciples. His death would not occur merely because of the **betrayer,** for the **Son of Man** had to die to complete God's plan **as the Scriptures declared long ago.**

But it would be **far better** for the betrayer **if he had never been born.** Jesus' words are reminiscent of Psalm 41:10-12, where the sufferer is vindicated by God and his enemies punished. Jesus knew that Judas was going to betray him, and he also knew that Judas would not repent.

26:25 Jesus' answer to **Judas** was ambiguous enough so that only Judas would know that Jesus had identified him as the betrayer. Luke wrote that "Satan entered into Judas Iscariot" before Judas went to the religious leaders (Luke 22:3); however, Satan's part in the betrayal of Jesus does not remove any of the responsibility from Judas. In God's sovereign will and according to his timetable, he uses sinful men, but that doesn't excuse their sin. All people will be held accountable for their choices and actions. Satan tried to end Jesus' mission and thwart God's plan. Like Judas, Satan did not know that Jesus' death and resurrection were the most important parts of God's plan all along.

26:26 As Jesus and the disciples were eating, Jesus took the **loaf** of unleavened bread, **asked God's blessing on it,** and **broke it in pieces.** Jesus took two traditional parts of the Passover meal, the passing of bread and the drinking of wine, and gave them new meaning as representations of his body and blood. He used the bread and wine to explain the significance of what he was about to do on the cross. Jesus told the disciples to **take it and eat** the bread for it was his **body.** Jesus portrayed the sacrifice he would make and the spiritual benefit that would be passed on to those who had a personal relationship with him. This was Jesus' pledge of his personal presence with all his disciples whenever they would partake of this meal.

26:27-28 Jesus **gave thanks** and gave the **cup** to the disciples, saying, **"Each of you drink from it."** As with the bread, Jesus spoke words in figurative language. **"This is my blood"** means "this wine represents my blood." Jesus' blood, shed on behalf of **the sins of many,** began a **covenant** between God and people.

In Old Testament times, God had agreed to forgive people's sins if they would bring animals for the priests to sacrifice. When this sacrificial system was inaugurated, the agreement between God and human beings was sealed with the blood of animals (Exodus 24:8). But animal blood did not in itself remove sin, and animal sacrifices had to be repeated day by day and year after year.

Jesus instituted a new covenant, or agreement, between humans and God. This concept is key to all New Testament theology and forms the basis for the name of the "New Testament" portion of the Bible. Under this new covenant, Jesus would die in the place of sinners. Unlike the blood of animals, Jesus' blood would truly remove the sins of all who would put their faith in him. And Jesus' sacrifice would never have to be repeated; it would be good for all eternity (Hebrews 9:23-28). The old covenant was a shadow of the new, pointing forward to the day when Jesus himself would be the final and ultimate sacrifice for sin. Rather than an unblemished lamb slain on the altar, the perfect Lamb of God was slain on the cross, a sinless sacrifice to **forgive sins** once and for all. Jesus explained that his blood would be **poured out,** referring to a violent death.

Those who accept Christ's sacrifice and believe in him receive forgiveness. Now all people can come directly to God through faith because Jesus' death has made us acceptable in God's eyes (Romans 3:21-24).

The Lord's Supper commemorates Christ's death on the cross in our place, paying the penalty for our sins, and it points to the coming of his Kingdom in glory. When we partake of it, we show our deep gratitude for Christ's work on our behalf, and our faith is strengthened.

26:29-30 Again Jesus assured his disciples of his victory over his imminent death and of a future in his **Father's Kingdom.** The next few hours would bring apparent defeat, but soon they would experience the power of the Holy Spirit, and they would witness the great spread of the gospel message. Because Jesus would be raised, so his followers will be raised, for he will drink that wine **with** his followers. One day we will all be together again in God's new Kingdom.

The **hymn** they sang was most likely taken from Psalms 115–118. John included a lengthy discourse that Jesus had with his disciples (John 13:31–17:26) before he and the eleven remaining disciples left the upper room and **went out to the Mount of Olives.**

JESUS AGAIN PREDICTS PETER'S DENIAL / 26:31-35 / 222
This is the second time in the same evening that Jesus predicted the disciples' denial and desertion (see Luke 22:31-34; John 13:36-38). The disciples would turn away from him. Jesus would go to the cross alone.

26:31-32 The disciples might have been tempted to think that Satan and his forces had gained the upper hand in this drama about Jesus' death. But God was in control, even in the death of his Son. Satan gained no victory—everything occurred as God had planned. Jesus himself explained that the disciples' desertion would also occur just as it had been predicted in Scripture, specifically Zechariah 13:7.

In Zechariah, God commanded that the **Shepherd** be struck down. As a result, the **sheep** would be **scattered.** Without a shepherd, the sheep would go through a period of great trial and be refined. The refining process would strengthen them and create a new, faithful people for God. The disciples would be staggered by what would happen to Jesus, but his death would ultimately produce their salvation and regather the sheep.

After predicting the disciples' desertion, Jesus predicted their reunion after his resurrection. Jesus promised that he would **go ahead** of them **to Galilee** and meet them all there.

26:33-35 Although all the disciples protested Jesus' words (26:35), **Peter,** always ready to speak up, declared that his allegiance to Jesus would prove to be much stronger than that of all the other disciples. He knew that Jesus had said to him, "Upon this rock I will build my church" (16:18), and may have assumed that he would be immune to such faithlessness.

Jesus' words to Peter were solemn. Instead of being the only loyal disciple, Peter would in fact prove to be more disloyal than the other ten. Not only would he desert Jesus, but he would also **deny** him **three times** before the night was over, that is before the **rooster** crowed at dawn's first light.

Peter did not think it possible for him to actually deny any relationship with Jesus. Not only Peter, but **all the disciples,** declared that they would **die** before denying Jesus. A few hours later, however, they all would scatter.

JESUS AGONIZES IN THE GARDEN / 26:36-46 / 223

After eating the meal, the disciples left Jerusalem and went out to a favorite meeting place (Luke 22:39; John 18:2). This gardenlike enclosure called Gethsemane, meaning "olive press," was probably an orchard of olive trees with a press for extracting oil. The garden was in the Kidron Valley just outside the eastern wall of Jerusalem and just below the Mount of Olives.

26:36 Jesus told eight of the disciples to **sit** down and wait, probably near the garden's entrance, while he went farther in to **pray.** The disciples must have been physically and emotionally exhausted from trying to comprehend what would transpire. Instead of watching, they gave in to their exhaustion and fell asleep.

26:37-38 Jesus then took the other three disciples, Peter, James, and John, farther into the garden with him. To these closest friends, Jesus revealed that he was **filled with anguish and deep distress** over his approaching death because he would be forsaken by the Father (27:46), would have to bear the sins of the world, and would face a terrible execution. The divine course was set, but Jesus, in his human nature, still struggled (Hebrews 5:7-9). As the time of this event neared, it became even more horrifying. Jesus naturally recoiled from the prospect.

Early in Jesus' ministry Satan had tempted him to take the easy way out (4:1-11); later Peter had suggested that Jesus did not have to die (16:22). In both cases, Jesus had dealt with the temptation soundly. Now, as his horrible death and separation from the Father loomed before him, he was **crushed with grief to the point of death.** So he asked Peter, James, and John to **stay** with him and keep **watch.** Jesus knew Judas would soon arrive, and Jesus wanted to devote himself to prayer until that time came.

26:39 Jesus went still farther into the garden to be alone with God. He threw himself on the ground before God in deep spiritual anguish, praying that **this cup of suffering** might be **taken away.** In the Old Testament, "cup" stood for the trial of suffering and the wrath of God (Isaiah 51:17). So Jesus referred to the suffering that he must endure as the "cup" he would be required to drink. This was a bitter cup. The physical suffering would be horrible enough (Hebrews 5:7-9), but God's Son also had to accept the cup of spiritual suffering—bearing our sin and being separated from God (27:46). Yet Jesus humbly submitted to the Father's will. He went ahead with the mission for which he had come. Jesus expressed his true feelings as a human being, but he was not denying or rebelling against God's will. He reaffirmed his desire to do what God wanted by saying, **"Yet I want your will,**

not mine." God did not take away the "cup," for the cup was his will. Yet he did take away Jesus' extreme fear and agitation. Jesus moved serenely through the next several hours, knowing that he was doing his Father's will.

26:40-41 Jesus got up from his prayer to return to the three disciples. He had told them to stay and keep watch. But instead of showing support for Jesus by remaining awake with him and praying for strength in the coming hours, they had fallen asleep. Jesus addressed Peter directly. Peter had said he would never leave Jesus; yet when Jesus needed prayer and support, Peter wasn't there for him. Thus, Jesus rebuked Peter for his failure to keep watch for even one hour.

Jesus told the disciples that this was the time to **keep alert and pray,** for very soon they would face difficult temptations. Jesus was not only asking that they pray for him, but also that they pray for themselves. Jesus knew that these men would need extra strength to face the **temptation** ahead— temptation to run away or to deny their relationship with him. The disciples were about to see Jesus die. Would they still think he was the Messiah? The disciples would soon face confusion, fear, loneliness, guilt, and the temptation to conclude that they had been deceived.

Jesus added, **"For though the spirit is willing enough, the body is weak."** Their inner desires and intentions would be, as they had previously boasted, to never deny Jesus and to die with him. Yet their human inadequacies, with all their fears and failures, would make it difficult to carry out those good intentions.

Jesus used Peter's drowsiness to warn him to be spiritually vigilant against the temptation he would soon face. The way to overcome temptation is to stay alert and to pray. This means being aware of the possibilities of temptation, sensitive to the subtleties, and morally resolved to fight courageously. Because temptation strikes where we are most vulnerable, we can't resist alone. Prayer is essential because God's strength can shore up our defenses and defeat Satan.

26:42-45 Jesus **left** the three disciples and returned to his conversation with the **Father** (26:39). Jesus **returned** to the three disciples and **found them**

sleeping. Despite his warning that they should be awake, alert, and praying not to fall to the coming temptations, **they just couldn't keep their eyes open.** Jesus **went back to pray a third time.** During these times of prayer, the battle was won. Jesus still had to go to the cross, but he would humbly submit to the Father's will and accomplish the task set before him.

After much time in prayer, Jesus was ready to face his **time,** which conveyed that all he had predicted about his death was about to happen (see John 12:23-24). The disciples had missed a great opportunity to talk to the Father, and there would be no more time to do so, for Jesus' hour had come. Thus, Jesus did not again tell them to pray. Jesus had spent the last few hours with the Father, wrestling with him, and humbly submitting to him. Now he was prepared to face his betrayer and the **sinners** who were coming to arrest him.

26:46 Jesus roused the three sleeping disciples (and perhaps the other eight as well) and called them together. His words **"Up, let's be going"** did not mean that Jesus was contemplating running away. Instead, he called the disciples to go with him to meet the **betrayer,** Judas, and the coming crowd. Jesus went forth of his own will, advancing to meet his accusers rather than waiting for them to come to him.

JESUS IS BETRAYED AND ARRESTED / 26:47-56 / 224

Judas, who had left the Last Supper at Jesus' request (John 13:27), had apparently gone to the religious leaders to whom he had spoken earlier (26:14-16). The religious leaders had issued the warrant for Jesus' arrest, and Judas was acting as Jesus' official accuser. Judas led the group to one of Jesus' retreats where no onlookers would interfere with them.

26:47 The **mob** came in the middle of the night when most of the people were asleep, so they could arrest Jesus without commotion. Although there were no crowds to worry about, Jesus was surrounded by eleven loyal followers who might put up a fight, so they came armed with **swords and clubs** in addition to lanterns and torches to light their way (John 18:3).

26:48-50 **Judas** had told the crowd to arrest the man whom he would **kiss.** A kiss on the cheek or hand was a common form of greeting in the Middle East, so this was not unusual. Judas would affectionately greet the man the guards were to arrest and lead away.

Jesus' use of the word **friend** for Judas was an act of love on Jesus' part, which shows that God's love never leaves even the apostate. But it carried a twist of irony in that both Jesus and Judas knew of the treachery. Jesus was still in charge, and his words **do what you have come for** amount to him giving permission for the event to take place.

The religious leaders had not arrested Jesus in the Temple for fear of a riot. Instead, they had come secretly at night, under the influence of the prince of darkness, Satan himself. Jesus offered no resistance and was duly **arrested.** Everything was proceeding according to God's plan. It was time for Jesus to suffer and die.

26:51 According to John 18:10, the person who **pulled out a sword** was Peter, who **slashed off** the right ear **of the high priest's servant** named Malchus. Peter was trying to demonstrate his loyalty as well as prevent what he saw as defeat. He wasn't going to let this crowd arrest Jesus without putting up a fight. Luke 22:51 records that Jesus immediately healed the man's ear and prevented any further bloodshed.

26:52-54 Jesus told Peter to **put away** his **sword** and allow God's plan to unfold. Peter didn't understand that Jesus had to die in order to gain victory. But Jesus demonstrated perfect commitment to his Father's will. His Kingdom would not be advanced with swords, but with faith and obedience.

Jesus' words here, recorded only by Matthew, stress the difference between people's tendency to take matters into their own hands (and suffer the consequences) and God's more far-reaching actions. The reason for putting the sword away was that **those who use the sword will be killed by the sword** (probably quoting a local proverb). To take revenge with one's own hands is to set oneself against the will of God. Jesus clarified this by stating that he could call on his Father who would at once make available to him **thousands of angels.** Jesus was stating that he was in control—thus, everything was happening with his permission.

Jesus knew the far-reaching results. If he were to call for protection from legions of angels, **how would the Scriptures be fulfilled that describe**

what must happen? Jesus' suffering would be necessary to God's plan; no one must stand in the way of God's will.

26:55-56 Jesus pointed out the ridiculous tactics of these people who had come to arrest him. They did not need to come against him with **swords and clubs,** for he voluntarily surrendered himself. Jesus was not a **dangerous criminal;** he was a religious teacher who had been teaching in the Temple **every day** during the past week. Instead, they came at night for fear of the crowds. Jesus also mocked their show of worldly power. He who could summon angels was not afraid of swords. Did the guards imagine that swords would intimidate Jesus? They didn't understand who he was.

Just hours earlier, these disciples had vowed never to desert Jesus (26:35). The "all" who promised total allegiance were now the **all** who **deserted him and fled.**

CAIAPHAS QUESTIONS JESUS / 26:57-68 / 226

The trial by the Council had two phases. This first phase occurred during the night (recorded here in 26:57-68); then another meeting was held early in the morning (27:1) to satisfy a law that allowed trials only during the daytime. That meeting was a mere formality held at daybreak, during which the verdict was given and Jesus was led off to the Roman procurator for sentencing. A death sentence had to be authorized by the Romans (John 18:31).

26:57 By then it was very early Friday morning, before daybreak. Jesus was taken under guard from the garden back into Jerusalem to **the home of Caiaphas,** the ruling **high priest.** That the **teachers of religious law and other leaders had gathered** shows that this was a trial by the Jewish Council. Because of their haste to complete the trial and see Jesus die before the Sabbath, less than twenty-four hours later, the religious leaders first met at Caiaphas's house at night to accomplish the preliminaries before their more formal meeting in the Temple at daylight. The leaders finally had Jesus where they wanted him, and they were determined to accomplish their plans as quickly as possible.

26:58 The high priest's residence was a palace with outer walls enclosing a **courtyard.** Although most of the disciples had fled when the soldiers arrested Jesus, two of them, **Peter** and another disciple (perhaps John) returned to where Jesus had been taken (John 18:15).

26:59-61 Upstairs in the high priest's palace, **the leading priests and the entire high council** had assembled before dawn. They wanted evidence to convict Jesus of a crime deserving death, but they did not find any. The obvious conclusion should have been that Jesus was innocent of any crime. But this was not a trial for justice; it was a trial to accomplish an evil purpose.

There was no shortage of witnesses; the problem was in finding two testimonies that agreed. During a trial, each witness would be called upon separately to give his testimony. But the stories these witnesses gave did not agree in the details. According to Moses' law, no one was to be put to death on the testimony of only one witness (Numbers 35:30); there had to be two or three agreeing witnesses (Deuteronomy 19:15). This must have been exasperating for the desperate religious leaders. They weren't going to let Jesus get away on a technicality!

Finally, two men were found who claimed that Jesus had said he could **destroy the Temple of God.** However, Jesus had not spoken in the first person ("I will destroy"); nor had he said anything linking his words with the Temple building. Instead, Jesus had spoken in the second person plural, issuing a command, "Destroy this temple, and in three days I will raise it up" (John 2:19). Jesus, of course, was talking about his body, not the building. Ironically, the religious leaders were about to destroy Jesus' body just as he had said, and **three days** later he would rise from the dead.

26:62-64 The legal code required that a defendant answer his accusers, so Caiaphas was getting frustrated. His only hope was to get Jesus to say something that would give them evidence to convict him. Caiaphas tried to make up in intimidation what was lacking in evidence. He asked Jesus to answer his accusers and then to explain the accusations against him. Jesus had nothing to say to the group of liars who had spoken against him, so he **remained silent.** This had been prophesied in Scripture (Isaiah 53:7). With Jesus' silence, the court proceedings ground to a halt.

But Caiaphas had another tactic up the sleeve of his priestly robe. He decided to ask Jesus point-blank, **"Tell us whether you are the Messiah, the Son of God."** The Council must have held its collective breath in anticipation. Would Jesus outrightly claim to be the Messiah?

To the first questions, Jesus made no reply because the questions were based on confusing and erroneous evidence. Not answering was wiser than trying to clarify the fabricated accusations. But if Jesus had refused to answer this question, it would have been tantamount to denying his deity and his mission. So Jesus answered without hesitation, **"Yes, it is as you say."**

Then Jesus gave a startling prophecy. The words **the Son of Man, sitting at God's right hand** refer to Psalm 110:1, and **coming back on the clouds of heaven** recall Daniel 7:13-14. The "clouds" represented the power and glory of God. Both verses were considered to be prophecies of the coming Messiah, and Jesus applied them to himself. As the one sitting at the right hand of power, he would judge his accusers, and they would have to answer to him (Revelation 20:11-13).

26:65-66 Blasphemy was the sin of claiming to be God or of attacking God's authority and majesty in any way. Caiaphas **tore his clothing** to signify his outrage at the audacity of the claims of this mere teacher from Nazareth. Jesus had identified himself with God by applying two messianic prophecies to himself. The high priest recognized Jesus' claim and exclaimed to the Council, **"You have all heard his blasphemy."**

Blasphemy was punishable by death (Leviticus 24:15-16). **"Why do we need other witnesses?"** asked Caiaphas without expecting any answer. They needed no more false witnesses. Jesus had finally said what Caiaphas needed, so he asked for the group's decision. They condemned him to **die.**

26:67-68 Then some of the members of the Council acted in a most brutish way. To **spit** in someone's **face** was the worst insult possible (see Numbers 12:14), but these religious men weren't content to stop at that. While Jesus was blindfolded, they took turns hitting him and then asking him to tell who it was that hit him. Yet even this had been prophesied in Scripture (Isaiah 52:14). Jesus suffered great pain, humiliation, and brutality to take away our sin.

PETER DENIES KNOWING JESUS / 26:69-75 / 227

Peter's experiences in the next few hours would revolutionize his life. He would change from an impulsive follower to a repentant and wiser disciple, and finally to the kind of person Christ could use to build his church.

26:69-70 This **servant girl** was actually guarding the gate to the inner courtyard (John 18:16). She had seen Peter enter and take a seat **outside in the courtyard** of the palace and recognized him as one who had been **with Jesus the Galilean.** This put Peter in a difficult position. Standing among the soldiers and servants right there in enemy territory, Peter did not necessarily want to be identified with the man in an upstairs room on trial for his life. So Peter made an impulsive response—he lied. Peter gave the answer that Jesus had predicted: He **denied** knowing Jesus. Temptation came when Peter least expected it, and this serves to warn us to be prepared. Peter had been ready to fight with a sword but not to face the accusations of a servant.

26:71-72 Once again Peter was put to the test. **Another servant girl noticed him.** She didn't question him; she just told those standing around that Peter **was with Jesus of Nazareth.** The accusation scared Peter, so once again he lied, this time **with an oath,** meaning he had invoked a curse on himself if he were lying. This was Peter's second denial.

26:73-75 About an hour passed (Luke 22:59), and another bystander noticed Peter's **Galilean accent.** While Peter may have hoped to seem a natural part of the group by joining in the conversation, instead he revealed, by his speech, that he did not belong there. This was too much for Peter, so he decided to make the strongest denial he could think of by denying with an oath, **"I don't know the man."** Peter was swearing that he did not know Jesus and was invoking a curse on himself if his words were untrue. He was saying, in effect, "May God strike me dead if I am lying." This was the third denial.

Immediately upon Peter's final words, **the rooster crowed.** Peter's denials fulfilled Jesus' words (26:33-35). When Peter heard the rooster crowing and saw Jesus look down at him from the upper story where the trial was being held (Luke 22:61), he was reminded of what Jesus had said to him earlier. Peter had indeed denied Jesus **three times** before the rooster crowed.

Peter **went away, crying bitterly,** realizing he had denied his Lord, the Messiah. Fortunately, the story does not end there. Peter's tears were of true sorrow and repentance. Later, Peter would reaffirm his love for Jesus, and Jesus would forgive him (see Mark 16:7; John 21:15-19). From this humiliating experience, Peter learned much that would help him later when he became

leader of the young church. The presence of this scene in all four Gospels shows its importance to the early church, both as a warning of the dangers of yielding to persecution and as an example of Jesus' power to forgive the most abject failure.

MATTHEW 27

THE COUNCIL OF RELIGIOUS LEADERS CONDEMNS JESUS / 27:1-2 / 228
At daybreak, the entire Council reached a decision. They had actually reached it before daybreak (26:66), but they had to pronounce the decision at a meeting during the daytime in accordance with their law.

27:1-2 Very early in the morning, the Council made it official that Jesus was worthy of **death.** The Jewish leaders had arrested Jesus on theological grounds—blasphemy; because this charge would be thrown out of a Roman court, however, they had to come up with a political reason for Jesus' death. Their strategy was to show Jesus as a rebel who claimed to be a king and thus a threat to Caesar. The charge against Jesus in the Roman court was treason.

Jesus was **bound** like a common criminal and sent off to **Pilate.** The Jewish leaders had to get permission from **the Roman governor** in order to carry out the death penalty. Pontius Pilate served as the Roman governor for the regions of Samaria and Judea from A.D. 26 to 36. Pilate happened to

be in Jerusalem because of the Passover festival. With the large crowds that flocked to the city for that celebration, Pilate and his soldiers came to help keep the peace. Pilate was a harsh governor who felt nothing but contempt for the Jews; they, in turn, felt the same about him. He seemed to take special pleasure in demonstrating his authority; for example, he had impounded money from the Temple treasuries to build an aqueduct and had insulted the Jewish religion by bringing imperial images into the city.

Pilate was not popular, but the religious leaders had no other way to get rid of Jesus than to go to him. So they imposed this on him early Friday morning, bringing a man whom they accused of treason against the hated Romans!

JUDAS HANGS HIMSELF / 27:3-10 / 229
The stories of Peter and Judas provide a dramatic contrast. We see in Peter the weakness of humanity and in Judas the guilt and spiritual consequences of rejecting Christ. Both had fulfilled Jesus' predictions (26:24 for Judas; 26:34 for Peter), yet they responded quite differently. Peter wept, repented, and was restored; Judas had remorse, but killed himself. Forgiveness was available from the Master, but Judas did not pursue it.

27:3-5 Judas, **filled with remorse** at having **betrayed** Jesus, went **back to the leading priests** (26:14-16). Jesus had been condemned to die, and Judas realized his sin, but it was too late. The religious leaders had Jesus where they wanted him, and they replied, **"What do we care?"** What a response from the religious leadership! The priests' job was to teach people about God and act as intercessors for them, helping them turn

from sin and find forgiveness. Judas returned to the priests, exclaiming that he had sinned. Rather than helping him find forgiveness, however, the priests didn't care. At that, **Judas threw the money onto the floor of the Temple. Judas then hanged himself.** Acts 1:18 says that he fell and burst open. Evidently, the limb from which he was hanging broke, and the resulting fall split open his body.

27:6-10 These chief priests felt no guilt in giving
Judas money to betray an innocent man, but when
Judas returned the money, the priests couldn't
accept it because it was **against the law to accept
money paid for murder.** True to character, they
refused to break certain laws while overlooking
their own gross sins as they planned the murder
of an innocent man! Because they could not put
the money into the **Temple treasury** (it was considered "unclean" money), they **decided to buy the**

**potter's field, and they made it into a cemetery
for foreigners.** Graveyards and tombs were considered by the Jews to be "unclean" places, so this
appeared to be a perfect use for this "unclean"
money. This fulfilled the prophecy in Zechariah
11:12-13, but it may also have been taken from
Jeremiah 18:1-4; 19:1-13; or 32:6-15. In Old
Testament times, **Jeremiah** was considered the collector of some of the prophets' writings. This may
account for why the quotation is attributed to him.

JESUS STANDS TRIAL BEFORE PILATE / 27:11-14 / 230
The region of Judea where Pilate ruled as governor was little more than a hot and dusty outpost
of the Roman Empire. The Roman government could not afford to put large numbers of troops
in all the regions under their control, so one of Pilate's main duties was to do whatever was
necessary to maintain peace. We know from historical records that Pilate had already been
warned about other uprisings in his region. Although he may have seen no guilt in Jesus and
no reason to condemn him to death, Pilate wavered when the Jews in the crowd threatened
to report him to Caesar (John 19:12). Such a report, accompanied by a riot, could cost him
his position and hopes for advancement. Would he set free this innocent man at the risk of
a major uproar in his region, or would he give in to their demands and condemn a man who,
he was quite sure, was innocent? That was the question facing Pilate that springtime Friday
morning nearly two thousand years ago.

27:11 The charge was treason, so Pilate asked Jesus
directly if he claimed to be **the King of the Jews.**
Jesus' answer was basically "yes" but with a qualification attached. Jesus did claim to be a king—to
remain silent would be like denying it (see also
26:64). But he wasn't claiming kingship in any way
that would threaten Pilate, Caesar, or the Empire.
Jesus' kingship was spiritual. Pilate could sense
that the Council's case was embarrassingly weak
and that the solemn rabbi standing before him
was unlikely to lead a revolt against Rome.

27:12-14 The Jewish leaders had to fabricate new
accusations against Jesus when they brought him
before Pilate (see Luke 23:1-5). The charge of blasphemy would mean nothing to the Roman governor, so they accused Jesus of three other crimes:
tax evasion, treason, and terrorism. Pilate knew that

the charges were preposterous, and he expected
Jesus to defend himself, but Jesus **remained silent.**
Jesus' silence had been prophesied in Scripture (Isaiah 53:7). It would have been futile to answer, and
the time had come to give his life to save the world.
Jesus had no reason to try to prolong the trial or
save himself. If Jesus did not answer, Pilate would
have to judge him guilty. Recognizing the obvious
plot against Jesus, Pilate wanted to let him go. John
recorded, in detail, Jesus' final answer to Pilate
regarding the nature of his messiahship (John
18:33-38). These words made Pilate realize that
Jesus was innocent of any crime against Roman law.
   Luke recorded that when Pilate found that
Jesus was from Galilee, he sent him off to Herod
Antipas, who was also in town for the Passover.
But Herod only mocked Jesus and returned him
to Pilate (Luke 23:6-12).

PILATE HANDS JESUS OVER TO BE CRUCIFIED / 27:15-26 / 232
In the custom of pardoning a criminal during Passover, Pilate saw an opportunity to avoid
responsibility for the death of a man whom he perceived to be innocent. That Jesus died for
Barabbas represents yet another example of the purpose of Jesus' death: to take the place not
just of one condemned man but of all who stand condemned before God's perfect standard
of justice.

27:15-16 Each year, during the Jews' **Passover celebration,** Pilate had made it a **custom to release one prisoner** they requested. Pilate may have instituted this custom to be on better terms with the people. The **notorious criminal** currently held was **Barabbas,** who had taken part in a rebellion against the Roman government. Although he had been arrested with those who committed a murder (Mark 15:7) and was now on death row, he may have been a hero among the Jews. He had no hope of acquittal, so he must have been surprised when the guards came to get him on that Friday morning. Ironically, Barabbas was guilty of the crime of which Jesus was accused. Pilate knew that Jesus was innocent of political sedition, so he sought a way to be free of the guilt of killing an innocent man. His custom of releasing one prisoner at Passover seemed like an obvious way out.

27:17-18 The proceedings of this hearing by Pilate were held in public, so a crowd heard all that transpired, and this crowd probably grew larger as news spread. Perhaps this was all part of the religious leaders' plan—to incite the crowd to ask that Pilate free a prisoner, but not Jesus. Pilate could see that this was a frame-up. Why else would these people, who hated him and the Roman Empire he represented, ask him to convict of treason and give the death penalty to one of their fellow Jews? Pilate knew very well that the Jewish leaders had arrested Jesus out of envy, so he suggested that Jesus, who is called the Messiah, be set free. Pilate thought the crowd would favor Jesus, a popular teacher, over a murderer.

27:19 This event is recorded only in Matthew. Again Matthew presented a contrast: The Jewish leaders clamored for Jesus' death, while a Gentile woman believed that Jesus was truly **innocent.** People of these times placed a great deal of importance on dreams. God was sending a warning to **Pilate** through **his wife,** but he didn't heed it.

27:20-21 The religious **leaders** went among the crowd, persuading the people to call **for Barabbas to be released.** Faced with a clear choice, the people chose Barabbas, a revolutionary and murderer, over the Son of God. Faced with the same choice today, people are still choosing "Barabbas." They would rather have the tangible force of human power than the salvation offered by the Son of God.

27:22-23 Pilate **asked** what to do with Jesus, **who is called the Messiah.** Perhaps Pilate hoped to let Jesus go as well, in an extra special offer at this Passover. Luke records that Pilate said he would punish and then release him (Luke 23:15-16). But the crowd **shouted, "Crucify him!"** This was a remarkable request—crucifixion was the Roman penalty for rebellion and abhorrent to the Jews. In their eyes, crucifixion would demonstrate that he was under God's curse (see Deuteronomy 21:23). He would die the death of a rebel and slave, not the death of the king he claimed to be.

27:24 This handwashing, performed as a gesture of innocence to show that one had nothing to do with a murder, was a Jewish custom, not a Roman one (Deuteronomy 21:6-9). In trying to excuse himself and place the responsibility for an innocent man's death on them, he followed the path already taken by the religious leaders as they dealt with Judas in 27:4, saying, **"The responsibility is yours!"** In making no decision, Pilate made the decision to let the crowds crucify Jesus. Although he washed his hands, the guilt remained.

27:25-26 The statement **"We will take responsibility for his death—we and our children!"** meant that the entire crowd, not just the leaders, willingly took responsibility for Jesus' death. This verse has been misused down through history to label the Jews as "Christ-killers," but this crowd had no authority to pledge the nation in responsibility for Jesus' death. It was merely the attempt of an unruly mob to persuade Pilate to do what it wanted. Similarly Pilate, by handing Jesus over, was just as guilty as anyone. Yet this rejection, and acceptance of the guilt of Jesus' death, signaled the end of the privileged status of the Jewish nation (see 21:43).

Pilate desired only to satisfy the crowd, so he rationalized in order to salve his conscience. For a leader who was supposed to administer justice, Pilate proved to be more concerned about political expediency than about doing what was right. So he **released Barabbas** and then **ordered Jesus flogged.**

The flogging that Jesus received was part of the Roman legal code, which demanded that flogging precede capital punishment. The Romans did it to weaken the prisoner so that he would die more quickly on the cross. The usual procedure was to bare the upper half of the victim's body and tie the hands to a pillar before whipping the victim with a **lead-tipped whip.** The continued lashing with these sharp instruments tore at the victim's skin, even baring the bones. After the flogging, Pilate handed Jesus **over to the Roman soldiers to crucify him** (see Isaiah 53:6-12).

ROMAN SOLDIERS MOCK JESUS / 27:27-31 / 233

27:27-30 Only the Romans were allowed to carry out execution, so the Roman soldiers took him from the post where he had been flogged and led him, beaten and bleeding, back inside **their head-quarters.** The **entire battalion** was probably about two hundred men who had accompanied Pilate from Caesarea. This whole event was a shameful mockery of Jesus by means of a cruel game. Some-one found a **scarlet robe,** probably one of the scarlet cloaks worn by the soldiers, and threw it around the shoulders of this supposed "king," pretending that it was a royal color. Someone else, with a brutal sense of humor, twisted some **long, sharp thorns** into a **crown** that was then jammed

onto Jesus' head. They **spit on him** and beat him. Such mockery of condemned prisoners was com-mon. This event, however, was fulfilling prophecy (Isaiah 50:6; see also 52:14–53:6).

27:31 In being led out **to be crucified,** condemned prisoners (who had already been flogged) would carry the crossbeam of their own cross. This cross-beam weighed about one hundred pounds and was carried across the shoulders. The heavy cross-beam was placed on Jesus' already bleeding shoul-ders (John 19:17), and he began the long walk out of Jerusalem. Usually execution sites were outside of the city.

JESUS IS LED AWAY AND PLACED ON THE CROSS / 27:32-44 / 234, 235

While the Crucifixion was meant to brand Jesus as cursed by God, for Christians, the Crucifix-ion pictures Jesus indeed taking God's curse against sin upon himself and allowing his people to be set free from sin.

27:32 Colonies of Jews existed outside Judea. **Simon** was from **Cyrene,** in northern Africa (see Acts 2:10), and was either on a pilgrimage to Jeru-salem for the Passover, or he was originally from Cyrene but resided in Palestine. Jesus started to carry his cross, but, weakened from the beatings he had received, he was physically unable to carry it. Roman soldiers had the power to enforce people to do tasks for them (see 5:41); so Simon, on his way into the city, was picked out of the crowd by the soldiers **to carry Jesus' cross.**

27:33-34 Golgotha is the Hebrew word for "skull." The familiar name "Calvary" is derived from the Latin **calvaria** (also meaning "skull"). Thus, it became known as **Skull Hill,** although some say its name was derived from its appearance, a hill with a stony top that may have looked like a skull. Gol-gotha may have been a regular place of execution. It was prominent, public, and outside the city along a main road. Executions held there served as examples to the people and as a deterrent to criminals.

The drink offered to Jesus was **wine mixed with bitter gall.** But Jesus **refused** to drink it. He would suffer fully conscious and with a clear mind.

27:35-36 Crucifixion, instituted by the Romans, was a feared and shameful form of execution. The victim was forced to carry his cross along the longest possi-ble route to the crucifixion site as a warning to bystanders. There were several shapes for crosses and several different methods of crucifixion. Jesus was

nailed to the cross; condemned men were some-times tied to their cross with ropes. In both cases, death came by suffocation as the person would lose strength and the weight of the body would make breathing more and more difficult.

Contrary to the discreet paintings of the crucifix-ion, Jesus was crucified naked. Roman soldiers had the right to take for themselves the clothing of those crucified, so they **gambled for his clothes by throwing dice.** This act had also been prophe-sied (Psalm 22:18).

27:37 A **signboard** stating the condemned man's crime would be placed on his cross as a warning. Because Jesus was never found guilty, the only accusation placed on his sign was the "crime" of calling himself **the King of the Jews.** This sign was meant to be ironic. A king, stripped and executed in public view, had obviously lost his kingdom forever. But Jesus, who turns the world's wisdom upside down, was just coming into his Kingdom. Few people reading the sign that bleak day under-stood its real meaning.

27:38 When James and John had asked Jesus for the places of honor next to him in his Kingdom, Jesus had told them that they didn't know what they were asking (20:20-22). Here, as Jesus was preparing to inaugurate his Kingdom through his death, the places on his right and on his left were taken by **two criminals** (Isaiah 53:12). As Jesus had explained to his position-conscious disciples, a person who wants to be close to Jesus must be prepared to suffer and die as he himself was doing. The way to the Kingdom is the way of the Cross.

27:39-40 Insult was literally added to injury when it came to public crucifixion. The people passing by **shouted abuse.** They taunted Jesus that if he could boast of building the Temple in three days, surely he had the power to save himself from the fate of the cross. Ironically, Jesus was in the very process of fulfilling his own prophecy. His body was being destroyed, but **in three days** he would rise again. Because Jesus was the Son of God who always obeyed the will of the Father, he did not come down from the cross to save himself. If he had done so, he could not have saved us. Their words, **"if you are the Son of God,"** recall Satan's temptations (see 4:3, 6), revealing that Satan was still at work attempting to get Jesus to give in to the suffering and fail to accomplish God's will. This incident recalls Psalm 22:7.

27:41-44 Apparently some religious **leaders** had followed the executioners out to Golgotha, eager to see their evil plot finally completed. Not content to have brought him to an unjust death, they also **mocked** him, that though he could save **others,** he couldn't **save himself.** The religious leaders had twice before asked Jesus to give them a miraculous sign so that they would believe in him, but Jesus had refused (12:38; 16:1). Here again they were saying, "Give us a sign," as they taunted, **"come down from the cross."** Their words echo Psalm 22:8. But Jesus would not renounce his God-appointed path. The lesson for all believers is that faith cannot be based on visible demonstrations of power; instead, faith is belief in things not seen (Hebrews 11:1).

Matthew, like Mark, recorded that **the criminals** also **shouted insults** at Jesus; but Luke states that later one of these robbers repented. Jesus promised that the repentant robber would join him in paradise (Luke 23:39-43).

JESUS DIES ON THE CROSS / 27:45-56 / 236
Jesus' death was accompanied by at least four miraculous events: early darkness (27:45), the tearing in two of the curtain in the Temple, a timely earthquake, and dead people rising from their tombs (27:52). Jesus' death, therefore, could not have gone unnoticed. Everyone knew that something significant had happened.

27:45 Jesus had been put on the cross at nine o'clock in the morning. Death by crucifixion was slow and excruciating. Three hours passed while Jesus put up with abuse from bystanders. Then, **at noon, darkness** settled over the land for three hours. We do not know how this darkness occurred, but it is clear that God caused it. Nature testified to the gravity of Jesus' death, while Jesus' friends and enemies alike fell silent in the encircling gloom. The darkness on that Friday afternoon was both physical and spiritual. All nature seemed to mourn over the stark tragedy of the death of God's Son. Some see a fulfillment of Amos 8:9.

27:46-47 Jesus did not ask this question, **"Why have you forsaken me?"** in surprise or despair. He was quoting the first line of Psalm 22, a prophecy expressing the deep agony of the Messiah's death for the world's sin. Jesus knew that he would be temporarily separated from God the moment he took upon himself the sins of the world because God cannot look on sin (Habakkuk 1:13). This separation was the "cup" Jesus had dreaded as he prayed in Gethsemane (26:39). The physical agony was horrible, but the spiritual alienation from God was the ultimate torture. Jesus suffered

this double death so that we would never have to experience eternal separation from God.

The **bystanders** misinterpreted Jesus' words and thought he was **calling for the prophet Elijah.** Because Elijah had ascended into heaven without dying (2 Kings 2:11), a popular belief held that Elijah would return to rescue those suffering from great trouble (Malachi 4:5).

27:48-49 John records that Jesus said he was thirsty (John 19:28-29). In response, one man soaked **a sponge with sour wine.** This was not the same as the drugged wine offered to Jesus earlier, but a thirst quencher that was there, probably for the soldiers to drink. This man, either in an act of kindness or further mockery, put the sponge on a long **stick** and held it up in order to reach Jesus' lips (again fulfilling prophecy, Psalm 69:21). The crowd, however, resuming its taunting, thought Jesus had called for **Elijah** (27:47), and said not to give Jesus any relief for his thirst, but instead to wait and see if Elijah would **come and save him.**

27:50-53 Jesus' loud cry may have been his last words, "It is finished!" (John 19:30). This cry climaxed the horror of the scene and showed his sudden death after over six hours on the cross.

Usually crucifixion caused a person to lapse into a coma from extreme exhaustion. Jesus, however, was completely conscious to the end, and then he **gave up his spirit.**

Some significant events symbolized what Christ's work on the cross had accomplished. The **Temple** had three main parts—the courts, the holy place (where only the priests could enter), and the most holy place, reserved by God for himself. It was in the most holy place that the ark of the covenant rested. The room was entered only once a year, on the Day of Atonement, by the high priest as he made a sacrifice to gain forgiveness for the sins of all the nation (Leviticus 16:1-34). The **curtain in the Temple** was between the holy place and the most holy place. Symbolically, that curtain separated the holy God from sinful people. By tearing the curtain **in two, from top to bottom,** God showed that Jesus had opened the way for sinful people to reach a holy God. The opening of the **tombs** and people being **raised from the dead** revealed that by Jesus' death, the power of death was broken.

27:54 A **Roman officer** had accompanied the soldiers to the execution site. He probably had done this many times. Yet this crucifixion was completely different. These Gentiles realized something that most of the Jewish nation had missed: **"Truly, this was the Son of God!"** Whether they understood what they were saying, we cannot know. They may simply have admired Jesus' courage and inner strength, perhaps thinking that he was divine, like one of Rome's many gods. They **were terrified** because of the other events (darkness and **earthquake**) that had surrounded this particular crucifixion, which they attributed to the wrath of God (or a

god). They certainly recognized Jesus' innocence. While the Jewish religious leaders were celebrating Jesus' death, a small group of Gentiles were the first to proclaim Jesus as the Son of God after his death.

27:55-56 There had been many people at the cross who had come only to mock and taunt Jesus or, like the religious leaders, to revel in their apparent victory. Some of Jesus' faithful followers were at the cross as well. Among the disciples, only John was there, and he recorded in his Gospel in graphic detail the horror he observed. **Many women** were also there, **watching from a distance.**

Mary Magdalene was from Magdala, a town near Capernaum in Galilee. She had been released from demon possession by Jesus (Luke 8:2). Another **Mary** is distinguished by the names of her sons who may have been well known in the early church. **Zebedee's wife** was the **mother** of the disciples **James and John.** Her name was Salome (20:20-21), and she was probably the sister of Jesus' mother. These women had been faithful to Jesus' ministry, following him and providing for his material needs (see Luke 8:1-3). John wrote that Jesus' mother, Mary, was present and that, from the cross, Jesus spoke to John about taking care of Mary (John 19:25-27).

These women could do very little, but they did what they could. They stayed at the cross when the disciples had not even come; they followed Jesus' body to the tomb; they prepared spices for his body. Because these women used the opportunities they had, they were the first to witness the Resurrection. God blessed their devotion, initiative, and diligence. As believers, we should take advantage of the opportunities we have and do what we can for Christ.

JESUS IS LAID IN THE TOMB / 27:57-61 / 237

27:57-58 The Sabbath began at sundown on Friday and ended at sundown on Saturday. Jesus died just a few hours before sundown on Friday (at about three o'clock, 27:46). It was against Jewish law to do physical work or to travel on the Sabbath. It was also against Jewish law to let a dead body remain exposed overnight (Deuteronomy 21:23).

So **as evening approached, Joseph of Arimathea asked for Jesus' body** so he could give it a proper burial. Arimathea was a town about twenty-two miles northwest of Jerusalem. Although an honored member of the Council (Mark 15:43), Joseph **was one of Jesus' followers.** Thus, not all the Jewish leaders hated Jesus. In the past, Joseph had been reluctant to speak

against the religious leaders who had opposed Jesus (John 19:38); at this time he went boldly **to Pilate** and Pilate released Jesus' body to him.

27:59-60 As evening and the Sabbath approached, Joseph had to hurry. Fortunately he had help. John wrote that Nicodemus, another member of the Council, brought spices in which to wrap Jesus' body (John 3:1; 19:38-42). Joseph brought a **long linen cloth.** The body was carefully taken down from the cross, washed, **wrapped** in layers of cloth with the spices in between, and laid in a tomb. Jesus was given a burial fit for a king.

This **new tomb** was unused (some tombs were large enough to hold several bodies). It had been **carved out of the rock,** so it was a man-made cave cut out of one of the many lime-stone hills in the area around Jerusalem. It was large enough to walk into (John 20:6). Joseph and Nicodemus placed Jesus' body in the tomb and **rolled a great stone across the entrance.** A wealthy person's tomb would often have a groove sloping down into the doorway, and a stone slab a yard in diameter would be rolled into it. The stone would be easy to roll in, but it would take several men to roll it up the slope to open the tomb.

27:61 Two of the women who had been at the cross (27:56), **Mary Magdalene and the other Mary,** followed Joseph and Nicodemus as they carried Jesus' body to the tomb. No mourning was permitted for those executed under Roman law, so they followed in silent grief. They wanted to know where the body would be laid because they planned to return after the Sabbath with their own spices to anoint Jesus' body (28:1).

GUARDS ARE POSTED AT THE TOMB / 27:62-66 / 238
Whereas the disciples in their despair had probably forgotten about Jesus' promise of resurrection, the leaders hadn't forgotten.

27:62-66 Apparently, **the leading priests and Pharisees** knew where Jesus was buried. Jesus may have died, but they remembered that he had said he would **be raised from the dead.** The religious leaders did not believe Jesus' claims, but they were afraid of fraud—after all, the body had been taken down by two followers of Jesus. The Pharisees wanted Pilate to **seal the tomb until the third day** to make sure that no one would steal Jesus' body and claim he had risen from the dead.

So they made sure the tomb was sealed and guarded. The tomb was made **secure** by stringing a cord across the stone that was rolled over the entrance. The cord was sealed at each end with clay. Pilate gave them permission to post **guards** at the tomb as a further precaution. These may have been some Roman soldiers or the Temple police who were at the Jewish leaders' disposal (see John 18:3). With such precautions, the only way the tomb could be empty would be for Jesus to rise from the dead. The Pharisees failed to understand that no rock, seal, guard, or army could keep them secure, nor could any power prevent the Son of God from rising again.

MATTHEW 28

JESUS RISES FROM THE DEAD / 28:1-7 / 239
The resurrection of Jesus from the dead is the central fact of Christian history. On it, the church is built; without it, there would be no Christian church today. Jesus' resurrection is unique. Other religions have strong ethical systems, concepts about paradise and afterlife, and various holy scriptures. Only Christianity has a God who became human, literally died for his people, and was raised again in power and glory to rule his church forever.

Why is the Resurrection so important?

- Because of the Resurrection, we know that the Kingdom of Heaven has broken into earth's history.
- Because of the Resurrection, we know that death has been conquered and that we, too, will be raised from the dead to live forever with Christ.
- The Resurrection gives authority to the church's witness in the world. The apostles' most impor-

tant message was the proclamation that Jesus Christ had been raised from the dead!
- The Resurrection gives meaning to the church's regular feast, the Lord's Supper. Like the disciples on the road to Emmaus, we break bread with our risen Lord.
- The Resurrection helps us find meaning even in great tragedy. No matter what happens to us

as we walk with the Lord, the Resurrection gives us hope for the future.

- The Resurrection assures us that Christ is alive and ruling his Kingdom.

Christians can look very different from one another, and they can hold widely varying beliefs about politics, lifestyle, and even theology. But one central belief unites and inspires all true Christians—Jesus Christ rose from the dead!

28:1 The women could not make the trip to the tomb until **early on Sunday morning** after the Sabbath. As dawn approached, **Mary Magdalene and the other Mary went out to see the tomb.** Both of them had been at Jesus' cross and had followed Joseph so they would know where the tomb was located (27:56, 61). Mark explained that they had gone back to the tomb to bring spices and perfumes to anoint Jesus' body because they had had no time to do so before the Sabbath (Mark 16:1). Anointing a body was a sign of love, devotion, and respect. Bringing spices to the tomb would be like bringing flowers to a grave today.

28:2-4 Again a supernatural event took place: **a great earthquake** occurred as **an angel of the Lord came down from heaven.** Mark records that the women were concerned about how they would get

into the tomb to anoint Jesus' body (Mark 16:3). They had seen Joseph put the stone at its entrance (27:60-61), although they may have been unaware of the sealing of the stone and of the guards who had been posted. When they arrived at the tomb, they saw that the large stone had already been **rolled aside.** An angel was sitting on the stone, whose **face shone like lightning** and **clothing was as white as snow.** For fear of him, the guards **fell into a dead faint.**

28:5-6 The **angel** spoke reassuringly to the frightened women. They were looking for Jesus, the human being who had been crucified on the cross. But Jesus was not there; he had risen. The angel invited the women to look into the inner burial chamber and **see where his body was lying.** Jesus had **been raised from the dead, just as he said would happen.**

28:7 The women who had come to anoint a dead body were given another task—proclaiming the Resurrection to the frightened **disciples.** The disciples had deserted Jesus in the hour of trial, but the angel's words held hope of renewal and forgiveness. The disciples had deserted Jesus, but they were directed to meet Jesus in **Galilee.** This was exactly what Jesus had told them during the Last Supper (26:32).

JESUS APPEARS TO THE WOMEN / 28:8-10 / 241

28:8. The women ran quickly from the tomb realizing that they had seen the results of an awesome miracle in the empty tomb and had been in the presence of an angel. This revelation from God had filled them with a mixture of fear and joy. They obeyed the angel's command and **rushed** to the eleven **disciples** with the good news.

28:9 As the women ran from the tomb, in their path appeared **Jesus** himself! The women **held his feet** (a Near Eastern custom of what a subject does in showing obeisance to a king) and **worshiped him,** giving homage to their Savior, Lord, and King.

28:10 By **brothers,** Jesus meant his disciples. This showed that he had forgiven them, even after they had denied and deserted him, and that he

raised them to a new level of fellowship—from disciples to "brothers" (see John 15:15). Jesus told the women to pass a message on to the disciples—that they should **leave for Galilee** as he had previously told them (26:32). But the disciples, filled with fear, remained behind locked doors in Jerusalem (John 20:19). So Jesus met them first in Jerusalem (Luke 24:36) and later in Galilee (John 21).

RELIGIOUS LEADERS BRIBE THE GUARDS / 28:11-15 / 242

28:11 Jesus' resurrection was already causing a great stir in Jerusalem. A group of women was moving quickly through the streets, looking for the disciples to tell them the amazing news that Jesus was alive. At the same time, guards were on their way, not to Pilate, but **to the leading priests.** If these were Roman guards, under Roman law, they would have paid with their lives for falling asleep on the job (28:13). Since they were assigned to the Jewish authorities, they went to the religious leaders badly in need of a cover-up.

28:12-15 The **religious leaders'** worst fears had been realized (27:63-64)—Jesus' body had disappeared from the tomb! Instead of even considering that Jesus' claims had been true and that he truly was the Messiah risen from the dead, the leaders **decided to bribe the soldiers** in order to explain that **Jesus' disciples came during the night** and **stole his body.** This may have seemed like a logical explanation, but they didn't think through the details. Why would Jesus' disciples, who already had run off on him at his arrest, risk a return at night to a guarded and sealed tomb in an effort to steal a body—an offense that could incur the death penalty? And if they had done so, would they have taken the time to unwrap the body?

If this had occurred **while** the guards **were sleeping,** how could the guards possibly have known what had occurred? If this truly happened, why didn't the religious leaders arrest the disciples in order to prosecute them? The story was full of holes and the guards would have to admit to negligence on their part, so getting them to spread this rumor required a bribe. The story circulated and many people believed the lie—also apparently not thinking through the information long enough to ask the obvious questions.

JESUS GIVES THE GREAT COMMISSION / 28:16-20 / 248

28:16-17 Jesus made several appearances to various people after his resurrection. **The eleven disciples** refers to those remaining after the death of Judas Iscariot. They went to Galilee, as Jesus had previously directed them (26:32; 28:10). Among the eleven who saw Jesus there were some who **still doubted.** Matthew may have been reporting some of the doubts and concerns still lingering in the minds of the eleven chosen disciples. Of course, they would all eventually be fully convinced and believe.

28:18-20 When someone is dying or leaving us, we pay close attention to his or her last words. Jesus left the disciples with some last words of instruction. God gave Jesus **complete authority** over heaven and earth. On the basis of his authority, Jesus told his disciples to **go and make disciples** as they preached, baptized, and taught. "Making disciples" means instructing new believers on how to follow Jesus, to submit to Jesus' lordship, and to take up his mission of compassionate service. **Baptizing** is important because it unites a believer with Jesus Christ in his or her death to sin and resurrection to new life. Baptism symbolizes submission to Christ, a willingness to live God's way, and identification with God's covenant people. To baptize **in the name of the Father and the Son and the Holy Spirit** affirms the reality of the Trinity, the concept coming directly from Jesus himself. He did not say baptize them into the "names," but into the "name" of the Father, Son, and Holy Spirit.

Whereas in previous missions Jesus had sent his disciples only to the Jews (10:5-6), their mission from here forward would be to go to **all the nations.** This is called the Great Commission. The disciples had been trained well, and they had seen the risen Lord. They were ready to **teach** people all over the world **to obey all the commands** that Jesus had given. This also showed the disciples that there would be a lapse of time between Jesus' resurrection and his second coming. During that time, Jesus' followers had a mission to do—evangelize, baptize, and teach people about Jesus so that they, in turn, could do the same. The Good News of the gospel was to go forth to all the nations.

With this same authority, Jesus still commands us to tell others the Good News and make them disciples for the Kingdom. We are to go—whether it is next door or to another country—and make disciples. It is not an option, but a command to all who call Jesus "Lord." As we obey, we have comfort in the knowledge that Jesus is **always with** us. This would occur through the Holy Spirit's presence in believers' lives. The Holy Spirit would be Jesus' presence that would never leave them (John 14:26; Acts 1:4-5). Jesus continues to be with us today through his Spirit. As this Gospel began, so it ends—Immanuel, "God is with us" (1:23).

The Old Testament prophecies and genealogies in the book of Matthew present Jesus' credentials for being King of the world—not a military or political leader, as the disciples had originally hoped, but a spiritual King who can overcome all evil and rule in the heart of every person. If we refuse to serve the King faithfully, we are disloyal subjects. We must make Jesus King of our lives and worship him as our Savior, King, and Lord.

Of the four Gospels, Mark's narrative is the most chronological—that is, most of the stories are positioned in the order they actually occurred. Though the shortest of the four, the Gospel of Mark contains the most events; it is action-packed. Most of this action centers in Galilee, where Jesus began his ministry. Capernaum served as his base of operation (1:21; 2:1; 9:33), from which he would go out to cities like Bethsaida—where he healed a blind man (8:22ff); Gennesaret—where he performed many healings (6:53ff); Tyre and Sidon (to the far north)—where he healed many, drove out demons, and met the woman from Syrian Phoenicia (3:8; 7:24ff); and Caesarea Philippi—where Peter declared him to be the Messiah (8:27ff). After his ministry in Galilee and the surrounding regions, Jesus headed for Jerusalem (10:1). Before going there, Jesus told his disciples three times that he would be crucified there and then come back to life (8:31; 9:31; 10:33-34). Jesus' earthly story begins in the town of Bethlehem in the Roman province of Judea (2:1). A threat to kill the infant king led Joseph to take his family to Egypt (2:14).

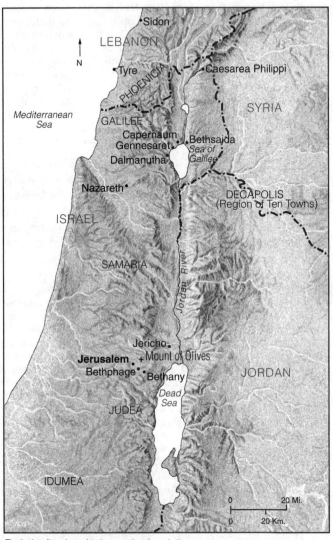

The broken lines (— · —·) indicate modern boundaries.

When they returned God led them to settle in Nazareth in Galilee (2:22-23). At about age thirty, Jesus was baptized in the Jordan River and was tempted by Satan in the Judean wilderness (3:13; 4:1). Jesus set up his base of operations in Capernaum (4:12-13) and from there ministered throughout Israel, telling parables, teaching about the Kingdom, and healing the sick. He traveled to the region of the Gadarenes and healed two demon-possessed men (8:28ff); fed over five thousand people with five loaves and two fish on the shores of Galilee near Bethsaida (14:15ff); healed the sick in Gennesaret (14:34ff); ministered to the Gentiles in Tyre and Sidon (15:21ff); visited Caesarea Philippi, where Peter declared him as the Messiah (16:13ff); and taught in Perea, across the Jordan (19:1). As he set out on his last visit to Jerusalem, he told the disciples what would happen to him there (20:17ff). He spent some time in Jericho (20:29) and then stayed in Bethany at night as he went back and forth into Jerusalem during his last week (21:17ff). In Jerusalem he would be crucified, but he would rise again.

MARK

INTRODUCTION

Action—moving, doing, helping, getting going, making things happen. Some people think, some talk, but a few get involved, not content to observe from the sidelines. They get into the game—they get into life! This is the picture of Jesus that Mark presents in this Gospel.

The Gospel of Mark is the shortest of the four records of Jesus' life, and it covers only three and a half years. On the first page, Mark jumps into the action, with John the Baptist's fiery preaching and the beginning of Jesus' public ministry. Then, moving swiftly through Jesus' baptism, temptation in the wilderness, and call of the disciples, Mark focuses his attention on Jesus' public ministry. He is interested in Christ's works, not just his words. In fact, Mark records eighteen of Jesus' miracles and only four of his parables. Although Mark presents events in chronological order, he gives little or no historical linkage between the events. Readers feel, "Jesus is on the move; we'd better stay alert or we'll miss something!"

Writing to a Roman audience, Mark did not have to recite Jesus' genealogy or refer to Old Testament prophecies that have been fulfilled. Gentiles don't need a Jewish history lesson; they need a clear picture of Christ. And the Romans believed in power and action. So Mark made sure they had a no-nonsense, concise, action-packed summary. Mark pictured Jesus as powerful—giving sight to the blind, raising the dead, calming stormy seas, restoring deformed bodies. But he showed Jesus using this mighty power to help others, taking the form of a servant, not a king. Mark wove the servant theme throughout his book and presented the servant Jesus as an example to follow: "And whoever wants to be first must be the slave of all. For even I, the Son of Man, came here not to be served but to serve others, and to give my life as a ransom for many" (10:44-45).

The Gospel of Mark is a short, action-packed account, bustling with life and focused on Christ's ministry. As you study Mark, be ready for nonstop action, be open for God's move into your life, and be challenged to move into your world to serve.

AUTHOR

Mark (John Mark): cousin of Barnabas (Colossians 4:10) and close friend of Peter (1 Peter 5:13)

The book of Mark names no one as author. Since the second century A.D., however, church leaders and scholars have accepted John Mark as the one who wrote this Gospel. (John is his Jewish name and Mark, "Marcus," his Roman name.) The early church fathers unanimously accepted Mark's authorship. Papias (A.D. 110) makes the earliest statement to this effect:

> Mark, who was the interpreter of Peter, wrote down accurately all that he remembered, whether of sayings or doings of Christ, but not in order. For he was neither a hearer nor a companion of the Lord; but afterwards, as I have said, he accompanied Peter, who adapted his instruction as necessity required, not as though he were making a compilation of the Lord's oracles. So then Mark made no mistake when he wrote down thus some things as he remembered them, for he concentrated on this alone—not to omit anything that he had heard, nor to include any false statement among them. (Eusebius, *Ecclesiastical History III*, p. 39)

Other church fathers, including Justin Martyr, Tertullian, Clement of Alexandria, Origen, and Eusebius, confirm this assessment of Mark as the writer of the Gospel. At the same time, they also affirm that Peter was the author behind the work. What this means is that Mark put Peter's oral accounts of Jesus' ministry into written form. Some believe that Mark took notes from Peter's preaching so that many stories in this Gospel were probably presented verbally before they appeared in written form. Perhaps Mark worked with Peter on the Gospel in those earlier years together but then released it for wider distribution after Peter's death. Whatever the case, we know that Matthew, Mark, Luke, and John are accurate accounts of the life and message of Christ. Through the Holy Spirit, God used these men to bring his word to the world.

Mark was young, perhaps in his teens, at the time of Jesus' death and resurrection. Evidently his mother, Mary, was a well-to-do widow who had come to faith in Christ. Many surmise that Mary's house was the site of the Last Supper (14:12-26) and the home where the disciples gathered at Pentecost (Acts 2:1-4); some believe that Mark was the young man who ran away naked when Jesus was arrested in the Garden of Gethsemane (14:51-52). Regardless of the truth of these speculations, Scripture clearly states that fourteen years after the tumultuous events leading to the Crucifixion, in about A.D. 44, the church gathered at Mary's house to pray. King Herod had begun to persecute believers; he had executed James, the brother of John, and he was keeping Peter in prison. The church was praying for Peter's release. Luke explains that after Peter had been miraculously released from prison, "After a little thought, he went to the home of Mary, the mother of John Mark, where many were gathered for prayer" (Acts 12:12). Mark was deeply involved in the drama of the Jerusalem church and was well-known to Peter and the other disciples.

In Colossians 4:10, Paul reveals that Mark was the cousin of Barnabas. Perhaps that is what motivated Barnabas and Paul to take Mark with them back to Antioch from Jerusalem (Acts 12:25). Soon thereafter, Barnabas and Paul were commissioned by the church in Antioch to begin their first missionary journey (Acts 13:1-3), and they included Mark as their helper (Acts 13:5). Early in the trip, however, at Perga, Mark abruptly left and returned to Jerusalem (Acts 13:13). Luke gives no reason for Mark's departure (perhaps he was homesick, fearful, or ill). Later, however, when Paul and Barnabas began to plan the second journey, Mark became the cause of a sharp disagreement between the two men. Barnabas wanted to include Mark again, but Paul was strongly opposed because Mark had "deserted" them on the previous trip. So Barnabas and Paul parted company. Barnabas sailed to Cyprus with Mark, while Paul chose Silas and traveled to Syria and Cilicia (Acts 15:36-41).

We know little else about John Mark. Evidently, he and Paul reconciled completely because later he joined Paul in Rome, during Paul's first imprisonment (A.D. 60–62), and was a comfort to him there (Colossians 4:10-11; Philemon 24). During Paul's second imprisonment and just before his death, he asked Timothy to bring Mark to Rome, "for he will be helpful to me" (2 Timothy 4:11). Mark must have matured emotionally and spiritually through the years and under the mentoring of cousin Barnabas.

Mark also enjoyed a very close relationship with Peter. In fact, Peter may have led Mark to Christ because he calls Mark "my son" (1 Peter 5:13). After Paul's release from prison in A.D. 62, Mark may have stayed in Rome (also called "Babylon"—1 Peter 5:13) to work closely with Peter. Mark probably left Rome in about A.D. 65 or 66, during Nero's intense persecution. Both Paul and Peter were executed by Nero in about A.D. 67 or 68. According to tradition, Mark died soon after.

John Mark provides a sterling example of how a young Christian can grow and mature. Perhaps basking in the attention of the spiritual giants Paul and Barnabas, and excited by the prospect of reaching the world with the gospel, he had sailed to Cyprus on the first missionary journey. A short time later, however, when the going got tough, Mark returned home. Whatever Mark's reason for leaving, Paul didn't approve; in fact, he wanted nothing to do with Mark after the incident. Yet fifteen years later, Mark was serving as a ministry companion to both Peter and Paul, and later he wrote the Gospel bearing his name. Little is known about Mark during those years, except that Barnabas took personal interest in him, encouraging Mark by continuing to work with him in ministry.

DATE AND SETTING
Written in Rome between A.D. 55 and 70

Dating the Gospel of Mark with accuracy is virtually impossible because the text contains few clues. We can only surmise that Mark was written before A.D. 70 because there is no mention of the destruction of Jerusalem, which had been predicted by Jesus (13:1-23). (Jerusalem was destroyed by Roman armies under the leadership of Titus, after a siege of 143 days. During this battle, 600,000 Jews were killed and thousands more taken captive.)

Rome is identified as the place of writing because both Paul and Peter mention Mark as being there (Colossians 4:10; 1 Peter 5:13—"Babylon" probably refers to Rome). All roads led to Rome, the capital of the vast and mighty Roman Empire. At that time, Rome was the largest city in the world, with a population of approximately one million. Wealthy and cosmopolitan, it was the diplomatic and trade center of the world, the epitome of power and influence. No wonder Paul and Peter were drawn to Rome—it was a strategic beachhead for the spread of the gospel.

We do not know who founded the church at Rome. It could not have been Peter because he ministered primarily to Jews and seems to have settled in Rome just after Paul's arrival in about A.D. 60. Also, it was not Paul, because in his letter to the Romans, he said as much (Romans 1:11-13; 15:23-24). Most likely, the church at Rome was begun by Jews who had traveled from Rome to Jerusalem for Pentecost in A.D. 30, had been converted through Peter's powerful sermon and the outpouring of the Holy Spirit (Acts 2:5-40), and then had taken their Christian faith with them back home to Rome. Soon those believers were joined by travelers like Priscilla and Aquila who had heard about Christ in other places.

Reading between the lines of the book of Romans, the church in Rome seems to have been strong, unified in worship and outreach, with no factions or divisions such as those that were plaguing other churches. Certainly the Roman church was strengthened even further through the ministry of Paul, as he boldly taught for two years during his first imprisonment (Acts 28:16-31).

The political climate in Rome was volatile with a litany of palace intrigue, assassinations, and egocentric emperors. Nero, the fifth Roman emperor, began to reign in A.D. 54 at sixteen years of age. The first few years of his reign were peaceful. During that time, Paul had appealed to Caesar at his trial in Caesarea (Acts 25:10-11) and thus had been taken to Rome to make his appeal (A.D. 60). Even as a prisoner, Paul was allowed to debate with Jewish leaders (Acts 28:17-28) and to preach and teach about Christ to all who came to see him (Acts 28:30-31). Evidently, after these two years, Paul was released. Soon, however, the tolerance for Christians would take a terrible turn.

After marrying Poppaea in A.D. 62, Nero became brutal and ruthless, killing his own mother, his chief advisers Seneca and Burrus, and many of the nobility in order to seize their fortunes and solidify his power. Eventually, Nero's thirst for publicity in the arts and sports pushed him into excessive acts of decadence, including chariot races, combat between gladiators, and the gory spectacle of prisoners thrown to wild beasts. In A.D. 64, fire destroyed a large part of Rome. Nero probably ordered the fire himself to make room for a new palace, but he deflected blame by accusing the Christians. Thus began the terrible persecution against the church—with torture, executions, and even Coliseum entertainment. Some followers of Christ were covered in animal skins and torn to pieces by dogs. Others were fastened to crosses and set on fire, serving as torches at night for the city.

During this reign of terror for Christians, Paul was taken prisoner again, apparently at Nicopolis, where he had intended to spend the winter (Titus 3:12). Transported to Rome, Paul was imprisoned in the Mamertine dungeon, in the center of Rome near the forum. There Paul wrote his final words. We know that Mark was not in Rome at this time because in 2 Timothy 4:11, Paul asked Timothy to bring Mark with him. If Timothy obliged, then Mark may have been in Rome when both Paul and Peter were martyred. According to tradition, soon after writing 2 Timothy, Paul was executed by beheading on the Ostian Way outside Rome, shortly before Nero's own death, by suicide, in A.D. 68. Peter also was martyred at this time.

What would cause Mark to return to Rome where Christians were hunted and killed like animals? What would strengthen Mark to courageously face his own death at the hands of the Romans? What would motivate Mark to write the story of Jesus? He knew the Truth, and the Truth had set him free (John 8:32). What keeps you from obeying God and living for Christ?

AUDIENCE
Roman Christians living in Rome
It is fairly certain that Mark directed his Gospel to Romans. One reason for this conclusion is that he took time to explain Jewish terms for his readers (see, for

example, 5:41). Mark also explained Jewish customs (7:3-4; see also 3:17; 7:11, 34; 14:12; 15:22, 34, 42). Gentile readers would need such phrases and customs explained. There are other indications that Mark wrote to Gentiles in general and Romans in particular: He used several Latin words, some of which do not appear elsewhere in the New Testament. (This is evident in the original text of Mark 5:9; 12:15, 42; 15:16, 39.) He referred to the Old Testament less than the other Gospel writers; he did not use the word "law," which was mentioned often by Matthew, Luke, and John; he used the Roman way of telling time (6:48; 13:35). All of this evidence points to a Roman audience.

It also seems clear that Mark was writing primarily to Christians. He used distinctively Christian terms such as "baptize" (1:4) and "Holy Spirit" (1:8) without explaining them. And Mark seems to have assumed that his readers were familiar with Jesus' background, with John the Baptist, and with the major events of Jesus' life.

So who were these Roman Christians to whom Mark directed his Gospel? At first the church at Rome was Jewish, consisting of Jews who had come to believe in Jesus as their Messiah. But over the years, many Christians from all parts of the Roman Empire had migrated to Rome, some of them Paul's converts and many of them Gentiles. In addition, many citizens of Rome had come to faith in Christ through the ministry of other believers and Paul while he was in prison (see Acts 28:30-31; Philippians 4:21-22; Colossians 4:10-12; 2 Timothy 4:21). Eventually the church had a majority of Gentiles, with an influential Jewish minority.

Being a Christian in Rome meant being part of a distinct minority, religiously and socially. Rome was filled with gods, and the prevailing thought was that all the gods were real. Thus, Jews and Christians were viewed as atheists because they believed in only one God and denied the existence of all the pagan deities. Christians also came into direct conflict with basic Roman values. To Roman citizens, the highest allegiance was to the state, but for Christians, God took priority. Roman citizens were very class conscious, and non-Romans were seen as distinctly inferior. But Christians believed that "there is no longer Jew or Gentile, slave or free, male or female. For you are all Christians—you are one in Christ Jesus" (Galatians 3:28). Believers also refused to participate in immoral activities (see Galatians 5:19-23). Christians stood out and eventually were singled out for terrible persecution. Mark wrote to men and women who could have felt overwhelmed by pressures and problems and needed a clear, fresh look at Christ.

In many ways, Roman culture resembles ours today. Certainly we live in an almost pagan society, filled with a wide variety of gods, both secular and religious, with true followers of Christ being a distinct minority. In addition, ours is a Gentile church, with believers from all races, nationalities, and walks of life. So Mark's Gospel translates easily to us today and provides a clear picture of Jesus.

OCCASION AND PURPOSE
To present a clear picture of Christ to Roman believers who were experiencing increased persecution

The exact occasion that spurred Mark to write this Gospel is unknown. Unlike many epistles written by Paul to counter heretical teachings or church divisions, Mark hints of no precipitating event or problem. It may have been that Mark simply felt led by the Holy Spirit to give Peter's eyewitness account of Christ, geared especially for the Roman people among whom they were ministering. Certainly the increasing pressure from the Roman government must have played a key role, because persecution can lead to doubts about the faith and discouragement. Believers needed assurance and hope. The Gospel of Mark gave them a close and personal look at Jesus, their Savior and Lord. They could be assured that the faith they were living and for which they were giving their lives was **true** and **reliable.** Jesus, the Son of God, had lived, served (1:1–13:37), suffered, and died for them (14:1–15:47). And he had risen from the grave (16:1-8)—their triumphant Savior was alive!

Today we enjoy the Bible, complete with Old and New Testaments. In fact, most Christians probably own several copies of the Scriptures. First-century believers did not have that privilege. The holy scrolls—ancient copies of the books of Moses, the prophets, and other Old Testament writers—were safely kept in the Temple and in synagogues, and were cared for and guarded by rabbis. These scrolls were studied and memorized and read on the Sabbath. As for the New Testament, most of the books and letters were just being written and circulated among the churches. Thus Christians had to rely on the teachings and eyewitness accounts of the apostles and others who had known Jesus. Members of the church at Rome, especially Gentiles, desperately needed to learn about Christ and what it meant to follow him. Thus, inspired by the Holy Spirit, Mark provided an accurate account of Jesus and the twelve disciples.

Like most new believers, the Romans also needed to know the cultural, social, and personal implications of their faith. How should they live in a hostile environment, in a society with values totally at odds with their own? Mark's Gospel presented Jesus, the Servant, as their model to follow.

Centuries later, we live in a secular culture whose predominant values are far from Christian, and where under the banner of **pluralism,** government officials strain to remove every vestige of historic Christian faith from public life. While usually not as violent as Roman persecution, our society still pressures Christians to forget Christ. In a society replete with aberrant and heretical religious beliefs, cults, and idols, true followers of Christ have become an absolute minority. As in Rome, it would be easy to become discouraged, dismayed, and doubtful. As with the Romans, we need a fresh look at Jesus of Nazareth, the Messiah, our Lord.

As you read Mark, look at Jesus and see him for who he is—God in the flesh, the suffering Servant, your Savior and model for how to live.

MESSAGE
Omitting the birth of Jesus, Mark begins with John the Baptist's preaching. Then, moving quickly past Jesus' baptism, temptation in the wilderness, and call of the disciples, Mark takes us directly into Jesus' public ministry. We see Jesus confronting a demon, healing a man with leprosy, and forgiving and healing the paralyzed man lowered into Jesus' presence by friends.

Next, Jesus calls Matthew (Levi) and has dinner with him and his disreputable associates. This initiates the conflict with the Pharisees and other religious leaders, who condemn Jesus for eating with sinners and breaking the Sabbath.

In chapter 4, Mark pauses to give a sample of Jesus' teaching—the parable of the farmer and the illustration of the mustard seed—and then plunges back into the action. Jesus calms the waves, drives out demons, and heals Jairus's daughter.

After returning to Nazareth for a few days and experiencing rejection in his hometown, Jesus commissions the disciples to spread the Good News everywhere. Opposition from Herod and the Pharisees increases, and John the Baptist is beheaded. But Jesus continues to move, feeding five thousand, reaching out to the woman from Syrian Phoenicia, healing the deaf man, and feeding four thousand.

Finally, it is time to reveal his true identity to the disciples. Do they really know who Jesus is? Peter proclaims him Messiah but then promptly shows that he does not understand Jesus' mission. After the Transfiguration, Jesus continues to teach and heal, confronting the Pharisees about divorce and the rich young man about eternal life. Blind Bartimaeus is healed.

Events move rapidly toward a climax. The Last Supper, the betrayal, the Crucifixion, and the Resurrection are dramatically portrayed, along with more examples of Jesus' teachings. Mark shows us Jesus—moving, serving, sacrificing, and saving!

The main themes in the Gospel of Mark are as follows: *Jesus Christ, Son of God; Jesus Christ, Servant; Discipleship; Miracles;* and *Evangelism.*

Jesus Christ, Son of God (1:1, 9-11, 21-34; 2:1-12, 23-28; 3:7-12; 4:35-41; 5:1-20; 8:27-31; 9:1-13, 30-32; 10:32-34, 46-52; 11:1-19; 13:24-37; 14:32-42, 60-65; 16:1-8). Jesus was God in the flesh. When Jesus lived on earth, he clearly told his followers, the crowds, the religious leaders, and his accusers that he was the Son of God (see 14:60-65). And he demonstrated this truth by forgiving sins (see 2:5-12), controlling the forces of nature (see 4:35-41), and overcoming disease, demons, and death (see 5:1-43). In addition, Mark affirmed the divinity of Jesus by reporting the voice from heaven at Jesus' baptism (1:11), the Transfiguration (9:2-10), and the Resurrection (16:1-8). Truly Jesus was and is the Son of God.

IMPORTANCE FOR TODAY. The truth that Jesus, the man, is also God means that Jesus has the authority to forgive sins and to change lives. In fact, he died in our place, paying the penalty for our sins. So we can trust in Christ for forgiveness and eternal life. It also means that he is Truth and our authority. Those who know Christ as Savior must obey him as Lord. Christ was fully man, but he was much more—he was, and is, fully God. Do you know him as Savior? Do you follow him as Lord?

Jesus Christ, Servant (1:40-45; 3:1-12; 7:31-37; 8:22-26, 34-38; 9:33-50; 10:13-45; 12:38-44; 14:17-26, 32-50; 15:1-5, 12-47). Jesus fulfilled the Old Testament prophecies about the coming Messiah by coming to earth. He did not come as the conquering king that the people expected, but as a servant, keeping the fact that he was the Messiah a secret. Eventually Jesus would reign as King of kings and Lord of lords, but first he would reveal himself as the Suffering Servant. Jesus served by telling people about God, healing them, and giving his life as the sacrifice for their sins. Jesus suffered by being born into a poor family and by being tempted, questioned, rejected, falsely accused and convicted, beaten, hit, spat upon, tortured, mocked, and crucified. Giving his life and becoming sin on the cross was the ultimate act of suffering and service.

IMPORTANCE FOR TODAY. Those who claim Christ as Savior and Lord should follow his example by serving God and others. Real greatness in Christ's Kingdom is shown by service and sacrifice. Instead of being motivated by ambition or love of power or position (as is true with most people), we should do God's work because we love him and his creation. What does it mean for you to be a servant? What can you do to serve God today? To whom in your home, neighborhood, school, place of employment, or church can you give a "cup of water" in his name (9:41)?

Discipleship (1:16-20; 3:13-19; 6:7-13; 8:27–10:52; 13:1–14:52; 15:42–16:8). Through the eyes of one of Jesus' closest followers, Peter, Mark described the disciples' difficulty in understanding Jesus' true identity. They didn't understand Jesus' parables (see 4:13, 34; 7:18), his miracles (see 4:35-41; 6:45-52), his teaching on divorce (10:10-12), and his predictions of his approaching death and resurrection (8:32-33; 9:9-13, 32). In fact, in this Gospel they never did fully grasp who Jesus really was (see Peter's response to Jesus in 8:31-32) and why he had come to earth. Jesus knew that his disciples wouldn't truly understand his identity and mission until after the Resurrection, and he wanted to keep his true identity partially concealed until it would be revealed publicly after he had been raised from the dead. Yet he continued to teach the disciples about the cost of following him (8:34-38), about humility and Kingdom living (9:33–10:31), and about the importance of serving others (10:35-45).

IMPORTANCE FOR TODAY. We live many centuries after Christ and have the benefit of reading about his life, death, and resurrection. But do we truly understand his identity as God and man, as Savior and Lord? And do we realize the cost of being his disciple? Following Jesus means dying to self, obeying him, and serving others (8:34-35). What kind of disciple are you?

Miracles (1:29-34, 40-45; 2:1-12; 3:1-12; 4:35-41; 5:1-43; 6:30-56; 7:24-37; 8:1-10, 22-26; 9:17-29; 10:46-52; 16:1-8). Mark records more of Jesus' miracles than sermons; in fact, every chapter until his final ministry in Jerusalem (chapter 11) and subsequent capture, trial, and execution contains at least one miracle. Mark's Roman readers could clearly see that Jesus was a man of power and action, not just words. Jesus performed miracles to release people from their sufferings (see 1:41-42), to convince the people who he was (see 2:1-12), and to teach the disciples his true identity as God (see 8:14-21).

IMPORTANCE FOR TODAY. The more convinced we become that Jesus is God, the more we will see his power and love. Christ's mighty works show us that he is able to save anyone, regardless of what he or she has done. His miracles of forgiveness bring healing, wholeness, and new life to all who trust him. Nothing is too big or too difficult for Christ to handle. We can give him all our needs and tell him all our problems. Are you struggling with doubts and fears? Trust Jesus. Are you hurting or suffering? Tell Jesus. Do you need a miracle in your life? Bring your request to Jesus.

Evangelism (1:2-8, 14-20, 38-39; 2:13-17; 3:13-19, 31-34; 4:1-34; 5:1-20; 6:1-13; 7:24-37; 9:33-41; 10:13-31; 12:28-34; 13:1-23, 32-36; 14:9). Jesus directed his public ministry to the Jews first (1:21-28, 38-39), but he also brought healing and the Good News to the non-Jewish world. Syrians (7:24-30) and other Gentiles (5:1-20; 7:31-37) were given the Good News. Jesus challenged his followers to take his message into all the world (6:7-13), preaching the gospel of salvation.

IMPORTANCE FOR TODAY. Jesus crossed national, racial, social, and economic barriers to spread the gospel. His message of faith and forgiveness is for the whole world, not just our church, neighborhood, community, or nation. We must reach beyond our own people and needs to fulfill Christ's worldwide vision that people everywhere might hear this great message and be forgiven of their sins and receive eternal life. Who do you know that needs to hear about Christ? What keeps you from sharing the Good News with them? What can you do today to begin to reach out beyond your circle of Christian friends?

OUTLINE OF MARK

I. Birth and Preparation of Jesus, the Servant (1:1-13)
II. Message and Ministry of Jesus, the Servant (1:14–13:37)
   A. Jesus' ministry in Galilee
   B. Jesus' ministry beyond Galilee
   C. Jesus' ministry in Jerusalem
III. Death and Resurrection of Jesus, the Servant (14:1–16:20)

MARK 1

JOHN THE BAPTIST PREPARES THE WAY FOR JESUS / 1:1-8 / 16

Reading Mark's first words, we can sense his excitement. His account doesn't give background biographical information because he wanted his readers to see Jesus in action as quickly as possible. The power of Jesus' ministry and character alone would impact the reader. Mark introduced his account as "the Good News." For Mark, the purpose of writing was to convey a crucial message, the life-changing Good News about Jesus Christ.

With Mark's help, we can picture ourselves in the crowd as Jesus healed and taught, imagine ourselves as one of the disciples, and respond to his words of love and encouragement. And we can remember that Jesus came for us who live today, as well as for those who lived two thousand years ago.

Before the curtain rises, already we can hear someone shouting. Words about a wilderness come from a man who would be called wild-looking in any age. He lived in a geographical wilderness, and he preached about a spiritual one. We meet John the Baptist as he sets the stage for Jesus' entrance.

1:1 The first verse, **here begins the Good News about Jesus the Messiah, the Son of God,** acts as both a title to the book and a summary of its contents. No mention is made of the author, generally considered to be John Mark. Mark was not one of the twelve disciples of Jesus but probably knew Jesus personally. For further information about Mark, see the "Author" section in the Introduction.

While we generally call this book the Gospel of Mark, the title correctly penned by Mark was **the Good News about Jesus the Messiah, the Son of God.** The first name, "Jesus," was a common name

in Israel (Matthew 1:21; Luke 2:21) as the Old Testament form of the name Joshua (meaning "Yahweh saves"). The second name, "the Messiah," is from the Greek word *Christos* meaning "the Anointed One." The Anointed One, the Messiah, would fulfill the Old Testament prophecies (see, for example, Genesis 49:10; Psalms 2; 110; Isaiah 9:1-7; 11:1-9; Zechariah 9:9-10).

Mark gave no genealogy because he presented Jesus as the servant. A servant needs no pedigree, but demonstrates his validity by the worth of the service he provides. The book portrays Jesus as a man who backed up his words with actions that proved he was the **Son of God.** Because Mark wrote the Gospel for Christians in Rome, where many gods were worshiped, he wanted his readers to know that Jesus was the one true Son of God. He is coeternal with God—and *is* himself God. He alone was fully man (Jesus), God's Anointed One (the Messiah), and fully divine (Son of God). Mark's Gospel fully develops Jesus' claims to be the Christ and the Son of God by showing how he was anointed by God's Spirit to carry out the divine plan of salvation.

1:2-3 Verses 2 and 3 are a composite quotation, taken first from Malachi and then from **Isaiah.** Malachi was a prophet to the Jews in Jerusalem who had returned to rebuild their beloved city after the exile. Isaiah was one of the greatest prophets of the Old Testament and one of the most quoted in the New. The second half of the book of Isaiah is devoted to the promise of salvation. Isaiah wrote about the coming of the Messiah and the man who would announce his coming, John the Baptist (Isaiah 40:3). Like Isaiah, John was a prophet who urged the people to confess their sins and live for God.

Although quoting from two prophets (Isaiah and Malachi), Mark simply applied the words to Isaiah. The theme in both references is the focus on a **messenger** who would **prepare** the **way.** With the help of the Holy Spirit, Mark understood the ministry of John the Baptist as fulfilling these promises. This messenger considered himself **a voice shouting** out to the people of Israel, **"Prepare a pathway for the Lord's coming! Make a straight road for him!"** How were they to do this? The picture could come from the Oriental custom of sending servants ahead of a king to level and clear the roads to make them passable for his journey. The people in Israel needed to prepare their minds—clear away the spiritual debris and straighten any "crooked" moral paths—in eager anticipation of their King and Messiah.

1:4 This **messenger** was **John the Baptist.** There had not been a prophet in Israel for more than four hundred years. It was widely believed that when the Messiah came, prophecy would reappear (Joel 2:28-29; Malachi 3:1; 4:5). Some people thought John himself was the Messiah. John spoke like the prophets of old, saying that the people must turn from their sin to avoid punishment and turn to God to experience his mercy and approval. This is a message for all times and places, but John spoke it with particular urgency—he was preparing the people for the coming Messiah.

Important Roman officials of this day were always preceded by an announcer or herald. When the herald arrived in town, the people knew that someone of prominence would soon arrive and they would be called to assemble. Because Mark's audience was comprised of primarily Roman Christians, he began his book with John the Baptist, whose mission was to announce the coming of Jesus, the most important man who ever lived.

John preached in the **wilderness** in the area near the Jordan River, but he did more than that. He urged his listeners to **be baptized.** Some scholars think that baptism by immersion (going down into the water) was a rite required by the Jews for Gentiles who wished to convert to Judaism. The ritual of immersion symbolized the death and burial of the old way of life; coming up out of the water symbolized the beginning of a new life. If so, then John took a known custom and gave it new meaning. While it was customary for Gentiles to be baptized in order to become Jews, John was demanding that *Jews* be baptized **to show that they had turned from their sins and turned to God to be forgiven.** John's baptism was immersion, and it was a visible sign that a person had decided to change his or her life, giving up a sinful and selfish way of living and turning to God. It was a public action signifying that a person had been cleansed of sin through repentance and had chosen a new way of life.

After Christ's death and resurrection, baptism became an outward sign for identifying with Christ and his resurrection and for signifying entrance into the Christian community. (See, for example, Romans 6:3-4; 1 Peter 3:21.) Baptism did not give forgiveness; baptism was a visible sign that the person had repented and received God's forgiveness for his or her sins. Matthew recorded that some of the Jewish religious leaders (Pharisees and Sadducees) came to be baptized and John angrily turned them away, for he knew there was no humble repentance in their hearts (Matthew 3:7-9).

1:5 From **Jerusalem** (the holy city of the Jews) and from **all over Judea,** a stream of people constantly flowed into the **wilderness** to **hear John** the Baptist preach. Why did John attract so many people? He was the first true prophet in four hundred years. He blasted both Herod and the religious leaders, a daring act that fascinated the common people. But John also had strong words for his audience—they too were sinners and needed to repent. **When they confessed their sins,** John **baptized them in the Jordan River.** Confession is more than simply acknowledging one's own sinfulness; it is agreeing with God's verdict on sin and expressing the desire to get rid of sin and live for God. Confessing means more than verbal response, affirmation, or praise; it means agreeing to change to a life of obedience and service.

1:6 John's **clothes** were much like the prophet Elijah (2 Kings 1:8) in order to distinguish him from the religious leaders, whose flowing robes reflected their great pride in their position (12:38-39). John's striking appearance reinforced his striking message. Elijah had also been considered a messenger preparing the way for God (see Malachi 3:1). His diet, **locusts and wild honey,** was common for survival in wilderness regions.

1:7 Although John was the first genuine prophet in four hundred years, Jesus the Messiah would be **far greater** than he. John saw himself as even lower than that **slave** in comparison to the coming Messiah (see John 3:30). What John began, Jesus finished. What John prepared, Jesus fulfilled.

1:8 John's baptism with **water** indicated immersion in the water of the Jordan River. John's baptism demonstrated repentance, humility, and willingness to turn from sin. This was the begin-

ning of the spiritual process. To be effective, it had to be accompanied by an inward change of attitude leading to a changed life. John's baptism did not give salvation; it prepared a person to welcome the coming Messiah and receive his message and his baptism.

John's statement, **He will baptize you with the Holy Spirit,** revealed the identity of the "one" coming after John as the promised Messiah. The coming of the Spirit had been prophesied as part of the Messiah's arrival (see Isaiah 44:3; Jeremiah 31:31-34; Ezekiel 36:26-27; Joel 2:28-29). The Old Testament promised a time when God would demonstrate his power among people and give special relationship and blessings to his people. This looked ahead to Pentecost (Acts 2). All believers, those who would later come to Jesus Christ for salvation, would receive the Holy Spirit. When Jesus would baptize with the Holy Spirit, the entire person would be transformed by the Spirit's power. Jesus would offer both forgiveness of sin and the power to live for him. We need more than repentance to save us; we need the indwelling power of the Holy Spirit.

THE BAPTISM OF JESUS / 1:9-11 / 17

Mark proceeded to describe Jesus' baptism by John. The signs of the voice and dove from heaven affirmed Jesus' identity as the Son of God and showed the uniqueness of Jesus' baptism. But the words of God the Father's declaration clearly signified who Jesus was. What Jesus was doing, including undergoing baptism by John, totally pleased God. Jesus was in no way "becoming" God's Son; instead, his true nature was being revealed. Jesus' baptism showed that he was identifying with sinful men and women without implying that he himself was a sinner.

1:9 The coming one was identified as **Jesus.** Although born in Bethlehem, Jesus moved to **Nazareth** when he was a young boy and grew up there (Matthew 2:22-23). Nazareth was a small town **in Galilee,** located about halfway between the Sea of Galilee and the Mediterranean Sea. The city was despised and avoided by many Jews because it had a reputation for independence. Nazareth was an unlikely hometown for so great a king as Jesus. Yet even Jesus' hometown demonstrated his humility and identification with ordinary people.

If John's baptism was for repentance from sin, why was Jesus **baptized?** While even the greatest prophets (Isaiah, Jeremiah, Ezekiel) had to confess their sinfulness and need for repentance, Jesus didn't need to admit sin—he was sinless (John 8:46; 2 Corinthians 5:21; Hebrews 4:15; 1 John 3:5). Although Jesus didn't need forgiveness, he

was baptized for the following reasons: (1) to confess sin on behalf of the nation (see Isaiah 6:5; Nehemiah 1:6; 9:1ff.; Ezra 9:2); (2) to fulfill all righteousness (Matthew 3:15) in order to accomplish God's mission and advance God's work in the world; (3) to inaugurate his public ministry to bring the message of salvation to all people; (4) to show support for John's ministry; (5) to identify with the penitent people of God, thus with humanness and sin; (6) to give us an example to follow.

Jesus, the perfect man, didn't need baptism for sin, but he accepted baptism in obedient service to the Father, and God showed his approval. We need this same attitude of humility, submission to God, and dedication to servanthood.

1:10 Apparently the action of the **Spirit descending** from heaven **like a dove** was a sign for John

that Jesus was the Messiah. The "splitting" of
the heavens presents God's intervention into
humanity in the human presence of God in
Jesus Christ. It was as if the heavens rolled back
to reveal the invisible throne of God (Isaiah
63:19–64:2).

The **dove** is used as a symbol for the Holy Spirit.
However, it is not the bird itself that was important, but the descent of the Spirit *like* a dove to
emphasize the way the Holy Spirit related to Jesus.
The Spirit descending portrays a gentle, peaceful,
but active presence coming to indwell Jesus. In the
same way, since Jesus has given us the Holy Spirit,
he is available to us as well.

1:11 The Spirit descended and **a voice came from
heaven** proclaiming the Father's approval of Jesus
as his divine Son. That Jesus is God's divine Son is
the foundation for all we read about Jesus in the
Gospels. This **voice** came from the heavenly realm
that had been briefly "split open" (1:10).

The voice said, **"You are my beloved Son."**

Jesus Christ has a unique relationship with God
because he is God's one and only Son. The phrase
"I am fully pleased with you," means that the
Father takes great delight, pleasure, and satisfaction
in the Son. Jesus did not become the Son or the
Messiah at this baptism. Jesus already had his
divinity from eternity past. The opened heavens,
the dove, and the voice revealed to John the Baptist
that Jesus was God's Son, come to earth as the
promised Messiah to fulfill prophecy and bring
salvation to those who believe.

In this event, we see all three members of the
Trinity together—God the Father, God the Son,
and God the Holy Spirit. The doctrine of the Trinity means that God is three persons and yet one in
essence. In this passage, all three persons of the
Trinity are present and active. This is one of God's
incomprehensible mysteries. Other Bible references
that speak of the Father, Son, and Holy Spirit are
Matthew 28:19; Luke 1:35; John 15:26; 1 Corinthians 12:4-13; 2 Corinthians 13:14; Ephesians 2:18;
1 Thessalonians 1:2-5; and 1 Peter 1:2.

SATAN TEMPTS JESUS IN THE WILDERNESS / 1:12-13 / 18

This temptation by Satan shows us that though Jesus was human and subject to temptations
such as we are, he was also divine because he overcame Satan and was ministered to by angels.
Jesus' temptation was an important demonstration of his sinlessness. He faced temptation and
did not give in. As his servants, we will also be prepared for discipleship by testing.

1:12 Jesus, empowered by **the Holy Spirit,** takes
the offensive against the enemy, Satan, by going
into the lonely and desolate **wilderness** to fight
temptation (see 1:13). The word for **compelled** is
very forceful in the Greek, conveying the meaning
of "thrown out" or "cast out." (Mark used the
same word to describe Jesus driving out demons,
as in 1:34, 39.) This does not imply that Jesus was
reluctant, but rather that God's Spirit was intensely
motivating him to go. As with Jesus' disciples, the
Spirit may have in mind to test us in order to prepare us for greater service.

1:13 Jesus remained alone for **forty days;** Matthew
and Luke add that Jesus fasted during that time
(Matthew 4:2; Luke 4:2). The Gospels of Matthew
and Luke describe in more detail the temptation
endured by Jesus. **Satan** is an angel who rebelled
against God. He is real, not symbolic, and he is
constantly working against God and those who
obey him. Satan tempted Eve in the Garden and
persuaded her to sin; he tempted Jesus in the
wilderness and did not persuade him to fall. The
verb **being tempted** describes continuous action
because Jesus was tempted constantly during the

forty days. Jesus' personal victory over Satan at
the very outset of his ministry set the stage for his
command over demons throughout his ministry,
but it did not dissuade Satan from continuing to
try to ruin Jesus' mission.

The **wilderness** was a dangerous and desolate
place, inhabited by **wild animals.** The wilderness
regions of Palestine had animals such as boars,
jackals, wolves, foxes, leopards, and hyenas. Mark
is the only Gospel writer to mention this, pointing out the hostile nature of the wilderness where
Jesus spent forty days being tempted. That **angels
took care of him** in no way lessens the intensity
of the temptations that Jesus faced. Angels, like
these who waited on Jesus, have a significant role
as God's messengers. These spiritual beings were
involved in Jesus' life on earth by (1) announcing
Jesus' birth to Mary, (2) reassuring Joseph,
(3) naming Jesus, (4) announcing Jesus' birth to
the shepherds, (5) protecting Jesus by sending
his family to Egypt, and (6) ministering to Jesus
in Gethsemane.

From Jesus' temptation we can learn that following our Lord could bring dangerous and intense
spiritual battles. It warns us that we won't always

feel good; there will be times of deprivation, loneliness, and hostility. It also shows that our spiritual victories may not always be visible to the watching world. Above all, it shows that we must use the power of God to face temptation, and not try to withstand it in our own strength.

JESUS PREACHES IN GALILEE / 1:14-15 / 30

Approximately one year elapsed between 1:13 and 1:14, which begins a new section. In this section Mark focuses on Jesus' choosing of his disciples. This section also tells how Herod removed John the Baptist from ministry while Jesus' public ministry was beginning (see John 3:30). Mark then includes a summary of Jesus' message. Jesus echoed John's call for repentance and added the challenge that each person must believe the Good News. From the beginning, Jesus did not allow himself to be only a topic for debate or even admiration. He expected those who approached him to believe or to reject him. He never allowed the middle ground of indecision.

1:14 Mark mentioned the arrest of John the Baptist as merely a signal for the ministry of Jesus into **Galilee,** his home region. Luke explained that **John was arrested** because he publicly rebuked King Herod for taking his brother's wife. John's public protests greatly angered Herod, so he put John in prison, presumably to silence him. The family of Herods were renowned for their cruelty and evil; it was Herod the Great who ordered the murder of the babies in Bethlehem (Matthew 2:16). The Herod who imprisoned John was **Herod Antipas;** his wife was Herodias, Herod Antipas' niece and formerly his brother's wife. The imprisonment of John the Baptist was only one evil act in a family filled with incest, deceit, and murder.

1:15 The Old Testament prophets often spoke of the future Kingdom, ruled by a descendant of King David, that would be established on earth and exist for eternity. Thus when Jesus spoke of the time and the presence of **the Kingdom of God,** the Jews understood him to mean that the Messiah had come to fulfill or inaugurate his long-awaited Kingdom. Jesus reassured them that God was in sovereign control. He had begun to act in a new and decisive way.

This caused great excitement among the people. The problem arose, however, in the misunderstanding of the nature of this Kingdom. The Kingdom of God began when God entered history as a human being. But the Kingdom of God will not be fully realized until all evil in the world has been judged and removed. Christ came to earth first as a Suffering Servant; he will come again as King and Judge to rule victoriously over all the earth. The Kingdom was as **near** as people's willingness to make Jesus king over their lives. Jesus began his ministry with the very words people had heard John the Baptist say: **Turn from your sins.** The message is the same today.

FOUR FISHERMEN FOLLOW JESUS / 1:16-20 / 33

Jesus confronted Simon and Andrew with a challenge beyond the one he presented in his public preaching. He called the crowds to repentance and belief. He invited Simon and the others to follow him. They had already repented and believed. Now they were being called into discipleship.

The Lord used their previous vocation as a metaphor of their new calling. The former fishermen would now be fishers of people. God finds a way to make good use of every past experience we have to help us serve him.

1:16 The **Sea of Galilee** is, in reality, a large lake—650 feet below sea level, 150 feet deep, and surrounded by hills. Fishing was the main industry for the approximately thirty fishing towns that surrounded the Sea of Galilee during Jesus' day. Fishing with nets was the most common fishing method. A circular **net** (ten to fifteen feet in diameter) was cast into the sea. Then it was drawn up, and the catch was hoisted into the boat.

The first pair of men Jesus called to follow him were brothers, **Simon** and **Andrew.** This was not the first time Simon and Andrew had met Jesus. Andrew had been a disciple of John the Baptist who, when introduced to "the Lamb of God," turned and followed Jesus (John 1:35-39). Andrew then brought his brother Simon to Jesus (John 1:42). These men understood and believed who Jesus was.

1:17 Jesus told Simon (Peter) and Andrew to leave their fishing business, **come** and be his **disciples,** and **fish for people** to also follow Jesus. These disciples were adept at catching fish, but they would need special training before they would become able to fish for people's souls. Jesus was calling them away from their productive trades to be productive spiritually by helping others believe the Good News and carry on Jesus' work after he was gone.

1:18 After their previous meeting with Jesus, Simon Peter and Andrew had returned to fishing. But when Jesus called them to follow him as disciples, **they left their nets at once.** Their lives had

changed; their allegiance was now to their teacher. Mark taught radical discipleship; a person must leave all behind to follow Jesus.

1:19 Not far down the beach was another pair of brothers, **James and John,** Simon Peter's partners (Luke 5:10). These men were sitting in their moored boat **mending their nets.** The weight of a good catch of fish and the constant strain on the nets meant that the fishermen had to spend a lot of time keeping their nets repaired and in good shape.

John had met Jesus previously. In his Gospel, John records his own and Andrew's discipleship with John the Baptist and then their turning to follow Jesus (John 1:35-39). James probably knew about Jesus from his brother, John. These men were ready for Jesus' call.

1:20 Both sets of brothers **immediately** left behind the lives they had known and embarked on an incredible adventure. Surely the impression Jesus made upon them must have been great, and the certainty of their call must have been strong for them to follow without hesitation.

JESUS TEACHES WITH GREAT AUTHORITY / 1:21-28 / 34

Earlier in chapter 1, Satan attacked Jesus in the wilderness. Then Mark directed our attention to Jesus' counterattack. He carried the spiritual warfare into the domain of Satan, to those controlled by evil spirits. As will be the case repeatedly, the battle took place in a synagogue on the Sabbath. Perhaps this shows that Satan can be active even in our houses of worship.

1:21 Capernaum, located on the northwestern shore of the Sea of Galilee, was the largest of the many fishing towns surrounding the lake. Jesus had recently moved to Capernaum from Nazareth (Matthew 4:12-13). Capernaum was a thriving town with great wealth as well as great sin and decadence. Because it was the headquarters for many Roman troops, heathen influences from all over the Roman Empire were pervasive.

The Temple in Jerusalem was too far for many Jews to travel for regular worship, so many towns had synagogues serving both as places of worship and as schools. Beginning in the days of Ezra, about 450 B.C., a group of ten Jewish families could start a **synagogue.** There, during the week, Jewish boys were taught the Old Testament law and Jewish religion (girls could not attend). Each Saturday, the Sabbath, the Jewish men would gather to hear prayers, the Scriptures read, and an interpretation from a teacher. Because there was no permanent teacher, it was customary for the synagogue leader to ask visiting teachers to speak. This is why Jesus often spoke in the synagogues in the towns he visited.

1:22 The people were completely **amazed** by Jesus' **teaching.** The Jewish **teachers of religious law** often quoted from well-known rabbis to give their words more authority. But Jesus didn't have that need. Because Jesus was the Son of God, he knew exactly what the Scriptures said and meant. He was the ultimate **authority.** The people had never heard such teaching. The **teachers of religious law** were the legal specialists in Jesus' day. They interpreted the law but were especially concerned about the *halakah* or "rules" for life that came to be as binding as God's written law in the Torah. Their self-assured authority, in fact, became a stumbling block for them, for they denied Jesus' authority to reinterpret the law, and they rejected Jesus as the Messiah because he did not agree with nor obey all of their traditions.

1:23-24 Evil spirits, or demons, are ruled by Satan. They work to tempt people to sin. They were not created by Satan, because God is the Creator of all. Rather, the evil spirits and demons are fallen angels who joined Satan in his rebellion and thus became perverted and evil. The **evil spirit** had entered the man's body and **possessed** him. Though not all disease comes from Satan, sometimes demons can cause a person to become mute, deaf, blind, or insane. But in every case where demons confronted Jesus, they lost their power. Thus God limits what evil spirits can do; they can do nothing without his permission. During Jesus' life on earth, demons were allowed to be very active to demonstrate once and for all Christ's power and authority over them.

The evil spirit knew two facts—that Jesus had indeed come to **destroy** demonic power and that Jesus was **the Holy One sent from God.** While the people in the synagogue were astounded at Jesus' teaching and wondered who this man could be, the demon knew. At this time, people believed that to know a person's precise hidden name was to be able to gain control over the person. Thus the demon's first attempt against Jesus was to state his divine identity in public. By including this event in his Gospel, Mark was establishing Jesus' credentials, showing that even the spiritual underworld recognized Jesus as God's Son.

1:25 Jesus simply and sternly commanded the demon to **be silent.** Two explanations may help us understand why Jesus asked this: (1) Jesus wanted to contain the enthusiasm for a political messiah. He did not wish to be the people's king in the way they desired, nor did he want to be a military leader; (2) To confess Jesus' deity without a proper understanding of his mission is partial and invalid. He did not want people to wildly proclaim him to be God's Son unless they understood the meaning of his death for them on the cross. This would explain why even his disciples lacked understanding until his resurrection.

To silence the demon was not enough, for Jesus wanted to free the man possessed by the demon. So Jesus next commanded, **"Come out of the man,"** again demonstrating his power and authority over Satan and his demons.

1:26 Without any recourse except to submit to a higher authority, the evil spirit **left** the man. But first, to show its anger and protest, the evil spirit **screamed and threw the man into a convulsion.** This could have been a severe spasm or a blow that thrust the man to the ground. With a final shriek, the demon left.

Many psychologists dismiss all accounts of demon possession as a primitive way to describe mental illness. Although throughout history mental illness has often been wrongly diagnosed as demon possession, clearly a hostile outside force controlled the man described here. Mark emphasized Jesus' conflict with evil powers to show his superiority over them, so he recorded many stories about Jesus driving out evil spirits. Jesus' power over demons reveals his absolute power over Satan, even in a world that seems to be in Satan's control. Satan is presently under God's authority; when God chooses to command, Satan must obey. Satan's workings are only within God's prescribed limits; he can do no more evil than God allows. In the end, Satan and all his demons will be tormented in the lake of fire forever (Revelation 20:10).

1:27 Jesus' display of his authority in the showdown with a demon caused **amazement** in the people. With a simple and stern command, the evil spirit obeyed and the possessed man was set free. The people called Jesus' teaching **new**; his teaching challenged them. Jesus taught with authority; he spoke to the powerful underworld with authority. Surely this man was someone to watch closely.

1:28 The people who left the gathering in the large synagogue in Capernaum had witnessed an authoritative and captivating new teacher with unheard-of power. The news **spread quickly** across the region of Galilee. Jesus' growing popularity becomes a major theme in chapter 1. This popularity among the common folk stands in glaring contrast to the religious leaders' opposition expressed in 2:1–3:6.

JESUS HEALS PETER'S MOTHER-IN-LAW AND MANY OTHERS / 1:29-34 / 35

After ending his clash with the demons in the synagogue, Jesus immediately healed Peter's mother-in-law of a fever. By the time evening arrived, there were many sick and demon-possessed crowding to Jesus for attention. Mark noted that Jesus was commanding the demons not to identify him. His goal was not to draw attention to himself, but to meet the real needs of others.

1:29 As the crowd hurriedly dispersed from the synagogue or continued talking among themselves, Jesus and the four disciples left for their own lodgings. They arrived at **Simon and Andrew's home.**

Jesus and the disciples probably stayed in this home during their visits to Capernaum (2:1; 3:20; 9:33; 10:10)

1:30-31 Simon's mother-in-law was sick in bed, burning with a **high fever.** Jesus went to the mother-in-law's **bedside, took her by the hand,** and **helped her to sit up.** Jesus' touch on the woman's hand brought instant and complete healing—**the fever suddenly left.** She went and **prepared a meal** as she had probably planned.

1:32-33 The people came to Jesus on Saturday **evening at sunset.** The day had been the Sabbath (1:21), their day of worship and rest, lasting from sunset Friday to sunset Saturday. Jewish law prohibited traveling and carrying burdens on the Sabbath, so they waited until sunset. After the sun went down, Sabbath was over, and the people searched for Jesus. The Greek word for **brought**

means "to carry." Many of the **sick and demon-possessed people** were literally carried to Peter's home so Jesus could heal them. The **crowd** was so **huge** that it appeared that **people from all over Capernaum** had **gathered** there. This was no unruly mob; the people had come on a mission and were there to stay until their mission was accomplished.

1:34 Jesus patiently **healed** all the sick people. No disease took Jesus by surprise, and no disease was beyond his ability to heal. Jesus' authority over the demons continued to be revealed as he **ordered many demons to come out** from the **victims** brought to him. Again, Jesus simply had to command the demon to come out, and it obeyed. However, this time Jesus **refused to allow the demons to speak** because **they knew who he was** (see 1:25).

JESUS PREACHES THROUGHOUT GALILEE / 1:35-39 / 36

Jesus had just spent a Sabbath in feverish activity. Early in the morning of the next day, he set aside a time of prayer by himself. By the time the disciples found him, he was ready to face the next challenge. We must follow Christ's example by making time for personal prayer. Those who help and serve on Sunday especially need to set aside time with God to restore their strength. Our ability to serve will be hindered if we neglect times of spiritual replenishment.

1:35 Before the sun came up, Jesus **went out alone into the wilderness to pray.** During his ministry on earth, Jesus was in constant prayer with the Father. Mark recorded three of these times of prayer: (1) after the successful ministry in Capernaum with the healing of many sick and demon-possessed people; (2) after the miracle of feeding more than five thousand people (6:46); (3) in Gethsemane, just prior to his arrest, trial, and crucifixion (14:32-42).

What did Jesus pray about? After his great successes with the crowds in Capernaum and on the mountainside, his prayers may have focused on fulfilling his mission as the Suffering Servant, when it seemed (at least humanly) more strategic to be a conquering king. Popularity was a temptation in itself, for it threatened to turn Jesus away from his mission. Jesus had a mission to fulfill—and death on the cross was the key, for only Jesus' death could accomplish salvation. Jesus, in his humanity, may have continued to face the temptation to turn away from the difficult path and take the easier one. He constantly needed strength from God. Going into the wilderness, alone with the Father, helped Jesus focus on his task and gain strength for what that task entailed.

1:36-38 Apparently the people in Capernaum continued to arrive at Simon Peter's house the next morning hoping to hear more of Jesus' teaching and see him perform more miracles. The disciples were surprised that Jesus would not follow up on his great success from the previous day's ministry in Capernaum, but instead disappeared before anyone awoke. So they **went out to find him** and bring him back. But Jesus had a mission to fulfill and a very limited time to accomplish it. Not only was Jesus not going to capitalize on his great popularity in Capernaum, he was not even going back into the city. Instead, he was leaving on an extended trip throughout the region. Many people needed to hear Jesus **preach** the Good News of the Kingdom of God (1:14-15), as Jesus explained, **"That is why I came."** Jesus would not be deterred from his mission to preach the Good News to as many people as possible. His primary mission was to bring people to a place of decision to have faith in God.

1:39 Jesus and the disciples left the early morning bustle of Capernaum behind and began a preaching and healing tour **throughout the region of Galilee.** The Romans had divided the land of Israel into three separate regions: Galilee, Samaria, and Judea. Galilee was the northernmost region, an area about sixty miles long and thirty miles wide. Jesus did much of his ministry in this area, an ideal place for him to teach because there were over 250 towns concentrated there, with many **synagogues.** Jesus' action of **expelling demons** verified his authority and power and showed compassion to those who had been possessed and, by Jesus' word, had been set free.

JESUS HEALS A MAN WITH LEPROSY / 1:40-45 / 38

Once the news was out that Jesus could heal diseases, people with serious needs converged from every direction. Perhaps the greatest handicap God accepted in coming to earth was to limit himself to space and time. He was a single individual with divine power in a sea of human needs. Even those he helped, like this man cured of leprosy, hampered Jesus by telling everyone of Jesus' miraculous power. By so doing, he drew attention to the sensational and miraculous aspect of Jesus' ministry and away from the need for repentance and faith that leads to a life of service.

1:40 Leprosy was a terrifying disease because of the social rejection and the devastating impact it had on its victims. In Jesus' day, the Greek word for leprosy was used for a variety of similar diseases; some forms were contagious, disfiguring, and / or deadly; some were as innocuous as ringworm. In keeping with the law in Leviticus 13 and 14, Jewish leaders declared people with leprosy (lepers) unclean. This meant that lepers were unfit to participate in any religious or social activity. Because the law said that contact with any unclean person made that person unclean too, some people even threw rocks at lepers to keep them at a safe distance. Even the mention of the name of this disabling disease terrified people because they were afraid of catching it. Lepers lived together in colonies outside their community. Most would remain there until they died. Sometimes, however, leprosy would go away. Then the person could return to the priest and ask to be declared "clean" before returning to the community.

That this man with leprosy **came** to Jesus reveals the man's great courage; that he **knelt** reveals his desperation and his humility; his words to Jesus reveal his faith. The priest would declare him clean, but only Jesus could make him clean. **"If you want to"** reveals the man's faith in Jesus' authority in this matter of healing. What this man wanted was to be made **well,** a huge request.

1:41 Jesus' love and power go hand in hand. Mark revealed Jesus' heart of compassion. While all people shunned lepers, Jesus **touched** this man covered with a dreaded, contagious disease. The fact that Jesus' touch precedes his pronouncement of healing indicates that Jesus disregarded the Jewish law not to touch a leper (Leviticus 5:3; 13:1-46; Numbers 5:2). This shows Jesus' compassion and his authority over the law. With the words, **"I want to . . . Be healed!"** the leprosy immediately disappeared. The words were simple but effective, revealing Jesus' divine authority over sickness.

1:42 We are not told the stage of this man's leprosy—he may already have lost portions of his body to the disease. But when Jesus spoke, the man's health was restored completely. The disease did not go into a type of "remission"—it **disappeared.** The man's becoming **healed** meant he had his life back. He could return to his community, to his family, and to worshiping in the synagogue.

1:43-44 When a leper was cured, he or she had to go to a **priest** to be examined. Then the leper was to give a thank **offering** at the Temple. Jesus adhered to these laws by sending the man to the priest. Jesus wanted this man to give his story firsthand to the priest to prove that his leprosy was completely gone so that he could be restored to his family and community. This would be done as **proof** of his healing.

Jesus also told the man: **"Don't talk to anyone along the way."** Why would Jesus ask this man not to tell anyone about his healing? Wouldn't this have been great advertising for Jesus, bringing more people to hear his message? While we might think so, Jesus knew better (John 2:24-25). Jesus' mission was to preach the Good News of the Kingdom of God. If crowds descended on him to see miracles accomplished or to benefit from his power, they would not be coming with the heart attitude needed to hear and respond to the gospel. Jesus did not want to be a miracle worker in a sideshow; he wanted to be the Savior of their souls.

1:45 The man disobeyed Jesus' strong warning. Perhaps the man thought he was helping Jesus' ministry; perhaps he just couldn't help himself.

In any case, he **spread the news.** His disobedience to Jesus' command, even if from good motives, hindered Jesus' work because the publicity Jesus received severely hampered his ministry in the synagogue. Jesus had planned to go into towns throughout Galilee and preach in the synagogues. But his notoriety as a healer made this

impossible. Mark recorded that Jesus **couldn't enter a town anywhere publicly**—probably crowds of people pressed on him, all seeking special favors. So Jesus **had to stay out in the secluded places.** But that did not hinder people in need of healing or desiring to see this healer. They still **came to him there.**

MARK 2

JESUS HEALS A PARALYZED MAN / 2:1-12 / 39

Chapter 1 draws the battle lines between Jesus and the power of Satan. Chapter 2 introduces a new factor in the conflict: resistance to Jesus by the religious establishment. The religious leaders, accustomed to giving lip service to the idea of a coming Messiah, found that Jesus threatened their power and prestige. Jesus challenged their authority, questioned their teachings, and trampled on their way of doing business. Mark illustrated their reactions and rejection of Christ with five clashes that form chapter 2 and the beginning of chapter 3.

2:1-2 Jesus returned to Capernaum, which had become his base of operations while he was in Galilee. Everyone in Capernaum had been looking for him (1:37), so when the people heard that he was back, they **packed** the house. Instead of healing, however, this time **he preached the word to them.** The basic message remained the same: The long-awaited Messiah had come to break the power of sin and begin God's personal reign on earth. The miracles Jesus performed served as a sign to Jesus' identity, as well as revealed his compassion and love for the people he had come to save.

2:3-4 As Jesus was preaching, **four men arrived carrying a paralyzed man.** The crowd had filled the house and the doorway (2:2), so the group **couldn't get to Jesus.** But these friends would not be deterred. Determined to get their friend to Jesus, **they dug through the clay roof above his head.** In Bible times, houses were built of stone and had outside stairways that led onto flat roofs. Roofs were made with joists covered with a mixture of mortar, tar, ashes, and sand. Thus they had to "dig" through the roof (see also Luke 5:19). They attached ropes to each corner of the pallet and carefully **lowered** the paralyzed man in front of Jesus.

2:5 We might expect a popular preacher in the middle of speaking to an expectant crowd to be annoyed at this intrusion. Obviously, several minutes were spent as the crowd watched these men take apart the roof above them. But Jesus saw **their**

faith acted out in their determination. If they could but get their friend within Jesus' touch, they knew their friend would be restored.

Among the first words Jesus said to the paralyzed man were **"My son, your sins are forgiven."** The man needed spiritual healing, so Jesus forgave his sins. Then Jesus healed the man.

2:6-7 These **teachers of religious law** were the legal specialists in Jesus' day. Jesus' teaching and his popularity had prompted special investigation by the powerful leaders of the Jewish faith. These teachers had been dispatched from Jerusalem to Capernaum (Luke 5:17) and had made their way into the crowd that filled this house. Jealous of Jesus' popularity and power, these men hoped to find something to criticize or even condemn in Jesus' teaching. When they heard Jesus tell the paralyzed man that his sins were forgiven, they were shocked. For Jesus to claim to **forgive sins** was considered blasphemy, defined as claiming to be God or to do what only God can do. In Jewish law, blasphemy was punishable by death (Leviticus 24:16). The religious leaders were correct in their statement that only God can forgive sins (Exodus 34:6-7; Psalm 103:3; Isaiah 43:25; Daniel 9:9), and they also rightly understood that Jesus was claiming to be God. But in labeling Jesus' claim to forgive sins as **blasphemy,** the religious leaders showed they did not understand that Jesus was God. Jesus had God's power and authority to heal bodies and forgive sins. Forgiveness of sins was a sign that the messianic age had come (Isaiah 40:2; Joel 2:32; Micah 7:18-19; Zechariah 13:1). Unfortunately, it did not occur to these Jewish leaders that perhaps this man *was* their Messiah.

2:8 Jesus **knew what they were discussing,** and their hostility and anger at Jesus' words could not be hidden. Jesus asked them, **"Why do you think this is blasphemy?"** Would the teachers of religious law respond, or did they too believe this man to be the Messiah? Jesus knew the teachers' dilemma and offered to prove his authority.

2:9 The teachers of religious law knew about Jesus' ability to heal, and they probably had expected Jesus to immediately heal the paralyzed man. Instead, Jesus forgave the man's sins. To the teachers, this sounded like blasphemy, and it also sounded like an easy out. Anyone can just *say* someone's sins are forgiven, but it would take someone with great power and authority to heal a paralyzed person. Jesus asked them the question that they were asking themselves. He wanted to show that he had the power to forgive sins by showing that he had the power to make a paralytic **pick up** his mat and **walk.**

2:10-11 By recording this incident, Mark hoped to prove to his audience beyond any doubt that Jesus was the Messiah. The Son of Man has the delegated authority of God the Father to forgive sins. The teachers asked, "Who but God can forgive sins!" (2:7). The answer is, "No human except one delegated that authority by God himself. And the Son of Man has that authority." However, people cannot "see" sins forgiven; they can see physical healing. Therefore, Jesus turned to the paralytic, still lying on the mat in front of him, and told him to **stand up** on his previously useless legs; **take** his **mat** with arms that may also have been previously useless; and **go on home.**

2:12 The man did not doubt Jesus' words; when Jesus told him to get up, he did so—before the **stunned onlookers** including Jesus' critics. The healing unmistakably showed Jesus' power and authority. The teachers of religious law who questioned Jesus' ability to forgive sins (2:6-7) saw the formerly paralyzed man get up and walk. Jesus' question in 2:9 forced their answer: Jesus had the power to make the paralyzed man walk; thus he also had the authority to forgive his sins. The people in Capernaum had already seen numerous healings by Jesus on his previous visit. But the crowd's amazement is expressed in Mark's words, **they all praised God.** While the religious leaders questioned and debated, the people recognized God's power and realized that Jesus had been given authority by God.

JESUS EATS WITH SINNERS AT MATTHEW'S HOUSE / 2:13-17 / 40

The next clash between Jesus and the religious leaders revolved around the company he kept. Not only had Jesus not separated himself from distasteful characters, he sought them out. Jesus was charged with befriending sinners. Just as Jesus entered the world to save sinners, he still enters sinful human lives to rescue those he loves.

2:13 Jesus left Capernaum and went back **to the lakeshore** (that is, the Sea of Galilee). A crowd of people **gathered,** and Jesus **taught** them. While Jesus often spoke in synagogues or homes, he also taught groups of people on hillsides (Matthew 5:1) or on the shore of the Sea of Galilee. The hillsides and sloping shoreline of the Sea of Galilee provided a convenient place for large crowds to gather and listen.

2:14 Levi (also called Matthew, and later the author of the Gospel of Matthew) was a Jew who worked for the Romans (specifically for Herod Antipas) as the area's tax collector. He collected taxes from the citizens as well as from merchants passing through town. (Capernaum was a customs post on the caravan route between Damascus to the northeast and the Mediterranean Sea to the west.) Tax collectors were expected to take a commission on the taxes they collected, but most of them overcharged and kept the profits. Thus, tax collectors were hated by most Jews because of their reputation for cheating and because of their support of Rome. A Jew who accepted such an office was excommunicated from the synagogue and shamed his family and friends. Thus, a Jewish tax collector was looked down upon for valuing money over reputation, respectability, purity before God, and concern for his own people, who had to pay extremely high taxes to the imperial power.

The **tax-collection booth** was an elevated platform or bench. Everyone knew who Levi was, and anyone passing through the city who had to pay taxes could find him easily. Levi's tollbooth taxed commercial goods being transported from the sea to land routes. This was probably not the first time Jesus saw Levi, for Jesus walked these shores many times.

Mark's words emphasize the brevity of Jesus' call and Levi's radical obedience. Jesus' words, **"Come, be my disciple,"** are in the imperative mood, meaning this was a command, not an invitation. Levi recognized that Jesus wasn't inviting him; Jesus was calling him. So Levi **got up and followed.**

Levi's radical obedience is amazing for the change it would effect in his life. Already ostracized by family and friends, following Jesus probably made no difference in this regard. But Levi was probably very wealthy—tax collecting was a lucrative occupation. Levi had been an outcast; now he was wanted as a member of a group. But he would have to learn to live in poverty.

2:15 Levi responded, as Jesus would want all his followers to do; he followed his Lord immediately, and he called his friends together to meet him too. He held a **dinner** for his **fellow tax collectors and many other notorious sinners** so they also could meet Jesus.

In Levi's house there gathered a crowd that Jesus could not reach in the synagogues. The tax collectors had been excommunicated. The term **sinners** referred to the common people who were not learned in the law and did not abide by the rigid standards of the Pharisees. The Pharisees regarded these people as wicked and opposed to the will of God because they did not observe the rituals for purity, which enabled them to eat with others. In any case, Jesus had attracted a following among these people. These people gathered at Levi's house, where they knew they had a welcome, and they too sat with Jesus and his disciples at dinner and listened to the message this marvelous teacher had for them.

2:16 Many of these **teachers of religious law** were also **Pharisees**—a strict religious group of Jews who also advocated minute obedience to the Jewish laws and traditions. Their job was to teach the Scriptures and the Law and to protect them against anyone's willful defiance. They saw themselves as righteous and everyone else as sinners. When Jesus sat down to a meal with these **"scum,"** the Pharisees were quite surprised. Here was a man who seemed to have the entire law at his fingertips, who taught with great authority, yet who stooped to the level of the poor, unlearned, common people (even sinners!). Thus the Pharisees pulled his disciples aside and asked why Jesus did this.

2:17 The question apparently made its way to Jesus' ears, and Jesus had an answer for the self-righteous, influential religious leaders. The first part of Jesus' answer was from a common proverb on the healthy and the sick. People who are well don't seek out a physician; the physician's waiting room is filled with people who are sick. They recognize their need and come to the one who can make them well.

Jesus carried the proverb a step further and explained his messianic mission. Jesus did not come to call **those who think they are already good enough** (used ironically—those, like these Pharisees, who thought they were righteous) to repentance, for the self-righteous did not recognize their sinfulness. But these **sinners** saw their need. This was Jesus' audience.

RELIGIOUS LEADERS ASK JESUS ABOUT FASTING / 2:18-22 / 41

At every turn, Jesus challenged the Pharisees' way of looking at life. They lived by appearance; he challenged motives. They constructed elaborate behavior patterns to indicate their holiness; Jesus taught that good behavior done for the wrong reasons has no spiritual value.

In response to their questions about fasting, Jesus turned the discussion from proper behavior to the reasons for fasting. Jesus made it clear that fasting was not a self-justifying action. It was right in its proper place, but there was also a proper place for feasting and joy. To further underscore this truth, Jesus added two other analogies (clothing repair and wineskin care). A worn item of clothing cannot be repaired with a new piece of cloth that shrinks when washed. A well-stretched wineskin filled with new wine will expand and burst when the wine ferments. So also the new spiritual age brought by Christ would not fit the old system; indeed it would burst the confines of the old system.

2:18 **John's disciples** refers to the remaining disciples of John the Baptist. These men and **the Pharisees** were fasting—that is, they were going without food in order to spend time in prayer repenting and humbling themselves before God. The Old Testament law set aside only one day a year as a required day of fasting for all Jews—the Day of Atonement (Leviticus 16:29). The Pharisees, however, fasted on Mondays and Thursdays (see Luke 18:12) as an act of piety, and most likely promoted this among the people.

John the Baptist was in prison, and his disciples erroneously sided with the Pharisees on this issue, fasting when they should have been feasting with Jesus. Naturally this caused a question: **"Why do John's disciples and the Pharisees fast, but your disciples don't fast?"**

2:19 The Pharisees fasted as a show of piety; the disciples of John the Baptist fasted as a sign of mourning for sin and to prepare for the Messiah's coming. But, like Jesus' disciples, they did not need to **fast** because the Messiah was with them! To be with Jesus the **groom** is as joyous as a wedding feast. Wedding guests do not mourn or fast; a wedding is a time of celebration and feasting. Likewise, Jesus' coming was a sign of celebration, not mourning and fasting. Jesus did not condemn fasting—he himself fasted (Luke 4:2). He emphasized that fasting must be done at the right time for the right reasons.

2:20 While Jesus walked the earth, his presence was a cause for celebration—the Messiah had come! The people did not need to mourn, they needed to rejoice. But Jesus knew that soon he (the groom) would be **taken away from them.**

The word **someday** refers to the day of Jesus' crucifixion. On that day, Jesus' disciples would indeed **fast** and mourn.

2:21 Jesus' arrival on earth ushered in a new time, a new covenant between God and people. The new covenant called for a new way of expressing personal faith. The newness of the gospel and its relationship to people could not be combined with the religion of Judaism any more than a piece of **unshrunk cloth** should be used as a patch on a worn-out garment. When the garment is washed, the patch will shrink, pull away from the old garment, and leave a bigger hole than before.

2:22 In Bible times, wine was not kept in glass bottles, but in goatskins sewn around the edges to form watertight bags called **wineskins.** New wine expanded as it fermented, stretching its wineskin. After the wine had aged, the old wineskin (that had gotten brittle with age and couldn't stretch anymore) would burst if more new wine was poured into it. **New wine,** therefore, **needs new wineskins.**

Like old wineskins, the Pharisees and indeed the entire religious system of Judaism were too rigid to accept Jesus, who could not be contained in their traditions or rules. They were the self-appointed guardians of the "old garments" and the "old wineskins." Christianity required new approaches and new structures.

THE DISCIPLES PICK WHEAT ON THE SABBATH / 2:23-28 / 45

Jewish life in Jesus' day revolved around the Sabbath. Elaborate laws had been designed so that everyone knew exactly how to "keep the Sabbath." The fourth clash between Jesus and the power of Satan recorded by Mark occurred on a Sabbath. The way Jesus kept the Sabbath irritated his critics to the point of fury. The religious leaders, by imposing a bewildering system of Sabbath laws, had in fact made themselves masters of the Sabbath and thus masters over the people. They made the seventh day dreaded rather than enjoyed.

By claiming the title "Lord of the Sabbath," Jesus was stating his own divinity. But this claim was also an affront to the position of the religious leaders. His remaking the Sabbath into a day of refreshment, worship, and healing pried open the tight-fisted control the Pharisees held on the people. No wonder Jesus' approach to the Sabbath led his enemies to plot his death.

2:23-24 Mark prepares us for a conflict with the opening words, **one Sabbath day.** Jesus, determined not to be confined to the Pharisees' petty rules, always seemed to be doing something against those rules on the Sabbath.

Jesus and the disciples were **walking through some grainfields.** As they walked, they **began breaking off heads of wheat** to eat. The **Pharisees**

(who apparently were following them around) pointed out that they were breaking the law against **harvesting grain on the Sabbath.** The Pharisees had established thirty-nine categories of actions forbidden on the Sabbath, based on interpretations of God's law and on Jewish custom. Harvesting was one of those forbidden actions. By breaking off heads of wheat to rub in their hands to eat, the disciples were technically harvesting, according to the religious leaders. However, Jesus and the disciples were picking grain because they were hungry (see Matthew 12:1), not because they wanted to harvest the grain for a profit. The disciples, who were not farmers, were not doing their daily work on the Sabbath. Neither were they stealing grain, for God's law allowed for this kind of sharing among his people (see Deuteronomy 23:25). Thus, though they may have been violating the Pharisees' rules, they were not breaking any divine law. The Pharisees, however, could not (and did not want to) see beyond their legalisms.

2:25-26 This story is recorded in 1 Samuel 21:1-6. Each week twelve consecrated loaves of bread, representing the twelve tribes of Israel, were placed on a table in the **house of God**, here meaning the Tabernacle. This bread was called the bread of the Presence. After its use, it was to be eaten only by priests. On one occasion, when fleeing from Saul, **David** and his men were given this **special bread** to eat by the **high priest.** The priest understood that the men's need was more important than ceremonial regulations. The loaves given to David were the old loaves that had just been replaced with fresh ones. Although the priests were the only ones allowed to eat this bread, God did not punish David because his need for food was more important than the priestly regulations.

The Pharisees knew the Scriptures thoroughly, yet Jesus' question, **"Haven't you ever read,"** reveals their ignorance of the true meaning of the Scriptures that they claimed to know so well. Yes, they had read this story many times, but they had obviously not discerned or applied its meaning.

Jesus justified his disciples' action on the grounds that they were hungry and that their need superseded the technicalities of ceremonial law. When Jesus compared himself and his disciples to David and his men, Jesus was saying, in effect, "If you condemn me, you must also condemn David." Jesus was not condoning disobedience to God's laws. Instead, he was emphasizing discernment and compassion in enforcing the ceremonial laws, something the self-righteous Pharisees did not comprehend. People's needs are more important than technicalities.

2:27 The Pharisees, having added all kinds of restrictions for the **Sabbath,** had completely forgotten God's purpose in creating the Sabbath. God mercifully provided the Sabbath as a day of rest for his people—a day to set aside the normal duties of the workweek and spend time resting and worshiping (Genesis 2:1-3). But the Pharisees had only succeeded in making the Sabbath an impossible burden. Jesus made clear that the Sabbath was **made to benefit people** by providing them a day of rest. God did not create people in order to place impossible restrictions and burdens on their lives.

2:28 Who created the Sabbath? God did. Therefore, because Jesus, the **Son of Man,** is God's Son, given authority and power by God himself, then he is **master even of the Sabbath.** By saying this, Jesus claimed to be greater than the law and above the law. To the Pharisees, this was heresy. They did not realize that Jesus, the divine Son of God, had created the Sabbath. The Creator is always greater than the creation; thus Jesus had the authority to overrule their traditions and regulations.

MARK 3

JESUS HEALS A MAN'S HAND ON THE SABBATH / 3:1-6 / 46
This episode completes a set of five escalating confrontations between Jesus and the religious leaders. Together, they summarize the points of tension leading to Jesus' rejection. The Pharisees were watching Jesus' actions on the Sabbath, anticipating that he might do something that would allow them to condemn him. Jesus thwarted their plan by involving them in the decision to heal the man. Their anger drove the Pharisees to break the Sabbath by plotting Jesus' murder. They committed the very sin they wanted to pin on him.

3:1-2 As was his regular custom (noted by the word **again**), **Jesus went into the synagogue** on the Sabbath (see 3:2). As Jesus entered, he **noticed a man**

with a deformed hand. Luke adds that it was the man's right hand (Luke 6:6). **Jesus' enemies** were the Pharisees (3:6). They were spying on Jesus with the intention of finding some fault in his actions so that they could **condemn him.**

Jesus' reputation for healing (even on the Sabbath, see 1:21-26) preceded him, but would he dare heal **on the Sabbath** with the Pharisees watching? God's law prohibited work on the seventh day of the week (Exodus 31:14-17); thus, the religious leaders allowed no healing to be done on the Sabbath unless the person's life was in danger. Healing, they argued, was practicing medicine, and a person could not practice his or her profession on the Sabbath.

3:3 Jesus didn't avoid a confrontation with his adversaries; he needed to make the important point that he would not be bound by the Pharisees' burdensome laws and that, as God, he would perform an act of kindness and healing, even on the Sabbath. So Jesus commanded the man with the deformed hand to **come** to the center of the crowd so everyone could see him and his deformity. The Pharisees would not miss anything of what Jesus was about to do.

3:4 To Jesus it didn't matter that this man's life was not threatened by the condition of his hand; it didn't matter that he could have waited until the next day to perform this healing legally. If Jesus had waited until another day, he would have been submitting to the Pharisees' authority, showing that their petty rules were equal to God's law. God is a God of people, not of rules.

So Jesus asked a rhetorical question: **"Is it legal to do good deeds on the Sabbath, or is it a day for doing harm?"** But the Pharisees **wouldn't answer him,** for to answer would have left them without an accusation to pin on Jesus. Their own laws allowed people to do good and to save life on the Sabbath—the farmer who could rescue his only sheep from a pit on the Sabbath knew that (see Matthew 12:11-12). How absurd, then, to refuse to allow a person to do good to another person on the Sabbath.

3:5 The religious leaders, the guardians of the Jewish faith, the keepers of the law, the teachers of the people—these men with **their hard hearts** were so spiritually and morally blind and hardened that they could not see who Jesus really was, and they could not even acknowledge a man's need and rejoice in his healing. No wonder Jesus was angry and **disturbed.** But the Pharisees' stubbornness didn't matter. Jesus planned to make his point and to heal this man. So Jesus told the man to **reach out** his hand.

In response to Jesus' command and with all eyes focused on him, the man stretched his hand out in front of him. The moment he did so, **it became normal again.** Jesus gave this man his life back. He could work again, and he no longer had to face the embarrassment of his deformity.

3:6 No particular action of Jesus is recorded; he told the man to move and with that movement, healing arrived. Jesus did nothing that could be called "work," but the Pharisees would not be swayed from their purpose. Jesus had embarrassed them. In their fury, the only option they saw was to kill him. Ironically, the Pharisees had accused Jesus of breaking their law about healing on the Sabbath, yet they themselves were discussing **plans for killing Jesus.** Their hatred, combined with their zeal for the law, drove them to plot murder—an act that was clearly against the law.

In an unlikely alliance, the Pharisees plotted with the **supporters of Herod** (or Herodians), a Jewish political party that hoped to restore Herod the Great's line to the throne. Their support of Rome's leadership over Palestine brought them into direct conflict with the Jewish religious leaders. These two groups had little in common—until Jesus posed a threat to them both. Jesus threatened the Pharisees' authority over the people; Jesus threatened the Herodians' political ambitions because his talk of a "kingdom" caused them to think that this popular and powerful man was planning to set himself up as a ruler. This would jeopardize their authority derived from Herod's power. To get rid of Jesus, the Pharisees needed the support of people with some influence with the secular leaders. Thus the Pharisees and Herodians, normally enemies, joined forces to discuss how to get rid of Jesus.

LARGE CROWDS FOLLOW JESUS / 3:7-12 / 47

In contrast to the rejection of Jesus by certain religious leaders, Mark described the attraction and adoration of Christ by the crowds. Mark's details provide us a picture of the context of Jesus' ministry. People were coming from literally every direction (from Tyre and Sidon in the north; from Judea, Jerusalem, and Idumea in the far south; from across the Jordan in the east). From this whirlwind of activity, Mark highlighted a number of smaller interactions between Jesus and those around him. The character of Jesus emerges under the constant scrutiny and demand of the crowds. Jesus was rarely alone.

3:7 Up to this point, Jesus had been aggressively confronting the Pharisees' hypocrisy. Then he decided to withdraw from the synagogue before a major confrontation developed, because it was not time for him to die. Jesus had many lessons still to teach his disciples and the people. So he **went out to the lake** (that is, to the Sea of Galilee), **followed by a huge crowd.** The actual twelve disciples had not yet been called, but those closest to Jesus were marked as following him. They had separated themselves from the religious establishment and were sharing in the glow of Jesus' popularity.

3:8 While Jesus was drawing fire from the religious leaders, he was gaining great popularity among the people—they came literally from all directions. News of Jesus had spread far beyond **Galilee.** People came from **Judea** (the southernmost region of Israel), **Jerusalem** (the key city of Israel, in Judea), **Idumea** (the region south of Judea), **east of the Jordan River** (which probably refers to Perea and Decapolis), and **Tyre and Sidon** (pagan cities to the far north on the coast of the Mediterranean Sea). The people came for various reasons with various motives. Some were simply curious, some sought healing, some wanted evidence to use against him, and others truly wanted to know if Jesus was the Messiah. Most of them could only dimly guess at the real meaning of what was happening among them.

3:9-10 Only Mark recorded this detail, suggesting that this was an eyewitness report from one of the disciples whom Jesus asked (possibly Peter). This **boat** was about the size of a rowboat. As Jesus walked along the shoreline with the crowds following, the little boat was rowed along close to the shore so it would always be ready in case the people **crowded** Jesus right into the water. Jesus'

reputation for healing had spread everywhere (see 3:8), and **many sick people** came from great distances just to **touch** Jesus and be healed. Picture people in the throng **crowding around** and shoving each other out of the way, reaching out at Jesus. They were so desperate to be healed that such rudeness made no difference.

3:11-12 Mark described a second encounter between Jesus and **evil spirits** (see also 1:23-24). The demons recognized who Jesus was, and whenever a possessed person saw Jesus, he or she would **fall down in front of him,** not in worship, but **shrieking** to everyone, **"You are the Son of God!"** The demons recognized Jesus and feared him (see James 2:19). They knew his power, and they were aware that he had the authority to cast them out of their lodgings (inside a person) and even to send them away permanently (see 5:9-10). Jesus didn't want or need the demons to endorse him. His true identity would be revealed at the right time, at his resurrection. Thus, he spoke sternly to the demons and **warned them not to say who he was** (see also note 1:25).

Ironically, the demons recognized who Jesus was; the people didn't. Jesus warned the evil (unclean) spirits not to reveal his identity because he did not want them to reinforce a popular misconception. The huge crowds were looking for a political and military leader who would free them from Rome's control, and they thought that the Messiah predicted by the Old Testament prophets would be this kind of man. Jesus wanted to teach the people about the kind of Messiah he really was, because he was far different from what they expected. Christ's Kingdom is spiritual. It begins, not with the overthrow of governments, but with the overthrow of sin in people's hearts.

JESUS CHOOSES THE TWELVE DISCIPLES / 3:13-19 / 48

Earlier in this Gospel, Jesus invited several persons to follow him (1:16-19; 2:14). Soon hundreds and thousands of others also tracked Jesus' steps. Some were curious, some critical, and some were committed. From among all of them Jesus chose twelve.

The better we know the disciples, the more we come to see that God might actually choose us, too. Grace does not make humanness a disqualifying characteristic. As disappointing as the disciples may have been, they leave room for us to hope. When we are aware of our unworthiness to merit God's mercy and love, we are in the best position to experience what he can do for us.

3:13 Jesus left the shore of the Sea of Galilee and **went up on a mountain** (probably referring to the hill country of Galilee instead of to one particular mountain). Luke records that Jesus "prayed to God

all night" (Luke 6:12) before calling **the ones he wanted to go with him**—that is, the twelve disciples. Jesus did not take volunteers; he chose and called those he wanted. Jesus *wanted* these men;

so he **called** them, and **they came to him.** They did not hesitate to obey.

3:14-15 Jesus had many disciples (learners), but he **selected twelve of them to be his regular companions, calling them apostles** (messengers). The apostles were Jesus' inner circle. He gave them special training, and he sent them out with his own authority. From the hundreds of people who followed Jesus from place to place, he especially selected these twelve to receive the most intense training. We see the impact of these men throughout the rest of the New Testament, for they started the Christian church.

The choice of twelve men is highly symbolic. The number twelve corresponds to the twelve tribes of Israel (Matthew 19:28), showing the continuity between the old religious system and the new one based on Jesus' message. Jesus looked upon this as the gathering of the true people of God. These men were the righteous remnant who would carry on the work the twelve tribes were chosen to do—to build the community of God.

Jesus did not choose these twelve to be his disciples because of their faith—it often faltered. He didn't choose them because of their talent and ability—no one stood out with unusual ability. The disciples represented a wide range of backgrounds and life experiences, but apparently they may have had no more leadership potential than those who were not chosen. The one characteristic they all shared was their willingness to obey Jesus.

The apostles remained with Jesus for the purpose of being trained, so that Jesus could then send them out as his ambassadors or representatives **to preach.** Their message was the Good News of salvation; they were to proclaim that message publicly and with the authority given to them by Christ himself. Not only did the disciples go out trained in the message of the gospel, they also had Jesus' **authority to cast out demons.** This power was given to the disciples by Jesus; it was delegated authority. The disciples could speak the word, and God's power would cast out the demons.

3:16 Mark listed these disciples by name or family name ("son of"). It is interesting to note the almost complete silence of the Gospels and the Epistles as to the future work of the vast majority of these twelve men. We know some about Peter, James, and John in the book of Acts; we know from 3:19 that Judas would betray Jesus. Otherwise, the Bible is silent about many of the disciples' activities. One reason for this silence is that many of the twelve apostles, according to tradition, went far beyond the regions focused on in the book of Acts and the Epistles.

The first name recorded was **Simon,** whom Jesus **renamed Peter** (see John 1:42). Jesus gave him a name in addition to the one he already had—he did not change Simon's name. Sometimes Peter is referred to as Cephas. "Peter" is the Greek equivalent of the Aramaic *Cephas*—a word meaning stone or rock. Peter had been a fisherman (1:16). He became one of three in Jesus' core group among the disciples. He also confessed that Jesus was the Messiah (8:29). Although Peter would deny ever knowing Jesus, he would eventually become a leader in the Jerusalem church, write two letters that appear in the Bible (1 and 2 Peter), and be crucified for his faith.

3:17 James and John had also been fishermen (1:19). James would become the first martyr for the Christian faith (Acts 12:2). John would write the Gospel of John, the letters of 1, 2, and 3 John, and the book of Revelation. They may have been related to Jesus (distant cousins); thus, at one point they requested special places in Christ's Kingdom (10:35, 37). These brothers were nicknamed **Sons of Thunder.** Scripture gives glimpses of these men, revealing that they were somewhat short-tempered and judgmental; for example, they wanted to call fire down from heaven on an inhospitable Samaritan village (Luke 9:52-56). Thus Jesus gave them an appropriate name.

3:18-19 Andrew was Peter's brother and also a fisherman (1:16). Andrew had been a disciple of John the Baptist. He left John to follow Jesus, and then brought his brother Simon Peter to Jesus (John 1:35-39). **Philip** was the fourth to meet Jesus (John 1:43). Philip probably knew Andrew and Peter because they were from the same town, Bethsaida (John 1:44). Philip then brought **Bartholomew** (also called Nathanael) as recorded in John 1:45-47. Bartholomew at first rejected Jesus because Jesus was from Nazareth. But upon meeting Jesus, his attitude changed (John 1:49). **Matthew** was also known as Levi. He had been a tax collector (Mark 2:14). He had been a despised outcast because of his dishonest career, but he abandoned that corrupt (though lucrative) way of life to follow Jesus. He would later write the Gospel of Matthew. **Thomas** is sometimes called "Doubting Thomas" because he doubted Jesus' resurrection (John 20:24-25). But he also loved the Lord and was a man of great courage (John 11:16). Thomas was tough and committed, even if he tended to be pessimistic. Thus, when the other disciples said that Jesus was alive, Thomas didn't believe them. However, when Thomas saw and touched the living Christ, doubting Thomas became believing Thomas. **James** is designated as **son of Alphaeus**

to differentiate him from James the son of Zebedee (and brother of John) in 3:17. **Thaddaeus** is also called "Judas son of James" (see Luke 6:16; Acts 1:13). **Simon** was probably not a member of the party of Zealots, for that political party did not appear until A.D. 68. Most likely the word **Zealot** used here indicates zeal for God's honor and not extreme nationalism; it was an affectionate nickname.

The name **Iscariot** is probably a compound word meaning "the man from Kerioth." Thus,

Judas's hometown was Kerioth in southern Judea (see Joshua 15:25), making him the only one of the Twelve who was not from Galilee. It was **Judas,** son of Simon Iscariot (John 6:71), who betrayed Jesus to his enemies and then committed suicide (Luke 22:47-48; Matthew 27:3-5).

Mark presents a paradoxical picture of the disciples. They doubted and they failed, yet they were used to build the church. Some died for him, one betrayed him. The message is, what kind of disciple will you be?

RELIGIOUS LEADERS ACCUSE JESUS OF GETTING HIS POWER FROM SATAN / 3:20-30 / 74

Mark never allowed his readers to get far from the fact that Jesus' ministry was constantly being opposed. He balanced Jesus' choice of disciples with the evolving group of opposition. The religious leadership chose to add the accusation of demon possession. He neutralized his enemies' charge with a counterattack. How, he asked them, could he possibly be serving Satan when his presence and his actions were causing such devastating damage to Satan's kingdom? Further, he pointed out that their failure to recognize the Spirit, under whose influence he was actually operating, indicated that they were committing the unforgivable sin. By identifying the Holy Spirit as Satan in Jesus' life, the religious leaders were committing unspeakable blasphemy.

3:20 The **house** Jesus entered was most likely in Capernaum and may have, once again, been Peter's house. As had happened twice previously, **crowds began to gather** (see 1:33; 2:1-2). Again, the demand of the people in the crowd made it impossible for Jesus and the disciples to have any quiet, to spend time in training, or even **to eat.**

3:21 Thinking Jesus had gone **out of his mind,** his family came to him. John recorded that Jesus' brothers did not believe in him (John 7:5), although some later did believe (Acts 1:14). In fact, Jesus' brother James became one of the leaders in the church in Jerusalem and the writer of the book of James. Mary believed that her son was special, but she didn't understand his mission. Perhaps she thought the situation was getting out of hand, and she needed to protect her son from himself, from the demands of his ministry, or even from the relentless crowds. Jesus' family decided that they needed to **take him home with them.**

3:22 These **teachers of religious law** probably had been summoned by the Pharisees and Herodians who were already in league to destroy Jesus (3:6). The teachers and Pharisees could not deny the reality of Jesus' miracles and supernatural power—he had indeed been driving out demons. But they refused to believe that his power was from God because then they would have had to accept him as

the Messiah. Their pride would not let them do that. So in an attempt to destroy Jesus' popularity among the people, the teachers accused him of being **possessed by Satan, the prince of demons.** That is why, they said, he was able to **cast out demons.**

3:23-26 Jesus first addressed their second accusation—that he was driving out demons by Satan's power—by simply asking, **"How can Satan cast out Satan?"** By the question, Jesus implied that it is impossible for Satan to cast out himself (or his own followers, demons). Why would Satan work against himself? Following the obvious conclusion of the accusation—that Satan was driving himself out of people—Jesus indicates that would then mean there was civil war in the kingdom of evil. No king would throw his own soldiers out of his kingdom; neither would Satan throw his soldiers out of his kingdom. His kingdom would then **collapse.** In the same way, a home, with people working against one another, is **doomed.** The answer to Jesus' question is that Satan doesn't and would not cast out his own, for to do so would mean the end of his power. **He would never survive.** The teachers' charge that Jesus was driving out demons by Satan's power was obviously false. But Jesus wasn't finished.

3:27 This picture reflects a situation in the ancient

world where wealthy people's homes were virtual fortresses, and their servants could form a small army. Jesus pictured Satan as the wealthy man and his demons as his servants and possessions. The only way those possessions could be carried off would be for someone to first tie up the strong man—the only way for the demons to be cast out is for someone to first limit Satan's power. Satan would not do that to himself.

Although God permits Satan to work in our world, God is in control. Jesus, as God, has "tied up" Satan; Jesus is able to drive out demons and end their terrible work in people's lives. As such, every exorcism was a binding of Satan; one day Satan will be bound forever (Revelation 20:10). Jesus was not in league with Satan, as the teachers of the law tried to claim; rather, he had overpowered Satan by refusing his temptations and by constantly freeing people held in Satan's grasp—either through demon possession or through the power of sin.

3:28-30 I assure you is a recurring phrase used only by Jesus prior to a solemn warning or pronouncement. No longer was Jesus reasoning with his accusers; he was giving them a solemn warning. Jesus had just been accused of being in league with Satan and had soundly refuted those charges. Here he had a few words for these so-called teachers of religious law, the Jewish leaders.

First he made the incredible promise that **any sin can be forgiven, including blasphemy.** Too often people miss this promise and worry about the warning in the next verse. But the fact is, those who believe in Jesus will be forgiven of all sins (evil acts, wrong actions, good actions not done, evil thoughts, evil motives, etc.) and of all blasphemies (evil words said against God). When there is

confession and repentance, no sin is beyond God's forgiveness.

There is one sin, however, that cannot be forgiven. **Anyone who blasphemes against the Holy Spirit will never be forgiven.** Blasphemy against the Holy Spirit refers not so much to a single action or word as to an attitude. Those who defiantly deny Jesus' divine power and instead attribute it to Satan are blaspheming the Holy Spirit (see also Matthew 12:32). Jesus was not talking about rejecting him, but of rejecting the power behind him. Jewish history tells us that Jesus' generation acknowledged that he performed miracles but that he did it by the power of the devil. Thus, the Jewish leaders rejected him as being the Messiah and thereby blasphemed the Holy Spirit.

Jesus' words were addressed directly to these teachers of religious law **because they were saying he had an evil spirit.** They had blasphemed the Spirit by attributing the power by which Christ did miracles to Satan instead of to the Holy Spirit. This is the unforgivable sin—the deliberate refusal to acknowledge God's power in Christ. It indicates an irreversible hardness of heart. Deliberate, ongoing rejection of the work of the Holy Spirit is blasphemy because it is rejecting God himself. The religious leaders accused Jesus of blasphemy (see also 14:63-64), but ironically they were the guilty ones when they looked Jesus in the face and accused him of being possessed by Satan.

Sometimes believers worry that they have accidentally committed this unforgivable sin. But only those who have turned their back on God and rejected all faith have any need to worry. Jesus said they can't be forgiven—not because their sin is worse than any other, but because they will never ask for forgiveness.

JESUS DESCRIBES HIS TRUE FAMILY / 3:31-35 / 76
Jesus turned his rejection by his family into a compassionate invitation to recognize his true nature. They came to claim him as their family member; he challenged them to be members of God's true family. The conflict between Jesus and his family continues in our lives. Do we avoid Jesus' claim on us as the powerful Lord by reducing him to friendship status? Jesus is our friend and brother, but he is also our Lord. By treating him as any less, we may be neutralizing his rightful ownership of our thoughts and actions.

3:31-33 This verse continues from 3:20-21 when Jesus' family arrived to take him home because he was "out of his mind." **Jesus' mother** was Mary (Luke 1:30-31), and his **brothers** were probably the other children Mary and Joseph had after Jesus (see also 6:3).

Apparently Mary had gathered her family, and they went to find Jesus. Mary hoped to use her personal relationship with Jesus to influence him. She saw her son occupied in a busy ministry that was taking its toll on him—to the point that he had no time to eat (3:20). They arrived at the house but could not get in. So they **stood outside** and sent their message in to Jesus. Obviously Jesus' family thought that their relationship with him precluded all others and that he would immediately answer their request.

Instead of immediately going outside to see what his family members wanted, Jesus looked at the crowd and asked an odd question, **"Who is my mother? Who are my brothers?"** Jesus knew why his family had come, and he wasn't about to be dragged home because they thought he'd gone crazy. So he used their visit as a lesson in discipleship. A relationship with Jesus is not limited to those in his immediate family. Jesus opened this relationship to all people.

3:34-35 Jesus looked at those seated around him (not the entire crowd, but probably his disciples who were seated closest to him) and answered his own question. The types of people who can have a relationship with him are those who listen, learn, believe, and follow. In these words, **"These are my mother and brothers,"** Jesus

explained that in his spiritual family, the relationships are ultimately more important and longer lasting than those formed in his physical family. The key to discipleship in Mark's Gospel is radical obedience to God's will. While Jesus looked upon his disciples seated around him as members of his family, he broadened the scope to include **anyone who does God's will.**

Jesus was not denying his responsibility to his earthly family. On the contrary, he was criticizing the religious leaders for not following the Old Testament command to honor their parents (Matthew 15:1-9). He provided for his mother's security as he hung on the cross (John 19:25-27). His mother and brothers were present in the upper room at Pentecost (Acts 1:14). Instead, Jesus was pointing out that spiritual relationships are as binding as physical ones, and he was paving the way for a new community of believers to be formed as Jesus' spiritual family. This family would be characterized by love; the members should desire to be together, work together, and share one anothers' burdens.

MARK 4

JESUS TELLS THE PARABLE OF THE FOUR SOILS / 4:1-9 / 77

In the first three chapters, Mark recorded the quick pace of Jesus' ministry. In this chapter, Mark turned his attention to the content of Jesus' teaching, including a series of stories. Jesus' stories entertained the many who were merely curious, while they enlightened the few who genuinely sought to know God. These earthy stories have profound spiritual applications. The story of the farmer, seed, and soils describes how the human heart responds to the truth.

4:1 Again Jesus **began teaching by the lakeshore** (of the Sea of Galilee). The crowd that gathered around him was so large that he **got into a boat** and sat in it out on the lake. Jesus **spoke from there.**

4:2-3 Jesus used many **stories,** or parables, when teaching the crowds. These stories used familiar scenes to explain spiritual truths. A parable compares something familiar to something unfamiliar. It compels listeners to discover truth, while at the same time conceals the truth from those too lazy or too stubborn to see it.

This story gave a familiar picture to Jesus' audience—a **farmer** planting **seed,** with the resulting increase dependent on the condition of the soil. In ancient Israel, seed was sown by hand. As the

farmer walked across the field, he would throw handfuls of seed from a large bag slung across his shoulders. No matter how skillful, no farmer could keep some of his seed from falling by the wayside, from being scattered among rocks and thorns, or from being carried off by the wind. So the farmer would throw the seed liberally, and enough would fall on good ground to ensure the harvest.

4:4-7 Some of the seeds **fell on a footpath.** The hard and compacted soil of the road made it impossible for the seed to penetrate. So it sat on top, as tempting morsels for **the birds that came and ate** the seeds. (In 4:15 we learn that these "birds" represent Satan.) Some of that seed **fell on shallow soil with underlying rock.** Unlike the wayside, the rocky places had some soil to accept the seed, but not much. The seed **sprang up quickly** in the shallow soil, but the sun took the moisture out so rapidly that the young plants **wilted**. Some of the farmer's seed **fell among thorns.** Thorns rob the sprouts of nutrition, water, light, and space. Thus, when the thorns grew up, the good seed was **choked** out.

4:8-9 However, some of the seed landed in **fertile soil.** This seed had the depth, space, and moisture to grow, multiply, and produce a crop. A farmer would be happy to see his crop multiply even ten times—**thirty, sixty,** or a **hundred times** would be an incredible yield for it would mean even more to plant and harvest in the coming year.

Jesus pointed out that "listening" makes fertile soil for the message of the Kingdom. If we bear fruit, it is proof that we have listened. If others bear fruit, it shows that the seed we have planted has taken root in their heart. Those **willing to hear** are those who will do a deeper kind of listening with the mind and heart that is necessary in order to gain spiritual understanding. Some people in the crowd were only curious about Jesus, a few were looking for evidence to use against him, and others truly wanted to learn and grow. Jesus' words were for the honest seekers. Those who honestly seek God's will have spiritual hearing, so they will be able to **listen and understand.**

JESUS EXPLAINS THE PARABLE OF THE FOUR SOILS / 4:10-25 / 78

The story of the soils was one of many Jesus used to create questions in the minds of his followers. Later, in a smaller group, Jesus explained why he used these stories, called parables, and what they meant. Although Jesus pointed out that the parables kept some people in ignorance, he willingly explained their meaning to the disciples. Any hearer who continued to be ignorant or confused did so because he or she refused to learn. Those who failed to understand the parables were not ready to obey the truth they taught.

4:10 When Jesus got away from the crowd and was alone with his true followers (the twelve disciples and the larger group of believers), a more intimate question-and-answer period followed. Perhaps these close followers did not want to reveal their ignorance about Jesus' words in front of the entire crowd. So, as soon as they were alone with Jesus, his followers **asked** him about the **stories** in general, and particularly the story of the four soils.

4:11 The **you** to whom Jesus spoke was the group of his true followers. They had been given a special gift by God, for only they—among the crowds around Jesus—**were permitted to understand the secret about the Kingdom of God.** They understood, though only partially, the **secret** that God's Kingdom had arrived among them in the person of Jesus. The Kingdom of God had been a "secret" to the prophets of the Old Testament because, though they wrote about it, they did not understand it (see Romans 16:25-26). The believers who knew Jesus personally received spiritual insight that illuminated the secret so that it was no longer a mystery to them.

Jesus was aware of the unbelief and outright hostility of many of his listeners. The **outsiders** have not yet accepted the message of salvation and may never do so. Thus, for them everything will remain concealed. Those "outside" (the religious leaders and the vast majority of the crowd) would

never comprehend the secret, for they would not come to God for the answer. Choosing not to believe in Jesus as their Messiah, they would not be able to understand his Kingdom. The parables allowed Jesus to give spiritual food to those who hungered for it; but for the others, Isaiah's prophecy would explain their situation.

4:12 God told Isaiah that people would **see** but not **perceive,** and **hear** but not **understand** (Isaiah 6:9); that same kind of reaction was witnessed by Jesus. The story of the farmer was an accurate picture of people's reactions to all of Jesus' stories. By quoting from the prophet Isaiah, Jesus was explaining to this inner group of followers that the crowd resembled the Israelites about whom Isaiah had written. God had told Isaiah that the people would listen but not learn from his message because their hearts had hardened beyond repentance. Yet God still sent Isaiah with the message because, even though the nation itself would not repent and would reap judgment, some individuals would listen. Jesus came to the Israelites hundreds of years after Isaiah, but the scenario was the same. Most would not repent because their hearts were hardened; but a few would listen, turn from their sins, and believe.

The deafness to the message did not mean the message was false or that the messenger was somehow at fault. It is not for us to understand why some believe and some do not; instead, we are simply to continue to trust in God and proclaim his message. Neither Isaiah's nor Jesus' audiences were denied the opportunity to **turn from their sins and be forgiven.** Instead, the point was clearly made that refusing to listen would mean inability to perceive and understand anything Jesus had to say.

4:13 People cannot see without the illumination of the Holy Spirit. To **understand** is like formerly blind eyes being made to see. By nature, humans are spiritually blind. But the spiritual insight given by the Holy Spirit illumines Jesus' stories and indeed all of God's word so that believers can truly "perceive" and "understand" what God has to say (4:9). Jesus was speaking to those to whom the "secret" had been revealed (4:11); thus, they shouldn't have needed any explanation at all.

4:14 The **farmer** was Jesus (see Matthew 13:37) and—by extension—anyone after him who would bring **God's message.** The seed that is sown is the word of God (4:3).

4:15 The story reveals people's varying responses to the gospel message. The attitude or condition of their hearts would govern their response. The word makes no impression on the **"hard-path"** people. **Satan** (like the birds, 4:4) **comes at once and takes it away.** Perhaps the person feels no need in his or her heart, no desire for anything other than this life, no guilt of sin or need of forgiveness. Satan has no trouble with these people.

4:16-17 The **"rocky-soil"** people **hear the message and receive it with joy** (4:5). These people receive the Good News of the gospel because of the promises offered. They initially show some promise of growth. These people understand some of the basics but do not allow God's truth to work its way into their souls and make a difference in their lives—**their roots don't go very deep** and thus **they wilt.** When trouble comes (the hot sun, 4:6), they fall away.

4:18-19 **"Thorny-ground"** people **hear and accept the Good News** and allow it to take root in their hearts, giving hope of a harvest. But "thorns" grow up and choke out the growing seed—distractions and conflicts rob new believers of time to reflect on and digest God's word in order to grow from it, as well as robbing guidance and support from interaction with other Christians. Jesus described the thorns: **cares of this life, lure of wealth,** and **desire for nice things.** Worldly cares (no matter how important or how minor), the false sense of security brought on by prosperity, and the desire for material things (including anything that serves

to distract a person) plagued first-century disciples as they do us today. Daily routines overcrowd and materialistic pursuits distract believers **so no crop is produced.**

4:20 But other people are like the **good soil**—they **hear, accept,** and **produce a huge harvest.** These are the true disciples—those who have accepted Jesus, believed his words, and allowed him to make a difference in their lives.

4:21 In ancient Israel, a **lamp** was a lighted wick in a clay bowl that was full of oil. The lamp was not lit and then put under a closed place. Instead, the lamp was lit and **placed on a stand, where its light will shine** and illuminate the room. The disciples may have wondered why Jesus seemed to be deliberately hiding the truth of the gospel through his stories. Perhaps they thought that if the word was going to fall on hard hearts, then why should they sow it so liberally? Shouldn't they just limit their teaching to those who were ready and eager to listen? "No," explained Jesus, "I am not deliberately trying to hide the truth from people. That would be like lighting a lamp and then putting it under a bowl. Why then light the lamp at all? If I am hiding the truth, there is no reason for me to teach." The purpose of the stories was not to conceal the truth, but to reveal it; the stories explained spiritual truths in everyday terms. Thus the stories do not obscure, they clarify—but only to those who are willing to listen and believe.

4:22 Jesus continued his explanation for his use of parables. Although the truth may be **hidden** or **secret** for a while, it will not remain so. One day the truth will be **brought to light.** This could refer either to Jesus' resurrection and ascension (when his followers would fully understand Jesus' words) or the Second Coming. Jesus' followers did not understand everything about Jesus at that time, but all their questions would be answered one day.

4:23 This saying, which repeats 4:9, often concluded Jesus' important statements. As explained in 4:9 above, Jesus spoke of a deeper kind of listening: hearing not with the ears, but with the mind and heart. Only then could the hearers gain spiritual understanding from his stories.

4:24 Because the stories are so important in what they teach, Jesus warned the people to **pay attention** to his words. We must treasure the words of Jesus. Those who heard, understood, and then shared with others would be given even more understanding to pass along. Believers are responsible to use well their God-given understanding, insight, and opportunities to share the gospel. Whether they have little or much, that is not nearly as important as what is done with what they have. "The more you do this, the more you will understand"—a person's openness and perception of the Kingdom message will bring great rewards. Ultimately, believers will receive eternal blessings in heaven.

4:25 The people who listen and understand are **those who are open to** Jesus' **teaching.** To them God will give **more understanding.** They will continue to grow because they let God's word make a difference in their lives. In contrast, **those who are not listening** will lose whatever they had. Jesus' words here may have been directed to the Jews who had no understanding of Jesus and would lose even what they had—that is, their privileged status as God's people. Or Jesus might have meant that when people reject him, their hardness of heart drives away or renders useless even the little understanding they had. Eventually, any opportunity to share in God's Kingdom will be **taken away** completely.

JESUS TELLS THE PARABLE OF THE GROWING SEED / 4:26-29 / 79

Many of Jesus' stories sprouted from similes. He focused on what people knew or saw and then pointed to a similarity between that and a characteristic of the Kingdom of God. The way Jesus made use of his surroundings demonstrates that all of creation is filled with lessons and pointers. This story teaches us that spiritual growth cannot be measured by a stopwatch. The Kingdom of God may be planted in us in an instant, but its growth becomes apparent only with the passing of time and the practice of faithfulness.

4:26-28 This story about the **Kingdom of God,** recorded only by Mark, reveals that spiritual growth is a continual, gradual process that is finally consummated in a harvest of spiritual maturity. We can begin to understand the process of spiritual growth by comparing it to the slow but certain growth of a plant. Even though the farmer did not understand the actual process of growth, his ignorance does not stop it from happening— **the seeds sprouted and grew.** In the same way, the Kingdom of God begins in a person's life with a seed of understanding that takes root in the good soil of a ready heart. That seed sprouts and grows into strong faith. But how that happens is God's responsibility.

The disciples, wondering about the difficult mission ahead of them, were being told by Jesus that they need not worry about how the Kingdom would grow. That part was up to God. Their job was to plant the seed. With his coming to earth, Jesus planted the Kingdom of God, and God would bring that harvest to fruition.

4:29 The farmer lets the seed grow in the fields and goes about his other work (4:26-27), but **as soon as the grain is ready,** he has work to do. **The farmer comes and harvests it with a sickle** (a curved blade mounted in a short handle). Likewise, the time will come when God will intervene decisively into the world's affairs.

JESUS TELLS THE PARABLE OF THE MUSTARD SEED / 4:30-34 / 81

Mark concluded this sampling of Jesus' stories with a second lesson about the Kingdom of God. He began the chapter with the story of the four soils, which illustrates the variety of responses to the gospel. The two following stories focus on what happens when the truth finds a receptive heart. The story of the growing seed illustrates the growth rate of the Kingdom of God. The story of the mustard seed illustrates the surprising size of the growth from such a small beginning.

4:30 As if repeating from 4:26, Jesus prepared again to explain the Kingdom of God in a story. No one story could completely describe God's Kingdom in all its aspects, so Jesus employed several of them. The crowds, and even some of the disciples, were expecting the Messiah to be a political leader who would free Israel from Rome. The only "kingdom" they could picture was an earthly one. So Jesus attempted to clarify his Kingdom even further for them.

4:31-32 In this story, Jesus stressed that his Kingdom would have a small beginning—indeed, it began with Jesus alone and, upon his ascension, was left in the care of twelve apostles and a few hundred other followers. Jesus compared this beginning to the **mustard seed**, which was the **smallest** seed a farmer used. The mustard seed was so small that it would take almost twenty thousand seeds to make one ounce. From this very tiny seed would grow a large shrub—the largest shrub among all the herbs that the farmer would plant in his garden. A mustard shrub could grow ten to twelve feet in just a few weeks. Jesus' point was that just as a tiny seed can grow into **one of the largest of plants,** so God's Kingdom can begin with a few people who truly believe and grow into such greatness that, upon Christ's second coming, it will overpower the entire earth and rule supremely forever. For the disciples, and for us, this story meant that size or relative power does not indicate final results. God's Kingdom would take root and grow across the world and through the years. This would be no political coup; the Kingdom would grow slowly but surely in people's hearts, making a difference in people's lives and preparing them for life to come in God's eternal Kingdom.

4:33-34 Mark made clear that he did not record all of Jesus' **stories**—there were probably too many to record. Jesus adapted his methods to his audience's ability and desire to **understand.** He didn't speak in stories to confuse people, but to challenge sincere seekers to discover the meaning of his words. As explained in 4:2-3, Jesus spoke in stories to the crowds (see also 4:1), but **when he was alone with his disciples, he explained the meaning to them** (see also 4:10). The disciples here are specifically the Twelve.

JESUS CALMS THE STORM / 4:35-41 / 87

In this section, Mark has described the intense encounters between Jesus and various groups (religious leaders, crowds, his own family) and given us a series of teaching stories. In this section, he recalled a series of miracles that demonstrated Jesus' power over the natural elements, the spiritual realm, and the human body. He presented a strong case for Jesus' startling uniqueness and divine nature.

Mark's details of Jesus calming the storm are absent in the accounts of Matthew and Luke. These details indicate that Mark used Peter as a source. He gives intimate facts that only an eyewitness would have known. Believers today profess trust in Jesus' power over the storms of life, but many fall short of demonstrating that trust when the storms arrive. Saying we believe that Jesus can help us takes on a whole new meaning when we actually depend on him for help.

4:35 When evening came, Jesus suggested that he and the disciples **cross to the other side of the lake**—that is, to the east side of the Sea of Galilee. The boat probably belonged to one of the fishermen in the group, most likely to Peter. For Peter to set sail in the evening was not unusual because he was used to fishing at night (see John 21:3). Fishing was best then; storms usually came in the afternoon.

Thus, when Jesus finished speaking, the disciples pulled up the anchor and set sail. Jesus' ministry was never without purpose. He was crossing the sea in order to enter a new area of ministry. Along the way, the disciples would be taught an unforgettable lesson about his power.

4:36 A few people in the crowd probably expected Jesus to come ashore to offer more healing or teaching. But Jesus, human as he was, needed rest. So he left the **crowds behind** when the boat set sail.

The detail that **other boats followed** is recorded only in Mark and signifies an eyewitness account—perhaps from Peter who sailed the boat and had to watch out for these other boats as they made their way out into the lake. (Josephus, an ancient historian, wrote that there were usually more than three hundred fishing boats on the Sea of Galilee at one time.) The other boats accompanying Jesus may have been filled with persistent followers. The tiny detail gives us a picture of God's grace—many people on these other boats were also saved when Jesus stilled the storm.

4:37 The Sea of Galilee is an unusual body of water. It is relatively small (thirteen miles long, seven miles wide); but it is 150 feet deep, and the shoreline is 680 feet below sea level. Because it is below sea level and surrounded by mountains, it is susceptible to sudden storms. Winds sweeping across the land come up and over the mountains, creating downdrafts over the lake. Combined with a thunderstorm that appears suddenly over the surrounding mountains, the water stirs into violent twenty-foot waves. The disciples had not foolishly set out in a storm. In fact, they usually didn't encounter storms at night and did not see this one coming. Even though several of these men were expert fishermen and knew how to handle a boat, they had been caught without warning by this **fierce storm.** Their peril was real as they battled huge waves that nearly swamped their vessel.

4:38 While this was happening, **Jesus was sleeping at the back of the boat.** How Jesus could sleep during this storm indicates his complete exhaustion and reveals his human nature. That the noise, the violent rocking of the boat, and the cold spray of the water didn't awaken him gives us a glimpse of the physical drain on Jesus throughout his earthly ministry.

The disciples had embarked on this journey at Jesus' request after a long day. They were probably tired too, but they had set sail anyway. Then, of all things, a storm blew in—one that was threatening to sink the boat and drown them. And Jesus was sleeping through it! They **woke him** and asked, **"Teacher, don't you even care that we are going to drown?"** Their words were more of a criticism than a call for help. How easy it is for us to complain and criticize God for not coming to our aid, rather than making our request and then trusting him to answer.

Although the disciples had witnessed many miracles, they panicked in this storm. Added to that, they revealed that they completely misunderstood their teacher. They had seen Jesus perform great miracles of compassion, but they dared to ask if he cared about them at all. Their question was rude; their misunderstanding was deep.

4:39 Jesus, abruptly awakened from a deep sleep, arose and without speaking to the disciples spoke instead to the elements. Standing in the stern of the rocking ship, Jesus **rebuked the wind and said to the water, "Quiet down!"** The disciples' were shocked at the power of their teacher to speak and control the ocean waves. But they should not have been surprised. The storm was out of control, their fears were out of control, but Jesus was never out of control. He has power over all the forces of nature, and he listens to the appeals of those who love him.

4:40 The disciples had seen Jesus do incredible miracles, but they hadn't taken their knowledge of his power and carried it to its logical conclusion. Jesus responded, **"Why are you so afraid? Do you still not have faith in me?"** They wanted him to do something; he wanted them to trust him! Despite all that the disciples had seen and heard thus far, and despite their belief in Jesus as the Messiah, they still had not grasped that Jesus was himself God, given God's power and authority over all of creation.

4:41 But the disciples still didn't understand, as betrayed by their question, **"Who is this man?"** They should have known because this miracle clearly displayed the truth of Jesus' divine identity. Being with the human, compassionate Jesus was fine; being with the powerful and supernatural Son of God was terrifying.

When we become Christians, we enter a cosmic struggle because Satan hates people to believe in Jesus. Satan's limited power is launched against believers individually and the church in general, hoping to sink us to the depths of the sea. But we have the ultimate power on our side, and the final victory is assured. Jesus should be our Savior, to whom we turn with all our needs and fears, knowing that he does care and will help.

MARK 5

JESUS SENDS DEMONS INTO A HERD OF PIGS / 5:1-20 / 88

Though we may emphasize the love for the world that God expressed through Christ, we sometimes fail to apply it to individual people. That Jesus permitted the demons to enter the large herd of pigs strikes us as odd, and we might be surprised by Jesus' disregard for personal property. Jesus' action, however, demonstrated the value of the man possessed by the demons. The demons, not Jesus, incited the pigs in their suicidal stampede.

By any standard, the value Jesus places on each one of us cannot be measured. He did not hesitate to present his own life in exchange for our salvation. The story about the herd of pigs dramatically contrasts the purposes of God and the purposes of Satan for people. To Jesus, the crazed man was worth saving. To Satan, he was a soul targeted for destruction. Upon entering the pigs, the demons immediately revealed their destructive intent. They accomplished in the pigs what they had been doing in the man.

5:1 The land of the Gerasenes was located southeast of the Sea of Galilee. The precise location is uncertain because this area is sometimes written as "Gerasenes," "Gergesenes," or "Gadarenes" in various manuscripts. However, some scholars cite evidence that favors "country of the Gerasenes," probably referring to a small town called Gersa (modern-day Kersa or Kours). Others prefer "Gadarenes," citing the town of Gadara, one of the most important cities of the region. Gadara was a member of the Ten Towns (see 5:20). These ten cities with independent governments were largely inhabited by Gentiles, which would explain the herd of pigs (5:11). The Jews did not raise pigs because, according to Jewish law, pigs were unclean and thus unfit to eat.

Whatever the exact location of their landing, the point is that Jesus had planned to go there. This was Gentile territory, revealing a new direction for his ministry.

5:2 It is difficult to picture the awful sight of this man, with an **evil spirit,** bloody (5:5), out of control, and apparently strong and frightening (5:4). Having an "evil" or unclean spirit means being demon possessed. Although we cannot be sure why demon possession occurs, we know that evil spirits can use the human body to distort and destroy a person's relationship with God. These evil spirits (5:9) had entered the man's body and were controlling him.

5:3-4 This demon-possessed man's condition was clearly hopeless without Christ. He no longer had contact with society, but **lived among the tombs.** This could refer to a type of graveyard with caves hewn into the rock. People with hopeless conditions, such as this man, could find shelter in the caves. People had tried to restrain his violent acts. The man had been **put into chains and shackles.** But he **snapped the chains** and **smashed the shackles,** indicating power not his own, but derived from the demons that held him. This man was so strong that no one could **control** (or overpower) him.

5:5 His **screaming** was more of a shriek—the voices of the demons (see also 1:26). The **hitting** of his skin with sharp **stones** refers to gashing and hacking at his body, leaving him bloody and covered with scars. These horrible actions occurred constantly. He was indeed a frightening creature.

5:6 The man did not run to escape Jesus, but ran to confront Jesus and scare him away as he would do to anyone else who ventured into his territory. When he came close to Jesus, the man **fell** on his knees, not in worship, but in grudging submission to Jesus' superior power. The demons immediately recognized Jesus and his authority. They knew who Jesus was and what his great power could do to them (see James 2:19).

5:7 The demon's first question was a request that Jesus leave them alone, showing the demons' ultimate rebellion. Jesus and the demons were as far separated as anything could be. Jesus' purpose was to heal and give life; the demons wanted to kill and destroy. But Jesus would not leave this man in such a condition.

Like the demon who had possessed the man in Capernaum (1:24), this demon tried using Jesus' divine name to control him. This demon referred to him as **Jesus, Son of the Most High God.** This is the highest title used for Jesus in Mark's Gospel and shows that the demons recognized Jesus as God's divine Son. The words "Most High God" appear in the Old Testament, and often were used by Gentiles when speaking of the superiority of Israel's God over any idol.

Then the demon had the audacity to ask for Jesus' mercy so that he would not be tortured in hell! The word for **torture** is graphic and correct. The Bible says that, at the end of the world, the devil and his demons will be thrown into the lake of fire (Revelation 20:10). The question revealed that the demons knew their ultimate fate; they hoped that Jesus would not send them to their fate early.

5:8-9 Jesus' first command was to one **evil spirit.** When that one did not obey, Jesus commanded the demon to give him its **name.** The answer revealed that there were **many** demons. A **legion** was the largest unit of the Roman army; it consisted of three thousand to six thousand soldiers.

5:10 The demons knew they had no power over Jesus; so when they saw Jesus, they **begged him again and again not to send them to some distant place** or into the Bottomless Pit (see Luke 8:31). Why didn't Jesus just destroy these demons—or send them away? Because the time for such work had not yet come. Jesus healed many people of the destructive effects of demon possession, but he did not yet destroy demons. In this situation, Jesus wanted to show Satan's destructive power and intent over the two thousand pigs. The same question could be asked today—why doesn't Jesus stop all the evil in the world? His time for that has not yet come. But it will come. The book of Revelation portrays the future victory of Jesus over Satan, his demons, and all evil.

5:11 According to Old Testament law (Leviticus 11:7), **pigs** were "unclean" animals. This meant that they could not be eaten or even touched by a Jew. This incident took place southeast of the Sea of Galilee in the region of the Gerasenes (5:1), a Gentile area. A normal herd of pigs would be 150 to 300 head. So this herd was unusually large.

5:12 The **evil spirits begged** Jesus not to send them away, but to send them **into those pigs.** The demons knew they had to submit to Jesus' power and authority, and they knew that he could seal their fate by returning them to the abyss or sending them far away. Notice that they did not ask to be sent into the city; they knew Jesus would not allow them to inhabit other people. But on the hillside were enough physical animal hosts for all these demons to inhabit.

5:13 Jesus did not command the demons to go into the pigs; he **gave them permission** to do what they requested. Satan has no final authority but can do only what God permits. While Jesus granted the demons' request to enter the pigs and destroy the herd, Jesus stopped their destructive work in people, and particularly the man they had possessed. Jesus also showed his disciples, the townspeople, and even us who read these words today the absolute goal of Satan and his demons. They desire total and complete destruction of their hosts.

The demons' action proves their destructive intent—if they could not destroy the men, they would destroy the pigs. Jesus' action, in contrast to the demons', shows the value he places on each human life. Some people might have difficulty with the fact that all the pigs died, but Jesus considered the man to be more important than the pigs.

5:14-17 When Jesus performed this miracle, he again gained immediate publicity. **The herdsmen,** astonished at what had happened, **ran** and told the amazing story. Their story seemed unbelievable: Two thousand pigs floating on the edge of the lake would certainly be a sight, so those who heard the story **rushed out to see for themselves.** The **crowd** saw the pigs in the water, they saw Jesus and the

disciples on the shore, and they saw the one who had been demon-possessed in his right mind. Jesus had restored this man's humanity; he was sane and self-controlled.

The people might have responded in several ways. They could have been overjoyed to see Jesus on their own shore, or they could have responded with joy that the demon-possessed man had been healed. However, Mark used one word for the people's response: **frightened.**

What were they afraid of? Perhaps such supernatural power as Jesus had displayed frightened them. Perhaps they thought Jesus would be bad for their economy (losing two thousand pigs in one day certainly cost someone). Perhaps they didn't want Jesus to change their status quo. In any case, their fear caused them to make a terrible mistake. They asked Jesus to **go away and leave them alone.** Unlike their own heathen gods, Jesus could not be contained, controlled, or appeased. They feared Jesus' supernatural power, a power that they had never before witnessed. And they were upset about losing a herd of pigs more than they were glad about the deliverance of the demon-possessed man. Unfortunately for them, Jesus did as they asked. And there is no biblical record that he ever returned. Sometimes the worst possible thing that can happen is for Jesus to answer one of our requests.

5:18-19 Having been freed, the man **begged to go** with Jesus. The man's request meant that he wanted to be one of Jesus' followers, with Jesus as a constant and close companion. But Jesus had other plans for him. As Jesus had done when he healed the leper (1:40-42) and the paralytic (2:11-12), Jesus gave this formerly demon-possessed man his life back. He could **go home,** something he could not do before. Certainly his family would rejoice to see him returned to sanity. When they would ask him what happened, the man was to **tell them** about the Lord's mercy.

Often Jesus asked those he healed to be quiet about the healing (1:43-45; 5:43), but he urged this man to "go and tell" what the Lord had done for him. Why the difference? This man was returning to his home in a Gentile region. Jesus knew the man would be an effective witness to those who remembered his previous condition and could attest to the miraculous healing. Through him, Jesus could expand his ministry into this Gentile area. Jesus would not remain in the region, but he did not leave himself without witness.

5:20 Although the man was healed and able to travel with Jesus, Jesus sent him on a mission. And the man wasted no time. He **started off to**

visit the Ten Towns of that region. Ten cities, each with its own independent government, formed an alliance for protection and for increased trade opportunities. These cities had been settled several centuries earlier by Greek traders and immigrants. Jews were a minority in the area. Many people from the area followed Jesus (Matthew 4:25). This former madman may have been known throughout the region. So when he returned to that same region, his testimony had results—everyone who saw and heard him was amazed.

JESUS HEALS A BLEEDING WOMAN AND RESTORES A GIRL TO LIFE / 5:21-43 / 89
Mark often wove together events in Jesus' life. On the way to see an ailing child, Jesus met a suffering woman. While he was dealing with her crisis, the message arrived that the sick girl had died. The account rings with lifelikeness. We are familiar with the jumble of urgency, delays, obstacles, and disappointments in life. Mark demonstrates that Jesus knew the same experiences. The conclusion of this episode reintroduces Jesus' efforts to control his publicity. His compassion motivated him to constant action, but God's plan required that Jesus resist the pull of growing public acclaim.

5:21 Jesus went back across the Sea of Galilee, probably landing back at Capernaum (4:35). As always, a large crowd gathered (see also 1:33; 2:2; 3:7, 20; 4:1). The contrast with Jesus just having been asked to leave the Gerasene region is unmistakable. Unfortunately, although he was popular with the people in Capernaum, they really were no more receptive to his message.

5:22-24 The synagogue was the local center of worship (see the explanation on 1:21), and Jairus was a lay person elected as one of the leaders. Jairus held a position of high esteem in the town. For him to fall down before Jesus and plead for him to come heal his daughter was a significant and daring act of respect and worship.

We do not know the nature of the young girl's sickness; apparently nothing had helped her and she would soon die. But Jairus remembered someone who could help—someone whose touch had healed many people in Capernaum (1:33-34). When Jairus heard that Jesus had returned to Capernaum, he was among the crowd on the seashore (5:21). He asked for Jesus' touch on his daughter, knowing that if Jesus were to come, his daughter would live. So Jesus went with him, with the curious crowd following along.

5:25-26 In the crowd that pressed on Jesus was another person in need of divine help. A woman who had had a hemorrhage (that is, bleeding; this may have been a menstrual or uterine disorder) for twelve years. The bleeding caused the woman to be in a constant condition of ritual uncleanness (see Leviticus 15:25-33). She could not worship in the synagogue, and she could not have normal social relationships, for anyone who came into contact with her would also become unclean. Thus, the woman was treated almost as severely as a leper. She had suffered and become destitute in trying to get a cure. There was no hope for alleviating her suffering, until she heard about Jesus.

5:27-28 The woman worked her way through the crowd and came up behind Jesus. She knew she only had to touch his clothing and she would be healed. The decision to touch Jesus' garment was due to the popular belief that the clothes of a holy man imparted spiritual and healing power (see 6:56; Acts 19:11-12). She may have feared that Jesus would not touch her if he knew her condition. Or she may have feared that if her disease became known to the crowd, the people who had touched her would be angry at having become unclean unknowingly. The woman knew she could be healed, but she tried to do it as unobtrusively as possible. She thought that she would just get healed and go away.

5:29 The moment the woman touched Jesus' garment, the bleeding stopped. The disease that had weakened her body for years suddenly disappeared. She felt the difference and knew not only that the pain had stopped, but that she was also completely healed of the disease. What a moment of incredible joy this must have been for this woman!

5:30 The healing had been immediate upon the woman's touch (5:29); Jesus' knowledge of the healing was also immediate. As the woman felt the healing of her body, Jesus felt the supernatural healing power go out of him. Someone had touched him in order to be healed, that person's faith had allowed the healing to take place, and Jesus perceived what had happened. Jesus' question, **"Who touched my clothes?"** had a definite purpose. Whether Jesus already knew who touched him or not is inconsequential. What mattered was that Jesus wanted to establish a relationship with this woman. She had hoped to go away undetected. Jesus, having healed her physically, wanted to heal her spiritually as well.

In the meantime, Jairus must have been exasperated; he was already in a hurry due to the severe illness of his daughter. No doubt the slow movement of the crowd was frustrating him. Then, of all things, Jesus stopped to ask a seemingly silly question. Little did Jairus know that through all these events, he would be learning a valuable lesson about Jesus' power.

5:31 The disciples were surprised by Jesus' question, so their reply seems almost rude. In effect they said, "How can you ask such a ridiculous question? Lots of people are touching you!" They did not understand that Jesus meant a different kind of touch.

5:32 Jesus looked around—the healed person could not have gone far, for Jesus had stopped immediately upon being touched. He knew that person was there. In his piercing gaze at the few people nearest him in the crowd was the unspoken demand that the person come forward. The crowd didn't understand what was happening, the disciples thought Jesus was being unreasonable, and Jairus was probably fuming. But one person *did* understand what Jesus meant by the question, and she knew she had no choice but to answer.

5:33 The woman **told him what she had done**— that she had been unclean and had come jostling through the crowd, that she had dared to touch him (a man) and did so in her unclean state, that she had hoped to remain undetected, and that she had been healed. To top it off, she had to say all of that in front of a crowd. No wonder the woman was **frightened** and **trembling**. According to Jewish law, a man who touched a menstruating woman became ceremonially unclean (Leviticus 15:19-28). This was true whether her bleeding was normal or, as in this woman's case, the result of illness. To protect themselves from such defilement, Jewish men carefully avoided touching, speaking to, or even looking at women. By contrast, Jesus proclaimed to hundreds of people that this "unclean" woman had touched him—and then he healed her. In Jesus' mind, this suffering woman was not to be overlooked. As God's creation, she deserved attention and respect.

5:34 Far from being angry, Jesus spoke to the woman in gentle words. She came for healing and received it. But she also received a relationship and peace with God himself because of her faith. Jesus explained that it was not his clothing that had healed her; rather, her **faith** in reaching out to the one person who could heal her had allowed that healing to take place. She not only had faith, but she had placed her faith in the right person.

The disciples, no doubt, received a profound lesson in the value of planting seeds in even the most unlikely places. The crowd, while seeming to be nothing more than a hindrance on the way, held one pocket of "good soil" in whom Jesus planted a seed.

5:35 The time taken by Jesus to seek out and speak to the woman was too long for the sick little girl at Jairus's house. During the delay, she died. The message was delivered to Jairus, undoubtedly calling him to come home. The opportunity for healing had passed, so the Teacher would no longer be needed.

5:36 Death did not make Jesus too late, however; instead, it meant that Jesus would do an even mightier miracle. Jairus must have looked in despair at Jesus, but Jesus made no indication of changing his plans. He turned in the direction of Jairus's house and told Jairus, **"Don't be afraid. Just trust me."** Jairus must have wondered what Jesus was going to do.

5:37 No doubt the curious crowd had every intention of staying with Jesus, having observed the healing of the diseased woman and hearing the words of the men from Jairus's house. What would Jesus do next? Sensitive to Jairus's pain, Jesus **stopped the crowd.** He planned to raise this little girl from the dead—a sign to his disciples of his true mission, of his power, and as a harbinger of his own resurrection. So he left the crowd and nine of his disciples behind, followed Jairus, and took along **Peter and James and John.** These three men became Jesus' inner circle—his closest followers, the only ones to see this miracle, observe the Transfiguration (9:2), speak about the end times on the Mount of Olives (13:3), and know of Jesus' agony in Gethsemane (14:33).

5:38 The five men finally reached Jairus's house, and the **commotion** of loud **weeping and wailing** filled the air. Such cries were customary at a person's death; lack of weeping and wailing was the ultimate disgrace and disrespect. Some people, usually women, made mourning a profession and were paid by the dead person's family to weep over the body. Jairus, the leader of the synagogue, was an important person in the town. Thus, at the death of his only daughter, the town demonstrated their great love and respect for Jairus and his family by their weeping and wailing.

5:39 Jesus' words, **"The child isn't dead; she is only asleep,"** probably made Jesus appear rather stupid—certainly anyone could distinguish death from sleep. Neither was she just in a coma from which Jesus would awaken her, as some have proposed. The girl was indeed dead, and everyone from the family to the paid mourners knew it. Jesus knew it too, but his words revealed to Jairus the hope beyond all hope of what Jesus was about to do. She was dead, but Jesus would bring her back to life, as if awakening her from sleep.

5:40 Jesus' words sounded ridiculous to the faithless crowd, so Jesus took charge in Jairus's house and used force to get rid of the jeering mourners. He had nothing further to say to them, and he had no use for their mourning or their scoffing.

Then Jesus **took the girl's father and mother** and the three disciples who had come (5:37) and went into an inner part of the house. Jesus had come to earth to conquer sin and death, and in this dramatic but quiet miracle, he would show his disciples that power. And two bereaved parents would receive back their beloved daughter.

5:41 Jesus did no incantations and spoke no magic words. He simply went to the girl's bedside and held **her hand.** The fact that Jesus touched the girl's hand would have amazed the proper synagogue leader and the disciples. Touching a dead body meant to become unclean. But Jesus had already dealt with a demon-possessed man and a woman with an incurable issue of blood and had touched and healed them. Touching the dead girl confirmed once again that compassion was more important than the letter of the law. Then Jesus spoke a simple command, **"Get up, little girl!"**

5:42 At Jesus' touch and command, the dead child awoke as if from sleep, **immediately** standing up and walking around. Just as the healings Jesus performed were always complete, so the rising of this young girl from the dead was complete. She didn't come back to life in the sick state in which she left; she came back well, whole, and able to walk around. The parents and the disciples were **absolutely overwhelmed.**

This was not the first time the disciples had witnessed the raising of a dead person. Luke 7:11-15 records Jesus raising a boy near the village of Nain. Yet, even in this instance, the disciples were amazed.

5:43 Jesus then gave two further commands. First, he **commanded them** (that is, the parents and the three disciples) **not to tell anyone what had happened.** Obviously the girl was not to be hidden for the remainder of her life; people would know she had recovered. Those in the unbelieving crowd would have to decide for themselves what had happened—no one would try to convince them. In fact, no one would even tell them what had happened.

Jesus told them to be quiet because he was concerned for his ministry. He did not want to be known as just a miracle worker; he wanted people to listen to his words that would heal their broken spiritual lives. Jesus' mission was to preach the Good News of the Kingdom of God. If crowds descended on him to see dead people raised, they would not be coming with the heart attitude needed to hear and respond to the gospel (see also 1:43-45). The disciples would talk about them and understand Jesus' miracles after his resurrection—then they could write them down for all of us to read and marvel as well.

Second, Jesus **told them to give** the girl **something to eat.** This is a good picture of Jesus' compassion and his understanding of human needs. The girl would be hungry and should be fed. This command also revealed to the parents and disciples that the girl was completely restored—she was well enough to eat.

MARK 6

THE PEOPLE OF NAZARETH REFUSE TO BELIEVE / 6:1-6 / 91

Following a section where great faith in Jesus is exhibited (5:21-43) is a story where there is great unbelief (6:1-6). Not only his own family, but Jesus' entire hometown, wondered what was wrong with their "son." Rather than offering welcome and expressing community pride, Jesus' townfolk were offended by his presence and his teaching. Familiarity bred contempt. As a result, their rejection limited his ministry.

6:1 After the previous incidents in Capernaum, where Jesus healed the bleeding woman and brought a dead girl back to life, Jesus **returned with his disciples to Nazareth** (1:9, 24), about twenty miles southwest of Capernaum.

Jesus had been born in Bethlehem, but raised in Nazareth (Matthew 2:19-23; Luke 2:39-40). This was not the first time he had spoken and taught in Nazareth; Luke 4:14-30 describes a visit when the people there had tried to kill him, but Jesus had walked away unharmed. Thus, this trip to Nazareth, recorded in Mark, is significant. The people of Nazareth were about to receive a second chance to believe; unfortunately, they again refused.

6:2 Synagogue services were conducted by lay people under the leadership of one or more synagogue "rulers" or leaders. For example, Jairus, the man whose daughter Jesus brought back to life, was a synagogue ruler (see 5:22). It was common for a visiting rabbi to be asked to speak in the local synagogue. Jesus, a well-known and popular speaker, had no trouble gaining an opportunity to teach **in the synagogue** on the **Sabbath**. As often happened when Jesus spoke, **many who heard him were astonished** (see also 1:22; 7:37; 10:26; 11:18) by **his wisdom** and his **miracles**.

6:3 Jesus was teaching effectively and wisely, but the people of his hometown saw him as only **the carpenter** whose family they also knew well. "He's no better than we are—he's just a common laborer," they said. Jesus was almost thirty years old before he began his public teaching ministry. For the years prior to that, he had been at home, learning the trade of carpentry from his father and probably helping to support himself and the family.

When the townspeople called him the **son of Mary,** it may have been a derogatory remark. While it may have been true that Joseph was already dead, in any normal situation Jesus would still have been called "son of Joseph." But Jesus was conceived prior to Joseph and Mary's wedding (while they were engaged, Matthew 1:18), and perhaps the townspeople had always regarded Jesus as not even being Joseph's son. Such was the stigma Mary continued to carry, even when Jesus was almost thirty years old. Apparently people saw Mary as less than honorable. Mary's obedience to God in carrying his

blessed Son had changed the course of her life (Luke 1:26-38).

The listing of the brothers (probably some of whom had come earlier to try to take Jesus by force in 3:21, 31) indicates that the people knew the family well. Apparently they were all ordinary people and Jesus had experienced an ordinary childhood. Thus for Jesus to claim to be someone special (especially with what they considered his less than honorable beginnings) caused them to be **deeply offended** by his words. Thus they **refused to believe in him.**

Jesus' brother **James** later became a believer, a leader in the Jerusalem church (Acts 15:13; Galatians 2:9) and the author of the book of James. **Judas** may have been Jude, author of the book of Jude. Nothing else is known of the other brothers and sisters.

6:4 Jesus used a common proverb found in rabbinic literature. It is significant that Jesus applied the word **prophet** to himself. The word refers not to one who foretells future events (although that may be part of a prophet's ministry), but to one who speaks God's message. Jesus was not the first prophet to be rejected **in his own hometown.** Jeremiah experienced rejection in his hometown, even by members of **his own family** (Jeremiah 12:5-6). Jesus also experienced rejection by **his relatives.** His family thought he had gone crazy (3:21) and most of them didn't believe until after his resurrection (John 7:5; Acts 1:14).

6:5-6 That Jesus **couldn't do any mighty miracles** in Nazareth does not mean a restriction on his power. Rather, Jesus could have done greater miracles in Nazareth, but he chose not to because of the people's **unbelief**—unbelief which **amazed** him. Jesus' mighty works were meant to further the Kingdom of God, not to try to convince a group of stubborn people who had already thoroughly rejected him. To do miracles would be of no value because the people did not accept his message or believe that he was from God. Apparently even in Nazareth, **a few sick people,** humbled by their need, did come to Jesus for healing. And Jesus, always compassionate, healed them.

Jesus left his hometown and **went out from village to village.** He visited all the villages in the environs of Nazareth. This sentence gives us a transition from Jesus' leaving Nazareth to preparing his disciples to continue his itinerant ministry.

JESUS SENDS OUT THE TWELVE DISCIPLES / 6:7-13 / 93

When Jesus gave his disciples their first commission, he included directions about conduct and content. Even while Jesus was still with the disciples, he helped them to discover what it would be like to function without him. Mark already mentioned two other mission circuits that Jesus traveled (1:14, 39), indicating that at least some of the disciples had experience in itinerant ministry. For these Galilean towns, the disciples' visit may have provided another opportunity for exposure to the gospel.

6:7 The **twelve disciples** had been trained in both the teaching they should give and the reception they could expect. It was time for them to do their "student teaching." Jesus could only travel so far and do so much. This sending out of six groups of disciples geographically multiplied his efforts (Jesus would later send out seventy-two others, also in pairs, see Luke 10:1-2). Jesus gave his disciples responsibility and authority to act as his representatives in both teaching and power. Jesus **sent them out** to witness. They also were given **authority to cast out evil spirits.** Matthew included the ability to cure disease and sickness (Matthew 10:1). This authority and power authenticated their message.

6:8-9 While these instructions—**no food, no traveler's bag, no money**—seem at first to be contrary to normal travel plans, they simply reveal the urgency of the task and its temporary nature. The disciples were sent out and then expected to return to Jesus with a full report. This was a training mission, and they were to leave immediately and travel light, taking along only minimal supplies. They were to depend on God and on the people to whom they were sent (6:10). Jesus allowed only the minimum: a **walking stick** and **sandals.** They were not even allowed to carry a bag because it was common for beggars to use such bags to solicit money. The disciples were not to be beggars, but were to live off the support of those who welcomed their message.

6:10 That a pair of disciples would **be a guest in only one home** meant that they had found a "worthy man" (Matthew 10:11)—a believer—and would either request or be invited to lodge in that person's home. By staying only in that home, they would not offend their hosts by even appearing to look for "better" lodging in a home that was more comfortable or socially prominent. To remain in one home would not be a burden for the host because the disciples' stay in each community would be short.

In a nutshell, Jesus instructed the disciples to depend on others while they went from town to town preaching the gospel. Their purpose was to blanket the area with Jesus' message, and by traveling light they could move quickly. Their dependence on others had other good effects: (1) It clearly showed that the Messiah had not come to offer wealth to his followers; (2) it forced the disciples to rely on God's power and not on their own provision; and (3) it involved the villagers and made them more eager to hear the message. Staying in homes was an excellent approach for the disciples' short-term mission; it was not intended, however, to be a permanent way of life for them. Yet the faith and simplicity that this way of life portrayed would serve them well in the future.

6:11 The disciples should also expect rejection, such as Jesus had faced in the Ten Towns (5:17) and in Nazareth (6:3). So Jesus further instructed that if any place did not **welcome** them (that is, take them in and offer hospitality) or **listen to** them, then they should **shake off its dust** from their feet as they left.

Shaking off dust that accumulated on one's sandals showed contempt for an area and its people, as well as the determination not to have any further involvement with them. Pious Jews shook dust from their feet after passing through Gentile cities or territory to show their separation from Gentile influences and practices. When the disciples shook the dust from their feet after leaving a **Jewish** town, it would be a vivid sign that they wished to remain separate from people who had rejected Jesus and his message.

Shaking off the dust of a place, Jesus said, would be a **sign** that the disciples had **abandoned that village to its fate** (see also 1:44). The act showed the people that the disciples had discharged their duty, had nothing further to say, and would leave the people to answer to God. By this statement, Jesus made it clear that the listeners were responsible for what they did with the gospel. The disciples were not to blame if the message was rejected, as long as they had faithfully and carefully presented it. Likewise, we are not responsible when others reject Christ's message of salvation, but we do have the responsibility to share the gospel clearly and faithfully.

6:12-13 The disciples went out as Jesus' representatives, continuing his message (1:14-15) and preaching that people should **turn from their sins.** The disciples not only brought the message of the gospel; they called for action in the form of repentance and belief. The gospel can only be life-changing if people allow it to change their lives. The change, for sinful humans, can begin only with turning from sin.

Jesus gave his disciples authority to **cast out demons** (3:15), as well as the power to heal the sick. Casting out demons extended Jesus' personal ministry, which was to confront Satan's power and destroy it. As the disciples went throughout Galilee, they would be announcing the arrival of the Kingdom of God through their preaching and healing.

Of all the Gospel writers, Mark alone included the words **anointing them with olive oil** in writing of the disciples' healing ministry. This "oil" was used often at that time as treatment (both internally and externally) for many illnesses. Medicines were few in these days, and olive oil had proven to have exceptional qualities.

HEROD KILLS JOHN THE BAPTIST / 6:14-29 / 95

The narrative about the disciples' preaching tour of Galilee continues at 6:30, interrupted with several verses telling the story of John the Baptist's death. John's imprisonment was mentioned in 1:14 when Jesus began his public ministry; 6:17-29 is a flashback. People were trying to explain Jesus' success. They were not ready to acknowledge him as the Son of God, but they were willing to call him a prophet. Some, like King Herod, were convinced that Jesus must be John the Baptist come back to life. Apparently, Herod was suffering pangs of guilt after ordering John's murder. He had gone along with his wife Herodias's scheme to take revenge on the irritating preacher by ordering him to be beheaded.

Told side by side, the success of the apostolic mission and the result of John's mission present a sobering lesson to those who obey God's calling: Sometimes discipleship means death.

6:14 The expanded ministry of the gospel by the disciples brought Jesus to the attention of King **Herod Antipas,** ruler over the territories of Galilee and Perea. **John the Baptist** had been arrested just prior to Jesus beginning his public ministry (1:14). The arrest marked the end of John's public ministry. He was imprisoned for some time prior to his death (see Matthew 11:2-6). At this point, the reader is to understand that John the Baptist had died at Herod's hands. (Mark will record the story in detail.)

The people, still trying to figure out where Jesus' miraculous powers came from, thought he was **John the Baptist** who had **come back to life.** Oddly enough, John had done no miracles; he had simply preached and prepared the way for Jesus. Among those who thought Jesus was John the Baptist was Herod himself (6:16). While Herod had succeeded in silencing John, he had not succeeded in silencing his own guilty conscience.

6:15 Others believed that Jesus was **the ancient prophet Elijah,** the great prophet who did not die but was taken to heaven in a chariot of fire (2 Kings 2:1-11). They applied the prophecy of Elijah's return in Malachi 4:5 to Jesus. (Later Jesus explained to his disciples that John had fulfilled Malachi's prophecy, see Mark 9:13.) Still others believed that Jesus was simply **a prophet,** someone in the tradition of Moses, Isaiah, or Jeremiah.

It was so difficult for the people to accept Jesus as the Son of God that they tried to come up with other solutions—most of which sound quite unbelievable to us. Very few found the correct answer, as Peter did (Luke 9:20). Many people today still cannot accept Jesus as the fully human yet fully divine Son of God, and they look for alternate explanations—a great prophet, a radical political leader, a self-deceived rabble-rouser. None of these explanations can account for Jesus' miracles or, especially, for his glorious resurrection; so these realities have to be rationalized. In the end, the attempts to explain away Jesus are far more difficult to believe than the truth.

6:16-17 Upon hearing about Jesus, Herod was certain that **John,** whom he had **beheaded,** had **come back from the dead.**

Mark explained how John's death came about. Herod, empowered by Rome over the region of Galilee, had simply **sent soldiers to arrest and imprison John.** The Jewish historian Josephus pinpointed this prison as Machaerus, a fortress (combination palace and prison) near the barren northeastern shore of the Dead Sea in the region of Moab. Herod did this **as a favor to Herodias.** She was Herod's brother Philip's wife. Herodias was the daughter of Aristobulus, another half brother. Thus Herodias was a half niece to both Philip and Herod (and they, in turn, were her half uncles). Herodias married her half uncle Philip and then divorced him to marry another half uncle, Herod. (Herod, meanwhile, had divorced his first wife.) Thus, in marrying, Herodias and Herod had committed adultery, as well as a type of incest. John the Baptist condemned Herod and Herodias for living immorally (6:18). Rebuking a tyrannical Roman official who could imprison and execute him was extremely dangerous, yet that is what John did.

6:18 John's denunciation of the marriage of Galilee's leader had been public as well as private. John had explained the obvious to Herod: It was against the law for Herod to be married to his **brother's wife** (not to mention that she was also his half niece). Leviticus 18:16 and 20:21 describe the laws that Herod was breaking. Herod was partly Jewish, and whether or not he cared about the Jewish law, he did care about a revolt against him by the Jews. John's public denunciation of the incest and adultery of Herod and Herodias was too much for them to bear, especially Herodias, whose anger turned to hatred.

6:19-20 **Herodias was enraged.** The phrase, in the imperfect tense, indicates that she never let up for one moment, but was waiting for her opportunity to have **John killed in revenge.** But **Herod respected John,** knowing that **he was a good and holy man.** So he protected John from Herodias's murderous intentions by locking him in prison. Perhaps he hoped that stopping John's public speaking would end the problem and quiet Herodias. Herod had little backbone. While he greatly respected John and **liked to listen to him,** he also kept John imprisoned for the sake of his evil wife and his incestuous and adulterous marriage. Herod was an evil man, so when he listened to John, he **was disturbed.**

6:21 That Herod had imprisoned John the Baptist was not enough for the angry Herodias. She continued to nurse her grudge against John for speaking publicly about her sins. Then on Herod Antipas's **birthday,** her **chance finally came.** Whenever we harbor guilt and hatred in our heart, Satan is busy creating opportunities for greater evil to happen. Herod **gave a party** for many notable men from governmental, military, and civil strata in Galilee. He hoped to entertain them, impress them, and win their respect and admiration by this elaborate party.

6:22-23 The **daughter** was a young woman in her middle teens. She **performed a dance** for Herod and his roomful of male (and probably drunken) dinner guests. She **greatly pleased them all,** so the king offered her **anything** she wanted. Herod continued to flaunt his power, desiring in this promise to show his ability to provide anything the girl might ask. Then he added that this gift could be **up to half** his **kingdom.** Herod and all his notables in the banquet hall knew that Herod had no kingdom to give. Herod's power came from Rome. Herod used a saying that revealed the scope of his offer but was not meant to be taken literally. But the young girl understood that she could ask for practically anything and receive it.

6:24-25 Any young woman might be prepared with a thousand possible suggestions to an offer such as Herod's, but the girl left the banquet hall to confer with her mother. Then she returned triumphantly with the gruesome request for **the head of John the Baptist.** Herodias wanted John killed and the gruesome proof of his death brought to the palace. Herod had no way out; John's death was sealed.

6:26-28 When the girl grandly gave her request to Herod in the hearing of all the important officials, Herod suddenly realized what he had done and was **very sorry.** Herod had made a promise (6:23). Such words were considered irrevocable. To **break his oath** would show his important guests that Herod was not a man of his word. So, out of regard for his reputation in front of the guests, Herod decided to show his power and authority by immediately fulfilling the girl's request. He **sent an executioner** to behead John and bring the grisly trophy back to the **girl,** who **took it to her mother.** Herodias had satisfied her lust for revenge.

Herod fulfilled his oath and saved face before his guests. But he had been shown up by his wife and was left with great fear over what he had done in killing a holy man. Herod's guilt could not be assuaged. Thus, when Jesus came upon the scene, he thought that John had come back to life (6:16).

6:29 John the Baptist apparently still had **disciples** (see Acts 19:1-5), even though many had left him to follow Jesus (John 1:35-37). When they heard that John had been beheaded, they came and **buried** him. They wanted to give their leader an honorable burial instead of having his body disposed of by the guards in the prison. Matthew added that after burying the body, "they told Jesus" (Matthew 14:12).

JESUS FEEDS FIVE THOUSAND / 6:30-44 / 96

The biographers of Jesus regarded the miraculous supply of food for a large crowd as a key event. Apart from the miracle of Jesus' resurrection, it is the only miracle recounted in all four Gospels. In Matthew and Mark, this miracle follows the account of Herod's tragic feast where John the Baptist was killed. The placement of the event creates a stark contrast between Herod's deadly orgy and the miraculous feast that Jesus provided for the multitude.

Like each of Jesus' miracles, the feeding of the five thousand demonstrated his control over creation, and it shows that God will provide when we are in need. Jesus was not transforming rocks into food, but multiplying bread and fish. He was doing instantly what he does constantly throughout nature. He was not breaking the "laws of nature," but was demonstrating that he was in control of these laws. Christ's power to feed a multitude, walk on water, and heal diseases all point to his identity as Lord of creation.

6:30 The word "apostle" means "one sent" as a messenger, authorized agent, or missionary. The word became an accepted title for Jesus' twelve disciples after his death and resurrection (Acts 1:25-26; Ephesians 2:20). Mark deliberately used the word because the **apostles** had completed their teaching mission (6:7-13) and thus were official "sent ones."

The pairs returned to Capernaum and reported to Jesus. This marked the first time the disciples had gone out on their own, so quite naturally, they were full of excitement upon their return. Jesus listened to their stories and answered their questions.

Perhaps it would be a great corrective for our furtive and sometimes foolish activities if we adopted the same practice of reporting our work to the Lord in prayer. We could ask him to sort out the wheat from the chaff, the important from the trivial. By so doing, we could seek his guidance for future activity.

6:31-32 Capernaum had never proven to be a place where Jesus and his disciples could find solitude. Indeed, **so many people** were **coming and going** that **Jesus and his apostles didn't even have time to eat.** Jesus knew that his disciples were weary, so he kindly suggested that they all go away **and rest.** So **they left by boat for a quieter spot.** Luke tells us that they went to Bethsaida (Luke 9:10), probably landing at a solitary harbor apart from the city, or else they went on foot into the hills.

6:33 Popularity and recognition have their own pitfalls. The disciples, now almost as well known as Jesus after their preaching mission, were seen and recognized along with Jesus, and the crowds would not let them get away. Either the people somehow heard where the boat was headed, or perhaps the boat sailed not quite out of sight along the horizon so that the people could follow it. In any case, a crowd **met them as they landed.**

6:34 As they drew near to shore, no doubt the disciples realized that their time alone on the boat was all the rest time they would have. A **vast crowd** waited on the shore, some having walked for miles in order to be there when Jesus and the disciples arrived. This would provide another lesson for the disciples. Far from feeling impatience and frustration toward these needy people, Jesus **had compassion on them.** He knew these people were as pitiful as **sheep without a shepherd.** Sheep are easily scattered and lost; without a shepherd they are in grave danger. The people needed a true Shepherd who could teach them what they needed to know and keep them from straying from God. While Jesus had hoped to be alone with the disciples for a time of rest, he did not send away this needy crowd. He had compassion for the people and took it upon himself to meet their needs.

6:35-37 Jesus had been teaching the people until **late in the afternoon** (after 3:00 P.M.). Sunset was approaching, and the disciples wondered what Jesus planned to do with this crowd that had come far from their homes to be with them. The place where Jesus had been teaching was **desolate,** far from any town or village. The disciples thought Jesus would be wise to let the people go before it got dark in order for them to find food and lodging for the night. So they brought their suggestion to Jesus: "Send the crowds away." No doubt, the disciples also hoped to soon get the rest they had anticipated when they had set out on this journey (6:31). Jesus' answer both astounded and exasperated them: **"You feed them."** The disciples summed up the situation and found it hopeless—**"It would take a small fortune to buy food for all this crowd!"** So what did Jesus mean, and why would he ask them to do something so obviously impossible?

6:38 In reply to their question about going and spending an extravagant amount of money on bread, Jesus told them first to check out their resources. John records that the **five loaves** (round barley cakes) and **two fish** they found were from the lunch of a young boy (John 6:9). Apparently, in their hurry, no one else in the crowd had thought to bring along food to eat, or they were unwilling to share it. The young boy offered his lunch to the disciples (specifically to Andrew, see John 6:8), but again the disciples could see only the impossibility of the situation.

6:39-40 Jesus did not answer the disciples, but set about organizing the people to **sit down in groups.** The men were probably separated from the women and children for the meal according to Jewish custom. So the people **sat in groups of fifty or a hundred.** In this wilderness, the Good Shepherd was about to feed his sheep (6:34).

6:41 Jesus, acting as the host of the soon-to-be banquet, **took the five loaves and two fish,** looked up to heaven, thanked God beforehand for the provision he was about to give, and then broke the loaves. As Jesus broke the loaves, the miracle occurred. The verbs in this verse are in different tenses in the Greek. The word **breaking** is in the aorist, implying an instantaneous act. The word **giving** is in the imperfect, implying a continuous act. Thus the miracle occurred in Jesus' hands. He broke the bread and then kept on giving it to his disciples to then **give to the people.** The same thing happened with the fish. The disciples acted as waiters to the groups of hungry people seated on the grass, taking bread and fish, distributing it, and then returning to Jesus to get more. They

continued to serve the crowd until everyone had had enough to eat (6:42).

The God who multiplied the bread was authenticating Jesus as his Son and portraying the Kingdom. Just as God provided manna to the Hebrews in the wilderness (Exodus 16), multiplied oil and meal for Elijah and the widow at Zarephath (1 Kings 17:7-16) and for Elisha (2 Kings 4:1-7), he was providing bread for the people on this day.

6:42-44 The five loaves and two fish multiplied so that **they all ate as much as they wanted.** Even the leftovers were more than they had begun with. The disciples picked up **twelve baskets** with the broken pieces of food. As if to cap off the record of this miracle, Mark added that **five thousand men had eaten from those five loaves!** If the readers weren't impressed already, now they should be astounded. The Greek word for men is *andres* meaning not "people," but "male individuals." Therefore, there were five thousand men **in addition to** the women and children. The total number of people Jesus fed could have been over ten thousand.

Jesus did what the disciples thought was impossible. He multiplied five loaves and two fish to feed over five thousand people. What he was originally given seemed insufficient, but in his hands it became more than enough. While we may feel that our contribution to Jesus is meager, he can use and multiply whatever we give him, whether it is talent, time, or treasure. When we give our resources to Jesus, they are multiplied.

JESUS WALKS ON WATER / 6:45-52 / 97

A long and stressful day was coming to a close. Jesus insisted that his disciples go on ahead in a boat while he dismissed the crowd. As people dispersed, Jesus went alone to pray. His time of silence and fellowship with his Father did not prevent his noticing the disciples struggling to make headway against the wind out on the lake. So Jesus ended his day (and began the next) by meeting the needs of his disciples as they floundered in the waves.

6:45 As soon as the crowd had been fed and the disciples had picked up the scraps, Jesus **immediately** got his disciples and the crowd moving. His sudden desire to dismiss the crowd and send the disciples off in their boat is explained in John's Gospel. Upon seeing the miracle of multiplied loaves and fish, the people "were ready to take [Jesus] by force and make him king," so Jesus "went higher into the hills alone" (John 6:15). Jesus' Kingdom would not be an earthly one, and he didn't want the enthusiasm of the crowd to

deter him or his disciples from fulfilling their true mission. Before the crowd could become an unruly mob, Jesus **made his disciples get back into the boat** and return to Bethsaida while Jesus **sent the people home.**

6:46 Jesus then **went up into the hills by himself to pray.** During his ministry on earth, Jesus was in constant prayer with the Father—he may often have gone off alone to pray, so his desire to do so may not have surprised the disciples who left in the boat as instructed. Jesus had just left a crowd that wanted to make him their king. Popularity was a temptation in itself, for it could threaten to turn Jesus away from his mission—death on the cross to accomplish salvation. Jesus, in his humanity, may have continued to face the temptation to turn away from the difficult path and take the easier one. He constantly sought strength from God. Going into the wilderness, alone with the Father, helped Jesus focus on his task and gain strength for what he had to do.

6:47 The disciples had left sometime before sunset, so by the time evening came, they were well out in the lake. The disciples often fished during the night, so sailing out into the night was not unusual. However, a storm blew in (see Matthew 14:24; John 6:18). Once again (as in 4:35-39), Jesus had sent them out to sea, when they were already bone tired, right into a storm. At least previously Jesus had been in the boat with them. This time, he **was alone on land,** and the disciples were left to fend for themselves.

6:48-50 The disciples took down the sails and tried to keep control of the boat by strenuous **rowing.** For the entire night they fought the storm.

As Jesus prayed on the mountainside, he **saw the disciples in serious trouble.** Jesus **came to them, walking on the water.** While some might try to explain away this miracle by saying Jesus was simply on the shore, Mark clearly states that Jesus walked **on** the water. Not only that, but he had walked a great distance. John records that the disciples had gone three or four miles by the time Jesus came to them (John 6:19).

Much confusion surrounds the phrase, **he started to go past them.** While the text sounds like Jesus meant to walk on by and leave the disciples to their fate, obviously that was not the case because he did help them. Interpretations on the meaning of this phrase include: (1) Jesus "meant to pass beside" them as in providing a divine manifestation so to reveal to them his divine presence; (2) Jesus "was about to pass by" as he waited for the disciples to see him and call out to him for

help; (3) the phrase was written from the disciples' standpoint (from Peter's eyewitness account) that, when they saw Jesus, it appeared to them that his intention was to "pass by them"; (4) the phrase means Jesus "intended to pass their way," that is, to go to them, which is exactly what he did. When they all saw Jesus walking on the water, the disciples thought he was a **ghost;** so they **screamed in terror.** Once again, Jesus was doing the unexpected, the impossible, and they were terrified.

Jesus called out to the disciples over the storm, telling them not to be **afraid.** The literal reading for **"I am here"** is "I am"; it is the same as saying "the I AM is here" or "I, Yahweh, am here" (see Exodus 3:14; Isaiah 41:4; 43:10; 52:6). Jesus, the "I AM," came with unexpected help and encouragement during the disciples' time of desperate need.

6:51-52 Jesus then **climbed into the boat** with the disciples. Then, as had occurred once before when the disciples had been tossed about by a storm at sea, **the wind stopped** (see also 4:39). Jesus had revealed to them his complete mastery over nature.

The disciples had seen Jesus perform numerous healings, calm a raging sea, multiply food to feed over five thousand people, and walk to them on the water. Their responses to the last miracle had been fear and then amazement. While they had seen the miracles, **they still didn't understand** them. They had seen the loaves multiplied, but they didn't realize who Jesus was and what he could do. Mark explained that **their hearts were hard.** This was not merely misunderstanding; it was a hard-hearted refusal to believe (the word is used elsewhere only when describing unbelievers, see 3:5; 10:5). But why wouldn't the disciples believe? Perhaps they simply couldn't bring themselves to consider that this human being was actually God's Son. Or maybe they thought that if and when the Messiah really did come, he wouldn't choose them for followers. The disciples needed a good healthy dose of faith in order to be able to see and understand what their Master, the Messiah, so beautifully and amazingly continued to teach them.

JESUS HEALS ALL WHO TOUCH HIM / 6:53-56 / 98

Jesus had achieved celebrity status. Wherever he and his disciples showed up, crowds gathered to watch. The sick flocked for healing. Jesus healed all those who were brought to him. Some who benefited from Jesus' healing touch went unchanged in other ways (Luke 17:11-19), but many were changed forever. Do you regard Jesus as an important, essential resource, yet still retain final control of your own decisions? Do you desire Jesus' help and friendship, but still want to be lord of your own life?

6:55 The storm had blown the disciples off course, and they did not land at Bethsaida as planned (6:45). They arrived at **Gennesaret,** a small fertile plain located on the west side of the Sea of Galilee as well as the name of a small town there. Capernaum (from where they had sailed that morning, 6:32) sat at the northern edge of this plain. Jesus was well known in the region of Galilee, and his presence always created great excitement. Immediately upon getting out of the boat, people **recognized** Jesus, and a flurry of activity began. There still would be no rest for the weary. The news of Jesus' arrival spread like wildfire through the area. As Jesus moved through the region, people **began carrying sick people to him** so that he might heal them.

People may seek Jesus to learn valuable lessons from his life or to find relief from pain. But we miss Jesus' whole message if we look to him for help only in this life, rather than for his eternal plan for us. Only when we understand the real Jesus Christ can we appreciate how he can truly change our lives.

6:56 In a day when medicines and medical help were few and limited, sickness was rampant and constant. As Jesus walked through Galilee, people **laid the sick in the market plazas.** Perhaps the story had spread of the woman in Capernaum who had been healed by touching Jesus' cloak (5:27-29), for now the people begged to **touch the fringe of his robe.** No one missed out on Jesus' loving compassion—**all who touched it were healed.**

MARK 7

JESUS TEACHES ABOUT INNER PURITY / 7:1-23 / 102

After the eye-opening demonstrations of Jesus' power in chapter 6, Mark provided a pause in the action by telling of another confrontation between Jesus and the Pharisees. Similar confrontations had already occurred (see chapters 2 and 3). Jesus' dramatic actions were met by determined resistance from groups that Mark identified as "Pharisees and teachers of religious law." Unable to overcome Jesus directly, their tactics shifted to the disciples. They were sure that the disciples were the weak point in Jesus' defenses.

7:1-2 Another delegation came from Jerusalem to investigate this new rabbi who was causing such a stir throughout the country. The **Pharisees and teachers of religious law** were ready to debate Jesus about the fact that his disciples did not follow all of the laws of the Pharisees' oral tradition. As these religious leaders scrutinized Jesus and his disciples, **they noticed that some of Jesus' disciples failed to follow the usual Jewish ritual of hand washing before eating.** This referred not to washing for cleanliness, but to a particular kind of washing that made a person "ceremonially clean" before eating.

7:3 Mark explained this "ritual of hand washing" for his Roman readers. The **Pharisees** did not **eat until they** had performed a ceremonial washing where water would be **poured over their cupped hands.** They did this so that they would not eat with "defiled" hands, for they believed that they then would become defiled. They scrupulously followed this law, thinking that this ceremony would cleanse them from any contact they might have had with anything considered unclean.

The origin of this ceremonial washing is seen in the laver of the Tabernacle, where the priests washed their hands and feet prior to performing their sacred duties (Exodus 30:17-21). That was part of God's law. But oral tradition extended this law to all Jews to be performed before formal prayers and then before eating. Thus, before each meal, devout Jews performed a short ceremony, washing their hands and arms in a specific way. But this was part of their **ancient traditions,** not a requirement of God's law.

Jesus discerned that the Pharisees' purpose was to keep up appearances, to demonstrate that they were not Gentiles, and to outdo the common people in priestly devotion. By their scrupulous observance of minute traditions and rituals, these religious leaders had completely lost their perspective on the reason the law of God had been given: to bring God's Kingdom to earth, to provide reconciliation between God and his people, and to bring peace.

7:4 Mark explained this Jewish ceremonial cleansing ritual a bit further for his Roman audience. The religious leaders were aware that in daily business they might unknowingly come into contact with a Gentile or an unclean Jew and thereby become defiled. If they were defiled, they would be unable to perform their religious duties. So they would not **eat** anything **from the market** before they had **immersed their hands in water**—another form of ceremonial washing. The devout leaders observed **many traditions,** including laws about how to wash their dishes. There were laws for everything; no wonder the common people didn't bother themselves with strictly following them. But the religious leaders kept all these laws because they believed their "cleanliness" equaled "godliness." In their minds, keeping these laws showed their devotion and service to God. But Jesus could not have disagreed more.

7:5 Picking up from 7:2, Mark continued the narrative. The religious leaders asked Jesus why his disciples did not follow the **age-old customs,** one of which was not eating **without first performing the hand-washing ceremony.** Their underlying question was, "If you are really a rabbi, as holy and righteous and versed in the law as we are, then you should know that we don't eat without first ceremonially washing our hands. That makes you no better than a common sinner, certainly not a rabbi whom all these people should be following!"

7:6-9 Jesus did not answer their spoken question, but their underlying one, by quoting the Scripture that they claimed to know so well. First, he called them **hypocrites.** A hypocrite is one who makes judgment from under a cover. The Pharisees pretended to be holy and close to God, thus judging all other people as sinners. But what they pretended on the outside was not true on the inside.

Jesus quoted from the prophet **Isaiah.** The Pharisees and teachers knew this Scripture. The prophet Isaiah criticized hypocrites (Isaiah 29:13), and Jesus applied Isaiah's words to these religious leaders. They might say all the right words and give lip service to God, but their hearts were far from him. Jesus attacked their true heart condition. The problem: **They replace God's commands with their own man-made teachings** and their **own traditions.** Their focus on minute rules of everyday life caused them to forget the scope of God's law and what it meant for the people. As leaders, they were especially culpable, for they should have been teaching the people about God. Instead, they looked down on the people as ignorant sinners and spent their time busily staying pure. Isaiah explained that **their**

worship was **a farce.** They worshiped for appearances, not out of love for God.

7:10-12 Next, Jesus gave an example to illustrate how the tradition could be (and was being) used to negate God's law. Jesus first quoted **Moses,** an especially relevant choice because the religious leaders traced the oral law back to him (see Deuteronomy 4:14). Jesus chose an example about people's duty toward their parents. One of the Ten Commandments, **Honor your father and mother** (Exodus 20:12), states that people are to respect their parents in honor of who they are and what they have done. The commandment did not apply just to young children, but to anyone whose parents were living. Honor includes speaking respectfully and showing care and consideration.

The same law is written negatively in Exodus 21:17, **Anyone who speaks evil of father or mother must be put to death** (see also Leviticus 20:9). Speaking evil of one's parents is the opposite of honoring them. It means to speak ill of, to ridicule, to abuse verbally. The natural result of such behavior is that the person will not honor his parents for who they are, will not speak respectfully, and will certainly show no care or consideration to them. Such action carried a severe penalty.

The religious leaders knew Moses' words, but they found a way to completely sidestep God's command to honor parents. The words **but you say** demonstrated their opposition to what Moses had written (7:10). What Jesus described here was the practice of "Corban" (literally, "offering") where a person could dedicate something to God for his exclusive use by withdrawing it from profane or ordinary use by anyone else. People could dedicate money to God's Temple that otherwise would have gone to support their parents (based on Deuteronomy 23:21-23 and Numbers 30:1-16). Thus, a man could simply take the vow of Corban, saying that he had **vowed to give to God what** he **could have given to** his parents. He could still use his money any way he chose, but could use his Corban vow as an excuse to **disregard** his **needy parents.** Corban had become a religiously acceptable way to neglect one's parents. Although the action—dedicating money to God—seemed worthy and no doubt conferred prestige on the giver, these religious leaders were ignoring God's clear command to honor parents.

7:13 The Corban vow effectively put tradition above God's word. To be able to exempt oneself from one of God's commandments by taking a human vow meant that the Pharisees had attempted to **break the law of God.**

Jesus added that the Pharisees did **many, many** things like that. This was only one example of the premeditated selfishness of these religious leaders who set themselves above all the people and, in effect, destroyed the laws that they took so much pride in keeping. In his example, Jesus clarified to these hypocritical religious leaders that God's law, not oral tradition, should be the true authority over people's lives.

7:14-15 Jesus addressed the crowd and the disciples regarding the true nature of "defilement." The people had listened to Jesus' stinging accusation of the religious leaders; here Jesus called the crowd to **listen . . . and try to understand,** for he would make his final point and have the final say in this debate. The Pharisees thought that to eat with defiled hands meant to be defiled (7:5). Jesus explained that the Pharisees were wrong in thinking they were acceptable to God just because they were "clean" on the outside. He explained that defilement is not an external matter (keeping food laws, washing ceremonially, keeping Sabbath requirements), but an internal one.

7:17-19 (Verse 16 is not in the earliest manuscripts.) In private, the **disciples** (specifically Peter, Matthew 15:15) **asked him what he meant.** Jesus explained that what goes into a person cannot defile that person. Thus, to eat food with hands that may have touched a "defiled" person or article did not mean that a person was ingesting defilement. Logically, as Jesus explained, food goes in the mouth, **passes through the stomach,** and then goes out. It has no effect whatever on the moral condition of the heart. Sin in a person's heart is what defiles (see 7:14-15).

The Roman Christians, the primary audience of Mark's Gospel, may have been confused about the Jewish food laws and whether they had to follow them. These words, **he showed that every kind of food is acceptable,** clarified this issue for them (although it took the early church several years to fully understand; see Acts 10 and 15).

The bottom line: People are not pure because of adherence to ceremonial laws and rituals.

We become pure on the inside as Christ renews our minds and transforms us into his image.

7:20-23 Defilement occurs because of sin. Sin begins in a person's heart—in the **thought life**—and what is in the heart comes out in words and actions. In Romans 6–8, Paul explained how this happens. Unless the Holy Spirit controls our sinful human nature, outbursts of the flesh will be prevalent. **Evil thoughts** begin within, in **a person's heart.** While most people work hard to keep their outward appearance attractive, what is in their hearts is even more important. When people become Christians, God makes them different on the inside.

Jesus listed a catalog of twelve "evil thoughts" that begin in the heart. Six are evil individual actions; six are evil attitudes or principles. Notice that the evil attitudes, whether acted upon or not, are still considered sin.

Sexual immorality—Various kinds of extramarital sexual activity
Theft—Taking something that belongs to another
Murder—Taking the God-given life of another person
Adultery—A married person having sex with someone other than his or her spouse
Greed—Relentless urge to get more for oneself
Wickedness—Doing evil despite the good that has been received (malice)
Deceit—To trick or mislead by lying
Eagerness for lustful pleasure—Immoral behavior that is neither restrained nor concealed
Envy—Desire for something possessed by another
Slander—To destroy another's good reputation
Pride—Making claims of superior intelligence or importance
Foolishness—Inability to discern between immorality and morality

All these vile things begin in a person's heart. It is those evil actions and attitudes that cause defilement. Many of the words Jesus used could have described the Pharisees.

JESUS SENDS A DEMON OUT OF A GIRL / 7:24-30 / 103

Jesus' actions never yielded to simple explanations. Those who thought they had him "figured out" were usually about to be stunned. His opponents tended to see the hurting people who came to Jesus as cases to be solved or examples of those who broke the law. Jesus treated them as valuable human beings, worthy of his attention. The presumption that Jesus was out to trample God's law might have led Jesus' opponents to expect him to quickly heal the daughter of this Gentile woman. But instead of adding this situation to his portfolio of unusual miracles performed, Jesus ignored the opportunity to make a statement; instead, he dealt with this woman as an individual whose own faith needed to be challenged and clarified.

7:24 Jesus traveled about thirty miles to **the region of Tyre** and then went to Sidon (7:31). These were port cities on the Mediterranean Sea north of Israel. Both cities had flourishing trade and were very wealthy. They were proud, historic Canaanite cities. In David's day, Tyre was on friendly terms with Israel (2 Samuel 5:11), but soon afterward the city became known for its wickedness. Its king even claimed to be God (Ezekiel 28:1ff.). Tyre rejoiced when Jerusalem was destroyed in 586 B.C. because without Israel's competition, Tyre's trade and profits would increase. Jesus and the disciples probably went to this Gentile territory thinking that they would be less well known and thus could obtain privacy and rest time. They went to someone's house (probably the home of a Jew who lived in that area) and did not want anyone to know they were there. But even in this Gentile territory, he couldn't keep his presence secret.

7:25-26 The word of Jesus' arrival had spread. One woman came to Jesus **right away** on behalf of her little girl who was **possessed by an evil spirit.** The woman **fell at Jesus' feet** and **begged him to release her child from the demon's control.** Mark added that this woman was a **Gentile.**

7:27 Jesus answered her in the language of a parable. Jesus used the word for **dogs** that referred to household pets. The simple parable meant that the children at the table are fed before the pets; it would not be right to take the children's food and throw it to the dogs. While it is true that in Jewish tradition Gentiles at times were referred to derogatorily as "dogs," that probably does not apply here. The Greek word used as a derogatory nickname applied to wild dogs or scavenger dogs, not household pets.

Jesus' ministry was first to his **own family, the Jews.** He would not take away from them to perform miracles for a Gentile. If that was what Jesus meant, we should realize that his words do not contradict the truth that God's message is for all types of people (Psalm 22:27; Isaiah 56:7; Matthew 28:19; Romans 15:9-12). Jesus was simply telling the woman that the Jews were to have the first opportunity to accept him as the Messiah because God wanted them to present the message of salvation to the rest of the world (see Genesis 12:3). Jesus may have wanted to test her faith, or he may have wanted to use the situation as another opportunity to teach that faith is available to all races and nationalities.

7:28 Unlike many of Jesus' Jewish listeners, this woman understood Jesus' parable. Her answer was wise, for she explained to Jesus, by extending his parable, that the children who love the pets often drop **crumbs** to them. Not all the Jews accepted Jesus, while some Gentiles chose to follow him. Why couldn't she have some of those "leftovers" that the Jews didn't "eat"? She adroitly pointed out that such "dogs" ate with (not after) the children. She did not ask for the entire meal, just for a few crumbs—or one crumb in particular—one miracle of healing for her daughter.

Ironically, many Jews would lose God's spiritual healing because they rejected Jesus, while many Gentiles, whom the Jews rejected, would find salvation because they recognized Jesus.

7:29-30 Jesus was delighted by the faith of the woman. He granted her request because of her humility and persistence. Her faith and understanding was in contrast to the misunderstanding of the disciples (6:52; 8:14-21). Her request had been made in faith that Jesus could perform the healing. His words had been meant to test her, and she had passed the test. She understood Christ's lordship and that, as a Gentile, she had no right to request mercy from Jesus. She also willingly accepted his conditions. On that basis, Jesus healed the woman's daughter. With his words, the demon left the little girl. This miracle showed that Jesus' power over demons is so great that he doesn't need to be present physically, or even to speak any word to the demon, in order to free someone. His power transcends any distance.

JESUS HEALS MANY PEOPLE / 7:31-37 / 104

The healing of the Gentile woman's daughter occurred during Jesus' northernmost travels. He concluded that mission by taking a long route back to Galilee. Then Jesus healed a deaf-mute.

Mark selected instances from Jesus' life to illustrate the many ways the Lord shows compassion for others. Mark seems to have made a connection between the deaf-mute here and the blind man in 8:22-26 with the deafness and blindness of the disciples described in 8:18. Jesus wants to open the ears and eyes of all who are deaf and blind so that they may receive the light of life.

7:31-32 The **Ten Towns** was a Gentile area, so this continues the emphasis of the previous miracle. Jesus had been in part of this region before (5:19-20). Mark alone recorded the miracle of the healing of this deaf and mute man. Apparently several of this man's friends brought him to Jesus; they had faith that Jesus could heal him. The key to Mark's recording of this miracle may be found in the Greek word translated **speech impediment.** That word is found only here and in the Greek Septuagint version of the Old Testament in Isaiah 35:6, where Isaiah wrote that one day "those who cannot speak will shout and sing." Mark saw the fulfillment of Isaiah's words in the healing ministry of Jesus.

7:33 Jesus wanted to heal this man, but again he wasn't looking for crowd acclaim in his healings. Thus, he took the man **to a private place** so they could be **away from the crowd** (see also 8:23). Jesus intended to deal with the man on a personal level—not use him as an advertisement of healing power.

Mark described this miracle in detail—apparently the disciples were with Jesus and the man. In this instance, Jesus **put his fingers into the**

man's ears and then spit onto his own fingers and **touched the man's tongue with the spittle.** Jesus often used touch in his healings. In addition, spittle was commonly recognized in the ancient world as having healing properties. The man responded in faith and desire for healing.

7:34-35 Jesus looked upward to God (the source of his power) and **sighed.** The sigh was probably in sympathy for the suffering man. Whether Mark recorded these details to describe what always happened in healings or whether this was unusual, is uncertain. In any case, the healing took place. Jesus commanded that the man's ears and mouth **be opened.** Immediately upon Jesus' speaking the word, the deaf man **could hear perfectly and speak plainly.**

7:36-37 Even though the miracle had been done in private (7:33), its results were obvious to the waiting crowd. The man, formerly deaf and barely able to talk, suddenly could hear and speak. Jesus asked the people not to talk about this healing because he didn't want to be seen simply as a miracle worker. He didn't want the people to miss his real message. But the people simply could not keep quiet, and **spread the news.**

MARK 8:1–9:1

JESUS FEEDS FOUR THOUSAND / 8:1-10 / 105

Differences in detail distinguish this miracle from the feeding of the five thousand described in chapter 6. At that time, those fed were mostly Jews. This time, Jesus ministered to a mixed crowd of Jews and Gentiles in the predominantly Gentile region of the Ten Towns. Jesus also began with different quantities of bread and fish, and he did not require his disciples to admit their own inability to solve the problem.

Even in Israel, Jesus took the gospel to a mixed audience. Jesus' actions and message had a significant impact on large numbers of Gentiles right from the start. Mark had his readers in mind when he recorded these facts. Examples of Jesus' compassionate ministry to non-Jews would be very reassuring to Mark's primarily Roman audience.

8:1-3 Jesus was ministering in the region of the Ten Towns (7:31), where he had healed a deaf and mute man, causing his popularity to spread throughout the area. It comes as no surprise, then, that **another great crowd had gathered.** In this episode, the crowd had been following Jesus for **three days,** listening to his teaching and observing his miracles. Whatever supplies they had brought along were depleted, so most of them had **nothing**

left to eat. Jesus was concerned about sending them away hungry. Although the disciples had seen Jesus feed five thousand people, they had no idea what Jesus would do in this situation.

8:4-5 As before, the crowd was **in the wilderness** (6:35), and the disciples asked the obvious question about **how** they were going to **find enough food** in such a place. Jesus had already found the resources in a previous remote place for an even larger crowd, and in this instance, when the disciples checked with the crowd, **seven** loaves were found. Yet the disciples were completely perplexed. Like the disciples, we often forget God's provision for us in the past.

8:6-9 Jesus **took the seven loaves** and gave thanks to God for the provision he was about to give. He **broke** apart the loaves and the disciples passed them out as before (6:41). The verbs could read, "Jesus kept on giving bread to the disciples and they kept on distributing it" to the crowd. **A few small fish were found** and after blessing them, Jesus ordered that these too should be distributed. As had happened before, each person in the crowd ate and was filled. The seven loaves

and few fish multiplied so that even the **scraps** were more than they had begun with. As before, the Greek word used here for **people** is *andres*, meaning "male individuals." Therefore, there were four thousand men; add to this number the women and children.

8:10 Once Jesus knew the people had eaten their fill and would not faint from hunger on their journey home (8:3), he sent them on their way. Jesus and the disciples once again got **into a boat** and sailed to **the region of Dalmanutha.** While there is no site identified as "Dalmanutha," it may have been another name for Magdala or Magadan (Matthew 15:39), a town located on the western shore of the Sea of Galilee. This was Mary Magdalene's hometown (Luke 8:2-3).

LEADERS DEMAND A MIRACULOUS SIGN / 8:11-13 / 106

Jesus had been able to escape the probing Pharisees for a while as he visited in Gentile areas (7:24–8:10). His last dealing with them had involved the issues of the law and ceremonial defilement, and Jesus had called the Pharisees hypocrites (7:6). But the Pharisees weren't going to give up in their relentless attempts to discredit Jesus before the crowds. So they constantly demanded "proof"—even more than they had already seen.

We can anticipate similar tactics in our own efforts to communicate the gospel. We may be asked to "prove" the existence of God. Such approaches are rarely honest; they are attempts to derail our message. These demands for proof, like the ones Jesus heard, are usually smoke screens covering up a refusal to believe. Though he was constantly under attack, Jesus always received those who were genuine seekers.

8:11 Upon Jesus' return to Jewish territory, the Pharisees **came to argue with him.** They demanded **a miraculous sign from heaven**—something beyond a mere miracle. A **sign** was used by God and his prophets to accomplish two purposes: (1) A sign showed trustworthiness or reliability—if a prophet said something would happen and it came to pass, it demonstrated that he was telling the truth from God. (2) A sign showed power—if a message was accompanied by a sign, it authenticated the power and authority of the prophet.

The Pharisees were asking for a sign to back up Jesus' claims and miracles. Perhaps they regarded his other miracles merely as random occurrences. Using the principle from Deuteronomy 13:1-3 and 18:18-22, the Pharisees were trying to draw Jesus into a trap. If he could not produce a sign, they could accuse him of being a false prophet. They had already seen and heard about many miracles, but that was not enough for them.

8:12-13 Jesus' sigh was a groan from the depths of his spirit. The obstinate rejection by those who should have been most able and eager to recognize him deeply distressed Jesus. His rhetorical question reveals his amazement that **this generation** (represented by these stubborn religious leaders) would ask for a **sign**—they had already seen many miracles and heard incredible, life-changing teaching. But they chose to reject Jesus. He knew that he could have done any type of spectacular cosmic miracle and they would not believe in him for they had already chosen not to believe in him.

Jesus did not come to earth to convince people to come to him by performing wonders; he came inviting people to come to him in faith, and as a response to their faith, he performed great miracles. But for these self-righteous religious leaders there was little hope. After this encounter, Jesus left abruptly, got into the boat, and departed back toward the northeastern shore of the Sea of Galilee. This event marked the end of his public ministry in the region of Galilee.

JESUS WARNS AGAINST WRONG TEACHING / 8:14-21 / *107*
Up to this point, Mark has conveyed the rejection of Jesus by his family and the religious leaders. At the same time, Mark has shown the inability of Jesus' closest followers to grasp his identity. With the two feeding miracles still fresh in their minds, the disciples failed to reach a conclusion about Jesus. The question Jesus asked the original disciples applies to us: "Don't you understand even yet?"

8:14-15 Jesus had left his confrontation with the Pharisees abruptly, and the disciples went along with him. Apparently, at some point out on the sea, they realized that **they had forgotten to bring any food.** As the disciples were worrying about bread, Jesus used the opportunity to teach of the danger of **the yeast of the Pharisees and of Herod.** Yeast is a key ingredient in bread, for it causes the dough to rise. "Yeast" in this passage symbolizes evil. Just as only a small amount of yeast is needed to make a batch of bread rise, so the evil teachings and hypocrisy of the religious and political leaders could permeate and contaminate the entire society. Jesus used yeast as an example of how a small amount of evil can affect a large group of people. The wrong teachings of the Pharisees were leading many people astray. Jesus warned his disciples to constantly **beware** of the contaminating evil of the religious leaders (see also 2 Corinthians 13:5; Galatians 5:9).

8:16 Jesus issued a warning, and the disciples quietly talked among themselves. They didn't understand the warning and interpreted Jesus' words in an odd manner. The phrase might also be translated, "But we have no bread at all." In other words, "How can we be in danger of their yeast if we don't even have any bread?" Their literal understanding missed Jesus' point entirely.

8:17-18 Jesus was saddened that the Jewish religious leaders, the people who should have rejoiced at Jesus' arrival, had completely rejected

him. It angered him that these religious leaders had the power to spread their unbelief throughout the nation. Jesus' disciples had not escaped the contamination, for even they consistently failed to realize who Jesus was. Jesus' rebuke in these verses is a series of questions focusing on the disciples' hardheartedness, blindness and deafness to the truth, and lack of memory regarding all that they had seen and experienced with Jesus. Each question was a stinging rebuke to the disciples.

8:19-20 Jesus quizzed the disciples further over their lack of perception. Did they even remember the feeding of the **five thousand?** When he had broken only **five loaves** and fed more than five thousand, how many baskets full of leftovers did they collect? They remembered that there were **twelve** baskets full. Then Jesus asked them what had just occurred when he had broken **seven loaves** and fed more than **four thousand.** The disciples knew that there were **seven** large baskets full. Both times they had collected more leftovers than food that they had at the beginning.

8:21 The disciples correctly answered Jesus' questions (8:19-20). In doing so, the conclusion should have been obvious. His question, **"Don't you understand even yet?"** was more of an appeal. The disciples needed to understand, and after all they had seen and heard, they should have reached the obvious conclusion that Jesus was their Messiah, the Son of God.

JESUS RESTORES SIGHT TO A BLIND MAN / 8:22-26 / *108*
The miraculous healing of the blind man from Bethsaida showed how Jesus responded with compassion to an obvious need, and gave an "acted-out parable" to demonstrate that insight seldom comes instantly. The disciples' struggle to grasp Jesus' identity parallels the blind man's experience of receiving his sight.

The healing of this blind man and the healing of the deaf-mute (7:31-37) are recorded only in Mark's Gospel. In both miracles, Jesus took the man away from the crowd before performing the miracle, used saliva, touched him, and did not publicize the event. This healing of the blind man is unique because it is the only record of Jesus healing in stages.

8:22 Jesus and the disciples went back across the sea to **Bethsaida.** The miracle recorded in this

section was recorded only by Mark and is a fitting story following the account of the disciples' persistent spiritual blindness in 8:14-21. Upon Jesus' arrival, some people **brought a blind man** and they **begged** Jesus to **touch** him.

8:23 Jesus led this blind man **out of the village.** Some have placed a great deal of symbolic significance on Jesus' special handling of this miracle, but the Bible text simply does not tell us for sure. It is uncertain why Jesus put saliva on the man's eyes. We do know that spittle was commonly recognized in these times as having healing properties. The Bible text also doesn't explain why Jesus did the healing in two stages. It may have been because of the man's lack of faith or to show that spiritual sight may be incomplete but can be restored gradually and fully by faith. We do know that Jesus was not faltering in his power or daunted by the man's blindness. He healed the man fully.

8:24 In response to Jesus' touch and question, the man replied that he saw **people** (the disciples and the people who brought him), but they were blurry, like **trees.** If the man had been blind from birth, he had never seen trees, but he knew the shapes from having touched them. The incomplete healing was not an indication of Jesus' inability to heal thoroughly the first time. Instead, it was a vivid teaching for the disciples. Sight was there, but it was not complete. The disciples too had spiritual sight, but it was far from complete. Jesus had rebuked the disciples for their lack of sight, but there was hope for them, just as there would be complete healing for this man.

8:25-26 After Jesus touched the man a second time, the man's sight was **completely restored.** Jesus told the blind man to return **home,** but not to go into village or tell anyone about what had happened. Obviously, people were going to find out, but Jesus did not want an immediate outpouring of sick people coming to him for healing. This gave Jesus time to move away from the area before the miracle was discovered. Jesus always had compassion on people in need, but he never lost sight of the fact that his mission was first and foremost the healing of people's souls.

PETER SAYS JESUS IS THE MESSIAH / 8:27-30 / *109*

The previous eight chapters recorded enough evidence to make Peter's confession, described here, reasonable. Further evidence in the Gospel reveals that Peter was saying more than he knew for sure. Matthew's parallel account of this incident includes Jesus' statement that Peter had made this declaration with the Holy Spirit's help. The final eight chapters of Mark's Gospel point to Jesus' death. From this point on, the journey leads to Jerusalem, and to Jesus' crucifixion and resurrection. The full impact of Peter's declaration would not be understood until Jesus' resurrection. With that event, the central spotlight of history came to rest on the person of Christ.

8:27 Caesarea Philippi was located about twenty-five miles north of Bethsaida. The city lay in the territory ruled by Philip (Herod Antipas's brother, mentioned in 6:17). The influence of Greek and Roman culture was everywhere. The city was primarily non-Jewish, known for its worship of Greek gods and its temples devoted to the ancient god Pan. When Philip became ruler, he rebuilt and renamed the city after Caesar Tiberius and himself. As Jesus and the disciples walked toward Caesarea Philippi, Jesus asked his disciples what they had heard from the people regarding his identity.

8:28 The disciples answered with the common view that Jesus was one of the great **prophets** come back to life. This belief may have stemmed from Deuteronomy 18:18, where God said he would raise up a prophet from among the people.

(For the story of **John the Baptist,** see 1:1-11 and 6:14-29. For the story of **Elijah,** see 1 Kings 17–21 and 2 Kings 1–2.) All of these responses were incorrect, revealing that Jesus' true identity was still unrecognized by the people. They didn't see that Jesus was the Messiah, the Son of God.

8:29 Mark's Gospel thus far has built up to this very question: **"Who do you say I am?"** Jesus had just recently asked the disciples, "Don't you understand even yet?" (8:21). Here they have their "final exam," their opportunity to show their understanding of Jesus, apart from what the crowds and religious leaders thought. Just as the disciples had to come to a personal understanding, acknowledgment, and acceptance of Jesus, so each person must do the same.

Peter, often the one to speak up, declared what

he had come to understand, **"You are the Messiah."** In his declaration, Peter revealed his belief in Jesus as the promised King and Deliverer. The problem now was to help these disciples understand the kind of king Jesus would be. Peter, and indeed all Israel, expected the Messiah to be a conqueror-liberator who would free the nation from Rome. Jesus would be a totally different kind of conqueror-liberator who would conquer sin and free people from its grasp.

From this point on, Jesus spoke plainly and directly to his disciples about his death and resurrection. He began to prepare them for what was going to happen to him by telling them three times that he would soon suffer and die and then be raised back to life (8:31; 9:31; 10:33-34).

8:30 Jesus told his disciples **not to tell anyone** that he was the Messiah because at this point they didn't fully understand the significance of Peter's confession—nor would anyone else. Everyone still expected the Messiah to come as a conquering king. But even though Jesus was the Messiah, he still had to suffer, be rejected by the leaders, be killed, and rise from the dead. When the disciples saw all this happen to Jesus, they would understand what the Messiah had come to do. Only then would they be equipped to share the gospel around the world.

JESUS PREDICTS HIS DEATH THE FIRST TIME / 8:31–9:1 / 110

Matthew, Mark, and Luke connect Peter's declaration that Jesus was the Messiah with the Lord's teaching about his crucifixion. This comes as no surprise. After all, messianic expectations were in the air. A strong consensus had developed about the political role the Messiah would play once he made himself known. The idea that the Messiah would "save people from their sins" had gotten lost among the list of social and political evils that the Christ would correct. Ultimately, the people wanted a Messiah who would crush the Roman occupation and raise Israel to prominence among the nations. Instead, Jesus explained that the Son of Man must die. Peter's response to Jesus clearly indicates how difficult it was for people to accept the idea of a suffering, dying Savior.

8:31 This was the turning point in Jesus' instruction to his disciples. From then on he began teaching clearly and specifically what they could expect, so that they would not be surprised when it happened. Contrary to what they thought, he would not yet be the conquering Messiah because he first had to **suffer, be rejected, be killed,** and **rise again.** But one day he would return in great glory to set up his eternal Kingdom.

Son of Man was Jesus' preferred designation for himself (see also 2:10, 28), and the name most often used other than "Jesus" in the New Testament. The title "Son of Man" emphasized Jesus as the vindicated, authoritative, and powerful agent of God.

Jesus' teaching that the Son of Man must **suffer** corresponds to Daniel's prophecies that God was in complete control of the plan for redemption (see Daniel 7:13-14; 9:26-27). The suffering also recalls Isaiah's prophecy of the Suffering Servant in Isaiah 53. The fact of his being rejected looks back to the rejected "stone" in Psalm 118:22. Jesus knew exactly from what quarter the rejection would come: the **leaders, leading priests,** and **teachers of religious law.** These three groups made up the Council, the Jewish supreme court

that ultimately sentenced Jesus to be killed (14:53, 64). Despite all this talk of impending death, a light shone through Jesus' words, for he also mentioned that he would be raised from the dead.

8:32 This was too much for **Peter.** Jesus had spoken **openly,** but his news was most unwelcome. If Jesus was going to die, what did this mean for the disciples? If he was truly the Messiah, then what was all this talk about being killed? So Peter took Jesus aside and **told him he shouldn't say things like that.**

8:33 Peter often spoke for all the disciples. In singling Peter out for rebuke, Jesus may have been addressing all of them indirectly. Peter had just recognized Jesus as Messiah; here, however, he forsook God's perspective and evaluated the situation from a **human** one. Peter was speaking Satan's words, thus Jesus rebuked Peter with the words, **"Get away from me, Satan!"** Unknowingly, the disciples were trying to prevent Jesus from going to the cross and thus fulfilling his mission on earth. The disciples were motivated by love and admiration for Jesus; nevertheless, their job was not to guide and protect Jesus, but to follow him.

Only after Jesus' death and resurrection would they fully understand why he had to die.

8:34 These words applied to the disciples and to all who want to follow Jesus. This statement offered special comfort to the Christians in Rome to whom Mark was writing, for they often faced persecution for their faith. Jesus invites every person to follow, but one who desires to follow him must have two attitudes: (1) a willingness to put aside selfish ambition, and (2) a willingness to take up his or her cross.

To **put aside selfish ambition** means to surrender immediate material gratification in order to discover and secure one's true self and God's interests. It is a willingness to let go of selfish desires and earthly security. This attitude turns self-centeredness to God-centeredness.

To **shoulder** one's **cross** was a vivid illustration of the humility and submission Jesus asked of his followers. When Jesus used this picture of his followers taking up their crosses to follow him, the disciples, the people, and the Romans (Mark's original audience) knew what he meant. Death on a cross was a form of execution used by Rome for dangerous criminals. A prisoner carried his own cross to the place of execution, signifying submission to Rome's power. Following Jesus, therefore, meant identifying with Jesus and his followers, facing social and political oppression and ostracism, and no turning back. For some, taking up the cross might indeed mean death. But Jesus' words meant that his followers had to be prepared to obey God's word and follow his will no matter what the consequences for the sake of the gospel (8:35). Soon after this, Jesus would take up his own cross.

The initial decision to **follow** Christ and be his disciple is a once-for-all act. From then on the believer is no longer his or her own; that person belongs to Christ. To follow Christ is also a moment-by-moment decision, requiring denial of self and taking up one's cross. Following Jesus doesn't mean walking behind him, but taking the same road of sacrifice and service that he took. The blessing for us is that we can fellowship with him along the way.

8:35-36 The Christian life is a paradox: to attempt to **keep your life** means only to **lose it.** A person who keeps his or her life in order to satisfy desires and goals apart from God ultimately loses life. Not only does that person lose the eternal life, he or she loses the fullness of life promised to those who believe. By contrast, those who willingly **give up** their lives for the sake of Christ and of the gospel actually **find true life.** To give up one's life for Christ's sake refers to a person refusing to renounce Christ, even if the punishment were death. To be willing to put personal desires and life itself into God's hands means to understand that nothing that we can gain on our own in our earthly lives can compare to what we gain with Christ. Jesus wants us to choose to follow him rather than to lead a life of sin and self-satisfaction. He wants us to stop trying to control our own destiny and to let him direct us. This makes good sense because, as the Creator, Christ knows better than we do what real life is about.

8:36-37 To reinforce his words in 8:35, Jesus asked his listeners a rhetorical question. What good would it be for a person to **gain the whole world** (that is, to have power or financial control over the entire world system of which Satan is the head) but to **lose** his or her **soul** (that is, to lose eternal life with God)? Every person will die, even those most powerful or most wealthy. If they have not taken care to "save" their lives for eternity with God, then they have gained nothing and have lost everything. A world of pleasure centered on possessions, position, or power is ultimately worthless. Whatever a person has on earth is only temporary; it cannot be exchanged for his or her soul.

8:38 Jesus constantly turned the world's perspective upside down with talk of first and last, keeping and giving up. Here he offered his listeners a choice. If they chose to be **ashamed** of Jesus, then Jesus would be **ashamed** of them at his Second Coming (they would be rejected from eternal life with him). By extension, those who were not ashamed of Jesus and his words, in spite of the **adulterous and sinful** culture surrounding them, would be accepted by Christ when he returns in **glory.** Many are fearless in business, battle, or sports but cower at potential ridicule. Speak up for your faith, for your convictions, and for Christ.

Jesus, the **Son of Man,** will judge when he comes with the **holy angels.** Jesus Christ has been given the authority to judge all the earth (Romans 14:9-11; Philippians 2:9-11). Although his judgment is already working in our lives, there is a future final judgment when Christ returns (see Matthew 25:31-46) to review and evaluate everyone's life. (See 1 Thessalonians 5:4-11 on how we are to live until Jesus returns and 2 Thessalonians 1:5-10 on how God will judge those who trouble us.) This judgment will not be confined to unbelievers; Christians too will be judged. Their eternal destiny is secure, but Jesus will review how they handled gifts, opportunities, and responsibilities in order to determine their rewards in the

Kingdom. At the time of judgment, God will deliver the righteous and condemn the wicked. Rejecting Christ may help us escape shame for the time being, but it will guarantee an eternity of shame later.

9:1 When Jesus said some would **not die** before seeing the **Kingdom of God arrive,** he may have been referring

- to Peter, James, and John, who would witness the Transfiguration a few days later
- to all who would witness the Resurrection and Ascension

- to all who would take part in the spread of the church after Pentecost

Jesus' Transfiguration, which immediately follows (9:2-8), was a preview of that coming glory. In the Transfiguration, Peter, James, and John saw Jesus' glory, identity, and power as the Son of God (see 2 Peter 1:16-18). Thus, certain disciples were eyewitnesses to the power and glory of Christ's Kingdom. Jesus' point was that his listeners would not have to wait for another, future Messiah because the Kingdom was among them, and it would soon come in power.

MARK 9:2-50

JESUS IS TRANSFIGURED ON THE MOUNTAIN / 9:2-13 / 111

Jesus revealed some of his most unusual demonstrations of power and divinity to his disciples alone. He stood up in their partly swamped boat and took command of the wind and the waves. He walked on water. On this occasion, he allowed three of them to witness his appearance without some of the limitations of his humanity. After teaching them the rigors of self-denial, he gave them a reassuring glimpse of his glory.

9:2-3 Rarely did Mark give exact times in his narrative, so his definite **six days later** is significant. This reference probably alludes to Exodus 24:16, where it is recorded that Moses waited for six days before meeting the Lord on Mount Sinai. The words also tie into 9:1, where Jesus probably was referring to his coming Transfiguration.

Jesus singled out **Peter, James, and John.** These three disciples comprised the inner circle of the group of Twelve. They were among the first to hear Jesus' call (1:16-19), they headed the list of disciples (3:16), they were present at certain healings where others were excluded (5:37), and they were with Jesus as he prayed in Gethsemane (14:33). Seeing Jesus transfigured was an unforgettable experience for Peter (see 2 Peter 1:16). Jesus took these three disciples **to the top of a mountain**—either Mount Hermon or Mount Tabor. Mount Hermon is about twelve miles northeast of Caesarea Philippi (where Jesus had been in 8:27); Mount Tabor is in Galilee. A mountain was often associated with closeness to God and readiness to receive his words (see Exodus 24:12-18; 1 Kings 19:8-18).

The Transfiguration was a brief glimpse of Jesus' true glory, God's divine affirmation of everything Jesus had done and was about to do. The Transfiguration clearly revealed not only that the disciples

were correct in believing Jesus to be the Messiah (8:29), but that their commitment was well placed and their eternity was secure. Jesus was truly the Messiah, the divine Son of God.

The Greek word translated **[Jesus']** appearance **changed** is *metamorphothe,* from which we get our word "metamorphosis." The verb refers to an outward change that comes from within. It was not a change merely in appearance, but it was a complete change into another form. On earth Jesus appeared as a man, but at the Transfiguration, Jesus' body was transformed into the glorious radiance that he had before coming to earth (John 17:5; Philippians 2:6) and which he will have when he returns in glory (Revelation 1:14-15). The glory shone out from him and his clothes **became dazzling white.** The white was not of this earth; it was a white that no human had seen. The words, unique to Mark's Gospel, reflect an eyewitness report (probably Peter's). These were the radiant robes of God, clothing "white as snow" (Daniel 7:9).

9:4 Elijah and Moses were considered the two greatest prophets in the Old Testament. Moses represented the law, or the old covenant. He had written the Pentateuch and had predicted the coming of a great prophet (Deuteronomy 18:15-19).

Elijah represented the prophets who had foretold the coming of the Messiah (Malachi 4:5-6). Moses' and Elijah's presence with Jesus confirmed Jesus' messianic mission to fulfill God's law and the words of God's prophets (Matthew 5:17). Their appearance also removed any thought that Jesus was a reincarnation of Elijah or Moses. He was not merely one of the prophets. As God's only Son, he far surpassed them in authority and power. Also, their ability to talk to Jesus supports the promise of the resurrection of all believers.

9:5-6 There is no indication that Peter was addressed, but he impetuously interrupted when he suggested making three **shrines,** one for each of them. Peter had forgotten (or was hoping to put aside) Jesus' words that suffering and death would come before glory. Peter saw the fulfillment of Christ's glory for a moment, and he wanted the experience to continue. Also, Peter mistakenly made all three men equal. He had missed Jesus' true identity as God himself. Peter called Jesus **"Teacher,"** obviously missing what Jesus was showing them by his revealed glory. His words, **"This is wonderful,"** revealed a further lack of understanding. He desired to prolong the experience, to keep Moses and Elijah there with them. But that was not the point of the experience nor the lesson to be learned by it. Peter had spoken impetuously, perhaps because the three disciples **were all terribly afraid.**

9:7 A **cloud** suddenly appeared and enveloped this group on the mountain. This was not a vapor cloud, but was, in fact, the glory of God (see also Exodus 13:21; 19:9; 1 Kings 8:10). God's **voice** came from the cloud, singling out Jesus from Moses and Elijah as the long-awaited Messiah who possessed divine authority. As he had done at Jesus' baptism, God was giving verbal approval of his Son (see 1:11). At that time, the message had been addressed to Jesus ("You are my beloved Son") and had benefited John the Baptist; here, the voice spoke to Peter and the other two disciples (**"This is my beloved Son"**). The voice then commanded Peter and the others to **listen** to Jesus and not to their own ideas and desires about what lay ahead.

9:8 Peter may have wanted to keep Jesus and Elijah and Moses there in glory on the mountainside, but his desire was wrong. The event was merely a glimpse of what was to come—no more. Thus, sud-

denly the glory came and went, and the prophets **were gone.** Jesus had been revealed as God's glorious divine Son, but his mission on earth still had to be completed.

9:9 Jesus told Peter, James, and John **not to tell anyone what they had seen,** presumably not even the other disciples because they would not fully understand it until after he **had risen from the dead.** After the Resurrection, these three disciples would understand the Transfiguration and be able to correctly interpret and proclaim it. They would then realize that only through dying could Jesus show his power over death and his authority to be King of all. They knew that Jesus was the Messiah, but they had much more to learn about the significance of his death and resurrection.

9:10 The three disciples **kept it to themselves,** but they didn't understand what Jesus **meant by "rising from the dead."** They certainly believed in a future resurrection, but Jesus clearly was speaking of some other event, something that would happen to only him. The necessity of Jesus' suffering and death was beyond their grasp.

9:11 The appearance of Elijah on the mountain caused a question in the disciples' minds. Based on Malachi 4:5-6, the Jewish **teachers** believed that **Elijah must return before the Messiah comes.** Elijah had appeared on the mountain, but he had not come in person to prepare the people for the Messiah's arrival (especially in the area of repentance). The disciples believed that Jesus was the Messiah, but they wondered where Elijah was.

9:12-13 Jesus answered that **Elijah** would come **first** and **set everything in order.** That the Messiah would **suffer and be treated with utter contempt** was **written** in Scripture (for example, Psalm 22:14, 16-17; Isaiah 53:1-12). Jesus explained that, in fact, Elijah had **already come.** Matthew explained that the disciples realized that Jesus meant John the Baptist (Matthew 17:13), who had taken on Elijah's prophetic role—boldly confronting sin and pointing people to God.

As "Elijah" then, John the Baptist **was badly mistreated.** Elijah was severely persecuted by King Ahab and Queen Jezebel and fled for his life (1 Kings 19). John the Baptist had been beheaded (6:14-29). All of this occurred **as the Scriptures predicted.**

JESUS HEALS A DEMON-POSSESSED BOY / 9:14-29 / 112

When they descended from the mountaintop of transfiguration to the flatland of common experience, the three disciples and Jesus found a scene of confusion. The other disciples had been asked to perform a miracle but had failed. This instance became a testing of faith, both for the child's father as well as for the disciples. Christ regards even our weak faith. After all, it is not the quantity of our faith that makes the greatest difference, but the quality of him in whom our faith rests.

9:14 Jesus, Peter, James, and John came down from the mountain and returned to the other nine disciples. **A great crowd** surrounded the **disciples** and **some teachers of religious law** in a heated argument. The nature of the argument is not stated, but perhaps the teachers were arguing with the disciples about their power and authority, or the power and authority of their Master, because the disciples had tried and failed to cast out a demon (9:17-18).

9:15-17 When Jesus unexpectedly arrived on the scene, the people **ran to greet him.** Usually the people were in awe of his teaching and miracles; here they were **in awe** at his very presence with them (see also 1:27; 5:20). Jesus asked, **"What is all this arguing about?"** The word for "arguing" means "disputing." The answer came from a man **in the crowd,** the father of the demon-possessed boy. He explained that he had come looking for Jesus to **heal** his son who was **possessed by an evil spirit,** making him unable to utter any sound (and he could not hear, see 9:25). This was not just a case of deafness and muteness; it was the work of an evil spirit, as the man explained.

9:18 The symptoms described by the father sound much like an epileptic convulsion, but the destructive intent of the demon described in 9:22 reveals that this was more than mere epilepsy. Having heard of Jesus' power to cast out demons, the father had come to Jesus, hoping for a cure for his son. Not being able to find Jesus, he had asked the disciples to **cast out the evil spirit,** an appropriate request since the disciples had been given this power and had recently returned from a preaching tour where they had demonstrated that power (6:7, 13). The disciples **couldn't do it,** however. This perplexed and upset them (Jesus explained why in 9:28-29). It also caused a commotion with the crowd and an argument with the Jewish leaders (9:14) who were seeking to discredit Jesus.

9:19 Jesus cried out in exasperation (see 3:5; 8:12). His unusual words carry a biting rebuke. They parallel Moses' frustration as intercessor for God's people (Deuteronomy 32:5, 20) and portray God's frustration with his people (Numbers 14:11; Isaiah 63:8-10). The disciples had been given the authority to do the healing, but they had not yet learned how to appropriate God's power. The disciples were not singled out for criticism because Jesus did not rebuke them (9:28-29), but merely answered

their question. Jesus would not leave the young boy in the power of the demon, so he told the father to **bring the boy.**

9:20-22 When the evil spirit saw Jesus, it knew that its rule over the boy would soon end. The demon responded with one last attack, throwing the boy **into a violent convulsion.** While it may seem odd that Jesus would ask **how long** the boy had been like this, Jesus asked it not for his own sake, but for the father's sake. By answering the question, the father was indicating just what a difficult and seemingly hopeless case this was. Jesus was truly the man's only hope. The boy had been possessed by the demon **since he was very small.** That this was not merely epilepsy is revealed in the demon's destructive intent as it made the boy **fall into the fire or into water, trying to kill him.** The poor father had probably saved his son's life numerous times, constantly having to watch the boy in order to protect him. Beyond that he had been unable to do anything. So he came to Jesus and pled, **"Do something if you can."**

9:23 Jesus repeated the father's words and turned them around to put doubt in the right place. In a sense, Jesus was saying that while he could do anything, it would depend on the father's belief. Spiritual power comes only when a person turns from self to God in faith. This father had placed limits on God's power, but with belief, **anything is possible.** Jesus' words do not mean that we can automatically obtain anything we want if we just think positively. Jesus meant that anything is **possible** if we believe because nothing is too difficult for God, even when our experience seems to indicate otherwise. We are free to ask whatever we want, as long as we realize that God will answer according to his will (1 John 3:21-22; 5:14).

9:24 Contrary to the patterns of confusion and unbelief the disciples had displayed, this father modeled the faith required of true discipleship. The father immediately understood Jesus' meaning. He had not meant to doubt the Master. **The father instantly replied, "I do believe,"** declaring his faith in Jesus power. Then he added honestly and humbly, **"Help me not to doubt!"** At the feet of the Master, the man cried out with tears, confessing both his faith and its weakness.

9:25-27 Jesus tried to keep the miracle from becoming a circus; so when he saw the crowd

growing, he quickly **rebuked the evil spirit,** commanding it to **come out** and never return. After crying out and convulsing him terribly, it came out, and the boy was like a corpse. After the terrible convulsion, probably prolonged by the angered demon, the child's exhausted body went limp as the demon left him. In fact, he was so still and quiet that most of the people in the crowd thought he was **dead.** Jesus took the child **by the hand and helped him to his feet.** That he **stood up** indicates not only that the demon had left, but that Jesus had given strength back to the child's body. As always, the cure was complete.

9:28-29 The disciples must have been very perplexed. They had cast out demons before (6:7, 13); why hadn't this demon responded? Jesus pointed to their lack of faith. Perhaps the disciples had tried to drive out the demon with their own ability rather than God's. If so, their hearts and minds

were not in tune with God, so their words had no power. Their question revealed their error; they centered on themselves ("we"), not on Christ. Jesus explained that **this kind can be cast out only by prayer,** and the disciples had not depended on God's power through prayer. God's power must be requested and relied upon in each instance. This presents a strong message to our present-day church: Arguing among ourselves disables (9:14); prayer enables. The disciples had been debating and not praying.

Prayer is the key that unlocks and reveals faith. Effective prayer needs both an attitude of complete dependence and the action of asking. Prayer demonstrates complete reliance on God. Thus, there is no substitute for prayer, especially in situations that seem impossible. Often the disciples would face difficult situations that could be resolved only through prayer. Their humiliation made this a painful lesson to learn.

JESUS PREDICTS HIS DEATH THE SECOND TIME / 9:30-32 / 113
Jesus clearly warned his disciples that he would eventually die. His assurance that death would only hold him three days did not allay the disciples' confusion.

9:30-31 Jesus and the disciples left **that region,** perhaps somewhere near Caesarea Philippi (see 8:27), and passed **through Galilee,** going toward Capernaum (9:33). Jesus had ended his public ministry and thus began his final journey toward Jerusalem. Jesus desired **to avoid all publicity** so that he would have time to focus on teaching the disciples. He needed to equip them to carry on the ministry when he returned to heaven and to prepare them for coming events so they would not be taken by surprise.

The disciples had persisted in their resistance to Jesus' predictions of his suffering and death. He had already told them that he would die (8:31), so this was the second time he clearly told the disciples that he would **be betrayed** and **killed.**

Whereas Jesus had spoken before about being rejected, this time he added the element of betrayal. He again said that he would **rise from the dead** after **three days.** There was always the assurance of victory, although the disciples seemed to miss this point in their concern over Jesus' talk of death.

9:32 The disciples **didn't understand** why Jesus would keep talking about dying because they expected him to set up a political kingdom. They didn't know that Jesus' death and resurrection would make his spiritual Kingdom possible. If Jesus died, the kingdom as they imagined it could not come. But they **were afraid to ask him what he meant.**

THE DISCIPLES ARGUE ABOUT WHO WOULD BE THE GREATEST / 9:33-37 / 115
Although this incident is included in the first three Gospels, each one recorded the exchange from a slightly different perspective. Though Mark does not record Jesus' comments about the humility of a little child, Jesus' use of the child as an example provided a clear rebuke to the petty arguments about status among his followers.

9:33-34 Jesus and the disciples arrived in **Capernaum.** Apparently the disciples had kept somewhat to themselves as they followed Jesus

along the road, but Jesus knew they were having a heated discussion. They had been **arguing about which of them was the greatest.** Apparently Jesus already knew what the disciples had been discussing; for even though he asked the question, **they didn't answer** him. But he then gave them an unforgettable lesson in true greatness.

9:35 Clearly Jesus had his work cut out for him in teaching these disciples who would be responsible to carry on his mission. So he **sat down** in the house and **called the disciples** to sit at his feet. In a sentence, he taught the essence of true greatness, **"Anyone who wants to be the first must take last place and be the servant of everyone else"** (see 10:45). Greatness is determined by servanthood. The true leader willingly serves, as Jesus exemplified in his life and in his death. Being a "servant" did not mean occupying a servile position; rather it meant having an attitude of life that freely attended to others' needs without expecting or demanding anything in return. Seeking honor, respect, and the attention of others runs contrary to Jesus' requirements for his servants. An attitude of service brings true greatness in God's Kingdom.

9:36-37 When Jesus took a little child **in his arms,** the explanation of greatness was made even more distinct. Only Mark mentions Jesus taking the child in his arms. When we receive Jesus, we actually

"enter" or are "received into" his Kingdom. The way into this Kingdom is to turn to God from sin in the same spirit of humility that a child exhibits when he shows simple trust in someone he loves. We must humbly recognize that Jesus already paid the price for our entrance into his Kingdom. Any greatness we might have comes only from humble service to our Savior and Lord.

The disciples had become so preoccupied with the organization of Jesus' earthly kingdom that they had lost sight of its divine purpose. Instead of seeking a place of service, they were seeking positions of advantage. Jesus used a child to help his self-centered disciples get the point. They were to have servant attitudes, being not "childish" (arguing over petty issues), but "childlike," with humble and sincere hearts.

In addition, Jesus taught the disciples to welcome children. This was a new approach in a society where children were usually treated as second-class citizens. Jesus equated the attitude of receiving children with a willingness to receive him. Hidden in this statement is a profound truth of Jesus' identity: **Anyone who welcomes me welcomes my Father who sent me.** Jesus and God the Father are one.

THE DISCIPLES FORBID ANOTHER TO USE JESUS' NAME / 9:38-41 / 116

Minor conflicts over leadership positions among the disciples also had their public aspect. In this case, the disciples displayed the tendency to become a closed group. They challenged the "credentials" of an outsider. But Jesus rebuked their attempt to be exclusive. We must welcome and encourage all who serve in the name of Christ. Having the same Lord covers a multitude of differences.

9:38 John, brother of James the son of Zebedee, one of the inner circle of three among the disciples, told Jesus of a recent event. They had seen a man casting out demons by using Jesus' name and had told the man to stop because he was not one of the group, that is, not one of the chosen Twelve. The incident has special irony considering that this unknown man apparently had success driving out demons while the disciples, who had been given special power to do so, had recently failed (9:18).

9:39 The disciples had been incorrect to stop the man from exorcising demons in Jesus' name; and incidentally, they were also incorrect in their supposition that they alone should have a monopoly on Jesus' power. Jesus explained that no one would do such a miracle as exorcising a demon in Jesus' name and then turn around and publicly **speak evil** against Jesus. The man, whatever his motiva-

tion, had at least done a deed of mercy for a possessed person and had stood against Satan. When Jesus had been accused of casting out demons because he was in league with Satan, he had said that Satan would not work against himself (3:22-29). The man, therefore, was on Jesus' side.

9:40 Jesus explained to his disciples, **"Anyone who is not against us is for us."** By this statement, he was pointing out that neutrality toward him is not possible. His followers would not all resemble each other or belong to the same groups. People who are on Jesus' side have the common goal of building up the Kingdom of God, and they should not let their differences interfere with this goal.

9:41 Not only did the man who exorcised demons serve Christ's Kingdom in his stand against Satan, but even someone who offered **a cup of water** to a person because he belongs **to the Messiah** was also serving the Kingdom. Good treatment of Christ's representatives is important to God (9:37). The Twelve did indeed have a special calling, but God willingly uses all people and all gifts for furthering his Kingdom. There are no "trivial" or unimportant services to God.

JESUS WARNS AGAINST TEMPTATION / 9:42-50 / 117

This teaching ties closely to the two preceding ones. In 9:33-37, Jesus held up a child as an example of servanthood and a standard for judging our openness. In 9:38-41, Jesus confronted exclusions of others who name Christ as Lord. Failure in any of the cases above puts believers in danger of causing others to lose faith (9:42).

9:42 While even small acts of kindness to believers carry great rewards, so acts of misguidance toward believers carry great penalties. **Little ones** could mean children or anyone considered to be insignificant or weak in faith. To cause a child or someone weak in the faith to **lose faith** means to purposely put a stumbling block in the way to make him or her trip and fall. Jesus warned that anyone who turns someone away from him will receive severe punishment. A **millstone** was a heavy, flat stone used to grind grain. To have a millstone **tied around** one's **neck** and then be **thrown into the sea** meant certain death. Even the horror of such a death was minor compared to what this person would face in eternity.

9:43, 45, 47 The Greek word for **to sin** is the same one used in 9:42 translated "to lose faith." In this verse, it seems as though Jesus was adding even more condemnation to the disciples' ambition. While prideful ambition is bad, Jesus' statement here includes **anything** that might cause another person to stumble.

All who desire to follow Jesus must remove any stumbling blocks that cause sin. Jesus did not mean to literally cut off a part of the body; he meant that any relationship, practice, or activity that leads to sin should be stopped. As a person would submit to losing a diseased appendage (**hand** or **foot**) or a sense (**eyes**) in order to save his or her life, so believers should be just as willing to "cut off" any temptation, habit, or part of their nature that could lead them to hold onto this world and turn away from Christ. Just cutting off a limb that committed sin or gouging out an eye that looked lustfully would still not get rid of sin, for that begins in the heart and mind. Jesus was saying that people need to take drastic action to keep from stumbling.

The reason? Jesus explained that it would be better to have lost some worldly possession, attitude, or action than to keep it and **be thrown into hell** because of it. This is true, radical discipleship. While none of us will ever be completely sin-free until we get new bodies, what God wants is an attitude that renounces sin instead of one that holds on to sin. (Verses 44 and 46 are not included in the best manuscripts.)

9:48 Still describing "hell," Jesus spoke of a place, like the garbage dump in the valley outside of Jerusalem, where **the worm never dies and the fire never goes out.** With these strange words, taken from Isaiah 66:24, Jesus pictured the serious and eternal consequences of sin and the absolute destruction of God's enemies (see also Matthew 3:12; 5:30). Worms and fire represented both internal and external pain. Hell will be a place of unbearable and unending torment reserved for those who refuse to believe in Jesus Christ and the salvation and eternal life he offers.

9:49 This verse, exclusive to Mark, has received dozens of interpretations. The most probable are included here. Some have suggested that **everyone** refers to every person. Thus, the meaning would be that every person will be **purified with fire** somehow—either with the unquenchable fire of hell or with the painful but life-giving power of self-discipline for the sake of the Kingdom.

Another view is that **everyone** refers to believers who will be purified with the fire of trials in order to purify them. The **fire** that purified them probably referred to trials and persecutions that made them fit for service (see Matthew 5:10-12; 1 Corinthians 3:13; 1 Peter 1:7; 4:12). This third view is most probable in light of the following verse.

9:50 Jesus carried on his metaphor from 9:49. Salt can purify; it also symbolizes the disciples and the work they were called to do.

"Salt is good for seasoning," Jesus said, for in the ancient world salt was both a condiment and a preservative for food. Jesus had said to the disciples, "You are the salt of the earth" (Matthew 5:13). They were to be life-producing agents in a dying world; they were to be preservatives in a world spoiled by sin. However, if salt **loses its flavor,** the flavor cannot be returned and it is of no value to anyone. Jesus stressed the responsibility of each disciple toward God. The disciples will be held accountable by God to maintain their "saltiness" (that is, their usefulness) by maintaining a close relationship with him. Finally, the disciples were told to **have the qualities of salt.** They must allow God's purifying work to be done in them. They, in turn, would be purifying agents in the community and in the world. The result, then, would be **peace with each other.** If the disciples had the "salt" in themselves, then they would not be arguing about

who would be the greatest in Christ's Kingdom (9:34). They must not allow the salt within them to be made useless by their wrangling over position and concerns of this world. Instead, they must serve Christ; then they would be doing their duty in the world and be at peace with each other. This peace among the disciples would be of vital importance after Christ's return to heaven (see 1 Thessalonians 5:13). The future of the gospel and of Christianity would be left in their hands.

MARK 10

JESUS TEACHES ABOUT MARRIAGE AND DIVORCE / 10:1-12 / 173

This chapter notes the geographic shift in Jesus' ministry from Galilee to Judea. The occasional travels to Jerusalem became a single-minded movement toward the Cross.

The religious leaders did not let up in their attempts to trap Jesus. This time they came with a question regarding divorce. The leaders defined this theological issue in all-male terms. Mark alone added the note that Jesus applied God's rules both to men and women. Jesus held men to a standard of conduct; he gave women dignity. He saw women not as property for keeping or disposal, but as full partners.

10:1 After a quiet time of teaching his disciples, Jesus continued his journey **southward** toward Jerusalem. They crossed **into the area east of the Jordan River,** arriving in the region of Perea. John the Baptist had ministered there, and crowds had come to Jesus from the region earlier (see 3:8). Jesus was already well known, and on his arrival there, crowds of people came to him, and he **taught them.**

10:2 The **Pharisees** hoped to **trap** Jesus by getting him to choose sides in a theological controversy and incriminate himself in the process. They came with a hot topic: **"Should a man be allowed to divorce his wife?"** If Jesus supported divorce, he would be upholding the Pharisees' procedures; they doubted that Jesus would do that. If Jesus chose sides in the controversy, some members of the crowd would dislike his position, for some may have used the law to their advantage to divorce their wives. Or, if he spoke against divorce altogether, he would appear to be speaking against Moses' law (which allowed divorce).

10:3 With these words, Jesus removed any possible condemnation of laxity about divorce or ignorance of God's law. Jesus turned the Pharisees from their

wrangling about his possible answers and sent them directly to the Pentateuch (the books of Genesis through Deuteronomy). He asked, **"What did Moses say about divorce?"** From their answer in 10:4, the Pharisees thought Jesus was referring to Moses' writing in Deuteronomy 24:1-4; but Jesus' response reveals that he was referring to Moses' words in Genesis about the ideal state of creation and particularly of marriage.

10:4 In their answer, the Pharisees summarized the law recorded in Deuteronomy 24:1-4. Moses **permitted** divorce, recognizing its presence and giving instructions on how it should be carried out. Because sinful human nature made divorce inevitable, Moses instituted laws to help its victims. Under Jewish law, only a husband could initiate and carry out a divorce. The civil laws protected the women who, in that culture, were quite vulnerable when living alone. Because of Moses' law, a man could no longer just throw his wife out—he had to write **an official letter of divorce** so she could remarry and reclaim her dowry. This was a radical step toward civil rights, for it made a man think twice before sending his wife away. Moses' words gave protection to the wife and limited abuses of divorce.

10:5 In Moses' day, as well as in Jesus' day, the practice of marriage fell far short of God's intention. Jesus said that Moses gave this law only because of the people's **hard-hearted wickedness;** in other words, they were completely insensitive to God's will for marriage. Many refused to follow through with their marriages as God had intended, so God allowed divorce as a concession to their sinfulness. Divorce was not approved, but it was preferred to open adultery. But God wants married people to consider marriage to be permanent.

10:6-8 The Pharisees quoted Moses' writings in Deuteronomy; Jesus also quoted from Moses' writings (Genesis 1:27; 2:24), but he went back to Genesis, **the beginning of creation,** to God's ideal in creating **male and female.** God's plan was that in marriage the husband and wife are **united into one,** an intimate closeness that cannot be separated. The wife is not property to be disposed of, but an equally created person. Jesus was drawing a distinction: God's creation of marriage and his absolute command that it be a permanent union versus the human injunction written hundreds of years later tolerating divorce because of people's sinfulness.

10:9 The Pharisees saw divorce as a legal issue rather than a spiritual one, regarding marriage and divorce as transactions similar to buying and selling land (with women being treated as property). But Jesus condemned this attitude, clarifying God's original intention—that marriage bring oneness that **no one** should **separate,** especially not the husband by simply writing a "letter."

Jesus recognized Moses' law, but held up God's ideal for marriage and told his followers to live by that ideal. Jesus also was saying to the self-righteous Pharisees who had hoped to trick him with the question, "True followers of God will hold his ideals above any laws—and especially those laws written as a concession to hardheartedness and sin."

10:10 Mark continued his theme of the disciples' misunderstanding of Jesus' teaching. Once they were again in privacy **in the house,** the disciples asked Jesus what he had meant in his answer to the Pharisees' question. Matthew records their comment that the standard Jesus upheld was so impossible that it would be better for people not to get married than to get into the unbreakable covenant of marriage (Matthew 19:10).

10:11-12 Jesus had clearly explained that divorce dissolved a divinely formed union. These people were divorcing in order to get remarried. Here he explained that marriage after divorce is adultery. To say that a man could commit adultery **against** his wife went beyond Jewish teaching and elevated the status of the wife to a position of equality. Women were never meant to be mere property in a marriage relationship; God's plan had always been a partnership of the two becoming "united into one" (10:8).

The rabbis' interpretation of Moses' law permitted remarriage after divorce, but Jesus said that was committing adultery. Matthew recorded the same words of Jesus but added that he gave one exception: "unless his wife has been unfaithful" (Matthew 19:9, see also Matthew 5:32). Scholars agree that Jesus' words refer to both husband and wife; that is, the unfaithfulness of one could be grounds for divorce by the other, because Jesus then added, **"And if a woman divorces her husband and remarries, she commits adultery."** These were earth-shaking words to Jewish ears. In Jewish society, only men had the right to divorce. Mark alone recorded these words, probably with his Roman audience in mind. They would not have been shocked, for in Roman society a woman could initiate a divorce.

God created marriage to be a sacred, permanent union and partnership between husband and wife. When both husband and wife enter this union with that understanding and commitment, they can provide security for each other, a stable home for their children, and strength to weather any of life's storms or stresses.

JESUS BLESSES THE CHILDREN / 10:13-16 / 174

There is a natural progression from Jesus' teaching on the permanence of marriage to his insistence on bringing children to him for blessing. Jesus declared the value of children and his love for them by his actions. And he used their receptivity as a guideline for the kind of response required of anyone who would want to enter the Kingdom of God.

Jesus' words forcefully confront parents and all those in contact with children: Are we helping or hindering children from coming to Christ? Are we, ourselves, receiving the Kingdom of God with childlike trust?

10:13 It was customary for people to bring their children to a rabbi for a blessing. Thus, people were bringing children to Jesus so that he could **touch them and bless them.** The disciples, however, thought the children were unworthy of the Master's time. In the first century, Jewish households were patriarchal—men came first, women and children next. Considering their inability to have any quiet time together, the disciples may have viewed these parents and children as another intrusion and drain of time and energy. So they told the parents **not to bother** Jesus. Once again Mark emphasized that the disciples misunderstood both Jesus' compassion and his mission.

10:14-15 When Jesus saw his disciples rebuking the people for bringing their children, he was **very displeased** with their insensitivity. They thought children were a waste of time, but Jesus welcomed them. He, in turn, rebuked the disciples, giving them in a double command to **let the children come** and **don't stop them.** Jesus explained that little children have the kind of faith and trust

needed to enter the **Kingdom of God.** Anyone of any age who exhibits **their kind of faith** and trust is promised access to Jesus and to the Kingdom. Children represent the essence of discipleship, coming to Jesus in humility and receiving his blessing as a gift. Unless we can completely trust in God, we **will never get into the Kingdom of God.**

10:16 One by one, Jesus took each child **into his arms, placed his hands on their heads** (rather than just "touching" them as he had been asked, 10:13), and **blessed them.** Jesus took time with each child. Jesus did not rush through the process or pass it off as unimportant. It probably brought him great joy to spend time with little children whose faith and trust were so pure and simple. The receptiveness of these children was a great contrast to the stubbornness of the religious leaders, who let their education and sophistication stand in the way of the simple faith needed to believe in Jesus, and the dullness of the disciples, whose self-centeredness continued to blind them to Jesus' true mission.

JESUS SPEAKS TO THE RICH YOUNG MAN / 10:17-31 / *175*

Jesus stopped in an unnamed town for several days. He was questioned about divorce and made a point to bless little children. But it was time to move on because he had an appointment with the cross. Jesus was on his way out of town when a young person flagged him down with a question. Apparently, this young man was trying his best but knew it wasn't enough. He lacked something and wanted Jesus to tell him what he had missed.

This episode with the rich young man contrasts sharply with the previous episode of Jesus' blessing of the children. The children are an example of faith and trust; they do nothing to gain eternal life, but they receive it because of their simple faith. The rich young man thought he could gain eternal life by what he did, only to find that he could not have it.

10:17 Jesus was continuing his journey toward Jerusalem when **a man came running up to** him. He called Jesus **"Good Teacher"** (not the more common "rabbi") and eagerly asked a pressing question. This rich young man wanted to be sure of **eternal life,** so he asked what he could **do to get** it. He viewed eternal life as something that one achieves. While he had kept the commandments (or so he thought, 10:20), he still had some concern about his eternal destiny. He thought Jesus would have the answer.

10:18 Jesus did not at first address the man's question, but instead challenged him to think about God. Goodness is not measured by one's works; in fact, **only God is truly good.** Jesus wanted the man to turn his attention from himself and from Jesus (whom he thought was merely a "Good Teacher") and think about God's absolute goodness. If he

truly did so, he would conclude that he could **do** nothing to inherit eternal life. Jesus was also saying, "Do you really know the one to whom you are talking?" Because only God is truly good, the man, without knowing it, was calling Jesus "God."

10:19 Having established the nature of true goodness (and recognizing that the man did not have a real understanding of God and how he gives eternal life), Jesus rehearsed six of the Ten Commandments—those dealing with people's relationships with one another. That the man kept these laws was the easily verifiable outward proof— an answer to what the man could **do.** Jesus' list showed that he was focusing on the man's actual lifestyle and not just his knowledge of these commandments. But Jesus would show the man that the law had far deeper meaning than just a list of rules to be kept.

10:20 The young man replied that he had **obeyed** all the commandments since his childhood. The man sincerely believed that he had not broken any commandments, so he wanted Jesus to guarantee his eternal life. Such is the condition of one who tries to attain eternal life or a relationship with God by his or her own merit. Even if it seems that the person has kept all the laws perfectly, he or she still needs assurance. Jesus would reveal to this man what he lacked.

10:21 Jesus lovingly broke through the young man's pride with a challenge that answered the question of what the man lacked: **"Sell all you have and give the money to the poor."** This challenge exposed the barrier that could keep this young man out of the Kingdom: his love of money. Money represented his pride of accomplishment and self-effort. Ironically, his attitude made him unable to keep the first commandment, one that Jesus did not quote: "Do not worship any other gods besides me" (Exodus 20:3; see also Matthew 22:36-40). The young man did not love God with his whole heart as he had presumed. In reality, the man's wealth was his god, his idol. If he could not give it up, he would be violating the first commandment.

The task of selling all his possessions would not, of itself, give the man eternal life. But such radical obedience would be the first step for this man to become a disciple. Jesus' words were a test of his faith and his willingness to obey. The man thought he needed to **do** more; Jesus explained that there was plenty more he could do, but not in order to obtain eternal life. Instead, he needed an attitude adjustment toward his wealth. Only then could he submit humbly to the lordship of Christ. By putting his **treasure in heaven** and "following" Jesus along the road of selflessness and service to others, the man could be assured of his eternal destiny.

10:22 This man's wealth made his life comfortable and gave him power and prestige. When Jesus told him to sell everything he owned, Jesus was touching the very basis of the man's security and identity. He could not meet the one requirement Jesus gave—to turn his whole heart and life over to God. The one thing he wanted, eternal life, was unattainable because he deemed the price too high. The man came to Jesus wondering what he could do; he left seeing what he was unable to do. No wonder he **went sadly away.** How tragic—to be possessed by possessions and miss the opportunity to be with Jesus.

10:23 Jesus looked at his disciples and taught them a lesson from this incident with the rich young man. Jesus explained that it is **hard** for **rich people to get into the Kingdom of God** (not impossible, but hard). This is true because the rich, with most of their basic physical needs met, often become self-reliant. When they feel empty, they can buy something new to dull the pain that was meant to drive them toward God. Their abundance and self-sufficiency become their deficiency. People who have everything on earth can still lack what is most important—eternal life. They have riches, but they don't have God's Kingdom.

This young man may have been very wealthy, but any of us who own anything could also be considered wealthy by someone else's standards. Whatever you own could become a barrier to entering the Kingdom if it comes between you and God.

10:24 Jesus' words **amazed** the disciples, and so he repeated them. As Jews, these disciples regarded wealth as a sign of God's blessing (see, for example, Job 1:10; 42:10; Psalm 128:18; Isaiah 3:10). Thus, they thought wealth came from God and would bring a person closer to God; it certainly did not pose an obstacle. The rich young man, with all his advantages, probably seemed like perfect "Kingdom material." Yet he went away empty-handed. What kind of Kingdom was this if those most blessed and advantaged would have difficulty entering? What did that mean for the disciples? It seemed to them that if the rich had a hard time, the disciples would never make it.

10:25 Jesus used a common Jewish proverb describing something impossible and absurd. With all their advantages and influence, rich people may find it difficult to have the attitude of humility, submission, and service required by Jesus. Thus Jesus explained that it would be easier to get a **camel** (the largest animal in Palestine) through the eye of a sewing **needle** than for a person who trusts in riches to get into the Kingdom of God.

10:26 The disciples were **astounded** almost to the point of exasperation. Again, they wondered what Jesus meant. If the rich—those who from the disciples' vantage point seemed to be first in line for salvation—cannot be saved, **then who in the world can be saved?**

10:27 In reality, it is not just the rich who have difficulty, for salvation is **impossible** for anyone from a human standpoint. No one can be saved by his or her wealth or achievements or talents. But the situation is not hopeless, for God had an entirely different plan: **Everything is possible with God.** No one is saved on merit; but all can be saved who humbly come to God to receive salvation.

10:28 Peter, once again acting as spokesman for the Twelve, contrasted the disciples with the rich young man. The disciples had **given up everything** to follow Jesus; they had done what the rich young man had been unwilling to do. Matthew recorded Peter's question to emphasize this fact: "What will we get out of it?" (Matthew 19:27). They had done the ultimate in self-denial and had followed Jesus' call. Wouldn't they then receive some great reward for having done so?

10:29-30 Peter and the other disciples had paid a high price—leaving their homes and jobs and secure futures—to follow Jesus. But Jesus reminded them that following him has its benefits as well as its sacrifices. Although they had to leave everything (10:28) to follow him, Jesus assured them that anyone who gave up something valuable for his sake would be repaid **a hundred times over,** although not necessarily in the same form. For example, someone may be rejected by his or her family for accepting Christ, but he or she will gain the larger family of believers with all the love it has to offer.

Along with these rewards, however, **persecutions** must be expected because the world hates God.

Jesus emphasized persecution to point out to the disciples that they must not selfishly follow him only for the rewards. This fact was also important for Mark's Roman readers who may have been facing persecution, or would soon be. The pressure of persecution did not mean that God wasn't keeping his promises or that the disciples had been wrong in putting faith in him. Rather, during persecution, God still blesses all those who believe in him.

Here was the answer to the rich young ruler's question about how to obtain eternal life (10:17). Jesus explained that by giving up anything that hinders following him, each person can have **eternal life.** For each person the sacrifice may be different, though no less difficult. We may have little or much, but are we willing to give it all up in order to have eternal life?

10:31 In the world to come, the values of this world will be reversed. Those who have desired to be Christ's disciples and have humbly served others are most qualified to be great in heaven. Rewards in heaven are given not on the basis of merit or "time served" or other earthly standards. What matters in heaven is one's commitment to Christ.

JESUS PREDICTS HIS DEATH THE THIRD TIME / 10:32-34 / 177
As if to underscore his destination, Jesus once again spoke to the disciples about his impending death. He included the Resurrection in his prediction. This prediction was the most graphic, which made it memorable when it was finally understood weeks later after the Resurrection.

10:32 Jesus and the disciples continued toward **Jerusalem.** This is the first mention in Mark of their destination. Jesus had just spoken to them about facing persecution and had told them of his impending death twice before. Thus, the disciples **were filled with dread** that he so steadfastly headed toward Jerusalem. This was the third time Jesus told the disciples about his impending death (see also 8:31; 9:30-31). This time he gave much more detail about what was coming.

10:33-34 Jesus' death and resurrection should have come as no surprise to the disciples. Here Jesus clearly explained that he would be **betrayed** (someone who had loved him would turn on him) to the Jewish leaders who would **hand him over**

to the Romans. Because Israel was occupied territory, they had to submit to Rome's authority in cases of capital punishment. They could punish lesser crimes, but only Rome could execute an offender. The Romans would show great contempt for their prisoner, mocking and beating him before killing him.

Jesus repeated that **after three days** he would **rise again,** but the disciples heard only his words about death. Because Jesus often spoke in parables, the disciples may have thought that his words on death and resurrection were another parable they weren't astute enough to understand. The Gospels include Jesus' predictions of his death and resurrection to show that these events were God's plan from the beginning and not accidents.

JESUS TEACHES ABOUT SERVING OTHERS / 10:35-45 / 178
Jesus devoted much of his final time on earth to two objectives: to prepare the disciples for his own death and resurrection, and to prepare the disciples for life together without his physical presence. James and John's special request provides another view of the disciples' overall state

of mind. They didn't understand what Jesus was saying; instead, they were convinced that great events were about to occur. They were jostling for position. Greatness, as defined and illustrated by Jesus' words and life, finds its clearest expression in service.

10:35-36 Two of Jesus' disciples, **James and John** (brothers who along with Peter made up the inner circle of disciples, 9:2) came to Jesus. They requested that Jesus promise to fulfill a **favor.** They may have misconstrued Jesus' promise that the twelve disciples would "sit on twelve thrones, judging the twelve tribes of Israel" (Matthew 19:28). Jesus was thinking about what he would face in Jerusalem and the death he knew awaited him there. Yet he showed remarkable patience with these two beloved disciples who came with a request. Jesus made no promises, but simply asked what they wanted him to do.

10:37 The disciples, like most Jews of that day, had the wrong idea of the Messiah's Kingdom as predicted by the Old Testament prophets. They thought Jesus would establish an earthly kingdom that would free Israel from Rome's oppression. As the disciples followed Jesus toward Jerusalem, they realized that something was about to happen; they certainly hoped Jesus would be inaugurating his Kingdom. James and John wanted to **sit in places of honor next to** Christ in his glory. In ancient royal courts, the persons chosen to sit at the **right** and **left** hands of the king were the most powerful people in the Kingdom. James and John were asking for the equivalent of those positions in Jesus' court. They understood that Jesus would have a Kingdom; they understood that Jesus would be glorified (they had seen the Transfiguration); and they approached him as loyal subjects to their king. However, they did not understand that Jesus' Kingdom is not of this world; it is not centered in palaces and thrones, but in the hearts and lives of his followers. None of the disciples understood this truth until after Jesus' resurrection.

10:38 Jesus responded to James and John that in making such a self-centered request, they did not know what they were asking. To request positions of highest honor meant also to request deep suffering, for they could not have one without the other. Thus, he asked first if they were **able to drink from the bitter cup of sorrow** that he would drink. The "cup" to which Jesus referred was the cup of suffering that he would have to drink in order to accomplish salvation for sinners. Then Jesus asked if they were **able to be baptized with the baptism of suffering** he would face. The reference to "baptism" picks up an Old Testament metaphor for a person being overwhelmed by suffering. The "cup" and the "baptism" refer to what Jesus would face on

the cross. In both questions, Jesus was asking James and John if they were ready to suffer for the sake of the Kingdom.

10:39-40 James and John replied confidently to Jesus' question. Their answer may not have revealed bravado or pride as much as it showed their willingness to follow Jesus whatever the cost. They said they were willing to face any trial for Christ. Jesus replied that they would indeed be called upon to **drink** from Jesus' cup and **be baptized** with his baptism of suffering: James died as a martyr (Acts 12:2); John lived through many years of persecution before being forced to live the last years of his life in exile on the island of Patmos (Revelation 1:9).

Although these two disciples would face great suffering, that still would not mean that Jesus would grant their request for great honor. Jesus would not make that decision; instead, those places were **prepared . . . for the ones he has chosen.** God's omniscience is revealed in the statement that he already knew who would gain those places of great honor.

10:41-42 The **ten other disciples** were **indignant,** probably because all the disciples desired honor in the Kingdom. The disciples' attitudes degenerated into pure jealousy and rivalry. Jesus explained to them the difference between the kingdoms they saw in the world and God's Kingdom, which they had not yet experienced. The kingdoms of the world (an obvious example being the Roman Empire) have **tyrants** and high **officials** who **lord it over** people, exercising authority and demanding submission.

10:43-45 Jesus' Kingdom had already begun right there in that group of twelve disciples. But the Kingdom was not set up with some who could lord it over others. Instead, the greatest person would be the servant of all. A real **leader** has a servant's heart, willingly helping out others as needed. Servant leaders appreciate others' worth and realize that they're not above any job. They aren't jealous about someone else's gifts, but gladly fulfill their duties. The disciples could not mistake Jesus' explanation that they were to serve sacrificially. Only with such an attitude would the disciples be able to carry out the mission of sharing the gospel across the world. Jesus was their perfect example of a servant leader because he **came here not to be served but to serve others, and to give [his] life**

as a ransom for many. Jesus' mission was to serve—ultimately by giving his life in order to save sinful humanity. His life wasn't "taken"; he "gave" it, offered it up as a sacrifice for people's sins. A ransom was the price paid to release a slave from bondage. Jesus paid a ransom for us, and the demanded price was his life. Jesus took our place; he died the death we deserved.

JESUS HEALS A BLIND BEGGAR / 10:46-52 / 179

The healing of Bartimaeus was the final event before the Passion Week. Chapter 9 focused on wrong perceptions of Jesus by the disciples and the crowds. Jesus responded, not to Bartimaeus's understanding of Jesus' lordship, but to the boldness of his faith. Bartimaeus believed, not because of the clarity of his sight, but as a response to what he heard. Blind Bartimaeus asked for mercy and received his sight.

10:46 Jesus and the disciples arrived in the city of **Jericho**. The Old Testament city of Jericho had been destroyed by the Israelites (Joshua 6:20). But during Herod the Great's rule over Palestine, he had rebuilt the city (about a mile south of the original city) as a site for his winter palace. Jericho was a popular and wealthy resort city, not far from the Jordan River, about eighteen miles northeast of Jerusalem. Jesus was on his way to Jerusalem (10:32), and after crossing over from Perea, he would naturally enter Jericho. Jesus passed through the city, accompanied by his disciples and a **great crowd** (probably made up of Jews also on their way to Jerusalem for the Passover). They came upon a **blind beggar** sitting by the roadside. Beggars often waited along the roads near cities, because that was where they were able to contact the most people.

10:47 The blind man could not see, but he **heard** that Jesus of Nazareth was at the head of the approaching crowd. **Bartimaeus** called Jesus **Son of David** because he, along with all Jews, knew that the Messiah would be a descendant of King David (see Isaiah 9:6-7; 11:1; Jeremiah 23:5-6). This blind beggar could see that Jesus was the long-awaited Messiah, while so many who witnessed Jesus' miracles were blind to his identity, refusing to open their eyes to the truth. Seeing with one's eyes doesn't guarantee seeing with the heart.

10:48 The crowd tried to get the man to **be quiet.** It was most natural for the people, even Jesus' disciples, to attempt to shield Jesus from being harassed by beggars. But this only caused Bartimaeus to shout **louder** in an attempt to gain Jesus' attention. And it worked.

10:49-50 Although Jesus was concerned about the coming events in Jerusalem, he demonstrated what he had just told the disciples about service (10:45) by stopping to care for the blind man. Blindness was considered a curse from God for sin (John 9:2), but Jesus refuted this idea when he told the people to call the man to him. Bartimaeus **threw aside his coat, jumped up, and came to Jesus.**

10:51-52 Obviously Jesus already knew what Bartimaeus wanted. Jesus' question was not to gain information, but to allow Bartimaeus to specify his need and, in the process, to declare his faith that Jesus could meet that need. **"I want to see"** is literally "I want to recover my sight." The blind man had at one time been able to see. The result of Bartimaeus's request was that he **could see.** His faith (evidenced in his persistence) had made him well. Bartimaeus then **followed** Jesus.

MARK 11

JESUS RIDES INTO JERUSALEM ON A DONKEY / 11:1-11 / 183

As in the other Gospels, the story slows now, from Jesus' entry into Jerusalem until his resurrection a week later. Until this point, the Gospels present a sampler of Jesus' life and ministry. But the closing chapters of each account present powerful details.

The crowd that accompanied the Lord into Jerusalem was made up of Jesus' followers and pilgrims on their way to Passover. Jesus raised Lazarus from the dead. The crowd joyfully escorted Jesus into Jerusalem, perhaps hoping that this would be the time when he would declare his political intentions and expel the Romans.

11:1-2 After passing through Jericho and healing the blind man (10:46), Jesus and the disciples **drew near Jerusalem** and **came to the towns of Bethphage and Bethany.** These two villages were about one mile apart, one and two miles respectively from the eastern wall of Jerusalem, and sat on the eastern slope of the Mount of Olives. Bethany was the home of Jesus' dear friends Mary, Martha, and Lazarus; he often stayed there with his disciples (see John 11:1). He may have returned to their home each night after his visits to Jerusalem during the days of this final week. The **Mount of Olives** is a ridge about two and a half miles long on the other side of the Kidron Valley east of Jerusalem. The view from the top of this twenty-nine-hundred-foot ridge is spectacular—one can see the whole city. From this site, Jesus discussed the coming destruction of the city and Temple (13:1-4).

They were probably in Bethphage when Jesus sent disciples to the other village (Bethany) to get the **colt** and **bring it** back. The specification that this be a colt **that has never been ridden** is significant in light of the ancient rule that only animals that had not been used for ordinary purposes were appropriate for sacred purposes (Numbers 19:2; Deuteronomy 21:3; 1 Samuel 6:7).

This was Sunday of the week that Jesus would be crucified, and the great Passover festival was about to begin. Jews came to Jerusalem from all over the Roman world during this week-long celebration to remember the great Exodus from Egypt (see Exodus 12:37-51). Many in the crowds had heard of or seen Jesus and were hoping he would come to the Temple (John 11:55-57).

11:3-6 Mark emphasized Jesus' supernatural knowledge and control in this incident. He knew the disciples would be asked why they were taking the colt. Donkeys and their colts were valuable; this could be compared to borrowing someone's car. By this time Jesus was extremely well known. Everyone coming to Jerusalem for the Passover feast had heard of him, and Jesus had been a frequent visitor in Bethany. **The Lord needs it and will return it soon** was all the two disciples had to say, and the colt's owners (Luke 19:33) would

gladly let them take the animal. The disciples went and found everything just exactly as Jesus had said.

11:7 The two disciples walked the colt back to Bethphage. The colt, having never been ridden (11:2), did not have a saddle, so the disciples **threw their garments** (coats) on its back so that Jesus could sit on it. The action of placing the garments on the donkey and Jesus riding it connotes majesty (see 2 Kings 9:13).

11:8 Crowds had already gathered on this stretch of road a mile outside of Jerusalem, going to the city for the Feast of Unleavened Bread and Passover. When Jesus mounted the colt and headed toward the city, they recognized that he was fulfilling the prophecy in Zechariah 9:9. All pilgrims walked the final ascent to Jerusalem; Jesus' riding was a clear sign. The crowd's spontaneous celebration honored Jesus. They **spread their coats on the road** for him to ride over, and **cut leafy branches** from the fields. These branches were used as part of the pilgrimage into Jerusalem.

11:9-10 The crowd chanted words from Psalm 118:25-26. "Long live the King" was the meaning behind their joyful shouts because they knew that Jesus was intentionally fulfilling prophecy. The expression, **the coming kingdom of our ancestor David,** recalls God's words in 2 Samuel 7:12-14. This was Jesus' announcement that he was indeed the long-awaited Messiah.

11:11 Jesus entered the great city and went to the Temple, entering its outer courts. Mark notes that Jesus **looked around carefully at everything.** This seems somewhat pointless until we read of Jesus' actions in the Temple the next day (11:15-17) and understand that Jesus had already cleared the Temple of these racketeers on an earlier Passover week (John 2:12-25), only to find here that they had returned. He and the disciples returned to Bethany for the night, perhaps to the home of Mary, Martha, and Lazarus. It was not safe for Jesus to stay in the city. His only night in the city was the night of his arrest. Jesus' dear friends must have been a great comfort to him during this final week.

JESUS CLEARS THE TEMPLE AGAIN / 11:12-19 / 184
Jesus was patient with ignorance, but he confronted arrogance. He was in constant conflict with those who knew better but did wrong. Jesus once again faced the desecration of the Temple by

the peddlers and parasites he had expelled during a previous visit had returned (see John 2:12-25). When a cleansed Temple isn't filled up with goodness, it is soon restocked with evil.

Mark bracketed this account of the Temple cleansing with the cursing of a fig tree. Jesus' cleansing of the Temple and cursing of the fig tree both demonstrate divine judgment on the apostasy of Israel.

11:12-14 This **next morning** was Monday. Jesus and the disciples got up and headed back into Jerusalem. They spent the nights in Bethany and went into Jerusalem during the day. Bethany was about two miles outside of Jerusalem.

Somewhere along the way, Jesus mentioned that he **felt hungry**. Fig trees were a popular source of inexpensive food in Israel. In March, the fig trees had small edible buds; in April came the large green leaves. Then in May the buds would fall off, replaced by the normal crop of figs. This incident occurred in April, and the green leaves should have indicated the presence of the edible buds which Jesus expected to find on the tree. However, this tree, though full of leaves, had no buds. The tree looked promising but offered no fruit.

Jesus did not curse this fig tree because he was angry at not getting any food from it. Instead, this was an acted-out parable intended to teach the disciples. They didn't know that Jesus was on his way to once again cleanse the Temple of the people who were desecrating it. By cursing the fig tree, Jesus was showing his anger at religion without substance. Jesus' harsh words to the fig tree could be applied to the nation of Israel and its beautiful Temple. Fruitful in appearance only, Israel was spiritually barren.

11:15-16 Jesus and the disciples arrived in Jerusalem and went straight to the Temple. He had some "cleansing" to do, and he **began to drive out** those who were buying and selling there.

People came to the Temple in Jerusalem to offer sacrifices. God had originally instructed the people to bring sacrifices from their own flocks (Deuteronomy 12:5-7). However, the religious leadership had set up markets on the Mount of Olives where such animals could be purchased. Some people did not bring their own animals and planned to buy one at the market. Others brought their own animals, but when the priests managed to find the animal unacceptable in some way (it was supposed to be an animal without defect, Leviticus 1:2-3), worshipers were forced to buy another. One such market was set up in the Court of the Gentiles, the huge outer court of the Temple. This was the only place Gentile converts to Judaism could worship, but the market filled their worship space with merchants. Because both those who bought and those who sold were going against God's commands regarding the sacrifices, Jesus drove them all out.

The **money changers** did big business during Passover. Those who came from foreign countries had to have their money changed into Jewish currency because this was the only money the merchants accepted and the only money accepted for payment of the Temple tax. The inflated exchange rate often enriched the money changers, and the exorbitant prices of animals made the merchants wealthy. Jesus became angry because God's house of worship had become a place of extortion and a barrier to Gentiles who wanted to worship.

11:17 Obviously Jesus' actions stunned the many people crowded into the Temple area. Jesus quoted from Isaiah 56:7 and explained God's purpose for the Temple: **a place of prayer for all nations.** These were important words in light of Jesus' concern for the Gentiles who had come to worship, and considering the Gentile audience to whom Mark was writing. God welcomed the Gentiles into his Temple to worship, but they were unable to do so because of the animals bellowing and merchants haggling.

Not only that, but all these merchants were no more honest than **thieves** who had turned the Temple into their **den.** This was a horrible desecration. No wonder Jesus was so angry.

11:18-19 The **leading priests** were mostly Sadducees (the wealthy, upper class, priestly party among the Jewish political groups); the **teachers of religious law** were usually Pharisees (legal experts). These two parties had great contempt for each other. That these two groups could agree on anything was highly out of the ordinary. But Jesus was becoming a real problem: undermining their authority in the Temple, performing great miracles of healing, and teaching the people in such an exciting manner. So these religious leaders **began planning how to kill him.** But Jesus was so popular with the crowds that they dared not make a move immediately. In short, **they were afraid of him.**

With the religious leaders plotting to kill him, Jerusalem would hardly be a safe place for Jesus to spend the night. So when evening came on that Monday night, Jesus and the disciples **left the city** and most likely returned to Bethany as before (because they passed the same fig tree the next morning, 11:13, 20).

JESUS SAYS THE DISCIPLES CAN PRAY FOR ANYTHING / 11:20-26 / 188

Mark split his account of Jesus cursing the fig tree into two parts: the curse itself as an acted-out parable about God's judgment of fruitless Israel, and the disciples' response. Our perspective tends to be different than that of the disciples. They accepted the cursing of the fig tree, but wondered how Jesus had caused the plant to wither. We take Jesus' power for granted but want to know why Jesus did it. The parallel between Jesus cursing the tree and cleansing the Temple reveals his motive. The power of faith and prayer can make us effective. For our prayers to be effective, we must have faith and we must forgive others.

11:20-21 The **next morning,** Tuesday, Jesus and his disciples passed by the same fig tree they had passed the day before (11:13-14). Jesus had cursed the tree, saying that no one would ever eat from it. By the next day, in the morning light, they could see that the tree had **withered.** This parable of judgment on spiritually dead Israel revealed a severe punishment. The early church later applied this parable to the total destruction of Jerusalem in A.D. 70.

11:22-23 Jesus did not explain why he cursed the fig tree, and we don't know whether the disciples understood Jesus' meaning. Yet his words to them could mean that despite the coming judgment on spiritual laxity in Israel, they would be safe if they had **faith in God.** Their faith should not rest in a kingdom they hoped Jesus would set up, in obeying the Jewish laws, or in their position as Jesus' disciples. Their faith should rest in God alone.

Jesus then taught them a lesson about answers to prayer. Jesus had cursed the fig tree; the fig tree had died; the disciples had expressed surprise. Then Jesus explained that they could ask anything of God and receive an answer. **This mountain** (referring to the Mount of Olives on which they stood) could be sent **into the sea** (the Dead Sea, that could be seen from the Mount). Jesus' point was that in their petitions to God they must **believe and not doubt** (that is, without wavering in their confidence in God). The kind of prayer Jesus meant was not the arbitrary wish to move a mountain; instead, he was referring to prayers that the disciples would need to endlessly pray as they

faced mountains of opposition to their gospel message in the years to come. Their prayers for the advancement of God's Kingdom would always be answered positively—in God's timing.

11:24 This verse was not a guarantee that the disciples could get **anything** they wanted simply by asking Jesus and believing. God does not grant requests that violate his own nature or will. Jesus' statement was not a blank check. To be fulfilled, requests made to God in prayer must be in harmony with the principles of God's Kingdom. They must be made in Jesus' name (John 14:13-14). The stronger our faith, the more likely our prayers will be in union with Christ and in line with God's will; then God would be happy to grant them. God can accomplish anything, even if it seems humanly impossible.

11:25 Jesus gave another condition for answered prayer—this one referring to believers' relationships with others. He told the disciples that when they stood praying, if one of them held **a grudge** against someone, he ought to first forgive that person before praying. Why would this matter? Because all people are sinners before God. Those who have access to him have it only because of his mercy in forgiving their sins. Believers should not come to God asking for forgiveness or making requests, all the while refusing to forgive others. To do so would reveal that they have no appreciation for the mercy they have received. God will not listen to a person with such an attitude. God wants those who are forgiven to forgive others.

RELIGIOUS LEADERS CHALLENGE JESUS' AUTHORITY / 11:27-33 / 189

At this point, Mark began an extended section (11:27–12:34) that shows Jesus under constant attack yet emerging victorious over his opponents. With the one exception of the teacher who asked Jesus about the greatest commandment (12:28), Jesus' opponents tried desperately to catch him in a wrong answer. In each case, Jesus turned their question around with a question of his own. He showed that their motives were evil and their premises were wrong.

11:27-28 The teaching recorded in 11:22-26 transpired on Tuesday morning, as Jesus and the disci-

ples were on their way back into Jerusalem. They returned to the **Temple,** where Jesus had thrown out the merchants and money changers the day before. The religious leaders were afraid to act on their plot to kill Jesus in the public surroundings of the Temple. He was safe in the Temple courts among the people with whom he was so popular.

But a delegation of religious leaders stopped Jesus to question him regarding his actions the day before. This group of leaders was already plotting to kill Jesus (11:18), but they couldn't figure out how to do it. His popularity was far too widespread and his miracle-working powers too well known. So they continued to try to trap him. They asked for his credentials and demanded that he tell them who gave him the **authority** to **drive out the merchants** from the Temple.

If Jesus were to answer that his authority came from God, which would be tantamount to saying he was the Messiah and the Son of God, they would accuse him of blasphemy (blasphemy carried the death penalty; see Leviticus 24:10-23). If Jesus were to say that his authority was his own, they could dismiss him as a fanatic and could trust that the crowds would soon return to those with true authority (themselves). But Jesus would not let himself be caught. Turning the question on them, he exposed their motives and avoided their trap.

11:29-30 To expose the leaders' real motives, Jesus countered their question with a question. Jesus' question seems totally unrelated to the situation at hand, but Jesus knew that the leaders' attitude about **John** the Baptist would reveal their true attitude toward him. In this question, Jesus implied that his authority came from the same source as John the Baptist's. So Jesus asked these religious leaders what they thought: Did John's authority to baptize **come from heaven,** or was it **merely human** authority?

11:31-33 The interchange recorded among these factions of the religious leaders revealed their true motives. They weren't interested in the truth; they didn't want an answer to their question so they could finally understand Jesus—they simply hoped to trap him. But they found themselves in a position of looking foolish in front of the crowd. If they answered that John's baptism had come **from heaven,** then they would incriminate themselves for not listening to John and believing his words. If they rejected John as having any divine authority, then they also were rejecting Jesus' authority and would be in danger of the crowd, **since everyone thought that John was a prophet.** If they accepted John's authority, they would then have to admit that Jesus also had divine authority. The leaders couldn't win, so they hoped to save face by refusing to take either alternative. Thus, Jesus was not obligated to answer their question. The religious leaders had already decided against Jesus, carrying on a long tradition of the leaders of Israel rejecting God's prophets. This is the point Jesus makes in the following parable (12:1-12).

MARK 12

JESUS TELLS THE PARABLE OF THE EVIL FARMERS / 12:1-12 / *191*
Jesus was presumably still in the Temple, where the Jewish leaders had come to question him. They had failed in their first attempt at tricking Jesus (11:27-33). In the parable of the wicked farmers, Jesus used a strong image of judgment from the Old Testament (Isaiah 5:1-7). Isaiah's ancient poem incriminated Jerusalem by name. The religious leaders immediately heard the charges leveled against them.

12:1 Jesus' **stories,** also called parables, always used something familiar to help people understand something new. This method of teaching compels listeners to discover truth for themselves. The moment Jesus spoke of a **vineyard,** the well-versed religious leaders surely recognized the correlation with Isaiah 5:1-7, where Isaiah described Israel as a vineyard. Isaiah's parable described judgment on Israel; Jesus' parable described judgment too. The situation pictured in this parable was by no means unusual. Galilee had many such estates with absentee owners who had hired **tenant farmers** to care for the fields and crops. The tenant farmers paid their "rent" by giving a portion of the crop to the landowner, who would send servants at harvesttime to collect it.

The main elements in this parable are (1) the man who planted the vineyard—God, (2) the vineyard—Israel, (3) the tenant farmers—the Jewish religious leaders, (4) the landowner's servants—the prophets and priests who remained faithful to God and preached to Israel, (5) the son—Jesus, and (6) the others to whom the vineyard was given—the Gentiles.

Israel, pictured as a vineyard, was the nation that God had cultivated to bring salvation to the world. The religious leaders not only frustrated their nation's purpose; they also killed those who were trying to fulfill it. They were so jealous and possessive that they ignored the welfare of the very people they were supposed to be bringing to God. By telling this story, Jesus exposed the religious leaders' plot to kill him, and he warned them that their sins would be punished.

12:2-5 When the grape harvest came, the absentee landowner sent **servants** to collect the rent—generally this amounted to a quarter to a half of the crop. All of these servants were either beaten up or killed. In Jesus' parable, the servants that were sent to the tenants refer to the prophets and priests whom God had sent over the years to the nation of Israel. Instead of listening to the prophets, the religious leadership had mistreated them and had stubbornly refused to listen.

12:6 With all the servants having been mistreated or killed, the landowner had only one messenger left—his beloved **son.** This son was sent to collect the fruit in hopes that the farmers would respect the son. This son refers to Jesus. This is the same description God used at Jesus' baptism (1:11) and at the Transfiguration (9:7). The son was sent to the stubborn and rebellious nation of Israel to win them back to God.

12:7-8 The tenants probably thought that the arrival of the son meant that his father (the landowner) had died. In Palestine at that time, "ownerless" or unclaimed land could be owned by whoever claimed it first. Thus they reasoned that if they **murdered** the son, they could **get the estate** for themselves.

12:9 What would the landowner do in this case? All agreed that the landowner would **come, kill** the tenants, and **lease the vineyard to others** who would care for it.

Over hundreds of years, Israel's kings and religious leaders had rejected God's prophets—beating, humiliating, and killing them. Most recently, John the Baptist had been rejected as a prophet by Israel's leaders (11:30-33). Next Jesus, the beloved Son of God, already rejected by the religious leaders, would be killed. Jesus explained that the Jewish leaders would be accountable for his death because in rejecting the messengers and the Son, they had rejected God himself.

God's judgment would be spiritual death and the transfer of the privileges of ownership **to others,** namely, the Gentiles (see Romans 11:25-32). In this parable Jesus spoke of the beginning of the Christian church among the Gentiles. God would not totally reject Israel; in ancient times he always preserved a remnant of faithful people.

12:10-11 Jesus quoted from Psalm 118:22-23. Like the son who was rejected and murdered by the tenant farmers, Jesus referred to himself as **the stone rejected by the builders.** The **cornerstone** is the most important stone in a building, used as the standard to make sure the other stones of the building are straight and level. Israel's leadership, like the builders looking for an appropriate cornerstone, would toss Jesus aside because he didn't seem to have the right qualifications. They wanted a political king, not a spiritual one. Yet God's plans will not be thwarted. One day that rejected stone will indeed become a "cornerstone," for Jesus will come as a king to inaugurate an unending Kingdom. And he had already begun a spiritual Kingdom as the cornerstone of a brand-new "building," the Christian church (Acts 4:11-12; 1 Peter 2:7). Jesus' life and teaching would be the church's foundation.

12:12 When the **Jewish leaders** realized that they were the wicked farmers in Jesus' parable, they **wanted to arrest him.** But the presence of all those people, hanging on Jesus' every word, caused these religious leaders to fear a riot if they were to forcibly take Jesus away. There was nothing to do but go away somewhere to gather new ideas and think of new questions to try to trap Jesus.

RELIGIOUS LEADERS QUESTION JESUS ABOUT PAYING TAXES / 12:13-17 / 193

The retreat mentioned in 12:12 was only temporary. Soon the attacks against Jesus resumed. The religious leaders sent a delegation with the purpose of trapping Jesus with the same kind of question he used on them earlier (11:29-33). They set up a conflict between the honor due to God and the honor due human authorities. By living under the authority and monetary system of the Romans, the people were obligated to follow through on their responsibilities under that human structure while still being accountable to God. Where they saw an impossible conflict, Jesus described parallel duties. They presented Jesus with a question that they were sure would trap him, but he snared them in their own trap.

12:13 The Jewish leaders would not be put off because they were so intent on killing Jesus. The **Pharisees** were a religious group opposed to the Roman occupation of Palestine. The **supporters of Herod** were a political party that supported the Herods and the policies instituted by Rome. These groups with diametrically opposed beliefs usually had nothing to do with each other. But these two groups found a common enemy in Jesus. Despite Jesus' solemn warning to the Jewish leaders in his previous parable, they didn't let up. More delegates arrived whose intent was to **trap Jesus into saying something for which he could be arrested.**

12:14 The men in this delegation, pretending to be honest men, flattered Jesus before asking him their trick question, hoping to catch him off guard. They asked, **"Is it right to pay taxes to the Roman government or not?"** Judea had been a Roman province since 63 B.C., but the Jews had fairly recently been forced to pay taxes or tribute to Caesar. This was a hot topic in Palestine. The Pharisees were against these taxes on religious grounds; the Herodians supported taxation on political grounds. The Jewish people hated to pay taxes to Rome because the money supported their oppressors and symbolized their subjection. This was a valid (and loaded) question, and the crowd around Jesus certainly waited expectantly for his answer. For Jesus, either a yes or a no could lead to trouble. If Jesus agreed that it was right to pay taxes to Caesar, the Pharisees would say he was opposed to God and the people would turn against him. If Jesus said the taxes should not be paid, the Herodians could hand him over to Herod on the charge of rebellion.

12:15-16 Jesus knew this was a trap. These leaders didn't care about Jesus' opinion; this was merely a **trick question.** But Jesus would answer. He asked someone to give him a **Roman coin,** probably a denarius, the usual day's wage for a laborer. It was a silver coin with Caesar's **picture and title** on it. The tax paid to Rome was paid in these coins.

12:17 Jesus said, **"Give to Caesar what belongs to him"**—that is, the coin bearing the emperor's image should be given to the emperor. In their question, the religious leaders used the word *didomi,* meaning "to give." Jesus responded with the word *apodidomi,* meaning "to pay a debt." In other words, having a coin meant being part of that country, so citizens should acknowledge the authority of Caesar and pay for the benefits accorded to them by his empire. The Jews may not have been happy about the situation, but God had placed Caesar on the throne and Judea under his rule. The Pharisees and Herodians tried to make it appear that it was incompatible to be a Jew and pay taxes to a pagan emperor who claimed to be divine. But Jesus explained that no such incompatibility existed because God was ultimately in control. They would lose much and gain little if they refused to pay Caesar's taxes (see Romans 13:1-7; 1 Timothy 2:1-6; 1 Peter 2:13-17).

However, paying the taxes did not have to mean submission to the divinity claimed by the emperor. The words on the coins were incorrect. Caesar had the right to claim their tax money, but he had no claim on their souls. The Jews had a responsibility to remember that **everything that belongs to God must be given to God.** While they lived in the Roman world, the Jews had to face the dual reality of subjection to Rome and responsibility to God. Jesus explained that they could do both if they kept their priorities straight. The tax would be paid as long as Rome held sway over Judea, but God has rights on people's souls. To Jesus, this was the crucial issue. Were they giving to God their lives? Were they loving God with all their heart, soul, mind, and strength (12:30)? These Jews (and especially the self-righteous Pharisees) claimed to be God's chosen people. But were they even "rendering" to God what truly belonged to him—themselves?

RELIGIOUS LEADERS QUESTION JESUS
ABOUT THE RESURRECTION / 12:18-27 / 194
No sooner had one delegation withdrawn from Jesus (in amazement) than another appeared to take up the cause. The Sadducees did not believe in the resurrection. They thought they had a thorny problem from God's word that would make the very idea of life beyond death ludicrous. This was probably a standard challenge posed by the Sadducees to those who believed in the resurrection, such as the Pharisees.

12:18 The **Sadducees** were at odds theologically with the Pharisees (the other major group of Jewish leaders) because they honored only the Pentateuch—Genesis through Deuteronomy—as Scripture, and because they rejected most of the Pharisees' traditions, rules, and regulations. The Sadducees said **there is no resurrection after death** because they could find no mention of it in the Pentateuch. Apparently, the Pharisees had never been able to come up with a convincing argument from the Pentateuch for the resurrection, and the Sadducees thought they had trapped Jesus for sure. But Jesus was about to show them otherwise.

12:19 Obviously, since the Sadducees recognized only the books attributed to Moses (Genesis through Deuteronomy), their question came from Moses' writings. In the law, Moses had written that when a man died without a son, his unmarried **brother** (or nearest male relative) **should marry the widow** and produce children. The first son of this marriage was considered the heir of the dead man (Deuteronomy 25:5-6). The main purpose of the instruction was to produce an heir and guarantee that the family would not lose their land. The book of Ruth gives us an example of this law in operation (Ruth 3:1–4:12; see also Genesis 38:1-26). This law, called levirate marriage, protected the widow (in that culture widows usually had no means to support themselves) and allowed the family line to continue.

12:20-23 The Sadducees took their hypothetical situation to a rather ridiculous length as they tried to show the absurdity of believing in the resurrection. The book of Tobit (an apocryphal book not accepted by Protestants as part of the Old Testament canon but highly regarded by Jewish scholars at that time) includes the story of a woman who was married to seven men successively without ever having children. In Tobit the men are not brothers.

The woman in the situation they described had been married seven times to seven different men, all according to the law. The Sadducees reasoned that since this was in the law, there could not be a resurrection. When all eight of them were resurrected (the seven brothers and the woman), **"Whose wife will she be?"** The Sadducees erroneously assumed that if people were resurrected, it would be back to a continuation of life on earth—and that would be too confusing to be possible. They were incapable of understanding that God could both raise the dead and make new lives for his people, lives that would be different than what they had known on earth. The Sadducees had

brought God down to their level. Because they could not conceive of a resurrection life, they decided that God couldn't raise the dead. And Moses hadn't written about it, so they considered the "case closed."

12:24 Jesus wasted no time trying to deal with their hypothetical situation, but went directly to their underlying assumption that resurrection of the dead was impossible. Jesus clearly stated that they were wrong about the resurrection for two reasons: (1) They didn't **know the Scriptures** (if they did, they would believe in the resurrection because it is taught in Scripture), and (2) they didn't **know the power of God** (if they did, they would believe in the resurrection because God's power makes it possible, even necessary). Ignorance on these two counts was inexcusable for these religious leaders.

12:25 Furthermore, Jesus said, **when the dead rise** (not "if" but *when*), they will not rise to an extension of their earthly lives. Instead, life in heaven will be different. Believers **will be like the angels in heaven** regarding marriage. Believers do not become angels, for angels were created by God for a special purpose. Angels do not marry or propagate; neither will glorified human beings. On earth where death reigns, marriage and childbearing are important, but bearing children will not be necessary in the resurrection life because people will be raised up to glorify God forever—there will be no more death. Those in heaven will no longer be governed by physical laws but will be "like the angels"; that is, believers will share the immortal nature of angels.

Jesus' statement did not mean that people will not recognize their partners in heaven. Jesus was not dissolving the eternal aspect of marriage, doing away with sexual differences, or teaching that we will be asexual beings after death. We cannot tell very much about sex and marriage in heaven from this one statement by Jesus. He simply meant that we must not think of heaven as an extension of life as we now know it. Our relationships in this life are limited by time, death, and sin. We don't know everything about our resurrection life, but Jesus affirmed that relationships will be different from what we are used to here and now. The same physical and natural rules won't apply.

12:26-27 Because the Sadducees accepted only the Pentateuch as God's divine word, Jesus answered them from the book of Exodus (3:6). God would not have said, "I am the God of your ancestors" if he thought of Abraham, Isaac, and Jacob as dead (he would have said, "I *was* their God"). Thus, from God's perspective, they are alive. This evidence would have been acceptable in any rabbinic debate because it applied a grammatical argument: God's use of the present tense in speaking of his relationship to the great patriarchs who had been long dead by the time God spoke these words to

Moses. God had a continuing relationship with these men because of the truth of the resurrection. Therefore, the Sadducees had **made a serious error** in their assumption about the resurrection.

RELIGIOUS LEADERS QUESTION JESUS ABOUT THE GREATEST COMMANDMENT / 12:28-34 / 195

Several defined groups had taken their best shot at Jesus. As each antagonist engaged him in debate, the others apparently looked on with mixed emotions. On one hand, they had a common purpose in destroying Jesus. On the other, each group wanted to claim supremacy by being the one who eliminated the troublemaker.

Matthew hints at the background tension (Matthew 22:34). He provides a brief account of this exchange between Jesus and the teacher. He reported only the original question and Jesus' response. Mark's version fills in the picture and adds a positive note to the conflict. Jesus' responses did not always antagonize his opponents. Often they expressed amazement (12:17) and even agreement (12:32). Jesus was looking for greater commitment from people, not that they merely knew the right answers. Jesus told this teacher that he had the truth but had not yet expressed his trust. Knowing God's requirement of wholehearted faith and surrendering ourselves to him are separate steps of entering into the Kingdom.

12:28 This discussion continued within the Temple courts. Jesus and the disciples were surrounded by a crowd of people, while various groups of religious leaders came and went with their questions. This time, however, a **teacher** (a Pharisee, Matthew 22:34-35) brought a sincere question: **"Of all the commandments, which is the most important?"**

The reference to "the commandments" focused on a popular debate about the "more important" and "less important" of the hundreds of laws the Jews had accumulated. The Pharisees had classified over six hundred laws and spent much time discussing which laws were weightier than others. As a Pharisee himself, the man had in mind the debates over the relative importance of ritual, ethical, moral, and ceremonial laws, as well as the positive versus negative laws. Jesus' definitive answer about the resurrection caused this man to hope he might also have the final answer about all these laws. He wouldn't be disappointed.

12:29-30 Among all the Gospel writers, only Mark recorded Jesus' quote from Deuteronomy 6:4, which is the first part of what the Jews know as the *Shema* (referring to the opening word of the sentence in Hebrew). The *Shema* is made up from Deuteronomy 6:4-9; 11:13-21; Numbers 15:37-41 and is the major creed of Judaism that was recited twice daily (morning and evening) by devout Jews. The teachers of the law could debate all they wanted, but Jesus brought them back to the basics by giving new life to the oft-repeated words, **The**

Lord our God is the one and only Lord. What mattered were not laws and their relative importance; what mattered was a relationship with the one true God.

Jesus then answered the man's question by explaining what those words should mean in the daily lives of the Jews. Because they believed that there was one God (as opposed to other religions, such as the Romans with their pantheon of gods), they ought to love the one true God with every part of their being: **"Love the Lord your God with all your heart, all your soul, all your mind, and all your strength"** (see also Deuteronomy 6:5). A person's total being must be involved in loving God. To love God in this way is to fulfill completely all the commandments regarding one's "vertical" relationship.

12:31 In addition to the law quoted in 12:30, there is a **second** and **equally important** law. This law focuses on "horizontal" relationships—our dealings with fellow human beings. A person cannot maintain a good vertical relationship with God (loving God) without also caring for his or her neighbor. For this second law, Jesus quoted Leviticus 19:18: **"Love your neighbor as yourself."** The word "neighbor" refers to fellow human beings in general. The love a person has for himself or herself (in the sense of looking out for oneself, caring about best interests, etc.) should be continued, but it should also be directed toward others.

The Ten Commandments and all the other Old

Testament laws are summarized in these two laws. By fulfilling these two commands to love God totally and love others as oneself, a person will keep all the other commands.

12:32-33 The man commended Jesus for his true and insightful answer. The man realized that after all the Pharisees' wrangling about the laws, the answer had been amazingly simple. The man reaffirmed the *Shema* (12:29) quoted from Deuteronomy, saying, **"There is only one God."** He then added, **"and no other,"** echoing Deuteronomy 4:35 (see also Exodus 8:10; Isaiah 45:21). This man understood that the laws of love for God and love for neighbor were **more important** than **all of the burnt offerings and sacrifices required in the law.** In other words, love was more important than all the ritual and ceremonial laws. This man, one of the few among the Pharisees, was able to see that loving God with all one's **heart, understanding** (substituted for "mind"), and **strength,** and to **love** one's neighbors revealed a level of love and obedience that went far beyond the offering of sacrifices.

12:34 Jesus was pleased by the man's response and told him that he was **not far from the Kingdom of God.** This man had caught the intent of God's law as it is so often stressed in the Old Testament— that true obedience comes from the heart. Because the Old Testament commands lead to Christ, the man's next step toward obtaining God's Kingdom was faith in Jesus himself. This, however, was the most difficult step to take.

The questions ended, for **no one dared to ask** any more. But this did not end the opposition. The leaders continued in their plot to kill Jesus.

RELIGIOUS LEADERS CANNOT ANSWER JESUS' QUESTION / 12:35-37 / *196*
Jesus did not settle for a silent, seething truce with the religious leaders. He continued to teach. He demonstrated that God's word had not been fully examined regarding the identity of the Messiah. His provocative questions brought delight to the crowds, thoughtfulness to the attentive, and continued anger to his enemies.

12:35 This was still Tuesday of Jesus' final week, and he was **teaching** in the **Temple.** The Pharisees expected a Messiah (the Christ, the Anointed One), but they erroneously thought he would be only a human ruler who would reign on King David's throne, deliver them from Gentile domination by establishing God's rule on earth, and restore Israel's greatness as in the days of David and Solomon. They knew that the Messiah would be a **son** (descendant) **of David,** but they did not understand that he would be more than a human descendant—he would be God in the flesh.

12:36 The Jews and early Christians knew the Old Testament was inspired by God, bearing his authority in its teachings. Jesus quoted Psalm 110:1 to show that **David,** speaking under the **inspiration of the Holy Spirit,** understood the Messiah to be his **Lord** (that is, one who had authority over him), not just his descendant. The Messiah would be a human descendant of David, but he would also be God's divine Son. That he sits at God's **right hand** means the Messiah will sit in the place of highest honor and authority in God's coming Kingdom. In ancient royal courts, the right side of the king's throne was reserved for the person who could act in the king's place. The picture of enemies humbled **beneath** his **feet** describes the final conquering of sin and evil.

12:37 If the great King David himself called the coming Messiah his **Lord** in Psalm 110:1, then how could he be merely David's **son** (meaning "descendant") **at the same time?** David himself didn't think the Messiah would be just a descendant; instead, David, under the inspiration of the Holy Spirit, realized that the Messiah would be God in human form and would deserve due respect and honor.

JESUS WARNS AGAINST THE RELIGIOUS LEADERS / 12:38-40 / *197*
This section offers a preview and provides a transition to the Olivet discourse in chapter 13. Here Jesus explained why such judgment will occur. As we read and think about Jesus' scathing evaluation of the teachers of religious law, we ought to keep our own behavior in mind. Some of the religious leaders liked the show. They were doing nothing more than playacting, pretending to be religious and righteous. Jesus confronted their lack of heartfelt obedience. What would he say about ours?

12:38-39 This denunciation of the religious leaders (specifically the **teachers of religious law**) probably occurred right in the Temple and was spoken to the surrounding crowd that had been "listening to him with great interest" (12:37). Matthew has an entire chapter of such denunciations—seven "woes" to the teachers of religious law and Pharisees whom Jesus unhesitatingly called "hypocrites" (Matthew 23). Mark recorded a shortened version, signaling Jesus' final break with the religious leaders.

Having silenced the questioning of the religious leaders, Jesus turned to the crowd and told them to **beware** of these men. While they had education and authority, Jesus denounced their conduct. Their actions revealed their desire for attention and honor. They had lost sight of their priority as teachers of religious law and were enjoying their position merely because of the "perks" it offered. Jesus condemned this attitude.

12:40 Not only did the teachers walk around expecting perks and honor, they also actively abused their position. Because they received no pay, they depended on the hospitality of devout Jews. It was considered an act of piety for people to help these teachers. That they **cheat widows out of their property** was a vivid picture of these religious men using their position to defraud the gullible. Some people would even go so far as to place all their finances in the teacher's control (especially widows who trusted them). As the nation's lawyers, these men were often employed in handling the money a widow received from her father's dowry. Some abused their trusted positions by unethically obtaining the dowry for the Temple and then keeping it themselves. They were in a position to exploit people, cheating the poor out of everything they had and taking advantage of the rich. How could they deserve anything but **punishment!**

A POOR WIDOW GIVES ALL SHE HAS / 12:41-44 / 200

Almost unheard in the clash of ideas and the noisy crowd, the ring of the widow's small coins became an eloquent example of truth. Her act sharply contrasted with the much more obvious giving of others and with the teachers who cheated widows such as she (12:40). But it also represented an alternative to business-as-usual in the Temple. All around her were large examples of meaningless worship, shallow honor given to God, frivolous giving, and downright evil. But this woman's act of sacrifice spoke volumes about herself and her faith.

12:41 Jesus completed his teaching and **sat** in the area of the Temple called the Court of Women. The treasury was located there or in an adjoining walkway. In this area were seven collection boxes in which worshipers could deposit their Temple tax and six boxes for freewill offerings. From his vantage point, Jesus **watched as the crowds dropped in their money.** A lot of money came into the Temple treasury during Passover; the increased crowds meant increased money amounts in the coffers. Surely the **large amounts** from the **rich people** clattered loudly into the boxes.

12:42 In contrast, a **poor widow** came with a freewill offering (that is, she was not paying a required tax, but rather giving a gift). As a widow, she had few resources for making money. If a widow in New Testament times had no sons, no protector, and remained unmarried, she was

often destitute. Since there was no social security or public aid for widows, a widow would often be without financial support. This widow's offering totaled only **two pennies.** Her small gift was a sacrifice, but she gave it willingly.

12:43-44 Jesus seized the opportunity to teach his disciples an important lesson in giving. In Jesus' eyes, the poor widow had **given more than all the others**—even the rich people who had contributed large amounts to the treasury. Though her gift was by far the smallest in monetary value, it was the greatest in sacrifice. The value of a gift is not determined by its amount, but by the spirit in which it is given. The rich had given **a tiny part of their surplus,** but she had **given everything,** trusting God to care for her. Jesus wanted the disciples to see this lesson in total surrender of self, commitment to God, and willingness to trust in his provision.

MARK 13

JESUS TELLS ABOUT THE FUTURE / 13:1-23 / *201*

Chapter 13 has a conversation between Jesus and his disciples as they left the Temple and Jerusalem, walking back to Bethany where they spent their nights. Jesus took advantage of this "teachable moment." A casual remark about the magnificent Temple by a disciple led Jesus to make a startling prophetic statement about the fate of the Temple. The group paused on the Mount of Olives, where they could glance back across the valley toward Jerusalem. Perhaps they watched the sun set behind the ancient city.

Several disciples chose that moment to ask two curious questions: When will these things happen? What will be the sign? With his answers, Jesus prepared his disciples for the difficult years ahead. He warned them about false messiahs, natural disasters, and persecutions. But he also assured them that he would be with them to protect them and make his Kingdom known through them. Jesus promised that, in the end, he would return in power and glory to save them.

13:1 Jesus and the disciples were leaving the Temple (this may have been either Tuesday or Wednesday evening of the week before the Crucifixion). This was Jesus' last visit to the Temple area. He would do no more preaching or public teaching. One of the disciples remarked on the incredible beauty of the Temple. Although no one knows exactly what this Temple looked like, it must have been magnificent, for in its time it was considered one of the architectural wonders of the world. This was not Solomon's Temple—it had been destroyed by the Babylonians in the seventh century B.C. (2 Kings 25:8-10). This Temple had been built by Ezra after the return from exile in the sixth century B.C. (Ezra 6:14-15), desecrated by the Seleucids in the second century B.C., reconsecrated by the Maccabees soon afterward, and enormously expanded by Herod the Great.

The Temple was impressive, covering about one-sixth of the land area of the ancient city of Jerusalem. It was not one building, but a majestic mixture of porches, colonnades, separate small edifices, and courts surrounding the Temple proper—hence the comment about the **tremendous buildings.** Outside these courts were long porches. Solomon's porch was 1,562 feet long; the royal porch was decorated with 160 columns stretching along its 921-foot length. The Temple's foundation was so solid that it is believed that some of the original footings remain to this day. The Jews were convinced of the permanence of this magnificent structure, not only because of the sta-

bility of construction, but also because it represented God's presence among them. The **massive stones** the disciple mentioned were huge white stones, some of them measuring twenty-five by eight by twelve feet and weighing more than one hundred tons.

13:2 Jesus made a startling statement: **These magnificent buildings** would be completely **demolished.** The destruction of the Jews' beloved Temple would be God's judgment against them for turning away from him. This happened only a few decades later when the Romans sacked Jerusalem in A.D. 70. Gazing at the massive stones, the disciples surely found it difficult to believe that not one of the stones would be **left on top of another.** Because the Temple symbolized God's presence among them, the Jews would be horrified to see it destroyed.

13:3-4 The **Mount of Olives** rises above Jerusalem to the east. As Jesus left the city to return to Bethany for the night, he would have crossed the Kidron Valley and then headed up the slopes of the Mount of Olives. From this slope, he and the disciples could look down into the city and see the Temple, with the sun setting behind it to the west. Four disciples came to Jesus **privately** because they wanted to understand what Jesus meant and when this terrible destruction would happen. Their question had two parts: (1) They wanted to know **when** this would happen (especially the destruction of the Temple), and (2) what **sign** would show that

Jesus' words **will be fulfilled.** The second part of their question referred to the end of the age. In the disciples' minds, one event would occur immediately after the other. They expected the Messiah to inaugurate his Kingdom soon, and they wanted to know the sign that it was about to arrive.

Jesus gave them a prophetic picture of that time, including events leading up to it. He also talked about far future events connected with the last days and his Second Coming, when he would return to earth to judge all people. Like much of Old Testament prophecy, Jesus predicted both near and distant events without putting them in chronological order. The coming destruction of Jerusalem and the Temple only foreshadowed a future destruction that would ultimately usher in God's Kingdom. Jesus was predicting the destruction of Jerusalem *and* the end times.

13:5-6 Jesus first answered the disciples' second question about the end of the age and the coming Kingdom. The disciples wondered what sign would reveal these things, but Jesus warned them against seeking signs, **"Don't let anyone mislead you."** Jesus knew that if the disciples looked for signs, they would be susceptible to being deceived. There would be **many** who would come **claiming to be the Messiah.** Jesus predicted that before his return, many believers would be led **astray** by false teachers claiming to be Christ.

In every generation since Christ's resurrection, certain individuals have claimed to be the Christ or to know exactly when Jesus would return. Obviously, no one else has been Christ, and no one has been right about the timing of the Second Coming. According to Scripture, the one clear sign of Christ's return will be his unmistakable appearance in the clouds, which will be seen by all people (13:26; Revelation 1:7). In other words, believers never have to wonder whether a certain person is the Messiah.

13:7-8 The key phrase in this verse comforts all believers, **"Don't panic."** As political situations worsen, as wars and rumors of wars ravage the world, Jesus instructed his disciples and all his followers not to be afraid that somehow God had lost control of his creation or that his promises would not come true. Just as false messiahs and religious frauds come and go, so do worldly crises. Even when the world's situation gets worse, God is in control. **These things must come** as part of God's divine plan. However, the wars and rumors of wars do not signal the end of the world. The disciples probably assumed that the Temple would only be destroyed at the end of the world as part of God establishing his new Kingdom. Jesus taught that

horrible events would happen, **but the end won't follow immediately.** Instead, this is **only the beginning of the horrors to come;** in other words, these would be preliminary sufferings. Jesus' words subtly explained to the eager disciples that there would be a span of time before the end of the age and the coming Kingdom—it would not happen this week, or immediately upon Jesus' resurrection, or even right after the destruction of Jerusalem. Instead, much suffering would occur as a part of life on earth, while history is moving toward a single, final, God-planned goal—the creation of a new earth and a new Kingdom (Revelation 21:1-3).

13:9 Jesus personalized his prophecy by explaining that the disciples themselves would face severe persecution; thus, they must be on their guard in order to stay true to the faith. Being **handed over to the courts** referred to the local Jewish courts held in the synagogues. They would also find themselves standing trial before Gentile **governors and kings.** But such trials would have a purpose— the disciples were to **tell them about** Jesus.

13:10 Jesus said that before his return, the **Good News** of the Kingdom (the message of salvation) would be **preached to every nation.** This was the disciples' mission—and it is ours. Jesus talked about the end times and final judgment to emphasize to his followers the urgency of spreading the gospel. By the time Mark's readers would hear these words, Jesus' prediction had already begun to happen. It occurred at Pentecost (Acts 2:5-11) and was spreading to all the world.

13:11 Not **if** the disciples would go on trial, but **when** they **are arrested and stand trial,** they were not to worry about defending themselves, but instead they were to concentrate on proclaiming the gospel. The **Holy Spirit** would give them God's peace and the words to say. These words would help the disciples be bold witnesses as they made their defense before the rulers (13:9). Notice that Jesus did not guarantee acquittal. James, one of the disciples here listening to Jesus, would be killed because of his faith (Acts 12:1-2).

13:12 Jesus warned that in the coming persecutions his followers would be betrayed by their family members and friends, as well as by religious and civil authorities. Certainly this was a reality for the Roman believers to whom Mark was writing. The fear of being **killed** for one's Christian faith would pit family members against one another.

13:13 Jesus' followers will face the reality that **everyone will hate** them because of their **allegiance to** Christ. For a Jew to convert to Christianity would soon become very dangerous because it would lead to hatred and ostracism. And Jesus' words looked forward to the time of the end when hatred of Christians would again occur. To believe in Jesus and **endure to the end** will take perseverance because our faith will be challenged and opposed. Severe trials will sift true Christians from fair-weather believers. Enduring to the end does not earn salvation for us; it marks us as already saved. The assurance of our salvation will keep us going through the times of persecution. While some will suffer and some will die, none of Jesus' followers will suffer spiritual or eternal loss.

13:14-18 Jesus warned against seeking signs, but as a final part of his answer to the disciples' second question (13:4), he gave them the ultimate event that would signal coming destruction. The **sacrilegious object that causes desecration** refers to the desecration of the Temple by God's enemies. Mark's phrase, **reader, pay attention,** may have been a sort of code for his Roman readers. A more precise explanation might have been dangerous for them if the Gospel fell into the wrong hands, so Mark urged them to understand Jesus' words in light of the prophecy from the Old Testament prophet Daniel (see Daniel 9:27; 11:31; 12:11). The **sacrilegious object** refers to pagan idolatry and sacrifice (see Deuteronomy 29:16-18; 2 Kings 16:3-4; 23:12-14). The sacrilege would occur in the Temple itself (**standing where it should not be**) and cause it to be abandoned.

The first fulfillment of Daniel's prophecy occurred in 168 B.C. by Antiochus Epiphanes. He sacrificed a pig to Zeus on the sacred Temple altar. This act incited the Maccabean wars. The second fulfillment occurred in A.D. 70 when the Roman army would destroy Jerusalem and desecrate the Temple. Some scholars say that the third fulfillment is yet to come. Jesus' words may also look far forward to the end times when the Antichrist will commit the ultimate sacrilege by setting up an image of himself in the Temple and ordering everyone to worship it (2 Thessalonians 2:4; Revelation 13:14-15).

Many of Jesus' followers (including Mark's readers) would live during the time of the destruction of Jerusalem and the Temple in A.D. 70. Jesus warned his followers to get out of Jerusalem and Judea and **flee to the hills** across the Jordan River when they saw the Temple being profaned. The Jewish historian Josephus wrote that from A.D. 66, Jewish Zealots clashed with the Romans. Many people realized that rebellion would bring the wrath of the Empire, so they fled to Pella, a town located in the mountains across the Jordan River. As Jesus had said, this proved to be their protec-

tion, for when the Roman army swept in, the nation and its capital city were destroyed.

The people were to leave immediately, without trying to pack bags or even to return from the field to the city to **get a coat** (a most basic necessity). They should leave everything behind as they fled from the coming crisis. Jesus expressed sympathy for those who will have difficulty fleeing because they are **pregnant** or have small children. Jesus told the disciples to pray that the crisis would not break **in winter.** Swollen rivers would make passage difficult across the usually small streams, as well as across the Jordan River.

13:19 Jesus gave this warning to get out quickly for these **will be days of greater horror than at any time since God created the world.** This language, while sounding like an exaggeration, is not unusual in Scripture when describing an impending disaster. The Jewish historian Josephus recorded that when the Romans sacked Jerusalem and devastated Judea, one hundred thousand Jews were taken prisoner and another 1.1 million died by slaughter and starvation. So many Jews were crucified that the hills were emptied of trees in order to build enough crosses.

While Jesus' words could be taken as referring to the coming destruction of Jerusalem by the Romans in A.D. 70, they are so emphatic and clear that they must point ultimately to the final period of tribulation at the end of the age, because, as he stated, **it will never happen again.**

13:20 Many interpreters conclude that Jesus, talking about the end times, was telescoping near future and far future events, as the Old Testament prophets had done. Many of these persecutions have already occurred; more are yet to come. While a certain amount of persecution happened in the destruction of Jerusalem, Jesus may also have envisioned the persecution of believers throughout history. The persecution will be so severe that **unless the Lord shortens that time,** that is, if it had not had a specific ending time, no one would survive. This refers to physical survival (as opposed to 13:13, which speaks of spiritual survival). The time would be cut short **for the sake of his chosen,** the believers. The shortening of the time will limit their duration so that the destruction will not wipe out God's people and thus their mission. God is ultimately in charge of history and will not allow evil to exceed the bounds he has set.

When the time of suffering comes, the important point for the disciples and all believers to remember is that God is in control. Persecution will occur, but God knows about it and controls how long it will take place. He will not forget his people.

13:21-23 The Old Testament frequently mentions **false prophets** (see 2 Kings 3:13; Isaiah 44:25; Jeremiah 23:16; Ezekiel 13:2-3; Micah 3:5; Zechariah 13:2) who claimed to receive messages from God, but they preached what the people wanted to hear, even when the nation was not following God as it should. There were false prophets in Jesus' day, and we have them today. They are the popular leaders who tell people what they want to hear—such as "God wants you to be rich," "Do whatever your desires tell you," or "There is no such thing as sin or hell." Jesus also said that **false messiahs** would come, and he warned his disciples, as he warns us, not to be deceived by whatever **signs and wonders** they might produce. They will be able to perform miracles designed to convince people that their claims are true. But their "power" will be by trickery or from Satan, not from God. Both false and true prophets can work miracles (see Deuteronomy 13:1-5;

2 Thessalonians 2:1-12; 1 John 4:1-3; Revelation 13:11-18).

Yet will they be so convincing that they might even lead **God's chosen ones** astray? Is it possible for Christians to be deceived? Yes, and Jesus pointed out the danger (see also Galatians 3:1). The arguments and proofs from deceivers in the end times will be so convincing that it will be difficult to be faithful. If we are prepared, Jesus says, we can remain faithful. With the Holy Spirit's help, believers will not give in and will be able to discern what the deceivers say as false.

Spiritual vigilance is a major theme of the Olivet discourse. Spiritual alertness and moral preparation are taught by Jesus and portrayed by Mark throughout chapters 13 and 14: Beware that no one misleads you (13:5); **watch out** (13:9, 23, 33); keep a sharp lookout (13:35); do not be found asleep (13:36); keep watch (14:34); keep alert and pray (14:38).

JESUS TELLS ABOUT HIS RETURN / 13:24-31 / 202

In the previous paragraphs, Jesus painted a picture of hardship, confusion, and waiting. But when it seems as though things can't possibly get any worse, they will. Heaven and earth will be irreversibly changed. There will be a sunset, but no sunrise. That completely dark stage will make the arrival of the Son of Man visible to all.

13:24-26 The phrase, **at that time,** signaled that Jesus was talking specifically about the end times. After the time of tribulation, nature itself would experience change. As taught in Romans 8 and 2 Peter 3, the entire universe became involved in humanity's sin predicament; thus, the entire universe will be changed when humanity is changed. The changes in the heavens will be an intended contrast to the pseudo "signs and omens" (13:22) of the false messiahs. These words also recall the words of the prophets (Isaiah 13:10; Joel 2:10-11) and what John saw in his vision (Revelation 6:12-14).

After these cosmic events, all the people on earth **will see the Son of Man arrive on the clouds.** Jesus' return will be unmistakable; no one will wonder about his identity. Jesus' Second Coming will not be as a humble, human carpenter, but as God's Son **with great power and glory.**

13:27 Upon his return to earth, Jesus will send out his angels to **gather together his chosen ones from all over the world.** The angels' gathering of the elect signifies the triumphant enthronement of the Son of Man, who will be revealed in

all his power and glory. When he comes, the whole world will know that Jesus is Lord, and Christians' hope and faith will be vindicated.

13:28-29 In the form of a parable, Jesus answered the disciples' question regarding when the events he spoke about would happen (13:4). So far in this lengthy discourse, Jesus has traced two key themes: (1) the disciples' suffering and (2) their need to be watchful.

The disciples, like anyone living in Palestine, knew how to interpret the coming of **summer** from the **buds** and **leaves** of the fig trees. In the same way, when the disciples see **the events** (described in 13:5-23), they would know that **his return is very near.** The fulfillment of Jesus' prophecy would assure the disciples that the other prophecies he had given regarding the end times would also come true.

13:30-31 There are three views of the meaning of this verse: (1) It refers only to those alive at this time who would be alive also at the destruction of Jerusalem; (2) it refers to the end times only; (3) it refers both to the destruction of Jerusalem and the end times.

Jesus singled out **this generation,** using the

Greek word *genea*, which can refer both to those living at a given time as well as to race or lineage (therefore, he was speaking of the Jewish race). That makes the third view above most likely. Jesus used "generation" here to mean that the events of 13:5-23 would occur initially within the lifetime of Jesus' contemporaries. Jesus explained that many of those alive at that time would witness the destruction of Jerusalem. In addition, the Jewish nation would be preserved and remain on earth, so Jews also would witness the end-time events.

There could be no doubt in these disciples' minds about the certainty of these prophecies. While **heaven and earth** as we know them would eventually **disappear,** Jesus' words (including all his teachings during his time on earth) **will remain forever.**

JESUS TELLS ABOUT REMAINING WATCHFUL / 13:32-37 / *203*

Regarding the "when," of his Second Coming, Jesus' answer was blunt. He then pointed out that the mark of a disciple was not having inside information, but serving Christ faithfully. Spiritual vigilance becomes the essential theme of the entire chapter. Jesus' servants must be so busy that they have no time to speculate about his schedule.

13:32-33 While Jesus had given general "signs" to observe regarding the coming of the end, he clearly explained to the disciples that the exact day or hour was not known by the **angels** or the **Son** (Jesus himself). When Jesus said that even he did not know the time of the end, he was affirming his humanity (see Philippians 2:5-8). Of course, God the Father knows the time, and Jesus and the Father are one. But when Jesus became a man, he voluntarily gave up the unlimited use of his divine attributes. On earth, Jesus laid aside his divine prerogatives and submitted to the Father's will. Thus, **only the Father** knows the exact time of Jesus' return. The emphasis of this verse is not on Jesus' lack of knowledge, but rather on the fact that **no one knows.** It is God the Father's secret to be revealed when he wills. No one can predict by Scripture or science the exact day of Jesus' return. Jesus was teaching that preparation, not calculation, was needed.

Because no one except the Father knows when Christ will return, Jesus explained that believers must **stay alert and keep watch,** ready for his return to happen at any moment. Christ's Second Coming will be swift and sudden. There will be no opportunity for last-minute repentance or bargaining. The choice that people have already made will determine their eternal destiny.

13:34-36 In this parable of watchfulness, Jesus described himself as **a man who left home to go on a trip** (Jesus would be returning to heaven). The disciples are **the employees** left behind to carry on their **work.** The **gatekeeper** is commanded to keep watch for the master's return. The employees understand that they are in charge of themselves, had their own work to do, and would not want the homeowner to return suddenly and find them being lazy. Because they **do not know when the homeowner will return,** these employees must **keep a sharp lookout** so as not to be found **sleeping.**

Jesus' followers would want to be found spiritually lax, but instead conscientiously going about the work given by God for them to do. Each of us has enough assigned work to do that we shouldn't be neutralized or paralyzed by fear or doubt. We do not need to worry about how other employees compare to us; instead, we should devote ourselves to doing what God has given us to do.

13:37 Jesus had spoken this discourse to only four of his disciples (13:3). Here he instructed them to carry these words to the rest of the disciples, for their truth was of vital importance. By extension, the words were meant for all believers. Even today, we do well to **watch for his return**—watching out for false teaching and watching expectantly for Christ's return as we do his work in the world.

MARK 14

RELIGIOUS LEADERS PLOT TO KILL JESUS / 14:1-2 / 207

Mark's account of the final acts in Jesus' ministry begins with a simple summary of the scene. It was almost Passover. Jesus' enemies were looking for a way to kill him. Their concern about timing had to do with keeping control of the people. They wanted to kill Jesus without anyone noticing. But God had a different purpose in the timing of events.

14:1-2 The **Passover** commemorated the night the Israelites were freed from Egypt (Exodus 12), when God "passed over" homes marked by the blood of a lamb. This was the last great plague on Egypt; in the unmarked homes the firstborn sons died. After this horrible disaster, Pharaoh let the Israelites go.

The day of Passover was followed by the seven-day **Festival of Unleavened Bread**. This, too, recalled the Israelites' quick escape from Egypt when, because they wouldn't have time to let their bread rise, they baked it without leaven (yeast). All

Jewish males over the age of twelve were required to go to Jerusalem for this festival (Deuteronomy 16:5-6). Jews from all over the Roman Empire would converge on Jerusalem, swelling the population from 50,000 to 250,000 people.

The Jewish leaders plotted secretly to kill Jesus. They had already decided that Jesus must die (see John 11:47-53); they just needed the opportunity. They did not want to attempt to arrest Jesus **during the Passover** because they feared that the crowd would **riot** on his behalf. They feared that such an uprising might bring the wrath of Rome.

A WOMAN ANOINTS JESUS WITH PERFUME / 14:3-9 / 182

Matthew and Mark put this event just before the Last Supper, while John included it just before the Triumphal Entry. Of the three, John placed this event in the most likely chronological position. Mark sandwiched this beautiful event between two sections dealing with the plot to eliminate Jesus. This act of devotion by Mary, who is a true heroine in this narrative, is contrasted with the treachery of the villains—the religious leaders and Judas.

14:3 Bethany was located on the eastern slope of the Mount of Olives (Jerusalem is on the western side). This town was the home of Jesus' friends Lazarus, Mary, and Martha (who were also present at this dinner, John 11:2). Jesus had been returning to Bethany from Jerusalem each night during this final week (11:11). This night, Jesus was a guest of **Simon.** He did not have **leprosy** at this time, for lepers had to live separately from people because of the extreme contagiousness of the disease. Jesus may have healed Simon.

This **woman** was probably Mary, the sister of Martha and Lazarus, who lived in Bethany (John 12:1-3). She brought **a beautiful jar of expensive perfume,** which she **poured** on Jesus' head. It was a common custom at some Jewish meals for the honored guests to be anointed with oil (see Luke 7:44-46), but it would not be so expensive. Such

an anointing, with expensive oil, pictured a royal (messianic) anointing.

14:4-5 Where Mark says **some,** John specifically mentions Judas (John 12:4-5). This indignation over Mary's act of worship would not have been based on concern for the **poor,** but on greed. Because Judas was the treasurer of Jesus' ministry and had embezzled funds (John 12:6), he no doubt wanted the perfume sold so that the proceeds could be put into his care. This event probably pushed Judas over the edge in his determination to betray Jesus.

14:6-8 Jesus reprimanded the disciples, but comforted Mary. The expensive ointment poured on Jesus had been **a good thing** to do for him—a beautiful, acceptable, appealing act of love and sacrifice—and Jesus declared it to be so. This was a unique act for a specific occasion—an anointing that anticipated Jesus' **burial** and a public declaration of faith in him as Messiah. Jesus was not saying that we should neglect **the poor,** nor was he justifying indifference to them. (For Jesus' teaching about the poor, see Matthew 6:2-4; Luke 6:20-21; 14:13, 21; 18:22.) Jesus was affirming Mary's unselfish act of worship. The essence of worshiping Christ is to regard him with utmost love, respect, and devotion, as well as to be willing to sacrifice to him what is most precious.

Jesus' purpose in these words was to explain that the opportunity to show him such devotion and to anoint him with oil (in preparation for burial) would soon be past. The phrase, **"I will not be here with you much longer,"** meant that Jesus would soon be gone from them physically. However, they could and should show kindness to the poor, and opportunities to do so would continue, **"You will always have the poor among you."**

Jesus' words should have taught Judas and the disciples the valuable lesson that devotion to Christ is worth more than money. Unfortunately, Judas did not take heed; soon he would sell his Master's life for thirty pieces of silver.

14:9 Mary's unselfish act would be remembered forever. This has come true because we read about it today. While the disciples misunderstood Jesus' mission and constantly fought about places in the Kingdom and while the religious leaders stubbornly refused to believe in Jesus and plotted his death, this one quiet woman so loved Jesus and was so devoted to him that she considered no sacrifice too great for her beloved Master. She is an example to us all of unselfish devotion to our Savior.

JUDAS AGREES TO BETRAY JESUS / 14:10-11 / 208

Each of the Gospel writers reported Judas's treachery with remarkable restraint. Their treatment of Peter's denial actually seems harsher than their references to the betrayer. Mark, the shortest account, conveys the simple facts. The enemies of Jesus were delighted. We're not told how Judas felt at this point. Since Mark was reflecting Peter's account, the reticence about Judas may indicate Peter's shame in recalling his own treatment of Jesus. We are much more likely to present a fair picture of the flaws and faults of others if we keep our own clearly in sight.

14:10 Why would **Judas Iscariot** want to **betray** Jesus? Very likely, Judas expected Jesus to start a political rebellion and overthrow Rome. As treasurer, Judas certainly assumed (as did the other disciples—see 10:35-37) that he would be given an important position in Jesus' new government. But when Jesus praised Mary for pouring out the expensive perfume, Judas finally began to realize that Jesus' Kingdom was not physical or political. Judas knew the **leading priests** had it in for Jesus, and he knew they would have the power to arrest Jesus. So that was where he went. Judas's greedy desire for money and status could not be fulfilled if he followed Jesus, so he betrayed him in exchange for money and favor from the religious leaders.

14:11 Obviously the **leading priests were delighted** to have discovered a traitor among Jesus' followers. They had been having difficulty figuring out how to arrest Jesus (14:1-2); so when an offer of help came from this unexpected corner, they took advantage of it. They promised Judas **a reward,** and Judas began looking for the right opportunity—when there would be no Passover crowds to prevent Jesus' capture and no possibility of a riot (14:2).

DISCIPLES PREPARE FOR THE PASSOVER / 14:12-16 / 209

Jesus and his disciples had been together long enough to celebrate Passover several times. Apparently, despite the gloominess of Jesus' predictions and the tension of constant scrutiny by the religious leaders, the disciples tried to keep a semblance of normality. They asked Jesus for instructions about Passover. His response indicates that he had planned their itinerary in advance.

14:12 The Passover took place on one night and at one meal, but the Feast of Unleavened Bread, which was celebrated with it, continued for a week. The first day of the feast was technically the day after Passover, but the two were often equated. Thus, this was either Wednesday night (the day before Passover) or Thursday of Jesus' last week (the night of the Passover meal). The highlight of the festival was the Passover meal, a family feast with the main course of lamb. The sacrifice of a lamb and the spilling of its blood commemorated Israel's escape from Egypt when the blood of a lamb painted on their door frames had saved their firstborn sons from death. This event foreshadowed Jesus' work on the cross. As the spotless Lamb of God, his blood would be spilled in order to save his people from the penalty of death brought by sin.

Jesus' disciples assumed that they would eat the Passover meal together with Jesus. However, the meal had to be eaten in Jerusalem, so the disciples asked Jesus **where** they should **go** in order to make preparations.

14:13 The **two** disciples Jesus sent were Peter and John (Luke 22:8). Whether Jesus had supernatural knowledge in this instance or if he had made arrangements in advance is unclear (as in the incident with his Triumphal Entry, see 11:1-6). It seems that in this instance this room had been reserved previously and kept secret— none of the disciples knew where they would eat this meal. Jesus already knew that Judas would be looking for an opportunity to betray him without crowds around, so Jesus may

have made these arrangements and kept them secret.

The two disciples were dispatched in the morning from Bethany to Jerusalem to prepare the Passover meal. Jesus told them that as they entered the city, they would meet **a man carrying a pitcher of water.** Ordinarily women, not men, went to the well and brought home the water. So this man would have stood out in the crowd. This may have been a prearranged signal, or Jesus may have supernaturally known that this man (most likely a servant) would be there and would lead them to the right house.

14:14-16 The owner of this home was probably one of Jesus' followers. He knew exactly who **the Teacher** was and probably knew the disciples by sight. Tradition says this may have been Mark's home, so this would have been Mark's father. Many homes had **upstairs** rooms large enough to accommodate Jesus and his twelve disciples. As before, when two disciples went to get the donkey for Jesus to ride into Jerusalem (11:1-6), these two disciples **found everything just as Jesus had said.** The preparations for the Passover would have included setting the table, buying and roasting the Passover lamb, and making the unleavened bread, sauces, and other ceremonial food and drink that were a traditional part of every Passover meal.

JESUS AND THE DISCIPLES SHARE THE LAST SUPPER / 14:17-26 / 211

We know from John's Gospel that a great deal was said during the Passover meal. But Mark mentioned only two central events that occurred during the supper itself. First, Jesus disclosed that there was a betrayer among them. Then he instituted the sacrament of the Lord's Supper.

14:17 On that **evening** (Wednesday or Thursday), **Jesus arrived** in Jerusalem **with the twelve disciples.** The meal was not to be eaten until after sunset and was supposed to be finished by midnight.

14:18-20 As Jesus and the disciples were **eating,** Jesus spoke the stunning words, **"One of you will betray me."** The betrayer was one of his own chosen twelve disciples, one with whom the meal was being shared. Jesus' words caused quite a stir among the disciples. They had heard Jesus tell them three different times that he would soon die, but that one of them would actually betray Jesus saddened them greatly.

Although the other disciples were confused by Jesus' words, Judas knew what he meant. Apparently Judas was not the obvious betrayer. After all, he was the one the disciples trusted to keep the money (John 12:4-6). So the disciples asked

Jesus who the betrayer was; **"I'm not the one, am I?"** each one asked in turn. Matthew records that even Judas asked this question (Matthew 26:25).

14:21 Jesus would indeed be betrayed and would indeed die as he had already told his disciples. His death would not occur merely because of the betrayer, for the **Son of Man** had to **die** to complete God's plan and fulfill Scripture (for example, Psalm 41:9-13; Isaiah 53:1-6).

But how terrible it will be for the one who betrayed Jesus. Again Jesus' words were reminiscent of Psalm 41, this time verses 10-12, where the sufferer was vindicated by God and his enemies punished. Jesus knew that Judas was going to betray him, and he also knew that Judas would not repent.

Luke wrote that "Satan entered into Judas

Iscariot" before he went to the religious leaders (Luke 22:3). However, Satan's part in the betrayal of Jesus does not remove any of the responsibility from Judas. In God's sovereign will and according to his timetable, he uses sinful men. But that doesn't excuse their sin. All people will be held accountable for their choices and actions. Whatever Judas thought, Satan assumed that Jesus' death would end Jesus' mission and thwart God's plan. Like Judas, Satan did not know that Jesus' death and resurrection were the most important parts of God's plan all along.

John records that upon this pronouncement, Jesus told Judas to "hurry. Do it now" (John 13:27). Then Judas went out into the night. He was not present for the remaining words Jesus spoke.

14:22 Jesus and the disciples were eating the bread, and Jesus took the loaf of unleavened bread, **asked God's blessing on it,** and **broke** it. Jesus told the disciples to **"Take it, for this is my body."** His words "this is my body" symbolize the spiritual nourishment believers obtain from a personal relationship with the Savior.

Christians differ in their interpretation of the meaning of the commemoration of the Lord's Supper. There are three main views: (1) The bread and wine actually become Christ's body and blood; (2) the bread and wine remain unchanged, yet Christ is spiritually present by faith in and through them; and (3) the bread and wine, which remain unchanged, are lasting memorials of Christ's sacrifice. No matter which view they favor, all Christians agree that the Lord's Supper commemorates Christ's death on the cross for our sins and points to the coming of his Kingdom in glory. When we partake of it, we show our deep gratitude for Christ's work on our behalf, and our faith is strengthened.

Just as the Passover celebrated deliverance from slavery in Egypt, so the Lord's Supper celebrates deliverance from sin by Christ's death.

14:23-24 The celebrations in the Christian church (Communion, Eucharist, the Lord's Supper) have first a sharing of bread (including a repetition of Jesus' words, "This is my body"), and then a sharing of wine (including a repetition of Jesus' words, **"This is my blood, poured out for many"**).

As with the bread, Jesus spoke words in figurative language. "This is my blood" means "This wine represents my blood." Jesus' blood, poured out on behalf of sinners, sealed **the covenant between God and his people.** In later manuscripts, the word "new" has been inserted before "covenant." This insertion is based on Luke 22:20 and 1 Corinthians 11:25, where the word "new" appears in all Greek manuscripts. The word "covenant" refers to an arrangement established by one party that cannot be altered by the other party. In other words, God established the covenant and humans can only accept or reject it; they cannot alter it in any way.

What did Jesus mean by a "new covenant"? In Old Testament times, God had agreed to forgive people's sins if they would bring animals for the priests to sacrifice. When this sacrificial system was inaugurated, the agreement between God and human beings was sealed with the blood of animals (Exodus 24:8). But animal blood did not in itself remove sin, and animal sacrifices had to be repeated day by day and year after year.

Jesus instituted a "new covenant," or agreement, between humans and God. This concept is key to all New Testament theology and forms the basis for the name of the New Testament portion of the Bible. Under this new covenant, Jesus would die in the place of sinners. The old covenant was a shadow of the new, pointing forward to the day when Jesus himself would be the final and ultimate sacrifice for sin. Rather than an unblemished lamb slain on the altar, the perfect Lamb of God was slain on the cross as a sinless sacrifice so that our sins could be forgiven once and for all. Those who accept Christ's sacrifice and believe in him receive forgiveness. Now all people can come directly to God through faith because Jesus' death has made us acceptable in God's eyes (Romans 3:21-24).

14:25 Again Jesus assured his disciples of his victory over his imminent death and of a future **in the Kingdom of God.** The next few hours would bring apparent defeat, but soon they would experience the power of the Holy Spirit and witness the great spread of the gospel message.

14:26 The **hymn** they sang was most likely taken from Psalms 116–118, the second part of the Hallel that was traditionally sung after eating the Passover meal. John included a lengthy discourse that Jesus had with his disciples (John 13:31–17:26) before he and the eleven remaining disciples left the upper room and **went out to the Mount of Olives,** located just to the east of Jerusalem. Leaving the room did not surprise the disciples, for they had not been staying in Jerusalem at night and had left the city every evening to return to Bethany. This time, however, Jesus went only as far as the southwestern slope, to an olive grove called Gethsemane, which means "oil press."

JESUS AGAIN PREDICTS PETER'S DENIAL / 14:27-31 / 222

Both Luke and John reported that Jesus predicted both the disciples' abandonment and Peter's denial while they were still having supper. True to form, Peter reacted strongly to Jesus' prediction. He could not imagine the disciples abandoning Jesus. Least of all himself. But before we criticize Peter, we should first see ourselves in him. Peter reminds us how easy it is to profess our faith and how difficult it is to remain loyal under pressure.

14:27-28 This was the second time in the same evening that Jesus predicted the disciples' denial and desertion, which probably explains their strong reaction (14:31). (For Jesus' earlier prediction, see Luke 22:31-34 and John 13:36-38.) That the disciples would **desert** him means that they would take offense at him and turn away. Fearing what would befall Jesus, they would not want to experience the same treatment. Jesus would go to the cross totally alone. The disciples' desertion would also occur just as it had been predicted in Scripture, specifically Zechariah 13:7. In Zechariah, God commanded that the **Shepherd** be struck down. As a result, **the sheep will be scattered.** Without a shepherd and on their own, the sheep would go through a period of great trial and be refined. The refining process would strengthen them and create a new, faithful people for God. The disciples would be overwhelmed by what would happen to Jesus, but Jesus' death would ultimately produce their salvation.

After his prediction of their desertion, Jesus then predicted their reunion after he would be **raised from the dead.** Jesus promised that he would go **ahead** of them into **Galilee** and **meet** them all there.

14:29-30 Peter, always ready to speak up at inopportune moments, declared that his allegiance to Jesus would prove to be much stronger than the others. Jesus explained, however, that instead of being the only loyal disciple, Peter would prove himself the least so. Not only would he desert Jesus, he would also **deny** him—not once, but **three times.** And this would happen in the space of the next few hours. Before the night was over, that is before the **rooster** crowed a second time, Peter would deny the Master to whom he claimed such loyalty. Only Mark recorded a second crowing of the rooster (see also 14:72). If Peter was, in fact, Mark's source for this Gospel, he certainly remembered this minor detail.

14:31 Peter did not think it possible for him to actually deny any relationship with Jesus. Perhaps he was worried that he was the betrayer Jesus had mentioned during their meal (14:18). Not only Peter, but **all** the disciples declared that they would **never deny** Jesus. A few hours later, however, they all scattered.

JESUS AGONIZES IN THE GARDEN / 14:32-42 / 223

Apart from the Cross itself, the moments in Gethsemane were the most intense in Jesus' life. He experienced the crushing weight of the task he was about to undertake. He witnessed the weakness that his disciples demonstrated by falling asleep. He saw the betrayer coming. And he sensed with anguish that the cup would not pass. He would drink it alone. The Cross did not catch Jesus by surprise. His self-sacrifice was deliberate, calculated, and undertaken with a great flow of human emotions that we can see in the garden.

14:32 After eating the meal, the disciples left Jerusalem and went out to **Gethsemane** (see John 18:1-2). The garden was in the Kidron Valley just outside the eastern wall of Jerusalem and just below the Mount of Olives. Jesus told eight of the disciples to **sit** down while he went farther in to **pray.**

Plenty of drama surrounds Mark's terse account. The elders of Jerusalem were plotting to kill Jesus and had already issued a warrant for his arrest. Jesus left Jerusalem under cover of darkness in order to pray. The disciples must also have been physically and emotionally exhausted from trying to comprehend what would transpire. Instead of watching, they gave in to their exhaustion and fell asleep.

14:33-34 Jesus took three disciples, his inner circle, farther into the garden with him. To these closest friends, Jesus revealed his inner turmoil over the event he was about to face. The divine course was set, but Jesus, in his human nature, still struggled (Hebrews 5:7-9). His coming death was no surprise; he knew about it and had even told the disciples about it so they would be prepared. Jesus knew what his death would accomplish. As the time of this event neared, it became even more horrifying. Jesus naturally recoiled from the prospect.

Jesus asked Peter, James, and John (14:33) to **stay** and **watch** with him. Jesus knew Judas would soon arrive, and Jesus wanted to devote himself to prayer until that time came.

14:35 Jesus went still farther into the garden to be alone with God. His agony was such that he threw himself on the ground before God in deep spiritual anguish, praying that if possible **the awful hour awaiting him might pass him by**—that his mission might be accomplished some other way. **Hour** figuratively refers to the entire event Jesus was facing. The "hour" and the "cup" were used synonymously. Yet Jesus humbly submitted to the Father's will. Luke tells us that Jesus' sweat resembled drops of blood. Jesus was in terrible agony, but he did not give up or give in. He went ahead with the mission for which he had come.

14:36 Abba was Aramaic for "father" and implied familiarity and closeness. Only Jesus could have used the word *Abba* in a prayer to God, because Jesus had a special Father-Son relationship with him. Jesus' using it showed his surrender to and faith in the Father's will. Children addressed their fathers as *Abba*, but the term was far too familiar for adult Jews to use in speaking to God. Paul used the term in Romans 8:15 and Galatians 4:6, showing that the early church picked up the term from this prayer of Jesus.

The words, **everything is possible for you,** indicate God's omnipotence. He could accomplish anything. Jesus was affirming God's sovereign control over the coming suffering (see 10:27). With the words, **take this cup of suffering away from me,** Jesus was referring to the agony, the separation from God, and the death he would have to endure in order to atone for the sins of the world. Jesus, as God's Son, recoiled from sin, yet part of his task would be to take the sins of the whole world upon himself. This was a cup he truly hated to drink. The physical suffering would be horrible enough, but what God's Son feared most was the cup of spiritual suffering—taking on sin and being separated from God (Hebrews 5:7-9). Yet Jesus reaffirmed his desire to do what God wanted by saying, **"Yet I want your will, not mine."**

God did not take away the "cup," for to judge the sins of the world was his will. Yet he did take away Jesus' extreme fear and agitation. Jesus moved serenely through the next several hours, at peace with God, knowing that he was doing God's will.

14:37-38 Jesus got up from his prayer to return to the three disciples. He had told them to stay and keep watch (14:34), but instead of showing support for Jesus by remaining awake with him and praying themselves for strength in the coming hours, they had fallen **asleep.** The hour was very late, perhaps after midnight.

Jesus spoke to Peter, calling him **Simon,** his name before he had met Jesus. Apparently Peter's recent boasting (14:31), present sleepiness, and coming denial rendered him less than Peter, the "rock" (see John 1:42). Peter had said he would never leave Jesus; yet when Jesus needed prayer and support, Peter had fallen asleep. Thus, Jesus rebuked him for his failure to keep watch for **even one hour.** Only Mark mentions the Lord's words to Peter. Perhaps Peter wanted Mark to tell this part of the story.

Jesus told the disciples that this was the time to **keep alert and pray,** for soon difficult **temptation** would come. Jesus wanted them to pray that their faith would not collapse. The word **temptation** can mean testing or trial. Jesus wanted his disciples to pray for strength to go through the coming ordeal. The disciples were about to see Jesus die. Would they still think he was the Messiah? The disciples' strongest temptation would undoubtedly be to think they had been deceived. Their **spirit** might be willing, but their **body** would be weak. Their inner desires and intentions would be, as they had previously boasted, to never deny Jesus and to die with him. Yet with all their human inadequacies, fears, and failures, the disciples would have difficulty carrying out those good intentions.

14:39-40 Jesus **left** the three disciples and went back to his previous **pleadings** with the Father (14:35-36). When **he returned to them,** they were asleep again. Despite his warning **they just couldn't keep their eyes open.** Apparently Jesus again awakened them, and in their embarrassment, **they didn't know what to say.**

14:41-42 Jesus went away to pray a **third time,** only to come back and find the disciples still asleep. The disciples had not taken the opportunity to pray, and there would be no more time to do so—**the time** had **come.** Thus Jesus did not again tell them to pray. Jesus had spent the last few hours dealing with the Father, wrestling with him, and humbly submitting to him. Now he was prepared to face his **betrayer** and the **sinners** who were coming to arrest him.

JESUS IS BETRAYED AND ARRESTED / 14:43-52 / 224

All four Gospels describe the moment of betrayal, but Mark's version is the shortest. He moved rapidly through the sequence of events. Mark alone added the description of a young man wrapped in a sheet who left his only covering behind in his hurry to escape. Many think this was Mark's own, somewhat humorous, signature to the Gospel.

In spite of all they had seen and heard with Jesus, when the moment of truth arrived, the disciples all fled. When we feel safe in our surroundings or we take life lightly, it is easy to consider ourselves prepared for anything. The disciples trusted in Jesus all right, but their trust came and went with what they saw and felt. As long as the Lord was in control, everything was fine. But when external circumstances changed, the weakness of their faith was revealed. Hardships open our eyes and enable us to deal with our true character.

14:43 Even as Jesus spoke to his disciples to rouse them from their sleep, **Judas arrived.** The leading priests had issued the warrant for Jesus' arrest, and Judas was acting as Jesus' official accuser. The **mob, armed with swords and clubs,** came in the middle of the night when most of the people were asleep and they could arrest Jesus without commotion. Although there were no crowds to worry about, Jesus was surrounded by eleven loyal followers who the Temple guards feared might put up a fight.

14:44 Judas had told the crowd to arrest the man to whom he would give **the kiss of greeting.** This was not an arrest by Roman soldiers under Roman law, but an arrest by the religious leaders. Judas pointed Jesus out, not because Jesus was hard to recognize, but because Judas had agreed to be the formal accuser in case a trial was called. A kiss on the cheek or hand was a common form of greeting in the Middle East, so this was not unusual.

14:45 Judas had expected to find Jesus and the disciples in Gethsemane. He entered the garden followed by the armed band and **walked up to Jesus.** In a friendly gesture of greeting and affection, Judas called Jesus **"Teacher"** and then gave him a **kiss** (on the cheek or on the hand), a sign of respect.

14:46 The religious leaders had not arrested Jesus in the Temple for fear of a riot. Instead, they had come secretly at night, under the influence of the prince of darkness, Satan himself. Jesus offered no resistance and was **grabbed** and **arrested.** Although it looked as if Satan were getting the upper hand, everything was proceeding according to God's plan. It was time for Jesus to die.

14:47 According to John 18:10, the person who **pulled out a sword** was Peter, who cut off the right **ear** of a **servant** named Malchus. Peter was trying to prevent what he saw as defeat. He wasn't going to let this crowd arrest Jesus without putting up a fight. Luke 22:51 records that Jesus immediately healed the man's ear and prevented any further bloodshed.

Jesus then told Peter to put away his sword and allow God's plan to unfold. Peter didn't realize that Jesus had to die in order to gain victory. But Jesus demonstrated perfect commitment to his Father's will. His Kingdom would not be advanced with swords, but with faith and obedience.

14:48-49 Jesus protested, not his arrest, but the way he was arrested. They did not need to come against him with weapons, for he was voluntarily surrendering himself. Jesus was not a **dangerous criminal** leading a rebellion; he was a religious teacher who had been teaching in the Temple daily during the past week. Jesus also mocked their show of worldly power. He who could summon angels was not afraid of swords. Did the guards imagine that swords would intimidate Jesus? They didn't understand who he was. Jesus knew why the events were unfolding as they were—**to fulfill what the Scriptures say.** Judas's treachery, the coming mockery of a trial against Jesus, and its ultimate outcome had all been prophesied (see, for example, Psalms 22:7-8, 14, 16-17; 41:9; Isaiah 50:6; 53:7-8).

14:50 Just hours earlier, these disciples had vowed never to desert Jesus (14:31). Judas's kiss marked a turning point for the disciples and Jesus' loyal disciples **deserted him and ran away.** The teacher who had held forth in the Temple was now under arrest. The treasurer had become a traitor. The garden sanctuary that had always been "safe" was turned into the place of confrontation. What confusion! The disciples' primary loyalty to Jesus should have kept them from running. But fear took its toll.

14:51-52 Only Mark records the incident of this **young man** who also fled the scene. Tradition says that this young man may have been John Mark, the writer of this Gospel, in whose home the Last Supper may have taken place. If that is true, at some point Mark had awakened from sleep (he had probably been sleeping in a **linen nightshirt** or had a sheet wrapped around him) and had followed the disciples to the garden. Perhaps soldiers had come to the house looking for Jesus and this young man had attempted to warn Jesus before the soldiers reached him. But in Gethsemane, the crowd had already arrested Jesus and the disciples had fled. Someone grabbed this young man, perhaps hoping to use him as a witness. At that, the young man **escaped and ran away naked.**

CAIAPHAS QUESTIONS JESUS / 14:53-65 / *226*

Only John records the events immediately following Jesus' capture. The other Gospels go right to the preliminary hearing at Annas's house. All of the accounts convey that the religious leaders had already decided Jesus' fate. Jesus' opponents merely wanted to solidify their case against him. The parade of false witnesses highlighted the murderous intent of the religious leaders. They eagerly acted out their hatred for Jesus with spitting, striking, and taunting. Injustice turned to brutality.

14:53 By now it was very early Friday morning, before daybreak. Jesus was taken under guard from the garden back into Jerusalem. First he was questioned by Annas, the former high priest and father-in-law of Caiaphas. Annas had been Israel's high priest from A.D. 6 to 15, when he had been deposed by Roman rulers. Then Caiaphas had been appointed high priest. He held that position from A.D. 18 to 36 / 37. According to Jewish law, the office of high priest was held for life, but the Roman government had taken over the process of appointing all political and religious leaders. Caiaphas served for eighteen years, longer than most high priests, suggesting that he was gifted at cooperating with the Romans. Caiaphas was the first to recommend Jesus' death in order to "save" the nation (John 11:49-50). However, many Jews still considered Annas to be the high priest. Annas may have asked to question Jesus after his arrest and was given first rights to do so. This hearing is described in John 18:12-24.

After that preliminary hearing, Jesus was taken to the **high priest's home.** That all the religious leaders had been speedily assembled shows that this was a trial by the Jewish council of religious leaders consisting of seventy members plus the high priest. Because of their haste to complete the trial and see Jesus die before the Sabbath, less than twenty-four hours later, the religious leaders first met in Caiaphas's home at night to accomplish the preliminaries before their more formal meeting in the Temple at daylight. They finally had Jesus where they wanted him, and they were determined to accomplish their plans as quickly as possible.

The trial by the Jewish leaders had two phases. This first phase occurred during the night (recorded here in 14:53-65); then another meeting was held "very early in the morning" (15:1) to satisfy a law that allowed trials only during the daytime. That meeting was a mere formality held at daybreak, during which the verdict was given and Jesus was led off to the Roman procurator for sentencing. The Jewish council was the most powerful religious and political body of the Jewish people. Although the Romans controlled Israel's government, they gave the people power to handle religious disputes and some civil disputes; so the council made many of the local decisions affecting daily life. But a death sentence had to be authorized by the Romans (John 18:31).

14:54 Although all the disciples had fled when the soldiers arrested Jesus, two of them, **Peter** and another disciple (perhaps John), returned to where Jesus was taken (John 18:15). The high priest's residence was a palace with **gates** and outer walls enclosing a **courtyard.** Here a charcoal **fire** was burning, around which the servants and **guards** were **warming** themselves against the early morning chill. Peter's story continues at 14:66.

14:55-56 Upstairs in the high priest's palace, **the leading priests and the entire high council** (meaning the group of seventy-one leaders of the Jews—priests and respected men) assembled in the middle of the night to get this trial under way, but they had a dilemma on their hands. They **were trying to find witnesses who would testify against Jesus, so they could put him to death,** but they couldn't find any—only **false witnesses** who **contradicted each other.** The obvious conclusion should have been that Jesus was innocent of any crime. But this was not a trial for justice; it was a trial to accomplish an evil purpose. These leaders held a trial, in keeping with all the trappings of their law, while their whole purpose was to kill Jesus. Ironically, these religious guardians of the law were breaking one of the Ten Commandments, "Do not testify falsely" (Exodus 20:16).

14:57-59 Finally they found **some men** who would **testify against him** with a lie regarding Jesus' words about the Temple. These men twisted

Jesus' words because their testimony, even on this same point, did not agree.

The witnesses claimed that Jesus had said he could **destroy** the **Temple** in Jerusalem—a blasphemous boast. Such a claim would bring wrath from even the Romans because destroying temples was considered a capital offense throughout the Roman Empire. However, Jesus had not spoken in the first person ("I will destroy"); nor had he said anything linking his words with the Temple building. Instead, Jesus had spoken in the second person plural, issuing a command, "Destroy this temple, and in three days I will raise it up" (John 2:19). Jesus, of course, was talking about his body, not the building. Ironically, the religious leaders were about to destroy Jesus' body just as he had said, and three days later he would rise from the dead.

14:60 Caiaphas, **the high priest,** was getting frustrated. Now his only hope was to get Jesus to say something that would give them evidence to convict him. The religious leaders had tried and failed on prior occasions to trap Jesus with trick questions (12:13-34); Caiaphas tried to make up in intimidation what was lacking in evidence. He asked Jesus to **answer** his accusers and then to explain the accusations against him.

14:61 Jesus refused to say anything. He had nothing to say to the group of liars who had spoken against him, and he had no reason to explain a bunch of false accusations. So he **made no reply.** This had been prophesied in Scripture (Isaiah 53:7). With Jesus' silence, the court proceedings ground to a halt. But Caiaphas had another tactic up the sleeve of his priestly robe. He decided to ask Jesus point blank, **"Are you the Messiah?"** The council must have held its collective breath in anticipation. Here was the question that could make or break the entire plot. Would Jesus outright claim to be the Messiah, **the Son of the blessed God?** We may wonder why Jesus refused to answer the first question and then chose to answer this one. Matthew's account points out that Caiaphas put Jesus under oath (Matthew 26:63) so that Jesus would be forced to answer by law (Leviticus 5:1); thus he would be forced to incriminate himself. Caiaphas's action was unlawful in trial proceedings, but no one voiced that fact to him. As mentioned above, this trial had nothing to do with justice; it was merely a ploy to get rid of Jesus.

14:62 To the first questions (14:60), Jesus made no reply because the questions were based on confusing and erroneous evidence. Not answering was wiser than trying to clarify the fabricated accusations. But if Jesus had refused to answer the second question (14:61), it would have been tantamount to denying his deity and his mission. So Jesus answered without hesitation, **"I am."** The two words, "I am," both answered the high priest's question and alluded to Jesus divinity ("I am" being God's self-designation, see Exodus 3:14).

Then Jesus spoke startling words: **the Son of Man, sitting at God's right hand,** refers to Psalm 110:1, and **coming back on the clouds of heaven** recalls Daniel 7:13-14. The clouds represented the power and glory of God. Both verses were considered to be prophecies of the coming Messiah, and Jesus applied them to himself.

14:63-64 Tearing one's clothing was an ancient expression of deep sorrow (see Genesis 44:13). The law forbade a priest from tearing his garments over personal grief (Leviticus 10:6; 21:10), but it was appropriate in an instance when **blasphemy** had been spoken in his presence. Blasphemy was the sin of claiming to be God or of attacking God's authority and majesty in any way. Caiaphas **tore his clothing** to signify his **horror** at the audacity of the claims of this mere teacher from Nazareth. These religious leaders thought that Jesus was leading the people astray and bringing dishonor to God's holy name. For any other human being, this claim would have been blasphemy; in this case, the claim was true.

Blasphemy was punishable by death (Leviticus 24:15-16). **"Why do we need other witnesses?"** asked Caiaphas without expecting any answer. Jesus had incriminated himself. Caiaphas asked for their **verdict.** The Jewish leaders had the evidence they wanted, so **they all condemned him to death.**

14:65 Next some of the members of the council acted in a most brutish way. Jesus was **blindfolded,** and they took turns hitting him and then asking him to tell who it was that hit him. When they finished with Jesus, the **guards** came and also beat Jesus. Yet even this had been prophesied in Scripture (Isaiah 52:14). Jesus suffered great pain, humiliation, and brutality to take away our sin.

PETER DENIES KNOWING JESUS / 14:66-72 / 227

As soon as Peter opened his mouth, he gave himself away. His accent was Galilean. He was an out-of-towner who couldn't explain his presence in the high priest's courtyard. The disciple's earlier brash confidence wilted under pressure. Each denial distanced Peter farther from Jesus:

First, he denied being with Jesus in any way; second, he denied being one of Jesus' followers; third, he strenuously denied even knowing Jesus.

Few of us get repeated opportunities, as Peter did, to profess or reject our allegiance to Christ. More often, our first denial of Jesus would keep away any further inquiries. But it is not our identification with Peter's weakness that helps us most. Rather, what happened later becomes our source of hope. Peter's repentance and the Lord's restoration of him give us confidence that God can handle our failures.

14:66-68 This **servant girl** was actually guarding the gate to the inner courtyard (John 18:16). She had seen Peter enter. Jesus' trial had been held in an upper story of the high priest's palace; thus, Peter was **below in the courtyard.** When the girl saw Peter's face more clearly in the light of the fire, she **looked at him closely** and recognized him as one who had been **with Jesus** (that is, one of Jesus' disciples). This put Peter in a difficult position. Standing among the soldiers and servants right there in enemy territory, Peter did not necessarily want to be identified with the man in an upstairs room on trial for his life. So Peter made a natural and impulsive response—he lied. He simply got out of this sticky situation by saying he didn't understand what the girl was talking about; then he scooted out into the **entryway,** away from the fire. Temptation came when Peter least expected it, and this warns us to be prepared. Peter had been ready to fight with a sword but not to face the accusations of a servant.

14:69-71 Once again Peter was put to the test. Another **servant girl** (Matthew 26:71) saw him. She didn't question him; she **began telling the others** around that Peter was indeed **one of them,** meaning one of Jesus' disciples. But he **denied it again.** This was Peter's second denial.

About an hour passed (Luke 22:59) and **some other bystanders** also recognized Peter by his Galilean accent (Matthew 26:73). Peter's dialect was closer to Syrian speech than to that of the Judean servants in that Jerusalem courtyard. While Peter may have hoped to seem a natural part of the group by joining in the conversation, instead he revealed, by his speech, that he did not belong there. Once again Peter lied, this time more vehemently. So Peter decided to make the strongest denial he could think of by denying with an oath, **"I swear by God, I don't know this man."** This was the third denial (14:30).

14:72 Immediately upon Peter's final words, **the rooster crowed the second time.** When Peter heard the rooster crowing and then saw Jesus look down at him from the upper story where the trial was being held (Luke 22:61), Jesus' previous words **flashed through** his mind. Peter had indeed denied Jesus three times before the rooster crowed.

Peter **broke down and cried,** not only because he realized that he had denied his Lord, the Messiah, but also because he had turned away from a very dear friend. Unable to stand up for his Lord for even twelve hours, he had failed as a disciple and as a friend.

Fortunately, the story does not end there. Peter's tears were of true sorrow and repentance. Peter reaffirmed his love for Jesus, and Jesus forgave him (see 16:7; John 21:15-19). From this humiliating experience, Peter learned much that would help him later when he became leader of the young church.

MARK 15

THE COUNCIL OF RELIGIOUS LEADERS CONDEMNS JESUS / 15:1 / 228

Mark's writing took on an added urgency as he neared the climax of his story. He stated the verdict of the council as an inevitable decision. The next steps the council took were mere administrative necessity. Because a death sentence required Roman approval, Pilate awakened one morning to the sounds of an angry mob outside his window.

15:1 The **entire high council** of Jewish leaders had already reached their verdict (14:64), but they had to make the decision at a meeting during the day-

time in accordance with their law. Thus **very early in the morning,** they made it official that Jesus was worthy of death. So Jesus was **bound** like a common criminal and sent off to **Pilate, the Roman governor.** The council had to get permission from Pilate in order to carry out the death penalty.

Pontius Pilate was the Roman governor for the regions of Samaria and Judea from A.D. 26–36. Jerusalem was located in Judea. Pilate's normal residence was in Caesarea on the Mediterranean Sea, but he was in Jerusalem because of the Passover festival. With the large crowds that flocked to the city for that celebration, Pilate and his soldiers came to help keep the peace. He stayed in his headquarters, called the Praetorium. Pilate was a harsh governor who felt nothing but contempt for the Jews; they, in turn, felt the same about him. Pilate was not popular, but the religious leaders had no other way to get rid of Jesus. So they interrupted his breakfast on this early Friday morning, bringing a man whom they accused of treason against Rome! Ironically, when Jesus, a Jew, came before Pilate for trial, Pilate found him innocent.

JESUS STANDS TRIAL BEFORE PILATE / 15:2-5 / 230

The Jewish leaders had arrested Jesus and desired his death on theological grounds—but their charge of blasphemy would be thrown out of the Roman court. They had to come up with a political reason for Jesus' death. Their strategy was to show Jesus as a rebel who claimed to be a king and thus a threat to Caesar. The charge against Jesus in the Roman court was treason.

15:2 Pilate asked Jesus directly if he claimed to be **King of the Jews.** Jesus' answer was **yes,** but with a qualification attached (see John 18:36). Jesus did claim to be a king—to remain silent would be denying it (see also 14:62). But he wasn't claiming kingship in any way that would threaten Pilate, Caesar, or the Empire. Jesus' kingship was spiritual. Pilate could sense that the council's case was embarrassingly weak and that the solemn rabbi standing before him was unlikely to lead a revolt against Rome.

15:3-5 Luke records the essence of these charges in Luke 23:1-2. The Jewish leaders had to fabricate new accusations against Jesus, so they accused Jesus of **many crimes.** These accusations were false, but the religious leaders were determined to have Jesus killed. Pilate knew the charges were preposterous, and he obviously expected Jesus to **say something** in self-defense against the false **charges.** But **Jesus said nothing.** Jesus' silence had been prophesied in Scripture (Isaiah 53:7). Jesus had no reason to try to prolong the trial or save himself. Nothing would stop Jesus from completing the work he had come to earth to do.

Luke recorded a middle phase in all of this action. When Pilate found that Jesus was from Galilee, he sent him off to Herod Antipas, who was also in town for the Passover. But Herod only mocked Jesus and returned him to Pilate (Luke 23:6-12).

PILATE HANDS JESUS OVER TO BE CRUCIFIED / 15:6-15 / 232

In the custom of pardoning a criminal during Passover, Pilate saw an opportunity to avoid responsibility for the death of a man whom he perceived to be innocent. That Jesus died for Barabbas represents yet another example of the purpose of Jesus' death: to take the place, not just of one condemned man, but of all who stand condemned before God's perfect standard of justice.

15:6-7 Each year, during the Jews' Passover festival, Pilate had made it a **custom to release** any prisoner they requested. **Barabbas** had taken part in a **murder during an insurrection** against the Roman government. Although he was a murderer, he may have been a hero among the Jews. Barabbas had no hope of acquittal, so he must have been surprised when the guards came to get him on that Friday morning.

15:8 The proceedings of this hearing by Pilate were held in public, so a crowd was hearing all that transpired, and the crowd probably grew larger as news spread. Perhaps this was all part of the religious leaders' plan—to incite the crowd to ask that Pilate **release a prisoner as usual,** but that it be someone other than Jesus.

15:9-10 Pilate asked if the people wanted **the King of the Jews** released. This is the second time Pilate used that title for Jesus (see 15:2), and he would use it again (see 15:12; see also 15:18 and 15:26), probably in mockery. In any event, Pilate could see that this was a frame-up. Why else would these people, who hated him and the Roman Empire he represented, ask him to convict of treason and give the death penalty to one of their fellow Jews? Pilate understood that the Jewish leaders had **arrested Jesus out of envy.**

15:11-12 The power of the religious leaders took precedence with the Jewish crowd who would hardly side with the Roman governor. **The leading priests stirred up the mob to demand the release of Barabbas.** This left Pilate wondering what to do with Jesus.

15:13 The people made their choice, stated their preference, and confirmed their sin. This is just what the Jewish religious leaders wanted. Only slaves or those who were not Roman citizens could be executed by crucifixion. If Jesus was crucified, he would die the death of a rebel and slave, not of the king he claimed to be. In addition, crucifixion would put the responsibility for killing Jesus on the Romans; thus, the crowds would not blame the religious leaders.

15:14 The region of Judea where Pilate ruled as governor was little more than a hot and dusty outpost of the Roman Empire. Because Judea was so far from Rome, Pilate was given just a small army. The Roman government could not afford to put large numbers of troops in all the regions under their control, so one of Pilate's main duties was to do whatever was necessary to maintain peace. We know from historical records that Pilate had already been warned about other uprisings in his region. Although he may have seen no guilt in Jesus and no reason to condemn him to death, Pilate wavered when the Jews in the crowd threatened to report him to Caesar (John 19:12). Such a report, accompanied by a riot, could cost him his position and hopes for advancement. Pilate became afraid. His job was in jeopardy. The last thing Pilate needed was a riot in Jerusalem at Passover time, when the city was crowded with Jews from all over the Empire. Pilate asked the people to specify some **crime** that would make Jesus worthy of death. But the mob kept on shouting more wildly to **crucify** Jesus.

15:15 Pilate decided to let the crowds crucify Jesus. Although Pilate washed his hands of responsibility (Matthew 27:24), the guilt would remain. Pilate had no good excuse to condemn Jesus, but he was wanted **to please the crowd.** So he **released Barabbas,** then **flogged** Jesus before handing him **over to the Roman soldiers to crucify him.**

The flogging Jesus received could have killed him. The usual procedure was to bare the upper half of the victim's body and tie his hands to a pillar before whipping him with a **lead-tipped whip.** The whip was made of leather thongs that connected pieces of bone and metal like a chain. The continued lashing with these sharp instruments tore at the victim's skin, even baring the bones. This torture by flogging always would precede execution; thus, Jesus was flogged before he was sent to the cross. The Romans did it to weaken the prisoner so he would die more quickly on the cross.

ROMAN SOLDIERS MOCK JESUS / 15:16-20 / 233

Jesus was placed in the hands of men who probably knew little or nothing about him other than the fact that he had just been condemned to die. In their eyes, Jesus represented the stiff-necked Jews who resented the power of Rome. Jesus had to endure their pent-up hatred. He was taunted, tortured, and killed by brutal and vulgar men who were ignorant of his true identity and mission. This makes it all the more remarkable that one of these soldiers later confessed, "Truly, this was the Son of God!" (15:39).

15:16 The Romans had to execute Jesus, so the soldiers took him from the post where he had been flogged and led him, beaten and bleeding, back inside the Praetorium (Pilate's **headquarters**). The **entire battalion** was called together, probably about two hundred men who had accompanied Pilate from Caesarea.

15:17-19 Someone found a **purple robe** and threw it around the shoulders of this supposed "king." Someone else, with a brutal sense of humor, twisted some **long, sharp thorns** into a **crown** that was then jammed onto Jesus' head. Matthew added that they put a stick in his hand, like a king's scepter (Matthew 27:29). They beat him, striking him on the head. They insulted him by spitting on him and kneeling down in mock worship. Yet even all of this had been prophesied (Isaiah 50:6; 52:14–53:6).

15:20 After having their fun, the soldiers took off the purple robe and put Jesus' **own clothes on him**

again. Then he was taken out to be **crucified.** Probably only four soldiers under the command of an officer (15:39) actually went out to the site to perform the execution because John mentions that the soldiers at the cross divided his clothing "among the four of them" (John 19:23).

JESUS IS LED AWAY TO BE CRUCIFIED / 15:21-24 / 234

Jesus bore our sins on the cross, but was unable to bear his cross to the crest of Golgotha. He had been flogged and abused repeatedly since his arrest the previous night. A stranger was drafted to carry the timber for Jesus. Meanwhile, the soldiers who had just nailed three men to crosses gambled for the meager possessions they took from the condemned. Their gambling for the worthless benefits from their grisly work stands in stark contrast to the immeasurable benefits the Lord was making available to them as he hung dying above their heads.

15:21 Colonies of Jews existed outside Judea. **Simon** was from **Cyrene,** in northern Africa (see Acts 2:10), and was either on a pilgrimage to Jerusalem for the Passover, or he was originally from Cyrene but resided in Palestine. His two sons, **Alexander and Rufus,** are mentioned as if Mark's readers in Rome knew them. Rufus may be the same man mentioned by Paul in Romans 16:13. If so, this could mean that Simon became a Christian through this incident. Simon, on his way into the city, was randomly picked out of the crowd and **forced to carry Jesus' cross.**

15:22 Some scholars say **Golgotha** (translated **Skull Hill**) derived its name from its appearance, a hill with a stony top that might have been shaped like a skull. *Golgotha* is the Hebrew word for "skull." The familiar name "Calvary" is derived from the Latin *calvaria* (also meaning "skull"). Golgotha may have been a regular place of execution in a prominent public place outside the city along a main road. Executions held there served as examples to the people and as a deterrent to criminals.

15:23 Wine drugged with myrrh was offered to Jesus to help reduce his pain. Myrrh is generally understood to be a narcotic that was used to deaden pain. Tradition says women of Jerusalem prepared and offered this drink to condemned men. This also may allude to Psalm 69:21. But Jesus **refused** to drink it. He chose to suffer fully conscious and with a clear mind.

15:24 Mark's words are simple and direct: **They nailed him to the cross.** Indeed, Mark's Roman readers needed no elaborate description; they knew it all too well. Crucifixion, instituted by the Romans, was a feared and shameful form of execution. Death came by suffocation as the person lost strength and the weight of the body made breathing more and more difficult.

Contrary to the discreet paintings of the Crucifixion, Jesus was crucified naked. Roman soldiers had the right to take for themselves the clothing of those crucified, so they **gambled for** Jesus' **clothes.** This act had also been prophesied (Psalm 22:18).

JESUS IS PLACED ON THE CROSS / 15:25-32 / 235

An execution could provide hours of grisly entertainment for spectators. The Gospels describe various responses within the crowd as Jesus was dying. Some openly taunted him. His opponents gloated. Those who had the most information about Jesus rejected his claims, while one prisoner who had very little information placed his trust in him (see Luke 23:40-43).

15:25-26 Jesus was placed on the cross at **nine o'clock in the morning.** A **signboard** stating **the charge against him** was fastened on his cross as a warning. Because Jesus was never found guilty, the only accusation placed on his sign was the "crime" of calling himself **King of the Jews.** This sign was meant to be ironic. A king, stripped and executed in public view, had obviously lost his kingdom forever. But Jesus, who turns the world's wisdom upside down, was just coming into his Kingdom. His death and resurrection would strike the deathblow to Satan's rule and would establish Christ's eternal authority over the earth. Few people reading the sign that bleak day understood its real meaning, but the sign was absolutely true. Jesus is king of the Jews—and the Gentiles, and the whole universe.

15:27 When James and John had asked Jesus for the places of honor next to him in his Kingdom, Jesus had told them that they didn't know what they were asking (10:35-39). Here, as Jesus was preparing to inaugurate his Kingdom through his death, the places on his right and on his left were taken by **two criminals.**

A person who wants to be close to Jesus must be prepared to suffer and die as he himself was doing. The way to the Kingdom is the way of the cross. If we want the glory of the Kingdom, we must be willing to be united with the crucified Christ.

15:29-30 Insult was literally added to injury when it came to public crucifixion. **People passing by shouted abuse at Jesus.** They again used the twisted accusation that had been brought against Jesus at the council (14:58), taunting him that if he could boast of building the **Temple** in **three days,** surely he had the power to **save** himself from the fate of the cross. Ironically, Jesus was in the very process of fulfilling his own prophecy. His body was being destroyed, but in three days he would rise again. Because Jesus is the Son of God who always obeys the will of the Father, he did not come down from the cross to save himself. If he had done so, he could not have saved us.

15:31-32 Apparently the religious leaders had followed the executioners out to Golgotha, eager to see their plot finally completed in Jesus' death. Not content to have brought him to an unjust death, they also **mocked** him as they talked among themselves. They mockingly dismissed his healings and miracles because even though he **saved others,** he could not **save himself.** They taunted him to **come down from the cross,** and if he did that, they would **believe him.** They did not believe that Jesus was the **Messiah,** nor the **king of Israel,** but they taunted him with these names. Obviously Jesus wasn't the Messiah, they thought, because he was dying just like the cursed robbers. Mark recorded that the **two criminals** also **ridiculed** Jesus; but Luke states that later one of these criminals repented (Luke 23:39-43).

JESUS DIES ON THE CROSS / 15:33-41 / 236

Mark recorded the final scene of Jesus' earthly life with graphic imagery. The dark sky was pierced by an anguished cry of abandonment. Those watching were gripped with awe.

15:33 Jesus had been put on the cross at nine o'clock in the morning. Death by crucifixion was slow and excruciating, sometimes taking two or three days. Three hours passed while Jesus put up with abuse from bystanders. Then, **at noon, darkness** settled over the land for three hours. We do not know how this darkness occurred, but it is clear that God caused it. Nature testified to the gravity of Jesus' death, while Jesus' friends and enemies alike fell silent in the encircling gloom. The darkness on that Friday afternoon was both physical and spiritual. All nature seemed to mourn over the tragedy of the death of God's Son.

15:34 Jesus did not ask this question in surprise or despair. He was quoting the first line of Psalm 22, a prophecy expressing the deep agony of the Messiah's death for the world's sin. Jesus knew that he would be temporarily separated from God the moment he took upon himself the sins of the world, because God cannot look on sin (Habakkuk 1:13). This separation was the "cup" Jesus dreaded drinking, as he prayed in Gethsemane (14:36). The physical agony was horrible, but the spiritual alienation from God was the ultimate torture. Jesus suffered this double death so that we would never have to experience eternal separation from God.

15:35 The **bystanders** misinterpreted Jesus' words and thought he was calling for **Elijah.** Because Elijah had ascended into heaven without dying (2 Kings 2:11), there was the popular belief that Elijah would return to rescue those suffering from great trouble.

15:36 John records that Jesus said he was thirsty (John 19:28-29). In response, one man **filled a sponge with sour wine** (this was not the same as the drugged wine offered to Jesus earlier). He put the sponge on a long **stick** and held it up so as to reach Jesus' lips. Thinking Jesus had called for Elijah (15:35), the people watched to see if Elijah would **come** to rescue Jesus.

15:37 Jesus' **loud cry** may have been his last words, "It is finished!" (John 19:30). Jesus' loud cry climaxed the horror of this scene and showed his sudden death after over six hours on the cross. Jesus did not die the normal death of a crucified person who would merely breathe his last breath. Usually crucifixion caused a person to lapse into a coma from extreme exhaustion. Jesus, however, was completely conscious to the end. His cry exclaimed his victory.

15:38 This significant event symbolized what Christ's work on the cross had accomplished. The

Temple had three main parts—the courts, the Holy Place (where only the priests could enter), and the Most Holy Place, a place reserved by God for himself. It was in the Most Holy Place that the Ark of the Covenant, and God's presence with it, rested. The room was entered only once a year, on the Day of Atonement, by the high priest as he made a sacrifice to gain forgiveness for the sins of all the nation (Leviticus 16:1-34). The **curtain in the Temple** was between the Holy Place and the Most Holy Place. Symbolically, the curtain separated the holy God from sinful people. By tearing the curtain **in two,** God showed that Christ had opened the way for sinful people to reach the holy God.

15:39 A **Roman officer** had accompanied the soldiers to the execution site. Undoubtedly, he had done this many times. Yet this crucifixion was completely different—the unexplained darkness, the earthquake, even the executed himself who had uttered words of forgiveness (Luke 23:34). The officer observed Jesus' alertness throughout the crucifixion and his relatively quick death. This Gentile Roman officer realized something that most of the Jewish nation had missed: **"Truly, this was the Son of God!"** Whether he understood what he was saying, we cannot know. He may simply have admired Jesus' courage and inner strength, perhaps thinking that Jesus was divine like one of Rome's many gods. While the Jewish religious leaders stood around celebrating Jesus' death, a lone Roman soldier was the first to acclaim Jesus as the Son of God after his death.

15:40-41 There had been many people at the cross who had come only to mock and taunt Jesus or, like the religious leaders, to revel in their apparent victory. But some of Jesus' faithful followers were at the cross as well. Among the disciples, only John was there, and he recorded in his Gospel in graphic detail the horror he observed. Several **women** were also there **watching from a distance.** John wrote that Jesus' mother, Mary, was present, and that Jesus spoke to John from the cross about taking care of Mary (John 19:25-27).

Mark mentions that **Mary Magdalene** was there. She had been released from demon possession by Jesus (Luke 8:2). Another **Mary** is distinguished (from Mary Magdalene and Mary Jesus' mother) by the names of her sons who may have been well known in the early church. **Salome** was the mother of the disciples James and John and was probably Jesus' mother's sister. These women had come from Galilee with Jesus for the Passover. They **had come with him to Jerusalem** and had witnessed the Crucifixion.

JESUS IS LAID IN THE TOMB / 15:42-47 / 237

Although Mark mentioned only Joseph of Arimathea, John mentioned both Joseph and Nicodemus, two secret disciples of Jesus who took action to ensure his burial (John 19:38-42). Their commitment to Jesus forced them out of hiding. The Gospels carefully note that Jesus was clearly dead. Pilate checked. One soldier made sure (John 19:34). Two men who had followed Jesus from a distance undertook the compassionate task of removing Jesus' body from the cross and placing it in a tomb, while several women watched.

15:42-43 The Sabbath began at sundown on Friday and ended at sundown on Saturday. Jesus died just a few hours before sundown on **Friday.** It was against Jewish law to do physical work or to travel on the **Sabbath,** so the day before was **the day of preparation** for the Sabbath. It was also against Jewish law to let a dead body remain exposed overnight (Deuteronomy 21:23). As **evening** and the **Sabbath** approached, **Joseph from Arimathea** (a town about twenty miles from Jerusalem) asked for Jesus' body so he could give it a proper burial. Although **an honored member of the high council,** Joseph was a secret disciple of Jesus (John 19:38). That he **was waiting for the Kingdom of God** suggests that Joseph was a Pharisee, who hoped for God's deliverance. Joseph **gathered his courage and went to Pilate to ask for Jesus' body** in order to bury it. He went directly to Pilate who alone could give permission to take down the body. He had to hurry; Sabbath was fast approaching.

15:44-45 Pilate was surprised that Jesus had died so quickly, so he asked an official to verify the report. He summoned the officer who had been at the execution site (15:39). Only Mark recorded Pilate's questioning of the officer, perhaps to show his Roman readers that Jesus' death had been verified by a **Roman military officer.** No officer so trained in execution could make such a basic error.

15:46 Joseph bought a linen cloth; Nicodemus brought spices (John 19:39). The body was carefully taken **down from the cross, wrapped** in layers of cloth with the spices in between, and **laid in a tomb.** Jesus was given a burial fit for a king.

This tomb was probably a man-made cave **carved** out of one of the many limestone hills in the area around Jerusalem. It was large enough to walk into (John 20:6). Matthew records that this was Joseph's own previously unused tomb (Matthew 27:60). Joseph and Nicodemus wrapped Jesus' body, placed it in the tomb, and **rolled a stone** across the **entrance.** The religious leaders also watched where Jesus was buried. They stationed guards by the tomb and sealed the stone to make sure that no one would steal Jesus' body and claim he had risen from the dead (Matthew 27:62-66). All of these actions give us verification that Jesus truly had died.

15:47 Two of the women who had been at the cross (15:40) followed these men as they carried Jesus' body to the tomb. They wanted to know **where Jesus' body was laid** because they planned to return after the Sabbath with their own spices to anoint Jesus' body (16:1).

MARK 16

JESUS RISES FROM THE DEAD / 16:1-8 / 239

The resurrection of Jesus from the dead is the central fact of Christian history. Jesus' resurrection is unique. Other religions have strong ethical systems, concepts about paradise and afterlife, and various holy scriptures. Only Christianity has a God who became human, literally died for his people, and was raised again in power and glory to rule his church forever.

Christians can look very different from one another, and they can hold widely varying beliefs about politics, lifestyle, and even theology. But one central belief unites and inspires all true Christians—Jesus Christ rose from the dead!

16:1 Mary Magdalene and the other **Mary** had been at Jesus' cross and had followed Joseph so that they would know where he had been buried (15:47). **Salome** had also been at the cross; she was probably the mother of the disciples James and John. The women went home and kept the Sabbath as the law required, from sundown Friday to sundown Saturday. So they **purchased burial spices** before returning to the tomb early Sunday morning. Anointing a body was a sign of love, devotion, and respect. Bringing spices to the tomb would be like bringing flowers to a grave today. Since they did not embalm bodies in Israel, they would use perfumes as a normal practice. The women undoubtedly knew that Joseph and Nicodemus had already wrapped the body in linen and spices. They probably were going to do a simple external application of the fragrant spices. Since Jesus' body was buried so rapidly after he was crucified, they had been unable to perform the anointing before Jesus' burial.

16:2 Sabbath had ended at sundown on Saturday, so **very early on Sunday morning,** the women left their homes, arriving at the tomb **just at sunrise.** They wasted no time. This further illustrates their misunderstanding of Jesus. He had told them that he would rise from the dead, yet they expected nothing.

16:3 Two of these women had seen where the body had been placed and knew that a huge stone had been rolled across the entrance to the tomb (15:46). Apparently, they were unaware that the tomb had been sealed and a guard set outside it (Matthew 27:62-66). So as they approached the tomb, they remembered that the stone would be a problem. They wondered aloud who might be able to **roll the stone away** so that they could get in.

16:4 The women needn't have worried about the stone. Jesus had said he would rise again after three days. In the Jewish reckoning of time, a day included any part of a day; thus, Friday was the first day, Saturday was the second day, and Sunday was the third day. When the women arrived at daybreak, Jesus had already risen.

When they arrived at the tomb, **they saw** that the large **stone had already been rolled aside.** Matthew records that there had been an earthquake and an angel of the Lord had descended from heaven, had rolled back the stone, and had sat on it.

16:5-6 The women **entered the tomb.** Once inside they were startled to see **a young man clothed in a white robe.** We learn from Matthew and John that this was an angel. When angels appeared to people, they looked like humans.

The angel spoke reassuringly to the women. They were looking for **Jesus the Nazarene**, the human being who had been **crucified**. But Jesus was not there; he had been **raised from the dead**.

The angel invited the women to **look** into the inner burial chamber and see **where they** (Joseph and Nicodemus, 15:46) **laid his body**. John records that the linen cloths that had been wrapped around Jesus' body were left as if Jesus had passed right through them. The handkerchief was still rolled up in the shape of a head, and it was at about the right distance from the wrappings that had enveloped Jesus' body (John 20:6-7).

16:7 The women who had come to anoint a dead body were given another task, that of proclaiming the Resurrection to the frightened disciples. The disciples had deserted Jesus in the hour of trial, but the angel's words held hope of renewal and forgiveness. The disciples were invited to meet Jesus in **Galilee**—there was work to do. The angel

made special mention of **Peter** to show that, in spite of Peter's denials, Jesus had not deserted him.

The angel told the disciples to meet Jesus in Galilee **just as he told you before he died**. This was exactly what Jesus had told them during the Last Supper, that he would go ahead of them into Galilee after his resurrection (14:28). But the disciples, filled with fear, remained behind locked doors in Jerusalem (John 20:19). Jesus met them first in Jerusalem (Luke 24:36) and later in Galilee (John 21).

16:8 The women **fled from the tomb**, realizing that they had seen the results of an awesome miracle in the empty tomb and had been in the presence of an angel. They either went straight to the disciples with the news, **saying nothing to anyone** along the way, or for a time they said nothing out of fear, perhaps expecting the response of disbelief that they eventually did receive from the disciples when they told the story (Luke 24:11).

JESUS APPEARS TO MARY MAGDALENE / 16:9-11 / 240

While the material included in 16:1-8 is universally regarded as being original to Mark's manuscript, the section of 16:9-20 is not considered to have been original. Most scholars believe that verses 9-20 were added sometime in the second century or later; whoever added these verses borrowed heavily from the resurrection accounts in the other Gospels. There are four other different additions to the ending of Mark as found in a few other ancient manuscripts. But the earliest and best Greek manuscripts do not contain these verses, and testimony of the early church fathers indicates that these verses were not part of the original text of Mark's Gospel. Most modern translations note that these verses are absent from our earliest manuscripts but include them anyway.

16:9-11 After the women had told the disciples about the Resurrection, and Peter and another disciple (presumably John) had gone to see for themselves (John 20:3-9), **Mary Magdalene** apparently had returned to the tomb and was weeping (John 20:11).

Although Mary Magdalene has been mentioned earlier in this Gospel as one of the women at the cross and at the tomb (15:40, 47; 16:1), Mark reminded his readers of the reason for her devotion to Jesus: He had **cast out seven demons**

from her (see also Luke 8:2). This devoted woman was **the first person who saw** the resurrected Christ.

Jesus told Mary to return and tell the disciples. The disciples did not believe the women who came to them; Peter and John saw the empty tomb and still did not understand what had happened. They continued their **grieving and weeping**. Mary returned to the disciples with the news that she had actually seen and talked to the risen Jesus, but **they didn't believe her**.

JESUS APPEARS TO TWO BELIEVERS TRAVELING ON THE ROAD / 16:12-13 / 243

Luke's description of Jesus' encounter with the two disciples on the road to Emmaus should be read when studying this brief paragraph—Luke 24:13-35.

16:12-13 At another point, Jesus appeared **to two** of the disciples who had disbelieved Mary's report of seeing the resurrected Jesus. They were

walking **from Jerusalem** to the small town of Emmaus (west of Jerusalem). These disciples knew that the tomb was empty but didn't understand that Jesus had risen. To compound the problem, they were walking in the wrong direction—away from the fellowship of believers in Jerusalem. They didn't recognize Jesus when he appeared beside them **because he had changed his appearance.**

After talking with these two disciples along the road and reprimanding them about their lack of knowledge of the Scriptures that described all that happened, Jesus revealed himself and then vanished (Luke 24:31). **When they realized who he was,** they immediately returned to Jerusalem and reported that they too had seen Jesus. But still, **no one believed them.**

JESUS APPEARS TO THOMAS / 16:14 / 245

The disciples' reluctance to believe was resolved by Jesus' appearance to them all at one time. The common theme in Mark's list of appearances was the disciples' reluctance to believe.

16:14 Jesus finally **appeared to the eleven disciples** together (Judas Iscariot, the betrayer, had killed himself). Jesus **rebuked them for their unbelief.** Jesus had foretold his own resurrection. Every time he had told them he would die, he had also told them that he would rise again. The Old Testament prophesied all that had happened to Jesus and also spoke of his resurrection. The disciples had no excuse for the stubborn refusal to believe.

JESUS GIVES THE GREAT COMMISSION / 16:15-18 / 248

This paragraph represents a change of scene. This was another post-Resurrection appearance, the last to the remaining eleven disciples and other followers. This paragraph outlines Jesus' final charge to his followers (see also Matthew 28:16-20). The Gospel of Mark is a record of the gospel (or Good News) from its beginning (1:1). As the book closes, the gospel does not end, but continues in the lives of Jesus' followers. Jesus' command is to go everywhere and preach the Good News.

16:15 This is the Great Commission. The disciples had been trained well, and they had seen the risen Lord. God had given Jesus authority over heaven and earth. On the basis of that authority, Jesus told his disciples to make more disciples as they preached, baptized, and taught. With this same authority, Jesus still commands us to tell **everyone everywhere** the **Good News.**

16:16 The disciples were commanded to baptize people because baptism unites a believer with Jesus Christ in his or her death to sin and resurrection to new life. It is not the water of baptism that saves, but God's grace accepted through faith in Christ. Because of Jesus' response to the criminal on the cross who died with him, we know it is possible to be saved without being baptized (Luke 23:43). Jesus did not say that those who were not baptized would be condemned, but that **anyone who refuses to believe will be condemned.** Baptism symbolizes

submission to Christ, a willingness to live God's way, and identification with God's covenant people.

16:17-18 As the disciples fulfilled their commission, and indeed as others believed and went on to spread the gospel, miraculous **signs** would accompany them. As with Jesus' miracles, these signs would authenticate the source of their power and draw people to belief. At times, God would miraculously intervene on behalf of his followers. While some people have misinterpreted the notion of "picking up snakes" as thinking that one's faith is demonstrated by handling rattlesnakes, the writer seems to have in mind incidents like the one described in Acts 28:1-6, where Paul was bitten by a poisonous snake without being harmed. The same could happen for someone who accidentally drank deadly poison. This does not mean, however, that we should test God by putting ourselves in dangerous situations.

JESUS ASCENDS INTO HEAVEN / 16:19-20 / 250

Even though it is questioned as having been from Mark's pen, this ending provides an effective closure to the book. Jesus resumed his place with God and was exalted to "the right hand of

God." Meanwhile, those who were left behind carried the gospel everywhere, accompanied by the Lord's presence.

16:19 These final verses end where the book of Acts begins. Luke wrote in Acts that Jesus appeared to various people over a period of forty days before he ascended (Acts 1:9). As the disciples stood and watched, Jesus **was taken up into heaven.** Jesus' physical presence left the disciples, but the Holy Spirit soon came to comfort them and empower them to spread the gospel (Acts 2:1-4). Jesus' work of salvation was completed, and he **sat down in the place of honor at God's right hand** where he has authority over heaven and earth (see also Romans 8:34; Hebrews 1:3; 8:1).

16:20 While Jesus' work on earth was completed, the disciples' work was just beginning. This verse compacts the book of Acts. These doubting, stubborn disciples turned into powerful preachers who **went everywhere and preached.** God **worked with them**—giving them peace, strength through persecutions, and confirmation of their message with **miraculous signs** (16:17-18; Hebrews 2:4).

Mark's Gospel emphasizes Christ's power, as well as his servanthood. Jesus' life and teaching turned the world upside down. The world sees power as a way to gain control over others. But Jesus, with all authority and power in heaven and earth, chose to serve others. He held children in his arms, healed the sick, acted patiently with his hardheaded disciples, and died for the sins of the world. Following Jesus means receiving this same power to serve. As believers, we are called to be servants of Christ. As Christ served, so we are to serve.

LUKE

INTRODUCTION

Precision. Accuracy. Truth.

Certain men and women make it their business to deal only with the facts. No hearsay. No speculation. No rumor.

Scientists belong in this category. Checking the data and conducting experiments, they test theories and draw conclusions. Detectives, too, work hard to discover the truth. Carefully gathering and analyzing evidence, they follow the clues to solve the crime. Add to the mix judges who weigh testimony, hear arguments, and consider the law before rendering just verdicts. Historians also strive to be accurate—to know precisely what happened at a certain time and place. And surely doctors stand with this group. With informative tests and diagnostic expertise, they examine patients, draw conclusions, and prescribe cures.

Luke wanted only the truth. As a historian, Luke's research would be meticulous, interviewing reliable witnesses and primary sources. As a doctor, a man of science, he would carefully consider all the facts before rendering an opinion. That is exactly what he did. Addressing Theophilus, Luke wrote, "Having carefully investigated all of these accounts from the beginning, I have decided to write a careful summary for you, to reassure you of the truth of all you were taught" (Luke 1:3-4). To "reassure" his friend and other believers who never had the opportunity to see Jesus themselves, Luke's investigation included reading "accounts about the events" (1:1) and analyzing "reports . . . from the early disciples and other eyewitnesses" (1:2). Thus, Luke sought and found the truth. Then he recorded it to affirm this truth in writing and to point his readers to the Truth, Jesus Christ.

As you read Luke's Gospel, carefully investigate the facts for yourself. Analyze the evidence presented, follow the clues, and render your judgment. No doubt, you too will discover that Jesus is Christ, the Savior, God's Son.

AUTHOR

Luke: doctor, Gentile Christian, traveling companion of Paul, and writer of the book of Acts

Although the texts of this Gospel and Acts make no mention of Luke, the early church fathers, without dispute or exception, identified him as the author. Justin Martyr (c. A.D. 100–165), Irenaeus (c. A.D. 175–195), and Tertullian (c. A.D. 160–230) all agree. Even the Muratorian Canon (c. A.D. 170–180), an early list of biblical books considered as inspired by God, includes Luke.

Luke begins his account in the Temple in Jerusalem, giving us the background for the birth of John the Baptist, then moves on to the town of Nazareth and the story of Mary, chosen to be Jesus' mother (1:26ff). As a result of Caesar's call for a census, Mary and Joseph had to travel to Bethlehem, where Jesus was born in fulfillment of prophecy (2:1ff). Jesus grew up in Nazareth and began his earthly ministry by being baptized by John (3:21-22) and tempted by Satan (4:1ff). Much of his ministry focused on Galilee: He set up his "home" in Capernaum (4:31ff), and from there he taught throughout the region (8:1ff). Later he visited Gerasa (also called Gadara), where he healed a demon-possessed man (8:36ff). He miraculously fed more than five thousand people on the shores of the Sea of Galilee near Bethsaida (9:10ff). Jesus always traveled to Jerusalem for the major festivals, and he enjoyed visiting friends in nearby Bethany (10:38ff). He healed ten men with leprosy on the border between Galilee and Samaria (17:11) and helped a dishonest tax collector in Jericho turn his life around (19:1ff). The little villages of Bethphage and Bethany on the Mount of Olives were Jesus' resting

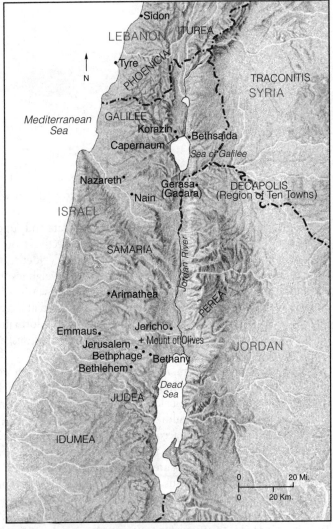

The broken lines (— · —·) indicate modern boundaries.

places during his last days on earth. He was crucified outside Jerusalem's walls, but he would rise again. Two of Jesus' followers walking on the road leading to Emmaus were among the first to see the resurrected Christ (24:13ff).

One of the oldest copies of this Gospel (Bodmer Papyrus XIV), dated to around A.D. 200, includes Luke in the title as the author.

What makes this unanimous testimony so remarkable is that Luke was a relatively unknown figure in the writings of the early church. Paul only mentions Luke three times (Colossians 4:14; 2 Timothy 4:11; Philemon 24). Most significant is the fact that Luke was not an original disciple, an eyewitness follower of Christ. This fact is freely admitted at the outset of the Gospel, as the author explains the necessity of relying on eyewitnesses for his investigation about Jesus' life (1:2-4). Assuming that Luke is the author, his close relationship to the apostle Paul and other church leaders undoubtedly would have given him access to a wealth of evidence about the life of Christ (see Acts 20:5-15; 27:1–28:16).

In addition to being one of Paul's traveling companions, Luke was a doctor (Colossians 4:14). Many have attempted to prove Luke's authorship of this Gospel by identifying medical terminology in it. In a few places, Luke presents more exact descriptions of diseases than Matthew or Mark. The Greek style of Luke does not prove that the author was a physician, but it does not disprove it and certainly seems consistent with what a doctor would write.

Luke is not included among the Jews in Paul's final greetings in Colossians (see Colossians 4:11, 14). From this omission, many have concluded that Luke was a Gentile, probably the only Gentile author of a New Testament book. A careful study of the Greek style of both Luke and Acts agrees with the conclusion that the author, Luke, was a Gentile. For example, these books consistently avoid Aramaic expressions, such as *rabbi*, and include, instead, words that would be more familiar to Gentiles, such as *teacher*.

Although Luke's historical accuracy has been called into question by critical scholars on certain points (especially the census of Quirinius in 2:1-2 and references to the priesthoods of Annas and Caiaphas in 3:2), it is clear that Luke, more so than Matthew and Mark, took great pains to verify the historical accuracy of the accounts that he was retelling. Historical references abound in the Gospel. For example, Luke dated Jesus' birth by mentioning the reigning Roman emperor and the local governor (2:1); he even dated the beginning of John the Baptist's ministry in the same way (3:1). This Gospel, along with the numerous details in Acts, reveals the careful and diligent research of a precise historian.

Although not much is known about Luke, it is evident that he was Paul's loyal and faithful friend. He quietly supported Paul, both when he was valiantly preaching the Good News and when he was sitting in prison. Toward the end of Paul's life, when everyone else had deserted him, Luke was by his side, encouraging and supporting the apostle during his last days (2 Timothy 4:11). Perhaps during these long hours at Paul's side, Luke quietly took up a pen and started writing down the results of his meticulous research of Jesus' life.

As you read Luke, look for the accuracy and precision with which Luke presents the teaching and ministry of Jesus. But also look beyond this to the Jesus whom Luke presents. Luke's careful research uncovered a person with a revolutionary message, a person who expressed love and compassion that could come only from God. Convinced of the truth of Jesus' message, Luke dedicated all his talents to furthering that message. What is your response to Jesus and his teachings? What can you do to spread the Good News?

DATE AND SETTING

Probably written from Caesarea, around A.D. 60–61.The best clue to the date for this Gospel is the last recorded event in the book of Acts, Paul's first Roman imprisonment. Acts ends on an unexpected note, with Paul a prisoner in Rome, awaiting his trial. It is an abrupt ending, with no mention of the trial's results and subsequent events. This seems to indicate that Luke was writing Acts right up to the present. If that is so, then Acts was probably written around A.D. 61–62 because Paul's first imprisonment is usually dated A.D. 62 and his second imprisonment and subsequent execution, much later. Clearly identifying his Gospel as the first of his two books (Acts 1:1), Luke probably wrote it around A.D. 60–61, perhaps when he was staying with Paul during his imprisonments in Caesarea (Acts 23:33) and in Rome (Acts 28:14-16).

After accompanying Paul on parts of his second and third missionary journeys, Luke remained with him when Paul was arrested in Jerusalem (Acts 21). Luke did not abandon Paul even when he was brought to Caesarea under heavy Roman guard (to protect him from his Jewish accusers, Acts 23:23-35). Also, Luke most likely endured, with Paul, the treacherous sea journey to Rome (Acts 27–28). It was during those long months, as Paul awaited trial, first before Felix (Acts 24:1-27), then Festus (Acts 25:1-22), then Agrippa (Acts 25:23–26:32), and finally Caesar himself (Acts 28:15-31), that Luke probably wrote this Gospel (and the book of Acts). Especially during the imprisonment at Rome, Paul enjoyed a measure of freedom. He lived in his own rented house, under the constant watch of a Roman guard, and welcomed guests and friends to tell them about the Good News concerning Jesus Christ and salvation (Acts 28:30-31). During this somewhat mild imprisonment, it appears that Luke stayed with Paul (Paul mentions Luke in the letters he wrote during that time—see Colossians 4:14 and Philemon 24).

In addition to staying with Paul and supporting him, Luke was diligently compiling the facts relating to Jesus' life—the testimonies of eyewitnesses, the written histories, and the stories of the Messiah's life that Paul had employed in his preaching. Luke wrote a history of Jesus' life that would become more influential than the Roman Empire itself. Luke's history would survive the fall of that powerful empire and would help establish the truth about Christ.

This date (A.D. 60–61) is fairly close to the time that the other two synoptic Gospels were written—Mark being the first, around A.D. 55–60, and Matthew following, around A.D. 60. Because of this proximity, some critics have maintained a later date for Luke and Acts—in the mid-eighties. Their reasons, however, are far from persuasive. The common assumption of these critics, that Luke would not have access to Mark's Gospel until several decades after Mark wrote it, is very doubtful because Paul mentioned in both Philemon 24 and 2 Timothy 4:11 that Luke and Mark were together. (Philemon was written in A.D. 60, and 2 Timothy was written in A.D. 66 or 67.)

In addition, Acts makes no mention of the destruction of Jerusalem which occurred in A.D. 70. Surely this catastrophic event would have been included in any history of the early church. In fact, Luke reported Jesus' predictions that Jerusalem would be utterly demolished (19:41-44; 21:20-24). Mentioning the fulfillment of Jesus' prophecy would have been especially appropriate since Luke wrote of Stephen's martyrdom (Acts 6:8–7:60) and Paul's arrest (Acts 21:26-36), both events having occurred in Jerusalem. Note also that Luke wrote of the fulfillment of Agabus's prophecy (Acts 11:28). Certainly the omission in Acts of the destruction of Jerusalem points to an earlier date for the Gospel.

Most likely, Luke took advantage of the prolonged imprisonment of Paul in both Casearea and Rome to collect information relating to Jesus' life and to record Paul's memories of his four missionary journeys that had spanned the previous decade.

AUDIENCE
Theophilus ("one who loves God"), Gentiles, and people everywhere

Luke addressed both of his books—the Gospel and the book of Acts—to Theophilus (1:1; Acts 1:1). Because "Theophilus" literally means "one who loves God" or "friend of God," some have speculated that the name does not refer to an actual person but, rather, to all people who love God. "Most honorable" (the words preceding the name), however, was a title often used in addressing a Roman official. This has led most scholars to conclude that Theophilus was an actual person, probably someone of rank in Roman society. Beyond that brief mention in Luke and Acts, however, nothing else is known of Theophilus. The name appears nowhere else in Scripture.

The name "Theophilus" suggests a Gentile. This is consistent with the content of both Luke and Acts, which seem to be written to a predominately Gentile audience. Luke took the trouble to explain common Jewish customs, such as the Passover, to his readers, who were apparently Gentiles (see 22:1-7). In addition, Luke omitted the teachings of Jesus that involved the intricacies of Mosaic law and Jewish customs, such as divorce regulations (see Mark 10:1-12), customs surrounding oaths (see Matthew 5:33-37), praying (see Matthew 6:5-6), and fasting (see Matthew 6:16-18). On the other hand, Luke underscored Jesus' mission to the Gentiles (2:32; 24:47) by tracing his genealogy back to Adam instead of just to Abraham (compare 3:23-38 with Matthew 1:1-17) and by highlighting the Roman soldier's remarkable faith (7:1-10). Luke's concern for Gentile inclusion into the community of faith becomes even more clear in the book of Acts, where he charted the spread of the gospel among the Gentiles (Acts 10:1–11:18; 13:46-48).

Although written to a specific individual, Luke probably also had a larger audience in mind. Certainly a new Christian questioning his or her faith would gain much from reading this Gospel. Jews and Jewish Christians would benefit from seeing that despite numerous invitations by God to participate in the new covenant, Israel had rejected God's invitations and their Messiah. Gentiles, especially, would benefit from this Gospel, especially those feeling out of place in what originally was a Jewish movement. Growing numbers of Gentiles were coming to Christ in Asia Minor and Greece, evangelized, for the most part, by Paul (as described in Acts). Luke offered reassurance that they belonged, as Christ's followers and God's people. Clearly, through Luke, God was communicating his message to all who love God.

What tensions do you face in your faith? What doubts about Jesus and the Christian faith nibble at the edges of your mind? Apparently Theophilus did not conceal his questions; instead, he went to his trusted and knowledgeable friend and asked for information and answers. Luke responded to Theophilus with two

8

books, filled with the results of his careful research about Jesus. As you read, dive into this God-inspired history of Jesus with your hard questions. You will find answers.

OCCASION AND PURPOSE
To present an accurate account of the life of Christ and to present Christ as the perfect man and Savior

Luke's purpose for writing is stated in his preface to the book. Luke wrote this account to provide Theophilus with a history of Jesus that could hold up to the standards of historical investigation. Luke knew that his account of Jesus' life must do more than report the Master's words and deeds. Jesus' actions certainly could speak for themselves. Healing the sick (5:12-16), exorcising thousands of demons (8:26-39), calming the waves (8:22-25), and raising people from the dead (8:40-56) surely could not be attributed to a mere human being. Only God could possess that type of control over nature, diseases, the spirit world, and even death. Yet Luke did not stop there. He connected Old Testament Scriptures with Jesus' actions, showing how Jesus fulfilled the prophecies concerning the Messiah (3:4-6; 7:22-23; 20:17). Jesus was the One about whom the prophets had spoken.

Luke did not leave Theophilus wondering how he should respond to Jesus. He described the various reactions of those who saw and heard Jesus—from amazement, joy, and wholehearted belief to fear, skepticism, and coldhearted rejection (compare 4:16-30 and 9:18-20). Luke highlighted the appropriate responses: fervent belief in Jesus as the Son of God (9:18-20) and willingness to sacrifice everything to follow him (9:23-27). Anyone who responded to the gospel message, repenting of sin and trusting in Christ, could become a member of the community of faith.

With two well-researched volumes, Luke answered Theophilus's hard questions about Christian faith. By retelling the life and teachings of Jesus, Luke presented Jesus as a real man, an extraordinary Jewish teacher in his own right. By recounting the miracles and the prophecies connected to Jesus' life, Luke portrayed him as a divine being, the Messiah sent by God. By tracing the growth of the Christian church throughout the known world at that time, Luke presented the Good News of salvation, applicable to every person—from the lowliest slave to the most respected nobleman, from orthodox Jews to pagan Greeks and Romans. When you sit down to read Luke, don't let your familiarity with the Gospel stories rob the freshness and vividness of Luke's account. Like Theophilus, approach Luke with questions. Who is Jesus? Why should I care about a Jewish teacher? Let Jesus' words speak directly to you, challenging you to repent and believe.

RELATIONSHIP TO THE OTHER GOSPELS
It is commonly accepted that Luke had access to Mark's Gospel when he was composing his account, for he seems to have adapted Mark's material in large blocks (see chapters 4, 5, 8, 9, 19–21; compare 18:15-17 and Mark 10:13-16 for the similar wording of the two Gospels). Parts of the rest of Luke's narrative have close affinities with portions of Matthew, but the striking differences at times suggest that Luke may not have had direct access to Matthew's Gospel. Around thirty percent of the Gospel is entirely unique. Most of this is parables:

Parables Unique to Luke:

The two debtors—7:41-50
The good Samaritan—10:25-37
The persistent friend—11:5-10
The rich fool—12:13-21
The barren fig tree—13:6-9
The foolish builder—14:28-30
The foolish king—14:31-33
The lost sheep—15:1-7
The lost coin—15:8-10
The lost son—15:11-32
The shrewd manager—16:1-8
The rich man and Lazarus—16:19-31
The humble servant—17:7-10
The persistent widow—18:1-8
The Pharisee and the tax collector—18:9-14

A theme emerges in a study of the parables unique to Luke: the emphasis on the spiritual importance of prayer and generosity. The parables of the persistent friend, the persistent widow, and the Pharisee and the tax collector all teach the power of prayer. Prayer is highlighted throughout Jesus' ministry—from his baptism (3:21) to his choosing of the disciples (6:12-13) to the night he was betrayed (22:40-46).

The parables of the rich man and Lazarus, the rich fool, the two debtors, the shrewd manager, and the good Samaritan emphasize the importance of generosity. Luke drives this point home by recording Jesus' straightforward confrontation of a rich man's spiritual arrogance (18:22).

Among all of the Gospel writers, Luke highlighted the high ethical demands Jesus made on his followers. Jesus did not mince words, commanding any who wanted to follow him that they had to take up the cross (9:23). As you read Luke, consider whether you are committed to taking up your cross each day. Do you dedicate time to God, praising him and praying for his will for your life? Have you committed all your resources to his purposes?

MESSAGE

Luke's story begins with angels appearing to Zechariah and then to Mary, telling them of the upcoming births of their sons. From Zechariah and Elizabeth would come John the Baptist, who would prepare the way for Christ. And Mary would conceive a child by the Holy Spirit and bear Jesus, the Son of God. Soon after John's birth, Caesar Augustus declared a census, and so Mary and Joseph traveled to Bethlehem, the town of David, their ancient ancestor. There the child was born. Angels announced the joyous event to shepherds, who rushed to the manger. When the shepherds left, they were praising God and spreading the news. Eight days later, Jesus was circumcised and then dedicated to God in the Temple, where Simeon and Anna confirmed Jesus' identity as the Savior, their Messiah.

Luke gives us a glimpse of Jesus at age 12—discussing theology with the Jewish teachers at the Temple (2:41-52). Eighteen years later Jesus went out in the wilderness to be baptized by John the Baptist before beginning his public ministry

(3:1-23). At this point, Luke traces Jesus' genealogy on his stepfather Joseph's side, through David and Abraham back to Adam, underscoring Jesus' identity as the Son of Man (3:23-38).

After the temptation (4:1-13), Jesus returned to Galilee to preach, teach, and heal (4:14ff). During this time, he began gathering his group of 12 disciples (5:1-11, 27-29). Later, Jesus commissioned the disciples and sent them out to proclaim the Kingdom of God. When they returned, Jesus revealed to them his mission, his true identity, and what it means to be his disciple (9:18-62). His mission would take him to Jerusalem (9:51-53), where he would be rejected, tried, and crucified.

While Jesus carried his own cross to Golgotha, some women in Jerusalem wept for him, but Jesus told them to weep for themselves and for their children (23:28). Luke's Gospel does not end in sadness, however. It concludes with the thrilling account of Jesus' resurrection from the dead, his appearances to the disciples, and his promise to send the Holy Spirit (24:1-53). Read Luke's beautifully written and accurate account of the life of Jesus, Son of Man and Son of God. Then praise God for sending the Savior—our risen and triumphant Lord—for all people.

The main themes in the Gospel of Luke include: *Jesus Christ the Savior, History, People, Social Concern,* and *the Holy Spirit.*

Jesus Christ the Savior (1:26-38; 2:1-52; 3:21-23; 4:1-44; 5:1-39; 6:1-11, 46-49; 7:1-50; 8:22-56; 9:18-45, 57-62; 10:16, 21-24; 11:14-32; 12:8-12, 35-59; 13:31-35; 14:15-35; 17:20-37; 18:18-34; 19:28-48; 20:1-47; 21:25-36; 22:14-71; 23:1-56; 24:1-53). Luke's Gospel describes how God entered human history. Jesus, the sinless Son of God was born of a virgin (2:1-7), grew and matured as a human boy and young man (2:52), resisted Satan's temptations (4:1-13), taught and ministered among the people (4:14–21:38), was betrayed by Judas and deserted by his closest followers (22:1-62), was convicted and executed as a common criminal (22:63–23:56), rose from the dead (24:1-49), and ascended into heaven (24:50-51). Jesus is an exemplar for all people. After a perfect ministry, he provided a perfect sacrifice for our sin so that men and women of all races and nations could be saved.

IMPORTANCE FOR TODAY. Jesus is the unique Son of God, humanity's perfect leader and only Savior. He offers forgiveness to all who will accept him as Lord of their lives and who believe that what he says is true. Christians know this profound truth. Christ has changed their lives, forever. They also have the great responsibility to share the Good News with others. The world is lost, with millions heading for eternal separation from God. These men, women, and children need to meet and know the Savior. If you know the truth about the Truth, your Lord and Savior Jesus Christ, what are you doing to share the gospel with others?

History (1:1-4; 2:1-3; 3:1-2, 23-38; 13:1-4; 23:6-7). Luke was a medical doctor and historian. He put great emphasis on dates and details, connecting Jesus to events and people in history. Luke made sure that what he was writing was historically accurate. He wanted believers, especially Theophilus, to be confident and secure in their faith. Inspired by the Holy Spirit, Luke faithfully recorded God's message for his first-century audience and for believers throughout the ages.

IMPORTANCE FOR TODAY. Christians today can believe in the reliability of Luke's history of Jesus' life. Even if approached as a secular document, this Gospel presents solid evidence for its historicity and accuracy. What is most important, however, is that the historical facts point to the divinity of Christ. When assailed by questions or doubts about your faith, open up and read Luke's Gospel. You can believe with certainty that Jesus is God.

People (4:42-44; 5:5-11, 27-32; 6:13-15, 27-42; 7:18-28, 36-50; 8:1-3, 19-21; 9:10-17, 47-48; 10:38-41; 12:1, 22-34; 18:15-17; 19:1-10; 21:5-24, 37-38; 23:42-43; 24:13-52). Jesus was deeply interested in relationships. He treated people with care and concern, not merely as potential converts. Jesus enjoyed strong friendships with his disciples, other followers, and special families (for example, Mary, Martha, and Lazarus, 10:38-42). He reached out to all types of people: outcasts such as lepers (17:12-19), alienated Samaritans (9:52), despised tax collectors (5:27; 19:1-10), women (8:1-3), and children (18:16). He showed warm concern for his followers and friends.

Of special note is Jesus' friendships with women. Luke seems to have made a point of highlighting this aspect of the Lord's ministry. Luke 8:1-3, for example, lists several women as close followers and supporters. This fits, of course, with Greek and Roman culture where women were active participants in business, politics, and household management (see, for example, Acts 16:13-15; 17:4, 12). It would have been almost scandalous, however, in Jewish culture where men and women were separated in the synagogue and only men could be taught by the rabbis.

IMPORTANCE FOR TODAY. Jesus' love for people is Good News for everyone. His message is for all people in every nation, and each person has the opportunity to respond to him in faith. In addition, Jesus' example teaches that his followers should love people, regardless of their sex, race, age, or worldly status. Christians should be known by their love. You may feel as if you are a second-class citizen in your community or neighborhood, but not in Jesus' eyes. Regardless of your status in society, know that you are important to him. Also, as you relate to neighbors, coworkers, and others, think of how you can show genuine concern and care for them and their families. Determine to reflect Christ in your life, to be known as a person of love.

Social Concern (4:31-41; 5:12-26; 6:6-10, 17-19; 7:1-17; 8:28-39, 41-56; 9:1-2; 10:25-37; 13:10-17; 14:1-6; 16:19-31; 17:11-19; 18:35-43; 22:50-51). As a perfect human, Jesus showed tender sympathy to the poor, the despised, the hurt, and the sinful. No one was rejected or ignored by him. Jesus healed the sick, diseased, and crippled. His compassion reached across racial lines and broke with convention (for example, healing on the Sabbath, 6:6-10). Luke paid special attention to Jesus' treatment of the poor and his teachings about poverty and wealth. Jesus also emphasized God's special interest in the poor and he commanded his followers to help the poor.

IMPORTANCE FOR TODAY. Obeying his teachings, Christ's followers should check their lives for materialism and love of money. Is financial security the focus of your life? Do you think more about what you can get or what you can give? Also, as they emulate their leader, Christ's followers should reach out to the hurting and disenfranchised in society, offering loving care, emotional support, and material assistance. What poor or infirm people can you help? Consider how you can "sell what you have and give to the poor," using your resources to make a difference in their lives. Finally, Jesus' compassion shows that he is more than an idea or teacher; he tenderly cares for each person. Know that only his kind of deep love can satisfy you. Whatever your need, bring it to the Savior.

The Holy Spirit (1:15, 35, 41, 67-79; 2:25-32; 3:16, 22; 4:1, 14; 10:21; 11:12). The Holy Spirit was present at Jesus' birth, baptism, ministry, and resurrection. Jesus lived in dependence on the Holy Spirit. This emphasis is carried over into Luke's sequel, the book of Acts, where we see Christians thoroughly immersed and motivated by the Holy Spirit.

IMPORTANCE FOR TODAY. The Holy Spirit was sent by God as confirmation of Jesus' authority. The Holy Spirit is given to enable people to live for Christ. Believers can now have the Holy Spirit's presence and power to witness and to serve. Don't try to live the Christian life in your own strength. Just as you trusted Christ to save you, rely on the Holy Spirit to give you the power to live for him.

OUTLINE OF LUKE

   I. Birth and Preparation of Jesus, the Savior (1:1–4:13)
  II. Message and Ministry of Jesus, the Savior (4:14–21:38)
     A. Jesus' ministry in Galilee
     B. Jesus' ministry on the way to Jerusalem
     C. Jesus' ministry in Jerusalem
 III. Death and Resurrection of Jesus, the Savior (22:1–24:53)

LUKE 1

LUKE'S PURPOSE IN WRITING / 1:1-4 / 1
Luke opens his Gospel with the explanation that, though he was not himself an eyewitness of Jesus' ministry, he wanted the eyewitness accounts to be preserved accurately and the foundations of Christian belief transmitted intact to the next generations. This is evident in his Gospel, for thirty percent of it is new information—not contained in the other three Gospels. As you read this Gospel, watch the way Luke carefully presents all the evidence surrounding Jesus' life, death, and resurrection to Theophilus, a Gentile Christian.

1:1-2 The first four verses of the Gospel of Luke are one sentence in Greek. Luke's sophisticated Greek writing style, revealed in this preface, set his work apart from the other three Gospels. The Gospels of Matthew and Mark were written at about the same time as Luke, and apparently **many** other witnesses and writers had also **written about the events that took place** during Jesus' life and ministry, using **as their source material the reports circulating** from the **disciples and other eyewitnesses.** Luke perceived a need to put the facts from these other written sources into an account written especially for a Gentile believer who needed to understand Jesus' story. Believers today owe the Gospels and the book of Acts to writers who, like Luke, took the carefully preserved oral information from eyewitnesses and wrote it down.

Theophilus literally means "one who loves God." While this may be a general term for all believers, it is a proper name and with the title, **most honorable,** indicates a person of some rank or distinction. The book of Acts, also written by Luke, is likewise addressed to Theophilus (Acts 1:1).

1:3-4 Luke, as an educated Gentile believer and a medical doctor, paid attention to details: he **carefully investigated all of these accounts from the beginning,** and then wrote **a careful summary.** Luke wanted to **reassure** Theophilus of **the truth** of all he had been **taught.**

AN ANGEL PROMISES THE BIRTH OF JOHN TO ZECHARIAH / 1:5-25 / 4

Luke started at "the beginning" (1:3). But for Jesus' life, the beginning was not his birth, but instead the announcement of the birth of John the Baptist—the person who would prepare the way for Jesus.

1:5 As a good historian should, Luke gave his readers the historical setting. The story begins **when Herod was king of Judea.** This was Herod the Great, confirmed by the Roman Senate as king of the Jews but never accepted by the Jewish people as their king (although half-Jewish, Herod was not part of the royal line of David). For the Jews living in Judea, this was a time of oppression. Although they were not in slavery, they were not completely self-governing either. Herod had expanded and beautified the Jerusalem Temple, but he had placed a Roman eagle over the entrance and also had built pagan Temples. When he helped the Jews, it was for political purposes—not because he cared about them or their God. Evil and ruthless, Herod the Great later ordered a massacre of infants in a futile attempt to kill the infant Jesus, whom some were calling the new "king of the Jews" (Matthew 2:1-2). Herod the Great ruled from 37–4 B.C.

Zechariah was a **priest,** a minister of God who worked at the Temple managing its upkeep, teaching the people the Scriptures, and directing the worship services. At this time there were about twenty thousand priests throughout the country. Priests were divided into twenty-four separate groups of about one thousand each, according to David's instructions (1 Chronicles 24:3-19). Zechariah was a member of the **order** (or division) **of Abijah.** Each division served in the Jerusalem Temple twice each year for one week.

Zechariah's wife, **Elizabeth, was also from the priestly line of Aaron.** Elizabeth descended directly from Aaron, brother of Moses and Israel's first high priest (Exodus 28:1). As a priest, Zechariah would have been required to marry a virgin Israelite, but not necessarily one from a priestly family. Zechariah was especially blessed to have a wife with such a background.

1:6-7 Zechariah and Elizabeth both **were righteous in God's eyes.** This does not mean that they were sinless, but that they loved God and obeyed him. But **they had no children.** To ancient readers, this would have seemed like a contradiction. Children were considered to be God's greatest blessings. Certainly such God-fearing and God-honoring people as Zechariah and Elizabeth should have been blessed with children. But **Elizabeth was barren.** Not only that, but Luke adds the detail that they **were both very old,** meaning that they could not expect any change in their situation. For Elizabeth, being childless in old age would be painful and lonely; but during this time she remained faithful to God.

1:8-9 Zechariah's division of priests was **on duty** in the Temple during this particular week (see 1:5). Each morning, one of the priests would enter the Holy Place **in the Temple** to **burn incense,** which was burned twice daily. Lots were cast to decide who would **enter the sanctuary,** and one day during that week Zechariah **was chosen by lot.** Offering the incense before the Lord was considered a great privilege. A priest was allowed to do so only once in his lifetime; many priests never had the opportunity. But it was not by chance that Zechariah was on duty and that he was chosen that day to enter the Holy Place.

1:10 The other priests and people would wait outside for the chosen priest to offer the incense and pray on behalf of the nation. When the people would see the smoke from the burning incense, they would pray. The smoke drifting heavenward symbolized their prayers ascending to God's throne. This **great crowd** were the faithful in Israel who were waiting and **praying** for deliverance. Faithful believers had been doing this since their captivity in Babylon six centuries before. This time, their prayers received a very special answer.

1:11 As Zechariah discharged his duty in the Holy Place, **an angel of the Lord appeared.** That the angel was **standing to the right of the incense altar** indicates a position of favor or blessing, perhaps indicating that the message was good. The exact location where the angel stood is a detail passed along by Zechariah himself and kept intact by writers (1:1-3). Gabriel (1:19) delivered a special message to Zechariah. This was not a dream or a vision; the angel was a royal herald of God. The angel appeared in visible form and spoke audible words to the priest.

1:12-13 Angels are powerful beings, certainly awesome in their appearance. No wonder **Zechariah was overwhelmed with fear.** So the angel's first words to him were, **"don't be afraid."** While Zechariah had been burning incense on the altar, he had also been praying, most likely for Israel's deliverance and for the coming of the Messiah. The angel's awesome words must have astounded him: **"God has heard your prayer."** Then the angel made a seemingly unrelated statement: **"Your wife, Elizabeth, will bear you a son."** The angel even told Zechariah what to name the baby. **John** means "the LORD is gracious." Through the birth of this son, God was gracious to Zechariah and Elizabeth, and ultimately to all people, for this son would prepare people's hearts for the Messiah.

1:14-15 The special son to be born to Zechariah and Elizabeth would fulfill a predetermined purpose before God. John was to be set apart for special service to God. He may have been forbidden to drink **wine** as part of the Nazirite vow, an ancient vow of consecration to God (see Numbers 6:1-8).

This is Luke's first mention of the **Holy Spirit,** the third person of the Trinity. Luke refers to the Holy Spirit more than any other Gospel writer does; it was a major focus for him (see 1:35, 41). That John would be **filled** with the Holy Spirit, **even before his birth,** indicates a special choice of this child. This also signals the restoration of the prophetic work of the Holy Spirit that had not been present in Israel for over four hundred years (since the days of the prophet Malachi).

1:16-17 John's role was to be almost identical to that of an Old Testament prophet—to encourage people to turn away from sin and back **to the Lord.** The angel explained to Zechariah that John would go before God **with the spirit and power of Elijah,** a great prophet who was known for not mincing words and for standing up to evil rulers (1 Kings 17–19; 2 Kings 2:9, 15; see also Matthew 11:14; 17:10-13).

John's mission would be **turn the hearts of the fathers to their children.** This phrase comes directly from the prophecy of the Messiah's forerunner found in Malachi 4:5-6. The meaning of the phrase is not immediately clear, but it may mean that John's messages of repentance would unify broken family relationships, help fathers in their parental responsibilities, or change the lives

of disobedient children so that their fathers would approve of them. In light of the Malachi reference, "fathers" may refer to the patriarchs, great men of faith who would be greatly displeased with their descendants' faithlessness toward God. John's call to repentance would **change the disobedient minds to accept godly wisdom** by bringing many of his contemporaries back to God.

1:18 Zechariah's response to the angel's word came perilously close to doubt. Zechariah wanted more than the word of this heavenly visitor, he wanted a sign: **How can I know this will happen?** Zechariah saw only the obstacle—he and Elizabeth were both past childbearing years, so he reminded the angel of this fact as if it had somehow been overlooked. Contrast his response with that of Mary who saw the opportunity and merely asked how God would perform the miracle (1:34).

1:19 The angel explained that he himself was sign enough for Zechariah. **"I am Gabriel,"** he exclaimed, **"I stand in the very presence of God."** Gabriel had come with an extremely important message—Gabriel himself described it as **good news.** The old priest ought not have doubted anything the angel said.

1:20 Unbelief ultimately results in punishment. Zechariah asked for a sign, and received it. He would be unable to speak **until the child is born** (in light of 1:62, it appears that he was deaf as well as mute). The angel's words would **certainly come true at the proper time,** whether Zechariah believed or not. God's plan had been set in motion, and nothing could stop it.

1:21-22 The people were waiting outside (1:10) for Zechariah to **come out** and pronounce the customary blessing upon them as found in Numbers 6:24-26. It seemed that the priest was taking an unusually long time in the Holy Place, so they became anxious. Finally, when Zechariah appeared, he could not pronounce the blessing because **he couldn't speak to them.** The angel's words had already begun to come true; the sign of fulfillment had taken place right in Zechariah's life. Apparently he made **gestures** to them and they realized that **he must have seen a vision.** Zechariah knew that God was moving forward in his plans to bring the Messiah to his people. But Zechariah would remain silent until his promised son arrived.

1:23-24 Zechariah completed his **term of service** (a week) and then **returned home** to the hill country (see 1:39) south of Jerusalem. The promise of a son to Zechariah and Elizabeth came even before this child was conceived. But, true to the angel's words, Elizabeth **became pregnant.** She may have gone **into seclusion** until her condition would be obvious to others.

1:25 Zechariah and Elizabeth had been childless for many years, but God was waiting for the right time to encourage them and take away their disgrace. Elizabeth realized that in this impossible pregnancy, God had performed a miracle. She praised God for taking away her **disgrace of having no children** (see 1:7).

AN ANGEL PROMISES THE BIRTH OF JESUS TO MARY / 1:26-38 / 5

Luke placed the story of the announcement of Jesus' birth right after the announcement of John's birth. By doing so, he highlighted the similarities and differences between the two births.

1:26-27 Six months after Gabriel delivered God's message to Zechariah (1:11-20), God sent the angel with another message, this time **to a virgin named Mary.** The angel Gabriel had also appeared to the prophet Daniel more than five hundred years earlier (Daniel 8:15-17; 9:21). Each time Gabriel appeared, he brought important messages from God. This time was no exception.

Nazareth in **Galilee** was Joseph's and Mary's hometown. Mary was not a prophet or a priest; she was not in God's Temple performing acts of service. Instead, she was simply a young woman who was living at home and planning her wedding, for **she was engaged to be married to a man named Joseph.** In ancient Jewish marriages, the word "engaged" (or "betrothed") had a different meaning than today. First, the two families would agree to the union and negotiate the betrothal, including a price for the bride which would be paid to the bride's father. Next, a public announcement would be made. At this point, the couple was "pledged" to each other. This is similar to engagement today, except that it was much more binding. At this point, even though the couple was not officially married, their relationship could be broken only through death or divorce. Sexual relations were not yet permitted. This second step lasted for a year. During that time, the couple would live separately, with their parents. This waiting period would demonstrate the bride's purity. If she were found to be pregnant during that time, the marriage could be annulled. After this waiting time, the couple would be married and begin living together. What Mary was about to hear from the angel would have significant impact on her engagement.

That Joseph was **a descendant of King David** is important for Joseph's journey to Bethlehem (2:1-4) and for the fact that Jesus would be born into the royal line of David. (Although Joseph was not his father, Jesus would be considered in the royal line through the rights of adoption.)

1:28-29 When Gabriel appeared to Mary, he called her **favored woman** because she would be a special recipient of God's grace. This young maiden was **confused and disturbed** as to why she was being greeted in such a way by this heavenly visitor.

1:30-33 Gabriel told Mary that **God** had **decided to bless** her. The words did not point out any special virtue in Mary—she was not sinless. God chose Mary, blessed her, and she humbly accepted his call to be the mother of Jesus. The result of this blessing came in God's choice of Mary to be the mother of Jesus. Gabriel explained that this child would grow in her womb, be born as all human children are born, and be named **Jesus.** This son **will be very great and will be called the Son of the Most High.** The word "Son" was a designation of the Messiah, the long-awaited Savior (Genesis 49:10; 2 Samuel 7:9-16; Psalm 2:7; Isaiah 7:14; 9:1-7; 11:1-3). *Jesus,* a Greek form of the Hebrew name Joshua, was a common name meaning "Yahweh saves." Just as Joshua had led Israel into the Promised Land (see Joshua 1:1-2), so Jesus would lead his people into eternal life. The symbolism of Jesus' name was not lost on the people of his day, who took names seriously and saw them as a source of power. In Jesus' name people would be healed, demons would be banished, and sins would be forgiven.

Centuries earlier, God had promised David that his kingdom would last forever (2 Samuel 7:16). This promise was fulfilled in the coming of Jesus, a direct descendant of **David** (1:27). Jesus was born in the line of David and thus could be a king to **reign over Israel forever.** His will be an eternal Kingdom that will **never end.** God had promised to continue the dynasty of David forever. David's earthly dynasty ended four centuries after his reign, but Jesus Christ, a direct descendant of David, was the ultimate fulfillment of this promise (Acts 2:22-36). Christ will reign for eternity—now in his spiritual Kingdom and in heaven, and later, on earth, in the new Jerusalem (Luke 1:30-33; Revelation 21).

1:34 Unlike Zechariah who desired a sign as proof of the angel's words (1:18), Mary's question displayed her faith. She merely asked how this miraculous event could occur because she was a **virgin**. She was engaged to be married and probably planned on having children. Engagements usually occurred when girls were in their early teens. Mary may have been as young as thirteen when this event took place. Her question reveals spiritual perceptiveness; she understood that Gabriel was referring to a miracle child to be born while she was still a virgin, prior to her marriage to Joseph. She naturally wondered how this was going to occur.

The birth of Jesus to a virgin is a miracle that many people find difficult to believe. Jesus' miracles, transfiguration, and resurrection were all actual, historical events that defy explanation. They were acts of God in a human world. Christians' faith, however, rests not on the virgin birth—indeed two of the four Gospels don't even mention it. Faith rests on the death and resurrection of Jesus Christ, not on his virgin birth. However, the virgin birth reveals two important facts: (1) In Jesus, God began a "new creation," for through Jesus' life, death, and resurrection, sin's power would be broken. In Jesus, people can come to God for a personal relationship and be freed from the power of sin. (2) Jesus was God's Son before he was even conceived in Mary's womb. He did not become God's Son at a later time. He was not accepted as God's Son because of good behavior or obedience. He was not a man promoted to that position. God's Son was born God's Son. In the birth of Jesus, God himself became human and entered the world—for fallen human beings! Therein lies the miracle! People are not meant to explain it, prove it, or ignore it—they are meant to believe it and worship God who made it happen.

1:35 Gabriel explained how Mary would become pregnant and yet remain a virgin. **The Holy Spirit will come upon you, and the power of the Most High will overshadow you**—these words picture the powerful presence of God coming upon Mary (see Matthew 17:5; Mark 9:7; Luke 9:34). This would indeed be a special baby, for he **will be holy.** Jesus was born without the sin that had

entered the world through Adam. He was born holy, just as Adam had been created sinless. Believers must be careful not to explain that Jesus was sinless simply because he did not have a human father. To do so would mean that Mary would have been sinless, which she was not. Jesus' sinlessness rests not on his miraculous birth to a virgin girl, but on the basis of his position with God. Through the birth of Jesus, God himself entered the world in human form.

The title, **Son of God,** shows that Jesus has a special role in God's purpose, and that he is the expected Messiah. The mention of the Holy Spirit gives the name greater significance for it shows that God, through the Spirit, has a special role in creating this child. The connection of "Son of God" to "Son of the Most High" states Jesus' divinity. In contrast to Adam, who disobeyed God, Jesus would completely obey his Father, enabling him to absolve the sins of the world (Romans 5:14-19).

1:36-37 Mary did not ask for a sign, but it seems that Gabriel gave her one by stating that Mary's relative **Elizabeth** was also **pregnant** as the result of God's grace. Gabriel gave Mary a person to whom she could go for support during what could prove to be a difficult time for Mary as she humbly fulfilled God's will. This also illustrated for Mary the fact that **nothing is impossible with God.**

1:38 God's announcement of a child to be born was met with various responses throughout Scripture. Sarah, Abraham's wife, laughed (Genesis 18:9-15). Zechariah doubted (1:18). By contrast, Mary submitted, knowing that she was merely **the Lord's servant.** She believed the angel's words and agreed to bear the child, even under humanly impossible circumstances, even with difficult social consequences. A young unmarried girl who became pregnant risked disaster. She risked losing Joseph, her family, and her reputation. And her story about being made pregnant by the Holy Spirit risked her being considered crazy as well. Still Mary said, despite the risks, **"May everything you have said come true."** She took the risk of faith, for she knew that God was asking her to serve him.

MARY VISITS ELIZABETH / 1:39-56 / 6

Mary is the type of woman who puts her faith into action. She not only says "Lord, your will be done" (see 1:38), but she also "hurries" to see God at work in the life of her relative Elizabeth. The journey to Judea that Mary undertook was not a simple drive to the next town; it was a difficult journey that would have taken at least three days at that time. Mary did not let that stop her from going to Elizabeth, rejoicing with her, and praising the Lord for fulfilling his promises.

1:39-40 Elizabeth and Mary were related (1:36). Perhaps Mary felt the need to take her news to someone who would understand. So Mary left Nazareth and **hurried to the hill country of Judea,** although **the town where Zechariah lived** is unknown. The trip from Nazareth to the hill country was probably fifty to seventy miles—a major trip for a young woman alone and on foot.

1:41 The visit from Mary no doubt came as a surprise, but the **Holy Spirit** made Elizabeth suddenly aware of both Mary's pregnancy and the identity of Mary's baby. The beautiful interweaving of the lives of Elizabeth and Mary before their children were born is a touching picture of God's grace upon his servants. Mary stayed with Elizabeth for three months (1:56). How they must have talked, wondering at what God was doing in their lives and what he was planning for their very special children.

1:42-45 Elizabeth had not even yet been told that Mary was pregnant. Elizabeth spoke words given to her by the Spirit (1:41) as she recognized Mary's **blessed** condition, knowing that Mary had been specially chosen by God, much as Elizabeth had. As Mary had rushed off to visit her relative, she must have been wondering whether the events of the last few days were real. Elizabeth's greeting surely strengthened her faith. Mary's pregnancy may have seemed impossible, but her wise relative believed in the Lord's faithfulness and rejoiced in Mary's condition. The Spirit also showed Elizabeth the identity of Mary's child, for she knew that this child was also **blessed**—God's Son, the promised Messiah, with a unique identity and role to fulfill. Mary would be **the mother of the Lord.** Only the Holy Spirit could have revealed this to Elizabeth. Mary and Elizabeth (and Zechariah—although he had been stricken deaf and mute, 1:20) were the first people on earth to see God's hand moving to fulfill hundreds of years of promises.

Under inspiration of the Spirit, Elizabeth interpreted the movement in her womb as the child's **joy** at hearing Mary's greeting. Elizabeth repeated that Mary was **blessed** because she **believed that the Lord would do what he said.**

1:46-50 This song is often called the "Magnificat," the first word in the Latin translation of this passage. Mary's song has often been used as the basis for choral music and hymns. Like Hannah, the mother of Samuel (1 Samuel 2:1-10), Mary glorified God in song for what he was going to do for the world through her. Notice that in both songs, God is pictured as a champion of the poor, the oppressed, and the despised.

As Mary journeyed from Nazareth to visit her relatives, she had much time to think about what she had heard from the angel and what she understood about God's plan for the Jewish people. When she arrived and Elizabeth spoke to her, Mary's joy overflowed and she could say with her whole heart, **"How I rejoice in God my Savior!"** Mary humbly understood that she was just a **lowly servant girl** chosen by God. She recognized that what he was doing in her life would have a profound impact on the world and future generations. Mary focused on God's power, holiness, and mercy. Her insight into God's character formed the basis for her confidence in him.

1:51-53 The **arm** of God is used in the Old Testament to describe his strength and power (see, for example, Exodus 6:6; Isaiah 51:5). Mary pictured God's strength being revealed to the sinful world as he **scatters the proud,** brings down the **princes,** and sends **the rich away with empty hands.** By contrast, God's power shows in his mercy to his own—lifting up **the lowly** and filling **the hungry with good things.** The tense of the verbs indicates that, while yet future, Mary was speaking prophetically of these events so certain to occur that they could be spoken of as having already happened.

1:54-55 The words **he has helped . . . Israel** are in the same verb tense as the previous verses—this is a future event so certain that it is mentioned in the past tense. This "help" for Israel is the Messiah, who will come according to the **promise** God made to the Jews' **ancestors,** specifically **Abraham** (Genesis 22:16-18). Jesus' birth fulfilled the promise, and Mary understood this as the Spirit revealed it to her. Some of God's promises to Israel are found in 2 Samuel 22:50-51; Psalms 89:2-4; 103:17-18; Micah 7:18-20.

1:56 Because travel was not easy, long visits were customary. Mary must have been a great help to Elizabeth, who was experiencing the discomforts of being pregnant in her old age. In addition, Elizabeth certainly helped Mary. During these **three months,** Mary surely discussed with Elizabeth how to handle what would be an extremely difficult social predicament. She would have to return home and explain her pregnancy to her family and her fiancé. Hopefully, when Mary **went back to her own home,** three months pregnant, she was even more strengthened in her faith by Elizabeth's faith (1:6), ready to face all that the future would hold.

JOHN THE BAPTIST IS BORN / 1:57-80 / 7

Zechariah's song prophesied about the coming Messiah—Jesus. He was the promised One from David's royal household, the One who would provide salvation for all of God's people. Zechariah's son, John, would be the one who would prepare the way for Jesus (1:76).

1:57-58 Elizabeth gave birth to a **boy,** just as the angel had said (1:13). From the wording of this verse, it seems that no one had known about Elizabeth's pregnancy. So when the **neighbors and relatives** heard that **the Lord had been very kind to her,** they rejoiced.

1:59-60 In observance of the law, **when the baby was eight days old,** he was circumcised. God had commanded circumcision when he was beginning to form his holy nation (Genesis 17:4-14), and he had reaffirmed it through Moses (Leviticus 12:1-3). The **circumcision ceremony** was an important event for the family of a Jewish baby boy. This ceremony was a time of joy when **relatives and friends came** to celebrate the baby's becoming part of God's covenant nation.

The day of circumcision was also the day when parents would formally announce the child's name. Family lines and family names were important to the Jews. The people naturally assumed the child would receive Zechariah's name or at least a family name. Thus, they were surprised that Elizabeth wanted to name the boy **John.** Apparently Zechariah had communicated to Elizabeth all that the angel had told him, so she knew what the child's name was to be (1:13). Zechariah and Elizabeth knew what family and friends did not know—that John had been given his name by God, and that he had a God-given mission to fulfill.

1:61-64 After Elizabeth gave the surprising name to her son, the relatives and friends took the situation to the head of the household who had been unable to speak since the day he had seen the vision in the Temple (1:20). It was customary to name a child after his father or grandfather, especially when they were esteemed men. The people could not believe that Elizabeth would choose a name that no one in the family had ever had. Apparently Zechariah had been stricken deaf as well, because they had to communicate to him **by making gestures,** asking him to name the child. In writing, Zechariah agreed with his wife in naming their son "John." After fulfilling God's command spoken through the angel that he name the child John, **instantly Zechariah could speak again.** With his first words, **he began praising God.** The last words Zechariah had spoken months before had been words of doubt; his first words when all was being fulfilled, even the name of the child, were words of praise to God for all God

had done and all he would do through this special child.

1:65-66 This baby's birth to an elderly couple, their strange insistence on an unusual name, the supernatural muteness and then the instantaneous cure caused **wonder** to fall **upon the whole neighborhood.** Unusual news travels fast, and as the story spread, everyone **reflected on these events.** Certainly this was a special child with a special destiny. It was obvious to everyone that **the hand of the Lord** was on John **in a special way.**

1:67-68 Zechariah praised God with his first words after months of silence. In a song that is often called the "Benedictus" after the first words in the Latin translation of this passage, Zechariah, **filled with the Holy Spirit** (see also 1:41) gave a **prophecy** of the coming of a Savior who would redeem his people. All the Old Testament prophecies were coming true—no wonder Zechariah praised God. These words were a common way to introduce a thanksgiving (see 1 Kings 1:48; 1 Chronicles 16:36; Psalms 41:13; 72:18; 106:48), thus Zechariah's words offered thanksgiving to God. Like Mary, Zechariah spoke of the coming redemption of Israel as though it was occurring: God **has visited his people and redeemed them.** Indeed, the Messiah was already on the way—although few people knew it. In Zechariah's song is a reminder that Jesus came as the fulfillment of all God's purposes and promises in the Old Testament.

The word **redeemed** literally means "accomplished redemption." In the Old Testament, "redemption" pictured the rescue by God of the Israelites from Egypt and their return from captivity in Babylon (see Deuteronomy 7:8; Jeremiah 31:11). "Redemption" means recovery of something or someone upon payment of a ransom. The climate of Israel in the first century was again a "captivity," for the Jews were subject to the Romans. The Jews were looking for a political Messiah to "redeem" them once again. But Messiah's redemption would be different from current expectations. Jesus would bring redemption from sin.

1:69-71 Zechariah praised God because **he has sent us a mighty Savior from the royal line of his servant David.** Again, Zechariah was speaking in the past tense about an event still future, albeit in the near future. The Messiah was already being "sent," for God had begun to set his plan into motion. The "royal line of . . . David" refers to the ancestral line through whom the Messiah was to come, as God had said through his holy prophets (see, for example, 2 Samuel 7:11-13, 26; Psalms 89; 132:17; Ezekiel 34:23-24; Amos 9:11-12; Hebrews 1:1).

The words, saved from our enemies and from all who hate us, clearly indicate what was happening in that society. Zechariah prophesied that the Messiah would bring deliverance. The Jews were eagerly awaiting the Messiah, but they thought he would come to save them from the powerful Roman Empire. They were ready for a military Savior, but not for a peaceful Messiah who would conquer sin. Zechariah's words would come true, but in a different manner than most expected. Thirty years later, when Jesus began his public ministry, he would be misunderstood and rejected for not being the mighty warrior for whom the Jews had been hoping.

1:72-75 Through the coming Savior, God has been merciful to the Jewish people and their ancestors by remembering his sacred covenant with them, specifically the covenant that he gave to Abraham. Recorded in Genesis 22:16-18, the oath to Abraham promised that the enemies of Abraham's descendants would be subdued and that blessing to his descendants would result from Abraham's obedience. God keeps his promises (see Micah 7:20). Yet the fulfillment of these promises means opportunity for God's people—that they might serve God without fear, in holiness and righteousness forever.

1:76-77 After recalling hundreds of years of God's sovereign work in history, beginning with Abraham and going on into eternity, Zechariah personalized the story. His son had been chosen for a key role in the drama of the ages. Although God has unlimited power, he chooses to work through frail humans who begin as helpless babies. Zechariah

proclaimed what the angel had told him (1:16-17), words that Zechariah had at first doubted. John will be called the prophet of the Most High. Zechariah speaks these same amazing words in a land where the voice of prophecy had been silent for over four hundred years. John would prepare the way for the Lord, as had been predicted by Israel's last prophet, Malachi (Malachi 3:1; 4:5-6), telling his people how to find salvation through forgiveness of their sins. The "salvation" referred to in 1:69-71 is here spelled out as "forgiveness of sins." John would explain this to people as he prepared the way for the Messiah. His message would be "repent," for only through repentance can sinners find forgiveness (see 3:3-18).

1:78-79 The light from heaven refers to that visitation of God to humanity in the form of the Messiah. These words echo Old Testament promises (Isaiah 9:2-3). This message of light to those who sit in darkness and in the shadow of death was fulfilled in the birth of Christ and the establishment of his eternal Kingdom. He came to deliver all people from their slavery to sin. (See also Isaiah 58:8, 10; 60:1-3.) He will also guide us to the path of peace. This peace would not merely be political, but spiritual. All of this would occur because of God's tender mercy and compassion on sinful humankind.

1:80 Luke briefly gave a glimpse of John's growing-up years. Became strong in spirit could refer to moral development, but could also refer to strengthening in God's Spirit. That John lived out in the wilderness refers to his isolation from people as he prepared for ministry. His parents, already old when he was conceived, presumably did not live very long into his growing-up years. John would have been on his own. Some scholars have suggested that John may have joined the community of the Essenes (a Jewish sect that required communal living) after his parents passed away. While possible, there is no direct evidence to support this.

LUKE 2

JESUS IS BORN IN BETHLEHEM / 2:1-7 / 9

Luke is the only Gospel writer who related the events he recorded to world history. His account was addressed to a predominantly Greek audience that would have been interested in and familiar with the political situation of those times.

2:1-4 The Romans ruled Palestine; Augustus, the first Roman emperor, was one of the greatest of all

Roman rulers. He was a good administrator and was fastidious about the financial accounting of his empire. Augustus ended the civil war in the land and brought peace and prosperity throughout the empire. He reigned from 27 B.C. to A.D. 14.

A Roman **census** (registration) was taken to aid military conscription or tax collection. The Jews didn't have to serve in the Roman army, but they could not avoid paying taxes. Augustus's decree went out in God's perfect timing and according to God's perfect plan to bring his Son into the world. No one had a choice about participating in the census. Thus **all returned to their own towns to register.** Joseph went to Bethlehem, a journey of about seventy or eighty miles. Bethlehem was where King David grew up (1 Samuel 16; 17:12; 20:6).

God controls all history. By the decree of Emperor Augustus, Jesus was born in the very town prophesied for his birth (Micah 5:2), even though his parents did not live there. Joseph and Mary went to Bethlehem because Joseph **was a descendant of King David.** In fact, both Joseph and Mary were descendants of David. Old Testament prophets predicted that the Messiah would be born in David's royal line (see, for example, Isaiah 11:1; Jeremiah 33:15; Ezekiel 37:24; Hosea 3:5).

2:5 Luke does not explain why Mary made this difficult trip with Joseph. Perhaps they simply both saw the outworkings of God's plan and traveled to Bethlehem where the promised child was to be born (Micah 5:2). At this point, Joseph and Mary were engaged.

2:6-7 In simple, direct language, Luke presented the Christmas story: no trees or lights, just a **manger** and animals and a too-crowded inn. It isn't surprising that there was **no room for them in the village inn** considering the number of travelers flocking to various cities during the time of this census.

At some time during their visit in Bethlehem, the promised child was born. Mary wrapped the baby in **strips of cloth,** which were bands of cloth that were used to keep a baby warm and give it a sense of security. These cloths were believed to protect its internal organs. This custom of wrapping infants is still practiced in many Mideastern countries. Then Mary **laid him in a manger,** an animal's feeding trough. She may have filled the manger with hay to make a soft bed. This mention of the manger is the basis for the traditional belief that Jesus was born in a stable. Stables were often caves with feeding troughs (mangers) carved into the rock walls. Despite popular Christmas card pictures, the surroundings were dark and dirty. Everything pointed to obscurity, poverty, and even rejection. Luke showed the King of kings born into poor and humble circumstances—born as a human, born to serve.

SHEPHERDS VISIT JESUS / 2:8-20 / 10
The angel Gabriel had announced the coming births of John and Jesus (1:5-20, 26-38); here a host of angels announced the "good news" of Jesus' birth to ordinary shepherds. The angels also gave the shepherds a sign. They would find their Savior in "a manger"—not only a sign of Jesus' identity but also his humble circumstances.

2:8 From the dirty manger, Luke moved to **the fields outside the village.** It was **night.** Shepherds were there, **guarding their flocks of sheep.** Among the occupations, shepherding had a lowly place. They were outcasts, not allowed in the city and not trusted by the general public, for often they were thieves. Luke gave this story about the shepherds for a reason. Jesus would come, not to the proud and powerful, but to the outcasts, the humble, those considered "last" on the social lists. To these men God brought the first news of his Son's arrival.

2:9-10 As these shepherds were living in the fields under the sky, suddenly a bright light broke through the darkness. **An angel of the Lord appeared among them, and the radiance of the Lord's glory surrounded them.** "Glory" refers to the majesty and splendor accompanying God's presence (see also Exodus 16:7; 24:17; Psalm 63:2; Isaiah 40:5).

The stunning display of God's glory and the appearance of the angel naturally **frightened** these shepherds. The angel encouraged the shepherds, saying he had come with **good news of great joy** for all people. This news comprised everything for which the Jews had been hoping and waiting—the Savior had come. Some of the Jews were waiting for a savior to deliver them from Roman rule; others hoped that the Christ (Messiah) would deliver them from physical ailments. But Jesus, while healing their illnesses and establishing a spiritual Kingdom, delivered them from sin.

2:11 The angel explained the substance of the "good news" that he brought: A child had just **been born in Bethlehem** (see commentary on 2:4).

The child is the **Savior,** a word used to refer to

Jesus only two times in the Gospels: here as the angels proclaimed his birth, and in John 4:42 by the Samaritans who came to believe in Jesus as "the Savior of the world." In the Old Testament, the same word (sometimes translated "deliverer" in some versions) is used for certain individuals, as well as for God (Judges 3:9, 15; 1 Samuel 10:19; 2 Samuel 22:2-3; 2 Kings 13:5; Isaiah 19:20). For the Greeks and Romans, the word "savior" could be applied to their gods as well as to great military or political leaders. Julius Caesar was called a "savior." The basic meaning of the word was readily understood by the Jews as well as Gentiles.

The title Messiah is Greek for "anointed one." To be anointed meant to be set apart for some special purpose. Moses anointed Aaron and his sons as the first priests of Israel (Exodus 28:41); the prophet Samuel anointed both Saul and David as kings of Israel (1 Samuel 10:1; 16:3). The title was applied to that future one whom God would raise up. The Jews were awaiting this special deliverer, one who would be the anointed one of God, the Messiah, the Christ.

The word **Lord** refers here to deity. That this tiny baby was the "Lord" means that God had arrived in human form. Thus the angel gave no doubt as to the identity of this child. He was the one for whom all Israel had been waiting.

2:12 The angel apparently expected the shepherds to immediately go looking for this child, so he told them what to look for. The baby would be **wrapped snugly in strips of cloth** and **lying in a manger.** Not only would this sign help the shepherds find the right baby, it would also attest to the truth of the angel's words to the last detail. While there might be other newborn babies in Bethlehem wrapped in strips of cloth, there would be only one "lying in a manger."

The shepherds were not told to look in a palace or in a wealthy home—indeed, they would not have gotten past the gates if they had. But they could go to the poor stable, receive acceptance from a poor couple, and discover the miracle baby.

2:13-14 After the angel gave the great news of God's arrival on earth, **suddenly** all heaven broke into praise, for **the angel was joined by a vast host of others—the armies of heaven.** John's vision of

heaven recorded in Revelation reveals that there are innumerable angels in heaven (Revelation 5:11). One of the angels' key roles is to offer continuous praise to God. The arrival of God's Son on earth caused all of heaven to join in an anthem of praise to God. **Glory to God** focuses the praise on the One who set these events in motion, the One who controls all events on earth. He is **in the highest heaven** and is sending **peace on earth to all whom** he **favors.** The peace referred to is the peace that only the Messiah can bring—not peace after war or conflict, but peace between sinful humanity and the holy God. Those whom God favors are those to whom he will graciously reveal his truth.

2:15-16 After their anthem of praise, the angels **returned to heaven** (see also 24:51; Acts 1:11), and the shepherds wanted to go and **see this wonderful thing that has happened.** They hurried into the village of **Bethlehem** to find the baby.

2:17-18 The **shepherds told everyone what had happened and what the angel had said**—thus becoming the first witnesses of the gospel message. They told about the child and all that the angels had said about him, and **all who heard . . . were astonished.** Most likely, the "everyone" and "all" refer to the people at the inn. Everyone was astonished at the shepherds' story.

2:19 Surely the shepherds told Mary and Joseph what the angels had said. **Mary quietly treasured these things in her heart.** "Treasured" means deep reflection, keeping in mind or safely storing up; that she **thought about them often** refers to mulling over, seeking to understand and interpret. Mary had a lot to think about as she gazed into the face of her tiny child. Gabriel had told her that the little boy would reign forever (1:31-33); the shepherds reported the angel's words—he is the Savior, Christ the Lord (2:11). As Mary held this tiny baby, she must have wondered at all that God was doing, and who her son would grow up to become.

2:20 The shepherds had to get **back to their fields and flocks** before their sheep wandered off into the night. As they did so, they were **glorifying and praising God.** They knew that they had received a special message and had been privileged to be the first to see the promised child.

MARY AND JOSEPH BRING JESUS TO THE TEMPLE / 2:21-40 / 11

Just as the story of John the Baptist's birth began in the Temple (1:5-25), so the story of Jesus' birth culminates in the Temple. In obedience to the dictates of Jewish law, Mary and Joseph presented Jesus to God (see Exodus 13:2-16), and they offered a sacrifice for the ritual purification of Mary (see Leviticus 12:2-6).

2:21 Every Jewish boy was circumcised and named on the eighth day after birth (Leviticus 12:3; Luke 1:59-60). Circumcision symbolized the Jews' separation from Gentiles and their unique relationship with God (Genesis 17:9-14). So **eight days later,** Mary and Joseph took the child to be **circumcised.** They **named** him **Jesus,** just as **the angel** had told Mary (1:31). They did not go to Jerusalem for this ceremony; instead, a local priest most likely performed it.

2:22-24 For forty days after the birth of a son and eighty days after the birth of a daughter, the mother was ceremonially unclean and could not enter the Temple. The **purification offering** was given at the end of her time of separation. Mary and Joseph were to bring an offering—a lamb for a burnt offering and a dove or pigeon for a sin offering. The priest would sacrifice these animals and declare the woman to be clean. If a lamb was too expensive, the **law** said that the parents could **sacrifice "either a pair of turtle doves or two young pigeons."**

In addition to the purification offering, another ceremony took place. A firstborn son was presented to God one month after birth (Exodus 13:2, 11-16; Numbers 18:15-16). The ceremony included buying back—"redeeming"—the child from God through an offering. Through this, the parents would acknowledge that the child belonged to God, who alone has the power to give life. Luke explained for his Gentile audience that this command came from **the law of Moses** (see Exodus 13:2, 12, 15; Numbers 18:15). So Mary and Joseph **took** Jesus **to Jerusalem to present him to the Lord.**

2:25-26 Luke introduced another person who would be divinely told of the Messiah's arrival and who would confirm the baby's identity. **Simeon** was spiritually in tune with God: **righteous, devout,** expecting **the Messiah to come.** He had all his life held on to God's promise of a coming deliverer, so through the **Holy Spirit,** God promised that Simeon would not die before seeing **the Lord's Messiah.**

2:27-32 When Mary and Joseph brought Jesus to the Temple to present him to the Lord (2:22), Simeon was there—having been **led** by the **Spirit** to be at the Temple on that particular day. God was ordaining this meeting, in keeping with his promise to Simeon (2:26).

Mary and Joseph arrived in the Temple **to present the baby Jesus to the Lord as the law required.** This obedience to the Old Testament law is mentioned several times in Luke. It points out Jesus' credentials as one who obeyed the law, even from birth, because his parents did exactly as they

were commanded. At the Temple, Mary and Joseph met an old man who took the baby Jesus **in his arms and praised God.** The Spirit led Simeon to recognize this baby as **the Savior.**

Simeon's song is often called the "Nunc Dimittis," the first words of its Latin translation. Simeon praised God that he had done what he promised. Luke, writing to Gentiles, pointed out that from the very beginning God's plan was to offer salvation to **all people**—Gentiles as well as to Jews.

2:33-35 Joseph and Mary were **amazed** that this stranger in the Temple recognized their small son as the Savior. Simeon **blessed** Mary and Joseph and then prophesied that Jesus would have a paradoxical effect on Israel. He would bring light and salvation, but his coming could also cause division. There would not be overwhelming acceptance of the promised Messiah—in fact, many would not recognize him and would reject him altogether. With Jesus, there would be no neutral ground: people would either joyfully accept him or totally reject him. Simeon told Mary that a **sword** would **pierce** her **soul.** As Jesus' mother, Mary would be grieved by the widespread rejection he would face; she would experience great pain when he died. Although she could not have known it and Simeon had only a hint of it, Mary would be the only person on earth who would witness both his birth and his death.

2:36-38 Another person who recognized this special baby arrived on the scene, as Simeon was giving his words of prophecy to Joseph and Mary. This was **Anna,** a **prophet,** indicating that she was close to God. Prophets did not necessarily predict the future. Their main role was to speak for God, proclaiming his truth. While the **tribe of Asher** does not stand out in Old Testament history (see Genesis 30:12-13; 35:26) and nothing is known of **Phanuel,** her father, apparently these details were important in establishing her credentials and her Jewishness. Anna had been a **widow** for most of her life; never remarrying but instead focusing her attention on **worshiping God with fasting and prayer.** That "she never left the Temple" means that she made her life occupation to be at worship whenever the doors of the Temple were open (see 24:53). Her lifestyle of worshiping, fasting, and praying indicates a woman of faith and strict devotion. While Luke did not record any exact words spoken by Anna, he wrote that **she began praising God.** As a second witness to the identity of this child, Anna praised God, as she perceived that this baby was the **promised King to come and deliver Jerusalem** (echoing Isaiah 52:9). Like Simeon, she, in her old age, was privileged to see the Messiah.

2:39 Luke again mentioned the fact that Joseph and Mary had **fulfilled all the requirements of the law of the Lord** (see 2:22-24). Jesus was the Son of God, but his earthly parents had fulfilled everything that God's law required regarding the birth of firstborn sons.

They then **returned home to Nazareth in Galilee,** from where they had come to register for the census (2:4). Did Mary and Joseph return immediately to Nazareth, or did they remain in Bethlehem for a time (as implied in Matthew 2)? Apparently there is a gap of several years between verses 38 and 39—ample time for them to find a place to live in Bethlehem, flee to Egypt to escape Herod's wrath (Matthew 2:1-18), and return to Nazareth when it was safe to do so (after Herod had died, Matthew 2:19-23).

2:40 Jesus' life gave the evidence of being filled with the Spirit. He **grew** physically, became **strong** spiritually, was **filled with wisdom,** and was the object of God's **favor.** Wisdom and God's favor indicated the presence of the Holy Spirit in his life. Jesus, like any child, developed from an infant to a toddler to a young child. He learned to crawl, sit up, walk, and finally to run. He learned to eat and talk. In many ways he was probably a typical child. Yet he was sinless in nature and certainly had uncanny wisdom for his years, as the next section reveals. For more on Jesus' growth, see 2:52.

JESUS SPEAKS WITH THE RELIGIOUS TEACHERS / 2:41-52 / 15

In first-century Israel, the age of twelve was considered the time when a child was beginning to reach adulthood. This section of Luke contains an incident at this crucial juncture in Jesus' childhood to give readers an indication of what Jesus' life would center on: the teachings of God, his true Father.

2:41-42 According to God's law, every male was required to go to Jerusalem three times a year for the great festivals (Exodus 23:14-17; Deuteronomy 16:16). In the spring, the Passover was celebrated, followed immediately by the week-long Festival of Unleavened Bread. Passover commemorated the night of the Jews' escape from Egypt when God had killed the Egyptian firstborn but had passed over Israelite homes (see Exodus 12:21-36). **Every year,** along with other Jewish families, Jesus and his parents **went to Jerusalem for the Passover festival.** Again there is attention to the law—Jesus grew up in a home where God's laws were obeyed and annual festivals observed. So, the year when **Jesus was twelve years old** was no different, and the family set off for the festival **as usual.**

2:43-44 Those who attended the festivals usually traveled in caravans for protection from robbers along the Palestine roads. It was customary for the women and children to travel at the front of the caravan, with the men bringing up the rear. A twelve-year-old boy conceivably could have been in either group, and both Mary and Joseph assumed Jesus was with the other one. Their caravan probably included a large number of people. So it was not until they were ready to strike camp that Mary and Joseph checked for Jesus among the other travelers, only to discover that he was not in the crowd but had **stayed behind in Jerusalem.**

2:45-47 When Mary and Joseph discovered that Jesus was not among the travelers, **they went back to Jerusalem to search for him.** The **three days** that elapsed probably refers to one day in travel away from the city, one day for them to return, then finding him on the third day. Certainly to their great relief, they found him **in the Temple.**

The Temple courts were famous throughout Judea as places of learning. At the time of the Passover, the greatest rabbis of the land would assemble to teach and to discuss great truths among themselves. The coming Messiah would no doubt have been a popular discussion topic, for everyone was expecting him. Jesus would have been eager to listen and to ask probing questions. It was not his youth, but the depth of his wisdom, that **amazed** these teachers.

2:48 Mary and Joseph knew the true identity of their son, yet that did not keep them from being typical concerned parents. Their son had been gone from them for three days, yet that seems not to have bothered him at all; he was absorbed in discussions at the Temple. Mary was worried, anxious, and overwhelmed by what had happened and her frustrating search for Jesus. Mary's words indicate a hint of scolding, **"Why have you done this to us?"** She explained that they had been **frantic** ever since he turned up missing.

2:49-50 Jesus surely felt bad that he had caused his parents distress, but it made perfect sense to him that he would be in his **Father's house,** that is, in the Temple. This is the first mention of Jesus' awareness that he was God's Son (he called God "my Father"). His relationship with his Father in heaven superseded his human family and even his human home. While he probably went to school and studied along with other boys in the synagogue in Nazareth, to be in the Temple with many learned teachers was a great opportunity for Jesus. He took full advantage of his time there, and it seems that he thought his parents would know where he would be.

Jesus' parents **didn't understand what he meant** about his Father's house. They didn't realize that he was making a distinction between his earthly father and his heavenly Father. Jesus knew that he had a unique relationship with God. Although Mary and Joseph knew he was God's Son, they didn't understand what his mission would involve. Besides, they had to rear him, along with his brothers and sisters (Matthew 13:55-56), as a normal child. They knew Jesus was unique, but they did not know what was going on in his mind. They had to learn and observe the complex outworkings of Jesus' special identity and calling even as he lived in their family.

2:51 Jesus **returned to Nazareth . . . and was obedient.** Jesus understood his identity with God, but also was not yet supposed to go about his earthly ministry (that did not happen until he was thirty years old). Jesus' behavior was not disobedient, but precociously acting out his true identity which he would one day fulfill. In the meantime, Jesus lived a human life, obeying his parents, growing up, studying, and learning. As she had with the words of the shepherds at Jesus' birth (2:19), Mary **stored all these things in her heart.** She did not completely understand her son, but she remembered these events, thought them over, and sought to find their meaning. One day, it all would be clear. One day her son would become her Savior, and she would understand.

2:52 The Bible does not record any events of the next eighteen years of Jesus' life, but Jesus undoubtedly was learning and maturing. As the oldest in a large family, he assisted Joseph in his carpentry work. Joseph may have died during this time, leaving Jesus to provide for the family. The normal routines of daily life gave Jesus a solid understanding of the Judean people.

The second chapter of Luke shows us that although Jesus was unique, he had a normal childhood and adolescence. In terms of development, he went through the same progression we do. He grew physically (**in height**) and mentally (**in wisdom**), he related to other people (**loved . . . by all who knew him**), and he was loved **by God.** A full human life is balanced. It was important to Jesus— and it should be important to all believers—to develop fully and harmoniously in each of these key areas: physical, mental, social, and spiritual.

LUKE 3

JOHN THE BAPTIST PREPARES THE WAY FOR JESUS / 3:1-18 / 16

When John began preaching in the wilderness, a group of eager listeners gathered around him. The Israelites considered John to be a great prophet. God had not sent a prophet to Israel for around four hundred years, so people noticed John.

3:1 Once again Luke gave his Roman audience a historical context for his narrative (as in 2:1-2). **Tiberius, the Roman emperor,** ruled from A.D. 14–37. **Pilate** was the Roman **governor** responsible for the province of **Judea** from A.D. 26–36. Originally, Archelaus, son of Herod the Great, had been assigned this portion to rule after his father died, but he ruled so poorly that his subjects petitioned for him to be removed. The Romans installed a governor in A.D. 6 and eventually Pilate held this post. **Herod Antipas, ruler over Galilee,** and his **brother** (actually half brother) **Philip,** were sons of the cruel Herod the Great. Herod Antipas was in power from 4 B.C. to A.D. 39. Philip ruled over the regions of **Iturea and Traconitis** from 4 B.C. to A.D. 33 or 34. **Lysanias, ruler over Abilene** is otherwise unknown. The region of Abilene was north of the other regions mentioned. Herod Antipas, Philip, Pilate, and Lysanias apparently had equal powers in governing their separate territories. All were subject to Rome and responsible for keeping peace in their respective lands.

3:2 Under Jewish law there was to be only one high priest. He was to be appointed from Aaron's line, and he would hold his position for life. Apparently the Roman authorities had deposed the Jewish-appointed **Annas** (who ruled from A.D. 6–15). Five of Annas's sons became high priest; **Caiaphas** was his son-in-law, who held the high priesthood from A.D. 18–36. Caiaphas, therefore, actually held the office, but Annas retained his title (see Acts 4:6) and probably much of the power and influence it carried.

It was during this time that **a message from God came to John.** There had not been a prophet in Israel for more than four hundred years. It was widely believed that when the Messiah would come, prophecy would reappear (Joel 2:28-29; Malachi 3:1; 4:5). With the arrival of John, prophecy returned to Israel, and this was a sign to the people. God gave John his message, and from that point, John brought that message to the people. The narrative here picks up from 1:80. John lived **in the wilderness** until he began his preaching.

3:3 News that a prophet had burst onto the scene excited the people. John **went from place to place on both sides of the Jordan River,** taking the message that God had given him (3:2). That message was that **people should be baptized to show that they had turned from their sins and turned to God to be forgiven.** "Baptism," "turning from sin," and "forgiveness" go hand in hand. John used an act to symbolize the cleansing from sin that occurs when one confesses and is forgiven: "baptism."

His baptism was new in that he was asking the Jews themselves to be baptized as a sign of repentance. They considered themselves "clean" as descendants of Abraham; only "unclean" Gentiles needed baptism. But John explained that sin makes everyone "unclean," and they all needed cleansing and forgiveness. For baptism, John needed water, so he remained in the region around the Jordan River.

3:4 In John's day, before a king took a trip, messengers would tell those he was planning to visit to prepare the roads for him. Similarly John told his listeners to make their lives ready so the Lord could come to them.

The prophet **Isaiah** also called his people to repentance. The second half of the book of Isaiah focuses on the promise of salvation—the coming of the Messiah and the arrival of a man who would announce this coming (Isaiah 40:3). John the Baptist was, in fact, that **voice shouting in the wilderness.** John was merely God's "voice" for the important message that God was sending to his people (3:2). What was that message? **"Prepare a pathway of the Lord's coming!"** Part of "prepar-

ing the pathway" is to **make a straight road for him.** John's audience, the people in Israel who came to see this prophet in the wilderness, were faced with a life-changing message. If they would prepare themselves—clear away the spiritual debris and straighten any "crooked" moral paths— the way would be ready for their King and Messiah to come.

3:5-6 While both Matthew and Mark quoted from Isaiah 40:3, Luke also quoted the two following verses, Isaiah 40:4-5. As the "pathway" is being prepared (3:4), seemingly impossible tasks must be done—such as **valleys** filled in and **mountains** leveled, **curves** straightened and **rough places** smoothed. The images of these words reflect a powerful construction force grinding up everything in its path. God's highway will roll over every obstacle of unbelief or idolatry. As people prepare for the King, they will "straighten out" their lives through repentance from sin. The important words quoted from Isaiah, **then all people will see the salvation sent from God,** showed Luke's non-Jewish audience that salvation was for all people, not just the Jews (see also Isaiah 52:10). John the Baptist called all humankind to prepare to meet Jesus.

3:7 John was the first prophet Israel had heard in over four hundred years. When news spread that a prophet was preaching in the wilderness, **crowds** came out to hear him, and apparently many also believed his message and **came for baptism.** This **sample** of his **preaching** sounds harsh; Matthew tells us that John spoke these words specifically to "Pharisees and Sadducees," distinguished men who had come to John not to be baptized but simply to find out what was going on (Matthew 3:7). John called them a **brood of snakes** (Jesus also used this term, see Matthew 12:34; 23:33), conveying how dangerous and cunning these religious leaders were and suggesting that they were Satan's offspring (see Genesis 3; John 8:44). John asked them, **"Who warned you to flee God's coming judgment?"** The Jews, and especially their self-righteous religious leaders, applied God's judgment to the Gentiles; John warned that judgment was coming on them. John's astonishing frankness made him popular with the people but unpopular with the religious establishment.

3:8 Confession of sins and a changed life are inseparable. Faith without deeds is dead (James 2:14-26). Those who believe must also truly turn from sin, proving by the way they **live** that they **have really turned** from their sin and **turned to God.**

The Jews thought that as **descendants of Abraham,** they were guaranteed God's blessings and that the promise given to the patriarchs was guaranteed to all their descendants, no matter how they acted. John explained, however, that relying on Abraham as their ancestor would not qualify them for God's Kingdom. John probably pointed at stones nearby and said, **"God can change these stones here into children of Abraham."** John may have used a play on the Aramaic words for "stone" and "children" in making his point that God can make a nation for himself from whomever he chooses.

3:9 God's message hasn't changed since the Old Testament—people will be judged for their unproductive lives. Just as a fruit tree is expected to bear fruit, God's people should produce a crop of good deeds (3:8). John said that people who claim to believe God but don't live for God are like unproductive trees that will be cut down. **The ax of God's judgment is poised** and **ready** to do its work, cutting down those trees that do not bear good fruit (see Psalm 74:5-6; Jeremiah 46:22). Not only will the trees be **chopped down,** but they will be **thrown into the fire,** signifying complete destruction.

3:10-11 John's preaching elicited responses from the crowd. Many asked, **"What should we do?"** in order to "produce good fruit" (3:8; see also Galatians 5:22-23). John responded that they could readily show compassion, such as sharing food and clothing with people in need. The word for **coats** is actually "tunic," referring to a short garment worn for extra warmth under the longer robe. The person with two tunics ought to share; the same with extra food, so that no one is hungry.

3:12-13 Tax collectors were notorious for their dishonesty. Romans gathered funds for their government by farming out the collection privilege. Tax collectors earned their own living by adding a sizable sum—whatever they could get away with—to the total and keeping this money for themselves. Obviously the Jews hated fellow Jews who were tax collectors. Yet, said John, God would accept even these men; God desires to pour out mercy on those who confess, and then to give strength to live changed lives. So when these men **came to be baptized,** they too asked what they should do to act on their repentance. John told them to **collect no more taxes than** was required by the government, to stop enriching themselves at the expense of their countrymen. John did not ask them to quit their jobs, only to do them honestly. Both Matthew and Zacchaeus were tax collectors (5:27-28; 19:2).

3:14 John's powerful message even reached **soldiers.** Luke does not specify, but most scholars agree that these were not Roman soldiers, but Jewish soldiers who served to help keep the peace. Like the tax collectors, they stood in a separate and privileged position over the common people, capable of using their power for good or for taking advantage of people. So when the soldiers asked what they should do, John told them to quit some of their activities—such as extorting money from people and accusing people of things they didn't do. As with the tax collectors, they were told to control their greed by being **content** with their pay.

3:15 John was obviously a great prophet, and people were sure that the eagerly awaited age of the Messiah had arrived. Some, in fact, **were eager to know whether John might be the Messiah.** John spoke like the prophets of old, saying that the people must turn from their sin to avoid punishment and turn to God to experience his mercy and approval.

3:16 John's baptism **with water** symbolized the washing away of sins. His baptism coordinated with his message of repentance and reformation. Baptism was an "outward" sign of commitment. To be effective, it had to be accompanied by an "inward" change of attitude leading to a changed life. John's baptism did not give salvation; it prepared a person to welcome the coming Messiah and receive *his* message and *his* baptism. Although John was the first genuine prophet in four hundred years, Jesus the Messiah would be infinitely **greater** than he. So much so that John would not even be **worthy to be his slave.**

The coming of the Spirit had been prophesied as part of the Messiah's arrival. **He will baptize you with the Holy Spirit and with fire** revealed the identity of the promised Messiah (see Isaiah 44:3; Jeremiah 31:31-34; Ezekiel 36:26-27; Joel 2:28-29). The Old Testament promised a time when God would demonstrate his purifying power among people (Isaiah 32:15; Ezekiel 39:29). The prophets also looked forward to a purifying fire (Isaiah 4:4; Malachi 3:2). This looked ahead to Pentecost (Acts 2). The baptism with fire also symbolizes the work of the Holy Spirit in bringing God's judgment on those who refuse to repent. The experience would not necessarily be like that recorded in Acts 2, but the outcome would be the same. This baptism would purify and refine each believer. When Jesus would baptize with the Holy Spirit, the entire person would be refined by the Spirit's fire.

3:17-18 Threshing was the process of separating the grains of wheat from the useless outer shell called chaff. This was normally done in a large area called a **threshing** floor, often on a hill, where the wind could blow away the lighter chaff when the farmer tossed the beaten wheat into the air. A **winnowing fork** is a pitchfork used to toss wheat in the air in order to separate wheat from chaff. The **grain** is the part of the plant that is useful; **chaff** is the worthless outer shell. Chaff is burned because it is useless; grain, however, is gathered.

"Winnowing" is often used in the Bible to picture God's judgment. Jesus used the same analogy in a parable (Matthew 13:24-30). John spoke of repentance, but he also spoke of judgment upon those who refused to repent. Those who refuse to live for God are chaff, the useless outer husk of the grain. By contrast, those who repent and reform their lives are like grain. Those who refuse to be used by God will be discarded because they have no value in furthering God's work. Those who repent and believe, however, hold great value in God's eyes because they are beginning a new life of productive service for him.

The **warnings** coupled with John's announcement of **the Good News** made John's message all that much more riveting.

HEROD PUTS JOHN IN PRISON / 3:19-20 / 26
John's courageous ministry in the wilderness led to his imprisonment and eventually his execution.

3:19-20 While John proclaimed the Good News and warnings of judgment, he also apparently had a no-nonsense attitude toward the morality of the day. He **publicly criticized Herod Antipas, ruler of Galilee** (see 3:2), because he had married **Herodias, his brother's wife.** Besides being his brother's wife, Herodias was also Herod's own niece. So Herod was committing both adultery and incest. John publicly protested these sins, as well as **many other wrongs** Herod **had done,** and so he greatly angered both Herod and Herodias. Herod **put John in prison,** presumably to silence him. The Herods were renowned for their cruelty and evil (Herod the Great had ordered the murder of the babies in Bethlehem, Matthew 2:16). Putting John in prison was simply **adding this sin to his many others.** The imprisonment of John the Baptist was only one evil act in a family filled with incest, deceit, and murder. (The full story is told in Matthew 14:1-12.)

THE BAPTISM OF JESUS / 3:21-22 / 17
Luke emphasized Jesus' human nature. This baptism recorded here was the first public declaration of Jesus' ministry. Instead of going to Jerusalem and identifying with the established religious leaders, Jesus went to a river and identified himself with those who were repenting of sin.

3:21-22 The words in 3:20, recording that Herod put John in prison, explained what would happen later in John's ministry as a result of his willingness to denounce sin where he saw it. In these verses, he was still out in the wilderness, preaching and baptizing (3:16). One day, when many people **were being baptized, Jesus** came for baptism too.

If John's baptism was for repentance from sin, why was Jesus baptized? Jesus didn't need to admit sin—he was sinless (John 8:46; 2 Corinthians 5:21; Hebrews 4:15; 1 John 3:5). Although Jesus didn't need forgiveness, he was baptized for the following reasons: (1) to confess sin on behalf of the nation, as Isaiah, Ezra, and Nehemiah had done (see Isaiah 6:5; Ezra 9:2; Nehemiah 1:6; 9:1ff.); (2) to fulfill all righteousness (Matthew 3:15) in order to accomplish God's mission and advance God's work in the world; (3) to inaugurate his public ministry to bring the message of salvation to all people; (4) to show support for John's ministry; (5) to identify with the penitent people of God, thus with humanness and sin; (6) to give an example to follow.

Jesus, the perfect human being, didn't need baptism for sin, but he accepted baptism in obedient service to the Father. God showed his approval, for **as he was praying, the heavens opened.** Then, **the Holy Spirit descended on** Jesus **in the form of a dove.** This emphasized the way the Holy Spirit related to Jesus. The descending Spirit portrayed a gentle, peaceful, but active presence coming to anoint Jesus. It was not that Jesus needed to be filled with the Spirit (as if there were any lack in him) because he had the Holy Spirit (1:35) since his conception. Rather, this was Jesus' royal anointing (see Isaiah 11:2; 42:1).

The Spirit descended and **a voice from heaven** proclaimed the Father's approval of Jesus as his divine Son: **"You are my beloved Son, and I am fully pleased with you."** The words spoken by the voice from heaven echo two Old Testament passages. First, Psalm 2:7, a messianic psalm that describes the coronation of Christ, the eternal King. The rule of Christ described in the psalm will begin after his crucifixion and resurrection and will be fulfilled when he comes to set up his Kingdom on earth. Second, Isaiah 42:1-17 describes the Servant-Messiah who would suffer and die as he served God and fulfilled his mission of atoning for sin on behalf of humanity. Thus, in the two phrases spoken, the voice from the throne of heaven described both Jesus' status as the Servant who would suffer and die for all people, and as the King who would reign forever.

Jesus did not become the Son or the Messiah at this baptism. Jesus already had his divinity from eternity past. The opened heavens, the dove, and the voice revealed to John the Baptist (and to readers of this story) that Jesus was God's Son, come to earth as the promised Messiah to fulfill prophecy and bring salvation to all who believe.

In 3:21-22, all three persons of the Trinity are named as present and active. The doctrine of the Trinity, which was developed much later in church history, teaches that God is three persons and yet one in essence. God the Father speaks; God the Son is baptized; God the Holy Spirit descends on Jesus. God is one, yet in three persons at the same time. This is one of God's incomprehensible mysteries. Other Bible references that speak of the Father, Son, and Holy Spirit are Matthew 28:19; John 15:26; 1 Corinthians 12:4-13; 2 Corinthians 13:13; Ephesians 2:18; 1 Thessalonians 1:2-5; and 1 Peter 1:2.

THE RECORD OF JESUS' ANCESTORS / 3:23-38 / 3

Although many Bible readers either skip over the extensive genealogies in the Bible or read through them quickly (Genesis 4–5; 1 Chronicles 1–9), it is important to pause at these genealogies and recognize their significance. Unlike Matthew, who provides a genealogy to Abraham (Matthew 1:1-17), Luke provides a genealogy that reaches back to the beginning of human history—to Adam himself (3:38). This is the point: Jesus is not only the fulfillment of the promises given to Abraham (3:34) and to King David (3:31), but the embodiment of perfect humanity.

3:23 Jesus **began his public ministry** at the time when he was baptized by John (3:21-22). He was **about thirty years old** at that time. Thirty was the prescribed age for priests to begin their ministry (Numbers 4:3).

Matthew included a genealogy of Jesus at the very beginning of his Gospel because his Jewish audience would have wanted to know Jesus' heritage. A person's family line proved his or her standing as one of God's chosen people, so Matthew showed that Jesus was a descendant of Abraham, the father of all Jews, and a direct descendant of David, fulfilling Old Testament prophecies about the Messiah's line. While it is impossible to completely harmonize the genealogies recorded by Matthew and Luke, believers can trust, as they can with all Scripture, that this is factual information obtained from different sources. While most of Matthew's names can be found in the Old Testament, Luke's names came from other sources, perhaps personal interviews or written registries of the day.

Luke's genealogy begins by saying that Jesus was known as the son of Joseph . . . the son of Heli. Genealogies were always traced through the fathers, so Luke begins with the man who was "thought" to be Jesus' father, Joseph. Although God was Jesus' Father, God had a reason for placing him in this particular line with Mary as his mother and Joseph as his legal father. According to Matthew 1:16, Joseph's father was Jacob. The answer to this apparent discrepancy may lie in the ancient custom of "levirate marriage" by which the widow of a childless man could marry his brother. A son born to that union would be considered the son of the deceased man.

3:24-25 Nothing is known of the men listed here. They should not be confused with Old Testament people with the same names.

3:26-27 There is Old Testament information on **Zerubbabel** who was born in Babylon during the Jewish captivity there, and then returned to Judah under the decree of Cyrus (Ezra 1:1–2:2). He led the first group of Jewish exiles back to Jerusalem and oversaw the rebuilding of God's Temple. The

Old Testament often lists him as Zerubbabel, **son of Shealtiel** (see, for example, Ezra 3:2, 8; 5:2; Nehemiah 12:1).

3:28-29 Again, nothing is known of any of these people. They should not be confused with Old Testament people with the same names.

3:30-31 The mention of **David** brings the line of Jesus Christ directly back to the great king of Israel to whom the promise of an eternal Kingdom had been made in 2 Samuel 7:16. David's story is recorded in 1 Samuel 16–1 Kings 2 (also 1 Chronicles 11–29). David himself was seen as an archetype of the coming Messiah King (Isaiah 9:6-7; 11:1-2; Ezekiel 34:23-24; 37:24-25). David's most famous son, Solomon, who sat on the throne, is referenced in Matthew's genealogy. Luke, however, has been tracing, up to this point, David's line through his third son, **Nathan.**

3:32-33 Jesse had several sons, one of whom had been anointed by the prophet Samuel to be the next king of Israel after King Saul (see 1 Samuel 16:5-13). The book of Ruth tells the story of **Boaz** and a young woman named Ruth, who had come to Israel from the nearby nation of Moab. Boaz married Ruth, and they became the parents of **Obed** (Ruth 4:13-17). Obed later became the father of Jesse (Ruth 4:21-22). See also 1 Chronicles 2:12.

Salmon is mentioned again only in the genealogy in Ruth 4:18-22. **Nahshon** and **Amminadab** are mentioned in Exodus 6:23 and 1 Chronicles 2:10-11. Nahshon is mentioned in Numbers 1:7 and 7:12-17. Not much is known about **Arni** and **Hezron.** Hezron is mentioned in Genesis 46:12, Numbers 26:21, and 1 Chronicles 2:5. Arni (or Ram) is mentioned in Ruth 4:19, 1 Chronicles 2:9-10. **Judah,** one of Jacob's sons, was patriarch of the tribe of Judah. His story is told in Genesis 29:35; 38:1-30; and 44:18-34. He actually had twin sons named **Perez** and Zerah (see also 1 Chronicles 2:4).

3:34-35 Judah had been one of the twelve sons of **Jacob.** Jacob had many sons by his wives Rachel and Leah. Jacob's twelve sons became the twelve tribes of Israel (see Genesis 49:1-28). Jacob's story is told in Genesis 25–50.

Jacob was the son of Isaac, who had been the miracle child, born to **Abraham** and Sarah in their old age, through whom God had promised to bless Abraham (Genesis 12:2-3). The line of Jesus would naturally go back through Isaac, this promised son. Jesus would ultimately fulfill God's promise to Abraham. Isaac's story is told in Genesis 17:15–35:29. Abraham's story is told in Genesis 11–25. (He is also mentioned in Exodus 2:24; Acts 7:2-8; Romans 4; Galatians 3; Hebrews 2; 6–7; 11.)

These three men—Abraham, Isaac, and Jacob—are often named together as the "patriarchs," fathers of the nation and receivers of God's covenant (see Genesis 50:24; Exodus 3:16; 33:1; Numbers 32:11; Deuteronomy 1:8; 6:10; 9:5, 27; 29:13; 30:20; 34:4; 2 Kings 13:23; Jeremiah 33:26; Matthew 8:11; Luke 13:28; Acts 3:13; 7:32).

For the names listed from **Terah** through Arphaxad (3:36), Luke seems to have drawn upon Genesis 11:10-26 and 1 Chronicles 1:24-27. Terah, father of Abraham, first took his family to Haran. There, God had called Abraham to travel to the land that would be given to his descendants. Apart from the listing of these names in the Old Testament passages noted above, nothing else is known of these men.

3:36-37 Cainan and **Arphaxad** are known only from the Old Testament passages that list their names. Arphaxad was the third **son of Shem.** Shem was one of the three sons of Noah from whom the Jews were descended. **Noah,** by his righteousness, spared his family from the flood that destroyed the earth (see Genesis 6–9). His sons and their wives repopulated the earth after the flood. Noah's father was **Lamech** (see Genesis 5:25, 28; 1 Chronicles 1:3). **Methuselah** reportedly lived 969 years, the longest anyone has ever lived (see Genesis 5:27; 1 Chronicles 1:3). **Enoch** was a righteous man who did not die but was taken up to heaven after walking with God for 365 years (Genesis 5:23-24; Jude 14). For **Jared,** see Genesis 5:15; 1 Chronicles 1:2. **Mahalalel** is also mentioned in Genesis 5:13 and 1 Chronicles 1:2. For **Kenan,** see Genesis 5:9; 1 Chronicles 1:2.

3:38 For the record of **Enosh,** see Genesis 4:26, 5:6 and 1 Chronicles 1:1. **Seth** was born to Adam and Eve after Cain killed Abel (Genesis 4:25). **Adam,** the first man, fathered the entire human race. Luke called him **the son of God.** While Jesus is God's true and only Son, all the human race is considered sons of God because they were created by him and owe their very existence to his divine will.

Luke accomplished his goal for this genealogy—to establish for his Gentile readers Jesus' direct connection, not only with the promises recorded in the Jewish scriptures, but also with the entire human race. Jesus came for all people.

LUKE 4

SATAN TEMPTS JESUS IN THE WILDERNESS / 4:1-13 / *18*
This section shows Jesus as the Son of God defeating Satan in open combat. No argument or temptation could daunt the Lord Jesus. This temptation by Satan also reveals that, though Jesus was human and subject to human temptations, he was perfect because he overcame all the temptations that Satan presented to him. The story of Jesus' temptation is an important demonstration of his power and sinlessness. He faced temptation and did not give in. His followers should trust in him as they face temptations that will test their faithfulness to God.

4:1-2 The word "then" picks up the story from 3:22. Jesus **left the Jordan River . . . to go out into the wilderness.** Jesus took the offensive against the enemy, **the Devil,** by going into the wilderness to face temptation.

The word "devil" in Greek means "accuser"; in Hebrew, the word "Satan" means the same. The Devil, who tempted Adam and Eve in the garden, also tempted Jesus in the wilderness. Satan is a real being, a created yet rebellious fallen angel, and not a symbol or an idea. He constantly fights against God and those who follow and obey God. Satan is not omnipresent, nor is he all-powerful. Through the evil spirits under his dominion, Satan works everywhere attempting to draw people away from God and into his own darkness.

The verb **tempted** describes continuous action; Jesus was tempted constantly during the **forty days.** The **Spirit** compelled Jesus into the wilderness where God put Jesus to the test—not to see if Jesus was ready, but to **show** that he was ready for his mission. Satan, however, had other plans; he hoped to thwart Jesus' mission by tempting him to do evil. Why was it necessary for Jesus to be tempted? Temptation is part of the human experience. For Jesus to be fully human, he had to face temptation (see Hebrews 4:15). Jesus had to undo Adam's work. Adam, though created perfect, gave in to temptation and passed sin on to the whole human race. Jesus, by contrast, resisted Satan. His victory offers salvation to Adam's descendants (see Romans 5:12-19).

During those forty days, Jesus **ate nothing,** so at the end he was **very hungry.** Jesus' status as God's Son did not make this fast any easier; his physical body suffered the severe hunger and pain of going without sustenance. The three temptations recorded here occurred when Jesus was at his most physically weakened state.

4:3 On the surface, this might seem to be a fairly harmless act, even a compassionate suggestion. Jesus was very hungry, so why not use the resources at his command and **change a stone into a loaf of bread?** In this case, however, the sin was not in the act but in the reason behind it. The Devil was trying to get Jesus to take a shortcut, to solve his immediate problem at the expense of his long-range goals, to seek comfort at the sacrifice of his discipline. Satan often works that way—persuading people to take action, even right action, for the wrong reason or at the wrong time. The fact that something is not wrong in itself does not mean that it is good for someone at a given time. Many people sin by attempting to fulfill legitimate desires outside of God's will or ahead of his timetable.

4:4 Jesus answered Satan with what **the Scriptures say.** In all three quotes from Deuteronomy, found in Luke 4:4, 8, and 12, the context shows that Israel failed each test each time. Jesus showed Satan that while the test may have caused Israel to fail, it would not work with him. Jesus understood that obedience to the Father's mission was more important than food. Making himself **bread** would have shown that he had not quite set aside all his powers, had not humbled himself, and had not identified completely with the human race. But Jesus refused, showing that he would use his powers only in submission to God's plan.

4:5-7 The Devil arrogantly hoped to succeed in his rebellion against God by diverting Jesus from his mission and winning his worship. Satan tempted Jesus to take the world as an earthly kingdom right then, without carrying out the plan to save the world from sin. For Jesus, that meant obtaining his promised dominion over the world without experiencing the suffering and death of the cross. Satan offered a painless shortcut. But Satan didn't understand that suffering and death were a part of God's plan that Jesus had chosen to obey.

That Jesus could see **all the kingdoms of the world in a moment of time** supports the view that this experience was visionary. The focus is not on the mountain, but on those kingdoms that were (and are) under Satan's dominion (John 12:31). Satan offered to **give** dominion over the world to Jesus. This challenged Jesus' obedience to God's timing and will. Satan's temptation was, in essence, "Why wait? I can give this to you now!" Of course, the offer had a catch: **"If you will bow down and worship me."**

4:8 Again, **Jesus replied** to Satan with Scripture. For Jesus to gain rule over the world by worshiping Satan would not only be a contradiction (Satan would still be in control), but it would also break the first commandment, **"You must worship the Lord your God; serve only him"** (Deuteronomy 6:4-5, 13). To accomplish his mission of bringing salvation to the world, Jesus would take the path of submission to God.

4:9-11 The **Temple** was the tallest building in **Jerusalem,** and **the highest point** was probably the corner wall that jutted out of the hillside. Whether the Devil physically **took** Jesus to Jerusalem, or whether this occurred in a vision is unclear. In any case, Satan was setting the stage for his next temptation.

Jesus had quoted Scripture in response to Satan's other temptations. Here Satan tried the same tactic with Jesus: he used Scripture to try to convince Jesus to sin! Satan was quoting from Psalm 91:11-12 to support his request. The psalm describes God's protection for those who trust him. Obviously Satan

was misinterpreting Scripture, making it sound as though God protects even through sin, removing the natural consequences of sinful acts. Jumping from the roof in order to test God's promises would not have been part of God's will for Jesus. In context, the psalm promises God's protection for those who, while being in his will and serving him, find themselves in danger. It does not promise protection for artificially created crises in which Christians call to God in order to test his love and care.

4:12 Jesus **responded** from **the Scriptures** again; however, he used Scripture with an understanding of the true meaning. The facts were that while God promises to protect his people, he also requires that they not **test** him. In the passage in Deuteronomy 6:16, Moses was referring to an incident during Israel's wilderness wanderings, recorded in Exodus 17:1-7. The people were thirsty and ready to commit mutiny against Moses and return to Egypt if he did not provide them with water. For Jesus to jump from the pinnacle of the Temple would have been a ridiculous test of God's power, and it would have been out of God's will. Jesus knew that his Father could protect him; he also understood that all his actions were to be focused on fulfilling his Father's mission.

4:13 This would only be the first of many encounters that Jesus would have with Satan's power. Jesus' personal victory over Satan at the very outset of his ministry set the stage for his command over demons throughout his ministry, but it did not dissuade Satan from continuing to try to ruin Jesus' mission. His defeat of the Devil in the wilderness was decisive but not final, for the Devil **left him until the next opportunity.**

JESUS' MINISTRY IN GALILEE / 4:14-15 / 30

Just as God's Spirit had led Jesus into the wilderness to be tempted (4:1), the Spirit next led Jesus to begin his teaching ministry among the people of Galilee. Luke did not yet mention anything that Jesus did in his ministry, but the other Gospels reveal much that had happened in the interim. Jesus already had his followers, he had turned water into wine (John 2:1-12), he cleared the Temple (John 2:12-25), and he had ministered in Samaria (John 4:1-42).

4:14-15 Jesus, **filled with the Holy Spirit's power,** returned to **Galilee.** He spoke often in Jewish **synagogues.** These gathering places for worship grew up during the exile when the Jews no longer had their Temple. Synagogues were established as places of worship on the Sabbath and as schools for young boys during the week. They continued to exist even after the Temple was rebuilt. Any town with at least ten Jewish families could have

a synagogue. The synagogue was administered by one leader and an assistant. Often the leader would invite a visiting rabbi to read from the Scriptures and to teach. Thus Jesus, traveling from town to town, teaching, preaching, and doing miracles, would be a popular person to invite into a town's synagogue. Everyone **praised** this new rabbi. His teaching was fresh—as Matthew recorded (Matthew 7:29).

JESUS IS REJECTED AT NAZARETH / 4:16-30 / *32*

Jesus' cruel rejection by the people of his hometown in Nazareth is highlighted to characterize Jesus' initial teaching ministry in Galilee. Isaiah 61, the passage Jesus read in the synagogue of Nazareth, speaks of the anointing of the Spirit on a prophet who would preach the Good News of salvation to the poor. This inaugural sermon at Nazareth is not recorded in the other Gospels. Luke begins his portrayal of Jesus' ministry with this account. It sets the tone for the importance of social concerns as found in the rest of Luke.

4:16 Jesus had been on a preaching tour of Galilee (4:14-15), and at last came to **Nazareth, his boyhood home.** Although Jesus had been born in Bethlehem (2:4-7), his parents had fled to Egypt to protect their son from King Herod (Matthew 2:7-18). After King Herod's death, Joseph had brought his family back to Israel, to the district of Galilee, to live in a town called Nazareth (Matthew 2:22-23).

Jesus **went as usual to the synagogue on the Sabbath.** Even though he was the perfect Son of God, Jesus attended services every week. As a visiting rabbi, Jesus was invited to **read the Scriptures.** The synagogue service usually included recitation of the Shema (Numbers 15:37-41; Deuteronomy 6:4-9; 11:13-21), benedictions, a psalm, a priestly blessing (Numbers 6:24-26), prayers, a reading from the Law (the Torah, Genesis through Deuteronomy) and then from the Prophets, and then an interpretation of the reading.

4:17-21 After the Law had been read, **the scroll containing the messages of Isaiah the prophet was handed to** Jesus. Scrolls were ancient "books" made of papyrus sewn together to make a long strip which was then wound around sticks at each end. Jesus **unrolled the scroll** until he found the place from which he wanted to read.

Jesus read from Isaiah 61:1-2. Isaiah's words pictured the deliverance of Israel from exile in Babylon as a Year of Jubilee, when all debts were to be canceled, all slaves freed, and all property returned to original owners (Leviticus 25). But the release from Babylonian exile had not brought the fulfillment that the people had expected; they were still a conquered and oppressed people. Isaiah was prophesying a future messianic age, a time when one would come in **the Spirit of the Lord** to do many wonderful things. This passage offered great expectations to an oppressed people. After reading, Jesus said, **"This Scripture has come true today before your very eyes!"** When Jesus spoke these words, he was proclaiming himself as the One who would bring this **Good News** to pass.

As Jesus read this passage from Isaiah to the people in the synagogue, he stopped in the middle of 61:2 after the words, **the time of the Lord's**

favor has come. (The next phrase in Isaiah 61:2, however, is "and with it, the day of God's anger against their enemies." This will not be fulfilled until Jesus returns to earth again. We are now under God's favor; his wrath is yet to come.)

4:22 The listeners in the synagogue that day were impressed by Jesus. They **spoke well of him,** meaning that at first they were impressed at his manner and his teaching. Their question, **"Isn't this Joseph's son?"** reveals their amazement that this man who had grown up among them was making such claims. This amazement, however, did not give way to faith.

4:23-24 Jesus understood what the people were thinking, so he quoted **that proverb, "Physician, heal yourself."** Nazareth was Jesus' hometown; shouldn't he most certainly take care of all the needs there—even before he did so in other cities? Jesus was right in thinking that the people wanted him to **do miracles** in Nazareth like those he did in Capernaum (John 4:46-54). Apparently, Jesus had already been through that city and done miracles, just as he soon would do more miracles there (Luke 4:33-41). If he were going to say that he was the one about whom Isaiah wrote—recovery of sight, releasing of oppression—then he ought to do so for them.

However, Jesus had not come to Nazareth to put on a show for all his friends and neighbors. In fact, his purpose was quite the opposite, for he understood **the truth** that **no prophet is accepted in his own hometown.** This was certainly true of many Old Testament prophets. Isaiah, Jeremiah, Ezekiel, Micah, and Amos suffered martyrdom.

4:25-26 Jesus stood in a long line of people sent by God specifically to Gentiles and rejected by their own countrymen. Jesus cited the experience of the prophet **Elijah** who was sent, not to any of the Israelite widows, but instead to **a widow of Zarephath—a foreigner in the land of Sidon** (1 Kings 17:8-16). Jesus' mission to the Gentiles is reemphasized here.

4:27 Elijah's successor, **Elisha,** met with similar guidance from God in one particular instance. God sent Elisha to cleanse only one person, **Naaman, a Syrian,** a hated Gentile (2 Kings 5). Syria was Israel's neighbor to the north. Syria had oppressed Israel, yet God had done a miracle for a commander in their army.

Jesus' message to the people was shocking. He did his work through lepers, Gentiles, and women just as Elisha did. Elijah and Elisha condemned Israel for their lack of faith; Jesus, too, confronted their unbelieving hearts. Israel often rejected the prophets and they were about to reject Jesus. Here Jesus implied that his work would be done outside his homeland among those who believe.

4:28-30 Why did the people of Nazareth react this way? Jesus' words made them **furious** because he was saying that God would reach out to Gentiles as well as to Jews. The Jews expected their Messiah to come and minister to them—free them from oppression, heal them, usher in a glorious Kingdom. They also expected that with his coming, the evil Gentiles would be vanquished. Instead, Jesus, who had just claimed to be the Messiah about whom Isaiah prophesied, illustrated his mission by way of the prophets who had shown kindness to Gentiles. Jesus' words implied that his hearers were as unbelieving as the citizens of the northern kingdom of Israel in the days of Elijah and Elisha, a time notorious for great wickedness. People became so angry that they tried to **push him over the cliff.** But it was not yet Jesus' time to die, so he simply **slipped away through the crowd.** There is no record that Jesus ever returned to Nazareth.

JESUS TEACHES WITH GREAT AUTHORITY / 4:31-37 / 34

In this second snapshot of Jesus' ministry in Galilee (the first being 4:14-30), the Gospel presents a glimpse of the cosmic battle that was occurring. A demon challenges Jesus. But Jesus—unruffled—commands the demon to leave. Jesus' teaching style was clearly different than the rabbis, who cited past religious teachers to bolster and support their various interpretations of Scripture. In contrast, Jesus taught straight from Scripture, applying it directly to his listeners' own lives.

4:31 Jesus left his home in Nazareth and **went to Capernaum,** about twenty miles farther north. Capernaum became Jesus' home base during his ministry in the northernmost region of Palestine, **Galilee.** Jesus had already been in Capernaum (as suggested in 4:23). It has already been established that Jesus' custom was to go to the **synagogue every Sabbath** (4:16). The setting was probably much the same as it had been in Nazareth. He would be invited to read a portion of the Scripture and then teach on it. The fact that this was a Sabbath day is important to the event to follow.

4:32 The people were completely **amazed** by Jesus' **authority** in his teaching. The Jewish teachers whom the people were used to hearing usually quoted from well-known rabbis or gave the opinions of predecessors in order to give their words more authority. Jesus did not merely give his opinion; he proclaimed his authority.

4:33-34 This is the first of Jesus' miracles that Luke recorded. Jesus was teaching the people **in the synagogue** on the Sabbath (4:31). **A man possessed by a demon** had also made his way into the synagogue. Demons are ruled by Satan. They work to tempt people to sin. They were not created by Satan because God is the Creator of all. Rather, demons are fallen angels who joined Satan in his rebellion. The demon had entered the man's body, had taken up residence, and controlled him. In every case where demons confronted Jesus, however, they lost their power. God limits what demons can do. During Jesus' life on earth, demons were allowed to be very active to demonstrate once and for all Christ's power and authority over them.

Luke emphasized Jesus' conflict with evil powers to show his superiority over them, so he recorded many stories about Jesus driving out demons. Jesus' power over demons reveals his absolute power over Satan. Jesus didn't have to conduct an elaborate exorcism ritual. His word was enough.

This demon inside the man knew two facts—that Jesus had indeed come to **destroy** them (and their power) and that Jesus was **the Holy One sent from God.** All demons, and Satan himself, knew that Jesus was the Messiah. While the people in the synagogue were astounded at Jesus' teaching and wondered who this man could be, the demon knew.

4:35 Jesus did not respond to the demon's comment, except to rebuke him by telling him to **be silent.** Why would Jesus want the demon to be silent—the demon knew more about who he was than the rest of Jesus' audience did. Jesus wanted to restrain any enthusiasm for a political messiah. He did not wish to be the people's king in the way they desired, nor did he want to be a military leader. Also, to confess Jesus' deity without a proper understanding of his crucifixion would be partial and invalid. Jesus did not want people to wildly proclaim him to be God's Son unless they understood the meaning of his death for them on the cross. Even Jesus' disciples lacked understanding until his resurrection.

To silence the demon was not enough, for Jesus wanted to free the man possessed by the demon. Jesus commanded the demon to **come out** of him. The demon **threw the man to the floor**. The

demon went, but not quietly. This could have been a severe spasm or a blow that thrust the man to the ground. This behavior reveals the true purpose of demons in their possession of people. Demons want only to do violence and destroy anything made in God's image. But this one **left** the man **without hurting him further**.

4:36-37 Jesus displayed power that no one had ever experienced before. He had **authority and power** so that with his words alone he could make a demon flee in fear. This **amazed** the people in the synagogue that day. Their amazement became headline news as the story **spread like wildfire**.

JESUS HEALS PETER'S MOTHER-IN-LAW AND MANY OTHERS / 4:38-41 / 35

After his clash with the demon in Capernaum, Jesus demonstrated his supernatural power to heal the sick by healing Peter's mother-in-law of a fever. Thus, by evening, the sick and demon possessed crowded Jesus, seeking his attention. Almost as an afterthought, Luke noted that Jesus was commanding the demons not to identify him. His goal was not to draw attention to himself, but to meet the real needs of others.

4:38 Jesus left the synagogue and **went to Simon's home**. Simon was another name for Peter. Obviously Jesus had met some of the men who would be his disciples. Luke did not write of the meeting, but Matthew and Mark recorded Jesus' call of the first four disciples (Matthew 4:18-22; Mark 1:16-20).

Simon Peter's **mother-in-law** was **very sick with a high fever**. There is no mention of a specific illness, but a malaria-type of fever was common to this region because of marshes near the mouth of the Jordan River. The Greek word for "fever" in the noun form is also the word for "fire"; thus, she was burning with a severe fever. Jesus' reputation for healing had spread so much that the people with him knew just what to do. They **begged** Jesus to **heal her**.

4:39 Jesus "rebuked" the fever, and **her temperature returned to normal** at his command. Jesus' power and authority were again emphasized as Luke pointed out what Jesus did with only a word. Jesus healed Simon's (Peter's) mother-in-law so completely that not only did the fever leave, but her strength was restored, and **she got up at once and prepared a meal for them**. Her healing was so complete it was as if she had never been ill.

4:40 The people came to Jesus **as the sun went down** because this was the Sabbath (4:31), their day of rest. Sabbath lasted from sunset on Friday to sunset on Saturday. The people didn't want to break the law that prohibited travel on the Sabbath, so they waited until the Sabbath hours were over before coming to Jesus.

News had spread quickly about Jesus' healing powers, so the people **brought sick family members to Jesus**. The verb is in the imperfect tense, signifying continuous action. A steady stream of sick and demon possessed people (4:41) were being carried to Jesus. Luke, the doctor, noted that **no matter what their diseases were**, they came to Jesus and **the touch of his hand healed every one**. No sickness stumped him, no disease was beyond his ability to cure; no sickness was too disgusting for the touch of his hand.

4:41 The **demons came out shouting** what they knew about Jesus. While their words were true, Jesus **told them to be silent** (see 4:35). The knowledge of the demons would soon become an ironic contrast to the misunderstanding of Jesus' own disciples, the fickleness of the crowds, and the stubborn blindness of Israel's own religious leaders.

JESUS PREACHES THROUGHOUT GALILEE / 4:42-44 / 36

Jesus had just spent a Sabbath day in feverish activity—healing the sick and exorcising demons. He had done practically everything except rest. Early in the morning of the next day, he set aside a time of prayer, by himself. He was careful to spend time maintaining his intimate fellowship with his Father. By the time the people found him, he was ready to face the next challenge. Believers should follow Christ's example by carving out time in their busy schedules for worship and prayer. Ability to serve will be hindered if believers neglect times of spiritual replenishment.

4:42 Early the next morning refers to the hours before the sun had come up because Mark wrote that it was still dark (Mark 1:35). Jesus **went out into the wilderness.** During his ministry on earth, Jesus was in constant contact with the Father. Jesus had to get up very early just to get some time alone. If Jesus needed solitude for prayer and refreshment, how much more is this true for Christians today?

Apparently the people in Capernaum continued to arrive at Simon Peter's house the next morning hoping to hear more of Jesus' teaching and see him perform more miracles. When Jesus didn't appear, **the crowds searched everywhere for him.** When the people finally tracked him down, **they begged him not to leave them.** Who would want to lose this kind man who could heal any sickness with just a word or a touch?

4:43-44 Jesus' primary mission was to bring people to a place of decision to have faith in God, not merely to remove their pain. The word **must** conveys Jesus' sense of call and urgency. **The Good News of the Kingdom of God** was the core of Jesus' teaching. This is the Kingdom where God reigns—it is a present reality and a future hope.

Today Jesus Christ reigns in the hearts of believers, but the Kingdom of God will not be fully realized until all evil in the world is judged and removed. Jesus came to earth first as a suffering Servant; he will come again as King and Judge to rule victoriously over all the earth. The Kingdom of God was good news! It was good news to the Jews because they had been awaiting the coming of the promised Messiah ever since the Babylonian captivity. It is Good News for people today as well because it means freedom from slavery to sin and selfishness. The Kingdom of God is here and now because the Holy Spirit lives in the hearts of believers. Yet it is also in the future because Jesus will return to reign over a perfect Kingdom where sin and evil no longer exist. The phrase **"That is why I was sent"** stresses Jesus' understanding of who was in charge.

Thus Jesus **continued to travel around.** Jesus had the call and the message; he had the power and authority. Wherever Jesus went, he also healed many people and cast out many demons. These miracles revealed Jesus to be the Messiah for whom the Jews had been waiting. The miracles also demonstrated Jesus' compassion for hurting people. Many people needed to hear Jesus proclaim the Good News of the Kingdom of God.

LUKE 5

JESUS PROVIDES A MIRACULOUS CATCH OF FISH / 5:1-11 / 37

Some scholars consider this incident to be the same as in Matthew 4:18-22 and Mark 1:16-20, which record Jesus' first encounter with the fishermen, Peter, Andrew, James, and John at the Sea of Galilee. Matthew and Mark then describe how Jesus called them to follow him. However, other scholars see Luke as giving an account of Jesus' second call to these disciples because there are several differences in the accounts. If Luke was recording a second call, the disciples must have gone back to their occupation of fishing in the interim. Some of the disciples did the same after Jesus' crucifixion and resurrection (see John 21:1-14).

5:1-3 Jesus continued his teaching tour, and **one day . . . was preaching on the shore of the Sea of Galilee.** Word about Jesus had spread everywhere (4:14), so **great crowds pressed in on him**

to listen to the word of God. Jesus could stand on the shore and the people could sit on the hillsides to listen. On this occasion, the crowds were pushing in and around him, practically backing him into the lake! Then **he noticed two empty boats; the fishermen had left them and were washing their nets.** Nets had to be kept in good condition, so they were washed to remove weeds and then mended in preparation for the next fishing expedition.

Jesus got **into one of the boats,** called to its owner, **Simon** (Peter), and asked him to **push it out into the water.** From this position, Jesus **sat** and **taught the crowds.**

5:4-5 Simon had spoken with Jesus and had even been called to be a follower (Matthew 4:18-22; Mark 1:16-20); he had seen Jesus perform great miracles. Even Simon's own family had benefited from Jesus' compassion and power (4:38-41). Jesus then suggested that they **go out where it is deeper** and do more fishing, Simon explained that they had **worked hard** all the **night** before and **didn't catch a thing.** Night fishing was very common on the Sea of Galilee. Fishing was usually best during the night while the fish were active and feeding closer to the surface where their nets could more easily trap them. If Simon and the others had been throwing out and pulling in nets over and over all night long and had caught nothing, surely they were tired and frustrated. Jesus said, however, **"You will catch many fish."** For Simon to answer Jesus, **"But if you say so, we'll try again,"** shows deference to Jesus and budding faith in what Jesus could do.

5:6-7 The words, **and this time,** occurred after Simon had rounded up his partners and other workers, put the huge net they had been cleaning (5:2) back into the boat, rowed out to the deeper water, spread the net, and then begun to row and draw the net together. Nevertheless, they followed Jesus' instructions and **their nets were so full they began to tear!** Simon and his workers began to haul in the catch of fish, but the weight of the nets was too much. So they shouted for help from **their partners in the other boat,** and pulling together they began to dump the fish into the both boats until they were **on the verge of sinking.** Obviously this was not an ordinary catch by any standards, judging from Peter's response in the following verse.

5:8 Simon had seen people cured and had heard Jesus' teachings, but this miracle reached directly into his life and grabbed him. Simon had been fishing all his life. When he saw what Jesus did in supplying such a huge haul of fish, he recognized Jesus as the Messiah. He had called him "Master" in 5:5, but here he called him **Lord.** Recognizing Jesus' identity and thus his inherent holiness made Simon painfully aware of his own sinfulness. Simon knew he was looking at the Messiah, and his sin and unworthiness caused him to fall **to his knees before Jesus** and ask him to **leave.** Simon realized that he had witnessed a true miracle and did not feel worthy to be in Jesus' presence or to be the recipient of Jesus' special favor.

5:9-11 The others with Simon included those who helped on the fishing boats, as well as Simon's **partners, James and John** (see Mark 1:19, 29). All were **awestruck by the size of their catch.** Jesus spoke reassuringly to Simon. Indeed, the central focus of this story is not so much the miraculous catch as it is the picture it gives of Jesus' call to Simon to be his disciple and begin **fishing for people.** While James and John also followed, Luke focused on Simon, as he did in much of this Gospel, most likely because Simon Peter figured prominently in the early church (Luke's second volume is the book of Acts) and because his Gentile readers would have been familiar with him.

When the fishing party landed, **they left** behind the biggest catch they had ever seen **and followed Jesus.** Jesus had not come along with them to give them a good catch and a good day's wage; Jesus had come to change their professions and priorities forever. They understood the picture he had given them of what he was calling them to do, and they left their ships and nets behind and followed.

JESUS HEALS A MAN WITH LEPROSY / 5:12-16 / 38

After recording the story of Peter's call, Luke placed a story of another person—this time, a leper—who with a spirit of brokenness ran to the mercy of Jesus, literally falling at his feet (5:8, 12).

5:12 This man took a great risk when he came near to Jesus because he had **an advanced case of leprosy.** Leprosy was a feared disease because there was no known cure for it, and some forms of it were highly contagious. Leprosy had a similar emotional impact and terror associated with it, as AIDS does today. (Sometimes called Hansen's disease, leprosy still exists today in a less contagious form that can be treated.) If a person contracted the contagious type, a priest declared him a leper and banished him from his home and city. This also excluded him from participating in any social or religious activities (according to the law in Leviticus 13–14). The leper went to live in a community with other lepers until the disease went into remission or he or she died. Quarantine was the only way the people knew to contain the spread of the contagious forms of leprosy. Because leprosy destroys the nerve endings, lepers often would unknowingly damage their fingers, toes, and noses. This man with leprosy had an advanced case, so he undoubtedly had lost much bodily tissue. The man believed that Jesus could heal every trace of the disease; he only wondered if Jesus would **want to.**

5:13 Lepers were considered untouchable because people feared contracting their disease. Yet Jesus **reached out and touched the man** who was covered with leprosy, assuring him that he did **want to** heal him. Then he spoke the words, **"Be healed!"** That Jesus' touch precedes his pronouncement of healing indicates his sovereignty over the Jewish law not to touch a leper (Leviticus 5:3; 13:1-46; Numbers 5:2). In touching the leper, Jesus became "unclean," but he did not worry about becoming ritually unclean when he could reassure this social outcast. Jesus also exposed himself to the disease. Most likely no one had touched this man in years. Jesus' touch showed great compassion. When Jesus spoke the words, **instantly the leprosy disappeared.**

5:14 Jesus healed the man, but also gave him two warnings: First, he was instructed **not to tell anyone what had happened.** Jesus' mission was to preach the Good News of the Kingdom of God;

he did not want the crowds descending on him to see miracles or to benefit from his power.

The law required a priest to examine a healed leper (Leviticus 14). Then the healed leper was to give an offering at the Temple. Jesus adhered to these laws by telling the man to **go right to the priest and let him examine** him, thereby demonstrating high regard for God's law. Jesus wanted this man to give his story firsthand to the priest to prove that his leprosy was completely gone. This would allow him to be restored to his family and community. Next the man was to **take along the offering required in the law of Moses for those who have been healed of leprosy.**

The man was not to proclaim his healing, but the priest's pronouncement would give **proof** to **everyone** that the man had been healed. Most important, however, the testimony would reveal that the one who heals lepers had come. People believed that healing leprosy was a sign of the Messiah's arrival (see Matthew 11:5).

5:15-16 Mark recorded that the man disobeyed Jesus' warning (Mark 1:45). Thus, **the report of** Jesus' **power spread even faster.** The healed man's disobedience to Jesus' command, even if from good motives, hindered Jesus' work because the publicity Jesus received severely hampered his ministry in the synagogues. **Vast crowds came to hear him preach and to be healed of their diseases;** Jesus' notoriety as a healer made it impossible for him to teach and speak because people pressed on him, seeking special favors. Instead of enjoying his newfound fame and success (at least according to the world's standards), **Jesus often withdrew to the wilderness for prayer.**

JESUS HEALS A PARALYZED MAN / 5:17-26 / 39

This is the first record in Luke of Jesus' interplay with the Jewish religious leaders of the day. Jesus was making headline news in ancient Israel, so obviously those in religious power wanted to see him for themselves.

5:17 Religious leaders came **from every village in all Galilee and Judea, as well as from Jerusalem** to listen to Jesus and see if everything they heard about him was true. Mark wrote that this event took place in Capernaum (Mark 2:1).

Two main groups of religious leaders, the **Pharisees** and the Sadducees, unofficially ran the religious affairs of the country. Although Palestine was occupied by Rome, the Jews had a certain amount of self-government, especially regarding their religion. By far the most influential, the Pharisees zealously followed the Old Testament laws,

as well as their own religious traditions. They were highly respected in the community, but unfortunately many became so proud of their "righteousness" that they felt set apart from the common people. They pledged to obey every minute detail, not only of God's law, but also of all the traditions and rules for life (over six hundred of these details came to be as important or more important than the word of God).

The **teachers of religious law** were the legal specialists of the day. Many teachers of the law were also Pharisees. They often handled correspondence for people or managed their financial accounts. By the time of Jesus, they had become a fairly powerful class.

Pharisees and teachers of religious law arrived to check out Jesus, and Luke immediately moved to the central point of this narrative, a healing. **The Lord's healing power was strongly with Jesus** (for more on Jesus' power, see 4:14; 6:19; 8:44-46). Through the Holy Spirit who had been given to Jesus, the power of God resided in him, which could flow out to those whom Jesus touched. Healing was one of the key signs of the Messiah (4:18-21; Isaiah 61:1-2). Jesus healed and these religious leaders saw it with their own eyes, but they refused to believe.

5:18-19 Jesus was teaching and the building was filled to capacity with people standing outside (Mark 2:2). **Some men came carrying a paralyzed man on a sleeping mat.** They wanted to gain access to Jesus. When they could not get in, **they went up to the roof.** In Bible times, houses were built of stone and had flat roofs made of mud mixed with straw. In addition, some homes had stone slabs underneath the mortar mixture—this was probably the case here, for the text mentions **tiles.** Outside stairways led to the roof. These men carried their friend up the stairs to the roof where they took apart a portion of the roof and **lowered the sick man down into the crowd, still on his mat, right in front of Jesus.**

5:20 Jesus saw **their faith** acted out in their determination—the faith of all the men who came, but he spoke directly to the paralyzed man, saying, **"Son, your sins are forgiven."** Jesus spoke first to the man's spiritual condition. All sickness and death are the result of evil and sin in the world. That does not mean that a person's spiritual health can be measured by looking at his or her physical health. It means that every person is sinful and that every person, whether healthy, sick, or paralyzed, needs forgiveness of sins. A healthy spiritual life with God is always far more important than a perfectly healthy body. The man needed spiritual healing, so Jesus forgave his sins.

5:21 When the **Pharisees and teachers of religious law** heard Jesus tell the paralyzed man that his sins were forgiven, they were shocked. **"Who does this man think he is?"** they asked incredulously. **"This is blasphemy!"** Blasphemy is the act of claiming to be God or to do what only God can do, as well as to curse, revile, or insult the name of God. In Jewish law, blasphemy was punishable by death (Leviticus 24:16).

Forgiveness of sins was a sign that the messianic age had come (Isaiah 40:2; Joel 2:32; Micah 7:18-

19; Zechariah 13:1), and these lifetime students of God's word should have known this. In labeling Jesus' claim to forgive sins as blasphemous, the religious leaders showed they did not understand that Jesus is God and that he has God's power to heal both the body and the soul. Because only God can **forgive sins,** Jesus was claiming to be God. Unfortunately, these religious leaders' reaction was anger and hatred, instead of honestly considering that perhaps this man was indeed their Messiah.

5:22-23 Jesus did not hear the men's amazed words, but he **knew what they were thinking** as part of his divine nature. While Jesus walked as a human on this earth, he never ceased to be God. As a man, however, Jesus was subject to place, time, and other human limitations. Yet he could still see each person's thoughts, intents, and motives. So Jesus asked them point-blank, **"Why do you think this is blasphemy?"**

The teachers knew about Jesus' ability to heal, and they probably had expected Jesus to immediately heal the paralyzed man. Instead, Jesus forgave the man's sins. To the teachers, this sounded like blasphemy. Anyone can just **say** someone's sins are forgiven, but it would take someone with great power and authority to heal a paralyzed person. Jesus would show that he had the power to forgive sins by also showing that he had the power to make a paralyzed person **get up and walk.** Jesus was offering to do an easier task (healing the man) as public evidence that the more difficult, "secret" task (forgiveness of sin) also had been accomplished.

5:24-25 The implied answer to the question Jesus asked in 5:23 is that it would certainly be easier to just say, "Your sins are forgiven" (who would know whether it had happened or not) than to perform a healing in public view. So to prove that he had power to forgive sins, Jesus showed them his power to heal. Speaking to the religious leaders, Jesus said, **"I will prove that I, the Son of Man, have the authority on earth to forgive sins."** Using the messianic title "Son of Man" (Daniel 7:13) gave them no doubt of who he claimed to be.

Turning back to the paralyzed man still lying on the mat in front of him, Jesus said, **"Stand up, take your mat, and go on home, because you are healed!"** Immediately he **jumped to his feet** and did as Jesus said. The religious leaders who had questioned Jesus' ability to forgive sins saw the formerly paralyzed man get up and walk. Such a healing would have been impossible apart from God's power. There could be no mistaking the connection—Jesus had the power to make the paralyzed man walk; thus, he also had the authority to forgive his sins.

5:26 The phrase, **everyone was gripped with great wonder and awe,** refers to the crowd in the house and implies amazement as well as fear. Such awe was appropriate in the presence of one who displayed the authority to heal and to forgive sins. As a result, the people **praised God.**

JESUS EATS WITH SINNERS AT MATTHEW'S HOUSE / 5:27-32 / 40

The next clash between Jesus and the religious leaders revolved around the company he kept. Not only was Jesus not separating himself from distasteful characters, he was seeking them out. Jesus wasn't accused of accepting sinners as his friends; he was charged with befriending sinners.

5:27 In Mark and Luke, Matthew is called **Levi.** Most people in this day had two or three names: a Jewish name, a Roman name, and possibly a Greek name. Levi was his Jewish name, Matthew his Roman name. Levi was a Jew who worked for the Romans as the area's **tax collector.** He collected taxes from the citizens as well as from merchants passing through town. Capernaum was a customs post on the caravan route between Damascus to the northeast and the Mediterranean Sea to the west. Most Jews hated tax collectors because of their reputation for cheating, their support of Rome, and their constant contact with "unclean" Gentiles. Tax collectors took a commission on the taxes they collected, so most of them overcharged the people and kept the profits.

Everyone in Capernaum knew Matthew, and anyone passing through the city who had to pay taxes could find him easily, for he sat at the **tax-collection booth,** an elevated platform or bench. This would not have been the first time that Jesus had seen Matthew, for Jesus had often walked along the shore of the Sea of Galilee. Certainly Matthew had seen Jesus before and, with the crowds, probably had been impressed and intrigued with this man. So one day when Jesus walked right up to Matthew's booth and said, **"Come, be my disciple!"** Matthew lost no time in responding. This was not a request, but a command; not an invitation, but a call to discipleship.

5:28 Levi responded as Jesus would want all his followers to do—he **got up, left everything, and followed him.** Levi left a lucrative tax-collecting business to follow the Lord. That Levi **left everything** was no small matter. Matthew was probably very wealthy, so when he walked away from his booth, he left behind a lifetime of potentially great wealth. Several of the other disciples could always return to fishing, but Matthew could never turn back.

5:29 Levi called his friends together to meet Jesus too. He **held a banquet in his home with Jesus as the guest of honor** so that his **fellow tax collec-** tors and other guests could meet Jesus. This was a crowd that Jesus could not reach in the synagogues, for they had been excommunicated (their profession was seen as traitorous). Jesus loved them and had a message for them too—the Good News of the Kingdom of God.

5:30 The religious leaders had apparently continued to follow Jesus all the way to Matthew's house and watched the feast. According to **the Pharisees and their teachers of religious law,** contact with such **scum** made a Jew unclean. The Pharisees regarded these people as wicked and opposed to the will of God because they did not observe the rituals for purity which enabled them to eat with others. Thus, to **eat and drink** with such people was particularly heinous. The Pharisees would have nothing to do with such people. But not so with Jesus. How could Jesus make the claims he did and hang out with the worst elements of society?

5:31-32 The disciples, perhaps wondering about this themselves, brought the question to Jesus. The first part of Jesus' answer was from a common proverb on the healthy and the sick. **Healthy people don't need a doctor**—the physician's waiting room is filled with **sick people.** They recognize their need and come to the one who can make them well. The Pharisees were appalled that Jesus ate with sinners and outcasts. Their love of principle and position motivated them to drive a wedge between God's law and common people. Jesus carried the proverb a step further and explained his messianic mission: **"I have come to call sinners to turn from their sins, not to spend my time with those who think they are already good enough."** Jesus was saying, "I am here because these are the people who realize their need and welcome me." This was Jesus' audience. Jesus, the Great Physician, healed people of physical illnesses, but he knew that all people are spiritually sick and in need of salvation. He was not lowering the standards; he was reaching out to seeking souls in order to bring them the salvation for which they sought.

RELIGIOUS LEADERS ASK JESUS ABOUT FASTING / 5:33-39 / 41

By this time, the Pharisees were constantly skirmishing with Jesus. Two confrontations have preceded this section: one over Jesus' authority to forgive sins (5:17-26) and the other over Jesus' friendship with unsavory characters (5:27-31). The parables of the cloth and the wineskins (5:37-38) apply to more than just fasting or to the Pharisees; they speak of Jesus' entire mission and the new era he inaugurated by his entrance into human history.

5:33 John the Baptist's disciples refers to the remaining disciples of John the Baptist; **the disciples of the Pharisees** were probably Pharisees-in-training who would observe the older men and attempt to also practice all the rules and regulations. The Pharisees wanted to know why their own followers, as well as those of John the Baptist, would **always fast and pray.** "Fasting" refers to going without food in order to spend time in prayer. The Old Testament law set aside only one day a year as a required day of fasting for all Jews—the Day of Atonement (Leviticus 16:29). The Pharisees, however, fasted on Mondays and Thursdays (see 18:12) as an act of piety, so their followers did the same. Jesus' disciples, however, were out of step.

5:34-35 In the Old Testament, people would fast in times of disaster and as a sign of their humility and repentance. Fasting represented mourning. During that time, the people approached God with humility and sorrow for sin (see, for example, Judges 20:26; 1 Kings 21:27; Ezra 8:21; Joel 1:14; Jonah 3:5). In the New Testament, the Pharisees fasted as a show of piety; the disciples of John the Baptist fasted as a sign of mourning for sin and to prepare for the Messiah's coming. Jesus' disciples, however, did not need to fast because the Messiah was with them!

Jesus compared himself to a **groom** and his time on earth as a time of feasting and celebration. His **guests** (those who had come to believe in him) did not need to fast while he was with them. Jesus did not condemn fasting—he himself fasted (4:2). He emphasized that fasting must be done at the right time for the right reasons.

Jesus also knew that **someday** the groom **will be taken away from** the people, referring to his death. **Then they will fast** in sorrow. Although Jesus was fully human, he knew he was God and why he had come—to die, paying the penalty for sin.

5:36 Jesus then told the questioning Pharisees a parable—a short story that uses familiar scenes and everyday objects and relationships to explain spiritual truths. Jesus' arrival on earth ushered in a new covenant between God and people. The New Covenant called for a new way of expressing

personal faith. The newness of the gospel could not be combined with the legalism of the Pharisees any more than a **piece of cloth from a new garment** should be used **to patch an old garment.** When the garment would be washed, the patch would shrink, pull away from the old garment, and leave a worse tear than before.

Jesus did not come to patch up the old religious system of Judaism with its rules and traditions. His purpose was to fulfill the law and start something new, though it had been prophesied for centuries. The "new" cannot fit with the "old" patterns of thought. Jesus Christ, God's Son, came to earth to offer people forgiveness of sins and reconciliation with God. The gospel did not fit into the old rigid legalistic system of religion. The gospel offered grace; Judaism offered law and rule keeping.

5:37-38 In Bible times, people would store wine in goatskins sewn around the edges to form water-tight bags (called wineskins). New wine expands as it ferments; thus **new wine must be put into new wineskins.** Old wineskins would become brittle and wouldn't stretch anymore; if someone put new wine into an old wineskin, the old wineskin would **burst** and spill the wine.

The Christian church was never meant to be a sect or adaptation of Judaism. Instead, Christ fulfills the intent of the Old Testament Scripture. The law reveals the nature and will of God; Jesus Christ reveals the nature and will of God. But while the law could only point out sin and condemn people, Jesus Christ gave his life to bring forgiveness of sin and salvation. These parables speak of Jesus' entire mission and the new era he inaugurated by his entrance into human history.

The **new wine** was the newness of the gospel as exemplified in the person of Jesus Christ (John 2:1-11). Like old wineskins, the Pharisees and indeed the entire religious system of Judaism had become too rigid to accept Jesus who could not be contained in their traditions or rules. Their understanding of faithfulness to the law had become unsuitable for the fresh, dynamic power of Christ's message. They were the self-appointed guardians of the "old garment" and the "old wineskins."

5:39 Jesus could have quoted another well-known parable for our day, "You can't teach an old dog new tricks." Jesus realized that many people are so content with the **old wine** that they don't even want to try the new wine. **"The old is better," they say.** Many tragically stick with the good when God wants to give them the best. Many of the Pharisees would investigate Jesus' teaching but cling to the old traditions. Many who check out Christianity will reject it, preferring their old ways. Loyalty to the old life may prevent people from believing and certainly will keep them from growing.

LUKE 6

THE DISCIPLES PICK WHEAT ON THE SABBATH / 6:1-5 / 45

The end of chapter 5 has the parables of the unshrunk cloth and the new wine. These were Jesus' explanation of how the message of the Good News could not be confined within the rigid rules and traditions of the Pharisees.

6:1-2 As these leaders continued to follow Jesus, they observed him one Sabbath day as he was walking through some grainfields. Roads often went right through fields. The disciples broke off heads of wheat, rubbed off the husks in their hands, and ate the grains. On any other day but the Sabbath, this would have been acceptable. God's law said that farmers were to leave the edges of their fields unplowed so travelers and the poor could eat (Deuteronomy 23:25). This day was a problem, however, because the religious leadership had set up strict laws regarding how to observe the Sabbath. They had set up thirty-nine categories of forbidden activities—and harvesting was one of them. According to the religious leaders, however, the disciples were technically "harvesting" because they were picking wheat and rubbing it in their hands. The disciples were not breaking God's law as recorded by Moses. Instead, they were only violating one of the Pharisees' many rules.

6:3-4 The Pharisees would have been taken aback by Jesus' question, **"Haven't you ever read in the Scriptures . . .?"** Of course they had read this story about **what King David did when he and his companions were hungry.** Jesus explained his disciples' action on the grounds that they were hungry and that their need superseded the technicalities of ceremonial law.

The story is recorded in 1 Samuel 21:1-6. Each week twelve consecrated loaves of **special bread,** representing the twelve tribes of Israel, would be placed on a table in the **house of God,** the Tabernacle. At the end of the week, the bread would be replaced with fresh loaves, and the old loaves were **reserved for the priests** to eat (Leviticus 24:9). On one occasion, the high priest gave this special bread to David and his men to eat as they were fleeing from Saul. The priest understood that their need was more important than ceremonial regulations. The loaves given to David were the old loaves that had just been replaced with fresh ones. Although the priests were the only ones allowed to eat this bread, God did not punish David because his need for food was more important than the priestly regulations.

By comparing himself and his disciples to David and his men, Jesus was saying, in effect, "If you condemn me, you must also condemn David." Jesus was not condoning disobedience to God's laws. Instead, he was emphasizing discernment and compassion in enforcing the ceremonial laws, something the self-righteous Pharisees did not comprehend. People's needs are more important than technicalities.

6:5 When Jesus said that he, calling himself **Son of Man,** was **master even of the Sabbath,** he was claiming to be greater than the law and above the law. Jesus meant that he had the authority to overrule the Pharisees' traditions and regulations because he had created the Sabbath—and the Creator is always greater than the creation. Jesus claimed the authority to correctly interpret the meaning of the Sabbath and all the laws pertaining to it. Who created the Sabbath? God did. Therefore, because Jesus, the Son of Man, is God's Son, given authority and power by God himself, he is also master of the Sabbath.

JESUS HEALS A MAN'S HAND ON THE SABBATH / 6:6-11 / 46

The ongoing debate about the Sabbath would continue to escalate as Jesus continued with his mission, regardless of the day of the week. Obviously Jesus taught and healed throughout the week, but the Gospel writers present several incidents that occurred on the Sabbath in order to highlight the animosity of the religious leaders. This healing is the last in a series of five confrontations with the Pharisees in this section. The Pharisees had already objected to Jesus forgiving sins (5:17-26), associating with "sinners" (5:29-32), and challenging their traditions involving fasting (5:33-39) and the Sabbath (6:1-5).

6:6-7 On another Sabbath day, Jesus was **in the synagogue . . . teaching.** At this particular time, **a man with a deformed right hand** came into the synagogue. There seems to be no question that Jesus could heal the man. The Pharisees were concerned only **to see whether Jesus would heal the man on the Sabbath.** What difference should that make? Luke explains that **they were eager to find some legal charge to bring against him.** How unfortunate that they could not rejoice in a healing; instead, they hoped to use the healing to bring a charge against Jesus. It was more important for them to protect their laws than to free a person from suffering. God's law prohibited work on the seventh day of the week (Exodus 31:14-17); thus, the religious leaders allowed no healing to be done on the Sabbath unless a person's life was in danger. Healing, they argued, was practicing medicine, and they had a law that a person could not practice this profession on the Sabbath.

The man's condition was not life threatening. Jesus could have avoided conflict by waiting until the next day to heal the man. But Jesus, as Lord of the Sabbath, had the authority to overrule the Pharisees' traditions and regulations. If he had waited another day, he would have been submitting to the Pharisees and showing that their made-up rules were indeed equal to God's law. But God's law for the Sabbath was never meant to keep people in bondage. When Jesus saw a need, he filled it, regardless of the day or time.

6:8 Again the text reveals the divine perception that Jesus retained while on earth: he **knew their thoughts** (see also 5:22). Jesus would make a public display of this healing, so **he said to the man with the deformed hand, "Come and stand here where everyone can see."** Jesus would make the important point that he could not and would not be bound by the Pharisees' burdensome laws.

6:9 Jesus' question should have been obvious— even to these religious leaders, **"Is it legal to do good deeds on the Sabbath, or is it a day for doing harm?"** The Pharisees' own laws allowed people to do good and to save life on the Sabbath—a farmer could rescue a sheep from a pit on that day, even though such an act would clearly be considered "work" (Matthew 12:11-12). How absurd, then, to refuse to allow a person to do good to another person on the Sabbath.

6:10 Jesus did not receive an answer to his question, so he turned his attention back to the man, telling him to **reach out** his hand. When the man did so, his hand **became normal again.** As with the leper (5:12-13) and the paralyzed man (5:24-25), Jesus gave this man new life.

6:11 No particular action of Jesus is recorded; he told the man to move, and with that movement, healing arrived. Jesus did nothing that could be called "work," but the Pharisees would not be swayed from their purpose. They became **wild with rage.** Jesus had looked them in the eyes and then had flouted their laws, overruled their authority, and exposed the hatred in their hearts to the entire crowd in the synagogue. When Jesus exposed their attitudes, he became their enemy, and they **began to discuss what to do with him.** Matthew and Mark state that their discussion focused on how they might kill Jesus (Matthew 12:14; Mark 3:6). Ironically, their hatred, combined with their zeal for the law, was driving them to plot murder—an act that was clearly against the law.

JESUS CHOOSES THE TWELVE DISCIPLES / 6:12-16 / 48

After a night dedicated to prayer, Jesus chose twelve men to be his apostles—his representatives. Whatever Jesus' specific reasons for choosing each disciple, as a group they were often hot-tempered, unbelieving, and "clueless" about the spiritual realities behind Jesus' ministry.

The better that Christians come to know the weaknesses of the disciples, the more they can see that God has freely chosen them, also.

6:12 Jesus' enemies had revealed their stubborn hearts and refusal to see him for who he was; his ministry was increasing as people crowded in to hear him. Jesus knew that he would not be long on the earth, so the continuing task of spreading the Good News of the Kingdom would be entrusted to a group of human beings whom he must choose. This was a daunting task and Jesus needed the Father's help. So **Jesus went to a mountain to pray, and he prayed to God all night.** This was not a quick call for help while Jesus followed his instincts; this was an intense conversation as Jesus sought his Father's guidance in this supremely important task.

6:13-14 At daybreak, after his night in prayer, Jesus **called together all of his disciples.** Of the many who were following him at this time, he **chose twelve of them to be apostles.** Jesus did not take volunteers; he chose those whom God had directed him to choose.

The choice of twelve men is highly symbolic. The number twelve corresponds to the twelve tribes of Israel (Matthew 19:28), showing the continuity between the old religious system and the new one based on Jesus' message. Jesus looked upon this as the gathering of the true people of God. These men were the righteous remnant who would carry on the work the twelve tribes were chosen to do—to build the community of God (see 22:28-30). The Gospels and Epistles stressed the ministry of the twelve men together and its significance. The number was so important that when Judas Iscariot killed himself, another man was chosen to replace him (see Acts 1:15-26). The apostles formed Jesus' inner circle. He gave them intense training and sent them out with his own authority. These were the men who started the Christian church. In the Gospels, these twelve men are usually called the disciples, but in the book of Acts they are called apostles. This is a rare instance of the term "apostles" in the Gospels.

The first name recorded was **Simon,** whom Jesus also called **Peter** (see John 1:42). He became one of three in Jesus' core group among the disciples, and he recognized that Jesus was the Messiah (9:18-20). Although Peter would deny ever knowing Jesus, this Gospel alone has Jesus' prayer on behalf of Peter that his faith would not fail (22:31-32). The risen Christ made a special appearance to Peter (24:34). He would become a leader in the Jerusalem church, write two letters that appear in the Bible (1 and 2 Peter), and be crucified for his faith.

Andrew was **Peter's brother** and also a fisherman (Matthew 4:18). Andrew had been a disciple of John the Baptist, and had accepted John the Baptist's testimony. He had left John to follow Jesus, and then had brought his brother Simon to Jesus (John 1:35-42).

James and **John** had also been fishermen and, incidentally, Peter and Andrew's partners (5:10). Along with Peter, the three of them became Jesus' inner circle. James would become the first martyr for the Christian faith (Acts 12:2). John would write the Gospel of John, the letters of 1, 2, and 3 John, and the book of Revelation.

John wrote about **Philip** (John 1:43). Philip probably knew Andrew and Peter because they were from the same town, Bethsaida (John 1:44). This is not the same Philip mentioned in Acts 7. Philip then brought **Bartholomew** (also called Nathanael) as recorded in John 1:45. Bartholomew was an honest man (John 1:47). Bartholomew at first rejected Jesus because Jesus was from Nazareth. But upon meeting Jesus, his attitude changed (John 1:49).

6:15 Matthew was also known as Levi. He had been a tax collector who, at Jesus' call, had given up everything in order to follow him (5:27-28). He would later write the Gospel of Matthew.

Thomas is often remembered as "Doubting Thomas" because he doubted Jesus' resurrection (John 20:24-25). Thomas loved Jesus and understood what Jesus' mission entailed (John 11:16).

This **James** was called **son of Alphaeus** to differentiate him from James the son of Zebedee (and brother of John) in 6:14.

Simon (the Zealot) was probably not a member of the party of Zealots, for that political party was not identified as such until A.D. 68. Most likely the word "Zealot" used here indicates zeal for God's honor and fervent nationalism that characterized Simon before he followed Jesus. Most likely, it was an affectionate nickname.

6:16 Judas (son of James) is also called Thaddaeus (Mark 3:18). He is also mentioned in Acts 1:13. Rounding out the list is **Judas Iscariot,** with the footnote that he is the one **who later betrayed** Jesus. The name "Iscariot" is probably a compound word meaning "the man from Kerioth." Thus, Judas' hometown was Kerioth in southern Judea (see Joshua 15:25), making him the only one of the Twelve who was not from Galilee. It might seem strange that Jesus would spend an entire night in prayer to pick this group, and then end up choosing Judas. Did Jesus make a mistake? No. The plan had been set in motion from the beginning of time, and this was part of the plan that would eventually come to its final conclusion in Judas' betrayal of Jesus and suicide. The betrayal fulfilled prophecy and helped to bring Jesus to the cross. There was no mistake. That was the way of salvation.

JESUS GIVES THE BEATITUDES / 6:17-26 / 49

This section is similar to the Sermon on the Mount (Matthew 5–7). It has been widely debated whether the two are the same sermon or different ones. It is very likely that Jesus taught the same truths twice, if not more.

6:17-19 Jesus' popularity had continued to grow, for there is not only **many of his followers,** but also **crowds.** People had come from **Judea** (the southernmost region of Israel), **Jerusalem** (the key city of Israel, in Judea), and **the seacoasts of Tyre and Sidon** (Gentile cities to the **far north** on the coast of the Mediterranean Sea). Word of Jesus' authoritative teaching and healing power had spread, so many had come long distances **to hear him, to be healed,** and to have Jesus **cast out evil spirits.** No one went away disappointed; **they were all cured.**

6:20 Most likely, Jesus gave these teachings primarily to the **disciples** with the crowds listening in. Jesus' newly chosen disciples, the twelve men who would be his closest associates, might have become tempted to feel proud and important. After all, Jesus' popularity continued to grow, as seen in the multitude with them at that moment. The disciples, riding on the wave of Jesus' popularity, needed to first understand the priorities of God's Kingdom. In addition, many of these disciples were confused about what exactly Jesus was going to do. The Gospels present a group of men who, while believing, never quite understood Jesus' coming death and resurrection until they witnessed it for themselves. So Jesus told them here, in no uncertain terms, that they should not expect fame and fortune in this world, for that is not what Jesus came to bring. They would indeed be "blessed," but by a different Kingdom's standards.

These verses are called the Beatitudes, from the Latin word meaning "blessing." They describe what it means to be Christ's follower. They are standards of conduct; they contrast Kingdom values with worldly values, showing what Christ's followers can expect from the world and what God will give them. They contrast fake piety with true humility; they show how Old Testament expectations are fulfilled in God's Kingdom. The word "blessed" means more than happiness; it means favored and approved by God.

The first "blessing" is reserved for **you who are poor.** These are the people who have nothing but God on whom to depend. They realize that they have nothing of their own to give to God and therefore must depend on his mercy. Jesus says, **"The Kingdom of God is given to you."** Notice that he does not say, "will be given," but "is given." Accepting Jesus into one's heart brings that person into the Kingdom, even as he or she lives on earth.

Jesus was not exalting poverty; instead, he was clarifying that these are the results of discipleship and that the disciples would ultimately be blessed because they could count on Jesus, the Son of Man. In these Beatitudes, Jesus was not cursing all that is part of life—such as laughter, fun, happiness, money, food—but if these become the focus of life without regard to God, then a person cannot be "blessed" by God.

6:21 The hunger about which Jesus spoke is a hunger based on poverty because of one's lot in life or for taking a stand with Christ. The word **hungry** pictures an intense longing that needs to be satisfied; people who do not get food will eventually die of hunger. Jesus' promise to those with this kind of hunger is **"you will be satisfied."** Jesus will completely satisfy those with spiritual hunger.

Jesus promises that those **who weep now . . . will laugh with joy.** Scholars differ on the exact nature of this "weeping." Jesus may have been referring to the nation of Israel weeping for its sins; others interpret this more personally, explaining that it refers to those who weep for their own sins or even for personal grief or oppression. Still other scholars see in the word "weeping" a picture of God's people who suffer because of their faith in him. Most likely it refers to people who are sensitive to the world's sin and resultant suffering. While their pain is real, they can know the end of the story and laugh.

6:22-23 To be surrounded by hateful people would hardly make a person feel like the object of blessing. But Kingdom values are the opposite of this world's values. Jesus explained to his disciples that not only would they, like anyone else, experience poverty and sorrow in this life, but they also would be actively persecuted. They would be **hated, excluded, mocked,** and **cursed**—the one common factor would be that this would occur because they believed in Jesus. Surely this must have sounded strange to the disciples on the mountainside, surrounded by literally a multitude of people desiring to get close to Jesus. Yet Jesus saw what the future held, and he warned them accordingly.

Jesus also comforted them by saying that when they faced persecution, they were to **rejoice.** No matter what those who hate Jesus attempt to do to his followers on earth, a **great reward awaits** them **in heaven.** Jesus placed his disciples in a long line of God's followers who lived righteously and spoke truthfully—only to suffer for it. The Jews held the **ancient prophets** of God in high esteem; to be placed among them was a great honor. Jesus explained that to live and speak for God in the face of unjust persecution, as did the ancient prophets, would bring great reward in heaven.

6:24 The next three verses contain **sorrows** that give the flip side of the "blessings" in the previous verses. While most in the world see riches as desirable and as a sign of God's blessing, Jesus says the opposite. He pronounces **sorrows** on those **who are rich.** Jesus probably addressed these comments to his audience at large. Jesus does not decry riches themselves but their effect on people. Riches cause people to feel self-sufficient and to feel that they have found the happiness for which they were seeking. Those who choose present comfort over God's way have their **only happiness now.** Those who try to find fulfillment through wealth will find that wealth is the only reward they will ever get and that it does not last.

6:25 The words **satisfied and prosperous** refer to those who have everything that this world offers. They lack nothing. Their material possessions and financial "security" cause them to think that they

have no need for God. One day, however, they will face **a time of awful hunger.** This may not occur in this life, but they will find that for eternity, when it really matters, they will be the ones who suffer. The Gospel later records a parable of a rich man and a poor man that illustrates this point (see 16:19-31).

In much the same way, those who **laugh carelessly** will one day face **mourning and sorrow** that will last for eternity. Jesus was not against laughter—indeed, laughter is one of the greatest gifts God has given to his people. Jesus was pointing at the same attitude carried by those who are rich and self-satisfied in this life and give superficial laughter at any mention of God or of eternity. They will find that they were wrong, and they will mourn and weep forever.

6:26 Jesus points out a serious problem facing those **who are praised by the crowds.** While being spoken well of is certainly a worthy goal, rarely can a person be spoken well of by everyone and have everyone completely agree with him or her on every topic. One cannot be pleasing to everyone in that way without sacrificing some principle here or another there. Such a person must waffle in all areas of life so everyone will like him or her.

One group in the Old Testament was **praised** by everyone, from the king to the common people—they were the **false prophets.** The **ancestors** of these Israelites listening to Jesus had spoken well of the false prophets. They were praised by kings and crowds because their predictions—personal prosperity and victory in war—were exactly what the people wanted to hear. Unfortunately, their words were shown to be lies as the nations of Israel and later Judah lost their freedom and their homeland when they were taken into captivity. Popularity is no guarantee of a person's truthfulness; human flattery does not bring God's approval. Sadness lies ahead for those who chase after the crowd's praise rather than God's truth.

JESUS TEACHES ABOUT LOVING ENEMIES / 6:27-36 / 57
While the Pharisees sought Jesus' death because he refused to keep their regulations regarding cleanliness and the Sabbath observance, Jesus was teaching standards of living that were far higher than anything the Pharisees could imagine. The difference was that the Pharisees were performing their acts in order to be good enough for God; Jesus knew the standards were impossible to reach on human strength alone. Jesus did not ask people to act this way in order to be good enough for God. But people who have accepted Christ as Savior have the Holy Spirit's help to accomplish what would otherwise be impossible.

6:27-28 Jesus taught that love must not be selective. His followers are to love all people, regardless of how unlovely or even hostile they may be. They also must act on that love by being willing to do good when it is in their power to do it. There are several words for love in Greek. The word used here is *agape*, meaning the kind of love shown even when the one loved has no merit for that love. It is love that must be chosen and willed.

All people have experienced *agape* from God. God loved the world even while people were sinful and rebellious. God willed to love his people and sent his Son to die for them, not because they deserved it or had any merit, but only because of God's love. Those who have experienced God's love understand what it means to be loved undeservedly. People who were once enemies of God and have joined his family can understand what it means to **love your enemies.** Only with the help of God's Spirit can his people **do good to those who hate** them, **pray for the happiness of those who curse** them, and **pray for those who hurt** them (see Romans 12:14-21). When believers are hated, cursed, and hurt, they are to respond with love.

6:29-30 How can anyone respond to persecution in love? Jesus offered a couple of examples. If you get slapped, **turn the other cheek.** The normal response would be to slap back, but Jesus offers another option—the attitude that says, "I will not seek revenge. In fact, if need be, I am ready to take another blow." The attitude is not so much to offer to be hit again as it is to offer forgiveness.

The same attitude is illustrated regarding the **coat** and the **shirt,** referring to the outer garment and the undergarment. If someone demanded the one, offer the other as well. The point is not so much being passive when being robbed as it is being compassionate for another's need. If someone needs to steal a coat, then perhaps that person also needs your shirt.

In fact, the more general principle could be stated: **Give what you have to anyone who asks you for it; and when things are taken away from you, don't try to get them back.** Such an attitude completely confounds the world. It doesn't understand non-retaliation, forgiveness, and a loose hold on possessions. But believers, citizens of a future heavenly Kingdom, are freed to forgive

and to give. The point is not that giving is always the correct answer, but that believers' actions are rooted first in love, not in regard for honor or possessions.

6:31 This is commonly known as the Golden Rule. Many religions teach a negative version of this statement. Confucius said, "What you do not want done to yourself, do not do to others." But Jesus stated this in a positive manner, making it even more powerful. While it may be possible to not do evil to others, it is much more difficult to take the initiative to actually **do for others as you would like them to do for you.** A person may be able to keep the negative form of the law by avoiding sin, but to keep the positive form requires action. This is the key to the radical discipleship that Jesus wants.

6:32-34 In these short statements, Jesus explained his commands that he had just given by showing how his followers must be different from **sinners,** that is, those who do not believe in him. How would God's people be any different from the world if they only loved people who love them? How would they be any different from the world if they only did good to people who could do good to them in return? Sinners love, sinners do good, sinners lend money—the difference is that God's people are willing to love, do good, and lend even when there is no promise of return. Such actions will mark Jesus' followers as different.

6:35-36 Because his followers are to be different, Jesus sums up their actions as **love your enemies, do good to them,** and **lend to them.** To make them different from the world, God's people will do those actions without expecting to get anything back. Their lives reflect the attitude of God himself; thus their **reward** will be great, and they will be **acting as children of the Most High.** God's people do these actions not so that they can be God's people, but because they *are* God's people. Their attitudes and values reflect God's attitudes and values. To **be compassionate** means to refuse to inflict just vengeance, as well as to show kindness.

JESUS TEACHES ABOUT JUDGING OTHERS / 6:37-42 / 63

Jesus not only commanded his disciples to be loving and compassionate, he also went on to explain to them what true love entails. First he emphasized that true love does not judge others or withhold forgiveness.

6:37 While the word "judge" can mean to evaluate or analyze, Jesus did not mean his people

should refuse to think critically or make decisions, nor was he attempting to abolish the legal system or disciplinary measures. Believers must be discerning and make certain judgments. Jesus was referring to the judgmental attitude that focuses on others' faults, criticizing and tearing them down.

The believers' special position with Christ does not give them license to take God's place as judge. Those who judge in that manner will find themselves **judged** by God. Neither should they criticize or they will face criticism. The practice of forgiveness leads also to forgiveness by God. Those who refuse to **forgive** show that they do not understand what God has done for them. God's children must be ready and willing to forgive, just as God has forgiven them.

6:38 Generosity in giving, both of material goods as well as love, compassion, and forgiveness of others will result in returned generosity. Jesus wants his disciples to be merciful and loving, not selfish or spiteful. He does away with retaliation and the concept of demanding an eye-for-an-eye recompense for wrongdoing. The picture is of blessings being returned in a bushel basket, filled to the brim, **pressed down** and **shaken together** to make room for more, then **running over.** Jesus wants our measure of mercy to overflow. Those who give easily will find goodness coming back to them. Those who are stingy and reluctant givers will receive in the same way.

6:39-40 In this parable, Jesus explained that, while his followers were to give, love, and refuse to be judgmental, they must also be discerning and careful whom they follow. Obviously, a **blind person** cannot lead a blind person because both of them will end up in **a ditch.** Then Jesus explained what he meant: **a student is not greater than the teacher.** Those who lead others must have clear vision, willingness to learn and understand, and no arrogance or self-righteousness. Such a standard would disqualify the Pharisees who, in this instance, were the blind guides leading people into disaster. Jesus explained that his disciples should not go beyond what they learned from him; instead, they should aim to be like him. Watch out whom you follow. No matter how many human teachers you may have, your ultimate authority must be Christ and his word.

6:41-42 How well Jesus understood human nature. He knew that human beings find it easy to **worry about a speck in** someone else's **eye,** but not be able to see **a log** in their own eye. It is easy for people to overlook their own sins yet easily spot sin in others. It's true that the sin that people most clearly see in others is also present in them. Sometimes they may offer help, but there is a crucial flaw, for they will do great damage when they **can't see past the log** still lodged in their eye. Jesus used hyperbole to show that someone attempting to help a brother or sister with a "speck" when that person is carrying around a "log" makes him or her a hypocrite. The person has criticized and found fault in another without applying the same standards to himself. Before that person can be of any assistance, he must **first get rid of the log** that is in his own eye, and then maybe he can **see well enough to deal with the speck** in the other person's eye.

JESUS TEACHES ABOUT FRUIT IN PEOPLE'S LIVES / 6:43-45 / 66

With a couple of proverbs derived from the agricultural setting of ancient Israel, Jesus showed his audience why hypocritically judging others (6:41-42) is foolish. Just as a good tree will eventually bear good fruit, so a person's heart will eventually bear fruit—a good heart producing good works and an evil heart bringing forth evil. Everyone's heart will eventually be exposed for what it is; and a strong indicator of the character of a person's heart is what one says.

6:43-45 Figs and **grapes** were two of the main agricultural products of Israel. A person knows a tree by its fruit. A **good** (or healthy) **tree can't produce bad fruit,** and likewise, a **bad** (or unhealthy) **tree can't produce good fruit.**

Claims are easier to make or fake than results. Even Jesus' claims would have been ludicrous if he hadn't backed them up with results. He pointed out that the principle applies universally: You can tell a lot about a tree from its fruit! Jesus warned that people are like trees: Examine their "fruit" closely. Jesus reminded his listeners that their **deeds** and speech (what they **say**) would reveal their true underlying beliefs, attitudes, and motivations. The good impressions people try to make cannot last if their hearts are deceptive. What is in the heart will come out in a person's speech and behavior.

JESUS TEACHES ABOUT BUILDING ON A SOLID FOUNDATION / 6:46-49 / 67

Jesus was not content with letting his audience ponder his profound thoughts. His teaching is not meant for academic discussion and debate. Instead, Christians should build their entire lives around his teachings, applying them to every facet of life. If they don't, they will not be able to withstand the pressures and temptations of this world and will be swept away to their destruction. Jesus calls believers to take the time they have now—before the floodwaters come—to reevaluate the way they live in light of his teachings.

6:46-47 To call Jesus **Lord** means to have committed oneself to following him and his teaching. Why would someone call Jesus "Lord" and then refuse to **obey** his teachings? Jesus' true followers not only hear his words, but they act on his words, allowing his message to make a difference in their lives. The following parable will **show** Jesus' listeners **what it's like** when a person **comes, listens,** and **then obeys.**

6:48 Jesus explained that his true followers were **like a person who builds a house on a strong foundation laid upon the underlying rock.** Jesus pictured Palestine's climate in these words. There were few rainfalls all year, but during the rainy season, heavy rains with excessive flooding could wash away poorly grounded homes. But those houses with their foundations on solid rock would be unaffected by the rising waters and beating winds. When the "storms of life" come (perhaps the hatred and persecution Jesus warned his fol-

lowers to expect) only the person who builds his or her life on the "strong foundation" of Jesus Christ will be able to "stand firm." When life is calm, the foundation doesn't seem to matter. But when crises come, the foundation is tested. Be sure your life is built on the solid foundation of knowing and trusting Jesus Christ.

6:49 In contrast is the person who **listens and doesn't obey.** While both of these people may have built houses that looked identical, the crucial difference was in the foundation. The person who won't listen to Jesus will be **like a person who builds a house without a foundation.** When the **floods sweep down against that house** it cannot stand firm. The sand beneath the house will be driven away and the house **will crumble into a heap of ruins.** As character is revealed by fruit (6:43-45), so faith is revealed by storms. The wise person, seeking to act upon God's word, builds to withstand anything.

LUKE 7

A ROMAN OFFICER DEMONSTRATES FAITH / 7:1-10 / 68

The story of the officer's extraordinary faith in Jesus reiterates a dominant theme in Luke's writings (this Gospel and the book of Acts): the inclusion of the Gentiles in the family of faith. The faith of this officer foreshadows the faith of another officer, Cornelius, the first Gentile convert to Christianity (see Acts 10).

7:1 Capernaum had become Jesus' "home base" while he was in Galilee. Located on the northwestern shore of the Sea of Galilee, Capernaum was the largest of the many cities surrounding the lake. Far more than just a fishing village, it was the economic center of Galilee and sat near a major trade route and thus was a wealthy city. The city housed a contingent of Roman soldiers.

7:2-3 A **Roman** army **officer** had a **highly valued slave** who was **sick and near death.** The officer

wanted him to be healed. Why so much concern about a slave? The Jewish historian Josephus wrote that Roman soldiers had many slaves who actually trained and fought with them. So this slave may have been the officer's personal attendant with whom he felt a close bond. The officer had **heard about Jesus,** so he certainly knew of Jesus' healing power. He sent a request for healing to Jesus apparently because he believed Jesus was sent from God. He may have known about the healing of the official's son (which probably occurred earlier, see

John 4:46-54). He knew that Jesus had the power to heal his slave. Matthew 8:5 says the Roman officer visited Jesus himself, while Luke says he sent **some respected Jewish leaders** to present his request to Jesus. In those days, dealing with a person's messengers was considered the same as dealing with the one who had sent them.

7:4-5 The animosity between the Jews and the Romans was no secret. The Jews hated the occupation army; the Romans, in turn, hated the Jews. Yet in this story we find a different sort of Roman soldier—a man who seems to have been a God-fearing man. He loved the Jewish people, and he **built a synagogue** (meaning that he funded it and certainly had genuine interest in it and the God worshiped there). That this officer could request a favor of these Jewish elders and have them respond so willingly would normally come as a surprise. That the elders **earnestly begged Jesus to come** on behalf of this officer was even more out of character with normal Jewish / Roman relations.

7:6-8 Jesus responded to the request brought by the Jewish elders and went with them. Just before they arrived at the house, the officer sent another message by way of some friends, "Lord, don't trouble yourself by coming to my home . . . Just say the word from where you are, and my servant will be healed." The officer understood that since he was a Gentile, he was considered unclean by the Jews. He may also have felt himself unworthy to have Jesus

enter his home. This Gentile understood more than most of the Jews of Jesus' day; he saw Jesus' superiority. He saw that Jesus' authority was greater than his own and that Jesus did not have to personally visit his home. Jesus' word would be enough.

The officer was accustomed both to obeying and to being obeyed. He may have understood that Jesus' power and authority came from God. When Jesus spoke, God spoke. Jesus did not need rituals or medicines or even his touch or presence to accomplish a healing. The officer applied his understanding of authority to Jesus.

7:9 The Jews who had been looking for Jesus couldn't see him for who he was, yet this Gentile did. Jesus **was amazed** and exclaimed **to the crowd** that he had not **seen faith like this in all the land of Israel.** This did not mean that no one in Israel had faith, but many did not accept the Good News (Romans 10:16). Without the benefit of really knowing the Old Testament Scriptures and learning from esteemed Jewish leaders, this Gentile man understood the need to depend totally on Jesus' power. He knew, without a doubt, that Jesus could do what seemed impossible. Such faith both astonished and pleased Jesus.

7:10 Luke did not even record another word spoken by Jesus, but emphasized that the officer's faith had been well placed. The **officer's friends returned to his house** and **found the slave completely healed.**

JESUS RAISES A WIDOW'S SON FROM THE DEAD / 7:11-17 / 69

With a touch and his word, Jesus gave life. He had already healed a number of maladies: demon possession (4:35), sin (5:20), and all kinds of diseases (5:13, 15). Here Jesus clearly demonstrated his power over death.

7:11-12 The **village of Nain** was a few miles southeast of Nazareth and about a day's journey from Capernaum. Upon approaching the **gate,** they came upon a **funeral procession.** A woman led the procession, followed by the dead man being carried out, and then **many mourners.** A funeral procession—the relatives of the dead person following the body that was wrapped and carried on a kind of stretcher—would make its way through town. As the procession passed, bystanders would be expected to join. In addition, hired mourners would cry aloud and draw attention to the procession. What made this funeral especially sad was that the dead boy **was the only son of a widow.**

7:13 This woman had already lost her husband, and here her only son was dead—her last means of sup-

port. The crowd of mourners would go home, and she would be left penniless and alone. The widow was probably past the age of childbearing and would not marry again. Unless a relative would come to her aid, her future was bleak. In the first century, it was very difficult for a woman to earn her own living. Without anyone to provide for the widow, she would be an easy prey for swindlers, and she would likely be reduced to begging for food. No wonder **when the Lord saw** this sad sight and the tearful woman, **his heart overflowed with compassion.** In fact, as Luke repeatedly emphasized, Jesus cares about people's deepest needs. As Jesus' crowd met the crowd of mourners, Jesus went to the woman and gently said, **"Don't cry."** This would be an empty statement under most circumstances; however, Jesus, Lord over death itself, was going to change the circumstances. Jesus has the power to bring hope out of any tragedy.

7:14 Jesus again reached out to someone in need with compassion, risking becoming unclean. To touch even the bier would have made him unclean. Risking ceremonial defilement according to the law (Numbers 19:11-22), Jesus **touched the coffin.** Jesus approaching the procession and touching the coffin was highly unusual, so **the bearers stopped.** Then Jesus spoke directly to the body, **"Get up."**

7:15 Suddenly the boy who had been dead **sat up and began to talk.** What he said is left to our imagination, but the important point is that **Jesus gave him back to his mother.** Jesus did the ultimate act of compassion—he did what no human being could have done. These words are almost identical to 1 Kings 17:23 when the great Old Testament prophet Elijah brought a widow's only son back to life.

7:16 The miracle of raising a widow's son to life brought to the people's minds the story of Elijah

and the widow of Zarephath. The people **praised God,** and exclaimed that **a mighty prophet** had arrived among them. The people thought of Jesus as a prophet because, like the Old Testament prophets, he boldly proclaimed God's message and performed great miracles. Both Elijah and Elisha had raised children from the dead (1 Kings 17:17-24; 2 Kings 4:8-37). The people were correct in thinking that Jesus was a prophet, but he was much more—he was God himself. That they recognized **the hand of God at work** probably does not mean that they recognized Jesus as God. Instead, they were using an Old Testament expression that often denoted blessing (as in Ruth 1:6; 1 Samuel 2:21).

7:17 The obvious result of Jesus' miraculous act of raising a dead person to life meant that **the report of what Jesus had done that day spread** everywhere. The town of Nain is actually in the region of Galilee, so the word **Judea** is used here not for the region, but for the entire "land of the Jews" (as in 4:44). Word about Jesus went all over the country and beyond.

JESUS EASES JOHN'S DOUBT / 7:18-35 / 70

At this time, John the Baptist was in prison (see 3:19-20). King Herod, also known as Herod Antipas, had married his own sister-in-law, and John the Baptist had publicly rebuked Herod's blatant sin. In an attempt to quiet him, Herod had imprisoned him (see also Matthew 4:12; 14:1-5). "Are you the Messiah we've been expecting?" (7:19). Luke used John the Baptist's simple question as a springboard for exploring Jesus' identity. He was not merely a prophet (as the people recognized in the preceding section; 7:16), he was *the* Prophet, the promised Messiah.

7:18-20 John the Baptist had his own **disciples** who apparently were keeping in touch with him during his imprisonment. They **told** him **about everything Jesus was doing**—healing people, raising some from the dead, and teaching about a coming Kingdom. This caused John to wonder, so he called **two of his disciples** and sent them back to Jesus with a question, **"Are you the Messiah we've been expecting, or should we keep on looking for someone else?"** John had baptized Jesus, seen the heavens open, and heard the voice of God (3:21-22), yet something caused him to doubt. Perhaps John was wondering why Jesus brought blessing but little judgment, for John had preached that Jesus would baptize with the Holy Spirit and fire and separate the "wheat" from the "chaff" (3:15-17). Jesus' peaceful teaching and healing ministry may not have seemed to measure up. Maybe John wondered that if Jesus was the promised Messiah, why he didn't just say so. John,

like the rest of the Jews, expected Jesus to be the conquering Messiah-King. What did all the parables and veiled teachings mean?

7:21 The acts listed here that Jesus was doing consist of observable deeds that Jesus' contemporaries had seen and have reported for people to read today. The prophets had said that the Messiah would do these very acts (see Isaiah 35:5-6; 61:1). These physical proofs helped John—and will help people today—to recognize who Jesus is.

7:22-23 Jesus answered John's doubts by telling John's disciples to **go back to John and tell him what you have seen and heard.** Jesus gave specific examples of miracles he had done—some are recorded in the Gospels, probably many more are not. Jesus' actions revealed who he was—and Jesus knew that by telling the messengers to say this, John would come to the right conclusion. Then, as if in a postscript, Jesus told the messengers to tell

John, **"God blesses those who are not offended by me."** The word for "offended" suggests closing a trap. God's blessing would come to those who accepted Jesus' credentials and believed in him rather than being "caught and trapped" by their false expectations and thus missing him completely.

7:24 After John's messengers left, Jesus **talked to the crowd about John.** In case anyone got the wrong impression of John or thought that Jesus was rebuking him, Jesus set the record straight by explaining John's ministry. In the following verses, Jesus asks three questions and gives three answers. When John the Baptist began his ministry, he was preaching out in the **wilderness,** and people went out to see and hear him (3:3). Jesus asked if the people had found a man **weak as a reed.** A "reed" is the cane-like grass that grows on the banks of the Jordan River. To compare a person to a reed was to say that the person was without moral fiber or courage, easily tossed about by various opinions, never taking a stand on anything. The people did not see a weak and fearful person. Instead, the people witnessed John's fiery preaching and willingness to speak out against sin.

7:25 In a second question, Jesus asked if the people had trekked out into the wilderness **expecting to see a man dressed in expensive clothes.** Again, Jesus gave the answer—John's rough attire made of camel's hair (Matthew 3:4) was hardly expensive or **beautiful.** Someone dressed like that would be found in **palaces, not in the wilderness.**

7:26-27 In this third question, Jesus pinpointed the reason that the people had gone into the wilderness—they went out to see **a prophet.** In fact, they had seen, Jesus said, **more than a prophet.** Jesus described John as "more" because John alone had inaugurated the messianic age and had announced the coming Kingdom of God. More than being a prophet, John had been the subject of prophecy, fulfilling Malachi 3:1. Jesus changed the words "before me" to "before you," showing that the wording refers to Jesus as the Messiah. John was the last to function like the Old Testament prophets, the last to prepare the people for the coming Messianic age. John came to announce the arrival of the Kingdom; with Jesus Christ, the Kingdom arrived.

7:28 Of all people, no one fulfilled his God-given purpose better than John the Baptist. His role as forerunner of the Messiah put him in a position of great privilege with **none greater.** Yet in God's Kingdom, all who come after John have a greater spiritual heritage because they have clearer knowledge of the purpose of Jesus' death and resurrection. The **most insignificant person in the Kingdom of God** is a faithful follower who participates in the Kingdom. John would die before Jesus would be crucified and rise again to inaugurate his Kingdom. Because they will witness the Kingdom's reality, Jesus' followers will have privilege and place greater than John's. Jesus was not contrasting the man John with individual Christians; he was contrasting life before Christ with life in the fullness of Christ's Kingdom.

7:29-30 The obvious contrast here cannot be missed. The words are simple but their significance is profound. **All the people,** referring to the crowds, and even the **tax collectors** had come to understand an important truth. When these common, ordinary people, and these evil, self-serving tax collectors heard Jesus' words, they **agreed that God's plan was right.** Certainly John had done his job—these people were ready to accept Jesus because they had been prepared. They had listened to John's preaching (3:7-18) and **had been baptized by** him.

But the group who should have been most ready and most accepting **had refused John's baptism.** They had refused the repentance and confession that John had required (probably because they felt themselves already righteous and did not need to do so). **The Pharisees and experts in religious law** had rejected the forerunner of Jesus; the obvious result was that they also had rejected their own Messiah. Luke explained that in so doing, they had **rejected God's plan for them.** While they may have understood God's law, they had missed his purpose.

7:31-32 This generation referred to the people, many of whom were the religious leaders (7:30), who had rejected John the Baptist and so also rejected Jesus. Jesus condemned their attitudes. No matter what Jesus said or did, they took the opposite view. Jesus compared them to **children playing a game** in the central part of town where the town's business was conducted. These children played games, perhaps copying adults in either celebrating as at a wedding dance or wailing as at a funeral. Some wanted to play "wedding" and calling out to others to join them, but their companions ignored their invitation and didn't want to play. Then the children suggested playing "funeral," but the others again refused to play. Nothing they did could get their friends to join them; neither extreme pleased them. Jesus' generation, like the children in the square, did not respond to the calls issued by John the Baptist and by Jesus.

7:33-34 The religious leaders criticized **John the Baptist** because he **didn't drink wine and he often fasted.** Because he was so different, the religious leaders assumed that he was **demon possessed.** By contrast, Jesus (here calling himself **the Son of Man**) would **feast and drink.** But that did not satisfy the Jews either. They simply labeled him as **a glutton and a drunkard** who hung out with the lowest sort of people. Many of the Jews in Jesus' generation, including most of the religious establishment, simply refused to listen to either John or Jesus. Neither John's asceticism nor Jesus' enjoyment of life could please

the stubborn people who chose not to believe, no matter what was offered.

7:35 God's **wisdom** is seen in Jesus' deeds. People could see the Kingdom's power through Jesus' miracles. These miracles proved Jesus' teaching to be **right.** People might reject both the miracles and the teaching, but that will not change their truth nor will it hinder the Kingdom's arrival. **Those who follow** wisdom are the followers of Jesus and John. These followers lived changed lives. Their righteous living demonstrated the validity of the wisdom that Jesus and John taught.

A SINFUL WOMAN ANOINTS JESUS' FEET / 7:36-50 / 72

In this section, Luke continued to explore the two radically different reactions to Jesus' ministry (see 7:29, 30). In this passage, the blatant arrogance of the Pharisees and the wise humility of a sinful woman stand side by side.

7:36 While Jesus did dine with tax collectors and others whom the religious elite thought to be "sinners" (5:29-30; 7:34), he also would share **a meal** with a Pharisee (see also 11:37; 14:1). This Pharisee was named Simon (7:40). When guests came to a home, they would remove their sandals; then their feet would be washed by servants.

7:37 This **immoral woman,** who may have been a prostitute, went to see Jesus. A meal such as this was not a private affair; people could come in, sit around the edges, watch what went on, and listen to the conversation. Thus, this woman could have gotten in, although her reputation would proceed her and she would not necessarily be welcome among this company of people. So it probably took her great courage. The woman **brought a beautiful jar filled with expensive perfume.** Many Jewish women wore a small perfume flask on a cord around their neck. This jar of perfume would have been valued very highly by this woman.

7:38 Although the woman was not an invited guest, she entered the house anyway and **knelt behind** Jesus **at his feet.** These people were reclining as they ate, so the woman anointed Jesus' feet without approaching the table. She began **weeping,** and as **her tears fell on his feet, she wiped them off with her hair.** This woman understood that Jesus was very special. Perhaps she, as a sinner, had come to Jesus with great sorrow for her sin. Perhaps she had followed John the Baptist and had confessed her sins. She may have been in the crowds that had been following Jesus and had come to believe in him. She may have come to Jesus grateful for being forgiven and so offering him the gift of her valuable

perfume. To wash Jesus' feet was a sign of deep humility—it was the job of a slave.

7:39 The **Pharisee** looked over from his meal and **saw what was happening**—that is, he saw this woman with a notorious reputation in his house, near his table, weeping and pouring perfume on the feet of his guest. Any self-respecting rabbi would have realized this woman's sinful nature and recoiled at being touched by her—for to be touched by a sinner would make Jesus unclean and the Pharisees avoided any contact with "uncleanness." This Pharisee concluded, **"If God had really sent Jesus, he would know what kind of woman is touching him"** and would have told her to go away.

This religious leader had no concern for this woman's plight, no desire to lift her from her sinful life, or to help her become a better Jewish woman. Instead, he judged her as a **sinner,** shoved her aside, and presumed that any other rabbi (and especially one who was a "prophet") would do the same.

7:40 Jesus knew the Pharisee's **thoughts** and so **spoke up and answered** them (see also 5:22; 6:8). Simon had already made a judgment of Jesus and probably felt morally superior to him as well. But Jesus had asked for his attention, so he acted like the good host. **"All right, Teacher,"** Simon **replied, "go ahead."**

7:41-43 This creditor had one man who owed him **five hundred pieces of silver,** and another who owed him **fifty pieces.** It would not be difficult for Simon to see which debtor would love the creditor more if he **forgave them both** their debts. **"That's right,"** Jesus said.

7:44-46 Simon had committed several social errors in neglecting to **wash** Jesus' feet (a courtesy extended to guests because sandaled feet got very dirty), offer him the **kiss** of greeting, and anoint his head with **oil.** The sinful woman, by contrast, lavished tears, expensive ointment, and kisses on Jesus. In this story it is the grateful prostitute, and not the self-righteous religious leader, whose sins were forgiven.

7:47 This woman's act of humility and love show that she had **been forgiven.** Jesus did not overlook her sins. He did, in fact, know that this woman was a sinner (7:39), and he knew that her sins were **many.** But the fact that her many sins were forgiven caused her to overflow with much love for Jesus. The woman's love did not cause her forgiveness, for no one can earn forgiveness. Her faith in Jesus, despite her many sins, saved her (7:50). By contrast, self-righteous people, like Simon, feel that they have no sins that need to be forgiven, therefore they also have little love to show for it.

7:48 Although it is God's grace through faith that saves, and not acts of love or generosity, this

woman's act demonstrated her true faith, and Jesus honored her faith by telling her in no uncertain terms, **"Your sins are forgiven."** Jesus supported this woman and treated her with dignity. Believers need to demonstrate Jesus' approach in dealing with people.

7:49-50 The Pharisees believed that only God could forgive sins, so they wondered why this man Jesus was saying that the woman's sins were forgiven. They asked each other, **"Who does this man think he is, going around forgiving sins?"** They did not grasp the fact that Jesus was God and therefore did have the authority to forgive sins. But Jesus simply looked at the woman and said, **"Your faith has saved you; go in peace."** This woman's humility did not save her, nor did her tears or her expensive perfume. It was her **faith,** her complete trust in the only one who could forgive her sins and save her. When people trust Christ, he changes their lives, gives them freedom from sin, and gives them peace with God.

LUKE 8

WOMEN ACCOMPANY JESUS AND THE DISCIPLES / 8:1-3 / 73

In a culture where women played invisible roles, the fact that Luke mentioned the support of three women and highlighted a number of women in his Gospel indicates the interest Luke took in showing how women were involved in Jesus' ministry.

8:1-3 Jesus continued his mission **to announce the Good News concerning the Kingdom of God** (see 4:43; 7:22). The **twelve disciples** (named in 6:13-16) traveled with him—Jesus poured much of his ministry into them. As Jesus traveled and preached the Good News, he was also training the Twelve, preparing them for future ministry. The picture of **women** traveling with Jesus and his disciples would have been completely uncharacteristic of rabbis in ancient times. Rabbis refused to teach women because they were generally considered to be inferior. Jesus, however, lifted women up from degradation and servitude to the joy of fellowship and service. By allowing these women to travel with him, Jesus was showing that all people are equal under God. These women supported Jesus' ministry with their own money. They owed a great debt to him because **he had healed** some of them and **had cast out evil spirits** from others.

Mary Magdalene was from a town called

Magdala or Magadan (see Matthew 15:39). Jesus had **cast out seven demons** from her. The number of demons indicates the severity of the possession from which Jesus freed her. Mary stayed at the cross, went to the tomb, and was the first person to see the resurrected Christ (24:10; Mark 15:40, 47; 16:1, 9; John 19:25; 20:1, 18).

Joanna was **the wife of Chuza,** who was **Herod's business manager** (or steward). He may have been in charge of one of Herod Antipas's estates. Joanna is also mentioned in 24:10 as one of the women, along with Mary Magdalene, who told the disciples the news of Jesus' resurrection. Otherwise, nothing else is known of her; Joanna's husband is mentioned only here. Perhaps Luke's Gentile readers knew of this man and the exact nature of the office that he held. **Susanna** is found nowhere else in Scripture, and nothing is known about her. Perhaps Luke highlighted these three women because they would have been known to his readers.

Besides these women there were **many others who were contributing from their own resources to support Jesus and his disciples.** This provides an insight into how Jesus and his disciples met their basic needs. John 13:29 reveals that Jesus and the disciples had a common pool of money from which they bought food and gave to the poor, and that Judas Iscariot acted as treasurer. This passage tells the origin of that pool of money. People, like the women listed here, gave money to Jesus and the disciples out of gratefulness for what Jesus had done for them.

JESUS TELLS THE PARABLE OF THE FOUR SOILS / 8:4-8 / 77

Jesus began teaching in parables to get his listeners to think. These parables hid the truth from those who had their minds made up, having already chosen to reject Jesus. Yet those who truly wanted to know Jesus could listen carefully and learn more about the Kingdom of God.

8:4 Jesus often communicated spiritual truth through short stories or descriptions that take a familiar object or situation and give it a startling new twist—often called "parables." Jesus' parables compelled listeners to discover the truth for themselves, and they concealed the truth from those too lazy or dull to understand.

8:5 In this parable, Jesus used a familiar picture to illustrate an important truth about the Kingdom of Heaven. In ancient times, when **a farmer went out to plant some seed,** he walked across the field and scattered handfuls of seed from a large bag slung across his shoulders. The farmer scattered the seed liberally—and **some seed fell on a footpath.** The hard and compacted soil of the path meant that the seed did not sink into the ground and so it sat on top **where it was stepped on** and where **the birds came and ate it.** In 8:12 Jesus explains that the devil comes and takes away the gospel message from hard hearts so that those people cannot hear or be saved.

Jesus was speaking to the crowds about the Kingdom, explaining through this parable that the religious leaders' rejection of the Messiah did not change the truth. Jesus and the gospel were truth; there was no problem with them as there was no problem with the farmer or his seed. The only variable was the land (or the hearts) where the seed (the message) fell.

8:6 Other handfuls of seed **fell on shallow soil with underlying rock.** The footpath had no soil at all. But on the shallow soil, the **seed began to grow.** This type of soil was probably found in every farmer's field—most of the land in Palestine is very

rocky, filled with stones of all sizes. Soil on top of rocks traps the moisture so that plants can grow quickly, but the roots cannot go deep. The hot sun then dries up the water, causing the young plant to wither and die **for lack of moisture.** In 8:13, Jesus explains that those with hearts like this may hear the word and at first receive it with joy. But, like the crowds who followed, when the going gets tough, they fall away.

8:7 Thorns rob sprouts of nutrition, water, light, and space. Thus, when the **thorns** grew (weeds grow faster than wheat), the good seed was **choked out** and could not grow to maturity. In 8:14, Jesus explains that those with "thorny" hearts may receive the message, but then find it choked out by life's worries and attractions.

8:8 Some seed may be lost, but **other seed fell on fertile soil.** This soil had been plowed by the farmer and the seed had ample sunlight, depth, and moisture to be able to grow. The seed **produced a crop one hundred times as much as had been planted.** Normal yield for good seed would be seven- to tenfold. Any farmer would be overjoyed at such a tremendous yield, for it would mean even more seed to plant and harvest during the next year. In 8:15 Jesus explains that "fertile soil" people are those disciples who hear the word, hold on to it, and share it with others.

Jesus understood that not everyone who heard him speak would **listen and understand,** referring to a different kind of hearing, a deep listening with the mind and heart that opens a person to spiritual understanding. Jesus' words, like the farmer's seed, fell on various types of hearts.

JESUS EXPLAINS THE PARABLE OF THE FOUR SOILS / 8:9-18 / 78

The meaning of the parable of the four soils reinforces Jesus' differentiation between those who are given the secrets of the Kingdom and those who are not. The secrets of God's Kingdom are for those whom God has prepared.

8:9-10 This explanation probably occurred after Jesus and the disciples were away from the crowd. **"Disciples"** here probably refers to the Twelve and other true followers, such as the women described in 8:1-3. As soon as they were alone with Jesus, his followers **asked him what the story** (told in 8:4-8) **meant.** Jesus' stories were not always easy to understand, even to those closest to Jesus. The disciples may have thought that they should have understood the story without an explanation.

Jesus explained first that understanding of **the secrets of the Kingdom of God** comes as a gift to those he has chosen. That this knowledge is **permitted** reveals God's sovereignty. The word translated **"secrets"** refers to the "hidden" revelation of God, given to his true people at the proper time. The Kingdom of God was like an unknown secret to the prophets of the Old Testament—they wrote about it, but they did not understand it (as Romans 16:25-26 explains). The believers received spiritual insight that illuminated the secret so that it was no longer a mystery to them.

The parables allowed Jesus to give spiritual food to those who hungered for it. Isaiah's prophecy explains the situation of the **outsiders.** God told Isaiah that people would hear without understanding, and see without perceiving (Isaiah 6:9). That kind of reaction confronted Jesus. By quoting the prophet Isaiah, Jesus was telling his inner group of followers that the crowd resembled the Israelites about whom Isaiah had written. God had told Isaiah that the people would listen but not learn from his message because their hearts had hardened beyond repentance. Yet God still sent Isaiah with the message because, even though the nation itself would not repent and would reap judgment, some individuals would listen. Jesus came to the Israelites hundreds of years after Isaiah, but the words to Isaiah still applied. Most would not repent because their hearts were hardened; but a few would listen, turn from their sins, and believe.

8:11-12 Jesus' closest followers may not have immediately understood the meaning of his parable, but that did not mean they were hard-hearted. Jesus explained that the **seed** that the farmer sowed represents **God's message** to the people—the Good News of the Kingdom. **The seed that fell on the hard path** represents those, like the religious leaders, who **hear,** but **the message** cannot penetrate their hearts. The element of spiritual warfare is revealed here because **the Devil** himself **comes and steals** the message **and prevents them from believing and being saved.** "Footpath" people, like many of the religious leaders, refused to believe God's message. Satan locked their minds

and hearts and threw away the key. Though not beyond God's reach, their hardness will make it very difficult for them to ever believe.

8:13 Those who are like **rocky soil** are **those who hear the message with joy.** These people **believe for a while,** but Jesus explains that **their roots don't go very deep,** so when difficulty comes, they fall away.

8:14 The same seed also fell in the **thorny ground.** These people **hear and accept the message.** But as they go on their way, **the message is crowded out by the cares and riches and pleasures of this life.** These distractions and conflicts rob new believers of growth—they do not spend time in God's word or with God's people. So even though the seed has grown, it can **never grow into maturity.** Daily routines overcrowd and materialistic pursuits distract them, choking out God's word so that it yields nothing.

8:15 Of course, some of the seed falls on **good soil** or the farmer would not plant in that area at all. Good soil can be found—hearts open to the gospel message wherever the seed of God's word is sown. Those with hearts like "good soil" are those who **hear God's message, cling to it, and steadily produce a huge harvest.** These people have truly believed and are willing to let Jesus make a difference in their lives. Because of this, they also "produce a harvest" because they are willing to share what Jesus has done for them.

Sometimes people's lives can represent several different types of soil at once. A person may react like good soil to God's teaching regarding one part of life, but be "thorny" in another area. Believers are called to be like "good soil" all the time in all areas of life. Then God can continue to teach them, they can continue to mature, and they can share the message with others.

8:16 These listeners would have understood Jesus' reference to a **lamp** as being a lighted wick in a clay bowl that was full of oil. It would be ludicrous to light a lamp and then **cover it up or put it under a bed.** A lit lamp is meant to light up the room.

8:17 Although the truth may be **hidden** or kept **secret** for a while, it will not remain so. One day the truth will be **brought to light and made plain to all.** Jesus was speaking of the days of his ministry as the time of using parables and being rejected by many. The time of revelation and coming to light could refer either to Jesus' resurrection and ascension (when his followers would fully understand his words) or the Second Coming. Jesus' followers did not understand everything about Jesus at that time, but one day all their questions would be answered.

8:18 Because the teachings in the parables were so important for his followers to understand, Jesus warned them to **pay attention.** They needed to listen with understanding and then apply what Jesus said to their daily lives. To the people who listen and understand, **more understanding will be given** because their openness and perception of the Kingdom message will bring great rewards. They will continue to grow because they let God's word make a difference in their lives. Ultimately, of course, they will receive eternal blessings.

Those who are not listening will lose whatever they had—it **will be taken away.** Jesus' words here may have been directed to the Jews who had no understanding of Jesus and would lose even what they had—that is, their privileged status as God's people. Or Jesus might have meant that when people reject him, their hardness of heart drives away or renders useless even the little understanding they had.

JESUS DESCRIBES HIS TRUE FAMILY / 8:19-21 / 76

Jesus' proverbial remark, that his true family members are those who listen to God's word and obey it, reinforces the point of the preceding sections (8:8, 15, 18). Studying the Bible and applying it to all aspects of our lives are important marks of faithful followers of Christ.

8:19-20 Jesus' **mother** was Mary (1:30-31), and his **brothers** were the other children Mary and Joseph had after Jesus was born (see also Mark 6:3-4). According to Mark, the reason Jesus' mother and brothers **came to see him** was because they thought he was out of his mind (Mark 3:21). His mother and brothers **couldn't get to him because of the crowds.** Apparently Mary had gathered her family, and they had gone to find Jesus. Mary was hoping to use her personal relationship with Jesus to influence him. Standing at the edge of the crowd, Mary and the brothers relayed a message to Jesus. They thought that because of their relationship with him, he would make his way out to see them.

8:21 Jesus gave a respectful rebuke to his overly concerned mother; he was not severing ties with his earthly family. Through this incident, Jesus gave another lesson to his followers by explaining that spiritual relationships are as binding as physical ones. This would be the basis for the new community that Jesus was building—the Christian family. Therefore, Jesus told them that his **mother** and **brothers,** that is, those closest to him, **are all those who hear the message of God and obey it.** Jesus offers people an intimate family relationship with him. The types of people who can have a relationship with Christ are those who do the Father's will. They listen, learn, believe, and follow.

Obedience is the key to being part of God's family. Knowledge is not enough—the religious leaders had that and still missed Jesus. Following is not enough—the crowd did that but still didn't understand who Jesus was. Those who believe are brought into a family. In these words, Jesus was explaining that in his spiritual family, relationships are ultimately more important and longer-lasting than those formed in one's physical family.

JESUS CALMS THE STORM / 8:22-25 / 87

Following a section emphasizing obedience and faith in God's word, Luke placed a powerful demonstration of Jesus' supernatural power. Only God controls nature (Psalm 107:23-32), and here Jesus demonstrated his complete control over the wind and the sea, leaving his disciples thoroughly dumbfounded.

8:22 Jesus asked his disciples to **cross over to the other side of the lake.** Capernaum sat on the northwestern shore of the Sea of Galilee (also called a "lake" because it is inland). So Jesus and the disciples got into a **boat** (perhaps Peter's fishing boat) and began to cross to the eastern shore. Jesus' ministry was never without purpose. He was crossing the lake in order to enter a new area of ministry. Along the way, the disciples would be taught an unforgettable lesson about his power.

8:23 Mark explained that it was evening when they finally set sail (Mark 4:35). Setting sail in the evening was not unusual because Peter was used to fishing at night (see John 21:3). As the boat set out, Jesus fell asleep.

That **a fierce storm developed** was not necessarily unusual. The Sea of Galilee is relatively small (13 miles long, 7 miles wide), 150 feet deep, and the shoreline is 680 feet below sea level. Storms appear suddenly over the surrounding mountains, stirring the water into violent twenty-foot waves. The disciples had not foolishly set out in a storm. They usually did not encounter storms at night and did not see this one coming. Even though several of these men were experienced fishermen and knew how to handle a boat, they had been caught without warning by this squall and **they were in real danger.**

8:24 The disciples were in great danger, so they went to Jesus, waking him to tell him that they were all **going to drown!** Jesus **rebuked the wind and the raging waves.** The verb "rebuked" may indicate that there was an evil force behind the storm because the Greek words are the same as

Jesus used when he told the demons to be silent. With his rebuke, **the storm stopped and all was calm.**

8:25 Jesus' words to the disciples, floating in their boat on the now-quiet sea, were simply, **"Where is your faith?"** They ought not to have been afraid—they were with Jesus. They had seen him heal people, but power over a furious storm may not have crossed their minds. But they should have readily made the connection and have come to Jesus in faith, not in fear. This demonstration of power **filled** them **with awe and amazement.**

They asked the question to which they should have known the answer, **"Who is this man?"** This miracle clearly displayed Jesus' divine identity. Yet despite all that they had seen and heard thus far, and despite their love for Jesus, they still did not grasp that he was himself God, and thus had power and authority over all of creation.

JESUS SENDS THE DEMONS INTO A HERD OF PIGS / 8:26-39 / 88

The elements of nature and the evil beings of the spiritual world do not ignore Jesus' command, but people do. The Pharisees rejected God's plan (7:30), and the Gerasenes were more concerned about the economic loss of a herd of pigs. But all was not lost, for the man who had been liberated from the clutches of demons listened—intently. His soul was the "good soil" about which Jesus had spoken. Knowing this, Jesus commanded this man to stay in this Gentile region, testifying to God's goodness and producing an abundant harvest of faith.

8:26 After Jesus had calmed the storm, the boat arrived at its intended destination, for Jesus wanted to go to **the land of the Gerasenes.** This region was **across the lake from Galilee,** a Gentile region probably southeast of the Sea of Galilee, home of the Decapolis, or the Ten Cities. These were Greek cities that belonged to no country and were self-governing. This was Gentile territory (there would not have been a herd of pigs in Jewish territory, for Jews considered pigs to be unclean, see 8:32 and Leviticus 11:7) and that Jesus had planned to go there. Luke would want to show his readers Jesus' desire to go into Gentile territory with his message.

8:27 As soon as Jesus **was climbing out of the boat,** he met with demonic opposition. A man **came out to meet him,** but not as a welcoming party, for he was **possessed by demons** who probably wanted to scare away Jesus and the disciples.

A demon-possessed person lived in isolation and agony. This man was **homeless.** (Mark's Gospel describes him as uncontrollable, so he could not live anywhere, see Mark 5:3-5.) He was **naked** and lived **in a cemetery.** In those days it was common for cemeteries to have many tombs carved into the hillside, making cave-like mausoleums.

There was enough room for a person to live in such tombs. Finally, the text says that he had been in this condition **for a long time.**

8:28-29 The demons saw Jesus and recognized him and his authority immediately. So the demons caused the man to fall down before Jesus, not in worship but in grudging submission to Jesus' superiority. The man **shrieked,** and demanded, **"Why are you bothering me?"** Such a question shows the demons' ultimate rebellion. Jesus and the demons were as far separated as anything could be. Jesus' purpose was to heal and give life; the demons' purpose was to kill and destroy. The demon used Jesus' divine name, **Jesus, Son of the Most High God** and begged Jesus saying, **"Don't torture me!"** Demons recognize Jesus, understand who he is, know his power, and also seem to know their ultimate fate. Jesus has the power to "torture" them (see also 8:31). Their "torture" will be no more than the consequences for the rebellion (see Revelation 20:10).

Jesus had already commanded the evil spirit to come out of him. The power of the demon is revealed in that when the man **was shackled with chains, he simply broke** them. Although Satan is not as powerful as God, for he is a created being, he still exerts great power over this world. Satan's demons (there were more than one in this man) could cause this man to break iron shackles that were intended to hold him. Then the demons would drive him into the **wilderness.** Finally, the story also shows Satan's cruelty. For all that Satan might promise (see what he wanted to give Jesus, 4:6), he is a cruel and ruthless master. Those under his control face complete ruin under a master bent on destroying even those who serve him.

8:30 Whether Jesus was asking this poor man for his name or asking the demon for its **name** is uncertain. But the demon answered, saying that its name was **Legion.** A "legion" was the largest unit in the Roman army, having between three thousand and six thousand soldiers. Thus this man **was filled with many demons.**

8:31 The demons undoubtedly knew that Jesus planned to free their prisoner. Their concern at this point was **where** Jesus would send them. They knew where they did **not** want to go. They also knew that they had no power over Jesus and would have to submit to him. When the demons realized that they were face-to-face with Jesus himself, they begged **Jesus not to send them into the Bottomless Pit.** Also mentioned in Revelation 9:1 and 20:1-3, the Bottomless Pit is the place of confinement for Satan and his demons.

Why didn't Jesus just destroy these demons— or send them far away? Matthew 8:29 says that the demons asked not to be sent to the Bottomless Pit before the appointed time. They knew their ultimate fate, but the time for such work had not yet come. The same question could be asked today— why doesn't Jesus stop all the evil in the world? His time for that has not yet come. But it will come. The book of Revelation portrays the future victory of Jesus over Satan, his demons, and all evil.

8:32-33 The Gospel of Mark reports that this **large herd of pigs** numbered about two thousand (Mark 5:13). The demons pled with Jesus to **let them enter into the pigs,** so **Jesus gave them permission.** Satan has no final authority but can do only what God "permits" for the short time that he is allowed to be "god of this world" (2 Corinthians 4:4). Why Jesus gave them permission is as uncertain as why the demons wanted to enter the pigs. While Jesus could have sent them away, he did not do so because the time for final judgment had not yet come. Yet it is clear from this story that Jesus valued this one man far more than any number of pigs. The demons' ultimate destructive intent cannot be missed in the picture of **the whole herd**

(about two thousand pigs!) running headlong **down the steep hillside into the lake, where they drowned.**

8:34 The **herdsmen** on the hill, responsible for the safety of the pigs, were astounded when their herd suddenly ran away, down the hill, and into the Sea of Galilee. Terrified, surprised, and afraid that they would somehow be blamed for the disaster, **they fled to the nearby city and the surrounding countryside, spreading the news as they ran.** Certainly those who heard the news had to go and see for themselves, so a crowd soon surrounded Jesus, the disciples, and the newly freed man.

8:35 One would think that the people would have rejoiced that this man who had terrorized them for so long had been completely cured. But their response was quite different. They did not respond in joy or relief or welcome—instead, **the whole crowd was afraid.**

8:36-37 There could be no mistaking it, **the demon-possessed man had been healed.** But the people, overcome with **fear** told Jesus that they wanted him to leave. If they were afraid because of the loss of their livestock, it was foolish for them to value possessions, investments, and even animals above human life. Unfortunately for them, Jesus did as they asked—**returned to the boat and left.** And there is no biblical record that he ever returned. Sometimes the worst that can happen is for Jesus to answer a poorly considered request.

8:38-39 While the townspeople wanted Jesus gone, the formerly possessed man **begged to go** with Jesus, meaning that he wanted to become one of Jesus' followers. Jesus had other plans for him, saying, **"No, go back to your family and tell them all the wonderful things God has done for you."** This man would be returning to his home in a Gentile region. Jesus knew that this man would be an effective witness to those who remembered his previous condition and could attest to the miraculous healing. Through him, Jesus' ministry would expand into this Gentile area. Jesus would not remain in the region, but he did not leave himself without a witness, for this man **went all through the city telling about the great thing Jesus had done for him.** The Gentiles may have sent Jesus away, but they could not send away his message or the irrefutable miracle evidenced by this healed man. Luke's Gentile audience would have been glad to know that although Jesus had been sent away from this Gentile region, Jesus still had compassion and a desire for their salvation by leaving behind this man to be his witness.

JESUS HEALS A BLEEDING WOMAN AND RESTORES A GIRL TO LIFE / 8:40-56 / 89
In this story, Jesus took the timid faith of a woman and transformed her into a powerful, public testimony of him. Then he gently encouraged the grief-stricken Jairus to believe in him.

8:40-42 Jesus returned across the Sea of Galilee, back to Jewish territory, probably landing at Capernaum. In contrast to the crowd on the eastern shore that had asked him to leave, here **the crowds received Jesus with open arms.** A man in the crowd had apparently been waiting for Jesus to return. **Jairus** was **a leader of the local synagogue.** The synagogue was the local center of worship, and Jairus was a lay person elected as one of the leaders. The leaders were responsible for supervising worship services, caring for the scrolls, running the daily school, keeping the congregation faithful to the law, distributing alms, administering the care of the building, and finding rabbis to teach on the Sabbath.

Despite his status, Jairus **came and fell down at Jesus' feet, begging him to come home with him.** This would have been an unusual scene, but Jairus was desperate because **his only child was dying, a little girl twelve years old.** Jairus's position as a loving father overshadowed his position as a leader. He put aside any concern for himself and went directly to the man who had healed so many (perhaps even in his own synagogue, 6:6-11). Jesus went with Jairus; as usual, the crowds went along.

8:43-44 One **woman** also had been awaiting Jesus' return. Perhaps she had hoped to reach out to him when he came back and thus be healed. But Jairus got to Jesus first, and now they were walking away from her. Perhaps she thought this would be her only chance—she might not be able to talk to Jesus, but she knew she wanted to be healed.

Luke, the physician, wrote that the woman **had had a hemorrhage for twelve years.** Many **doctors** had tried to cure her, but with no success (Mark 5:26). The bleeding caused the woman to be in a constant condition of ceremonial uncleanness (see Leviticus 15:25-33). She could not worship in the synagogue, and she could not have normal social relationships, for under Jewish law, anyone who touched her also would become unclean. Thus, the woman had been treated almost as severely as a leper. That she was in the crowd at all was a courageous move on her part. If all those people bumping against her in the crowd had known her condition, she would have been in for some rough treatment.

Nevertheless, she also desperately needed Jesus.

So she pressed her way through the crowd, **came up behind Jesus and touched the fringe of his robe** for she believed, as did many people, that the clothes of a holy man imparted spiritual and healing power (see Mark 6:56; Acts 19:11-12). She may also have feared that Jesus would not touch her if he knew her condition because she would make him unclean. And she certainly did not want the pressing crowd to know that she had ventured among them. So she hoped to touch Jesus and then get away as unobtrusively as possible. The moment that she touched Jesus, **the bleeding stopped. Immediately** her pain was gone and she knew that she was healed.

8:45 The woman had hoped to disappear into the crowd. But Jesus knew about the healing the moment it happened. He asked the seemingly absurd question, **"Who touched me?"** While the **whole crowd** had been **pressing up against** him, no one close by had deliberately touched him. It wasn't that Jesus didn't know who had touched him. He wanted the woman to step forward and identify herself. Jesus wanted to teach her that his cloak did not contain magical properties, but that her faith in him had healed her.

8:46 Jesus persisted. He stopped the entire crowd, determined to find out who touched him. Jesus was talking about a different kind of touch— not the press of a person in the crowd but the deliberate touch of someone who wanted to be healed. Jesus knew it because **power** had gone **out from** him.

8:47 The woman realized that to try to slip away at that point would have been impossible. The woman came forward, trembling, and fell down before Jesus. She explained to the crowd **why she had touched him.** This was not a simple act— for she would have to explain how she—unclean and filled with a dreadful disease—had come in among the crowd, had reached out and touched a man (a rabbi) in her unclean state, and had hoped to slip away. All these were huge infractions of social laws and would have probably been grounds for anger from any other rabbi and any other crowd. But this was no ordinary rabbi, for she also explained that when she had touched Jesus, **she had been immediately healed.**

8:48 The woman may have been afraid of an angry backlash for her actions, but Jesus spoke to her in gentle words. She came for healing and received it, but she also received a relationship and peace with God himself because of her faith. Jesus explained that it was not his clothing that had healed her; rather, her **faith** in reaching out to the one Person who could heal her had allowed that healing to take place. Not only did the woman have faith, but she had also placed her faith in the right person.

The words **"Go in peace"** are more literally, "Go into peace." With this healing, Jesus gave this woman her life. Her cure was permanent. Jesus wished her peace of both body and soul— renewed health for her body and eternal salvation for her soul.

8:49 During this interval, Jairus had been waiting. Jesus **was still speaking** to this woman who had interrupted his walk to Jairus's house when **a messenger arrived.** What Jairus feared most had happened. His dear little girl had died. It was too late for the Teacher to heal her, so there was no longer any reason to bring Jesus to his home. Apparently Jairus hadn't heard that Jesus could raise the dead (7:11-15)—or perhaps he thought it would be too much to ask.

8:50 Upon hearing the news, Jairus surely reacted in great sorrow. It seemed that the delay had been too long, and it was now too late. But Jesus turned to the grieving man and said, **"Don't be afraid. Just trust me."** In the presence of Jairus, the woman had been commended for her faith. Here in the presence of the woman, Jairus was told to have faith. He had believed that Jesus could heal his daughter; Jesus wanted him to continue to believe that his daughter would **be all right.** The fact that the daughter had died did not change anything for Jesus.

8:51 Apparently Jairus did continue to believe, for he led Jesus the rest of the way to his house. The crowd still followed, perhaps all the more curious wondering what Jesus would do in this seemingly impossible situation. **When they arrived at the house,** however, Jesus took control and made everyone stay outside. The only people who entered with him were **Peter, James, John,** and the child's parents. These three particular disciples had become Jesus' inner circle to whom he gave special teaching and consideration (they were the only ones to see his transfiguration, see Matthew 17:1; also Mark 13:3; 14:33).

8:52-53 The house full of people probably included relatives and neighbors, as well as professional mourners who may have already arrived. Lack of **weeping and wailing** was the ultimate disgrace and disrespect. Jairus, the leader of the synagogue, was an important person in the town. Thus, at the death of his only daughter, the townspeople demonstrated their great love and respect by their intense grief. Yet their weeping turned to derisive laughter at Jesus' words that the girl was not dead, **only asleep.** She was indeed dead, but Jesus would bring her back to life, as if awakening her from sleep. Jesus used the image of sleep to indicate that the girl's condition was temporary and that she would be restored. For Jesus, death is nothing more than sleep, for he has power and authority over death.

8:54-55 Again Jesus went against all ceremonial law and **took** the dead girl **by the hand.** Touching a dead body would make a person unclean, but Jesus often would go past such laws in order to show compassion on those in need. He could have raised the girl without touching her (as he did Lazarus, John 11:43-44), but in this case, he chose to take her hand. Jesus' words were simple and direct, **"Get up, my child!"** While Mark recorded the words in Aramaic (Mark 5:41), as Jesus most likely said them, Luke translated for his Gentile audience. With those words, **her life returned.** She came back well, whole, and able to walk around. She was even well enough to eat, for Jesus gave her parents instructions to **give her something to eat.**

8:56 The young girl's **parents were overwhelmed** and certainly overjoyed. Jesus told the parents **not to tell anyone** about their daughter's healing because he knew that the facts would speak for themselves. Jesus was not attempting to keep this a secret, for the crowd outside was waiting and would see what had happened. Jesus was concerned for his ministry. He probably was asking them to keep to themselves the details of what he had done. He did not want to be known as just a miracle-worker; he wanted people to listen to his words that would heal their broken spiritual lives. Jesus' mission was to preach the Good News of the Kingdom of God. If crowds descended on him to see dead people raised, they would not be coming with the attitude needed to hear and respond to the gospel.

LUKE 9

JESUS SENDS OUT THE TWELVE APOSTLES / 9:1-6 / 93

After giving examples of Jesus' pattern of preaching about the Kingdom of God and of his power through all types of miracles, Luke reported how Jesus sent out the Twelve to continue this work. This begins two missionary trips (9:1; 10:1). Luke is the only Gospel writer that includes two trips, and the disciples probably were sent on other trips as well. Jesus gave the Twelve some instructions and then sent them on a "training mission." They would soon be the ones left to carry on Jesus' work after he was gone.

9:1-2 Jesus had chosen twelve disciples for special training (6:13-16). The men had traveled with Jesus, observed him, and listened to his teaching. Now they were to take a more active part in Jesus' ministry; they themselves would go out to **tell everyone about the coming of the Kingdom of God.** More than that, Jesus also **gave them power and authority to cast out demons and to heal all diseases.** That was important because these miracles backed up the message. Jesus sent out **his twelve apostles** and gave them this power. The message of the Good News was of primary importance, but the healings showed God's great compassion and fulfilled the ancient prophecies of the Messiah's arrival (4:18-19).

9:3-4 The disciples were to travel light. The urgency of their task required that they not spend time preparing for the trip. Besides, it was to be a short trip after which they would come back and report to Jesus. As disciples sent by God, they were to depend on him and on the people to whom they ministered to meet their needs. In addition, whatever **home** showed them hospitality was the home where they were to stay until they left that town. The disciples were not to offend their hosts by moving to a home that was more comfortable or socially prominent. To remain in one home was not a burden for the homeowner because there would only have been two together at a time and their stay in each community would be short.

The disciples were instructed to depend on others while they went from town to town preaching the gospel. This had a good effect: (1) it clearly showed that the Messiah had not come to offer wealth to his followers; (2) it forced the disciples to rely on God's power and

not on their own provision—they carried no outward symbols of authority, only the inward power that Christ gave them; (3) it involved the villagers and made them more eager to hear the message. This was an excellent approach for the disciples' short-term mission; it was not intended, however, to be a permanent way of life for them. Jesus' instructions pertained only to this particular mission, so this would not be a command for missionaries today. Different times and situations would call for different measures, both then and now.

9:5 The disciples could be sure of finding hospitality from some people, but Jesus told them to also expect places where they would not be welcomed. Jesus' instructions for such a town was that as the disciples were leaving, they were to **shake off its dust** from their feet. Shaking off dust that had accumulated on one's sandals showed extreme contempt for an area and its people, as well as the determination not to have any further involvement with them. Pious Jews would do this after passing through Gentile cities to show their separation from Gentile practices. If the disciples shook the dust of a *Jewish* town from their feet, it would show their separation from Jews who rejected their Messiah. This action also showed that the disciples were not responsible for how the people responded to their message.

9:6 Six teams of two **began their circuit of the villages**—perhaps going back to villages in which Jesus had already preached, or going where he did not have time to go (4:14-15, 43-44). They went with Jesus' authority and power—**preaching the Good News and healing the sick.**

HEROD KILLS JOHN THE BAPTIST / 9:7-9 / 95
The ministry of Jesus and his disciples was effective. The gospel message even reached Herod, leaving him questioning: "Who is this man?"

9:7-8 Herod Antipas was the king who had imprisoned and executed John the Baptist, and he would later hear Jesus' case before the crucifixion (23:6-12). Herod was **worried and puzzled** because a man and his disciples were traveling around doing miracles and teaching a message that, once reported to Herod, sounded eerily like the message that John the Baptist had taught. In addition, some were saying that John had **come back to life again.** Herod thought that John had come back to life to trouble him some more. Others thought that **Elijah or some other ancient prophet** had **risen from the dead.** While John the Baptist had been widely regarded as a prophet (and the first prophet to the nation in over four

hundred years), the people had refused to listen to him.

9:9 For the story of how Herod had **beheaded John,** see Matthew 14:1-12 and Mark 6:14-29. Herod may have had some guilt-pangs, for he had beheaded an innocent man who had done no more than speak the truth. So it bothered Herod that this good man, considered by everyone to be a prophet, may have come back to life. This certainly caused Herod to think twice about this man and try **to see him—** perhaps Herod thought he might be able to recognize him or talk to him. Luke did not include the details surrounding John's death, focusing instead on Herod's question, **"Who is this man about whom I hear such strange stories?"**

JESUS FEEDS FIVE THOUSAND / 9:10-17 / 96
Apart from Jesus' resurrection, this is the only miracle that appears in all four Gospels, showing its importance to Jesus' ministry and to the early church. While many people have tried to explain away the incident, it is clear that all the Gospel writers saw this as a marvelous miracle.

9:10 The word "apostle" means "one sent" as a messenger, authorized agent, or missionary. The word became an accepted title for Jesus' twelve disciples after his death and resurrection (Acts 1:25-26; Ephesians 2:20). The **apostles** had completed their teaching mission (9:6) and thus were official "sent ones." They **returned** to Capernaum and **told Jesus everything they had done.** Jesus wanted to hear how their training mission, their "student teaching," had gone. In order to do this, he needed to get them away from the crowds. So they withdrew by themselves to **the town of Bethsaida.**

9:11 The disciples needed rest; Jesus wanted quiet teaching time with them, but this was not to be. **The crowds found out where he was going, and they followed him.** Matthew wrote that they had gone by boat, and the crowds went on foot and met Jesus when he landed (Matthew 14:13-14). Far from being upset by the interruption of their plans, Jesus **welcomed** the people, using the opportunity afforded by their interest to teach them **about the Kingdom of God.**

9:12 Jesus' teaching about the Kingdom of God (9:11) lasted until the evening. As the day was drawing to a close, the disciples certainly wondered when they would have time alone with

Jesus. So they went to Jesus and suggested that he **send the crowds away** so they would have time to get food and lodging in the surrounding villages. The place where Jesus had been teaching was **deserted,** far from any town or village. It was near Bethsaida, east of the lake about four miles from Capernaum.

9:13 These disciples, already tired, meant to be compassionate in their request for Jesus to send the crowd away to get food before nightfall. Jesus' response certainly surprised them, for he said, **"You feed them."** A check of the resources had yielded **five loaves of bread and two fish**—John's Gospel explains that these belonged to a boy (John 6:9). The disciples had just come back from a teaching tour in which they had used Jesus' authority to preach and heal. But apparently they couldn't see past the obvious in this situation.

9:14-15 No wonder the disciples were a little dismayed at Jesus' command to feed this crowd. Luke fills us in on the detail that **there were about five thousand men there.** The Greek word translated "men" is *andres,* meaning not "people" but "male individuals." Therefore, there were five thousand men in addition to the women and children.

The disciples didn't understand what Jesus wanted them to do, so he gave them a job and prepared to show them that little is much when God is in charge. The disciples followed Jesus' instructions to have everyone **sit down on the ground in groups of about fifty each.** The people, perhaps realizing that this would be worth staying for, **all sat down.**

9:16 Jesus took the small lunch provided by the boy and **asked God's blessing on the food.** Then he gave the **bread and fish to the disciples to give to the people.** As Jesus broke the loaves, a miracle happened. The disciples began serving the groups of people, and the supply never diminished.

This miracle certainly helped a hungry crowd, but it had a higher purpose and theology. God, who multiplied the bread, was authenticating Jesus as his Son and portraying the munificent blessings

of the Kingdom. Just as God had provided manna to the Hebrews in the wilderness (Exodus 16), had multiplied oil and meal for Elijah and the widow at Zarephath (1 Kings 17:7-16) and for Elisha (2 Kings 4:1-7), and had multiplied twenty loaves to feed one hundred men (2 Kings 4:42-44), he was providing bread for the people on this day. This also points to the prophesied feast that the Messiah will abundantly provide for people in the wilderness (see also 13:29; 14:15-24; Isaiah 25:6, 9).

9:17 The disciples continued serving food, and the food continued to be supplied in abundance. **They all ate as much as they wanted.** Not only that, but there were enough **leftovers** to fill **twelve baskets.** The disciples collected the leftovers and may have taken them along for their own provision for a couple of days. While Jesus could have, he did not make a habit of supplying food out of nothing for himself and the disciples.

PETER SAYS JESUS IS THE MESSIAH / 9:18-20 / 109

Peter's confession that Jesus is the Christ, the promised Messiah, marks a turning point in this Gospel. Luke had been meticulously recording the reactions of people to Jesus and his message and their questions revolving around Jesus' identity. Peter gave a clear answer to Jesus' identity.

9:18 Apparently the disciples and Jesus did at times get to be alone, for here we find Jesus and his disciples together, away from the crowds. **Jesus was alone, praying.** That the Son of God often took time to pray was certainly an example to his disciples, as well as to all who follow him (see also 3:21; 6:12; 11:1).

Then he asked his disciples, **"Who do people say I am?"** What had the disciples heard—perhaps this information would come from what they had learned on their preaching tour (9:6).

9:19 The disciples' answer echoes what the crowds had been saying and what Herod had heard (9:8). This belief may have come from Deuteronomy 18:18, where God said he would raise up a prophet from among the people. (For the story of **John the**

Baptist, see Mark 1:1-11; 6:14-29. For the story of **Elijah,** see 1 Kings 17–21 and 2 Kings 1–2.) All of these responses were incorrect, revealing that the people still didn't recognize Jesus' true identity.

9:20 People may have had various opinions and ideas about Jesus' identity, but Jesus was concerned about what his chosen twelve believed about him. So he asked, **"Who do you say I am?"** The word "you" is plural; Jesus was asking the entire group. But Peter, who often acted as their spokesman, answered. Peter's ready answer reveals a deep insight into Jesus' identity, for he said, **"You are the Messiah sent from God!"** Peter did not understand the exact nature of Jesus' ministry, but he knew one fact for sure—Jesus was the Messiah.

JESUS PREDICTS HIS DEATH THE FIRST TIME / 9:21-27 / 110

Jesus responded to Peter's confession that he was the Messiah with a prophecy of his own death and resurrection. Most Jews at this time were expecting a political messiah, a person who would deliver them from their subjection to the Romans. To correct this, Jesus depicted his suffering and death at the hands of the religious leaders (see 9:43-45).

9:21-22 Jesus **warned** his disciples **not to tell anyone** that he was the Christ because at this point they

didn't fully understand the significance of that confession of faith. Even though Jesus was the Messiah, he still had to **suffer many terrible things, be rejected,** and **be killed.** Jesus then added that after all those tragic events occurred, **three days later** he would **be raised from the dead.** When the disciples saw all this happen to Jesus, they would understand what the Messiah had come to do and the kind of Kingdom he was preparing. Jesus here called himself **Son of Man,** a title emphasizing that he had power and authority from God himself. The Son of Man was the figure prophesied by Daniel to come as God's agent to gather his people and to be their judge. Only then would they be equipped to share the gospel around the world.

9:23 Jesus didn't make following him sound very easy. To his disciples who may have been hoping to have special positions in Jesus' earthly kingdom (22:24), these would have been hard words to hear. Denying one's personal desires and taking up a cross in order to follow this man was not what most of them had bargained for.

To **put aside** one's **selfish ambition** means a willingness to let go of selfish desires and earthly security. "Self" is no longer in charge; God is. Too often this has been interpreted to mean that believers should have no self-esteem. Some discipleship or "deeper life" strategies have advocated stripping oneself of all dignity or anything that contributes to a sense of self-worth. Jesus' view of denial was immediate and practical. They would need this attitude in the days ahead. They would need a willingness to set aside their own desires in order to spread the Good News.

To **shoulder** one's **cross daily** means to follow Jesus to the death if necessary. When Jesus used this picture of his followers taking up their crosses, everyone knew what he meant. Death on a cross was a form of execution used by Rome for dangerous criminals. A prisoner would carry his own cross to the place of execution, signifying submission to Rome's power. Following Jesus, therefore, meant identifying with Jesus and his followers, facing social and political oppression and ostracism, and no turning back. And this would not be a once-for-all deal—believers would need to be willing to take up this cross "daily" as they faced new situations, new people, new problems.

To **follow** Jesus means recognizing that belief is only the beginning of discipleship. Following Jesus doesn't mean walking behind him, but taking the same road of self-denial and self-sacrifice. Because Jesus walks ahead, he provides an example and stands with his followers as encourager, guide, and friend.

9:24 As the Messiah must suffer and die (9:21-22), so his followers must realize that they must not grasp selfishly onto their own lives. Those who want to **keep** life for themselves strive to get only the best for themselves. Such people will try to hold on to earthly rewards and security only to find that in the end, they **lose.** By contrast, however, those who generously **give up** their lives, willing to lose them if necessary for the sake of Jesus and the Kingdom, **will find true life.** That person will have given up in order to gain, and what is gained is of greater value indeed for it is eternal. Those who invest their life for Christ and his Kingdom will receive eternal life, as well as the satisfaction of serving God on earth. Those who give up control to God find that he fills their lives with himself.

9:25 Many people are willing to turn away from Christ in order to stay in a relationship, hold on to a sin, or stay on a career path. Jesus explained, however, that even if someone could **gain the whole world,** it would be of no **benefit** if it means losing his or her **soul in the process.** The answer to Jesus' question, then, is that nothing is so valuable that it can be exchanged for one's soul. In order to gain the whole world, one would have to worship the ruler of this world—Satan—because this is the offer he made to Jesus (4:5-7). Even if a person could gain the whole world, that person would lose his or her soul—and the soul counts for eternity.

9:26 If people are **ashamed** of Jesus and his **message,** he **will be ashamed** of them at his second coming (they would be rejected from eternal life with him). In the Bible, "ashamed" means more than embarrassment. It refers to the judgment of God (Isaiah 44:11), repentance (Ezekiel 43:10), or submission before God (Micah 7:16). When Jesus judges unbelieving people, his "being ashamed of them" means that he will reject them when he returns in **glory.** This indicates the Second Coming—the time of future judgment when present life ceases and everyone will be judged for their decisions about Jesus Christ.

9:27 When Jesus said that some of those who were with him would **not die** before seeing **the Kingdom of God,** he may have been referring to: (1) Peter, James, and John, who would witness the Transfiguration eight days later, or in a broader sense (2) all who would witness the resurrection and ascension, or (3) to all who would take part in the spread of the church after Pentecost. Jesus' listeners would not have to wait for another, future Messiah—the Kingdom was among them, and it would soon come in power. Jesus' Transfiguration, which follows, previewed the Kingdom of God.

JESUS IS TRANSFIGURED ON THE MOUNTAIN / 9:28-36 / *111*

Drowsily, Peter, James, and John awoke to an extraordinary sight—Moses and Elijah, with Jesus, standing together in a moment of glorious heavenly splendor. Stunned—Peter blurted out that he would build three shrines. Peter's instant reaction was to commemorate this moment of glory, at this very site. But God himself answered Peter. No shrines were needed; instead the disciples needed to recognize Jesus' unique identity—that he was God's Son—and obey what he told them to do.

9:28 Three of Jesus' disciples did indeed get a glimpse of the Kingdom of God within days of Jesus' pronouncement (9:27). Jesus singled out **Peter, James, and John** for this special revelation of his glory and purity. These three disciples comprised the inner circle of the Twelve (see 8:51; Mark 14:33). Jesus took them with him and went **to a mountain to pray.** This "mountain" is traditionally considered to have been either Mount Hermon or Mount Tabor.

9:29 As Jesus **was praying, the appearance of his face changed, and his clothing became dazzling white.** This revealed Jesus' true glory and purity. While Luke avoided the word "transfiguration," what occurred was an outward change that came from within—he appeared glorious because he was divine. On earth, Jesus appeared as a man; at this time, he was transformed into the glorious radiance that he will have in heaven.

9:30-31 Moses and Elijah appeared with Jesus. Both of these men had, during their time on earth, met with God on a mountain (Exodus 24; 1 Kings 19). Both men also had departed from this earth in an unusual way—Elijah was taken up into heaven in a whirlwind (2 Kings 2:11); Moses was buried by the Lord (Deuteronomy 34:6), and the location of his body became a matter of great speculation (Jude 9). These men represented the sweeping vista of God's plan of salvation across the ages. Moses represented the Law, or the Old Covenant. He had written the Pentateuch and had predicted the coming of a great prophet (Deuteronomy 18:15-19). Elijah represented the prophets who had foretold the coming of the Messiah (Malachi 4:5-6).

These men were **speaking of how** Jesus **was about to fulfill God's plan by dying in Jerusalem.** Jesus' death would accomplish true freedom for all people who believe in him. It would happen according to God's divine plan (see 1 Peter 1:19-20).

9:32-33 Apparently Jesus had been spending a long time in prayer; Peter, John, and James **had fallen asleep.** The display of dazzling glory awakened them. When it seemed that Elijah and Moses were going to leave, Peter spoke up and suggested making **three shrines.** Peter wanted to keep Moses and Elijah with them. But this was not what God wanted. While these three disciples got a glimpse of Jesus' future glory, they had to realize that this did not erase Jesus' previous words of suffering and death for himself (9:21-22). Peter also mistakenly treated these three men as equals—he was missing Jesus' true identity as God himself. He called Jesus **Master** (meaning "Teacher"), when this glorious display should have shown him that Jesus was far more. No shrines would be built; no one was going to stay. Moses and Elijah would return to glory; Jesus would walk back down the mountain and head toward Jerusalem. There would be no shortcuts.

9:34-35 Even as Peter was blurting out words that he shouldn't have been saying, **a cloud came over them** and **covered them.** This "cloud" was actually the glory of God—the same glory that had guided Israel out of Egypt (Exodus 13:21), had appeared to the people in the wilderness (Exodus 16:10; 24:15-18; 34:5; 40:34-38), had appeared to Moses (Exodus 19:9), and had filled the Temple (1 Kings 8:10). No wonder **terror gripped** the three disciples. Then, as had happened at Jesus' baptism, a **voice** came from **the cloud**—the voice of God himself (3:22). God gave divine approval of his Son, separating him from Moses and Elijah by saying that Jesus was the **Son,** the **Chosen One** and that the disciples must **listen to him.** The voice affirmed, both at the Baptism and at the Transfiguration, that Jesus was the one sent by God and the one whose authority came directly from God.

9:36 The glory disappeared, the cloud went away, the voice finished speaking, Moses and Elijah left, and Jesus looked once again like an ordinary man. **Jesus was there alone** with his disciples. Jesus would return to glory, but he would first follow the path of suffering and seeming defeat on this earth. Only then could he fully accomplish the plan of salvation.

The three disciples kept quiet about this entire

experience, not telling anyone **what they had seen until long after.** Matthew and Mark wrote that Jesus ordered the disciples not to tell anyone about this until he had risen from the dead—then they could talk about it, presumably because then they would better understand it (Matthew 17:9; Mark 9:9).

JESUS HEALS A DEMON-POSSESSED BOY / 9:37-43A / 112

Luke closely tied the Transfiguration to this healing of a demon-possessed boy. The ignorance and unbelief of the disciples was the same issue that God had spoken about on the mountain. He had commanded Peter, James, and John to "listen" to Jesus. There was no reason for the disciples to be defeated by any demon; all they needed to do was to believe in Jesus and dedicate themselves to prayer (see Matthew 17:20; Mark 9:29).

9:37 Jesus, Peter, James, and John came down from the mountain. **A huge crowd met Jesus.** This crowd included the rest of Jesus' disciples, some teachers of religious law, and a group of followers and onlookers. Mark wrote that the disciples and the religious leaders were in an argument (Mark 9:14), which probably focused on the fact that the disciples had tried and failed to cast out a demon (9:40). The religious leaders may have been questioning the disciples' power and authority.

9:38-39 A man had brought his **only son** who was possessed by **an evil spirit.** While the symptoms described by the father sound much like an epileptic convulsion, the destructive intent of the demon was described by the father—the demon was **injuring** his son. This was more than mere epilepsy; it was indeed a case of demon possession. Mark's Gospel reveals that the boy could neither speak nor hear (Mark 9:17, 25).

9:40 This desperate man wanted his child to be freed from the demon, so he brought his son to Jesus and his disciples (the disciples had been given authority to heal demon possession, 9:1). But the disciples **couldn't do it.** The text does not explain the reason for their failure. Matthew explained it as the disciples' lack of faith (Matthew 17:19-20), Mark as a need for prayer (Mark 9:28-29). The disciples certainly tried, but the demon did not respond.

9:41 Jesus saw the failure of the disciples to cast out this demon as merely one more indication of the stubbornness and faithlessness surrounding him. The disciples were not singled out for rebuke, but they reflected an attitude prevalent in their society. Jesus would not stay with them forever; one day he would leave and the Spirit would come. The Spirit could help soften stubborn hearts. In the meantime, Jesus would battle this unbelief, but he would not leave this young boy in his horrible condition, so Jesus told the father to **bring** his son.

9:42-43a As if to show its anger that Jesus was now involved, the demon **knocked** the boy **to the ground and threw him into a violent convulsion.** It did not yell Jesus' name as did other demons, for this one was mute (4:34; 8:28; Mark 9:17), but it showed its displeasure. Jesus, however, simply **rebuked the evil spirit,** and it had no choice but to obey. As the boy was **healed** and returned to his father, the people realized that this was a **display of God's power** and they were filled with **awe.**

JESUS PREDICTS HIS DEATH THE SECOND TIME / 9:43B-45 / 113

While Jesus was still in the limelight, while the people were still marveling over his recent exorcism, Jesus took time to reiterate to his disciples that the path he was traveling was the way of suffering—the way of the cross (9:23-27). Jesus calls all his followers to that path.

9:43b-44 Jesus did not let this healing fill him with pride, for he knew that the path ahead did not hold earthly glory and honor. As the crowd murmured their wonder at Jesus, he turned to **his disciples** and reminded them a second time (see 9:21-22 for the first) that he was going to die. This time he added the element that he would **be betrayed.**

9:45 The disciples **didn't know what** Jesus **meant** about his death. They still thought of Jesus as only an earthly king, and they were concerned about their places in the Kingdom that he would set up (9:46-48). If Jesus died, the Kingdom as they imagined it could not come. Consequently, they preferred not to ask him about his predictions.

THE DISCIPLES ARGUE ABOUT WHO WOULD BE THE GREATEST / 9:46-48 / 115

This argument among the disciples about who would be the greatest highlights how they did not understand Jesus' mission (9:45). Jesus was trying to prepare these men for the suffering and rejection that would come. At the same time, however, the disciples were enjoying all the attention and even disputing with each other over who was the greatest. So Jesus called over a little child—considered the most lowly person in first-century society—to show them their false priorities.

9:46 Apparently this argument among the disciples was occurring away from Jesus, but they could not hide it from him (9:47). The disciples, still not understanding the true nature of Jesus' mission, were having **an argument . . . as to which of them would be the greatest.** Either they ignored Jesus' words about his death as they planned for the coming Kingdom, or they took his words to heart and wondered who would be in charge after he had died.

9:47-48 Jesus used this opportunity to teach his disciples a lesson about the "greatness" about which they were so concerned. He **brought a little child** as a visual aid. Jesus suggested that he and this child were peers—**"Anyone who welcomes a little child like this on my behalf welcomes me."** Jesus equated the attitude of welcoming children with a willingness to welcome him. This was a new approach in a society where

children were usually treated as second-class citizens. Jesus equated the attitude of receiving children with a willingness to receive him. Even more important is the profound truth of Jesus' identity—**"Anyone who welcomes me welcomes my Father who sent me."** Jesus was saying that he and God the Father were one.

The disciples had become so preoccupied with the organization of Jesus' earthly kingdom that they had lost sight of its divine purpose. Instead of seeking a place of service, they were seeking positions of advantage. Jesus used a child to help his self-centered disciples get the point. They were to have servant attitudes, being not "childish" (arguing over petty issues), but "childlike," with humble and sincere hearts. Greatness would be measured by attitude toward service—**"Whoever is the least among you is the greatest."** True greatness means to deny oneself, willingly serve others, and then follow and obey the Master.

THE DISCIPLES FORBID ANOTHER TO USE JESUS' NAME / 9:49-50 / 116

Here the disciples displayed their tendency to be a closed group. Jesus rebuked their attempt to be exclusive. His ministry was to empower and encourage all those who do good, not to limit and restrict. Christians must welcome and encourage all who serve in the name of Christ. Having the same Lord should cover a multitude of differences.

9:49-50 John was one of the inner circle of three, along with his brother James and Peter. Apparently he needed to clear something with Jesus— he may have felt concerned that they had done wrong, especially after this illustration about greatness through serving. They had seen someone using Jesus' **name to cast out demons** and they had tried to stop him. This was not an evil man, for apparently God was blessing him—the man was having success (as opposed to the disciples, nine of whom had just failed, 9:40). But the disciples stopped the man for one reason—**he isn't in our group.**

Jesus explained that they should not stop such a person; instead, they should have been thrilled

that there were other people through whom God was working, others who were on Jesus' side. Jesus made the point that with him there would be no middle ground—**"Anyone who is not against you is for you."** The disciples had been wrong to stop the man from exorcising demons in Jesus' name; and they were also wrong to think that they alone had a monopoly on Jesus' power. Jesus explained that no one would do such a miracle as exorcising a demon in Jesus' name and then turn around and publicly speak against Jesus. The man, whatever his motivation, had at least done a deed of mercy for a possessed person and had stood against Satan in so doing.

JESUS TEACHES ABOUT THE COST OF FOLLOWING HIM / 9:51-62 / *122*

Luke began an extended section of his Gospel presenting the teaching and parables of Jesus that, for the most part, focus on the cost of discipleship and the coming suffering that Jesus would endure. Jesus was preparing his disciples for the rejection, suffering, and death that he would experience.

9:51 Jesus knew that his time on earth was ending and that **the time drew near for his return to heaven.** In other words, Jesus knew that he would soon die and that this death awaited him in Jerusalem. As if needing to arrive on time for a pre-planned appointment, **Jesus resolutely set out for Jerusalem.**

9:52-53 Jesus was journeying from Galilee to Jerusalem, so he had to travel south. Samaria lay between Galilee and Judea, thus he would have to travel through that region. The animosity between the Jews and the Samaritans was so great that many Jews would go out of their way not to travel through Samaria, instead opting to cross the Jordan River and travel on the other side until they could recross. Jesus held no such prejudices, so he **sent messengers ahead** to go into a **Samaritan village** and **prepare for his arrival** (presumably to secure lodging for Jesus and the Twelve). Because the men were heading toward **Jerusalem,** however, the people in the Samaritan village **refused** to welcome him.

9:54-56 When the messengers reported back, **James and John** were furious. The disciples had been told that if they faced rejection in a certain town, they were to shake the dust from their feet as a testimony against the people (9:5). James and John did not want to stop there—they asked Jesus if they should **order down fire from heaven to burn them up.** Jesus **rebuked** their suggestion. The point here was that the village was not consciously rejecting Jesus; instead, they were rejecting this group of thirteen or more because they were Jews on their way to Jerusalem (9:53). The disciples were to take this rejection in stride and go **on to another village.** Whether this other village was in Samaria is unknown. There was no stopping Jesus; he continued resolutely toward Jerusalem.

9:57-58 Someone approached and wanted to **follow** Jesus. Matthew wrote that this man was a teacher of religious law (Matthew 8:19). Most of these leaders became Jesus' enemies, but at least one apparently recognized Jesus' authority and wanted to be his disciple. Jesus' reply, however, pointed out to the man the cost of becoming a disciple. Jesus did not grab onto disciples, eagerly taking anyone who wanted to follow. Those who truly wanted to be his disciples needed to understand that it would cost them something. While most of God's creatures have warm places in which to live and to sleep, the Son of Man had no home of his own, no place to lay his head. To be Jesus' disciple, a person must willingly put aside worldly security. The words are recorded for believers' benefit. Have you counted the cost of following Jesus? Do you understand that following Jesus is far more valuable than anything this world offers?

9:59-60 The previous man came on his own to Jesus (9:57-58); this time, however, Jesus asked another man to be his **disciple.** But this man explained that he **first** needed to **return home and bury** his **father.** The man was asking for permission to wait until his father died—an indefinite delay. The reason is not given, but whatever it was, the man wanted to do it "first." Whether his concern was fulfilling a duty, having financial security, keeping family approval, or something else, he did not want to commit himself to Jesus just yet.

Jesus' response: **"Let those who are spiritually dead care for their own dead"** points out that those who want to follow him should count the cost and set aside any conditions they might have. In other words, let those who are spiritually dying (those who have not responded to the call to commitment) stay home and handle responsibilities such as burying the dead. This may sound insensitive, but it had precedents. A high priest and those who had taken the Nazirite vow were required by the law to avoid the corpse of even a parent (Leviticus 21:11; Numbers 6:6-8). A later Jewish precedent says that if there were enough people in attendance, a student of the Torah should not stop his studying to bury the dead. Jesus placed commitment to God even above these precedents. As God's Son, Jesus did not hesitate to demand complete loyalty. Even family loyalty was not to take priority over the demands of obedience to the command to **go and preach the coming of the Kingdom of God.** Jesus' direct challenge forces believers to evaluate their priorities.

9:61-62 A third person approached and this one, like the first, expressed his desire to **follow** Jesus. However, this man also had something he wanted to do **first.** Jesus ascertained in this potential follower a sense of reluctance and an unfortunate willingness to put something else ahead of following Jesus. This was not the type of follower Jesus needed.

The picture of a person putting **a hand to the plow** and looking back can be compared with Elijah's call of Elisha in 1 Kings 19:19-21. Elisha was called to be a prophet right in the middle of plowing a field—and he never looked back. In fact, he slaughtered the oxen so that there would be no temptation to return. Elisha then moved wholeheartedly into the ministry to which he had

been called. Jesus explained that service in the Kingdom of God was of such vital importance that his followers must make it their top priority. They must step out in faith to serve him, without looking back.

What does Jesus want from his followers? Total dedication, not halfhearted commitment. His followers must accept the cross along with the crown, judgment as well as mercy. They must count the cost and be willing to abandon everything else that has given them security. Nothing should distract them from service for the Kingdom.

LUKE 10

JESUS SENDS OUT SEVENTY-TWO MESSENGERS / 10:1-16 / 130

Luke is the only Gospel to record the sending out of seventy-two disciples. In this passage, Luke highlighted and anticipated the universal mission of Jesus—the gospel would go to all people.

10:1 Far more than twelve people had been following Jesus. According to 1 Corinthians 15:6, Jesus had at least five hundred followers by the time he had finished his ministry. A group of 120 of these followers went to Jerusalem to begin the church there (Acts 1:15). Here Jesus designated a group of **seventy-two** to prepare a number of towns for his later visit.

The number 72 is found in the earliest Greek manuscripts. This number is significant for it was, according to Genesis 10, the traditional number of nations in the world, according to the Septuagint. Other Greek manuscripts read 70. This alternative reading may have been influenced by the Hebrew Old Testament, which lists seventy names in Genesis 10. By choosing and sending out seventy-two disciples, Jesus was symbolically showing that all nations in the world would one day hear the message. This would include the Gentiles—an important point for Luke's Gentile audience.

10:2 Jesus was sending thirty-six teams of two to reach the many towns and villages that he had not yet been able to visit. Jesus compared this work to a **harvest**—the gathering of new believers into his Kingdom (see also John 4:35). To have a harvest, however, one must have **workers** in the field. So many people need to hear the message, but there are so few workers willing to gather it in. Even as Jesus had sent the Twelve, and now seventy-two more, he told them to **ask** the Lord **to send out**

more workers for his fields. In Christian service, there is no unemployment. God has work enough for everyone. No believer should sit back and watch others work because the harvest is great.

10:3 The world into which these seventy-two were going was not a pleasant place. The harvest was going to involve intensive labor and possibly danger. Jesus commanded them to **go,** explaining that they were going out **as lambs among wolves.** The use of the word "lambs" refers to their vulnerability (see Isaiah 11:6; 65:25). But the important point is the four words, **"I am sending you."** If Jesus were not sending them, then they would be attempting to go on their own plans, their own power, their own itinerary, being lambs among wolves would be like asking to be slaughtered. But because Jesus was sending them, they might face danger from the opposition. Their very defenselessness would cause them all the more to depend on God.

10:4 These instructions are basically the same as those given to the Twelve in 9:3-4. The reason was the same—they were to travel light, spend no time preparing for the trip, and depend upon God and those to whom they ministered to meet their basic needs. So urgent is their task that they are not to **stop to greet anyone on the road.** Jesus did not mean for them to be impolite to people whom they passed, but rather that they were not to spend precious time on dallying by the wayside. They had to remain focused on their task.

10:5-6 The **home** that a pair of disciples would **enter** would be the home from which they would receive hospitality during their stay in a particular town. When they entered a house, they should give the characteristic **blessing.** This blessing conveyed the messianic peace promised in the Old Testament and stressed the authority based on power from God that was behind the missionary. If the householders **were worthy** (had a proper attitude toward God), then **the blessing** would **stand.** Such people would be open to the gospel message. But if the people were **not** worthy, the blessing would **return** to the one who had given it.

10:7 Jesus had also directed the Twelve to remain with their original hosts in any town (9:4). This instruction avoided certain problems. For the two disciples to **move around from home to home** could offend the families who first took them in. In addition, by staying in one place, the disciples would not have to worry continually about getting good accommodations. They could settle down and do their appointed task. The disciples were to willingly eat and drink what their hosts provided **because those who work deserve their pay.** Jesus told his disciples to **accept hospitality** graciously because their work entitled them to it. Ministers of the gospel deserve to be supported, and it is believers' responsibility to make sure they have what they need.

10:8-9 When the pairs of disciples entered a town, received a welcome, and entered a home, Jesus told them to **eat whatever is set before** them. It may well be that they would be welcomed into non-Jewish homes where the meals might not satisfy all the ceremonial laws of the Jews. Jesus told them not to be sidetracked about what they ate. Instead, they should do what they came to do—**heal the sick** (which was a signal that the Kingdom had arrived) and proclaim to the people that **the Kingdom of God is near** (see also 10:11; 21:31). This "nearness" meant both "already here" and "soon to come." The Kingdom Jesus began on earth would not overthrow Roman oppression and bring universal peace right away. Instead, it was a Kingdom that began in people's hearts and was as near as people's willingness to make Jesus king over their lives.

10:10-11 Jesus also gave instructions if the disciples should enter a town and not be welcomed. He made it clear that they would face rejection in some places. But the rejection of their message would not change the message. Even if the people refused it, the Kingdom of God was still near, but those who refused it would miss it. Jesus repeated the instruction of wiping **the dust** of that town

from their **feet** as a **public announcement of** their **doom** (9:5).

10:12 Sodom was a **wicked** city that God destroyed because of its great sinfulness (Genesis 19:24-28). The city's name is often used to symbolize evil and immorality. Sodom will face God's wrath at judgment day, but cities that rejected the Messiah and his Kingdom will face even worse wrath from God. A city as evil as Sodom would be **better off** than these towns because they had been given the opportunity to believe the Messiah—they had seen great miracles and had the Good News preached to them—but they had turned away and had refused salvation.

10:13-14 The mention of cities that might reject the Messiah (10:10-11) leads to a message of those who already had. **Korazin and Bethsaida** were cities near Capernaum, at the north end of the Sea of Galilee. Jesus had concentrated his ministry in and around Capernaum, so he must have performed **miracles** in these cities. These miracles are not recorded in the Gospels—there is much about Jesus' ministry that is unknown. **Tyre and Sidon** were pagan cities in Phoenicia, the territory north of Galilee. They had rebelled against God and had been judged and punished for their wickedness and opposition to God's people (see Isaiah 23:1-18; Jeremiah 25:22; 47:4; Ezekiel 26–28; Joel 3:4-8; Amos 1:9-10). Yet Jesus explained that, though these people were evil and rebellious, if he had come to them and had done miracles, they **would have sat in deep repentance.** The mention of **sackcloth** and **ashes** depicts mourning and repentance. A person humbled himself or herself by wearing only this rough cloth made of goat hair and sitting in a pile of ashes. Tyre and Sidon had not had that opportunity, while Korazin and Bethsaida had been visited by the Messiah who had done miracles among them; yet they rejected him. The punishment these cities would suffer on **the judgment day** would be far worse than what Tyre and Sidon experienced.

10:15 Capernaum was Jesus' base for his Galilean ministry (Matthew 4:13; Mark 2:1). Jesus had performed many miracles there, and apparently the people were feeling a certain amount of pride in their connection with Jesus. But many people of Capernaum did not understand Jesus' miracles or believe his teaching. Instead of being **exalted to heaven** as they might have thought because Jesus chose to live among them, they would **be brought down to the place of the dead** because they had seen the Messiah and rejected him. The language is reminiscent of Isaiah 14:12-15, where the prideful attitude of the king of Babylon is condemned. The

Greek word translated, "place of the dead," is *Hades*, the dwelling place of the condemned wicked people (16:23; Revelation 20:13-14). This pictured fiery judgment on this city that rejected Christ. Today the site of ancient Capernaum is desolate—a stunning picture of Jesus' words here.

10:16 Jesus' messengers are important people. They are sent with authority. In ancient times, when a person dealt with a messenger, it was the same as dealing with the person who had sent him (for example, see 7:3 and commentary). Therefore, people who accepted the message of Jesus' disciples were **accepting** Jesus. Likewise, people who rejected Jesus' disciples' message were **rejecting** Jesus. Because Jesus and God are one, anyone who rejects Jesus **is rejecting God who sent** him. These messengers could take their mission seriously because Jesus did—he was sending them out with his message and his authority.

THE SEVENTY-TWO MESSENGERS RETURN / 10:17-24 / 131

This passage continues the theme of discipleship (started at 9:51). Here the seventy-two returned, rejoicing. Jesus rejoiced with them, praising God for the defeat of Satan and the fact that he had chosen to use these humble followers to advance his Kingdom.

10:17 Some time had passed between 10:16 and 10:17. The **seventy-two disciples** completed their mission to various towns and villages (10:1) and returned with joy. They had seen tremendous results as they ministered in Jesus' name and with his authority. They were elated by the victories they had witnessed—that even the **demons** had submitted to them in Jesus' name. Probably they were able to heal demon-possessed people, and this thrilled them.

10:18-19 This could mean that Jesus **saw,** as in a vision, **Satan falling from heaven as a flash of lightning** (that is, from a place of power) during the ministry of these disciples. Satan suffered a notable defeat as these thirty-six pairs of men went around the countryside casting out demons.

Satan might attempt to discourage and harm Jesus' disciples, but when they were on this mission, nothing could harm them. Jesus had given them **authority over all the power of the enemy.** To **walk among snakes and scorpions** may allude to Psalm 91:13 where snakes are listed among dangerous creatures from which God protects the people of Israel. See also Deuteronomy 8:15 where scorpions and snakes are connected.

10:20 Such power and authority can be a heady experience, so the disciples were warned not to **rejoice just because evil spirits** had obeyed them. The main reason to rejoice was that their **names** were **registered as citizens of heaven.** Their ministry was not to become an experience of power leading to pride, but an experience of servanthood out of love for God and out of the desire for more people to join them in the Kingdom.

10:21 Jesus praised God, his **Father,** for making spiritual truth available **to the childlike.** Those who willingly submit themselves to God and do not depend upon their own wisdom will have the truth revealed to them. So often **the wise and clever** in this world refuse to submit themselves to God. They may not see their need for him, or they may think that their wisdom and learning have placed them in a separate class. These words of Jesus reveal God's sovereignty and initiative regarding who will receive divine truth. God has chosen to hide it from those who refuse and reject it (see 8:10), and instead reveals it to those who may not seem wise and learned but have trusting hearts (like little children, 9:47-48).

10:22 Jesus further identified his special and unique relationship with God the Father. So close and intimate, so completely trusting, that Jesus said, **"My Father has given me authority over everything."** The Father and the Son have an exclusive relationship that humanity at large cannot fathom. (Luke brought it up again in 20:41-44; 22:69; Acts 2:29-38.) Jesus' mission was to **reveal** God the Father to people. His words brought salvation down to earth. He explained God's love through parables, teachings, and, most of all, his life. By examining Jesus' actions, principles, and attitudes, those chosen by him are enabled to understand God more clearly. As used here, the word **chooses** does not refer to predestination; rather, it refers to Jesus' divine status and authority to reveal saving knowledge to people.

10:23-24 Old Testament men of God such as David and the prophet Isaiah made many God-inspired predictions that Jesus fulfilled. As Peter later would write, these prophets wondered what their words meant and when they would be fulfilled (1 Peter 1:10-13). In Jesus' words, they **longed to see and hear** what the disciples were seeing and hearing, **but they could not.** Despite their privileged positions as part of God's people and God's plan, many **prophets and** **kings** were not as blessed as this little band of disciples or all the "simple" people who came in faith to Jesus.

JESUS TELLS THE PARABLE OF THE GOOD SAMARITAN / 10:25-37 / *132*
Jesus had just praised God for hiding the secrets of the Kingdom from the wise and learned (10:21). Next an expert in Old Testament law asked Jesus a question that revealed the lawyer's profound ignorance about central issues of the faith—eternal life and the basic command to love one's neighbor.

10:25 This **expert in religious law** was a man who had made it his business to know and understand the details of the Jewish religion. He had studied the Scriptures (the Old Testament—the Law, the Psalms, and the Prophets). He also knew all the traditions. The fact that this man wanted to **test Jesus** does not necessarily indicate hostility. He wanted to know what he had to **do to receive eternal life.**

10:26-28 This expert in the law obviously would have known **the law of Moses.** In his answer, he quoted from Deuteronomy 6:5 and Leviticus 19:18. He correctly understood that the law demanded total devotion to God and love for one's neighbor. To love God in this way is to fulfill completely all the commandments regarding one's "vertical" relationship. But another command from the law says to love your neighbor. This refers to "horizontal" relationships—among people. A person cannot maintain a good vertical relationship with God without also caring for his or her neighbor. The word "neighbor" refers to fellow human beings in general.

The expert in the law had it right. Jesus explained that people only needed to obey these commands; in doing so, they would fulfill all the rest of them. But with these abrupt words, Jesus was subtly making the point that no one can obey these commands. **Do this and you will live** sounds simple—in reality, however, those commands are impossible to keep in our human strength alone. This would be the lifestyle of Kingdom people—but they would not have to "do" it in order to be saved. Instead, they would be saved and then enabled by the Holy Spirit to obey these impossible demands. Jesus would show this to the man in the following story.

10:29 The expert in the law would not leave the encounter there. He wanted to **justify his actions.** It is unclear if he wanted to justify the question he had asked by asking the teacher to delve deeper into the topic, or whether he wanted Jesus to give an answer that he could then say he had fulfilled.

He may have been attempting to pin down and limit the law's demand, thereby limiting his responsibility. So he pressed Jesus further, **"And who is my neighbor?"**

10:30 Jesus answered this legal expert by telling a story. The rest of his listeners could easily picture this **Jewish man** who was **traveling from Jerusalem to Jericho.** The distance was about seventeen miles on a road that was notoriously dangerous because it curved through rocky and desolate terrain with many hiding places for **bandits.** As the listeners may have anticipated, the man in this story, who was traveling alone, **was attacked** and left **half dead.**

10:31-32 Jesus told a story about three different people, also traveling alone on this road. This **priest** served in the Temple and probably offered sacrifices. The **Temple assistant** also served in the Temple. Both of these servants of God **saw the man lying there,** but both **passed by** without helping. Perhaps it was concern over defilement, for a Jew would become "unclean" if he came into contact with a dead body. This would render him unable to worship. The man on the road may have appeared dead, so they did not want to risk defilement if there was nothing they could do. Either way, they deliberately refused to help.

10:33-35 The next person to come along was a **despised Samaritan.** Jews hated Samaritans, so when Jesus introduced this Samaritan man into the story, the Jewish listeners would not have expected him to help a Jewish man. But in great detail, Jesus described all that the Samaritan did for this man. This Samaritan is pictured as understanding what it meant to help someone in need, to be a neighbor, regardless of racial tensions.

10:36-37 Having finished the story, Jesus asked the expert in the law who had been a **neighbor** to the wounded man. The legal expert had no choice but to answer that **the one who showed him mercy**—the Samaritan—had been the true "neighbor." The

Samaritan traveler and the Jewish man were far apart in distance and spiritual heritage, but the Samaritan had loved his neighbor far better than the hurt man's own religious leaders. Jesus said that the legal expert had answered correctly and should **go and do the same.** Jesus taught that love is shown by action, that it must not be limited by its object, and that at times it is costly.

JESUS VISITS MARTHA AND MARY / 10:38-42 / 133

This short story follows the parable of the good Samaritan because it involves another reversal. Mary was sitting at Jesus' feet listening to his teaching, while Martha was busying herself fixing a meal. Although intently listening to Jesus was Mary's way of expressing her love and devotion to God, in the first century, this would be quite unusual for a woman. Learning at a rabbi's feet was a privilege typically reserved for young men. Thus, Martha assumed that Jesus would honor her request that he rebuke Mary. Instead, Jesus commended Mary, welcoming her to learn from him.

10:38 The **village** where these people lived was Bethany, located about two miles outside of Jerusalem. **Martha** had a sister named Mary (10:39, who was probably younger because this home is described as belonging to Martha) and a brother named Lazarus (whom Jesus later raised from the dead, John 11).

10:39-40 Jesus did not come alone—he had twelve disciples with him who all needed to have their feet washed, to be made comfortable, and to have a meal prepared for them. A respectable hostess in the ancient world would extend all of these courtesies to his or her guests. The impression here, however, is that Martha was overdoing it. She wanted something extra special for the Master, but she let herself get to the point where she was **worrying,** overworked, and unable to enjoy these guests. In attempting to serve Jesus, she did not understand or attend to Jesus' reason for being there. Mary, however, **sat at the Lord's feet, listening to what he taught.** She was taking advantage of the opportunity to hear Jesus. Martha, for her part, wanted to give her guests the royal treatment—and she should not be criticized for that. However, she allowed her worry to turn to irritation. She went to Jesus and asked him to tell Mary to get up and get to work. There is a touch of reproach in her words.

10:41-42 Jesus did not blame Martha for being concerned about preparing the meal, nor did he scold her for attempting to make him and his disciples welcome. But he did want her to understand that because she was **so upset,** she was not making time for what was most important, shown in Mary's attitude. Jesus wanted Martha to rearrange her priorities. It is possible for service to Christ to degenerate into mere busywork that is no longer full of devotion to God. There was nothing wrong with Martha's desire to serve—someone had to do it or no one would have eaten. Perhaps she could have laid out a less lavish feast so that she too could have had time to sit at Jesus' feet and digest his teaching. But Jesus was not going to send Mary away to attend to housework. She had chosen to be at Jesus' feet, and Jesus knew that he would not be on this earth forever. His time would be short, and he would not send away those who wanted to listen and learn.

LUKE 11

JESUS TEACHES HIS DISCIPLES ABOUT PRAYER / 11:1-13 / 134

This passage highlights one of Luke's most prominent themes: prayer (see 1:9-10; 3:21; 6:12; 9:18, 28-29). Here the disciples asked Jesus about prayer—interestingly enough, it was after Jesus had been praying. Jesus gave them an example of a prayer and two stories that emphasize the importance of seeking God in prayer.

11:1 Once again, Jesus had **been out praying.** Luke has presented several instances where Jesus was praying, making it clear that prayer was a regular part of his life (3:21; 5:16; 6:12; 9:18, 28-29; 18:1; 22:41, 44). Something about Jesus' prayer life prompted **one of his disciples** to approach him **as he finished.** He wanted Jesus to teach them to pray, **just as John taught his disciples.** It was common for religious leaders to teach their followers how to pray. To be able to pray as their Master prayed would give them assurance of expressing themselves correctly to God.

11:2 The prayer Jesus taught his disciples was not a formulaic prayer; rather, it was a "how to" prayer. These were not meant to be magical words prayed like an incantation over and over. Instead, he was giving the disciples a pattern. Luke's form of the Lord's Prayer is shorter than Matthew's (Matthew 6:9-13). Most likely they were two distinct prayers on two different occasions. The differences in the prayers show that Jesus did not utter a rote prayer every time he prayed. Different occasions call for different utterances.

Notice the order in this prayer. First Jesus praised God; then he made his requests. The first person plural pronouns indicate that the believers could pray this prayer corporately. The pattern of praise, intercession, and request helps believers understand the nature and purpose of their personal prayers in their relationship with their Father. Because Jesus taught it to his followers, it is a prayer pattern for believers today as well.

The phrase, **Father, may your name be honored,** focuses on God as majestic and transcendent and says that the person praying is committed to honoring God's holy name. Christians, God's children who bear his name, must be responsible to "honor" God in every aspect of their lives. When believers pray for God's name to be "honored," they pray that the world will honor his name and look forward to the day when that will be a reality.

May your Kingdom come soon refers to God's spiritual reign. To say this is to pray that more and more people will enter the Kingdom; it is also a petition for all evil to be destroyed and for God to establish a new heaven and earth, thereby revealing his glory to all nations.

11:3 This request, **give us our food day by day,** is for a personal need to be met. "Food" could refer to spiritual "food." The words "day by day" reveals that God's provision is daily, and that believers do not need to worry from one day to the next. Christians dare not be self-satisfied. Instead, believers should live in a state of continual dependence on God.

11:4 As God's people need daily provision, they also need daily forgiveness. When Jesus taught his disciples to pray, he made forgiveness the cornerstone of their relationship with God. God has forgiven believers' **sins;** they must now **forgive those who have sinned against** them. To remain unforgiving shows that the person has not understood that he or she deeply needs to be forgiven. The meaning of this sentence focuses on the true repentance of a believer who understands the greatness of the forgiveness that he or she has received. This believer willingly extends such forgiveness to others for their wrongs. To refuse to forgive others can impede the forgiveness needed daily from God (see 6:37; Matthew 6:14-15; 18:23-35; Mark 11:25).

Finally, there is the request that God would help believers refuse to **yield to temptation.** The Greek word translated "temptation" means "enticement" or "test" or "trial." This is a request for spiritual protection from trials and temptations.

11:5-6 This parable points out, with a touch of humor, that God's people must persist in their prayers, and that God is always ready to give. The setting is **midnight.** A journeying friend has arrived, presumably unexpected. Social custom dictates providing food, but the bread is gone and the person has **nothing for him to eat.** The person knows that another friend has some bread, so he goes to him and asks to borrow **three loaves of bread.**

11:7-8 The friend would not be happy to be interrupted at this late hour, having already gone to bed. Jesus explained that although the friend might not get up for the sake of the friendship, **if you keep knocking long enough, he will get up.** Because of the persistence of the person knocking, the request will be answered.

Boldness in prayer overcomes the praying person's apathy, not God's perceived insensitivity. To practice persistence changes the hearts and minds of those praying, and it helps them understand and express the intensity of their need. Persistence in prayer helps them recognize God's work. By praying persistently, believers are not trying to get a reluctant God to answer their prayers; instead, they are showing that they are very serious about their request.

11:9-10 Highlighting the importance of persistent and consistent prayer, Jesus encouraged his disciples, who wanted to be taught to pray (11:1), to **keep on asking, keep on looking,** and **keep on knocking.** Only through prayer can believers stay in contact with God, know what he wants them to do, and then have the strength to do God's will in all areas of life. God will answer believers who persistently ask, look, and knock. In all these cases,

God is accessible and willing to respond. Jesus promised, **"For everyone who asks receives. Everyone who seeks, finds. And the door is opened to everyone who knocks."** (See also Jeremiah 29:13). Believers must not take Jesus' words as a blank check however; prayer is not a magical way to obtain whatever we want. Requests must be in harmony with God's will, accepting his will above our desires.

11:11-13 Jesus explained that his followers can depend on God to answer their prayers. If human beings who are **sinful** would not think of giving a child a **snake** instead of a **fish,** or a **scorpion** instead of an **egg,** then how much more will a holy God

acknowledge and answer Christians' requests? In these words, Jesus revealed the heart of God the Father. God is not selfish, begrudging, or stingy; his followers don't have to beg or grovel when they come with their requests. He is a loving Father who understands, cares, comforts, and willingly gives **the Holy Spirit to those who ask him.** Because the Holy Spirit is God's highest gift and he will not refuse giving him to those who ask, believers can trust in God's provision for all their lesser needs as well. How much better the perfect heavenly Father treats his children! The most important gift he could ever give is the Holy Spirit (Acts 2:1-4), whom he promised to give all believers after his death, resurrection, and return to heaven (John 15:26).

JESUS ANSWERS HOSTILE ACCUSATIONS / 11:14-28 / 135

In this passage, Luke underscores two different negative reactions: (1) those who reject Jesus, accusing him of being associated with the Devil, and (2) those who sit on the fence, waiting for yet another sign. Jesus confronted those who rejected him, by clearly asserting that his miracles were evidence of his connection to God. There is no middle ground, no room to withhold judgment. A person is either against him or for him.

11:14-15 On another occasion, **Jesus cast a demon out of a man who couldn't speak,** thus enabling the man to speak. But **some** in the crowd said that Jesus was casting out demons because he got **his power from Satan, the prince of demons.** Jesus exposed the absurdity of this accusation.

11:16 Some wanted to make accusations, but others wanted **to test Jesus.** As if all the healings and miracles and sending demons from people were not enough, they **asked for a miraculous sign from heaven to see if he was from God.** If they thought that the exorcism just witnessed might be by the power of Satan, then they felt that they needed something "from heaven" as proof of Jesus' identity. The irony, of course, is that no matter what kind of sign Jesus might have given, they would have stubbornly refused to believe (see Matthew 12:38-42).

11:17-18 Jesus' first response was to the accusation recorded in 11:15. He explained that **any kingdom at war with itself is doomed,** and likewise with **a divided home.** If Jesus were driving out demons by Satan, then the conclusion would be that **Satan is fighting against himself.** If that were true, it would mean civil war in the kingdom of evil. No king would throw his own soldiers out of his kingdom; neither would Satan throw his soldiers out of a person they had possessed. Such a kingdom could not stand.

11:19-20 Jesus was not the first person to exorcise demons. In the first century, exorcism was thriving in both Jewish and pagan societies (Mark 9:38; Acts 19:13-14). Many Jewish exorcists were Pharisees. Jesus asked, **"If I am empowered by the prince of demons, what about your own followers"** who were also casting out demons? If it took Satan's power to drive out demons, then those Pharisees who drove out demons were also working under Satan's power.

But if it isn't by Satan's power that demons were fleeing, then it had to be by **the power of God.** Jesus' exorcisms were specific evidence of the presence of Kingdom power. They showed that the hoped for time of God's Kingdom had come in the power of Jesus' authority. That Jesus was powerfully casting out demons and plundering Satan's kingdom revealed that **the Kingdom of God** had **arrived.**

11:21-22 Jesus explained his words in 11:19-20 with a parable. Here Satan is fully armed with all kinds of demons guarding his **palace.** This whole scene changes, however, when **someone who is stronger attacks and overpowers him,** as Jesus had just done in sending the demon out of the man (11:14, and had done many times previously). Satan cannot stand against God or against Christ. Jesus overpowers Satan.

11:23 The line has been drawn. There are two king-doms—God's and Satan's. Satan is active and pow-erful in the world, but God's Kingdom is far stronger and will eventually triumph. People can-not be neutral in this matter. Either they choose to side with God, or they do not. That is the meaning of Jesus' ominous words, **"Anyone who isn't help-ing me opposes me."** In this battle, if a person is not on God's side, he or she is on Satan's.

11:24 To further illustrate the danger of attempting to be neutral about him, Jesus explained what can happen to such people. Unfilled and complacent people are easy targets for Satan. The **evil spirit** was not "cast out," but for some reason had left a person. The **desert** was believed to be the habita-tion of demons. Because demons need a resting place (that is, someone or something living that they can enter and torment), this demon returned to **the person** it **came from.** Jesus was making a serious point about people's spiritual destiny—they must make a decision about him.

11:25-26 In the demon's absence, the **home** (the person's life) had been **swept** and made **clean,** but it is still empty. In fact, the accommodations are now so inviting that the demon **finds seven other spirits more evil than itself, and they all enter the person and live there.** The "owner" of the "house" is now filled with eight demons instead of one; definitely, **that person is worse off than before.**

Jesus was illustrating an unfortunate human tendency—personal desire to reform often does not last long, and attempts to take care of life end in disaster. It is not enough to be emptied of evil; the person must then be filled with the power of the Holy Spirit to accomplish God's new purpose in his or her life (see also Matthew 12:43-45; Galatians 5:22).

11:27-28 Jesus was speaking to people who highly valued family ties. Their genealogies guaran-teed that they were part of God's chosen people. A man's value came from his ancestors, and a woman's value came from the sons she bore. Jesus' response to the woman meant that a person's obedience to God is more important than his or her place on the family tree (see 8:21).

JESUS WARNS AGAINST UNBELIEF / 11:29-32 / 136
After admonishing his listeners to follow him (11:23), Jesus clearly described the consequences of not believing him. The request for a sign revealed wicked unbelief.

11:29-30 Here Jesus was responding to the request made in 11:16. The people had asked Jesus for a sign from heaven to prove that he was from God. Instead of giving a sign (beyond the miracles and healings he had performed), Jesus explained that no **miraculous sign** would be given except **the sign of the prophet Jonah.** God had asked Jonah to preach repentance to the Gentiles (non-Jews)—he had been sent by God to the Assyrian city of Nineveh (see the book of Jonah). Jonah preached to the city and saw it repent. With the words, **"what happened to him was a sign to the people of Nineveh that God had sent him,"** Jesus was affirming Jonah's mes-sage. Salvation is not only for Jews, but for all people. The "sign" granted to them may refer to the Resurrection, for Jesus said, **"What happens to me will be a sign that God has sent me, the Son of Man, to these people."** Jesus' resurrection would prove that he was the Messiah. Three days after his death Jesus would come back to life, just as Jonah had been "brought back" to life after spending three days in the fish. Jonah's presence was a sign to the people of Nineveh; they repented at his teaching. Jesus' return to his people after his death would also be a sign to the people of his generation. Some would repent; many would not.

11:31 **The queen of Sheba** had traveled from southern Arabia to **hear the wisdom of Solomon** (1 Kings 10:1-10). **Someone greater than Solo-mon** was there with the people—the Messiah himself—but they refused to believe. As a result, this queen **will rise up** at the **judgment** and **con-demn** the people of Jesus' generation. She, an unbelieving Gentile, had recognized true wisdom when it was presented to her, unlike Jesus' audi-ence who refused the truth and wanted signs instead.

11:32 The cruel, warlike men of **Nineveh,** capital of Assyria, **repented at the preaching of Jonah**— even though Jonah did not care about them. By contrast, Jesus, the perfect Son of God, had come to people that he loved dearly—but they were rejecting him. Thus God's chosen people were making themselves more liable to judgment than a notoriously wicked nation. The people of that nation **will rise up** at the **judgment** and **con-demn** Jesus' generation.

JESUS TEACHES ABOUT THE LIGHT WITHIN / 11:33-36 / 137

Jesus next exhorted each person to focus his or her eyes on the light: Jesus himself. The people had requested a sign (11:16, 29), but Jesus explained that the light of his perfect life should be enough of a sign.

11:33 These words are very close to 8:16; however, in 8:16 the "lamp" that had been lit refers to the person who hears Jesus' message, responds to it, and spreads it to others. In this teaching situation, it seems that Jesus was describing his own ministry and message as lighting **a lamp** that was not hidden or put **under a basket**, but was done in public with a message available for all to accept. **All** refers to Jesus' mission to reach all the world, not just the Jews.

11:34 The **lamp** is Christ's message, and "light" is the truth of his revelation and guidance (11:33); the **eye** represents spiritual understanding and insight that is filtered through the "good" or the "bad" in a person. When eyes are **pure**, that is, when they are operating properly, the illumination makes it easy for the body to function. Those with "pure eyes" are those true disciples who listen and respond to Jesus' guidance. By contrast, when eyes are **evil**, that is, when they are not operating properly, the result is impaired functioning for the rest of the body. Those with "evil eyes" are those who reject Jesus' words; all they have is the darkness and futility of their own evil ways.

11:35-36 To have the **light** within actually be **darkness** would be a dismal condition. That would mean that no goodness would be left, for even what might have been light would actually be dark—what good should have been there would actually be evil. But with Jesus, and with the filling of the Holy Spirit, a person can be **filled with light, with no dark corners.** This cannot happen from within—for the light does not originate there. It has an outside source, **as though a floodlight is shining on you.**

JESUS CRITICIZES THE RELIGIOUS LEADERS / 11:37-54 / 138

Placed after Jesus' teaching about the inner light is an example of those caught in darkness: the Pharisees and the experts in religious law. These religious leaders had meticulously cleaned the outside of the "cup," but had not bothered to look at the filthiness of their souls.

11:37-38 Again Jesus was invited to **a meal** with a Pharisee (see also 7:36). Jesus offended his host, however, because he did not first perform **the ceremonial washing.** This washing was done not for health reasons but as a symbol of washing away any contamination from touching anything unclean. Not only did the Pharisees make a public show of their washing, but they also commanded everyone else to follow a practice originally intended only for the priests.

11:39-40 Obsessed about ceremonial "purity," the Pharisees neglected their own internal defilement. They washed on the **outside,** like one would wash a **cup** or a **dish,** but they left the inside **full of greed and wickedness,** never bothering to deal with those sins. They were no more pure than a dirty cup. Jesus condemned the Pharisees and religious leaders for outwardly appearing saintly and holy but inwardly remaining full of corruption. Jesus accordingly castigated these Pharisees as **fools.** God who made the **outside** of each person also made **the inside.** In other words, God is just as concerned with the inside as with the outside. He is not only concerned about what you do, but also about who you are.

11:41 The Pharisees loved to think of themselves as "clean," but their stinginess toward God and the poor proved that they were not as clean as they thought. Jesus wanted to stress the importance of the inward over the outward, here focusing on the importance of a right attitude when giving to the poor. The inner attitude must match the outward act in order for them to be **clean all over.**

11:42 Jesus pronounced **how terrible** it would be for the **Pharisees** because although they were keeping the tiniest details of law, ceremony, custom, and tradition, they were forgetting **justice and the love of God.** Jesus did not condemn the practice of tithing, even of small amounts if one chose to do so. Jesus condemned the Pharisees for being scrupulous in less important matters while completely neglecting the larger issues that were far more **important**—such as dealing correctly and fairly with people and building a relationship with God.

11:43 Jesus condemned the **Pharisees** for their love of public importance and honor. The elders sat on the **seats of honor in the synagogues,** at the front, near the place where the scrolls of the Torah were kept. Those seats faced the congregation. To receive **respectful greetings** was a highly treasured honor. Jesus condemned the attitude that focused on the "perks" of position, while they forgot their responsibility to be teachers. The Pharisees loved to receive honor and deference from ordinary people; yet they did not love or desire to serve those people. Instead, they often showed contempt for them as "lower" than themselves.

11:44 This third condemnation pictures the Pharisees, for all their ceremonial cleanliness, as actually typifying the worst sort of uncleanness. The Old Testament laws said a person who touched a grave was unclean (Numbers 19:16). Sometimes a body might be buried in an unmarked grave, causing an unwary traveler to become ceremonially unclean by walking over it. Jesus accused the Pharisees of actually being **hidden graves** who made others unclean by their spiritual rottenness. Like graves hidden in a field, the Pharisees corrupted everyone who came in contact with them.

11:45-46 Jesus did not back down from what was being taken as insults, nor did he leave these legal experts without condemnation. Jesus condemned them for crushing people **beneath impossible religious demands.** These "demands" were the details the Pharisees had added to God's law. To the commandment, "Remember to observe the Sabbath day by keeping it holy" (Exodus 20:8), for example, they had added instructions regarding how far a person could walk on the Sabbath, which kinds of knots could be tied, and how much weight could be carried. Instead of teaching God's law so that people could love, understand, and obey the God who gave it, they turned the law into such a confused maze of do's and don'ts that it had become a burden to the people. The legal experts refused to **lift a finger to help** the people.

11:47-48 The **tombs** of the **prophets** were revered. People even decorated the graves of those long dead who seemed worthy of such honor. Building tombs over the graves of the martyrs was ironic because most of these prophets had been **killed** by the **ancestors** of this present religious establishment. In essence, these religious leaders were agreeing with the

deeds of their ancestors in killing these prophets. Jesus was saying that these leaders were no different from their ancestors who had killed God's messengers because, in a sense, they were simply completing their work. The attitude of hatred for God's messengers would carry through, and Jesus himself would face it as well.

11:49-51 God's prophets have been persecuted and murdered throughout history. But this generation was rejecting more than a human prophet—they were rejecting God himself. This quotation is not from the Old Testament. Jesus, the greatest Prophet of all, was directly giving them God's message.

Jesus gave two examples of martyrs in the Old Testament. **Abel's** death is recorded in Genesis 4:8—he was the first martyr, the first to die because of his faithfulness to God. **Zechariah's** death is recorded in 2 Chronicles 24:20-22 (the last book in the Hebrew canon). Zechariah is a classic example of a man of God who was killed by those who claimed to be God's people. The current religious establishment would be guilty of all of their deaths, for they would be guilty of murdering the Messiah and would face judgment for that act. The destruction of Jerusalem in A.D. 70 was a partial fulfillment of Jesus' words.

11:52 The **experts in religious law** were effectively locking people out of God's Kingdom. Their rejection of Jesus and emphasis on their petty demands had the effect of making them unable to enter the Kingdom and then preventing those who might otherwise want to enter. Anyone who might have gotten in through a saving relationship with God was stopped short by their erroneous interpretations of Scripture and their added man-made rules. Then, as they prided themselves in their "understanding," they themselves missed God's message. Caught up in a religion of their own making, they could no longer lead the people to God. They had closed the door of God's love to the people and had thrown away the keys.

11:53-54 It may come as no surprise that these leaders were **furious** at Jesus. He had challenged these professed experts, so they hoped to trip him up and arrest him for blasphemy, heresy, or lawbreaking. They had to find a legal way to get rid of Jesus, so they **grilled him with many hostile questions, trying to trap him.** Jesus had pointed out the blatant hypocrisy of so much of Israel's leadership, and there would be no turning back. The opposition was mounting; Jesus had become a threat to the establishment.

LUKE 12

JESUS SPEAKS AGAINST HYPOCRISY / 12:1-12 / 139

After denouncing the religious leaders for hypocrisy, Jesus warns his disciples of the same pernicious problem. With the limelight of fame shining on them, they were beginning to follow the Pharisees on a path of hypocrisy—acting religiously superior and judging others, while harboring jealousy, greed, and pride within their souls. This type of hypocrisy was utterly repugnant to Jesus.

12:1 Even as Jesus began to infuriate the religious leaders, his popularity continued to grow, for the **crowds grew** into the **thousands**. As Jesus watched the huge crowds waiting to hear him, he **warned** his **disciples** against **hypocrisy**—trying to appear good when their heart was far from God. Just as yeast works its way through dough, so a small amount of evil can affect a large group of people. The **yeast of the Pharisees**—their hypocrisy— could permeate and contaminate society, leading the entire nation astray.

12:2-3 Hypocrisy can happen when certain actions or attitudes are hidden. One day, however, **everything will be revealed.** The Pharisees could not keep their attitudes hidden forever. Their selfishness would act like "yeast" (12:1), and soon they would expose themselves for what they really were—power-hungry impostors, not devoted religious leaders. The time of this "revelation" could be the final judgment day when the true attitude of these hypocrites will be exposed (see Romans 2:16; 1 Corinthians 4:5).

12:4-5 Jesus explained that his followers (his **dear friends**) might face death for their faith in him, but he also told them not to **be afraid** of people who could **kill** them or even of death itself. Evil people may be able to **kill the body**, but they **cannot do any more.** Jesus knew that fear of opposition or ridicule could weaken their witness for him because the natural human tendency is to cling to peace and comfort, even at the cost of one's walk with God. Jesus said that there is only one whom all people should **fear**—God alone. He controls eternal consequences. It is more fearful to disobey God than to face martyrdom.

The word translated **hell** here is *Gehenna*. The name was derived from the Valley of Hinnom, south of Jerusalem, where children had been sacrificed by fire to the pagan god Molech (see 2 Kings 23:10; 2 Chronicles 28:3; Jeremiah 7:31; 32:35).

12:6-7 While Jesus' followers should "fear" God because of his awesome power, they are not to **be afraid** of him because they are **more valuable to him than a whole flock of sparrows.** A person could buy **five sparrows** for a small amount of money; they were the cheapest type of living food sold in the market. Even so, **God does not forget a single one.** God loves his people so much that he cares about the smallest details of their lives— down to knowing the number of **hairs** on their heads.

12:8-9 God sent his Son to die for people worldwide, and salvation is offered to all people. But individuals still must choose whether or not to accept God's offer. Jesus clearly explained that anyone who **publicly** confesses faith in and allegiance to him will find that **the Son of Man will openly acknowledge that person in the presence of God's angels.** By contrast, the person who **denies** any relationship to Jesus will face denial by Jesus in heaven. These words refer to those whose lack of allegiance will be revealed under pressure. Most likely, this does not refer to an incident where lack of courage might cause a believer not to speak up, but rather to a person who totally rejects Christ and lives a life of denial. The astounding statement is that each person's standing before God is based on his or her relationship to Jesus Christ.

12:10 While 12:8-9 deals with apostasy, 12:10 focuses on people who have not yet come to believe. These words mean that speaking against the person of Jesus can be forgiven because the insult may be based in ignorance of his true identity (before the resurrection, not even Jesus' disciples completely understood who he was). But **anyone who speaks blasphemies against the**

Holy Spirit—continually rejects the Holy Spirit's message about Jesus and his convicting influence—will never be forgiven because he is beyond redemptive help. Whoever rejects the prompting of the Holy Spirit removes himself from the only force that can lead anyone to repentance and restoration with God. That act has eternal consequences.

This sin of blasphemy against the Holy Spirit has worried many sincere Christians. The unforgivable sin means attributing to Satan the work that the Holy Spirit accomplishes. Thus the "unforgivable sin" is deliberate and ongoing rejection of the Holy Spirit's work and even of God himself. A person who has committed this sin has shut himself off from God so thoroughly that he is unaware of any sin at all. A person who fears

having committed this sin shows by his very concern that he has not sinned in this way.

12:11-12 Jesus told the disciples that when (not "if") they would be brought to trial in the synagogues and before rulers and authorities, they need not worry about what to say in their own defense. They would not be left unprepared—Jesus promised that the Holy Spirit would supply the right words at the very moment they were needed. This promise of the Spirit's help, however, does not compensate for lack of preparation. Remember that these disciples had three years of teaching and practical application. Study God's word, then God will bring his truths to mind when you most need them, helping you present them in the most effective way.

JESUS TELLS THE PARABLE OF THE RICH FOOL / 12:13-21 / 140

Perhaps because of Jesus' constant insistence on justice (11:42), a person from the crowd asked him to arbitrate a dispute. Instead of addressing the injustice, Jesus exposed the greedy motives of the man and revealed God's perspective on the foolishness of greed. The simple parable Jesus told describes a person who is solely concerned with himself—his welfare, pleasure, and security. He possessed no gratitude toward God or a willingness to share with those less fortunate. His ingratitude invoked God's anger and led to the man's downfall.

12:13 A person in the crowd appealed to Jesus as an authority. He wanted Jesus to settle a dispute over his father's estate. The Old Testament laws covered most cases (see, for example, Numbers 26–27; 33:54; 36; Deuteronomy 21:17), but sometimes an issue would arise that needed intervention in order to make a decision. Problems like this were often brought to rabbis for them to settle (see 10:38-42).

12:14-15 Jesus used the man's request as an opportunity to teach his listeners about the pitfalls of being greedy. "Greed" is the excessive and consuming desire to have more possessions or wealth. He explained that the good life has nothing to do with being wealthy; real life is not measured by how much we own. This man apparently thought that the division of the inheritance would solve his problems. But Jesus wanted him to deal with deeper issues.

12:16-18 Jesus proceeded to illustrate his point that life consists of more than wealth and possessions. This story includes a rich man who had a productive year on his farm. He tore down his barns and built bigger ones so that he could store everything. While there was nothing wrong with the man's rejoicing in his crop or building to

make storage, his basic flaw was in focusing completely on his wealth and on his own enjoyment. In Greek, this story includes the word "my" four times and the word "I" eight times. As this story reveals, the man's joy came from his things—but things do not last forever.

12:19-20 The rich man was concerned for no one else, and he had no care for God. With no eternal perspective, the man's life was completely focused on the temporal. His goal to take it easy and to eat, drink, and be merry reveals his desire for mere self-indulgence. He thought that, with his barns storing up mountains of wealth for the future, he had everything completely under control. The rich man had made a fatal flaw: he had forgotten to put God at the center of his life. Concerned for no one but himself, when the time came for him to stand before God, he was nothing more than a fool.

12:21 The moral of the story: fools spend all their time storing up earthly wealth but neglect to have a rich relationship with God. The turning point is for whom the treasures are being accumulated. If for oneself, then the evils of wealth will be turned loose. Being rich toward God means using wealth as he provides it to fulfill his priorities. People who are "rich" in this way love God and are filled with a passion to obey and serve him and to give to others. In this way, the "treasures" a person may gain in this life can be gladly handed back over to God for his use in furthering his Kingdom.

JESUS WARNS ABOUT WORRY / 12:22-34 / *141*

Luke placed Jesus' teaching about believers and possessions right after the negative example of the rich fool (12:13-21). Instead of hoarding possessions, believers should give them away. Such generosity builds an eternal inheritance in God's Kingdom. Christians should completely trust in God's loving provision for them; this should free them to show generosity.

12:22-23 Jesus continued to highlight the priorities of those who want to follow him. Again, these words were directed not to the crowd in general, but **to his disciples.** Just as their attitude toward money should differ from the world's (12:15), so their life view should be different. All the goals and worries in life can be entrusted to the loving heavenly Father who promises to meet every need. The command, **don't worry,** does not imply lack of concern, nor does it imply that people should be unwilling to work to supply their own needs and thus have to depend on others. Instead, Jesus was saying that worrying about **food and clothing** should never take priority over serving God. Worriers immobilize themselves and focus on their worries. They refuse to trust that God can supply their most basic needs.

12:24 Jesus had already explained that God's care for the sparrows shows that he cares for his people (12:6-7). Here Jesus explained God's care for people's basic needs by asking the disciples to **look at the ravens.** The birds don't have elaborate farming systems by which to supply food for themselves; **God feeds them.** God makes sure that the birds, who do no worrying about their food supply, always have food to eat. The raven (or crow) was considered to be "unclean" (Leviticus 11:13-15), yet even unclean animals received God's care. The conclusion, of course, is that God's people are **far more valuable to him than any birds.** God's children can know that their Father will care for their needs as well.

12:25-26 Worry accomplishes nothing; it is wasted effort. While worry cannot **add a single moment** to a person's life, it can damage that person's health, cause the object of worry to consume one's thoughts, disrupt productivity, negatively affect the way the person treats others, and reduce the ability to trust in God.

12:27-28 Like the ravens who do not store up food for themselves in barns, neither do the **lilies** work to array themselves. If God feeds the birds and clothes the earth with beauty that surpasses the fine garments of King **Solomon,** then will God not also clothe his people?

Jesus was not condoning laziness while waiting for God to provide. He wanted his disciples to understand that they should place their lives in God's hands, refusing to worry about basic needs. It shows **little faith** to worry over what God has promised to provide.

12:29-30 Eating and drinking are necessary for survival, but God's people know that life is more than what they eat or drink, more than their clothing or possessions. If they **worry about** these things, they will find themselves motionless for God, accomplishing nothing for the Kingdom. God's people are to be different. Believers have an eternal perspective that is focused on the Kingdom to come; they trust their **Father** to know their **needs** for their time on the earth.

12:31 Jesus told his disciples to **make the Kingdom of God** their **primary concern.** This means to submit to God's sovereignty today, to work for the future coming of his Kingdom, to represent God here and now, and to seek his rule in our hearts and in the world. So many spend their time worrying about the basics of life, but Jesus says to think about the Kingdom first, and God **will give you all you need from day to day.** Christ's promise is not that Kingdom seekers will get everything they desire, but that the necessities for faith and service will be in abundance. When God's children have their priorities right, they can trust that God will always care for them. They may not become rich, but they will not lack what they need.

12:32 The **Kingdom** is worth making a priority (12:31), for one day God the Father will **give** it to those who faithfully follow him. The Kingdom is a certain reality, so God's people need not **be afraid.** Fear and worry will be constant companions to those who devote their lives to getting, achieving, and protecting what they have. No bank and no medical plan can protect a person from death or from present harm. Only those whose true treasure is in heaven (12:33-34) can be truly secure. Not only does God promise to give believers his Kingdom, but it is his **great happiness** to do so. God the Father (12:30) wants to share his Kingdom with them.

12:33-34 Because of their eternal perspective (12:29-30) and because of the future Kingdom they will possess, God's people are free to give. They can hold their possessions lightly. In fact, they can **sell** them and **give to those in need**. In so doing, they will provide for themselves **treasure** that cannot disappear, for it rests **in heaven**. Jesus was not telling his followers to

sell all their possessions, but rather to sell whatever they could to make giving to the poor possible. This "treasure" in heaven includes, but is not limited to, tithing money. Believers add to it as they bring others to Christ and act out their obedience to God. The "treasure" is the eternal value of whatever is accomplished on earth. Acts of obedience to God, stored in heaven, cannot be stolen nor will they decay. Nothing can affect or change them; they are eternal. **Wherever your treasure is, there your heart and thoughts will also be** means that whatever occupies a person's thoughts and consumes his or her time—that is the person's "treasure." The heart will be with the treasure.

JESUS WARNS ABOUT PREPARING FOR HIS COMING / 12:35-48 / 142
The teaching about the end times in Luke does not entail a detailed description of what will occur, but it portrays a secure conviction that the Son of Man will return in judgment. This knowledge should motivate Christians to be faithful servants or stewards, to do what God has commanded them to do, and to use their talents and resources effectively.

12:35-38 Because of the certainty of the Kingdom coming and because it would be coming in the future, waiting for it requires both faith and vigilance. God's people must **be dressed for service and well prepared.** Faithful servants would stay awake while waiting for their master's return from **the wedding feast.** They are dressed so that they can do service for him should he require it. No matter how late the master may come, the servants are prepared to **open the door** immediately upon his arrival. In the same way, God's people must be awaiting his arrival so they too can welcome him the moment he arrives. Servants who are **ready and waiting** for the master's arrival will be rewarded. The master will be so pleased upon his arrival that he will **serve them.** Such a reversal of roles likely will not happen in the world, but in God's Kingdom such a welcome will await those who were ready.

12:39-40 This story describes the need for constant vigilance as believers await the Kingdom. A **homeowner** does not know when a burglar is coming to break into the house; if the homeowner did, he would be ready and **would not permit** it to happen. Likewise, God's people **must be ready all the time.** Jesus referred to himself as **the Son of Man** and left no doubt that he would be the one who **will come when least expected** (1 Thessalonians 5:2; 2 Peter 3:10; Revelation 16:15). God's people should be ready and waiting.

Christ's return at an unexpected time is not a trick by which God hopes to catch his people off guard. In fact, God is delaying his return so that more people will have the opportunity to follow him (see 2 Peter 3:9). Before Christ's return, believers have time to live out their beliefs and to reflect Jesus' love as they relate to others. Christians have time to bring more people with them into the Kingdom.

12:41-42 Peter wondered to whom Jesus was addressing the previous parable about being prepared for the Kingdom's arrival. Perhaps Peter was wondering about the disciples' responsibilities. They still did not understand what this Kingdom would be like. Peter wondered what their roles would be in comparison with the crowds in general.

Jesus answered Peter's question with another question that focused the disciples' attention on what it meant to be put in charge, and what their roles should be as leaders. They should be like a **faithful, sensible servant,** left in charge by **the master.** In this story, there is one faithful servant (12:42-44) and three unfaithful ones (12:45-48).

12:43-44 The **master** is Jesus, who would leave his servants in his household (the earth) to serve while he would be gone. All the servants must work, although some are given more responsibility and thus more accountability (12:48). Those servants who have **done a good job** when the **master returns** will have a **reward** and be given more responsibility.

12:45-46 However, with the master gone, a slave might think to himself that he can do as he likes, taking advantage of his position of authority. The master would **return unannounced**, catch him in the act, and **banish him** for being irresponsible to his task in the master's absence. The words **with the unfaithful** probably pictures the end-time judgment, wherein the faithful enter God's Kingdom and the unfaithful are sent away (Matthew 25:31-46).

12:47-48 Those who fail to do their duty can expect punishment. More responsibility, and thus more severe punishment, however, will come to those who **knew** their **duty** but **refused to do it**. Those **who are not aware that they are doing wrong will be punished only lightly.** Each per-son is responsible to seek out God's will and to obey; however, God will demand more from those who have been given many gifts and entrusted with much responsibility for the Kingdom. Clearly, leadership in God's Kingdom—no matter how small or large one's responsibilities in comparison to others—is taken very seriously by God. Those placed in positions where they will guide, influence, and care for others have been **given** much, and therefore **much more is required** for their moral, spiritual, and ethical lives. They must show themselves to be examples and must stay close to the Lord so he can guide them. Their responsibilities involve the eternal destinies of others—a job description that should cause them to be ever vigilant and watchful of God's will.

JESUS WARNS ABOUT COMING DIVISION / 12:49-53 / 143
These verses introduce a section in which Jesus calls the Jews to accept him before their time runs out (12:54–13:8). It is a quick summary of Jesus' earthly mission. Jesus came to earth to bring division, not peace. That is because Jesus confronts everyone with a choice. Will you side with him? There is no middle ground (11:23).

12:49-50 **Fire** stands for God's judgment and the coming of the Holy Spirit (see 3:16-17 for more on Jesus' baptism being one of Spirit and fire). Judgment is coming, and Jesus is the one to bring it. Jesus' arrival has caused upset and division among people across the centuries. No one can sit on the fence about Jesus; decisions have to be made to believe or not to believe, inevitably dividing even families (see 12:51-53). Jesus wished that his **task were already completed,** meaning that he desired that God's purpose for the earth already be fulfilled. Judgment would come through Jesus and after that he would reign. But Jesus waits for God's timing.

Here Jesus anticipated the outworking of God's plan through **a terrible baptism,** which here refers to his coming suffering at the cross. Despite Jesus' distress, he knows that through it the work of salvation can begin in people's hearts.

12:51-53 Jesus promises **peace,** but it is not the kind of peace the world gives or tries to give (John 14:27). Peace on earth, universal peace, will not come until Jesus' second coming when evil is destroyed and he reigns forever. Instead, Jesus' first coming and the time now as believers await his return is a time of **strife and division** between God's forces and Satan's forces. There is no middle ground with Jesus. Because he demands a response, family groups may be torn apart when some choose to follow him and others refuse to do so. Loyalties must be declared and commitments made, sometimes to the point of severing relationships with those who reject Jesus or who try to substitute him with someone else.

JESUS WARNS ABOUT THE FUTURE CRISIS / 12:54-59 / 144
"Hypocrites!" With this harsh word, Jesus tried to startle his listeners to the urgency of their plight, which was terrible. But Jesus, God's only Son, was offering them a way out—the free gift of salvation to all who believe in him. In effect, Jesus was saying, "Wake up! Destruction is around the corner. Come to me for salvation."

12:54-56 Jesus turned back **to the crowd** and spoke to them. For most of recorded history, the world's principal occupation has been farming. Farmers depend directly on the weather for their livelihood. They need just the right amounts of sun and rain to make a living. Such people were skilled at interpreting natural signs. The people knew that **clouds** forming **in the west** over the Mediterranean Sea would bring rain. **Wind** blowing in from the desert to the **south** would bring hot weather. People interpreted these signs and then prepared themselves accordingly.

But these same people were ignoring the signs of the coming Kingdom. Thus Jesus said, **"You hypocrites!"** Jesus was announcing an earthshaking event that would be much more important than the year's crops—the coming of God's Kingdom. Like a rainstorm or a sunny day, there were signs that the Kingdom would soon arrive. While people could successfully discern the signs of the weather by watching the sky and predicting fair weather or storms,

they were intentionally ignoring the signs of the times.

12:57-59 With the signs of the Kingdom around them and as Jesus stood among them, he asked his listeners, **"Why can't you decide for yourselves what is right?"** Why weren't they taking advantage of this opportunity to make peace with God? They ought to do so, for waiting could be disastrous, just as the man on his way to court would be wise to settle the matter beforehand. In Jesus' day, a person who couldn't pay a debt would be **thrown in jail.** How much better to attempt to settle the matter **on the way to court** (under Roman law, the plaintiff went with the defendant to court) than to wait for the judge's verdict to be handed down.

God's judgment is irreversible. Each person must decide what to do about Jesus. That decision should be made now.

LUKE 13

JESUS CALLS THE PEOPLE TO REPENT / 13:1-9 / *145*

In Jesus' previous exhortation, he admonished the people to realize their predicament, that judgment was around the corner. Here Jesus took the sudden and terrifying deaths of some innocent people to illustrate their tragic situation. Still stunned by the grisly murders, the people were, in effect, told by Jesus that they faced a similar fate—eternal death, much worse than physical death.

13:1 Pilate was last mentioned in 3:1. The city of **Jerusalem,** the site of the Jews' **Temple,** lay in his jurisdiction. While no other historical source refers to this incident where **some people from Galilee** were **murdered** at Pilate's orders, it is completely in character for this man. Galilee was a hotbed for fanatics who sought to bring down Rome by force. Galilee was out of Pilate's jurisdiction, but when some Galileans arrived in Jerusalem, they were murdered.

13:2-3 Jewish theology attributed individual suffering to individual sin. While the Pharisees would also have liked to see Israel freed from Roman control, they were against the use of force that many in Israel (such as a group called the Zealots) were advocating. Some people, such as the Pharisees and their followers, would have thought that these Galileans that were murdered must have been **worse sinners than other people from Galilee** because they had **suffered.** The Pharisees,

who were opposed to using force to deal with Rome, would have said that the Galileans deserved to die for rebelling.

Jesus explained, however, that suffering has nothing to do with one's spiritual state. In fact, all people are sinful and, unless people repent, they all will **perish.** This doesn't mean that everyone will be killed in such a manner. It could mean that death will be sudden with no second chance to repent, or it could mean that Jesus' listeners would suffer at the hands of the Roman conquerors (which the entire nation did in A.D. 70 when Jerusalem was destroyed and millions of Jews were killed).

13:4-5 Just as suffering is no indicator of one's spiritual state, neither is tragedy. The Pharisees would have seen the previous incident as God's judgment on the Zealots, but the Zealots would have seen this incident as God's judgment against those who had compromised with Rome. Again, popular thought would have concluded that the

eighteen men who died when the Tower of Siloam fell on them must have been the eighteen **worst sinners in Jerusalem,** otherwise they would not have suffered such a fate. The Zealots, a group of anti-Roman terrorists, would have said that the aqueduct workers deserved to die for cooperating. The Zealots would have considered Jews working on a Roman project such as this as traitors and deserving of God's punishment.

Again, Jesus explained that all people are sinners who must repent or they too will **perish**—spiritual death with eternal consequences. He said that neither the Galileans nor the workers should be blamed for their calamity. Instead of blaming others, everyone should consider his or her own day of judgment. Whether a person is killed in a tragic accident or miraculously survives is not a measure of righteousness. Everyone has to die; that's part of being human.

13:6-7 After highlighting the need for repentance, Jesus used an **illustration** to show the people that while God is gracious in giving people time to repent, come to him, and grow in him, that patience will not go on forever. In the Old Testament, a fruitful tree was often used as a symbol of godly living (see, for example, Psalm 1:3 and Jere-

miah 17:7-8). Jesus pointed out what would happen to the other kind of tree—the kind that took valuable time and space and still produced nothing for the patient gardener. In this way, Jesus warned his listeners that God would not tolerate forever their lack of productivity. (See 3:9 for John the Baptist's version of the same message.) A **fig tree** in fertile soil should certainly have produced fruit—a tree that did not produce for **three years** was probably not going to produce at all. The farmer gave the command to **cut it down** so another, more fruitful tree, could be planted in its place.

13:8-9 The **gardener** intervened and asked the owner to **give** the tree **one more chance.** He even offered to give it **special attention** and **fertilizer.** Jesus had come to the nation; the time for repentance had come. The extra attention and love had been showered on the nation in the presence of their Messiah. God's judgment had been graciously held back. But if the people continued to refuse to "bear fruit" for God—if they continued to refuse to live for and obey him—the end would come. The tree would be cut down. There would be no more chances. God is merciful toward sinners. But for those who reject him, he will not be merciful forever. They will be punished.

JESUS HEALS THE CRIPPLED WOMAN / 13:10-17 / 146

The story of healing this woman is unique to Luke. It reveals the unfruitfulness of the nation of Israel to which Jesus' parable of the unfruitful tree alludes (in the previous passage, see 13:6-8). Instead of finding love, justice, humility, and mercy among God's people, Jesus found an arrogance that didn't even allow healing a woman on the Sabbath, the day set aside for the God of mercy.

13:10-11 Jesus had already come into conflict with the religious leaders over how the Sabbath should be used. At this particular time, as Jesus looked over the crowd, he saw a woman who had been **bent double for eighteen years.** The text explains that this was the work of **an evil spirit.** She may not have been demon-possessed, because a demon didn't speak and Jesus did not cast out any demon. Instead, this woman's painful affliction is attributed to Satan's work (see 13:16).

13:12-13 The woman did not ask; instead, Jesus **called her.** He **touched her** and she was **instantly** healed. She stood up **straight** for the first time in eighteen years. No wonder her first response was to praise and thank God!

13:14 Jesus had performed a great miracle with God's power; a woman had been set free from

years of suffering and was praising God! But the synagogue **leader** was **indignant.** Why? Because Jesus had healed her on the Sabbath. The synagogue leader, who was addressing his remarks **to the crowd** and not to Jesus, could not see beyond the law to Jesus' compassion in healing this crippled woman. He simply concluded that if Jesus wanted to heal people, he should reserve his healings for the other **six days of the week.** Jesus did not need to abide by those laws, for they did not fulfill God's intention for the Sabbath and were burdensome on the people.

13:15-16 Jesus shamed this synagogue ruler and the other leaders by pointing out their hypocrisy. They would untie their animals and care for them on the Sabbath. Yet these same people refused to see that care for humans is far more important. Jesus attributed the woman's illness to **Satan** and **bondage** by him. Whatever the immediate cause of an illness, its original source is Satan, the author of all the evil in the world. The good news is that Jesus is more powerful than any devil or any disease. He often brings physical healing in this life; and when he returns, he will put an end to all disease and disability.

13:17 When Jesus made this point, **all the people rejoiced.** They probably appreciated a rabbi who stood up for them against the burdensome laws that the religious leaders had placed on them in every area of life. Jesus had **shamed his enemies.** This humiliation would cause such intense hatred that they would plot to kill him.

JESUS TEACHES ABOUT THE KINGDOM OF GOD / 13:18-21 / 147

First-century Jews expected the Kingdom of God to come all at once, in great glory and power. But Jesus corrected their perception, by the illustrations of the mustard seed and yeast. Both are small; but one grows into a huge tree and the other eventually permeates an entire loaf. Jesus' ministry began small, but the gospel would eventually grow to cover the entire globe (a story Luke begins to tell in the book of Acts).

13:18-19 Jesus used a variety of parables to describe what the **Kingdom of God is like.** Nothing on earth can completely explain the Kingdom or give us an adequate picture of it, for the Kingdom will be far beyond anything anyone could ever imagine. Jesus used this parable to explain that his Kingdom would have a small beginning. The general expectation among Jesus' hearers was that the Messiah would come as a great king and leader, freeing the nation from Rome and restoring Israel's former glory. But Jesus said that his Kingdom was beginning quietly. The **mustard seed** was so small that it would take almost twenty thousand seeds to make one ounce. From one tiny seed would grow a **tree.** A mustard shrub could grow ten to twelve feet in just a few weeks. No other seed so small produced such a large plant. While that is not technically a "tree," Jesus used its rapid growth to stress both the insignificance and magnificence of the Kingdom. Like the tiny mus-

tard seed that becomes a large plant, the Kingdom of God would eventually push outward until the whole world would be changed.

Jesus' mention of **birds** added color and showed how large the shrub could become, but they probably had no allegorical meaning. Some commentators, however, think the birds may represent the Gentiles becoming part of God's Kingdom (see prophecies such as Ezekiel 17:22-24; 31:6).

13:20-21 Another symbol of something small producing something much larger occurs with **yeast.** In some Bible passages, "yeast" is used as a symbol of evil or uncleanness (12:1). Here it pictures positive growth. Although yeast is a minor ingredient (only a small amount is used), it is responsible for the dough rising. Although God's Kingdom had small beginnings, it would grow to have a great impact on the world.

JESUS TEACHES ABOUT ENTERING THE KINGDOM / 13:22-30 / 153

Jesus answered a person who asked whether only a few would be saved. Jesus turned this theoretical question into a practical question. Instead of letting the questioner analyze who would be entering heaven, and by implication judge the process and then those who would enter, Jesus asked that person: "Are *you* saved?"

13:22 This is the second reminder that Jesus was intentionally **pressing on toward Jerusalem** (the other time is in 9:51). Jesus knew he was on his way to die, but he continued traveling and **teaching.** The prospect of death did not deter Jesus from his mission.

13:23-27 The question about whether **only a few** or many people would **be saved** was a topic of

debate and much speculation among the rabbis. Jesus refused to be drawn into taking a side in this argument; instead, he urged his listeners to be among those who would be saved, no matter what the final number might be. He told his audience to **work hard to get in.** The word "work" means to put one's whole self into the task of listening and responding. Jesus did not explain the **narrow door,** but the picture is of a way that one must seek out and then enter into while it is still open. Although many people know something about God, only a few have acknowledged their sins and accepted his forgiveness. Just listening to Jesus' words or admiring his miracles is not enough—all must turn from sin and trust in God for salvation. Regardless of how many would be saved, Jesus said that **many will try to enter,** but **it will be too late.** The time for decision would pass them by.

Familiarity with Jesus will not count when God's Kingdom arrives and people rush to be a part of it. When the **door** is **locked,** the time for salvation will have passed, and they will not be able to enter. While many will claim to have eaten with him and listened to his teaching, they had not turned to him in faith for salvation. Such people will be utterly rejected, for Jesus will simply say, **"I do not know you."** Such words will be the final pronouncement of rejection on those who rejected him. They will be sent **away** from God and the Kingdom.

13:28 When the door is shut and they are sent away, there will be intense sorrow (**weeping and gnashing of teeth**). Jesus pictured them looking in the windows at the ancestors on whom they had depended for their salvation—

the patriarchs **Abraham, Isaac,** and **Jacob.** They will also see **all the prophets,** many of whom had been slain for speaking God's messages. These men had not had the opportunity to see the Messiah, but they had loved God, believed his promises, and trusted that he would accomplish what he said. Thus, they received places in the **Kingdom.** By contrast, many of these Jewish people, who did have the opportunity to eat and drink with and then listen to the teachings of the Messiah himself (13:26), subsequently rejected him. For such rejection they would be **thrown out** of the Kingdom.

13:29-30 God's Kingdom will include people from **all over the world.** Israel's rejection of Jesus as Messiah would not stop God's plan. True Israel includes all people who believe in God (see Isaiah 49:12). The inclusion of Gentiles in God's Kingdom had been prophesied, but it still would have astounded Jesus' Jewish audience to hear of the Gentiles being involved in God's Kingdom at all. This was an important fact for Luke to stress because he was directing his Gospel to a Gentile audience (see also Romans 4:16-25; Galatians 3:6-9). Even worse for these Jews, however, was the statement that some of them might not have places at the feast.

JESUS GRIEVES OVER JERUSALEM / 13:31-35 / 154
Luke placed Jesus' grieving over Jerusalem right after a discussion about salvation, those being first (the Jews who were chosen by God) being placed last (or excluded from God's heavenly Kingdom). Jesus mourned Jerusalem's rejection of God's message and salvation.

13:31 The motives of these **Pharisees** remain unknown. Perhaps they were simply trying to get him out of their area. They thought that telling Jesus of Herod's plan (whether true or not) would cause Jesus to be afraid and run. **Herod Antipas** had killed John the Baptist and had been perplexed about who Jesus was (9:7-9). It is highly possible that he did want to kill Jesus. But Jesus' life, work, and death were not to be determined by Herod or the Pharisees. His life was planned and directed by God himself, and his mission would unfold in God's time and according to God's plan.

13:32 Jesus was hardly going to run in fear of Herod; in fact, the message he sent to him was filled with contempt, calling Herod **that fox.** Jesus clearly explained that Herod would have absolutely no control over Jesus' life and ministry. Jesus would continue doing miracles

until the day when he would **accomplish** his **purpose.**

13:33-34 Jesus knew that he **must proceed on** in his ministry until the very moment appointed for his death. The words, **it wouldn't do for a prophet of God to be killed except in Jerusalem,** have a stinging sound—Jesus knew he was to die and he knew he would die in Jerusalem. Jerusalem had a history of rejecting God's prophets (1 Kings 19:10; 2 Chronicles 24:19-21; Jeremiah 2:30; 26:20-23), and it would reject the Messiah just as it had rejected his forerunners. Thus Jesus mourned for the city. Jesus' emotional words reveal his compassion and love for the people to whom he had come. Like a mother **hen** who **protects her chicks beneath her wings,** Jesus would have gathered and protected his people. Several places in the Old Testament picture the loving God protecting his people under his "wings" (see Ruth 2:12; Psalms 17:8; 36:7; 57:1; 61:4; 63:7; 91:4). But they **wouldn't let** him.

13:35 **House** could refer to the city itself or to its Temple. The nation had rejected their promised Messiah and invited the final result of such rejection. They would be **empty** (or forsaken). In Jeremiah 12:7, Jeremiah prophesied the coming destruction of the Temple by the Babylonians. The nation's sin had sealed their punishment, and God's presence had left the Temple. When Jesus Christ came, God himself again stood in the Temple. But the people's refusal to accept him would have severe consequences, for he would leave again. The Temple stood for the people's relationship with God; an empty Temple meant separation from God (see Matthew 23:38).

The Jews understood their Temple to be the dwelling place of God on earth. The city was intended to be the center of worship of the true God and a symbol of justice to all people. No wonder Jesus loved the city and grieved over it. But the people had become blind to God. They had killed the prophets and would put to death the One about whom the prophets had testified. In that very city, the Messiah would be rejected and put to death (13:33). God's presence would leave what was supposed to have been the holy city. The city would not see him again until the words of Psalm 118:26 would be fulfilled, **"Bless the one who comes in the name of the Lord!"** While some take this to refer to Jesus' Triumphal Entry, Matthew recorded these same words as being spoken after the Triumphal Entry (Matthew 23:39). The solemn prediction of desolation would come true, but as always, God would have compassion. A day would come when some of God's people would recognize him as their Messiah (Romans 11:25-26).

LUKE 14

JESUS HEALS A MAN WITH SWOLLEN LIMBS / 14:1-6 / 155

To illustrate how Israel rejected Jesus (13:31-35), Luke recorded another example of the Pharisees' opposition to Jesus. In the face of repeated miracles, the Pharisees stood stone-faced. They did not rejoice with the healed man; instead, they accused and condemned Jesus, for having compassion and doing good.

14:1-3 A **leader of the Pharisees** invited Jesus to his home, but **the people were watching** Jesus **closely.** It may be surprising to see Jesus on the Pharisees' turf after he had denounced them so many times. Perhaps this Pharisee actually wanted to learn from Jesus or was interested in a discussion with him. But the fact that Jesus was being watched seems to reveal that the religious leaders were hoping to trip up Jesus. Because it was another **Sabbath**, perhaps they again hoped to find Jesus violating their Sabbath rules, for it seems quite suspicious that **a man** was there in front of Jesus **whose arms and legs were swollen.** This certainly makes one wonder if this man were not there on purpose—as if planted by the religious leaders so they could again catch Jesus in the act of healing on the Sabbath. It is also possible that the man was an outsider who came in near Jesus, as had the woman who had anointed Jesus' feet at another Pharisee's house (7:37-38). Also called "dropsy," this disease had an abnormal accumulation of fluid in bodily tissues and cavities causing swelling.

Jesus knew what his "watchers" were thinking, so he asked them the question that had caused friction between him and them before, **"Is it permitted in the law to heal people on the Sabbath day, or not?"** (For more on Sabbath healings, see commentary on 6:1-9; 13:10-17.)

14:4-6 The religious leaders **refused to answer** Jesus' question. Why didn't they explain that it was not lawful and then patiently tell him why? Because they knew Jesus would heal the man and because they were hoping to use it against him. The men had no more concern for their rules at this moment than Jesus did. The rules did not serve the purpose, so they refused to answer. So Jesus **touched the sick man and healed him and sent him away.** Jesus explained that when it served their purposes, these religious leaders did work on the Sabbath. They could go pull a **son** or a **cow** out of a pit if need be, but they were ready to condemn Jesus for touching a man and healing him from a disease. Jesus pointed this out to them, but **they had no answer.**

JESUS TEACHES ABOUT SEEKING HONOR / 14:7-14 / 156
Jesus wasn't one to mince words; he didn't wait for a discreet time to teach and preach. In the midst of his enemies (the Pharisees were carefully watching him to see if they could trap him in any way), Jesus admonished them for their arrogance.

14:7-9 In Jesus' day, Jewish custom at a dinner was to arrange couches in a U shape with a low table in front of them. Guests reclined on the left elbow, and they would be seated according to status, with the place of honor being the seat at the center of the U. The seats would decline in status the farther away from that seat of honor. If arrivals had placed themselves in the **best seat** and then **someone more respected** arrived, they would be asked to move to lower seats. By then, the only seat that would still be open would be **at the foot of the table.**

This may seem like an odd bit of social manners given by Jesus, but his meaning went much deeper. This **wedding feast** pictures the Messiah's Kingdom. Those who seek honor for themselves will be disgraced. Jesus explains that honor cannot be taken, it must be given by God. He will not honor those who seek to honor themselves.

14:10-11 Jesus explained that people should **sit at the foot of the table.** This would show that the person had not overestimated his or her own importance. Then, the host may ask that person to move to **a better place.** Then, instead of being disgraced, the person would be **honored.** The principle would be true in that situation, and in the Kingdom of God—**the proud will be humbled, but the humble will be honored.** The host, God himself, will make the final seating arrangements in his Kingdom. People dare not presume upon their own importance; how much better to be honored by God.

14:12-14 While guests ought not presume upon their importance in the eyes of their host (14:7-11), hosts should not be exclusive about whom they invite. Jesus explained that they shouldn't invite only people who can pay them back. Instead, they should **invite the poor, the crippled, the lame, and the blind.** When God's people can do good, without expecting reward or repayment, they will have truly served him unselfishly. **God will reward** those who so willingly serve him.

JESUS TELLS THE PARABLE OF THE GREAT FESTIVAL / 14:15-24 / 157
The tie between this parable and the previous one is the resurrection. The host who invites the poor, the crippled, the lame, and the blind will be rewarded at the resurrection. Jesus went on to explain that God himself, the heavenly host of the messianic banquet, would offer the same invitation.

14:15 Jesus' words about the resurrection sparked a comment from **a man sitting at the table** (apparently a Pharisee or teacher, 14:1-3). This Pharisee assumed that he and his fellow Pharisees and other leaders would have the **privilege** to **share in the Kingdom of God.** They counted on their ancestry and their law-keeping to have reserved places for them. Jesus would shatter this preconception.

14:16-17 It was customary to send two invitations to a party—the first to announce the event. Thus, this man **prepared a great feast and sent out many invitations.** It does not appear that anyone had declined, so the man made final preparations in order to have enough for everyone. The second invitation told the guests that everything was ready. In this case, the man's **servant** personally notified all the guests that **it was time for them to come.**

14:18-20 The guests in Jesus' story insulted the host by making **excuses** when he issued the second invitation. The guests decided that other matters were more important at the time. The point is that nothing should become an excuse to put off joining God's Kingdom. All pursuits, no matter how valid they seem, can rob people of the great celebration with Jesus. Let nothing stand in the way of following Christ.

14:21-23 Upon learning how his invitations had been snubbed, the master of the house **was angry.** But his banquet was ready, the food had been prepared. Instead of abandoning the whole prospect, he sent his servant to bring into the banquet hall **the poor, the crippled, the lame, and the blind** (see also 14:13). This done, the servant reported back that there was still **room for more.** So the master again dispatched the servant to go throughout the **country lanes and behind the hedges** and fill the house. This story would seem scandalous to Jesus' audience. No ancient wealthy person would ever invite the poor. This startling statement told Jesus' hearers that God's Kingdom is especially for the poor. Not a morsel of food was to go to waste. If the previously invited guests would not accept the hospitality of the master, then he would invite those who would.

14:24 In Israel's history, God's **first** invitation came from Moses and the prophets; the second came from his Son. Jesus' listeners, the religious leaders, accepted the first invitation. They believed that God had called them to be his people. But they insulted God by refusing to accept his Son. They would miss the banquet completely because they refused to accept the Son's invitation—they would not **get even the smallest taste of** what had been prepared for them. Thus, just as the master in the story sent his servant into the streets to invite the needy to his banquet, so God was sending his Son to the whole world of needy people (Jews and Gentiles) to tell them that his Kingdom had arrived and was ready for them.

JESUS TEACHES ABOUT THE COST OF BEING A DISCIPLE / 14:25-35 / 158
This collection of Jesus' teachings about discipleship suggests a turning point in Luke's narrative of the journey to Jerusalem begun at 9:51. From this point to the end of this "Jerusalem section" around chapter 18, the Gospel contains materials that focus on discipleship.

14:25-26 Great crowds were still **following Jesus.** Perhaps all these casual followers considered themselves "disciples" of this popular teacher. Jesus explained what it meant to truly be his disciple. His disciples had to **love** him **more than** their own family members. Certainly this caused a stir among the people. Who would possibly ask his followers to love him that way?

Jesus was not going against the fifth commandment to honor father and mother (Exodus 20:12). Nor was he attempting to subvert the natural love that exists among family members. Instead, he was saying that his followers' love for him should be so complete and wholehearted that their love for family members and for life itself would pale in comparison. In first-century Jewish family settings, deciding for Jesus could mean alienation from the family. Jesus warned the would-be disciples that they must be clear about their true allegiance. Those who cannot make that kind of commitment **cannot be** his **disciple.**

14:27 Besides being willing to love Jesus more than any others and more than life itself, the true disciple must be ready to **carry** his **own cross and follow** Jesus (see also 9:23 and commentary there). Jesus gave this teaching to get the crowds to think through their enthusiasm for him. He encouraged those who were superficial either to go deeper or to turn back. Following Christ means total submission to him—perhaps even to the point of death.

14:28-30 Jesus promised his followers a Kingdom, but he also said that they would face diffi-

culty and suffering because of their faith. Those on the fence needed to **count the cost.** When a builder doesn't count the cost or estimates it inaccurately, his building may be left half-completed. What are those "costs" to believers? Christians may face loss of social status or wealth. They may have to give up control over their money, time, or career. They may be hated, separated from their family, and even put to death. All people must carefully count the cost of becoming Christ's disciple so that they will know what they are getting into and won't be tempted to turn back when the going gets tough.

14:31-32 In this second example, Jesus described a wise king's decision to consider whether his **ten thousand** soldiers could defeat twice that number coming against him. He has to act, but should he fight or ask for peace? To rush out with his soldiers, without first discussing the options, would invite disaster for his nation. Far better to think it through beforehand. So those who want to follow Jesus should carefully consider their decision.

14:33 The cost to be counted is **giving up everything** for Jesus. To be preoccupied with money or possessions is to miss the demands and joys of true discipleship, as with the people who refused the host's invitation to the Kingdom (14:18-20). Again Jesus painted no rosy picture of a high-paying job with all the benefits. He said that the way would be rough and would be a way of self-sacrifice. Oddly enough, however, this is the only way to true fulfillment and satisfaction.

14:34-35 In the ancient world, **salt** was used as a seasoning and as a preservative. The salt came mostly from salt marshes in the area southwest of the Dead Sea. This impure salt was susceptible to deterioration and could lose its flavor, leaving only useless crystals. Such salt was simply **thrown away.** Jesus' question, **"How do you make it salty again?"** did not require an answer—for once salt has deteriorated, nothing is left but worthless residue.

Many Christians blend into the world and avoid the cost of standing up for Christ. But Jesus says if Christians lose their distinctive "saltiness," they become worthless. Just as salt flavors and preserves food, Christ's disciples are to preserve the good in the world, help keep it from spoiling, and bring new flavor to life. This requires careful planning, willing sacrifice, and unswerving commitment to Christ's Kingdom. Being "salty" is not easy, but if Christians fail in this function, they fail to represent Christ in the world. The person **who is willing to hear** should be able to **understand** these words and apply them.

LUKE 15

JESUS TELLS THE PARABLE OF THE LOST SHEEP / 15:1-7 / 159

This passage of Luke begins with the opposition of the Pharisees, just like the previous section (14:1). Here the Pharisees grumbled about Jesus consorting with "sinners," as they had done before (5:30; 7:39). Luke placed three parables together that speak of the joy of God at the repentance of a single sinner. For Christians today, this parable of the lost sheep is not only an invitation to rejoice with God at the repentance of sinners but a reminder to follow Jesus' example in searching for the lost.

15:1-2 Jesus' association with **notorious sinners** in the eyes of the Pharisees has already been documented (5:30; 7:34). **Tax collectors** were Jews who worked for the Roman Empire in collecting Rome's taxes from their countrymen. Yet these people **came to listen to Jesus teach.** These were the very people Jesus had come to reach—those who needed help. In that culture, sitting down and having a meal with a person showed a certain amount of identification and welcome. If Jesus were eating with such horrible people, then he was guilty by association. The Pharisees would not even go near such people, not even to teach them the law or point them to God.

15:3-5 The religious leaders were to picture themselves as shepherds (in reality, as leaders of the nation, they should have been serving as shepherds of God's people). Each shepherd has **one hundred sheep**—a typical number for the average flock of sheep. Shepherds counted their sheep every night, for sheep would easily stray away and get lost. When this shepherd counted, he was missing one sheep. Jesus used the shepherd's concern for each sheep to set up the question, **"Wouldn't you leave the ninety-nine** others to go and search for the lost one?"** The answer was obvious to these listeners—any caring shepherd would do so. He would search, find the lost sheep, carry it back to the flock, and rejoice.

God's love for each individual is so great that he seeks each one out and rejoices when he or she is "found." Jesus associated with sinners because he wanted to bring the lost sheep—people considered beyond hope—the Good News of God's Kingdom. Just as the shepherd took the initiative to go out and find the sheep, so Jesus actively seeks lost souls. These tax collectors and sinners (15:1) with whom Jesus was associating were like sheep who had strayed away from God and needed to be returned. More than that, they needed the salvation that Jesus offered.

15:6-7 The shepherd did not rejoice alone. He even called his **friends and neighbors to rejoice** with him that he found his lost sheep. In reality, the shepherds would not have had a party over one found sheep. Jesus used this element in the story to stress his Kingdom's reality and the value of one lost person. God rejoices when **one lost sinner** is found and **returns to God.**

JESUS TELLS THE PARABLE OF THE LOST COIN / 15:8-10 / 160

In this parable, Jesus portrays God's love for someone who falls into a life of sin. They are lost, disconnected from their true owner, God himself. But their owner doesn't give up on people. Instead, he compassionately searches for them, freely offering them forgiveness through his Son, Jesus Christ.

15:8-9 Palestinian women would often receive **ten silver coins** as a wedding gift. Besides their monetary value, these coins held sentimental value like that of a wedding ring; to lose one would be extremely distressing. The ten coins could have been this woman's life savings, meant to support her in a time of need. Upon discovering that one of the coins was missing, the woman would **light a lamp** in order to see into the dark corners, and **sweep** every part of the dirt-packed floor in hope of finding it. Although the woman still had nine coins, she would not rest until the tenth was retrieved. Her search was rewarded. Like the shepherd, she shared her joy with her friends and neighbors so they could rejoice with her.

15:10 Just as a shepherd would rejoice over finding a lost sheep and a woman would rejoice at finding her lost coin, so all heaven rejoices over a repentant sinner. Each individual is precious to God. He actively seeks those lost ones, and when they are found, **there is joy in the presence of God's angels.** Through these two parables, Jesus was explaining to his detractors that, while they were not pleased with him, God was pleased that Jesus was seeking the lost souls and bringing them the Good News of the Kingdom.

JESUS TELLS THE PARABLE OF THE LOST SON / 15:11-32 / 161

The previous two parables—the one of lost sheep and the lost coin—build up to the climax, the parable of the lost son, a parable that is unique to Luke. Through the parable of the lost son, Jesus presents a vivid illustration of God and his mercy for repentant sinners.

15:11-12 Jesus continued with another parable **to illustrate the point further** that God rejoices when lost sinners repent and find forgiveness. **A man had two sons,** the younger of whom wanted his share of his father's **estate** (inheritance). This would have been one-third of the total estate, with the older son receiving two-thirds, a double portion of the other as prescribed by the law (Deuteronomy 21:17). In most cases, the son would have received this at his father's death, although fathers sometimes chose to divide up their inheritance early and retire from managing their estates. What is unusual is that the younger son initiated the division of the estate. This showed arrogant disregard for his father's authority as head of the family.

15:13-14 Within just **a few days,** the younger son was on his way—indicating that this had been his plan when he had asked for his inheritance in the first place. He **packed all his belongings** and traveled **to a distant land.** The young man apparently had wanted to live his own way, be his own master, get out from under the rules of his home and his father. Money was his ticket out, so he took it and ran.

In this distant land, he **wasted all his money on wild living.** But then **his money ran out.** To make matters worse, **a great famine swept over the land** and the boy did not even have money for food.

15:15-16 The young man became so desperate that he began to work feeding **pigs.** According to Moses' law, pigs were unclean animals (Leviticus 11:2-8; Deuteronomy 14:8). To protect themselves from defilement, Jews would not even touch pigs. For a Jew to stoop to feeding pigs would have been a great humiliation. The **pods** were the seeds of the carob tree, which grows around the Mediterranean Sea. That **no one gave him anything** shows that he was neglected and insignificant; he had truly sunk to the depths.

15:17-19 Sitting among pigs that were better fed than he was, he reflected on life back home. With no money, no dignity, and, so he thought, no claim to sonship in his father's household, he decided to **go home** to his **father,** confess his sin, and ask to be taken on **as a hired man.** At least there he would not go hungry. The key lies in the words that he planned to say to his father, **"I have sinned against both heaven and you."** He wanted to tell his father he was sorry. He wanted to repent of the selfishness that had led him to leave and spend all the money that his father had set aside for his future. Even if it meant living as a hired man in his own home, he would return there in order to say these things to his father.

15:20-21 So the son **returned home to his father,** not knowing what to expect—the best he could anticipate was a cold shoulder, a halfhearted welcome, or a chance to be hired as a slave. The father, however, seemed to have cast his eyes on the horizon many times since his son had left, hoping one day to see him returning. Finally, **his father saw him coming** even while he was far away. The father ran, embraced, and kissed his son. He was **filled with love and compassion** at the sight of his son who had come home. The son began to give his father the speech he had prepared (15:19), but he didn't even get to the part about asking to be hired, for the father wanted to welcome his son back into his home with a grand celebration.

In the two preceding stories, the seeker actively looked for the sheep and the coin, which could not return by themselves. In this story, the father watched and waited. He was dealing with a human being with a will, but he was ready to greet his son if he returned. In the same way, God's love is constant and patient and welcoming. He will search and give people opportunities to respond, but he will not force them to come to him. Like the father in this story, God waits patiently for people to come to their senses.

15:22-24 The father immediately restored this destitute and humbled young man as his son. Then the **calf** that was being fattened up for the time when a special feast should be prepared was to be killed—the father could think of no more fitting celebration. His son had been as good as **dead** to him, but now had **returned to life.** He had been **lost,** but now was **found.** As the shepherd celebrated upon finding the lost sheep (15:6), and the woman upon finding her lost coin (15:9), so this father celebrated at "finding" his "lost" son.

15:25-27 The **older son,** according to tradition, would have received a double inheritance. He probably had continued to be under his father's authority, working on the estate. While he would inherit it, this would not take place until his father's death. So he **was in the fields working,** being responsible to do the work that he should do, patiently following the typical plan for passing on the family inheritance. Imagine this other brother's surprise at returning from a day of hard work to the sound of a grand celebration going on in the house. Naturally he wondered **what was**

going on. The servant simply replied with the facts—the wayward brother had returned, the calf had been killed, the feast had been prepared, and everyone was celebrating the brother's **safe return.**

15:28-30 At the report of the news, the older brother **was angry and wouldn't go in** to join the celebration. The older son was quite reasonable in his list of complaints. The father could have consented, pacifying his older son with additional gifts and rewards. But relationships prosper on love, not on fairness. Love is the dynamic that sweeps "reasonable claims" into secondary concerns here. When relationships need love, we often must let fairness take a second seat.

While the resentment of this older brother is easy to understand, his volley of words reveals the same sort of self-righteousness that afflicted the religious leaders of Jesus' day. The key to understanding this story is found in the context of 15:1-2. The younger son stands for the tax collectors and sinners, the waiting father is God, and the older brother represents the religious leaders. The younger son had lived as a notorious sinner, so the brother wanted nothing to do with him. Yet the loving father, who had gone out to meet his younger son, also **came out** to plead with his elder one who would not take a moment to understand that he would inherit everything that he was working for and that he was dearly loved by his father. He only felt angry that his father was celebrating for an irresponsible person.

The religious leaders, claiming how hard they "slaved" for God, were attempting to keep myriad rules and regulations, many of which God never even demanded. They had the Father's love, but had chosen to reject it in favor of hard work and self-denial. So when God eagerly welcomed the sinful, common people into the Kingdom, the religious leaders were refusing to join the celebration. But God rejoiced that these sinful people had come "home," and he invited even these religious leaders to join the party. They had only anger and resentment that their efforts had not earned a party.

15:31-32 The father spoke kindly to his overheated son; the son had not been displaced as the first-born—he had his relationship with his father (who obviously loved him very much), and he still had his inheritance. The younger son had squandered his, and had gone through great suffering before coming to his senses. The wild life the younger son had sought had brought him only to ruin, and he returned home with no inheritance, humbled from having suffered some hard knocks. The older son needed to get his perspective, be grateful that he had not had to go through such pain, and **celebrate this happy day** of his brother's safe return.

Desperate sinners, notorious outcasts, difficult people—all have been offered salvation. God's people must not stand aside and above, but must join in heaven's celebration when those who were lost have been found.

LUKE **16**

JESUS TELLS THE PARABLE OF THE SHREWD MANAGER / 16:1-18 / *162*

This passage of Luke begins a section dealing with the wise use of one's possessions. This parable is one of the most difficult to interpret, but it explains how Jesus' followers ought to use worldly wealth. Jesus was pointing out that everyone, fully warned of the coming divine judgment, should follow this manager's example. All people are in a worse predicament than this manager because their eternal destinies hang in the balance. Instead of frantically holding on to possessions which soon will disappear, possessions should be given away, especially to those in need (12:33). Money will not last, but people, God's word, and his Kingdom will. Will your investments reap eternal dividends?

16:1-2 This **manager** handled financial matters for the **rich man.** He had extensive authority over the rich man's financial affairs, even the ability to make contracts in the master's name. A person in such a position should have complete integrity. Unfortunately, this manager did not. He **was thoroughly dishonest.** Having been informed of the problems, the rich man **called him in** and demanded a financial **report.** As a consequence, the rich man would strip the manager of his authority, but first he required that the steward prepare the documents. This would take some time, and the manager used this time to his advantage.

16:3-4 The manager just lost his livelihood, but he had a window of time before being fired. So he thought about how best to handle his coming unemployment. Having been a manager, he did not want to **dig ditches,** he had too much pride to **beg,** and his mismanagement of his master's funds would cause no one else to hire him for such a position. So he came up with a plan whereby others would **take care** of him. By plying upon the code of reciprocity, the manager could find food and housing and possibly a job from those whose debts were reduced.

16:5-7 Much discussion has arisen around exactly what this money manager was doing in this situation. Some commentators suggest that what the manager was doing was removing the interest and his own earnings from each of the debts. Most likely, this manager was acting very shrewdly in figuring out a way to put his master's debtors in his own debt. The debts here involved are very high, thus these probably would have been commercial transactions—perhaps involving lease arrangements on pieces of land. The manager summoned all his master's debtors and reduced their debts by a substantial amount. In this fraudulent way, the manager earned their good will. Once the debts had been dishonestly reduced, the master could do nothing, but social custom would require these debtors to reciprocate such kindness to the manager.

16:8-9 The commendation for the **dishonest rascal** raises questions. Why would dishonesty be commended? The manager had cut down the debts, legally made them binding with a third party, and indebted others to him. Thus, there was nothing left for the master to do than to commend the manager for his shrewdness. He had solved his problem—albeit at expense to his master. The commendation seems odd, unless the master was simply appreciating the farsightedness of the plan.

Actually, Jesus did not want his listeners to focus on the details as much as on the lesson to be learned, which he includes here. **The citizens of this world are more shrewd than the godly are. Citizens of this world** refers to unbelievers, who are neither committed to God nor his eternal standards. **The godly** refers to the disciples and followers of Jesus. The shrewd manager sized up his situation, made some decisions, came up with a strategy, and did what was needed. Jesus was not commending dishonesty, but rather the manager's foresight and diligence to follow through and make friends. The manager did not profit directly in reducing the debts, but he used the principle of reciprocity to gain favor with the debtors. By doing a favor for them, the manager could require a favor from them.

Then Jesus added, "I tell you, use your worldly resources to benefit others and make friends. In this way, your generosity stores up a reward for you in heaven." Believers are to make wise use of their financial opportunities, not to earn heaven, but to use their resources to make friends by helping the poor. If believers use their money to help those in need or to help others find Christ, their earthly investment will bring eternal benefit. Those who obey God will find that the unselfish use of their possessions will follow. Soon Jesus would spell out some of the applications for gaining friends (16:10-13).

16:10-12 How people handle their **worldly wealth** shows their trustworthiness. If a person can be trusted with a little bit, if he or she maintains integrity even in small matters, then that person has proven trustworthiness for large matters. The reverse is also true—the one who would willingly steal a dollar may also be willing to steal thousands. Trustworthiness goes to a person's very core.

16:13 Money often takes the place of God in people's lives. How a person handles money indicates how much mastery money has attained in that person's life. Jesus explained that **no one can serve two masters.** From a spiritual standpoint, all people will serve someone or something; here Jesus spoke of two choices, **God and money.** People can choose to serve money—in essence, this means serving themselves and all the pleasure and power money can buy—or they can choose to serve God. But no one can do both, for the two choices are diametrically opposed. No one can seek selfish pleasure and be able to give money away. When money is one's master, there can be no room for God who requires single-hearted obedience and devotion.

Avoid mistaken judgments here. Many rich people are genuine, mature Christians. Wealth is not the issue. Many mature Christians work hard and expect to be paid. That's not the issue either. Money for these people is only a means to an end. Yet some people tragically have made wealth an end in itself—the thing to serve, their god. For Christians, money is always a means of service, never an ultimate goal. Money is God's loan to you for smart stewardship, never a measure of your real worth.

16:14-15 Because the Pharisees **loved their money,** they **scoffed** at Jesus' teaching. They may not have thought that they were serving money (16:13), but their laughing at Jesus' words shows that Jesus had touched a sensitive area. The Pharisees acted piously to get praise from others, but **God** knew their **evil hearts.** They considered their wealth to be a sign of God's approval. God detested their wealth, however, because it caused them to abandon true spirituality. **What this world honors is an abomination in the sight of God.** People who focus their lives on outward appearance and impressing others serve the wrong master and therefore cannot serve God.

16:16-17 Jesus emphasized that his Kingdom fulfilled the **law;** it did not cancel it (Matthew 5:17). **The Good News of the Kingdom of God** was not a new system but the culmination of the old. The same God who had worked through Moses was working through Jesus. **John the Baptist's** ministry was the dividing line between the Old and New Testaments (John 1:15-18). Up until his time, the only revelation of God available to people came through the **laws of Moses and the messages of the prophets.** The Good News was the culmination of all that the Law demanded and the Prophets foresaw. Those who recognized his true identity realized that the Kingdom had come and were **forcing their way in,** so desiring to be part of it.

16:18 Jesus had just made the point that his coming fulfilled the law and the prophets. That did not mean, however, that the law was no longer valid. In fact, in many cases, Jesus took the law and required even higher standards for those who would follow him (Matthew 5:21-22, 27-28, 33-35, 38-39, 43-44). Divorce was a hot topic of debate. Stricter than any of the then-current schools of thought, Jesus' teachings shocked his hearers (see Matthew 19:10), just as they shake today's readers. Jesus stated in no uncertain terms that marriage is a lifetime commitment, and he explained that divorce dissolves a divinely formed union. He also explained that marriage after divorce is **adultery.** (Matthew 19:9 gives one exception: marital unfaithfulness.) While the application of Jesus' words requires interpretation to specific situations, one truth is inescapable: God created marriage to be a sacred, permanent union and partnership between husband and wife. Anyone who takes this lightly forgets God's law and his plan for marriage from the very beginning.

Through this statement about divorce, Jesus was showing the unbelieving religious leaders that his words do not violate the law. He also wanted to point out to them their hypocrisy in attempting to keep the letter of the law while failing to fulfill its moral obligations.

JESUS TELLS ABOUT THE RICH MAN AND THE BEGGAR / 16:19-31 / *163*
In Jesus' parable of a rich man and a poor man, their fortunes were exactly reversed at death:
the poor man went to paradise, while the rich man suffered in hell. In agony, the rich man
cried out for help, asking Abraham to send Lazarus to warn his brothers of this tragic, irreversible fate.

16:19-21 Finally, regarding the Pharisees' attitude
toward money (they "dearly loved" it, 16:14), Jesus
gave an illustration that vividly portrays the value
of money in light of future judgment. This **Lazarus**
should not be confused with the Lazarus whom
Jesus raised from the dead in John 11. Incidentally,
this is the only person in any of Jesus' stories who
is given a name. The **rich man** in this parable lived
out the lifestyle afforded to the wealthy who lived
in the Roman Empire. Splendid clothing, delicious
food of all types, and days lived in **luxury** could be
had by those with enough money.

In contrast, there is a poor **diseased beggar.**
Ancient Rome had no middle class—there were
the very rich and the very poor. Often the poor
were reduced to begging in order to survive. This
man, Lazarus, was sick, hungry, and abandoned,
so he **lay** at the rich man's door, **longing for
scraps from the rich man's table.** Leftovers were
all he desired, and the rich man could easily have
shared from his extravagance by sending a servant
out with a plateful. But the rich man chose to
spend his money on himself, refusing to share,
probably not even taking notice of the poor man
at his door. His wealth was not sinful, but his selfishness was. While he had everything he could
possibly want, Lazarus lay hungry with even the
dogs licking **his open sores.**

16:22-23 In time, both the rich man and Lazarus
died, for death takes everyone regardless of social
station or wealth. The rich man ended up in **torment** in **the place of the dead**, the destiny of
those who have refused to believe. The "torment"
is described in 16:24 as "flames." Added to the
torment was the rich man's ability to see paradise,
with Abraham and Lazarus in peace and luxury.
The role reversal is obvious—as Lazarus once lay
in pain outside the door of the rich man's house
watching him feast, so here the rich man was in
torment watching the joy far away in heaven.

In contrast, Lazarus must have been a God-
fearing man, despite the fact that God had not
allowed him an easy or pleasant lifetime on earth.
When Lazarus died, **the angels** carried him to **be
with Abraham,** another way of describing the
Kingdom.

A theology of heaven and hell should not be

based on Jesus' words here. Pressing the details
too much will take us away from the main point
of the illustration, which is to teach about the
danger of pursuing wealth, as well as the finality
of God's judgment.

16:24-25 Not only could the rich man in this story
see into heaven's bliss from his torment, but he
could call out to those in paradise as well. He
spoke to **Father Abraham,** a title any Jew would
use for Abraham, the father of their nation (John
8:39). The request for Abraham to send Lazarus to
dip the tip of his finger in water shows that the
rich man's basic attitude had not changed. For all
his deference to Abraham, he still thought of Lazarus as no more than a messenger who could be
sent by Abraham to do the rich man a favor.

Abraham sent an answer, but not the one that
the rich man wanted or even expected. The rich
man may have thought there was a mistake. He
had been rich, and if wealth was a sign of God's
blessing, why would he be in agony? Abraham
explained that, during their time on earth, the rich
man had **everything,** but **Lazarus had nothing.**
While the rich man could have helped the poor
within his reach (such as Lazarus), he chose only
personal pleasure. The roles for eternity would be
reversed. Lazarus went from pain and hunger to
comfort; the rich man went from pleasure and
merriment to **anguish.** This would have unnerved
the Pharisees who were listening to this parable.
To them, wealth was a sign of God's blessing,
poverty a sign of God's disfavor. So they enjoyed
their wealth and did not attempt to bridge the
chasm that separated them from the "disfavored
ones." But Jesus was explaining that another chasm
would develop, and they would find themselves
on the wrong side.

16:26 Abraham explained to the rich man that he
couldn't send Lazarus because between them and
him was **a great chasm** and **no one** can **cross over.**
The ultimate fates cannot be changed. God's decision upon death is final. There is only one life on
this earth, and that is the time of decision. People
cannot wait until eternity to make their relationship right with God—it will be too late. The judgment will have been made on the basis of their
choices, and it will be irreversible.

16:27-29 The rich man still thought Lazarus could be sent on messenger duty. If Lazarus could not come to help him, then he wanted Lazarus sent to warn his **five brothers** about the **place of torment** so they wouldn't have to go there when they died. Abraham simply explained that they could read the words of **Moses and the prophets** (that is, the Old Testament) and there find the warnings about the place of torment. If those brothers hadn't heeded the major message of God in his word, they would not heed a messenger.

16:30-31 Perhaps the rich man knew his brothers only too well. The suggestion that they read God's word (or listen to it read in the synagogue) met with a **no.** It just wouldn't happen—probably for the same reasons that the rich man himself never had heeded the warnings therein. So the rich man begged that someone **from the dead** go back to them. Surely, then, they would **turn from their sins.** Abraham answered that if these brothers did not **listen to Moses and the prophets,** then **they won't listen even if someone rises from the dead** and appears to them.

Notice the irony in Jesus' statement; on his way to Jerusalem to die, he was fully aware that even when he had risen from the dead, most of the religious leaders would not accept him. They were set in their ways, and neither Scripture nor God's Son himself would shake them loose.

LUKE 17

JESUS TELLS ABOUT FORGIVENESS AND FAITH / 17:1-10 / *164*

After the parable of the rich man and Lazarus, Luke collected four of Jesus' teachings that involve discipleship. In these teachings, Jesus addressed his followers' relationship with each other and their relationship with God. They are sharp words of truth from the Savior—a firm prod to reevaluate all of life in light of these principles.

17:1 Since 16:14, Jesus had been focusing his comments toward the Pharisees. The following samples of teaching, whether chronological or not, were focused toward **his disciples.** Because people are sinful and because people live in relationship with one another, they will tempt each other to sin. The Greek word *skandala* used here denotes any hindrance that causes another person to fall into sin, whether through temptation or false teaching. Jesus explained that while there would **always be temptations,** that did not excuse **the person who does the tempting.** Jesus may have been referring to the religious leaders who taught their converts their own hypocritical ways (see Matthew 23:15). These leaders were perpetuating an evil system through their false teaching. A person who teaches others has a solemn responsibility (James 3:1).

17:2 Leading another person astray is very serious. Jesus explained that the consequences were so severe that it would be **better** to have a **millstone** tied around one's neck and be **thrown into the sea** than for a person to face God after causing others to stumble. A "millstone" was a heavy, flat stone used to grind grain. To have a millstone tied around the neck and be dumped into the sea pictured a horrifying death by drowning. Even such a death would be minor, however, compared to what this person would face in eternity. Jesus used the term **little ones** to refer not just to children but to his followers. Those who turn people away from God will receive severe punishment.

17:3-4 Careful leadership is important for Jesus' followers, but so is constant forgiveness. When there is sin among God's people, they are responsible to **rebuke** one another. To "rebuke" does not mean to point out every sin, for Jesus also warns against being judgmental (6:37). To "rebuke" (always in love) means to bring sin to a person's attention with the purpose of restoring that person to God and to fellow humans. In context here, this refers to sin that could pull that person or others away from God, and thus result in the horrible judgment Jesus spoke of in 17:2. When a person feels that he or she must rebuke another Christian for a sin, it is wise for that person to check his or her attitudes and motivations first. Unless rebuke is tied to forgiveness, it will not help the sinning person. Jesus explained, in fact, that if the other person repents, the rebuker must **forgive.** And that forgiveness extends constantly.

17:5-6 The disciples told Jesus, **"We need more faith."** Jesus didn't directly answer their question because the amount of faith is not as important as its genuineness. What is faith? It is total dependence on God and a willingness to do his will.

A **mustard seed** is small, but it is alive and growing. Like a tiny seed, a small amount of genuine faith in God will take root and grow. The apostles didn't need more faith; a tiny seed of faith would be enough, if it were alive and growing.

Jesus pointed to a nearby **mulberry tree** and said that even small faith could uproot it and send it **into the sea.** Mulberry trees grow quite large (as high as thirty-five feet). Matthew's Gospel records a similar teaching when Jesus said that a mountain could be told to throw itself into the sea (Matthew 21:21). It is the power of God, not faith, that uproots trees and moves mountains, but faith must be present for God to work. Even a small "seed" of faith is sufficient. There is great power in even a little faith when God is there

17:7-10 When Jesus' followers **obey,** they have only done their **duty** and should regard it as a privilege. They should not expect thanks, for they were only doing what they were supposed to do. Jesus used the example of a slave who renders service and does not expect to be thanked. Obedience is not something extra done for God; it is the duty of anyone who desires to be Christ's follower. Before God, all people are sinners, saved only by God's grace, but believers *are* saved and therefore have great worth in God's Kingdom. They must lay aside selfishness and treat others with respect and common courtesy.

With these words, Jesus was not rendering service as meaningless or useless, nor was he doing away with rewards. He was attacking unwarranted self-esteem and spiritual pride—perhaps such as many of the religious leaders were exhibiting, or what the disciples themselves might be tempted to fall into as they would seek to serve God. Jesus' followers focus their eyes on God with their goal only to serve and please him. They don't work for recognition or rewards or even for God to praise them for their hard work. They understand that their duty is to serve the Master.

JESUS HEALS TEN MEN WITH LEPROSY / 17:11-19 / *169*

Ten lepers were healed, but only one leper—a Samaritan—returned to thank Jesus. This story, unique to Luke, highlights the faith of a foreigner in Israel. One of the major themes of Luke is the remarkable faith of Gentiles. Although many of the Jewish religious leaders rejected Jesus, a number of foreigners wholeheartedly placed their trust in him (7:1-10).

17:11-13 Jesus was traveling along the **border between Galilee and Samaria.** Galilee was Jewish; Samaria was occupied by Samaritans who were despised by the Jews. The exact location is unknown, but that Jesus was near the border accounts for a Samaritan in the group of lepers. People who had leprosy were required to try to stay away from other people and to announce their presence if they had to come near. Thus these **ten lepers** were standing at a **distance,** outside the city, and they were **crying out** to Jesus for mercy. They called Jesus **Master**—they knew who he was and what he could do for them. They did not try to get close, however, perhaps because of the crowd that was probably still following Jesus (14:25).

17:14 Jesus sent the ten lepers to the priests (as prescribed by the law, Leviticus 14) before they were healed, **and as they went, their leprosy disappeared.** Jesus did not touch these men or even speak words of healing as he had done for most of his healings. This time he simply gave them the command to **go show** themselves **to the priests.** Jesus was asking the men to respond in faith so that, by their obedience, what they desired would happen. All the men responded in faith, and Jesus healed them on the way.

17:15-16 Jesus healed all ten lepers, but only **one of them** returned to thank him. It is possible to receive God's great gifts with an ungrateful spirit—nine of the ten men did so. Only the thankful man, however, learned that his faith had played a role in his healing; and only grateful Christians grow in understanding God's grace. God does not demand that his people thank him, but he is pleased when they do so. And he uses their responsiveness to teach them more about himself. The surprise of this story is that this **Samaritan,** used to being despised by Jews (except perhaps for his fellow lepers), would dare to go to this Jewish healer and prostrate himself before him. But this man's faith went deep enough that he saw God's hand in the healing. Once again Luke was pointing out that God's grace is for everybody.

17:17-19 Jesus had been distressed many times with his own people's lack of acceptance and faith (7:9; 8:25; 12:28). This time was no different. **Ten men** had been healed, but only one, the **foreigner** (referring to the man from Samaria), came back to **give glory to God.** Jesus was not so much concerned about being thanked as he was about the men's understanding of what had happened. The other nine went off, free from leprosy but not necessarily free from sin through the salvation Jesus could offer. This one man was freed, so Jesus sent him on his way with the knowledge that his **faith** had made him well. He not only had a restored body, his soul had been restored as well.

JESUS TEACHES ABOUT THE COMING OF THE KINGDOM OF GOD / 17:20-37 / 170

Here Luke placed a series of Jesus' teachings about the Kingdom of God in order to present a concise summary of it. This passage, plus 21:15-38, parallel the Olivet discourse of Matthew 24 and Mark 13. In answering the Pharisees' question about the Kingdom, Jesus pointed out that the Kingdom was already among them. With his ministry, Jesus had already inaugurated the Kingdom of God. But Jesus also warned his disciples (17:22) that the complete realization of the Kingdom of God was still in the future.

17:20-21 Up to this point in the chapter, Jesus was explaining how his followers should live. From 17:20–18:8, as a response to a question brought by the **Pharisees,** Jesus discussed **when the Kingdom of God** would **come.** The Pharisees did not understand that the Kingdom of God had already arrived with Jesus. Jesus had made this clear in 11:20. In 19:11-27, he will explain that the full expression of God's Kingdom is yet to come (and is still to come). These are the days "between"—the Kingdom has arrived in Jesus Christ, yet it has not arrived in its fullness. Believers are waiting for it, as Jesus has already described (12:35-48), knowing that it could come at any moment. So Jesus' words here explain the nature of the Kingdom now.

Jesus explained that the Kingdom **isn't ushered in with visible signs;** in other words, no one can project when it will come by looking for supernatural signs. Nor will anyone be able to point to anything that proves that the Kingdom is **here** or **there.** The Kingdom of God **was among** the people because Jesus was among them. When Jesus returned to heaven, the Kingdom remained, and continues today, with the work of God's Spirit in people's lives and in relationships. Still, today, believers must resist looking to institutions or programs for evidence of the progress of God's Kingdom. Instead, they should look for what God is doing in people's hearts. Rather than looking for signs or trying to figure out timetables, each person should look into his or her own heart to be sure to be ready. When the Kingdom arrives, will you be ushered in or sent away?

17:22 Jesus turned his attention back to his disciples and explained that days would come when they would **long to share in the days of the Son of Man,** but they **won't be able to.** We are not certain whether this longing on the disciples' part would be for the return of the days when Jesus was among them physically (for he would soon be gone physically), or if their longing looked ahead to the "days" of the end times when the Kingdom would arrive and Jesus would return. Most likely their "longing" would be looking ahead for what had been promised (because the following verses concern the Second Coming). That they won't be able to share in it means that they would not see his arrival in their lifetimes. There would be an intervening time between Jesus' first and second comings.

17:23-24 In these intervening days, after Christ has returned to heaven and as his followers await his return, there will be much speculation. Some will attempt to pinpoint exactly when Jesus will return; others will attempt to mock believers' expectations. Some will claim to be the Messiah; others will say that Jesus has returned—and people will believe them. Jesus warned believers never to take such reports seriously, no matter how convincing they may sound. When Jesus returns, his power and presence will be evident to everyone, like **lightning** that **flashes across the sky.** No one will need to spread the message because all will see for themselves.

17:25 Before this great return occurs, however, Jesus would return to heaven from earth. In order for that to occur, he would **suffer terribly and be rejected,** and then be crucified. This would happen soon, for it would be **this generation** who would do it, specifically this generation of religious leaders who would arrange for Jesus to be put to death (9:21-27, 37-44; 18:31-34).

17:26-27 To illustrate the suddenness of his return, Jesus used two examples, the first being the flood (see Genesis 6–7). In the days before the flood, life went on as usual for most people, with the exception of **Noah** who had been building a huge boat for many years. Then, it began to rain, **the flood came,** and everyone drowned.

Jesus was warning against false security. Although life will continue as usual until the day of Christ's return, believers must always be ready to go at a moment's notice. When Christ returns, there will be no second chances. Some will be taken to be with him; the rest will be left behind.

17:28-29 The second example of the suddenness of Christ's return is the destruction of the city of **Sodom** (recorded in Genesis 18–19). Sodom, along with the nearby city of Gomorrah, was destroyed by God because of their great wickedness. **Lot,** Abraham's nephew, had chosen to settle in the city of Sodom (Genesis 13:11-13). The people of Sodom, wicked as they were, **went about their daily business.** Then, **the morning Lot left Sodom,** the city was destroyed. The destruction came so suddenly that only Lot and his family escaped. Angels came and spared Lot and his family from the fire and burning sulfur.

In the time between Christ's first and second comings, some may be lulled into complacency by the fact that life continues with its normal activities. Many today see life moving ahead with no interruptions. But Jesus made it clear that judgment would come, unexpectedly, without warning, in the middle of what would begin as a routine day.

17:30-32 When the **Son of Man returns,** there will be no time to return home for anything. Those outside should not go back inside to try to **pack;** those working out in the **field must not return to town.** Jesus exhorted his listeners to **remember what happened to Lot's wife!** When angels led Lot and his family out of the city, the angels warned them not to look back (Genesis 19:17). Surely the sound of destruction reached their ears, but they were not to turn around. Lot's wife looked back, and she became a pillar of salt (Genesis 19:26). Clinging to the past, she was unwilling to completely leave the evil of the city and the comfort of her possessions.

The time for deciding about Christ will pass in a single moment. Those who were waiting and longing to see that day (17:22) will rejoice at its arrival. Those who did not believe it would happen will not have time to do anything about it. It will be too late.

17:33 Christ's return will cause great upheaval and danger. This is described in other prophecies regarding the end times, such as chapter 21 and the book of Revelation. The person looking for the Kingdom will be able to run with joy to welcome it, willingly forfeiting home and possessions in order to have eternal life. However, **whoever clings to this life will lose it,** for nothing in this life will remain. When God's Kingdom comes, everything will change. Clinging to this world is foolish, for it will pass away. Clinging to life is foolish, for it too will pass away. Jesus said much the same thing in 9:24 (see commentary there). (See also Matthew 10:39; 16:25; Mark 8:35; John 12:25.)

17:34-35 The sudden return of Christ and the sudden end of all chances to change one's decision about him will result in sudden separation of his followers from those who chose not to follow. People may be close enough in this world—even sleeping in the same bed or working together at the same job. (Note: The best manuscripts do not include 17:36.) While these people may have looked no different from the outside, one difference will separate them forever. When Jesus returns, he will take his followers to be with him (see 1 Thessalonians 4:14-17).

17:37 Those listening to Jesus' words of warning wanted to know **where** all of this would take place. To answer the disciples' question, Jesus quoted a familiar proverb. One vulture circling overhead does not mean much, but a **gathering of vultures** means that a dead body is nearby. Likewise, one sign of the end may not be significant, but when many signs occur, the Second Coming (**the end) is near.**

LUKE 18

JESUS TELLS THE PARABLE OF THE PERSISTENT WIDOW / 18:1-8 / 171

This parable, unique to Luke, illustrates the importance of prayer for Christians (a theme of Luke's, see 5:16; 6:12; 11:1-13). In the same way as the widow, Christians should not give up praying to God even when facing indifference and powerful opposition.

18:1 The **need for constant prayer** and the injunction to **never give up** should be interpreted in light of the preceding chapter and its focus on the coming Kingdom. Jesus had been discussing with his listeners the aspects of the "in between" time as they lived in a sinful world and awaited the Kingdom. The problem of evil and suffering and the need for justice would plague Jesus' followers as they experienced pain and awaited vindication. As they wrestled with these difficulties, they could know that their heavenly Father listened and understood and that the answer to their prayers for relief and justice is coming in his time.

18:2-5 Jesus was not comparing God to this unjust and contemptuous judge, as though he would treat believers in this manner. Instead, this story shows that if even an evil man can be made to deal justly by a persistent woman, how much more would God, who loves his people, care for their requests.

The scene pictures a **judge** who is **godless** and contemptuous. He should have been championing those who needed justice, but when **a widow** came for help, he **ignored her.** Widows and orphans were among the most vulnerable of all God's people, and both Old Testament prophets and New Testament apostles insisted that these needy people be properly cared for. (See, for example, Exodus 22:22-24; Isaiah 1:17; 1 Timothy 5:3; James 1:27.) This woman had little hope of gaining the justice she sought, so she used the only weapon she had—persistence. With nothing to lose, she made herself an irritant to the judge. To get rid of her, he saw to it that **she got justice.**

18:6-8 If an unjust judge will respond to constant pressure, how much more will a great and loving God respond to his people? They know he loves them; they can believe he will hear their cries for help. They can trust that one day God will give a **just decision in the end.** As God's people seek to be obedient in this sinful world, they can know that God will not **keep putting them off.** It may seem for a time that their cries go unheard. But one day, God **will grant justice to them quickly.** But Christ has not yet returned. Jesus had made it clear that there would be an intervening time. This would be the church age, the present time. During these years, God's people help others find the Kingdom and are themselves strengthened in their faith. Their needs cause them to be on their knees constantly, knowing that God alone is their help. Jesus gave no indication of how long this intervening time would last or when he would return. Indeed, he said no one knows (Matthew 24:36), so believers are always to be ready. But Jesus asked, **"When I, the Son of Man, return, how many will I find who have faith?"** Will people have persisted in faith? Will they be ready and waiting when he comes?

JESUS TELLS THE PARABLE OF TWO MEN WHO PRAYED / 18:9-14 / 172
After encouraging the disciples to be persistent in prayer (18:1-8), Jesus taught them, with a parable, how to pray. This parable sharply contrasts the prayer of a Pharisee with that of a tax collector.

18:9-10 Prayer is important (18:1-8), but the attitude of prayer is vitally important. The people **who had great self-confidence and scorned everyone** were the Pharisees and other religious leaders who saw themselves as the only ones righteous enough to be acceptable to God. To these people, Jesus told a **story** about **two men** who **went to the Temple to pray.** These two men were as different as could be: the one was a law-keeping and religious **Pharisee,** and the other was **a dishonest tax collector.**

18:11-12 This Pharisee's actions and his prayer provide a picture of his life and occupation—he was a separatist, but his separatism and desire to remain clean before God had hardened into a lifestyle of self-righteousness. He **stood by himself and prayed.**

The words of this prayer, however, while probably true, were not prayed in the correct attitude of humility before God. He thanked God that he was **not a sinner like everyone else.** While the Pharisee was probably not like everyone else in a lot of ways, he erred in thinking that he was "not a sinner." This Pharisee knew that he was far better than the **tax collector** he saw praying across the way. Tax collectors were not noted for their honesty, so this Pharisee compared himself favorably, telling God that he himself had never cheated or sinned or committed adultery. And, by the way, he also fasted **twice a week** and tithed from his income.

This Pharisee was confident of himself and his righteousness, while at the same time despising this other man, even though he too was in the Temple praying to the same God. The Pharisee did not welcome the tax collector who may have been seeking God; instead, the Pharisee gloated that he was so much more righteous.

18:13-14 The focus shifts to the **tax collector** who had come to the Temple and seems to have known full well the extent of his sin. He felt so low that he did not think he could **even lift his eyes to heaven** into God's face; instead he **beat his chest** (a sign of sorrow), praying for God to **be merciful to him.** He recognized himself as **a sinner.** He had been convicted of his sin and had come to the one place where he could find forgiveness. He had come to God, humbly recognizing that he did not deserve mercy.

Surprisingly enough, only the tax collector

returned home justified before God. The word "justified" means God's act of declaring people "not guilty" of sin. Only the tax collector recognized his sin; therefore, he was the only one God justified. The self-righteous Pharisee had said that he had no sin; therefore, there was nothing for God to justify for him. He returned home no different than when he had entered.

The principle is that no one has anything of value to bring to God in order to deserve salvation, mercy, justification, or even a second glance from God. **The proud will be humbled, but the humble will be honored.** Acceptance before God cannot be achieved by good deeds, piety, or any amount of self-proclaimed righteousness.

JESUS BLESSES THE CHILDREN / 18:15-17 / *174*
Jesus used a child's humility as a striking picture of the appropriate attitude with which to approach God. That type of humility was demonstrated by the tax collector in the previous parable (18:9-14).

18:15 In the first century, Jewish households were patriarchal—men came first, followed by women and children. Adult men were the key members of society, women quite secondary, and children were to be seen but not heard. It was customary, however, for parents to bring their children (the Greek word for "children" is *paidia,* meaning children ranging in age from babies to pre-teens) to an elder or a scribe **so he could touch** (or lay hands on) **and bless them.** The disciples apparently viewed this as an intrusion and a drain of time and energy. So they **told** the parents **not to bother** Jesus.

18:16-17 Instead of being too busy for children, Jesus **called for** them and wanted them to come to

him. No one should be stopped from coming to Jesus, no matter how young or old. Jesus explained that **the Kingdom of God belongs to such as these,** not meaning that heaven is only for children but that people need childlike attitudes of trust in God. The receptiveness of little children was a great contrast to the stubbornness of the religious leaders who let their education and sophistication stand in the way of a simple faith. **Anyone who doesn't have their kind of faith will never get into the Kingdom of God.** Childlike faith means trusting God no matter what, always knowing that he has your best in mind. You love him because he loves you. You trust completely because the One you trust is completely trustworthy.

JESUS SPEAKS TO THE RICH YOUNG MAN / 18:18-30 / *175*
This episode with the rich young man differs greatly with Jesus' blessing of children in the previous section. The children are an example of innocent faith and trust. The rich young man thought he could gain eternal life by what he did, only to find that he could not have it.

18:18-19 This **religious leader** addressed Jesus as **good teacher** (not the more common "rabbi") and eagerly asked a question about what he should **do to get eternal life.** He viewed eternal life as something that a person could achieve or earn through certain works or good deeds, and he wanted to make sure that he did everything necessary.

Instead of answering the man's question, Jesus first took issue with the way the man addressed him. This may have been no more than a flippant attempt at flattery, but Jesus forced the man to think about it. Because **only God is truly good,** the man had made a statement about Jesus that he probably did not even realize. By asking this question, Jesus was saying, "Do you really know the one to whom you are talking?" The man was correct in calling Jesus good for he was good and also God.

18:20-21 Regarding the man's question, Jesus at first pointed him back to the **commandments** (meaning the Ten Commandments). Jesus listed only five of them—those dealing with human relationships. He did not list any of the first four commandments that deal with a person's relationship to God. All of the ones listed could be easily identified—the man probably could honestly say that he had not committed adultery or murder, had not stolen or lied, and had honored his parents. To keep the letter of these laws would be relatively easy for a wealthy young Jewish man. Yet he still felt strongly that something was lacking in his life. So he asked if there were more he should do. The point is that even if a person could keep all these commandments perfectly, which this man claimed to have done, there would still be a lack of assurance of salvation.

18:22-23 The man saying that he had kept all the commandments led Jesus to focus on the man's relationship to his material possessions (alluding to the last commandment not to covet) and on his relationship to God (the first four commandments that Jesus had not mentioned). Jesus perceived an area of weakness—his wealth—and so said that it was the money itself that was standing in the way of his reaching eternal life. So Jesus told him to **sell** everything he owned, **give** away his **money to the poor,** and then **follow** him. This challenge exposed the barrier that would keep this man out of the Kingdom: his love of money. Ironically, his attitude made him unable to keep the first commandment: "Do not worship any other gods besides me" (Exodus 20:3). The young man did not love God with his whole heart as he had presumed. In reality, his many possessions were his god.

The task of selling every possession would not, of itself, give the man eternal life. But such radical obedience would be the first step. The emphasis was not so much on "selling" as on "following." Jesus' words to this rich young man were a test of his faith and his willingness to obey. The man thought he needed to do more; Jesus explained that there was plenty more he could do but not in order to obtain eternal life. Instead, he needed an attitude adjustment toward his wealth; only then could he submit humbly to the lordship of Christ. By putting his **treasure in heaven** and following Jesus along the road of selflessness and service to others, the man could be assured of his eternal destiny. But the young man **became sad** when he heard this.

Jesus does not ask all believers to sell everything they have. He does ask each person, however, to get rid of anything that has become more important than God. If your basis for security has shifted from God to what you own, you may need to get rid of those possessions.

18:24-25 Offered discipleship, the man chose to return to his possessions. Jesus sadly pointed out to his disciples that it is **hard** for **rich people to get into the Kingdom of God.** This was contrary to conventional wisdom. Most Jews believed that wealth was a sign of God's blessing on people. Here Jesus explained that riches can often prove to be a stumbling block. Rich people often don't feel the deep spiritual hunger needed to seek out and find God. They can use their money to buy possessions, trips, and helpers so that they don't perceive any needs in their lives. With all their advantages and influence, the rich often find it difficult to have the attitude of humility, submission, and service required by Jesus. Because money represents power and success, the rich often miss out on the fact that power and success on earth cannot provide eternal salvation. Even if they use their money to help good causes, they can still miss out on God's Kingdom.

Jesus used a well-known Jewish proverb to describe the difficulty faced by the rich; he said, **"It is easier for a camel to go through the eye of a needle than for a rich person to enter the Kingdom of God."** The Greek word refers to a sewing needle. Jesus' image was for hyperbolic effect. The camel, the largest animal in Palestine, could get through the eye of a sewing needle easier than a rich person could get into God's Kingdom. These are indeed sobering words for those whose money and possessions are extremely important to them.

18:26-27 Because the Jewish people saw riches as a sign of God's special blessing, they were astounded when Jesus said that riches actually worked against people finding God. So they asked, **"Then who in the world can be saved?"**

Jesus answered that **what is impossible from a human perspective is possible with God.** People cannot save themselves, no matter how much power, authority, or influence they buy. Salvation comes from God alone. Both rich and poor can be saved, and human impossibilities are divine possibilities. The rich need to hold their riches loosely, remembering that every penny comes from God. And they should willingly use what God has given to advance his Kingdom. This does not come easily for anyone, rich or poor. Money can be a major stumbling block, but God can change anyone.

18:28-30 Peter and the other disciples had paid a high price—leaving their homes and jobs—to follow Jesus. They had done what the rich man had been unwilling to do. They had abandoned their former lives.

Jesus reminded Peter that following him has its benefits as well as its sacrifices. Any believer who has had to give up something to follow Christ will be **repaid** in this life as well as in the next. For

example, if you must give up a secure job, you will find that God offers a secure relationship with himself now and forever. If you must give up your family's approval, you will gain the love of the family of God. For each person the sacrifice may be different, though no less difficult. No matter how much or how little you have, no matter how difficult the sacrifice may be, are you willing to do whatever it takes to have eternal life?

JESUS PREDICTS HIS DEATH THE THIRD TIME / 18:31-34 / *177*

For the third time, Jesus predicted his death; this time, he graphically described his rejection by the religious leaders and even predicted his own resurrection. Luke placed these predictions within his long section that recounts Jesus' journey to Jerusalem. He placed the first two predictions at the beginning of the journey (9:22, 43-45) and this third prediction toward the end, showing that Jesus was heading to Jerusalem to fulfill these predictions (see 12:50; 13:32-33; 17:25).

18:31 As a warning to his disciples, he gathered them around himself and explained that when they arrived in Jerusalem **all the predictions of the ancient prophets concerning the Son of Man will come true.** Some of those predictions about what would happen to Jesus are in Psalm 41:9 (betrayal); Psalm 22:16-18 and Isaiah 53:4-7 (crucifixion); Psalm 16:10 (resurrection). Jesus explained that the plans had already been in place for thousands of years and soon would be fulfilled.

18:32-34 The first time Jesus told of his impending death, he focused on his rejection by Israel's leaders (9:21-27); the second time, he added the element of betrayal (9:44-45). Here Jesus mentioned the foretelling of these events by the prophets and the

involvement of the **Romans.** While the Jewish leaders would reject Jesus (as reported in 9:21-27), they had to submit to Rome's authority in cases of capital punishment. They could punish lesser crimes, but only Rome could call for and enact an execution.

So sad were these words that it seems the disciples didn't even hear the last sentence—on the **third day,** he would **rise again.** Their ignorance and blindness were simply because they could not grasp the scope of God's plan in Jesus. The disciples **didn't understand** Jesus, apparently because they were focusing on what he said about his death. Even though Jesus spoke plainly, they would not grasp the significance of his words until they had seen the risen Christ face-to-face (see 24:13-35).

JESUS HEALS A BLIND BEGGAR / 18:35-43 / *179*

The healing of the blind man is the last miracle before the Passion Week. On his approach to Jerusalem, Jesus went through Jericho. Here a blind man, a person considered insignificant by others, cried out for mercy and expressed his faith in Jesus as the Messiah who could save him. His bold faith was rewarded.

18:35-36 Continuing on their journey toward Jerusalem, Jesus and the disciples **approached Jericho.** The Old Testament city of Jericho had been destroyed by the Israelites (Joshua 6:20), but during his rule over Palestine, Herod the Great had rebuilt the city (about a mile south of the original city) as a site for his winter palace. Jericho was a popular and wealthy resort city, not far from the Jordan River, about eighteen miles northeast of Jerusalem.

They came upon a **blind beggar** who was **sitting beside the road.** Beggars often waited along the roads near cities because that was where they were able to contact the most people. Usually disabled in some way, beggars were unable to work for a living. Thus, beggars had little hope of escaping their degrading way of life.

18:37-39 When the blind man heard that **Jesus of Nazareth was going by,** he shamelessly cried out for Jesus' attention. He called **"Son of David,"** a title for the Messiah (Isaiah 11:1-3). This means that the blind man understood Jesus to be the long-awaited Messiah. The crowds **tried to hush the man,** perhaps trying to keep Jesus from being harassed by beggars. But that only made the blind man more persistent.

18:40-41 Any normal human being, heading toward certain death, would be extremely preoccupied and probably not necessarily in the mood to help others. But Jesus did not reject the man as the crowd had done. He **ordered that the man be brought to him,** then asked him to voice his request. The man replied unhesitatingly, **"I want to see!"** How many times in his life had he voiced that desire? Probably thousands. But here he stood before the one person in the universe who could actually make his desire a reality. And

he would not have asked if he had not believed that it could be so.

18:42-43 Jesus recognized the man's faith. As a result of such faith, Jesus healed him. All Jesus did was speak the words and **instantly the man could see.** He immediately joined the crowd of followers, staying with Jesus, and **praising God.** This was also the response of the people in the crowd. There were no healings of the blind recorded in the Old Testament, so the Jews believed that such a miracle would be a sign that the messianic age had begun (Isaiah 29:18; 35:5). Jesus healed other blind people as well, so these people knew something special was happening. A poor and blind beggar could see that Jesus was the Messiah, and the crowds understood that God was to be praised for such miracles. But the religious leaders who saw his miracles were blinded to his identity and refused to recognize him as the Messiah.

LUKE 19

JESUS BRINGS SALVATION TO ZACCHAEUS'S HOME / 19:1-10 / 180
In Jericho, Jesus invited himself to the home of Zacchaeus, the chief tax collector. Apparently Zacchaeus was a corrupt tax collector. Although he was despised and hated, he became an impressive example of a rich man coming to salvation. With Zacchaeus, Jesus accomplished the impossible. He sought out a wealthy sinner and called him to repentance and salvation.

19:1-2 After healing a blind man outside the city (18:35-43), **Jesus entered Jericho. Zacchaeus** was a tax collector, **influential** and **very rich.** To finance their great world empire, the Romans levied heavy taxes on all nations under their control. The Jews opposed these taxes because they supported a secular government and its pagan gods, but they were still forced to pay. Some of their own countrymen became tax collectors, lured by the wealth such a position promised.

19:3-4 Zacchaeus, like the rest of the people in Jericho, was curious to see this man whose healings and teachings had been astounding people all over the country. Moments earlier, a blind man sitting on the side of the road had been healed (18:42-43). The news had spread, and Zacchaeus wanted to **get a look at Jesus.** The text reveals another detail about this wealthy tax collector: he was so **short** that he could not see over the people in the crowd. Zacchaeus would not be put off. He ran on down the road and

climbed a sycamore tree. The sycamore tree was easy to climb, it was like an oak tree with wide lateral branches.

19:5-7 Up in the tree, Zacchaeus watched the approaching crowd. He wanted to see Jesus, and apparently Jesus wanted to see him. Many places in Luke reveal Jesus having knowledge of people's inner thoughts and needs (see 5:22; 6:8; 7:39-40; 8:46; 9:47). As always, every act of Jesus was part of a divine plan—he said he **must** go to Zacchaeus's home. Zacchaeus climbed down **quickly** and took Jesus home.

But why Zacchaeus? In fact, many in the crowd were unhappy with Jesus' choice of hosts: **the crowds were displeased** that he had **gone to be the guest of a notorious sinner.** Zacchaeus must have been a pretty bad character, for the crowd reacted with great displeasure that Jesus would have chosen him out of everyone. No one else in the crowd could have known that Jesus' visit would change this tax collector's life.

19:8 Some grumbled, but Jesus knew that Zacchaeus was ready for a change in his life. After Jesus took the initiative with him, Zacchaeus took the initiative to follow wherever the path of obedience to Jesus might lead. The rich young man had come asking and had gone away empty, unable to give up his money and possessions (18:18-23). Zacchaeus, however, was able to give away his wealth in order to follow Jesus. This is the heart attitude that Jesus was looking for. Perceiving it in Zacchaeus, he quickly brought this man the Good News. So eager was Zacchaeus to rid himself of the shackles of wealth that he said he would pay back **four times as much** of the overage that he had charged people. His attitude was correct, and his actions showed his inner desire to obey. Zacchaeus was setting his priorities right and he would be ready for the Kingdom.

19:9-10 This tax collector was perceived as a traitor by his people, so they would not have considered him a **son of Abraham.** Yet, by opening his heart to Jesus, he proved himself to be not only a son of Abraham in the sense of a Jew looking for the Kingdom, but also a son of Abraham in the truest sense of the word because he experienced **salvation.** Salvation came to Zacchaeus, not because he did good deeds, but because he truly believed in Jesus and set aside anything that might get in the way of obeying him. To the grumblers, detractors, and self-righteous, to those who thought they were saved simply because they were descendants of Abraham, Jesus explained his mission—he came **to seek and save those like Zacchaeus who are lost.**

JESUS TELLS THE PARABLE OF THE KING'S TEN SERVANTS / 19:11-27 / 181

Because the crowd was expecting the coming Kingdom of God, Jesus told them a parable that corrected their misunderstanding about the nature of the Kingdom. Here, as in 12:35-40 (the parable of the servants waiting for their master), Jesus tied responsible stewardship of resources to the coming Kingdom of God. The first parable emphasized the importance of being alert and watchful, for the master may return suddenly and at any time. This parable encourages listeners to wisely use their resources for the master's benefit. The implication is clear. Christians are accountable to Jesus for the way they use their time, money, and abilities.

19:11 The people still hoped for a political leader who would set up an earthly Kingdom and get rid of Roman domination. The fact that Jesus had been steadily heading toward Jerusalem fueled speculation that he was going there to begin **the Kingdom of God.** So Jesus wanted to **correct** this wrong **impression.** This story showed Jesus' followers what they were to do during the time between Jesus' departure and his second coming. Because believers today live in that time period, it applies directly to them as well. Christians have been given excellent resources to build and expand God's Kingdom. Jesus expects them to use these talents so that the Kingdom grows.

19:12-13 In the world of the Roman Empire, when a man was going to become king, he would go to Rome to receive the appointment, and then return to his land to begin his rule. This **nobleman was called away.** Since this trip could take several months, the man in this parable made sure that his financial situation did not become stagnant while he was gone. He gathered **ten servants** and gave them **ten pounds of silver to invest for him while he was gone,** each servant receiving one pound.

In these words, Jesus was making it clear that

there would be a time interval between his presence with them and the time when he would come to set up his Kingdom. Like this king, he would go away to a distant country (heaven) and would be gone for an undetermined amount of time. In the meantime, his servants here would be given responsibilities to handle.

19:14-15 The king in this parable had subjects who **hated him** and did not want him made king. After his return, he **called in the servants** to give an accounting for **what they had done with the money and what their profits were.** He fully anticipated that they had made more money with his money through wise business and investments.

19:16-17 The first servant **reported a tremendous gain**—he took the money entrusted to him and made **ten times** the original amount. The king, knowing that his servant had been trustworthy and wise with that fairly small amount of money, told this servant he would be entrusted with far more responsibility. So the king made him **governor of ten cities.** The servant would share in his master's rule because he had shown faithfulness with the **little** that had been **entrusted** to him (see also 16:10).

A time of accounting will come for all believers. Christians can know they are saved and will be with God in his Kingdom, but they will be judged for how they have used what God has entrusted to them during his absence and their time on earth. God will reward faithful servants.

19:18-19 The second servant also had a gain—not as much as the first, but still he had done a fine job and was commended by the king. This servant also was rewarded in proportion to his ability—**five cities** for earning **five times the original amount.**

19:20-21 We are not told of the other seven servants, but this third servant received mention because of his failure to do what his master had expected of him. There would have been only two groups: those who used the master's money well (the amount they made seems to have been inconsequential), and those who did nothing, as this servant here who **brought back only the original amount.** He had **hid it and kept it safe.** This servant was **afraid** of the master, and that fear had led him to inactivity. He was afraid that his master expected too much, so he did nothing at all. Perhaps there was a bit of anger that he had to do all the work, while the master took the profits—**taking what** wasn't his.

19:22-23 If the servant had been so afraid, he should have at least put the money in the **bank** in order for it to earn some **interest.** There were several reasons for his failure and for the king's anger. The king punished the man because he didn't share his master's interest in the Kingdom; he didn't trust his master's intentions; his only concern was for himself; and he did nothing to use the money.

Like the king in this story, God has given you gifts to use for the benefit of his Kingdom. Some people, like this servant, don't mind being identified in a nominal way with Jesus, but when given responsibility or expectations, they refuse to do anything and do not want to be made accountable to God. Are you willing to use faithfully what he has entrusted to you? The results, the "earnings," are ultimately in God's hands, but believers are responsible to use what they have to glorify God.

19:24-27 The king took the money away from the faithless servant and gave it to the one who had proved to be responsible with it. Although the others standing around wondered why the king would give more to the one who already had the most, the king was acting wisely in giving more resources to the most effective servant. **To those who use well what they are given, even more will be given** so they can continue to produce. Those who **are unfaithful** because they refuse to take advantage of any opportunities they have—will end up losing even what they had been given.

The parable ends with the ultimate judgment on those who had actively rebelled against the king. They would be slaughtered. When Jesus returns, his enemies will be judged and sentenced to eternity without him.

JESUS RIDES INTO JERUSALEM ON A DONKEY / 19:28-44 / 183

Until this point, Luke presented a sampling of Jesus' ministry—his teaching and his miracles. But with this description of Jesus' final entry into Jerusalem, Luke, just like the other Gospel writers, slowed down his narrative, taking time to present the powerful details of Jesus' final week leading up to the cross.

19:28-31 Jesus and the disciples approached **Bethphage and Bethany,** two towns about one mile apart, situated **on the Mount of Olives** to the east of Jerusalem. Bethany was the home of his friends Mary, Martha, and Lazarus whom Jesus had visited before (10:38; see also John 11:1). When Jesus spoke these words, they were probably in Bethphage, sending two disciples to bring a **colt.** By this time Jesus was extremely well known. Everyone coming to Jerusalem for Passover had heard of him, and, for a time, the popular mood was favorable toward him. **The Lord needs it** was all the disciples had to say, and the colt's owners gladly turned their animal over to them. The specification that this be a colt **that has never been rid-** den is significant in light of the ancient rule that only animals that had not been used for ordinary purposes were appropriate for sacred purposes (Numbers 19:2; Deuteronomy 21:3; 1 Samuel 6:7).

19:32-35 The two disciples did as they were told, and found the colt exactly as they were told. Donkeys and colts were valuable; what the disciples did amounted to coming along and taking someone's car. But they said what Jesus told them to say. Mark wrote that Jesus also said the colt would be returned (Mark 11:3). The owners let the colt go, and the disciples brought it to Jesus. In Matthew, a donkey and a colt are mentioned (Matthew 21:2). This was the same event, but Matthew focused on the prophecy in Zechariah 9:9 which indicates a donkey and a colt, thus affirming Jesus' royalty. The disciples then **threw their garments** over the colt, making a seat for Jesus. With this act of entering Jerusalem on a donkey's colt, Jesus was fulfilling prophecy and affirming his messianic royalty. He came in royal fashion, not as a warring king on a horse or in a chariot, but as a gentle and peaceable king on a donkey's colt.

19:36-37 The custom of spreading coats on the ground ahead of a royal personage can also be seen in 2 Kings 9:12-13. This was Sunday of the week that Jesus would be crucified, and the great Passover festival was about to begin. Jews would come to Jerusalem from all over the Roman world during this week-long celebration to remember the great Exodus from Egypt (see Exodus 12:37-51). Many in the crowd had heard of or had seen Jesus and were hoping he would come to the Temple (John 11:55-57). People lined the roads, and Jesus already had a crowd of followers who, when they saw what he was doing, **began to shout and sing as they walked along.** According to the other Gospels, many others joined the celebration of praise. The Gospel of John (12:13) also describes the people cutting down branches from the trees, probably from olive or fig trees, to wave in welcome.

19:38 The expression **"Bless the King who comes in the name of the Lord"** may have been recited as part of the Passover tradition—as a blessing given by the people in Jerusalem to the visiting pilgrims (see Psalm 118:25-26). The people lined the road, praising God, waving branches, and throwing their cloaks in front of the colt as it passed before them. "Long live the King" was the meaning behind their joyful shouts because they knew that Jesus was intentionally fulfilling prophecy.

19:39-40 The **Pharisees** thought that the crowd's words were sacrilegious and blasphemous. They asked Jesus to keep his people quiet. But Jesus said that if the people were **quiet, the stones** would **burst into cheers** (see Habakkuk 2:11).

19:41-42 Only Luke recorded this lament by Jesus. In contrast to the great joy of the crowd, the man on the donkey **began to cry** at the sight of the city. The name of the city has "peace" as part of its meaning (Hebrews 7:2), but the people of the city did not know what would bring them **peace.** The "city of peace" was blind to the "Prince of Peace" (Isaiah 9:6). If the people had known what was truly happening and had recognized it for what it was, they could have found peace. But the Jewish leaders had rejected their Messiah (19:39, 47); they had refused God's offer of salvation in Jesus Christ when they were visited by God himself. Now the truth would be **hidden,** and soon their nation would suffer.

19:43-44 About forty years after Jesus said these words, they came true. In A.D. 66, the Jews revolted against Roman control. Three years later Titus, son of the Emperor Vespasian, was sent to crush the rebellion. Six hundred thousand Jews were killed during Titus's onslaught. This would occur as judgment because though some of the people believed (such as the disciples and other faithful followers), most **had rejected the opportunity God offered** them. But God did not turn away from the Jewish people who obeyed him. He continues to offer salvation to both Jews and Gentiles.

JESUS CLEARS THE TEMPLE AGAIN / 19:45-48 / 184
Jesus directly confronted those who dared to try to make an exorbitant profit in the very Temple of God. He had expelled these people before (John 2:12-25). Here Jesus again stood for what was right, confronting those who dared to participate in wickedness under the guise of religiosity.

19:45-46 This is the second time that Jesus cleared the Temple and drove **out the merchants from their stalls.** These "merchants" were the people who sold goods to worshipers. Jesus told them, in no uncertain terms, why he was so angry and why he acted as he did in throwing these merchants out of the Temple. He quoted from Isaiah 56:7 explaining that God's purpose was for the Temple to be **a place of prayer,** but the merchants had turned it into a **den of thieves.** Their treatment of pilgrims who had traveled and needed to count on them for service, their exorbitant rates, and their cheating of the customers had made them no better than thieves hiding out together in a "den." But this "den" was God's Temple—no wonder Jesus was angry.

19:47-48 During his last week on earth, Jesus was still busy—teaching **daily in the Temple.** He traveled into the city each morning, then retired out to the environs, perhaps to the home of Mary, Martha, and Lazarus in Bethany (Matthew 21:17; Mark 11:11). Jesus had many enemies who kept looking for a way to **kill him.** These enemies were the Jewish religious leaders themselves—the people who, above everyone else, should have been the first to recognize and rejoice in the arrival of their Messiah. The **leaders of the people** probably included wealthy leaders in politics, commerce, and law. They had several reasons for wanting to get rid of Jesus. He had damaged business in the Temple by driving the merchants out. In addition, he was preaching against injustice, and his teachings often favored the poor over the rich. Further, his great popularity was in danger of attracting Rome's attention, and the leaders of Israel wanted as little as possible to do with Rome.

Despite their plans, however, these people could not do anything. The man they wanted to kill came daily to the Temple, but he was far too popular with the people.

LUKE 20

RELIGIOUS LEADERS CHALLENGE JESUS' AUTHORITY / 20:1-8 / 189

With Jesus' entrance into Jerusalem (19:28-44), Luke began an extended section (19:45–21:4) that highlights the growing controversy between Jesus and the Jewish religious leaders. In this first clash after Jesus' cleansing of the Temple, the representatives of the Jewish council struck at the heart of the issue between them: Who had the authority? Jesus was implicitly asserting his own authority over the Temple, a challenge to the council's power.

20:1-2 Soon after Jesus' cleansing of the Temple, Jesus returned to the Temple to teach and preach. While he was there, a delegation of **leading priests, teachers of religious law,** and **other leaders** stopped Jesus. These were representative of the three groups that made up the Jewish ruling council (Jesus already had predicted that the Jewish religious authorities would reject him, see 9:22). Apparently the council had met after the clearing of the Temple, enraged by Jesus' actions, but unable to decide how to handle him. They then sent this representative group to question Jesus regarding his actions, hoping he would say something treasonous or blasphemous. They demanded to know **by whose authority** he had thrown out the **merchants from the Temple.**

20:3-4 Jesus countered the Jewish religious teachers' question with a question. Jesus knew that the religious leaders' attitude toward John the Baptist would reveal their attitude toward him. With this question, Jesus was implying that his authority came from the same source as John the Baptist's. John had called the people to repentance, and the people had expressed their repentance through baptism, a symbol of the cleansing of one's sins. So Jesus asked these religious leaders what they thought: **Did John's baptism come from heaven,** thus, from God, **or was it merely human?**

20:5-8 These leaders weren't interested in Jesus' authority or in the truth. They really didn't want an answer; instead, they wanted to trap Jesus. But they found themselves looking completely foolish. If they answered that John's baptism had come **from heaven** (with God's authority), then they would be incriminating themselves for not listening to John. On the other hand, if they rejected John as having any divine authority and said that his baptism was **merely human,** they would infuriate the crowd. So they remained silent, but their silence spoke volumes. Because they refused to answer, Jesus said that he too would refuse to answer their question. By his silence, Jesus had already answered. His authority was the same as John the Baptist's. John was clearly a prophet of God, and Jesus also was commissioned by God to call all who would listen to him.

JESUS TELLS THE PARABLE OF THE EVIL FARMERS / 20:9-19 / 191

After his confrontation of the Jewish religious leaders, Jesus told a parable that revealed the spiritual realities behind his conflict with them. The parable indirectly answered their question about his authority, showed them that he knew about their plan to kill him, and revealed the judgment that awaited them.

20:9 The characters in this story are easily identified. The owner of the vineyard is God; the vineyard is Israel; the tenant farmers are the religious leaders; the servants are the prophets and priests God sent to Israel; the son is the Messiah, Jesus; the others are the Gentiles. The comparison of Israel to a vineyard is common in the Old Testament (Psalm 80:8-13; Isaiah 5:1-7; Jeremiah 12:10; Hosea 10:1). It pictures God's work (someone has to plant a vineyard) and patient care in tending and caring for his people.

Jesus described a common business method of the time—an absentee owner who hired tenant farmers to care for the fields and crops. The tenant farmers paid their "rent" by giving a portion of the crop to the landowner, who would send servants at harvest time to collect it. Tensions often arose; records exist of bitter disputes between landowners and their tenants.

20:10-12 When the grape harvest came, the landowner **sent one of his servants to collect** the "rent"—namely **his share of the crop.** The "servants" represented the prophets and priests whom God had sent over the years to the nation of Israel. The picture of angry farmers beating the landowner's servants and sending them on their way without any "rent" pictured the religious leaders who were entrusted with the care of the vineyard. Instead of listening to the prophets, they had **treated** them **shamefully** and sent them away, stubbornly refusing to listen. Some had been beaten (Jeremiah 26:7-11; 38:1-28), and some had been killed (tradition says that Isaiah was killed; John the Baptist had been killed, Matthew 14:1-12), and some had been stoned (2 Chronicles 24:21). Jesus was reminding the religious leaders that God's prophets often had been ridiculed and persecuted by God's people.

20:13 The fact that this landowner had not already punished the farmers for their treatment of his servants shows a man of great patience. This pictures God, who has been very patient with his people over the centuries, even when they stubbornly refused to listen to his messages through the prophets. So the landowner sent his **son** to collect the fruit of the vineyard in hopes that the farmers would give him due honor and respect. This "son" refers to Jesus (see also 3:22; 9:35). With these words, Jesus implicitly answered the religious leaders' question regarding the source of his authority (20:2). Like the son in this parable, Jesus had been sent on behalf of the Father. He was acting with God the Father's authority. The son had been sent to the stubborn and rebellious nation of Israel to win them back to God.

20:14-16 The historical situation behind this section reflects the law that property would go to anyone in possession of it when the master died. The tenants probably thought that the arrival of the son (**the heir**) meant that his father had died. They reasoned, therefore, that if they killed the son, they could claim the property (**the estate**) as their own. So they **murdered** the son. With these words, Jesus was revealing to the religious leaders his knowledge of their desire to kill him.

Jesus asked his listeners what they thought the **owner** would do to his tenant farmers when he found out that they had killed his son. The answer: **He will come and kill** those tenants. Over hundreds of years, Israel's kings and religious leaders had rejected God's prophets—beating, humiliating, and killing them. Most recently, John the Baptist had been rejected as a prophet by Israel's leaders. Finally Jesus, the beloved Son of God, already rejected by the religious leaders, would be killed. Jesus explained that the Jewish leaders would be punished for his death because in rejecting the messengers and the Son, they were rejecting God himself.

Jesus added that not only would the wicked tenant farmers be killed, but that the owner would **lease the vineyard to others.** God's judgment on the Jewish people who rejected him would result in the transfer of the privileges of ownership "to others," namely, the Gentiles. Jesus was speaking of the beginning of the Christian church among the Gentiles.

20:17-18 Quoting Psalm 118:22, Jesus showed the unbelieving leaders that even their rejection of the Messiah had been prophesied in Scripture. Psalm 118 was a key part of the Passover Service—all the pilgrims coming to Passover would recite 118:25-26 as they came to Jerusalem. The religious leaders had been reciting this passage for years without understanding or applying it (see John 5:39-40). In Jesus' quotation, the "son" of the parable became the **stone** of this prophecy; the "tenant farmers" of the parable became the **builders.** Rejecting the **corner**stone was dangerous. A person could be tripped or crushed (judged and punished).

Jesus used this metaphor to show that one stone can affect people different ways, depending on how they relate to it (see Isaiah 8:14-15; 28:16; Daniel 2:34, 44-45). Ideally they will build on it; many, however, will trip over it. Although Jesus had been rejected by many of his people, he would become the "cornerstone" of his new building, the church (see Acts 4:11 and 1 Peter 2:6-7).

20:19 This delegation that had been sent to demand answers from Jesus (20:1-2) realized that Jesus **was pointing at them—they were the farmers in the story.** They would have arrested Jesus on the spot, but he was still surrounded by crowds of eager listeners, and **they were afraid there would be a riot.** There was nothing to do but go away to gather new ideas and think of new questions to try to trap Jesus.

RELIGIOUS LEADERS QUESTION JESUS ABOUT PAYING TAXES / 20:20-26 / 193
Although the religious leaders had been outwitted by Jesus once (20:1-8), they did not give up. They returned with another carefully thought-out question to trap him. This new question related to taxation: to pay or not to pay taxes to Rome. If Jesus answered in the affirmative either way, he would be in a predicament. It was a perfect trap, or so the Pharisees thought.

20:20 The religious leaders continued their attempts to **get Jesus to say something that could be reported** to the authorities. They **sent secret agents pretending to be honest men.** These men addressed Jesus as if he were a mediator, inviting him to settle their dispute regarding whether or not to pay taxes to Caesar.

20:21-22 Pretending to be honest men (20:20), these spies flattered Jesus before asking him a question that was a hot topic in Palestine at the time, **"Is it right to pay taxes to the Roman government or not?"** Obviously it was lawful according to Caesar, but was it lawful according to God's law? The Jews hated having to pay taxes to Rome. If Jesus said they should pay taxes, they would call him a traitor to their nation and their religion. But if he said they should not, the religious leaders could report him to Rome as a rebel. The crowd waited expectantly for Jesus' answer. Jesus' questioners thought they had him this time, but he outwitted them again.

20:23-25 Jesus asked someone in the crowd to show him **a Roman coin.** This would have been a silver coin with a **picture** of the reigning Caesar on it. The tax paid to Rome was paid in these coins. The **title** referred to Caesar as divine and as "chief priest." The Caesars were worshiped as gods by the pagans, so the claim to divinity on the coin itself repulsed the Jews. In addition, Caesar's image on the coins was a constant reminder of Israel's subjection to Rome.

Jesus' answer surprised everyone: **"Give to Caesar what belongs to him. But everything that belongs to God must be given to God."** Having a coin meant being part of that country, so citizens should acknowledge the authority of Caesar and pay for the benefits accorded to them by his empire (for example, peace and an efficient road system). They would lose much and gain little if they refused to pay Caesar's taxes (see Romans 13:1-7; 1 Timothy 2:1-6; 1 Peter 2:13-17).

Paying the taxes, however, did not have to mean submission to the divinity claimed by the emperor through the inscription on the coins. Caesar had the right to claim their tax money, but he had no claim on their souls. The Jews had a responsibility to give to God what was his. While they lived in the Roman world, the Jews had to face the dual reality of subjection to Rome and responsibility to God. Jesus explained that they could do both if they kept their priorities straight. The tax would be paid as long as Rome held sway over Judea, but God had rights on eternity and on their lives.

20:26 In his reply, Jesus did not show rebellion against Caesar, nor did he show any disloyalty to God and his law. This answer **amazed** and **silenced** Jesus' questioners. Their amazement showed that Jesus had been victorious over his opponents. They had tried to trap him, but he stayed one step ahead of them (see also 20:39-40).

RELIGIOUS LEADERS QUESTION JESUS ABOUT THE RESURRECTION / 20:27-40 / 194
Jesus had already evaded two traps laid by the Jewish religious leaders—one involving his authority and then one on Roman taxation. They were determined to embarrass Jesus. The Sadducees used a standard theological question they had often used to discredit the idea of a resurrection, which was a belief of the Pharisees. Jesus rose to this occasion, as well, and he exposed the Sadducees' ignorance of the Scripture and of God's infinite power.

20:27 No sooner had one delegation withdrawn from Jesus in amazement than another appeared to take up the cause. The **Sadducees** were a group of conservative Jewish religious leaders who honored only the Pentateuch—Genesis through Deuteronomy—as Scripture. They did not believe in a **resurrection** of the dead because they could find no mention of it in those books.

20:28 In the law, **Moses** had written that if a man were to die without a son, his unmarried brother (or nearest male relative) should marry the widow and produce children. The first son of this marriage would be considered the heir of the dead man (Deuteronomy 25:5-6). The main purpose of the instruction was to produce an heir and guarantee that the family would not lose their land. The book of Ruth gives an example of this law in operation (Ruth 3:1–4:12; see also Genesis 38:1-26). This law, called "levirate" marriage, protected the widow (in that culture widows usually had no means to support themselves) and allowed the family line to continue.

20:29-33 In order to show what they perceived as the absurdity of believing in the resurrection, the Sadducees offered a hypothetical situation in which the same woman married and outlived seven brothers, but never had any children. This particular woman would have had a real problem because when she and her seven husbands would be resurrected, the Sadducees asked, **"Whose wife will she be?"** Their problem lay in their view of resurrection, and the God who, throughout Scripture, promised it. The Sadducees had brought God down to their level and decided that because they could not make sense out of resurrection life, God couldn't raise the dead. They did not consider for a moment that God, Creator and Sustainer of all life, could not only raise the dead, but create entirely new lives that would be different from what people had on this earth.

20:34-36 Jesus pointed out that there are differences between life in this age and life in the age to come. The resurrection life in heaven will not be merely a continuation of life on this earth. Here in this world, people marry and are given in **marriage.** However, those who do get to heaven will find that their lives are not merely extended into eternity, but that everything is different. They won't be marrying or being given in marriage (as per the Sadducees question). **They will never die again.** Believers anticipate a resurrection to a life of no more tears or sorrow (Revelation 21:4).

In the new heaven and new earth, marriage will no longer be needed. Inheritance laws and property rights will be irrelevant. It is important

to human beings in this world, but it will not be a needed feature of the Kingdom. In addition, marriage is needed in this world in order to produce children and thereby continue the human race. This also will not be needed in the Kingdom because no one can die there. Death will have been banished and will not affect people in the Kingdom (Revelation 20:14).

Believers will be **like angels** regarding marriage. Having been raised to new life, those in heaven will no longer be governed by physical laws but will be **like angels;** that is, believers will share the immortal and exalted nature of angels, living above physical needs.

Jesus was not teaching that people will not recognize their spouses in heaven, thereby dissolving the eternal aspect of marriage. Nor was he doing away with sexual differences or teaching that people will be asexual beings after death. Nor was he teaching that the angels are asexual. Little can be learned about sex and marriage in heaven from this one statement by Jesus. His point was simply that people must not think of the next life as an extension of life as they now know it. Relationships in this life are limited by time, death, and sin; in the new heaven and new earth they will be different from here and now.

20:37-38 After addressing their question about marriage, Jesus answered the Sadducees' assumption about the resurrection which was the real issue. Jesus based his answer on the writings of Moses, an authority the Sadducees respected. **Even Moses proved** that there is a resurrection for **when he wrote about the burning bush,** he wrote of the patriarchs as though they were still alive (Exodus 3:6). Thus, from God's perspective, they were alive. God had a continuing relationship with these men because of the truth of the resurrection. In Matthew and Mark, the entire quote from Exodus 3:6 is used, with God saying, "I am the God of . . ."—with the argument being that God, speaking in the present tense, was affirming his continuing relationship with these men. Therefore **he is the God of the living, not the dead.** God continues his relationship with them because **they are all alive to him.** Death separates people from their loved ones on earth, but it cannot separate believers from God.

20:39-40 The **teachers of religious law** (Pharisees), who also had been attempting to trick Jesus, had to congratulate Jesus on this answer to the Sadducees. This question had probably stumped the Pharisees for some time, and at last the Sadducees had been duly silenced. At this time, the questions ended, for **no one dared to ask any more.**

RELIGIOUS LEADERS CANNOT ANSWER JESUS' QUESTION / 20:41-44 / 196

Jesus had already emerged victorious over his opponents on three separate occasions (20:1-8, 20-26, 27-40). Jesus took the offense, challenging his opponents with a question of his own: Who is the Son of David? With this question, Jesus identified the weakness of the religious teachers' thinking. They had not sufficiently examined what the Scripture said about the coming Messiah.

20:41-44 Jesus asked the leaders a question about the Messiah's identity. He turned to Psalm 110:1 and asked how **the Messiah is said to be the son of David.** Jesus quoted these words, explaining what the religious leaders should have understood. David wrote, **"The Lord said to my Lord."** The first "Lord" is **Yahweh,** the Hebrew name for God the Father. The second "Lord" in Hebrew is **Adonai** and refers to David speaking of the coming Messiah as his "Lord." The phrase, **sit in honor at my right hand,** means that the Messiah would sit at the right side of God's throne, the place of highest honor and authority in God's coming Kingdom. **"Until I humble your enemies"** describes the final conquering of sin and evil. There is an inherent problem in the prophecy because it makes no sense that David would call the Messiah "Lord" when the Lord was also his "son." The only way to understand this is to see the Messiah as more than a mere human being (see Romans 1:2-4). David himself didn't think the Messiah would be just one of his descendants; instead, David, under the inspiration of the Holy Spirit, said that the Messiah would be God. The answer to Jesus' question is that David was clearly saying the Messiah was his Lord. By this statement, Jesus was revealing his divine identity. The divine Messiah had, indeed, come in human form; he was standing among them.

JESUS WARNS AGAINST THE RELIGIOUS LEADERS / 20:45-47 / 197

Luke, like the other Synoptic writers (see Matthew 23:1-12; Mark 12:38-40), concluded this section, which describes the confrontation between Jesus and the religious leaders (19:45–21:4), with Jesus' severe condemnation of the teachers of religious law. Their concern for outward appearances over the condition of their own hearts, especially their total inattention to justice and mercy, was despicable in God's eyes.

20:45-47 The **teachers of religious law** loved the benefits associated with their position, and they sometimes cheated the poor in order to get even more benefits. Jesus warned his followers to **beware** of them. They were supposed to be just what their title implied—teachers who led people into the truth of God; instead, they loved the "perks" of their position and did just the opposite. They led people away from God.

The reference to parading in **flowing robes** and being bowed to in the marketplaces pictured these religious leaders who went through the market in their long robes receiving bows of respect from everyone. These actions were motivated by vanity. They loved the **seats of honor in the synagogues and at banquets** because those seats were reserved for the most important people. The accusation of cheating **widows out of their property** pictured the teachers' abuse of their trusted position. Because they received no pay for their services, they depended on the hospitality of devout Jews. It was considered an act of piety for people to help them. But some of these religious men were using their position to defraud the gullible. They were in a position to exploit people, cheating the poor out of everything they had, and taking advantage of the rich. How could they deserve anything but condemnation! Their lengthy public prayers, Jesus said, amounted to no more than a **cover up.** Their long prayers were not conversations with the Lord, but were merely ploys to make people think they were especially holy. Through their pious actions they hoped to gain status, recognition, and respect.

The punishment for these leaders would be especially severe because as teachers they were responsible for shaping the faith of the people. Jesus solemnly announced, **"Their punishment will be the greater."**

LUKE 21

A POOR WIDOW GIVES ALL SHE HAS / 21:1-4 / 200
After warning his disciples about the greed of the teachers of religious law (20:46), Jesus pointed out a poor widow as an example of extraordinary faith.

21:1-2 Jesus spent much time during his last week on earth in the Temple, teaching, preaching, and dealing with religious leaders (19:45–20:47). At some point during one of his days there, Jesus watched people put **their gifts** into the **collection box** for the Temple treasury. Jesus was in the area of the Temple called the court of women. The treasury was there or in an adjoining walkway. Seven boxes were in this area. Worshipers could deposit their Temple tax in these boxes. In addition, six boxes more collected freewill offerings like the one this woman gave. A lot of money came into the Temple treasury during Passover.

The **rich people** put their gifts into the treasury—large gifts that clattered into the boxes. Then **a poor widow** came and dropped in **two pennies.** As a widow, she had few resources for earning

money, and may have been without financial support. But she put her coins into the freewill offering box, meaning that this was not a required tax, but a gift.

21:3-4 Jesus judged the poor woman's gift not by how much she gave, but by how much she had left after giving. The rich did well to give out of their abundance, but they had plenty left. Yet she gave **everything** and therefore had **given more than all the rest of them.** The widow could have kept back one coin, but she willingly gave both coins. She gave everything and trusted God to care for her. Jesus wanted the disciples to see this lesson in total surrender of self, commitment to God, and willingness to trust in God's provision. For more on giving, see 1 Corinthians 16:1-4; 2 Corinthians 8:1-5.

JESUS TELLS ABOUT THE FUTURE / 21:5-24 / 201
A disciple's casual remark concerning the splendor of the Temple gave Jesus the opportunity to make an alarming prophecy about the Temple and the end times. This section, along with 17:20-37, parallel the Olivet discourse given in Matthew 24:1-25 and Mark 13:1-23. Jesus spoke of the end times in order to realign his disciples' priorities and to caution them about being deceived.

21:5-6 Jesus and the disciples would leave Jerusalem every evening of that final week and walk the couple of miles back to Bethany. As they left the city on one of those evenings, some of the disciples commented on the beauty of the Temple itself. The Temple that the disciples were admiring was not Solomon's Temple—that had been destroyed by the Babylonians in the seventh century B.C. This Temple had been built by Ezra after the return from exile in the sixth century B.C., desecrated by the Seleucids in the second century B.C., reconsecrated by the Maccabees soon afterward, and enormously expanded by Herod the Great over a forty-six-year period. It was a beautiful, imposing structure with a significant history. Although no one knows exactly what it looked like, it must have been magnificent,

for in its time it was considered one of the architectural wonders of the world.

Jesus used the disciples' comments about the Temple to give them a prophetic statement about the fate of the Temple: it will be **completely demolished.** This happened only a few years later when the Romans sacked Jerusalem in A.D. 70. The Romans fulfilled Jesus' words to the letter. After fire raged through the Temple, Emperor Titus ordered the leveling of the whole area so that no part of the original walls or buildings remained. Titus considered this punishment for the Jewish rebellion in A.D. 66. The Temple has never been rebuilt; the stones that we can see today, commonly called the "wailing wall" are part of the foundation. Truly the Temple was leveled.

21:7-9 The disciples' question had two parts. They wanted to know when the destruction would take place and if there would be any sign ahead of time. Jesus first answered the disciples' second question about signs. Jesus warned them against false messiahs. He knew that if the disciples looked for signs, they would be susceptible to deception. Many false prophets would display counterfeit signs of spiritual power and authority. Jesus predicted that before his return, many believers would be misled by false teachers coming in his name—that is, claiming to be the Messiah. Jesus said clearly, **"Don't believe them."** According to Scripture, the one clear sign of Christ's return will be his unmistakable appearance in the clouds that will be seen by all people (Matthew 24:30; Revelation 1:7). Believers never have to wonder whether a certain person is the Messiah. When Jesus returns, believers will know beyond a doubt because he will be evident to all.

Just as false messiahs and religious frauds come and go, so do political and natural crises. However, these do not signal **the end** of the world. The disciples probably assumed that the Temple would be destroyed only at the end of the age as part of God establishing his new Kingdom. Jesus taught that horrible events would happen, but the end **won't follow immediately.** Believers should not **panic.** God will not lose control of his creation, and his promises will come true.

21:10-11 Jesus' words indicated that there would be a span of time before the end of the age and the coming Kingdom. First, much suffering would occur as a part of life on earth, including wars and natural disasters. These, along with **miraculous signs in the heavens,** will mean only that history is moving toward a single, final, God-planned goal—the creation of a new earth and a new Kingdom (Revelation 21:1-3). Today we must guard against preoccupation with signs, such as frequency of earthquakes. Instead, we must focus on doing God's will.

21:12 Without hesitation, Jesus explained that his followers would not escape suffering. **Persecution** soon began; Luke recorded such in the book of Acts. Jesus didn't say it, but the disciples would learn that loyalty to Christ meant separation from Judaism. Not only would Jesus' followers be in trouble with Jews, they would also find themselves standing trial before Gentile **kings and governors** because of being Jesus' **followers.**

21:13-15 These trials in the synagogues and before Gentile rulers would give the disciples an **opportunity** to testify about Jesus. Standing before Jewish or Roman leadership would be intimidating, but

Jesus explained that they could trust him to give them **words** and a **wisdom** that would astound their opponents. Notice that Jesus did not guarantee acquittal. James, one of the disciples here listening to Jesus, would be killed because of his faith (Acts 12:1-2).

21:16-19 Not only would the disciples face hatred from religious and civil leaders, as well as their own families, they also would be hated by **everyone.** For Jews to convert to Christianity would soon become very dangerous because they would be hated and ostracized. Jesus' words also looked forward to the time when hatred of Christians would again occur. Jesus gave a promise however: **"But not a hair of your head will perish! By standing firm, you will win your souls."** This does not mean that standing firm earns salvation; instead, it marks those who are already saved. Assurance of salvation will keep believers going through the times of persecution.

What assurance was Jesus giving in light of the eventual martyrdom of James and Peter? Some have taken the reality of the words about being put to death (21:16) and not a hair of one's head perishing to mean that some will be taken and others will be preserved. But this seems to nullify the whole tone of assurance. Most likely, "not a hair of your head will perish" refers to ultimate deliverance and salvation in Christ's Kingdom. Some will suffer and some will die, but none of Jesus' followers will suffer spiritual or eternal loss. On earth, everyone will die, but believers in Jesus will be saved for eternal life.

21:20 Luke 21:20-24 refers not to the end times (the warning for that is recorded in 17:30-36), but to the coming destruction of the city of Jerusalem that would occur in A.D. 70. The verb **surrounded** pictures the coming siege of the city. Jesus' words in the next verses explain what the people should do quickly before the city would be completely surrounded and put under siege.

21:21-22 With the armies coming to surround the city, the people who are outside should **flee to the hills,** those in the city should **escape,** those in the country **should not enter** the city. This was the opposite of the usual advice—generally, in time of war, the people outside would go to the city for protection. But not this time. The time **of God's vengeance** will have arrived; the city would face the full punishment for its history of unfaithfulness and rebellion against God.

Many of Jesus' followers would live to see this happen. The Jewish historian Josephus wrote that from A.D. 66, Jewish Zealots clashed with the Romans. Many people realized that rebellion would bring the wrath of the Empire, so they fled to Pella, a town located in the mountains across the Jordan River. As Jesus had said, this proved to be their protection, for when the Roman army swept in, the nation and its capital city were destroyed.

21:23-24 Jesus expressed sympathy and concern for those who would have difficulty fleeing because they were **pregnant** or had small children. These people literally would be running for their lives from the **great distress.** If they didn't get away, they would **be brutally killed by the sword or sent away as captives.** According to the historian Josephus, ninety-seven thousand people were taken prisoner during the war and over one million were killed.

Jerusalem, the holy city, **will be conquered and trampled down by the Gentiles until the age of the Gentiles comes to an end.** These would have been horrifying words to any Jew. The "age of the Gentiles" began with Babylon's destruction of Jerusalem in 586 B.C. and the exile of the Jewish people. No longer an independent nation, Israel was under the control of Gentile rulers. In Jesus' day, Israel was governed by the Roman Empire, and a Roman general would "trample" the city in A.D. 70. Jesus was saying that the domination of God's people by his enemies would continue until God decided to end it. The "times of the Gentiles" refers not just to the repeated destructions of Jerusalem, but also to the continuing and mounting persecution of God's people until the end.

JESUS TELLS ABOUT HIS RETURN / 21:25-33 / 202
After predicting Jerusalem's destruction, Jesus described his second coming (21:27). It will be accompanied by all kinds of cosmic signs, instilling terror in those who are unprepared for the end but inspiring hope in those who are anticipating his return. Don't be caught unprepared; commit yourself to follow Jesus wholeheartedly and to pray fervently (21:34-36).

21:25 The disciples had asked if there would be a sign (21:7); here Jesus gave the answer. Jesus spoke of his return in full glory without any of the limitations he had taken on by becoming human. Jesus was not speaking of his immediate resurrection but of his eventual, glorious return. Some of the signs would be in nature, for nature itself would experience change. As taught in Romans 8 and 2 Peter 3, the entire universe had become involved in humanity's fallen predicament; thus, the entire universe will be changed when humanity is changed. There will be a variety of changes—the **sun** going dark, the **moon** not being seen, **stars** falling, heavenly bodies being shaken (see Matthew 24:29). **Roaring seas** shows that nature will be in chaos from one end of the earth to the other (see Psalm 46:2-4; Isaiah 17:12). These words also recall the words of the prophets (Isaiah 13:10; Joel 2:10-11). What Jesus described here, John saw in his vision (Revelation 6:12-14).

21:26 Persecutions and natural disasters will cause great sorrow in the world—**people will falter.** When believers see these events happening, they should realize that the return of their Messiah is near and that they can look forward to his reign of justice and peace. Rather than being terrified by what is happening in the world, believers should confidently await the Lord's return, an event that will shake the very heavens.

21:27 The signs will occur, and afterwards **everyone will see the Son of Man arrive on the clouds with power and great glory.** Jesus' return will be unmistakable. To the Jews, clouds signified divine presence (Exodus 13:21; 19:9; Psalm 97:1-2; Daniel 7:13). Jesus will return as the powerful, glorious, and divine Son of Man. There will be no doubt as to his identity.

21:28 When believers see these events happening, they will know that the return of their Messiah is **near,** and they can look forward to his reign of justice and peace. Rather than being terrified by what is happening in the world, believers should confidently await Christ's return to bring justice and restoration to his people.

21:29-31 Here Jesus answered the disciples' other question about "when" the events would occur (21:7). People knew when summer was coming by looking at **the fig tree.** Seeing the dry, brittle branches becoming tender, filled with sap, and beginning to bud, people knew **that summer was near.** Just as people can interpret the seasons by watching the signs in nature, so they can know that when they see **the events** he has been describing **taking place,** then **the Kingdom of God is near.** The second coming of Jesus is both certain and near. The fulfillment of Jesus' prophecy would assure the disciples that the other prophecies he had given regarding the end times would also come true.

21:32 There are three main views of the meaning of **this generation will not pass:** (1) It refers only to those alive at the time Jesus spoke and who still would be alive at the destruction of Jerusalem; (2) it refers only to those who would experience the end times; (3) it refers both to the destruction of Jerusalem and the end times— the destruction of Jerusalem contains within itself the elements of the final end times and thus serves as a precursor. The Greek word for

"generation" is *genea;* it refers both to those living at a given time as well as to race or lineage (therefore, Jesus would have been speaking of the Jewish race). This makes the third view most likely.

21:33 Everything may change, and eventually everything will **disappear.** But one truth is absolutely, eternally certain: Jesus' words **will remain forever.** Everything he said will come true.

JESUS TELLS ABOUT REMAINING WATCHFUL / 21:34-38 / 203

Jesus concluded his teaching on the end times (21:5-38) with a grave warning to his disciples. They were to guard against letting the worries of this life or the pleasures of the world distract them from the truth—especially, the truth that the Son of Man would return, in judgment. They were to be always prepared for his return. They could be fully prepared by praying that God would help them persevere in faith until Christ's return.

21:34-36 Believers know that Jesus will indeed return. But because no one knows when this great event will occur (Matthew 24:36), Jesus told his followers to **watch out,** and not let the temptations or worries of this life distract them from being ready. That day will come unexpectedly, and it will **come upon everyone**—no exceptions. There will be no opportunity for last-minute repentance or bargaining. The choice that each person has already made will determine his or her eternal destiny.

For Jesus' followers to **keep a constant watch** and **pray** pictures an attitude toward life that seeks to stay away from evil and to follow and obey Jesus. Both watching and praying are voli-

tional actions—as believers await Jesus' return, they work to further his Kingdom. Only with a focus on him can believers **escape** the **horrors** to come. Only through obedience to him will they be able to **stand before the Son of Man** when he returns.

21:37-38 During this final week on the earth, Jesus went **every day** to the **Temple** to teach the people (samples of that teaching have been recorded in chapters 20–21). He left the city in the evening and spent the **night on the Mount of Olives,** probably in the city of Bethany (Matthew 21:17). He returned the next morning, and already crowds of people had gathered to hear him.

LUKE 22

RELIGIOUS LEADERS PLOT TO KILL JESUS / 22:1-2 / 207

Luke began the final section of his Gospel (22:1–24:53) with a short statement of the evil intentions of the chief priests and the teachers of religious law. They were diligently looking for an opportunity to have Jesus arrested and executed.

22:1 All Jewish males over the age of twelve were required to go to Jerusalem for **Passover.** This would be followed by a seven-day festival called the **Festival of Unleavened Bread** (Exodus 12:15-20). For these festivals, Jews from all over the Roman Empire would converge on Jerusalem

to celebrate one of the most important events in their history. Passover took place on one night and at one meal, but the Festival of Unleavened Bread would continue for a week. The Passover celebration commemorated the night the Israelites were freed from Egypt (Exodus 12).

22:2 The religious leaders' opposition to Jesus had grown to such a point that they **were actively plotting Jesus' murder.** There is a certain irony in seeing these leaders celebrating the Exodus while plotting to kill one of their own at the same time. But they had a problem: **they greatly** **feared** the people. Jesus was a popular teacher, and there were many Galileans in the city who would have rioted if Jesus had been taken captive. The religious leaders felt that they had to kill him because of his growing popularity (20:19; 22:6).

JUDAS AGREES TO BETRAY JESUS / 22:3-6 / *208*
The Jewish religious leaders had opposed Jesus from the beginning (6:7; 7:29-30; 11:53; 19:47), and their opposition had grown more fierce in the last couple of days (see 20:1-8, 20-26, 27-40). But here the plot thickened. Judas struck a deal with the Jewish council to betray Jesus for money.

22:3-4 The leaders' opportunity to get to Jesus came in a manner they least expected. One of Jesus' twelve disciples came to them willing to act as betrayer and accuser. Luke explained that Satan entered into Judas Iscariot (see also John 12:6; 13:2, 27). Satan assumed that Jesus' death would end Jesus' mission and thwart God's plan. Like Judas, Satan did not know that Jesus' death and resurrection were the most important parts of God's plan all along.

22:5-6 Naturally these leaders were **delighted** at this unexpected defection from Jesus' ranks. Matthew alone recorded the exact **reward**—thirty pieces of silver, the price of a slave (Exodus 21:32; Matthew 26:15). The religious leaders had planned to wait until after the Passover to take Jesus, but with Judas's unexpected offer, they accelerated their plans. Judas, in turn, **began looking for an opportunity to betray Jesus** when there would be no Passover crowds to prevent Jesus' capture and no possibility of a riot.

DISCIPLES PREPARE FOR THE PASSOVER / 22:7-13 / *209*
Jesus and the disciples were one group out of thousands needing a place to celebrate the Passover meal in Jerusalem. Jesus' instructions to Peter and John reveal God's complete control over all the events surrounding Jesus' final days on earth. The room where the disciples would celebrate the Last Supper had been prepared (22:12), and Jesus knew every detail, even how Peter and John would find the room (22:10).

22:7-8 Jesus and his disciples had been together long enough to celebrate Passover several times. Disciples often ate this celebratory meal with their teacher, so it was not unusual for Jesus to send **Peter and John** to **prepare the Passover meal** for him and his disciples.

22:9-11 Peter and John needed to know **where** they should go to **prepare the Passover meal.** They would need a location big enough for Jesus and the twelve disciples. Jesus' answer indicates that he had, in advance, made many of these preparations. Jesus knew that he needed safety and security in order to avoid being taken prematurely. The time in the upper room was a precious time for Jesus and his disciples, as the record of the conversation and teaching shows (recorded in John 13–17).

As the two disciples entered Jerusalem, they would see **a man carrying a pitcher of water.**

Ordinarily, women, not men, went to the well and brought home the water. So this man would have stood out in the crowd. They should follow this man to his **house,** and the owner of that house would show them to the room where they would eat together. This private location kept the plans secret—even Judas would not know their destination until they arrived.

Tradition says that this may have been Mark's home (the writer of the Gospel). If this speculation is true, the owner of the house would have been Mark's father and one of Jesus' followers. He knew exactly who **the Teacher** was and probably knew the disciples by sight. The disciples did as Jesus directed and made preparations for the others.

22:12-13 The owner of the house would take Peter and John **upstairs to a large room** already **set up.** Many homes had large upstairs rooms, sometimes with stairways both inside and outside the house. This room was large enough to accommodate Jesus and his twelve disciples for a banquet at a large table with reclining couches. It seems that Jesus had prearranged this because he already knew what the room looked like—it was large, furnished, and ready.

As before, when two disciples went to get the

donkey for Jesus to ride into Jerusalem (19:29-32), they **found everything just as Jesus had said.** The preparations for the Passover would have included setting the table, buying and roasting the Passover lamb, and making the unleavened bread, sauces, and other ceremonial food and drink that were a traditional part of every Passover meal.

JESUS AND THE DISCIPLES SHARE THE LAST SUPPER / 22:14-30 / *211*
Although the Gospel of John goes into great detail recounting what Jesus said and did during his last Passover meal (see John 13:1–17:26), Luke's Gospel merely highlights Jesus' institution of the Lord's Supper (22:17-20), his prediction of his betrayal (22:21-23), his teaching on service (22:24-27), and his prediction of Peter's denial (22:31-34).

22:14 Peter and John had been sent ahead to prepare the meal, then at the appointed time to eat, **Jesus and the twelve apostles** arrived and assumed their seats at the table. The Passover meal was supposed to be eaten in Jerusalem after sunset and finished before midnight. The disciples and Jesus took their places on the reclining couches around the table. During such an important meal as the Passover, everyone would recline at the table, symbolizing the freedom the people had gained after the very first Passover and their subsequent release from slavery in Egypt.

22:15-16 Jesus had **looked forward to** this quiet time with his disciples. We know from John's Gospel that a great deal was said during the Passover meal. These would be Jesus' "last words"—thus words of vital importance to these to whom he was entrusting the carrying on of his work. Jesus knew that his time of **suffering** would soon come, and that he would not celebrate this event again **until it comes to fulfillment in the Kingdom of God.** The mention of "fulfillment" reveals the complete and ultimate significance of the entire Passover celebration. While Passover commemorated a past event, it also foreshadowed Jesus' work on the cross. As the spotless Lamb of God, his blood would be spilled in order to save his people from the penalty of death brought by sin. At that time, those who belong to Christ will sit down at a glorious banquet (see 13:29; 14:15-24; Isaiah 25:6-8; Revelation 19:7-9). Jesus will not celebrate Passover until God's plan is complete.

22:17-18 This Gospel mentions two cups of wine. In the traditional Passover meal, the wine is served four times. A fourth cup of wine would conclude the meal. Jesus made the vow to abstain from wine before the fourth cup. Jesus reserved the drinking of this cup for the future restoration. Because Jesus

would be raised, so his followers will be raised. One day all believers will be together again in God's new Kingdom (see 11:2) The **Kingdom of God** refers to the time of the complete fulfillment of the rule of God. When Jesus celebrates with his people, all God's promises, power, and authority will be fully realized.

22:19 Jesus **took** the **loaf** of unleavened **bread, thanked God, and broke it.** Because bread was considered a gift from God, it was irreverent to cut bread with a knife, so bread would be torn (or broken) with the hands. Jesus gave the bread **to the disciples** to eat with the sauce. As he did so, he gave this Passover practice an entirely new meaning. Just as the Passover celebrated deliverance from slavery in Egypt, so the Lord's Supper celebrates deliverance from sin by Christ's death. Jesus told the disciples: **"This is my body, given for you."** Jesus used literal terms to describe a figurative truth. Just as he had so many times said, "I am" the door, the bread, the light, the vine, so the bread symbolized Jesus' work of salvation on behalf of humanity. That his body would "be given" pictures the cross on which Jesus gave his body in death, allowing it to be broken so that believers could receive life.

Jesus told the disciples to eat the broken bread **in remembrance of me.** He wanted them to remember his sacrifice, the basis for forgiveness of sins, and also his friendship that they could continue to enjoy through the work of the Holy Spirit.

22:20 As noted above, in a traditional Passover meal, wine is served four times. Most likely, the cup mentioned in this verse was the third cup; the words of 22:17-18 were spoken about the fourth and final cup that Jesus did not drink, vowing first to complete his mission before drinking again of wine. Jesus took this cup and explained, **"This wine is the token of God's new covenant to save you."**

In Old Testament times, God agreed to forgive people's sins if they brought animals for the priests to sacrifice. When this sacrificial system was inaugurated, the agreement between God and sinful humanity was sealed with the blood of animals (Exodus 24:8). But animal blood did not in itself remove sin (only God can forgive sin), and animal sacrifices had to be repeated day by day and year after year. Jesus instituted a "new covenant" or agreement between humans and God. Under this new covenant, Jesus would die in the place of sinners. Unlike the blood of animals, his **blood** would seal the **agreement** between God and people to remove the sins of all who put their faith in him.

22:21 Verses 3-6 revealed that the **man who will betray** Jesus is Judas Iscariot. Although the other disciples were confused by Jesus' words, Judas knew what he meant. The betrayer was there among them, joining them in the meal, one of Jesus' chosen twelve disciples. Jesus' words allude to Psalm 41:9.

22:22 Jesus' death was part of the divine purpose; Jesus recognized that. But this does not remove responsibility from the **betrayer.** Judas allowed his desires to place him in a position where Satan could manipulate him (22:3). In betraying Jesus, Judas made the greatest mistake in history. But the fact that Jesus knew Judas would betray him does not mean that Judas was a puppet of God's will. Judas made the choice. God knew what that choice would be and confirmed it. Judas didn't lose his relationship with Jesus; rather, he had never found Jesus in the first place. Judas, by his own choice, betrayed God's Son into the hands of soldiers, but Judas's betrayal was part of God's sovereign plan (Psalm 41:9; Zechariah 11:12-13; Matthew 20:18; 26:20-25; Acts 1:16, 20).

It must be remembered that while Judas betrayed him, all the disciples fled, and Peter even denied ever knowing Jesus. But all those disciples came to Jesus for forgiveness; Judas never took that opportunity. Instead, he killed himself (Matthew 27:3-5).

22:23 Apparently, Judas was not obvious as the betrayer. After all, he was the one the disciples were trusting to keep the money (John 12:4-6). So **the disciples began to ask each other which of them would ever do such a thing.** Only Judas knew that Jesus had identified him as the betrayer. Judas had been able to keep his treachery a secret from everyone, except the one he would betray.

22:24 The most important event in human history was about to take place, and the disciples were still arguing about their prestige in the Kingdom! The disciples, wrapped up in their own concerns, did not perceive what Jesus had been trying to tell them about his approaching death and resurrection. The disciples had already had this discussion (9:46) and Jesus had told them that they should be like children—the least among them would be the greatest (9:48). As before, they were either ignoring his words about his death, or they were wondering who would take over when Jesus died.

22:25-26 The world's system of leadership varies greatly from leadership in God's Kingdom. But among Christians, the **master** is to be **like a servant.** There are different styles of leadership— some lead through public speaking, some through administering, some through relationships. Whatever the style, every Christian leader needs a servant's heart. Jesus immediately corrected his disciples' attitudes, for they would be unable to accomplish their mission if they did not love and serve one another.

22:27 Jesus did not come to sit at the table and be served; he came as a **servant.** Greatness is determined by servanthood. The truly great leader places his or her needs last, as Jesus exemplified. Because Jesus served, his disciples must also seek to serve, not seeking to occupy better positions. Being a "servant" did not mean occupying a servile position; rather, it meant having an attitude of life that freely attended to others' needs without expecting or demanding anything in return. An attitude of service brings true greatness in God's Kingdom.

22:28-30 The disciples had **remained true to** Jesus throughout the three years of ministry and the hardships it often entailed (9:58). They had been willing to be servants, sharing the gospel message and healing people through Jesus' power (9:1-6). The words, **"I now grant you the right to eat and drink at my table in that Kingdom,"** refer to Jesus' promise that because of their faith in him, they would enjoy the promised messianic banquet with him. This would happen, not immediately, but in due time. They would receive all that he had promised. In addition, they would also **sit on thrones, judging the twelve tribes of Israel.** The "thrones" and "tribes" can be understood in different ways. (1) If taken literally, the twelve apostles will rule the tribes of Israel at Christ's return (although this leaves open the question of Judas's betrayal, the addition of Matthias as a disciple to replace Judas, and the role of Paul's apostleship). (2) If not taken literally, then the disciples will oversee the church, which will have a prominent place in God's plan. (3) This may be a promise to Jesus' closest disciples (probably Paul would be included), who will have a special place of authority in God's Kingdom. But the entire church, meaning all believers, is included.

The second understanding (the disciples will oversee the church) seems likely. Jesus Christ gave the Kingdom to the new Israel, his church—all faithful believers. His coming ushered in the Kingdom of God with all believers as its citizens. God may allow persecution to continue for a while, but the destiny of his followers is to possess the Kingdom and live with him forever. The apostles, and all believers, can trust that Jesus will surely accomplish all that he promised.

JESUS PREDICTS PETER'S DENIAL / 22:31-38 / 212

After describing the disciples' glorious roles in the Kingdom of God (22:29-30), Jesus turned to the immediate trials they would face. First, Jesus warned Peter of his future denial. Second, Jesus warned them all to prepare themselves for the coming troubles.

22:31-32 Luke alone recorded these solemn words to **Simon** (Peter) and described Satan's role in the upcoming difficulties **all** the disciples, but especially Peter, were soon to face. Satan **asked** to **sift** them **like wheat,** meaning a severe trial. These words recall when Satan asked God for permission to test Job (Job 1:7; 2:2). Satan wanted to crush Simon Peter and the other disciples like grains of wheat. He hoped to find only chaff and blow it away. But Jesus assured Peter that although his faith would falter, it would not be destroyed, **"But I have pleaded in prayer for you, Simon, that your faith should not fail. So when you have repented and turned to me again, strengthen and build up your brothers."** Jesus prayed for faith, not the removal of the test. Apparently, he knew that Peter would fail; otherwise, there would be no need for Peter to repent. Yet Jesus was confident of this turning back, and also understood that, having faced this trial, Peter would be able to strengthen fellow believers. Indeed, the book of 1 Peter deals entirely with encouragement for believers who are undergoing trials and difficulties. Peter became a source of strength to many who needed it.

22:33-34 Peter seemed to ignore Jesus' words regarding intercession on his behalf and simply answered with bravado. Peter considered his loyalty to exceed anyone's, for he declared that suffering and death could not dissuade him. Peter surely wanted to believe that his loyalty to Jesus would be strong, but Jesus already knew that Peter would initially fail the test. Instead of being the only loyal disciple, Peter would, in fact, prove to be more disloyal than the other ten. Not only would he desert Jesus, but he would also deny **three times** that he even knew Jesus. And this would happen before the night was over.

22:35-36 Here Jesus would reverse his earlier advice regarding how to travel (9:3). Before, Jesus had sent the disciples out without extra resources, wanting them to depend on God and on other believers to meet their basic needs. The disciples remembered that they did not **lack anything** during that preaching tour. **But now,** Jesus explained, the situation was different. His followers needed to be prepared.

22:37-38 Jesus quoted from Isaiah 53:12 and said that those very words were about to be **fulfilled.** Jesus would take the place of transgressors, taking their punishment for them. Because of all that was about to happen to Jesus, the disciples would be in danger too. The disciples did not understand. The "fulfillment" of which Jesus spoke referred to his death, but the disciples were busy checking for arms with which to defend themselves. They came up with **two swords,** hardly enough to defend them all. But Jesus said, **"That's enough,"** meaning either that this was not the time to think of using swords or that he'd had enough of their discussion. In either case, mention of a sword vividly communicated the trials they soon would face.

JESUS AGONIZES IN THE GARDEN / 22:39-46 / 223

Throughout his Gospel, Luke highlighted Jesus' consistent prayer life. This section provides an intimate look at Jesus' dependence on prayer, right before his greatest hour of need. For Jesus, prayer was not an escape, but a respite; not a way to avoid difficulty, but a way to strengthen himself to endure it.

22:39 The disciples and Jesus finished the Passover meal and the lengthy teaching recorded in John (John 13:31–17:26); then they **left the upstairs room and went as usual to the Mount of Olives.** Apparently, this was a favorite place for Jesus and the disciples. Up to this point, Jesus and the disciples had been returning each night to Bethany; but this time, Jesus only went as far as the Mount of Olives, located just to the east of Jerusalem. Jesus went up the southwestern slope to an olive grove called Gethsemane.

22:40 Jesus asked the disciples to pray that they would **not be overcome by temptation** because he knew that he would soon be leaving them. Jesus also knew that they would need extra strength to face the temptations ahead—temptations to run away or to deny their relationship with him. They were about to see Jesus arrested and then crucified. The disciples' strongest temptation would undoubtedly be to think that they had been deceived.

22:41-42 Jesus **walked away, knelt down, and prayed.** Jesus exposed his dread of the coming trials, but he also reaffirmed his commitment to do what God wanted. In deep anguish, he asked the Father to let the mission be accomplished some other way not requiring the agony of crucifixion, when he would become sin and be separated from the Father. The **cup of suffering** meant the terrible agony he knew he would endure—not only the horror of the crucifixion but, even worse, the total separation from God that he would have to experience in order to die for the world's sins. The "cup" in the Old Testament could be a symbol of blessing (Psalms 16:5; 23:5) or of cursing (Psalms 11:6; 75:8). A whole nation could "drink a cup" of either blessings or curses (Isaiah 51:22; Jeremiah 25:15; 49:12; Ezekiel 23:31-33).

Jesus was not trying to get out of his mission, however. He reaffirmed his desire to do what God wanted by saying, **"Yet I want your will, not mine."** Jesus' human will was distinct from God's will, but it did not oppose God's will. His prayer reveals his terrible suffering, but he willingly placed himself in his Father's hands.

22:43-44 *This portion is often bracketed and/or noted in most modern English versions because it does not appear in many of the earliest manuscripts.* Here an angel from heaven appeared and strengthened Jesus. Angels are God's emissaries, sent to do his bidding, ministering to people on earth. God sent an angel to be with Jesus in this horrible time of fear, and perhaps even temptation far worse than what Satan tried. In his humanity, Jesus suffered terribly during this night, battling what he knew to had happen. Jesus was in extreme agony; his prayer reveals his terrible suffering. Luke was speaking metaphorically. Jesus did not sweat blood, but rather the emotional agony he felt caused the perspiration to fall like clotted blood. The focus of this prayer was probably not so much on the painful death but on the agony of being separated from God. God did not take away the "cup," for the cup was his will. Yet he did take away Jesus' extreme fear and agitation. Jesus moved serenely through the next several hours, at peace with God, knowing that he was doing his Father's will.

22:45 Jesus got up **at last** from praying—how long he struggled in prayer is not revealed, but the hour was late. Matthew wrote that Jesus went back and forth three times between praying and checking on the disciples, each time finding them asleep (Matthew 26:40-45). Jesus needed his friends to support him with their prayers, but they were **asleep, exhausted from grief.** It had been a long day and the reality of Jesus' impending death left them emotionally exhausted.

22:46 Jesus told the disciples that this was the time to **get up and pray,** for very soon they would face the temptation to run away or to deny their relationship with him. They would need extra strength so that these temptations would not **overpower** them. The word "temptation" can mean testing or trial. Jesus wanted his disciples to pray for strength to go through the coming ordeal.

JESUS IS BETRAYED AND ARRESTED / 22:47-53 / 224

Despite all of Jesus' warnings about the coming trouble, the disciples were unprepared for it when the moment arrived. Judas, formerly one of them, appeared and betrayed Jesus with a kiss. The disciples attempted to defend Jesus, and then fled, as Jesus gave himself over to an illegal arrest.

22:47 Even as Jesus spoke the words about not being overcome by temptation (22:46), **a mob approached.** The leader was **Judas,** who had gone to the Jewish religious leaders in order to betray Jesus (22:3-4). He was at the Last Supper with Jesus and the other disciples (Matthew 26:25) and then had abruptly left, apparently to let the leaders know where to find Jesus (John 13:27). Judas came up to Jesus **and greeted him with a kiss.** Judas had told the crowd to arrest the man whom he would kiss (Matthew 26:48).

22:48 With this kiss of greeting, Judas showed himself to be the ultimate traitor. He had eaten with Jesus only hours before, and here he used a sign of friendship and affection in his betrayal. Apparently Jesus understood that this greeting had been designated as a signal. Jesus asked, **"Judas, how can you betray me, the Son of Man, with a kiss?"** This was the height of disloyalty and hypocrisy.

22:49-51 Apparently the arrival of the mob had awakened the sleeping disciples, and they came fully awake and ready to fight. **One of them slashed at the high priest's servant and cut off his right ear.** The Gospel of John reveals that the man who cut off the servant's ear was Peter and that the servant's name was Malchus (John 18:10). Peter may have thought that this was the time to fight, the time to defend themselves, but Jesus told

Peter, **"Don't resist anymore."** Peter should put away his sword and allow God's plan to unfold. Jesus' time of prayer had made him serene in God's will. He would comply with God's plan. So he **healed** the man's ear. Even as Jesus was being led away to face what would be the most difficult of trials, he first stopped to care for this member of the mob, restoring his ear.

22:52-53 Apparently many of the religious leaders had come together to take part in this arrest. Jesus pointed out the ridiculous picture of all these men coming after him **with swords and clubs.** Jesus also pointed out the basic cowardice in their actions. He had been among them **every day** in the **Temple,** but they had not laid a hand on him. We know from 20:19 and 22:2 that they had not arrested Jesus in the Temple for fear of a riot. Instead, they came secretly at night, under the influence of the prince of darkness, Satan himself. Although it looked as if Satan was getting the upper hand and that **darkness** was in control, everything was proceeding according to God's plan. It was time for Jesus to die.

PETER DENIES KNOWING JESUS / 22:54-65 / 227
Peter's confidence and courage had wilted under pressure. Only several hours before, he had courageously asserted that he would follow Jesus to prison—or even to death. At this point, however, he was repeatedly denying any association with Jesus. Each denial distanced Peter further from him. The best part of this sad story is that it did not end here.

22:54 Jesus did not resist arrest, his disciples had turned and run (Mark 14:50), so Jesus was led away **to the high priest's residence,** even though it was not yet daylight. The Jewish leaders were in a hurry because they wanted to complete the execution before the Sabbath and get on with the Passover celebration. The high priest's residence was a palace with outer walls enclosing a courtyard. That this trial should occur here was unprecedented. Normally the council would meet in a large hall in the Temple area. They could have met there because during the Passover, the Temple opened at midnight rather than at dawn. This meeting at Caiaphas's home may have been to aid in a hasty assembly; however, they still could just as easily have met in a normal location. Most likely, it was their desire to avoid a riot that led them to this more private setting. **Peter** followed the mob from **far behind,** along with John (John 18:15).

22:55 As mentioned above, this **courtyard** was probably in a central area of the buildings that made up the high priest's residence. In the court-

yard, **the guards lit a fire,** around which the servants and soldiers were warming themselves against the early morning chill. **Peter joined** the others around the fire.

22:56-57 John wrote that this **servant girl** was acting as a guard at the gate to the inner courtyard (John 18:16). She apparently noticed Peter **in the firelight, staring at him.** Then the girl realized where she had seen Peter before—he was **one of Jesus' followers.** This put Peter in a difficult position. Standing among the soldiers and servants right there in enemy territory, Peter did not necessarily want to be identified with the man held in an upstairs room, on trial for his life. So Peter made a natural and impulsive response—he lied. **"Woman . . . I don't even know the man!"** Temptation came when Peter least expected it. This serves as a warning to all believers to be prepared. Peter had been ready to fight with a sword, but not to face the accusations of a servant girl.

22:58 Peter could run, but he couldn't hide. He got away from the questioning servant girl only to run into **someone else** who also recognized him as **one of them** (one of Jesus' followers). But Peter again denied it.

22:59-60 This time, another bystander heard Peter's Galilean accent which was closer to Syrian speech than to that of the Judean servants in the Jerusalem courtyard. Thus the group concluded that Peter must have been with the **Galilean** on trial inside the palace. Peter again replied in the negative, claiming to not even know what they were talking about. These three denials did not occur quickly, one immediately after another. Time elapsed in between, yet Peter could not control himself. As he spoke these words of his third denial, **the rooster crowed**, signaling the early morning hour.

22:61-62 Peter's denials fulfilled Jesus' words to him (22:34). When Peter heard the rooster crowing and then saw Jesus turn and look at him (either from the upper story where the trial was being held or as he passed through the courtyard between visits with Annas and Caiaphas), **Peter remembered** what Jesus had said to him earlier (12:9). Peter had indeed denied Jesus three times before the rooster crowed.

Peter **left the courtyard, crying bitterly.** His tears were not only because he realized that he had denied his Lord, the Messiah, but also because he had turned away from a very dear

friend, a person who had loved and taught him for three years. Peter had said that he would go to prison or even death for Jesus (Mark 14:29-31; Luke 22:33-34). Fortunately, the story does not end there. Peter's tears were of true sorrow and repentance. Later, Peter would reaffirm his love for Jesus, and Jesus would forgive him (see Mark 16:7; John 21:15-19).

22:63-65 After the preliminary meeting in Caiaphas's house, the men adjourned to await daybreak and the arrival of the entire council for the more formal meeting in the Temple. Matters had really already been decided during the night, but the full trial would be held early in the morning to satisfy a law that allowed trials only during the daytime. This would be a formality to carry out the sentence that already had been decided.

Apparently Jesus was left in the care of **guards** who proceeded to mock and beat him. Evidently, the charge of Jesus being a prophet had come up, so the guards took advantage of their prisoner by playing on this claim. **They blindfolded him, hit him,** and asked that he say who had hit him. In addition, they **threw all sorts of terrible insults at him.** Matthew and Mark wrote that these guards were only following the example of the religious leaders themselves who had already beaten and insulted Jesus (Matthew 26:67-68; Mark 14:65). None of this surprised Jesus (see 18:32).

THE COUNCIL OF RELIGIOUS LEADERS CONDEMNS JESUS / 22:66-71 / 228

Luke's presentation of Jesus' trial before the council is much shorter than Matthew or Mark's (see Matthew 26:57-68; Mark 14:53-65). In retelling the story of the trial, Luke's clear purpose was to get at the heart of the matter: Who is Jesus?

22:66 As stated above, the **leaders assembled** during the day in order for the trial to be legal. So they met immediately **at daybreak,** keeping such trivialities of the law while holding a trial that was completely illegal.

22:67-69 They already knew what they planned to do with Jesus, so this meeting was merely a formality. They asked him to tell them if he was **the Messiah.** For Jesus to answer in the affirmative would incriminate himself. To answer in the negative would have been to lie. Jesus knew this was their plan, for he said, **"If I tell you, you won't believe me."** The council had already proven that they had no intention of believing Jesus to be their Messiah. Jesus also knew that if he questioned them, they would not answer (as already seen in 20:1-8). Jesus was in a no-win situation, but he told them the

truth, **"The time is soon coming when I, the Son of Man, will be sitting at God's right hand in the place of power."** To say this was to say that yes, he was the Messiah and to boldly claim his own exaltation to the place of highest honor in heaven.

22:70-71 The religious leaders understood exactly what Jesus was saying. He was indeed claiming to be **the Son of God**—but they needed him to be a bit more clear. So they asked again. Jesus agreed, saying, **"You are right in saying that I am."** Jesus identified himself with God by using a familiar title for God found in the Old Testament: "I am" (Exodus 3:14). The council recognized Jesus' claim and realized that they needed no **other witnesses.** He had accused himself. Their accusation against him was blasphemy—claiming equality with God (Matthew 26:65; Mark 14:64). For any other human this claim would have been blasphemy, but in this case it was true. Blasphemy was punishable by death (Leviticus 24:16). The council could condemn Jesus to death, but they could not carry out the death penalty under Roman law. The Romans would have to condemn him. So Jesus was led to trial before the local Roman leader—Pontius Pilate.

LUKE 23

JESUS STANDS TRIAL BEFORE PILATE / 23:1-5 / 230

Early that morning, Jesus' accusers rushed him to Pilate. To the high priests and the teachers of religious law, Jesus was very dangerous. He simply had to be eliminated. Therefore, they did not shrink from presenting completely false charges against Jesus. Pilate saw through their blatant lies. He knew Jesus was innocent.

23:1 The Jewish **council** had already decided that Jesus should die, but they could not, under Roman law, carry out the death penalty. Jesus would have to be tried and convicted in a Roman court. Thus, they **took Jesus over to Pilate, the Roman governor.** Pilate was the governor of Judea, where Jerusalem was located. Pilate's normal residence was in Caesarea on the Mediterranean Sea, but he happened to be in Jerusalem because of the Passover festival. With the large crowds who had flocked to the city for that celebration, Pilate and his soldiers came to help keep the peace. He stayed in his headquarters, called the Praetorium.

23:2 The Jewish leaders had arrested Jesus on theological grounds—blasphemy; but they had to come up with a political reason for executing Jesus. The charges against Jesus in the Roman court were rebellion and treason. The irony is that the first accusation—that Jesus was **leading the people to ruin**—was completely unfounded. The second accusation—that Jesus told the people **not to pay their taxes**—was an outright lie (see 20:20-26). The third charge, that he was claiming to be **the Messiah, a king,** was absolutely true.

23:3-4 Pilate focused on the accusation about Jesus claiming to be a king, for that could amount to treason and be grounds for a death sentence. So **Pilate asked** the prisoner, **"Are you the King of the Jews?"** This question is identical in all four Gospels, and in all four the word "you" is emphatic. Jesus answered the question, **"Yes, it is as you say."** To have said otherwise would have been to lie. Jesus was a king, but his kingship was not a threat to Pilate or to Caesar. At some point, Pilate realized that the religious leaders simply wanted to get rid of this man, so he said **"I find nothing wrong with this man!"** Pilate's reluctance to prosecute Jesus was undoubtedly due more to his contempt for the Jews than for any particular consideration of Jesus.

23:5 The Jews' plan was unraveling. Pilate wasn't playing into their hands as they had hoped, and **they became desperate.** So they came up with more trumped-up charges. They claimed that Jesus was **causing riots everywhere.** Because Pilate was mainly charged with keeping peace, he would be interested in dealing with a man who was causing riots. If this charge were true, Pilate would have heard about Jesus long before this.

JESUS STANDS TRIAL BEFORE HEROD / 23:6-12 / 231

Herod was ecstatic that he would be able to see Jesus. He had heard so much about this mysterious, miracle-working man from Galilee. But Herod was severely disappointed. Jesus remained silent. He would not answer Herod's questions, much less perform any miracles.

23:6-7 When the religious leaders mentioned that Jesus had been in Galilee, Pilate wanted to know if Jesus was **a Galilean.** Jesus had grown up in Nazareth and later had made Capernaum his base; he was indeed **under Herod's jurisdiction.** This was the Herod who had killed John the Baptist. Herod, also called Herod Antipas, was himself **in Jerusalem** that weekend for the Passover celebration, mainly as a tactic to please his subjects. Pilate hoped to pass Jesus off on Herod.

23:8-9 Herod may have been **delighted** to finally **see Jesus,** but he had already closed his window of opportunity to hear the message. John had spoken to him; Herod had killed John. Herod's motivation here was only to see Jesus **perform a miracle.** He apparently saw Jesus as no more than an amazing traveling sideshow. When Jesus was brought before him, Herod asked him questions, **but Jesus refused to answer.** Herod is the only person to whom Jesus said nothing at all. Herod had not listened to John; Jesus had nothing to add to what John had said. Cold and cruel, Herod had a hard heart. Jesus knew this and remained silent.

23:10 The religious leaders had hoped for a quick sentence from Pilate so they could return to their religious duties during this important Passover celebration. But they had already had to trek with

Jesus from Pilate's residence over to Herod's palace, and now Herod was wasting more time. So they shouted **their accusations,** probably with more of the same kinds of lies (23:2, 5). They hoped their accusations would sway Herod, so they would get a verdict from him that would be as good as one from Pilate.

23:11-12 With this prisoner refusing to answer, and looking very little like a great miracle worker, **Herod and his soldiers began mocking and ridiculing Jesus.** Angry at Jesus' refusal to even answer questions for him, Herod resorted to mocking Jesus. To make fun of Jesus' claim to be a king, Herod **put a royal robe on him.** Herod did not even take the charge seriously. So he neither released the prisoner nor made a judgment about his guilt. He simply **sent him back to Pilate.** Herod and Pilate had a rather tenuous relationship. But because neither man knew what to do in this predicament, their common problem made them **friends that day.**

PILATE HANDS JESUS OVER TO BE CRUCIFIED / 23:13-25 / 232
According to the Roman custom of releasing a criminal during the Passover season, Pilate presented Jesus to the people. Pilate did not want to bear the responsibility of putting an innocent man to death. But the crowd insisted on Barabbas's freedom. That Jesus literally died in Barabbas's place vividly illustrates the ultimate significance of Jesus' death. He took the place of not only Barabbas but all who stand condemned before God's perfect standard and trust in Christ for salvation.

23:13-14 Pilate thought he had gotten rid of his problem, only to have Jesus sent back. The decision still rested on his shoulders. So he attempted to let this innocent man go by telling Jesus' accusers that he found him **innocent.**

23:15 Pilate could back up his decision with Herod's conclusion about Jesus. Herod had mocked Jesus, but apparently had sent back word to Pilate that he could find nothing worthy of the **death penalty.** Jesus was tried a total of six times, by both Jewish and Roman authorities, but he was never convicted of a crime. Even when condemned to execution, he had been convicted of no felony.

23:16 The word **flogged** may not indicate the severe flogging that Jesus received after being sentenced, prior to the crucifixion (as noted in Matthew 27:26; Mark 15:15), although John 19:1 reports Jesus being flogged and then brought before the crowd. Pilate may have hoped that the flogging would appease the crowd, and they would pity the man and let him go. Pilate was planning

to **release** Jesus, but first he would punish him— to pacify the Jews and teach the prisoner a lesson to stay out of trouble in the future. (Verse 17 does not exist in most modern English versions because it does not appear in any of the earliest Greek manuscripts.)

23:18-19 The suggestion that Pilate was going to release Jesus (23:16) sent the leaders into a frenzy. Pilate had wanted to release Jesus as the Passover gift (Mark 15:8-9). This had been a public announcement, so many people in **the crowd** cried out that Jesus must be put to death. The prisoner they wanted set free was a man named **Barabbas,** who may have been somewhat of a hero among the Jews for his acts of rebellion against Rome. He was a true rebel and revolutionary and had even committed **murder.** The religious leaders had tried to pin this accusation on Jesus in order to have him put to death, but they chose a man who had done such acts and wanted him set free. Clearly their actions had no logic. They merely wanted

Jesus put to death and would go to any lengths to make sure it happened.

23:20-21 Pilate really **wanted to release Jesus.** Matthew recorded that even Pilate's wife had experienced a dream about Jesus and had urged Pilate to let Jesus go (Matthew 27:19). Pilate must have been in a tight spot, because for some reason he put himself in the position of bargaining with the crowd. He had the authority to let Jesus go and then get on with his day; instead, he **argued with them,** but to no avail. They wanted Jesus to be crucified.

23:22 Pilate tried for the **third time.** He could not fathom why the crowd so badly wanted this man's death. Jesus had not committed any crime, so there was **no reason to sentence him to death.** There are two reasons why Luke stressed these three attempts Pilate had made to release Jesus. First, Luke wanted to show through his Gospel the innocence of Jesus before Roman law. Luke was giving evidence to prove the acceptability of Chris-

tianity to his Gentile readers. Second, he was establishing the Jewish mob's guilt for Jesus' death.

23:23-24 Pilate wanted to release Jesus, but the crowd **shouted louder and louder,** so Pilate **sentenced Jesus to die.** No doubt Pilate did not want to risk losing his position, which may already have been shaky, by allowing a riot to occur in his province. As a career politician, he knew the importance of compromise, and he saw Jesus more as a political threat than as a human being with rights and dignity.

23:25 Pilate **released Barabbas** and **delivered Jesus over to them to do as they wished.** Matthew's Gospel explains that Pilate took water and washed his hands in front of the crowd to symbolize his innocence in condemning Jesus (Matthew 27:24), but this act was no more than self-deception. Jesus may have been surrendered to the will of the mob, but this was still a purely Roman execution. Pilate had to command it in order for it to happen.

JESUS IS LED AWAY TO BE CRUCIFIED / 23:26-31 / 234
Severely beaten and worn out from the previous night's ordeal, Jesus could not carry his cross to the crest of Golgotha. So Simon was drafted to carry Jesus' cross. The image of Simon shouldering the cross graphically pictures what every follower of Christ should be willing to do: to take up his or her own cross daily to serve Christ (see 14:27).

23:26 Jesus was led away from Pilate and out to the place where he would be executed. Condemned prisoners had to carry the crossbeam of their own cross on their shoulders through the streets of Jerusalem and to the execution site outside the city. Jesus started to carry his cross, but, weakened from the beatings he had received, he was physically unable to carry it all the way. A man named **Simon** from the country of **Cyrene** (in northern Africa, see Acts 2:10) was coming into the city. He may have been a Jew coming on a pilgrimage to the city for the Passover, or he may have been from Cyrene but resided in Palestine. Soldiers were free by law to coerce citizens at any time. So this stranger **was forced to follow Jesus and carry his cross.**

23:27-28 Luke alone wrote of the Jewish women shedding tears for Jesus while he was being led through the streets to his execution. Not everyone wanted Jesus to die. Seeing him on his way to be executed caused many, especially women along the way, to mourn and wail for him. Jesus told them not to **weep** for him but for themselves and for their **children.** He knew that in only about forty years they would face great suffering and would

then mourn, weep, and wail, for at that time Jerusalem and the Temple would be destroyed by the Romans. This was Jesus' third lament for the city of Jerusalem (see also 13:34-35; 19:41-44).

23:29-31 The days are coming indicates a key time in God's judgment about to unfold (21:23). While being **childless** was normally a curse, the coming days in Jerusalem would be so difficult that it would be considered a blessing not to have had children. Punishment would be so great that people would want the **mountains** and **hills** to fall on them and kill them. Death would be preferred to the judgment that they would face and its accompanying misery.

This proverb about the green wood and dry wood is difficult to interpret. Some think it means that if the innocent Jesus (green wood) suffered at the hands of the Romans, what would happen to the guilty Jews (dry wood)? The "green wood" is hard to burn, so if fire burns it up, what chance has dry wood? God would not spare the rebellious hard-hearted Jewish nation from judgment. Thus, Jesus expressed his grief over the nation for the last time.

JESUS IS PLACED ON THE CROSS / 23:32-43 / 235

Even during the final hours of Jesus' life, when he struggled in agony for his last gasp of air, people reacted to him in a variety of ways. Even the two men who were being crucified with Jesus had starkly different reactions to Jesus.

23:32-33 Jesus was not the only "criminal" executed that morning. **Two others** were also led out to be crucified. In his death, Jesus truly was numbered among transgressors (22:37; Isaiah 53:12). The place called **The Skull** may have been a regular place of execution. It was prominent, public, and outside the city along a main road. Executions held there served as examples to the people and as deterrents to criminals.

The words are direct, but the full meaning was horrific: **all three were crucified there.** Instituted by the Romans, crucifixion was a feared and shameful form of execution. It was designed to prolong the gruesome pain. There were several shapes of crosses and several different methods of crucifixion. Death would come by suffocation as the person would lose strength and the weight of the body would make breathing more and more difficult. Crucifixion was the harshest form of capital punishment in the ancient world.

23:34 Jesus spoke only a few times from the cross, and his prayer of forgiveness were the first words he said. Jesus asked his Father to **forgive** his killers. Jesus lived and died by the words he preached: "Love your enemies" (6:27-28). **They don't know what they are doing** refers most likely to the Jews, not the Roman soldiers, although all who participated in Jesus' death were included in his prayer for forgiveness. The Jews made a serious mistake, for they failed to realize God's plan for their nation.

Roman soldiers customarily would divide up the clothing of executed criminals among themselves. When they **gambled** for Jesus' clothes, they fulfilled the prophecy in Psalm 22:18. Jesus was crucified naked. John recorded that four soldiers divided the garments (John 19:23).

23:35 These men, hanging in extreme pain and humiliation on their crosses, provided hours of grisly entertainment for spectators. Luke pointed specifically at **the leaders** who had followed Jesus to the execution site, watched him be crucified, and now **laughed and scoffed** at him. Jesus had gone about the countryside healing people, but he could ᵇᵒᵘᵗ They assumed that if he truly had as he had claimed, then he get himself out of his present pre-

dicament. Jesus' position there on the cross proved to them that he was not any kind of Messiah. Unfortunately, they missed the fact that this entire episode had been prophesied (Psalm 22:6-8) and was all proceeding exactly as God had planned.

23:36-37 The **soldiers** (presumably the Roman soldiers who had carried out the execution) had the duty that day of sitting and waiting until the men on the crosses died. They had already divided up the clothing, and then began mocking the man on the cross who had claimed to be a king. Only Luke wrote of this offer of sour wine as part of the soldiers' mockery. They too called up to him to **save** himself, if he were indeed **the King of the Jews.**

23:38 This **signboard** stated the condemned person's crime and was placed on the cross as a warning. According to John, Pilate wrote this sign in three languages: Aramaic, Latin, and Greek. The three languages meant that people of any nationality passing that way would be able to read the sign. Because Jesus was never found guilty, the only accusation placed on his sign was the "crime" of calling himself **King of the Jews.** Perhaps this was another way for Pilate to show contempt for the Jews—here was their king, stripped and executed in public view.

23:39 One of the criminals scoffed at Jesus, even though the three of them were facing the same horrible deaths. One of them seems to have picked up on the taunts of the religious leaders: if Jesus were indeed **the Messiah,** then he should save himself and them. Obviously these words were no more than barbed sarcasm. All three were beyond hope, beyond the point of being saved—physically.

23:40-43 The other criminal, however, **protested,** pointing out that they deserved their sentence, but Jesus did not. There, on the cross, receiving punishment for what his deeds deserved, this criminal faced himself, feared God, and said: **"Jesus, remember me when you come into your Kingdom."** And Jesus replied, **"I assure you, today you will be with me in paradise."** The dying criminal had more faith than all the rest of Jesus' followers put together. By all appearances, the Kingdom was finished. How awe-inspiring is the faith of this man who alone saw beyond the present shame to the coming glory!

JESUS DIES ON THE CROSS / 23:44-49 / 236

It seemed to most onlookers that day that a poor, deluded man had been executed without good reason. But on that Friday, a huge spiritual battle was being waged unseen. Satan rejoiced that Jesus was going to die. The angels in heaven looked on in sorrow, held back from intervening by the hand of God. God himself looked away from his Son as the sins of the world descended upon him. But Jesus was actually gaining a huge victory. His death and resurrection would strike the deathblow to Satan's rule and would establish Christ's eternal authority over the earth. Few people reading the sign that bleak afternoon understood its real meaning, but the sign was absolutely true. All was not lost. Jesus is King of the Jews—and the Gentiles, and the whole universe.

23:44 Jesus had been placed on the cross at nine o'clock in the morning. Three hours had passed, hours of excruciating pain and physical agony. Then, **it was noon,** and at the height of the day, an eerie **darkness fell across the whole land** for three hours. How this darkness occurred is unknown, but it is clear that God caused it to happen. All nature seemed to mourn over the stark tragedy of the death of God's Son. The darkness was both physical and spiritual—for while nature mourned, this was also the time when darkness reigned (22:53).

23:45 Obviously the darkness that covered the land meant that somehow **the light from the sun was gone.** Luke did not explain it, but clearly God controlled these events. Most significant and symbolic was an event that occurred in the city of Jerusalem, in the Temple, right in the inner area called the Holy Place.

The Temple had three parts: the courts for all the people; the Holy Place, where only priests could enter; and the Most Holy Place, where the high priest alone could enter once a year to atone for the sins of the people (Leviticus 16:1-34). In the Most Holy Place, the ark of the covenant and God's presence rested. As Jesus suffered on the cross and as darkness covered the land, **the thick veil hanging in the Temple was torn apart.** The veil (curtain) that was torn was the one that closed off the Most Holy Place from view. Symbolically, that curtain separated holy God from sinful people. The writer of Hebrews saw this tearing of the curtain as God's way of removing the barrier between himself and humanity. Now sinful people could approach the holy God directly through Christ (Hebrews 9:1-14; 10:19-22). From then on, God would not reside behind a curtain in the Temple, he would take up residence in his people.

23:46 In committing his **spirit** to the Father, Jesus died, fulfilling the words of Psalm 31:5. Jesus did not faint; he did not become unconscious only to be revived later—he **breathed his last.** Jesus died as a human being—voluntarily, sacrificially, in the place of sinners.

23:47 Matthew, Mark, and Luke all point to the head Roman soldier, **the captain,** who had apparently been in charge of carrying out this execution. Upon seeing **what had happened,** he realized that Jesus had been no ordinary person. Presumably this soldier had carried out other such executions, but never had he experienced what he did at this one. This Gentile soldier understood something that most of the Jewish nation had missed: **Surely this man was innocent.** The captain understood that Jesus had not deserved what he received, yet Jesus had borne it all with dignity, courage, and even words of forgiveness.

23:48 Miracles had occurred out there on the hill—darkness, an earthquake, dead people walking, and the torn veil in the Temple that no one had probably heard about yet. Perhaps the crowd expected, through all that, to see Jesus come down off the cross and be their Messiah. But he didn't. He died. The onlookers in the crowd, who had come to see the spectacle of this execution **went home in deep sorrow.**

23:49 The women who had followed Jesus **from Galilee** are named in 8:2-3. John wrote that besides himself, Jesus' mother was also there, as well as others (John 19:25-26). Perhaps Jesus' mother, watching **at a distance,** finally understood Simeon's words from years before (2:35). Among Jesus' disciples, only John was at the cross.

JESUS IS LAID IN THE TOMB / 23:50-56 / 237

Sometimes the worst circumstances bring out the best in people. In this case, two secret disciples—Joseph of Arimathea and Nicodemus (according to John 19:38-39)—openly expressed their allegiance to Jesus. Joseph was a member of the council, and Nicodemus was a Pharisee.

23:50-51 The scene shifts away from the cross to a man, **a member of the Jewish high council** who **had not agreed with the decision and actions of the other religious leaders.** Apparently the death sentence for Jesus had not been a unanimous vote. Joseph had been against it, as had another member of the council named Nicodemus (John 3:1; 19:38-42). Both of these men came to bury Jesus' body. Their commitment to Jesus forced them out of hiding.

Joseph **was from the town of Arimathea,** about twenty-two miles northwest of Jerusalem. Joseph was a secret disciple of Jesus (John 19:38) who was **waiting for the Kingdom of God to come** (suggesting that he was a Pharisee, not a Sadducee). The disciples who had publicly followed Jesus had fled, but Joseph boldly took a stand that could cost him dearly. He cared enough about Jesus to ask for his body so he could give it a proper burial.

23:52 Joseph had to go **to Pilate** to ask if he could have **Jesus' body** in order to give it a proper burial. Apparently Pilate alone could give this permission, and this may not have been an easy thing to do—going back to Pilate who was already furious at the Jewish leaders. Mark recorded that Pilate was surprised that Jesus was already dead and asked the Roman captain for verification (Mark 15:44-45).

23:53 Joseph had to hurry; Sabbath was fast approaching. Fortunately he had help. John wrote that Nicodemus, another member of the council, brought spices for the burial. Probably along with the help of several servants, Jesus' body was carefully taken down from the cross, washed, wrapped in layers of **linen cloth** with the spices in between, and laid in a tomb. Jesus was given a burial fit for a king.

The **tomb** was likely a man-made cave cut out of one of the many limestone hills in the area around Jerusalem. Such a tomb was large enough to walk into. Some caves were large enough to hold several bodies, but this tomb had never been used—in fact, it was owned by Joseph himself (Matthew 27:60). Such tombs were for wealthy people. So Jesus had a proper burial. After Jesus' burial, a large stone was rolled across the entrance to the tomb (John 20:1).

23:54 Friday of every week was **the day of preparation for the Sabbath**—all necessary work had to be completed before Sabbath began at sundown on Friday. Sabbath ended at sundown on Saturday. Jesus died just a few hours before sundown on Friday. Joseph had to hurry in order to complete this burial before the Sabbath began.

23:55-56 The **women from Galilee** who had been at the cross followed Joseph to the **tomb.** This way, they would know exactly where to find Jesus' body when they would return after the Sabbath with their **spices and ointments.** Anointing a body was a sign of love, devotion, and respect. Bringing spices to the tomb would be like bringing flowers to a grave today. Since bodies were not embalmed in Israel, perfumes were normally used. The women undoubtedly knew that Joseph and Nicodemus had already wrapped the body in linen and spices. They were probably going to do a simple external application of the fragrant spices. After seeing where the body was laid, they went home and **rested** as **the law** required, planning to return at first light on Sunday morning.

LUKE 24

JESUS RISES FROM THE DEAD / 24:1-12 / 239

Jesus' awful death on the cross was not the end of the story. Within three days, Jesus rose from the tomb. Even though Jesus had predicted his own resurrection (9:22; 18:32-33), no one believed it would happen.

Today Jesus still lives, at the right hand of God the Father (Acts 2:33). The Resurrection still stands as the foundation of the Christian faith. Christians can have complete confidence that Christ is alive, guiding the church and individual Christians through the Holy Spirit. His own resurrection is a guarantee of the future resurrection; death has already been conquered. Moreover, the same power that brought Christ's body back from the dead is available to every Christian today, bringing each spiritually dead person back to life (1 Corinthians 15:12-28).

24:1-2 In the Jewish reckoning of time, a "day" included any part of a day; thus, Friday was the first day, Saturday was the second day, and Sunday was the third day. When the women arrived at daybreak, Jesus had already risen. Jesus had died on Friday; Joseph had taken his body and had prepared it for burial just before the Sabbath began at sundown on Friday. The Sabbath had ended at sunset on Saturday; so the women ventured out **very early on Sunday morning.** They brought **spices** to the tomb, just as people today would bring flowers—as a sign of love and respect. When they arrived, **they found that the stone covering the entrance had been rolled aside** (see Matthew 28:2). The stone was not rolled away so that Jesus could get out, for he was already gone. It was rolled aside so others could get in and see for themselves that Jesus had indeed risen from the dead, just as he had said he would.

24:3 The stone had been rolled back, and the women went in expecting to accomplish their task with the spices. Many tombs were large enough to walk into, so these women went into the tomb, **but they couldn't find the body of the Lord Jesus.** Of course, the body was not there because Jesus had been raised, just as he said. But Jesus' followers did not expect this. They had been told at least three times, but they had not come to truly believe (9:21-27, 44-45; 18:31-34).

24:4-7 Matthew and John reveal that these **two men** in **dazzling robes** were angels. When angels appeared to people, they looked like humans. These men at the tomb surprised the women, and their dazzling appearance frightened them. The women reacted in humility, bowing before these men. The angel asked the obvious question, **"Why are you looking in a tomb for someone who is alive?"** Then one angel spoke the words that have thrilled every believer since that first resurrection morning, **"He isn't here! He has risen from the dead!"** The angels then reminded the women that Jesus had accurately predicted all that had happened to him.

24:8-9 These women must have been among Jesus' faithful followers and had heard Jesus' predictions of his death, for Luke says **they remembered** that Jesus **had said** those things, and suddenly everything came together. Everything had occurred just as Jesus had said. So these women left the tomb and **rushed back to tell his eleven disciples** (disciples, minus Judas Iscariot) **and everyone else** among Jesus' followers who may have been in hiding since the Crucifixion. Matthew and Mark say that the angel told them to go and tell the disciples what had happened. The women obeyed, running with the great news to the sorrowing and bewildered disciples.

24:10-11 The women are named here, probably because some of the later believers may have known them or about them. **Mary Magdalene** had been a loyal follower—Jesus had cast seven demons out of her (8:2). All the Gospels place her at the cross and at the tomb. Jesus' first appearance to any human after his resurrection was to this woman (Mark 16:9; John 20:11-16). **Joanna** was previously mentioned among the women who followed Jesus (8:3). **Mary the mother of James** is also mentioned in Mark 15:40; 16:1 (she may be "the other Mary" of Matthew 28:1). The **several others** includes Salome (Mark 16:1) and other unnamed persons—all women.

They brought their story back to **the apostles**—giving them the message that the angel had told them. The fact that the message was carried by women gives credibility and persuasive force to Luke's account. No ancient person making up such a story would have women as the official witnesses. By Jewish law, women could not do so.

Amazingly, the disciples did not believe it—**the story sounded like nonsense.** Apparently Jesus' words about dying and rising again had gone past all of them. Many skeptics have tried to write off the Resurrection as a story made up by a group of overzealous disciples. But here the opposite occurred. The disciples were not anxiously looking for any reason to believe that Jesus had risen; in fact, they were not anticipating it. When told of the Resurrection, they refused to believe without concrete evidence. Even a missing body was not enough to convince them.

24:12 John 20:3-4 reveals that another disciple **ran to the tomb** with **Peter.** That other disciple was almost certainly John, the author of the fourth Gospel. When Peter arrived at the tomb, he bent over and **peered in.** He **saw the empty linen wrappings.** Peter went away, **wondering what had happened.**

JESUS APPEARS TO TWO BELIEVERS TRAVELING ON THE ROAD / 24:13-34 / *243*
Luke was the only Gospel writer who described in detail Jesus' encounter with the two disciples on the road to Emmaus (Mark briefly mentioned this encounter in Mark 16:12-13).

24:13-14 This event occurred on Sunday, the **same day** as the Resurrection. Two followers of Jesus were leaving Jerusalem and walking the seven miles **to the village of Emmaus.** Little is known of these disciples; one was named Cleopas (24:18), and the other was not one of the eleven disciples, as noted by 24:33. During their walk, **they were talking about everything that had happened.**

24:15-16 The two men were deep in discussion as they walked along. Apparently a man walking in the same direction drew up beside them (they knew he had been in Jerusalem, 24:18). This man was **Jesus himself,** but they were **kept from recognizing him.** In other appearances after the Resurrection, Jesus was also not recognized at first (John 20:14; 21:4). Here, God prevented these men from seeing Jesus until Jesus was ready to reveal himself to them (24:30-31). God's divine sovereignty kept them from understanding until the full reality of the bodily resurrection of Jesus could be understood.

24:17 Jesus, who had walked up behind these men during their **deep discussion,** asked what they were **so concerned about.** At Jesus' question, they **stopped short** in their **sadness.** Apparently, in their discussion they had been unable to come to any understanding, so they were still sad and upset about what had occurred.

24:18 Jesus had apparently walked up behind these men, so they assumed that he too was a pilgrim traveling home from **Jerusalem.** If he had been in Jerusalem, how could he not have known what had happened there?

24:19 Jesus asked **what things** had occurred. They answered that much had happened to a man named **Jesus.** The two followers described him as **a prophet who did wonderful miracles** and **a mighty teacher.** They had heard Jesus teach and had seen him perform miracles of healing; but, as far as they knew, he had died like all the other prophets before him.

24:20 The telling item in this statement is that these two disciples knew who was responsible for Jesus' death. The Romans may have actually done the executing, but the Jews' (they said **our**) **leading priests and other religious leaders arrested him and handed him over.** If all of Jerusalem knew what had happened, then the religious leaders' plan to try to blame the execution on the Romans had failed. Everyone knew the leaders' role in Jesus' death.

24:21 The disciples from Emmaus had **thought** that Jesus could **rescue Israel.** Most Jews believed that the Old Testament prophecies pointed to a military and political Messiah who would free the nation from Roman tyranny. Jesus had come to redeem, however, and had indeed paid a huge price—his life. No one comprehended this yet. They didn't realize that the Messiah had come to redeem people from slavery to sin. When Jesus died, therefore, they lost all hope. Their report that **that all happened three days ago** reveals a bit of expectation at Jesus' promises regarding the "third day" after his death. As far as they knew, however, nothing had changed.

24:22-24 Another insight found in this statement is that these two men had left Jerusalem, hopeless and downcast, **after** having heard **an amazing report.** The women who had been to the tomb and heard the angels' words said that Jesus' **body was missing** and that angels had said **Jesus is alive.** Then some **men** (Peter and John, 24:12; John 20:3-4) verified what the women had said. Yet there was still gloom, as noted by these disciples who had all this information, but had left the city still believing that all their hopes in Jesus had been dashed.

24:25-27 Why did Jesus call these disciples **foolish?** Even though they well knew **all that the prophets wrote in the Scriptures,** they failed to understand that Christ's suffering was his path to glory. The prophets had said that Christ would have to **suffer** before **entering his time of glory.** Beginning with the **writings of Moses and** then moving through **all the prophets,** Jesus explained to these bewildered disciples **what all the Scriptures said about himself.** Jesus pointed out all the Scriptures and how what had happened to Jesus had fulfilled everything that had been prophesied regarding the Messiah.

24:28-29 They approached Emmaus and the journey's end for the two travelers. Jesus would not have stayed with them if he had not been invited. But they were impressed with all that Jesus had been telling them—probably answering many of the questions the two of them had been discussing before this man had joined them. They wanted to talk further, so they invited Jesus to **stay.**

24:30-31 At the meal, Jesus took **bread, asked God's blessing, broke it,** and **gave it to them.** When he did so, **their eyes were opened, and they recognized him.** These two disciples had not been at the Last Supper, so this was not what sparked recognition. This was the exact time God wanted them to recognize Jesus. God had kept them from understanding (24:16), and now he opened their eyes through the teaching of the word (24:27) and the breaking of the bread. His mission accomplished with these two disciples, Jesus **disappeared.**

24:32 Jesus had vanished as quickly as he had come, and the two disciples were left to discuss how their hearts were stirred as Jesus had talked with them and had opened the Scriptures to them. Jesus' presence had almost imperceptibly changed their mood from despair to **hearts** feeling **strangely warm.** Their hope had been confirmed; their doubts dispelled.

24:33-34 Evening may have been coming on (24:29), but their news was too exciting to wait until morning. **Within the hour** the two disciples **were on their way back to Jerusalem.** When they got there, they found that Jesus had already **appeared to Peter.** Paul also mentioned that Jesus appeared to Peter alone (1 Corinthians 15:5). This appearance is not further described in the Gospels. Jesus showed individual concern for Peter because Peter felt completely unworthy after denying his Lord. But Peter repented, and Jesus approached him and forgave him. Soon God would use Peter in building Christ's church (see the first half of the book of Acts).

JESUS APPEARS TO HIS DISCIPLES / 24:35-43 / 244

The disciples, who had gathered in Jerusalem, were already talking with excitement about what had occurred. The tomb was empty. Jesus had appeared to Peter and to two of them on the way to Emmaus (24:33-35). In the excitement and confusion of it all, Jesus appeared in the room, wishing them "peace."

24:35 The two disciples then told their story of how Jesus had appeared and talked to them and how they had recognized him. Why Jesus chose certain people to whom to appear at first and not others is unknown. Peter apparently needed an extra personal encounter; Mary Magdalene's love and devotion accorded her the opportunity to see Jesus first. Whatever the reason for Jesus to have spent a lengthy time with these two disappointed followers on the road to Emmaus, the story stands as a beautiful treasure of Jesus' compassion and love for those who, when discouraged and confused, needed his presence and wisdom to comfort them.

24:36 As Jesus' followers discussed his recent appearances, suddenly **Jesus himself was standing there among them.** He appeared among them behind locked doors (John 20:19). Jesus could do this because his resurrection and glorification had altered his bodily form. In this new body he was able to transcend all physical barriers.

Jesus' first words to the group of disbelieving and bewildered followers and disciples, all of whom had deserted him in his time of greatest

need were: **"Peace be with you."** This was a standard Hebrew greeting, but here it was filled with greater meaning. Jesus brought a greeting of peace, and his presence brought peace.

24:37-39 These people in the locked room were still wrestling with the fact that Jesus' body was missing, and then they heard amazing stories of his appearances to several people of their group. Jesus appeared among them suddenly, and they were **frightened, thinking they were seeing a ghost.** But Jesus' body wasn't a figment of the imagination; they weren't seeing a ghost. Jesus encouraged them to look and touch. He had flesh and bones and could even eat food (24:43). On the other hand, his body wasn't a restored human body like Lazarus's (John 11)—he was able to appear and disappear. Jesus' resurrected body was glorified and immortal.

24:40-43 Jesus showed them his **hands** and his **feet** so as to reveal the wounds inflicted by the nails that had held him to the cross (see John 20:25). His resurrected body still bore these wounds as a testimony to his followers that this was the same man whom they had loved, followed, and seen die. This was too good to be true—and they experienced the conflicting emotions of disbelief, doubt, joy, and wonder that any person would have when a most desired, but seemingly most impossible,

wish actually comes true. Jesus stood there among them, alive, even eating **a piece of broiled fish** to show that he was not a ghost. He was real; he came back to life just as he had told them he would.

JESUS APPEARS TO THE DISCIPLES IN JERUSALEM / 24:44-49 / *249*

Jesus did not come back to Jerusalem after his resurrection to provide a spectacular show or to seek revenge on his enemies. Instead, he returned to teach his disciples. He had already instructed them while he was with them, but they had not completely understood him (see 9:45; 18:34). During his final days, he taught them again. This time, he opened their minds, so that they could understand the truth: his life, death, and resurrection all fulfilled Scripture. He taught them so they could teach others, telling what they had seen Jesus do and heard him say. They were to be Jesus' witnesses (a theme Luke continued in the book of Acts, see Acts 1:4-5, 7-8).

24:44-45 Many days may have elapsed between 24:43 and 24:44 because Jesus and his followers traveled to Galilee and back before he returned to heaven (Matthew 28:16; John 21). Acts, Luke's second book, reveals that Jesus spent forty days with his disciples between his resurrection and ascension.

As he had already done with the two men on the road to Emmaus, Jesus **opened their minds to understand** the **Scriptures** and explained how everything that had been written about the coming Messiah had been fulfilled in him. Writings of **Moses, the prophets,** and **the Psalms** encompass the entire Old Testament. In other words, the entire Old Testament points to the Messiah.

24:46-48 Not only had the Old Testament Scriptures been fulfilled in Jesus' life, death, and resurrection, but the Old Testament went much further—speaking of **repentance** and **forgiveness of sins.** Luke was writing to the Greek-speaking world. He wanted them to know that Christ's message of God's love and forgiveness should go

to all the nations—and that this had been God's plan from the very beginning. Christ's gospel has a worldwide scope. God wants all the world to hear the Good News of salvation. They would begin right where they were—in Jerusalem and then be **witnesses of all these things** throughout the world (see Acts 1:8).

24:49 This task of being witnesses was not to be carried out in the disciples' own strength. Obviously these followers, hiding behind locked doors in fear of the Jews right there in Jerusalem, hardly seemed like the kind of people who could take the message across the world. But Jesus was not expecting them to do it on their own—he would send what his Father had promised—**the Holy Spirit** (John 14:15-27; 16:5-15). Jesus instructed them to **stay in the city** (that is, in Jerusalem) until they were filled **with power from heaven.** Jesus promised them the power (the Spirit in them) which would enable them to be witnesses (Acts 1:8). After his exaltation at his ascension, the power would be given to them (Acts 2:1-4).

JESUS ASCENDS INTO HEAVEN / 24:50-53 / *250*

Luke concluded his Gospel with a brief account of Jesus' ascension. In Acts, he provided a more complete description of it (see Acts 1:6-11). After watching Jesus ascend into heaven, the disciples returned to Jerusalem to praise God, the only appropriate response to Jesus' glorious life and his message of salvation.

24:50 Jesus took his followers out of Jerusalem **to Bethany,** the village only a couple of miles away on the slopes of the Mount of Olives. Jesus lifted his **hands** and **blessed** his followers. At this time,

he would leave them, never to return until the time of the Second Coming. They would never be able to walk and talk with him physically as they had done during those three years of ministry. But they would soon receive the Holy Spirit who would fill them and be with them always.

24:51 In the act of **blessing** his followers, Jesus **left them and was taken up to heaven.** Jesus' physical presence left the disciples (Acts 1:9), but the Holy Spirit soon came to comfort them and empower them to spread the gospel of salvation (Acts 2:1-4). Today Jesus' work of salvation is completed, and he is sitting at God's right hand, where he has authority over heaven and earth.

24:52-53 The sight of Jesus returning to glory in heaven called for a response of worship from those who watched. Then they **returned to Jerusalem filled with great joy.** As yet, they did not separate themselves from their Jewish roots, but **spent all of their time in the Temple, praising God.** There were no more closed and locked doors for these followers. Jesus told them to stay in Jerusalem, so they did. Acts 1 gives some idea of their activity as they awaited the promised Holy Spirit. But they openly went to the Temple to praise God for all that he had done.

Luke's Gospel portrays Jesus as the perfect example of a life lived according to God's plan. The Greeks had a difficult time understanding the spiritual importance of the physical world. To them, the spiritual was always more important than the physical. To help them understand the God-man who united the spiritual and the physical, Luke emphasized that Jesus was not a phantom human but a real human being who healed people and fed them because he was concerned with their physical health as well as the state of their souls.

Believers today, living according to God's plan, should obey their Lord in every detail as they seek to restore people's bodies and souls to the health and salvation God has in store for them. To know how to live a perfect life, look to Jesus as the perfect example.

John's story begins as John the
Baptist ministers near Bethany
east of the Jordan (1:28ff). Jesus
also begins his ministry, talking
to some of the men who would
later become his twelve disciples. Jesus' ministry in Galilee
began with a visit to a wedding
in Cana (2:1ff). Then he went
to Capernaum, which became
his new home (2:12). He journeyed to Jerusalem for the
special festivals (2:13) and
there met with Nicodemus, a
religious leader (3:1ff). When
Jesus left Judea, he traveled
through Samaria and ministered to the Samaritans (4:1ff).
Jesus did miracles in Galilee
(4:46ff) and in Judea and Jerusalem (5:1ff). We follow him as
he fed 5,000 near Bethsaida
beside the Sea of Galilee (6:1ff),
walked on the water to his
frightened disciples (6:16ff),
preached through Galilee (7:1),
returned to Jerusalem (7:2ff),
preached beyond the Jordan in
Perea (10:40), raised Lazarus
from the dead in Bethany
(11:1ff), and finally entered
Jerusalem for the last time to
celebrate the Passover with his
disciples and give them key
teachings about what was to
come and how they should act.
His last hours before his crucifixion were spent in the city
(13:1ff), in a grove of olive trees
(the Garden of Gethsemane)
(18:1ff), and finally in various
buildings in Jerusalem during
his trial (18:12ff). He would be
crucified, but he would rise
again as he had promised.

The broken lines (— · —·) indicate modern boundaries.

JOHN

INTRODUCTION

He spoke, and galaxies whirled into place, stars burned the heavens, and planets began orbiting their suns—the words of awesome, unlimited, unleashing power. He spoke again, and the waters and lands were filled with plants and creatures, running, swimming, growing, and multiplying—words of animating, breathing, pulsing life. Again he spoke, and man and woman were formed, thinking, speaking, and loving—words of personal and creative glory. Eternal, infinite, unlimited—he was, is, and always will be the Maker and Lord of all that exists.

And then he came in the flesh to a tiny spot in the universe called planet Earth—the mighty Creator becoming part of his creation, limited by time and space and susceptible to age, sickness, and death. Propelled by love, he came to rescue and save, offering forgiveness and life.

He is the Word: he is Jesus Christ.

It is this truth that the apostle John presents in this book. John's Gospel is not a life of Christ; it is a powerful argument for the incarnation, a conclusive demonstration that Jesus was, and is, the very heaven-sent Son of God and the only source of eternal life.

AUTHOR

John the Apostle, son of Zebedee and Salome, and younger brother of James.

Thunder evokes fear and images of a pending storm. We would expect someone nicknamed Son of Thunder to be powerful, loud, and unpredictable. That's what Jesus named two of his disciples—Zebedee's sons, James and John (Mark 3:17)—for he knew their tendency to explode. Sure enough, when Jesus and the Twelve were rebuffed by a Samaritan village, these rough fishermen suggested calling down fire from heaven to destroy the whole village (Luke 9:52-56). Just before that incident, John had told Jesus that he had tried to stop a man from driving out demons because he was not a disciple. Jesus had explained that he didn't have an exclusive club (Luke 9:49-50).

In addition to being forceful and angry, James and John also seem to have been quite self-centered. They requested seats of honor and power in the Kingdom. When the other disciples heard about what James and John had said, they became indignant (Mark 10:35-44). Yet Jesus also saw potential in these thundering brothers—he knew what they would become. So Jesus brought both, with Peter, into his inner circle, allowing them to see him transfigured on the mountain (Mark 9:2-13). And as Jesus was dying on the cross, he entrusted Mary, his mother, to John's care (John 19:26-27).

John was following in his father Zebedee's footsteps as a fisherman when Jesus called him (Matthew 4:21; Mark 1:19-20). His mother was Salome (Matthew 27:55-56; Mark 15:40). His brother, James, was also one of the Twelve and the first apostle to be martyred (Acts 12:2). They fished on the Sea of Galilee with Peter and Andrew.

One might predict that someone with a personality like John's would self-destruct. Certainly this person would die in a fight or in a clash with the Roman government. At the very least, he would be discarded by the church as self-seeking and power-hungry. But such was not the case. Instead, John was transformed into someone who was strong but gentle, straightforward but loving, courageous but humble. There is no dramatic event to account for John's transformation—it must have come from being with Jesus, being accepted, loved, and affirmed by the Lord, and then being filled with the Holy Spirit. So overwhelmed was John by Jesus that he did not mention himself by name in the Gospel that bears his name. Instead, he wrote of himself as "the disciple Jesus loved" (John 13:23; 19:26; 20:2; 21:20, 24). What a humble change for one who, at first, had wanted power and recognition.

John stands as a great example of Christ's power to transform lives. Christ can change anyone—no one is beyond hope. Jesus accepted John as he was, a Son of Thunder, and changed him into what he would become, the apostle of love.

JOHN'S MINISTRY

John was a Palestinian and a Galilean. Many believe that John was first a disciple of John the Baptist. His mentor pointed him to Jesus when Jesus passed by. Then Jesus and John spent the day together (1:35-39). At that time, John must have become a part-time disciple, for later we find him back fishing with his brother, James, and their father, Zebedee. But the next time Jesus called them, John and James left everything, father and boat included, and followed him.

As a member of the Twelve, John was an eyewitness to the miracles, an "ear-witness" to the parables and confrontations with the Pharisees and other leaders, and a student of Jesus' special words of instruction. John was at the Last Supper and in the Garden of Gethsemane. And he was the only one of the Twelve at the cross. John also saw the empty tomb and was in the upper room, on the beach, and at the Ascension.

Beyond being a leader in the Jerusalem church (as mentioned in Galatians 2:9), little is known of John's ministry. When John wrote his epistles (1, 2, and 3 John), he simply identified himself as "the Elder." So it is thought that John must have been the only surviving apostle at that time. He wrote those letters from Ephesus about A.D. 85–90, just before writing his Gospel. In about A.D. 94, John was banished to the island of Patmos during the reign of Domitian. There, this wise and elder apostle received the dramatic vision of the future from Jesus, given to us as the book of Revelation. John probably returned to Ephesus during Nerva's reign and then died there during the reign of Trajan, around A.D. 100.

John provides a powerful example of a lifetime of service to Christ. As a young man, John left his fishing nets to follow the Savior. For three intense years he watched Jesus live and love, and listened to him teach and preach. John saw Jesus crucified and then risen! John's life was changed dramatically, from an impetuous, hot-tempered youth, to a loving and wise man of God. Through it all, John remained faithful, so that at the end of his life, he continued to bear strong witness to the truth and power of the gospel.

How strong is your commitment to Christ? Will it last through the years? The true test of an athlete is not in the start but the finish. So too with faithfulness to Christ—how will you finish that race?

DATE AND SETTING
Written between A.D. 85–90 from Ephesus, after the destruction of Jerusalem (A.D. 70) and before John's exile to the island of Patmos

The Gospel of John contains no references concerning where it was written. But according to the earliest traditions of the church, John wrote his Gospel from Ephesus. The church at Ephesus had been founded by Paul on his second missionary journey in A.D. 52 (Acts 18:19-21). The church grew under the ministry of Apollos, Priscilla, and Aquila (Acts 18:24-26). Paul returned to Ephesus on his third missionary journey and had an incredible ministry there (Acts 19:1–20:1). Later, during his first Roman imprisonment, Paul wrote the letter to the Ephesians (about A.D. 60). That church is described in Revelation 2:1-7.

We don't know how old John was when Jesus called him. But assuming that John was a little younger than Jesus, John would have been in his eighties when writing this Gospel, which was quite old for a time when the life expectancy was much shorter. And considering the fact that all the other apostles had died as martyrs, John was indeed the church's elder statesman. We can imagine him teaching and counseling the Christians in this well-established church, as well as doing some writing.

AUDIENCE
New Christians and searching non-Christians.

John does not reveal his audience directly, but several characteristics of the book provide insight into the people he was trying to reach.

1. The Gospel of John differs greatly from the other three Gospels in content and approach. Matthew, Mark, and Luke (the Synoptic Gospels) present much historical data with few explanations or interpretations. John, however, selected key events and took time to explain and apply them. In addition, John chose to write about a few important, miraculous signs (20:30-31) in order to give a clear picture of the person of Christ.
2. John illustrates the tension between faith and unbelief and emphasizes the importance of responding to Christ. He states this fact at the very beginning and carries it throughout the book (1:12).
3. John uses simple vocabulary but chooses special words and loads them with meaning—for example, *word, truth, light, darkness, life, and love.*
4. John repeats four main points: the true identity of Jesus, the necessity of responding to Christ in faith, the gift of eternal life, and the church's mission to the world.
5. John explains his purpose clearly (20:31).

John presents the evidence for Jesus as the God-man and the Savior of the world, and he challenges readers to follow his Lord. So we can conclude that John wrote to unbelieving Asian Jews and Gentiles.

But John also wrote to Christians, to help strengthen their faith. John was the last surviving apostle and one of the few still living who had seen Jesus in the flesh. It would be easy for young believers—removed from Christ's life, death, and resurrection by a generation and surrounded by a hostile government and unbelieving neighbors—to have doubts and second thoughts about their faith. Remember, this is the late eighties, after the terrible persecutions by Nero (A.D. 54–68) and the total destruction of Jerusalem (A.D. 70). The church had flourished under persecution, but believers needed reassurance of the truth of Christianity. John, the venerable eyewitness to all that Jesus had done and faithful follower of his Lord, would give that assurance through his personal account of the gospel story.

OCCASION AND PURPOSE

John gives a clear and straightforward statement of his purpose for writing this book: "But these are written so that you may believe that Jesus is the Messiah, the Son of God, and that by believing in him you will have life" (20:31). To achieve this purpose, John shows, throughout the Gospel, that Jesus was, in fact, the Christ, the Son of God, the prophesied one, and the only source of salvation. This is the dominant theme of the entire book.

The Gospel of John was written to convince those who had not seen Jesus to believe in him, to help believers deepen their faith, and to convince unbelievers to trust in Jesus Christ as their Savior. In addition, John had several other emphases worth noting. John showed that the Jewish leaders were completely wrong in rejecting Jesus as the Messiah. John continues this emphasis throughout the book. John also emphasized that Jesus is much greater than John the Baptist. It may be that some followers of John the Baptist were still claiming that he was more important than Jesus. Whatever the reason, John declared the preeminence of Christ and John the Baptist's special role in preparing the way for him (see 1:6-8, 15-18, 19-27, 35-38; 3:25-30).

John focused on the deity and humanity of Jesus. It is possible that he did this to confront a docetic heresy promoting the false notion that Jesus only seemed to be living a human life—that he was not fully human. John also mentioned Jesus' family ties (2:12; 7:3-5), stated that Jesus became tired (4:6), and showed that Jesus really died on the cross (19:33-34). John clearly presented Jesus as the God-man. John also described the work of the Holy Spirit, assuring believers of the presence of the risen Christ. Through the Holy Spirit, Christians have Christ with them; they don't have to face life alone. John spoke of the work of the Holy Spirit more than any other Gospel writer.

John reminded the believers that unbelief and opposition to God and his plans do not surprise God or thwart his purposes. This includes the betrayal by Judas (foretold by prophets and known by Jesus—6:64; 13:18; Psalm 41:9), the death of Jesus on the cross (a necessary part of God's salvation plan—3:14-18), and the rejection of Christ by unbelievers (1:10-11). Although conflicts are inevitable, God is sovereign and in control, and his goals will be accomplished.

Because of John's special purpose for writing this book, he described many incidents in the life of Christ that are not recorded in the other Gospels. These events include: John the Baptist declaring Jesus to be the Messiah, Jesus turning water into wine, Nicodemus visiting Jesus at night, Jesus talking to a Samaritan woman at the well, Jesus healing a government official's son, Jesus healing a lame man by the pool, Jesus' brothers ridiculing him, Jesus healing the man who was born blind, Jesus raising Lazarus from the dead, Jesus teaching about the Holy Spirit, Jesus teaching about the vine and the branches, and Jesus appearing to Thomas and reinstating Peter after his resurrection.

MESSAGE

John discloses Jesus' identity with his very first words, "In the beginning the Word already existed. He was with God, and he was God. He was in the beginning with God" (1:1-2); and the rest of the book continues the theme. John, the eyewitness, chose nine of Jesus' miracles (or miraculous signs, as he calls them) to reveal his divine/human nature and his life-giving mission. These signs are (1) turning water to wine (2:1-11); (2) healing the official's son (4:46-54); (3) healing the lame man at the pool of Bethesda (5:1-9); (4) feeding the 5,000 with just a few loaves and fish (6:1-14); (5) walking on the water (6:15-21); (6) restoring sight to the blind man (9:1-41); (7) raising Lazarus from the dead (11:1-44); (8) Jesus' own resurrection (20:1-29), and, after the Resurrection; (9) giving the disciples an overwhelming catch of fish (21:1-14).

In every chapter Jesus' deity is revealed. And Jesus' true identity is underscored through the titles he is given—the Word, the only Son, Lamb of God, Son of God, true bread, life, resurrection, vine. And the formula is "I am." When Jesus uses this phrase, he affirms his preexistence and eternal deity. Jesus says, I am the bread of life (6:35); I am the light of the world (8:12; 9:5); I am the gate (10:7); I am the good shepherd (10:11, 14); I am the resurrection and the life (11:25); I am the way, and the truth, and the life (14:6); and I am the true vine (15:1).

The main themes in the Gospel of John include: *Jesus Christ, Son of God; eternal life; believing; Holy Spirit;* and *resurrection*—because John's purpose was to convince people to believe in Christ, it's not surprising that his message follows the themes listed here. In order to trust Christ, a person must understand Jesus' true identity, the promise of eternal life, the necessity of faith, and the resurrection of Christ. And to live for Christ, a person must understand the person and work of the Holy Spirit.

Jesus Christ, Son of God (1:1-18; 2:1-11; 4:46-54; 5:1-15; 6:5-14; 6:16-21; 9:1-12; 11:1-44; 19:1–20:30). Because this is a "Gospel," the entire book tells about Jesus. But in relating the life of the Lord, John chose nine "signs" (miracles) that illustrate and prove Jesus' true identity as God's Son. These chosen signs (seven miracles plus the Resurrection) display Christ's glory and reveal his true nature: (1) turning the water into wine (2:1-11); (2) healing the royal official's son (4:46-54), (3) healing the invalid by the pool at Bethesda (5:1-15); (4) feeding the 5,000 (6:5-14); (5) walking on water (6:16-21); (6) healing a man blind from birth (9:1-41); (7) raising Lazarus from the dead (11:1-44); (8) rising from the dead (20:1-29); (9) giving the disciples an overwhelming catch of fish (21:1-14). John shows us that Jesus is unique as God's special Son, yet he is fully God. Because he is fully God, Jesus is able to reveal God to us, clearly and accurately.

IMPORTANCE FOR TODAY. Because Jesus is God, he has the nature, ability, and right to offer eternal life. When he died on the cross, he was the perfect sacrifice and only mediator between God and people (14:6). Because Jesus became a man, he identified fully with us, enduring temptation, persecution, hardship, and suffering. Through the Incarnation, the infinite, holy, and all-powerful God demonstrated his love for us. As believers in Christ, we must affirm both sides of his nature and not exclude or diminish one side in favor of the other. Jesus is fully God and fully man.

Eternal Life (3:15-16, 36; 4:14, 36; 5:24, 39-40; 6:27, 40, 47, 54, 58; 8:51; 10:10, 27-30; 11:25-26; 12:25, 49-50; 20:30-31). Jesus came to bring us life, eternal life. This life begins now, on this earth, through faith in Christ. Jesus said, "My purpose is to give life in all its fullness" (10:10). The life that Christ offers also continues beyond death. Obtaining eternal life is not automatic or magic. People aren't saved just because Jesus became a man and died and rose again. Individuals must believe in Jesus; they must trust in him. John presents Jesus as the Good Shepherd who lays down his life for the sheep (10:11, 15, 17). His death is said to be a saving death—he is the Lamb of God who takes away the sin of the world (1:29, 36). But his sacrifice is applied only to those who repent and believe (1:12; 2:11; 3:15-16, 18, 36; and many other passages).

IMPORTANCE FOR TODAY. Life on earth is short, and filled with struggles, suffering, and hardships. Of course, there are moments of ecstasy and joy, but for many those moments are very few. And because all human beings are mortal, eventually everyone dies. That description is not mere pessimism, but truth. But God offers hope amidst the suffering—eternal life. Through faith in Christ, we have abundant life now and life unending after we die. The assurance of eternal life gives hope, meaning, and purpose as we live each day. Jesus offers eternal life to us. We are invited to begin living in a personal, eternal relationship with him that begins now. Although we must grow old and die, we can have a new life that lasts forever by trusting Jesus.

Believing (1:12, 50; 2:11, 23; 3:15-18; 4:39-42, 48-53; 5:24-47; 6:30, 47, 64; 8:24, 31; 9:38; 10:25-42; 11:25-27; 12:37-46; 14:11-14; 16:9; 17:8, 20; 20:25-30). Belief in Jesus as the Messiah and Son of God is the central theme of this book and the desired response from all who read it. Knowing that Jesus is the Son of God and that eternal life is available only through him, people must believe in Jesus as their Savior and Lord. The first step toward eternal life is to believe the facts about Jesus. But having saving faith ("believing") involves much more than mental assent to the truth. John emphasizes Jesus' strong teaching that those who truly believe in Christ turn from their sin, follow him closely, and obey his teachings. The person who puts his or her faith in Christ (believes the facts about him, trusts him, follows close to him, and obeys his commands) is forgiven and gains eternal life.

IMPORTANCE FOR TODAY. Believing is active, living, and continuous trust in Jesus as God. When we believe in his life, his words, his death, and his resurrection, we are cleansed from sin and receive power to follow him. But we must respond to Christ by believing. This believing begins with the facts about Jesus, but it must go deeper, involving total commitment to him. Do you truly believe in Jesus? Remember, too, that we also live in a world of skeptics. Most people won't believe that something is true simply because we tell them, especially regarding religion. They need to see Jesus in action, to read about his claims and his miracles, and to understand his teachings. As we explain to relatives, friends, neighbors, and coworkers about how they can have eternal life, we need to present the evidence that Jesus is the Son of God and their only hope.

Holy Spirit (1:32-34; 3:5; 6:63; 7:39; 14:16-26; 15:26; 16:7-15). The first mention of the Holy Spirit in the Gospel of John is John the Baptist's statement at Jesus' baptism: "I saw the Holy Spirit descending" (1:32). He adds that Jesus will baptize "with the Holy Spirit" (1:33). We know, therefore, that Jesus possessed the Spirit. The main teaching about the Holy Spirit in the Gospel of John, however, describes him as the Counselor. This Holy Spirit would come and abide in the disciples after the departure of Jesus, to teach them, remind them of his words (14:26), and show them the truth (16:13). The Holy Spirit would bear witness to Jesus through the disciples before the world (15:26-27) and will do his convicting work in the hearts of men and women in the world (16:7-11).

All of these actions of the Holy Spirit are parallel to the work of Jesus on earth. Jesus claimed to be the way, the truth, and the life (14:6), and he preached about sin (8:24), righteousness (8:42-47), and judgment (9:39). Jesus taught his disciples that the Holy Spirit would come after he left the earth. The Holy Spirit would then indwell, guide, counsel, and comfort those who follow Jesus. Through the Holy Spirit, Christ's presence and power are multiplied in all who believe.

IMPORTANCE FOR TODAY. God has sent the Holy Spirit into the world to draw people to himself and to work in the lives of believers. As we read and study God's word, the Holy Spirit will guide us into the truth (16:13), helping us understand about Christ and about God's principles for living. One of our responsibilities as believers is to testify about Christ in the world (15:27), passing on what the Holy Spirit tells us (15:26). As we do this, we can be confident that the Holy Spirit will be working in the lives of men and women, convicting them of their sin and their need to trust Christ as Savior (16:7-11). We must know the Holy Spirit to understand all Jesus taught. We can experience Jesus' love and guidance as we allow the Holy Spirit to work in us.

Resurrection (20:1–21:23). The greatest sign presented by John of the divinity of Jesus is his resurrection from the dead. Just as Jesus really lived as a man on the earth, he really died on the cross. The witnesses to Jesus' death were many: the Roman soldiers (19:23-24, 32-34), the chief priests and other Jewish religious leaders (19:21), the crowd (19:20), a small collection of his loyal followers (19:25-27), and those who buried him, Joseph of Arimathea and Nicodemus (19:38-42).

But Jesus' death was not the end of the story. He arose, triumphant over death. Mary Magdalene, John, and Peter found the tomb empty (20:1-9). Then Mary Magdalene met the risen Christ face to face (20:10-18). Later, the disciples saw Jesus alive (20:19-29; 21:1-23). The fact of the Resurrection changed the disciples' lives—from fearful men who fled danger to courageous witnesses who took the gospel to every corner of their world, from discouraged and disillusioned followers to hopeful and joyful "Christ-ones" (i.e., "Christians"—ones belonging to Christ). The fact that Jesus rose from the dead is the foundation of the Christian faith.

IMPORTANCE FOR TODAY. The resurrection of Christ from the dead is important for us for several reasons. Because Jesus rose from the dead, we know that he is, in fact, the Son of God and that all he taught is true. Jesus taught that whoever believes in him will have eternal life (3:16-18). Because Jesus is God and truthful, we know that his promise of eternal life is also true. Jesus is alive, therefore we worship and serve a living Savior. We can be changed as the disciples were and have the confidence that some day our bodies will be raised to live with Christ forever. The same power that raised Christ to life can give us the ability to follow him each day.

OUTLINE OF JOHN

   I. Birth and Preparation of Jesus, the Son of God (1:1–2:11)
  II. Message and Ministry of Jesus, the Son of God (2:12–12:50)
      A. Jesus encounters belief and unbelief from the people
      B. Jesus encounters conflict with the religious leaders
      C. Jesus encounters crucial events in Jerusalem
 III. Death and Resurrection of Jesus, the Son of God (13:1–21:25)
      A. Jesus teaches his disciples
      B. Jesus completes his mission

JOHN 1

GOD BECAME A HUMAN / 1:1-18 / 2

John starts at the "beginning," with the first eighteen verses of John, called the **prologue.** Many commentators consider the prologue to be a poem or, at least, rhythmical prose. Some commentators suggest that verses 1-5, 10-12, and 14-18 may have been parts of one or several early Christian hymns. Others have thought that verses 14-18 were used as an early church confessional statement, to which John added his stamp of approval. John's goal and guiding purpose in writing can be found in almost every phrase of his work. In the rest of the Gospel, John expanded and illustrated each of these from Jesus' life and ministry.

1:1 When John wrote of **the beginning,** he was paralleling the words of the creation account. John called Jesus, **"the Word."** John did not identify this person immediately, but described his nature and purpose before revealing his name (see 1:17). As **the Word,** the Son of God fully conveys and communicates God.

Theologians and philosophers, both Jews and Greeks, used the term "word" in a variety of ways. The Greek term is *logos*. It could mean a person's thoughts or reason, or it might refer to a person's speech, the expression of thoughts. As a philosophical term, *logos* conveyed the rational principle that governed the universe, even the creative energy that generated the universe. In the Hebrew language of the Old Testament, "the Word" is described as an agent of creation (Psalm 33:6), the source of God's message to his people through the prophets (Hosea 1:2), and God's law, his standard of holiness (Psalm 119:11).

John may have had these ideas in mind, but his description shows clearly that he spoke of Jesus as a human being he knew and loved (see especially 1:14), who was at the same time the Creator of the universe, the ultimate revelation of God, and also the living picture of God's holiness. Jesus as the *logos* reveals God's mind to us.

By using the expression, **he was with God,** John

was explaining that the Word (the Son) and God (the Father) already enjoyed an intimate, personal relationship in the beginning. The last verse of the prologue (1:18) tells us that the Son was at the Father's side; and in Jesus' special prayer for his followers (chapter 17), he expressed that the Father loved him before the foundation of the world.

Not only was the Son with God, **he was** himself **God.** John's Gospel, more than most books in the New Testament, asserts Jesus' divinity. One of the most compelling reasons to believe the doctrine of the Trinity comes from the fact that it was revealed through a people most likely to reject it outright. In a world populated by many gods, it took the tough-minded Hebrews to clarify the revelation of God's oneness expressed through "three-in-oneness."

1:2 The second verse of the prologue underscores the truth that the Word, the Son, **was in the beginning with God.** A wrong teaching called the "Arian heresy" developed in the fourth century of Christianity. Arius, the father of this heresy, was a priest of Alexandria (in Egypt) during the reign of Emperor Constantine. He taught that Jesus, the Son of God, was not eternal but was created by the Father. Therefore, Jesus was not God by nature. Arius's views gained some support. At the Church Council in Nicea in A.D. 325, Athanasius defeated Arius in debate and the Nicene Creed was adopted, which established the biblical teaching that Jesus was "one essence with the Father." Yet this controversy raged until it was defeated at the Council of Constantinople in A.D. 325. This heresy still exists, however, in several cults. Yet John's Gospel proclaims simply and clearly that the Son of God is coeternal with the Father.

1:3 The New Testament portrays the Son of God as the agent of creation, for all things were **created** through him (see 1 Corinthians 8:6; Colossians 1:16; Hebrews 1:2). Everything came into being through Christ and ultimately depends upon him.

1:4 Creation needs to receive life from the Word—for **life itself was in him.** Christ gives physical life to all. But he also gives eternal life to all those who believe in him. The Greek term used for "life" is *zoe*; it is always used to describe the divine, eternal life in the Gospel of John. Jesus used this specific term during the Last Supper when he told his disciples, "I am the way, the truth, and the life" (14:6).

The divine **life** embodied in Christ **gives light to everyone**—revealing divine truth and exposing their sin. Everywhere Christ went, he brought light (see 3:21; 8:12). **Light** means understanding and moral insight, spiritual vision. But more than just shining or reflecting, the light of Jesus penetrates and enlightens hearts and minds. Everyone who comes into contact with Christ can be enlightened. When Christ's light shines, we see our sin and his glory. We can refuse to see the light and remain in darkness. But whoever responds will be enlightened by Christ. He will fill our minds with God's thoughts. He will guide our path, give us God's perspective, and drive out the darkness of sin.

1:5 John used the past tense in the previous sentence, saying that Jesus *was* the light of all people by virtue of being their Creator; but John shifted to the present tense: **the light shines through the darkness.** The timeless light has invaded our time, and we can see it in our darkness. As the light shines, it drives away the darkness, for the unsaved world is blinded by the prince of this world (2 Corinthians 4:4; Ephesians 5:8). Christ's light shined to a hardened, darkened humanity—and he continues to shine. But **the darkness can never extinguish it.** This statement indicates the struggle between the darkness and the light. Unregenerate humanity under the influence of Satan, the prince of darkness, has not accepted the light and even resists the light. Thus, "darkness" indicates ignorance and sin, active rejection of God's will. Those in darkness reject Christ, his light, and his followers. But no matter how deep the darkness, even a small light can drive it back. The power of Christ's light overcomes any darkness in the world.

1:6-8 John abruptly introduces Jesus' forerunner and herald, **John the Baptist.** God sent John the Baptist to prepare the way for the Messiah. John the Baptist has a prominent position in the prologue because his ministry prepared the way for the Messiah—he pointed people to Jesus. John the Baptist's function was **to tell everyone about the light so that everyone might believe because of his testimony.** He was the first to point people to Christ, so in a very real sense, all who have come to believe have done so because of his witness. **John himself was not the light,** but he came as **a witness to the light.** He was first in a line of witnesses that stretches through the centuries to this day.

1:9 The word **everyone** here could be nationalistically inclusive, referring to both Jews and Gentiles, or it could refer to all individuals. Every person has life from God, thus they have *some* light; creation reveals God's power and divinity (1:3; Acts 14:17; Romans 1:19-20; 2:14-16); and our conscience also bears witness to God's existence. The Gospel writer's description captures the transition between the ministry of John the Baptist as herald and the ministry of Jesus, **the true light.** Jesus, as opposed to any other "luminaries," is the true and exclusive revelation of God to man. Because of this, we can count on him.

1:10 John notes one of the greatest tragedies: **the world**—humankind—**didn't recognize** its own Creator. They were blinded and could not see his light. Although Christ created the world, the people he created didn't recognize him. He was denied the general acknowledgment that should have been his as Creator.

1:11 In Greek this reads, "He came to his own things"—that is, he came to that which belonged to him. The expression can even be used to describe a homecoming. This phrase intensifies the description of Christ's rejection. Jesus was not welcome in the world, or even his home. **His own land** and **his own people** refer to God's chosen nation, Israel, which was particularly Christ's. **He was not accepted** by those who should have been most eager to welcome him. As a nation, they rejected their Messiah. This rejection is further described at the end of Jesus' ministry (12:37-41). Isaiah had foreseen this unbelief (Isaiah 53:1-3). In spite of the rejection described here, John steers clear of passing sentence on the world. Instead, he turns our attention on those who did welcome Christ in sincere faith.

1:12-13 Though the rejection of Christ was universal, individuals did respond personally—some **believed him and accepted him** as the Son of God, the Savior. To them **he gave the right to become children of God.** In Greek **right** means "authority or permission." In this context, it speaks of God granting the right or giving the privilege for the new birth. No one can attain this new birth by his or her own power, merit, or ability. Only God can grant it. One is not in God's family because he or she is a Jew by **physical birth** (or even born into a Christian family). The new birth cannot be attained by an act of **human passion,** and it has absolutely nothing to do with any human **plan.** It is a gift of **God.**

Many believed superficially in Jesus when they saw his miracles, but they did not believe in Jesus as the Son of God. They "believed" in him while he fulfilled their expectations of what the Messiah should be, but they left him when he defied their preconceived notions. We must believe in Jesus as Jesus, the Son of God; we must wholeheartedly believe in Jesus, not limiting him to our ideas and misconceptions; we must regard Jesus as the Bible truly presents him.

1:14 Returning to the powerful term used at the beginning of the Gospel, John continues the theme of the prologue. The first thirteen verses summarize "the Word's" relationship to the world as its rejected Creator, Visitor, Light, and Savior. Yet throughout the opening paragraph, John does not identify **the Word** as being human, except in the personal pronouns.

The phrase, **became human,** is striking and arresting, despite its familiarity. Understanding its meaning simply increases our wonder. When Jesus was born, he was not part man and part God; he was completely human and completely divine (Colossians 2:9). Before Christ came, people could know God partially. After Christ had come, people could know God fully because he became visible and tangible (Hebrews 1:1-3). Christ is the perfect expression of God in human form. The two most common errors that people make about Jesus are minimizing his humanity or minimizing his divinity. Jesus is both divine and human (see Philippians 2:5-9). God, in Jesus, **lived on earth among** people. The man living with the disciples was God incarnate! John was overwhelmed with that truth. He began his first letter by describing the experience of seeing, touching, and hearing this Word who became flesh and was with them (1 John 1:1-4). In Christ, God came to meet with people; through Christ we can come to meet with God. John described him as **full of unfailing love and faithfulness.**

Glory refers to Christ's divine greatness and shining moral splendor. (For a specific instance of "seeing his glory," see 2:11.) This is perhaps the clearest example of what John was thinking when he and two other disciples saw Jesus' Transfiguration (see Matthew 17:1-13. Peter spoke of it specifically in 2 Peter 1:16-18). This was **the glory of the only Son of the Father.** The Son was the Father's one and only, his unique Son. Although all believers are called "children" (1:12-13), Jesus is one of a kind and enjoys a special relationship with God. Eastern thought teaches a cycle of reincarnation. Many Hindus believe that Jesus was one in a series of reincarnations of Krishna. But John teaches that Jesus, as the unique Son of God, has a special glory and an unrivaled, unparalleled, and unrepeatable place of honor.

1:15 John the Baptist declared that Christ **is far greater than I am, for he existed long before I did.** Although Jesus was humanly born after John the Baptist, Jesus existed from eternity past. For this reason, Jesus outranked John the Baptist.

1:16 The **rich blessings** indicate superabundance and completeness. When John spoke of Jesus' benefiting his people with **one gracious blessing after another,** he was affirming that he had never found Jesus lacking in any way. John's description conveys a subtle invitation for us to trust Jesus' ability to meet our needs.

That **we have all benefited** includes all the

believers, not just John and the apostles. All believers receive Christ's blessings, but nothing can deplete Christ—no matter how much the believers receive of him, he keeps on giving. His strength is not diminished by helping us. Believers do not need to seek any other source of spiritual power but Christ. Christ himself fulfills our Christian life; we do not need to seek anything beyond him. The blessings given by Christ can never be exhausted.

1:17 John introduced one of the central questions Jesus would answer: Because **law** and **God's unfailing love** seem to contradict, what action should people take? Both law and love express God's nature. **Moses** emphasized God's law and justice, while Jesus Christ came to highlight God's mercy, love, and forgiveness. Moses could only be the giver of the law, while Christ came to fulfill perfectly the law (Matthew 5:17). The law revealed the nature and will of God; now **Jesus Christ** reveals the nature and will of God. Rather than coming through cold stone tablets, God's revelation now comes through a person's life. As we get to know Christ better, our understanding of God will increase.

1:18 This statement, **no one has ever seen God,** seems to contradict passages like Exodus 24:9-11, which says that the elders of Israel "saw God." What then does John mean? Very likely, he is affirming the fact that no human being has seen the essential being of God. Some men experienced "theophanies" (special appearances of God in various forms), but no one saw the essential being of God. Only the **Son, who is himself God,** can communicate his glory to us. The Son **is near to the Father's heart,** picturing the Son as a child in close dependence on his Father—enjoying a close and warm relationship with him. It also reflects the image of two close companions enjoying a meal together. According to an ancient custom, the one who reclined next to the master at a meal was the one dearest to him. This is the Son who **has told us about** God. The Son is God's explainer; he came to earth and lived among people to explain God to us—with his words and by his person. No one can know God apart from Christ, God's explainer. Again, this mirrors verse 1, where the Son is called "the Word"—the expression of God, the communicator of God.

JOHN THE BAPTIST DECLARES HIS MISSION / 1:19-28 / 19
His stirring summary accomplished, John launched into telling the gospel. He had already introduced John the Baptist in the prologue. His overall description of the wilderness preacher leaves out the physical notes of the other Gospels (see Mark 1:1-11; Luke 1:5-25, 57-80; 3:1-20) but focuses instead on his unique role as herald of the Messiah. The messianic expectations of the time, combined with his initial success in attracting large crowds, made John the Baptist the subject of speculation: Could he be the Messiah?

1:19-21 John the Baptist's calling in life was described to his father even before John was conceived (Luke 1:13-17). John's mission was to give **testimony** to Jesus Christ (1:7). He was Christ's first and most important witness. John disavowed any personal status; he constantly pointed men to Christ. **The Jewish leaders, priests,** and **Temple assistants** were respected religious leaders in Jerusalem. The leaders who came to see John were Pharisees (1:24), a group that both John the Baptist and Jesus often denounced. Many Pharisees outwardly obeyed God's laws in order to look pious, while inwardly their hearts were filled with pride and greed.

These leaders came to see John the Baptist **to ask him whether he claimed to be the Messiah.** Their question indicates that the Jews were looking for the Messiah. John **flatly denied** that, making it perfectly clear that he was not the Christ; rather, he was one who prepared the way for the Christ.

John's role and actions reminded these religious leaders of what had been written of **Elijah** (see 2 Kings 2:11). The Old Testament predicted that Elijah would come to prepare the way for the Messiah (see Malachi 3:1; 4:5-6). John the Baptist, in the spirit of Elijah (Luke 1:17), had come to prepare the way for the Christ, but he did not claim to be Elijah. So then they asked him if he was **the Prophet** foretold by Moses (Deuteronomy 18:15). Again he said **no.**

1:22-23 His questioners wanted John to claim a special identity; he was perfectly content in his role. He simply called himself, in the words of the Old Testament prophet Isaiah, **"I am a voice shouting in the wilderness, 'Prepare a straight pathway for the Lord's coming!'"** (Isaiah 40:3). John quoted Isaiah 40, a portion that introduces the Messiah's forerunner and herald. In Isaiah 40:3-11, this herald announced the coming of the divine Shepherd. In ancient times, a herald (or forerunner) would go before a dignitary to announce his coming and to clear the way before him. John was the Messiah's herald and forerunner; he came on the scene to announce Jesus' coming and to exhort people to prepare the way to receive him.

The leaders kept pressing John to say **who** he was because people were expecting the Messiah to come (Luke 3:15). But John emphasized only why he had come—to prepare the way for the Messiah. Those sent by the religious leaders of Jerusalem confronted a man sent by God; they had run out of stereotypes and were ready to listen. Although their attentiveness was hostile, John gave them an answer.

1:24-25 John was being grilled by **those who were sent by the Pharisees.** They wanted to know what **right** he had **to baptize** if he wasn't **the Messiah or Elijah or the Prophet.** John had not invented baptism. Gentiles converting to Judaism were baptized as an initiation rite. But John was calling upon **Jews** to be baptized. Since this was new, the leaders demanded an explanation from John.

1:26-28 It was John's function to provide the means for God's cleansing through **water** baptism; it would be Jesus' function to provide the people with an infusion of the Spirit. John was merely helping the people perform a symbolic act of repentance. But the one who would be able to truly forgive sins was there **in the crowd.** The Son of God had taken up his abode among his own people, the Jews; but they did not realize it. John said that he was not even worthy to be that man's **slave.** John knew who he was in comparison to Jesus. This took place at **Bethany** to the **east of the Jordan River,** a site that has never been determined. This is different than the Bethany Jesus visited during his ministry.

JOHN THE BAPTIST PROCLAIMS JESUS AS THE MESSIAH / 1:29-34 / 20

The opening portion of John's narrative provides two witnesses to Jesus Christ's identity. The first witness is John the Baptist; this is covered in verses 19-36. John the Baptist's witness had been briefly mentioned in the prologue (1:7, 15) and is here expanded. The second witness comes from Jesus' first disciples—John (the Gospel writer), Andrew, Peter, Philip, and Nathanael. Both John the Baptist and the disciples declare and affirm that Jesus is the Christ, the Son of God.

1:29 The title **Lamb of God** would be associated in the minds of the Jews with the Passover lamb (Exodus 12) and the lambs used in the daily sacrifices for the sin offerings (see Leviticus 14:12, 21, 24; Numbers 6:12). Every morning and evening, a lamb was sacrificed in the Temple for the sins of the people (Exodus 29:38-42). Isaiah 53:7 prophesied that the Messiah, God's servant, would be led to the slaughter like a lamb. To pay the penalty for sin, a life had to be given—God chose to provide the sacrifice himself. When Jesus died as the perfect sacrifice, he removed the sin of the world and destroyed the power of sin itself. Thus God forgives our sin (1 Corinthians 5:7). In calling Jesus the Lamb of God, John pointed to Jesus as the substitutionary sacrifice provided by God.

Jesus **takes away the sin of the world.** The Greek word for "takes away" can also mean "take up." Jesus took away our sin by taking it upon himself. This is the image depicted in Isaiah 53:4-9 and 1 Peter 2:24. The "sin of the world" means the sin of each individual. Jesus paid the price of our sin by his death. We claim the forgiveness he provided by first taking ownership of our sin.

1:30 This verse, which reiterates 1:15, is here put in its chronological context. Although John the Baptist was a well-known preacher who attracted large crowds, he was content that Jesus take the higher place. John demonstrated true humility, the basis for greatness in preaching, teaching, or any other work we do for Christ. Accepting what God wants us to do and giving Jesus Christ the honor for it allows God to work freely through us.

1:31 Since John and Jesus were cousins, John must have known Jesus before this time. But this statement means that John had not realized that Jesus was God's Son, the Messiah, until God provided the sign of the Spirit descending upon Jesus. Though John had not yet clearly seen the Messiah, he knew that the Messiah was coming and that his mission was to **point him out to Israel.** But, as John would soon explain, he had been instructed to baptize, and as he was baptizing he saw a sign that indicated the arrival of the one he had come to announce.

1:32-34 Evidently, the action of **the Holy Spirit descending like a dove from heaven** was a sign for John. Only John and Jesus saw this (see Matthew 3:16). The other Gospel writers tell us that a voice accompanied this divine sign (Matthew 3:17). God had sent John to baptize and to prepare the way for the Messiah. This same God promised to reveal the Messiah to John by the Holy Spirit upon him.

In well-known prophetic passages, the Messiah was depicted as having the Spirit resting upon him (see Isaiah 11:1-2; 61:1ff.). The statement that **he is the one who baptizes with the Holy Spirit** foretells Jesus' divine mission. It does not just point to the day of Pentecost on which Jesus sent the Holy Spirit to baptize the disciples (see Luke 24:49; Acts 1:8; 2:4); it characterizes Jesus' entire ministry. Jesus came to give eternal life to those who believe in him. But no one could actually receive that life apart from receiving the life-giving Holy Spirit.

John the Baptist's baptism with water was preparatory because it was for repentance and symbolized the washing away of sins. Jesus, by contrast, would baptize with the Holy Spirit, imparting not only forgiveness but also eternal life. He would send the Holy Spirit upon all believers, empowering them to live and to teach the message of salvation. This outpouring of the Spirit came after Jesus had risen from the dead and ascended into heaven (see 20:22; Acts 2). All true believers have been baptized by Jesus in the Holy Spirit (see Romans 8:9). As such, we have been immersed in Jesus' Spirit. Now we can experience the life-giving Spirit and enjoy his presence day by day.

John was declaring Jesus' special position with God. God had told John that he would reveal his sent one to John—the Spirit would descend upon the Messiah and remain upon him. John **saw this happen to Jesus** and declared his belief in Jesus as God's identified Son.

THE FIRST DISCIPLES FOLLOW JESUS / 1:35-51 / 21

This last section of John 1 records how the earliest believers became disciples of Jesus; it is a drama of salvation revealing the formation of Jesus' first band of disciples. Andrew and John became Jesus' followers through the testimony of their teacher, John the Baptist. Peter, Andrew's brother, became a follower through the testimony of Andrew. Philip became a disciple by Jesus seeking him out and calling him to follow him. And Nathanael became a believer through the testimony of Philip and the revelation Jesus gave to him. This progression provides a model for evangelism.

1:35-36 These **disciples** of **John** the Baptist were Andrew (see 1:40) and John, the writer of this Gospel. Both these men had followed John the Baptist until he pointed them to the Lamb of God, Jesus Christ. Why did these disciples leave John the Baptist? Because that's what John wanted them to do—he was pointing the way to Jesus, the one John had prepared them to follow. This was the second time that John declared that Jesus was **the Lamb of God** (see comments on 1:29).

1:37 These disciples **followed Jesus** in two ways. They literally turned and walked after him, and they also became two of Jesus' close followers, or disciples. This was a great tribute to John the Baptist's preaching—they heard John and followed Jesus.

1:38-39 Those coming to Christ, whether for the first time or each day in worship, should ask themselves this question— "What do I want? What do I expect to receive from Jesus?" The question,

"Where are you staying?" indicates that John and Andrew were serious followers. They wanted to know where to find Jesus. This indicates a commitment, not an experiment. John recalls the exact time he first stayed with Jesus. It must have been a special opportunity for John and Andrew—a time never to be forgotten. We can only imagine their wonder as they spent **the rest of the day** alone with Jesus. From this time forward, these two men became his disciples.

1:40-42 After spending a day with Jesus, **Andrew** immediately went to find his brother **Simon** (who would later be named **Peter**) and tell him that he had found the **Messiah** (the Hebrew term), or **the Christ** (the Greek translation of "Messiah," meaning "Anointed One"; see Isaiah 61:1).

Andrew brought Simon to meet Jesus. Andrew appears two more times in this Gospel; each time he is bringing people to Jesus (see 6:4-9; 12:20-22). Jesus changed Simon's name to **Cephas,** the Aramaic word for "stone," because Jesus foresaw that Peter would become a pillar and a foundation stone in the building of the first-century church (see Matthew 16:16-18; Galatians 2:9; Ephesians 2:20; 1 Peter 2:4-5).

1:43 Jesus' first two disciples (Andrew and John) sought out Jesus. Andrew brought the third disciple, Peter, to Jesus. Jesus sought out the fourth disciple, **Philip.** Jesus looked for him, found him, and called him to be his **disciple.**

1:44-46 Philip must have known Andrew and Peter before he began to follow Jesus for they all were from **Bethsaida.** Earlier, Andrew had found Simon (his brother) and had brought him to Jesus. Philip does the same with **Nathanael.**

In the list of disciples in the other Gospels, Philip and Bartholomew are listed together (Matthew 10:3; Mark 3:18); here, Philip and Nathanael are paired up. Thus, it stands to reason that, since Bartholomew is not mentioned in the fourth Gospel and Nathanael is not mentioned in the Synoptic Gospels, Nathanael is none other than Bartholomew.

In saying **we have found** the promised one, Philip was probably referring to himself, Andrew, and Peter. If this was the case, the first five disciples (John, Andrew, Peter, Philip, and Nathanael) may have been acquainted or even friends. What a delightful experience for a Christian to witness a circle of friends or to see a family be drawn to Jesus.

The language referring to Jesus as **the very person Moses and the prophets wrote about** indicates that Philip was also a thoughtful seeker— one who read the Old Testament Scriptures and was looking for the Messiah. Moses had written about the Messiah in the Law (see Deuteronomy 18:15-18), and the prophets had foretold his coming. That Jesus is called **the son of Joseph** refers to Jesus' family line; in other words, this was how Jesus was known among the people (see Luke 3:23—it was supposed that Jesus was Joseph's son). In reality, Jesus was not Joseph's son; he was (and is) God's Son.

Nathanael's statement about **Nazareth** does not necessarily mean that there was anything wrong with the town. Nazareth was possibly despised by the Jews because a Roman army garrison was located there. Some have speculated that an aloof attitude or a poor reputation in morals and religion on the part of the people of Nazareth led to Nathanael's harsh comment. Nathanael's hometown was Cana, about four miles from Nazareth. Nathanael's expression seems to indicate that he did not expect that anything related to God's purpose could come from that place because Nazareth is not mentioned in the Old Testament. The prophets, moreover, never said that the Messiah would come from Nazareth. The Messiah was to be born in Bethlehem (Micah 5:2); and, in fact, Jesus *was* born in Bethlehem. But his parents' flight to Egypt and soon return to Galilee, where Jesus was raised, gave Jesus the reputation of being a Galilean, even a Nazarene. This was offensive to many Jews because they could not accept a Messiah who had not come from Bethlehem.

Philip did not argue with Nathanael about Jesus; he just said, **"Come and see for yourself."** Fortunately for Nathanael, he went to meet Jesus and became a disciple. If he had stuck to his prejudice without investigating further, he would have missed the Messiah! We must not let people's stereotypes about Christ cause them to miss his power and love. We must invite them to come and meet Jesus themselves.

1:47 Jesus' statement about **Nathanael** reveals that Nathanael was an **honest man.** Jesus' direct, intimate knowledge of him must have taken Nathanael by surprise. He was not offended, just intensely curious. If we remember that God's grace and love come to us even though he knows all about us, we may find ourselves being even more grateful to him.

1:48-49 Here Jesus unveiled his omniscience to **Nathanael.** Jesus had been aware of Nathanael's exact location before Philip called him. According to Jewish tradition, the expression **"to sit under the fig tree"** was a euphemism for meditating on the Scriptures. Thus, Jesus had seen Nathanael studying the Scriptures before **Philip** had called him to come and see Jesus. Instantly, Nathanael realized that Jesus is **the Son of God** (see Psalm 2:7) and **the King of Israel** (see Psalm 2:6; Zephaniah 3:15).

The early disciples of Jesus were well versed in the Scriptures. Life in the small towns of Israel revolved around the synagogue, where the Old Testament was constantly read, taught, and argued. Unlike many of the studied religious leaders of the day, these simple men understood the Scriptures, and knew what to look for. So when the Messiah came, they recognized him!

1:50-51 Jesus now speaks to all the disciples there present. He says that they would thereafter see the **angels of God going up and down upon the Son of Man.** These words allude to Jacob's dream of the ladder connecting heaven and earth upon which the angels of God were ascending and descending (Genesis 28:12). As such, Jesus is the fulfillment of this dream: he is the vehicle of communication between heaven and earth.

JOHN 2

JESUS TURNS WATER INTO WINE / 2:1-12 / 22
The miracle of turning water into wine was Jesus' "first display of his glory" (2:11). After his death and resurrection, Jesus would be fully glorified—and all people would (or should) know that he is the Son of God. But until that time, Jesus would reveal his identity by miracles—even though he would have preferred for people to believe in him because of his words. Transforming the water into wine revealed Jesus' glory by showing his tremendous power. This small display of his divine power was enough to convince the disciples of his identity and initiate their trust in him (2:11), though later events demonstrated that they only partially understood Jesus' purpose.

2:1-2 A **wedding celebration** could last as long as a week (see Genesis 29:27-28). **Cana** was a town about nine miles north of Nazareth. The only references to the town of Cana are found in John's Gospel. Two of Jesus' miracles are connected with that location: creating wine from water (2:1-11) and healing an official's son (4:46-54). Nathanael, one of the twelve disciples, is described as a native of Cana (21:2). The town has not survived into the present but is thought to have been between Nazareth and Capernaum, in the northwest region of the Sea of Galilee.

Jesus' mother, Mary, was a guest, and Jesus and his disciples were also invited. When a wedding was held, the entire town was invited, and most made the effort to come (it was considered an insult to refuse an invitation to a wedding). Cana was Jesus' home region, so he may have known the bride and groom. In any case, his presence was intentional.

Jesus' attendance and his actions at this wedding indicate his approval of the celebration. (See Jesus' comments about marriage in Matthew 5:31-32; 19:3-9.) Images of Jesus as a dour-faced Messiah, passing judgment on all in his path simply fail to account for the biblical evidence that he was completely at home in festive occasions. In fact, part of his rejection by religious leaders was based on their perception that he enjoyed being with sinners more than was appropriate (see Mark 2:15-16 and Luke 5:30). Jesus' life is the most profound statement ever made against joyless spirituality.

2:3-4 The week-long weddings in Jesus' time must have had about the same impact on family budgets as weddings do today. Banquets were prepared for many guests, and everyone spent several days celebrating the new life of the married couple. To accommodate the guests, careful planning was needed. Running out of **wine** meant more than embarrassment; it broke the strong unwritten laws of hospitality. Jesus was about to respond to a heartfelt need. Mary told Jesus of the predicament, perhaps expecting him to do something about it. Some believe Mary was not assuming that Jesus would perform a miracle; she was simply hoping that her son would help solve this major problem and find some wine. Tradition says that Joseph, Mary's husband, was dead, so she probably was used to depending on her son's help in certain situations. Although Mary did not know what Jesus was going to do, she trusted him to handle the problem. Others point out that Mary had known for a long time about her son's divine commission. Perhaps she wanted Jesus to do something in the presence of her relatives and/or friends (who may have heard some reports about Jesus) that would prove he was the Messiah. The tension between Jesus' verbal response, **"How does that concern you and me?"** and his later actions leaves the question of Mary's expectations undecided. But Mary's trust is unmistakable!

In any case, Jesus made it clear to his mother that his life was following a different timetable, that he lived to carry out his Father's business, according to his Father's plans. Whatever Jesus' intended response to the problem at hand, he expressed to his mother a firm reminder that his priorities were different from hers—his **time** had **not yet come.** The "time" to which Jesus referred was the time of his glorification, when he would receive his true place and position, not as an earthly king, but as the Messiah, God's Son, Savior of mankind, seated at God's right hand (see 7:30, 39; 12:23-24; 17:1). This glorification would occur after his death and resurrection, for it would be only through death and resurrection that Jesus could accomplish what he came to earth to accomplish—to offer salvation to all people.

2:5-6 Mary was not promised any kind of action but realized that Jesus might do something about the situation, even though his remark in verse 4 must have limited her expectations. Nevertheless, Mary's words to the **servants** to **do whatever** they are told show her respect for Jesus' authority.

The **six stone waterpots** were normally used for the **ceremonial** washing of hands as part of the Jewish purification rites before and after meals (see Matthew 15:1-2). When full, each jar would hold **twenty to thirty gallons.**

2:7-8 This filling **to the brim** showed that nothing could be added to the **water.** When Jesus performed the miracle, **all** the water was changed to wine; wine was not added to the water. It portrays the abundance of Christ's gracious work; it also indicates the wholeheartedness of the servants' obedience. The servants dipped into the jars and drew out the water that had been miraculously changed to wine. Jesus instructed them to **take it to the master of ceremonies.**

2:9-10 It was customary to give the **best wine first** and the poorer wine last because people's taste buds grow less sensitive with more and more drinks. The water turned into wine was of such quality that the **master of ceremonies** made a point of mentioning this to the **bridegroom,** who also probably reacted in surprise. Neither of them knew where this wine came from, but Mary, the servants, and the disciples were aware of what had happened.

This miracle illustrated the emptiness of the Jewish rituals versus what Jesus came to bring (see 4:13; 7:38-39). The water of ceremonial cleansing has become the wine of the messianic age. Have we tasted the new wine?

2:11 The Gospels record thirty-five **miraculous signs** performed by Jesus. In the Gospel of John, each miracle was a sign intended to point people

to the truth that Jesus is the divine Son of God come down from heaven. These signs were remarkable actions that displayed the presence and power of God. According to John's Gospel, this was Jesus' first sign—and it was performed in **Cana in Galilee** (his own region). His second was also performed in Galilee (see 4:46-54).

Many have wondered why Jesus would "waste" his powers on performing a miracle of providing wine for a wedding feast, a party. But all of Jesus' miracles had a purpose beyond alleviating suffering; they were a **display of his glory.** The miracles recorded in John's Gospel (and indeed all the miracles recorded by the other Gospel writers) demonstrated God's great love for people and his concern for their individual needs. But on a deeper level, Jesus' unique, divine nature was portrayed in such a way as to claim our loyalty and reverence. The sign of turning water into wine was a partial unveiling of Jesus' full identity. His power over nature, death, sin, and evil revealed him to be the promised Messiah.

Up to this point, the **disciples** (those who had been called thus far) were following Jesus for their own reasons. Others may have been questioning who Jesus was and were following him to find out. John says that when the disciples saw the miracle, they **believed in him.** The miracle demonstrated Jesus' power over nature and revealed the way he would go about his ministry—helping others, speaking with authority, and being in personal touch with people. God may confront us in any number of ways with our need to believe in his Son. We will be held accountable for whether or not we have believed.

2:12 Capernaum became Jesus' home base during his ministry in Galilee. Located on a major trade route, it was an important city in the region, with a Roman garrison and a customs station. At Capernaum, Matthew was called to be a disciple (Matthew 9:9). The city was also the home of several other disciples (Matthew 4:13-19) and a high-ranking government official (4:46). It had at least one major synagogue. Although Jesus made this city his base of operations in Galilee, he condemned it for the people's unbelief (Matthew 11:23; Luke 10:15).

JESUS CLEARS THE TEMPLE / 2:13-25 / 23
The magnificent Temple that Jesus entered with his disciples was the one rebuilt by the remnant of Israelites who had returned from Babylon under Ezra and Nehemiah; it was later enlarged by Herod. The Jews considered the Temple to be God's house. But the arrival of Jesus and the beginning of his ministry signaled a change. The glory of God, which had filled the

holy shrine since the days of the Exodus and the Tabernacle, was no longer in the building; that glory was in Jesus, though veiled within his humanity.

2:13 The **Passover celebration** took place yearly at the Temple in **Jerusalem.** Every Jewish male was expected to make a pilgrimage to Jerusalem during this time, so **Jesus went** (Deuteronomy 16:16). This was a week-long festival—the Passover was one day, and the Feast of Unleavened Bread lasted the rest of the week. The entire week commemorated the freeing of the Jews from slavery in Egypt (Exodus 12:1-14).

2:14 The **Temple** was on an imposing hill overlooking the city. Solomon had built the first Temple on this same site almost one thousand years earlier (949 B.C.), but his Temple had been destroyed by the Babylonians (2 Kings 25). The Temple was rebuilt in 515 B.C., and Herod the Great had recently remodeled it.

God had originally instructed the people of Israel to bring from their own flocks the best animals for sacrifice (Deuteronomy 12:5-7). This would make the sacrifice more personal. But the Temple priests instituted a market for buying sacrificial animals so the pilgrims would not have to bring their animals on the long journey. In addition, the **merchants** and **money changers** were dishonest. The businesspeople selling these animals expected to turn a profit. The price of sacrificial animals was much higher in the Temple area than elsewhere. In order to purchase the animals, travelers from other lands would need local currency, and the Temple tax had to be paid in local currency; so money changers exchanged foreign money, but made huge profits by charging exorbitant exchange rates. Jesus was angry at the dishonest, greedy practices of the money changers and merchants, and he particularly disliked their presence on the Temple grounds. They had set up shop in the Court of the Gentiles, making it so full of merchants that foreigners found it difficult to worship—and worship was the main purpose for visiting the Temple. With all the merchandising taking place in the area allotted for the Gentiles, how could they spend time with God in prayer? No wonder Jesus was angry!

2:15 Jesus' response to the desecration of the Temple was deliberate and forceful. He was intent on scouring the Temple. This cleansing was significantly appropriate during Passover because that was the time when all the Jews were supposed to cleanse their houses of all leaven (yeast). During the Feast of Unleavened Bread, no leaven was used in any baking and, in fact, was not even to be found in the Israelite homes (Exodus 12:17-20).

Jesus did not lose his temper; his action expressed anger, but he was clearly in control of himself. Jesus was zealous for the reverence due to God the Father, and he knew that the irreverent marketplace within the very courts of God's Temple would not be expelled without the use of force. He **made a whip** and **chased them all out of the Temple.**

2:16 Jesus saw the Temple as his **Father's house.** His own rightful claim to ownership was unmistakable. But the religious leaders of that day were trespassers—turning it into a place of business and money-making—no more than a **marketplace.** People had created an environment that, in essence, put a price on what God intended to be free. Access to God is not for sale. According to the other three Gospels, Jesus visited the Temple again and cleansed it during his final visit to Jerusalem during the Passover, just prior to his crucifixion (see Matthew 21:12-17; Mark 11:15-19; Luke 19:45-46).

2:17 This quote from Psalm 69:9 was thought to refer not only to the psalmist but also to the coming Messiah. His incredible zeal for God and for purity of worship would endanger his life. In fact, Jesus was perceived as a threat to the religious establishment, and this was a direct cause of his death. The **disciples,** probably as much as any of the people then present, must have been shocked at Jesus' display of anger. But John reported that they remembered God's word and saw the action as God-ordained, having been prophesied in **the Scriptures.**

2:18-19 The hardhearted people of Jesus' day continually required Jesus to give them some **miraculous sign** to prove his **authority from God.** However, Jesus would not give his generation the kind of sign they demanded; he himself was the sign, for he was the Son of God come from heaven to earth. This would be known to all after his resurrection. This would be the ultimate sign he would give Israel and all mankind. So Jesus answered the Jewish leaders' challenge with a counter-challenge that the disciples later understood to be a prediction of his own death and resurrection (2:22). Jesus' opponents saw only the absurdity of his claim. His sign to them was, **"Destroy this temple, and in three days I will raise it up."** Jesus' ambiguous statement is a good example of how he encouraged people to think and inquire more deeply. Along with his parables, these statements accomplished the dual task of frustrating the halfhearted and self-righteous while at the same time piquing the curiosity of those who were sincere seekers.

This would be the sign the Jews required, even if they did not recognize it. They would destroy his body, and he would raise it up in three days. At another time when the Jews asked Jesus for a sign, he told them that the only sign he would give them was that of Jonah the prophet, who spent three days and three nights in the belly of a great fish before God delivered him (see Matthew 12:39-40). In like manner, Jesus would be killed and after three days rise from the dead.

2:20-21 The Jews understood Jesus to mean the **Temple** where he had just driven out the merchants and money changers. This was the Temple Zerubbabel had built more than five hundred years earlier, but Herod the Great had begun remodeling it, making it much larger and far more beautiful. It had been **forty-six years** since this remodeling had started (20 B.C.), and it still wasn't completely finished. They understood Jesus' words to mean that this imposing building could be torn down and rebuilt in **three days,** and they were openly skeptical.

2:22 The **Scriptures** probably means the whole Old Testament as it testifies to Christ's death and resurrection (passages such as Psalm 22:7-17).

After Christ's resurrection, the Spirit illuminated these Scriptures (14:26), so the disciples **remembered** and **believed.** As Jesus predicted, they did destroy his body (the Temple), and he did raise it up in three days.

2:23-25 This was during the same week that Jesus purged the Temple in Jerusalem (see 2:13ff.). It was the week-long Feast of Unleavened Bread that followed the day of **Passover.** John did not recount any of the **miraculous signs** Jesus performed in Jerusalem; he simply said that **many people were convinced that he was indeed the Messiah.** But, as the next verse indicates, this belief was not complete. The people believed in Jesus as a miracle worker or a political Messiah, but not necessarily as the true Messiah, the Son of God.

John used the Greek verb *pisteuo* to make a wordplay. In 2:23, John said that many believed (*episteusan*) in him; in 2:24, John said that Jesus did not entrust (*episteusen*) himself to them. The reason for Jesus' lack of trust then follows—**he knew what people were really like.** Jesus was realistic about the depth of trust in those who were now following him. Some would endure; others would fall away (6:66). Jesus was discerning, and he knew that the faith of some followers was superficial. Some of the same people who claimed to believe in Jesus at this time would later yell, "Crucify him!"

JOHN 3

NICODEMUS VISITS JESUS AT NIGHT / 3:1-21 / 24
It would be difficult to find any other portion of Scripture as well known as John 3:16 or any other statement of Scripture more applied than "You must be born again" (3:7). When Jesus revealed the necessity of the new birth to Nicodemus, he exposed mankind's ultimate hope. This evening interview is the first of a series of individual encounters between Jesus and persons who fit the description given at the end of chapter 2—those who approached Jesus with an inadequate faith. Nicodemus (3:1-15), the Samaritan woman (4:1-42), and the nobleman from Capernaum (4:43-54) illustrate a certain view of who Jesus was and what he could do. But meeting Jesus face to face changed their views. It also changed their lives.

3:1-2 Nicodemus was **a Jewish religious leader,** a **Pharisee**—the most strict Jewish sect of those times. The Jewish religious leaders were divided into several groups. Two of the most prominent groups were the Pharisees and the Sadducees. The Pharisees separated themselves from anything non-Jewish and carefully followed both the Old Testament laws and the oral traditions handed down through the centuries. As a "leader," he was a member of the Jewish ruling council. Although the Romans controlled Israel politically, the Jews were given some authority over religious and minor civil disputes. The Jewish ruling body was the council made up of seventy-one of Israel's religious leaders.

What motivated Nicodemus to come to Jesus? Very likely Nicodemus was both impressed and curious about Jesus and chose to form his opinions about him from firsthand conversation. It is possible that he did not want to be seen with Jesus in broad daylight because he feared reproach from his fellow Pharisees (who did not believe in Jesus as the Messiah). But it may not have been fear that brought Nicodemus **after dark;** it is also possible that he chose a time when he could talk alone and at length with the popular teacher who was often surrounded by people.

Nicodemus respectfully addressed Jesus as a **teacher** who had been **sent by God.** While true, the title reveals Nicodemus's limited understanding of Jesus. He was far more than just another rabbi. At least Nicodemus identified Jesus' **miraculous signs** as a revelation of God's power.

3:3 Jesus' words are unmistakable and to the point: **"Unless you are born again, you can never see the Kingdom of God."** That a person must be **born again** speaks of spiritual birth, but Nicodemus understood Jesus as referring to a physical rebirth. What could Jesus expect Nicodemus to know about the Kingdom? From the Scriptures he would know that the Kingdom would be ruled by God, it would eventually be restored on earth, and it would incorporate God's people. Jesus revealed to this devout Pharisee that the Kingdom would come to the whole world (3:16), not just the Jews, and that Nicodemus wouldn't be a part of it unless he was personally born again (3:5). This was a revolutionary concept: the Kingdom is personal, not national or ethnic, and its entrance requirements are repentance and spiritual rebirth. Jesus later taught that God's Kingdom has already begun in the hearts of believers (Luke 17:21). It will be fully realized when Jesus returns again to judge the world and abolish evil forever (Revelation 21–22).

During Jesus' earthly ministry, the Kingdom of God was present with him (Luke 17:21). To "see" the Kingdom of God means, in part, to have a special perception or insight concerning God's absolute control. But a sense of belonging, or citizenship, is also included. The "seeing" is not simply for purposes of examination; it represents participation. To "see," then, is to be a citizen without yet being able to exercise all the rights and privileges of that citizenship. Nicodemus was being taught that Israel was a chosen people to be a vehicle of God's message to the world, not to be the only beneficiaries of that relationship.

3:4 Nicodemus either stopped listening after Jesus' opening phrase, or he chose to address the first curious statement he heard. These questions that focused solely on birth—whether spoken sincerely or sarcastically—show that Nicodemus did not perceive the spiritual intent of Jesus' words. He saw only the literal meaning and questioned its absurdity: **"How can an old man go back into his mother's womb and be born again?"** But with all his learning he should have understood that God can and will give spiritual rebirth. The prophets had spoken about this spiritual regeneration (see Ezekiel 36:25-27; see also Jeremiah 31:31-34; Joel 2:28-32).

3:5 This statement has perplexed and divided commentators for many centuries. Some traditions have taught that the **water** denotes physical birth (referring to the "water" of amniotic fluid or even semen) and **Spirit** to spiritual birth—in which case Jesus would be saying that a person has to have two births: one physical and the second, spiritual. This view builds upon the preceding context when Nicodemus referred to physical birth. It also points to the parallel Jesus makes in verse 6. According to this position, Jesus would have been granting the Pharisee's point in order to highlight the nature of the second birth as spiritual. Two strengths of this interpretation are that it avoids making the physical act of water baptism a necessity and that it avoids bringing almost a "third birth" idea into the discussion. If **water** doesn't refer to natural birth, say its defenders, then Jesus seems to be saying that a person must be born of their parents, born of water, and born of the Spirit.

Other traditions have taught that the **water** refers to baptism and the **Spirit** to spiritual regeneration—thus, Jesus would have been saying that a person must both be baptized and receive the Spirit in order to enter the Kingdom of God. This view is at times influenced by the belief that the sacrament of baptism is itself a requirement for salvation.

A parallel view makes **water** refer to baptism but places the emphasis on teaching two steps of baptism; one by water, the other by the Spirit. For support, these views point to the larger context in John where John the Baptist and water baptism are mentioned just preceding the events in Cana and following this encounter with Nicodemus. They also rely on the tendency of previous generations of Christians to equate the mention of water with baptism. But in the first seven chapters of John, water appears in some way (naturally or symbolically) in each chapter. To associate water and baptism too closely makes baptism a higher priority than the Scriptures give it. Here, for instance, if Jesus was speaking of two completely separate acts, two baptisms, it is odd that the rest of the discussion between Jesus and Nicodemus never again refers to the subject but revolves entirely around the work of God's Spirit.

Still other traditions have taught that Jesus' reference to **water** is not physical in either the sense of birth or baptism. The term water is simply another description of the Spirit—or the Spirit's activity of cleansing and giving life (see John 7:37-39).

3:6 Humans can produce only more human beings; this answers Nicodemus's question in verse 4. Only God the **Holy Spirit gives new life from heaven.** At the same time God puts his Spirit into us, we are given a new regenerated human spirit. It is God's Spirit, not our effort, that makes us children of God (1:12). Jesus' description corrects human hopes that we might somehow inherit goodness from parents, or earn it by good behavior, church background, or correct associations. At some point we must be able to answer the question: Have I been born of the Spirit?

3:7 Jesus' statement to Nicodemus that evening has been heralded to all the world ever since. Both Jew and Gentile have heard the divine mandate: **You must be born again.** Without the new birth, one cannot see or enter into the Kingdom of God. In those words, millions have heard Jesus speaking directly to their hearts. Behind Jesus' challenge is his invitation to each of us—"You must be born again; allow me to do that for you."

3:8 Perhaps at this moment in the evening a soft wind rustled the leaves outside the house or in the garden where they were talking. Jesus used the illustration of the **wind** to depict the effect of the Spirit in the person **born of the Spirit.** In Greek the same word (*pneuma*) can have several meanings: "Spirit," "wind," and "breath." God's Spirit, like the wind, has free movement and, like reviving breath, has power. Jesus used this illustration to show that the reality of the Spirit living in a person is evidenced by the effect of the Spirit on that person's life. People can control neither the wind nor the movement of God's Spirit. The image Jesus used describes the wonderful experience we can have of realizing that God actually moves in and through us by his Spirit. Just as we do not know the origin or the destination of the wind, we do not know or control the Spirit. What we do know are the effects of the wind and of the Spirit. Life in the Spirit is as radical and unexpected as being born of the Spirit.

3:9-10 In response to Nicodemus's continued question, Jesus called him **a respected Jewish teacher** and expressed amazement at his lack of understanding. Having such a position, Nicodemus should have known what Jesus was talking about,

for the new birth is not a topic foreign to the Hebrew Scriptures (see, for example, 1 Samuel 10:6; Isaiah 32:15; Jeremiah 31:33; Ezekiel 36:25-27; 37; Joel 2:28-29). Jesus' question must have exposed Nicodemus, who perhaps thought that he and Jesus were teachers who would discuss spiritual matters from an equal level of learning and understanding (see 3:2). This Jewish teacher of the Bible knew the Old Testament thoroughly, but he didn't understand what it said about the Messiah.

3:11-12 Commentators do not agree as to whom the pronoun **we** refers to. Most likely, it refers to all those prophets who have spoken to Israel; it may also refer to Jesus and his Father. **Things that happen here on earth** such as the wind, can be "sensed"—that is, felt and heard. Jesus has spoken in an "earthly" analogy, and if Nicodemus could not **believe** that, **how** could he **possible believe** if Jesus were to tell him **what is going on in heaven?** These are the truths that pertain to the heavenly realm and heavenly Kingdom (for example, the more abstract theological topics such as the Trinity or Jesus' coming glory).

3:13-15 This statement, following the last part of verse 12, tells us why Jesus was uniquely qualified to speak about heavenly matters. His authoritative message about heaven was based on personal experience. He came to **earth and will return to heaven.** Heaven was the home he left on his mission to rescue us. No other man could claim the same. **The Son of Man** is the term Jesus always used as his self-designation (1:51; see also Daniel 7:13; Matthew 26:64).

The Son of Man came from heaven and became flesh in order to die—but his death would have special importance. That significance had been "taught" by God throughout the experiences of his chosen people. To illustrate this, Jesus compared his coming death to a story well known to Nicodemus, for it came from Jewish history. According to Numbers 21:6-9, while the Israelites were wandering in the wilderness, God sent a plague of snakes to punish the people for their rebellious attitudes. But God also gave the remedy for the poisonous snakebites—he told Moses to erect a **pole** upon which he was to attach a **bronze snake.** Those bitten by the poisonous snakes could be healed by obeying God's command to look up at the elevated bronze snake and by believing that God would heal them. Their healing came when they looked upon this lifted-up, bronze snake.

Jesus used this incident to picture his coming salvation work on the cross. To be **lifted up** in Jesus' time—according to the usage in John (see 8:28; 12:32-34)—was a euphemism for death on the cross (the victim was literally lifted up above the earth); it also spoke of his subsequent glorification. In Numbers 21:6-9, the perishing Israelites looked upon the lifted-up snake and lived. Similarly, salvation happens when we look up to Jesus, believing he will save us. God has provided this way for us to be healed of sin's deadly bite. The Israelites were spared their lives; the believer in Jesus is spared eternal destruction and given **eternal life.**

3:16 The entire gospel comes to a focus in this verse. God's love is not just to a certain group of individuals—it is offered to **the world.** God's love is not static or self-centered; it reaches out and draws others in. Here God's actions defined the pattern of true love, the basis for all love relationships—when you love someone, you are willing to sacrifice dearly for that person. Sacrificial love is also practical in seeking ways to meet the needs of those who are loved. In God's case, that love was infinitely practical, since it set out to rescue those who had no hope of rescuing themselves. God paid dearly to save us; **he gave his only Son,** the highest price he could pay.

This offer is made to **everyone who believes.** To "believe" is more than intellectual agreement that Jesus is God. It means putting our trust and confidence in him that he alone can save us. It is to put Christ in charge of our present plans and eternal destiny. Believing is both trusting his words as reliable and relying on him for the power to change.

Jesus accepted our punishment and paid the price for our sins so that we would **not perish.** Perish does not mean physical death, for we all will eventually die. Here it refers to eternity apart from God. Those who believe will receive the alternative, the new life that Jesus bought for us—**eternal life** with God.

3:17 All people are already under God's judgment because of sin—specifically the sin of not believing in God's Son (16:9). The only way to escape the condemnation is to believe in Jesus, the Son of God, because **God did not send his Son into the world to condemn it, but to save it.** He who believes in him is saved from God's judgment. And God wants people to believe (2 Peter 3:9).

When we consider ways to communicate the gospel, we should follow Jesus' example. We do not need to condemn unbelievers; they are condemned already. We must tell them about this condemnation, and then offer them the way of salvation—faith in Jesus Christ. When we share the gospel with others, our love must be like Jesus'—willingly giving up our own comfort and security so that others might join us in receiving God's love.

3:18-20 What follows describes the grounds for **judgment.** Those who **trust** in Jesus have **no judgment awaiting** them. But those who don't believe **have already been judged for not believing in the only Son of God.** The arrival of the **light from heaven** signals that with the coming of Jesus we have: (1) an absolute source of truth; (2) condemnation of sin; (3) guidance for our daily decisions; and (4) illumination to learn about God more clearly.

What a tragedy that people have turned away from God's offer, embracing instead the **darkness** in hopes of covering up evil actions. There is probably no more painful moment than when we honestly confront our tendency to love darkness, to twist or withhold the truth. The Son did not come to judge, but in the light of his character the sharp shadows of our sinfulness stand out. The people who **hate the light** are those who **want to sin in the darkness.** Evil deeds are revealed by the light, so people who want to do evil must do it in the dark so they cannot be **exposed** and caught in the act.

3:21 According to the context, to **do what is right** is to come to Christ, the light; the result of coming to the light and living in the light will be clearly seen in believers' lives. Christ's life in us will make our lives able to stand exposure to bright light, for our deeds will be honest, pure, and truthful. John wrote about this at length in 1 John 1:5-7.

JOHN THE BAPTIST TELLS MORE ABOUT JESUS / 3:22-36 / 25

This section begins with an abrupt change of scene to Aenon, near Salim, in the land of Judea. Both Jesus and John—the two prominent figures in the new movement of God—were gathering disciples; but more were coming to Jesus than to John. This seems to have troubled John's disciples. As for John, he was perfectly aware of what his position was in God's plan. He was the herald of the Messiah-King—to put it in his own words, the friend of the bridegroom (3:29). John was content to prepare for the bridegroom and then fade quietly into the background while the bridegroom received all the attention. John knew that he would become less important and less noticed and that Jesus would receive increased recognition and importance. John rejoiced to see this happen.

3:22-23 These verses tell us that two groups were baptizing at the same time: one in **Judea**, the other at **Aenon, near Salim**, which may have been in northern Samaria. Aenon, which means "a place of many springs," helps explain the statement, **there was plenty of water.**

While John was baptizing in northern Samaria, the disciples of Jesus under his direction (for Jesus himself did not baptize, according to 4:2) were also baptizing. Since John's baptism prepared the way for people to come to the Messiah, we can postulate that Jesus' disciples carried out the same kind of baptism as did John—one that prepared people to receive Christ and enter into his Kingdom.

3:24 This was occurring **before John was put into prison**, clarifying the chronology of events. At the time John wrote this Gospel (A.D. 90s), his readers may not have known when John the Baptist's ministry ended—especially in relationship to Jesus' ministry.

3:25 Given the immediate context, the argument over **ceremonial cleansing** probably involved some debate about the authority of John's baptism and how it related to the baptisms connected with Jesus. This topic was still controversial years later during one of the final confrontations between Jesus and the teachers of religious law (Luke 20:1-8). The Jews sought cleansing through various sacrifices and washings prescribed by God through Moses. But centuries of human "adjustments" had transformed the way of humility before God into a hopeless maze of human effort. The huge system was bent on self-preservation rather than in truly serving God. Thus, for many religious leaders, John's effrontery in preaching simple repentance and requiring public baptism was unacceptable as a form of cleansing.

3:26 John's disciples exposed their competitive spirit—this is certain because of the way John responded to them in the following verses. These disciples of John must have lost sight of their mission—which was to join John in preparing people for Christ. They should not have been surprised (much less, dismayed) that people were **going** to Christ—they were supposed to!

Why did John the Baptist continue to baptize after Jesus came onto the scene? Why didn't he become a disciple too? John explained that because God had given him his work, he had to continue it until God called him to do something else. John's main purpose was to point people to Christ. Even with Jesus beginning his own ministry, John could still point people to Jesus.

3:27 John's reply to his disciples was the response of a man who knew his place in God's plan. He knew that a person is not able to do anything unless it has been given to him or her from God: **"God in heaven appoints each person's work."** If all the people were going to Christ, if Christ's ministry was expanding, then it must be God's plan. John exemplifies the kind of exuberant endorsement that ought to come from us when we hear that someone is being effective as a servant of Christ.

3:28 Here John reiterated what he had told the disciples earlier: **"I am not the Messiah"** (1:20). John had always been forthright in declaring his position; he did this so that the distinction between himself and the Messiah would be unmistakably clear. His job had always been **to prepare the way for him—that is all.**

3:29 John employed a beautiful metaphor to depict the way he saw his relationship with Jesus the Christ. He described himself as being the **bridegroom's friend**—or, as we would say today, "the best man." As the best man, John enjoyed seeing his friend, the bridegroom, honored. He insisted that all the attention should go to the bridegroom and his bride.

3:30 What a realization John had! He knew that his work was destined to **become less and less**—he himself would have to decrease. John's willingness to decrease so that Jesus would increase reveals unusual humility. It also reveals how much he was like Jesus in character.

3:31 John's statement revealed his attitude about Christ's superiority and preeminence over him. The same word (*anothen*) that appears here was used in 3:3. Jesus is the one who **has come from above**, while we are people who must be "born from above" if we hope to see the Kingdom of God. John, whom Jesus himself called the greatest man born among men (Matthew 11:11), was still a man **of the earth** (see 1 Corinthians 15:47). Christ's heavenly origin gives him superiority over every person.

3:32 Throughout his Gospel, John emphasized the fact that Jesus spoke what he had **seen and heard** from the Father (8:14-30). He was the Father's representative in word and action. But **few would believe what he tells them.** This is a great condemnation upon mankind—especially upon the people who lived when Jesus did, for they were the ones who heard his testimony and rejected it (see 1:10-11; 3:11; 12:37ff.).

3:33 By way of contrast with verse 32, this verse indicates that some did receive Jesus' testimony.

Those who believe him discover that God is true. They believed that he was the Son of God come from heaven, the Messiah. Their belief in his testimony was their "stamp of approval" on the truthfulness of God's action (sending his Son). In other words, they tested the testimony and found it to be true. It was true whether or not anyone else ever witnessed to its truth. The gospel is the invitation from God to add ourselves to those who have staked their lives on Christ, the Truth.

3:34 This statement authenticates what was said in verse 32. God's Son, Jesus Christ, **is sent by God** and **speaks God's words** because **God's Spirit is upon him without measure or limit.** God gave the immeasurable Spirit to his Son. As such, the Son was the recipient of the immeasurable Spirit for his prophetic ministry (see Isaiah 11:1ff.). But unlike the Old Testament prophets who were anointed with the Holy Spirit only when they were speaking for God, Jesus always had the Spirit and therefore always spoke the words of God. We can trust the words of Jesus.

3:35 The Father committed all of his divine plan to the care of his beloved Son: **The Father loves his Son, and he has given him authority over everything.** What a glorious privilege and awesome responsibility! By the end of his ministry, Jesus told the Father that he had accomplished everything the Father had wanted him to do (17:1-4).

3:36 Believers need not wonder whether or not they have eternal life (or wait for the future judgment to see if eternal life will be granted or not). **All who believe in God's Son have eternal life.** Thus, eternal life begins at the moment of spiritual rebirth. The question for individual believers, then, is: How does our way of living demonstrate the fact that we expect to live eternally?

In contrast, **those who don't obey the Son will never experience eternal life.** There are only two groups in the end—those who have eternal life, and those who do not. To disobey the Son is to reject him. To reject the Son's testimony and the gospel is to cut ourselves off from the benefits available only through him. Those people will experience **the wrath of God.**

John, the author of this Gospel, has been demonstrating that Jesus is the true Son of God. Jesus sets before us the greatest choice in life. We are responsible to decide today whom we will obey (Joshua 24:15). God wants us to choose him and life (Deuteronomy 30:15-20). God's wrath is his final judgment and rejection of the sinner. To put off the choice is to choose not to follow Christ. Indecision is a fatal decision.

JOHN 4

JESUS TALKS TO A WOMAN AT THE WELL / 4:1-26 / 27
Jesus had to pass through Samaria on his way to Galilee. In Jesus' encounter with the Samaritan woman and with the Samaritans in Sychar, he revealed that he is the expected Messiah (4:25-26). Furthermore, Jesus pointed the Samaritans to the truth about salvation, God's nature, and the worship of God: Salvation comes from among the Jews (the Messiah is a Jew), God is spirit, and God must be worshiped in spirit and in truth.

4:1-2 Jesus realized that his popularity had come to the attention of the **Pharisees.** They had scrutinized the activities of John the Baptist and sent emissaries to question him about his identity (1:19-28). John always pointed his followers to a greater one, the coming Messiah. Because the greater one had come and was in fact drawing the crowds away from John, the Pharisees began to watch Jesus closely.

Jesus had gained many more disciples than just the Twelve. We know that he had at least seventy-two committed disciples (Luke 10:1-17).

We are also told that various disciples came and went, especially when times were difficult or when Jesus predicted troubles ahead (Luke 9:57-62; John 6:66).

Part of the information received by the Pharisees was incorrect because **Jesus didn't baptize** anyone—**his disciples did.** This parenthetical remark helps to explain John the Baptist's statement in 1:33 that the Messiah would baptize in the Holy Spirit—in contrast to John who baptized in water. Thus, Jesus never personally performed water baptism; his disciples continued to perform that task during the early years of the church. These baptisms, still following the pattern set by John the Baptist, indicated repentance and confession of sin (see Matthew 3:6).

4:3 Knowing that the Pharisees (in Jerusalem) had heard about his popularity and that they would begin watching him closely, and at the same time knowing that his "hour" had not yet come (see also 2:4), Jesus wisely decided to withdraw from possible conflict by leaving **Judea** and returning to **Galilee**. Thus, Jesus' first Judean visit had come to an end—a visit begun by his coming to Jerusalem for the Passover (see 2:13). The other Gospels do not record this visit.

4:4 The territory of Samaria lay between Judea and Galilee—thus Jesus' itinerary meant that **he had to go through Samaria on the way.** Since the Samaritans were hated by the Jews, many of the strict Jews traveling from Judea to Galilee took a route around Samaria (through Perea, east of the Jordan River), even though that route took more time. But for those who were trying to make the best time, it was faster to go through Samaria to Galilee. The context does not indicate that Jesus was in a hurry to get to Galilee (see 4:40, 43). Thus, the necessity must be understood in a different way: Jesus went to Samaria to give the Samaritans what he had given to Nicodemus—the offer of eternal life by being born again. And, furthermore, by going to Samaria and bringing the gospel to the despised Samaritans, he showed that he was above the Jewish prejudices.

Where did these prejudices come from? Samaria was a region between Judea and Galilee where Jews of "mixed blood" lived. In Old Testament days, when the northern kingdom of Israel, with its capital at Samaria, fell to the Assyrians, many Jews were deported to Assyria. King Sargon of Assyria repopulated the northern kingdom with captives from other lands to settle the territory and keep the peace (2 Kings 17:24). These captives eventually intermarried with the few Jews who remained in the land to form a mixed race of people who became known as Samaritans. The Jews hated the Samaritans because they were no longer "pure" Jews. The Jews who lived in the southern Kingdom felt these Jews had betrayed their people and nation through intermarriage with foreigners. And the hatred continued down through the years. The Samaritans had adopted the Pentateuch as their Scriptures and set up a place for worship on Mount Gerizim using for their guidelines Deuteronomy 11:26-29; 27:1-8. Although they knew about a coming Messiah, they were far from having an accurate knowledge of the truth.

4:5-6 According to Genesis 33:19, **Jacob** purchased a piece of land in this vicinity and then later gave **Joseph** some land in Shechem (Genesis 48:22). Joshua 24:32 says that Joseph was buried on that land (the Jews had brought Joseph's bones with them when they made their Exodus from Egypt). **Jacob's well was there** indicates that the land must have included the parcel on which Jacob's well was dug. Thus, this well was highly valued by the Samaritans who claimed Jacob (also called Israel) as their father (4:12), just as the Jews do. The trip made Jesus **tired.** He had walked from Judea to **Sychar**— a trip that probably took two days. Jesus' weariness shows his true humanity. He waited while his disciples, more rested, or hungrier, than he, went to find food. He never seemed to worry that the limitations he took in becoming human might somehow undermine his claims to be the Son of God. Such expressions about Jesus' humanity help us identify with him. So he **sat wearily beside the well** at about **noontime,** the hottest part of the day.

4:7 Two facts are unusual about the woman's actions: (1) she could have gone to a closer well (scholars have identified wells that were closer to Sychar); (2) women generally drew water later in the day, when the temperature was cooler. This woman, whose reputation seems to have been well known in the small town (4:18), probably chose the well farther away from home and came to that well at an unusual hour in order to avoid contact with other women. It was also highly unusual for a man to address a woman, but Jesus said, **"Please give me a drink."** Again, this statement reveals Jesus' true humanity; he was really thirsty. Even though such a request startled her (4:9), it drew her into a conversation with Jesus.

4:8 This statement serves to inform the reader that Jesus was alone with this woman. Jesus could not ask his disciples to help him get water, for they had gone into Sychar to **buy food.** Thus, we see Jesus, weary from his journey, depending on others for food and drink.

4:9 The **Samaritan woman** was very surprised— first, that a **Jew** would even speak to a Samaritan; second, that a Jewish male would speak to a Samaritan woman (she also had a bad reputation and this was a public place); third, that a Jew would drink from a Samaritan's cup. The Jewish ceremonial laws described not only certain people as ceremonially unclean, but also anything they touched. In strict religious terms, many Jews of Jesus' time considered the Samaritans to be permanently unclean.

4:10 The woman was ignorant of **the gift God** had for her—the gift of life, represented by **living**

water—and she did not know the giver, Jesus the Messiah. Jesus makes an extraordinary offer to this woman—living water that would quench her thirst forever.

4:11-12 Jesus' remark concerning "living water" produced several practical questions in the mind of the Samaritan woman. Like Nicodemus, she did not immediately sense the depth of Jesus' words. Obviously, if this **living water** was at the bottom of the well, Jesus was in no position to offer it because he had no **rope** or **bucket** for drawing it. She began to wonder if Jesus had access to some source of water other than Jacob's well. She asked if he thought he was **greater than** their ancestor Jacob and could somehow **offer better water.** Perhaps the woman sensed in Jesus' words a possible dishonoring of the well provided by their great ancestor. Or perhaps the woman was beginning to have some inkling of who Jesus was claiming to be. He certainly accepted her in a way that must have challenged her thinking.

4:13-14 People need water daily because they **soon become thirsty again.** The water from Jacob's well would indeed satisfy the woman's thirst, but only temporarily. So also are all the other "drinks" of life—they never satisfy. Some of them even create more thirst. The human needs for love, food, sex, security, and approval, even when met, do not give complete satisfaction. Attempts to find full satisfaction will lead only to disappointment and despair. But the **water** Jesus offers **takes away thirst altogether.** Jesus' "water" continually satisfies the desire for God's presence because **it becomes a perpetual spring within them, giving them eternal life.** The gift that Jesus gives—this **perpetual spring**—suggests the availability, accessibility, and abundance of the divine life for believers.

4:15 The woman's response reveals that she took Jesus' words literally. The woman must have been thrilled to think that this man could give her water that really quenches thirst and would not have to be drawn from a well. Obtaining water was hard work—requiring trips to the well twice a day and carrying heavy jars full of water home. If she had **some of that water,** she would **never be thirsty again** and wouldn't have to **haul water** every day.

4:16-18 Jesus abruptly shifted the subject from his living water to her style of living. The woman perceived her need for living water at one level; Jesus knew that her need was far deeper, so he turned the conversation to reveal his knowledge

of her personal life—and her sin of adultery. By asking her to **go and get** her **husband,** Jesus wanted to make this woman see her sin and her need for forgiveness and then offer her the living water—salvation. She must have realized that this was not a man who could be fooled, for she answered transparently, **"I don't have a husband."** The woman spoke the truth without any explanation.

Although he confronted the woman's sinful life, Jesus managed to affirm her truthfulness. He did not accuse or excuse; he simply described her life so that she could draw some clear conclusions about the mess in which she was living. The conclusions we reach without knowing the facts will usually err in one of two directions: We will accuse others and raise their defenses, or we will excuse others and enable their denial. We see in Jesus' communication with this woman that when faced with an accepting confrontation, people will often respond positively. When we speak to others about themselves, we must limit our words to what we know.

4:19 The woman acknowledged the truthfulness of Jesus' remarks about her life. At the same time, she recognized that he must be a **prophet** who had the power to "see" the hidden past as well as the future. The theme of people "seeing" Jesus appears several times in John (especially in chapter 9). The persons Jesus encountered saw him many different ways, but he consistently directed their attention to recognize him for who he really was—their Savior.

Many commentators have pointed out that the woman may have been purposely attempting to avert any further disclosure of her personal, sinful life by shifting the conversation to religion. Notice how Jesus responded to her change of direction. He was not presenting a system or a gospel outline; he was having a conversation with someone who needed the living water. Jesus made no attempt to turn the discussion back to her lifestyle; rather, he entered into a dialogue about the true place of worship. Jesus kept the woman's interest by demonstrating his willingness to let her direct the discussion.

4:20 The unspoken question is, If you are a prophet, who's right? The Samaritans had set up a place for worship on **Mount Gerizim,** basing their authority to do so on Deuteronomy 11:26-29; 27:1-8; the Jews had followed David in making **Jerusalem** the center of Jewish worship. The split had come in the days of Ezra and Nehemiah (Ezra 4:1-2; Nehemiah 4:1-2) when the Samaritans had offered to help rebuild the Temple in

Jerusalem but had been rebuffed. So there was an ongoing debate between the two groups as to who was correct. The Scriptures authenticated Jerusalem as the place of worship (Deuteronomy 12:5; 2 Chronicles 6:6; 7:12; Psalm 78:67-68); thus, the Jews were correct and the Samaritans in error. The Samaritan woman wanted to hear what a Jewish prophet had to say about this.

4:21 Both the Jews and the Samaritans were convinced the correct way to worship God depended on a particular geographical location. But Jesus pointed to a new realm—not at Mount Gerizim or in Jerusalem, but in the Spirit of God. He also knew that the Temple in Jerusalem soon would be destroyed. The first readers of John would have known this as a historical fact because it would have already happened!

4:22 The **Samaritans** worshiped, but their system of worship was incomplete and flawed because it had no clear object. Because the Samaritans only used the Pentateuch (Genesis through Deuteronomy) as their Scriptures, they did not know what the rest of the Old Testament taught about worship. The **Jews,** with whom Jesus explicitly identified himself here, did know whom they worshiped, for they had the full revelation in the Old Testament Scriptures. These Scriptures revealed that **salvation comes through the Jews,** for the Messiah would come from the Jewish race (Genesis 12:3). The message is: "You are demonstrating a good quality in desiring to worship, but your worship is misdirected; the perfect object to be worshiped, the Messiah, has come." The living water that comes from Christ and is ever present in the believer makes the idea of continual worship a possibility. Worship becomes, at least in part, the enjoyment of our relationship with Christ wherever we are at any moment.

4:23-24 The new worship **is already here** among Jesus' followers (including both Jews and Samaritans who are united in Christ), although the end of worship in the Temple or on Mount Gerizim is still future—**is coming.** Jesus announced that a new time had come, a time in which **true worshipers will worship the Father in spirit and in truth.** True worshipers are to be recognized by the way they worship. After making the place of worship and order of worship secondary to our spiritual relationship with God, Jesus defined real worship. According to him, worship would take on two new aspects: It would be **in spirit** and **in truth** (see also 4:24).

The expression "in spirit" refers to the human spirit—the immaterial, inner being in each person, the God-breathed entity that corresponds to the nature of God himself, who is Spirit. Using the terms of Jesus' conversation, worship involves the person's awareness of that personal "spring of living water" that God has planted in him or her. God indwells believers—that is where true worship takes place. Our body can be anywhere, yet worship occurs as our attention and praise are turned toward God. We need to consciously focus on God when we are in a house of worship because we easily assume that our presence in church is all that we need in order to worship. We can usually remember how long the worship service lasted, but can we remember exactly when we actually worshiped the Lord?

The phrase **in truth** means "in a true way" or "with genuineness." This would speak to all people—Jews, Samaritans, and even Gentiles; all need to worship God by recognizing God's character and nature as well as our common need for him. We worship in truth because we worship what is true.

In the Greek text, the word **Spirit** comes first for emphasis: "Spirit is what God is." Here is a simple yet sublime definition of the nature of God. He is Spirit. God is not a physical being limited to place and time as we are. He is present everywhere, and he can be worshiped anywhere, anytime.

4:25 Talk of a new kind of worship must have reminded the Samaritan woman about the coming of the **Messiah.** Her comment was only loosely related to what Jesus had just said. She probably uttered it with a sigh, revealing her uncertainty about an unknown future. The Samaritans believed in the coming of "the Prophet" predicted by Moses (Deuteronomy 18:15-18), whom they called "the Restorer." The Samaritans may have also heard of the coming Messiah from John the Baptist who had been baptizing in northern Samaria (3:23). They, as with the Jews, probably did not consider "the Prophet" and "the Messiah" to be the same person. Either way, both groups were expecting someone who would be a political liberator. They could not accept the idea that the long-awaited one would be a suffering servant before he would become the conquering king.

The woman had already perceived that Jesus was a prophet (4:19); his comments made her wish for the coming Prophet who would **explain everything.**

4:26 Although Jesus avoided telling the Jews directly that he was the Christ, he told this Samaritan woman that he, the one who sat there with her on the well, was the promised **Messiah.**

JESUS TELLS ABOUT THE SPIRITUAL HARVEST / 4:27-38 / 28

The sudden arrival of the disciples interrupted the conversation. Jesus seems to have made no effort to continue the exchange. He had placed himself before the woman as the one she was expecting. What the woman would have said in response to Jesus' revelation is unknown. But what she did is clear. She immediately went and told her neighbors that she had just encountered a unique and wonderful person whom they should also meet.

4:27 The disciples returned from getting food (4:8) and were **astonished to find** Jesus **talking to a woman.** Jesus had broken two cultural taboos: (1) Jews did not speak with Samaritans, and (2) a male did not normally speak with a female stranger. Yet the disciples did not query him concerning his motives, for they must have come to realize that all of his motives were good. Anyone else would have been called to account.

4:28 Beyond displaying the woman's excited state of mind, her action of leaving **her water jar beside the well** as she **went back to the village** has several significant explanations: On the one hand, it speaks of the woman leaving behind her water jar representing her thirst for true life and satisfaction; on the other hand, it also reveals her intention to return. The water jar was a valuable and practical household object. But as useful as it was to get water from the well, it was useless for obtaining the water of life. However, she had just met someone who promised living water and who had displayed intimate knowledge of her life and profound understanding of spiritual truths. We can't be sure how much she understood of what Jesus had told her, but she was convinced that everyone in town ought to hear what he had to say.

4:29-30 In essence, the Samaritan woman was saying that Jesus *could have* told her everything about her life, for in telling her about her relationships with various men, he revealed his knowledge about her history. She made no promises about what Jesus might know about everyone else, but she appealed to their curiosity. What was it about this stranger that could make a woman who had every reason to be ashamed of her life now speak publicly about her experience of transparency before him? Yet she said to the townspeople, **"Can this be the Messiah?"** Her invitation proved irresistible. She probably knew that her reputation preceded her, and any assertion on her part regarding her belief in this man would go unheeded. But her question did serve to stir up curiosity and had the desired effect— **the people came streaming from the village to see him.**

4:31-33 After the woman left for the town, the disciples urged their master to eat. His response was baffling: **"I have food you don't know about."** The disciples thought he was talking about physical food; instead, Jesus was saying that he was spiritually satisfied by having shared the Good News with the Samaritan woman.

4:34 This statement shows that Jesus lived to please his Father and in so doing found spiritual **nourishment** (17:4). **Doing the will of God** meant that Jesus submitted himself to the Father's plan and enjoyed carrying out his Father's desires. Satisfying the Father gave Jesus true satisfaction. **Finishing** God's **work** speaks of completing the task—all the way from sowing the seed to reaping the harvest (see following verses). According to 17:4, Jesus accomplished all that the Father wanted him to do before leaving this earth. Preeminently, Jesus had revealed the Father to the world.

4:35 For farmers, approximately **four months** elapsed between the end of sowing and the beginning of reaping. From Jesus' spiritual perspective, the time for harvesting had already arrived. The Samaritans, who were coming from town, were ready to be harvested. In telling the disciples to **look around** and see the **vast fields,** Jesus may well have been directing them to look at the approaching Samaritans.

4:36-38 The **harvester** of this spiritual harvest derives satisfaction from bringing others to experience eternal life. This parallels Jesus' experience with the Samaritan woman; he was satisfied by offering her the gift of life. Jesus also here mentions the **planter** in addition to the **harvester.** Jesus, as both, sowed the seed through a single Samaritan woman and reaped a **harvest** from many in a Samaritan city. This sowing and reaping transpired so quickly that the planter and harvester could rejoice together.

The planter and the harvester do not have the same role—the point of the next verse: **"One person plants and someone else harvests."** This saying may have come from verses like Deuteronomy 20:6; 28:30; Micah 6:15; Job 31:8, but it is not a direct quotation of any known biblical passage.

That the disciples would **harvest where** they **didn't plant** probably refers to the coming harvest of Samaritan believers reaped by Jesus and his disciples, as well as to the harvest that would come

after Pentecost (see Acts 1:8; 2:41; 9:31; 15:3). The **others** who labored may have been some of the Old Testament prophets or, more likely, John the Baptist and his followers (see 3:23).

MANY SAMARITANS BELIEVE IN JESUS / 4:39-42 / 29

As a result of Jesus' conversation with the Samaritan woman, her bold witness in town, and the people's curiosity, many became believers. Jesus' proof was compelling. John was convinced and believed; the Samaritans were convinced and believed; so have millions of others. The unavoidable question each person must ask is, "Have I believed in Jesus?"

4:39-42 Many of the **Samaritans** who believed in Jesus were first drawn by the testimony of the **woman** about the mysterious man who told her everything she had ever done. **They begged** Jesus to **stay at their village,** and because of that, others believed when they heard Jesus for themselves.

Many Samaritans had come to know absolutely and positively that Jesus was **the Savior of the world.** This last statement is the climax of this passage (4:1-42), for it speaks of how Jesus had come to be, not just the Jews' Messiah, but the world's Savior as well.

JESUS PREACHES IN GALILEE / 4:43-45 / 30

After his wonderful experience in Samaria, Jesus went to Cana in Galilee, where he healed a government official's son. But along with the healing came Jesus' rebuke that the people's belief was based on seeing signs and wonders, not on trusting in Jesus himself. These events stand in contrast to Jesus' experience in Sychar (4:1-42), where without miracles and through an unexpected witness, many placed their trust in him.

4:43-44 According to verse 3, Jesus left Judea and headed for Galilee. He passed through Samaria on the way and stayed there for two days (4:40). So after those two days, **Jesus went on into Galilee,** called **his own country,** as he had been raised in Nazareth, a town in Galilee. Jesus went to the Galileans, knowing that they would welcome him as miracle-worker but not as a **prophet,** much less as the Messiah.

4:45 This statement that **the Galileans** had **seen all his miraculous signs** refers to 2:23, which says that the people assembling in Jerusalem (among whom were these Galileans) during the **Passover** believed in Jesus because of the signs they saw him perform.

JESUS HEALS A GOVERNMENT OFFICIAL'S SON / 4:46-54 / 31

The story of Jesus turning water into wine was still news in Cana when he returned. The local welcome was tinged with interest over what new wonders he might perform. The opportunity would soon come. A child in nearby Capernaum lay sick, and an anxious father came to Jesus, begging for help.

4:46-50 Jesus **arrived** in **Cana** where he had done a miracle (see 2:1-11). Jesus' name was known there, and so this **government official** went to find him. This man was very likely an official in Herod's court, serving in some capacity in **Capernaum,** about twenty miles from Cana. Although this miracle bears similarities with the one recorded in Matthew 8:5-13 and Luke 7:2-10 (both

deal with the healing of a soldier's servant), they seem to be different incidents. All the Gospel writers imply that the miracles they recorded were nothing more than samples of Jesus' work.

When the government official requested that Jesus **heal his son, who was about to die,** Jesus responded, **"Must I do miraculous signs and wonders before you people will believe in me?"**

Jesus took the opportunity to address all the Galileans (2:23; 4:45) and reprimand them for being sign-seekers. But this Galilean was not merely a sign-seeker. He had a need, and he truly believed Jesus could meet that need. As a result, his need was met. The man believed the word that Jesus spoke, **"Go back home. Your son will live!"** and started on his way. The official believed Jesus' word, and the healing was performed. He was the type of man whom Jesus would later call "blessed," for he had not seen and yet he believed (see 20:29). Jesus' word is a life-giving word (see 5:24-25; 6:68).

4:51-53 The details given in these verses tell the reader that the healing occurred at exactly the time Jesus spoke the words, **"Your son will live!"** Although the official's son was twenty miles away, he was healed when Jesus spoke the word. Distance was no problem because Christ has mastery over space. This miracle produced faith in **the officer and his entire household** (including family members or servants). There are cultures where the word or belief of the head of the household represents what each member of the house believes. New Testament evidence points to these kinds of responses in more than one case (Acts 10:2; 16:15, 33).

4:54 The first sign was changing the water into wine at the wedding in Cana (2:1-11). The **second miraculous sign** was healing a dying child. According to the Gospel of John, Jesus' miracles were "signs"—pointing the people who witnessed them to the one who performed the signs, Jesus, the Messiah, the Son of God. If the miracle produced faith in Jesus only as a miracle worker and not as the Son of God, then the people missed the miracle as the sign it was intended to be.

JOHN 5

JESUS HEALS A LAME MAN BY A POOL / 5:1-15 / 42

God gives salvation freely through Jesus Christ. But to receive salvation, a person must **believe**. The lame man by the pool at Bethesda had to want to be healed. Then Jesus approached him later to explain to him that he needed to believe and receive spiritual healing as well. God makes the offer and God performs the miracle, but we must respond to his offer and accept it.

5:1 All Jewish males were required to come to Jerusalem to attend three feasts: (1) the Festival of Passover and Unleavened Bread, (2) the Festival of Weeks (also called Pentecost), and (3) the Festival of Shelters. Though this particular holy day is not specified, the phrase explains why Jesus was in **Jerusalem.**

5:2-4 Readers familiar with Jerusalem would have known about the **Sheep Gate** (it is mentioned in Nehemiah 3:1, 32; 12:39). Recent excavations show that this site had two pools with **five covered porches.** These were open structures with roofs that allowed some protection from the weather. A multitude of sick people lay on the porches. People made pilgrimages to the **pool of Bethesda** to receive the healing benefit of the waters.

Verse 4 is not included in the best manuscripts. Where it does occur in later manuscripts, it is often marked in such a way as to show that it is an addition. The passage was probably inserted later by scribes who felt it necessary to provide an explanation for the gathering of disabled people and the stirring of the water mentioned in verse 7. The water would stir and it was believed that an angel disturbed it. The superstition was that the first person into the pool after the water stirred would be healed.

5:5-8 A man lay there who **had been sick for thirty-eight years.** Jesus **knew how long he had been ill** and asked him, **"Would you like to get well?"** Jesus' question shows us that he will not force himself upon anyone. He seeks permission before intervening in that person's life. The man indirectly answered Jesus by telling how he had not been able to be healed because others would get into the water before he did. But in making this statement, the man admitted that he needed help. His hope for healing was stuck behind his hopelessness of ever having help to get to the water in time.

Jesus offered help, but not the kind of help the man expected. Jesus simply said, **"Stand up, pick up your sleeping mat, and walk."** And the man responded immediately.

5:9 This miracle should have revealed to the Jews in Jerusalem that the Messiah was finally present, for Isaiah had prophesied this (Isaiah 35:5-6). Instead, they chose to focus on another issue: **This miracle happened on the Sabbath day.** Presumably, if the waters had been stirred on the Sabbath and he had been healed by getting in, the Jews would not have argued against his healing. But these religious leaders would not allow God in the flesh to break their rules by healing this man directly.

5:10 There is nothing in God's law making it **illegal to carry** a **sleeping mat** on the Sabbath. But the man broke the Pharisees' legalistic application of God's command to honor the Sabbath. The regulation against carrying something on the Sabbath was the last of thirty-nine rules in the "tradition of the elders" that stipulated the kinds of work prohibited on the Sabbath. This was just one of hundreds of rules the Jewish leaders had added to the Old Testament law.

5:11-13 In this exchange between the man who was healed and the Jewish leaders in Jerusalem, the man said he **didn't know** who had **healed** him. The man's ignorance is quite possible, for Jesus had not identified himself and had immediately **disappeared into the crowd.** At the same time, however, the healed man seemed to be more eager to blame the healer for having him walk around with his mat than to shout about his healing.

5:14-15 Perhaps the man had gone to the **Temple** to give thanks to God for his healing. When Jesus found him, he told him, **"Stop sinning, or something even worse may happen to you."** This statement leads to the conclusion that the man's sickness was in some way caused by sin. This does not contradict what Jesus said in 9:3 about the man born blind because Jesus did not say the blind man never sinned; rather, he was pointing out that sin had not caused his blindness. One of the results of sin is suffering, but not all suffering is the result of personal sin.

In this case, Jesus sought out the healed man to warn him that though he was healed physically, his thirty-eight years as an invalid would be nothing compared to something worse—that is, eternity in hell. The man needed to stop sinning and come to salvation in Christ. He had been lame, but now he could walk. This was a great miracle. But he needed an even greater miracle—to have his sins forgiven. The man was delighted to be physically healed, but he had to turn from his sins and seek God's forgiveness to be spiritually healed.

After this encounter, the man told the Jewish leaders what he could not tell them before: **It was Jesus who had healed him.** This report triggered the Jews' persecution of Jesus—a persecution that continued from that day onward.

JESUS CLAIMS TO BE THE SON OF GOD / 5:16-30 / 43

The Jewish leaders were faced with a mighty miracle of healing and a broken rule. They threw the miracle aside as they focused their attention on the broken rule. As is common with those who assume authority that is not rightfully theirs, these leaders instinctively felt their power threatened by Jesus' actions, thus they resented him.

5:16-17 Jesus was being harassed **for breaking Sabbath rules.** But Jesus told these leaders, **"My Father never stops working, so why should I?"** With this statement Jesus challenged the notion that God himself was somehow literally subject to the Sabbath rules. If God stopped every kind of work on the Sabbath, nature would fall into chaos and sin would overrun the world. Genesis 2:2 says that God rested on the seventh day; he rested from the work of creation but began the work of sustaining the creation. God has been at work and continues to work; so does his Son, Jesus. With this claim, Jesus affirmed his equality with God. Furthermore, Jesus was teaching that when the opportunity to do good presents itself, it should not be ignored, even on the Sabbath.

5:18 The Jews realized that Jesus' words revealed his very personal relationship with God. In saying, "my Father," he was clearly claiming to be God's Son, thus **equal with God.** For a human to claim equality with God was blasphemy; and blasphemy was a sin carrying the death penalty (Leviticus 24:15-16). People regularly misunderstood Jesus, and he was constantly correcting them. Jesus never attempted to correct the understanding that he was claiming to be God, for that was exactly what he meant. Thus the Jewish leaders **tried all the more to kill him.**

5:19-20 Jesus did not say that he **would not** do anything independent from the Father, but that he **cannot:** **"The Son can do nothing by himself. He does only what he sees the Father doing."** The Son performs the tasks the Father wants done because they are of one spirit. The Father and the Son know and love each other completely. Because of their transparent relationship, the Son always knows what the Father is doing and works in harmony with him to see it accomplished. Because of his unity with God, Jesus lived as God wanted him to live. Jesus promised to **do far greater things.** According to the following verses, this refers to the Son's ability to give life to the dead and to execute judgment.

5:21 This statement would have shocked Jesus' audience because it ascribes to the Son—Jesus himself—what was seen as exclusively the activity of God the Father. God alone can **raise from the dead anyone he wants to.** That God gave that power to the Son is demonstrated in Jesus' raising of Lazarus from the dead (see 11:41-44).

5:22-23 The certainty of our salvation is in the hands of the Son because God entrusted him with judicial and executive authority to judge. Thus, he has equal dignity and honor with the Father— **"everyone will honor the Son, just as they honor the Father."** The flip side is that those who **refuse to honor the Son** are not **honoring the Father who sent him.** Here Jesus was referring to that time when everyone will recognize his lordship. The tragedy will be that many will then recognize Jesus' true nature but will have lost the opportunity to receive his saving help. Those unwilling to honor Christ now will discover that they have not been honoring the Father either. People should not say they believe in God while ignoring the power and authority of his Son.

5:24 True hearing results in believing. The gospel usually stresses believing in Jesus himself; but Jesus points to believing **in God who sent** him. The statement affirms the unity of the Father and the Son. To believe in the Father is to believe in the Son he sent to earth. This belief gives **eternal life.** Believers have eternal life as a present possession. Because of that, **they will never be condemned for their sins, but they have already passed from death into life.** The judgment has passed. Belief in Jesus provides the only escape from this judgment.

5:25 When Jesus spoke of a **time** that **is coming,** and **is here,** he saw God's wonderful future plan as happening in the present. Christ makes the same power that will resurrect the dead at his return available to all who are spiritually dead—the woman at the well, the paralyzed man, and each one of us.

In the future, the physically **dead** will hear the voice of the Son of God. Jesus was speaking about two kinds of life-giving power. On one level, he was speaking of the power to give life as we know it; on the other, he was speaking of the power to give life

as he knows it. In saying that the dead could **hear** his **voice,** he was referring to the power to return physical life to those who had died. In fact, Jesus raised several persons who had died while he was on earth (11:38-44), though at some point they would die again. But he was also referring to the spiritually dead who hear, understand, and accept him. Those who accept God's Word **will live,** even though they may still experience physical death (11:25-26).

5:26 Human beings do not have life in themselves; they receive it from God. God does not receive his life from any exterior source; he is the source and Creator of life. In eternity past, the Father gave his Son the same capacity—**to have life in himself** (see 1:4). God does not share this uniquely divine characteristic with any created being. Because Jesus exists eternally with God the Father, he too is "the life" (14:6) through whom we may live eternally (1 John 5:11). God's gift of life comes through Christ alone (Deuteronomy 30:20; Psalm 36:9).

5:27 This statement seems to contradict 3:17, where Jesus is said not to have come into the world to judge it, but 8:15-16 offers an explanation. Jesus did not come to judge, but his coming led to judgment because his coming forced decision—and decision results in judgment for those who reject Jesus. **Because he is the Son of Man,** Jesus, as man, will **judge all mankind** (see Daniel 7:13-14). In this way, the Father has given all **authority** to the Son, for everyone must answer to him (see Philippians 2:5-11). Jesus always kept before his audience, in word and deed, his unique dual nature as God-man.

5:28-29 Verse 28 speaks only about a future event— **the time is coming when all the dead in their graves will hear the voice of God's Son, and they will rise again.** Every person will be resurrected when the Lord returns, with one of two results: one will be **life,** the other will be **judgment.** God grants eternal life to those who have come to the Light and have believed in Jesus Christ. But God will judge and condemn those who rebelled against Christ by refusing to come to the Light. God's judgment has already come upon them and will be completely executed by the Son of Man after the resurrection (see 3:18-21).

5:30 Even though the Father committed to the Son the task of executing judgment, the Son cannot and will not perform on his own authority and by his own initiative. The distinctions within the persons of the Trinity allow each to perform certain specific functions, but the divine unity of God means that Father, Son, and Holy Spirit each do what the others would do if the roles were changed.

JESUS SUPPORTS HIS CLAIM / 5:31-47 / 44

Jesus claimed to be equal with God (5:18), to give eternal life (5:24), to be the source of life (5:26), and to judge sin (5:27). These statements make it clear that Jesus claimed to be divine—an almost unbelievable claim. So he called upon several witnesses to his divine being: (1) John the Baptist (5:33-35), (2) Jesus' works (5:36), (3) the Father himself (5:37), (4) the Scriptures (5:39-40), and (5) Moses (5:45-47). Any of these witnesses should have been enough, but together they supplied a compelling testimony to Jesus' claims. But many of the ones listening to Jesus were examples of how a hard heart can nullify even the most powerful argument.

5:31-32 According to the Jewish law, truth or validity had to be established by two or three witnesses (Deuteronomy 17:6; 19:15). Therefore, Jesus' **testimony would not be valid** by itself. For these Jewish leaders, he needed the witness of another. So Jesus said that **someone else** was **testifying about** him, referring to his Father (see 5:36).

5:33-35 Further witness came from **John the Baptist** (see 1:6-8). His testimony that Jesus was the Christ was necessary for the Jews, not Jesus. They all knew **he preached the truth.** He **shone brightly for a while,** and some of the Jews enjoyed the light he brought them. But they did not really understand his message or receive the illuminating revelation concerning the one to whom John gave witness—Jesus, the Son of God.

5:36-38 The **teachings** and **miracles** testified **that the Father** had sent Jesus. The Father **testified about** his Son at Jesus' baptism (Matthew 3:16-17), on the Mount of Transfiguration (Matthew 17:5), before his crucifixion (12:28), and in his resurrection (Romans 1:3-4). The Jews to whom Jesus was speaking had **never heard** God's **voice or seen him face to face.** Yet, here they had the greatest of all God's manifestations standing right before their eyes—Jesus, the Word, the visible expression of God to people. But they did not **have his message in** their **hearts** because they were refusing to **believe** in Jesus. Even though the Jews to whom Jesus was speaking had not received the kinds of revelations some of their ancestors had, they still possessed the Word of God. If that Word had been abiding in their hearts (see 8:31; 15:7), they would have recognized the one to whom the Scriptures give testimony.

5:39 The Jewish teachers devoted their lives to studying **the Scriptures**—not so much to search for the truth but to analyze the minutia of the law. And the "scholars" studied, Jesus said, because they thought that by doing so they would possess **eternal life.** But by studying the Scriptures they should have seen the source of life: **"The Scrip-**

tures point to me!" If we fail to see this testimony, we miss the very purpose for which the Scriptures exist. If there were no such person as Jesus Christ, the Scriptures would have little value. The Bible's chief value lies in its testimony to him.

5:40 To **refuse to come** to Jesus is to reject **life** because Christ is the giver of eternal life (1:4; 5:25; 14:6). Religious zeal—even involvement with the Scriptures—does not bring a person eternal life. The religious leaders knew what the Bible said but failed to apply its words to their lives. They knew the teachings of the Scriptures but failed to see the Messiah to whom the Scriptures pointed. They knew the rules but missed the Savior. Entrenched in their own religious system, they refused to let the Son of God change their lives.

5:41-43 Just as Jesus did not receive (or need) the testimony from people (5:34), he does not need to receive **approval** from them. Jesus knew the condition of the people; they did not really **have God's love within** them—they loved their religion. Therefore, they could not receive the Son of God. Jesus came as the Father's personal representative (see 14:7-11), but many of the Jews could not accept his claims of being the one sent by the Father. The **others** that were accepted may have been other persons who claimed to be the Messiah. Because they fit the mistaken image of what the Messiah was supposed to accomplish (political liberation), people eagerly received them. Many men made such a claim. For example, in A.D. 132 Simeon ben Kosebah claimed to be the Messiah, and his claim was upheld by Akibah, the most eminent rabbi of the day.

5:44 This condemning word exposes why the Jewish religious leaders could not **believe:** They were so dependent on group acceptance that an individual could hardly make a stand that differed from the rest. Instead of seeking what would honor God and bring glory to him—which, in this case, would be to believe in his Son—they continued to seek acceptance from their peers.

5:45 The verb tenses here reveal that Jesus wouldn't have to go to the Father and accuse these religious leaders because they were already being accused by **Moses.** This could mean that Moses was in the presence of God in heaven accusing them (Matthew 17:3), or it could mean what Moses wrote, as is indicated in the next two verses. To be told that Moses was accusing them was a great blow. The Pharisees prided themselves on being the true followers of their ancestor Moses. They followed every one of his laws to the letter and even added some of their own. Jesus' warning that Moses was accusing them stung them to fury.

5:46-47 Moses had written about Christ (see Genesis 3:15; Numbers 21:9; 24:17; Deuteronomy 18:15-18; see also Luke 24:44), but since they did not believe in Christ when he came, they did not really **believe** in the writings of Moses. This was Jesus' final condemnation in this section.

JOHN 6

JESUS FEEDS 5,000 / 6:1-15 / 96

Once again in this Gospel, John selects a particular place for presenting a spiritual truth about Christ. Earlier, the well in Samaria was an excellent setting for Christ to teach about the fountain of living water. Here, in chapter 6, the multiplication of the loaves provides a way for Christ to present himself as the Bread of Life.

6:1 Jesus **crossed over the Sea of Galilee,** a great body of water (which is actually a lake, thirteen miles by seven miles) given the name **the Sea of Tiberias** by Herod Antipas in honor of the Roman emperor Tiberias in A.D. 20.

6:2-4 Jesus was popular, and **a huge crowd kept following him,** mainly because of his **miracles as he healed the sick.** Presumably to continue teaching, **Jesus went up into the hills** (the Sea of Galilee is surrounded by hills) **and sat down with his disciples.** John mentions three **Passover** celebrations in this Gospel: the first in 2:13 (when Jesus was in Jerusalem), the second here (when Jesus remained in Galilee), and the third in 12:12 (when Jesus went to Jerusalem and was crucified shortly thereafter).

6:5-6 The crowds followed Jesus right up into the hills. As Jesus saw them, he asked **Philip** where they should **buy bread to feed all these people.** If anyone knew where to get food, Philip would because he was from Bethsaida, a town about nine miles away (1:44). Jesus was testing Philip to strengthen his faith. By asking for a human solution (knowing that there was none), Jesus highlighted the powerful and miraculous act that he was about to perform.

John clues us in: Jesus **was testing Philip, for he already knew what he was going to do.** In usual use, the word "test" (*peirazo*) has a neutral meaning. It refers to a proving experience like Jesus' testing in the wilderness or Abraham's test over the sacrifice of Isaac. In all these cases, God allowed the test to occur, not expecting failure, but placing the person in a situation where his or her faith might grow stronger. Jesus did not want Philip to miss what he was about to do.

6:7-9 Philip realized that with the number of people climbing in their direction, **it would take a small fortune to feed them.** But, in fact, Philip did not really answer Jesus' question. The Lord had asked him to consider where they could get food; Philip responded with what he perceived as the larger problem—the money it would take to supply the food.

At this point, **Andrew** (who is usually presented in the Gospels as **Simon Peter's brother** and takes a subordinate position to him) took advantage of an opportunity to join the discussion. Apparently a **young boy** who had overheard the conversation pulled out his lunch and made it available. It was Andrew who inadvertently answered Jesus' original question. He pointed out that the only available food was the boy's lunch: **five barley loaves and two fish.** (Barley loaves and fish were food for the poor.) Then Andrew added the disclaimer: **"But what good is that with this huge crowd?"** Whether Andrew was speaking in humor or hyperbole we can't be sure, but we can be fairly certain that he did not expect what followed.

6:10-13 What was offered was enough for Jesus. He told the disciples to have **everyone sit down.** The **men** (the Greek word means "male individuals") **numbered five thousand.** So with women and children, there were many more. **Then Jesus took the loaves, gave thanks,** and **passed them out to the people.** The **fish** were also distributed in like manner. After all had eaten and were **full,** they still had **leftovers;** the disciples filled **twelve baskets** with the pieces of the five barley loaves left over. This miracle and these leftovers reveal Jesus once again as the all-sufficient Lord. Our needs and problems are not obstacles to him, for his abundant power transcends any need or problem we place before him.

6:14 The people saw and filled their stomachs as a result of this sign—who could have missed it?—and this led them to believe that Jesus was **the Prophet** whom Moses had predicted (Deuteronomy 18:15-18). John does not say the people were wrong to think of Jesus as "the Prophet," but the next verse shows that they thought this Prophet should be a political leader. In this they were wrong.

Elisha foreshadowed this Prophet (who was one in the same as the Messiah) to come. According to 2 Kings 4:42-44, Elisha fed one hundred men with twenty loaves (a 5:1 ratio). But Jesus fed five thousand with five loaves (a 1000:1 ratio)! In Isaiah 25:6-9, the prophet said that the Messiah would prepare a great feast for all people, Jews and Gentiles. This miracle shows Jesus to be the Messiah.

6:15 During Jesus' ministry, nationalistic fervor was high; the people wanted a **king,** a leader who would free Israel from Rome. The people expected this of the coming Messiah-King. When Jesus realized their intentions, he left. Jesus' Kingdom would not be an earthly one; his Kingdom would not be established by a groundswell of popularity. This same opportunity for political power had already been offered to Jesus by Satan in the wilderness (Matthew 4:1-11). Jesus knew that the immediate opportunity was nothing compared to what God had planned (see Daniel 7:13-14).

JESUS WALKS ON WATER / 6:16-21 / 97

Of the three Gospel accounts of this miracle, John's includes the fewest details. He understates the action, and apart from a brief mention of the disciples' fright, he makes little emphasis on this event. Matthew described Peter's walk on (then in) the water. Mark mentioned the difficulties being created by the wind and waves as well as the fact that when the disciples saw Jesus, he was passing by them. The focus of Matthew and Mark highlighted the miracle and its effects on those who participated in it; John included the miracle as yet another indication of the true identity of Jesus.

6:16-18 Jesus had gone up to a mountainside to be alone (6:15). The disciples **went down to the shore to wait for him.** Though it was late in the day, many of the disciples were experienced boatmen who would have felt comfortable sailing at night as well as in daylight. Jesus had called Peter to follow him after Peter and his partners had been out all night fishing (Luke 5:1-11). As it got dark and **Jesus still hadn't come back,** the disciples decided to head out **across the lake toward Capernaum.** This lake, the Sea of Galilee (or Sea of Tiberias, see 6:1), is very large. It is 650 feet below sea level, 150 feet deep, and surrounded by hills. These physical features make it subject to sudden windstorms that cause extremely high waves. Sailors expected such storms on this lake, but the storms could still be very frightening. Such a sudden storm arose as **a gale swept down upon them.**

The Sea of Galilee is about seven miles across at its widest point, and the disciples were rowing the boat through **rough** waters that the wind had stirred up at the north end. They had recently encountered a bad storm in similar circumstances, except that at that time Jesus was in the boat with them (Mark 4:35-41). This time they noticed his absence.

6:19-21 They had gone **three or four miles.** According to Mark 6:45, it had taken the disciples all evening to row this short distance—evidently because the headwind was so strong. Suddenly, **they saw Jesus walking on the water toward the boat.** Not only was Jesus walking on the water, he had walked a great distance over raging seas! Understandably, the disciples were **terrified,** but Jesus called over the wailing wind, **"I am here! Don't be afraid."** The disciples thought they were seeing a ghost (Mark 6:49).

JESUS IS THE TRUE BREAD FROM HEAVEN / 6:22-40 / 99

To understand the action in these verses, we must back up and trace the movements of all the characters. Jesus performed the miracle of feeding the five thousand somewhere on the eastern shore of the Sea of Galilee (6:1). That evening, his disciples boarded a boat headed west toward Capernaum (6:17) without Jesus, who had gone up into a mountain to be alone (6:15). Then Jesus came to the disciples during the storm (6:21). So Jesus and the disciples arrived together at Capernaum (presumably before dawn). On the opposite shore, the crowd that had seen the disciples leave knew that Jesus hadn't gone with them and that the disciples had taken the only boat. The next morning they discovered that Jesus was gone, but they knew that he had not gone with the disciples. They assumed that he must have left to join his disciples.

6:22-25 At some point during the day, several boats arrived from **Tiberias.** Though it is not stated, the implication is that the **crowds** may have heard of Jesus' whereabouts from someone on the boats. So people from the crowd used those boats, which were probably going to head back across the sea toward Tiberias anyway, to cross to **Capernaum** to search for Jesus.

6:26-27 The crowd, being satisfied once by what Jesus had done for them, wanted to see what else Jesus could do for them (maybe he'd provide more free meals?). But they did not realize what the miracle actually revealed to them. Jesus refused to encourage them in their desire for the material satisfaction he could provide. His beginning response in effect was, "You were so intent on being **fed** that you haven't yet seen who provided the food." The people may not have known it, but their needs went much deeper. Jesus' signs were given to reveal that he could meet those deeper needs.

Thus, Jesus told them: **"Spend your energy seeking the eternal life that I, the Son of Man, can give you."** The bread that fills the stomach, whether produced by a miraculous sign or made at the bakery, is not spiritual or eternal. Jesus was saying that the people should not be following him because he provided free bread, but because he provides spiritual "bread"—bread that can give them eternal life. He wanted the people to look to him as the one who could provide the food that endures to eternal life. He himself is that food. By coming to him and receiving him by faith they would partake of the Bread of Life. That is why **God the Father** sent him.

6:28-29 The crowd missed Jesus' words about how he would **give** the food that lasts for eternal life. So they asked, **"What does God want us to do?"** Jesus gave a straightforward answer: **"This is what God wants you to do: Believe in the one he has sent."** The only "work" God requires from us is to believe

in his Son. But for some reason, we feel better somehow "earning" God's favor rather than accepting it as a gift. Eternal life is a gift; it cannot be earned; the only work to be done is to believe in Jesus.

6:30-31 Amazingly, the crowd then asked Jesus to do a **miraculous sign** if he wanted them to **believe in** him. The crowd had just seen the miracle of the multiplication of the loaves, but they wanted more—not just one day's supply of bread, but a guarantee of continuous supply. Their argument was that their **ancestors ate manna** in the **wilderness**—which, of course, was available every day for nearly forty years. And they cited their **Scriptures,** quoting from such verses as Exodus 16:4 and Psalm 78:24-25. A Midrash (Jewish commentary) on Exodus 16:4 says that just as the former redeemer (Moses) caused manna to descend from heaven, so also the latter Redeemer will cause manna to descend. They expected this from Jesus if he was the Messiah.

6:32-33 Moses hadn't performed the miracle, the Father had. And the God who gave the manna to the Israelites for forty years now gives the **true bread from heaven**—Jesus. Just as the Israelites ate manna every day, so God provides **the true bread of God** for daily sustenance. God had given them his Son—**the one who comes down from heaven and gives life to the world**—as the true heavenly bread to meet their daily spiritual needs. The present tense indicates the continual supply.

6:34-35 The Jews did not grasp that Jesus spoke about himself as the Bread of Life; they wanted a daily supply of physical bread, saying, **"Give us that bread every day of our lives."** Like the woman at the well who asked Jesus to give her the living water so she wouldn't be thirsty again, this crowd wanted what Jesus could give so their lives could be made easier. They missed the point. So Jesus told them directly, **"I am the bread of life."** If people wanted this bread, they must come to

Jesus and believe in him. When Jesus used the words "I am," he was pointing to his unique, divine identity. In essence this statement says, "I the Lord God am here to provide you with everything you need for your spiritual life." For Jesus to say he is the Bread of Life is for him to say, "I am the sustenance of your life." Just as bread supplies our bodies with strength and nourishment, Jesus, the true Bread from Heaven, had come to strengthen and nourish his people, so that they would never **be hungry again** and **never thirst.**

6:36 According to some manuscripts, the reading is: **"You have seen me."** This emphasizes that the crowds had **seen Jesus,** the very Bread of Life, standing before them, and yet they had not **believed** in him. Other manuscripts read, "You have seen and still you do not believe." This emphasizes that the crowds had seen the miracles Jesus did and still they did not believe. They had not only seen but eaten the multiplied bread and fish, but they resisted the necessary conclusion that he was divine.

6:37 In the Greek, the word **those** is neuter singular, indicating the total body of believers for all time. The Father gives this collective group to the Son (see also 17:2, 24). Only those selected by God can come to the Son and believe in him. God's Spirit enables them to come. All those who have been invited to come to Jesus and have done so can rest assured that God was at work in their lives.

While the first part of this verse speaks of the collective group of believers, this second part speaks about the individual: **"I will never reject**

them." God's word assures us that Jesus will always welcome the sincere seeker, and the seeker who comes to believe will never be rejected (10:28-29).

6:38 Jesus did not work independently of God the Father, but in union with him: he came **to do the will of God.** This should give us even more assurance of being welcomed into God's presence and being protected by him. All who respond positively to God's call can be assured of his protection (see 17:11). The protection covers them in this life and for eternity. Our spiritual hunger and thirst are satisfied in this life, and we know in the future that we will be raised from the dead to live with Jesus forever. Yet the guarantee does not apply to superficial attachment. We must follow him wholeheartedly and commit our lives to him.

6:39-40 As in verse 37, the Greek word for **all those** is neuter singular; they indicate the total collective entity of all believers. All those who are among this group of believers can be assured of God's promise of eternal life. Christ will not let his people be overcome by Satan. They will not be lost, and he will **raise them to eternal life at the last day.** However, this commitment must not be superficial, as was the "commitment" of those disciples who turned away (see 6:66). But those who **believe** will **have eternal life.** God values each person. Jesus demonstrated how valuable we are by his teaching: God sent the Son to earth; the Son came to earth; the Son promised to both preserve and to resurrect the ones he received from the Father.

THE PEOPLE DISAGREE THAT JESUS IS FROM HEAVEN / 6:41-59 / 100
Many of the crowd in Capernaum that day could not believe their ears. They knew this man's family, yet he claimed to be the Son of God. To them, Jesus' delusion seemed obvious. In their minds, Jesus was a local product with interesting powers and unusual authority, but was audacious when it came to speaking about himself. Jesus responded with uncompromising directness. He required then, as he requires now, an unconditional acceptance of his lordship. Any attempt to soften his claim amounts to rejection of his central message.

6:41-43 The **people** had some **disagreement** with Jesus. They knew **his father and mother,** so how could he say he **came down from heaven?** What they concluded was logical, but they really didn't know Jesus' parentage. Jesus had moved from Nazareth to Capernaum at the beginning of his ministry (see Matthew 4:13; Mark 1:21; John 2:12). Most likely, his parents and siblings had gone with him. The Jews in Capernaum knew Jesus' parents, and therefore they thought they

knew who Jesus was—the son of Joseph. But Jesus told the people to stop grumbling and complaining about what he had said. Not one of them could know his true identity if the Father had not revealed it to him. Jesus relied on this revelation.

6:44-46 A person cannot come to Jesus if he has not been drawn by the **Father,** taught by the Father, heard from the Father, and learned from the Father. God, not the person, plays the most active role in salvation. When someone chooses to believe in Jesus Christ as Savior, he or she does so only in response to the urging of God's Holy Spirit. Thus no one can believe in Jesus without God's help.

When Jesus quoted from the prophets saying, **"They will all be taught by God,"** he was alluding to an Old Testament view of the messianic Kingdom where all people would be taught directly by God (Isaiah 54:13; Jeremiah 31:31-34). He was stressing the importance of not merely hearing, but learning. We are taught by God through the Bible, our experiences, the thoughts the Holy Spirit brings, and relationships with other Christians. Are you open to God's teaching?

Jesus' previous statement about people being taught by God (and listening to and learning from the Father) does not mean that any person could actually see God the Father. **Only** Jesus has come from God's presence, and only he has seen the Father. This last statement in itself implies divine privileges—for no man has ever seen God (see 1:18; 1 Timothy 6:15-16).

6:47 Jesus makes it plain that the believer **has eternal life,** starting now. The verb **"believes"** in these verses means "continues to believe." We do not believe merely once; we keep on believing in and trusting Jesus.

6:48-50 Jesus then declared again (6:35), **"Yes, I am the bread of life!"** This is one of Jesus' remarkable "I am" declarations recorded in John's Gospel. No one but Jesus is the Bread that gives eternal life. The people earlier had spoken of the manna their ancestors ate in the wilderness (6:31), using that event as a standard for measuring Jesus. Jesus refused their challenge. **Manna** was a physical and temporal bread. The people ate it and were sustained for a day. But they had to get more bread every day, and this bread could not keep them from dying.

Without demeaning Moses' role, Jesus was presenting himself as the spiritual Bread from Heaven that satisfies completely and leads to **eternal life.** Again, the personal effectiveness of this Bread comes not from seeing it or from recognizing its heavenly origin, but from taking it in—eating it.

6:51 To offer his **flesh** meant Jesus gave over his body to death on the cross, so that by his death

people could **live forever.** To eat the living **bread** means to accept Christ into our lives and become united with him. We are united with Christ in two ways: (1) by believing in his death (the sacrifice of his flesh) and resurrection and (2) by devoting ourselves each day to living as he requires, depending on his teaching for guidance, and trusting in the Holy Spirit for power. Just as the Jews depended on bread for daily strength and relished it as a main part of their diet, so we should depend on and desire the living Christ in our daily lives.

6:52-53 Instead of directly answering their question about how he could give them his **flesh to eat,** Jesus reemphasized the necessity of eating his flesh and also drinking **his blood.** No one could receive his life until the giver died by shedding his own life's blood. Thus, Jesus wants us to accept, receive, even assimilate the significance of his death in order to receive **eternal life.** Christians do this frequently when they commemorate the Lord's Supper. But Christians should not limit this to only the celebration of the Lord's Supper (or Eucharist); Christians can partake of Jesus anytime.

6:54-55 Those who **eat** Jesus' **flesh** and **drink** his **blood have eternal life.** Those who accept by faith Jesus' sacrificial death receive **eternal life.**

6:56 This is the first mention in this Gospel of "mutual indwelling" (that is, a simultaneous indwelling of two persons in each other, also known as "coinherence"). When we receive Jesus, we **remain** in him and he remains in us.

6:57 Here Jesus pointed to his relationship with the Father as a model of the vital union he would share with each believer. Jesus said that he lives **by the power of the living Father who sent** him, so **those who partake of** Jesus **will live because of** Jesus.

6:58-59 This verse summarizes the discourse and repeats the major points of Jesus' message. He again contrasted himself as the **true bread from heaven** that gives life with the **manna** that could not give eternal life to those Israelites who ate it. Jesus gave this **teaching in the synagogue in Capernaum** to the Jews gathered there for worship.

MANY DISCIPLES DESERT JESUS / 6:60-71 / *101*

Those listening to Jesus were experiencing a crisis in their determination to follow him. Many of his actions thus far had been attractive, though sometimes curious. But all this talk of consuming his body and blood was difficult to stomach. Jesus' claims forced his followers to examine their real motives and the depth of their commitment.

6:60 At this time in Jesus' ministry, he had several followers who could loosely be called **his disciples** (see 4:1). These "disciples" were not the Twelve, and many of them would not receive his message. They pointed out that it was **hard to understand.** The motive behind Jesus' harsh words is not difficult to see—he wanted people to count the cost of following him (Luke 14:25-33). His words shocked and challenged. They were not comfortable half-truths, but hard-edged truth. Those who follow Jesus in hopes of feeling good will always be disappointed sooner or later. Only those who find in Jesus the rock-solid truth will be able to weather the difficulties of living in this fallen world

6:61 Jesus, knowing that his listeners were **complaining,** asked, **"Does this offend you?"** or more literally, "Does this cause you to stumble?" (The Greek word *skandalizo* means "to ensnare, to trap, to cause to stumble"; it is often used to indicate a falling away into unbelief. See, for example, Matthew 13:21; 24:10; Mark 6:3; Romans 14:20-21.) Jesus was keenly aware that those not ready to respond fully to him would stumble over him or be offended by him. Remember that it is possible to be offensive in the way we communicate the gospel, for which we would be at fault. But if we present Jesus lovingly and honestly, we must neither be shocked nor feel guilty if the Good News offends someone.

6:62 They didn't believe that Jesus came down from heaven. If they saw him **return to heaven,** would they then believe? According to verse 65, they would not, for they were not true believers. Jesus had been purposely harsh so as to separate the true believers from those who were accompanying him for the wrong reasons. Some sought a new political party; others thought Jesus might lead a revolt against Rome; still others were simply fascinated with theological discussions. All of these thoughts were potential starting points of interest in Jesus, but they were not enough to make people real disciples.

6:63 This statement gives us the key to interpreting Jesus' discourse. His hearers had not understood the spiritual intent of his message. A fleshly interpretation of his words would yield nothing; one must apply a spiritual interpretation to Spirit-inspired words. Human effort that begins with the desires and objectives of human wisdom **accomplishes nothing.** Instead, **it is the Spirit who gives eternal life.** Jesus' very words are **spirit** and **life;** therefore, we must depend on the life-giving Spirit to appropriate Jesus' words. Peter was one such believer who came to realize that Jesus had the words of eternal life (see 6:68).

6:64 From the beginning of his ministry Jesus knew that some of the ones following him were not believers in his true identity as the Son of God come from heaven.

Jesus also knew from the first **who would betray him.** This was Judas, the son of Simon Iscariot (6:70). For a moment, John interrupts with a brief word of explanation for his original readers and us. Jesus included Judas in every facet of his ministry, knowing all the time that he would not respond to the living truth. Jesus' treatment of Judas was consistent with his own character, despite that which Judas deserved for his unwillingness to believe.

6:65 This repeats what Jesus had declared before (see 6:44-45). The signs in themselves, no matter how remarkable, are not completely convincing. Some believe through seeing and others believe though not seeing, but all require God's assistance (20:29).

6:66 Jesus was saying tough things, and this caused **many of his disciples** to not follow anymore. Within sight of the Kingdom of Heaven, privileged with a taste of the bread of life, and watching the living water flow, they nevertheless walked away. In a short sentence, John captured one of the saddest moments in the ministry of Jesus.

6:67-68 According to the Greek, this question expects a negative answer. Jesus knew their weaknesses and how little they really understood. He knew that one of them would not only go away, but betray him also. Yet he also knew that God had chosen eleven to believe in him.

We can't stay on middle ground about Jesus. When he asked the disciples, **"Are you going to leave, too?"** he was showing them that he was not taking their faith for granted. Jesus never tried to repel people with his teachings. He simply told the truth. The more the people heard Jesus' real message, the more they divided into two camps—the honest seekers wanting to understand more, and those rejecting Jesus because they didn't like what they heard.

Peter replied, **"To whom would we go?"** In his straightforward way, Peter answered for all of us—there is no other way. Though there are many philosophies and self-styled authorities, Jesus alone has **the words that give eternal life.** People look everywhere for eternal life and miss Christ, the only source. There is nowhere else to go.

6:69 Peter's declaration parallels the one he made at Caesarea Philippi, but each of the synoptic Gospels gives a slightly different version of Peter's words (see Matthew 16:16; Mark 8:29; Luke 9:20). Peter was actually saying more than he knew. The descriptive words he blurted out to tell Jesus how he and the other disciples felt about him conveys both Peter's impulsive nature and his genuine impression of Christ. First, he called Jesus "Lord" (6:68). To this he added: (1) there's no one else like you; (2) you have the truth about eternal life; (3) we have believed; (4) we know that you are **the Holy One of God.** Peter was doing the best he could to describe Jesus in a category separate from anyone else who ever lived.

Like Peter's, our own understanding of Jesus must expand as we live for him. When we first believe in Jesus as Savior and Lord, our understanding will be real but limited. But as time passes, our awareness of the breadth and depth of Jesus' saving work and his lordship ought to grow.

6:70-71 Peter may have thought he was speaking for the Twelve, but not so. One among them—Judas Iscariot—was a **devil,** the traitor who would betray Jesus. According to 13:2 and 27, Satan put the idea into Judas's heart to betray Jesus and then entered Judas to instigate the actual betrayal. *Diabolos* (6:70) means "slanderous, devilish," and having Satan's nature and qualities. Judas gave into evil thinking and came under the control of the devil.

John reminded his first readers about what was at stake. Almost every word of teaching uttered by Jesus was given in the context of intense spiritual drama. Heaven must have held its breath as humans tried to figure out Jesus' true identity.

JOHN 7:1-52

JESUS' BROTHERS RIDICULE HIM / 7:1-9 / 121

From this chapter forward, John shows Jesus as the suffering Messiah—suffering the unbelief of his own family, the divided opinions of the crowd, and the persecution of the Jewish religious leaders in Jerusalem. By portraying Jesus' rejection, John provided his first readers and us with a realistic picture of the costs of being a disciple. Those who followed did so knowingly and willingly. John encourages us to believe, to stand firm, and to resist being like those who opposed and doubted Jesus while he lived on earth.

7:1 Because the Jewish religious leaders in Jerusalem **were plotting his death** (see 5:18), Jesus **stayed in Galilee** for the next twelve months. He was not afraid of the Jewish leaders; rather, he knew that his time to die had not yet come (see 7:8). When God's intended time came, he would willingly give his life. According to the synoptic Gospels, during this time Jesus ministered actively throughout Galilee (with Capernaum as his home base).

7:2 The **Festival of Shelters** occurred about six months after the Passover celebration mentioned in 6:4. This festival commemorated the days when the Israelites wandered in the wilderness and lived in tents (Leviticus 23:43). Celebrated in the month of Tishri (September/October in our calendar), it marked the gathering of the autumn harvest including the grapes (see Exodus 23:16). During this time many Jews went to Jerusalem and built shelters in which they would live for a full week while enjoying the festivities in the city (see Leviticus 23:33ff.). These simple dwellings helped the

people remember their days of misery in the wilderness.

7:3-5 Jesus' **brothers**, the sons of Joseph and Mary, did not believe that their brother was the Messiah (see Mark 3:21, 31-35). Apparently, they did not become believers until after Jesus' resurrection. After his resurrection, Jesus appeared to his brother James (1 Corinthians 15:7), who believed and eventually became the leader of the church in Jerusalem (Acts 15:13) and the author of the book of James. The prayer meeting that followed Jesus' ascension included his family (Acts 1:14). The brothers were James, Joseph, Simon, and Judas (Matthew 13:55). Judas (Jude) later wrote the book of Jude. Matthew writes that Jesus also had half sisters (Matthew 13:56).

Jesus' brothers **scoffed** at him. The **followers** refers to the crowds, not the Twelve. Jesus' brothers asked why he would remain in relative obscurity (in Galilee, at home with them) when he was trying to show **the world** he was the Messiah. They urged him to prove his identity by showing his wonderful **miracles** in Jerusalem, so that the world could see that Jesus was who he claimed to be. But because of their unbelief, they missed the point. The miracles had pictured Jesus' power and glory. He would reveal his true glory and power through his death and resurrection, and the time for that revelation was coming.

7:6 Jesus explained that **now** was **not the right time** for him **to go.** Jesus was simply indicating that the freedom to go up to Jerusalem had not yet come for him. As events unfolded, he did eventually go to the festival, but according to God's timetable. Jesus added that his brothers could use time as if it was theirs to squander, basing their decisions about time only on immediate opportunities, and showing no apparent desire to fit into God's plan. But Jesus' time belonged to the Father; he lived according to a different and predetermined schedule. His every step on this earth had a purpose; he would only act according to God's timetable. Whether he would go to this festival, and when he would go, would be determined by God alone, not by harassing relatives or waiting crowds.

7:7 The world at large hates Jesus because his testimony (as the Light of the World) exposes the world's evil (see 3:19-21). By **the world** John means this nonbelieving world's system of values and all those in it who have no love for or devotion to God. The world hated Jesus for accusing it **of sin and evil.** At this time Jesus' brothers were one with the world in not believing in Jesus; therefore, the world could not **hate** them. Rebellion loves company. People do not realize that indifference to Christ makes them partners with those who hate Christianity.

7:8-9 Jesus would do nothing by coercion or persuasion of others. Whatever he did would be done for his Father's glory and on his Father's timetable. In this incident, Jesus' brothers seem to be trying to taunt him into proving he is the Messiah. But Jesus knew his mission. No one, not even his taunting brothers, would turn him away from what he had come to do and from the way he had chosen to do it. True to his word, Jesus did not go up to Jerusalem when his brothers wanted him to. He **remained in Galilee** until after they left.

JESUS TEACHES OPENLY AT THE TEMPLE / 7:10-31 / *123*

Throughout this chapter John highlights the various opinions the Jews had about Jesus. Before Jesus appeared at the festival, opinions about him were swirling through the visiting crowd. Some of these Jews may have seen Jesus' miracles or heard him teach; others may have only heard of what he had done both in Jerusalem and in Galilee. That particular year, Jesus was the hot topic of conversation during the Festival of Shelters.

Meanwhile, Jesus was leaving Galilee for the last time. Events were moving rapidly toward "his time," and he would have no further opportunities to travel back to the area where he had spent his childhood. This visit marked the third appearance of Jesus in Jerusalem during his ministry (2:13; 5:1).

7:10-12 After Jesus' mocking **brothers left for the festival** in Jerusalem, Jesus **also went, though secretly.** Jesus would not go up to Jerusalem for the purpose of showing himself to be the Christ (which was what his brothers had told him to do, see 7:3-4). In fact, Jesus could not be found during the first few days of the festival (see 7:11, 14).

In the events that follow, a lot happened behind the scenes. Not only did Jesus travel to Jerusalem in secret, but intrigue and subterfuge were at work everywhere. The crowds were buzzing with opinions about Jesus, yet there was no clear consensus. The Jewish leaders were busily conferring and watching for the right time to legitimately arrest him. The tension-laden atmosphere fostered both excitement and treachery.

7:13 The **Jewish leaders** had a great deal of power over the common people. Apparently these leaders couldn't do much to Jesus at this time, but they threatened anyone who might publicly support him. They could use excommunication from the synagogue as a reprisal for believing in Jesus (9:22). Jews considered this a severe punishment. Jesus' listeners had their opinions but were **afraid** to express them. This created a power stalemate between the religious leaders and the crowds.

7:14-15 Midway through the festival, Jesus came out from secrecy and **began to teach** in public, in the extremely visible outer court of the Temple. Jesus' delay in arriving and the crowd's divided opinion created an anticipation for his appearance and teaching. The atmosphere was tense and excitable.

When the **Jewish leaders heard** Jesus, they **were surprised** at his knowledge, having never been trained as a rabbi in their schools. In other words, Jesus had no official human certification. He spoke with authority without relying on license or degree to legitimize his teaching. From what follows this statement about the amazement of the crowd, we understand that the unrest among the people about Jesus' identity continued to develop. After the crowd's initial amazement, they grew restless over the issues of Jesus' identity and began to take sides.

7:16-18 Jesus' teaching was authoritative because it originated from **God**, not from himself. Those who knew God and sought to **do the will of God** would **know whether** his **teaching** was **from God** or was his own. Unlike those who **present their own ideas** and are **looking for praise for themselves,** Jesus sought **to honor the one who sent** him. Jesus determined to bring God's message of salvation to humanity and thereby to bring him glory. Therefore, Jesus could rightfully claim about himself that he is **good and genuine.** And only those who want to do God's will can recognize Jesus for who he is—God's Son. Jesus was saying that those who examine his teaching or the signs that accompanied his ministry must be open-minded and desire to respond to God's will once it is known. Some people who demand more evidence may be covering up their refusal to submit to God. Every believer who desires to know God's will must seek it with the intention of obeying it once it has been found.

7:19 Beginning with verse 19, Jesus alluded to the debate he had with the Jews during his last visit to Jerusalem (see 5:18ff.). Because Jesus had healed a man on the Sabbath and then directly implied his own equality with God, his Father, the Jewish religious leaders wanted to **kill** him for Sabbath-breaking and blasphemy. The Pharisees tried to achieve holiness by meticulously keeping the rules that they had added to God's laws. Jesus' accusation that they didn't obey **the law of Moses** stung them deeply. In spite of their pompous pride in their accomplishments and their rules, they did not measure up, for they were living far below what the law of Moses required. By enforcing their own laws regarding Sabbath-breaking and blasphemy, they were about to break one of the Ten Commandments: "Do not murder" (Exodus 20:13). But they didn't see this error; they so hated Jesus that they were blind to their own sin.

7:20 In response to Jesus' charge that they were **trying to kill** him, the people responded with an accusation of their own and a question. We cannot

know how widely spread the plot against Jesus was. But verse 25 records the fact that a certain "they" were trying to kill him, and their intentions were widely known. At this point, the crowd wanted to know whether Jesus could identify the people behind the plot. But this crowd also blasphemed against Jesus by charging him with being **demon possessed.** Mark records an earlier incident (Mark 3:22-30) when a similar charge was leveled against Jesus. It was a particularly effective tactic on the part of the religious leaders to admit the spirituality of Jesus, but then define it as evil. This time Jesus did not even bother refuting the obvious dishonesty of the allegations.

7:21-24 Because Jesus was in Jerusalem, he most likely was referring back to the miracle in 5:1-15—the healing of the paralyzed man. Jesus mentioned that he had healed on the **Sabbath,** the point of contention surrounding the miracle. Jesus reminded the people again that their spiritual priorities were wrong. He noted that, according to **Moses' law, circumcision** was to be performed eight days after a baby's birth (Genesis 17:9-14; Leviticus 12:3). This rite demonstrated the Jews' identity as part of God's covenant people. If the eighth day after birth fell on a Sabbath, they still performed the circumcision (even though it was considered work). By referring to **Abraham** performing circumcision, Jesus was pointing to an authority and principle prior to Moses. By healing the whole person, Jesus demonstrated that his creative power was equal to God's and superior to Moses'.

The point was that while the religious leaders allowed certain exceptions to Sabbath laws, they allowed none to Jesus, who simply showed mercy to those who needed healing. He demonstrated from their own practices that they would overrule a law when two ceremonial laws came into conflict. But the Jewish leaders were so engrossed with their regulations about Sabbath-keeping that they failed to see the true intent of Jesus' actions. Their superficial but tenacious adherence to their own traditions would cause them to miss the Messiah, to whom their Scriptures pointed.

7:25-27 Some of the people of **Jerusalem** had heard that the religious rulers were **trying to kill** Jesus. But since he was **speaking in public** and none of the rulers attempted to stop him, they wondered if the rulers had reconsidered and had recognized that Jesus **really** was **the Messiah.** But this seemed improbable to the crowds because even they could think of some objections.

Their reasoning? **"We know where this man comes from. When the Messiah comes, he will** simply appear; no one will know where he comes from." The people thought they knew where Jesus came from—Nazareth of Galilee. They saw him as a man, a neighbor, a carpenter, but they did not have a close relationship with him. They did not know that he had come from God and had been born of a virgin, heralded by angels, recognized as divine by shepherds and then by wise men from the East, and greeted joyfully as the Messiah by two aged prophets (Luke 2). Instead, the people were convinced that no one was supposed to know where the Messiah came from. There was a popular tradition that the Messiah would **simply appear.** It was just as mistaken as the belief that the Christ would be a military/political leader who would restore Israel's greatness. Those who believed this tradition were ignoring the Scriptures that clearly predicted the Messiah's birthplace (Micah 5:2). The popular tradition about the origin and appearance of the Messiah probably came from what is recorded in 1 Enoch 48:6; 4 Ezra 13:1ff., books that were not included in our Bibles because they were not considered authoritative. (They were, however, valued for personal study.)

7:28-31 Knowing that the people did not believe in him, Jesus said: **"Yes, you know me, and you**

know where I come from." Some versions render this sentence as a question rather than a statement. The people did indeed know where he was from geographically (he grew up in Galilee), but they really did not know because, as Jesus went on to say: **"I represent one you don't know, and he is true. I know him because I have come from him, and he sent me to you."** Jesus was declaring his divine origin and divine commission. From Jesus' proclamation we can gather that it is important to know, not from **where** Jesus came, but **from whom** he came. To recognize this origin requires revelation. But the people did not know Jesus because they did not know the one who sent him.

This was too much for the **leaders who tried to arrest him.** This was the first spontaneous attempt to restrain Jesus. A little later there was an official attempt described in verse 32. But Jesus could not be detained, for **his time had not yet come.** The verse between the two attempted arrests says that **many believed.** There was turmoil in the crowd about Jesus' true identity. People were taking sides. Some people believed and others did not. For a while there had been general confusion. But the confusion was resolving into belief and unbelief. Those who believed Jesus concluded that he had presented the true credentials of the Messiah.

RELIGIOUS LEADERS ATTEMPT TO ARREST JESUS / 7:32-52 / 124

Nicodemus tactfully confronted the Pharisees with their failure to keep their own laws. The Pharisees were losing ground—the Temple guards came back impressed by Jesus (7:46), and one of the Pharisees' own, Nicodemus, was defending him. With their hypocritical motives being exposed and their prestige slowly eroding, the Pharisees renewed their efforts to protect themselves. Pride would interfere with their ability to reason, and soon they would become obsessed with getting rid of Jesus just to save face. What was good and right no longer mattered.

7:32-34 Aware that the Jewish religious leaders had **sent Temple guards to arrest** him, Jesus alluded to his coming death: **"I will be here a little longer. Then I will return to the one who sent me."** No one would be taking Jesus' life from him; rather, he would depart this life according to the preordained time and then return to his Father. Jesus' statement also served as a calm warning to those who were plotting against him that their efforts would only succeed subject to God's plan. At that time, says Jesus, **"You will search for me but not find me. And you won't be able to come where I am."** Another way to say this is, "You will seek me and not find me because your unbelief has rendered you unable to understand where I am." Even after Jesus

(the true Messiah) left, the Jews would continue to seek for the coming of the Messiah but would never find him—because he had already come!

7:35-36 The **Jewish leaders**, not understanding that Jesus' statement referred to his death, wondered if he was speaking about **going to the Jews in other lands** or **even to the Gentiles.** The Dispersion or *Diaspora* is a technical term referring to the large number of Jews who were "dispersed" (or scattered) throughout the Roman Empire and beyond. Some of the Jews were dispersed among the Gentiles. The Jews listening to Jesus wondered if he was about to depart Judea and go to these Jews.

7:37-39 The **last day, the climax of the festival,** was the eighth day. During the Festival of Shelters, the Jews celebrated the memory of how God protected their ancestors in their travels across the wilderness to the Promised Land, guiding them on their way and providing them with manna and, on one occasion, water from a rock (see Exodus 17:1-7). Every day during this festival, except for the last day, a priest stood in front of the Temple with a golden pitcher of water and poured the water on a rock. This commemorated the water flowing out of the rock that gave the Israelites water to drink. They performed this ceremony each day of the festival except the eighth, when they offered public prayers for continued rain.

Thus, on the last day when the water was not poured out, Jesus stood and said in a loud voice, "If you are thirsty, come to me! If you believe in me, come and drink! For the Scriptures declare that rivers of living water will flow out from within." Jesus' words, "Come and drink," allude to the theme of many Bible passages that talk about the Messiah's life-giving blessings (Isaiah 12:2-3; 44:3-4; 58:11). By promising to give the Holy Spirit to all who believed, Jesus was claiming to be the Messiah, for that was something only the Messiah could do. There is no particular verse in the Old Testament that exactly says "rivers of living water will flow out from within." Jesus was either paraphrasing a verse like Psalm 78:16 or Isaiah 58:11.

John provided an explanatory note: He was speaking of the Spirit, who would be given to everyone believing in him. At that time, the Holy Spirit had not yet been given to all believers. That happened after Jesus entered into his glory through the resurrection and ascension (see 16:7-16). The availability of the Spirit is linked with the glorification of Jesus, for it was after Jesus' glorification through death and resurrection that the Spirit became available to believers (see 20:22).

7:40-44 Jesus' exclamatory invitation generated faith in some of the hearers. Some said, **"This man surely is the Prophet"** (meaning the Prophet predicted by Moses in Deuteronomy 18:15-18); others said, **"He is the Messiah."** But others could not believe. They were convinced that the Messiah would not **come from Galilee.** They argued correctly from **the Scriptures** that he was to be **born of the royal line of David, in Bethlehem** (see Psalm 89:3-4; 132:11; Isaiah 9:6-7; 11:1; Micah 5:2). And, in fact, Jesus was David's son (see Matthew 1:1-18; Romans 1:3-4) born in Bethlehem (see Matthew 2:1-6; Luke 2:1-11). But soon after his birth, Jesus' parents took him to Egypt to protect his life. Later, they brought him to Nazareth of Galilee (the hometown of Joseph and Mary),

where he grew up (see Matthew 2:13-23). Thereafter he was identified as a Galilean and a Nazarene, not a Judean or a Bethlehemite. However, Jesus never once tried to explain that his birthplace was Bethlehem. Instead, he always pointed to his divine, heavenly origin. If a person knew God, he would know that Jesus was the Christ.

As the crowd argued about Jesus' identity, they were **divided** and **some wanted him arrested.** But his time had not yet come, so **no one touched him.**

7:45-49 The **Temple guards** were very likely police under the jurisdiction of the Jewish religious rulers, not the Romans. Some of the Levites were probably assigned this duty. Although the Romans ruled Palestine, they gave the Jewish religious leaders authority over minor civil and religious affairs. The religious leaders supervised their own Temple guards and gave the officers power to arrest anyone causing a disturbance or breaking any of their ceremonial laws. But these Temple guards couldn't find one reason to arrest Jesus. And as they listened to Jesus to try to find evidence, they couldn't help but hear his wonderful words.

Although sent by **leading priests and Pharisees** with specific orders to **arrest** Jesus, the guards returned empty-handed. When asked why they did not bring Jesus, they said, **"We have never heard anyone talk like this!"** When the guards heard Jesus, they recognized that they were listening to a man like no other, for, in fact, they were listening to the Son of God (see Matthew 7:29; Luke 4:22).

But the Pharisees rejected this simple testimony. They asked these guards if they, like the crowd, were also **led astray.** If Jesus really were the Messiah, they argued, at least some of the religious rulers would believe in him. And since not **a single one** of them did, then this man could not be the Messiah. Maybe the crowds believed in him, but the **crowds** were **ignorant.** But in judging the people for their supposed ignorance, the Pharisees were judging themselves, for they were ignorant of God and did not know the one he sent.

7:50-52 Nicodemus, who had gone to Jesus earlier and who was one of their own number (see 3:1-21), asked, **"Is it legal to convict a man before he is given a hearing?"** Nicodemus attempted to make his fellow Pharisees adhere to the law they claimed to know and to act fairly and justly. An accused person, according to Deuteronomy 1:16, must first be heard before being judged.

This passage offers additional insight into Nicodemus, the Pharisee who visited Jesus at night (chapter 3). Apparently Nicodemus had become a secret believer (see 12:42). Since most of the Pharisees hated Jesus and wanted to kill him, Nicodemus risked his reputation and high position when he spoke up for Jesus. His statement was bold, and the Pharisees immediately became suspicious. After Jesus' death, Nicodemus brought spices for his body (19:39). That is the last time Nicodemus is mentioned in Scripture.

But these Pharisees would not listen even to one of their own. The depth of their real allegiance to the law became clear when their position was threatened by the truth. They retorted sarcastically, **"Are you from Galilee, too? Search the Scriptures and see for yourself—no prophet ever comes from Galilee!"** The Pharisees and religious leaders were confident that they could reject Jesus as having any claim as the Messiah because of his Galilean origin. But they were wrong on three counts: (1) Jesus was born in Bethlehem, the city of David (Luke 2:4-11; also Micah 5:2); (2) The Scriptures do speak of the Messiah as a "great light" for Galilee (Isaiah 9:1-2); (3) Jonah (2 Kings 14:25) and Elijah (1 Kings 17:1) came from this region. The leaders may have been referring to the Prophet of Deuteronomy 18:15. They were proud and certain that he would come from their territory, Judea.

JOHN 7:53–8:59

JESUS FORGIVES AN ADULTEROUS WOMAN / 7:53–8:11 / 125

The earliest manuscripts of John's gospel do not include the story of the adulterous woman. It does not appear in any Greek manuscript until the fifth century, and no Greek church father comments on the passage prior to the twelfth century. Even then, the comments state that the accurate manuscripts do not contain this story. When it was inserted in later manuscripts, the story of the adulterous woman appeared in different places: after John 7:52, after Luke 21:38, at the end of John; and when it does appear it is often marked off by asterisks to signal doubt about where it belongs. The story is part of an oral tradition that was circulated in the Western church, eventually finding its way into the Latin Vulgate, and from there into later Greek manuscripts.

The evidence against John having included this particular story in his Gospel is conclusive. First, many scholars point out that the vocabulary used in this passage does not match the rest of John. Second, although the setting is plausible (other similar confrontations between Jewish leaders and Jesus occurred in Jerusalem), the insertion of the story at this point in John (after 7:52 and before 8:12) disrupts the narrative flow. Third, since the account does not appear in writing until later manuscripts, its "orphan" status is evidenced by it being in several locations, as mentioned above.

However, even though the passage was not written by John, it still may be regarded as a true story. The actions and words of Jesus are consistent with what we know of him from the rest of the Gospels. There is no new or unusual information in the passage that adds evidence against its inclusion. The encounter appears as an added snapshot of Jesus in John's collection, though we can tell that someone else probably took the picture. The event deserves at least consideration in teaching and preaching as an act that Jesus did at some point in his ministry, for it illustrates Jesus' compassion for sinful people (which includes us all) and his willingness to forgive any sinner; but the story should not be given the same authority as Scripture.

7:53–8:3 The teachers of religious law and Pharisees brought a woman they had caught in the act of adultery. The religious leaders did not bring this woman to Jesus to promote justice; they used her to try to trap Jesus. Though indignant toward this woman's sin, the religious leaders brought her to Jesus with political, not spiritual, motives in mind. They forgot the obvious fact that catching someone in the very act of adultery involves catching two people. Their devaluation of the woman (while ignoring the man's sin) made her no more than a pawn in their efforts to trap Jesus.

8:4-6 The Jewish leaders had already disregarded the law by arresting the woman without the man (Leviticus 20:10; Deuteronomy 22:22). Both were to be stoned. But the proceedings before Jesus had little to do with justice. The leaders were using the woman's sin as an opportunity to trick Jesus and destroy his credibility with the people. If Jesus were to say that the woman should not be stoned, they could accuse him of violating Moses' law. If he were to urge them to execute her, they would report him to the Romans, who did not permit the Jews to carry out their own executions (18:31). But Jesus was aware of their intentions and did not give either of the expected responses to the dilemma they placed before him. He simply **stooped down and wrote in the dust with his finger.** Many have speculated what he wrote: maybe he was listing the names of those present who had committed adultery (and scaring them to death that he knew it); he might have been listing names and various sins that each person had committed; maybe he was writing out the Ten Commandments to point out that no one could claim to be without sin. In any case, Jesus made the accusers uncomfortable.

8:7-8 The religious leaders could have handled this case without Jesus' opinion. Jesus was fully aware that the woman was only brought to him so the Pharisees could test him. Jesus' statement of permission, **"All right, stone her,"** balanced several crucial points of truth. He upheld the legal penalty for adultery (stoning), so he could not be accused of being against the law. But by requiring that only **those who have never sinned throw the first stones,** Jesus exposed what was in the accusers' hearts. Without condoning the woman's actions, he highlighted the importance of compassion and forgiveness and broadened the spotlight of judg-

ment until every accuser felt himself included. Jesus knew the execution could not be carried out.

How are we to apply Jesus' statement about only sinless persons rendering judgment? Jesus was not saying that only perfect, sinless people can make accurate accusations, pass judgment, or exact a death penalty. Nor was he excusing adultery or any other sin by saying that everyone sins. This event illustrates that wise judgment flows out of honest motives. Jesus resolved an injustice about to be committed by exposing the hypocrisy of the witnesses against the woman. By making the accusers examine themselves, he exposed their real motives.

Jesus did confront the woman's sin, but he exercised compassion alongside confrontation. As with the woman at the well (chapter 4), Jesus demonstrated to this woman that she was of greater importance than what she had done wrong.

8:9-11 When Jesus invited someone who had not sinned to throw the first stone, the leaders **slipped away one by one,** from **oldest** to youngest. Evidently the older men were more aware of their sins than the younger. Age and experience often temper youthful self-righteousness. We all have a sinful nature and are desperately in need of forgiveness and transformation. None of us would have been able to throw the first stone; none of us can claim sinlessness. We, too, would have had to walk away.

Jesus was left in the middle of the crowd with the woman. Apparently no one could claim sinlessness so as to stone this woman. Jesus had exposed their hypocrisy and embarrassed them, and there was nothing for them to do but go back and try to think of some other way to trap Jesus.

No one had accused the woman, and Jesus kindly said that he would not condemn her either. But there was more—she was not simply free to go her way. Jesus didn't just free her from the Pharisees, he wanted to free her from her sin, so he added, **"Go and sin no more."** Jesus didn't condemn her, but neither did he ignore or condone her behavior. Jesus told the woman to leave her life of sin.

JESUS IS THE LIGHT OF THE WORLD / 8:12-20 / 126
This section ties in closely with the previous section (7:45-52) where Nicodemus had recommended that the religious leaders first hear Jesus before passing judgment on him. In this section Jesus is heard, and he affirms the validity of his testimony based on his divine identity. In no other chapter of the Bible does Jesus make so many declarations about himself.

8:12 In the earliest manuscripts of John, this verse immediately follows 7:52. Chapters 7 and 8 record the dialogues that Jesus had with the Jewish leaders in Jerusalem during the Festival of

Shelters. In addition to the ceremony with water, huge lamps in the Court of Women in the Temple were lit in commemoration of the pillar of fire that led the Israelites in their wilderness journey

(Numbers 9:15-23). The light from those lamps lit up much of Jerusalem. In declaring himself to be **the light,** Jesus was claiming divinity. In the Bible, "light" symbolizes the holiness of God (see also Psalm 27:1; 36:9; Acts 9:3; 1 John 1:5). As the light, Jesus illumines the truth, gives people spiritual understanding, and reveals to us God himself and what he has done for us.

In claiming to be the light **of the world,** Jesus defined his unique position as the one true light for all people, not just the Jews (Isaiah 49:6). Death brings eternal darkness; but to follow Jesus means not **stumbling through the darkness,** but having **the light that leads to life.** Believers no longer walk blindly in sin, rather his light shows sin and the need of forgiveness, gives guidance, and leads into eternal life with him.

8:13-14 After Jesus said this, **the Pharisees replied, "You are making false claims about yourself!"** But they did not know anything about Jesus. They assumed he was talking with no valid testimony from anyone else. Jewish law says that two witnesses are needed for a valid testimony in a capital offense, as their charge of blasphemy was (5:31; also Deuteronomy 19:15). Jesus claimed that his testimony was true because Jesus knows God the Father, and the words that Jesus spoke were from the Father himself. Therefore when Jesus spoke, not only was he testifying for himself, but because he spoke the words of God, God was testifying for him as well.

8:15-16 The religious leaders did not know Jesus' divine origin and considered him to be no more than a fake Messiah; that is, they were judging him **with all** their **human limitations.** While they did that, Jesus was **not judging anyone.** Jesus meant that while his accusers judged by human standards, he did not. Jesus reserved for himself the right to judge, though that was not

the primary reason for his presence. Jesus did not come to judge, but to save. He had already told a noted Pharisee (Nicodemus), "God did not send his Son into the world to condemn it, but to save it" (3:17). But as the Son of man, he has been given the authority to judge; and when the future day of judgment comes, Jesus' **judgment** will **be correct in every respect** because he will judge according to the Father's will (see 5:27, 45). Therefore, it could be said that while Jesus did not come to judge, his coming led to judgment because it forced a decision—and a rejection of Jesus led to judgment.

8:17-18 The religious leaders did not understand that the Father and Son lived in each other and were with each other (see 10:38; 14:9-11; 17:21). Therefore, even though the Son came from the Father (8:14) and was sent by the Father (8:16, 18), he was not separate from the Father—for the Father who sent the Son came with him and provided testimony for him. His confirming **witness** was God himself. Jesus and the Father made **two** witnesses, the number required by the law.

8:19-20 In asking to see his **father,** the leaders might as well have been saying, "Bring on the other witness; we wish to question him." If his father was the other witness, then where was he? In their very presence, Jesus affirmed that they knew neither him nor his Father. Their unwillingness to "know" him when he was among them also kept them from knowing the Father, who was just as truly among them.

Jesus had already told them that his Father was with him, but their question showed that they did not know the Son or the Father—for **"if you knew me, then you would know my Father, too."** When Jesus speaks, the Father speaks. But this was completely lost on these religious leaders.

JESUS WARNS OF COMING JUDGMENT / 8:21-30 / *127*

With chilling brevity, Jesus predicted the fate of those who fail to find him. The Pharisees continued to respond to Jesus out of rigid human standards. Because of this, they continued to be denounced by Jesus. But in this case, Jesus' hardness proved to be compassion. Only the bluntness of Jesus' vision of their condition finally broke through to some.

8:21-22 Speaking again to the Jewish religious leaders, Jesus declared, **"You will search for me and die in your sin."** If the Jewish religious leaders would not believe in Jesus while he was with them, they would run the risk of not having any further opportunity to receive eternal life. Jesus predicted that they would continue to look for a messiah,

though the real one had already been among them. The leaders' fatal sin would be in rejecting the only one who could save them.

His statement, **"You cannot come where I am going,"** refers to his death and return to his Father—the religious leaders could not follow him there. The opportunity to speak with Jesus was limited; soon he would leave them having been rejected by them. Those who rejected Jesus would die without having their sins forgiven and would therefore literally not be able to go where Jesus would be.

As in 7:34-36, the Jews could not comprehend Jesus' words. They surmised that he must be speaking about committing **suicide**. In Greek, the question expects a negative answer. Instead of responding to their tentative interpretation, Jesus explained why they were unable to comprehend his statements.

8:23-24 Those **from below** and **of this world** are earthly, born of the flesh, incapable of understanding heavenly and spiritual realities (see 3:6; 1 Corinthians 2:14-15). The Pharisees were set in their faulty perspective and were unwilling to consider that they might be wrong. They were looking very hard—in the wrong place. Therefore, Jesus told them, **"Unless you believe that I am who I say I am, you will die in your sins."** By refusing to acknowledge Jesus as the divine Son of God, these people were committing spiritual suicide. To die in our sins is the worst that can happen, for it is to die without ever repenting of our sinful lifestyle or having our guilt and sin covered by the blood of Christ. Jesus confronted the leaders with their crucial need to recognize or reject his divinity. People today face that same need.

8:25 The Pharisees decided to try the direct approach; they asked Jesus, "Tell us who you are." When the Pharisees pressed Jesus to declare his identity, he answered, **"I am the one I have always claimed to be."** Jesus simply refused to answer their question, for to do so would have created an endless argument. Jesus had already revealed his identity to them through his speeches, his miracles, and the Father's testimony about him. But the Pharisees were unable to understand because they were deaf to his word (8:43).

8:26 Jesus could have said more to them in way of judgment, but he would speak only what his Father commanded. The Pharisees claimed they

wanted him to explain his identity, but Jesus knew they were simply heaping judgment on themselves. Instead of continuing an argument with these religious leaders who had already made up their minds not to believe, Jesus would say nothing more to **condemn** them. Rather, he would speak only what he **heard from the one who sent** him—and he would speak, not just to the Jews, but to the world. And whatever he says is the Father's word; thus it is **true**, reliable, and valid (see also 8:16).

8:27 The Pharisees **still didn't understand that he was talking to them about his Father.** They mentally blocked out the possibility that Jesus had come from God the Father and was still accompanied by God the Father, even though Jesus mentioned this twice. Jesus was not alone; the Father who had sent him had come with him (see 8:16, 29). Jesus had not come on his own, and he did not do anything of his own initiative (see 8:28, 42). He lived to please his Father.

8:28-30 The Jews in Jesus' day understood the expression **lifted up** to signify crucifixion. That the religious leaders would realize who Jesus was does not mean that they would believe in him. Rather, it means that Jesus' claims would be proven through the Crucifixion and Resurrection. **"I am he"** refers immediately to the title **"Son of Man."** Jesus was pushing his hearers to recognize his full identity. Jesus was not on his own mission to gain glory for himself; he had come to fulfill the Father's will by dying **on the cross.** Jesus' death on the cross exhibited his absolute submission to the Father's will. He summed it up thus: **"I always do those things that are pleasing to him."**

The passage concludes with a crack in the wall of resistance to Jesus. **Many who heard, believed.** Even among those most unyielding to Jesus were some who surrendered to his character and words. Groups may be labeled as being solidly against Christ, but God specializes in plucking out believers from the most unexpected sources.

JESUS SPEAKS ABOUT GOD'S TRUE CHILDREN / 8:31-47 / 128

Next Jesus singled out the group of people who recently had believed in him. They formed part of the scattered response from among the crowd listening to Jesus in 8:30. Difficulties with this passage arise from the fact that John called them believers in verses 30 and 31, but they proved to be faithless. Their belief in Jesus turned out to be merely superficial. Jesus tested their commitment with his first instructions; their response demonstrates their unwillingness to actually follow the one in whom they had recently declared their faith.

8:31-32 To those who **believed in him,** Jesus said, **"You are truly my disciples if you keep obeying my teachings."** As the following verses demonstrate, some of these new believers did not remain his followers for long. But Jesus urged those who really wanted to remain his disciples to hold to, or continue in, his teachings. John's report of the failure of one group of followers is a strong lesson. We need to count the cost of following Jesus (see Luke 14:25-35). A true and obedient disciple will **know the truth** by knowing the one who is the truth, Jesus himself (1:17; 14:6). This knowledge frees people from their bondage to sin (see 8:34). When Jesus spoke of "knowing the truth," he was speaking of knowing God's revelation to people. This revelation is embodied in Jesus himself, the Word; therefore, to know the truth is to know Jesus. The truth is not political freedom or intellectual knowledge. Knowing the truth means accepting it, obeying it, and regarding it above all earthly opinion. Doing so offers true spiritual freedom from sin and death. Believers become truly **free** because they are free to do God's will, and thus fulfill God's ultimate purpose in their lives. As believers, we have the Holy Spirit living within us and guiding us on our journey through life.

8:33 The Jews thought that Jesus' words about their needing freedom devalued their ancestry and unique position with God, so they gave Jesus a little history lesson: **"We have never been slaves to anyone on earth."** Yet the crowd's denial of the obvious seems apparent even to us. The Jewish ancestors of these people had been enslaved by the Egyptians, the Assyrians, and the Babylonians. And they were ruled by the Romans at the moment Jesus spoke. Though not actually in slavery, they were under foreign domination, and were looking for the Messiah to free them from Roman rule. But they insisted that as Abraham's descendants they were free people who did not need to be **"set free."** They also claimed that Abraham's righteousness guaranteed their righteousness. Their spiritual superiority made them blind to their real slavery to sin. Jesus bluntly challenged their claims.

8:34-38 Not only was the crowd wrong about their national history, they were also wrong about the meaning of Jesus' earlier statement. Jesus spoke of a different liberation—that of the soul set free from sin. He pointed out that they did indeed need to be set free, because, **"Everyone who sins is a slave of sin."** Jesus went on to explain the difference between a **slave** and a **son.** A slave has no permanent standing in the master's household because he or she can be sold to a different master (in the Roman Empire slaves had no legal status).

But a son always has a place in the family. The Jews had a false sense of security because they claimed to be **descendants of Abraham**—and thus thought this guaranteed them a permanent place in God's family and household (heaven). But Jesus explained that they, along with all people, were slaves to sin. As such, they had no permanent standing in the Father's house. The Son of God alone has the power and authority to free people from their bondage to sin. Jesus can free people from the slavery that keeps them from becoming the people God created them to be. Jesus is the source of truth, the perfect standard of what is right. Jesus does not give people freedom to do what they want, but freedom to follow God.

The Jews were Abraham's descendants only in the physical sense, not spiritually or morally, because they were **trying to kill** Jesus. In doing so, these leaders revealed that they were not Abraham's spiritual children. If they had been, they would have recognized their Messiah. Instead, they were **following the advice of** their **father,** namely the devil (8:44). Jesus made a distinction between hereditary children and **true** children. The religious leaders were hereditary children of Abraham (founder of the Jewish nation) and therefore claimed to be children of God. But their actions showed them to be true children of Satan, for they lived under Satan's guidance.

8:39 The Jews said that their **father** was **Abraham,** but Jesus said that if they really were children of Abraham, they would **follow his good example.** Sons copy their fathers, but the Jewish leaders did not behave like the one whom they claimed as their father. Jesus specifically pointed to their sin of wanting to kill him because this proved that they were not Abraham's true children. Abraham believed in and obeyed God (see Genesis 12:1-4; 15:6; 22:1-14) and welcomed God's messengers (Genesis 18:1-8).

8:40-41 They could not claim to have Abraham as their father when they were seeking to kill the one who brought them truth from God, for **"Abraham wouldn't do a thing like that."** Instead, they were obeying their **real father.** Jesus was speaking of Satan as being their father, but they did not understand this. Instead, they said, **"We were not born out of wedlock."** Some commentators have said that this retort was a slur on Jesus' own birth, but they would not have known about his unusual origins. They all assumed Jesus was Joseph's son. Rather, they could have been claiming to be unlike the Samaritans, who were not purebred Jews or claiming to be devout monotheists untainted by spiritual fornication with other gods. Since their appeal to Abrahamic privilege was either deflected or challenged by Jesus (see explanation of translation above), they appealed to their position with God: **"Our true Father is God himself."** Their retort shows that they took offense at being told that their ancestry did not automatically place them in a privileged moral standing before God. But they did not truly know the one God they claimed as their Father because they did not recognize his Son who had come to give them the truth and to set them free from sin.

8:42 Jesus forcefully challenged the leaders' claim that they were God's children. **"If God were your Father, you would love me."** If those people truly loved God as their Father, then they would recognize and love the Son. And he repeated for them his origin and mission: **"I have come to you from God. I am not here on my own, but he sent me."** Jesus came as the one sent by the Father to bring God's word to his people.

8:43 Jesus knew that they could not **understand** because they were **unable to do so.** They had already made up their minds about him, and thus could not hear and accept what Jesus had to say. Understanding was not the problem; being willing to hear and accept it as the truth was their barrier.

8:44 Jesus told these self-righteous people, **"You are the children of your father the Devil, and you love to do the evil things he does."** A person's actions reveal what is in his or her heart (see 1 John 3:8). The Devil was a murderer from the beginning and has always hated the truth. In short, the Devil is the father of lies. The intent to murder comes from the Devil. The Devil was the instigator of Jesus' murder (6:70-71; 13:27) and

the perpetrator of the lies that the Jews believed about Jesus. The attitudes and actions of the Jewish leaders clearly identified them as followers of the Devil, though they may not have been conscious of this. But their hatred of truth, their lies, and their murderous intentions indicate how much control the Devil had over them. They were Satan's tools in carrying out his plans; they spoke the very same language of lies. Satan still uses people to obstruct God's work (Genesis 4:8; Romans 5:12; 1 John 3:12).

8:45-46 In contrast to the Devil, who habitually lies, Jesus speaks only **the truth**—and for that reason was not believed. In the end, Jesus was rejected not only because the Jews judged him to be a Sabbath breaker and blasphemer (5:18), but also because his words to them were very harsh and exposing. In light of his character and words, they could not stand to see and hear the truth about themselves.

If there was a chink in Jesus' armor, his next question would have been their golden opportunity to destroy him. Jesus left himself completely open for a direct attack, **"Which of you can truthfully accuse me of sin?"** Of course, no one could. People who hated him and wanted him dead scrutinized his behavior but could find nothing wrong. And they were grasping at straws trying to make him anything but what he claimed to be. Jesus proved he was God in the flesh by his sinless life. He was speaking the truth, but they refused to believe.

8:47 Although some in his audience had heard and become believers (8:30), most remained deaf because their hearts were hardened (see 12:39-40). They refused to listen to (or obey) the words of God because they were not **God's children.**

JESUS STATES HE IS ETERNAL / 8:48-59 / 129

At this point, the dialogue between Jesus and his Jewish audience took a decidedly angry turn. Since they had no answer for his clear diagnosis of their spiritual sickness, Jesus' audience reacted with a verbal attack against him. Up until this point, Jesus' opponents reserved one final accusation against him: blasphemy. But as Jesus responded to their angry tirade he finally led them to realize the full extent of his claims. He used the "I am" phrase in 8:58 to state his unequivocal claim to divinity. He left no more room for debate. The crowd took up the stones to carry out judgment for blasphemy, but Jesus removed himself from that place. He would choose the time and place for final confrontation.

8:48-50 This is the only instance in the Gospels where Jesus is charged with being a **Samaritan.** These expressions were filled with great anger. The Samaritans were considered beneath the Jews

because of their intermarriage with heathens and their religious impurity. The Jews leveled this charge at Jesus because he, a fellow Jew, had accused them of not being true descendants of

Abraham (see 8:37-44). Elsewhere in John, Jesus was accused of being **possessed by a demon** (see 7:20; 8:52; 10:20).

Jesus did not respond to the charge of being "a Samaritan devil"; he did refute the charge of being demon-possessed. Jesus told the leaders that they were dishonoring him by such a charge because Jesus always sought to honor and glorify his Father. Jesus was not seeking any glory for himself. The Father would seek glory for his Son and judge those who dishonor him.

8:51 Obeying Jesus' **teaching** includes relying on the character, ability, strength, and truth of what he promised. When Jesus said that those who obeyed would **never die,** he was talking about spiritual death, not physical death. Even physical death, however, will eventually be overcome. Those who follow Christ will be raised to live eternally with him.

8:52-53 For Jesus to claim that he could prevent death was for him a claim to be **greater than the prophets**—indeed, it meant he was claiming to be divine. These Jews were convinced that only a madman (someone who was **possessed by a demon**) would make such a claim.

8:54-55 Again, Jesus deferred the matter of his divine identity to his relationship with his **Father.** He could never make the kind of claims he made apart from his union with the Father. If he had come of his own accord, his glory would be worthless. But the Father had sent him, and the Father would glorify him— even if the Jews didn't. The crux of the matter was that the Jews did not **know** the Father from whom Jesus came, even though they claimed to know him. The one who really knew the Father and kept his word knew that these Jews were lying.

8:56 Jesus referred to **Abraham** as their **ancestor,** but he meant it only in the physical sense. Abraham, by some revelation not directly recorded in Genesis, **looked forward to** the Messiah's **coming** (Hebrews 11:8-13). Several possibilities have been proposed: (1) According to rabbinic tradition, Abraham was

given foresight about the future of his descendants. Jesus, perhaps knowing this tradition, pinpointed the one event that would have made Abraham rejoice—the day when the Messiah, his descendant, would come to deliver the world; (2) Genesis 17:7 mentions God's establishment of an everlasting covenant with Abraham's offspring, which some take to be a messianic promise; (3) Genesis 22:8 records Abraham's prophetic words that "God will provide a lamb," which received their complete fulfillment in Jesus. Of the three interpretations, the first makes the most sense because the text speaks of "my coming"—that is, the time of Christ's presence on earth.

8:57 Jesus had not claimed to be a contemporary with Abraham or that he had **seen Abraham;** instead, he said that Abraham had foreseen Jesus' coming. The comment about Jesus being not yet **fifty years old** is a roundabout way of saying that he was not yet an old man.

8:58-59 Jesus astounded them with his answer: **"The truth is, I existed before Abraham was even born!"** Abraham, as with all human beings, had come into existence at one point in time. But Jesus never had a beginning—he was eternal and therefore God. He was undeniably proclaiming his divinity. No other religious figure in all of history has made such claims. Either Jesus was God or he was a madman. His claim to deity demands a response. It cannot be ignored.

This was too much for the Jews; these words so incensed them that they **picked up stones to kill him** for blasphemy in accordance with the law (Leviticus 24:16). The leaders well understood what Jesus was claiming; and because they didn't believe him, they charged him with blasphemy. In reality, they were really the blasphemers, cursing and attacking the God whom they claimed to serve!

But Jesus hid himself or "was hidden" (perhaps meaning he was hidden by God). John doesn't say it, but by now we know it—Jesus escaped their attempted stoning because his "time had not yet come."

JOHN 9

JESUS HEALS THE MAN WHO WAS BORN BLIND / 9:1-12 / 148
All of Jesus' miracles also pointed to who he was. John follows Jesus' discourse about being "the light of the world" (8:12; 9:5) with the account of Jesus restoring sight to a man born blind. This story illustrates the spiritual truth of Christ being the Light of the World. As the

blind beggar comes to "see" that Jesus is the Messiah, so Jesus offers us spiritual sight to enable us to see him as our Savior and Lord. We too are born spiritually blind and need the gift of sight that only the Light of the World can provide. The Light of the World becomes our light when we put our faith in Jesus Christ.

9:1-3 In ancient cultures, **blind** people had no choice but to be beggars. This man probably was very poor and was begging along the roadside, thus Jesus saw him as he passed by. The disciples believed, based at least partly on Old Testament texts like Exodus 34:7, that a disability such as blindness was a punishment for sin. Many people around the world believe that suffering results from sin. People tend to believe that displeasing God leads to punishment; therefore, they assume that whenever a person seems to be undergoing punishment, there is reason to suspect wrongdoing. This assumption, for example, drove Job's friends to treat him with heavy-handed judgment.

But if suffering always indicates sin, what do we say about babies born with deformities or handicaps? This man was **born blind,** so they asked, **"Was it a result of his own sins or those of his parents?"** The disciples were thinking about what caused the blindness. Jesus shifted their attention away from the cause to the purpose. Jesus demonstrated **the power of God** by healing the man. Instead of worrying about the cause of our problems, we should instead find out how God could use our problem to demonstrate his power. Jesus explained that the man's blindness had nothing to do with his sin or his parents' sin. God allowed nature to run its course so that the victim would ultimately bring glory to God through the reception of both physical and spiritual sight (see 9:30-38).

9:4-5 Jesus was speaking of himself and his disciples as coworkers. He wanted them to learn from him because they would continue his work as his sent ones (see 20:21). Jesus included the disciples in this work (although they actually did nothing for this blind man) because they would be the ones doing the work of God on earth after his resurrection and ascension. What a privilege to be called Christ's coworkers (see 1 Corinthians 3:9; 2 Corinthians 5:21; 6:1).

While Christ was in the world, light was in the world. However, there was **little time left before the night** would fall and **all work** would come **to an end.** The night would come, that is, Jesus would soon die, and would no longer be in the world in physical form. The coming of the night speaks of the shortness of time Jesus had left to fulfill his purpose on earth. But while he was **still in the world,** Jesus would be **the light of the world.** The healing of the blind man affirmed Jesus' identity as the Messiah, for the Old Testament predicted that the Messiah would come to heal the blind (Isaiah 29:18; 35:5; 42:7).

9:6-7 This is not typical of the way Jesus performed miracles, according to John. But Mark records two incidents of miraculous healing where Jesus used his saliva—to cure a deaf and dumb man and to heal a blind man (Mark 7:33; 8:23). John's account, however, provides the only record of Jesus spitting on the ground and forming mud from it.

From antiquity, **spit** or saliva was thought to have medicinal power. But the Jews were suspicious of anyone who used saliva in healing because it was associated with magical arts. It is worth noting, however, that the role of Jesus' saliva in the healing was primarily in making the **mud.** As has been pointed out before (see section on 2:6-8), Jesus did not use random objects without a specific purpose.

First, Jesus used the mud to help develop the man's faith (he had to do as Jesus said, which was to **go and wash** in a certain pool). Second, Jesus kneaded the mud with his hands in order to put it on the man's eyes. This constituted "work" on a Sabbath day and would upset the Pharisees. Jesus had much to teach them about God and his Sabbath.

Siloam is a Greek translation of the Hebrew name, *Shiloah,* meaning "sent." The pool of Siloam had been built by King Hezekiah. His workers had built an underground tunnel from the Spring of Gihon in the Kidron Valley outside of Jerusalem. This tunnel channeled the water into the pool of Siloam inside the city walls. Located in the southeast corner of the city, the tunnel and pool were originally built to help Jerusalem's inhabitants survive in times of siege. The man **went and washed, and came back seeing!** He did as he was told, and his faith healed him.

9:8-12 These verses record the various reactions of the blind man's neighbors to his healing. Some thought he looked like the one who used to sit and beg. Others positively identified him as the same man. Still others objected that this only looked like that blind man. In response, the healed man insisted, **"I am the same man."** Finally realizing that the person who once was blind had received his sight, they asked, **"Who** healed you?"** The formerly blind man testified to the healing power of Jesus by recounting the story of how he had been healed.

RELIGIOUS LEADERS QUESTION THE BLIND MAN / 9:13-34 / 149

Because the people discovered both a miracle and a mystery surrounding the healing of the blind man, they took him to what they considered the most dependable place for exploring such matters. The Pharisees quickly concluded that whatever else the healer might be, he certainly wasn't from God, for otherwise he would not work on the Sabbath. In their quest for "truth," these Pharisees tried a number of explanations to invalidate the miracle: (1) perhaps the blind man had not been blind from birth or had not been totally blind; (2) perhaps God did this miracle directly (but they would recognize no human agent). When the formerly blind man pointed out the obvious answers that they had been so studiously avoiding, they responded by viciously berating him and expelling him from their presence. The astonishing fact of the man's newly given vision eluded this group as if they were blind. Later Jesus pointed this out as their problem, over their strenuous objections.

9:13-15 Why did the people bring him **to the Pharisees?** The possible answer: **Jesus had healed the man on a Sabbath.** The people had realized that Jesus had performed another miracle on the Sabbath and that the Pharisees would want to know about this event. This miracle was news because it was very unusual (9:32). Healing, along with many other actions defined as work, was strictly controlled on the Sabbath. Healing was only to occur in cases of life and death, for which the blind man did not qualify because he had been living with his blindness since birth.

The Pharisees wanted to know how this man had received his sight, and the man explained it in the simplest of terms. Because the man was still blind during the interview with Jesus, he really didn't know who Jesus was. He could only exclaim that he **could see.**

9:16-17 Jesus' actions of kneading the mud, anointing the man's eyes, and healing the man (whose life was not in danger) were all considered work and therefore were forbidden. Jesus may have purposely made the mud in order to emphasize his teaching about the Sabbath—that it is right to care for others' needs even if it involves working on a day of rest. But because Jesus broke their petty rules, they immediately decided he was **not from God.**

But some other Pharisees questioned this condemnation: **"How could an ordinary sinner do such miraculous signs?"** There is no indication that these men were inclined to believe in Jesus; more likely, they were protecting themselves from the charge of obvious bias. Thus, **there was a deep division among them.** While the Pharisees conducted investigations and debated about Jesus, people were being healed and lives were being changed. The Pharisees' skepticism was not based on insufficient evidence, but on jealousy of Jesus' popularity and his influence on the people.

The staunchest Pharisees attacked the healed man with a renewed attempt to break down his testimony. But this newly sighted beggar responded with even more praise for his healer than he had offered previously—he called Jesus **a prophet.**

9:18-21 The **Jewish leaders wouldn't believe** that the man **had been blind,** so they called in the man's **parents** in the hope that they would refute their own son's testimony. Failure to reach quick agreement on the case meant they needed to review the "facts." They asked the parents if this man was really their son, and if he was really born blind. The Pharisees were exasperated: **"How can he see?"** they asked, although we may wonder what they expected the parents to answer.

They knew their son, and they knew his previous condition, but how he could see they didn't know. They responded, **"Ask him."** The parents did not deny their son's story, but neither did they support his claim.

9:22-23 The reason for the parents' fear was that to say **Jesus was the Messiah** would cause them to be **expelled from the synagogue.** Jewish regulations stipulated two kinds of excommunication: one that would last for thirty days until the offender could be reconciled, and one that was a permanent "ban" accompanied by a curse. Because the synagogue controlled every aspect of life (civic, recreational, legal, and religious), an individual cut off from the synagogue would suffer severe isolation.

But why would such a harsh punishment be given people who followed this Jesus, whom the Pharisees had proclaimed as a fake Messiah? The Pharisees were facing a politically dangerous situation. If the crowds were to take Jesus by force and make him king, Rome would respond quickly and forcefully to suppress such a revolt. Roman intervention would cause incredible troubles for the Jews. So the religious leaders decided on the harsh punishment of being put out of the synagogue for anyone who dared believe in Jesus.

9:24-25 Not content with their cross-examination of the healed man, the Pharisees called him in a **second time** with a command, **"Give glory to God by telling the truth."** The Pharisees tried to make the man confess his wrong in proclaiming Jesus as a prophet and to make him agree with them that **Jesus** was **a sinner.**

But the healed man would not give in; he would not say whether or not Jesus was a sinner. What he would say was what he had experienced: **"I know this: I was blind, and now I can see."**

9:26-27 The Pharisees relentlessly asked who did the healing and how it happened. Perhaps they hoped the man would contradict his earlier story so they could accuse him. The religious leaders were making such extensive inquiry about Jesus' identity that it would appear they wanted to follow him—when actually they had no intention of becoming his **disciples.**

The religious leaders were unable to throttle the healed beggar's willingness to testify for Jesus. In fact, the more the Pharisees questioned this man who had received his sight, the stronger and clearer he became about Jesus. At first, the man recognized his healer as "the man they call Jesus" (9:11); then he knew Jesus was "a prophet" (9:17); then he saw Jesus as one who was "from God" and had performed a miracle never done before (9:32-33). Finally, when confronted by Jesus, he believed that Jesus is the "Son of Man" (the Messiah), worthy of worship (9:35-38).

9:28-29 While the Pharisees questioned and **cursed** the man, they persistently defended their adherence to **Moses** (they were confident that God had spoken to Moses). But Jesus had already told them that if they really knew Moses and understood his writings, they would know the Messiah, for Moses wrote of him (5:45-47). But **as for** Jesus, they said they didn't **know anything about him.** It is ironic that the Pharisees claimed not to know where Jesus was from, for that was one item they believed would be true about the Messiah: "No one will know where he comes from" (7:27). They refused to accept Jesus' words or believe that the signs he did validated his claims. They chose to reject him.

9:30-31 This reasoning (and probably their insults too) astonished the **healed** man, so he tried to explain to them that the act of giving him sight proved that Jesus was a man whom God listened to: **"God doesn't listen to sinners, but he is ready to hear those who worship him and do his will."** There are many Scriptures that support this man's statement (see, for example, Job 27:8-9; 35:12-13; Proverbs 15:29; Isaiah 1:15). As a boy, this healed man certainly had been taught the Scriptures, and he pointed out this fact to these supposedly "learned" Pharisees. God does not listen to the requests of sinners, only to the requests of those devoted to him.

9:32-34 Jesus had done the unprecedented, but not the unpredicted. In their fury, the Pharisees were blind to the Old Testament descriptions that specifically speak of the Messiah as being **able to open the eyes of someone born blind** (see Isaiah 29:18; 35:5; 42:7). Indeed, many thought the healing of the blind would be the messianic miracle *par excellence* because there was never any record of such a healing in the Old Testament. Obviously, Jesus had healed him, so Jesus must be **from God.**

The healed man's condemnation of the Pharisees' irrational rejection of Jesus proved too much for them to take, so **they threw him out of the synagogue.**

JESUS TEACHES ABOUT SPIRITUAL BLINDNESS / 9:35-41 / 150

Unless we have suffered rejection for our faith, we may not be able to identify with the state of this blind man whom Jesus healed. In a single day he went from being a disabled outcast to a celebrity who had miraculously received his sight, then to being a witness in court where he was treated like a criminal, and finally to being outcast again (literally) for simply telling the truth as he clearly saw it. At this point, Jesus intervened again. The man's understanding of the one who had healed him had already expanded considerably. Here was his chance to really see Jesus.

9:35-38 Since **Son of Man** is a title of the Christ, Jesus was asking the man if he believed him to be the Messiah. Perhaps the man instantly recognized Jesus by his voice. He expressed immediate desire to believe, which here means not intellectual recognition, but wholehearted trust.

When the man asked who the Son of Man was, Jesus responded, **"You have seen him."** The man could physically see Jesus with his healed eyes, and he could spiritually see because he understood that Jesus was the Messiah. The man acted on his newfound belief—he **worshiped.** He may have just been excommunicated from the synagogue, but he had found true worship. His personal belief is the culmination of the narrative. His belief sharply contrasts with the blindness of the religious leaders (9:40-41).

9:39-41 Do Jesus' words here contradict his statement in 3:17: "God did not send his Son into the world to condemn it." Jesus did not execute judgment during his years on earth, although he would do that in the future. However, his words here reveal that, as the light of the World, he sees and reveals people's innermost thoughts and deepest motives. In so doing, he "judges" or separates those who claim to have great spiritual knowledge when in fact they are blind, from those who humbly seek to follow God and who thus find the Savior.

Christ spoke these words to the healed man in the presence of the **Pharisees who were standing there.** The **blind** are those who realize their need for the Savior and humbly come to him for salvation. They will receive **sight.** But **those who think they see** are the self-righteous who think they have all the answers and have no need of the Savior. They **are blind** because they have rejected the "light of the world" (8:12).

The Pharisees quickly understood that Jesus had directed this statement toward them, but they were not fully sure of the meaning of his words. They assumed that with their learning, reputation, and high standing, they certainly would not be counted among the "blind."

Jesus expanded his statement with the rather cryptic condemnation: **"If you were blind, you wouldn't be guilty, but you remain guilty because you claim you can see."** In contrast to the man who had received his sight, the Pharisees had sight but no light. They were spiritually blind, though they claimed to see. Those who admitted blindness could receive the light and see, but those who thought they saw would remain in their darkness. And their guilt remained, whether they felt guilty or not.

JOHN 10

JESUS IS THE GOOD SHEPHERD / 10:1-21 / 151

This chapter begins with an extended figure of speech or illustration (10:6), similar to a parable, about shepherds and sheep. John provides two aspects of the illustration: the "gate" (10:1-3) and the "shepherd" (10:3-5), each with its own interpretations—the "gate" is interpreted in 10:7-10, and the "shepherd" in 10:11-18.

The entire passage calls to mind the imagery of Ezekiel 34, where the prophet castigated the false shepherds (Israel's evil leaders) and predicted that the true Shepherd (the Messiah) would come and provide God's people (the sheep) with genuine care and leadership. In comparison to the Pharisees, who were bad leaders of God's people, Jesus was the true Shepherd of all God's people. The healed man who believed in Jesus (in the previous chapter) represented all believers who would come out of Judaism to follow Jesus, as sheep follow their shepherd.

10:1-2 At night, the shepherd often would gather the sheep into a fold to protect them from thieves, bad weather, or wild animals. A **sheepfold** could be a cave, shed, or open area surrounded by walls made of stones or branches, eight to ten feet high. Sometimes the top of the wall was lined with thorns to further discourage predators and thieves. The fold's single entrance made it easier for a shepherd to guard his flock. Often several shepherds used a single fold and took turns guarding the entrance. In towns where many people each owned a few sheep, the combined herd was watched over by a shepherd. Mingling the animals was no problem since each flock responded readily to its own shepherd's voice.

The **gate** is the main entrance. Jesus explained that anyone who tried to get in any other way besides going through the gate would be **a thief**—that person would be up to no good. Most likely this "gate" represents the position of Messiah because Jesus went on to say, **"A shepherd enters through the gate."** Only the shepherd has the right to enter the sheepfold and call his own sheep out to follow him.

Jesus rebuked those who would claim to lead God's people without regarding the Messiah (who is in their midst, but unrecognized by them). Such leaders have false ambitions, selfish desires, and evil intentions.

10:3-5 When the shepherd arrived, he would call **his own sheep by name.** Because sheep recognize the voice of their shepherd, they come and **follow him** out to pasture.

The "sheepfold" of Judaism held some of God's people who had awaited the coming of their Shepherd-Messiah (see Isaiah 40:1-11). When the Shepherd came, believing Jews recognized his voice and followed him. It is said that shepherds in the East could name each sheep and that each sheep would respond to the shepherd calling its name. True believers, as sheep belonging to the true Shepherd, would never follow a **stranger** pretending to be their shepherd (5:43).

10:6-7 This illustration was meant to communicate spiritual truths, but many **didn't understand.** So Jesus **explained** the symbolic meaning of "the gate" (10:7-10) before identifying the "shepherd" (10:11-18). The shepherd has called together his flock and taken them to the pasture. Near the pasture is another enclosed place for the sheep. Here the shepherd sits in the doorway, acting as the "gate." The sheep can go out to the pasture or stay inside the walls of the enclosure. To go out or in is to pass by the shepherd's watchful eye.

Having realized they had not grasped what he is teaching them, Jesus said to his listeners, **"I am the gate for the sheep."** As the gate, Jesus is the only way to salvation and eternal life (10:9; 14:6), and his sheep are under his watchful care.

10:8-9 The reference to **all others who came before** was not directed at Old Testament saints and prophets, but at those who had come on the scene pretending to be the Christ (see 5:43), or who had led the people away from God. By immediate context, we see that Jesus was also

referring to those evil Jewish religious leaders who cared nothing about the spiritual welfare of the people, but only about their petty rules and their reputation (see Matthew 23:13; 24:5). Their treatment of Jesus had made it clear that they were far more committed to their system than to God's word. They had invented their own gateway and had appointed themselves gatekeepers. Jesus reminded them that any other supposed "gate" to salvation is false.

Though false teachers, leaders, and messiahs do have their followings, the **true sheep** of God do **not listen** to any of them because none of them possess the authentic voice of the Shepherd. Because Jesus was the genuine Messiah, the sheep could enter through him to be **saved,** pointing to spiritual salvation and spiritual security. The sheep **find green pastures** not as a result of their diligent searching, but through the gracious provision of the Shepherd.

10:10 The **thief** (like false messiahs) has evil intentions. Jesus pictured a heartless individual who began by taking all he could and then killing what he couldn't have. Anything else he destroyed. God's people, Israel, had suffered through more than their share of evil leaders, false prophets, and false messiahs (see, for example, Jeremiah 10:21-22; 12:10; Zechariah 11:4-17). By contrast, Jesus gives **life in all its fullness** to his sheep. This speaks of the gift of divine, eternal life, a life which becomes the possession of every believer for now and for eternity. Jesus would provide his sheep with this eternal life, and it would cost him his own life.

10:11 Jesus is the devoted and dedicated Shepherd—**the good shepherd.** As described in the verses that follow, there are four characteristics that set this Good Shepherd apart from the false or evil shepherds:

1. He approaches directly—he enters at the gate.
2. He has God's authority—the gatekeeper allows him to enter.
3. He meets real needs—the sheep recognize his voice and follow him.
4. He has sacrificial love—he is willing to lay down his life for the sheep.

By repeating it four times, Jesus pointed out that the most important trait of the good shepherd is that he **lays down his life for the sheep** (10:11; see also 15, 17, 18). According to the imagery in this chapter, a shepherd's life could at times be dangerous. Wild animals were common in the countryside of Judea. A good shepherd may indeed risk his life to save his sheep.

10:12-13 The **hired hand** does not have a particular parallel, but is in the story as a contrast with the good shepherd. Because he is doing the job only to be paid, he does not have an investment in the sheep. When **the wolf attacks,** he's not about to risk his life—he **runs away!** Very likely, "the wolf" refers to false prophets or others who take advantage of God's people, the sheep (see Acts 20:29).

What a difference between the good shepherd and the thief and the hired hand! The thief steals, kills, and destroys; the hired hand does the job only for money, but readily flees when danger comes. The good shepherd is committed to the sheep. Jesus is not merely doing a job; he is committed to loving us and even laying down his life for us.

10:14-15 Just as the shepherd calls his sheep and they follow only him, so Jesus knows his people. And his followers, in return, **know** him to be their Messiah, and they love and trust him. Such knowing and trusting between Jesus and his followers is compared to the relationship between Jesus and the Father: **"just as my Father knows me and I know the Father."** And Jesus repeated his point—that he is the Good Shepherd and that he will **lay down** his life for the sheep.

10:16 Jesus had already spoken of leading out his sheep from the fold of Judaism. All of his disciples came out of this fold, as did all those Jews who came to believe in him as their Messiah. Jesus knew, however, that he had **other sheep** that were not from Judaism. These are Gentile believers. Jesus came to save Gentiles as well as Jews. This is an insight into his worldwide mission—to die for sinful people all over the world. The Good Shepherd came to gather together God's people into one flock (Ezekiel 34:11-14, 23). The new Gentile believers and the Jewish believers who left Judaism would form one flock that would be altogether outside of Judaism. The flock would have **one shepherd.** Furthermore, Jesus' words here foreshadow those he uttered in his prayer for the oneness of all those who would believe in him through the disciples' message (17:20ff.)

10:17-18 The Father loved the Son for his willingness to die in order to secure the salvation of the believers. Jesus laid down his life of his own accord; and yet of his own accord he would also take up his life again in resurrection. When Jesus said, **"I lay down my life voluntarily"** and that he had **"the power to take it again,"** he was claiming authority to control his death and beyond. John's original readers needed to remember that Jesus specifically foretold his death and resurrection. We need the same reminder. Jesus **gave up** his life; it was not taken from him. The Son's authority to lay down his life and take it up again did not originate with himself; it came from **the Father.**

10:19-21 Some of the unbelieving Jews who heard Jesus pronounced a twofold judgment against him: **"He has a demon, or he's crazy."** Jesus had already been accused of being demon-possessed (7:20; 8:48), but this is the first and only time in John's Gospel that Jesus is accused of being crazy. It was commonly believed that insanity went hand-in-hand with demon-possession.

Some other Jews in Jesus' audience were impressed with both Jesus' words and miraculous deeds. They had not yet forgotten the healing of the blind man (chapter 9). Thus, they disagreed with those who charged him with demon-possession.

RELIGIOUS LEADERS SURROUND JESUS AT THE TEMPLE / 10:22-42 / 152

As this section begins, there has been a temporary stalemate between Jesus and his opponents. They have become divided, so they are unable for a time to mount an effective attack against him. It must have been a period of intense frustration for the Jewish religious leaders. Finally, an opportunity for confrontation developed one day while Jesus was visiting the Temple.

10:22-23 A couple of months had passed since Jesus' last teaching to the people in 7:1–10:21. That teaching had occurred during the Festival of Shelters in September/October; the coming words occurred at the celebration of **Hanukkah** in December, in **winter.** This celebration was not one of the official festivals in the Old Testament. It was instituted by Judas Maccabeus in 165 B.C. to commemorate the cleansing of the Temple after Antiochus Epiphanes had defiled it by sacrificing a pig on the altar of burnt offering (see 1 Maccabees 4:36-59; 2 Maccabees 1:9; 10:1-8). This is also the present-day Feast of Lights called Hanukkah.

Jesus was in Jerusalem walking through **Solomon's Colonnade,** a roofed porch with tall stone columns located on the east side of the Temple. It was named for Solomon because it was believed to rest on portions of the original Temple built by Solomon. These were common places for teaching, so it would have been an appropriate place for Jesus to be walking and probably teaching as he walked.

10:24 Many people who ask for proof do so for wrong reasons. Jesus had never plainly told the Jews in Jerusalem that he was the **Messiah** because it connoted a military leader or political liberator for them. Therefore, Jesus wisely avoided using that term. Most of these questioners didn't want to follow Jesus in the way that he wanted to lead them. They hoped that Jesus would declare himself the Messiah, but only if he intended to get on with their political agenda and drive out the Romans. So they wanted to hear an open declaration from Jesus' lips: **"If you are the Messiah, tell us plainly."**

It is doubtful, however, that a plain declaration would have convinced them, for they had already made up their minds on the issue. Some of them hoped he would identify himself so they could accuse him of telling lies or catch him in the act of blasphemy (see 10:31, 33, 39).

10:25-26 Although Jesus had never told them "I am the Messiah," he had clearly indicated his unity with God the Father (5:17ff) and his heavenly origin (6:32ff). Besides, the **proof** was in what he was doing **in the name of** his **Father.** Jesus' miracles should have convinced them he was the Messiah (see Isaiah 35:3-6).

John refers to the illustration Jesus used months earlier regarding Jesus as the "good shepherd" (10:3-9, 16). Here, Jesus told the Jewish leaders surrounding him, **"You don't believe me because you are not part of my flock."** Only those who were given to Jesus by the Father (10:29) were his sheep.

10:27-29 Of those who do believe Jesus and do belong to his sheep, Jesus says, "My sheep recognize my voice; I know them, and they follow me. I give them eternal life, and they will never perish. No one will snatch them away from me." In this grand statement, Jesus summarized the blessings of those who truly listen to and believe the gospel. The believer in Jesus knows him personally, has eternal life, will not perish, and is secure in his care. But many of those who heard had no intention of truly listening. It is also true that those refusing to listen to Jesus' voice are not his sheep. We recognize Christ's voice when he speaks to us through the Bible. Are we truly listening for it? They cannot be snatched away because the Father has given them to Jesus, and the Father is more powerful than anyone else. God's power guards and preserves the flock for salvation.

10:30 There is no mistaking Jesus' meaning: **"The Father and I are one."** Jesus did not mean that he and the Father are the same person, because the word for "one" in Greek is neuter. The Father and the Son are two persons in the Trinity, but they are one in essence. Given this essential oneness, the Father and Son act as one—what the Father does, the Son does, and vice versa. This is one of the clearest affirmations of Jesus' divinity in the whole Bible. Jesus is not merely a good teacher—he is God. His claim to be God was unmistakable. The religious leaders wanted to kill him because their laws said that anyone claiming to be God should die for blasphemy. Nothing could persuade them that Jesus' claim was true.

10:31-33 For the third time (see 5:17-18; 8:58-59), these Jews wanted to **kill** this "blasphemer" (Leviticus 24:11-16). But Jesus withheld their violent act by asking them, **"For which one of these good deeds are you killing me?"** The Jews answered that they were not stoning him for any **good work,** but because he, **a mere man,** had made himself **God.** Though they didn't believe him, they understood that he was claiming equality with God.

10:34-36 The term "law" is often used in the New Testament to encompass the entire Old Testament. By saying **"your own law,"** Jesus was claiming common ground with his accusers, for they all agreed that **the Scriptures cannot be altered.** Jesus used Psalm 82:6, where the Israelite judges are called **gods** (see also Exodus 4:16; 7:1) to counter the Jews' charge of blasphemy. In Psalm 82, the supreme God is said to rise in judgment against those whom he calls "gods," because they had failed to be just to the helpless and oppressed. These "gods" were those who were the official representatives and commissioned agents of God; they were the judges executing judgment for God. If they were called "gods," how was it blasphemous **when the Holy One who was sent into the world by the Father** calls himself **the Son of God.** This is especially important when, in fact, he was the one the Father sanctified and sent into the world.

10:37-39 This statement underscores Jesus' claim to oneness with the Father: **"The Father is in me, and I am in the Father"** (see 14:10-11; 17:21). Jesus told them to not believe unless he was doing the Father's work. But if they saw him doing his work, then they should believe in what he was doing, even if they didn't believe his words. Jesus' explanations did not change the Jews' minds; they had been intent on stoning him for blasphemy (10:31). But when they attempted to arrest him, **he got away.** Once again Jesus demonstrated that his fate would not be determined by the will of crowds or human priorities. Even when "his time" would come, God would still be ultimately in control. John's readers, who may have faced persecution, would have been encouraged by this report. And we need the same encouragement to know that God cares for us.

10:40-42 Jesus went to the east side of the **Jordan** (see 1:28). It was his final preaching mission out in the countryside and the final opportunity for many

people to respond. Jesus did not return to Jerusalem again until the day he made his Triumphal Entry.

The ministry of **John** the Baptist had left a permanent impression on those who had heard him speak of the coming Messiah. What they heard here and saw in Jesus confirmed in their minds the genuineness of his forerunner's proclamations. As a result of hearing John's prophetic ministry and then seeing the Messiah himself, **many believed in him.**

JOHN 11

LAZARUS BECOMES ILL AND DIES / 11:1-16 / *165*

The Gospels tell us that Jesus raised others from the dead, including Jairus's daughter (Matthew 9:18-26; Mark 5:41-42; Luke 8:40-56) and a widow's son (Luke 7:11-17). These people represent a cross section of ages and social backgrounds to whom Jesus gave back human life. All of them, including Lazarus, were raised but eventually died again. Lazarus's story stands out because John used it as a **sign** of Jesus' ultimate life-giving power and a picture of his own coming resurrection. And, as with all the miracles recorded in this gospel, it glorifies God. From John's perspective, this miracle was the turning point; it caused the Jewish leaders to take decisive action against Jesus.

11:1-3 Though John only introduces us to the family of **Mary, Martha,** and **Lazarus** at the end of Jesus' ministry, Jesus and the disciples often visited their home. Jesus enjoyed their close friendship and hospitality on his visits to Jerusalem, for **Bethany** was a village just outside of the city. At this time, Jesus was on the other side of the Jordan River, also in a town called Bethany. The events described in Luke 13:22–17:10 occurred between chapters 10 and 11 of John.

John identified Mary with an event described in the next chapter (12:1-7) because Mary's display of love for Christ was well known to the first-century Christians (Matthew 26:6-13; Mark 14:3-9). **Lazarus was sick,** so the sisters contacted Jesus, their friend who had healed so many.

11:4 When Jesus heard of Lazarus's sickness, he said it **will not end in death.** He knew Lazarus would die, but the end of the story would not be death. His disciples understood him to mean that the illness was not serious. Again, we see the parallel between Jesus' response here and in 9:3. In the former passage, Jesus spoke of the man's blindness as an opportunity for God's works to be seen. Lazarus's death was an opportunity for **the Son of God**

to **receive glory.** God strategically placed some miracles in human history to demonstrate his wise providence and his sovereignty.

11:5-7 This statement of Jesus' love for the family explains that it was not lack of love that kept Jesus from going to them. Humanly speaking, Jesus would have wanted to go to them immediately. But he was constrained by the Father's timing. When God's time came, Jesus headed back into **Judea** to be with his dear friends in their sorrow. God's timing is always perfect, whether in guiding his Son through his ministry on earth, or in guiding us today and answering our prayers.

11:8-10 The disciples couldn't understand why Jesus would want to go into **Judea,** when the **Jewish leaders** there just recently had been seeking to kill him (see 10:31ff.). Why leave a place where people believe in you and welcome you (10:42) to go back to certain death? But Jesus was not afraid, for he knew that he had to die and that his death would only occur in the Father's timing.

The disciples worried about what the Jewish leaders might do. Jesus pointed to an unlimited sphere— the sovereignty of God, who transcends the limits of time and over whom people have no control. As

Jesus obeyed his Father, he was as confident about the victorious outcome as he was that every day contained **twelve hours of daylight.** We should remember that God's sovereignty extends to each moment of our life; otherwise, our trust in him will be limited to only those times when he meets our expectations. We will repeat the disciples' mistake—attempting to limit God to the sphere of human effort.

Jesus' answer mentioned an expected number of "hours" during which **people can walk safely.** It also clearly implied that time would run out. After twelve hours of daylight the **night** comes. Our Lord's "day" (his time on earth) was approaching its final hour. But Jesus still had tasks to accomplish, and he would not be sidetracked from his mission. The simple lesson of using daylight to walk safely illustrates our deeper need to trust in the "light" of Jesus' presence and God's guidance. Jesus had already used the phrase "the light of the world" to refer to his own presence among people. While he was among them, he was their light (see 1:4; 8:12; 9:5). As long as they did their work in the light of Christ's presence they would not stumble. Sadly, those who live in the dark, without the presence of Jesus' light in them, will stumble.

11:11-15 The disciples missed Jesus' meaning when he said, **"Lazarus has fallen asleep."** They assumed he was **getting better.** Jesus explained: **"Lazarus is dead."** Lazarus died so that Jesus could show his power over death to his disciples and others. He would go and **wake him up,** thus giving the disciples **another opportunity to believe.** The raising of Lazarus displayed Christ's power— the resurrection from the dead is a crucial belief of Christian faith. Jesus not only raised himself from the dead (10:18), but he also has the power to raise others.

11:16 We often remember **Thomas** as "the doubter" because he doubted Jesus' resurrection (20:24-25). But he also loved the Lord and was a man of great courage. The disciples knew the dangers of going with Jesus to Jerusalem, so they tried to talk him out of it. Thomas merely expressed what all of them were feeling. When their objections failed, they were willing to go and even die with Jesus. They may not have understood why Jesus would be killed, but they were loyal. We may face unknown dangers in doing God's work. It is wise to consider the high cost of being Jesus' disciple.

JESUS COMFORTS MARY AND MARTHA / 11:17-37 / *166*

Although we get many glimpses of Jesus' compassion throughout the Gospels, his tender conversations with Mary and Martha are the most moving. His words reveal patient pastoral concerns. Elsewhere we see him confront people with the truth; here we see him console as the gentle Master. Jesus did not ridicule or belittle grief. He affirmed our need for comfort by providing it to the sisters without hesitation. It is a tribute to the family that many from Jerusalem came to Bethany to pay their respects and offer their support to the sisters.

11:17-19 Lazarus had already been in his grave for four days by the time **Jesus arrived.** In the warm climate of Palestine, a dead body would decompose quickly, so a person's body was often buried the same day of death. When Jesus and the disciples arrived in Bethany, many Jews from **Jerusalem** had gathered to console Lazarus's family, and some of those who had arrived were religious leaders. In Jewish society, prolonged mourning for the dead was considered an essential part of every funeral.

11:20-24 Upon seeing Jesus, **Martha** said to him, **"Lord, if you had been here, my brother would not have died."** Martha probably realized that Jesus could not have arrived much earlier, but she was confident that Jesus' presence would have prevented Lazarus's death. Mary makes the same comment later (11:32). Despite their pain and sorrow, their faith in Jesus did not waver. The implication

for us is that we should not quickly assume that God has let us down when we are in the midst of difficulties. Then she added, **"But even now I know that God will give you whatever you ask."** Perhaps Martha thought Jesus would bring her brother back to life. But her reply in verse 24 and subsequent protests at the tomb (11:39) suggest otherwise. She did not realize, understand, or dare to hope that Jesus would ask God to give Lazarus back his physical life and be returned to his family. Instead, she reaffirmed her trust in his power even though she thought Jesus had missed an opportunity to display it by healing her brother.

When Jesus said, **"Your brother will rise again,"** she attributed it to the future resurrection— **"When everyone else rises, on resurrection day."** But Jesus did not mean an eventual, distant resurrection, he meant that Lazarus would rise again that very day!

11:25-26 To the woman at the well (4:25-26), Jesus identified himself as the Messiah; to the blind man (9:35-37), he disclosed himself as the Son of Man; but here he enlarged the picture by revealing himself as the source of resurrection life.

To understand Jesus' statement, we need to see it in two parts. First, Jesus explained the resurrection: **"I am the resurrection . . . Those who believe in me, even though they die . . . will live again."** Then he explained the life: **"I am . . . the life . . . They are given eternal life for believing in me and will never perish."**

The believer will not experience eternal death. Lazarus had been a believer in Jesus; therefore, even though he died, he would live. Every believer who has died will yet live, and everyone who is still living and believing will die, but not eternally. Christ did not promise the prevention of physical death; he guaranteed in himself to give abundant life, including resurrection and eternity with him. Christ did not prevent Lazarus's physical death (after being raised, Lazarus would eventually die again), but Lazarus had the guarantee of eternal life.

11:27 Martha is best known for being too busy to sit down and talk with Jesus (Luke 10:38-42), but here we see her as a woman of deep faith. When asked if she believed his words about resurrection, she replied, **"I have always believed you are the Messiah, the Son of God, the one who has come into the world from God."** Her statement of faith is exactly the response that Jesus wants from us. This confession presents a high point in John's Gospel, for here we see a believer acknowledging

that Jesus is the Messiah, the Son of God. In recognizing Jesus as the Messiah, she saw him to be God's envoy appointed to deliver God's people; in recognizing Jesus as the Son of God, she saw his divinity.

11:28-32 Martha spoke to **Mary** secretly so that the visiting Jews would not follow her to where Jesus was—somewhere outside the village. However, when Mary arose quickly to go to Jesus, she was **followed** by the mourners. Mary met Jesus and repeated Martha's statement (11:21). They were both convinced that Jesus would have been able to do something had Lazarus still been living. But they had no idea that death might be reversible.

11:33-37 The Greek word for **deeply troubled** can mean "intensely agitated." Jesus may have been troubled by the excessive sorrow of the mourners, by Martha and Mary's limited faith, or by the general unbelief. Even more so, Jesus was angry at the power of death, man's ultimate enemy (1 Corinthians 15:26). Among the commotion and the loud wailing of the mourners, **Jesus wept.** What made Jesus cry? Was it his love for Lazarus? Was it the presence of sadness and death? Or was it the faithless grief that surrounded him? For whatever the reason, the situation caused Jesus to shed some tears. The Jews' interpreted Jesus' tears as a sign of Jesus' great love for Lazarus. They assumed that Jesus wept in frustration and sorrow that he had not arrived earlier in order to heal Lazarus. Following Martha and Mary, others also asked, **"This man healed a blind man. Why couldn't he keep Lazarus from dying?"** (referring to Jesus' previous miracle—see 9:1-7).

JESUS RAISES LAZARUS FROM THE DEAD / 11:38-44 / 167

As this chapter opens, we see Mary, Martha, and the crowd expressing conditional belief in the power of Jesus. They believed that Jesus could have worked a miracle if Lazarus had still been alive. But death intervened, and they thought it was irreversible. Little did they know that what they considered impossible would soon be overcome by God's power.

11:38-39 John once again tells us that Jesus was **deeply troubled** (see 11:33). Lazarus was buried in **a cave with a stone rolled across its entrance.** Tombs at this time were usually caves carved in the limestone rock of a hillside. A tomb was often large enough for people to walk inside. Several bodies would be placed in one tomb. After burial, a large stone would be rolled across the entrance to the tomb. This burial spot was much like the one in which Jesus would be buried. Jesus said to the crowd, **"Roll the stone aside."** When Jesus asked that the stone be removed, Martha protested.

11:40 The purpose of the whole event was for Jesus to exhibit **God's glory.** Jesus had proclaimed this from the moment he heard about Lazarus's sickness (11:4). In order for the miracle to occur and for God to be glorified through it, the sisters would have to **believe** enough to order the stone to be removed from the tomb's entrance.

11:41-44 While the crowd waited beside the tomb—with the **stone** now rolled **aside** from its entrance—Jesus praised his Father aloud, publicly, so that, upon witnessing the miracle of resurrection, the people might believe in Jesus. His prayer was not a petition, but a prayer of thanks to the Father. Jesus knew that his request would be answered.

Then **Jesus shouted, "Lazarus, come out!"** The voice of Jesus is potent and life-giving. Lazarus provided proof of Jesus' earlier words: "The dead will hear my voice . . . and those who listen will live" (5:25). At Jesus' words, **Lazarus came out.** He was completely **bound in graveclothes.** There was no question that a dead man had come back to life. The miracle was not only Lazarus' resuscitation. After four days, the body would have seriously decayed. Lazarus' body was raised and restored. Jesus told them, **"Unwrap him and let him go!"**

RELIGIOUS LEADERS PLOT TO KILL JESUS / 11:45-57 / *168*

Some eyewitnesses to the raising of Lazarus reported to the Pharisees in Jerusalem, only a couple of miles away. This fresh evidence of Jesus' power threw the Pharisees into a panic. What followed is a priceless opportunity for us who know the full story to see how badly mistaken people can be in their assessment of events.

11:45-46 Jesus' words and works, even today, divide people into two camps—believers and unbelievers. Many people can see the same miraculous event, yet walk away being affected differently. The raising of Lazarus was stunning to many, so that **many** of the witnesses **believed in Jesus** as the Messiah. Yet other Jewish onlookers did not believe; they brought word of what had happened to the **Pharisees,** who were looking for a reason to kill Jesus (7:1, 19, 25; 8:37, 40).

11:47 The **high council** was the highest ruling authority among the Jews in Judea. It was composed of seventy-one members: The high priest presiding over seventy religious leaders, the majority of whom were Sadducees and the minority, Pharisees. **"What are we going to do?"** they asked. The dialogue that follows points clearly to the Jewish leaders' single-minded opposition to Jesus. John captured the irony of their conversation as they used every true statement to lead to wrong conclusions.

11:48 It was Rome's custom to allow conquered people to carry on their religious practices as long as they did not lead to rebellion against Rome. Jesus' miracles, however, often would cause a disturbance. If all the Jewish populace would **follow** Jesus as their Messiah-King, the leaders feared that the **Roman army** would take away their limited privileges of self-rule, as well as destroy the **Temple** and the **nation** (see Acts 6:13; 21:28).

11:49-52 Caiaphas led the Sadducees, the elite, educated, and wealthy Jews, who stood on fairly good terms with Rome. Jesus was a special threat to their quiet and secure positions in leadership over Judea's religious life. Caiaphas was proud and ruthless. His usual policy was to remove any threats to his power by whatever means necessary.

For him, Jesus' death was not an "if" but a "when, where, and how."

Since Caiaphas served as a high priest for eighteen years (A.D. 18 to 36), the expression **that year** refers to that one year in which Jesus was crucified. The office of high priest was originally instituted by God to be a lifetime position (Numbers 35:25); but the Romans did not want any one person to become too powerful, so they appointed high priests and placed a new one in position whenever they wanted. Caiaphas was convinced that nothing short of destroying Jesus would save Israel from being destroyed by Rome. The life of one person was considered cheap and expendable as an alternative to endangering the nation. God used his words to express an unwitting prophecy of universal proportions: **"Let this one man die for the people."** One man did have to die in order that the world might be saved.

The words of **Caiaphas** were really a **prophecy.** Though his intent was sinful, God used him to indicate that Jesus **should die for the entire nation.** In addition, Caiaphas **didn't think of it himself; he was inspired to say it.** The irony of Caiaphas's statement that John didn't want his readers to miss was that Jesus' death, intended to spare the nation of Israel from physical destruction, was actually to spare Israel from spiritual destruction. In the end, Jesus' death was **for the gathering together of all the children of God scattered around the world.**

11:53 The **Jewish leaders** missed the prophetic implications of Caiaphas's statement, and **began to plot Jesus' death.** But evil leaders, no matter how long they have power or how evil their actions, are always under God's control.

11:54 Aware of the plot against his life, Jesus **went to a place near the wilderness. Ephraim** may have been the same place as Ophrah, near Bethel (see 2 Chronicles 13:19). Jesus and his disciples stayed there until the time of the Passover.

11:55-57 This **Passover** probably occurred in A.D. 30, the year of Jesus' death. Everyone in Jerusalem during the Passover celebration knew that the chief priests and Pharisees wanted to arrest Jesus. Furthermore, they were under strict orders to report Jesus' whereabouts. Into this tense scene Jesus would make his triumphal entry (12:12ff.).

JOHN 12

A WOMAN ANOINTS JESUS WITH PERFUME / 12:1-11 / 182

The chapter opens with a portrayal of Mary anointing Jesus, accompanied by a wide range of reactions. This anointing concurs with the one described in Matthew 26:6-13 and Mark 14:3-9; but it is different from the one depicted in Luke 7:36-50, which occurred much earlier in Jesus' ministry. The tender attention given to Jesus by his three friends in Bethany contrasts with the treachery Judas planned to commit by the week's end.

12:1-2 Another **Passover** was coming, and **Jesus arrived in Bethany six days** beforehand. John last placed him in Ephraim, where he had gone to be alone with his disciples (11:54). From there, they returned to Galilee for a while. This was Jesus' final visit with his friends at Bethany because he was on his way to Jerusalem where, as he had already told his disciples he would die. Only a few weeks had gone by since Jesus had raised Lazarus from the dead. He was back in **the home of Lazarus.** According to parallel accounts of this story (see Matthew 26:6-13; Mark 14:3-9), this meal was held at the home of Simon the leper, who also lived in Bethany and was very likely healed of his leprosy by Jesus. A **dinner** had been **prepared** in Jesus' honor.

12:3 This **perfume** was made from an aromatic herb (**nard**) from the mountains of India, and it was imported in alabaster bottles. This expensive imported item carried such value that people used it for investment purposes, as gold is often used today. When supper was finished, Mary took this pure, expensive perfume and **anointed Jesus' feet.** Nard was used to anoint kings; Mary may have been anointing Jesus as her kingly Messiah. Many centuries later we are still humbled by the extravagance and the appropriateness of Mary's gift. She poured out the very best she could find. Price is not the central issue, but the sincere expression of faith and love.

12:4-6 According to Matthew and Mark, all the disciples were offended that Mary had "wasted" this expensive ointment (Matthew 26:8; Mark 14:4). But in John's Gospel, **Judas Iscariot** verbalized the offense. **"The perfume was worth a small fortune. It should have been sold and the money given to the poor."** Judas's motive was not to care for the poor. Judas was a **thief** who had been entrusted with the **disciples' funds** (see 13:29). Judas often dipped into the money **for his own use.** Undoubtedly, Jesus knew what Judas was doing (2:24-25; 6:64), but he never did or said anything about it.

12:7-8 Jesus pointed out that Mary was not wasting this perfume on him. Certainly, the money could have been given to the poor; there would **always** be opportunities to care for the **poor.** But they would not always have Jesus. Mary understood how special Jesus was. Her anointing was like an ointment put on his body **in preparation for burial** (Matthew 26:12; Mark 14:8). (Later Nicodemus and Joseph of Arimathea would actually wrap Jesus' body with linen and spices, 19:39.)

This act and Jesus' response to it do not give us permission to ignore the poor. Rather, Jesus explained that his followers would have many opportunities to help the poor, but only a short time to love and honor the Messiah. Mary's loving act was for a specific occasion—an anointing that anticipated Jesus' burial and a public declaration of her faith in him as the Messiah. Jesus' words should have taught Judas a valuable lesson about the worth of money. Unfortunately, Judas did not learn it. In contrast to Mary's sacrificial gift to Jesus, Judas sold his master's life for thirty pieces of silver (Matthew 26:14-16), the price one paid a slave owner if one's ox killed one of his slaves (see Exodus 21:32).

12:9-11 Jews were arriving from all over the world for the Passover celebration. Many had heard of the miracle of Lazarus's resurrection. When they discovered that **Jesus** had returned to Bethany to be with **Lazarus,** they came to see both of them.

However, the leading priests decided to kill Lazarus too, for it was because of him that many of the people had deserted them and believed in Jesus. The chief priests' blindness and hardness of heart caused them to sink ever deeper into sin. One sin led them to another. From the Jewish leaders' point of view, they could accuse Jesus of blasphemy because he claimed equality with God. But Lazarus had done nothing of the kind. They wanted Lazarus dead simply because he was a living witness to Jesus' power.

JESUS RIDES INTO JERUSALEM ON A YOUNG DONKEY / 12:12-19 / 183

John's description of the Triumphal Entry, mentioned in all four Gospels, is the most brief of the accounts. John's objective seemed to be to sketch the events, relating them to Old Testament prophecies and explaining that those present did not fully understand all that was going on. He pointed out that these events intensified the animosity of the leaders toward Jesus. In the other Gospels, we are left with the impression that the crowd's reaction to Jesus was largely spontaneous. John, however, helpfully explained that those who had witnessed the raising of Lazarus had been busily telling others. The news created great anticipation in Jerusalem of Jesus' arrival.

12:12-13 The day after the feast in Bethany, Jesus made his triumphal entry into Jerusalem. Given the importance of the approaching Passover, the road into the holy city would have been clogged with pilgrims. Among them would have been many people from Galilee, familiar with Jesus from his years of ministry there.

Not only was **Jesus** part of the large crowd moving toward Jerusalem, others came out to meet him from the city itself. Expectations that something marvelous was soon to happen must have been at fever pitch! The crowd began to shout. As they shouted **"Praise God,"** they thought that their conquering King had finally come to liberate them from Roman rule. They believed that **the one who comes in the name of the Lord** was **the King of Israel** (see Psalm 118:25-26; Zephaniah 3:15; John 1:49). Therefore, the Jews thought they were hailing the arrival of their King! But these people who were praising God for giving them a king had the wrong idea about Jesus. They were sure he would be a national leader who would restore their nation to its former glory; thus they were deaf to the words of their prophets and blind to Jesus' real mission. When it became apparent that Jesus was not going to fulfill their hopes, many people turned against him.

12:14-15 Indeed, their King came to them—but not the kind of king they had expected. He did not arrive as a political ruler might, on a mighty horse or in a chariot. Rather, Jesus came to them in the way prophesied by Zechariah: **"Don't be afraid, people of Israel. Look, your King is coming, sit-**

ting on a donkey's colt." The Old Testament prophet Zechariah had prophesied the arrival of a great king, possibly Alexander the Great, in Zechariah 9:1-8. Then contrasting that, he had prophesied the arrival to Jerusalem's people of their King (see Zechariah 9:9). In this coming, Israel's King would be a humble servant, not a conqueror. He would not be exalted to a throne, but lifted up on a cross.

12:16 The same kind of statement was made in 2:22. After Christ's resurrection and subsequent glorification, the disciples **remembered** these events and understood what they signified. Prior to Jesus' resurrection, his followers did not understand the significance of his triumphal entry into Jerusalem. The Holy Spirit would open their eyes to the meaning of the Old Testament Scriptures, Jesus' **fulfillment of prophecy,** and remind them of this and other messianic predictions (14:26; see also Luke 24:25-35, 44-48).

12:17-19 The crowd that was with him when he called **Lazarus back to life** continued to spread the word. **That was the main reason so many went out to meet him.** This statement emphasizes the superficial enthusiasm that possessed most of the cheering throng. They flocked to Jesus because they had heard about his great miracle in raising Lazarus from the dead. Their adoration was short-lived and their commitment shallow, for in a few days they would do nothing to stop his crucifixion.

The Pharisees were exasperated by such exultation. They were hoping to find some sly way to get hold of Jesus and get rid of him while they knew his whereabouts, but it was impossible with the huge adoring crowds surrounding him. Their state-ment, **"the whole world has gone after him!"** is ironic—for most of those people did not really believe in Jesus.

JESUS EXPLAINS WHY HE MUST DIE / 12:20-36 / *185*

As if to confirm the fears expressed in verse 19, this section begins with a group of Gentiles trying to approach Jesus. We are not told if their request for an audience with Christ was ever granted, but Jesus replied to their interest with some instruction on the necessity of his own death.

This passage also includes the third instance of God speaking audibly during the ministry of Jesus. The first was at the baptism of Jesus (Matthew 3:13-17; Mark 1:9-11; Luke 3:21-22); the second at the Transfiguration (Matthew 17:1-13; Mark 9:2-13; Luke 9:28-36). God the Father broke the silence of heaven to encourage his Son in the final days of his mission on earth. Jesus himself emphasized again the brief time that remained during which the light would still be present.

12:20-22 Indeed, it seemed as if the "whole world" had gone after Jesus, as illustrated by these **Greeks** who came to the **Passover** and sought a meeting with him. These people were either visitors from Greece or Greek-speaking Jews. They may have been Jewish proselytes or simply God-fearing Gentiles. These Greeks proba-bly selected **Philip** as their emissary to Jesus because, though Philip was a Jew, he had a Greek name. And Philip was from Bethsaida, a town in Galilee near the Greek territory on the eastern side of the Sea of Galilee called Decapolis. The city of **Bethsaida** itself had a large Greek popula-tion, and Philip may have been able to speak Greek.

For a moment, Philip hesitated to approach Jesus with the Greeks' request. So first, **Philip told Andrew** (with whom Philip is often associ-ated—1:40-44; 6:7-8; Mark 3:18). Then, **they went together to ask Jesus.** The very inclusion of Greeks in the events of the final week has great significance. John continued his pattern of including Gentiles (the world) all along the way (1:12; 3:16). His readers, who may have been Gentiles struggling with their acceptability to God, would have gained encouragement from this incident and Jesus' response. We Gentiles also ought to be grateful that Christ includes us in his offer of salvation.

12:23-24 Jesus' words to Philip and Andrew and perhaps to the other disciples as well were not addressed to the crowd. The crowd (probably including the Greeks) is not mentioned again until verse 29. Jesus explained, **"The time has come for the Son of Man to enter into his glory"** through death and resurrection. The

"whole world" had gone after Jesus (12:19); even the Greeks wanted to see him (12:20ff). Yet it is exactly at this point, when by human standards Jesus was in a perfect position to consolidate his forces and overwhelm the opposition, that he faced the heart-troubling time that was upon him. Until this moment, the "time" had always been a future event. But here Jesus declared that it had arrived.

The picture of **a kernel of wheat** reveals the necessary sacrifice of Jesus. When a grain of wheat is buried in the ground, it actually **dies** before becoming a mature blade producing **many new kernels.** In the same way, Jesus, by his death, produced more fruit than could have been gained had he become the king of Israel on an earthly throne. Indeed, by being lifted up on the cross, Jesus would draw all people to himself. In his pic-ture of the dying grain, Jesus spoke directly about his own life. He does not necessarily require us to literally give up our lives in sacrificial death as the only way to be fruitful. God does call some believ-ers to die for him. But he calls many more to stay alive for fruitful service (see Romans 12:1-2).

12:25-27 True followers of Jesus must have their priorities in order; if they choose to **love their life** more than their Master, they **will lose** the very life they seek to maintain. True disciples must be willing to suffer and experience rejection, even unto death if need be. To serve and **follow** Jesus means making radical lifestyle changes. To follow Jesus means going the way he went—not the way of earthly power and honor—but the way of humility and death. Everything Jesus did was for God's glory. When we choose to follow him, we must live for God's glory alone. This does not mean we have no fun, no joy, no security. Rather, it simply means we live to honor God and then **the Father will honor** us.

The honor from God that Jesus promises may, in fact, be partly experienced in this life, but never entirely. And for many believers, what God has planned by way of honor we can only guess. Meanwhile we can derive real comfort and security from knowing that God observes and remembers each and every act of service we do in his name. None will be forgotten.

Unlike the synoptic Gospels, John does not record Jesus' agony in the Garden of Gethsemane prior to his crucifixion (Matthew 26:36-46; Mark 14:32-42; Luke 22:39-46). The record of Jesus being **deeply troubled** is the only indication in John that Jesus was troubled by that approaching hour. His agony proves the genuineness of his humanity. Jesus refused to ask the Father to **save** him from the cross (see Romans 8:32) because he knew he had been sent for the very purpose of dying on the cross. Jesus knew his crucifixion lay ahead, and because he was human, he dreaded it.

12:28-30 Jesus now turns his thoughts back to the **Father** and back to the purpose for which he had come to earth: to **bring glory** to him. Thus, the Father responded in a **voice** from **heaven, "I have already brought it glory, and I will do it again."** God would glorify his name through the obedience of his Son (13:31-32) and then would glorify his name again when he would be reunited (17:5) with his Son after his resurrection.

The Father's voice was audible but not correctly perceived by the multitude standing around. Some in the crowd said that it was **thunder.** Others thought it was **an angel.** Whatever their interpretation of the sound, it could not be denied that the phenomenon was supernatural. Jesus made it clear that **he** did not need this "voice" (he knew that the Father would glorify him); the voice had come for the **benefit** of the people. However, only a few (such as John who recorded this event) understood what was said and who said it. To the others it was merely thunderous noise.

12:31-33 Anticipating his glorification through death and resurrection, Jesus proclaimed: **"The time of judgment for the world has come, when the prince of this world will be cast out."** From our perspective we see how Christ's death brought judgment on those who had the upper hand in the world's system: Judas, Caiaphas, Pilate, and the Jewish religious leaders. But the Son had ultimately come to destroy the works of Satan, who controlled the minds of people,

producing unbelief. Therefore, the world would be judged in the sense that Satan, the ruler of the world (see 14:30; 16:11; 2 Corinthians 4:4; Ephesians 2:2; 6:12; Revelation 12:9), would be cast out—his final and ultimate weapon, death, was about to be overcome (see 1 Corinthians 15:26; Hebrews 2:14).

As he did earlier, Jesus spoke about his death in terms of being **lifted up** (see 3:14; 8:28). John's explanation makes it clear that this expression signified **how he was going to die**—the cross onto which Jesus would be nailed. Jesus knew that he would not die by stoning, something the Jews had already tried to do (8:59), but by crucifixion.

That Jesus **will draw everyone** to himself does not mean that everyone will ultimately be saved. Jesus has already made it clear that some will not be saved (5:28-29). Rather Jesus was saying that his offer of salvation extends to all people, not just to the Jews. Jesus' incredible love, expressed in his death for all people, will draw and unify those who believe, so that sin, evil, and death (the weapons of the prince of this world) will be powerless.

12:34 The people had **understood from Scripture that the Messiah would live forever** (see Psalm 72:17; Isaiah 9:6-7; Ezekiel 37:26-28). They had believed that Jesus had been making a claim to be the Messiah, and here they were waving palm branches for a victorious Messiah who they thought would set up a political, earthly kingdom that would never end. So it was difficult for them to believe that Jesus was the Messiah when he spoke of his imminent death—and that on a cross. Therefore, they wanted clarification about what Jesus meant when he used the term **the Son of Man.** Was this Son of Man someone different than the Messiah?

12:35-36 Jesus did not attempt to clear up the people's confusion about the Messiah. Rather, he admonished them to **walk** in the **light** while he was still with them (see also 1:5-9; 3:18-21; 8:12; 9:4-5). The ones enlightened by God would recognize their Messiah. The light of Jesus' physical presence on earth was about to be extinguished, and the **darkness** of Satan's evil influence and sin would overtake those who would refuse to accept Jesus' light. To walk in Satan's darkness is to **stumble** through life with no guidance, no help, no protection, no understanding, no ultimate goal or meaning. So Jesus urged the people to **believe in** him, who is the **light,** and become his children. The opportunity was available to all, but Jesus was about to depart this world.

MOST OF THE PEOPLE DO NOT BELIEVE IN JESUS / 12:37-43 / 186

As he does persistently, John never allows his readers to avoid the decision about what to do with Jesus Christ. For those ready to respond, no obstacle will keep them from belief. For those whose hearts are hardened, even the most compelling reasons for faith become obstacles. John soberly reminds us that many of those who believe in Jesus still allow the pressures and fears of people to hinder their faith. Hidden faith may avoid a confrontation with others, but it seldom pleases God.

12:37-41 Jesus had performed enough **miraculous signs** to cause people to believe in him. The greatest of all signs—raising Lazarus from the dead—should have been enough to elicit faith from all those who saw it and even heard about it. Yet **most** of the **people** still **did not believe** that Jesus was the Messiah.

This unbelief had been predicted by **Isaiah.** In the opening of his chapter on the suffering Savior, Isaiah asked, **"Who has believed our message? To whom will the Lord reveal his saving power?"** (Isaiah 53:1). It took revelation from God to know that Jesus was the one through whom God demonstrated his saving power. **Isaiah was referring to Jesus when he made this prediction, because he was given a vision of the Messiah's glory.** But the Jews lacked this understanding. Why? Because it was prophesied. Isaiah wrote: **"The Lord has blinded their eyes and hardened their hearts."** The entire quotation (taken from Isaiah 6:9-10) appears quite often in the New Testament because it provides a prophetic explanation for why the Jews did not perceive Jesus' message nor receive him as their Messiah (see also Matthew 13:14; Mark 4:12; Luke 8:10; Acts 28:26). And because they **would not** believe, they eventually **could not** believe. As a result, the Jews remained unenlightened and hardened.

12:42-43 At these words, **some of the Jewish leaders believed** in Jesus, but they **wouldn't admit it,** afraid the **Pharisees** would **expel them from the synagogue.** John made the point that their faith was weak, and he described the reason: They were still subject to the lure of **human praise** (see 5:44). But John primarily warned his readers that secret faith does not ultimately please God. Secrecy may be prudent at times (witness the presence of secret believers and churches in repressive societies like China and the former Romanian state), but that usually comes from a courageous strategy. All too often we remain silent at the very times we ought to be confessing our faith in Christ.

JESUS SUMMARIZES HIS MESSAGE / 12:44-50 / 187

John closes this section in his Gospel about Jesus' public ministry with a summary of Jesus' entire testimony. The shared Passover meal will take up the next several chapters. But John leaves his readers with the cry of Jesus' final public speech ringing in their ears. It is an ultimatum set before the crowds: Believe in Jesus, the Light of the World, or live in darkness under God's judgment.

12:44-45 Jesus left the crowds temporarily (12:36-37), but in one final public appearance he appealed to his hearers to believe in him (see also 5:17-44; 6:27-65; 7:16-18; 8:14-58; 10:14-18) and thereby walk in his light. In this appeal, he affirmed his union with the Father: **"If you trust me, you are really trusting God who sent me. For when you see me, you are seeing the one who sent me."** Because the Son sent by the Father is the visible expression of the Father to all people (see 14:9-11), those who believe in the Son also believe in the Father. Jesus *is* God. If you want to know what God is like, study the person and words of Jesus Christ.

12:46 Those who believe in Jesus have left Satan's **dark** kingdom and influence in the **world,** and they have entered the **light** of God's Kingdom. Some people in the church act as though they still **remain in the darkness.** Jesus died so that we might be transformed. If our life is not changing, we may not have begun to really follow the light.

12:47-48 Jesus repeated the important truth that he came **not to judge** the world but **to save** it (see also 3:17; 8:15-16); but his rejected words would condemn all unbelievers in the judgment at the last day (see 3:31-36; 5:22-23, 26-30; 9:39).

The purpose of Jesus' first mission on earth was not to judge people, but to show them the way to find salvation and eternal life. On the day of judgment, those who have accepted Jesus and lived his way will be raised to eternal life (1 Corinthians 15:51-57; 1 Thessalonians 4:15-18; Revelation 21:1-8), but **all who reject Jesus and his message will be judged at the day of judgment by the truth** Jesus had **spoken** (Revelation 20:11-15). Decide now your future fate, for the consequences of your decision will last forever.

12:49 Jesus' mission was to faithfully convey the words of God to all who would truly listen. He knew that those who rejected those words would be rejecting life. God himself **gave** Jesus **instructions as to what** he **should say.** Jesus did not change that message. Some, like the Jehovah's Witnesses, have used verses like this to say that Jesus was not God because he was subordinate to the Father. But Jesus' essential, divine being was not subordinate to the Father—in all things he was equal with God (Philippians 2:5-6); rather, Jesus coordinated his will to fully comply with the Father's will. Thus, to respond to Jesus is to respond to God. To believe in Jesus is to believe in God. To reject Jesus is to reject God. To hear Jesus' words makes each person responsible before God for what he or she does with them.

12:50 Jesus closed his message with one final appeal to accept the words he had spoken as having come from the Father. To accept those words is to receive **eternal life** (3:16-17, 35-36; 5:24-29, 39-40).

JOHN 13

JESUS WASHES THE DISCIPLES' FEET / 13:1-20 / *210*
The pace of John's writing slowed remarkably beginning with chapter 13. The first twelve chapters cover three years; the next six chapters cover one night.

13:1-2 Because Jesus was fully aware that **his hour had come to leave this world and return to his Father,** he devoted his last hours to instructing and encouraging his disciples. Jesus continued his devotion to his disciples until the very end of his life, showing them in this last night **the full extent of his love.** Before he left them, he wanted to express his love to them, one by one—and this he would do in a way that would surprise them.

The **supper** was probably the official Passover meal, indicated by verse 1. And this was a special Passover, for it was the last meal Jesus would eat with his disciples. During this meal he would institute the "Lord's Supper" (see Matthew 26:17-30; Mark 14:12-26; Luke 22:7-39). The context indicates that the food was being placed before them, but the meal itself had not been eaten (see 13:26, 30).

Jesus had already called **Judas** "a devil" in 6:70 because Jesus knew that Judas would cooperate with the **Devil** in perpetrating Jesus' death. Thus, the Devil and Judas corroborated in Jesus' betrayal. Indeed, Satan entered Judas to **carry out** the actual betrayal (see 13:27).

13:3-5 Jesus, the Son of God, knew his origin and his destiny. He knew that he would soon be return-ing to his Father. Being assured of his own destiny, he focused his attention on the disciples and showed them what it meant for him to become their Servant and for them to serve one another. At the time so near to the revelation of Jesus' true identity and glory, he set aside what was rightfully his and expressed his character through an act of humility. He **got up, took off his robe,** and **wrapped a towel around his waist** like an apron. He then **poured water into a basin** and **began to wash the disciples' feet.**

Jesus was the model servant, and he showed his servant attitude to his disciples. Foot washing was a common act in Bible times. People traveled mostly on foot in sandals across the dusty roads of Judea. When entering a home, it was customary to wash one's feet. To not offer to wash a guest's feet was considered a breach of hospitality (see Luke 7:44). Washing guests' feet was a job for a household servant to carry out when guests arrived (1 Samuel 25:41). It was a subservient task. What was unusual about this act was that Jesus, the Master and Teacher, was doing it for his disciples, as the lowliest slave would do.

13:6-9 All the disciples accepted the washing until Jesus came to **Peter,** who questioned Jesus: **"Lord,**

why are you going to wash my feet?" Jesus did not provide Peter with an explanation, other than that Peter would understand the significance of the washing some time in the future. Later in the New Testament, Peter explains his understanding of what Jesus had done (1 Peter 5:5-6). Peter came to realize that humble service meant obedience to Christ. When Jesus washed the disciples' feet, he was demonstrating his ultimate sacrificial act— giving his life for them on the cross.

But at this moment, Peter didn't understand: **"You will never wash my feet!"** he protested. Seeing the Master behave like a slave confused Peter. And Peter did not feel worthy that his Master should be acting like a slave toward him! This was not an expression of arrogance but of confusion. Peter felt he should be washing the Master's feet— not the other way around.

Jesus responded: **"But if I don't wash you, you won't belong to me."** There are two possible meanings for this sentence: (1) Jesus meant that unless he washed away Peter's sins by his death on the cross, then Peter could have no relationship with him. (2) Jesus meant that unless Peter submitted to him and allowed Jesus to minister in this way, Peter would never learn the lesson of humility. Either way, Peter seemed to grasp the significance of Jesus' words, for he then wanted to be bathed completely.

13:10-11 After one has **bathed,** another bath is not necessary at the end of the day. The person is still clean—except for the feet, which are constantly soiled by the dust of the ground. A clean and bathed person just needs to have his or her feet rinsed. According to the customs of those times, once a person had bathed, he or she needed only to wash his or her feet upon entering a person's home.

To be bathed by Jesus meant to be washed by his living word. To receive Jesus, nothing is required of the believer except humble acceptance of what Jesus has done. Peter had to sit and humbly allow Jesus to wash his dirty feet in order to understand that to accept the salvation Jesus offers means to humbly accept his death on the cross for all sins.

When Jesus said, **"You are clean, but that isn't true of everyone,"** he was referring to Judas Iscariot (see 13:18) and suggesting that Judas was not a true believer. Though Jesus had washed Judas's feet, Judas was not clean, for he had not come to believe in Jesus as the Messiah, the Son of God. Jesus already **knew** that this man would be used by Satan to bring about the events that unfold in the final chapters of this Gospel.

13:12-16 Jesus' act of washing the disciples' feet demonstrated love in action. Jesus was their

Teacher and **Lord,** meaning he was on a higher level than they; yet he assumed a position of humility and service because he loved those he served. Jesus commanded his disciples to **wash each other's feet**—to serve one another in love according to the example he set. To refuse to serve others, to refuse to humble yourself, no matter how high your position, is to place yourself above Jesus. Such arrogant pride is not what Jesus taught.

These disciples would soon be sent out as the **messengers** for the Christian church. They would be leaders in many places—indeed, James, John, and Peter became the leaders of the Christian church in Jerusalem. Jesus taught these soon-to-be leaders that as they labored to spread the gospel, they first and foremost had to be servants to those whom they taught. The disciples must have remembered this lesson often as they labored with the problems, struggles, and joys of the early believers. How many times they must have remembered that they were called to serve. And what a difference it made! Imagine how difficult the growth (even existence) of the early church would have been if these disciples had continued vying for spots of greatness and importance! Fortunately for us, they took Jesus' lesson to heart.

13:17 We are blessed (happy, joyful, fulfilled), not because of what we **know,** but because of what we **do** with what we know. God's grace to us finds its completion in the service we, as recipients of his grace, perform for others. We will find our greatest **blessing** in obeying Christ by serving others.

13:18-19 Jesus' previous statements about serving and loving one another did **not** apply to **all** of his disciples because, in fact, one of his disciples (Judas) was about to betray him. However, this betrayal was not an unexpected event, for Jesus had known from the beginning that one of the men he chose would betray him (6:70-71). Jesus' betrayal was necessary to fulfill Scripture—specifically, Psalm 41:9. Jesus drew from Psalm 41 because it describes how one of David's friends **turned against** him. This may have referred to the story of David's trusted companion, Ahithophel, who betrayed David and then went and hanged himself (see 2 Samuel 16:20–17:3, 23). Judas, who had been with Jesus and was a trusted companion (Judas was keeper of the money), would betray Jesus and then hang himself.

Jesus had known all along that Judas would betray him (see 6:64, 70-71; Matthew 17:22-23; 20:17-19), but he predicted the betrayal in the presence of his disciples so that they would realize, when the betrayal actually occurred, that it had been prophesied in Scripture (see Acts 1:16). This would strengthen their faith.

13:20 This verse follows the thought of verse 16, where Jesus spoke of being a servant to the one who sent him. He would send forth his disciples so that whoever would welcome them would welcome Jesus and, in turn, welcome the one who sent Jesus—God the **Father.**

JESUS AND THE DISCIPLES SHARE THE LAST SUPPER / 13:21-30 / 211

At this point in the dinner, the mood shifted, partly as a reflection of the ominous tone Jesus used in verse 18. Apparently the food was on the table, and they may have already been eating. Moments later, in answer to John's direct question, Jesus indicated his knowledge of Judas's betrayal by handing him the bread that he had dipped in the bowl. The rest of the disciples could not understand the meaning of Judas's abrupt departure.

13:21-26 Jesus was in great anguish of spirit over the coming betrayal, even though he knew that the betrayal had been foreordained. His inner turmoil was expressed when he said, **"The truth is, one of you will betray me!"** Jesus' pronouncement caused great consternation among the disciples. It was not obvious who the betrayer was. Judas, as keeper of the money, may have been the one they would least suspect.

Peter motioned to the one who was sitting beside Jesus to ask who the betrayer was. So that disciple, **the one Jesus loved** (identified as John, the author), asked Jesus, **"Lord, who is it?"** Jesus identified the betrayer as **"the one to whom I give the bread dipped in the sauce."** Jesus dipped the piece of bread into a dish filled with a sauce probably made of dates, raisins, and sour wine. Having said this, Jesus **dipped** the piece of bread and **gave it to Judas.** Ironically, a host offering a piece of bread to a guest was a sign of friendship. Jesus' act of friendship was his identification of the betrayer. Later, in the Garden, Judas would identify Jesus to the guards with another sign of friendship—a kiss (Luke 22:47-48).

13:27-30 After **Judas** ate the bread, **Satan entered into him.** Thus the betrayal was set in motion.

Satan would use Judas as his tool to accomplish his evil plan. But Satan's part in the betrayal of Jesus does not remove any of the responsibility from Judas. Judas may have been disillusioned because Jesus was talking about dying rather than setting up his Kingdom. Or perhaps Judas didn't understand Jesus' mission and no longer believed that Jesus was God's chosen one. Whatever Judas thought, Satan assumed that Jesus' death would end his mission and thwart God's plan. Like Judas, Satan did not know that Jesus' death was the most important part of God's plan all along.

Jesus said to Judas, **"Hurry. Do it now."** No one else at the table understood, but Judas did. Jesus identified Judas so tactfully that all the disciples missed the significance of the act: they did not connect Jesus' earlier statement ("One of you will betray me") with his present exchange with Judas. Despite the disciples' misunderstanding, the stage was quickly being set: **Judas left at once, going out into the night.** The last statement recounts the actual time yet also symbolizes the spiritual condition of Judas. He was in darkness, under the control of the prince of darkness, Satan.

JESUS PREDICTS PETER'S DENIAL / 13:31-38 / 212

After Judas's departure, Jesus spoke of his own glorification and referred to the brief time they would still have together. With a sense of urgency, he commanded them to love each other. He indicated that this single characteristic would set them apart from the world as his disciples. Peter wanted to know where Jesus was planning to go that they could not go with him. Jesus simply restated that his destination would not be theirs until later.

Ironically, Peter came close to the truth when he suggested that he would not even allow death to keep him from following Jesus. With profound compassion, which Peter could not possibly fathom until later, Jesus pointed out that Peter was not ready to lay down his life. That disqualified Peter from going with Jesus at this time. Peter would, in fact, shortly deny that he even knew Jesus.

13:31-32 When **Judas** was gone, Jesus said, **"The time has come for me, the Son of Man, to enter into my glory."** As Judas was on his way to betray Jesus into the hands of those who would crucify him, Jesus looked past the cross to his glorification at the resurrection. Jesus had allowed Judas to leave and carry out his murderous plans. By this act, Jesus committed himself to following through on what he had come to do. Thus he could say, **"God will bring me into my glory very soon."** Jesus framed his words based on his knowledge that his glorification through death and resurrection already had been accomplished. He anticipated how his resurrection would bring about his spiritual union with the disciples. This is the key to interpreting the following discourse (13:31–17:26). Now that Judas had left to complete his treachery, nothing would stop the events leading to the final hour. God's magnificent moral splendor is displayed by Jesus' act of obedience, so **God will receive glory** in Jesus. At the same moment, Jesus is glorified as he resumes the glory he had with the Father before the foundation of the world.

13:33-35 Jesus told his **dear children** that the time of his departure was nearing. Jesus would be going to the Father (14:6, 28) to rejoin him in the glorious fellowship that the Father and Son enjoyed from all eternity (see 17:5, 24). The disciples would not be able to participate in that fellowship just yet.

Jesus would be gone, and they would not be able to **come to** him for a while. In the meantime, they were to follow this commandment: **Love each other.** A command to love one another is not a new commandment; it had been mandated in the Old Testament (Exodus 20:12-17; Leviticus 19:18, 33-34; Deuteronomy 5:16-21; 22:1-4; see also Matthew 5:38-48; 7:12; 23:36-40; Luke 10:25-37). The new-

ness of Jesus' command pertains to the new kind of love that Christians have for one another because they have each experienced the love of Christ.

Jesus commanded his followers to love one another **"just as I have loved you."** This was revolutionary, for believers are called to love others based on Jesus' sacrificial love for them. Jesus was a living example of God's love, as we are to be living examples of Jesus' love. This love would be the mark of distinction: **"Your love for one another will prove to the world that you are my disciples."** One of the major themes in John's first letter is brotherly love (see 1 John 3–4).

13:36 Simon Peter, ever the one to voice his thoughts and questions, asked, **"Lord, where are you going?"** Again, Jesus answered that where he was going they could not go until **later.** Peter would later follow Jesus in the way of death (see 21:15-19) and would also follow Jesus into glory.

13:37 Peter loved Jesus intensely, and he wanted to be with Jesus always. He did not understand any need for Jesus to die; in fact, he planned to protect Jesus with his life if necessary. As with the footwashing incident, Peter would much rather **die for** Jesus than think that Jesus would die for him. Peter's brave and proud response resounds across the centuries like many who proudly refuse to accept Jesus' act on their behalf, preferring instead to do something in order to obtain salvation. However, obeying Jesus means more than the intention or the promise to obey. No one can do anything to obtain salvation.

13:38 When the time of trial came, **three times** Peter would say that he didn't **even know** Jesus (see also Matthew 26:69-75; Mark 14:66-72; Luke 22:54-62). The disciples may have started to wonder if Peter (instead of Judas) was the betrayer.

JOHN 14

JESUS IS THE WAY TO THE FATHER / 14:1-14 / 213

After predicting Peter's denial (13:38), Jesus spoke to the deep concerns of the disciples. They were confused; he encouraged them to trust. They needed to anchor that trust in Jesus. He indicated that he and the Father would prepare a place for them while he was gone, but that he would return to gather them.

After this intimate opening dialogue, the Last Supper discourse began. The next several chapters have been among the most treasured of those who follow Jesus. They not only draw us close to him; they also give us compelling reasons to invite others into that fellowship with our Savior.

14:1 Jesus spoke to Peter (whose denial of Jesus had just been predicted—see 13:38) and to all the other disciples, telling them, **"Don't be troubled. You trust God, now trust in me."** All of the disciples must have been troubled about Jesus' predictions of betrayal, denial, and departure. After all, if Peter's commitment was shaky, then every disciple should be aware of his own weaknesses. Jesus urged his disciples to maintain their trust in the Father and in the Son, to continue trusting through the next few very difficult days

14:2 The traditional interpretation of this phrase teaches that Jesus is going to heaven to prepare **rooms** or "mansions" for his followers. Based on that imagery, entire heavenly subdivisions and elaborate "mansion blueprints" have been described. Many commentators think that Jesus was speaking about his Father's house in heaven, where he would go after his resurrection in order to prepare rooms for his followers. Then he would return one day to take his believers to be with him in heaven. The day of that return usually has been regarded as the Second Coming.

The other view is that the passage primarily speaks of the believers' immediate access to God the Father through the Son. The **place** Jesus was preparing has less to do with a location (heaven) than it does with an intimate relationship with a person (God the Father). This interpretation does not deny the comfort of heaven's hope in this passage, but it does remove the temptation to view heaven purely in terms of glorious mansions. Heaven is not about splendid accommodations; it is about being with God. The point of the passage is that Jesus is providing the way for the believers to live in God the Father. As such, the way he prepared the place was through his own death and resurrection and thereby opened the way for the believers to live in Christ and approach God.

According to this view, the Father's house is not a heavenly mansion, but Christ himself in whom all the believers reside. By expansion, the Father's house is Christ and the church (see 1 Corinthians 3:16-17; Ephesians 2:20-22; Hebrews 3:2). The believers don't have to wait until the Second Coming to live in this house; once Christ rose from the dead he brought them into a new, living relationship with God (see 20:19-23). He would be the means whereby the believers could come to dwell in the Father and the Father in them. As such, the promise in 14:2-3 relates to the corporate fellowship that would be possible through Christ's departure and return in the Spirit. In this view, the **many rooms** would be the many members of God's household. Christ went to prepare a place for each member in God's

household (1 Chronicles 17:9)—the preparation was accomplished by his death and resurrection.

14:3 There are three ways to understand the words, **"I will come and get you"**: (1) Jesus' coming again to the disciples would be realized in a short while. When Jesus said, "I will come," that coming again occurred on the day of his resurrection. (2) Jesus' coming is the Second Coming. (3) This "coming" refers to both the Resurrection and the Second Coming—the former foreshadowing the latter. Those who hold this view, therefore, extract a double meaning from Jesus' words in verses 2 and 3; they say the passage speaks both of the believers being brought into the risen Christ as the many "rooms" in the Father's house and of the believers being brought by the returned Christ into the Father's house in heaven. It does seem that both meanings merge. Christ has us completely in his care.

14:4 Jesus said, **"You know where I am going and how to get there."** This statement anticipated Thomas's question (in the next verse) and prepared the groundwork for what Jesus was about to teach regarding himself. Jesus was not naively hoping his disciples understood; he was inviting them to declare their ignorance so they might receive the truth.

14:5-6 Clearly, the disciples didn't know what Jesus meant. Thomas expressed the obvious by asking, **"We haven't any idea where you are going, so how can we know the way?"** Like us, the disciples thought in terms of this world—time and space. So **going** must mean physically moving from one place to another. Jesus replied: **"I am the way, the truth, and the life. No one can come to the Father except through me."** Jesus' response shows that the destination is not a physical place but a person (the Father), and that the way to that destination is another person (the Son). Jesus is the **Way** to the Father; Jesus is the **Truth** (or reality) of all God's promises; and Jesus is the **Life** as he joins his divine life to ours, both now and eternally. Jesus is the way that leads to the truth and life.

Jesus' exclusive claim is unmistakable. It forces an unconditional response. Jesus invites people to accept or reject him, making it clear that partial acceptance is rejection. His self-description invalidates alternative plans of salvation. Some would say that a single way is entirely too restrictive. But that attitude fails to see the desperate state of the human condition. That there is **a way** at all is evidence of God's grace and love. The state of human rebellion can be seen in this: We are like people drowning at sea who are graciously thrown a life-saving rope but who respond by insisting that we deserve a choice of several ropes along with the option of swimming to safety if we so choose.

14:7 In verses 2-6, Jesus told the disciples that he provides the one and only way to the Father. In verses 7 and following, he tries to explain that he is the visible manifestation of the Father. To know Jesus is to know the Father (see 1:18; Colossians 1:15; Hebrews 1:3). Jesus shifted the questioning from the future to the present. Instead of being preoccupied with Jesus' going and how they could get there, they were to realize that Jesus opened the way to the Father right now. The disciples needed to discern the meaning of Jesus' time on earth and then respond to him as their Savior. Jesus holds the way open for us today—**from now on,** we can begin a relationship with the Father by accepting Jesus Christ as our Savior and Lord. The disciples had not yet thoroughly understood this incredible truth, for the death and resurrection of Jesus had not yet occurred (although Jesus had spoken about them), and the Holy Spirit had not yet arrived to help them understand.

14:8-9 Philip was not **satisfied**—he wanted to see **the Father.** But Jesus explained that to see him is to see the Father, for Jesus is God in human form (see 1:14, 18). Philip and the disciples, after their years with Jesus, should have come to know and recognize that the one among them was God in human, physical form. He is the visible, tangible image of the invisible God. He is the complete revelation of what God is like. Jesus' answer contains no rebuke; he explained to Philip, who wanted to see the Father, that to know Jesus is to know God. The search for God, for truth and reality, ends in Christ. (See also Colossians 1:15; Hebrews 1:1-4.)

14:10-11 This statement conveys the complete unity between Jesus and the Father (see 10:30, 38; 17:21-24). This unity ensures that Jesus truly and completely revealed God to us. This unity goes far deeper than Jesus being of one mind with the Father—merely reflecting the intentions of the Father. Jesus and God were one in essence and purpose. Because of this oneness, Jesus said, **"The words I say are not my own, but my Father who lives in me does his work through me."** If believing in this oneness is too difficult for you just now, Jesus told the disciples, **"at least believe because of what you have seen me do."** God's power was revealed through Jesus' works.

14:12 Very likely Jesus gave this promise specifically to his disciples concerning evangelism—"bearing much fruit" (see 15:7-8). There are two parts to the **greater works:** There would be a greater number of converts, and there would be a greater scope to the converts. Jesus performed some truly impressive miracles during his earthly ministry; his disciples would perform even greater ones after his resurrection. Furthermore, the disciples, working in the power of the Holy Spirit that would be sent to them after Jesus went to the **Father,** would carry the gospel of God's Kingdom out of Palestine and into the whole world and thus to the Gentiles.

14:13-14 To pray "in Jesus' name" is to pray in union with Jesus' person and purpose because the "name" of a person symbolized his essence and destiny. We have the promise of answered prayer described in these verses if we properly understand the context of Jesus' last discourse. Jesus promised the disciples that their requests concerning fruit bearing would be answered because it would bring **glory** to God (see 4:41; 7:18; 8:50, 54). The next chapters clarify this (15:7-8, 16; 16:23-24).

When Jesus says we can **ask for anything,** we must remember that our asking must be **in** his **name**—that is, according to God's character and will. God will not grant requests contrary to his nature or his will, and we cannot use his name as a magic formula to fulfill our selfish desires. If we are sincerely following God and seeking to do his will, then our requests will be in line with what he wants, and he will grant them. (See also 15:16; 16:23.)

JESUS PROMISES THE HOLY SPIRIT / 14:15-31 / *214*

The second half of chapter 14 includes Jesus' teaching on the resources of discipleship. Jesus prepared his followers for his physical absence by telling them that they would experience his presence more fully and intimately because the Counselor, the Holy Spirit, would take up residence in them.

14:15-17 Prior to this, Jesus had urged the disciples to love one another. Then he spoke of their **love** for him. Truly loving Jesus requires that we do what he commands. Eternal life is a gift that we cannot work for or earn. Once we begin that life in Christ, loving and obeying Christ's commands become the evidence that he is in us. This is John's emphasis in his first epistle (see 1 John 5:2-3).

Various translations use different words for the **Holy Spirit** here: Advocate, Helper, Comforter. The Greek word *parakletos* denotes the Helper or Counselor who is always there to give special care in times of need. But the Holy Spirit is more than a Comforter, Helper, and Counselor; he is also an Advocate and an Encourager. In this context, it is also clear that the Holy Spirit is the Son's "Representative," even as the Son was the Father's "Representative."

The expression **another Counselor** means "another counselor of the same kind as the first." This implies that Jesus was the first Counselor (see 1 John 2:1), and that the Spirit would be the same kind of Counselor. When Jesus would no longer be with the disciples physically, the Holy Spirit would be their constant companion to guide, help, and empower them for the tasks ahead. Jesus identified the Counselor as the one **who leads into all truth** because he is the Spirit who reveals the truth about God.

It may seem, at first, that **the world at large cannot receive** the Spirit because of its sin and disobedience. But if that were the case, no one could accept the Spirit, for all of us sin and are disobedient. Instead, the world cannot receive this Spirit of truth because the world **isn't looking for him and doesn't recognize him.** In the same way that Jesus was not accepted by the world (see 1:11-12), the Spirit would also not be received. But the disciples (and all believers) can receive the Spirit, for Jesus said, **"But you do, because he lives with you now and later will be in you."** The disciples, sinful men, not clear in their understanding at this point, even somewhat greedy in their quest for positions in God's Kingdom, would be able to know the Spirit, for the Spirit would come to live in them, helping them understand and empowering them to do great works for God. The world has refused to know Jesus; but any sincere seeker, no matter how sinful or how ignorant, who humbly comes to Jesus, can receive this gift of the Spirit.

14:18-19 This statement showed Jesus' fatherly care for his own, those whom he loved (see 13:1); it also affirmed Jesus' presence with the disciples through the Spirit of truth, for he said, **"I will come to you."** After Jesus' resurrection, he appeared to the disciples in his glorious resurrection body and spoke to them prior to returning to the Father (20:19–21:25). At that time, he breathed into his disciples the Holy Spirit (20:22). This assured the disciples that Jesus would come to them when the Spirit was given to them. This coming would be **in just a little while,** during which time Jesus would experience crucifix-

ion, burial, and resurrection (see 16:16-23). The disciples and many of Jesus' followers saw him in his resurrection appearances (see 20:20, 26; 21:1, 14). Through the Resurrection, the living Jesus became the disciples' life because they became united to him like branches in a vine. This is the intent behind the words: **"For I will live again, and you will, too."** As the Son's life is dependent upon the Father's life (5:26; 6:57), so the believer's life is dependent on the Son's life. The reality of the Resurrection becomes the basis for our hope of eternal life.

14:20 After Jesus was **raised to life again,** the disciples would realize by their own experience that Jesus lived in his Father, they lived in Jesus, and Jesus lived in them. In other words, they would begin to know what it meant to live in God and have God live in them.

14:21 We who **love** Jesus demonstrate our love by keeping Jesus' commands. Love means more than words; it requires commitment and action. If we love Christ, then we must prove it by obeying what he says in his word. In return, the Father and Jesus himself love us. Furthermore, Jesus reveals himself to those who love him. Since the Greek word translated **reveal** means "to appear," it is likely that Jesus was speaking of his appearances to the disciples after his resurrection. But the statement extends beyond that special time to include believers of all time. To all those who love and **obey** him, he reveals himself as an invisible, spiritual presence (see 20:29; 2 Corinthians 4:6).

14:22 John clarified for us that this is **not Judas Iscariot,** but **Judas** the son of James (see Luke 6:16). This disciple asked Jesus how he would **reveal** himself **only** to the disciples and **not to the world.** The disciples may still have been expecting Jesus to establish an earthly kingdom and overthrow Rome; they found it hard to understand why he did not tell the world at large that he was the Messiah. Or at least they felt that if he was going to rise from the dead, everyone should see it and know about it, for surely then they would believe. But Jesus explained that such a revelation to the world was not in the plans—at least not then. Not everyone would understand Jesus' message, and a hardened and unbelieving world would not believe even someone who had come back from the dead (Luke 16:31). Ever since Pentecost, the gospel of the Kingdom has been proclaimed in the whole world, and yet not everyone is receptive to it. Jesus reveals himself most deeply to those who love and obey him.

14:23 In effect, Jesus' response reassured Judas and the disciples that neither he nor the Father would be abandoning them. At first, it must have seemed to the disciples that they had no advantage over everyone else—Jesus would die and leave them. In answering Peter's question in the previous chapter, Jesus had explained that, as opposed to the Jewish leaders who had been told they could not go where Jesus was going, the disciples eventually would be able to be with Jesus, but it would be later (see 7:32-34; 13:36). Here Jesus offered the best comfort of all—there wouldn't really be any separation from him for these disciples. Because Jesus would return to the Father, the Holy Spirit would be made available, allowing every believer constant access to the Father and the Son. To those who **love** Jesus, the Son and the Father would **come to them and live with them.**

14:24 Obedience comes from love and trust. Thus a person who **doesn't love** Jesus will not obey him. A sobering way of stating Jesus' point is to say, "The quality of our obedience is a direct reflection of our love for Jesus." Jesus repeated that all he said was from God himself (see also 12:49; 14:10).

14:25 Jesus gave his last words to his disciples. The coming days would bring horrifying, then glorious, events, but Jesus would not be able to talk to his disciples during those events. Before the disciples could understand any more, Jesus' death and resurrection would have to take place. Then, the disciples' understanding would be heightened by the coming of the Holy Spirit.

14:26 The **Counselor,** the **Holy Spirit,** would be sent as Jesus' **representative** The Spirit would continue Jesus' ministry of teaching. The Spirit would also **remind** the disciples of what Jesus had **told** them. The apostles remembered and wrote with the help of the Spirit. John's Gospel, even the entire New Testament, would not exist if not for this reminding work of the Holy Spirit.

In the case of the disciples, the reminding role of the Holy Spirit uniquely guided the recording of the New Testament. However, the process is still in place. The disciples first heard Jesus speak; we discover Jesus' words in Scripture. Reading, studying, memorizing, meditating, and obeying place Christ's words firmly inside us, and the Holy Spirit reminds us of their further application as we move through life.

14:27 This verse echoes the first verse of the chapter. Jesus' **peace** would not guarantee the absence of trouble—for Jesus himself faced excruciating spiritual, physical, and emotional struggles in the coming hours. Instead, Jesus' peace supplies strength and comfort for the burdens we are called to carry. Jesus gave the disciples peace that would help them through their own time of trial ahead. After three days, the risen Jesus would come to them and again bestow his peace upon them (20:19).

The peace Jesus offers his disciples **isn't like the peace the world gives.** It is his peace, the peace he modeled every day of his life. Jesus' peace did not flee conflict, pain, or death. In fact, the more intense the difficulties, the more apparent Jesus' peace became. Jesus derived his peace from his relationship with the Father.

Sin, fear, uncertainty, and doubt work to make us **troubled** and **afraid.** The peace of God moves into our hearts and lives to restrain these hostile forces and offers comfort in place of conflict. Jesus says he will give us that peace if we are willing to accept it from him. The Holy Spirit's work in our lives brings deep and lasting peace. We have confident assurance in any circumstance; with Christ's peace, we have no need to fear the present or the future.

14:28 Jesus repeated what he had said in 14:3. Although Jesus was sad to leave his disciples, he was glad to return to his Father. If the disciples truly loved Jesus, they would understand this and **be very happy for** him—instead of feeling sorry for themselves. In saying that **the Father** is greater than he, Jesus was asserting his role as the Father's servant, for the Son was the one sent to do the Father's will. This does not deny his equality with God (see 10:30); rather, it affirms Jesus' humble attitude about his relationship with the Father.

14:29 Jesus told the disciples about his imminent departure and return so that they would recognize these events, realize that he knew about them, and believe that Jesus upholds his claims. Jesus gave them the tools and resources to understand later events even though at the time he gave them, they did not appreciate their value.

14:30-31 The hour was at hand; Jesus was about to leave his disciples and go to the cross. In so doing he would face **the prince of this world** (12:31) who has the power of death (Hebrews 2:14). Although Satan was unable to overpower Jesus (Matthew 4), he still had the arrogance to try. Satan's power exists only because God allows him to act. But because Jesus is sinless, Satan has **no power over** him. Satan would not be able to exert this power over Jesus because Jesus would conquer death. Jesus faced death as one who did so out of **love** for his **Father,** for his Father had sent him to die for the sins of the world. Ironically, when Jesus died, Satan thought he had won the battle. He did not realize that Jesus' death had been part of the plan all along. In dying, Jesus defeated Satan's power over death, for Jesus would rise again (16:11; Colossians 2:15).

The words, **"Come, let's be going,"** suggest that chapters 15–17 may have been spoken en route to the Garden of Gethsemane. Another view holds that Jesus was asking the disciples to get ready to leave the upper room, but they did not actually do so until 18:1. However, it is also likely that these words are spoken, not as a separate sentence, but as an ending to the discourse above. He has just said that the prince of this world is coming, and perhaps by this sentence he is saying, "Let us rise and be ready to meet him." This conveys more of a spiritual movement and preparation than a physical one.

JOHN 15:1–16:4

JESUS TEACHES ABOUT THE VINE AND THE BRANCHES / 15:1-17 / *215*

Jesus knew that his physical presence with his precious disciples would soon end. He also knew that these men would need a clear understanding of their position with God, as well as what was expected of them. So he consciously filled their minds with pictures and ideas to help them survive the days to come. But these same lessons also provide vital resources for preparing future generations of disciples to grow in their faith.

15:1-2 The grapevine is a prolific plant; a single vine bears many grapes. In the Old Testament, grapes symbolized Israel's fruitfulness in doing God's work on earth. The prophets had written of Israel as God's vine, carefully planted and cared for. But the vine was a disappointment because it yielded only rotten fruit; that is, they refused to give him love and obedience. This is very graphic and poignant in Isaiah 5:1-7, a passage Jesus seems to have drawn upon here (see also Jeremiah 2:2, 21; 6:9; Ezekiel 15; 17:5-10; 19:10-14; Hosea 10:1; 14:7). Jesus, with all believers "abiding" in him, is the **true vine**—the true fulfillment of God's plan for his people (see Psalm 80:8-17). The new society of God's people—Christians—originates from Christ and is united to him as branches to a vine. God is the **gardener,** the cultivator of the vine and the **branches.** Believers, both sincere and false, are pictured here as the branches.

The fruitful branches are true believers who, by their living union with Christ, produce much fruit. But this union can be broken. The Father **cuts off every branch that doesn't produce fruit.** Those who become unproductive—those who turn back from following Christ after making a superficial commitment—will be separated from the vine (see 15:6 for more discussion on the specific identity of the unproductive branches). Unproductive followers are as good as dead and will be cut off and tossed aside. **Fruit** is not limited to soul winning. In this chapter, answered prayer, joy, and love are mentioned as fruit (15:7, 11-12). Galatians 5:22-24 and 2 Peter 1:5-8 describe additional fruit, explained as qualities of Christian character.

In contrast, **he prunes the branches that do bear fruit so they will produce even more.** Successful gardeners know that pruning, cutting back the branches, increases fruit bearing. Each spring vinedressers cut back each vine to its root stock to enhance its fruitfulness. Sincere believers, the fruitful branches, will be "pruned," meaning that God must sometimes discipline us to strengthen our character and faith. But branches that don't bear fruit are "cut off" at the trunk and are completely discarded because they are worthless and often infect the rest of the plant. People who won't bear fruit for God or who try to block the efforts of God's followers will be cut off from his life-giving power.

15:3-4 Jesus' illustration here shifts to a different level. This pruning is spiritual, taking away the contamination of sin. This verse indicates that the disciples **have already been pruned** because they had accepted the Lord's **message;** they were ready for **greater fruitfulness.** But not so with Judas, the betrayer; he was not clean—therefore, he was one of those branches that had been cut off.

Believers are to **remain** in Jesus, the vine, and he **will remain in** us. A vine branch can survive and produce foliage for a while after it has been **severed,** but it cannot **produce fruit** unless it is connected to a root stock. As Jesus had a living dependence on the Father (see 6:57), so believers in Jesus need to have a living dependence on him. "Remaining," for the disciples and for all believers today, means to make a constant, moment-by-moment decision to follow Christ. And we must not be passive—believers don't just sit and "remain" until they die. Instead, we must be active—we have a lot to do.

15:5-6 Each branch that continues to **remain** in the vine will **produce much fruit.** This "fruit" could be new converts (15:5), or "the fruit of the Spirit" (see Galatians 5:22), or both. The fruit of the Spirit displayed in our lives should attract people to Jesus and thereby make them new members of God's vine. Jesus' emphasis here was not to dwell on our glaring inadequacies, but to remind us of the incomparable adequacy that comes from our relationship with him. **Apart from** him, we **can do nothing.**

Each branch that does not continue to remain in the vine is removed from the vine. The branch seems physically attached, but it is not organically part of the plant because it does not participate in the life-giving flow of the vine. Sooner or later, that branch will drop off and have to be **thrown away.** Three traditional interpretations have tried to identify who these **useless branches** might represent:

1. For some, these branches are true believers who have lost their salvation because they were cut off from Christ.
2. For others, these burned branches are Christians who will lose rewards but not salvation on the day of judgment (1 Corinthians 3:15). But this is probably not true because Jesus was speaking of dead branches.
3. For still others, these burned branches refer to those professing to be Christians who, like Judas Iscariot, are not genuinely saved and therefore are judged. Judas, a disciple of Jesus, seemed like a branch, but he did not truly believe. Therefore, he was cut off; his fate was like that of a dead branch. Given John's concern to make committed disciples of his readers and Jesus' goal to bring people into a continuing relationship with himself, this view provides a healthy balance. It keeps the decision of destiny as God's responsibility while preserving an emphasis on our responsibility to "remain" in the relationship. In any case, the verse is not so much aimed at creating discomfort and doubt as it is in teaching the importance of daily connectedness with Christ.

15:7-8 True disciples do more than just believe what Jesus says; they let Jesus' **words remain in** them. Then they can **ask any request** of him and **it will be granted.** In this passage and in 14:13-14,

"asking God" is connected with fruit bearing and doing greater things for God. When a believer remains in Christ and Christ's words remain in him, that person's prayers will be answered. This does not mean that all requests are granted—for the context suggests that the prayers should pertain to fruit bearing (either helping others believe, or showing more of the fruit of the Spirit in one's life) and glorifying the Father. An essential part of being a disciple requires bearing fruit for the Lord. And in order to pray for results, a person must remain in Christ. For when we remain in him, our thoughts and desires conform to his, and we can pray "in his name" (14:13), knowing that our requests please God. We can be assured then that whatever we ask will be done.

A vine that produces **much fruit** glorifies God, for daily he sends the sunshine and rain to make the crops grow, and he constantly nurtures each plant and prepares it to blossom. What a moment of glory for the Lord of the harvest when the harvest is brought into the barns, mature and ready for use! He made it all happen! This farming analogy shows how God is glorified when we come into a right relationship with him and begin to "bear much fruit" in our lives.

15:9 Believers must remain in Jesus (15:4), remain in his words (15:7), and **remain in** his **love.** For the Son to love us in the same way that his Father loves him means we receive the greatest love possible. We should respond with total dedication, commitment, and obedience.

15:10 We can **remain** in Jesus' **love** by obeying his commands—just as he obeyed his Father's commands. If we do so, we will experience the daily joy of obedience to our Lord. Jesus himself modeled two important behaviors for true disciples: (1) since he obeyed his Father's commands, we can **obey** his; (2) and he loved them, so they should love one another. Jesus not only tells us what to do; he shows it through his life.

15:11 Jesus does not call Christians to a dull existence of being hated by the world, obeying commands, and waiting to get to heaven. Instead, he offers us fullness of **joy!** Nothing else in all the world can bring the joy that we find in serving, abiding in, and obeying Christ.

15:12-13 Jesus commanded his followers to **love each other** as he loved them. The highest expression of **love** people could have for others is to **lay down their lives for** them—just as Jesus did for those he loved. We must love each other sacrificially, as Jesus loved us. He loved us enough to give his life for us (see Romans 5:7-8). We may not have to die for someone, but we can practice sacrificial love in many other ways: listening, helping, encouraging, giving. We do not need to feel love for everyone. Some people will be difficult to love, but still we are commanded to act lovingly toward our fellow believers.

15:14-15 In those days, the disciples of a rabbi were considered his **servants**. Jesus changed that relationship; the disciples were not his servants but his **friends**. Jesus considered them his friends because he had told them everything he had heard from the Father. This showed that Jesus trusted them to receive these communications and then pass them on to others as the gospel. In fact, he had chosen and appointed them for this task.

15:16 Jesus **chose** these disciples and **appointed** them to spread the gospel and **produce fruit** for God's Kingdom. The Lord chooses each believer to be a branch in the vine—a branch that bears **fruit that will last.** The remaining, or lasting, fruit means either new believers whose faith perseveres, or the enduring quality of the fruit of the Spirit— especially brotherly love.

Then, Jesus speaks of making requests to the Father: **"That the Father will give you whatever you ask for, using my name."** As in verses 7-8, Jesus linked the request making with the fruit bearing. The Father would answer their requests in order to help them accomplish the mission he gave them—to produce "fruit that will last."

15:17 This verse capsulizes the theme that Jesus introduced in verse 12 and yet also serves as a contrast for what follows. The disciples must **love each other** because they would take Jesus' message to a world that despised them. Christians get plenty of hatred from the world; from each other we need love and support.

Jesus legislated love. He required his disciples to make peace with one another, to place the interests of others above their own, and to solve differences quickly. He knew they were diverse in background, but he ordered them to love each other. Jesus knew that setting this high standard was essential to preserving the unity of the church. If he required it, the believers would accept and live out this standard. Backbiting, disrespect, and bitterness toward fellow believers strips the church of its power.

JESUS WARNS ABOUT THE WORLD'S HATRED / 15:18—16:4 / 216

Jesus called the disciples to abide in him and to love one another. But their relationship with the world would be entirely different. Because they loved Christ and were so like him, the world would transfer its hatred of Christ to the disciples. Yet they must take the Good News to the world. This section explains how the disciples, with the help of the Counselor, would continue Jesus' work of glorifying the Father in a hostile world.

15:18-19 Jesus was **hated** from the very beginning (when Jesus was a young child, King Herod sought him out to kill him—Matthew 2:13-16). He was hated at the end when the people rejected him as the Savior and called for his crucifixion. The same **world** would surely hate those who proclaim allegiance to the crucified Lord. Jesus wants believers to be distinctive; he sets us apart from the world. His choosing and setting us apart makes us holy and helps us grow. Our very separation from the world arouses the world's animosity. The world would prefer that we were like them; since we are not, they hate us (see 1 Peter 4:3-4).

15:20-21 Jesus had told the disciples this earlier that evening (13:16; also Matthew 10:24). He had been speaking of their need to imitate his acts of humble service. They also needed to understand that, if their Lord was not respected or honored by the world, they should expect even harsher treatment. To **persecute** believers is to persecute Christ

because believers are an extension of Christ, as branches are an extension of the vine. Yet despite certain persecution, believers are called to share the gospel—this includes not just telling the story, but giving the invitation to accept Jesus as Savior and Lord. While they will face those who **hate** them because they **belong to** Christ, it would also be true that those who would have **listened** to Jesus will **listen** to the disciples.

15:22-25 Jesus said that the Jews would not have been **guilty** of rejecting God if they had not rejected Jesus Christ—who was God in the flesh. But since they did reject Jesus, who came to reveal God the Father to all humanity, they had **no excuse for their sin.** Their rejection of Jesus caused their sin to be fully exposed because, as Jesus said, **"Anyone who hates me hates my Father, too."** They actually hated the Son and the Father—even after seeing the marvelous works Jesus performed.

The entire nation should have recognized and

responded to the Messiah. Ironically, their own Scriptures predicted this rejection and hatred. Jesus knew the hatred **fulfilled what the Scriptures said** (see Psalm 69:4). The Jews had no reason to hate Jesus—he came as their Savior, fulfilling their Scriptures, doing **miraculous signs,** and promising eternal life to those who believed in him. Yet the people thought they were serving God by rejecting Jesus, when in reality, they were serving Satan (8:44).

15:26-27 In 14:26 Jesus had said that the Father would send the **Counselor,** the **Spirit of truth.** The word **Counselor** conveys the helping, encouraging, and strengthening work of the Spirit as he represents Christ. **The Spirit of truth** points to the teaching, illuminating, and reminding work of the Spirit. The Holy Spirit ministers to both the head and the heart, and both dimensions are important. The Spirit would **come** to the disciples and **tell** them **all about him.** These disciples were the vital link between Jesus Christ and all subsequent believers. They would need the Holy Spirit to remind them so that as they preached, taught, and wrote, they would spread the **truth** of the gospel. The Holy Spirit would see to it that their witness would not be impaired by persecution. Jesus has already forewarned these men about the persecution to come so that they would not be surprised.

The disciples would **tell others** that Jesus is the Messiah. The Holy Spirit would testify by preparing people's hearts and minds, persuading them of the truth of the gospel, and enabling them to receive the message. By application, this verse extends to all Christians. All Christians are called to testify of Jesus, allowing the Holy Spirit to help them through times of persecution and to remind them of the truth of God's word and work in the hearts and minds of their listeners.

16:1-2 Jesus warned and safeguarded the disciples against the trials that awaited them. He did not want them to be caught off guard, to stumble, or to fall when trials came. Jesus wanted them to remember that he had predicted his own persecution and theirs in order to fortify them for the difficult times to come. He also wanted them to remember the rest of his teaching (**these things**). His accurate predictions would increase their trust in his instructions.

In 9:22 and 12:42 we are told that the religious leaders had decided that anyone who confessed Jesus as the Messiah would be **expelled from the synagogues.** Jesus predicted that this would happen to the disciples. By the time John's Gospel was recorded, Christians were already frequently barred from the synagogues. The prophecy that some would be killed would come true very soon. An early deacon in the church, Stephen, would become the first martyr for the faith (Acts 7:54-60). James, one of the disciples present with Jesus during this teaching, would be put to death by King Herod (Acts 12:1-2). Saul of Tarsus—before his conversion—went through the land hunting down and persecuting Christians, convinced that he was serving God by killing those who proclaimed Jesus as their Messiah (Acts 9:1-2; 26:9-11; Galatians 1:13-14; Philippians 3:6).

16:3-4 Those who would persecute believers would do so out of ignorance. They had **never known the Father or** Jesus. They did not understand that God was at work through Jesus; so, when they rejected Jesus, they also rejected God. When the persecutions would actually occur, they would be prepared because they would **remember** what Jesus had said. Jesus' predictions hold today. The world is still hostile toward Jesus and his disciples. When a tree in the forest stands taller than the rest it must endure the full force of the wind. When Christians take a stand for Christ in their cultures, they will experience the full force of the opposition. Jesus waited until the very last evening to warn his disciples because he himself had been their protection from the beginning. Jesus had deflected any criticism and opposition away from the disciples. But after Jesus was crucified, the persecution would shift to his followers and would focus on these men, his inner circle.

JOHN 16:5-33

JESUS TEACHES ABOUT THE HOLY SPIRIT / 16:5-15 / 217

Not all the news for the disciples was grim. There would be persecution, but Jesus comforted his followers with the promise that they would not be alone; he would send them the

Counselor, the Spirit of truth. John highlighted five important tasks of the Holy Spirit: (1) to convict the world of its sin and call it to repentance, (2) to reveal the standard of God's righteousness to anyone who believes because Christ would no longer be physically present on earth, (3) to demonstrate Christ's judgment over Satan, (4) to direct believers into all truth, and (5) to reveal even more about Jesus Christ.

16:5-6 The verb tense for **has asked** is present; otherwise, this statement would contradict 13:36 and 14:5. The disciples **had asked** (past tense) where Jesus was going. In this verse, Jesus was looking for an immediate reaction to his words about his departure. But instead of asking, "Where are you going?" at that time when Jesus was ready to answer, they were **very sad.** Although the disciples had previously talked with Jesus about his death (see 7:33-34), they had never truly understood its meaning because they had been mostly concerned about themselves. If Jesus went away, what would become of them? If they had asked where Jesus was going, and then had understood that he was going to the Father, they would not have been filled with such sorrow—they would have realized that Jesus' departure was for their good.

16:7 Without Jesus' death and resurrection we could not be saved. His death made it possible for him to remove our sins. Before Jesus could defeat death by his resurrection, he had to submit to death. And if he would not go back to the Father, the **Counselor,** the Holy Spirit, would not **come** in the way God had planned (7:39). After his glorification—through the process of crucifixion, resurrection, and ascension—Jesus could **send** the Spirit to the believers. Christ's presence on earth was limited to one place at a time. His leaving meant he could live, through the Holy Spirit, in every believer in the whole world. Thus, it was for their good that he had to go away. The Spirit would carry Jesus' work to a more intense level during the history of the church. By the Spirit the gospel would go out to all the world.

16:8-11 To **convince** means "to expose the facts, to convince someone of the truth, to accuse, refute, or to cross-examine a witness." **The world's sin is unbelief in** Jesus. The greatest sin is the refusal to believe in Jesus (3:18). Those who reject Jesus are in danger of eternal separation from God.

Righteousness is available to people **because** Jesus goes to the Father. The Spirit's function will be to show all people that Christ alone provides the standard of God's righteousness. The Holy Spirit must make unbelievers recognize God's perfect standard before they will admit their own deficiency. This can also mean that the Spirit will show the world the futility of religious self-

righteousness. The Holy Spirit will show the inadequacy of ceremony and ritual in making one right with God (see Matthew 5:20; Romans 10:3; Philippians 3:6-9).

The Spirit will show that, through Jesus' death and resurrection, **the prince of this world has already been judged** and condemned. Though Satan still actively attempts to harden, intimidate, and delude those in this world (1 Peter 5:8), we are to treat him like a condemned criminal, for God has determined the time of his execution (see Revelation 20:2, 7-10).

Convincing us of our sin, convincing us of God's righteousness, and convincing us of Satan's (and our) impending judgment describes three approaches that the Holy Spirit uses. We do not all require all three in order to be convinced that we need God's grace. The Holy Spirit does not crush those who only require prodding. Some are simply more stubborn and resistant than others. God demonstrates his grace by approaching each of us with that level of conviction necessary for our response.

16:12 Having indicated what the Spirit would be doing in the world (16:7-11), Jesus then related to the disciples what the Spirit would be doing in believers. But most of what Jesus told the disciples would be unclear to them until after the events of the Crucifixion and Resurrection. Thus Jesus wanted to tell them more, but they couldn't **bear it** then.

16:13 The prominent role of the Spirit of truth is to guide the believers **into all truth.** By truth Jesus meant the truth about his identity, the truth of his words and actions, and the truth about all that was to happen to him. In time they would fully understand that he was the Son, come from the Father, sent to save people from their sin. But only after these events occurred, and only through the Holy Spirit's guidance, would the disciples be able to understand. The Holy Spirit is the true guide for all believers; his primary task is to instruct us about the truth (1 John 2:20).

The disciples were not given power to predict the future, but the Spirit would give them insight into **the future**—that is, the events of the Crucifixion, Resurrection, Ascension, and perhaps the Second Coming. The disciples would not fully understand until the Holy Spirit had come after Jesus' death and resurrection. Then the Holy Spirit would reveal truths to the disciples that they would write down in the books that now form the New Testament.

16:14 The Spirit does not glorify himself; rather, he brings **glory** to the Son. The Spirit takes what the Son is and reveals it to believers. In so doing, he individualizes the teaching of Christ and calls people to obey. The Holy Spirit makes us want to apply, teaches us to apply, and then helps us apply Christ's words!

16:15 Jesus explained that the Holy Spirit works in complete submission to, and in harmony with, the Son and the Father. The Spirit reveals the Son to the believers. Yet as he reveals the Son, the Spirit is also revealing the Father because all the attributes of the Son are the attributes of the Father: **"All that the Father has is mine."** Thus the Spirit reveals to believers **whatever he receives from** the Son, who, in turn, expresses the Father. This verbal picture of what cannot be fully seen by finite humans helps us understand the profound unity of God.

What we call the doctrine of the Trinity is a summary of what Jesus taught about his relationship to the Father and the Spirit. Without in any way diminishing the awesome revelation of God as one, Jesus demonstrated that God's oneness is at the same time a threeness: Father, Son, and Holy Spirit. God exists in perfect, unbroken harmony while at the same time functioning in the person of the Father, the Son, and the Holy Spirit. They are one; yet they relate to one another. They are beyond our complete grasp; yet they have graciously revealed themselves to us so that we may trust and be saved!

JESUS TEACHES ABOUT USING HIS NAME IN PRAYER / 16:16-33 / 218

Jesus explained to the disciples that his departure would only last "a little while" (actually only three days), for he would see them again on the day of his resurrection. Then a new relationship between the disciples and Jesus' Father would begin. They would then be able to approach God the Father as his children and bring to him their requests through prayer. Jesus concluded this section with yet another prediction and teaching to prepare them. He informed the disciples that, while they thought they believed, within hours they all would abandon him. Jesus did not berate them for their weakness but prepared them to endure in spite of it.

16:16-19 Jesus was referring to his death (**"I will be gone"**), only a few hours away, and his resurrection (**"You will see me again"**) three days later. But the disciples didn't understand this, so they were grieved and perplexed. They kept asking each other what he could possibly mean. Jesus had already told the disciples that he would go to the Father and return to them after his resurrection (chapter 14), but they didn't understand.

16:20-22 Following his explanation of the time between his departure and return, Jesus used a figure of speech to depict how quickly the disciples' **grief will suddenly turn to wonderful joy:** **"It will be like a woman experiencing the pains of labor. When her child is born, her anguish gives place to joy."** The disciples would **grieve** for their crucified Master, and the **world** (the mass of people opposed to Jesus) **will rejoice** that this "madman" had finally been silenced. But the disciples' grief would turn to joy when they would see their resurrected Lord. In addition, the Holy Spirit would help them understand the true purpose of Jesus' crucifixion and resurrection—that it meant salvation from sin and eternal life for everyone who believes! Indeed, they would **rejoice, and no one** would be able to **rob them of that joy.**

16:23-24 At that time refers to the time subsequent to Jesus' resurrection. From that day forward, when they had a request, the disciples could **go directly to the Father and ask him** (see 14:13-14; 15:7). This was another reminder that Jesus would not remain on earth indefinitely after he rose from the dead. Requests asked in Jesus' name are requests that the believer knows Jesus would be pleased to answer, requests that are in accordance with the Father's will. Any such request will be given. Answered prayer brings **abundant joy**—just ask any believer! Jesus encouraged the disciples to ask, so that they might **receive** and have full and complete joy (see also 1 John 5:13-15).

16:25-27 Specific predictions about future events would have been too much for the disciples at this point (16:12-13), so Jesus spoke to them in **parables.** After Jesus arose, however, the disciples were given a new, living relationship with the Father (see 20:19). Through the Holy Spirit, Jesus would **tell** them **plainly all about the Father** (16:13-15). The disciples would have direct, personal access to the Father. Jesus would not have to make their requests for them; instead, they would go straight to God, asking in Jesus' name. Jesus was not withdrawing from representing us before the Father. He still makes intercession for us (Romans 8:34; Hebrews 7:25). Jesus was preparing the disciples for the reality that his death would allow them direct access to the Father in prayer and that they ought to make use of it (Hebrews 10:19-25)! The Father would respond to the disciples because, as Jesus said, **"The Father himself loves you dearly because you love me and believe that I came from God."** All who love Jesus and believe in him as God's Son are loved by the Father. Why? Because they have loved him whom the Father dearly loves. God remembers our faithfulness to his Son, Jesus Christ. Jesus not only encouraged the disciples to love him and remain faithful, but he also reminds us how essential our faithfulness really is.

16:28-30 In this sentence, Jesus plainly described his entire mission—he was incarnated (**came from the Father**), he was made a human being in order to secure the salvation of human beings (**into the world**), and he would be resurrected from death and ascend back to the glory from which he came (**return to the Father**).

The disciples finally realized that Jesus had been speaking of his departure to the Father. Then they said, **"We believe that you came from God."** Jesus' repeated predictions of his imminent death, resurrection, and ascension (7:33; 10:11-18; 12:23-24, 30-36; 13:18-38; 14:1-5, 15-31; 16:5-7) finally left their mark on the disciples. Now they were convinced that Jesus' knowledge about future events marked him unquestionably as the Son of God come from God. The disciples believed Jesus' words because they were convinced that he knew **everything.** He even knew the questions on their minds before they asked them (16:19). They were making a claim, not about their own knowledge, but about his. Jesus' omniscience was another

proof of his divinity. But their belief was only a first step toward the enduring faith they would receive when the Holy Spirit came to live in them.

16:31-32 The implied exasperation in the statement is conveyed better by "You believe at last!" The disciples had taken a small but real step forward in understanding. Jesus continued to tell them what was going to happen so that their faith would be strengthened in the end: **"But the time is coming— in fact, it is already here—when you will be scattered, each one going his own way, leaving me alone."** **Scattered** alludes to the prophecy in Zechariah 13:7. As predicted, the disciples abandoned Jesus when he was arrested (Matthew 26:56; Mark 14:50). Even though Jesus was abandoned by his disciples, he was not completely alone. As Jesus said previously (8:29), here he says, **"Yet I am not alone because the Father is with me."**

16:33 In a final note of encouragement, Jesus promised the disciples **peace** through their union with him—for he would **overcome the world** by rising from the grave. The world, Satan's system that is opposed to God, will give the believers **many trials and sorrows.** But Jesus has beaten Satan's system, won the victory, and overcome the world. Before his own trial, Jesus could already speak of an accomplished task. This adds impact to his victory over Satan since he not only accomplished it, he predicted it! The disciples could constantly rejoice in the victory because they were on the winning team.

Jesus summed up all he had told them this night, tying together themes from 14:27-29, 16:1-4, and 16:9-11. With these words he told his disciples to take courage. Despite the inevitable struggles they would face, they would not be alone. Just as Jesus' Father did not leave him alone, Jesus does not abandon us to our struggles either. If we remember that the ultimate victory has already been won, we can claim the peace of Christ in the most troublesome times. Jesus wants us to have peace.

JOHN 17

JESUS PRAYS FOR HIMSELF / 17:1-5 / 219

John 17 contains Jesus' great intercessory prayer. It is not the prayer of agony in the Garden of Gethsemane but an open conversation with the Father about his followers. This prayer brings to a close Jesus' discourse in 13:31–16:33. It expresses the deepest desires of Jesus' heart for his return to the Father and for the destiny of his chosen ones. Jesus asked the Father to grant the believers the same kind of unity that he and the Father enjoyed from eternity—a unity of love.

17:1 Jesus began his petition by praying for himself: **"Father, the time has come. Glorify your Son so he can give glory back to you."** Jesus knew that his "hour" of suffering had come—several times previously in the Gospel, John had pointed out that Jesus' time had *not* come (2:4; 7:6, 8, 30; 8:20). But the time for Jesus' glorification had arrived. If the Father would glorify the Son in the Crucifixion and Resurrection, the Son could, in turn, give eternal life to the believers and so glorify the Father. Jesus asked the Father to restore to him the full rights and power as Son of God (as described in Philippians 2:5-11).

17:2 Jesus made his requests to the Father, knowing that from eternity past the Father had **given him authority over everyone in all the earth** so that he could give **eternal life** to **each one** the Father had given him.

17:3 Jesus defines **eternal life** as **to know** experientially **the only true God, and Jesus Christ, the one** he sent to earth. We find eternal life only by knowing the one true God. This knowledge is ongoing and personal (see also Matthew 11:27).

17:4 In this statement, Jesus affirmed that he had **brought glory to** the Father **on earth** by **doing everything** God wanted him to do. The last phase of Jesus' revealing work was about to be accomplished through his death on the cross. Jesus spoke of his work as though it had already happened—his obedience to death on the cross was a certainty. Jesus requested again to be returned to glory based on the certainty of his completing the work of the cross.

17:5 Looking beyond the Cross to his resurrection and ascension, Jesus asked the **Father** to restore **the glory** he had **shared** with the Father **before the world began.** In saying this, Jesus gives us a glimpse of his relationship with the Father before the beginning of time. Jesus wanted to return to the glory he had with the Father before the world was created (see 1:1, 18). Jesus would enter into that glory as the crucified and risen Lord Jesus Christ. Thus, Jesus' return to God was not simply a return to his preincarnate state, since Jesus would have his resurrected body. Jesus' resurrection and ascension—and Stephen's dying exclamation (Acts 7:56)—attest that Jesus' prayer was answered. He returned to his exalted position at the right hand of God.

JESUS PRAYS FOR HIS DISCIPLES / 17:6-19 / *220*
This prayer is one of several mentioned in the Bible that focused on the disciples. Before choosing the Twelve, Jesus spent the night in prayer (Luke 6:12). During their ministry together (John 6:15; Luke 10:18-22), we assume Jesus' prayers included his disciples. We know that before the final days, Jesus had been praying specifically for Peter (Luke 22:32). The Scriptures also tell us that part of Jesus' present activity is to pray for us (Romans 8:34; Hebrews 7:25). Jesus made it clear that although we have direct access to the Father (16:26-27), we are still the objects of his loving concern.

17:6 After praying for his own glorification, Jesus turned the direction of his petition to his disciples. These were the men God had selected to give to his Son as his disciples (see 15:19). To **these men,** given to him by the Father out of **the world,** Jesus had expressed the reality of the Father's person to them (see 1:18). And they had **kept** his **word.** Their faith wasn't perfect, and they would fail their Savior in the coming hours; but their commitment was in the right place, and they would return to this faith and to obedience to God.

17:7-8 The disciples had received Jesus' words as coming from God; as a result, they had come to believe that Jesus had been sent from the Father (see 16:28-30). Before Jesus instituted God's plan of salvation by dying on the cross, he introduced it to his disciples. They had to believe the words of Christ to benefit from the work of Christ. Jesus effectively demonstrated that what he said came from God. The disciples were not in a position to accept the saving purpose of Jesus' death until they had accepted the fact that God had sent him. Once they knew God had sent Jesus, they were ready to learn that God had sent him to die! Jesus was declaring that the disciples were ready for the next lesson, as difficult as it might be.

17:9 We know that God loves the world (3:16), but at this time Jesus was focusing on the disciples, not the world. These disciples were the object of Jesus' affection and Jesus' prayer. He was not praying **for the world,** because the world was hostile and unbelieving. Instead, he was praying for **those** the Father had **given** him.

17:10 Jesus' words reveal his oneness, closeness, and equality with God the Father. These disciples belonged to both him and the Father, and they were the ones in whom Jesus would be glorified on earth after he had returned to the Father. The disciples' lives would reveal Jesus' essential character to those who had not yet believed, so Jesus was present in the world through them.

17:11 Jesus would be **departing the world** to rejoin the Father; the disciples would stay **behind** to carry out God's plan by spreading the good news of salvation. Such a mission would arouse great hostility from the evil one, so the disciples needed special protection. Jesus asked that the **Holy Father** would **keep them and care for them.** The prayer itself indicates confidence in God's ability to "keep" his children, while at the same time allowing the disciples to hear Jesus' desire for how they are to be kept. Jesus prayed that they would **be united just as** he and the Father are united. They should have a unified desire and purpose to serve and glorify God. Then they would have the strongest of all possible unions.

17:12 Jesus' physical presence had provided the obvious point of unity for the disciples. The more they were "in Christ," the more they were united and protected. Jesus had **kept them safe** as a precious gift given to him from the Father; here he gave an account of the job he had done. All of the disciples had been **guarded—not one was lost, except the one headed for destruction, as the Scriptures foretold.** The one was Judas Iscariot who, by his own volition, betrayed Jesus. Thus, Jesus sadly identified Judas as one who had rejected the protection offered.

The place of Judas among the disciples and his choice to betray Jesus highlight the balance that we find throughout the Bible between the awesome sovereignty of God and the freedom he allows people to exercise. We would tip the balance toward error if we would say that Jesus intentionally withheld his protection of Judas to expose him to the temptation of Satan so that the betrayal could happen. We would also be in error if we would say that the temptation of Satan was stronger than Jesus' ability to protect Judas. Judas was not a puppet on a string. Judas shared the protection offered by the presence of Jesus all during their time together. Judas made his decision to betray Jesus, and by so doing he removed himself from Christ's protection. He passed the point of no return and thereby fulfilled the scriptural prediction.

The extent of God's protection over us every single day is beyond our comprehension. His sovereignty is complete, including his choice to allow us to actually be able to effectively reject him. God could have created persons whose choices didn't really matter. Instead, because of his love for us, he created us with enough freedom to live in relationship with him.

17:13 Jesus had **told** his disciples **many things** about his coming death—hardly a joyful topic. But after these events would take place—especially after the Resurrection—the disciples **would be filled with joy,** for they would then understand that Jesus had conquered death and Satan and had brought eternal life to all who believe in him.

17:14 The **world hates** Christians because Christians' values differ from the world's, and because Christians expose the world's values for what they are—absolutely worthless. Because Christ's followers don't cooperate with the world by joining in their sin, they are living accusations against the world's immorality. The world follows Satan's agenda, and Satan is the avowed enemy of Jesus and his people (see 15:18; 16:2).

17:15-16 Jesus did not pray that God would **take them out of the world** to protect them from the hatred and persecution to come, rather that they would be kept **safe from the evil one**—that through difficult circumstances they would not fall prey to the devil. The only way believers can be witnesses *to* the world is to be witnessing for Christ *in* the world. We must carry our message, trusting God for his protection. Jesus was not a part of the world's system, headed by Satan (indeed, he had been tempted to that end and had refused—see Matthew 4:1-11). Neither are believers a part of the world because they have been born again (3:3).

17:17 Three distinct views have emerged to explain what Jesus meant by **"make them pure and holy by teaching them your words of truth."** (1) The truth found in God's word will make us pure and holy. (2) The central truth of God's saving love sets into motion God's work in us. (3) The process of passing on (preaching, teaching) God's truth would have a purifying effect in the disciples' lives. These views are actually complementary, describing different aspects of becoming pure and holy (called **sanctification**): the second view highlights the initial pouring of God's grace into our lives through the truth of the gospel; the first view summarizes the ongoing effects of the applied truths from God's word; and the third view emphasizes that progress in sanctification will be seen in our desire and practice of communicating the gospel. God's word, then, works as a divine cleansing agent that God uses to bring about our sanctification.

17:18 Jesus came **into the world** on a mission for the Father; so he sent these disciples **into the world** on a mission by the Son. That mission was to make God known. This is an important and exciting theme in John's Gospel. The Father sent the Son into the world, the Father and the Son sent the Spirit to the disciples, and the disciples are sent by the Father and Son into the world.

It is up to us to carry on Jesus' mission—to make God known to others. Because Jesus sends us into the world, we should not try to escape from the world, nor should we avoid all relationships with non-Christians. We are called to be salt and light (Matthew 5:13-16), and we are to do the work that God has sent us to do.

17:19 Jesus set himself apart to do the Father's will like a priest consecrating himself to make the sacrifice. His final act of dedication was his offering himself on the cross (see Hebrews 10:10). The purpose of that death was so that the disciples (and all believers) **might be entirely** God's possession. Jesus died to set us apart for him.

JESUS PRAYS FOR FUTURE BELIEVERS / 17:20-26 / 221
The pattern of Jesus' prayer provides a helpful outline for us. He prayed for himself, for those close to him, and for those beyond his immediate sphere who would be affected by the ministry of his friends.

17:20 After praying for his **disciples**, Jesus prayed for **all who** would **ever believe in** him **because of their testimony.** In a sense, everyone who has become a Christian has done so through the apostles' message because they wrote the New Testament and were the founders of the Christian church. So Jesus was praying for all the believers who would ever exist. He was praying for you and others you know. And he was praying for those he wants us to reach! Knowing that Jesus prayed for us should give us confidence as we work for his Kingdom.

17:21 There are three requests in verse 21, and they hinge on one another. In the first request, the Lord asked for unity—**that they will be one.** This all-encompassing petition includes all the believers throughout time. This oneness does not readily fit the idea of one unified church structure. Rather, this unity becomes most visible through love, obedience, and commitment to the Father's will.

In the second request, Jesus prayed for a unity among the believers that is based on the unity of Jesus and the **Father.** Christians can be unified if they live in union with God. For example, each branch living in union with the vine is united with all other branches (see 15:1-17); or each part of the body is united with the other parts so that when one hurts, they all hurt, and when one rejoices, they all rejoice (1 Corinthians 12:12-27).

This union with the Father and Son would result in people all over the **world** believing that Jesus had been **sent** by God as the world's Savior—and not only believing, but receiving this Savior as their own. This is the third request.

17:22-23 Jesus further explained this oneness in terms of mutual indwelling: **"I have given them the glory you gave me."** Jesus was still referring to all his followers, not just the immediate disciples. The phrase is a promise. Jesus gave all true believers his glory by completing his mission of revealing God (17:4-6). Jesus' work was not only to speak and model the character of God. His ultimate purpose was to present both the splendor and character of God (God's glory) in such a way that God would become personally real to the disciples. They, in turn, were to pass on what they had received to others who would also believe. Those who, in fact, received the glory would become unified by their shared relationship with Christ. Complete and perfect unity between God and believers results in worldwide belief. When we demonstrate this oneness, we will convince the world that the Father sent the Son, and that the Father loves believers deeply and eternally, just as he loves the Son.

17:24 Jesus wants all believers (the eleven disciples and all others) **to be with** him where he is so they can **see** his **glory.** What wonderful assurance Jesus' prayer gives us to know that the Lord of heaven wants us to be with him. This request impacts our present experience and future hope. In the present, we unite with Christ in God the Father (see 14:6; Colossians 3:3). In the future, we will be with Christ in eternal glory and enjoy with him the love he experienced with the Father forever.

17:25-26 Jesus addressed his Father as **righteous Father** because God's righteous judgment reveals that the world's knowledge of God is incorrect and that the disciples' knowledge is correct. Just as Jesus had chosen the name "Holy Father" (17:11) to present his request for protection of the disciples, so here Jesus added **righteous** as a highlight to the gulf that exists between the world and God. Jesus knew he was the living connection between the lost world and his loving, righteous Father.

The world failed to recognize that Jesus was God's communication to them. The **disciples** did recognize this, for they had come to believe that Jesus was the one sent from God. Jesus, who knew the Father personally and intimately, had revealed the Father to his disciples and would continue to do so. Thus, Jesus could say, **"I have revealed you**

to them and will keep on revealing you." Finally, Jesus asked the Father to love the disciples with the same love he (the Father) had for his Son.

Jesus asked that the Father's **love** would be **in** believers and that he himself (Jesus) would be **in them.** This expresses the heart of the Father's desire, which is to have his Son in his people: "I . . . in them." And because it is the Father's desire, he will make sure it is accomplished. How do you understand your relationship with God the Father? Is his love in you?

JOHN 18:1-37

JESUS IS BETRAYED AND ARRESTED / 18:1-11 / 224

After the prayer recorded in John 17, Jesus again predicted Peter's denial (Matthew 26:31-35; Mark 14:27-31). The synoptic Gospels then record Jesus' agony in the Garden of Gethsemane (see Matthew 26:36-46; Mark 14:32-42; Luke 22:39-46). Here is a summary of that section: After arriving in Gethsemane, Jesus sat his disciples down and told them to wait for him while he went and prayed. Then he took Peter, James, and John aside, expressed his great distress to them, and asked them to stay awake with him. How touching that Jesus, in this great hour of distress, sought human companionship from his closest friends—just someone to stay awake and be with him.

18:1 To get to the Garden of Gethsemane, Jesus and the disciples had to cross the **Kidron Valley,** a ravine that starts north of Jerusalem and goes between the hill where the Temple is built and the Mount of Olives, then moving on to the Dead Sea. During the rainy season, the valley filled with water torrents, but at this time it was dry.

18:2 Though **Judas** had left the group while they were still in the upper room (13:26-31), he calculated that Jesus would go to Gethsemane with his **disciples** because that seemed to be a favorite place for Jesus and the disciples to get away from the crowds when they were in Jerusalem (see Luke 21:37).

18:3-4 Judas acted as a guide to two groups: (1) **a battalion of Roman soldiers** (about 600 men), and (2) **Temple guards** who were Jewish Temple police. The Jews were given authority by the religious leaders to make arrests for minor infractions. The soldiers probably did not participate in the arrest but accompanied the Temple guard to make sure matters didn't get out of control. The **leading priests and Pharisees** may have asked the Romans for help in arresting Jesus

because their ultimate intention was to obtain assistance in executing Jesus. The police and the guards were prepared to meet violent resistance, for they carried **blazing torches, lanterns, and weapons.** It was still night—Judas's departure into the night to go and betray Jesus had occurred only hours earlier (13:30). John did not record Judas's kiss of greeting (Matthew 26:49; Mark 14:45; Luke 22:47-48), but the kiss marked a turning point for the disciples. They ran away (Matthew 26:56).

Jesus' betrayal, arrest, and crucifixion transpired according to the prearranged, divine plan—he **fully realized** what was happening. The betrayer, Judas Iscariot, had been selected by Jesus. He knew from the beginning that Judas was a devil and would be his betrayer (see 6:64, 70). The time of his arrest was predetermined; it would happen during Passover, not before or after. The method of execution (crucifixion) was predetermined, so Jesus knew that he would be lifted up on the cross (see 12:32-33).

18:5-6 Jesus' response is literally only **"I am."** With these words, he declared his deity (as in

8:58; see Exodus 3:14). The reaction this utterance produced in those who were there to arrest him (including **Judas**) indicates that Jesus' words startled this mass of armed men, for **they all fell backward to the ground.** Because some Temple guards were among the Roman soldiers, quite possibly they understood the significance of Jesus' claim. Or perhaps they were overcome by his obvious power and authority. Among them may have been some of those who earlier (7:46) had concluded that, "We have never heard anyone talk like this!" The response of the guards shows that Jesus could have exercised his power to thwart his arrest, but chose not to.

18:7-9 Jesus was willing to turn himself over to the soldiers, but he asked them to **let these others go**, referring to the eleven disciples who were with him. By this action, he fulfilled **his own statement, "I have not lost a single one of those you gave me."** Jesus was referring to words recorded in 6:39 and 17:12. Jesus was the Good Shepherd who would lay down his life for the sheep (10:11).

18:10-11 Peter had promised to die for Jesus (Matthew 26:33-35), and he wasn't going to let Jesus be taken without a fight. Peter's **sword** was probably a dagger. Luke mentions that the disciples had two swords among them (Luke 22:38). Peter **slashed off the right ear of Malchus, the high priest's servant.** Luke added that Jesus then healed the servant's ear (Luke 22:50-51).

Jesus was determined to do his Father's will. (This is the only mention of the **cup** of suffering in John's Gospel. See Mark 14:36.) In the Old Testament, the "cup" often referred to the outpouring of God's wrath (see Psalm 75:8; Isaiah 51:17; Jeremiah 25:15; Ezekiel 23:31-34). For Jesus, the cup meant the suffering, isolation, and death that he would have to endure in order to atone for the sins of the world. Peter may have shown great loyalty, but he missed the point. All that was happening was part of God's plan.

Immediately after the same reference to the cup of suffering, both Matthew and Mark mention that all the disciples deserted Jesus and fled (Matthew 26:56; Mark 14:50).

ANNAS QUESTIONS JESUS / 18:12-24 / 225

Once the religious leaders had Jesus in their power, the events began to move with planned precision. Since the point of the effort was to kill Jesus, determining his guilt or innocence was a mere formality. To the leaders, the issue of timing the death was more important than asking whether Jesus deserved to die.

18:12-13 The Jews and the Romans **arrested Jesus and tied him up** like a common prisoner. Jesus was immediately taken to the high priest's residence even though it was the middle of the night. The religious leaders were in a hurry—they wanted to complete the execution before the Sabbath and get on with the Passover celebration. **First they took him to Annas, the father-in-law of Caiaphas, the high priest that year.** Both Annas and Caiaphas had been high priests. According to Jewish law, the office of high priest was held for life. But the Romans didn't like such concentration of power under one person, so they frequently changed the high priest. However, many Jews still considered Annas to be the high priest and still called him by that title. But although Annas retained much authority among the Jews, Caiaphas made the final decisions.

18:14 Caiaphas was the one who had advised the Jews that it was better to have **one** person die for **all** (see 11:49-52). Caiaphas said this because he feared the Romans. The Jews had limited religious freedom so long as they kept the peace. The Jewish

leaders feared that Jesus' miracles and large following would cause Rome to react and clamp down on them. So better that Jesus die than that many be endangered by an uprising.

18:15-18 Although all the disciples had fled when the soldiers arrived, two of them returned and decided to follow Jesus. So these two disciples followed Jesus to Annas's house. This house was more like a compound surrounded by walls with a guarded gate. Only one disciple was identified: **Peter;** the other was apparently a disciple who was an acquaintance of the **high priest.** This other disciple only entered with Jesus into the **courtyard** of the high priest.

Some scholars think the other disciple was John because of similar references to himself in 20:2 and 21:20, 24. But many scholars argue that John, the son of Zebedee from Galilee, would not have been known by Annas. Whoever this disciple was, he secured permission for Peter to enter the courtyard.

Immediately Peter was put on the defensive. Just as he entered, the **woman** who was **watching the gate** (actually a servant) asked Peter, **"Aren't you** one of Jesus' disciples?" In striking contrast to Peter's earlier declaration that he would lay down his life for his Lord (13:37), Peter denied it: **"I am not."**

It was a spring evening, and the city of Jerusalem sits 2,500 feet above sea level. The **charcoal fire** kept the **cold** at bay. Peter's story continues at 18:25.

18:19 Meanwhile **the high priest** wanted to know **what** Jesus **had been teaching** his **followers.** If a rebellion was feared by the authorities, Annas may have wanted to know how many disciples Jesus had gathered so as to estimate the force of their retaliation. Or Annas may have wanted to question the disciples about what Jesus had taught them. Jesus said nothing about his disciples, so as to protect them (as in 18:8), but was willing to talk about his teaching.

18:20-23 Jesus was not the leader of a cult or secret organization. He was not planning a religious coup. Instead, Jesus noted that everything he taught had been taught **in public.** Even the quiet and private talks with his disciples included no secret or subversive teachings. Everything he said

to the disciples was told to the crowds, but they refused to understand. If Annas wanted to know the substance of Jesus' teachings, he could ask anyone who had heard Jesus speak on several occasions. Interrogating the disciples would not be necessary. So Jesus turned the questioning back to Annas: **"Why are you asking me this question? Ask those who heard me. They know what I said."**

This incited anger. **One of the Temple guards,** seeing Jesus' answer as a sign of contempt for the high priest, **struck Jesus on the face** (probably a good hard slap). Jesus defended himself, for he had been slapped unjustly. This incident is similar to that recorded in Acts 23:2-5, where Paul was struck for not answering the high priest "correctly." Jesus denied that he **said anything wrong.**

18:24 After being interrogated by **Annas,** Jesus was sent on to **Caiaphas,** the ruling **high priest.** Mark records that this questioning before Caiaphas included the entire Jewish council (Mark 14:53-65). The religious leaders knew they had no grounds for charging Jesus, so they tried to build evidence against him by using false witnesses.

PETER DENIES KNOWING JESUS / 18:25-27 / 227
While Jesus was countering the questions of Annas (see 18:19-24), who was trying to gather information against the disciples, Peter denied knowing Jesus three times. Jesus displayed his great moral character by not disowning his disciples, even though they had denied him. John captured the pathos of the moment by merely reporting that Peter's final denial was made with the rooster crowing in the background.

18:25 These verses are a continuation of verses 15-18. **Peter** was still in the courtyard of Annas's house and was standing beside a **fire** with several other people. Again Peter was asked: **"Aren't you one of his disciples?"** Peter denied it saying, **"I am not."** The vehemence of Peter's denial may have caught the attention of several others who were gathered around the fire. To at least one of them, Peter looked very familiar.

18:26-27 This, the third denial, happened exactly as Jesus had predicted (see 13:38; Mark 14:30). The other three Gospels say that Peter's three

denials happened near a fire in the courtyard outside Caiaphas's palace. John places the three denials outside Annas's home. This was very likely the same courtyard. The high priest's residence was large, and Annas and Caiaphas undoubtedly lived near each other. This time a **household servant** who happened to be **a relative of the man whose ear Peter had cut off, asked, "Didn't I see you out there in the olive grove with Jesus?"** But for the third time, **Peter denied it.** A crowing **rooster** and the piercing look of Jesus (Luke 22:61-62) made Peter realize how quickly he had abandoned his Lord.

JESUS STANDS TRIAL BEFORE PILATE / 18:28-37 / 230
The same rooster that announced the third denial of Peter also welcomed the day that Jesus was to be crucified. John gives us none of the details of Jesus' further questioning before Caiaphas, since the two parts of the preliminary "trial" were perfunctory and repetitious. The

faces changed, but the false accusations remained the same. Early morning found Jesus and his accusers at Pilate's gate demanding an audience. Pilate quickly concluded that the charges against Jesus were groundless. But he was also clearly puzzled that Jesus refused to defend himself. The imperial representative of Rome found himself uncomfortably pressed between a rock and a hard place.

18:28-29 By now it was the **early hours of** Friday **morning.** This **headquarters** was also called the Praetorium, where **the Roman governor** resided when he was in Jerusalem. By Jewish law, entering the house of a Gentile would cause a Jewish person to be ceremonially defiled. As a result, a Jew could not take part in worship at the Temple or celebrate the feasts until he or she was restored to a state of "cleanness." Afraid of being defiled, Jesus' **accusers** stayed outside the house where they had taken Jesus for trial. They kept the ceremonial requirements of their religion while harboring murder and treachery in their hearts. Because the Jews were outside, **Pilate went out** to them and asked, **"What is your charge against this man?"**

Pilate was in charge of Judea (the region where Jerusalem was located) from A.D. 26–36. Pilate was unpopular with the Jews. He resided in Caesarea, but came to Jerusalem during the major feasts in order to handle any problems that could arise with so many people in the city during the festival. Passover was a very important feast to the Jews as they remembered their freedom from bondage in Egypt.

To go to Pilate, these Jewish leaders must have been really desperate to get rid of Jesus. Normally, the Jews would never turn one of their own people over to the hated Romans.

18:30-31 Pilate realized that something wasn't normal about this case. He must have sensed the jealousy of the Jewish leaders who brought this popular teacher to him. Pilate certainly had seen or at least had heard about Jesus' glorious entry into Jerusalem only a few days earlier, so he understood the motives of these religious leaders. Therefore, Pilate demanded that they provide a bona fide legal charge against Jesus. The Jewish leaders answered as vaguely as possible: **"We wouldn't have handed him over to you if he weren't a criminal!"**

But Pilate, uninterested in the constant squabbling among the Jews, was satisfied that this potential troublemaker was in custody. He had no reason to push the trial any farther, so he tried to dismiss them: **"Take him away and judge him by your own laws."**

But the Jewish leaders persisted and gained Pilate's attention by insinuating that they had already found reasons in their own law for Jesus'

execution. But the Jews needed Pilate to give Jesus a trial because **only the Romans** were **permitted to execute someone.** Being under Roman rule, the Jews were not permitted to carry out the kind of execution they were planning without the sanction of the Roman government. It seems that "spontaneous" executions like the stoning of Stephen or the woman taken in adultery were overlooked by the Romans. But in the eyes of the Jewish leaders, Jesus needed to be executed publicly. Thus, the Jews needed the Romans to execute Jesus for them.

18:32 Jesus knew all along that his would be a Roman execution, for he had predicted that he would die on a cross. Capital punishment for the Jews was by stoning and for the Romans by crucifixion. Jesus had always foretold his death in terms of crucifixion, not stoning (Matthew 20:19).

18:33-34 Since Jesus' enemies had accused him of sedition against Rome (Luke 23:1-2), Pilate asked Jesus if he really was **the King of the Jews.** Jesus then asked Pilate where the question came from. If Pilate was asking this question in his role as the Roman governor, he would have been inquiring whether Jesus was setting up a rebel government. But the Jews were using the word "king" to mean their religious ruler, the Messiah. Israel was a captive nation, under the authority of the Roman Empire. A rival king might have threatened Rome; a Messiah could have been a purely religious leader.

18:35-36 Pilate's response indicates that his interrogation was motivated by the Jews. The impression is that he was merely performing his task. Jesus explained that he was not a threat to Rome because he was **not an earthly king.** Instead, his **Kingdom** was **not of this world.** Jesus was referring to all he had done and would do as God's Son and all that is under his authority. When believers are born again, they become subjects of this Kingdom—a spiritual Kingdom.

18:37 Pilate tried to get his original question answered (see 18:33): **"You are a king then?"** Jesus explained that he was indeed a king, and **born for that purpose.** But he was the king of a different realm, a king who had come to **bring truth to the world.** Jesus did not enter the world for any political purpose; instead, he came to testify to the truth. There seems to have been no question in Pilate's mind that Jesus spoke the truth and was innocent of any crime. It also seems apparent that while recognizing the truth, Pilate chose to reject it. It is a tragedy when we fail to recognize the truth. It is a greater tragedy when we recognize the truth but fail to heed it.

JOHN **18**:38—19:42

PILATE HANDS JESUS OVER TO BE CRUCIFIED / 18:38–19:16A / 232

Pilate mused on the possibility of truly comprehending "truth" and then declared Jesus "not guilty." He had no basis for a charge against Jesus and certainly no evidence that required a death penalty. But it wouldn't be that easy.

18:38 Pilate was cynical; he thought that all **truth** was relative—it could be whatever Rome wanted it to be. To many government officials, truth was whatever the majority of people agreed with or whatever helped advance their own personal power and political goals. When there is no basis for truth, there is no basis for moral right and wrong. Justice becomes whatever works or whatever helps those in power. In Jesus and his word we have a standard for truth and for our moral behavior.

At that point, Pilate had the power and authority to simply set Jesus free because Jesus was **not guilty of any crime.** But he lacked the courage to stand by this conviction in the face of opposition from these Jews and a possible ensuing riot. Problems like that could mean that Pilate would be removed from his position because of being unable to keep the peace. So Pilate tried first to pass Jesus off on Herod, who was ruler of Galilee, the region of Jesus' hometown (Luke 23:6-7). But Herod only mocked Jesus and then sent him back to Pilate.

18:39-40 Pilate hoped to escape passing judgment on Jesus by allowing the Jews to determine Jesus' fate. As a **custom,** Pilate had released **someone from prison each year at Passover.** He hoped they would ask for **the King of the Jews.**

The screaming Jewish officials demanded that a convicted rebel, **Barabbas,** be pardoned instead of Jesus. Barabbas was a rebel against Rome (Mark 15:7), and although he had committed murder, he was probably a hero among the Jews. Barabbas, who had led a rebellion and failed, was released instead of Jesus, the only one who could truly help Israel.

19:1 Pilate handed Jesus over to the soldiers to be **flogged.** This was another attempt by Pilate to set

Jesus free. Pilate knew that Jesus was innocent of any crime, and he desperately wanted Jesus freed to quiet his own conscience. So Pilate thought the flogging would appease the Jews. This was ruthless but not intended to kill him. Nevertheless, it was not uncommon for prisoners to die of floggings. Some of the whips used for flogging were designed to inflict terrible damage to the human body. The leather thongs that formed the striking surfaces were **lead-tipped** so that victims were both bruised and cut severely. Punishment was applied to the bared upper body of a bound prisoner. Apparently, Pilate thought this flogging was a humane alternative to crucifixion. He was avoiding condemning Jesus to death.

19:2-3 The Roman **soldiers** jammed a **crown of long, sharp thorns** onto Jesus' **head** and obtained a **purple robe** (purple was the color of royalty) in order to mock Jesus' supposed kingship. The Roman soldiers **mocked** Jesus further by bowing before him and striking him. This had been prophesied in Isaiah 50:6 (see also 52:14–53:6).

19:4-7 After Jesus' beating and the display of mockery, Pilate, for the second time (see 18:38), declared Jesus **not guilty**—that is, not guilty of a crime warranting death. Pilate hoped the sight of this beaten, bloody person would elicit pity and make the crowd realize that there could be no possible threat from this poor fellow. The tone of these words implies ridicule, as if he said, "How can you possibly believe this pitiful man's claim to be a king?"

But the bloodthirsty chief priests and officials responded: **"Crucify! Crucify!"** That they demanded crucifixion reveals their intense hatred of Jesus. Crucifixion was a shameful death reserved for criminals, slaves, and rebels. Jesus was none of these, and Pilate knew it. But the Jewish enemies of Christ wanted not only to kill him but also to discredit and humiliate him thoroughly.

Pilate dared the Jewish leaders to usurp the exclusive Roman authority of capital punishment by crucifying their "King" themselves. The leaders responded that Jesus **ought to die because he called himself the Son of God.** The law they were referring to is Leviticus 24:16. For anyone to claim to be God (as Jesus did) was a clear case of blasphemy and thus required that the person be put to death. The irony here is that Jesus was not violating the law, for what he had said was true! The Jews just didn't believe it.

19:8 Pilate's fear may have had its origin in a combination of three factors:

1. Romans were inclined to believe in human deities; so Pilate may have sensed that the man in his presence was a god.
2. According to Matthew 27:19, Pilate's wife may have influenced his thoughts about Jesus, for she had had a troublesome dream, and had sent word to Pilate to leave Jesus alone.
3. Pilate may well have been concerned that a riot was about to break out among the Jews. Hatred for Romans and the extremely crowded conditions in Jerusalem created a powder keg of unrest that needed only a good spark to become explosive.

19:9-11 Pilate asked Jesus about his origin: **"Where are you from?" But Jesus gave no answer.** Some commentators see Jesus' silence as fulfilling Isaiah 53:7. Pilate, astounded by Jesus' silence, reminded Jesus: **"Don't you realize that I have the power to release you or to crucify you?"**

Pilate's power did not intimidate Jesus because God's authority overrules all human authority. Instead, **the one who** had **brought** Jesus to Pilate had **the greater sin.** Jesus referred to Caiaphas, the high priest, who handed Jesus over to the Romans, not to Judas, who had betrayed him to the Jews. For a Jewish high priest to deliver the Jews' King and Messiah over to the Romans for execution was an even more heinous sin than for the Roman governor to sentence him to death. Pilate was merely a pawn in a very elaborate game, but the high priest would be more severely judged because he should have known better. Caiaphas turned from the "light" in order to side with the darkness and made excuses for disobeying God's law. However, Jesus was at the same time clearly charging Pilate with sin. Pilate was responsible for his choices.

19:12 By this time Pilate was apparently convinced that Jesus was some kind of extra-special, supernatural person, so he **tried** still another time to **release him.** But the **Jewish leaders** were not about to let Jesus escape. In a final desperate ploy, they played their trump card: **"If you release this man, you are not a friend of Caesar."** Since the Jews despised Roman rule, this was blatant hypocrisy. But these Jews hated Jesus so much that to get rid of him they were claiming their allegiance to Rome and to Caesar! Their strategy worked—very likely Pilate was afraid that he would be reported to Caesar as having released a man who had been charged with claiming to be a king. Historical records indicate that the Jews had already threatened to lodge a formal complaint against Pilate for his stubborn flouting of their traditions. Most likely such a complaint would have led to being recalled by Rome, losing his job, or even losing his life. The Roman government could not afford to put large numbers of troops in all the regions under its control, so one of Pilate's main duties was to do whatever was necessary to maintain peace.

19:13-14 Pilate **brought Jesus out** and **sat down on the judgment seat.** Although the text does not explicitly state that Pilate passed judgment on Jesus, the fact that Pilate seated himself on the judgment seat indicates that the judgment originated from him; thus, he was responsible. But the judgment was very indirect. Perhaps Pilate was too guilt-ridden to summarily condemn Jesus, and he was angry at having his hand forced against his better judgment. So his words ring with anger and mockery at these Jews by saying to them: **"Here is your king!"**

19:15-16a But the Jews continued with their shouting: **"Away with him—crucify him!"** Again Pilate retorted, **"What? Crucify your king?"** His repetition of Jesus as "your king" angered the leaders all the more, to the point where they made a ludicrously hypocritical statement: **"We have no king but Caesar."** Nothing could be farther from the truth than this pronouncement of loyalty to Caesar from the Jewish **leading priests.** These religious men, in the heat of the moment and in their blindness, had forgotten their faith—the Jews were God's people. God was their King (Judges 8:23; 1 Samuel 8:7). But perhaps the words rang with truth, for in their murderous plans against Jesus, God's Son, they showed that God was no longer their king. And if that was the case, they, the Jewish leaders, were committing blasphemy. **Pilate gave Jesus to them to be crucified,** but Roman soldiers actually carried out the crucifixion.

JESUS IS LED AWAY TO BE CRUCIFIED / 19:16B-17 / 234

We must never forget the reason Christ died. Unless we recognize the eternal tragedy that would have occurred to the human race without the Cross, we will not be able to see the Cross as our victory. At great personal cost, Jesus won eternal life for us. He paid the price for our sin with his own life. That he offers us life as a free gift ought to give us deep joy. We must be touched by Christ's death, for he died in our place!

19:16b-17 Jesus was **led away**, forced to carry his **cross by himself.** But he became weak because of the flogging, and Simon was commanded to take over (see Matthew 27:32; Mark 15:21; Luke 23:26). Jesus was taken to **Skull Hill.** This hill may have been called this because of its stony top or because it was shaped like a skull. **Golgotha** is the Hebrew word for "skull." The familiar name "Calvary" is derived from the Latin *calvaria* (also meaning "skull").

As the drama of the cross unfolds, John's writing captures the simple ironies of the tragedy. The soldiers who escorted Jesus to Calvary didn't know who he was; they were just doing their duty. Pilate knew that Jesus wasn't guilty of death, but he still didn't understand who Jesus was. The people, roused to a fever pitch by the religious leaders, didn't take the time to care about who Jesus was (even though they had hailed him as their king a few days earlier. Obviously, they were disappointed by the mocking display of him as a pitiful king). The chief priests perhaps were the most blind of all, for they had totally lost sight of everything they stood for, seeking Jesus' death only to hold onto their precious positions and to stop the teachings that were threatening their status quo.

JESUS IS PLACED ON THE CROSS / 19:18-27 / 235

Jesus knew his destiny (see 18:37), and he approached death boldly and courageously. Jesus endured the shame of crucifixion, the ridicule of the crowd, and the insults of those who cast lots for his clothing as he died. Though he was in agony, his thoughts included the care of his aged mother, whose care he entrusted to the disciple he loved. The Jews and the Romans were not taking Jesus' life from him; he was laying it down of his own accord.

19:18-22 The **others** were criminals (see Matthew 27:38; Mark 15:27; Luke 23:32). This again fulfilled prophecy (see Isaiah 53:12). Luke records that one of the criminals insulted Jesus, while the other turned to Jesus and asked to be saved (Luke 23:42). To which Jesus replied, "Today you will be with me in paradise" (Luke 23:43).

Pilate had a **sign** prepared and fastened to the cross. It read, **"Jesus of Nazareth, the King of the Jews."** Pilate wrote this notice in three languages so that anyone passing into or out of the **city** would be able to read it: **Hebrew** (or, Aramaic—the language of the Jews), **Latin** (the Roman language, the official language), and **Greek** (the *lingua franca*, the common tongue).

Probably bitter over his political defeat at the hands of the Jewish leaders, Pilate posted a sign over Jesus that was meant to be ironic. The sight of a humiliated king, stripped of authority, fastened naked to a cross in public execution could only lead to the conclusion of complete defeat. But the irony that Pilate hoped would not be lost on the Jews pales before the irony that God wanted to communicate to the world. The dying King was actually taking control of his Kingdom. His death and resurrection would strike the death blow to Satan's rule and would establish Jesus' eternal authority over the earth. Few people reading the sign that bleak afternoon understood its real meaning, but the sign was absolutely true. Jesus was King of the Jews as well as the Gentiles, the universe, and you. This sign became a universal proclamation, an unconscious prophecy, that Jesus is the royal Messiah.

The **leading priests** wanted Jesus' crime posted as a false claim to kingship, but no persuasion from the chief priests could induce Pilate to change his mind. He dismissed them by saying, **"What I have written, I have written."**

19:23-24 Contrary to the paintings depicting the Crucifixion, Jesus died naked, another horrible part of his humiliation. The Roman soldiers who performed the Crucifixion **divided** the victim's **clothes** among themselves. Clothing was not a cheap commodity in those days as it is today. Thus this was part of the "pay" the executioners received for performing their gruesome duties. But his **robe** was not divided because **it was seamless.** So they threw **dice**

to see who would get it. In so doing they fulfilled the Scripture: **"They divided my clothes among themselves and threw dice for my robe"** (quoted from Psalm 22:18).

19:25 The four women, in contrast to the four soldiers, are the faithful; they stayed with Jesus until the end. Even more so, in contrast to the disciples who had fled after Jesus was arrested, these women followed Jesus to the cross and became eyewitnesses of his crucifixion. The first woman mentioned is **Jesus' mother** (see 2:1ff.). Imagine her incredible grief, helplessly watching her son suffer and die unjustly. Indeed the prophet Simeon, who had spoken to her in the Temple just after Jesus' birth, had been correct when he had told her, "A sword will pierce your very soul" (Luke 2:35). Surely Mary was feeling that "sword" at that very moment.

The other women mentioned here have not appeared earlier in John's Gospel. Mary's **sister** could have been Salome (see Matthew 27:55ff.; Mark 15:40ff.), the mother of John (the Gospel writer) and James. If this is true, Jesus, John, and James were cousins. **Mary (the wife of Clopas)** was the mother of James the younger. **Mary Magdalene** is mentioned here for the first time in this Gospel. She will be a prominent figure in the next chapter—for Jesus appears first to her after his resurrection.

19:26-27 Seeing his **mother** and **the disciple he loved** (John, the Gospel writer), Jesus directed his disciple John to take care of Mary, his mother, in his absence. Mary had apparently been widowed and was being cared for by Jesus himself. Even while suffering in agony, Jesus demonstrated his care for his mother.

JESUS DIES ON THE CROSS / 19:28-37 / 236

As he had stated in 17:4, Jesus knew he had carried out the mission his Father had given him. His success was complete at the moment of his death. He was about to surrender his life to his Father who would carry out the crowning touch of the plan by raising the Son from the grave.

19:28-30 Some scholars believe this fulfilled Scripture is Psalm 69:21, "They offer me sour wine to satisfy my thirst." Thus, Jesus said, "I thirst." This emphasizes Jesus' humiliation. Others point to Psalm 42:2, "I thirst for God, the living God." This affirms Jesus' submission to the Father. In either case, Scripture was fulfilled.

This **sour wine** was not the same as the drugged wine offered to Jesus earlier (Mark 15:23). Jesus did not take the wine earlier because he wanted to be fully conscious through the entire process. Jesus **tasted it,** and then said, **"It is finished!"** According to the Greek, the one word, *tetelestai*, means "it is accomplished," "it is fulfilled," or even, "it is paid in full." Jesus' death accomplished redemption— "paid in full"; and his death fulfilled all the Old Testament prophecies. It was time for Jesus to die (see 4:34; 17:4).

Up to this point, sin could be atoned through a complicated system of sacrifices. Sin separates people from God, and only through the sacrifice of an animal, a substitute, and faith in God's promise could people be forgiven and become clean before God. But people sin continually, so frequent sacrifices were required. Jesus, however, was the final and ultimate sacrifice for sin. With his death, the complex sacrificial system ended because Jesus took all sin upon himself. Now we can freely approach God because of what Jesus did

for us. Those who believe in Jesus' sacrificial death and resurrection can live eternally with God and escape the penalty that comes from sin.

Then Jesus **bowed his head and gave up his spirit.** The language describes Jesus voluntarily yielding his spirit to God. Luke records Jesus' last words from the cross: "Father, I entrust my spirit into your hands" (Luke 23:46, echoing Psalm 31:5). Jesus' life was not taken from him; he gave his life of his own free will (see 10:11, 15, 17-18; 15:13). This shows Jesus' sovereignty over all— he was even in control of his death!

19:31-34 The **Jewish leaders** were concerned that the dead bodies would remain on the crosses during the **Sabbath.** The Sabbath began on Friday evening—and this was **a very special Sabbath** because it coincided with the **Passover** festival. The Jews did not want to desecrate their Sabbath (Deuteronomy 21:22-23) by allowing the bodies of three crucified Jews to remain hanging on crosses overnight. Thus, **they asked Pilate to hasten their deaths by ordering that their legs be broken.** A person being crucified could use his legs to lift up his body in an attempt to take more oxygen into his collapsing lungs. To break the legs of one being crucified would, therefore, speed up the death. Pilate agreed with the request.

However, when the soldiers came to Jesus, they saw that he was dead already, so they didn't break his legs. Instead, one of the soldiers pierced his side with a spear, and at once blood and water flowed out. This piercing would make sure that Jesus was really dead. Medical experts have tried to determine what was punctured to create a flow of blood and water. Some think the pericardial sac was ruptured. John's testimony of this occurrence was important to affirm a major argument in this Gospel against the Docetists who were denying Jesus' humanity. Jesus was indeed a man composed of blood and water. He actually experienced death as a human being (see 1 John 5:6-7). The mention of the blood and water also answers the argument by some that Jesus did not really die but fell into some type of coma from which he later awakened in the tomb. But the eyewitness account of the blood and water refutes that. The piercing itself would have killed Jesus, but he was already dead as the separation of blood and water reveal. Jesus did indeed die a human death. In addition, the Roman soldiers, who had participated in numerous crucifixions, reported to Pilate that Jesus was dead (Mark 15:44-45).

19:35 The **eyewitness** who saw the Crucifixion and witnessed the issue of blood and water is John the apostle (see 20:30-31 and 21:24-25). Luke's prologue (Luke 1:1-4) and John's words demonstrate that the Gospel writers were writing reliable history, not just a subjective description of what they felt (see also 2 Peter 1:16-18).

19:36-37 Without knowing it, the soldiers fulfilled two biblical prophecies when they lanced Jesus instead of breaking his bones: (1) **Not one of his bones will be broken.** Exodus 12:46 and Numbers 9:12 speak of the bones of the Passover lamb that are not to be broken. Because Jesus was the final sacrifice, these verses apply to him; and (2) **They will look on him whom they pierced.** This is from Zechariah 12:10; see also Revelation 1:7. The risen Christ bore this mark in his side (20:19ff.).

JESUS IS LAID IN THE TOMB / 19:38-42 / 237

Two secret disciples of Jesus came forward to take care of Jesus' burial. They both had feared persecution from the Jewish religious leaders, so they had not openly declared their faith in Jesus as the Messiah (see 12:42).

19:38-39 Joseph was from **Arimathea,** a town not exactly pinpointed today but generally considered to have been about twenty miles northwest of Jerusalem. He was a **secret disciple.** Matthew's Gospel says Joseph was a rich man (Matthew 27:57); Mark describes him as "an honored member of the high council" (Mark 15:43); and Luke adds further that he was "a good and righteous man," who had "not agreed" with the council regarding Jesus (Luke 23:50-51).

Joseph would not have been able to stop the council's planned murder of Jesus, but he did what he could afterwards by boldly going to **Pilate** to ask for **Jesus' body** so he could give it a proper burial. He had to ask for permission because the Romans usually left the bodies exposed without burial, both as a lesson to anyone passing by, and as a final humiliation for those executed. So Joseph went to ask Pilate, and Pilate agreed to let him take and bury the body.

Jesus had talked at length with **Nicodemus** about being born again (3:1ff.), and Nicodemus had stood up for Jesus among the leading priests and Pharisees (7:50-52). Nicodemus joined Joseph in embalming and wrapping Jesus' body in regal style. The **seventy-five pounds of embalming ointment** was an extraordinarily large amount and must have been extremely expensive.

Perhaps the action of Joseph and Nicodemus points to a lesson in teamwork. Both men were naturally cautious. Perhaps they had been chastised repeatedly for not openly rejecting Jesus. But when the moment for boldness came, they worked together. When we join with other believers we can often accomplish what we would not dare to try alone. Though Joseph and Nicodemus were probably each very much afraid, they nevertheless acted courageously. Obedience will often require us to act in spite of our fears.

19:40-42 The **Jewish custom of burial** did not include mummifying or embalming; instead, they washed the body, then **wrapped** it in a **cloth** soaked with aromatic oils and spices. According to Matthew 27:60, this **new tomb** was Joseph's own that he gave up for Jesus (see also Luke 23:53). Such rock-hewn tombs were expensive. Even in burial, Jesus fulfilled prophecy (see Isaiah 53:9). It was fortuitous that Joseph had a tomb nearby and that he wanted to put Jesus' body there; the burial had to happen quickly **because it was the day of preparation,** prior to the coming of the Sabbath. So they **laid Jesus there.**

JOHN 20

JESUS RISES FROM THE DEAD / 20:1-10 / 239

The truth of Christianity rests heavily on the Resurrection. If Jesus rose from the grave, who saw him? How trustworthy were the witnesses? Those who claimed to have seen the risen Jesus went on to turn the world upside down. Most of them also died for being followers of Christ. People rarely die for halfhearted belief. Chapter 20 of John's Gospel contains the record of Jesus' resurrection, the first appearances to his followers, and John's personal discovery of the empty tomb.

20:1-2 Mary Magdalene was one of several women who had followed Jesus to the cross, watched his crucifixion (19:25), and then remained to see where he was buried (Matthew 27:61). She, along with other women, was an early follower of Jesus who traveled with him and helped provide for the financial needs of the group (Luke 8:1-3). Mary was obviously grateful to Jesus for freeing her from the torment of demon possession. She was from Magdala, a town near Capernaum in Galilee.

Because of the short interim between Jesus' death and the coming of the Sabbath on Friday evening, the women who had stood by the cross had not had time to anoint Jesus. When the Sabbath arrived with the sunset on Friday, they had to go to their homes and rest. But after sundown on Saturday, the end of the Sabbath, they probably purchased and/or prepared the spices, then **early Sunday morning** Mary Magdalene came to anoint the body of Jesus with certain spices. According to the other Gospel accounts, she was joined by Mary the mother of James, Salome (Matthew 28:1; Mark 16:1), and perhaps other women as well.

Mark records that as the women were on their way to the tomb, they were discussing how they would remove the stone that had been rolled across the entrance (Mark 16:3). But this would not be a problem, because as they approached they **found that the stone had been rolled away.** The other Gospel accounts record that angels spoke to the women.

Mary Magdalene, and the other women, **ran and found Simon Peter and the other disciple, the one whom Jesus loved** (probably John).They had been in the tomb, the body was gone, and they assumed that someone had **taken the Lord's body.**

20:3-5 Though John's youthful legs carried him more swiftly to the grave, once he was there he **stooped and looked in,** but he waited for Peter's arrival before entering the cave. Resurrection would not have been their first thought. None of the possible natural explanations for the missing body were of any comfort. If Jesus' body had been stolen or moved by the religious leaders, the disciples would have reason to worry about their own fate.

20:6-7 Close examination revealed that the **linen wrappings** had been left—perhaps as if Jesus had passed right through them. The **cloth that had covered Jesus' head** was rolled up separately from the other wrappings that had enveloped Jesus' body. A grave robber couldn't possibly have made off with Jesus' body and left the linens as if they were still shaped around it. The neatness and order indicated that there was not a hasty removal of Jesus' body. Rather, Jesus arose and left the wrappings lying there, empty.

20:8-9 When John **saw** the empty tomb and the empty graveclothes, he instantly **believed** that Jesus must have risen from the dead. The text stresses the importance here of John "seeing and believing" to affirm the eyewitness account of an apostle. Most believers would not have this opportunity; they would have to base their faith on what these witnesses reported. John explains that **until then they hadn't realized that the Scriptures said he would rise from the dead.** Though Jesus had told them, it took the experience for them to understand. Some of the Scriptures that foretold this included Psalm 16:10 and Isaiah 53:11.

John's account also demonstrates that the disciples couldn't have "invented" the Resurrection in order to fulfill the Old Testament prophecies because they did not immediately see any Old Testament connection. The fact of the Resurrection opened the disciples' minds to see that God had foretold his plan through the prophets.

20:10 Perplexed, John and Peter left and **went home.** They "believed" in something miraculous; that is, they did not fear that Jesus' body had been stolen, as Mary had, but they did not know for sure what they believed or what they should do next. So they just went home. Later, they joined with the other disciples behind locked doors (see 20:19).

JESUS APPEARS TO MARY MAGDALENE / 20:11-18 / 240

We see Jesus' humility in his resurrection, as well as in his crucifixion. Jesus did not rise and then march into the Temple to confront the religious leaders or Caiaphas; he did not dash to the Praetorium to say to Pilate, "I told you so!"; he did not go stand in the center of Jerusalem to impress the crowd. Instead, Jesus revealed himself only to believers. The first person to see him was a woman who had been healed and forgiven and who tearfully stayed at the cross and followed his body to the tomb. As Jesus demonstrated throughout his life, he responded to those who waited attentively and faithfully. Jesus dissolved the perplexities of the disciples. He dried their tears. He dispelled their doubts. Jesus knows how similar we are to his original disciples, and he does not overpower us either. Even though our faithfulness wavers, Jesus faithfully stays with us.

20:11-12 Mary apparently followed Peter and John back to the **tomb.** When the two disciples left, she was there alone, still **crying,** still hoping that somehow she could discover where Jesus' body had been taken, but fearing the worst. Then **she saw two white-robed angels.** The angels actually looked like humans—not beings with halos and wings. The angels had appeared to the women and then sent them to spread the good news that Jesus was alive (Matthew 28:1-7; Mark 16:1-7; Luke 24:1-12), but apparently they were not in the tomb when Peter and John arrived. Yet they are here again to speak to Mary.

20:13 The angels asked Mary, **"Why are you crying?"** Under normal circumstances this would seem to be an odd question. People might be expected to be crying beside the tomb of a loved one. However, the angels knew why the tomb was empty. They also knew that if these people had listened to Jesus' words about his resurrection while he was alive, they would not be sad and confused; instead, they would be leaping for joy. So the angels' question was not odd, but obvious. It was not meant as a rebuke, but as a reminder of heaven's perspective. Mary simply answered the angels' question with her fears, **"Because they have taken away my Lord and I don't know where they have put him."**

20:14-15 Something caused Mary to look **over her shoulder,** probably a feeling that a person was **standing behind her.** And indeed, next to the tomb stood Jesus, but Mary **didn't recognize him.** Perhaps this was the same kind of blindness that afflicted the two who walked with the risen Jesus on the road to Emmaus (see Luke 24:15-16). Or perhaps Mary's eyes were so full of tears and her grief so intense that she literally could not see who was standing there. Jesus repeated the angels' question and added an additional question, asking Mary to specify her request. **"Who are you looking for?"**

Mary was trying to grasp what might have happened to Jesus' body, so thinking Jesus was **the gardener,** she asked if he knew anything. If only she could find him, she herself would go get him.

20:16-17 Mary had been looking for the body of her dead Lord; suddenly, to her amazement, she stood face to face with her living Lord. Jesus spoke her name, and immediately she recognized him. Imagine the love that flooded Mary's heart when she heard her Savior saying her name!

Mary's immediate response was to touch Jesus and cling to him. But Jesus stopped her. Perhaps Mary wanted to hold Jesus and not lose him again. She had not yet understood the Resurrection. Perhaps she thought this was his promised Second Coming (14:3). But Jesus was not to remain on this earth in physical form. If he did not ascend to heaven, the Holy Spirit could not come. Both he and Mary had important work to do.

Prior to his death, Jesus had called the disciples his "friends" (15:15). But here, because of the Resurrection, Jesus' disciples had become his **brothers.** Christ's resurrection creates this new level of relationship because it provides for the regeneration of every believer (see 1 Peter 1:3). After Jesus **ascended** to his **Father,** he would come to his disciples and give them this new life and relationship by breathing into them the Holy Spirit. Thus, for the first time in the Gospel, it is made clear that Jesus' Father is our Father, that Jesus' God is our God. The death and resurrection of Jesus ushered in a new relationship between believers and God.

20:18 Mary was the first person to see the risen Christ. She obeyed Jesus and **found the disciples, telling them, "I have seen the Lord!" Then she gave them** Jesus' **message.** Jesus' words should have been a great comfort to the disciples. Despite their deserting him in the Garden, he was calling them his "brothers" and explaining that his Father was theirs, his God was theirs. But this report was no more believed by the disciples than the women's report of the angels' words (see Mark 16:10-11; Luke 24:10-11). The disciples were still hiding behind locked doors, for fear of the Jews.

JESUS APPEARS TO HIS DISCIPLES / 20:19-23 / 244

Mary's announcement (20:18) must have stunned the disciples. Later the news that the Lord was alive came from two travelers who had unknowingly spent the day walking to Emmaus with Jesus (Luke 24:15-16). Confused, elated, doubtful, and fearful, the disciples stayed close together, hoping to endure the waiting in one place. They were huddled behind locked doors when Jesus appeared to all of them.

20:19 The **disciples** were still perplexed and apparently had gotten together that night **behind locked doors.** They probably were discussing the women's reported sighting of angels, what Peter and John saw at the tomb, and Mary's astounding claim that she had seen Jesus. At some point during the day, Jesus had appeared to Peter (Luke 24:34), and the women had reported the angel's words that the disciples were to go to Galilee and meet Jesus there (Matthew 28:7). But for some reason, they did not go; instead they stayed in Jerusalem, **afraid of the Jewish leaders. Suddenly, Jesus was standing there among them.** Jesus could do this because his resurrection and subsequent glorification had altered his bodily form. In this new spiritual form, he was able to transcend all physical barriers. He gave the standard Hebrew greeting, **"Peace be with you,"** but here it was filled with deeper meaning (see 14:27; 16:33). Jesus would repeat these words in verse 21.

20:20 Due to Jesus' sudden, miraculous appearance among them, the disciples at first thought he was a ghost (Luke 24:37). Jesus needed to convince them that he, including his touchable physical body, was present with them, so **he held out his hands** and **showed them his side.** When they realized who he was, they rejoiced. Jesus had said, "Your grief will suddenly turn to wonderful joy when you see me again" (16:20). Indeed, **they were filled with joy.**

20:21-23 Jesus gave his **peace** to them and then commissioned them to be his representatives, even as he had been the Father's (see 17:18). Jesus again identified himself with his Father. He told the disciples by whose authority he did his work. Then he gave the task to his disciples of spreading the gospel message around the world. They were sent with authority from God to preach, teach, and do miracles (see Matthew 28:16-20; Luke 24:47-49)—in essence, to continue across the world what Jesus had begun in Palestine. Whatever God has asked you to do, remember: (1) Your authority comes from God, and (2) Jesus has demonstrated by words and actions how to accomplish the job he has given you. As the Father sent his Son, Jesus sends his followers . . . and you. Your response is to determine from day to day those to whom the Father has sent you.

Before the disciples could carry out this commission, however, they needed the power of the **Holy Spirit.** And Jesus gave them this power by breathing into them the Holy Spirit. This act reminds us of what God did to make the first man come alive—he breathed into him and he became a living soul (Genesis 2:7). There is life in the breath of God. Man was created but did not come alive until God had breathed into him the breath of life (Genesis 2:7). God's first breath made man different from all other forms of creation. Here, through the breath of Jesus, God imparted eternal, spiritual life. With this breathing came the power to do God's will on earth.

Jesus gave the disciples their Spirit-powered and Spirit-guided mission—to preach the Good News about him so that people's sins might be forgiven. The disciples did not have the power to forgive sins (only God can forgive sins), but Jesus gave them the privilege of telling new believers that their sins have been **forgiven** because they have accepted Jesus' message. All believers have this same privilege. We can announce the forgiveness of sin with certainty when we ourselves repent and believe. Those who don't believe will not experience the forgiveness of sins; their sins will be retained (i.e., not forgiven).

JESUS APPEARS TO THOMAS / 20:24-31 / *245*

Thomas was not with the other disciples for Jesus' first visit in 20:21-23. Consistent with his character elsewhere in the Gospel (see 14:5), Thomas was skeptical toward his friends' report about seeing Jesus. He epitomized hardheaded realism by insisting that seeing and touching Jesus for himself would be the only proof that would satisfy him. When Jesus did appear to him, Thomas realized the inappropriateness of his demand.

Jesus made it clear that our faith must be based on the testimony of those who were with him. Insisting on seeing and touching Christ ourselves would indicate a reluctance to believe. We have no right to require God to prove himself; but he has every right as our Creator to expect our belief and obedience. The fact that God blesses those who believe is simply an added gift of his grace.

20:24-25 When the disciples told **Thomas** that Jesus had appeared to them, he did not believe. Thomas insisted that he see the Jesus who had been crucified. He wanted bodily proof—to **see** and touch the nail scars in Jesus' hands and to **place** his **hand into the wound in Jesus' side.** Sometimes people overemphasize the doubtful part of Thomas's character. John 11:16 reveals Thomas as tough-minded and committed, even if he tended to be pessimistic. And Matthew points out (Matthew 28:17) that all the disciples shared Thomas's skepticism. It was part of his character to put the group's feeling into words. Most of the other disciples (with the exception of John—20:8) did not believe until they saw Christ face-to-face.

20:26-28 After **eight days,** Thomas got his chance. This time he was present when Jesus appeared. The disciples were still behind locked doors when Jesus appeared among them as he had before and gave the same greeting, **"Peace be with you!"** But this time he spoke directly to Thomas, supernaturally knowing of Thomas's doubt and what he needed in order to be convinced. Jesus told him to touch and **see** his **hands** and **side.** Jesus' resurrected body was unique. It was no longer subject to the same laws of nature as before his death. He could appear in a locked room; yet he was not a ghost or apparition because he could be touched and his wounds were still visible.

When he saw Jesus, "doubting" Thomas became believing Thomas. His response rings through the ages as the response of many doubters who finally see the truth, **"My Lord and my God!"** This clear affirmation of Jesus' deity provides a good conclusion to John's Gospel, which continually affirms Jesus' deity (see 1:1, 18; 8:58; 10:30).

20:29 Though Thomas proclaimed Jesus to be his Lord and God, Jesus reproved Thomas because he had to see before he could **believe.** The **blessed** ones are they who **haven't seen** and yet **believe.** Some people think they would believe in Jesus if they could see a definite sign or miracle. But Jesus says we are blessed if we can believe without seeing. We have all the proof we need in the words of the Bible and the testimony of believers.

20:30-31 In the last two verses of the chapter, John explains why he wrote this Gospel: to encourage belief in Jesus as the Christ and as the Son of God. All the **miraculous signs** in this Gospel point to Jesus as being the Christ and God's Son, who came to give life to all those who believe. Most likely, John wrote this Gospel to encourage those who already believed to continue in their faith. We who believe are encouraged to read and reread John in order to continue in our belief. And this Gospel has also been used far beyond that as a powerful tool for evangelism, bringing people to faith in Christ.

To understand the life and mission of Jesus more fully, all we need to do is study the Gospels. John tells us that his Gospel records only a few of the many events in Jesus' life on earth. But the Gospels include everything we need to know to believe that Jesus is the Christ, the Son of God, through whom we receive eternal life.

JOHN 21

JESUS APPEARS TO SEVEN DISCIPLES / 21:1-14 / *246*

Chapter 21 is an epilogue to John's narrative. Very likely, John decided to add this chapter some time after he completed his Gospel in order to clarify the misconception about the relationship between his (John's) death and the Lord's return. The rumor that John would not die before the Lord's return (21:23) had to be corrected; otherwise, the church might experience great trouble at his death before the Lord's return. John, therefore, decided to add a chapter that would make it clear that Jesus did not say that he would return before John died.

21:1-3 This chapter records Jesus' appearance to the disciples beside the **Sea of Galilee.** Jesus had made at least six appearances in (or around) Jerusalem. After the Jerusalem appearances, the disciples evidently had returned to Galilee. Jesus made several appearances in this region: to five hundred believers (1 Corinthians 15:6); to James, his brother (1 Corinthians 15:7); and the appearance recorded here.

Prior to his resurrection, the Lord had told his disciples that he would meet them at an appointed place in Galilee after he arose (Matthew 28:10; Mark 14:28). But due to the disciples' unbelief and fear, they had remained in Jerusalem. After Jesus appeared to them behind locked doors, they did as they had been told and returned to Galilee. But as they waited there, they remained unsure, confused. So they did what they knew how to do best—they went **fishing.** Seven **disciples** were together at this time:

Having returned to Galilee, the disciples did not know what to do next, so it was natural for some of them to return to their occupation. Simon, Andrew, and James and John (the sons of Zebedee) had been fishermen (see Mark 1:16-20). Peter took the lead, and the other six disciples went with him. Although fishing was often good during the **night** while the fish were active and feeding closer to the surface, the disciples **caught nothing.** When daybreak arrived, they were tired, hungry, and probably more than a little frustrated.

21:4-6 Jesus had come to make another appearance to the disciples, especially to Peter. Perhaps because of the distance, haze over the water, or lack of light at **dawn,** the men in the boat did not recognize the man on the shore. He **called out, "Friends, have you caught any fish?"** They were only about a hundred yards out (21:8) and called back, **"No."**

The man then said, **"Throw out your net on the right-hand side of the boat, and you'll get plenty of fish!"** The disciples, tired as they were, responded to the obvious authority in the voice, and cast their nets to starboard—and a miracle occurred! This recalls Luke 5:1-11, another occasion where Peter and the other disciples were fishing, catching nothing. Jesus gave a command to go out into the deep water. Peter, though doubtful, followed Jesus' orders. When they obeyed, a miracle occurred! When Peter saw the first miracle, he recognized beyond Jesus' power a holiness that was not part of his own life.

On this occasion, Peter is again a central character. Jesus identified himself by his unexpected and seemingly useless request. The fishermen's actions involved them in another miracle. If the request did not give them a clue, the results unmistakably pointed to the power of their Lord: **They couldn't draw in the net because there were so many fish in it.** Both John and Peter recognized that Jesus was behind the overwhelming catch of fish.

21:7 John (**the disciple whom Jesus loved**) may have immediately recognized the repeated miracle, for he was part of the incident recorded in Luke 5. As John peered through the morning mist, he recognized that the man on the shore was **the Lord.** Peter immediately **jumped into the water** to swim to Jesus. Though his love for Jesus was very great, Peter may have thought a barrier still existed between the Lord and him because of his denial.

21:8-9 We can only guess what Peter did when he came out of the water, dripping wet, facing the one he had denied. He may have been at a loss for words. Peter must have appreciated the **fire** that Jesus had burning; there he dried off while he felt the inward chill of remembering what he had done the last time he had stood by a fire warming himself. If any words were said, they were kept between Jesus and Peter, since the others were still too far away to hear.

21:10-11 The miraculous catch of fish must have affected Peter profoundly. Peter did not say a word as he **dragged** the heavy **net** full of **153 large fish** to shore and then, with the other disciples, ate the breakfast of bread and fish the Lord had prepared even before they caught the fish.

The number of fish probably has no other significance than that it was a very large amount of large fish—especially after having caught nothing all night. And the exact number is recorded simply as a matter of historical fact. It was the usual procedure for a group of fishermen to count the day's catch and then divide it among themselves. Once again, John observed that when Christ takes action, the results bring overabundance.

21:12-13 Any question or any comment seemed trite at that moment. They stood around in awed silence before this one who, as always, was doing the serving, inviting them to **have some breakfast.** This special meal with the risen Jesus had a profound effect on these seven disciples. Peter would later make claim to his reliability as a witness of Jesus (see Acts 10:41). John does not record that Jesus ate anything, but Luke 24:41-43 describes an appearance of Jesus where he did eat some fish.

21:14 This was the **third time Jesus had appeared to his disciples;** the first two times had been behind locked doors in Jerusalem. Jesus had come to them to encourage these disciples, especially Peter, concerning their future work. The text seems to imply that Jesus had come to remind them that they were not to return to their old life of fishing. He had called them to be fishers of people (Luke 5:10) and to start the church (Matthew 16:19). Peter, the leader among them, needed to be ready for the responsibilities he soon would assume. He would lead and feed the flock—not with physical food (which Jesus would provide) but with spiritual food.

JESUS CHALLENGES PETER / 21:15-25 / 247

After the meal, Jesus and Peter had a talk. During their conversation, Jesus led Peter through an experience that would remove the cloud of guilt that came from Peter's denial. The Master-Teacher conveyed both forgiveness and usefulness to this disciple who must have concluded he was beyond being useful to Jesus.

21:15-17 Simon son of John was the name Jesus had said when he first met this man who would become his disciple (1:42). But Peter had not yet proven himself to live up to that name—Peter, "the rock." According to Luke 24:34, Jesus had probably met with Peter previously. Jesus' first question to Peter, **"Do you love me more than these?"** could be translated in three ways: (1) "Do you love me more than these men love me?" (2) "Do you love me more than you love these men?" (3) "Do you love me more than these things?" (that is, the fishing boat, nets, and gear). Of the three options, the first seems the most appropriate because Peter had boasted that he would never forsake Jesus, even if all the other disciples did (see Matthew 26:33; Mark 14:29; John 13:37). This was the same as saying that he had more love for Jesus than the others did.

Peter did just the opposite of what he boasted: He denied Jesus three times. As a consequence, Jesus asked Peter three times, **"Do you love me?"** to affirm Peter's love and commitment. Each time Peter told Jesus, **"I love you,"** Jesus exhorted Peter to care for his flock: **"Feed my lambs"** (21:15); **"Take care of my sheep"** (21:16); **"Feed my**

sheep" (21:17). Lambs and sheep can be taken as words of endearment. Jesus' love and concern is for all believers—the entire "flock" that would grow as a result of the apostles' ministry.

21:18-19 Jesus used a proverbial statement about old age to depict Peter's death, which was by crucifixion. From this day onward, Peter knew what death lay before him. Peter never forgot this prophecy from Jesus; Peter referred to it in his Second Epistle when he spoke about his imminent death (see 2 Peter 1:14). Peter was crucified in Rome under Nero around A.D. 65–67. By his words, **"Follow me,"** Jesus was reinstating and restoring Peter as his disciple. What assurance these words must have been for Peter. Despite what glory or trial or death lay ahead, he would always be under the Savior's care, for he would be following Jesus.

Three years earlier, along the same lake, Jesus had said the same words to Peter—"Follow me." These words mean "Keep on following." Stripped of pride, impulsiveness, and false expectations of leadership, Peter was ready to follow Christ in a new way because of new experiences and a clearer picture of himself. "Follow Me" means consistent discipleship and steadfast pursuit of Christ, even if that requires martyrdom. It means continuing Christ's work in the way he wants it done, not in a way we want it done.

21:20-23 Having been told his destiny, Peter wanted to know what would happen to John (called **the disciple Jesus loved**). In this profound but loving rebuke, Jesus explained to the impulsive Peter that he was not to be concerned about God's plans for anyone else but himself. Indeed, Peter's contribution to the beginnings of the Christian church would be astounding (from his sermon on Pentecost in just a few weeks, to his leadership of the Jerusalem church, to his being the first to understand that Gentiles too could become Christians), and both his miraculous escape from death (Acts 12:1-19) and his death by martyrdom would be heroic. John, although he would remain alive, would be called to a different kind of service, even through exile on a remote island—for John would write this incredible Gospel, three letters, and the astounding account of the triumphant return of the Son of God in the book of Revelation. Peter, the impulsive one, would write two epistles to encourage patience while we wait for Christ's return. Peter and John were called to different kinds of service for their Lord; neither was to question why.

Jesus' statement to Peter had been interpreted to mean that John **wouldn't die,** but would remain alive on earth until the Second Coming. John had to correct this **rumor.** If John died and the Lord still had not come, this tiny rumor could throw many believers, and the church itself, into confusion. John insisted that Jesus' words had been misunderstood. Jesus had not said that John would not die; rather, if Jesus were to want him to **remain**

alive, it wasn't any of Peter's business. The point is that the decision was up to Jesus—not John or Peter. What Jesus was communicating to Peter was that it was not for Peter to be concerned about what would become of John's life. He, Peter, was responsible to follow the Lord according to what the Lord had revealed to him. And so was John.

21:24 The last two verses of John's Gospel contain the finishing touch to the book that attests to the truth of John's written testimony. The testimony is trustworthy because John was an eyewitness of Jesus Christ. After many years of experience and reflection, John wrote an account that reflects his spiritual insight into the life of Jesus Christ (see 1:14; 1 John 1:1-3).

The statement, **"We all know that his account of these things is accurate"** is probably from some of John's contemporaries who knew that what John wrote was true. Some scholars think these contemporaries were the Ephesian elders, who had been told and/or read the preceding narrative. Early church history reports that after John spent several years as an exile on the island of Patmos (see Revelation 1:9), he returned to Ephesus where he died as an old man, near the end of the first century.

21:25 This final statement is not mere hyperbole. It is an affirmation of the fact that John's one book is far from being exhaustive because John recorded only some of the things that Jesus had done. If John had covered every event, how many more **books** would be required to contain all the material? Some of this material can be found in the other three Gospels. But there is so much more that could have been said about Jesus. Nonetheless, what was written has provided believers with a true biography of the greatest person who ever lived: Jesus Christ, the Son of God.

ACTS

INTRODUCTION

Acts has it all—supernatural intervention, astounding miracles, powerful preaching, breathtaking escapes, harrowing journeys, life-and-death decisions, courtroom dramas, thrilling rescues, action, mystery, and adventure! Acts will grab your attention, trigger your imagination, and tug at your emotions. It's a terrific story and a great read . . . and it's true.

As you flip through the pages, however, don't miss the story behind the stories. Underlying the stimulating sermons and the display of miracles, look for God at work in individuals. In fact, as much as Acts could be called the story of the early church, it could also be titled "The Miracle of Changed Lives."

Consider this: When we last saw the disciples, they were running scared and abandoning their Lord (Matthew 26:56). Fleeing, denying, disillusioned, and crying, these men seemed the least likely candidates to be boldly proclaiming the gospel. Yet that's what happened. Peter, James, John, and the rest had been transformed from cowardly to courageous, argumentative to articulate, and selfish to selfless. Then they were joined by Paul, whom God also miraculously transformed.

What made the difference? Acts reveals the profound answer. This is their story—the history of the early church and the changed men and women who changed the world.

As you read of the Holy Spirit, the gifts, persecution and power, Paul's dramatic conversion, and the rapid spread of the gospel beyond Jerusalem and Judea to the ends of the earth, look for yourself in the stories. Ask God to transform you into the kind of person he can use to change *your* world.

AUTHOR

Luke: doctor, Gentile Christian, traveling companion of Paul, and writer of the Gospel according to Luke.

Luke was a close friend and companion of Paul. He is listed as the writer of the Gospel bearing his name by nearly all the ancient church fathers, including Justin Martyr (A.D. 100–165), Irenaeus (c. A.D. 120–200), and Tertullian (A.D. 160–230).

The text of the book of Acts clearly reveals the same author as the Gospel of Luke. Both books are addressed to "Theophilus" (Luke 1:1; Acts 1:1). It makes sense, as well, in light of Luke's commitment to recording the facts, that Acts be seen as a continuation of the story, a second volume detailing what happened subsequent to Christ's death and resurrection.

Although the writer does not identify himself by name anywhere in the book, he does use the pronoun "we" beginning with 16:10, thereby indicating that the

Modern names and boundaries are shown in gray.

The apostle Paul, whose missionary journeys fill much of this book, traveled tremendous distances as he tirelessly spread the gospel across much of the Roman Empire. His combined trips, by land and sea, equal more than 13,000 air miles.

Judea Jesus ascended to heaven from the Mount of Olives outside Jerusalem, and his followers returned to the city to await the pouring out of the Holy Spirit, which occurred at Pentecost. Peter gave a powerful sermon that was heard by Jews from across the empire. The Jerusalem church grew, but Stephen was martyred for his faith by Jewish leaders who did not believe in Jesus (1:1–7:60).

Samaria After Stephen's death, persecution of Christians intensified, but it caused the believers to leave Jerusalem and spread the Good News to other cities in the empire. Philip took the gospel into Samaria, and even to a man from Ethiopia (8:1-40).

Syria Paul (Saul) began his story as a persecutor of Christians, only to be met by Jesus himself on the road to Damascus. He became a believer, but his new faith caused opposition, so he returned to Tarsus, his home, for safety. Barnabas sought out Paul in Tarsus and brought him to the church in Antioch of Syria, where they worked together. Meanwhile, Peter had received a vision that led him to Caesarea, where he presented the gospel to a Gentile family, who became believers (9:1–12:25).

Cyprus and Galatia Paul and Barnabas were dedicated by the church in Antioch of Syria for God's

work of spreading the gospel to other cities. They set off on their first missionary journey through Cyprus and Galatia (13:1–14:28).

Jerusalem Controversy between Jewish Christians and Gentile Christians over the matter of keeping the Law led to a special council, with delegates from the churches in Antioch and Jerusalem meeting in Jerusalem. Together, they resolved the conflict, and the news was taken back to Antioch (15:1-35).

Macedonia Barnabas traveled to Cyprus while Paul took a second missionary journey. He revisited the churches in Galatia and headed toward Ephesus, but the Holy Spirit said no. So he turned north toward Bithynia and Pontus but again was told not to go. He then received the "Macedonian call" and followed the Spirit's direction into the cities of Macedonia (15:36–17:14).

Achaia Paul traveled from Macedonia to Athens and Corinth in Achaia, then traveled by ship to Ephesus before returning to Caesarea, Jerusalem, and finally back to Antioch (17:15–18:22).

Ephesus Paul's third missionary journey took him back through Cilicia and Galatia, this time straight to Ephesus in Asia. He visited other cities in Asia before going back to Macedonia and Achaia. He returned to Jerusalem by ship, despite his knowledge that arrest awaited him there (18:23–23:30).

Caesarea Paul was arrested in Jerusalem and taken to Antipatris, then on to Caesarea under Roman guard. Paul always took advantage of any opportunity to share the Good News, and he did so before

many Gentile leaders. Because Paul appealed to Caesar, he began the long journey to Rome (23:31–26:32).

Rome After storms, layovers in Crete, and shipwreck on the island of Malta, Paul arrived in Sicily and finally in Italy, where he traveled by land, under guard, to his long-awaited destination: Rome, the capital of the empire (27:1–28:31).

---

writer had joined Paul in his journeys in Troas at that point. As such, Luke must have become one of Paul's coworkers, which is what Paul explicitly acknowledges in Philemon 1:24.

Although Luke had a major role in the formation of the early church through his writing and through his ministry with Paul, he is only mentioned in three of Paul's letters (Colossians 4:14; 2 Timothy 4:11; Philemon 1:24). It is significant that Luke was not a Jew but a Greek and not one of the original disciples of Christ. Thus he was not a member of the inner circle of Jesus' followers nor one who saw Jesus as his long-promised Messiah. Luke must have been a convert, convinced of the truth of the gospel message and determined to spread the message to others. Perhaps little is said of Luke because he chose not to give himself a prominent place in the text of his books.

Luke's research into what had already been written about Jesus gave him a start. And his close relationship to the apostle Paul (20:5-15; 27:1–28:16) undoubtedly gave him access to an abundance of information concerning Christ, thus helping him write the Gospel. Certainly there also could be no better person to record the history of the early church than an eyewitness of the tremendous spread of the gospel (himself a convert) and a close friend of the church's greatest missionary.

For more about Luke, see the Author section in the Introduction to the Gospel of Luke.

DATE AND SETTING
Written between A.D. 63 and 65 from an unknown location.

The final event of Acts—Paul's ministry in Rome—provides a clue to the date and setting of the book. Christianity, perceived as a sect of Judaism, was tolerated by the Roman authorities before A.D. 65, but then Nero began persecuting followers of the Christian faith. Yet Acts makes no mention of this persecution. It also does not comment on the destruction of Jerusalem in A.D. 70, something that would surely have been mentioned if Luke had written in the 70s. The Gospel records Jesus' words regarding the destruction of the temple (Luke 19:41-44; 21:20-24), so Luke certainly would have mentioned in Acts the prophecy's fulfillment. Noting that the gospel account, probably written A.D. 60–61, was the first of his two books to Theophilus (1:1), the two books probably were written within a short time of each other, possibly during Luke's stays with Paul while in prison in Caesarea (23:33) and Rome (28:14-16).

Biblical scholars suggest a number of possible places where Luke may have written Acts. Because Luke is traditionally associated with Antioch, some believe that Luke penned the book in that city, where the disciples were "first called Christians"

(11:26). Rome is another option because the book of Acts concludes with Paul's ministry there. A third option is the city of Ephesus because the book focuses on many events in that Greek city, including Paul's farewell to the leaders of the church. In summary, there is no consensus among scholars about where Luke actually wrote the follow-up to his gospel account.

AUDIENCE
Theophilus ("one who loves God"), Gentiles, and people everywhere.

Both the Gospel of Luke and Acts name Theophilus (Luke 1:1; 1:1) as the addressee. Because the literal meaning of "Theophilus" is "lover of God" or "friend of God," some have thought that the books were addressed generally and written to anyone who loves God, not a specific, first-century individual. Others note that "most excellent" is attached to "Theophilus" in Luke 1:3. In that day, this title was used only when addressing a Roman officer, thus leading to the conclusion that Theophilus was a Gentile and possibly someone of high rank in Roman society. Beyond those inferences, little is known—the name Theophilus appears nowhere else in Scripture. Many biblical scholars think that Theophilus was a new believer who was having some difficulty with the Christian faith. Thus Luke wrote the gospel account in order to provide solid answers to Theophilus's questions.

Luke also elaborated in Acts about a subject that he had mentioned in his Gospel account—that the Gentiles are heirs of God's salvation together with the Jews. The Gospel records stories of Jesus healing non-Jewish people and proclaiming his message to them (Luke 7:1-10; 8:26-39). Acts describes the spread of Christianity among the Jews and then well beyond, to the vast Gentile world. Clearly, then, Gentile Christians would have been eager readers of this book.

OCCASION AND PURPOSE
To give an accurate account of the birth and growth of the Christian church.

After reading what Luke had written in his gospel account, Theophilus may have had unanswered questions. So Luke wrote Acts to answer those questions and to underscore the truth of the gospel. By tracing the growth of the Christian church throughout the known world at that time, Luke demonstrated that God's good news of salvation applies to every person—from the lowliest slave to the most respected nobleman and from the Jews to the Greeks and Romans.

Luke probably had other purposes in mind for writing the book of Acts. These are mentioned below.

Historic. In writing his Gospel, Luke wanted to present "a careful summary" (Luke 1:3). Thus, he took great pains to verify the historical accuracy of the events he was recording, because his purpose was to write a careful and accurate account of what he had researched and seen. Evidence of his accuracy can also be seen throughout Acts. For example, the Roman famine prophesied by Agabus is confirmed and dated through a parenthetical note by Luke that the prophecy had come true during Emperor Claudius's reign (11:28).

These facts, along with the numerous details in Acts, reveal the careful and diligent research of a precise historian. In Acts, Luke was writing history.

Kerygmatic. The Greek word *kerygma* literally means "that which is preached"— i.e., the message. An important purpose of the book of Acts is to highlight the *kerygma,* the core of the gospel message proclaimed by the apostles. The good news of Jesus' death and resurrection, proclaimed fearlessly in streets, synagogues, and prisons, changed thousands of lives and the course of history. Paul's three missionary journeys and voyage to Rome provide solid evidence that the gospel was being proclaimed to the ends of the earth (1:8).

Apologetic. The word "apologetic" refers to a rational defense of the faith, a presentation of solid evidence that the gospel is true. Because of the rapid spread of the Way (i.e., Christianity) across the Roman Empire, Luke wanted to assure readers that Christianity was not a political movement or threat but the reality of God becoming flesh and the fulfillment of Israel's hope of a Messiah.

Roman law defined religions as either *licitia* (legal) or *illicita* (illegal). Even though Christianity was the offspring of Judaism, it was having difficulty acquiring *licitia* status because the Jewish establishment considered it a breakaway sect. Thus, Luke may have written this as an apology to the Roman government. Because Luke probably wrote this book while Paul was awaiting trial in Rome, the intended audience may have included Paul's trial judge. Acts includes several defenses presented both to Jews (see 4:8-12) and Gentiles (see 25:8-11).

Conciliatory. The early church contained two dominant factions—Jewish believers and Gentile believers. Paul had become the champion of reaching the Gentiles, while in many ways Peter had been leading the charge for ministering to the Jews. The council at Jerusalem was held to discuss the issue, and the matter was resolved amicably (15:1-35). But old ways are hard to change, so the same issues were raised again and again. Each time, Paul would write to the church to try to defuse the potential explosion and to keep believers focused on the truth (see, for example, Galatians).

The book of Acts presents a noteworthy parallel between Peter and Paul. Each conceded specific aspects of the church to the other. For example, Peter conferred upon Paul a second mode of apostolic authority as well as approval for reaching out to Gentiles, not on the merits of the law. At the same time, Paul conceded primacy in the church to Peter and apostleship to the Twelve, due to their earthly relationship with Christ.

In many ways, the church struggles today with the same issues: new believers need encouragement and assurance, nonbelievers need to know that the Christian message is true, and the church needs to avoid petty wrangling and unite around the core of the gospel message.

As you read Acts, recommit to unity in the church, working together with Christian brothers and sisters to spread the gospel throughout the world. And thank God for his grace, which extends salvation to all kinds of people, even you.

MESSAGE

The book of Acts begins with the outpouring of the promised Holy Spirit and the commencement of the proclamation of the gospel of Jesus Christ. This Spirit-inspired evangelism began in Jerusalem and eventually spread to Rome, covering most of the Roman Empire. The gospel first went to the Jews, but they, as a nation, rejected it. A remnant of Jews, of course, gladly received the Good News. But the continual rejection of the gospel by the vast majority of the Jews led to the ever-increasing proclamation of the gospel to the Gentiles. This was according to Jesus' plan: The gospel was to go from Jerusalem, to Judea, to Samaria, and to the remotest part of the earth (1:8). This, in fact, is the pattern that the Acts narrative follows. The glorious proclamation began in Jerusalem (chapters 1–7), went to Judea and Samaria (chapters 8 and following), and to the countries beyond Judea (11:19; 13:4 and on to the end of Acts). The second half of Acts is focused primarily on Paul's missionary journeys to many countries north of the Mediterranean Sea. He, with his companions, took the gospel first to the Jews and then to the Gentiles. Some of the Jews believed, and many of the Gentiles received the Good News with joy. New churches were started, and new believers began to grow in the Christian life.

The main themes in the book of Acts include: *Church beginnings; Holy Spirit; Church growth; witnessing;* and *opposition.*

Church Beginnings (1:4-8, 12-26; 2:1–8:40). Acts is the history of how the Christian church was founded and organized as well as how the early church solved its problems. Led by outspoken and courageous apostles, the community of believers grew as individuals put their trust in the risen Christ. Filled with the Holy Spirit, they were empowered to witness, to love, and to serve. Although pressured and persecuted, they continued to preach, considering it a privilege to suffer for Christ. And the church thrived.

IMPORTANCE FOR TODAY. New churches are continually being founded, but true Christian churches preach the crucified and risen Christ. Although believers continue to be pressured to give up or give in, by faith in Jesus Christ and in the power of the Holy Spirit, the church can be a vibrant agent for change. God wants to work in you and through you. Filled with his Spirit, as a courageous witness, you also can share the Good News with the world—with *your* world.

The Holy Spirit (1:5, 8; 2:1-13, 17-18, 33, 38-39; 4:8, 25, 31; 5:3, 9, 32, 6:3, 5; 7:51, 55; 8:15-24, 29, 39; 9:17, 31; 10:19, 38, 44-47; 11:12-18, 24, 28; 13:2-12, 52; 15:8, 28-29; 16:6-7; 19:2-6, 21; 20:22-28; 21:4, 10-12; 28:25). The church did not start or grow by its own power and enthusiasm. The disciples were empowered by God's Holy Spirit. He was the Comforter and Guide promised by Jesus and sent when Jesus went to heaven. The Holy Spirit came upon the assembled believers at Pentecost and continued to fill those who trusted in Christ as Savior. Through the Spirit's power, the gospel was preached, and people were healed.

IMPORTANCE FOR TODAY. The filling of the Holy Spirit at Pentecost demonstrated that Christianity was supernatural. As a result, the church became more Holy Spirit-conscious than problem-conscious. Then, led and empowered by the Spirit, they changed the world. Everyone who trusts in Christ as Savior receives the Holy Spirit. By faith, therefore, any believer can claim the Holy Spirit's power to do Christ's work. Allow God to fill you with his Spirit; then follow the Spirit's leading as you live and minister in this world.

Church Growth (2:37-47; 4:1-4, 32-37; 5:12-16, 42; 6:1-7; 8:12, 40; 9:31-35, 39-42; 10:44-48; 11:19-21, 24; 12:24; 13:42-43, 44-49; 14:1, 21-28; 16:4-5, 13-15, 29-34; 17:1-4, 10-12, 32-34; 18:7-8; 19:17-20; 28:23-31). Jesus had told his disciples to take the gospel to all the world (Matthew 28:19-20). He also had said that they would be his witnesses in Jerusalem, Judea and Samaria, and to the ends of the earth. Acts shows the fulfillment of this prediction, presenting the history of a dynamic, growing community of believers from Jerusalem to Syria, Africa, Asia, and Europe. In the first century, it spread from believing Jews to non-Jews in thirty-nine cities and thirty countries, islands, or provinces.

IMPORTANCE FOR TODAY. The Holy Spirit brings movement, excitement, and growth. He gives believers the motivation, energy, and ability to spread the gospel. God still loves the world (John 3:16)—the whole world. And he wants men and women everywhere to hear his wonderful, life-changing message. Consider how you are part of God's plan to expand the Christian gospel.

Witnessing (1:8; 2:4-40; 3:12-26; 4:8-15; 5:29-32, 42; 6:7; 7:1-56; 8:4-40; 9:20-22, 28-29; 10:34-43; 11:4-17, 20-21; 13:4-6, 16-47; 14:1, 6-7, 14-17, 21; 16:9-15, 25-34; 17:2-4, 22-34; 18:4-11, 19-20, 24-28; 19:8-10; 20:7, 20-27; 22:1-21; 23:1, 6; 24:10-21, 24-26; 26:1-23, 28-29; 28:17-31). Peter, John, Philip, Paul, Barnabas, and thousands more witnessed to their new faith in Christ. By personal testimony, preaching, or defense before authorities, they told the story with boldness and courage to groups of all sizes. Paul, in particular, took every opportunity to tell others about Jesus' life, death, and resurrection, and Paul told how God had changed his life. Whether in a synagogue (17:10) or lecture hall (19:9), on a riverbank (16:13) or in prison (16:31-32), or in the public square (17:17), in front of a mob (21:40) or in front of rulers (24:10), Paul courageously spoke the truth.

IMPORTANCE FOR TODAY. We are God's people, chosen to be part of his plan to reach the world. We have the truth, the good news about the only way to God, and the message of eternal life. Like the apostles and early believers, we must share this message with boldness and love. And God has promised that the Holy Spirit will help us as we witness or preach. Witnessing is also beneficial to us because it strengthens our faith as we confront those who challenge it. To whom has God called you to share his message of forgiveness and hope? Who needs to hear from you about Christ? What can you do to take the Good News to the world?

Opposition (4:1-22, 29-30; 5:17-42; 6:8-14; 7:54-60; 8:1-3; 9:1-2, 22-30; 12:1-19; 13:50-52; 14:1-7, 19-20; 16:16-39; 17:5-9, 13-15; 18:12-17; 19:9, 23-41; 21:26-36; 22:22-29; 23:2, 7-10, 12-21; 24:1-9; 25:2-7). Through imprisonment, beatings, plots, and riots, Christians were persecuted by both Jews and Gentiles. Countless numbers suffered financial loss and physical and emotional pain, and many died. Although Christ's message focused on love and forgiveness, it threatened the pagan establishment and brought furious opposition. But this opposition became a catalyst for the spread of Christianity as believers, convinced of the truth of the gospel, courageously continued to hold on to the faith and to share it with others. This showed that the Christian movement was not the work of humans but of God.

IMPORTANCE FOR TODAY. Christ still threatens the establishment because he identifies sin and calls people to repent and to turn to him. And Jesus' claim to be the only way (see John 14:6) is said to be impossibly narrow and politically incorrect. So believers continue to be threatened and persecuted for believing in Christ and telling others about him. But God can work through any opposition, and persecution can help spread his word. When severe treatment from hostile unbelievers comes, realize that it is because you have been a faithful witness. Then look for the opportunity to present the Good News. Stay focused on Christ, and seize the opportunities that opposition brings.

OUTLINE OF ACTS
  I. PETER'S MINISTRY (1:1–12:25)
     A. Establishment of the church
     B. Expansion of the church
 II. PAUL'S MINISTRY (13:1–28:31)
     A. First missionary journey
     B. The council at Jerusalem
     C. Second missionary journey
     D. Third missionary journey
     E. Paul on trial

ACTS 1

THE PROMISE OF THE HOLY SPIRIT / 1:1-5

The book of Acts, written by Luke, picks up where Luke's Gospel left off, providing details of the birth and early years of the church that Jesus had promised to build. Together the two books, Luke and Acts, form a seamless account of how the followers of Jesus turned the world upside down.

Before documenting this rapid spread of the gospel, however, Luke asserted two important truths in what serves as an introduction to the book of Acts: (1) the indisputable fact of Christ's resurrection; and (2) the indispensable presence of the Holy Spirit. Apart from these two strong foundations, the church would be without hope and without power. What was true in the first century is still true today.

1:1-2 Luke's opening statement ties this volume to his **first book**, the Gospel of Luke. That book was also addressed to **Theophilus**, whose name means "one who loves God." While some scholars have argued that this is a general term for all believers, it is more likely a proper name. When addressing Theophilus in Luke 1:1, Luke called him "most honorable." A proper name with a title indicates that this was probably a real person, someone who belonged to the nobility, possibly as a high-ranking Roman official. Most likely Theophilus was a Roman acquaintance of Luke's with a strong interest in the new Christian religion.

Whether or not Theophilus was a believer, he had apparently learned some of the facts, but he may have needed further clarification. Luke set out to explain the entire gospel story to Theophilus, telling him **about everything Jesus began to do and teach until the day he ascended to heaven after giving his chosen apostles further instructions from the Holy Spirit.** The book of Acts would show the continuation of his work on earth through his church, his body.

1:3 During the days after Christ rose from the dead, **he appeared to the apostles from time to time.** The word **proved** refers to demonstrated, decisive evidence. Jesus' resurrection had not been sleight of hand or illusion, with Jesus being merely a ghostly presence. Instead, these were solid, visible, and undeniable proofs of the fact that Jesus was **alive.**

During Jesus' post-Resurrection appearances, the main subject of Jesus' remarks was **the Kingdom of God.** Throughout the Gospels the Kingdom was always on Jesus' lips, for this unified his teachings and activities (see, for example, Luke 13:18-21; 17:20-37). When Christ came to earth, he brought

God's Kingdom, but it was not an earthly kingdom. The promised Kingdom is present now only in part. The New Testament writers confirmed that through his death and resurrection, Christ bound Satan (Colossians 2:15; 1 Peter 3:22), provided forgiveness and holiness to sinners (Romans 3:21-26; Hebrews 9:11-12; 10:10), and is now enthroned as Lord over all (Acts 2:33-36; 5:31; Ephesians 1:20-22). Believers become participants of this Kingdom through God's power (Matthew 19:24-26; John 3:3), by repentance and trust in Jesus (Matthew 4:17; John 14:6; Acts 8:12). His Kingdom began in the hearts of his followers. When Christ returned to heaven, God's Kingdom remained in the hearts of all believers through the presence of the Holy Spirit. God promised, however, that he would ultimately reign over all and bring about the end of all death and disease. The ultimate culmination of the Kingdom of God will not be fully realized until Jesus Christ comes again to rule, defeat his enemies, and consummate the Kingdom (Matthew 24:29-31; 25:31-46; John 14:1-3). Before that time believers are to work to spread God's Kingdom across the world.

1:4-5 As the risen Christ met with his disciples, here **eating a meal with them,** he surely told them many things. Luke records only a handful of sentences from those forty days of instruction, so they certainly are important words. Christ first told his followers to stay and **not leave Jerusalem until the Father sends you what he promised.** This points back to Luke 24:49. He had spoken **about this before,** at the Last Supper: "And I will ask the Father, and he will give you another Counselor, who will never leave you. He is the Holy Spirit" (John 14:16-17).

This would be a new kind of baptism. **John baptized with water,** said Jesus, but these believers would **be baptized with the Holy Spirit.** John the Baptist had baptized people as a sign of repentance. They had confessed their sins and had determined to live as God wanted them to live. Baptism was an outward sign of commitment. To be effective, it had to be accompanied by an inward change of attitude leading to a changed life. John's baptism did not give salvation; it prepared a person to welcome the coming Messiah and receive **his** message and **his** baptism (Matthew 3:11).

The Old Testament promised a time when God would demonstrate his purifying power among people (Isaiah 32:15; Ezekiel 39:29). The prophets also looked forward to a purifying fire (Isaiah 4:4; Malachi 3:2). This looked ahead to Pentecost (Acts 2:1-6), when the Holy Spirit would be sent by Jesus in the form of tongues of fire, empowering his followers to preach the gospel. All believers, those who would later come to Jesus Christ for salvation, would receive the baptism of the Holy Spirit and the fire of purification (in the Greek one article precedes these words, indicating that they were not two separate baptisms). This baptism would purify and refine each believer. When Jesus baptized with the Holy Spirit, the entire person would be transformed by the Spirit's power.

If Jesus had stayed on earth, his physical presence would have limited the spread of the gospel because physically he could be in only one place at a time. After Christ was taken up into heaven, he would be spiritually present everywhere through the Holy Spirit. The Holy Spirit was sent so that God would be with and within his followers after Christ returned to heaven. The Spirit would comfort them, guide them to know his truth, remind them of Jesus' words, give them the right words to say, and fill them with power. As promised by Christ in the upper room (John 13–17) and by the Father (see Peter's speech in Acts 2:17 and following), the Holy Spirit would be the next great event in the life of the church. Many believe it to be the very birth of the church.

THE ASCENSION OF JESUS / 1:6-11

When would the risen Lord set up his Kingdom? This was the question uppermost in the apostles' minds. They were eagerly hoping for a glorious earthly kingdom free from Roman rule. Christ, however, sidestepped these questions about earthly kingdoms and divine timetables. Instead, he reminded his followers of their calling to be Spirit-filled witnesses who would take the gospel message everywhere. A spiritual revolution needed first to take place in the hearts and minds of people. With this final charge on the top of the Mount of Olives, Christ ascended into heaven. Moments later divine messengers appeared and assured the apostles that the Lord would one day return in similar fashion.

1:6 The average Jew of Jesus' day was looking forward with great anticipation to the literal coming of the Messiah's earthly kingdom and with it the restoration of the fortunes and military might that the nation had enjoyed under King David. Jesus had certainly taught a great deal about his coming Kingdom in his ministry with the disciples. During this forty-day instruction period, the disciples had questions about the promised Kingdom, for their anticipation had been heightened with their Master's resurrection from the dead. Fully expecting Jesus to bring in his Kingdom on earth at that moment, the **apostles** asked: **"Are you going to free Israel now and restore our kingdom?"**

The coming of the Kingdom was closely associated with the coming of the Holy Spirit (as implied in passages such as Isaiah 32:15-20; 44:3-5; Ezekiel 39:28-29; Joel 2:28–3:1; Zechariah 12:8-10). When Christ told the disciples of the imminent coming of the Spirit, therefore, they were even more likely to assume the coming of the Kingdom would also be at hand. During the years of Jesus' ministry on earth, the disciples continually had wondered about the coming of the Kingdom and what their roles would be in it. In the traditional view, the Messiah would be an earthly conqueror who would free Israel from Rome. But the Kingdom about which Jesus spoke was first of all a "spiritual" Kingdom established in the hearts and lives of believers (Luke 17:21); behind it was the earthly kingdom that Christ promised to institute at his return.

1:7 The **dates** of the restoration of the Kingdom were not the disciples' business. These are **set** by the **Father.** Later revelation through Paul and others would help clarify the issue (1 Thessalonians 5:1-2). What **should** concern and consume the disciples, however (notice the contrastive word "but" that begins 1:8), was the loaded statement that follows.

1:8 This is the last recorded statement of Christ on earth. It is thus final, authoritative, and of utmost importance. The **Holy Spirit** is a major theme in Luke and Acts and is the major point of continuity between the life of Jesus and the ministry of the church.

Who is the Holy Spirit? God is three persons in one—the Father, the Son, and the Holy Spirit. God became a man in Jesus so that Jesus could die for our sins. Jesus rose from the dead to offer salvation to all people through spiritual renewal and rebirth. When Jesus ascended into heaven, his physical presence left the earth, but he promised to send the Holy Spirit so that his spiritual presence would still be among mankind (see Luke 24:49). The Holy Spirit first became available to all believers at Pentecost (Acts 2). Whereas in Old Testament days the Holy Spirit empowered specific individuals for

specific purposes, now all believers have the power of the Holy Spirit available to them. For more on the Holy Spirit, read John 14:16-28; Romans 8:9; 1 Corinthians 12:13; and 2 Corinthians 1:22.

When the Spirit comes, he told his followers, **you will receive power.** To do what? To **tell people about** him. They were to start right there in **Jerusalem** (1:4). **Judea** was the region surrounding Jerusalem (possibly including Galilee). **Samaria** was Judea's hostile next-door neighbor, a more difficult but equally important place to take the gospel. The **ends of the earth** may have referred to Rome or the Roman Empire, the world power at that time. The direction was of primary importance: Beginning from where you are at this moment, take the message of Christ outward, like ripples caused by a pebble thrown into a pond, not stopping at just your city or state but moving on beyond regional influence to the very "ends" of the earth. In other words, reach it **all!**

The disciples took Jesus at his word and went about their task exactly as he directed: they began in Jerusalem (1–7), spread to Judea and Samaria (8–12), then filtered out across the world to the imperial capital, Rome (13–28).

1:9 After giving this important charge, Jesus was **taken up into the sky while they were watching, and he disappeared into a cloud.** This cloud symbolized the glory of God. In the Old Testament, we read that a cloud led the Israelites through the wilderness (Exodus 13:21-22) and that God made his presence known to the people by appearing in a cloud (Exodus 16:10; 19:9, 16; 24:15-18; 33:9-10; 34:5; 40:34-35). A cloud also enveloped Jesus and three of his disciples at the Transfiguration (Luke 9:34-35) as a visible symbol of God's presence. So when Jesus returned to glory, he returned in a cloud.

The disciples needed to see Jesus make this transition. The Ascension confirmed for them that Jesus truly was God. In addition, they witnessed the fact that he had physically left earth and had returned to his heavenly home; thus, the remaining work would be done by the witnesses he had left behind, operating in the power of the promised Holy Spirit.

1:10-11 While the disciples were **straining their eyes,** staring into the sky, two angelic messengers appeared **among them.** The angels confirmed what had just happened: indeed, Jesus had been **taken away into heaven.** They also reminded the disciples of Jesus' promise: **"Someday, just as you saw him go, he will return!"** Most likely, this refers to Jesus' coming in a cloud to show his glory (see Matthew 24:30; 26:64; Mark 13:26; Luke 21:27).

MATTHIAS REPLACES JUDAS / 1:12-26

Having been instructed to wait for the coming of the Holy Spirit, the disciples withdrew to an upstairs room in Jerusalem. There they wisely spent time praying. It was during this lull that the apostles, under Peter's leadership, filled the vacancy in their ranks created by the defection of Judas. It was important for them to have twelve apostles, representing the twelve tribes of Israel, to position the church as the fulfillment of the righteous remnant (see 1:21). Practical and simple steps in organization often play an important part in God's Kingdom plan.

1:12-13 Following the instructions of Christ (1:4), the disciples stayed in **Jerusalem.** The **upstairs room** seems to have been a specific and well-known place (the noun has the definite Greek article). This may have been the same room in which they had eaten the Last Supper with Christ (Luke 22:12), as well as the location of many of the post-Resurrection appearances. At this time it became the first meeting place of the church.

This list of names of the eleven disciples parallels the lists in the Gospels (Matthew 10:2-4; Mark 3:16-19; Luke 6:14-16).

1:14 Luke took special note of the fact that the disciples were joined by **Mary the mother of Jesus** and **several other women,** likely the ones who had been present at the Crucifixion and at the empty tomb (Luke 8:2-3; 23:49; 23:55–24:10). Also present were **the brothers of Jesus.** During his lifetime, Jesus' brothers (Mary and Joseph's other sons) did not believe he was the Messiah (John 7:5) and actually thought he was out of his mind (Mark 3:21-35). But Jesus' resurrection must have convinced them otherwise. Jesus' special appearance to James, one of his brothers, may have been an especially significant event in James's conversion (see 1 Corinthians 15:7). This gathering may have included all of Jesus' other brothers— Joses (or Joseph), Judas (or Jude) and Simon (see Matthew 13:55-56; Mark 6:3).

The main emphasis, however, is not who was present but what they were doing—praying! **Prayer** begins to appear as a mark of the early church. When they were fearful, they prayed. When they were confused, they prayed. When they were waiting for God to fulfill his promise to them, they prayed. When they needed an answer to a question (such as who was to be the twelfth apostle), they prayed!

1:15-16 The group was a little larger than the previous verses seem to indicate. During this "waiting" period, evidently, the meetings in the upper room were regular (**during this time**), repeated (**on a day when**), and growing in size (**about 120 believers** attended this particular meeting). **Peter,** who had taken a prominent role among the disciples

throughout the Gospels, continued in that leadership role.

Peter put the events concerning Judas's betrayal and suicide into biblical perspective by explaining how **it was necessary for the Scriptures to be fulfilled,** and then he called the believers to the task of choosing Judas's replacement, something he likewise said was necessary (1:21). Peter gave a great lesson in healthy biblical leadership: it is a combination of insight from the word of God and corresponding practical action. Peter's reference to **King David** refers to the Spirit-led predictions recorded in some of David's psalms, such as Psalm 69:25 and Psalm 109:8.

1:17-19 It is hard to believe that someone who had been with Jesus daily could betray him. Judas had received the same calling and teaching as everyone else. Though **chosen to share in the ministry** by Christ himself, Judas hardened his heart and joined in the plot with Jesus' enemies to put him to death. Judas remained unrepentant to the end, and he finally committed suicide. Although Jesus predicted this betrayal and bitter end, it was Judas's choice. Those privileged to be close to the truth are not necessarily committed to the truth.

The section set off by parentheses was not part of Peter's speech but rather was an insertion by Luke explaining the suicide of Judas, the resulting spread of the news, and the naming of the place where it happened. Matthew reports that Judas hung himself (Matthew 27:5); here Luke says that he fell. The traditional explanation proposed by Augustine of this seeming contradiction is that both reports are true: when Judas hung himself, the rope or branch broke, Judas fell, and his body burst open.

1:20 The psalms picture the Messiah as the ideal king. Thus, the enemies of King David (addressed in certain psalms where curses are called on God's enemies) are a prototype or foreshadowing of the enemies of the Messiah. Peter applied the meaning in those psalms to the enemies of Jesus, particularly here to Judas. Peter saw Psalm 69:25 as a prediction of Judas's horrible end, the **desolate** name of the place of his demise. Peter then quoted Psalm 109:8 as the basis of the necessity of choosing someone to replace Judas. Thus Peter's Spirit-led application of David's Spirit-inspired prediction became the basis for the gathered believers' first significant decision—replacing Judas.

1:21-23 The main reason for this process was to make sure that there were twelve apostolic witnesses. They also believed that a twelfth disciple would be necessary to fulfill such promises as Matthew 19:28 and Luke 22:28-30 (the twelve disciples sitting on twelve thrones in the Kingdom government). The church was regarded as a fulfillment of the Old Testament righteous remnant, those faithful to God, and so must assure its rightful place. The Twelve were needed to lead. Because Judas betrayed Christ, he had to be replaced because twelve faithful leaders were needed. James was not replaced after his death (12:2) because he had not defected from the faith. Even after James's death, he still was regarded as one of the Twelve.

Peter pointed out the qualifications of the one who was to be chosen. Notice that it had to be someone who had been with Jesus and the other disciples throughout Jesus' ministry on earth. Such eyewitness involvement was absolutely necessary for the credibility of the person bearing witness to the words and the works of Christ. This one would join the other apostles in being **a witness of Jesus' resurrection.** What this witness said would be a testimony to the credibility of the life of Christ and the words of Christ. It is clear that, in addition to the twelve disciples, many others had consistently followed Jesus throughout his ministry on earth. The Twelve were his inner circle, but many others shared deep love for and commitment to Jesus. It was now simply a matter of finding the one who would be elevated to the title of apostle. In answer to Peter's request, the eleven apostles **nominated two men** who met the qualifications of 1:21-22.

1:24-25 As **they all prayed** for direction in this decision, the apostles reminded themselves of God's omniscience. God knew that Judas would betray Christ and subsequently take his own life. God also knew the hearts of all the people in that room. All these believers needed God to **show** them which one—either Matthias or Barsabbas— he had already **chosen.**

1:26 The final phase of this choosing process was that **they cast lots.** This casting of the lots was not done casually or flippantly, for the apostles had carefully chosen two candidates according to certain qualifications (1:21-22) and then had spent time in prayer (1:24-25). The final process of casting the lots was likely done by writing the two names on two stones and then placing them into a container. The first stone to fall out when the container was tipped would be considered God's choice. Proverbs 16:33 mentions this practice. It is also similar to the use of the Urim and Thummim in the Old Testament (see Leviticus 8:8; 1 Chronicles 26:13; Ezra 2:63; Nehemiah 7:65).

As far as we know, this practice did not continue after Pentecost because the "Guide," the Holy Spirit, had come to indwell the hearts and minds of God's people. Later the elders would select the leaders at the various churches, but not with lots. Christians—then as now—were encouraged to search the Scriptures and to know the will of the Lord (Ephesians 5:17-18; Colossians 1:9; 1 Thessalonians 4:1; 2 Timothy 3:16-17).

Matthias was chosen to be the twelfth apostle. That may seem odd because Paul (who is also called an "apostle") is not mentioned here. Remember that all of this occurred prior to Paul's conversion. Paul's calling was unique. To begin with, he did not meet the qualifications spelled out by Peter. Thus, though Paul was not technically one of the Twelve, he clearly was designated an apostle with authority equal to any of them.

ACTS 2

THE HOLY SPIRIT COMES / 2:1-13

In Old Testament times, the Spirit of God came upon isolated individuals or smaller groups, only on special occasions, and only in a temporary way to help them accomplish God's purposes (Exodus 31:3; Judges 14:6; 1 Samuel 16:13). As the apostles were gathered together in Jerusalem for the feast of Pentecost, the time had come for the fulfillment of Christ's promise to send his

Spirit completely and permanently upon all believers (Luke 24:49; John 14:16-17, 26; 16:5-15). This marvelous outpouring of God provided the supernatural power for believers to take the life-changing message of the gospel to the ends of the earth (Acts 1:8). This is the day Christ made good on his promise to send the Helper, the Comforter, the Holy Spirit who would take up permanent residence in those who put their faith in Christ. And what a day it was! God's individualized pouring out of his Spirit into the lives of 120 believers resulted in the effective pouring out of his story, changing the lives of three thousand people in one day!

2:1 The day of Pentecost was an annual feast celebrated on the day after the seventh Sabbath after Passover (Leviticus 23:15-16). Since the date was determined by the passing of a "week" of weeks (seven weeks), it was often called the Festival of Weeks. The word "Pentecost" means "fifty," so named because this festival was celebrated fifty days after Passover. Pentecost was one of three major annual festivals celebrated by the Jews (along with Passover, fifty days earlier, and the Festival of Shelters about four months later). Jesus was crucified at Passover time, and he ascended forty days after his resurrection. The Holy Spirit came fifty days after the Resurrection, ten days after the Ascension.

The **believers** were the 120 mentioned in 1:15. The **one place** where they were **meeting** was likely the same upper room mentioned in 1:13. Most likely the believers were praying, as had been their regular practice during the period since the Ascension (1:14). What happened this day would forever change the world.

2:2 Suddenly, as the believers were gathered, they heard a **sound from heaven like the roaring of a mighty windstorm.** The wind is a good analogy for the Spirit: it is not seen, though its effects are, and it can be found everywhere in never-ending supply. The sound **filled the house where they were meeting.** The "house" probably refers to the upper room mentioned in 1:13 where the believers had been meeting and praying.

2:3 To the great sound of wind was added a visual image: **what looked like flames or tongues of fire appeared and settled on each of them.** Why tongues of fire? It may be that "tongues" symbolized speech and the communication of the gospel. "Fire" symbolizes God's purifying presence, which burns away the undesirable elements in people's lives and sets their hearts aflame to ignite the lives of others.

At Pentecost God confirmed the validity of the Holy Spirit's ministry by sending fire. And while at Mount Sinai fire had come down on one place, at Pentecost fire came down on many believers, symbolizing that God's presence is available to all who believe in him. This event certainly fulfilled John the Baptist's words about the Holy Spirit baptizing

with fire (Luke 3:16). Peter declared that this event had been prophesied by Joel (Joel 2:28-29). Note, too, that every believer in the room received this blessing; no one was excluded. It was clear to all present that God was at work.

2:4 At this point in this wonderful scene, Luke recorded that **everyone present was filled with the Holy Spirit and began speaking in other languages.** The "filling" that occurred on Pentecost is called a "baptizing" (1:5 and 11:16) and a "receiving" (10:47). "Baptizing" or "filling" can be used to describe the basic act of receiving the Spirit. It can be understood to refer to the first occurrence of the Spirit indwelling a believer. Acts 1:5 looks forward to this day; Acts 11:15-16 refers back to it. Here, four short verses record it.

In principle, the filling of the Holy Spirit can be distinguished from the term "baptism" of the Spirit. "Baptism" is the theological, objective term referring to the Spirit's initial work in a believer's life, beginning the relationship, and—like water baptism—is not a repeated act (Acts 11:15-16; Romans 6:3; 1 Corinthians 12:13; Colossians 2:12). The believer who has taken this initial step of Spirit baptism must, however, continue to take advantage of the Spirit's active work in his or her life. That phenomenon is described in the New Testament as the Spirit's filling (see Acts 4:8, 31; 6:3, 5; 7:55; 9:17; 13:9, 52; Galatians 5:16; Ephesians 4:30; 5:18).

At Pentecost (2:1-4) the Holy Spirit was made available to all who believe in Jesus. Believers receive the Holy Spirit (are baptized with him) when they trust in Jesus Christ for salvation. The baptism of the Holy Spirit must be understood in the light of his total work in Christians:

- The Spirit marks the beginning of the Christian experience. No one belongs to Christ without his Spirit (Romans 8:9); no one is united to Christ without his Spirit (1 Corinthians 6:17); no one is adopted as God's child without his Spirit (Romans 8:14-17; Galatians 4:6-7); no one is in the body of Christ except by baptism in the Spirit (1 Corinthians 12:13).
- The Spirit is the power for the new life. He begins a lifelong process of change as believers

become more like Christ (Galatians 3:3; Philippians 1:6). Those who receive Christ by faith begin an immediate personal relationship with God. The Holy Spirit works in them to help them become like Christ.

- The Spirit unites the Christian community in Christ (Ephesians 2:19-22). The Holy Spirit can be experienced by all, and he works through all (1 Corinthians 12:11; Ephesians 4:4).

These people literally spoke in "other languages" (see comments on the following verse)—a miraculous attention-getter for the international crowd gathered in town for the feast. All the nationalities represented recognized their own languages being spoken. Jews believed that spoken prophecy had ceased with Malachi, the last of the writing prophets. They believed that from that point on, God spoke through the Torah as interpreted by scholars and teachers. So this was truly a remarkable day for the church, fulfilling Ezekiel 37:11-14.

The believers could speak in these other languages because **the Holy Spirit gave them this ability.** This is the clear teaching of the New Testament—that the Holy Spirit sovereignly determines which gift(s) a believer will have (1 Corinthians 12:7, 11). Furthermore, these gifts are meant to be used to build up the body of Christ.

2:5-8 Such an event could not help but attract attention, and a crowd must have quickly gathered. The **godly Jews from many nations** who **were living in Jerusalem at that time** were the Jews among the *Diaspora* (the Greek word for "scattering"), whose families had been driven from Jerusalem and forced to live in other nations but had since returned to Jerusalem to live. These people had been born and raised in other nations, so among them many different languages were spoken. Thus, **they were bewildered to hear their own languages being spoken, languages of the lands where** they **were born!** As the international, multilingual crowd gathered, they were astonished to hear their native tongues spoken by these Galileans. At this point, "tongues" was not the ecstatic or heavenly utterance to which Paul referred in 1 Corinthians 12-14; these were languages people understood.

This gathering of the nations was a perfect platform for launching the worldwide mission of the church. This event told the Jerusalem church that God intended the gospel for all the nations in their own languages.

2:9-11 This list includes the many lands from which Jews came to Jerusalem—some living in Palestine and others who had been dispersed throughout the world through captivities and persecutions. The list begins from the east of the Roman Empire and sweeps to the south and west. Very likely, some of the Jews who responded to Peter's message then returned to their homelands with God's Good News of salvation (for example, see Acts 8). Through this divine manifestation of languages, therefore, God prepared the way for the spread of the gospel across the world. Throughout the book of Acts, it is clear how often the way was prepared for Paul and other messengers by people who had become believers at Pentecost. The church at Rome, for example, was probably begun by such Jewish believers. The list of countries reads mostly from East to West geographically, but why they are cited and why in this order is not known.

The content of these speeches in each language was **the wonderful things God has done.** The subject of discussion was not sin, repentance, judgment, not even the gospel, but rather the proclamation of the mighty works of God. This was a sign for unbelieving Israel that the Messiah had come.

2:12-13 These two verses describe a typical response of the crowd, leading up to Peter's speech. The crowd continued to be **amazed** (see 2:7), but their amazement led them to be **perplexed** and to try to figure out what was happening. Some **were mocking.** Others were speculating that the believers were **drunk.** Such confusion and the drawing of such wrong conclusions was just the prodding Peter needed to clear things up. There will always be those who misunderstand the working of God, who mock it and call into question its integrity. Christians can either wring their hands and worry or, like Peter, seize the opportunity to tell the watching world about the work of God in their midst.

PETER PREACHES TO A CROWD / 2:14-42

In Luke's history of the church, there is always a close connection between the activity of God's Spirit and the proclamation of the gospel. Time and again those who experience the baptism of the Spirit begin immediately speaking with others about God and his Son, Jesus Christ (1:8; 2:4, 17; 4:8, 31; 6:10; 10:44-46; 13:9; 19:6).

2:14 Peter, the early spokesman for the Twelve, seized the opportunity and **shouted to the crowd.** Peter explained to the people why they should listen to the testimony of the believers: because the Old Testament prophecies had been entirely fulfilled in Jesus (2:14-21), because Jesus is the Messiah (2:25-36), and because the risen Christ could change their lives (2:37-40).

2:15-18 Peter answered the accusation that they were all **drunk** (2:13) by saying it was **too early** in the day for that. He then proceeded to tie the event the crowd had just witnessed to the words of the **prophet Joel,** quoting from Joel 2:28-32. Not everything mentioned in Joel 2:28-32 was occurring that particular morning. The **last days** include all the days between Christ's first and second comings; it is another way of saying "from now on." Peter was reminding these Jewish listeners that from prophecies like this one recorded by Joel, **I will pour out my Spirit upon all people,** they should recognize the event they had just witnessed as the work of the Spirit. It would be to all kinds of people—Jews and Gentiles, rich and poor—not just to kings and priests.

The "prophesying" mentioned by Peter is likely not only prediction of the future but also declaration of the nature and will of God. The **visions** and the **dreams** were common means that God used to reveal himself to all people. The point was that the insight into these visions and dreams would be the product of the Spirit's work.

At Pentecost the Holy Spirit was released throughout the entire world—to men, women, slave owners, slaves, Jews, and Gentiles. Everyone can receive the Spirit. This was a revolutionary thought for first-century Jews. Pentecost was designed to be a clear indication—to Jew and Gentile alike—that the messianic age had arrived. The Messiah had come!

2:19-20 Not everything mentioned in Joel 2:28-32 was happening that particular morning. This part of Joel's prophecy probably refers to the future period surrounding the second coming of Christ, placing the period of the church age (between Christ's ascension and his return) between verses 18 and 19 (see Revelation 6:12). These events bear more resemblance to the phenomena of the Tribulation period as spelled out by many other Old Testament prophets, as well as Jesus himself (see Matthew 24:14, 21, 29-30 and the judgments of Revelation 8, 9, and 16).

It is possible that Peter was quoting the entire prophecy from Joel—even some of the parts that are still future—in order to avoid being accused of improper use of Scripture (the crowd would certainly know the Joel passage) and to get all the way through Joel's passage to its final sentence, quoted in the next verse.

2:21 This is Peter's punch line. This salvation is available to **anyone.** Any person **who calls on the name of the Lord will be saved.** God's special relationship with Israel will continue, but it has been broadened to include everyone who calls on the name of the Lord. God's plans for Israel had their climax in Christ. Access to God—for all people—now comes through Jesus Christ. With these words Peter witnessed to the crowd, as Jesus had predicted (1:8).

It would be a while before these new believers understood that the "anyone" included Gentiles. God had to work in a special way to make Peter understand that the message was meant for the whole world, not just the Jews (see Acts 10).

2:22 The coming of the Messiah, the miracles, and the events described by Joel were all well-established concepts to these **people of Israel** (the Jews). Now all that remained was for Peter to connect those events to **Jesus of Nazareth**—the teacher many of them had heard and seen, the teacher who had been crucified. Peter began this sermon by stating that God himself had **publicly endorsed** Jesus by **doing wonderful miracles, wonders, and signs through him.** Certainly many of the gathered crowd had seen or heard of the famous ministry of Jesus.

2:23 With little forewarning Peter suddenly accused his Jewish audience of an awful participation in the Messiah's death. This is a perfect presentation of God's sovereignty and people's responsibility—both in the same sentence. God's prearranged plan was his sovereign will to bring salvation to people through the death and resurrection of Christ. Though God's will is sovereign, he works through people and events of history (see 4:28). Even putting Jesus to death fulfilled God's plan. **God's prearranged plan** led to Christ's death, but people were culpable. The **lawless Gentiles** (the Romans) had been involved, but they had been merely "helping." Ultimately, the Jews had been responsible. Whether or not anyone in this audience had literally participated in the trials, accusations, and crucifixion (many in the crowd **could** have been involved) was not important. Peter was saying that they were at least culpable because, as Jews, they had missed their Messiah and had allowed their leaders to kill him. Thus, they were guilty by their relationship to the actual murderers. Peter was pointing his finger at the crowd and shouting, **"You nailed him to the cross and murdered him."**

2:24 But the murdered Messiah had not stayed dead. God **raised him back to life again,** and many people could testify to having seen the risen Christ. This was a powerful statement because many of the people listening to Peter's words had been in Jerusalem fifty days earlier at Passover and may have seen or heard about the crucifixion of this "great teacher." Jesus' resurrection was the ultimate sign that what he said about himself was true. Without the Resurrection, no one would have any reason to believe in Jesus (1 Corinthians 15:14). Peter phrased it appropriately: **death could not keep him in its grip.**

2:25-28 Peter continued his witness to Jesus' Messiahship by quoting from Psalm 16:8-11, written by **King David.** He explained that David was not writing about himself because David had died and was buried (2:29); his audience would have walked right past his tomb many times in their pilgrimages to Jerusalem. This quote from Psalm 16 and the one from Psalm 110:1 (2:34-35) were both prophesying Jesus' resurrection (2:24). The emphasis is that Jesus' body had not been left to **rot in the grave,** but had been, in fact, resurrected and glorified. Peter wanted his audience to realize that David was not speaking of himself in these psalms but rather of the Messiah.

2:29-31 The Old Testament spoke of the resurrection of the Messiah—and this was very important for Peter's Jewish listeners to understand. Peter argued that the words of this psalm could not have been referring to David himself, for David **died and was buried.** The reference to **his tomb** may have been a site on the south side of Jerusalem, near the pool of Siloam.

If David was not speaking of himself, then he was speaking as **a prophet;** he was writing about one who would be resurrected from the dead. The **oath** looks back at Psalm 132:11 and 2 Samuel 7:15-16, recording the promises God made to David that one of his **descendants would sit on David's throne as the Messiah.** David did have children who ruled, but this promise was for someone to be on the throne for eternity. The Jewish listeners of Peter's day understood the words of this psalm, as well as others, as referring to the Messiah.

2:32 Having begun by tying these Old Testament references to Jesus of Nazareth, here Peter again made it clear that David's **prophecy was speaking of Jesus.** The resurrection of Christ had taken place less than two months previously. The post-Resurrection appearances and instruction sessions of the forty days prior to Christ's ascension must have caused a stir around the city. Peter pointed

out that he and the others with him—who had just experienced this Spirit's coming—had been **witnesses** to the predicted resurrection of Christ.

2:33 Peter had one more major point to make: this crucified one, the resurrected one, is now the exalted one, who occupies **the throne of highest honor in heaven, at God's right hand** (see 5:30-31; Ephesians 1:20; Colossians 3:1; Hebrews 1:3; 8:1; 10:12; 12:2; 1 Peter 3:22). Not only is Christ the predicted one in the Psalms, not only had he risen from the grave, but he now sits in the most authoritative, sovereign position in the universe. That is why Jesus had the authority to **pour out** the Spirit with results that the audience could **see and hear.**

2:34-35 In Psalm 110:1, again David was not speaking of himself but of Christ. This verse is the most frequently quoted Old Testament passage in the New Testament (thirteen times) and was the primary text used to explain the exaltation of Christ. The Jews believed that this psalm referred to their coming Messiah. All three synoptic gospels—Matthew 22:41-46; Mark 12:35-37; Luke 20:41-44—report that Jesus applied this verse to himself as the one having the highest authority because he would be instructed to **sit in honor at God's right hand.** The victory belongs to Christ and not to any created being. The greatest archangels stand before God (Luke 1:19; Revelation 8:2), but none are allowed to sit, for sitting next to God would indicate equality. Jesus' sitting also indicates the completion of his task, the successful accomplishment of his mission. God promised to make Jesus' enemies **a footstool.** This pictures Christ as completely victorious over his enemies.

2:36 Peter concluded his message with a solid review of his main point: **So let it be clearly known by everyone in Israel** that Jesus was **both Lord and Messiah.** In the prophesied plan of God, this Jesus of Nazareth had been **crucified** by the Jews, raised from the dead, and exalted to the throne of God.

2:37 That these people were **convicted deeply** speaks of genuine pain. It means to "strike, prick violently, sting sharply, stun." The crowd was stunned! They asked the question that warms the heart of any messenger of the gospel: **"What should we do?"** Peter was ready with the answer.

2:38 In answer to the people's question, Peter presented a fourfold challenge:

1. Turn from your sins—In other words, "repent." It is a basic and wholehearted change of mind that results in a change of purpose, direction,

and values. The words, **each of you,** remind the listener (and modern reader) that this message is for all. Everyone needs to make a decision about Christ. His offer is the only effective solution for the sin problem that plagues every descendant of Adam.

2. Turn to God—In addition to turning from sin, people must turn to God. It does no good to turn from sin without turning then to the one who can solve the sin problem.

3. Be baptized in the name of Jesus Christ for the forgiveness of your sins—For believers, baptism is visible proof of repentance and commitment to follow Jesus, the Messiah. The idea of baptism for the forgiveness of sins does not mean that baptism results in forgiveness of sins but rather that forgiveness of sins as a result of accepting Jesus as Savior should result in a baptism—an outward display of an inner conviction. Repentance, not baptism, is what brings forgiveness.

4. Receive the gift of the Holy Spirit—Only through the coming of the Holy Spirit into believers' hearts can they truly experience forgiveness of sin. The "gift of the Holy Spirit" (not multiple or varied gifts but rather a singular gift) is the Spirit himself. The Holy Spirit is a gift from God. As Jesus had promised, he is the Comforter and the one who guides his people.

2:39-40 The truths presented in the previous verses here find their universal application. This **promise** of the work of the Spirit in the life of the believer has a personal application (**to you**), a generational application (**to your children**), and a global application (**even to the Gentiles**). Luke recorded no more of Peter's words to the gathered crowd except to say that Peter kept talking for a long time, warning and pleading with the people to be saved.

2:41 What a response! **Three thousand** people **believed** and took the step of faith in Christ and were baptized—they took that first step of obedience, publicly identifying themselves with Christ. And they were **added to the church;** that is, they immediately joined the fellowship of believers.

2:42 This first report of the newborn church describes early church worship in the first decade of the church. The three thousand new believers **joined with the other believers.** That is, they gathered with others of like mind and faith. **Devoted themselves** implies that they were regularly, continually persisting in the activities that follow. These activities form a practical map for not only the day-old church but for any church of any age.

The **apostles' teaching** was central to the content of what was to be studied. The apostles, the eyewitnesses of all Jesus had done, would be the ones whom the Holy Spirit would remind of the crucial truths by which the church would be directed for centuries to come (John 14:17, 25-26; 16:13). From the beginning the early church was devoted to hearing, studying, and learning what the apostles had to teach.

The **fellowship (koinonia)** means association and close relationships. This was more than just getting together, certainly more than just a religious meeting. It involved sharing goods, having meals together, and praying together.

Sharing in the Lord's Supper refers to communion services that were celebrated in remembrance of Jesus and patterned after the Last Supper, which Jesus had eaten with his disciples before his death (Matthew 26:26-29). It likely included a regular meal shared together (Acts 2:46; 20:7; 1 Corinthians 10:16; 11:23-25; Jude 1:12).

Prayer is joined with the expression "sharing in the Lord's Supper" to explain the word "fellowship." These are at least two of the activities that were part of their regular meetings. Prayer has always been a mark of the believers' gatherings.

THE BELIEVERS MEET TOGETHER / 2:43-47

Books about church planting, church health, and church growth are popular. Seminars about the church abound, with pastors and church boards eager to copy the techniques of a successful pastor or a fast-growing congregation. The following paragraph is a snapshot of the church a few days old. At Pentecost, after the coming of the Holy Spirit, the gathering of 120 exploded! In one day three thousand people came to faith in Christ. Now what do they do? This handful of verses provides a concise summary of what the early church was about; it provides a model that can be applied to the modern church, as well.

2:43 The word **awe** is the Greek word *phobos*, literally translated "fear." This awe was partly caused

by the **many miraculous signs and wonders** performed by the apostles. The "wonders" *(terata)* were fabulous miracles that evoked awe in those who saw them. The "miraculous signs" *(semeia)* were given to authenticate the message and the messenger, pointing observers toward a divine source of the miracle or a divine truth. Here these signs and wonders authenticated the apostles' message, identifying it as divine truth.

2:44-45 Of the thousands of Jews who had made the pilgrimage to Jerusalem for Pentecost, many may have come as early as Passover (fifty days earlier). Now they were extending their stay in Jerusalem even longer to learn the basics of this newfound Christian faith. Many would likely need financial or physical help from those who lived in Jerusalem to be able to remain this long. When a need arose, believers would sell **their possessions** to help **those in need.** This practice of sharing **everything they had** was likely a response to that specific need.

2:46-47 With these words this marvelous chapter comes to a close. Luke pointed out the everyday nature of the church's meetings. Believers were gathering both **at the Temple** (that is, in large groups, possibly for apostolic teaching) and **in homes** to celebrate the **Lord's Supper** and, presumably, for fellowship, the sharing of needs, and prayer.

A common misconception about the first Christians (who were Jews) was that they rejected the Jewish religion. But these believers saw Jesus' message and resurrection as the fulfillment of everything they knew and believed from the Old Testament. At first the Jewish believers did not separate from the rest of the Jewish community. They still went to the Temple and synagogues for worship and instruction in the Scriptures. But their belief in Jesus created great friction with Jews who didn't believe that Jesus was the Messiah. Thus, believing Jews were forced to meet in private homes for communion, prayer, and teaching about Christ. By the end of the first century, many of these Jewish believers were excommunicated from their synagogues.

We also see here one of the repeated themes of the book of Acts: *joy.* The early church was marked by joy. Two final statements reveal two significant results of the presence of this regularly meeting, money-sharing, miracle-working, Bible-studying, God-praising group:

1. The watching community was favorably impressed (the believers were **enjoying the goodwill of all the people**).
2. The watching community was coming to faith (and each day the Lord added to their group those who were being saved).

These are two measurable results of any church that is living like the early church. Note, too, that the credit for the salvation of souls is not given to Peter's preaching, the apostles' miracles, or the Spirit's manifestations—it was the Lord who was adding to their number daily.

ACTS 3

PETER HEALS A CRIPPLED BEGGAR / 3:1-11
Commissioned by Christ to preach the Good News to all the earth (Matthew 28:18-20), the apostles had his authority. Miracles such as healing the sick (9:34; 19:11-12; 28:8), liberating the demon possessed (5:16; 8:7), even raising the dead (9:36-42; 20:7-12) highlighted their ministries. These supernatural signs authenticated the message being preached and drew people to the Savior. The first eleven verses record a miracle. Peter's ensuing sermon explains the point of the miracle, particularly for the Jewish audience who witnessed it.

3:1 The Jews observed three times of prayer— morning (9:00 A.M.), afternoon (3:00 P.M.), and evening (sunset). At these times devout Jews and Gentiles who believed in God often would go to the Temple to pray. **Peter and John** were going to the **Temple** for the **three o'clock prayer service.** Note that Peter and John were still living, for the most part, as obedient Jews, keeping the appointed times of prayer, though they now had a significantly different mission.

3:2-3 Beggars would often wait in places where they would have the most traffic—such as along the roads near cities or, as here, at the entrance to the Temple. The **Beautiful Gate** was one of the favored entrances into the Temple complex, and many people passed through it on their way to worship. Since giving money to beggars was considered praiseworthy in the Jewish religion, the **lame** man wisely had himself placed where he could catch the almsgivers headed both to and from religious gatherings. As **Peter and John** entered the Temple area, the lame man called out to them and **asked them for some money.**

3:4-6 Peter demanded the man's attention, and the beggar gave it, obviously **expecting a gift.** What was offered, however, was not **money,** but rather something far more valuable. Peter commanded the beggar to **get up and walk.** Note that the command was not by Peter's authority but rather **in the name of Jesus Christ of Nazareth,** calling on Christ's power and authority. The apostles were doing this healing through the Holy Spirit's power given to them by Christ, not their own (see Luke 10:17).

3:7-8 To encourage the lame man to begin walking, Peter reached for him to help him up. The terms that follow here reflect Luke's medical orientation—**the man's feet and anklebones,** which to this point had never been able to support the man, **were healed and strengthened.** Not only could he

stand, but he also immediately tried out his new legs at full throttle, moving quickly from standing, to beginning to walk, to ultimately **leaping.** In the midst of his excitement and this obviously emotional moment, he praised God, who had given him a new lease on life.

3:9-10 This must have been some scene. The beggar, known for years for his crippled condition danced into the Temple area with words of praise to God. There could be no doubt about who he was or about what had happened. Nor could there be any doubt about whom the beggar thought should get the credit for the miracle. The people, quite appropriately, **were absolutely astounded.**

3:11 The scene broadened as the beggar, almost like a young child, was pictured clinging to Peter and John. Even more people came running **to Solomon's Colonnade,** a covered porch or entrance with columns that stood just east of the outer court of the Temple. The reference to this site would remind the Jews of the golden days of Israel's history, making the healing here all the more poignant.

For the Jewish observers and readers, the sign here was too spectacular to overlook. Isaiah had written of such a time: "The lame will leap like a deer, and those who cannot speak will shout and sing!" (Isaiah 35:6).

PETER PREACHES IN THE TEMPLE / 3:12-26

A good sermon introduction is supposed to capture attention, raise a need, and orient listeners to the subject at hand. Peter and John's healing of the lame man in the Temple courts did all those in a powerful way. It drew a huge crowd of awed spectators. It prompted these onlookers to want to know how such a miracle was possible. It gave the apostles an open door to declare plainly that Jesus, crucified and resurrected, was the long-awaited Messiah who fulfilled all the predictions of the prophets.

3:12-13 Peter took advantage of a gathered, attentive crowd, and he addressed them by making it clear that this miracle was not the product of his personal **power** or **godliness.** Rather, this miracle had been performed by God himself, for a very explicit purpose. Peter wanted to make it clear to this Jewish crowd that this miracle was the handiwork of the very God they claimed to follow, **the God of Abraham, the God of Isaac, the God of Jacob, the God of all our ancestors.** The miracle also had purpose: to bring **glory to his servant Jesus.** God the Father was exalting the Son through this miracle. The term "servant" called to mind the Servant of Yahweh in Isaiah 42:1; 49:6-7; 52:13; 53:11. Peter wanted Jesus identified with the Servant-Messiah of the Old Testament. Then, as his

audience was thinking about this connection, he pressed home the brutal truth—Peter told them point-blank that they were responsible for Jesus' death.

The Roman leader, **Pilate,** had decided to **release** Jesus, but the Jews had **rejected** Pilate's offer and had clamored to have Barabbas, a murderer, released instead (see Luke 23:13-25). When Peter said, **Jesus whom you handed over,** he meant it literally. Jesus' trial and death had occurred right there in Jerusalem only weeks earlier. All Jews were there (and thus guilty) through their representative leadership.

3:14-15 Note the number of times in the balance of the sermon Peter used the words "you" or "your." This was a pointed condemnation of those who stood before him: **You** handed over. . . . **You** rejected. . . . **You** killed. Peter called Jesus the **holy** and **righteous** one. This clearly identified Jesus' equality with God. But the Jews had **rejected** him. The horrendous nature of their deed was made all the worse by the contrasting character of the **murderer** (Barabbas) whose release they had **demanded.** Not only had the Jews rejected him, but they had **killed** him. With a ring of irony, Peter stated that they had killed **the author of life,** the one who had written the book on life, the Creator (John 1:1-4; Colossians 1:16).

The sense of outrage here is heightened by the use of three strong contrasts in three straight verses: (1) 3:13—the Jews had delivered Jesus to be killed, though Pilate had decided to free him; (2) 3:14—they had rejected Jesus, and requested the release of a murderer; (3) 3:15—they had killed Jesus, though God raised him from the dead. The one the Jews had killed was presently alive, raised by God himself! Peter and hundreds of others were witnesses of that (see 1 Corinthians 15:5-8).

3:16 Peter referred to the miracle that had gotten everyone's attention. As before, he took no credit for himself or his companions but, instead, credited the **name of Jesus** with the healing. As in his earlier use of the "name," Peter was referring to the full identity of Jesus. Jesus was the Healer.

3:17-18 The concluding ten verses record Peter's plea to his audience to make a change. He acknowledged that their actions were done **in ignorance,** as were the actions of their **leaders** (see also 17:30; Ephesians 4:18; 1 Peter 1:14).

That **God was fulfilling what all the prophets had declared** probably refers to such prophecies as Psalm 22, Isaiah 50:6, and Isaiah 53:1-12. The Jews had not expected a suffering Messiah; instead, they had anticipated a great ruler, a conquering king. When he arrived as a lowly carpenter and then died a criminal's death, they missed it. But Peter explained that it wasn't too late. They may have acted in ignorance, but now they could understand that Jesus was exactly what **the Messiah** had been prophesied to be.

3:19 They had rejected, despised, and killed Jesus, but they could still **turn** from their sins, **turn to God,** and **be cleansed.** They could change their minds about Jesus. The words "turn from your sins" are the standard Greek term (*metanoeo*) for repentance. The verb means to turn away from a former way of life and toward a new way of life. The term "cleansed" (*exaleiphthenai*) is often used in Greek as a figure of speech, meaning to erase, especially of writing.

3:20-21 The "turning" of 3:19 promises two results: (1) the coming of **wonderful times of refreshment,** and (2) the return of **Jesus your Messiah to you again.** In other words, the repentance of Peter's audience would have a part in bringing in the marvelous events of the end times. This **final restoration** likely refers to the final era of salvation—the Second Coming, the promised coming Kingdom of God, the Last Judgment, and the removal of sin from the world.

3:22-23 This quote from Moses in Deuteronomy 18:15 refers to Christ. The Messiah would come with deliverance, just as Moses had. Most Jews thought that Joshua was this prophet predicted by Moses. Peter explained that the **Prophet** who would be **from among** the Jews was Jesus Christ. Jesus had fulfilled this prophecy, for he was their long-awaited Messiah! Moses had warned the people that they should **listen carefully to everything** he would tell them. Those who refused to listen would be **cut off** from the true people of God—the believers.

3:24 The prophet **Samuel** lived during the transition between the judges and the kings of Israel, and he was the first in a succession of prophets. Samuel had anointed David as king and had spoken clearly of the establishment of David's kingdom (1 Samuel 13:14; 15:28; 16:13; 28:17; see also 2 Samuel 7:12-16). Peter wanted his audience to come to understand that from the inception of the prophetic office—down through the whole order of the prophets—**every prophet** had spoken of what was **happening** right then.

3:25 The Jews to whom Peter was speaking were **the children of those prophets.** God had promised **Abraham** that he would bless the world through Abraham's descendants, the Jewish race (Genesis 12:3), from which the Messiah would come. They were **included in the covenant,** for God intended the Jewish nation to be a separate and holy nation that would teach the world about God, introduce the Messiah, and then carry on his work in the world. Through them, because of the Messiah coming from them, **all the families on earth** would be **blessed.** Israel had been given the promise of one who would come from the line of Abraham and sit forever on David's throne.

3:26 The message of salvation came first to the **people of Israel,** the descendants of Abraham, Moses, Samuel, and the prophets. They—of all people—should have known the prophecies and recognized him when he came. They were to have been the prime beneficiaries of the blessings of the covenant.

Notice that the primary nature of the blessing was to turn them **back from** their **sinful ways.** Christ's work, at its core, is to turn lives around, taking individuals on sinful paths and turning them from those paths to the path of blessing. Israel had every reason to turn to Jesus—history, heritage, bloodline, centuries of warning from prophetic messengers. And they had not recognized him.

ACTS 4

PETER AND JOHN BEFORE THE COUNCIL / 4:1-22

Evidently a large crowd had gathered at Solomon's Colonnade (3:11) where Peter began to preach. While Acts is a record of powerful sermons, astounding miracles, and the rapid spread of the Christian church throughout the world, it is also a reminder of the truth of spiritual warfare. Whenever believers are seeking to impact their culture, whenever the gospel is preached in power, wherever the church is growing and making inroads, the enemy stirs up fierce opposition.

4:1 This crowd in the Temple drew the attention of the religious leaders, who **came over** to see what was going on. The **leading priests** were mostly **Sadducees.** The Sadducees were members of a small but powerful Jewish religious sect that did not believe in the resurrection of the dead. They were the religious leaders who stressed cooperation with the Roman Empire. They also rejected the idea of a coming Messiah, believing that he was an ideal, not a person who would intervene in history.

The **captain of the Temple guard** was also a high-ranking Sadducee. He was the leader of the guards who ensured order in and around the Temple. The captain was considered second in authority only to the high priest himself. The Temple guard had arrested Jesus in the Garden of Gethsemane (see Luke 22:52-54).

4:2 Imagine these Sadducees, who did not believe in the resurrection of the dead, listening to Peter **claiming,** right there in the Temple, the **resurrection of the dead.** No wonder **they were very disturbed.** Peter and John were refuting one of the Sadducees' fundamental beliefs and thus threatening their authority as religious teachers. The religious leaders had thought this uprising would be finished with the death of its leader, so it disturbed them to find Jesus' followers teaching the people in the Temple.

4:3 Even though Israel was under Roman rule, the Sadducees had almost unlimited power over the Temple grounds. Thus, they were able to arrest Peter and John for no reason other than teaching something that contradicted their beliefs.

Assuming that the healing of the crippled man occurred as Peter and John made their way to the 3:00 P.M. prayer time (3:1) and that Peter's sermon to the gathered masses followed this miracle, it would have been too late in the day (**already evening**) to gather the necessary religious leaders to hold an official inquiry.

4:4 The Jewish religious leaders were able to arrest (at least for one night) Christ's messengers; they could not, however, stop the spread of Christ's message. The miraculous healing of the crippled man in such a visible place, combined with the powerful preaching of the apostles, sent spiritual shock waves through Jerusalem. This brought the total number of believers to **about five thousand men, not counting women and children.** God was mightily using Peter, for at his first sermon, three thousand people had become believers (2:41)! Estimates of Jerusalem's population at this time range from twenty-five thousand to eighty-five thousand. Josephus recorded that there were a total of six thousand Pharisees in Palestine. Thus, a total of five thousand Jewish Christian men (not counting women and children) was a very high percentage of the population!

4:5 The **rulers, elders,** and **teachers of religious law** made up the Jewish **council**—the same council that had condemned Jesus to death (Luke 22:66). This council acted as the ruling government of Israel. They handled the local problems and religious questions but had to work under Rome's supervision. For crimes that carried capital punishment, they had to obtain Rome's approval. For instance, the council had condemned Jesus to death, but it could not carry out the sentence; the Roman leader in the area alone had the authority to order an execution. That is why the religious leaders had taken Jesus to Pilate, the Roman leader in the Jerusalem area (Luke 23:1).

The council had seventy members plus the current high priest, who presided over the group. The Sadducees held a majority in this ruling group. These were the wealthy, intellectual, and powerful men of Jerusalem. Jesus' followers stood before this council, just as he had.

4:6 **Annas** had been deposed as high priest by the Romans, who then had appointed **Caiaphas,** Annas's son-in-law, in his place. But because the Jews considered the office of high priest a lifetime position, they still called Annas by that title and gave him respect and authority within the council. **John, Alexander, and other relatives of the high priest** were also there, supporting the power base of the high priest's office. Annas and Caiaphas had played significant roles in Jesus' trial (John 18:24, 28). It did not please them that the man whom they thought they had sacrificed for the good of the nation (John 11:49-51) had followers who were just as persistent and who promised to be just as troublesome as he had been.

4:7 The council asked Peter and John **by what power, or in whose name,** they had healed the man (see 3:6-7). "In whose name" refers to exorcism practices. They wanted to know what formula Peter and John had used. Their concern was more about the apostles' teaching, but they began their questioning with the miracle, for the healed man was there as well (4:14). The actions and words of Peter and John threatened these religious leaders who, for the most part, were more interested in their reputations and positions than in the glory of God.

4:8-10 Peter, the rough ex-fisherman, stood before a room of disapproving, scowling faces and, **filled with the Holy Spirit,** began to speak. There are two kinds of courage: reckless courage that is unaware of the dangers it faces, and the courage that knows the peril and yet is undaunted. Peter's boldness is of the latter variety as he **clearly** stated in whose name they had healed and how they could do so.

4:11 Peter quoted a familiar Old Testament passage—Psalm 118:22—and gave it new meaning. Most Jews regarded their nation, Israel, as the stone chosen by God but rejected by the nations. Jesus had referred to himself as the **stone** that the builders **rejected.** The cornerstone was the most important stone in a building, used as the standard to

make sure that the other stones of the building were straight and level. Israel's leadership, like the builders looking for an appropriate cornerstone, would toss Jesus aside because he didn't seem to have the right qualifications. They wanted a political king, not a spiritual one. Peter made it clear that **you builders** were the Jewish religious leaders.

Yet God's plans will not be thwarted. One day the rejected stone will **become the cornerstone,** for Jesus will come as King to inaugurate an unending Kingdom. He already had begun a spiritual Kingdom as the cornerstone of a brand-new "building," the Christian church (see also 1 Peter 2:7). Jesus' life, teachings, death, and resurrection would be the church's foundation.

4:12 The resurrected Jesus had healed the crippled man physically. That same Jesus, the long-awaited Messiah, can heal all people spiritually. Salvation does not come from being a descendant of Abraham (Luke 3:8) or by following the law of Moses (John 6:32-33). The clear gospel teaching is that **there is salvation in no one else** but Jesus (John 14:6; 1 Timothy 2:5).

4:13 **Peter and John,** fishermen by trade, had never received formal theological or rhetorical training in the rabbinical schools; they were **ordinary men who had had no special training.** Yet they were bold, composed, confident, and undaunted in their defense. As the apostles stood there with the healed cripple, speaking with authority, the members of the council **recognized them as men who had been with Jesus.** Their boldness was possible only because they were filled with the Holy Spirit (4:8; cf. 4:29, 31; 9:27-28; 13:46; 14:3; 18:26; 19:8; 26:26; 28:31).

4:14-15 In the same way that the words and works of Jesus had often left the Jewish leaders speechless (Mark 12:34), the council had **nothing to say** in the face of this supernatural healing and preaching. The **council chamber** was cleared so that the leaders could decide on a course of action. How Luke knew what went on in this closed discussion has been debated. Possibly a sympathizer among the council "leaked" the information. Perhaps Gamaliel, a member of the council, told his student Paul, who later told Luke (5:34; 22:3).

4:16-17 The council was in a quandary. The apostles had performed an undeniable, widely publicized **miraculous sign.** The masses were gravitating toward this new sect. How could the religious leaders save face (in light of the obviously healed man), discourage further teaching and healing in the name of Jesus, and preserve the status quo? Their solution was to order the apostles **not to**

speak to anyone in Jesus' name again. It seems as though they thought that their power and position could convince these men to be silent.

4:18 Because Peter and John had not broken any laws and were enjoying popular support among the people, the Jewish council's best attempt at damage control was to summon the apostles and try to scare them into silence with vague warnings. They were **told never again to speak or teach about Jesus.** Jewish law specified that at the first instance of wrong or illegal action, the guilty were to be warned and released. The second time they did wrong, they were to be beaten with rods (5:28, 40). With this official order, the council would have legal grounds to impose more punishment in the future should the apostles choose to disobey.

4:19-20 Commanded by Christ to be witnesses (1:8) and utterly convinced of the truth of the gospel, **Peter and John** announced their rejection of any such ban on speaking in the name of Jesus. In effect, the apostles' response accused the council of being at odds with the will of God. The apostles already knew the answer, so they asked the council members to judge for themselves whether they should obey the council's orders or God's. This principle of obeying God rather than people is a major Christian ethical principle (see commentary at 5:29).

These men had indeed "been with Jesus" (4:13), and he had completely transformed their lives. They had lived with him; they had witnessed his resurrection; they had experienced the filling of the Holy Spirit. And so they said, **"We cannot stop telling about the wonderful things we have seen and heard."** To have obeyed the council's command would have been to disobey God.

4:21-22 Stunned by the courage of Peter and John and fearful of their popularity among the masses, the religious leaders could do nothing more than threaten them and **let them go.** One would think that these leaders would be thrilled that the people were **praising God.** But that was not the case. Luke's comment heightens the significance of the miracle—the man had been healed of a forty-year condition.

THE BELIEVERS PRAY FOR COURAGE / 4:23-31

After being sternly threatened by the same group of men who had orchestrated the crucifixion of Jesus only six weeks earlier, the followers of Jesus gathered and prayed. Their prayers weren't for an end to persecution or for easy times. Rather, the believers asked God for the boldness necessary to continue proclaiming the good news about Jesus. God gave them what every church needs: a reminder of his power and a fresh outpouring of the Holy Spirit.

4:23-24 Upon their release, the apostles **found the other believers** and shared with them the details of their experience. In the face of this recent persecution, the believers spontaneously joined **in prayer** to acknowledge God's sovereign control (see Psalm 146:6; Isaiah 37:16). This appeal to the God of creation shows that God, who had power to create the universe, will have power over their enemies. Everything in heaven and earth is subject to God and his will.

4:25-26 The group's prayer cited Psalm 2, a messianic hymn written by King David. Psalm 2 describes the rebellion of the nations and the coming of Christ to establish his eternal reign. David may have written these words during a conspiracy against Israel by leaders of some of the surrounding nations. Chosen and anointed by God, David knew that God would fulfill his promise to bring the Messiah into the world through his bloodline (2 Samuel 7:16; 1 Chronicles 17:11-12). This psalm is also cited in other places in the New Testament (see 13:33; Hebrews 1:5-6; 5:5; Revelation 2:26-27; 12:5; 19:15) because of its prophetic description of Jesus, the Messiah. The believers saw the Jewish leaders' opposition to Jesus (and to them, his appointed representatives) as fulfilling this ancient prophecy.

4:27 In fulfillment of the prophecy in Psalm 2, **kings** and **rulers** had gathered against the **Messiah. Herod Antipas** ruled over the territory of Galilee. **Pontius Pilate** was the Roman **governor** over Judea who had bowed to pressure from the mob of **Gentiles and the people of Israel** in Jerusalem. All of these had conspired against Jesus, God's **anointed.**

4:28 While it seemed that Satan had gotten the upper hand when the Son of God was crucified on the cross, in reality **everything occurred according to God's eternal will and plan.** The believers declared that God is the sovereign Lord of all events; he rules history to fulfill his purpose. What his will determines, his power carries out. No army, government, or council can stand in God's way.

4:29-30 The apostles prayed not for divine vengeance but that God would **hear** the **threats** that had been leveled against them. The believers did not pray that God would remove the threats, take away the possibility of persecution, or even protect them. Instead, they prayed that God would **give** the believers, his **servants, great boldness in their preaching.** They also asked for displays of power to confirm their message.

These believers were not afraid to ask God for great power and wonders in order that his name would be glorified.

4:31 God's answer of the apostles' prayer was both swift and powerful. When the **building shook,** the believers realized that God had not only heard their prayer, but he also was pleased with it. The believers received a fresh filling **with the Holy Spirit,** which renewed their courage to go out and preach **God's message with boldness,** just as they had requested (4:29).

THE BELIEVERS SHARE THEIR POSSESSIONS / 4:32-37

The final verses of chapter 4 provide a glimpse into the inner workings of the early church. The first-century Christians enjoyed a sense of closeness and unity that caused the world to sit up and take notice. It's one thing to talk of loving others; it's quite another to sell one's valuable possessions and give the proceeds to those less fortunate. Yet that kind of generosity was common in the early church. And that kind of selflessness is the essence of true fellowship.

4:32 In summarizing the daily activities of the early church, Luke noted the believers' unselfishness. Surely the church's spiritual unity (**all the believers were of one heart and mind**) prompted this material generosity. No one was required to contribute to the needs of others; this "communal purse" was voluntary. Yet the believers willingly **shared everything they had,** not holding tightly to possessions.

Differences of opinion are inevitable among human personalities and can actually be helpful if handled well. But spiritual unity is essential— loyalty, commitment, and love for God and his word. Without spiritual unity, the church could not survive. The early church was able to share possessions and property as a result of the unity brought by the Holy Spirit working in and through the believers' lives. This way of living is different from communism because the sharing was voluntary, didn't involve all private property but only as much as was needed, and was not a membership requirement in order to be a part of the church. The spiritual unity and generosity of these early believers attracted others to them. This organizational structure is not a biblical command, but it offers vital principles for us to follow.

4:33 Ignoring the threats of the council (4:18), the apostles **gave powerful witness.** God worked powerfully among them (see 6:8) to empower their witness and to meet their material needs. Jesus had told his disciples, "Your love for one another will prove to the world that you are my disciples" (John 13:35). As the outside world saw the believers' generosity with one another, their care for the needy, and their powerful witness, they were drawn to the Lord Jesus.

4:34-35 So widespread was the generosity of the Jerusalem believers that **there was no poverty among them.** Lavish gifts from the sale of land or houses were brought to the apostles for distribution **to others in need.** Such gifts were exceptional expressions of social concern for those in need. These good times, however, would not last. A famine (see the prophecy of Agabus in 11:28) would eventually result in the Jerusalem church becoming dependent on the gifts of believers in Asia (see Romans 15:25-28; Galatians 2:10).

4:36-37 Barnabas (Joseph) is introduced here because he gave money from the sale of **a field** to the apostles to give to those in need. Barnabas would prove to be a respected and important leader in the life of the early church. He was a Levite by birth (a member of the Jewish tribe that carried out Temple duties) but a resident of **Cyprus.** This may explain why he was a landowner (Levites were forbidden to own land in Israel—see Numbers 18:20-24 and Deuteronomy 10:9; 18:1-2). Barnabas would later travel with Paul on Paul's first missionary journey (13:4). John Mark (author of the Gospel of Mark) was his cousin. "Barnabas" means **Son of Encouragement,** and it would prove, over and over, to be most appropriate.

ACTS 5

ANANIAS AND SAPPHIRA / 5:1-11

Acts 5:1–8:3 tells of internal and external problems facing the early church. Inside, there were dishonesty (5:1-11) and administrative headaches (6:1-7); outside, the church was being pressured by persecution. Ananias and Sapphira, a married couple in the Jerusalem church, concocted a plan whereby they hoped to give a little to God but get credit for a lot. Their scheme was dishonest, and God's judgment was swift and severe. As you ponder their story, ask yourself the question, What are my motives for serving and giving?

5:1-2 The word **also** ties back to 4:36-37, where Barnabas was introduced as a man who had generously given to those in need. At the inception of the church, the practice of selling one's possessions in order to give money to those in need showed the believers' willingness to help other believers. Not everyone was liquidating everything, nor was there pressure to do so (Mary, John's mother, still owned her home—12:12). This was a freewill offering, and it appears to have been practiced only here in the early Palestine church.

It seems that the positive response of the church to gifts from people like Barnabas became a source of envy for **Ananias** and **Sapphira**. They also **sold some property.** They could have given any amount of the selling price, but because they apparently desired the esteem that Barnabas had received, they pretended to give **the full amount** they had received for the field. Instead, however, they kept back **part of the money.**

5:3-4 Given insight by the Holy Spirit, **Peter** saw through Ananias's lie. Apparently involved in the new church, Ananias and Sapphira had succumbed to temptation and allowed **Satan** into their hearts. Their sin was lying to God and God's people— saying they gave the whole amount but holding back some for themselves and trying to make themselves appear more generous than they really were. This act was judged severely because dishonesty, greed, and covetousness are destructive in a church. All lying is bad, but when people lie to try to deceive God and other believers about their relationship with him, they destroy their testimony.

5:5-6 When **Ananias** realized that Peter knew all about his scheme, **he fell to the floor and died.** The Greek word *ekpsucho* literally means "to breathe one's last, to die" and usually connotes

death by divine judgment (see 5:10; 12:23; 1 Corinthians 10:6; 1 John 5:16). Peter didn't kill Ananias, nor did he ask the Holy Spirit to kill him. Peter condemned the lying, and the Spirit of God executed judgment.

5:7-8 Sapphira showed up **about three hours later.** She didn't know **what had happened** to her husband. Peter's questions to Sapphira exposed her complicity in the deed. Peter gave her the opportunity to tell the truth, but she told the same lie that her husband had told. In so doing she revealed a hardness of heart that had not been touched by the grace of God.

5:9 To test God is to see how much one can get away with before God will respond or act according to his word (see Exodus 17:2; Deuteronomy 6:16; Matthew 4:7; Luke 4:12 for further passages on testing God). The entire direction of this lie by Ananias and Sapphira was wrongheaded, self-serving, church-destroying, and sinful. Ananias and Sapphira had conspired together to mock God, to lie and think they could get away with it as if God would not know. They had tried to **test the Spirit of the Lord,** referring to the Holy Spirit in the body of believers—specifically the apostles before whom this lie was told (John 16:8).

5:10 Like her husband, Sapphira **fell to the floor and died.** As she and Ananias had been joined in their "testing" of God (5:9), so they were joined in death. This is more than just a historical record of events in the early church. This serves as a warning that no one should trifle with the Holy Spirit or take lightly the importance of telling the truth.

5:11 This is the first appearance of the term **church** (*ekklesia*, meaning "assembly") in the book of Acts. It will become the regular word for the universal church and the local church in the remainder of the book (7:38; 8:1; 9:31; 11:22; 13:1; 14:23; 15:22, 41; 16:5; 20:28). God's judgment on

Ananias and Sapphira produced **great fear** among the believers, making them realize how seriously God regards sin in the church.

THE APOSTLES HEAL MANY / 5:12-16

Even as word spread of the sudden deaths of Ananias and Sapphira, the apostles continued to preach boldly about Jesus right in the Temple courts. Large crowds continued to gather. Miraculous healings and exorcisms gave credence to the message. Because of the power of God and the faithfulness of his people, the gospel was spreading, taking root, and bearing fruit in lives.

5:12 Solomon's Colonnade was part of the **Temple** complex built by King Herod the Great in an attempt to strengthen his relationship with the Jews. A colonnade is an entrance or porch supported by columns. Jesus taught and performed miracles in the Temple many times. When the believers met **regularly at the Temple,** they were undoubtedly in close proximity to the same religious leaders who had conspired to put Jesus to death. God granted the apostles power to perform **miraculous signs and wonders.** The miracles were from God, but administered through the hands of the **apostles.** These healings were not random acts of kindness by a benevolent God, but rather sign-miracles intended to convince Jewish onlookers of the credibility of the Christian message and movement.

5:13-14 Although many people **had high regard for** the apostles and the other believers, few "outsiders" **dared to join them** in the Temple or in their faith. The watching community respected these believers (2:47) but likely found God's direct

and obvious work through them to be intimidating. Some may have been afraid to face the same kind of persecution the apostles had just faced (4:17), while others may have feared a fate similar to the one that fell on Ananias and Sapphira. In what seems like a contradiction, Luke added that **more and more people believed and were brought to the Lord.** Genuine seekers were still coming to faith in Christ. The thousands who joined the first day (2:41) were daily joined by more (see 2:47; 4:4; 6:1, 7; 9:31).

5:15-16 The word was beginning to spread beyond Jerusalem, drawing people **from the villages around Jerusalem.** In the same way that healing had "flowed" from Christ during his ministry on earth (see Mark 5:25-34), here it was Peter whose **shadow** simply had to **fall across** the **sick and those possessed by evil spirits,** and they would be **healed.** These miraculous signs confirmed the validity of the apostles' witness and connected their work to Christ's healing ministry (see Luke 4:33-37; 8:26-39).

THE APOSTLES MEET OPPOSITION / 5:17-42

Smarting from the apostles' refusal to heed their threats, and in light of the growing popularity of the Christian movement, the Jewish authorities clamped down. They arrested and jailed Peter and his colleagues. When God miraculously freed his spokesmen in the night, the apostles went straight back to the Temple and resumed their preaching!

5:17-18 The religious leaders did not listen and learn the gospel message that focused on their own Messiah; instead, they reacted to the apostles with **violent jealousy.** Peter and the apostles were already commanding more respect than the religious leaders had ever received. In addition, the apostles could do the most amazing miracles, a power the **high priest** and his fellow **Sadducees** lacked. (For more on the Sadducees, see commentary on 4:1.) This event was occurring only weeks after Jesus' trial and crucifixion, so the high priest

would still have been Caiaphas, who had condemned Jesus to death, and the other men on the council (Sadducees and Pharisees) would also be the same. It was the jealousy of the Sadducees that drove the events of this chapter, the first being that the leaders **arrested the apostles and put them in the jail.**

5:19-21 The jealous religious leaders thought they could silence the apostles by throwing them into jail. But God would not allow his servants to be silenced. In a startling moment, **an angel of the Lord came at night, opened the gates of the jail, and brought them out.** The **angel of the Lord** refers to God's presence (see also 8:26; 12:7, 23; Matthew 1:20, 24; 2:13, 19; 28:2; Luke 1:11; 2:9). What made this incident even more remarkable was that the Sadducees, who had sent the apostles to jail (5:18), did not believe in angels!

The angel of the Lord gave the apostles the necessary encouragement to continue in their task despite this latest opposition. The angel's charge to the apostles was to go back out to the **Temple** and keep preaching. Without a moment's hesitation, the **apostles** did just exactly as commanded by the angel of the Lord. The **Temple** at **daybreak** was a busy place. Many people stopped there to pray and worship at sunrise. The apostles were already there, ready to tell them the Good News.

The scene that follows with the **high council** is filled with irony. The **high priest, his officials,** and **all the elders of Israel** must have prepared for this meeting, during which they would reprimand their prisoners. **They sent for the apostles to be brought for trial.** But the council would be surprised.

5:22-24 The prisoners were being called for trial, so **the Temple guards went to the jail** to get them. However, they returned rather dumbfounded, reporting that the door of the cell **was locked,** the **guards** were faithfully **standing outside** at their posts, and when they opened the cell door, **no one was there!** So complete was the miracle that no one could deny that God's power was behind it. Yet these leaders were **perplexed** about how these men had escaped from a locked cell.

5:25-26 In the middle of their deliberations, the leaders received a report that the escaped prisoners were right back where they were first arrested, doing the very thing for which they had been arrested! So the officers arrested them again, **but without violence, for they were afraid the people would kill them.** They did not want a riot to break out. The same concern had been expressed with respect to arresting Jesus (Matthew 21:46).

5:27-28 The **apostles** went peaceably with the Temple guard to appear **before the council.** In Caiaphas's remarks, note that he would not even mention the name of the one in whose authority the apostles were teaching; instead, he reminded them that they had been ordered **never again to teach in this man's name.** He was also angry that the apostles blamed the religious leaders for Jesus' death. The Jewish leaders wanted the apostles to stop teaching in Christ's name and to stop accusing them of culpability in Christ's death. Both prob-

lems would surface again quite clearly in the words of Peter, recorded in the next four verses.

5:29 With this comment Peter stated the primary necessity of obeying God first and foremost. These words are almost identical to his earlier ones in 4:19-20. The New Testament makes it clear that believers are to obey governmental authority (Romans 13:1-7 and 1 Peter 2:13-17), but not when the authority requires believers to sin. It would have been sinful for these apostles to obey the leaders' mandate not to speak when they had been clearly commanded by God himself to speak (5:20). God is the highest authority and rules in the highest court anywhere. Our first obedience is always to him. In that case, they had to **obey God rather than human authority.**

5:30 When Peter, the Galilean fisherman turned preacher, spoke to this group of religious leaders, he identified their common heritage with the phrase **the God of our ancestors.** These words tied the miracles these leaders had been hearing about to the Old Testament miracles, with which they were thoroughly familiar. The God who had parted the Red Sea and had led the Israelites to the Promised Land had also **raised Jesus from the dead.** Peter repeated his accusation, **you killed him by crucifying him.** Jesus, whose name the high priest would not even speak (5:27-28), had been killed by the Jewish leaders, but he had been raised from the dead by God himself.

5:31 Not only had God raised Jesus, he also had **exalted him to his own right hand,** the place of highest honor and authority. Through his death, Christ had given **the people of Israel an opportunity to turn from their sins and turn to God.** With these words Peter was offering salvation to the very people who had crucified the Savior. They, along with all the rest of Israel, could find forgiveness through the crucified and risen Christ.

5:32 Standing before the council, the apostles explained that they had been **witnesses of these things.** They had seen the risen Christ, and they had seen the exalted Christ as he had been taken into heaven. Peter's inclusion of the **Holy Spirit** as part of the witness points back to the Spirit's coming in power on the day of Pentecost, an event with which the present audience would have been familiar. Peter wanted them to know that this same Holy Spirit was still at work among them because the Spirit was being **given by God to those who obey him.** This gift of the Holy Spirit, given to those who accept Christ as their Savior, was described by Paul as "God's guarantee that he will give us everything he promised and that he has purchased us to be his own people" (Ephesians 1:14).

5:33-34 The high council listened to the apostles' words and became so **furious that they decided to kill them.** Except for one lone and wise voice from an unlikely source, this council surely would have gotten rid of these followers just as they had gotten rid of their leader. The previous night God had used supernatural means to free the apostles from jail; here he used a less "flashy" but just as miraculous means—a **Pharisee** defending the church! The Pharisees were the other major party in the high council with the Sadducees. They were the strict keepers of the law—not only God's law but hundreds of other rules they had added to God's law. They were careful about outward purity, but many had hearts full of impure motives.

Gamaliel was an unexpected ally for the apostles, although he probably did not support their teachings. He was a distinguished member of the council. He **stood up** to speak to the assembly, but first he ordered that the apostles be taken **outside** so the situation could be discussed.

5:35-37 Gamaliel's point was that revolutions come and revolutions go. It would not be wise to get embroiled in this one too deeply, for if it was like the others, it would disappear of its own accord. There is controversy over Gamaliel's references to **Theudas** and **Judas of Galilee** regarding the historical data. Josephus, the Jewish historian, mentions a "Theudos" who persuaded many to take their possessions and move with him to the Jordan River area. He posed as a second Moses who promised to lead the Jews out of Roman oppression. He was unsuccessful. The revolt to which Josephus alluded, however, was likely larger and later than the one mentioned by Gamaliel. Judas the Galilean likely had led a religious and nationalist revolt against Caesar that had been crushed by Rome. Some think his movement was continued by other insurrectionists. The Zealots were an active group at this time but did not come into full, organized force until 60–70 A.D. In both cases, when the leader was **killed**, his followers disbanded. If this "Christ-movement" were like these others, with Jesus dead and gone (so they thought), his followers would soon disperse and disappear.

5:38-39 Gamaliel offered sound **advice.** With the leader gone, this new movement would **be overthrown** if the apostles were acting **merely on their own.** If, however, this movement truly was **of God,** then even these religious leaders would

be unwise to fight against it, because not only would they **not be able to stop them** (the apostles), but they would end up **fighting against God.** Gamaliel's logic prevailed. He spoke these words probably not because he was a church sympathizer nor a secret follower of Christ but rather because he had confidence in the sovereign operation of God in the affairs of people.

5:40 The council accepted Gamaliel's sound **advice** and decided not to put the apostles to death (5:33). But they were not going to let the apostles off easily. The council **had them flogged.** In a flogging, leather thongs made into whips were beaten against the bared upper body of the bound prisoner. The prisoner would be made to kneel, then the triple-strap whip would be beaten across both chest and back, with two beatings on the back for every one on the chest. This punishment would be given to people judged guilty of crimes (Deuteronomy 25:2-3). This flogging fulfilled Jesus' words to his followers in Mark 13:9. Once again, the leaders gave the foolish order, which likely none of them even believed would be carried out, that the apostles **never again speak in the name of Jesus** (see 4:18).

At least one of Luke's purposes for including this incident was to inform readers of the sad but consistent path the Jewish leadership had taken (and the nation with them) in the total rejection of Jesus as Messiah. Much more is included in the chapters that follow.

5:41 These apostles had endured tremendous pain, yet they left the council, **rejoicing that God had counted them worthy to suffer dishonor for the name of Jesus**—the name that the high priest would not even say (5:28), the name in which they had been forbidden to speak (5:40). Notice the attitude of the early church toward difficulty: they were imprisoned, threatened, beaten. Their response was to rejoice—not because they had all these bad things happen but because they had been "counted worthy" of disgrace from their association with Christ.

5:42 Instead of making the apostles fearful, the suffering they had endured at the hands of the Jewish leaders only made them more courageous. **Every day, in the Temple and in their homes, they continued to teach and preach.** These apostles wanted everyone to know that Jesus was the fulfillment of all the Old Testament prophecies—he was the promised **Messiah!** The threat of prison, beatings, and even death would not deter this group of witnesses from their appointed task. The heat was on, but it was only spreading the fire!

ACTS 6

SEVEN MEN CHOSEN TO SERVE / 6:1-7

From arrests at the hands of the Jews to the attempted deception within the congregation, the early days of the church seemed difficult. Yet the growth was phenomenal! Chapter 6 returns to an internal problem—some apparent discrepancies in the distribution of goods to the needy widows in the congregation. The result: complaints from those who thought they were being discriminated against and a rising tide of anger. It was a potential disaster. But the Spirit-filled apostles wisely solved the young church's problem.

6:1-2 The number of believers in Jerusalem made it necessary to organize the sharing of resources. People were being overlooked, and some were complaining. The believers **who spoke Hebrew** were the native Jewish Christians, "locals" who spoke Aramaic, a Semitic language. The believers **who spoke Greek** were the Grecian Jews from other lands who had been converted at Pentecost. They could not speak Aramaic, the native tongue of the Jews living in Israel. They were probably at least bilingual, speaking their native tongue and Greek but not Aramaic. There had developed a class distinction between the two groups, similar to racism. Though all were Christians, their backgrounds and outlooks were different.

The Greek-speaking Christians **complained that their widows were being discriminated against in the daily distribution of food.** There were many more widows than usual since many of the widows who came from other Greek-speaking countries had returned to Jerusalem to live out their years and be buried with their ancestors. Their money may have run out, and they needed help. Widows in general needed help since property was passed on from father to son, and the son was responsible to care for the mother. She had no wealth of her own. This "discrimination" against the Greek-speaking believers was more likely caused by the language and class barrier. So **the Twelve called a meeting of all the believers.** They noted that they needed to be **preaching and teaching, not administering a food program.** From both physical energy and time restraints, it would be impossible for them to do both. The reason was not that the apostles thought that they were "above" that job; rather, they knew that they had been called to preach and teach the word of God, and that had to be their priority.

6:3-4 Five requirements were clearly spelled out for the candidates: (1) believers (**among yourselves**); (2) **men** (*andras*—a specific Greek term for males); (3) **well respected**; (4) **full of the Holy Spirit;** (5) full of **wisdom**—demonstrating their ability to apply God's truth appropriately to life situations. **Seven** was the typical number of men used to handle public business in a Jewish town, the official council.

6:5 Seven men were chosen, though how this was done was not recorded. **Stephen** and **Philip** were likely placed first because they are the only two whose ministries will be explained later in Acts (chapters 7–8). All seven of these names are Greek, which means that the men were probably Hellenistic Jews. This would lay a good foundation for the future spread of the gospel to the Greek world.

6:6 Spiritual leadership is serious business and must not be taken lightly by the church or its leaders. In the early church, those chosen to serve would be ordained or commissioned (set apart by prayer and laying on of hands) by the apostles. Laying hands on someone, an ancient Jewish practice, was a way to set a person apart for special service (see Numbers 27:23; Deuteronomy 34:9). That the apostles **laid their hands on them** was a common gesture used in the commissioning of individuals to a task or office. It was also a granting of some sort of authority (see 8:17-19; 13:3; 19:6; 1 Timothy 4:14; 5:22; Hebrews 6:2). The apostles were hereby identifying themselves with the seven men and granting them a portion of their authority, at least for the task at hand.

6:7 The word of God was spreading in **ever-widening circles.** Jesus had told the apostles that they were to witness first in Jerusalem (1:8). In a short time, their message had infiltrated the entire city and all levels of society. Even some **Jewish priests** were being converted (as many as eighteen thousand priests may have been living in Jerusalem at the time)!

The work increased, and the word spread, at least in part because the apostles were dedicating more of their energies to that ministry. They could not have imagined, however, an explosion of the magnitude that lay just around the corner in the short but significant ministry of the church's first martyr.

STEPHEN IS ARRESTED / 6:8-15

Around the world, the gospel has most often taken root in places fertilized by the blood of martyrs. Before people can give their lives for the gospel, however, they must first live their lives for the gospel. One way that God trains his servants is to place them in insignificant positions. Their desire to serve Christ translates into the reality of serving others. Stephen was an effective administrator and messenger before becoming a martyr. For faithfully discharging his duties as a believer, Stephen was arrested.

6:8 Stephen was one of the managers of food distribution in the early church (6:5). The most important prerequisite for any kind of Christian service is to be filled with God's **grace** and the **power** of the Holy Spirit. By the Spirit's power, Stephen was a wise servant (6:3), miracle worker (6:8), and evangelist (6:10). Stephen is the first non-apostle to whom miracles are ascribed, as well as the first non-apostle whose sermon is recorded, in the book of Acts. It is unknown how long Stephen's ministry continued before the events of this chapter and the next occurred, but he obviously had a powerful, visible, and influential ministry.

6:9-10 The **Synagogue of Freed Slaves** was probably a group of Jewish slaves and children of Jewish slaves who had been freed by Rome and had formed their own synagogue in Jerusalem. **Cyrene** was in northern Africa, as was **Alexandria** (in Egypt). **Cilicia** was Paul's home province, so he may be one of those mentioned here.

Besides being a man of high character as well as one who was used of God in doing great works of power (see 6:8), Stephen was also a skilled debater. Notice the combination of Stephen's **wisdom** and the empowering work of the **Spirit** (6:3-5).

6:11-12 Some men lied about **Stephen,** causing him to be **arrested** and brought **before the high council** (before whom the apostles had just recently appeared—4:5-7; 5:26-27). The group falsely accused Stephen of blaspheming Moses, partly because they knew that the Sadducees, who controlled the council, believed only in Moses' laws. In their view, to **blaspheme Moses** was a crime. The entire council is mentioned here as being **roused** against Stephen. The **crowds** were riled up as well.

6:13-14 Similar to the way that Jesus had been handled, Stephen was the victim of a lying conspiracy. When Stephen was brought before the council, the accusation against him was the same that the religious leaders had used against Jesus (Matthew 26:59-61). As it was with Jesus and here with Stephen, this was not a wholesale fabrication but rather a subtle misrepresentation of Stephen's actual words. They twisted his comments into making him say that **Jesus of Nazareth will destroy the Temple and change the customs Moses handed down.** Jesus did not nullify Moses' law, but rather he completely fulfilled it. The religious leaders did not see this, however, and only saw someone seeming to make changes to what Moses had spoken. To them, that was blasphemy.

6:15 After the false witnesses had finished twisting Stephen's teaching, everyone turned to Stephen for his reaction. They found his face shining **as bright as an angel's** (see Judges 13:6; Luke 9:28-29). Stephen's "glowing face" would certainly call to mind the experience of Moses after being with God (Exodus 34:29, 35). The avid followers of Moses among his accusers (especially the Sadducees) would have made the connection.

Stephen's glowing face, like Moses', was likely a literal reflection of God's glory, a sign of having been in God's presence. Maybe Stephen had been given a glimpse of the vision that would be more evident at the moment of his death (7:55). Maybe his change in countenance was in part because of the fullness of the Spirit, a characteristic that had marked his life and ministry. Whatever it was, the moment was at hand for the first witness of Christ to lose his life for the faith.

ACTS 7

STEPHEN ADDRESSES THE COUNCIL / 7:1-60

This chapter records the first major speech of a non-apostle in the book—as well as the longest speech of anyone in Acts! It also records the first believer to die for his faith. Stephen—one of the seven men chosen to distribute food in the young church—was falsely accused by the Jewish religious leaders of committing blasphemy and inciting rebellion against the Temple. Then he was dragged before the Jewish authorities. In his speech to them, he spoke little in his own defense but said a great deal about Israel's historical tendency toward missing what God was doing. Their response to Stephen was typical of the Jews' response to every prophet throughout their history, down to and including Jesus himself: violence. This blunt and pointed sermon sent the Jewish leaders into a rage and resulted in the first martyrdom of the church.

7:1 This **high priest** was probably Caiaphas, the same man who had questioned and condemned Jesus (John 18:24) and had just recently interrogated the apostles (4:6-7; 5:26-28). He was high priest from 18–36 A.D. He gave Stephen a chance to speak in his defense by asking him, **"Are these accusations true?"** just as Caiaphas had asked Jesus, "Aren't you going to answer these charges? What do you have to say for yourself?" (Matthew 26:62).

7:2-3 Stephen launched into a speech about Israel's relationship with God. From Old Testament history, he showed that the Jews had constantly rejected God's message and his prophets and that the current Jewish leaders had rejected the Messiah, God's Son. He made three main points: (1) Israel's history is the history of God's acts in the world; (2) people worshiped God long before there was a Temple because God does not live in a Temple; and (3) the Jewish leaders' rejection of Jesus was just one more example of Israel's rebellion against and rejection of God.

Before the council, Stephen began his response to the accusations by reviewing the call of the Jewish patriarch **Abraham** from **Mesopotamia.** One of the themes of the speech is that God has been creatively and sovereignly directing his Kingdom program through many different people and in many different places. God's revelation was not limited to the land or people of Israel.

7:4-5 At God's call, **Abraham left the land of the Chaldeans,** referring to Mesopotamia, mentioned in the previous verse. The first stop on Abraham's journey to the land of Canaan was at **Haran,** a large city in the upper Euphrates valley.

Even after settling in the Promised Land (curiously referred to as **the land where you now live**), Abraham owned no property. Only very late in his life, when he needed a place to bury Sarah, did he buy any property there (Genesis 23). Stephen referred to both the **land,** of which Abraham owned **not even one square foot,** and the promised **descendants**—none of whom had even been born yet, both crucial aspects of the covenant promise God had given Abraham. He had to believe the unfulfilled promises of God. He had to look ahead in faith to what God was doing, not to what seemed best or most logical.

7:6-7 Abraham's faith was tested further when he was told that **his descendants would be mistreated as slaves for four hundred years.** This mention of "four hundred years" is the first of a number of difficulties in this speech concerning historical numbers, sequences, and biblical quotations. For example, see the discrepancies between the numbers in Genesis 15:13, the numbers in Exodus 12:40, and Paul's reference in Galatians 3:17 as to the length of time of the Egyptian enslavement. In these issues and others, readers must remember that Stephen may have been referring to traditional reckonings by the scholars of the day (some of whom were listening to this speech) or perhaps even to popular writings of the day. Often Stephen appears not to be strictly quoting a particular passage of Scripture but alluding to the interpretations that were common to the thinking of the day.

The Hebrews did eventually **come out** of slavery **and worship** God in Israel. But God had been with them in Egypt—still revealing himself to them, still guiding them, and still blessing them. The key was God, his will, and his guidance, not the place of the blessing.

7:8 **Circumcision** was a sign of the promise or **covenant** made between God, Abraham, and the entire nation of Israel (Genesis 17:9-13). Stephen pointed out that God always had kept his side of the promise, but Israel had failed, again and again, to keep its side. Although the Jews in Stephen's day still circumcised their baby boys, they failed to obey God. The people's hearts were far from him. Their lack of faith and lack of obedience meant that they had failed to keep their part of the covenant.

Isaac was Abraham's son, born to him in his old age (see Genesis 20–28 for Isaac's story). **Jacob**, in turn, was one of Isaac's twin sons, born with Esau (see Genesis 25–35; 46–49 for Jacob's story). These three men formed the foundation of the nation of Israel; God is called "the God of Abraham, Isaac, and Jacob" (see Exodus 3:16). **Jacob was the father of the twelve patriarchs;** this means that Jacob's twelve sons became the ancestors of each of the twelve tribes of Israel (see Genesis 49).

7:9-10 Stephen's speech moved to a brief summary of the life of **Joseph.** His brothers **were very jealous** and **sold him to be a slave in Egypt.** The story is recorded in Genesis 37:12-36. But **God was with** Joseph. Genesis 39–50 records Joseph's ups and downs in Egypt—yet he always remained faithful to God. In the end, **God gave him favor before Pharaoh** himself. As the following verses demonstrate, Joseph become the savior of his people.

Notice how often God is mentioned in this verse: God was with him; God gave Joseph favor; God gave Joseph unusual wisdom; God was working in an unusual way in an unusual place (outside of Israel). A wise student of history would expect God to intervene again.

7:11-13 When a **famine** struck, the leaders in **Egypt** were not caught off guard, for Pharaoh had foreseen it in a dream from God, which God had given Joseph the ability to interpret. As a result Joseph had wisely suggested that during the good years before the famine, extra grain be collected and held so that when the famine years came, there would be food for everyone (Genesis 41). **Jacob** sent his sons to Egypt to get food, and Joseph recognized them immediately. He did not reveal himself, however, for he wanted to find out first if their characters had improved since that day they had sold him as a slave.

It was on the brothers' **second** visit that Joseph revealed himself to them, having thoroughly tested them for changes in their attitudes. In what has to be one of the most emotional scenes in all of Scripture (Genesis 45), Joseph revealed himself to his brothers. This opened the door for moving the entire patriarchal band to Egypt. This was all part of God's sovereign plan to provide for Israel's needs in the famine and to move them to Egypt, as had been predicted to Abraham (Genesis 15:13).

7:14-15 Joseph had not forgotten his faith, his roots, or his beloved father, despite a change of fortune and culture! Stephen said that there were **seventy-five persons** who made the trek to Egypt. He must have been using the Septuagint when he made this quote or citing a Hebrew text different than the Masoretic Text, which reads "seventy" (see Genesis 46:27; Exodus 1:5). (One Dead Sea Scroll manuscript of Exodus 1:5 says "seventy-five" persons.)

7:16 There is a problem with Stephen's apparent reference to the location of Abraham's tomb. Genesis states that **the tomb that Abraham had bought** was located in Hebron (Genesis 49:29–50:13). Evidently, the bodies that were **taken to Shechem** referred to Joseph and his family and does not include Abraham, Isaac, and Jacob and their wives, who were buried in Hebron.

7:17-19 The four hundred years had almost passed, and so **the time drew near when God would fulfill his promise to Abraham** (Genesis 15:13-15). The **number** of the Israelite **people in Egypt greatly increased** (from seventy-five to likely over 2 million—see Exodus 12:37), and they experienced great prosperity until Egyptian dynasties changed and **a new king** arose **who knew nothing about Joseph.** The reference to abandoning **their newborn babies** is a reminder of the events of Exodus 1:15-22; Pharaoh ordered the Hebrew midwives to kill every male newborn. The slaughter of the innocents by Herod at the birth of Jesus Christ a few short decades earlier should have been ringing a bell in the minds of Stephen's listeners.

7:20-22 During the days when the Hebrew midwives were under orders to kill Hebrew baby boys, **Moses was born.** God did not choose a convenient time for the child to be born; instead, he chose the worst of times. During this horrible time in Israel's history, the nation's first real "deliverer" was born. The story is told in Exodus 1–2. Moses was a great figure of the nation of Israel, greater in the estimation of many than even the founding father, Abraham. Moses was the vehicle God used for the salvation of the nation, for letting in so much of his light through the revelation on Mount Sinai, and for bringing the nation to the very edge of entrance into the Promised Land.

Again, Stephen emphasized that God was working in the nation, but through some very odd circumstances (adoption by an Egyptian princess) and in a strange location (outside the borders of geographic Israel).

7:23-25 Moses' first attempt to lead his people came when he tried to save an Israelite who was being mistreated by an Egyptian. Moses, the prince, came to the **defense** of his fellow Israelite and **avenged him, killing the Egyptian.** Apparently, Moses knew his calling and **assumed his brothers would realize that God had sent him to rescue them.** Unfortunately, **they didn't.**

This is the first of four direct references to the fact that Israel had totally missed the work of a "redeemer" sent by God (see 7:27, 35, 39). Such a pattern of behavior was replayed many times in Israel's history and was happening again in the first century, as the Jews were missing their Redeemer, Jesus.

7:26-28 The incident with the **two men of Israel** who were fighting presents an even more compelling case for the absurdity of Israel's initial rejection of Moses as deliverer. The two fighters questioned Moses as he interceded in their argument, **"Who made you a ruler and judge over us?"** The Jewish council showed the same belligerence concerning Stephen's speech, in effect saying, "What makes you think this Jesus of Nazareth should be ruler and judge over us?" The parallels between the nation's rejection of Jesus and its early rejection of Moses should have been another wake-up call.

7:29-30 Rejected by his own people and fearing for his life because he had killed an Egyptian, Moses **fled the country and lived as a foreigner in the land of Midian** (northwest Arabia). For **forty long years,** he served his father-in-law as a shepherd. Eighty years of his life were gone—it seemed that Moses had spent most of his life waiting. But the wait soon would be over. There in the **desert,** after what must have seemed an eternity, God spoke to him.

Stephen reminded his audience of the incredible moment when **an angel appeared to Moses in the flame of a burning bush** (see Exodus 3–4). God was working. God was speaking. God was about to deliver his people. There was no Temple here, no Tabernacle, and they were nowhere near Jerusalem. God had chosen to speak from a bush in the desert!

7:31-32 As Moses approached the burning bush, **the voice of the Lord called out to him.** The mention of **Abraham, Isaac, and Jacob** would connect this present revelation to all that had been said and done through the patriarchs. As God had spoken to Abraham in a foreign land, as he had led Jacob and his family to a foreign land, so now in the desert of Midian, God was speaking to Moses, preparing him to lead his people to the next stage of their salvation journey. Stephen wanted his audience to remember how amazed Moses was and how unusual were the

timing, place, and form of revelation that God used. It was entirely unexpected and without historical precedent in God's dealing with his people.

7:33-34 The command to remove the **sandals** from his feet and God's designation of the place as **holy ground** was significant in Stephen's argument. It reminded his audience that God can speak from wherever he wishes and that any place becomes "holy ground" when God is there. God has worked in the past and will continue to work in the future outside of the boundaries of the Holy Land or any building called holy (such as a sanctuary).

God reminded Moses that though eighty years had passed in his life and though four hundred years had passed in Israel's life in Egypt, God would intervene at this point in history and **rescue them.** But God would not be doing the rescue alone. He planned to send Moses back **to Egypt—** surely the last place that Moses wanted to go.

7:35 This verse summarizes Stephen's talk and wraps up this review of Moses' life. The man **sent back** to Egypt as Israel's **ruler and savior** was the same man they had **previously rejected.** The word translated "savior" conveys the idea of redemption and is used only of Moses in the New Testament. In the succeeding verses, Stephen also notes that Moses was a Prophet (7:37) and mediator (7:38). Stephen's point seems to be that even greater than Moses, the lawgiver who "saved" Israel from Egyptian bondage, was Jesus, the grace-giver who offered eternal freedom from the sin of slavery. If Moses was beloved and revered, Jesus should be to an infinitely greater degree.

7:36 So much of what God had revealed, so many of the miracles God had performed, and much of what lay behind the intricate system of sacrifices (which he would show Moses), would help God's people recognize the coming Messiah. God wanted his people to be ready to recognize and receive the ultimate Deliverer (the one who would deliver people from their sins) when he came.

The reminder of the journey **back and forth through the wilderness for forty years** was yet another example of Israel ignoring the command of God and rejecting his direction of them. For forty years they wandered through the wilderness, burying the entire older generation (with the exception of Moses, Joshua, and Caleb—see Numbers 14:21-45). It was Israel's stubborn, Holy Spirit-resisting (see 7:51) refusal to recognize the leading of God that got them excluded from experiencing his blessing in the land. Stephen's current generation would do well to remember their forefathers' propensity to miss what God was saying and doing.

7:37-38 The Jews originally thought this **Prophet** was Joshua. But Moses had been prophesying about the coming Messiah (Deuteronomy 18:15). Peter also had quoted this verse as referring to the Messiah (3:22).

Stephen used the word *ekklesia* (translated **assembly**) to describe the congregation or people of God **in the wilderness.** This word means "called out ones" and was used by the first-century Christians to describe their own community or "assembly." Stephen's point was that the giving of the law through Moses to the Jews was the sign of the covenant. By obedience, then, would they continue to be God's covenant people. When they disobeyed (7:39), however, they broke the covenant and forfeited their right to be the chosen people—God's congregation.

7:39 Stephen again stated what had become an obvious theme, especially from the life of Moses. The Jewish ancestors of the audience and of the speaker (**our ancestors**) had **rejected Moses**—his message, his leadership, and his claim to be speaking for God. Incredibly, they **wanted to return to** the slavery and idolatry of **Egypt** (Numbers 14:1-4).

7:40-41 The Jews' ancestors had not only rejected Joseph and Moses, but at one crucial point in their history they had also rejected God! While Moses was up on Mount Sinai receiving the Law, the children of Israel got tired of waiting. They forgot about God and decided that they needed a new leader and a new god. They asked Aaron to construct a god for them. In one sorry, sinful deed, the children of Israel blatantly, publicly, and corporately defied God. This "invisible" God and "absent" Moses were too much to bear. They wanted something they could see, even if it was the product of their own hands. Stephen's wording highlights the idiocy of it all, as he pictured them bringing sacrifices to **an idol shaped like a calf.** The story is told in Exodus 32.

7:42-43 The Israelites' worship of the golden calf was the beginning of a downward spiral. At times they returned to God, but far more often they were running after the gods of the evil nations surrounding them. This quote from Amos (Amos 5:25-27) supports Stephen's accusation that Israel had a history of idol worship. **Molech** and **Rephan** were planetary divinities. Molech was an Ammonite deity associated with child sacrifice, while Rephan was a god "borrowed" from Egypt. Both became popular options for Israel's idolatry as her history progressed.

The ancestors of Stephen's current audience, the audience who stood in rejection of Jesus Christ, had a history of rejecting not only God's messengers but even of turning from God himself to their own handmade gods. The cost for their idolatry had been **captivity far away in Babylon.** No one within the sound of Stephen's voice could have any doubt about the historical accuracy of that statement.

7:44 Suddenly, the subject switches to this intriguing section concerning the **Tabernacle.** Having sufficiently denied the charge against him that he had blasphemed Moses (6:11), Stephen proceeded to address the charge that he had blasphemed God. The Tabernacle was a movable worship center used by the Israelites prior to the construction of the Temple by Solomon. The detailed instructions for constructing the Tabernacle were spelled out for Moses and the people of Israel (see Exodus 25-31). The construction plans were **shown to Moses by God** himself. This large and mobile tent was suitable for the wilderness wanderings because it could be taken apart and moved easily from location to location. It was the place where, after the nation left Mount Sinai, Moses would meet with God (Exodus 29:42; 30:6, 36; Numbers 17:4).

7:45 When the people finally moved into the land of Canaan under Joshua's leadership, **the Tabernacle was taken with them** and remained with them as they settled the land and had many **battles against the Gentile nations.** Stephen reminded his audience that **God drove** the Gentiles out of the Promised Land. This temporary and mobile Tabernacle remained with the people **until the time of King David,** when Jerusalem was made the capital city and David began making plans for a Temple.

7:46-47 King **David found favor with God and asked** to build a permanent **Temple.** He desired this so much that he wrote about it in Psalm 132:2-5. Second Samuel 7:1-16 relates God's answer to David's request. David's son **Solomon,** the next king of Israel, would oversee construction of a glorious Temple to God in Jerusalem (1 Kings 5-8).

7:48-50 Only in Christ, however, would this vision of David and promise of God ever be realized. God **doesn't live in Temples made by human hands.** To support this, Stephen quoted from **the prophet Isaiah: "Heaven is my throne, and the earth is my footstool"** (Isaiah 66:1-2a). The Temple was a building and **just** a building. As in Jesus' ministry, the religious leaders were more intent on scrupulously guarding the Temple building and their traditions than they were in exhibiting the virtues of justice, mercy, and faithfulness (see Matthew 23:23-24).

7:51 Stephen moved to the critical point of his speech. He had responded brilliantly to the accusations against him. All that remained was to drive the point of application home to his audience. Those who stood before him had not broken the cycle of sin that had been passed down to them by their **ancestors.**

7:52-54 Indeed, many of their prophets had been persecuted or killed: Uriah (Jeremiah 26:20-23), Jeremiah (Jeremiah 38:1-6), Isaiah (tradition says he was killed by King Manasseh; see 2 Kings 21:16), Amos (Amos 7:10-13), Zechariah (not the author of the Bible book, but the son of Jehoiada the priest, 2 Chronicles 24:20-22), and Elijah (1 Kings 19:1-2). Jesus had made the same charges against the Jews (Matthew 23:37; Luke 11:47-48). Jesus had also told a parable about how the Jews had constantly rejected God's messages and had persecuted his messengers (Luke 20:9-19). See Hebrews 11:35-38 on the killing of the prophets.

Not only had the Jews killed the prophets who had **predicted the coming of the Righteous One** (the **Messiah,** Jesus Christ), but they had **betrayed and murdered** their Messiah. The children of Israel had rejected their deliverer, Moses, from the start to the finish of his ministry. They had **deliberately disobeyed God's law, though** they had **received it from the hands of angels.** God himself had been rejected in their ancestors' constant forays into idolatry. God's Messiah, the Righteous One, the Savior of the world, was the latest victim of their rebellion. These final words so enraged his hearers that **they shook their fists in rage.**

7:55-56 In contrast to their rage, Stephen was still in control, **full of the Holy Spirit,** the ultimate source of strength and courage (see also 6:3, 5, 8, 15). The text tells us that as the maddened crowd drew nearer, Stephen kept his gaze **steadily upward.** In the process he **saw the glory of God, and he saw Jesus standing in the place of honor at God's right hand.** Just before his death, how-

ever, Stephen saw Christ standing. In this scene, as the church experienced the first (of many) to die for faith in Christ, Luke wanted his readers to know martyrs do not die alone—as if out of the gaze of their Savior. Christ was not only present at the right hand of the Father, but he also was (at least in Stephen's case) standing to receive his faithful servant home. There can be no greater nor more honorable reception than to have the **Son of Man standing** at one's entrance into his presence.

Stephen saw **the heavens opened.** This is a very important term for the presence of God and a sign of his revelation. The heavens opened at the baptism of Jesus (Luke 3:21-22) as a sign of affirmation of Jesus' deity. It was accompanied by the voice of God and the descending of the Spirit.

7:57-58 This pictures a violent mob taking the law into their own hands. The wording of this scene—covering **their ears,** shouting loudly, rushing together, and dragging Stephen out of the city—leads one to the conclusion that this was a sudden, impassioned, violent (and probably illegal) action.

With dramatic style Luke gave what would seem to be a passing piece of information about the one who kept the **coats** while the stoning occurred: **a young man named Saul.** This, of course, was Paul (see 13:9), the great missionary who wrote many of the letters in the New Testament. Saul was his Hebrew name; Paul, the Greek equivalent, was used as he began his ministry to the Gentiles.

7:59-60 As they were in the process of stoning Stephen, he made two fascinating statements, both reminiscent of Christ's words on the cross. The first, **"Lord Jesus, receive my spirit,"** is similar to Christ's final words in Luke 23:46 (in some manuscripts). The second is a word of forgiveness: **"Lord, don't charge them with this sin!"** Stephen had obviously learned from his Master some important lessons about how to live and how to die.

ACTS 8

PERSECUTION SCATTERS THE BELIEVERS / 8:1-3

After the martyrdom of Stephen, the Jews stepped up their persecution of the followers of Christ. The man introduced as Saul (8:1) proved to be a major leader in this widespread campaign of intolerance and terror. From a human perspective, this was a dreadful turn of events; from a divine perspective, it produced a far greater good. The Christians who had been in Jerusalem were now forced to migrate to the surrounding regions of Judea and Samaria.

8:1 In the final words of Luke's record of Stephen's martyrdom, Saul was introduced subtly into the text as a young man in charge of keeping the coats of those who were stoning Stephen (7:58). The opening verse of this chapter adds the information about Saul's current attitude: he was not just there by accident or just passing by. **He was one of the official witnesses at the killing of Stephen.** Saul was a native of Tarsus, a city in Cilicia (modern-day south-central Turkey), and may have entered into the controversy with Stephen at the synagogue in Jerusalem where Stephen had been debating (6:9-10). Luke mentioned him only in passing here, before recording the details of his conversion in chapter 9. When we get to chapter 13, Paul's ministry will be the entire focus of the book and the main instrument for the church's outreach to the Gentile world.

Stephen's martyrdom was the impetus for an immediate increase of persecution against those who followed Christ. The persecution forced the Christians out of **Jerusalem** and into **Judea and Samaria**—thus fulfilling the second part of Jesus' command (see 1:8). Evidently, they had become somewhat comfortable sticking close to Jerusalem. All of that was instantly changed with Stephen's death and the resultant persecution.

Not every Christian left Jerusalem, for a church remained there for the balance of the New Testament era. Why the **apostles** stayed in Jerusalem instead of scattering with the others is a matter of speculation. Leadership of the Christian movement continued from the Jerusalem church for quite some time (see chapter 15). Eventually, the major missionary center moved north to Antioch (chapter 13 and following). Paul would regularly return to Jerusalem to report and to bring monetary support to the suffering Jerusalem saints from the Asian and European churches (16:4; 21:15-20).

8:2-3 What a contrast between this verse and the next one! **Godly people came and buried Stephen with loud weeping,** while **Saul was going everywhere to devastate the church.** Obviously the loss of a person so important, respected, and needed in the church would be a huge blow. Evidently spurred on by the Jewish council's murder of Stephen, Saul zealously went on the attack. Saul passionately tried to protect the Jewish faith (see 9:1, 13). He later described these activities thoroughly in his testimony before King Agrippa (26:9-11). Saul was **dragging out both men and women** and putting them in **jail.** Evidently, Saul had been given legal authority to carry out this persecution (see comments on 9:1-2).

PHILIP PREACHES IN SAMARIA / 8:4-25

This is the second step of the Gentile mission in Acts 1:8—"to Samaria." Philip's trip into Samaria and his ministry there reveal the marvelous truth that Jesus, the promised Jewish Messiah, was also the king and Savior of Gentiles. The message of Christ is a worldwide gospel. All nations and languages are invited and included (see Isaiah 56:3; Daniel 7:14) in the Kingdom of God.

8:4 The persecution caused the **believers who had fled Jerusalem** to scatter into other nations. As they went, they were **preaching the Good News about Jesus.** The gospel message was spreading like wildfire! Satan had attempted to defeat the young church, but all he did was encourage the spread of the gospel.

8:5 Israel had been divided into three main regions—Galilee in the north, Samaria in the middle, and Judea in the south. The **city of Samaria** (in the region of Samaria) had been the capital of the northern kingdom of Israel in the days of the divided kingdom, before it was conquered by Sargon of Assyria in 722 B.C. During that war, Sargon had taken many captives, leaving only the poorest people in the land and resettling it with foreigners. These foreigners had intermarried with the Jews who were left, and the mixed race became known as Samaritans. The Samaritans were considered half-breeds and religious apostates by the "pure" Jews in the southern kingdom of Judah, and the two groups hated each other. But Jesus went into Samaria (John 4), and he commanded his followers to spread the gospel there (1:8).

Philip is not the apostle Philip (John 1:43-44) but a Greek-speaking Jew; he was one of the seven men who had been chosen to help distribute food in the Jerusalem church (6:5). Philip went into Samaria **and told the people there about the Messiah.**

8:6-8 The effectiveness of Philip's ministry is highlighted here as **crowds** gathered and saw Philip perform **miracles** that authenticated the message.

Evil spirits were cast out of people. Their **scream-ing** revealed their rage at encountering a power greater than their own. Demons are never pleased to be told to leave their human dwellings, but they have no choice but to submit to the higher authority (see Mark 9:25-26). Philip also **healed.** As a result of the healings and the message he brought, **there was great joy in that city.**

8:9-11 The balance of this chapter reports two significant experiences of Philip as he faithfully spread the gospel. The first incident involved a **sorcerer** named **Simon.** Evidently, Simon had quite a following in the region and was using his **magic** to draw crowds of his own. In the days of the early church, sorcerers and magicians were numerous and influential. They worked wonders, performed healings and exorcisms, and practiced astrology, but they utilized the power of Satan (Matthew 24:24; 2 Thessalonians 2:9). Simon had done so many wonders that some even thought that he was **the Great One—the Power of God** (in other words, the Messiah).

8:12-13 In sharp contrast to Simon and his magic is Philip and the **message of Good News concern-ing the Kingdom of God.** People believed in Jesus Christ and **were baptized.** Even the sorcerer him-self appeared to believe and was baptized. So now the man who had previously had a large and diverse following was **following Philip wherever he went,** himself being **amazed by the great mira-cles and signs** that Philip, in the power of Christ, was performing. Simon may have found it easy to believe when it was exciting and everyone else was caught up in the excitement. There is some question, however, about the sincerity of his pro-fession of faith and the genuineness of his conver-sion. In his conversation with Peter (see 8:18-24), the description of Simon does not have the sound of one who truly had come to faith.

8:14 **Peter and John** were sent to **Samaria** as apos-tolic representatives to find out whether or not the Samaritans were truly becoming believers. The Jewish Christians, even the apostles, were still unsure whether Gentiles (non-Jews) and Samari-tans (half-Jews) could receive the Holy Spirit.

8:15-16 This was a crucial moment for the spread of the gospel and for the growth of the church. Peter and John had to go to Samaria to help keep this new group of believers from becoming sepa-rated from other believers. There was deep-seated hostility between Jews and Samaritans that went back centuries. The Jews looked down on the Samaritans for not being pure Jews; the Samaritans resented the Jews for their arrogance. However,

Samaritans were coming to faith in Christ through Philip's preaching, and there could be no denying that they should be included among the believers. So **they prayed for these new Christians to receive the Holy Spirit.**

It may seem odd that **the Holy Spirit had not yet come upon any of them.** Many scholars believe that God chose to have a dramatic filling of his Spirit as a sign at this special moment in history—a "Samaritan Pentecost" paralleling the Pentecost that the apostles had experienced in chapter 2. Normally, the Holy Spirit enters a per-son's life at conversion; it is then that the Spirit baptizes, seals, and indwells that person. But this was a special event. The pouring out of the Spirit would happen again with Cornelius and his family (10:44-47), a sign that the uncircumcised Gentiles could receive salvation.

With the verification by Peter and John that the Samaritans' faith was genuine, these new believers were incorporated into the church. When the Samaritans were converted, they received the Spirit, as was essential for regeneration, but their partici-pation in the church was needed for the full expression of the gifts of the Spirit.

8:17 These Samaritan believers **received the Holy Spirit** through the laying on of the apostles' **hands.** One of the likely reasons for the delay between water baptism and the baptism of the Spirit was to keep the Samaritan church united with the Jewish church. Because of the historical conflict between these two groups, it would be crucial to have an apostolic presence for this significant event. The presence of apostles, especially two with such a high profile—**Peter and John**—would give unquestionable credibility to the Samaritan spiritual movement. These two apostles, through whom the Samaritans first received the Holy Spirit, would confirm to the rest of the Jerusalem church that indeed God was doing the same thing among the Gentiles that he was doing among the Jews. This Samaritan Pentecost also demonstrated to the Jerusalem church God's expansion plans for the Gentiles and the ever-widening scope of the gospel ministry. Chapters 7–12 are a careful record of that first critical move of Christianity out of the confines of Jerusalem—and, more importantly, beyond the confines of the Jewish faith.

8:18-19 Evidently there were some visible manifes-tations of the **power** of the Holy Spirit that accom-panied this laying on of hands, possibly similar to those present at Pentecost in chapter 2 (such as the violent wind and the tongues of fire). **Simon** was the sorcerer from 8:9-13 who had supposedly believed and been baptized. But he was more interested in miracles than in Christ. So **when Simon saw that the Holy Spirit was given when the apostles placed their hands upon people's heads,** he wanted to have that power as well. Simon foolishly believed that Peter and John were in the same business as he had been (sorcery and magic), so he **offered money** for the power.

8:20-23 Peter's stern answer was a stinging rebuke. Simon's errant **thinking** had led him to believe that **God's gift** could **be bought.** Simon's **heart** was **not right before God;** his behavior was called **wickedness;** his thinking was called **evil;** he was said to be **full of bitterness;** and, in the most sweeping of condemnations, Peter said that Simon was still, despite his supposed conversion, **held captive by sin.** The implication was that Simon had not genuinely come to Christ.

8:24 Simon was apparently terrified. He seemed to respond well to the rebuke, asking Peter to **pray for** him. It is hard to tell whether his outcry was simply a fear of **terrible** consequences for having insulted these powerful visitors or a genuine change in heart toward God. It may well be that Simon was a typical pseudoconvert, a make-believer, rather than a genuine one (notice that he didn't pray himself but asked Peter to pray).

8:25 Encouraged by what they had just experienced in Samaria, Peter and John made their way back to Jerusalem **testifying and preaching the word of the Lord, the Good News,** in **many Samaritan villages.** As Peter and John continued to learn God's strategy for reaching the world, the rest of the apostles would also be enlightened, and through them, so would the church back in Jerusalem.

PHILIP AND THE ETHIOPIAN EUNUCH / 8:26-40

This passage is set carefully and strategically **after** the initial work in Jerusalem and **before** the conversion of Paul, the apostle to the Gentiles (chapter 9). This is the third step of expansion to the uttermost parts of the world (1:8). The gospel of Christ was leaving a purely Jewish audience and beginning to be spread to the world. In the story of Philip and the Ethiopian eunuch, we have a wonderful picture of God's global love and his surprising plan to get the good news of Christ to those who have never heard.

8:26-28 An **angel of the Lord** appeared at various times in Scripture giving directions to people. In this instance, **Philip** was told to **go south.** In the sovereign strategy of God, Philip was sent to the side of the road, where **he met the treasurer of Ethiopia** traveling home from a pilgrimage to Jerusalem. Ethiopia is located in Africa, south of Egypt. The **eunuch** was obviously dedicated to God, because he had traveled such a long distance to **worship** in Jerusalem. This man may have been a Gentile convert to Judaism. That he had a copy of **the book of the prophet Isaiah** points to that probability. To own a scroll of the Scriptures (handwritten and thus rare) likewise indicated wealth.

8:29-30 The Holy Spirit directed Philip to go over and walk along beside the carriage. Again, Philip immediately complied. He heard the man reading from the prophet Isaiah. After observing for a moment, Philip asked: "Do you understand what you are reading?" In so doing, Philip exhibited two of the most important characteristics of an effective evangelist: The first is patience. He waited to find out where the man was in his understanding before diving in with the gospel. A second characteristic is the power of observa-

tion. Philip looked for an opportunity to engage the man at a meaningful level.

8:31-34 The court official expressed the frustration that every Bible student throughout the ages has felt from time to time: **"How can I** understand this passage unless someone explains it to me?" This perfect lead-in to the gospel was made even better considering the passage he was reading. As Philip was invited to join the eunuch in the chariot, he discovered which **passage of Scripture** the eunuch was reading—Isaiah 53. Here God continued his sovereign work. There is no better place to be reading in the Old Testament for a picture of Jesus Christ than Isaiah 53. The passage is Isaiah's prophecy about the great suffering Servant—his rejection, his silence before his accusers, his death with wicked men, the substitutionary nature of his suffering, his burial in a rich man's grave, and his ultimate resurrection.

8:35 Philip began with this same Scripture, added to it **many others,** and told the eunuch **the Good News about Jesus.** It is important to note that Philip began where the man was; only then did he directly and clearly take him to where he needed to go. This means he listened, thought, adapted the message to his audience, and then explained the Good News.

8:36 Whatever Philip said to the court official, it is obvious that he came to faith. Evidently included in what Philip had taught was the fact that being **baptized** was the next step of obedience in this newfound faith. Philip began where the Ethiopian was, but he did not stay there. Philip gave the Ethiopian the rest of the story—maybe the rest of Isaiah 53—including the coming of Christ, his substitutionary death, his resurrection, and his offer of eternal life. Most of the earlier Greek manuscripts do not include verse 37.

8:38 After commanding **the carriage to stop,** the official and Philip **went down into the water.** There **Philip baptized him.** The witnesses to the baptism included at least Philip and the carriage driver, though a man of such high position may have been traveling with a sizable entourage.

Commanded by Christ (Matthew 28:18-20), water baptism was an outward, visible sign of one's identification with Christ and with the Christian community. This was one of the first acts of new converts in the early church. In submitting to baptism, this official was proclaiming his faith in Christ publicly. Deeply symbolic and meaningful, baptism sends a powerful message to onlookers about one's obedience to Christ.

8:39-40 Philip was suddenly transported by **the Spirit of the Lord** to a different city (likely his next job site). **Azotus** is Ashdod, one of the ancient Philistine capitals, about twenty miles north of Gaza. This miraculous sign may be here to show the urgency of spreading the message to the Gentiles. Philip **preached the Good News.** Philip disappears from the Acts story at this point, but ultimately he ended up in **Caesarea.** The only other mention of Philip is in 21:8-9. Twenty years later, Philip was still at Caesarea with four daughters, all of whom were prophetesses.

Nothing else is recorded about the newly converted eunuch, other than this wonderful report that he **went on his way rejoicing**—clear evidence of the Spirit's work in this new believer's life (Galatians 5:22).

ACTS 9

SAUL'S CONVERSION / 9:1-19A

Acts 1:8 seems to be a concise outline for the entire book. Chapters 1–7 describe the gospel being preached in Jerusalem. Chapter 8 shows believers, under threat of persecution, taking the Good News of Jesus to Judea and Samaria.

Chapter 9 records a monumental event in the history of the church—the conversion of Saul of Tarsus. Saul (later known as Paul) would be God's apostle to the Gentiles (Galatians 2:8; Ephesians 3:8). He would lead the church in spreading Christianity "to the ends of the earth" (1:8). Therefore Paul, more than any other person, figures prominently in chapters 10–28.

9:1-2 Saul (later called Paul, the equivalent of "Saul" in Greek), first mentioned as a participant in the stoning of Stephen (see 7:58; 8:1), was so zealous for his Jewish beliefs that he began a persecution campaign against all who believed in Christ, all who were **followers of the Way** (see Paul's testimony in Philippians 3:6). This name implied "the way of the Lord" or "the way of salvation."

Why would the Jews in Jerusalem want to persecute Christians as far away as Damascus? There are several possibilities: (1) to seize the Christians who had fled; (2) to prevent the spread of Christianity to other major cities; and (3) to keep the Christians from causing any trouble with Rome.

The **letters** requested by Saul would not only introduce him, but they would provide him with the high priest's authorization to seize followers of Christ and bring them **back to Jerusalem.** Most synagogues in Syria probably recognized this right of extradition. Not only was Saul going to pursue them, he also was going to arrest **both men and women** and bring them back **in chains.**

9:3 Damascus, a key commercial city, was located about 175 miles northeast of Jerusalem in the Roman province of Syria. Several trade routes linked Damascus to other cities throughout the Roman world. Damascus was one of the ten cities known as the Ten Towns (see Mark 5:20; 7:31). Saul may have thought that by stamping out Christianity in Damascus, he could prevent its spread to other areas.

Nearing his destination, at about noon, when the sun was at its full height (see 22:6; 26:13), Saul suddenly found himself awash in a **brilliant light.** Though the text does not overtly state that Saul saw Christ, that fact is implied, since seeing the resurrected Lord was a requirement of New Testament apostleship (see 1 Corinthians 9:1; 15:8). Also, the testimonies of Ananias (9:17) and Barnabas (9:27) confirm an eyewitness encounter.

9:4-5 Not only did Saul witness the brilliant glory of the Lord, but he also **heard** the **voice** of Jesus Christ. (For the rest of what Jesus said, see 22:8, 10, 17, 21; 26:15-18.) Saul thought he was pursuing heretics, but according to the voice, his actions were tantamount to attacking Jesus himself—**I am Jesus, the one you are persecuting.** Anyone who persecutes believers today is also guilty of persecuting Jesus (see Matthew 25:40, 45) because believers are the body of Christ on earth. This is a powerful statement about the union that exists between Christ and his church.

As he lay there in the dust, Saul must have been reeling from the realization that Jesus, the crucified founder of this detested sect, had been resurrected by God and exalted in divine glory. Saul was not serving God, as he had thought, but opposing him!

9:6 According to Paul's own testimony in 26:16-18, Christ gave him, at this moment, a brief preview of his future as an apostle to the Gentiles. Further details would come once he made his way into the city of Damascus.

9:7 Those accompanying Saul heard **the sound of someone's voice** and saw some kind of light (see 22:9), but they didn't understand the full significance of this encounter. **They saw no one,** nor had they heard the specific words spoken to Saul (26:14).

9:8-9 Saul was temporarily blinded by this revelation (an event with Old Testament precedence— see Genesis 19:11; 2 Kings 6:17-20), **so his companions led him by the hand to Damascus.** Saul's subsequent fast (going **without food and water**) was most likely motivated by shock as he tried to ponder the full significance of his experience. Typically, fasting indicated a period of mourning or repentance.

Saul certainly had a lot to think about during those **three days.** He realized that despite his zeal for God, his recent activity of arresting Christians

had been in direct opposition to God—otherwise, he would not have received this rebuke. Suddenly, all that Saul had believed was being torn down and replaced with a new truth—the very truth that he had been seeking to extinguish. As Saul was thinking about all this, he was also praying (9:11).

9:10-12 As Saul waited for further directions, the Lord began speaking to **Ananias,** a Jew who had become a **believer** in Christ. Ananias responded to the call of God. The meeting between Saul and Ananias was divinely arranged. **Straight Street** was and still is one of the main thoroughfares of Damascus. Ananias was directed to the street and **to the house of Judas.** The Lord gave specific instructions to Ananias about where to go and for whom to look; in a separate vision, he told Saul to expect Ananias's arrival. Such divine revelation with separate individuals having similar visions would be repeated again in 10:1-23.

9:13-14 Ananias was understandably shaken by the Lord's command to go and find Saul of Tarsus. Christians wanted to stay far away from Saul. His reputation as an enemy of the church was well documented, and the intent of this particular mission to Damascus was widely known. Ananias knew that Saul had been **authorized by the leading priests to arrest every believer in Damascus.** Fearful of what might happen, Ananias began to protest. Despite his protests, however, Ananias was up to the task.

9:15-16 Ananias's protest was met with a divine statement that Saul was God's **chosen instrument.** What irony that the most zealous Jew and most anti-Gentile would be the chosen witness to **take** God's **message to the Gentiles and to kings, as well as to the people of Israel.** For the rest of his life, Saul marveled that he would be the recipient of such mercy and grace, as well as be the appointee for such a noble task. Saul, who had caused horrible suffering for so many Christians, would find that he, too, **must suffer.** The remainder of the book of Acts, as well as the many letters that Saul wrote, chronicle the words of this verse: Saul would find himself witnessing for Christ in front of Gentile audiences, Jewish audiences, and even kings. He also would suffer severely for his faith.

9:17-19a Ananias's actions fulfilled at least two purposes. First, he functioned almost in a prophetic role, serving as God's confirming mouthpiece in the commissioning of the great apostle. Second, his visit served as a ministry of personal encouragement. Saul must have been encouraged when he heard Ananias greet him as **brother.** Ananias told Saul that Jesus had sent him so that Saul could **get his sight back and be filled with the Holy Spirit.** Evidently, the Holy Spirit filled Saul when he received his sight and was baptized. Upon the conclusion of this experience, **something like scales fell from Saul's eyes, and he regained his sight.** Saul was **baptized,** presumably by Ananias, and he ended his three-day fast (9:9).

SAUL IN DAMASCUS AND JERUSALEM / 9:19B-31

The change in Saul was instantaneous. In less than one week, he went from being eager to destroy the Lord's followers (9:1) to preaching about Jesus in the synagogues (9:20). The believers were understandably suspicious, but Saul's powerful and persistent preaching, coupled with efforts by the Jewish leaders to kill him (9:23), finally convinced the apostles that his conversion was genuine. According to Galatians 1:17-18, Saul spent three years in Arabia between the time of his conversion (9:3-6) and his journey to Jerusalem (9:26).

9:19b-20 Saul obeyed his new calling immediately, for **immediately he began preaching about Jesus in the synagogues.** Saul could do this so soon after his conversion because his experience on the road to Damascus had been unmistakable. Saul knew that Jesus was alive, Jesus was **the Son of God,** and Jesus was the Messiah.

9:21 The change in Saul caused his hearers to be **amazed.** They had expected Saul to show up and begin arresting followers of Jesus for they knew that was why he had come to Damascus in the first place. Yet here was this enemy of Christianity preaching the Christian message! Surely these Jews made this information known to their leaders back in Jerusalem (9:23).

9:22 Saul's **preaching** was **powerful,** filled with **proofs that Jesus was indeed the Messiah.** The word "proofs" as used here means "to put together." Essentially, what Saul was doing was taking Old Testament prophecies of the Messiah and putting them together with the facts of Jesus' life, thus proving that Jesus was the one to whom the Scriptures pointed.

9:23-25 According to Galatians 1:17-18, Saul left Damascus and traveled to Arabia, the desert region just southeast of Damascus, where he lived for three years. It is unclear whether his three-year stay occurred between verses 22 and 23 or between verses 25 and 26. Some commentators say that **after a while** could mean a long period of time. They suggest that when Saul returned to Damascus, the governor under Aretas ordered his arrest (2 Corinthians 11:32) in an effort to keep peace with influential Jews. The other possibility is that Saul's night escape occurred during his first stay in Damascus, just after his conversion, when the Pharisees were especially upset over his defection from their ranks. He would have fled to Arabia to spend time alone with God and to let the Jewish religious leaders cool down.

Regardless of which theory is correct, there was a period of at least three years between Saul's conversion (9:3-6) and his trip to Jerusalem (9:26). What is clear is that Saul's preaching had made such headlines that **the Jewish leaders decided to kill him.** But God had plans for Saul, and so he protected him. **The other believers,** too, convinced of Saul's transformed life, were willing to help him escape the city. They **let him down in a large basket through an opening in the city wall** so that he could bypass the **city gate,** where people were watching for him in order to **murder him.** In some of the ancient walled cities, houses were built right on the city walls (see Joshua 2:15). It would not have been too difficult, therefore, for one of the believers who lived in such a house to use a window in his home for Saul's escape.

9:26 After his three-year sojourn in Arabia, **Saul arrived in Jerusalem** only to find himself in a delicate situation. Word had come from Damascus about Saul's shocking conversion, for the Jewish leaders had already tried to kill him (9:23). But the believers **were all afraid of him.** This shows how terrible Saul's persecution had been. Clearly, the believers viewed this unexpected turn of events as part of a plot to infiltrate the church and do more harm.

9:27-28 Barnabas, in keeping with his nickname ("Son of Encouragement"—see 4:36), encouraged Saul by acting as his "sponsor." He vouched for the genuine transformation of Saul's life. Galatians 1:18-19 explains that Saul stayed in Jerusalem only fifteen days and that he met only with Peter and James (the brother of Jesus). Barnabas told these two apostles about Saul's experience on the Damascus road, as well as about his work in Damascus.

These facts seem to have convinced the apostles of the genuineness of their former enemy's conversion. Paul began **preaching boldly in the name of the Lord.**

9:29-30 While in Jerusalem, Saul felt led to witness to the very same audience that had masterminded the stoning of Stephen—**some Greek-speaking Jews** (6:9-10). As might be expected, he encountered furious opposition. Saul was, in their eyes, a turncoat and a traitor, so **they plotted to murder him.** In these short sentences, we can see two characteristics of Saul, even as a new believer in Christ: he was bold, and he stirred up controversy. These would characterize Saul's ministry for the rest of his life. With the help of **the believers,** Saul escaped to **Caesarea,** where he

then made his way **to his hometown of Tarsus.** Saul's departure helped quiet conflicts with the Jews. Galatians 1:21-24 probably refers to Saul's continued ministry both in Caesarea and Tarsus.

9:31 After Saul, the most zealous persecutor, was converted, the **church** enjoyed a brief time of **peace.** After every crisis the power of God was present, and the church grew. The gospel was spreading, and the church was growing in **Judea, Galilee and Samaria.** It was now time for the message of Christ to be taken to the "ends of the earth" (1:8).

Saul now disappears from the record until Acts 11:25, several years later. In the interim, Saul had some experiences that are not recorded in Acts but are referred to in 2 Corinthians 11.

PETER HEALS AENEAS AND RAISES DORCAS / 9:32-43

After describing Saul's astounding conversion, Luke focused again on the ministry of Peter, specifically on the miraculous signs that accompanied his preaching. Capitalizing on the newfound climate of religious tolerance (the result of Saul's conversion and departure to Tarsus), Peter began an itinerant ministry intended to strengthen and encourage believers scattered throughout Israel.

9:32 Peter, the leader of the apostles, was last mentioned in 8:25 returning from Samaria to Jerusalem with John. He came to **Lydda,** a predominantly Gentile community about twenty-five miles west of Jerusalem. Lydda was a fairly large town and commercial center at the intersection of highways connecting Egypt to Syria and Joppa (on the Mediterranean coast) to Jerusalem. The gospel likely came to Lydda as a direct result of the mass conversion at Pentecost (chapter 2) or from those who had fled the Jerusalem persecution (8:1).

9:33-35 Nothing more is known about **Aeneas** other than this fact of his miraculous healing from an eight-year crippling illness. The healing was done by **Jesus Christ,** and it was immediate. This miracle was not an end in itself but a confirming sign of the truth of the gospel. The phrase, **the whole population,** was probably not meant to be taken literally; rather, it was Luke's way of reporting that a vast number of people **turned to the Lord** and were saved, including not only those in Lydda but in the whole area of **Sharon,** a coastal plain about ten miles wide and fifty miles long stretching north from Lydda toward Carmel.

9:36-37 The important harbor city of **Joppa** sits 125 feet above sea level, overlooking the Mediterranean Sea. Joppa was the town into which the cedars of Lebanon had been floated to be shipped

to Jerusalem and used in the temple construction (2 Chronicles 2:16; Ezra 3:7). The prophet Jonah had left the port of Joppa on his ill-fated trip (Jonah 1:3).

It was customary to bury corpses before sundown. The believers had only **prepared her for burial and laid her in an upstairs room,** suggesting that they believed that she could be raised. The church had not previously experienced miracles of this nature, though such signs had occurred during the life and ministry of Christ. Perhaps word about the healing of Aeneas had reached Joppa from Lydda, because the believers dispatched two men to find and bring Peter (9:38).

9:38-39 Joppa was only about ten miles northwest of Lydda. To go and find Peter and bring him back would have taken these **two men** six to eight hours. Once located and presented with the need in Joppa, Peter **returned with them.** The text indicates the haste with which all this was accomplished. Arriving, Peter was immediately ushered to **the upstairs room.** There he met a group of mourning **widows.** Clearly, this woman's death was a major blow to the church in Joppa.

9:40-43 After getting down on his knees to pray, Peter told Tabitha to **get up.** Then **she opened her eyes.** Peter presented this back-from-the-dead saint to her overjoyed friends. As a result of this startling miracle, **many** citizens of Joppa **believed in the Lord. Peter stayed a long time in Joppa,** at the home of **Simon,** probably in order to teach the people more thoroughly the full implications of the gospel.

It is significant that Peter stayed with a man who was, by vocation, **a leatherworker** who made animal hides into leather. This occupation involved contact with dead animals, and Jewish law considered it an "unclean" job. Peter was already beginning to break down his prejudice against people who were not of his kind and customs that did not adhere to Jewish religious traditions. This would set the stage for what is reported in the next chapter.

ACTS 10

CORNELIUS CALLS FOR PETER / 10:1-8

In the history of the early church recorded in the first nine chapters of Acts, this saving work of God's Spirit was mostly confined to the Jews. Suddenly, Acts 10 describes the Spirit's sovereign activity in a Gentile army officer stationed on the Mediterranean coast. The book of Acts continues with its steady, singular message: God is directing the expansion of his church, founded on the crucified and resurrected Christ. The conversion of Cornelius, the first Gentile convert recorded in Acts, portrays a significant step in the process of expansion. The word was spreading and the church was on the threshold of a whole new phase of Jesus' promised progress (1:8).

10:1-2 This **Caesarea,** sometimes called Palestinian Caesarea, was located on the coast of the Mediterranean Sea, thirty-two miles north of Joppa. The largest and most important port city on the Mediterranean in Palestine, Caesarea was the capital of the Roman province of Judea. This was the first city to have Gentile Christians and a non-Jewish church.

This **Roman army officer,** although stationed in Caesarea, would probably have had to return soon to Rome. Thus his conversion may have helped to spread the gospel to the empire's capital city. Because of frequent outbreaks of violence, Roman soldiers had to be stationed to keep peace throughout Israel. But most Romans, hated as conquerors, did not get along well in the nation. As an army officer, **Cornelius** was in a difficult position. He represented Rome, but he lived in Caesarea. During Cornelius's years in Israel, he had been conquered by the **God of Israel.** With a reputation as a **devout man,** Cornelius was respected by the Jews. Cornelius's faith had hands—he was regularly involved in activities that displayed his interest in serving others.

10:3-4 The time—**about three o'clock**—was likely one of Cornelius's regular times of prayer. This was one of the hours of prayer at the Temple.

Cornelius may have prayed faithfully for many years before this day when **an angel of God** came to speak to him. Later, Cornelius would describe this angel as "a man in dazzling clothes" (10:30). Even this veteran soldier was terrified. God saw Cornelius's sincere faith. His prayers and generous giving had **not gone unnoticed by God.** God answers the sincere prayers of those who seek him by sending the right person or the right information at the right time.

10:5-6 God told Cornelius to send for **a man named Simon Peter** because Peter would give him more knowledge about the God he was already seeking to please. Cornelius was directed to **Joppa** (thirty-two miles south of Caesarea) to find Peter.

10:7-8 Cornelius obeyed the message of the angel and sent his most trusted aides to get Peter. Three men were sent—**two household servants** and a **devout soldier,** the latter of whom is described as **one of his personal attendants.** Obviously, the godly character of Cornelius had made an impact on those closest to him. The word used to describe Cornelius's account of **what had happened** is the word from which we get the term "exegesis" (*exegesamenos*), meaning to "explain" clearly and in detail.

PETER VISITS CORNELIUS / 10:9-33

Even as Cornelius's messengers were on their way to get Peter, the apostle was having a divine vision of his own. In this vision, three times Peter was commanded to kill and eat a number of unclean animals. Of Jewish descent, Peter was both horrified and confused by this strange dream. The meaning of the vision slowly became clear, however, when the messengers arrived and told their story (10:17-23).

10:9-10 Like Cornelius, Peter prayed daily. Morning and evening were the common times to pray, and evidently Peter made it a habit to pray in the middle of the day as well (see Nehemiah 1:4-11; Psalm 55:17; Daniel 6:10). This significant opening of the door to the Gentiles was God-directed, but note that the two men were devout, God-dependent, regular seekers of God through prayer. It is no coincidence that Peter and Cornelius were both found praying when God revealed more of himself to them.

Peter **went up to the flat roof to pray.** Houses in Bible times usually had flat roofs accessed by an outside staircase. The roof would have given Peter privacy. As he prayed, he **was hungry** and evidently **fell into a trance** while he was waiting for lunch to be prepared. During this trance God spoke to him.

10:11-14 Peter saw **something like a large sheet** being **let down** to earth from heaven. The **voice,** obviously that of someone in authority (probably God himself), told Peter that he was free to **kill and eat** the **animals,** including **reptiles** and **birds.** According to Jewish law, these particular foods were forbidden (see Leviticus 11). Peter, always ready to voice his opinion, expressed his conviction not to eat anything **forbidden by** the **Jewish laws.** The point of this vision, as was about to be made clear, was that God was working outside of Israel, beyond Israel, and if Peter was to be a part of what God was doing, he needed to understand that nothing was unclean.

10:15-16 This educating of Peter, as with the educating of most believers, took a little repetition— **three times** in this case. God was revealing something that would be startling to Peter's Jewish mind; God was basically nullifying the Jewish dietary laws and, by analogy, God was preparing Peter to meet an unclean Gentile.

10:17-20 Peter was very perplexed, and his confusion is understandable. For centuries the dietary restrictions had been in place for devout Jews. As Peter reflected over what **the vision** meant, his God-sent visitors arrived to provide an opportunity for Peter to apply what the voice from heaven had said. Peter was to **go with them without hesitation,** for

they would take him to see the real meaning behind the vision of the sheet and the animals.

10:21-22 Peter was greeted by three men at the door (10:19-20) who introduced the one they represented. Cornelius's godly character had obviously built him a good reputation. Peter was informed of the heavenly message that Cornelius had received, and he recognized it as being somehow related to his own. The openness of Cornelius to whatever **message** Peter would have to say was a beautiful foreshadowing of the coming Gentile openness to the message of the Cross.

10:23-24 Peter had been staying at the house of Simon the leatherworker. Peter continued to remove barriers: not only was he staying in a place that his prejudices would have previously prohibited (see commentary on 9:42-43), he went a step further by inviting Gentiles into that home **to be his guests.** This kind of fellowship would have been unacceptable to a strict Jew. A sheet had been let down from heaven, and Peter's eyes were being opened.

Peter was wise to take with him **some other believers from Joppa** (six believers, according to 11:12). Some things, particularly changes as radical as Peter suspected were on the horizon, were better observed firsthand rather than explained secondhand. Possibly Peter knew that it was easier for him to accept this new Gentile openness to the gospel because he had been present at the "Samaritan Pentecost" (8:15-17). If God were truly doing something new, it would be best that other believers could see it as well. The eagerness and expectation of Cornelius was obvious, for he **called together his relatives and close friends,** probably many, considering Cornelius's reputation for kindness and piety.

10:25-27 The reaction of Cornelius to Peter's arrival was that of one who felt he was in the presence of a messenger of God. Peter's statement, **"I'm a human being like you,"** was profound. Certainly these words would be spread throughout the Gentile world, that the great apostle had equated himself with a Roman centurion.

10:28-29 Peter acknowledged his breaking of Jewish laws to enter this **Gentile home,** but he continued and gave the gathered audience the benefit of God's vision of the sheet from heaven. Peter had gotten the message. The vision was not primarily about food; the dietary issues were secondary to the human ones. The vision was from **God** and was about people, specifically those people whom the Jews (and, as a carryover, the Jewish Christians) still considered "unclean." Without reserve, Peter stated that God had shown him that he **should never think of anyone as impure.**

10:30-32 Cornelius recounted his experience for the sake of Peter and his gathered guests. Luke recorded it because it is a very important vision, and in each retelling, more details were added or emphasized. This will be repeated again by Peter

in the next chapter (11:4-14). Here Cornelius added to his description of the angelic messenger, saying that he had been wearing **dazzling clothes.** Cornelius recounted to Peter what the angel had told him to do. Surely the specifics that had been given to Cornelius about Peter's whereabouts showed how God was behind this meeting.

10:33 Cornelius stated that those present were in a holy convocation—**waiting before God**—and that their sole purpose was **to hear the message the Lord** had given Peter. Cornelius had sure, solid confidence that God was about to speak to them through Peter, and on behalf of all those gathered there, he expressed eagerness to hear what God had to say. If ever there was an ideal audience for a preacher or teacher, this was it.

THE GENTILES HEAR THE GOOD NEWS / 10:34-43

Having been sovereignly (even miraculously) guided to the home of Cornelius and having been impressed by the truth that God doesn't show partiality (10:34), Peter took the keys of the Kingdom of Heaven given him by Christ (Matthew 16:19) and, in an epoch-changing moment, opened the door of salvation to the Gentiles.

10:34-35 Peter's words—**God doesn't show partiality, every nation, he accepts those who fear him**—express Peter's clear understanding of the universal application of Christ's work on the cross and the subsequent universal offer of the gospel. For more on God's acceptance of all kinds of people, see Ephesians 6:9; Colossians 3:25; James 2:1, 9; 1 Peter 1:17. Because God doesn't discriminate on the basis of race, economics, or sex, neither should any believers.

10:36 Assuming that his audience had already **heard** much of the information about the coming of Christ and the birth of the church, Peter proceeded to tell the story of Christ's life and death in detail. This is a beautiful summary of the teaching of the apostles, and it perfectly parallels the Gospel of Mark (who probably received much of his information from Peter). This verse expresses the clear purpose of the gospel—to provide an opportunity for people to experience **peace with God.** The means by which that happens is **through Jesus Christ,** to whom Peter referred here by the powerful title, **Lord of all.**

10:37-38 Peter started where Mark's Gospel does—with **John the Baptist.** He mentioned Christ's ministry, including the good works and **healing** Jesus had done. Peter's audience would likely have been familiar with most of these events. The miracles and the healings were a

demonstration of Jesus' power over **the Devil** as well as the fact that **God was with him** and in fact had **anointed** him **with the Holy Spirit and with power** (Isaiah 61:1-3; Luke 4:16-21). The anointing of which Peter was speaking had occurred at Jesus' baptism, when the Holy Spirit, in the form of a dove, had descended upon him (Mark 1:9-11; Luke 3:21-22).

10:39-41 In short order, Peter stated the fact that he and others had been **witnesses** to the ministry of Jesus, including his crucifixion and his resurrection. Peter acknowledged that there was no general appearance of Christ to the **public** but rather to those who had been chosen by God. In no way should that diminish the magnitude of the miracle or the credibility of the testimony of the witnesses. The fact that they had eaten and had drunk with him should squelch any rumor that Jesus had appeared in some "phantom" form. This was solid, decisive proof of Christ's resurrection and was confirmed by one who had been there, had seen it, and had participated fully in it.

10:42 Christ came to judge (see 2 Timothy 4:1; 1 Peter 4:5). The command of the resurrected Christ was for these witnesses **to preach everywhere and to testify that Jesus is ordained of God to be the judge of all.** He is the one before whom ultimately all people (Jew and Gentile alike) will stand and give account. For Christ's commands to the disciples, see Acts 1:8, also Matthew 28:18-20; Mark 16:15-18; Luke 24:47-48.

10:43 Christ came to forgive sin. In contrast to the preceding verse, Peter turned to the **prophets'** testimony for the flip side of judgment—salvation. Jesus Christ was the long-awaited Savior who would offer forgiveness of sins to **everyone who** **believes in him** (John 3:16). Two examples of prophets testifying about Jesus and his forgiveness of sins are Isaiah (see Isaiah 52:13–53:12) and Ezekiel (see Ezekiel 36:25-26).

Note again that Peter made it clear that this message is for **everyone**, not just the Jews. **Everyone** sins. **Everyone** needs to be saved. **Everyone** needs forgiveness. All that is needed is faith.

THE GENTILES RECEIVE THE HOLY SPIRIT / 10:44-48

To confirm the Gentiles' acceptance by God and their full inclusion in his Kingdom as heirs of grace, Luke recorded these new converts' experience of the Holy Spirit. Luke recorded the original Pentecost in chapter 2. Chapter 8 told of the "Samaritan Pentecost." This event could be called the "Gentile Pentecost." The Spirit came upon all those in attendance.

10:44 Peter's sermon was interrupted by **the Holy Spirit,** who **fell upon all who had heard the message.** Unlike the Samaritan believers who had waited between belief and the baptism of the Spirit, which had come by the laying on of apostolic hands (see 8:17-18), the Spirit **fell** on these Gentile believers, just as he had at the first Pentecost—no laying on of hands, no praying for the Spirit to fall; God just did it!

10:45-46a The **Jewish believers** who had accompanied **Peter** (10:23) **were amazed** that the same phenomena of Pentecost were being demonstrated on **the Gentiles.** As at Pentecost, reported in chapter 2, these Gentiles experienced **speaking in tongues and praising God.** This was a powerful testimony to Peter and his Jewish contingency of the necessity of fully accepting Gentile believers into the body of Christ. Whatever lingering questions Peter may have had about his vision of a sheet and animals or about Cornelius's visit by an angelic messenger would have been put aside in light of this event.

10:46b-48 In this case the believers were **baptized** after they received the Holy Spirit, publicly declaring their allegiance to Christ and identification with the Christian community. Peter's words (**received the Holy Spirit just as we did**) reveal the impressiveness of what they had just seen. It was undeniable, irrefutable evidence that God had come to the Gentiles. They were now full-fledged, Spirit-indwelled members of the body of Christ. These new Spirit-baptized believers were then **baptized in the name of Jesus Christ.** Peter was invited by his new Christian friends to **stay with them for several days,** presumably for further instruction on what had just happened and what was next in this new life in Christ.

ACTS 11

PETER EXPLAINS HIS ACTIONS / 11:1-18

Word of Peter's eating with Gentiles caused a negative reaction among the Jewish believers back in Jerusalem. The incident violated Hebrew customs and presuppositions. Following a detailed explanation of events by a persuasive and changed Peter, however, the others became convinced that God had ordered these surprising circumstances. The Jerusalem church began to accept the Gentile mission.

11:1-3 Most **Jewish believers** thought that God offered salvation only to the Jews because God had given his law to them (Exodus 19–20). A group in Jerusalem believed that **Gentiles could**

be saved, but only if they followed all the Jewish laws and traditions—in essence, if they became Jews before they became Christians (this would be the topic of discussion at the Jerusalem council—chapter 15). Thus, when **Peter arrived back in Jerusalem,** he was **criticized** for entering a Gentile home and then eating a meal with Gentiles. Both practices were terribly offensive to devout Jews who feared accidentally breaking one of their strict dietary regulations.

11:4-7 Peter then repeated to his critics **exactly what had happened** (see comments at 10:30). Evidently, he thought the best defense against his critics would be simply to tell the story as it happened. Peter wanted this potentially hostile (already critical) audience to know that he had been **praying** at the time that he saw the vision.

11:8-10 Peter repeated for his audience his refusal to "kill and eat" (11:7) these animals as instructed by the Lord. He quoted the response of the **voice from heaven,** instructing him that when **God says something is acceptable** not to **say it isn't.** Finally, he noted the threefold repetition of this dialogue between himself and the Lord, and the pulling of the sheet back up to heaven again. This event and all the effects of it in Cornelius's life became a primary argument for the Gentile mission in the early church.

11:11-12 Peter spoke of the arrival of the **three men from Caesarea.** Upon the command of no one less than the **Holy Spirit,** Peter had accompanied them, citing the Spirit's command **not to worry about their being Gentiles.** He had taken **six** fellow believers with him to witness what was to happen and help recall it accurately. Peter understood that God was at work and deduced that something controversial (or potentially divisive) might take place. The potential for misunderstanding was evidently great enough for these men to have also accompanied Peter back to Jerusalem to report to the apostles. Jewish law only required two witnesses. Peter's having six witnesses reveals the gravity of the issue and the significance of the event.

11:13-14 In two sentences Peter summarized the experience of Cornelius, which has already been recorded twice (see 10:1-7 and 10:30-32). It would be important to the Jewish audience to hear that an angelic messenger had also appeared to the principle Gentile figure in the drama.

Peter added a significant statement that had been excluded from the other accounts of Cornelius's experience: the angel had told Cornelius that he and **all his household will be saved.** In other words, God's intent from the start was to bring

this Gentile soldier, along with his friends and family, to Christ.

11:15-17 Peter described that crucial moment in recounting his meeting with the Gentiles when **the Holy Spirit fell on them, just as he fell on** the Jewish believers **at the beginning,** referring to Pentecost (chapter 2). The Holy Spirit had come on these Gentile believers just as he had come on the Jewish believers. There was no difference between the two "Pentecosts" other than that the Jews' experience had come first. These subsequent events, parallel to Pentecost, proved to the Jerusalem church that they must accept each new group of converts (the Samaritans, the Gentiles) because God had put his guarantee on them by repeating Pentecost.

Peter added what he had been thinking when the event had occurred, for he remembered something the risen Christ had said right before his ascension: **"John baptized with water, but you will be baptized with the Holy Spirit"** (1:5). Up until the event in Cornelius's house, Peter (along with the rest of the Jewish believers) must have thought that the baptism of the Holy Spirit was reserved exclusively for Jewish believers. Having witnessed the baptism of the Holy Spirit on Gentile believers, Peter realized that Jesus' words had a much broader application. Jesus had also demonstrated clearly that he and his message were for all types of people. He had preached in Samaria (John 4:1-42), in the region of the Gerasenes (populated by Greeks, Mark 5:1-20), and had even reached out to Roman citizens (Luke 7:1-10). The apostles shouldn't have been surprised that they were called to do the same.

11:18 The theological discussion stopped with the report that God had given the Holy Spirit to the Gentiles. This was a turning point for the early church. They had to accept those whom God had chosen, even Gentiles.

The response was one of **praising God** as the congregation remarked on the fact that **God has also given the Gentiles the privilege of turning from sin and receiving eternal life.** This is a remarkable example of the spiritual health of this young church. Though steeped in centuries of Jewish rules and regulations, they had seen enough of God's wonders over the past few months to know that God was moving in some new ways. Even though they had the words and example of Christ pointing them toward the Gentile world (Matthew 28:19; Acts 1:8), they had to overcome enormous inertia. The fact that they were so open to what God was doing and so responsive to Peter's leadership speaks well of the work of the Spirit in their lives.

THE CHURCH IN ANTIOCH OF SYRIA / 11:19-30

The closing verses of chapter 9 and the record in chapter 10 describe Peter's preparation for the universal dissemination of the gospel; and the opening verses of chapter 11 describe the apostles' preparation for the universal nature of the gospel, then these final verses of chapter 11 describe the preparation of the church at Antioch for the same thing. The focus of the church is shifting to the north, to this incredible missionary church in Antioch of Syria. The balance of this chapter gives a close-up view of a church that can be used mightily of God to change an entire empire and, beyond it, the world.

11:19 As Peter was dealing with this new issue of Gentiles entering the church, God was at work elsewhere. **Meanwhile,** the seeds of missionary work were being sown after Stephen's death, for many believing Jews were persecuted and scattered, settling in faraway cities and spreading the gospel. The **Good News** was being preached, **but only to Jews.**

There was a large Jewish population in **Antioch of Syria.** When persecution against Christians broke out in Jerusalem after the death of Stephen, many Christians fled there—three hundred miles north of Jerusalem. An important commercial center and the third largest city in the Roman Empire (population 500,000), the city of Antioch was located fifteen miles inland from the Mediterranean Sea on the Orontes River. Under the Roman Empire, Antioch became the capital of the province of Syria. The city was beautified by Caesars Augustus and Tiberius, with the help of Herod the Great. The city enjoyed a beautiful location and abundant water supply. But Antioch was a horribly corrupt city and was the center of worship for several pagan cults that promoted sexual immorality and other forms of evil common to pagan religions. This city would be home to the church that would be the sovereignly chosen group to fund and direct the next decade of church expansion under a new missionary, Paul.

11:20-21 Cyprus is an island off the Mediterranean coast from Antioch, and **Cyrene** was a city in northern Africa. Fortunately, these **believers** had the courage to spread the gospel of **the Lord Jesus** outside of the confines of Judaism. When these believers spoke, **the power of the Lord was upon them, and large numbers of these Gentiles believed and turned to the Lord.**

Evidently, this small beginning turned Antioch into a place where the believers aggressively preached to the Gentiles. Philip had preached in Samaria (8:5), but the Samaritans were part Jewish. Peter had preached to Cornelius, but he already worshiped God (10:2). Believers who were scattered after the outbreak of persecution in Jerusalem spread the gospel to other Jews in the lands where they had fled (11:19). Finally, the believers began actively sharing the Good News with Gentiles, with great results.

11:22-24 Word of the happenings in **Antioch** prompted the leaders of the Jerusalem church to send someone to investigate. **Barnabas** was the emissary. He was a wise choice for a number of reasons. From Cyprus, he would have had a natural national connection with the evangelists who had started the movement in Antioch. **Barnabas was a good man, full of the Holy Spirit and strong in faith.** His name means "Son of Encouragement" (4:36), and he lived up to it as **he encouraged the believers to stay true to the Lord.** The ministry of the gospel was thriving—**large numbers** believed.

11:25-26 Saul had been sent to his home in **Tarsus** for protection after his conversion caused an uproar among the Jewish religious leaders in Jerusalem (9:26-30). He stayed there for several years before **Barnabas brought him back to Antioch.** Evidently, the work at Antioch had grown so that it was too much for Barnabas to handle alone. Barnabas and Paul's ministry in Antioch was marked by their **teaching.** Those who became believers were consistently and systematically instructed by these two teachers in the basics of their newfound faith.

The young church at Antioch was a curious mixture of Jews (who spoke Greek or Aramaic) and Gentiles. It is significant that this was the **first** place where the believers were called **Christians** ("Christ's ones"—the ending "-ian" means "belonging to the party of"). There has been a great deal of debate about who gave them the name "Christians." It is not likely that the believers themselves invented the name, because they had other terms for themselves like "disciples" or "saints" or "brothers." Certainly, the Jews would never want their term "Messiah" *(christos)* associated with this new movement. It is likely, therefore, that the term "Christian" was invented by the non-Christian culture of Antioch. One of the earliest extrabiblical occurrences of the term comes from a remark made by Emperor Nero. Whatever the case, the believers in Christ were becoming an identifiable group, distinct from Judaism and, at least in Antioch, primarily Gentile in composition.

11:27-28 Prophets were not limited to Old Testament times (see 13:1; 15:32; 21:9). God appointed certain people to be prophets to the church, and Paul ranked "prophets" second only to apostles in his list of those gifted by the Holy Spirit (1 Corinthians 12:28). The Jews believed that prophecy had ceased during the time of the exile but would resurface as a sign of the Messiah's coming. Peter had quoted the prophet Joel in his sermon at Pentecost: "Your sons and daughters will prophesy" (2:17). Prophets had special gifts in ministering God's messages to his people. At times, they would foretell the future (as Agabus did here), but the gift of prophecy was also valued for its role in exhorting, encouraging, and strengthening God's people (1 Corinthians 14:31). God spoke through prophets, inspiring them with specific messages for particular times and places.

In the early church, these prophets seem to have traveled from place to place. **Agabus** predicted **that a great famine was coming upon the entire Roman world.** Agabus later would predict Paul's arrest in Jerusalem (see 21:10-11). What happened was actually a series of famines during the **reign** of Emperor **Claudius** (41–54 A.D.). This enigmatic pair of verses seems to introduce the reason for the Antioch church's support of the "mother" church in Jerusalem, mentioned in 11:29-30.

11:29-30 Because there were serious food shortages during this time due to the famine, **the believers in Antioch** assisted the church in Jerusalem. The daughter church had grown enough to be able to help the mother church. The solid reputation for the spiritual integrity of **Barnabas and Saul** is affirmed by the fact that they were the ones entrusted with the money. This visit was most likely the second visit of Paul to **Jerusalem,** occurring in about A.D. 46. This visit corresponds to Galatians 2:1-10. His first visit was in Acts 9:26-29, and that correlates with Galatians 1:18-20.

This is the first mention of **elders** in the New Testament (see 15:4, 6; 16:4; 21:18). Not much is known about their role in those days, but clearly, at least part of their responsibilities included managing the church's financial affairs. See 1 Timothy 3:1-7 and Titus 1:5-9 for a later listing of their qualifications; see 1 Peter 5:1-4 and Acts 20:28-32 for some clues as to their responsibilities.

The chapter ends with a very healthy picture of this burgeoning, young, and mostly Gentile church. They had two high-quality teachers, Barnabas and Saul. They had a solid contingency of giving saints—donating enough money to tend to the local needs of the congregation **and** send something to the "mother church" at Jerusalem. The idea of a Gentile-Christian congregation sending help to a Jewish-Christian church highlights the quality of its spiritual character.

ACTS 12

JAMES IS KILLED AND PETER IS IMPRISONED / 12:1-5
The rapid growth of the church in Jerusalem (6:1) brought fierce opposition (8:1). Persecution often accompanies progress. Unable to stop the masses from embracing this new faith, the Jews launched a direct attack upon the Christian leaders. Beyond mere threats and warnings (see 4:18-21; 5:40), this time Herod had James executed and Peter arrested.

12:1 The church was growing dramatically, but the king was increasing the persecution. This was **King Herod Agrippa I,** the son of Aristobulus and grandson of Herod the Great. His sister was Herodias, who had been responsible for the death of John the Baptist (see Mark 6:17-28). Herod Agrippa I was partly Jewish. The Romans had appointed him to rule over most of Palestine, including the territories of Galilee, Perea, Judea,

and Samaria. He **began to persecute** the Christians in order to please the Jewish leaders who opposed them, hoping to solidify his position. Agrippa is mentioned in the Bible only in this chapter. He died suddenly in A.D. 44 (see 12:20-23), a fact also recorded by the historian Josephus.

The Christian movement created an unexpected opportunity for Herod to gain new favor with the Jews. Gentiles began to be accepted into the church in large numbers. Many Jews had been tolerating this new movement as a sect within Judaism, but its rapid growth alarmed them. Persecution of Christians was revived, and even the apostles were not spared.

12:2 **James** and **John** were two of the original twelve disciples who followed Jesus. They had asked Jesus for special recognition in his Kingdom (Mark 10:35-40). Jesus said that to be a part of his Kingdom would mean suffering with him. James and John did indeed suffer—Herod had James **killed with a sword** (John was later exiled, Revelation 1:9). These two brothers were the first and the last apostles to die.

There is a great deal to be learned here from what did not happen to James and what did happen to Peter later in this chapter. Imagine being a part of both prayer meetings. The church surely had prayed as fervently for James as they did for Peter. Peter was miraculously set free; James was executed. Was there something wrong with the way the believers prayed for James as opposed to Peter? The wrong words? Scriptures? Posture? Was there not enough faith? Did God love Peter more than James? The answer to all these questions is, of course, no, but they are the kinds of questions Christians invariably ask when faced with such a clear example of the contrasting will of God for

two lives. The sovereign choices of God in the lives of these two apostles—equally loved by God, needed by the church, and missed by their friends and family—should teach believers to trust God more.

12:3-4 Herod, in the self-serving spirit of the previous Herods of the New Testament, took special delight in the positive political benefits he received from executing James. Since James's execution **pleased the Jewish leaders,** Herod Agrippa then **arrested Peter** during the **Passover.** This was a strategic move since more Jews were in the city than usual, and Herod could impress the most Jews by imprisoning the most visible of the church leaders.

Peter was well guarded by **four squads of four soldiers each**—each squad would have guarded Peter for one-fourth of a day! Evidently, Herod knew of Peter's previous escape (5:19-24) and wanted to be sure that such would not happen this time. Luke stressed this detail to set the scene for the mighty power of God. No one could escape under human power alone.

12:5 Herod undoubtedly was planning to execute Peter, but the believers were praying **earnestly** for Peter's safety. The earnest prayer of the church significantly affected the outcome of these events. The believers are here called **the church,** a clearly identified entity in Jerusalem.

PETER'S MIRACULOUS ESCAPE FROM PRISON / 12:6-19
James was already dead. Peter was in prison. From a human perspective, the situation appeared terribly grim, but from a heavenly perspective, this was just another opportunity to display the infinite power of God.

12:6 Luke carefully recorded the location of the soldiers (12:4) in charge of making sure this reputed jail-breaking apostle (5:19-24) did not slip away again and leave Herod with a serious public-relations problem. **Two soldiers** were **chained** to Peter, one on either side, and **others** were **standing guard at the prison gate.** Luke again stressed the power of God over earthly rulers.

12:7-8 This same type of jailbreak had happened to the apostles before, as recorded in 5:19-24, but more detail is given here. From his sleep, Peter was roused by an **angel of the Lord** and was told to **get up.** The command was accompanied by his **chains** falling **off his wrists.** The term for "falling off" comes from a Greek word meaning to "drop away." Neither the angel nor Peter touched the chains—they came off because God was setting Peter free.

Nothing is written about the whereabouts of the guards, who were likely not the only prison guards around. A couple of them would have been posted at every gate, every door, and at any possible escape route from the prison. The soldiers may have been dazed, asleep, or blinded from the whole event. In the end, it would be a deadly miracle for them (12:19).

12:9-10 Peter seemed dazed as he followed the angel's instructions because **he thought it was a vision.** Peter thought this was similar to his experience with the sheet let down from heaven, recorded in chapter 10 (the same word is used here for "vision" that was used for his vision at Joppa in 10:17). They passed two **guard posts** before arriving at **the iron gate** which led to **the street.** With dramatic effect, the gate mysteriously, miraculously **opened** (the Greek is *automate*—"automatically"). The angel stayed with Peter a little longer, then **suddenly left** Peter alone.

12:11 Peter finally realized what had happened. He realized that the Lord had **saved** him. He knew Herod's plans to use Peter's incarceration (and possible execution) as another way to ingratiate himself to the **Jews**. Peter's awareness of his life-threatening situation, particularly in light of the recent execution of James (see 12:2), made his peaceful sleep in the prison cell all the more marvelous. Peter had seen enough to trust that the Father was in control of his life.

12:12 Once he realized that he was not dreaming, Peter **went** directly to **the home of Mary, the mother of John Mark.** Mentioned here in passing, John Mark was the author of the Gospel of Mark and became an important character on the first journey of Paul (see 13:5, 13; 15:37-39).

Mary's house was large enough to accommodate a meeting of many believers. An upstairs room in her house may have been the location of Jesus' last supper with his disciples (Luke 22:8) and/or the place where the 120 earliest believers met for prayer (1:15; 2:1). Evidently Mary's home was a common place of meeting for the Jerusalem church (or part of it), at least for prayer. This particular night, with their beloved Peter in prison and the apostle James recently martyred, a large group had **gathered for prayer.**

12:13-15 Peter **knocked** and **Rhoda, a servant girl,** answered the door. Mary's house must have had a vestibule or hallway to the street with an outer door at the street and an inner door opening into the house. Rhoda was so excited to hear **Peter's voice** that she forgot to open the door! Meanwhile, the sober, serious saints, hard at the work of praying for Peter's release, failed to realize that the answer to their prayer was **standing at the door,** trying to get in! They even went so far as to accuse the poor girl of being crazy. At her insistence, they speculated that maybe Peter's **angel** was at the door, indicating they thought that he must have been executed already.

12:16 One wonders what was going through this usually impatient apostle's mind at this point. Certainly, his absence from prison would be noticed soon. The guards would likely know exactly where to look for him. The servant girl had recognized Peter's voice, but the others, so busy praying for Peter's release, wouldn't come to the door to let the freed apostle into the house! If ever people should stop praying and do something, that was the time! As **Peter continued knocking,** someone **finally** went to the outer door and **opened** it. Everyone was **amazed.**

12:17 The pandemonium was so loud that Peter had to **quiet** the crowd. He recounted the story of his escape and instructed that the information be passed on to **James and the other brothers.** This James was Jesus' brother, who became a leader in the Jerusalem church (15:13; Galatians 1:19). The James who had been killed earlier (12:2) was John's brother and one of the original twelve disciples. Peter's instruction to inform James indicates that James may have already been recognized as one of the leaders (if not *the* leader) of the Jerusalem church. Perhaps through this very series of events and this statement before the gathered church, Peter was officially moving out of direct leadership of the Jerusalem believers. Possibly he sensed that this latest brush with Herod was God's sovereign shifting of him to plow another field.

In short order, likely because of his certainty that Herod's soldiers would be after him, Peter **went to another place.** It is unknown exactly where he went.

12:18-19 Meanwhile, back at the prison, **there was a great commotion.** Under Roman law, guards who allowed a prisoner to escape were subject to the same punishment the prisoner was to receive. After a **thorough search** for Peter, these sixteen guards were **sentenced to death.**

Herod's departure to **Caesarea** sets up the next scene. The Jews considered Jerusalem their capital, but the Romans made Caesarea their headquarters in Palestine. That was where Herod lived. (For more on Caesarea, see commentary on 10:1.)

THE DEATH OF HEROD AGRIPPA / 12:20-25

Herod Agrippa's fate should not surprise us. The Scriptures proclaim that pride goes before a fall. By foolishly setting himself against God and refusing to give him glory, Herod guaranteed his own disastrous demise.

12:20 Tyre and Sidon, coastal cities on the Mediterranean, were free and self-governing but economically dependent on Judea. It is unknown why **Herod was very angry** with them, but representatives from those cities were trying to appease him, probably through a bribe. Presumably, through **Blastus,** they asked for **peace,** needing the benefit of the Galilean market **for their food.**

12:21-22 Herod, bedecked in his **royal robes,** addressed the people of Tyre and Sidon, who were trying to get a trade agreement out of him. This was A.D. 44 and may have been just before Passover, approximately one year after Peter's escape from prison. The people had already bribed Herod's personal assistant, but here they also resorted to ridiculous flattery—**shouting** out to the ego-driven Herod that his voice was **the voice of a god, not of a man.** The Greek historian Josephus also recorded this event in his **Antiquities of the Jews** (19.334).

12:23 While neither account (Luke's or Josephus's) described Herod Agrippa's response to the crowd, Luke explained that God acted, and he did so **instantly. An angel of the Lord** was God's vehicle to strike Herod with a horrible illness, described in gory detail: **So he was consumed with worms and died.** Some scholars suggest that the worms were intestinal roundworms, which grow ten to sixteen inches long and rob the body of nutrients while causing intense pain.

The reason for this judgment was that Herod **accepted the people's worship instead of giving the glory to God.** God knew what was going on in Herod's heart and refused to share his glory with any earthly potentate. Pride is a serious sin. God chose to punish Herod's pride immediately. God does not immediately punish all sin, but he will bring all to judgment (Hebrews 9:27). Those who set themselves against God are doomed to ultimate failure.

12:24 In great contrast with the verse above, Luke described quite a different scenario for the church. **God's Good News was spreading rapidly.** The death of James, the imprisonment of Peter, and other persecutions had not slowed the steady expansion of the church.

12:25 This verse picks up from the story in 11:27-30, where **Barnabas and Saul** had been sent with the famine relief funds from the church at Antioch for the believers in Jerusalem. That had been **their mission.** Barnabas and Saul were probably not in Jerusalem for the events of this chapter; instead, they made the trip some time after Herod's death. Luke, in his arrangement of his materials, chose to put the events of Peter and Herod at this point in the story.

Upon the completion of their mission, Barnabas and Saul **returned to Antioch,** having picked up **John Mark** in the process. John Mark was also Barnabas's cousin (Colossians 4:10). His mother, Mary, often would open her home to the church (12:12), so John Mark would have been exposed to most of the great teachers and teachings of the early church. He had become a believer and had the great opportunity to travel with these two men of God.

ACTS 13

BARNABAS AND PAUL ARE SENT OUT / 13:1-3

Luke's history of the church changes focus to the Gentile ministry and the subsequent spread of the church around the world. Beginning in chapter 13 with the Spirit's selection of Paul and Barnabas to become special missionaries, Paul replaces Peter as the central figure in the book of Acts as the church continued its Spirit-led penetration farther out into the world beyond Jerusalem.

13:1 The **church at Antioch of Syria** became the sending center of the mission to reach the world (the last part of Jesus' commission in 1:8). This first verse gives us an idea of its truly international makeup and of the broad spectrum of people who were being reached by the gospel.

Until this point it appeared that Barnabas and Paul had been the principle teachers in the church of Antioch (11:26). This list shows, at least, these three others who were said to have had the gifts of being **prophets and teachers. Barnabas** appears first on the list because he was likely the leader of the group. **Simeon,** because of his **black** skin, has caused some speculation that this was the same Simon of Cyrene who carried the cross of Christ (Mark 15:21), but that is unknown. The next name on the list is a man from **Cyrene** by the name of **Lucius.** Cyrene was in North Africa. Lucius was probably among the Cyprian and Cyrenian men who first preached the gospel to Gentiles in Antioch (see 11:20-21). The fourth individual was **Manaen, a childhood companion** of King Herod Antipas. Saul was a highly trained rabbinic Jew and a Roman citizen. His name closes the list of this very diverse group. The social, geographic, and racial variety of these people shows that the Spirit of God had been moving rapidly and over a broad geographic area. Not only had the Good News spread to these areas, but the Spirit of God used cosmopolitan Antioch to put together a diverse team for the next "phase" of Kingdom expansion.

13:2-3 These believers **were worshiping the Lord and fasting** when God sent them a special message. Just as both Peter and Cornelius received messages while praying (chapter 10), so God spoke to these believers as they were seeking him. "Fasting" means going without food for a specified period of time in order to focus on the Lord. People who are fasting can set aside the time of preparing and eating meals

and use it to worship and pray. Also, their hunger pangs will remind them of their complete dependence upon God (see also 2 Chronicles 20:3; Ezra 8:23; Esther 4:16; Matthew 6:16-18).

The Spirit spoke—possibly through one of the members of this group (there were prophets among them—13:1). The Spirit told them to **dedicate Barnabas and Saul for the special work** God had for them. The laying on of **hands** was a symbolic act that indicated public recognition of calling and ability as well as the association of a particular congregation with a ministry. The roots of the practice are found in the Old Testament, where it was used to set someone aside for an office (Numbers 27:23), bless someone (Genesis 48:14), or dedicate something to God (Leviticus 1:4). The church at Antioch was identifying itself with these two men and with their mission. With that, they **sent them on their way.**

PAUL'S FIRST MISSIONARY JOURNEY / 13:4-12

Having been chosen by God to embark on what came to be called the "first missionary journey," Paul and his entourage (Barnabas and John Mark, at the very least) set sail. The target of this evangelistic thrust was the Gentile population of Asia Minor. They followed the communication routes of the Roman Empire—this made travel easier. They first visited Barnabas's home country. Then they visited key population and cultural centers to reach as many people as possible.

13:4 The **Holy Spirit** was the central force in sending **Saul and Barnabas** (along with John Mark—13:5) on their journey. **Seleucia** was a seaport of Antioch, a few miles north of the city at the mouth of the Orontes River. **Cyprus,** an important island in the Mediterranean, was about one hundred miles to the southwest.

13:5 Salamis, the leading city on Cyprus, was their first stop. It was located on the east coast of the island and was the seat of government. As would become his custom for years, Saul began his witness in **the Jewish synagogues** (Romans 1:16). Saul's credentials as a highly trained Pharisee— a former student of Gamaliel (22:3)—would have been more than enough to prompt an invitation to speak, at least until his reputation for bringing such a radical message began to precede him.

John Mark was on the trip **as their assistant.** The nature of Mark's job is not spelled out, though the word used here *(hupereten)* has led to speculation that he instructed the new converts and also was in charge of practical needs.

13:6-7 The missionary team traveled the length of the island from east to west (about one hundred

miles), arriving at the town of **Paphos,** a regional center of government. There **they met a Jewish sorcerer** (Greek: *magos*—which means "magician"). **Bar-Jesus** is further described as a **false prophet.** The **governor, Sergius Paulus** received news of the traveling Jewish evangelists and wanted to hear what they had to say. For Paul and Barnabas, presenting the gospel to the governor was a great opportunity (see 13:12).

13:8 Trouble was brewing, however, because Bar-Jesus realized that if Sergius Paulus believed in Christ, he would no longer need a sorcerer. Apparently Bar-Jesus' Greek name was **Elymas** (meaning "sorcerer" or "magician"), and he was going to do his best to stop any influence Barnabas and Saul might have on the governor.

13:9-11 At this point Luke noted that **Saul** was also known as **Paul.** The implication is that he already had both names but began to go by the latter, preferring to use his Roman name for the balance of his Gentile-oriented mission. After this, Paul is always called by his Roman name in Luke's record.

Paul was **filled with the Holy Spirit,** a phrase reminiscent of the way the apostles were used earlier in Acts (see 2:4; 4:8, 31; 7:55), as well as one of the requirements for the choosing of the "seven" in chapter 6. For the first time, Paul took center stage. Evidently this was a big turning point in Paul's leadership of the mission.

Not intimidated by his spiritual rival, Paul boldly exposed the source of his sorcery. In Aramaic the name Bar-Jesus means "son of Jesus," so Paul played on that name to confront him (in the presence of the listening Sergius Paulus) with the accusation that Bar-Jesus was actually a **son of the Devil.** This is the first recorded presentation of the word of God to the Roman world, and it would be crucial that a clear distinction be

made between Christianity and the perverted spiritualism so prevalent in the Empire. Paul's rhetorical questioning of the sorcerer turned to an announcement of judgment, telling him that the Lord's **punishment** was on him. **Instantly** Bar-Jesus was struck with **blindness.**

13:12 This miracle was all it took to convince Sergius Paulus. **He believed.** Notice also that his astonishment was not at the powerful act he had just witnessed but rather **at what he learned about the Lord.** Sergius Paulus is the highest ranking converted official recorded in the New Testament.

PAUL PREACHES IN ANTIOCH OF PISIDIA / 13:13-43

Leaving the city of Paphos on the island of Cyprus, Paul and his companions sailed north, arriving at Perga. For an unknown reason, John Mark abruptly left the venture at that time and returned to Jerusalem. Paul and Barnabas continued inland to Antioch of Pisidia.

13:13 Having traveled Barnabas's homeland (Cyprus) from coast to coast, the party boarded a ship for the mainland. They arrived at the province of **Pamphylia,** landing in the **port town of Perga.** Why **John Mark left them** is never explained. Perhaps:

- he was homesick;
- he resented the change in leadership from Barnabas (his cousin) to Paul;
- he became ill (an illness that may have affected all of them—see Galatians 4:13);
- he was unable to withstand the rigors and dangers of the missionary journey;
- he may have planned to go only that far but had not communicated this to Paul and Barnabas.

Paul implicitly accused John Mark of lacking commitment, and, therefore, Paul refused to take Mark along on another journey (see 15:37-38). John Mark's story does not end here, though. It is clear from Paul's later letters that Paul grew to respect Mark (Colossians 4:10) and that he needed him in his work (2 Timothy 4:11). Somewhere along the way, John Mark was restored completely to usefulness even in the ministry of Paul. He later wrote the Gospel that bears his name.

13:14 This is **Antioch of Pisidia,** not Antioch of Syria, home of the sending church where the ministry was flourishing (11:26). This Antioch, in the region of Pisidia, was a hub of good roads and trade and had a large Jewish population. It had been founded in 281 B.C. by Seleucius I, and he had named it after his father, Antiocus. It had been declared a Roman colony city and became the most

important city of southern Galatia. It had a mix of Romans, Greeks, Orientals, and Phrygians.

When they went to a new city to witness for Christ, Paul and Barnabas **went first to the synagogue.** They would go **on the Sabbath,** taking advantage of the Jewish custom of inviting itinerant teachers to speak (Jesus also did this—see, for example, Luke 4:16). Paul and Barnabas did not separate themselves from the synagogues but tried to show clearly that the very Scriptures the Jews studied pointed to Jesus.

13:15 In a synagogue service, first the "Shema" would be recited (this is Deuteronomy 6:4, which Jews would repeat several times daily). Then certain prayers would be spoken, followed by a reading from **the books of Moses** (Genesis through Deuteronomy), a reading from the **Prophets** (intended to illustrate the law), and a sermon. The invitation from **those in charge** was to speak a **word of encouragement.** Such an invitation was all Paul needed.

13:16 Paul's sermon, which continues from here to 13:41, probably was included as a typical example of what Paul would say to a synagogue gathering. It shows how Paul first preached the Good News to a Jewish congregation. The opening address to the **people of Israel** and to the **devout Gentiles who fear the God of Israel** covered both groups of possible worshipers—Jews by birth and Gentile God-fearers (see remarks about Cornelius at 10:2).

13:17-18 Paul began his message by emphasizing God's covenant with Israel. This was a point of agreement because all Jews were proud to be God's chosen people. His review of Israel's history is like Stephen's lengthy review of the same in his sermon to a Jewish crowd in Jerusalem (chapter 7). This was a common form of address known as a "historical retrospect"—a sketch of the course of God's work in the nation's history. Paul would move quickly from Abraham to Moses, Samuel, and David and eventually come to Jesus (13:23).

After the implied mention of Abraham (**chose our ancestors**), Paul moved on to **Egypt**. Moses' name is not mentioned, but rather, God is pictured leading Israel out of **slavery**.

13:19-21 He did not name the **seven nations in Canaan** whose land had been given **to Israel as an inheritance**—these were well known to Paul's audience (see Deuteronomy 7:1 for the list). The **450 years** was an inclusive figure for all the events that had occurred so far in Paul's survey—from the move to Egypt (four hundred years), the wandering in the wilderness (forty years), through the distribution of the land under Joshua (ten years). Paul summarized the period of the judges with two words, **judges ruled**, leading up to the time of the prophets, beginning with **Samuel**, who was considered the first prophet. Israel's kingdom period began with **Saul** (1 Samuel 9:1-2), who was the first king.

13:22 Saul, of course, had been **removed** from the throne because of his disobedience (see 1 Samuel 13:1-14; 15:1-25). Then **David** had become the new king, replacing the rejected Saul, who did not possess the same **heart** for God (1 Samuel 13:14).

13:23 A large jump over Old Testament history occurred here, as Paul went from King David directly to one of his **descendants, Jesus**. Paul described Jesus as **God's promised Savior of Israel**. This is the only place recorded in Acts where Paul called Jesus "Savior." Peter used the same term in 5:31.

13:24-25 John the Baptist was the last of the prophets, the one who would prepare the way for the coming of the Messiah. Yet even this great prophet had not considered himself **worthy to be Jesus' slave**. John's whole thrust was to try to turn Israel to the Savior by preaching that people should **turn from sin and turn to God and be baptized**. Turning away from sin and to God means an about-face from a sinful life to a life lived for God. Baptism with water was a way of publicly showing one's commitment to turn away from sin and toward God.

13:26 With this direct address to his Jewish **brothers**, Paul appealed for them to come to faith in Jesus Christ—the one to whom all the prophecies of their Scriptures pointed. The **salvation** that

Christ offers is for both Jews (**sons of Abraham**) and **devout Gentiles** (fearers of God who aligned themselves to worship in the Jewish community).

13:27 Paul joined Peter and Stephen in blaming the Jews who rejected Christ (**the people in Jerusalem and their leaders**) for killing Jesus. Yet this had **fulfilled prophecy** (see Psalm 118:22; Isaiah 53:3). The failure of the Jews to **recognize him** as **the one the prophets had written about** was made all the worse by the fact that they had sat **every Sabbath** and had heard the **prophets' words read**. They had been exposed to the prophecies but had missed the fulfillment of those prophecies (see Luke 24:46; Acts 3:18).

13:28 Although the Jewish leaders **found no just cause to execute him**, they still **asked Pilate to have him killed**. Because of the Roman occupation of the land of Israel, the Jewish leaders could not carry out the execution. So, after the Jews had condemned Jesus, they had to get permission from the Roman ruler of their province—and that was Pilate. Pilate had even pointed out to the Jewish accusers the fact that they had no grounds for execution, but he gave in to their demands (Luke 23:4, 14-15, 22).

13:29-31 Jesus' death **had fulfilled all the prophecies**. Oddly enough, the very Jews who had killed Jesus were the ones who would have been the most well versed in all those prophecies. In their blindness they killed Jesus because they had refused to believe that he was their Messiah—all the while fulfilling the Scriptures about the death of their Messiah! After Jesus had been crucified on **the cross**, he had been **placed in a tomb** (Luke 23:44-56). But the tomb was not the end of the story. In this note of triumph, Paul reported what most would think impossible—**God raised him from the dead** (Luke 24). Without the Resurrection, there would be no gospel, no salvation, no Good News to spread. But Paul, though he had not been among the apostles to witness the Resurrection, had seen the risen Christ and, thus, could testify to the truth of this statement (9:1-6). The credibility of the Resurrection had also been affirmed by **witnesses** who had seen the resurrected Christ **over a period of many days**.

13:32-33 Paul tied together all of the events that he had been recounting to that moment when he and **Barnabas** were standing before them as the bearers of **this Good News**. The **promise** God had made to their common **ancestors** had **come true**. After centuries of waiting, watching, and wanting, the Messiah had come. His name is **Jesus**. To support this statement, Paul quoted from three Old Testament texts already considered by most Jews to have been referring to the Messiah—Psalm 2:7; Isaiah 55:3; and Psalm 16:10. In these verses, Psalm 2:7 pictures God the **Father** as speaking to his **Son.** This moment had been publicly recognized (although it already was a reality) in Christ's life on the day of his baptism (Luke 3:22; 9:35).

13:34 A more direct proof for the Resurrection came from Isaiah 55:3, which promised **sacred blessings.** This prophecy by Isaiah was a reference back to the covenant first promised to **David** by Nathan the prophet in 2 Samuel 7:6-16. The eternal throne did not find fulfillment in David. But in Jesus Christ, who rose from the dead, there is an eternal King who will reign forever.

13:35-37 Psalm 16:10 also offers proof of the promised Resurrection. This argument was the same one Peter had used on the day of Pentecost (see comments at 2:27) and was a strong promise of resurrection for the **Holy One** of God. Judging from the popularity of its use, this psalm must have been one of the strongest cases to the Jewish audience for the necessity of the resurrection of the Messiah. The words could not have referred **to David,** because David **died and was buried, and his body decayed**—many in Paul's audience had likely been to the site of David's tomb in Jerusalem. Therefore, Paul was saying that David must have been writing prophetically of one who would come after he had died, **someone whom God raised and whose body did not decay.** That person was Jesus of Nazareth.

13:38-39 With his scriptural support for the Resurrection stated, Paul explained the spiritual significance of what Christ had done; then he called his audience to believe. With Christ's substitutionary death and the approval of God as demonstrated in

the Resurrection (Romans 1:4; 4:25), **forgiveness** of **sins** has been made available. This proclamation included the necessity of belief and the promise of being **declared right with God,** something that **the Jewish law could never do.** The law could not make people right with God. Because God is holy, he cannot accept people by simply disregarding or ignoring their sins. Nor can he accept his own people, the Jews, merely on the basis of their relationship to Abraham or by their trying to follow the law of Moses, for the sinful human nature had to be dealt with. God did this through the sacrificial death of his Son. Because of Christ's shed blood on the cross, people no longer have to bear the penalty for their sin—death (Romans 6:23). Jesus paid it all.

13:40-41 Paul's final words were words of warning. He drew from a common theme sounded by many of the prophets—**Be careful.** Paul cited Habakkuk 1:5 as a representative passage in which the prophet warned Judah of its impending judgment—the exile to Babylon. In the same way that their ancestors had failed to recognize what God was doing among them, Paul's audience was about to miss what God was doing in its day.

13:42-43 After the sermon the reception must have been positive, for **Paul and Barnabas** were invited to **return** the following **week.** But this warm welcome would not last long. The two groups addressed twice by Paul—**Jews and godly converts** (see remarks at 13:16, 26)—followed them out of the synagogue. These were probably the ones who were ready to respond to the message or perhaps even already had. The simple message from these two missionaries was to urge them, **"By God's grace, remain faithful."** That is, they should continue in the direction they were headed.

PAUL TURNS TO THE GENTILES / 13:44-52
Declaring boldly the death and resurrection of Christ and the forgiveness that is possible only through him (see 13:38-39), Paul and Barnabas drew huge crowds on their second Sabbath in Antioch of Pisidia. Among those gathered were a number of jealous Jewish leaders (13:45). Despite efforts by these leaders to discredit Paul and his message, the assembled Gentiles eagerly embraced the gospel. This further enraged the Jewish leaders, who were eventually able to stir up a mob that ran Paul and Barnabas out of town.

13:44-45 In one short week, the news had spread through the city of Antioch so that **almost the entire city turned out to hear** what Paul and Barnabas had to say. This huge and unusual turnout was likely due to a Gentile influx rather than a Jewish one, since the Jewish attendance at the synagogue probably was fairly constant. The **Jewish leaders** in

attendance **were jealous** and so they **slandered Paul and argued** with him, although it must have been difficult taking on this brilliant rabbi in a debate.

13:46-47 In answer to this jealous and abusive response from the Jews, Paul and Barnabas explained that **it was necessary** for them to go first to the Jews. God planned that through the Jewish nation, all the world would come to know him (Genesis 12:3). They, of all people, should have been the most ready for the fulfillment that had come in Christ. Paul quoted Isaiah 49:6. God had made the Jew to be a light to the Gentiles. He wanted them to be the privileged announcers of salvation. But it was not to be. They rejected the Good News, thereby judging themselves unworthy of eternal life. The evangelistic thrust was thus turned to Gentiles. God had planned for Israel to be the light (Isaiah 49:6). But Israel had forsaken that task, so it was given to the church to carry out.

13:48-49 Contrast this Gentile response to that of the Jews. They were very glad and thanked the Lord for his message. In a strong statement about the sovereign hand of God, Luke wrote: and all who were appointed to eternal life became believers. The Greek verb for "appointed" is *tetagmenoi* from *tasso*, a military word meaning to "arrange" or "assign." Various people were "assigned" to eternal life by him (the unmentioned "Appointer"). The significance, of course, is the fact that these "appointed" were Gentiles.

Thus was set the pattern that would surface again and again—the Jews reject, the Gentiles respond in great numbers, and, in turn, the Jews become belligerent and often physically violent against the Christians. But still the Lord's message spread.

13:50 The Jews used their contacts in high places—influential religious women and the leaders of the city—to drive Paul and Barnabas out of their part of the country. Christianity was not an official religion like Judaism, and these women and men may have feared that Paul would disturb their fragile relationship with the Roman government. This was a sad moment: those so desperately in need of salvation driving from their city the bearers of the Good News—news of forgiveness, of justification before God.

13:51 Often, Jews would shake off the dust of their feet when leaving a Gentile town, on the way back to their own land. For Paul and Barnabas to do this to Jews demonstrated that Jews who reject the Good News are not truly part of Israel and are no better than pagans. It was a gesture of utter scorn and disassociation. Jesus had told his disciples to shake from their feet the dust of any town that would not accept or listen to them (Mark 6:11). This symbolized cleansing themselves from the contamination of people who did not worship God. The disciples were not to blame if the gospel was rejected, as long as they had faithfully presented it.

13:52 In contrast with the paranoid, politicking Jews working hard to rid themselves of the gospel messengers, the believers, most of whom were Gentiles, were filled with joy and with the Holy Spirit. Like the coming of the Holy Spirit in Jerusalem at Pentecost (2:3-4), in Samaria at the laying on of the apostles' hands (8:17), and in Caesarea during Peter's preaching (10:44-46), the believers here were "filled with joy"—the kind of inexplicable and overflowing joy of one freshly filled with the loving, forgiving Spirit of God.

ACTS 14

PAUL AND BARNABAS IN ICONIUM / 14:1-7

Chased out of Antioch of Pisidia (13:50), Paul and Barnabas journeyed southeast to the region of Galatia, stopping first in the city of Iconium. Again the missionaries went straight to the synagogues, where they preached the Good News with great power and saw many believe in Christ.

14:1-2 Iconium was located about sixty miles east and a bit south of Antioch of Pisidia. What happened there confirmed the fact that the mighty movement of God in Antioch was no fluke—God was working with such power that a great number of both Jews and Gentiles were coming to faith. As in Antioch, Paul and Barnabas began in the synagogue, presumably preaching upon the invitation of the leaders there. But also as in Antioch, the Jews in Iconium opposed the gospel. They spurned God's message, rousing the Gentiles and stirring up distrust against Paul and Barnabas.

14:3-4 The persecution seems to have partially been the reason that Paul and Barnabas stayed in Iconium. As had been the case everywhere they had gone, God **proved their message was true by giving them power to do miraculous signs and wonders**—probably healing the sick and casting out demons. In Acts, signs and wonders are key to revealing the work of salvation in Christ and to proclaiming the gospel. They authenticated the apostles' authority. Even so, a rift developed and **the people of the city were divided.** Some believed the rumors and **sided with the Jews,** while others sided **with the apostles.**

14:5-7 A **mob** of **Gentiles and Jews** decided to **attack** the apostles **and stone them.** Fortunately, the apostles heard of the plan and **fled for their lives.** The opposition did not stop their message. Paul and Barnabas **went to the region of Lycaonia.** The next stop was **Lystra,** a smaller city about twenty miles south of Iconium. Paul may have picked this smaller place in order to let the storm of opposition quiet down a bit. The events that occurred in **Derbe** are recorded in 14:21.

PAUL AND BARNABAS IN LYSTRA AND DERBE / 14:8-20

At Lystra, the missionaries healed a man crippled from birth. The pagan Gentiles of the area saw this miracle and concluded that Paul and Barnabas must be Greek gods. Despite an immediate rejection of this foolish notion and loud explanations to the contrary, the apostles could barely convince them. Then the fickle mob turned murderous, prodded by some angry Jews from nearby Antioch and Iconium. Together they stoned Paul, dragged him out of Lystra, and left him for dead. Then, in one of most amazing moments of New Testament history, the bloody apostle got up and went back into the city. His joyful perseverance in the face of extreme persecution is testimony to the power of the Holy Spirit in a believer's life.

14:8 In contrast to what had been mostly a preaching ministry so far (although there is a reference to signs and wonders in Iconium—14:3), the major event of Lystra involved **a man with crippled feet.** This verse has the identical wording used in Luke's description of the lame man healed by Peter in 3:2. The fact of his being **that way from birth** assures that the healing was real. The people of the area would **know** beyond a shadow of a doubt that this person had a lifelong physical ailment that could not be cured.

14:9-10 Paul recognized the fact that this man **had faith to be healed,** so he addressed the man with authority. **"Stand up!"** the apostle commanded, and the man **started walking** for the first time ever. This is a wonderful example of how God changes lives. When Paul was sensitive to the moment, when he made himself available to be used by God, and when the crippled man put his faith in the power of God, then God worked a miracle! God wants to do big things in and through his people, but they need to live with a sense of eager expectancy. To see changes in their lives, believers must trust fully in God (Matthew 13:58).

14:11-13 Evidently, the crowd that witnessed this miracle was large. The response was immediate and emotional. Concluding that these men were **gods in human bodies,** they went so far as to decide that Paul was **Hermes** and Barnabas, **Zeus.** According to Greek and Roman mythology, Zeus and Hermes (the Roman names were Jupiter

and Mercury) had once visited this city and, according to the legend, no one offered them hospitality except an old couple. So Zeus and Hermes killed the rest of the people and rewarded the old couple.

When the citizens of Lystra saw the miracles of Paul and Barnabas, they assumed that the gods were revisiting them. Remembering the story of what had happened to the previous citizens, they immediately honored Paul and Barnabas, showering them with gifts. The matter quickly got out of hand. The **priest** of the **temple of Zeus** was in the process of bringing **oxen** for a **sacrifice.** He would not want to be caught up short with such noble visitors in town!

14:14-15 Barnabas and Paul were horrified by news of an impending sacrifice on their behalf, so they **tore their clothing,** a common Jewish gesture of horror or sorrow. Paul and Barnabas affirmed the fact that they were not visiting gods but **merely human beings** just like the residents of Lystra. They immediately took advantage of the startled, gathered, and attentive crowd to preach the **Good News.** These sincere, excited believers in Zeus had been ready to spend the time, money, and effort to worship a god that didn't exist. So Paul directed them to **the living God, who made the heaven and the earth.** The residents of Lystra needed to redirect their affection and attention from **these worthless things** (referring to their pantheon of gods) to the one true God.

14:16-17 Contrast this sermon to a crowd of idol-worshiping pagans with Paul's sermon in chapter 13 to the Scripture-literate Jews. This message was perfectly designed for a crowd accustomed to superstitious worship built around the various gods of nature. This is one of two speeches to Gentiles recorded in Acts (see also 17:22-31) and differs from Jewish sermons in its absence of Old Testament references. This shows Paul's creative adaptability.

God had been trying to get the people's attention. The first **witness** these people should have noticed was the **reminders** that God had made and had given abundantly to all—the **rain**, the **good crops, food,** and even **joyful hearts.** This general revelation was in place to encourage all observers to seek God.

14:18 The impact of the miracle of the healed man was almost too strong to counter. The worshipers of Zeus refused to be deterred from worshiping these two "miracle workers." In spite of the message of the apostles, they **could scarcely restrain** what appeared to be a sacrificial ceremony. It is further testimony to the character of Paul and Barnabas that such was not allowed to happen.

14:19 A small Jewish contingent in Lystra may have informed **Jews** from **Antioch and Iconium** of the presence of these "troublemakers." The healing miracle would only have deepened the jealousy and heightened the resolve to take drastic action to rid themselves of them. The Jews **turned the crowds into a murderous mob.** Paul was **stoned** and **dragged** out of the city, left for **dead.** According to Scripture records, this is the only time Paul was stoned (2 Corinthians 11:25). Nothing is said about what they did to Barnabas.

14:20 This is one of the most powerful moments in the whole book. Paul, surely bloody and bruised from the stoning he had just endured, surrounded by **believers** (maybe some who had just come to faith through his ministry), **got up and went back into the city.** This courageous messenger, who had faithfully preached the Good News and had been hounded for it at every turn, got up, dusted himself off, and went back to work. Others would have quit, but not Paul. **The next day he left** for the next stop on his missionary journey—the town of **Derbe.**

PAUL AND BARNABAS RETURN TO ANTIOCH OF SYRIA / 14:21-28

Following a successful evangelistic campaign in Derbe, the missionaries backtracked through all the cities visited on their missionary journey. The goal was to strengthen the believers and to appoint elders in the churches. Having done this, Paul and Barnabas returned to their home base in Antioch of Syria and reported to the church there. This brief passage not only demonstrates God's grace and faithfulness, it also sets the stage for the coming controversy over the presence of newly converted Gentiles in a previously all-Jewish church.

14:21-22 Paul and Barnabas once again preached **the Good News,** this time **in Derbe.** The phrase, **making many disciples,** shows that there was more than just an evangelistic campaign in progress. There is no mention of opposition in Derbe. Perhaps that is why they were able to get to the discipleship phase of ministry.

Having reached the easternmost part of this first journey, as incredible as it must seem, Paul and Barnabas retraced their footsteps, returning to **Lystra, Iconium, and Antioch of Pisidia,** even to places where they had experienced rejection of the most violent sort! What a courageous pair! They went home the hard way! The purpose of this return trip was mainly to strengthen **the believers** and encourage **them to continue in the faith.** Apparently, the believers left behind in these cities were facing persecution from the sources that had attacked Paul and Barnabas, for Paul had to tell them that **they must enter into the Kingdom of God through many tribulations.**

14:23 To evangelism and discipleship was added organization. The apostles established healthy churches in the areas where people responded to the gospel. They **appointed elders** (Greek *presbuterous*—the first reference to such in church history) **in every church.** The prayer and fasting recall the way this missionary team had been commissioned (13:3) and the meticulous spiritual process by which they proceeded through every major decision. The commissioning **(turning them over to the care of the Lord)** probably involved laying on of hands.

14:24-25 Paul and Barnabas had faced stoning in Lystra (14:19), a violent mob of Gentiles and Jews in Iconium (14:5), and a jealous, manipulating coalition of influential Jews in Antioch of Pisidia (13:50). Yet they retraced their footsteps exactly, returning to each place they had been. It seems that they had not preached **in Perga** on the outward leg of the journey. The record states only that

John Mark had left them there (13:13). They may have left that region quickly and gone into higher ground because of sickness that had affected them. (This may have been the cause of John Mark's departure.) On the way back, however, they did minister in Perga.

14:26 From the port city of Attalia, they sailed back to **Antioch of Syria, where their journey had begun.** The road-weary travelers had **completed** the work for which they had been sent.

14:27-28 Paul and Barnabas returned to their sending church in **Antioch** and **called the church together** to report about their trip. Even though Paul and Barnabas had been the active subjects of the story, they made it clear that the real work had been done by God, who **had opened the door of faith to the Gentiles.** Paul and Barnabas had witnessed it with their own eyes.

Paul and Barnabas **stayed there with the believers in Antioch for a long time.** This journey had probably taken the better part of a year and had aroused the interest of the Jerusalem church, who would want the apostles' report as well (see the next chapter).

Paul probably wrote his letter to the Galatians while he was staying in Antioch (A.D. 48 or 49) after completing his first missionary journey. There are several theories as to what part of Galatia Paul was addressing, but most agree that Iconium, Lystra, and Derbe were part of that region for whom the letter was intended. Galatians was probably written before the Jerusalem council (chapter 15) because, in the letter, the question of whether Gentile believers should be required to follow Jewish law was not yet resolved. The council would meet to solve that problem, as recorded in the next chapter.

ACTS 15

THE COUNCIL AT JERUSALEM / 15:1-21

As many Gentile believers came into the church, legalistic Jews demanded that these new converts be circumcised. Fierce arguing about this issue resulted in the first church council. At Jerusalem, the apostles and elders convened to consider the relationship between Jewish Christians and Gentile Christians, between Moses' law and the gospel of grace.

The council concluded, based on the Old Testament book of Amos (as expounded by James, leader of the proceedings), and in light of the experiences of both Peter and Paul, that Gentiles were accepted. Further, the council ruled that salvation depended solely on simple belief in Jesus, not on keeping the law of Moses.

15:1 These **men** were of a group called the Judaizers (see comments on 15:5). They came **from Judea** (perhaps from Jerusalem) to Antioch; they held the opinion that Gentiles could not be saved **unless** they kept **the ancient Jewish custom of circumcision taught by Moses.**

God had originally made the covenant of circumcision with Abraham (Genesis 17). This covenant was a sign of Abraham's and his descendants' obedience to God in all matters, and it signified the Jews as God's covenant people. More than any other practice, circumcision separated God's people from their pagan neighbors. Circumcision became part of the law of Moses. The problem described in this verse involves the terms under which Gentiles could be admitted into the church. These Jews from Judea were not disputing that

Gentiles could be saved. They were insisting, however, that Gentiles must adhere to the laws of Moses, including the physical rite of circumcision. In effect, this was tantamount to saying that Gentiles must first become Jews before they could become Christians.

To understand the Judaizers' actions, we need to understand their mind-set. In the early days, all of the believers were Jews. In fact, the early church was viewed as a sect within Judaism. The Judaizers concluded that Christianity was not intended to **bypass** Judaism but to **build** on it. Judaism, with its centuries of history and tradition, was the prerequisite. They saw Jesus (and his message) as the final step in the long process. The Judaizers were afraid that soon there would be more Gentile than Jewish Christians. Also, they were afraid that moral standards among believers would be weakened if they did not follow Jewish laws.

15:2 This was no small difference of opinion. The Greek words for **disagreeing** and **argued forcefully** convey the idea of great strife, discord, disunion. This debate over circumcision and keeping the law was a major dispute, a serious theological and ecclesiastical crisis. If not handled wisely, the debate could have split the church. So **Paul and Barnabas were sent to Jerusalem, accompanied by some local believers.** They would meet with the **apostles and elders** in Jerusalem **about this question.**

15:3 On their journey to **Jerusalem** (a trip of about three hundred miles), Paul and Barnabas paid visits to several congregations. The church in **Phoenicia** was founded by believers who had fled from Jerusalem (11:19); **Samaria** had been evangelized by Philip (8:5). Rather than being alarmed at the news of the conversion of Gentiles, these believers expressed much **joy.**

15:4 The language of the text suggests a public meeting. This group **welcomed** Paul and Barnabas who then **reported** to the church that the events in question were things **God had been doing through their ministry.** The implication is that divine activity must indicate divine will. God surely would not be drawing the Gentiles to himself if he did not want them in his church or if they still had to fulfill other requirements before they could be saved.

15:5 These Christians had been **Pharisees before their conversion** (like Paul). They found themselves having compatible views with Christianity because Pharisees believed in resurrection and in a Messiah, but many were reluctant to accept anyone who did not adhere to the oral tradition of law in addition to the Scriptures (Torah). Since only God knows the human heart, it is impossible to make a blanket statement regarding the eternal "destination" of this group. Probably some were sincere believers in the resurrection of Christ and his claim to be the Messiah (though obviously confused about the relationship between law and grace). Others likely were blindly trusting in their own moralistic efforts to make them acceptable to God. Still others may have been infiltrators with evil motives. Whatever these believers' individual status before God, the common concern of all in the Judaizer camp was that all Gentile converts **be required to follow the law of Moses,** especially regarding circumcision.

15:6 The exact makeup of this council is unknown. Other apostles (besides Peter, Paul, and James)

may have been summoned and present. Verses 12 and 22 indicate that this discussion took place in the presence of the entire congregation. But the clear implication is that the church leaders, **the apostles and church elders** (and not the whole assembly), deliberated and decided this volatile issue.

15:7 The Gentile question prompted **a long discussion.** After lengthy interaction, **Peter** shared his experience of how God had used him **to preach to the Gentiles.** Specifically, he was referring to the incident described in chapter 10, where God had sovereignly led him to share the Good News with the Gentile Cornelius. If the Jerusalem council took place in about A.D. 50, then Peter was referring to an event that had occurred about ten years earlier.

15:8-9 Jews considered Gentiles impure and required them to undergo proselyte baptism in order to convert to Judaism. Peter made it clear that God had purified Cornelius and his family as a result of faith alone. God had **made no distinction between** them as Gentiles and the Jewish believers (see 10:34-48). All kinds of people have access to forgiveness and eternal life through their faith in Christ.

Peter bolstered his argument by noting God's outpouring of the Spirit. The Gentiles had received the **Holy Spirit** when they believed (**through faith**), not because they had done any works of the law (see 10:44-46; Galatians 3:2). The presence of the Spirit in them was the clearest evidence of their acceptance by God (Romans 8:9).

15:10-11 Peter warned that by making strict adherence to the law a prerequisite for salvation, the church would be guilty of **questioning God's way** (that is, doubting his wisdom and plan and thus arrogantly pursuing a different course of action). Furthermore, the Jewish believers would be putting an unbearable **yoke** on the Gentiles. The word "yoke" was a common figurative term for religious "obligations." It was the heavy wooden harness used by oxen to pull carts or plows. Here it suggests less of a religious duty and more of an onerous burden (see Matthew 23:4; 11:28-30).

If the law was a yoke that **neither** the Jews of that day nor their **ancestors** had been **able to bear,** however, how did having the law help them throughout their history? Paul wrote that the law had been a guide that had pointed out their sins so they could repent and return to God and right living (see Galatians 3:24-25). It was, and still is, impossible to obey the law completely. That would be a burden too hard for any human being.

In effect, Peter urged the council not to advocate

a double standard. Salvation—whether for Jew or Gentile—is **by the special favor of the Lord Jesus** (see Ephesians 2:8-9). What the law could never do, God did through Jesus Christ (Romans 8:1-4). No one deserves to be saved, and no religious, intellectual, or moral effort can earn salvation because it comes only from God's mercy and love. To receive God's salvation, people must acknowledge that they cannot save themselves and that only God can save them. Then they must trust in Christ.

15:12 In much the same manner as Peter, **Barnabas and Paul** related their recent experiences in ministry among the Gentiles. What gave their presentation added authority was the report of **miraculous signs and wonders God had done through them among the Gentiles.** The missionaries gave full credit to God for these miracles. The clear implication is that these supernatural events signified God's endorsement and blessing of their ministry to non-Jews (see commentary on 14:3).

15:13-14 James was Jesus' half brother (Galatians 1:18-19) and the writer of the Epistle of James (perhaps already written and distributed prior to this council). James became the leader of the church in Jerusalem (12:17). We don't know how James attained that important position (Clement of Alexandria wrote that he was chosen for the office by Peter and John), but clearly he was the leader. When this controversy over Gentile believers threatened to divide the church, Barnabas and Paul met with the elders and apostles in Jerusalem and submitted their authority to James as the moderator, spokesman, and announcer of the final decision.

The phrase, **God first visited,** is important because it underlines the truth that God had already made clear his plan to include Gentiles in the church before Paul and Barnabas ever went on the first missionary venture. The phrase, **to take from them a people for himself** (previously used only of the Jews as the people of God), here describes the Gentiles. This would have been heard as a remarkable statement by James.

15:15-18 Recognizing the need to base any forthcoming decision on something more substantial than mere experience, James went to the Scriptures. He demonstrated how the **conversion of Gentiles agrees with what the** Old Testament **prophets predicted.** This was the ultimate test.

Scholars have long wondered about this passage of Acts and the Old Testament quote it contains. James's quote includes a text of Amos 9:11-12 different from the Hebrew text and even

from the Septuagint (an ancient Greek translation of the Old Testament). It is not clear why James did this, but it is obvious how he understood and applied this passage to the crisis facing the early church. In God's judgment **the kingdom of David** had **fallen** and was reduced to **ruins.** God's covenant with David stated that one of David's descendants would always sit on his throne (2 Samuel 7:12-16). The exile of the Jews made this promise seem impossible. But God would **rebuild** and **restore** the kingdom to its promised glory. This was a promise to both Israel and Judah, not to be fulfilled by an earthly, political ruler but by the Messiah, who would renew the spiritual Kingdom and rule forever. James quoted these verses, finding this promise fulfilled in Christ's resurrection and in the presence of both Jews and **Gentiles** in the church. When God brings in the Gentiles, he is restoring the ruins. After the Gentiles are called together, God will renew and restore the fortunes of the new Israel. All the land that was once under David's rule will again be part of God's nation.

Even though James quoted just one prophet, Amos, he said "prophets" (plural), perhaps alluding to other written Scriptures, like Isaiah 2:2; 11:10; 25:8-9; and Zechariah 8:23. His main point was that Gentile salvation apart from the law does not in any way contradict the Old Testament Scriptures.

15:19-21 Without explicitly mentioning circumcision, James echoed Peter's argument by ruling that **we** (referring to the leaders in the church who were Jewish) **should stop troubling the Gentiles.** This was, in effect, a rejection of the circumcision requirement. But this judgment did include the stipulation that the Gentile converts should **abstain from eating meat sacrificed to idols.** This was a problem in the New Testament churches whereby meat was first sacrificed to idols and then sold in butcher shops (see 1 Corinthians 8:1-13; 10:18-33). They were also to abstain **from sexual immorality,** which was often a part of idol worship, although this probably referred to the common Gentile violation of Levitical matrimonial laws against marrying close relatives. The prohibition here was probably meant regarding prohibited marriage relationships like incest and homosexuality (see Leviticus 18:6-20). Finally, they were to abstain from **consuming blood or eating the meat of strangled animals.** This reflected the biblical teaching that life is in the blood. Strangling an animal would keep the blood in the circulatory system and not drained away, thus causing blood to be eaten with the meat (see Genesis 9:4; Leviticus 17:10-14).

If Gentile Christians would abstain from these practices, they would please God and get along better with their Jewish brothers and sisters in Christ. Of course, there were other actions inappropriate for believers, but the Jews were especially concerned about these. This ruling reflected the law of love (described by Paul in 1 Corinthians 8–10). There was a sense in which the Jews needed to be patient with these new Gentile believers who were not familiar with all the Old Testament laws and rituals. And there was a sense in which the Gentiles needed to be sensitive to the Jews who were there first—being careful not to offend.

THE LETTER FOR GENTILE BELIEVERS / 15:22-35

The Jerusalem council summarized in a letter its decision regarding Gentile circumcision. This letter was carried to Antioch of Syria by Judas and Silas. Paul and Barnabas accompanied these specially chosen messengers. This directive brought joy to the believers at Antioch. The Jerusalem entourage stayed for a while, strengthening the believers and teaching the word of the Lord.

15:22 The **apostles** did not hold a church office but a position and function based on specific gifts (see 1 Corinthians 12:28). **Elders** were appointed to lead and manage the local church. In this meeting, the apostles submitted to the judgment of an elder—James, Jesus' half brother.

A representative from the Jewish believers and one from the Gentile believers were appointed as **delegates** to go with Paul and Barnabas to deliver the council's decision to **Antioch of Syria** and the surrounding churches. **Judas** was a Jew; **Silas** was a Greek. Their presence together would give credence to the council's ruling. Later, Silas would accompany Paul on the second missionary journey in place of Barnabas, who would visit different cities with John Mark. Peter referred to Silas as the coauthor of 1 Peter (1 Peter 5:12), but it is not known when he joined Peter.

15:23 This letter concisely summarized the findings of the Jerusalem council. It would serve to validate the verbal report that Paul, Barnabas, Judas, and Silas would be delivering **to the Gentile believers in Antioch, Syria, and Cilicia.**

15:24-27 In this letter, the Jerusalem church disassociated itself from those **men** who had **troubled** the Gentile converts regarding circumcision. They had received **no such instructions** from the apostles and had been acting without their approval. They were not to be regarded as spokesmen for the church. Rather, the men bringing the letter (Paul, Barnabas, Judas, and Silas) had been chosen as **representatives** of the church, with authority to speak on behalf of the elders and apostles.

15:28-29 The letter implies a clear leading of God in the decision rendered (**it seemed good to the Holy Spirit**). Two of the council's requirements involved issues of morality (avoiding idolatry and sexual immorality), and two involved issues of food. The dietary restrictions were because the early church often shared common meals (similar to modern-day church potluck dinners). Sometimes called "love feasts" and held in conjunction with the Lord's Supper (see 1 Corinthians 11:17-34), these meals would bring Jews and Gentiles together. In such settings, a Gentile might horrify the Jewish Christians by eating meat that was not kosher. In this compromise agreement, legalistic Jews no longer insisted that the Gentiles had to be circumcised to be saved, and the Gentiles accepted a change in their eating habits. These decisions should not be regarded as divine ordinances but rather as stipulations for fellowship between the two parties. Their concerns were not so much theological as practical. For more discussion on these four stipulations, see comments at 15:19-20.

15:30-31 Luke painted a picture of a teachable, eager church in Antioch. Whereas the false teaching of the legalists had been burdensome and a source of great confusion, the divine wisdom behind the ruling of James and the elders resulted in a joyful, encouraged congregation. The law obligates; the gospel liberates.

The end result of the potential crisis was **great joy.** It's easy to see why. First, a wise and careful approach to conflict resolution had been followed. Second, the leaders had ruled only after lengthy discussion and leading by the Spirit. Third, the members of the church had submitted to their God-appointed leadership. Churches today would be much happier and more peaceful if they followed these principles when handling conflict.

15:32-33 Judas and Silas remained in Antioch and used their prophetic gifts (see commentary on 11:27-28) **encouraging and strengthening** the believers' **faith.** They then returned to Jerusalem. Several of the more reliable, ancient manuscripts do not contain verse 34.

15:35 The length of Paul and Barnabas's stay in **Antioch** is not known. The fact, however, that **many others** were **teaching and preaching** there opened up the opportunity for Paul to attempt another missionary endeavor.

PAUL AND BARNABAS SEPARATE / 15:36-41

When the time came for a second missionary journey, Barnabas and Paul had a sharp disagreement concerning John Mark. Barnabas wanted to take this young man, his nephew, but Paul refused, citing John Mark's desertion during the first evangelistic endeavor. This incident demonstrates the sovereignty of God as two missionary teams were formed: Paul and Silas, and Barnabas and Mark. Even though no further word is given regarding the results of Barnabas and Mark's evangelistic efforts, we see Kingdom messengers departing Antioch in two directions.

15:36 Paul wanted to take another trip, primarily to revisit the churches that had been established on the first missionary journey. Evangelism would prove to be a major component of Paul's mission, but establishing and equipping the **new believers** were his primary objectives (see Ephesians 4:11-12).

15:37-39 The grand plan of Paul and Barnabas to launch a follow-up campaign quickly unraveled when the topic of **John Mark** came up. The men disagreed over the inclusion of this young believer on another missionary trip. Paul adamantly did not want to take him along. Because he had **deserted** them on the first journey (13:13), Paul felt that he would be an unreliable person to have along. The debate between the old colleagues became heated—they **disagreed strongly** and ended up separating. Each formed his own missionary team. **Barnabas took John Mark** and sailed west to **Cyprus.** These two are

not mentioned again in the book of Acts. It is important to note that the disagreement was not about theology. Both men would continue to teach the true gospel message. Through this disagreement God doubled the missionary effort.

15:40-41 Paul's second missionary journey, this time with **Silas** as his partner, began approximately three years after his first one ended. The two visited many of the cities covered on Paul's first journey, plus others. This journey would lay the groundwork for the church in Greece.

Silas had been involved in the Jerusalem council; he was one of the two men chosen to represent the Jerusalem church by taking the letter and decision back to Antioch (15:22). Paul, from the Antioch church, chose Silas, from the Jerusalem church, and they traveled together to many cities to spread the Good News. This teamwork demonstrated the church's unity after the decision at the Jerusalem council.

ACTS 16

PAUL'S SECOND MISSIONARY JOURNEY / 16:1-5

Acts 16 records Paul and Silas embarking on what is called the second missionary journey. A few verses describe a quick trek over the cities of the first journey and a series of divine prohibitions about going in certain directions. Then Paul had a vision of a man in Macedonia calling out for help, and God's door swung wide open in a new direction.

16:1 Acts 14:6-21 describes the rough treatment Paul and Barnabas had received during their last

visit to the city of **Lystra.** That was where Paul had been stoned (likely the only stoning of his ministry), dragged out of the city, and left for dead. Paul had already gone back to that city once (14:21), and on this second journey, he returned again. If anyone ever doubted Paul's courage or tenacity, this verse ought to change that opinion! So concerned was Paul for the believers in these cities that he risked his life to make sure they were growing in the faith.

In Lystra lived **a young disciple** named **Timothy.** He probably had become a Christian after Paul's first visit to Lystra. Timothy had already had solid Jewish training in the Scriptures from his mother (a Jewish believer) and grandmother (see 2 Timothy 1:5; 3:15). When Paul arrived on this second journey, Timothy had grown into a respected disciple of Jesus. Verses 1 and 3 mention that Timothy's **father was a Greek;** verse 3 explains why that mattered.

16:2-3 Timothy's excellent reputation in the church and, evidently, Paul's need for an assistant compelled Paul to invite Timothy **to join them on their journey.** Apparently, Timothy wanted to go, for he submitted to being **circumcised before they left**—clearly a mark of his commitment. Timothy was the son of a Jewish mother and Greek father. Under Jewish rabbinic law, since his mother was Jewish, Timothy was Jewish and needed to fulfill the covenant. So Paul asked Timothy to be circumcised in order to remove some of the stigma that might have hindered his effectiveness in ministering to Jewish believers. Timothy's mixed Greek/Jewish background could have created problems on their missionary journeys because many of their audiences would contain Jews who were concerned about keeping this tradition. Timothy's submission to the rite of circumcision helped to avoid that potential problem.

Paul may appear to be inconsistent here with his teaching in Galatians 2:3-5, where he refused to let Titus be circumcised. This is easily resolved when considering the difference in the circumstances of the two situations. In Galatia, circumcision was being proclaimed (heretically!) as a method of justification. Paul wanted to clarify that it was not, so he intentionally left Titus uncircumcised to make his point. Here in Lystra, early on in his evangelistic endeavors, Paul was more intent on avoiding any potential offense that might hinder the spread of the gospel (see Romans 9:32-33; 1 Peter 2:8; 1 Corinthians 1:23; 9:19-23). Although the Jerusalem council had just ruled that circumcision was not necessary for Gentiles, Paul apparently thought that Timothy's mixed religious background might hinder his effectiveness. So, because Timothy was partly Jewish, he was circumcised. This was merely for effectiveness in spreading the gospel, not as a prerequisite for salvation.

16:4-5 At least one of the new items on the agenda of this trip was **explaining** the **decision regarding the commandments that were to be obeyed,** as had been **decided by the apostles and elders** at the **Jerusalem** council (Acts 15). The Jewish/Gentile issues that had been decided at the council would likely arise again in the largely Gentile areas where Paul was traveling.

Rapid growth was important to this first part of the "Gentile" thrust of the gospel. Critics of Paul's Gentile-oriented ministry (especially the Jewish element) would be waiting greedily for an opening with which to shut Paul down or at least diminish his influence. Yet here, in the first real penetration of the gospel into the Gentile world, the church thrived in exactly the same way the mostly Jewish church had in its early days.

A CALL FROM MACEDONIA / 16:6-10
Forbidden by the Holy Spirit to go into the provinces of Asia and Bithynia, Paul and his companions were directed instead past Mysia to the city of Troas. There Paul had a divine vision instructing him to go to Macedonia. These supernatural events served to underline the sovereign guidance of God in Paul's evangelistic efforts. Sometime during the events described in this passage, Luke became part of Paul's entourage (see the pronoun "we" in 16:10).

16:6 The regions of Phrygia and Galatia included much of modern-day Turkey, yet God, for reasons known only to him, did not allow the missionaries to go **into the province of Asia at that time.** "Asia" referred not to the continent but rather to the Roman province that was the western part of what is today called Asia Minor. Ephesus probably would have been the leading city in this region.

16:7-8 The travelers moved on **to the border of Mysia** and **headed for the province of Bithynia,** a province just to the northeast of Asia, but again they were prohibited by God himself. The **Spirit of Jesus** is another name for the Holy Spirit (see Romans 8:9; Galatians 4:6; Philippians 1:19). The Holy Spirit had closed the door twice for Paul, so Paul must have wondered which geographical direction God wanted him to take in spreading the gospel. Paul and Silas **went on through Mysia to the city of Troas.** There, at last, God opened the door.

16:9-10 Finally God spoke. During the **night, Paul had a vision** in which he saw **a man from Macedonia** who was **pleading, "Come over here and help us."** (See 9:10, 12; 10:3, 17; 18:9; 22:17 for other references of God communicating through visions.) Macedonia had been a Roman province since 146 B.C. and was located in what is today northern Greece.

The group **decided to leave** right away, knowing that **God was calling** them. In the first of many sections where this occurs, Luke unobtrusively introduced his presence on this part of the journey by the simple use of the plural pronouns *we* and *us*. The traveling group consisted at least of Paul, Silas, Timothy, and Luke. Clearly, Luke had experienced what he wrote.

LYDIA OF PHILIPPI BELIEVES IN JESUS / 16:11-15

In response to the Macedonian call, Paul and his associates immediately boarded a ship at Troas and sailed across the Aegean Sea, landing at Neapolis, the port city for Philippi (in what is now northern Greece). Acts 16 highlights the stories of three individuals who became believers through Paul's ministry in Philippi: Lydia, the influential businesswoman (16:14), the demon-possessed slave girl (16:16-18), and the jailer (16:27-30). The gospel was affecting all strata of society, just as it does today.

16:11-12 The travelers made their way across the upper portion of the Aegean Sea from **Troas** to **Samothrace** (a small island in the Aegean), then on to **Neapolis,** the port city for **Philippi.** From Neapolis, Philippi was a ten-mile journey inland.

Philippi was **a major city of the district,** although it was not the capital. With mountains on every side and its port city of Neapolis on the Aegean Sea, Philippi had originally been a strategic site in the Greek Empire. Gold had been discovered at Mount Pangaeum to the west, tempting settlers from the Aegean island of Thasos to seize the area. They founded a city near the site of Philippi, naming it Krenides (meaning "spring") for the spring-fed marshlands in the valley. When Philip II of Macedon (the father of Alexander the Great) ascended the throne of the Greek Empire, he captured the city (in about 357 B.C.), enlarged and strengthened it, and gave it his name. Philip used the yield of the gold mines to outfit his army.

In 168 B.C., the Romans conquered Macedonia. The mountain's gold was exhausted, and the city declined. On the plains surrounding the city, Augustus defeated Brutus and Cassius (assassinators of Julius Caesar). In 42 B.C., Augustus gave the city the status of a **Roman colony** to celebrate his victory. A colony was considered a part of Rome itself. Its people were Roman citizens (a standing that carried high privilege), had the right to vote, were governed by their own senate, and had Roman laws and the Latin language. Later, the city received the right to the Law of Italy, giving it many privileges and immunities—most significantly, immunity from taxation. Philippi was also a garrison city with a Roman garrison stationed there to keep it secure. The Philippians were proud of their Roman heritage and standing. Philippi also boasted a fine school of medicine. Luke may have attended medical school in Philippi. Later, Paul would write a letter to the church he started in this city—the book of Philippians (probably from prison in Rome around A.D. 61). The letter is personal and tender, showing Paul's deep friendship with the believers there. The ministry in Philippi would be significant. The positive response to the gospel in this city, as described in the next few verses, was likely the reason for the missionary team remaining there for **several days.**

16:13 Inscribed on the arches outside the city of Philippi was a prohibition against bringing an unrecognized religion into the city; this may have been the reason for the prayer meeting being held outside the city, on **a riverbank.** Ten Jewish males were necessary in a location to establish a synagogue. It appears there was no synagogue in Philippi, forcing Paul and his companions to search for the seekers of God elsewhere. They **supposed that some people met for prayer** at a location by the river (the Gangites River was a mile or so west of the city), and they did find and **speak with some women** there who had gathered for prayer. Jews typically gathered by rivers for prayer when a local synagogue was not available.

Paul's first evangelistic contact in Macedonia was with a small group of women. Paul never allowed gender or cultural differences to keep him from preaching the gospel. He presented the gospel to these women, and Lydia, an influential merchant, believed. This opened the way for ministry in that region. In the early church, God often worked in and through women.

16:14 Lydia was **a merchant of expensive purple cloth,** a valuable and expensive material often worn as a sign of nobility or royalty. Lydia may have been a wealthy businesswoman. She was obviously a person of means, since she had guest rooms (16:15) and servants. Greek women of Lydia's day held elevated status and were able to conduct business and hold honorary public titles. **Thyatira** was a city known for its commerce, so Lydia may have brought her business to Philippi from there.

Lydia was **a worshiper of God.** This is similar to the almost technical description of Gentiles who were not official proselytes to Judaism but who did worship the God of Abraham (see the commentary on Cornelius at 10:2). Lydia was sincerely seeking

the Lord, and the Lord was about to meet her. God was at work, for he **opened her heart** to respond.

16:15 After Lydia's conversion, **she was baptized along with other members of her household.** These same words are used to describe other conversions in Acts—Cornelius in 10:24, 44; the Philippian jailer in 16:31; and Crispus in 18:8 (see also Romans 16:10-11; 1 Corinthians 1:16). The other members of Lydia's household may have included servants as well as children. It is assumed, of course, that only those who truly had come to believe in Christ were baptized. As is commonly the case, however, the Lord may have reached whole families through the salvation of one of the members who shared the Good News with the other family members. Lydia's sincerity and the genuineness of her conversion appear in her invitation to the missionaries to use her house as their home base while in Philippi. Lydia **urged** the travelers to stay at her home.

PAUL AND SILAS IN PRISON / 16:16-40

While in Philippi, Paul's missionary team encountered a demon-possessed slave girl who continually attempted to disrupt their ministry. When an exasperated Paul commanded the evil spirit to come out of her, the girl lost her fortune-telling ability. This infuriated her masters, who had Paul and Silas dragged before the city authorities and thrown in prison. God used an earthquake to free his servants and bring about the salvation of the Philippian jailer and his family. The next day, after the city officials learned that they had unlawfully beaten and jailed two Roman citizens, they apologized and begged Paul and Silas to leave the city. They did so after a final visit with Lydia and the believers at her home. Despite opposition, the gospel continued to spread powerfully to all the strata of society.

16:16 Luke continued his firsthand account of the events in Philippi with the word **we.** Evidently, the **place of prayer** by the river continued as the spot where Paul and his companions would meet on a regular basis. There were likely many contacts, but Luke chose to describe only two others.

The next recorded contact by Paul came from a significantly different level of society. This verse describes the missionaries meeting a **slave girl.** Worse still, she was **demon-possessed** (see commentary on 5:15-16 for more on demon possession). Fortune-telling was common in Greek and Roman culture. People used many superstitious methods for trying to see the future—from interpreting omens in nature to communicating with the spirits of the dead. This young slave girl had an evil spirit, and she made her masters rich by interpreting signs and by fortune-telling. **Her masters** were exploiting her unfortunate condition for personal gain.

16:17 What the slave girl said was true, although the source of her knowledge was a demon. Paul and his companions indeed were **servants of the Most High God** and, in fact, were telling others **how to be saved.** Why did a demon announce the truth about Paul, and why did this annoy Paul? If Paul accepted the demon's words, he would appear to be linking the gospel with demon-related activities, not to mention the prophecy-for-profit approach that this girl's owners had taken. Such association would damage the message of Christ.

16:18-21 Evidently, the young girl followed them every day as they made their way from Lydia's home to the place of prayer down by the river (or wherever else they went). **Finally Paul got so exasperated** that he directly rebuked **the demon** that was abusing the girl. Using the powerful **name of Jesus Christ,** Paul commanded the demon to depart. This angered her **masters** who had been using the servant girl and her demonic powers. With cold heartlessness, they were not arguing about the young girl's cure but were infuriated that their business venture had been ruined. So they **dragged Paul and Silas before the authorities at the marketplace.** The charge was not that they had performed an exorcism on a slave girl, but rather that these men were **Jews** and were **teaching the people to do things that are against Roman customs.** These two government officials would be interested in keeping the peace (an important aspect of their job in a Roman colony) as well as enforcing the laws against foreign religions proselytizing Romans in a Roman colony. They were interpreting the law to say that the exorcism was proselytizing Judaism. Thus, the accusations were effective.

16:22-24 The twisting of the truth by these accusers was effective enough to motivate **a mob** to assemble **quickly.** Wanting to keep the peace, the **city officials ordered** Paul and Silas to be **stripped and beaten with wooden rods.** Rods were wooden poles bound together and carried by these magistrates. This was not the only time that such had happened (or would happen) to Paul. He wrote in 2 Corinthians 11:25 that it happened three times—at least three up until the writing of that letter to Corinth.

After being **severely beaten,** Paul and Silas were thrown in prison, and Luke subtly introduced the next unsuspecting convert to Christianity—**the jailer**—who was ordered to **make sure they didn't escape.** Perhaps the stories of Christians mysteriously escaping from jail (12:3-17) or even of guards losing their lives (12:18-19) had made it as far as Philippi. Whatever the case, the jailer imposed his version of maximum security—taking them to the **inner dungeon** and there fastening **their feet in the stocks.**

"Stocks" were made of two boards joined with iron clamps, leaving holes just big enough for the ankles. The prisoner's legs were placed across the lower board, and then the upper board was closed over them. Sometimes both wrists and ankles were placed in stocks. Paul and Silas, who had committed no crime and were peaceful men, were put in stocks designed for holding the most dangerous prisoners in absolute security.

16:25 What an incredible scene this must have been! **Paul and Silas** were barely into their first stop on what promised to be a wildly effective Macedonian evangelistic campaign—God had verbally called them there (16:9-10). In short order, however, they found themselves the victims of false and prejudicial charges, locked up in the depths of a Roman jail, in stocks! So what did they

do? Moan? Whine? Blame God? Give up? No, their jail term was marked by only two activities: **praying and singing hymns to God.**

The other prisoners were listening as Paul and Silas sang and prayed. The Greek word for "listening" *(epekroonto)* is a strong word implying that the prisoners were listening intently. It is a reminder to all believers that the world is watching when they suffer. There is intrigue, interest, and even openness to believers' "answers" when they respond so unnaturally—so supernaturally—to difficulties. How believers respond to their troubles can play a major role in how others will respond to the Savior.

16:26-28 The answer to the prayers of Paul and Silas came with suddenness and authority in the form of a **great earthquake,** shaking the **foundations** of the prison, bursting open doors, and breaking loose the **chains of every prisoner.** Guards were responsible for their prisoners and would be held accountable for their escape. The punishment was usually the same sentence that would have been the prisoner's. Sometimes the guards were even executed (see 12:19). Possibly in order to avoid a Roman execution or perhaps to avoid having to live with the shame of his career failure, the jailer **drew his sword to kill himself.**

Paul intervened, shouting, **"We are all here!"** Paul was not speaking of just himself and Silas but of all the prisoners. All the prisoners were still there, sitting in a wide open jail, without chains. The other prisoners had listened intently to all that had been prayed and sung (16:25). They knew that the earthquake surely had something to do with the praying and singing of the two prisoners.

16:29-32 The jailer **called for lights** and torches lit the prison in the middle of the night. Once inside, the jailer **fell down before Paul and Silas.** Then he **brought them out,** evidently from the inner recesses where the stocks were located. He asked the question, the most profound and important question in life, **"What must I do to be saved?"** The answer is **"Believe."** This is not just faith for faith's sake; it is faith with a very serious object. It is belief **on the Lord Jesus.** The result is that **you will be saved.** Paul and Silas **shared the word of the Lord** with the jailer's **household.**

16:33-34 The jailer's conversion, like Lydia's, was followed by clear, demonstrated deeds reflecting the reality of the life-change that had occurred internally. The terms **that same hour** and **immediately** show that the new convert did not waste any time about changing his life or about making his public profession of allegiance to Jesus Christ through baptism. The **entire household rejoiced because they all believed in God.** Who in that household could ever have dreamed that one of their father's prisoners, bound in chains, would one day bring a message that would set them all free from their sin?

16:35-36 What brought the **city officials** to the decision of freeing the prisoners is not stated. Maybe it was the way the officials had let the mob determine their actions. Perhaps it was the brutal nature of the punishment of two with so little evidence against them. Maybe it was the earthquake that shook some sense into the governing authorities. Whatever the case, Paul and Silas were told by the jailer, who had become a brother in Christ: **"You and Silas are free to leave."**

16:37 That would not be the last word, however. Paul had often been unfairly treated, beaten, and stoned—all illegally in light of his Roman citizenship. Yet here he chose to speak up. He may have wanted to give the new young church in Philippi some breathing room from the local authorities. The word would spread that Paul and Silas had been found innocent and freed by the leaders, expressing the truth that believers should not be persecuted—especially if they were **Roman citizens,** as were Paul and Silas.

16:38-39 Roman citizenship had certain privileges. These Philippian authorities were alarmed because it was illegal to flog **Roman citizens.** In addition, every citizen had the right to a fair trial—which Paul and Silas had not been given. Roman citizens were allowed to travel throughout the Empire under Rome's protection. They were not subject to local legislation or local legislators! No wonder the **city officials were alarmed** when they heard that Paul and Silas both were Roman citizens. The officials' jobs (and lives) were in jeopardy, in the very hands of the ones they had treated so unfairly. So they personally, politely, contritely **came to the jail and apologized** to Paul and Silas. Then **begged them to leave the city.**

16:40 Paul and Silas left the prison and **returned** to Lydia's home. As had been their custom everywhere they had been, they spent time meeting with the new believers **and encouraged them** for a while longer before they took their message to the next city.

Note that Luke returned to the third person "they" in this verse, as the first "we" section of Acts ends (see Introduction and note on 16:9-10). This may indicate that Luke stayed behind in Philippi to continue the work while Paul and Silas moved on toward Athens. The next "we" section begins at 20:5.

The book of Philippians stands as a testimony to the health of this first church in Europe. Lydia's generosity and the jailer's kindnesses exemplified the solid, spiritual character of the early days of the Philippian church. Who could have known what their influence would be? A few years hence, when Paul was sitting out a trial in Rome, he would write them a note and, in it, commend them for supporting him (see Philippians 1:5, 7; 4:16-19).

ACTS **17**

PAUL PREACHES IN THESSALONICA / 17:1-9

Leaving Luke in Philippi, Paul, Silas, and Timothy journeyed in a southwesterly direction along the Grecian coast, eventually arriving at Thessalonica. There Paul repeated his usual procedure: go first to the synagogue and preach to the Jews and God-fearing Greeks there. The response was typical—a revival among the Greeks, a riot at the hands of the Jewish leaders!

17:1 Thessalonica was about one hundred miles from Philippi, along the Egnatian Way toward Athens. **Amphipolis** was about thirty miles from Philippi, and **Apollonia,** an additional thirty miles. No record is given of any ministry occurring in these towns, though surely the missionaries would have taken every opportunity to speak about Christ.

Thessalonica was one of the wealthiest and most influential cities in Macedonia, with a population of over 200,000. This is the first city where Paul's teachings attracted a large group of socially prominent citizens. The most important Roman highway (the Egnatian Way)—extending from Rome all the way to the Orient—went through Thessalonica. This highway, along with the city's thriving seaport, made Thessalonica one of the wealthiest and most flourishing trade centers in the Roman Empire. Recognized as a free city, Thessalonica was allowed self-rule and was exempted from most of the restrictions placed by Rome on other cities in the Empire. With its international flavor, however, came many pagan religions and cultural influences that challenged the faith of the young Christians there.

After his ministry in Thessalonica, Paul would write two letters to the Thessalonian believers (1 and 2 Thessalonians), encouraging them to remain faithful and to refuse to listen to false teachers who tried to refute their beliefs.

17:2-3 Paul spent **three Sabbaths** ministering to the Jews in the **synagogue.** This does not mean he spent only three weeks in Thessalonica. Paul probably was there for much longer (a time period that occurred between 17:4 and 17:5). He had to have been there long enough to do everything mentioned in his letter to the Thessalonians, such as work at his trade (1 Thessalonians 2:7-9), win converts, instruct new believers in the Christian life (1 Thessalonians 4:1-2), and form a strong bond of love with these believers (1 Thessalonians 2:17-20). Paul's letter to the Philippians indicates that he was in Thessalonica long enough to receive from the Philippians financial help "more than once" (Philippians 4:16).

17:4 The response at Thessalonica was typical of the response Paul had experienced from the beginning days of his missionary travels. **Some who listened were persuaded,** probably referring to Jews. In addition, **a large number of godly Greek men** also joined, as well as **many important women.** These were influential women in the upper class (see 16:14; 17:12).

17:5 So far, Paul's ministry was following its usual course. The gospel was preached in the synagogues with meager response from the Jews. The Gentiles, however, were responding in great numbers (both worshipers in the synagogues and others). Then, as had been the custom, the **Jewish leaders** became **jealous** and set their sights on running these "heretics" out of town or worse. They **gathered some worthless fellows from the streets to form a mob and start a riot.** They went to **the home of Jason,** an early Thessalonian convert who, like Lydia, had convinced the travelers to stay in his home.

17:6-7 The mob had not found Paul and Silas at Jason's house. Perhaps Paul and Silas had been informed and had hurried away from the dangerous crowd. So the mob grabbed **Jason and some of the other believers** and brought them before the **city council.** Their accusations, like all good lies, bore some resemblance to the truth but were presented in their worst light. Paul and Silas were not **guilty of treason against Caesar** just because they declared allegiance to the King of kings, for Christ's Kingdom is of an entirely different sort than Caesar's was.

17:8-9 The manipulative accusations threw **the city officials** and the **people** into **turmoil.** Because there was no substantive case, however, and because **Jason and the other believers** had done little more than house the accused, they were **released** after posting **bail,** cash for their freedom. In Paul's first letter to this church, his statement about Satan blocking a future trip (1 Thessalonians 2:18) may refer to the events described here.

PAUL AND SILAS IN BEREA / 17:10-15

God continued to use persecution and opposition to spread the good news of forgiveness and eternal life through Jesus Christ. The uproar in Thessalonica forced Paul and Silas to journey to Berea, where they found a very teachable and receptive Greek audience. In a short time, however, hostile Jews came from Thessalonica to attack Paul's work in Berea. But this succeeded only in getting the great evangelist to Athens!

17:10-12 Paul and Silas had probably been in hiding from the riot in Thessalonica, and then went on **to Berea.** There they would begin again in the **synagogue.** Berea was about forty-five miles south of Thessalonica. The people of Berea **were more open-minded than those in Thessalonica.** The Greek word for "open-minded" is *eugenesteroi,* meaning "noble" or "generous—free from prejudice." Instead of hurling attacks, **they listened eagerly to Paul's message.** Instead of

forming a mob to run the missionaries out of town, they **searched the Scriptures day after day** to confirm whether or not Paul and Silas were **teaching the truth.** Here, in contrast to so many cities before, **many Jews believed,** as well as **prominent Greek women and many men.** See 17:4 for comparison with prominent people in Thessalonica. God honored the fact that these leading men and women of the city were searching for the truth.

17:13 What began as a wonderful situation did not last, however. Though there appeared to be no trouble at all from the Berean Jews, trouble followed Paul from **Thessalonica**. When the Jews there heard of Paul's ministry **in Berea**, they **went there** to stir up trouble.

17:14-15 Again, **the believers** rushed to protect Paul, sending him **on to the coast**.

Fortunately, the gospel message was so identified with Paul that it caused most of the Jewish anger to be directed at him, leaving his traveling companions more freedom to build up the churches. Thus, **Silas and Timothy** were able to stay **behind** in Berea. Those who were **escorting Paul** took him **to Athens**. He instructed them to tell **Silas and Timothy to hurry and join him**.

PAUL PREACHES IN ATHENS / 17:16-34

Paul's brief stay in Athens is a remarkable case study in the universality of the gospel. This chapter deals with the early stages of Paul's second missionary journey. He and his fellow travelers worked their way down the peninsula of modern-day Greece. Luke recorded Paul's message to the idol-worshiping academicians at Athens at length. That message revealed Paul's God-led wisdom for dealing with those who knew very little about the true God but who felt very secure in their intellectual abilities.

17:16 What can be viewed today in Athens as wonderful works of art and architecture were, in their day, the worshipful expression of a culture steeped in godless idolatry. Athens was named after the goddess Athena, and there were temples in Athens for all the gods in the Greek pantheon. Paul was **deeply troubled** by all the idolatry he saw **everywhere in the city**. Athens, with its magnificent buildings and many gods, was a center for Greek culture, philosophy, and education. Philosophers and educated people were always ready to hear something new—thus their openness to hear Paul speak at their meeting in the Areopagus (17:18-19). Athens had been the political, educational, and philosophical center of the world in its prime, the home of men such as Plato, Socrates, Aristotle, Epicurus, Zeno. But that was four hundred years before Paul's visit. When Paul arrived, it was a small town (ten thousand or so residents), reliving the glory days and filled with intellectuals spending their days philosophizing.

17:17 Paul had a balanced and adaptive approach to his ministry in Athens. In **the synagogue**, he debated with the Jews and worshiping Gentiles, likely using the arguments recorded at other places in the book of Acts (for example, 13:16-41), seeking to prove to them that Jesus was the long-awaited Messiah. Between his Sabbath debates with the worshipers in the synagogues, however, Paul **spoke daily in the public square** (the agora, which was the central marketplace) to whomever would listen.

17:18 The **Epicurean** philosophers, followers of Epicurus (341–270 B.C.), believed that the chief purpose for living was pleasure and happiness. If God existed, he didn't interfere in human affairs. Epicurians are similar to modern-day materialists and hedonists. The **Stoic** philosopherss were followers of Zeno (320–263 B.C.), who taught on a porch or patio called a *stoa*, hence the name "Stoics." The Stoics were pantheistic and felt that a great "purpose" was directing history. Humans' responsibility was to align themselves with that purpose through duty and self-discipline. This, quite logically, led to pride and self-sufficiency ("I am the master of my fate!").

These philosophers characterized Paul's arguments as "babbling." In the same way that a bird collects seeds, or a junk collector gathers trash, Paul was accused of collecting little pieces of knowledge that wouldn't take him anywhere. They were saying that his ideas were not as well thought through or as valid as theirs. Others of these philosophers recognized in Paul's teaching **about Jesus and his resurrection** that he was **pushing some foreign religion**.

17:19-20 Paul's dialogue in the marketplace led to an invitation to address the **Council of Philosophers**, also known as the **Areopagus**, which had been the judicial and legislative seat of government of Athens. By Paul's time, however, their responsibilities involved little more than overseeing certain areas of religion and education.

These intellectuals, ever interested in hearing new ideas, wanted to hear **about this new religion** that Paul was presenting. They wanted to **know what it** was **all about**. The word "know" will surface a good deal in the verses that follow. Here the descendants of the most influential thinkers in Western civilization, who had been on a centuries-long quest for knowledge, were given an opportunity to receive the ultimate knowledge about God entering the human race to redeem fallen humanity and put them in a position to know the person of Jesus Christ.

17:21 Luke parenthetically explained this predisposition of the **Athenians** and many who were residing there **(foreigners)** to spend days at a time **discussing the latest ideas.** Evidently, these were somewhat highbrow intellectuals, who loved to hear and discuss the latest fads in philosophy and theology. The picture is that they rarely actually did anything they discussed; they just enjoyed tossing around ideas.

17:22-23 Paul was well prepared to speak to this group. He came from Tarsus, an educational center, and had the training and knowledge to present his beliefs clearly and persuasively. Paul was a rabbi, taught by the finest scholar of his day, Gamaliel, and he had spent much of his life thinking and reasoning through the Scriptures.

Luke recorded this sermon in more detail than many of the others, likely as a sample of how Paul addressed the typical lost, intellectual Greek. Rather than arguing the Scriptures as he would with a Jewish audience, he adapted his message and backed up a step or two to speak of a Creator; then he moved toward speaking about a Savior and Judge.

Paul began his address by affirming the **religious** nature of his audience by explaining what he had seen in their city. He chose a starting point, a place where they could agree, rather than starting with their differences. The Athenians had built an idol **to an Unknown God** for fear of missing blessings or receiving punishment. The Athenian philosophers were either polytheistic (worshiped many gods) or pantheistic (believed all nature was god), so it would be natural for them to build an altar, superstitious that they might have overlooked a god. Archaeological finds have shown many such altars with the inscription, "to the unknown god(s)." Paul's opening statement to the men of Athens was about their "unknown god." Paul was not endorsing this god but using the inscription as a point of entry for his witness to the one true God.

17:24-27 The central body of Paul's speech is a presentation of God as the Creator, **who made the world and everything in it.** This Creator **doesn't live in man-made temples,** even spectacular wonder-of-the-world Greek structures like the one a few hundred yards up the hill from where they sat on

the Acropolis. God does not need anything from humans since **he has no needs.** From general characteristics of the Creator God, Paul moved to the more specific Judeo-Christian claims that God created all life and all nations **from one man.** This would likely rub proud Greeks the wrong way, since they believed themselves to be racially superior to all other nations (whom they called "barbarians").

This "unknown god" is not only knowable, **he is not far from any** person. This contrasted to the Greek gods, which lived in seclusion and could not be approached. The need that motivated the construction of an altar "To an Unknown God" (17:23) could be realized in Christ, for he was very near and available—to be known!

17:28 To illustrate and support his point, Paul quoted first from Epimenides, a Cretan poet from 600 B.C. (whom he also quoted in Titus 1:12): **In him we live and move and exist.** The next quote is from Aratus (a Stoic poet from Cilicia, 315–240 B.C.) in a line from his work *Phainomena:* **We are his offspring.** Both of these statements from well-known and accepted literary sources of the day served Paul's purpose well in arguing for the fact that the creation and sustaining of life was in the hands of the one God whom they did not know but who was very near and very knowable. The sense of humanity being God's "offspring" means that all receive life and breath from him.

17:29-30 Paul began to wrap up his message, building this statement on all that he had presented thus far and gently correcting where the Greeks had been incorrect: **And since this is true,** they needed to make some changes. Their thinking had been incorrect. They should not **think of God as an idol** who could be constructed by human hands. God is profoundly bigger than any idol.

Also, the Athenians had to understand that although God had **overlooked people's former ignorance** (not in the sense that he condoned it but rather that he had not yet judged it—see Acts 14:16; Romans 3:25), he now commanded **everyone everywhere** to turn from idolatry and **turn to him.** This was a serious and somber word to the gathered Athenians. They would do well to hear it and respond. Whatever the nature and consequences of their former failure to respond to God, it was nothing compared to ignoring what was being offered in the finished work of Christ.

17:31 Paul confronted his listeners with Jesus' resurrection and its meaning to all people—either blessing or punishment. The Greeks had no concept of judgment. Most of them preferred worshiping many gods instead of just one. And though their gods became angry from time to time, there was no real accountability in the way that Paul was presenting.

God **has set a day for judging the world,** however, and the judge had been selected. All judgment had been given to the one who was raised **from the dead**—Jesus Christ (see John 5:22)—the one Paul had been proclaiming in Athens since the day he had arrived (see 17:18).

To the Greek mind, the concept of resurrection was unbelievable and offensive, but on this issue the whole gospel hinged (1 Corinthians 15:13-14). Although Paul knew it would offend their precious philosophies, he did not hold back the truth. Paul often would change his approach to fit his audience, as he did with this one, but he never would change his basic message.

17:32 The mention of **the resurrection** would, of course, draw an immediate reaction from this group of intellects. **Some laughed,** yet there

were others who seemed intrigued and asked if they could **hear more about this later.** The latter group may simply have been patronizing this fellow scholar and visiting lecturer. Paul's speech was not in vain, however, as the next verse shows.

17:33-34 Though the discussion had ended with a few sneers and a polite invitation to return, Paul's time had not been wasted. **Some joined him and became believers,** one of them even a **Council member** named **Dionysius.** Only one other convert is named, **a woman named Damaris,** though we are told there were **others.**

Although there is no record of a church being founded in Athens and Paul soon moved on to Corinth (chapter 18), his visit to Athens was not a failure. The responsibility of the messenger is to present the message, and Paul certainly did that (and did so brilliantly). The fruit was God's responsibility.

ACTS **18**

PAUL MEETS PRISCILLA AND AQUILA IN CORINTH / 18:1-17

The spread of the gospel requires a team effort by individuals with different gifts. In Corinth, Paul met Priscilla and Aquila, a married couple (and fellow tentmakers) who proved to be faithful partners in the gospel (see Romans 16:3; 1 Corinthians 16:19; 2 Timothy 4:19). Paul's ministry in this decadent city was long and fruitful (18:11). Not even a concerted effort by the Jews could stop him from teaching the word.

18:1 Ancient **Corinth** had been destroyed by the Romans in 146 B.C., but it had been rebuilt by Julius Caesar in 46 B.C. because of its strategic seaport. By Paul's day (A.D. 50), the Romans had made Corinth the capital of Achaia (present-day Greece). Only fifty miles from Athens, Corinth by this time was regarded as the most influential city of Greece. The population was about 650,000—250,000 free citizens and 400,000 slaves. Corinth was a major center of commerce. Located on a narrow strip of land near two bustling seaports, and at a busy crossroads for land travelers and traders, the city was wealthy and very materialistic. Corinth was a center of culture. Though not a university town like Athens, there was great interest in Greek philosophy and wisdom. The city was permeated with religion—at least twelve temples were located there. The most infamous of these temples was

dedicated to Aphrodite, the goddess of love, and featured one thousand "sacred" prostitutes. Another temple, dedicated to Apollo, employed young men whose job was to fulfill the sexual desires of male and female worshipers. Largely due to this fact, the city was notorious for its immorality. So brazen was the unbridled licentiousness that a new Greek verb was eventually coined: to "Corinthianize" meant to practice sexual immorality. When Plato referred to a prostitute, he used the expression "Corinthian girl."

From a human point of view, Corinth was not the type of place where one would expect to launch a thriving ministry, but Paul didn't view things from an earthly perspective. He saw Corinth as both a challenge and a great ministry opportunity. Later he would write a series of letters to the Corinthians dealing in large part with the problems of immorality. First and Second Corinthians are two of those letters.

18:2-3 Aquila and **Priscilla** had just been expelled from **Rome** by **Claudius Caesar's order.** Trained as **tentmakers,** Aquila and Priscilla had packed up the tools of their trade and had made their way to Corinth. There they met Paul, who joined them in the business of tentmaking.

Jewish boys were expected to learn trades from which they could earn their living, so Paul learned tentmaking. Tents were much in demand because they were used throughout the Empire to house soldiers. Tentmakers also made canopies and other leather goods. It is highly likely, therefore, that the Roman army was a major purchaser of Paul's tents. As a tentmaker, Paul had a transportable livelihood that he could carry with him wherever God led him. Since ancient craftsmen did not compete as merchants do today but rather formed cooperative trade guilds and often lived in close proximity, it is not surprising that Paul and Aquila worked together. Because many of the trade guilds had adopted pagan practices, two God-fearing artisans would have been delighted to work together.

Paul chose to work to support himself during his stay in Corinth. The presence of so many religious promoters in Corinth may have added an incentive for Paul to earn his own living. Paul wanted to disassociate himself from those teachers who taught only for money. As Paul lived with Priscilla and Aquila, he must have shared with them his wealth of spiritual wisdom. They likely were already believers (or else Luke, it seems, would have mentioned their conversion). Perhaps they had embraced the gospel through the ministry of the Roman natives who had been in Jerusalem at Pentecost (see 2:10). They may even have been founding members of the church of Rome.

18:4 Paul never veered from this ministry philosophy. Because of his great burden for his lost Jewish brothers (see Romans 9:2-3), Paul would go **each Sabbath** to the **synagogue** (9:20; 13:5, 14; 14:1; 17:2, 10, 17; 18:19; 19:8). There he would speak to both **Jews and Greeks** (Gentiles who had converted to Judaism).

18:5 Upon the arrival of his colleagues, Paul was able to set aside his tentmaking and devote himself to **full time preaching. Silas and Timothy** must have brought with them a financial gift from the believers in Macedonia (see Philippians 4:15). They also brought a good word about the perseverance of the believers in Thessalonica (1 Thessalonians 3:6-8). Paul must have been encouraged by all these factors.

18:6 Some **Jews** in Paul's audience **opposed** and **insulted** Paul. That he **shook the dust from his robe** was a dramatic gesture separating him from even the dust found in such a rebellious synagogue. His pointed statement, **"Your blood be upon your own heads!"** is a reference to the Jews' own responsibility for their eventual spiritual destruction and brings to mind the sobering warning of Ezekiel 33:4. Paul was telling the Jews that he had done all he could for them. Because they continued to reject Jesus as their Messiah, he would turn his attention **to the Gentiles,** who would prove to be more receptive.

18:7-8 The home of **Titius Justus** became Paul's base of operations, and its proximity to the synagogue gave the apostle convenient and ongoing contact with both Jews and God-fearing Greeks. As the synagogue **leader, Crispus** would have been responsible for maintenance of the synagogue complex and the services held there. Such a position would have made him a prominent and well-to-do person in the community. Thus, his conversion (and that of his household) was a significant breakthrough for the church.

18:9-11 Apparently, the conversions of Crispus and other Corinthians (18:7-8), together with the formation of a growing "house church" right next door to the synagogue, must have provoked great controversy and opposition. But in contrast to his treatment elsewhere (see 17:5, 13), **no one** would **harm** Paul—he would not endure bodily harm during this time in Corinth. As a result of this divine word of assurance, Paul spent eighteen months in Corinth preaching and teaching. During that **year and a half,** Paul established a church and wrote two letters to the believers in Thessalonica (1 and 2 Thessalonians).

18:12-13 God's promise was that Paul would not be personally harmed (18:9); this guarantee did not preclude an attack on his ministry. In time, the **Jews** would successfully manage to have Paul charged with promoting a religion not approved by Roman **law.** Such behavior amounted to treason. But Paul was not encouraging obedience to a human king other than Caesar (see 17:7), nor was he speaking against the Roman Empire. Instead, he was speaking about Christ's eternal Kingdom.

This sequence of events took place when **Gallio,** the brother of Seneca the philosopher, was **governor of Achaia** (modern Greece). He had come to power in A.D. 51-52, and he enjoyed a good reputation among his people as a pleasant man.

18:14-15 This was an important judicial decision for the spread of the gospel in the Roman Empire. Judaism was a recognized religion under Roman law. As long as Christians were seen as a sect within Judaism, the court could **refuse** to hear cases brought against them. Gallio's decision proved to be extremely beneficial for the emerging Christian church for the next ten years. His ruling became a legal precedent used in Paul's trial in Rome. If Gallio had found Paul guilty, every governor in every province where Paul or other missionaries traveled could arrest the Christians. By not ruling against Paul, the Romans were including Christianity (as a sect of Judaism) as one of the legal religions *(religio licita)* of the Roman Empire. Gallio, in effect, helped spread the gospel throughout the Empire.

18:16-17 The fact that Gallio had Paul's Jewish accusers driven **out of the courtroom**, rather than merely sent away, reveals his irritation with what he evidently felt were petty, trumped-up charges. The gathered crowd, however, became unruly and erupted in violence. This **mob** may have been Greeks venting their feelings against the Jews for causing turmoil, or it may have included some Jews. If the latter is true, **Sosthenes,** the newly designated **leader of the synagogue** (after the conversion of Crispus, see 18:8) became the focal point of the mob's anger and frustration probably because he was seen as the one responsible for losing the case against Paul and leaving the synagogue worse off than before. A man named Sosthenes is mentioned in 1 Corinthians 1:1, and this may be the same man. If so, he would later become a convert and a companion of Paul.

PAUL RETURNS TO ANTIOCH OF SYRIA / 18:18-23
Leaving Corinth, Paul set sail for Syria with Priscilla and Aquila. He made a brief stop in Ephesus, leaving his faithful colleagues there, and hoping to return later. From there he continued in a southeastward direction to Caesarea, where he visited the church at Jerusalem to report on his activity. Then he traveled north to Antioch. This marked the end of Paul's second missionary journey.

18:18 Following the failure of the Jewish plot against him, Paul continued ministering in **Corinth.** The **vow** Paul took at **Cenchrea** (the seaport for the city of Corinth) may have been a temporary Nazirite vow, which would end with shaving the head and offering the hair as a sacrifice (Numbers 6:18). Or it could have been a personal vow of thanksgiving, offered in light of God's providential protection while in Corinth. **Paul, Priscilla,** and **Aquila** then **sailed for the coast of Syria** and Paul's sending church.

18:19-21 Arriving at **Ephesus,** the missionary team disembarked. Paul paid a quick visit to the Jewish synagogue, but Priscilla and Aquila settled in Ephesus (18:23-28). Though the **Jews** were receptive to Paul's message, he apparently felt a pressing need to return to Antioch. A few ancient manuscripts imply that Paul was also eager to arrive in Jerusalem in time to celebrate the Feast of the Passover. If this is accurate, Paul probably wanted to take advantage of the evangelistic

opportunities presented by such a gathering of devout Jews. He promised to return to them, "God willing" (see James 4:15).

18:22 With the five-hundred-mile voyage from Ephesus completed, Paul went to **Jerusalem,** then **to Antioch.** Having been away from Antioch of Syria for some two years, Paul had much good news to report to his fellow believers. This verse marks the end of Paul's second missionary journey.

18:23 This verse marks the beginning of Paul's third missionary journey, which lasted from A.D. 53 to 57. Leaving the church at **Antioch,** Paul headed toward Ephesus, but along the way he revisited the churches in **Galatia and Phrygia.** The heart of this trip was a lengthy stay (two to three years) in Ephesus. Before returning to Jerusalem, Paul also visited believers in Macedonia and Greece. As Paul set out, one of his priorities was **helping** the believers **to grow.** Such was Paul's regular practice—to keep checking up on those he had led to Christ and the churches he had founded.

APOLLOS INSTRUCTED AT EPHESUS / 18:24-28
Left in Ephesus by Paul, Priscilla and Aquila met a gifted speaker named Apollos, who had great passion for Christ but an incomplete knowledge of the gospel. Equipping him with a

more accurate message, they sent him on to Achaia, where he was used powerfully by God. This small investment in one life by the faithful Priscilla and Aquila resulted in enormous eternal dividends!

18:24 From **Alexandria,** the second most influential city in the Roman Empire, came **a Jew named Apollos.** Growing up in that Egyptian city's university atmosphere, Apollos was highly cultured and trained in philosophy and rhetoric. As a Jew, he also **knew the Scriptures well.** It is not stated what prompted him to move to **Ephesus.**

18:25 Apollos was an eloquent and powerful speaker. He had an accurate though incomplete message. While he had knowledge of the Old Testament, he **knew only about John's baptism** (referring to John the Baptist). In all likelihood, Apollos's preaching was a more polished version of John's message: "Turn from your sins and turn to God" (Matthew 3:2). John had focused on repentance from sin and on water baptism as an outward sign of commitment to and preparation for the Messiah's Kingdom. Apollos was probably urging people in a more eloquent fashion to do the same. Apollos needed to get the entire picture, and then he would be a powerful witness for Christ.

18:26 The eloquent, fiery young man who was so ably interpreting and applying the Old Testament messianic Scriptures in the synagogue was quickly noticed by **Priscilla and Aquila.** Upon hearing Apollos preach, they immediately recognized the deficiencies in his message. Consequently, they

took him aside (probably to their home) and **explained the way of God more accurately,** telling him about the life of Jesus, his death and resurrection, and the coming of the Holy Spirit. As Aquila and Priscilla set forth the historical facts of the gospel, Apollos must have seen many Old Testament prophecies become clear. The reports of his subsequent ministry suggest that he was filled with new energy and boldness after he received the complete gospel message.

18:27 With his more complete theology, Apollos, who **had been thinking about going to Achaia,** was encouraged to do so by **the Christians in Ephesus.** They sent along a glowing letter of introduction, asking the **believers in Achaia** to **welcome him.** He quickly became the verbal champion of the Christians in Achaia (probably Corinth), debating the opponents of the gospel in public. Read what Paul says of Apollos's impact in 1 Corinthians 4:1, 6.

18:28 Apollos proved to be a master debater. His arguments for the messiahship of Jesus were so powerful and logical that the Jews could not oppose him. His reputation spread far and wide (1 Corinthians 1:12; 3:4-6; 4:6), and Paul came to view him as a trustworthy coworker in the gospel (1 Corinthians 16:12; Titus 3:13).

ACTS 19

PAUL'S THIRD MISSIONARY JOURNEY / 19:1-7

After the parenthetical story of Apollos, Luke continued his record of Paul's third missionary journey, begun in 18:23. Evidence from Paul's epistles suggests the great apostle launched out on his third missionary trip in an attempt to undo the damage caused among the churches by numerous opponents of the gospel. Beginning at Antioch, Paul journeyed in a northwesterly direction through Galatia and Phrygia (18:23), eventually coming to Ephesus on the west coast of Asia Minor.

19:1 Paul traveled an interior road across Asia Minor, arriving in **Ephesus,** a hub of sea and land transportation, ranking with Antioch in Syria and Alexandria in Egypt as one of the great cities on the Mediterranean Sea. The population of Ephesus during the first century may have reached 250,000.

The temple to the Greek goddess Artemis (Diana is her Roman equivalent) was located there. The worship of Artemis was also a great financial boon to the area because it brought tourists, festivals, and trade. Upon his arrival, he promptly found a group of **several believers.**

Paul would stay in Ephesus for about three years. Ephesus had great wealth and power as a center for trade. It was a strategic location from which to influence all of Asia. From Ephesus he would write his first letter to the Corinthians to counter several problems that the church in Corinth was facing. Later, while imprisoned in Rome, Paul would write a letter to the Ephesian church (the book of Ephesians).

19:2 Paul's question to this group of Ephesian men underlines the truth that apart from the **Holy Spirit,** there is no salvation (Romans 8:9, 16; 1 Corinthians 12:13; Ephesians 1:13). The Spirit is the one who imparts life (John 3:5). Perhaps the men were unaware that the time of the Spirit's outpouring had come at last. Whatever the case, like Apollos (18:24-26), these men needed further instruction on the message and ministry of Jesus Christ.

19:3-4 John's **baptism** was a sign of turning **from sin** only (Matthew 3:2, 6, 8, 11; Mark 1:4-5; Luke 3:8), not a sign of new life in Christ. John's ministry had been preparatory. His baptism had anticipated something greater, pointing forward, toward **Jesus,** the fulfillment of all things. After adequate explanation, these men **were baptized into the name of the Lord Jesus.** Given Paul's remarks in 1 Corinthians 1:14-17, it may be that an unnamed associate of Paul actually performed this ceremony. This is the only place in the New Testament where we find an instance of rebaptism.

19:6-7 When Paul laid his hands on these **twelve** disciples (either to greet them as brothers or as a final part of the baptism rite), **the Holy Spirit came on them** in a similar fashion as at Pentecost. Pentecost was the formal outpouring of the Holy Spirit on the then mostly Jewish church, and it included outward, visible signs of the Holy Spirit's presence. Similar supernatural manifestations had occurred when the Holy Spirit first had come on Gentiles (see 10:45-47). The other outpourings in

the book of Acts were God's way of uniting other (mostly Gentile) believers to the church. The mark of the true church is not merely right doctrine but right actions, the true evidence of the Holy Spirit's work.

In Acts, believers received the Holy Spirit in a variety of ways. Usually the Holy Spirit would fill a person as soon as he or she professed faith in Christ. Here that filling happened later because these believers had not fully trusted in Christ as Savior. God was confirming to these believers, who did not initially know about the Holy Spirit, that they were a part of the church. The Holy Spirit's supernatural filling endorsed them as believers and showed the other members of the group that Christ was the only way.

What was the significance of the speaking in **tongues** among these Ephesian men? Perhaps to show that Paul had the same apostolic authority as did Peter to bestow the Spirit (see chapters 2 and 8). In any event, this is the final recorded instance of speaking in tongues in the book of Acts.

In order to interpret (and apply) the work of the Holy Spirit in Acts, believers must remember several truths. First, Acts is a book of transitions—documenting the end of the "old covenant" age of Israel and the law and the beginning of the "new covenant" age of the church and grace. Second, Acts is a history book that describes what did happen, not necessarily a doctrinal manual intended to prescribe what is supposed to happen. Third, there really is no set pattern for the reception of the Spirit in Acts. Sometimes people received the Spirit at baptism (2:38; 8:38), sometimes after baptism (8:15), and sometimes before baptism (10:47). The instances of tongues-speaking in Acts are erratic, not the general rule (see 2:4; 10:44-46; cf. 8:39; 13:52; 16:34). In Acts, Luke was primarily describing the spread of the gospel and its inclusiveness. In the epistles, the apostolic witnesses presented a more comprehensive doctrine of the Holy Spirit.

PAUL MINISTERS IN EPHESUS / 19:8-20

Paul was making good on a promise. He had paid an earlier visit to this synagogue in Ephesus at the end of his second missionary journey, while on his way back to Antioch and Jerusalem (18:19-21). Though his visit had been brief, he had found a receptive group of Jews and had pledged to return at the first opportunity. Paul's ministry in Ephesus lasted more than two years and was marked by an obvious movement of God's Spirit.

19:8-9 Given Paul's volatile history with the Jews (and his rather blunt preaching about Jesus as Messiah), it is surprising that he was able to minister at

the synagogue for **three months** before the Jews **publicly spoke against the Way** (a common name for early Christianity—see 9:2; 19:23; 24:14).

Consequently, Paul moved his ministry to a nearby **lecture hall** (school). Such halls were used in the morning for teaching philosophy, but they were empty during the hot part of the day (about 11:00 A.M. to 4:00 P.M.). Because many people did not work during those hours, they would come to hear Paul's preaching.

19:10 Paul faithfully labored in Ephesus. His lectures were "daily" (19:9) and continued **for the next two years.** These were two of the most fruitful years for the expanding church. **The province of Asia** refers to Asia Minor or modern-day Turkey. During this time, spiritually hungry Asians must have traveled to Ephesus to hear Paul speak.

19:11-12 Paul's ministry in Ephesus was accompanied by **unusual miracles**—long-distance healings as well as exorcisms. The miracles had a threefold purpose: (1) to demonstrate God's ultimate power and authority (in a city where Satan had a stronghold; see 19:18-19); (2) to authenticate Paul as an apostle and a spokesman for the one true God (Mark 16:20; Romans 15:18-19; 2 Corinthians 2:12; Hebrews 2:1-4); and (3) most obviously, to demonstrate compassion and mercy to those in great need.

19:13-14 This **team of Jews** was making a living by claiming to heal and drive out demons. This was a common occurrence in Israel (see Luke 11:19). Often such people would recite a list of names in their incantation to be sure of including the right deity. Here they were trying to use Jesus' name in an effort to match Paul's power.

Many Ephesians engaged in exorcism and occult practices for profit (see 19:18-19). The

sons of Sceva were impressed by Paul's work, obviously more powerful than their own. But they failed to see that Paul's power to drive out demons came from God's Holy Spirit, not from incantations and magic formulas. These men were calling on the name of Jesus without knowing him personally.

19:15-17 The self-proclaimed exorcists were so overpowered by one **evil spirit** in a man that they all were **attacked** and **badly injured.** Eventually, they fled for their lives, feeling fortunate that they had lost only their clothes. Here is a clear incident that demonstrates the truth that knowing about Jesus is not the same as knowing him. The surprising knowledge and great strength of a demon-possessed person is recorded in other places (Luke 4:33; 8:28). The report of the encounter between the sons of Sceva and the evil spirit spread quickly throughout the area. The **name of the Lord Jesus** came to be viewed as the most powerful name and not one to be taken lightly.

19:18-20 Ephesus was a center for black magic and other occult practices. Superstition and sorcery were commonplace. Many of the Ephesian converts had been involved in these dark arts. However, the demonstrated power of the name of Jesus over evil spirits became the impetus for a spiritual spring cleaning in the lives of many of the new believers in Ephesus. Specifically, they renounced their fascination with all occult practices. Then, taking the remnants of their pagan pasts, they **brought their incantation books and burned them at a public bonfire.** Making a clean break with sin was costly—the magic books alone were worth **several million dollars.**

THE RIOT IN EPHESUS / 19:21-41

In the great cosmic conflict for the souls of men, every intrusion of good is met by the fierce resistance of evil. Such was the case in Ephesus. A silversmith named Demetrius, who manufactured small idols of the Greek goddess Artemis, became alarmed by the mass conversion of Ephesians to Christianity. Gathering his fellow tradesmen, he convinced them that Paul and his message were a serious threat to their livelihood.

19:21-22 Wherever Paul went, he could see the influence of **Rome.** Paul wanted to take the message of Christ to the world's center of influence and power. Paul had already decided to depart from Ephesus before the trouble recorded in 19:23-41 broke out. But **he stayed awhile longer,** sending **Timothy and Erastus** ahead to do advance work in **Macedonia.**

19:23-24 Artemis was a **goddess** of fertility. She was represented by a carved female figure with many breasts. A large statue of Artemis (see 19:35) was in the great temple at Ephesus. That temple was one of the wonders of the ancient world. Supported by 127 pillars each six stories tall, the edifice was about four times larger than the Parthenon in Athens. The religious and commercial life of Ephesus reflected the city's worship of this pagan deity.

After a period of relative peace and steady growth for the Ephesian church, the gospel became offensive and intolerable to the city's **craftsmen** because it was undermining their ability to sell silver idols of Artemis. Converts to Christianity were no longer buying these products. Consequently, for economic and religious reasons, **the Way** (a reference to those who followed Christ) came under scrutiny, suspicion, and eventually attack. **Demetrius,** a prominent member of the silversmiths' guild, was the instigator of this trouble.

19:25-26 In the first century, craftsmen united with one another to form professional trade guilds. Similar to modern-day unions, these groups adhered to self-prescribed standards and practices. In this instance, Demetrius, perhaps the leader of this powerful guild, gathered not only the silversmiths who produced the miniature images of Artemis for sale at the temple but also **others employed in related trades.** (Archaeologists have also located images of the goddess made out of terra-cotta and gold.)

During the months that Paul had preached in Ephesus, Demetrius and his fellow craftsmen had not quarreled with his doctrine. They only became concerned when his preaching threatened their profits. Because they derived major income from making and selling silver statues of the Ephesian goddess Artemis, the craftsmen knew their livelihood would suffer if people started believing in Jesus and discarding the **handmade gods.**

19:27 Demetrius's strategy for stirring up a riot was to appeal to his fellow workmen's love of money and then to encourage them to hide their greed behind the mask of patriotism and religious loyalty. It would be difficult to get Ephesian citizens worked up about the slumping sales of a group of idol makers. However, it would be easy to rally the masses behind a noble campaign to defend the **prestige** of the **goddess** and her magnificent shrine.

19:28-29 The ploy of Demetrius worked perfectly. In short order, the gathered crowd **boiled** with anger at the Christians in their city and the subversive message of the gospel. They began to cry out, **"Great is Artemis of the Ephesians!"** As the gathering became an unruly mob, they **rushed to the amphitheater,** apparently to stage a large demonstration. Archaeologists have determined that this open-air auditorium, cut into the western slope of Mount Pion, could seat nearly twenty-five thousand people.

As the crowd rushed along, fueled by their fury, they managed to seize two of Paul's known **traveling companions—Gaius and Aristarchus.** (Aristarchus,

a native of Thessalonica, would later accompany Paul on other journeys—see 20:3-4; 27:1-2; Gaius is probably not the same Gaius mentioned in Romans 16:23 or 1 Corinthians 1:14.)

19:30-31 Paul **wanted** to go to the theater, most likely to speak up and defend his companions but also to have the opportunity to preach to such a large crowd. But the other believers, fearing for his safety, wouldn't let Paul go. These **officials of the province** were the most prominent men of the province of Asia, responsible for the religious and political order of the region. Clearly, Paul's message had reached all levels of society, crossing all social barriers and giving Paul **friends** in high places. Out of a dual concern for both public order and the well-being of their Jewish Christian friend, these powerful authorities begged Paul **not to risk his life by entering the amphitheater.**

19:32 Luke's observations about many in the rioting crowd not even knowing **why they were there** would have brought a chuckle to his original readers, for Greek playwrights and authors commonly mocked human foibles. Irony and parody were common elements in Greek comedy. The scene in the theater was one of total **confusion.**

19:33-34 This **Alexander** may have been pushed forward by the **Jews** as a spokesperson to explain that the Jews were distinct from the new religion that was causing economic problems for the silversmiths. An uninformed mob might vent their anger on the Jews since they were well known for their monotheistic refusal to believe in pagan deities like Artemis. But the attempt was futile. The gathering had become anti-Jewish as well as anti-Christian. Reasoning with a hysterical mob that has whipped itself into a frenzy is impossible. They shouted down Alexander by chanting, **"Great is Artemis of the Ephesians,"** and keeping it up **for two hours!**

19:35-36 Into the chaos stepped **the mayor** of Ephesus. Perhaps fearing Roman reprisal—specifically the suspension of Ephesus's privileges as a "free" city with its own elected assembly—this respected leader somehow managed to get the attention of the angry mob. The mention of the **image** that **fell down** to the Ephesians **from heaven** was likely a reference to a meteorite that was regarded as divine and placed in the Ephesian temple for the purposes of veneration. The presence of this mysterious object from above was considered proof that Artemis was a great and powerful goddess. In short, the mayor's argument was that the citizenry need not (for religious reasons) fear the intrusion of Christianity and should not (for political purposes) degenerate into incivility and disorder. Law and order, he was suggesting, should prevail in this instance.

19:37-39 With the crowd quiet and under some semblance of emotional control, the mayor briefly reiterated the facts of the case involving the Christians. First, they had **stolen nothing from the temple,** nor had they **spoken against the goddess.** Given that, if this was a conflict involving economic matters, Ephesus had an adequate legal system through which personal grievances could be addressed. Consequently, the mayor urged **Demetrius and the craftsmen** to pursue their dispute with the Christians **through legal channels.**

19:40-41 The city of Ephesus was under the domination of the Roman Empire. The main responsibility of the local city leaders was simply to maintain peace and order. If they failed to control the people, Rome would remove the appointed officials from office. The entire town could also be put under martial law, taking away many civic freedoms. The mayor's straightforward reminder must have had a sobering effect on the Ephesian populace, for they **dispersed.**

The riot in Ephesus convinced Paul that it was time to move on. But it also showed that the law still provided some protection for Christians as they challenged the worship of the goddess Artemis in the most idolatrous religion in Asia.

ACTS 20

PAUL GOES TO MACEDONIA AND GREECE / 20:1-6

This chapter records the conclusion of Paul's third missionary journey. Paul was heading for Jerusalem, intending to arrive before Pentecost. On the way, he took time in Troas to encourage the believers, then he had a tearful farewell with the elders of the church in Ephesus.

20:1 When **it** was over referred to the riot in Ephesus (19:26-41). Paul then **sent for the believers,** presumably those he had been teaching in Ephesus for two years. After he **encouraged them,** he **left for Macedonia** to continue his ministry of encouragement.

20:2-3 Second Corinthians 2:12-13 and 7:5-7 give a few more details about this journey. Second Corinthians was written somewhere during this part of the journey. On this trip Paul likely retraced many of his steps, revisiting many of the churches he had established on his second journey (see 16–18) and arriving ultimately in **Greece** (specifically Corinth), **where he stayed for three months.** From Corinth Paul wrote the letter to the Romans. Although he had not yet been to Rome, believers had already started a church there (2:10; 18:2). Paul wrote to tell the Roman believers that he planned to visit them.

Paul's three-month stay was brought to a close in typical fashion: a Jewish **plot** was **discovered** against the apostle, causing him to decide to **return through Macedonia** instead of sailing **back to Syria.**

20:4-5 This is an unusually complete listing of those who **were traveling with** Paul on this

section of the journey. The company provided accountability. Paul was carrying the offering from the Asian churches for the suffering church at Jerusalem (see 2 Corinthians 8–9). Paul would not want the Jerusalem church to think he handled the money by himself, without others to account for it.

These men who were traveling with Paul also represented churches that Paul had started in Asia: (1) Galatia—**Gaius** and **Timothy;** (2) Asia—**Tychicus** and **Trophimus;** (3) Macedonia—**Sopater, Aristarchus,** and **Secundus.** Having the men deliver the gifts to Jerusalem gave the gifts a personal touch and strengthened the unity of the universal church. This was also an effective way to teach the church about giving, because the men were able to report back to their churches the ways in which God was working through their giving. Paul discussed this gift in one of his letters to the Corinthian church (see 2 Corinthians 8:1-21).

20:6 The **Passover** was here a calendar marker, telling when all these things occurred. The use of **we** shows that Luke again had joined the group. The last "we" section was 16:10-40.

PAUL'S FINAL VISIT TO TROAS / 20:7-12

In Troas, the believers gathered on Sunday, and Paul preached a lengthy, late-night sermon. A young man by the name of Eutychus fell asleep and fell to his death out of the third-floor window in which he was sitting! Paul calmly restored Eutychus to life, and the church resumed its worship service.

20:7-8 The gathering of this group was **on the first day of the week.** This is one of the clearest New Testament references to the church meeting on Sunday rather than on Saturday, the Sabbath. Because Paul and his companions were **leaving the next day,** Paul had an extended teaching time, talking **until midnight.** Paul did not want to leave Troas until he had made the most of every minute he had with the believers.

The **many flickering lamps** were candles in lanterns. The combination of the heat from the candles and the gathered number of people in an upstairs room probably made the room very warm. This no doubt helped Eutychus fall asleep.

20:9-10 Paul **spoke on and on,** and **Eutychus,** likely sitting on the **windowsill** because of the crowd in the room, **sank into a deep sleep.** He **fell** out of the window, **three stories.** Luke, the physician, confirmed the fact that Eutychus was dead. Paul went to the boy and **took him into his arms.** Paul addressed the concerned flock. **"Don't worry,"** he said. Then, with those powerful Resurrection-reminiscent words, he added: **"He's alive!"**

20:11-12 Following this amazing miracle, the meeting was resumed **upstairs** where they celebrated the **Lord's Supper,** followed by Paul's continuing to teach **until dawn.** The believers were **greatly relieved** (literally, "encouraged")— a repeated feature of Paul's ministry.

PAUL MEETS THE EPHESIAN ELDERS / 20:13-38

Traveling south to Miletus, Paul summoned the elders of the Ephesian church in order to bid them farewell. In his charge to them, Paul reviewed his ministry among them, described the Spirit's leading him to Jerusalem, and challenged them to shepherd the church in their care. This discourse reveals Paul's pastoral heart (20:18-20, 31, 36-37), reiterates Paul's preoccupation with preaching the Kingdom of God (20:24-25), and records the presence of a well-trained group of disciples who would be able to carry the message of Christ throughout Asia.

20:13-15 Paul traveled ahead **by land to Assos,** which was about twenty miles away, a much shorter distance than a ship had to travel. The rest of the party **went on ahead by ship.** At Assos, the party was reunited, and Luke faithfully recorded the inland passage trek of their ship—**to Mitylene,** then past **the island of Kios and Samos,** eventually arriving **at Miletus.** Miletus was situated at the mouth of the Maeander River on the Aegean Sea (in modern-day Turkey).

20:16 Paul had missed attending the Passover in Jerusalem, so he was especially interested in arriving on time for **Pentecost,** which is fifty days after Passover. He was carrying gifts for the Jerusalem believers from churches in Asia and Greece (see Romans 15:25-26; 1 Corinthians 16:1-4; 2 Corinthians 8:1–9:15). The **Jerusalem** church had been experiencing difficult times.

20:17-19 Paul wanted to meet with **the elders of the church at Ephesus,** so he sent word for them to come meet him at **Miletus.** Paul's message to the elders is an example of a typical address of Paul to the spiritual leaders of the churches he had begun. Paul described his ministry among the Ephesians, reminding the elders that they had observed his character. As wildly successful as Paul's ministry was—the miracles, decisions, baptisms, and successfully discipled believers and planted churches—he did not boast. Under his ministry there, the word of the Lord had spread widely (19:20). The glory, however, was consistently given back to the one directing it all—it was the **Lord's work,** not Paul's. Another characteristic of Paul's ministry to the Ephesians was the presence of **tears.** In other words, his work was done with passion and compassion. Paul's ministry also showed endurance. He spoke of the **trials** that he had endured.

20:20-21 Paul's ministry in Ephesus exuded boldness in **telling the truth.** The mention of **homes** may refer to house churches. Paul had **one message** for all. Both **Jews and Gentiles** alike were included in his mission, and both needed the central message of **turning from sin and turning to God.**

In this day of growing complexity, the church often falls prey to the temptation to become sophisticated and complicated, to fit into the culture. Believers must never let the message get lost in the trappings of the ministry (buildings, programs, schedules, calendars) or the ever-present busyness of church activities. The message must not be prejudiced—it's applicable to Jews and Gentiles alike. It is not optional, and it must not be overly complicated. It is just one message: turn from sin, turn to God, and believe in Jesus Christ.

20:22-23 Paul's message to the Ephesian elders shifted from a description of his past work among them to a description of the present and immediate future for him. That future would begin in **Jerusalem,** where Paul said he was being **drawn there irresistibly by the Holy Spirit.** The Holy Spirit **told** Paul that he would be imprisoned and experience **suffering.** Even knowing this, Paul did not shrink from fulfilling his mission. His strong character was a good example to the Ephesian elders—as well as to all Christians, many of whom would suffer for Christ.

20:24 Paul's statement of his priorities and values is a great perspective for any believer of any age. Self-preservation must be subservient to the faithful completion of **the work assigned by the Lord Jesus.** Paul was a single-minded person, and the most important goal of his life was **telling others the Good News** (Philippians 3:7-13). No wonder Paul was the greatest missionary who ever lived.

20:25-27 Paul may have been convinced that **none** of these men would **ever see** him **again.** It is unknown if he ever did, but at this somber moment, Paul was saying good-bye to a group, most of whom were led to Christ by him and probably all of whom had been taught by him. In a solemn declaration, Paul claimed his innocence of anyone's **damnation.** He was likely referring to the people of Ephesus before whom he had boldly and thoroughly proclaimed what they needed to know to be saved and to grow in Christ. All of God's purpose that had been revealed to Paul, he had taught to them.

20:28 Paul outlines the philosophy of the ministry that pastors and church leaders should follow

as he charged these **elders** in Ephesus to **beware**—first for themselves and then for the **church.** Although Paul had likely chosen and trained most of them, the operative force behind everything had been the **Holy Spirit.** Those who lead God's people must beware by keeping a careful watch over themselves and the flock. The leadership (elders, pastors, deacons) would be the first line of attack from the enemy (the "wolves" mentioned in the next verse). Before the flock could be protected, the shepherds must protect themselves! These leaders were also to **feed and shepherd God's flock.** They were to guide, direct, protect, feed, and help the flock to grow into its full potential (see Psalm 23; Ephesians 4:11; 1 Peter 5:1-4).

20:29-30 With a vivid, colorful shepherding image, Paul forewarned the Ephesian elders of the coming attack on the **flock** by **vicious wolves.** Some would attack from outside the church. These **false teachers** would invade the church after the departure of Paul and, like wolves, ruthlessly attack the flock. They would bring with them their fine-sounding words, **not sparing** a soul who would believe and follow them.

Other attacks would come from inside the church (**even some of you**). Paul warned that some of their own members, in order to build a **following,** would **distort the truth** and lead away a portion of the flock to their own doom. False teachers did, in fact, hound the church at Ephesus. This is confirmed in the later books of the New Testament (1 Timothy 1:6-7, 9-20; 4:1-3; 2 Timothy 1:15; 2:17-18; 3:1-9; Revelation 2:1-7).

20:31 Paul's final warning is simply, **"Watch out!"** The leaders needed to **remember** Paul's example of wakefulness, his **constant watch and care** over them. Since the vicious enemy is always around (both inside and outside the church) and always looking for victims, the shepherd must never let down his guard.

Paul pointed to his own **three years** of shepherding of the Ephesian church as an example. The few incidents recorded in chapter 19 serve as examples of how constant and vicious the attacks could be. This is a good word for every church leader and person who seeks to live for Christ.

20:32 Paul pronounced a benediction of sorts to this group into whom he had poured so much of his life; he entrusted them to **God** and to **the word of his grace.** This was evidently a common parting phrase, as it occurs elsewhere in the book (14:23, 25; 15:40). The **message** had two essential characteristics: (1) it was **able to build** them **up,** and (2) it was able to **give** them **an inheritance**

with all those he has set apart for himself (26:18; Ephesians 1:18; Colossians 1:12; 1 Peter 1:4). This message is the word of God, by which the believers would be built up in the faith.

20:33-35 Returning to remarks similar to those with which he opened (20:18-20), Paul reminded the elders of three more characteristics of his ministry: (1) contentment and self-restraint—he had not **coveted** anyone's **money or fine clothing;** (2) diligence—he had **worked to pay** his **own way,** and that of his companions as well; and (3) selflessness—he had **been a constant example** of how to **help the poor by working hard,** following Jesus' words concerning the advantage of giving over receiving.

These words of Jesus, **"It is more blessed to give than to receive,"** are not recorded in the Gospels. Obviously, since not all of Jesus' words were written down (see John 21:25), this saying must have been passed on orally through the apostles. Cer-

tainly the theology of this statement is found abundantly in Christ's teachings.

20:36-38 Paul's relationship with these believers is a beautiful example of genuine Christian fellowship. He had cared for them and loved them, even **wept** with them in their needs. They responded with love and care for him and sorrow over his leaving. They **prayed** together and comforted one another.

Like Paul, all believers can build strong relationships with other believers by sharing, caring, sorrowing, rejoicing, and praying with them. And—like Paul—the best way to gather others around is by giving oneself away to them and to the gospel. It is not surprising that these men **accompanied him down to the ship.** They may have stood, wept, and prayed until the mast of their beloved shepherd's ship disappeared over the Aegean horizon, and only then returned to Ephesus, determined more than ever to shepherd their flock with the passion of the one who had so lovingly shown them the way.

ACTS 21:1–22:29

PAUL'S JOURNEY TO JERUSALEM / 21:1-14

Upon making his way to Tyre, Paul was urged by the believers not to go to Jerusalem. Nevertheless, the apostle pressed on. At Caesarea further prophecies were given, warning Paul of certain imprisonment if he journeyed to Jerusalem. Unmoved, Paul adamantly determined to complete his mission. God's sovereignty was at work. This becomes more apparent upon viewing how this Jerusalem visit ultimately paved the way for Paul's trip to Rome!

21:1-3 Having said **farewell to the Ephesian elders** at Miletus, Paul continued his journey to Jerusalem. The stops along the way—**Cos, Rhodes,** and **Patara**—were a normal day's run for the smaller ship they were on. At Patara they boarded a different ship, possibly a larger vessel that could make the longer, open-sea trip to **Phoenicia.** Luke recorded the sighting of **Cyprus** in their transit of the Mediterranean—surely sparking memories for Paul of his first journey with Barnabas. How many miles and memories had passed since then, not to mention how many souls had found the Savior! The ship put in at **Tyre, in Syria,** its destination, giving Paul and his group a week's rest before they shipped out again.

21:4 A church had been founded in Tyre, probably soon after the dispersion of believers from Jerusalem following Stephen's martyrdom (8:1; 11:19). Paul

and his traveling companions (see 20:4) **found the local believers** and **stayed with them a week.**

Certain believers who had the gift of prophecy **prophesied through the Holy Spirit,** warning Paul **not** to go **to Jerusalem.** Was Paul disobeying the Holy Spirit by continuing his journey to Jerusalem? More likely, the Holy Spirit warned these believers about the suffering that Paul would face in Jerusalem. They drew the conclusion that he should not go there because of that danger. This is supported by 21:12-14, where the local believers, after hearing that Paul would be turned over to the Romans, begged him to turn back. Acts 20:22 and 21:14 show that Paul determined that it was God's will for him to go to Rome, as does the fact that God directly told him that he was supposed to go to Rome (23:11). Paul said that he was "drawn irresistibly" by the Holy Spirit to go to Jerusalem (20:22). But Paul's importance to the church organizationally, and their love for him personally, compelled these believers to interpret the certainty of danger to mean he should stay safe. But, like his Savior before him, Paul "resolutely set out for Jerusalem" (Luke 9:51).

21:5-6 After the week was over, the **congregation** of believers, **including wives and children,** went down to the **shore** to see them off. As at Miletus (20:36-38), the farewell from Tyre was a tender time of prayer. Whenever someone says that Paul was cold or harsh (based on the stinging rebukes he passed out to churches like those in Galatia and Corinth or to individuals like Barnabas and even Peter), lead the person to passages such as these. Whether it was from the elders at Ephesus or the believers at Tyre, there was a warm, loving response to his ministry virtually everywhere he went.

21:7 Ptolemais was the only stop between Tyre and Caesarea, and there the stay was much shorter—**only one day.** Still, Paul and his companions **greeted the believers.** As with Tyre, there is no record of how or by whom the church had been planted in the area.

21:8-9 In **Caesarea** lived **Philip,** called here **the Evangelist.** The last record of his activities is found in 8:26-40. Philip had been **one of the seven men chosen** to serve the tables in the early days of the church at Jerusalem (6:5). Philip **had four unmarried daughters,** and they all **had the gift of prophecy.** From this text we learn that the gift of prophecy was given to both men and women. Several women are noted for their active participation in God's work (2:17; Philippians 4:3). Other women who are recorded in the Bible as prophesying include Miriam (Exodus 15:20), Deborah (Judges 4:4), Huldah (2 Kings 22:14), Noadiah (Nehemiah 6:14), Isaiah's wife (Isaiah 8:3), and Anna (Luke 2:36-38).

21:10-11 Fifteen years earlier, **Agabus** had predicted the famine in Jerusalem (11:27-29). He arrived at Philip's home **from Judea** and gave a graphic display of what lay ahead for Paul, giving more detail as to what the previous prophecies had been warning. Agabus gave the information of Paul's impending arrest—naming **the Jewish leaders** as the cause and adding that he would be **turned over to the Romans.**

21:12-14 Spurred along by the graphic and foreboding prophecy of Agabus, the believers in Caesarea **begged Paul not to go on to Jerusalem.** Even Paul's traveling companions (**we**) added their voices to the crowd. Why would he go to certain imprisonment in Jerusalem? The answer was that Paul knew God wanted him to go. No one enjoys pain, but a faithful disciple wants above all else to please God. Paul was not ignoring the warnings. He was not suicidal. Paul simply disagreed with his brothers and sisters in Christ as to whether the prophesied difficulties outweighed the potential progress that could be made for the gospel. And the ultimate issue—the will of God—was the one to which Paul's friends finally resigned themselves: **"The will of the Lord be done."**

PAUL ARRIVES AT JERUSALEM / 21:15-25

At long last, Paul reached his destination—Jerusalem. He was warmly welcomed by the believers there. Aware, however, of the strong Jewish animosity toward Paul, James and the elders encouraged the apostle to participate in a public Jewish ceremony of purification at the Temple. Such an act, they felt, would quell the false rumors circulating about Paul—that he was actively undermining the Mosaic law.

21:15-17 The trip from **Caesarea** to **Jerusalem** was about sixty-five miles—a two-day journey on horseback. **The home of Mnason** may have been in Jerusalem or at some point along the journey there. Mnason was **from Cyprus** and was **one of the early disciples.** He may have been converted during Paul and Barnabas's first missionary journey (13:4-12), or he may have been a convert from even earlier than that—perhaps one of the original Jerusalem disciples from the few weeks following that miraculous Pentecost (chapter 2).

Upon their arrival in Jerusalem, Paul and his friends were **welcomed cordially,** a testimony to the growing reputation of the apostle and gratitude for the generous gift he was bringing from the churches (see 24:17; Romans 15:25-27; 1 Corinthians 16:1-4; 2 Corinthians 8:13-14; 9:12-13). Paul had not forgotten the charge of the Jerusalem church from years ago to remember the poor (Galatians 2:10). The Jerusalem elders had never thought that they would be the beneficiaries of Paul's obedience to their charge; much less had they imagined that the support would come from predominantly Gentile churches. How that must have bonded the Jewish and Gentile segments of the church!

21:18-19 James, Jesus' brother, was the leader of the **Jerusalem church** (15:13-21; Galatians 1:19; 2:9). It was not only an influential church, but it had also been a horribly persecuted church (since Stephen's day), and at this particular time, it faced famine and poverty. This was obviously an important gathering, since **all the elders were present.** They listened to Paul's **account of the things God had accomplished among the Gentiles through his ministry.**

The "we" section ends here and will not appear again until 27:1. It is unclear whether Luke was no longer with them (an unlikely event) or whether he just changed his literary style.

21:20-22 There were great tensions in Jerusalem during this period. The ancient Jewish historian Josephus described this time period (approximately A.D. 56 or 57) as being filled with political unrest and strong Jewish nationalism. There were several uprisings by Jews against their Roman leaders—all of which had been brutally put down by Felix, the Roman procurator. This caused even more anger from the Jews and intensified their hatred for Gentiles. Paul, missionary to the Gentiles, entered the city with news of vast Gentile conversions.

The elders informed Paul of the large contingency of **Jews** who had **believed.** The problem, however, was that **all** of those Jews took **the law of Moses very seriously** (15:5), meaning that they probably would not be rejoicing in the success of Paul's ministry among the Gentiles. The Jewish Christian "zealots" had **been told,** through rumors, that Paul was **teaching all the Jews** he had contacted who lived **in the Gentile world to turn their backs on the laws of Moses.** Not only that, but they had heard that Paul was minimizing the rite of circumcision and allowing the Jews to stop following **Jewish customs.**

The Jerusalem council (chapter 15) had settled the issue of circumcision of Gentile believers. Evidently, there was a rumor that Paul had gone far beyond the council's decision, even **forbidding** Jews to circumcise their children. It was true that Paul was downplaying the importance of circumcision and did not require keeping the Jewish customs, but that was for the Gentiles, not for the Jews. Paul had Timothy circumcised because his mother was Jewish (see commentary on 16:2-3). Paul taught both Jews and Gentiles that salvation did not depend on keeping the law (Galatians 3:24-29; 5:1; Colossians 2:11-17). He taught Gentiles not to get circumcised (1 Corinthians 7:18-19), but there is no evidence that he taught Jews to abandon the practice.

21:23-24 The rumors about Paul, of course, were not true, but Paul willingly submitted to this Jewish custom to show that he was not working against the council's decision and that he was still Jewish in his lifestyle. (Sometimes believers must submit to authorities to avoid offending others, especially when such offense would hinder God's work.)

The Jerusalem elders suggested that Paul join **four men** among their number who had **taken a vow.** The details are unknown, but they seem to have taken the Nazirite vow (Numbers 6:13-21). Paul was to join them in the **purification ceremony** and **pay** their expenses. Often a Jew who had been in Gentile territory for a lengthy time would undergo ritual purification upon returning to his homeland. The time period for this purification was seven days. This may have been what the elders were asking Paul to do.

There seems to have been a definite lack of resolve in this decision by the Jerusalem elders as they tried to appease the Jews. A far more appropriate response by the leaders would have been to tell them that the Jerusalem council had made an authoritative decision (probably at least eight years ago by this time) and communicated it in written form. Paul agreed to abide by the ruling, and had been doing so. It seems absurd that this hardworking apostle, who had just brought to Jerusalem a generous offering from his Gentile ministry, should be asked for some of his hard-earned money to placate that group. But when asked, Paul graciously gave the money and went along with the leaders' suggestion.

Those who think Paul was wrong for going along with this request by the elders forget one of the marks of Paul's ministry: "When I am with the Jews, I become one of them so that I can bring them to Christ. When I am with those who follow the Jewish laws, I do the same, even though I am not subject to the law, so that I can bring them to Christ" (1 Corinthians 9:20). This was one of those times when it was not worth offending the Jews, so Paul wisely chose to comply.

21:25 Here, quoting almost word for word, the elders stated the past ruling of the Jerusalem council (see 15:19-21). One wonders if any of these individuals had seen a copy of Paul's letter to the Romans or the Galatians. It is not clear who this restatement of the council ruling was for—themselves, Paul, or those among them who may have been wavering. Perhaps this statement is best understood as given to assure Paul that they were not changing the ruling or adding anything to what had been decided years earlier.

PAUL IS ARRESTED / 21:26-36

Paul's attempt to placate his enemies was an utter failure. A group of Jews from Asia spotted him in the Temple and incited a crowd to seize him. Dead set in their determination to reject the message of salvation in Christ, these opponents of Paul refused to look objectively at the facts. Instead, they whipped the mob into a frenzy by making a series of false and highly inflammatory accusations against the apostle. Only the quick action of a detachment of Roman soldiers saved Paul from being beaten to death.

21:26-29 Paul's agreement **to their request** was a sign of his greatness. In submission to their political sensitivity, he paid for a ceremony in order to appease the religious zealots. He **went through the purification ritual** with the four others and proceeded to the **Temple**. But Paul's gracious action appeased none of his detractors. The opposition appears to have come from unbelieving (that is, non-Christian) **Jews** from **Asia**, who recognized him **in the Temple** during the time of his completion of the purification ritual. These Jews, present for Pentecost, must have recognized Paul from his ministry in their area. Since they recognized **Trophimus**, they likely were from **Ephesus** and may have even been a part of the riot there (19:28-41).

These Jews **roused a mob** that began to shout against Paul. Contrary to their emotional accusation, Paul had not been teaching against the Jews or telling **everybody to disobey the Jewish laws**, nor had he spoken **against the Temple**. The pinnacle of this argument was the accusation that Paul had brought **Gentiles** into the Temple. Luke explained that the Jewish accusers **had seen** Paul in the city with Trophimus, whom they knew to be **a Gentile**. Then, without any investigation whatsoever, **they assumed Paul had taken him into the Temple,** reporting this as if it had actually happened (21:28)!

21:30-31 The city was thrown into **an uproar,** and **a great riot followed.** In mob-like fashion, Paul was **dragged out of the Temple,** and **the gates were closed behind him.** These were the gates between the inner court and the Court of the Gentiles. The Temple guards (Levites) shut the gates to prevent the mob from coming inside. How ironic that the final scene at the Temple in the book of Acts is the gates slamming shut to keep Paul out. Evidently, the mob probably was going to try to beat him or stone him to death. Because

Jerusalem was under Roman control, an uproar in the city would quickly be investigated by Roman authorities. The **commander of the Roman regiment** at this time was Claudius Lysias (see 23:26).

21:32-33 Lysias **called out his soldiers and officers.** The quick action of Lysias and the close proximity of the garrison (the Antonia Fortress was adjacent to the Temple area) were all that saved Paul's life. The seizing of Paul by the crowd was superseded by the seizing of Paul by the Roman soldiers.

Paul actually was fortunate to be **arrested** and **bound.** Luke, ever the one for details, wrote that Paul was bound with **two chains.** The chains handcuffed him to a Roman soldier on each side. This would be normal treatment for a criminal. After seizing Paul, the **commander** asked the crowd who the chained man was and what crime he had committed.

21:34-36 The commander could not get a direct answer because the crowd could not agree on what the issues were—of course, that had not stopped them in their murderous course a few moments earlier. Because the commander **couldn't find out the truth,** he **ordered Paul to be taken to the fortress,** probably the safest place for the apostle in all Jerusalem! This was the Fortress of Antonia, built by Herod the Great to defend the Temple area. It was located northwest of the Temple and connected by stairs to the Court of the Gentiles. The fortress housed nearly one thousand soldiers.

In the process of moving their prisoner, the mob, supposedly seeing the object of their anger being safely whisked away, **grew so violent** that Paul had to be carried by the soldiers! The murderous mob pursued, all the while shouting, **"Kill him, kill him!"** These were almost identical to the words another murderous crowd had shouted to Pontius Pilate concerning Jesus of Nazareth just a few decades earlier (Luke 23:18; John 19:15).

PAUL SPEAKS TO THE CROWD / 21:37–22:23

Paul's defense before the Jewish mob in the Temple courts is a textbook example of how to communicate to a hostile audience. He disarmed the Roman commander by speaking to him in Greek. Then he established common ground with the Jews gathered below him by speaking to them in their own language. Presenting his credentials as a devout Jew trained under the highly respected rabbi Gamaliel, Paul then described his unlikely encounter with the risen Christ on the Damascus Road. The crowd listened attentively until Paul mentioned "Gentiles." At that word, the mob erupted in anger. Although Paul knew his statement would cause controversy, he refused to dilute the truth.

21:37-38 By speaking in **Greek,** Paul showed that he was a cultured, educated man and not just a common rebel starting riots in the streets. The language grabbed the commander's attention and gave Paul protection and the opportunity to give his defense.

The historian Josephus wrote of an **Egyptian** who had led a revolt of thousands of Jews in Jerusalem in A.D. 54 (just three years previous). This self-proclaimed prophet had convinced his fanatical followers to accompany him to the nearby Mount of Olives. He said that, at his word, the walls of Jerusalem would collapse and this miraculous event would precipitate the destruction of the Roman Empire. Governor Felix had dispatched troops to deal with this insurrection. Hundreds of Jews were either killed or captured, and the Egyptian ringleader of this sect had disappeared **into the desert.** Lysias apparently assumed that Paul was this rebel, returning to make more trouble.

21:39-40 All these events took place outside the Fortress of Antonia, the Roman garrison that adjoined the Temple area on the northwest side. From the headquarters of Claudius Lysias, two flights of stairs led down into the outer court of the Temple. The staircase would prove to be an excellent platform from which Paul could **talk to these people.**

The commander agreed to Paul's request. The text does not tell us why. Perhaps he was convinced that Paul was not some insurrectionist or rabble-rouser. He was a Jew and a proper citizen. The commander may have thought that Paul could explain to the crowd what had happened, and hopefully they would disperse peacefully. So he **agreed** to let Paul speak.

Paul looked out on an enraged mob, and his heart broke. He ached for his people to understand the truth about Christ. He had been just like them—spiritually blind—and he wanted his Jewish brothers to experience this same salvation. When Paul began speaking to the assembled crowd, he **addressed them in their own language, Aramaic,** the common language among Palestinian Jews. He spoke in Aramaic not only to communicate in the language of his listeners but also to show that he was a devout Jew and had respect for the Jewish laws and customs.

22:1-2 With this courteous salutation, Paul began the first of five defenses recorded by Luke in the book of Acts. He commanded the mob's attention by speaking Aramaic, **their own language,** because many Jews of the Dispersion (that is, Hebrews who were born or reared outside of Palestine) could not speak Greek or Hebrew. The mob would have assumed that Paul, an outsider, could speak only Greek. Paul's ability to speak Aramaic gave his Jewish credentials even more weight and helped win him a hearing.

22:3 Paul began his defense with a brief personal history. The statement, **I am a Jew,** declared Paul's brotherhood with the crowd. Though **born in Tarsus,** Paul had been **educated in Jerusalem.** Not only that, but **under Gamaliel,** the most honored rabbi of that time. Gamaliel was well known and respected as an expert on religious law and as a voice for moderation (5:34). At Gamaliel's feet, Paul had **learned to follow our Jewish laws and customs very carefully.** The Pharisees were legendary for their rigorous keeping of the most minute details of the law (see Matthew 23). This statement by Paul was intended to refute the allegation in 21:28 that he had been telling everyone to disobey the Jewish laws.

In saying he was **zealous to honor God in everything,** Paul was alluding to his former prominent role in the persecution of Christians. He recognized the sincere motives behind their desire to kill him and that a few years earlier, he had shared that same well-meaning but misguided passion.

22:4-5 Having commended his Jewish audience for their zeal, Paul described how his passion for Judaism and against Christianity had been even more intense. Beyond merely accosting Christians on the Temple grounds, Paul had sought their **death** (see 7:54-60; 26:10). Furthermore, he had been authorized **to bring Christians** all the way from **Damascus** back to **Jerusalem, in chains, to be punished.** These were widely known, indisputable facts, making Paul's testimony extremely powerful.

22:6-9 Paul's conversion is recorded in chapter 9. Here Paul told the story himself, making it clear that his conversion was not an issue of defection but a matter of divine intervention! Paul had been about his business, intent on his mission (rounding up the followers of Jesus)—and apparently very content and settled in his pro-Jewish, anti-Christian state of mind. Suddenly **Jesus** himself intervened and spoke to Paul. Without referring to a single Old Testament prophecy or launching into a theological discourse, Paul used his personal experience to press the points that Jesus was both alive and glorified.

22:10-13 Blinded, confused, shocked, scared— Paul's mind must have been reeling as he lay in the dust. He had responded with a humble question, **"What shall I do, Lord?"** Paul related to his audience the physical effects of this divine revelation. He had been unable to see and had to be **led into Damascus** by others. There Jesus had told him that he would receive further instructions.

To give further credence to his testimony before such a zealous Jewish mob, Paul described the role **Ananias** had played in his conversion, mentioning Ananias's stellar reputation among the **Jews of Damascus.**

22:14-16 Paul reported that he had heard through the lips of this respected, devout Jew his unexpected, unsought commission. **Ananias** had made it clear that the supernatural events being experienced by Paul were the sovereign work of none other than **the God of our ancestors.** In zealously opposing Jesus and his followers, Paul had assumed that he had been serving and honoring the God of Abraham, Isaac, Jacob, and Moses. Through the announcement of Ananias, he had learned the truth. The God of the Hebrews—far from leading Paul to fight Christianity—was selecting him to become the leading spokesman for this new faith! Paul would **take his message everywhere.** So Paul was **baptized** right then—a powerful outward sign of Paul's inward cleansing from sin and his embracing of the truth.

22:17-18 Paul continued to answer the mob's accusations. He stated, in effect, that he was not anti-Temple (see 21:28). By praying and worshiping there, he demonstrated his continued respect for the Temple—even as a follower of Jesus.

While he was **praying in the Temple,** Paul received a heavenly **vision.** The Greek word for trance is *ekstasei,* the same root used to describe Peter's dreamlike encounter on the rooftop in Joppa (10:10; 11:5). In this vision, Jesus appeared and

warned Paul to promptly **leave Jerusalem** because the Jews would not accept his **testimony.**

In 9:29-30, Luke reported that Paul departed Jerusalem upon the advice of his Christian brothers. This apparent discrepancy is easily resolved by viewing Paul as led by both human counsel and divine revelation. The advice from worried believers probably came first, later being confirmed by that other, stronger, more irresistible voice (20:22).

22:19-20 Never one to run from controversy or trouble, Paul protested mildly. He obviously felt convinced that his conversion from a notorious persecutor of Christians into an ardent evangelist for the Way would impress his Jewish accusers. Surely, they would marvel at the change in his life. He could not and would not have done such a complete about-face without compelling reasons. Perhaps implicit in Paul's rejoinder was the thought that preaching to such a volatile audience might in some way make up for the damage he had done to the church—especially assisting in and approving of the killing of **Stephen.**

22:21 Paul's appeal to the Lord was unsuccessful. For Paul's own safety and for the fulfillment of God's eternal plan, Paul needed to **leave Jerusalem.** A plot on his life was in the works (see 9:22-23). Specifically, the Lord was commissioning Paul to take the message of salvation **to the Gentiles.**

22:22-23 These people had **listened** intently to Paul, but the word "Gentiles" brought out all their anger and exposed their pride. They were supposed to be a light to the Gentiles, telling them about the one true God, but they had renounced that mission by becoming separatist and exclusive. Did the Jews hate the Gentiles? No. Continual efforts were made by the Jews to try to convert the Gentiles. The implications of Paul's testimony and Christian gospel were clear, however. He was suggesting that the Gentiles could be saved and made right with God without first subscribing to the law and submitting to Jewish circumcision. In effect, Paul was claiming divine approval for the idea that Jews and Gentiles could have equal standing before God. This message collided head-on with the blindness, pride, and prejudice of the Jews. The results were explosive.

PAUL REVEALS HIS ROMAN CITIZENSHIP / 22:24-29
Irritated at Paul for having created such a ruckus, and eager to force some sort of confession, the Roman commander ordered the apostle flogged. Paul barely escaped this sentence by mentioning his Roman citizenship. Here is yet another instance of God's sovereign control over lives and events. Who knows how the spread of the gospel might have been hindered had Paul not been a Roman citizen?

22:24-25 The **commander,** who only minutes before had been impressed enough with Paul to give him the opportunity to speak to the crowd, suddenly became annoyed. Weary of the continual upheaval surrounding Paul, he ordered the apostle to be **lashed with whips.** He believed this examination by torture would **make him confess his crime** or at least an explanation about what was really going on.

Paul, ever the shrewd servant of the Lord, resorted to his civic privilege. By law, a **Roman citizen** could not be punished without first having a trial, nor could a Roman citizen be interrogated by beating or torture. Paul knew the law. He knew the answer to that question. It was most certainly not legal. There had been no trial, hearing, or formal charges presented.

22:26-28 Paul's question stunned and scared his captors. They had come dangerously close to violating strict Roman laws. In quizzing Paul, the commander learned that Paul was **a citizen by birth** (apparently his father had somehow achieved this status). The commander admitted that he had been forced to purchase his citizenship. Buying one's citizenship (actually bribing the right people in power) was a common practice and a good source of income for the Roman government. Bought citizenship was considered inferior to citizenship by birth.

22:29 Paul's revelation about himself effectively ended the proceedings. The text does not state so explicitly, but Roman laws prohibited even the fettering of Roman citizens. The commander realized how close he had come to breaking the law himself. Paul was likely freed from his chains immediately but still detained for the night at the Fortress of Antonia (for his own protection, given the volatile nature of the crowd).

ACTS 22:30–23:35

PAUL BEFORE THE HIGH COUNCIL / 22:30–23:11

Having been saved from the murderous mob at the Temple the previous day, Paul was brought before the Jewish high council. When he sensed the charged atmosphere (he was slapped after uttering the first sentence of his defense!), Paul decided to focus the council's attention on something even more controversial than himself—the theological debate concerning the resurrection of the dead. Immediately, the Pharisees and Sadducees began to argue, and Paul was led back to the safety of his cell. There the Lord appeared to him in a comforting vision, assuring him that he would preach the Good News in Rome. No amount of human opposition can thwart God's plan and purposes.

22:30 In an unusual move, the Roman **commander** removed Paul's chains, then **ordered the leading priests into session with the Jewish high council** to hear Paul's case (for more on the Jewish high council, see commentary on 4:5). If Paul were found innocent there, the commander could release him. If found guilty by the Jewish court, however, then the commander would see that Paul, a Roman citizen, went before the Roman governor (and, if necessary, on to Rome).

23:1 With clear, solid eye contact, the first words Paul said to the assembled Jewish religious leaders were, **"I have always lived before God in all good conscience!"** Two times in Acts (here and in 24:16) and twenty-one times in his letters (see, for example, 1 Corinthians 4:4; 2 Corinthians 1:12; 1 Timothy 1:5; 2 Timothy 1:3), Paul referred to his clear conscience. He wanted his audience to know that he was committed to his spiritual and moral choices that had resulted in his trial before them. He was ready to stand before God and be accountable for his choices and actions. Inherent in Paul's statement, of course, was the challenge: were **they** ready?

23:2-3 Almost as soon as Paul began speaking, he was slapped **on the mouth.** Obviously, Paul had already offended **Ananias the high priest,** his accuser! Ananias became high priest in A.D. 48, and he reigned through A.D. 58 or 59. Josephus, a respected first-century historian, described Ananias as profane, greedy, and hot-tempered. He was hated by many of his Jewish contemporaries because of his pro-Roman policies.

Paul's outburst came as a result of the illegal command that Ananias had given. Ananias had violated Jewish law by assuming that Paul was guilty without a trial and by ordering his punishment (see Deuteronomy 19:15). Paul had not yet been charged with a crime, much less tried or found guilty.

Paul's use of the term **whitewashed wall** also recalls Jesus' similar description of the Pharisees in Matthew 23:27. This amounted to calling Ananias a hypocrite. "Whitewashed wall" may refer to the practice of whitewashing gravestones. This created a clean and positive appearance for what contained death and corruption.

23:4-5 When Paul was given the information that he did not know, that the one whom he had rebuked was the **high priest,** he apologized—not to the individual but to the office. It is clear that Paul was submitting to the word as he quoted the appropriate passage from Exodus 22:28, a verse that prohibits speaking **evil of anyone who rules over you.** Paul's ministry and his life had been marked by his obedience to God. Here he exhibited again, even in a very difficult situation, that God's word mattered.

Paul may not have recognized Ananias as the high priest because of poor eyesight. Or perhaps his words were ironic, expressing his amazement that one who would behave so badly (and illegally!) toward him could be the high priest. Most likely, Paul simply did not know who the high priest was or even that he was present at the trial. Because Paul had been in Jerusalem only sporadically for about twenty years, he may have never seen Ananias, maybe only knowing him by name or, more likely, by reputation. This meeting had been called by the Roman commander, not the council members, so the members may not have been in their official robes, which would have identified the high priest (22:30).

23:6 The **Sadducees** and **Pharisees** were two groups of religious leaders but with strikingly different beliefs. The Pharisees believed in a bodily resurrection, but the Sadducees did not. The Sadducees adhered only to Genesis through Deuteronomy, which contain no explicit teaching on resurrection. Paul's statement about his **hope** moved the debate away from himself and toward the religious leaders' festering controversy about **the resurrection of the dead.**

By identifying himself as a **Pharisee** and the descendant of Pharisees, Paul utilized three tactics: (1) he opened the door for inserting the Good News of the resurrected Christ, at least with the part of the council who believed in the Resurrection; (2) he got some sympathy and support from a part of the coun-cil; (3) he surfaced an ongoing controversy that would embroil the council in hopeless debate.

Paul's sudden insight that the council was a mixture of Sadducees and Pharisees is an example of the power that Jesus promised to believers (Mark 13:9-11). God will help his people when they are under fire for their faith. Like Paul, believers should always be ready to present their testimony. The Holy Spirit will give them power to speak boldly.

23:7-8 Paul's tactic worked. The council was **divided.** Their historic argument about **resurrection, angels,** and **spirits** came to the surface. This was the same issue over which the Sadducees had tried to trap Christ (Matthew 22:23-33), but without success. It is not likely that Paul was simply causing a distraction, though that was the result. Rather, he was utilizing this opportunity, maybe his last with his Pharisee "brothers," to tell them the truth, to introduce them to his Savior. His primary motive was to tell them the truth: "I know you believe in resurrection, and I have a resurrection that you have to investigate!"

23:9 The dispute caused **a great clamor.** As expected, the Pharisees came to the vigorous defense of one who spoke so positively about one of their valued positions—resurrection. Paul had, in fact, stated that resurrection was the reason that he was on trial at all (23:6)! The Pharisees alluded to another area of their differences between them and the Sadducees by speculating on the fact that **a spirit or an angel** may have spoken **to him.** They may have drawn this conclusion based on some of Paul's remarks to the crowd at the Temple court the day before (22:17-18). The Sadducees would have argued strongly that such communication was not possible because they didn't believe in the existence of spirits and angels.

23:10 Finally the disagreement became so heated that the Roman **commander** had to step in. Evidently, Paul was in the middle of it all and had to be removed by the Roman troops. From there he was safely brought **back to the fortress.** Just as had been Paul's experience for the last decade of ministry, he was once again attacked by the Jews and treated kindly by the Gentiles—locked in a Roman prison in order to protect him from the high court of the Jews!

23:11 When **night** came, **the Lord appeared to Paul,** telling him to **be encouraged.** He praised Paul for faithfully telling **the people about me here in Jerusalem.** Then he gave Paul a word of promise—**you must preach the Good News in Rome.** God, in essence, promised Paul safe passage to another field of ministry.

THE PLAN TO KILL PAUL / 23:12-22
The morning after God had pledged to deliver Paul safely to Rome, a group of Jews gathered to plot the murder of the apostle. Paul's nephew learned of the plot and revealed it to the Roman commander in Jerusalem.

23:12-13 The Lord himself had come to Paul in prison and essentially had promised him safe passage to Rome. Meanwhile, these zealous Jews **bound themselves with an oath to neither eat nor drink until they had killed Paul.** They put themselves under a solemn vow, like a curse, if they did not fulfill what they said. Paul had already been granted safe passage to Rome by God himself. Luke must have chuckled as he was writing these words, knowing that these sincere but misguided **Jews (more than forty of them)** would have to go without food for a long time. It would be ten years or so before Paul's death in Rome!

23:14-15 This group of over forty men announced their oath to **the leading priests and other leaders.** Their plan was to get the **high council** to have Paul returned to a meeting with them under the guise of examining **his case more fully.** And, exposing their contemptible character, they planned to **kill him on the way.** Evidently, the Jewish leaders thought this was a good idea and went along with it! To these leaders, politics and position had become more important than God. They were ready to plan another murder, just as they had done with Jesus. This also revealed the flimsiness of their case against Paul. They knew they had no case, but they so desperately wanted to get rid of him that they were willing to stoop to any means to do so. As always, however, God, not the council, was in control.

23:16-19 This is the only biblical reference to Paul's family. Some scholars believe that Paul's family disowned him when he became a Christian. Paul wrote of having suffered the loss of everything for Christ (Philippians 3:8). **Paul's nephew,** who is never named, was evidently able to visit Paul, even though Paul was in protective custody. Roman prisoners were often accessible to their relatives and friends who could bring them food and other amenities. How the nephew heard of the plan is not stated. Once Paul received the information, he immediately sent his nephew to the **commander.** Although God had told Paul that he would go to Rome, God did not explain how he would be kept safe. There is a healthy balance here of Paul trusting in God's sovereignty and yet wisely utilizing the God-sent provisions that would come his way—his Roman citizenship, the Roman soldiers, the Roman prison, and now, a piece of important information from a relative. Paul trusted God, but he kept his eyes open to see just how the Father would deliver him.

23:20-22 Paul's nephew gave a detailed report of the plot (23:12-15). The lad even knew about the oath. How he obtained the information is unknown, but there is no doubt about its accuracy. Evidently, the ambush was already in place, simply waiting for the commander's order to send the prisoner to the council chambers. The commander wisely told Paul's nephew to keep his silence on the report he had given. After this, the only member of Paul's family mentioned anywhere in the New Testament disappeared into the silence of unrecorded history.

PAUL IS SENT TO CAESAREA / 23:23-35
Guarded by an armed escort of almost five hundred Roman soldiers, Paul was transferred to Caesarea and the jurisdiction of Governor Felix. He would be safe there until it was time for him to leave for Rome. God's sovereignty is visible in both the actions of these secular authorities and in the resulting spread of the Good News.

23:23-24 There were 470 men dispatched to guard one prisoner—**two hundred soldiers, two hundred spearmen, and seventy horsemen.** The commander knew that the forty assassins would fight to the death, and he did not want to have to explain the assassination of a Roman citizen under his protection. The zealous desire to kill Paul on the part of the Jews in ambush was more than matched by the extent to which the Romans went to protect him.

Instead of returning Paul to the Jewish council, the commander sent him to **Caesarea,** sixty miles to the northwest. Jerusalem was the seat of Jewish government, but Caesarea was the Roman headquarters for the area. There the judicial process would be continued before the Roman court (**Governor Felix**), a process that was begun when Paul had exercised his rights as a Roman citizen (22:25).

23:25-26 Felix was the Roman governor or procurator of Judea from A.D. 52 to 59. This was the same position that Pontius Pilate had held. While the Jews had been given much freedom to govern themselves, the governor ran the army, kept the peace, and gathered the taxes.

How did Luke know what was written in the letter from **Claudius Lysias**? In his concern for historical accuracy, Luke used many sources to make sure that his writings were correct (see Luke 1:1-4). This letter was probably read aloud in court when Paul came before Felix to answer the Jews' accusations. Also, because Paul was a Roman citizen, a copy may have been given to him as a courtesy.

23:27-30 This letter seems to be a formal description of the events as well as the careful wording of a subordinate commander (Claudius Lysias) to his superior (Governor Felix). It must be noted that in his first sentence, the commander carefully rearranged the order of events, leaving out the fact that he had chained Paul and had been in the process of having him flogged when the information about his Roman citizenship was brought to light—a careful cover-up to protect himself (see 22:23-28).

Claudius stated that Paul was charged with **nothing worthy of imprisonment or death.** For the early readers of Acts, these would be encouraging precedents and may have helped them in their own struggles with the Jews or with Roman law.

23:31-32 The **soldiers took Paul as far as Antipatris**—more than thirty-five miles. At that

distance from Jerusalem (and at that speed), the prisoner would certainly be safe from pursuers, so the soldiers had been released to return to Jerusalem, leaving Paul with the seventy **horsemen** to accompany him the final twenty-five miles to **Caesarea.** The last few miles into Antipatris provided excellent terrain for an ambush, so that was likely part of the reason that the larger contingent went so far before turning back.

23:33-35 And so Paul and his Roman escort **arrived in Caesarea** and were **presented** to Governor Felix. The governor ascertained Paul's province—**Cilicia**—and agreed to hear the case when his **accusers** arrived.

Felix was the governor (procurator) of Judea from about A.D. 52 to 59, holding the position that Pontius Pilate had held during Jesus' day. Felix had married Drusilla (24:24), a sister of Herod Agrippa II, the Agrippa mentioned in chapter 25. A man of low birth, Felix rose to power through the influence of his well-connected brother Pallas and his politically expedient marriages. He also married the granddaughter of Antony and Cleopatra. The historian Tacitus, however, described Felix's career with a stinging epigram: "He exercised the power of a king with the mind of a slave." He was regarded as a poor governor. He dispensed justice arbitrarily and served his own ends. Jewish revolts increased under his administration.

Thus, the platform was set for Paul to speak before the leading rulers of the area (recorded in the next three chapters). When God has a willing person, there will be no end to the places he or she can be used, with phenomenal opportunities for effective work.

ACTS 24

PAUL APPEARS BEFORE FELIX / 24:1-27

The next three chapters provide a look at an interesting trio of politicians—Felix, Festus, and Agrippa. All three were at the top of their profession, holding significant offices in the Roman regime that dominated their world. All three were known as intelligent, effective leaders. All three came face-to-face with the gospel of Jesus Christ through the testimony of none other than the apostle Paul. As determined from the text, all three rejected Christ. The reasons were different, but the results were the same.

24:1 The accusers arrived (24:35)—**Ananias, the high priest,** and **the lawyer Tertullus,** along with

several **Jewish leaders.** They had traveled sixty miles to Caesarea, the Roman center of government, to bring their false accusations against Paul. Their murder plot had failed (23:12-15), but they were persisting in trying to kill him.

24:2-4 Tertullus began the religious leaders' case against Paul before the Roman governor **Felix** (see commentary at 23:33-35). The case, which surely is only summarized here, began with gushing flattery, which seems to have taken up almost as much time as the case itself! The flattery is even more sickening, given the historical record of Governor Felix, who is remembered as a violent and corrupt ruler and was hated by the Jews.

24:5-9 Finally, Tertullus got to the case. He made three accusations against Paul: (1) he was a **troublemaker, inciting riots and rebellions;** (2) he was the **ringleader** of an unrecognized **sect,** which was against Roman law; (3) he had tried to **defile the Temple.** The religious leaders hoped that these accusations would persuade Felix to execute Paul in order to keep the peace in Palestine.

If Felix would not prosecute Paul on the basis of his disruption of the peace, maybe he would do so if Paul were seen as a leader of a religious sect or cult that was not sanctioned by the state. This designation of Christians as **Nazarenes** was probably used of Jewish Christians from the earliest days of the church, but it is unknown what Felix may have known about them or what opinion he may have had. Surely Tertullus was using the term to put the church in its most controversial light.

The charge of defiling the Temple was designed to push Felix toward allowing the Jews to put Paul to death. It was one of the few offenses for which the Jews could still exact the death penalty. There seems to be a slight modification of the charge against Paul in this area (see 21:28). Originally, Paul had been charged with actually bringing a Gentile (Trophimus) into the temple area, thus desecrating it. Here the charge was modified to read that Paul "tried" to desecrate the temple—an attempted desecration rather than an actual one. Evidently the accusers knew they had no proof of the actual desecration (and maybe they did have solid proof of the exact opposite), so they had to shift their strategy to say that they had **arrested him** in order to prevent the desecration. When Tertullus finished his remarks, **the other Jews chimed in,** affirming the truthfulness of their legal counsel's case.

Most modern versions do not include verse 7, because it is not found in the most ancient manuscripts.

24:10 The **governor** gave the apostle permission to speak, so **Paul** began his defense. Tertullus and the religious leaders seemed to have made a strong argument against Paul, but Paul would refute their accusations point by point.

Paul's introductory remarks were much more cursory and to the point, in contrast to Tertullus's flowing flattery. Paul simply alluded to the fact that Felix had **been a judge of Jewish affairs for many years,** thus making him a good person before whom to make his **defense.** This is likely the only accomplishment on which Paul could compliment him—that he had been around long enough and had tried enough cases involving Jewish affairs to be familiar with the nature of what was before him.

24:11-13 Paul answered the first charge (stirring up riots) by stating the easily verifiable trip he had made to **Jerusalem no more than twelve days** previously. The implication here was that he had not been in Jerusalem long enough to stir up trouble. Also, he stated that he had come to Jerusalem for the purpose of **worship.** Paul's statement of easily provable or not provable evidence made a strong case. His accusers could not **prove the things** they had accused him of doing. He knew his accusers could not present a shred of evidence that he had defiled the Temple.

24:14 In this verse, Paul began to answer the second accusation—that of being a ringleader of a Nazarene sect. His answer to this accusation continues through 24:16 and provides the opening for the gospel. Paul affirmed that he followed **the Way,** which his accusers called a **sect.** "The Way" was the earliest name for the Christian church. It probably came from Isaiah 40:3, 10-11, referring to God's people led on God's way. It also had analogies to Matthew 7:14, "the way of salvation," and to John 14:6, where Jesus referred to himself as "the way."

Paul took this opportunity to tie the roots of the Christian movement to the God of the Jewish people—**the God of our ancestors**—and particularly to the Old Testament Scriptures. He affirmed before Felix his firm belief in **the Jewish law and everything written in the books of prophecy.** It would be hard to make the "heretic" or "sectarian" label stick with an argument as strong as this one. Paul was still worshiping the same God and holding to the same moral code as his accusers. He would soon get more specific.

24:15-16 Paul went straight to the issue of resurrection and judgment. He stated, first of all, his **hope** of a resurrection of **both the righteous and the ungodly** (see Daniel 12:2). This is, of course, the proclamation he had made in his case before the Jewish council that had won him support from the Pharisees and attack from the Sadducees (see 23:6-9).

Because of this resurrection of both the

righteous and the wicked, Paul sought to **maintain a clear conscience before God and everyone else** (see comments at 23:1). Here is the strong personal testimony of one who expected to stand before his Maker and give account for his life. In stating it this way, Paul not only bore witness to the fact that he was ready to meet God but also—by implication—that all people must get ready for such a meeting of their own.

24:17 Paul finally moved to the last accusation, that he had tried to defile the Temple. Paul stated the main purpose of his Jerusalem trip—to bring **money to aid** his **people and to offer sacrifices to God.** This is the only mention, at least in the book of Acts, of the collection for the saints in Jerusalem. Paul's letters refer to it several times (Romans 15:25-28; 1 Corinthians 16:1-4; 2 Corinthians 8:13-14; 9:12-13; Galatians 2:10), but, for the most part, it is left out of the Acts record.

24:18-19 As to the charge of defilement—Paul had been **completing a purification ritual** when he was discovered in the Temple courts. As to the charge of causing an uproar, he stated that there had been **no crowd** and **no rioting.** The problem came when **some Jews from the province of Asia** showed up. They, in fact, had caused the uproar, not Paul. This was a strong point in Paul's defense, one that his accusers simply could not refute.

24:20-21 Paul suggested that Felix ask those members of the **Jewish high council** who were present what **wrongdoing** they found in him. Paul explained that he had made a controversial remark by claiming to **believe in the resurrection of the dead** (23:6). Paul knew it was unlikely that any of his accusers would attack that statement in Felix's presence, and they kept their silence. This, of course, gave Paul a chance to present the Resurrection again, this time before Felix and his court, as well as to those Pharisees (accusers) who had been present at Paul's meeting with the Jewish Council in Jerusalem. Thus the charges verbalized by Tertullus had been answered, and all that remained was for Felix to respond.

24:22-23 Felix had been governor for six years and was **quite familiar with the Way.** The Christian movement, which had involved thousands of people from the first day on (2:41, 47; 4:4), would have been a topic of conversation among the Roman leadership. Hopefully, too, the Christians' peaceful lifestyles had already proven to the Romans that Christians didn't go around starting riots. Felix's knowledge of and exoneration of the church seemed very important to Luke, and for good reason. Luke wanted the original readers of his book to have a solid record (and one of precedence) that found Christians innocent, even as they experienced ongoing persecution all over the Roman Empire. That is probably why Luke went to such lengths to record Roman court decisions from Gallio (18:14-15), Felix, Festus, and Agrippa (chapters 24–26).

Felix decided to delay the hearing until the **commander, Lysias,** could get there to give his testimony as to what had transpired. It is not recorded whether Lysias came to Caesarea or not. Likely he did, but as the next few verses indicate, for various political and fiscal reasons, Felix did not want to complete Paul's trial. It appears that this postponement became indefinite.

Paul was kept **in custody,** but, evidently, he was given a great deal of **freedom** by Governor Felix. Paul had a number of Christian brothers and sisters in Caesarea who loved him dearly and would readily visit him and take care of him (21:8-14). Such freedom was likely the result of Paul's being a Roman citizen against whom no crime had yet been proven.

24:24 After an unnamed period of time, **Felix** and **his wife Drusilla** sent for Paul and **listened as he told them about faith in Christ Jesus.** Drusilla was the daughter of Herod Agrippa I (see chapter 12) and the sister of Herod Agrippa II, making her part **Jewish.** At this time, she was likely only twenty years old. She had left a previous husband to marry Felix, which she did contrary to Jewish law, since Felix was a Gentile.

24:25-26 Paul's discourse with Felix and Drusilla included an interesting trio of topics—**righteousness, self-control, and the judgment to come.** Like Paul's remarks earlier in the trial (see 24:15-16), these three areas track with Jesus' description of the convicting work of the Holy Spirit (John 16:8) and would likewise be areas of great conviction for Felix. As stated earlier, Felix's career was marked by brutality and injustice; thus, the subject of righteousness and judgment would likely be more than a little uncomfortable. History also records that Drusilla was Felix's third wife, and he had to break up her previous marriage in order to free her for himself. Thus, a discourse on self-control would likely not have been something he would have enjoyed hearing.

Felix responded like an individual under conviction: **"Go away for now."** Felix was **terrified.** Paul confronted Felix, forcing him to deal with its full convicting message. And Felix wanted no part of it. Notice, too, another example of Felix's poor character. He frequently sent for Paul, hoping the apostle **would bribe him,** supposedly to buy his freedom. He **talked** to Paul **often** and, so, was regularly exposed to the truth. Felix seems to be a sorry example of one who "went to church" with regularity, listening to a personalized message from none other than the apostle Paul. Yet there is no record of Felix's ever coming to faith.

24:27 Two years went by in this way as Felix toyed with the apostle Paul. For two years this apostle to the Gentiles was out of commission, out of the pulpit, and serving as Felix's personal spiritual conversationalist.

By keeping Paul in prison, Felix could **gain** **favor with the Jewish leaders.** Eventually, **Porcius Festus** took over as governor of the region. He was a welcome successor. After Felix mishandled a political situation between the Jews and Greeks at Caesarea in A.D. 60, where he took unnecessarily harsh military action against the Jews, he was called back to Rome. Josephus wrote that things would have gone badly for him there, had not his brother, Pallas, interceded for him.

Festus is recorded in history as a more just ruler than Felix, although he was not on the scene very long. When Festus came into office, he inherited the imprisoned apostle and the Jewish leaders with a definite agenda.

ACTS 25:1-22

PAUL APPEARS BEFORE FESTUS / 25:1-22

When Felix was replaced by Porcius Festus, the Jews once again made their case against Paul. During this trial before the new governor, Festus, Paul, using his rights as a Roman citizen, asked for and received the promise of a hearing before Caesar. This legal decision thwarted the final action of Paul's Jewish enemies.

25:1-2 The new governor, **Festus,** wasted no time; after just **three days** on the job, he went to Jerusalem. Festus was procurator or governor of Judea A.D. 58–62. Little is known about Festus, though most of it is favorable, particularly in contrast with Felix whom he succeeded. In Jerusalem, the Jewish leaders **met with him and made their accusations against Paul.** God had allowed his most effective instrument for Gentile evangelism and church planting to sit in custody for two years, the apparent victim of Roman bureaucracy. But this was not God's perspective. The gospel would not be stopped simply by imprisoning Paul. Most likely, Paul was leading those around him to Christ, even in his chained condition.

25:3 Although two years had passed, the Jewish leaders still were looking for a way to kill Paul. The plot had expanded from the original forty-plus leaders (23:12-13) to all the Jewish leaders. They tried to convince **Festus** to **transfer Paul to Jerusalem** (so they could prepare an ambush). The ruthless Jews had obviously abandoned all hope of a conviction of Paul by the Romans, so they decided to take matters into their own hands. This request was likely a clever political move, and we can only imagine how these politically savvy Jewish leaders tried to explain how such a favor early on in Festus's administration would do wonders for their working relationship in the future.

25:4-5 By God's intervention, Festus decided to leave Paul in **Caesarea.** The trial would not be moved, so Festus informed the Jewish leadership that those **in authority** could **return with** him. In Caesarea, in his courtroom, they would be allowed to make their **accusations.**

25:6-7 After a few days, Festus **returned to Caesarea,** where on the very next day, the case of this Roman citizen, alleged troublemaker for the Jews, began again. As before, the **Jewish leaders from Jerusalem gathered around and made many serious accusations they couldn't prove**—probably all the same baseless accusations from two years before.

25:8 Paul succinctly denied all the charges that had just been blasted at him again. He applied his denial to the three main areas of accusation: the **Jewish laws, the Temple,** and **the Roman government** (see 21:28; 24:5-6).

25:9-11 Only about two weeks into this new procuratorship, Festus wanted to get off to a politically healthy start with the people he was governing. The Jews were known as a difficult people to govern, and many Roman political careers had been dashed at this Judean outpost (including that of Festus's immediate predecessor, Felix). It is not surprising that Festus would wish **to please the Jews.** Catering to what he knew they desperately wanted, he asked Paul if he would be **willing to go to Jerusalem** to **stand trial** before him (Festus) there. Festus knew that the Jews had no case against Paul, but either he wasn't willing to aggravate and enrage them further or he simply didn't know how to investigate such religious matters (see 25:20).

Whatever Festus's motive behind this offer to switch the location of the trial, it became irrelevant at Paul's next words: **"I appeal to Caesar!"** Every Roman citizen had the right to appeal to Caesar. This didn't mean that Caesar himself would hear the case but that the citizen's case would be tried by the highest courts in the Empire—it is much like appealing to the Supreme Court. This right of appeal to the emperor provided Roman citizens protection in capital offense trials carried out by local judges in the provinces. It was normal for a Roman judge to set up a group of advisors in a case. Festus might have proposed to have members of the council serve. Thus, there would be no fair trial in Jerusalem. Paul insisted on a court made up of a jury of all Roman citizens. He appealed to Emperor Nero, who in A.D. 60 had not yet started the persecution of Christians. To go to Rome as a prisoner was better than not to go there at all.

25:12 Festus probably felt enormous relief at having a way out of this difficult situation. Paul's request led Festus into a conference **with his advisers** (these were his legal experts and higher officials), giving what seems to be a quick reply: **"To Caesar you shall go!"**

Humanly speaking, it is probably better that it happened this way. If Festus had ruled on the case, he likely would have set Paul free—free to make his own way (without an armed escort) back to Antioch or on to Rome. The bloodthirsty group of Jewish leaders would have done their best to make sure that Paul didn't live to see another day. Instead, Paul would have an armed guard all the way to his next preaching stop. Though he would have a few more audiences with whom to share the gospel between there and Rome, few were more prestigious than the one he was about to meet.

25:13-15 King Agrippa was Herod Agrippa II, son of Herod Agrippa I, and a descendant of Herod the Great, the last of the Herod dynasty that ruled parts

of Palestine from 40 B.C. to A.D. 100. Like great-grandfather, like grandfather, like father, like son—Agrippa inherited the effects of generations of powerful men with flawed personalities. Each son followed his father in weaknesses, mistakes, and missed opportunities. Each generation had a confrontation with God, and each failed to realize the importance of his decision.

At this time (A.D. 60) Agrippa II was a young man of about thirty-three. He ruled the territories northeast of Palestine, bearing the title of "king." With power over the Temple, he controlled the Temple treasury and could appoint and remove the high priest. **Bernice** was his sister. When she was thirteen (A.D. 41), she had married her uncle, Herod Chalcis, who died in A.D. 48. Then she became a mistress to her brother, Agrippa II. In A.D. 63, she married King Polemon of Cilicia, but in the early 70s, she became mistress to Emperor Vespasian's son, Titus. Here Agrippa and Bernice were making an official visit to Festus, **to pay their respects.**

Agrippa and Festus were anxious to cooperate in governing their neighboring territories. The relationship between the Herodian dynasty and the Roman governors had always been sticky (remember Herod Antipas and Pontius Pilate, for example, sending Jesus back and forth—Luke 23:1-12). This state visit was an extended one, giving Festus an opportunity to discuss **Paul's case with the king.** Agrippa, of Jewish descent, could help clarify Paul's case for the Roman governor.

25:16-17 Festus described the details of the case with some embellishment. He included at the outset, for example, a statement about how he **quickly pointed out** to the Jewish leaders that **Roman law does not convict people without a trial** and how the accused **are given an opportunity to** face their accusers and **defend themselves.** Festus was accurate, however, when he reported that he saw **the case the very next day** after the arrival of the Jewish leaders (the ones who would have Agrippa's interest).

25:18-22 Quickly reviewing the facts, Festus explained that he had **expected** a different set of **accusations.** He did not anticipate that it would concern **something about their religion and about someone called Jesus who died, but whom Paul** was insisting was **alive.** Festus admitted that he didn't know **how to conduct an investigation.** Particularly confusing seems to have been the part about the "dead man" being allegedly alive. But because Paul had **appealed to the emperor,** so he was kept in custody until arrangements could be made to get him to Rome.

Festus's quick review of the facts had its desired

result: **Agrippa** wanted to **hear the man** himself. Paul's audience with Agrippa was set for the following day. It would be a golden opportunity for all those present—Festus, Agrippa, Bernice,

the royal entourage, the high-ranking officials (see 25:23)—to hear more from this ex-Pharisee about the "dead man named Jesus" who he claimed had come back to life!

ACTS 25:23–26:32

PAUL SPEAKS TO AGRIPPA / 25:23–26:32

King Agrippa, in Caesarea with his sister Bernice for a political visit with the new governor, Festus, became embroiled in the controversy over Paul. Festus, mindful of Agrippa's familiarity with Jewish law and practice and needing to prepare some kind of legal paperwork for Caesar, arranged a special audience with Paul. Festus found Paul's testimony absurd; Agrippa found it pointed and a bit too personal. Nevertheless, Paul took advantage of this situation to tell about his encounter with Christ and his fervent belief in the truth of the gospel.

25:23 Into the **auditorium** came **Festus, Agrippa and Bernice,** and a controversial prisoner. While they arrived **with great pomp,** the real royalty in the room was the prisoner, the born-again child of the King of kings.

25:24-25 Festus, as the Roman governor in charge of the court at Caesarea, opened the proceedings. Luke certainly wanted to include this concise exoneration of Christianity by an esteemed representative of the Roman Empire. Festus explained that the **local** Jewish leadership and **those in Jerusalem** were demanding Paul's **death.** In his judgment of the case, however, Paul had **done nothing worthy of death.** That would be a significant check to those who were chasing, imprisoning, and prosecuting Christians around the Roman world. Because Paul had **appealed his case to the emperor,** he would be sent to Rome.

25:26-27 Festus went on to explain how he was at a loss for what to **write** in his report to **the emperor.** He was required to prepare a legal brief, detailing the charges, that had to be sent along with the appeal to Emperor Nero. Explaining his reason for the gathering, Festus explained that he wanted **King Agrippa** to help him put into words **the charges against** Paul.

26:1-3 After hearing Festus's opening remarks, Agrippa ordered Paul to **speak** in his own **defense.** What follows is an excellent example of Paul's powerful oratory skills and the most complete statement of his defense. The thoroughness of the record of this speech and details like this hand motion indicate that Luke must have been present.

The accusing Jewish leaders, however, were not present, so Paul would not be responding to specific charges. The absence of a strict prosecutorial air allowed the apostle to freely express his thoughts. Paul aimed his remarks most directly at Agrippa (26:1-28), though other very important people were in the audience. Agrippa's verdict, though not a formal judicial one in Paul's case, would be important for Paul and, thus, for all of Christianity. Agrippa not only was an **expert on Jewish customs and controversies,** he was also a very influential government figure for Israel.

26:4-5 Paul began with his early life, which had been spent in **thorough Jewish training.** Paul's contemporaries, including some on the Jewish council who were attacking him, knew of his solid Jewish heritage and the fact that he had **been a member of the Pharisees, the strictest sect.** By saying this, Paul established that there could be no doubt about the thoroughness, seriousness, or excellence with which he pursued his Judaism. Being a Pharisee meant that Paul was already committed to the importance of the resurrection from the dead—a major tenet of the Pharisees, one that prompted their ongoing debate with the Sadducees, who did not believe in a resurrection (see 23:6-9). Of course, this issue would take on much more significance as Paul's message unfolded.

26:6-7 Paul used the rich heritage of **God's promise** to his and Agrippa's common **ancestors** as a connection to Agrippa and to the Jews (**the twelve tribes of Israel**). They all shared **the same hope,** that God would keep the promise he had made to his people, a hope that was inextricably tied up with the resurrection of the dead (see 23:6; 24:15). If any Jew—from Abraham forward—had any hope for the fulfillment of any promise that God had made, it must be tied to a belief that he would be resurrected in some form at some time, or the whole concept of God's promises would be ludicrous. That was Paul's point. The absurdity was that Paul was being attacked for holding to this hope that was shared so adamantly by his Jewish brothers.

26:8 While he was addressing the king singularly concerning their ancestral "hope" in 26:7, Paul addressed his question to the whole audience, which was mostly Gentile. He asked them why it was so **incredible** (literally, "unbelievable") to any of them **that God can raise the dead.**

Since so much of the Jewish hope was tied to a belief that God raises people to continued life beyond this one, why were the Jews arguing with Paul about resurrection? The reason, of course, was one well-documented case of a certain resurrection that had been confirmed by hundreds of eyewitnesses. This had become the lifework of those who had been closest to the scene of this resurrection. In addition, many had already given their very lives for the cause—a cause whose whole credibility rested on the veracity of the resurrection of this one whom Paul was about to name.

26:9 Paul named himself as one who theoretically believed in the resurrection of the dead as a solidly educated Pharisee but who vigorously opposed the movement that believed in the resurrection of Jesus. He not only refused to believe that **Jesus of Nazareth** had been resurrected, he also thought he should **do everything** he **could to oppose** the movement.

26:10-12 With the authorization of the **leading priests,** Paul had captured **believers in Jerusalem** and sent them to **prison.** He even went so far as to **cast** his **vote against** Christians **when they were condemned to death.** Much of Paul's work was done through the **synagogues,** where Paul found most of the Christians in the early days of the movement. This would remind Agrippa that the Christian movement had Jewish roots. In the synagogues Paul would have believers **whipped** in order to try to force them to **curse Christ.** Paul was so passionate, **so violently opposed** to those who knew Christ, that he **hounded them in distant cities of foreign lands.** He took his campaign of terror on the road, headed **to Damascus.**

26:13-14 About noon, Paul saw **a light from heaven brighter than the sun,** blazing around him and his traveling companions. The presence of this

bright light from heaven is mentioned in all three accounts—in chapter 9 (the actual event), in chapter 22, and here. The voice from heaven is also central to all three accounts. The revealed word of the risen Christ to the apostle Paul is the centerpiece of the story. **In Aramaic,** Paul had been addressed and asked, **"Why are you persecuting me?"** Notice, as has been the case in every account, Jesus made it clear that Paul had not been persecuting heretics but, rather, Christ himself.

One important addition to Christ's words here is not included in either chapter 9 or 22. Paul added that Christ had said, **"It is hard for you to fight against my will."** Paul's passion and his conviction were commendable, but he was not headed in the direction that God wanted him to go.

26:15-16 Upon Paul's inquiry as to the identity of the speaker, the voice answered: **"I am Jesus, the one you are persecuting."** The information to follow is also unique to this particular recounting of the Damascus road experience. From his prostrate position, Paul was commissioned by Christ himself. He was to be Christ's **servant** (1 Corinthians 4:1) and Christ's **witness** (the ongoing theme of Acts predicted in Christ's words in 1:8). Paul would **tell the world** about not only **this experience** at Damascus but also about the other times that Christ would **appear** to him. Paul was to be the recipient of a great deal of God's "light" to both Jews and Gentiles.

26:17-18 When Jesus said, **"I will protect you,"** inherent in this statement was the promise of danger from which Paul would need protection. The two sources of the danger would be his **own people** (the Jews) **and the Gentiles,** in whose court he stood. Christ's words of commission to Paul sound like the work predicted of the Messiah in places like Isaiah 35:5; 42:7, 16; 61:1. Paul was to **turn** many people **from darkness to light,** which he did (see 2 Corinthians 4:4; Ephesians 4:18; 5:8; Colossians 1:12-13). Paul was to be God's instrument of turning Gentiles **from the power of Satan to God,** inviting them to **receive forgiveness for their sins,** which he did (13:38; Ephesians 1:7; Colossians 1:14). Paul was also to offer Gentiles **a place among God's people** (Romans 8:17; Colossians 1:12). Paul took every opportunity to remind his audience that the Gentiles had an equal share in God's inheritance. This inheritance is the promise and blessing of the covenant that God made with Abraham (Ephesians 2:19; 1 Peter 1:3-4).

26:19-20 From that point, Paul had been obedient to the **vision from heaven** (1 Corinthians 9:1, 16). He had begun **in Damascus,** then gone to **Jerusalem, Judea,** and beyond. Ultimately, his field of endeavor, under the sovereign leadership of God, was **the Gentiles.** Though the locations changed and the nationalities changed, the message was the same at every stop. This message, of course, tied Paul to John the Baptist (Matthew 3:2, 8), Jesus (Matthew 4:17), and Peter (Acts 2:38). They all called for personal conversion— a change of heart and mind that showed itself in a change of direction.

26:21-23 For his simple obedience to this incredibly powerful calling, for his faithful presentation of this gospel message, Paul had been **arrested.** Attempts had even been made on his life. But God had been true to his promise to protect him (26:17) so that he could **tell these facts to everyone,** including those before whom he was standing. Then Paul summarized what he had said in front of every Jewish audience so far in his ministry: **I teach nothing except what the prophets and Moses said would happen** concerning the suffering Messiah and the promise of his resurrection (see 13:27-41 for a sample). This resurrection, which followed the rejection and murder of the Messiah, would serve as a beacon, **a light to Jews and Gentiles alike.**

26:24 Festus could not stand it anymore, and he erupted. The message of this suffering Messiah was one thing, but to actually believe that he had been killed by his own people and then had been raised from the dead as a light to the world was too much for the humanistic mind of the Roman governor. He decided that Paul must be **insane.**

26:25-27 Paul affirmed to the governor that he was **not insane,** but was instead **speaking the sober truth** that had the most important of implications for all those within its hearing. Paul turned to Agrippa for confirmation of what he had just presented, stating his certainty that **these events** were **all familiar.** Agrippa's responsibilities for the Temple activities at Jerusalem would surely have caused him to cross paths with the activities of the church. He would likely have been familiar with not only the Old Testament Scriptures but also the basics of Jesus' life and the start of the church in the wake of Jesus' crucifixion and claimed resurrection.

Paul's statement that this was **not done in a corner** is simply an idiomatic way of reminding his audience that Christianity had been a very public movement from the moment of the inception of the church on that first Pentecost, when three thousand people had been converted in the temple courts at Jerusalem in one day (chapter 2).

Next, Paul got very personal and direct with King Agrippa, asking and then answering his own question about Agrippa's knowledge of and belief in the prophets. Agrippa could provide, if he were so inclined, plenty of information to Festus on the subject of Judaism, the Messiah, Jesus, and the Way. He could corroborate what Paul had said so far and confirm that his message was not far removed from mainstream Judaistic theology. But Agrippa did not.

26:28 Paul's direct question probably embarrassed Agrippa in front of this powerful crowd. His response, in what appears to be a condescending fashion, was to shoot back. It is difficult to tell whether Agrippa's tone of voice was harsh or joking, though the desired effect was to brush Paul off.

If Agrippa were to say that he did *not* believe the prophets, he would have lost influence with his Jewish constituency. If he were to say that he *did* believe the prophets, then he would have played into the hands of Paul the evangelist, who then would say that Agrippa would have no reason not to believe in Christ. So Agrippa just retaliated quickly, reminding the apostle who was the prisoner and who was the potentate: **"Do you think you can make me a Christian so quickly?"** The question may have been a jab at Paul and his message, saying that he would not be as easily persuaded as Paul's other converts had been.

26:29 The passion of the apostle and the universal need of the gospel message comes through in Paul's response to Agrippa's brusque statement. Notice how Paul changed the tone of the exchange. This was not Paul the debater; this was Paul the evangelist with a tender heart for the lost souls in need of finding the Savior. Paul explained that it didn't matter to him whether Agrippa believed **quickly or not;** he simply prayed that Agrippa, along with the entire **audience,** would become just like him, **except** for the **chains.** That is, Paul wanted them to find the Messiah who had found him that day on the road to Damascus.

26:30-31 Agrippa may have been getting uncomfortable with the way the conversation had turned. Maybe he was moving toward conviction. Perhaps he had simply heard all he needed to hear to know what he thought of it all. In any case, Agrippa decided that the meeting was over.

Festus and Agrippa discussed the case and agreed that Paul was innocent. King Agrippa, a Jewish sympathizer and well versed in Jewish issues, added his legal vindication of the Christian movement. This word would be of great comfort and usefulness to believers around the Empire who were experiencing increasingly intense pressure from those who wanted to prosecute the Christian movement as being anti-Jewish and anti-Roman.

26:32 Paul's appeal **to Caesar**, of course, had pretty much taken the matter out of the jurisdiction of Festus and Agrippa. Paul had to go to Rome. Though he could have been **set free**, Paul was instead free from the murderous Jews and setting out on an all-expense-paid trip to Rome.

ACTS 27

PAUL SAILS FOR ROME / 27:1-12

At long last, Paul boarded a boat for Rome, probably in October (A.D. 59). He was accompanied, at the very least, by Luke and Aristarchus. This was too late in the fall to be on the open seas. And, sure enough, bad weather made for rough sailing. Paul sensed real danger ahead and encouraged the crew to find safe harbor for the winter. Nevertheless, the leaders of the voyage pressed on.

27:1-2 The first person plural pronoun *we* indicates that Luke had again joined Paul (for the first time since chapter 21). Perhaps Luke accompanied the apostle to Rome so as to serve as his personal physician. **Aristarchus** may have been acting as Paul's personal attendant or servant. Aristarchus was the man who had been dragged into the theater at the beginning of the riot in Ephesus (19:29; 20:4; Philemon 1:24). It is not stated whether the centurion **Julius** was a believer, but he took good care of Paul (see 27:3). Later, Julius would single-handedly protect Paul and the other prisoners from being executed during the shipwreck. He is one of several Roman centurions in the New Testament who are portrayed favorably (Luke 7:1-10; Luke 23:47; Acts 10:1-48).

27:3 Sidon was about seventy miles north of Caesarea, where this journey had begun. A brief stop in Sidon permitted the Christians there to provide food and supplies for Paul's needs. The Christian community there probably originated with the dispersion of believers from Jerusalem after the death of Stephen (see 11:19). The Roman officer allowed Paul to **go ashore to visit with friends.** Julius may have been advised by Festus to give preferential treatment to Paul.

27:4 The most direct route from Sidon to Myra would have directed the ship south and west of Cyprus (the same route Paul had traveled when he had returned from his third missionary journey). The summer and early autumn winds, blowing from the west and northwest, however, required the ship to remain close to the coast, sailing **north of Cyprus between the island and the mainland.**

27:5-6 Rounding the northeast peninsula of Cyprus, Paul's vessel would have once again faced the strong headwinds from the west and northwest. But by hugging the coastline and (most likely) taking advantage of the gentler night breezes, the ship was able to dock at **Myra.**

In this port city on the southern coast of Asia Minor (modern-day Turkey), Julius located an **Egyptian ship** sailing **for Italy.** This was a large grain ship (big enough to carry 276 passengers—see 27:37-38). Egyptian grain was a Roman staple at this time in history, and Myra was a key hub of the imperial grain service.

27:7-8 With the favorable travel period quickly coming to a close, the captain of the Alexandrian ship pushed westward in an attempt to reach Italy before winter. But the elements were already beginning to make sailing west difficult.

Cnidus, with its two harbors and ample accommodations, would have made an excellent stopping point from which to wait for favorable winds. But the weather conditions made it difficult to put in there. Thus the ship's captain chose to head south toward **Crete,** which is the largest island in the Aegean Sea. In better weather, captains would sail to the north of Crete. With winter fast approaching, however, the northern route was suspect. The northern coast had few suitable harbors and left ships unprotected against the often dangerous winds; therefore, Paul's ship journeyed to the eastern tip of Crete and then west along the southern coast, where harbors were more available. The small harbor at **Fair Havens** (probably modern-day Limeonas Kalous) did not afford much protection. Nevertheless, since the coastline just beyond Fair Havens veers sharply northward and exposes vessels to the full force of the northwesterly winds, the ship put in there to wait for the wind to shift.

27:9-10 Waiting for favorable weather at Fair Havens, the ship's anxious commanders had a decision to make: Should they stay put and find winter quarters in Fair Havens (or nearby Lasea)? Or should they push on westward in an attempt to complete their journey to Italy before winter? A guiding principle of sailing was that it was **dangerous** from mid-September to mid-November and disastrous from mid-November to mid-February.

Luke did not record whether or not this decision was the subject of a public discussion. Nevertheless, Paul made his prediction known to the **ship's officers** that to continue the trip would result in **trouble** and **danger.** Paul's warning may have been stimulated by his own experience. Prior to this voyage, he had written, in 2 Corinthians 11:25, that he had already survived three shipwrecks. Paul probably was exhibiting common sense from the weather/sailing calendar. In ancient times ships had no compasses and navigated by the stars, so Paul understood that overcast skies and strong northwesterly winds made sailing west all but impossible and very dangerous.

27:11-12 Apparently, by this time the worsening weather conditions had eliminated any remaining hopes of reaching Italy. Although the weather was not ideal for sailing, the **captain** and the **owner** of the ship didn't want to spend the winter in **an exposed harbor** like **Fair Havens.** The ship departed for **Phoenix,** only a few miles west along the southern **coast of Crete.**

THE STORM AT SEA / 27:13-26

Leaving the relative safety of Fair Havens, Paul's vessel encountered a violent storm. The crew tried valiantly to weather the storm but eventually gave up all hope of saving their lives, much less the battered ship. Paul gathered the ship's crew and encouraged them with two promises of God: (1) that he (Paul) had been guaranteed safe arrival in Rome; and (2) that everyone sailing with him would be protected from harm. One truth stands clear in the middle of this nerve-racking voyage: Life may get messy, complicated, or even frightening, but God's will cannot be thwarted!

27:13-15 Favorable winds and weather at that moment caused the captain to proceed with the journey. Had these conditions continued, the ship would have brought the passengers and crew to their destination within hours, certainly less than one day. But the air currents suddenly **changed** (a common occurrence in these waters), and the resulting **"northeaster"** coming down off the mountains of southern Crete was deadly! In describing this wind, Luke used the Greek word from which we get our English word *typhoon.* The opposing currents of air created a whirling motion of both clouds and sea, but then the wind began to blow steadily in one direction.

Ancient ships lacked much ability to tack (i.e., follow a charted zigzag movement so as to make optimal use of unfavorable winds). When contrary winds arose, ships were mostly at their mercy and were left to **run before the gale.**

27:16-17 The tiny island of **Cauda** (some twenty-three miles south) provided a temporary cover from the storm as the ship moved behind (south of) it. The sailors used this brief respite to tie everything down and prepare for the worst. The **lifeboat** they managed to hoist aboard was an important tool in ancient sailing. It was typically used for landings and to maneuver the ship for primitive attempts at tacking. No doubt it was filled with water and was on the verge of breaking loose or crashing into the mother ship; the lifeboat had to be brought on board. Anyone who has ever attempted to right an overturned canoe filled with water can appreciate the difficulty of such a task. Another emergency measure was "banding" **the ship with ropes.** This involved passing ropes (or chains) under the ship to hold it together. Pulled tightly in a transverse fashion, such cables would hopefully help hold the timbers against the tremendous force of stormy waves.

Even though **Syrtis,** on the northern coast of Africa (Libya), was some four hundred miles away, the sailors began to fear the prospect of being driven there. The legendary quicksand and shoals in the southern Mediterranean were treacherous even in normal weather—so much so that Alexandrian ships would sail northward to Asia and then west to Italy to avoid this area. To combat this possible drift, the sailors **lowered the sea anchor.** This had the effect of giving the ship a dragging resistance to the wind and waves. By putting the ship on a starboard tack (her right side to the wind) and by utilizing storm sails, the ship would have been able to drift slowly in a westerly direction.

27:18-20 Despite all the emergency measures taken, the ship was being battered, perhaps even beginning to take on water. Crew members began **throwing the cargo overboard** (the grain) to make the ship lighter. When this proved inadequate, the sailors **threw out the ship's equipment.** Such actions indicate the crew's absolute desperation. The severity of the storm obscured the **sun** and **stars** (by which sailors navigated). The ship was being driven and tossed by the winds. It probably was leaking. A bleak sense of doom and despair permeated the passengers and crew.

27:21-24 The passengers and crew probably had not **eaten** due to fear, busyness, depression, or seasickness. They may have been fasting, or supplies may have been depleted (and were being rationed) due to the extra length of the journey. Paul reminded the crew that, with God's guidance, he had prophesied this very problem (27:10). Because he had been right in the past, they should listen to him now and have hope. Paul told them, **"None of you will lose your lives."** For no one to die in a shipwreck would be considered a great miracle in the ancient world. Standing under dark skies on the deck of a ship that was bobbing like a cork, Paul stated the reason for his unlikely confidence. The previous night he had been visited by **an angel** of his God, who told him that he would get safely to Rome, along with **everyone sailing with** him.

27:25-26 After relating this encouraging vision to his despairing shipmates, Paul admonished them to **take courage.** Having faith means taking God at his word. It means relying wholeheartedly on the clear-cut promises of God. The issue isn't whether a person has great faith but whether he or she has faith in a great God. This was true of Paul. A shipwreck would not normally be considered good. Knowing about it in advance, however, would make the experience less terrifying for the passengers and crew.

THE SHIPWRECK / 27:27-44

God had revealed to Paul that a shipwreck was inevitable (27:26). Sure enough, the ship ran aground and began to break apart just off the coast of Malta. Though the experience proved to be harrowing, all 276 people on board were able to swim safely ashore. Repeatedly during this grim experience, Paul had proclaimed his faith in God. Now, during this end of Paul's two-week-long nightmare at sea, God demonstrated his faithfulness and mercy.

27:27-28 In the two weeks that had passed since departing Fair Havens, the Alexandrian ship found itself adrift in the **Sea of Adria** (here a reference to the central part of the Mediterranean Sea between Italy, Crete, and the northern coast of Africa). Perhaps **the sailors sensed land was near** because they heard the sound of breakers in the night. **Soundings** were made by throwing a weighted, marked line into the water. When the lead hit the bottom, sailors could tell the depth of the water from the marks on the rope.

Calculating a conservatively estimated rate of drift of some thirty-six miles per day (given the inclement weather conditions), a ship would, in two weeks' time, be very close to what is known as St. Paul's Bay at Malta. This calculation corresponds to the recorded soundings both cited by Luke and demonstrated by modern oceanographic research.

27:29 If breakers were being heard in the distance, to continue to push toward land in the dark would have been foolhardy. Anchors acted as a kind of primitive braking device; ships had many anchors (from five to fifteen). Therefore, the crew **threw out four anchors** to keep the ship off the rocks and to keep the bow pointed toward the beach. They **prayed for daylight** so they could see where they were going.

27:30-32 In the night, a group of sailors, not convinced by Paul's earlier assurances that all aboard would be saved, **tried to abandon the ship.** Under the guise of going out in the ship's dinghy to drop additional **anchors** and stabilize the vessel, the men intended to head for shore. Somehow Paul discerned their real intentions. He may have been divinely warned or merely suspicious because of his own sailing experience. He alerted the **commanding officer,** Julius, and the Roman **soldiers** of the plot, implying that their own safety would be in jeopardy if these sailors were allowed to carry out their plan. Unlike the situation at the beginning of the voyage, Paul had the officer's attention and was functioning almost as the commander of the ship. Paul's words were followed completely, even when they went against common sense. The soldiers derailed the sailors' plan by cutting the lifeboat free. Without this smaller boat to ferry passengers to shore, everyone aboard was forced to depend on the Lord.

27:33-35 With a voice-of-experience and sense of the arduous task just ahead (making it to shore in cold, choppy waters), Paul encouraged his fellow travelers to gain strength and sustenance by eating. They had barely eaten for **two weeks** (due to a combination of fear, forced rationing, fasting, seasickness, and preoccupation with just surviving the storm). Again, Paul assured everyone of God's promise of safety. There, in the midst of dire circumstances, Paul presided over a traditional Jewish meal.

27:36-38 The passengers and crew were **encouraged** and **began eating.** There was no need to ration what was left or save it for later, for they knew they would soon be on land. Had they not eaten, they might not have had the strength to swim to shore. In the first instance of jettisoning (see 27:18), some of the cargo had to be kept for ballast, lest the ship become completely unmaneuverable. Now, by lightening the load even more, the ship would ride higher in the water and be able to get closer to shore before running aground.

27:39-41 The disoriented sailors had no idea where they were. The geography and topography of what is now known as St. Paul's Bay on the northeast shore of modern Malta fits this description. They prepared to run the ship ashore. The sailors **cut off the anchors,** thus eliminating any kind of "braking action." Before reaching land,

however, the ship **hit a shoal and ran aground** (modern research has confirmed between St. Paul's Bay and the island of Salmonetta the existence of a shallow channel only one to three hundred yards wide). Striking this underwater barrier between the two seas, the ship could go no further. Fierce waves began to strike the exposed rear of the vessel. Already weakened from a two-week pounding on the open seas, the ship quickly **began to break apart.**

27:42 Roman soldiers were charged with the safekeeping and safe delivery of any prisoners in their care. The law required them to pay with their own lives if any of their prisoners escaped (see 12:19; 16:27). In the certain chaos of a shipwreck, it would be relatively easy for prisoners to slip away. The soldiers' instinctive reaction was to **kill the prisoners** so as to prevent this from happening.

27:43-44 Despite the potential for risk, the **commanding officer** was impressed enough with Paul to keep the soldiers from carrying out their plan. As the highest ranking official, he had the full authority to make this decision. Some swam; others floated ashore on pieces of the collapsing ship. The evacuation plan worked, because **everyone escaped safely ashore.** No prisoners are recorded as having escaped. This sequence of events preserved Paul for his later ministry in Rome and fulfilled his prophetic utterance that everyone on the ship would be saved (27:22). In the minds of both Greeks and Romans, surviving a disaster at sea was evidence of a person's innocence. The powerful sea gods were not believed to spare the guilty.

ACTS 28

PAUL ON THE ISLAND OF MALTA / 28:1-10

Detailed plots on his life, angry mobs, storms at sea, shipwrecks—all the forces of hell seemed to have been intensifying their efforts to keep Paul from reaching Rome. Now, on the island of Malta, the attack continued—Paul was bitten by a poisonous snake. Paul not only survived the snake attack unharmed, but he turned around and healed a number of sick people on the island. During the three-month stay in Malta (see 28:11), Paul was showered with hospitality. What the Devil intended for evil God turned into good.

28:1-2 In about two weeks, the storm had pushed Paul's ship some 470 miles west of Fair Havens, Crete. Only when the crew and passengers came ashore did they realize that they had reached

Malta, an island 60 miles south of Sicily and 320 miles from Rome. The islanders there were of Phoenician ancestry and had given the island its name (taken from the Canaanite word for "refuge"). Malta had excellent harbors and was ideally located for trade. Many Roman soldiers retired there.

28:3-4 In cold weather, reptiles become lethargic. Lying in a bundle of twigs and brush, a snake might easily go unnoticed. Apparently, the jostling of Paul's walking, combined with the warmth of the fire, caused the **poisonous snake** to become roused. It struck Paul on the hand.

The Maltese people quickly tried to make sense of these events by using their pagan presuppositions. Steeped in Greek legends and stories of gods relentlessly bringing wrongdoers to justice, they concluded that Paul must have been guilty of murder. Though Paul had somehow escaped divine retribution in the shipwreck, Nemesis, the Greek goddess of retribution, must have orchestrated this additional means of punishing him.

28:5-6 To the amazement of the Maltese observers, Paul not only did not drop dead, he did not even exhibit any swelling or discomfort. God had promised safe passage to him (27:23-25), and nothing could prohibit his reaching Rome. When these superstitious pagans saw that Paul was unhurt by the poisonous snake, they did a complete about-face in their assessment of him. They had assumed that Paul was a murderer (28:4); now they decided he was a **god.** A similar appraisal is reported in 14:11-18 when Paul ministered at Lystra. It is rea-

sonable to assume that Paul deflected any idolatrous comments in the same manner as he had done previously.

28:7 Apparently wealthy, this **chief official,** named **Publius,** had a large estate. Whether he invited all 276 people to his home or whether he invited only Paul (and Luke) is unclear. In view of the miracle on the beach (the snakebite), Paul's "divine" reputation, and the illness afflicting Publius's father, it is likely that Publius entertained only Paul and his immediate entourage (perhaps also Julius and the ship's owner).

28:8-10 Malta **fever and dysentery** is now known to be caused by microbes in goats' milk. This illness seems to have been common on the island. A person could be ill for a few months to two or three years. When Paul learned that **Publius's father** was suffering from this disease, he visited him, laid hands on him, and prayed over him. The man's complete healing followed. The news of this miracle spread quickly, and soon everyone with any kind of disease or ailment came to Paul to be cured.

Three months passed (see 28:11), because the shipwreck survivors had to wait for the passing of winter and arrangements to complete their journey on another vessel. When the time came to leave the island, the grateful Maltese people inundated Paul and his friends with gifts and provisions for the remainder of their trip of 320 miles to Rome.

PAUL ARRIVES AT ROME / 28:11-16

The last leg of Paul's journey to Rome was almost anticlimactic—smooth sailing, a warm reception by some Italian believers, his own private lodging (house arrest rather than imprisonment in a Roman penal facility). The stage was now set for Paul to begin ministering in the most influential city in the world.

28:11-12 Ships began sailing again between mid-February and mid-March, depending on the weather. Sailing vessels often would be named in honor of certain deities. These deities were thought to serve as protectors and would be called upon in times of trouble. The **twin gods** referred to the sons of Zeus, the patrons of navigation. Their constellation (Gemini) was considered by sailors to be a sign of good luck. This **Alexandrian ship** was also likely a grain ship. It promptly (perhaps in one day's time) arrived in **Syracuse,** the chief city of Sicily.

28:13-14 Rhegium is modern-day Reggio on the "toe" of Italy. **Puteoli** is now called Pozzuoli and is located some 150 miles south of Rome. Situated in the Bay of Naples, Puteoli was the preferred

point of entry for Alexandrian wheat ships (prior to the building of larger port facilities at Portus, near Ostia, during the reign of Claudius).

At Puteoli, Paul and his colleagues **found some believers** and stayed with them for **seven days** (apparently while the ship was being unloaded or while the centurion, Julius, was conducting other official business).

28:15 The **believers in Rome** heard about Paul's imminent arrival, probably due to messengers sent by the believers in Puteoli. Eager to meet and greet the great apostle, an entourage headed south and intercepted Paul's party **at the Forum on the Appian Way,** a town about forty-three miles from Rome. A second welcoming committee of Roman believers encountered Paul at **The Three Taverns,**

thirty-five miles south of Rome. Paul's entrance to Rome was more like a victor's triumphal entry than a prisoner's march. A "tavern" was a shop or a place that provided food and lodging for travelers. The Appian Way, a main thoroughfare to Rome from the south, featured many such inns. Paul was grateful for this warm Italian reception; he **thanked God and took courage.**

28:16 At last Paul **arrived in Rome,** the most influential city on earth. This was the fulfillment of a long-term desire (Romans 1:10-16). Paul's **private lodging** was a rented house (see 28:30). Though **guarded** around the clock (in four-hour shifts) **by a soldier** (perhaps members of the Praetorian— or palace—guard, see Philippians 1:13), Paul had much more freedom than a typical prisoner.

PAUL PREACHES AT ROME UNDER GUARD / 28:17-31

Paul's first act in Rome was to call together the Jewish leaders. He wanted to declare his innocence of the charges brought against him in Jerusalem. But more than this, he wanted to proclaim the gospel to his Hebrew brothers.

28:17 The decree of Claudius expelling Jews from Rome (18:2) happened eleven years previously (A.D. 49–60), so by the time of Paul's arrival, Jewish leaders were back in Rome. These Jews were likely an unofficial gathering of the leaders of various synagogues, not an official ruling body.

After **three days,** Paul **called together the local Jewish leaders** because he did not have the freedom to visit them in their synagogues. Beginning his presentation, Paul stated his innocence in the charge of violating Jewish laws or customs.

28:18-19 Paul reiterated the Romans' inability or unwillingness to execute him. On three separate occasions, statements had been made to the effect that Paul had done nothing to deserve a **death sentence** (Claudias Lysias in 23:29; Festus in 25:25 and 26:31).

Paul emphasized that he had appealed **to Caesar** (25:11) because the Jewish leaders had adamantly and unjustly continued to pressure the authorities for a conviction. He felt he had no other recourse. And he further assured the Jews of his own motives in appealing to Caesar—not because he was trying to harm his own countrymen but solely to be declared innocent and set free.

28:20 The phrase, **the hope of Israel,** has been mentioned several times by Paul (see 23:6; 24:15; 26:7; 28:20). For Paul, the messianic hope meant the fulfillment of God's messianic prophecies first given to the patriarch Abraham. For all of its history, the nation looked forward to a time when God's anointed one would rule over a heavenly Kingdom. Because of his conviction that Jesus of Nazareth was that long-awaited **Messiah** and because of Christ's resurrection from the dead, Paul was adamant that his message and theology were consistent with Jewish hope through the ages. Paul wanted his countrymen to come to see (as he had) that this relatively new entity known as the Christian church was not a dangerous sect or departure from traditional orthodox Judaism but simply the next phase in the unfolding plan of God that had been first announced to Abraham.

28:21-22 The Jewish leaders had not heard specific allegations about Paul and his case, but they had heard a steady stream of negative comments about the **Christians.** There was a growing group of these people right there in Rome. The people who **denounced** Christianity may have been Jews who kept up with events in Israel, together with skeptical Romans, because Christians believed in one God, whereas the Romans had many gods, including Caesar. The Christians were committed to an authority higher than Caesar.

28:23-24 A meeting was arranged, and when the time for that appointment came, **a large number** of Roman Jews came to hear from Paul. It was an all-day affair, during which Paul used the Old Testament **Scriptures** to explain the gospel to the Jews. In essence, Paul reminded the Jews of the many Old Testament prophecies and references to the Messiah; then he skillfully demonstrated how Jesus, in his coming, living, dying, and rising, exactly fulfilled every divine promise and every Jewish hope. The effect of this long discourse and discussion was simply that **some believed and some didn't.**

28:25-27 In this interchange, Paul had the final word, and it was a strong rebuke. He compared the departing, arguing Jewish leaders to the long-ago audience of **Isaiah the prophet** (see Isaiah 6:9-10). Those Jews had heard the very word of God and had seen the spokesman of God, but because of stubbornness and pride, they had been unable to understand and perceive the deeper, life-changing implications of the divine revelation that was being extended to them. Rather than submitting to judgment by the truth, they had sat in judgment of truth. The great irony is that these Jews viewed themselves as religiously successful and slated for divine commendation, when in truth they were spiritually blind, deaf, and under divine condemnation!

28:28 As he had done on several prior occasions (see 13:46; 18:6; and 19:8-10), Paul announced a turning from the unresponsive, hard-hearted Jews to the receptive **Gentiles.** From that point on, the non-Jews would be given priority when it came to evangelical witness. At some future point, Paul apparently expected a change of heart by his countrymen (see Romans 11:25-32), but for the immediate future Paul would direct his ministry to those who were eager to embrace the truth about Christ.

Verse 29 is not included in most of the ancient manuscripts.

28:30-31 While Paul was under house arrest **for the next two years,** he did more than speak to the Jews. He wrote letters, commonly called his Prison Epistles, to the Ephesians, Colossians, and Philippians. He also wrote personal letters, such as the one to Philemon. This ending shows the gospel going forward to Rome, as the great commission had directed. It had now reached the international capital of the Gentiles.

He **welcomed all who visited him,** and that list was surely long. Luke was with Paul in Rome (2 Timothy 4:11). Timothy often visited him (Philippians 1:1; Colossians 1:1; Philemon 1:1), as did Tychicus (Ephesians 6:21), Epaphroditus (Philippians 4:18), and Mark (Colossians 4:10). Paul witnessed to the whole Roman guard (Philippians 1:13) and was involved with the Roman believers.

Tradition says that Paul was released after two years of house arrest in Rome and then set off on a fourth missionary journey. Five reasons for this tradition are as follows: (1) Luke does not give us an account of his trial before Caesar—and Luke was a detailed chronicler; (2) the prosecution had two years to bring the case to trial, and time may have run out; (3) in his letter to the Philippians, written during his imprisonment in Rome, Paul implied that he would soon be released and would do further traveling; (4) events and places mentioned in the Pastoral Epistles indicate that Paul's journeys continued after those recorded in Acts 28; (5) early Christian literature talks plainly about other travels by Paul. During Paul's time of freedom, he may have continued to travel extensively, even going to Spain (see Romans 15:24, 28) and back to the churches in Greece. The books of 1 Timothy and Titus were written during this time. Later, Paul was imprisoned again, probably in Rome, where he wrote his last letter (2 Timothy).

During this first Roman imprisonment, he spoke **with all boldness** and **no one tried to stop him.** The Greek word *akolutos* ("without hindrance") is the last word of Acts, thus ending the book on a triumphal note. Many readers, however, have thought that the book ends too abruptly, especially in that it doesn't relate what happened to Paul. But it must be remembered that the book is not about the life of Paul but about the spread of the gospel, and that had been clearly presented by Luke. God apparently thought it was not necessary for someone to record the entire history of the early church. Now that the gospel had been preached and established at the center of trade and government, it would spread across the world.

ROMANS

INTRODUCTION
The courtroom is filled with intense drama as the lawyer for the plaintiff states the case for guilt and the lawyer for the defendant builds the case for innocence. Judge and jurors listen carefully in preparation for their verdict. Although Romans was not presented in court, this letter from Paul to the Roman believers reads like a lawyer's brief as Paul slowly and skillfully presents the case for the gospel. Paul was a scholar and a world traveler. He was a Pharisee and a Roman citizen. But most important, Paul was a follower of Jesus Christ. Because Paul had not visited Rome, he wrote this letter to introduce himself to the Roman believers and to prepare the way for his coming. And so, under the inspiration of the Holy Spirit, he clearly outlined the Christian message. His readers would know that this Roman citizen was *first* a citizen of the Kingdom of Heaven, a brother in Christ.

AUTHOR
Paul (Saul of Tarsus): Pharisee, apostle, pioneer missionary of the church.

Paul was a Jew, culturally and religiously, by birth and by choice. We know little of his early years except that he was from Tarsus, far north and west of Jerusalem, in Cilicia. When he comes onto the biblical scene at the confrontation with Stephen (Acts 7:58), we see Paul as a young Pharisee, zealous for the faith and giving his approval to Stephen's death. Later, we learn that Paul had been trained by Gamaliel, the most respected rabbi of the day (Acts 22:3). Paul was so Jewish, in fact, that he became obsessed with eliminating the young Christian sect that he viewed as heretical (Acts 8:1-3; 9:1-2).

Paul was Jewish, but he was also a Roman citizen (Acts 22:28). The mighty Roman Empire extended well beyond Italy, through Macedonia and Asia, all the way to the limits of Judea. Although all who lived in the conquered territory were under Roman domination, not everyone was a Roman citizen. That was a special privilege. A person could become a Roman citizen by birth (born to parents who were citizens) or by purchase. And with Roman citizenship came certain rights and guarantees (for example, the right to a fair trial and the right of passage).

So Paul had dual citizenship—in Israel and in Rome—and both were important to him. But Paul was a citizen of yet another nation, the Kingdom of God. As this zealous Jew, armed with authority from the high priest, had journeyed to Damascus to root out and capture Christians, he was confronted by Christ (Acts 26:12-18). From that moment on, Paul had a new Emperor, a new Commander-in-chief.

Paul's Ministry. After his conversion to Christ (Acts 9:1-19), Paul spent three

When Paul wrote his letter to the church in Rome, he had not yet been there, but he had taken the gospel "from Jeru-salem clear over into Illyricum" (15:19). He planned to visit and preach in Rome one day and hoped to continue to take the gospel farther west—even to Spain.

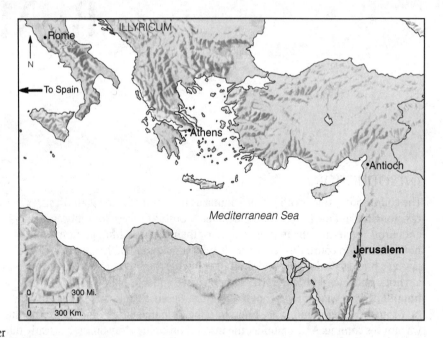

years in Damascus with Ananias and the other disciples in that city (Galatians 1:18). There his ministry began (Acts 9:20-23). Paul then returned to Jerusalem, sponsored by Barnabas, who encouraged him and presented him to the apostles. But after attempts on Paul's life by his former associates, zealous Jews, he was sent by the apostles to Tarsus. (It would be fourteen years before he would return to Jerusalem—see Galatians 2:1.)

Paul remained in the northern region for about eight years, becoming established in the faith and teaching in the churches, especially in Antioch (Acts 11:25-26). The church at Antioch then commissioned Paul and Barnabas, sending them on the first missionary journey (Acts 13:2-3), to Cyprus, Pamphylia, and Galatia (Acts 13:4–14:28). This trip occurred in A.D. 46–48. At each town, first Paul would attempt to reach the Jews with the gospel; then he would reach beyond the synagogue to the Gentiles, who responded in great numbers. The response of the Gentiles further enraged the Jews and even caused the apostles and other believers to question Paul's ministry. But the issue of taking the gospel to non-Jews was somewhat resolved at the Council of Jerusalem in A.D. 50 (Acts 15).

Paul took two other missionary trips, establishing churches in Ephesus, Philippi, Thessalonica, Corinth, and other cities along the Mediterranean coast and inland. These trips occurred in A.D. 50–52 and A.D. 53–57. While on his third missionary journey, Paul became determined to return to Jerusalem to deliver the money he had collected for believers there, even though he knew that enemies were waiting for him (Acts 20:22-24).

Paul's arrival in Jerusalem was peaceful at first (Acts 21:17-19), but when he was recognized at the Temple, a violent mob seized him and tried to kill him

(Acts 21:27-32). This led to his conversation with the commander and the beginning of his series of trials that eventually brought Paul to Rome in A.D. 59 (Acts 28:11-16).

Although under Roman guard in a house, Paul was able to continue his ministry while in Rome, teaching all who came to visit and listen. In addition, he was able to write the Prison Epistles: Ephesians, Philippians, Colossians, and Philemon. This arrangement lasted two years (Acts 28:17-31).

According to tradition, Paul was released after those two years. Some reasons for this tradition are as follows: (1) Luke does not give an account of Paul's trial before Caesar, and Luke was a detailed historian; (2) the prosecution had two years to bring the case to trial, and time may have run out; (3) in Paul's letter to the Philippians, written during his imprisonment in Rome, he implied that he would soon be released and would do further traveling; (4) Paul mentioned several places where he intended to take the gospel, but he never had visited those places in his first three journeys; and (5) early Christian literature talks plainly about other travels by Paul.

After his release, Paul probably left on another missionary journey, through Ephesus where he left Timothy (1 Timothy 1:3), then to Colosse (Philemon 22), and on to Macedonia. He may also have realized his goal of going to Spain (Romans 15:24, 28). Eventually he probably journeyed east and visited Crete (Titus 1:5), where he left Titus to organize and lead the church. During this time of freedom, Paul wrote 1 Timothy and Titus.

Eventually, Paul was arrested a second time and returned to Rome. This prison experience differed greatly from his first—this time Paul was isolated and lonely, awaiting execution (2 Timothy 4:9-18). However, he was able to write 2 Timothy. Paul was martyred in the spring of A.D. 68.

From beginning to end, Paul's ministry was focused on taking the good news of Christ to the world. Despite continual harassment and violent persecution, he courageously took every opportunity to tell others about the Savior, teaching, preaching, making his defense in court, and sharing one-to-one. Paul's identity and citizenship were found in Christ. He was committed to obeying God, his true Emperor, no matter what.

When Paul wrote to the church in Rome, therefore, he was writing first as a citizen of heaven. Yet Paul also was writing as a Roman citizen to people who lived at the apex of worldly power—the capital of the Roman Empire. Paul had felt the tension between those allegiances; he knew the conflicts that his readers must be facing.

DATE AND SETTING
Written from Corinth in A.D. 57.

During Paul's ministry in Corinth, he met Aquila and Priscilla, Jews who had left Rome following an order from Emperor Claudius (Acts 18:2). They were tentmakers, a trade that Paul also knew. While in Corinth, Paul stayed and worked with Aquila and Priscilla and had a tremendous effect on their spiritual growth (Acts 18:3). Later, this godly couple returned to Rome and became leaders in the church there (Romans 16:3-5).

During this journey, Paul was collecting money for the church in Jerusalem, which was poor and struggling through a devastating famine. For three years of this trip, Paul ministered in Ephesus. But after a riot (Acts 19:23-41), he left for Greece, where he stayed for three months (Acts 20:2-3) before leaving for Jerusalem with the money he had collected (Romans 15:25-26). Much of the three months was spent in Corinth. That's when Paul wrote the letter to the Romans. Note the reference to Gaius, a Corinthian believer (1 Corinthians 1:14) who was known to the believers in Rome (Romans 16:23).

Although Paul had never been to Rome, he longed to go there (Romans 1:9-13). He was planning to visit the church on his way to Spain, after delivering the money to Jerusalem (Romans 15:25-29).

AUDIENCE
Christians in Rome.

The city of Rome. Rome was the capital city of the vast and mighty Roman Empire, an empire that stretched from Britain to Arabia. Truly, all roads led to Rome. It would be natural, then, for Paul to want to visit this great city, not merely as a dutiful citizen or a curious tourist, but as a gifted evangelist who desired to reach the world for Christ.

Founded in 753 B.C., Rome was strategically located on the Tiber River at a ford that was indispensable for traveling between northern and southern Italy. In Paul's day, Rome was the largest city in the world, with a population of approximately one million. Wealthy and cosmopolitan, it was the diplomatic and trade center of the world. The Roman Empire provided stability, order, and the rule of law for the conquered countries. The Roman peace made travel safe; Roman roads made it relatively swift and easy.

There is evidence for a Jewish colony in Rome dating to the second century B.C. The colony was small until Judea was incorporated into the Roman Empire in 63 B.C., when Pompey called for the deportation of Jews to Rome. Then the Jewish population expanded. In 59 B.C., Cicero wrote that the Jews of Rome were a large, powerful, and influential group.

During the period of the Roman Republic (527–509 B.C.), the Romans adopted and "Romanized" Greek gods. Thus Zeus, the king of the gods, became Jupiter, Hera became Juno, Poseidon became Neptune, Hermes became Mercury, and Aphrodite became Venus. Emperor worship also was encouraged. This worship was enforced in varying degrees, depending on the emperor's disposition. Devout Jews had very different worship patterns and would never worship the emperor, so the Jewish community was often persecuted and was expelled from Rome several times. Aquila and Priscilla were driven from Rome by an edict from Claudius in A.D. 49. Each time, the expulsion edict would lapse and the Jews would return. This was the case with Claudius's edict.

What was it like to be a Christian in Rome? It was like being a distinct and oppressed minority. In many ways, Rome was a secular city, consumed with financial and political concerns. But Rome was also a very religious city. Its pagan religion centered around Jupiter and other gods and included many superstitions. Thus, Jews and Christians who insisted on *one* God were viewed as atheists because they denied the existence of all the other deities.

At first Christianity was tolerated in Rome, as a sect of Judaism. But in the last few years of Emperor Nero's reign (A.D. 54–68), he authorized hunting down, torturing, and killing Christians. In A.D. 64, a large part of Rome was destroyed by a fire, thought by many to have been ordered by the emperor himself. Nero, however, accused the Christians in the city, giving him the excuse for any number of terrible atrocities. The secular historian Tacitus wrote:

> Their death was made a matter of sport; they were covered in wild beast's skins and torn to pieces by dogs; or were fastened to crosses and set on fire in order to serve as torches by night. . . . Nero had offered his gardens for the spectacle and gave an exhibition in his circus, mingling with the crowd in the guise of a charioteer or mounted on his chariot (*Annals* 15.44).

During these terrible persecutions, Christians were forced to choose between the emperor and Christ; those who chose Christ often died for their faith. Both Peter and Paul are thought to be victims of Nero's terror.

The church at Rome. The founders of the church at Rome are unknown. It was not started by Peter—his ministry was to Jews, and he seems to have settled in Rome just after Paul's arrival in about A.D. 60. And the church was not founded by Paul—he admits to not having been there (Romans 1:11-13; 15:23-24). Most likely, the church was begun by Jews who had been in Jerusalem for the Passover celebration and had been converted through Peter's powerful sermon and the outpouring of the Holy Spirit in A.D. 30 (Acts 2:5-40). These new believers were soon joined by travelers like Aquila and Priscilla, who had heard the Good News in other places and had brought it back to Rome.

At first, of course, the Roman church was Jewish; that is, the members were Jews who had come to believe in Jesus as their Messiah. But over the subsequent twenty-seven years, many Christians from all parts of the Roman Empire had migrated to Rome, some of them Paul's own converts and many of them Gentiles. The recipients probably were a loosely knit fellowship of believers and not a highly organized church. That is, there were no ordained leaders by any title. And the Roman Christians worshiped in various homes and other meetings places, rather than in one church location (16:5, 14-16). But organized or not, this church had become large and influential—"your faith in God is becoming known throughout the world" (1:8). The membership of the church reflected Roman society; that is, it was a cosmopolitan mix of believers from a wide variety of backgrounds and walks of life.

OCCASION AND PURPOSE

The main purpose for Paul writing this letter at this time was to prepare the way for his visit to Rome, to let the believers in Rome know of his plans to come, and to enlist their support for his future ministry in Spain. Paul had longed to visit Rome, and, God willing, he would be there soon (1:10-13). He knew that Rome was the most important city in the empire, with influence spreading far and wide—ministering there would be strategic.

Paul also wanted to counteract any misunderstanding of his goals and his message—there was widespread slander directed at him by some fellow Christians and many Jews (for example, see 1 Corinthians 3 and 2 Corinthians 10–12). To most Roman Christians, Paul was just a name; they had never met him and had only heard about him. So Paul took time to build his credibility and authority by carefully setting forth his theology. It's as if Paul were saying, "Here's who I am, and here's what I believe."

Another purpose for Paul's writing was to solidify the Romans in their faith, since they had no apostolic leaders or teachers. He knew the inevitable conflicts that would arise for citizens of Christ's Kingdom in the greatest city of the Roman Empire. This was a church without a whole Bible—they had the Hebrew Scriptures (the Old Testament), but the Gospels hadn't been written, and the other Epistles had been sent to other churches. This letter, therefore, was the first piece of strictly Christian literature that these believers would see. So, under the inspiration of the Holy Spirit, Paul clearly and carefully crafted this theological masterpiece with the strong message of the sovereignty of God and justification by faith.

MESSAGE
After a brief introduction, Paul presents the facts of the gospel (1:3) and declares his allegiance to it (1:16-17). He continues by building an airtight case for the lostness of humanity and the necessity for God's intervention (1:18–3:20). Then Paul presents the Good News: Salvation is available to all, regardless of a person's identity, sin, or heritage. We are saved by unearned, undeserved favor from God through complete trust in Christ and his finished work. Through him we can stand before God justified, "not guilty" (3:21–5:21). With this foundation Paul moves directly into a discussion of the freedom that comes from being saved—freedom from the power of sin (6:1-23), freedom from the domination of the Law (7:1-25), freedom to become like Christ and discover God's limitless love (8:1-39).

Speaking directly to his Jewish brothers and sisters, Paul shares his concern for them and explains how they fit into God's plan (9:1–11:12). God has made the way for Jews and Gentiles to be united in the body of Christ; both groups can praise God for his wisdom and love (11:13-36).

Paul explains what it means to live in complete submission to Christ: Use spiritual gifts to serve others (12:3-8), genuinely love others (12:9-21), and be good citizens (13:1-14). Freedom must be guided by love as we build each other up in the faith, being sensitive and helpful to those who are weak (14:1–15:4). Paul stresses unity, especially between Gentiles and Jews (15:5-13). He concludes by reviewing his reasons for writing, outlining his personal plans (15:22–33), greeting his friends, and giving a few final thoughts and greetings from his traveling companions (16:1–27).

The main themes in the book of Romans include: *Sin, Salvation, Spiritual Growth, Sovereignty,* and *Service.*

Sin (1:18–3:20). Before announcing the Good News, Paul gives the bad news: The whole human race stands condemned as sinners deserving God's wrath and punishment. Since Adam's rebellion against God, our nature is to disobey him. Our sin cuts us off from God. Sin causes us to want to live our own way rather than God's way. Because God is morally perfect, just, and fair, he is right when he condemns sin. All human beings are sinners. All human beings are guilty—deserving the death penalty.

IMPORTANCE FOR TODAY. It is easy to point judgmental fingers at others, noting their sins and almost gleefully condoning their certain punishment. In doing so, we often compare ourselves to them and thus excuse our own disobedience and shortcomings. But the terrible truth is that every person has sinned, either by rebelling against God or by ignoring his will. Compared to God's standard of perfection, we fall woefully short. Thus we stand condemned, no matter how religious we are. Regardless of our background or how hard we try to live a good moral life, we cannot earn salvation or remove our sin. Only Christ can save us.

Salvation (3:21–5:21). The Romans had a smorgasbord of gods and religious beliefs from which to choose. In our pluralistic society, which holds tolerance and open-mindedness in high regard, a popular idea is that all religions are essentially the same and equally effective. Christians, therefore, are often seen as narrow-minded and dogmatic when insisting that Christ is the *only* way to God. But that is what Jesus taught, and it is the truth that Paul affirms here in Romans.

IMPORTANCE FOR TODAY. Although we may lose popularity for insisting that salvation comes only through faith in Christ, we must be steadfast in our commitment to the gospel because it is the truth. And we must explain that the exclusiveness of the message is far from being closed or narrow-minded—it is Good News. After recognizing our utter lostness in our sins, we can say, "Thank God there is *one* way!" By believing in Jesus Christ and accepting him as Savior, men and women can enter into a wonderful new relationship with God.

Spiritual Growth (6:1–8:17). New followers of Christ must mature in their relationship with God, continually turning away from sin and obeying God. Paul explains that by God's power, believers are freed from the cycle of sin and death and are sanctified—made holy. This means they are set apart from sin and enabled to obey and to become more like Christ (6:1–7:6). Although breaking free of sin's grasp can be a struggle, Christians can be freed totally because of the work of Christ and through the power of the Holy Spirit (7:7-25). And when believers are growing in their relationship with Christ, the Holy Spirit frees them from the demands of the law and from fear of judgment (8:1-17).

IMPORTANCE FOR TODAY. Because we are free from sin's control, the law's demands, and fear of God's punishment, we can grow in our relationship with Christ. By trusting in the Holy Spirit and allowing him to help us, we can overcome sin and temptation (8:1-2).

Sovereignty (8:18–11:36). One word that would epitomize the Roman government is **power.** Into this milieu, Paul sent the message of God's sovereignty. This is a crucial truth for the Roman Christians to understand and believe, for it is at this point that the Kingdom of God and the kingdom of Rome will come into the greatest conflict. Soon believers will have to choose between allegiance to Rome and allegiance to Christ. Knowing that God reigns triumphant will make that choice much easier.

IMPORTANCE FOR TODAY. Our world is also obsessed with power—in politics, business, and relationships. Power means control, influence, security, and ease. In the face of this lust for power, Christians can feel isolated and alone. And as a powerless minority, we can feel discriminated against and persecuted. Like the Roman believers, we need to hear Paul's message reaffirming the sovereignty of God, reminding us that our allegiance is not to the puny gods of this world and their hollow offers of power and prestige. No, we belong to the Sovereign of the universe.

Service (12:1–15:13). Paul's final theme is service: serving God and the other members of the body of Christ, the church. Although Christians made up a small minority of the population of Rome, still they could make a difference for Christ. How? By living as "transformed" men and women (12:2). During these difficult days, with all the pressures and temptations of the surrounding society, it was important for Christians to be a unified (15:5) and loving body. If men and women truly honor Christ as Lord, it will show in their lives. They will be known for their love, in the community and in the church.

IMPORTANCE FOR TODAY. If believers are going to make any kind of impact in this world for Christ, we must love as Christ loved, helping those in need and serving with humility and grace. This example of love must begin in our churches. Unity, encouragement, and support should be our goal, rather than the much-publicized arguments, splits, and even lawsuits. People will take seriously the claims of Christ when they see what he was done in the lives of those who bear his name—Christians.

OUTLINE OF ROMANS

   I. What to Believe (1:1–11:36)
      A. Sinfulness of mankind
      B. Forgiveness of sin through Christ
      C. Freedom from sin's grasp
      D. Israel's past, present, and future
   II. How to Behave (12:1–16:27)
      A. Personal responsibility
      B. Personal notes

ROMANS 1

GREETINGS FROM PAUL / 1:1-7

Paul opens his letter to these Roman believers, most of whom he had never met, by explaining who he is and what his credentials are. Almost immediately, he directs their attention to the Lord Jesus Christ. Paul knew that the resurrected Christ was the most important common denominator for him and the believers in Rome. From that common ground he introduces his plan to visit them and then plunges into one of the most detailed explanations of the Christian faith found in the Bible.

1:1 Paul had friends in Rome, as Romans 16 shows, but he had not personally visited that church. So he begins his letter by formally presenting his credentials. He first calls himself **Christ's slave,** meaning one who is subject to the will and wholly at the disposal of his master. Paul, in using the term, expresses his absolute devotion and

subjection to Christ Jesus. For a Roman citizen to identify himself as a servant was unthinkable. Paul could have introduced himself to these Romans as a Roman citizen, but instead he chose to speak of himself only as completely dependent on and obedient to his beloved Master.

Paul then notes two important roles to characterize his life. Paul was **chosen by God to be an apostle** and **sent out to preach his Good News.** His calling occurred when he saw the Lord Jesus on the road to Damascus (Acts 9:1-19). His assignment was to teach the Good News of salvation—especially "to the Gentiles" (Galatians 1:16).

The title "apostle" designated authority to set up and supervise churches and discipline them if necessary. Even more than a title of authority, apostle means one sent on a mission, like an envoy or an ambassador. Paul represents himself with the credentials and responsibilities given to him by the King of kings as an ambassador to evangelize the Gentile world.

1:2 The **Good News** had been **promised long ago by God** and was not a new religion made up by Paul or anyone else. It was rooted in God's promises in the Old Testament to his people **through his prophets.** The gospel that Paul preached was in perfect continuity with God's earlier words in the Scriptures to his people, Israel. Both the Jews and Gentiles in the church of Rome needed to be reminded that the gospel is an ancient message of God's plan for his creation. This was on Paul's mind and is a recurring theme throughout the letter.

Even though the church in Rome consisted mostly of Gentiles and former converts to the Jewish faith, Paul reminded them all that, in their acceptance of the gospel, they were not casting off **the holy Scriptures** in order to embrace Jesus as the Christ. Rather, they were discovering and responding to the out-working of God's eternal plan. The prophets in the Old Testament announced the coming fulfillment of God's grace in Christ.

1:3 After introducing the messenger (himself), the message (gospel), and the source (God), Paul turns to the subject of the message. In verses 3-5, Paul summarizes the **Good News** about Jesus Christ. The central focus of the gospel is **Jesus,** God's **Son,** who was both human and divine (see Luke 3:31; 2 Timothy 2:8). Jesus was **born into King David's royal family line,** in Bethlehem, and of David's tribe (Judah). King David was promised a kingdom without end (2 Samuel 7:12-16). In the birth of Jesus Christ, the eternal King of kings, that promise was fulfilled.

In Christ's humanity we see his identification with us and his excellence as our example. In Christ's divinity we see his worthiness to take our place in receiving the punishment for sin that is due us. We separate Christ's human and divine natures for understanding and discussion, but in fact, they cannot be separated. Jesus is and will always be the God-man, our Lord and Savior.

1:4 Jesus' entire life, from his human conception to his resurrection, was planned, promised, and fulfilled by God. His nature as God's Son was made clear **when God powerfully raised him from the dead by means of the Holy Spirit.** He was, is, and will always be the Son of God. Christ's resurrection unmistakably revealed that truth to the world. At the time of his resurrection, Christ was glorified and restored to his full rights and status as Son of God in power (Philippians 2:4-9).

1:5 Christians have both **privilege** and **authority.** Paul and the apostles received forgiveness (grace) as an undeserved privilege. But they also were given the authority to share the message of God's forgiveness with others. God also graciously forgives our sins when we repent and put our trust in Christ. In doing this, we are committing ourselves to begin a new life. God's call may take many forms and many directions, but he does call each believer to be an example of the changed life that Jesus Christ has begun and to spread the word.

In Paul's case, God's direction became very clear. He was **to tell Gentiles everywhere what God has done for them** (Acts 9:15). Paul did carry the Good News across the known world, speaking in synagogues, convincing the Gentiles, and even standing before kings. Paul understood his calling, for in Romans 11:13 he states, "God has appointed me as the apostle to the Gentiles." Paul makes it clear that the gospel is the working out of God's plan first revealed to the Jews. He also makes it clear that the gospel offered hope to the Gentiles.

The desired response to the gospel message was that people **will believe and obey him, bringing glory to his name.** Faith and obedience are inseparable. Real faith will always lead to obedience; real obedience comes from faith.

1:6-7 Having stated the scope of his ministry, Paul goes on to include the believers **in Rome** in God's plan. These believers may not have been called as apostles, as Paul was, but they certainly had been **called to belong to Jesus Christ,** to be **his very own people.** Paul was reminding the Romans that the message of the gospel is larger than its messengers. Even though he had not been able to visit them personally, he was fully aware that they were among those God had intended to reach. The reality of this invitation rests on the truth that **God loves** people **dearly.** Before believers are called, they are loved.

The church in Rome was primarily made up of Gentiles (1:5-6, 13; 11:13; 15:15-16), although there were a number of Jewish Christians as well. Part of the church may have been Jews who became believers at Pentecost and returned to

Rome with the Good News. Acts 2:10-11 states that among the great crowd in Jerusalem who heard Peter's speech were "visitors from Rome (both Jews and converts to Judaism)." In addition, travelers who had heard the Good News in other places brought it back to Rome (for example, Priscilla and Aquila—Acts 18:2; Romans 16:3-5).

Grace is the unmerited favor God gives to the believers; **peace** refers to the peace that Christ made between us and God through his death on the cross. Only God can grant such wonderful gifts. Paul wants his readers to experience God's grace and peace in their daily living. In these two words of greeting Paul is combining expressions from Jewish and Gentile customs. Jews wished each other peace *(eirene* or the Hebrew *shalom);* Gentiles wished each other grace *(charis).* Each of these common expressions gained considerable value in Christian use.

GOD'S GOOD NEWS / 1:8-17

After formally introducing himself, Paul expresses his feelings toward the Roman believers and his reasons for wanting to visit them. This would disarm objections that might be raised to his coming. Some believers in Rome might think that he was arrogant in trying to extend his influence all the way to the capital of the empire; others might think he was presumptuous in planning to teach the gospel to those who had already heard it; others might even be concerned that he lacked integrity for often expressing his desire to come to Rome but never getting there. Paul does not leave the Romans guessing—he tells them exactly why he wants to come.

1:8 Living in the Western world's political power center, Roman Christians were highly visible. Fortunately, their reputation was excellent; their strong faith was **becoming known throughout the world.** To have a thriving church in Rome and to have Christians living pure lives in an evil city bore strong testimony to their faith! For this Paul thanked God.

1:9 Paul was a man of prayer. Paul prayed for the Romans the same way that he prayed for the Ephesians (Ephesians 1:15-16), the Philippians (Philippians 1:3-4), the Colossians (Colossians 1:3-4), and the Thessalonians (1 Thessalonians 1:2-3). We would expect Paul to pray for his own converts and the churches he helped establish, but these words show that he also prayed for those outside his immediate acquaintance and responsibility. Paul had not personally visited these believers, so he had not yet been able to prove his love for them, but he appeals to God as his witness, confirming his constant prayers for the believers in Rome.

1:10-11 Paul also prayed that he could visit these believers. For a long time, Paul had wanted to visit the empire's capital city, but he had been prevented from doing so (see also 1:13; 15:22; Acts 19:21; 23:11; 28:14-16). Here Paul expresses his continued desire to go, but only if God willed it. Having prayed so often for them, he wanted to visit them in order to minister to them. Paul proposed a trip to Rome to serve, not to be served. He fully intended that his visit would benefit the believers there.

What **spiritual blessing** did Paul want to **share?** This was not a particular empowering to do something; rather, it was an insight or teaching based on the needs that Paul would find when he got to Rome. It would help them **grow strong in the Lord.** This letter to them certainly worked toward that end, but Paul also hoped that the spiritual effects of his intended visit would be powerful and mutual.

1:12 Paul prayed for the chance to visit these Christians so that he could **encourage** them with his gift of faith and **be encouraged** by theirs. As God's missionary, he could help them understand the meaning of the Good News about Jesus. As God's devoted people, they could offer him fellowship and comfort. Paul makes it clear that he will not come as simply the teacher and giver—he will be open to be given to and encouraged as well. When Christians gather, everyone should give and receive. Our mutual faith gives us a common language and a common purpose for **blessing** one another.

1:13 As noted above, Paul had tried to come to Rome, but had been **prevented.** Paul's original plan was to include Rome in his missionary efforts. Although the church had been established there without his efforts, that fact did not discourage Paul from wanting to visit and **work among** the believers in order to see more **Gentiles** become believers and join the church. He had done this in many other cities, and hoped to do so in Rome. By the end of his third missionary journey, Paul had traveled through Syria, Galatia, Asia, Macedonia, and Achaia. The churches that he had begun in these areas consisted mostly of Gentile believers. Paul could make statements like these without a hint of pride. He is making it clear that God directed him into ministry to the Gentiles and that the **good results** came from God.

1:14 Paul's **obligation** was to proclaim Christ's salvation to all types of people in different **cultures,** crossing cultural, social, racial, and economic lines. **The educated and uneducated** referred to the classes in Rome versus the peoples of other "uncivilized" places. No barrier would stop Paul from bringing the Good News.

1:15 Paul had already visited some of the most beautiful cities of the world—Athens, Corinth, Ephesus—yet he carried an unfulfilled desire to minister in one of the most populated, corrupt places on earth. Neither the power nor the hostility of **Rome** intimidated Paul. He was convinced that the Good News must be taken everywhere, specifically to the large and needy metropolitan areas of the world. Paul knew that the gospel had already gained a foothold in Rome—the believers to whom he was writing had heard and had responded. But Paul wanted to **preach God's Good News** more fully. This letter to the Romans is the introductory statement of all that Paul wanted these believers to understand more fully.

1:16 Verses 16 and 17 summarize the thrust of the rest of Paul's letter and give the reason behind Paul's missionary zeal. Paul was ready, even eager (1:15), to preach at Rome. And he was **not ashamed of this Good News about Christ,** even though the gospel was held in contempt by those who did not believe and even though those who preached it could face humiliation and suffering. Paul was not intimidated by the intellect of Greece nor the power of Rome. Paul was not ashamed, because he knew from experience that the gospel had the **power** to save **everyone who believes** and then to transform their lives. The Greek word for power *(dunamis)* is the source for our words dynamite and dynamic. Dynamite was not invented by Nobel until 1867, so it is obvious that Paul did not have that specific picture in mind. Instead, the inventor of the explosive took its name from the Greek. But the parallel is instructive. The Good News, as the power of God, can be like spiritual dynamite. Under certain circumstances it has a devastating, even destructive effect, demolishing world views and traditions—paving the way for new construction. Placed inside a stone-hard heart that is resistant to God, it can shatter the barrier.

God's power in the gospel is not only explosive; it also overcomes evil.

The only way to receive salvation is to believe in Christ. This offer is open to all people. The gospel is powerful because the power of God resides in it by nature. The Good News is the inherent power of God that gives salvation to all who accept it. Salvation can only happen when a person believes.

The **Jews** were given **first** invitation because they had been God's special people for more than 2,000 years, ever since God chose Abraham and promised great blessings to his descendants (Genesis 12:1-3). God did not choose them because they deserved to be chosen (Deuteronomy 7:7-8; 9:4-6), but because he wanted to show his love and mercy to them, teach them, and prepare them to welcome his Messiah into the world. For centuries Abraham's descendants had been learning about God by obeying his laws, keeping his sacrifices and feasts, and living according to his moral principles. Often they forgot God's promises and requirements and had to be disciplined; but still they had a precious heritage of belief in the one true God. Of all the people on earth, the Jews should have been the most ready to welcome the Messiah and to understand his mission and message—and some of them were. The disciples and Paul were faithful Jews who recognized in Jesus God's most precious gift to the human race (see Luke 2:25, 36-38). The Jews were given the first opportunity to receive the Messiah during his ministry on earth (John 1:11) and during the days of the early church (Acts 1:8; 3:26). Although Paul was commissioned as the apostle to the Gentiles (Acts 9:15), even he followed this pattern. Whenever Paul went to a new city, he recognized his obligation to carry the Good News to the Jews first (Acts 13:45-46; 28:25, 28).

1:17 The message of the Good News tells us how we, sinners as we are, can be made **right** in God's sight. It tells how God, who is righteous, can vindicate sinful people. Righteousness is an aspect of God's character, his standard of behavior, and a description of all that he wishes to give to us. Our righteousness begins because of God's faithfulness to his promises; it moves on in our response of faith and is a continuing process through life. Thus it is **accomplished from start to finish by faith.** Faith—unconditional trust—is the appointed way of receiving God's righteousness. Faith in what? Faith in the fact that Jesus Christ took our sins upon himself, taking the punishment we deserved, and, in exchange, making us righteous before God. By trusting in Christ, our relationship with God is made right both for now and for eternity.

To nail his point, Paul quoted from Habakkuk 2:4, **"It is through faith that a righteous person has life."** Righteousness by faith was not a new idea; it is found in the writings of the prophets, with which the Jewish believers would be familiar. This expression means that Christians will live because of God's faithfulness and because of their response of faith in God;

as a result, they will have eternal life and experience fullness in life.

- Faith is personal trust in God.
- Faith is the source of the believer's new life in Christ.
- Faith justifies us, saves us, and gives us new life and a new lifestyle.

GOD'S ANGER AT SIN / 1:18-32
The remainder of the first chapter paints a picture of the human predicament before a holy God. These verses, when they are read aloud, sound like a list of charges being read in court. All people everywhere deserve God's condemnation for their sin. They know they are not acknowledging their creator and are deliberately disobeying his standards. The consequences have been disastrous. Sin continues to increase. Before detailing God's way of salvation, Paul first sets out to convince people of their lost condition and their need for a Savior.

1:18 As God's righteousness was revealed (1:17), so was his wrath. The flip side of God's righteousness is his wrath against evil. Certain aspects of human character elicit God's wrath. It is the response of his holiness to all wickedness and rebellion.

Why is God angry with sin? Because **sinful, wicked people** have pushed **the truth away from themselves,** substituting the truth about him with a fantasy of their own imagination (1:25). They have suppressed the truth God naturally reveals to everyone in order to believe anything that supports their own self-centered lifestyles. Once humans have abandoned God, it will not take long for the effects to be felt in their relationships with each other.

God cannot tolerate sin because his nature is morally perfect. He cannot ignore or condone such willful rebellion. He wants to remove the sin and restore the sinner, but the sinner must not distort or reject the truth. **But God shows his anger from heaven** against those who persist in sinning.

While we do not have many idol-worshiping religions in our neighborhoods, we do find those who suppress the truth about God. These people

- replace God with the worship of success, property, and wealth,
- demote God by elevating their own homespun philosophies, and
- ignore God by devoting themselves to family, leisure, and career—rejecting his claim on their lives.

1:19-20 The **truth about God** has been clearly revealed by God. The clues to God's existence and character have traditionally been called general

revelation. God could have kept humans in ignorance about himself. But he chose to reveal himself, generally in nature and specifically through the Scriptures and Jesus Christ. Because God has made certain facts about himself **known instinctively,** people will someday have to give an account before God of why they chose to ignore his existence and his character.

But how could a loving God send anyone to hell, especially someone who has never heard the Good News of Jesus? In fact, says Paul, **people have seen the earth and sky and all that God made**—therefore, **they can clearly see his invisible qualities.** Also, everyone has an inner sense of what God requires, but they choose not to live up to it. Put another way, people's moral standards are always better than their behavior. If people suppress God's truth in order to live their own way, they have **no excuse.** They know the truth, and they will have to endure the consequences of ignoring it.

The paradox can't be missed—all people can "clearly see" God's "invisible qualities." How? God created the world with natural processes, with cause and effect. In the same way that observing a painting leads a person to conclude that there is an artist, so to observe the tremendous creation is to conclude that there is a supreme Creator, one with eternal power and divinity. This is part of the truth that unsaved people are suppressing.

One look at creation in all its splendor tells people that a mighty power made this world—but not just an abstract, impersonal force; rather, a personal God (Psalm 19:1-4). Thus, creation shows both God's eternal power and his divine nature. Indeed, nature reveals a God of might, intelligence, intricate detail, order, beauty, and power; a God who controls powerful forces. God's qualities are revealed through creation (Acts 14:17), although creation's testimony has been distorted by the Fall. Adam's sin resulted in a divine curse upon the whole natural order (Genesis 3:17-19), thorns and thistles were an immediate result, and natural disasters have been common from Adam's day to ours. Nature itself is eagerly awaiting its own redemption from the effects of sin (8:19-21; Revelation 22:3).

Then why do we need missionaries if people can know about God through nature (the creation)?

- Although people know that God exists, they suppress that truth by their wickedness and thus deny him. Missionaries can point out their error.
- Although people may believe there is a God, they refuse to commit themselves to him. Missionaries can help persuade them.
- Missionaries can convince people who reject God of the dangerous consequences of their actions.
- Though nature reveals God, people need to be told about Jesus and how through him they can have a personal relationship with God.
- Missionaries are needed to help the church obey the great commission of our Lord (Matthew 28:19-20).

Knowing that God exists is not enough. People must learn that God is loving. They must understand what he did to show that love to us. They must be shown how to accept his forgiveness of their sins. (See also 10:14-15.)

1:21 People's denial of their own awareness of God is what left them without excuse. When Paul says that **they knew God,** he is not describing a knowledge that could save them but a knowledge that simply recognized God's existence. He was describing an awareness of God, that, if not suppressed, would be nurtured by God. But since human beings have, in fact, suppressed the truth about God, the following calamities ensued: (1) **they wouldn't worship him as God;** (2) they couldn't **give thanks;** (3) in the void, **they began to think up foolish ideas of what God was like;** and (4) in the end **their minds became dark and confused.**

When people refuse to recognize God as Creator, they will also fail to glorify or thank him for his gifts—food, clothing, shelter, even life itself. When they neglect God, they open the door to evil. To omit what is good inevitably leads to committing what is evil. Ingratitude may seem like a small thing, but it begins the downward spiral into

depravity. To forget to thank God for all he is and all he has done reveals a dangerous self-centeredness. This causes futile thinking and planning, darkness, pride, blindness, and finally total departure from God that bursts into a flood of sin.

1:22 Without answers based on the reality of God, people seek heroes among those who claim **to be wise** and will boldly say there are no answers. Under such circumstances, it is seen as a sign of sophistication and intelligence to refuse to acknowledge God's existence. But by biblical definition, people who refuse to believe in God are **utter fools** (Psalm 14:1). The evidence of God's existence is so plain and clear that to ignore it is totally foolish.

To some people, statements like these by Paul appear to be intolerant of other religions and views. The objection is often voiced in a question: "Well, after all, the point is that people are naturally somewhat religious; so isn't the most important thing not what religion you follow, but that you follow some religion?" The fallacy behind the question is that it still assumes that man is at the center, not God. The emphasis is not on believing what is true but on believing. Paul was speaking in a world that was inundated with gods. He would have been horrified to think that anyone would understand him to be saying that a little religion is a good thing! To Paul, even a lot of religion was bad if it was not true.

1:23 Whether they claim it or not, people are religious beings. By their very nature, they are bound to worship and serve something beyond themselves. It may be another idea of God, a person, a thing, or even some false notion that no God exists. Anyone who rejects the Creator will end up worshiping the creature. And how foolish that they turn their backs on the **glorious, ever-living God** in order to worship **idols**—things created by humans. Because they were created by humans, they owe their existence to humans. This places people in control of their own gods.

How can intelligent people turn to idolatry? Idolatry begins when people reject what they know about God. Instead of looking to him as the Creator and sustainer of life, they see themselves as the center of the universe. They soon invent gods that are convenient projections of their own selfish plans and decrees. These gods may be wooden figures, or they may be things we desire—such as money, power, or comfort. They may even be misrepresentations of God himself—a result of making God in their image, instead of the reverse. The common denominator is this: Idolaters worship the things God made rather than God himself.

1:24 God left those who spurned him to their own desires. Without his guidance, they degenerated into ruinous moral practices. This rush into sinful patterns can be seen in societies as well as in individuals. When people and nations refuse to repent, sin takes over and draws people into a life where there is no sense of right and wrong. Without God's remedy, his righteousness, the end is destruction.

Here Paul introduces the subject of sexual impurity. He returns to it in verses 26 and 27. The context indicates that he is referring in part to cultic prostitution and the fertility cults that made use of temple prostitutes in their rites. Throughout history, paganism has shown a remarkable capacity for substituting the pursuit of sexual pleasure for the pursuit of holiness. Rejection of God is often accompanied by deification of sex or reproduction. Because people ignored their innate awareness of godly restraints, personal desire became the standard of behavior. Paul did not hesitate to point out the devastating effects of sin on the most personal aspects of human life. Without God's righteousness, wrong rules.

1:25 Just as people exchanged the glory of God for lackluster images (1:23), they also traded **what they knew was the truth about God** for **lies**. These people have completely turned their back on God and replaced him with **things** that they then **worshiped**. Although many may refuse to acknowledge God's existence, that doesn't change the truth of his existence and the fact that he will indeed be **praised forever**. God's worthiness to be praised is not affected by human beings' rebellion or their poor choices. God will be praised forever, though there are many who, by their deliberate exchange of truth for lies, will not be present to participate.

1:26-27 There have always been those willing to believe that human desires are self-regulating. They do not believe that any action they enjoy could possibly be wrong. When the desire for the true God is rejected, other gods are raised up. When the desire for God is rejected, **shameful desires** take control. When people refuse God and his standards, when they are left to themselves as their own gods, nothing can stop them from seeking to fulfill their passions. Perversions of sex became rampant. God's plan for natural sexual relationships is his ideal for his creation. It is the height of foolishness to think that any sex act is acceptable as long as "no one gets hurt."

Paul's treatment of homosexual behavior falls in the middle of two other major areas at which God shows anger (1:18). The first is sinful worship; the third is a whole list of personal and relational sins.

It is important to note that Paul is using homosexual practices to indicate the extent to which sin has brought chaos into every area of life. Homosexuality (to exchange or abandon natural relations of sex) was as widespread in Paul's day as it is in ours. Many pagan practices encouraged it. God is willing to receive anyone who comes to him in faith, and Christians should love and accept others no matter what their background. But homosexual behavior is strictly forbidden in Scripture (see Leviticus 18:22). Homosexuality is considered an acceptable practice by many in our world today—even by some churches. But society does not set the standard for God's law. Many homosexuals believe that their desires are normal and that they have a right to express them. But God does not obligate nor encourage us to fulfill all of our desires (even normal ones). Desires that violate God's laws must be controlled. God offers freedom from those sins through Jesus Christ and power to control our desires through the Holy Spirit.

Sin has a **penalty**, and the punishment is in keeping with the offense. The exact consequences of sin are not predictable, but they are inevitable. These people cannot call themselves helpless victims; a sinful choice was made, and it carries its penalty. Unfortunately, the due penalty also has a way of spilling over into other lives. The connectedness of everything in creation makes it almost impossible to confine sinful penalties. Often a truly painful consequence is seeing how a sin we unleashed affects others.

1:28 Humans sat in judgment on God to decide whether he fit the qualifications of a God that would be to their liking; they decided he did not meet those qualifications and so **refused to acknowledge** him. They had the knowledge (they were not ignorant), but they did not want to use it. In our own times we have seen a belittling of God as no more than a pale extension of our wishful thinking, someone made in our image. Yet those most vocal in condemning the authoritative Christian view of God have been busy at work creating people who think of themselves as gods. Paul's discussion is not out-of-date. The same rebellion against God is alive in the human heart.

When people choose to reject God, he allows them to do so. Their minds become depraved, and they lose the ability to distinguish between right and wrong. Their **evil minds** lead them to **do things that should never be done,** indicating acts not just offensive to God, but also offensive by human standards. God does not usually stop us from making choices against his will. He lets us declare our supposed independence from him, even though he knows that in time we will become slaves to our own rebellious choices—we will lose our freedom not to sin. Does life without God look like freedom to you? Look more closely. There is no worse slavery than slavery to sin.

1:29-31 That these people's **lives became full of every kind of wickedness** suggests a state of being filled to the point of overflowing. Once the mind of man had become depraved (1:28), it followed that the creative power of thought was turned to the pursuit of evil. Paul listed over twenty different ways in which the mind can be focused once it has turned away from God. (For similar lists, see 1 Corinthians 6:9-10; Galatians 5:19-21; and Colossians 3:5.) The catalog of sins may not be in any particular order, but it emphasizes the extent of the evidence against humanity. Who cannot find in himself more than one among these qualities?

1:32 In the previous verses Paul pointed out several results when God abandons people to pursue their evil desires. He was convinced that each person in rebellion against God perceives the final outcome of that rebellion. But even the finality of death is ignored by many.

How are people **fully aware of God's death penalty?** Human beings, created in God's image, have a basic moral nature and a conscience. This truth is understood beyond religious circles. Psychologists, for example, say that the rare person who has no conscience has a serious personality disorder, one that is extremely difficult to treat. Most people instinctively know when they do wrong—but they may not care. Not only have they turned their backs on God and realized that their deeds deserve the ultimate penalty of death, they also are continuing in their sin and encouraging it in others.

The cause for the appalling condition of our world—the horrible perversions and the rampant evil—lies in people's rebellion against God. Although knowledge of God is accessible, people turn their backs on it, close their minds to it, and go their own way, worshiping whatever they choose. With this stroke, Paul places the final touches on the dismal picture of man's condition apart from God. From here, he will move on to deal with those who might use their knowledge of God as an excuse for missing his righteousness.

ROMANS 2

GOD'S JUDGMENT OF SIN / 2:1-16
Having painted in large strokes the fate of humankind apart from God, Paul abruptly switches his attention to a new audience. He shapes his next thoughts in a style used widely at that time, called the diatribe. In a diatribe, the writer verbally attacks and attempts to destroy the ideas of the opposition. The anticipated questions or objections of the opposition are expressed or noted and then answered or refuted. Paul probably did not have an individual, but a character type in mind as he began his diatribe.

2:1 The critic here is Jewish, for Paul is focusing primarily on Jews. Paul had criticized the horrible evil of the Gentiles, their sins of idolatry and homosexuality and their general lifestyle. This Jewish critic nodded in agreement and assumed that he was free from such vices. Many Jews believed that their national heritage would save them; they thought their privilege of birth ensured entrance into God's Kingdom (Matthew 3:8-9). They went to great lengths to separate themselves from "unclean" Gentiles. So when Paul finished his list of characteristics of those whom God will judge (chapter 2), Paul knew that his Jewish listeners would agree that such

people are **terrible** and deserve to **be punished.** But then Paul says that the Jews have no right to pass judgment, because they are **just as bad.** They are not guiltless and therefore have **no excuse.** Their attitude freely condemned others' sins but somehow overlooked those sins in themselves (see Matthew 7:2-3).

2:2 Paul assumes that all his readers will agree with him regarding God's judgment. Human judgment is based on prejudice and partial perception; God's judgment is based on the truth—he judges on the basis of the facts about what we do. And there is no doubt that God **will punish** sinners.

2:3 Seven times in the first three verses, Paul used various forms of the Greek word for judgment *(krima).* Though human beings pass judgments, their judgments are judged by God. When we stand condemned before God, we have no higher court of appeal.

Paul ridicules the idea that a person might escape God's judgment by correctly analyzing the wrong in others. Those Jews, who were guilty of the same sins for which God would **judge and condemn** the Gentiles, would not escape God's judgment. All people, Jews and Gentiles, have sinned, and all stand condemned before God. Paul repeats this theme over and over.

2:4 God is **kind** in giving us life and its fullness to enjoy; he is **tolerant** and **patient** as he bears our ingratitude and sin. He postpones punishment in order to give people **time to turn from** their **sin** (see 2 Peter 3:15). But Paul was concerned that these Jews, overconfident in their special status with God and unwilling to repent of sin, were showing contempt for God's blessings. So Paul reminds them that God's kindness is also meant to lead them to repentance, because all people need to repent!

2:5-6 This kind of person has sat in self-righteous judgment of others for too long and has lived as described in verse 4—by showing contempt for all God has given (see also Deuteronomy 10:16 and Jeremiah 4:4). People receive blessings but stubbornly continue in sin, refusing to repent. It is difficult for self-righteous people to repent. Paul's readers who boasted of their faith yet refused **to turn from** their **sin** were **storing up terrible punishment** when God's wrath would be poured out upon them.

Though we do not know exactly when that will occur, we do know that no one will escape that **day of judgment when God, the just judge of all the world, will judge all people according to what they have done.** In the end, what matters most is not exactly when in history the day of God's wrath arrives, but that the clock is ticking. "It is destined that each person dies only once and after that comes judgment" (Hebrews 9:27). We do not know the day of the Lord, nor the day of our own death. We will treat both days with more respect if we call them "near."

God's judgment will be impartial, and it will be according to what people have done. Final judgment will be based upon character. All people will be held accountable for the truth that was available to them and what they did with it. (See also Job 34:11; Psalm 62:12; Proverbs 24:12; Jeremiah 17:10; 32:19; Matthew 16:27; 2 Corinthians 5:10; Revelation 20:12; 22:12.)

2:7 This **doing what is good** is a result of new life in Christ. Real faith generates good works in a believer's life. To **persist** in this is a characteristic of the growing and progressing Christian (see Luke 8:15; Hebrews 12:1; James 1:3). Again Paul is emphasizing God's impartial treatment of all people (Ephesians 2:8-10).

Persistence and hope in God are rewarded by meeting the goal—**glory, honor,** and **immortality** in **eternal life.** In the end, people will receive what they really want. If we desire to be with God, he will gladly fulfill our wish; but if our inmost desire is to keep God at arm's length, the distance will be preserved forever. Many people want it both ways: They think that eternal life might be nice as long as God doesn't interfere with their present life. But we must choose. Will we persist in wanting our own way, or in wanting God's way?

2:8 Paul still has in mind the self-confident, self-righteous person, who through his own self-seeking has actually turned away from the truth and resisted the gospel, and is following his own evil path. God's **anger and wrath** are promised to those who have turned from him, yet are claiming to have a special place with him. They will receive the wrath and anger that they thought would fall on others.

2:9 God's impartiality and our behavior ensure the final results. There will be **trouble and calamity** for those who reject God. In simple terms, Jews or Gentiles who do evil, even if they don't perceive it that way, will receive the consequences of final judgment. Just as the gospel and salvation came first for the Jew and then for the Gentile (1:16), so will judgment by God. Those self-righteous Jews who thought they were somehow protected from judgment because of their heritage will not only find that they will be judged; they will be first in line!

2:10 In contrast to verse 9, Jews or Gentiles **who do good** (those who fulfill the law in Christ), no matter how incomplete they may feel that goodness to be, will receive a reward. As with the consequences of evil, there may be immediate benefits of a right relationship with God, but the full measure of **glory, honor,** and **peace** is for the future. Paul's main point is that God's judgment is based on truth and results, not on who we are, where we came from, our upbringing, or our intentions. The final question will be, What did you do with what you knew?

2:11 God does not show favoritism for Jew over Gentile when it comes to judgment for sin, no matter what the Jews had come to assume or expect.

This personally addresses those who adopt Israel's mind-set that religious heritage guarantees salvation. This verse answers the most common perception on how God will judge. God is usually pictured as the deity who grades on the curve. Those holding this idea almost always express the hope that they are somehow just above the passing line, but they have no way of really knowing. They blatantly hope that God will show favoritism. This verse obliterates that hope. There is no passing line. Instead, sin has created a moral chasm over which no one can leap. The gospel gives us a way to reach the other side. God offers us something far better than favoritism. He offers grace. Having Christian parents or attending the church of our ancestors does not guarantee one's salvation. Salvation is given to individuals on the basis of personal faith in Jesus Christ.

2:12 Gentiles will be judged on the basis of the knowledge available to them. They won't be condemned for failing to conform to a code of laws they knew nothing about. They will not perish because they didn't have the Jewish law; they will perish because they have sinned. The **Jews** will be judged by God's written law because they had been trained in it. They will be judged for sinning against the **law** that they knew so well. People are condemned not for what they don't know, but for what they do with what they know. Those who know God's written word and his law will be judged by them. Those who have never seen a Bible still know right from wrong; they will be judged guilty because they did not keep even the standards of their own conscience.

2:13 Those faithful Jews who attend the synagogues every Sabbath and hear God's law read over and over may consider themselves to be righteous, but just hearing is not enough, because **it is not merely knowing the law that brings God's approval.** Those who do good (2:10) and those who **obey the law will be declared right in God's sight**—this includes both Jews and Gentiles (see also Leviticus 18:5 and James 1:22-25). The obedience that Paul describes is perfect and well beyond our reach. Our being made right with God must be sought and found elsewhere. Paul effectively closes many appealing doors while he describes the only one that leads to eternal life.

2:14 Some **Gentiles** who did not know anything about **God's written law** had moral sensitivity and lived as though following it. They had the law of conscience. The knowledge of God's character was available to them, for they knew **right from wrong.** Their moral awareness will serve in place of the law to judge them.

Paul does not attempt to prove that people are incapable of any good. His point is that not one of us is capable of perfect goodness. At the human level, we all behave more or less in line with the standards of our society. But righteousness is not determined by what most people do, or even by what most people think might be possible for someone who tries very hard. Righteousness is God's standard, God's character. Comparisons with others are of no help when we measure ourselves before God's standard. Ultimately, whatever our background, we will be held accountable by God for our life.

2:15 All cultures and nations, no matter how different, have a common recognition that some things are **right** and others are wrong. Gentiles who do not know God's law have a moral sensitivity in their hearts that matches what God's law requires. A conscience is an inward monitor that lets us know when we have done wrong. What the law does for the Jew, the conscience does for the Gentile, acting as **God's law written within them.**

2:16 The only way to truly judge a person is to judge his or her **secret life.** Some actions that appear good may be wrongly motivated; other, less visible actions may be done with good intentions. In this manner, both Jews and Gentiles will be judged. In the end, **God will judge.** Nothing will have to be explained to God. His judgment will be perfect, based on his perfect knowledge of every action and every motive. God will judge through Jesus Christ (see John 5:27). The gospel Paul preached included the wonderful message that though judgment is inevitable, it will be conducted through Christ's mediation. For those who are trusting in Christ for their righteousness, God's judgment does not include the fear of exposure and punishment. As Paul later says joyfully, "There is no condemnation for those who belong to Christ Jesus" (8:1).

THE JEWS AND THE LAW / 2:17-29

Paul knew that among those in Rome who would vigorously agree with his first chapter, there would be legalistic Jews, proud of their heritage as God's chosen people. But their agreement with his case would surely turn to anger as they realized that they were being included in the judgment, as equal members in the fallen human race. Possessing God's law increased both privilege and responsibility. Because these Jews knew more, they were expected to do more. At first they thought they were Paul's allies, but suddenly they were confronted by him.

Those of us who have grown up in a Christian family are the religiously privileged of today. Paul's condemnation applies to us if we do not live up to what we know.

2:17 Paul pointed out that Jews had **God's law,** worshiped the one true God, knew right from wrong, and yet regarded themselves better than all those who didn't have the law (i.e., were not Jews). **"You boast that all is well between yourself and God."** The kind of knowing and boasting described here is a sham without a life that demonstrates the knowledge. Paul was bluntly asking, "If you claim to be Jewish, why don't you live up to the name?" We who claim to be Christians, do we live up to this name?

2:18 Knowing **what** God **wants** and knowing **right from wrong** are the result of having been **taught his law.** God's word is not only a record of God's will; it is also a guideline to determine what course of action is best for us. Through God's word we can be trained or instructed in how to appreciate what is good. Yet how often do we, surrounded by a wealth of spiritual resources, live no differently than our pagan neighbors! We need to put our knowledge into action.

2:19 Paul saw these people as dangerously self-confident. It was apparent from their lives that they could not back up their claims. Paul's sarcasm here parallels Jesus' words to the Pharisees, "How terrible it will be for you teachers of religious law and you Pharisees. For you cross land and sea to make one convert, and then you turn him into twice the son of hell as you yourselves are" (Matthew 23:15). A Jew would see himself as **a guide for the blind,** but Jesus repeatedly called them "blind guides" (Matthew 15:14; 23:16, 24). They claimed to be **a beacon light,** but were unwilling to recognize the light of the world (John 9:5, 39-41).

2:20 The Jews that Paul had in mind considered themselves not only separate from the Gentiles, but also capable of teaching those whom they considered **ignorant** in spiritual matters. These people knew they had the truth and were proud of it! But assuming the teaching role carries with it heavy responsibility, especially in spiritual training (James 3:1). Knowing what ought to be taught is only one part of being an effective teacher. Practicing what is taught is the clearest test of a teacher. If you are a teacher, can you pass this test?

2:21-23 Anyone proud of his spiritual background should take a careful look at himself. The Jews were called to be guides of the Gentiles, and salva-

tion is of the Jews (John 4:22), but their response to God's plan for them had made them arrogant. The Jew of whom Paul was thinking possessed the law and was confident that this position allowed him to teach all those who were ignorant without the law. However, Paul's questions were designed to force the listener to realize that not all Jews could claim such superiority. Many did not understand God's law, had false confidence in it, and could not apply it readily to their daily life. Without God's Spirit and the gospel, they had neither superiority nor all the answers. Having, knowing, and reading the law are not enough.

The Jews needed to **teach** themselves, not others, by their law. The law is more than legalistic minimum requirements—it is a guideline for living according to God's will. It is also a reminder that we cannot please God without a proper relationship to him. The general principle is that it is much easier to tell others how to behave than to behave properly ourselves. As Jesus pointed out, even withholding what rightfully belongs to someone else is stealing (Mark 7:9-13); and looking on another person with lustful, adulterous intent is **adultery** (Matthew 5:27-28). Before we accuse others, we must look at ourselves and see if that same sin, in any form, exists within us. The question, **do you steal from pagan temples,** may be making the contrast between condemning **idolatry** while in private valuing them so highly that they become worth stealing. By **knowing** God's law and then **breaking it,** the Jews had given God great **dishonor.** The unmerited honor that God had given Jews by choosing them was being treated with unhealthy pride and outright disrespect.

Each of the questions touches on matters in the Ten Commandments. Theft, adultery, idolatry, and dishonoring God were all prohibited. His assumption is not that every reader would answer yes to each question, but that each reader would find his life spotlighted at least once.

2:24 Those who glory in God's law and brag about their relationship to him and then live in disobedience bring God into disrepute among nonbelievers. Paul quotes from Isaiah 52:5, written about Israel's exile to foreign lands. It was the Jews' rampant evil and flouting of God's law that led to the exile. They had boasted about being God's chosen people, but because of their sin, their nation was destroyed. The Gentiles despised a God who, it appeared, could not save his own people. Paul's parallel was that Jews were again resting with false confidence on their being "chosen" and their possession of God's law. Their sins were still causing Gentiles to blaspheme a God who would choose such a nation.

2:25 Circumcision was fundamental to the Jews— it symbolized the covenant between God and Abraham's descendants (Genesis 17:9-14). It was the expression of Israel's national identity and was a requirement for all Jewish men. Circumcision was a physical reminder to Jews of their national heritage and privilege. Many were confident that it sealed their position with God. But just as having the law did not make a person right before God, neither was circumcision in itself a cause for confidence. To be circumcised was **worth something only if you obey God's law** (see Galatians 5:3). To be circumcised and yet break God's law was no better than not being circumcised at all. What God desires is a pure and obedient heart.

Symbols require some sense of reality in order to be significant; otherwise they are empty. Signing a contract does not take the place of doing the work. In fact, signing a contract and then refusing to carry out its terms is considered a serious breach. It is worse than a failure. It is a deception.

2:26-27 Paul had already pointed out that circumcision was a valuable part of a system governed by obedience. Where there was no obedience, circumcision was of no value. By the same logic, when obedience was present, the real objective was accomplished, even though circumcision had not occurred. In other words, **Gentiles** who **obey God's law** are as good in God's sight as a law-abiding, circumcised Jew and could receive **the rights and honors of being** God's **own people.** A Gentile who kept the law would be in a position to condemn a Jew who broke it, no matter how well that Jew knew the law. The Jew who required strict observance to every letter of the law, but was not a doer of the law, was actually a transgressor of that law because he had missed the point.

We must keep in mind that Paul is dealing here with absolutes. Obedience is not a matter of degrees. James saw this clearly: "The person who keeps all of the laws except one is as guilty as the person who has broken all of God's laws" (James 2:10). The sharp division that the law creates reveals the startling nature of the gospel. The righteousness we might try to create by living up to the law, circumcised or not, leads to hopelessness. Perfect obedience is beyond us.

2:28-29 Paul is adamant: The **circumcision** that God wanted was not cutting the flesh, and cutting the flesh did not fulfill the law. Paul is not inventing new theology, but urging his readers to reexamine the testimony of the Old Testament Scriptures. To be one of God's children—**a true Jew**— was not merely to be a circumcised Jew, but to be one who loved God and followed his laws. The kind of Jews God wanted were not those people tied to a heritage, rather people whose lives were pleasing to God. It was a matter of the **heart.** The person whose heart is right with God because of God's Holy Spirit will be of great value to God. A Jew transformed by God's Spirit would be living up to his name, for he would be praiseworthy in God's eyes. He would fulfill what the law required but was powerless to produce.

ROMANS 3

GOD REMAINS FAITHFUL / 3:1-8

Having firmly described the shared sinful condition of humankind, Paul turns to several thoughts about the unique benefits of being Jewish. He wants to remind his Jewish brothers that their lack of faith has not hindered God's plan. Paul does not want his people to miss the significance of God's faithfulness. In spite of their failures, God still allows them to be the people of the Messiah. In fact, the Jews' lack of faith is a clear witness to the absolute need for a Savior. Neither they nor we can save ourselves. God's faithfulness is our only hope.

3:1 Paul's conversation with his Jewish critic continues into this chapter. At the end of chapter 2, Paul had clearly stated that true "Jewishness" is not a matter of heritage, but a matter of one's relationship with God, and that true circumcision is not on the body, but on the heart. The Jewish response might have well been, **"Then what's the advantage of being a Jew? Is there any value in the Jewish ceremony of circumcision?"** Paul gives his response.

3:2 Paul answers **yes**, there are advantages for those members of God's chosen nation. **The Jews were entrusted with the whole revelation of God** (Exodus 19–20; Deuteronomy 4:8). That great privilege alone made the Jews even more responsible to live up to God's requirements. Paul himself was a Jew, and even though he became a dynamic Christian, he did not turn his back on his heritage. In fact, he realized that the prophets, the law, and God's plan all pointed to fulfillment in Jesus Christ. Therefore, he could confidently state that being a Jew and being circumcised did have meaning, but only as part of God's total plan. The Jews were entrusted with God's words, preserving them until the coming of Christ, who was the fulfillment of the prophetic Scriptures.

3:3 While it was true that many Jews **were unfaithful** to God or to what they had been entrusted, that didn't change the fact of God's faithfulness. Many Jews rejected the gospel and thus failed to understand their own Scriptures. But Israel's unfaithfulness did not determine God's faithfulness. God had always been faithful to Israel, despite the nation's failings, and God would continue to be faithful to his covenant with them.

3:4 In the strongest terms he could use, Paul wanted to drive home the point that the combined self-justification of the whole world could not stand up to God's truth. If God and every person were to disagree, there still would not be any doubt about who was right. The fact that many people are unfaithful (see Psalm 116:11) by suppressing the truth (1:18), exchanging the truth for a lie (1:25), and rejecting the truth (2:8), doesn't change the deeper fact that **God is true.** God's purpose for Israel and his plan for all people remained unshaken.

Paul quoted from one of the profoundly confessional passages in the Old Testament (Psalm 51:4). It records the repentance of David following his confrontation with the prophet Nathan over his sin with Bathsheba. In the revelation of his sin David realized, as all of us must, that there is no denial before God. He sees even those things that we hide so well in ourselves and perhaps even come to believe never happened. Kings were used to getting their way. We tend toward

the same arrogance. Before God it carries no weight at all.

3:5-6 The apologist in Paul can foresee further objections arising. He poses them in the question of this verse. He understands that people are usually more willing to rationalize than repent, and that their minds will be pondering ways to elude God's righteous judgment. Paul knows they are thinking, "If my sinfulness makes God look so good, then why should he punish me? I'm actually helping him out!" This was an attempt to make it seem **unfair for God to punish** sinners.

Many believe that God's wrath contradicts his loving nature. But God judges based on his own character, not on society's norm for fairness. God is not accountable to some external, vague notion of fair play. His personal moral uprightness is the standard by which he judges.

Eventually the final day of reckoning will come when God "will judge all people according to what they have done" (2:6). God must and will judge sin—he has the right to judge the world because he is God, and he is holy and just. Paul answers by reaffirming God's character. **If God is not just, how is he qualified to judge the world?** No person can be an exception to God's laws; that would violate God's character and disqualify him as the Judge.

3:7 This is the same question from verse 5, posed with different words. The root problem is in people's misunderstanding of God's righteousness when he is patient to both unfaithful Jews and sinful Gentiles. Jews cannot condemn Gentiles; both are in the same predicament. Both need to rely on God's righteousness in his dealings with them and then choose to trust him or face his inevitable wrath for their sins.

3:8 The gospel Paul preached was being misconstrued because he argued that obeying the law would not bring salvation. Paul, and possibly the Roman Christians, had heard this objection from Jews who were accusing him of teaching lawlessness. If Jews or Gentile Christians interpreted Paul's words that God is faithful despite people's faithlessness to mean that God's laws need not be followed, then they could reach the incorrect conclusion that **the more we sin the better it is.** Paul dismisses this perverse reasoning with the terse words, **"Those who say such things deserve to be condemned."**

ALL PEOPLE ARE SINNERS / 3:9-20

Paul applies the concept of depravity he taught in 1:18-32 to the Jews in these verses. Paul now brings to a close the lengthy introduction of the charges against humanity that he began back in 1:18. He continually maintains that everyone stands guilty before God. Every person must accept that he or she is sinful and liable for God's condemnation. Only then can they understand and receive God's wonderful gift of salvation.

3:9 To the question of whether there was any value in being a Jew, Paul had said yes (3:2). But to the question as to whether **Jews are better** than Gentiles, Paul answers **no**. The reason? Jews and Gentiles alike are **under the power of sin**. Both need God's grace. Gentiles have no excuse (1:20), and neither do Jews (2:1).

3:10 There can be no more argument about special privileges for the Jews, for from their own Scriptures Paul strings together a series of verses outlining universal indictment. The advantage of being a Jew does not apply to salvation. All have sinned; no one is righteous. **No one** can earn right standing with God.

As is the pattern throughout the New Testament, writers do not always quote word for word from the Old Testament. Their notions about making exact citations were less stringent than ours. And because writers were probably working from memory as often as they were working with a text before them, their quotations tend to be allusions more than they are direct references. At other times their quotes may have been exact to the translation they did have before them, such as the Greek version of the Old Testament.

3:11-12 The phrase **no one is seeking God** is from Psalm 14:2. Seeking is a way of expressing what is most important to us. This kind of seeking means training ourselves to turn to God first for help, to fill our thoughts with his desires, to take his character for our pattern, and to serve and obey him in everything. The phrase **all have turned away from God; all have gone wrong** is from Psalm 14:3. The failure to seek God does not leave a person immobilized; rather, it sets him or her on a course of destruction. Whatever does not include the seeking of God ends up leading people in the wrong direction.

3:13-14 From Psalm 5:9 comes the statement that **their talk is foul, like the stench from an open grave.** Jesus made it clear that the indications of sinfulness come from inside of us (Matthew 15:11). Up until this verse, the evidence of rebellion has been mainly evident between a person and God. Here Paul begins to point out that sinfulness corrupts human relationships too. The gift of communication becomes twisted into a weapon to deceive others.

From Psalm 10:7 comes the picture of sinful people's **mouths full of cursing and bitterness.**

Eventually, rebellion against God shows itself by tainting the way a person speaks. Cursing and bitterness may strike us first as offensive expressions, but they are also clues about a person's inward condition.

3:15-17 Isaiah 59:7-8 states that rebellion against God leads to violence against others. The shameful milestones of history are marked with bloodstains from the atrocities committed by those who freed themselves from God. There is always talk of peace, but apart from God, there can be no real peace.

3:18 Quoting from Psalm 36:1, Paul states the bottom line condition of these people: **they have no fear of God to restrain them.** To fear the Lord is to recognize God for who he is: holy, almighty, righteous, pure, all-knowing, all-powerful, and all-wise. When we regard God correctly, we gain a clearer picture of ourselves: sinful, weak, frail, and needy. When we recognize who God is and who we are, we will fall at his feet in humble respect. Only then will he show us how to choose his way.

Paul's brief tour of truth ends almost full circle. He began with the fact that no one is like God (who is righteous), and he ends with the parallel truth that we lack fear of God. Some people lack this fear out of ignorance, while others, through familiarity with God, lose the sense of humble awe that ought to characterize a person's attitude before God.

3:19 The verses above quoted from the Scriptures condemn all people, but especially those under **the law,** the Jews. Those who read the verses above are silenced. There are no more excuses to be made, no more self-defenses uttered. No one has any **excuses;** everyone is liable for **judgment.** And if the Jews—God's special chosen people— can say nothing in their own behalf, then no one can.

In the silence filling the court, one thought is clear: guilty as charged. That accountability of guilt must be answered, even though every explanation and excuse had failed. We are held accountable to God because he is our Creator, the personal source behind the standard (law), and the faithful Judge. We owe our existence and obedience to this One.

3:20 With this all-inclusive statement, Paul closes his opening arguments that describe the state of human lostness. The purpose of the law is not to bring salvation, but to make us aware of sin.

The only way people can be **made right in God's sight** is for God to declare them so. No one can do it by trying to do **what** God's **law commands,** meaning keeping certain traditions, such as circumcision, in order to be identified as a Jew and so remain under God's covenant promises. These traditions have to do with identifying with God's people and maintain-ing one's relationship within that people. Again Paul drives the point home: being a knowledgeable, faith-ful, and law-keeping Jew doesn't make a person righ-teous. The law was not meant to become something the Jews boasted about; rather, it was given to elimi-nate anyone's boasting and to make all people aware of sin and their constant need for God's grace. The law only makes it painfully clear that people **aren't obeying it.**

CHRIST TOOK OUR PUNISHMENT / 3:21-31

Like the swelling waves of the tide, Paul's argument rolls over the predicament of the human race. After each wave of the gospel, the waters recede to reveal a new aspect or depth of the problem of sin. This wavelike approach to Paul's letter provides a number of views of the same issues, with slightly different emphases. Having stated such a strong case for our universal indictment under the law, Paul now turns to God's gracious alternative plan.

3:21 The words **but now** present an important shift in subject. Whereas the law was God's righ-teous standard, the righteousness required to live up to it was not within man's capacity. God, the measure of righteousness, had to provide a means of righteousness—of **being right in his sight.** The gospel is not a recent creation by God to respond to human failure. It was **promised in the Scriptures long ago.** Whereas the law pro-vided a measurement of the distance between God and his creatures, this righteousness from God has been provided in **a different way.** There is a way to be righteous before God. It is not by obeying the law, by being "Jewish" (see 3:20), yet it has always been in the Law and the Prophets, for they pointed to it.

3:22 The way to being **made right in God's sight** is the way of faith in **Jesus Christ to take away our sins.** Trusting in Jesus Christ means putting our confidence in him to forgive our sins, to make us right with God, and to empower us to live the way he taught us. God's solution is avail-able to all of us regardless of our background or past behavior. And this way is open to all who believe—both Jews and Gentiles.

Trusting in Jesus Christ is the only way **we all can be saved.** We all begin in the same place spir-itually, and there is only one way. Faith in Jesus Christ doesn't mean we understand everything that Christ has done for us, but it does mean that we believe he has done everything for us!

3:23 Paul has made it clear thus far in his letter that there is no difference between Jews and Gentiles when it comes to final judgment—**all have sinned.** If the law measures the distance between God and his creatures, then human righ-teousness is our attempt to bridge that distance by our own efforts. Paul is correct— we **all fall short.** But what is this **glorious standard** that we do not reach on our own? The word glory *(doxes),* from which we derive the word doxology, refers to the wonderful and awe-inspiring but indescrib-able presence of God himself. Sin keeps us from the presence of God.

Sinning confirms our status as sinners, and sin cuts us off from our holy God. Furthermore, sin leads to death (because it disqualifies us from living with God), regardless of how great or small each sin may seem. Sins are deadly, but sinners can be forgiven. There are no distinctions: we have all sinned; we all need a savior; Jesus Christ is the Savior; through faith we can receive his salvation.

3:24 Just as there is no distinction in our fallen-ness, Paul writes, so there is no distinction in the source of our justification. God justifies us; he **declares us not guilty** for our sins. When a judge in a court of law declares the defendant "not guilty," all the charges are removed from the person's record. Legally, it is as if the person had never been accused. When God forgives our sins, our record is wiped clean. From his perspective, it is as though we had never sinned. We do not have to anxiously work while hoping that in the end we will have been good enough to meet God's approval. Instead, those who believe in Jesus Christ and his sacrifice on the cross are freed—**Christ Jesus** has taken **away our sins.** Our righteousness before God depends entirely on him and can only be accepted as a gift from him. God **in his gracious kindness** assures us of our acceptance and then calls us to serve him as best we can out of sheer love for him.

3:25-26 In describing how God provided us with undeserved righteousness, Paul alludes to the sacrificial system in the Old Testament (see Leviticus 17:11). Only now, the life offered as sacrifice is not a spotless animal, but Christ. God **sent Jesus to take the punishment for our sins.** That punishment involved his death—he **shed his blood** for sinners. Because of what Jesus did on the cross, God can accept those who put their trust in Jesus.

Why did the punishment require shed blood? God had said from the beginning, "For the life of any creature is in its blood . . . It is the blood, representing life, that brings you atonement" (Leviticus 17:11). But the blood Paul mentions here is a particular blood—it is Christ's blood. Only the sacrificial death of Christ on the cross was the effective atonement for our sins. Christ stands in our place, having paid the penalty of death for our sin, and he could **satisfy God's anger against us.**

If God **did not** eternally **punish those who sinned** before Christ lived, then why did Christ die? Paul shows that, at the cross, God forgave the sin of all who believe—Old Testament believers looked forward in faith to Christ's coming and were saved, even though they did not know Jesus' name or the details of his earthly life. Unlike the Old Testament believers, we know about the God who loved the world so much that he gave his own Son (John 3:16). The question to answer is, Have you put your trust in him?

God is **entirely fair and just,** both in his inherent character, and in his dealings with sinners. Christ's death relates to both the past and the present. God did not completely reject his people, the Jews, even though they constantly rejected him. He was not being unfairly generous; rather, he was looking forward to the time when Jesus' death would be effective for all those who believed in God before Jesus came, as well as those who come after. The only answer to humanity's plight—that is, death because of sin—was given by God in the death and resurrection of Jesus Christ. This action fulfilled God's own law and his promises to Israel. The way to receive this answer for ourselves is through faith in Jesus Christ.

3:27-28 In conclusion, Paul writes that there is no room for personal pride. There can be no boasting heritage, law, or works. God's **acquittal is not based on our good deeds. It is based on our faith.** Why are we **made right with God through faith?**

- Faith eliminates the pride of human effort, because faith is not a deed that we do.
- Faith exalts what God has done, not what people do.
- Faith admits that we can't keep the law or measure up to God's standards—we need help.
- Faith is based on our relationship with God, not our performance for God.

Most religions prescribe specific duties that must be performed to make a person acceptable to God. Christianity is unique in teaching that the good works we do will not make us right with God. No amount of human achievement or progress in personal development will close the gap between God's moral perfection and our imperfect daily performance. So there can be no basis for pride. Good deeds are important, but they will not earn us eternal life. We are saved only by trusting in what God has done for us through Jesus Christ (see Ephesians 2:8-10).

3:29-30 Again, the **Jews** cannot claim sole propriety of God or deny that **Gentiles** can also receive God's saving grace. The Old Testament consistently recorded God's inclusion of the Gentiles in his plans. God had promised Abraham, "All the families of the earth will be blessed through you" (Genesis 12:3). Paul simply states the logical necessity. Because there is only one true God, then he is God of all his creation and calls both Jews and Gentiles to faith in him. The question of being **right with** God will not be settled according to those who have and have not been circumcised, but rather by their **faith,** whatever their physical lineage.

3:31 Paul envisions the Jewish critic raising a valid question: **If we emphasize faith, does this mean that we can forget about the law?** Paul answers, **Of course not! In fact, only when we have faith do we truly fulfill the law.** The law is not something that only the Jews can "do" for God; the law is for both Jews and Gentiles and can only be "done" through faith in Christ. Faith returns the law to its proper place and role in God's plan for people. Faith does not wipe out the Old Testament; rather, it makes God's dealings with the Jewish people understandable. (See also 5:20-21; 8:3-4; 13:9-10; Galatians 3:24-29; 1 Timothy 1:8.)

ROMANS 4

THE FAITH OF ABRAHAM / 4:1-25

In order to show the priority of faith, Paul turns his readers' attention to the origins of the Jewish race. He invites Abraham to make a contribution to the discussion by providing proof that faith was already the sole requirement between God and his creatures long before the law was given. Paul knows that if he can make a convincing case for Abraham's justification by faith, Jews might be more open to considering the claims of the gospel. After all, if the ancestral father of the Jewish nation did not attempt to earn his way into God's favor, neither should his offspring. Paul was anxious that his fellow Jews discover what he and their father Abraham had discovered—that justification comes by faith.

4:1 Paul continues his conversation with his Jewish questioner by mentioning **Abraham,** the great **founder** of the **Jewish nation.** Paul wants to make it clear that Abraham is forefather to all believers, whether Jews or Gentiles.

According to Jewish tradition, Abraham had been chosen by God for his unique role in history because he was the only righteous man alive at the time. Abraham was the epitome of what it meant to be a Jew, and he was the first Jew, the father of all Jews. John the Baptist had warned that being descendants of Abraham did not settle matters with God (see Luke 3:7-9). Jesus had anticipated the broader application of Abraham's faith (John 8:39). Clearly there was more to being a child of Abraham than simply being able to trace one's genealogy back to him. Abraham, too, had experienced **being saved by faith.**

4:2 If Abraham was **accepted** by God because of his **good deeds,** then **he would have had something to boast about.** This was the traditional rationale for religious pride that Paul expects from his Jewish questioner. Many Jews saw Abraham as being made right by God because of his obedience, especially to God's command to sacrifice Isaac. They believed that he had every reason to boast in his relationship with God. As Abraham's descendants, they believed that they also had reasons for pride. But Paul knocks down that argument by saying that **from God's point of view Abraham had no basis at all for pride.** To underscore his point, Paul quotes directly from Genesis 15:6, **"Abraham believed God, so God declared him to be righteous."** Abraham's works or obedience were not credited as righteousness, but his faith was.

4:4-5 Paul illustrates the difference between faith and work by describing the process of employment. An employer does not call an employee's wages **a gift;** instead, the **workers earn what they receive.** The employer is obligated to pay for work that has been completed. The wages are the agreed-upon amount, not a gift. If a person could earn right standing with God by his or her works (doing good, obeying the law), salvation wouldn't be free; it would be God's obligation, like payment for our efforts.

In contrast to the wage earner are the sinners (the ungodly) who trust in God. These people do not work—in other words, they have come to God because of faith and have not performed any rituals or followed any laws. Yet these **people are declared righteous because of their faith, not because of their work.** How could God do this?

4:6-8 Paul quotes from Psalm 32 (written by **King David**) to develop his explanation of how God can declare **an undeserving sinner** as **righteous.** David had written of the **joy of those whose disobedience is forgiven, whose sins are put out of sight.** God's forgiveness of sins by his sheer grace is the same as declaring people to be righteous apart from their works. He will explain this in coming verses.

4:9-10 Does **this blessing** (referring to 4:6-8) refer only to the **Jews, or is it for Gentiles** as well? Back to **Abraham** who was **declared righteous by God because of his faith.** It was Abraham's faith, not his faithfulness to certain rituals, that made him righteous. The critical question is: **Was he declared righteous only after he had been circumcised, or was it before he was circumcised?** Paul uses the term "circumcised" to refer to the whole of the law, because circumcision implies a desire to live under the demands of the law.

Paul immediately answers his own question—**God accepted him first, and then he was circumcised later!** God called Abraham in Genesis 12, declared him righteous in Genesis 15, then introduced the circumcision ceremony in Genesis 17.

4:11-12 Abraham's **circumcision** sealed the righteous standing he **already** had with God because of his **faith**. God said, "This will be a sign that you and they have accepted this covenant" (Genesis 17:11). **God had already accepted him and declared him to be righteous—even before he was circumcised.** So, **Abraham is the spiritual father of those who have faith but have not been circumcised.** He is the father of those who **are made right with God by faith.** That makes him the father of Gentiles who have believed in Jesus Christ as Savior. But he is also **the spiritual father of those who have been circumcised,** meaning the Jews. But this only applies to those Jews who **have the same kind of faith Abraham had before he was circumcised,** faith in God, not in their own goodness.

Abraham is father of all who believe in God. He is father of uncircumcised believers because he was uncircumcised when he was considered righteous; he is the father of circumcised believers not simply because of common Jewish heritage, but because they both had faith in God.

4:13 The **promise to give the whole earth to Abraham and his descendants** is found in Genesis 12:2-3 and Genesis 15:5. This promise was made to Abraham many years before the requirement of circumcision, and hundreds of years before the giving of the Ten Commandments (Exodus 20). Abraham believed God's promise, even though it was also made when he was almost one hundred years old and did not yet have any children. The promise was based on his **faith** not his **obedience** to a set of laws that did not yet exist.

4:14-15 If people must **obey God's law** and be **good enough** in order to be saved, then **faith is useless.** That, in turn, would make God's **promise also meaningless.** If the law does not bring righteousness, then why does it exist? **The law brings punishment.** In other words, in a world where people can make real choices, the law's presence automatically includes the possibility of failure and the consequences that would follow. The law's function is to help people realize their great sinfulness and to impose penalties on those who transgress it. **The only way to avoid breaking the law is to have no law to break.** If no one defines right and wrong, then no one knows the difference, and no one can sin.

4:16 What God gives by grace can only be accepted by **faith.** The promise given to Abraham that he and his countless offspring would inherit the world (4:13) refers to his spiritual offspring, those who follow his example of faith. Abraham had pleased God through **faith** alone, before he had ever heard about the **customs** that would become so important to the Jewish people. We too are saved by faith plus nothing. That makes Abraham **the father of all who believe,** not just of the Jewish nation.

4:17 The promise (or covenant) that God gave Abraham said that Abraham would be the **father of many nations** (Genesis 17:2-4) and that the entire world would be blessed through him (Genesis 12:3). This promise was fulfilled in Jesus Christ, who was from Abraham's line. Not only was Abraham the physical father of God's chosen nation, the Jews, he was also the father of God's people today, the church. Paul points out that the promise to Abraham to be the father of many nations extends beyond Israel to all the nations of the world.

Paul switches quickly into a description of God. Abraham and Paul believe in the same God, so what is the character of the God in whom they believe? Paul answers this question because believers need to have a clear understanding of the God being trusted. Paul's words here may seem awkward to us, but they were very familiar to the Jews. God is Creator—the giver and sustainer of life. He **brings the dead back to life** and **brings into existence what didn't exist before** (see also Deuteronomy 32:39; 1 Samuel 2:6). God has demonstrated his power. We know he can do the impossible!

4:18-19 Abraham **believed** God's promise that **he would become the father of many nations.** He believed it against all hope; that is, beyond any possible natural hope, because he was **too old to be a father at the age of one hundred** and his wife was well past childbearing age and **had never been able to have children.** Yet Abraham realized that God's ability to fulfill his promises outweighed the circumstances. So, **Abraham's faith did not weaken** even when they, a childless couple, had been promised **descendants** as **numerous as the stars.** It was **impossible,** but Abraham believed in God.

4:20 Abraham **never wavered in believing God's promise** because he was able to take God at his word. Abraham persisted in believing; thus, **his faith grew stronger.** He was able to trust in God to do what seemed humanly impossible, and even to glorify God before the results were apparent.

In spite of all this, Abraham was clearly human and imperfect. He had his weaknesses (fears) and bad habits (lying under pressure). The Bible describes Abraham with all his flaws, but as a man of faith. Thus, Abraham's faith could not have been anything but simple trust in God. Yet God honored that. Abraham is a model not just for the Jews, but for all people as a person of faith who realized he was totally dependent on his Creator for all things, even life itself.

4:21 Surrounded by a society fully immersed in paganism, where gods came by the dozens and were subject to human manipulation, Abraham dared to trust a God he could not control. Abraham did not say, "Well, we'll see what happens." Instead, **he was absolutely convinced that God was able to do anything he promised.** Abraham's faith was in God alone. And Abraham never doubted that God would fulfill his promise.

4:22 Abraham's faith, detailed above, was exactly the kind of faith God wanted and accepted when he **declared** Abraham **righteous** (4:3). It was this "absolutely convinced" faith that Paul called for when he preached the gospel—faith that relies on nothing but God; faith in God, who gives life, sustains life, and has power to keep his promises.

4:23-24 That Abraham's faith was credited to him as righteousness (Genesis 15:6) describes not

only how Abraham became righteous, but also how all his descendants (spiritual descendants, see 4:16) can become righteous before God. He will **declare us to be righteous if we believe in God, who brought Jesus our Lord back from the dead.** What makes us acceptable to God is not our works, but simply exercising the kind of faith Abraham had.

Abraham had to simply trust in God. That trust was confirmed in the immediate promises Abraham witnessed God fulfill in his lifetime. But he faced death without seeing all the promises fulfilled, nor understanding how God would fulfill them. The writer of Hebrews described the quality of this faith in glowing terms: "All these faithful ones died without receiving what God had promised them, but they saw it all from a distance and welcomed the promises of God" (Hebrews 11:13). Now Paul directs his readers to the same Abrahamic faith, but clearly focused on God's fulfillment of the great promise, the blessing of the entire world through the gift of Jesus.

4:25 Jesus died **because of our sins,** taking the penalty we deserved, according to God's plan (see 3:23-26). Just as God brought life from Abraham and Sarah (even though they thought they were "dead" and unable to have children), so God **raised Jesus from the dead.** His resurrection made us **right with God.**

ROMANS 5

FAITH BRINGS JOY / 5:1-11
Paul introduces some difficult concepts in this chapter. He demonstrates the truth of the gospel in ways that stretch our thinking. To begin to understand the next four chapters, it helps to keep in mind the two-sided reality of the Christian life. On the one hand, we are complete in Christ (our acceptance with him is secure); on the other hand, we are growing in Christ (we are becoming more and more like him).

5:1 With the word **therefore,** Paul indicates a conclusion based on his previous argument. In chapter 4, Paul showed how sinners, both Jews and Gentiles, are justified by faith. Here he begins to describe how having **been made right in God's sight by faith** affects our relationship with God. First, **we have peace with God because of what Jesus Christ our Lord has done for us.** Having peace with God means there is no more

hostility between us and God, no sin blocking our relationship with him. More than that, a new relationship has been established, so we no longer dread the outcome of judgment but live under the protection established by God.

5:2 Not only has Christ made us right with God, but he also has given us personal access to God, bringing **us into this place of highest privilege**

where we now stand. We have been brought into a place of favor with God. Instead of being his enemies, we are his friends—in fact, his own children (John 15:15; Galatians 4:5). Mankind was created for glory, but because of sin, had fallen "short of God's glorious standard" (3:23). It is God's purpose to recreate his image, his glory, fully in us so that we can **confidently and joyfully look forward to sharing God's glory.** Anticipating our future with God ought to bring great joy. We stand in God's grace, and the outcome of our lives is secure in his hands. We no longer need to be haunted by thoughts of judgment; now we can reflect upon and respond to his grace.

5:3-4 Problems and trials were a normal experience for first-century Christians. On their first missionary journey, Paul and Barnabas preached in several cities, and many people became believers. But, as was always the case, there was an immediate backlash of persecution against believers. For Christians, suffering does not negate the reality of God's love, but provides the occasion to affirm and apply it. This character quality of learning to **endure** is not an end in itself (see 1 Peter 1:6-7). It is one step in a process. **Endurance develops strength of character.** The word character *(dokime)* includes the idea of "approved as a result of testing." A person with this kind of character is known for his or her inward qualities rather than any outward appearances. The end result of this chain reaction is **confident expectation of salvation**—confidence that God is in control and will see us through. The difficulties of life are not random, meaningless, or wasted when we are trusting God.

5:5 Our **expectation** that God will keep his promises will never **disappoint us.** When our trust is in God, we are absolutely assured that he will fulfill all that he has promised—we will be resurrected to eternal life and will be with him in glory. Why? Because he has already **given us the Holy Spirit to fill our hearts with his love.** The Holy Spirit continues to encourage us, reminding us **how dearly God loves us.** He loves us and will do as he has promised. (See also John 7:38; Romans 8:35; 2 Corinthians 5:14; Titus 3:5-6.) We can have hope in God because of the nature of his love.

5:6 God's plan, from the beginning, was to send his Son to die for us, **at just the right time,** referring to both the timing in history and the timing in God's plan (see Galatians 4:4). In the face of our helplessness, God was fully in control. The events in human history did not determine the plan of salvation; the plan of salvation was designed by

God to happen at just the right time. We are saved only because God took the initiative and demonstrated his incredible grace and love by sending his own Son to take the punishment we deserved.

5:7-8 The highest expression of human love is when someone gives his or her life so that another person can continue to live. People are able to understand sacrificial love, even though it is rarely practiced. This kind of sacrificial gesture is almost always dependent on a relationship that already exists between the one sacrificing (parent, sibling, spouse, fellow soldier) and the one benefited. Even so, people do not readily die for others. But God's love stands in stark contrast to even the deepest expression of human love because **God showed his great love for us by sending Christ to die for us while we were still sinners.** Christ's death is the highest manifestation of God's love for us. While we were rebellious and despicable, Christ died for us so that we could come to God, find peace with him, and become heirs of his promises. Christ did not die so that we could be made lovable; Christ died because God already loved us and wanted to bring us close to himself.

5:9 God made us **right in** his **sight** through the **blood of Christ** shed on the cross (see 3:25). Because God is holy, he could not accept us by simply disregarding or ignoring our sins. Instead, those sins had to be dealt with. And God did this through the sacrificial death of his Son. Again, this justification is God's approval, given to us only on the basis of what Christ did. It is an acquittal that sets free all of us who were otherwise hopeless prisoners of sin. If Christ's blood was shed on our behalf, then his blood will **certainly save us from God's judgment.**

5:10-11 We were **enemies** because we were rebels against God. Because of Christ's death, we **were restored to friendship with God by the death of his Son.** Because Christ's death accomplished this, so **his life**—his present resurrection life—delivers us **from eternal punishment** and insures our salvation. Knowing all that God has accomplished should cause us to **rejoice.** Paul has already told his readers that they should rejoice in sharing God's glory (5:2) and in their problems (5:3). Now he exclaims that they should rejoice in God. We rejoice in God because Christ took our sins upon himself and paid the price for them with his own death, instead of punishing us with the death we deserve. Through faith in his work, we become his **friends** and are no longer enemies and outcasts.

ADAM AND CHRIST CONTRASTED / 5:12-21

Having linked Jews and Gentiles through Abraham to the promises of God, Paul now shows how the gospel applies to all humankind. Paul made important points by going back to Abraham; but by going back to Adam, he will draw conclusions that affect the fate of every person.

5:12 Sin came into the world through one man. **Adam sinned** against God causing a domino effect: **sin entered the entire human race,** then **sin brought death.** Because **everyone sinned,** then everyone also died (Genesis 2–3). Death is the consequence of being under the power of sin. It was not in God's original plan for human beings to die, but it was the result when sin entered the world. Inevitably, the gift of life we bequeath to our children includes with it the sting of death. All human beings have two characteristics in common: They are sinners, and they will die.

5:13-14 God's **law** was not **given** until the time of Moses, so the people who lived between Adam and Moses did not have any specific laws to obey or **break.** But sin that was in the world was the power or force that causes people to act independently of God. All people are under the power of sin, and all people act in rebellion against God. Sin was in the world from the beginning, but it came into sharp focus when the law was given.

Adam disobeyed **an explicit commandment of God** (5:12). His descendants who lived prior to the time of Moses could not break any specific laws because there were none. But they still sinned, witnessed by the fact that **they all died.** Adam's descendants had sinned with Adam (5:12). Death is the result of Adam's sin and ours, even if our sins don't resemble Adam's. For thousands of years, the law had not been explicitly given, and yet people died. The law was added (5:20) to help people see their sinfulness, to show them the seriousness of their offenses, and to drive them to God for mercy and pardon. This was true in Moses' day and in Paul's day, and it is still true today. Sin is a deep rupture between who we are and who we were created to be. The law points out our sin and places the responsibility for it squarely on our shoulders, but it offers no remedy.

The **contrast between Adam and Christ** is that Adam's one act determined the character of the world; Christ's one act determined the character of eternity. In modern terminology, we could say that Adam was a flawed prototype, but Christ was the perfect original. Just as Adam was a representative of created humanity, so is Christ the representative of the new, spiritual humanity.

5:15 God's **generous gift of forgiveness** through Christ (justification) has a greater but opposite

effect than the trespass of Adam and its consequences. Yet in each case, the act of one affected the lives of **many.** Because of Adam's sin, **death** entered the human race, and since then all people have died (with the Bible's exceptions of Enoch and Elijah). All people will die until the end of this age. Because of **Jesus Christ,** however, we can trade judgment for **forgiveness.** We can trade our sin for Jesus' goodness. Jesus offers us the opportunity to be born into his spiritual family— the family line that begins with forgiveness and leads to eternal life. If we do nothing, we have death through Adam; but if we come to God by faith, we have life through Christ.

5:16 God passed judgment on Adam's one sin of disobedience. As a result, Adam and the entire human race received **condemnation.** Everyone since Adam has sinned, and yet Christ overcame those many trespasses and brought righteousness to those who accept him, **even though** they **are guilty of many sins.** The result of sin is death; the gift of God—his justifying sinners—results in reigning forever with Christ.

5:17 By capitulating to sin, **Adam caused death to rule over** the whole human race. Death is inescapable; it comes to every living thing. We all live close to the valley of the shadow of death. And the reign of death over creation began because of Adam's sin. However, there is a remedy. Those who **receive God's wonderful, gracious gift of righteousness will live in triumph over sin and death.** What a promise this is to those who love Christ! We can reign over sin's power, over death's threats, and over Satan's attacks. Eternal life is ours now and forever. Though this promise has its greatest fulfillment in the future, it also has a significant immediate impact. In Christ, death loses its sting (see 1 Corinthians 15:50-57). We are still subject to the physical suffering and death brought by sin in the world, but we are free from the eternal spiritual separation that we would experience outside of Christ. Also, in the power and protection of Jesus Christ, we can overcome temptation (see 8:17 for more on our privileged position in Christ).

5:18-19 The same statement is made in different words in these two verses. Paul emphasizes the contrasting roles of two single agents, Adam and Christ.

Adam's one sin brought condemnation on the human race; this **one person disobeyed God** causing all people to become **sinners**. But **Christ's one act of righteousness**, done because he **obeyed God**, opened the way for **all people** to be **made right in God's sight** and given eternal **life**.

5:20 This statement is certainly not what Paul's Jewish readers expected to hear. The **law was given so that all people could see how sinful they were.** Paul is winding up the argument he has been carrying on through the first five chapters of his letter. The purpose of the law for his own people, the Jews, had been to make them aware of their need for salvation. Sin was present from Adam, but the giving of the law was like having a huge spotlight turned on—the sinfulness of people became all the more defined. The solution to sin was not law, but grace. No matter how much people sin, **God's wonderful kindness** is greater. When our awareness of sin increases, we need to ask God to help us see that his grace is always greater in its capacity to forgive than our capacity to sin.

5:21 Our age is characterized by sin and inevitable death; but the age to come will be characterized by grace, righteousness, and eternal life. It is common to call the ultimate struggle that is going on in the universe "the conflict between good and evil." Paul was picturing here the outcome of the war between the Kingdom of grace and the kingdom of sin. Until Christ, the war appeared to be decided, because **sin ruled over all people.** But Christ's death and resurrection provided the decisive victory by which **God's wonderful kindness rules.** Under the reign of grace, a **right standing** is declared that will bring **eternal life.**

This ends the first section of Paul's letter and his explanation of the law and its relation to salvation. But the law is not set aside as old and worthless. Paul will explain, in coming chapters, the role of the law for believers.

ROMANS 6

SIN'S POWER IS BROKEN / 6:1-14

Up to this point in his letter, Paul has shown people's need for salvation, God's gift of that salvation through the death of his Son, and God's grace in forgiving the sins of all who accept him. This next section of the letter (chapters 6–8) deals with God progressively separating believers from sin and making them more like himself. The key point to realize is that all believers have a new nature and the Holy Spirit within, yet they also have the old, human nature with its capability to sin. These opposites are in constant tension, yet God promises help and victory.

6:1-2 Paul realized that his statements about God's wonderful kindness to sinners could be interpreted to suggest that people ought to **keep on sinning so that God can show us more and more kindness and forgiveness.** "If God loves to forgive, why not give him more to forgive?" would be their erroneous reasoning. Paul answers with an emphatic, **"Of course not!"** The availability of God's mercy must not become an excuse for careless living and moral laxness. The idea that someone would claim to believe the gospel while planning to continue in sin is preposterous to Paul. The point of the gospel was not to find an excuse for sin, but to give freedom from sin.

To make his answer clear, Paul introduces a new concept—believers have **died to sin.** How?

• In the legal sense, we died in the sight of God's judgment.

• In the conversion sense, believing in Christ is dying to sin.
• In the baptismal sense, that burial implies we have died with Christ.
• In the moral sense, sinful desires may be present, but they are mortally wounded.
• In the resurrection sense, we exchange our sinful life for Christ's resurrection life.

Paul speaks of this death as fact and concludes, therefore, that believers cannot **continue to live in it.**

6:3-4 Baptism is a picture of a spiritual truth. In the very early church, baptism followed a person's decision to trust in Christ (see, for example, Acts 2:41; 8:37; 9:18; 10:48), marking these first generation believers as followers of Christ, members of the Christian community. Paul assumes that these

Roman believers were baptized at conversion and would vividly recall the experience. Those who believe in Christ are baptized into him and baptized into his death; in other words, they are **baptized to become one with Christ Jesus.** As he died, we die to our old, sinful lifestyle, and a new life begins. Immersion may have been the form of baptism—that is, new Christians were completely buried momentarily in water. They understood this form of baptism to symbolize being **buried with Christ,** thus the death and burial of the old way of life. Coming up out of the water symbolized resurrection to new life with Christ, as well as the promise of a future bodily resurrection—**as Christ was raised from the dead,** so too believers **may live new lives.**

If we think of our old, sinful life as dead and buried, we have a powerful motive to resist sin. We can consciously choose to treat the desires and temptations of the old nature as if they were dead. Then we can continue to enjoy our wonderful new life with Jesus (see also Galatians 3:27; Colossians 3:1-4).

6:5 **United** literally means, "we have become grown together." Our baptism painlessly acts out the union that Christ painfully made real. God's plan was that in Christ's **death,** believers would also die (to sin and to rebellion against God). Dying to sin is a lifelong process. When we accept Christ and die to our old nature, we begin a life of continually dying to the enticements of the world and living to please the One to whom we belong. Also as Christ was **raised,** believers also will be raised from death to eternal life with God. What people do with Christ now will greatly influence what happens to them later.

6:6 The **old sinful selves** describe believers before they trusted Christ, people who were ruled by sin and rebellion (5:10). That old self was **crucified with Christ**—believers have died the same death as Christ when Christ was crucified. Why? This was the only way that **sin might lose its power** in people's lives, the only way our sinful nature could be set aside so that God's nature could live through us.

As a result, believers **are no longer slaves to sin.** Those who have accepted God's gracious gift of emancipation will be able to participate fully in a new life of obedience. As slaves to sin, we are set free by Christ before we can begin to live free. The power and penalty of sin died with Christ on the cross. We are no longer slaves to our sinful nature; we can choose to live for Christ.

6:7-8 During slavery, freedom was rare except through death. Death brings about a release that cannot be reversed. In the same way, **when we**

died with Christ we were set free from the power of sin. We are not yet sinless, but sin no longer has control over us. With our death to sin, we are free to begin our **new life** in Christ. This new life in Christ (this side of physical death) is already the beginning of resurrected living. Getting used to this new life requires that believers exchange old habits and patterns for new ones.

6:9 Jesus experienced physical death and **rose from the dead, and he will never die again.** His resurrection was a victory over death, so **death no longer has any power over him.** Paul concluded that dying with Christ, then, ends the power of death over us as well.

6:10 Christ **died once to defeat sin,** emphasizing the finality and completeness of Christ's work. When Christ groaned from the cross, "It is finished!" (John 19:30), he knew that the sacrifice was complete, once for all (see Hebrews 7:27). Unlike Christ, we will still fall into sin's traps now and then; but like Christ who **now lives for the glory of God,** we can focus on living for God. God's great plan was to liberate us from sin's ruling power. Thus our perspectives, attitudes, relationships, and desires will change, in light of the incredible events that have taken place on our behalf—death to sin and the ability to come to God and live for him.

6:11 If we have identified with Christ, what is true for him can be true for us. This identification starts in our minds by an act of mental reckoning or accounting. We can **consider** ourselves **dead to sin.** In other words, just as a dead body cannot respond to temptations or enticements, neither can we respond to them. Thus we are **able to live for the glory of God through Christ Jesus** because we have been given new life, a new lifestyle, and the sure promise of eternal life (see also Ephesians 2:5; Colossians 2:13).

6:12 If we are dead to sin, how can **sin** still **control** us? We have died to sin, but we are constantly being freed from sin. When sin is in control, people have no choice but to **give in to its lustful desires** because they are its slaves (6:6). Believers have died to sin, but as long as we live in our mortal bodies, we will have the compulsion to sin. But only because we have died to sin do we have the power to no longer let it control us. We are, in fact, free from our slavery. But each day we must reject our old slave ways.

6:13 While we are in our bodies, there will always be the chance that some actions will be sinful or used as a **tool** to distort our relationship with God or with others. Because our bodies are mortal (decaying and dying), we should not yield to sinful desires and temptations. Why yield to a decaying master? Why offer the parts of our bodies to sin, something to which we have died? Instead, Paul tells believers, **give yourselves completely to God** and **use your whole body as a tool to do what is right.** We have a choice. We have been given new life by God; thus, our bodies are to be given to him to use for promoting righteousness. We are to refuse sin and instead be wholly committed to living for God. We make these choices moment by moment.

6:14 Sin cannot and will not ever again be our **master** because we **are no longer subject to the law.** What does it mean that we are not under the law?

- We are not under the law's demands, as were the people of the Old Testament.

- We are not under curse implied by the impossible standard of the law (see Galatians 3:10-14).
- We are not under its system of requirements, the ceremonial laws that had to be meticulously kept.
- We are not under the fear of failing the just standard of the law.

If believers were still under the law, then the sin would have to be master. By itself, the law produces both the proof and the acute awareness of sin but cannot direct or motivate a person to do what is right. Instead, believers **are free by God's grace** because only grace can overcome sin. Only by living in that grace can we defeat the power of sin in our lives. When our lives are under the law alone, sin is our master. But when we live under grace, our master is God.

FREEDOM TO OBEY GOD / 6:15-23

Paul begins this section in almost the same way as the last one. He wants to make sure there is no misunderstanding of the nature of grace. It is not the chance to do anything we want. Rather, it is the opportunity to live the way God wants us to live. Ultimately, there are only two masters: sin and the Lord Jesus Christ. The choice is clear and required. The only rightful master is our Creator!

6:15 Paul's wording in verse 14—that seems to set the **law** against **grace**—probably surprised his readers. It would look as though Paul was replacing the law with grace, thus giving people no law and, therefore, freedom to sin. This almost repeats the question in verse 1, and Paul's response is the same: **Of course not!** As the argument develops, however, there is clearly a different matter at stake. In verse 1, Paul was challenging the crude assumption that sinning will give God the opportunity to exercise more grace. Here, Paul is guarding against the assumption that because sin is no longer our master, we can indulge in sin without fear of being controlled by it. Being under grace and under the mastery of Christ allows us the freedom not to sin. Any attitude that welcomes, rationalizes, or excuses sin is not grace, but slavery to sin itself.

6:16 All human beings are enslaved. While this idea clashes with our goal of independence, the fact is that we were created for interdependence. Paul is using an "illustration" (6:19) to make an important spiritual point: You are a slave to whomever or whatever you commit yourself to obey. This means that friendships, goals, employment, citizenship, membership, education, career, debt, and marriage all include aspects of slavery.

We should choose our slavery wisely. When **sin** is our **master,** we have no power except to do what it bids us, with the end being **death.** But when we **choose to obey God,** the one who created us, we become slaves to obedience and will **receive** God's **approval.**

There are only two choices and no middle ground. This is as Jesus said, "No one can serve two masters" (Matthew 6:24). To refuse to allow God to be master over your life is to choose slavery to sin. While service to sin leaves us powerless and leads to death, service to God leads to righteousness and eternal life.

6:17 Before accepting the salvation offered through Christ, all believers **were slaves of sin.** But now they have a new master because they **have obeyed** the **new teaching** from God, referring to the Good News of salvation (see 1 Corinthians 11:2; 2 Thessalonians 2:15; 3:6). This message abolished the slavery to sin that they had lived under, and it outlined a new way of living—under grace.

6:18 It is impossible to be neutral. Every person has a **master**—either **righteousness** or **sin.** A Christian is still able to sin, but he or she is no longer a slave to sin. This person belongs to God. Believers are set free from the control of their evil desires and their selfish habits, free to become enslaved to righteous living. We serve the righteous God who is in the process of transforming us to become more like him so that we can one day share in glorious resurrection to eternal life. That's not a bad master to have!

6:19 Paul emphasizes that he is using an **illustration** in case any of his readers fail to understand his meaning. Anyone living in Rome knew about **slaves and masters.** There were more slaves than citizens in the empire. When people are **slaves of impurity and lawlessness,** they are held in bondage to a master who seeks their destruction. But to **choose to be slaves of righteousness** is very different. God does not keep us in his service against our will—rather, we desire to please him in everything we do. Then we are becoming **holy,** referring to the progressive goal of salvation, our growth into persons who exhibit more and more of the character of Christ in the way we live.

6:20-21 The freedom that people experience when they are **slaves of sin** is the antithesis of genuine freedom. It is such a distortion of the meaning of liberty that it causes people to be glad that they are not **concerned with doing what** is **right.** That is ultimately the worst kind of slavery. And the **result** is that people end up **shamed of the things** they **used to do.** Paul was teaching the Roman Christians that it was appropriate for them to feel ashamed of their pre-Christian actions, and Paul was encouraging them to seek the benefits of high moral living now that they served Christ.

6:22 The benefits are immeasurable for those who are **slaves of God** and set **free from the power of sin.** Faith makes us righteous in God's eyes and challenges us to realize that righteousness in practical living—doing **those things that lead to holiness and eternal life.** Holiness is gained as a process over our entire life wherein we become more Christlike and set apart for his service; eternal life begins at conversion and, despite the physical death we will inevitably face, continues beyond the grave.

6:23 This result of **sin** is not just physical **death**— everyone dies physically, believers and nonbelievers alike. This refers to eternal separation from God in hell. This is the wage that a person receives for his or her rebellion against God. Those in hell will find no comfort in the truth that they have been paid exactly what they earned.

But instead of wages, those who believe receive a **free gift** from God—**eternal life.** Eternal life does not mean endless life on earth, but resurrection from death to eternal glory with God. Because eternal life is a gift, we cannot earn or purchase it. It would be foolish for someone to offer to pay for a gift given out of love. To be a gift, it must be given and received freely. A more appropriate response to a loved one who offers a gift is grateful acceptance. Our salvation is a gift of God, not something of our own doing (Ephesians 2:8-9). He saved us because of his mercy, not because of any righteous acts on our part (Titus 3:5). How much more we should accept with thanksgiving the gift that God has freely given to us.

ROMANS 7

NO LONGER BOUND TO THE LAW / 7:1-6

In chapter 6, Paul explained how Christ delivered us from sin: when he died, we also "died" to sin. But while we are alive in our bodies, we must continue to deal with our sin nature and its attempts to control our thoughts and actions. To describe this tension between our old and new natures, Paul used the analogy of slavery to sin versus slavery to God. He begins chapter 7 by arguing the same point, using the analogy of marriage: Just as death breaks the marital vow, so death with Christ breaks our "marriage" to sin. We were bound to sin because we failed to keep the law. The problem is not with the law; it is within us.

7:1 Obviously, the **law** can only apply **to a person who is still living**—a dead body cannot be expected to follow any laws, nor can it make restitution for sins committed. Paul's rhetorical question creates a chilling afterthought. Death brings an end to the authority of the law, but what remains is judgment. Death removes a person from the frying pan of the law, but then drops him or her into the fire of judgment. But if a person can get out from under the authority of the law without coming under the judgment of law, that would be good news!

7:2-3 The **marriage** vows bind a woman to her husband while he lives. **If he dies,** however, she is free from her vows to him. However, if a wife leaves her **husband** for another man, she is **committing adultery.** If this woman is widowed, **she is free from that law** to marry another man and **does not commit adultery.**

Again, Paul was developing an analogy from common living to emphasize his lesson. Having begun the theme of marriage, Paul wants his readers to remember that under normal circumstances any breaking of the marriage vows would be adultery. Having stated that fact, Paul explains its significance.

7:4 Just as death breaks the bond between a husband and wife, so a believer's "death" (death to his old self) breaks the **power** of the **law.** The old contractual arrangement had to be completely severed before the new one could begin. This had to be as final as death. Jewish believers could not live with a dual allegiance. They could not be under the lordship of Christ and the lordship of the law. Total commitment to Christ cannot coexist with a total commitment to the law. That would be spiritual adultery. A believer belongs fully to Christ. This happens because of Christ's death on the cross and the believer's being **united with** him

in his death and resurrection. The result is **good fruit.** Only by belonging to Christ can we do **good deeds** and live a life pleasing to God. This is how we serve in the new way of the Spirit (7:6). (See also Galatians 5:22-23; Philippians 1:11.)

7:5 Paul reminds his readers that the law did little more for them than fuel their **evil desires,** referring to the human tendency to be dominated by desire and sin (see 8:7; Galatians 3:3; 5:24). They were **controlled by** their **old nature.** The only fruit produced by a life that is under the law are **sinful deeds** and **death.** The law restrains us and teaches us God's will, but it also reveals and stimulates our sinful nature. At the same time it identifies sin, it also generates sin.

7:6 This statement anticipates the spiritual solution to the problems Paul will address in this chapter. Because **we have been released from the law,** we no longer have to serve **in the old way by obeying the letter of the law.** In other words, the law is not erased, but it is no longer to be obeyed on the superficial level of "works" (the way of obedience familiar to the Jews). Nor are we freed from all responsibility to serve. God still desires our moral obedience, but we are to serve Christ by focusing on his desires, not on a list of commands. We have been released so that we can serve **in the new way, by the Spirit** living within us, guiding us, and showing us how to please God. We are still called to serve, but our master is gracious, and we are no longer trapped by the cycle of effort, failure, and guilt.

GOD'S LAW REVEALS OUR SIN / 7:7-13

But where does the law fit into all this? In this section, Paul shows that the law is powerless to save sinners (7:7-14) and lawkeepers (7:15-22). Even a person with a new nature (7:23-25) experiences ongoing evidence of the law's inability to motivate him or her toward good. The sinner is condemned by the law; the lawkeeper can't live up to it; and the person with the new nature finds that his or her obedience to the law is sabotaged by the effects of the old nature. Once again, Paul declares that salvation cannot be found by obeying the law. No matter who we are, only Jesus Christ can set us free. Yet the law, because it is God's law, is not then cast aside as useless. In the next chapters, Paul grapples with the complexity of life under grace and the believer's relationship to God's law.

7:7-8 Because the law arouses evil desires (7:5) and because we have been released from the law (7:6), does that mean **the law of God is evil?** Paul again answers his own question, **Of course not!** The law itself is not evil, but it does tell us what evil is. Paul uses coveting (Exodus 20:17; Deuteronomy 5:21) as an example—**I would never have known that coveting is wrong if the law had not said, "Do not covet."**

Paul deliberately chose the last commandment as an example. That particular commandment was unique among the laws in the Decalogue, and it obviously had a significant effect on Paul himself. The tenth commandment focuses entirely on our inward nature. At a superficial level, we may claim to have lived up to the first nine, but the last commandment exposes our intentions with shameful clarity. Paul claims that no sooner had he discovered that commandment than it **aroused all kinds of forbidden desires** within him. In telling him not to covet, the law had introduced Paul to the darkest desires. But still Paul could maintain his firm belief that God's law itself was sinless. The bright light that revealed a world of filth was not itself evil for having done so. Without the law, sin goes unnoticed, unknown. Some sins may not even present a problem until they are prohibited.

7:9-10 Before we realize the seriousness of the law and of sin, we believe ourselves to be **fine.** But when we **understand what the law** really demands, then we also come to understand that we have **broken the law,** we are sinners, and we are **doomed to die** eternally. The commands, given to **show** people **the way of life,** instead show merely that all people have been given **the death penalty.**

7:11 Sin fooled people by misusing the law. It is filled with false promises and deceptions:

- Sin promises to satisfy our desires even more than the last time.
- Sin promises that our actions can be kept hidden, so no one will know.
- Sin promises that we won't have to worry about consequences.
- Sin promises special benefits: wisdom, knowledge, and sophistication.
- Sin promises power and prestige in exchange for cooperation.

In the Garden of Eden (see Genesis 3), the serpent deceived Eve by taking her focus off the freedom she had and putting it on the one restriction God had given. Since that time we have all been rebels.

7:12 Although it gave him the death penalty, Paul could not speak against the law. **The law itself is holy and right and good** because it reflects the character and will of God himself, who is holy. The commandments define sin but are not sin (7:7). The purpose of the law is to teach us right from wrong, to give us guidelines, and to show sin for what it is. The law helps us live for God, but it cannot save us.

If the law causes so much difficulty, what useful purpose does it serve? (1) It is a revelation of the nature, character, and will of God. (2) Its ethical components were incorporated in Christ's teaching. (3) It teaches us about sin. (4) It demolishes self-righteousness.

7:13 Paul asks, **"Did the law, which is good, cause my doom?"** Again he answers his own question, **Of course not!** The law was given by God; it tells us what God desires of us, and it is good. It is sin, not the law, that brings death, and it is only through the law that **we can see how terrible sin really is.** Sin **uses God's good commandments** to continue to produce death in people because people cannot keep the law in their own strength. But, by using the commandments as instruments of death, sin reveals itself in all its ugliness.

STRUGGLING WITH SIN / 7:14-25

Paul's intense desire to view the law with high esteem helped fuel his next thoughts. He made every effort to clarify the tension between the holy law and the sin that uses the law for its deadly purposes. The law comes from God, has his character, and tells his will for his people. But as the majesty of the law fills Paul's mind, along with it comes the vision of his own standing before the law. Paul wants to make the point that sin does not besmirch the law. But he also realizes that he must clarify his own ongoing relationship to the law.

7:14 How can we be free from sin and yet continue to do wrong? In Christ, we are free from the penalty of sin (judgment) and the power of sin (hopelessness). But while still in the flesh, we are not free from the presence of sin (temptations) and the possibility of sin (failures). Paul never claimed that being under grace instead of under the law meant that a believer was somehow above the law. In fact, having described such a great distance between the law and sin, he realized that he was still far more acquainted with the reality of sin than the righteous standard of the law.

So, Paul writes, **the trouble is not with the law**

but with me, because I am sold into slavery, with sin as my master. The law has an uncanny capacity for reminding us of what we once were, and of how captivating that old life can still appear. Our hope never shifts back to the law. We must daily focus on Christ.

7:15 By introducing his personal dilemma, Paul invites us to consider how well we understand our own behavior. As long as believers live in this world as men and women of flesh and blood, they will face a constant tension—the conflict between their sinful nature and their new spiritual life. Paul wrote to the Galatians, "The old sinful nature loves to do evil, which is just opposite from what the Holy Spirit wants. And the Spirit gives us desires that are opposite from what the sinful nature desires. These two forces are constantly fighting each other, and your choices are never free from this conflict" (Galatians 5:17).

Paul shares three lessons that he learned in trying to deal with his old sinful desires. (1) Knowledge of the law is not the answer (7:9). (2) Self-determination (to **want to do what is right**) doesn't succeed (7:15). (3) Becoming a Christian does not stamp out all sin and temptation from a person's life (7:22-25).

Being born again starts in a moment of faith, but becoming like Christ takes a lifetime. Paul compares Christian growth to a strenuous race or fight (1 Corinthians 9:24-27; 2 Timothy 4:7). Thus, as Paul has been emphasizing since the beginning of this letter, no one in the world is innocent; no one deserves to be saved—not the pagan who doesn't know God's laws, nor the Christian or Jew who knows them and tries to keep them. All of us must depend totally on the work of Christ for our salvation. We cannot earn it by our good behavior.

7:16-17 We want to obey God's law, yet we still fail. Our failure is not the law's fault, nor is it our own fault: **It is sin inside me that makes me do these evil things.** If sin did not exist, then the law would give us guidelines for living perfectly. But sin perverts everything. Paul is not abdicating responsibility for his sin; instead, he is making the point that his desires and the sin within him are in constant conflict. Sin is a power that, at times, can still win because his redemption is not yet complete.

7:18-20 In our sinful nature, there is nothing good. Paul sees this as part of being human. Although we belong to Christ and have died to sin, we still live in a sinful world and have a **sinful nature** that is **rotten through and through.** The tension continues—trying to do good and not being able to do it. Paul describes the person who knows what is good and might even desire to do it, but this person lacks the power. Believers still have a sinful nature that pulls them to do what they **don't want to do.** The seeming contradiction of "I do—I don't do" emphasizes how difficult it is to identify the sources of our sinful behaviors. Without the Holy Spirit's help, the person is dominated by the power of sin and continues to do evil when he actually desires to do good.

7:21 The **fact of life** at work here is the reality that evil is within us, even when we **want to do what is right.** In fact, it is when we most want to do good

that we become most acutely aware of our propensity not to do so. A swimmer has no idea how strong the current is until she tries to swim upstream. When she faces the current, she finds this law at work: the current is against her.

7:22-23 Believers **love God's law** (referring to the path of obedience to God that the entire Old Testament presents) because they long to know it and do it and thus to please God. This is one of the marks of wisdom (Psalm 1:2). The problem is that there is **another law at work within.** That other law is the law of sin. Sin is constantly **at war** because it will not give up the control over us that it lost when we came to faith in Christ. Sin fights against our **mind** because our mind is where we make our decisions and our moral judgments. We cannot resist our sin nature in our own power. When we try, we will be defeated.

Paul does not say that these powers are equal, but he knows they are both there. We must realize the same. One power must be resisted while relying on the other. When we fail to rely on Christ's strength for our daily strength, we in essence provide sin with more power over us. Sin's power will not have grown, but our relative weakness will make it seem that way. Sin's power is not an excuse for us to drift spiritually, or openly give in to temptation. Believers must not forget that they have already won because the Spirit within is greater than the spirit in the world (1 John 4:4).

7:24 Our bodies are mortal; they are bodies of death. As long as we live on this earth in our human bodies, we will face this conflict with sin. Our place of residence is our place of least resistance. And, as seen above, as long as we are confined to this world, we will experience a measure of struggle and defeat. But, we are not left in **miserable** defeat, **dominated by sin**—rescue will come!

7:25 The triumph is sweeter because the struggle is real. In the last few verses, we have glimpsed the struggle of a genuine believer. Now the answer is shouted in exclamation.

Many who claim to know Christ never see themselves well enough to appreciate as deeply as Paul did what they actually have in Christ. Because of Jesus Christ, we are assured of a great future. We will one day join him in eternity with a new body that is free from sin. In the meantime, however, we must realize that we remain in the **sinful nature** as slaves **to sin.** But the **answer** to who will set us free **is in Jesus Christ our Lord.** The battle ends with a shout of victory. The winners know who really won. The winners also know the war isn't over. But in the meantime, there are more lessons to learn, and there is more freedom to experience.

ROMANS 8

LIFE IN THE SPIRIT / 8:1-17

At the end of chapter 7, Paul assures all believers of having power to overcome sin and the assurance of final deliverance from this evil world. But he includes the reminder that during this lifetime, there will be constant tension because in the sinful nature, even a believer is "a slave to sin" (7:25). The question arises, So, are we to spend our entire lives defeated by sin? The answer is a resounding no! In this chapter, Paul describes the life of victory and hope that every believer has because of Christ Jesus.

8:1 We feel condemned because Satan uses past guilt and present failures to make us question what Christ has done for us. Our assurance must be focused on Christ, not our performance. No matter how we may feel, **there is no condemnation for those who belong to Christ Jesus.** Because we have been rescued by Christ (7:24-25), we are not condemned. To belong to Christ Jesus means to have put our faith in him, becoming a member of his body of believers. Jesus said, "I assure you, those who listen to my message and believe in God who sent me have eternal life. They will never be condemned for their sins, but they have already passed from death into life" (John 5:24).

8:2 The **life-giving Spirit** is the Holy Spirit, who was present at the creation of the world as one of the agents in the origin of life itself (Genesis 1:2). He is the **power** behind the rebirth of every Christian, and the one who helps us live the Christian life. The Holy Spirit sets us free, once and for all, from **the power of sin** and its natural consequence, **death.** How did this happen?

8:3 Freedom over sin never can be obtained by obedience to the law. The law of Moses could not save us, because of our sinful nature. But what the law can't do, God did by sending his own Son in a human body like ours, except that ours are sinful. Jesus was completely human (John 1:14), with the same desires that yield to sin, yet he never sinned (see 2 Corinthians 5:21; Hebrews 2:17-18; 4:14-16). Christ took on humanity in order to be a sacrifice for our sins. Because Christ was sinless, his death passed the "death sentence" on sin for all of us, destroying sin's control over us.

In Old Testament times, animal sacrifices were continually offered at the temple. These animals brought to the altar had two important characteristics: they were alive, and they were without flaw.

The sacrifices showed the Israelites the seriousness of sin: innocent blood had to be shed before sins could be pardoned (see Leviticus 17:11). But animal blood could not really remove sin (Hebrews 10:4); and the forgiveness provided by those sacrifices, in legal terms, was more like a stay of execution than a pardon. Those animal sacrifices could only point to Jesus' sacrifice that paid the penalty for all sin. Jesus' life was identical with ours, yet unstained by sin. So he could serve as the flawless sacrifice for our sins. In him, our pardon is complete. The tables are turned so that not only is there "no condemnation for those who belong to Christ Jesus," but also the very sin that guaranteed our condemnation is itself condemned by Christ's sacrifice.

8:4 The **requirement of the law** is holiness (see Leviticus 11:44-45; 19:2; 20:7); but the law is powerless to make us holy because of our innate sinfulness. Only through Christ's death and the resulting freedom from sin can we **no longer follow our sinful nature but instead follow the Spirit** and thus fulfill the righteous requirements of the law. The Holy Spirit is the one who helps us become holy. The Holy Spirit provides the power internally to help us do what the law required of us externally.

It is the Spirit who produces "fruit" in us; only in this way can we fulfill the requirements of the law. But Paul has already made it clear that the law is powerless to save. So why do its requirements still need to be met? The law is God's law and was never meant to be cast aside. Paul makes a distinction between two kinds of obedience to the law. He speaks against the obedience to the law that stays merely at the level of the flesh (such as being circumcised because the law required it) and the obedience that depends on God's Holy Spirit. Only the latter fulfills the law. When we live according to the Spirit, we actually do meet the requirements of the law.

8:5 We will struggle constantly with sin and its temptations until the resurrection. People who decide to follow their **sinful nature** will be **dominated** by it and **think about sinful things.** But believers do not need to live in sin because they can now live **controlled by the Holy Spirit,** so they can **think about things that please the Spirit.** We must follow Christ daily in every area of our life, in our choices and moral decisions. Will you follow your former sinful nature or the Spirit's leading?

8:6 The **mind** refers to our mind-set, our goals. Choosing to let the **sinful nature** be in control will result in **death,** both spiritual and physical. Choosing to let the **Holy Spirit** control our minds will bring us full **life** on earth, eternal life, and **peace** with God. Elsewhere in Scripture we find the characteristics of a mind under the Spirit's control. It will be a mind directed toward truth, aware of the Spirit's presence (John 14:17). It will be a mind seeking to please the Holy Spirit (Galatians 6:8). It will be a mind active in memorizing and meditating on the words of Christ (John 14:26). It will be a mind sensitive to sin (John 16:7-11). It will be a mind eager to follow the Spirit's guidance (Galatians 5:16-22). The control of the Holy Spirit begins with voluntary commitment and submission to Christ.

8:7-8 The **sinful nature** cannot submit to God because it is the seat of indwelling sin and is **always hostile to God.** Living in sin, following one's own desires, and disregarding God boils down to hostility to him. Every person not united to Christ is thoroughly controlled by sin's power. Thus, **those who are still under the control of their sinful nature can never please God** because they are interested only in themselves and have cast aside the one and only power that can defeat sin. The mind directed by the sinful nature can only be devoted to its own self-gratification, which will lead to destruction.

Every human being has a sinful nature. But believers in Christ have access to the Holy Spirit. In fact, Paul says, "The Spirit of God lives in you" (8:9). Believers are still in the flesh, but because they are born again, they also have God's Spirit. The question is which will be in control.

8:9-11 In contrast to those still controlled by the sinful nature, believers **are not controlled by** our **sinful nature** when we have yielded control to **the Spirit of God.** To **not have the Spirit of Christ** means to not be a Christian. Christ's Spirit lives within our human spirits, but our fleshly bodies are still infected by **sin** and **will die.** Sin has been defeated by Christ, but sin and death still claim their hold on our mortal bodies. Yet in these bodies we are **alive** spiritually and can live by the Spirit's guidance. In addition, we are promised the physical resurrection of our bodies into eternal life. **The Spirit of God who raised Jesus from the dead** will also **give life** to us. So there is wonderful hope even for our prone-to-decay bodies.

8:12 Because of all that Christ has done and is going to do for us, we are under **no obligation whatsoever to do what** the sinful nature urges us to do. We are to refuse the drives and desires of our still attractive but crucified sinful nature, to say no to ungodliness and worldly passions. The old, sinful nature may present its demands, based upon the past, but we have no obligation to cooperate.

8:13-14 Our sinful nature shows itself through the vehicle of the body. Therefore, we must **turn from** following the sinful nature and its **evil deeds,** the practices and habitual responses of the sinful nature. This is an action to be done, a moral decision to be made—every day we are to turn away from the desires that draw us away from God. The Jews already considered themselves to be **children of God** because of their heritage; but Paul explains that the term has new meaning. True children of God are those **who are led by the Spirit of God** as evidenced in their lifestyle. Believers not only have the Spirit (8:9); they are also led by the Spirit.

8:15-16 This slavery to fear most likely refers to life under the law, obedience that was concerned for scrupulous exactness with a constant fear of failure. Paul implies that believers are **not** to **be like slaves** who cower in fear before their master. Instead, we are **adopted** children who can call God our **Father.** We can know this is true because the **Holy Spirit** within tells us it is so. The Holy Spirit not only adopts us as God's children, but he also assures us of our family status (see Galatians 4:6). The Spirit within changes our obedience to God from slavery to a relationship where God is both our Master and our loving Father. The Scriptures indicate that believers can expect inward confirmation of the faith by the Spirit. Our very capacity and desire to approach God as our Father is itself evidence of the Spirit's witness with our spirit that we are children of God. We are motivated by the Spirit.

8:17 The Jews were convinced that they were the Lord's inheritance, and that as such they would inherit the Promised Land. Paul explains that God's promise includes all who believe in Christ—both

Jews and Gentiles. Because we are God's **children, we are his heirs and will share his treasures.** The Jews thought this was to be the Promised Land— instead, it is another "land," God's Kingdom.

We are God's children only because of Christ's suffering on our behalf. As believers, therefore, **if we are to share his glory, we must also share his suffering.** We will enjoy our future inheritance if our relationship with Christ is genuine enough so that we will face suffering for his sake.

THE FUTURE GLORY / 8:18-30

The preceding paragraph ended with the shared connection between suffering and glory. Sharing in the glory of Christ will come only after sharing in his sufferings (8:17). For Paul, this matter of glory has cosmic proportions, for the glorious destiny of believers will signal a new day for all of creation. He wants his readers to realize that sin has imprisoned all people and the entire environment. We must wait for God's timing to be free, depending on the Spirit, who helps us in ways we can hardly describe.

8:18 In verse 17, Paul stated that believers will share in Christ's sufferings. He completes that thought with this verse, concluding that the sufferings we now face are **nothing compared to the glory he will give us later.** The present suffering is temporary, while the future glory is eternal. Paul had written to the Corinthians, "For our present troubles are quite small and won't last very long. Yet they produce for us an immeasurably great glory that will last forever!" (2 Corinthians 4:17). Suffering is part of the process of sharing in Christ's death; it will culminate in sharing his glory.

8:19 Human beings and the rest of creation presently face suffering, and both will be glorified in the future. When Adam sinned, God sentenced all of creation (Genesis 3:17). Since then, the world has suffered decay and pollution, largely because people have forgotten or ignored their responsibilities as stewards of the earth. The created order functions in spite of its flaws. But diseases, deformities, and suffering constantly remind us that all is not right with us or with the world. **All creation is waiting eagerly for that future day when God will reveal who his children really are.** This will occur at the second coming of Christ when he returns for his people. The entire universe is looking forward to the conclusion of God's plan.

8:20-21 When Adam sinned, **everything on earth was subjected to God's curse;** that is, to futility, change, and decay. Creation is cursed because it is unable to attain the purposes for which it was made. The perfect order in the world was marred by sin; therefore, fallen people had to live in a fallen world. Yet **all creation anticipates the day when it will join God's children in glorious freedom from death and decay.** Revelation 22 describes the future removal of the curse from the earth.

Adam and Eve were the first polluters of the environment when they sinned. Their act of rebellion affected the entire world. It has taken many centuries to realize the interrelatedness of this global village, but the Bible begins with that assumption. Having the same Creator links us with the rest of the created order. But as much as we do personally and corporately to clean up and care for the environment, we must realize that creation will require the same kind of transformation that we require in order to be set straight again.

8:22-23 Paul pictures the fallen **creation as groaning as in the pains of childbirth.** Consider earthquakes, floods, fire, drought, famine—these are surely not what creation was meant to be, but sin and evil now rule. Just as the pains of childbirth end at the birth of the child, so the groaning and pain of the creation will end at the birth of the new earth. Creation groans and longs for its release and transformation into the new heaven and new earth. We **Christians** also **groan to be released from pain and suffering,** longing for our own release from the cycle of sin and decay (8:23). We long for redemption **when God will give us our full rights as his children, including the new bodies he has promised us.** In this process we are not alone, for the **Holy Spirit** groans with us, expressing our unutterable longing to God and giving us a **foretaste of future glory.** But until the time of our release and redemption, we must groan, wait, and hope.

8:24-25 When we put our faith in Christ as Savior, we **are saved** and we can **eagerly look forward to the freedom** we will have at Christ's return. We already have the presence of the Holy Spirit, who is unseen, but we must eagerly wait for our new bodies, which are also unseen. Our full redemption has not yet happened; it will happen when Christ returns. That is why it is still a **hope** for believers. Our salvation is both present and future. It is present because the moment we believe in Jesus Christ as Savior we are saved (3:21-26; 5:1-11; 6:1-11, 22-23); our new life (eternal life) begins. But at the same time, we have not fully received all the benefits and blessings of salvation that will be ours when Christ's new Kingdom is completely established. While we can be confident of our salvation, we still **look forward** with hope and trust toward that complete change of body and personality that lies beyond this life.

Waiting for things **patiently** is a quality that must be developed in us (see Romans 5:3-4; James 1:3-4; 5:11; Revelation 13:10; 14:12). Patience is one of the Spirit's fruit borne in our lives. It includes fortitude, endurance, and the ability to bear up under pressure in order to attain a desired goal.

8:26 In the same way that our "hope" gives us fortitude, the **Holy Spirit helps us in our distress.** At times, our weakness is so intense that **we don't even know what we should pray for, nor how we should pray.** At those times, the Spirit voices our requests for us. He intercedes by appealing to the only one who can help us, God himself. We may not know the right words to say, but the Holy Spirit does. His **groanings** to God become effective intercession on our behalf.

The companionship of the Spirit in prayer is one of the themes of this chapter. Here, the Spirit literally "joins in to help" us, expressing for us what we can't fully express for ourselves. How should we pray?

- Utilize all the forms prayer takes: adoration, confession, petition, thanksgiving, and meditation. As we pray, we should trust the Spirit to make perfect what is imperfect.
- Listen during prayer. We should ask the Spirit to search our hearts and minds, and then we should be silent.
- Practice prayer as a habit.
- Combine prayer with other regular spiritual disciplines (see Philippians 4:4-8).
- Confess sins that the Spirit points out.

8:27 The Father **knows all hearts** and he **knows what the Spirit is saying** (see 8:26). God can look deep, past our inarticulate groanings, to understand the need we face, our hidden feelings. Even when we don't know the right words to pray, the Holy Spirit prays with and for us, always **in harmony with God's own will.** With God helping us pray, we don't need to be afraid to come before him.

8:28 Because the Spirit's efforts on our behalf are carried out in full agreement with God's will,

everything that happens to us in this life is directed toward that goal. What happens may not itself be "good," but God will cause **everything to work together for the** ultimate **good** of his children, to meet his ultimate **purpose** for their maturity. The point is, God works all things for good, not "all things work out." Suffering will still bring pain, loss, and sorrow, and sin will bring shame. But under God's control, the eventual outcome will be for our good.

God works behind the scenes, ensuring that even in the middle of mistakes and tragedies, good will result for those who love him. At times this will happen quickly, often enough to help us trust the principle. But there will also be events whose results for good we will not know until eternity. Our ultimate destiny is to be like Christ. God's design is more than just an invitation; God summons us with a purpose in mind: we are to be like Christ and share his glory.

8:29-30 Believers are those people whom God **knew in advance.** God's foreknowledge refers to his intimate knowledge of us and our relationship with him based on his choosing us. God **chose** believers to reach a particular goal: **to become like his Son.** When all believers are conformed to Christ's likeness, the resurrected Christ will be the **firstborn** of a new race of humans, who are purified from sin. Because we are God's children, we are Christ's **brothers and sisters.**

What does it mean to be chosen? What keeps foreknowledge and predestination from being determinism? How can belief in predestination avoid leading someone to despair over the futility of any human choice? God's foreknowledge does not imply determinism—the idea that all our choices are predetermined. Since God is not limited by time as we are, he "sees" past, present, and future at the same time. Parents sometimes "know" how their children will behave before the fact. We don't conclude from these parents' foreknowledge that they made their children act that way. God's foreknowledge, insofar as we can understand it, means that God knows who will accept the offer of salvation. The plan of predestination begins when we trust Christ and comes to its conclusion when we become fully like him. Receiving an airline ticket to Chicago means we have been predestined to arrive in Chicago.

To explain foreknowledge and predestination in any way that implies that every action and choice we make has been not only preknown, but even predetermined, seems to contradict those Scriptures that declare that our choices are real, that they matter, and that there are consequences to the choices we make. What is clear is that God's purpose for human beings was not an afterthought; it was settled before the foundation of the world. Humankind is to serve and honor God. If we have trusted Christ as Savior, we can rejoice that God has always known us. His love is eternal. His wisdom and power are supreme. He will guide and protect us until we one day stand in his presence.

God's plan for the salvation of those who believe in Christ has three steps: **chosen, called,** and glorified. When we are finally conformed to the image of Christ, we will share his **glory.**

NOTHING CAN SEPARATE US FROM GOD'S LOVE / 8:31-39

Alongside the theme of glory in the Christian life is the theme of victory. We get to be on the winning side, though our contribution is almost insignificant. We are protected by a God whose love cannot be measured and from which, as Paul will eloquently explain, absolutely nothing can separate us. Paul's questions fall into three categories: (1) Will opposition from people or Satan be too great (8:31-32)? (2) Will we fail because of our tendency to sin (8:33-34)? (3) Will we be overcome by difficult times (8:35-39)?

8:31-32 Satan and those under his power are **against us,** but in the end, God promises the victory. How much is God **for us?** So much that he **did not spare even his own Son but gave him up for us all.** The word for "spare" is the same word for "withheld," used in Genesis 22:12, when God said to Abraham, **You have not withheld even your beloved son from me.**

Our major struggle with prayer is not that God doesn't answer. What upsets us is that he seldom answers in line with our plans or schedule. At those times we may think that God is intentionally withholding something from us. But God has already given us the greatest gift of all. Remembering God's gift will help us see that God is working for our good even when we can't immediately see it. God sacrificed his Son to save us; will he now invalidate that sacrifice by refusing to help and guide believers? No, instead, he promises to give us **everything else** to bring us to the ultimate goal—our sanctification and glorification.

8:33-34 If God did not withhold his Son, and if God will give us everything to make us complete, **will God** then **accuse us?** Paul's emphatic answer is **no!** God **is the one who has given us right standing with himself,** and he is also the Judge who has already declared us "not guilty." So **who then will condemn us?** Will it be Jesus—for we surely have offended him. But **no,** it won't be him **for he is the one who died for us.** To condemn us would then make his death of no value. Jesus would not condemn those for whom he died. Instead, Jesus, who **was raised to life for us** is at God's side **pleading for us** in heaven (see also Psalm 110:1; Mark 12:35-37; Hebrews 4:14-16). The Spirit intercedes for us (8:27) and Christ intercedes for us. How much more advocacy do we need?

8:35 The next questions help seal our assurance in God. Nothing can **separate** us from **Christ's love** for us. Then Paul lists several situations we might think could come between us and God. Paul knew from experience that these could not separate believers from God—he had already experienced them (see 2 Corinthians 11:23-28). This means that the love of Christ doesn't separate us from these experiences, but that even in the most devastating of these, the love of Christ is with us.

8:36 Paul quotes from Psalm 44:22 to remind the believers that people who trust in God must expect to face persecution, even death. In that psalm, the poets made the specific point that difficulties and suffering were coming to people who had been faithful. Believers who suffer are the rule, not the exception.

8:37 No, instead of being separated from Christ through all these things (the trials and hardships mentioned in 8:35), we have **overwhelming victory.** This does not mean that we will be superheroes, but that our victory will be intensified by virtue of our union with Christ.

8:38-39 Yes, we are secure in Christ—Paul was **convinced** of this, and so should we be. **Nothing can ever separate us from** God's **love** for us (8:39). In both **death** and the trials of **life** in this evil world, we will be in God's presence. No spiritual forces, such as **angels** or **demons,** are powerful enough to undo what God has done for us. Nothing in the sphere of time itself (**fears** and **worries**) can threaten us; nothing that can happen in the present and nothing that can happen in the future, such as persecution and hardship, would cause God to leave us. No **powers** that exist (Satan, human governments, etc.) are more powerful than God; they can have no effect on our relationship with him. Nothing in space, from **high above** or **in the deepest ocean,** can take us away from God's love. **Nothing in all creation** can take us away from God's love or thwart his purposes for us.

Paul's point is simple and compelling: once in

his care, it is impossible to be separated from Christ. His death for us is proof of his unconquerable love. Nothing can stop his constant presence with us. God tells us how great his love is so that we will feel totally secure in him.

ROMANS 9:1-10:4

GOD'S SELECTION OF ISRAEL / 9:1-29

The end of chapter 8 marks the conclusion of the first major section of Romans. Paul has discussed the doctrines of our being made right with God and our ultimate future. But before Paul moves on to address practical concerns of local church life (in chapters 12–15), he feels compelled to speak about God's plan for the Gentiles and the Jews, Paul's very own people.

9:1-3 The words Paul writes bear the truth—he did **not lie** as his **conscience and the Holy Spirit confirm.** Paul reveals his depth of feeling here; as the apostle to the Gentiles, with his great zeal for preaching to the Gentiles, he was probably often accused of turning his back on his own people. Though his commission to preach the gospel took him outside Jewish boundaries, Paul never lost his love for his **Jewish brothers and sisters.** Paul's **sorrow** was so intense that he was willing to be **cursed** and **cut off from Christ** if, by doing so, the Jews would be saved. For his people's sake, Paul would have borne the curse himself if it would have ensured their salvation. Of course, he knew it would be impossible for God to curse him, but his expression shows the intensity of his affection for his people.

9:4-5 Paul lists the benefits of being a Jew. They were God's chosen nation. As such, they had witnessed his glory, received his covenants and his law, worshiped him, and received his promises. The ancestors had been **great people of God** and **Christ himself was a Jew** in fulfillment of all the promises. Christ was more than just a Jew, however, **he is God, who rules over everything and is worthy of eternal praise.** This was where the Jews got hung up.

9:6 The Jewish nation as a whole did not respond to the gospel, even though God's gifts had made them better prepared than any other nation to receive Christ. On the surface, it might seem that God has **failed to fulfill his promise to the Jews.** But that is not the case: Human beings failed. Earlier in this letter, Paul clarified that **not everyone born into a Jewish family is truly a Jew**—that is,

not all Jews are part of spiritual Israel (see 2:28-29; 11:5-6; Galatians 3:7-9). Israel's history demonstrates that God was fulfilling his promises, apart from human failures and misunderstandings. Paul illustrates this from three Old Testament events: (1) verses 7-9, the lineage passing from Abraham to Isaac, rather than Ishmael (see Genesis 16–21); (2) verses 10-16, the lineage passing from Isaac to Jacob, rather than Esau (see Genesis 25–28); (3) verses 17-18, the hardening of Pharaoh's heart (see Exodus 7–12).

9:7-9 Paul's first illustration of God's sovereign choice is **Abraham** and his children. Just being Abraham's physical descendants did not guarantee an inheritance. The line of natural descent was not the same as the line of promise. Abraham had children by three different women (Isaac, by Sarah—see Genesis 21:1-7; Ishmael, by Hagar—see Genesis 16; and six sons by Keturah—see Genesis 25:1-4). But God made it clear that **Isaac** was the **son** through whom Abraham's **descendants will be counted.** God made a sovereign choice regarding who among Abraham's physical descendants would carry the line of promise, the line that would result in the Messiah. God did not choose Isaac because he was better than his half brothers; the choice was made before Isaac was even born. Instead, it was simply God's sovereign choice. Therefore, **Abraham's physical descendants are not necessarily children of God. It is the children of the promise who are considered to be Abraham's children.**

God's sovereignty, not people's works or character, is the basis for election. The Jews were proud of the fact that their lineage came from Isaac, whose mother was Sarah (Abraham's legitimate wife), rather than from Ishmael, whose mother was Hagar (Sarah's maidservant). Paul asserts that no one can claim to be chosen by God because of his or her heritage or good deeds. God freely chooses to save whomever he wills. The doctrine of election teaches that it is God's sovereign choice to save us by his goodness and mercy, and not by our own merit.

9:10-12 Paul's second illustration of God's sovereign choice focuses on **Isaac** and **Rebekah's** twin sons, Jacob and Esau. God chose to continue the line of blessing through the **younger son**, Jacob, rather than Esau (Genesis 25:23). This was quite unusual in the Hebrew culture, where the firstborn son was highly honored. In Abraham's case, Isaac and Ishmael were sons of different women—each was a firstborn, so a choice had to be made. But Isaac and Rebekah were the parents of children over whom God had a sovereign purpose. Again, this had nothing to do with either son's character, because the choice had already been made. Jacob's future conduct does not even enter into the discussion because it was unrelated to God's choice.

Was it right for God to choose Jacob, the younger, over Esau? God chose Jacob to continue the family line of the faithful because he knew that Jacob was teachable. But he did not exclude Esau from knowing and loving him. We must remember what God is like: he is sovereign; he is not arbitrary; in all things he works for our good; he is trustworthy; he will save all who believe in him. When we understand these qualities of God, we will know that his choices are good even if we don't understand all his reasons.

9:13 The words **"I loved Jacob, but I rejected Esau,"** refer to the nations of Israel and Edom rather than to the individual brothers (see Malachi 1:2-3). God chose Jacob to continue the family line of the faithful. God did not exclude Esau from knowing and loving him. God was not rejecting Esau's eternal salvation; he was choosing Jacob to lead the nation.

Paul answers the concern voiced in verse 6 and shows that God's word has not failed. The Jews have simply misunderstood it. They missed the truth that God's election never has anything to do with works of the law, rituals, even family or community ties. They misunderstood their own election as God's people. They settled on enjoying the benefits of God's promises, rather than fulfilling their role as emissaries for sharing God's promises with the world. While we enjoy the gracious benefits of our salvation, we must not ignore the others whom God wants to reach through us.

9:14-16 God chose Isaac over Ishmael and Jacob over Esau, not because of their character or their actions, but simply because that was his choice. **"Was God being unfair?"** we might ask. "Surely those Jews who are working so hard to follow all of God's laws should be chosen. Isn't it rather arbitrary of God to just choose some and reject others?"

Paul's wording of the question in Greek expects a negative answer, which he emphatically supplies: **Of course not!** If God gave anyone exactly what they deserved the results would be disastrous! Both Isaac and Jacob were scoundrels. God demonstrated unexpected grace when he chose these men in spite of their weaknesses and failures. God is absolutely sovereign. He had explained to Moses, **"I will show mercy to anyone I choose, and I will show compassion to anyone I choose"** (see Exodus 33:19). We might still be tempted to say, "Doesn't that seem a bit unfair?" But by asking such a question we are claiming a higher understanding of fairness than God himself. We must remember that God has no obligation to show mercy or compassion to any of us—not one of us deserves his slightest concern. For God to even choose anyone is evidence of his great mercy. These words of God reveal that he does show mercy and compassion, but they are by his sovereign choice.

We tend to read God's statement to Moses (which was a response to Moses' request to see God's glory) as if it were an expression of God's withholding mercy rather than a statement of his merciful generosity. In the context of this statement in Exodus, God was not justifying himself, but saying in effect, "I will have mercy on people you would not expect, and I will have compassion in ways that will surprise you, especially when I am compassionate with you!" No one can know the heart of a person in the way that God knows. No individual, court of law, or group can perfectly assess the righteousness of a person. So we must leave the choosing and judging to God.

9:17-18 For a third illustration of God's sovereign choices, Paul recalls **Pharaoh.** God had purposely placed that particular Pharaoh in that particular position at that particular time in history so God's great **power** would be displayed (through the miracles witnessed in Egypt and by the incredible release of the Hebrew slaves), and so God's **fame** would be **spread throughout the earth.** God put up with Pharaoh's fickleness and defiance for quite some time, but all for the same purposes. Pharaoh became mired in his own rebelliousness. In fact, part of God's judgment on Egypt was the hardening of Pharaoh's heart. Eventually, those nations who heard what God had done for his people in Egypt greatly feared the Israelites and their God (see Joshua 2:10-11; 9:9; 1 Samuel 4:8).

Again, someone might ask, "Doesn't it seem a bit unfair that God would just use somebody to glorify himself?" But Paul answers the implicit question as before: God has mercy on whomever he chooses; and conversely, **he chooses to make some people refuse to listen.** God's judgment on Pharaoh's great sinfulness was to "harden" his heart, to confirm his disobedience so that the consequences of his rebellion would be his own punishment. "Hardening" occurs when a person has a track record of disobedience and rebellion. From the human perspective, it is difficult to know exactly at what point God confirms our own resistance as hardness. Paul's implicit warning is to avoid attitudes that lead to hardness of heart (see 1 Corinthians 10:6; Hebrews 3:8).

Everything comes from God's sovereign choices. Israel, as God's chosen people, had made a grave mistake in acting with superiority over others who were not of God's "chosen" nation. It was that pride that made them misunderstand their own Scriptures that said that God would offer salvation beyond Israel, to people from all nations.

9:19 Paul probably had countless discussions with fellow Jews about these issues. So he can anticipate their questions. If God simply chooses those on whom he will have mercy and those whom he will harden, **why does God blame people for not listening? Haven't they simply done what he made them do?** Occasionally these questions are asked by those who are genuinely seeking to understand God and his ways with people. Usually, however, they are used to excuse certain behavior—"It's not my fault, God; it's your fault!" In either case, as Paul explains, the answer is the same. We ourselves are to blame because we are guilty of trying to reject or resist God.

9:20 Paul has little patience for such questions, and he supposes that God doesn't either. When it comes down to it, **a mere human being** cannot **criticize God.** He is absolutely sovereign. We are extremely privileged to have any relationship with him at all. His dealings with all the world are not to be judged by us. Quoting from Scripture, Paul illustrates the absurdity of such questions. This passage was taken from Isaiah 29:16 and/or Isaiah 45:9; in context it expresses God's response to his rebellious people.

While God welcomes our sincere questions and concerns (see for example, John the Baptist in Matthew 11:1-6, and Thomas in John 20:24-29) and patiently answers us, he will not allow sin-

ners to question his sovereignty. The **thing that was created** has no right to sit in judgment on the Creator.

9:21 To further illustrate God's sovereignty, Paul compares God to a **potter** (a very common and necessary vocation in ancient times, since most cooking and storage was done in various types of clay pots). The potter has every **right** to take one large lump of clay and use part of it to make a **jar for decoration** and another part of it to make a **garbage** can. Neither item has any right to complain and ask why the potter did what he did. The lesson of the potter points to equal worth among lumps of clay, while the artist's purpose and design may differ. The proper attitude for clay is to be pliable rather than stiff, receptive rather than rebellious, and grateful for the potter's touch rather than resentful of the potter's purpose for us.

9:22 The **objects of his judgment** are nonbelievers, and especially, in context, Jewish nonbelievers (1:18). God has been **patient** with their antagonism, rebellion, blasphemy, and hatred because he is giving them time to repent (2 Peter 3:9). But those who refuse to repent are **fit only for destruction.** Their doom is coming. They have rebelled and refused to turn to God for salvation, and thus have taken responsibility for their own destruction. **God has every right to exercise his judgment and his power.** Without God's mercy and great patience, shown to us completely apart from our performance, we would have no hope at all. If God did not do this for his own purposes, we would be instantly destroyed.

9:23-24 In contrast, **the objects of his mercy** are believers, both **Jews** and **Gentiles.** To these he will **pour out the riches of his glory.** This is God's sovereign choosing when he works with "pots" prepared for destruction (9:22) or with "pots" prepared for glory. The key point to remember is that all this has been in God's plan from the beginning. When God's dealings with his creation have been summed up, there will not be a shred of doubt about his wrath, power, and glory. God did not change his plans just because his people were disobedient. Instead, God knew all that would happen to both Jews and Gentiles, and God does everything to display his great mercy.

Believers still may wonder why they would be chosen while others were rejected. Paul's point is that God is sovereign and that no one has any claim on his mercy. He prepared us in advance by his gift of salvation, and he will reveal his glory when we are finally with him for eternity. Instead of focusing on God choosing some and rejecting others, we should stand in awe at God's offer of grace to any of us. Thus, no one can demand that God explain why he does what he does. He makes all the rules. But he loves to show mercy to us—what an amazing God he is!

9:25-26 To back up the statement that God also calls the **Gentiles,** Paul quoted two verses from the prophet **Hosea.** Several hundred years before Jesus' birth, Hosea told of God's intention to bring Gentiles into his family after the Jews would reject his plan. God was not surprised by Israel's rejection. Israel thought that they alone were God's chosen because of their lineage and their laws. But God's plan never was to save only the Jews. His call was for people from all nations. Verse 25 is a quotation from Hosea 2:23, and verse 26 is from Hosea 1:10.

Hosea's situation and his children's names pictured God's attitude toward Israel—they had turned away from him and were no longer called his people or his loved ones. But God would not let this situation remain forever; one day he would call Israel back to himself. God would also turn to the Gentiles, those who are outside his chosen nation. Some day, many Gentiles would be considered God's people, his loved ones, his children. Paul saw that while God's plan had always made room for the Gentiles, with the advent of Christ, the doors to the Kingdom were opened wide. Those not known as God's people were becoming his people by God's mercy and grace, shown through Christ.

9:27-29 But the Jews (here called **Israel**) will not be forgotten. God's sovereign choice always includes some Jews, but his promises were not a blanket guarantee for all Israel. Isaiah prophesied that **only a small number** of God's original people **will be saved.** Paul saw this happening in every city where he preached. Even though he went first to the Jews, relatively few ever accepted the gospel message. Continuing the quote from Isaiah (Isaiah 10:23), God will punish his people for turning away from him. In the captivity and the exile, much punishment had been meted out. If God had **not spared** a small number of faithful believers, all of Israel would have been destroyed. But God always saved some. Having chosen Israel, God remained faithful to her. If he had not, Israel **would have been wiped out as completely as Sodom and Gomorrah,** the ancient cities that were completely destroyed by God for their horrible wickedness (see Genesis 19:24-29; Isaiah 1:9). Nothing was left of Sodom and Gomorrah. But God never completely destroyed his people.

Today the Gentiles are the majority in the church, but one day, many Jews too will come to their Savior. There is a final judgment to come, and God will carry it out. There is no time to delay. A few will be saved—who of God's people, the Jews, will become part of that small number? Paul explores this further in chapter 11.

ISRAEL'S UNBELIEF / 9:30–10:4
This section provides a summary in the middle of Paul's exposition on God's sovereign plan and an expanded explanation of the present position of the Jews. He realized that his teaching was creating a paradox, especially for his Jewish audience. How could it be that the acknowledged experts in righteousness would find their way to God barred, while those who were ignorant of righteousness were welcomed by God as long-lost children? Paul here contrasts the way of faith with the way of the law. Israel, following after a law of righteousness, did not attain it—while the Gentiles, not seeking righteousness by the law, found it by faith in Christ.

9:30 The gospel was preached to both Jews and Gentiles, but it was being accepted by far more Gentiles than Jews. The **Gentiles** did not have God's law, did not even know God, and were not even **seeking him,** yet they were being **made right with God.** Why? Because they were coming in **faith.**

9:31-32 In contrast to the Gentiles, the **Jews tried to get right with God by keeping the law,** only to fail. They had incorrectly understood righteousness in terms of works. They could not keep the law perfectly, therefore they could not keep it at all.

They tried to achieve right standing with God the wrong way—by **keeping the law and being good.** Thus some of them became more dedicated to the law than to God. They thought that if they kept the law, God would have to accept them as his people. But God cannot be obligated by us. The Jews did not see that their Scriptures, the Old Testament, taught salvation by **faith** and not by human effort—the point Paul made in the first part of this letter. As a result, they **stumbled over the great rock in their path**—the Lord Jesus Christ (see 1 Peter 2:4-8). Jesus was not what they expected, so they missed him. In so doing they missed their only way of salvation. Jesus is a stumbling block to Jews and to all who by pride would rather have recognition for doing it on their own than for trusting Christ and his goodness.

Some people still stumble over Christ because salvation by faith doesn't make sense to them. They would rather try to work their way to God, or else they expect him simply to overlook their sins. Others stumble over Christ because his values are the opposite of the world's. Christ asks for humility, and many are unwilling to humble themselves before him. He requires obedience and many refuse to put their will at his disposal. The "rock" has caused them to stumble. They heard about Christ and misunderstood, so they tripped over the one thing that could have saved them.

9:33 Paul quotes from Isaiah 28:16. Isaiah declared God's warning of destruction to Israel by Assyria. Then he said, **"I am placing a stone in Jerusalem that causes people to stumble."** This stone refers to the righteous few and to Christ. Some will stumble over him, but those who put their trust in him need never fear that their trust is misplaced. When we have placed our feet on the Rock of Zion, the Lord Jesus Christ himself, we **will not be disappointed.**

10:1 Paul's concern for **the Jewish people** is genuine and heartfelt; his **longing** and **prayer** is that they **might be saved** (see also 9:1-3). Paul worked hard and sacrificed much to teach Jews about Jesus Christ. Because Jesus is the most complete revelation of God, no one can fully know God apart from knowing Jesus; and because God appointed Jesus to bring God and human beings together, no one can come to God by another path. The Jews,

like everyone else, can find salvation only through Jesus Christ (John 14:6; Acts 4:12). Just as Paul did, we should wish that all Jews might be saved. We should pray for them and lovingly share the Good News with them. In fact, we should ask ourselves, Who do I desire to be saved, and am I regularly praying for them?

10:2 The Jews certainly had **enthusiasm** in their devotion to God and their practice of the law—Paul knew that from his own experience. However, it was **misdirected zeal.** The people Paul loved (the Jews) were so busy trying to keep the law that their zeal was actually keeping them from understanding God's way of salvation. This was exactly Paul's state of mind before Christ confronted him. He was so zealous for God and for his religion that he persecuted Christians (see Acts 9:1-2; 22:3-5; 26:4-11). His zeal was based on a misunderstanding of God's word, and so was the zeal of his fellow Jews.

10:3-4 The Israelites did not understand the extent of God's righteousness, how it would be achieved, and how it would be made available to all people (the point Paul explained in chapters 3–6). Instead, they were **clinging to their own way of getting right with God by trying to keep the law.** They were not creating some new kind of righteousness; rather, they wanted to achieve God's righteousness by observing the law and their rituals. Once their minds were set, they could not see **God's way**—that righteousness had been provided for them through faith in Jesus Christ, that the **whole purpose of the law** had been **accomplished** in him. Christ fulfills the purpose and goal of the law (Matthew 5:17) in that he perfectly exemplified all that the law requires.

ROMANS **10**:5-21

SALVATION IS FOR EVERYONE / 10:5-21

Why did God give the law when he knew people couldn't keep it? According to Paul, one reason that the law was given was to show people how guilty they are (Galatians 3:19). In addition, the law was a shadow of Christ—that is, the sacrificial system educated the people so that when the true sacrifice came, they would be able to understand his work (Hebrews 10:1-4). The system of ceremonial laws was to last until the coming of Christ. The law points to Christ, the final sacrifice for sin, the reason for all those animal sacrifices.

10:5 Paul quotes freely from Moses. The first quote is from Leviticus 18:5, a section in Leviticus that gives God's instructions to the people for how they

should live in the Promised Land. They were to obey the law for it would separate them from the pagan nations around them. But the statement, the law's way of making a person right with God requires obedience to all of its commands reveals the law's fatal flaw. In order to be right with God, one would have to obey the law perfectly, not sinning once—and that is impossible (see James 2:10). Righteousness that comes from the law is the ideal way of life, but it cannot be achieved well enough to merit God's acceptance. For that level of righteousness, supernatural help is needed.

10:6-8 Moses also wrote about **getting right with God through faith.** In verses 6-8, Paul recalls phrases from Deuteronomy 30. The book of Deuteronomy includes Moses' final speeches to Israel as they were about to enter and subdue the land that God had promised to them many years before. Moses recited the blessings they could look forward to for their obedience to God, as well as the curses they could expect if they disobeyed and turned away from him.

At the conclusion of his third address to the people, Moses explained that the people knew what they had to do to please God (Deuteronomy 30:11-14). The **message** was as near as their **lips** and **heart.** No one would have to **go to heaven** or **to the place of the dead** to get it so that they would know what to obey. No one has to go up to heaven to bring Christ down as though he had never been incarnated; Christ himself has already come in the flesh (John 1:14). No one has to go into the grave to bring Christ up from the dead; Christ has already been resurrected.

Just as God's message was already clear to the people of Moses' day, so it is as near as the lips and hearts of Paul's readers, including us. The words convey an immediate opportunity to respond. It is as close and available to us as it can possibly be without overruling our will. What message is that? **Salvation comes from trusting Christ,** and it is **within easy reach.**

10:9 The word is near—as near as your lips and heart (10:8; Deuteronomy 30:14). To **confess** means to "give verbal affirmation,"—in this case to acknowledge with your mouth that **Jesus is Lord** and was **raised** for you. When we confess that Jesus is Lord, we are acknowledging his rank or supreme place. We are pledging our obedience and worship; we are placing our life under his protection for safekeeping. We are pledging ourselves and our resources to his control for direction and service.

Anyone can say he or she believes something, but God knows each person's heart. In this confession, it is not enough to merely utter the words; they must be declared, professed, proclaimed from the **heart,** expressing our full conviction. The gospel message in a nutshell is confess and **believe**

and **you will be saved.** There is no reference to works or rituals.

10:10 You must first believe **in your heart**—that belief makes you **right with God** (God declares you "not guilty" for your sins). By prayer to God, you confess **with your mouth** your belief in God and what he has done for you. As in verses 8-9 above, belief and confession lead to salvation. To believe and to confess involve whole-person commitment. They are two parts of a single step, just as lifting the foot and then placing it back down are two movements in the one act of taking a step.

10:11 To summarize the transaction that he has just described, Paul quotes again from Isaiah 28:16, as he did at the end of chapter 9. **"Anyone who believes in him will not be disappointed."** Paul is not saying that Christians will never be disillusioned or disappointed. At times people will let us down and circumstances will take a turn for the worse. Paul is saying that God will keep his side of the bargain—those who call on him will be saved. God will never fail to provide righteousness to those who believe.

10:12 The "anyone" of verse 11 includes both **Jew and Gentile.** God's salvation is available to all who believe for **they all have the same Lord.** Every person is confronted with the need to acknowledge Jesus as Lord. Because sin is a universal condition, the remedy of justification by faith universally applies. Those who are saved will be richly blessed with God's great **riches**—in this world (although not always materially, as some might hope or expect), and most certainly in the world to come.

10:13 A final quotation taken from the Hebrew Scriptures (Joel 2:32) serves well for Paul's conclusion. God's special relationship with Israel will continue, but it has been broadened to include **anyone who calls on the name of the Lord.** God's plans for Israel had their climax in Christ. Access to God, for all people, now comes through Jesus Christ. With this last reference, Paul neatly lays the foundation for the necessity of worldwide evangelism. Joel 2:32 is an Old Testament mandate for missions. To call on the Lord is to ask the Lord to come to you and be real to you. Those who call on Jesus as their Lord want him to be their Lord and Savior.

10:14-15 If God's salvation is for anyone who calls, how can people **call** on God **to save them** if they have not been moved to **believe in him?** How can they believe **if they have never heard about him?** There can be no call, no belief, if these people have not heard about God ("heard" means a hearing that understands the significance of the words and realizes that a response is required), and been given the offer of salvation. And **how can they hear about him unless someone tells them?** There can be no call, no belief, no hearing, unless there are those **sent** to share the Good News.

All believers are sent to announce this Good News. The process of salvation begins with the one who tells another the Good News. Like Paul and the early Christians, who spread the message of Christ despite persecution and even death, we should be eager to share this Good News of salvation to all who will listen. In the verse quoted from Isaiah 52:7, the herald is bearing **good news** to Judah about the end of their exile in Babylon and their return to their own land. His **feet** were **beautiful** to them, for his good news was so welcome. The message was what he brought, but it was those worn and dusty feet that brought him. Those feet were beautiful because they represented the messenger's willingness to be sent with good news. Only now the message was not just for Israel, but for the whole world.

10:16 Many Jews did not welcome the gospel of Jesus Christ—they heard it but refused to believe and submit to it. The failure of Jews to respond to God's warnings of impending judgment was true in Isaiah's day, **"Lord, who has believed our message?"** It was true while Jesus preached (John 12:37-41), and it was true in Paul's day. We can expect the same today. Bringing people good news does not guarantee a welcome. But having been changed by the message ourselves ought to change the way we see those who have not yet heard. We are not held responsible for how others respond, but we are expected to carry the Good News.

10:17 This statement expresses the main theme of this section. People need to hear the Good News of salvation in Christ in order to believe it (10:14). Faith does not respond in a vacuum or respond blindly. **Faith** is believing what one has been told about God's offer of salvation and trusting the one who has been spoken about.

10:18 Some might argue that the Jews weren't given enough chances to hear or that somehow the message should have been made clearer for them. Perhaps Isaiah's complaint ("Who has believed?" 10:16) was the fault of the messenger. But Paul emphatically responds that of course they heard. The message had been preached far and wide, first to the Jews and then to the Gentiles (see 1:16). Then Paul quotes from Psalm 19:4: **"The message of God's creation has gone out to everyone, and its words to all the world."** When Luke ended the book of Acts with Paul in Rome, this was probably considered a culmination of the great commission to take the gospel to the ends of the earth (Acts 1:8). At this time in history, the Good News had

been preached to Jews and Gentiles for about twenty years, and it had spread throughout the Mediterranean areas where Jews lived. There may have been some Jews who truly had not yet heard, but to use that as an excuse for the large number of Jews who had rejected the gospel did not sit well with Paul (see also Romans 1:18-20).

As the loopholes close for the Jews, they close for everyone else, too. If the Jews are not excused for their unbelief, how can the rest of us think there might be some excuse for us? In the end, some may wish they had heard more, but God will declare that what they heard was enough. In the meantime, those of us who have heard have little excuse for our apathy in passing on the Good News!

10:19 Someone might then argue, "Okay, so the Jews heard, but perhaps they didn't **really understand** that God's message was salvation not by the law, but by faith, and that it was for the Gentiles too." Paul didn't like that excuse either. The Jews' knowledge of their own Scriptures should have led them to believe in Christ. He quotes again from their Scriptures to answer the argument. First, from Deuteronomy 32:21: **"I will rouse your jealousy by blessing other nations. I will make you angry by blessing the foolish Gentiles."** The Gentiles were not a single nation; they consisted of everyone who was not part of the Jewish nation. The Jews would be envious that God would offer salvation to the world at large and not just to his chosen people. They would be angry that the pagan peoples whom they considered to have no understanding would be accepted by God. In all of this, God's purpose would not be to reject his people, but to cause them to return to him.

10:20 The second quote is from Isaiah 65:1. The **people who were not looking for** God were the Gentiles. Although they had previously ignored God as simply the God of Israel and so had never sought him out, the Gentiles would recognize God as the one true God, and God would reveal himself to them.

10:21 Finally, from Isaiah 65:2, Paul explains that God had been gracious to his people, patiently holding out his **arms** to them and calling them, only to have them disobey and argue with him. God's invitation was spurned and his gifts were rejected.

The disobedience of Israel was judged by God's welcome to the Gentiles (even though that was in his plan all along). But he will still accept his chosen people if they will only return to him. He remains faithful to his promises to his people, even though they have been unfaithful to him. God still holds out his arms.

ROMANS 11

GOD'S MERCY ON ISRAEL / 11:1-24

In this section Paul points out that not all Jews have rejected God's message of salvation. He draws upon the experience of Elijah to show that there had always been a faithful remnant among the people. In Paul's day, there was still a remnant living by faith, under the law (11:5). After all, Paul was a Jew; so were Jesus' disciples and nearly all of the early Christian missionaries. Part of God's sovereign choice involves bringing a remnant of his people back to himself. This truth forbids any hint of anti-Semitism—God's plan still includes the Jews.

11:1 The Jewish nation had heard words of rejection before. In the depths of their sinfulness when King Manasseh ruled the northern kingdom of Israel, God said he would forsake his people because of their sin (2 Kings 21:14-15). Indeed, Jeremiah had warned the people that God had abandoned them (Jeremiah 7:29). With this question Paul expresses a deep concern—has God finally grown tired of Israel's constant disobedience and **rejected** them forever?

Paul responds, **Of course not!** One proof of this is Paul's experience. Paul had received salvation, and he was **a Jew, a descendant of Abraham and a member of the tribe of Benjamin.** Paul is a full-blooded Jew (who had even gone so far as to persecute Christians before he became a believer). Surely if God was going to reject someone, Paul would have been a good choice. But God, in his sovereignty, called Paul and rearranged his entire life.

11:2-3 God did not reject his people in the days of Moses, nor in the days of the prophets. And he is not rejecting them now. Regardless of Israel's unfaithfulness, God always keeps his promises. God **chose** Israel to be the people through whom all other nations of the world could know him. He made this promise to Abraham, their ancestor (Genesis 12:1-3). Israel didn't have to do anything to be chosen. God had given them this privilege because he wanted to, not because they deserved special treatment (Deuteronomy 9:4-6). God knew beforehand that Israel would be unfaithful; if God's faithfulness to Israel was going to be dependent on their faithfulness, God would never have chosen them in the first place. God will remain faithful to his promises to Israel, despite Israel's failure.

Paul then reminded his readers of a time when all Israel had deserted God, but God had preserved some for himself. After Elijah's stunning demonstration of God's power over Baal's prophets at Mount Carmel (and the killing of all of Baal's prophets), **Elijah** fled for his life from the wrath of Israel's evil Queen Jezebel who threatened to have him killed. He ran for many miles and then stopped to rest. In his terror and exhaustion, he cried out to God, **"Lord, they have killed your prophets and torn down your altars. I alone am left, and now they are trying to kill me, too."** "They" actually refers to the evil leadership in the northern kingdom of Israel, but Elijah was holding the entire nation responsible for the actions of many. He had concluded that he was the only person left in Israel who believed in God.

11:4 God shared some very important information with Elijah, replying that Elijah was **not the only one left**—God had **seven thousand** believers who had not turned to idol worship. That was not a large number, but it was a faithful "remnant." Notice that God reserved these faithful followers for himself—the remnant existed because of his sovereign choice.

11:5-6 Just as God had preserved a few of his people when almost the entire nation had turned to idolatry, so **today,** God has **a few** who **are being saved as a result of God's kindness in choosing them.** The Jewish believers in this faithful few are proof that God has not rejected his people (2 Kings 19:4, 19). These few, **saved by God's kindness** realize that they were not saved by **good works.** Jews who believe in Christ are not denying their faith or their heritage; instead, they are discovering what these were truly meant to be. If God's grace in choosing us depended on our works or obedience to the law, it would not be **free and undeserved.** "God saved you by his special favor when you believed. And you can't take credit for this; it is a gift from God. Salvation is not a reward for the good things we have done, so none of us can boast about it" (Ephesians 2:8-9).

11:7-10 This verse provides an excellent summary of Romans 9–11. The nation had **earnestly** sought **the favor of God** by doing works of the law (see 10:2-3). But God did not accept them. Instead, he accepted the **few** who had been **chosen.** Israel's failure was foreseen by God and, in fact, brought about by him (see 9:22-23, 33). Their being **made unresponsive** was confirmation of their inability to understand and their insensitivity to God's word and God's call. When God judged them, he removed their ability to see, hear, and repent; thus they would experience the consequences of their rebellion. But this is not the same as rejection; rather, it confirms their response to God. Paul illustrates this from two passages in Scripture (as follows).

Quoting from Deuteronomy 29:4 and Isaiah 29:10, their unresponsiveness was like a **deep sleep.** When people repeatedly refuse to listen to God's Good News, they eventually will be unable to hear and understand it. Israel's present misinterpretation of their Scriptures and refusal to accept Christ as their Messiah is a continuation of their tendency to misunderstand God's plans and purposes for them. Paul saw this happening in the Jewish congregations he visited on his missionary journeys.

Next, Paul quoted from Psalm 69:22-23 (a psalm thought to be prophetic about the suffering of the Messiah). These words of David were originally a curse directed at Israel's enemies. Paul turns the curse around and points it at the Jews! These blessings should have drawn Israel to God and thus led them to Christ; instead, they became **a snare, a trap.** Israel's blessings had led to pride that led them away from God. Thus, not only did they miss the Messiah when he came, but they also persecuted and killed him.

11:11 This is the tenth time in this letter that Paul has asked a question only to respond in a strong negative. No, Israel's stumbling did not cause them to **fall** so that God has declared the nation **beyond recovery.** Their blindness is not permanent (11:8); their fall is not fatal. Israel's stumbling means that **salvation** has come **to the Gentiles.** Israel's rejection of Christ was a part of God's plan all along, as essential as God's sovereign choice of Jacob over Esau (9:10-13) and his hardening of Pharaoh (9:17-18). But the salvation of the Gentiles is not the end of the story. It too has a purpose—to make the **Jews jealous.** The blessings offered to the Gentiles would spur Israel to end their hostility toward the gospel and ultimately bring them to faith. God desires to restore Israel to himself.

11:12 God took the riches that the Jews should have received and offered them to the Gentiles, who gladly received them. The **Gentiles were enriched**—those who received the gospel received great riches for eternity; and believers, in turn, have an influence for good on the rest of the world. Paul looks beyond the present to a future time when **the Jews** will **accept** the riches of salvation that God offers (see 11:26). Israel's acceptance does not mean that the riches given to the Gentiles will be taken away; rather, when the Jews are saved, the Gentiles will enjoy even **greater** blessings along with them.

11:13-14 We can almost sense the intensity of Paul's words as he defines his audience. If we are not Jews, we know that the next words are meant for us. Paul singles out the Gentile believers to listen carefully to what he is going to say. They (and we) are being given an opportunity to understand their role in the divine plan. Paul will explain that the salvation of the **Gentiles** both depends on Israel and contributes to Israel's salvation.

All of the apostles were preaching both to Jews and non-Jews, but Paul had been specially **appointed** by God to go to the Gentiles (Acts 9:15; Galatians 2:3-10). Throughout this ministry he had been a strong (and at first lone) advocate for Gentile freedom from the Jewish law. Beyond that, Paul hoped that **the Jews** would **want what** the Gentiles had been given, and so they would be saved. Paul hopes to cause the Jews to recognize that God greatly blessed the Gentiles when they believed in the Jews' own Messiah. The Jews might then realize that those blessings are still promised to them as part of God's covenant with them, but they can only be obtained by faith in Jesus Christ. Again Paul is revealing his great desire to see his people be saved (see 9:1-3; 10:1).

11:15 Israel's **rejection** by God meant that **God offered salvation to the rest of the world.** God had always planned to include the Gentiles, even if that meant a temporary setting aside of the Jews. When the chosen people, who were designated as the vehicles of God's blessing to the world, actually blocked that message from getting through, God made sure that the message arrived anyway. When Jews come to Christ and God accepts them back, there will be great rejoicing, as if **dead** people had come back to **life.**

Though we may not grasp all the nuances of Paul extensive argument, his purpose is unmistakable. He wants to give Gentiles every reason possible to welcome their Jewish brothers and sisters in the faith with open arms. At the same time, he wants to help his Jewish brethren reciprocate that welcome. Neither group is to claim supremacy in the church. The message is: God has made room in his family for both of you, so you must get along together.

11:16 Paul believes that Israel's refusal to accept Christ is temporary and that one day the nation will be brought back to God. He explains this in an illustration. The **roots**, obviously, are the first part of a tree, and form the "character" of the **branches**. **Abraham's** faith was like the root of a productive tree, and the Jewish people are the tree's natural branches. As a result of God's choice and Abraham's response, the nation that descended from him was **holy.**

Paul extends the principle to cover the fate of his people. If the remnant of Jews who had lived by faith were called holy by God, then there is still hope for the whole, proving that God has not rejected them. If the root, the tree of justification by faith, is holy, then any branch attached to and nourished by that root will also be holy.

11:17 God did not tear down the entire tree, but **some** of the branches were **broken off** because of sin and unbelief. These branches are Jews who failed to respond in faith to God's mercy. In their place, the Gentile believers are likened to **branches from a wild olive tree** that have been **grafted in.** Grafting involves inserting a bud or shoot of one plant into a slit in the stem or trunk of another plant. The shoot shares in the nourishment from the main stem or trunk (here pictured as **God's rich nourishment**) and grows, receiving the same blessings that the natural branches had.

11:18 But the Gentiles, the wild olive shoots who have been grafted into the cultivated olive tree (Israel), have no grounds for bragging. The Gentile "branches" need to remember that they are just as dependent on "the root," for their survival as the Jewish branches. God has not changed his original plan; salvation stems from the promise to Abraham and God's choice of Israel. Both Jews and Gentiles share the tree's nourishment based on faith in God. For Paul, the only appropriate attitude for any "branch" is humble thankfulness. Any attitude of superiority is to be avoided, for it might indicate that grafted-in branches are candidates for the same fate as the original ones that had been broken off (see 11:21).

11:19 A Gentile believer might make this argument. It is true that it was necessary to break off some branches in the grafting process. But it would

be a mistake to assume that Paul is limiting God's acceptance, as if there was only so much room on the tree for branches. The point is not so much replacement as opportunity. The idea is not that Jews were **broken off** so that we could take their place; but rather that they were broken off so that the Gentile opportunity for justification by faith might become clear. This is underscored by Paul's assertion that even broken off branches can be grafted back in (see 11:23).

11:20 The real reason some of the branches of the tree, some of the nation of Israel, were broken off was because of their stubborn unbelief. The Gentiles that were grafted in are only there by their faith and by God's grace. Thus they are warned, **Don't think highly of yourself, but fear what could happen.** Those who are arrogant cherish proud thoughts about themselves; they do not have a proper fear and respect for God. Our relationship with God is to be one of humble dependence (see 12:3).

Jesus used many of these images to explain his own role as the vine (John 15:1-8). He spoke of his Father, the Gardener who cuts off every branch that is unproductive. He also reminded the disciples that a branch cannot survive on its own, but is entirely dependent on the vine for its survival and nourishment. The branches serve their purpose in bearing fruit.

11:21 God willingly set aside Israel because of their stumbling and blindness to the Good News. The Gentiles should remember that God will set them aside as well if they became arrogant—he will **not spare** them **either.** According to the context, it is not absolutely clear whether Paul is referring to those who have fallen away from the faith or those whose faith was never real. What is clear is that he is warning Gentiles not to arrogantly think that their being grafted in is irreversible. The only way they can remain in the tree is by continuing to trust in God's grace.

11:22 God sovereignly decided to put Israel aside for a time and offer salvation through faith to all the world. This was a **severe** act, but it was done in judgment **to those who disobeyed** (9:32-33). He has been **kind** to the Gentiles, but Gentile believers must **continue to trust in his kindness.** This refers to steadfast perseverance in faith—continual and patient dependence on Christ. Steadfastness is a proof of the reality of faith. If Gentile believers do not continue in their perseverance in faith, they **will be cut off,** just as the natural branches were cut off because of their unbelief. This does not mean individual believers can lose their salvation and be cut off from God; rather, Paul is speaking from a generalized standpoint, picturing Gentiles as a group turning away from God as the nation of Israel had. God's sternness was demonstrated in that faith was not automatic for the chosen people; and his kindness was demonstrated in providing Gentiles with the opportunity for faith.

11:23-24 Returning to Israel, Paul says if they will **turn from their unbelief, God will graft them**

back into the tree again. If, contrary to nature, wild olive shoots can be grafted into a cultivated olive tree, certainly the natural branches can be grafted back into root stock of the cultivated tree. We become part of God's "tree" by faith; we forfeit any potential relationship with God by unbelief. Gentiles are orphans graciously adopted into God's family. A wayward Jew who discovers the faith of Abraham is coming home.

GOD'S MERCY IS FOR EVERYONE / 11:25-36

As difficult as it may be for us to understand, God's handling of the Jews and the Gentiles is intended to expose all of us to his mercy. Paul wraps up his argument by saying that in the end there will be room for both Jews and Gentiles in the plan of God. The details of exactly how God will do all this are aptly called a mystery!

11:25 The temporary stumbling of Israel is part of what Paul calls a **mystery**—the word here means a truth that has been unrevealed up to this point but is now being made known. The mystery reveals, for example, that Israel's stumbling has always been part of God's plan. God put Israel aside for a time in order to offer salvation to the Gentiles. Paul reviews this mystery so the Gentiles **will not feel proud and start bragging.** Conceit would be a sign that they were ignorant of God's master plan that included everyone (see 11:32).

Some of the Jews have hard hearts, but this is only temporary, because it will only be experienced **until the complete number of Gentiles comes to Christ**—that is, when all the elect of the Gentiles have come to salvation (see Acts 15:14). God knows the size of that number of Gentiles who will be grafted into God's tree of faith. We only know that the number will be complete. As many will have come in as are going to come in.

11:26-27 This statement, **all Israel will be saved,** has provoked a variety of interpretations. The most widely held are as follows:

- The majority of Jews in the final generation before Christ's return will turn to Christ for salvation.
- Paul is using the term Israel for the "spiritual" nation of Israel made up of everyone—Jew and Gentile—who has received salvation through faith in Christ. Thus all Israel (or all believers, the church) will receive God's promised gift of salvation.
- Israel as a whole will have a role in Christ's Kingdom. Their identity as a people won't be discarded. God chose the nation of Israel, and he has never rejected it. He also chose the church, through Jesus Christ, and he will never

reject it either. This does not mean, of course, that all Jews or all church members will be saved. It is possible to belong to a nation or to an organization without ever responding in faith. But just because some people have rejected Christ does not mean that God stops working with either Israel or the church. He continues to offer salvation freely to all.
- **And so** means "in this way" or "this is how," referring to the necessity of faith in Christ.

These explanations do not exclude one another, and they all serve to underscore Paul's clear intention: to demonstrate that God had not rejected Israel. Indeed, Paul believed the nation of Israel would be restored to God. Both Jews and Gentiles will make up the flourishing tree that stands for the Kingdom, as well the brush pile of broken branches prepared for burning that represents those who have rejected God's gracious offer of forgiveness.

To confirm his statement, Paul quotes from Isaiah, first from 59:20-21. Jesus Christ is the **Deliverer** who **will come from Jerusalem.** For the first and only time in this letter, Paul speaks of the second coming of Christ. At that time, Christ **will turn Israel from all ungodliness** (see also Psalm 14:7; 53:6). God also promises to **take away their sins** (see also Jeremiah 31:33-34).

11:28 Paul is still speaking to the Gentiles in his audience (11:13). In order for God to bring the gospel to them, he had to set the **Jews** aside—as if they were his **enemies** for having rejected the **Good News.** But as far as God's choice, his election, is concerned, **the Jews are still his chosen people because of his promises to Abraham, Isaac, and Jacob.** Because God chose those men through whom he would carry out his promises, he will keep his promises to their descendants.

11:29 The privileges and invitation given to Israel **can never be withdrawn.** God will not take back his **gifts** or withdraw his **call.** He will keep his promises. While God will not take back what he has offered, we are certainly able to reject it. Paul is making an application from God's characteristic faithfulness to the Jews that anyone can rely on. God will do what he promises.

11:30 The **Gentiles were rebels** before they knew God, but they received God's mercy and offer of salvation because of Israel's disobedience. Having received from God something that they had lacked previously, they could expect to keep on enjoying God's mercy. By the same logic, however, the Jews could also expect God to be consistent with his promises, even though they had, for a time, rejected his mercy.

11:31 From Paul's time onward, Israel has been rebellious to God because of their refusal to accept salvation in Christ. Though they began with an advantage due to God's gracious choice of them as his people, by being disobedient, the Jews had proved themselves equally needing God's mercy. And Israel will receive mercy because as soon as all the elect of the Gentiles have come (see 11:25), then God's **mercy** will again be directed to Israel.

In these verses, Paul shows how the Jews and the Gentiles benefit each other. Whenever God shows mercy to one group, the other shares the blessing. In God's original plan, the Jews would be the source of God's blessing to the Gentiles (see Genesis 12:3). When the Jews neglected this mission, God blessed the Gentiles anyway through the Jewish Messiah. He still maintained his love for the Jews because of his promises to Abraham, Isaac, and Jacob. But someday the faithful Jews will share in God's mercy.

11:32 When Adam sinned, all humanity sinned with him (5:19). We are all sinners (3:23). When people choose to follow their own passion and desires, they are **imprisoned** in their **disobedience.** People who deliberately choose to disobey God imprison themselves. It is those who understand that they have been saying no to God who are in the best position to say yes to him. God then is willing to **have mercy** on all who come to him. For a beautiful picture of Jews and Gentiles experiencing rich blessings, see Isaiah 60.

11:33-35 Here Paul bursts into a song of praise as he concludes his entire treatise in chapters 1–11 on God's sovereign plan for our salvation. It is **impossible for us to understand.** Paul quoted from Isaiah 40:13, pointing out that God alone knows the plan. In his unsearchable wisdom he designed it. No human being was, is, or will ever be involved in giving him advice or making new suggestions. Then Paul quotes loosely from Job 41:11 to point out that God is in sovereign control. He is not in our debt, we are in his!

11:36 God is the Creator, Sustainer, and Omega of all life. Everything **comes from him** and is for him to use for **his glory.** God is almighty and all-powerful, but even more, he cares for us personally. No person or power can compare with God.

Paul began his letter with the statement that God left his imprint on the world he created, but that the human beings of that creation had chosen rebellion. In the past eleven chapters, Paul has examined God's marvelous plan for bringing the rebels home. God has chosen to "have mercy on everyone" (11:32). What more can any believer, saved by grace, say than, **to him be glory evermore. Amen.**

ROMANS 12

A LIVING SACRIFICE TO GOD / 12:1-21

Next, Paul moves from a doctrinal discussion to a practical discussion, for Christian doctrine translates into action. The first eleven chapters of this letter reveal God's mercy to sinners in that he sent his Son to die on the cross for our sins. The last five chapters explain our obligation to God. If the early message of the letter is the way we all can come to God through Christ, then the closing part of the letter is the way we all can live for God in Christ. In view of all God has done for us, how can we respond in a way that is pleasing to him?

12:1 And so, because of God's great compassion on both Jews and Gentiles in offering salvation

through Christ, Paul urges believers to please God in their daily lives. The evil world is full of temptation and sin. Paul helps believers understand how they can live for God.

Paul had already told the Roman believers to offer themselves to God so that their whole bodies would be for his glory (6:13). Our **bodies** are all we have to offer—we live in our bodies. The body enfolds our emotions, our mind, our thoughts, our desires, and our plans. Thus, the body represents the total person; it is the instrument by which all our service is given to God. In order to live for God, we must **give** him all that we are, represented by our body. If our body is at God's disposal, he will have our free time, our pleasures, and all our behavior.

When sacrificing an animal according to God's law, a priest would kill the animal, cut it in pieces, and place it on the altar. Sacrifice was important, but even in the Old Testament God made it clear that obedience from the heart was much more important (see 1 Samuel 15:22; Psalm 40:6; Amos 5:21-24). God wants us to offer ourselves as living sacrifices—daily laying aside our own desires to follow him, putting all our energy and resources at his disposal, and trusting him to guide us (see Hebrews 13:15-16; 1 Peter 2:5). Our new life is a thank-offering to God. Offering our body as **a living and holy sacrifice** to be completely set apart for God and dedicated to his service.

12:2 When believers offer their entire self to God, a change will happen in their relation to the world. Christians are called to a different lifestyle than what the world offers with its **behavior and customs,** which are usually selfish and often corrupting (Galatians 1:4; 1 Peter 1:14). Christians are to live as citizens of a future world. There will be pressure to conform, to continue living according to the script written by the world, but believers are forbidden to give in to that pressure.

But refusing to conform to this world's values must go even deeper than the level of behavior and customs—it must go to the transforming of the **way** we **think.** Believers are to experience a complete transformation from the inside out. And the change must begin in the mind, where all thoughts and actions begin. Much of the work is done by God's Spirit in us, and the tool most frequently used is God's word. As we memorize and meditate upon God's word, our way of thinking changes. Our minds become first informed, and then conformed to the pattern of God, the pattern for which we were originally designed. When believers have had their minds transformed and are becoming more like Christ, they **will know what God wants** and they will want to do it for it is **good, pleasing** to God, and **perfect** for them.

12:3 Paul is here speaking as **God's messenger,** an apostle (see 1:5). The authority he was about to exercise was not his own by right, but was an evidence of God's grace. He warned the believers that inflated pride has no place in a believer's life (see 3:27; 11:18, 20). This is especially significant in light of Paul's teaching up to this point in his letter. The Jews are not better than the Gentiles; the Gentiles are not better than the Jews. Rather, all are dependent on God's mercy for their salvation, thus there is no room for pride. Any such pride would undermine the oneness vital to the growth of the church.

Each believer's personal appraisal ought to be **honest.** Neither an inflated ego nor a deflated person is free to obey. God has given each believer a measure of **faith** with which to serve him. This expression refers to the spiritual capacity and/or power given to each person to carry out his or her function in the church. The concept of **measuring your value** is described further in 12:6, where Paul uses the terminology "different gifts, according to the grace given us." It is God's discernment, not ours, that gives out the measure for service. Whatever we have in the way of natural abilities or spiritual gifts—all should be used with humility for building up the body of Christ. If we are proud, we cannot exercise our faith and gifts to benefit others. And if we consider ourselves worthless, we also withhold what God intended to deliver to others through us.

12:4-5 Replacing the national identity that had once set apart God's people, Paul gives a new picture of the identity of God's redeemed people. They are like a **body.** Each of us has **one body,** but it has **many parts**—eyes, ears, fingers, toes, blood vessels, muscles. And **each part has a special function.** Not every part of our body can see; not every part hears. But all must work together if the body is going to move and act correctly. (See also 1 Corinthians 12:12-27.) Just as our physical bodies are composed of many parts, so **Christ's body** is made up of many believers who all perform **different work.** And as our bodies cannot be taken apart, so **we belong to each other.** The members work together to make the body work. When it is not done, the body suffers.

We must be humble and recognize our partnership in the body of Christ. Only then can our gifts be used effectively, and only then can we appreciate others' gifts. God gives us gifts so we can build up his church. To use them effectively, we must:

- realize that all gifts and abilities come from God
- understand that not everyone has the same gifts nor all the gifts

- know who we are and what we do best
- dedicate our gifts to God's service and not to our personal success
- be willing to utilize our gifts wholeheartedly, not holding back anything from God's service.

12:6 The emphasis here is that **God has given** these abilities to his people. These are God's gifts to his church, and he gives faith and power as he wills. Our role is to be faithful and to seek ways to serve others with what Christ has given us.

The gifts Paul mentions in this list fall into two categories: speaking and serving. Gifts are given that God's grace may be expressed. Words speak to our hearts and minds of God's grace; acts of service show that grace in action. This list is not exhaustive; there are many gifts, most of them hidden from the public—those "behind the scenes" words and actions that serve and magnify God.

The ability to prophesy, according to the New Testament, is not always predicting the future. Often it means effectively communicating God's messages (1 Corinthians 14:1-3). These gifts are not for having, but for using. In other words, God's gifts fulfill their value as they are utilized for the benefit of others.

12:7-8 If a person has the gift of **serving,** then he or she should use it where and when it is needed, and use it to its best and fullest capacity. The same goes for the other gifts that Paul mentions: teaching, encouraging, sharing, leading, showing kindness. Whatever gift a believer has, he or she should faithfully use it in gratitude to God. By focusing on the application of the gifts, Paul is removing the tendency toward unhealthy self-congratulation in the discovery of gifts. If we are busy using our gifts, we will be less taken up with concerns over status and power. Genuine service controls pride.

This list of gifts is representative, not exhaustive. It would be difficult for one person to embody all these gifts. An assertive prophet usually would not make a good counselor, and a generous giver might fail as a leader. When people identify their own gifts and their unique combination of gifts (this list is far from complete), they should then discover how they can use their gifts to build up Christ's body, the church. At the same time, they should realize that one or two gifts can't do all the work of the church. Believers should be thankful for each other, thankful that others have gifts that are completely different. In the church, believers' strengths and weaknesses can balance each other. Some people's abilities compensate for other people's deficiencies. Together all believers can build Christ's church. But all these gifts will be worthless if they are used begrudgingly out of duty, or if they are exercised without love (see also 1 Corinthians 13:1-3).

12:9 The key ingredient in interpersonal relationships is **love**—God's love *(agape)*. This kind of love is a self-sacrificial love, a love that cares for the well-being of others. All the gifts that are exercised in the body should be expressed in this love.

To **hate what is wrong** means turning toward what is **good** and clinging to it. This principle is practiced when we are able to detest an evil act while practicing compassion toward the one who has done it. This principle is also important regarding the exercise of spiritual gifts. Believers must always be careful that the use of their gifts does not lead them to unloving or evil motives, attitudes, or actions.

12:10 Paul's charge goes against the value of rugged individualism—the attitude of "doing it all by myself." Believers are to show brotherly **love** to fellow believers, and respect all the gifted people in the church, not just those whose gifts are visible. That's the only way that the body of Christ can function effectively and make a positive impact on the unbelieving world. The Greek word for **genuine affection** pictures the type of loyalty and affection that family members have for one another. This kind of love allows for weaknesses and imperfections, communicates, deals with problems, affirms others, and has a strong commitment and loyalty to others. Such a bond will hold any church together no matter what problems come from without or within.

God's command for us to **delight in honoring each other** involves love. To honor means to give a person high value and respect. As Christians, we honor people because they have been created in God's image, because they are our brothers and sisters in Christ, and because they have a unique contribution to make to Christ's church (see also Ephesians 5:21; Philippians 2:3).

12:11 As believers who **serve the Lord enthusiastically,** it follows that we would never want to be **lazy.** Paul is not advocating activity for activity's sake. Rather, we should consistently use our spiritual gifts to serve the body. We have been called (1:6-7), challenged (12:1-2), and equipped (12:4-6) for serving the Lord. Fatigue may be part of the cycle of service, but apathy (lack of zeal) should not be part of a believer's life. Christians must fight against discouragement, depression, and negativeness; they must do their utmost to keep their spiritual temperature high.

12:12 This means that we should look forward with happy anticipation to all that **God is plan-**

ning for us. We don't have to fear our future when it is in God's hands. Christ is the reason that we can be joyful. When we face **trouble** or persecution, we are to **be patient,** for we know God is in control (see also 5:2-5). A trademark of believers is prayer, for it is our lifeline to God. We must **always be prayerful,** both individually and corporately.

12:13 For believers, the challenges of the Christian life are constantly shifting between what we experience personally and what we experience because we are part of the body of Christ. Gifts, love, hope, patience, and prayer are valuable, but they do not take precedence over other believers' needs. Because we are members of Christ's body, we must **help** those who **are in need.** This was another trademark of believers, and it was often what drew nonbelievers to Christianity (see Acts 2:44-45; 4:34-37; 11:27-30).

To **get into the habit of inviting guests** refers to hospitality. Christian hospitality differs from social entertaining. Entertaining focuses on the host—the home must be spotless; the food must be well prepared and abundant; the host must appear relaxed and good-natured. Hospitality, in contrast, focuses on the guests. Their needs—whether for a place to stay, nourishing food, a listening ear, or acceptance—are the primary concern. Hospitality can happen in a messy home. It can happen around a dinner table where the main dish is canned soup. Believers should not hesitate to offer hospitality just because they are not wealthy enough to entertain.

12:14 Paul now broadens his perspective to the world where the believers live—in this case, the capital of the empire, Rome itself. The community of believers was a tiny segment, vulnerable to the edicts of pagan emperors and persecution by any who disagreed with them. Paul, aware of these realities, counsels believers to avoid trouble by refusing to retaliate when persecuted and to respond with good when they are treated with evil, as Jesus had instructed as well (Matthew 5:44).

12:15 Christians should **be happy** with others, with no hint of jealousy; and they should **share** the **sorrow** of fellow believers, offering kindness, concern, compassion, and a shoulder to cry on if needed. The believers needed to have this as they dealt with the ups and downs of daily life in their surroundings.

Following Jesus will mean that believers will pass through a kaleidoscope of experiences in life. Christianity is neither denying life's hardships, nor dulling life's excitements. Our perspective of eter-

nity in Christ can free us to enter into the full variety of living. Both laughter and tears are appropriate before God. Each has an important place in representing our feelings. Identifying with the joys and heartaches of others is also an important way to show them our love.

12:16 In order to **live in harmony** with others, and especially with fellow believers, we must not **act important** or think we **know it all.** Instead, we are to **enjoy the company of ordinary people.** James leveled a scathing indictment on believers who were practicing favoritism and elitism in the church (James 2:1-9). People of low position are only identified as such by the world's standards. Christ thought they were worth dying for, and so we can associate with them.

12:17 The commands in verses 17-21 relate mainly to dealings with nonbelievers. When people do evil against us, we are **never** to **pay back evil for evil,** as much as we might like to (see also 1 Peter 3:9). Instead, we are to **do things in such a way that everyone can see** we are honorable (see 1 Peter 2:11-12). Paul's standard for behavior was not common consensus, but godliness. The point being made here is that the behavior of believers must be such that no one can rightfully make a claim of wrongdoing. To commit the same evil that was committed against us makes us indistinguishable from the original offenders.

12:18 Paul counsels believers to have as peaceful relations **as possible** with their unbelieving neighbors and associates. In a perfect world, all people could live peacefully together. Realistically this is impossible in our imperfect world. However, believers, as the salt of the earth, should **do their part to live in peace with everyone.** They certainly are not to be the cause of dissension. Believers should do their utmost to seek reconciliation.

12:19 Quoting from Deuteronomy 32:35, Paul reminds us that though we may want to **avenge** ourselves, we must **leave that to God.** Refusing to take revenge avoids grudges and feuds. God will ensure that his just vengeance will be given.

12:20 The opposite of repaying with evil and taking revenge is caring for our **enemies.** Believers are not simply expected to abstain from evil; rather, they are expected to actively pursue opportunities to care for an enemy's needs. God invites us to observe our enemies and at the very points of weakness, where a counterattack of revenge might be most effective, we should mercifully meet that need. This will make them **ashamed** of their actions toward us.

12:21 Do not give in to your desire to take revenge or retaliate with evil; instead, act in a positive way. Paul comes full circle back to his point of verse 9. To hate evil is to **conquer** it **by doing good.** When we hang on for dear life to those things that are good and to God, we will be overcoming evil. All of this will be accomplished to the degree that we allow God to create in us sincere love.

ROMANS 13

RESPECT FOR AUTHORITY / 13:1-7

Paul ends chapter 12 by exhorting his readers about their Christian lifestyle as they relate to unbelieving neighbors, employers, and others. In chapter 13, he discusses how Christians should relate to the government. Remember, Paul's immediate audience was in Rome, the capital city of the mighty Roman Empire.

13:1 Paul says that believers are to **obey the government.** These were wise words to this small group of believers living within the massive structure of the Roman Empire. It wouldn't take much for an imperial edict to fall on a group who might become known for causing unrest within the empire. Their quiet submission would not guarantee peace, but at least it might allow them to continue to spread the gospel freely for a time.

Paul does not recommend either of the two possible extreme responses to the presence of a hostile authority. He does not favor believers becoming like the Zealots, Jewish rebels who fought (often violently) for freedom from Rome; neither does he suggest that they withdraw to the desert to set up their own community far from the evil city. Instead, Paul explains how Christian should live within the structure. Only then would they be able to share the gospel and transform society.

Why should they do this? Because **all governments have been placed in power by God.** He allows all governments and leaders to function under his sovereign will. Government is ideally in place to protect and serve its citizens. When governments distort or betray this function, those who run them will answer to God. They are under God's constraint and under his final judgment (see also Psalm 2; Daniel 4:34-35).

13:2 Citizens of any government should respect their government and obey its laws. If they **refuse to obey the laws of the land,** they are ultimately **refusing to obey God** and can expect **punishment.** For hundreds of years, however, there have been at least three interpretations of how we are to do this.

1. Some Christians believe that the state is so corrupt that Christians should have as little to do with it as possible. Although they should be good citizens as long as they can do so without compromising their beliefs, they should not work for the government, vote in elections, or serve in the military.
2. Others believe that God has given the state authority in certain areas and the church authority in others. Christians can be loyal to both and can work for either. They should not, however, confuse the two. In this view, church and state are concerned with two totally different spheres—the spiritual and the physical—and thus complement each other but do not work together.
3. Still others believe that Christians have a responsibility to make the state better. They can do this politically, by electing Christian or other high-principled leaders. They can also do this morally, by serving as an influence for good in society. In this view, church and state ideally work together for the good of all.

None of these views advocates rebelling against or refusing to obey laws or regulations unless those laws clearly require a person to violate the moral standards revealed by God. Wherever we find ourselves, we must be responsible citizens, as well as responsible Christians.

Are there times when we should not submit to the government? Paul does not address this question here, but other passages of Scripture give guidelines and examples. The government can demand respect, obedience, taxes, and honor from its citizens inasmuch as God appoints governments to protect people. When a government demands allegiance that conflicts with a believer's loyalty to God, Christians must respond in a different way. Believers should never allow the government to force them to disobey God. Jesus and his apostles never disobeyed the government for personal reasons; when they disobeyed, they were following their higher loyalty to God (Acts 5:29). Their disobedience was not cheap; they were threatened, beaten, thrown into jail, tortured, and executed for their convictions. If we are compelled to disobey, we must be ready to accept the consequences (see 1 Peter 2:13-14; 4:15-16).

13:3-4 These verses focus on officials who are doing their duty. Society needs leadership and positive constraints in order to ensure the safety and well-being of its citizens. When these officials are just, people who are doing right have nothing to fear. Governments that serve well facilitate and encourage citizens to do right. Christians are not to use their freedom in Christ as a handy excuse for disobeying the laws of the state. Civil disobedience should come only after submission to authority has been practiced. We should be informed and willing to question the motives of those who govern us, but we should be more demanding and more suspicious of our own motives. We must be careful not to be ruled by our sinful desires. Our protest may not be spiritual but rooted in our offended pride or hatred of any authority. This response is not directed by Christ or the Holy Spirit.

Rulers are in their position only because God has placed them there (Proverbs 21:1). All earthly governments are temporary—only Christ's reign will be eternal. To rebel against them is to rebel against their God-given authority. In practice, the responsibilities and opportunities of the politically powerful and the politically powerless will differ. For believers in a hostile environment, cooperation may be the most realistic approach. Believers who have the opportunity to affect change must challenge, speak out, offer solutions, and confront the power structure.

13:5 Believers have two good reasons to submit to their government: **to keep from being punished and to keep a clear conscience.** Believers know

in their consciences that obeying the authorities pleases God. However, a believer's conscience answers to a higher, divine authority; if ever the human authority contradicted the divine authority, a believer must be true to his conscience in following the higher authority.

True citizenship is rarely rewarded. Faithfully carrying out our small duties may not gain recognition. But Paul reminds the Romans that God notices every action. When we obey the government because it serves God, God knows our real motives.

13:6 Believers are called not only to submit to authorities, but also to support them by paying **taxes** (see also Matthew 22:21; Mark 12:17). Taxes pay the salaries for **government workers so they can keep on doing the work God intended them to do.** This was a heated topic at the time Paul wrote—he does not refer to this in any other letter. Government taxation, and abuses of taxation, were causing great unrest in the city. Christians might be thinking that they could get away with not paying the inflated taxes, but that would inevitably draw the attention of the authorities and put the believers at unnecessary risk. So Paul says to pay. In this regard Paul followed Jesus, who told Peter to pay taxes so as not to offend the governing authorities (Matthew 17:24-27). Paul is not teaching that all the authorities in Rome are God's servants in the same sense as the believers are God's servants. The powers in Rome were arbitrary and often self-serving. But they were God's servants, ultimately responsible to the one who set them in place.

13:7 Christians are not exempt from fulfilling the expectations of any government. This verse also prepares for Paul's idea of debt in the next section. We must certainly pay taxes to the government, but our obligation also extends to others to whom we may **owe** a debt of **respect and honor.**

LOVE FULFILLS GOD'S REQUIREMENTS / 13:8-14
Paul's practical directions for Christian living have a distinct pattern. Each time he focuses on a set of applications, whether it is gifts (chapter 12), government (chapter 13), or personal convictions (chapter 14), Paul always anticipates the question, Why should we do this? In this section, Paul teaches that love is an urgent requirement for believers. Love is not to be withheld for later. We must live as if this were our last day on earth. One day will be the last day—will Christ find us loving others?

13:8-10 If we owe something, we should **pay** the debt. But we must ask, Is Paul against home

mortgages and school loans? Paul is not teaching against borrowing, except as it applies to borrowing things or money that we cannot hope to repay. Careless or deceitful debt is not acceptable behavior among believers. To this point Jesus adds the command that his followers ought to be known as willing lenders and givers (Matthew 5:42). We are to be responsible to make payments and not borrow beyond our ability to pay. One debt should never be paid in full, however. We should **never finish paying** our **debt of love for others** (see also John 13:34-35; Galatians 5:22; Ephesians 5:1-2; 1 John 3:11-24; 4:7-21).

The commandments against **adultery, murder, stealing,** and **coveting** that Paul quotes are directly from the Ten Commandments. They apply to our relationships with others (see Exodus 20:13-15, 17). Paul lists them to show that they all fit under a broader commandment: **"Love your neighbor as yourself,"** quoted from Leviticus 19:18. When we love others, we will not purposely harm or do evil to them, **so love satisfies all of God's requirements.**

Christians must obey the law of love, which supersedes both religious and civil laws. It is easy to excuse our indifference to others merely because we have no legal obligation to help them, and even to justify harming them if our actions are technically legal! But Jesus does not leave loopholes in the law of love. Whenever love demands it, we are to go beyond human legal requirements and imitate the God of love.

13:11 Paul wants believers to realize their constant need to show love, especially considering the time—Christ's return is near. New Testament passages on the return of Christ center on our responsibility to be morally prepared, spiritually alert, and diligently serving (1 Peter 4:11; James 5:8; 1 John 2:18). Believers must be vigilant, alert, and not caught unaware. Paul knows that the old sinful nature will still cause problems from time to time, but he requires believers to **wake up.** Remaining too long in a state of spiritual lethargy, where sin is tolerated and good works are not pursued, can lead to a spiritual coma, rendering us unresponsive to God (see Ephesians 5:14; 1 Corinthians 15:34).

The return of Christ and our ultimate and final **salvation is nearer now than when we first believed.** Each day that passes brings us closer to the time of Christ's return, when we will be taken to heaven to be with him forever. (See also Mark 13:13; Luke 21:28; 1 Thessalonians 5:4-11; Hebrews 9:28.) **Time is running out** so we need to make every minute count for **right living.**

13:12 The **night** refers to the present, evil time. The **day** refers to the time of Christ's return. Believers in Paul's day, as well as believers today, are living in the night, the time of darkness characterized by Satan's evil work (see 2 Corinthians 4:4; Ephesians 2:2). Believers must **get rid of** their **evil deeds** and **clothe** themselves **with the armor of right living.** As Paul explains in Ephesians 6:10-17, this armor represents all the features that make up God's gift of justification by faith (see also John 12:36; Ephesians 5:8; 1 Thessalonians 5:4, 5; 1 John 1:7; 2:10). We should depend on God's strength and use every resource that he has given us.

13:13 To put on the armor of light (13:12) means to **be decent and true in everything we do, so that everyone can approve of our behavior.** The world is still in darkness, but we are to behave decently, in a way that will stand up to examination. For believers, the surrounding darkness is no excuse for indecent behavior.

The **wild parties and getting drunk,** the **adultery and immoral living,** the **fighting and jealousy** are examples of what does not please God; actions, activities, and attitudes that belong to the darkness. These have no place in the believer's life. (See also Galatians 5:19-21.)

Some people are surprised that Paul lists fighting and jealousy with the gross and obvious sins of drunkenness and sexual immorality. Like Jesus in his Sermon on the Mount (Matthew 5–7), Paul considers attitudes to be as important as actions. Just as hatred leads to murder, so jealousy leads to strife, and lust to adultery. When Christ returns, he wants to find his people clean on the inside as well as on the outside.

13:14 So how do we clothe ourselves "with the armor of right living" (13:12)? How can we "be decent and true" (13:13)? The answer: We **let the Lord Jesus Christ take control** of us (Ephesians 4:24; Colossians 3:10). This is deliberate, conscious acceptance of the lordship of Christ, so all our desires and actions are under his control. Letting him have control means avoiding indulging our **evil desires.** Sinful actions and sinful attitudes all start with a single thought. Just as in violent crimes, where premeditation is a factor, premeditation is the first step toward gratifying our desires. A temptation becomes an opportunity to plan to sin. But as harmless as imagination may seem to be, it actually impels us toward our desires. If we don't make plans, we can't carry them out.

ROMANS 14

THE DANGER OF CRITICISM / 14:1-23

Paul has already established the equality of Jewish and Gentile believers. In this chapter he continues to discuss how that equality could work out in daily living. Paul focuses on two issues: dietary restrictions and observance of special days. Next to circumcision, diet and calendar were the most sensitive issues that separated Jews from all Gentiles. Now, as Jews and Gentiles attempted to work out their distinctive character as Christians, these issues had to be resolved.

14:1 The key word is **accept,** which also means "receive" or "welcome." Believers in the church in Rome came from a wide variety of backgrounds. As we've already seen, the major differences were between Jewish believers and Gentile believers. But there were other differences. Some believers were slaves, some were masters; some were wealthy, most were poor. In addition, they were all at different stages of spiritual maturity. Growing in the spirit is like growing physically—everyone grows at different rates as God works in each life. So the first instruction Paul gives the church is to accept, welcome, and love one another without judging or condemning—no matter how weak, immature, or unlearned someone's faith may seem. Acceptance creates room for growth to continue; rejection stunts growth.

Who is **weak in faith,** and who is strong? Every believer is weak in some areas and strong in others. A person's faith is strong in an area if he or she can survive contact with sinners without falling into their patterns. The person's faith is weak in an area if that individual must avoid certain activities, people, or places in order to protect his or her spiritual life. Paul advises that those strong in an area should not **argue with** those who are weak **about what they think is right or wrong.** This refers not to doctrines essential to salvation, but to discussions about differences of lifestyle. Paul says we are not to quarrel about issues that are matters of opinion. Differences should not be feared or avoided, but accepted and handled with love. We shouldn't expect everyone, even in the best church, to agree on every subject. Through sharing ideas we can come to a fuller understanding of what the Bible teaches. Our basic approach should be to accept, listen to, and respect others. Differences of opinion need not cause division. They can be a source of learning and richness in our relationships.

14:2 Believing **it is all right to eat anything** may refer to freedom from certain Jewish dietary restrictions. When Jews became Christians, many still would be concerned about the proper preparation of food according to their laws. Some believers were more **sensitive** and would **eat only vegetables,** most likely for fear that meat might have been improperly prepared or offered to idols.

How could Christians end up eating meat that had been offered to idols? An ancient sacrificial system was at the center of religious, social, and domestic life in the Roman world. After a sacrifice was presented to a god in a pagan temple, only part of it was burned. Often the remainder was sent to the market to be sold. Thus a Christian might easily, even unknowingly, buy such meat in the marketplace or eat it at the home of a friend. Some thought there was nothing wrong with eating meat that had been offered to idols because idols were worthless and phony. Others carefully checked the source of their meat or gave up meat altogether to avoid a guilty conscience. This problem was especially acute for Christians who had once been idol worshipers. For them, such a strong reminder of their former paganism might weaken their newfound faith (see also 1 Corinthians 8).

Paul is speaking about immature faith that has not yet developed the strength it needs to stand against external pressures. For example, if a person who once worshiped idols were to become a Christian, he might understand perfectly well that Christ saved him through faith and that idols have no real power. Still, because of his past associations, he might be badly shaken if he knowingly ate meat that had been used as part of a pagan ritual. The same would be true for a Jew whose strict observance to the law would cause him to be concerned about the preparation of the meat.

14:3 When believers differ over scruples or matters of opinion, they **must not look down on** or **condemn** each other. The Greek for look down on means "despise" (see) or "reject with contempt." The stronger one faces the temptation to despise the weaker brother or sister. The weaker one is in danger of condemning the stronger brother or sister. Neither attitude is acceptable. Believers should not condemn each other for their different opinions, because God does not; instead, **God has accepted them** both.

Paul responds to both brothers in love. Both are acting according to their consciences, but their honest scruples do not need to be made into rules for the church. Our principle should be: In essentials, unity; in nonessentials, liberty; in everything, love.

14:4 Every believer will be judged by God alone (14:10); therefore, believers have no right to **condemn** one another. Each person is accountable to Christ, not to others (see also Matthew 7:3-5; Luke 6:37, 41-42; 1 Corinthians 4:3-5). While the church must be uncompromising in its stand against activities that are expressly forbidden by Scripture (such as adultery, homosexuality, murder, theft), it should not create additional rules and regulations and give them equal standing with God's law. Often Christians base their moral judgments on opinion, personal dislikes, or cultural bias, rather than on the Word of God. When they do this, they show that their own faith is weak, and they demonstrate that they do not think God is powerful enough to guide each of his children. When we stand before God's judgment seat (14:10), we won't be worried about what our Christian neighbor has done (see 2 Corinthians 5:10).

14:5 For Jews, this **holy** day would have probably been the Sabbath; for Christians, the Lord's day (Sunday). The believers had differing opinions about the sacredness of certain days. For example, if a Jew who once worshiped God on the required Jewish holy days were to become a Christian, he might well know that Christ saved him through faith, not through his keeping of the law. Still, when the feast days came, he might feel empty and unfaithful if he didn't dedicate those days to God. Other believers might not have any concern about that and might think that **every day is alike**—in other words, every day is holy to the Lord. (See also Colossians 2:16-17.)

The position of each is no matter to Paul, but he does add that **each person should have a personal conviction about this matter** through prayer and careful thought examining whether that action is what he or she believes God wants

him or her to do. People must decide for themselves before God and be convinced of the rightness of their position, even if it means disagreeing with other believers. Believers can disagree on some points and can still be acceptable to God.

14:6 When it comes to differences of opinion between believers on matters of conscience, each believer should respond to the Lord, doing as his or her conscience dictates. This great principle of freedom should guide us: we are to dedicate our actions, attitudes, and habits to the Lord. Thus whether we are setting aside a day to honor God, or eating different kinds of food, or refusing to eat certain kinds of food—in all cases we must **want to please the Lord.** The questions that others ask us about our convictions should cause us to ask, "Am I doing this out of respect for God?"

14:7-8 We do not live in a vacuum; everything we do affects others. We need to consider our responsibility to others. We can demand freedom for ourselves, but we must also allow other believers that same freedom. If demonstrating our freedom causes us to act in an uncaring, hurtful way toward other believers, we are not yet free. Ultimately **we are not our own masters.** Our entire life, from beginning to end, belongs **to the Lord.** We **live** to him and **die** to him. Our relationship with the Lord is more important than life or death, and life and death are more important than religious observances. So all our discussions must never interfere with our relationship to Christ, who is our Lord. It is the Lord's judgment that matters. With respect to the way we treat other believers, we ought to consider the question, "Am I treating people as though they also belong to the Lord?"

14:9 Christ **died** to free us and to deliver us from judgment. He alone is our judge. For any believer to claim to have the authority to tell others how they should think or act in matters of opinion is to usurp the position that Christ alone holds.

14:10 Believers are not to **condemn** one another, because all of us will be judged by Christ. **Each of us will stand personally before the judgment seat of God** to give an account of our actions. This is not where God judges the eternal destiny of all people, but where believers' lives will be judged for what they have done (see also Matthew 12:36; 1 Peter 4:5).

14:11 Quoting from Isaiah 45:23, Paul explains that a time of judgment will come. Isaiah referred to the day when **every knee will bow** before God. It was God's original intention to bring all the people to himself through Abraham, but the Jews had discarded God's message to the Gentiles. We must never participate in rejecting those whom God has accepted. We must be convinced that we will be held responsible for our own lives before God. Each person will give an account for himself or herself (14:12; Matthew 12:36). We are to confront one another in love, concern, and truth, but not in judgment.

14:12 Each believer **will have to give a personal account to God.** Each of us will have enough to explain without adding condemning or mocking attitudes toward other believers. We need each other, so we simply cannot afford to be undercutting each other. If anything, we ought to be busy helping ourselves and our fellow believers so that we can give a good account of ourselves to God. In the front lines of a battle, all the soldiers on your side look good.

14:13 Believers are to not judge one another regarding their convictions on matters of opinion. Here Paul directs his words to the "strong" believers, explaining that they need to be sensitive about how their convictions affect other believers. Each believer, though free to have his or her own convictions, must also be careful that those convictions don't **put an obstacle in another Christian's path.** And if they do, then those freedoms must be reevaluated.

Both "strong" and "weak" Christians can cause their brothers and sisters to stumble. A stumbling block or obstacle refers to something that might cause someone to trip or fall into sin. The strong but insensitive Christian may flaunt his or her freedom, be a harmful example, and thus offend others' consciences. The scrupulous but weak Christian may try to fence others in with petty rules and regulations, thus causing dissension. Paul wants his readers to be both strong in the faith and sensitive to others' needs. Because we are all strong in certain areas and weak in others, we constantly need to monitor the effects of our behavior on others (see also 1 Corinthians 8:9).

14:14 Referring back to the issue of **food** (14:2-3, 6), Paul states his own conviction that **no food, in and of itself, is wrong to eat.** But not all believers felt the same way. At the Jerusalem council (Acts 15), for example, the Jewish church in Jerusalem asked the Gentile church in Antioch not to eat meat that had been sacrificed to idols. Paul accepted this request, not because he felt that eating such meat was wrong in itself, but because this practice would deeply offend many Jewish believers. Paul did not think the issue was worth dividing the church over; his desire was to promote unity. So, he concludes, **if someone believes it is**

wrong, then for that person it is wrong (see also Mark 7:14-23). Paul's practice was to honor, as far as possible, the convictions of others.

Believers are called to accept one another without judging our varied opinions. However, when the situation has to be faced, how should we deal with those who disagree with us? Paul's response is that all believers should act in love so as to maintain peace in the church.

14:15-16 If one believer has no scruples about where meat comes from or how it is prepared, but flaunts his or her belief in order to cause one who is concerned to be **distressed,** then the stronger individual is **not acting in love.** The conduct of stronger believers is not to be decided by what they feel is their better insight into the Scriptures, or what they feel would "strengthen" those weaker ones. Rather, it is to be decided by love and sensitivity. The stronger believer must not let what he or she wants to do, when it is a minor matter such as whether to eat meat or not, become a stumbling block that could **ruin someone for whom Christ died.** If Christ gave his life for that person, surely no believer has the option to ruin him or her because of food!

Mature Christians shouldn't flaunt their freedom; otherwise, they might **be condemned for doing something** that is **all right** simply because their doing it destroyed another believer. Mature believers should be sensitive to younger converts whose faith can be destroyed by such freedom. For example, a young Christian addicted to gambling may be damaged by our freedom to play cards. Some activities may be all right in and of themselves, but not around weaker new converts.

14:17-18 After all, says Paul, if we let those little scruples become major points of contention, we have forgotten what the Kingdom of God is all about. It has nothing to do with **what we eat or drink** (Matthew 6:31, 33). Instead, it is **living a life of goodness and peace and joy in the Holy Spirit.** Arguing over scruples does not contribute to that. Believers need to concern themselves with doing what is right in the essentials, maintaining harmony, and sharing God's joy, not in forcing their scruples and lifestyles on others. Those who **serve Christ** by doing right before God, maintaining peace among the believers, and sharing joy with others are the ones who will accomplish the acceptable service to Christ—they will **please God and people.**

14:19 Christian fellowship should be characterized by **harmony** and building **each other up** (see also 1 Thessalonians 5:11). False believers and immature Christians have been known to use the "weaker brother argument" to support their own opinions, prejudices, or standards. "You must live by these standards," they say, "or you will be offending the weaker brother." In truth, the person would often be offending no one but the speaker. While Paul urges us to be sensitive to those whose faith may be harmed by our actions, we should not sacrifice our liberty in Christ just to satisfy the selfish motives of those who are trying to force their opinions on us. Strong believers need not judge their own liberty by the troubled consciences of the weak. Each believer is to follow Christ.

14:20-21 Food and our feelings about it, or any scruples that are not specifically condemned in Scripture, are not worth arguing about, flaunting, or judging—these should never be allowed to tear down other believers or tear apart the church. It is wrong for one believer to insist on his or her freedom when it causes others to **stumble.** If it causes someone else to fall, then put it aside for the other's sake (see also 1 Corinthians 10:23-24, 31-32). Therefore, mature believers must not **eat meat or drink wine or do anything else if it might cause another Christian to stumble.** Truly strong believers can restrict their freedoms for the sake of others.

14:22 In those areas of disagreement, Paul counsels the believers to keep their beliefs **between** themselves and **God.** The brother or sister who believes in certain freedoms should not be trying to influence others with scruples to "loosen up." Those bothered by some actions should not be judging or condemning those with freedom, nor should they be trying to force their scruples on the entire church. Instead all believers should seek a clear conscience before God. The believers who do so are **blessed** and **do not condemn themselves by doing something they know is all right.** This person has a good, but not insensitive, conscience.

14:23 If a believer does something that he or she has **doubts about whether** it is right or wrong, that action will bring condemnation. Believers ought to try to steer clear of actions forbidden by Scripture, of course, but sometimes Scripture is silent. Then we should follow our conscience. To go against a conviction will leave a person with a guilty or uneasy conscience. When God shows us that something is wrong for us, we should avoid it. But we should not look down on other Christians who exercise their freedom in those areas.

ROMANS **15**

LIVING TO PLEASE OTHERS / 15:1-13
Paul continues his discussion from chapter 14 on how believers should relate to one another, especially when there are disagreements on matters of opinion. There is no question that a variety of opinions on many matters will be represented in any church—and the church in Rome was no exception. Paul uses "strong" and "weak" to describe the believers. "Strong" believers are those who understand their freedom in Christ and who are sensitive to the concerns of others. They realize that true obedience comes from the heart and conscience of each individual. "Weak" believers are those whose faith has not yet matured so as to be free of some of the rituals and traditions. "Strong" believers can function in a variety of situations and be influences for good; "weak" believers find that they need to stay away from some situations in order to maintain a clear conscience. But both are still believers, and both are still seeking to obey God.

15:1 Paul identifies himself as one of the "strong" who knows that **these things** (issues of food and drink) **make no difference** when it comes to salvation. But yet these strong believers are not to live just **to please** themselves. They have an obligation to **be considerate of the doubts and fears of those who think these things are wrong.** They may find themselves frustrated by the failings of

the weak—their concerns and worries over what, to the strong, seems trivial. But the responsibility lies with the strong to maintain harmony in the church by bearing with these brothers and sisters (see Galatians 6:1-2). The stronger believers demonstrate their spiritual strength precisely at those moments when they are practicing compassion for those who are weaker. The kind of strength modeled by Christ allowed him to put up with our failings. We ought to do the same for one another.

15:2 The strong believer must never be self-centered, but must be concerned for the spiritual welfare of his neighbor—the weaker person beside him or her in the congregation. To **please others** is done with a goal in mind—to encourage and **build up** that other believer in the faith. There is a fine line to walk—the stronger person should not push the weaker one to change his or her ways before he or she is ready; neither should the stronger person pander to the scruples of that weaker one by allowing such scruples to become rules for the church. Instead, the stronger believers should bear with (15:1) and work to help the weaker believers in their faith; this will benefit the church as a whole.

15:3 Christ was the "strongest" human who ever lived—he **didn't please himself,** but did God's will. Certainly death on a cruel cross was not the path he would have chosen to please himself, but his mission was to please God (see John 4:34; 5:30; 8:29). Strength is not independence from God, but total dependence on God. Strength in the church doesn't come from each believer being completely independent, but from mutual interdependence. Truly strong believers are those who are willing to limit their freedoms in order to care for and love their weaker brothers and sisters. Paul quotes from Psalm 69:9. This messianic psalm prophesied the Messiah's coming into the world and what would happen to him. Christ faced reproach and insults because he did not choose to please himself; instead, he chose to do what God had called him to do. How much more should we, who are called by his name, also choose to please God rather than ourselves.

15:4 The **Scriptures** (here referring to the Old Testament) were written and preserved for future generations. Our scriptural knowledge affects our attitude toward the present and the future. The more we know about what God has done in years past, the greater will be our confidence in what he will do in the days ahead. We should read our Bible diligently to increase our trust that God's will is best for us.

How does the Bible **give us hope and encouragement?** (1) God's attributes and character constantly remind us in whom our hope is based (Psalm 46:1-2). (2) The biographies of saints who overcame great obstacles give us examples of what can be done with God's help (Hebrews 11). (3) The direct exhortation of Scripture calls for endurance and speaks encouragement (James 1:2-4; Hebrews 12:1-2). (4) The prophetic statements support our hope for a wonderful future planned for us in eternity (Romans 5:1-5).

Paul admonishes strong believers not to please themselves but to please God and others. Scripture records stories of those who pleased God, those who didn't, and those who failed but learned from their mistakes. We are to endure as Christ endured and be encouraged by the examples of other believers. This gives us hope as **we wait patiently for God's promises.**

15:5-6 The **patience and encouragement** received from the Scriptures (15:4) have their ultimate source in **God,** for the Scriptures are his. Paul asks God to give the believers an attitude of **harmony—** Jews and Gentiles, weak and strong—as they seek to follow Christ. This prayer is strikingly similar to the one Jesus prayed with his disciples at the end of his final meal with them (John 17:22-23). Harmony is not an optional behavior for believers. They must have the **attitude of Christ Jesus** toward one another. Doing so would allow all believers to **join together with one voice, giving praise and glory to God.** This should be the ultimate purpose of each believer and of the entire church.

15:7 If our goal is to glorify God, we cannot be caught up in dissension, disagreements, or arguments, especially about trivial matters. Instead, we should **accept each other just as Christ has accepted** us—there is to be no one-sided acceptance. All are to accept one another and live in harmony. At one time, we all were weak. And many strong believers are still weak in some areas. Christ is our model of what acceptance means. When we realize that Christ accepted us, as unlovely and sinful and immature as we were when we came to him (see 5:6, 8, 10), then we will accept our brothers and sisters. The world sits up and takes notice when believers of widely differing backgrounds practice Christlike acceptance. In this, **God will be glorified.**

15:8-9 Having referred to harmony again, Paul feels compelled to remind his readers that the greatest example of harmony brings both Jews and Gentiles under the lordship of Christ. Jesus **came as a servant to the Jews to show that God is true to the promises he made to their ancestors.** At the same time, Christ **came so the Gentiles might also give glory to God for his mercies to them.** The promises, the covenants, were made to the patriarchs of the Jewish nation alone, but God, in his mercy, made them available to the Gentiles as well. God's offer of salvation to the Gentiles would cause them to glorify him for his mercy. Without God's mercy, the Gentiles could never receive his blessings and his salvation.

To offer final proof, Paul quoted four Old Testament passages, taken from the three divisions of the Old Testament—the Law, the Prophets, and the Psalms. The Old Testament pictured the Gentiles as receiving blessings from God. First, Paul quotes from Psalm 18:49 and 2 Samuel 22:50. In this psalm and the parallel passage in 2 Samuel 22, David, **the psalmist,** praises God for delivering him from his enemies and from King Saul who was trying to kill him. He writes that he would praise God **among the Gentiles,** not just among his own people.

15:10 The next quote is from Deuteronomy 32:43, sometimes called "The Song of Moses," where Moses poetically recites a brief history of Israel, reminds the people of their mistakes, warns them to avoid repetition of those mistakes, and offers the hope that comes only in trusting God. Moses calls the **Gentiles** to **rejoice** with the **Jews.**

15:11 In this quote from Psalm 117:1, the psalmist calls the **Gentiles** to **praise** God. It must have been startling, at times, for Jews to be reminded from their own Scriptures that the God who had chosen them was not theirs alone. Since God's unlimited love has been extended to all people, Jewish Christians should accept the Gentile Christians as full-fledged participants in God's Kingdom.

15:12 Paul quotes from **the prophet Isaiah** in Isaiah 11:10. The **heir to David's throne** refers to Christ. He **will rule over the Gentiles** who will **place their hopes on him.** Isaiah prophesied that the Gentiles would also hope in or believe in the Messiah.

In the foregoing quotations, Paul demonstrated that the Old Testament spoke of the Gentiles being included in the messianic Kingdom. Since Christ would rule over both the Jews and the Gentiles, they should accept each other as members of God's family.

15:13 Paul again prays for the believers (as in 15:5). This time Paul prays **that God who gives hope** will also **keep** them **happy and full of peace** as they anticipate what God has in store for them. Then, the believers can **overflow with hope through the power of the Holy Spirit.** It is by the power of the Holy Spirit that God accomplishes his care for his people—giving them endurance, encouragement, unity (15:5), hope, joy, and peace. Hope comes as a by-product of the Holy Spirit's work. It does not come from our own senses or experiences. This is Paul's benediction to his letter. What follows from this point are his personal plans and greetings.

PAUL'S REASON FOR WRITING / 15:14-22

Although Paul referred briefly to his reason for writing earlier in the letter, here in his closing remarks, he says more about his reasons for writing. He also explains his writing style. In these verses, we feel the heartbeat of Paul's missionary zeal.

15:14 Although Paul had never met most of the believers in Rome, he was **convinced** (most likely from reports he had heard of them) that they were spiritually mature. Paul knew they were doing good and living to please God, that they had a full understanding of the truth of the gospel, and were able to counsel and help guide one another. Paul was practicing the kind of encouragement that he had just asked them to use with each other.

15:15-16 Paul knew these believers were mature, but he wrote this lengthy letter on the basics of Christianity to remind them. It may have seemed **bold** of him to write in this manner to a church he had not founded, but he was the apostle to the Gentiles, and it was in that capacity that he wrote to them. (See also 2 Peter 1:12; 3:1-2.) He is qualified to write to them because God had allowed him the special privilege of being **a special messenger from Christ Jesus to** the **Gentiles.** Paul viewed his ministry to the Gentiles as a priestly duty. He faithfully proclaimed the gospel to the Gentiles so that they would receive the Good News, and become acceptable to God, **pure and pleasing to him by the Holy Spirit.** Paul's missionary work was an act of worship. He viewed the Gentile church as a **fragrant sacrifice** which he presented to God for his acceptance.

15:17 Paul did not glory in what he had done, but in what God had done through him. He was not proud, but he was **enthusiastic.** This caused him to glory in his service because of what Christ was accomplishing through him. We should reevaluate our attitudes in service and ministry. How often do we view our efforts as giving glory to God?

15:18-19 Being proud of God's work is not a sin—it is worship. Paul knew that all the glory for his ministry went to Christ alone, for it was Christ who was accomplishing the work of bringing **the Gentiles to God.** But Paul well understood that he was the vessel through whom God was working because the mission to the Gentiles was being accomplished by what Paul had said and done. Paul had, by the power of God's Spirit, done **miracles** and **signs** to verify the authority of his words. Because of the Holy Spirit's empowerment, Paul had taken the Good News from **Jerusalem** to **Illyricum.** Also known as Dalmatia (see 2 Timothy 4:10), Illyricum was a Roman territory on the Adriatic Sea between present-day Italy and Greece. It covered much the same territory as present-day Yugoslavia. (See the map in the Introduction.)

15:20 The reason for the extent of Paul's ministry was the driving ambition to share Christ in territories **where the name of Christ has never been heard.** Paul saw his mission as moving into the centers of population, starting a church, being sure it had a good foundation, then allowing it to continue the work of evangelization in its area while Paul moved on to areas uncharted by the gospel. Other preachers would have brought the gospel to some areas that Paul had not gone to; they would be involved in the follow-up and spiritual growth of the believers there. Paul did not want to move into those areas when it was more important for him to preach where people had not yet heard the Good News.

15:21 Paul quoted from part of Isaiah 52:15 to show that those who had been ignorant of God's word would respond positively to the Messiah. Isaiah predicted how surprised the Gentile nations would be when they saw the humiliation and exaltation of God's Servant, the Messiah. Paul uses this prophetic word to affirm the need for his missionary efforts to the Gentiles.

15:22 Because of his driving force to bring the gospel to people who had not yet heard, Paul had been **delayed** from going to Rome. He had much territory to cover in Asia Minor and around Greece, so it seems likely that he postponed his trip to Rome because there was already a strong church there.

PAUL'S TRAVEL PLANS / 15:23-33

It is quite evident that Paul was not aware that his plan to go to Rome was about to be accomplished in a way he did not foresee. His imprisonment in Jerusalem and in Caesarea and his eventual travel to Rome was completely at the expense of the Roman Empire.

15:23 At this point, Paul felt that enough local churches have been established throughout the area (not just by him, but by the other apostles and other missionaries) that these churches could complete the work of evangelization. Because he feels that his work in the **regions** of Jerusalem and Greece has been **finished,** and because of his great desire to meet the believers in Rome, he will **visit** them on his next trip. The fact that he knows so many of them personally is reason enough for his desire (see chapter 16). But up to this point, his pioneering missionary work has taken all his time.

15:24 The planned destination of Paul's next trip is **Spain.** On the way, he will **stop off in Rome** to **fellowship** with the believers there. Apparently Paul did not plan to stay long in Rome, but he hoped that the believers there would **send** him on his way as he continued on to Spain. This statement should dispel any concern that Paul would try to assume some sort of permanent leadership position or take advantage of the church's hospitality. Instead, he was planning to move through, to the next uncharted territory for the gospel, at the western limit of the Roman Empire.

Spain was a Roman colony, and there were Jews there. Paul wanted to take the Good News there. Also, Spain had many great minds and influential leaders in the Roman world (Lucan, Martial, Hadrian), and perhaps Paul thought Christianity would advance greatly in such an atmosphere.

15:25 Paul was indefinite about exactly when he would visit Rome because he was busy with another matter at present. Paul was on his way **to Jerusalem** from Corinth (from where he had most likely written this letter; he had been in that city for about three months, see Acts 20:3) with a delegation of men chosen by each church **to take a gift** from those churches **to the Christians** in Jerusalem (see Acts 24:17; 1 Corinthians 16:1-4; 2 Corinthians 9:13). Paul considered his delivery of this offering as an act of worship. Indeed, it was a fitting climax to his ministry in the east before he moved west.

15:26-27 Paul had collected voluntary offerings from various churches, including the ones in **Greece,** and would be taking that **offering** to the poor **Christians in Jerusalem** who were **going through such hard times.** The Gentile believers had collected an offering for the Jewish believers in Jerusalem. These Gentile churches **were very glad to do this because they felt they** owed **a real debt** to the Jewish church in Jerusalem. The Gentiles had received the gospel **(spiritual blessings)** originally from Jerusalem (where Christianity began), so they wanted to offer financial help to the needy poor there.

Not only that, but Paul hoped that such generosity and caring among the churches would strengthen the ties between them. The Jerusalem church, obviously made up mostly of Jews, at first had a difficult time even accepting ministry to the Gentiles (see Peter's situation in Acts 10:1–11:18). Some were still concerned about these mostly-Gentile churches. Gentile churches helping to meet the needs of the Jerusalem church was a sure way to maintain harmony among the believers and strengthen the bond of brotherhood.

This was not the first time a collection was taken to the church in Jerusalem. About ten years earlier, Paul and Barnabas brought a collection from the church in Antioch of Syria to help the Jerusalem church during a time of famine (Acts 11:30; 12:25). It seems that being Christian and being poor went together if one lived in Jerusalem. Christianity was not well accepted by the Jewish authorities, and when Jews became Christians they were often cut off from family and friends. The Jerusalem church probably had little means of support, so help from the other churches was needed and greatly appreciated.

15:28 After making sure the church in Jerusalem received the offerings from the other churches, Paul would take his anticipated trip. He was looking forward to taking the gospel to new lands west of Rome. But even the best-laid plans may not happen as we anticipate. Eventually Paul got to Rome, but it was after having his life threatened, becoming a prisoner of Rome, enduring a shipwreck, getting bitten by a poisonous snake on the island of Malta, and landing finally in Rome under arrest (see Acts 27–28)! Tradition says that Paul was released for a time, and that he used this opportunity to go to **Spain** to preach the Good News. This journey is not mentioned in the book of Acts.

15:29 Paul knows that when he arrives in Rome, he will come with **a great blessing** to share. The sense of this verse can be read in two ways: Paul will be bringing a fresh awareness of all the benefits of being united with Christ; or Paul is expecting to experience with the Romans a rich time of fellowship in Christ. The benefits of spending time with other believers, even those we do not know, are very real. From time to time, Christians should worship in unfamiliar places, just to be reminded

how oneness in Christ overcomes the barrier of meeting strangers.

15:30 Paul asked his readers to pray for him, a request he made in many of his letters (Ephesians 6:19-20; Colossians 4:3-4; 1 Thessalonians 5:25; 2 Thessalonians 3:1-2; Philemon 22). Paul needed their intercessory prayer; he needed them to join him in promoting the cause of Christ. The Greek term for **join me in my struggle** was often used in connection with athletic events where a team had to put forth a great, concerted action. Though the Roman believers could not be physically with Paul, they could join his efforts by **praying** for him. This is a subtle but effective emphasis that Paul was not an independent agent. He was part of the body, and he needed the body's help.

15:31 Paul's specific prayer requests pertain to his return to Jerusalem. Paul knew of the potential danger awaiting him there (see Acts 20:22-24; 21:27ff.), so he asked them to pray for his safety. Paul was still regarded as a traitor to his faith, and some of his fellow Jews might have considered it their religious duty to get rid of him for good. He also asked the Roman Christians to pray that **the Christians** in the Jerusalem church would **be willing to accept the donation** he was **bringing.** He may have been fearing that the church would not want to accept the money.

15:32 If all went well in Jerusalem, Paul hoped to then visit the church in Rome, finally to be able to relax with them and be refreshed. Paul's anticipation of being with other believers puts to shame our halfhearted efforts at preparing for worship and looking forward to the time we spend with other believers. Could it be that most of the lack of vitality in church life is created by the very ones who notice its absence? If we don't mentally prepare ourselves to be with Christ and his people, how can we expect to be refreshed by those encounters?

15:33 Paul closes this section of the letter with another personal benediction for the believers. The **God who gives us his peace** was a Jewish benediction, and Paul offers it here to his Jewish and Gentile Christian readers. This phrase sounds as if it should signal the end of the book, but the epistle continues on for another chapter. However, this benediction pronounces the end of Paul's teaching—the last chapter is an extended salutation. His greeting at the opening of the letter was "Grace and peace to you" (1:7). Most of the letter had explained the nature and results of God's grace. It was natural, then that he close by referring also to the God of peace.

ROMANS 16

PAUL GREETS HIS FRIENDS / 16:1-16

Rome was the capital of the empire. As Jerusalem was the center of Jewish life, Rome was the world's political, religious, social, and economic center. As Paul preached in the eastern part of the empire, he went first to the key cities—Jerusalem, Antioch in Syria, Philippi, Corinth, Athens, Ephesus. Along the way he met many believers who eventually ended up in Rome. The fact that Paul knew the whereabouts of so many of his friends and coworkers gives us a glimpse into the interest this great missionary had in the people to whom he ministered and who ministered to him. This final chapter reveals a treasury of friends Paul expected to see in Rome.

16:1-2 Phoebe was known as a servant or **deacon in the church in Cenchrea.** Apparently she was a wealthy person who helped support Paul's ministry. Phoebe was highly regarded in the church. Furthermore, because Paul specifically says that she would **be coming** to Rome, it is likely that she delivered this letter from Corinth to Rome. This provides evidence that women had important roles in the early church, as well as important roles in business. Cenchrea, the town where Phoebe lived, was the eastern port of Corinth, six miles from the city center (see Acts 18:18). The church here was probably a daughter church of the one in Corinth. Paul asked that the believers **receive** Phoebe **as one who is worthy of high honor** and to **help her** in any way they could. Believers who traveled from one place to another could always be assured of a warm welcome and kind hospitality from other believers. How Phoebe helped Paul and others is unknown, but those she helped were obviously very grateful. Life within the body of Christ is a constant exchange of help. Those who are helped one day are given the privilege in Christ of being the helpers the next day. We need to make sure we are participating in both roles in the local church where we worship.

16:3-5a Priscilla and Aquila were a married couple who had become Paul's close friends. They, along with all other Jews, had been expelled from Rome in A.D. 49 by Emperor Claudius (Acts 18:2-3) and had moved to Corinth. There they met Paul while he was on his second missionary journey, and they invited him to live and work with them. At some point, they moved back to Rome when they were allowed to return (the Emperor Claudius died five years after issuing the edict expelling Jews from Rome, so it is possible

that many returned then). Later, they went back to Ephesus (2 Timothy 4:19). Paul was indebted to these dear friends, even explaining to the others that they **risked their lives** for him. What they did is no longer known, but Paul had faced plenty of danger and had heard many threats against himself. This was certainly true in Ephesus (see Acts 18:6-10; 19:28-31; 1 Corinthians 15:32). Somehow Priscilla and Aquila intervened at one time to save Paul. He was grateful that they saved his life, and the **Gentile churches** would also be grateful that Paul's life was spared.

A common characteristic of the early church was that the believers met in people's homes. Priscilla and Aquila had also had a church in their home in Ephesus (1 Corinthians 16:19).

16:5b Whoever **Epenetus** was, Paul calls him **my dear friend,** and he has the legacy of being **the very first person to become a Christian in the province of Asia!** Paul was in Asia on his third missionary journey (Acts 19:10); he had wanted to travel there during his second missionary journey but had been prevented (Acts 16:6).

16:6 Paul would not know firsthand who had worked hard among the believers in Rome, so he is probably speaking from information given him by others, possibly Priscilla and Aquila. So he sent **greetings to Mary** who apparently was a hard worker in the church.

16:7 Andronicus and Junia may have been a husband and wife team. Junia (or "Julia," which is the reading in certain ancient manuscripts) was a widely used female name at the time. Paul's references to them as **relatives** could mean that they were also Jews, possibly from the same tribe. When they were **in prison** with him is not known, because Paul had been imprisoned numerous times (see 2 Corinthians 11:23). Andronicus and Junia distinguished themselves **among the apostles.** They belonged to that larger group of apostles who had seen the risen Christ (a credential of an apostle—see Acts 1:22; 1 Corinthians 15:5-8). If Andronicus and Junia were believers **before** Paul was, they would have been Christians for about 25 years.

16:8-9 Ampliatus was a common Roman name at this time period, and it often showed up in the imperial household. It is possible that this man was part of Caesar's household because the gospel had reached even there (Philippians 4:22). Another common Roman name, **Urbanus** is greeted as a **coworker**—most likely another missionary for the early church. The name **Stachys** was not so common; some people in association with the imperial household were named Stachys.

16:10 Apelles is a typical Jewish name, common among the Jews in Rome. **Aristobulus** may have been related to the Herods, perhaps a brother of Herod Agrippa I. He lived in Rome as a private citizen. To greet a **household** would mean greeting both the family and the servants.

16:11 Herodion was probably a fellow Jew, and a **relative** by tribe, not family. To **greet the Christians in the household of Narcissus** may mean that some in Narcissus's household were not believers. This person has been identified as Tiberius Claudius Narcissus, a wealthy and powerful man during the reigns of emperors Tiberius and Claudius. But he was executed under Nero (sometime after A.D. 54). At that point, all his possessions, including slaves, would have been confiscated and become imperial property. So Paul sent his greetings to the believers among Narcissus's household who are now the property of Rome.

16:12 Tryphena and Tryphosa probably were sisters, maybe even twins because of the close relation of the names. The name **Persis** has appeared both among slaves and wealthy people, but never in connection with the imperial household.

16:13 Rufus is an extremely common name, but it is possible that this is the same Rufus as mentioned in Mark 15:21. If so, then this is a son of Simon of Cyrene, and thus a North African. If Rufus is the same as the one mentioned in Mark's Gospel, Paul may have met his **mother** in Antioch of Syria. Rufus's father, Simon, has been identified as the Simeon who was a teacher in the church there (Acts 13:1). Paul was brought to Antioch of Syria by Barnabas, where they spent a year (Acts 11:25-26). Perhaps Paul lived with them, and Rufus's mother had special concern and love for Paul—seeming like a mother to him.

16:14 Perhaps these men were leaders of other house churches. The names are common names, especially among slaves.

16:15 These people may have been other leaders and servants in various house churches.

16:16 The **churches** Paul was referring to would most likely be those who were joining together in delivering the offering to Jerusalem (see 15:25-27).

Taken together, the list above represents a cross-section of Roman culture, from slaves to those of high social status. The church to whom Paul was writing had all the potential for unity in Christ in spite of every possible barrier. Even this list serves as another example of the theme of Paul's letter: God's plan includes the entire world. Justification by faith is the greatest proof of the truth of the theme, but the repeated theme of this letter is the great news that the Good News is for everyone!

PAUL'S FINAL INSTRUCTIONS / 16:17-27

Jesus had told the disciples that false teachers would come (Matthew 24:11; Mark 13:22-23). Just as false prophets had contradicted the true prophets in Old Testament times (for example, see Jeremiah 23:16-40; 28:1-17), telling people only what they wanted to hear, so false teachers were twisting Christ's teachings and the words of his apostles. These teachers were belittling the significance of Jesus' life, death, and resurrection. Some claimed that Jesus couldn't be God; others claimed that he couldn't have been a real man. These teachers allowed and even encouraged all kinds of wrong and immoral acts, especially sexual sin. This was a problem throughout the early church and Paul often warned the churches about it.

16:17 Paul had not yet been to Rome, but he certainly realized that the ubiquitous false teachers would make their way there. He urged believers to

watch out for people who cause divisions by **teaching things that are contrary** to the truth. They should **stay away from them.** The severe problem of false teaching in some of the other churches Paul visited caused him to include this in the closing lines of his letter, for he knew it could certainly become a problem.

16:18 Teachers should be paid by the people they teach, but false teachers were attempting to make more money by distorting the truth and saying what people wanted to hear. They were more interested in **serving their own personal interests,** motivated by a desire to gain power and prestige. In contrast, genuine Christian teachers are motivated by sincere faith and a desire to do what is right. Both Paul and Peter condemned greedy, lying teachers (see 1 Timothy 6:5).

Paul warned the Roman believers that when they listen to teachers, they should check the content of what is said and not be fooled by **smooth talk** or **glowing words.** Many cult leaders have led Christians astray by teaching things that sound like truth but are actually falsehoods. Christians who study God's word will not be fooled, even though superficial listeners may easily be taken in. For an example of those who carefully checked God's word, see Acts 17:10-12.

16:19 Paul quickly adds that he knows the Roman believers are not naive (16:18) because their obedience to God is well known. Believers are to be wise in their understanding of what is good, that is, in what God wants them to do. On the reverse, they are to be **innocent** about evil.

16:20 This language echoes Genesis 3:15, wherein God declares that the serpent's head would be crushed by the seed of the woman. These false teachers, servants of **Satan,** would try to sow discord in the churches, but God is the **God of peace.** The false teachers will be destroyed when Christ establishes his peace upon his return (see Revelation 20:1-6).

16:21 Timothy was a key person in the growth of the early church, traveling with Paul on his second missionary journey (Acts 16:1-3). Later Paul wrote two letters to him (1 and 2 Timothy) as Timothy worked to strengthen the churches in Ephesus. Acts 20:4 places Timothy with Paul prior to Paul's departure to Jerusalem. These other men

are fellow Jews, not family relations. These names are also mentioned in other places: Acts 13:1; 17:5-9; 20:4.

16:22 Tertius was Paul's secretary, who wrote the letter as Paul dictated it. He included his **greetings.**

16:23 This is most likely not the same **Gaius** who was from Macedonia (Acts 19:29), nor the one from Derbe (Acts 20:4), nor the one addressed in 3 John. It is probably the Gaius whom Paul baptized in Corinth (1 Corinthians 1:14). As the **city treasurer, Erastus** would have been a powerful and influential man. A civic official of this name is mentioned on the inscription on a marble paving-block in Corinth. The name was common enough that he need not be identified with the Erastus mentioned in other places (Acts 19:22 and 2 Timothy 4:20). **Quartus** is unknown other than that he is **a Christian brother.**

There is no verse 24 in most modern translations because it is not found in the most trusted Greek manuscripts. It is a scribal addition repeating the words of 16:20.

16:25-27 Paul had explained his gospel at length in this letter to the Romans (see 2:16). Paul's **Good News** was the proclamation of **Jesus Christ and his plan for** the **Gentiles.** Paul knew that the gospel and Christ himself would **make** these believers **strong** in the faith. The plan had been **kept secret from the beginning of time.** The **prophets** who wrote various books of the Old Testament were not fully aware of the meaning of their own words; but they wrote, at God's command, much about the fulfillment of the mystery—the coming of the Messiah, the salvation of the Gentiles, and the return of the Jews (see 11:25). Now, after the coming of Christ and the growth of the church, what they wrote is being understood (1:2). (See also Luke 24:44-45; 1 Peter 1:10-12.)

Paul exclaims that it is wonderful to be alive when the mystery, God's secret—his way of saving the Gentiles—is becoming known throughout the world! All the Old Testament prophecies are coming true, and God is using Paul as his instrument to tell this Good News. For that we must give **God** the **glory forever through Jesus Christ.**

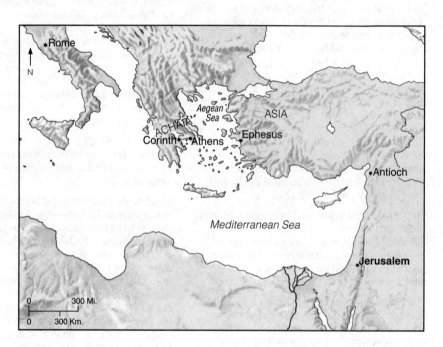

Paul wrote this letter to Corinth during his three-year visit in Ephesus on his third missionary journey. The two cities sat across from each other on the Aegean Sea—both were busy and important ports. Titus may have carried this letter from Ephesus to Corinth (2 Corinthians 12:18).

1 CORINTHIANS

INTRODUCTION

Lawsuit.

Split.

Scandal.

Tragically, contemporary headlines often trumpet bad reports from local churches. News of leaders' sexual escapades, disgruntled and disgraced members' lawsuits, unethical and irresponsible fiscal practices, and blatant heresies seems to parade weekly across television screens. Jesus had told the Twelve that his followers would be known by their love (John 13:35). Yet, today, many who claim to follow him are marked by anything but love. Instead of standing apart from the world, the church has taken the appearance of other, secular institutions and has blended in.

What would God say to these errant believers, to churches and individuals who have strayed from obeying his commands? He said it nearly 2,000 years ago through Paul to Christians in decadent Corinth, a city similar to many communities today. Paul wrote letters, now known as 1 and 2 Corinthians, urging believers to focus on Christ, forsake immorality, settle their differences, reject false teachers, unify, and love. As you read these personal and powerful epistles written first to ancient Greeks, know that the words and principles apply to this generation as well.

AUTHOR

Paul (Saul of Tarsus): former Pharisee, apostle, pioneer missionary of the church.

Paul visited Corinth on his second missionary trip. At the time of Paul's visit, Corinth was a bustling commercial city, a center of Mediterranean trade. It is no wonder that Paul easily found work as a tentmaker (most likely working with goat's-hair cloth, a prominent trade of Paul's native region, Cilicia). In his spare time, Paul began to speak about Christ to Jews at the local synagogue, but he received a cold reception. Undaunted by opposition, Paul began teaching next to the synagogue in Titius Justus's house. This infuriated the Jews. Paul's congregation probably included many God-fearing Gentiles who used to attend the synagogue right next door. Because these Corinthian Jews hated Paul, they presented an official complaint to Gallio, the governor of Achaia. Gallio refused to hear his case, however, because he viewed the early Christians as simply another sect of Judaism. Ironically, this mistaken perception protected the infant church from being rigorously persecuted by the Romans. With his opponents defeated, Paul was free to stay in Corinth for a year and a half (around A.D. 50–52), one of Paul's longest stays in any one city during his missionary journeys. Perhaps he envisioned Corinth as a center of evangelism for all of Greece.

The two letters to the Corinthians preserved in the Bible are evidence that Paul took special interest in the spiritual welfare of the Corinthian church. His long stay in the city made it painful for him to hear of the problems that had begun to plague the church there. Paul himself had established the church. He had endured much ridicule in order to preach the gospel. He had worked hard in order to preach free of charge. As these two letters make clear, however, the Corinthian church struggled in Paul's absence.

Paul's authorship of 1 Corinthians has never been seriously questioned by Bible scholars. In the very first verse of 1 Corinthians, he identifies himself as the author and Sosthenes as his secretary. This evidence, along with the Pauline emphasis on the believer's freedom in Christ (10:23-33), is enough to convince most scholars.

For more about Paul, see the Author section in the Introduction to the book of Romans.

DATE AND SETTING
Written from Ephesus around A.D. 55.

Near the end of 1 Corinthians, Paul reported the details of his recent travel plans and revealed that he was writing from the city of Ephesus (16:8). On his third missionary journey, Paul stayed in Ephesus for three years. Ephesus, a bustling seaport town in Asia Minor (present-day Turkey), was a strategic city for the spread of the gospel message in Asia Minor. Located at the intersection of two ancient overland routes (the coastal road running north to Troas and the western route to Colosse, Laodicea, and beyond), Ephesus became a customary stopping point for ships sailing through the Aegean Sea. Thus, the city became known as the gateway to Asia. During the first century, however—the time period of Paul's ministry—the harbor began filling up with silt. This condition caused a slight economic downturn.

The numerous visitors who came to Ephesus every month kept revenue flowing into the town. The magnificent temple to Diana (the goddess of fertility, also called Artemis) was located in Ephesus. Four times larger than the Parthenon, this marble temple was considered one of the wonders of the ancient world. People from throughout the Roman Empire came to worship Diana there. In addition to the temple of Diana, Ephesus boasted an immense amphitheater that could seat twenty-five thousand and an equally huge stadium that hosted all types of gladiator fights. A sparkling marble street flanked by colonnades ran through the city, directing all visitors to the amphitheater. Because of its temples to pagan gods and goddesses, Ephesus was one of the great tourist capitals of the ancient world. It was no wonder that the craftsmen of that city became alarmed at the spread of Christianity among the populace (see Acts 19:21-41).

Perhaps it was because the city was such a center for tourism and trade that Paul spent three full years there—teaching the gospel in the lecture hall of Tyrannus. According to Luke, the author of Acts, this lecture hall became a gathering place for people from all over the province of Asia Minor who were interested in the Good News of Jesus Christ (see Acts 19:9-10). During this extended stay in Ephesus, Paul wrote 1 Corinthians.

AUDIENCE
The church in Corinth.

Along with Rome and Alexandria, Corinth was one of the major cities of the Roman Empire. Its prominence and wealth were derived from the extraordinary amount of shipping and commerce that passed through its harbors. The location of Corinth on a four-and-a-half-mile isthmus that connected mainland Greece and Achaia made it an ideal shipping hub. Ships were placed on wooden platforms and dragged across a stone road on the isthmus between the two ports of Corinth-Lechaeum and Cenchrea. A canal would have been ideal, but the Romans never built one. The lack of a canal, however, did not impede the ship traffic across the isthmus. It was easier and safer for a ship captain to pay the fees to have his ship dragged across the isthmus than to sail around Achaia, a two-hundred-mile journey known for its severe and unpredictable storms.

Although the Romans destroyed Corinth in 146 B.C. for taking a leadership role in a rebellion, Julius Caesar rebuilt the city in 46 B.C. The city quickly regained its former prominence, and by 27 B.C., it was named the capital of a senatorial province of Achaia. By the first century A.D., the city was the most influential commercial center in Greece. In addition to being a commercial center, Corinth was a manufacturing center for bronze, a metal used in the construction of many of the Roman amphitheaters. The prestige of Corinth was elaborately displayed at the biennial Isthmian games in that city (a series of games equivalent to the Olympic games). Paul drew upon the images of the athletes and awards in these games to illustrate the nature of the Christian life (9:24-27).

The wealth accompanying commercial success often breeds moral laxity; that certainly was the case in Corinth. Throughout the ancient world, the city was known for its moral decadence. Plato used the term "Corinthian girl" to refer to a prostitute; and Aristophanes used the verb "to act like a Corinthian" to refer to fornication. The magnificent temple of Aphrodite (the goddess of love, fertility, and beauty) stood on the mountain that overlooked Corinth as a monument to this immoral lifestyle. That temple was the center of many varieties of religious prostitution.

As a strong commercial center, Corinth drew a substantial number of people from every corner of the Roman Empire, so the city was ethnically and religiously diverse. In addition to the temple of Aphrodite, Corinth contained a temple for Asclepius, the Greek god of healing, as well as sites to venerate Issi, the Egyptian god of seafarers, and Poseidon, the Greek counterpart to Issi. There is even archeological evidence of a Jewish synagogue dating back to the third century. The diversity of the city was reflected in the makeup of the Corinthian congregation (12:13).

Corinth was the last city Paul visited on his second missionary journey (Acts 18:1-18). He stayed in Corinth for eighteen months, establishing a church there. Apollos, who had been taught the basics of the Christian faith by Aquila and Priscilla in Ephesus, visited the church at a later time, encouraging the believers (1:12).

Unfortunately, the Corinthian church not only reflected the city's multiethnic character, but also its moral depravity. Paul's exhortations against incest (5:1-5) and against soliciting prostitutes (6:9-20) indicate that members in the church were struggling to resist the pervasive immorality of their city. But Paul wouldn't compromise the high standards of Christian conduct for the church in Corinth. Being surrounded by ubiquitous immorality did not make the Corinthians an exception. Instead, he called them to a pure life, set apart for God. He even compared their bodies to God's temple (6:18-20). Even with its numerous problems, the Corinthian body of believers became a strategic church for the propagation of the gospel. Its location on the major trade routes of the Roman Empire made it a key outpost for spreading the gospel in Achaia (present-day Greece).

OCCASION AND PURPOSE
To answer some questions about church order, to identify some problems in the Corinthian church, and to teach the believers how to live for Christ in a corrupt society.

In his travels throughout the Mediterranean world, Paul had visited numerous towns and seaports, establishing small cells of committed believers in almost every place he visited. During his travels Paul had dealt with a wide variety of people—from mad mobs to subtle philosophers—and with various situations—from fierce persecution to moral laxity. Throughout all this, he showed keen interest in the spiritual welfare of every person with whom he came in contact. His letters frequently recount how he wrestled in prayer for a church or an individual (2 Corinthians 13:7; 1 Thessalonians 3:10). This genuine concern prompted Paul to write letters to his converts, instructing them in the faith, and it compelled him to visit churches again and again. Corinth was no exception.

The very first letter that Paul wrote to the Corinthian believers has been lost. First Corinthians 5:9 mentions this previous letter. Obviously, it could not have been 1 Corinthians. The exact contents of this letter are unknown; 1 Corinthians 5 implies that Paul had warned the Corinthians in that letter not to associate with so-called Christians who engaged in sexual immorality.

The problems in Corinth. Near the end of his stay in Ephesus, Paul wrote a second letter, the epistle entitled 1 Corinthians. He wrote this letter in response to a message delivered by Stephanas, Fortunatus, and Achaicus (16:17). Stephanas and his companions had asked Paul a series of questions, mostly concerning church order. In his long letter in response, Paul answered the questions related to Christian marriage (7:1-16), food sacrificed to idols (8:1-13), spiritual gifts (12:1-31), and the procedure for collecting money for the relief of the Jerusalem church (16:1-14). This is why 1 Corinthians is arranged topically. Instead of a theological treatise, with a central thesis and a number of arguments supporting the main point, 1 Corinthians is a practical letter addressing a variety of issues faced by the church.

In addition, Paul addressed problems that had surfaced in an unofficial report from Chloe's household in Corinth (see 1:11). According to that report, persistent problems had been plaguing the church. Specifically, members were quarreling with each other and forming cliques around various teachers— especially Paul, Peter, and Apollos (1:10-17). Corinthian believers were even suing each other (6:1) and arguing when they met to celebrate the Lord's Supper (11:17-22). Even more disturbing was the report of a case of incest in the church that had not been confronted by the church leaders (5:1). Paul responded to each of these very serious issues. In fact, 1 Corinthians seems to almost follow Chloe's report as an outline, as it answers the problems and issues raised.

The Gentile heritage. At first, many of the conflicts addressed in 1 Corinthians seem to be unrelated and disconnected. A careful analysis of all the problems and disputes, however, reveals a predominantly Gentile church. First, sexual permissiveness in the church would have been more a problem for Gentiles than for Jewish believers, who were already familiar with Old Testament restrictions on their sexual appetites (6:12-20). Second, numerous lawsuits would not have been a problem among Jewish Christians, for Jews were forbidden to use heathen courts and were expected to resolve their differences with the elders of the local synagogue (6:1-11). Only Gentile Christians would be inclined to sue each other in Roman courts. Third, Paul's extensive discussion on the wisdom of the Spirit compared to the foolishness of people confirms that his audience was primarily composed of Gentile Christians. Greek philosophers would demonstrate their so-called wisdom with lavish rhetoric. That's why Paul had to explain his reason for not presenting the gospel with "lofty words" but instead with the power of the Holy Spirit (2:1-4).

First Corinthians clearly shows that some of the philosophies of the Greek and Roman world were coloring the Corinthians' perception of their newfound faith in Jesus. This letter was written to a group of believers who were still influenced by philosophical dualism. Ever since Plato, much of Greek philosophy had been based on the belief that the spiritual and the material were completely separate spheres of human existence. According to this view, the material or physical side of human nature was inherently corrupt and doomed for destruction. By contrast, the spiritual side could gradually lose its connection to the material and ascend to God, the pure Spirit. This type of thinking was absorbed by Gnostics in the second century and probably formed the foundation of the Corinthians' denial of a bodily resurrection (see Paul's defense of Jesus' resurrection in 15:12-34).

Philosophical dualism led to two opposite extremes. Some people concluded that because the physical/material was irredeemable, what a person did in his or her body was irrelevant. Only the spirit mattered. This type of thinking justified all types of immorality. It would also explain why Paul had to emphasize to the Corinthians that their physical bodies were in fact members of Christ (6:12-20).

This dualism between body and spirit could also lead to asceticism. Some denied their physical bodies any pleasure in order to ascend to spiritual heights. This also is an emphasis in 1 Corinthians, where Paul had to confront the asceticism of some church members—those husbands and wives who were denying each other the physical joys of marriage (7:5).

Paul's relationship with the Corinthians. Tragically, Paul's passionate appeal for Christian love and holy living in 1 Corinthians fell on deaf ears. Paul must have been aware of the difficult situation that was developing in Corinth, for he sent his trusted assistant, Timothy, there (4:17; 16:10). Perhaps he hoped that Timothy would deal with some of the problems in person, explaining Paul's letter and modeling Christian love to the believers.

These efforts, however, must have been futile, for at the time that Paul wrote 2 Corinthians, about a year later, the situation had deteriorated even further. Paul had made a quick visit to Corinth, during which time some church members had challenged his authority (2 Corinthians 2:1; 12:14, 21; 13:1-4). After that trip, Paul may have written another letter to the Corinthians, a letter alluded to in 2 Corinthians 2:1-4; 7:8. In this letter, Paul sternly warned them to correct the abuses in the church. Around that time, he sent Titus to monitor the spiritual progress of the church. Finally, in his fourth letter to the Corinthians (2 Corinthians), Paul rejoiced in the good news brought to him by Titus. The Corinthians had disciplined some of their members, as Paul had instructed. Unfortunately, however, the reform was not completely sincere. Some members continued to challenge Paul's authority to instruct them in Christ's ways. So Paul wrote 2 Corinthians to encourage them to continue in their obedience and to warn those who were still opposing his authority.

The book of Acts reports that Paul finally did make it to Corinth on his third missionary journey (Acts 20:1-3). Perhaps at that time, the tear in the relationship between Paul and the Corinthians was finally mended. Not much else is known about the Corinthian church until A.D. 95. In that year, Clement of Rome wrote the Corinthians a letter urging them to stop arguing among themselves and to unite under Jesus' leadership. Clement's letter reveals that the division in the Corinthian church had persisted, despite Paul's severe warnings.

The central problem in Corinth. Why were there persistent divisions among the Corinthians? One group, associated with one teacher, wanted to achieve prominence in the church over another group, associated with another teacher. The situation had deteriorated so much that church members were boasting about their immorality. In Corinth, pride ran rampant. Even the display of spiritual gifts—teaching, preaching, and prophesying—had become an occasion for competition and a subject of boasts (12:21-30). Paul told the Corinthians to stop bragging and to love each other (12:1-11; 13:1-13). Only when they put their differences aside and united in a spirit of love would Jesus be able to use them for his holy purposes (1:2; 15:58). Today, that same lesson must be learned. Just as in Corinth, many modern churches are divided. Conflicts over personalities, agendas, and even the color of the church carpet arise from pride. One side will not give in to the other. Believers must unify around Christ and love each other.

MESSAGE
After his customary greeting (1:1-3), Paul begins by affirming the great truths of the gospel: God had given the Corinthian believers grace through Christ Jesus (1:4); God had enriched them greatly (1:5); God had given them every spiritual

gift (1:7); the Lord Jesus Christ would soon return (1:7); God would give them the power to be strong and blameless (1:8); God is faithful (1:9).

But then Paul punches out the rest of the story, beginning with a discussion of the divisions among believers and a strong appeal for unity (1:10– 4:21). Next he moves swiftly to condemn a specific illicit relationship in the church (5:1-2), lawsuits between Christians (6:1-11), and sexual immorality (6:12-20). Then, Paul softens a bit as he teaches about marriage and the single life (7:1-40), the relationship between conscience and freedom in Christ (8:1–10:33), order in worship services (11:1-34), spiritual gifts (12:1–14:40), and the reality and power of the Resurrection (15:1-58). Each of these teachings, however, brings the implication of a problem. Evidently marriages were in trouble; strong and weak Christians were in conflict; worship, Communion, and spiritual gifts were being abused; and wrong doctrine was being introduced. So Paul says, "Come to your senses" (15:34).

Paul closes with a reminder of the collection for the church in Jerusalem (16:1-4), his plans to visit the Corinthians (16:5-9), and miscellaneous comments and encouragements (16:10-24).

As you read this first letter from Paul to the church at Corinth, look for yourself and your church in the text, and between the lines. If God were writing a letter specifically to you, what would be your "good news" and "bad news"? Then look again; he has something poignant to say to each one of us.

The main themes in the book of 1 Corinthians include: *Loyalties, Immorality, Freedom, Worship, Body of Christ*, and *Resurrection*.

Loyalties (1:10-31; 2:1-5; 3:1-15; 4:1-21; 9:1-27). The Corinthians were rallying around various church leaders and teachers—Peter, Paul, and Apollos. Others, in an attempt at spiritual superiority, were claiming to "follow Christ." These loyalties led to intellectual pride and created a spirit of division in the church.

IMPORTANCE FOR TODAY. Personal loyalty to human leaders or human wisdom must never divide Christians into camps. Believers should care for each other, not compete for prominence. Christ unifies those who trust in him; he doesn't divide believers from each other. Like Christians in Corinth, contemporary believers often cluster around popular preachers and teachers. And the result is just as divisive as in the first century. Instead of dividing over personalities, worship styles, and theological minutiae, we need to focus on Christ. He will unify us. Give your allegiance to no one but Christ. Let him lead you.

Immorality (1:8; 5:1-13; 6:1-20; 7:1-40; 9:24-27; 10:1-13; 16:13). Paul had received a report of rampant immorality in the Corinthian church: uncorrected sexual sin and lawsuits between believers. The people were indifferent to the immorality in their community and in the church and were thinking only of themselves. This blunted the witness of the church and led to misconceptions about Christian living, especially sexual freedom and marriage. Highlighting the necessity for moral living and for bodies dedicated to serving God, Paul confronted the Corinthians with their sin and called them back to Christ-centered lives and marriages.

IMPORTANCE FOR TODAY. Although contemporary culture denigrates marriage and promotes sexual promiscuity and frivolous lawsuits, Christians must keep their focus on God and his word and never compromise with sinful ideas and practices. Believers should not blend in with society. It won't be easy to go against the flow, but you should determine to live up to God's standard of morality. Refuse to condone immoral behavior, especially among believers.

Freedom (8:1-13; 9:19-27; 10:23-33; 11:1). Paul taught freedom of choice on practices not expressly forbidden in Scripture. Some believers felt certain actions, such as buying meat taken from animals used in pagan rituals, were sinful by association. Others felt free from the law to do such actions. Paul taught that those who were stronger, who felt free to eat meat that had been offered to idols, should refrain from eating it in order to not become a stumbling block for a weaker believer. He also taught, however, that those with more sensitive consciences should not judge others and force them into a rigid "meat-less" lifestyle.

IMPORTANCE FOR TODAY. Although eating meat usually is not a controversial issue among believers today, other practices divide our churches. Paul clearly teaches that we are free in Christ, yet we must not abuse our Christian freedom by being inconsiderate and insensitive to others. We must never encourage others to do wrong by anything we do. Whatever the behavior controversy in your church and community, let love be your guide. Avoid judging other believers, and be sensitive to those with more sensitive consciences.

Worship (11:2-34; 14:1-40). Paul addressed disorder in worship. People were taking the Lord's Supper without first confessing sin. And many were using it as an occasion to eat and drink to excess. In addition, there was misuse of spiritual gifts and confusion over the role of women in the church. Paul gave explicit instructions for bringing order and focus back to their worship services. These instructions center around taking God's presence seriously.

IMPORTANCE FOR TODAY. Certainly there is no greater privilege than to stand in the presence of almighty God. Thus, worship is an awesome and sacred task and should be carried out properly and in an orderly manner. Although worship styles will vary from culture to culture and church to church, all worship of God should be done in a manner worthy of his high honor. Make sure that worship in your church is Christ-centered, harmonious, useful, and that it builds up all believers.

Body of Christ (12:1-31; 13:1-13; 16:1-3). Corinthian believers were confused about their roles in the church. And, evidently, many were seeking to possess the more noteworthy, public gifts (for example, preaching, teaching, speaking in tongues). But Paul emphasized that every member and every gift is essential for the life of the body of Christ. Just as with a physical body, the church has many parts, and each part has a special role to play; thus, God has given each member of the body a unique set of spiritual gifts. Instead of minimizing one's own role and usefulness or envying the more glamorous gifts that others may possess, each member should discover and use his or her own God-given spiritual gifts. Although great diversity exists in the body, expressed in the wide range of personalities and gifts, the church finds unity in Christ. And the greatest gift of all is love.

IMPORTANCE FOR TODAY. Contemporary churches often divide over the exercise of specific spiritual gifts. Instead, believers should recognize that God gives all his children special gifts that should be used to build up and unify the church. Analyze your giftedness in light of God's word, and consult with fellow believers to discover your spiritual gifts. Don't worry if your gifts seem minor and insignificant; you have a vital role to play in the church. Use your gifts to build up the body and to glorify Christ. And above all else, reflect Christ's love.

Resurrection (15:1-58). Some people were denying that Christ had risen from the dead. Others taught that people would not physically be resurrected. Refuting these ideas, Paul proclaimed the reality of the Resurrection. In fact, Christ's resurrection assures believers that they will have new, living bodies after they die. The hope of the Resurrection gives Christians assurance and confidence to live for Christ daily.

IMPORTANCE FOR TODAY. Since we will be raised again to life after we die, our lives are not in vain. We must stay faithful to God in our morality and our service. We are to live today knowing we will spend eternity with Christ. When you stand at the graveside of a loved one, or when you struggle with your own mortality, remember the Resurrection. Because he lives, you, too, shall live and be reunited with all the other believers who have gone before you.

OUTLINE OF 1 CORINTHIANS

I. Paul Addresses Church Problems (1:1–6:20)
   A. Divisions in the church
   B. Disorder in the church
II. Paul Answers Church Questions (7:1–16:24)
   A. Instruction on Christian marriage
   B. Instruction on Christian freedom
   C. Instruction on public worship
   D. Instruction on the Resurrection

1 CORINTHIANS 1

GREETINGS FROM PAUL / 1:1-3
Through various sources, Paul had received reports of problems in the Corinthian church, including jealousy, divisiveness, sexual immorality, and failure to discipline members. Churches today also address many of the same problems. Believers can learn a great deal by seeing how Paul handled these delicate situations.

1:1 Following the style of first-century letters, Paul began his letter to the Corinthians by introducing himself as the writer: **This letter is from Paul.** Then he described himself as **chosen by the will of God to be an apostle of Christ Jesus.** God chose Paul for special work among the Gentiles (Acts 9:15). Paul was not one of the original twelve disciples (later called apostles), but the risen Christ Jesus had confronted him on the road to Damascus and had called him to preach the gospel to both Jews and Gentiles (Acts 9:3-19). The apostles' mission was to be God's representatives: They were envoys, messengers, and delegates directly under the authority of Jesus Christ. They had authority to set up and supervise churches and to discipline them if necessary (which Paul did in these two letters to the Corinthian church).

The **brother** named **Sosthenes** may have been Paul's secretary, who had written this letter as Paul had dictated it. He was probably the Jewish synagogue leader in Corinth (Acts 18:17) who had been beaten during an attack on Paul and then later became a believer. Sosthenes was well known to the members of the Corinthian church, so Paul included his familiar name in the opening of the letter.

1:2 Paul wrote this letter **to the church of God in Corinth** while he was visiting Ephesus during his third missionary journey (Acts 19:1–20:1). Corinth and Ephesus faced each other across the Aegean Sea. Paul knew the Corinthian church well because he had spent eighteen months in Corinth during his second missionary journey (Acts 18:1-18). While in Ephesus, he had heard about problems in Corinth (1:11). About the same time, a delegation from the Corinthian church had visited Paul to ask his advice about their conflicts (16:17). Paul's purpose for writing was to correct those problems and to answer questions that church members had asked in a previous letter (7:1). For more about the city, see the Setting section in the Introduction.

Corinth, a giant cultural melting pot with a great diversity of wealth, religions, and moral standards, had a reputation for being fiercely independent and as decadent as any city in the world. Yet out of this moral wasteland God formed a church through Paul's ministry. Paul recognized this group of believers as **called by God to be his own holy people.** The term "called" means designated by God. God had identified them to serve him and not to serve their own purposes. To be **made holy** means to be cleansed of sin, separated from the world, and belonging to God. This can only happen through salvation in **Christ Jesus,** for only his death on the cross could accomplish this for sinners. Jesus did this not just for the Corinthians, but for **all Christians everywhere.** The Corinthian church must have included a great cross section of believers—wealthy merchants, common laborers, perhaps former temple prostitutes, and middle-class families. Because of the wide diversity of people and backgrounds, Paul took great pains to stress the need for both spiritual unity and Christlike character.

1:3 Grace means God's undeserved favor, his kindness shown clearly in his free gift of salvation given in Christ. Receiving it brings **peace,** the peace that Christ established between believers and God through his death on the cross. Paul used "grace and peace" as a standard greeting in all of his letters. **God our Father and the Lord Jesus Christ** makes a distinction between two of the persons in the Trinity—the Father and the Son. They are separate but equal in essence (see also 1 Thessalonians 3:11).

PAUL GIVES THANKS TO GOD / 1:4-9

The problems in the Corinthian church shaped almost every word Paul wrote in his letter. He realized that the believers were struggling with internal, as well as external, problems. They were forgetting to whom they belonged. When correcting others, draw their attention to what God has already accomplished in them and for them. The same process can guide your own reflections on the condition of your relationship with God.

1:4 In this letter, Paul would include strong words to the Corinthians, but he began on a positive note of thanksgiving. Paul affirmed their privilege of belonging to the Lord, **thanking God for all the generous gifts he** had given to the Corinthian believers because of their faith in **Christ Jesus.** Paul usually would begin his letters with a word of thanks for the believers to whom he was writing (see, for example, Romans 1:8; Philippians 1:3-7; Colossians 1:3-8).

1:5-6 God had **enriched** the Corinthian **church.** However, the Corinthians may have been putting too much emphasis on possessing the **gifts** of the Spirit and not enough emphasis on God, who gave those gifts to them, or on Christ, who enabled them to have those gifts. They had been enriched in their **eloquence** in speaking about God and in their **knowledge** of him. Greeks attached great importance to oratory and knowledge. God's grace had increased their ability to speak about their faith, as well as their spiritual knowledge and understanding. These facts—both seen by Paul himself and reported to him by others—served to confirm his testimony about Christ to the Corinthian believers. The changed lives of these believers validated the truth of the gospel message that had been preached to them.

1:7 The Corinthian church members had **every spiritual gift** they needed to live the Christian life, to witness for Christ, and to stand against the paganism and immorality of Corinth. These gifts would help the church battle sin both inside the congregation and outside in the world. These believers in Corinth lacked nothing—they had every spiritual gift—and because of this they more **eagerly** looked forward in faith and hope to **the return of our Lord Jesus Christ.** This statement refers to the second coming of Christ. The spiritual gifts God has given to believers here on earth are merely a foretaste of what is to come.

1:8 There will be an **end** to the eager waiting of believers (1:7), because Christ will return. Not only have the believers received gifts for building up the church and standing against sin, but Christ would also keep them **strong** until the day the

Lord Jesus Christ returns. Because Christ has died for believers, given them spiritual gifts, and promised to return for them, Paul guaranteed these believers that God would also consider them **free from all blame** (see Romans 8:33-34; Ephesians 1:7-10). This guarantee was not because of their great gifts or their shining performance, but because of what Jesus Christ accomplished for them through his death and resurrection.

1:9 Believers need never doubt God's grace, his gifts, or his promise to give them eternal life because God **always does just what he says.** God has promised, and because he cannot lie (Titus 1:2), believers can be certain that all of his promises will come true. God himself had **invited** each of the Corinthian believers into **friendship with his Son** and that call will never be rescinded.

DIVISIONS IN THE CHURCH / 1:10-17

In this large and diverse Corinthian church, the believers were favoring different preachers. Because the whole New Testament had not yet been written, the believers depended heavily on preaching and teaching for spiritual insight into the meaning of the Old Testament. However, they had split into factions—each following their favorite preacher or leader, even though the leaders spoke the same message and apparently had no knowledge of these factions. Paul admonished the believers to remember the singular message that had brought them to faith, and to stop comparing messengers. Believers today should also focus on the truth of the message, not the style of the messenger.

1:10 Paul had founded the church in Corinth on his second missionary journey. Eighteen months after he had left, arguments and divisions had arisen, and some church members had slipped back into an immoral lifestyle. Paul wrote this letter to address the problems, to clear up confusion about right and wrong, and to remove the immorality among them. Because Paul was an apostle (1:1), he had the right to **appeal by the authority of the Lord Jesus Christ.** Paul simply told the Corinthian believers to **stop arguing** over factions or **divisions** that had developed in the church itself, with various believers aligning themselves behind various teachers (1:12-13). Thus, Paul here was pleading with the believers to **let there be real harmony** and for them to **be of one mind, united in thought and purpose.** To be perfectly united does not mean that Paul required everyone to be exactly the same. Instead, he wanted them to set aside their arguments and focus on what truly mattered—Jesus Christ as Lord and their mission to take the light of the gospel into a dark world. The internal divisions

would only cause strife and hinder the gospel, as well as make the church look ridiculous to those outside.

1:11 This woman named **Chloe** is unknown. Apparently, she was well-to-do, with servants (**members** of her **household**) traveling and handling the family's interests between Ephesus and Corinth. It is unknown if she was a believer, but some members of her household were. Paul was writing this letter from Ephesus, and Chloe may have lived in Ephesus with some of her servants having been to Corinth. There they would have heard about what was going on in the Corinthian church and would have reported this back to Paul. Or Chloe may have lived in Corinth; thus, when her servants had come to Ephesus, they had given Paul the details. In either case, these first-hand observers **told** Paul about the **arguments** that were going on in the Corinthian church.

1:12-13 The factions in the Corinthian church threatened to destroy it. These factious groups followed different preachers for different reasons.

Some of the believers followed **Paul,** who had founded their church. Others chose to follow **Peter.** A Jew and one of the twelve disciples of Jesus, Peter probably attracted many of the Jewish believers. A third group chose to follow **Apollos,** an eloquent and popular preacher who had had a dynamic ministry in Corinth (Acts 18:24; 19:1; Titus 3:13). Apollos was from Alexandria and had become distinguished for his speaking ability. Oratory and eloquence were highly valued in the culture of the day, so Apollos probably attracted the highly educated and distinguished believers in the congregation. Finally, a fourth group claimed to **follow only Christ.** This group may have boasted a special relationship to Christ, or they may have been positioning themselves above the fray, saying that they had chosen to follow Christ alone, not any human leader (see 2 Corinthians 10:7).

Paul asked whether Christ could be **divided.** This is a graphic picture of what happens when the church (the body of Christ) quarrels. Then Paul asked if he, himself, had been **crucified** for them. No, because only One had been crucified for the believers—indeed, only One *could* be crucified to pay the penalty for sins. Were the believers **baptized in the name of Paul** (or even of Peter or Apollos)? Again, the answer was no.

1:14-16 Paul's question about baptism in 1:13 led him to note that he had baptized very few people in Corinth. He saw this as providential and thanked God that he had baptized only

Crispus (perhaps the same man mentioned in Acts 18:8), **Gaius** (perhaps the same man noted in Romans 16:23), and **the household of Stephanas.** While Paul certainly had many converts in the city, he had not baptized them all. No one could claim that Paul had been baptizing people in order to obtain their loyalty as their special leader. Clearly he was not attempting to make disciples for himself.

Believers are not baptized "into" different preachers—they are baptized into the family of believers. Baptism replaced circumcision as the initiation rite of the new order, the new covenant. Christians need only "one baptism" by which they publicly acknowledge their one faith in one Lord. Far from it being divisive, baptism is a key unifying factor in the church.

1:17 When Paul said **Christ didn't send me to baptize,** he was not minimizing the importance of baptism. Instead, he was pointing out that his gift was to **preach the Good News** (see Acts 9:15). But even preaching could be cause for division. In fact, this was already happening in Corinth, with the believers lining up behind different preachers for different reasons. Paul pointed out that neither he, nor the other apostles and preachers, spoke **with clever speeches.** They did not depend upon the rhetoric or philosophical arguments so admired by the Greeks. To do so would have emptied the message of its **power,** and it would have drawn people to the preachers rather than to the message of salvation in Christ.

THE WISDOM OF GOD / 1:18-31

The Greeks highly valued wisdom. Paul showed in the following verses, however, that there is the kind of "wisdom" that the world worships, and there is the true wisdom that comes from God alone.

1:18 Paul preached **the message of the cross—** Jesus Christ crucified on behalf of sinners. Such a message always has two results, for ultimately all of humanity will end up in one of these two classes. (1) The gospel message sounds **foolish** to those who desire worldly wisdom. "Who wants a crucified king?" they might ask. (2) But for those **who are being saved,** the gospel message is **the very power of God.** Only with such power can the gospel message redeem sinful people and transform them into God's people.

1:19 Paul summarized Isaiah 29:14 to emphasize a point that Jesus often made: God's way of thinking is not like the world's way (normal human

wisdom). **Human wisdom** and **brilliant ideas** refer to world-centered wisdom and intelligence. These are not wrong, but they are worthless as a means of salvation. People can spend a lifetime accumulating human wisdom and yet never learn how to have a personal relationship with God. They must come to the crucified and risen Christ to receive eternal life and the joy of a personal relationship with the Savior.

1:20 No human wisdom or intelligence can either discover or disprove God. No human reasoning can bring salvation. So all those who have lived by their own wisdom will be left with nothing. God had already made them all **look foolish** and showed that their "wisdom" was no more than **useless nonsense.** For all their learning, God would show them to be fools. Their wisdom would be "useless" because it could do nothing to provide salvation. That can come only through the cross.

1:21 In his complete sovereignty and **wisdom,** God decided that people **would never find him through human wisdom.** Instead, he chose a crucified Savior and a message of salvation preached by weak and fallible human beings **to save all who believe.** This looks like absurdity to the "high and mighty" of this world. Many people of Paul's time, and many today, mocked the message of the gospel. In their human wisdom, they wanted to reason "above and beyond" and experience more than what they felt was offered in the **foolish preaching** of believers. In reality, the worldly wise will not find God; those who accept the message of the cross will find him and be saved.

1:22-24 Many **Jews** considered the Good News of Jesus Christ to be **foolish** because they thought the Messiah would be a conquering king who would give them **a sign from heaven.** Although Jesus had performed many miracles during his ministry on earth, many Jews who observed his miracles firsthand had refused to believe (Matthew 12:38-39; 16:1-4; Mark 8:11-12; Luke 11:16; John 6:30). Jesus had not restored David's throne in the way that they had expected. Besides, he had been executed as a criminal (Deuteronomy 21:23)—how could a criminal be the Savior? This proclamation of **Christ crucified offended** them.

The **Greeks** (also called **Gentiles**) did not believe in a bodily resurrection; they did not see in Jesus the powerful characteristics of their mythological gods, and they thought no reputable person would be crucified. To them, death was defeat, not victory. It did not make sense—in their **own wisdom**—that any god would do such a thing as come to earth to be killed. The gospel message was **all nonsense.**

While some Jews and Greek tripped over the message, it was a different story for **those called by God to salvation**—those who embraced and believed the gospel. Many people, **both Jews and Gentiles,** will not stumble over the message but will find that it is **the mighty power of God and the wonderful wisdom of God.**

1:25 This verse provides the key to Paul's words in chapters 1–3. The message of Christ's death for sins sounds **foolish** to those who don't believe. But **human plans** and **human strength** cannot

begin to compare to God. What the world sees as foolishness (Christ's death for our sins as a display of God's power) is God's truth. The "foolish" people who simply accept Christ's offer are actually the wisest of all, because they alone will live eternally with God.

1:26-27 Having shown the difference between God's wisdom and what people of this world call wisdom, Paul urged his readers to **remember** that few of them had any worldly achievements **when God called** them. Few would have been considered **wise in the world's eyes, powerful,** or **wealthy.** By using these three terms, Paul was pointing out that intellectual, political, and social position are not qualifications for being chosen by God. In fact, just the opposite was true. Yet they *had* been called by God. Clearly, God does not seek out the people whom the world admires; instead, he reveals himself to humble and searching hearts, regardless of their worldly position. But God **chose** what **the world considers foolish to shame those who think they are wise.** He chose the **powerless to shame those who are powerful.** Why would God not choose leaders and influential people who could make sweeping reforms and be followed by the masses? God does not choose as people choose. His sovereign choice is not based on anything that people can do or achieve.

1:28-29 God chose the foolish and the weak, **things despised by the world,** so that those chosen can never **boast in the presence of God.** God chooses those who are **counted as nothing at all** by the world and turns them into great people for him. People's abilities, social standing, or knowledge have nothing to do with God's choice. Skill and wisdom do not get a person into God's Kingdom—faith in Christ does— so no one can boast that his or her achievements helped him or her secure eternal life.

1:30-31 Here Paul reminded the Corinthian believers that **God alone made it possible** for believers **to be in Christ Jesus.** God is the source of believers' existence and the reason for their personal and living relationship with Christ. Because salvation is completely by God's grace, any boasting before God is sheer nonsense. If believers must boast, they must **boast only of what the Lord has done.** These words come from Jeremiah 9:23-24 and refer to saved people glorying in the Lord's acts on their behalf. So the redeemed people of the New Testament boast not in their salvation, but in God alone, who provided that salvation through his grace alone.

1 CORINTHIANS 2

PAUL PREACHES WISDOM / 2:1-16

The Corinthians were confusing the gospel by creating artificial standards of faith. They were using wisdom as the gauge. The more wisdom someone claimed, the more spiritual that person became. Standards were determined by teachers. They were arguing and dividing over which teacher had the deepest spirituality. For Paul, the gospel—God's wisdom—was a pool of clear water. Believers were urged to go deeper, but they would find living water no matter how deep they dove.

2:1-2 The words, **when I first came to you,** refer to Paul's first visit to Corinth during his second missionary journey (A.D. 51), when he founded the church (Acts 18:1-18). As Paul had explained in chapter 1, the gospel message, by its very simplicity, appears foolish to those who think themselves wise by human standards. Paul was a brilliant scholar and could have overwhelmed his audience in Corinth with **lofty words and brilliant ideas.** While this may have led to a measure of intellectual assent, it may not have led them to saving faith. Faith that depends on clever arguments and bright oratory can be undermined if another logical argument or better orator comes along. Faith grounded in the power of the Holy Spirit, however, cannot be undermined. So Paul **decided to concentrate only on Jesus Christ and his death on the cross.** Paul shared the simple message of Jesus Christ, who had been crucified for the world's sins, and let that simple message move into the Corinthians' hearts by the power of the Holy Spirit (2:4).

2:3-4 Paul came to Corinth not as a powerful preacher and debater ready to take on the city but, rather, **in weakness—timid and trembling.** His attitude was not fearful, but utterly dependent upon God for the important task of bringing the gospel into this wicked and idolatrous city. He did not depend on using **wise and persuasive speeches** to change people's hearts. That would happen only by the work of the **Holy Spirit** among them. The power of their conversion was not through him and his preaching but through the Holy Spirit.

2:5 Paul deliberately chose not to use the style of persuasion and oratory that so fascinated those in the Greek world. Instead, he brought a simple message that depended upon the Holy Spirit's power for its effectiveness. Paul did not want his listeners

focusing on the speech he gave, or how he presented it, or whatever other brand of **human wisdom** might have been used to persuade the Corinthians to believe. Instead, Paul wanted them to trust in the simple message and so **trust the power of God** for their salvation.

2:6-7 The Corinthians were accustomed to philosophical debate—whether engaging in it or simply listening to it. But, as Paul already noted, he did not come to them with philosophy; he came with the simple gospel message. When Paul did not entertain his listeners with philosophical debate, many probably criticized him, considering him unlearned and his message unimportant. Paul was not teaching a philosophy, however, nor was he debating speculative notions, for these never saved anyone. **The kind of wisdom that belongs to this world** offers nothing. Paul didn't bother with the worldly wisdom in order to impress anyone.

Instead, when he was **among mature Christians,** Paul did **speak with words of wisdom,** but this was the highest wisdom because it came from God. The "mature" Christians were not those with advanced training but those who had been enlightened by the Holy Spirit and had received salvation, as contrasted with those who had rejected it (1:21-23; 2:14). Because of the Holy Spirit's guidance, believers could grasp this **secret wisdom of God,** referring to God's offer of salvation to all people made available through Jesus' death on the cross. This plan was "secret" because only through God's wisdom and the insight given by his Spirit can people begin to comprehend it. Attempting to understand this plan with human wisdom and through philosophical discussions will take people nowhere. Only God, through the Holy Spirit, can reveal it (2:10).

This plan had been made **before the world**

began. God knew the entire cycle of the creation, fall, and salvation through his Son before he made the earth and placed Adam and Eve on it. This reveals God's great plan for the human race—that despite their downfall, he would bring some to glory.

2:8 This "secret wisdom" had not been revealed to **the rulers of this world** (those who are impressed by worldly wisdom, 2:6). "Rulers" refers to the rulers in Palestine (the Pharisees, Sadducees, King Herod) and the Roman rulers (such as Pilate and the soldiers under his command). If these leaders had truly understood who Jesus was and the eternal consequences of rejecting him, **they would never have crucified our glorious Lord.** This is at the heart of Paul's irony: The very ones who were trying to kill Jesus were actually carrying out God's will. Thinking they were getting rid of a nuisance—Jesus of Nazareth—they were really crucifying the very Lord of glory, God incarnate. Jesus was misunderstood and killed by those whom the world considered wise and powerful.

2:9-10 Paul generalized an Old Testament theme, including references such as Psalm 31:20; Isaiah 52:15; 64:4; 65:17. Paul's point is that humans cannot begin to comprehend **what God has prepared for those who love him.** The future blessings that believers will enjoy in eternity are beyond human understanding; nevertheless, Christians believe and trust in these promises because **God has revealed them.** Believers have received the Holy **Spirit** and, thus, can understand from Scripture the wonderful future that God is preparing for them. Paul was explaining to the Corinthian believers that they had become very different from their unbelieving neighbors—essentially different because of the entrance of the Holy Spirit into their lives. The Holy Spirit, as God, reveals God to people. Human beings, through the Holy Spirit, can get some glimpses of what God has planned for his people.

Who is the Holy Spirit? God is three persons in one—the Father, the Son, and the Holy Spirit. God became a man in Jesus so that Jesus could die for our sins. Jesus rose from the dead to offer salvation to all people through spiritual renewal and rebirth. When Jesus ascended into heaven, his physical presence left the earth, but he promised to send the Holy Spirit so that his spiritual presence would still be among mankind (see Luke 24:49). The Holy Spirit first became available to the apostles on the day of the Resurrection (John 20:22) and then to more believers on the day of Pentecost (Acts 2). In the Old Testament, the Holy Spirit empowered specific individuals for specific purposes, but now all believers have the power of the Holy Spirit available to them. The statement, **the Spirit searches out everything and shows us even God's deep secrets,** means that only the Spirit can reveal to believers God's profound nature and wonderful plan, especially that formerly hidden mystery that is now revealed—salvation through Jesus' death and resurrection.

2:11 Paul compared the Spirit's understanding of God with a person's understanding of himself or herself. Just as a person cannot penetrate another person's thought processes, so **no one can know God's thoughts except God's own Spirit.** The only way to know God is to know his Holy Spirit, to have him in one's life. The only way to obtain the Holy Spirit is to accept, by faith, the sacrifice of Christ on the cross. The Holy Spirit is a distinct person, yet one in essence and function with God the Father.

2:12 The words **us** and **we** contrast the believers with nonbelievers. The rest of the verse contrasts their source of power and wisdom. Believers do not depend on worldly wisdom (**the world's spirit**); instead, they have received God's **Spirit** (Galatians 3:5). Jesus had told his disciples that God would send the Spirit after his return to heaven. When the Spirit came, believers would **know the wonderful things God has freely given** them. What God "freely gave" was salvation through the death of his Son. The understanding of the salvation that had been accomplished through Jesus' death would come to the believers as the Holy Spirit revealed it to them.

2:13 Paul may have had some critics in Corinth—the philosophers and orators who had been unimpressed with his message. Here Paul explained that the gospel message had not been given with **words of human wisdom** because no human wisdom can adequately explain God's wisdom. In order to speak the Spirit's message, believers must **speak words given by the Spirit.** In order to **explain spiritual truths,** believers must use **the Spirit's words.** Paul's words are authoritative because their source was the Holy Spirit. Paul was not merely giving his own personal views or his personal impression of what God had said. Under the inspiration of the Holy Spirit, he was writing the very thoughts and words of God. Today, all believers pass along the gospel message—trusting in God's Spirit to speak the spiritual truths.

2:14 The gospel sounded foolish to many in Corinth, just as it is scoffed at by many today. This should not come as a surprise. Non-Christians cannot fully understand God; thus they cannot grasp the concept that God's Spirit lives in believers.

Just as a tone-deaf person cannot appreciate fine music fully, the person who rejects God cannot understand God's beautiful message. With the lines of communication broken, a person is not able to hear what God is saying to him or her. Paul highlighted these truths about **people who aren't Christians: They can't understand these truths;** the spiritual truths all sound **foolish to them.**

Unbelievers simply cannot comprehend Christ's work on the cross, see the beauty and compassion of God's divine plan, or desire to know God at all. All of these mysteries remain as mere foolishness to them because the ability to comprehend, love, and glory in these realities comes directly from the Holy Spirit.

2:15-16 Because believers have the Spirit, they **understand these things.** They are able to make right judgments—not necessarily about all matters, but certainly about spiritual matters such as salvation or God's future blessings, and they will be able to make the necessary discernments regarding them. Paul quoted from Isaiah 40:13 to show that a Christian is not subject to nonbelievers' judg-

ments about spiritual matters because nonbelievers **can't understand.** For them to judge believers' faith in salvation by the cross is to judge the Lord's wisdom. Paul wondered who was ready to take human wisdom up against God's wisdom. Who among the detractors knew the mind of the Lord so as to bypass the simple message of the cross?

In contrast to those who do not have the Spirit and do not know the mind of the Lord, believers do **have the mind of Christ.** Believers understand fully, as did Christ himself, the significance of the cross and what it meant for mankind's salvation.

No one can completely comprehend God (Romans 11:34), but through the guidance of the Holy Spirit, believers can understand spiritual truths. Believers have insight into some of God's plans, thoughts, and actions because, with the Spirit within, they have access to the mind of Christ. Through the Holy Spirit, believers can begin to know God's thoughts, talk with him, and expect his answers to their prayers. Paul could allow his detractors in Corinth to jeer at him, for they had no right to make judgments on him or his message—because he had the mind of Christ and they did not.

1 CORINTHIANS 3

PAUL AND APOLLOS, SERVANTS OF CHRIST / 3:1-23
The Corinthians needed to mature in their spiritual lives. They were allowing themselves to be divided into factions regarding which preacher they liked better. These divisions in the church threatened the unity they would need in order to stand for the truth against false teachers and persecution.

3:1 Paul reproved the believers for their lack of maturity in the faith. Instead of growing in the faith, they had let themselves be diverted into quarrels and factions so that Paul could not even talk to them as he **would to mature Christians.** He had to talk to them in his letters as though they **belonged to this world** or as though they **were infants in the Christian life.** Paul was not accusing the Corinthians of being carnal (or "worldly"); he was saying that their behavior was sinful in comparison to that of the mature believers. They were indwelt by the Spirit, for they could not be Christians without the Holy Spirit (see Romans 8:9; Galatians 3:2-3). But these "infants" had not grown in the faith because they were acting like the world around them. The proof was that they quarreled like children, allowing divisions to distract them.

3:2-3 These believers in Corinth should have long since grown out of the "infant" stage and been maturing in their faith. Instead, they were still acting like "infants" (3:1), so Paul had to continue to **feed** them (teach them) the basics of the faith instead of being able to teach them deeper truths (Hebrews 5:12; 1 Peter 2:2). Just as babies drink only **milk** because they cannot eat **solid food,** so these "baby Christians" had to keep relearning the basics. Paul longed to teach them deeper truths, but he realized that they weren't ready because they were still influenced by the world. Their **sinful desires** indicated that their mind-set was worldly, not characterized by the desires of the Spirit. Their jealousy and quarreling proved it. Instead of acting different from the world because of their salvation through Christ, they continued to act **like people who don't belong**

to the Lord. They were believers, but they were spiritually immature. By remaining immature and allowing that immaturity to divide them, they were wreaking havoc on the church.

3:4-5 As already mentioned in 1:12-13, the cause of the divisions and quarrels had to do with loyalty to different teachers. In 1:12, Paul also mentioned Peter; here he focused on the two men who had actually preached and taught in Corinth—himself and Apollos. The believers had split up, some being followers of **Paul,** others preferring **Apollos.** Paul was pointing out that to act that way was to act **like those who are not Christians.** Apollos and Paul were no more than **servants** of God who brought the message of salvation to the Corinthians. As mere servants of the Lord, they had pointed the people toward Christ, not toward themselves.

3:6-7 Part of the reason for the factions may have been the different jobs Paul and Apollos had done in Corinth (3:5). Paul planted **the seed** of the gospel message in the believers' **hearts.** He was a missionary pioneer, the first to bring the message of salvation, and the founder of the church in Corinth. Apollos had **watered** that seed, helping the believers grow stronger in the faith. Unfortunately, some of the believers in Corinth had split into factions that pledged loyalty to Paul, the "planter," or to Apollos, the "waterer."

Paul explained to these loyal believers that they had misplaced their loyalties. Paul and Apollos had only done what God had told them to do. In fact, compared to God's role in the process, they were unimportant, for God **is the one who makes the seed grow.** Paul, Apollos, Peter, and any missionary or minister of the gospel is nothing more than God's instrument. God alone brings the seed to fruition. Thus, there is no room for pride on the part of these leaders, and there is no room for divisive loyalty toward these leaders on the part of the followers.

3:8-9 While each servant has various functions, each one was a **team** member **with the same purpose**—to bring people into God's Kingdom and to see them mature in their faith. Yet, that being said, each servant is still individually responsible for his or her work—**they will be rewarded individually, according to their own hard work.** (For more on how God rewards our work, see 4:5. Paul will explain this comment in more detail in the following verses. For more on how God rewards believers, see 4:5; Ephesians 6:8; Colossians 3:23; Hebrews 11:6.) Paul and the other preachers and teachers of the true gospel message worked together **as partners who belong to God.** Their ministry belonged not to them, but to God.

3:10-11 Paul had been called by God to be an apostle and to take the gospel message to the Gentiles (see 1:1; Acts 9:15). God gave him the grace for this message, and, **like an expert builder,** he was doing what God had called him to do. He **laid the foundation,** meaning that he took the message of Jesus Christ to these people. The foundation of the church—of all believers—is **Jesus Christ.** Whoever builds on that foundation **must be very careful.** All true believers have the gospel message as their foundation, and each one is building on that foundation. This "building" probably refers to the church, to sound teaching, and to each individual's Christian character. Only the truth can build strong character in the believers and thus build a strong church. The foundation may be strong, but a variety of materials might be chosen in the building process, as Paul describes further.

Jesus ended his Sermon on the Mount with the same picture Paul used here (Matthew 7:24-27). Jesus compared two kinds of life: one constructed on the knowledge and application of his words; the other constructed without regard for Christ. Both houses can be built, but only one will stand up to the winds and storms of life.

3:12-13 The foundation for the building is Jesus Christ (3:11); Christians build on this foundation with a variety of materials of different quality. There is little value in attempting to find a meaning behind each of the materials Paul mentioned; most likely, he was dividing the materials into two basic classes—the valuable building materials, which were imperishable (here called **gold, silver,** and **jewels**), and the worthless building materials, which probably symbolize worldly wisdom (here called **wood, hay,** and **straw**). This **time of testing** that is coming **at the judgment day** refers to Christ's second coming. At that time, believers will be separated from unbelievers, with believers receiving their promised reward in heaven (1 Thessalonians 5:2-9). Believers will not be judged regarding their salvation—their salvation is sure—but they will be judged **to see what kind of work** they have done. **Everyone's work will be put through the fire to see whether or not it keeps its value.** "Fire" pictures a scorching test that will reveal the value of the "building." Those made with gold, silver, and jewels will stand up to this test; those thrown together with wood, hay, and straw will go up in flames and be destroyed.

Christ will evaluate each person's contribution to the life of the church, and the judgment day will reveal the sincerity of each person's work. God will determine whether or not each person has been faithful to Jesus' instructions. Good work will be rewarded; unfaithful or inferior work will be burned up.

3:14-15 Because the foundation is Jesus Christ, everyone who builds on that foundation **will be saved.** But these believers will present to God the lives that they have lived for him. Some of them will present lives of gold, silver, and jewels— lives built on the truth of the gospel and spent in sacrifice and service to God. These builders **will receive a reward** (see 3:8). Some will present lives that amount to no more than wood, hay, and straw, and all that they did and accomplished in this world will be **burned up.** These builders will be saved, but only as if they jumped out of a burning building and lost everything but their lives. They will enter heaven but will not receive the same reward as those who built well.

3:16 God's people, all believers in Jesus Christ, **are the temple of God.** Not only that, but **the Spirit of God lives in** them. While it is true that each individual is a "temple of the Holy Spirit" (6:19), Paul was teaching here about the nature of the church or Christian community. This is a common theme in the New Testament (2 Corinthians 6:16; Ephesians 2:22; Hebrews 3:6; 1 Peter 2:5).

Corinth boasted many pagan temples and shrines, but there was only one temple for God— the Corinthian Christians were it! The "Spirit of God" is the Holy Spirit, whom Jesus promised would come and live in his followers (John 14:17-20; 16:7). The Holy Spirit draws all believers together as Christ's body on earth; he provides the unity that should characterize them. Because every believer is a temple for the Holy Spirit (a dwelling place for him), the believers ought not be dividing into warring factions because that destroys the temple.

3:17 In the Old Testament, the penalty for defiling God's dwelling (whether the tabernacle or the temple) was death (Leviticus 15:31) or separation from the nation (Numbers 19:20). The penalty for bringing **ruin upon** God's spiritual temple—found in his people individually and in the church collectively—is no less severe. How might anyone attempt to destroy God's temple? False teaching that undermines believers' faith, rivalry that creates dissension and rips churches apart, and weak discipleship that promotes easy-believism are all problems that weaken the church. In 3:15, Paul wrote of the builder who, though he or she builds shoddily on the foundation, will yet be saved. This verse focuses on those who, already unsaved, set out to destroy those who are saved—such as the false teachers. God will destroy them because of their sin.

3:18 Thus far, most of Paul's letter has focused on the difference between the world's wisdom and God's wisdom (see 1:17–2:16). Paul admonished the believers to **stop fooling** themselves. If they continued to think that they were **wise by this world's standards,** they were fooling themselves.

Some people have used Paul's teaching here to rail against any study of philosophy or even higher learning in general. But Paul was not promoting the abandonment of reason. Paul was countering the Corinthians' use of rhetoric and debate (the "world's standards") to uphold their own divisive positions. He was warning them that God's way of thinking is infinitely more valuable, even though it may seem foolish to the world (1:27). They would need to empty themselves of their pride in human wisdom in order to be filled with God's wisdom.

3:19-20 Two Old Testament Scriptures back up Paul's statement that **the wisdom of this world is foolishness to God.** The first comes from Job 5:12, where God is the one who **catches those who think they are wise in their own cleverness.** The other reference comes from Psalm 94:11, again speaking of the worldly-wise ones, warning them that **the Lord knows the thoughts of the wise— they are worthless.** God knows the thoughts of everyone. What these wise people will accomplish is futile because it concerns this world alone and will pass away.

3:21-23 Therefore, the Corinthian believers ought not **take pride in following a particular leader;** instead, they must follow Christ Jesus alone. The phrase **everything belongs to you** underscores the fact that all believers have everything because they have **Christ.** They need not boast about following any particular leader because they would be limiting themselves. Indeed, all those leaders already belonged to them, as did everything else, because they **belong to Christ, and Christ belongs to God.**

The "whole world" refers to the physical world, not to the ethical system (as in 1:20). Believers have true "life" because life only has meaning when lived for Christ. While nonbelievers are victims of life, swept along by its current and wondering if there is meaning to it, believers can use life well because they understand its true purpose. Even "death" belongs to believers because it holds no terrors. Nonbelievers can only fear death. Believers, however, know that Christ has conquered death; death is the entranceway into an eternity with God. The present and the future belong to believers because they belong to the One who holds the present and the future.

Believers ought never settle for faithfulness to a human leader or human ideas; they ought never

break into factions quarreling over their respective loyalties. And this should especially not occur since believers have been given everything from God's gracious hand.

1 CORINTHIANS 4

PAUL AND THE CORINTHIANS / 4:1-21

The discussion in chapter 3 regarding the status of ministers of the gospel led Paul to further explain how believers should regard their ministers. The leaders (himself, Apollos, Peter, or others) were never to be the focus of anyone's loyalty. They do not have supernatural powers, nor do they advance their own doctrines. Their authority is given and limited by the Master—Jesus Christ.

4:1-2 The believers ought not to be boasting about "their" leader (3:21). Instead, Paul wrote that he and **Apollos** were **mere servants of Christ,** doing what he told them to do—**explaining God's secrets.** These **secrets** refer to the plan of salvation (2:7). Ministers of the gospel message are merely God's servants. As servants who have been entrusted with much responsibility, they should **be faithful.**

4:3-4 The Corinthians battled over the preacher whom they judged to be the best, but Paul dismissed their judgment entirely. Human judgment was as worthless before God as human wisdom (2:6). Because he had been called by God to serve, Paul owed allegiance to God alone, and he looked to God alone to **examine** his performance. As a servant serves the master of the estate, so Paul served God. Paul did not concern himself with what any group of people thought of his teaching style or his message. Paul did not even depend on his own self-evaluation. When he did look within, Paul could honestly say that he had a **clear conscience,** but he was accountable to God and would be judged by God alone.

4:5 The Corinthian believers had expended much energy on making judgments concerning various leaders. Paul explained that God alone could judge the leaders because he alone knows the **deepest secrets** and **private motives.** Human beings cannot do that, so they should **be careful not to jump to conclusions before the Lord returns as to whether or not someone is faithful.** People can see only the outside, but God can discern a person's heart (1 Samuel 16:7).

4:6 Because the Corinthians had split into various cliques, each following its favorite preacher, Paul

used their loyalties to himself and Apollos to illustrate what he was saying about God's ministers. The groups were not to boast about being tied to a particular preacher because each preacher was simply a humble servant who had suffered for the same message of salvation in Jesus Christ. No preacher of God has more status than another. If they would **pay attention to the Scriptures,** focusing on what God has said, they wouldn't be bragging about one leader over another. If they read and understood the Scriptures and what they say about God's sovereignty and the role of spiritual leaders, the factions would dissolve.

4:7 Paul's words about God's ministers merely illustrate the larger truth that believers ought not make judgments about one another either. Apparently, each faction that followed a different leader also placed itself above the others. But Paul asked the rhetorical questions so they could see the silliness of their prideful positions against one another. No one was **better than anyone else.** Everything they had, everything they accomplished, every gift they received—all came from God. No one has any right to **boast** about anything.

4:8 With biting sarcasm, Paul derided the rampant pride in the Corinthian church. The believers proclaimed loyalties and set themselves against one another, and many looked down even on the apostle Paul for his lack of wealth or great oratory (see 2:1-5). These believers apparently already had all they wanted. They thought they had the Kingdom's riches, and they reigned in their little groups as though they had **become kings.** Believing that they possessed all the great wisdom and knowledge they needed, they felt qualified to judge others. Paul marveled that they were able to accomplish all of this apart from those who had brought the gospel truth to them. With great irony, Paul explained that he wished he could be a king along with them, for apparently they had surpassed the apostle in wisdom and knowledge and had already reached full maturity.

4:9 While some of the Corinthian believers lived as though they were kings, the apostles apparently had been passed up for such honor. How odd that the apostles, who had been called to minister the gospel message across the world, were not reigning as kings but instead were **like prisoners of war** who had been **condemned to die.** For almost all of the apostles, that was in fact what happened. While these new Christians were attempting to reign, their spiritual leaders were facing an entirely different sort of life—one filled with suffering for the sake of the gospel.

4:10-13 Surely Paul's sarcasm shamed his readers. He pointed out the strangeness of their supposed wisdom, strength, and honor while God's apostles were considered as foolish, weak, and without honor. To further elaborate on the warped viewpoint of the proud Corinthian believers, Paul described the hardships that he and the other apostles continued to face in their ministry. Far from being honored for their preaching and fawned over as kings, they faced severe suffering. The world saw these men as no more than **trash,** because they did not meet up to worldly standards of success. Paul willingly took this abuse in order to bring the message of eternal life to any and all who would believe. Most Christians today want careers that give them comfort, money, and prestige. Very few are willing to accept work that takes away "necessary" comforts, earns little money, and/or causes people to look down on them— even if it is for the cause of the gospel.

4:14-16 Paul's previous sarcasm had not been meant to **shame** these believers **but to warn** them because they were his **beloved children** in the faith. Paul portrayed a special affection for these believers—he was their **spiritual father.** In an attempt to unify the church, Paul appealed to his relationship with them. By "father," Paul meant that he was the church's founder because he had originally **preached the Good News to** them. Because Paul had started the church, he could be trusted to have its best interests at heart, and he had the authority to warn them of their sinful ways. Paul's tough words were motivated by love—like the love a good father has for his children (see also 1 Thessalonians 2:11). Because the church could trust him, they could also imitate

him, so he boldly explained that they could **follow** his **example.**

4:17 Timothy had accompanied Paul on his second missionary journey (see Acts 16:1-3) and was a key person in the growth of the early church. Timothy probably arrived in Corinth shortly after this letter (see 16:10)—the bearers of the letter possibly being Stephanus, Fortunatus, and Achaicus (see 16:17). It is clear that Timothy was not with Paul at this letter's writing because he is not mentioned in either the greeting or the closing. Most likely Timothy was notified by Paul to travel on to Corinth from Macedonia (Acts 19:22). Timothy's role was to **remind** the Corinthians of the faith they had received. Afterward, Timothy was to return to Paul and report on the church's progress.

4:18-19 In their eagerness to set themselves up as leaders, the false teachers had said that Paul would not be coming back to Corinth—probably pointing out weakness, fear, or some other inadequacy (see 9:1-3; 2 Corinthians 1:17; 10:10). They assumed, therefore, that they could do as they pleased. But Paul explained that he had every intention of going back to Corinth **soon,** if this was the Lord's will. At that time, Paul would expose the **arrogant people** for who they really were. They were **big talkers,** but did **they really have God's power?** The answer would be obvious to everyone.

It is not known whether Paul ever returned to Corinth, but it is likely. In 2 Corinthians 2:1, he wrote that he decided not to make "another painful visit," implying that he had had a previous painful confrontation with the Corinthian believers—sometime after he wrote 1 Corinthians.

4:20 Being a big talker is one thing, but **living by God's power** is quite another. Some people talk a lot about faith, but that's all it is—talk. They may know all the right words to say, but their lives don't reflect God's power. Paul says that the **Kingdom of God is not just fancy talk,** it is to be lived. A person can live only by God's power when he or she has the Holy Spirit within (see John 3:3-8; 2 Corinthians 5:17).

4:21 Paul wrote that when he came—and he would come, barring divine intervention (4:19)— he would come with his authority from God as their spiritual father. Far from being afraid or weak, he would arrive ready to deal with the situation as it was. This letter would precede him, and the Corinthian believers would have time to **choose** to continue in their arrogance and therefore receive **punishment and scolding,** or to make the necessary changes and therefore receive **love and gentleness.** It would be up to them.

1 CORINTHIANS 5

PAUL CONDEMNS SPIRITUAL PRIDE / 5:1-13

The pride that characterized the Corinthian church (see 4:10, 18) had so blinded the believers that they were allowing flagrant sexual immorality to take place in their fellowship. Their pride may have been such that they refused to admit this sin and deal with it, or they may have been proud that this man was one of their spiritual people, honored for his "knowledge" or "wisdom." Paul condemned the believers for allowing this sin to go on unchallenged in their midst. Believers today can learn from this passage about how the church must deal with flagrant and unrepented sin.

5:1 A report had been delivered to Paul regarding **sexual immorality going on among** the believers in Corinth. The Corinthian church had been unwilling to discipline this man. Paul prefaced his pronouncement of knowledge of this situation by saying that the problem was **so evil that even the pagans don't do it**—quite an indictment on these believers. Most of the believers knew about the sinful relationship already, but apparently they had been unwilling to admit it, so Paul described the sin point-blank: A man in the church was **living in sin with his father's wife**. This man was having an affair, already a sinful act deserving discipline. But his sexual activity outside of marriage had taken place with his "father's wife" (probably his stepmother). Whether the man had seduced this woman away from his father, or whether the woman was divorced or widowed is unclear. In any case, even the pagans would have shuddered at this, but the church members were trying to ignore the situation.

5:2 The problem of arrogance in the Corinthian church had spilled over to the point where they were tolerating flagrant sin. Instead of being **proud** of themselves, they should have been **mourning in sorrow and shame**. Then, they should have **removed** the man from the **fellowship**. The church must discipline flagrant sin among its members—such sins, left unchecked, can divide and paralyze a church. This "removal" of the person was not meant to be vengeful but to help bring about a cure.

Today, tolerance has become such a battle cry in the media and in political and educational circles that it has affected even the church. It is very difficult for people to discipline sin in church members because everyone is trying to be accepting of others. People say, "Who am I to judge? I have sin in my life." So they want all sin excused, including their own. We must not let modern-day low standards determine what is true and right for the church.

5:3-5 While those in the Corinthian church had failed to do anything about this man's sin, Paul himself would tell them what had to be done. Paul had weighed the matter and had **passed judgment.** As an apostle and the spiritual father of this church (4:15), Paul had the authority to deal with the matter and he understood the danger to the church if the sin were to remain undisciplined. Paul told the church, in no uncertain terms to **call a meeting of** the whole congregation so they would witness and support the action. As they met, Paul would **be there in spirit,** because he carried the authority as an apostle, and **the power of the Lord Jesus** would also be with them as they met. The entire situation was under the mighty power of the Lord Jesus to deal with the man's spirit and to bring him to repentance.

Paul explained the discipline that should be carried out: **Cast this man out of the church and into Satan's hands.** This would mean excluding him from the fellowship of believers (see 1 Timothy 1:20). Without the spiritual support of Christians, this man would be left alone with his sin and Satan, and hopefully this emptiness would drive him to repentance. The church could not literally give him to Satan, for only God can consign a person to eternal judgment. It was meant to force him to see the consequences of sin by living in Satan's sphere of influence—the world apart from Christ and the church.

That his sinful nature will be destroyed meant

that the exclusion from the fellowship would help the man to face his sinful, selfish nature (flesh), repent, and return to the church. Paul wanted this sinner to experience the crucifixion of his sinful nature (Romans 7:5-6; Galatians 5:24). It may take such drastic measures to deal with the sinful nature, but how much more important for the man that he face this and repent in order that he would **be saved** in the end. Paul hoped that this harsh disciplinary action might be of eternal benefit to the man.

Churches today need the spiritual determination to deal with sins such as these that affect the whole church. But excommunication as a form of discipline should be used rarely and carefully. It should be an action of the church body, not just one or two people. Its purpose should be redemptive and restorative, not vengeful or vindictive.

5:6-7 Paul was writing to those who wanted to ignore this church problem. They boasted, but they had no grounds to **boast about** their **spirituality** because they were allowing a horrible sin to exist in their fellowship. They had to expel this sinful man from the fellowship so that his sinning would not affect everyone. For them to **stay pure** did not mean that without this man they would be sinless (Paul would address other problems in the rest of this letter). Instead, Paul understood that this kind of sin, left unchecked, would work evil in the church; thus, it needed to be disciplined by excommunication so that the believers could see the serious consequences of sin.

Indeed, they ought not forget that Christ gave his life so that people could deal with sin. By not dealing with this man's sin, they were making Christ's death of no effect. They should remember, said Paul, that **Christ, our Passover lamb, has been sacrificed** (see Exodus 12:15; 13:7). Continuing in sin shows disregard for Christ's sacrifice.

5:8 The words **let us celebrate the festival** are a figurative way of picturing what Christ is to believers. In Paul's day, the Passover was celebrated with a ceremonial search throughout one's home for yeast and then destroying the yeast before the Passover lamb was slain in the temple. Because Christ, the Passover Lamb, has already been sacrificed, all yeast (that is, all evil) should be removed from among his people. The old life **(the old bread)** was characterized by **wickedness and evil;** these have no part in Christ's church. Believers, characterized by being born again, have cleansed the evil from their lives and are like **the new bread,** living in **purity and truth.** A small piece of fermented dough eventually affects the whole loaf. Boasting, as well as immo-

rality, hurts the whole church. Christianity is not a private lifestyle.

5:9-11 The words **when I wrote to you before** refer to Paul's earlier letter to the Corinthian church, often called the "lost letter" because it has not been preserved. In that letter, he had told the Corinthians **not to associate with people who indulge in sexual sin.** Either the Corinthians had misunderstood what Paul meant, or they had avoided his command by pointing out the impossibility of not associating with sinners in a sinful world. So Paul made it clear here that he **wasn't talking about nonbelievers,** for they, by nature, are involved in sexual sin, greed, swindling, and idol worship. Believers cannot disassociate themselves completely from nonbelievers—they **would have to leave this world to avoid people like that.** In addition, with no contact with nonbelievers, believers would not be able to carry out Christ's command to tell them about salvation (Matthew 28:18-20).

Paul meant that believers were **not to associate with anyone who claims to be a Christian** and yet has a sinful lifestyle. Believers must separate themselves from those who claim to be Christians yet indulge in sins explicitly forbidden in Scripture and then rationalize their actions. By rationalizing their sin, these "believers" harm others for whom Christ died, and they tarnish the image of God in their lives. The church has a responsibility to rebuke, correct, and restore those in the fellowship who claim to be believers but live like nonbelievers.

5:12-13 The difference between believers and nonbelievers lies in their relationship to Jesus Christ. The **outsiders** (referring to nonbelievers) are to be met where they are (even in their sinful lifestyles, 5:9-11) and offered the gospel message. Yet the believers are not responsible to **judge** them because God will.

In the church, however, believers need to make such judgments. The Bible consistently says not to criticize people by gossiping or making rash judgments. At the same time, however, believers are to **judge** and deal with those who claim to be believers but are living sinful, rebellious lives. Paul's instructions for this sinful man—**remove him**—come from Deuteronomy 17:7. This instruction should not be used to handle trivial matters or to take revenge; nor should it be applied to individual problems between believers. These verses are instructions for dealing with open sin in the church, with a person who claims to be a Christian and yet who sins without remorse. The church is to confront and discipline such a person in love.

1 CORINTHIANS 6

AVOIDING LAWSUITS WITH CHRISTIANS / 6:1-8
In chapter 5 Paul explains what to do with open immorality in the congregation. In chapter 6 he explains how the congregation should handle smaller problems between believers.

6:1 While there are certain cases that, by law, have to be submitted to the legal authorities, disputes between Christians should be handled by qualified Christian leaders in the church. Paul declared that disagreeing Christians should not have to **file a lawsuit and ask a secular court** to resolve differences among them. Why did Paul make this point? (1) If the judge and jury were not Christians, they would not likely be sensitive to Christian values. (2) The basis for going to court is often revenge; this should never be a Christian's motive. (3) Lawsuits make the church look bad, causing unbelievers to focus on church problems rather than on its purpose.

6:2 By going to pagan authorities to settle disputes, the Christians were acting beneath their dignity. They should be able to settle these disputes among themselves because **someday** (at the Second Coming) **Christians** (who are coheirs with Christ) **are going to judge the world** (see also 2 Timothy 2:12; Revelation 3:21; 20:4). Because of this truth, believers should not take their disputes into the world, because it would be a poor witness and would show a lack of unity in the church.

6:3 Christians will also **judge angels.** The use of the word "angels" without an article leaves the meaning unclear. This could mean that Paul was referring to Christians' part in judging the Devil and his demons (evil angels) at Christ's second coming (see 2 Peter 2:4; Jude 1:6; Revelation 19:19-20; 20:10). Or it could mean that the Christians will "judge angels" in the sense that they will preside over angels when they (the Christians) reign with Christ. Paul's point was that, in light of the privilege that will belong to believers in the future, they should be able to **resolve ordinary disagreements here on earth.**

6:4-6 Repeating his concern stated in 6:1, Paul asked why the Corinthian Christians were taking their disputes **to outside judges** who were not Christians. That they were **not respected by the church** does not mean that the believers were showing no respect. Instead, these pagan judges lived by an entirely different standard than the Christians; therefore, their judgments could not be in accordance with the spiritual laws by which the Christians lived. Surely someone in the church was **wise enough to decide** their disagreements. Apparently, they had been acting with great pride (4:8), yet they couldn't handle their own **arguments.** Instead of using the wisdom and discernment from the Holy Spirit, which was available to them as believers, they were suing each other, **right in front of unbelievers.** What kind of witness was this for the church? How much better for the believers to live "above" such matters, dealing with them in their own congregation with the help of respected leaders, so that nothing would hinder their witness for Christ in the world.

6:7-8 The basic problem went back to the Corinthian congregation. If they had been maturing in their faith, they would not have become so riddled with sin that the believers would actually have to bring lawsuits against one another. That these believers had to resort to lawsuits to settle disputes among them was **a real defeat** for them. It showed that they were still immature. Paul explained the direction in which they needed to grow—they needed to willingly **accept injustice** if that would mean protecting the church. Believers should never be wronged and defrauded by other believers in the first place. Mature believers would not act in that manner. If they were wronged by other believers, mature believers should be willing to "turn the other cheek" (Matthew 5:39).

AVOIDING SEXUAL SIN / 6:9-20
If the Corinthian church truly realized their high calling, they would live in a completely different manner, and they would not have the problems involving lawsuits (6:7-8). Paul

seized upon this opportunity to remind the Corinthian believers that their lives must change. They should not practice such evil acts because evil people cannot inherit the Kingdom of God.

6:9-10 In these verses, Paul gives a strong proclamation about those who will not have a **share in the Kingdom of God.** The Christians could not call themselves followers of Jesus and allow any kind of evil to permeate their lives. They will not share in the Kingdom because these people persisted in their evil practices with no sign of remorse. Such people—if they think they are believers—need to reevaluate their lives to see if they truly believe in Christ.

Male prostitutes refers to those who practice homosexuality. Some people attempt to legitimize homosexuality as an acceptable alternative lifestyle. Even some Christians say that people have a right to choose their sexual preference. But the Bible specifically calls homosexual behavior sin (see Leviticus 18:22-29; Romans 1:18-32; 1 Timothy 1:9-11). Christians must be careful, however, to condemn only the practice, not the people. Those who commit homosexual acts are not to be feared, ridiculed, or hated. They can be forgiven, and their lives can be transformed. The church should be a haven of forgiveness and healing for repentant homosexuals without compromising its stance against homosexual behavior.

6:11 The list of sins may seem unduly long (6:9-10), but apparently Paul was being complete in listing what kinds of lives and lifestyles from which the Corinthian believers had come. Even the writings of pagan authors and historians attest to the rampant immorality in the city of Corinth. Many of the believers had come out of a lifestyle where sexual perversion was part of their "worship." When Paul had come to Corinth, he met people with the lowest morals. Yet the power of Jesus Christ had changed them.

Paul stressed that all sin can be forgiven. When the Corinthians received Jesus Christ, their **sins** had **been washed away.** This refers to a cleansing process that had washed away their sins through the blood of Jesus (Hebrews 10:22; Revelation 7:14). They were sanctified, **set apart for God** (John 17:17; 1 Corinthians 1:2; 1 Thessalonians 4:3; 5:23). And they were **made right,** meaning that God had declared that these believers were righteous and just in his sight **because of what the Lord Jesus Christ and the Spirit of our God** had done for them. In this verse, the Trinity is represented—God the Father, Jesus Christ the Son, and the Holy Spirit all taking part in transforming people from their sinful lives to a new way of living in obedience to God.

6:12 The phrase **"I am allowed to do anything,"** appears to have been a catchphrase, as it appears twice in this verse and twice again in 10:23. Apparently, the Christians in Corinth had been using this phrase as a license to live any way they pleased. Perhaps Paul had used the statement when he preached to them about their freedom in Christ, but they had wrongly interpreted it. Paul never meant disregarding basic Christian morality and ethics. Some Christians in Corinth apparently were using this to excuse their sins, saying Christ had taken away all sin, so they had complete freedom to live as they pleased; or what they were doing was not strictly forbidden by Scripture.

Paul answered both of these excuses. While Christ has taken away sin, this does not mean **everything** a person might do would be **good.** While some actions may not be specifically forbidden in Scripture, believers should know that these actions and their results would not be beneficial to themselves or to the church. Believers should be using their Christian freedom to share the gospel and show love for others instead of looking for ways to gratify themselves. In addition, while some actions are not sinful in themselves, they are not appropriate because they can control believers' lives and lead them away from God. Believers should not do these actions because they do not want to become enslaved to anything.

Freedom is a mark of the Christian faith—freedom from sin and guilt, and freedom to use and enjoy all things that come from God. But Christians should not abuse this freedom and hurt themselves or others. Many people have misinterpreted the phrase today to mean, "I will not be mastered by any rule of ethics, law, or Bible principle," rather than, "I will not be mastered by any besetting sin." Christians who have been in the church for many years can easily excuse sins such as gossip, bitterness, an unforgiving spirit, lust, or withholding money from God's work. We must be on alert for those desires that can master us. What God has allowed his children to enjoy must not grow into a bad habit that controls them. For more about Christian freedom and everyday behavior, read chapter 8.

6:13 Another saying, **Food is for the stomach, and the stomach is for food,** had apparently been used as an illustration to explain the Corinthians' warped understanding of Christian freedom. They seemed to believe that because the physical activity of eating and digesting food had no effect on one's Christian life, neither would other merely physical activities—such as sexual sin.

Paul stated that it was **true** that what one eats does not affect the spiritual life. In fact, so transitory is this physical realm that one day **God will do away with both** stomachs and food. However, he also stated that one could not compare eating to sexual activity. Humans are a combination of material and spiritual. Just as the spirit affects the body, so too the physical body affects the spirit. People cannot commit sin with their bodies without damaging their souls because their bodies and souls are inseparably joined. While the stomach was made for food, people's **bodies were not made for sexual immorality.** Stomachs and food will pass away, but believers' bodies will be transformed and glorified.

The Greek word for "body" used here refers to the whole being and personality, not to the worldly flesh. These bodies **were made for the Lord, and the Lord cares about our bodies.** Christianity takes very seriously the realm of the physical. God created a physical world and pronounced it good. He promises a new earth where real people have transformed physical lives. At the heart of Christianity is the story of God himself taking on flesh and blood and coming to live with people, offering both physical healing and spiritual restoration.

6:14 God's care and concern for the physical bodies of his children began at Creation. Jesus was put to death, but God **raised** him. Likewise he **will raise our bodies from the dead.** That God would bring his Son back in a body shows the value that God places on his children's physical bodies.

6:15-16 This teaching about sexual immorality and prostitutes was especially important for the Corinthian church because the temple of the love-goddess Aphrodite was in Corinth. This temple employed more than a thousand prostitutes, and sex was part of the worship ritual. Paul clearly stated that Christians should have no part in sexual immorality, even if it is acceptable and popular in the surrounding culture.

His reason? Because the believers' **bodies** were **actually parts of Christ.** They obviously should **never** think of taking a part of Christ and joining **it to a prostitute.** Sex is more than a mere physical act; instead, it unites a man and a woman in such a way that they become **one body** as it had been planned in the beginning, quoting the **Scriptures** in Genesis 2:24.

Paul was not denying the beauty of sex between a married man and woman, nor was he saying that any sexual union is an exact comparison of believers' union with Christ. Paul wanted his readers to see the perversion of using their God-given bodies for such wickedness as sexual sin with a prostitute (perhaps even a temple prostitute, thus making the sexual sin a form of idol worship). These sins are not merely physical, having no effect on a person's spiritual life. They are deeply emotional and even mystical, in the case of the union created between sexual partners. This must not be taken for granted. But for the person who has sexually sinned in the past, there is forgiveness, healing, and renewal.

6:17 A person who commits sexual sin with a prostitute is "united" (joined) with him or her. By contrast, **the person who is joined to the Lord becomes one spirit with him.** The same verb is used both times in the Greek, describing the oneness that believers have with the Lord who is spirit (see 2 Corinthians 3:17-18).

6:18 Sexual sin is a violation of one's own body. Paul described it as a sin that affects the body like no other. As in 6:13, the word **body** refers not to the flesh, but to the whole being and personality. This sin has disastrous effects. But what an enticement it can be for all people, and believers are not exempt. Clearly other sins also affect the body, such as gluttony or drunkenness, but no other sin has the same effect on the memory, personality, or soul of a person as sexual sin. Paul argues that in intercourse, people are united (6:16-17). Their spirits are not involved in quite the same way in other sins. Also Paul argues that our bodies are the temple of God (6:19-20). In sexual sin, a person removes his or her body from God's control to unite with someone not in his plan. Thus, those people violate God's purpose for their bodies. Satan gladly uses sexual sin as a weapon, for he knows its power to destroy. Thus, Paul says, don't walk, but **run away from sexual sin.** Believers need to exercise alertness and awareness to stay away from places where temptation is strong, and they need to use strong, evasive action if they find themselves entrapped.

6:19-20 The words **your body** in this verse refer not to the corporate "body of Christ," but to each believer's individual, physical body. Each believer should view his or her body as a **temple of the Holy Spirit,** who was living in them. Jesus Christ died to pay the **high price** that purchased sinful people's freedom (Ephesians 1:7; 1 Peter 1:18-19). His blood provided the sacrifice that made believers acceptable to God. Because of Jesus' death and resurrection, the Holy Spirit came to indwell those who believed in him—he took up residence **in** their bodies. This Holy Spirit had come into them when they had believed. Believers, therefore, **do not belong to** themselves. God bought them, so they **must honor God with** their bodies. They must "honor God" by showing their gratefulness for Jesus' sacrifice by their worship, obedience, and service (see Romans 12:1-2).

1 CORINTHIANS 7

INSTRUCTION ON CHRISTIAN MARRIAGE / 7:1-40

After discussing disorder in the church, Paul moved to the list of questions that the Corinthians had sent him, including those on marriage, singleness, eating meat offered to idols, propriety in worship, orderliness in the Lord's Supper, spiritual gifts, and the resurrection. Questions that plague churches today are remarkably similar, so we can receive specific guidance in these areas from this letter.

7:1 The Corinthian believers had written to Paul, asking him several questions, or perhaps even taking issue with some of his principles, relating to the Christian life and problems in the church. Apparently this first question regarded whether people should stay married or if those previously married should remain celibate.

Christians in Corinth were surrounded by sexual temptation. The city had a reputation even among pagans for sexual immorality and religious prostitution. To this sexually saturated society, Paul was delivering these instructions on sex and marriage. The Corinthians needed special, specific instructions because of their culture's immoral standards. Some believers were teaching total sexual abstinence within marriage because of a mistaken notion that sexual relations were sinful; some were proposing separating from or divorcing spouses in order to stay pure. To the first question, Paul answered that **it is good to live a celibate life.** At first glance this may seem to contradict God's words in Genesis 2:18, "It is not good for the man to be alone." Paul maintained a high view of marriage (Ephesians 5:25-33), and here was simply explaining that celibacy was normal, and that it may be God's will for some to remain single. Paul's advice may have been directed at the "present crisis" referred to in 7:26; he thought it would be easier to face persecution as a single person. But, as Paul would explain later in this chapter, his words do not mean that married couples should divorce or that Christians ought not marry. For those whom God calls to celibacy (such as Paul himself), the lifestyle is in accordance with God's will for them. They should see it as a gift to be used to further God's Kingdom (7:7).

7:2 God created marriage, so it cannot be bad. Those who can remain celibate should do so, but the believers in Corinth ought not deprive themselves of being married and try to enforce celibacy. That would set them up for failure **because there is so much sexual immorality.** As noted above, sexual immorality was pervasive in Corinth, invading even the worship of some of their gods and goddesses. Many of the believers had come out of very immoral lifestyles. Paul advised, therefore, that those men and women not given the gift of celibacy from God should go ahead and marry. Then they would be able to fulfill their sexual desires in the God-honoring institution of marriage.

7:3 In the same way that God created marriage, he also created sex with which the human race could procreate as well as find great enjoyment. Just as with anything else that God created, however, sinful humanity can find a way to dirty it. God created sex to occur only between a man and a woman, and only within the confines of the marriage commitment. The Corinthians were surrounded by sexual temptations. Such temptations can be difficult to withstand because they appeal to the normal and natural desires that God has given to human beings.

Some people in the ancient world reacted against the extreme immorality by doing just the opposite—becoming ascetics and abstaining from sex altogether. Apparently, some married people, who saw or experienced the evil of sex wrongly used, began to believe that all sex was immoral, so they should abstain even in their marriages. While celibacy should be the rule for those who choose to remain single (7:1), Paul explained that it should not have any place in the marriage relationship. Marriage provides God's way to satisfy natural sexual desires and to strengthen the partners against temptation. Married couples have the responsibility to care for each other; therefore, husbands and wives should not **deprive** each other but should fulfill each other's needs and desires. The reference to the wife's **right as a married woman** as being equal to the man's right was revolutionary in this culture of male domination. Paul stressed equality of men and women in their rights as marriage partners to give and receive from each other.

7:4 A person's body belongs to God when that person becomes a Christian (see 6:19-20). Physically, their bodies belong to their spouses. God designed marriage so that through the union of husband and wife two become one. The sexual relationship makes two people "one flesh" (6:16; also Genesis 2:24). The unity given to the married couple through their sexual relationship makes them no longer independent beings; they have become "one flesh." So Paul said to these married believers that sex is not immoral because God created it; therefore, they should not deprive their spouse.

7:5 The only time the spouses should abstain from sexual intimacy would be if they mutually agree, **for a limited time,** to abstain from sex in order to devote themselves to **prayer.** Times of devoted prayer to God are vital for all believers; some may feel that they should do this with total focus on God and thus abstain from sex (or even food if it is a time of fasting). This is laudable, but Paul also explained that it should not be a habit. Because those married are already "one flesh," they must maintain that union and **come together again.** Otherwise, they would leave themselves open for Satan's temptations.

7:6 Most likely, this refers to all that Paul had said thus far concerning his answer to their marriage question (7:1). Marriage is desirable, and certainly needful in order to procreate under God's guidelines, but marriage is not commanded by God. However, this **suggestion** could just as easily conclude his statement in 7:5—which he doesn't want to them to understand as if it were a command.

7:7 Paul made a personal note, further explaining that celibacy is acceptable, by stating that he wished **everyone could get along without marrying** just as he did. Paul well knew that his lifestyle—itinerant travel, difficult work, not having a permanent home, danger, often being mocked and ridiculed, sometimes being beaten and jailed, all for the sake of the gospel—was not one that he could easily adhere to with a wife and children along. Paul thanked the Lord for his gift of being able to remain celibate by doing what God wanted

him to do with the freedom that a married man would not have. He wished that others could serve the Lord with such complete abandon.

Paul also realized, however, that if everyone remained unmarried, there would be no Christian children and no furthering of the Christian faith to the next generation. Thus **God gives** some people **the gift of marriage,** and they can serve God well in that capacity. To others **he gives the gift of singleness** so they can fulfill other roles in the furthering of his Kingdom. Because these are gifts from God, one should not try to force either one on anyone's life.

7:8-9 Paul laid down the general principles regarding marriage in the previous verses; here he began to speak to various people's situations specifically. First, he wrote instructions **to those who aren't married and to widows** (and widowers). Paul's single-minded focus was always on God's Kingdom and service for it, so his advice to these believers in Corinth is couched in his concern for their ability to bear up under persecution for their faith and to serve the Lord wholeheartedly (see 7:26, 32-35). (Note that in a different place and situation, Paul counseled the younger widows to marry. See 1 Timothy 5:14.) So he suggested to those presently not bound in marriage that it would be **better to stay unmarried** as he himself was. However, if they found that they couldn't **control themselves, they should go ahead and marry.**

The Corinthians seemed to have a problem with self-control—as suggested by the kind of sexual immorality so common in the city. The believers came out of that lifestyle, yet probably many still were struggling with their sinful natures in that area. Paul did not suggest enforced celibacy on such people. Instead, he told married people to give themselves to each other (7:3-4); he told single people to try to use their singleness as an opportunity to give all to the Lord (7:7-8). Yet, he also understood that those who struggled with self-control should not put themselves in the position of enforced celibacy, for Satan would use many temptations right there in the city to bring them down. Instead, Paul said these people should **marry** so as not to **burn with lust.** This is not a put-down of marriage as being no more than a legitimate way to release sexual pressure; instead, it is tied with the gifts of marriage and singleness that Paul had mentioned in 7:7. Those who do not have the gift of singleness, and thus have a passion that will need a proper release, ought to marry. It would be difficult to live with such a desire without having been given the grace to do so.

7:10-11 Having spoken to the unmarried people in 7:8-9, Paul here turned his attention to the **married.**

He explained to the Corinthian believers the Christian view of divorce, given as a **command from the Lord.** Jesus had taught about divorce during his time on earth (see Matthew 5:31-32; 19:3-9; Mark 10:2-12; Luke 16:18), saying that married people were not meant to be divorced. While divorce was permitted as a concession, it was not God's plan for married people.

Paul explained, therefore, that **a wife must not leave her husband.** Apparently it was possible in the Greco-Roman culture for a wife to leave her husband (in Jewish culture, divorce laws focused on the husband separating from his wife). If a woman has already separated from her husband, she should **remain single** or **go back** to her husband. She does not have the option to marry another man. In the same way, **the husband must not leave his wife.** Although Paul gave an exception in 7:15, the ideal remains.

7:12-13 Next, Paul turned his attention to **the rest of you**—the people who were married but felt "single" because their spouses were unbelievers. Undoubtedly, there were many such couples in the Corinthian church. About this particular situation, Paul said he did **not have a direct command from the Lord.** So he did what all believers must do when Scripture doesn't state exactly what must be done in a particular situation—he inferred what should be done from what Scripture *does* say. Paul based his advice on God's commands about marriage and applied them to the situation the Corinthians were facing.

Because of their desire to serve Christ, some people in the Corinthian church thought they ought to divorce their pagan spouses and marry Christians. But Paul affirmed the marriage commitment. God's ideal is for marriages to stay together—even when one spouse is not a believer. To leave the marriage—even for the noblest of goals in serving the Lord—would actually be to disobey God's express command regarding marriage (Mark 10:2-9). Instead, the believing spouse should try to win the other to Christ (7:16). It would be easy to rationalize leaving; however, Paul makes a strong case for staying with the unbelieving spouse and being a positive influence on the marriage. Paul, like Jesus, believed that marriage is permanent. Paul commanded this for the believers in the church whose unbelieving spouses were **willing to continue living with** them. He gave other advice to those whose unbelieving spouses wanted to dissolve the marriage *because* the husband or wife had become a Christian (see 7:15).

7:14 The reason for these couples to stay together (7:13-14) is that the **Christian** spouse **brings holiness** to the **marriage.** There are two views of how

holiness is applied to the unbeliever. One view is that there is a moral influence on the unbeliever as the Christian spouse bears witness to Christ and lives obediently to God. The other view is that the Christian, now blessed by God, includes his or her spouse in the promised blessings of the covenant as they overflow to the unbeliever. "Holiness" does not carry the meaning of "salvation"; that is, the unbelieving husband is not "saved" through his wife's salvation. More likely, the Corinthians had heeded Paul's advice in 5:9-11 not to associate with unbelievers. They had interpreted Paul to mean that sex with an unbelieving marriage partner would defile them. Paul affirmed the opposite. When believers have sexual relations with their unbelieving spouse, the unbelievers are blessed in a certain way. The marriage and its sexual relations set up or lead into the possibility of the conversion of the unbeliever.

The blessings that flow to believers don't stop there but extend to others. Among those most likely to receive benefits from the **godly influence** of believers' lives are their **children.** God regards the marriage as "holy" by the presence of one Christian spouse. Paul calls the children of such a marriage **set apart** because of God's blessing on the family. The believing parent, called upon to raise his or her children in the faith, will hopefully have such an influence that the children will accept salvation for themselves.

7:15 While the believing spouse must not leave the marriage if the unbeliever wants to stay married (7:12-13), the opposite may also happen. The unbeliever may decide that, because his or her spouse has become a Christian, the marriage should be dissolved. In this case, the believer's only choices would be to deny faith in Jesus Christ in order to maintain the marriage, or maintain faith in Christ and let the marriage be dissolved. As difficult as it might be, and as much as marriage is sanctified by God, the high calling of God must not be denied for any reason. So the believer must let the unbeliever go. This may be the second exception to remarriage, along with adultery (see Matthew 5:31-32). So the Christian man or woman can allow the divorce to happen and not be disobeying God.

7:16 Another reason for believers to try not to dissolve their marriage to an unbeliever is that they can be a good influence on their spouse. The intimacy and day-to-day-ness of marriage provide ample opportunity for the Christian to be a powerful witness to his or her spouse. So powerful can it be, Paul reminded them, that the unbelieving wife or husband **might be converted** because of the faithful testimony of the believing wives and husbands.

7:17-19 Christ makes changes from within and calls people from all walks of life. While some changes are made in behavior and attitudes, the believers ought not make some kinds of changes. For example, they ought not change marriage partners. They need not even try to change jobs (unless the job was dishonoring to God). Instead, **accept whatever situation the Lord has put you in, and continue on as you were when God first called you** because God can use his faithful followers in all areas of life. This was not Paul's advice just to the church in Corinth but his **rule for all the churches.**

For example, the ceremony of circumcision was an important part of the Jews' relationship with God. For the Jews, circumcision was the sign of their covenant with God (Genesis 17:9-14); the Greeks, however, looked down upon it as the mark of lowly people. Some Jews, in an attempt to become more acceptable in Greek culture, could attempt to surgically reverse the marks of a circumcision. To add to the confusion, the Judaizers (a group of false teachers) were claiming that Gentiles had to be circumcised before they could become Christians. Paul pointed out that, in God's Kingdom, **it makes no difference.** Jewish Christians did not need to reverse their circumcisions, and Gentile Christians did not need to be circumcised (Romans 2:25, 29; Galatians 5:6). Instead, they should stay exactly as they were when they became believers; any outward change would make no difference. The inner change and desire to **keep God's commandments** is all that matters.

7:20-21 Paul repeated what he had said in 7:17 for emphasis and because he had said this was his rule for all the churches. The believers **should continue on** as they were **when God called** them. From religious variations in the church (between those circumcised and those uncircumcised), Paul moved on to the varied social states of the believers. The church in Corinth also included people from every station in life—many of them slaves. Therefore, if a believer was a **slave** when he became a Christian, he could continue as a Christian slave, doing his work as for the Lord (Ephesians 6:5-9). Of course, they also were free to seek freedom, but in the meantime, they should obey God in their position.

7:22-23 Slavery was common throughout the Roman Empire, so many of the believers in Corinth were slaves **when the Lord called** them. Paul said that although the Christian slaves remained enslaved to other human beings, they were **free from the awful power of sin** in their lives (Romans 6:18, 22). These slaves had been made free. In the same way, if a person was free

when the Lord called him, he was **now a slave of Christ.** Because God paid a **high price** to bring his people to himself, he has complete authority over their lives.

7:24 This passage repeats Paul's statement of 7:17 and 7:20. God can use people from all areas of life, so **whatever situation** God found them in, they should **stay there** in their **new relationship with God.** They should serve God from that position, seeking to share the gospel with those who might not otherwise hear it.

7:25-26 Paul began addressing another matter about which the Corinthian church had asked. In their culture, a young woman's parents usually would make the decision about whether or not their daughter would marry. So these parents had written wondering what decisions to make regarding their unmarried daughters. Paul did **not have a command from the Lord,** but he would **share** some God-given **wisdom.**

Paul advised the young women to **remain** as they were, unmarried. He reasoned that it would be easier on them to be single than married during **the present crisis.** There has been discussion among scholars regarding the nature of this "crisis." Some have suggested that Paul expected the Lord's return and was referring to the certain calamities that would take place prior to the Second Coming. More likely, however, Paul foresaw the impending persecution that the Roman government would soon bring upon Christians. He gave this practical advice because being unmarried would mean less suffering and more freedom to throw one's life into the cause of Christ (7:29), even to the point of fearlessly dying for him. Paul's advice reveals his single-minded devotion to spreading the Good News. He wanted these unmarried believers to consider the times in which they were living and how well they could follow the will of God for them in their unmarried state as compared to being married.

7:27 Paul expanded his advice for everyone, both men and women, married and single. A married person should **not end the marriage;** an unmarried man should not **get married.** Paul's reasoning rested with what he had said in 7:26. It would be difficult to be a Christian in the Roman Empire in coming days. Paul was advising church members to stay focused on the Lord and on the business of sharing the gospel.

7:28 Lest he be misunderstood, Paul explained that he was not saying that it would be sinful for these young unmarried women to get married. That would be inconsistent with all of Scripture. Instead,

Paul was **trying to spare** them **the extra problems that come with marriage.** Life holds plenty of difficulties—and in the first-century Roman world, one of those difficulties would be persecution of Christians. Paul wanted the believers in Corinth to be able to let go of everything in their faithfulness to God—that would be much easier without the attachment of marriage. Thus, he advised the unmarried to remain that way. If they chose to marry, however, that would **not be a sin.**

7:29-30 As Paul had challenged the unmarried to consider their situation in light of the call of God on their lives and their brief time on earth to accomplish it, so he challenged all the brothers and sisters to look at life and realize that **the time that remains is very short.** Paul probably did not have the Second Coming in mind here; rather, he probably was thinking of coming persecutions and the resulting curtailment of the believers' freedom to witness for their faith. Paul urged the believers not to regard marriage, home, or financial security as the ultimate goals of life. As much as possible, they should live unhindered by the cares of this world that might keep them from doing **God's work.** Married men and women, as Paul pointed out (7:33-34), must take care of earthly responsibilities—but they should make every effort to keep them modest and manageable. Paul's focus, as always, was that believers make the most of their time before Christ's return.

7:31 Believers must live detached from this world. Those who have been blessed with **the things of the world should make good use of them without becoming attached to them.** Material blessings can be used to further God's Kingdom. Believers who have been blessed with material wealth must always remember that they have been blessed in order to bless others. Paul did not want the believers to be "attached" to anything in this life as if that were all there is—to do so would be to forget that **this world and all it contains will pass away** (see also 1 John 2:8, 17).

7:32-34 Marriage is a tremendous responsibility for each of the spouses involved. For a marriage to be successful, husband and wife must work at their relationship—they will both have to be concerned about **earthly responsibilities** and about **how to please** each other. This is good and important for those who are married. Paul was simply pointing out that unmarried people can focus their energies elsewhere.

7:35 Paul gave the advice in the previous verses for their **benefit,** but **not to place restrictions** upon the believers. These were not regulations that the

churches had to follow. Instead, this advice came from Paul's heart, to help the struggling believers in Corinth to **serve the Lord best.** This would be helpful as they lived their Christianity in the midst of the gross immorality of Corinth and as they anticipated persecution for their faith.

7:36-37 A young man should marry if he **thinks he ought to.** But if he **has decided firmly not to marry,** he should let the young woman go. That **there is no urgency** means that he does not have outside pressure such as from parents or through a prior agreement. Such a man can thus make his own decision.

7:38 When Paul wrote that **the person who doesn't marry does even better,** he was referring to the potential time available for service to God. The single person does not have the responsibility of caring for a spouse and raising a family. Singleness, however, does not ensure service to God—involvement in service depends on the commitment of the individual.

7:39 The Bible teaches that marriage is a lifelong contract between a man and a woman. The relationship was not to be dissolved for any reason. If the woman's husband were to die, however, the marriage contract would be void, and **she is free to marry whomever she wishes,** providing that this person were a Christian so that the **marriage** would be **acceptable to the Lord.** This also applied to men whose wives had died.

There may have been some teaching in either Jewish or Greek society stating that a widowed woman could not remarry because she was bound forever to her husband, even if he had died. Paul stated clearly that this was not to be the case. But the widow or widower should still be very careful about whom he or she chooses to marry.

7:40 While the widow *can* remarry (7:39), that doesn't necessarily mean that she *should.* In fact, Paul's opinion was that **it will be better for her if she doesn't marry again** for the same reasons he said that the unmarried people might think about remaining single (7:25, 28, 32-34).

When Paul stated, **I think I am giving you counsel from God's Spirit,** there was nothing tentative in his meaning. At times he gave these believers commands from the Lord because he could bring words directly from Jesus or from the Old Testament; at other times, he gave them his "advice" or "counsel," but this still carried the weight of divine inspiration. Paul's advice came from the Holy Spirit, who gave him the words he needed to answer the Corinthian church's questions.

1 CORINTHIANS 8

FOOD SACRIFICED TO IDOLS / 8:1-13

The discussion regarding whether the Corinthian believers should eat food that had been sacrificed to idols begins here and continues through 11:1. Most likely, this first section deals with meals served in the pagan temples, and the discussion in 10:23–11:1 deals with food purchased in the marketplace and served in private homes. The Corinthians had written to Paul with questions regarding these issues, but their exact questions are unknown. The believers concluded that their knowledge of God and the fact that the idols had no power allowed them to continue to eat meals in the temple. Paul dealt with that issue in this first section.

8:1 The Corinthian believers had sent another question to Paul (see 7:1)—this one regarding **food sacrificed to idols.** Their question pertains to the idolatry with its sacrifices that permeated the Greek and Roman cultures of the day. (Paul also dealt with this issue in his letter to the Roman believers—see Romans 14). One might think that believers should obviously not have contact with idolatry in any form. Paul had prohibited such contact in 5:9-11, and the Jerusalem council had forbidden the Christians to eat meat offered to idols (Acts 15:29). For believers in Corinth, however, staying clear of any contact with idolatry was nearly impossible for two main reasons. First, people often ate meals in temples or in places associated with idols. This was accepted social practice for public or private gatherings. To cut oneself off from such gatherings would be like not attending weddings or other social celebrations today. So this caused much concern for the believers. At such gatherings, a sacrifice was made to the idol. When such meat was sacrificed, the priest would divide it into three portions: One would be burned up, one would be given to the priest, and one would be given to the offerer. If the priest did not use his portion, it would be sent to the marketplace. This caused the second concern for the believers. The meat, after being sacrificed to an idol and sold in the market, would then be bought and served in private homes. So the Corinthian believers wondered if the meat had been contaminated by its having been offered on a pagan altar, and, if by eating it, they would be participating in idol worship. Paul answered both of these concerns; most likely, the advice in 8:1-13 deals with temple-sponsored meals, while 10:23–11:1 deals with meat sold in the marketplace.

The words **you think that everyone should agree with your perfect knowledge** may refer to the wording in the Corinthians' letter to Paul. This **knowledge** probably refers to knowledge that there is one true God and knowledge that idols are worthless and have no power. The conclusion, then, is that believers can eat anything because God created it, so a ceremony in front of a worthless idol could do nothing to contaminate it. Since they didn't believe in idols, and God doesn't regard idols, Corinthian believers could eat with their friends without problems. Some believers understood this fact. Others, however, felt very strongly that to eat such meat would be wrong; their consciences bothered them. This must have become a divisive issue, because the question had come to Paul.

Paul took the opportunity to tell them that **love builds up the church.** Those who might be taking pride in their knowledge of Christ would only be "puffed up" and could end up dividing the church. In this situation, acting on knowledge alone—even accurate knowledge—without love for other believers, would harm the church.

8:2-3 Knowledge without **love** leads to a pride that will eventually fall under its own weight. Love without knowledge, however, can lead to sentimentalism, wherein people love everyone without regard for truth. The following verses explain that true knowledge of God leads Christians to willingly support and help weaker believers so as not to cause them to stumble—in this context by not eating food sacrificed to idols. But the principle can apply to any situation in the modern world where some believers experience freedom in certain areas where others do not.

8:4 Paul returned to the question at hand, **Should we eat meat that has been sacrificed to idols?** The believers in Corinth had come to believe **that there is only one God and no other** out of a culture that embraced many gods. The idols had no substance, authority, power, or ability to curse or bless.

8:5-6 Paul acknowledged that many people believed the **so-called gods** to be real. Idolatry takes away from God the worship he is due. There is **one God** and there is **one Lord, Jesus Christ,** who **made everything.** God is creator. He is not himself part of the cosmos but is the source of everything created. Christ is the "Lord," a name that the Old Testament uses only in reference to God. Through Jesus Christ, God created and redeemed the world.

8:7 Basic Christian theology focuses on the fact that there is one God, who created everything, and that idols are nothing. But **not all Christians realize this.** They believe in the all-powerful God of the Christian faith but are not thoroughly convinced that the other gods do not exist at all. In their hearts and consciences, they have difficulty because they are **accustomed to thinking of idols as being real.** Therefore, when they eat meat that had been sacrificed as part of a religious ceremony, they cannot separate the meat from the ceremony. They had **weak consciences.** A "weak" conscience regards as wrong an act that is not wrong, or is still unclear about whether it is wrong or not. The possibility exists for new converts to fall back into old obsessions by seeing other believers exercise their freedom. Old patterns may link the activity (such as playing cards) with an old obsession (such as gambling). The Corinthians' weak consciences could not discriminate between right and wrong regarding food offered to idols, so when they ate such meat, they **violated** their consciences and so believed that they were sinning against God.

8:8-9 Food is neutral—neither good nor evil, regardless of whether or not it has been sacrificed in a pagan temple to an idol. There would be nothing inherently wrong with eating such meat because food has nothing to do with one's relationship with God. Paul said that the strong believers should not push the weak but, instead, be willing to love them. These "strong" believers (as opposed to those whom Paul described as "weak") knew Scripture and stood strong on God's commands and prohibitions but were free from minor, legalistic constraints. Yet, they must **be careful** with their **freedom** so that it would **not cause a brother or sister with a weaker conscience to stumble.** Since it really doesn't matter what kind of food believers eat, the strong believers should live on the side of love for the sake of the weaker believers.

A "stumbling block" refers to something that might cause someone to trip or fall into sin. The strong but insensitive Christian may flaunt his or her freedom, be a harmful example, and thus offend the consciences of others. The overscrupulous but weak Christian may try to fence others in with petty rules and regulations, thus causing dissension. Paul wanted his readers to be both strong in the faith and sensitive to others' needs. Because all believers are strong in certain areas and weak in others, they constantly need to monitor the effects of their behavior on others.

8:10 Paul offered an example of what might happen. The **weak Christians** (those with "weak consciences" as explained in 8:7) think that **it is wrong to eat** food that has been sacrificed to an idol. Strong Christians **know there's nothing wrong with** eating such food, so they go to **the temple of an idol** and eat there. As noted in 8:1, this would not have been an uncommon occurrence, for most social and cultural events happened in the temples. When weak believers see their fellow Christians eating in the idol temple, the weak believers would **be encouraged to violate their conscience** by doing the same. If a weak believer does something that he or she is not sure is right or wrong, that action will bring condemnation (see also Romans 14:23).

If one believer has no scruples about where meat comes from or how it is prepared but flaunts his or her belief in order to cause one who is concerned to be distressed, then that stronger individual is not acting in love. The conduct of stronger believers is not to be decided by what they feel is their better insight into the Scriptures or what they feel would "strengthen" those weaker ones. Rather, it is to be decided by love and sensitivity. Paul was pointing out how the strong believers ought to use their freedom in public—the situation he described here was very public. If these strong believers ate meat that had been offered to idols in the privacy of their homes because they knew such meat was not tainted in any way, they could do so with liberty and without concern for the scruples of the weaker believers. Strong Christians ought to, at times, restrain their freedom for the sake of the weak, but they need not come into bondage to the consciences of weak believers.

8:11 The stronger believer must not let what he or she wants to do (when it is a minor matter such as whether to eat meat or not) become a stumbling block that could destroy a weaker brother or sister. The strong believers know they are free from concern about meat offered to idols, but that **superior knowledge** must not cause them to harm other believers. The Greek verb translated **destroyed**

means "to bring about destruction." It could also mean a "ruin" of one's conscience if the weaker believer goes against his or her scruples. To ruin a person's conscience would be total destruction. Therefore, strong Christians are to act in love. That other person, no matter how much the strong believer disagrees with him or her, is still someone for whom Christ died. If Christ willingly gave up his life, Christians ought to be willing to give up their freedoms occasionally so as not to harm another.

Mature Christians shouldn't flaunt their freedom. They should be sensitive to younger converts whose faith can be destroyed by such freedom. For example, a young Christian addicted to gambling may be damaged by the strong Christian's freedom to play cards. Some activities may be all right in and of themselves but not around weaker new converts. Weak believers ought not do anything against their consciences, but they must grow in the faith and, at the same time, not pass judgment on their stronger brothers and sisters.

8:12 Throughout this passage, Paul has been addressing stronger believers. So when he wrote **and you,** he was referring to these people. If they were insensitive to their weaker brothers and sisters **by encouraging them to do something they believe is wrong,** then they would be **sinning** both **against Christ** and **against other Christians.** Because all believers are temples of the Holy Spirit (6:19), no one believer has the right to sin against any other believer—to do so would be to sin against Christ himself.

8:13 Paul willingly followed his own advice, stating that if what he ate would **make another Christian sin,** he would never eat meat again. Strong believers can restrict their freedoms for the sake of others. In areas of disagreement, Paul counseled the believers to keep their beliefs between themselves and God. The brother or sister who believes in certain freedoms should not be trying to influence others with scruples to "loosen up." Those bothered by some actions should not be judging or condemning those with freedom, nor should they be trying to force their scruples on the entire church. Instead, all believers should seek to have a clear conscience before God.

1 CORINTHIANS 9

PAUL GIVES UP HIS RIGHTS / 9:1-27

At the end of chapter 8, Paul said that he would gladly give up his right to eat meat if that would help a weaker believer not to stumble. What follows in this chapter is Paul's defense of his apostleship and of his freedom to exercise, or not to exercise, his rights as a believer who is free in Christ.

9:1-2 In defending his apostleship, Paul reestablished his authority for some in Corinth who doubted that they should listen to him (9:3). So Paul presented his credentials as **an apostle.** In Greek, these four questions are rhetorical—they expect a "yes" answer. Only a small group of believers were "apostles." In order to have the authority of an apostle, the person had to show the following three evidences: (1) A commission directly from Jesus Christ in the sight of witnesses, or confirmed by others. To qualify as a true "apostle," a person had to have personally seen the Lord Jesus after his resurrection. For Paul, this occurred in Acts 9:3-18 (see also 1 Corinthians 15:8). (2) Ability to perform signs, wonders, and mighty acts to confirm their message (Acts 13:9-12; 2 Corinthians 12:12). (3) Evidence of a successful ministry

(Acts 18:1-17). Such credentials make the advice he gives in this letter more persuasive. Second Corinthians 10–13 defends Paul's apostleship in greater detail.

9:3-4 Earlier in this letter, Paul rebuked the Corinthians for their factions and their overly zealous loyalty to different preachers (3:1-22). Those who were not loyal to Paul apparently had been questioning his **authority.** It seems that they questioned Paul because he was not taking advantage of the rights accorded to apostles. Evidently in the Greco-Roman world of Paul's day, it was quite an issue how missionaries, traveling teachers, or philosophers were supported. They could charge fees, beg, work, or accept gifts by patrons. In Philippi, Paul accepted Lydia's support (Acts 16:15), but since then had abandoned that practice. Because other church leaders continued to accept patronage, the issue arose: Maybe Paul did not get support because his status as an apostle was in question. Paul was asserting his right to get support (which he had voluntarily laid aside so as not to bring the gospel under suspicion).

9:5 That the apostles had **the right to bring a Christian wife along** means that their wives could travel along with them, supported financially by the churches. Others in the church who were considered to be apostles had wives who had come to believe in Jesus. The **Lord's brothers** (referring to Jesus' physical half brothers) had not believed in Jesus at first (John 7:3-5), but after the Resurrection, they believed and attained leadership status in the church at Jerusalem (Acts 1:14). James (one of the "Lord's brothers"), for example, led the way to an agreement at the Jerusalem council (Acts 15) and wrote the book of James. **Peter** was a prominent apostle in the early church; his wife is not mentioned elsewhere, but the Gospels record a time when Jesus healed Peter's mother-in-law (Matthew 8:14-15; Mark 1:30; Luke 4:38).

9:6-7 Barnabas had traveled with Paul during the first missionary journey (Acts 13:1–14:28). Barnabas was also considered to be an apostle (Acts 14:3-4, 14). This may mean that Paul and Barnabas were the only apostles who made it a habit to work and earn their living as they traveled to spread the gospel (4:12; Acts 18:2-3). Because these two men had refrained from taking money from the churches, some were saying that they were not apostles (see 9:3-4). They questioned whether Paul had the same authority as other apostles because they looked down on him for working with his hands. Paul asserted that he and Barnabas had the authority of apostles, even though they did not take advantage of the rights they deserved.

9:8-10 Paul's argument held the authority of Scripture. The **law of Moses** states, in Deuteronomy 25:4, **"Do not keep an ox from eating as it treads out the grain."** In ancient times, grain was often "threshed" by placing sheaves on a hard surface and then allowing oxen to drag something heavy back and forth across it. The law said that the oxen should be allowed to eat some of the grain while they worked. This law was not made to protect oxen but to illustrate a point. God's people were to care for their animals by allowing oxen to eat while they worked, but this applied to people as well. Just as farm workers who plow fields and thresh the grain expect a share of the harvest, **Christian workers should be paid by those they serve.**

9:11-12 Those who had **planted good spiritual seed** in Corinth would not have been expecting **too much** in wanting **support** from the Corinthian believers. Then, added Paul, since they were supporting others, then most certainly those who originally had brought the gospel message **have an even greater right to be supported.** Paul and others had not demanded support, however; they had worked to earn their own living and not be a burden to the church. Paul was not required to work this way, but he chose to **put up with anything** rather than **put an obstacle in the way of the Good News about Christ.** He put up with the hardships of "working two jobs" so that no pagan inquiring about Christianity would be put off by the financial obligation of supporting a missionary.

9:13 Paul gave two more examples of his right to receive support. It was everywhere understood that those who had sacred jobs (such as serving **in the Temple** or **at the altar**) were "working" and therefore derived their livelihood from the job. They did not have to go elsewhere. As part of their pay, priests in the Temple would receive a portion of the **offerings** as their food (see Numbers 18:8-24). This was true in the pagan temples, as well.

9:14 Paul's explanation that God's ministers should be supported by the churches came as an order from the Lord. The churches were required to honor **those who preach the Good News,** and those who served among the believers should be supported by **those who benefit from** their ministry. This command from God allowed traveling missionaries and local ministers to focus entirely on the spread of the gospel and the growth of the church, and not be concerned about making money.

9:15 The churches were commanded to support God's ministers, and the ministers had a right to expect such support, but Paul had **never used any of these rights** in Corinth because he felt that doing so would hinder the spread of the gospel in that city. Paul did accept gifts from some churches, such as the Philippian church (see Philippians 4:14-19). He must have felt, however, that to take any money in Corinth would have caused some to think he was after money instead of souls! So Paul willingly set aside his rights as an apostle. Paul hastened to add that he was not writing all this in the hopes that now the Corinthians **would** begin to give him support. Instead, he wanted them to know that he would continue to preach without expecting support.

9:16 Paul may have "boasted" in his desire to serve the Corinthian believers freely, but he could not

boast about that service. Paul was **compelled** to preach. This compulsion did not mean that Paul did not enjoy this duty (see Romans 1:5; 11:13; 15:15-16; Galatians 1:15-16); instead, it means that, like a slave serving a beloved master, Paul served his Lord by faithfully doing the duties God had given him (see Acts 9:15-16).

9:17 Paul perceived his call by God as a **sacred trust;** therefore, he felt that he could freely serve God as an apostle without expecting **payment.** Far from not deserving to be paid, as his detractors were saying, Paul did not feel that he deserved payment for an honored duty that he had been commanded to do. In this matter, he felt that he had **no choice** but to serve these believers without financial support.

9:18 Paul did receive **pay** in the form of **satisfaction** from **preaching the Good News without expense to anyone.** His pay came in being able to show the genuineness of his love and concern for these Corinthian believers.

9:19 Paul's goals were to glorify God and to bring people to Christ. Thus he stayed free of any philosophical position or material entanglement that might sidetrack him while he strictly disciplined himself to carry out his goals. For Paul, both freedom and discipline were important tools to be used in God's service.

9:20 Paul never compromised the doctrines of Scripture, never changed God's word in order to make it more palatable to people in any given place. He never went against God's law or his own conscience. In matters that did not violate any principle of God's word, however, Paul was willing to **become one** of his audience in order to **bring them to Christ.** Three groups are mentioned in these verses: Jews, Gentiles, and those with weak consciences.

When speaking to the **Jews,** Paul conformed his life to the practices of **those who follow the Jewish laws,** even though he himself was no longer **subject to the law** (because of his freedom in Christ; see Acts 16:3; 18:18; 21:20-26). If, however, Paul had gone into a Jewish synagogue to preach, all the while flouting the Jewish laws and showing no respect for their laws and customs because of his "freedom in Christ," he would have offended the very people he had come to tell about Jesus Christ. But by adapting himself to them, by conforming to their regulations and restrictions (Paul had been a Pharisee), he had gained an audience so that he might bring them to Christ. Again, Paul was careful never to violate any of God's commands in his attempts to serve his listeners. He

never conceded that those regulations had to be kept in order for people to become believers, but he conformed to the laws to help the Jews come to Christ. The line was a difficult one to walk, for the book of Galatians records a time when Paul rebuked Peter for acting like a Jew among the Gentiles (see Galatians 2:11-21).

9:21 As Paul conformed himself to the Jews, he also conformed to **Gentiles, who do not have the Jewish law.** Paul met them on their own turf, fitting in as much as he could. This did not mean that Paul had thrown aside all restraints and was living like a pagan in hopes of winning the pagans to Christ! As he explained, he did **not discard the law of God.** Paul lived according to God's law and his conscience, but he did not put undue constraints on his Gentile audiences. Unlike some false teachers of the day, called Judaizers, Paul did not require the Gentiles to follow the Jewish laws in order to become believers (see Acts 15:1-21). Instead, he spoke a message that would **gain their confidence and bring them to Christ** (see, for example, Acts 17:1-34).

9:22-23 The **oppressed** refers to those with a weak conscience, a subject Paul had discussed in chapter 8. In that chapter, Paul had explained that believers who were free in Christ ought to set aside certain freedoms in the presence of another believer with a more sensitive conscience. Paul followed his own advice, saying that he shared **their oppression** (meaning that he had set aside his freedoms and had lived by their restraints for a time) so that he might **bring them to Christ.** The "weak" were already believers, but they needed to grow into a deeper knowledge of Christ and a deeper understanding of their freedom in Christ. Paul did this delicately, becoming as they were in order to gain their listening ears. He chose to **find common ground with everyone** (the Jews, the Gentiles, and those with weak consciences, 9:20-22) in order that some might be saved. Paul never compromised the gospel truth, God's law, or his own conscience; in other matters, however, Paul was willing to go to great lengths to meet people where they were. He had one focus: **to spread the Good News.** Paul's life focused on taking the gospel to an unbelieving world.

9:24-25 Paul's exhortations in the previous verses—for the believers to give up their own rights, to think of others first, to be wholehearted in their focus on bringing others to Christ— called upon the Christians to deny themselves as they looked forward to future reward. Paul compared this to **a race,** picturing the ancient "games." The Olympics were already operating in Paul's time. Second in popularity only to the Olympic games, the Isthmian games were celebrated every two years at Corinth. Athletes would come from all over Greece, and the winners of the games were accorded the highest honor. To get into the games, and especially to emerge as victors, required that athletes **practice strict self-control.** Typically, for ten months prior to the games, the athletes-in-training denied themselves many ordinary pleasures. Each put forth his greatest effort during the contest, setting aside all else in order to win the **prize.**

When Paul told the believers to be like those athletes, he did not mean that the believers were all running against each other with only one actually winning. Instead, he wanted every believer to **run in such a way that you will win.** In other words, every believer should be putting out the kind of effort for the reward of God's Kingdom that an athlete puts out to merely win a wreath. Believers, therefore, ought to willingly practice self-control with a focus on bringing others to Christ because they are running toward **an eternal prize.** They have all already "won"; the prize is not dependent on how they run the race. Because they already are assured of the prize, they should live for God with as much focus and enthusiasm as did the ancient runners at the games.

9:26-27 Paul not only preached the gospel message and encouraged the believers to self-discipline and self-denial, he also practiced what he preached. He also had to live by the gospel, and he also practiced self-denial like the athletes just described. Paul did not run the race aimlessly, nor was he **like a boxer who misses his punches.** Instead, he kept his eyes focused on **the goal,** running **straight** for it, **with purpose in every step.** He did not allow himself to be sidetracked and he did not waste time becoming lazy. He kept on, disciplining and **training** his body. Paul pictured life as a battle. Believers must not become lazy—for Satan seeks to cause them to stumble, sin continues to buffet, and sorrow and pain are a daily reality (see Romans 7:14-25). Instead of being bound by their bodies, believers must diligently discipline themselves in their Christian lives in order to stay "in shape."

When Paul said he **might be disqualified,** he did not mean that he feared losing his salvation, only that he would be disqualified from receiving rewards from Christ. This passage describes the spiritual maturation process, the period of growth during believers' lives on earth when they are living "in" the world while not being "of" it. The time between a person's acceptance of Christ as Savior and his or her death is the only time when growth in Christ can occur. Paul wanted to grow diligently and receive a reward from Christ at his return. Paul did not want to be like the person who builds his or her life with shoddy materials, only to be saved "like someone escaping through a wall of flames" (3:15).

1 CORINTHIANS 10:1–11:1

WARNINGS AGAINST IDOLATRY / 10:1–11:1

This chapter continues Paul's argument concerning the lifestyle of the believers and the need for self-discipline, as recorded in chapters 8 and 9. Some of the Corinthian believers thought that because they had professed faith, went to church, and joined in the Lord's Supper, they could then live as they pleased. But this was a false belief, as Paul would show through the example he used from Israel's history.

10:1 A perfect Old Testament example of believing the false notion that one can be saved and then live a faithless, Godless life can be seen in **what happened to** the Jews' **ancestors in the wilderness long ago.** The book of Exodus contains the record of their miraculous escape from slavery in Egypt by the intervention of God (see Exodus 1–12). God gave them a leader (Moses), set them free (through great miracles), and then **guided all of them** as they moved out of Egypt and headed toward the land God wanted to give them (the Promised Land). God's presence was with them in the form of a **cloud** by day and fire by night (Exodus 13:21-22). When they came to the Red Sea, God **brought them all safely through the waters of the sea on dry ground** (Exodus 14).

The emphasis in 10:1-4 is on the word **all,** which Paul used four or five times. Paul was making the point that all of the Israelites experienced the miracles of God's protection and guidance. Yet, later, so many turned away. Many thought that their place among God's people assured them the Promised Land. Assuming themselves secure, they refused the life of self-discipline, self-denial, and obedience to God. Because of that, many were "disqualified" from entering the Promised Land.

10:2 The Israelites were **baptized** in that they shared the blessing and gracious deliverance of God. By their experience of passing through the Red Sea, they were united **as followers of Moses.** The **cloud** represented God's presence and glory among them (Exodus 14:19-22), indicating his leadership and protection. The **sea** represented God's salvation of his people through the Red Sea as they crossed safely to escape the Egyptians. **All** of the Israelites experienced this "baptism." However, the common experience of this baptism did not keep most of them faithful to God in the days that followed.

10:3-4 Further miracles sustained the Israelites as they journeyed through the wilderness. God provided **miraculous food** in the form of "manna" that came from heaven (Exodus 16:4, 14-31). **Miraculous water** was obtained from a rock—a provision directly from God. Moses got water from a rock both at the beginning and at the end of Israel's journey (Exodus 17:1-7; Numbers 20:2-13). This had given rise to a rabbinic interpretation of Numbers 21:16-18 that a well, known as Miriam's Well and shaped like a rock, had **traveled with them,** providing water wherever they went. Paul referred to **Christ** as **that rock** who had actually accompanied and sustained the people, meeting their needs during their travels. The Old Testament often refers to God as a "rock" (see, for example, Genesis 49:24; Deuteronomy 32:4; 2 Samuel 22:32). Paul's reference to Christ as the spiritual "rock" would have connected Christ with Yahweh of the Exodus, thereby indicating the deity of Christ.

10:5 God had performed great miracles for his people, but **most of them** rebelled against God. The word "most" is actually an understatement; of the thousands who stood at the very edge of the Promised Land, only two men (Joshua and Caleb) had faith enough in God to enter (Numbers 14:5-12, 30). Because of their lack of faith, God caused the people to turn back from the land and wander for forty years in the wilderness. God **destroyed them in the wilderness** by causing them to wander until they died. This was God's punishment on them for their disobedience and rebellion.

10:6-7 Far from being irrelevant to New Testament Christians, the stories of people in the Old Testament provide **a warning** from which the believers can learn **not to crave evil things as they did.** Clearly, the Israelites' status as God's people and recipients of his love and provision did not mean that all of them loved and served God in return. Instead, many actually desired evil and turned away from God. The incident of **pagan revelry** occurred when the Israelites made a golden calf and worshiped it in the wilderness (Paul quoted Exodus 32:6). If those people who had witnessed the miracles of the escape from Egypt could so easily be tempted to turn to idolatry, then the Christians in Corinth, who were surrounded by idols, should also be on their guard.

10:8 This incident, when **23,000** Israelites died **in one day** is recorded in Numbers 25:1-9. The Israelites worshiped a god of Canaan, Baal of Peor, and engaged in **sexual immorality** with Moabite women. Because of their sin, God punished them harshly. For the believers in Corinth, the comparison would have been inescapable. Much of the idol worship there focused on ritual prostitution and sexual immorality of all kinds. God would not go lightly on those who claimed to be his but still engaged in idol worship or sexual immorality.

10:9 Paul had already affirmed that **Christ,** as the spiritual Rock, accompanied them in their wilderness journeys (10:4), so the Israelites' sins were indeed against Christ. This verse recalls Israel's complaining about having been brought out into the wilderness (Numbers 21:5). They were testing the Lord's patience to see what he would do, and he punished them by sending poisonous snakes among them. Many **died from snakebites.** Those who claim to be God's people will not test the Lord to see how much they can get away with. True believers will seek to stay near to God in order to constantly live in obedience to him (see also Hebrews 3–4).

10:10 This incident of grumbling occurred when the people complained against the leadership of Moses and Aaron—an event that actually happened several times. The phrase, **God sent his angel of death to destroy them,** could refer to when the Israelites grumbled at Kadesh, refusing to enter the Promised Land. God punished them with a plague (Numbers 14:2, 36-37). This could also refer to the incident recorded in Numbers 16 when a group rebelled against Moses, and God sent a plague that killed the rebels. Grumbling against God or against his leaders results in divine punishment. God does not take this sin lightly either. This was another problem that the Corinthian church was facing (3:1-9).

10:11 When the Israelites disobeyed, they received punishment. Likewise, when people who claim to be Christians sin with no repentance, no desire to change, and no concern for God's laws, they too will receive punishment.

10:12 Paul warned the Corinthian Christians that if they began to take it for granted, if they thought they were **standing strong,** that was the time to be most careful not to **fall.** The Corinthians were very sure of themselves, almost prideful. Paul said that if the Israelites fell into idolatry, so could some in the Corinthian church. No human being is ever beyond temptation. Paul warned the believers not to let down their guard.

10:13 Temptations come into every believer's life—no one is exempt. Temptation is not sinful; the sin comes when the person gives in to temptation. Believers must not be shocked or discouraged, or think that they are alone in their shortcomings. Instead, they should realize their weaknesses and turn to God to resist the temptation. Enduring temptation brings great rewards (James 1:12). But God does not leave his people to Satan's whims. Instead, **God is faithful.** He will not always remove the temptation, because facing it and remaining strong can be a growing experience; however, God does promise to **keep the temptation from becoming so strong that you can't stand up against it.** The secret to resisting temptation is to recognize the source of the temptation and then to recognize the source of strength in temptation.

Not only that, but God also promises to **show you a way out so that you will not give in** to the temptation and fall into sin. It will take self-discipline to look for that "way out" even in the middle of the temptation and then to take it when it is found. The way out is seldom easy and often requires support from others. One of the God-given ways of escape from temptation is common sense. If a believer knows that he will be tempted in certain situations, then he should stay away from them. Another way out of temptation is through Christian friends. Instead of trying to deal with temptation alone, a believer can explain her dilemma to a close Christian friend and ask for support. This friend can pray, hold the person accountable, and give valuable insights and advice.

The truth is that God loves his people so much that he will protect them from unbearable temptation. And he will always give a way out. Temptation need never drive a wedge between believers and God. Instead, a believer ought to be able to say, "Thank you, God, for trusting me that much. You know I can handle this temptation. Now what do you want me to do?"

10:14-15 The Corinthian believers needed to be aware that any dabbling at the edges of their former lives of idol worship might lead them back into sin. How much wiser, instead, to **flee from the worship of idols.** The Corinthian believers needed to be wise enough to know that, because of past association, they should run from some temptations. It might not be wise for believers to go to feasts where meat had been offered to idols, because it could draw them back into former sins. Even if one person were strong against such temptation, he or she might be a stumbling block for a weak person—actually becoming a temptation for someone who might not be as strong against the temptation to return to idolatry (see 8:9). Because they were **reasonable people,** Paul trusted that they could **decide** if what he had to say were true.

10:16-17 Christians participate in Christ's once-for-all sacrifice when they share **the cup** (symbolizing Christ's **blood**) and eat the **bread** (symbolizing his **body**) at the Lord's Supper. Sharing in this meal signified **sharing** in its **benefits.** Since the early days of the church, believers have celebrated this special meal. Taking part in sharing the **one loaf** with other believers symbolized their unity in **one body** with Christ.

10:18 In Old Testament days, when Jews offered a sacrifice, they ate a part of that sacrifice as a way of restoring their unity with God, against whom they had sinned (Deuteronomy 12:17-18; 14:22-27). By offering the **sacrifices** and then eating a portion of the gift that had been offered, they were **united;** that is, they were fellowshiping with God, to whom they had brought their gifts.

10:19-20 Paul's advice here seems to focus on believers taking part in actual religious celebrations (not mere social functions) at an idol's temple. Because both Christian communion and the Jewish system of sacrifice provided a mystical relationship between God and the participants, then, by extension, to take part in a pagan sacrificial feast would provide a similar mystical union—not with **idols** (for they are nothing but wood and stone), but with the **demons** that the idols represent. Therefore, taking part in such a religious ceremony was not a neutral activity; it amounted to them becoming **partners with demons.**

10:21-22 Eating **at the Lord's Table** means communing with Christ and identifying with his death (10:16-17). Eating **at the table of demons** means identifying with Satan by worshiping or promoting pagan (or evil) activities (10:19-20). Obviously, Christians cannot do both. To do so is to **rouse the Lord's jealousy.** When ancient Israel turned to idols, God punished them severely (10:7-8). Because believers are not **stronger** than God, they should not think that they can withstand the Lord's anger for their sin of idolatry (see Deuteronomy 32:21).

10:23-24 The issue of eating meat offered to idols led Paul to three conclusions in the matter that can be applied to the broad spectrum of Christian liberties:

- While eating such meat is essentially unimportant to one's faith, and while it is **allowed** (not against God's law, see also 6:12), it may not necessarily be **helpful** to the believer. The Christian has the freedom to eat such meat because he or she knows it doesn't matter (8:6-8). Just because something is not against the law, however, doesn't mean that it is helpful.
- While believers are free to practice their freedom in Christ in matters that are allowed, some practices of freedom do not necessarily work to build up individual believers, others, or the church.
- Therefore, Christians are to use their freedoms, not for their **own good**, but to **think of other Christians and what is best for them.** As Paul had concluded at the end of chapter 8, all Christians, free in Christ, should humbly set aside their freedoms in order to win more people for the Kingdom. Nothing should ever impede a believer's witness for Christ. It is always more important to avoid unhelpful actions than to assert freedoms.

10:25-26 Regarding the specific example of meat offered to idols, Paul offered this advice. First of all, the believers should feel free to **eat any meat that is sold in the marketplace.** As noted in the commentary on 8:1, meat that arrived for sale in the marketplace may have been left over from a sacrifice at a pagan altar. But it was impossible to know if such meat had been part of a sacrifice. Paul told the believers simply not to ask because it didn't matter. Whatever happened to the meat in a pagan temple, the believers knew that all food was created by God and is a gift from God—**the earth is the Lord's, and everything in it** (quoted from Psalm 24:1). And if they didn't ask, then they wouldn't know whether it was offered to idols. Then they wouldn't have to worry about their consciences.

10:27 In the same way as suggested in 10:26, if the believers were invited to the home of an unbeliever for dinner, they could go. In the homes of unbelievers, the Christians might well be served meat that had been offered to idols. Paul's advice, as with buying meat in the market (10:25-26) is to **eat whatever is offered** and **don't ask any questions.** It would probably have been a breach of hospitality to ask about the food and then to refuse to eat it. How much better to just enjoy the host's hospitality and be a witness to his family than to raise questions of **conscience** and so lose that opportunity.

10:28-31 But the situation could arise that several believers are eating a meal at the home of an unbeliever. One of these believers (the **someone** referred to here, who was a "weaker" believer, see 8:10) **warns** his fellow believers that the meat they had been served had been **offered to an idol.** At that point, then, the stronger believers, although they know that this really makes no difference, should refrain from eating the meat **out of consideration for the conscience** of that weaker believer because of the clear association with temple worship. (This weaker believer feels that in eating that meat, the Christians would be sanctioning idol worship.) This is the same advice Paul gave in chapter 8.

Paul's question, **"Why should my freedom be limited by what someone else thinks?"** is in the context of his discussion regarding strong believers acquiescing to weaker believers in matters of conscience. The only real way to hold on to that freedom, because it is freedom, is to use or not use it freely, depending on the situation. Strong believers must not allow their freedom to be limited or condemned by weaker believers, so they should not use their freedom when that could happen. Simply because these strong believers can **thank God for the food and enjoy it,** no matter where it came from, they should not allow themselves to be condemned for using that freedom. It is better, said Paul, to set aside one's freedom in those situations. The bottom line is that all that believers do should be done **for the glory of God.** If these strong believers had to set aside their liberties in order to win others to Christ, they should do so because this would bring glory to God.

10:32-33 Paul wanted these believers to understand that the liberty God gave them was not to be used to **give offense;** rather, as Paul described in 8:13, his entire life focused on winning others to Christ. If need be, he would never eat any meat again if it would keep others from stumbling. In things that did not really matter, Paul tried **to please everyone.** Always, Paul's focus was to do what was best for others **so they may be saved.** Nothing, not even liberty in Christ, should cause believers to lose sight of their desire to win others to Christ.

11:1 This verse belongs at the conclusion of chapter 10, not at the beginning of chapter eleven, where it has been traditionally placed. Paul had just told the Corinthians that his goal was to seek the best for others, not himself. In this regard, Paul called upon them to **follow** his **example.** As in 4:15-16, Paul's words were not prideful. He had just spent three chapters explaining how the Corinthian believers needed to deal with the issue of eating meat that had been offered to idols. His conclusion of the matter balanced freedom in Christ with responsibility to love the "weaker" believers. All Christians should be so focused on

bringing others to Christ that nothing stands in the way of that goal. Paul followed his own advice (see 8:13; 10:33) and encouraged the believers to follow his example. The reason they could do so? Because he followed Christ's example.

Christians owe much to others who have taught them and have modeled for them what they need to know about the gospel and Christian living. They should continue following the good examples of those who have invested themselves in them by investing their own lives through evangelism, service, and Christian education. They, in turn, become models worth imitating.

1 CORINTHIANS 11:2-34

PROPER WORSHIP / 11:2-16

This section focuses primarily on proper attitudes and conduct in worship, not on the marriage relationship or on the role of women in the church. While Paul's specific instructions may be cultural (women covering their heads in worship), the principles behind his specific instructions are timeless—for they instruct believers to show respect for their spouse and to have reverent behavior in worship. If a believer's actions offend members and could divide the church, then the believer should change his or her ways to promote church unity. Paul told the women who were not wearing head coverings to wear them, not because it was a scriptural command, but because it kept the congregation from dividing over a petty issue that took people's focus off Christ.

11:2 Apparently, in their letter to Paul, the Corinthian believers had told him that they were **following the Christian teaching** that Paul had **passed on to** them. This teaching was what Paul had received from the other apostles of Christ or even from Christ himself through special revelation. It was truth, not anything Paul had thought up on his own (which the false teachers did); so the believers could trust and follow it.

11:3 Paul had been answering specific questions; apparently a question had arisen about head coverings in worship—see 11:10. The Corinthians may have adopted cultural patterns of male-female relationships into their worship that (as some scholars argue) had blurred the distinction between males and females. It may have been customs of dress regarding hair coverings, or perhaps it involved issues of hairstyle (short or long hair for men and women). Paul began to answer the Corinthians' question by first giving the general principle of how relationships in the church had been instituted by God: **A man is responsible to Christ, a**

woman is responsible to her husband, and Christ is responsible to God. In the language of 11:9-12, the phrase, "a woman is responsible to her husband" focus on their relationship. Paul was not concerned, as some have argued, for the submission of women, but rather that the completeness or glory of their relationship not be diminished (see 11:7).

In the phrase "Christ is responsible to God," Paul was not teaching that Christ was inferior to God or lesser in any way (see 8:6). Nor was he thinking that Christ was the offspring of God with regard to his eternal being. Paul was referring to the incarnation of Christ. Through Christ's coming to earth, believers receive forgiveness and are united with God and with one another (3:22-23). From this theological base, Paul will address the issue of head coverings.

11:4-5 In this section Paul's main concern is irreverence in worship. The praying and prophesying mentioned here were in the context of public worship. When a man prayed or prophesied, he was to do so **without** his head covered. In contrast, when a woman prayed or prophesied, she was to do so only **with** her head covered. We do not know conclusively what the historical situation was. A woman uncovering her head could have meant (1) that she was not wearing a veil; (2) that she was not wearing a shawl or true head covering; or (3) that her hair was loosened and hanging down.

Remember that Paul gave these instructions in response to a question that had been sent to him by the Corinthian believers. Paul explained that the men were not to cover their heads because they are "God's glory" (11:7); to do so would be to shame their head—Christ. So in worship, the men should not veil themselves because that would dishonor God. Women were allowed to pray and prophesy in public worship (a great freedom for them); Paul's only stipulation for the Corinthian women was that they should cover their heads when doing so.

While the general principle of propriety and distinctions between men and woman still stands, the cultural advice given here about head coverings need not be considered as binding to all the churches for all time. Indeed, when Paul wrote to Timothy with advice about the women in the church in Ephesus, he did not tell Timothy to make sure the women covered their heads. Instead, his advice focused on modesty in their dress (see 1 Timothy 2:9-10). The situation in Corinth may have been that women were coming to church with their heads uncovered and this was causing disruption. Although the reason for the problem is unknown, we can gather that Paul's concern was that nothing disrupt worship. So he advised the Corinthian women to cover their heads in public worship much as he advised the Christians not to eat meat offered to idols in public situations. The women were certainly free to not cover their heads just as they were free to eat meat offered to idols. Neither of these mattered regarding their salvation. However, Paul always advised that Christians show deference to others in order to promote unity.

The statement that for a woman to have her head uncovered in worship would be **the same as shaving her head** is cultural and, again, the reason for the statement is unknown, although 11:6 hints that a shaved head was a disgrace. Some commentators believe that a woman with a shaved head may have been a temple prostitute or the dominant mate in a lesbian couple. Such women who became Christians not only needed to grow out their hair (11:15) but also to cover their heads in worship in recognition of their relationship to God and to their Christian brothers under God.

A modern example might be a Christian woman living in an Eastern culture. While that Christian is certainly "free" to wear shorts and a T-shirt (and would not have any problem doing so in the United States), she should set aside that freedom out of respect for the culture in which she lives. She should dress modestly and cover what should be covered. She will have far more acceptance by doing that than by flaunting her freedom to dress in a certain way that would be acceptable elsewhere.

"Praying" refers, as noted above, to public prayer during worship. "Prophesying" refers not just to telling of future events as revealed to a person by God but also to public speaking about religious truths, witnessing for Christ, and bringing God's word of encouragement to the congregation (see 14:31). Both men and women could do this in the early church. The spiritual gifts, given by the Holy Spirit, do not discriminate between men and women.

11:6 To further make the point that women should cover their heads in public worship, Paul wrote that if a woman **refuses** to cover her head, thus disgracing herself, then she might as well cut or shave off all of her hair because that too was **shameful.** Therefore, if the "uncovered" head (short or shaved hair) is a disgrace, then she ought to willingly cover her head during worship. Paul was not here referring to the woman's hair as her covering; the covering was a sort of veil worn over the head.

11:7-9 The reason that **a man should not wear anything on his head when worshiping** is because he **is God's glory, made in God's own image.** Women are also made in the image of God (Genesis 1:27), but she **is the glory of man.** By praying and prophesying with her head uncovered, she would be dishonoring and shaming man whose glory she was supposed to be. Paul does not say what he means by using the word "glory" here. It could be that man and woman together reflect the image of God (glory) and that by uncovering her head, the woman was taking something away from the identity of the man, thus depleting his part in the reflection of God's glory. Paul reasoned this back to the order of creation: **the first woman came from man.** Genesis also explains that man was not created for woman, **but woman was made for man** (Genesis 2:18).

11:10 Because God's people are to glorify him, **a woman should wear a covering on her head as a sign of authority.** There are two basic views of this verse: (1) that the head covering represents the woman's submission to male authority; or (2) that the head covering represents the God-given authority (enablement) for a woman to function this way in the church. Most likely, Paul meant the second option. It is important to understand that while

4

the stipulation of head covering is upheld in Corinth, the main point is that these Christian women had an equal status with men because of their union with Christ. They were free in Christ, equal before God, and able to pray and prophesy in the worship services. They were no longer to be regarded as inferior, which would have been their previous status in both Greek and Jewish cultures (see Galatians 3:27-28). The head covering was not a sign of subjection but a sign of women's willingness to be under the authority of God, just as men were under the authority of God.

The other reason for women wearing this sign of authority is **because the angels are watching.** It was proper for women to wear head coverings in the worship of God because the angels would be present during this worship. Hebrews 1:14 states that angels watch over believers and care for them. Because the angels observe God's people at worship, his people should be sensitive to follow God's commands in worship. The angels live to serve God; likewise God's people, who have been saved by his grace, should live in obedience to his commands.

11:11-12 Paul acknowledged women's roles in praying and prophesying, and their authority in doing so. But he reminded the Corinthians that all people

relate to each other and to God. Clearly God created men and women as interdependent. Even though Adam was created before Eve, and even though Eve came from Adam, ever since then **all men have been born from women.** No one is completely independent. Finally, **everything comes from God,** who is the Source of all that exists.

11:13-15 Paul's point in these verses is that men and women are different; they were created differently. He pointed out custom, propriety, and the way culture operates. Men should live as and look like men; women should live as and look like women. Anything that blurs their God-given distinctions in the culture or ruins their ability to share their faith has to be put aside. In the culture of Corinth, it was **obvious** to these believers that long hair on a man was disgraceful, while short hair on a woman was equally disgraceful. No one knows the details as to why, except that this may have had to do with the looks of heathen priests and priestesses, homosexuals, or temple prostitutes.

11:16 In this statement Paul admonished the contentious ones at Corinth to behave appropriately in church meetings. Calling upon the other churches as examples of such orderliness, Paul urged anyone who might **argue** with him that the other churches would stand with Paul in this matter.

ORDER AT THE LORD'S SUPPER / 11:17-34
A second abuse of worship existed in the Corinthian church regarding how to celebrate the Lord's Supper. Apparently, there was a division between the rich and the poor during both the love feast and the celebration of Communion itself. This lack of unity caused the believers to lose the real meaning behind what they were remembering—the sacrifice of Jesus' body on the cross.

11:17 At the beginning of the last section (11:2), Paul commended the Corinthians for remembering what he had taught them. Concerning this **next issue** in his letter, however, he had no **praise** for them. In this situation, their meetings were doing **more harm than good.**

11:18-19 When people in a church develop into self-willed **divisions** (such as class distinctions, or the factions described in 3:4), these are destructive to the congregation. Apparently, Paul was referring to class (economic) distinctions here, because these divisions were hurting a time of fellowship that should have been drawing the believers together, not separating them.

11:20-21 The **Lord's Supper** was instituted by Jesus before he died (Matthew 26:26-29). Jesus and his disciples ate a meal, sang psalms, read

Scripture, and prayed. Then Jesus took two traditional parts of the Passover meal, the passing of bread and the drinking of wine, and gave them new meaning as representations of his body and blood. He used the bread and wine to explain the significance of what he was about to do on the cross. The Lord's Supper was celebrated from the earliest days of the church. This celebration included a feast or fellowship meal followed by Communion. At the fellowship meal in the church in Corinth, it seems that people brought food to share, with the rich bringing more food than the poor. Instead of sharing equally among everyone, some went **hungry while others** got **drunk.** They were merely satisfying their hunger, not **concerned** about celebrating Communion. Paul condemned these actions and reminded the church of the real purpose of the Lord's Supper.

11:22 Some in the Corinthian church had turned the fellowship meal into a gluttonous feast where some ate too much and others got nothing. This had made a mockery of the Lord's Supper. In addition, by the rich separating themselves from the poor who could not bring as much food, the rich were humiliating those who had nothing. Obviously there was nothing for Paul to **praise** in this behavior. Instead, he advised the believers to eat and drink in their **own homes.** Then, when they came to share in the feast, no one would be ravenous, but they could, with self-control, wait for one another and eat only a little so there would be enough for everyone (11:33-34).

11:23-24 Paul had passed on to them **what the Lord himself said** regarding the celebration of the Lord's Supper. This probably does not mean that he had a divine, direct revelation because the tradition of the Lord's Supper had been in circulation among the churches through the teaching of the apostles ever since the church first began. Paul and the Gospel writers drew upon the same apostolic tradition.

Christians posit several different interpretations for what Christ meant when he referred to his **body** and his **blood.** Some believe that the wine and bread actually become Christ's physical blood and body (transubstantiation). Others believe that the bread and wine remain unchanged, but Christ is spiritually present with the bread and wine (consubstantiation). Still others believe that the bread and wine symbolize Christ's body and blood (symbolization). Christians generally agree, however, that participating in the Lord's Supper is an important facet of Christian worship and that Christ's presence, however they understand it, strengthens them spiritually. By eating "the body of Christ," believers receive, through faith, the power and benefits of Christ's body broken for sin and glorified forever. Because the Lord's Supper is commemorated **in remembrance** of the body and blood of Jesus given for the redemption of sinful people, it must never be taken lightly. Hence, Paul's instructions in the remainder of the chapter.

11:25 The **cup** represented **the new covenant between God and** people, **sealed by the shedding of** his **blood.** What is this new covenant? In the old covenant (the promise of God with his people before Christ came), people could approach God only through the priests and the sacrificial system. God would forgive people's sins if they would bring animals for the priests to sacrifice. When this sacrificial system was begun, the agreement between God and human beings was sealed with the blood of animals. The people of Israel first

entered into this agreement after the Exodus from Egypt (Exodus 24). But animal blood did not in itself remove sin (only God can forgive sin), and animal sacrifices had to be repeated day by day and year after year.

Jesus' death on the cross ushered in the new covenant (or agreement) between God and humanity. This concept is key to all New Testament theology. Under this new covenant, Jesus died in the place of sinners. Unlike the blood of animals, Jesus' blood truly removed the sins of all who put their faith in him. And Jesus' sacrifice will never have to be repeated; it is good for all eternity (Hebrews 9:23-28). The new covenant completes, rather than replaces, the old covenant, fulfilling everything the old covenant looked forward to (see Jeremiah 31:31-34). Now people can personally approach God and communicate with him. Eating the bread and drinking the cup shows that God's people are remembering Christ's death for them and renewing their commitment to serve him.

11:26 The eating of the bread and drinking of the cup are to be done on a continual basis in the churches **until he [Jesus] comes again.** By observing this special meal, the believers **are announcing the Lord's death.** By partaking of the body and blood of Christ, they personally show their participation in the Christian community and their faith in the Lord Jesus Christ as Savior. The periodic, solemn celebration of the Lord's Supper among believers reminds them of Christ's suffering on their behalf and of his imminent return when he will take them with him.

11:27-28 The solemn occasion of the Lord's Supper was to be celebrated carefully and entered into with spiritual readiness. When Paul said that no one should take the Lord's Supper **unworthily,** he was speaking to church members who were rushing into it without thinking of its meaning. Those who did so would be **guilty of sinning against the body and the blood of the Lord.** To treat the symbols of Christ's ultimate sacrifice irreverently is to be guilty of irreverence toward his body and blood shed on sinners' behalf. Instead of honoring Christ's sacrifice, those who ate unworthily were sharing in the guilt of those who crucified him.

The very nature of the rite calls for introspection. Therefore, Paul told the believers to **examine** themselves. No one should partake of the Lord's Supper who had not accepted Jesus' sacrifice on the cross for salvation. Neither should they come to the table drunk, angry with others, or with known but unrepented sin in their lives. Coming to the Lord's table "in an unworthy manner" means to come without a solemn understanding of what is being remembered, and without a repentant and humble spirit before the Lord.

11:29-30 The seriousness of the matter is revealed in these words. To take Communion **unworthily, not honoring the body of Christ** means coming to the Lord's table and not honoring the body of Christ sacrificed for our sins. To take the Lord's Supper—to eat the bread and drink the wine—as though it were no more than a regular meal to assuage hunger is to miss the sanctity of this special rite. Those who did so were eating and drinking **God's judgment** against themselves. This "judgment" was severe, one of the most severe in the New Testament. The judgment was disciplinary in nature (11:32); that is, this did not refer to eternal judgment, but it was severe enough as to cause **many** of the believers to be **weak and sick,** while some had even **died.** That some of the people had died may have been a special supernatural judgment on the Corinthian church. This type of disciplinary judgment highlights the seriousness of the Communion service. The Lord's Supper is not to be taken lightly; this new covenant cost Jesus his life. It is not a meaningless ritual, but a sacrament given by Christ to help strengthen believers' faith.

11:31 If the believers took time to **examine** themselves (11:28) before taking the Lord's Supper and so came to it with humble and repentant hearts— they would **not be examined by God and judged in this way.** This "judgment" refers to what Paul had just described in 11:29-30. While no one can

come to the Lord's Supper "worthy" of Christ's redemptive work, all believers can come with the right attitude and the right motivation to thank and praise God for what he has done.

11:32 Paul hastened to add that the judgment of 11:29-30 was disciplinary in nature and not eternal. The judgment sent by God is meant to bring believers back to a right understanding of the Lord's Supper so they can celebrate it correctly. The discipline will draw them back so that they can worship the Lord and **not be condemned with the world.** The world will face eternal condemnation because it has rejected Christ.

11:33-34 To solve the problem in Corinth, Paul advised the believers, when they gathered to celebrate the **Lord's Supper,** to **wait for each other.** They should come to this meal desiring to fellowship with other believers and to prepare for the Lord's Supper to follow, not to fill up on a big dinner. If they were hungry, they should **eat at home,** so they would come to the fellowship meal in the right frame of mind. As Paul had already explained, to come with the wrong attitude would **bring judgment** upon themselves. How sad to turn a blessed time of unity and thanksgiving into a time of division and judgment. Paul did not want this to be the case in Corinth.

Apparently there were other questions that needed Paul's **instructions,** but these questions were not urgent enough for him to take up in this letter. He would talk with the believers about these when he arrived in Corinth.

1 CORINTHIANS 12

SPIRITUAL GIFTS / 12:1-11

Spiritual gifts had become symbols of spiritual power, causing rivalries in the church because some people thought they were more "spiritual" than others because of their gifts. This was a terrible misuse of spiritual gifts because their purpose is always to help the church function more effectively, not to divide it. We can be divisive if we insist on using our gift our own way without being sensitive to others. We must never use gifts as a means of manipulating others or promoting our own self-interest.

12:1 The Corinthians had apparently asked Paul to answer a question **about the special abilities the Holy Spirit gives to each** believer. Also called "spiritual gifts," these are freely bestowed by God to enable his people to minister to the needs of

the body of believers and to enable them to do extraordinary work for God. Paul did not want the believers to have **misunderstandings** about these gifts, but, rather, to understand and use them for God's glory.

12:2 To contrast the work of the Holy Spirit, Paul reminded the believers of the influence of evil spirits (see 10:20-21). When they were **pagans** (non-Christians), they had been **led astray and swept along in worshiping speechless idols.** Evil spirits had done the "influencing." Evidently, in the cult religions, evil spirits "spoke" through their followers in what was called "ecstatic" or "inspired" speech. Evil forces were at work in the world, and the Corinthians would need to understand that what they had experienced as "tongues" or "inspired speech" in their pagan religion was completely different from the "speaking in tongues" that the believers might experience through the Holy Spirit.

12:3 The way to **discern** whether a person was speaking **from God** was to listen to what he or she said about Jesus Christ. Those who proclaimed and believed that **Jesus is Lord** were speaking by the Spirit, for only **by the Holy Spirit** can a person acknowledge the lordship of Christ. Some false teachers might be able to say those words and not mean them, but the truth would eventually come out. The Holy Spirit within believers helps them to truly believe and publicly confess Jesus Christ as Lord.

12:4-6 The answers that Paul has given to the Corinthians' questions thus far in this letter have focused on unity among believers, order in the church, and exaltation of Jesus Christ. So with the concern about spiritual gifts, Paul was concerned that the Corinthians' focus on any particular gift, such as "tongues," or ecstatic speech, would tear them apart. While the specific question is unknown, Paul clearly wanted the believers to understand that tongues had their place but should not be sought by everyone. In the broad context of spiritual gifts, the gift of tongues was just one gift. **There are different kinds of spiritual gifts, different kinds of service in the church, and different ways God works in our lives.** God's people receive many kinds of gifts, and no one gift is better than another. All the gifts come from one source and are to be used for one purpose—the building up of the body of Christ.

These gifts are just that—gifts. They are not earned. They are not given to believers asking for a specific one. They are not chosen by people. God alone administers the gifts among his people. God, not believers, controls the gifts. Each believer, then, is responsible to seek God's guidance in discovering his or her particular gift(s) and then discovering how best to use them for God's purposes.

12:7 Each believer has at least one **spiritual gift** to be used **as a means of helping the entire church.** Some people have interpreted this verse to imply that each person must have a gift; therefore, each believer must identify it and insist on using that gift. It may be true that every believer has a gift (12:11), but this statement was meant to counter those in Corinth who believed that every person *had* to speak in tongues. Such a view is wrong. What Paul stressed was the manifestation of the Spirit, the great variety and diversity of the gifts of the triune God (12:4-6), and the importance of using the gifts to help others.

12:8 To illustrate that there are a wide variety of gifts from the Holy Spirit, Paul gave a list. This list was not meant to be exhaustive; it merely illustrates many of the different kinds of spiritual gifts. The Spirit gives many gifts; the Bible contains no definitive list of all the gifts.

All believers are given wisdom from the Spirit (2:15-16), but some are given **the ability to give wise advice.** That this particular gift does not occur on any of the other lists of gifts has led some scholars to think that this gift was especially important (and more prominent) for the believers in the Greek city of Corinth, where the issue of "wisdom" was causing much discussion. Another person is given **the gift of special knowledge.** People may think they have all kinds of wisdom and knowledge, which leads to pride, but true wisdom and knowledge are found in Christ alone. But to some people the Spirit gives extraordinary knowledge. This could mean a special knowledge of spiritual realities (see 13:2, 8-12; 14:6) or knowledge given to teachers who are training others in Christian truth.

12:9 All Christians have faith because the faith that brings a person to salvation is the work of the Holy Spirit. Some people, however, have the spiritual gift of **faith,** which is an unusual measure of trust in the Holy Spirit's power. This kind of faith is a supernatural trust in God's miraculous power for specific situations. This gift of faith could also be manifested in believers' willingness to face persecution and martyrdom without renouncing what they believed.

The next two gifts (healing and miracles) are visual manifestations of the Spirit. **The power to heal the sick** had been manifested through Peter, Paul, and the other apostles (see, for example, Acts 3:6-8; 5:15-16; 9:33-34; 14:8-10). The gift of healing is given, not to the person healed, but to the person who does the healing. Some people want to say they have received the gift of healing for an illness they have, but the gifts are given to be used to benefit others.

12:10 As with the gift of healing (12:9), the Spirit will give to some an extraordinary power to **perform miracles.** While performing a healing would be considered a miracle, the inclusion of this gift separately from healings refers to other miraculous manifestations of the Spirit (see Galatians 3:5).

The rest of the gifts mentioned in this passage focus on verbal manifestations of the Spirit. To some people, the Spirit gives a special **ability to prophesy.** "Prophesy" does not just refer to predicting the future; it can also mean giving a message received from God to the community of believers. As with the gift of faith, the ability to share one's faith with power is available to everyone (see 14:1-5), but to some the Spirit gives a special measure of this gift.

Because there are many false teachers who claim to "prophesy" for God, some in the church are given **the ability to know whether it is really the Spirit of God or another spirit that is speaking.** While some believers have a special gift to discern what is really from God's Spirit and what is not, all believers are expected to have discernment. Since the gift mentioned here is also described in 14:29, this kind of spiritual discernment pertains specifically to oracular manifestations in Christian meetings. Paul's mention of this shows his concern for the protection of the truth in the worship service. Those given the gift of special discernment can help separate truth from error.

Opinions differ over exactly what Paul meant by **unknown languages.** Some believe that this refers to earthly languages that a person did not know before (the same as the gift described in Acts 2:4, 7-8). Other scholars say that this refers to an "ecstatic" language, a "heavenly" language. Most likely the second view is correct. Probably

the only time that the word "tongues" refers to other earthly languages is when describing Pentecost (Acts 2:4, 7-8). The rest of the time in the New Testament, the word refers to ecstatic languages unknown to anyone—thus another is given the gift **to interpret what is being said.** Speaking in tongues *is* a legitimate gift of the Spirit. The exercise of the gift demands some guidelines (as noted in chapter 14) so that the purpose of the gift—to help the body of Christ—is not lost. Those who speak in tongues should follow the guidelines; those who do not speak in tongues ought not seek the gift as a sign of salvation or as a sign of special closeness with God, for it is neither. It is a gift of God, given only to whomever God chooses. If a person has not experienced the gift of tongues, he or she ought not seek it but seek what gifts God *has* given.

12:11 The **Holy Spirit distributes these gifts,** and they are to be used for God's divine purpose. Because the Holy Spirit **alone decides which gift each person should have,** there is no place for rivalry, jealousy, or pride among believers regarding their gifts. God, through his Spirit, gives to every person in the community of believers exactly the right gifts for him or her to provide the needed services for the church and for God's Kingdom.

Whatever the practice of different churches, believers must realize that the Holy Spirit does not submit to any view of methodology. He cannot be limited or confined to cultural or contemporary views of propriety. All believers need to be open to God's gracious power in their lives and in their worship.

ONE BODY WITH MANY PARTS / 12:12-31

Using the analogy of the body, Paul emphasized the importance of each church member. If a seemingly insignificant part is taken away, the whole body becomes less effective. Thinking that one's gift is more important than someone else's is an expression of spiritual pride. Devaluing the gift offends the Giver. We should not look down on those who seem unimportant, and we should not be jealous of others who have impressive gifts. Instead, we should use the gifts we have been given and encourage others to use theirs. If we don't, the body of believers will be less effective.

12:12 Paul followed his section describing the diversity of gifts that the Holy Spirit gives to the church by providing an analogy of a **body** (see also 10:17). Just as a body **has many parts,** so the church is made up of many people with different gifts. It seems that the Corinthians all wanted to speak in tongues or desired more spectacular manifestations of the Spirit's power. Paul explained, however, that while not everyone has the same gift, they still **make up only one body**—the body of Christ.

12:13 What gives believers their unity is the **one Spirit**—the very same Spirit who also gives their diversity through the many and varied gifts. As believers live out their diversity through the gifts, they must never forget the basic fact that unites them—they **have all received the same Spirit.** All believers receive the same Holy Spirit at the time of their conversion. This distinguishes them from nonbelievers and unites them with one another.

12:14-15 Having established that the church, the worldwide community of believers, is indeed one body—the body of Christ—Paul went on to show the necessary diversity in that body. For a body to function, such diversity is essential. Individual members cannot separate themselves without harming the body. Just as a **foot** cannot decide to leave the body because it is not a **hand,** so a believer who does not have a particular gift cannot decide that he or she is not a part of the church. Apparently, some believers in Corinth were discouraged that they did not have a particular gift—probably one of the more spectacular gifts, such as the gift of tongues—so they believed that they could not truly be a part of the body unless they experienced that particular gift. But Paul explains, through this metaphor, that all the different gifts given by the Spirit to believers must be utilized in order for the church to function well.

12:16 As with the foot and the hand (12:15), so it is with the **ear** and the **eye.** The parts of the body should desire to perform only the functions for which they were made, not seeking other parts. Each believer should discover his or her spiritual gift and then use it to its fullest capacity for the Lord.

12:17 Every spiritual gift from the Holy Spirit is vital to the functioning of the body. Thus, the gifts are not given at whim and will not be changed according to people's preferences. If everyone wanted to be **an eye,** then the body might see very well, but it would not be able to **hear.** If the whole body were an **ear,** there would be no sense of **smell.**

12:18-20 As God created human bodies to function with their **many parts** working together, so the body of Christ—the church—needs all the various gifts working in harmony. The picture of a body with **only one part** illustrates the absurdity of a church with everyone trying to have the same gift. It would not be a body at all, and it would be unable to function. While **there are many parts,** there is **only one body,** because God ordained it that way. All believers are placed right where God wants them so that they might serve effectively together.

12:21 Not only should each individual part realize its own importance, but all the other parts should realize their interdependence as well. One part of the body **can never say** it doesn't need another part. Those in the church who have the more spectacular gifts should not look down on or dismiss those with other gifts because, in reality, all are needed.

12:22 The more honored members must not look down on the more humble members (12:21); in fact, those who **seem weakest and least important are really the most necessary.** These people may not be always visible, always up front exercising their gifts, but they are in the background. If they are using their God-given gifts, they are actually most necessary to the body. Those with the visible gifts could not function to their full capacity without the other members utilizing their gifts. The pastor in a church may be well versed and eloquent, but he will not be effective if the other members are not utilizing their gifts to greet newcomers warmly, to make sure the building is maintained and clean, to plan the worship service, to make sure equipment is working properly, to follow up on people with needs, or to pray faithfully for the ministry. The church needs the visible members, but it needs everyone. In reality, the less visible members are the most necessary ones.

12:23-26 The parts we regard as less honorable refers to the sexual parts of the body, the parts that **we carefully protect from the eyes of others.** The point of this verse is that appearances are deceiving; all parts of the body are necessary, even the ones that **should not be seen.** No one should dismiss anyone else as unimportant in the body of Christ; neither should undue prominence be given to anyone. Doing this **makes for harmony among the members, so that all the members care for each other equally.** The harmony Paul wanted had already been discussed in 1:10. Such harmony happens only when all the members—the weak and the strong, the flamboyant and the quiet, the up-front and the behind-the-scenes—use their gifts, appreciate one another, and share in one another's honors and suffering. As with the physical, human body, one part's suffering causes every part to suffer. When the head aches, the whole body suffers. When a thumb is hit with a hammer, the whole body knows it. Believers should share one another's burdens in order to help lighten them. There is no room for jealousy or strife when one person receives praise; instead, all should be glad.

12:27 The words **all of you together** refer to all believers across the world. All believers together **are Christ's body.** As new believers come to salvation in Jesus Christ, they join that body, receive a gift from the Holy Spirit, and are used by God. Therefore, each and every believer in the body of Christ **is a separate and necessary part of** that body. No believer is unimportant—each one has a gift to share in order to make the body function that much more effectively.

12:28 Having established believers' unity in their diversity, Paul went on to describe this diversity by a list (not complete) of various offices and gifts. The order of these gifts in this verse is important. The first three gifted people listed are those who proclaim the gospel and teach the truth. These are important gifts, for there would be no church without those who bring the message and teach the truth. Thus, Paul specifically ranked them as **first, second, and third** to show their prime importance above all the other gifts.

The **apostles** include the eleven men Jesus called (without Judas Iscariot), plus others who are called apostles—such as Paul himself (Romans 1:1), Matthias (Acts 1:26), Barnabas (Acts 14:14), Jesus' brother James (Galatians 1:19), Silas (1 Thessalonians 2:6), and Andronicus and Junias (Romans 16:7). It seems that the qualifications for being an apostle were to have seen the risen Christ, to have been sent out by Christ to preach the gospel, and to work on behalf of the Kingdom, building its foundation. Paul also noted "signs, wonders, and miracles" as marks of a true apostle (2 Corinthians 12:12). There were only a few apostles who brought the gospel message to the world.

God also appointed **prophets** to the church. These people had special gifts in ministering God's messages to his people. At times they would foretell the future (Acts 11:28; 21:9, 11), but more often they exhorted, encouraged, and strengthened God's people (Acts 15:32; 1 Corinthians 14:29). God spoke through prophets, inspiring them with specific messages for particular times and places.

While the apostles and prophets had a universal sphere of function (the church as a whole), the **teachers** probably served in the local churches. They needed to be trustworthy and faithful stewards of the truth of the gospel. People in that day did not have their own Bibles to read, so the teachers in the local congregations continued to teach the believers in the truth after the apostles had moved on to other cities.

The rest of this list reveals other gifts. Some of these have been noted earlier in this chapter. Some **do miracles** (12:10), some **have the gift of healing** (12:9), some **help others** (perhaps unusual compassion and caring), and others **can get others to work together** to help the church run smoothly. It is significant that Paul places last the gift of speaking **in unknown languages**. This was the one gift that seemed to have caused so much consternation and division in the Corinthian church (12:1-3, 10). Paul placed it as a relatively unimportant gift when compared with those who share the gospel or serve in more tangible ways.

12:29-30 These rhetorical questions demand a "no" answer. Not everyone in any church falls into one of these categories. Not everyone in the church has the same gift, nor can anyone claim to have all the gifts. Believers in the church must see themselves, not as individual plants, but as an entire garden under the cultivation of God's Spirit. His purpose involves not simply the production of a single gift but all the gifts, each becoming ripe as it is needed. Believers should be thankful for each other, thankful that others have gifts that are completely different. In the church, believers' strengths and weaknesses can balance each other. Some people's abilities compensate for other people's deficiencies. Together all believers can build Christ's church. But all these gifts will be worthless if they are used begrudgingly, out of duty, or if they are exercised without love (see also 13:1-3).

12:31 The believers **should desire the most helpful gifts.** In other words, in the desire to be helpful in the body of Christ, they should seek the power of the Spirit. Too often this verse is only applied individually when the emphasis should be on the church as a body. The church ought to desire the most helpful gifts so that it can function well. It would be incorrect to interpret Paul as saying "desire the most helpful gifts" to mean "seek the gifts from the top of the list" (12:27-28). Paul had been stressing diversity of gifts and the necessity for the gifts to be interactive within the body. He could not have thereby excluded healing or tongues as lesser gifts. In addition, he could not have meant for the people to desire to be apostles—that was impossible, because only a few chosen men could claim that title.

The believers should earnestly desire gifts that benefit everyone (as opposed to an unintelligible tongue that, without interpretation, helps no one but the speaker). The Corinthians had to get their focus off of the gift of speaking in ecstatic languages; instead, they needed to see the value in all the gifts, especially those that helped others. Paul's saying, **let me tell you about something else that is better than any of them,** leads into chapter 13.

1 CORINTHIANS 13

LOVE IS THE GREATEST / 13:1-13

In chapter 12, Paul gave evidence of the Corinthians' lack of love in the utilization of spiritual gifts; chapter 13 defines real love; and chapter 14 shows how love works. While spiritual gifts are important to the functioning of the body (12:12-31), they lose their value if love is not behind them.

13:1 Great faith, acts of dedication or sacrifice, miracle-working power, or the ability to **speak in any language in heaven or on earth** will produce very little without **love**. Without love, speaking in a heavenly language, although a gift of the Spirit, becomes nothing more than **meaningless noise**. The gift of tongues, used without love, is as valueless as pagan worship. Without love, the gifts do not build up other believers, so they are useless. Christians must not exalt gifts over character. Love is far more important. The word for "love" used here is *agape*. The Greeks had different words that described different kinds of love. The word *agape* connotes a deep, abiding, self-sacrificing love—the kind that looks out for the other person first.

13:2 The **gift of prophecy** was described in the commentary on 12:10 as a gift that might enable the person to see events in the **future** but mainly to bring God's message to the church under the direction of the Holy Spirit (see also 14:1-25; 1 Thessalonians 5:19-20). Some people have been given a special measure of this gift with the ability to know **everything**. Such understanding and even the ability to share it with others, however, are worth nothing without **love**.

The **gift of faith** was described in 12:9. This does not refer to saving faith, whereby people come to believe in Jesus Christ as Savior; instead, this is an unusual measure of trust in the Holy Spirit's power to do mighty works, much like Elijah received in 1 Kings 18. If a person has faith that could move mountains but does not have **love**, the faith is **no good to anybody**.

13:3 True **love** produces willingness to give sacrificially and to suffer. Acts of charity and self-sacrifice can be done for the sake of an ideal or with pride as a motivation. But they are of no value for the Kingdom, wrote Paul, unless they are done from the foundation of **love** for **others**.

13:4 Because love is so important among the believers, Paul described that love in more detail. How does such love look when lived out in the lives of believers? First of all, **love is patient,** the opposite of being short-tempered. Patience (sometimes translated "long-suffering" or "slow to anger") is an attribute of God (see Exodus 34:6; Numbers 14:18; Romans 2:4; 1 Peter 3:20). In many places, God's people are called upon to be patient (see, for example, Ephesians 4:2; Colossians 3:12; 1 Thessalonians 5:14). Patience is a fruit of the Spirit (Galatians 5:22). Such love bears with certain annoyances or inconveniences without complaint. It does not lose its temper when provoked. It steadily perseveres.

Love is also **kind.** Kindness takes the initiative in responding generously to others' needs. The psalms and writings of the prophets say much about God's kindness (Psalm 18:50; Isaiah 54:8; Jeremiah 9:24). Because believers have received kindness, they ought to act with kindness toward others. Such love is considerate and helpful to others. Kind love is gentle and mild, always ready to show compassion, especially to those in need.

Love is not jealous. The jealous person desires what another person has. This seems to have been a particular problem in Corinth—those with "lesser" gifts envied those with "greater" gifts. The seed of envy can lead to seething anger and hatred. Those who are too busy envying each other's gifts are unlikely to be using their own gifts in loving service to God and others. When there is love, believers will gladly use whatever gifts they have been given to work together for the advance of God's Kingdom. They will be glad that others have different gifts so that the entire job can get done.

Love is not **boastful or proud.** While some believers may have a problem with envy, those with the "greater" gifts might have a problem with boasting or pride. Again, it seems that this may have been a problem in Corinth. While some pride can be positive, this kind of pride takes credit for an undeserved gift. Gifted believers who are caught up in pride and boasting over their gifts are unable to serve. Without love, they may feel that by using their gifts, they are doing someone a favor, that others should be grateful to them, and that they are far superior.

13:5 Love is not **rude.** This refers to actions that are improper, impolite, discourteous, or crude. Believers who use their gifts with love will be careful to act in a manner worthy of their calling before God. They will never humiliate others. This may also have been a problem in Corinth, especially in their worship services (see 11:2-16).

Love **does not demand its own way.** Love looks out for others, seeks their best interests, willingly gives up its own for the sake of another. A person who wants his own way may use his gifts but not with a serving attitude or a desire to build the Kingdom. Instead, the gifts are only used if they can somehow benefit the self-seeking person. This is not God's way. Instead, because of love, the believers use their gifts to benefit others first, without "self" or selfish desires getting in the way.

Love is not **irritable,** meaning easily angered or touchy. Such people let things get on their nerves. One believer, in the process of exercising his or her gifts, may irritate another believer. These "easily angered" believers may not like the style or manner in which these others exercise their gifts. This is not the way of love. When believers exercise their gifts in love, they will be able to give one another some latitude to follow God as they see fit. They will not let themselves be easily provoked over disagreements, but they will be able to always respond in a loving manner.

Love **keeps no record of when it has been wronged.** Such people will remember every offense against them as though it were written in a book and tallied. These "wrongs" are not sins that need to be dealt with in the congregation (such as that described in chapter 5) but minor offenses or misunderstandings between believers. Those who keep record of these wrongs and personal injuries will harbor resentment against other believers. Love, however, makes allowances for people's foibles and flaws and willingly forgets when wrongs were done. This frees all believers to grow and mature in Christ and to grow in their ability to serve and use their gifts. When mistakes are made, love overlooks them and allows believers to continue to serve with the gifts God has given them. God does not keep a record of believers' wrongs (2 Corinthians 5:19).

13:6 Love **is never glad about injustice but rejoices whenever the truth wins out.** When

believers show love, they do not show superior morality by taking pleasure in another's fall. Love does not take pleasure in any kind of injustice. Instead, love does the exact opposite. Through their relationship with Jesus Christ, believers possess the one and only truth (John 14:6). Those who love should remain untainted by evil. Instead, they ought to always seek truth, desire that truth wins out, protect the truth, and proclaim the truth whenever possible.

13:7 After explaining what love does not do (13:4b-6), Paul listed four positive attributes of love. **Love never gives up,** but willingly protects others. The word in Greek means "cover" or "hide by covering." This does not refer to hiding hurtful sin but to protecting someone from embarrassment, gossip, or any other such harm. When believers love one another, they refuse harmful gossip and protect one another from those who would try to inflict harm.

Love **never loses faith.** It is willing to think the best of others. It does not mean that believers must be gullible, trusting everyone; instead, it means that they are willing to think the best as opposed to the worst of others. Love gives the benefit of the doubt. With real love, believers can deal with conflict lovingly. When everyone willingly thinks the best of everyone else, people are freed to be honest and open.

Love **is always hopeful.** Believers who love look forward, not backward. They seek for growth and maturity in the church, knowing that God is working in every person.

Love **endures through every circumstance.** Believers who love are active and steadfast in their faith. They hold on, no matter what difficulties they face. Hardship and pain do not stop love. When believers persevere, they face suffering within the body. They face persecution. They hang on when the going gets tough. They strive to save their marriages despite disappointment, to continue to trust God despite setbacks, and to continue to serve God despite fear or sorrow. When believers truly persevere, nothing can stop them.

13:8-10 All the spiritual gifts will eventually **disappear,** but **love will last forever.** On this earth, outside of heaven, everything is imperfect. No matter how much people may know, they **know only a little.** No matter how much prophecy is given, it still **reveals little.** Not until the arrival of God's Kingdom (**the end**) will everything be made perfect and complete. At that time, all the **special gifts** of the Spirit will **disappear.** Because gifts are given for the building up of the body of Christ, they will no longer be needed. The body will be complete, and God's Kingdom will have arrived. Yet love will continue (13:8), because love is the very essence of God himself. "God is love," wrote John (1 John 4:8, 16). God's love caused him to reach out to undeserving humanity and send a Savior. His love saved people and will bring them into his Kingdom to be with him forever. The Kingdom rests on God's love.

13:11 The contrast between believers' spiritual understanding now, when they know only a little, and their lives in the future Kingdom, when everything will be made clear, is illustrated in human terms. A child talks, thinks, and reasons like a **child.** His or her understanding is incomplete. But when a child grows up, he or she matures in speech, thought, and reason, putting **away childish things.** So now believers know only a little, like children, but one day they will be able to put their present understanding behind them because they will understand clearly.

13:12 By way of further metaphor, believers' present spiritual understanding is like a reflection **in a poor mirror.** They see very poorly now; what they know **is partial and incomplete.** While believers' knowledge is still growing and maturing, God already knows each person **completely.** Instead of boasting about their spiritual gifts, the Corinthian believers

should realize that these gifts were nothing compared to what they would experience in heaven.

13:13 Paul was showing that love is a spiritual reality of a different kind, like hope and faith, and not to be considered as one of the spiritual gifts. In eternity, the gifts will drop away in significance, but faith, hope, and love will **endure.**

Faith sometimes refers to a spiritual gift (12:9; 13:2) or to saving faith that God has forgiven sins. In this context, it refers to trust in the goodness and mercy of the Lord. Such trust will see believers through until they live face-to-face in God's presence. Believers also **hope;** they look forward to the arrival of God's promised Kingdom in its fullest form, knowing that God will deliver them in times of suffering.

Paul added that **the greatest of these is love.** How is love "the greatest"? Paul already had established that love would abide forever (13:8). Love is the greatest because it is one quality of the Christian life that will be fully active both in the present and for eternity. Believers' faith in God will be realized when they see God face-to-face—for where there is sight, faith is no longer needed. Similarly, the believers' hope will be fully realized. Love will endure forever as those in the new heaven and new earth continue to love God and his people.

1 CORINTHIANS 14

THE GIFTS OF TONGUES AND PROPHECY / 14:1-25

The previous chapter, known as the "love chapter," is nestled purposefully into this section on tongues. As beautiful as it is standing alone, chapter 13 serves as a transition from chapter 12 (regarding the various gifts of the Spirit) to chapter 14 (focusing on the abuse of one particular gift, the gift of tongues). When spiritual gifts are properly used, they help everyone in the church. Much of the controversy over spiritual gifts today is because the gifts have been abused in some Christian circles (strikingly similar to the Corinthian problems), while at the same time they have been almost completely ignored in other Christian groups. In your church, seek balanced biblical teaching.

14:1 Having described love as the most valuable of all the gifts given by the Holy Spirit, Paul concluded here that believers should **let love be** their **highest goal.** Then, from that foundation, they should **desire the special abilities the Spirit gives.** To **desire** the gifts means literally "to pursue, strive for, seek after, aspire to." The **special abilities** that Paul wanted the Corinthians to seek were those

that edified the church. **The gift of prophecy** (see also 12:10) had not so much to do with predicting future events as it had to do with bringing some message from God under the direction of the Holy Spirit to the body of believers. This gift provides insight, warning, correction, and encouragement (see 14:3). The Corinthians were eager for gifts, especially tongues, but Paul wanted them to be eager for the gifts that edify—namely, prophecy. The Reformers (Calvin, Luther) believed that sermons are the exercise of the gift of prophecy. Other scholars say that "prophecy," as used here by Paul, means spontaneous, Spirit-inspired messages that are orally delivered in the congregation for the edification and encouragement of the body of Christ.

14:2 The gift of prophecy should be desired more than the gift of tongues because **the ability to speak in tongues** does not help other people **since they won't be able to understand you.** The "tongues" mentioned are not earthly languages (such as the gift described in Acts 2:4-12). Instead, this refers to an "ecstatic" or heavenly language, unknown to the speaker or to anyone else. Through this special gift, the believer talks **to God but not to people;** talking to God primarily involves prayer and praise. Because "tongues" is a true spiritual gift, the speaker is **speaking by the power of the Spirit,** but the words are **mysterious.**

As wonderful as this gift is, Paul wanted the Corinthian believers, in particular, to stop overemphasizing it. They needed to keep its value in perspective. Paul's goal, as always, was the unity and edification of all the believers. In light of this, Paul made several points about the gift of speaking in tongues:

- The gift of speaking in tongues is a spiritual gift from the Holy Spirit (12:28; 14:2, 39).
- Speaking in tongues is a desirable gift, but it is not a requirement of salvation or of being filled with the Spirit (12:30-31).
- The gift of tongues is less important than prophecy and teaching (14:4).
- The gift of tongues must be accompanied by some rules regarding its best use in public settings (14:26-28).

14:3-4 Although Paul himself spoke in tongues (14:18), he stressed prophecy because it benefits the whole church. In context, speaking in tongues primarily benefits the speaker. Public worship must be understandable and edifying to the whole church. The purpose of "prophecy" is **helping others grow in the Lord, encouraging and comforting them,** and the one who **speaks a word of prophecy strengthens the entire church.** Through prophecy, believers are taught more about the Lord and their faith so they can grow as a body.

The **person who speaks in tongues,** however, **is strengthened personally in the Lord.** Such personal edification is truly a blessing for the one who has received this gift, but a person who prays in a tongue for personal edification should not be doing so in public worship because, while it strengthens him or her, it does not strengthen anyone else. Paul would

give some guidelines for the use of tongues in public worship later in this chapter.

14:5 Paul never wrote disparagingly of the gift of tongues, only the Corinthians' overemphasis of it. In fact, he even wished that they **all had the gift of speaking in tongues,** for the gift has great value for individuals in their private communication with God. But the issue at hand was that the Corinthian believers were seeking that gift above all others, when other gifts were actually more helpful to the church as a whole. Repeating his emphasis in 14:1, Paul stated that **prophecy is a greater and more useful gift than speaking in tongues.** The one who prophesies helps others to grow and encourages and comforts them (14:3). The one speaking in tongues realizes a wonderful relationship with the Lord but has edified no one else **unless someone interprets** what has been said **so that the whole church can get some good out of it.** (For more on interpretation, see 12:30; 14:13, 22-25.) With interpretation, therefore, the gift of tongues *can* edify the church. Apparently, the Corinthian believers were exhibiting the gift of tongues in public worship without interpretation, and that was helping no one.

14:6 In Corinth, the gift of tongues was being used as a barometer of spirituality. Therefore, Paul described the natural inferiority of a gift that does not edify. For example, if, on his next visit to the Corinthian church, he was **talking in an unknown language,** would that help the young church grow in Christ? However, **revelation, knowledge, prophecy,** or **teaching** would be helpful to them.

14:7-8 Paul argued his point with three different pictures. First, **musical instruments** make only noise if no one can **recognize the melody.** If an instrument is to make beautiful sounds that benefit the listener, the sounds must be **played clearly.** For example, the bugler was important in a battalion of soldiers. With different note combinations, the bugler would sound the call to wake up, to retire for the evening, or the call to battle. **If the bugler doesn't sound a clear call,** however, the soldiers would be left in confusion, not knowing whether or not **they are being called to battle.** Mere sounds are not beneficial; only sounds that make sense and are understood by the hearers are helpful.

14:9 People from many lands converged in a busy city like Corinth. The residents were certainly familiar with foreigners who could not speak their language. As mere sounds mean nothing without some sort of plan and pattern of understanding (14:7-8), so human language, when not understood, is like **talking to an empty room.**

14:10-12 Just because someone doesn't understand a certain language doesn't mean that the language has no meaning. But when two people who speak different languages attempt to communicate, one is not able to **understand** the other. Just as two foreigners cannot understand each other's language, so those speaking in tongues cannot be understood by the congregation. Thus, their speaking is not beneficial to the church.

Because the Corinthians had been so **eager to have spiritual gifts,** Paul admonished them to **ask God for those that will be of real help to the whole church** (see Ephesians 4:12). The church as a whole should strive to have the gifts that build up its members. It should support those who serve in those capacities, and it should redirect its zeal from a desire to speak in tongues to a desire to serve the Lord in the best way that will build up the church.

14:13-14 The simple conclusion to the matter is that **anyone who has the gift of speaking in tongues should pray also for the gift of interpretation** of what he or she says in the unknown language. Up to this point, Paul had been explaining that the gift of speaking in tongues was of no value to the congregation as a whole, only to the person who speaks to God in the unknown tongue. But if the person also has the gift of interpretation, the tongue could be used in public worship if the one praying (or someone else with the gift of interpretation) would then interpret **in order to tell people plainly what has been said.** That way, the entire church would be edified by this gift.

Paul intimates in 14:2 and 14:4 that the gift of speaking in tongues provides a person with glorious communion with God. Most likely, however, this communion results not from understanding what the person is saying but from drawing closer to God through the power of the Spirit. Yet the person who prays that way is not expected to be able to interpret his or her own words immediately. Paul wrote, **if I pray in tongues, my spirit is praying, but I don't understand what I am saying.** That is part of the mysterious beauty of this particular gift.

14:15 Paul states in 14:18 that he himself speaks in tongues, so he wrote in the first person here, including himself in this situation. His answer is that he will do both—he will **pray** and **sing** in tongues with his **spirit,** and he will pray and sing in words he will **understand.** Praying in tongues was, for Paul, a practice that edified him even if he did not understand what he was saying (see 14:13-14 commentary). Praying with the spirit (see "spiritual songs," Ephesians 5:19) may be

charismatic singing in the Spirit or singing spontaneously to previously composed songs. Paul may also have had in mind a private/public distinction. In his private prayers and singing, he could do so in tongues. In public, however, he would speak in Greek so that the congregation would understand and be edified.

14:16-17 Those with the gift of tongues could continue to speak in tongues privately, but they needed to focus more on praying and singing in their own language in corporate worship. The reason is simple. If a person were praising God **in the spirit** (meaning in an unknown tongue), no one could praise God along with him. If the rest of the people in the congregation have no clue what a tongues-speaker has said, how can they express agreement with it? The bottom line on the corporate use of a spiritual gift is that it should **help the other people present.** That is the purpose of corporate worship, and believers must be sensitive to one another in that context—keeping out anything that would interfere with spiritual growth.

14:18-19 Paul had been downplaying the value of tongues because of the Corinthian overemphasis on that particular gift, but he added that he himself had that gift. But he understood the limitations of the gift of tongues when it came to edifying the body of believers. Instead of impressing people with the gift of tongues, Paul said that he would rather speak **five understandable words** to instruct others than **ten thousand words in an unknown language** because only words that are understood can instruct. The implication is that the believers in Corinth who were gifted with tongues should do the same.

14:20 Children prefer excitement to instruction, but adults ought to know better. The Corinthians had been acting like children, enjoying the excitement that tongues offered in their assembly without realizing that they were obtaining no solid instruction from them. It is all right to be as **innocent as babies when it comes to evil,** but there is no place for constant immaturity in the Christian life. Believers are to be growing and maturing so that they can understand these issues for themselves and make wise decisions concerning them.

14:21 Paul's use of Scripture comes from Isaiah 28:11-12. He may have been adapting the passage or generalizing from it, since it is not an exact quote from either the Greek (Septuagint) nor the Hebrew text available at that time. Paul's point in quoting this passage was to set up his conclusion in 14:23. The people in Isaiah's time did not listen to the prophets who spoke in their language, and when people of other languages spoke to the Jews, they still did not listen. So Paul was saying that speaking in tongues will convince no one.

14:22 The Corinthians argued that **speaking in tongues** was supposed to be a **sign** to **unbelievers,** as it was in Acts 2. But Paul argued that after speaking in tongues, believers were supposed to explain what was said and give the credit to God. The unsaved people would then be convinced of a spiritual reality and be motivated to look further into the Christian faith. **Prophecy,** the teaching of God's word, will **benefit the believers.**

14:23 The way the Corinthians were speaking in tongues was helping no one. If **everyone** in the church is **talking in an unknown language** all at one time without interpretation, people who don't understand or unbelievers who come in **will think they are crazy.** They will not sound as though they are praising and praying, but rather one would think that they are all insane. This will edify no one, scare off unbelievers, and hurt the witness of the church.

14:24 Paul had already stated the value of **prophesying** over speaking in tongues (14:1-6). The unbelievers or people who don't understand should come into the meeting and be able to learn something. Here Paul highlighted the specific speaking that would help lead people to repent of their sins. **Convicted of sin** means reproved or rebuked through the probing work of the Holy Spirit, who exposes and convinces people of sin (Ephesians 5:12-13; 1 Timothy 5:20; 2 Timothy 4:2). Unbelievers would also be **condemned,** meaning "judged," "held to account," "examined."

14:25 Having one's **secret thoughts laid bare** will lead both to conviction and condemnation. Obviously, the Corinthian believers would be far less convicted to have everyone speaking in tongues. They all would feel very spiritual, with no one having to face any sin. But when Spirit-inspired, intelligible words of truth are spoken, those who truly **listen** will find God right there among the congregation. The listeners **will fall down on their knees and worship God** (see Isaiah 45:14; Zechariah 8:23). And that is ultimately what the church should desire—to reach out and draw in the unbelievers, bringing them to saving faith in Jesus Christ and then helping them grow to maturity.

A CALL TO ORDERLY WORSHIP / 14:26-40

Paul reviews the guidelines for tongues and prophecy as exercised in corporate worship. He restates the importance of everyone being able to understand, of orderliness, and of edifying each participant.

14:26 This verse is not to be taken as Paul's recommendation of an order of service; his point is that various activities can happen in corporate worship. While all of this occurs, however, **everything that is done must be useful to all and build them up in the Lord.** Also, all believers should show love (chapter 13), and everything should edify (14:1-25).

14:27-28 Tongues can be edifying to everyone, if a few simple rules are followed. First, if tongues are spoken **no more than two or three** should do so, they must **speak one at a time,** and there must be someone who can **interpret.** That Paul should have to say that they should speak "one at a time" seems to be a corrective—apparently they were not doing so. Not only were the Corinthians overemphasizing this gift, but they were allowing it to dominate their church gatherings. Thus, Paul corrected this error. If those with the gift of tongues know that they do not have the gift of interpretation, and if no one else in the congregation is known to have that gift, then they should **be silent.** Paul was not forbidding believers from using their gift, but instructing them to pray silently, speaking to **God privately.** That way they would be blessed by the use of their gift, but they would not in any way hinder the assembly.

14:29 Having just explained certain regulations on the use of tongues in the assembly, Paul also placed regulations on prophetic speaking. Although this was the particular gift that Paul had recommended to the believers (14:1-5), he also realized that its use had to be regulated by love, edification, and order. Just as only two or three people should be allowed to speak in tongues (14:27-28), so only **two or three** should **prophesy.** It is unclear who **the others** are—they could be "others" who also have the gift but exercise it at that time, not by speaking but by evaluating **what is said.** Or "the others" could refer to the congregation as a whole, discussing a prophet's words to make sure that they agreed with Scripture. People in the church should never accept the words of any person, gifted or not, without careful discernment and personal knowledge of God's word; otherwise, false teachers could easily obtain a hearing and lead people astray.

14:30-32 In order for the worship service to continue in an orderly manner (14:40), further guidelines were needed. These words might have been directed at those who would have a tendency to dominate. One who is speaking should willingly defer to another who has received a prophecy. That **a revelation** would come suddenly to a person describes this gift and its use in a worship service. It, too, could get out of control if the speakers were not careful to take turns and defer to one another as the Spirit leads each to speak. As always, the worship service should be for the edification of the believers. This gift, like the gift of tongues, does not put people out of control, unable to stop their mouths. The message, given by the Spirit, is subject to the person's spirit. He or she can control when to speak and when to defer to another. This gift could also be exercised in a controlled, appropriate, and orderly way.

14:33 The reason that the church service must be controlled and orderly is that **God is not a God of disorder but of peace.** In worship, everything must be done in harmony and with order. Even when the gifts of the Holy Spirit are being exercised, there is no excuse for disorder or disturbances. To contradict God's own character in worship does not honor him. When everyone in the Christian assembly is truly in tune with the Holy Spirit, there will not be disorder, but harmony and "peace" that pleases God and encourages his people.

14:34-35 Does this mean that women should not speak in church services today? It is clear from 11:5 that women often prayed and prophesied in public worship. It is also clear in chapters 12–14 that women are given spiritual gifts and are encouraged to exercise them in the body of Christ. So what did Paul mean? It would be helpful to understand the context and the use of the word **silent.**

In the Greek culture, women were discouraged from saying anything in public, and they were certainly not allowed to confront or question men publicly. Apparently, some of the women who had become Christians thought that their Christian freedom gave them the right to question the men in public worship. This was causing division in the church. In addition, women of that day did not receive formal religious education as did the men.

The Greek word for "silent" used here is also used in 14:28, referring to the silence commanded on the one who desired to speak in tongues but without an interpreter present. Obviously, that did not mean that this person was never to speak in the church, only to remain silent when certain conditions were not met so that the church service

would not be disrupted. The same Greek word is also used in 14:30 for the prophet who is asked to stop speaking ("be silent" in the Greek) when another has been given a revelation. Again, this obviously does not mean that the prophet was never to speak. This would negate his or her gift. Because women as well as men were gifted with tongues, interpretation, or prophecy, they would need to speak in order to exercise their gifts.

The "speaking" to which Paul referred was the inappropriate asking of questions that would disrupt the worship service or take it on a tangent. Therefore, the **women should be silent during the church meetings,** not because they were never to speak, but because they were not to speak out with questions that would be ineffective in edifying the entire church. **If they have any questions,** says Paul, **let them ask their husbands at home.** That **they should be submissive** compares with Paul's words in 11:7-12—to keep the believers in obedience with God's commanded lines of authority (**just as the law says**). There is no clear reference to an Old Testament passage. Paul may have been referring to a generally accepted interpretation of Genesis 3:16. Apparently, the women believers in Corinth, newly freed in Christ to be able to learn and take part in worship, had been raising questions that could have been answered at home without disrupting the services. In this entire chapter, Paul had been dealing with various forms of disorder and confusion taking place in the Corinthian church in particular. His words are corrective. In this instance, Paul was asking the Corinthian women not to flaunt their Christian freedom during worship. The purpose of Paul's words was to promote unity, not to teach about the role of women in the church.

14:36 This entire chapter corrects the Corinthian believers regarding their insistence on the gift of tongues as a sign of being "filled with the Spirit" and allowing it to overtake their church services. They have been guilty of taking off on a tangent and leaving the gospel behind. So Paul asked, sarcastically, **Do you think that the knowledge of God's word begins and ends with you?** The Corinthian church was out of line with what was acceptable behavior in the churches (14:33), and they needed to make some changes.

14:37-38 The authority of Paul's words was not to be questioned. As an apostle, Paul was writing **a command of the Lord,** and they all should treat his words as such. Any true **prophet** among them would **recognize** this; anyone who claimed to be a prophet but did **not recognize** Paul's words as authoritative was **not to be recognized.** The lines of authority went from "apostles" to "prophets" (12:28). Paul was an apostle, so his authority was not to be questioned. Those who claimed to be "prophets" would prove it by their acceptance of Paul's words.

14:39-40 Paul truly loved these believers and sought to correct their errors so that they could continue to grow in the Lord and not be sidetracked by anything. They were to **be eager to prophesy** (14:1) because that is the more

powerful tool for the edification of the believers, but they should not **forbid speaking in tongues** because that is a bona fide gift of the Holy Spirit. They must **be sure that everything is done properly and in order**—and that would happen if they followed his instructions as outlined in this chapter. Worship services should be intelligible and marked by mutual respect and proper behavior. They should be organized in a way to enhance communication but not so as to stifle the spontaneous work of the Spirit.

1 CORINTHIANS 15

THE RESURRECTION OF CHRIST / 15:1-11

In this final section of the letter, Paul gave a masterly defense of the resurrection of Christ and its importance to the Christian faith. The struggles in the Corinthian church made it clear to Paul that they needed to refocus their attention on the gospel. He brought his letter to a close with a vigorous proclamation of the resurrection of Jesus Christ.

15:1-2 The gospel message that he had **preached to** them, that they had **welcomed,** on which they had taken their stand was the message that had saved them. Paul wanted to remind them of that gospel, because apparently some (probably false teachers) had been distorting it. In fact, some of the Corinthians had come to believe that there would be no resurrection of the dead (15:12). Not only was the church in Corinth having problems with unity (as Paul tried to clear up in the previous chapters), it was also dealing with basic problems of theology. This, too, would tear apart the church. As an apostle who had himself seen the risen Christ (15:8), Paul took these Corinthian believers back to the basics of the message that they had welcomed and received.

15:3-4 The central theme of the gospel is given here. It is the key text for the defense of Christianity. The three points that are **most important** are as follows:

1. **Christ died for our sins.** Without the truth of this message, Christ's death was worthless, and those who believe in him are still in their sins and without hope. However, Christ as the sinless Son of God took the punishment of sin, "dying for sin" so that those who believe can have their sins removed. The phrase **as the Scriptures said** refers to the Old Testament prophecies regarding this event, such as Psalm 16:8-11 and Isaiah 53:5-6. Christ's death on

the cross was no accident, no afterthought. It had been part of God's plan from all eternity in order to bring about the salvation of all who believe.

2. **He was buried.** The fact of Christ's death is revealed in the fact of his burial. Many have tried to discount the actual death of Christ, from the false teachers of Paul's day to false teachers today. But Jesus Christ did die on the cross and was buried in a tomb.

3. **He was raised.** Christ came back to life from being a dead person in a grave **on the third day** as noted in the Gospels (Friday afternoon to Sunday morning—three days in Jewish reckoning of time). This also occurred **as the Scriptures said** (Psalm 16:8-11; 110; Jonah 1:17).

15:5 Jesus made several appearances to various people after his resurrection. Paul first mentioned the appearance to **Peter** noted in Luke 24:34 (see also Mark 16:7). Peter had denied his Lord and then had wept bitterly (Mark 14:72). Jesus had also been seen **by the twelve apostles.** The expression "twelve apostles" was a title for the original disciples. These appearances are recorded in Mark 16:14; Luke 24:36-43; John 20:19-31.

15:6 This event is recorded nowhere else. It most likely occurred in Galilee, and the sheer number of eyewitnesses, **more than five hundred,** should cause doubters to stop and think before dismissing the Resurrection accounts of a few followers. All these people saw him **at one time,** and at the time of Paul's writing, **most of** them were still alive. Paul could appeal to their testimony to back up his own.

15:7 This **James** is Jesus' brother (actually, half brother), who at first did not believe that Jesus was the Messiah (John 7:5). After seeing the resurrected Christ, he became a believer (as did Jesus' other brothers, Acts 1:14). This next mention of **all the apostles** must describe an event separate from that recorded in 15:5, as well as designating the James mentioned here from the two apostles of that name.

15:8 One of the credentials to be an apostle was to have been an eyewitness of Jesus Christ. Paul could call himself an apostle (1:1) because he had also seen Jesus. This event is recorded in Acts 9:3-6. Paul's opportunity to see Jesus Christ was a special case. The other apostles saw Christ before the Resurrection; they lived and traveled with him for nearly three years. Paul was not one of the original twelve apostles, yet Christ appeared to him.

15:9 As a zealous Pharisee, Paul had been an enemy of the Christian church—even to the point of capturing and persecuting believers (see Acts 9:1-3). Here Paul reminded the Corinthian believers of the magnificent grace of God in drawing sinners out of sin and into his Kingdom. By calling himself **the least** of the apostles, Paul was not putting himself down (see 2 Corinthians 11:5; Galatians 2:11). Instead, he realized that although all of the apostles had been drawn from sin, Paul had actively **persecuted the church of God.** He fully realized the depth of the error and sin from which he had been saved, so much so that he knew he was **not worthy to be called an apostle.** Only God's grace had handed him such a privilege and responsibility.

15:10-11 Neither Paul nor any of the apostles could take credit for achieving the position of apostle. They had all been called to that position. Only by God's **special favor** was Paul saved and enabled to serve. And Paul certainly did so! He wrote of having **worked harder than all the other apostles.** This was not an arrogant boast because he knew that his hard work was a result of God **working through** him. Because of his previous position as a Pharisee (Acts 23:6; Philippians 3:5) and his previous occupation of persecuting Christians, Paul's conversion made him the object of even greater persecution than the other apostles; thus he had to work harder to preach the same message. They all brought the same message and the apostles never strayed from that message. This is what they **believed,** so they must not stray from the message that had brought them salvation.

THE RESURRECTION OF THE DEAD / 15:12-34

Christians attempting to share their faith are often shocked by the world's denial of the possibility of the Resurrection. The gospel remains an irritating and upsetting challenge to the commonly held views of life and death. Christians are convinced that Jesus' Resurrection *did* happen, and that it changed everything. The Christian faith comes from Christ's experience, not people's individual feelings or desires. The conviction of the Resurrection gives believers hope for the future.

15:12 The gospel message the Corinthians had received and believed included the basic fact of the Resurrection—a fact central to the Christian faith. But apparently some were **saying there will be no resurrection of the dead.** Such a belief contradicted the entire gospel message. This may have come from the Greek view that matter was evil and, therefore, no physical body would rise. The church at Corinth was in the heart of Greek culture. Thus, many believers had a difficult time believing in a bodily resurrection. Paul wrote this part of his letter to clear up this confusion about the Resurrection.

15:13-14 Paul argued that **if there is no resurrection of the dead,** then Jesus is still in the grave. If Jesus is still in the grave, then the apostles' **preaching is useless** because they preached a risen Savior. **If Christ has not been raised,** the believers' faith is also **useless.** Why believe in a dead "Savior"? If Jesus is still dead, then his sacrifice did not appease God for believers' sin, and believers have no advocate with the Father (Hebrews 7:25; 8:1). They also have no Comforter in the Holy Spirit, for he was to come when Christ returned to glory (John 16:5, 13-15). They have no hope of eternal life, if not even their Savior gained eternal life.

15:15-16 If Christ has not been raised from the dead, the apostles would all be lying about God because they had said that God raised Christ from the grave. However, if resurrection is impossible, if there is no resurrection of the dead, then Christ has not been raised. This point is repeated from 15:13 to drive home the point. The Corinthians had to understand the logical implications of the position they had chosen. To no longer believe in the physical resurrection was to throw away the entire gospel message. They could not claim to be Christians without believing in the Resurrection.

15:17 Refusing to believe that Jesus rose from the grave means that Christians are **still under condemnation for** their **sins.** If Jesus died and was never raised, then his death did nothing to accomplish justification. God's raising him from the dead showed acceptance of Christ's sacrifice. If God left Jesus in the grave, then the sacrifice was not accepted and no one has received cleansing from sin. The condemnation for sin is death (Romans 6:23). To still be under condemnation means that all people will be given the ultimate penalty for their sins.

15:18-19 Christians carry with them, even through persecution and death, the promise of eternal life with God. Yet if Christ was never raised from the dead, and if there is no hope of resurrection, then **all who have died believing in Christ have perished!** Paul pointed out the silliness of the argument—**if we have hope in Christ only for this life, we are the most miserable people in the world.** If the only promise of the Christian faith applies to this life, then why believe in it? Why believe in a faith that brought—in this culture and even still in many places in the world—persecution, sorrow, death, ostracism, separation? Without the resurrection, there would be no hope for final judgment and justice or hope for a final dwelling place with God. If the end is the same for everyone, why not live like the pagans in sensual pleasure (15:32)?

15:20 However, the above argument is moot because **the fact is that Christ has been raised from the dead.** The hypothetical "if" statements in the previous verses concede to the certain facts of history. Christians may indeed face difficulty, but the fact of the Resurrection changes everything. Because Christ was raised from the dead, **he has become the first of a great harvest of those who will be raised to life again.** Christ was the first to be raised to never die again. He is the forerunner for those who believe in him, the proof of their eventual resurrection to eternal life.

15:21-22 Death came into the world as a consequence of the sin of one man, **Adam** (Genesis 3:17-19). Adam sinned against God and brought alienation from God and death to all humanity. All human beings are **related to Adam** and have

two characteristics in common: they are sinners; and they will die. Adam's sin brought condemnation and death to all; Christ's sinless sacrifice and resurrection brought **resurrection from the dead** to **all who are related to Christ** through accepting his sacrifice on their behalf. Those who believe in him **will be given new life.**

15:23 Paul wanted to clarify, however, that **there is an order to this resurrection.** It had not already happened, as perhaps some of the false teachers were claiming. Rather, **Christ was raised first.** The "harvest" will be taken in when **Christ comes back** at his second coming. At that time, **his people,** those who believed in him as Savior, **will be raised** from death to eternal life.

15:24-25 At the time of Christ's second coming, **the end will come,** and the resurrected Christ will conquer all evil, including death. (See Revelation 20:14 for words about the final destruction of death.) At Christ's resurrection, Christ began the destruction of Satan and all his dominion. At the resurrection of the dead, all Satan's power will be broken. Christ **must reign** because God has ordained it so; what God has said cannot be changed. Christ will reign as the ultimate ruler, having put **all his enemies beneath his feet.** This phrase is used in the Old Testament to refer to total conquest (see Psalm 110:1). Because the resurrection of Christ is an accomplished fact and because the promise of the resurrection is a future fact, the promise of Christ's ultimate and final reign can be trusted as fact and anticipated by every believer.

15:26 Death is every living being's **enemy,** the common fate of all humanity. Death is the last enemy that always wins. But Christ will destroy death! At the Cross and through the Resurrection, Christ has already defeated death. Yet people still die. For those who believe in Christ, however, death is merely a doorway into eternal life.

15:27 As noted in 15:24-25, the one ultimately in charge is God the Father. This verse sounds very much like Psalm 8:6, **"God has given him authority over all things."** God gave the Son supreme authority over everything, except God himself.

15:28 When the Son has toppled all evil powers and when God has placed everything under the Son's feet, **the Son will present himself to God.** "God" here refers to "God the Father." No one can take God's place, not even the Son. This must happen **so that God will be utterly supreme over everything everywhere.** Some have used this verse to attempt to prove the inferiority of Christ (that he was not equal with God). But this verse is not about the person, nature, or being of God (his essence) as it relates to

Christ. Instead, this verse is speaking of the work or mission of Christ, whereby he willingly obeyed the Father by subjecting the government of the world first to himself, then symbolically and willingly placing it under God's control. In these words, Paul was not attempting to take the three persons of the Trinity and decide their relative importance. Their essential nature is always one and the same; however, the authority rests through the work each has accomplished. God sent the Son; the Son will finish the work and then will turn redeemed humanity back over to God.

15:29 To further emphasize his point about the fact of the resurrection, Paul returned to his conditional "if" clauses. **If the dead will not be raised, then what point is there in people being baptized for those who are dead?** Apparently, some believers had been baptized on behalf of others who had died unbaptized. Nothing more is known about this practice, but it obviously affirms a belief in resurrection. Corinthian believers may have been practicing a sort of vicarious baptism for the sake of believers who had died before being baptized. The "dead" certainly referred to those who had come to faith, not to unbelievers who had died, or Paul would have condemned the practice. Paul was not promoting baptism for the dead; he was continuing to illustrate his argument that the resurrection is a reality. Paul's apparent lack of concern over this situation probably means that the practice was basically harmless. Paul could have written disapprovingly of this practice, but pointing out the glaring inconsistency of their rejecting the afterlife while baptizing for the dead was sufficient. Paul had deeper theological issues to straighten out—at this point, the fact of the resurrection. If there is a resurrection, then all believers will be raised (and all who truly believed will be saved whether they have been baptized or not). If there is no resurrection, however, as some had contended, then why bother with this ritual?

15:30-31 If there is no resurrection, why should the apostles risk their lives, **facing death** for the sake of

the gospel message. Why would any sane person do this for the sake of a gospel that only ends in death, just like anything else? This constant danger **is as certain as** Paul's **pride in what Christ** had done for the Corinthians. Despite all that Paul had to correct and rebuke in them, he genuinely loved the Corinthian believers and boasted of their faith.

15:32 The human enemies that Paul had faced in **Ephesus** had been as vicious as **wild beasts** (see Acts 19). **If there will be no resurrection from the dead,** then **what value was there in** standing up for his faith against those in Ephesus who wanted to kill him (Acts 19:31)? Why bother standing for anything at all? If there is nothing more to look forward to than simply to one day die and return to dust, then why deny oneself? Instead, it would make far more sense for everyone to **feast and get drunk** (see also Isaiah 22:13). Life with no meaning leaves one with the need to simply indulge oneself and get all one can for enjoyment here and now.

15:33 Those who denied the resurrection could not possibly be true believers, for this entire chapter explains why the resurrection is central to the Christian faith. Paul told the Corinthian believers not to **be fooled** by those who denied the resurrection. The quote is from a proverb in a comedy by the Greek playwright Menander, titled *Thais*; it was used by Paul to make a point to his Greek audience. The bit of worldly wisdom, **"bad company corrupts good character,"** means that keeping company with those who deny the resurrection will corrupt true believers and hurt the testimony of the church.

15:34 Paul's final words about this issue were simply that the Corinthians should **come to** their senses. To deny the resurrection amounted to **sinning,** for it denied the truth of the claims of Christ and the promises of God. It was to their **shame** that some among them did not **even know God.** To not understand and believe the doctrine of the resurrection meant to not understand anything about God, for the doctrine is central to all that God has done for sinful humanity.

THE RESURRECTION BODY / 15:35-58

Our present bodies have been wonderfully designed for life in this world, but they are perishable and prone to decay. In a sense, each person lives as a prototype of his or her final body version. Our resurrection bodies will be transformed versions of our present bodies. Our spiritual bodies will not be weak, will never get sick, and will never die. The very possibilities inspire anticipation, excitement, and praise to the God who can do all things!

15:35-37 Paul had already argued for the truth of the resurrection. Those who might still be skeptical

may have further questions about this resurrection, so Paul asked two such questions himself in order to answer them: (1) **How will the dead be raised?** (2) **What kind of bodies will they have?** To Paul, these were **foolish** questions. The answers should have been obvious from nature itself. Paul compared the resurrection of believers' bodies with the growth in a garden. A seed placed into the ground - **doesn't grow into a plant unless it dies first.** The plant that grows looks very different from the seed because God gives it a new "body." New bodies will not be obtained until the earthly bodies have died. And those new bodies will be different from the present bodies.

15:38-39 There are different kinds of bodies— for people, animals, fish, birds. Paul was preparing the foundation for his point that bodies before the resurrection can be different from bodies after the resurrection.

15:40-41 Furthermore, the **heavenly bodies** (the sun, moon, and stars) differ greatly from **earthly bodies.** Each kind of body has its own kind of substance created and controlled by God. Each is appropriate to its sphere of existence, and each has its own kind of **glory** or radiance. God made many different types of bodies; certainly he can arrange and govern the existence of the resurrection body.

15:42-44 Like a seed that is sown and then grows into a glorious new plant, **it is the same way for the resurrection of the dead.** Believers' present physical bodies will be different from their resurrection bodies. First, **earthly bodies die and decay,** but **resurrected** bodies **will never die.** Death eventually takes everyone. Those raised with Christ, however, will have bodies that will live forever. Physical bodies **disappoint us,** but resurrection bodies **will be full of glory.** Physical bodies are **weak** but resurrection bodies will **be full of power.** Physical bodies are **natural** and **human,** but resurrected bodies **will be spiritual.**

The "natural" body is suited to life in the present world; however, such a body is not fit for the world to come. That future world, where Christ will reign in his Kingdom, will require a "spiritual" body. Paul did not mean that this will be "spiritual" as opposed to physical or material, for that would contradict all that Paul has just written about resurrected bodies. Believers will not become "spirits." Instead, "spiritual" refers to a body that suits a new, spiritual life.

15:45 Paul quoted **the Scriptures** to point out the difference between these two kinds of bodies. Genesis 2:7 speaks of **the first man, Adam,** becoming **a living person.** Adam was made from the dust of the ground and given the breath of life from God. Every human being since that time shares the same

characteristics. However, **the last Adam, Christ, is a life-giving Spirit.** Just as Adam was the first of the human race, so Christ is the first of those who will be raised from the dead to eternal life.

15:46-47 People have **natural** life first; that is, they are born into this earth and live here. Only from there do they then obtain **spiritual** life. Paul may have been contradicting a particular false teaching by this statement. He illustrated this point by continuing that **Adam, the first man, was made from the dust of the earth, while Christ, the second man, came from heaven.** Christ came as a human baby with a body like all other humans, but he did not originate from the dust of the earth as had Adam. He "came from heaven."

15:48-49 Because all humanity is bound up with Adam, so **every human being has an earthly body just like Adam's.** Earthly bodies are fitted for life on this earth, yet they have the characteristics of being limited by death, disease, and weakness (15:42-44). Believers can know with certainty, however, that their **heavenly bodies will be just like Christ's**—imperishable, eternal, glorious, and filled with power (15:42-44). At this time, all are **like Adam;** one day, all believers will be **like Christ** (Philippians 3:21; 1 John 3:2).

15:50 The resurrected bodies have to be different from these present, physical bodies because **flesh and blood cannot inherit the Kingdom of God.** These bodies cannot go into God's eternal Kingdom because these present bodies were not made **to live forever**—otherwise they would. So God has prepared new bodies that will live forever. The resurrection is a fact; new bodies ready for life in eternity is also a fact.

15:51-52 With great emphasis Paul passed on to these Corinthians a **secret**—knowledge given to him by divine revelation from Christ. The phrase **not all of us will die** means that some Christians will still be alive at the time of Christ's return. They will not have to die before they get their new resurrection bodies. (For further discussion of these new bodies, see 2 Corinthians 5:1-10.) Instead, they **will all be transformed,** immediately (see 1 Thessalonians 4:13-18). A **trumpet** blast will usher in the new heaven and earth. Christ will return, the dead **will be raised** out of the graves **with transformed bodies.** Those still alive **will be transformed,** also receiving their new bodies. This change will happen instantly for all Christians, whether they are dead or alive. All will be made ready to go with Christ.

15:53 Because "flesh and blood cannot inherit the Kingdom of God" (15:50), and because Christians are promised eternal life in God's Kingdom, then their present **perishable earthly bodies must be transformed into heavenly bodies that will never die.** Each person will still be recognizable, will still be the person God created him or her to be, but each will be made perfect with a body that will be able to live forever in the Kingdom.

15:54-55 The ultimate enemy of every human body is **death.** For those who have no hope in Christ, death is the end of everything. Christians have been given an entirely different perspective. For believers, death is not the end; it is merely a doorway into eternal life. Most Christians will experience death; some who are alive at the time of Christ's return will not themselves face death but will have known plenty who did. But **when our perishable earthly bodies have been transformed into heavenly bodies that will never die,** then the final victory over death will have been accomplished. Death was defeated at the resurrection of Christ, but total victory over death will not be accomplished until human beings—made from the dust of the earth, just like Adam—are given bodies that defy death. When this happens, **the Scriptures will come true.** Paul quoted from Isaiah 25:8 and Hosea 13:14— God's promises that one day death itself will no longer carry **victory** or **sting** because death will be no more (Revelation 21–22).

15:56-57 If it were not for **sin,** then there would be no **sting that results in death.** If it were not for **the law,** then sin would have no **power.** But the law declares sin, and the wages of sin is death (see Romans 6:23; 7:7-20). Because the law set standards that cannot be reached, all people are condemned as sinners. For those who have not had their sins pardoned at the cross of Christ, death is not a passage to eternal life but an enemy with a terrible "sting." It is not annihilation or nothingness, it is the doorway to judgment. But those who have come to Christ as Savior have been given **victory over sin and death.**

15:58 Because of these promises—of future resurrection, of living eternally in the Kingdom, of preparation for that Kingdom with new bodies that will be fashioned by God himself—believers have motivation and responsibilities for life now lived in their perishable bodies. The time on earth is valuable—we have much work to do for the Kingdom. Others must be invited to join; believers must be taught to grow in the Lord. Nothing done for the Lord **is ever useless.** So believers should **be strong** in their faith, not wavering or doubting; they should be **steady,** not listening to the whims of false teachers; and **always enthusiastic about the Lord's work,** serving him to the utmost, knowing that great reward awaits.

1 CORINTHIANS 16

THE COLLECTION FOR JERUSALEM / 16:1-4
Paul had just said that no good deed is ever in vain (15:58). In this chapter, he mentions some practical deeds that have value for all Christians. The Corinthians had been asked to join with Christians in other areas to support the church in Jerusalem. Paul could hardly have found a more practical example of the unity of the body of Christ (12:12-13) than in his desire that all the churches give to help a suffering body of believers.

16:1 The words **now about** indicate that this was another topic about which the Corinthians had asked (see also 7:1; 8:1; 12:1). Paul must have spoken or written to them earlier about this, so that they knew they would be giving and to whom. Their questions apparently focused on how to go about collecting the **money for the Christians in Jerusalem.**

The Christians in Jerusalem were suffering from poverty. While the reason is unknown, it may have had to do with a famine, such as the one mentioned in Acts 11:28-29 when the believers in Antioch had sent help to the church in Jerusalem. That collection had been carried by Paul himself and Barnabas (Acts 11:30). Apparently, the Jerusalem church was still suffering, so Paul continued to collect money from other churches to send to Jerusalem (see Romans 15:25-31; 2 Corinthians 8:4; 9:1-15). Paul advised the Corinthian believers to **follow the same procedures** that he had given **to the churches in Galatia.** This collection was a widespread effort involving many of the churches.

16:2 The first procedure that the Corinthian believers should implement right away was to ask each person (or family) to **put aside some amount of money**. This was to be done **on every Lord's Day**. Some have suggested that this offering was to be kept at home, but Paul's mention of setting it aside on Sunday (the day when the believers met together for worship—see Acts 20:7) probably means that the believers were to bring the amount that had been set aside that week and place it in a special **offering** at church. That offering, in turn, would be held until Paul's arrival. Paul stipulated that everyone must give (**each of you**); no one was exempt. But he did not stipulate how much everyone should give; instead, each should give **in relation to what** he or she had earned. By implementing this plan, the money would be ready and waiting whenever Paul arrived (which at this point was still an uncertain date), and they would not have to **try to collect it all at once.**

16:3-4 To further distance himself from the offering, Paul suggested that the Corinthian church **choose** their own **messengers to deliver** the **gift to Jerusalem**. These men are listed in Acts 20:4. Paul would **write letters of recommendation** for those messengers, so that when they arrived at the Jerusalem church their mission would be heralded by Paul himself and the church could readily welcome them. Paul might end up traveling with them if it seemed **appropriate.**

PAUL'S FINAL INSTRUCTIONS / 16:5-18
As the Corinthians awaited Paul's next visit, they were directed to be on their guard against spiritual dangers, stand firm in the faith, behave courageously, be strong, and do everything with kindness and in love. This list could be called a Christian's job description. Today, as believers await the return of Christ, they should follow the same instructions.

16:5-7 Paul was writing this letter near the end of his three-year ministry in Ephesus. It may have been tempting for Paul to take the next ship across the Aegean Sea from Ephesus to Corinth in order to deal with the problems and squelch those who said he was avoiding them (4:18); however, Paul explained that he would indeed visit with them after passing through **Macedonia** (see Acts 20:1-2). In the meantime, he would send Timothy (4:17; 16:10) and Titus (2 Corinthians 7:13). But when he did arrive, he would **stay** with them for a time, perhaps even spending the entire **winter** there. These were not the words of a man afraid to deal with the problems in Corinth. He would **stay awhile** if the Lord permitted it. Paul made plans, but he always knew that at any moment God could intervene and make changes. Paul would go wherever God sent him (16:6).

16:8-9 Paul was writing from **Ephesus** and wanted to stay there until **Pentecost**. That meant that Paul was planning to stay well into the spring in Ephesus, travel through the summer in Macedonia (16:5), and then spend the winter in Corinth (16:6). Paul wanted to go to Corinth, but he had pressing work in Ephesus and knew that he needed to be there to take advantage of **a wide-open door for a great work** there. Oddly enough, Paul also wanted to stay in Ephesus because of many who were opposing him. Who these were is unknown, although Acts 19 gives a clear picture of the opposition he faced in Ephesus. Paul was not afraid of the opposition; instead, because God had opened the door, Paul would stay to complete the ministry God had given.

16:10-11 As Paul was writing, **Timothy** (and another believer named Erastus) were traveling ahead of him through Macedonia (Acts 19:22). Paul expected Timothy to also arrive ahead of him at Corinth (4:17). Paul respected Timothy and had worked closely with him (Acts 16:1-3; Philippians 2:22; 1 Timothy 1:2). Although Timothy was young, Paul encouraged the Corinthian church to welcome him because he was **doing the Lord's work.** With all the problems that had been brewing in the Corinthian church, Paul wanted to make sure that young Timothy would be treated with **respect.** Paul stated that Timothy should be accepted by the churches in the same way that they would accept Paul himself. After Timothy stayed among the Corinthians for a while, they should send him back to Paul **along with the other brothers.** The identity of these men is unknown, although one of them may have been Erastus, who had been sent along with Timothy on this particular trip (Acts 19:22). Paul knew of the tensions in the church and had sent Timothy to remind the church of his instructions in case any animosity toward him would spill over to Timothy. Paul did not want Timothy to be mistreated.

16:12 Another question posed by the Corinthians had to do with **Apollos.** Perhaps they wondered about Apollos and wanted him to come and visit. He had preached in Corinth, was doing evangelistic work in Greece (Acts 18:24-28). He **was not willing** to go to Corinth right away, but he would do so when he had the chance. Perhaps Apollos's reluctance had to do with the factions in the Corinthian church (1:12; 3:4-5) and a desire not to make the problem any worse. Paul could "send" Timothy, but he could only urge Apollos, who apparently worked independently of Paul although preaching the same message (3:5-6; 4:1).

16:13-14 Paul's final words to the church in Corinth sum up what he has written in this letter.

- They were to **be on guard,** constantly watchful for spiritual enemies that might slip in and threaten to destroy them, whether it be divisions (1:10-17; 11:18), pride (3:18-21), sin (5:1-8), disorder (14:40), or erroneous theology (15:12).
- They needed to **stand true** to what they believed—the gospel that had brought them salvation (15:1-2).
- They had to **be courageous** so that they could stand against false teachers, deal with sin in the congregation, and straighten out the problems that Paul had addressed in this letter.

- They should **be strong** with the strength given by the Holy Spirit.
- They should do everything **with love** (13:1-13), because without love, they would be no more than prideful noisemakers.

16:15-16 Stephanas and his household were mentioned in 1:16 as people whom Paul had baptized. Paul held them up as an example of Christian living. Exactly what they were doing is unknown, but Paul made it clear that they were **spending their lives in service to other Christians.** These people were examples to the rest of the believers in Corinth, exhibiting practical Christian faith.

16:17-18 Stephanas himself had come to Ephesus to see Paul, along with two other men, **Fortunatus** and **Achaicus,** who are mentioned only here. These men may have delivered the letter that contained all the questions that Paul had been answering (see 7:1). These words give a glimpse into Paul's genuine joy at being able to commune with other believers. These men were **a wonderful encouragement** to Paul as representatives of the larger congregation. Paul wanted them to be treated with **proper honor** as well. They had taken time to serve the church by finding Paul and getting the answers to questions so that the church could deal with some difficulties. These men's concern for the church in Corinth was honorable indeed.

PAUL'S FINAL GREETINGS / 16:19-24

As Paul had traveled across the Roman Empire, he started churches in many cities. Although far apart geographically, the churches were united in their relationship to Jesus Christ, and Paul emphasized this unity each time he would send greetings from one church to another.

16:19 The phrase **the churches here in the province of Asia** would have referred to the Roman province of Asia located in what is now part of Turkey. There were churches in Ephesus (Ephesians 1:1), Colosse, Laodicea, and Hierapolis (Colossians 1:2; 4:13, 16).

Paul also sent greetings from **Aquila and Priscilla.** The church in Corinth would have known this married couple, for they had lived in Corinth. Both were tentmakers (or leatherworkers) whom Paul had met during his stay in Corinth (Acts 18:1-3). Aquila and Priscilla had followed Paul to Ephesus and had lived there with him, helping to teach others about Jesus. They even risked their lives for Paul, although the exact event is unknown (Romans 16:3-5). The great preacher Apollos, whom so many of the Corinthian believers admired, had been taught the Christian faith by this couple (Acts 18:26).

Apparently, Aquila and Priscilla had opened their home **for church meetings.**

16:20 Finally, Paul sent greetings from all the **other believers.** To **greet each other in Christian love** was encouraged by Paul to help break down the divisions in this church.

16:21 Usually Paul would dictate his letters to a scribe, and often he would end with a short note in his own handwriting (see also Galatians 6:11; Colossians 4:18; 2 Thessalonians 3:17; Philemon 1:19). This is similar to adding a handwritten postscript (PS) to a typewritten letter. It assured the recipients that false teachers were not writing letters in Paul's name (as apparently had been a problem—see 2 Thessalonians 2:2; 3:17). It also gave the letters a personal touch.

16:22 Paul had addressed many problems in this letter, hoping to help the believers straighten out their attitudes and actions and then to bring them back in line with the truth. Some of the problems existed because of pretenders in the church, people who did **not love the Lord.** Paul's final word for such people is that they be **cursed.** The word means to be placed under God's wrath (see also commentary on 12:3). These words were written in Paul's own handwriting (16:21), adding emphasis to these serious words toward any who would attempt to hurt the church of God.

As always, Paul's focus was on the coming Kingdom, so he added the Aramaic word *maranatha* (translated for modern readers as **"Our Lord, come!"**). Paul never wanted believers to forget that this was what they were looking forward to and working toward.

16:23-24 As Paul began this letter (1:3), so he ended it. Paul's final prayer was for **the grace of the Lord Jesus** to remain with them. Paul often ended his letters this way, asking his readers to continue to experience God's undeserved kindness and love every day of their lives and then to pass along that grace to others.

Although this had been a difficult letter to write, with many issues to be handled and sins to be corrected, Paul closed by reaffirming his **love** for these believers **in Christ Jesus.** Through Christ alone they had all been saved from the darkness and brought into the light; through him alone they had been joined together in his service. Paul loved these believers, cared for them, prayed for them, and longed to see them.

2 CORINTHIANS

INTRODUCTION

Educational background, personal experience, completed projects, satisfied customers, special qualifications—people list a variety of credentials to prove their competency and reliability. Credentials are important. Before hiring a plumber or entrusting your life to a surgeon, you want to make sure the crucial person is well qualified. Not to do so would be foolish or irresponsible. But credentials can seem superfluous, especially in a close relationship. You probably wouldn't ask a friend for proof of his reliability, nor would you ask a relative for references. You know the person well, and that's good enough.

It comes as a surprise, then, to find Paul presenting his credentials to the believers at Corinth. He had lived among them, had led many of them to Christ, and had established the church in that important Greek city. But false teachers had infiltrated the church and were trying to undermine his authority. They questioned his apostleship and veracity, especially considering the harsh words of his previous correspondence.

So Paul reiterated his qualifications, refuting phony preachers (2:17), false teachers (3:1), and false apostles (11:5, 13) in the process. This was awkward for Paul, but it was necessary to regain the Corinthians. Paul cared for the church, and he knew it was vital that they follow his Spirit-led instructions.

Second Corinthians reveals the heart of a concerned pastor. Paul had heard of the Corinthians' problems. They had even sent him a delegation with questions about church order. With concern similar to a father who is sending his son to college for the first time, Paul wrote a long letter that he hoped would put the Corinthian church on track. He had invested so much of himself into them that he couldn't bear to see the church disintegrate over petty matters and lax discipline.

As you read 2 Corinthians, consider what you would say to counteract the lies of false teachers today, using the power and authority of this inspired letter and the rest of God's word.

AUTHOR

Paul (Saul of Tarsus): Pharisee, apostle, pioneer missionary of the church.

Second Corinthians is, for the most part, an autobiographical letter. In it, Paul described to the Corinthians the details of his recent missionary trip. The letter includes intriguing specifics about Paul's life, such as the time he faced his imminent death in Asia Minor (1:8-10) and his irritating "thorn in the flesh" (12:7). These explicit details substantiate the fact that Paul wrote 2 Corinthians, for no other person could provide such an intimate portrait. Furthermore, in

2 Corinthians, Paul made the concept of God's grace central (God's grace in Paul's preaching—1:12; God's grace to the Corinthians—9:8, 14; God's grace in Paul's weakness—12:9) as he did in his other well-known letters (see, for example, Galatians 1:6). For these reasons, no one has effectively challenged Paul's authorship of 2 Corinthians.

Although Paul's authorship has gone unchallenged, scholars have debated whether 2 Corinthians is actually one letter. Because of the fluctuations in tone and word choice, some Bible commentators have asserted that 2 Corinthians is actually two, three, or even four letters placed together by an editor. In their zeal to divide 2 Corinthians, these scholars have overlooked the overall consistency of the letter. As just mentioned, grace remains a central theme of the letter. Furthermore, there is a focus throughout on Paul's authority to preach the gospel (for example, 1:3-23; 2:14-17; 10:1-18) and his sufferings for the cause of Christ (for example, 6:3-13; 11:16-33). The obvious changes in tone in 2 Corinthians can be explained without suggesting that the book is actually a series of letters. For instance, a change in tone could reflect a lengthy pause in Paul's writing, at which time he received additional information on the state of the Corinthian church.

Second Corinthians can be viewed as a single, unified letter written by Paul to a troubled and divided church. The church at Corinth needed both encouragement to continue doing what was right and exhortation to discipline those who were still misleading people in the congregation. Second Corinthians is a passionate letter from a pastor who was extremely concerned about his congregation. Paul rejoiced in the triumphs of his congregation, but he expressed sorrow over the problems that persistently plagued them.

For more about Paul, see the Author section in the Introduction to the book of Romans.

DATE AND SETTING
Written from Macedonia around A.D. 55–57.

In this letter, Paul repeatedly stated that he was writing from Macedonia (7:5; 8:1; 9:2). The exact city is unknown, but the subscriptions on some manuscripts of 2 Corinthians read "written from Philippi." (The subscriptions were comments inserted at the conclusion of ancient letters.) There is no way to verify whether Paul was actually at Philippi, however; and this location has been questioned by a number of scholars.

What is known for certain is that Paul was in Macedonia. This region—along with Corinth in Greece—was evangelized on Paul's second missionary trip. Congregations were established in Philippi, Thessalonica, Berea, and Athens. On his third missionary journey, Paul stayed in Ephesus for over two years. During that time he wrote 1 Corinthians. After the riot at Ephesus (Acts 19:21-41), Paul traveled through Asia Minor and into Macedonia, encouraging the congregations he had established on his second missionary journey. In Macedonia, Paul experienced severe persecution, the type of hardship the churches in that region were already experiencing (see 2 Thessalonians 1:3-12 for Paul's earlier encouragement of a Macedonian church to stand firm in the faith in the face of persecution). In Macedonia, however, Paul's thoughts were not only on the horrible conditions there (see 1:8-9; 7:5) but on the spiritual battles the Christians at Corinth were fighting. Titus, Paul's assistant, was supposed to meet him in Troas with the news from Corinth. Somewhere in Macedonia, they got together. There Titus delivered a mixed report. The church in Corinth had obeyed Paul's earlier directives to discipline some of its members, but at the same time some were questioning his authority (by delaying his visit, 1:12-24, and by not confronting them in person, 10:1).

Thus, in Macedonia—in the middle of troubles and difficulties—Paul wrote this letter to the divided congregation at Corinth. He praised the believers for their obedience, but he also reasserted his authority to preach the gospel to the Gentiles. Paul warned them that he was on his way to Corinth. Then he sent Titus ahead with the letter to prepare the congregation for his visit (8:16; 13:1-3). When Paul finally did make it to Corinth, he stayed in that region for three months (see Acts 20:1-3).

AUDIENCE
The church in Corinth. (See the Audience section in the Introduction to 1 Corinthians.)

OCCASION AND PURPOSE
To affirm Paul's ministry, defend his authority as an apostle, and refute the false teachers in Corinth.

Every letter has a context. A mother in her letter to a daughter may allude to the girlfriend they were discussing in the previous letter. The same is true for letters preserved in the Bible. Second Corinthians is no exception. To understand 2 Corinthians, it is useful to understand the long and complicated relationship between Paul and Corinth, a relationship that has taken some time for scholars to unravel. In fact, some of the details surrounding Paul's painful visit (2:1) and his severe letter to the Corinthians (2:1-4; 7:8) are still debated by scholars. It is possible, however, to sketch an outline of Paul's difficult relationship with the Corinthians.

1. *Evangelizing Corinth.* On Paul's second missionary journey, Paul traveled into what is known today as Greece. After a cold reception by the philosophers and thinkers who gathered in Athens, Paul went on to Corinth (Acts 18). Initially, Paul worked with Aquila and Priscilla as a tentmaker. But eventually he received enough financial support from Macedonian Christians to preach the gospel full-time. After being rejected by many of the Jews, Paul focused his missionary work on the Gentiles and stayed with the Gentile God-fearer Titius Justus. In a vision one night, God encouraged Paul to keep on preaching in Corinth (Acts 18:9-11), so he stayed for a year and a half (A.D. 50–52).

2. *Paul's stay at Ephesus.* Around A.D. 52, Paul left Corinth to report back to his home church in Antioch and the elders in Jerusalem (Acts 18:18-22). On his next missionary journey, Paul made his headquarters at Ephesus, at the lecture hall of Tyrannus (Acts 19:8-10). There, he preached for a little over two years. Evidently, he sent many of his students to the surrounding region, for Luke reported in Acts "that people throughout the province of Asia—both Jews and

Greeks—heard the Lord's message" (Acts 19:10). It was at Ephesus that Paul wrote several letters to the Corinthians.

3. *The first letter to the Corinthians.* Around this time, Paul wrote his first letter to the Corinthians. This is the letter to which Paul alluded in 1 Corinthians 5:9. Evidently the letter warned the Corinthians not to associate with those who called themselves Christians and yet persistently participated in sexual immorality (1 Corinthians 5:9-13). Although some scholars consider 6:14–7:1 to be a fragment of that letter, most believe that this letter was not preserved.

4. *The second letter to the Corinthians.* Toward the end of his stay at Ephesus (around A.D. 54–55), Paul wrote his second letter to the Corinthians, known today as 1 Corinthians. Earlier Paul had received a letter from the Corinthian church delivered by Stephanas, Fortunatus, and Achaicus (1 Corinthians 16:17). This letter had been filled with questions about church order. In 1 Corinthians, Paul answered these questions. The questions involved Christian marriage (1 Corinthians 7:1), food sacrificed to idols (1 Corinthians 8:1), spiritual gifts (1 Corinthians 12:1), and the collection of money for the relief of Christians in Jerusalem (1 Corinthians 16:1). In addition to these questions, Paul addressed a number of concerns arising from the unofficial report from Chloe's household. In particular, he was concerned with the reports of incest (1 Corinthians 5:1), lawsuits between members of the church (1 Corinthians 6:1), and drunkenness, gluttony, and arguments at the Lord's Supper (1 Corinthians 11:17-22).

5. *Paul's painful visit.* Shortly after sending 1 Corinthians, Paul most likely visited Corinth himself. The situation with the church concerned him so much that he traveled there to rectify the problems that had emerged. According to what can be gathered from 2 Corinthians, Paul's authority was challenged by a particular church member (perhaps leading others) during this visit. In response, Paul warned the church to discipline its immoral members before he had to do it himself (see 2:1; 12:14, 21; 13:1-4).

6. *The severe letter to the Corinthians.* After this painful visit, Paul wrote a "severe letter" to the Corinthians, evidently encouraging the Corinthians to discipline their errant member and/or members (see 2:1-4; 7:8). Most Bible commentators consider this letter to be Paul's third letter to the Corinthians, which is now lost. It has become generally accepted that 1 Corinthians was not the "severe letter," primarily because 1 Corinthians as a whole does not reflect the extreme sorrow that Paul described as being behind his severe letter.

7. *The fourth letter to Corinthians.* In A.D. 55, Paul left Ephesus for an evangelism trip to Troas (Acts 20:1-6). Evidently, he was supposed to meet Titus there in order to receive a report on the Corinthian church. Although there were some promising opportunities to share the gospel in Troas, Paul went on to Macedonia to find Titus because of his concern about the spiritual condition of the Corinthians (2:12-13). He met Titus somewhere in Macedonia and heard the good news that the Corinthians had disciplined the offender just as Paul had instructed (2:5-11; 7:2-16). Titus gave Paul a report that was, on the whole, encouraging (2:14; 7:5-7). However, other problems were surfacing in Corinth. Many were grumbling about Paul—the fickleness of his travel plans (1:12–2:4) and whether he truly possessed the authority of an apostle (3:1-18).

Paul wrote his fourth letter, 2 Corinthians, to encourage the Corinthians in their obedience (7:8-15), to defend his own authority (10:1-18), and to refute the false teachers that were still among them (11:1-15). In this letter, he revealed his earnest concern for the Corinthians. False teachers were trying to steal them away from Christ's teaching and from Paul himself. With a passion unmatched in any of his other letters, Paul revealed his entire life to the Corinthians. Even though he was reluctant to do so, he paraded his suffering for the cause of Christ as his official credential as Christ's ambassador to them (6:3-13). Would the Corinthians open their hearts to him, the person who had told them about Christ in the beginning? That was Paul's fervent plea (6:13). If they didn't remedy the problems in their church, Paul warned that he would come to do so himself (13:1-10). But his wish was to build them up in Christ instead.

MESSAGE

Second Corinthians begins with Paul reminding his readers of (1) his relationship to them—Paul had always been honest and straightforward with them (1:12-14), (2) his itinerary—he was planning to visit them again (1:15–2:3), and (3) his previous letter (2:4-11). Paul then moves directly to the subject of false teachers (2:17), and he reviews his ministry among the Corinthians to demonstrate the validity of his message and to urge them not to turn away from the truth (3:1–7:16). Paul then turns to the issue of collecting money for the poor Christians in Jerusalem. He tells them how others have given, and he urges them to show their love in a tangible way (8:1–9:15). Paul then gives a strong defense of his authority as a genuine apostle while pointing out the deceptive influence of the false apostles (10:1–13:10).

The main themes in the book of 2 Corinthians include: *Trials, Church Discipline, Hope, Giving,* and *Sound Doctrine.*

Trials (1:3-11; 2:1-11; 6:1-13; 12:1-10). Paul experienced great suffering, persecution, and opposition in his ministry. He even struggled with a personal weakness—a "thorn in the flesh." Through it all, Paul affirmed God's faithfulness. Despite the pain, he trusted in his loving Father and stayed true to his call.

IMPORTANCE FOR TODAY. God is faithful. His strength is sufficient for any trial. When trials come, they keep us from pride and teach us dependence on God. He comforts us so we can comfort others. When persecuted or pressured, it is easy to lose heart or to doubt. When struggling with pain, it is easy to question God's goodness. Like Paul, however, we must focus on God's faithfulness and love and then persevere. Regardless of what you are going through, God is with you. Keep focused on him and his love.

Church discipline (2:1-17; 5:11-21; 7:2-16; 10:1-18; 11:1-33; 12:1-21; 13:1-4). Paul defended his role in church discipline. And because of mounting opposition to his leadership, Paul presented his credentials as an apostle of Christ. Neither immorality nor false teaching could be ignored, so Paul hit the issues head-on. The church was to be neither lax nor too severe in administering discipline. The church was to restore the corrected person when he or she repented.

IMPORTANCE FOR TODAY. The goal of all discipline in the church should be correction, not vengeance. For churches to be effective, they must confront and solve problems, not ignore them. In everything, we must act in love. We must also beware of those who would rationalize sinful behavior or unjustly criticize spiritual leaders. We must clearly present God's word, live by it personally, and hold the church to it corporately. If you are a church leader, don't neglect church discipline, but do so with care. Also, submit yourself to the discipline of your church.

Hope (3:7-18; 4:1-18; 5:1-10). To encourage the Corinthians as they faced trials, Paul reminded them that they would receive new bodies in heaven. This would be a great victory in contrast to their present suffering. This world is not the final home of the believer. What a profound and life-changing truth.

IMPORTANCE FOR TODAY. To know we will receive new bodies offers us hope. No matter what adversity we face, we can keep going. Our faithful service will result in triumph. We must also resist becoming too tied to this world and its values. Hope can be found *only* in Christ. That's our salvation and our message. Find your hope in Christ. In him and him alone is life.

Giving (8:1-24; 9:1-15). Paul organized a collection of funds for the poor in the Jerusalem church. Many of the Asian churches gave money. Paul explained and defended his beliefs about giving. And Paul was not shy about asking for money, as he urged the Corinthians to give generously and follow through on their previous commitment.

IMPORTANCE FOR TODAY. God's work should be supported by his people. In addition, believers should take the lead in helping the needy, feeding the hungry, and curing the sick. Like the Corinthians, we should follow through on our financial commitments. Our giving should be generous, sacrificial, according to a plan, and based on need. Our generosity not only helps those in need but enables them to thank God. Give generously to support your local church and God's work all over the world. And look for ways to reach out to needy folks in your community.

Sound Doctrine (6:14-18; 7:1; 13:5-14). False teachers were challenging Paul's ministry and authority as an apostle. So Paul listed his credentials and asserted his authority in order to preserve correct Christian doctrine. His sincerity, his love for Christ, and his concern for the people were his defense.

IMPORTANCE FOR TODAY. We should share Paul's concern for correct teaching in our churches. But in so doing, we must share his motivation—love for Christ and people. For us, sound doctrine begins with a study of the Bible, God's word.

OUTLINE OF 2 CORINTHIANS

I. Paul Explains His Actions (1:1–2:11)
II. Paul Defends His Ministry (2:12–7:16)
III. Paul Defends the Collection (8:1–9:15)
IV. Paul Defends His Authority (10:1–13:13)

2 CORINTHIANS 1:1–2:4

GREETINGS FROM PAUL / 1:1-2

This letter was probably one of the more difficult letters for Paul to write. Although Paul wanted to rejoice with the Corinthians in their spiritual growth, he didn't shrink from asserting his authority and disciplining those who needed it.

1:1 It was appropriate for **Paul** to mention his apostleship here, for his authority is a major theme of this letter. A group of false apostles (11:13) had infiltrated the Corinthian church. This distressed Paul greatly because he had founded the church himself on his second missionary journey. To gain a foothold in Corinth, these false apostles had systematically discredited Paul's missionary work. Paul wrote 2 Corinthians to defend his apostolic authority and to refute the false teachers and their accusations.

An **apostle** was "sent forth" by **Christ Jesus** with the mission to make disciples in his name (Matthew 28:18-20). The disciples—the Twelve who followed Jesus during his earthly ministry, learning from him and witnessing his miracles—became the apostles. Yet Paul was also included among the apostles because he had been **appointed by God** to preach the Good News to the Gentiles (Acts 9:15). This call gave Paul the authority to establish churches throughout the known Mediterranean world and to teach the believers who gathered in these churches. Paul's apostleship was confirmed by the apostles in Jerusalem (Acts 9:28), and his message was confirmed at the Council of Jerusalem (Acts 15:1-21).

Timothy was Paul's assistant. He had grown up in Lystra, a city in the province of Galatia. Paul had visited Galatia on his first missionary journey (Acts 14:8-21). During that trip, he most likely met Timothy's mother, Eunice, and his grandmother, Lois (2 Timothy 1:5). On his second visit to Lystra, Paul asked young Timothy to travel with him (Acts 16:1-5).

In 1 Corinthians, Paul not only informed the Corinthians that Timothy would come to them, he also endorsed Timothy's message (1 Corinthians 4:17). It becomes clear in 2 Corinthians that the Corinthian church—or some group within the church—had rejected Paul's authority, so some scholars have suggested that Timothy was

the one who was rejected. It is significant, therefore, that Paul mentions Timothy at the outset of his letter as a **brother** in Christ—a person on an equal level, instead of a subordinate. Paul may have done this to bolster Timothy's authority among the Corinthians.

Paul founded the **church in Corinth** around A.D. 50 on his second missionary journey. The core of this church was a group of Gentiles who would gather at Titius Justus's house to hear Paul preach. For more information on the city and church in Corinth, see the Audience section in the Introduction. Paul addressed this letter not only to the Corinthian church, but also **to all the Christians throughout Greece** because he viewed Corinth as the center of Christianity for that province. Paul would make it clear to every Christian in that region what his stance was with respect to the controversial issues in the Corinthian church. Furthermore, Paul wrote this letter with general spiritual principles in mind. Paul's passionate defense of his apostolic authority (10:1-18) and his eloquent comparisons of the new covenant to the old covenant (2:12–3:18) could benefit all Christians.

1:2 This was the standard greeting Paul used in his letters, and a Christian adaptation of the common letter-writing practice of his day. **Grace** is God's undeserved favor. God's graciousness is preeminently shown by the fact that he sent his own Son, Jesus Christ, to die on the cross. The Greek word for **peace** is based on the common Hebrew greeting *shalom* meaning well-being, wholeness, and inner tranquillity. For Paul, Christ's death on the cross was the only event that restored true peace.

By identifying **God** and the **Lord Jesus Christ** together, Paul was asserting that both the Father and the Son had granted these wonderful gifts of grace and peace. Paul was pointing to Jesus as a full person in the Godhead.

GOD OFFERS COMFORT TO ALL / 1:3-11

Paul would typically begin a letter by thanking God for the believers to whom he was writing. In 1 Corinthians, Paul praised God for giving the Corinthians spiritual gifts of eloquence and knowledge. But in 2 Corinthians, Paul had no praise for the Corinthians. In its place, however, he did not blame them; rather, he tried to encourage them.

1:3 All praise was owed only to the **God** who had sent Jesus to die on the cross for our salvation. Paul used the Greek word for **Lord**, which means "master" or "owner," with the name **Jesus**, to express Jesus' complete authority over believers. **Christ**, on the other hand, was the Greek word for "Messiah." Thus Paul was identifying Jesus as both his Master and the promised Messiah of the Old Testament. God was the **Father** of Jesus in the sense that Jesus had come from God the Father, not that Jesus had been created by God the Father.

Paul had dramatically experienced God's **mercy** in his recent travels through Asia. God alone is the **source.** This sentence was probably recited by the believers in their churches. That God **comforts** people means he encourages them. The word does not imply that God rescues his people from every discomfort but that he gives them the tools, the necessary training, and the essential guidance to endure the problems of this life.

1:4 Paul had an extremely difficult letter to write to the Corinthians. Although they had not necessarily been hard-pressed by external persecution, the Corinthian church had gone through a lot of internal dissension. God would **comfort** the Corinthians through these difficult times. When the troubles passed and the Corinthians emerged faithful, then they would be able to **comfort others** who needed the **same comfort.** Trials are never easy. But it is through trials that God can shape and mold our character. Often, it is only through trials that we can learn about God's loving care for us.

1:5 Paul expected to **suffer,** just as Christ had suffered on this earth, enduring the ultimate humiliation—a criminal's death on a cross (John 19:19-37). Jesus had warned his disciples that they could expect the same (John 15:20). His warning was an apt one, for the early church experienced strong opposition and persecution. It was clear to Paul that God doesn't protect his people from suffering. According to Paul, suffering—especially trials and discomfort associated with the advancement of Christ's Kingdom—is God's way of allowing Christians to become more like Jesus (Philippians 1:29; 3:10). Peter agreed with Paul: Christians should rejoice when they suffer, for in their own suffering

they will in some small way experience what it meant for Jesus to suffer for their sins (1 Peter 4:12-13). In the midst of difficulties, Christians can be confident that God is present. He knows their pain, and would **shower** his people **with his comfort through Christ.** Such comfort will help believers persevere through any hardship.

1:6 This letter relates Paul's own suffering for the cause of the gospel in order to remind the Corinthians of their unity with Paul as a fellow Christian. Paul and his fellow travelers had been **weighed down with troubles,** but this resulted in the Corinthians' **benefit and salvation.** Because Paul and his fellow travelers had been comforted by God, they could **be an encouragement to** the Corinthians. This life will bring suffering and trials, but Christians should encourage the suffering person. And when the sufferer perseveres, that person will gain renewed insight, which will enable that person to encourage others who experience similar difficult situations. Then those people **can patiently endure the same things.**

1:7 Paul knew the Corinthian church was struggling and **suffering,** but his confident hope was that their struggles were for the cause of the gospel, just as he was struggling for the advancement of the gospel in Asia Minor. Their steadfastness to the gospel of truth and their perseverance through difficulties would enable them to **share God's comfort**—a reward that was worth the agonizing struggle.

1:8-9 Next, Paul moved from the general principle—that God encourages Christians in their trials—to his particular situation. He didn't explain to the Corinthians the details about what happened to him in **Asia,** only that it involved fearing for his life. Commentators have suggested a number of different scenarios: (1) Paul was afflicted with a serious illness, perhaps loosely connected to his "thorn in the flesh" (see 12:1-10). (2) Paul was imprisoned in Ephesus, an event to which Paul might have been alluding when he wrote of fighting "wild beasts in Ephesus" (see 1 Corinthians 15:23-31). (3) Paul had feared for his life during the riot instigated by the Ephesian silversmiths (see Acts 19:31).

Of course, Paul's trials stemming from the

Ephesian riot is the most documented of the three possibilities. This very well could have been the life-threatening situation to which Paul was referring, but this is not certain. Paul and his companions **thought** they **would never live through it** for they were **crushed and completely overwhelmed.** Their despair was real and so deep that they **expected to die.** No person could save them. Paul's only hope was in God. Through their despair, they **learned not to rely** on anyone **but on God who can raise the dead.** God's power to raise from the dead was a doctrine some of the Corinthians were doubting (see Paul's extended explanation of the doctrine of the resurrection in 1 Corinthians 15:1-56). In 2 Corinthians, Paul repeatedly emphasized the temporary nature of human existence (4:16; 5:1) in order to highlight the importance of the Christian hope in eternal life. Without a confident hope in the resurrection, the Christian faith would be useless (see 1 Corinthians 15:14).

Paul wrote that any amount of suffering is worth enduring, for suffering makes God's people realize that God is the only One on whom they can rely. If suffering in your life produces nothing more than a fervent dependence on God and a renewed prayer life, then in God's eyes the suffering may have been well worth the pain.

1:10 God, who holds the ultimate power between life and death, had rescued him. His prayer was answered. The same God who raised Jesus Christ from the dead delivered Paul and his companions **from mortal danger.** God had not only protected them from death, but he had also given them the courage to trust that he would **continue to deliver** them in the future. Just like Paul, we should recount the times God has rescued and delivered us in the past.

1:11 Paul showed an untiring belief in the effectiveness of intercessory prayer. Often he would ask churches to pray for him (see Romans 15:30-32; Ephesians 6:18-20). Here Paul thanked the Corinthians for **praying for** them. Reports of the suffering of Paul and his companions had driven the Corinthians to prayer. In response to their prayers, God had delivered them and, no doubt, would **rescue** them yet. Past deliverance gave Paul the opportunity, in turn, to write a letter to share the news, which would strengthen the Corinthians to face any difficulties they might encounter. This type of reciprocity was what Paul was trying to illustrate with his recent trial. There is no such thing as a self-reliant Christian. The whole church is inextricably joined together in its spiritual growth toward God. Because God had delivered him, Paul could encourage the Corinthians to **give thanks to God because** their **prayers for** the **safety** of Paul and his companions had been answered. The Corinthians' praise would inspire many others and teach them of God's faithfulness.

PAUL'S CHANGE OF PLANS / 1:12–2:4

After praising God for the comfort the Lord had shown him in his most recent trials, Paul started to explain his most recent travel plans to the Corinthians. In 1 Corinthians, Paul had told the Corinthians that he would visit them after traveling through Macedonia (see 1 Corinthians 16:5-7). Since that time, he had altered his travel plans. He planned to visit Corinth twice, stopping there first before traveling through Macedonia and then again on his way back east (see 1:15-16). Paul made the first of these two visits. But since this visit was extremely "painful," Paul decided not to return to Corinth immediately. Instead, he most likely went straight to Ephesus from Macedonia. There, he wrote a letter to address the difficult issues that the Corinthian church had to handle (see 2:3).

1:12 With **confidence and a clear conscience,** Paul could say that he and his companions had been **honest and sincere.** Paul did not want to bring reproach on the gospel with his behavior. For this reason, he was extremely careful. Paul tried to be completely sincere, and he tried to act in a way that was beyond criticism. In this way, he would draw attention to the truthfulness of his message instead of to his own behavior. In addition to his conduct, Paul pointed to the rea-

son for his good behavior and the source of his teaching: It did not come from **earthly wisdom,** but from **God's grace.** Paul had already delineated the difference between human wisdom and God's wisdom in 1 Corinthians. Although most people look either for eloquent speeches or awe-inspiring signs to authenticate the truth of a message, God chooses to use foolish and weak messengers to shame the wise with his powerful message of truth (1 Corinthians 1:18–2:14). Paul wasn't relying on his own wisdom and knowledge when he visited Corinth with the truth of the gospel. Instead, he was relying on God's enabling power—something that should have been clear to all the Corinthians.

1:13-14 Apparently, the Corinthians were questioning Paul's sincerity. Some in the church were claiming that he wrote one thing and then said another (see 10:9-10). Here Paul defended his sincerity, especially his honesty in his previous letters. If the Corinthians were not convinced of his genuine intentions, Paul could only **hope**— that is, confidently expect—that his sincere intentions would be revealed **when our Lord Jesus comes back again.** On that day, Paul expected that his actions and words would be shown for what they were: blameless and true. Indeed, the genuineness of the Corinthians' faith would be a matter of great joy for Paul on that day. They would be able to **be proud** of having had Paul as their teacher, and he would then be proud having had them as his converts.

1:15-16 Paul had based his travel plans on his confidence that the Corinthians were taking pride in him, just as he was in them (see 1:14). He had made a quick, unscheduled visit to Corinth. But when he had arrived, he had found quite a different atmosphere at that church. At least a portion of its members had rejected him and repudiated his authority. Paul would later call this a "painful visit"—one that caused a breach in the Corinthians' intimate relationship with him (see 2:1). This "painful visit" was quick because Paul had to hurry on to visit the churches in Macedonia. But while he was in Corinth, he had promised to visit the Corinthians on the way back.

Paul changed his travel plans, however. Instead of visiting Corinth on the way back through Macedonia and Achaia (present-day Greece), Paul most likely sailed directly to Ephesus. Paul had made his original plans thinking that the church had solved most of its problems. When the time came for Paul's scheduled trip to Corinth, however, the crisis had not been fully resolved (although progress was being made in some areas; see 7:11-16). So Paul wrote a letter instead (2:3-4; 7:8). He believed that another visit would only make matters worse. The fact that Paul first made an unscheduled visit and then canceled his second scheduled visit to Corinth gave his opponents another reason to criticize him.

1:17 Paul's change of plans had given his accusers at Corinth reasons to complain about his conduct—and even to criticize his authority. By criticizing him for his erratic travel plans, Paul's

opponents were implying that he couldn't be trusted. If Paul couldn't be trusted, then how could they believe his message?

The allegation that Paul was no different than the **people of the world** meant that he was no more reliable than anyone else. A worldly person governed by pure self-interest and selfish desires would say yes when it was convenient, but then renege on that promise when some other better opportunity afforded itself. Paul's opponents at Corinth had used Paul's own sharp distinction between the world and the Spirit against him. They had labeled his actions as being motivated by the world's standards. This accusation was in direct contradiction to Paul's own claim in 1 Corinthians that his preaching was not from himself or any other human authority but from the Spirit of God (see 1 Corinthians 2:4). Labeling his actions as coming from worldly reasoning was a direct assault on Paul's spiritual authority. These serious accusations circulating in Corinth were the reason why Paul had to write 2 Corinthians. In essence, this letter is a passionate defense of Paul's apostolic authority and the truth of his message.

1:18-19 Instead of immediately answering his opponents' criticisms of his behavior, Paul addressed the fundamental problem at Corinth: The believers in Corinth were questioning the veracity of Paul's message to them. Paul clearly saw what was at stake. Questioning the motives and honesty of the messenger would eventually lead to questioning the truth of the message. Instead of defending himself, Paul reminded the Corinthians of God's faithfulness. He does not waver **between yes and no.** All of God's promises concerning the Messiah, or the Savior of Israel, were fulfilled in Christ. Thus **he is the divine Yes.** Jesus is the embodiment of God's faithfulness. If Jesus had proved himself faithful, then Jesus' appointed messengers—Paul, **Timothy,** and **Silas**—would certainly be faithful and trustworthy. Paul had shown his faithfulness as a messenger of Christ by not wavering in his preaching. The fact that Paul consistently preached Christ—as he had with them—meant he would be trustworthy in the smaller things—such as travel plans.

1:20 This verse reiterates Paul's point: **all of God's promises have been fulfilled in** Christ. His earthly ministry is an example of God's faithfulness to his people. God had promised he would provide a Savior, and he did. Christ obediently and faithfully said "yes" to God and his great promises.

The Hebrew word **Amen** conveys a firm agreement with what has been said. The Israelites used this word to express their agreement to God's law and its blessings and curses (see Deuteronomy 27:15). In this verse Paul explained why Christians use the word. It is the way Christians acknowledge that Jesus has fulfilled all of God's promises. Jesus is the great "Amen" (Revelation 3:14) because he has been faithful to God. When Christians say "Amen," they are joining Jesus in saying "Yes" to God. By doing this, Christians everywhere bring **glory** to God. They give God the proper respect and honor that he deserves. With this type of reasoning, Paul made it clear that his own integrity stood on Christ's integrity because his message was consistently Christ's gospel.

1:21-22 In these two verses, Paul described how he, his coworkers—Timothy and Silas—and the Corinthians themselves were all tied together. They had all received the **Holy Spirit,** an indication they all belonged to God through Christ.

These verses use four key terms to describe how God made them all part of his family. The first, **stand firm,** is derived from legal terminology. In the first-century Mediterranean world, this was a technical word for a legal guarantee that would confirm a sale as valid. Paul used the word to express that it is God himself who guarantees the salvation of those who believe in Jesus. Having the guarantee or confirmation of God Almighty would be the best security a person could ask for—especially since the Lord God had already proven his faithfulness to his promises in the life of Jesus Christ.

The second refers to all the believers being **commissioned** (literally, "anointed"). In the Old Testament, prophets, priests, and kings were anointed to signify their commission to be representatives of God to the Israelites (see Exodus 28:41; 1 Samuel 15:1; 1 Kings 19:16). The Holy Spirit comes upon believers making them God's representatives to the world.

Third, God **identifies** his people **by placing the Holy Spirit in** believers' **hearts.** God himself has given us his mark of ownership when he gave his Spirit to live in us (see Paul's use of this word in Ephesians 1:13; 4:30).

Finally, Paul described the Spirit as **the first installment of everything** God will give us. This "installment" is like a down payment that a buyer will give a seller to declare the intent of paying the full amount. God gives his Spirit to his children as a down payment. It is only a foretaste of the glorious joy they will experience in heaven—the full payment that God has promised.

With these four key terms, Paul reiterates again and again to whom he, along with the Corinthians, belongs. These four assurances are the basis for a believer's certainty that he or she is saved and will live with God forever in heaven. It is the Spirit of God, not a Christian's works, that guarantees a believer's salvation.

1:23 This verse has a common legal expression, **I call upon God as my witness,** that was used to summon a witness to a trial. In other words, Paul was subpoenaing God. Since no other person could testify to his motives, Paul was appealing to God as a witness that Paul was **telling the truth.** Paul saw his whole life—including his innermost thoughts—as an open book to God.

In this case, Paul wanted to make it clear that his decision to cancel his second visit to Corinth had been made out of consideration for the spiritual welfare of the Corinthians. He hadn't made the decision for selfish reasons, as his opponents had claimed (1:17). His motive had been to **spare** the Corinthians the sorrow that another visit would produce. Apparently, Paul wanted to give the Corinthians time to resolve some of the problems that had surfaced on his last visit.

1:24 This verse protects Paul from any misunderstanding with the Corinthians by explaining what he meant by "sparing them a severe rebuke" in his previous statement. Paul wasn't acting as a judge or governor over the Corinthians' **faith** in Christ. Paul couldn't give them their faith—that is, their confident belief in God and in Jesus, their Savior—much less control it. Their faith was a gift from God (Romans 12:3; Ephesians 2:8), not subject to anyone's control except God's. In this respect, the Corinthians were subject to no one except the ultimate Judge (Romans 14:1-4). As a result of this gift of faith, the Corinthians were to **be full of joy** and **stand firm.** Paul wasn't their taskmaster. Instead, he was a fellow worker, pointing out how they could experience the joy God wanted to give them. This is a potent image for any spiritual leader—from a pastor to a Sunday school teacher. A spiritual leader should be less of a master and more of a friend—a person who works along with others and gives them joy.

2:1-2 From the two letters that have been preserved—1 and 2 Corinthians—we know that the Corinthians not only had problems with incest (1 Corinthians 5:1-2) and adultery (1 Corinthians 6:9), but they were also troubled by incessant arguing (1 Corinthians 1:10), disruptions during the worship service (1 Corinthians 11:17-22), and even lawsuits between believers (1 Corinthians 6:1-8). Moreover, a group of false teachers were preoccupied with criticizing Paul's actions and authority (11:1-11). Apparently, on Paul's last visit, a member of the Corinthian church had publicly challenged Paul (2:5). Paul issued a severe warning to those who were persistently sinning in the church (13:2). On his last visit, apparently the problems had not been dealt with, and their time together had been **painful**. Paul decided not to visit the Corinthians again because he didn't want to cause unnecessary sorrow. He had already rebuked the church on his last visit (13:2). He wanted to give them more instruction on how to correct some of the abuses in the church (see Paul's description of his letter in 2:3-4), but he also wanted to give them some time to resolve the issues amongst themselves, for their faith would ultimately stand on God—not on Paul or his efforts to reform them (see 1:24). Appropriately, Paul gave the Corinthians some time to work out what putting their faith in action meant.

2:3 The identity of Paul's **last letter** has been a subject of much scholarly debate. Traditionally, the letter Paul referred to here was considered 1 Corinthians. Proponents of this theory identified the sinner who Paul forgave in the next passage (2:5-11) with the incestuous man of 1 Corinthians 5:1-5.

However, it has become generally accepted that 1 Corinthians is not the "last letter," primarily because 1 Corinthians as a whole does not reflect the extreme sorrow described by Paul in these following verses. Furthermore, the details described in the next passage (2:5-11) do not seem to fit the situation with the incestuous man of 1 Corinthians 5:1-5 but instead someone who had personally offended Paul on his last trip to Corinth (see 2:5). For these reasons, many Bible commentators consider the letter referred to in this verse to be lost. Apparently, Paul wrote this severe letter to the Corinthians

soon after his "painful visit" with them. In this lost letter, he had exhorted the Corinthians to discipline their errant members—specifically, the ones who were publicly opposing his authority (see 2 Corinthians 2:1-4; 7:8). God, according to his sovereign plan, preserved all of Paul's letters he wanted to include in the Bible—God's inspired Word. According to his plan, this letter was not preserved for later generations to read and study.

This verse reiterates that Paul's own **joy** depended on the spiritual condition of the Corinthians. The first part of 2 Corinthians emphasizes the interdependence of Paul and the Corinthians—the community of faith that existed between them (see 1:11-14). Paul's own spiritual success was intimately connected with the Corinthians' spiritual success. This verse (2:3) again emphasizes that the Corinthians provided part of Paul's motivation. In fact, their strong faith and their **happiness** was one of the reasons he could courageously face the trials of an evangelist (see 7:4).

2:4 Paul passionately expressed how he felt when he wrote **that letter**. Although he was sorry that his letter would **hurt** the Corinthians, he had sent it anyway. In 7:8-12, Paul explains his reasons in more detail. His severe reprimand in this letter was aimed at securing a change of heart in the Corinthian believers. He knew it would cause much sorrow, but he was hoping that it would lead to repentance. That is why Paul claimed here that his motive was **love**. Sometimes the most loving action a person can do for a fellow Christian is to confront him or her with the truth. The truth often hurts. Confronting a person in the wrong with the truth, however, can be the best thing a friend can do.

2

2 CORINTHIANS **2**:5-11

FORGIVENESS FOR THE SINNER / 2:5-11

After explaining in general terms why he had delayed his visit to Corinth (see 1:12–2:4), Paul addressed the specific confrontation that most likely had led to his decision to cancel his visit. Paul doesn't name the offender who had caused the trouble the last time he was in Corinth, but he does instruct the church on how to handle this man. It was essential that the church act quickly to forgive and restore this man, while he was still repentant. Church discipline should always seek the restoration of the offender. Two mistakes in church discipline should be avoided—being too lenient by not correcting mistakes and being too harsh by not forgiving the sinner. There is a time to confront and a time to comfort.

2:5 These verses emphasize that the reason Paul was concerned about this man's offense was not to correct an injury Paul had suffered. The man had **hurt** the **entire church** far more than he had offended Paul. Most likely, the offender's actions had amounted to a direct attack on Paul's apostolic authority. The teachings of the "false apostles," who had infiltrated the Corinthian church and had started discrediting Paul's authority, might have inspired this man to challenge Paul's authority in public (see Paul's censure of these "false apostles" in 11:1-15). Paul would perceive this not only as an attack on his authority but also an insult to the entire church, which had been founded on the gospel message that Paul had delivered to them.

Paul's concern in all of this was to assure the Corinthians that he wasn't trying to defend himself. This wasn't a personal vendetta; instead, it touched on the foundations of the Christian faith. The distinction expressed in this verse should be made in churches today. Personal agendas or preferences should not block the clear proclamation of the gospel. But when an issue touches on the authority of Jesus or the truth of the gospel, that issue must be taken seriously, for it affects the life of the entire church. We, too, need to muster the courage to pass judgment on quarrelsome, selfish ambition in our churches, just as Paul did in the first century (see Philippians 2:3; James 3:14).

2:6 Apparently, the majority of the Corinthians had realized that tolerating this man and the sin he encouraged would ruin the congregation. They couldn't function as the holy people of God with such a rebel among them. It is not clear what action the Corinthian church took against this offender. The main point is that **most** of the believers in the church **were united in judgment against** this man. This united front showed the man the seriousness of his sin and, no doubt, helped lead him to repentance.

2:7-8 Evidently, the reproof that the Corinthians had meted out was sufficient. The offender had realized the seriousness of his actions. Paul was extremely concerned that the Corinthians **forgive** and **comfort** the offender at the appropriate time so he would not **become so discouraged** that he couldn't **recover.** Paul's image here was of the disciplined person drowning in sadness. Paul wasn't concerned for his own vindication in this distressing incident but instead for the offender's spiritual welfare. Then the believers should **show** that they **still love him.**

Knowing the appropriate time to rebuke and the appropriate time to forgive is the key to compassionate church discipline. This type of discernment is cru-

cial for a church plagued with problems, as the Corinthian church was. Christians in positions of authority must consistently check their motives when it comes to church discipline. They must ask: Am I keeping the spiritual welfare of my church members—especially that of the offender—in mind?

2:9 Paul reiterated his reason for writing the severe letter to the Corinthians. First of all, he hoped the letter would rectify the troublesome situation before he arrived (see 2:3). When he visited them, he wanted to encourage them in their faith instead of correcting them. Second, he wanted to **find out how far** they **would go in obeying** him.

Later in 2 Corinthians, Paul unequivocally will assert his authority as an apostle to punish disobedience. He had been empowered by Christ with apostolic authority (10:4-6). But Paul's authority didn't involve commanding obedience to himself but, instead, to Christ and the gospel. When Paul defended his apostolic authority to the Corinthians, he was careful to explain that he possessed the authority to build up the church, not to tear it down (see 10:8; 13:10).

The good news was that the Corinthians were obedient to the gospel. Titus's report from Corinth revealed that they had listened to Paul's rebuke and had obeyed his instructions. Their complete obedience in these matters caused Paul to rejoice (7:13-16).

2:10-11 The word for **forgive** is derived from the Greek word for "grace." For Paul, forgiveness was the central point of the gospel. It is only through God's grace—that is, his undeserved favor—that anyone is saved at all (Ephesians 2:5, 8). So the Corinthians' forgiveness of the offender among them was fundamentally based on Christ's forgiveness of them (Ephesians 4:32; Colossians 3:13).

This verse downplays Paul's own part in the entire incident. Since the offense was primarily directed against Paul (see 2:5), he should have been the first to pronounce forgiveness. Instead, he emphasized that it was the Corinthians who should forgive. He would merely agree with their verdict. In this way, he was reiterating the point that the offense had been against the entire church, not merely himself (see note at 2:5). In downplaying his own authority in this situation, Paul was pointing to the ultimate **authority: Christ** himself. It was before Christ that the church would forgive the offender, and it was before Christ that Paul—hundreds of miles away—would forgive the same offender. In this way, **Satan** would not **outsmart them.**

Paul spoke of Satan more in his letters to the Corinthians than in any other of his New

Testament letters. He saw the telltale signs of a demonic attack on the church at Corinth. Second Corinthians unambiguously identifies the "false apostles" in the Corinthian church with the clever deceptions of **Satan** (see 11:14). Moreover, Paul identifies Satan as the one who was tempting some in the church into sexual immorality (see 1 Corinthians 5:1-5; 6:12-20) and others to participate in the idolatrous feasts of their pagan neighbors (see 1 Corinthians 10:18-22).

This passage identifies another one of Satan's evil schemes. In their zeal to purge sin from the church, the Corinthians could punish the offender without keeping in mind the purpose of discipline: to inspire repentance and promote reconciliation to God. Under Satan's influence, the offender's sorrow could easily be turned into resentment (see 2:7) instead of repentance. Paul pleaded with the Corinthians to guard against such a tragic outcome.

2 CORINTHIANS 2:12–3:18

MINISTERS OF THE NEW COVENANT / 2:12–3:6

Paul spent the first two chapters of 2 Corinthians chronicling his ministry. He had suffered severe affliction in Asia (1:8-10). Criticism of his integrity plagued him in Corinth (1:17-20). The situation was so bad that some person had publicly confronted Paul during a visit. In response, with sorrow and tears, Paul had to write a stern letter of warning (2:1-4). Then, because he was plagued with concern over Titus's welfare and the status of the Corinthian church, Paul had to pass over a definite opportunity to preach the gospel in Troas (2:12-13). Most missionaries would hesitate to write such a report to their supporters. Opposition, conflict, and distress faced Paul at every turn. Paul interrupted this sad tale with a burst of heartfelt praise. One of the clear emphases of 2 Corinthians is God's ability to transform suffering and weakness into victory for the gospel.

2:12 Troas was a large seaport on the Aegean Sea, ten miles away from the well-known, ancient city of Troy. It was near the straits of Dardanelles, which led to the Black Sea. Paul had visited this bustling seaport on his second missionary journey. He most likely had met Luke, the author of Luke and Acts, at that time. In this city, Paul had a vision of a Macedonian man asking him to share the gospel with him. Paul took this as a sign from God and immediately went to Philippi, a prominent town in Macedonia (see Acts 16:9-10). But Paul is not referring to this visit to Troas in this letter. Paul wrote 2 Corinthians on his third missionary journey, not his second. Apparently, while Paul was traveling through Asia Minor on his third missionary journey, **the Lord** gave him **tremendous opportunities** to preach the gospel.

2:13 This is the first time that Paul mentioned Titus's role in the complex relationship between Paul and the Corinthians. As it becomes clear in this letter, **Titus** played a crucial role in reconciling Paul and the Corinthians (see also 7:6, 13-14; 8:6, 16-17, 23; 12:18). Titus was a Greek

convert whom Paul greatly loved and wholeheartedly trusted (Galatians 2:3). For more information on Titus, see the Introduction to the book of Titus.

Paul had already sent Timothy to Corinth, where, apparently, Timothy had run into some difficulties. So after being personally and publicly challenged during his visit to Corinth, Paul had sent Titus with his severe letter. Apparently, Titus had the courage and resolve to go to this rebellious church with a letter from Paul commanding them to correct the abuses in their church. Paul was anxiously awaiting word on how his stern letter had affected the troublesome situation in Corinth. This was the same letter that he had cried over (2:4), so it was natural that he **couldn't rest** until Titus arrived back **with a report** from Corinth. Uncharacteristically, Paul abandoned an opportunity for evangelism at Troas because he was so troubled about the situation in Corinth. Apparently, Paul had made some arrangements to meet Titus in Troas. But when Paul couldn't find him there, he **went on to Macedonia to find him.**

2:14 In a Roman **triumphal procession,** a Roman general would drive his captives and the spoils of war before him down the main thoroughfare of Rome. He would be greeted by the loud cheers of Roman citizens, and a cloud of incense would be burned for the gods as they paraded to the temple of Jupiter. To the Romans, the aroma was the sweet smell of victory. To the captives in the parade, it was the smell of abject slavery and perhaps even death.

Though it is clear that this verse alludes to this Roman practice, the exact nature of Paul's analogy has been widely disputed. It is unclear whether Paul was implying that Christians are victorious partners with Christ or whether he was implying that they are God's willing captives. Some commentators insist that **leads us along in Christ's triumphal procession** means that Christians are like the Roman soldiers being led by the victorious general. These commentators point to the context of the passage. Paul was emphasizing God's power to triumph over Paul's weaknesses. The triumph was God's and the gospel's. Other commentators insist that this means "to lead someone as a captive in a procession." As such, Paul was comparing himself and all Christians to the captives in a Roman triumphal procession. He, along with all Christians, were former enemies of God. Hence, when Christians become believers, God takes them as captured enemies. In the final analysis, the general meaning seems to be that Christ will eventually triumph over all evil. No opponent, setback, or weakness can stop Christ's victory. It has already been accomplished on the cross. The triumphal procession of Christ is on its way.

2:15-16 These verses expand the analogy of the Roman processional incense, burned to the god Jupiter. But Paul's Jewish readers, steeped in Old Testament language, would immediately recognize Paul's language as being similar to Leviticus 23:18, where the burnt offerings are said to be an aroma pleasing to the Lord.

Unlike these settings, where physical smells were presented to God (or in the Roman case, to Jupiter), Paul told the Corinthians that the holy **lives** of Christians **are a fragrance presented by Christ to God.** In addition to being something that pleases God, a holy life dedicated to God brings glory to him. Through Christians (**those being saved**), the precious aroma of God's grace is spread throughout the world. When Christians preach the gospel message, however, it is good news to some (**life-giving perfume**), but **to those who are perishing,** it is the **fearful smell of death and doom.** Those who are being drawn by the Spirit immediately recognize the life-giving power

of the message. Those who stubbornly refuse to believe, however, smell something foul—the judgment of death that awaits them.

The answer to the rhetorical question posed here, **"Who is adequate for such a task as this?"** is not entirely clear. The implied answer may be that no one is competent for the task. God was the One who commissioned Paul (Acts 9:1-22) and empowered him to be an ambassador to the Gentiles (Galatians 2:7; Ephesians 3:8); he made Paul competent for the enormous task of preaching the gospel (3:5; 1 Corinthians 15:10).

2:17 In reality, no one is competent to preach the gospel message. God did not need anyone's professional services. No one could claim to be qualified for the task of handling God's truth. Paul saw these high-priced preachers as mere **hucksters** preaching **to make money.** It is obvious from 1 Corinthians that Paul did not object to preachers earning a living wage for their work in sharing the gospel. He had gone to great lengths to defend the right of preachers to ask for money in 1 Corinthians 9:3-10. On the other hand, Paul himself passed up that right. He strove to present the gospel free of charge in order to show his **sincerity.**

3:1 Just as people use résumés today to introduce themselves to a prospective employer, in Paul's day traveling preachers and evangelists introduced themselves with **letters of recommendation** from various churches. Paul had written letters of recommendation on behalf of Phoebe (Romans 16:1-2) and Timothy (1 Corinthians 16:10-11). These letters helped Paul's trusted companions and friends find a welcome in various churches.

Apparently, some false teachers had started using letters of recommendation to gain a speaking platform in the Corinthian church (see 11:13-15). These traveling hucksters of the Word of God, as Paul called them (2:17), had come to Corinth with these letters—perhaps authentic, perhaps forged— and were asking the Corinthians to recommend them to other churches. The letters gained for them hospitality from members of other churches, an opportunity to speak, and even reimbursement.

Apparently, some of these false teachers had begun to criticize Paul's authority by subtly asking if he had presented any letters of recommendation. Justifiably, Paul was annoyed that he would have to explain his apostolic credentials to the church he had founded.

3:2-3 In a clear and forceful way, Paul stated that he did not need any letters. The changed lives of the believers to whom he and his companions had preached were **recommendation** enough. Any discipleship program should be judged by the quality of those who have been discipled. With the statement, **your lives are a letter written in our hearts,** Paul might have been trying to express his own participation in the lives of the Corinthians (a theme of this letter, see 1:6-7, 11; 2:5-6). As an evangelist to them, Paul was inextricably intertwined with them. Their success was his; their sorrows were also his. In this way, their lives of faith were etched in his heart and the hearts of his coworkers, Silas and Timothy. Just as the **lives** of the Corinthians were an open book to all, the intimate connection between the Corinthians and their founder, Paul, was manifest to all. So anything that the Corinthians did would also reflect on Paul and his ministry, and vice versa.

If the Corinthians were Paul's letter of recommendation, then this letter was from **Christ** himself. In contrast to the false teachers at Corinth, Paul's ministry was authorized by Jesus. Paul's letter of recommendation had been written by Christ himself. This "letter" of Christ had been delivered by Paul and his coworkers; they were messengers for God and his glorious Good News of salvation. It was **written not with pen and ink, but with the Spirit of the living God** on the hearts and lives of those who believed. The Holy Spirit, who was working in the Corinthians' hearts and was a guarantee of the Corinthians' glorious inheritance in heaven, affirmed the authenticity of Paul's message.

Next, Paul compared this letter from Christ written on the Corinthians' hearts to the Ten Commandments written by the finger of God on **stone.** Paul's point is clear: The signs of the Spirit's work in a person's life are superior to any kind of writing, whether it was a church's recommendation or the law of God etched on stone (see Exodus 31:18). The imagery of writing **on human hearts** comes from the prophet Ezekiel. This Old Testament prophet had predicted that one day God himself would remove Israel's heart of stone and replace it with a heart of flesh, a heart that would follow God's decrees because God himself had written his law on it (Jeremiah 31:33; Ezekiel 36:26-27). Paul was declaring to the Corinthians that the day Ezekiel had predicted had come. The Holy Spirit was writing God's law on their hearts and changing them on the inside.

3:4-5 Paul did not want to have anything to do with vain boasting (see 3:1; 5:12; 10:18). Yet he expressed his confidence and assurance (see 1:15; 5:6, 8) in his own ministry, not because of his own eloquence or sophistication, but because **God through Christ** had commissioned Paul as an apostle on the Damascus road (see Acts 9:15-19).

Paul had asked who was competent (or adequate) for the task of preaching the Good News (2:16). In this verse, Paul answered his own question: Only those who are called by God will have **power** and **success.** This might have been a slight snub to Paul's opponents in Corinth. They had boasted of their wisdom (see 1 Corinthians 2:1), their eloquence (11:6), their superior Jewish ancestry (11:12), and, as it has become clear in this passage, their letters of recommendation. In contrast, Paul refused to boast in himself. Instead, he boasted in Christ's strength, which had become evident through his weaknesses (11:30) and the trials he had endured for the cause of Christ (11:16-27; see also Ephesians 3:7-8; 1 Thessalonians 2:4; 1 Timothy 1:12, 14).

3:6 God had **enabled** Paul and his companions to **represent** the **new covenant.** This is one of the two times that Paul used the Greek words for "new covenant." The other reference to the new covenant is Paul's quote of Jesus' words concerning the "cup of the new covenant" (1 Corinthians 11:25). Most likely, Paul was using the terminology of Jeremiah 31:31-33 in this passage. The prophet Jeremiah spoke of a new covenant when God would write his law on his people's hearts (see 3:2).

This verse ends with a short adage—**the old way ends in death; in the new way, the Holy Spirit gives life.** "The old way" refers to the Old Testament Scriptures, the summary of the law of Moses. Paul's letter to the Romans shows that Paul unequivocally denied that following the law can achieve salvation. Instead, the law only makes people conscious of their sin, the sin that ultimately leads to death (Romans 2:29; 3:19-20; 6:23; 7:6). Trying to be saved by keeping Old Testament laws will end in death. Only by believing in the Lord Jesus Christ can a person receive eternal life through the Holy Spirit. No one but Jesus has ever fulfilled the law perfectly; thus, the whole world is condemned to death. Under the new way, eternal life comes from the Holy Spirit. The Spirit gives new life to all who believe in Christ.

THE GLORY OF THE NEW COVENANT / 3:7-18

Paul recalled the stone tablets on which God had written the old covenant. He identified the law, although lethal, as nonetheless glorious because it is God's provision and proof of his intervention in the life of his people. But that which was summarized on stone is nowhere near as glorious as what is yet to come. The Spirit creates a new life in us. He is the Holy Spirit who was present at the creation of the world as one of the agents in the origin of life itself (Genesis 1:2). He is the power behind the rebirth of every Christian and the one who helps us live the Christian life.

3:7-8 Paul used the story of the giving of the Ten Commandments to illustrate the difference between his ministry and the ministry of Moses. The story can be found in Exodus 34:29-35. After receiving the Ten Commandments written by God himself, Moses came down from Mount Sinai with the tablets. Although Moses did not realize it, his **face shone with the glory of God.** When Moses returned to the Israelite camp, the people saw his radiant face and were afraid to approach him. Moses called the people to gather around him so he could tell them all that God had commanded them to do, so he put a veil over his face. Whenever Moses would enter the Most Holy Place in the tabernacle to be in the Lord's presence, he would take the veil off his face to speak with God. Then, he would stand before the people with his face uncovered and tell them what God had commanded. After he finished speaking, Moses would once again slip the veil over his face.

Paul seized Moses' habit of putting a veil over his face and then taking it off as a symbol of the difference between the old and new covenants. **The old system of law etched in stone** brought condemnation because it pointed out sin and its tragic consequence: death. In contrast, the new covenant brings **life** through **the Holy Spirit.** This was more glorious—literally, reflecting more of the brilliance of God—than the law. To make his point even more forceful, Paul described the glory of Moses' face as a **fading** glory. The Old Testament passage does not record this fact. It seems that Paul interpreted Moses' action of covering his face with a veil as an effort on Moses' part to divert attention from the fading brilliance of his own face in order to focus the people's attention on the law. Paul saw this fading glory as another sign of the temporary nature of the old covenant.

3:9-11 The **old covenant** could give only **condemnation,** but the **new covenant** can make people **right with God.** Paul's letter to the Romans explains in detail how the old covenant brings condemnation. The law carries a verdict of guilty because it points out sin in people's lives (Romans 3:19-20; 5:12-13). No one is righteous before God (Romans 3:10). But God mercifully gives his own righteousness to those who believe in his Son (Romans 5:17). This way, all those who believe in Jesus are declared right with God (Romans 3:20-22). This sentence, therefore, sums up the difference between the old covenant and

the new covenant Paul had preached to the Corinthians: The old, by pointing out sin, brings God's judgment; but the new, through Jesus' innocent life and death, brings God's righteousness to the believer.

The old covenant was **glorious.** Not only did Moses' face shine, but thunder, lightning, earthquakes, dense clouds, blazing fire, and a deafening trumpet blast accompanied its inauguration at Mount Sinai (Exodus 19:16-20).But that **was not glorious at all compared with the overwhelming glory of the new covenant.** The new ministry of the Spirit is even more glorious. The changed hearts and lives of believers is an even more miraculous work of God than lightning, thunder, and earthquakes. In fact, this greater glory was eclipsing the glory of the old covenant. Just as the bright light of the sun makes a flashlight useless, so the surpassing glory of the new covenant renders the lesser glory useless. The old covenant was temporary, had **been set aside,** and was being superseded by the new covenant, **which remains forever.**

3:12-13 From his discussion on the superiority of the new covenant over the old, Paul concluded that the new inspires believers to **be very bold.** The Greek word translated "boldness" is the word that the Greeks used to speak of the right to free speech. Here Paul used this word to indicate the public nature of his ministry. He would boldly preach the mysteries of salvation. Paul's boldness was an outgrowth of his **confidence** in the new covenant— the glorious, permanent ministry of the Holy Spirit in the lives of believers. This type of confidence in the faithfulness of God inspired Paul to publicly proclaim the Good News of salvation. Paul could act with greater confidence than the spiritual giant **Moses,** for Paul had been given an eternal message to proclaim to all nations. Paul did not need to worry about its **glory fading away.**

3:14-16 Paul's common practice when he first went to a city was to preach to the Jews who would gather in the local synagogue (as he did in Corinth, see Acts 18:1-4). But the Jews rejected his message of salvation (Acts 18:6-7). At times, Jews even pursued Paul to other cities to try to silence him (see Acts 14:1, 19). Paul most frequently found welcome with the God-fearing Gentiles (Acts 17:4).

In his letter to the Romans, Paul focused on why the Jews had rejected Jesus, to whom all of the Scriptures (the Old Testament) pointed. Jesus was

Israel's Messiah, the person who fulfilled God's promises to Israel. The Jews, if anyone, should be rejoicing. Instead, their **minds were hardened** to what was occurring (see Romans 9–11, especially 10:1-3). It was as if **a veil** were covering **their minds** so that they could not **understand the truth.** But **by believing in Christ,** the veil is miraculously lifted. Just as Christ had opened Paul's spiritual eyes to the truth about Jesus, the Holy Spirit would also open believers' eyes to how Jesus fulfilled the Scriptures. Moses and his veil illustrate the fading of the old system and the veiling of the Jews' minds by their pride, hardness of heart, and refusal to repent. The veil kept many Jews from understanding the references to Christ in the Scriptures they heard every week.

Whenever anyone turns to the Lord and becomes a Christian, Christ removes the **veil,** giving that person not only understanding of the true meaning of the Scriptures but also eternal life and freedom from trying to be saved by keeping laws. Christ saves the person not only from sin but from the ignorance that his or her sin has created.

3:17-18 Next, Paul introduced another reason why the new covenant is better than the old: It is a ministry of **freedom.** Christ's death on the cross bought freedom for anyone who believes (1 Corinthians 6:20). He frees us from sin and the condemnation that results from trying to obey the law (Romans 8:1-4; Galatians 3:21-24). He frees us from the fear of death, the penalty for our sins (Romans 5:17-18). Jesus even frees us from the evil powers of the age (Galatians 1:4). Christ frees believers from the same mental veil that

covered many of the Jews to whom Paul was preaching (3:14).

When we trust Christ to save us, Jesus removes that heavy burden of trying to please him. His light dispels our ignorance, giving us a clear understanding of the gospel. By trusting Christ, we are loved, accepted, forgiven, and freed to live for him.

Just as Moses took off his veil when he went into the Lord's presence, so too all Christians can behold God's glory with **that veil removed.** Unlike the Jews, who had to rely on priests to mediate between them and God, Christians through Christ's saving work on the cross have direct access to the Father (Ephesians 2:18). Thus, under the new covenant, all believers **can be mirrors that brightly reflect the glory of the Lord.** In contrast, under the old covenant only Moses had access to the Lord's presence and thus could reflect his glory. But now all Christians can be like Moses. Thus, when Christians, who are given access to the Father through Christ's work, look at God's glory, they begin to reflect his holy character in their lives, becoming **more and more like him.** As a result of this encounter with God, they are forever changed. The Holy Spirit works through believers' lives, step by step, helping them come closer to God's perfect way of living. It occurs little by little as the Holy Spirit points out more areas of our lives that need to be submitted to God's will; and we, then, freely submit to God. The Holy Spirit works through the preaching of God's word, the reading of Scripture, our prayer life, and the wise guidance of other mature believers to lead believers on God's wonderful path of righteousness.

2 CORINTHIANS 4

TREASURE IN PERISHABLE CONTAINERS / 4:1-18

Paul was under attack at Corinth. His authority and honesty were being questioned. Charges of duplicity were circulating in the church. Paul was facing a church in revolt. How did Paul handle opposition? At every step, he deflected criticisms of his abilities. He simply refused to defend himself. He even submitted to his opponents a list of his weaknesses and the trials he had endured. Why did Paul do this? He knew that this list would focus the Corinthians on what was important: God's glorious plan of salvation.

4:1 In the last chapter, Paul painted an appealing picture of what it means to be a Christian minister. This chapter comes down to reality. What does all

this mean for everyday life? Why would Paul keep going—even in the face of trials and suffering?

First of all, because **God** gave Paul and his companions their **wonderful ministry,** they would **never give up.** The Greek for this phrase can mean anything from not becoming discouraged to not acting like a coward. In other words, the glorious plan of God gave Paul hope and courage to face his day with great confidence in God (see 3:4, 12; 5:6-8).

4:2 This verse contrasts the way Paul preached with the methods of some of the traveling preachers who had come to Corinth. These preachers had sought a platform on which to speak and ask for money (2:17). Paul categorically denied using any dubious techniques in his preaching. He and his fellow evangelists had rejected **all shameful and underhanded methods.** This expression denotes methods, motives, and actions that are shrouded in secrecy because they are intrinsically scandalous. The implication is that some of the preachers who had visited Corinth had greedy motives. Paul could perceive their hidden motives because of the havoc and confusion these men were causing in Corinth. One of the telltale signs of the impure motives of these preachers was the way they handled God's word. Instead of a straightforward presentation of the truths of the gospel, they used tricks to captivate their audience. In so doing, they would **distort the word of God.**

Paul had rejected such deceptive and cunning ways when he preached to the Corinthians. He had "walked" by faith instead of placing his trust in the ingenious, deceptive ways of the world (see 5:7). In other words, Paul always reminded himself of the spiritual realities that were behind his ministry. When he preached the truths of God's word, he reminded himself that he was preaching it **before God.** He stood in the presence of God. The Lord God, the One who knows all secrets, could look into Paul's heart and discern his motives. Because God was always watching him, Paul was careful to preach for the right reasons. He consciously submitted his motivations to God's scrutiny, so that no shameful act or motive could disqualify him as a minister. Paul opened up his entire life and honestly told the Corinthians the **truth.** He hid nothing.

4:3-4 Although the **Good News** Paul preached was a clear presentation of salvation, he admitted that the gospel would be **veiled,** or obscure, to some. He explained that there are two types of people—those who will receive eternal life and **those who don't believe.** Paul's description here of the way **Satan** has **blinded the minds** of unbelievers is reminiscent of his conversion experience on the Damascus road. Although Paul could see perfectly well, he had been blinded to spiritual truth. Naively and zealously, he had persecuted the Christians, vowing to destroy them in any

way possible. Unknowingly, Paul had been an instrument of Satan. In one magnificent moment, however, Christ had broken through Satan's deception and had revealed the truth to Paul. A glorious vision of Christ finally had opened Paul's eyes to the truth. Appropriately, Paul had been physically blinded for a while (Acts 9:1-18).

Instead of being blinded by Satan like unbelievers are, believers recognize that Jesus is **the exact likeness of God** (see also Colossians 1:15). God the Father as spirit is invisible (1 Timothy 6:16). God's Son, however, is God's visible expression. Jesus not only reflects the Father, but, as God, he reveals God to us (John 1:18; 14:9; Hebrews 1:1-2). Christ's glory expresses divine **glory.**

4:5 The focus of Paul's preaching was on **Christ Jesus** and not himself. Since his own authority was under attack, Paul could have written that he was their God-appointed leader and teacher (as he did in 1 Timothy 2:7). Instead, Paul emphasized that he and his fellow evangelists were the Corinthians' **servants.** Paul was not trying to exercise arbitrary authority over their faith (1:24). On the contrary, Paul was merely serving them as Christ's appointed messenger, faithfully delivering the truths of the gospel to them.

4:6 Paul returned to the image of **light** and **darkness,** which he had introduced in 4:4. The image symbolizes the stark difference between good and evil, between God and Satan. This imagery came from the Creation story itself (Genesis 1:2-5). Just as **God** had brought order out of the chaos of darkness by ordering, **"Let there be light in the darkness,"** so God was piercing the chaos of evil with the light of his truth. The light of Christ exposes falsehood and evil for what it is: a perversion of the good (Ephesians 5:13-14). Those who believe in Jesus become children of the light. They live in the light, allowing it to judge all of their actions (see Ephesians 5:8; 1 Thessalonians 5:5).

This passage emphasizes that **this light is the brightness of the glory of God that is seen in the face of Jesus Christ.** The light of Christ illumines a believer's understanding. Only those who allow their minds to be clouded by Satan's dark deceptions think the message is obscure. God illumines the minds of believers so that they know with certainty that in Jesus' face they see the glory of God. The implication is that those who look for God's glory only in the old covenant, in the face of Moses, are being deceived by Satan (compare with 3:15-17).

4:7 People keep treasures in safety deposit boxes and vaults. But God places his **precious treasure**—the message that frees people from sin—in perishable containers; that is, in human beings. The message of freedom that God had entrusted to them would last much longer than their frail bodies. Why would God do this? Because he delights in empowering the **weak** in order to confound the strong. The Lord loves to answer the prayers of the needy and bring down those who take pride in themselves (see Luke 1:51-55; Jeremiah 20:13). God works through the weak and powerless so that it is clear that the **power** comes from God alone (1 Corinthians 2:3-4).

4:8-9 Paul recounted how weak he, as a human being, really was. He freely admitted he had been **crushed** and **perplexed.** Few teachers would admit to being perplexed because they might lose the respect of their audience. Then he added the words, **God never abandons us.** The Lord did not abandon Paul to his own inadequacies. God had saved Paul from being **crushed and broken** by his responsibilities and from reaching utter despair.

The next two entries speak of external opposition: Paul had been **hunted down** and **knocked down.** Paul had received most of his opposition from Jews. They had persecuted him, even following him to different cities to malign him (see Acts 14:19). Through it all, God never abandoned him.

4:10-12 Jesus himself was Paul's model. Although Jesus had all the glories of heaven—all of its power and privilege—he gave it all up to suffer humiliation, insults, and finally death (see Philippians 2:5-11). Paul saw his own sufferings for the cause of Christ as sharing **in the death of Jesus.** Of course, Jesus' suffering was of a qualitatively different nature. Jesus died on the cross to save believers from their sins. Yet Jesus had warned his followers they could also expect suffering and hardship (John 15:20-21). The suffering of Jesus' followers would be merely an extension of Jesus' own suffering. So Paul lived **under constant danger of death** for Jesus' sake so that people would see **the life of Jesus.**

Paul lived **in the face of death,** but he knew that something greater than life on this earth was working through him. His sufferings and death would never spell the end for the life-giving message of the gospel. In fact, God was working so that Paul's suffering would result in **eternal life for** those who believe in Jesus. This passage reminded the Corinthians that Paul's sufferings, which the Corinthians were presently ashamed of, had brought the message of eternal life to them in the first place. Paul had courageously endured the insults of the Jews in order to deliver the gospel to them—the message that would result in their eternal salvation (Acts 18:6).

4:13-14 In this passage, Paul identified himself with the writer of Psalm 116. Paul, like the **psalmist,** had experienced fear of death (Psalm 116:3). In the midst of troubles and in the face of death, Paul, like the psalmist, had cried out to God (Psalm 116:4). The psalmist believed that God would answer his prayers (Psalm 116:1), so he vowed to pray as long as he had breath (Psalm 116:2). His prayers were not the only expression of his **faith** in God; he also promised to thank and praise God, telling others of what God had done for him (see Psalm 116:14, 17-18). In this psalm, Paul saw an extraordinary expression of faith, which he endeavored to imitate. The psalmist had refused to let his circumstances dictate to him what he should believe.

Although Paul was experiencing the sufferings and death of Christ on this earth (4:10-12), he **believed in God.** Although Paul was facing suffering, he wasn't discouraged, because he knew that Jesus would return. At that time, Paul and the Corinthian believers would celebrate their Savior in his presence because God would also raise them **with Jesus.** The believers in Corinth had been struggling with the doctrine of the Resurrection, so Paul had written much to explain why the Resurrection is a central doctrine of the Christian faith. With his sights always set on the glories of God's Kingdom, Paul didn't have any reason to be ashamed (Romans 1:16; see also Hebrews 12:2). Instead, he boldly and confidently could preach the gospel and tell others of what God had done for him (4:1).

4:15 All of the trials and difficulties he had endured were for their **benefit.** As more people heard of and accepted **God's grace**—that is, God's gift of salvation—more people would join the grand celebration before God. **Thanksgiving** would begin to overflow toward God. This would benefit the Corinthian Christians, for—through their prayers—they also had participated in Paul's work of spreading the gospel (see 1:11). Ultimately, God would be glorified through all this. All praise and **glory** would be solely his, for he is the One who sacrificed his own Son for the benefit of all who believe.

4:16 Paul and his colleagues would **never give up** because they knew the great power behind their message (3:16-18). Even though the things of this life—their **bodies**—were deteriorating, moving daily toward death, their **spirits,** in contrast, were **being renewed every day.** The hardships of Paul's ministry were real and were having their effect. Paul, however, did not gripe or complain about how much he was giving up in order to preach the gospel. Instead, he knew that every trouble, hardship, and difficulty endured for Christ's sake was making him spiritually new. This occurred day by day, trouble by trouble. Paul saw every difficulty as an opportunity to mature in the faith.

4:17-18 Paul knew that the hardships he endured were really **quite small** and wouldn't **last very long** in comparison to how long he would enjoy God's presence—the **immeasurably great glory that will last forever.** What really matters— what is eternal and permanent—cannot be seen, touched, or measured. Only with the eyes of faith can people **look forward to what** they **have not yet seen.** Only with eyes of faith can they begin

to understand, with God's help, the eternal significance of their actions. A believer's hope is not in this world. A Christian's hope is not in the power and wealth that can be accumulated on earth. Instead, a Christian's hope is in Christ—someone who cannot be seen at the present moment (Romans 8:24; Hebrews 11:1). Nevertheless, Jesus Christ and his significance to every person's life is real enough. That is why Paul encouraged the Corinthians to live by faith and not by sight (5:7). The Corinthians were to take their eyes off of this world—for **the troubles will soon be over.** Instead, they should fix their eyes on the Almighty, the One who possessed all power, for he will bring **joys to come** that **will last forever.**

2 CORINTHIANS 5:1–6:2

NEW BODIES / 5:1-10

As a Christian evangelist in the first century, Paul was insulted, ridiculed, and taunted. For the cause of the gospel, he faced angry mobs, irate local officials, and conceited philosophers. He spent many anxious nights in prayer and long hours working to support himself and studying the Scriptures. He received no applause, no reward, no appreciation. Why did he do this? Paul answered this question for the Corinthians. He measured all of his troubles in the light of eternity. Paul knew that he would experience infinite happiness and unending joy in the next life. This confident hope was Paul's motivation to never stop preaching the truth to all who would listen.

5:1 In the middle of discussing his own sufferings for the gospel, Paul once again broached the subject of the resurrection. His confident hope that he would be given an **eternal body** by God inspired him to consider his present troubles as nothing, in light of the heavenly glory he would enjoy forever and ever (see 4:17-18). Paul compared his present earthly body to a **tent,** a temporary structure designed to be dismantled (see also 2 Peter 1:13-15). When this earthly tent **is taken down**— a reference to physical death—believers will be given **a home in heaven,** made by **God himself.** The contrast is clear. Our earthly bodies are like temporary, flimsy tents, while our eternal bodies will be permanent buildings. In the same way, earthly troubles are temporary, while the glory and joy of heaven are eternal (compare with 4:17-18).

5:2-3 Paul was loaded down and **weary** with all sorts of troubles in this world (see 1:8; 4:8, 16-17), but his troubles inspired him to **long for the day** when he would receive his **heavenly** body **like new**

clothing. This image depicts the glorious truth that the earthly bodies of Christians will be transformed into eternal, heavenly bodies. The believers in Corinth probably had been influenced by the Greek idea that death would free the soul from the prison of the body. This idea was probably the reason some Corinthians had begun to deny a bodily resurrection in the first place (1 Corinthians 15:12). This verse clearly repudiates the idea that believers will become **spirits without bodies.** Instead, believers' earthly bodies would be transformed into **new heavenly bodies.**

5:4 This verse adds another image to this list of images about the heavenly body. While we **groan and sigh** in our present bodies, we don't look forward to a time of having **no bodies at all.** As Jesus' own resurrection body shows, believers will have bodies that to some degree correspond with their own physical bodies. Their bodies will be redeemed (Romans 8:24). Through Christ's saving work, their resurrected bodies will be better than they can imagine. We will **slip into** these **new bodies** and will have **everlasting life.**

5:5 Paul's yearning for his heavenly body was not a desperate hope. God had determined long ago that believers in his Son would inherit eternal glory. This picks up the idea expressed in 4:17 that the Lord God had planned not only to justify believers through his Son's sacrificial death, but he also had planned to glorify them with heavenly bodies.

Part of God's wonderful plan to save those who believe in his Son includes the **Holy Spirit** as proof of his and their eternal destiny with God the Father. The Spirit is a **guarantee** that he will one day pay up in full. Paul envisioned Christ, on one glorious day, coming to complete the process that had already begun, with the help of the Holy Spirit, within the Corinthians' lives (see 4:16; see also Romans 8:23; Ephesians 1:13-14). Through his death, Jesus will not only save believers, he will also clothe them in heavenly glory so that they can celebrate their salvation in God's presence (Romans 8:30; 9:23). The Holy Spirit within believers is a trustworthy guarantee that God will give Christians everlasting bodies at the resurrection (1:22). Christians have eternity within them now!

5:6-7 Paul was not afraid to die because he was **confident** of spending eternity with Christ. In fact, being in these earthly bodies only means that believers are not yet **at home with the Lord.** Of course, facing the unknown may cause anxiety, and leaving loved ones hurts deeply. But because Christians believe in Jesus, they can share Paul's hope and confidence of eternal life with Christ. Because of that confidence, believers **live by believing and not by seeing.** Christians believe there is a greater spiritual reality that determines how they will live in eternity. To base life on what can be seen—the realities of this world—would be foolish indeed. This world will pass away, but the truth of God's word will never pass away (Matthew 24:35; 2 Peter 3:10).

5:8 This verse straightforwardly asserts that to be **away from these bodies** means being **at home with the Lord.** Paul also wrote in his letter to the Philippians that departing from this life means to "be with Christ" (Philippians 1:23). These passages have been the subject of much debate over the exact state of believers at death—what theologians call the "intermediate state" between being at home in the body (5:6) and at home with the Lord. There are four main views of the "intermediate state":

1. Soul sleep—This view is held by Seventh-Day Adventists and Jehovah's Witnesses. They believe that the soul rests in unconsciousness or oblivion until the resurrection. They base this view on verses where death is referred to as "sleep." Some have modified this view to say that believers are "with Christ," but not in a conscious state. However, Scripture teaches the believer's immediate presence with the Lord at death (Luke 23:43; Acts 7:56, 59).

2. Purgatory—This is the Roman Catholic view that at death those who have died in their sins and rejected Christ go to Hades for eternal punishment; those who died in a perfect state of grace go directly to heaven. Those who are not spiritually perfect go to purgatory for a refining process and purification of sin. This view has developed largely from church theologians and church councils rather than the Bible itself, although 1 Corinthians 3:15 has been used by Catholics to justify this view.

3. Immediate resurrection—This view states that at death there is an immediate separation from the earthly body and an immediate reclothing or reconstituting of the resurrection body. Proponents teach that in 1 Corinthians 15 and 1 Thessalonians 4, Paul believed in the resurrection of the body at the Second Coming and fully believed that believers would see it in their lifetime. After Paul's brush with death and the reality that he might die before Christ returns, Paul explained what would be the case for those who died in the interval. Romans 8:19 and Colossians 3:4 are used to argue that believers are already resurrected but will be "revealed" or glorified at the Second Coming.

4. Incomplete resurrection—This view is the most commonly accepted view of Paul's words in the New Testament. There is a conscious, personal existence for the believer after death. At death, a believer goes to a place and condition of blessedness. The time interval between the believer's death and the full resurrection of the body will be imperceptible to the Christian. No anxiety or discomfort will mar this condition. Most do not believe this will be a bodiless existence because of Paul's teaching (5:3-4). However, it is true that the body will not be in its complete and final form because Paul points to a future resurrection as a specific event (Philippians 3:20-21; 1 Thessalonians 4:16-17), as does Jesus (John 5:25-29). At death we will assume a different expression or condition of the bodily self; then, at the Second Coming, this will be exchanged or reconstituted as the resurrection body.

In the final analysis, Christians can only affirm exactly what the Bible says: When a believer dies, he or she will be with Jesus (see also Philippians

1:23). Believers will not float in a limbo state. Instead, they will have a personal encounter with the Savior. Then, when Jesus returns in all his glory, all believers will be given heavenly bodies that will be perfect and will last forever (see 1 Corinthians 15:51-54; 1 Thessalonians 4:16-18). A believer's life in eternity will involve some type of bodily existence. We have the example of our Lord's resurrected body as he appeared on earth. The Spirit imparted to believers in this life not only guarantees that they will be resurrected to eternal glory but also begins that transformation within believers' souls (see 4:16; 5:5).

Although this verse, along with others, has provoked much speculation, Paul's point is abundantly clear: A believer's destination—his or her eternal home with Jesus—should inspire confidence and courage in the face of life's difficulties. Although Christians may moan under the strain of persecution, their problems should never push them to despair. Like a woman in labor, believers endure the pain and suffering joyfully, because they know it is temporary and will lead to something much better: a perfect and eternal home.

5:9-10 Knowing that when you die you will be with Jesus should inspire you to live **to please** your Lord and Savior, Jesus Christ **always.** Just as you live for Christ's sake on this earth, you will continue to live for him in heaven. The transformation that the Holy Spirit is working within you now will finally be completed: You will become like Jesus (Romans 8:29-30). Eternal life is a free gift given on the basis of God's grace (Ephesians 2:8-9), but Christians' lives will still be **judged** by Christ. Salvation is never obtained by works (Romans 4:4-5), and this judgment before Christ will not determine believers' eternal destiny. Instead, at this judgment, Christ will reward Christians for how they have lived on earth. God's gracious gift of salvation does not free Christians from the requirement of faithful obedience to Christ. All Christians must give an account for how they have lived in this body.

Throughout 2 Corinthians, Paul tells the Corinthians how he had been careful about his speech and behavior among them because he knew Jesus was hearing what he had said and was judging it (1:14; 2:10, 17; 3:18; 4:2, 14). This passage warns the Corinthians that their speech and behavior will also be judged, and they would **receive whatever** they deserved **for the good or evil** they had **done in** their **bodies.** This is a sober reminder to all Christians that we must evaluate all we do from God's perspective. The fact that we, as Christians, will meet Jesus should inspire both joy and a holy fear—joy that we will finally be with our Savior and fear that Jesus will hold us accountable for our actions.

WE ARE GOD'S AMBASSADORS / 5:11–6:2

After reminding the Corinthians that everyone will appear before Christ's judgment seat, Paul explained that he had evaluated his own motives and actions in light of this sobering fact. He knew—and reminded himself of the fact—that God saw his motivations. His life was an open book to God. Paul didn't have to prove to God that he was sincere, for God already knew it. Paul hoped that the Corinthians, also, would understand that his actions were motivated by a healthy respect for God—not by greed or any other sinful motivation.

5:11 Paul had a **solemn fear of the Lord.** Many skip over fear as a motivation for serving God and instead emphasize how love should motivate Christians (see 5:14). But many forget that fear isn't fundamentally bad. Fear keeps people from jumping out of airplanes without a parachute. Fear of God means having a proper respect for his perfect nature and great power. For those who have persisted in evil and rebellious ways, contemplating God should inspire dread. Their ways have been condemned by God, and their path leads to death (see 2:14-16). Believers who contemplate God should be filled with reverential awe, standing in wonder and amazement at his greatness. Knowing God's perfection and that he will judge everyone's actions should spur Christians to **work hard to persuade others** to know God. This Paul did, with all sincerity.

5:12 In this letter, Paul has been extremely cautious about bragging about himself to the Corinthians. Several times he has explicitly denied doing any such thing (see 3:1; 10:18). Paul knew that in the process of patting himself **on the back,** he could easily fall into the trap of doing just what the false preachers were doing: bragging about their own spirituality and their own accomplishments.

Paul's Corinthian critics were more concerned about getting ahead in this world (see 2:17). They were preaching the gospel for money and popularity. They were bragging **about having a spectacular ministry:** eloquent speeches (11:5; 1 Corinthians 2:1), formal letters of recommendation (3:1), and impressive presentations (see 10:10-11). In contrast, Paul and his companions were preaching out of **a sincere heart before God** with concern for eternity and to please the ultimate Judge, God himself. The Corinthians had been dazzled by these magnificent and impressive shows. They had been captivated by their astonishing rhetoric. Subtly, they had given up striving to find God's perspective.

5:13 Exactly what Paul meant by being **crazy** is not entirely clear. Perhaps the Corinthians had begun to think that Paul had a mental problem. He welcomed all kinds of trials, difficulties, and sufferings and even listed them (see 4:7-9). Later, Festus would call Paul mad because of his unquenchable zeal to preach the gospel (see Acts 26:22-24). Paul had already warned the Corinthians in 1 Corinthians that the gospel and its messengers would appear foolish to the wise of this world (1 Corinthians 2:7-16). If this was the idea that Paul was trying to express, then he was saying that he was acting like a fool because of his zeal for God and the gospel. Although Paul didn't clarify his meaning, his point is abundantly clear. Paul's actions were not motivated by self-interest or a quest for power. Everything he did—whether crazy or in **right mind**—was **to bring glory to God** and to **benefit** the Corinthian believers.

5:14-15 Everything that Paul and his companions did was to honor God. Not only did fear of God motivate them (see 5:11), but **Christ's love** controlled their actions. Out of his great love, Jesus had given up his life for their sakes. He had not acted out of his own self-interest, selfishly holding on to the glory of heaven that he already possessed (Philippians 2:6). Instead, Jesus had willingly **died for everyone.** Those who **believe that** also believe that they have **died to the old life.** They should be willing to abandon their old, selfish ways in order to live a **new life** for Christ (Romans 6:6-14; Galatians 2:20; Colossians 2:20). Like Paul, we should no longer live to **please** ourselves. We should die to ourselves and live for Christ, who is alive today and interceding with God on our behalf (Romans 6:22).

5:16-17 At one time, Paul had evaluated Jesus **by what the world** thought about him. As an educated Jew, Paul was looking forward to the Messiah. But the Jews of his time were looking for a political Messiah, a powerful person who would free them from Roman rule. Instead, Jesus had died, even suffering the Romans' most cruel punishment: crucifixion.

According to human standards, Jesus was **merely a human being,** an insignificant man who died like a criminal. But that changed at Paul's encounter with the risen Christ on the Damascus road (Acts 9:1-15). In the same way, believers are changed when they meet Christ. **Christians** are **new** people. The Holy Spirit gives them new life, and **they are not the same anymore.** Christians are not reformed, rehabilitated, or reeducated—they are recreated. At conversion, believers are not merely turning over a new leaf; they are beginning a new life under a new Master. The **old life** of sin and death has gone; the selfish, sinful human nature has been dealt a death blow (see Galatians 5:16-21, 24). Old ways of thinking, old distinctions, have been abolished. In its place, **a new life has begun.**

5:18-19 This **newness of life** is not of any human doing. **God** himself has begun the work. Only God can allow people to approach him. Only God can satisfy his own righteous demands. Only God can save. God is the Author and Finisher of salvation (see Hebrews 12:2). God **brought** his people **back to himself through what Christ did.** When they trust in Christ, believers are no longer God's enemies. Through Christ's self-sacrificial work on the cross, God has made believers part of his family. Jesus died in our place so that we might enjoy fellowship with God (1 Corinthians 15:3). Because believers have been reconciled to God, we have been **given the task of reconciling people to him.** Since Paul experienced reconciliation through Christ, it became his mission to preach that message. Just in case the Corinthians had forgotten the heart of Paul's message to them, he repeated it to them: **God was in Christ, reconciling the world to himself, no longer counting people's sins against them.** God, through Christ's death on the cross, was bringing back all people—Jews and Greeks alike—who had fallen (Romans 5:10; Ephesians 2:14-17). Although we were enemies of God, Christ reached out to us, saving us from certain destruction. He even washed us in order that we might approach God with clean hearts (Colossians 1:21-22). That is indeed a **wonderful message.**

5:20-21 Ambassadors are official representatives of one country to another. Paul described himself and his coworkers as **Christ's ambassadors,** representatives of Christ to the world (5:19). **God** was **using** them **to speak to** the Corinthians the message that they **be reconciled to God**—accept God's free gift of reconciliation. Paul did not announce this message halfheartedly. He implored—even urged and pleaded—everyone who would listen to him to accept God's free gift of salvation. It was extremely urgent, for it would change their eternal destiny.

And it was a gift that had an expensive price tag. **For God made Christ, who never sinned, to be the offering for our sin, so that we could be made right with God through Christ.** Christ bore the consequences of, or punishment for, our sins. God made Jesus, who was completely innocent and perfect, identify himself with sin so he could take it away.

In life, rarely will anyone claim perfection. Sin is a part of life, so much so that many people simply expect to encounter dishonesty, self-centeredness, and greed in other people. If they don't, they are surprised. That is why many people in Jesus' day expressed surprise at Jesus' life. They could not find anything wrong with him (see Pilate's words in Luke 23:4-22, the centurion's words in Luke 23:41-48, and God's testimony in Matthew 3:17; 17:5). The disciples, Jesus' closest friends and followers, did not find any evil in his actions (see Peter's testimony in 1 Peter 2:22 and John's testimony in 1 John 3:5). Jesus never knew what it meant to sin: He always followed God's ways. Yet Jesus bore the consequences of believers' sin for their sakes. Since Jesus, who was perfect and innocent, took on the penalty of sin, death itself, Jesus can make those who believe in him right with God. His perfect righteousness can cover our corrupt and imperfect lives. When people trust in Christ, they make an exchange—their sin for his righteousness. Believers' sin was placed on Jesus at his crucifixion. His righteousness is given to believers at their conversion. This is what Christians mean by Christ's atonement for sin.

6:1-2 Paul and his fellow **partners** with God in sharing the salvation message begged the Corinthians **not to reject** it. They should take God's grace seriously and live up to the gospel's demands. Paul was imploring the Corinthians, who had already accepted Jesus, to live up to their profession of faith (see 5:14).

The prophet Isaiah predicted a **time** of God's own choosing when he would save his people: God would release them from bondage and clear a path for them to return to their land and restore their fortunes (see Isaiah 49:8-12, 23-26). God would do all this so that the whole world would know that he was Israel's Savior and Redeemer (Isaiah 49:26). The Hebrews who had heard Isaiah's message long ago would have understood this as a prediction that God would one day bring the Israelites back out of their exile in Babylon. This did occur (see Ezra 1).

Paul, however, understood Isaiah's prediction as also being fulfilled in his day. God had sent Jesus to the earth. It was **the day of salvation.** So Paul, being God's messenger just as Isaiah was, echoed Isaiah's message with even more urgency. Paul announced that what Isaiah was looking forward to had occurred. God offers salvation to all people. Many people put off making a decision to receive God's salvation, thinking that there will be a better time—but they could easily miss their opportunity altogether. **Today is the day of salvation.** There is no time like the present to receive God's forgiveness.

2 CORINTHIANS 6:3 – 7:1

PAUL'S HARDSHIPS / 6:3-13

Paul had demonstrated his willingness to suffer all kinds of hardships—beatings, imprisonments, poverty, and even insults—for Jesus. He had a single-hearted commitment to Christ. This extraordinary commitment, demonstrated by the sufferings he had endured, was proof of his apostolic authority. Instead of submitting a list of successes and accomplishments, Paul submitted a list of difficult situations that he had endured for Christ.

6:3-5 Paul knew that unbelievers and believers alike were watching his life. God had entrusted Paul with the message of truth; he, in turn, had to live up to God's ways. That is why he was careful to be straightforward, honest, and upright (see 1:12). Any wrongdoing—or anything that was perceived to be wrong—might distract from the gospel message (4:2; 1 Corinthians 1:17). Paul did not want anyone to **be hindered from finding the Lord** or to give people cause to **find fault with** their **ministry.** The last thing he wanted to do was bring ridicule on God's glorious plan of salvation. So **in everything** he and his fellow workers did, they tried **to show that** they were **true ministers of God.** The Corinthians, however, had begun to doubt Paul's credentials and, more importantly, his authority over them (see 12:11). So Paul listed the different situations in which he had served God. Similar to his weaknesses in 4:8-10, this list includes **troubles, hardships, and calamities** that most preachers would not catalog for their audiences.

For preaching Christ, Paul had been **beaten.** In 11:23-25, Paul recalls that he had been whipped five times by the Jews. He also had been beaten with rods by the civil authorities on three separate occasions. Luke recorded in the book of Acts that Paul and Silas suffered this punishment at Philippi (see Acts 16:23-24).

Paul had **been put in jail** in Philippi (Acts 16:23). In almost every city, Paul had **faced angry mobs,** usually stirred up by resentful Jews. In Pisidian Antioch, Jews stirred the high-ranking men and women of the city to expel him from that city (Acts 13:49-52). In Iconium, the citizens plotted to stone Paul to death (Acts 14:5-6). In Lystra, an angry mob did stone him, and, miraculously, he survived it and went to the next town to preach the Good News (Acts 14:19). At Philippi, a mob seized Paul and Silas and had them imprisoned (Acts 16:19-24). At Thessalonica, a crowd looking for Paul surrounded Jason's house (Acts 17:5). At Ephesus, an enraged mob of silversmiths seized Paul's traveling companions (Acts 19:23-41). Even during Paul's ministry among the Corinthians, the Jews of Corinth seized Paul and brought him before the governor (see Acts 18:12-17). Everywhere Paul preached the gospel, he was met with incensed mobs. He expected opposition, but he also expected Jesus to see him through those difficult situations (see 1:3-7).

After listing some of the involuntary hardships he faced, Paul mentioned the hardships he had endured voluntarily in order to further the cause of the gospel. Paul not only dutifully faced all kinds of opposition for Christ, he also made personal sacrifices so that he could continue to announce the Good News. Paul had **worked to exhaustion** so as not to become a burden to the people he was preaching to, especially the Corinthians (see 11:9). In Thessalonica, he worked night and day; perhaps this caused some of those **sleepless nights** Paul **endured** (1 Thessalonians 2:9; 3:8). Perhaps some of those voluntary sleepless nights were not spent in physical labor but in prayer for all the churches. Moreover, Paul had **gone without food.** He may have done this in order to not be a financial burden for the people to whom he was ministering (see 11:7-10).

6:6 In the middle of his list of the difficult situations he faced for the cause of Christ, Paul listed five character traits of an effective minister of the gospel.

First, he and his coworkers had acted in **purity.** To be pure means to be free of any contamination.

Paul's actions (1 Timothy 5:22) and thoughts (Philippians 4:8) were pure. Paul may have had in mind a phony preacher's motivations—such as greed and self-interest—which were contaminating the messages of many preachers who had visited Corinth (see Paul's description of these traveling preachers in 4:2).

Second, he and his coworkers had **understanding** of the gospel message. Christ had revealed to Paul the mysteries of salvation (Ephesians 3:6). Paul understood the gospel and knew he had to communicate it clearly (1:12).

Third, they had **patience.** Paul had learned patience through all of these difficult situations. In the end, however, any patience he had was from the Holy Spirit, for in Galatians Paul explicitly stated that "the fruit of the Spirit is love, joy, peace, patience, kindness, goodness, faithfulness, gentleness and self-control" (Galatians 5:22-23). **The Holy Spirit** empowered all of their efforts.

Fourth, they treated others with **kindness.** Through the Spirit's power, Paul had learned to consider others' needs above his own. Realizing how much God had done for him, Paul sought to show that same type of mercy to others.

Finally, they had **sincere love.** The self-sacrificial love that Jesus had shown to the Corinthians when he died for them on the cross (see Romans 5:5) was the type of love Paul attempted to emulate in his ministry.

6:7 Although they had encountered all kinds of opposition when they preached the Good News, Paul and the others continued to **faithfully** preach **the truth.** Although traveling preachers were deceiving the Corinthians with a false gospel (see 4:2; 11:4), they had **God's power working in** them to continue to bring that truth. Even more, they had **righteousness as** a **weapon** with which they could **attack and defend** themselves. A Roman soldier would arm himself with a full-length shield in his left hand and a spear in his right hand. No Roman soldier was fully prepared for battle without both weapons: his shield on his left and his spear on his right. Ephesians 6:10-18 lists, along with **righteousness,** the other spiritual weapons. They consist of the gospel message itself, the truth of God's word, and faith. In order to resist the Devil, Christians need to not only immerse themselves in the truths of God's word and the gospel itself, they need to put their faith into action. The righteousness God gives Christians through faith in Christ should be evident in the way they live. Then Christians will be able to withstand Satan's attacks.

6:8-10 A pastor's job is to confront people with the truths of the gospel. But sometimes this responsibility is neglected because a pastor is more concerned about being liked. The traveling preachers in Corinth were like this. They had told the Corinthians what they wanted to hear.

Instead of worrying about the reaction of his audience, Paul focused on whom he was serving: God (6:4). He would **serve God whether** he was honored or despised, whether he was slandered or praised. No flattery or insult would distract Paul from preaching the Good News.

This passage contrasts how God evaluated Paul's ministry with how his critics saw it. God's evaluation mattered most to Paul, for he had his sights set on eternity, not on the temporary conditions of the present (see 5:1-10). The paradox was that though Paul and his coworkers were completely **honest,** they were still being accused as **impostors.** They had renounced all deceptive means to communicate the holy message of God (see 4:2). They used no tricks or games. Instead, Paul preached the truth with a genuine frankness and with the power of God himself (see 1 Corinthians 2:4).

Paul's preaching and actions were **well known,** but he was **treated as unknown.** Some considered his message as foolishness (see Acts 17:18-21, 32-33; 18:14-17; 1 Corinthians 2:6-10). Second Corinthians began with an explanation of how Paul had faced **death** in Asia Minor (present-day Turkey; see 1:8). But he was **still alive.** Paul had been **beaten** on numerous occasions for preaching the gospel (see 6:5; 11:23-24). In the first century, often people would die of a beating at the hands of the authorities. The Jews used whips with metal pieces, which would tear into the flesh. The Roman authorities beat offenders with rods. Both beatings could be severe enough to kill a person.

In addition to hardships, Paul's ministry involved mental anguish. Paul had agonized over the Corinthians' spiritual welfare, as well as the welfare of other churches. He had spent night and day in prayer, committing these churches and their

congregations to the Lord (see Romans 10:1; Philippians 1:9; 1 Thessalonians 3:10; 2 Thessalonians 1:11). Although the **hearts** of him and his coworkers would **ache** over the churches, they were filled with **joy** because they knew what their spiritual struggles would accomplish. Being **poor** was another hardship. Through his deprivation, however, Paul had learned to be content with what God had given him (Philippians 4:12) for Paul knew that he already possessed **everything**—that is, the riches of a Kingdom that would last forever (see Matthew 6:19-21).

6:11-13 Paul had been completely straightforward with the Corinthians. His transparent honesty is mentioned at numerous places in this letter (1:12-13, 23-24; 2:17; 4:1-2; 5:11). But critics at Corinth were accusing Paul of some sort of deception. Paul hoped that the very fact that he was cataloging his own weaknesses and sufferings before the Corinthians would testify to his openness. Paul had revealed his true feelings for the Corinthian believers—he and his coworkers had no **lack of love.** The Corinthians, however, were withholding their **love from** them. As Paul would explain in this letter, any harsh words he had for the Corinthians came from his deep love for them (see 7:8-13). He wanted them to grow in the faith. Paul hoped his sincerity in this letter—the way he opened up his life to the Corinthians' examination—would prompt them to also **open** their **hearts** to him.

As founder of the church, Paul had fatherly affections for the Corinthians. He had spent hours agonizing over the believers' spiritual welfare (11:28) and had worked hard for them. But like rebellious **children,** the Corinthians had returned Paul's concern with a cold heart. Although Paul could have commanded and disciplined them, he merely pleaded with them. He wanted to give them a chance to reform their ways (see Paul's attitude in 2:1-4; 13:5).

THE TEMPLE OF THE LIVING GOD / 6:14–7:1

The unique Greek writing style of this section indicates that Paul most likely was quoting an early Christian sermon, perhaps even a Jewish sermon. He had already exhorted the Corinthians to be reconciled to God (5:20-21; 6:1-2) and was pleading with them to open their hearts to him as God's messenger (6:11-12). In this short sermon quote, Paul was reminding the Corinthians what reconciliation to God means. If they were to open their hearts to him as God's messenger (6:13), they had to separate themselves from the wickedness of unbelievers. Their pagan neighbors would only tempt them to reject God's word and God's ways.

6:14-15 After passionately appealing to the Corinthians to open their hearts to him, Paul exhorted

them, **"Don't team up with those who are unbelievers."** He urged them not to form binding relationships with nonbelievers because this might weaken their Christian commitment, integrity, or standards.

Earlier, Paul had explained that not associating with unbelievers did not mean isolation from nonbelievers (see 1 Corinthians 5:9-10). The Corinthians were even to remain with their unbelieving spouses (1 Corinthians 7:12-13). In order to witness to their neighbors, believers were to adopt some of the customs of the people to whom they were witnessing (1 Corinthians 9:2).

So what did it mean to avoid "teaming up"? The picture is of teaming up two animals, such as an ox and a mule, to plow a field. However, because the plow would be pulled unevenly or the weight being carried would be spilled, it wouldn't work out (see Deuteronomy 22:10). In the same way, a believer and an unbeliever are categorically different. Teaming up with unbelievers would lead to disaster. The Corinthian church was having a difficult time separating themselves from the immoral practices of their unbelieving neighbors. Paul was telling the Corinthians to avoid any situation that would compromise their faith or their Christian morals. Why? Because **goodness** cannot **partner with wickedness; light** cannot **live with darkness; Christ and the Devil** cannot live in **harmony.** Therefore, **how can a believer be a partner with an unbeliever?** While this verse applies to all partnerships and alliances, marriage certainly comes under this teaching.

6:16-18 As building blocks of **God's temple,** each individual had to maintain a holy life, set apart to God. There was no room for any mixed loyalties. No compromise or agreement had been made between the true God and **idols.**

Several Old Testament quotes illustrate how the church at Corinth was a fulfillment of God's promises long ago. When God brought the Israelites out of Egyptian bondage, he made them his holy people. He had them construct a tabernacle, where his glorious presence would reside in its inner sanctuary. In this sense, God would **live in them**—even **walk among them.** He wasn't going to be a far-off God, who watched the Israelites from a distance. The Israelites were his **people,** and he would be **their God** (see Leviticus 26:11-12).

The prophet Ezekiel also prophesied of a time when God would live among his people forever (see Ezekiel 37:26-28). By quoting this passage, Paul was saying that Ezekiel's prophecy was being fulfilled in the Corinthian church. Jesus, a descendant of David and the Son of God himself, had defeated Satan. He had begun his reign as the King of a heavenly Kingdom. As believers, the Corinthians were part of this spiritual Kingdom. Jesus, as God in human form,

had literally shown people what God was like (Matthew 1:23; John 1:14). In a real sense, God had lived among his people. After Jesus' resurrection and ascension, God sent his Holy Spirit to the believers who had gathered in Jerusalem on the Day of Pentecost. From that day to the present, every believer has God living within his or her spirit (Romans 8:9; 1 Corinthians 6:19; 2 Timothy 1:14).

After telling the Corinthians not to partner with unbelievers, Paul quickly gave them a positive command. Instead of partnering with unbelievers, they were to **separate** from anything that was sinful. To emphasize his point, Paul strung together several Old Testament quotes. He loosely quoted Isaiah 52:11. Originally this was a command for the exiles to come out of Babylon and to abandon any object associated with pagan worship. In this passage, Paul interpreted this command as also a command to Christians to separate themselves from the immorality of the pagan peoples around them.

Paul continued his comparison of the Corinthian Christians with the returning Israelite exiles. The phrase **"I will welcome you"** is an adaptation of Ezekiel's prophecy that God would gather all of Israel's exiles together (see Ezekiel 20:34). Finally, Paul adapted God's promise to be the Father of David's Son (see 2 Samuel 7:14; see also Hebrews 1:5, where the author interpreted this verse as a prophecy about Jesus) to also refer to believers. Christians would become the **sons and daughters** of God (see Isaiah 43:6 where Isaiah prophesied of a time when God would gather all his sons and daughters together). Through Christ's death, believers have become part of God's loving family (see Galatians 4:1-7).

7:1 Because God has given **these promises:** to live with his people (6:16), to welcome them as his people (6:17), and to act like a loving Father toward them (6:18), Christians are to **cleanse** themselves of **everything that can defile.** The Corinthians were to have nothing to do with paganism. They were to make a clean break with their past and give themselves to God alone. **Work toward complete purity** means "becoming mature" or "becoming complete." Thus, Paul wasn't suggesting that the Corinthians could become sinless in this life. Instead, he was prodding the Corinthians to work at maturing in their faith. God had provided them with all the resources they needed, and Christ's Spirit would empower them to become Christlike (see Romans 8:2).

Paul exhorted the Corinthians to pursue purity out of **fear** of **God.** "Fear" means to keep respect or awe for God. He is the almighty Creator. Obeying God's commands and pursuing spiritual maturity are the best ways to show respect for God.

7

2 CORINTHIANS 7:2-16

PAUL'S JOY AT THE CHURCH'S REPENTANCE / 7:2-16

Paul here resumed his story about his recent travel plans (7:5) Concerned about the accusations against his authority and his ministry circulating in Corinth, Paul spent these chapters (2:14–7:4) explaining and defending his ministry to the Corinthians. He ended this extended defense by appealing to the Corinthians to not only reconcile themselves to God but also to reconcile themselves to himself as God's messenger (see 6:13 and 7:2). So this (7:3) was a logical place to resume a description of his latest travels (from 2:13), for Titus had told Paul of the Corinthians' steps at reconciling themselves to Paul. The joy of meeting Titus had been accompanied by an even greater joy: Paul had been delighted to hear that the Corinthians were sorry about the distressing incident that occurred on his last visit and that they longed for him to visit them again (see 7:7). This was not only a reunion between Titus and Paul, but also a spiritual reunion between Paul and the Corinthians.

7:2-3 This repeats Paul's plea in 6:13 for them to **open** their **hearts** to Paul and his coworkers. This appeal logically follows Paul's exhortation to the Corinthians to separate themselves from relationships with unbelievers that would compromise their loyalty to Christ (see 6:14–7:1). This appeal is coupled with three denials. Most likely, Paul was responding to accusations that the Corinthians had been repeating. Not one person among the Corinthians had been wronged, led astray, or taken advantage of. All three words are translations of Greek words that were commonly used for deceitful and exploitative financial dealings. Paul's critics may have been criticizing the collection for the Jerusalem church (see 8:1-7). The end of this letter contains a strong defense against this charge—that is, the charge of financially exploiting the believers (12:13, 17-18).

Paul had spent considerable time defending his ministry (see the previous verse and 1:23; 3:1-6; 4:1-2, 8-10; 5:6-10; 6:3-13). The believers at Corinth may even have thought that Paul was abandoning them or dismissing them as genuine Christians. Here Paul assured the Corinthians that this was not his intent. On the contrary, Paul considered himself so intimately connected to the Corinthians that not even death could separate them. In Christ, he would **live** with the Corinthians and even **die** with them.

7:4 Like a loving father, Paul had boasted to Titus of the Corinthians and hoped to boast about them before Jesus (see 1:14; 7:14). Paul possessed **the** **highest confidence** in them, and that hope had been realized by Titus's recent report (see 7:14). Moreover, even though Paul had recently faced many **troubles,** knowing that the Corinthians were maturing in the faith had **encouraged** him and made him **happy.**

7:5-7 Here Paul resumed the story that he left off in 2:13 of how he had forsaken some exciting evangelistic opportunities in Troas in order to look for Titus in **Macedonia.** He knew that Titus had visited Corinth and would have some news of how the Corinthians were progressing in their faith. So like a father who was anxious to hear news of his children, Paul had hurried ahead to find out how the Corinthians were doing.

On leaving Troas, Paul continued to face **conflict.** Paul's first visit to Macedonia had been a tumultuous one, and it appears that this one was also. On his first visit, a group of Jews from Thessalonica had followed him all over the province of Macedonia, opposing his teaching (see Acts 17:13). Perhaps it was those determined opponents in Thessalonica who harassed Paul on this journey. Paul's letters to the Thessalonians reveal that the church was enduring much persecution (see 1 Thessalonians 1:6-8; 2 Thessalonians 1:4). Paul was also beset by **fear.** He had already told the Corinthians that he was concerned about Titus's and the Corinthians' welfare (see 2:13). But God had **encouraged** him at the right time with **the arrival of Titus.** Being reunited with a fellow laborer in Christ brought Paul **joy.**

But more than that, **the news he brought** from Corinth was cause for joy. Titus had been sent on a difficult mission. He had to deliver a stern letter from Paul that exhorted the Corinthians to right some wrongs. No one knew—especially Paul, who was greatly concerned about the whole matter (see 2:13)—how the Corinthians would react. Titus brought word that the Corinthians had welcomed him and his unpleasant message. He had been welcomed as an emissary of Paul.

Moreover, the Corinthians had given Titus **encouragement;** as a result, Titus could encourage Paul. According to Titus's report, the Corinthians were truly **sorry** about the incident and wanted to reaffirm their commitment to Paul and let him know of their **love** for him. They were even **looking forward** to Paul's next **visit.** Naturally, such a report would encourage any leader. After a rocky period between Paul and the Corinthians, the church was correcting some of the problems that had arisen in their congregation. They were ready for Paul to visit them.

7:8-9 Paul's previous **letter** to the Corinthians was the one he had cried over because he had to censure them (see 2:1-4 for a discussion of this letter). It has become generally accepted that 1 Corinthians was not the letter to which Paul was here alluding, primarily because 1 Corinthians as a whole does not reflect the extreme sorrow described by Paul here and in 2:4. In this letter, he had exhorted the Corinthians to discipline their members who persisted in error—specifically, the one who had publicly opposed Paul's authority (see 2:1-4; 7:8; 13:1-4). At first, Paul was **sorry** that he had sent that letter. He had written it with a great amount of anguish (see 2:4), knowing that his tone and his message would be **painful** to the Corinthian believers. But Titus's report that they were still anxiously awaiting his visit and had reaffirmed their loyalty to him had caused Paul to change his mind. The letter had produced its desired effect. Although harsh, it had produced a change of heart in the Corinthians, the repentance that God desired.

The repentance Paul wanted was not merely anguish over the acrimonious situation or a regret that it had ever happened. Godly repentance implies a reorientation of the entire person away from sins and toward God's ways. It is a "turning around." The type of **remorse** that compels a person to **change** his or her direction is what God wants—not "sorrow" that paralyzes or becomes resentful. To Paul's great joy, the disciplinary letter had **not harmed** the church.

7:10 Many people are sorry only for the effects of their sins or for being caught. In the original Greek,

sorrow without repentance literally means "the sorrow of the world." When people do not channel their grief over their behavior into life-changing actions, it is unproductive grief. It leads to self-pity. But **godly sorrow** is practical and action-oriented. When a person realizes what he or she has done wrong, that person should not only regret the error but also turn back to God. Only God can empower people to change their ways. Only God can save people from the way sin imprisons them and paralyzes them. Only God can **help us turn away from sin and seek salvation.**

Compare the stories of Peter and Judas. Both handled the events surrounding Jesus' death in a wrong way. Judas brazenly betrayed Jesus with a kiss (Mark 14:43-46). Peter denied knowing Jesus three different times (John 18:15-27). Both were overcome with grief over their actions (Matthew 26:75; 27:3). Although Peter was distraught, he had the humility and the courage to admit his failure, reform his behavior, and rededicate his life to Jesus' cause (see John 21:15-19). In contrast, Judas let his remorse eat at his soul. Eventually overcome by guilt, he committed suicide. Judas wasn't able to learn from his sin and repent. He didn't submit his sins to Christ and beg to be forgiven. He was too proud to cry out for salvation, so his stubbornness led to death.

7:11 Titus's encouraging report from Corinth gave Paul the evidence that the Corinthians had responded appropriately to his stern letter—with **godly sorrow.** That sorrow **produced earnestness** and a **concern to clear** themselves. Titus had explained the Corinthians' reaction to Paul's letter step-by-step; and Paul listed those steps here, approving each one. The letter had inspired appropriate **indignation,** or displeasure, about what had been happening among them. It had also caused **alarm.** Perhaps the Corinthians were fearful of God's divine judgment or Paul's discipline. Their intense **longing** and great **zeal** to restore their damaged relationship with Paul had led them to take prompt action **to punish the wrongdoer.** Paul praised them in glowing terms. Their zeal to **make things right** was exactly the kind of behavior God's holy people should exhibit.

7:12-13 Paul's primary purpose was to save the deteriorating relationship between himself and the Corinthians; and according to the previous verse, the letter had done just that. Although the Corinthians knew **who did the wrong** and **who was wronged,** Paul discreetly didn't mention names because more than likely his letter would be circulated in all the churches of southern Greece. Since Paul was instructing the Corinthians to restore this man to Christian fellowship, Paul didn't want his name to be unnecessarily despised. What was more important to Paul than exactly who the offender was and what he had done was the furtherance of the cause of the gospel in Corinth. Paul reminded the Corinthians that their relationship to him wasn't trivial. Everything he did would benefit them in some way; their prayers and actions would, in turn, encourage him in his task of preaching the gospel (see 1:6-7, 11; 7:4). They were so interdependent because everything each of them did was **in the sight of God**—in fact, in his presence (2:10, 17; 3:4; 4:14). They were all part of God's family.

The Corinthians' appropriate reaction to Paul's disciplinary letter had **encouraged** Paul. In addition, he was encouraged by the way **Titus** had been **welcomed**. Even though the church in Corinth was

in turmoil, Titus had taken on the challenge of delivering the disagreeable news to the Corinthians. No one—not even Paul—knew how the Corinthians would respond. Yet Titus was pleasantly surprised. The Corinthians welcomed him and his message.

7:14-16 Even though the Corinthians had caused Paul so much pain and grief (see 2:4; 8:16; 11:28), Paul still was **proud** of his spiritual children. He refused to focus on their weaknesses and failures; instead, he praised their strengths (see how he praised the Corinthians at 8:7; 1 Corinthians 14:12). Paul was glad that his **boasting** about them to Titus had **proved true**. Their treatment of him had, in turn, moved Titus to care for them **more than ever.** Paul's confidence had not been misplaced.

2 CORINTHIANS 8

A CALL TO GENEROUS GIVING / 8:1-15

About a year before the writing of 2 Corinthians, the believers in Corinth had started collecting money for the poor in Jerusalem (see 8:10). First Corinthians instructed the Corinthians to set aside money every week for the offering (see 1 Corinthians 16:1-4). But that collection had floundered (see 8:10-11). It appears that greedy, traveling preachers (2:17) had suggested that Paul had invented the collection to extort money from the congregation. They asserted this, even though Paul had taken no money from the Corinthians to support his own ministry (7:2; 11:7-9; 12:14-17). He had supported himself as a tentmaker when he was in Corinth (Acts 18:1-4). These traveling preachers may have very well wanted to divert the money to themselves (2:17). In any case, one of the purposes of 2 Corinthians was to encourage the Corinthians (in a diplomatic way) to finish the collection they had started a year ago (8:10-11; 9:1-3).

8:1 Paul's great tact with the Corinthians should be noted. Although Paul planned to ask the Corinthians to collect money for the impoverished Jerusalem Christians, he first presented them with an illustration of admirable generosity: the giving of the **churches in Macedonia.**

8:2 Paul had founded the Macedonian churches on his second missionary journey. Although Jesus had called Paul and his fellow evangelists to Macedonia, they had experienced opposition to the preaching of the gospel at every turn (see Acts 16:6-10). From Paul's letters to the Thessalonians and to the Philippians, it appears that this persecution did not subside after Paul's initial visit. In spite of their **trouble and hard times,** the Mace-

donian Christians had grown in their Christian faith, endeavoring to imitate Jesus in every situation (see Philippians 1:29-30; 1 Thessalonians 1:6; 2:1-2, 14). And despite their **deep poverty,** they still gave generously. They were filled with **wonderful joy** because they possessed the message of salvation (see 1 Thessalonians 1:6) and had faith in God (see Philippians 1:25-26). Their joy **overflowed in rich generosity.** They considered their monetary gifts to the Jerusalem Christians as a small token of their appreciation to God for their eternal salvation.

8:3-4 Paul continued to praise the Macedonians for their attitude about giving. Apparently, the Macedonians had calculated how much they could give and then tried to exceed that amount. Their giving was **far more** than what Paul expected. In fact, Paul had been reluctant to ask for money for the Jerusalem Christians. It was the Macedonians who, of their own **free will**, had **begged** to be a part of the **privilege of sharing** in this gift.

8:5 The Macedonians' giving was not motivated by a desire for praise from Paul or others. Their generosity was fundamentally motivated by their desire to serve the Lord. They **first** dedicated themselves to God and expressed the desire to follow **whatever directions God might give them.** They gave because they knew they were God's. Everything they had—even their very souls—were God's. Knowing this, they devoted themselves to serving Jesus and his Kingdom in any way they could.

8:6 Titus would **return** to Corinth and **encourage** the believers to **complete** their **share in this ministry of giving**—in other words, to finish the collection efforts there. On a previous visit, Titus had encouraged the Corinthians to continue collecting sums of money every week for the Jerusalem church as Paul had instructed (1 Corinthians 16:1-4). Apparently, the Corinthians' giving had dwindled.

8:7-8 The Corinthian church had a great amount of spiritual gifts—they excelled in **faith, gifted speakers, knowledge,** and **love.** Paul placed **giving** alongside other gifts, asking that the Corinthians **excel** in that **ministry** as well. Giving is a natural response of Christian love. Paul did not order the Corinthians to give; he encouraged them to **prove** the sincerity of their **love** for Christ. When you love someone, you want to help that person. You want to give your time, your attention, and your possessions to enrich that person. If you refuse to help, your love is not as sincere as you say it is.

8:9 The Corinthian church—a wealthy church— had pledged a great deal of money, but they had not yet given any of it. Paul was concerned that they might never get around to giving what they had promised, so he gave them two models of generous giving. Paul had given them the first model: the poor Macedonian Christians who had enthusiastically given beyond what they could afford. Then in this verse, Paul gave another model: Jesus himself. Although the Macedonians had shown a great amount of generosity, their sacrifice couldn't compare with Jesus' giving of himself. Jesus' action was the ultimate model for the Corinthians.

Jesus became **poor** for the Corinthians' **sakes** by generously giving up his rights as God and becoming human. He even voluntarily surrendered himself to death on a cross—the most cruel and

humiliating death known at that time. Yet by doing so, he made all who believe in him **rich.** Christians have not only been saved through his self-sacrificial actions, they have also been accepted into God's family (5:8, 18). That means that they have a glorious, eternal inheritance in heaven (4:18; 5:1).

8:10-11 Paul was careful not to command the Corinthians (8:8), but he strongly suggested that they **finish** what they had **started a year** before. This passage appeals to the Corinthians' competitive spirit (see also 8:1-2, 6-8). They had been the **first** in two ways: They were the first to suggest this collection, and they were the first to contribute substantially to the fund. Now they should **carry this project through to completion.** He challenged the Corinthians to **give whatever** they could **according to what** they had. Four principles of giving emerge in the following verses:

1. Your willingness to give cheerfully is more important than the amount you give (8:12; 9:5).
2. You should strive to fulfill your financial commitments (see also 9:5).
3. If you give to others in need, they will, in turn, help you when you are in need (8:14).
4. You should give as a response to Christ, not for anything you can get out of it (8:9; 9:13).

How you give reflects your devotion to Christ. Don't rush into a commitment to give. Evaluate your finances so that you will be able to keep your promise.

8:12 Paul wasn't concerned about the total amount the Corinthians would raise, but he wanted them to be **eager** in giving. When he spoke of the Macedonians' giving, he did not tell the Corinthians **how much** the Macedonians had given but **how** they had given: with great joy out of their devotion to Christ (8:2-5). Paul was more concerned about the Corinthians' attitude than whether he reached a certain goal in his fund-raising.

Although what the Corinthians possessed was a gift from God in the first place (1 Corinthians 4:7), Paul asked them to **give** of what they had, **not what** they didn't have. Sacrificial giving must be responsible.

8:13-14 Paul wanted the Corinthians to give generously but not to the extent that those who depended on the givers (their families, for example) must **suffer from having too little.** Give until it hurts, but don't give so that it hurts your family or relatives who need your financial support.

The Jerusalem Christians had been poor for some time. About a decade before this collection, the believers in Antioch had sent Paul and Barnabas with some monetary relief for the church at Jerusalem. Palestine had been hit with a severe famine, and apparently the believers in Jerusalem were in great need (see Acts 11:27-30). Most likely, the Jerusalem Christians remained extremely poor because of their social ostracism. Apparently, the Christians in and around Jerusalem had limited ways to support themselves—even a decade later. Paul considered the poverty of the Jerusalem Christians as an opportunity for Gentile believers. They could dispel any doubts about the genuineness of their faith by demonstrating it through giving generously to the Jerusalem church—the church that had sacrificed in the beginning to send evangelists throughout the Roman world (see Paul's explanation of the collection in Romans 15:25-27). Paul hoped their generosity would smooth over some of the hesitancy of some Jewish Christians to accept Gentiles into the church.

In the end, the giving and the receiving of money would tie the entire church together. Each would be dependent on the other. Just as the Gentiles had been dependent on the Jewish Christians for the wonderful message of salvation, the Jews would be dependent on the Gentiles for financial support. **In this way, everyone's needs will be met.** Paul appealed to the principle of **equality.** Each church should provide for other churches as the need arose.

Each church should help the others out of the resources God had given it. If one church was wealthy, it could meet the others' needs. When conditions reversed, the formerly poor church might be able to return the favor.

8:15 Paul quoted Exodus 16:18 to illustrate how everyone's needs would be met. In the wilderness, the Israelites could not find enough food to feed all of their number. So God provided food from heaven: manna. These thin, white flakes appeared on the ground every morning. God told the Israelites to gather as much as they needed for the day. Some gathered more than others, but each had enough for the day. Those who were greedy tried to store the manna for the next day. They didn't trust God for what they needed. Their lack of trust was rewarded with a smelly, maggot-ridden mess (see Exodus 16:19).

Although God didn't supply the first-century Christians' needs the same way, Paul saw the same principles at work. God would provide everyone with what they needed. Although some had more and others had less, everyone's needs would be met in the end. God wanted the wealthy to give out of their surplus so that the needy could have enough. It wasn't a matter of exact equality; instead, it was a matter of fairness or justice.

TITUS AND HIS COMPANIONS / 8:16-24

The rest of chapter 8 is, in essence, a letter of recommendation for Titus and two anonymous "brothers." Titus was an official representative of Paul, while the "brothers" were representatives of churches that had contributed to the Jerusalem fund (see 8:18, 22).

8:16-17 Paul first commended **Titus** to the Corinthians. He had already emphasized how encouraged Titus was after his initial visit with them (see 7:13-15). The Corinthians had welcomed Titus, had respected his message to them, and had even provided for his needs (see 7:7, 15). When Paul asked Titus to visit Corinth again, he **welcomed** Paul's **request.** Titus had been **eager to go and see** them. He had the same **enthusiasm** Paul did in wanting to spur the Corinthians to excel in giving (see 8:7).

8:18-19 Paul took some steps to guard the integrity of the Jerusalem collection. A **brother** had been **appointed by the churches** to ensure that the money would be given to its intended recipients. Paul didn't want any allegations of financial impropriety. This brother would function as a representative for the churches to ensure that the money of the Jerusalem collection would be handled properly. Paul did not want anyone to accuse

him of mishandling this gift for the Jerusalem Christians, for that would defeat his entire purpose. The gift was to promote unity in the early church, not division.

8:20-21 Paul didn't want anyone to be suspicious of his handling of the money. Therefore, he was **careful** that his actions were not only **honorable before the Lord,** who saw all things, but also before people, who look on the appearance of things (see Proverbs 3:4). In order to finish the collection without **any suspicion,** Paul continued to refrain from collecting the money himself. Instead, he sent someone whom the Corinthians respected and trusted: Titus. Accompanying Titus were two other representatives from the churches who contributed to the fund to oversee how the money was handled.

8:22 Paul recommended the third **brother** to the Corinthians in these verses. Although Paul didn't mention this person's name, he made it clear that the man had proven himself. This man's zeal for Christ had been **thoroughly tested** and he had passed these tests. Besides, this man had evidently heard about the Corinthians from Paul and Titus, and he possessed the same **confidence** that Paul had in them (see 7:13-16).

8:23 The last two verses of this chapter summarize Paul's recommendation of Titus and his two traveling companions. He called Titus his **partner** to emphasize Titus's authority among the Corinthians. Titus was Paul's official representative to the Corinthians to collect the money for the relief of the Jerusalem Christians (8:6). The two **representatives of the churches** who accompanied Titus were also recommended by Paul to the Corinthians (the

complete list of representatives is given in Acts 20:4). The Greek for "representatives" is *apostoloi*— literally, apostles. In the Gospels, this Greek word is only used for the Twelve. Paul in his letters, however, used the term for any representative of a church commissioned for some special task.

8:24 Paul told the Corinthians to shower their Christian **love** on these fellow believers, just as they had welcomed Titus before (see 7:7, 13). These men were representing the other **churches;** therefore, the Corinthians should conduct themselves in an appropriate way, for their conduct would be broadcast to other churches by these representatives. Paul wanted the believers to **prove** that his boasting about them was **justified.**

2 CORINTHIANS 9

THE COLLECTION FOR CHRISTIANS IN JERUSALEM / 9:1-15
This passage reminds the Corinthians of their initial enthusiasm for the Jerusalem collection, their delight that God could use them to help other believers. Their enthusiasm was contagious. The Macedonians had heard of their eagerness and had also eagerly responded to the appeal for money. As Paul was preparing to collect the last of the contributions, however, the Corinthians' enthusiasm had waned. The collection had ground to a halt. Paul was worried that when he came to Corinth the Corinthians would give grudgingly. God wants cheerful givers and enthusiastic team players (9:7). He can do without selfish and disgruntled givers.

9:1-2 Paul was not sending Titus and his representatives to Corinth (8:16-24) in order to explain the collection and how it would benefit the Jerusalem Christians. A **year** before, they were one of the first to **begin helping.** In fact, Paul had been **boasting** to the Christians in Macedonia about the Corinthians' **enthusiasm** that had incited others to give. Paul was, in effect, prodding the Corinthians to rekindle their initial enthusiasm for giving. Paul wasn't naive about human behavior. The start and end of a marathon are much more thrilling than the miles in between. It takes stubborn determination and perseverance to keep on running.

9:3 Paul didn't want his boasts about the Corinthians to be proven **wrong.** That was why Paul decided to send Titus with two other **brothers.** In several months, Paul would return to Jerusalem with the money (see Acts 20:1-5, 22-24; 24:17); therefore, the final contribution had to be **ready** when he came to Corinth (9:4). Titus's job was to inspire the Corinthians to diligently set aside

money as Paul had instructed them in his earlier letter (see 1 Corinthians 16:1-4). The representatives who accompanied Titus, on the other hand, were to ensure that all the money was collected. In sharp contrast to the false teachers who had infiltrated the Corinthian church, no underhanded methods would be used (2:17). Respected and trustworthy representatives from the churches would witness the entire process (see 8:20).

9:4 Paul **had told** the Macedonians how the Corinthians had eagerly wanted to give from the beginning (about a year ago). But since then, much had changed. Paul was taking precautions just in case the Corinthians were to challenge his apostolic authority on this visit (see 13:1-4). These **Macedonian Christians** would act as witnesses to how Paul had handled any confrontation that might occur. Paul was giving the Corinthians plenty of warning about his coming. In this passage, he skillfully warned the Corinthians of how he would be **humiliated** if the Corinthians were unprepared for his visit. On the surface, Paul was speaking about the Jerusalem collection, but he certainly may have been warning the Corinthians of his other concerns. Paul was hoping that the Macedonians would not find the Corinthian church in spiritual disorder. That would be even more embarrassing. The end of this letter will state it more bluntly, where Paul would sternly warn the Corinthians to prepare themselves for his visit by examining their hearts before God.

9:5 Paul wanted this money to be **a willing gift, not one given under pressure** by trying to pull it together in a short time period. Otherwise, his appearance at Corinth would be associated with frenzied collection efforts. If the money was raised in a short time, it might give the appearance of some type of scam. Paul wanted the Corinthians to remember that they were giving to God. This required some advance planning. Titus and the two traveling **brothers** would go to Corinth before Paul's visit to **make sure the gift** was **ready.** Proper preparation would ensure that the people gave cheerfully.

9:6 The people of this time were intimately familiar with the principles of an agricultural economy. Planting, weeding, and harvesting were common, everyday tasks. Keeping more seeds in storage might appear to be wise, a way to ensure against future disasters. But the farmer who scattered his seed meagerly inevitably would have a small harvest. A farmer who refused to risk his grain on the next year's harvest would lose. This piece of agricultural wisdom contains a profound truth about Christian giving (see Proverbs 11:24-26; 22:8-9 for similar sayings). Like the foolish farmer, he **who plants only a few seeds**—who refuses to trust God with their future financial security—will inevitably lose out on God's rich blessings. He who sows **generously will get a generous crop.** The eternal harvest will exceed their expectations.

9:7 Each Corinthian believer was to **make up** his **own mind as to how much** would be given to this collection. It wasn't to be an impulsive decision but a deliberate one. They were to assess their own ability to give and plan accordingly. Paul didn't want to use urgent appeals or pressure tactics to coerce the Corinthians to give. Even though he was the one appealing for the money, he was careful to give the Corinthians enough time to think and to pray about how much God wanted them to give. Paul didn't want anyone giving **reluctantly or in response to pressure.** Paul knew that God weighs the heart and not the amount of money; he looks at the giver and not the gift. One **who gives cheerfully** out of a sincere gratitude for what God has

done, is the type of giver God cherishes. God multiplies those gifts beyond measure (9:11).

9:8 The biggest obstacle that people have to overcome in order to give is worry. What if I will not have enough money next year for my retirement? What if some emergency comes up? What if I lose my job? These verses reassure the Corinthians that God is able to **generously provide all** their needs. The purpose of God's overwhelming blessing is always to equip his people to have **plenty left over to share with others.** This text doesn't imply that Christian giving is a contract with God, where the one who gives gets. Instead, it says that God will provide whatever a Christian needs to do good. Thus, in the end, a Christian's good works will bring praise and glory to God.

9:9 Just as a farmer has to scatter the seed on the ground in order to reap an abundant harvest, so Christians must **give generously to the poor** in order to reap God's blessing. Paul already made it clear that God's blessing does not always include an increase of riches. All of God's gifts, both spiritual and material, are intended to help a Christian do good works (9:8). This quote from Psalm 112:9 demonstrates this truth. Although the psalmist does speak of material blessings for the righteous person in that psalm (Psalm 112:3), Paul quotes a line that emphasizes the spiritual benefits of generosity to the poor. Those who are blessed by God with financial resources should give generously to help those with less. These **good deeds will never be forgotten.** Those who receive this person's gifts will remember the generosity for a long time, but, more importantly, God will never forget the person's benevolence.

9:10 God **gives** both the **seed** and the **bread,** both the surplus to invest and the resources to support one's family every day. The resources that God gives Christians are not to be hoarded, foolishly devoured, or thrown away. God gives gifts to his people for their own use and for investing back into God's work. Instead of squandering these gifts, Christians need to cultivate them in order to produce more good works (9:8).

God does not limit himself to merely giving more resources—in other words, more seed. He blesses what you sow. He showers the seed with gentle rain. He gives the seed that is sown everything it needs to grow into a healthy, thriving plant. Although the seed is small, it has great potential if it has the right conditions to grow. In the same way, God blesses believers' feeble efforts at generosity so that they **produce a great harvest.** This harvest does not consist of personal wealth and riches. It is a harvest **of generosity.** God will take inadequate efforts at good works and increase them so that they bless many people. All a person has to do is give.

9:11-12 Giving generously to those in need causes **two good things** to **happen.** First, through those **gifts** given **to those who need them,** God meets their **needs** (here, specifically, the needs of the **Christians in Jerusalem**). Second, the recipients of these generous gifts will **joyfully express their thanksgiving to God.** Their celebration over these gifts will lead to heartfelt praise to God, for they will know that it is God who enables the giver to give in the first place.

9:13 In addition to the normal advantages that come through Christian giving (see 9:11-12), Paul hoped that the Jerusalem collection would have extra benefits: He hoped that through this gift from Gentile Christians, Jewish and Gentile believers would be drawn closer together in Christian fellowship. Paul viewed the collection for the destitute Jerusalem believers as concrete evidence that the Gentile believers were **obedient to the Good News of Christ.** One of the directives of the Jerusalem council was that Gentile Christians shouldn't forget the poor (see Galatians 2:10). The Gentiles' generous gift to the Jerusalem poor would prove that they were obeying this directive. Paul never viewed the Jerusalem collection as a rite of initiation for the Gentiles. He was always perfectly clear that salvation came only through faith in Jesus

(Galatians 3:26). Giving back to God, however, is one of many signs that a person's faith is authentic (see also James 2:14-18).

9:14 The collection for the Jerusalem believers would not only demonstrate the sincerity of the Corinthians' faith, it would also tie the Christian community of faith closer together. Jewish Christians would view the monetary gift as an indication of God's **wonderful grace** working in the Corinthians' lives. This generous gift might be the one thing that would prompt these Jews to start praying for the Corinthian believers for the first time. Just as the Corinthians' prayers for Paul made them partners with him in sharing the gospel (1:11), so these prayers of Jewish Christians would make them partners with Gentile believers. Through this, the entire community of faith—Jewish and Gentile Christians—would be built up in love.

9:15 Paul ended his appeal for giving with fervent praise to God. The source of all this—the ability to give, the desire to give, even the reconciliation that would occur between Jewish and Gentile believers—was solely from God's hands. God is the ultimate Giver. He gave **a gift too wonderful for words**—the gift of **his Son.** God's extraordinary gift of salvation should motivate you to give generously to others. Spend time meditating on how much God has given you. Then evaluate your generosity in light of God's generosity to you.

2 CORINTHIANS 10

PAUL DEFENDS HIS AUTHORITY / 10:1-18

Clearly, chapter 10 introduces a drastic change of tone in 2 Corinthians: from conciliatory to severe. In the first nine chapters, Paul was careful to congratulate the Corinthians for their obedience to his latest directives (2:5-11; 7:2-15). The last four chapters, however, warn the Corinthians in no uncertain terms to reform their ways (10:6, 11; 13:2, 5). The first half of the letter uses diplomatic language (see 3:1; 5:12), while the second half contains scathing sarcasm (11:7-8, 19).

10:1 Although most of the Corinthian congregation sided with Paul (as is evident from 7:8-16), a persistent minority continued to slander him. The group impugned Paul's integrity by pointing out that he was **bold** in his **letters** but **timid in person**—in other words, reluctant to exercise any authority when he visited them. Paul's critics saw this as duplicity and an indication that Paul truly

didn't possess the spiritual authority he claimed. Chapters 10 through 13 are Paul's direct response to his critics in Corinth.

This harsh section of 2 Corinthians (chapter 10 through 13) begins with kind and gentle words. Paul had the authority to command, yet he consciously refused to exercise his authority in an overbearing manner. Instead, he pled with them.

Christ was Paul's model in the approach he took here. Although Jesus possessed complete heavenly authority, he came to this earth as a servant (Philippians 2:5-11). Instead of commanding obedience and respect, Jesus simply asks for people to believe in him. Following Christ's example, the apostle Paul, who possessed full authority from Jesus (2:17; 5:19), merely pleaded with the Corinthians. In this way, Paul was showing them Christ's **gentleness and kindness.** The Greek word for "gentleness" has the idea of "forbearance"—like that of a benevolent judge being lenient on the guilty. "Kindness" speaks of friendliness and cheerfulness. In other words, Paul wasn't going to act like a harsh and overbearing judge.

10:2 Here Paul explained why he was writing this letter. He was hoping and praying that when he came, everything would be in order in the church (see 13:7). He wanted to give the Corinthians enough time to deal with the difficulties in their church on their own. This verse also clearly identifies Paul's critics: **those who think we act from purely human motives.** Apparently, Paul's opponents in Corinth were accusing him of making decisions and preaching according to worldly standards instead of God's holy standards. In the first chapter of 2 Corinthians, Paul had already defended his recent travel plans from just such an accusation (see 1:17).

10:3 Of course, Paul was **human,** thus susceptible to all kinds of difficulties, oversights, and weaknesses. Yet he said that he and his fellow workers did not **wage war with human plans and methods.** Paul equated the Christian life to a war. This war isn't against "flesh and blood, but against the . . . authorities of the unseen world" (Ephesians 6:12). The Christian life is a spiritual battle against spiritual forces aligned against Christ. Fighting this spiritual battle with weapons of the world—with physical strength, worldly strategies, and material wealth—would be foolish. A spiritual battle requires spiritual weapons that can only come from God.

10:4-5 According to Paul's letter to the Ephesians, **God's mighty weapons** are faith, truth, righteousness, the gospel message, and the word of God. The Holy Spirit equips Christians for the struggle, providing the weapons they need (see 6:6; Ephesians 6:10-20). **Worldly weapons**—wealth, fame, and political might—may wield some power on this earth, but they are useless in spiritual battles. **The Devil's strongholds** included **every proud argument that keeps people from knowing God** and **rebellious ideas.** The world of ideas is the real battleground for God and the Devil. Many com-

plex theories and philosophies try to block people from knowing the truth about God and worshiping him. These false philosophies that divert glory from God and hide the truth are the Devil's strongholds. In Corinth, where advances in Greek philosophy were held in high esteem, the believers were tempted to evaluate the gospel with the various tools of Greek philosophy. In an earlier letter, Paul had already told the Corinthians that the gospel would appear as foolishness to those who saw the world through the lenses of secular Greek philosophy (see 1 Corinthians 1:22). Just as an army would attack a fortress, so Christians must take apart and defeat these false and evil arguments.

10:6 Paul wouldn't hesitate on his next visit to use those spiritual weapons entrusted to him to **punish those who remained disobedient.** But notice how Paul attached a condition to his exercising of his authority. He would not do so until **the rest of** the Corinthian believers recommitted themselves to be **obedient** to the gospel. According to Titus's recent report, the majority of the Corinthians had already done this. They had been filled with godly sorrow about the recent problems in their church and had made the necessary steps toward reconciling themselves to Paul (see 7:7-13). From the way Paul carefully defended his ministry in this letter (see 1:12-18; 3:1-5; 5:11-17), it is clear that there was still a rebellious minority in the church (see 2:17). At the end of this letter, Paul promised to deal sternly with this minority on his next visit.

10:7 Paul encouraged the Corinthians to adjust their perspective. They had been making their **decisions on the basis of appearance.** They were listening intently to the false teachers who were boasting of their own authority (10:12-13), their perfect Hebrew heritage (11:21-22), and their visionary experiences (12:11-12). All of their loud boasts and extravagant displays of power had dazzled the Corinthians so much that they had become blind to the simplicity of the gospel message that Paul had preached to them in the first place (1 Corinthians 2:1-3). While these teachers would **proudly declare** that they belonged to Christ, the Corinthians had to remember that so did Paul and his companions. Paul challenged those who were doubting his authority to consider carefully the evidence for Paul's own relationship to Jesus: First, the undeniably changed lives of people who believed in the message he preached (3:1-5); second, the integrity with which he faithfully presented the gospel message (4:1-5); third, the hardships he had endured for the cause of Christ (6:3-10; 11:23-29); and finally, the fact that Christ himself had commissioned him to be an apostle to the Gentiles (1:21-22; 5:20-21; 6:1-2; 10:8; 12:2-4).

10:8 Although Paul's opponents had portrayed him as weak and powerless, Paul reminded the Corinthians that he did possess God-given **authority** (see 1:21-22; 5:20-21). False teachers were encouraging the believers to ignore Paul, but he maintained that what he had written in his letters was to be taken seriously. Paul possessed the authority from **the Lord** to exhort the Corinthians. Although he would not boast in himself or compare himself to other preachers, he would boast in the Lord and in the authority that Jesus had given him to preach the gospel that saves (see 10:12-13, 17-18; see also 1 Corinthians 1:31). Unlike the false teachers who had come to Corinth, Paul knew the limits of his authority (compare with 10:13-14). He wasn't given the authorization to **tear down** the church. Paul's mission was constructive, not destructive. Thus he would not sit by and allow his **work** in Corinth to be **destroyed.**

10:9 Apparently, Paul's critics at Corinth had attacked Paul's letters as not only being hard to understand (see Paul's defense of the straightforwardness of his letters in 1:13) but also written **to frighten** them. Paul's last letter to the Corinthians had been harsh. Paul had even cried over it (2:3-4). The letter was necessary, however, because Paul had to work through some troublesome situations in the church.

10:10 Greece was known for its eloquent and persuasive orators. Corinth, a prominent Greek city at this time, was filled with trained speakers. Apparently, some of the Corinthian believers (perhaps encouraged by the false teachers among them) were judging Paul's speaking ability. He had already admitted to the Corinthians that he had consciously avoided dependence on rhetoric or human philosophy when he had presented the gospel of salvation to them (see 1 Corinthians 2:1-3). He wanted the message to speak for itself, unencumbered by such distractions.

10:11 In the past, Paul had refrained from disciplining members of the Corinthian church in person. He had warned them to stop sinning (see 13:2) on several occasions and had written letters encouraging them to discipline persistent sinners (see 1 Corinthians 5:1-5). Paul had used these indirect methods to encourage the leaders of the Corinthian church to take charge of the situation and discipline their own members. Paul even had promised to go along with the judgments they made (see 1 Corinthians 1:5; see also 2:6-10). Because his more accommodating approach wasn't working with the Corinthians, however, Paul assured them that on his next visit he would be **demanding and forceful** (13:3-4), punishing

those who had not taken his warnings to heart earlier (13:1-2).

10:12 Here Paul went on the offensive. Although his critics had dared to tell everyone **how important they are,** Paul would not **dare** compare himself with them or anyone else. Any ability he possessed was a gift from God; therefore, God deserved the full credit for it. Yet Paul's opponents in Corinth didn't shrink from measuring and comparing themselves **with each other.** Because the Corinthians tended to focus on appearances (see 5:12, 16; 10:7), they had been successfully duped by the false teachers' slick presentation (11:4, 19-20). Meanwhile, Paul, who appropriately refrained from any boasting, was accused by the Corinthians of being "unimpressive" (10:10). Although the Corinthians claimed to be wise, they didn't recognize that the pretentious boasts of Paul's opponents was **foolishness** (10:17-18). Because of the power these false teachers were consolidating in the congregation, Paul was finally forced to spell it out: These teachers were foolish, loud-mouthed braggarts!

10:13 Because the Corinthians had listened to these false teachers, they were forcing Paul to **boast** in order to silence his critics (see 11:1–12:13). Here Paul explained the grounds on which he was boasting. To boast in himself and in his own accomplishments would have been entirely inappropriate. Only God deserved honor, for he had given Paul his abilities. What could Paul boast about? Paul could only boast in God and in the tasks God had assigned him. Paul regarded his assignment at Corinth as within his proper **boundaries.**

10:14 Paul and his companions had been the **first to travel all the way to** Corinth **with the Good News of Christ.** He was the founder of the Corinthian church, and as such could **claim authority over** the congregation. That should have been obvious to the believers in Corinth. Paul had welcomed in the past any teacher of the truth, such as Apollos, to build on the foundation he had laid (see 1 Corinthians 3:5-13). In the final analysis, however, the Corinthians had only one founder: Paul himself (see 1 Corinthians 4:14-16). If anyone could claim authority over the Corinthian congregation, he could. Ironically, it was his authority that was being called into question.

10:15-16 Paul refused to **claim credit for the work someone else** had **done,** as the false teachers were doing with the Corinthians (the fruit of Paul's hard labor among them). Unlike the traveling preachers who had come to live off the Corinthian congregation (see 2:17), Paul envisioned his evangelistic ministry as expanding into unevangelized regions. He would never plan on invading regions that had already been evangelized by some other teacher. In order to do this, however, the Corinthians' **faith** had to increase. As they matured in the faith, his work would be **greatly enlarged.** Paul might have been implying that as the Corinthians matured in their faith, he could spend less time guiding them in their Christian walk. As mature Christians, they would not only be less dependent on Paul to solve their congregation's problems, but they would also start supporting Paul as he launched evangelistic missions **beyond** them into completely unevangelized areas. From Paul's letter to the Romans, we know that Paul's vision included reaching Spain with the Good News (see Romans 15:24).

10:17-18 The following chapters list some of Paul's ministerial credentials and accomplishments. Paul was extremely cautious about boasting about himself; first of all, so that he might not rob the honor

that God deserved (11:30-31), and second so that he might not be misunderstood as praising himself (see 5:12-13; 10:13; 11:16-18). The situation in Corinth, however, had forced Paul to set aside his scruples about boasting in order to save the Corinthian church from ruin. By touting his credentials—the credentials the Corinthians should have recognized in the first place—Paul hoped to discredit the false teachers who had infiltrated the church (11:12).

Paul paraphrased Jeremiah 9:24 in order to emphasize to the Corinthians that he knew he was treading on shaky ground. The Old Testament passage was especially relevant because it was an indictment against false teachers who took pride in their wisdom and their speaking abilities. Only those who seek after God and make it a priority to know and love him are commended by God. Only those who bring honor and praise to God, instead of themselves, are those people in whom God delights; and, in the end, only God's approval counts. In light of eternity, it really doesn't matter how other people judge us.

2 CORINTHIANS 11

PAUL AND THE FALSE APOSTLES / 11:1-15

Because the Corinthians were easily impressed by résumés (11:21-23), articulate and persuasive speakers (11:6), and shows of spiritual power (12:12), they had been duped by a group of false teachers. By consistently criticizing and accusing Paul, this group of upstart teachers had undermined Paul's authority in Corinth. Paul felt obligated to respond to their criticisms, point by point (11:21). He had founded the church and had the responsibility to keep the church on the right course (1 Corinthians 4:15).

11:1 Paul asked the Corinthian believers to **be patient** and **bear with** him as he spoke of his apostolic credentials. He felt foolish repeating his credentials because it was through his evangelistic efforts that he had founded the Corinthian church. There shouldn't be any reason for the Corinthians to question him; he was their father in the Christian faith (see 1 Corinthians 4:15). But because the Corinthians had been mesmerized by the rhetoric of these false teachers, dazzled by their claims to ecstatic spiritual experiences, and duped by their logic, Paul was forced to talk like a **fool,** to remind them of what he had done for the cause of Christ. It was against his principles to do this, for all honor, glory, and even boasts belonged to God (see 10:17). Yet Paul was in a dilemma. If he didn't speak up, the false teachers in Corinth might con-

tinue to lead the Corinthian believers astray. Paul had hoped that the believers would discern the emptiness of these false teachers' boasts, but they had not. As a spokesman for the truth, therefore, Paul couldn't stay silent; he had to speak up. In this case, speaking up for the truth meant defending his own credentials. If his own ministry was discredited, the gospel he preached would also be discredited.

11:2 Paul was anxious that the Corinthian church's love should be reserved for Christ alone, just as a chaste virgin saves her love for her groom. In the first century, an engagement was a serious commitment, similar to a contract. If the **bride** wasn't a virgin on the wedding day, it was considered a breach of the engagement contract. Ensuring the bride's purity and virginity until the wedding day was partially her father's responsibility.

Paul had already described himself as the Corinthians' spiritual father (see 1 Corinthians 4:15). This passage depicts his concern for the Corinthians as a father's concern for the purity of his daughter. Paul had already **promised** the Corinthians **to one husband, Christ.** He was anticipating that wonderful day when he would present them proudly to Jesus. That day when Christ returns will be like a great wedding feast, an image that Jesus himself had used for his second coming (see Matthew 25:1-11). To guarantee that he would not be embarrassed at Christ's return, Paul took the necessary steps to discourage the Corinthians not to stray from their pure devotion to Christ (11:3). Thus, the **jealousy** that motivated Paul was a godly jealousy for the Corinthians: that they might wholeheartedly follow Christ, their Savior (11:3-4).

11:3 This passage compares the serpent's temptation to the temptation of the false teachers' enticing message. The Corinthians had begun their Christian walk with a sincere and pure devotion to Christ. But false teachers were luring Corinthian believers away from the truth. Paul didn't want the believers' **pure and simple devotion to Christ** to be corrupted. Sin begins with thoughts. The **serpent** first tried to convince **Eve** that God's law was not the best for her, that the advantages of disobeying God outweighed the advantage of obeying him. The serpent's deception was primarily directed against what Eve thought about God and his instructions (Genesis 3:1-6). Satan knew that once the mind was convinced, actions would soon follow. Eve was persuaded by Satan's lies and subsequently reached out to pluck the forbidden fruit. In the same way, the false teachers were Satan's servants, deceiving the Corinthians to abandon their wholehearted devotion to Christ (see 11:14-15).

11:4 The false teachers who had come to Corinth had distorted the truth about Jesus and ended up preaching **a different Jesus, a different Spirit** than the Holy Spirit, and **a different kind of gospel** than God's way of salvation. Because of the sparse amount of evidence in 2 Corinthians, the exact form of the false teachers' erroneous teaching cannot be known. But whether it was a heresy dealing with the Jewish law or a heresy dealing with Greek wisdom and knowledge (see 1 Corinthians 1:21-25), clearly the teaching was different than what Paul preached. The false teachers were distracting the Corinthians from the grace of God, the only thing that could save them (see Paul's emphasis on grace in 1:12; 6:1; 9:8; 12:9). These

false teachers' rhetoric, reasoning, and boasts were drawing attention to themselves instead of pointing the Corinthians to God.

11:5-6 Paul, a brilliant thinker, was not trained in Greek rhetoric. He probably wasn't a spellbinding speaker. Although Paul's preaching ministry was effective (see Acts 17), he had not been **trained** in the Greek schools of oratory and speechmaking, as the false teachers evidently had been. In fact, Paul avoided fine-sounding arguments and lofty ideas in order to preach the simple gospel message (see 1 Corinthians 1:17). Some of the Corinthians had begun to think that Paul's plain speaking style indicated a simple-mindedness. Despite what his accusers (the **super-apostles**) said, Paul knew **what** he was **talking about,** for it was the message of salvation.

11:7 The Corinthians evaluated a speaker by how much money he demanded from his audience. A good speaker would charge a large sum; a fair speaker would be cheaper; a poor speaker would speak for free. Since Paul hadn't asked for money when he preached in Corinth, some were accusing him of being an amateur speaker.

The reason why Paul hadn't asked for support when he first came to Corinth was because he thought he would be misunderstood. Many teachers traveled the Roman Empire hoping to make a good profit from their own speaking abilities (2:17), and Paul thought that he might appear like one of them. Instead of asking for a fee, as a professional speaker would do, Paul supported himself by manual labor, working as a tentmaker with Priscilla and Aquila (see Acts 18:1-3). Prominent Greeks considered manual labor as beneath them. The sophisticated teachers at Corinth attacked Paul for doing this, trying to discredit his ministry by drawing attention to this fact. So Paul asked how he had done **wrong** to the believers **by preaching God's Good News without expecting anything in return.**

11:8-9 Paul's language in these verses evokes a military metaphor. The Greek word for **robbed** is a military term that depicts how a first-century soldier would "strip bare" his enemies. Thus, Paul was saying that in order to **serve** the Corinthians he had, in effect, plundered the churches in **Macedonia** for his wages. Why did Paul accept support from the Macedonian Christians and refuse it from the Corinthians? Part of the answer to this question is that the Macedonians were giving cheerfully (8:1-5), while the Corinthians were using their money to gain influence and power. So there would be no question about his motivations, Paul would continue to refuse compensation. The Macedonians weren't questioning his authority, but the Corinthians were.

11:10-11 Paul knew that the fact he hadn't taken any money from the Corinthians was the strongest rebuttal to the false teachers, for their whole purpose in preaching was to gather a following who would support them (see 2:17). More than likely, they were the ones who had slowed the collection for the Jerusalem Christians in order to divert the funds to themselves. Paul hoped that his consistent integrity with money would be one of the indicators that he was a preacher of the truth, while his opponents were greedy peddlers of falsehoods (2:17). Why did Paul refuse support? Why did he boast in his own integrity? Why did he oppose the false teachers? It was because of his deep **love** for the Corinthians. As the founder of the church of Corinth, Paul was concerned for the Corinthians' spiritual welfare. He was jealous for their spiritual purity (1:6, 23; 2:10).

11:12 In order to set the record straight, Paul wouldn't stop boasting that he had preached the gospel free of charge (see 6:10; 7:2; 11:27; 12:16-18; 1 Corinthians 9:3-18). Eventually, the Corinthians would wake up to the fact that these false teachers, unlike Paul, were more interested in the money of the Corinthians than in their spiritual welfare. Although Paul was being forced to boast foolishly about his own ministry, it was his consistent honesty and integrity—the way he had conducted himself around the Corinthians—that would silence his critics and answer their charges against him. They weren't willing to suffer, as Jesus had, to present the gospel free of charge.

11:13 Paul reserved some of the harshest language for those who were boasting about their ministry among the Corinthians: They were **false apostles.** One of the first signs that a teacher is false is that that teacher tries to discredit true Christian teachers and preachers. A second sign is self-serving methods. The teachers at Corinth were boasting of their own credentials, comparing themselves to Paul (3:1; 10:12). Their methods (their loud boasts)

should have been a clue that these teachers were not looking out for the Corinthians' spiritual welfare but instead for their own financial welfare. A third sign that these teachers were false and deceitful is that their methods were causing division and conflict in the church. The final sign that these were false teachers is the message they preached. A careful analysis would have revealed that it was "different" from the true gospel that Paul, Silas, Timothy, and Apollos had preached (11:4-5).

The Corinthian believers should have tested the teachers to see whether they believed Jesus is the Son of God (1 John 4:1-2). The Corinthians had failed to do this and had even let these teachers wreak havoc in their congregation. Paul was disappointed with the Corinthians' lack of discernment (11:4, 19-20).

11:14 Paul wasn't amazed that false teachers were disguising themselves as preachers of God, for **Satan** himself had deceived God's people in similar ways. Nothing could be more deceitful than Satan, the prince of darkness (Ephesians 6:12; Colossians 1:13), disguising himself as **an angel of light.** In the same way, false teachers, claiming to represent the truth, are extremely deceptive.

11:15 The false apostles were **servants** of Satan. Their actions betrayed them. Instead of bringing glory to God, they were boasting in their own achievements (10:17-18). Instead of preaching in response to God's call (compare 2:17 with 4:1-2, 5; 5:20), they were preaching for money. Instead of guarding the spiritual welfare of their followers, they were consolidating power over their followers (compare 1:23-24; 10:8; 11:21 with 11:18-20). Instead of preaching the gospel of Jesus Christ clearly (11:6-7), they were preaching a twisted gospel of another Jesus (11:4). In the **end,** their fraud would be exposed for what it was and they would receive the **punishment their wicked deeds deserved.**

PAUL'S MANY TRIALS / 11:16-33

If the greedy teachers of Corinth questioned Paul's authority, he questioned their devotion to Christ. They were enjoying the luxuries of one of the most prominent cities in the Roman Empire, while Paul, as he noted in this passage, was enduring all kinds of hardships to preach the gospel to those who hadn't heard it. These teachers had been careful to collect correct references, respected credentials, and impeccable recommendations; but they, unlike Paul, had failed to offer their entire lives in service to Christ, wherever that brought them. Paul's long list of hardships he had endured couldn't be matched by any of the teachers who were criticizing him.

11:16-18 Clearly, Paul was extremely reluctant to **boast.** But faced with the persistent faultfinding of his critics, Paul felt compelled to list his

accomplishments for the Corinthians. He wasn't primarily concerned with his own reputation but, instead, with the spiritual welfare of the

Corinthian believers. If his critics' attacks went unanswered, the believers might turn away from Christ (11:3-4, 12). Paul had to speak up in order to quiet the gossip and slander circulating in the Corinthian church. Even though Paul knew he had to defend himself, he was extremely careful. He cautiously explained to the Corinthians that he was going to act **like a fool** in order to silence those false teachers.

11:19 With biting sarcasm, Paul reprimanded the Corinthians for putting up with these arrogant false teachers. They thought they were being **wise** when they welcomed itinerant teachers and listened to their new ideas. If these teachers were godly, like Apollos, Paul applauded this generous hospitality. The most recent teachers, however, were introducing a different gospel and were discrediting Paul in the process (11:4). Apparently, the Corinthians enjoyed **listening to fools.**

11:20 The Corinthians continued to listen to the false teachers even when it became clear that they were trying to enslave the Corinthians. Paul went on to explain the nature of this enslavement, with four evocative images of exploitation.

Take everything is a translation of a Greek verb commonly used to describe how animals devour their prey. **Take advantage** is from a Greek verb used to describe how a hunter catches animals with a trap or a bait. The imagery of a hunter and prey suggests that the false teachers' primary sin was their motives. They were traveling preachers looking for a gullible group of people to support them. They were literally preying on the Corinthians, trying to exploit the relationship for all that it was worth. Ironically, the Corinthians thought they were wise by welcoming these teachers when, in reality, these itinerant teachers were making the Corinthians into **slaves.** With arrogant boasts, they paraded their credentials and achievements. **Put on airs** is literally "to lift up" high. They were slapping the Corinthians **in the face** by their actions.

11:21 Paul was probably quoting what his critics said about him when he wrote that he was **not strong enough** to take advantage of the Corinthians, to take their money, and to physically discipline them. Even though Paul would refrain from doing that, he was going to **dare to boast,** just as his opponents did. Once again, Paul issued a disclaimer. He felt foolish talking as he did, listing his accomplishments.

11:22 These statements address the charges Paul's opponents had leveled against him point by point. First of all, these traveling preachers from

Judea were bragging about being **Hebrews** and **Israelites**—God's chosen people. Paul had been born in Tarsus; and thus, in his opponents' eyes, he had a questionable heritage. Paul was one of the **descendants of Abraham** through the tribe of Benjamin. He had been circumcised eight days after he was born—a physical sign of his Israelite heritage. He had been trained by one of the most respected Pharisees of that day, Gamaliel. As a Pharisee, he had spent hours poring over the Hebrew Bible and had been scrupulously careful to observe Jewish law (Philippians 3:4-6). No one could question Paul's credentials as a Jew and as an expert in the Hebrew Scriptures.

11:23 Although Paul had conceded to his opponents their Jewish heritage, he would not agree with them that they served **Christ.** To prove his point, Paul listed all the trials he suffered for Christ. Could his opponents, who boasted in achievements, accomplishments, and credentials, produce an even more extensive list of suffering and persecution endured for Christ's name? Were they willing to follow Jesus' way of the cross, his life of suffering? Were they willing to take up their crosses daily for Christ (Matthew 10:38)? Paul had suffered the hardship of imprisonment, including being **whipped** (Acts 16:22-24). He had faced **death** on a number of occasions (see Acts 14:19, when Paul was stoned by a crowd). Since this letter was written during Paul's third missionary journey (Acts 18:23–21:17), his trials weren't over. He would experience further difficulties and humiliations for the cause of Christ (see Acts 21:30-33; 22:24-30). Paul was sacrificing his life for the gospel, something the false teachers would never do.

11:24 According to the Jewish law, forty lashes was the maximum number the Jews could prescribe (Deuteronomy 25:3). The rabbis, however, would only allow **thirty-nine,** so that if the flogger miscounted he wouldn't accidentally sin by administering more than forty. These beatings were carried out in the synagogues and were for either moral or religious offenses. The lashes were made of several straps of leather, sometimes with bone or metal tied to the ends to inflict more pain. In Paul's case, the punishment would have been for preaching the gospel, what Jews commonly considered blasphemy. He faced this **five different times.** None of these beatings are recorded in Acts, but the adamant opposition of the Jews to the gospel message is recorded (Acts 13:45, 50; 14:2; 18:6, 12).

11:25 Only the Romans could administer beatings with rods. Yet Paul **was beaten with rods** at

Philippi (Acts 16:22). Apparently, government officials had beaten him on two other occasions (these weren't recorded in the book of Acts, however). At Lystra, Paul had survived being **stoned** (Acts 14:8-20). Sea travel was not as safe as it is today. Paul had been **shipwrecked three times,** and he would face another accident on his voyage to Rome (Acts 27). By this time, Paul had probably made at least eight or nine voyages; thus, given the danger of first-century sea travel, he could have certainly experienced that many disasters at sea. The fact that Paul survived twenty-four hours **adrift at sea** would have been considered miraculous in the first century, a sign of God's hand on his life.

11:26 The sea did not present the only **danger** Paul faced on the many **weary miles** he had **traveled** as he took the gospel all over the Mediterranean world. **Robbers** were a constant problem in the ancient world. In addition, Paul's **own people, the Jews,** were trying to orchestrate his downfall. When Paul first visited Corinth, the Jews had dragged him before the governor of Achaia in order to stop him from preaching (Acts 18:12-17). The **Gentiles** also had opposed Paul in Philippi and in Ephesus (Acts 16:19-24; 19:23-31). Paul's list of dangers climaxes in **men who claim to be Christians but are not.** His point is abundantly clear. Since he had bravely faced all sorts of dangers for Christ, he certainly would have enough courage to face those false teachers who were discrediting his authority and his name in Corinth. On past visits, Paul had not been as aggressive with those who opposed him (10:1). He was planning to confront his critics on his next visit (13:1-5).

11:27 In order to place his ministry beyond reproach, Paul had supported himself by working at a manual trade. Working two jobs had caused **weariness and pain and sleepless nights.** Because of the low wages of itinerant laborers and the hardships of first-century travel, Paul was often **hungry, thirsty,** and **cold.** But Paul had endured all these hardships cheerfully to preach the gospel, to tell men and women all over the Roman Empire that Jesus could save them from their sins.

11:28 Every day Paul thought about the spiritual health of the **churches** he had founded. There were so many pitfalls and traps into which a young congregation could fall. Persecution could force the church to compromise its theology; quarreling and inner strife could distract the church from its purpose; false teachers could deceive a church. Paul was concerned that the

churches wouldn't persevere in the faith. One indication of his **burden** was his dedication and persistence in praying for them.

11:29 If Paul heard of any individual who was **weak** in the faith, he sympathized with that person. He encouraged stronger believers to help weaker ones (1 Thessalonians 5:14). If any individual was **led astray** from the faith, Paul would **burn with anger** at the ones who had caused it.

11:30 Although the Corinthians had forced Paul to defend his own integrity and his apostolic authority, this letter focuses on **how weak** Paul was. Paul paraded his sufferings, trials, and weaknesses before his opponents. He didn't **boast** in his accomplishments, as they did; thereby, he defused some of their criticisms. The only way Paul could show his authority was to point out how God had worked through his weaknesses. These were the telltale signs of God's work in his life.

11:31 Paul had already called on **God** as a witness to his truthfulness three other times in this letter: when he asserted his integrity in his recent travel plans (1:18), when he denied taking any money from the Corinthians (11:10), and when he asserted his genuine love for them (11:11).

11:32-33 Most likely, the Roman Emperor Caligula (A.D. 37–41) had given **King Aretas IV,** the king of the Nabateans from 9 B.C. to A.D. 40, the authority to appoint a **governor** to oversee the Nabatean population in **Damascus.** The Jews in Damascus had been able to enlist this governor to help them try to **catch** Paul (see Acts 9:22-25). The way the passage builds up to this story indicates that Paul saw this as a seminal event. Paul had come to Damascus with his head held high. The high priest had given him the authority to arrest Christians in that city. After his conversion, Paul was forced to sneak out of the city under the cover of darkness. He couldn't even walk through the city gates, much less command the authority and respect of the city elders (compare Acts 9:1-2 with 9:23-25).

Although Christ had predicted that Paul would suffer much for him (Acts 9:15-16), this was probably the first time Paul had realized to what extent he would have to suffer. Hunted as a common criminal, he couldn't stand up to his accusers and defend himself with integrity. Instead, he had to run away. For Paul, fleeing would have been considered a coward's reaction. This was probably one of the weakest moments he had experienced in his life, and admitting this to his opponents in Corinth would have been extremely difficult for him to write.

2 CORINTHIANS 12

PAUL'S VISION AND HIS THORN IN THE FLESH / 12:1-10

God had granted Paul a vision of the highest heaven. Paul had heard words that couldn't be repeated and had seen sights that couldn't be recounted. But because of this experience, God had given him a "thorn"—a weakness that continually reminded him of his utter dependence on God. Paul had experienced what others would never experience in this life. Instead of being able to boast about it, Paul had to suffer because of it.

12:1 Paul felt compelled to move to the next category about which his opponents had been boasting: **visions and revelations.** It is clear from the frequency of disclaimers about boasting in this section (11:30; 12:1, 5-6, 9-11) that Paul thought of bragging about revelations as the height of folly. A revelation by definition was purely God's work. Yet apparently, Paul's critics were boasting in revelations. In effect, they were saying that they had been judged worthy of these revelations. Only a fool boasts in something that is so clearly the work of God.

12:2 Although Paul didn't give many details about this ecstatic experience, he did write that he was **caught up into the third heaven.** In Paul's day, the notion of multiple heavens—from three to seven heavens—was common. Scholars who have systematically analyzed the use of the words "heaven" and "heavens" in the Old and New Testament believe that the Scriptures use the word "heaven" to refer to three separate places. The first heaven is the earth's atmosphere (see Acts 1:9-10); the second heaven is the entire universe, which contains all the stars (see Genesis 1:14). The third heaven, beyond these two heavens, is where God himself lives (1 Peter 3:22). This is the "heaven of heavens" (Nehemiah 9:6; Psalm 68:33). Whether or not Paul had this three-fold division of the heavens in mind, it is clear that he considered the third heaven as the highest heaven. Paul saw his revelation as an extraordinary and unique revelation (12:7).

It was **fourteen years ago** that Paul experienced this revelation. Although Luke records a number of visions and trances Paul received (Acts 9:3-7; 16:9; 22:17-21), including the one Paul experienced while visiting Corinth (Acts 18:9-10), none of those visions fit the description here. Paul described this revelation as such a rapturous experience that he heard words he could not repeat (12:4). The fact that Paul couldn't express what he heard might explain the silence about this revelation in the book of Acts.

Fourteen years before the writing of 2 Corinthians would be around A.D. 40, close to the beginning of Paul's ministry. Paul may have experienced this revelation when he was in Arabia (see Galatians 1:17; 2:2), or when he was in Antioch (Acts 13:1-3), or when he was stoned outside of Lystra and assumed dead (Acts 14:19-20).

12:3-4 In two sentences, Paul repeated that he had actually been transported to heaven, though he didn't know how—whether his **body** had been there or just his **spirit.** Jesus also had used the word **paradise** as a synonym for heaven (Luke 23:43). Then, in Revelation 2:7, Jesus promised the tree of life, the one in paradise, to all those who overcome. Given the extraordinary nature of this revelation (12:4), this is a surprisingly brief description of it. All Paul revealed was that he had been transported to heaven and had heard some **things so astounding that they cannot be told.** What Paul saw and heard in heaven was meant for his own edification. Most likely, God was strengthening and encouraging him for the extraordinary trials and suffering he would have to face in order to preach the Good News (see Acts 9:15-16). Paul mentioned it here only to invalidate the claims of his opponents in Corinth.

The emphasis here is instructive. Although accounts of revelations and visions typically focus on what a person has seen, Paul highlighted what he had heard. For Paul, listening to God and responding to his word was extremely important (see Romans 10:14, 17; Galatians 3:5; Ephesians 1:13).

12:5-7 Paul sensed he was on shaky ground when he started referring to a revelation that he couldn't describe. He didn't want anyone to mistakenly think that he was boasting about himself in this revelation. Therefore, he once again issued a disclaimer that he wasn't boasting in himself. Paul turned attention away from his vision and to his **weaknesses.** In fact, to keep him from **getting puffed up** about the extraordinary privilege of the visions he had seen, Paul was **given a thorn in** his flesh. The exact nature of this is not known, because he never reveals it. Because the Greek word for "flesh" can refer either to one's physical body or one's carnal self, there have been numerous conjectures concerning what the "thorn in the flesh" was.

The Greek word for "thorn" can also mean "stake." The word is used in the Greek Old Testament for Israel's neighbors who had become a temptation and a snare to the Israelites (Numbers 33:55). Some interpret Paul's use of the word here as a veiled reference to people who opposed the gospel—whether the false teachers who were deceiving the Corinthians or the Jews who were actively opposing his preaching.

Others argue that this type of external opposition wouldn't have humbled Paul, as he clearly stated the thorn did. According to these commentators, the thorn had to be some type of temptation of the flesh. Medieval commentators usually suggested a sexual temptation, while commentators of the Reformation suggested a spiritual temptation. In any case, this sort of explanation suggests that Paul would have viewed this temptation as a hindrance to the gospel and would have been humbled by his weakness.

Another set of commentators insist that the thorn in the flesh is a reference to a physical weakness, not to a persistent temptation. The earliest commentators on 2 Corinthians suggested that this ailment could have been severe headaches. These interpreters viewed the thorn in the flesh as a description of symptoms. In other words, "it feels like a bar going through my head." Some doctors think Paul may have had recurrent malarial fever, a disease that includes migraine headaches.

Many commentators, however, continue to insist that the thorn in the flesh is simply a general metaphor for Paul's physical weaknesses (especially in his eyes), and not a description of the symptoms. Some see hints in Paul's letter to the Galatians of a type of eye disease that impaired his vision (Galatians 4:14-15). Whatever the thorn was, it is clear that it was a chronic and debilitating problem, which at times kept Paul from working and attending to his ministerial responsibilities.

Yet this passage in 2 Corinthians does not focus on the exact problem Paul faced—he purposely didn't explain the nature of the problem in detail. The important point was why the thorn was given

to him. Jesus had given Paul **plenty to boast about.** But to keep Paul from getting arrogant about the **wonderful revelations from God** he had received, God had allowed **Satan** to **torment** him with some hardship or temptation. This thorn continually reminded Paul of his dependence on God and steered him away from pride, arrogance, and self-sufficiency. In this way, God would use Satan's evil designs for good, just as he had with Joseph and his brothers (Genesis 50:19-20).

Paul had to explain the reason for his thorn, because the Corinthians valued success instead of failure, power instead of weakness. Those who are so often dazzled by success need to learn the same lesson. Christ loves to work through weakness (1 Corinthians 1:26-29).

12:8 Because this thorn was a hindrance to his ministry, Paul saw it as caused by Satan (12:7). Appropriately, Paul responded to these demonic-inspired attacks with prayer, the chief weapon of the Christian against evil (Luke 22:40; Ephesians 6:12, 18). Paul prayed **three different times** for the thorn's removal so he could be free to preach the Good News and build up others in the faith. In his wisdom, however, the Lord did not remove the problem (see 12:9). Sometimes he denies requests so that his people will depend on his abundant grace.

12:9 Jesus' answer to Paul's prayer is the theme of 2 Corinthians: Christ's **gracious favor** is what empowered Paul's ministry, despite his own inadequacies and failures. Although Paul's request wasn't granted, Jesus assured him that he would continue to work through Paul **in his weakness.** In fact, Christ's **power** worked best there. So in response, Paul accepted that Jesus, in his divine wisdom, knew what was best for him. Paul would not boast in being healed, but he would **boast about** his **weaknesses,** for it was through his weaknesses that Christ could powerfully work through him.

12:10 Although Christ did not remove Paul's affliction, he promised to demonstrate his power in Paul's **weaknesses.** Knowing this, Paul saw **insults, hardships, persecutions, and calamities** in a different light. When he had no options left, he would be forced to run to Jesus. Paul's utter dependence on Christ came into clear light. Christ's clear manifestation of his power in Paul's weakness would become a source of inspiration and a reason to praise and glorify Jesus. Truly when Paul was **weak** was really when he was **strong.**

The fact that Christ's power is displayed in weak people should give believers courage. Instead of relying on their own energy, effort, or talent, they should turn to Christ for wisdom and strength. Weakness not only helps a person develop Chris-

tian character; it also deepens that person's worship, because admitting weakness affirms Christ's inexhaustible strength.

PAUL'S CONCERN FOR THE CORINTHIANS / 12:11-21

Toward the end of 2 Corinthians, Paul begins to sound like a father who is profoundly disappointed in his children. Paul was disappointed that the Corinthians hadn't defended him when others had maligned his reputation (12:11-12). He was disappointed that they were questioning his motives (12:16-18). He was disappointed that they hadn't shown him the same kind of love he had showered on them (12:15). Paul was planning to visit Corinth, but he was clearly apprehensive about it. Would he find all kinds of disorders, just as if the Corinthians were his children running wild? Would he find them arguing and fighting (12:20)? Paul hoped that everything would be in order; then he could congratulate the Corinthians instead of disciplining them.

12:11 The Corinthians should have been **writing commendations for** their founder when malicious rumors about him had begun to circulate. After all, Paul was their spiritual father (1 Corinthians 4:15; 9:1; 11:2-4). The very existence of the gathering of believers, whose lives had been changed by the Holy Spirit, was evidence of Paul's faithfulness to the truth (3:1-5). Instead, Paul had to **act like a fool**, boasting about himself in order to deal with the issues at hand. Paul made it clear that he definitely wasn't the least of those who called themselves **super-apostles**, for they weren't the true apostles of Christ but false apostles sent by Satan (see 11:13-14). Paul never thought he would have to defend himself against these conniving preachers, but the Corinthians had forced him to do so.

12:12 When Paul was in Corinth, he had acted according to his calling as an apostle of Christ. He had been careful to be completely honest in all his dealings so that no one could impugn his name (1:12). He had faithfully preached the gospel (5:11, 19-21; 1 Corinthians 1:23; 9:16-18), and his preaching in Corinth had been accompanied by **signs and wonders and miracles.** Through these signs, the Spirit of God had clearly demonstrated to the Corinthians Paul's apostolic authority and the truthfulness of the gospel message he preached (Romans 15:17-19; 1 Corinthians 2:4).

12:13 The only practice Paul refrained from doing that these "super-apostles" did and that he did at **the other churches** was charging money for his teaching. Building on the Greek notion that manual labor was beneath teachers and preachers, these false teachers had asserted that one of the signs of an apostle was demanding payment for his services (2:17). The fact that Paul had spent long hours sewing tents together disqualified him as an

apostle in the eyes of these false teachers. Paul hadn't taken advantage of this right because he didn't want to owe anything to any one person. He wanted the freedom to preach the gospel to everyone—no matter if they were Jew or Greek, slave or free (1 Corinthians 9:19-23). So he sarcastically asked that he be forgiven **for this wrong.**

12:14-15 Paul had founded the church in Corinth on his first visit there (Acts 18:1). He had subsequently made a short and painful visit. That second visit was when he had warned those who were persistent in sinning to repent of their sin (2:1; 13:2). After this visit, he had abandoned plans for another visit and had instead written a stern letter, warning the Corinthian congregation that it was the church's responsibility to punish the wrongdoer (2:1-4; 7:8-13). Now he was planning to visit them a **third time.**

Paul explained that, as on his previous visits, he didn't want to be paid or fed. The Corinthian church was too divided; accusations might result from him accepting any money. Paul didn't want what they had anyway; he wanted their allegiance and friendship. Paul had been their spiritual parent. As a parent naturally loves his or her child, so Paul loved the Corinthians, desiring to **supply food** for them, in the form of spiritual food. Yet it seemed that the **more** he loved them, **the less** they loved him.

12:16-18 But still, it seemed Paul couldn't win. While some would **admit** that Paul had never been a financial **burden** to them, they then decided that he must have gotten money in some other **sneaky** way. Finally, Paul asked the Corinthians a legitimate question: How could he trick them out of their money? Had one of his coworkers taken **advantage** of them. Had **Titus?** Of course, they both knew that the answer was **no.** If they had found nothing wrong with Titus's conduct, how could they find anything wrong with Paul, whom Titus was representing? Titus had learned what **steps** to take from Paul. How could Paul's own steps be any different? This appeal would have been even more persuasive because Titus himself was delivering the epistle known as 2 Corinthians. His impeccable behavior among them would be a continual rebuttal to the gossip of those who were discrediting Paul.

12:19 Paul was worried that the Corinthians might get the impression that he was trying defend his own reputation. Here Paul corrected this impression, if it existed. It wasn't before the Corinthians that Paul was speaking, it was before **God** himself. Paul was confident that he would pass God's judgment because God knew that all that he had done was for the Corinthians' **benefit.** Paul's chief concern was for the Corinthians, that they become firmly grounded in the faith. Paul knew that God himself could see his motives, that everything he did was out of love for the Corinthians (11:11) and concern for their spiritual welfare (11:2-3).

12:20 On his last visit to Corinth, Paul had warned those who were persisting in sin to repent of their ways (13:2). Paul was still apprehensive that the church might not be ready for his visit. He was concerned that the Corinthians might not have taken the appropriate steps to rid their church of sin. He worried that the Corinthians might still be **quarreling** (in Greek, the word can mean "strife" or "contention"; the word is also used in the list of sins in Romans 1:29; 13:13). In his earlier letter, Paul had already warned the Corinthians of dividing into factions and competing for power in the church (see 1 Corinthians 1:10-13; 3:3). One of the key problems in the church was the Corinthians' **jealousy** of each other (1 Corinthians 3:3-5). Instead of concentrating on what they could each do for God, they were enviously eyeing one another, coveting the abilities and resources God had given their fellow brothers and sisters in Christ (see also Romans 13:13). These evil attitudes were resulting in **outbursts of anger** in the church. Evidently, tempers were short because of the division and jealousy in the Corinthian church. Instead of growing into a supportive community of faith (1 Corinthians 12:12-13), the Corinthians were dividing into factions and fighting each other. In the process, they were tearing down the church, the very temple of God (1 Corinthians 3:16-17).

Also, it was the Corinthians' **selfishness** (literally, in the Greek, their "selfish ambition"; see also Galatians 5:20) that was also causing problems in the church. In 1 Corinthians 4:6-7, Paul had

described how they were boasting in themselves, and he had already warned them to focus their energies on preserving Christ's honor—not their own reputation.

These disputes were not one-time affairs. They were ongoing quarrels, where church members on each side began **backstabbing** each other. The Greek word used by Paul here literally means "evil speech" or "slander" (see Romans 1:30 and James 4:11 for more on slander). In this way, the Corinthians were impugning the reputation of their fellow brothers and sisters in Christ (1 Corinthians 5:11; 6:10).

Not only were they slandering each other, but they did so in secret. They continued to maliciously **gossip** about each other—and also, presumably, Paul (see 1 Corinthians 5:11; 6:10). The Greek word for "gossip" is literally "whisperer" (see Paul's use of the word in Romans 1:29).

Instead of building each other up in the Christian faith (1 Corinthians 12:7), the Corinthians were simply growing conceited (see 1 Corinthians 4:6; 8:1). The Greek word Paul used for **conceit** means "inflated." The Corinthians had become inflated with pride (see Paul's similar description in 1 Corinthians 8:1). Finally, Paul warned the Corinthians of **disorderly behavior,** just as he had done in 1 Corinthians (6:1-8; 11:20-22, 33-34; 14:32-33, 40). Paul was speaking about any behavior that disrupted worship services or contributed to the disunity of the church.

12:21 Paul had already told the Corinthians that he was concerned that he might be humiliated when he came to Corinth. Some Macedonian Christians were accompanying him. If Paul found the church in disorder and the Corinthians refusing to participate in the Jerusalem collection, then Paul would be humiliated in the presence of the devout Christians from Macedonia (see 9:3-5). Paul hinted here that finding the Corinthian congregation in disorder would mean more than his own humiliation. He would also have to **grieve** over those who stubbornly refused to repent of their sins.

The sins Paul listed here are sexual sins (as compared to sins relating to pride in 12:20). The Greek for **impurity** means "unclean," referring to uncleanness before God. The Greek for **sexual immorality** is *porneia* (the word is the root for the English word "pornographic"), referring to illicit sexual intercourse and is commonly translated "fornication." Finally, the Greek for **eagerness for lustful pleasure** means "excess" or "absence of restraint." The word connotes shameful conduct, the type of sexual deviance that occurred at religious orgies in Corinth.

Paul was afraid that his directions had not been heeded. The fact that he would have to grieve over those who hadn't repented of their sexual sins implied that Paul was going to carry out the discipline he had told the Corinthians to impose. On his visit, he would have to remove these people from fellowship. He didn't want to discipline them, for it would cause him great sorrow.

2 CORINTHIANS 13

PAUL'S FINAL ADVICE / 13:1-10

True Christian love sometimes demands confrontation. Paul had spent most of the letter taking the time to address the Corinthians' concerns and their accusations (1:12-14, 17, 23; 4:1-2; 5:11-13; 6:11-12; 12:16-18). But at the end of this letter—in this last chapter—Paul didn't hesitate to warn the Corinthians sternly that everything they did was before God, the great Judge. If they wouldn't take his advice, he encouraged them to examine themselves. Did they measure up? Were they living as if Christ was living in them?

13:1-2 This would be Paul's **third time** he would **visit** (see also 12:14). Paul quoted Deuteronomy 19:15 as a stern legal summons to the Corinthians. Throughout 2 Corinthians, he had explained and defended his actions (see 2:1-4; 11:22-31). Finally here, at the end of his letter, Paul stopped defending himself and directly confronted the Corinthians. He wasn't coming to them in a "timid" manner, as he had done before (10:1). He wouldn't merely issue warnings. Instead, he would exercise his apostolic authority in full measure.

The exact reason why Paul quoted Deuteronomy 19:15 has been the subject of some debate among commentators. During his ministry, Jesus had endorsed the Old Testament principle that all accusations had to be established on the **testimony of two or three witnesses** (Matthew 18:15-17). By quoting this law, Paul may have been implying that this time he would be coming to the Corinthians as a judge. He would settle their disputes and quarrels, but everything had to be done in a proper order: All disputes would have to be presented to him with two or three witnesses.

Other commentators suggest that Paul was quoting Deuteronomy 19:15 because he considered his third visit as the final witness against the Corinthians. He had visited them on two separate occasions and had warned them at least two times—during his last visit and also in this letter, 2 Corinthians. He had taken the appropriate steps before disciplining them. He had warned them enough times and had waited long enough for repentance. His next visit would be the third one, the time he would **not spare** the sinners.

In the final analysis, Paul may have been quoting Deuteronomy 19:15 to indicate both ideas, that he had already given them three warnings and that they could bring disputes before him with three witnesses. Jesus' teaching in Matthew 18:15-17 supports both interpretations. Jesus had instructed his disciples to confront a fellow Christian with three warnings—one in private, one with two other witnesses, and one in front of the church (Matthew 18:15-17). There were to be not only three different witnesses before anyone could pass judgment on a believer but also three separate occasions when the believer was to be warned of his or her sin.

13:3 Some of the Corinthians had been asking for **proof** that Paul was truly speaking on behalf of **Christ,** that he was truly an apostle. Paul directly challenged the Corinthians. If they were looking for proof and **mighty power,** then they would most assuredly experience Christ's power on his next visit. Jesus' power among them, however, would not be the type of power the Corinthians were expecting. He wouldn't present spectacular wonders through Paul so that the Corinthians could sit back, watch, and judge them. When Christ came in mighty power, he wouldn't be coming to prove himself to the Corinthians but instead to judge the false teachers among them.

13:4 Paul's consistent message to the Corinthians was that Christ **died on the cross** (1 Corinthians 1:23), a message of Christ's **weakness.** Paul reminded the Corinthians that **the mighty power of God** had been demonstrated through weakness, not through power (12:9). Christ's own life was testimony of this fact. Through Christ's weakness, God worked in a powerful way. Through Christ's death on the cross, God provided salvation for all those who believe (John 3:16-18).

Just as God had demonstrated his power through Christ's weakness, he was doing the same in Paul's life. It was through hardships, persecutions, and even a stoning that God had shown his **power.** The power that God gave Paul was the strength to serve the church.

13:5 The Corinthians had insisted on testing Paul, the one who had introduced them to the gospel of salvation in the first place. Now that Paul had withstood their investigation, he asked the Corinthians to **examine** themselves, to **test** whether their **faith** was **genuine.** If they couldn't find evidence of **Jesus Christ among** them, then they would fail the test.

13:6 Paul had founded the Corinthian church. Although it was completely absurd for the Corinthian church to question their own founder, they were doing just that! Here Paul tactfully reminded the Corinthians that their Christian faith was a result of his ministry, and they had to recognize that he had **passed the test** and was **approved by God.**

13:7-8 Paul was a man of prayer. He was deeply concerned about the spiritual growth of the Christian church (11:28), so he spent his nights and days praying about those who had accepted Christ as a result of his ministry. Although the Corinthi-

ans had caused him much trouble and grief (2:4), Paul had never stopped praying for them. He prayed that God might give them the wisdom and the power to do what was right. He wasn't praying for their success, so that, in turn, he would appear **successful.** His prayer was for the Corinthians' success, even if it meant that people might consider him to have **failed.** Just as Christ was willing to suffer insults and die on a cross in order to serve all of humanity, Paul was willing to become a failure in order to serve the Corinthians and the **truth** of the gospel (13:4).

13:9 Just as parents will make great sacrifices for their children's welfare, so Paul didn't hesitate to make sacrifices for the Corinthians. Paul wanted the Corinthians to grow in the faith and to become **strong** Christians and be restored to **maturity.** If he had to exhaust himself, deplete his own resources, and appear **weak,** he would do so for their sakes (see also 1:6; 12:14-15).

13:10 Just as a concerned parent would warn an out-of-control child before the child gets hurt or severely punished, so Paul was warning the Corinthians before it was too late. Paul didn't want to **deal harshly** with them, but he would be forced to take drastic measures if certain ones persisted in sin (13:2-3). Paul was hoping that this letter would prepare the Corinthians for his visit. He wanted to be able to use his **authority** to **build** them up, not discipline them.

PAUL'S FINAL GREETINGS / 13:11-13

Paul typically would end his letters with a short list of exhortations (see Colossians 4:2-6; 1 Thessalonians 5:12-22). In 2 Corinthians, he did the same.

13:11 He wanted these believers to be able to **rejoice.** Then he said they must **change** their **ways.** Foremost in Paul's mind was that the church leaders of the Corinthian congregation would take charge by disciplining the unrepentant (13:2), silencing the false teachers in their congregation (11:13), and restoring the repentant to church fellowship (2:7). Paul knew that the disruption the false teachers had caused in the Corinthian church would create disunity—they needed instead to **encourage each other.** They should seek opportunities to build each other up in the faith (1 Corinthians 1:10; 12:7, 12-14). With his brief commands to **live in harmony and peace,** this verse sums up Paul's exhortations in his earlier letter for the Corinthians to unite as one congregation under **the God of love and peace** (see 1 Corinthians 12:27). They were to put their

disputes aside and join together under Christ's leadership to advance his heavenly Kingdom.

13:12 Paul encouraged the Corinthians to **greet each other in Christian love.** By alluding to the **greetings** of **all the Christians,** Paul was reminding the Corinthians that other congregations throughout the Roman Empire were trying, along with the Corinthians, to be unified under Christ. There were congregations across the eastern Mediterranean that shared the same faith and the Spirit that the Corinthians had. Although these believers were miles apart, all Christians were united through the Holy Spirit under Jesus Christ's authority.

13:13 Paul's final blessing on the Corinthians invokes all three members of the Trinity—**God the Father, Jesus Christ,** and the **Holy Spirit.**

Although the term "Trinity" is not explicitly used in the Bible, verses such as this one show that early Christians believed that there were three persons in the Godhead (see Matthew 3:17; 28:19; Luke 1:35).

With this final Trinitarian benediction, Paul was giving the Corinthians a model from the Godhead of how to be unified in love. Through the Spirit's empowering, they, too, could begin to imitate in their congregation the grace, love, and fellowship that the Godhead already enjoyed. It was by Paul's commitment to the Corinthians—through good times and bad, through rejection and acceptance—that Paul hoped to bring the Corinthians back into the full enjoyment of Christ and Christian unity.

GALATIANS

INTRODUCTION

Slavery comes in many forms. Historically, slaves were men and women forced to serve their conquerors or captors. But there are other ways to become enslaved. Some men and women, trapped by destructive habits, struggle under the control of drugs or alcohol. Others, trapped in destructive relationships, struggle to live with an abusive spouse or parent. Still others, trapped in dead-end jobs or systems, struggle to extricate themselves from financial and emotional strangleholds. And all who do not live in Christ are slaves to sin.

Yet all slaves share a common dream—to be free!

As a world traveler, Paul had seen and known many slaves—men and women subjugated by powerful governments, powerful leaders, and powerful personalities. In fact, Paul himself had been a slave to religious zealotry and legalism. But Paul also knew what it meant to be free, to know true liberty in Christ. And since meeting his Liberator on the road to Damascus, Paul had spent his life spreading the news of that freedom.

Having seen both sides, nothing bothered Paul more than seeing people return to bondage. That's what he learned about his friends in Galatia: Men and women, who had found freedom in Christ, were being pressured and persuaded to return to the slavery of religious rules and regulations. Paul's response was quick and strong—don't desert Christ (1:6), don't be foolish (3:1), don't be cursed (3:10), don't be a prisoner (3:23), and don't be a slave (4:8); instead, be free (4:7), be free (4:31), be free (5:1), BE FREE (5:13)!

Paul's letter to the Galatians is called the charter of Christian freedom. In it Paul proclaims the reality of believers' liberty in Christ—freedom from the law and the power of sin, and freedom to serve the living Lord.

Are you trapped in sin? You can be a child of God through faith in Christ Jesus, an heir to the promise, and free (3:26-29). Are you trapped in legalism, trying to earn favor with God by doing good and being good? Don't be burdened again by a yoke of slavery—stand firm and free in Christ (5:1). Are you unsure how to channel the energy from your newfound liberty? Use your freedom to serve others with love (5:13).

AUTHOR

Paul (Saul of Tarsus): Pharisee, apostle, teacher, church planter, evangelist.

The very first line of this letter names Paul as the author (1:1). He is also mentioned in 5:2, "I, Paul, tell you this . . ." In addition to this internal evidence, Paul's authorship of Galatians is affirmed by many early church fathers, including

Paul visited several cities in Galatia on each of his three missionary journeys. As widely as he traveled, Paul may well have considered the Galatian churches to have been his home town neighbors. Raised in Tarsus, just southeast of the Galatian province, the apostle probably knew the area well.

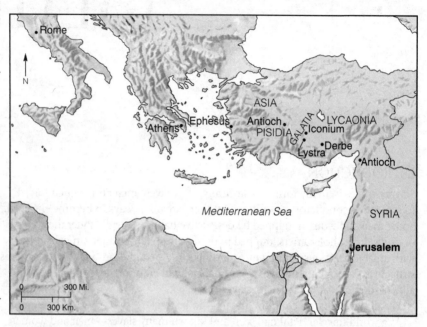

Tarsus had a well-known port and was situated on a main east/west overland route through Asia Minor. A heavily used pass through the Taurus mountains was located just north of the city.

On his first journey, Paul went through Antioch in Pisidia, Iconium, Lystra, and Derbe, and then retraced his steps. On his second journey, he went by land from Antioch in Syria through the four cities in Galatia. On his third journey, he also went through those cities on the main route to Ephesus.

Clement of Rome, Irenaeus, and Tertullian. Paul's authorship of Galatians has been widely accepted by virtually all biblical scholars, including Bible critics. Galatians traditionally has been recognized as the standard for measuring other documents' claims to Pauline authorship.

Paul's intense desire to tell others about Christ led him to make three extensive missionary journeys. The first began in A.D. 46, when he and Barnabas were commissioned by the church at Antioch and sent to Cyprus, Pamphylia, and Galatia (Acts 13:4–14:28). At each town, they first would try to reach Jews with the gospel; then they would reach beyond the synagogue to the Gentiles, who responded in great numbers. During this time, they established several churches in Galatian cities, including Lystra, Derbe, Iconium, and Antioch of Pisidia.

Evidently, upon returning from the first missionary journey, Paul heard of the influence of certain Judaizers on the Galatian converts. Judaizers were Jewish Christians who believed strongly that converts to Christ must keep Jewish laws and follow Jewish rites and rituals, especially circumcision and dietary laws. In other words, they were teaching that Gentiles had to become "Jewish" in order to become Christian. Judaizers acknowledged Jesus as Messiah but still looked for salvation through the works of the law. These teachers were undermining Paul's authority and the message he preached. So Paul wrote to vindicate his apostleship, to refute the Judaizers, and to build the Galatian believers in their faith.

For more about Paul, see the Author section in the Introduction to the book of Romans.

DATE AND SETTING
Written from Antioch in A.D. 49.

Dating Paul's letter to the Galatians depends for the most part on the question of its destination. Galatia covered a large area that extended almost from the coast of the Black Sea to the coast of the Mediterranean, through the mountains and plains of central Turkey. In Paul's day, the word *Galatia* could be understood in two different ways. Geographically, it could refer to the northern territory inhabited by Celtic tribes. If Paul had visited this area, it would have been on his second or third missionary journeys. Thus, the letter to the Galatians would have been written around A.D. 57–58.

But *Galatia* could also be interpreted politically, referring to the Roman province in the south, which included Lycaonia, Isauria, and parts of Phrygia and Pisidia. Paul's Galatian letter would have been addressed to churches in Derbe, Lystra, Iconium, and Antioch in the southern part of Galatia. These churches were founded on the first missionary journey (Acts 13:3–14:26). The letter was most likely written to the believers in this area. The main reason for that conclusion is that the issue addressed at length in this book (how Gentiles become believers) was officially resolved at a council held in Jerusalem (see Acts 15). Because Paul does not appeal to that council decision (made in A.D. 50), then the letter was probably written prior to that, but after the first missionary journey. Therefore the date of A.D. 49 is most probable.

AUDIENCE
The churches in southern Galatia founded on Paul's first missionary journey.

The Galatian people were Gauls who had migrated to that area from western Europe. In fact, the term *Galatia* is derived from Gaul ("Gaul-atia").

Paul first visited South Galatia, the Roman province, during his first missionary journey. In Antioch of Pisidia, Paul and Barnabas went to the synagogue where they presented Jesus as the Christ (Acts 13:13-41). At first, they were warmly received, but then many jealous Jews began to speak against them. So Paul and Barnabas announced that they would take God's word to the Gentiles (Acts 13:42-47). "When the Gentiles heard this, they were very glad and thanked the Lord for his message; and all who were appointed to eternal life became believers" (Acts 13:48). The gospel spread rapidly throughout the area, but the Jews were able to have Paul and Barnabas expelled from the city (Acts 13:49-52).

Next, they traveled to Iconium, where they again spoke in the Jewish synagogue and had a very positive response. Soon opposition arose again, but this time Paul and Barnabas were able to stay in the city for a while, speaking boldly for the Lord (Acts 14:1-3). Their message divided Iconium, however, and upon learning about a plot to stone them, they left the city and traveled to Lystra (Acts 14:4-7).

In Lystra they encountered a man who had been crippled from birth. When God healed the man through Paul, the crowd thought that Paul and Barnabas were gods and began to honor them as such (Acts 14:8-13). Paul and Barnabas tried to convince the people that they were only human, but many still tried to worship them

(Acts 14:14-18). Eventually, some Jews from Antioch and Iconium turned the crowd against Paul and Barnabas. In fact, they stoned Paul and left him for dead outside the city (Acts 14:19). "But as the believers stood around him, he got up and went back into the city" (Acts 14:20). The mention of "believers" implies that many in that area had responded to the gospel message and had trusted Christ as Savior.

In Derbe, Paul and Barnabas had a very good response and encountered little opposition to their message. After ministering there, they retraced their steps through Lystra, Iconium, and Antioch, strengthening and encouraging the new believers in those cities and appointing elders in each church (Acts 14:21-23).

From the way the Galatians responded to Paul and Barnabas, it is clear that they were easily swayed. On one hand, they were warmhearted and generous (Acts 13:42-43, 48; 14:11-18; Galatians 4:15); on the other, they were fickle and quickly misled (Acts 13:50; 14:4-5, 19; Galatians 1:6). On the positive side, the Galatians were ready to listen and respond, able and willing to work hard for their religion, and very sincere. But they were easily impressed and influenced because they were not rooted in faith and grace. No wonder Paul could call them "foolish" (3:1).

It's easy to judge the Galatians for their fickle ways, wanting to worship Paul and Barnabas as gods and then suddenly turning and trying to kill them, committing themselves to Christ but then being deceived by the Judaizers. Yet many in churches today act similarly. Eager, at first, to learn about Christ and God's word, they soon tire of Bible study and personal application and are swept along by the latest religious fad. Instead of becoming rooted in the faith, they remain shallow and are easy victims of modern false teachers. Don't be fooled by those who claim to be authorities or by new ideas that sound good; stay true to God's word, focus on Christ, and deepen and strengthen your faith.

OCCASION AND PURPOSE
After finishing their very successful missionary journey on which they had seen hundreds come to faith in Christ and had established several new churches in Asia and in the Roman province of Galatia, Paul and Barnabas returned to Antioch (in Syria). Upon their return, however, they found that some false teachers, called Judaizers had gone to the new believers in Galatia and taught that the legalistic commands in Scripture were linked to salvation, and made the covenant restrictions more important than the cross. They were promoting circumcision and food laws. In short, these Judaizers were teaching that in order for Gentiles to be saved, they first had to become Jews.

Evidently, Paul also learned that Judaizers had been spreading their false teachings in Galatia and that many of the believers there had been influenced. In fact, these doctrinal debates were splitting the churches apart (5:25; 6:1, 3) and causing believers to become discouraged (6:9). To enhance their own authority as Bible teachers and spiritual leaders, these Judaizers had undermined and minimized the authority of Paul, representing him as an inferior teacher and apostle.

When Paul heard this news, he wrote immediately to the Galatian believers, denouncing the Judaizers and their false teachings and emphasizing his credentials as an apostle (1:1, 11-24), teaching and ministering with the blessing of the apostles in Jerusalem (2:1-10). Next, he had to show that both Jews and Gentiles come into a right relationship with God the same way—through faith, not works

(3:1-14, 26-29). In fact, all legalistic versions of the gospel are perversions of it (5:2-6, 11-12); salvation is by grace through faith in Christ alone. Nothing needs to be added; in fact, nothing can be added. Believers are free, not bound to the law.

In addition to refuting the Judaizers and emphasizing the truth of salvation by faith alone, Paul also sought to show that with Christian freedom comes responsibility. In other words, believers should use their freedom in Christ to love and serve each other and to obey Christ by living under the control of the Holy Spirit and not giving way to the sinful nature (5:13-14; 6:22-23).

Even today, many Christians swing to either of those extremes: legalism or libertinism. That is, some, like the Judaizers of the first century, seek to find God's approval through doing good works—church attendance, Bible reading, "full-time" Christian service, tithes—and refraining from bad activities. They judge others who fail to meet their behavioral standards or their particular interpretation of devotion or dedication. In so doing, they become slaves to the law. Others, however, go to the other extreme, emphasizing their freedom and easily rationalizing self-indulgence and lack of commitment to the church. But Paul's message to us is the same as to the Galatians: "You are free from the law; salvation is by faith alone. But that means you are free to serve Christ. Don't leave the slavery of the law only to become slaves of sin!"

MESSAGE

After a brief introduction (1:1-5), Paul addresses those who were accepting the Judaizers' perverted gospel (1:6-9). He summarizes the controversy, including his personal confrontation with Peter and other church leaders (1:10–2:16). He then demonstrates that salvation is by faith alone by alluding to his conversion (2:17-21), appealing to his readers' own experience of the gospel (3:1-5), and showing how the Old Testament teaches about grace (3:6-20). Next, he explains the purpose of God's laws and the relationship between law, God's promises, and Christ (3:21–4:31).

Having laid the foundation, Paul builds his case for Christian liberty. We are saved by faith, not by keeping Moses' law (5:1-12); our freedom means that we are free to love and serve one another, not to do wrong (5:13-26); and Christians should share each other's troubles and be kind to each other (6:1-10). In 6:11-18, Paul takes the pen into his own hand and shares his final thoughts.

The main themes in the book of Galatians include: *the Law, Faith, Freedom, Sinful Nature,* and *Holy Spirit.*

The Law (1:6-8; 2:15-21; 3:1-25; 5:2-6; 6:12-16). A group of teachers had traveled from Jerusalem to Galatia and were insisting that non-Jewish believers must obey Jewish laws and traditions. They taught that a person was saved by following the law of Moses (with emphasis on circumcision for males, the sign of the covenant), in addition to faith in Christ. In other words, Gentiles had to first become Jews in order to become Christians. Some Galatians had been convinced by these teachings, and many had become confused. Paul opposed the false teachers (Judaizers) by showing that the law is powerless to save anyone. Only God's grace through personal faith in Christ makes people right with God.

IMPORTANCE FOR TODAY. No one can be saved by keeping the Old Testament laws, even all the Ten Commandments. The law served as a guide to point out people's need to be forgiven, as a straightedge to show people how crooked they are. Even the most loving, generous, kind, and moral person falls short of God's standard. But Christ fulfilled all of the obligations of the law for us. We must turn to him, and him alone, to be saved. Don't be fooled by those who suggest that performance of certain works or religious rituals are necessary to obtain eternal life. Only Christ can make a person right with God!

Faith (2:15-21; 3:6-18, 23-29). If people cannot be saved by keeping the Jewish laws or by living good, moral lives, how can they be saved? Paul answered this question by reminding the Galatians of Abraham's faith and pointing them again to Christ. Salvation is a gift from God, made available to human beings through Christ's death on the cross. Individuals receive God's salvation by faith— trusting in Christ—not by anything else. Becoming a Christian is in no way based on a person's initiative, wise choice, or good character. A person can become right with God only by believing in Christ. This common faith in Christ unites all believers, everywhere—Jews, Gentiles, men, women, slaves, and those who are free; all are true descendants of Abraham and children of God.

IMPORTANCE FOR TODAY. A person's acceptance with God comes only by believing in Christ. We must never add to or twist this truth. We are saved by faith, not by the good that we do. And we must never exclude anyone because of sex, race, or social standing from the Good News of Christ. All can come through faith. What or whom are you trusting for salvation? Have you placed your whole trust and confidence in Christ? He alone can forgive you and bring you into a relationship with God.

Freedom (4:1-31; 5:1, 13-15). In answering the Judaizers, Paul emphasized the believers' freedom in Christ. Christians were neither under the authority of Jerusalem nor under the jurisdiction of Jewish laws and traditions. Faith in Christ brings true freedom from sin and from legalism—the futile attempt to be right with God by keeping the law. Paul also emphasized that the freedom in Christ must not be abused or flaunted. Believers' freedom must be used to serve one another in love and to submit to the Holy Spirit's control. So we have this paradox: Believers are freed from sin in order to be slaves of Christ.

IMPORTANCE FOR TODAY. When a person trusts Christ as Savior, he or she becomes a new person, forgiven, empowered, free from the bondage of sin. Yet this freedom is a privilege, with responsibility. Christians are not free to disobey Christ or practice immorality; they are free to serve the risen Christ. Before trusting Christ you were a slave to sin, but now you are forgiven and free from sin's power and penalty. Use your freedom to love and serve, not to do wrong.

Sinful Nature (5:13, 16-21; 6:7-8). The tendency of human beings to sin is inherited from Adam. This sinful nature continues to trouble believers and cooperates with the world and Satan to stifle their effectiveness. The sinful nature affects the body and also the mind.

IMPORTANCE FOR TODAY. Our sinful nature opposes the Spirit and becomes more active when we try to live by the Spirit, hindering our relationship with God. The sinful nature is not limited to sensual desires and often is more dangerous as pride or apathy. There is a constant battle between our sinful nature and the Holy Spirit in us. But we can overcome the flesh by recognizing its presence and yielding our lives to God's Spirit. Don't be surprised or discouraged by how easily you are influenced by the sinful nature. Then yield to the control of the Holy Spirit daily, moment by moment.

Holy Spirit (5:16-26; 6:1-10). People become children of God, regenerated, through the work of the Holy Spirit. He brings new life, and even the faith to believe in Christ is his gift. Then, after conversion, the Holy Spirit continues to live in believers, instructing, guiding, leading, and giving power. Paul told the Galatians that if they would submit to the Holy Spirit's direction, he would produce love, joy, peace, and many other wonderful changes in them.

IMPORTANCE FOR TODAY. When a Christian allows the Holy Spirit to work, the Spirit produces his fruit in him or her. Just as becoming a Christian was a work of God in us through faith, so too is living the Christian life and the process of spiritual growth. The secret is in submitting to his leadership, trusting him to guide us, and then, by faith, following his guidance. Do you live by the Spirit? Instead of submitting again to the desires of your sinful nature, daily submit to the Holy Spirit. He will produce heavenly by-products in your life, transforming you into the person God wants you to be.

OUTLINE OF GALATIANS

   I. Authenticity of the Gospel (1:1–2:21)
  II. Superiority of the Gospel (3:1–4:31)
 III. Freedom of the Gospel (5:1–6:18)

GALATIANS 1

GREETINGS FROM PAUL / 1:1-5

The year was probably A.D. 49. Paul and Barnabas had just completed their first missionary journey (Acts 13:2–14:28). Following a brief stay on the island of Cyprus, they had visited Iconium, Lystra, and Derbe, cities in the Roman province of Galatia (present-day Turkey). In their travels they had met with both wholehearted response and deep-seated resistance.

Shortly after their return to Antioch, some Jewish Christians arrived from Judea. These Judeans claimed that the Antioch church and its missionaries were diluting Christianity to make it more appealing to Gentiles, and they challenged Paul's authority as an apostle. Some of Paul's accusers went to the Galatian churches and insisted that the Gentile converts had to be circumcised and follow all the Jewish laws and customs in order to be saved. According to these people (called **Judaizers**), Gentiles had to first become Jews in order to become Christians. This caused much confusion in the churches that Paul and Barnabas had planted in Galatia.

In response to this threat, Paul wrote this letter to the Galatian churches. In it, he explained that following the Old Testament laws or the Jewish laws would not bring salvation. A person is saved only by grace through faith. Most likely, Paul wrote this letter shortly before the meeting of the Jerusalem council in A.D. 50, which settled the law-versus-grace controversy (Acts 15).

1:1 First-century letters often began by introducing the writer, although this "writer" often dictated his letters to a scribe. Paul used a secretary for most, if not all, of his letters (see Romans 16:22), usually writing the last few lines in his own hand to authenticate his message (6:11).

Paul was called to be **an apostle** by **Jesus Christ and God the Father.** Paul was not one of the original twelve disciples (later called apostles), but Jesus had specially called him on the road to Damascus to preach the gospel to Jews and Gentiles (Acts 9:3-19). The apostles' mission was to be God's representatives; they were envoys, messengers, and delegates who were directly under the authority of Jesus Christ. They had authority to set up and supervise churches and discipline them if necessary. Paul presented his credentials as an apostle at the beginning of this letter because his authority was being undermined in the churches in Galatia.

No human had **appointed** Paul; Jesus Christ, the one who had been **raised** from the dead, had spoken to Paul (Acts 9:4-5). Paul explained his apostleship in these words, not to separate himself from the original Twelve, but to show that his apostleship rested on the same basis as theirs. If the believers in Galatia questioned Paul's apostleship, then they also should question the apostleship of Peter, John, James, and all the others—and such questioning would be absurd. All the apostles were called by Jesus Christ and God the Father, and they answered to God as their final authority.

1:2 Paul's fellow **Christians** in Antioch joined him in **sending greetings** to the Galatian believers. These coworkers in Antioch were a sizable group, including Barnabas, Titus, Timothy, and some of the men listed in Acts 13:1 (see also Acts 19:29; 20:4).

This letter is an example of Paul writing to a region or group of churches. In Paul's time, **Galatia** was the Roman province located in the center section of present-day Turkey. Much of the region was on a large and fertile plateau; many people had moved to the region because of its favorable agriculture. During his missionary journeys, Paul planned to visit regions with large population centers in order to reach as many people as possible and to plant churches in those centers. This letter was to be circulated among the **churches** planted by Paul and Barnabas during the first missionary journey—in Derbe, Lystra, and Iconium.

1:3 Paul used **grace and peace** in all his salutations, wishing his readers the benefits of both. "Grace" was the Greek greeting, as "peace" was the Jewish greeting. Jointly used in the context of the gospel, these two words gained great depth. The word **grace** reminded Paul's readers of God's kindness in offering salvation to undeserving people. **Peace** reminded the readers of Christ's offer of peace to his disciples as they lived out their faith in an evil world (John 14:27). Christian letters not only expressed the wish for peace, but identified the source of peace. If "grace" summarizes God's gift to us, then "peace" summarizes the personal results of that gift (see John 14:27; 16:33).

True peace comes only from a right relationship with God because peace comes **from God our Father and from the Lord Jesus Christ.** As in verse 1, the connecting of "God" and "Jesus" reveals their oneness (John 10:30). God is called "Father," a name Jesus taught his disciples to use in the Lord's Prayer (Matthew 6:9). Jesus Christ is identified as "Lord," a title given to him after his resurrection and ascension that reveals him as worthy of worship (see John 20:28; Acts 2:36; Philippians 2:9).

1:4 Jesus **died for our sins,** not his own, for he was sinless. Jesus' sacrifice was ultimate, voluntary, and substitutionary. This is called "substitutionary atonement." Christ died for *our* sins, in *our* place, so we would not have to suffer the punishment we deserve (see 1 Peter 2:24). This was not an accident; it occurred just **as God our Father planned.** God made a way of salvation—the ultimate sacrifice of sending his only Son to die on the cross, taking the penalty for humanity's sins. People can only be saved through Christ.

The result of Jesus' gift of himself was **to rescue us from this evil world.** This rescue or deliverance does not remove believers from the world (at least not yet); instead, it gives us the blessings of our future eternity with Christ and offers us his guidance and presence as we serve him in **this evil world.** Indeed, if all the early believers had been rescued out of the evil age in which they lived, there would have been no hope for us. To use Jesus' expression, though we are still "in" the world, we are no longer "of" the world (see John 17:15-18).

1:5 Thoughts of God's love, mercy, and guidance, and Christ's ultimate sacrifice on our behalf evoke words of praise and thanks. Does the glory of God lead you to give such praise? **Glory belongs to God** alone. Even if God had not done so much for us, he would still be the only one deserving glory from his creation. As believers, we will be able to glorify our God **through all the ages of eternity** because of the promise of eternal life with him.

With a decisive **Amen** ("Let it be so," "Let it come to pass"), Paul closed his introduction to this letter. In these first five verses, Paul touched on what would be the intent of his letter: his authority as an apostle, and the fact that salvation is not by works but by grace through faith in Christ alone.

THERE IS ONLY ONE GOOD NEWS / 1:6-10

Paul was amazed at how easily the believers in the Galatian churches had given up the Good News of the gospel of Christ for the "bad news" that the false teachers had brought them. Paul's concern was not over alternative viewpoints of interpretation; he was warning Galatian Christians about turning from the truth to lies, from what was right to what was wrong.

1:6-7 Paul immediately expressed shock at the Galatians' behavior. He found it difficult to comprehend that the believers were **turning away so soon from God.** They had been **called,** but they were throwing aside that privilege in order to try to earn their salvation. Paul was **shocked** that someone would insist on attempting to pay for a free (and priceless) gift! Those who turned to this **different way** would no longer be Christians. This different way only pretended **to be the Good News,** but it was **not the Good News at all.** The false teachers, Judaizers, were teaching that to be saved, Gentile believers had to follow Jewish laws and customs, especially the rite of circumcision. Faith in Christ was not enough. They may have included in their teachings the need for faith in Christ for salvation, but they taught that additional requirements had to be met before true salvation could occur. This twisted and changed the truth, and it infuriated Paul. Whether or not the Judaizers were sincere, their teaching **fooled** these new churches and had to be countered. They were loading down people with the requirements of the "law" instead of encouraging them to live by grace in joyful obedience to Christ.

Jesus Christ has made the gift of salvation available to all people. Faith in Christ is the only requirement for salvation. Beware of people who say that we need more than simple faith in Christ to be saved. When people set up additional requirements for salvation, they deny the power of Christ's death on the cross (see 3:1-5).

1:8-9 Paul denounced the Judaizers' perversion of the gospel of Christ. Using strong language to deal with this life-or-death issue, Paul said that **God's curse** should **fall on anyone,** even himself, **who preaches any other message than the one** originally brought to them. In fact, **even if an angel comes from heaven and preaches any other message,** that angel should **be forever cursed.** (This passage strongly refutes the claim by Mormons regarding the source of Joseph Smith's teaching, that the angel Moroni appeared to him.) If the truth is changed, the teacher is false, regardless of his or her qualifications, accomplishments, or experience. Paul has already noted that there is no other gospel (1:7), thus **any other message** would be false. The gospel teaching must not be changed, for the truth of the gospel never changes. Paul's repeated use of the condemnation of **God's curse** conveys the most severe penalties imaginable for distorting the truth of the gospel. Paul and Barnabas preached; the Galatians accepted. That decisive experience did not need to be added to by certain actions required by the false teachers. The acceptance of the message alone had accomplished their salvation.

1:10 Undoubtedly the Judaizers had accused Paul of compromise, saying that he taught freedom from the Jewish law to the Gentiles in order to **be a people pleaser** and thus win as many converts as possible. But Paul explained that his purpose was always to **please God.**

Paul's use of the word **still** offers a glimpse into his inner self and his past life as a Pharisee. Paul understood that by living a strict, law-abiding, judgmental, and appearance-focused life of a Pharisee, his goal had really been to please people. Religious and pious people may receive mountains of praise for their supposed character and good works. Christians are rarely accorded such praise. Thus if Paul were **trying to please people,** he would **not be Christ's servant.** As there is no compromise with the truth, there is no compromise for the Christian with "this evil world" (1:4). The life of serving Christ does not put people in the limelight, offer great material rewards, or promise worldly security. Thus, if Paul wanted to please people, he could have chosen many other routes or stayed a Jewish Pharisee.

Much of church growth philosophy centers on a "market" approach, discovering what people want and need. For a culture that treats God and the Bible as irrelevant, this approach may be the only way to break through barriers. But we must have our motives clearly understood. If our desire is to please people, our packaging of the gospel may take priority over the content. If our purpose is evangelism, then reaching people through felt needs can be legitimate. We must not forget that our allegiance to Christ comes first. We must never water down his authority in the life of a believer in order to bring him or her into a church.

PAUL'S MESSAGE COMES FROM CHRIST / 1:11-24

Having pointed to the uniqueness of the gospel in the last paragraph, here Paul turned his attention to his authority as an apostle. Why should the Galatians have listened to Paul instead of the Judaizers? Paul answered this implicit question by furnishing his credentials: His message was received directly from Christ (1:12); he had been an exemplary Jew (1:13-14); he had had a special conversion experience (1:15-16; see also Acts 9:1-9); he had been confirmed and accepted in his ministry by the other apostles (1:18-19; 2:1-9). Paul also presented his credentials to the Corinthian and Philippian churches (2 Corinthians 11–12; Philippians 3:4-9).

1:11 In verse 1, Paul had introduced himself as appointed by God. As Paul launched into a repudiation of those who would refuse to recognize his authority as an apostle, he began at the beginning. Paul wanted the Galatian believers to be assured that he was an apostle—called separately from the Twelve and received as an equal by the Twelve.

The **Good News** that Paul preached was the true gospel, not any false gospel, as he had discussed in verses 6-9. The gospel Paul taught was **not based on mere human reasoning or logic**—that is, it was not a belief or doctrine handed down to him through Jewish tradition.

1:12 The Judaizers, refusing to acknowledge Paul as an apostle, most likely claimed that Paul owed his salvation and gospel knowledge to Peter and James in Jerusalem and that he had to turn to them for approval and support of his teaching. But, as Paul would point out, he had become a believer before he ever met these leaders in the Christian church. Nor was Paul **taught** the gospel. As a young man, Paul had sat at the feet of Gamaliel, learning by rote and repetition the Hebrew Law and Scriptures. But that was not the gospel, nor could it give salvation.

Instead, the message Paul preached **came by direct revelation from Jesus Christ himself.** We do not know the extent or manner of this revelation. Paul could be referring to his vision of Christ on the road to Damascus (Acts 9:3-6), to the time after Ananias returned Paul's sight (Acts 9:17-19), to the three years spent in Arabia (Galatians 1:17-18), or to his ongoing contact with Christ in his ministry (Acts 9:19-22; 22:17-18). Paul was probably referring to something more than his Damascus road experience.

Paul didn't say it, but he implied at this point: "How can anyone doubt my authority? How can anyone doubt the divinely revealed truth about Jesus Christ?"

1:13-14 To further support his apostolic claim, Paul showed how radically Christ had transformed him from a persecutor of the church to an apostle of the church. When he **followed the Jewish reli-gion,** he was one of the most religious Jews of his day. He scrupulously kept the law and also **violently persecuted the Christians,** seeking to **get rid of them.** So adamant was he for upholding the traditions of his faith, so convinced was he that Christianity was a false religion deviating from Judaism, that he wanted to see it annihilated (see Acts 7:57–8:1; 9:1-2; 26:9-11). He called himself **one of the most religious Jews** of his age, working hard **to follow all the old traditions** of the Jewish religion. Before his conversion, Paul had been even more zealous for those traditions than the Judaizers themselves could ever claim to be! Paul's intense study under one of the most respected teachers of his day helped to establish his credentials. Paul wrote about himself, "I was circumcised when I was eight days old, having been born into a pure-blooded Jewish family that is a branch of the tribe of Benjamin. So I am a real Jew if there ever was one! What's more, I was a member of the Pharisees, who demand the strictest obedience to the Jewish law" (Philippians 3:5, see also Acts 22:3-13; 26:4-18). Paul had been sincere in his zeal, but wrong. Militant Judaism was in Paul's past—it was his "previous" way of life. When he met Jesus Christ, his life changed. He then directed all his energies toward building up the Christian church.

1:15 What changed Paul's life from persecutor of the church to preacher of the faith? The little phrase, **but . . . God,** reveals what happened. God got hold of Paul's life. Paul's conversion happened only because **it pleased God.** And God used every part of Paul's life, even prior to his conversion, to prepare Paul for the ministry.

God had chosen Paul **even before** he **was born.** God's designs on Paul's life clearly began before his birth. Similarly, Jeremiah was divinely informed that God had called him even before he was born to do special work (Jeremiah 1:5). Paul's expression recalls the profound awe described by the psalmist in Psalm 139 in recognizing the scope of God's awareness of us. The context indicates that Paul was humbled by God's grace in calling him to be an apostle rather than proud about any personal qualifications that made him noticeable to God. The fact that God would accomplish his work through any of us ought to inspire deep humility.

The understanding that Paul and all believers are chosen before birth by God is referred to as the doctrine of election. This was a key part of Paul's theology (see, for example, Romans 8:29-30; 9:11-29; Ephesians 1:4-5). In the Bible, election refers to God's choice of an individual or group for a specific purpose or destiny. God's sovereignty, not people's works or character, is the basis for election.

Election—being "chosen" before we're born— is like receiving an invitation for a wonderful banquet. But the invitation comes to us unearned and unmerited. No friendship, political pull, or effort makes it necessary that we be on the invitation list. The guest list is purely the host's choice. After all, it is *his* banquet. The invitation comes with the traditional RSVP. God's gracious invitation does require our response and attendance. Only those who respond to God's call receive the gift of salvation; it is "by invitation only." It comes to us completely undeserved so that we might have no basis for pride. When we understand God's sovereignty as well as his mercy, we respond with humility and gratitude that God would be merciful to even us.

Believers still may wonder why or how they could be chosen while others might be rejected. God is sovereign and, in reality, no one has any claim on his **mercy**. It is completely **undeserved**. He prepared us in advance by his gift of salvation, and he will reveal his glory when we are finally with him for eternity. Instead of focusing on God choosing some and rejecting others, we should stand in awe at God's offer of grace to any of us. Thus, no one can demand that God explain why he does what he does. He makes all the rules, but he loves to show his mercy to us. What an amazing God he is! What may seem to us to be an inconsistency on God's part actually reveals our own inability to see as God sees.

1:16 When God called Paul on the road to Damascus, Paul accepted the gracious invitation of salvation. Part of that call was that God **revealed his Son** to Paul. When Paul heard the voice of the resurrected and living Jesus Christ (Acts 9:4-6), this confirmed the fact of the Resurrection. In his appearance to Paul, God revealed who Jesus really was—the Jews' promised Messiah, the Savior. The revelation of Jesus carried with it the command to go with the message to others. The little phrase **so that** carries great weight. Paul was saved "so that" he could serve God.

Paul understood exactly what that service was to be: **proclaim the Good News about Jesus to the Gentiles** (see Acts 9:15-16). **Gentiles** were non-Jews, whether in nationality or in religion. In Paul's day, Jews thought of all Gentiles as heathens. Jews avoided Gentiles, believing that contact with Gentiles brought spiritual corruption. Although Gentiles could become Jews in religion by undergoing circumcision and by following Jewish laws and customs (they were called "proselytes"), they were never fully accepted.

Many Jewish Christians had difficulty understanding that the gospel enabled both Jews and Gentiles to have equal standing before God. But God planned to save both Jews and Gentiles. He had revealed this plan through Old Testament prophets (see, for example, Genesis 12:3; Isaiah 42:6; 66:19), and he had fulfilled it through Jesus Christ. Paul was called to proclaim this message to the Gentiles (see also Acts 13:46-47; 26:20; Romans 11:13; 15:16; Ephesians 3:8; 1 Timothy 2:7).

Paul's personal encounter with Jesus was so compelling that no further confirmation was required. Paul **did not rush out to consult with anyone else** about doctrine, theology, the Old Testament Scriptures, or the specifics of the gospel message. Repeating the thought from verse 12, Paul emphasized that his authority did not come secondhand. The Judaizers were attacking Paul's authority by saying he could be no more than a student of the apostles. But Paul never even spoke to any of the apostles about the gospel until three years after his conversion. His understanding of the gospel message had come from God himself.

1:17 The twelve apostles **were apostles before** Paul became an apostle, but beyond that, there was no difference between them. When he finally did go to Jerusalem to meet with the church leaders, he went as an equal. The other apostles recognized him as such.

Although the book of Acts doesn't seem to allow time for this retreat **into Arabia,** here Paul explained that he went away for three years (1:18) in order to spend time alone with God. This was vital for the newly converted Jewish Pharisee and persecutor of Christianity. Paul was converted; he needed time to rethink his former position against Christianity in light of the truth of the gospel that had been revealed to him. During this interim, Paul probably studied the Scriptures, prayed, and thought about the meaning of Christ's crucifixion and resurrection in relation to the Old Testament that he knew so well. God revealed to Paul the meaning of the gospel, and from Paul's time of study, we today have the New Testament letters that focus on explaining God's plan (especially the doctrinal book of Romans). Paul's point in explaining this itinerary was to show that he formed his theology, not from consulting with any other believers, but alone, with God's guidance. After his time in Arabia, Paul **later returned to the city of Damascus.**

Although the sequence of events making up this part of Paul's life appears clear, fitting it into the chronology of the book of Acts presents some challenges. Luke did not mention a three-year time period similar to Paul's account. The primary accounts covering this time period are Acts 9:1-31 and Galatians 1:13-24. The following presents a suggested chronology:

• On his way to Damascus to imprison Christians, Saul was confronted by Christ and converted.
• Journeying on into Damascus, Paul waited until he was contacted by Ananias, who prayed for his healing and arranged for his baptism.
• Paul began preaching about Jesus in the synagogues of Damascus (Acts 9:20). He left clear evidence of his conversion before he went into Arabia.
• Paul retreated into Arabia (Galatians 1:17). This retreat into solitude consolidated and integrated the central change in his life with the rest of his experience and training.
• Three years pass. During that time, Paul left Damascus twice: first to spend time alone in Arabia, second to avoid plotters against his life and visit Jerusalem. Paul's escape from Damascus fits better at the end of the three-year time period than shortly after his conversion. The Pharisees were probably upset by Paul's desertion from their ranks and the effect that he had on their numbers within the city after a while.

1:18 Paul's visit to **Jerusalem** was his first as a Christian. This was where the church began, and this was where some of the apostles lived and worked, specifically **Peter,** whom Paul went to see. Paul explained that he wanted to **visit** with Peter; he did not get instruction from Peter nor was he commissioned by Peter. While Paul does not mention the reason for the brevity of the visit (**fifteen days**), we are told by Luke that the opposition had plans in motion to kill Paul. Perhaps because of concerns for his life, as well as for the ongoing safety of believers in Jerusalem, Paul was given safe conduct by the believers to Caesarea, where he set out toward his home in Tarsus (see Acts 9:30).

1:19-20 To further repudiate the Judaizers' claim that Paul needed the twelve apostles' instruction and approval, Paul pointed out that during his time in Jerusalem, **the only other apostle** he **met** was **James.** Paul's intention to meet with Peter

implies a self-perception of equality with the apostle who was acknowledged as the leader among Jesus' disciples. Paul planned an apostolic summit with Peter. But there was no general apostolic meeting to confirm Paul, no official gathering to approve this new convert and missionary. Instead, Paul talked only with Peter and James, the Lord's brother. This was not James the apostle (one of the Twelve) whom Herod put to death (see Acts 12:2); it was James, Jesus' younger half-brother. During Jesus' ministry on earth, James did not believe that Jesus was the Messiah. But after the Resurrection, Jesus appeared personally to James (1 Corinthians 15:7), and James believed. He became the leader of the Jerusalem church. Interestingly, James is here called an **apostle** although he, like Paul, also was not one of the original Twelve. Assuring his readers **before God** of the truth of his words, Paul made clear that any assumption on anyone's part that he was taught and/or commissioned by the twelve apostles was absurd.

1:21 Paul's arrival in Jerusalem had caused real problems. His preaching stirred up a hornet's nest of opposition. Paul's life was in danger. Many of the believers were hesitant to accept his roadside conversion. His presence may have also caused added persecution for other believers. Those who did accept Paul were committed to keeping him alive. So Paul was urged to leave after only fifteen days. His departure eventually took him to his hometown of Tarsus in Cilicia (see Acts 9:30; 22:3). On his way, while in **the provinces of Syria and Cilicia,** Paul most likely continued preaching the gospel. These small details serve to emphasize Paul's claim of direct authority from Jesus, apart from the equal authority of those in Jerusalem. In the remote areas Paul mentioned, he had no opportunity to receive instruction from the apostles or have his ministry overseen by them. Thus, he was not part of the Judean authority structure.

1:22 Although Paul was known to the Christians in Jerusalem at this time, because of both his personal visit and his brief ministry there, **the churches in Judea,** outside the city limits of Jerusalem, **didn't know** Paul **personally. Judea** was the name of the Roman district where the city of Jerusalem was. There were identifiable groups of believers meeting in towns throughout Judea.

1:23 Paul was unknown to the churches in Judea, yet they recognized the message he preached and glorified God because of it (1:24). Paul was making the point that his authority and ministry were recognized by people who had never even seen him, yet the Galatians had met him, listened to him, and believed his message, only to turn around and doubt him! The Judean Christians heard what **people were saying** (perhaps as the Galatians had, 1:13): **The one who used to persecute** believers was now preaching **the very faith he tried to destroy.**

1:24 The Jewish Christians in Judea were rejoicing and glorifying God **because of** Paul—his conversion, his message, his ministry. How ironic that the Judean Christians had given Paul full status and recognition without ever seeing or hearing him, but the Galatian Christians, who had no reason to doubt Paul or his message, were beginning to join the Judaizers and thus to undermine Paul. They needed to cast aside their doubts, get back to the truth, and get on with what God wanted them to do.

GALATIANS 2

THE APOSTLES ACCEPT PAUL / 2:1-10

To defend himself against the Judaizers' charges, the apostle pointed to his fourteen years of independent ministry between his first two visits to Jerusalem following his conversion. He functioned directly under Jesus' authority during that time, not under the official body at Jerusalem. He helped the Galatians understand the complex relationship existing between himself and the apostles in Jerusalem. So when Paul wrote about his visit to the mother church, he showed both his independence from the other apostles' authority and his respect for them. Paul gave four significant aspects of his visit that established his credentials: (1) the companions on his journey; (2) the content of his message; (3) the confirmation of his ministry; and (4) his commission to come to Jerusalem.

2:1 Paul continued the itinerary from 1:21 and explained that he went to the regions of Syria and Cilicia; afterward he **went back to Jerusalem.** The book of Acts records five visits to Jerusalem by Paul: (1) the visit to get acquainted with Peter (around A.D. 35, Acts 9:26-30; Galatians 1:18-20); (2) the visit to deliver a gift to the Jerusalem church for famine relief (around A.D. 44, Acts 11:27-30); (3) the visit to attend the Jerusalem council (around A.D. 49 / 50, Acts 15:1-30); (4) the visit at the end of the second missionary journey (around A.D. 52, Acts 18:22); and (5) the visit that resulted in his being imprisoned and sent to Rome (around A.D. 57, Acts 21:15–23:35).

The visit to Jerusalem mentioned here is most likely the second visit, when he delivered the famine relief gift to the Jerusalem church. It would not be the third visit, because Paul spends time in this letter dealing with questions that the Jerusalem council ultimately settled, so the council could not yet have taken place.

The **fourteen years** are probably dated, not from the last mention in his itinerary (that is, from his time in Syria and Cilicia), but rather from his conversion. The first and fourteenth years were partial years. Like history itself, Paul tended to divide and orient his life around the time "before Christ" and "after Christ." Paul was converted around A.D. 32, dating this visit at A.D. 44/45. Paul was pointing out that he had been preaching to the Gentiles for a long time, and thus had a specific message that could be discussed with the church leaders in Jerusalem. Following this visit, Paul then took the first missionary journey (Acts 13:1–14:28), wrote this letter to the Galatians in response to the troubling news of spiritual desertion by the new believers, and later attended the Jerusalem council that settled many of the issues discussed in this letter to the Galatians.

According to the book of Acts, **Barnabas** recognized Paul's sincerity as a truly converted former persecutor and introduced Paul to the apostles. Many believers, even the apostles themselves, may have feared that Paul simply was acting in some extravagant ruse in order to find out and capture more Christians. But Barnabas was not afraid (Acts 9:27). His name means "Son of Encouragement," and Paul knew firsthand about Barnabas's kind encouragement. Barnabas accompanied Paul on the famine relief visit to Jerusalem (Acts 11:27-30) and traveled with him on the first missionary journey, during which Galatia was evangelized (Acts 13:2-3). Thus, Barnabas was well known to the Galatian Christians to whom Paul was writing.

Titus, a Greek, was one of Paul's most trusted and dependable coworkers. Paul called him "a true child in the faith" (Titus 1:4), so he was probably one of Paul's converts. This trip to Jerusalem with Paul became the first of many journeys for Titus, who would later become a true right-hand man to Paul. Exactly why Paul brought Titus along to Jerusalem is unclear. Possibly because Titus was a pure Gentile convert, he was presented as a "test case" to the church leaders (2:3-5).

2:2 God told Paul, through a revelation, to confer with the church leaders in Jerusalem so they would **understand** the message he **had been preaching to the Gentiles.** Paul's point here was that his visit to Jerusalem was not because the apostles had summoned him or because he had felt a need to talk to the apostles about his ministry among the Gentiles.

This revelation may have been to Paul personally, or it may have come through someone else. It is probable that Paul was referring to the prophecy made by Agabus, who had predicted that a severe famine was coming (Acts 11:28), for we are told that this prophecy led to Paul and Barnabas being sent to Jerusalem and Paul using that God-given opportunity to then talk to the church leaders.

Remember that one reason Paul wrote this letter was to combat the false teaching of the Judaizers who were trying to undermine Paul's authority as an apostle. Paul did not go to Jerusalem at the call of the apostles, and he did not go to get approval for the gospel he preached. Instead, Paul went to set his message before them **to make sure they did not disagree** (which was really the only response they could have). Paul didn't need approval because the gospel had been revealed to him by God himself. The essence of the gospel Paul preached to both Jews and Gentiles was that God's salvation is offered to all people regardless of race, sex, nationality, wealth, social standing, educational level, or anything else. All types of people can be forgiven by trusting in Christ (see Romans 10:8-13; Galatians 3:28).

The language Paul used here may seem harsh or even boastful, but it preserves an important distinction. Paul believed and taught the principle of mutual submission among believers (Ephesians 5:21). But the truth does not submit. Paul voluntarily came before the leaders in Jerusalem and calmly presented to them the message he was preaching. He was maintaining accountability and solidarity with other Christian leaders, without for a moment assuming that what Christ had given him was open to their approval. Paul discussed the gospel he was preaching among the Gentiles in a private meeting with **the leaders of the church**— probably James, Peter, and John (2:9).

The meeting in privacy was not, as the Judaizers hoped to claim, for the purpose of correcting Paul's message. Instead, Paul met privately to make sure they were all in agreement, or his **ministry would have been useless.** If the apostles incorrectly disagreed with him and agreed with the Judaizers (that to be Christians, people first had to become Jews and follow all the laws and customs—especially regarding circumcision), this would have caused severe damage to the work that Paul had already done for years among the Gentiles and hurt future missionary efforts. Paul realized the momentous importance of the decision that needed to be made regarding the relationship of Gentiles and Jews on the common meeting ground of Christianity. Paul had no doubts about the message Christ had given him, but he appeared before the other apostles as an equal expecting their wholehearted support.

2:3 Paul's message preached among the Gentiles was tested in the treatment of the young Greek convert whom Paul brought along to Jerusalem— Titus. Paul's message to the Gentiles was that God accepted anyone who believes, regardless of race or religious background. Titus's presence gave the entire church an opportunity to practice what they intended to preach. The gospel clearly applied to Titus without requiring his circumcision. The development was a major loss for the Judaizers (the "false Christians," 2:4), for it showed that the Jerusalem church had accepted Paul's policy.

Circumcision was a big issue for the Jews because the custom dated back to the days of Abraham and their birth as a nation. More than any other practice, circumcision separated God's people from their pagan neighbors. In Abraham's day, this was essential for developing the pure worship of the one true God. Whether the Judaizers were intentionally trying to undermine Christianity with this requirement, or whether they sincerely believed that as an outgrowth of Judaism, Christianity should fulfill Jewish requirements, they were wrong.

The apostles did **not demand** that **Titus be circumcised, though he was a Gentile.** They agreed with Paul that circumcision was an unnecessary rite for Gentile converts. Several years later, Paul did circumcise Timothy, another Greek Christian (Acts 16:3). Unlike Titus, however, Timothy was half Jewish. Paul did not deny Jews the right to be circumcised; he was simply saying that Gentiles should not be asked to become Jews before becoming Christians.

2:4 Here Paul called the Judaizers **so-called Christians . . . false ones.** They were most likely from the party of the Pharisees (Acts 15:5), the strictest religious leaders of Judaism. Some of these Judaizers **came to spy on** the believers. These people somehow were planted into the Christians' ranks. If they got into the private meeting Paul had with the church leaders, someone of power may have been behind the controversy. The Pharisees would have been most interested in observing what was going on in the Christian camp, especially regarding freedom from **Jewish regulations.** Indeed, their very existence involved detailed obedience to Jewish law and traditions—and making sure everyone else did the same. The philosophy of the Judaizers was something like, "If you can't beat them or join them, then try to change them by absorbing them." The status quo of Judaism, which Jesus repeatedly confronted during his ministry, did not give up easily. Those still committed to that system **wanted to force** the believers **to follow** all the Jewish regulations, to make them **slaves** under the religious legal system. Circumcision, with its inherent significance (see 2:3 above), was a good first step. Obviously, they did not see themselves as trying to enslave anyone, but Paul understood that this was the ultimate end of required obedience to all the Jewish laws and traditions.

2:5 The **truth of the Good News** was at stake. Paul sought to protect the truth that the gospel is for all people who can accept it by faith alone. Paul was convinced that circumcision, a rite he himself had undergone, was not part of the essential truth of the gospel. Paul fought to protect that gospel **for you,** specifically referring to the Galatian Christians to whom he wrote. But it also applies to any believer today who has not come out of a Jewish background. We have received salvation without having to ascribe to a whole set of Jewish laws because Paul had the foresight and wisdom to fight for protection of the gospel of grace regarding this issue.

2:6 Paul's wording here was not meant disrespectfully toward the apostles and church leaders. Paul was walking a fine line between asserting his independence from the apostles, and yet his unity with them. Paul was not in awe of the apostles; who they were **made no difference** to him in that sense. Paul wanted to make it clear that both his gospel and his apostleship were of supernatural origin. Because **God has no favorites** between him and the recognized apostles, then neither should anyone else (see also Ephesians 6:9). The apostles **had nothing to add to what** Paul **was preaching**—they did not correct Paul's message or try to add anything to it (such as the need for circumcision). Instead, they accepted Paul as an equal and accepted his message to the Gentiles as "gospel truth."

2:7-8 What the apostles **saw** was most likely the convincing success that God had given to Paul's ministry **of preaching the Good News to the Gentiles.** This is compared to **Peter** who had been having a dynamic ministry **of preaching to the Jews.** Peter also had had contact with Gentiles (see Acts 10), probably a key point in the approval of Paul and Barnabas's ministry. Peter's encounter with Cornelius had demonstrated God's acceptance of the Gentiles. This prepared Peter to accept the legitimacy of Paul's special call. Peter and Paul represented God's ongoing covenant with all of humanity under the saving grace made possible by Jesus. Each of them had valid ministries, ordained and authorized by Christ, because **the same God** was working through both men.

Both Paul and Peter preached the same gospel. Though their audiences were vastly different, the message did not, could not, and would not ever change. The gospel that remains unchanged today is that salvation is by God's grace alone for anyone who believes.

2:9 The men mentioned were **James,** half brother of Jesus and leader of the Jerusalem church, and two of Jesus' original disciples and part of his inner circle of three—**Peter and John.** These three noted leaders **accepted** Paul and Barnabas **as their coworkers**—giving their blessing and encouragement in their ministry among the Gentiles. These **pillars of the church** had **recognized the gift God had given** to Paul. There was evidence of God's saving grace in Paul's own life and the results flowing from his ministry among the Gentiles. Paul was a walking, talking advertisement for the gospel. So Paul and Barnabas were **encouraged to keep preaching to the Gentiles,** while the apostles in Jerusalem and Judea would continue **their work with the Jews.** This referred to each group's main focus; it was not exclusive. The apostles ministered to many Gentiles; Paul and his team always spoke to Jews, as well. Yet always their message was the same: the gospel of salvation.

2:10 Although the ministry and message of Paul and Barnabas had been accepted, the entire issue had not been handled because the Judaizers had not been silenced. It would take the council of Jerusalem (Acts 15) to block the efforts to bring the gospel back under the law. In the meantime, much effort would be required to promote unity at the grass roots level between Jewish and Gentile Christians. The apostles realized that one immediate and practical way to bridge this possible gap would be to **remember to help the poor.**

Paul assured them that he had **been eager to do that.** Paul never forgot this understanding. He continued to be eager to help the poor believers in Jerusalem. On his missionary journeys (especially the third journey), Paul gathered funds to help the poor Jewish believers in Jerusalem (see Acts 24:17; Romans 15:25-28; 1 Corinthians 16:1-4; 2 Corinthians 8-9).

PAUL CONFRONTS PETER / 2:11-21

With the speed of a remote control switch, the scene changed as Paul began to explain another time when his authority as an apostle had been confirmed. The setting switched from Jerusalem (2:1-10) to Antioch, a Gentile city familiar to the Galatians (2:11-21). In Antioch, Paul had faced another conflict over his authority. At that time, however, he openly opposed the actions of the apostle Peter himself.

Peter had arrived in Antioch and had been warmly welcomed by the church. He, Paul, Barnabas, and the rest of the leadership fellowshiped, taught, and ate together regularly. Then a delegation arrived from Jerusalem, and almost immediately Peter's treatment of the Gentile Christians changed. He kept his distance from them. Others, including Barnabas, followed Peter's example. But Paul leaped into the breach with a ringing confrontation.

2:11 This **Antioch** was in Syria (as distinguished from Antioch in Pisidia). Antioch was a major trade center in the ancient world. Heavily populated by Greeks, it eventually became a strong Christian center. In Antioch the believers were first called Christians (Acts 11:26). Antioch in Syria became the headquarters for the Gentile church and was Paul's base of operations.

When **Peter** made this trip to Antioch is uncertain; there is no reference to it in the book of Acts. It may have occurred soon after Paul, Barnabas, and Titus had returned to Antioch from Jerusalem after delivering the famine relief. Perhaps Peter wanted to see for himself the ministry taking place in Antioch. During this visit, Paul **had to oppose** Peter **publicly.** Peter's actions were **very wrong,** and Paul, an apostle with the right to speak with authority, had to confront Peter. The event involved an emotional, face-to-face showdown. Peter was caught in a glaring inconsistency that might have gone tragically unresolved if not for Paul's boldness. He always focused on the purity of the gospel truth; whenever it was threatened, Paul acted.

2:12 When Peter arrived in Antioch, he saw that Jewish and Gentile Christians enjoyed fellowship at mealtimes without concern over Jewish dietary laws. His setting aside long-established taboos against Jews sharing board and room with Gentiles showed nothing less than his acceptance of freedom in Christ. Peter accepted these practices; he himself had received a vision from God about food laws and Gentiles in the new world of the gospel. Indeed, Peter had been the first to receive the understanding about God's acceptance of the Gentiles, and he was the first to preach to Gentiles. Peter understood from this vision that he should not look upon the Gentiles as inferior people whom God would not redeem. After Peter had this vision, a Gentile Roman officer named Cornelius asked him to come and share the gospel message with him and his household. Peter did so, without the hesitation he would have felt before the vision, and Cornelius and his household became believers.

Thus, when Peter arrived in Antioch, he already knew that God had broken down the barriers between Jews and Gentiles, and he understood the true meaning of Christian freedom. So he gladly **ate with the Gentile Christians.** The imperfect tense of the verb indicates that this was not one occasion but a repeated pattern, meaning that Peter joined with the other Jews in eating with their Gentile brothers and sisters in Christ on a regular basis. This pattern undoubtedly went beyond sharing common meals and included taking the Lord's Supper together.

But all that was before **some Jewish friends of James came.** These men were the legalists and most likely *not* sent by James. The wording here means they came "from James's group," that is, from the Jerusalem church. James, as leader of the Jerusalem church, had a vast range of people to deal with, and these men were part of the legalistic group of his church. Among the entourage from Jerusalem, there must have been certain men who frowned on fraternizing with Gentiles. These may have been rigid and legalistic Jewish Christians, but they were probably associated with the same "false Christians" who had disrupted Paul's visit to Jerusalem.

Though this group probably tried to trade on James's authority, he later firmly denied sending them. In the letter sent back to the Gentile Christians in Antioch after the Jerusalem council, James wrote,

"We understand that some men from here have troubled you and upset you with their teaching, but they had no such instructions from us" (Acts 15:24).

Apparently, the mere appearance of this group caught Peter by surprise. When these legalists arrived, they may have expressed shock at Peter's conduct. Peter surely knew these men, as they came from the Jerusalem church, and he was influenced by their presence to the point that he **wouldn't eat with the Gentiles anymore.**

Why was this action "very wrong" (2:11)? By his actions, Peter was implying that there really was a difference between Jewish and Gentile believers— a difference that could not be bridged. The notion that the body of Christ had to be divided between Jews and Gentiles was nothing other than heresy. Peter was being hypocritical. Perhaps he was motivated by the desire to keep peace between the legalists and the law-free gospel group. Peter's error was that he gave in because he was **afraid of what these legalists would say.** Peter must have known that he had gone against God's revelation. By the very nature of Peter's stature as an apostle, his actions confused and hurt other believers—thus Paul's strong face-to-face opposition to Peter's actions.

2:13 As Peter acted on his fear, the other Jews, meaning those not already committed to the policy of separation, went along with his **hypocrisy.** They, too, gradually stopped joining with the Gentiles in eating and fellowshiping. These **other Jewish Christians** were the Jewish believers who lived in Antioch and were members of the church there. In that setting, they were most likely in the minority.

Paul mentioned **Barnabas** separately, probably because Paul was especially surprised that Barnabas would be so **influenced.** Barnabas was Paul's traveling companion; together they preached the gospel to the Gentiles, proclaiming Jews' and Gentiles' oneness with Christ. Barnabas was not from the Jerusalem church and would not have had the personal and relational stake in this that Peter had. Yet, like Peter, Barnabas was human, and for some unknown reason he followed Peter's example.

Paul boldly pointed out the hypocrisy. A hypocrite says one thing but does another. Peter, Barnabas, and the Jewish believers knew that God accepted everyone equally, that salvation was available to all, that there should be no separation in the body of Christ. Yet their actions implied just the opposite. If Paul had opted for peace and allowed these actions to go unrebuked, the Christian church would have divided into two distinct groups going their separate ways. But this was not God's plan, nor was it consistent with "the truth of the Good News," as Paul would explain in the next verse.

2:14 This was the crux of the matter—**they** (Peter, Barnabas, and the Jewish believers in Antioch) **were not following the truth of the Good News.** This truth was that Jesus Christ had died and had risen again to offer salvation to all people—Jews and Gentiles alike. Both groups are equally acceptable to God; thus, they must be equally acceptable to each other. Jewish believers separating themselves implied that they were superior because of their race, traditions, or law keeping. The Good News clearly shows, however, that people do not become accepted by God for anything they do.

Paul did not oppose Peter in order to elevate himself. Paul recounted this story in this letter to the Galatians to show that he was a full apostle and could speak authoritatively, even in opposition to another apostle if the truth of the gospel were at stake. This was not a secondary issue blown out of proportion. The confrontation fit the crisis.

Paul spoke to Peter publicly **in front of all the others**—that is, in front of the Jewish believers, the Gentile believers, the legalists, and Barnabas. Those who want to attribute other motives to Paul might ask why he didn't go to Peter privately. Wouldn't that have been more "peace loving"? more "Christian"? But Peter's actions had started a domino effect; and, because of his authority as an apostle, his actions had confused the believers. A private solution to this problem was not an option. Peter's action was public, with public consequences; the rebuke had to be public. As a leader of the Jerusalem church, Peter was setting public policy.

Paul recorded his exact words here. Obviously, everyone knew Peter's Jewish background; Paul's wording indicates they also knew that Peter had set aside Jewish rituals and ceremonial laws (especially the food laws that made fellowship between Jews and Gentiles almost impossible) because of his freedom in Christ, thus **living like a Gentile** and not like a Jew. Certainly the visions Peter had seen and his experience with Cornelius had cured him of any prejudice against Gentiles (see Acts 10).

But how could Paul say that Peter was **trying to make these Gentiles obey the Jewish laws?** By siding with the Judaizers who were visiting Antioch, Peter was playing into their hands, appearing as if he agreed with them and actually supported their insistence that Gentiles should follow Jewish customs. By separating himself from the Gentiles, Peter was supporting the Judaizers' claim that Jews still were better than Gentiles.

Alongside the theological problems that Peter's actions caused, a practical question must have surfaced. While Peter's change in policy about having meals with Gentiles was harmful, the change in the policy for the Lord's Supper must have been

disastrous. If this group was divided over the sharing of common meals, it is inconceivable that they
would be able to assemble together for the Lord's
Supper. Without Paul's immediate and forceful
intervention, the church in Antioch might have
been crippled and destroyed.

2:15 Both Paul and Peter were **Jews by birth,** as
were, obviously, all the Jewish Christians. Yet
being Jews by birth was not enough for salvation.
Paul's phrase, **"sinners" like the Gentiles,** was
said ironically because this was the scornful name
Jews applied to Gentiles. Peter's actions had conveyed some sort of "holier than thou" attitude
in line with the teaching that Gentiles were still
"sinners" unless they became Jewish. But both
Peter and Paul knew better.

2:16 All people stand as condemned sinners before
God: God-fearing, law-keeping Jews, and "Gentile
sinners" alike. But all are made **right with God,
not by doing what the law commands, but by
faith in Jesus Christ.** This is the doctrine of "justification." God justifies people despite their guilt,
pardons them, and then makes them his children
and heirs. The law to which he was referring could
mean Jewish Scripture, plus the laws added by the
Pharisees. If people could be saved by obeying the
law, then Christ did not have to die. But the reality
is, **no one will ever be saved by obeying the law.**

2:17 In this verse, Paul responds to one objection
that might be raised by his opponents. They might
say, What if we seek to be made right with God
through faith in Christ and then find out that we are
still sinners? Has Christ led us into sin? How could
Paul claim that justification by faith is effective
when Christians still sin? To say that the law doesn't
matter is to say that standards and morality don't
matter. This leaves the door open for people to
become believers and then live any way they choose.

But Paul's reply is vehement: **Of course not!** Sin
does not result because people are justified; Christ
is not responsible for promoting sin. Obviously,
those who have been justified—Christians—can
and do sin, for that, unfortunately, is part of our
human nature (Paul details his own struggle with
sin in Romans 7). But the sin led to the need for
justification, not the other way around. The
Judaizers saw Christianity as an excuse to get out
from under Jewish law. But Paul (and the Jewish
Christians who had experienced justification)
knew that while offering freedom from the restrictive law, justification by faith demanded lifestyle
and behavioral changes. When God truly gets hold
of a life, nothing can remain the same. Grace does
not abolish the law with its standards and morality; rather, it moves it from an external standard

impossible to keep to an inner motivation for
living a pure and God-honoring life.

2:18 Justification by faith **tore down** the Pharisees'
"merit system" with all its laws and good deeds that
attempted to rack up points with God. To **rebuild**
that, to be justified by faith and then return to that
legal system as a basis for one's relationship with
God, would erroneously imply that Christ's death
was not sufficient. Paul saw the situation in Antioch
with Peter as a clear illustration of the unnecessary
burden that some wanted to place on Gentile believers. Peter, through his act of pulling away from the
Gentile fellowship, was giving law a place of authority that it no longer held.

Justified people will sin, but they are moving
onward and upward. The real sinner is the one who
is justified and then returns to the law. Ironically,
that person is actually **guilty.** People under the law
are more precisely described as lawbreakers than as
law-keepers! The law cannot give salvation because
no one can keep it perfectly. The best the law can do
is prove our sinfulness and how much we need the
Savior and his gracious offer of justification by faith.

2:19 The law itself could not save because no one
can keep its perfect standards. The law thus cannot
earn God's approval; instead, it offers only failure
and death. So what is its usefulness? The law was a
necessary instrument to show people the ultimate
futility of trying to live up to God's standard on their
own. But that very hopelessness created by the law
can have a positive impact if it leads a person to the
true hope, Christ himself. Christ took upon himself
that death penalty—the death we deserved for being
lawbreakers. When Paul understood that the law
was completely incapable of giving salvation, and
when he embraced the one who could give salvation, he knew he could never go back to the law.
Paul felt this so intensely that he expressed it in
terms of death, **I died to the law.** The perfect tense
of the verbs indicates something that happened
in the past but influences the present. Paul "died
to the law" by being **crucified with Christ.** Christ
completely fulfilled the law (past tense); this act
influenced Paul in the present (who, as an imperfect
human, could not keep the law). Yet because of
Christ's death, the law no longer had a hold on
either of them. The cross of Christ shows that
although the law had to be kept, it was fulfilled by
a perfect human. Christ paid sin's penalty for imperfect humans. Being crucified with Christ refers to
the conversion experience, a once-for-all transaction
that has ongoing results.

Paul knew he had to die to the law before he
could **live for God.** There can be no middle ground.
It makes no sense to accept salvation by faith and

then work for it, just as it makes no sense to accept a gift and then offer the giver money for it. We must deny that our own efforts can accomplish anything in order to be able to humbly accept the gift that Christ offers. By identifying with Christ, we can experience freedom from the law that he procured for us by dying on our behalf.

2:20 Paul claimed he had been "crucified," but he was still alive. Paul had died with Christ, but it was his "old self" that had died: **I myself no longer live.** The self-centered, Jewish Pharisee, Christian-persecuting, law-abiding, violent, and evil Paul "no longer" lived. That person's sinful life had been crucified with Christ on the cross. This is the "I" of the flesh (see 5:13-24), of sinful human desires, of works and pride. Paul was released, not only from the tyranny of the Mosaic law, but also from the tyranny of self.

Instead, Paul was a "new person" (2 Corinthians 5:17) because, he explained, **Christ lives in me.** In other words, Paul had turned over his life to Christ. Each of the phrases is a crucial aspect of the sequence of salvation: We relinquish our old life and turn to Christ for his life. The self-centered self now becomes the Christ-centered self. It is as if Paul was saying, "My old life, my old goals and plans, even old relationships were nailed to the cross with Christ. Now I have a new life because Christ came in and filled the empty spaces all those old pursuits could not fill.

Now he lives in me and is the focus of my life." To accomplish this, there must be a radical cleansing of our old selfish nature. But there must also be a turning to the empowering of Christ. Just as in repentance we turn away from sin and toward Christ, we must turn from the self in the flesh to the self hidden in Christ.

Paul no longer focused his life on trying to please God by obeying laws; instead, with Christ in him, **I live my life in this earthly body by trusting in the Son of God, who loved me and gave himself for me.** Believers live in their bodies that are prone to sin while they remain on earth. But with Christ in charge, they are new creations, living life by faith. This faith is an attitude, a lifestyle.

2:21 Paul's message of salvation by faith (without works of the law) did not treat **the grace of God as meaningless.** Instead, that is exactly what the Judaizers' teaching did—they "set aside" or "nullified" God's grace. For **if we could be saved by keeping the law,** then the logical conclusion is that **there was no need for Christ to die.** However, it was because no one could obey God's law perfectly that Christ came to both obey it, fulfill its penalty, and then set it aside as a means to salvation. That was the ultimate picture of God's love and grace for sinful humanity. The basis of Christianity is God's grace and Christ's death for sin. Without these there is no faith, no gospel, and no hope of salvation.

GALATIANS 3:1 – 4:7

THE LAW AND FAITH IN CHRIST / 3:1-14

With the heartfelt words affirming his personal commitment to the Galatians, Paul spoke of his ministry with his Galatian friends. He remembered how clearly he had shared the message and how openly they had responded. Since they had been launched so beautifully in the Christian faith, how could they have run aground so quickly? Paul was convinced that those who influenced the Galatians acted like friendly harbor pilots. They promised to guide the Galatians' faith by adding to their understanding of Christ an "essential component" of the law. But, instead, these pilots put the Galatian ship of faith in great danger.

Paul was adamant in his response to all of this. Whatever role the law might play in a believer's life, it did not add to or improve the salvation provided freely in Christ. To be acceptable to God, we must be justified by faith in Jesus Christ alone. The point needed to be hammered home, and Paul did this repeatedly in this letter.

3:1 In 1:11 Paul had called the believers in Galatia "friends"; in this verse, he used a much more impersonal **Galatians** to address his converts. He

preceded it with a strong adjective reprimanding their behavior—they were **foolish.** The Greek word does not mean that they were mentally deficient;

rather, it suggests the behavior of people who are intelligent yet are not using that intelligence to perceive the truth (the same Greek word is used in Luke 24:25; Romans 1:14; 1 Timothy 6:9; and Titus 3:3). The Galatians had shifted from believing in the death and resurrection of Christ for salvation to believing that they must obey the law in order to be fully saved. Such illogical thinking implied that "Christ died for nothing" (2:21).

Paul sarcastically thought that perhaps a **magician** had **cast an evil spell on** them. The Galatian believers had become fascinated by the false teachers' arguments, almost as though they had been hypnotized. How else could this nonsense be explained? He was questioning, not their intelligence, but their lack of discernment. They were being fooled by arguments that they should have been able to refute.

Paul's preaching of Christ crucified was so clear and vivid, it was almost as if they had seen it with their own eyes, as if Paul had **shown** them **a signboard with a picture of Christ dying on the cross.** By turning their eyes from the Cross to the law, they were confusing the very simple facts of salvation.

3:2 To rectify the Galatians' confused thinking, Paul returned to the basics. Four simple questions in the following verses will reveal their foolishness.

Paul's first question was most basic, for it focused on how their Christian life had begun. The Galatians' shift to following the law for salvation was completely contrary to their initial experience of the Christian faith at Paul's preaching. So he asked, **"Did you receive the Holy Spirit by keeping the law?"** The Galatians had accepted the gospel and had received the Holy Spirit (see also 4:6). Did this happen because they obeyed the law or because they believed the gospel Paul preached to them? The Galatian believers, mostly Gentile in background, didn't even have or know the law, so the answer was painfully obvious. Their salvation began by faith. Law keeping had nothing to do with it.

Paul mentioned as an indisputable fact that **the Holy Spirit came upon** the Galatian believers **only after** they had **believed the message** Paul had told them **about Christ.** The apostle could point to their reception of the Spirit at the time of their conversion as proof that God had accepted them—based solely on their acceptance of the gospel message. God's Spirit had been within them long before the Judaizers had entered the scene.

3:3 The Galatians had started their **Christian lives in the Spirit,** so why would they now try **to become perfect by** their **own human effort?** Paul highlighted how completely inconsistent it was to

receive a gift and then try to earn it. But Paul had heard that those in Galatia were attempting just that—trading freedom in Christ for slavery to tradition.

3:4 Paul's next question asked the Galatians to apply their past experience to their immediate situation. The words, **you have suffered so much for the Good News,** probably included actual suffering at the hands of nonbelievers.

Paul and Barnabas certainly had faced great suffering as they preached in the region of Galatia on the first missionary journey (see Acts 13:45-50; 14:2-33). It may be that the new believers in each of these cities had been treated the same. **"Are you now going to just throw it all away?"** In other words, "If you were willing to suffer so much for your newfound faith at the hands of the Jews, why would you now turn back to obeying the Jewish laws?" This too was foolish. Even as he said it, he was unwilling to believe it, for he added: **"Surely it was not in vain, was it?"** Paul did not feel it was hopeless to try to bring the Galatians back to true faith.

3:5 Paul had yet another rhetorical question. **"Does God give you the Holy Spirit and work miracles among you because you obey the law of Moses?"** The similar question in verse 2 is in the past tense, reminding the Galatians of their initial response of salvation and what happened because of that response. This verse, however, is in the present tense, focusing on what God continued to do for the Galatians. He "gives" his Spirit and "works" miracles among them every day. Was this happening because the Galatians were carefully observing the Jewish law or because they believed in Christ and proclaimed that opportunity to others? Again, the answer was painfully obvious. God's continual blessings come just as salvation came—through belief in **the message** they **heard about Christ,** not through law keeping.

3:6 The previous questions pointed to the Galatians' experience; then Paul turned to an example from Scripture to support his teaching of salvation by faith alone. For the Jews, there could hardly be a more important and influential person than **Abraham,** the father of their nation. But how did the Galatian Gentiles know about Abraham? It could be that the Galatian converts had heard about Abraham from the Gentile converts to Judaism in the church (there were many Jews in southern Galatia). Another possibility is that the Judaizers were hammering away at the need for Gentiles to become "children of Abraham" (3:7) through circumcision (see notes on 2:3). The Judaizers would focus on passages like Genesis 17:1-14 (where God gave Abraham the covenant of circumcision) to teach that only those who were circumcised and kept Jewish laws would be acceptable to God. Thus, the Gentile believers knew Abraham's name.

The covenant of circumcision was given to Abraham (Genesis 17), but after the words quoted in this verse from Genesis 15:6, where Abraham **believed God, so God declared him righteous because of his faith.** Abraham, the founder of the Jewish nation, was considered righteous, not by works, but because he "believed God."

To be "declared righteous" means accepted by God. Abraham did not have Moses' law, nor did he have the cross of Christ, the gospel, or salvation as offered in the New Testament. But he was God's servant, acceptable to God and considered righteous because he believed what he knew of God.

3:7 The Judaizers had argued that to be a Christian a person had to first become a Jew, a descendant of Abraham, and subsequently obey the Jewish laws. Jews, including these Judaizers, were extremely proud of their lineage traced back to Abraham. At the heart of Jewish salvation theology was the concept of being "children of Abraham." The Jews believed that they were automatically the people of God because of their heritage. But from Abraham's own example, Paul showed that **the real children of Abraham are all those who put their faith in God,** those who believe in Christ and the salvation he offers. As Abraham was saved by faith, so each person is saved by faith. As Abraham was declared righteous because of his faith in God, so both Jews and Gentiles who believe are declared righteous because of their faith in Christ. Belief is the first and only step to salvation.

3:8 Although Paul had made his point, he added a further devastating application of **the Scriptures** against the Judaizers' false teaching: not only are Gentiles and Jews saved by faith, but it was God who planned from the beginning to **accept the Gentiles on the basis of their faith.**

God had **promised this Good News to Abraham.** God's promise that **all nations will be blessed through** Abraham encompassed God's plan for the ages. **All nations** would be blessed through Abraham because his descendant, Jesus, would bring salvation to all who believe. The blessing promised to Abraham was intended, from the beginning, to be given by God to all nations, not just to the Jews. This blessing, both to Abraham and to the nations, was promised by God before any laws or works were given or required. Thus, God would justify the Gentiles, not by works of the law, not by circumcision, but by faith. Salvation is the ultimate blessing, a gift simply to be

believed and received. All believers in every age and from every nation share Abraham's blessing.

3:9 Faith did not begin in the New Testament; rather, it has been the key requirement for all believers from the beginning. God's relationship with his children has always been based on faith. Abraham, the father of the Jewish nation, exemplified faith in God, even though his faith faltered at times. Abraham clearly stands out among those before and after him who lived by faith. **All who put their faith in Christ** and in the salvation we have been so graciously offered, **share the same blessing Abraham received because of his faith.** While it is true that "all nations" would be blessed, there is a qualifier—only the people in those nations **who put their faith in Christ** would receive the blessing of salvation.

3:10 Having shown that justification by faith is true according to the Scriptures, Paul here made the opposite point, that justification by the law is false according to the Scriptures—in fact, according to the law itself. Paul quoted Deuteronomy 27:26 to prove that, contrary to what the Judaizers claimed, obeying the law cannot justify and save— it can only condemn. **Cursed is everyone who does not observe and obey all these commands that are written in God's Book of the Law.** They are **cursed** because no one can obey the law perfectly and because breaking even one commandment brings a person under condemnation. Trying to achieve salvation through obedience to the law is a no-win situation. The law demands perfection—an impossibility for sinful humans.

The law cannot save; neither can it reverse the condemnation (Romans 3:20-24). But Christ took the curse of the law entirely upon himself when he hung on the cross (Deuteronomy 21:23). He did this so we wouldn't have to bear our own punishment. The only condition is that we accept Christ's death on our behalf by faith as the means to be saved (Colossians 1:20-23).

3:11 Trying to be **right with God** by keeping **the law** doesn't work. The law could not save, but faith could. Paul pointed to Habakkuk's declaration in Habakkuk 2:4, **"It is through faith that a righteous person has life."** A **righteous** person is not one who keeps the law, but one who is in a right relationship with God. This expression means Christians will have **life** because of God's faithfulness and because of their response of faith in God; as a result, they will have eternal life and experience fullness of life.

3:12 When we have faith, we do not need the law. Quoting again from the law (Leviticus 18:5), Paul supported his statement, **"If you wish to find life by obeying the law, you must obey all of its commands."** The law itself says that only perfect obedience can gain approval from God—one can "live" by the law only by obeying it completely, without fail. The problem is, no one can do that—it is humanly impossible.

3:13 Because the law sets forth requirements that are impossible to fulfill, it serves as a **curse.** But there is hope because **Christ has rescued us.** How did Christ take **upon himself the curse for our wrongdoing?** Paul answered the question by yet another Old Testament quotation, **"Cursed is everyone who is hung on a tree"** (Deuteronomy 21:23). To be hanged on a tree signified to the Jews that a person had been cursed. Christ willingly allowed himself to become cursed for all humanity, and thus endured the Crucifixion. At the cross, the curse of the law was transferred from sinful humanity to the sinless Son of God. Christ took on himself the penalty for sin.

3:14 The **blessing** refers to justification by faith (as discussed in 3:8-9), to be offered to Gentiles as well as to Abraham's descendants, the Jews. Through trust in Christ's redemption on the cross, God's promise to Abraham (see 3:8) could be made a reality to all who believe.

Then **we Christians** (Jews and Gentiles together), having been justified through faith, will **receive the promised Holy Spirit through faith.** If all persons are eligible to benefit from Christ, then the Holy Spirit, God's deposit, must also be available to all (see Ephesians 1:13-14).

The Holy Spirit was present at the creation of the world as one of the agents in the origin of life. He is the power behind the rebirth of every Christian and the one who helps us live the Christian life. The Holy Spirit sets us free, once and for all, from sin and its natural consequences. The Holy Spirit provides the power to help us do what the law requires of us externally. The Holy Spirit directs the entire course of our lives. He will guide our actions, daily behavior, and moral direction. Choosing to follow the Spirit's leading brings us full life on earth, eternal life, and peace with God. The Holy Spirit lives in us, taking control of our sinful human desires. Romans 8:14-15 says that we have received the Spirit of sonship. The true sons of God are not those of Jewish birth but those who are led by the Spirit of God as evidenced in their lifestyles. Romans 8:16 says, "His Holy Spirit speaks to us deep in our hearts and tells us that we are God's children." The Holy Spirit strengthens us and sustains us through times of trial. These wonderful benefits of the Holy Spirit come to believers by faith, not by keeping the law.

THE LAW AND GOD'S PROMISES / 3:15-23
Paul turned to an illustration from the Galatians' daily experience to help them understand the principles of law and grace. He found parallels in the making and executing of human agreements to the way that God deals with us. In 3:15-18 he used the Judaizers' own arguments against them. They had argued that Moses' law was a fuller and more complete expression of the covenant given to Abraham. Paul reversed their train of thought and showed that God's promise to Abraham was a promise made prior to Moses.

3:15 Paul anticipated a question the Judaizers might raise at this point, and summarily answered it. While the Judaizers might go so far as to agree with Paul that Abraham was justified by his faith, they would then add that the coming of the law changed the basis for gaining salvation. Paul wanted to clarify that nothing would change the promise that God made to Abraham.

Paul turned to **an example from daily life.** People know that in an **irrevocable agreement, no one can set aside or amend** any part of it. If that is the case with human contracts, how much more is it true of divine contracts? God's promises always stand, no matter what changes occur. He always keeps his promises. Paul's point was not that God couldn't change his covenant with us, but

that God **didn't** ever change the covenant established between himself and us, as illustrated by his specific dealings with Abraham. God's divine promise was made to Abraham long before the giving of the law to Moses. As such, it was a binding agreement not to be changed or annulled.

3:16 This verse would probably make more sense in the flow of the text if it appeared in parentheses. If the promise was meant for Abraham and his many descendants alone (to all his "children"), then it might appear that the promises had already been fulfilled, and that the law had come as a new phase in God's dealing with his people. But the promises had been given to **his child**—that is, Abraham's most famous descendant, Christ, who came many years after both Abraham and the law. The law has an important function, but salvation by grace through faith was God's promise from the beginning of time.

The Jews had always believed that God's promises would be fulfilled in a single person, the Messiah. God's promise remained intact even though Abraham himself only had one descendant through Sarah. Further, the promises were not fulfilled prior to the giving of the law, nor by the giving of the law. Instead, they were fulfilled when **Christ** came. Christ alone fulfilled the messianic aspects of God's covenant and showed that God's promises are in effect for all time.

Many claimed to be rightful heirs to God's promises to Abraham by their being his offspring, but Paul pointed out the only true, rightful heir was Jesus. The covenant that God shared with Abraham had been reaffirmed many times, but only Christ fulfilled the Abrahamic covenant as the unique child. The Jews certainly enjoyed many privileges and responsibilities as part of the Abrahamic covenant, but blessing the nations was the Messiah's role. The promises to Abraham go just to Christ. (They don't reside in the Jewish people.) In and through Christ they go to individual believers. Christ is our hope of blessing.

3:17 Moses received the law and gave it to God's people **430 years later.** While there is debate about the exact period of these 430 years, the point is not the number of years, but rather that the law came "later" than God's promise to Abraham. For four centuries God had been blessing Abraham and his descendants on the basis of their faith, not by Moses' law, for it did not yet exist. When the law was given, it did not cancel God's agreement with Abraham; otherwise **God would be breaking his promise.** The giving of the law itself was an integral part of God following through on his covenant. God had preserved his people in Egypt and had overseen their Exodus. Then, through Moses, God had provided the law as a written standard of his own legitimate expectations of those in covenant with him.

The law neither replaced nor improved the covenant of promise (by faith through grace). As Paul would later develop (see 3:23-25), the law's main function is to demonstrate how crucial the covenant of faith is in allowing people any hope at all. As a paragraph in God's gracious covenant, law provides guidance; but taken alone the law becomes a grinding foe, constantly pointing to our shortcomings. In other words, the Judaizers were wrong. The promise of justification by faith is still in effect; the law does not set that aside or annul it.

3:18 There is yet another reason why salvation cannot be through law, or through faith plus law. The words **law** and **promise** are opposites in nature. Like oil and water, they cannot be combined. **Inheritance** here refers to believers' enjoyment of what they receive through the promise: salvation, eternal life, and removal of the curse. Thus, if our salvation and enjoyment of God's gifts depend on obeying the law, then they cannot depend on a promise, for it cannot be both ways. People do not need to work to attain what has been promised to them.

Instead, **God gave it to Abraham as a promise.** God gave the promise because he loved Abraham, not because Abraham deserved it. God "gave" the promise—the verb implies something that is both free (or unearned) and permanent. That way of salvation was still in effect in Paul's day, as well as in our own. God in his grace gives us salvation by our faith alone. He grants graciously and generously, not reluctantly; in love and compassion, not in judgment; abundantly and without reservation.

3:19 In the previous verses, Paul made four distinct observations about the law: (1) The law could not give the Holy Spirit (3:1-5); (2) the law could not give righteousness (3:6-9); (3) the law could not justify, it could only condemn (3:10-12); and (4) the law could not change the fact that righteousness always comes by faith in God's promises (3:15-18). Paul's opponents, and especially the Judaizers, could still be expected to raise the question, **Why was the law given?** Paul's arguments could sound as though he believed the law had no purpose whatsoever and that he was actually opposed to it. So Paul explained the true purpose behind God's giving of the law and its place in the plan of salvation.

The law had two functions. First, it had a negative function: **It was given to show people how guilty they are** (meaning that God had given the law to punish sin). Second, it had a strong positive function: The law reveals the nature and will of God and shows people how to live; it guarded and protected people until they could believe in Christ (see 3:23).

The little word **until** indicates that the law was meant as a temporary measure, and certainly not as the permanent and final means of salvation. The law was in place until **the coming of the child to whom God's promise was made.** When Jesus Christ came, the law was finally fulfilled (see Matthew 5:17-20).

God's promise to Abraham dealt with Abraham's faith; the law focuses on actions. The covenant with Abraham shows that faith is the only way to be saved; the law shows how to obey God in grateful response. Faith does not annul the law; but the more we know God, the more we will see how sinful we are. Then we will be driven to depend on Christ alone for our salvation.

To show the inherent inferiority of the law, Paul explained that while God personally gave the promises to Abraham; the law, however, was given **to angels to give to Moses, who was the mediator between God and the people.** This was not a new idea made up by Paul; it was already a Jewish belief. Although it is not mentioned in Exodus, Jews believed that the Ten Commandments had been given to Moses by angels (see Acts 7:53; Hebrews 2:2).

3:20 To have a **mediator** obviously means that **two people** are involved in the **agreement.** A mediator works between two or more parties to aid in communication, effect an agreement, or settle a dispute. Moses, implied in 3:19, was the mediator who communicated between God and Israel. God (through angels) mediated the law to Moses, who then gave it to the people. The law could be compared to a contract, which is valid only as long as both sides keep their sides of the agreement. While God kept his, the people of Israel could not keep theirs.

However, **God acted on his own when he made his promise to Abraham.** There was no mediator. The promises were given and would be kept by God, regardless of the actions of people. Thus, the promise is superior to the law because the promise is from God alone, meant for eternity, and would not be broken. The law and its mediator, Moses, were temporary, preparatory arrangements designed to confirm the truth of God's ultimate desire to relate directly with his creatures. Paul did not put down Moses, but showed the primacy of Christ's way of faith over the law.

3:21 Paul raised another question that might have been troubling his listeners: **Is there a conflict between God's law and God's promises?** The Judaizers might have even concluded that Paul was inferring that the law was evil. Paul answered with an emphatic, **Absolutely not!** Both the promises and the law were given by God; both are important, but for different reasons. God offered eternal life through the promises. Paul's use of the phrase, **new life,** refers to spiritual life as illustrated by such other passages as John 6:63; Romans 8:11; 1 Corinthians 15:22, 36; and 2 Corinthians 3:6. The law's purpose

was never to give that kind of life (as explained in 3:19 above). If a law could have been given that people could obey perfectly, then the law would have given life and **we could have been made right with God by obeying it.** The law is not evil; it is very good. But not for salvation.

3:22 Sin affects all of humanity without discrimination; **we are all prisoners of sin.** By **Scriptures,** Paul may have had in mind Deuteronomy 27:26 or the series of verses that he later quoted in Romans 3:10-18, which describe the universal sinfulness of mankind (Psalms 5:9; 10:7; 14:1-3; 36:1; 140:3; and Isaiah 59:7-8). Or he may have been thinking of the Pentateuch as the biblical context of the law itself, filled with the record of unrelenting rebelliousness against God. What must be understood, however, is that the Scriptures speak with one voice when describing the human condition—we are sinners. Through Scripture we discovered that we could not earn a right relationship with God by our good works because our works were not good enough— they were always tainted by sin. But just like a dot of light shining into a dark prison cell, a ray of hope shone for us. The law showed us our hopelessness on our own, caused us to look elsewhere for hope, and directed us to the Savior, Jesus Christ. We missed the promises by trying to keep the law, but we found that **the only way to receive God's promise is to believe in Jesus Christ.**

3:23 Faith, as spoken of in the Scriptures, does not refer to some innate human power that, when used to its greatest capacity, gives us merit with God no matter what the actual content or object of that faith. The central point of the gospel is in whom our faith is placed—that is, **in Christ.** Abraham was justified by his faith and, along with other Old Testament believers, had to trust in God's grace without knowing much of God's plan; but their faith was **in the coming Savior.**

Until people could put their faith in that Savior, the law **kept** them in a kind of **protective custody.** In a sense, it kept people out of trouble, kept them away from the evil into which their natures might otherwise have led, until faith in Christ would be revealed. That faith then sets people free from the law but leads into the desire to obey God wholeheartedly out of love for him.

GOD'S CHILDREN THROUGH FAITH / 3:24–4:7

While maintaining that the law was useful, Paul pointed out what a severe taskmaster it could be for those who failed to learn about grace received through faith. At this point in the letter, he shifted from a legal to a familial point of view. Once we have gained a right relationship with God, our dealings with people will be entirely different.

3:24 In Greek culture, a **guardian and teacher** was a slave who had the important responsibility for the children in a family. A wealthy family might have one guardian for each child. This slave strictly disciplined the child, conducted the child to and from school, cared for the child, taught the child manners, and gave the child moral training. The guardian's role was temporary—he or she was responsible for the child until the child reached adult age (probably age sixteen).

The picture of the law serving as a **guardian and teacher** shows that the law was a temporary measure meant **to lead us until Christ came.** This leading was meant in the sense of the law watching over us until we could receive our "adulthood," our full relationship with the Father, through Christ's coming.

What was the ultimate purpose of the law? Paul repeated it in the last phrase, that **through faith in Christ, we are made right with God.** The law had its usefulness in pointing out the wrong and providing constant reproof. The law, through imprisonment and discipline, taught us (though negatively) that justification with God really is through faith alone.

3:25 Once the child came of age, he or she no longer needed the services of the **guardian.** Since Christ arrived, offering salvation by faith alone, people **no longer need** the supervision of **the law.** The law teaches the need for salvation; God's grace offers that salvation. However, the Old Testament still applies today. In it God has revealed his nature, his will for humanity, his moral laws, and his guidelines for living. The law still serves as a demanding instructor to those who have not yet believed. But we cannot be saved by keeping that law; **now that faith in Christ has come,** we must trust in Christ.

As Paul will immediately demonstrate, the arrival of faith was not a static experience. Faith had its most basic work in our being "crucified with Christ," but it immediately pursues its ongoing task: "I live my life in this earthly body by trusting in the Son of God" (2:20). This living by faith will be the theme of much of the remainder of this letter.

3:26 The change to **you** shows Paul's return to focusing on the Galatian believers. They did not need to be children under the care of the guardian (the law); instead, they were **all children of God.** They received this status **through faith in Christ Jesus.** Those who are truly God's children have been justified by faith in Christ and receive a new relationship with God—that of adopted children.

What does it mean to be **children of God?** As he

did in most of his letters, Paul was moving from the initial section of teaching passages to the application of what he had been developing. Here the first application is unmistakable: Our relationship with each other has its common principle in how we are related to God. We are children of the same family if we have the same heavenly Father. From this point, Paul will first develop applications regarding how we should see ourselves and others. Later in the letter he will discuss how we should treat each other.

3:27 The reference to **baptism** here does not mean that Paul was replacing the rite of circumcision with baptism. Baptism does not save anyone any more than circumcision does. If Paul was referring to water baptism, he was recognizing the fact that, in the early church, new converts usually were baptized (see Acts 2:41; 8:36-38; 9:18; 10:47-48; and 16:33 for some examples of new converts being baptized). Baptism demonstrated their faith—people "believed and were baptized"—not the other way around. It also demonstrated identification with the body of believers, the Christian church.

Paul may have been referring to the baptism of the Holy Spirit. When a person believes, the Holy Spirit comes to dwell within. Jesus promised this (John 14:16-17). The Holy Spirit also supernaturally makes us a part of the body of Christ (1 Corinthians 12:12-13).

Most likely, Paul referred to the theology behind water baptism expressed as an early form of liturgy. Paul restated for emphasis his claim to the Galatians that they were children of God. The purpose of baptism ultimately confirms the connection between us and Christ. We are **united with Christ** in baptism. The context certainly implies an active, informed faith whose object is Jesus Christ. Our faith rests, not on any form of baptism, but in Christ.

Being **united with Christ** leads to our ongoing experience of being **made like** Christ. By becoming Christians and being baptized, the Galatian believers were becoming spiritually grown up and ready to take on the privileges and responsibilities of the more mature. The person who is being made like him is a "new" person, with a new lifestyle and new aspirations.

3:28 In the first part of this verse, discrimination and barriers are eliminated. In the second part, unity is established. If all believers are being made like Christ, if all believers have professed faith and joined the body of Christ, then this unity sets aside all other superficial distinctions. While it is true that in the body of Christ, Jews, Gentiles, slaves, free people, men, and women do still have individual identities, Paul exalts their unity—**you are one in Christ Jesus.** All labels become secondary among those who share Jesus in common.

Some Jewish males would greet each new day by praying, "Lord, I thank you that I am not a Gentile, a slave, or a woman." The prejudice toward all three categories was real and strong. As discussed throughout this letter to the Galatians, a **Jew** who believes in Christ is no different from a **Gentile** who believes. Unity in Christ transcends racial distinctions. Next is the barrier of social status. A **slave** and a **free** person must treat each other like brothers and sisters in the body of Christ. To take it even further, when it comes to faith and God's promises, there really is no gender distinction. Both **male** and **female** alike are acceptable in the body of Christ. Our equal standing in Christ gives us equal access not only to salvation but to the full gifts of the Spirit and to all avenues of service.

The barriers broken down in this verse may not seem so radical to our day, but they were astounding in ancient Roman culture. This made Christianity unique and attractive—it valued each individual, yet it provided a unified body. All believers are one in Christ Jesus. All are equally valuable to God. Differences arise in gifts, in function, in abilities, but all are one in Christ (Ephesians 2:15).

3:29 Becoming God's children (3:26) and one in Christ (3:28) means that those who **belong to Christ . . . are the true children of Abraham.** Jews believed that they were automatically God's people because they were Abraham's descendants. Paul concluded that Abraham's spiritual children are not the Jews, nor are they those who have been circumcised. Abraham's children are those who respond to God in faith as Abraham had done. The only difference is that our response is to Christ as Savior. Because we have responded, we are **heirs.** In other words, **all the promises God gave to** Abraham **belong to** us. By responding to Christ in faith, we have followed in the ancient way of Abraham, one of the early ones justified by faith. He trusted God, and so do we. But to us has been added the opportunity to appreciate what price Christ paid to ensure our share in the promise.

4:1 To further illustrate the spiritual immaturity of those who insist on remaining under the law, Paul used an example from Roman law and custom. In ancient times, the "coming of age" of a son carried tremendous significance. This did not occur at a specific age (such as twelve or thirteen), as it did among Jews and Greeks; rather, the "coming of age" was determined by the father. In Rome this event was usually marked on March 17 by a family celebration known as the *Liberalia.* During this event, the father formally acknowledged his son and heir. The son received a new "grown-up" toga and entered into adult responsibilities.

Paul pointed out, however, that while the **young children** and heirs are still minors (not yet of age), they are **not much better off than slaves until they grow up.** Although they are the future owners of an estate and a fortune, while they are young, they have no claim to it nor any right to make decisions regarding it. In the eyes of the Roman law, the young heirs were no different than slaves. Paul's application of the illustration reveals that when we were under the law, we were no better off than slaves.

4:2 In this analogy Paul focused on the legal rights and status of the children. These **guardians** are different from the ones described in 3:24—these are more like trustees. But Paul's meaning was the same. The law performed its function of "keeping us out of trouble" and disciplining us during our "immaturity" until God offered us "maturity" through our acceptance of salvation by grace. Paul's words imply that the time of this "coming of age" differed for every child. In Rome, the father set the time for his son's coming of age and adulthood. So too, God set the time for terminating our guardianship under the law and making us his children and heirs by faith. The date was the time of Christ's coming into the world.

Faith, then, initiates the believer into maturity and full rights. Paul was dumbfounded that the Galatians would choose to revert to slavery when Christ had given them freedom. They were behaving like children who had inherited an estate but still insisted on remaining in a dependent, servile role.

4:3 Paul alluded to slavery in order to show that before Christ came and died for sins, people were **slaves to the spiritual powers of this world,** in bondage to whatever law or religion they chose to follow. Thinking they could be saved by their deeds, they became enslaved to trying—and failing—to follow even the basics.

The phrase, **"spiritual powers of this world,"** has been translated several ways. Most likely, Paul was referring to these "powers" as the elementary stages of religious practice, whether under the law of the Jewish religion, or the rites and rituals in any heathen religion (see also 4:9 and Colossians 2:20). In other words, the statement referred to any religious experience prior to accepting Christ as Savior. Paul was pointing out that trying to reach God through any religion or any worldly plan brings failure. The "powers" of the world (whether religious or moral) suggest that a solution is needed, but do not offer that solution. Paul compared religious rituals to slavery because they force a standard that people can never achieve. But, with the proclamation of the gospel, grace in Christ replaced those worldly religious practices.

4:4 Everyone was enslaved under the "spiritual powers of this world," **but** . . . That little word offered hope to humanity. God's intervention into human history changed the world.

When the right time came, God sent his Son to earth. Why did Jesus come when he did? The "why" may be unanswerable, except that God knew it was the right time. Several factors present in the Roman Empire certainly aided the quick spread of the message of the gospel. The Greek civilization provided a language that had spread across much of the known world as the main language for all people. The Romans had brought peace throughout their empire and built a system of roads that made land travel quicker and safer than ever before. The Jews were expectant, eagerly awaiting their Messiah. Messianic fervor was at its height. Into this world came Jesus.

Just as a Roman father would set the date for his son to reach maturity and attain freedom from his guardians (4:2), so God had set the date when he would send his Son to free people from the law, to become his children (see 4:5). Guided by a sovereign God, historical events worked in harmony to prepare for the predecided moment of Jesus' arrival on earth (see also Psalm 102:13; Mark 1:15; and Ephesians 1:10).

Jesus was **born of a woman**—he was God yet also human (Genesis 3:15; Luke 1:26-38; John 1:1, 14). Paul balanced his amazing claims about Jesus' divine nature with his reminder of Jesus' human character. Jesus was a human and **subject to the law;** thus he was voluntarily subject to the structured universe that he had created (John 1:3-5) and that had been marred by human rebellion. More significantly, Jesus lived as a Jew, subject to God's revealed law. In keeping with this, Jesus was both circumcised and presented at the Temple (Luke 2:21-32). Yet while no other human being has been able to perfectly fulfill God's law, Jesus kept it completely (Matthew 5:17; Hebrews 4:15). Thus, Jesus could be the perfect sacrifice because, although fully human, he never sinned. His death bought freedom for us who were enslaved to sin, offering us redemption and adoption into God's family.

4:5 Jesus was himself born "subject to the law" (4:4) so that by his living and dying he could accomplish two purposes: (1) **to buy freedom for us who were slaves to the law,** and (2) to allow those "freed" people to be adopted **as his very own children.** Through his life, Jesus demonstrated his unique eligibility to **buy** our freedom. Through his death, Jesus paid the price to release us from slavery to sin. When Christ redeemed those **who were slaves to the law,** he did not redeem the Jews alone. His death set people free from bondage to any law or religious system (see 4:3)—offering, instead, salvation by faith alone. But because the law was God's clearest revelation of his justice, being born under the law and keeping it perfectly proved that Jesus was the perfect sacrifice. He took upon himself the curse the law required in order to set believers free of that curse.

In these verses, Paul continued to respond to the foolishness of the Galatians. If Christ had fulfilled the law, taking upon himself the curse of the law, and had freed people from the law, why would the Galatians try to keep requirements already fulfilled by Christ? The question appears again plainly in 4:9. Meanwhile, Paul was building a case that would make the question entirely rhetorical.

Redemption had an ongoing purpose—**so that he could adopt** these believers as his children. Until Christ bought us (that is, paid the ultimate price by taking the penalty for our sins), we could never have been acceptable to God. Even our good works or religious rituals could bring us no closer to a relationship with him. But Christ gave freedom from the slavery people faced before and brought them into a new relationship with God the Father. Believers' new position in Christ goes beyond mere acceptance by God. So close is that relationship that Paul called it "adoption." In Roman culture, a wealthy, childless man could take a slave youth and make that slave his child and heir. The adopted person was no longer a slave. He became a full heir to his new family, guaranteed all legal rights to his new father's property. He was not a second-class son; he was equal to all other sons, biological or adopted, in his father's family. That person's origin or past was no longer a factor in his legal standing. Likewise, when a person becomes a Christian, he or she leaves the slavery of trying to please God through works and gains all the privileges and responsibilities of a child in God's family.

4:6 This verse and the next are central in the apostle's entire argument. Focusing again on the Galatians, Paul added, **you Gentiles have become his children,** part of God's family. Despite their doubts and confusion at that time, God still regarded the Galatian believers as his children. How did Paul know this? How could the Galatian believers claim this? Because **God has sent the Spirit of his Son into** their **hearts.** The Spirit cannot be earned or obtained, as if he were the result or reward of some system of works or discipline. Instead, God sends the Holy Spirit as a gift. Having the Spirit of Christ meant that they belonged to Christ.

A person cannot have a personal relationship with laws or rituals. But believers have an intimate relationship with God: they **can call God** their **dear Father.** As God's adopted children, we can approach him with love and trust. As God's adopted children, we share with Jesus all rights to God's resources. As God's heirs, we can claim what he has provided for us—our full identity as his children.

4:7 To conclude his argument from this analogy, Paul explained briefly that each Galatian believer was **no longer a slave** to any law or religious ritual or even to Satan. Instead, each person had entered into God's family, being adopted as **God's own child.** Belonging to God as his child also means that **everything he has belongs to** the child, for God has promised the inheritance of eternal life and his riches and blessings to all his children. We need no further preparation. No system can fill in or stand in for Christ. Being a child and being an heir are inseparable realities in God's family.

GALATIANS 4:8-31

PAUL'S CONCERN FOR THE GALATIANS / 4:8-20

What do Christians mean when they claim to "know God"? As strange as the concept may sound to modern ears, the Scriptures speak confidently of our ability to know God intimately. Paul turned to the Galatians' seeming denial of their relationship with God. Though they had met God, their present course of action (living by the law) amounted to a sad betrayal of God's grace.

4:8 As in 3:23 and 4:1, Paul reiterated the former enslaved condition of the Galatians to the **so-called gods that do not even exist.** Before they came to know the one true God, the Galatians believed in other gods (such as Zeus and Hermes—read about Paul's experience in Lystra, a city in Galatia, in Acts 14:8-18). These "beings" had no divine power. These "gods" could also refer to the principles and pursuits of life that so easily change from being possessions to possessing us. The people's ignorance of God made them **slaves** of something less than God. There is only one God; to worship anything else means false worship and slavery to sin. As Paul explained in 4:1-7, anyone who has not discovered freedom in Christ remains a slave. In this verse, Paul was simply restating the preconversion predicament of the Galatians.

4:9 The Galatian believers had been enslaved, but then Paul introduced them to God. They **found God** (although, as Paul points out, it was **God** who **found** them). Paul was astonished that after getting to know God personally, the Galatians would **go back again and become slaves once more to the weak and useless spiritual powers of this world.** Who, after tasting freedom, would return to slavery? Why, after meeting God, would the Galatians **become slaves once more?** Was that what they truly wanted?

4:10 As an example of this law keeping the Galatians had been attempting, Paul pointed out their observance of special holidays. The **days** referred to keeping the Jewish Sabbaths or other specified dates in the Jewish calendar. The observance of **months** would be the new moon celebrations of the Jews. **Seasons** would refer to the festivals that lasted several days. For the Jews this could be the three main feasts: Unleavened Bread, Pentecost, and Shelters. **Years** of celebration for the Jews were the Year of Jubilee and Sabbath years.

Paul did not condemn the celebration of the Jewish events—for he himself kept the Sabbaths and still traveled to Jerusalem for certain festivals (see also Colossians 2:16). He would have condemned the Gentile Galatians celebrating the Jewish holidays in order to somehow receive more merit before God or fulfill some legal duty in doing so. The God-honoring festivals were not bad in themselves; but when used as a way to earn salvation or "score points" with God, they became nothing more than slavery.

4:11 If the Galatians continued in their law-centered approach to Christianity, setting aside God's grace in order to obey codes, customs, and rituals, then Paul feared that all his **hard work** among them and his suffering on their behalf (see 3:4 explanation) would be **worth nothing.** Paul was not saying that the Galatians would lose their salvation but that their very turning away from the truth would render them unfruitful and their faith "dead," as if Paul had never visited them at all.

4:12 Paul had become **like the Gentiles** (specifically these Galatians) in the sense that he was **free from the law,** as they had been before they ever knew about the law. They had accepted the gospel; here Paul asked that they simply remain in **freedom.** He was convinced that they would realize in an instant the folly of what was being offered to them if they would only reflect on the change that had actually occurred in their lives when they had trusted Christ.

Paul reminisced about how the Galatians had received him on his first visit to them (see Acts 13–14). They **did not mistreat** him, even receiving him in his physical weakness. Paul had depended on them in ways that were as important as their own dependence on the gospel that he had delivered to them.

4:13 Many attempts have been made to identify the illness to which Paul referred here. Some commentators suggest that Paul's illness was some sort of an eye disorder (inferred from the reference to eyes in 4:15). Others think that Paul may have contracted some form of malaria on the coast after landing in Perga in Pamphylia (see Acts 13:13). Or he may have had epilepsy, so he and his traveling companions had headed for the highlands where Paul could recuperate. Still others point to the physical abuse and beating Paul had received in Lystra and the resulting care of the believers as his wounds had healed (Acts 14:19). Whether this sickness was the same as Paul's "thorn in the flesh" referred to in 2 Corinthians 12:7 is also unknown. Whatever the illness, it did not completely incapacitate Paul, for while in Galatia, he had **brought the Good News of Christ** to the Galatians.

While it would be interesting to identify this illness, we can know for certain from Paul's words that he remembered the illness as the cause of his encounter with the Galatians. Their relationship with each other had not begun with Paul as a confident herald of the gospel but rather as a weak person in need of help. Paul had depended on the Galatians before they had come to depend on his message and his Lord.

4:14 The Galatians could have refused Paul any reception because his **sickness was revolting** to them. Apparently his need had been a genuine imposition; perhaps Paul's resulting appearance had made him difficult to look at, or his weakness had made him an extra burden on those who cared for him. The trial may simply have been the temptation to treat him with contempt or scorn because of his illness. To the Galatians' credit, they welcomed the ill Paul with open arms, ready to care for him and to listen to his words. Paul compared their reception to how they might have received **an angel from God or even Christ Jesus himself.** The Galatians had respected Paul very highly, although they had never met him before.

4:15 The Galatians had received Paul with open arms and joyfully received the message he had preached among them. So Paul asked, **"Where is that joyful spirit?"** The Galatians loved and respected Paul greatly. Paul knew they would have given him their **eyes** if they could have. This may be a reference specifying Paul's particular illness, or it may be a figure of speech meaning that the Galatians would have given their most precious possessions to Paul out of love and respect for him.

4:16 But Paul was now being treated like an **enemy.** Why? The only possible reason would be that the Galatians didn't want to hear the **truth.** The Galatians needed to realize that they were in real danger of believing a lie rather than the truth of the gospel.

4:17 While Paul had spoken only the truth from pure motives (to bring the Galatians to salvation), the Judaizers had less than honorable motives. The **false teachers** were claiming to be religious authorities and experts in Judaism and Christianity, but they had selfish motives. They were **anxious to win** people's **favor,** but their only desire was to win the people over to their side—and at the same time alienate the people from Paul, and thus from Christ. Once the Galatians became committed to the false teachers, the roles would be reversed and the Galatians would be forced to pay **attention** to and even provide money and lodging for them. They would be in bondage to the false teachers and all their wrong teachings.

4:18 Paul acknowledged that eagerness helps, especially when a leader cannot be with them but can depend on their faithfulness. But eagerness needs the right goal or object. Paul worried that his Galatian friends were becoming eager over the lie that human moral and ethical efforts can satisfy God's perfect standard. The false teachers were eager to win over the Galatians in order that the Galatians would be eager to support them.

4:19 While the false teachers simply sought a larger following, Paul saw these believers as his **dear children.** Obviously his motives differed from those of the false teachers, for he loved the Galatians dearly, as a mother loves her children. Paul compared the **labor pains** of childbirth to the pain he felt at their turning from the faith.

Paul's concern would **continue until Christ** would be **fully developed** in their lives. Paul wanted each of his children to reach spiritual maturity in the faith. They would do so by having the likeness of Christ portrayed in their lives. "Fully developed in your lives" refers to a mother carrying an embryo until it is developed enough to be born. Having Christ becoming fully developed

in their lives emphasizes the personal changes necessary to become like Jesus.

4:20 As with any confusion or misunderstanding, face-to-face talk accomplishes more than written correspondence. Paul could not pick up and dash off to Galatia. If he could go, he might change his tone but not his message or his expectations—those would always remain the same, for they were true and correct. Paul wrote this one-sided letter because he didn't know **what else to do.**

ABRAHAM'S TWO CHILDREN / 4:21-31

The final paragraph of Galatians 4 records an extended allegory. Hagar and Sarah, Abraham's wives-in-conflict, illustrate the conflict between law and grace. The Judaizers, indeed all Jews, took great pride in their descent from godly Abraham. However, as John the Baptist and Jesus pointed out, merely being descended from Abraham was not enough to secure salvation (see Matthew 3:9; John 8:37-44). Paul made the same point in this section, though from a slightly different angle.

4:21 Under the influence of the false teachers (the Judaizers), the Galatians wanted **to live under the law.** Paul wanted to turn them back to accepting salvation by grace alone. He confronted them directly by saying, **"Do you know what the law really says?"** The Galatian believers, most of them *not* from a Jewish background and thus with little more than an elementary understanding of the Jewish law, may have answered an indignant "yes." Hopefully they would have halted long enough to realize the impossible standards under which they were placing themselves.

4:22 Paul turned to an argument from the Jewish Scripture and the life of **Abraham,** father of the Jewish nation (see also 3:6-29), to illustrate his point. The story, originally recorded in Genesis 16 and 21:1-21, was summarized by Paul as a fundamental spiritual lesson demonstrated by Abraham, his **two sons,** and his two wives. In ancient times, a mother's status affected the status of her children. Paul reminded his readers that Abraham had two types of sons—one born of a **slave-wife** and one born of his **freeborn wife.** Paul wanted the Galatians to consider which type of descendant these Judaizers were more like and then decide which they themselves desired to be like.

4:23 Besides the contrast in the status of the mothers, the two boys were different in another important way. Abraham's son by the slave woman **was born in a human attempt to bring about the fulfillment of God's promise** of descendants for Abraham. Ishmael's birth was engineered by Abra-

ham and Sarah to "make the promise come true" by their own plans and efforts, rather than waiting on God's timing.

However, Abraham's son by the **freeborn wife was born as God's own fulfillment of his promise.** When Abraham was ninety-nine years old and Sarah was ninety years old (Genesis 17:1, 17), God appeared to Abraham and promised Isaac's birth (Genesis 17:15-16, 19).

4:24 By using this **illustration,** Paul was showing that what happened to Sarah and Hagar pictures the relationship between God and mankind. Though perhaps difficult for us to follow, this was a common type of argument in Paul's day. Paul was pointing to a great spiritual truth illustrated by this story, namely, the superiority of Christianity over Judaism.

The two women, Hagar and Sarah, represent **God's two covenants.** The two well-known covenants were made with Abraham and with Moses. The one covenant with Moses had begun at **Mount Sinai** with the giving of the **law** (see Exodus 19:20). **Hagar** was a **slave-wife** (Genesis 16:1); thus, her children would be slaves, for a child's status equaled the status of his or her mother.

Although both sons had the same father, their mothers were different and their descendants became two different races—Ishmael, the Ishmaelites (Genesis 21:18; Psalm 83:1-6); Isaac, the Jews (Genesis 22:16-18). The Jews proudly considered themselves children of God's covenant. However, Paul refuted the claim, reminding them of the "two covenants" and explaining that because of their behavior, the

Jews were actually children of the covenant with Moses, the covenant of the law. The Judaizers claimed superiority for their point of view by claiming that the blessings of the covenant came to descendants of Abraham through Isaac. Gentile Christians could be "adopted" into Abraham's covenant group by accepting circumcision. Paul contradicted the Judaizers by showing that those who promote the law for salvation or sanctification demonstrate the characteristics of slavery to the law. Paul claimed that they were products of the Sinai covenant, not Abraham's covenant. Trying to win salvation by obeying the law leads to slavery, and as the Jews persisted in this pattern, they showed themselves to be enslaved to their law. Although the Jews had descended from Abraham and Isaac, as they tried to piously obey their laws, they were actually slaves to it. As slaves, they were more like Ishmael than Isaac.

4:25-26 Not only do the women and their children represent two covenants (4:24), they also represent two Jerusalems. Hagar represents the old covenant given at Mount Sinai. She also represents the present city of Jerusalem, which was enslaved to Rome and, as the center of the Jewish religious and legal system, was filled with people **in slavery** to the Jewish law.

Sarah, on the other hand, **represents the heavenly Jerusalem,** the promise of faith and freedom. Sarah was mother of the promised miracle-child, Isaac, and corresponds to the covenant of Abraham (inferred in 4:24). This covenant promised a future "new covenant" that would begin at the death of Jesus Christ on the cross. Paul used the concept **she is our mother** to show that faith, not adherence to the law, is the source of our salvation. Paul was offering the Galatians the opportunity to claim that they were descendants of Abraham through faith, and that they possessed citizenship in the spiritual Jerusalem. For Gentiles to be included in this way would be as miraculous as the birth of Isaac.

4:27 Paul quoted from Isaiah's prophecy (Isaiah 54:1). Isaiah's words had comforted the Jewish exiles in Babylon. To be **childless** in ancient days meant great shame and disgrace for a woman. Israel had been unfruitful, like a childless woman, but God would give great blessings and would change their mourning into rejoicing.

Paul applied the comparison of former-versus-later blessings, prophesied by Isaiah, to his Hagar/Sarah analogy. Sarah, who had been barren, was blessed with Isaac. Her child was a gracious gift, not the result of work. Because God had promised to bless Abraham and his descendants, she ultimately would have **more** children **than all the other women** (the Christian church grew rapidly

and is still growing). While the Jews knew (or should have known) from their own Scriptures that Gentiles would turn to God, two changes astounded them: (1) The Gentiles did not have to become Jews first; and (2) so many Gentiles would become believers that they would outnumber Jewish believers.

4:28 The Galatians who had become Christians under Paul's ministry, fit into the analogy as **children of the promise, just like Isaac.** Just as Isaac's birth was a miracle of God, so Christianity, offering people the opportunity to be born again, is a miracle of God (John 3:3). Just as Isaac's mother was free, so Isaac was free, and so Christianity offers true freedom because it depends not on our actions but on God's unchangeable promises to us. Paul hammered home his point to the Galatian believers: "As children of the promise, you never need to be enslaved to the Jewish laws. You are like Isaac!"

4:29 Paul reminded his readers of the story in Genesis 21. Abraham had held a feast on the day Isaac was weaned. Isaac was probably about two years old; thus, Ishmael would have been a teenager. Ishmael had teased his younger half brother—Paul called this persecution. Paul explained that the persecution of the older brother on the younger was continuing to play itself out in the later animosity between the nations that had descended from them (Israel and Edom, Psalm 83:1-6), and on into the persecution of those who want people **to keep the law** (the Jews) toward those **who are born of the Holy Spirit** and thus are freed from the law.

4:30 The first question is: What happened when Ishmael persecuted Isaac at this feast? As Scripture says in Genesis 21:9-10, Sarah saw this happen, went to Abraham, and demanded that Hagar and Ishmael be sent away.

The second question refers to the application: So what happens to Ishmael (the Jews) and Isaac (Christians) today? Judaism and Christianity could not coexist as paths to the same goal any more than Ishmael and Isaac could share Abraham's inheritance. Perhaps most ironic was Paul's bold clarification of this old story. The Jews had long held that this verse described God's rejection of the Gentiles. But Paul turned the tables: "You had it wrong. Jews and Gentiles are included together in God's inheritance when they become believers, or 'Isaacs.' Those who reject grace lose their share in the inheritance, whether unbelieving Jews or unrepentant Gentiles. Those are the 'Ishmaels.'" Those in slavery to the law **will not share the family inheritance** with those who have experienced freedom in Christ and salvation by faith alone.

4:31 Paul tied up his allegory, and indeed all the points he proved with it, with the simple word, **so.** He repeated that **we** (that is, all believers of all time) **are children of the free woman, acceptable to God because of our faith.** That freedom must be treasured because of the price paid for it.

GALATIANS 5

FREEDOM IN CHRIST / 5:1-15

Paul's application of the Genesis account of Sarah and Hagar exposed the real danger facing the Galatians—they were on the brink of losing their freedom in Christ. Paul expressed dismay at the report that though the Galatians had been growing in their faith, they were being influenced by those trying to destroy God's work of grace in them. In this paragraph, Paul had two objectives: (1) exposing what would actually happen if the Galatians returned to the slavery of the law, and (2) confronting the Judaizers with the fruitlessness of their system.

5:1 We have freedom from slavery to our sinful desires and to the Jewish law. But the freedom came at great price. In order for us to enjoy ultimate freedom, someone had to set us free, and that someone was Christ Jesus (John 8:32, 36). Because **Christ has really set us free,** we should **stay free.** Christ has set us free from legalistic formulas, from God's judgment upon sin, from all man-made rules, and from the subjective experiences of fear and guilt. We are to live it out, practice it, and rejoice in it! To turn back to the law and try to earn what Christ has already given mocks his sacrifice.

5:2 Paul gave a serious warning, and he didn't want any of his hearers to miss it. If the Galatian believers were to follow the Judaizers' teaching, **counting on circumcision to make** them **right with God** (the tense of the verb reveals that the Galatians had not yet taken the step, but were considering it), **then Christ** would not be able to **help** them. How could this be? What could be the harm in circumcision?

Obviously, only men could be circumcised, but more than circumcision was at stake (see 5:6). Paul was confronting the Galatians because they were trying to fulfill the Jewish law. Insistence on circumcision had become the most prominent feature of the Judaizers' thinking. They taught that the gospel needed the Jewish law system to make it perfect. But God's way was different—salvation through Christ by grace alone. We can't mix and match works and grace. God has an exclusive arrangement. The Galatians were about to be circumcised as a requirement to "complete" their salvation. But Paul explained that by that very act

they would be saying that Christ's sacrifice by his death had not been enough to save them.

5:3 Choosing circumcision would cause them to lose the value of the free gift of salvation given through Christ. It also would have another devastating effect. Choosing circumcision would mean choosing law keeping (legalism). To choose law keeping meant that one **must obey all of the regulations in the whole law of Moses.**

Paul might well have repeated his question from 4:21. Did the Galatians have any idea what their choice to obey all the Jewish laws would entail? Chances are, the Judaizers had not spelled that out—yet. They may have told the Galatians about some of the food laws (2:12) and about the festivals and holy days (4:10). But to any Jew, circumcision was the first act of obedience to a law that would, from then on, rule every detail of his life. Did the Galatians understand that "the person who keeps all of the laws except one is as guilty as the person who has broken all of God's laws" (James 2:10, see also Deuteronomy 27:26)? By becoming circumcised, the Galatians were submitting themselves to an entire system—one that doomed them to failure.

5:4 Those who try **to make** themselves **right with God by keeping the law** are, in fact, **cut off from Christ.** God allows no middle ground—it is Christ *or* law, not both. Anyone deciding to be justified by law has **fallen away from God's grace.** Christ cannot save those who persist in saving themselves. Paul's words should not be taken out of context to mean that salvation can be lost. **Grace** did not mean salvation, but refers to the means of salvation. To decide on legalism as the way of salvation is to "fall away" from grace. It's like throwing away the life preserver when lost at sea.

5:5 In this short verse Paul gave his doctrine of justification by faith: **we** (all believers, even the wavering Galatians) **who live by the Spirit** (not through anything we can do or have done, and not through the law) **eagerly wait to receive** (we don't work for righteousness; we wait for God to grow his righteousness in us) **everything promised to us** (a certain event that has not yet occurred) **who are right with God** (Christian perfection that God helps us reach in our lives and then grants completely in glory) **through faith** (in Christ and his faithfulness, and not in works or even the strength of our believing).

The words "faith" and "Spirit" provide the keys to this verse, for these words separate the Judaizers' approach to God from the Christian approach to God. The Judaizers' emphasis on circumcision showed that they were trying to gain salvation "in the flesh." But Paul pointed out that Christian faith comes "by the Spirit." The Judaizers' emphasis on the law contrasted sharply with Christianity's emphasis on faith. Christianity's basic doctrine showed the Judaizers to be wrong—dead wrong.

5:6 If Paul clearly told the Gentile Galatian believers *not* to be circumcised, what would he say to the Jews, who were already circumcised? Paul made the point that **it makes no difference to God whether we are circumcised or not circumcised** (see also 3:28; 6:15; Colossians 3:11). Paul's conviction rested on the importance of all it means to **place our faith in Christ Jesus.** Each aspect of salvation and every component of the life we live after conversion are rooted in Christ.

So what does matter? Paul didn't hesitate: **What is important is faith expressing itself in love.** To the faith discussed in chapter 4, Paul added the clarification that it must be faith expressed in love. We are saved by faith alone; but for these Galatian believers who seemed to want so desperately to work, Paul was saying, "OK, work, but don't try to earn your salvation. Instead, let your salvation by faith result in loving and kind works done to serve others." Genuine faith in Christ is expressed in love for others.

5:7 The Galatian believers had accepted the gospel of salvation and were living out their faith—they were **getting along so well.** But despite their good start, someone had **interfered,** holding them **back from following the truth.** Although Paul asked **who** had done this, he already knew the answer. Paul knew that the problem was the Judaizers. Paul warned the Galatians that the Judaizers, instead of helping them along, were actually hindering their

faith. Instead of opening up new truths to the Galatians, they kept the Galatians from following the truth. The Judaizers represented the interests of Satan. They wanted to keep the Galatians enslaved to the law and derail the new believers.

5:8 The Galatians needed to realize that it was not **God** who was holding them back, for he had **called** them **to freedom** in the first place. God had called the Galatians (1:6), but he had called them to salvation by his grace, not by their works (see also Romans 9:11; 1 Thessalonians 2:12; 5:24).

5:9 Yeast is put into bread to make it rise, and it takes only a little to affect **the whole batch of dough.** Jesus used yeast as an example of how a small amount of evil can affect a large group of people (see Matthew 16:5-12). Even **one wrong person** among the Galatian believers could **infect all the others,** putting the entire Galatian church at risk.

5:10 In spite of his obvious concern over the Galatian believers and the dangerous situation they faced, Paul believed that they would come to their senses. His confidence was based on **trusting the Lord to bring** them **back** to the faith they knew to be true.

Paul also was confident that the **person** who had been **troubling and confusing** the Galatian believers would receive due punishment. While Paul knew that the troublemakers were a group of Judaizers, he singled out the leader of this group, whom he probably did not know (see 5:7). Paul suspected that this man carried a certain amount of weight as a leader. **Whoever it is** does not so much stress Paul's ignorance of this person's identity as the worthlessness in Paul's eyes of any status he might carry. "Whoever he may be, however high in leadership or however revered by the Jews, this man is teaching wrong doctrine," Paul was saying. And by the same token, no matter what this leader's position, he would pay the penalty for his wrong teaching.

5:11 Paul asked a personal question; apparently he was reminded of an accusation against him. If Paul were **preaching** that people needed to be **circumcised** in order to be saved, then why were the Judaizers still persecuting him? He would be preaching the same message they preached! But the fact that he was **still being persecuted** was proof that he was **still preaching salvation through the cross of Christ alone.**

Why was Paul persecuted for this message? To human nature, and especially to Jews brought up to love and revere their law, the concept of needing someone else's death in order to be saved was offensive. The very thought of describing the Messiah as an executed convict disgusted them. But the impact of Christ's cross on their pride was the greatest stumbling block. As Paul described to the Corinthians, "When we preach that Christ was crucified, the Jews are offended, and the Gentiles say it's all nonsense" (1 Corinthians 1:23). Paul had witnessed the rejection of the gospel by both Gentiles and Jews, each for different reasons.

5:12 Paul's words here, though very harsh, were not meant in jest. He wanted to make another point regarding circumcision. **Those troublemakers** referred again to the false teachers, the Judaizers, who were preaching that the believers needed to be circumcised. In effect, Paul said that if the false teachers were so concerned about zeal for the law, maybe they shouldn't stop at circumcision but go the whole way and **mutilate themselves.** According to their own logic, wouldn't this make them even holier? The comparison to pagan rituals was probably not lost on the Galatians. Pagan priests of the prominent cult of the goddess Cybele in Asia were eunuchs, castrated as a part of a sacred ritual. By making this statement, Paul placed circumcision as no better than the pagan rituals of cutting parts of the body.

5:13 When Paul ministered among the Galatians, he did not give his converts a new set of rules to obey (as the Judaizers had done), for that would have made them slaves to the law. Instead, the Galatians **were called to live in freedom.** Paul was the messenger, but they "were called" by God himself, the author of the gospel.

Some of Paul's critics may have condemned his preaching of Christian freedom, saying that it would lead to people living without restraint or guidelines. Paul had an immediate and forceful answer, explaining that freedom was not to be used **to satisfy** the **sinful nature** (see also 5:16-17, 19, 24). Satan and the flesh use our freedom from law as an opportunity to enflame our desires. Sinful human desires lead to the problems mentioned in 5:26 (conceit, provoking one another, and envy) and to the lack of mutual help described in 6:1-10. When we indulge the sinful nature, we open the door to these kinds of behaviors and attitudes (see 1 Peter 2:16; 2 Peter 2:8-10; Jude 4). The demands of our human nature present a constant threat to our real freedom in Christ. We need his ongoing help to keep our "flesh" under control.

Christian freedom is **freedom to serve one another in love.** Love for other believers flows outward from what God has done in each believer's heart. The Greek word for love *(agape)* refers to selfless, self-giving love. Christian freedom does not leave believers wandering through life without laws, rules, restraints, or guidelines. Instead, they freely live according to God's standards and glorify God through loving service to others.

5:14 In fact, Christian servanthood ultimately does what slavery to the law cannot do—it fulfills the law! Quoting from Leviticus 19:18 (from the law), Paul explained that **the whole law can be summed up in this one command: "Love your neighbor as yourself."** Jesus made this same point (Matthew 22:35-39; Luke 10:25-28). In fact, the entire law is fulfilled as the Christian community acts in love toward one another through the power of the Holy Spirit.

Paul made it clear through this letter (and others) that the law cannot save anyone. But he did not cast aside the law as worthless. Believers must still be concerned with it; otherwise Paul would not have made this statement. No one could ever completely fulfill the law; but if someone could, the Christians (not the Judaizers) would most resemble that person because of their love for one another.

5:15 Paul used the present tense in these verbs, indicating that these problems were occurring as he wrote. Such conflict threatened to tear the church apart. The verbs increase in intensity—**biting, devouring,** and ultimately, **destroying one another.** The source of the conflict went back to the false teachers and the confusion they were causing among the believers (5:10). The presence of the conflict supports the theory that factions were developing in the church—some people going with the law-centered teachers, some staying with Paul and the gospel, and some deciding to pursue their every sinful whim based on the "freedom" they had in Christ. Such continued confusion would ruin their faith, their testimony, and ultimately the church itself. While some differences of opinion would be natural, the Galatians had gone beyond that. They disagreed on foundational issues. Like piranhas, they were destroying one another.

LIVING BY THE SPIRIT'S POWER / 5:16-26

Paul turned to the personal, spiritual lives of the Galatians. He had warned them not to follow the teaching of the Judaizers. Here he warned them about following their own wishes and desires. Slavery was a threat from the outside influence of the false teachers, but it was an equal threat from the inside desires of the sinful nature. Paul wanted them to replace self-indulgence with loving service to others.

In this section, Paul explained that the secret to loving our neighbor as ourselves is by living in the Spirit and not giving in to our sinful human desires. He contrasted the characteristics of a life motivated by the sinful nature and a life motivated by the Spirit.

5:16 The word **so** ties in with verses 13-15. The strategy for removing the divisiveness that marred the Galatian church was to **live according to** the new life given to them by **the Holy Spirit.** God sent the Holy Spirit to be with and within his followers after Christ had returned to heaven (see John 14–16).

The phrase conveys the meaning of the literal translation "by the Spirit keep on walking." Walking means "living" in this context, and it emphasizes the moment-by-moment contact with and guidance by the Holy Spirit for daily decisions and activities. Living "according to the Spirit" should be a daily, continuous action by Christians. He is always present, but we must be in touch with him and stay open to his guidance and correction.

The result? **You won't be doing what your sinful nature craves.** When we become believers, our sinful nature still exists. But God asks us to place our sinful nature under the control of the Holy Spirit so that he can transform it. This is a supernatural process. We must never underestimate the power of our sinful nature, and we must never attempt to fight it in our own strength. Satan is a crafty tempter, and we have a limitless ability to make excuses. Instead of trying to overcome sin by our own willpower, we must take advantage of the tremendous power of Christ. God provides for victory over our sinful nature—he sends the Holy Spirit to live in us and give us power. But our ability to restrain the desires of the sinful nature depends on how much we're willing to "live according to" the Holy Spirit. For each believer, this daily process requires moment-by-moment decisions.

5:17 While believers live in this world, they face constant tension between their **old sinful nature** and **what the Holy Spirit wants.** We must not infer from Paul's words that our personality has two selves, nor that we have two equal and opposite forces struggling to gain control. In Christ and in the Holy Spirit, we have a victorious new resurrection life. The Holy Spirit in us guarantees our future total redemption and change. Though we have new life in Christ, we still have a mind and body prone to rebel and enticed by sinful desires. We must resist those desires.

We often experience resistance when we follow the Spirit's leading. Satan serves as a persistent teacher of rebellion, and humanity has had centuries of practice. Whatever path we choose, we will hear the whispers of opposition—our **choices are never free from this conflict.** Whenever we set out to do what the Holy Spirit instructs, we can expect our sinful nature to flare up in opposition. When we decide to share the gospel, our sinful human nature will make us feel foolish. When we decide to commit ourselves to some service, evil desires hinder us, trying to thwart the leading of the Spirit. Conversely, each time we follow our sinful human nature, we will receive (through our consciences, God's word, or even other believers) reminders not to follow those sinful desires. True believers realize the deadly power of sin. No longer their master, sin now attacks like a powerful enemy. These **two forces** within **are constantly fighting each other.** Sinful desires still pop up, like guerrilla forces, attacking us when we least expect it.

5:18 Freedom from the law does not imply freedom to do whatever we please (5:13). Neither do we live in the Spirit in some sort of "middle ground." Instead, we live on another plane altogether—we have truth as opposed to falsehood; we have grace as opposed to works; we act out of love as opposed to being **subject to the law;** we are supervised by the Spirit as opposed to being supervised by the law.

5:19-21 Paul contrasted the **desires of** the **sinful nature** and the works of the Spirit-filled life in 5:19-21 and 5:22-23. Paul's list of sins falls into four categories. These particular sins were especially prevalent in the pagan world, and the Galatians would have readily understood them. With few exceptions, we recognize these sins as present in our own time as well.

In the first category three sexual sins are mentioned:

- **Sexual immorality**—Any form of illicit sexual relationship. The term serves to spotlight forbidden sexual behavior between people or indirect participation as an audience.
- **Impure thoughts**—Moral uncleanness. Perhaps no sexual act has taken place, but the person exhibits a crudeness or insensitivity in sexual matters that offends others. An example today

would be the excessive use of sexual humor (or what is supposed to be humor) where people make statements with a sexual double meaning.

- **Eagerness for lustful pleasure**—Open and excessive indulgence in sexual sins. The person has no sense of shame or restraint. This is the outworking of sexual immorality and impurity.

The next two sins are religious sins particular to pagan culture:

- **Idolatry**—Worship of pagan idols. A person creates substitutes for God and then treats them as if they were God. This person is giving in to sinful human desires.
- **Participation in demonic activities**—Involvement with the powers of evil, at times using potions and poisons. With idolatry, a person acts in a submissive role in relation to evil; with demonic activity, the person is an active agent who serves the powers of evil.

The next eight sins pertain to conduct toward people (interpersonal relations) that has been motivated by sinful desires. It's sad to note, but many of these social sins are often seen in our churches today:

- **Hostility**—A condition of fixed enmity between groups. This may be real, unresolved conflict whose cause has been forgotten but which has yielded a harvest of bitterness.
- **Quarreling**—Competition, rivalry, bitter conflict—the seeds and the natural fruit of hatred.
- **Jealousy**—A feeling of resentment that someone else has what another feels he or she deserves.
- **Outbursts of anger**—Selfish anger. The plural form conveys the meaning of continual and uncontrolled behavior.
- **Selfish ambition**—The approach to life and work that tries to get ahead at other people's expense. Not only might this refer to what we call "workaholism," it also implies a mercenary, aggressive attitude toward others in the pursuit of one's goals.
- **Divisions**—Strong disagreements or quarrels. The situation that can quickly develop between people when a disagreeable attitude prevails.
- **The feeling that everyone is wrong except those in your own little group**—Dissension created among people because of divisions. This describes the tendency to look for allies in conflict. The almost spontaneous generation of cliques demonstrates this characteristic of sinful human desires.
- **Envy**—A desire to possess something awarded to or achieved by another. Or even the twisted logic that cries "Unfair!" about another's circumstances and expresses the wish, "If I can't have that, they shouldn't get it either!"

Finally Paul lists two sins, common to pagan cultures, that are often connected with the rituals of idol worship:

- **Drunkenness**—Excessive use of wine and strong drink.
- **Wild parties**—Drunken, carousing "parties," often filled with sexual promiscuity, were associated with festivals of some pagan gods. The feasts in honor of Bacchus were particularly infamous for their immorality.
- **And other kinds of sin**—Paul added an "etc." to show that the list was by no means complete.

Anyone living that sort of life refers to the lifestyle of people who habitually exhibit these characteristics. This does not mean that believers who lapse into any of these sins will lose their salvation and their inheritance. But people who habitually exhibit these characteristics reveal themselves to be enslaved to sinful human nature. They are not children of God; thus, they cannot have any part in the inheritance in the Kingdom of God. People who have accepted Christ and have the Holy Spirit within them will manifest that new life by making a clean break with such sins as listed above.

5:22-23 Paul's introduction of the word **fruit** is filled with meaning. By it Paul conveyed the meaning of a full harvest of virtues. **Fruit** is a by-product; it takes time to grow and requires care and cultivation. The Spirit produces the fruit; our job is to get in tune with the Spirit. Believers exhibit the fruit of the Spirit, not because they work at it, but simply because **the Holy Spirit controls** their **lives**. The fruit of the Spirit separates Christians from a godless, evil world, reveals a power within them, and helps them become more Christlike in their daily lives. In contrast to the list it follows, Paul did not describe these characteristics as obvious. The previous ones reside in us; the following ones come as a result of the Spirit's presence.

Again, the characteristics fall into categories. The first three are inward and can come from God alone:

- **Love**—Love as shown by Jesus, whose love is self-sacrificing and unchanging, and as demonstrated by God who sent his Son for sinners (Romans 5:5). Love forms the foundation for all the other fruit listed. Elsewhere, Paul breaks love itself down into various components (see 1 Corinthians 13), so that "love" turns out to bear little resemblance to the emotional meaning so often given to the word.

- **Joy**—An inner rejoicing that abides despite outer circumstances. This characteristic has little to do with happiness and can exist in times of unhappiness. It is a deep and nourishing satisfaction that continues even when a life situation seems empty and unsatisfying. The relationship with God through Christ remains even in the deserts and valleys of living.
- **Peace**—An inner quietness and trust in God's sovereignty and justice, even in the face of adverse circumstances. This is a profound agreement with the truth that God, not we, remains in charge of the universe.

The next three concern each believer's relationships with others:

- **Patience**—Patiently putting up with people who continually irritate us. The Holy Spirit's work in us increases our endurance.
- **Kindness**—Acting charitably, benevolently toward others, as God did toward us. Kindness takes the initiative in responding to other people's needs.
- **Goodness**—Reaching out to do good to others, even if they don't deserve it. Goodness does not react to evil but absorbs the offense and responds with positive action.

The last three present more general character traits that ought to guide a believer's life:

- **Faithfulness**—Reliable, trustworthy.
- **Gentleness**—Humble, considerate of others, submissive to God and his word. Even when anger is the appropriate response, as when Jesus cleared the Temple, gentleness keeps the expression of anger headed in the right direction. Gentleness applies even force in the correct way.
- **Self-control**—Mastery over sinful human desires and their lack of restraint. Ironically, our sinful desires, which promise self-fulfillment and power, inevitably lead us to slavery. When we surrender to the Holy Spirit, initially we feel as though we have lost control, but he leads us to the exercise of self-control that would be impossible in our own strength.

God gave the law to make people aware of their sin and to restrain evil. But no one would make a law against these fruit (virtues), for they are neither sinful nor evil. Indeed, a society where all people acted thus would need very few laws at all. Because God who sent the law also sent the Spirit, the by-products of the Spirit-filled life harmonize perfectly with the intent of God's law. A person who exhibits the fruit of the Spirit fulfills the law far better than a person who observes the rituals but has little love in his or her heart.

5:24 Paul made it clear that the sinful nature and the Holy Spirit oppose each other. Believers, while receiving the Holy Spirit, also have sinful desires within. So how do believers gain the victory? The answers lie in these last three verses.

Those who belong to Christ Jesus (believers) have victory over the sinful desires to the degree that they have **crucified** the **passions and desires of their sinful nature.** Believers know that this does not mean our sinful nature really dies—life would be so much easier if it did! Instead, our sinful human nature continues to persuade and seduce us. Like a real crucifixion, the death of our sinful human desires is slow and painful . . . and lifelong. In many ways, our sinful human desires may need to be "recrucified" daily. But the picture conveyed by this "crucifixion of the sinful nature" shows us that God has broken the power of sin at work in our body. That remains a fact even when it may not feel that way to us. We need no longer live under sin's power or control. God does not take us out of the world or make us robots; we will still experience the temptation to sin, and sometimes we will sin. Before we were saved, we were slaves to our sinful desires, but now we can freely choose to live for Christ (see also Colossians 2:11; 3:9).

But what happens when we sin? Christ's death made forgiveness available to us. As believers continue to repent of sin, they will always receive God's forgiveness—all because of Christ's death on the cross on our behalf. We can experience victory over our sinful human desires because we are united with Christ in his death, having "crucified" that sinful nature. Our evil desires, our bondage to sin, and our love of sin have been nailed to his cross. Now, united by faith with him, we have unbroken fellowship with God and freedom from sin's hold on us. Our conduct and attitudes change, and the fruit of the Spirit grows within us because of what Christ did for us.

5:25 Because it is the Holy Spirit who gives new life, believers ought to **follow the Holy Spirit's leading in every part of** their **lives.** Apart from the working of the Holy Spirit, a person cannot please God. When the Holy Spirit leads, believers must follow. Since believers have been made alive by the Holy Spirit, he ought to direct the course of their lives. Unless we actively pursue contact with the Holy Spirit and obey his leading, we will be unable to resist the passions and desires of our flesh.

5:26 This verse seems like a last-minute addition to a section that could have easily ended with verse 25. Paul probably focused on particular problems in Galatia. He explained that if they would "follow the Holy Spirit's leading," step-by-step, they could solve any attitude problems in the church. Perhaps even living by the Spirit might be used by some as an occasion for pride.

The apostle mentioned three particular problems. They are the opposite of serving, and they remain three prevalent sins in the church today. (1) Some were being **conceited;** they had an excessively favorable opinion of their own ability or importance. It could be that those who had not fallen prey to the Judaizers were acting this way, or those who had followed the Judaizers were acting conceited because they believed they were "more spiritual." In any case, conceit causes problems where it flourishes. (2) Paul did not

want them to **irritate one another;** they were causing annoyance and anger, the opposites of the virtues the Holy Spirit desired. Some people can't resist starting verbal fights in church. (3) Finally, they were **jealous of one another;** they wanted to have what others had earned or achieved, whether recognition, status, money, or even spirituality. This also could do nothing more than divide the believers and ruin the church's unity in Christ. Don't give in to envy.

Pride makes us perpetually vulnerable to temptation. When Satan can't stop our spiritual growth, his tactic immediately changes to using pride. As soon as we notice progress, we should expect pride to set in. This will especially be true if we measure our growth against the progress others are making. Growth should be cause not for pride but for humility and thanksgiving because it comes from God.

GALATIANS 6

WE REAP WHAT WE SOW / 6:1-10

The flow of thought from chapter 5 to chapter 6 reminds us that the original letter that Paul wrote had no breaks. In the last verses assigned to chapter 5, Paul had already begun to urge the Galatians to express the "fruit of the Spirit" in their relationships. In 5:25-26, Paul offered practical counsel for living "by the Spirit: keeping in step with the Spirit on the one hand while avoiding pride and envy on the other. In this section, Paul spelled out in practical terms what a "life in the Spirit" should look like.

6:1 Paul addressed the problem of individual sin by explaining corporate (group) responsibility. A Christian may sin alone, but because he or she participates in the body of Christ, his or her sin affects the whole. Our reaction to other Christians' sins ought not to be how we can rid the church of these sinners. Rather, we should help our brothers and sisters who are fellow members of the body of Christ.

The phrase, **if a Christian is overcome by some sin,** pictures a believer being trapped or caught by sin. No church, indeed no believer, is completely free of sin, for sinful human desires still exist in believers (as Paul explained in 5:16-18). We must not report every sin or point out each person's failings. While Paul didn't explain the word **sin,** he focused on the type of sin that entraps a person, refusing to let him or her go and causing damage to his or her faith.

The believers may have wondered how the church should deal with members who have fallen

into sin. Should the sin be overlooked in the name of love? Should the sin be exposed to everyone? If not, who needs to know, and what should they do about it? Paul did not recommend ignoring unrepented sin because, no matter how well hidden, sin will eventually cause problems in the church. Neither did Paul recommend a public humiliation of the sinner, for that would not achieve the objective of restoring the person to the fellowship. Paul recommended action, but he gave advice as to who should act and how the action should be taken.

First, action should be taken only by those **who are godly.** Who are these people? Paul was referring to men and women who walk in the Spirit in the sense that Paul had explained at the end of chapter 5. Only those mature in the faith (see also Hebrews 5:13-14) and mature enough to handle this situation properly should deal with it. In other words, the new, immature believers should not deal with the delicate subject of sin (and sinners) in the church. In addition, mature believers should discern when to confront sin (see Matthew 18:15-20). Every person's fault need not be dragged into the light for all to see, but persistent sin that destroys the person and hurts the fellowship must be resolved.

Next, Paul clarified what the spiritually mature should do for the one caught in sin: **gently and humbly help that person back onto the right path.** When leaders confront a person caught in sin, they should avoid humiliating, punishing, or using the person as a public example. Instead, the leaders' purpose should be to restore the person to the fellowship of believers (see 2 Timothy 2:24-26). Mature believers should help get the person on the right track, encourage repentance and accountability, offer assistance if needed, and warmly accept the repentant person back into the church. All church discipline aims at this goal.

The church has a duty to help erring believers, but each individual believer must take responsibility for dealing with sin and temptation. In situations such as the apostle was describing, those who restore a fallen one could face two temptations: (1) They might be tempted to have spiritual pride, or (2) they might **fall into the same temptation** faced by the one they are trying to correct.

6:2 As used in this verse, **troubles and problems** refer to the heavy or oppressive burdens that a believer cannot carry alone. It could be financial burdens; it could be burdens of temptation. We must help **share** the loads that others find too heavy to carry alone. However, we must not regard this load as a burden, but a joy. Like people hiking a trail, we not only shoulder our own backpacks, but we help out with other people's loads when the trail gets too steep, they get too tired, or their feet get blistered—whenever they need assistance.

To share one another's troubles also obeys **the law of Christ.** How so? As Paul had explained in 5:14, "For the whole law can be summed up in a this one command, 'Love your neighbor as yourself.'" Jesus told his disciples on the night before his crucifixion, "I am giving you a new commandment: Love each other" (John 13:34, see also John 15:12). The **law of Christ** is his "new commandment" summed up when we show love for others. In a sense Paul was saying, "If you insist on carrying burdens, don't carry the burden of the law; instead, in love, carry one another's burdens. Then you not only help one another out and build unity among yourselves, you also fulfill the law of Christ!"

6:3 However, some believers either would refuse to follow Paul's command to help share one another's troubles or would do so in order to be noticed and receive praise. Both motives come from conceit. Those people may have regarded themselves as **too important** to dirty themselves with others' problems and failings. Paul was anxious to warn the Galatians not to tolerate any form of spiritual superiority, no matter how cleverly disguised. Paul explained that these people's lack of love for others revealed both their worthlessness to the body of Christ and also their bankrupt spiritual state. This person may think he is important, but he is **really a nobody.** The true "somebodies" in the church produce the Holy Spirit's fruit in their lives, and these people won't even be concerned about their status. They will be busy helping others.

6:4-5 While some people may be conceited regarding their burden bearing, others may feel as though they can't "share troubles" as well as others. Some might be afraid of grief or pain; some others might get tongue-tied in trying to offer encouragement; others may be so shy as to be unable to approach needy people. Conversely, some may have experienced others who, under the pretense of helping, exploit the vulnerability of a person in trouble or violate a trust that was placed in them regarding very personal matters. Both our abilities and motives need healthy, ongoing examination.

Here Paul offered the solution. People should **do what they should,** and then they could **enjoy the personal satisfaction of having done** their **work well.** Each person is **responsible for** his or her **own conduct.** We should compare ourselves to God's standard, not **to anyone else.** Good pride is being able to say, "I have lived up to the potential God gave me." We will not be judged on the basis of how we have matched up to others, but on how we have met God's expectations for us. The danger of comparing ourselves with others is that we either come out ahead (a cause for false pride) or behind (leading to lowered self-esteem and the danger of not doing any more for others at all). Christians have different gifts and abilities, but God does not excuse us from sharing others' troubles. We are not responsible to do everything or to make the same contributions as others; we are responsible to accomplish what God has called us to do.

6:6 After describing how the Holy Spirit helps believers in their relationships with others, Paul explained how the Holy Spirit would affect their use of money. Paul's first admonition prescribed support of Christian **teachers** (the true teachers as opposed to the false teachers) in the Galatian churches. These teachers were serving full-time in preaching and teaching. The congregations (**those who are taught the word of God**) should voluntarily and generously provide for the teachers' needs.

This included financial support and sharing material items and services, as well as personal encouragement. While the radical giving and sharing of the early church in Jerusalem (recorded in Acts 2:44-45) was a model, all churches were not required to follow it. Instead, Paul recommended a spirit of giving among the believers in the churches that he had founded, especially regarding their care for those who were devoting their time to ministry.

6:7 This sentence, inserted within Paul's flow of thought regarding money, gives a general principle about the attitudes of kindness, giving, and sharing. While people can deceive one another, and even themselves, about their motives and attitudes for giving, they cannot deceive God. Paul said that these believers themselves must not **be misled.** People **can't ignore God and get away with it.** What they **sow, they will reap.** Sow means "spread, utilize, invest." Whatever we use as key values determines the course of our life. Jesus taught the importance of investing our time and utilizing our resources wisely for the Kingdom (Matthew 6:19-21).

While believers have received God's special blessings and promises, God does not change the positive and negative of the natural law that people will reap what they sow. From farming to finances, this saying holds true (Proverbs 22:8). A farmer plants corn and grows corn; he should not expect nor desire anything else. Believers must decide what crop they want and plant accordingly, for what they get back will be directly related to what they put in, as Paul explains in the next verse.

6:8 Believers who use their lives and **sow** their resources **to satisfy their own sinful desires** will earn a harvest of **decay and death.** Those who live like this will not inherit the Kingdom of God (5:21). When we sow to the flesh, we bring these seeds of destruction into our life. Believers who sow their resources and invest their lives **to please the Spirit** have a far different harvest. They will reap **everlasting life.**

How do we sow "to please the Spirit"? When we use our resources to grow spiritually and to support the Lord's work so that others can enter the Kingdom and grow spiritually, we are sowing to please the Spirit. Why? Because our harvest results in spiritual growth and souls reached for the Kingdom; thus, our harvest lasts forever. This kind of stewardship of our resources can only be done through the power of the Holy Spirit. When the Holy Spirit controls a believer's life, the results are amazing. As 5:22-23 pointed out, the fruit borne in a believer is life-changing. That change will affect the believer's handling of money, use of talent, and investment of time.

6:9 While good works will never earn salvation, Paul did encourage believers to persist in **doing what is good.** While we do good, we should not **get discouraged and give up.** To continue the analogy of sowing and reaping, a farmer will have no harvest to reap if he becomes too weary to labor in the fields or if he gives up altogether. The harvest will not reap itself. Every aspect of farming, planting, maintaining, and finally the harvesting takes hard work. So, too, believers must not become discouraged and give up when they follow the Holy Spirit's guidance, grow spiritually, and do good for God's Kingdom. While it may seem at times like a losing battle, we are assured that **we will reap a harvest of blessing at the appropriate time.**

What kind of harvest did the apostle have in mind? A Christian will reap a harvest of present blessings: the fruit of the Spirit, well-instructed believers, restored sinners, and mutual support. But ultimately he or she will reap the harvest of eternal life in the Holy Spirit (6:8). Though the **appropriate** time is the time of God's own choosing, Paul was most likely referring to the time of the fulfillment of God's promises at Christ's second coming (1 Timothy 6:15).

6:10 Every time **we have the opportunity** to do good, **we should** do it. The timing for doing good is always right. The opportunity is not optional. We are to treat it as strategically placed by God in our path. Our settings may continually change, but each one will bring a fresh opportunity for helping and serving.

God calls believers to **do good to everyone,** believers and nonbelievers alike. The fruit of the Holy Spirit must be shared with both the Christian and the non-Christian world. Some fields may be very difficult to "work," but our purpose should be to sow goodness anyway!

If Paul still had in mind our financial responsibility, we should be willing to help others financially whenever we are able. But we should focus particularly on the needs of **our Christian brothers and sisters.** The Christian family extends far beyond the walls of a particular church or the limits of a particular denomination to include all true believers.

When Paul told individual believers to "do good," he spoke to their responsibility in the community as well as in the church. The church is not meant to become merely a social agency, but individual believers can work together in meeting social needs, giving time and resources as God calls and enables them. Sowing seeds of kindness to those in need expresses Christ's love and prepares hearts to receive the gospel.

PAUL'S FINAL ADVICE / 6:11-18

We can hardly imagine how Paul felt as he dictated this letter. Perhaps he took up the parchment and reread his arguments and instructions. Some time may have passed since the original dictation. The letter was complete, but Paul decided to add some final thoughts, shaping the words in large and forceful movements of the pen and praying that this letter would be used by God to get his Galatian brothers and sisters to the truth.

He left the Galatians with a strong word-picture of the cross of Jesus Christ. The decision that faced his readers was not really between two competing voices of authority; rather, the choice was between denying the Cross or finding through it the only true way of life.

6:11 Up to this point, Paul had probably dictated the letter to a scribe. Then he took the pen and closed the letter in his **own handwriting.** Paul did this in other letters as well, to add emphasis to his words and to validate that the letter was genuine (see 1 Corinthians 16:21; Colossians 4:18; 2 Thessalonians 3:17). Paul pointed out his **large letters,** perhaps because the contrast in the original letter was obvious. Paul's scribe, if trained in writing, would have written in well-formed Greek characters. Paul, a preacher and not a scribe, had a less precise writing style. Another theory is that Paul wrote in large letters due to poor eyesight (see 4:13-15). Most likely, however, Paul wrote in large letters for emphasis, as these last verses reiterate the main points of this epistle. They were his signature.

6:12 As Paul concluded the key points of his letter, he referred again to the Judaizers, the false teachers who were causing all the trouble and confusion in Galatia. Those who were **trying to force** the Galatian believers **to be circumcised** were only doing it because they didn't **want to be persecuted for teaching that the cross of Christ alone can save.**

The Judaizers had brought legalistic issues to the surface, but their rejection of the death of Christ ran deeper. To accept that the Cross alone can save includes accepting certain beliefs: that people are sinners under God's curse, that a personal sacrifice was required, that only the death of Christ on the cross could secure people's salvation, and that people can do nothing to obtain that salvation but to accept Christ's sacrifice on their behalf. People don't want to be told they are sinners who can do nothing but accept someone else's help. Human nature would much prefer to earn salvation, if only to be able to have pride along with the accomplishment. To preach anything else would incur persecution, as Paul would learn over and over again.

6:13 In addition to attacking the Judaizers' motives to make a good impression and escape persecution, Paul attacked them because all they wanted to do was **brag about it and claim** the Galatians

as their disciples. In other words, they wanted to report the number of circumcisions back to their superiors. For the Judaizers to "sell" Judaism to the Christians meant selling them a worthless product. The Judaizers compelled the believers to be circumcised, as they had been, thereby bringing them under the law with them. Yet the Judaizers themselves did not and could not **really keep the whole law.** If the Jews themselves couldn't keep the law, how futile it was to compel new Christians to accept circumcision that would bind them to that same law. Worse yet, the Judaizers did this for the sake of pride—personal pride, religious pride, national pride—yet pride all the same. Not a very strong base for dealing with someone's eternal destiny!

6:14 To **boast** with puffed-up pride would be sinful arrogance. While the Judaizers sought to please people, escape persecution, and boast in statistics, Paul's boasting was never of anything **except the cross of our Lord Jesus Christ.** Paul could boast about the Cross because of what the Cross had accomplished in his life. For Paul, it was as though his **interest in this world** had **died** and vice versa. Paul had no need of the earthly and selfish motives and ambitions. His only boast was **the cross** (the only way of salvation) of **our** (that is, salvation belongs to every believer personally) **Lord Jesus Christ** (the only God, Savior, and Messiah).

6:15 Paul, a circumcised Jew, knew that his circumcision counted for nothing as a means to salvation. Neither was uncircumcision a detriment to salvation. Neither of these outward markings makes any difference to God regarding salvation. The cross of Christ made such distinctions valueless and put all people on equal ground. When Jews or Gentiles become believers, they are **changed into new and different people.** That is **what counts;** the only thing that matters is being born again. How do we know if we have been changed? By believing on the Lord Jesus Christ and what he accomplished on the cross, being born again by the power of the Holy Spirit, and living by his transforming power.

6:16 This sentence underlined Paul's entire argument. **This principle** refers to the gospel message Paul had defended throughout this letter—that we receive salvation by grace through faith alone. Paul might have said, "To those who believe this principle"; however, he chose the words **live by** to emphasize the Galatians' problem. They had initially believed, but they hadn't "followed" or "walked" or "grown" in that belief and thus had fallen prey to false teachers.

But to those who did follow (and he hoped this would include all the Galatian believers), Paul wished **mercy** and **peace.** "Peace" was a common greeting and benediction (see, for example, Psalms 125:5 and 128:6). At the beginning of this letter, Paul had greeted the Galatians with "grace and peace" (1:3). Here he chose "mercy and peace." These two characteristics would return in great force if the Galatians would follow through on their original commitment to Christ. The exit of the Judaizers and the renewed commitment to share each other's troubles would yield a harvest of mercy and peace. He saved "grace" for his final phrase in the letter (6:18). These believers **are the new people of God.** No longer are the promises focused on the Jews alone—instead, the people of God are those who have accepted Jesus Christ as their Savior.

6:17 Paul ended his letter with a request that this trouble stop. Paul had aptly argued against the Judaizers' teaching in this letter, ending the need for more to be said about them. He expected the Galatian Christians to return to the faith and stand up for themselves against the false teachers. He had provided the ammunition; they should use it.

The suffering he had endured for the faith should be enough to encourage these believers to remain steadfast against false teaching. Paul bore on his body **the scars** that showed that he belonged **to Jesus.** This referred, not to circumcision, but to the scars Paul received when he was persecuted for the sake of the gospel. Some of these he received while he was in Galatia (recorded in Acts 13–14; see also Philippians 3:10; Colossians 1:24).

6:18 Unlike many of Paul's other letters, Paul included no personal greetings or remarks as he concluded this letter. Perhaps he did not want to lighten the solemnity of the letter's contents, but wanted to close the letter in a way that would cause the Galatians to think of nothing but acting upon Paul's words. Instead, he closed as he had begun in 1:3, wishing **the grace of our Lord Jesus Christ** on these believers. Grace was exactly what Paul hoped would be the result of his entire urgent letter to them—that they would return to the gospel of salvation by God's grace alone.

EPHESIANS

INTRODUCTION

What builds a friendship? Certainly common values, ideals, and experiences help. But friendship also needs mutual appreciation and respect, vulnerability, and spending many hours together. And shared experiences bond people—especially experiences of suffering together and working together to reach a common goal.

Of all the churches planted and visited along Paul's missionary journeys, he enjoyed a very close relationship with the church at Ephesus. Paul first visited the city briefly on his way home to Jerusalem (A.D. 53), but he promised to return (Acts 18:19-21). He did, just one year later, on his third missionary journey. This time, Paul lived and ministered in the city for three years (Acts 20:31). During these stays in Ephesus, Paul developed close relationships with the believers there. Paul taught about the Holy Spirit (Acts 19:1-7), encountered opposition in the synagogue (Acts 19:8-9), and held an open forum in a lecture hall for seekers from all over the province of Asia (Acts 19:9-10). He healed the sick and cast out demons (Acts 19:11-12). Many confessed their sins and turned to Christ (Acts 19:13-20). Paul became a controversial figure, incurring the anger of many Greek businessmen and Jews. In fact, the silversmith Demetrius stirred up a riot against Paul and his traveling companions (Acts 19:23-41). Paul's enemies were as ferocious as wild beasts (1 Corinthians 15:32). No wonder Paul and the Ephesian believers were close.

As you read Ephesians, see this book as more than an important, theological document for an ancient church. It is the Holy Spirit-inspired letter to followers of Christ with whom Paul had lived and worked for three years. He was committed to them and to the churches in that area. This is a letter bathed in love.

How committed are you to those whom you have taught and led? What can you do to encourage them in their walk with Christ?

AUTHOR

Paul: apostle of Christ, courageous missionary, gifted teacher, articulate apologist, and Christian statesman.

Two major headings in this book (1:1 and 3:1) show that this epistle claims to have been written by Paul the apostle. This claim is confirmed by many church fathers, including Polycarp, Origen, Irenaeus, Clement of Alexandria, and Tertullian. Most scholars throughout the history of the church have affirmed the same. For more about Paul, see the Author section in the Introduction to the book of Romans.

Ephesus was a strategic city, ranking in importance with Alexandria in Egypt and Antioch of Syria as a port. It lay on the most western edge of Asia Minor (modern-day Turkey), the most important port on the Aegean Sea on the main route from Rome to the east.

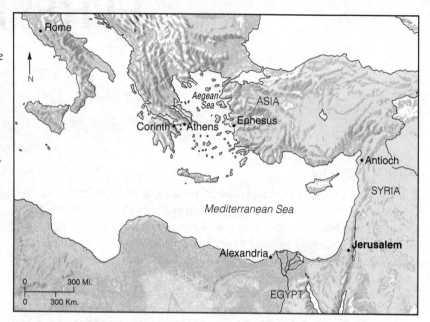

DATE AND SETTING

Written about A.D. 61, from Rome, during Paul's imprisonment there.

Paul had been a Christian for nearly thirty years by the time he wrote this letter. He had taken three missionary trips and had established churches all around the Mediterranean Sea. At the end of his third journey, he was arrested in Jerusalem for causing a riot with his preaching. Paul was committed to going to Rome (Acts 19:21), and God told him that he would go there and preach the gospel (Acts 23:11). So, upon his arrest, Paul appealed to Caesar and eventually did arrive in Rome, the capital of the empire (read the story in Acts 21:27–28:31). Paul probably hadn't planned on being in prison during his ministry there, but that didn't stop him from preaching and teaching.

In Rome, Paul was under house arrest—meaning that he was not really in a prison but probably under guard in a minimum security situation while awaiting trial. There was no threat of his trying to escape; Paul was right where he wanted to be. People from all over the empire made their way to Rome. Though a prisoner, Paul was free to have visitors and to write letters (see Acts 28:16ff.). Those who heard the gospel could take it, for Paul, to the ends of the earth (Acts 1:8). While under house arrest, Paul preached to Jews and Gentiles alike, witnessing to the whole Roman guard (Philippians 1:13) and helping Roman believers grow in their faith. He also wrote four letters that are commonly called his Prison Epistles: Ephesians, Colossians, Philippians, and Philemon. Timothy often visited Paul (Philippians 1:1; Colossians 1:1; Philemon 1), as did Tychicus (Ephesians 6:21), Epaphroditus (Philippians 4:18), and Mark (Colossians 4:10).

Tychicus and Onesimus were sent by Paul to Colosse. Tychicus carried the two epistles to the two churches respectively (Ephesians 6:22; Colossians 4:7)—Ephesians as an encyclical and Colossians as a specific letter. Onesimus carried a letter of recommendation from Paul to Philemon, his former master, residing at Colosse.

The date was probably about four years after Paul's parting with the Ephesian elders at Miletus (Acts 20), about A.D. 61. From 6:19-20 it is plain that although he was a prisoner, Paul had some degree of freedom in preaching. This agrees with Acts 28:23, 30-31. Paul's house arrest began in A.D. 60 or 61 and lasted two whole years (Acts 28:30) at least, and perhaps longer.

AUDIENCE

The churches in Ephesus and the surrounding area.

The city. Outside of Rome, Ephesus was the most important city that Paul visited. Located at the intersection of two ancient, major overland routes (the coastal road running north to Troas and the western route to Colosse, Laodicea, and beyond) at the western edge of Asia Minor (now Turkey), with easy access to the Aegean Sea, Ephesus had become a political, commercial, and religious center. It had been one of the main routes either by sea or by land from Rome to the east. Ephesus had a harbor on the Cayster River, which emptied into the Aegean Sea, so the city, at one time, was known as "the Landing Place," and the citizens were proud of its role as a port city and a gateway to Asia. By the first century, however, the harbor was nearly filled with silt, thus causing some economic decline.

A strong source of income for Ephesus was the great temple of Artemis (Diana), the fertility goddess. Four times larger than the Parthenon, this shrine, considered one of the seven wonders of the ancient world, was reverenced throughout Asia and the world (Acts 19:27). The temple stood outside the city walls and faced east. Built completely of marble, it was 324 feet long and 164 feet wide and took 220 years to erect. The image of the goddess stood, surrounded by curtains, in the center of the temple.

In addition to the temple, Ephesus had an immense amphitheater (see Acts 19:27-29) that could seat more than twenty-five thousand spectators. The city was positioned between two mountainous ridges. The eastern ridge formed the foundation for this theater, as it had been cut out of the mountainside. Nearby stood the stadium, or race course, where fights between wild animals or between men and animals were held. A great marble street, the main street of Ephesus, ran northwest from the theater to the harbor. The street was flanked on both sides by an elaborate colonnade.

The city's commercial life and prosperity came to depend on the many thousands of tourists and worshipers visiting the temple, theater, and stadium annually. No wonder the populace became alarmed, and then enraged, when told that Paul's teachings would undermine the worship of Artemis and thus endanger their livelihood and the city's economy (Acts 19:23-41).

The church. As was his custom, Paul began his ministry in Ephesus among Jews, in the synagogue (Acts 19:8). When the Jewish leaders refused to listen, Paul left and taught in a rented lecture hall (Acts 19:9-10). During the next two years, many Jews and Greeks came to hear the gospel and believed (Acts 19:11, 17). At the writing of this letter, the church consisted mostly of Gentiles (2:11-19; 3:1).

The church at Ephesus flourished and became a strong spiritual community. Apollos had taught there and had been instructed by Priscilla and Aquila (Acts 18:24-28). Paul left the Ephesian church under the care of competent elders (Acts 20:17), and later, he commissioned Timothy to minister there (1 Timothy 1:3).

Scholars believe that the apostle John wrote his letters and his Gospel from Ephesus (A.D. 85–90). After John's exile on Patmos, he returned to Ephesus for his final years (A.D. 100). Irenaeus (A.D. 120–202) wrote, "Afterwards, John, the disciple of the Lord, who also had leaned upon his breast, did himself publish a gospel during his residence at Ephesus in Asia."

In addition to having hosted these great spiritual leaders, the church in Ephesus is mentioned in the book of Revelation. God commends the believers, but also warns them" (Revelation 2:2-5). Certainly this was a remarkable church.

The recipients. Most likely, this letter was addressed to several churches in the district around Ephesus—namely, the Roman province of Asia (commonly known as Asia Minor). The letter was not really intended to be only for the church at Ephesus. Most modern scholars are convinced that it was an encyclical (circular letter) meant for many churches in Asia, including Ephesus. It is possible that this letter was the one mentioned by Paul in Colossians 4:15-16, wherein Paul encourages the church in Colosse to exchange letters with the church in Laodicea—exhorting the church in Colosse to read the letter from Laodicea. This doesn't mean that this epistle was written by the Laodiceans or that it was written from Laodicea, just that it was circulating among the churches in Asia Minor and would naturally come to Colosse after Laodicea. The two cities are just a few miles apart.

This situation helps us understand why Paul's message in this letter is both intimate and global. Intimate—because of his close association with the Ephesians. Global—because the truths he wanted to communicate were for all the churches. And this is why Ephesians has had such an appeal to all believers throughout the church age. Next to Paul's letter to the Romans, this is the one epistle that could also be called a treatise rather than an occasional letter. Ephesians presents the grand picture of God's eternal purpose for the Christian church.

OCCASION AND PURPOSE

To strengthen the believers in their Christian faith by explaining the nature and purpose of the church, the body of Christ.

Paul felt keenly responsible for the spiritual health of the churches that he had planted. His deep concern led him to revisit many of those churches on subsequent travels, and it certainly motivated him to write letters and to send other teachers and leaders after him. In Paul's parting words to the Ephesian elders, he urged them to be on guard for false teachers (Acts 20:28-31). Paul knew that young believers, like little lambs, would be easy prey for false teachers and egotistical preachers who could devastate the flock. So Paul wrote to strengthen and mature his Christian brothers and sisters in their faith by explaining the purpose and power of the church—helping them see the big picture—and by calling believers to sound doctrine and holy living.

The Epistle to the Ephesians can be considered Paul's treatise on the universal church, the body of Christ. Thus, unencumbered with local problems, his description soars high above any mundane affairs and takes us into heaven, where we are presented with a heavenly view of the church as it fits into God's eternal plan.

Paul wanted his readers to see God's eternal purpose for the church. With such a high calling and privilege, believers, as individuals and as a local group, should settle for nothing less. In addition, Paul claimed to have received a revelation about the church that had never before bee.. known—that the church would be comprised of both Jewish and Gentile believers, sharing equal status in the body as coheirs, comembers of the body, and joint partakers. He wrote about this revelation so that all the believers could understand the secret plan (see 3:1-9).

Today, many Christians take their faith and their church for granted. Thus, they become critical of fellow believers, the worship services, and church leaders, and often they become susceptible to wrong doctrines. As you read Ephesians, examine your attitudes in light of Paul's description of the church, the body of Christ. And consider how you might encourage and strengthen fellow believers and spiritual leaders.

MESSAGE
After a warm greeting (1:1-2), Paul affirms the nature of the church—the glorious fact that believers in Christ have been showered with God's kindness (1:3-8), chosen for greatness (1:9-12), marked with the Holy Spirit (1:13, 14), filled with the Spirit's power (1:15-23), freed from sin's curse and bondage (2:1-10), and brought near to God (2:11-18). As part of God's "house," we stand with the prophets, apostles, Jews, Gentiles, and Christ himself (2:19–3:13). Then, as though overcome with emotion by remembering all that God has done, Paul challenges the Ephesians to live close to Christ, and he breaks into spontaneous praise (3:14-21).

Paul then turns his attention to the implications of being in the body of Christ, the church. Believers should have unity in their commitment to Christ and their use of spiritual gifts (4:1-16). They should have the highest moral standards (4:17–6:9). For the individual, this means rejecting pagan practices (4:17–5:20), and for the family, this means mutual submission and love (5:21–6:9).

Paul then reminds them that the church is in a constant battle with the forces of darkness and that they should use every spiritual weapon at their disposal (6:10-17). He concludes by asking for their prayers, commissioning Tychicus, and giving a benediction (6:18-24).

The main themes in the book of Ephesians include: *God's Purpose, Christ the Center, the Living Church, the New Family,* and *Christian Conduct.*

God's Purpose (1:3-14, 18-23; 2:6-10). According to God's eternal and loving plan, he directs, carries out, and sustains our salvation. God chose believers before the world began (1:4-5). Everything happens according to God's eternal purpose (1:11). Using his Son as the model and prototype, God decided to make more sons just like his beloved Son. This decision emanated from a deep desire in the heart of God to have many children who would be like his beloved Son. In love, he predestined many people to participate in this "sonship"—not by their own merits but by virtue of being in the Son (1:4-5).

IMPORTANCE FOR TODAY. Knowing that we have been chosen before Creation to receive God's salvation and eternal life and to be his very own children should energize our gratitude and boost our self-esteem. Think of it—we have been chosen by God! Knowing of God's plan and work should not fill us with pride, however, for his choice of us was totally by grace. We had no credentials, characteristics, or good works that could earn his favor. Instead, the proper response is thanksgiving and humility. The reality of God's perfect plan should also motivate us to trust him in every area of life, with his purpose becoming our mission. How have you responded to God's sovereign plan? Have you committed yourself to fulfilling God's purpose?

Christ the Center (1:19-23; 2:19-22; 3:10-11, 20-21; 4:7-16). Christ is exalted as the central meaning of the universe and the focus of history (1:20-23). He is the head of the body, the church (2:19-22; 4:15-16). He is the Creator and Sustainer of all creation (1:22-23). Ephesians presents the church as God's masterpiece (2:10), his most splendid work of art. God did not create with clay or canvas and paint. No, everything was created in Christ. God's Son is the substance of this masterpiece. And everything in God's new creation was created **for Christ**—he is the recipient of God's masterpiece.

IMPORTANCE FOR TODAY. Because Christ is central to everything, he must be central in us—our highest value and the focus of our lives. In our high-tech, materialistic, relationship-driven, and sex-oriented society, many idols and values compete for our devotion. It becomes easy to be enticed and drawn away or to have our lives cluttered by trivial pursuits. But Christ must be at the center, receiving our total devotion and ordering our priorities. Keep your focus on him and place all your interests, relationships, desires, possessions, and goals under his control. What competes with Christ for your attention? What can you do to keep him at the center of your life?

The Living Church (1:2-23; 2:1-22; 4:4-6, 11-16). Ephesians includes a masterful and profound description of the church. The church, under Christ's control, is a living body, a family, a dwelling. And God gives believers, by his Holy Spirit, spiritual gifts—special abilities to build the church. The church is Christ's body to carry out the work he began on earth. He is the head of his body, directing it and motivating it to complete his ministry on earth (1:22-23). As such, the church is the continuation of Christ's incarnation—in the sense that Christ, through another human body, still lives and works on earth among human beings in a tangible, palpable way. But it takes all the members of the body working together in harmony to fulfill the designs and desires of the head (4:4-6, 15-16). This is why there are so many appeals in this epistle for unity and collective maturity. The body must match the head so that Christ can be fully expressed!

IMPORTANCE FOR TODAY. Paul's presentation of the church reached its pinnacle in this epistle. The church he pictured with words was the church in ideal perfection, the church as seen from heaven—but not yet manifested on earth in fullness. As part of Christ's body, we believers must live in vital union with him. Our conduct must be consistent with this living relationship. People in the world should be able to see Christ by looking at Christians, seeing their values, lifestyles, and loving acts of service.

What do people know about Jesus by watching how you relate to other Christians? In what ways can you use your God-given abilities to equip believers for service? Fulfill your role in the living church.

The New Family (1:5; 2:11-19; 3:1-6; 4:1-6; 5:21-33). Because God through Christ paid the penalty for our sin and forgave us, we have been reconciled—brought near to him. We are a new society, a new family. Being united with Christ means that we are to treat one another as family members. God's many sons and daughters compose his divine family (3:14-15). They are his inheritance and his glory (1:11, in the Greek; 2:19), for he has invested everything into them. He gave them his Son and created them anew in his Son. In the final days, when the time comes for God to display his glory to the whole universe (both visible and invisible), he will make a grand spectacle of all his children who, through transformation, will bear the image of Jesus Christ. God will be glorified, not just through Jesus Christ, but also through the church (3:10). His family is also his household and dwelling place. Those among whom he lives are also those in whom he lives (2:20-22).

IMPORTANCE FOR TODAY. As a believer in Christ, you have a place where you are accepted and welcomed, where you belong—the church. You also have the responsibility to accept and welcome other believers, regardless of race, sex, occupation, nationality, ability, physical characteristics, social status, or personality type. And if you have a conflict with another believer, you should resolve the conflict as quickly as possible, maintaining unity and harmony. How well do you relate to the other members of your Christian family? What can you do to help unify your church?

Christian Conduct (2:1-10; 3:14-19; 4:1-3, 17-32; 5:1-33; 6:1-18). Ephesians encourages all Christians to wise, dynamic Christian living, for with privileges goes family responsibility. As a new community, we are to live by Christ's new standards. God provides his Holy Spirit to enable us to live his way. The Holy Spirit, as the third person in the Trinity, is often described as God in action. When God moves and acts, he does so in and through the Spirit. Believers are called upon to live in the Spirit, to worship in the Spirit, to please the Spirit, and to maintain unity by the Spirit (4:3, 30; 5:9, 18-19). The church should display the full activity of the life-giving Spirit, or it is nothing more than a dead corpse.

IMPORTANCE FOR TODAY. Christians are under attack today as at no other time in history. Satan is working within the church to cause conflict and to divide, and he is moving against individuals, especially spiritual leaders, to prompt them to engage in self-centered sin. So we need all of our spiritual armor to win our spiritual battles. In addition to the armor, God gives us power through his Spirit. To utilize the Spirit's power, we must lay aside our evil desires and draw upon the power of his new life. Are you ready for the battle? Do you know how to dress in your spiritual armor? Have you submitted your will to Christ?

OUTLINE OF EPHESIANS

I. Unity in Christ (1:1–3:21)
II. Unity in the Body of Christ (4:1–6:24)

EPHESIANS 1

GREETINGS FROM PAUL / 1:1-2

Paul wrote to the believers in Ephesus and the surrounding churches to give them in-depth teaching about how to nurture and maintain the unity of the church. He wanted to put this important information in written form because he was in prison for preaching the gospel and could not visit the churches himself. Paul apparently received reports that the Ephesian church held up well against false teachers. However, perhaps the love, care, and unity Paul had called for were lacking. Thus, this letter speaks much of love and unity and the out-workings of these in relationships in the home and in the church. Paul knew that such teaching was needed not only in Ephesus but in every church—again pointing to the probable circular nature of this letter. Indeed Paul's words applied in Ephesus and in all the Asian churches—and they apply to our churches today.

1:1 Paul was a Jew from the tribe of Benjamin. He was raised as a strict Pharisee (Philippians 3:5), grew up in Tarsus, and was educated under a well-known teacher, Gamaliel (Acts 22:3). However, he was also a Roman citizen, a fact that he used to great advantage at times (Acts 22:27-29). Out of this diverse background, God formed and called a valuable servant, using every aspect of Paul's upbringing to further the gospel. He was not one of the original twelve disciples (later called apostles), but the risen Christ Jesus confronted him on the road to Damascus and called him **to be an apostle** (Acts 9:3-19). The apostles' mission was to be God's representatives: They were envoys, messengers, delegates, directly under the authority of **Christ Jesus.** They had authority to set up and supervise churches and to discipline them if necessary, which Paul did on all three of his missionary journeys and after his release from this first imprisonment in Rome. God chose Paul for special work, saying that Paul would be his "chosen instrument to take my message to the Gentiles and to kings, as well as to the people of Israel" (Acts 9:15). Paul did not seek this apostleship; instead, **God** had **chosen** him.

Paul wrote this letter to the Ephesian believ-ers—**God's holy people in Ephesus,** the **faith-ful followers of Christ Jesus.** The words "in Ephesus" are not present in the three earliest manuscripts. Therefore, this was very likely a circular letter, meaning the name of each local church would be filled in as the letter circulated from church to church. Ephesus, the leading church in the region of Asia Minor, was probably the first destination for this epistle. Paul men-tioned no particular problems or local situations, and he offered no personal greetings as he might have done if this letter were intended for the Ephesian church alone. (For more about Ephesus, see the Audience section in the Intro-duction.)

Clearly, Paul had a deep love for the church in Ephesus. His last words to the Ephesian elders focused on two items: (1) warning them about false teachers (Acts 20:29-31), and (2) exhorting them to show love and care toward one another (Acts 20:35).

1:2 Grace means God's undeserved favor. It is through God's kindness alone that anyone can become acceptable to God. **Peace** refers to the peace that Christ established between believers and God through his death on the cross. True peace is available only in Christ (John 14:27).

Paul used "grace and peace" as a standard greeting in all of his letters. He wanted his readers to experience God's grace and peace in their daily living. Only **God our Father and Jesus Christ our Lord** can grant such wonderful gifts. By mentioning Jesus Christ along with God, Paul was pointing to Jesus as a full person of the Godhead. He recognized Jesus' deity and lordship over all of creation. Both God the Father and Jesus Christ the Lord are coequal in provid-ing the resources of grace and peace.

SPIRITUAL BLESSINGS / 1:3-14

Here begins a lengthy passage that praises God for what he has done for us in Jesus Christ. Paul, writing in Greek, wrote one long sentence from 1:3 to 1:14 (which is not reflected in English). It forms the longest sentence ever found in ancient Greek. In this sentence, Paul introduced most of the themes he develops in this epistle. This complex sentence is very difficult to analyze. Paul heaped praise upon praise, one thought leading into another, which then would remind him of another. This section forms a blessing, in Hebrew called a *berakah*, frequently used in Jewish liturgy. It is a eulogy for God and for all the blessings he gives his people.

1:3 Paul first praised God, saying that all believers **praise God.** God alone is worthy of praise and worship. He is **the Father of our Lord Jesus Christ.** Because believers **belong to Christ,** God **has blessed us.** The verb "blessed" occurs hundreds of times in the Old Testament, revealing that God enjoys blessing his people. Here Paul used the past tense ("has blessed"), indicating that this prospering of believers had already occurred— even from eternity past. God has blessed us by allowing us to receive the benefits of Christ's redemption (1:7) and resurrection (1:19-20). God blessed us through Christ's death on the cross on our behalf.

Because by faith **we belong to Christ,** we have **every spiritual blessing**—that is, every benefit of knowing God and everything we need to grow spiritually. These are spiritual blessings, not material ones. Because God has already blessed believers, we need not ask for these blessings but simply accept them and apply them to our lives. Because we have an intimate relationship with Christ, we can enjoy these blessings now and will enjoy them for eternity.

The phrase **heavenly realms** occurs five times in this letter (1:3, 20; 2:6; 3:10; 6:12) and refers to the sphere beyond the material world—the place of spiritual activity where the ultimate conflict between good and evil takes place. This conflict continues but has already been won by Christ's death and resurrection. This is the realm in which the spiritual blessings were secured for us and then given to us. Our blessings come from heaven, where Christ now lives (1:20), and Christ's gift of the Holy Spirit, the source of all spiritual blessings, came as a result of his ascension to heaven (4:8). Paul was making the point that these blessings are spiritual and not material; thus, they are eternal and not temporal.

1:4 That God **chose us** forms the basis of the doctrine of election—defined as God's choice of an individual or group for a specific purpose or destiny. The doctrine of election teaches that we are saved only because of God's grace and mercy; as believers we are not saved by our own merit. It focuses on God's purpose or will (1:5, 9, 11), not on ours. God does not save us because we deserve it but because he graciously and freely gives salvation. We did not influence God's decision to save us; he saved us according to his plan. Thus, we may not take credit for our salvation or take pride in our wise choice.

The doctrine of election runs through the Bible, beginning with God's choosing Abraham's descendants as his special people. Although the Jews were chosen as special recipients and emissaries of God's grace, their opportunity to participate in that plan arrived with the coming of Christ, their promised Messiah. But many didn't recognize Christ and so rejected him. God's "chosen" and elected people are now Christians, the body of Christ, the church—all who believe on, accept, and receive Jesus Christ as Messiah, Savior, and Lord. Jesus himself called his followers "the chosen ones" (see Matthew 24:22, 24, 31; Mark 13:20, 22, 27).

God chose his people **before he made the world.** The mystery of salvation originated in the timeless mind of God (2 Thessalonians 2:13; 2 Timothy 1:9). Before God created anything, his plan was in place to give eternal salvation to those who would believe on his Son. Before God created people, he knew sin would occur, he knew a penalty would have to be paid, and he knew that he himself (in his Son) would pay it.

Election is **in Christ** because of his sacrifice on our behalf. We have blessings and election only because of what Christ has done for us. Election is done for a specific purpose—that we would **be holy and without fault in his eyes.** What God began in eternity past will be completed in eternity future. God's purpose in choosing us was that we would live changed lives during our remaining time on earth. To be "holy" means to be set apart for God in order to reflect his nature. God chose us, and when we belong to him through Jesus Christ, God looks at us as though we had never sinned. Our appropriate responses are love, worship, and service—in thankfulness for his wonderful grace. We must never take our privileged status as a license for sin.

1:5 In his infinite love, God chose **to adopt us** as his own children. People were created to have fellowship with God (Genesis 1:26), but because of their sin, they forfeited that fellowship. Through Jesus' sacrifice, God brought us back into his family and made us heirs along with Jesus (Romans 8:17). God did not do this as an emergency measure after sin engulfed creation; instead, this has been his **unchanging plan** from the beginning. Under Roman law, adopted children had the same rights and privileges as biological children. Even if they had been slaves, adopted children became full heirs in their new family. Paul used this term to show the strength and permanence of believers' relationship to God. This adoption occurs **through Jesus Christ,** for only his sacrifice on our behalf enables us to receive what God intended for us.

1:6 God's goal in the election of believers was that they would **praise** him. Therefore, the ultimate purpose of believers' lives is to praise God because of his **wonderful kindness.** Without it, we would have no hope, and our lives would be nothing more than a few years on earth. Instead, we have purpose for living and hope of eternal life. His kindness was **poured out on us.** It was a free gift, not something we could earn or deserve. God's favor to us is realized by our union with **his dearly loved Son.** We could say that God's love for his only Son motivated him to have many more sons—each of whom would be like his Son (Romans 8:28-30) by being in his Son and by being conformed to his image.

1:7 All people are enslaved to sin, but God, so **rich in kindness, purchased our freedom through the blood of his Son.** Jesus paid the price to redeem us, to buy our freedom from sin. The purchase price was his blood. To speak of Jesus' blood was an important first-century way of speaking of Christ's death. Our freedom was costly—Jesus paid the price with his life. Through his death, Jesus released us from slavery and **our sins are forgiven.** When we believe, an exchange takes place. We give Christ our sins, and he gives us freedom and forgiveness. Our sin was poured into Christ at his crucifixion. His righteousness was poured into us at our conversion. God's forgiveness means that he no longer even remembers believers' past sins. We are completely forgiven. Jesus became the final and ultimate sacrifice for sin. Instead of an unblemished lamb slain on the altar, the perfect Lamb of God was slain on the cross, a sinless sacrifice so that our sins could be forgiven once and for all.

1:8 God's **kindness** is **showered** on believers. When God gives, he gives abundantly and extravagantly. In the phrase **with all wisdom and under-** standing, the word "wisdom" is the ability to see life from God's perspective. Proverbs 9:10 teaches that the fear (respect and honor) of the Lord is the beginning of wisdom. The word "understanding" could also be translated "insight," referring to the ability to discern the right action to take in any given situation. Wisdom and understanding are given to believers for them to know God's will.

1:9 Paul had been praising God's wonderful kindness in 1:7-8. Thoughts of kindness led Paul to praise God for the entire plan of salvation. God had purposed to offer salvation to humanity "before he made the world" (1:4). How this would happen had not **been revealed** (made clear, understood) until the death and resurrection of Jesus Christ.

What God "revealed" was his plan to bring people (both Jews and Gentiles) back into fellowship with himself through their faith in Christ and then to keep them with him for all eternity. Paul called this **the secret plan** which was **centered on Christ.** The word "secret" has two meanings in Hellenistic Greek. One meaning referred to something known to only a select few. The word described heathen religions or "mystery religions" with their secret rites and practices. As used in the Septuagint (a Greek version of the Jewish Old Testament writings), a second meaning of the word describes what God reveals (as in Daniel 2:19). The Jews used the word to describe some secret plan that God would reveal at the end of the age. In the New Testament, the word refers to a truth formerly hidden but now made known to people—in this case, **to us,** meaning all believers. As with our being chosen (1:4), so the revelation of the secret plan of salvation is **according to** God's **good pleasure.**

1:10 The Greek word *oikonomia* (translated **bring everything together)** refers to the management of a household or estate. In this context, it refers to large-scale management, as in administration or economy. In God's timing, God brings everything together **under the authority of Christ.** With his first coming, Christ completed part of this mystery, but there are promises yet to be fulfilled. The mystery of salvation does not end with a person's acceptance of Jesus Christ—God promises a glorious future in a glorious Kingdom (see Revelation 21–22). This time is unknown to everyone but God.

God is planning a universal reconciliation—all of creation will be reinstated to its rightful owner and creator. Just as Christ administered God's plan of redemption by carrying it out as a human on this earth, so he will ultimately be in charge of **everything in heaven and on earth.** All of creation (spiritual and material) will be brought back under one head.

Sin holds people in bondage. That fact is clearly established throughout Paul's letters. Sin has also caused all creation to fall from the perfect state in which God created it. The world physically decays and experiences conflict so that it cannot fulfill its intended purpose. One day God will liberate and transform all creation. Until then, it waits in eager expectation for **the right time.** Christ provided the means for this restoration. When the time arrives, all of creation (meaning every created thing and being) will be as God created it to be—perfect, eternal, and fulfilling its intended function to praise God.

This verse does not teach that God will eventually save everyone, although many would like to believe this. The doctrine of Universalism, as this belief is called, seems to make God a little easier to understand and a little less harsh on sinners. In the end, every knee will bow, but for some, it will be too late. Christ will bring those elected and saved, and all creation with them, to be united under him in this glorious Kingdom. Those who have refused to believe (whether Jews or Gentiles) will face the consequences of their unbelief (Matthew 25:31-46).

1:11 Up until this verse, Paul was speaking to Jews and Gentiles alike. In 2:11, Paul made a distinction between the backgrounds of the Jewish believers and Gentile believers. In verses 11-14, however, he identified the two separate groups with the pronouns he used. The wording in these verses includes both the first person (we, our) and the second person (you). The word "we" refers specifically to Jewish believers (Paul being one of them). While it is true that believing Jews and Gentiles alike will receive God's blessings, the Jews were called first (Romans 1:16); they were chosen. Christ will be the Head of all things (1:10), including a body of believers made up of Jews ("we") and Gentiles ("you," 1:13).

The Jews were chosen **from the beginning** and had **received an inheritance from God** that would ultimately be accomplished in Jesus Christ (born into the nation of Israel) and finalized at the end of time. God chose the Jews to be the people through whom the rest of the world could find salvation. But this did not mean that the entire Jewish nation would be saved; only those who receive Jesus Christ as their Messiah and Savior will receive God's blessings (see Romans 9–11). When God offered salvation to the Gentiles, he did not exclude the Jews. God's Kingdom will include all Jews and Gentiles who have accepted the offer of salvation. Both Jews and Gentiles will also make up the group that does not believe and so receives

God's punishment. The inclusion of Jewish believers in salvation was the plan of God, for **all things happen just as he decided long ago.** In the same way that God planned for Israel to be the elect nation, he planned for the spiritual Israelites, the believers in Christ, to be an eternal gift to himself. As a refrain carried through from 1:5 and 1:9, Paul repeated that everything is under God's sovereign control. The words reinforce the certainty of these events. Because God controls everything, he will carry out his plan according to his purpose and will, bringing it to completion in his time.

1:12 The word **we** refers to Jewish believers—those who recognized their promised Messiah. The Jews **were the first to trust in Christ.** This could mean that ages before the arrival of Christ, the Jews had set their hope on their coming Messiah (see Acts 28:20), or it could mean that the Jews were the first to believe in Christ because the gospel was preached first to them (see, for example, John 1:11; 8:30; Acts 1:8; 3:26; 13:45-46).

1:13 Because the word "we" in 1:12 most likely refers to Jews, the words **you also** refer to Gentile believers who were **identified as** Christ's **own** along with the Jewish believers. The believers, both Jews and Gentiles, **heard the truth** (see also Colossians 1:5; 2 Timothy 2:15; James 1:18), also called **the Good News.** These people **believed** and were given **the Holy Spirit.** God marks his people as his own through the presence of the Holy Spirit in their lives. The Holy Spirit fills us with a sense of God's love (Romans 5:5), assures us that God has adopted us as his children (Romans 8:15-16), and helps us to manifest our Christlikeness. The Spirit is a once-and-for-all identification that gives us continued assurance that we are God's children, entitled to his riches and goodness, now as well as in eternity.

The Holy Spirit had been **promised** in the Old Testament (Isaiah 32:15; 44:3; Joel 2:28;) and was promised by Jesus to his disciples (John 14:16-17, 25-26; 15:26; 16:7-15; Acts 1:4-5; 2:38-39). After Christ returned to heaven, he would be spiritually present everywhere through the Holy Spirit. The Holy Spirit came so that God would be within his followers after Christ returned to heaven. At Pentecost (Acts 2) the Holy Spirit came upon all who believed in Jesus. Believers received the Holy Spirit when they received Jesus Christ. The transformation that the Holy Spirit makes in a believer's life (as described in Galatians 5:22-23) undeniably marks God's presence in and ownership of that life.

1:14 The word **guarantee** was used in ancient times to describe a down payment, promising that the buyer would complete the transaction and pay the full amount. The guarantee was binding. In the same way, the Holy **Spirit is God's guarantee that he will give us everything he promised.** He is the first payment of all the treasures that will be ours because he has **purchased us to be his own people.** The presence of the Holy Spirit in us demonstrates the genuineness of our faith, proves that we are God's children, and secures eternal life for

us. His power works in us to transform us now, and what we experience now is a taste of the total change we will experience in eternity.

As a final ringing note echoing 1:6 (praising God) and 1:12 (praising Jesus Christ), Paul declared that the Holy Spirit's presence in believers is **one more reason for us to praise our glorious God.**

PAUL'S PRAYER FOR SPIRITUAL WISDOM / 1:15-23

As verses 3-14 are one long sentence in the Greek, so are verses 15-23. As verses 3-14 are an extended eulogy, verses 15-23 are an extended thanksgiving. Verses 15-16 are the thanksgiving proper; verses 17-19 are an intercessory prayer; verses 20-23 are a confession of praise for God's power.

1:15-17 After describing the glorious blessings given to believers (1:3-14), thoughts of the great promises of God led Paul to give praise and to pray for the church—the people chosen to receive those blessings. The phrase **ever since I first heard of your strong faith in the Lord Jesus** could mean that Paul had heard a good report of the Ephesians' growth in the faith. It could also be a way of including the believers in the surrounding churches. Paul knew the Ephesian church well but not all the surrounding churches. Yet he may have heard a positive report of all the churches in the area, and thus he could thank God for their faith and remember them in his prayers.

Paul **never stopped thanking God for** these believers. That Paul prayed for them **constantly** demonstrates personal attention. Paul was truly a prayer warrior—remembering the churches in his personal prayers: for example, the Romans (Romans 1:9), the Philippians (Philippians 1:3-4), the Colossians (Colossians 1:3-4), and the Thessalonians (1 Thessalonians 1:2-3). Paul kept asking on behalf of these believers that God would give them **spiritual wisdom and understanding.** The Holy Spirit gives "wisdom" (see also 1:8)— the ability to see life from God's perspective, to have discernment. He also gives "understanding," which refers to enlightened understanding in their **knowledge of God** and the mysteries of divine truth. (See 1 Corinthians 2:14, 16 and Colossians 1:9.)

1:18 For the Jew, the heart was the core of personality, the total inner person, the center of thought and moral judgment. The imagery of **hearts flooded with light** pictures an ability to see the reality of our **wonderful future.** Believers look forward to a **glorious inheritance** (Colossians 1:5) as well as blessings in this present world (1:19;

Colossians 1:27) because of an action by God in the past (**those he called**).

1:19-21 Paul prayed that the believers would **begin to understand the incredible greatness of** God's **power** on behalf of those **who believe him.** Because of his power, believers know that:

- God is on their side, ready to help them meet each and every obstacle
- God's power is never stagnant or out of commission—it is always actively working on their behalf
- God is always fighting against the forces of evil on believers' behalf
- no human strength or spiritual power from the evil world (not even Satan himself) can deter or change God's inherent power.

Only God's power can change weak human beings into strong believers who are willing to sacrifice everything for the God who loves them. After impressively describing the completeness of God's power, Paul pointed out three instances of God's power: (1) he **raised Christ from the dead,** (2) he **seated** Christ **in the place of honor** in the **heavenly realms,** and (3) he **is far above any ruler or authority.** Christ has no equal and no rival. He is supreme over all other beings. These words ought to encourage believers, because the higher the honor of Christ, the Head, the higher the honor of his people.

1:22-23 Paul probably had a psalm in mind as he wrote these words. This alludes to Psalm 8:6, a kingly messianic psalm describing sovereign power and enthronement. Christ is the obvious application for the verse. Just as the psalm writer described people as having dominion on earth, so Paul described Christ as having **authority** over all of creation—**all things** (1 Corinthians 15:20-28). **The church** receives the **benefit** of his universal headship because **the church is his body.** Paul used the analogy elsewhere when he wrote about the interrelationships of believers in the church (Romans 12:4-5; 1 Corinthians 12:22-27; Colossians 1:18-19). This passage focuses on Christ as the head of that body, the church (see also 4:4, 12, 16; 5:30). The church is not a building (or all the church buildings on earth)—it includes all believers in a living, growing, moving, working organism deriving existence and power from Christ. The church obeys Christ's commands to carry out his work in the world.

All believers, as part of Christ's body, are **filled by Christ who fills everything everywhere with his presence.** Christ fills all things with himself and with his blessings, bringing all believers to the state of obedience and praise for which God created them (as in 1:10; 4:10, 13, 16). The church is being filled with and by Christ, who fills all things totally. Thus, Christ, who is the fullness of God (Colossians 1:19), finds full expression in the church.

By Christ's resurrection and exaltation, he is head over all things for the church. Christ fills the church and then uses the gifts he bestows to fulfill his mission—revealing himself to the world and drawing people to himself by that witness. The image of the body shows the church's unity. Each member is involved with all the others as they go about doing Christ's work on earth. We should not attempt to work, serve, or worship on our own. We need the entire body.

EPHESIANS 2

MADE ALIVE WITH CHRIST / 2:1-10

The style of using lengthy sentences continues from chapter 1 into this chapter, in which verses 1-7 are one sentence in the Greek. To help understand the first seven verses, note that the subject of that Greek sentence is "God" (2:4) and that there are three main verbs: (1) "gave us life" (2:5), (2) "raised us from the dead" (2:6), and (3) "seated with" (2:6). The object of each of these verbs is "us," referring to believers. God has made us alive, raised us up, and seated us with Christ.

2:1 This verse is a continuation of 1:19-23, which speaks of the resurrection power imparted to Christ's body, the church. These believers **once were dead** and **doomed** before they met Christ. This refers not only to eventual physical death or to the sinners' ultimate eternal state; it also refers to a very real "death" in this life. People who are spiritually dead have no communication with God. These people are physically alive, but their **sins** have rendered them spiritually unresponsive, alienated from God, and thus incapable of experiencing the full life that God could give them.

2:2-3 Sin reveals spiritual death but is acted out by people who are physically alive. Before the believers came to Christ, they **used to live** in their sins. They could not and did not follow God. Paul described three marks of unbelievers:

1. They lived **like the rest of the world,** referring to the world's accepted, but immoral, lifestyles and godless motives. People who live like the world that is **full of sin** cannot also follow Jesus (Romans 12:2; Galatians 1:4).

2. They **obeyed Satan.** The passage focuses on Satan's reality as an evil power with a certain amount of control in the world. The Bible pictures Satan as ruling an evil spiritual kingdom—the demons and those who are against Christ. He is the **mighty prince of the power of the air** referring to the space around the earth, and thus, this is Satan's sphere of influence. Though Satan's influence is great among unbelievers, his power is limited because he is a defeated enemy. He cannot separate believers from the love of God. Satan is also called **the spirit at work in the hearts of those who refuse to obey God.** People who have not surrendered to God or decided to obey are energized by the power of evil. The force of the evil spirit is seen in those who actively disobey God both in faith and action (2 Thessalonians 1:8). These people live in constant rebellion and opposition to God.

3. They followed **the passions and desires of their evil nature. All of us** (Jews and Gentiles alike) were at one time separated from God because of disobedience, **born with an evil nature.** That nature puts us **under God's anger.** When we become believers, our sinful nature still exists. But when we submit our lives to the Holy Spirit, he transforms us and our sinful natures. This is a supernatural process. We must never underestimate the power of our sinful nature, and we must never attempt to subdue it in our own strength. God provides for victory over sin—he sends the Holy Spirit to live in us and give us power. But our ability to restrain the desires of the sinful nature depends on how much we're willing to depend on God and his mercy (2:4-5).

2:4-5 The first three verses of this chapter present a hopeless humanity—trapped in sin, under Satan's power, unable to save itself. Then follow the small but glorious words **but God.** Behind those two words lies a cosmic plan so huge in scope and so vast in love that the human mind cannot fully comprehend it—all we can do is humbly receive it. Instead of leaving sinful humanity to live worthless and hopeless lives ending only in death, God acted on behalf of humanity because he **is so rich in mercy.** As God is rich in kindness (1:7), so he is rich in mercy. The word "rich" indicates the bountiful nature of God's mercy—beyond our comprehension, an inexhaustible storehouse. What is "mercy"? It is an attribute of God, sometimes called "loving-kindness" or "compassion." This word describes the outworking of God's love toward people and is shown in his lovingkindness toward them even though they do not deserve it (Psalm 51:1; Jeremiah 9:24; Hosea 2:19; Jonah 4:2).

God also acted on behalf of humanity because **he loved us so very much.** The Greek word for love, *agape,* is used. It means the selfless love that seeks the best for others. While God could have simply destroyed all people because of their sin, he chose instead to show mercy and love. While we once were **dead because of our sins** (2:1), God **gave us life when he raised Christ from the dead.** That we have been given life means that we are "saved" (this phrase is repeated in 2:8 and elaborated on there). When Christ rose from the dead, so did all the members of his body by virtue of God's uniting them with Christ. The only way spiritually dead people can have a relationship with God is to be made alive. And God is the only person who can accomplish that, which he did through his Son, Jesus Christ. Christ defeated sin and death through his death and resurrection, thus offering spiritual life to those dead in sins.

The verb form **have been saved** refers to a past event (accomplished by Christ because of **God's special favor**) with present and ongoing results. Believers have already passed from death to life. Salvation is not something to be waited for but something that has already been delivered.

2:6 In addition to being given life (2:5), believers are also **raised from the dead.** Christ was raised from death and left the tomb—an act accomplished by God's power alone. Believers have also been "raised." In addition to assurance of physical resurrection and glorification at the end of the age, believers participate in a new "resurrection" life from the moment they believe (see Colossians 2:12).

Finally, believers are **seated with him in the heavenly realms.** Christ has taken his seat at the right hand of the Father, indicating his finished work and his victory over sin. Christ has been exalted by God's great power (1:20). Christians have tended to see this seating with Christ as a future event, based on Jesus' words in Matthew 19:28 and Luke 22:30 as well as other verses that point to our future reign with Christ (such as 2 Timothy 2:12; Revelation 20:4; 22:5). Yet Ephesians teaches that we are seated with Christ *now.* We share with Christ in his victory *now.* This view of our present status should help us face our work and trials with greater hope! Believers, as heirs of the Kingdom along with Christ, are spiritually exalted from the moment of salvation. We have a new citizenship—in heaven, no longer just on earth: The power that raised and exalted Christ also raised and exalted his people because **we are one with** him. That same power works daily in believers, helping us live and work for God during our time in the world.

2:7 Here is the final and definitive reason for God's action on behalf of humanity, his reason for making us alive, raising us, and seating us along with his Son in the heavenly realms. God wants quite simply to **point to us as examples of the incredible wealth of his favor and kindness.** The Greek word for "point to" comes from legal terminology. God closes the case by presenting the astounding evidence of his church, his people. The church could only exist by God's love; the fact of its existence, the fact that people have been offered salvation, reveals the abundance of God's favor and kindness (see also 1:7; 2:4). Again, this was accomplished only **through Christ Jesus.** Without Christ's sacrifice, there would be no hope for a relationship with God.

2:8 Our salvation comes from God's **special favor** alone. It was appropriated **when** people **believed.**

However, lest anyone should think that belief is a necessary work that must be performed in order to receive salvation, Paul added that people **can't take credit for** believing, for it too **is a gift from God.** Paul is firm that absolutely nothing is of our own doing—not salvation, not grace, not even the faith exercised to receive salvation. Instead, everything is the gift of God. Salvation does not come from our self-reliance or individualism but from God's initiative. It is a gift to be thankfully accepted (see Romans 3:24-28; 1 Corinthians 1:29-31; Galatians 2:16).

2:9 We can't take credit for our **salvation** (2:8), and it is **not a reward for the good things we have done.** In other words, people can do nothing to earn salvation, and a person's faith itself also is not to be considered a "work" or grounds that anyone should **boast.**

People find it difficult to accept something so free, so willingly given, so available to anyone. We want to feel as though we did something, that we somehow earned our salvation by our merit. That was how the Judaizers (false teachers who said Christians had to obey all the Jewish laws) regarded their laws and why they tried to impose them on the Gentiles—there had to be a certain amount of law keeping and goodness on people's part in order for them to receive salvation. But Paul's words are unmistakable—if salvation is by God's grace and is accepted through faith, then it is "not a reward." If salvation could be earned by good works, then people would, by nature, "boast" about their good works, compare the goodness of their works to others' good works, and do good only to boast about it. Then, what would be "good enough" for salvation? But no one could ever be good enough to please a holy God. He casts aside all human effort and pride by offering salvation for free to all people by simple acceptance. People are given salvation on the grounds of God's grace alone.

2:10 But wait, there's more. **We are God's masterpiece.** Salvation is something only God can do—it is his powerful, creative work in us. People are re-created into new people, and those new people form a new creation—the church.

The verb **created** is used only of God—for only God can truly create. As he created the universe from nothing, so he creates new, alive, spiritual beings from the old, dead, sinful creatures we were (2 Corinthians 5:17). Then God forms believers into a unified body, his church (see 2:15; 4:24; Colossians 3:10). **In Christ Jesus** emphasizes the source of this creation, as in 2:6-7—Christ has provided it.

People become Christians through God's undeserved favor (his grace), not as the result of any efforts, abilities, intelligent choices, personal characteristics, or acts of service. Out of gratitude for this free gift, however, believers will seek to do **good things**—to help and serve others with kindness, love, and gentleness. While no action or work we do can help us obtain salvation, God's intention is that our salvation will result in acts of service. We are saved not merely for our own benefit but to serve Christ and build up the church (4:12). This solves the so-called conflict between faith and works. Works do not produce salvation but are the evidence of salvation (see James 1:22; 2:14-26).

The Greek word translated **do** means "to walk about in." We move ahead in this life of grace doing the good works that God **planned for us long ago.** The new life that God gives cannot help but express itself in good works. This does not necessarily mean that God has set up all the specific good works each person will do—although there would be no point arguing against the possibility of our omniscient God doing just that. Just as God planned salvation in Jesus Christ before the foundation of the world, so he planned that believers should do good to others (see 1 Timothy 6:18; Titus 2:7; 1 Peter 2:12).

ONENESS AND PEACE IN CHRIST / 2:11-18

Christ Jesus set individuals free from sin and death by making them alive through faith in him (2:1-10), but there is more to the story. Jesus saved individuals of all races and backgrounds in order to bring them into unity as his body, his church. There existed a huge gulf between Jews and Gentiles (non-Jews). God was going to bring these two distinct groups together by drawing believers in Christ from among the Jews *and* from among the Gentiles.

2:11 The Jews had the privilege of being God's chosen nation to whom he had given his covenant promises (Deuteronomy 7:6). One of the signs of his covenant was circumcision. God required circumcision as a sign of obedience to him, as a sign of belonging to his covenant people because once circumcised, the man would be identified as a Jew forever, and as a symbol of "cutting off" the old life of sin, purifying one's heart, and dedicating oneself to God. More than any other practice, circumcision separated God's people from their Egyptian and Canaanite neighbors.

Pious **Jews** considered all **Gentiles** to be **outsiders** because they were **uncircumcised.** The Jews erred in being **proud of their circumcision** and believing that circumcision was sufficient to make them godly without the necessity of inner renewal; in other words, **it affected only their bodies and not their hearts** (see Paul's discussion of this in Romans 2:25-29; also see Galatians 5:6). In this section in Ephesians, Paul focused on the Gentiles, calling the Gentile Christians not to **forget** their former condition.

2:12 Compared to the Jews, the Gentiles had five distinct disadvantages:

1. They were **living apart from Christ,** having had no expectation of a Messiah to save them.
2. They were **excluded from God's people, Israel.** Gentiles could never fully partake of the spiritual privileges promised to Israel, God's chosen people. While Gentiles could become Jews after an extensive training period, followed by circumcision and baptism, the sense of "exclusion" was never fully removed. Gentiles could never truly be citizens of Israel.
3. They **did not know the promises God had made** to Israel. For Paul, the covenant promises were the basis for Israel's distinctive. The Gentiles were "foreigners," meaning that they had no share or part in the promises.
4. They were **without God.** The Gentiles had many gods, but they were without the one true God. They lived entirely and only in this evil world. Without God, the world was all they had.
5. They were **without hope.** There was no hope for the Gentiles to find the one true God or to obtain anything beyond physical life in this world. The pagan philosophers' theories about life after death were at best vague and supplied no way to atone for evil committed during a person's life. They had no "divine promise" and, thus, no basis for hope.

This was a bleak description indeed. Fortunately, it does not end here, for God himself intervened.

2:13 The two little words **but now** reveal God's intervention from heaven to earth and the entire story of redemption. The words **far** and **near** describe the position of Gentiles and Jews in relation to God. To take those who were far away and bring them **near to** him could only happen **because of the blood of Christ.** Salvation could come only through Jesus' death. "Without the

shedding of blood, there is no forgiveness of sins" (Hebrews 9:22).

2:14 Christ Jesus, through his death, destroyed the barriers that had separated **Jews** and **Gentiles,** making **peace** between both groups. Even more than making peace, Christ reconciled them both to God. Those who believed in him would be made into **one people,** Christians. Paul described the peace that Christ had made between Jews and Gentiles as breaking down **the wall of hostility that used to separate** them. It was no secret that hostility existed between the two groups, a cultural and religious hostility that no one could bridge— no one but God. This "dividing wall" alludes to the wall in the Jewish Temple that separated the court of the Gentiles from the Temple proper, which only Jews could enter. The Jewish historian Josephus wrote that on this wall was an inscription in Greek and Latin: "No foreigner may enter within the barricade that surrounds the sanctuary and enclosure. Anyone who is caught doing so will have himself to blame for his ensuing death" (see Acts 21:28-29). This "breaking down" refers symbolically to Christ's reconciliation.

2:15-16 The "dividing wall" (2:14) was also pictured in the Jewish law itself, for the **law** was the means by which the Jews justified themselves before God and excluded the Gentiles (Deuteronomy 31:11-13; Isaiah 51:7-8). Christ himself said that he did not come to abolish the law but to fulfill it (Matthew 5:17). Christ fulfilled the Old Testament law because that law (especially the ceremonial law with its regulations for sacrifices) foreshadowed his coming. In his life on earth, he obeyed and supported the intent of the law as God's revelation and standard for people's behavior (see Matthew 5:21-48). Paul also supports the moral and ethical purpose of the law as valid to guide us (Romans 3:19-31; Galatians 3:24). But in his death and resurrection, Jesus annulled the law—that is, he made it ineffective. The law was annulled because of its ineffectiveness to make people right with God.

All have sinned; neither Gentiles nor Jews are capable of keeping God's law. All need a Savior. That Savior came, died, and rose again, fulfilling and abolishing the law as the way of salvation. Jesus then opened to both Jews and Gentiles a way to God by faith in him (John 14:6). By offering salvation to all kinds of people, Christ could create **one new person from the two groups.** In Christ there are no longer Jews and Gentiles but a mixture of Jews and Gentiles, combined as Christians, who make up the body of which he is the Head. By doing so, Christ also could **make peace**

between Jews and Gentiles—that is, in the church. This reconciliation could occur only **by means of his death** because Jesus' death was the substitutionary sacrifice fulfilling the demands of the law, taking its punishment in our place. Not only were Jews and Gentiles reconciled to God, but they were also reconciled to each other, for Jesus' death on the cross **put to death** any remaining **hostility** between them. There was no necessity for further hostility other than their refusal to accept Christ's reconciliation.

Because Christ broke down the dividing wall, believing Jews and Gentiles can have unity with one another in Christ. Because of Christ's death, believers are one (2:14); we are reconciled to one another (2:16); we have access to the Father by the Holy Spirit (2:18); we are no longer foreigners or aliens to God (2:19); we are all being built into a holy temple with Christ as our chief cornerstone (2:20-21).

2:17 Continuing the theme of 2:14-16, this **peace** preached by Christ includes peace with God and peace between Jews (the chosen people, those **who were near**) and Gentiles (those **who were far away** and without God, 2:12). In these words, Paul may have been alluding to Isaiah 52:7 and Isaiah 57:19. According to the sequence of the previous verses, Jesus bringing **this Good News** referred to (1) Jesus' coming after the resurrection to preach to the apos-

tles directly (see Luke 24:36; John 20:19, 21, 26); and (2) Jesus' coming through the Spirit to preach to all people. The Jews were **near** to God because they already knew of him through the Scriptures and worshiped him in their religious ceremonies. The Gentiles were **far away** because they knew little or nothing about God. Because neither group could be saved by good deeds, knowledge, or sincerity, both needed to hear about the salvation available through Jesus Christ. Both Jews and Gentiles are now free to come to God through Christ.

2:18 It is only **because of what Christ has done for us** (through Jesus' sacrifice on the cross) that **all of us** (referring to believing Jews and Gentiles) **may come to the Father through the same Holy Spirit.** The words "may come" picture being presented to a king in his throne room. Through Christ, the believer is ushered into God's very presence (see 3:12). The One we come to see is not only the King but "the Father"—the One who has adopted us as his very own children (Romans 8:15; Galatians 4:6).

Christ provides the access to the Father by one Spirit (the Holy Spirit), who helps us when we pray (Romans 8:26-27) and who baptizes and unifies us into one body (1 Corinthians 12:13). Note the three distinct persons of the Trinity mentioned in this verse. All people can come to God through Christ by means of the Holy Spirit.

A TEMPLE FOR THE LORD / 2:19-22

All believers are citizens of God's Kingdom and members of his household. Many barriers divide us from other Christians: age, appearance, intelligence, political persuasion, economic status, race, theological perspective. One of the surest ways to stifle Christ's love is to be friendly only with those people who are similar to us. Fortunately, Christ has knocked down the barriers and has placed all believers into one family. His cross should be the focus of our unity. The Holy Spirit helps us look beyond the barriers to the unity we are called to enjoy. People can see that God is love and that Christ is Lord as we live in harmony with each other and in accordance with what God says in his Word.

2:19 The **Gentiles are no longer strangers and foreigners.** These words describe people who live in a country other than their own without any of the rights of citizenship in that country. The Gentiles were "outsiders" in relation to the Jews, as well as to any hope (without Christ) for a relationship with God (2:12). That was their old position. Because of Christ, however, the Gentiles became **citizens** with all who have been called to be **God's holy people.** Jews and Gentiles who put their faith in Jesus Christ as their Savior become **members of God's family.** (See Philippians 3:20; Hebrews 3:2-6.)

2:20 God's **house** is **built** on a solid **foundation**—the apostles and the prophets. Paul used a common metaphor to describe **Christ**—the **cornerstone.** This alludes to Psalm 118:22 and Isaiah 8:14; 28:16 (see also Romans 9:32-33; 1 Peter 2:4-8). Paul expanded the metaphor, describing the apostles and prophets as the "foundation." Every well-built structure with a firm foundation has a cornerstone. A cornerstone is a valued architectural piece. Stonemasons choose just the right rock. The cornerstone anchors the building and gives all the walls their line. Jesus is the cornerstone of God's building.

The "prophets" here are probably the New Testament prophets (see 3:5; 4:11) because "apostles" are listed first. These apostles and prophets received and believed in Jesus Christ as their Messiah; then they took the gospel message out to the world.

2:21 The body of believers, the church, has been **joined together** and continues to rise (or grow). Each part of the building, each believer, fits perfectly into the building, all the pieces being aligned with the cornerstone. The structure is not yet complete; it will not be complete until the day that Christ Jesus returns. The building's purpose is also described: it is **a holy temple for the Lord.** The church becomes a holy temple because of the presence of the holy God. The word used for "temple" here refers to what was the inner sanctuary (the Most Holy Place) in the Jewish Temple. The union

of God with people, and the unity of previously alienated people with one another, could only occur through Christ.

2:22 It is only **through** Christ that the **Gentiles** could be **joined** with Jewish believers **as part of this dwelling where God lives by his Spirit.** In the Old Testament, God's "dwelling" referred either to the nation of Israel or to the Tabernacle or Temple. But in the New Testament, this dwelling is the whole body of believers, the church, made up of both Jews and Gentiles. There would not be two "churches"—one made up of Jewish believers and one of Gentile believers. Instead, there should be no barriers, no divisions, no basis for discrimination. We all belong to Christ and share fully in his blessings. He lives in us (corporately and individually) **by his Spirit.**

EPHESIANS 3

GOD'S SECRET PLAN REVEALED / 3:1-13

Paul had been arrested in Jerusalem and, eventually, had been imprisoned because he took a stand for the equality of Jews and Gentiles as Christians (believers in Christ). The Jewish antagonists saw Paul's teaching as radical and destructive to Temple practices. Thus, Paul was writing here that he had been imprisoned for the sake of Gentiles.

3:1 The religious leaders in Jerusalem, who had felt scandalized by Jesus' teachings and didn't believe he was the Messiah, pressured the Romans to arrest Paul because he was **preaching** salvation to the **Gentiles.** The Jews brought Paul to trial for treason and for causing rebellion among the Jews. They used Trophimus, the Ephesian Gentile convert, as a ploy to arrest Paul. Paul had appealed for his case to be heard by the emperor, and he was awaiting trial (see Acts 21:21, 28; 28:16-31). Yet Paul knew that his imprisonment was by God's will—therefore, he called himself **a prisoner of Christ Jesus**—not of the Jews, not of the Romans, but of Christ Jesus himself (see 1 Corinthians 4:1; Philippians 1:1; 2 Timothy 1:8).

3:2-3 Verses 2-13 are a parenthesis; he completes his thought from 3:1 in 3:14. Here Paul explained more fully his ministry to the **Gentiles.** Paul knew that the Ephesians and the believers in surrounding cities knew that God had given Paul **this special ministry of announcing his favor to** the Gentiles. God had assigned to Paul the special work of preaching the Good News to the Gentiles (Acts 9:15).

That the Gentiles could be included in God's grace is called a **secret plan** (Paul described this amazing new truth at length in 2:11-22). This "secret plan" was at one time hidden but now **revealed** (see 1:9). The plan was hidden, not because only a few could understand it, but because it was hidden until Christ came. God had revealed this secret plan to Paul in a direct communication. Paul had refused to believe in Christ and had persecuted anyone who did (Acts 9:1-2). God got hold of Paul and revealed that Jesus Christ truly was the promised Messiah of the Jews and the light to the Gentiles too. Both Jews and Gentiles would be included in the church.

3:4 When a church received a letter from Paul or one of the other apostles (such as the letters from Peter, James, and Jude), a church leader would read the letter aloud to the assembled congregation. Paul wrote to this leader and to the congregation, explaining that as he **read what** Paul had **written,** the listeners would **understand what** Paul knew **about this plan regarding Christ.**

Why did Paul have such insight into this secret plan about Christ, and how could he explain it so clearly? Because it had been revealed to him by God himself!

3:5 God's method of communicating with the Israelites was to reveal his words to a chosen prophet, who would in turn teach the people. The **previous generations** in the time of the Old Testament prophets did not clearly understand the secret plan which has now been **revealed by the Holy Spirit to his holy apostles and prophets.** God's plan was hidden from previous generations, not because God wanted to keep something from his people, but because he would reveal it to everyone in his perfect timing (see also Colossians 1:25-26). God planned to have Jews and Gentiles comprise one body, the church. These "prophets" are New Testament prophets (see also 2:20; 4:11). The phrase "by the Holy Spirit" focuses on divine revelation and inspiration. The revealing of this plan to one of the "holy apostles" is recorded in Acts 10. Peter received a dream making clear to him that the gospel message was meant not for the Jews alone but also for Gentiles.

3:6 In case anyone missed his point, Paul explained exactly what that **secret plan** entailed. While the early prophets had written of the inclusion of **Gentiles** with **Jews** (see, for example, Isaiah 49:6; 56:6-7;), their writings were interpreted that the Gentiles could become proselytes. The extent of this inclusion and the radical change—the Jews and Gentiles having **an equal share**—was not even considered. No one ever knew this until God revealed it to Paul and the other New Testament apostles and prophets. This inclusion of Gentiles with Jews can happen because both **have believed the Good News.** Also, **both are part of the same body** and so are united into one unit under Christ, the Head. Finally, both **enjoy together the promise of blessings through Christ Jesus.** They will be fellow partakers and copartners in receiving the coming blessings promised in God's Kingdom (2 Timothy 1:1).

3:7 The unity Paul described above can only happen when the gospel message is preached and believed. **This Good News** refers to the message of Jesus Christ as Messiah and Savior of all who believe—whether Jews or Gentiles. Paul had been **given the wonderful privilege of serving** God by spreading that message. Paul did not seek this job description, nor was it given to him on the basis of earned degree or merit.

Paul explained that his servanthood was **by God's special favor and mighty power.** Paul had actually been working for the "other side" when God called him—Paul had rejected Jesus as the Messiah and had actively persecuted Christians. Obviously God had not called Paul on the basis of his goodness or apparent faithfulness! God made Paul a key messenger of the gospel in the early days of the church. Yet Paul realized that he could not have fulfilled this mission without God's favor and power within him.

3:8 When Paul described himself as **the least deserving Christian there is,** he meant that God's favor alone had saved him, the one who had hated and persecuted all who followed Jesus. Nothing in Paul merited such favor; Paul knew this and was utterly amazed at what God had done. God had chosen him and had saved him for the **special joy of telling the Gentiles about the endless treasures available to them in Christ.** Paul considered telling others about Christ to be like sharing "treasures." To the Gentiles, who had been excluded by the Jews from participation in God's Kingdom (2:12-13), these treasures were unfathomable.

3:9 Paul's job was **to explain to everyone this plan** (see 3:2). All people were to know that it pleased God at this time to make known or bring to light his secret plan (explained in 3:6). The carrying out of this explanation of the mystery occurred as Paul and the other apostles taught God's great purpose in Christ and as the church itself took root and grew. For Paul, explaining God's plan was at the core of his selection as an apostle. Paul understood that he was born at a specific time to fulfill a specific purpose—revealing this mystery that God knew the plan all along but had kept it a **secret** until the appropriate time. God, **the Creator of all things,** was at work both in the former creation and the new creation. The same God is at work, and his plan was in place before the creation of the world.

3:10 God's plan was to build a church by uniting Jews and Gentiles as believers in Jesus Christ. Through this joining of believers **together in his church, God's purpose** would be powerfully displayed. God would **show his wisdom in all its rich variety,** making it known **to all the rulers and authorities in the heavenly realms.** "Rulers and authorities" refers to both good and evil angels. (In 1:21, the words referred to angelic powers; in 6:12, they refer to demonic powers.) All powers in the heavenlies, whether evil or good, will receive their understanding of God's great mystery from humans. God builds his church on earth from saved sinners, who, through God's grace and mercy, received their salvation through Jesus Christ's death on the cross. No angel or demon can comprehend what God has done.

3:11 God, "Creator of all things" (3:9), has always been in control of his creation. The plan of salvation, the secret plan of the church, and the revelation of his wisdom across all the realms of creation will occur according to **his plan from all eternity.** God's plan did not arise as an emergency measure when Adam sinned; it did not occur because God somehow lost control. God has always been in control, and his eternal purposes will always be accomplished. The central theme of this letter is God's great work of joining Jews and Gentiles together in a unified body—the church. God could only accept sinful people through a sacrifice that would cover their sins. Jesus Christ gave that sacrifice—himself—through his death on the cross.

3:12 Only **because of Christ** and people's **faith in him** can they approach the holy God. Paul described the most awesome privilege any mere human could have—to be able to **come fearlessly into God's presence.** Most of us would be apprehensive in the presence of a powerful ruler, but faith gives us confidence. The Greek word translated "approach" implies a formal introduction into the presence of a king. Thanks to Jesus Christ, Christians can enter directly into God's presence through prayer, **assured of his glad welcome** (see also Hebrews 4:16; 10:19-22).

3:13 Because of the tremendous scope of God's plan and because God gave believers access to him in freedom and confidence (3:12), Paul asked his readers to not **despair** because of his **suffering.** Paul had been imprisoned for championing the ministry of the gospel to the Gentiles (Acts 21:27-36). He could truly say to these Gentile believers that his sufferings were **for you,** but he asked that they not be discouraged. Instead, they should **feel honored and encouraged.** Why should Paul's suffering make the Ephesians feel honored? If Paul had not preached the gospel, he would not be in jail—but then the Ephesians might not have heard the Good News and been converted. Just as a mother endures the pain of childbirth in order to bring new life into the world, Paul endured the pain of persecution in order to bring new believers to Christ.

Obeying Christ is never easy. He requires you to take up your cross and follow him (Matthew 16:24). That means being willing to endure pain so that God's message of salvation can reach the entire world. We should feel honored that others have suffered and sacrificed for us so that we might reap the benefit. Because he understood that the Creator God was completely in control, Paul also understood that God was working his will even through his imprisonment and suffering. In this, the Ephesian believers could "glory."

PAUL'S PRAYER FOR SPIRITUAL EMPOWERING / 3:14-21
Paul's prayer for the Ephesians is that they be united by the Spirit, indwelt by Christ, and filled with all the fullness of God's love.

3:14-15 The phrase, **when I think of the wisdom and scope of God's plan,** actually continues the thought begun in 3:1. Overwhelmed by the blessings given to Jews and Gentiles and the privilege of sharing this newly revealed "secret plan," Paul exclaimed, **I fall to my knees.** The following words are his prayer for the Ephesians. While it was common among Jews to stand in prayer, kneeling revealed the earnestness and humble submission that Paul felt as he spoke these words (see Luke 22:41; Acts 7:60; 9:40; 20:36).

Paul praised God as both **the Father** and **the Creator of everything.** When his children kneel before him in prayer, they come to the God who is in complete and ultimate control. These words set the tone for the prayer that follows.

3:16 This beautiful prayer for the Ephesian believers (3:16-21) includes some of the most loved

verses in the New Testament. Paul knelt before the Father (3:14); then he prayed that God would grant certain petitions made on behalf of these Christians. Paul had previously written of the immeasurable riches of God in 1:7 and 2:7; here he prayed that **from his glorious, unlimited resources,** God would grant his requests. Because the riches of God's glory are without measure, Paul prayed that the answers would be given to believers without measure and beyond their comprehension.

Paul first prayed that God would grant **mighty inner strength** to these believers. The Greek word for "strength" is the opposite of "despair" in 3:13. We find the source of this strength in the Holy Spirit. God sent the Holy Spirit to be with and within his followers after Christ had returned to heaven. The Spirit would comfort them, guide them to know his truth, remind them of Jesus' words, point out when they did not obey, give them the right words to say, and fill them with power to do good (John 14–16). After Pentecost (Acts 2:1-4), God made the Holy Spirit available to all who believed in Jesus. We receive the Holy Spirit when we believe in Jesus Christ as Savior. The Spirit provides power for our new lives.

3:17-18 The Greek word translated **at home** conveys the idea of settling down, taking up permanent residence. Christ finds his home in believers' **hearts.** The "heart" in the Bible always refers to the center of a person's emotions and will. Christ takes up permanent residence, changing a person's "heart" and, consequently, his or her words and thoughts. Christ takes up residence in the hearts of those who **trust in him.** Christ's indwelling presence and the Spirit's strengthening power also help believers' **roots** to **go down deep into the soil of God's marvelous love.** In Greek, this clause connects with 3:18, suggesting that by being "rooted" we will then be able to understand the magnitude of God's love. "Rooted" brings to mind the stable image of trees.

Paul prayed that this firm rooting of love would give all believers **the power to understand** the vastness of Christ's love. Christ's love is total, complete, eternal, and all-encompassing. It reaches every corner of our experience. This passage shows that even as we seek to grasp an understanding of Christ's love, we will never understand it completely, for it is beyond our comprehension. It is **wide**—covering the breadth of our own experience and reaching out to the whole world. It is **long**—continuing the length of our lives and on into eternity. It is **high**—rising to the heights of our celebration and elation. His love is **deep**—reaching to the depths of discouragement, despair, and even death.

3:19 Paul prayed in 3:18 that the believers might "understand" Christ's love. Here he prayed that they might **experience** it. Paul also recognized that Christ's love **is so great** that people will **never fully understand it.** Believers cannot rationally explain Christ's love; they can only know it by experiencing it. This knowledge requires a continuous growing experience.

As believers get to know Christ better, they **will be filled with the fullness of life and power**

that comes from God. This "fullness" means that there is nothing lacking in our relationship to the Father. God pours his love and power into believers, making us complete for this life and readying us for the life to come. This "fullness" is fully expressed only in Christ (Colossians 2:9-10). We need not look anywhere else. The ultimate goal is for believers to become Christlike individuals, filled so totally with Christ that he is seen in us.

3:20 Our thoughts include more than we dare to ask in our prayers; our dreams exceed what we consciously desire. God answers prayer; he even answers unspoken prayers. God can act beyond our ability to ask or even imagine. Paul uses superlatives to drive home his point: God is able to do **infinitely more than we would ever dare to ask or hope**—more than we would dare to imagine. God is far above and beyond our finite minds. God **is able** because of his **mighty power.** To the unfathomable depths of Christ's love is added the exceeding abundance of his power. Believers can claim Christ's great love (3:19) and know that his power is **at work within us** through the Holy Spirit.

3:21 God alone deserves **glory,** for he alone is glorious. The word "glory" refers to the wonderful and awe-inspiring but indescribable presence of God himself. Glory is given to God **in the church.** The church, God's creation, exists to glorify him. The church is the sphere of the outworking of God's plan here on earth (3:10). The ability to give glory to God comes only **in Christ Jesus,** for he brought the church into existence through his sacrifice for sin and his resurrection from the dead. This glory will be made known **through endless ages.**

This doxology—prayer of praise to God—ends part 1 of Ephesians. Some have thought that this doxology was originally the end of this letter. More likely, Paul simply broke into spontaneous words of praise growing out of his prayer (3:14-19). In the first section, Paul described the timeless role of the church. In part 2 (chapters 4–6), he explained how church members should live in order to bring about the unity God wants. As in most of his books, Paul first laid a doctrinal foundation and then followed with practical applications of the truths he presented.

EPHESIANS 4

UNITY IN THE BODY OF CHRIST / 4:1-16

Here the focus changes from theological to practical. Paul has explained to his readers God's great mystery and plan for his church, and he has prayed an awe-inspiring prayer that they might know all of Christ's love and all of his blessings. The remainder of the letter contains Paul's plea to live out the grace and unity the believers had received through Christ. Verses 1-6 are on unity; verses 7-16 are on diversity in the church. The challenges for churches today parallel the challenges that faced first-century churches like the one in Ephesus. We must remain unified as believers, incorporating our diversity so that we can serve and glorify our Lord.

4:1 The word **therefore** connects this sentence to Paul's words in the previous chapters—the great plan God has revealed. Paul was imprisoned in Rome **for serving the Lord** (that is, his imprisonment was a result of his preaching the gospel, see Acts 21:27–22:22). Despite the chains that bound him physically and kept him from traveling, Paul continued to write, in this case urging the Ephesian believers to **lead a life worthy of your calling** and to remember that they had been **called by God** (1:4). Their "call" to salvation was accomplished through Christ's humble act of dying on the cross for our sin. It was also a "call" to service for God.

How can one live **worthy** of the calling? The Greek word for "worthy" refers to a balance, as on scales. Thus, believers are to live "in balance" with their calling. How they act should match what they believe. Remembering Christ's sacrifice should cause believers to live for his glory in every area of their lives. The following verses describe how to do this.

4:2 This verse lists four characteristics of a person who is "worthy of the calling." Believers make up the church, the body of Christ. Thus, believers, by privilege of their responsibility, must be together, serve together, and worship together. The following characteristics help create and maintain smooth relationships among people.

Both the Greek and Roman cultures considered humility and gentleness to be weak character traits showing a lack of self-respect. The Old Testament, however, paved the way for a positive connotation for humility because God "lives with" the **humble** (Isaiah 57:15). Jesus exalted humility as a virtue (John 13:13-15). Christ expected his followers to be humble not only before God but toward one another—serving one another and not putting

themselves "above" anyone else. Christ is our example; thus, we must also be humble.

Believers are also to be **gentle.** Humility is an attitude, and gentleness is the action derived from it. Gentle people do not attempt to grab for positions of importance or assert authority over others. Gentle people accept God's dealings with them without arguing or resisting. Gentle people are considerate of others. If everyone in a church had the characteristics of humility and gentleness, conflicts would disappear and members would have strength and power in their service.

Patience conveys the quality of being able to handle one another's faults and failures and refusing to avenge wrongs. No one is ever going to be perfect here on earth, so believers must **be patient with each other** despite their faults.

Making allowance for each other's faults is the action side of patience, emphasizing the willingness to forgive. To show patience requires **love,** which ought to be the guiding principle for all of a believer's actions, even when natural differences and clashes occur. Bearing with one another presupposes that, at times, loving others will be a burden. Believers must be willing to carry the load without expecting reward, thanks, or return.

4:3 For believers to be **united** is only possible when the **Holy Spirit** acts in believers' lives— the Spirit originates and sustains oneness among believers. Love for each other, which the presence of the Spirit causes, makes peace possible. To **bind** themselves **together with peace** includes the idea of uniting the members into one body. This "bond" holds people together, like string or twine. Peace functions as the "binding twine" of unity. God gives it to us, producing equality and understanding.

Paul knew that maintaining unity among believers would take hard work and continual diligence. Believers face many attempts to tear apart their unity. False teachers would arise, even from within their ranks, attempting to divide the people; persecution would attempt to frighten the church and send it scattering. The believers in each of the churches in and around Ephesus would need to work diligently to maintain their unity. Churches today need the same quality of diligence.

4:4 Believers diligently maintain their unity (as described in 4:3) because Christ desires it—there is only **one body** and all believers **have the same Spirit.** The repetition of the word "one" in verses 4-6 emphasizes this unity. Regardless of all that can divide the believers—racial background, social status, and gender, to name a few—Christians belong to one body through one Holy Spirit (see also 1:13-14; 2:11-22; 3:6). In a pagan culture, people can choose from any number of cults to join and gods to worship. For Christians, however, there is only one body, unified by one Spirit.

The unity in the body of believers occurs because one Spirit indwells them. The Holy Spirit lives in all Christians and gives to the church its true oneness (2:18). Without the Spirit, the body could not exist. Christianity is not a club to join, nor is it some mystical but unreal entity. Instead, true Christianity is a spiritual relationship with Christ as well as with other believers. Through the Spirit, all believers are united in one universal body. The "one Spirit" guarantees that all believers have been **called to the same glorious future**—that is, to eternal life in God's Kingdom.

4:5 This verse focuses on Christ. **One Lord** refers to Jesus Christ, whose lordship (headship) forms the basis of unity in the body. Christians worship one Lord. There are not many real gods from which to choose; there is only one—the Lord Jesus Christ. Believers are one body because of this **one faith.** This faith alone saves; this faith is the one and only "way" (John 14:6). This one faith binds all believers together.

The act of believing is manifested through the act of baptism, the symbol of being brought into the body. (Faith and baptism are similarly connected in Mark 16:16 and Colossians 2:12.) Paul's inclusion of this **one baptism** reveals the great importance that baptism held for the early church. Baptism replaced circumcision as the initiation rite of the new order, the new covenant. "Baptism" refers here to baptism in water, as opposed to baptism by the Spirit, because of the word's placement in this verse. This expression of faith through baptism brings unity to believers.

4:6 This verse focuses on God the Father. There are not many gods, as in the pagan culture; **there is only one God.** As the only God, he alone deserves our worship and praise. **Father** of all means that he is the Creator. All people were made in his image (Genesis 1:26). The sovereign God completely controls his creation. Christians understand themselves as God's creation and as God's "called." God **is over us all**—supreme, transcendent, the ruler over all of his creation. God is **in us all**—actively present and pervasive in every part of his creation. God is **living through us all**—he himself lives within his people. Any view of God that violates either his transcendence, pervasiveness, or immanence does not paint a true picture of God. Paul did not teach pantheism ("God is in everything, so we can worship nature") or universalism ("God is Father of all and will therefore save everyone"). Rather, he taught about the omnipotent, omnipresent, and omniscient God, ruling over creation and exercising his power through his followers on behalf of the church.

4:7 Although the church is one unified body, each of its members has **a special gift** to be used for the good and growth of all. No one is overlooked; everyone is important to building up the community. God in his wisdom did not make believers photocopies of one another. Instead, each believer has at least one special ability, given **according to the generosity of Christ,** to be used to accomplish the work of the Kingdom.

4:8 Psalm 68:18 pictures God as conqueror as the Ark of the Covenant was being brought up to Zion in triumph by David (2 Samuel 6; 1 Chronicles 15). It had been removed in battle. As David returns the Ark to Jerusalem, he also brings the tribute of war extracted from the captured foes. Some of the spoil was given to the Temple, and some was distributed among the warriors.

Paul used that picture to refer to Christ's ascent into heaven. The work and authority for apportioning spiritual gifts rightly belongs to the ascended Christ. Paul's development of this theme prepares readers for his thoughts in 4:11. In the psalm, the victory is over David's foes. In Paul's reference, Christ, the Son of David, is triumphant in destroying his foe Satan. In the psalm, the conqueror receives gifts and, as was the custom, distributes a portion of the spoils to his people. Paul's reference means that God began to give special gifts to people following Christ's return to heaven.

The statement **he led a crowd of captives** could mean: (1) He led the captured ones (as one would lead a train of vanquished foes) into their captivity, or (2) he captured the captors (that is, he reversed the captivity; he enslaved the enslavers). Both meanings imply that Christ vanquished our enemies (such as death, Satan, and sin) and captivated them. He returned in triumph to heaven (**ascended to the heights**) and, in turn, **gave gifts to his people.**

Paul used the picture from this psalm to explain how Christ conquered his enemies, returned to glory, and bestowed gifts on his church. The gifts God gave to his church (in the form of people called to special functions) are described in 4:11-12.

4:9-10 Paul reasoned that Christ's ascent implies a previous descent. The phrase **lowly world** represents the earth, the place where the Son came in his incarnation. The "captives" (4:8) then would be either Satan and his hosts or the saints who were taken "captive" or "called" (a reference to election).

The same Christ **who came down is the one who ascended higher than all the heavens.** As a result of his descent and ascent, nothing is hidden from him. All things are subject to him; no realm in heaven or earth is beyond his control. That Christ will **fill the entire universe** refers to his power and control over all of his creation. Christ is Lord of the whole universe—past, present, and future. He fills all things with himself as their sovereign Head, yet he fills the church, his body, with the blessings of his Spirit, grace, and gifts (see also 1:10, 23).

4:11 This expands on the thought begun in 4:7-8 regarding the gifts Christ **gave.** In this context, these gifts are actually people who have been called to special functions. Not all people have all the gifts, for Paul was clear to explain that some would be gifted in one area and some in another. The list given here is by no means complete (for other types of gifts, see Romans 12; 1 Corinthians 12). According to the Greek, all the people listed are direct objects of "gave," indicating that God gave these people to the church as gifts. The offices listed here focus mainly on those who proclaim the gospel and teach the truth.

First listed are the **apostles.** They are the foundation for Christ's temple (see 2:20 and 3:6). "Apostles" included the eleven men Jesus called (without Judas), plus others who are called apostles—such as Paul himself (Romans 1:1), Matthias (Acts 1:26), Barnabas (Acts 14:14), Jesus' brother James (Galatians 1:19), Silas (1 Thessalonians 2:6), Andronicus, and Junias (Romans 16:7). It seems that the qualifications for being an apostle were to have seen the risen Christ, to have been sent out by him to preach the gospel, and to be working on behalf of the Kingdom, building its foundation

(as noted in 2:20). Paul also notes "signs and wonders and miracles" as marks of a true apostle (2 Corinthians 12:12).

God also gave **prophets** to the church. These people, also laborers on the church's "foundation" (2:20), had special gifts in ministering God's messages to his people. At times they would foretell the future (Acts 11:28; 21:9, 11), but more often their job was to exhort, encourage, and strengthen God's people (Acts 15:32; 1 Corinthians 14:29). God spoke through prophets—inspiring them with specific messages for particular times and places.

The **evangelists** were the traveling ministers, similar to the missionaries of today. They went to non-Christian people and proclaimed the gospel to them, often being the first to start a church in a particular area (Acts 21:8; 2 Timothy 4:5).

Next, God gave **pastors and teachers.** These two gifts are likely the same. While the apostles, prophets, and evangelists had a universal sphere of function (the church as a whole), the pastors and teachers probably served in the local churches. Like shepherds, they tended God's "flock," handling the day-to-day affairs of their congregation—administering, counseling, guiding, feeding.

4:12 These specially gifted people (4:11) were given to the church for one ultimate goal: **to equip God's people.** The word for "equip" means to make right, like the setting of a broken bone, or to bring to completion by training or restoring. The apostles, prophets, evangelists, pastors, and teachers furnish and equip the believers to do the work of the ministry, which results in building **up the church.** The church builds itself in the faith as the members care for one another, show love, and generally manifest the other gifts God gives (as mentioned in Romans 12 and 1 Corinthians 12). Yet the church also builds itself as it reaches out to its surrounding community with the love of Christ, drawing others into the fold. God has given his church an enormous responsibility—to make disciples in every nation (Matthew 28:18-20). This involves preaching, teaching, healing, nurturing, giving, administering, building, and many other tasks. Fulfilling this command solo would be impossible. But God calls us as members of his body. No one should be a bystander, an observer.

4:13 The word **until** indicates that the process described in 4:12 must continue until a certain end is achieved—when all believers **come to** (arrive at, attain) **unity in our faith.** This means a unity of belief in Christ himself, and this belief relates intrinsically to our knowledge of him. The goal includes making a united effort to live out and proclaim this faith.

Unity in our **knowledge** refers to fuller and more complete experiential knowledge. Every believer must have a personal, intimate relationship with Jesus Christ. Paul here called him **God's Son,** showing that this knowledge includes an appropriate understanding of the new relationship with the Father that has been provided by the Son (Romans 8:10-17).

This unified body of believers is called to **be mature and full grown, measuring up to the full stature of Christ.** The focus is on **we** in this verse—every believer as part of the entire body. This metaphor means that the church, as Christ's body, must match the Head in growth and maturity. This does not speak of perfection (impossible in this life) but of growth—such as children growing into adults, which ties into the following advice regarding this growth.

4:14 Because believers will be mature in the faith (4:13), they **will no longer be like children** (or like helpless infants) who are easily led astray. People who are "children" in their faith and knowledge must grow up and mature (4:13). Otherwise, they are susceptible to false teaching. They will be unstable, rootless, without direction, and susceptible to manipulation, **forever changing** their **minds about what** they **believe.** Immature believers, like children, are unable to discern when they are being **lied to** because the lie sounds **like the truth.** Uncritical acceptance of new teachings will keep their minds in as much turmoil as a stormy sea. Indeed, false teaching was a major problem in the early church (see, for example, Galatians 1:6-9; 3:1-14; Colossians 2:6-23). Believers must be growing toward maturity in true faith. Only then will they be able to discern false doctrines; only then will they stay the course and reach the goal of maturity (4:13).

4:15 Believers are not to be like immature children (4:14). In their witness for Christ, they need not resort to trickery and scheming as do the false teachers (4:14). Instead, their continuous objective should be to **hold to the truth in love, becoming more and more in every way like Christ.** Believers should want to be like Christ, the truth (John 14:6), and be strengthened by the Holy Spirit, who guides the church, the Spirit of truth (John 16:13). Satan, by contrast, is the father of lies (John 8:44). As followers of Christ, we must be committed to the truth. This means that our words should be honest and that our actions should reflect Christ's integrity. Speaking the truth in love is not always easy, convenient, or pleasant, but it is necessary if the church is going to do Christ's work in the world.

4:16 Christ is head of this body of believers (4:15) and its source; without him there could be no body, no church. From him alone the **other parts grow, so that the whole body is healthy and growing and full of love.** The reference to growing refers not so much to increased size as to increased faith and spiritual strength. This increase can occur because Christ, as head, supplies all the needs of the body. The description of believers as **fitted together perfectly** describes the bond in Christ that holds the church together. Believers from different backgrounds, nations, and languages, who make up **the whole body,** are held together by a strong bond and have the goal of growing spiritually. This happens **as each part does its own special work.** Members of the body receive exactly what they need and are responsible to use what they have for the good of the whole. We receive gifts not for our own prestige or acclaim but to help build up other believers in the church.

LIVING AS CHILDREN OF LIGHT / 4:17-32

People should be able to see a difference between Christians and non-Christians because of the way Christians live. The section from 4:17-24 appeals to believers to leave behind the old life of sin because they are followers of Christ—which should result in a radical change in their behavior. This change is further detailed in the section from 4:25-32, which lists negative characteristics that have no place in the church and positive characteristics that will reflect Christ's character.

Living the Christian life is a process. Although we have a new nature, we don't automatically think all good thoughts and express all right attitudes. But if we keep listening to God, we will be changing all the time. We must trust God to change us on the inside—our character, values, attitudes, perspective, and motives.

4:17 Believers are to be maturing in their faith and using their gifts to benefit the church (4:11-16).

The believers in Ephesus must **live no longer as the ungodly do.** He insisted that the Ephesian believers abandon what had been their former way of life, not living any longer as the other ungodly around them because they were **hopelessly confused**, referring to the natural tendency of human beings to employ intellectual pride, rationalizations, and excuses (Romans 1:21). Their thinking was "confused" because their lives were being wasted on worthless objects (idols), untrue teachings, and immoral behavior.

4:18 This describes the unfortunate state of the unbelievers surrounding this core of believers in the church. The unbelievers had **closed minds** that were **full of darkness**, while the believers had found the light of Christ and were given his wisdom. The unbelievers were **far away from the life of God,** while the believers had been made one with him through Christ. The unbelievers had **shut their minds and hardened their hearts,** while the believers had received access to the full knowledge of the truth and had welcomed Christ into their hearts.

4:19 These unbelievers **don't care anymore about right and wrong;** they have no feeling about their degenerate condition. Such people are beyond feeling either shame for their evil or hope for anything better concerning their condition before God.

The logical next step for people who have lost all conscience is that they **have given themselves over to immoral ways, filled with all kinds of impurity and greed.** While these terms seem strong, we must understand the culture that surrounded the believers in and around Ephesus. The temple to the goddess Artemis (the Roman name was Diana) stood in Ephesus. Artemis was the goddess of fertility in women, animals, and nature. Her temple had a hierarchy of religious personnel, including eunuch priests, young virgins, and prostitute priestesses. One month every year was devoted to ceremonies honoring Artemis. A carnival atmosphere that included concerts, feasts, athletic games, and plays created opportunities for immorality, drunkenness, and sensuality. To the Jews, worship at the temple of Artemis was extremely corrupt. Christians, as well, were not to take part in its practices.

4:20 In great contrast to the unbelieving Gentiles (referred to as "they" in the previous verses) stands the word **you** in this verse. The Ephesian believers had **learned about Christ** from Paul himself as well as from other teachers. To know Christ is the greatest knowledge that anyone can have. That knowledge is the truth; that knowledge opposes what the evil world teaches and applauds. Therefore, what the Ephesians and the other believers were taught should make all the difference in their lifestyles.

4:21-22 Jesus is the **truth** (John 14:6). This is the truth that the Ephesians heard and believed. This is the truth that brings salvation. While unbelievers live in darkness and sensuality, believers were taught a whole new manner of living, which must **throw off** the old evil nature and the **former way of life.** The "old nature" describes each person before he or she comes to know Christ. The old nature was **rotten through and through, full of lust and deception** (which Paul described in 4:17-19 above). Like a cancer, the evil nature spreads and destroys. The person was enslaved to sin, bound to the world, and without hope. Those who have accepted Christ are still susceptible to temptations and the evils of the sinful nature. Paul does not distinguish between two parts or two natures within a person. The old self describes those areas of rebellion against God. We must forsake this former lifestyle. To "throw off" that old nature will take conscious, daily decisions to remove anything that supports or feeds the old self's desires.

4:23-24 We cannot get rid of the old evil nature without putting on a **new nature.** Believers must follow with two specific actions: (1) **there must be a spiritual renewal of your thoughts and attitudes,** and (2) they **must display a new nature.**

While we are still on this earth, we will struggle with our old way of life. Paul understood this struggle clearly (see Romans 7:14-25). In explaining these concepts, some people have wrongly given the idea that there are two selves or two equal-but-opposite poles in our life (old and new) warring against each other. This is not how the New Testament used these words. Christ sees his people as redeemed. Transformation begins in the mind and results in renewed behavior. How are believers to be renewed in their thoughts and attitudes? They must:

- be involved in activities that renew their minds (Philippians 4:8-9)
- desire to pattern themselves after God, not the world (Romans 12:2)
- study and apply God's word so that it changes their behavior from within (2 Timothy 3:15-16).

This **new person** is created according to the **likeness** of God—**righteous, holy, and true.** We have a right relationship with God that results in right behavior, creates an aversion to sin, and prompts us to devote ourselves to his service. These qualities are "true," meaning they cannot be faked. This is totally opposite of the old way of living characterized by sin and corruption. Finally, the new person refers not to a split in one's personality; instead, it pictures the new direction, attitude, and mind-set away from self and toward God and his will.

4:25 The general character of the new nature will lead to specific ways of acting. Because believers in the church are righteous, holy, and true (4:24), they must **put away all falsehood.** This may refer to various forms of falsehood—anything that pertains to the old lifestyle and is not part of Christ's truth. They must put on the willingness to **tell the truth** to their **neighbor.** This is a quote from Zechariah 8:16. We do this **because we belong to each other.** Paul stressed our mutual responsibility. Because we are all members of Christ's body, our words and actions must not be destructive to the body. Lying to each other disrupts unity by creating conflicts and destroying trust. It tears down relationships and leads to open warfare in a church. Truthfulness, however, opens the door to understanding. To maintain unity, the believers must be completely truthful with one another.

4:26-27 Another characteristic of the old nature that has to be put off is bad temper, or a lifestyle characterized by anger. The words, **don't sin by letting anger gain control over you,** are quoted from Psalm 4:4. The Bible doesn't tell us that we shouldn't feel angry, but it points out that it is important to handle our anger properly. We must not indulge our angry feelings or let them lead to pride, hatred, or self-righteousness. Jesus Christ became angry at the merchants in the Temple, but this was righteous anger and did not lead him to sin. Believers must follow Jesus' example. We ought to reserve our anger for when we see God dishonored or people wronged. If we get angry, we must do so without sinning. To do this, we should deal with our anger before the **sun** goes **down.** According to Deuteronomy, sunset was the time by which wrongs against God and against others should be made right (Deuteronomy 24:13, 15). Anger that is allowed to smolder and burn over time can eventually burst into flame and give **a mighty foothold to the Devil,** causing people to sin as they become bitter and resentful. It is so much better to deal with the situation immediately; perhaps the previous admonition to lovingly speak the truth can solve the problem.

4:28 In most cases, a reference to **stealing** or to **a thief** in the New Testament concerns a bandit or a person who engages in stealing as a livelihood. Paul explained that such a person who became a believer had to "throw off" that old lifestyle and make a change, turning to **honest work** in order to make a living. Stealing and idleness go together; thus, Paul's charge was not only to stop stealing but also to begin honest work. In addition, slaves were often prone to stealing from the households they served; many slaves became Christians, and

Paul may have been speaking to them. All believers should work hard, do their part in the community, hold their own, and not expect anyone else to support them.

Even then, the Christian's goal for his or her labor differs from the world's. We work not to enrich ourselves, but so that we can **give generously to others in need.** Giving is at the heart of Christianity. We hold lightly to our possessions because we have our treasure in heaven (Matthew 6:19-21; Romans 12:13; 2 Corinthians 8–9).

4:29 Believers must also be careful about what they say. As part of Christ's body, filled with his righteousness and holiness, they must not **use foul or abusive language.** Such speech is worthless, spreads worthlessness, and leads hearers to think about worthless matters. Not only should our speech be kept clean and truthful, but we should also speak words that are **good and helpful,** words of **encouragement.** We must be sensitive to the situation and the needs of anyone with whom we converse, and we must be wise in choosing our words, for even good words, unless used appropriately, can be destructive instead of useful. God can work through our words to help others and bring his grace to them.

4:30 That the Spirit can be caused **sorrow** points to the personality of the Spirit. The **Holy Spirit** is a person who can be saddened by the way we live. Paul has already explained that the Holy Spirit's power within gives new life to believers. While we continue to battle with our sinful nature, we should be living for Christ each day. To refuse to do so, to constantly give in to lying, anger, stealing, and foul talk is to bring him sorrow. Paul reminded the readers that the Holy Spirit within them gives both a privilege and a responsibility. Their responsibility is to not disappoint him by the way they live; their privilege is their promised future, for through the presence of the Spirit, they have been given a guarantee that they **will be saved on the day of redemption.**

4:31 The sins listed in this verse picture the former way of life, the old nature (4:22). None of these attitudes and activities have any place in a believer's Holy Spirit-filled life; indeed, they foster dissension today and are the opposite of how believers should be characterized (see 4:32). In their lives and in their churches, the believers must **get rid of:**

- **Bitterness**—a spirit that refuses reconciliation.
- **Rage**—outbursts of anger or quick temper for selfish reasons. This could mean continual and uncontrolled behavior.

- **Anger**—a continuous attitude of hatred that remains bottled up within. This could refer to what is under the surface, while "rage" refers to what bursts out. Anger would destroy harmony and unity among believers.
- **Harsh words**—loud self-assertions of angry people determined to make their grievances known.
- **Slander**—destroying another person's good reputation by lying, gossiping, spreading rumors, etc. Malice often manifests itself through slander. This defamation of character destroys human relationships.
- **Malicious behavior**—doing evil despite the good that has been received. This word is a general term referring to an evil force that destroys relationships, and it can mean anything from trouble to wickedness. It is a deliberate attempt to harm another person. Thus, **all types** of malice must be destroyed.

4:32 The previous way of life must be put off (4:31) and the new life put on. Believers ought to **be kind to each other.** Kindness means acting charitably and benevolently toward others, as God has done toward us. Kindness takes the initiative in responding generously to others' needs. The Psalms and writings of the prophets say much about God's kindness. Because believers have received kindness, we ought to act with kindness toward others.

The word for **tenderhearted** is also translated "compassionate." Compassion is genuine sensitivity and heartfelt sympathy for the needs of others. Compassion characterizes God.

Believers must also be constantly **forgiving one another.** In what way? **Just as God through Christ has forgiven you.** Though Christ has bridged the gap between us and God so that we are forgiven once and for all, we only experience God's forgiveness in personal, practical ways as we learn to forgive others from day to day. Having received forgiveness, we will pass it on to others. Those who are unwilling to forgive have not patterned their lives after Christ, who was willing to forgive even those who crucified him (Luke 23:34).

EPHESIANS 5

LIVING IN THE LIGHT / 5:1-14

In 4:17-24 Paul described, in general terms, the putting off of the old self and the putting on of the new; in 4:25-31, he described particular sins of speech and personal animosities. He continued here in 5:3-4, further describing actions that are unsuitable among the Christian community. Paul understood that this is a process. Because of our relationship with God through Christ and the power given us through the Spirit, we are to become Godlike in our characteristics and obedient disciples in our lifestyles.

5:1 Just as **children** imitate their parents, believers should **follow God's example.** His great love for us led him to sacrifice his Son so that we might live. We can do that by following his example in Christ, emulating his attributes in our lives (see 1 Peter 2:21).

5:2 How we live our lives should be characterized by our oneness with Christ. Paul explained that we are to **live a life filled with love for others.** Our love for others should be of the same kind that Christ showed to us—a love that goes beyond affection to self-sacrificing service. Christ loved us so much that he **gave himself as a sacrifice to take away** our sins. Christ gave himself in death as a sacrifice on our behalf. The **sweet perfume** relates to the acceptability of the sacrifice. God was not bound to accept any offering (Genesis 4:5); he did so only on the basis of the attitude of the giver. This focuses on God's pleasure with Christ's sacrifice. Because God accepted Christ's sacrifice, we who believe are acceptable to God. Because of this, our love ought to also be self-sacrificial. Jesus had told his disciples, "Love each other in the same way that I love you" (John 15:12).

5:3 Sexual immorality includes any kind of sexual perversion. Sexual immorality was tolerated in the pagan Roman society (see Romans 1:24-32), but it should not exist in the Christian community. Neither should there be any **impurity.** As in 4:19, "impurity" is aligned with a lifestyle bent on fulfilling every indulgence, so the focus in this verse is probably on sexual indulgence.

Greed refers to an inordinate desire for anything—wanting something so much that one sacrifices everything to get it. Again, this verse may focus on sexual immorality and indulgence—the greed to have what one should not have. Such desires are idolatrous.

These sins **have no place among God's people** because they have been called to be holy. God's people should exhibit his attributes. These activities are the opposite of what God desires from his people.

5:4 Obscene stories, foolish talk, and coarse jokes are so common that we begin to take them for granted. Paul cautioned, however, that improper language should have no place in a Christian's conversation because it does not reflect God's gracious presence in us. This use of language by believers sometimes stems from their desire to remain inconspicuous by sounding like the people who surround them. Principle is sacrificed to the convenience of the particular occasion.

Throughout this section, Paul told the believers not to just get rid of some types of attitudes and activities but to replace them with others. So here, impure talk is to be replaced by **thankfulness to God**. In this way, our words will build up and benefit others (4:29). Giving thanks brings about the real joy of the spirit that the worldly people try to achieve with their style of humor and communication. Paul did not mean that all other talk is vulgar; rather, he commanded against the foolish and vulgar talk that harms the spiritual life.

5:5 Immorality, impurity, and greed (described in 5:3) are compared to idolatry because those who consistently engage in these types of activities are idolaters. Because they have allowed their desires to run their lives, those desires are their gods. Anyone who has made anything more important than God will not **inherit the Kingdom of Christ and of God**. In the Greek, the words "of Christ and of God" emphasize the complete unity of the Father and the Son, consistent with the doctrine that Christ is completely God (John 10:30). Sin, no matter what its form or category, separates people from God. Unrepentance leaves people without hope and without inheritance. Only by forsaking sin, accepting Christ's sacrifice, and allowing him to be Lord of our lives can we believers obtain our inheritance in God's glorious Kingdom (1:14, 18).

5:6-7 This verse builds on 4:14. False teachers had begun infiltrating the early church, teaching that "freedom in Christ" meant freedom "from" laws and rules, freedom to live as one pleased. The false teachers taught their false doctrines, probably even trying to make evil seem less serious. The false teachers made up a doctrine that allowed for sinful lifestyles. Paul did not want the believers to be deceived by **those who try to excuse sin**. The believers should be on guard, **for the terrible anger of God comes upon all those who disobey him**. Those who thought they could continue in sin as a part of their "freedom" would discover that they were never free but were all the time enslaved to their sin. And they would face God's wrath both in the present and in the future.

Therefore, Paul told the believers not to **participate in the things** those people were doing. This "participating" refers to joining them in their sinful activities or in justifying sin. To do so would be to mock the sacrifice Christ made in order to take away sin.

5:8-9 There can be no clearer distinction between the new life and the old life than to compare them to light and darkness. Light and darkness cannot coexist, so a life redeemed by the blood of Christ and brought into the light of his truth must not continue in the darkness of a sinful lifestyle. Paul had already described unbelievers as "full of darkness" due to ignorance, hard-heartedness, and lack of sensitivity (4:18-19). This darkness is part of every believer's past; all Christians **were once full of darkness**. But when they heard the gospel message and received salvation through Jesus Christ, they became **full of light from the Lord**. Christians are not merely "enlightened" to God's truth; they are also filled with light and their **behavior should show it, reflecting the light of his holiness and truth. The natural outcome of such a lifestyle—good and right and true** are the opposites of the characteristics described in 4:25-29 and 5:3-5. In other words, believers who live in God's light are above reproach morally, spiritually, and ethically.

5:10 Every believer is responsible to **find out what is pleasing to the Lord**—how he or she ought to live full of the light. Thus, each person must study God's word, pray, and seek counsel in order to find out how God would have him or her act in every situation. This "finding out" naturally goes with "living out" because the knowledge must be put into practical use—doing what God calls us to do in every situation every day.

5:11 Light and darkness cannot coexist, so children of the light (5:8) must **take no part in the worthless deeds of evil and darkness.** Believers must separate themselves from sin, having no part of it. This does not mean that believers must be separate from unbelievers, but they must "take no part" in their sinful actions. It is important to avoid activities that result in sin, but we must go even further. Paul instructed believers to **rebuke and expose** these deeds because silence may be interpreted as approval. Just as the light shines into darkness and exposes what is hidden, so the light of Christ, through a believer, should shine into the darkness of sin and expose it for what it is. God needs people who will take an active and vocal stand against sin and permissiveness in all its forms (see Leviticus 19:17). Christians must lovingly speak out for what is true and right.

5:12-14 While believers should stand for the truth, they ought not get caught up in empty talk and gossip about the **shameful** actions of sinful people. We should not promote or dignify sin by even so much as discussing it. What the **ungodly people do in secret** becomes clear for **how evil it is**—all it takes is some **light**. Nothing can hide from the light piercing through darkness. Believers are the "rays" of that light. By our actions (5:8-12), we become

instruments of light, exposing the dark acts of sin. Believers who shine out in a dark world will expose evil. Their mission is to invite unbelievers to renounce their life of sin and come into Christ's light so that they, too, can step into the light.

This quotation is not a direct quote from Scripture but may have been taken from a hymn well known to the Ephesians. The hymn could have been part of a baptismal hymn that was sung by the congregation for a new convert when he or she emerged from the baptismal waters. For the new believer, coming out of spiritual death is like awaking from sleep, and coming into spiritual life is like greeting the sunshine—who is Christ. The hymn seems to have been based on Isaiah 26:19; 51:17; 52:1; and 60:1. As the prophets appealed to Israel to awaken from its state of darkness and death, so Paul was appealing to the Ephesians to stay **awake,** stay alert, and realize the dangerous condition into which some of them had been slipping by listening to false teachings.

LIVING BY THE SPIRIT'S POWER / 5:15-20

Because of believers' responsibility to live in the light (5:8) and to expose evil, they must be careful how they live. Their lives must please God (5:10), and they must conduct themselves before unbelievers so as to shine with Christ and draw others to him.

5:15 Paul encouraged the believers to live **not as fools but as those who are wise.** In other words, they must take their knowledge of Christ and apply it to their everyday lives and be especially aware of their conduct with unbelievers. Paul wrote to the Colossians, "Live wisely among those who are not Christians" (Colossians 4:5). Wisdom has been made available to believers; they need only ask for it (1:17; James 1:5; 3:17).

5:16 The Greek phrase translated as **make the most of every opportunity for doing good** conveys the idea of "buying from time" or "redeeming time." The believers should carefully use their time, making use of opportunities for doing good (see Galatians 6:10). This implies that we should not allow ourselves to be controlled by our circumstances; rather, we should make use of time as a valuable commodity or resource, as a master does with his servant. We should not read into this verse that God expects or condones workaholics. God has given us periods of both work and rest. We must never find in Scripture an excuse to neglect our physical needs or the needs of our families. Why be so concerned about using every opportunity to help draw people from darkness to light? Because these are **evil days,** wrote

Paul. He was communicating his sense of urgency because of evil's pervasiveness.

5:17 Believers must not waste their time acting **thoughtlessly.** We have a job to do, and our lives must reflect our motivation and our goal—to serve our Lord, to share his gospel message, and to be ready for his Kingdom. We should not be foolish and silly but instead **understand what the Lord wants** us **to do.** We have not only intellectually comprehended God's will, as taught in his Word, but we are also continually learning and growing in our understanding as we walk with him. What is the will of the Lord? Ultimately, it is to be holy (1 Thessalonians 4:3). As his servants, we ought to do everything we can to work toward his will for us.

5:18 These words should be considered in light of the whole section (4:17–5:20) in which Paul has contrasted the "before and after" of the believers' lives. Getting **drunk with wine** was associated with the old way of life and its selfish desires and will ultimately end in **ruin.** This has no place in the lives of believers. Besides, we don't need alcohol, according to Paul, for we can **let the Holy Spirit fill and control** us. Paul contrasted getting drunk with wine, which produces a temporary "high," to being filled with the Spirit, which produces lasting joy. The focus of Paul's words here is not so much the prohibition against drunkenness, for the believers probably already understood that, but his urging that they continually be filled by and live in the Spirit. When a person is drunk, everyone can tell. His or her actions make it obvious. In like manner, our lives should be so completely under the Spirit's control that our actions and words show beyond a doubt that we are filled with the presence of God's Holy Spirit.

5:19-20 Just as drunkenness is evidence of too much wine, so Spirit-filled worship should be evidence of the Holy Spirit's presence. From this exhortation came much of the style of historic corporate Christian worship that is still a part of our worship today. Believers can encourage one another and give praise to God through music. Paul mentioned **psalms**, such as the psalms of the Old Testament, as well as new ones written in the old style. The psalms were usually accompanied by a harp. **Hymns and spiritual songs** were written by the believers and could be used in praise to God. Some fragments of these hymns may exist in some of Paul's letters (see Philippians 2:5-11; Colossians 1:15-18; 1 Timothy 3:16). Although the early Christians had access to the Old Testament and freely used it, they did not yet have the New Testament or any other Christian books to study. Their stories and teachings about Christ were sometimes set to music to make them easier to memorize and pass on from person to person. Believers are to be full of the Holy Spirit when they sing. Grounded in God's word and correct doctrine, music can be an important part of Christian worship and education.

Paul encouraged the believers to **sing** and make **music** that comes from hearts that praise God. This makes a contrast between the music of Christians, sung together in praise to God, and the music of unbelievers, done purely for entertainment or self-praise. The primary focus of our singing is to **give thanks to God the Father in the name of our Lord Jesus Christ.**

SPIRIT-GUIDED RELATIONSHIPS: WIVES AND HUSBANDS / 5:21-33

Paul presented concepts governing household behavior. Household codes were common among Jewish and Greek communities. As Christianity spread, it aroused suspicion. Tensions grew between Christians and the rest of society. This required Christians to have high standards for their behavior. Paul outlined God's plan for Christian behavior in the home.

5:21 People often misunderstand the concept of submitting to another person. It does not mean becoming totally passive. Christ—at whose name every knee will bow (Philippians 2:10)—submitted his will to the Father, and we honor Christ by following his example. When we submit to God, we become more willing to obey his command to submit to others, that is, to subordinate our rights to theirs. In Paul's day, women, children, and slaves were to submit to the head of the family—slaves would submit until they were freed, male children until they grew up, and women and girls their whole lives. Paul emphasized the equality of all believers in Christ (Galatians 3:28), but he counseled all believers to **submit to one another** by choice. This kind of mutual submission preserves order and harmony.

Submission provides evidence that we have Spirit-controlled relationships, and it requires the Holy Spirit's guidance and restraint (4:2-3). In the church, the believers should be willing to learn from, serve, give to, or be corrected by others in the fellowship. Such submission can allow growth both individually and corporately as the believers seek to follow Christ. Our motive should be **reverence** (literally, "fear") for Christ. We should not treat one another rightly just because it is expected or because we will be well regarded but because one day we must give account to Christ of how we have lived.

5:22-24 Submission in the church should follow from submission in the home. The home, the foundation for relationships and personal growth, must be an example of peaceful submission. In a marriage relationship, both husband and wife are called to submit. The relationships between husbands and wives are a microcosm of the larger picture of church relationships.

Paul spoke first to the **wives**, explaining that they were to **submit** voluntarily to their **husbands** as they would **to the Lord,** meaning "as is fitting to the Lord." This does not mean that the husband is "lord" over the wife. Our concept of submission must come from that which exists between Christ and the church: Christ loves the church, and the church submits to him. We must not base it on either a feminist or chauvinist view. Christian marriage involves mutual submission, subordinating our personal desires for the good of the loved one and submitting ourselves to Christ as Lord. The wife's submission to her husband is one way that she can demonstrate her submission to Christ. She does this voluntarily out of love for her husband and for Christ.

Paul explained that **a husband is the head of his wife as Christ is the head of his body, the church.** In other words, the husband is the spiritual head of the family, and his wife should acknowledge his leadership. Real spiritual leadership involves service and sacrifice. Christ as head of the church is also its **Savior.** Christ gave his life for the church. So, **as the church submits to Christ, so the wives must submit to their husbands in everything.** A wise and Christ-honoring husband will not take advantage of his leadership role, and a wise and Christ-honoring wife will not try to undermine her husband's leadership. Either approach causes disunity and friction in marriage. For the wife, submission means willingly following her husband's leadership in Christ. For the husband, it means putting aside his own interests in order to care for his wife. Submission is rarely a problem in homes where both partners have a strong relationship with Christ and where each is concerned for the happiness of the other.

5:25-26 Paul also had words for **husbands**—to **love their wives.** Why did Paul tell wives to "submit" and husbands to "love"? Perhaps Christian women, newly freed in Christ, found submission difficult; perhaps Christian men, used to the Roman custom of giving unlimited power to the head of the family, were not used to treating their wives with sacrificial respect and love. Of course, both husbands and wives should submit to each other (5:21) just as both should love each other. Thus, "submission" reaffirms the new covenant of equality as well as the affirmation of marriage in which the partners voluntarily and joyously submit in order to seek each other's best.

Some Christians have thought that Paul was negative about marriage because of his counsel in 1 Corinthians 7:32-38. These verses in Ephesians, however, show a high view of marriage. Here marriage is not a practical necessity or a cure for lust but a picture of the relationship between Christ and his church! Husbands are called to love their wives **with the same love Christ showed the church.** That Christ **gave up his life** for the church indicates a sacrificial, substitutionary surrendering of himself to death. Christ sacrificed himself for the church because of his love for it. Husbands, then, should be ready to make whatever sacrifices are necessary for their wives. Marriage is a holy union, a living symbol, a precious relationship that needs tender, self-

sacrificing care. How should a man love his wife? (1) He should be willing to sacrifice everything for her. (2) He should make her well-being of primary importance. (3) He should care for her as he cares for his own body. No wife needs to fear submitting to a man who treats her in this way.

Paul further explained that Christ gave himself up for the church **to make her holy and clean, washed by baptism and God's word.** Christ's death sanctifies and cleanses the church. He cleanses his people from the old ways of sin and sets them apart for his special sacred service. Baptism is a picture of the cleansing that has occurred because of Christ's sacrificial death. Through baptism we are prepared for entrance into the church just as ancient Near Eastern brides were prepared for marriage by a ceremonial bath. It is God's word that cleanses us (John 17:17; Titus 3:5).

How does this apply to marriage? Probably the details need not be carried too far; Paul was quoting a hymn and did not mean for each detail to correspond to the marriage relationship. But this does paint the picture of mutual sanctification and self-sacrifice. Indeed, Paul had that thought in mind when he wrote in 1 Corinthians 7:12-16 that the unbelieving partner may be drawn to God by the believing partner. Paul was telling husbands to draw their wives closer to Christ and be a part of his sanctifying process. Peter applied the same thought to wives (1 Peter 3:1-2).

5:27 Continuing from 5:26, probably as part of an early Christian hymn, this verse explains why Christ gave himself up for the church in order to make the church holy—**to present her to himself as a glorious church without a spot or wrinkle or any other blemish.** The "presentation" pictures a future wedding; this is like the betrothal period, which for the Jews was as binding as marriage. The church age is the interim before the "wedding" when the church will at last be presented to Christ as his "bride" (Revelation 19:7). During this time, the church is making itself ready, as a bride would be preparing for her wedding. It was traditional for a bride to take a ritual bath just before her wedding as a symbol of her chastity. Similarly, the sacrament of baptism demonstrates the Christian's desire that God should find him or her pure and faithful when Christ returns to claim his bride, the church. The church does not make itself **holy and without fault;** instead, it has already been made so through the blood of Christ.

5:28 In the same way means that there exists between the husband and the wife the same union as between Christ and the church. Following from 5:27, husbands should be as concerned for their wife's spiritual growth and closeness to the Lord as Christ is for the church. Paul expressed this unity in physical terms, for the husband and wife become "one flesh" through marriage (Genesis 2:24; see 5:31 below, where Paul quoted this verse). So Christ and his church become "one" through spiritual union (see 4:4). As such, the church is Christ's body: "Now you are the body of Christ, and each one of you is a part of it" (1 Corinthians 12:27). Christ gave himself for the church (5:25), so **husbands ought to love their wives as they love their own bodies.** The spiritual and physical union between a husband and wife is as total and complete as the union a person has with his or her own body. When a man **loves his wife,** he **is actually loving himself** for she is so much a part of him. This is a beautiful picture of the mutuality that should be a part of every marriage. This picture shattered the cultural norms of the day, in which a wife was often considered no more than "property." No, Paul says, in fact, the relationship is so deep and intimate that the husband and wife are a single being. The husband loves his wife not as an extension of self-love but because it is advantageous both to her and to himself. The Greek word for "love" is *agapao*, referring to that giving love that seeks the highest good for the other. When a husband loves his wife with this kind of love, they both will benefit. A wife need not worry about submitting to a husband who treats her this way.

5:29-30 The fact that **no one hates his own body** refers not to self-centeredness but to self-preservation, the natural self-concern that causes people to feed and care for themselves. As a man **cares for** his own body, he should also do the same for his wife, who is one with him. Why? Again Paul draws on the example given by Christ, who nourishes and cares for **his body, which is the church.** As Christ nourishes and cares for believers, so husbands must imitate Christ in their loving concern and care for their wives. But more than just an example, Christ provides the basis for the husband's loving attention to his wife's needs. For the husband, and indeed every believer, receives this loving attention from Christ because **we are his body.** He cherishes and nourishes us as living parts of his body. (See John 15:1-8, where Jesus used the analogy of the vine and the branches to teach this concept.) The union of husband and wife reflects the union of the body of Christ; Christ is the life of both relationships (1:22-23; 4:12, 16).

5:31 The creation story tells of God's plan for husband and wife to be one (Genesis 2:24); Jesus also referred to this plan (Matthew 19:4-6). The union of husband and wife merges two persons in such a way that little can affect one without also affecting the other. Oneness in marriage does not mean one person's losing his or her personality in the personality of the other. Instead, it means that each person cares for the other as though caring for himself or herself, learning to anticipate the other's needs, helping the other person reach his or her potential.

5:32 The union of husband and wife, although sometimes imperfect, provides the best picture to describe the union of Christ with his church. The picture we experience in marriage is an analogy of the relationship of Christ and believers. The words in Genesis take on a more profound meaning as we contemplate Christ and his church. **This is a great mystery** pictures a profound hidden truth. As Paul contemplated the mutual love and loyalty, loving headship of the husband and loving submission of the wife, riches bestowed, intimacy and oneness, and self-sacrifice that should describe every marriage, he saw in these a picture of **Christ and the church.**

5:33 This verse returns to the commands about human marriage, summarizing the attitudes that are to be shown by both husband and wife. Here Paul addressed husbands first: **each man must love his wife as he loves himself.** This is the core of Christian marriage. Each **wife,** in turn, **must respect her husband.** How many marriages could be made healthy and strong if both husband and wife would fulfill these simple yet profound instructions?

EPHESIANS **6**

CHILDREN AND PARENTS / 6:1-4

If our faith in Christ is real, it will usually prove itself at home, in our relationships with those who know us best. Children and parents have a responsibility to each other. The fact that Paul took the time to directly address those who were regarded by some as the "lower" and "less important" members of society (wives, children, and slaves) shows that he raised them to a level of importance and responsibility in the body of Christ. All Christians are to be responsible in their positions, living as Christ would have them live.

6:1 Continuing the theme of Christian submission, Paul turned next to **children.** He assumed that children would be in the congregation of believers as this letter was read. By even addressing them—a segment of society that was considered to be virtually without rights—Paul elevated them and invested them with dignity and worth unheard of in the Roman world at the time. His command to them is simple: **Obey your parents.** This is not an absolute command; when a parent tells a child to do something unbiblical, immoral, or unethical, the law of God supersedes the will of the parent. But aside from those extremes, children are to obey their mothers and fathers. This is the way God intends it. It's easy to see the immediate practical benefits of this for both children and parents because parents usually really do know best.

The Greek word for "children" *(tekna)* refers to young children living at home (see also Colossians 3:20, where the same word is used). The word "obey" conveys a stronger demand than the submission required of wives (5:22). God requires children to obey because children need to rely on the wisdom of their parents. Jesus himself submitted to the authority of his earthly parents, despite his authority as the Messiah (Luke 2:51). All young children will, at times, disobey and test their parents' limits. As they get older, they will understand why God wants them to obey. Obedience that recognizes parents' authority can carry over into recognizing God's authority. God's plan for his people includes solid family relationships where there exists respect, obedience, submission, and love for one another. When both parents and children love God, all of them will seek to obey and please him.

6:2-3 Paul added the authority of the revealed law to the natural law described in 6:1, quoting the fifth commandment, recorded in Exodus 20:12, **Honor your father and mother.** Obeying and honoring are different. To obey means to do what another says to do; to honor means to respect and love. Children are to obey while under their parents' care, but they must honor their parents for life. This command **ends with a promise,** that of **a long life, full of blessing.** How is this the first commandment with a promise? It is neither the first commandment, nor the first with a promise, since the second commandment carries a promise with it. Commentators offer many explanations. Two are most helpful: (1) This is the first commandment (after the first four, which are general commandments) that deals with social involvements and codes for behavior. (2) More likely, this is the first or primary commandment for children to follow, but it holds a promise applicable to them. As children obey the command to honor their parents, they show an attitude of love and respect that they carry over into their relationship with God. Such an attitude provides a community that helps provide for and protect the aged. On the individual level, as each person cares for older people, the elderly live longer, and the younger people help pass the values down to the next generation.

6:4 Parental discipline should help children learn, not exasperate and make them **angry.** In Colossians 3:21, Paul gave the same advice, adding that if children are disciplined in unloving and irresponsible ways, they may become discouraged and resentful. In families of Paul's day, the father had full legal rights over his children and often ran his household with rigid control. In Jewish families, the fathers were responsible for the education of the children. Paul did not have to establish the fathers' authority; rather, his aim was to set the limits on harsh treatment. Parenting is not easy—it takes lots of patience to raise children in a loving, Christ-honoring manner. But frustration and anger should not be causes for discipline. Parents can remove the exasperating effect of their discipline by avoiding nagging, labeling, criticizing, or dominating. Don't goad your children into resenting you. Paul wrote specifically to **fathers** because, in that culture, fathers were the absolute head of the home, with complete control and authority. For Paul to say that they needed to treat their children as human beings and consider their feelings was revolutionary. As Christ changed the way husbands and wives related, so he changed the way parents and children related.

Parents ought not provoke their children, and neither should they abandon their responsibility to guide, correct, and discipline them. Parents still have a job to do for their children—to **bring them up with the discipline and instruction approved by the Lord.** The words "bring up" imply nourishing and cherishing. "Discipline" includes punishment for wrongdoing combined with persistent love (see Proverbs 13:24; 22:6, 15; 23:14), all as part of the "instruction" of a child.

SLAVES AND MASTERS / 6:5-9

Slaves played a significant part in this society as well as in most societies of that day. No ancient government ever considered abolishing slavery as it was such an instrumental part of the Mediterranean economy. There were several million slaves in the Roman Empire at this time. People could become slaves by being born to a woman who was a slave, by being made a slave as punishment for a crime, by being kidnapped from another land, and by being conquered by another nation (slave dealers would buy captured prisoners and send them to the slave markets to be sold for a profit). Sometimes, however, parents would sell their children into slavery. And some would voluntarily become slaves in order to pay a debt. Usually those with financial means owned slaves. Slave owners had absolute power over their slaves.

Because many slaves and owners had become Christians, the early church had to deal straightforwardly with the question of master/slave relations. Masters and slaves had to learn how to live together in Christian households. They were to be treated equally in the church. In Paul's day, women, children, and slaves had few rights. In the church, however, they had freedoms that society denied them.

6:5 Paul used the same word for **obey** here that he used in 6:1. Slaves were to obey the commands and desires of their masters; this was their duty because of the authority of the master. Paul addressed the slaves who had become Christians and needed to understand how their new faith affected their service to human masters. Paul advised the slaves to treat their **earthly masters with deep respect and fear** (referring to an attitude of reverence and honor, a desire to do right). These slaves had been set free from slavery to sin, but they were not freed from serving their masters. They should serve their masters in the same way they would **serve Christ.**

6:6 Slaves were to **work hard** for their masters, not only when they were being watched and hoping for a reward, but at all times. They should work not only for human approval but also to **do the will of God** with all their hearts. Why? Because they were **slaves of Christ** as well as of human masters. They should work hard to do their job well in this world, while at the same time working hard for Christ as they look forward to the next world, where all believers will serve Christ in his Kingdom. All believers, as slaves of Christ (whether slaves or free in this world), should do the **will of God** with all their hearts, wholeheartedly, not halfheartedly, doing their work well enough to pass God's inspection.

6:7-8 Slaves had a variety of tasks—running errands, caring for or teaching children, cleaning, preparing meals, or doing menial work. Paul gave their jobs a new dignity, telling these slaves to **work as though they were working for the Lord rather than for people.** Our true Master, the Lord Jesus, knows the state of our hearts and knows if we are shirking the job that we, as his slaves, have been given to do. We should also faithfully serve our earthly masters in this way. The Christian slave should obey as an expression of his or her commitment to the Lord. In the end, all people, slaves and free, will be rewarded by the Lord.

6:9 Paul also had words for the **masters,** for those who had become Christians needed guidance in relationships with their Christian slaves. Paul advised them to treat their slaves **in the same way.** In other words, the masters should have the same concern for God's will and for the slaves' well-being as the slaves were expected to show toward God and their masters.

In those days, slaves may have been conquered peoples from foreign lands or people sold into slavery to recover debts. It was difficult for a slave to rise from that social caste. Often slaves were treated as less than human, thus Paul's advice to masters, **Don't threaten them.** Without attempting to overturn the social structure of a worldwide empire, Paul applied Christ's inward transforming principles to the system. Paul did not advise the Christian masters to free their slaves; in fact, in some cases, setting them free might not have been the best action. Instead, Paul told the masters to remember that both the master and the slave had **the same Master in heaven.** Although Christians may be at different levels in earthly society, we are all equal before God. He does not have **favorites;** no one is more important than anyone else. Paul's letter to Philemon stresses the same point: Philemon, the master, and Onesimus, his slave, had become brothers in Christ.

THE WHOLE ARMOR OF GOD / 6:10-20

In this letter, Paul explained the need for unity in the body of believers; here he further explained the need for that unity—there will be inevitable clashes with evil, and the church must be ready to stand and fight. In the Christian life, we battle against rulers and authorities (the powerful evil forces of fallen angels headed by Satan, who is a vicious fighter, see 1 Peter 5:8). To withstand their attacks, we must depend on God's strength and use every piece of his armor. Paul was not only giving this counsel to the church, the body of Christ, but to all individuals within the church. The whole body needs to be armed. As you battle against evil, fight in the strength of the church, whose power comes from the Holy Spirit. What can your church do to be a Christian armory?

6:10 Be strong with the Lord's mighty power refers to strength derived from God, not strength we humans have to somehow obtain. The words "be strong" describe continual empowering of the Christian community. God's strength and power are part of the Kingdom blessings available to God's people. The power that raised Christ from the dead empowers God's people as they prepare for the spiritual battle they must face on this earth.

6:11 God empowers his people, but he does not send them into battle unarmed. God's people must **put on all of God's armor** (see also Romans 13:12). The *panoplia*, or full armor, means complete equipment, head-to-toe protection, both defensively and offensively. This gear was for hand-to-hand combat. This "armor of God" was mentioned in the Old Testament. Isaiah 59:17 describes God as wearing the breastplate of righteousness and the helmet of salvation. Paul wrote this letter while chained to a Roman soldier. Certainly the soldier's armor must have brought this metaphor to mind. Paul described a divine and complete "outfit" that God gives believers in order to provide all we need to **stand firm against all strategies and tricks of the Devil.** The Devil rules the world of darkness, the kingdom opposed to God. "Stand against" was a military term meaning to resist the enemy, hold the position, and offer no surrender. The Devil will not fight fair; he uses subtle tricks and schemes. Our ability to stand firm depends on our use of the armor.

6:12 Christians are **fighting** against evil—describing hand-to-hand combat. But we are not in an earthly military campaign—our battle is not **against people made of flesh and blood.** Instead, we battle the demons over whom Satan has control. Demons work to tempt people to sin. They were not created by Satan because God is the Creator of all. Rather, the demons are fallen angels who joined Satan in his rebellion and thus became perverted and evil. The descriptive words

reveal the characteristics of these enemies as well as their sphere of operations. **Rulers** and **authorities** are cosmic powers, or demons, mentioned in 1:21. These spiritual beings have limited power. They are invisible to us, operating in **the unseen world.** The **mighty powers** refers to those spiritual powers who aspire to world control. They are evil (of the **darkness**) and they currently **rule this world.** The **wicked spirits in the heavenly realms** refers to the demons' dwellings, planets and stars, from which the demons control the lives of people. Paul used the names of groups of evil powers not so much to establish classes or distinguish demonic powers as to show the full extent of Satan's warfare.

Here is a host of spiritual forces arrayed against us, requiring us to use God's full armor. These are real and powerful beings, not mere fantasies. Believers must not underestimate them. The Ephesians had practiced magic and witchcraft (Acts 19:19), so they were well aware of the power of the darkness. We face a powerful army whose goal is to defeat Christ's church. When we believe in Christ, the satanic beings become our enemies, and they try every device to turn us away from him and back to sin. Although believers are assured of victory, we must engage in the struggle until Christ returns because Satan constantly battles against all who are on God's side.

6:13 Believers' response to the reality of this warfare should be to **use every piece of God's armor.** The armor is available, but the believer-soldier must use it. We would be neglectful to do otherwise, for the battle is real, and we are Satan's targets. Only with the armor will believers be able to be **standing firm,** a word describing standing against great opposition; indeed, it would be impossible to stand on our strength alone. Christian soldiers must be able to hold their ground and not flee or surrender under Satan's attacks. **The time of evil** refers to the hours of trial that have within themselves the seeds of the last and greatest trial. Christians must be prepared for every day's conflicts with the forces of evil.

6:14 In order to **stand** their **ground** in the heat of battle, believers need every piece of God's armor. The order of the pieces listed in the following verses is the order in which a soldier would put them on. First, fasten **the sturdy belt of truth** around your waist. This belt, also called a girdle, was about six inches wide. Probably made of leather, it held together the clothing underneath as well as holding the other pieces of armor in place, such as the breastplate and the sheath for the sword. It may have contained a "breechclout," an apron that protected the lower abdomen. It may have also braced the back in order to give strength. When the belt was fastened, the soldier was "on duty," ready to fight. A slackened belt meant "off duty." Christians, however, must face each day with a fastened belt, ready to fight the battle when needed. As the belt formed the foundation of the soldier's armor, the truth is the foundation of the Christian life. When the enemy, the father of lies (John 8:44), attacks with his lies, half-truths, and distortions, we believers can stand firm in the truth.

Next, the soldier must put on **the body armor of God's righteousness.** The body armor was a large leather, bronze, or chain-mail piece that protected the body from the neck to the thighs. Protecting the vital organs, no soldier would go into battle without his body armor. Often this had a back piece too, protecting the body from hits from behind. Righteousness provides a significant defense; it gives the evidence that we have been made right with God and that this righteousness has been given us by the Holy Spirit. Satan seeks to thwart righteous living. When the enemy, the accuser (Revelation 12:10), tries to convince us that we are not really saved, that we just keep on disappointing God, and that we're "poor excuses" for Christians, we can stand up to him because of the righteousness we have been promised through our faith in Jesus Christ.

6:15 A soldier wore special sandals or military shoes that protected his feet without slowing him down. Roman soldiers had special shoes made of soft leather with studded soles. This allowed them to march farther and faster as well as giving them facility of motion in battle—they could dig in and hold their ground when in hand-to-hand combat.

Believers also need special **shoes—peace that comes from the Good News.** Believers can stand firm, with peace, even in hand-to-hand combat, because they know that they are doing right and that they are on the winning side. Christians are in the battle both with the inner peace Christ has already given and the desire to produce that peace in the hearts of others. This can only happen as they share this "gospel of peace" with those who have not yet heard and accepted it. When the enemy, the deceiver (Revelation 12:9), offers false ways to peace or tries to get us to focus on our concerns and fears, we Christian soldiers can stand up to him.

6:16 The soldier needed to also carry extra protection in the form of a **shield.** The image was taken from the Roman shield, a large oblong or oval piece, approximately four feet high by two feet wide, made of wood and leather, often with an iron frame. Sometimes the leather would be soaked in water to help extinguish **fiery arrows.** The ancient "flaming arrow" or "fire dart" was made of cane with a flammable head that was lighted and then shot so as to set fire to wooden shields, cloth tents, etc. For Christians, this shield is **faith**—complete reliance on God. Faith means total dependence on God and willingness to do his will. It is not something we put on for a show for others. It means believing in his promises even though we don't see those promises materializing yet. When the enemy, the ruler of this world (John 12:31), sends his fiery arrows of temptation, doubt, wrath, lust, despair, vengeance, problems, and trials into our lives, we can hold up our shields and **stop** them. Faith gives us the strength to stand against Satan with firm courage, even when he uses his most fearsome weapons.

6:17 The **helmet** protected the soldier's head. Helmets were made of leather and brass, or sometimes bronze and iron—no sword could pierce a good helmet. Isaiah 59:17 describes God wearing a helmet of **salvation.** Believers' salvation, already accomplished, will be consummated when Christ comes to claim his own. With the assurance of salvation protecting their minds, Christians can stand against Satan's attacks. As a blow to the head often means death, so a person without hope of salvation will be easily defeated by the enemy. When the enemy, the Devil (1 Peter 5:8), seeks to devour and destroy God's people with empty or evil thoughts, trying to get us to doubt our salvation, we can trust in the protection of the helmet. Our salvation will be accomplished, for God has promised it.

Finally, the soldier takes **the sword of the Spirit**—the only offensive weapon mentioned. This refers to the short sword used in close combat. The sharp, short sword was one of Rome's great military innovations. The Roman army was called the "short swords" because of its use of the short swords in winning battles. The sword's double edges made it ideal for "cut and thrust" strategy. The Spirit makes the **word of God** effective as we speak it and receive it. The Spirit gives the word its penetrating power and sharp edge. Jesus' use of God's word in his temptation prompts our use of it against Satan (Matthew 4:4, 7, 10). With the Holy Spirit within, believers have the constant reminder of God's word to use against Satan's temptations. When the enemy, the tempter (Matthew 4:3-4; 1 Thessalonians 3:5), tries to tempt us to do evil, we have the power to send him away with the word of God. The Spirit will bring the words to mind.

6:18 This verse, although not naming another "weapon" in the believer's armor, does continue the thought of 6:17. As we take the sword of the Spirit, God's word, we must also **pray at all times and on every occasion in the power of the Holy Spirit.** Praying in the Spirit means that the Spirit helps us when we pray (Romans 8:26); the Spirit prays on our behalf (Romans 8:27); the Spirit makes God accessible (Ephesians 2:18); the Spirit gives us confidence when we pray (Romans 8:15-16; Galatians 4:6). He inspires and guides us when we pray. He helps us communicate with God and also brings God's response to us.

Paul was not calling prayer a weapon; instead, he was giving the how-to's for taking up the armor described in the previous verses. We must not underestimate Satan's forces. He will strike in different ways at different people; thus, we need to pray "all kinds" of prayers, allowing for all kinds of requests. Satan will attack at various times, but he will always be attacking someone. Satan will attack when we least expect it, so we need to

stay alert to prayer needs when they arise. Satan will rarely let up if he thinks he can win the battle, so believers must **be persistent** in praying, no matter how long it takes. No believer is exempt from being Satan's target—Satan demands battle against his enemies (believers). Thus **all Christians everywhere** need our prayer support.

How can anyone pray at all times? Make quick, brief prayers your habitual response to every situation you meet throughout the day. Order your life around God's desires and teachings so that your very life becomes a prayer. You can make prayer your life and your life a prayer while living in a world that needs God's powerful influence.

6:19-20 After asking the believers to pray for one another in the battle, he asked them to pray also for him. Paul wrote this letter as a Roman prisoner, yet his ministry could be virtually unhindered if he continued to speak the gospel message clearly. Undiscouraged and undefeated, Paul wrote powerful letters of encouragement from prison. He did not ask the Ephesians to pray that his chains would be removed but that he would continue to **boldly explain God's secret plan** even as he wore his **chains.** The "secret plan" refers to God's plan through the ages to draw both Jews and Gentiles to himself in one body, the church (see 1:9; 3:3, 6, 9; 5:32). Indeed, it was that very message that had landed Paul in prison in the first place (see Acts 22:17–23:11). Yet he considered himself **God's ambassador,** a political term for a government's legal representative. Paul realized that in being taken to Rome as a prisoner, he was actually acting as an ambassador for another "nation," God's Kingdom.

FINAL GREETINGS / 6:21-24
Paul closed this letter to the Ephesians and the surrounding churches by sending greetings from Rome and the Christians there. The Roman Christians and the Ephesian Christians were brothers and sisters because of their unity in Christ. Believers today are also linked to others across cultural, economic, and social barriers. All believers are one family in Christ Jesus.

6:21-22 Tychicus is also mentioned in Acts 20:4; Colossians 4:7; 2 Timothy 4:12; and Titus 3:12. He carried this letter to the Ephesians, as well as the one to the Colossians (and probably the one to Philemon as well). Tychicus brought news about Paul to the Ephesian church, which would be very interested in hearing how Paul was doing. Paul had lived in Ephesus for three years and had become very close to the believers there (see Acts 20:17-38). Paul did not write of all those details in his letter because this letter was meant to go to several churches in the area (see the Introduction). Instead,

he would allow Tychicus to give the Ephesian believers the details of how he was **getting along.**

Paul wanted Tychicus to **encourage** the believers, for it seems that they were discouraged by Paul's imprisonment (3:13). Paul wanted them to know that his imprisonment was resulting in great things for the worldwide church.

6:23 Paul closed his letter with a prayer that they would have **peace** (1:2; 2:14-15, 17; 4:3; 6:15). He knew they had **faith,** but he prayed that **love** would accompany it (1:4, 15; 2:4; 3:17-19; 4:2,

15-16; 5:2, 25, 28, 33). The source of peace, love, and faith is **God the Father and the Lord Jesus Christ.**

6:24 As he began his letter (1:2), so he ended it. Paul's final prayer was for **God's grace** upon his readers, a topic he had also written about in this letter (see also 1:6; 2:5, 7-8; 3:2, 7-8; 4:7). God's grace can only be upon those **who love our Lord Jesus Christ with an undying love.** Such love for our Lord is a taste of the eternal life of love that is our guaranteed inheritance.

Philippi sat on the Egnatian Way, the main transportation route in Macedonia, an extension of the Appian Way, which joined the eastern empire with Italy.

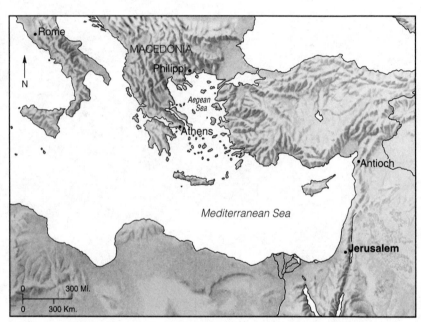

PHILIPPIANS

INTRODUCTION

Picture a baby, rested, fed, and lying in his mother's arms. Looking down with unspeakable love into those precious eyes, Mommy begins to talk to her son and gently strokes his cheek, evoking a sudden smile.

Or imagine a three-year-old playing with his father on the living room floor. With Dad's wrestling moves transformed into tickles, the little boy begins to giggle, and both end up laughing hysterically.

That's joy—contentment, security, and unbridled laughter.

But joy can also be discovered in the pain and struggles of life—at a funeral, knowing, through tears, that your loved one now lives with God; in a hospital bed, knowing that the Lord stands near; at the unemployment office, knowing that God will provide all your needs. True joy runs deep and strong, flowing from confident assurance in God's loving control. Regardless of your life's situation, you can find joy, true joy, in Christ.

Joy dominates this letter to the believers at Philippi. In fact, the concept of "rejoicing" or "joy" appears sixteen times in four chapters. The pages radiate the positive, triumphant message that because of Christ's work for us (2:6-11; 3:12), because of the Holy Spirit's work in and through us (1:6, 12-14, 18-26; 2:12-13; 4:4-7, 10-13), and because of God's plan for us (1:6, 9-10, 3:7-14, 20-21; 4:19), we can and should REJOICE!

As you read Paul's letter from prison to his beloved friends in Philippi, note all that you possess in Christ, and find your joy in him.

AUTHOR

Paul (Saul of Tarsus): Pharisee, apostle, teacher, church planter, evangelist.

Evidence for Paul's authorship of Philippians comes from the letter itself, as the very first sentence states: "This letter is from Paul and Timothy" (1:1). Although Timothy's name also appears in the greeting, it soon becomes obvious that Paul alone is writing since he uses the first person throughout the letter. In addition, the personal references in 3:4-11 and 4:10-16 clearly apply to Paul. The early church fathers Polycarp, Irenaeus, Clement of Alexandria, Eusebius, and others affirmed Paul's authorship.

For more about Paul, see the Author section in the Introduction to the book of Romans.

DATE AND SETTING

Written from prison in Rome in approximately A.D. 61.

Paul wanted to get to Rome (Acts 19:21), not only to teach and fellowship with the believers there (Romans 1:8-13), but also because Rome stood as the center of the civilized world. It was a strategic city for the spread of the gospel. To reach the Roman Empire, the gospel had to reach Rome.

In God's sovereign plan, Paul did sail to Rome, but not as a prominent citizen, missionary statesman, or even itinerant preacher. He arrived, rather, as a prisoner, in chains (Acts 28:11-16). Even as a prisoner, however, Paul was free to teach, preach, and write (Acts 28:17-31). During these years of house arrest, Paul wrote what have come to be known as the "Prison Epistles"—Ephesians, Philippians, Colossians, and Philemon.

It is clear that Paul was a Roman prisoner when he wrote this letter because of his words in 1:12-17. He wrote of being "in chains" (1:13, 17) and of being a witness for Christ to "all the soldiers in the palace guard" (1:13). Paul's imprisonment at that time and place fits the statement about his needs (4:17-18), allows time for the trips to and from Philippi, and makes sense of his references to the palace guard (1:13) and Caesar's palace (4:22).

All that is known of Paul's place of confinement in Rome at this time is that it was his own rented house. Thus, Paul's prison was considerably more comfortable than the environment in which he wrote 2 Timothy. In that prison, the Mamertine dungeon, Paul was suffering and chained like a criminal (2 Timothy 2:9). He had been deserted (2 Timothy 4:10, 16), he was cold (2 Timothy 4:13), and he was expecting to die (2 Timothy 4:6-7, 18). In this setting, however, although guarded constantly, Paul enjoyed great freedom to welcome visitors (Acts 28:17-30) and to preach and teach (Acts 28:31).

Paul was imprisoned in Rome for two years—approximately A.D. 60–62. He wrote Philippians in about A.D. 61. Evidently, this was the last letter written from prison because 1:21-28 seems to indicate that Paul was expecting a decision about his fate very soon.

AUDIENCE
The believers in Philippi

The Macedonian (northern Greece today) city of Philippi was named after Philip of Macedon (the father of Alexander the Great). Surrounded by mountains and close to the sea, Philippi became a strategic city in the Greek empire. In 167 B.C. it became part of the Roman Empire, but it did not achieve real importance until after 31 B.C. when Octavian defeated Antony at the battle of Actium. After that decisive battle, Philippi received a number of Italian colonists who had favored Antony and had been dispossessed of their property. The colony was then renamed Colonia Iulia Philippensis to honor Julius Caesar. Later, in 27 B.C., when Octavian was designated Augustus, the colony's name was changed again to Colonia Augusta Iulia (Victrix) Philippensium, equating the cause of Augustus with that of Caesar. At that time, Philippi was given the right to the Law of Italy together with many rights and privileges, including immunity from taxation. The residents of Philippi were very conscious and proud of their Roman citizenship and heritage (see Acts 16:20-21). Philippi also boasted a fine school of medicine.

Paul visited Philippi on his second missionary journey, in A.D. 51, about ten years previous to this letter. By the time of Paul's visit, Philippi had become a thriving commercial center because of its strategic location as the first city on the Egnatian Way, an important ancient highway linking the Aegean and Adriatic Seas. Travelers to Rome would cross the Adriatic and then continue up to Rome on the Appian Way. Thus, Philippi was the gateway to the East. Although thoroughly colonized by the Romans after 31 B.C., Philippi was still more Greek in culture than Roman. Luke refers to Philippi as "a major city of the district of Macedonia and a Roman colony" (Acts 16:12). Although Philippi was not the capital city of the region (subprovince of Macedonia), it certainly was a "major city." Luke's statement also reflects civic pride in his hometown.

The church at Philippi in ancient Macedonia was the first European church founded by Paul. Thus, it represents the first major penetration of the gospel into Gentile territory (see Philippians 4:14-15).

Acts 16:9-40 tells how the church began. On the second missionary journey in about A.D. 51, prevented by the Holy Spirit from preaching in Asia and in Bythinia, Paul and Silas traveled to Troas, the farthest Asian port on the Aegean Sea. While there, God spoke to Paul through a vision, telling him to take the gospel to Europe. In this vision, a Greek man begged, "Come over here and help us" (Acts 16:9). Immediately, Paul and his traveling companions set sail for Samothrace and Neapolis, continuing on to Philippi.

In every city, Paul and his party would go to the synagogue to share the gospel with the Jews. So on their first Sabbath in Philippi, Paul and Silas probably looked for a synagogue. Instead, they found a group of women who had gathered outside the city on the banks of a river. The fact that Philippi had no synagogue indicates that there were few Jews in that city. Therefore, from its inception, the church at Philippi consisted mainly of Gentiles. Acts 16:14-34 tells of two of the first converts in Philippi: Lydia, a businesswoman who may have been a Jew or a Jewish proselyte; and a Roman jailer. The response of these two provided a clear demonstration that God's Good News was for all classes, sexes, races, and nationalities.

Luke also mentions that when Lydia responded to Paul's message, so did the members of her household (Acts 16:15). The same was true for the jailer—his family responded with him (Acts 16:34). No other specific converts are mentioned in this account in Acts, but the chapter concludes with: "Paul and Silas . . . met with the believers" (Acts 16:40). The plural seems to indicate that a small but vital group of believers had been forged. Clement, Euodia, and Syntyche may have been won to Christ during this time (see 4:2-3).

When Paul and Silas departed from Philippi, they left Luke there, in his hometown, to carry on the ministry. A few years later, at the end of his third missionary trip, Paul visited Philippi prior to spending the winter in Corinth. When Paul wrote this epistle, the church in Philippi was thriving, and he felt very close to the believers there.

OCCASION AND PURPOSE
To thank the Philippians for their gift and to strengthen the believers in their faith.

This is a very personal epistle. It is obvious from Paul's opening comments that he enjoyed a close friendship with the Philippian believers. During their visit to Philippi, Paul and Silas had witnessed an immediate and dramatic response to their message. And despite the fact that they were attacked and imprisoned, they had seen the church begin and then grow into a strong core of believers (Acts 16:40). During the course of Paul's ministry, the Philippian believers had continually come to his assistance through their gifts (4:15-18). At this time, nearly ten years later, the Philippians had again sent a gift to Paul to help him in his time of need (4:10, 14). Perhaps their donated funds were helping to pay for the rented house to which Paul was confined (Acts 28:30). In response to this gift and to their relationship over the years, Paul wrote to express his deep appreciation for their love, faithfulness, and generosity.

Paul also took the opportunity of this letter to deal with important issues in the church. He had heard of divisive rivalry and selfish ambition (2:3-4), so he gave strong counsel and even named names (4:2). Paul knew that the Judaizers could be a problem, so he gave clear instructions to avoid those men (3:2-3). He also warned of those who would go to the opposite extreme and live totally without the law or any personal discipline (3:17-19). None of these issues were full-blown problems that were threatening the life of the church, but Paul knew their destructive pattern. So he warned his beloved Christian brothers and sisters, encouraging and challenging them to continue to stand strong and united and to live for Christ (1:27; 4:1, 4-9).

Paul's sensitivity to the needs at Philippi stands as a great example. He didn't wait for a crisis; instead, he confronted potential problems early, before they could fester and infect the whole body. When we see a fellow believer begin to struggle or stray, we should follow Paul's example and lovingly confront that person, urging him or her to stay on track.

MESSAGE

Philippians is Paul's joy letter. The church in that Macedonian city had been a great encouragement to Paul. The Philippian believers had enjoyed a very special relationship with Paul, so he wrote them a personal expression of his love and affection. They had brought him great joy (4:1). Philippians is also a joyful book because it emphasizes the real joy of the Christian life. The concept of **rejoicing** or **joy** appears sixteen times in four chapters, and the pages radiate this positive message, culminating in the exhortation to "Always be full of joy in the Lord" (4:4).

In a life dedicated to serving Christ, Paul had faced excruciating poverty, abundant wealth, and everything in between. He even wrote this joyful letter from prison. Whatever the circumstances, Paul had learned to be content (4:11, 12), finding real joy as he focused all of his attention and energy on knowing Christ (3:8) and obeying him (3:12, 13).

The main themes in the book of Philippians include: *Joy, Humility, Self-sacrifice, Unity,* and *Christian Living.*

Joy (1:3-6, 12-26; 2:1-4, 17-18; 3:1; 4:4-13). Although Paul had suffered much for the cause of Christ and was writing this letter as a prisoner of Rome, still he was filled with joy because of what God had done for him, because of his hope in God's plan for the future, and because of the faithfulness of the Philippian believers. Paul knew that his beloved brothers and sisters in Christ would be tempted and tested, so he urged them to stay strong in their faith, to be content, and to rejoice always. Regardless of the circumstances, believers can have profound contentment, serenity, and peace. This joy comes from knowing Christ personally, depending on his strength, and trusting in his plan for our lives.

IMPORTANCE FOR TODAY. Most people are discontent and continually seeking meaning and peace. But true, lasting contentment comes only through knowing Christ. With sins forgiven, our future secure, and our lives in God's control, we can be content . . . and have joy. Yes, we can have joy, even in hardship. Joy does not come from outward circumstances but from inward strength. In addition to discontent, Paul highlights other joy-stealers: selfish ambition (1:17; 2:3), complaining and arguing (2:14), self-centeredness (2:21), hedonism (3:18-19), anxiety (4:6), and bad thoughts (4:8). What steals your joy? Rely on Christ within you to give you joy, not on what you own, who you know, or what you experience.

Humility (1:15-18; 2:5-11; 3:7-14). If anyone had the right to boast, it was Paul. Yet he continued to lay aside personal ambition and glory in order to know Christ (3:7-11) and to glorify him (3:12-14). Paul knew that Jesus had left glory to come to earth in order to live as a man and to die on the cross. Paul held up Jesus as the example to follow, urging the Philippians to humble themselves as Christ had done. Jesus showed true humility when he laid aside his rights and privileges as God to become a human being (2:5-11). He poured out his life to pay the penalty that we deserve. Laying aside self-interest is essential to being Christlike.

IMPORTANCE FOR TODAY. As Christ's representatives, believers should live as he would. This means putting others first and renouncing personal recognition. It also means serving others and looking out for their best interests. When we give up our self-interest, we can serve the Lord with joy, love, and kindness. True humility is a by-product of seeing ourselves from Christ's perspective and recognizing that we are nothing without him. What can you do to see yourself and the world from Christ's point of view? What can you do to give your life for others?

Self-sacrifice (1:15-26; 2:4, 17, 25-30; 3:7-14; 4:14-19). Christ suffered and died so that all who believe might have eternal life. Following Christ's example, with courage and faithfulness, Paul sacrificed himself for the ministry, taking every chance to tell others God's Good News, preaching and teaching even while in prison. For Paul, living meant opportunities for serving the Lord, but dying would mean going to live with the Lord (1:20-24). So Paul lived with his goal always before him, motivating him to forget the past and press on to win the prize (3:13-14).

IMPORTANCE FOR TODAY. Reaching people for Christ, helping those in need, and changing our world will involve personal sacrifice. Christ gives us the power to do that. We must follow the example of Jesus and of godly leaders like Paul who demonstrate self-denying concern for others. What will it take—what sacrifices will you have to make—for you to be an effective witness for Christ in your neighborhood? at work? What will it take for your church to make a difference for Christ in your community?

Unity (1:15-18, 27-30; 2:1-4, 14-16; 4:2-3). In every church, in every generation, controversial issues, personality conflicts, and other divisive issues arise.

The tendency toward arguments and division intensifies during hard times, when people can turn against each other. Although the church at Philippi was strong, it was not immune to these problems and, in fact, had experienced some internal conflicts. Paul encouraged the Philippians to get along, agree with one another, stop complaining, and work together.

IMPORTANCE FOR TODAY. Christians should contend against their common enemy—Satan and his work in the world—and not against each other. We need all our resources, focus, and energy for the battle. When we are unified in love, Christ works through us, and we can make a difference for him. We need to keep before us the ideals of teamwork, consideration of others, and unselfishness. What tends to break your unity with other believers? What issues threaten to divide your church? Keep your focus on Christ and his mission in the world; don't be sidetracked by petty jealousies, competition, hurt feelings, or minor irritations. Work together with your brothers and sisters in Christ to make a difference in the world.

Christian Living (1:6, 9-11, 21-29; 2:12-13; 3:12-21; 4:4-13). Paul could not stay in Philippi, teaching the new believers, encouraging them to live for Christ, and holding them accountable. When he was with the Philippians, they were careful to obey the Lord (2:12) because they were aware of Paul's powerful example and strong encouragement. But now, in his absence, they should be even more careful to live the Christian life (work out their own salvation—2:12). They could be confident that God was with them and in them, changing them from the inside out (2:13). Certainly God would complete his good work in them (1:6).

IMPORTANCE FOR TODAY. In this day of media evangelists, celebrity Bible teachers, and articulate preachers, it can be easy to depend on others for our spiritual nourishment and motivation. Yet the Christian life always depends on the relationship an individual believer has with the Lord Jesus. Instead of relying on others for our "faith," we must depend on Christ and the Holy Spirit working within us. And instead of expecting growth to happen because we have a strong Christian environment, we must keep our focus on Christ, discipline ourselves to pray and to read the Bible, and apply God's word to our lives. On whom do you depend for your motivation to live for Christ? Where do you find your spiritual nourishment? Christian living depends on Christ living in you and you then living in obedience to him.

OUTLINE OF PHILIPPIANS

I. Joy in Suffering (1:1-30)
II. Joy in Serving (2:1-30)
III. Joy in Believing (3:1–4:1)
IV. Joy in Giving (4:2-23)

PHILIPPIANS 1

GREETINGS FROM PAUL / 1:1-2

As Paul wrote this letter, he was under house arrest in Rome. When the Philippian church had heard about Paul's imprisonment, they had sent Epaphroditus (who may have been one their elders) to Rome to visit and encourage him. Epaphroditus had arrived with words of affection from the church, as well as a financial contribution that would help make Paul's confinement more comfortable. Paul wanted to thank the believers for helping him during his time of need. He also wanted to tell them why he could be full of joy despite his imprisonment and upcoming trial. He wanted them to remain strong in the faith, realizing that although he was in chains for the gospel, God was still in control and the truth of the gospel remained unchanged. In this uplifting letter, Paul counseled the Philippians about humility and unity and warned them about potential problems they would face.

1:1 The undisputed author of this letter is the apostle **Paul,** missionary to the Gentiles, imprisoned in Rome for preaching the gospel. Paul had founded the church in Philippi, so the recipients of the letter were his dear friends and children in the faith (see Acts 16:11-40).

Paul wrote this letter from Rome. He had arrived there through a series of unusual circumstances. He had been arrested in Jerusalem by the Romans for seemingly inciting a riot. As a prisoner being unjustly tried, Paul used the opportunity to get to Rome by appealing his case to Caesar (Acts 25:12). Paul had wanted to preach the gospel in Rome, and he eventually got there—in chains, through shipwreck, and after many trials (Acts 27–28).

In Rome, Paul was under house arrest. This meant that he could receive visitors and write and receive letters. Paul had to finance his imprisonment. Acts 28:30 states that Paul had to pay for his own rented apartment in Rome; plus he had to pay for the guards as required by Rome. Although Paul's normal policy was not to accept support from the churches so that he could not be accused of having a "profit motive," he did accept a gift from the Philippians for his support in prison (see 4:10-18).

Paul had arrived in Rome around A.D. 59 and had spent two years under house arrest. The letter to the Philippians was probably written toward the end of Paul's imprisonment there, in A.D. 61.

Timothy was a frequent visitor during Paul's imprisonment in Rome (Colossians 1:1; Philemon 1) and was with Paul when he wrote this letter. Then Timothy went as Paul's emissary to the church in Philippi (2:19). Timothy had a special interest in

the Philippians (2:20), for he had traveled with Paul on his second missionary journey when the church at Philippi had begun (Acts 16:1-3, 10-12). Although he is mentioned in the salutation, Timothy is not considered a coauthor. Paul wrote in the first person throughout this letter.

Paul and Timothy had developed a special bond, like father and son (2:22). Paul had led Timothy to Christ during his first missionary journey. Timothy would become an important leader in the early church and, like Paul, eventually would be imprisoned for his faith (Hebrews 13:23).

While Paul usually used the designation "apostle" in the beginning of his letters, here he referred only to his and Timothy's role as **slaves of Christ Jesus.** The Philippians had been an encouragement to Paul, readily accepting his position and message. Apparently, Paul did not feel the need to mention his apostleship or to present his credentials as in some of his other letters. By the word **slaves,** Paul expressed his and Timothy's absolute devotion and subjection to Christ Jesus.

At the time of Paul's visit, **Philippi** was a thriving commercial center at the crossroads between Europe and Asia. During Paul's second missionary journey, he tried to continue his ministry northward into Bithynia and Mysia, only to be stopped by the Spirit. In Troas, the Holy Spirit led Paul to Macedonia (Acts 16:9). Thus in about A.D. 50, Paul, Silas, Timothy, and Luke crossed the Aegean Sea from Troas and landed at Neapolis, the port of Philippi (Acts 16:11-40). For more about Philippi, see the Audience section in the Introduction.

While Paul greeted **all of God's people,** meaning

the entire church, he singled out the church's leadership for greetings as well. **Elders** were in charge of the church, overseeing it—watching over, nourishing, and protecting the spiritual lives of the believers. The sheer number of churches meant that neither Paul himself, his companions, nor all the apostles could administer the day-to-day workings of each church. So Paul wisely set up groups of leaders, allowing church members to govern themselves with guidance from the apostles. The qualifications and duties of the elders are explained in detail in 1 Timothy 3:1-7 and Titus 1:5-9.

Deacons were selected to handle the church's external concerns. Some scholars think that the office of deacon first arose in response to a need in the Jerusalem church (Acts 6:1-6). These men functioned as deacons because they were responsible for specific administrative details of the church. The qualifications and duties of deacons are spelled out in 1 Timothy 3:8-13.

1:2 Paul used **grace** and **peace** as a standard greeting in all his letters. **Grace** is God's undeserved favor—his lovingkindness shown to sinners whereby he saves them and gives them strength to live for him; **peace** refers to the peace that Christ made between sinners and God through his death on the cross. Peace also refers to that inner assurance and tranquility that God places in the heart, producing confidence and contentment in Christ. Only God can grant such wonderful gifts. Paul wanted his readers to experience God's grace and peace in their daily living.

The phrase **God our Father** focuses on the family relationship among all believers as God's children. By using the phrase **Lord Jesus Christ,** Paul was pointing to Jesus as a full person of the Godhead and he was recognizing Jesus' full deity. God the Father and Christ the Lord are coequal in providing the resources of grace and peace.

PAUL'S THANKSGIVING AND PRAYER / 1:3-11

Following the convention of first-century letter writing, Paul extended his greeting by expressing thanksgiving and saying a prayer for the believers. Paul's words in this section are tender and sincere; he was genuinely thankful for the Philippians' gifts and partnership in the gospel, and he was confident that they would continue in the faith. Paul's prayer for this church gives us an example for a prayer we can pray for our church and for believers around the world.

1:3 Every time Paul thought about the Philippians, he gave **thanks** to God for them. The Philippian church had brought Paul much joy and little pain. Some of the churches had developed severe problems, and Paul's letters had focused on dealing with the problems. Paul's letter to the Philippians, while mentioning some concerns and giving some advice, could be considered a beautiful thank-you note for their unwavering support.

Paul probably visited Philippi on three separate occasions: (1) on the second missionary journey, when the gospel was planted (Acts 16:12); (2) on his journey from Ephesus through Macedonia on his way to Greece, where he stayed for three months; and (3) on his way back to Jerusalem (Acts 20:6). While the length of time of each stay is uncertain, his time with the Philippians had cemented a strong relationship.

1:4-5 The words, **I always pray for you,** are in the present tense, meaning that Paul was praying for them continually. Paul planted churches and then kept those churches in prayer as he continued in his ministry. When Paul prayed for the Philip-

pians, he thanked God for them, and he prayed **with a heart full of joy.** This is the first of many times that Paul used the word "joy" in this letter. Coming from an itinerant preacher imprisoned for his faith, joy would be the last attitude one would expect. Paul had joy despite his imprisonment and the uncertain decision on his case. True joy rises above the rolling waves of circumstance; true joy keeps us on an even keel no matter how happy or sad we might feel. One reason for Paul's joy was that the Philippians had been his **partners in spreading the Good News** through their generous contribution to Paul's ministry.

1:6 The verb tense indicates that Paul had been **sure** from the first, and he was still **sure** to that very day, of God's continued work to transform the lives of the Philippian believers. The **good work** refers to God's salvation and continued perfecting of the believers. God who began a good work of redemption **will continue his work until it is finally finished** when believers meet **Christ Jesus** face to face when he **comes back again.** Paul was describing the process of Christian growth and maturity that begins when people accept Jesus.

Nothing in this life or after death can stop God's good work in us (Romans 8:28-39). Despite any persecution the church in Philippi might face, Paul was confident that God would continue his good work in them.

1:7 Paul knew that his feeling of confidence in the Philippians was **right** because of his personal relationship with them and knowledge of their sincere faith in Christ. These believers held a **special place** in Paul's heart (see also 1:8; 4:1). All the believers shared **the blessings of God** (see 1:2). As Paul sat imprisoned in Rome, he knew that the Philippians suffered as well because of their deep concern and love for him. Paul knew that the church was constantly praying on his behalf. The Philippians also shared **in defending the truth and telling others the Good News** through their support of Paul's ministry across the world both when he was **in prison** and when he was **out.**

1:8 Paul, separated by his imprisonment from his dear friends in Philippi and uncertain of whether he would see them again during his life on earth, experienced intense longing for fellowship with them. He called God as his witness to the truth of his statement; Paul's **love** for the Philippians was so strong that it was deeper than human emotion; it was **the tender compassion of Christ Jesus** himself.

1:9 While Paul's travels were hindered by his imprisonment, his prayers were not. Paul prayed that their **love** for God and for **each other will overflow more and more.** But Paul wasn't talking about gushing sentimental or emotional affection. He was praying that their love would overflow, first in the **knowledge** of God and his ways, and then in their **understanding.** The church in Philippi was experiencing several problems in its fellowship, such as pride and fault finding (see 2:1-18 and 3:10–4:1). Before giving any admonition, Paul tactfully revealed that he was praying that the believers would have **understanding** in their words and actions.

1:10 The Philippians should have both knowledge and understanding so that, in their Christian lives and in their dealings with one another, they would **understand what really matters.** They should have the ability to differentiate between right and wrong, good and bad, healthy and dangerous, vital and trivial; but they should also have the discernment to decide between acceptable and right, good and best, and important and urgent.

Paul prayed that the Philippians would be **pure.** The word derives from the Greek words for "sunlight" and "judgment." The Philippians' transformation should be so thorough that the resulting purity could pass the toughest scrutiny— the light of God's judgment (see 2 Corinthians 5:10).

Paul also prayed that they would be **blameless.** The Greek word also means "not causing others to stumble." Believers ought to be blameless with God (keeping their relationship with him up-to-date and personal) and with people (that their behavior would not lead others into sin).

1:11 Finally, Paul prayed that the believers would be **filled with the fruit of** their **salvation**—that "fruit" being all of the character traits flowing from a right relationship with God. The phrase refers to **the good things that are produced** in a person's life **by Christ Jesus.** There is no other way for believers to gain this fruit than through a personal relationship with Jesus Christ. Only his life through us can help us live in ways that often go against our human nature. See Galatians 5:22-23 for a listing of this fruit. Such filling and the results revealed as "fruit" in people's lives always **bring much glory and praise to God.** Believers' lives ought to glorify and praise God, for it is by his grace alone that sinful human beings can obtain righteousness.

PAUL'S JOY THAT CHRIST IS PREACHED / 1:12-19

Paul explained to the Philippians that they shouldn't despair over his imprisonment because what had happened to him was helping to spread the gospel. Paul's example encouraged many believers to willingly take a stand for Christ and preach the Good News regardless of the consequences. Paul himself never stopped preaching, even in his confinement. The soldiers guarding Paul heard the gospel and they learned that he was in prison not for being a criminal, but for being a Christian.

1:12 The Philippians were certainly concerned for Paul's well-being (expressed by their financial gift), but they were also concerned that Paul's imprisonment had slowed down the spread of the gospel. By the time of this writing, Paul had been in prison about two years. Paul even may have questioned

God's reason for his lengthy imprisonment, for it effectively put him out of commission for further traveling and preaching. But Paul had come to understand, and he wanted the Philippians to **know** beyond any doubt, that **everything that** had **happened** had actually **helped to spread the Good News.** Although one of Christianity's most tireless missionaries had been imprisoned, God's work could not be slowed down.

1:13 Paul's long arrest had allowed him to share the gospel with the very soldiers who guarded him. As a result, **all the soldiers in the palace guard** (the elite troops housed in the emperor's palace) and **everyone** else knew that Paul was **in chains** only **because** of his belief **in Christ** and teaching of the Good News, not for being a criminal. Paul's example, fervent love for Christ, and manner of life, even in prison, had allowed others to see the gospel in a whole new light. The custom of the time was for a prisoner to be guarded by a soldier who would be replaced every four hours. These soldiers certainly heard Paul's words to those who visited, as well as his message spoken to them personally. Paul was confident that the message of the gospel was infiltrating the Roman army and the palace itself (see comments on 4:22).

1:14 Not only was the gospel being spread by Paul through his contacts in prison, but his efforts were being multiplied outside the prison. Paul's faith, confidence, and patience in spite of his imprisonment helped his fellow believers gain **confidence.** Whatever the reason for their lack of confidence before—whether they had been afraid to speak up, whether they left all the mission work to Paul because they lacked his boldness, or whether they wondered if faith in God was worth the price—they saw Paul's faith and it strengthened their own. They became **more bold in telling others about Christ.** With more and more believers gaining boldness in telling the gospel of Jesus Christ, more and more people heard the message and had the opportunity to accept it. This gave Paul great joy. He passed this good news on to his friends in Philippi, that they might know how God was working through his difficult situation.

1:15 Paul had been made aware that some of the brothers and sisters who had been newly emboldened to speak about Christ were doing so **out of jealousy and rivalry.** But others were preaching Christ **with pure motives.** They wanted to help others to faith and they wanted to glorify God.

This comment by Paul provides an interesting look into people's motives. All of those who preached Christ were sincere believers—they had the right doctrine and they acted upon it by shar-

ing it with others. While the end result might be the same (people hearing the Good News), some actually had wrong motives in their preaching. Now that the great missionary Paul had been virtually silenced in prison, some of these brothers were hoping to make a name for themselves in the vacuum that Paul left. Perhaps they hoped for great notoriety, trying to turn people's eyes away from Paul and toward themselves. These people had no personal love for Paul. They even hoped that their planting churches and gaining converts would upset Paul and make his imprisonment even more frustrating.

1:16 Those who preached Christ "with pure motives" (1:15) did so **because** of their **love** for Paul. They knew Paul was in prison, not because of any criminal act, but because **the Lord brought** him there **to defend the Good News** (see 1:7). Paul had landed in prison because of his devotion to Christ and his zeal to spread the gospel. Yet his fellow believers in Rome, some of whom may have been his spiritual children, fearlessly picked up where he left off, continuing and expanding his ministry.

1:17 Those who were preaching Christ "out of jealousy and rivalry" (1:15) were doing so because of their own **selfish ambition,** making their motives less than pure. These preachers were not so much interested in their message as they were in their reputation. Apparently their doctrine was sound—these were not false teachers—Paul never tolerated any kind of false teaching (see 2 Corinthians 11:4; Galatians 1:6-9). The error was in motive, not in content. These self-seeking opportunists hoped that Paul would be angered at the notoriety of new and powerful preachers who took his place while he was in prison. These men did not understand Paul's sincere love for God and his single-minded focus on spreading the gospel.

1:18-19 Paul rejoiced that **whether or not their motives were pure . . . the message about Christ** was **being preached.** Some Christians serve for the wrong reasons. Paul wouldn't condone, nor does God excuse, their motives, but we should be glad if God uses their message, regardless of their motives. Paul had no concern for his own reputation or success; he had dedicated his life to glorifying God. He understood that God was being glorified even as he sat in chains; thus, Paul could **rejoice.**

Paul had been able to rejoice during his two years in prison, could rejoice that good results could come from preachers with bad motives, and would **continue to rejoice** no matter how long he would remain in prison or how long he would live. Paul knew that all that had happened (resulting in his imprisonment, see also 1:12) would end in his **deliverance.**

What kind of deliverance did Paul envision? While most scholars agree that Paul was quoting from Job 13:16, "This is what will save me" (some versions say, "this will be for my deliverance"), they disagree on what Paul meant. Some scholars argue that Paul was referring to his upcoming trial, believing that he would be acquitted and freed (which did happen). However, this is unlikely because of Paul's words in the next verse that reveal his uncertainty about the outcome of his trial. Others believe that, like Job, Paul was focusing on his relationship with God—that whether he lived or died, his stand for Christ would be vindicated. Still others think Paul was referring to his apostleship in the face of the envious preachers. As Job sought to prove his integrity, so Paul was seeking to vindicate his

standing, despite his chains. A final option, and most likely, is that Paul was referring to his ultimate deliverance in salvation. That is, whether or not he would be delivered by the Roman court, he would be delivered from God's judgment.

Paul's confidence came from two sources: human and divine. Paul knew that the Philippians' constant prayers had sustained him. As Paul consistently prayed for the churches (1:4-5), so he petitioned their prayers on his behalf (Romans 15:30; 2 Corinthians 1:11; Colossians 4:3; 1 Thessalonians 5:25; 2 Thessalonians 3:1-2). In addition, Paul depended upon **the Spirit of Jesus Christ,** the Holy Spirit, who makes Christ's presence real in true believers. The prayers of the church and the support of the Holy Spirit sustained Paul through a difficult trial and, in the end, no matter what the outcome, Paul would ultimately be "delivered."

PAUL'S LIFE FOR CHRIST / 1:20-26

This was not Paul's final imprisonment in Rome, but he didn't know that. Awaiting trial, Paul knew that he could either be released or executed; however, he trusted Christ to work it out for his deliverance. If the verdict were to go against him, Christ would be glorified in Paul's martyrdom. If Paul was to be released, he would welcome the opportunity to continue serving the Lord. As it turned out, Paul was released from this imprisonment but arrested again two or three years later. Only faith in Christ could sustain Paul in such adversity.

1:20 The Greek word translated **eager expectation** pictures a person straining his neck to see what is ahead. In Romans 8:19, Paul used the same word as he described looking forward to the revelation of God's children, as God had planned from the beginning of creation. **Hope** and expectation are linked together. Paul looked forward to the final fulfillment. He was not concerned about the verdict of his trial, but for the testimony he would leave. Paul hoped he would **never do anything that** would **cause** him **shame.** He was not worried about his own humiliation, but he prayed for courage to **be bold for Christ** and to **always honor Christ.** When standing trial, Paul wanted to speak God's truth courageously and not be timid or ashamed. The words, **whether I live or I die,** reveal that Paul was uncertain about the outcome of his trial. He faced the possibility of execution.

1:21 To those who don't believe in God, life on earth is all there is, and so it is natural for them to strive for this world's values—money, popularity, power, pleasure, and prestige. For Paul, however, **living** was **for Christ**—Paul's life focus was to develop eternal values and to tell others about Christ, who alone could help them see life from

an eternal perspective. **For to me** indicates Paul's firm resolve and unshaken faith. The essence of life was Christ and having a vital spiritual union with him. Everything Paul desired or attempted was inspired by his devotion for Christ.

With that attitude, **dying** would not be a tragedy but, instead, a realization of Paul's hope and expectation (1:20). To live would continue Paul's ministry of spreading the gospel; to die would be **even better** because Paul's martyrdom would glorify Christ and bring him face to face with the Savior. Paul's faithful and fearless witness even unto death would enhance the reputation of the gospel. Christ would be magnified as much in Paul's death as he had been in Paul's life.

1:22 Paul poured out his heart to his friends in Philippi. If the verdict should go for Paul and he should be released, that would mean more **fruitful service for Christ**—further missionary travels, more churches planted, more converts, the strengthening of fellow believers, more opportunities to serve Christ. Certainly that would be a happy result. Yet if the decision to either live or die were up to him, he wouldn't **know which is better.** How many of us are so dedicated to God that if the choice were given, we would choose to be in God's presence?

1:23-24 Two choices were equally compelling: (1) the desire to die and be with Christ himself and (2) the desire to stay alive and so continue his fellowship with and service to the believers. While Paul lived in intimate communion with Christ during his (Paul's) service on earth, being **with Christ** in heaven would be even closer and more intimate than any human could imagine. These words reveal Paul's understanding of death—believers being immediately present with the Lord (2 Corinthians 5:2-8). Paul had no question that death would be **far better** because in death he would reach his ultimate goal (to be with Christ) and finally have eternal fellowship in God's presence.

Paul was prepared and ready to die at any moment for his faith, and he actually looked forward to death because of the certainty of being with the Lord forever. But he knew that his personal desires had to be subordinated to God's will. Paul felt that his ministry on earth was not yet complete and that he needed to **live** to help the churches grow and solidify. Paul placed his fellow believers' needs above his own desires.

1:25 This verse seems to reveal a new confidence. At times, Paul felt that death was certain (1:20; 2:17). At times, he was **convinced** that God still had work for him to do. In this verse, Paul expressed confidence that this imprisonment, at least, would not end in his death. Paul would remain alive, return to Philippi (Philemon 22), and work among them so they would **grow and experience the joy of** their **faith.** Perhaps Paul wrote these words thinking that if he was released, their joy would know no bounds (1:26) and their faith would certainly be strengthened.

1:26 Paul's **return** would reassure the Philippians as they saw God answering their prayers for Paul's safety (1:19). They could **have even more reason to boast about what Christ** had done for Paul. Paul's safe return would cause the congregation that loved him so much to boast in Christ Jesus because of answered prayer.

LIVE AS CITIZENS OF HEAVEN / 1:27-30

While Paul focused his letter to the Philippians on his thankfulness for their partnership and gifts to him, he also focused on problems that were brewing in the congregation. Paul encouraged the believers to be unified and to always remember that Christ is their example. We must follow Christ because of who he is and what he has done for us.

1:27-28 While Paul felt confident that God still had work for him on earth, he did not know for sure the outcome of his trial. So he urged the Philippians that whether he would return to them or whether he would be martyred, they would **live in a manner worthy of the Good News.** Paul called them **citizens of heaven,** and said they should live that way. Philippi was a Roman colony, and its citizens were proud of all the privileges gained by their Roman citizenship (see Acts 16:20-21). While the Philippians enjoyed the privileges and fulfilled the responsibilities of their Roman citizenship, Paul asked the Philippian Christians to remember that they were also citizens of another Kingdom and that they ought to live as citizens of heaven, with all the responsibilities their status entailed.

Being a believer is indeed a high calling. To live **worthy of the Good News** does not mean that one must live perfectly before being accepted into God's family—for such a life is impossible outside of the Holy Spirit's help. Instead, believers ought to live differently because of the grace they have received. When we believe, we become God's children, heirs of his promises, and members of Christ's body. And this privilege was bought at a price—the precious blood of Jesus Christ. Believers ought to reflect humility, gentleness, patience, understanding, peacefulness, strength, endurance, and gratitude to God in every aspect of their lives on earth.

News got around. Whether by letter or personal contact through key people (such as Timothy, Silas, Epaphroditus, and Luke), Paul knew what was happening in the churches. Thus, even though Paul hoped to return to the Philippian church, if he didn't, he would inevitably **hear about** the believers there, and he wanted to hear that they were **standing side by side.** The Holy Spirit unites Christians into one spiritual group. If they can stand side by side in the Spirit, they can overcome small differences among individual members and work forcefully toward a common goal—to withstand external persecution.

Paul also wanted to hear that the believers were **fighting together for the Good News.** Like athletes on a team, they were to work together with one mind focused on one goal—to help advance the faith that comes through the preaching of the gospel. In order to face opposition, they needed to be unhindered by internal dissension, jealousies, and rivalries (2:1-18).

Finally, he told them not to be **intimidated by their enemies.** Paul had faced severe opposition in many cities, including Philippi. If he was persecuted for his faith, the Christians ought to expect similar treatment. Christianity's **enemies** included the Roman Empire, the pagan Philippian populace (whom Paul had encountered, Acts 16:16-24), and false teachers who had infiltrated many Christian circles and whom Paul blasted in many of his letters. The church would need to be strong within the fellowship in order to live out these three attributes. How sad that much time and effort are lost in some churches by people's fighting against one another instead of uniting against the real opposition! It takes a courageous church to resist infighting and to maintain the common purpose of serving Christ.

The opposition the believers faced at that time and would face in the future gave them proof of two things: (1) the destruction of their opponents and (2) the salvation of the believers (see 2 Thessalonians 1:5-10). Doom would be sealed for those who persecuted the believers; salvation is assured for God's people. Like Paul, whether the believers witnessed through their lives or through their deaths, they would ultimately be saved because of God's control of the entire situation. Again Paul focused on the assurance of eternal salvation for those who believe.

1:29 The believers had received a high calling (1:27-28). By God's grace alone and by the sacrifice of Jesus Christ, they had **been given** the **privilege of trusting in Christ.** They also had another privilege: that of **suffering for him.** Paul considered it a privilege to suffer for Christ. Paul wanted the believers in Philippi to understand that suffering persecution was not punishment for their sins, nor was it accidental (that somehow God had gotten sidetracked and had forgotten to protect them). Instead, suffering for the faith was to be considered a high honor.

1:30 Paul and the Philippians faced the same **great struggle**—suffering for spreading the gospel. The Philippian believers had encouraged Paul through his suffering; Paul wanted to encourage them in the same manner. Paul had faced that struggle in Philippi on his first visit there (Acts 16:12, 19; 1 Thessalonians 2:2), and he still faced it in his imprisonment. Like the Philippians, we are in conflict with anyone who would discredit the saving message of Christ. All true believers are in this fight together, uniting against the same enemy for a common cause.

PHILIPPIANS 2

UNITY THROUGH HUMILITY / 2:1-4

Verses 1-18 continue the thought from 1:27-28. Paul wanted unity in the Philippian church so they could carry on the ministry of the gospel; but such unity would only be possible by being united with Christ so that there would be harmonious relationships among the believers themselves.

2:1 Paul asked four rhetorical questions. These conditions already existed in the Philippian church. It had some problems to deal with, but the church had proven itself to be strong and unified. Paul asked if there was **any encouragement from belonging to Christ.** The word translated "encouragement" is the same word when he spoke of the Holy Spirit as the Counselor or Comforter (John 14:16). Every believer has received encouragement, exhortation, and comfort from Christ. That common experience ought to unite the Philippians.

The Philippian believers had **comfort from his love.** The common experience of Christ's love should unite them (Ephesians 5:25). In turn, their common love for Christ should cause them to love one another. They had **fellowship together in the Spirit.** When a person believes in Jesus Christ as Savior, he or she receives the Holy Spirit. Each believer has personal fellowship with the Holy Spirit in his or her private life; all the believers are united by the same Spirit in times of fellowship. Because there is only one Spirit, there can be only one body

(Ephesians 4:4); factions or divisiveness have no place in the body of Christ. (See also 2 Corinthians 13:14.)

They also had **hearts** that were **tender and sympathetic.** When the Holy Spirit works in believers' lives, fruit is produced (Galatians 5:22-23). "Tenderness" refers to sensitivity to others' needs or feelings; "sympathy" means feeling the sorrow of another person and desiring to help alleviate it. Such concern for one another unifies a body of believers.

2:2 The four results of unity listed above are here joined by four goals for harmony in the church. The Philippians had given Paul great joy (1:4). Yet Paul was aware of a lack of unity in the Philippian church. For example, believers were demonstrating a false sense of spiritual superiority over others (2:3), and some were not working harmoniously with others (4:2). Paul knew that even the beginnings of divisiveness could cause major problems unless the "cracks" were repaired quickly.

Because of their common experience in Christ and their common fellowship with the Holy Spirit, they should be **agreeing wholeheartedly with each other.** This does not mean that the believers have to agree on everything; instead, each believer should have the mind (or attitude) of Christ, which Paul describes at length in 2:5-11.

Paul also wanted the church to be **loving one another.** Christ's love sent him from heaven, into humble humanity, to death on a cross on behalf of sinners. Although believers cannot do what Christ did, they follow Christ's example when they express the same love in their dealings with others (see Galatians 5:22).

Jesus had prayed for future believers, "that they may be one" (John 17:22). The church ought to be **working together with one heart.** Paul's thought was the same as he wrote in 1:27. The Holy Spirit should unite the believers into one body.

As they stand firm in the Spirit, they overcome small differences and work forcefully toward one **purpose**—a common goal (3:14-15). The church's goal was to spread the gospel.

A unified church is a formidable fortress against any enemy. The very unity of the Philippian church would ensure that it could stand against any persecution or false teaching that might come its way.

2:3 Members in the Philippian church were causing discord by their attitudes or actions. They desired recognition or distinction, not from pure motives, but merely from being **selfish** (see also 1:17). Those kind of people cannot work with others in the church in like-mindedness and love (2:2). When people are selfishly ambitious and trying only to **make a good impression,** they ruin a church's unity.

While selfish ambition and conceit can ruin unity, genuine humility can build it. Being **humble** involves having a true perspective about ourselves in relation to God (see Romans 12:3), which in turn gives us a correct perspective on our relationships with others. Being humble does not mean that we should put ourselves down. Instead, humility is a healthy respect for who God is, and then a healthy respect for ourselves because of what God did on our behalf. **Thinking of others as better than** ourselves means that we are aware of our own failings and are thus willing to accept failings in others without looking down on them.

2:4 Each believer should not be completely absorbed in his or her **own affairs,** but should also **be interested in others,** noting their good points and qualities. A sure cure for selfish ambition is appreciative recognition of others' good qualities and their walk with the Lord. It is easy to get caught up in competition, aggressive acquiring, and vying for our own rights and needs. But compared to knowing Christ, those interests seem shallow. We need Christ's attitude of self-sacrifice to look beyond ourselves to the needs of others.

CHRIST'S HUMILITY AND EXALTATION / 2:5-11

If anyone didn't understand what Paul meant by acting out of humility (2:3) and looking first to others' concerns (2:4), then Paul made it clear by giving an example to follow. The believers should adopt the same attitude or frame of mind that was found in Jesus Christ, their Lord.

2:5 Many people feel that they can't control their moods or attitudes. But Paul doesn't accept the fact that Spirit-filled Christians are slaves to their attitudes. **Christ Jesus** had a particular **attitude;** so must we. One of the great myths of popular psychology that has drifted into the church today

deals with impulsive behavior based on emotions. Those who accept Jesus Christ as Savior enter a community of believers, the church. Believers are to obey their Savior because of who he is and what he has done on their behalf. Paul eloquently describes this in the following verses.

2:6 Most scholars believe that verses 6-11 are from a hymn sung by the early Christian church. Paul was using this hymn to show Jesus as a model of servanthood. The passage holds many parallels to the prophecy of the Suffering Servant in Isaiah 53. As a hymn, it was not meant to be a complete statement about the nature and work of Christ. It is not known if Paul wrote it or merely quoted it.

This verse describes the status of Christ as he existed before the creation of the world—that is, his preincarnate state. Jesus Christ **was God.** Everything God is, Christ is; the equality is in essential characteristics and divine attributes. But Jesus did not **demand and cling to his rights as God,** but set them aside for a time in order to become human. When Christ was born, God became a man. Jesus was not part man and part God; he was completely human and completely divine. Christ is the perfect expression of God in human form. As a man, Jesus was subject to place, time, and other human limitations. What made Jesus' humanity unique was his freedom from sin. He did not give up his eternal power when he became human, but he did set aside his glory and his rights. In his full humanity, we can see everything about God's character that can be conveyed in human terms.

2:7 Christ voluntarily gave of himself, making **himself nothing.** The Incarnation was the act of the preexistent Son of God voluntarily assuming a **human** body and human nature. He did not give up his deity to become human. Yet upon his birth as a human being, he **took the humble position of a slave.** What appeared on earth was not a prince in a palace, or a royal king, or a wealthy and scholarly teacher; instead, Jesus' entire life was devoted to serving others (Isaiah 53:2; Mark 10:45). Jesus' glory and divinity were veiled by his humanity and mortality.

2:8 When Jesus took on a **human form,** he then **humbled himself** to accomplish that task for which he had come—to die for sinful humanity in order that they might have eternal life. He died a **criminal's death,** but he was not a criminal. He took on that humiliation so that we might be saved. He died by the worst possible torture— death by crucifixion. Death **on a cross** was the form of capital punishment that Romans used for notorious criminals. It was excruciatingly painful and humiliating. Prisoners were nailed or tied to a cross and left to die. Death might not come for several days, and it usually came by suffocation when the weight of the weakened body made breathing more and more difficult. Jesus died as one who was cursed (Galatians 3:13).

But why did Jesus have to become human and have to die? A holy God cannot overlook sin. The sinfulness of humanity had to be punished. In the Old Testament, God required his people to sacrifice animals ("perfect" animals, healthy and whole) to atone for their sins. The costly sacrifice of an animal's life impressed upon the sinner the seriousness of his or her sin before God. When animals' blood was shed, God regarded the people's faith and obedience, cleansed them, and made them **ceremonially** clean.

Why blood? There is no greater symbol of life than blood; blood keeps us alive. Instead of sending all humanity to eternal punishment, God took the punishment himself (Romans 8:3). Jesus shed his blood—gave his life—for our sins so that we wouldn't have to experience spiritual death and eternal separation from God.

2:9 Because Christ willingly set aside his glory to totally obey the Father's will, God **raised him up to the heights of heaven.** God did not leave Christ in the grave but raised him from the dead, brought him back up to heaven, and glorified him (see Acts 2:33; Ephesians 1:20-22; Hebrews 1:3). God gave Jesus all authority (Matthew 28:18; John 5:27) and made him the Lord of both the dead and the living (Romans 14:9).

That Jesus' name **is above every other name** refers not to Jesus' title, but instead to his name that signifies his person. In the Bible, names often reveal a person's character. Jesus' dignity and honor are above all others. Because Jesus did not cling to his equality with God (2:6) but willingly obeyed God in order to carry out the plan of salvation, God honored that obedience by giving Jesus this name above all names.

2:10 In keeping with Jesus' exaltation and power, one day **every knee will bow** before him. **In heaven** refers to the angels; **on earth** means all humanity; **under the earth** refers to the underworld—possibly to unsaved people who have died or to demons. Those who love Jesus will bow in adoration and worship; those who refused to acknowledge him will bow in submission and fear (see also Ephesians 4:9-10; Revelation 5:13). This will take place at Jesus' second coming when the forces of evil will be completely defeated and God will form a new heaven and a new earth (Revelation 19:20-21; 21:1).

Paul purposely quoted Isaiah 45:23 here and in Romans 14:11. In so doing, he applied those powerful words to Jesus Christ. Isaiah, proclaiming the unique greatness of God, had said that the same God who would not share his glory with another would receive the homage of every living being. Paul equated that position of God with

clean and innocent and holding tightly to the truth as they reached out to a depraved world, he would be **proud** that his **work** among them **was not useless.** Paul had been the first to bring the gospel to Philippi; the church existed because of his preaching. Paul's boasting was not prideful, as if he had built the church with his own hands. Instead, his boasting would be like that of a parent over a child who has done well.

2:17-18 Paul's reference to being **poured out like a drink offering** was an allegory for martyrdom. The drink offering was an important part of the Jewish sacrificial system. It involved wine being poured out on an altar as a sacrifice to God (see Genesis 35:14; Exodus 29:40-41; Numbers 28:24). Because the Philippian church had little Jewish background, Paul may have been referring to the wine poured out to pagan deities prior to important public events. Paul regarded his life as a suitable offering **to complete the** Philippians' **sacrifice** of **faithful service,** and he willingly offered it for the sake of Christ's gospel and for the many who had believed in Christ because of his preaching.

Yet even through these somber words a ray of light was shining. If Paul were indeed to die, he would **rejoice** and desire that they would **share** his **joy.** Paul was content, knowing that he had helped the Philippians live for Christ. Paul was able to have joy, even though he faced possible execution. When you are totally committed to serving Christ, sacrificing to build the faith of others brings a joyous reward. Paul considered it a privilege to die for the faith, and he wanted the Philippians to take the same attitude in the case of his death.

PAUL COMMENDS TIMOTHY / 2:19-24

Paul had nothing but praise for two of his coworkers—Timothy and Epaphroditus (2:25-30). Both had proven themselves to be faithful in the ministry and sincere in their love for fellow believers. Because he could not go to Philippi, Paul would soon send Timothy.

2:19 Timothy was with Paul in Rome when Paul wrote this letter, although Timothy was not imprisoned. He had traveled with Paul on his second missionary journey when the church at Philippi was begun, so the Philippians knew Timothy. Paul could not visit the Philippians, thus he hoped to send Timothy on his behalf. Timothy had traveled to various churches as Paul's representative at other times (see 1 Corinthians 4:17; 16:10; 1 Thessalonians 3:2). Epaphroditus would leave immediately and deliver Paul's letter (2:25-30); then Timothy would arrive later after Paul learned the verdict of his trial (2:23). Paul hoped that in the meantime the Philippians would take to heart his call to unity in their church and would iron out their difficulties. Timothy would be able to see their progress and then could come **back** to Rome with news that would bring Paul good **cheer.**

2:20 Timothy **genuinely** cared about the Philippian believers because he had traveled with Paul on his second missionary journey when the church at Philippi had been begun (Acts 16:1-3, 10-12). The phrase **no one else like** him literally means "no one of equal soul." These words of praise reveal that Timothy had become a dependable coworker and friend.

2:21 This sentence could mean that Paul had spoken to others about possibly taking this trip to Philippi on his behalf, but all of them were more concerned **for themselves** than for **what matters to Jesus Christ.** Or Paul may not have been indicting his fellow Christians; rather, he may have been reflecting on the state of a selfish world where few truly selfless people can be found. More likely, Paul was using hyperbole. He could not have meant that Luke, Titus, and other disciples cared only for themselves. Rather, he meant that Timothy cared so deeply that the concern of others paled by comparison. While many believers might express concern, too often they are too preoccupied with their own activities to act on that concern. Timothy was concerned for the Philippians' welfare, and he was willing to act on the concern by dropping what he was doing in Rome to make the lengthy and tiring trip to Philippi. Once in Philippi, he might have to deal with problems in the church—certainly not an enviable task. Timothy's willingness to go to Philippi reveals a spirit of selfless service. Here was a man who exemplified what it meant to put others' interests ahead of his own (2:4).

2:22 Timothy had been with Paul during Paul's ministry in Philippi. The Philippian church well knew Timothy's value, sound character, and worthiness. The church knew that Timothy's coming would be equal to that of the arrival of Paul himself, for Timothy had served with Paul **like a son with his father.** Paul and Timothy had developed a special bond; Paul had led Timothy to Christ during his first missionary journey. In the first century, the Greeks valued highly the service a son gave to his father. Yet Paul realized that both he and Timothy were servants of Jesus Christ; thus he wrote that Timothy had **helped** him **in preaching the Good News** across the empire.

2:23-24 Paul was in prison (awaiting his verdict) for preaching about Christ. He planned to **send** Timothy to Philippi (2:19) and hoped to do so when he learned of the court's decision. Even if Paul were to be released from prison, he would send Timothy to Philippi with the news, and then Paul would **come to see** them **soon** after.

PAUL COMMENDS EPAPHRODITUS / 2:25-30

Timothy would come after Paul found out the verdict of his trial; but Paul thought it was necessary to send Epaphroditus along immediately. Paul explained that Epaphroditus had fulfilled the mission for which the Philippian church had sent him. While in Rome, he had become extremely ill (2:27, 30). After his recovery, Paul sent him back to Philippi, carrying this thank-you letter and news of Paul to share with them.

2:25 Epaphroditus had come from Philippi to Rome, acting as their **messenger** to deliver a financial gift from the Philippians to Paul and to care for Paul on the Philippians' behalf. Epaphroditus may have been an elder in Philippi (2:25-30; 4:18).

Epaphroditus had come not just to deliver money, but to minister to Paul's spiritual needs. He may have been sent to Rome to remain with Paul indefinitely, ministering to and encouraging the imprisoned apostle. Like Timothy, he put another's **need** ahead of his own (see 2:4). Epaphroditus came to serve Paul, but Paul felt it necessary to **send Epaphroditus back** to Philippi with this letter to assure the Philippians of Paul's well-being after his severe illness (see 2:26)

Paul wanted the Philippians to know how highly he regarded Epaphroditus, so he characterized him with three names: (1) **true brother,** meaning fellow believer; (2) **faithful worker,** which means he too was working for God's Kingdom; (3) **courageous soldier,** referring to the solidarity among believers who are fighting the same battle.

2:26 Communication happens so quickly in our world, but Epaphroditus couldn't just pick up the phone or send an e-mail saying all was well. The Philippians had heard that Epaphroditus **was ill,** and word of their concern about him had gotten back to Rome (again, weeks elapsed as the news traveled the forty-day journey between the two cities). When he recovered, Epaphroditus was **longing to see** his friends and family in Philippi so they would know he was well. So Paul figured the best way to do that would be to send him **home again.**

2:27 The Philippians' concern about Epaphroditus's illness had been well founded, for he had been so **ill** that he **almost died.** While the apostles had been given the ability to heal, it was not a permanent gift to be used at will; otherwise, Paul would surely have healed his friend. Instead, Paul could do nothing but pray. Epaphroditus recovered because **God had mercy on him** as well as on Paul, who would have faced **unbearable sorrow** at the death of his friend. What illness Epaphroditus had and how he regained his health are unknown. To Paul, these details were less important than the significance of the healing. God had mercy on both his servants—on Epaphroditus by healing him and returning him to ministry; on Paul by not adding the sorrow of bereaving a friend's death on top of other sorrows rendered by his imprisonment.

2:28 With Epaphroditus's unexpected return, the church might think that his mission to minister to Paul had failed. They might be concerned that Epaphroditus was leaving Paul alone in Paul's most desperate time of need. Instead, Paul took full responsibility for Epaphroditus's return to Philippi and encouraged the believers to rejoice that he had come back to them. As he planned to do with Timothy (2:19), Paul willingly sent away those closest to him, if their ministry were required elsewhere. Epaphroditus had certainly been an encouragement to Paul, as Paul's description of this brother indicates (2:25). Yet Paul knew that the Philippians needed to see Epaphroditus for themselves. This would ease Epaphroditus's distress (2:26) and **lighten** Paul's **cares.**

2:29-30 While Epaphroditus had not been able to remain in Rome to encourage Paul as the Philippian church had hoped, Paul wanted the believers to **welcome him** back and give him great **honor** for what he had done. Paul let the Philippians know that Epaphroditus had not failed in his mission, and that he should be given great honor.

Epaphroditus had **risked his life for the work of Christ** by helping Paul on behalf of the Philippian church. Paul needed personal encouragement; the church couldn't give it because they **were far away.** But Epaphroditus had taken that responsibility and had risked his life to help the apostle in his time of need. Epaphroditus had done his work so well that he could report back to Philippi and bring Paul's letter of thanks and encouragement along with him.

PHILIPPIANS 3:1 – 4:1

THE PRICELESS GAIN OF KNOWING CHRIST / 3:1-11

Paul warned the Philippian believers to stay clear of the false teachers who taught that what people did (like being circumcised), rather than the free gift of grace provided through Christ, made them believers. Are you depending on Christian parents or church affiliation, or are you just being good to make you right with God?

3:1 The tone of Paul's letter to the Philippians is joyous—and as he prepared his final words to them, he exhorted them to let **the Lord give** them **joy.** He would say this again at the real end of his letter (see 4:4). In this short epistle, a form of the word joy occurs twelve times. What is true joy? Often happiness is mistaken for joy, but the two are very different. Inward joy comes from knowing and trusting God; happiness comes as a result of pleasant circumstances. Inward joy is lasting; we can feel joy in spite of our deepest troubles; happiness is temporary because it is based on external circumstances.

Paul was able to rejoice in spite of his suffering because he knew and trusted God. He did not let his circumstances discourage him. To remain joyful, we should remind ourselves daily of God's love for us and our ultimate life with him in heaven. The joy of knowing Christ kept Paul level-headed, no matter how high or low his circumstances (see also 4:12). Paul **never** got **tired** of **telling** the believers this, because it was **for their own good.** An attitude of joy would help the believers safeguard against the practices Paul so vehemently warned against: dissension, grumbling, and attitudes of superiority. If we lose the joy of the Lord, we are susceptible to these attitudes. Joy acts as a barrier against them. It guarantees the safety of our Christian hope.

3:2 Paul warned the believers to **watch out** for a particular group of people he described using three different derogatory terms. (1) **Dogs** were regarded by Jews as despised and unclean creatures; it was common for orthodox Jews to refer to Gentiles as "dogs"; however, here Paul switched the designation to refer not to Gentiles but to an extreme faction of Jews. (2) He also called them **wicked men.** The Jews regarded themselves as holy, not evil, because they kept the law. But their reliance on the law lessened their reliance on God. (3) Finally, he called them **mutilators.** Some Jewish Christians wrongly believed that it was essential for Gentiles to follow all the Old Testament Jewish laws, saying that the Gentile believers had to **be circumcised to be saved.** Those who taught this wrong doctrine were called Judaizers; they were a severe problem for Paul. The Judaizers' main argument was that Gentiles had to first become Jews before they could become Christians.

Circumcision was an important covenant for the Jews—God had established it with Abraham (Genesis 17:9-14). While there was nothing wrong with circumcision itself, Paul maintained that it *was* wrong to teach circumcision as a requirement for salvation. Paul criticized the Judaizers because they looked at Christianity backwards—thinking that what they *did* (especially circumcision) made them believers rather than the free gift of grace given by Christ. What believers do is a **result** of faith, not a **prerequisite** to faith. The teaching of these Judaizers threatened the new churches and had to be countered. Paul was concerned that **nothing** get in the way of the simple truth of his message—that salvation, for Jews and Gentiles alike, comes through faith in Jesus Christ alone.

The early church had already confirmed Paul's teaching at the Jerusalem Council eleven years earlier (see Acts 15). However, this didn't stop many of the Judaizers, who were motivated by spiritual pride. Because they had invested so much time and effort in keeping their laws, they couldn't accept the fact that all their efforts couldn't bring them a step closer to salvation. And the age-old hatred of Gentile "dogs" didn't make it any easier for them to accept Gentiles as brothers in the faith. Whether or not they had come to Philippi as yet, Paul knew it was only a matter of time, and he wanted the Philippians to be forewarned.

3:3 Circumcision had been a requirement under the old covenant God had made with Abraham— a physical sign to God's people of their relationship with him. It also had spiritual application, for the physical mark was to be a sign of a spiritual relationship with God (Deuteronomy 30:6). At one time the physical sign of circumcision had set God's people, the Jews, apart from the Gentiles. After Jesus Christ, all people could become part of God's family by believing in Jesus as Savior. True believers **are the only ones who are truly circumcised.** They have three common characteristics that prove their standing before God:

First, they **worship God in the Spirit.** Believers worship by means of God's Spirit and in God's Spirit. The Holy Spirit, the third person of the Trinity, is vital to all aspects of our Christian life. Whatever outward forms may or may not be used, worship is always inspired by the Holy Spirit.

Second, they **put no confidence in human effort.** The Judaizers depended on their obedience to the Jewish law, and especially the covenant of circumcision, to make them acceptable to God. By contrast, true believers did not place their confidence in anything they did or didn't do, but in what God through Jesus Christ had done for them.

Finally, they **boast about what Christ Jesus has done.** The word translated "boast" could better be translated "exult." Paul explained that true believers exult, not in their works as if they somehow saved themselves, but in Christ Jesus alone. Only because of Christ's sacrifice on the cross are believers saved. Any believer who understands the incredible significance of Christ's death cannot help but respond with exultation.

3:4 The Judaizers believed that their accomplishments would earn their salvation, thus giving them reason for having **confidence in their own efforts.** Paul challenged any false teachers to a credentials "showdown." If anyone could have confidence in worldly achievements, Paul could; in fact, he probably had **even more** than any of those Judaizers who so adamantly opposed Paul's teaching of salvation by faith alone.

3:5 The Judaizers focused on circumcision as the way to be right with God. The first item on Paul's list of credentials in which he at one time placed confidence was the fact that he, too, had been **circumcised** when he was **eight days old.** If anyone would have known about the true value of circumcision, Paul would. But Paul knew that his being circumcised could not give him salvation. Next Paul's list included his membership among God's elect race, the chosen people. Paul's parents were both true Jews, and Paul could trace his heritage back to Abraham (see Romans 11:1; 2 Corinthians 11:22). He was **pure-blooded.** As part of the people of Israel, Paul described his membership in one of Israel's twelve tribes— **Benjamin**—a heritage greatly esteemed among the Jews. Though the tribe of Benjamin was one of the smaller tribes, it had a special place of honor throughout its history. The patriarch of the tribe, Benjamin, was the only one of Joseph's brothers born in the Promised Land. Along with the largest tribe, Judah, the tribe of Benjamin remained loyal to David's line when the monarchy split. Paul was an Israelite by birth, a genuine Jew through and through—**a real Jew if there ever was one!**

These were Paul's qualifications by birth and heredity. Next he turned to his qualifications gained by study and zeal for his faith. Paul was also **a member of the Pharisees,** the most devout and orthodox Jewish sect. Pharisees demanded **the strictest obedience to the Jewish law**—the Old Testament laws as well as their own numerous rules and traditions thought to be the revealed oral law of God (see Acts 5:34; 22:3; 23:6; 26:5). At one time, Paul had believed, like the Judaizers, that salvation came from perfect obedience to the law.

3:6 How much more **zealous** could anyone be than to outright persecute the church? No Judaizer could boast of traveling hundreds of miles in order to find Christians, bring them back in chains to Jerusalem, and cast a vote for their deaths (Acts 9:1-2; 22:3-5; 26:9-11). No Judaizer had stood by holding the coats of those who stoned an early Christian leader (Acts 7:59–8:1). Paul **persecuted the church** because he thought that Christianity was heretical and blasphemous. Jesus did not meet the expectations of what the Messiah would be like, so Paul and many Jews with him had assumed that Jesus' claims were false—and therefore wicked (Acts 26:9).

As a Pharisee, Paul had to follow the Old Testament law in addition to hundreds of rules and traditions. Paul had **obeyed** the laws **so carefully that** no one could find any **fault.** He took his position as a Pharisee seriously—whether it included detailed law-keeping or zealous persecution of heretics.

Any of the Judaizers would have loved to have had Paul's qualifications. Such a list would have given certain confidence in salvation according to their teachings. But Paul, who seemingly had it all, listed his advantages and then set them aside as disadvantages.

3:7-9 Paul had **once thought** those great qualifications listed above were so **very important** for his salvation; now, however, he considered them **worthless.** All the qualifications no longer mattered **because of what Christ has done.** Paul had learned that nothing he could do would earn him salvation—all his hard work and meticulous law-keeping and zeal for the Jewish faith had gained him nothing. Doubtless Paul's meeting with Christ on the road to Damascus had sealed this change in Paul. When Paul understood **the priceless gain of knowing Christ Jesus,** his accomplishments became nothing more than **garbage** by comparison. The Greek word for "knowing" here speaks of a personal, experiential, and progressive knowledge. The Judaizers might have their rituals and rules, but Paul (and all true believers) had a wonderful personal relationship and fellowship with Christ Jesus himself (Colossians 2:2-3). Such a relationship far surpasses the value of anything else.

When Christ returned or when Paul died, Paul wanted **to become one with** Christ, that is, living in union with Christ. But his **own goodness** or **ability to obey God's law** would not be enough to **save** him. Not even Paul, with all his credentials and accomplishments, could have been good enough. The only way for people to be made **right with** God is through **faith.** Believers are made righteous by their faith in Christ's sacrifice on the cross on their behalf. Being made right with God is his gift to us; it cannot be earned. God secured the gift and then offered it to us. Because of Jesus' death on the cross, God can exchange our sin and shortcomings for his complete righteousness. Believers are offered a gift; all we have to do is accept it. We are considered righteous at the moment we believe, and we gradually work out the fruit of our righteous life on a day-to-day basis as we live in Christ and he lives through us.

3:10 The word for **know** here is the same form used in 3:8, referring to personal, experiential knowledge. To know **Christ** is more than merely to know facts or doctrine about him. It should be the goal of every believer to know Christ more fully and personally, and that can be a lifelong process.

Paul also wanted to **experience the mighty power that raised him from the dead.** The power of the Holy Spirit that brought Jesus back from the dead is available to all believers to raise them from spiritual death now (Ephesians 1:19-20) and from their physical death in the future (Romans 8:11). Paul wanted to know this power, personally and experientially, for that power assures Christians of their justification (Romans 4:25; 1 Corinthians 15:17) and of their regeneration as they identify with Christ in resurrection (Romans 6:4; Colossians 2:12; 3:1, 10).

Paul also wanted to **learn what it means to suffer with him, sharing his death.** Paul was not referring to sharing Christ's death on the cross; that suffering could not be shared because it was Christ's alone. But Paul wanted to participate with Christ, as a believer, in suffering for the gospel (1:29). Even as Paul had already suffered greatly for the gospel and was suffering in prison at the writing of this letter, he still wanted to know, firsthand, what it meant to suffer for Christ. He was willing to experience more in order to serve Christ, who had suffered so much for him (Colossians 1:24). Believers share his death as they "die" to sin and to the old nature. In a transaction we cannot completely understand, when Jesus died on the cross, we died to our former life. Christ took our punishment on himself, so God looks at us as though we have died to sin and then have been raised, along with Christ, to newness of life.

When we are united with Christ by trusting in him, we experience the power that raised him from the dead. That same mighty power will help us live morally renewed and regenerated lives. But before we can walk in newness of life, we must also die to sin. Just as Christ's resurrection gives us his power to live for him, his crucifixion marks the death of our old sinful nature. We can't know the victory of the Resurrection without personally applying the Crucifixion.

3:11 When Paul wrote, **"so that, somehow, I can experience the resurrection,"** he was not implying uncertainty or doubt that he would be resurrected. Rather, this was a way of humbly stating that he trusted in God for his complete salvation—from regeneration to resurrection. Paul did not doubt the fact that he would be raised, but how he would experience the resurrection was within God's plan and power and not his own. Confident of God's care and blessing, Paul runs toward salvation as if he is in a marathon. He wanted to attain the finish line without quitting. Paul was not making a point about eternal security in his wording; rather, he was announcing his dramatic and full commitment to persevere in the footrace of spirituality, never giving up until the finish line, where Jesus stands ready with a crown.

PRESSING TOWARD THE GOAL / 3:12–4:1

Paul's goal was to know Christ, to be like Christ, and to be all Christ had in mind for him. This goal absorbed all his energy. This provides a helpful example. We should not let anything take our eyes off our goal—knowing Christ. With the single-mindedness of an athlete in training, we must lay aside everything harmful and forsake anything that may distract us from being effective Christians. What is holding you back?

3:12 Paul saw the Christian life as a process. While believers are considered righteous when they accept salvation, their entire lives are marked by growth toward Christlikeness. Complete **perfection** will not be obtained until Christ's second coming, when he will take his people with him. While Paul may have seemed like a nearly perfect Christian to his Philippian friends, he emphasized that he had not **achieved** perfect knowledge of Christ, the power of his resurrection, or the sharing of his suffering and death (3:10). All of these were part of the process of sanctification— of **working toward that day** when we can **be all that Christ Jesus saved** us to be and **wants** us to be.

3:13 Unlike the Judaizers, Paul did not consider that he had achieved spiritual maturity; he was **not all** that he knew he **should be,** but he lived in absolute confidence of his ultimate salvation. Christians know they will be saved, yet they must have perfection as their goal (Matthew 5:48) while not pretending that sin does not exist (1 John 1:8). Like Paul, they should be **focusing on one** goal: **forgetting the past and looking forward to what lies ahead.** The past should not be used as a barrier to the future, as an excuse for dropping out, or for avoiding proper spiritual conduct in their relationship with God. Paul would forget his past with all its credentials and accomplishments (and sins) and, like a runner in a race with his whole body reaching for the finish line, would press on toward the goal (3:14).

3:14 As a runner straining toward the finish line, Paul pressed on **to reach the end of the race and receive the prize.** While Paul didn't identify **the prize,** it seems from his writing above that the prize refers to gaining full knowledge of Jesus Christ (see also 1 Corinthians 9:24; 2 Timothy 4:7-8). Paul aimed to win the prize, but all who finish the race win it as well. The full knowledge of Christ is the final prize for which believers gladly lay aside all else.

For this prize, **Christ Jesus is calling us up to heaven.** Some think this refers to the rapture; others say that it means the call to be saved; still others connect it to the high purpose or high vocation of Paul as apostle. Yet because of Paul's use of the metaphor of athletic games, it seems more natural to understand the "call" as the calling of athletes up to the winner's stand. Thus, the heavenly call is the summons to win the victor's prize of salvation.

3:15 After Paul described his spiritual goals, he explained to the Philippians that all **mature Christians** should **agree on these things**. That is, they too ought to be pressing on toward the goal. Mature believers would understand that they could not, in their own humanity, gain perfection and acceptance by God (as opposed to the teachings of the Judaizers). Yet because of their love for Christ, they willingly pressed on to follow his example in order to become more like him in life, all the while knowing that they were promised to know him fully upon their death (or his return).

The phrase, **if you disagree on some point,** betrays some of the problems that faced the Philippian church. Paul made clear that those who were truly mature were those who realized their dependence on God. They pressed on, not to make themselves good enough or to gain credentials by their accomplishments; rather, they pressed on to know their Savior better. Whatever problem of pride may have threatened to divide the Philippian church, Paul stopped it. This was the final word on the matter; Paul invoked the illumination of **God** himself to **make plain** the truth of his words.

3:16 Christian maturity involves acting on the guidance that we have already received. The believers were in different stages, but everyone needed to **obey the truth** they had **learned already.** As they pressed on toward the goal, they should not use their lack of complete knowledge as an excuse for taking lightly what they knew or for getting sidetracked. They should continue to learn and grow, while at the same time governing their lives by the light they had already received.

3:17 Paul used these two key words for discipleship: **pattern** and **example.** Paul challenged the

Philippians to pursue Christlikeness by following Paul's own example and the examples of others whose lives were based on his (those "mature" believers in 3:15). This was not egotism on Paul's part, for Paul always focused on Jesus Christ and urged the believers to also follow the example of others who followed Christ. They should not follow false teachers or the enemies of the cross (3:18). Instead, as Paul focused his life on being like Christ, so should they. The Gospels may not yet have been in circulation, so Paul could not tell them to read the Bible to see what Christ was like. Therefore he urged them to imitate him as a practical guide for conduct. That Paul could tell people to follow his example is a testimony to his character. Can you do the same? What kind of follower would a new Christian become if he or she imitated you?

3:18 The reason for Paul's admonition to follow his example was to turn the believers away from following the bad examples of the false teachers, the Judaizers, and any others who claimed to be believers but refused to live up to Christ's model of servanthood and self-sacrifice. These people focused on their own attainments, thus making them **enemies of the cross of Christ.** Paul had warned the Philippians about false teachings, and he continued to do so with **tears.**

3:19 Four characteristics were true of these "enemies of the cross" (3:18). (1) Because they refused to accept Christ's sacrifice on their behalf, they could not be saved. Their only alternative was **eternal destruction**—separation from God. (2) **Their god is their appetite,** meaning they worshiped those temporal elements that satisfy only physical desires. (3) **They brag about shameful things.** They gloried in themselves, when they should have been ashamed so that they could turn to God for salvation. (4) **All they think about is this life here on earth.** They depended on credentials, accomplishments, law-keeping, etc., for salvation.

3:20 While the false teachers had their minds on earthly matters (3:19), believers ought to be yearning for their home. Paul's speaking of being **citizens of heaven** struck a chord with the Philippians. Philippi was a Roman colony; those who lived in Philippi had their citizenship in far-off Rome, although most of the Philippians had never been there. Roman citizenship was highly prized during Paul's time. The Christians in Philippi, as proud as they had been of their Roman citizenship (Acts 16:20-21), should have valued even more highly their citizenship in heaven **where the Lord Jesus Christ lives.** The believers should have thought of themselves as "resident aliens" living temporarily in a foreign country with their home elsewhere. One day they would experience all the special privileges of their heavenly citizenship because Christ would **return** as their **Savior.** Believers are expecting the Savior to return from heaven to earth at his second coming. While on earth, believers were citizens of their country (the Philippians were citizens of Rome itself and thus under Caesar's rule), yet absolute loyalty was to the one and only true Savior, the Lord Jesus Christ, who rules in heaven, where all believers hold their ultimate citizenship.

3:21 When Christ returns, he will **conquer everything, everywhere.** There will be no more sin, no more evil rulers, no more persecution of believers. Christ will be King of kings and Lord of lords, ruler over all (Revelation 19:11-16; 21:22-27; see also Psalm 8:6; 1 Corinthians 15:24-28; Hebrews 2:8-9). With that same power, he will transform all believers' **weak mortal bodies** into **glorious bodies** like Christ's resurrected body. Our identities will not change, but our bodies will be **like** Jesus' glorified body. This won't be an external resemblance, but we will share his nature and life. (For a more detailed discussion of our new bodies, see 1 Corinthians 15:35-55 and 2 Corinthians 5:1-10.)

4:1 Because of these amazing and certain promises, the believers in Philippi ought to **stay true to the Lord**—standing against false teaching or divisiveness from within and persecution from without. Paul referred to the Philippians as his **joy** and **reward,** proof that his labor had not been in vain (2:16). This congregation was dear to his heart. His words to them were of vital importance, for he cared about their very souls. How he longed **to see** them again; but during this time of his imprisonment, the yearning words of his letter, carried to them by a mutual friend, would have to suffice.

PHILIPPIANS 4:2-23

PAUL'S FINAL THOUGHTS / 4:2-9

In 4:1, Paul had urged the Philippian believers to "stay true to the Lord." In order to stay true against false teaching, divisiveness, and persecution, the believers needed to develop certain attitudes in their lives.

4:2 Paul not only warned the Philippian church of doctrinal errors (3:1–4:1), he also addressed some relational problems. Two women, **Euodia** and **Syntyche,** had been workers for Christ in the church—perhaps deacons. Their broken relationship was no small matter: Many had become believers through their efforts (see 4:3), but their quarrel was causing dissension in the church. We do not know the reason for the **disagreement,** but Paul pled with them to **settle** it. He expected them to work it out themselves. The unity of the church was to be their highest concern.

4:3 The identity of this **true teammate** remains a mystery. The reference may have been obvious to the Philippian believers. Paul knew that he could count on this man to **help these women** work out their disagreement so they could once again fellowship with one another and be good examples in the church.

Euodia and Syntyche had **worked hard with** Paul **in telling others the Good News.** In many of the churches Paul visited, men were the key players, but women played a key role in founding the churches of Macedonia (see Acts 16:14, 40; 17:4, 12). At Philippi, women were the first to hear the gospel, and Lydia was the first convert. Those who were among the first to understand the gospel would be asked to teach. Thus, Euodia and Syntyche were to take an active part in teaching. Their quarrel was highly visible and threatened to disrupt the unity of the church. This intermediary was asked to help.

The mention of the women's help reminded Paul of **Clement** and other **coworkers** who had also labored along with Paul. While the names of the rest of the coworkers are not listed, we can be sure that each person's name is **in the Book of Life.** The names of all believers are registered there. In the Old Testament this referred to a register of God's covenant people (see Exodus 32:32-33; Psalm 69:28; 139:16). The "book" symbolizes God's knowledge

of who belongs to him (see Luke 10:17-20; 12:8-9; Hebrews 12:22-23; Revelation 3:5; 20:11-15).

4:4 Paul returned to writing to the church at large: **Be full of joy . . . rejoice!** It seems strange that a man in prison would be telling a church to keep on rejoicing. But Paul's attitude teaches us an important lesson: Our inner attitudes do not have to reflect our outward circumstances. Paul was full of joy because he knew that no matter what happened to him, Jesus Christ was with him. While believers often will encounter situations in which they cannot be happy, they can **always** rejoice and delight **in the Lord.**

4:5 Joy isn't always visible to others, but acts toward others are readily seen. So Paul encouraged the Philippians to **let everyone see that** they were **considerate.** They should have a spirit that is reasonable, fair-minded, and charitable. Believers are motivated to joy and consideration of others by remembering that their **Lord is coming soon.** The promise of the Lord's second coming encourages careful conduct by his followers.

4:6 Attitudes of joy and gentleness, combined with constant awareness of Christ's return, should dispel any **worry.** Believers should not set aside life's responsibilities so as not to worry about them; Paul was focusing on believers' attitudes in daily life and as they faced opposition and persecution. Christians are to be responsible for their needs and their families and to care about and be concerned for others, but they are *not* to worry (Matthew 6:25-34).

Worrying is bad because it is a subtle form of distrust in God. When believers worry, they are saying that they don't trust that God will provide and they doubt that he cares or that he can handle their situation. Paul offered prayer as an antidote to worry. **Instead, pray about everything.** Prayer combats worry by allowing us catharsis. We can off-load our stress onto God. Paul said to take all the energy that is used in worrying and put it into prayer. This includes praying about **everything.** No request is too small, difficult, or inconsequential to God. Paul encouraged the believers to pray about what they **need** and then to **thank** God **for all he has done.** It may seem impossible not to worry about anything, but Paul explained that this can happen if believers truly give their worries to God. Worry and prayer cannot coexist.

4:7 If the Philippians would take to heart Paul's words in 4:4-6, then they will turn from anxiety to prayer and be filled with **God's peace.** This peace is different from the world's peace. It is peace that Jesus promised his disciples and all those who would follow him (John 14:27). True peace is not found in positive thinking, in absence of conflict, or in good feelings; it comes from knowing that God is in control. Believers are given peace *with* God when they believe (Romans 5:1), and they have the inner quiet of the peace *of* God as they daily walk with him.

God's peace **is far more wonderful than the human mind can understand.** Such peace cannot be self-generated; it comes from God alone; it is his gift to us in a difficult world. As with so much of God's dealings with humanity, we cannot understand it, but we can accept and experience God's peace because of his great love for us.

Why does God give his people peace? Because it will **guard** their **hearts and minds.** The Greek word for "guard" is a military term that means to surround and protect a garrison or city. The Philippians, living in a garrison town, were familiar with the Roman guards who maintained watch, guarding the city from any outside attack. God's peace is like soldiers surrounding believers' hearts and minds (that is, emotions and thoughts), securing them against threatening and harmful outside forces.

4:8 If one is to have this inner peace from God and maintain a life free of worry, then certain steps must be taken, notably in his or her thoughts. This list describes what should pervade believers' minds. Believers should **fix** their **thoughts on** things that are:

True. Truth includes facts and statements that are in accordance with reality (not lies, rumors, or embellishments), sincere (not deceitful or with evil motives), and loyal, faithful, proper, reliable, and genuine. Truth is a characteristic of God.

Honorable. These matters are worthy of respect, dignified, and exalted in character or excellence.

Right. Thoughts and plans that meet God's standards of rightness. They are in keeping with the truth; they are righteous.

Pure. Free from contamination or blemish; unmixed and unmodified; wholesome. Paul probably was speaking of moral purity, often very difficult to maintain in thoughts.

Lovely. Thoughts of great moral and spiritual beauty, not of evil.

Admirable. Things that speak well of the thinker— thoughts that recommend, give confidence in, afford approval or praise, reveal positive and constructive thinking. A believer's thoughts, if heard by others, should be admirable, not embarrassing.

Excellent. Moral excellence; nothing of substandard quality.

Worthy of praise. This phrase may be restated as "anything that deserves the thinker's praise" or "anything that God deems praiseworthy."

4:9 Paul had lived out and was continuing to live out his words, so he could urge the believers to put **into practice** what they had **learned** from him (from his teaching and training). The Scriptures were not compiled into a Bible until later, so the standards of belief and behavior were embodied in the teachings and example of those in authority. Paul could speak confidently; people could follow his example because he was following Christ's example (1 Corinthians 11:1). If the believers would keep on practicing the virtues that Paul cited above, they would experience **the God of peace.** God is the source of peace for all believers.

PAUL'S THANKS FOR THEIR GIFTS / 4:10-20

Although Paul had already thanked the Philippians for their partnership with him in spreading the gospel (1:5), in this section he specifically thanked them for their monetary gift. Paul never asked any of the churches to support him, yet the believers in Philippi had sincerely wanted to give, so Paul accepted.

4:10 Epaphroditus had been sent to Rome from Philippi with a generous financial gift for Paul, and it had come during a time of need. Paul's words sound harsh, but that harshness is absent in Greek.

The second phrase explains that the church had **always been concerned for** Paul, but **didn't have the chance to help.** Whatever the reason for that lack of opportunity, Paul rejoiced not only at the gift and God's wondrous provision for his needs, but also for the church who cared so much about him and had not forgotten him.

Though Paul never asked for money for himself, he accepted the Philippians' gift because they gave it willingly and because he was in need. In 1 Corinthians 9:11-18, Paul wrote that he didn't accept gifts from the Corinthian church because he didn't want to be accused of preaching only to get money. But Paul maintained that it was a church's responsibility to support God's ministers (1 Corinthians 9:14).

4:11 At this point, Paul took pains to make sure that his words were not misunderstood. The fact that the Philippians had not sent help sooner did not mean that Paul had been disappointed in them or that he had been put in desperate straits at that time. Instead, he had learned an important secret to the Christian life—that he could **get along happily** with whatever he had, whether **much or little.** Paul had **learned** this—such contentment is not a natural human response. Paul explained that his sufficiency was in Christ alone, who provides strength to cope with all circumstances.

How do we get to that lofty goal of contentment? It is important for believers to realize that biblical "contentment" is not fatalism or acquiescence to one's lot in life. Such thinking would smother God's ongoing guidance. Rather, contentment involves one's perspective on life. To have real contentment, remember that everything belongs to God and what we have is a gift from him. Be thankful for what we have, not coveting what others have. Ask for wisdom to use wisely what we do have. Pray for grace to let go of the desire for what we don't have. Trust in God to meet our needs.

4:12 The following verses give a bit of Paul's personal testimony. Paul knew what it was like to **live on almost nothing** (see also 1 Corinthians 4:11-13; 2 Corinthians 6:4-10). Although he taught that the churches should support their leaders, Paul himself did not demand salaries from the churches that he had planted. This kept him above criticism (see 2 Corinthians 11:7). Thus with travel and food costs, Paul probably had very little to live on. Paul also knew how to live **with everything.** Literally, the meaning of the Greek word is "to overflow." This might refer to Paul's pre-Christian days as a fairly wealthy and influential Pharisee.

Whether Paul had plenty or little, he could keep life on an even keel because of contentment. What an important lesson for all believers to learn! No wonder Paul called it a **secret.**

4:13 Paul's contentment was not gained through stoic self-discipline. Instead, it was through Christ alone. In context, the word **everything** refers to the list in 4:11-12. In every possible circumstance, Paul could truly be content because he did not let outward circumstances determine his attitude. Christ was giving him the **strength** to continue with his ministry and the work of spreading the gospel whether he had plenty or was in need. Paul had complete confidence that, no matter what the circumstance, Christ would give him the strength to meet it.

This verse can be divided into two halves. The first half is, "I can do everything." To stop there and pull the words out of context would imply the idea of self-reliance, cocky self-assuredness. That's the kind of message we often hear from motivational speakers: "You can do anything you want if you put your mind to it." But that's not what the verse says. The last half reveals the source of our strength: Christ. God wants us to accomplish much for him in this world, but only through Christ. Instead of trusting our own strength and abilities, we must rely on Christ and his power.

Paul's confident words can be spoken by every Christian. The power we receive in union with Christ is sufficient to do his will and to face the challenges that arise from our commitment to doing it.

4:14 The Philippians shared in Paul's financial support while he was in prison, thus communicating their sympathy with him. The sense of this phrase, lost in the English translation, is a closeness between the apostle and the Philippian believers. That they had been willing to **share** in his **present difficulty** refers to having fellowship in them, identifying with the apostle on behalf of his work for the gospel. Paul commended them for this.

4:15-16 The "sharing" the Philippians had done with Paul refers to their partnership with him, revealed in the practical expression of financial support (see 4:10). **Only** the Philippian church had been ready to give **financial help** to Paul while he was ministering to them, and then when he **traveled on from Macedonia** to minister in other places. It seems that other churches did support Paul's ministry later (see 2 Corinthians 11:8) but that the Philippians had been especially attentive and generous, sending gifts not only while Paul was in **Thessalonica,** but later when he was in Corinth (2 Corinthians 11:9).

4:17 Paul made it clear that his thankfulness for the Philippians' generosity was not a veiled request for more. Instead, Paul focused on what their good works on his behalf were benefiting them in heaven. He knew that they would receive **a well-earned reward because of** their **kindness.** When we give to those in need, we benefit as well as the receiver, as we grow in the grace of giving (2 Corinthians 8:1, 6-7; 9:14). Paul appreciated the Philippians' spirit of love and devotion more than their gifts.

4:18 This was Paul's acknowledgment that he had received the Philippians' most recent **gifts** and that **Epaphroditus** had faithfully fulfilled his mission (see 2:25). Their generous gift was **more than** Paul needed. Surely the Philippian church rejoiced that they had been able to meet Paul's needs.

Paul described the Philippians' gift as a **sweet-smelling sacrifice.** Their very gifts were acts of worship, and **God** was the true recipient. They had given in faith, not so much to Paul as to God. That should be the ultimate goal of every act of love, care, concern, and charity—to help, but also to please God (see 2 Corinthians 5:9; Hebrews 13:16).

4:19 The **same God** who had taken **care** of Paul would also **supply all** their **needs.** The Philippian church was not wealthy. God had met Paul's need through the generosity of the Philippian church. God would more than repay that generosity by supplying the need of the Philippian church. Not only would God supply all their needs, but he would do it **from his glorious riches.** Believers cannot begin to comprehend God's riches in glory—his riches are limitless, infinite. If it is from that storehouse that believers' needs are met, then the Philippian believers could rest assured that God would indeed meet every need, no matter how large, desperate, or hopeless it seemed.

4:20 God the **Father** was both Paul's God and the Philippians' God—and he is also our God. God who supplied Paul's needs and met the Philippians' needs is the same yesterday, today, and forever, and he promises to meet our needs. To God belongs all **glory forever and ever.** Paul broke into a doxology of praise as he remembered God's great love and provision. God alone deserves all glory from his creation. **Amen,** so be it.

PAUL'S FINAL GREETINGS / 4:21-23
Paul closed his letter by sending greetings from Rome and the Christians there to the believers in Philippi. The gospel had spread to all strata of society, linking people who had no other bond but Christ.

4:21 Paul sent his personal **greetings to all the Christians** in the Philippian church; he probably knew each by name. In addition, the **brothers** with Paul in Rome (his coworkers, such as Timothy) also sent their **greetings** to the Philippians.

4:22 Paul expanded his message to include a greeting from **all the other Christians**—that is, all the believers in the Roman church, some of whom are probably listed in Romans 16:1-15.

The mention of **those who work Caesar's palace** offers an interesting sidelight. There were many Christians in Rome; some were even in Caesar's palace. This probably did not refer to Emperor Nero's family or members of his court, but rather to Christians in civil service (perhaps some soldiers—especially those who guarded Paul!) or on the imperial staff as slaves or servants. Because Philippi was a Roman colony, there may have been a link between some on the imperial staff in Rome

and those in some civil capacity in Philippi. Paul rejoiced because the gospel had infiltrated even into the emperor's household.

4:23 This letter to the Philippians begins and ends with **grace** (see 1:2). Paul had experienced God's undeserved favor, and he never tired of praying that others would also experience that grace.

In many ways the Philippian church was a model congregation. It was made up of many different kinds of people who were learning to work together. Paul recognized, however, that problems could arise, so in this thank-you letter, he prepared the Philippians for potential difficulties they might encounter. Though a prisoner in Rome, Paul had learned the true secret of joy and peace—imitating Christ and serving others. By focusing our minds on Christ we will learn unity, humility, joy, and peace. We will also be motivated to live for him.

Paul had no doubt been through Laodicea on his third missionary journey, as it lay on the main route to Ephesus, but he had never been to Colosse. Though a large city with a significant population, Colosse was smaller and less important than the nearby cities of Laodicea and Hierapolis.

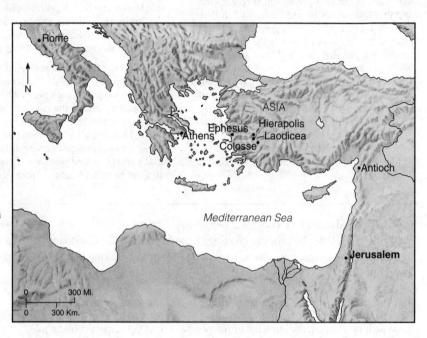

COLOSSIANS

INTRODUCTION

The human brain is amazing. God has created us with the ability to think, react, reason, consider, meditate, learn, imagine, understand, philosophize, know, perceive, evaluate, theorize, reflect, predict, and communicate. Enamored with the incredible power of our minds, however, we can become complacent in our wisdom, proud of our mental abilities, and reliant on ourselves.

To be complimented as "smart," "a genius," or "very intelligent" feels great. Beyond this, to have special knowledge feels even better. We like to be seen as experts and sought out, as though we have a secret formula or inside information.

The philosophical system of Gnosticism emphasized the mind and taught that salvation could be obtained through knowledge *(gnosis)* instead of faith. This "knowledge" was esoteric and could only be acquired by those who had been initiated into the mysteries of the Gnostic system, not by study or the normal process of learning. With a strong appeal to human pride (who wouldn't want to be on the "inside," the recipient and owner of secrets and mysteries?), Gnosticism distorted Christian theology and twisted biblical truths in order to support its concepts. Perhaps the most foundational of these false teachings was that matter is inherently evil and only the spiritual or non-material is good. This led to denying the doctrines of Creation and the Incarnation ("How could God take on an 'evil' body?"), elevating the role of angels, and reducing Christianity to just one of many religions (Gnosticism sought to combine the "best" of all religions).

A kind of proto-Gnosticism was gaining popularity in Colosse; it was a combination of Gnostic concepts and Judaism. Full-fledged Gnosticism did not appear until the second century. In any event, Paul wrote to refute the error and to get the believers back on track. To do so, Paul highlighted the preeminence of Christ and the importance of godly living.

As you read Paul's letter to the Colossian believers, use your God-given mind to evaluate your own belief system. Is it based on God's word and centered on Christ? Or do you rely on human philosophy and your ability to think?

AUTHOR
Paul

Colossians identifies both the sender and receiver of this letter (1:1-2). This opening line also mentions Timothy, but in the rest of the epistle Paul often writes in the first person. As with Philippians, Paul's authorship was affirmed by the early church fathers and has not been seriously disputed through the centuries.

One of the strongest arguments for Paul as the author of Colossians is this letter's relation to Philemon. Both letters, sent to the same city, probably by the same messenger, contain many of the same names: Paul, Timothy, Onesimus, Archippus, Epaphras, Mark, Aristarchus, Demas, and Luke.

DATE AND SETTING
Written from a Roman prison in approximately A.D. 60. Colossians was written in the same year as Ephesians and Philemon. According to the reference in 4:3 to being in chains, in 4:10 to fellow prisoner Aristarchus, and in 4:18 to his chains, clearly Paul was in prison when he wrote this letter. Evidently Epaphras, who was visiting Paul or was imprisoned with him (Philemon 23), told him of the problems in Colosse (1:7).

AUDIENCE
The believers in Colosse.

Colosse lay about one hundred miles east of Ephesus, in the Lycus River valley in Phrygia, a district of Asia Minor (Turkey) that had been incorporated into the Roman province of Asia in the second century B.C. Located on the great east-west trade route linking the Aegean Sea and the Euphrates River, Colosse thrived as a center of commerce. At one point the city also may have been a military base. Colosse was known for the distinctive, glossy, deep purple wool from the sheep that grazed in the surrounding hills. By the time of Paul's missionary journeys, the trade route had changed, placing Colosse off the beaten path. Thus, Colosse had been surpassed in power and importance by Laodicea and Hierapolis (see 4:13), neighboring towns in the Lycus Valley. Colosse was further reduced by an earth-quake at about the same time this letter was written.

The population of Colosse was diverse, including native Phrygians, Greek settlers, and Jews descended from Jewish families who had fled to the area during the persecutions of Antiochus the Great (223–187 B.C.).

Although Paul had traveled through Phrygia on his second and third missionary journeys (Acts 16:6; 18:23) and had lived for three years in Ephesus (Acts 19:1–20:1), it seems that he had never visited Colosse (see 1:9; 2:1-5). Yet Paul considered Colosse, as well as Laodicea and Hierapolis, to be in his area of responsibility, probably because the churches in these cities had been indirectly founded by him during his powerful ministry in Ephesus (see Acts 19:10, 26). Quite possibly both Epaphras and Philemon had been converted to Christ during that time (see Philemon 19, 23).

The church may have been started by Epaphras who had been sent by Paul to preach to the Colossians (1:7). Epaphras probably began the work in Laodicea and Hierapolis as well (see 4:12-13). The church in Colosse was comprised mainly of Gentiles (including Apphia—Philemon 2). Archippus may have been the church's pastor (4:17). Philemon and his slave Onesimus lived there. In fact, the church met in Philemon's home (Philemon 2). Another group met in Nympha's house (4:15).

OCCASION AND PURPOSE
Word had come to Paul of false teaching in Colosse, so Paul wrote to encourage the believers in Colosse and to combat errors in the church.

Although Paul was a Roman prisoner, his prison was a rented house (Acts 28:16, 30-31). He was allowed to entertain many visitors and to preach and teach. One of Paul's visitors was Epaphras (although he may have been a prisoner as well—Philemon 23). Epaphras reported on the situation in Colosse, including word of false teaching that was threatening the church (1:8; 4:12). Paul wrote quickly to warn the believers of the dangers of this heresy. Paul also wanted to send a letter to Philemon, along with his runaway slave, Onesimus. He was able to send both letters with Tychicus (4:7-9). Paul had learned from Epaphras that the church at Colosse was threatened by false teaching, partly pagan and partly Jewish (2:8, 16, 18, 20). In fact, it seems to have been a mixture of Jewish and pagan religions.

The Jewish element asserted that true believers had to observe certain days, deny themselves certain foods, and follow certain rituals. The pagan element emphasized self-denial, the worship of angels, and a mystical "wisdom." This probably was an early form of Gnosticism, a complex belief system that would become very prevalent in the second century. Gnosticism emphasized the supremacy of knowledge and that salvation came through knowledge, not by faith. This knowledge was attained through astrology and magic and was available only to those who had been initiated into the Gnostic system. Another Gnostic belief, that all matter is inherently evil and only the spiritual and nonmaterial is of itself good, led to the idea that God could not have created the world and would have no contact with it. Therefore they taught that God, in Christ, never could have become a human person. If matter is evil, how could God ever be united with a human body? Thus they denied either the humanity or the divinity of Christ (in their view, he couldn't have been both).

The heretical poison in Colosse was a deadly Judaic-Gnostic combination. So Paul wrote to warn the Colossian Christians of these errors of doctrine and practice:

- He warned against ritualism that had strict rules about permissible food and drink, religious festivals (2:16-17), and circumcision (2:11; 3:11).
- He warned against asceticism—the idea that the body is evil and that through self-torture or self-denial a person can attain exalted spirituality (1:22; 2:20-23).
- He warned against relying on human philosophy, knowledge, and tradition (2:4, 8).
- He warned against trying to obtain secret knowledge (2:18; see also 2:2-3).
- He warned against the worship of angels (2:18-19).
- He warned against making Christ any less than the divine Son of God, Lord of the universe, and Head of the church (1:13-20; 2:2-3, 9-10, 17).

Paul recognized that the most dangerous element of this heresy was the deprecation of Christ, so he focused much of his attention on Christ's supremacy. In fact, Colossians is the most Christ-centered book in the Bible.

Today we don't hear much about Gnosticism, but this heresy's false doctrines still abound: secret knowledge, mysticism, human philosophy, and syncretism. In fact, Jesus is seen as just one of many great historical religious leaders, not the unique Son of God and the only way to heaven (John 14:6).

Don't be deceived. These ideas may be popular, but they are wrong. Keep Christ,

God's only Son and your Savior, at the center of your life. Follow only him, the God-man, your crucified and risen Lord.

MESSAGE

Paul's introduction to the Colossians includes a greeting, a note of thanksgiving, and a prayer for spiritual wisdom and strength for these brothers and sisters in Christ (1:1-12). He then moves into a doctrinal discussion of the person and work of Christ (1:13-23), stating that Christ is "the visible image of the invisible God" (1:15), the Creator (1:16), "head of the church" (1:18), and "the first of all who will rise from the dead" (1:18). His death on the cross makes it possible for us to stand in the presence of God (1:22).

Paul then explains how the world's teachings are totally empty when compared with God's plan, and he challenges the Colossians to reject shallow answers and to live in union with Christ (1:24–2:23).

Against this theological backdrop, Paul turns to practical considerations—what the divinity, death, and resurrection of Jesus should mean to all believers (3:1–4:6). Because our eternal destiny is sure, heaven should fill our thoughts (3:1-4), sexual impurity and other worldly lusts should not be named among us (3:5-8), and truth, love, and peace should mark our life (3:9-15). Our love for Christ should also translate into love for others—friends, fellow believers, spouses, children, parents, slaves, and masters (3:16–4:1). We should constantly communicate with God through prayer (4:2-4), and we should take every opportunity to tell others the Good News (4:5-6). In Christ we have everything we need for salvation and for living the Christian life. Paul had probably never visited Colosse, so he concludes this letter with personal comments about their common Christian associations, providing a living lesson of the connectedness of the body of Christ.

The main themes in the book of Colossians include: *Christ's Divinity*, *Christ as Head of the Church*, *Union with Christ*, and *Man-made Religion*.

Christ's Divinity (1:15-20; 2:2, 9-12). Jesus Christ is God in the flesh, Lord of all creation, and Lord of the new creation. He is the expressed reflection of the invisible God. He is eternal, preexistent, omnipotent, and equal with the Father. He is supreme and complete. Jesus is God!

IMPORTANCE FOR TODAY. Because Christ is divine and the Lord of all creation, our lives must be centered around him. We must honor him as our God and our Lord; we must not accept any substitutes, tolerate any additions, or entertain any thoughts of a diminished role. This means regarding our relationship with him as most vital and making his interests our top priority. Is Christ the number one priority, the Commander in chief, the Lord of your life? Do you honor and worship him as God?

Christ as Head of the Church (1:15-20; 3:15-17, 23-24). Because Christ is God, he is the head of the church. Christ is the founder, leader, and highest authority on earth. As such, he expects his followers to listen to him carefully and obey him completely. Christ requires first place in all of their thoughts and activities.

IMPORTANCE FOR TODAY. To acknowledge Christ Jesus as our head, our Lord, we must welcome his leadership in all we do or think. No Christian individual, group, or church should regard any loyalty (to family, friends, country, employer, church, or denomination) more important than loyalty to Christ. Many voices vie for our attention and loyalty. We can feel pressure from peers and even from loved ones to think or act contrary to God's word. But only Christ should have our total allegiance. We should obey him regardless of what anyone else thinks or says. He is our head. In what ways are your loyalties divided? What can you do to better acknowledge Christ as your leader?

Union with Christ (1:13, 21-23; 2:6-15, 20; 3:1-4, 11, 15-17). Because believers' sins have been forgiven and they have been reconciled to God, they are united with Christ. That union can never be broken. Being united with Christ means being identified with his death, burial (2:20), and resurrection (3:1).

IMPORTANCE FOR TODAY. Because we have been united with Christ, we can have assurance of our salvation. Because we have been united with Christ, we should focus on heaven (3:2). And we should live as those who have been raised with Christ, ridding ourselves of all sinful habits related to life before Christ (3:8-11) and committing ourselves to good works (3:12-17).

Man-made Religion (2:8, 16-23). False teachers were promoting a heresy that stressed keeping rituals and rules (legalism). They also taught that spiritual growth was attained by discipline of the body (asceticism) and visions (mysticism). Emphasizing human knowledge, they missed God's wisdom; focusing on human philosophy, they didn't understand God; attempting to combine a variety of religious viewpoints, they lost sight of Christ.

IMPORTANCE FOR TODAY. We must not hold on to our own theories and ideas and try to blend them into Christianity. Nor should we allow our hunger for a more fulfilling Christian experience to cause us to trust in a teacher, group, or system of thought more than in Christ and in God's word. Don't be swayed or moved away from Christ by smooth-talking teachers, and don't be confused by attractive arguments and sophisticated philosophies. Keep your focus on Christ, and live by God's word.

OUTLINE OF COLOSSIANS

COLOSSIANS 1:1-23

GREETINGS FROM PAUL / 1:1-2

Colosse had early been a stopover along the main road from the east on the way to Ephesus. However, under the Roman Empire, the preferred route was through Laodicea, so Colosse declined in importance although it was still a large and busy city. As a trading center it was a crossroads for ideas and religions. Colosse had become the home of many Jews who had fled there when they were forced out of Jerusalem under the persecutions of Antiochus III and IV, almost two hundred years before Christ. The church in Colosse had been founded by Epaphras (1:7), one of Paul's converts. Although Paul had not yet visited this church, he wanted to write this letter to refute heretical teachings about Christ that were confusing many of the Christians there.

1:1 As at the beginning of all of his letters, **Paul** identified himself by name. But because Paul did not know the Colossian believers and because he needed to write to them about some specific doctrinal issues, he identified himself as **an apostle of Christ Jesus.** The word "apostle" means "one who is sent." Because Paul was not one of the original twelve disciples (who were called apostles after Jesus' resurrection), some doubted his credentials; yet Jesus had appeared to Paul personally and had commissioned him (Acts 9:1-6; 26:12-18). Thus, he was an apostle **chosen by God.** Paul's apostleship was not a matter of his own personal aspirations.

  Timothy was the young man Paul had met in Lystra on the second missionary journey. Paul wanted Timothy to accompany him (Acts 16:1-3). Timothy probably came to believe in Christ through Paul, for Paul later calls him his son in

the faith (1 Timothy 1:2). Timothy became Paul's assistant and emissary—traveling with him and sometimes for him. Timothy was not imprisoned with Paul, but he stayed in Rome to encourage Paul and to help with ministry needs. Thus, Paul's letter to the church in Colosse includes greetings from Timothy, a **brother** in the faith.

1:2 God's holy people were the believers. The city of **Colosse** was one hundred miles east of Ephesus on the Lycus River, and over one thousand miles from Rome, from which Paul was writing this letter. Paul often began his letters with greetings of **grace and peace. Grace** means God's unmerited favor; **peace** refers to the peace that Christ made between us and God through his death on the cross. Only **God our Father** can grant such wonderful gifts. Paul wanted his readers to experience God's grace and peace in their daily living.

PAUL'S THANKSGIVING AND PRAYER / 1:3-14

Paul made it a habit to pray for the churches—some he had visited, some he had not. He knew that the churches had to withstand difficulties from without and within. Paul wasn't able to go to the churches, and his letters would take weeks to arrive, but he could pray—regularly and persistently—for the strength and growth of the believers. Never underestimate the power of intercessory prayer. Who prays regularly for you? For whom do you regularly pray?

1:3 One characteristic of Paul was his constant prayers for the churches—those he knew well and those he did not. The word **always** could modify **give thanks,** or it could modify **pray,** referring to Paul always praying for the churches (and specifi-

cally the Colossian church) during his regular prayer times (see also 1:9). Picture Paul and Timothy (and others who might have joined with them) regularly kneeling in fervent prayer on behalf of specific congregations and even individual believers who sought

to grow in their faith, sometimes in hostile environ-
ments. In those prayers, the believers thanked
God—Paul explained what they gave thanks for
in the following verses.

1:4-5 Paul had not been to Colosse; he had **heard** of
their **trust in Christ Jesus** from Epaphras (1:7). He
had also heard that they loved **all of God's people**
and acted upon that love. Trust in Jesus refers to the
vertical component of the Christian life; love refers
to the horizontal relationships with other believers.
The Colossians' trust in Christ Jesus and love for
others had reason: they were **looking forward to
the joys of heaven.** Why have faith in Jesus Christ
if there is no hope for a glorious future? Why love
others if it doesn't matter in the end? But looking
forward to heaven makes all the difference. These
believers have been looking forward to heaven **since**
they **first heard the truth of the Good News.** Paul
brought them the "truth" of the gospel as opposed
to the heresy of the false teachers. No matter what
interesting teaching or ideas they heard, the believers must hold on to the truth as it was taught to
them, rejecting anything that contradicted that truth.
They could trust Paul's teaching because they could
trust the truth of the gospel.

1:6 Paul spoke of the **Good News** as an entity unto
itself—something alive, growing, spreading, bearing fruit, and spreading some more. Paul was not
exaggerating when he wrote the words, **all over
the world.** He did not mean that every location
on earth had been evangelized, but that the gospel
was making headway across racial, national, and
geographical barriers throughout the Roman
Empire. Indeed, nothing could stop it from **changing lives everywhere.** Not only was the gospel
growing and bearing fruit across the known world,
it was doing the same right in the city of Colosse.
When Epaphras first brought them the Good News
of the gospel (1:7; 4:12-13), the Colossians **heard
and understood the truth about God's great
kindness to sinners.**

Here, in short summary, Paul emphasized
what makes the Christian gospel so wonderfully
helpful to us and so different from every other
religion in the world. Through that gospel, God
enabled us human beings to understand, with our
limited ability, his grace upon us—his unmerited
favor to his lowly creation. Of all the world religions, Christianity alone offers salvation without
demands for pious works. Followers of Christ set
down their load of sin and guilt at the cross and
begin a life of pleasing God, who lovingly guides
and directs them. Who can resist such an opportunity? Who can say no to such a God? Who would
desire something other?

1:7 Epaphras had founded the church at Colosse
while Paul was living in Ephesus (Acts 19:10).
Epaphras may have been converted in Ephesus
and then had returned to Colosse, his hometown.
Paul called Epaphras a **much loved coworker,** a
faithful servant, and a "fellow prisoner" (Philemon
23). The letter to the Colossians and the personal
letter to Philemon were written at about the same
time and sent to the same destination (the Colossian church met in Philemon's house). It is unclear
from this verse whether Epaphras was actually in
prison with Paul, or if Paul's words were metaphors
of warfare or "captivity to Christ." It is more likely
that Epaphras was with Paul voluntarily and would
return to Colosse. The Colossian believers could
trust Epaphras, and they could trust his message.
Paul was saying that Epaphras was speaking on
behalf of the apostle himself. Epaphras's authority
gave them good reason to *not* accept teachings that
had come to them later and which were contradictory to Epaphras's teaching.

1:8 Undoubtedly, Epaphras had told Paul all
about the church in Colosse. Some concern from
Epaphras about the false teaching that had come
into Colosse prompted Paul's response through
this letter. But Epaphras had also told Paul about
the character of the church—they had **great love**
for one another, they showed love outside the
fellowship, and they loved the well-known Paul
as a brother in Christ, even though they had never
met him. Such love comes from our relationship
with Christ and the indwelling of the **Holy Spirit**
because this love is a fruit of the Spirit. Christian
love comes from the Holy Spirit (see Galatians
5:22). The Bible speaks of it as an action and attitude, not just an emotion. Love is a by-product
of our new life in Christ (see Romans 5:5; 15:30;
1 Corinthians 13).

1:9 In 1:3, Paul had already mentioned that he con-
tinued praying for these believers (as he did for all
the churches; see for example Romans 1:8-9 and
Philippians 1:3-6, 9-11). Paul didn't know about a
church in Colosse until he had **heard about** it from
Epaphras, and Paul rejoiced to be able to pray for
another growing church. Paul did not stop at saying
that he prayed constantly for the Colossian believers; he went on to explain exactly what he prayed
for them. He asked God that they have **complete
understanding** of God's will for their lives. He
asked that they be made **wise with spiritual wisdom.** These are not abstract concepts; instead, Paul
was referring to the true wisdom and understanding
made available by God's Holy Spirit. The Colossians
needed to be filled with this type of spiritual wisdom and knowledge, leaving no room for any

other type of false "knowledge" advocated by Gnostic heretics. Wisdom and understanding refer to discretion and discernment. When believers possess those, they will be able to discern the truth from false teaching.

1:10 True understanding and wisdom of God's will is inseparable from living in harmony with it. True knowledge leads to obedience; complete obedience cannot occur without the knowledge of God's will given by the Holy Spirit. The Colossian believers should **live always** to **honor and please the Lord.** By so doing, they **will continually do good, kind things for others.** Their behavior should match their status as God's holy people. They ought to be following God closely—their lives being transformed to Christlikeness. A Christian must be active in order to grow spiritually and to live worthy of the Lord.

Is it possible for Christians to **please** God? Apparently so, for Paul prayed exactly that for the Colossian believers. Perfection will not be achieved in this life, yet believers press on toward the goal of God's high calling (Philippians 3:12-14). In the meantime, believers can be fully pleasing to God by virtue of their relationship with him and their attempts to "live in order to please" him in all areas of life (1 Thessalonians 4:1).

1:11-12 The Colossians' growth in the knowledge of God and the resultant fruit would help to strengthen them. Paul continued his prayer for the believers, asking God that they **be strengthened with his glorious power**. One can hardly pray a more wonderful prayer. To be made strong with God's power is to be given incredible strength—it was God's glorious power that created the universe and that brought Jesus back to life. One can hardly imagine more power. In fact, Paul's words here show the inadequacy of describing God's power— it is beyond our words or our human minds to comprehend. Yet that power is available to believers and to the church so they can fulfill their mission in the world. Paul wanted the Colossian believers to be strengthened with God's power so they would not be pulled away from their faith and their witness to the world.

This power would give them **all the patience and endurance** they would **need. Patience** is the ability to stand firm against opposition without giving up; it is often used in describing one's dealings with difficult people. **Endurance** is the ability to continue toward a goal regardless of the obstacles; it is often used in relation to difficult circumstances. Both would be needed by the believers in Colosse, and both come from the empowerment of God's glorious strength. Paul reminded the

Colossians that even when they were surrounded by persecution and false teaching, they had the strength to continue toward the goal of their faith and to stand firm against the opposition. It is God's power that helps believers endure and be patient even as they are **filled with joy** that overflows in **always thanking the Father.**

Why? Because Jesus Christ made it possible for the believers to **share the inheritance that belongs to God's holy people.** By using the word **inheritance,** Paul was alluding to the inheritance of the Promised Land, first promised to Abram for his faithfulness to God (Genesis 13:14-17). God's people, the Old Testament saints, inherited a portion of a bountiful land (Numbers 26:52-56; 34:2, 13). God's people in the New Testament are the very sons of God, and as such they have the right to inherit Christ and a glorious eternity in **the light.** The promise of land is broadened to include the whole creation (Romans 4:14; 8:17-25). Paul was most likely setting up the contrast between the state of "light" that the believers have been transferred to from their previous state of "darkness" as described in 1:13.

1:13 This verse continues the thought from 1:12; Paul still had in mind the analogy of Israel inheriting the Promised Land. The book of Exodus tells the story of how God **rescued** (or delivered) his people from Egypt (typifying Satan's **kingdom of darkness**) and took them to the Promised Land (typifying the **Kingdom of his dear Son**). (See Exodus 6:6; 12:27; 14:30.) Jesus referred to the **kingdom of darkness** at his arrest in the Garden of Gethsemane (Luke 22:53), describing the forces of evil that he had to combat in his final hours. In Scripture, "darkness" is a metaphor for evil; it is the dominion of those who are without God. True believers, however, have been transferred from darkness to light, from slavery to freedom, from guilt to forgiveness, and from the power of Satan to the power of God. We have been rescued from a rebel kingdom to serve the true King. That King, the Son God loves, is described in the following verses (1:15-20).

1:14 Believers are able to be in Christ's Kingdom because through Jesus Christ, **God has purchased our freedom with his blood and has forgiven all our sins.** That is the way God chose to buy sinful people back—he offered his Son in exchange for us. Paul was reminding the Colossian believers that they were not saved by knowledge or by good works or by inclusion in some sort of secret religious cult; they were saved by the blood of Jesus Christ. Through him alone had they received the forgiveness of sins.

If we want to be freed from the deadly consequences of our sins, a tremendous price must be paid. But we don't have to pay it. Jesus Christ, our substitute, has already redeemed us by his death on the cross. Our part is to trust him and accept his gift of eternal life. Our sins have been paid for, and the way has been cleared for us to begin a relationship with God.

CHRIST IS SUPREME / 1:15-23
In the Colossian church there were several misconceptions about Christ that Paul directly refuted in this section:

- Believing that matter is evil, false teachers argued that God would not have come to earth as a true human being in bodily form. Paul stated that Christ is the image—the exact likeness—of God and is himself God, and yet he died on the cross as a human being.
- They believed that God did not create the world because he would not have created evil. Paul proclaimed that Jesus Christ, who was also God in the flesh, participated in the creation of the universe.
- They said that Christ was not the unique Son of God but rather one of many intermediaries between God and people. Paul explained that Christ existed before anything else and is the firstborn of those resurrected.
- They refused to see Christ as the source of salvation, insisting that people could find God only through special and secret knowledge. In contrast Paul openly proclaimed the way of salvation to be through Christ alone. Paul continued to bring the argument back to Christ.

1:15 Many New Testament scholars believe that this section was based on a hymn written before Paul wrote his letter to the Colossians. If this was a hymn, we can assume that it was known to the church at Colosse and to other Christians. Paul would not have quoted something unknown to them. However, Paul was very capable of writing such poetic lines, as demonstrated in passages such as Romans 8:37-39 and 1 Corinthians 13:4-8. These verses are regarded as some of the most important verses in the New Testament establishing the deity of Jesus Christ.

Christ is the visible image of the invisible God—the verb is present tense, describing Jesus' position now and forever (John 10:30, 38; 12:45; 14:1-11). God as Spirit is invisible and always will be (1 Timothy 6:16). God's Son is his visible expression. He not only reflects God, but, as God, he reveals God to us (John 1:18; 14:9; Hebrews 1:1-2).

Christ existed before God made anything at all. Thus he is **supreme over all creation.** He has all the priority and authority of the firstborn prince in a king's household (Hebrews 1:2). He came from heaven, not from the dust of the earth (1 Corinthians 15:47), and he is Lord of all (Romans 9:5; 10:12; Revelation 1:5; 17:14). Christ is supreme over all creation, including the spirit world.

Paul explained in no uncertain terms that the Colossian believers had to focus on the deity of Jesus Christ (that Jesus is God) or their Christian faith would fall prey to false teaching. To put Jesus any lower is to lose the central truth of Christianity.

1:16 All things were created **through** Christ (John 1:3). Just as all the fullness of Deity is in him (1:19), so in him are all the creative powers that make him the supreme Lord. Because the false teachers believed that the physical world was evil, they thought that God himself could not have created it. If Christ were God, they reasoned, he would be in charge only of the spiritual world. But Paul explained that **everything in heaven and earth** was created by Christ, **things we can see and the things we can't see,** the visible and invisible world (physical government and spiritual forces). Christ has no equal and no rival. Because Christ is the Creator of the world, all powers, whether the spiritual forces the Colossians wished to study or any material force, were under Christ's final authority.

Paul's words here refuted the false teaching that Christ was one of many intermediaries and that the angels were to be worshiped. All angelic and celestial powers in heaven and on earth are subject to Christ. He is the Lord of all.

1:17 Christ **existed before everything else began.** He is not only the Creator of the world, he is also its Sustainer. By him everything came to be, and by him everything **holds together.** In him, everything is held together, protected, and prevented from disintegrating into chaos (see Acts 17:28). Because Christ is the Sustainer of all life, nothing in creation is independent from him. In him alone and by his word, we find the unifying principle of all of life (Hebrews 1:2-3). The Colossians, and all believers, are his servants who must daily trust him for protection, care, and sustenance.

1:18 While 1:15-17 unveiled the Son's relationship to the "old creation" (the world), this verse describes his relationship to the "new creation"— that is, **the church.** The church (meaning the **body** of believers) existed because Christ was its beginning, its source, its **head.** Just as the parts of the body function under the direction of the brain, so Christians are to work together under the command and authority of Jesus Christ.

Paul repeated that Christ is **the first of all who will rise from the dead.** He was the first to die and come back to life. He was "first" both in time and rank; there will be many more who will live forever after physical death (1 Corinthians 15:20). All who trust in Christ will also defeat death and rise again to live eternally with him (1 Corinthians 15:20; 1 Thessalonians 4:14). This makes him **first in everything.**

Jesus' resurrection is the cornerstone of the Christian faith, the reason that the church even exists. Only Christianity has a God who became human, died for his people, and was raised again in power and glory to rule the old creation and the new creation (the church) forever. The Resurrection assures believers that Christ is not a legend; he is alive and ruling his Kingdom. Because Christ is spiritually supreme in the universe, surely we should give him first place in all our thoughts and activities.

1:19-20 The little word **for** explains why Christ will have first place in everything. **God** wanted his **fullness** (meaning "completeness" or "totality") to **live** (meaning "live permanently") **in Christ.** Paul wanted to explain to the Colossians that Christ is God's dwelling place; therefore, Christ is divine, sovereign, and preeminent. Christ perfectly displays all the attributes and activities of God: Spirit, Word, wisdom, glory.

By this statement, Paul was refuting the Greek idea that Jesus could not be human and divine at the same time. Christ is fully human; he is also fully divine. Nor is there more than one God; this one God, in all his fullness, resides in Christ. Christ has always been God and always will be God. All of God (including his attributes, charac-

teristics, nature, and being) indwells the Son. When we have Christ we have all of God in human form. Any teaching that diminishes any aspect of Christ—either his humanity or his divinity—is false teaching.

God's fullness dwells in Christ and in that fullness he **reconciled everything to himself.** This reconciliation was accomplished through Christ's **blood on the cross.** "Reconciliation" means reestablishing a relationship, causing a relationship to become friendly and peaceable when it had not been so. Because Christ is Creator and Sustainer of everything (1:17), his death on the cross provided reconciliation for **everything.** But what did Paul mean by "everything"?

First, consider what this reconciliation means for humanity. There can be no peace between sinful humans and a holy God. Because people are born into sin, they cannot become good enough to be acceptable to God. In Old Testament times, God accepted symbolic offerings. Jesus had not yet been sacrificed, so God accepted the life of an animal in place of the life of the sinner. When Jesus came, he substituted his perfect life for our sinful lives, taking the penalty for sin that we deserve. The penalty for sin is death. We are guilty and culpable, but Jesus took the punishment. Thus, he redeemed us from the power of sin and reconciled us to God.

Second, does this reconciliation of "everything" mean that everyone will be saved? From other passages, we know that Paul understood salvation to be something accepted or rejected by humans, who are given the choice (for example, see 2 Thessalonians 1:5-10). The scope of God's reconciliation is universal—it is offered to all people. But reconciliation is accomplished only for those who accept Christ as Savior (2 Corinthians 5:17-18).

Third, what does this reconciliation mean for "everything" (besides humans)? Just as all of creation fell when Adam sinned, so all of creation will be reconciled. Sin has caused all creation to fall from the perfect state in which God created it. Thus, the world is subject to decay so that it cannot fulfill its intended purpose. One day, all creation will be liberated and transformed (Romans 8:19-21).

In addition, Paul's reference to things **in heaven and on earth** was meant to be another blow to the false teachers. Nothing in the universe escapes Christ's reach. There is no neutral ground; everything falls under his power. No alien force of darkness can undermine his work or his church. Satan and demons **will not** be reconciled to God; instead, their end is certain (see Revelation 20:7-10).

1:21-22 Paul gave the reason why we need reconciliation. The believers in Colosse had, at one time, been **far away (separated,** estranged) from God and they were his **enemies.** Their thoughts and behaviors had revealed, not apathy or ignorance, but hostility toward God because of sin. They were strangers to God's way of thinking. Wrong thinking leads to sin, which further perverts and destroys thoughts about him. When people are out of harmony with God, their natural condition is to be totally hostile to his standards.

God made peace by **his death on the cross in his own human body** (1:20). In order to answer the false teaching that Jesus was only a spirit and not a true human being, Paul explained that Jesus' fleshly, physical body actually died. Jesus suffered death fully as a human; thus, we can be assured that he died in our place. Since Jesus, as perfect God, faced death, we can be assured that his sacrifice was complete and that he truly removed our sin.

What is the goal of this reconciliation? He wants to bring his people **into the very presence of God, holy and blameless, without a single fault.** Believers can be called **holy and blameless** because they have been acquitted of all charges (Ephesians 5:27; Jude 24). Christ's act of reconciliation put believers in perfect standing with God. By Christ's death on the cross, God already dealt with sin. His goal is to make believers his holy people, to transform their character so they can live consistent with their faith. The pattern is the perfect life lived by Jesus Christ. The process of living the Christian life will end with the resurrection and will result in believers being presented to God as his dear and beloved children.

1:23 The certainty of believers' present and future status with God should not be an excuse for careless living or dabbling in heresy. Paul warned the Colossian believers to **continue to believe this truth and stand in it firmly.** As they built their lives upon the foundation laid by the gospel, they ought to build carefully through obedience. Then their "building" would stand firm. The Colossians should not wander off into false teaching that contradicted the gospel they had heard and the hope they had believed for salvation.

As Paul closed his introductory section, he made one final stab at the doctrine of the false teachers by proclaiming that the gospel **has been preached all over the world.** Spiritual reality was not, as the false teachers claimed, available only to a select group of intellectually elite people. The hope of the gospel is available to the whole world. And the writer, **Paul,** had been **appointed by God to proclaim** that message. This was the gospel to which Paul had become a servant; this was the only true gospel. This was what the Colossians had heard and believed. There ought to be no excuse for wandering away into false teaching.

COLOSSIANS 1:24–2:23

PAUL'S WORK FOR THE CHURCH / 1:24–2:5

Paul was combating a false teaching in the Colossian church similar to Gnosticism (from *gnosis,* the Greek word for knowledge). Though Gnosticism did not become fashionable until the second century, even in Paul's day these ideas sounded attractive to many, and exposure to such teachings could easily seduce a church that didn't know Christian doctrine well. We combat heresy by becoming thoroughly acquainted with God's word through personal study and sound Bible teaching. In this chapter, Paul wanted to help the Colossian believers guard against those who would undermine the simple faith and sufficiency they had found in Christ.

1:24 Sitting in his prison in Rome and suffering for his faith, Paul was able to say **I am glad** even as he suffered. Paul was honored to be suffering, and he rejoiced at what God was doing in the churches and in the believers who were gaining courage and faith by watching Paul's example. Perhaps the false teachers had pointed to Paul's imprisonment as proof that his leadership and his teachings were in question. Paul explained that, instead, his imprisonment proved the truth of his words, and he could rejoice in that imprisonment knowing that it was all part of God's plan, **for his body, the church.**

Paul's words, **"I am completing what remains of Christ's sufferings,"** did not mean that Christ's suffering was inadequate to save people.

Paul believed that Christ's suffering on the cross alone paid for believers' salvation from sin (Romans 3:23-25). (See also 1 Corinthians 1:18-31; 2 Corinthians 5:16-21; Galatians 1:4; Colossians 2:13-14.)

While we know what Paul did *not* mean by these words, we must consider several interpretations regarding what he *did* mean. There are three main views:

1. One view comes from the Jewish belief that an anointed ruler would come and God's people would be called upon to suffer (Daniel 12:1). However, God would set a limit to these sufferings. Paul saw himself as suffering on behalf of the church, thereby completing what remained of that set amount of suffering. Some commentators consider that Paul thought that by his suffering he actually was saving others from suffering. This view seems unlikely, however, because Paul was tying suffering to the spread of the gospel, not to preparation for the end times.
2. Referring to Paul's words in Philippians 3:10 where Paul wanted to suffer with Christ, he may have meant that he wanted to complete in himself what was lacking in his understanding of Christ's suffering. This also seems unlikely in this context, however, because Paul was emphasizing the believers' completeness in Christ.
3. Another view refers to the mystical union between Paul and Christ and between Christ and the church. What Paul suffered, Christ suffered, because Paul was a member of Christ's body on earth. What Christ began as suffering with his persecution and rejection on earth, all believers complete in his continuing body on earth. This view seems most likely because it stresses that the cause of the suffering would be the extension of the gospel to all the world. Paul shared the suffering of the Messiah as he brought the Messiah's message to the world.

Jesus had warned his followers to expect affliction (John 15:20-21). This suffering would not be limited to Paul. By identifying themselves with Christ, all believers would face affliction. Not all would face imprisonment, as Paul did, but all would have varying degrees and kinds of suffering simply because they have allied themselves with Christ in a world hostile to Christ. But this suffering should be cause for rejoicing. Suffering does not mean that Christ is losing ground, but that he is gaining it and that the present age is passing away to eventually herald in the age to come when Christ will reign.

1:25-26 Paul explained that **God** had **given** him the **responsibility of serving his church by proclaiming his message in all its fullness to you Gentiles.** When Paul was commissioned by God, the focus of his ministry was made clear—he would go to the Gentiles (Acts 9:15). Paul was keenly aware of who had commissioned him, to whom he had been commissioned, and what he had been called to do. Paul's ministry among the Gentiles was to fully make known the word of God and to bring the preaching of the word of God to completion. Without Paul's ministry concerning God's plan for Christ and the church, God's word, the revelation of his will, would be unfinished. The heresy in Colosse focused on mystical knowledge, and only a few could find the "fullness of knowledge" needed for inclusion in their special group. Thus, when Paul wrote of making God's word fully known to all the believers, he was pointing out once again that God's word is for all people. They could have all the wisdom they needed to be saved and to grow in Christ.

Making God's word fully known meant revealing a **message** that had been **kept secret for centuries and generations past.** This message was hidden, not because only a few could understand it, but because it was hidden until Christ came. With Christ's coming and the beginning of Christianity, that message is no longer hidden; it **has been revealed** to those who believe, that is, **his holy people.** God's plan was hidden from previous generations, not because God wanted to keep something from his people, but because he was going to reveal it in his perfect timing. Paul was explaining that God's time for action was then and there.

What is that hidden message? Paul wrote the answer in Ephesians 3:1-6. The mystery hidden throughout the ages was that one day Jews and Gentiles would be joined together in one body because of their common belief in Jesus Christ as Savior. The Old Testament revealed that the Gentiles would receive salvation (Isaiah 49:6), but it was never explained that Gentile and Jewish believers would become **equal** in the body of Christ, with no divisions between them. In the Old Testament, Gentiles could convert to Judaism but would always be considered "second-class" Jews, not pure Jews. With the coming of Christ, however, and the new union he created through his church, all believers were joined together in Christ's body.

1:27 God's hidden message is not a puzzle to solve; instead, it is like a treasure chest filled with **the riches and glory of Christ,** and the message is that the riches are available to the **Gentiles.** These words would have been joyful to Paul's Gentile audience, that God was **pleased** to offer salvation to them. They did not need to acquire some secret knowledge in order to find God; God had reached down to them because he wanted to save them.

God made the **secret** available to Jews and Gentiles alike, and the secret is **Christ lives in you.** Jews and Gentiles will have that oneness in Christ's body because God had planned from the beginning of time to have Christ live in the heart of each person who believes in him. The indwelling Christ gives believers **assurance that** they **will share in his glory** in his eternal Kingdom. Believers are in Christ; Christ is in them; therefore, believers can look forward to sharing Christ's glory.

1:28-29 The word **we** includes Paul and his coworkers, particularly Epaphras and Tychicus who served the Colossian church. Paul and his coworkers were telling the Good News about **Christ,** who at present was dwelling in them as well as in the Colossian believers, making all of them one body awaiting a glorious future.

Their proclaiming of Jesus Christ included both warning and teaching. The word **warn** (also translated "admonishing") connects with repentance and refers to a person's conduct and heart attitude. **Teach** is connected to faith and doctrine and refers to a person's intellect. Paul needed both, and **all the wisdom God** had **given** him, especially when dealing with false teachers.

The warning and teaching always had one goal in mind: **we want to present** the believers **to God, perfect in their relationship to Christ.** This "presentation" would be when Christ returned. Believers are not to remain like babies in the faith, easily led away by something new (see also 1 Corinthians 3:1-2). Instead, they are to grow up into spiritual maturity so that they cannot be enticed by false teachings. God makes this possible only through a personal relationship with Christ. This relationship with Christ, empowered by the indwelling of the Holy Spirit, helps believers grow in faith and maturity until the day when Christ returns. Paul worked **very hard** for this goal. His task was not simple. He struggled against false teaching, persecution, and questions about his qualifications. He bore heartache and concern on behalf of the churches because he had his goal always before him. Not only did he want people to accept the gospel, but he also wanted them to mature in their faith. Thus he wrote letters, prayed constantly, traveled to many churches, stayed and worked and taught in some places, sent emissaries on his behalf, wrote more letters upon the reports of these emissaries in order to deal with specific situations facing some churches, and sent emissaries back for reports.

Paul did not struggle with his own strength alone, however. He depended **on Christ's mighty power** that worked **within** him. Paul needed God's supernatural power, and God supplied it.

2:1 Paul's labor and struggle were not limited to those churches he had planted or even to people he knew **personally.** Paul also worked on behalf of those who had never met him. He **agonized** for the Colossians in prayer and with the concern that had prompted the writing of this letter. Paul struggled, knowing that the false teaching threatened to keep the Colossian believers from maturing in their faith.

Laodicea was located a few miles northwest of Colosse. Like the church at Colosse, the Laodicean church was probably founded by one of Paul's converts while Paul was staying in Ephesus (Acts 19:10), perhaps even Epaphras, who had founded the Colossian church. The city was a wealthy center of trade and commerce, but later Christ would criticize the believers at Laodicea for their lukewarm commitment (Revelation 3:14-22). The fact that Paul mentioned this city and either wanted this letter to be passed on to the church there or wrote a separate one (4:16), indicates that false teaching may have spread there as well.

2:2-3 Paul wanted those he had not been able to visit to know that he was interested in them and was praying diligently for them. He simply prayed that the Colossians would **be encouraged** and that they would be **knit together by strong ties of love.** These two characteristics would help them resist false teaching.

Paul also wanted these churches to **have full confidence because they have complete understanding of God's secret plan, which is Christ himself.** Christ is the secret, yet he is a secret revealed to those who believe. This complete understanding obtained through a personal relationship with Christ himself assures believers of the truth and helps them recognize and avoid heresy. Everything anyone wants to know about God and his purposes in the world is answered in the person of Christ. The secret is revealed because it is Christ in whom **lie hidden all the treasures of wisdom and knowledge.** True wisdom is found only in Christ; true knowledge is found only in Christ. Knowledge is often described as good judgment, wisdom as application of that good judgment in the form of good actions. The false teachers claimed to have a higher knowledge than what ordinary believers possessed. Against this, Paul argued that all wisdom and knowledge were in Christ and that Christ's treasures were accessible to every believer. **Hidden** does not mean concealed but rather that they were laid up or stored away to be made available to those who desire a relationship with Christ.

Certainly these words greatly comforted the Colossian believers who did not have to look any farther for wisdom and knowledge than to their Savior, Jesus Christ. The believers already possessed all wisdom and knowledge, yet they had a long way to go to attain maturity and complete understanding.

2:4 The believers in Colosse already knew what they needed to know to be saved; they already knew the One they needed to know to have eternal life. But they needed to grow to maturity in the faith they had received. That way **no one** would **be able to deceive** them **with persuasive arguments.** The false teachers did a good job of making their teachings sound plausible and of using persuasive tactics to cause the believers to question their faith. When believers are fully committed to the truth in Jesus, they will not be easily deluded.

2:5 Paul couldn't go to Colosse due to his imprisonment, but his **heart** was with them. He knew that they were **living** as they should and had **strong faith in Christ.** These two characteristics caused Paul to be **happy,** for they meant that the Colossians had not succumbed to the false teaching. They were a unified body, steadfast in their faith.

FREEDOM FROM RULES AND NEW LIFE IN CHRIST / 2:6-23
Paul rejoiced in the Colossians' unity and steadfast faith because these proved they had not given ground to the heresy. But Paul wanted to insure that they wouldn't give in and believe the lies of the false teachers. So he launched into a full-scale rebuttal of the false teaching.

2:6 The Colossians had not merely accepted the doctrines of Christ, they had **accepted Christ** himself **as Lord.** The verb **accepted** means more than the moment a person asks Christ into his or her heart. Paul most likely used the word, taken from Judaism, to describe the transmitting and safeguarding of traditions and teachings from one person or generation to another. Thus when Paul reminded the Colossians of when they received Christ Jesus, he was reminding them of their receiving the proclamation and teaching, and their confession of faith, their baptism, and their new status as members of Christ's body.

Because Christ dwells within all believers through the Holy Spirit, they should **live in obedience to him.** The past event of receiving Christ should be a present reality in the believers' daily lives.

2:7 Paul used several metaphors in these verses. Each metaphor has a specific and profound point for Christian living. First, the Colossians were to **let** their **roots grow down into** Christ. Just as plants draw nourishment from the soil through their roots, so the believers should **draw up nourishment** from Christ. The more they would draw strength from Christ, the less they would be fooled by those who falsely claimed to have life's answers.

Second, the Colossians were to **grow in faith.** Like a plant, they were "rooted" once and for all, but they had to grow continuously. Or like a building, they had a solid foundation, but had to keep on building with solid materials in order to be strong.

Third, the Colossians were to be **strong and vigorous in the truth.** This too is continuous action, an ongoing process. The **truth** which these Colossian believers had been **taught** should be a source of abundant **thanksgiving.** True understanding of what Christ has done on behalf of believers can lead to no other response than gratefulness.

2:8 Paul strongly warned about the heresy's effect on those who believed it. They would be led **astray.** According to Paul, the heresy amounted to nothing more than **empty philosophy and high-sounding nonsense.** The word translated "philosophy" occurs only here in the New Testament, so this may have been a significant feature of this heresy. In Greek, the word "philosophy" means "love of wisdom." Paul was a gifted philosopher, so he was not condemning education or the study of philosophy. Instead, he was condemning false philosophy, the kind that is deceptive because it keeps people from seeing the truth.

Paul was so disparaging toward this heresy because it came **from human thinking and from the evil powers of this world.** No man-made religion can lead to the truth, for truth can be found only in Christ. True philosophy will focus on Jesus Christ—it will not put Christ in any lower position, nor will it focus on human endeavor.

2:9 Again Paul asserted Christ's divine nature (see 1:19). **In Christ** designates a local or spatial relationship rather than a mystical relationship. God's saving action happens in the person of Jesus Christ. In 2:9-15, every verse contains the word "Christ," showing that Christ is the center of God's saving activity. **The fullness of God** refers to all the divine attributes. God's nature and person are in Christ's **human body.** The false teaching said that Christ could not have been both man and God. But Paul clearly stated that this was indeed the case. Paul made two significant points in this sentence: (1) Christ was not another deity along with God; instead, God's fullness was dwelling uniquely and supremely in Christ. (2) Christ was not less than God.

2:10 Not only does all the fullness of the Deity dwell in Christ, but all believers have been given fullness (been made **complete) through** their **union with Christ.** The Colossians lacked nothing outside of Christ; in him they had everything they needed for salvation and right living. But what does this "completeness" mean? It means that there is nothing lacking in a believer's relationship with God. God pours his love and power into believers, giving them fullness for this life and readying them for the life to come. Believers need not look anywhere else. Christ is the unique source of knowledge and power for the Christian life.

Christ is not just one of many intermediaries or angels who must be worshiped, as the heresy maintained. Instead, **he is the Lord over every ruler and authority in the universe.** Because Christ is the head and is superior to any angel or archangel, it would be absurd to worship or venerate any angel. Again this countered the false teaching.

2:11 Jewish males were circumcised as a sign of the Jews' covenant with God (Genesis 17:9-14). Circumcision was an expression of Israel's national identity and was a requirement for all Jewish men. Circumcision (cutting off the foreskin of the penis) was a physical reminder to Jews of their national heritage and privilege. It symbolized "cutting off" the old life of sin, purifying one's heart, and dedicating oneself to God (Deuteronomy 10:16; Jeremiah 4:4; Ezekiel 44:7). Bodily circumcision was no longer necessary to be identified as God's people. Paul explained that all believers **were circumcised, but not by a physical procedure.** Instead, their circumcision involved **cutting away** the **sinful nature.** The Colossian believers had become God's children. The sign of their new life was not a cutting of the flesh, but a **cutting away** of the sinful nature. Their commitment to God had been written on their hearts, not on their bodies. Only Christ could perform this **spiritual procedure,** for only by accepting him as Savior can people be saved.

2:12 Baptism parallels the death, burial, and resurrection of Christ, and it also portrays the death and burial of the believer's sinful way of life. In the church of Paul's day, many people were **baptized** by immersion—that is, new Christians were completely **"buried"** in water. They understood this form of baptism to symbolize being buried with Christ, thus the death and burial of the old way of life. When Christ died, our old nature died with him also. This was a spiritual circumcision (2:11). Baptism also portrays the death of our old nature.

Coming up out of the water symbolized being **raised to a new life** with Christ. It also symbolized the future bodily resurrection. Believers' faith is in the **mighty power of God** that **raised Christ from the dead,** and thus it is faith in the power that will one day raise us from the dead.

2:13 The Colossians were Gentiles, so they were uncircumcised, but that was not the cause of their spiritual death. It was their uncircumcised **sinful nature** that made them **dead in their sins** (see 2:11-12). In Deuteronomy 10:16, Moses told the people of Israel to circumcise their hearts. He wanted the people to go beyond physical surgery; they needed to submit to God in their hearts as well as in their bodies. Jeremiah echoed that teaching in Jeremiah 4:4. In Romans 2:29, Paul taught, "true circumcision is not a cutting of the body but a change of heart produced by God's Spirit." The Colossians, as Gentiles, had been dead in sin and outside the scope of God's mercy.

To defeat death, God made us alive; to deliver us from sin, he made us **alive with Christ.** Because God raised Christ, those who belong to Christ are raised as well. The penalty of sin and its power over believers were miraculously destroyed by Christ on the cross. Through faith in Christ, believers are acquitted, or found not guilty, before God, their judge. How did this happen? The answer is simple: **He forgave all our sins.** If our sinful nature caused us to be dead, then that sinful nature had to be dealt with before God could make us alive. The word "forgave" is in the past tense, referring to Christ's work on the cross. God's forgiveness opens the way for believers to experience new life in Christ.

2:14 In forgiving all our sins, Christ **canceled the record that contained the charges against us.** This record was like a handwritten ledger of our trespasses against the law. Humanity could not pay the debt for these offenses, so God wiped out the record of our sin for us by **nailing it to Christ's cross.** In so doing, our debts were canceled; what stood against us can no longer hinder us. Christ set us free by his sacrificial death on the cross.

2:15 Not only did Christ's death on the cross pay humanity's debt to God, his death also meant his triumph over **the evil rulers and authorities.** Who are these? Several suggestions have been made, including (1) demonic powers, (2) the gods of the powerful nations, (3) the government of Rome, or even (4) angels (highly regarded by the heretical teachers). Since Paul did not identify who these powers and authorities were, it could be any one of them, or all four. What Christ **disarmed** on the cross was any embodiment of rebellion in the world—whether that be Satan and his demons, false idols of pagan religions (as in 2:16), evil world governments, or even God's good angels when they become the object of worship (as in the Colossian heresy).

This "disarming" occurred when Jesus died on the cross. The word for "disarmed" is literally "stripped," as in stripping a defeated enemy of armor on the battlefield. The powers and authorities of this evil world stripped Christ of his clothing and popularity, made a public spectacle of him on the cross, and triumphed over him by putting him to death. Ironically, the victory belonged to Christ. Actually **he shamed them publicly by his victory.**

2:16 Because Christ had canceled the written code (2:14) and had disarmed evil powers (2:15), believers have been set free from legalistic rules about what they **eat or drink** or what festivals they observe. Although it is most likely that Paul was referring to Jewish laws about diet and festival observances, pagan food laws and celebrations, or a combination of the two, cannot be excluded as a possibility. Paul's point was that the believers should not give up their freedom for legalism. They must not let anyone **condemn** them by saying that certain actions would exclude them from God's people. If the Colossians submitted to any of the regulations imposed by the false teachers, they would be saying that evil powers still held authority over them. They needed to remember that Christ had set them free.

2:17 Paul did not condemn the keeping of some Old Testament dietary laws or observing some of the celebrations. Instead, he condemned doing so in order to somehow earn credit with God. The Old Testament laws, holidays, and feasts were **shadows of the real thing.** The law pointed to the future—to **Christ himself.** Anything that is not Christ or found in Christ is, by contrast, a shadow or unreal. At one time these laws were needed as God prepared a nation for himself. These people would be keepers of his laws and ancestors of his Son. The ceremonial and civil regulations of Judaism set God's people apart from

the world. Through Christ, however, God was preparing a new people for himself—a worldwide family. What the Old Testament promised, Christ fulfilled. If we have Christ, we have what we need in order to know and please God.

2:18 By turning the Colossian believers away from the reality back to the shadow, the false teachers served only to **condemn** the believers. Paul did not mean that the believers would lose their salvation, but that they would lose their prize (that is, their rewards; see also 1 Corinthians 3:10-15).

The false teachers were **insisting on self-denial,** meaning that not only did they enjoy their pretense of humility, but they also attempted to impose it on the Colossian believers. The false humility, revealed by self-abasement and self-denial, came from observances of rituals and regulations that had no bearing on salvation. This sort of humility was self-absorbing and self-gratifying, a kind of pretentious piety.

In addition, these teachers' false humility said that the people could not approach God directly—he could be approached only through various levels of angels. They taught, therefore, that people had to **worship angels** in order to eventually reach God. This is unscriptural; the Bible teaches that angels are God's servants, and it forbids worshiping them (Exodus 20:3-4; Revelation 19:9-10; 22:8-9). The false teachers took great pride in what they had seen in **visions**—most likely these were part of an initiation rite that climaxed in some sort of vision that supposedly revealed great secrets of the universe. While the false teachers may have thought that they had a "corner on God," their thoughts and actions betrayed a mere human origin. Their desire for attention from others showed that, in reality, they were **proud.** They were putting their confidence in their visions and rule keeping, and not in Christ.

2:19 The fundamental problem with the false teachers was that they were **not connected to Christ,** the **head of the body** of believers. If they had been joined to him, they would not have taught false doctrine or lived immorally. Just as a limb that is detached from the body loses life, so these false teachers, detached from the body of Christ and no longer under his headship, had lost the most vital connection. The **sinews,** by connecting all the members of the body to one another, allow body to get **nourishment and strength** and thus to **grow.** The body of Christ can only grow when the believers are connected to one another under Christ.

2:20-22 Believers have **died with Christ** and are no longer under the power of the **evil powers of this world**—the evil spirits and demonic powers that work against Christ. Their "death" released them from their previous slavery. Paul wondered, somewhat incredulously, why these Colossian believers would even think about submitting themselves to the regulations of a conquered power. These **rules** about what to **handle, eat,** or **touch** had nothing to do with God's holy laws. The focus was on how well a person could keep the rules and then congratulate himself or herself for rule keeping. There were two problems with this: (1) These were **mere human teaching** and (2) they were **about things that are gone as soon as** they are used. In these words we hear an echo of Christ when he explained himself to the Pharisees (Matthew 15:11, 17).

2:23 To the Colossians, the discipline demanded by the false teachers seemed good. Actually, forms of legalism still attract many people today. Following a long list of religious rules requires **strong devotion, humility, and severe bodily discipline.** But such people are empty shells, only seeming **wise.** True wisdom is found only in Christ, the source of all wisdom. But all this piety and asceticism was worthless. No amount of religious rules can change a person's heart; they have no value in **conquering a person's evil thoughts and desires.** Only the Holy Spirit can do that. Therefore, all human attempts at religion are worthless. By extension, then, the heresy with all its positive-sounding rules was also worthless.

COLOSSIANS 3:1 – 4:1

LIVING THE NEW LIFE / 3:1-17

Whereas chapter 2 was mostly a criticism of false teachers, this section affirms the Christian's new position in Christ. In chapter 2, Paul exposed the wrong reasons for self-denial. In chapter 3, Paul explains true Christian behavior—putting on the new self by accepting Christ and regarding the earthly nature as dead. We change our moral and ethical behavior by letting Christ live within us, so that he can shape us into what we should be.

3:1 The Greek words in the phrase, **since you have been raised,** express certainty. Once dead in their sins, these believers had been raised from death, just as Christ had been raised from the dead by God's power. They had received **new life** from God through the power of the Holy Spirit. They did not need to struggle and work to attain that life, as the false teachers were trying to tell them; they already had new life! What remained was to work out its implications in daily life. Because they had been raised, they had a clear responsibility to Christ, who had raised them.

First, they must **set** their **sights on the realities of heaven.** The Greek word for "set" means to seek something out with a desire to possess it. The other religious teachers stressed "heavenly things" also, but Paul was appealing to the highest reality of all, the exalted Christ. The believers must take their focus off the world and turn it to Christ, who **sits at God's right hand in the place of honor and power.** Christ's seat at God's right hand reveals his power, authority, and position as both judge and advocate. The Colossian believers already had experienced this exaltation; they needed to set their sights there so that they

would live out their lives on earth as citizens of heaven.

3:2 Letting **heaven fill** their **thoughts** meant concentrating on the eternal rather than the temporal, letting their thoughts dwell in the realm of Christ. They were to focus on the Lord Jesus. Thoughts can influence actions, so if the believers would place their thoughts above and not **only here on earth,** their actions would please God. The **things** on earth refers to the legalistic rituals, the false methods used to achieve holiness, and even to the basic principles of the world described in chapter 2. But how were they to fill their thoughts with heaven? Paul had explained this in another letter: "Fix your thoughts on what is true and honorable and right . . . pure and lovely and admirable . . . excellent and worthy of praise" (Philippians 4:8; see also Colossians 3:12). They were not to live as ascetics in some mystical, visionary realm; rather, Paul was saying that, by setting their thoughts above, their lives on this earth would be pleasing to God and would help accomplish Christ's work.

3:3-4 The Greek aorist tense in the phrase, **for you died** connotes that we died when Christ died. It happened at a point in history. In Christ's death, all believers died (2:20). Then, like a seed buried in the earth, a believer's **real life is hidden** from the world, just as Christ's glory is hidden, only to be revealed when he returns (3:3-4). The spiritual lives of believers are **hidden** inner lives that are in union **with Christ** who has brought them to be with him **in God.**

One day, when Christ **is revealed** in his glory, believers will also **share in all his glory.** The divine life of Christ will be revealed fully and will glorify us (reveal our true potential as children of God). Christians look forward to the new heaven and new earth that God has promised, and they wait for God's new order that will free the world of sin, sickness, and evil. In the meantime, they go with Christ into the world, where they heal people's bodies and souls and fight the evil effects of sin. Christ gives us power to live for him now, and he gives us hope for the future—he will return. In the rest of this chapter Paul explains how Christians should act *now* in order to be prepared for Christ's return.

3:5 While Paul opposed the false teachers' asceticism and regulations, he still forbade certain activities that had no part in believers' lives. If the Colossian believers were to live as examples of Christ, they had to **put to death** certain aspects of the **sinful earthly things lurking within** them—the sinful nature, the old self. Again, Paul was describing the "already" and "not yet" of believers' lives. Although they had died with Christ and had been raised with him, they were still susceptible to temptation and the evils of the sinful nature.

Two sets of sins are listed. The first five refer to sexual sin; the second five to sins of speech. These first five were related to the cultural background of the Colossians and were particularly deadly to the life of the church:

Sexual sin. Any form of illicit sexual relationship. The term serves to spotlight forbidden sexual behavior between people or indirect participation as an audience. We derive our term "pornography" from this Greek word. In contrast to the loose morals of the ancient Greek world, believers ought to show self-discipline and obedience to God in this area.

Impurity. Moral uncleanness. Perhaps no sexual act has taken place, but the person exhibits a crudeness or insensitivity in sexual matters.

Lust. Evil sexual passion that leads to excessive sexual immorality and perversion. (See Romans 1:26; 1 Thessalonians 4:5.)

Shameful desires. Wanting something that is sinister and vile in order to satisfy one's desires (see also Galatians 5:16).

Greed for the good things of this life, for that is idolatry. Relentless urge to get more for oneself. In this context, Paul may have been focusing on greed for satisfying evil desires and for sexual immorality. The greed is described as idolatry because its focus is on filling desires rather than on God.

3:6 God's terrible anger refers to God's judgment on these kinds of behavior. God does not reveal his wrath arbitrarily; his perfect moral nature will not permit sin and wickedness to go unpunished. While wrath occurs at present in the natural consequences of sinful behavior, the final culmination of God's **will comes** with future and final punishment of evil. People may try to get around it, but there is punishment for evil for those who have not believed in Christ as Savior.

3:7-8 The Colossian believers **used to do** the actions described above. They had been dead in their sins (2:13), but that all changed when they came to know Christ. Because of their new life in Christ, the believers were to **get rid of** those things listed above and others listed below. "Get rid of" means to put off or disrobe. The old, filthy clothes must be taken off before the new clothes can be put on. The believer "removes" the old life of sin and "puts on" the new life of Christ. The Colossian believers had experienced this; Paul asked that they act it out in their lives.

Not only did they need to deal with sexual immorality in all its variations, they also needed to deal with misused anger that often spilled over into evil speech.

Anger. A continuous attitude of hatred that remains bottled up within. This could refer to what is under the surface, while "rage" (below) refers to what bursts out. Anger would destroy the harmony and unity Paul called for among the believers.

Rage. Outbursts of anger or quick temper for selfish reasons. This could mean continual and uncontrolled behavior.

Malicious behavior. Doing evil despite the good that has been received. This word is a general term referring to an evil force that destroys relationships. It can mean anything from trouble to wickedness. It is a deliberate attempt to harm another person.

Slander. Destroying another person's good reputation by lies, gossip, spreading rumors, etc. Malice often manifests itself through slander.

Dirty language. Crude talk, abrasive language, expletives. Paul admonished the believers that such language must be caught and stopped before it escapes their mouths.

These behaviors have no place in any Christian or in any church. These are part of the "old life" before knowing Christ. Christians must resolutely "put off" these repulsive sins of anger and speech so that they can "put on" Christ's attitudes and actions.

3:9-10 Because Jesus Christ is "the truth" (John 14:6), believers ought to practice truth in all areas of life. They should not **lie to each other.** Lying to others disrupts unity by destroying trust. It tears down relationships and may lead to serious conflict in a church. Lying can take place in words said as well as words left unsaid. Believers should not exaggerate statistics, pass on rumors or gossip, or say things to build up their own image at others' expense. Instead, because they **have stripped off the old evil nature and all its wicked deeds,** they should be committed to telling the truth.

The "old nature" was each person before he or she came to know Christ. The person was enslaved to sin, bound to the earth, without hope. But believers have **clothed** themselves **with a brand-new nature that is continually being renewed.** The "new nature" from Christ frees us from sin, sets our hearts on "things above" (3:1), and gives us the hope of eternity. Paul was appealing to the commitment the believers had made, urging them to remain true to their confession of faith. Every Christian is in a continuing education program. Renewal is constantly needed in the believer's battle against sin and the old nature. What we **learn** is personal knowledge of Christ **who created this new nature within** us. The goal of the learning is Christlikeness. The more believers know of Christ and his work, the more they are being changed to be like him. Because this process is lifelong, we must never stop learning and obeying.

3:11 There should be no barriers of nationality, race, education level, social standing, wealth, gender, religion, or power (see also Galatians 3:26-28; 6:15). Paul pointed out four groupings that were of particular importance in the Greek culture:

1. Racial or national distinctions, such as between **Jew** and **Gentile.** The spread of the Greek culture and civilization meant that a Greek person (regardless of his or her country of origin) could feel pride in a privileged position and would look down on the Jews and their persistent clinging to an ancient culture. The Jews, meanwhile, would look down on Greeks as heathen, immoral, and outside of God's grace for the chosen nation.
2. Religious distinctions, such as between those who have been **circumcised** (Jews) and those who are **uncircumcised** (Gentiles).

Circumcision, the physical mark of the male Jew, was prized as part of the covenant of God with his chosen people. If practiced at all by Gentiles, it was as part of a heathen cult; most often, the Gentiles were uncircumcised, and they mocked the seriousness of the rite for the Jews.

3. Cultural distinctions, such as between **barbaric** or **uncivilized** peoples (contemptuous names used for people unfamiliar with Greek language and culture) and cultured peoples.
4. Economic or social distinctions, such as between a **slave** and a **free** person. Slavery was common in the ancient world. Paul would have special words for the relationships between masters and slaves (3:22–4:1).

How could these barriers possibly be removed? Paul's answer: because **Christ is all that matters, and he lives in all of us.** The Colossian church was probably made up of all kinds of people. No believer should allow prejudices from pre-Christian days to be carried into the church. Christ broke down all barriers; he accepts all who come to him. Believers, as Christ's body, must do the same. Nothing should divide believers; nothing should keep them from experiencing unity. Each believer is responsible to get rid of the sinful practices of whatever life he or she led and become a new person in Christ. Then, as part of God's body of believers on earth, each person should work as part of the whole to advance God's Kingdom.

3:12 In the Bible, God's **holy people** are chosen by God for a specific purpose or destiny. No one can claim to be chosen by God because of his or her heritage or good works. God freely chooses to save whomever he wills. The doctrine of election teaches that it is God's sovereign choice to save us by his goodness and mercy and not by our own merit. To have received such incredible grace from God ought to cause all believers to gladly lay aside their sinful desires in order to **clothe** themselves with a nature that pleases God. In contrast to the vices listed above, Paul offered a list of virtues to be adopted as believers' strategy to live for God day by day in the social activities of life. These include:

Tenderhearted mercy. Genuine sensitivity and heartfelt sympathy for the needs of others. This is an attribute of God, who is described as compassionate and who acted so on our behalf.
Kindness. Acting charitably, benevolently toward others, as God has done toward us. God's kindness is a continual theme in the Psalms and Prophets. Kindness takes the initiative in responding generously to others' needs. Because

believers have received kindness, we ought to act that way toward others. This does not come naturally; it is a fruit of the Spirit (Galatians 5:22-23).

Humility. An attitude of self-esteem that is neither puffed up with pride, nor self-depreciating. It is a true understanding of one's position with God. As Christ humbled himself (Philippians 2:6-11), so believers ought to humble themselves in service to the Lord and Savior.

Gentleness. Humble, considerate of others, submissive to God and his Word. Gentleness is not to be confused with weakness; instead, it means consideration for others and a willingness to give up one's rights for the sake of another. Again, Christ is our example.

Patience. Long-suffering, or putting up with people who irritate. The person might have the right to retaliate, but chooses patience instead. The Holy Spirit's work in us increases our endurance.

3:13 Clothing ourselves with the new nature affects how we treat others. Paul called the believers to **make allowance for each other's faults.** To **forgive** implies continual, mutual forgiveness of the problems, irritations, and grievances that occur in the congregation. The church had enough enemies and troubles dealing with the outside world; they didn't need infighting or energy wasted on grievances or grudges (either held over from pre-Christian days or arising in the church) that could be worked out with forbearing and forgiving. The key to forgiving others was for the believers to (1) remember how much **the Lord forgave** them, and (2) realize the presumption in refusing to forgive someone God had already forgiven. Remembering God's infinite love and forgiveness should help the Colossian believers love and forgive one another.

3:14 All the virtues that Paul encouraged the believers in Colosse to develop were perfectly bound together by **love.** As they clothed themselves with these virtues, the last garment to put on was love, which, like a belt, **binds** all of the others in place. Love pulls together the other graces in perfect, unified action. To practice any list of virtues without practicing love will lead to distortion, fragmentation, and stagnation. In any congregation, love must be used to unify the people and build them up. Those who would desire to be mature in Christ must make love a top priority.

3:15 Putting on all the virtues, with love binding them together (3:14), would lead to **peace** between individuals and among the members

of the body of believers. The Colossian Christians should let the peace **that comes from Christ rule in their hearts.** To live in peace would not mean that suddenly all differences of opinion would be eliminated, but it would require that they work together despite their differences. This kind of tranquility and cooperation can't come from mere human effort. It requires God's help to arbitrate and enable people to get along.

The word **rule** comes from the language of athletics: Paul wanted the believers to let Christ's peace be umpire or referee in their hearts. Peace would arbitrate, decide any argument, and thereby restrain any of the passions of the old nature that might threaten. Peace would settle any friction and strife so the believers could remain strong and unified.

When believers have an overriding attitude of thankfulness and when they have constant gratitude in their hearts for all that God has done for them in giving salvation and making them part of Christ's body, then other virtues to which Paul called them would be much easier to live out. Being **thankful** would also make other relationships easier, as Paul explained in the following verses (3:18–4:6).

3:16 The **words of Christ** referred to the message proclaimed by Christ (the gospel). For us, this means the Bible. This teaching should **live** (reside permanently) in believers' **hearts** by their study and knowledge of God's word, making them **wise.** To **teach and counsel** refers to the whole congregation and their responsibility to teach the Word—including the life, ministry, and teachings of Jesus Christ—as a means to warn and correct one another.

The **psalms, hymns and spiritual songs** were a vital part of this teaching and admonition. Although the early Christians had access to the Old Testament and freely used it (thus, Paul's reference to "psalms"), they did not yet have the New Testament or any other Christian books to study. Their stories and teachings about Christ were sometimes set to music to make them easier to memorize and pass on from person to person. Grounded in God's word and correct doctrine, music can be an important part of Christian worship and education.

While music can teach, its primary function may be to praise God. As believers sing, they ought to do so **with thankful hearts** (see 4:2). Again, the word "heart" refers to a person's entire being. Gratitude to God overflows in praise.

3:17 Earlier Paul listed a few vices and virtues to give the Colossian believers an idea of what was expected of them in their attitudes toward one another, but he did not want to regulate every area of life with a list of rules. So Paul gave this general command to cover every area of life.

Everything the believers said and everything they did should be done **as a representative of the Lord Jesus,** realizing his constant presence and bringing honor and glory to him in every aspect and activity of daily living (see also 1 Corinthians 10:31). To act in someone's name

is to act on his authority; believers act as Christ's representatives.

Paul echoed the need for **giving thanks,** as he had in 3:15 and 3:16. All we do for Christ should be done with the spirit of thankfulness for all he has done for us. Believers are not enslaved to rules about every word they speak or deed they do; instead, they freely put themselves under the Lord's guidance because they love him, have accepted his salvation, and live to glorify him.

INSTRUCTIONS FOR CHRISTIAN HOUSEHOLDS / 3:18–4:1

In Paul's day, women, children, and slaves were to submit to the head of the family—slaves would submit until they were freed, male children until they grew up, and women and girls for their whole lives. Paul emphasized the equality of all believers in Christ (Galatians 3:28), but he did not suggest overthrowing Roman society to achieve it. Instead, he counseled all believers to submit to authority by choice. Paul gave rules for three sets of household relationships: (1) husbands and wives, (2) parents and children, and (3) masters and slaves. In each case, there is mutual responsibility to submit and love, to obey and encourage, to work hard and be fair. Examine your family and work relationships. Do you relate to others as God intended?

3:18-19 Why **must wives submit** to their husbands—and why is that **fitting for those who belong to the Lord?** This may have been good advice for Christian women, newly freed in Christ, who found submission difficult. Paul told them that they should willingly follow their husbands' leadership in Christ. But Paul had words for husbands as well: **husbands must love** their **wives and never treat them harshly.** It may also have been true that Christian men, used to the Roman custom of giving unlimited power to the head of the family, were not used to treating their wives with respect and love. Real spiritual leadership involves service. Just as Christ served the disciples, even to the point of washing their feet, so the husband is to serve his wife. This means putting aside his own interests in order to care for his wife. A wise and Christ-honoring husband will not abuse his leadership role. At the same time, a wise and Christ-honoring wife will not try to undermine her husband's leadership. There must be mutual love and respect. Husband and wife must accept mutual subordination in God's hierarchy. The Lord Jesus is the criterion for our duty. He, not society, defines what is "fitting."

Although some people have distorted Paul's teaching on submission by giving unlimited authority to husbands, we cannot get around it. The fact is, Paul wrote that wives should submit to their husbands. The fact that a teaching is not popular is no reason to discard it. According to the

Bible, the man is the spiritual head of the family, and his wife should acknowledge his leadership. There should not be a constant battle for power in the relationship. Our concept of submission must come from the Bible, demonstrated by the church to Christ (as Christ loved the church and submitted to God, 1 Corinthians 15:28; Ephesians 5:21). We must not base it on either a feminist or chauvinist view. Christian marriage involves mutual submission (Ephesians 5:21), subordinating our personal desires for the good of the loved one, and submitting ourselves to Christ as Lord. Submission is rarely a problem in homes where both partners have a strong relationship with Christ and where each is concerned for the happiness of the other.

Submitting to another person is an often misunderstood concept. It does not mean becoming a doormat. Christ submitted his will to the Father; we honor Christ by following his example.

3:20-21 God's design for family relationships continues in this verse. **Children** (*tekna,* "young children living at home") are to **obey** their **parents.** While all young children will at times be disobedient and test their limits with their parents, as they get older and understand what they are told, God wants them to obey. Such obedience reveals an understanding of authority that can carry over into understanding God's authority and all believers' responsibility to obey him. A child's obedience to his or her parents **pleases the Lord.**

Children's obedience is balanced by Paul's next command: **Fathers, don't aggravate your children,** or they will become **discouraged.** The command for children to obey does not give parents license for harsh treatment. Children must be handled with care. They need firm discipline administered in love. **Fathers** refers to both parents. Parents must not discourage their children by nagging and deriding. Belittling children, or showing by words or actions that they are unimportant to the parents, should have no place in Christian families. Discipline administered in derision ultimately discourages children, destroys their self-respect, and causes them to **quit trying.**

The purpose of parental discipline is to help children grow, not to exasperate and provoke them to anger or discouragement. Parenting is not easy—it takes lots of patience to raise children in a loving, Christ-honoring manner. But frustration and anger should not be causes for discipline. Instead, parents should act in love, treating their children as Jesus treats the people he loves. This is vital to children's development and to their understanding of what Christ is like.

3:22 Paul used the same word for **obey** here as he used in 3:20 for children to obey their parents. **Slaves** were also to obey the commands and desires of their **masters,** not just when they were being watched and hoping for a reward, but at all times. They should no longer merely work for human approval, they should work hard and well **because of** their **reverent fear of the Lord.** Believers who were slaves were not set free from serving their masters, but they were set free from slavery to sin. Their ultimate Master was God himself. Paul explained that God wanted the slaves to fulfill their responsibilities in this world even as they looked forward to the next.

Slaves played a significant part in this society, with several million in the Roman Empire at this time. Slavery was sanctioned by law and was part of the empire's social makeup. Because many slaves and slave owners had become Christians, the early church had to deal straightforwardly with the question of master/slave relations. While neither condemning nor condoning slavery, Paul told masters and slaves how to live together in Christian households. In Paul's day, women, children, and slaves had few rights. In the church, however, they had freedoms that society denied them. Paul tells husbands, parents, and masters to be caring.

3:23-24 Slaves had a variety of tasks—running errands, caring for or teaching children, cleaning, preparing meals, or doing menial work. Yet Paul gave their jobs a new dignity because these slaves would do their work **for the Lord, serving** the Lord **Christ.** Slaves had little, if any, opportunity to get out of slavery, and they received little, if any, monetary compensation for their work. Obviously, they had no **inheritance** in this world, but Paul reminded the Christian slaves that they would ultimately be rewarded by Christ with their deserved inheritance as children of the true, eternal King. (See Luke 6:35 and Ephesians 6:7-8 for more on the Lord's reward.)

3:25 Echoing his words in 3:6, Paul once again explained that judgment would be coming. Whether master or slave, the wrongdoer **will be paid back,** and those who do right will receive the inheritance as their reward (3:24). At the Judgment, God will judge without partiality. Paul explained the responsibilities of the believers. Both the Christian slave with the harsh and ruthless master and the Christian master with the lazy and untrustworthy slave knew how they were to act as believers. They also knew that God would judge wrongdoing without favoritism.

4:1 Whether the master's slaves were believers or not, Christian masters were responsible to be **just and fair** to all their **slaves.** Without attempting to overturn the social structure of a worldwide empire, Paul applied Christ's inward transforming principles to the system (see the discussion on 3:22). Paul did not say that Christian masters should free all slaves; in fact, in some cases, setting them free might not have been humane. Instead, Paul explained that Christian masters should do what is just and fair, treating their slaves as human beings. To some masters, this would mean freeing their slaves; to others, it would mean treating the slaves better in terms of living quarters, remuneration, time to rest, and tone of voice.

Why should Paul command this of Christian slave masters? Because the slave masters themselves had someone to report to—their **Master in heaven.** The slave masters could hardly expect to be treated rightly and fairly by God if they refused right and fair treatment to those in their charge.

Masters and slaves who followed Paul's advice would be able to serve or be served in their daily routines, and yet come together to worship as brothers and sisters in the Lord without any disruption.

COLOSSIANS 4:2-18

AN ENCOURAGEMENT FOR PRAYER / 4:2-6
As he began to draw his letter to a close, Paul turned his focus back to the church as a whole, reminding the Colossians of their corporate responsibilities.

4:2 The believers were responsible to pray; prayer was their lifeline to God. To **devote** themselves **to prayer** meant that they should be persistent and unwilling to give up even though their prayers may seem to go unanswered. Paul's advice to "keep on praying" (1 Thessalonians 5:17) has the same meaning. Their devotion to prayer did not mean that they should spend all their time on their knees, but that they should have a prayerful attitude at all times. This attitude would be built upon acknowledging their dependence on God, realizing his presence within them, and determining to obey him fully. Then they would find it natural to pray frequent, spontaneous, short prayers. A prayerful attitude is not a substitute for regular times of prayer but should be an outgrowth of those times.

Having an **alert mind** may have been referring to not dozing off, to being alert in their devotion, or to being alert for God's answers and then thankful when they came. More likely, he was focusing on the anticipation of the Lord's coming. The Lord could return at any time, so believers should be found alert and waiting.

As Paul had mentioned several times (in 1:3, 12; 2:7; 3:15-17), the believers ought always to be **thankful.** Thankfulness implies understanding all that God has done and anticipating what he promises.

4:3 The Colossian believers could have a part in Paul's worldwide ministry by praying for him and his coworkers. Paul requested prayer for **opportunities to preach** in spite of his imprisonment, so that he could continue to proclaim God's **secret plan—** that the message is also for the **Gentiles.** Although Paul was **in chains** for preaching the gospel, the chains could not stop the message.

4:4 Paul asked for the ability to **proclaim** the **message clearly.** In other words, Paul wanted to

be able to "reveal" the mystery so that many could hear and believe. This was his compulsion; he had been called (Acts 9:15; 26:17-20).

4:5 Paul reminded the believers of their responsibility to be wise in the way they acted toward **those who are not Christians.** Paul was observing that while the Christian fellowship does (and should) make some allowances for the mistakes of its own, the world will not. Christians' behavior toward unbelievers should be above reproach. The believers were not to hide from the world in a secret organization; instead, they were to live in the world. They were to **make the most of every opportunity** to share the gospel with unbelievers. Paul was communicating a sense of urgency (see Galatians 6:10; Ephesians 5:15-16).

4:6 The spoken word would be the communication method; therefore, the believers should be wise in how they spoke. Speech that is **gracious** is kind and courteous. Speech that is **effective** is interesting (as opposed to dull), invites interaction (as opposed to refusing to listen and discuss), adds "spice" to a discussion (by penetrating to deeper levels), and is pure and wholesome (as opposed to "filthy language," 3:8). Believers should always be ready to answer questions about their faith and be ready to share words of personal testimony (see also 1 Peter 3:15-16).

No Christian should have a dull, tiresome, know-it-all monologue of his faith. Instead, Christians, who have the most exciting news in the world to share, should be able to share that message with excitement, ability to invoke interest, an understanding of the basics, a willingness to listen and discuss, and a desire to answer everyone's questions graciously.

PAUL'S FINAL INSTRUCTIONS AND GREETINGS / 4:7-18
Paul often closed his letters by sending personal greetings from himself and others with him to individuals in the church to whom he wrote.

4:7 Tychicus had accompanied Paul to Jerusalem with the collection for the church there (Acts 20:4). He later became one of Paul's personal representatives. Paul sent him to Ephesus a couple of times (Ephesians 6:21-22; 2 Timothy 4:12), and he sent him to Colosse with this letter for the Colossian church. Tychicus also may have been sent to Crete (Titus 3:12). Tychicus would give the believers news about Paul that Paul did not include in this letter. Paul trusted Tychicus, making good use of his freedom and faithfulness to continue the ministry of the gospel while Paul was imprisoned.

4:8 In spite of the fact that Paul had never been to Colosse, he and the believers there had a bond because of their unity in Christ. This letter, bearing important information needed by the church in Colosse, was entrusted to a brother who would be sure to deliver it and ensure that its contents were understood. Paul also sent Tychicus to tell the believers how he was doing in prison and to **encourage** them. This personal letter and Paul's continued faithfulness to spread the gospel in spite of his imprisonment would encourage and strengthen the Colossian believers.

4:9 Onesimus was a native of Colosse. He was a slave who had run away from his master, Philemon (an elder in the church at Colosse), and was saved through Paul in prison. The letter to the Colossians and the letter to Philemon were written at the same time and carried by these men back to Colosse. Paul referred to Onesimus as a **much loved brother** both here and in Philemon 16. Onesimus would accompany Tychicus and also bring news of Paul's circumstances. Tychicus probably provided moral support to Onesimus as Onesimus returned to his master in hopes of being restored. He was also returning to the church, not merely as a fellow Colossian, but also as a fellow Christian.

4:10 Aristarchus was from Thessalonica and had accompanied Paul on his third missionary journey. He had been arrested, along with Gaius, during the riot at Ephesus (Acts 19:29). He and Tychicus were with Paul in Greece (Acts 20:4); Aristarchus had traveled to Rome with Paul (Acts 27:2).

Mark (also called John Mark) was not yet well known among the churches, although apparently Barnabas was (see, for example, 1 Corinthians 9:6; Galatians 2:1, 9, 13), for Mark is noted as **Barnabas's cousin.** Mark wrote the Gospel of Mark (see the Author section there for more information). Apparently Paul wanted the Colossians to know that he had confidence in Mark; instructions concerning Mark had already been conveyed by some-

one. Apparently Mark was making good efforts to show himself to be an effective and productive worker. In any case, the Colossians were to **welcome** Mark if he were to arrive at their church.

4:11 Jesus was a common Jewish name, as was the name **Justus** (which means "righteous"). Apparently Aristarchus, Mark, and Justus were the only ones among Paul's fellow workers who were **Jewish Christians.** These men had proven to be **a comfort** to Paul. Paul had been called as a missionary to the Gentiles, yet he had kept his concern for the lost of his own nation, Israel. Yet Paul's very mission to the Gentiles had alienated him from many of his fellow Jews; thus, the hard work on behalf of the gospel by these faithful Jewish Christians was especially comforting to Paul.

4:12 Like Onesimus (4:9), **Epaphras** was from Colosse. He may have been converted in Ephesus under Paul's teaching, for Paul had stayed in Ephesus for three years, teaching and preaching (Acts 20:31). Epaphras, then, had returned to Colosse, his hometown, where he had founded the church there, and probably the churches in Hierapolis and Laodicea as well (1:7; Acts 19:10). Later, he apparently visited Paul in Rome, perhaps to get the apostle's advice on dealing with the false teachers. His report to Paul caused Paul to write this letter. Like Paul (1:23) and Tychicus (4:7), Epaphras was **a servant of Christ Jesus,** who had been responsible for the missionary outreach to these cities.

Epaphras was a hero of the Colossian church, one of the believers who had helped keep the church together despite growing troubles. His earnest prayers for the believers show his deep love and concern for them. Epaphras's prayers focused on the Colossian believers' growth in the faith— that they would become **strong** spiritually (as in 1:28; 2:2; 3:14) and be **perfect, fully confident of the whole will of God** (filled with everything that is God's will). We have already been filled with Christ, but we must go on to fulfill what has been given us. Such strength and assurance of faith will help believers of any time period stand against false teaching.

4:13 Epaphras **agonized** in prayer, not only for the believers in Colosse, but also for those in the other cities in the Lycus Valley. **Laodicea** was located a few miles northwest of Colosse, also on the Lycus River, and was a stopover along the main road from the East to Ephesus. The city was named for Laodice, queen of Antiochus II. **Hierapolis** was about five miles north of Laodicea. Epaphras was truly a zealous missionary in this particular portion of the Roman Empire.

4:14 Doctor Luke had spent much time with Paul. He had accompanied Paul on most of the third missionary journey. He also remained beside Paul through this imprisonment, as well as Paul's final imprisonment (see 2 Timothy 4:11). The good doctor certainly had helped with Paul's health (especially after the beatings Paul received during his travels, as well as other ailments that plagued Paul in prison). Luke was also a prolific writer, authoring the Gospel of Luke and the book of Acts. Since Paul had explained that the only three Jewish Christians with him were Aristarchus, Mark, and Justus, it has been assumed that Luke was a Gentile or a Greek-speaking Jew. Apparently, **Demas** was faithful at this time (see also Philemon 24), but later he deserted Paul (2 Timothy 4:10).

4:15 Paul turned his attention from sending everyone else's greetings to sending his own. He asked that the Colossian church relay his greetings to the church (that is, to the **brothers and sisters**) in **Laodicea** (ten miles to the west). This gives an interesting sidelight to church life in the first century—it seems that the churches had fellowship with one another, as the sending of greetings and sharing of letters would indicate (4:16; 1 Thessalonians 5:27). Another sidelight is the picture of believers meeting in private homes. It wasn't until the middle of the third century that churches began to own property and build public places of worship. So during this time, individual believers opened their homes for worship services. Here Paul greeted those who met in **Nympha's** home. In Colosse, the believers met in Philemon's house (Philemon 2). Lydia opened her home to the believers in Philippi (Acts 16:40). Gaius offered his home to the believers in Corinth (Romans 16:23). Aquila and Priscilla, a husband and wife team, opened their home while they lived in Rome (Romans 16:5) and in Ephesus (1 Corinthians 16:19).

4:16 After this letter had been **read** to all the believers in Colosse in a worship service, they were to send it on to **Laodicea.** Apparently the heresy was a problem for that church as well, and they needed Paul's advice and encouragement. At this time, no New Testament had been assembled—indeed, most of the New Testament books were still being written. So the churches circulated these letters from Paul (1 Thessalonians 5:27), Peter (1 Peter 1:1), James (James 1:1), and other key Christian leaders.

The Colossians, in turn, were to read **the letter** Paul had written to the church in Laodicea. Most scholars suggest that the letter may have been the book of Ephesians because the letter to the Ephesians was to be circulated to all the churches in Asia Minor. It is also possible that there was a special letter to the Laodiceans, which we do not have.

4:17 Paul's letter to Philemon is also addressed to **Archippus** (Philemon 2), where Paul called him a "fellow soldier." Archippus may have been a Roman soldier who had become a member of the Colossian church, or he may have been Philemon's son. In any case, Paul called upon the members of the church to encourage Archippus to **carry out** some **work** that **the Lord gave** him. Paul singled out Archippus for making sure his job was completed. Paul saw nothing wrong in challenging believers to attempt more in ministry and to go beyond their current level of achievement.

4:18 Paul usually dictated his letters to a scribe, and he often ended with a short **greeting** in his **own handwriting** (see also 1 Corinthians 16:21; Galatians 6:11; 2 Thessalonians 3:17; Philemon 19). This assured the recipients that false teachers were not writing letters in Paul's name (as apparently had been a problem, see 2 Thessalonians 2:2; 3:17). It also gave the letters a personal touch, especially to this congregation Paul had never visited.

Paul asked that the believers continue to pray for him during his imprisonment (see also 4:3, 10). This reference to his **chains** also reminded the believers that the letter had been written to them while he was in prison. Paul had been remembering them; he wanted them to remember that he was a prisoner for the gospel's sake, a gospel he would not stop preaching regardless of his chains. Paul was in prison because he refused to set aside one iota of his faith; he hoped that the Colossian believers would remember that when they encountered the false teachings.

Just as Paul had begun his letter with **grace** (1:2), so he ended it with the benediction that the believers would continue to experience God's unmerited favor. Ultimately, God's grace would strengthen and defend the church.

To understand the letter to the Colossians, we need to realize that the church was facing pressure from a heresy that promised deeper spiritual life through secret knowledge. The false teachers were destroying faith in Christ by undermining Christ's humanity and divinity. Paul makes it clear in this letter to the Colossian believers that Christ alone is the source of our spiritual life, the Head of the body of believers. Christ is Lord of both the physical and spiritual worlds. The path to deeper spiritual life is not through religious duties, special knowledge, or secrets; it is only through a clear connection with the Lord Jesus Christ. We must never let anything come between us and our Savior.

Paul visited Thessalonica on his second and third missionary journeys. It was a seaport and trade center located on the Egnatian Way, a busy international highway. Paul probably wrote his two letters to the Thessalonians from Corinth.

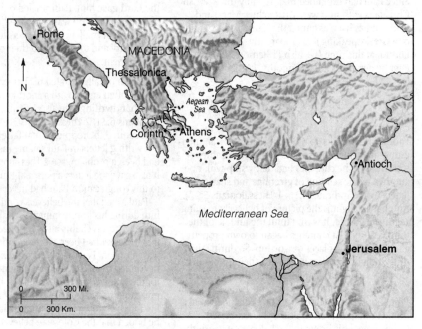

1 THESSALONIANS

INTRODUCTION

"You won't learn unless you ask questions!" Countless teachers and parents have explained that truth to children as they begin their educational experience. Those who desire to train others and impart knowledge don't mind responding to queries. Questions help them know what students are thinking and learning. Those who don't verbalize their doubts, voice their concerns, or seek to clarify what they have heard often harbor misunderstanding, go the wrong way, or live in ignorance.

Paul wrote this epistle, his first to the church at Thessalonica, to answer believers' questions and to commend them on their faith and commitment to Christ. The Thessalonians had questions . . . and they asked them. As you read this short, personal letter, look for answers for yourself. Also, think of questions that you will ask your spiritual mentor . . . and then learn.

AUTHOR

Paul (Saul of Tarsus): apostle of Christ, missionary, church planter, and gifted teacher.

The first verse of this letter identifies Paul as the author. Paul's traveling companions—Silas and Timothy—are mentioned as well, but Paul is clearly the primary author because the pronoun "I" is used so often.

As he had done on other occasions, Paul most likely dictated this letter to a scribe. Timothy, Paul's trusted assistant, may have been the one who actually transcribed the words. Also, Silas, who assisted Paul in founding the Thessalonian church, would have been very interested in this letter and may have offered suggestions on what to say.

Because Paul's time in Thessalonica had been so limited, he was concerned that he hadn't been able to teach the young believers the details of Christian doctrine and to adequately model the Christian faith. Later, when Timothy returned from Thessalonica with the believers' questions, Paul wrote to encourage and instruct them.

For more about Paul, see the Author section in the Introduction to the book of Romans.

DATE AND SETTING

Written from Corinth around A.D. 51.

Paul and Silas's nighttime escape from Thessalonica inaugurated their quick tour of Macedonia and Achaia (northern and southern Greece, respectively). Their next stop was Berea, where Timothy rejoined them. When Paul's enemies from

Thessalonica followed him there, he was quietly escorted to Athens. At this intellectual center of the Greek world, Paul was allowed to present the gospel to the philosophers who had gathered at Mars Hill (Acts 17:19-34). Although most of his audience rejected and even mocked his message, a few were persuaded and became believers (Acts 17:32-34).

Silas and Timothy soon joined Paul there (Acts 17:15). While at Athens, Paul probably sent Timothy back to Thessalonica to see how the believers were doing (see Paul's reference to this in 3:1-4). Paul then traveled to Corinth, where he spent a full year and a half establishing a church. During that time, Timothy returned from Thessalonica (Acts 18:5) with a favorable report on the Thessalonian believers and with their questions. In response to Timothy's report, Paul dictated 1 Thessalonians.

AUDIENCE
The believers in Thessalonica.

The city of Thessalonica. Thessalonica was a bustling seaport on the Aegean Sea. The Roman road that connected the major cities of Macedonia—the Egnatian Way—was the main road through Thessalonica. The Arch of Galerius, which spanned the Egnatian Way in Paul's day, still stands today.

In 315 B.C. Cassander, a military commander of Alexander the Great, founded the city and named it after his wife, Thessalonica, the half sister of Alexander the Great. The strategic location of the city allowed it to grow rapidly in wealth and influence. By 146 B.C., Thessalonica had been named the capital of Macedonia. The Romans even allowed the Thessalonians to govern themselves (in 42 B.C., Anthony and Octavia rewarded the city for supporting them in the Battle of Philippi by making it a free city). During Augustus's reign, Thessalonica was the most populous town in Macedonia. Thus, when Paul entered the city, it was the commercial and political center of Macedonia.

The church. As was his custom, Paul first went to the Jews in Thessalonica. For three Sabbaths he taught in the synagogue, explaining the gospel and showing that Jesus was the Christ, the Messiah—the one about whom the prophets had foretold. Some were persuaded (Acts 17:1-4). Among these was Jason, who offered his home to the missionaries, and Aristarchus, who later became Paul's traveling companion (see Acts 19:29; 20:4; 27:2). A number of God-fearing Greeks (Greeks who attended the synagogue services) and prominent women of Thessalonica were also persuaded.

But the Jewish leaders of the synagogue grew jealous of Paul's success and thought he was stealing the prominent members of their congregation. In attempting to stop him, they rounded up some rough characters in the marketplace and started a riot in the city. The mob broke into Jason's house, looking for Paul and Silas. When they couldn't find them, they brought Jason before the city officials (Acts 17:6). They accused Jason of housing preachers who had been asserting that Jesus, instead of Caesar, was king (Acts 17:7). Treason was a serious charge. The Romans didn't tolerate any sign of defiance to their rule. Moreover, the city officials probably had heard of Claudius's recent expulsion of the Jews from Rome (around A.D. 49). The historian Suetonius wrote that Claudius threw the Jews out of Rome because of the "tumults instigated by Chrestus" (see also Acts 18:1-2).

Some scholars believe that "Chrestus" is a misspelling of Christ; if so, the Jewish riots would have occurred in response to the preaching of the gospel of Jesus Christ. Although the city officials of Thessalonica probably didn't understand why the Jews were rioting or whose fault it was, they certainly had been apprised of the Jewish rioting that had occurred throughout the Roman Empire and didn't want their city to be thrown into turmoil.

Given the social instability of Thessalonica, the believers decided to send Paul and Silas to nearby Berea. Paul's opponents in Thessalonica were not so easily deterred and soon followed Paul and Silas there, stirring up a riot against them in that city as well (Acts 17:13). Once again Paul had to flee. This time, he went to Athens—the center of Greek culture (Acts 17:15).

The church at Thessalonica was birthed in an atmosphere of persecution. The band of believers had to withstand not only the determined opposition of the Thessalonian Jews but also city officials who could be manipulated by the Jews. The small group who gathered around Paul was primarily made up of God-fearing Greeks and former pagans.

The Thessalonian church was a gathering of enthusiastic new believers. Within months, their courage, determination, eagerness, and devotion had become well known. They still had much to learn about the Christian faith, for Paul could only instruct them for a short while. Yet their courage in the face of persecution formed them into a church filled with extraordinary promise.

OCCASION AND PURPOSE
To strengthen the Thessalonian Christians in their faith and assure them of Christ's return.

First Thessalonians is primarily a letter of praise and thanksgiving. In this letter Paul rejoiced over the Thessalonians' progress in the Christian faith. Timothy had given Paul an encouraging report on the Thessalonian believers. Their faith in Christ had remained strong. Although severely tested, they had withstood persecution. Having accepted Paul's message with great joy, they had been eagerly looking forward to Christ's return. Their eager response was a clear sign that the Holy Spirit had been working in their hearts. This letter celebrates this great news. Although Paul's ministry with them had been short, they had thrived. He wrote to congratulate them and to answer their questions about the faith.

The small and young Thessalonian church faced powerful and determined enemies. Paul wasn't concerned about the power of the enemies, however, as much as the strength of the Thessalonians' faith. Would they continue to seek God? Would they continue to love and encourage each other? Would they spurn the temptations of life in a cosmopolitan city? This letter explains exactly how the believers could endure persecution and opposition.

MESSAGE
Paul begins this letter with a note of affirmation, thanking God for the strong faith and good reputation of the Thessalonians (1:1-10). Then Paul reviews their relationship—how he and his companions brought the Good News to them (2:1-12), how they accepted the message (2:13-16), and how he longed to be

with them again (2:17-20). Because of his concern, Paul sent Timothy to encourage them in their faith (3:1-13).

Paul then presents the core of his message—exhortation and comfort. He challenges them to please God in their daily living by avoiding sexual immorality (4:1-8), loving each other (4:9-10), and living as good citizens in a sinful world (4:11-12).

Paul comforts the Thessalonians by reminding them of the hope of the resurrection (4:13-18). Then he warns them to be prepared at all times, for Jesus Christ could return at any moment. When Christ returns, those Christians who are alive and those who have died will be raised to new life (5:1-11).

Paul then gives the Thessalonians a handful of reminders on how to prepare themselves for the second coming: Warn the lazy (5:14), encourage the timid (5:14), help the weak (5:14), be patient with everyone (5:14), do good to everyone (5:15), always be joyful (5:16), keep on praying (5:17), be thankful (5:18), examine everything that is taught (5:20-21), and keep away from evil (5:22). Paul concludes his letter with two benedictions and a request for prayer.

The main themes in the book of 1 Thessalonians include: *Persecution, Paul's Ministry, Hope,* and *Preparation for the Second Coming.*

Persecution (1:6; 2:1-2, 14-16; 3:3-8). Paul and his associates had been hounded and finally driven out of Thessalonica during their short visit to that city. The new Christians Paul left behind were being persecuted because of their faith in Christ.

IMPORTANCE FOR TODAY. Believers in any age can expect to be persecuted. They need to stand firm in their faith in the midst of trials, being strengthened by the Holy Spirit, who helps them remain strong. We may experience threats or overt slander and physical opposition, or the persecution and oppression may be more subtle. Whatever the case, we must remain strong in faith through the power of the Spirit, showing genuine love to others and maintaining our moral character.

Paul's Ministry (1:5-6; 2:1-20; 3:1-8). Some in Thessalonica were suggesting that Paul and his associates were preaching with selfish motives. Paul denied these charges by reminding the believers of his ministry among them and throughout the area. Paul was determined to share the gospel despite being slandered and facing other difficult circumstances.

IMPORTANCE FOR TODAY. Paul not only delivered his message, he also gave of himself. In addition, Paul didn't allow persecution or slander to deter him from obeying the Lord and fulfilling his calling. In our ministries, we must become like Paul—faithful and bold, yet sensitive and self-sacrificing.

Hope (1:3, 10; 2:19; 4:13-18). Paul encouraged the Thessalonian Christians by reminding them that one day all believers, both those who are alive and those who have died, will be united with Christ. Christians who die before Christ's return have hope—the hope of the resurrection of the body and life everlasting with the Lord.

IMPORTANCE FOR TODAY. All who believe in Christ will live with him forever. All those who belong to Jesus Christ—throughout history—will be present with him at his Second Coming. No matter how bad the situation or bleak the outlook, we can take heart, knowing that our future is secure in Christ. We can be confident that at death or at the Second Coming, we will be with loved ones who also have trusted in Christ.

Preparation for the Second Coming (1:3, 9; 2:19-20; 3:13; 4:1-12; 5:1-28).
No one knows the time of Christ's return—it will come suddenly, when people
least expect it. Thus, believers should live moral and holy lives, ever watchful for
his coming, not neglecting daily responsibilities, but always working and living
to please the Lord.

IMPORTANCE FOR TODAY. The Good News is not only what we believe but
also what we must live. The Holy Spirit helps us to be faithful to Christ, giving us
strength to resist lust and fraud. Live as though you expect Christ's return at any
time. Don't be caught unprepared.

OUTLINE OF 1 THESSALONIANS
  I. Faithfulness to the Lord (1:1–3:13)
 II. Watchfulness for the Lord (4:1–5:28)

1 THESSALONIANS 1

GREETINGS FROM PAUL / 1:1

Thessalonica was the capital and largest city (population: about two hundred thousand) of the
Roman province of Macedonia. The most important Roman highway (the Egnatian Way)—
extending from Rome all the way to the Orient—went through Thessalonica. This highway,
along with the city's thriving seaport, made Thessalonica one of the wealthiest and most flourishing trade centers in the Roman Empire. Recognized as a free city, Thessalonica was allowed
self-rule and was exempted from most of the restrictions placed by Rome on other cities in
the empire. With its international flavor, however, came many pagan religions and cultural
influences that challenged the faith of the young Christians there.

1:1 Paul began this letter by introducing three men
well known to the Thessalonian church. **Paul** was
the head of this missionary team and key writer of
this letter. **Silas** was a prophet (Acts 15:32) who
was held in high esteem by the Jerusalem church.
Silas accompanied Paul on his second missionary
journey (Acts 15:36–17:15) and helped him establish the church in Thessalonica (Acts 17:1-9). The
young Christian named **Timothy** joined Paul and
Silas during Paul's second missionary journey.
The account in the book of Acts describes the
preaching of Paul and Silas in **Thessalonica** (Acts
17:4). Envious and angry Jewish leaders watched
many from their synagogue follow Jesus Christ.
When a riot broke out, Paul and Silas had to leave
under cover of darkness.

Paul wrote to the **church** in Thessalonica.
The Greek word for church is *ekklesia,* meaning
"assembly." These people were part of the assembly in Thessalonica that belonged to **God the
Father and the Lord Jesus Christ**. This set them
apart from all the other "assemblies" that may
have been meeting in Thessalonica.

Paul combined expressions from Jewish and
Gentile customs. Jews wished each other **peace**
(Greek *eirene* or Hebrew *shalom*); Gentiles
wished each other **grace** *(charis)*. When Christians used these words in greeting, the meaning
was significant. Christ offers grace to handle
life's difficulties; he offers peace that gives
inner calm—no matter what the outward
circumstances.

THE FAITH OF THE THESSALONIAN BELIEVERS / 1:2-10

Paul and his companions probably arrived in Thessalonica in the early summer of A.D. 50. They planted the first Christian church in that city but had to leave in a hurry because their lives were threatened (Acts 17:1-10). At the first opportunity, probably when he stopped at Corinth, Paul sent Timothy back to Thessalonica to see how the new believers were doing. Timothy returned to Paul with good news: the Christians in Thessalonica were remaining firm in the faith and were unified. But the Thessalonians did have some questions about their new faith. Paul had not had time to answer all their questions during his brief visit; in the meantime, other questions had arisen. So Paul wrote this letter to answer their questions and to commend them on their faithfulness to Christ.

1:2 In many ancient letters, an introduction would be followed by a word of encouragement; Paul often followed this pattern. In most of his letters he would **thank God** for the believers. Paul told the Thessalonians, a young church facing persecution, that he and the other apostles **always** thanked God **for all of** them and prayed for them **constantly.** Paul was not depending on his great skills or his teaching to carry the young believers; instead, he was trusting in God to guide and protect them. Paul spent much time traveling and preaching, but apparently he spent much time on his knees praying for the believers.

1:3 The Thessalonian believers had stood firm when persecuted (1:6; 3:1-4, 7, 8). Paul commended these young Christians for their **faithful work, loving deeds,** and **continual anticipation** of Christ's return. Their **work** had been produced by faith. Paul made it clear that believers are saved by faith alone (Ephesians 2:9), but then faith should produce good works in the believers. The Thessalonians' good **deeds** had been prompted by love. The believers were willing to give of themselves (even if it meant hardship) in service to others. Only God's kind of love could prompt such willing labor. Their **anticipation** of the Lord's return helped them to be strong in the face of opposition and difficulty because they know that God sees all and one day will make everything right.

1:4 Paul, Silas, and Timothy could resolutely say to the believers in Thessalonica that God **chose** them. That God "chooses" his people forms the basis of the doctrine of election—defined as God's choice of an individual or group for a specific purpose or destiny. The doctrine of election teaches that believers are saved only because of God's grace and mercy, not because of their own merit. God does not save anyone because that person deserves to be saved; rather, he graciously and freely gives salvation to whomever he chooses.

1:5 Paul knew that these believers had been chosen by God because his presentation of the **Good News** brought great results. Paul and his companions had **brought** the message to Thessalonica. There were no believers when they arrived; when they left, a strong church had been planted. This was not a source of pride for the apostles, however. When Paul brought the message to people, he spoke with **words,** and God used those words to ignite the Thessalonians to understand and believe that message. God had used Paul's words by enveloping them in divine **power** (see also 1 Corinthians 2:1-5; Ephesians 6:17). Paul's words alone could not persuade anyone to believe or open a needy heart to hear the message. But his words—combined with the power of the **Holy Spirit** to convince, enlighten, and comfort the listeners—could help many to believe what Paul was saying and give their hearts and lives to Christ for salvation.

The last half of this verse points to chapter 2 where Paul discusses his ministry with them. The Thessalonians could see that what Paul, Silas, and Timothy were preaching was true because these men **lived** it. They demonstrated their willingness to face opposition, travel under adverse conditions, and work without being paid while dealing with severe frustrations.

1:6 The **message** of salvation, though welcomed with great **joy,** brought the Thessalonian believers **severe suffering** because it led to persecution from both Jews and Gentiles (3:2-4; Acts 17:5). By doing so, they **imitated both** the apostles (Acts 16:16-40; 2 Corinthians 11:16-33) and **the Lord** (John 15:18-19, 20, 21). The same **Holy Spirit** who empowered the gospel message also opened hearts to receive the message and then gave joy to the hearers. The Holy Spirit works in those presenting the message and those hearing and accepting it. He gives "joy" (see Galatians 5:22).

1:7-10 The Thessalonians had followed the example of the apostles and of the Lord himself (1:6), and they, in turn, had become **an example**

to all the Christians in Greece. Paul praised this church (no other church received this particular type of praise) because not only were they model believers to an unbelieving world, but they were also examples to other believers. These Thessalonian believers had a worldwide reputation and were an example to all the other churches. The message of these believers' lives had an effect even beyond Greece, their faith was known everywhere. So well known was the Thessalonians' faith that Paul did not need to tell about it—believers in other places brought it up first! Any believer from any church might be found talking about what was going on in Thessalonica. The other churches knew how some people in Thessalonica had turned away from idols to serve the true and living God. In fact, they were suffering severely for this change of faith and life (1:6). The impact of this may slip past modern ears. The idols, the Greek "gods," were considered to be extremely powerful. For these Thessalonians, living barely 50 miles from Mount Olympus where the Greek gods were said to live, to "turn from" their many false idols to

the one true God had caused significant change in all areas of their lives. No wonder they faced persecution.

In addition to turning and serving, the Thessalonians were waiting. The Christian life doesn't end at death. All believers await God's Son from heaven. All believers look forward to the Second Coming when Jesus Christ will take his followers to be with him, rescuing them from the terrors of the coming judgment. This refers to the time when God will display his anger toward a sinful world and destroy all evil (see 5:9; 2 Thessalonians 1:6-10). God's wrath is a certainty, for he will not let sin continue unabated forever. Believers, however, can trust in their Savior who rescues them.

Paul emphasized Christ's Second Coming throughout this book. Because the Thessalonian church was being persecuted, Paul encouraged them to look forward to the deliverance that Christ would bring. A believer's hope is in the return of Jesus, the great God and Savior (Titus 2:13). Just as surely as Christ was raised from the dead and ascended into heaven, he will return (Acts 1:11).

1 THESSALONIANS 2 :1-16

PAUL REMEMBERS HIS VISIT / 2:1-16

Paul and Silas had been driven out of Thessalonica by their enemies, who then slandered Paul to the young believers in the new church there. This letter answers the accusations of Paul's enemies by describing what the believers already knew—the truth of Paul and Silas's message, the sincerity of their motives, and the proof of both by their actions among them. Paul was totally committed to the growth of those who had come to faith through his preaching.

2:1 This refers to Paul's first visit to Thessalonica recorded in Acts 17:1-10. The ministry in Thessalonica had begun calmly enough, but it had ended with Paul and Silas leaving under cover of darkness because a riotous mob attempted to turn the city against them. And the Jews' slander did not end after Paul and Silas had left the city. Not only had the Jews followed them to Berea to stir up trouble there (Acts 17:13), but evidently they had continued to speak against the apostles to the Thessalonian believers. The Jews seemed to have taken the occasion of Paul and Silas's hasty departure to try to convince the believers that they had been defrauded. The following verses seem to reflect Paul's response to what the Jews had said against him and Silas.

Some may have thought that the visit to Thessalonica was a failure, but the believers there knew that it was not a failure (meaning ineffective or worthless). Paul and Silas had arrived in a city with no believers. They left a strong church that was alive, growing, standing up to persecution, and becoming an example to believers across the world. Lives had been changed.

2:2 The Thessalonians knew that Paul and Silas had indeed been treated badly in Philippi, for they ended up in prison. Despite severe suffering for sharing the Good News of Christ, Paul explained that God had given him courage to go on to Thessalonica and declare God's Good News. Only such supernatural courage could help the men boldly face persecution because the threat of opposition had not been left behind in Philippi. The apostles continued to be **surrounded by many who opposed** them. In Thessalonica, their enemies had started a riot against Paul and Silas and their teachings. The Jewish leaders had claimed that Paul and Silas were "guilty of treason against Caesar" because they were professing "allegiance to another king, Jesus" (Acts 17:7). In reality, their only "crime" was proclaiming the Good News of salvation in Jesus Christ. In addition, the Thessalonians had sent a delegation to Berea to follow Paul and Silas in order to stir up trouble against them (Acts 17:13).

2:3 The words **so you can see** seem to indicate that Paul was answering accusations. Perhaps some of the Jews who had caused the riot in Thessalonica had told the Thessalonian believers that Paul and Silas had been defrauding them (Acts 17:5). But Paul pointed out that he had just left severe persecution in Philippi before his arrival in Thessalonica. Then he had experienced persecution in Thessalonica, causing he and Silas to leave secretly. How then could they have been preaching with any other motive than to obey God? If they had wanted to make money and please the crowds with their preaching, they had certainly gone about it the wrong way! Instead, they had faced persecution and then, with courage (2:2), had continued to face more persecution. No preacher hoping for an easy buck and popularity would take such a path. People only willingly suffer for something they believe in. Such was the case for Paul.

Paul mentioned three ways in which he and his companions **were not preaching**. First, they did not preach **with any deceit.** They were not trying to lead the Thessalonians down the wrong path. They did not preach with **impure purposes.** The word "impure" may point to accusations of sexual sin or sensuality, a trait common among traveling preachers. The "impure purposes" could also refer to another trait such as greed or pride. Again, these were common among some traveling preachers. The believers knew that this accusation was not true, for they knew Paul and his companions. Also, they were not using **trickery.** They had not hidden any of the truth from those to whom they ministered.

2:4 Paul and his companions did not seek anything for themselves. Instead, they spoke only **as messengers who have been approved by God to be entrusted with the Good News.** This was their commission; this was why they presented the Good News in the face of persecution. These men had been approved because God had examined

their **motives** and had seen what he needed in these willing servants. God knew that they wanted to **please God, not people.**

Gaining the approval of others will distract believers from pleasing God. As they do God's will, they must resist the desire to please people. The clarifying question of the believer should always be, "Who am I really serving?" If the answer is "people," then the believer will be tossed back and forth by conflicting demands and expectations. But if the answer is consistently "Christ," the believer will only have one person to please and not have to worry about how much or how little he or she is pleasing others.

2:5-6 The accusers could say what they wished, but the believers in Thessalonica could attest to the fact that Paul and the others with him had never used **flattery,** referring to language in order to cajole someone. Paul had no such intentions when he preached the gospel. He sought only to bring people to salvation in Christ.

The Thessalonians also knew that Paul and his fellow apostles had not been preaching for **money.** Many false teachers traveled about the ancient world willingly saying whatever an audience would pay to hear. **God** himself was **witness** of Paul and Silas's motives and mission. They had not even desired **praise** from anyone. They didn't need people to compliment their hard work and eloquent speeches in order to feel that they had accomplished much. They didn't need anyone to praise them, for they sought approval from God alone.

2:7-8 The **apostles** included the eleven men Jesus called (without Judas Iscariot), plus others, including Paul himself. The qualifications for being an apostle were to have seen the risen Christ, to have been commissioned by Christ to preach the Good News, and to be working on behalf of the Kingdom. Paul also noted signs, wonders, and miracles as marks of a true apostle (2 Corinthians 12:12).

As apostles, Paul and Silas **certainly had a right to make some demands** of the believers—such as expecting a certain amount of monetary help. In fact, most traveling teachers depended entirely on donations from their listeners. Paul practiced a trade (tentmaking) so as not to be a burden to his listeners (see also 2 Thessalonians 3:7-10). He also did not want to appear to be preaching for money. While he had a "right" to expect compensation (1 Corinthians 9:7-14), he did not always exercise that right. It was far more important to him that the gospel reach unbelievers. Paul and Silas **were as gentle among** the Thessalonian believers **as a mother feeding and caring for her own children.** Some traveling teachers may have breezed into various towns with superior airs and high-minded attitudes. But this was not the case with God's apostles. They had come with the authority of the God of heaven, yet they had served among the people because they truly **loved** them. Far from being preachers who used their audiences for self-aggrandizement, Paul and Silas **gave** both **God's Good News** and their **own lives.** Such sharing showed Paul and Silas's deep commitment to the gospel message and to the people with whom they shared it.

2:9 Although Paul had the right to receive financial support from the people he taught, he supported himself as a tentmaker (Acts 18:3; 20:34; 1 Corinthians 4:12). Each Jewish boy would learn a trade and try to earn his living with it. As a tentmaker, Paul was able to go wherever God led him, carrying his livelihood with him. Paul modeled self-reliance, the opposite of those false teachers and opportunists who sold "religion" in the marketplace. Paul didn't want to burden the young congregation by requiring financial support. The "double duty" of earning a living while trying to preach, teach, and build up a body of believers in Thessalonica called for them to toil **night and day.** But Paul and Silas gladly did it so that their **expenses would not be a burden** to the believers.

2:10 Again Paul appealed to what the Thessalonian believers knew about Paul and Silas. The believers themselves were **witnesses** of how these apostles had conducted themselves (see John 15:26-27; Acts 5:32). Paul could not make these claims before the Thessalonians and before **God** if the claims were not true. The accusing Jews could say what they liked, but everyone knew that Paul and Silas had conducted themselves in a **pure and honest and faultless** manner. This consistent example of right living surely affected the Thessalonians. If Paul and Silas had shared the gospel message but had lived carelessly, their message would have had little impact. But they preached through both their words and their lives.

2:11-12 Paul had already compared himself and Silas to a gentle and caring "mother" (2:7) in describing how they had brought the gospel message to the Thessalonians. The verses go on to describe their role among the Thessalonians as being like a **father** in matters of teaching and raising these "baby believers." As a father **treats his own children,** so the apostles dealt with the new believers one by one—the phrase **each of you** is emphatic. Paul and Silas had a personal relationship with each believer in Thessalonica. With pleading, encouragement, and urging, they had taught the believers to conduct their daily activities

in a way that God would consider worthy (see also Romans 16:2; Ephesians 4:1; Philippians 1:27; Colossians 1:10). To live worthy of God means to live consistent with his commands and character.

2:13 Paul thanked God for how the Thessalonians had received the message. When Paul and Silas had **preached,** the people had recognized **the words** as being more than human ideas, and they had **accepted** the gospel message **as the very word of God** (2:9). The gospel message reveals its divine origin and power as it transforms people's lives. The Thessalonians were experiencing how **this word continues to work** in those **who believe.** Through his word, God works in believers' lives, transforming them, guiding them, cleansing them.

2:14 One evidence of God's work had been the believers' fortitude when they had **suffered persecution from** their **own countrymen**—the Greeks in Thessalonica. But the believers in Thessalonica had good company, for in that persecution they had actually **imitated the believers in God's churches in Judea.** Not that they had planned on this imitation—but in the way they faced and withstood persecution, they were just like the churches in Judea who had also suffered **because of their belief in Christ Jesus,** and they had also **suffered from their own people, the Jews.** It had been persecution in Judea that had driven the believers out of that country to various places— and the gospel went with them. The book of Acts relates some of the early persecution that was going on in Jerusalem and Judea. This suffering is described in the following verses. When Paul referred to the "Jews" causing all kinds of persecution, he was speaking of specific Jews who were opposing his preaching of the gospel. He did not mean all Jews. Many of Paul's converts were Jewish, and Paul himself was a Jew (2 Corinthians 11:22).

2:15-16 Paul's most recent relationship with the Jews had been when he had been **persecuted** in Philippi (Acts 16:22-24) and had been **driven out** of Thessalonica (Acts 17:5-6, 10). Persecution did not surprise Paul, for Jesus himself had warned that his followers would face just such animosity (John 15:18). The churches had grown to expect persecution from both hostile Jews and Gentiles. Paul would later write to Timothy, "Everyone who wants to live a godly life in Christ Jesus will suffer persecution" (2 Timothy 3:12).

Why were the Jews so hostile to Christianity? The Jewish people had a history of killing **their own prophets** (Matthew 23:29, 31, 34-35, 37). Despite the Jews' constant watching for the arrival of their promised Messiah, they missed him when he came, and **even killed** him (see Matthew 27:25). The Jewish leaders thought Jesus was a false prophet; they didn't want his teachings to spread, so they opposed all who preached about him (Acts 4:18).

The Jewish opposition to Christianity continued after Jesus' death. Although the Jewish religion had been declared legal by the Roman government, it still had a tenuous relationship with the government. At this time, Christianity was viewed as a sect of Judaism. The Jews were afraid that reprisals leveled against the Christians might be expanded to include them. In addition, the Jewish leaders feared that if many Jews were drawn away into Christianity, their own political position might be weakened. The leaders were also very proud of their special status as God's chosen people, and they resented the fact that the Christians were **preaching the Good News to the Gentiles** and including Gentile believers as full members in the church. The Jews' natural animosity against Gentiles extended to fearing that **some might be saved.** As the people who should have recognized the Messiah and welcomed all who would come to the one true God, the Jewish leaders had failed miserably—they actually feared that others might find salvation. The inevitable consequence of this attitude would be **the anger of God.** The words, **has caught up with them at last,** has several views:

1. It could refer to a coming event. Writing this letter in A.D. 50, Paul may have been referring to the severe famine in Judea in A.D. 45-47 (Acts 11:27-28), the massacre of Jews in the Temple area in A.D. 49 (recorded by Josephus), or the expulsion of Jews from Rome by Emperor Claudius (Acts 18:2).
2. Paul may have been foreseeing disastrous coming events, such as the destruction of Jerusalem in A.D. 70. The Jews' continued rejection of the gospel message would spell destruction.
3. Most likely, Paul was using language conveying the "dramatic present." He was talking about the future as though it had already happened. Because of their continual rejection of Jesus as the Messiah and persecution of his followers, the Jews were not only piling up their guilt, they were hardening their hearts to the point of no return.

These must have been difficult words for Paul, a Jew from birth, to write about his countrymen. In another letter Paul wrote, "The longing of my heart and my prayer to God is that the Jewish people might be saved" (Romans 10:1). Paul understood that the Jews were God's chosen people and that many of them *would* come to salvation in Christ. He also knew, however, that many would flatly reject the truth. This pained him greatly.

2

1 THESSALONIANS 2 : 17 – 3 : 13

TIMOTHY'S GOOD REPORT ABOUT THE CHURCH / 2:17–3:13

Paul had been explaining to the Thessalonian believers why he and Silas had been unable to return to them. It had not been, as their detractors had said, because of fear or because they had been lying. Instead, Paul and Silas had wanted to come back but had been prevented by evil spiritual forces (2:18). However, they did not leave the young believers in Thessalonica without help—as the following verses explain.

2:17-18 The accusers had attacked Paul and Silas's methods and message (Paul refuted the accusations in the previous verses). The accusers also had pointed out the sudden departure of the apostles and the fact that they had not soon returned, implying that Paul and Silas had lied and were too scared to return. So Paul explained that the separation had not been desired (they did not separate themselves but **were separated from** them). The word "separated" can also be translated

"torn away." In addition, while physically separated, the apostles kept the believers in their hearts. They had **tried hard to come back** and had an **intense longing** to be back in Thessalonica with the believers. Far from being afraid to return, Paul and Silas **wanted** to go back to Thessalonica.

Yet they could not return because **Satan prevented** them. What exactly blocked Paul and Silas from returning to Thessalonica—opposition, illness, travel complications, or a direct attack by

Satan—is unknown. But, somehow, Satan had been able to keep them away more than once.

Spiritual warfare is real. Satan and God are constantly at war. Satan actively works to keep people from accepting Christ. He also works to hinder God's people from advancing God's Kingdom. Some of the difficulties that prevent believers from accomplishing God's work can be attributed to Satan (see Ephesians 6:12). Satan will bring sexual temptation on those who lack self-control (1 Corinthians 7:5). He will attempt to cause division among believers (2 Corinthians 2:11). He will bring in false teaching to lead believers astray (2 Corinthians 11:3). Satan can even disguise himself as an angel of light (Galatians 1:8). Satan will also attempt to hurt the community of believers through persecution (1 Thessalonians 3:1-5). While God is more powerful than Satan and sometimes intervenes and overrides, he does not always do so. Therefore, Christians must be vigilant and faithful to Christ.

2:19-20 With overflowing love for this young church, Paul asked a question and then answered it himself. What was the **hope, joy,** or **crown** in which Paul and Silas would have **much joy?** It would be the Thessalonian believers! The word **hope** describes Paul's confidence in these believers. The word **joy** pictures his own inner feelings when he imagined them presented to the Lord and welcomed into the Kingdom. The **crown** pictures a victor's wreath—the believers were like a victory crown, giving Paul joy in having "run the race" for their sakes (1 Corinthians 9:25; Philippians 4:1). One day, all will stand together before the Lord Jesus **when he comes back again.**

3:1-3 Because Paul could not return to Thessalonica (2:18), he **sent Timothy** as his representative. According to Acts 17:10, Paul left Thessalonica and went to Berea. When trouble broke out in Berea, some Christians took Paul to **Athens,** while Silas and Timothy stayed behind (Acts 17:13-15). Then Paul directed Silas and Timothy to join him in Athens. Later, Paul sent Timothy to encourage the Thessalonian Christians to be strong in their faith in the face of persecution and other troubles.

Paul's inability to return to Thessalonica and to support the new church weighed heavily upon him. All three of the letter's senders—Paul, Silas, and Timothy (1:1)—**could stand it no longer.** The apostles had no idea what was happening to these young believers. The Jews had chased the apostles out of the city, so it was fair to assume that the new Christians were under attack, as well. Concern for the believers caused Paul and his companions to take action. Paul really wanted to go back himself;

because he could not go, however, at least his **coworker for God** could go in his place.

Timothy had three main tasks for his return to Thessalonica—to **strengthen** the believers, **encourage** them, and **keep** them **from becoming disturbed by . . . troubles.** In addition, Paul wanted him to find out about their faith (3:5). Paul was concerned that the opposition had caused disruption in the church, so he wanted Timothy to find out how their faith was holding up against persecution. Though Paul had been convinced of the genuine conversion experience of these believers (1:5), he also knew the importance of follow-up and discipleship. He also wanted the believers to know that their **troubles** were not unusual.

3:4 Paul had never taught that Christ would make life easy; instead, he had constantly faced persecution for his faith, and he explained that any believer would do likewise. The Thessalonians could attest to this fact—for Paul and Silas had **warned** them that **troubles would soon come.** They saw it firsthand as the apostles had been run out of town for preaching the Good News (Acts 17:5-10).

3:5 Because persecution had occurred against the apostles—Paul **sent Timothy to find out whether** their **faith was still strong** and if they were persevering in the face of difficulty. The words **I was afraid** focus not so much on fear as on concern that **the Tempter** (Satan) **had gotten the best of** them. Paul was concerned that the new and struggling believers might turn away from their faith.

3:6 At the writing of this letter, **Timothy** had just **returned** with **good news.** Their **faith** was solid, their **love** strong, and they remembered Paul and Silas with affection. What relief Paul must have felt! Far from having been beaten by the opposition and turned against the faith, the believers had stayed strong; they even longed to see Paul and Silas as much as Paul and Silas longed to see them.

3:7-8 Paul's certain relief and joy at the good news from Thessalonica was matched by great comfort that they had **remained strong** in the faith. Paul and Silas had continued to experience **crushing troubles and suffering,** but this report from Timothy encouraged and inspired them with **new life**—renewed energy (see also 4:18; 5:11; Romans 1:12).

3:9-10 It brings **great joy** to a Christian to see another person come to faith in Christ and to mature in that faith. Paul experienced this joy countless times. He thanked God for those in Thessalonica who had come to know Christ and had held strong in the faith. Paul had been forced to leave while they were still infant Christians with incomplete knowledge. Yet they had held on to their faith despite opposition and persecution and had come through unscathed. No wonder Paul thanked God!

In the presence of God refers to the context of prayer. Paul also **earnestly** prayed, **night and day,** or constantly, for their continued growth. He also asked God to let them return to Thessalonica. Thus far, Satan had hindered them, but Satan's hindrances only happen with God's permission. So Paul asked God to allow them to go back **to fill up anything that may still be missing in** their **faith.** Paul wanted to give them further teaching, move on to deeper doctrines, and help these believers mature in Christ.

3:11 The first half of the letter closes with Paul praying that he might enjoy a reunion with the Christians in Thessalonica. Paul has made it clear in this letter that he really wanted to return to Thessalonica (2:17-18; 3:6, 10). He repeated his desire—breaking into prayer, calling upon God to **make it possible for** Paul and Silas to return to the Thessalonians. The double subject, God the Father and the Lord Jesus, is followed by a singular verb—clearly indicating Paul's understanding of the oneness of God and Christ.

It is unclear whether Paul ever returned to Thessalonica, but he traveled through Asia on his third journey and was joined by Aristarchus and Secundus, who were from Thessalonica (Acts 20:4-5).

3:12 Whether Paul could return or not, he knew that the church needed to sustain itself. A key ingredient would be **love** among the believers— as opposed to disunity, factions, or disagreements. The church would need love to survive. Although Paul had received good news from Timothy of the Thessalonians' love (3:6), he knew that love can always be strengthened and deepened with God's

help. So Paul prayed that **the Lord** would make the believers' love **overflow.** The word for love, *agape,* describes the selfless love that comes from God. Such love looks out for the best interests of those loved—caring for fellow believers and reaching out to unbelievers.

3:13 That God would **make** their **hearts strong** refers to Paul's desire for the Thessalonians to continue to have inner strength. In Scripture, the "heart" refers to the inner sphere of emotion, desire, and will—the personality. Such strength would be seen in one's character—and so Paul prayed that they would be **blameless and holy.** Complete perfection is not attainable in this life, but the process of sanctification brings believers ever closer to perfection. One day, the process will be over, and all believers will be made perfect when we **stand before God our Father.** The phrase, **when our Lord Jesus comes with all those who belong to him,** refers to the Second Coming of Christ when he will establish his eternal Kingdom. There are two views about the identity of these "holy ones." Some think it refers to believers; others say it refers to angels (see Matthew 25:31; Mark 8:38; 13:26-27; Luke 9:26; 2 Thessalonians 1:7). Most likely, both are true because the words "holy ones" are used in the Bible to describe angels (Deuteronomy 33:22), as well as believers. Note that Paul used the inclusive word "all" to describe this group. Therefore, it seems that Paul was saying that those who will come with Christ at his Second Coming will be the angels and those believers who will have already died by that time.

At that time, Christ will gather all believers, those who have died and those who are alive, into one united family under his rule. All believers from all times, including these Thessalonians, will be with Christ in his Kingdom.

1 THESSALONIANS **4**:1-12

LIVE TO PLEASE GOD / 4:1-12
The first three chapters of this letter focus on looking back at Paul's visit with the Thessalonians and defending his ministry with them against his critics. The final two chapters look ahead to the future of the church—giving advice for certain areas of Christian conduct that he felt needed to be addressed. The end of chapter 3 is a prayer that Christ would make these believers strong, blameless, and holy before God (3:13). That is a process of walking in faith and learning to live to please God. Effective faith should show itself in every area of a believer's life.

4:1-2 The word **finally** signals a change in subject, as Paul moved on to practical application of faith. Apparently, Timothy's report (3:6) had brought Paul great joy regarding the believers' faith but also included a few noteworthy concerns, for Paul gave instructions for right living in some very specific situations.

The believers had been **taught** from Paul and his companions **to live in a way that pleases God.** The apostles had set an example for them of how Christ-like living looks. Evidently, they had learned, for Paul said that they were **doing** just that; but he wanted them to **do so more and more.** Living to please God is every Christian's priority. Knowing Jesus as Savior brings salvation and should prompt every believer to please God. Through obedient believers, God works in the world. Obedience pleases God. Believers cannot claim to know and love God if they do not seek to please him.

4:3-5 The phrase, **God wants you to be holy,** refers to a process called "sanctification." This process continues throughout every believer's lifetime on earth. God takes the old patterns and behaviors and transforms them to his standards and will. Those who are being sanctified have accepted Christ as Savior and are allowing the Holy Spirit to work in their lives, making them more and more like Christ.

Because God wants his people to become holy, believers need to uphold certain standards here on earth. Christianity is not a list of do's and don'ts but a relationship in which the believers desire to please their heavenly Father (2:4; 4:1). To please him requires obedience to *his* standards. Apparently the area of **sexual sin** was plaguing the church in Thessalonica, as it was plaguing the Roman Empire as a whole. The many idols worshiped in the regions across the empire often had an emphasis on sex—some temples even employed prostitutes for the pleasure of "worshipers." In general, people regarded any kind of sexual activity as acceptable. It was quite common for a man *not* to limit his sexual relationship to his wife. Homosexuality was common. Incest was overlooked. Slaves were kept and used for sex.

God's standards are the opposite. Paul taught abstinence from sexual immorality. This included any kind of illegitimate sexual intercourse or relationship outside of marriage. We live in a society similar to the one in which Paul lived and taught. Every kind of sexual activity, including violence and abuse of children, has become commonplace. Unbridled expression of all desires has become the norm. As Christians, we must uphold the sanctity of sexual expression within the loving commitment of the marriage relationship.

These believers were not being exhorted to **keep clear** of all sex but of all sexual sin. God created sex to be a beautiful and essential ingredient of marriage, but sex outside the marriage relationship is sin. These believers had to "keep clear" of all forms of sexual sin—stay away or even run away if need be (see also 1 Corinthians 6:13-20; 2 Corinthians 12:21). Therefore, Paul taught that believers must **control** their bodies **and live in holiness and honor—not in lustful passion as the pagans do, in their ignorance of God and his ways.** Sex should be kept in the context of marriage between a man and woman; honorable conduct is contrasted with an evil, lustful attitude that can contaminate even a marriage. People who live by "lustful passion" are ignorant of God because they have chosen to ignore the knowledge of him that they have been given (Romans 1:19-20, 24-27) and to ignore his messengers who had brought the Good News to them.

4:6 Paul focused here on the men among the believers. Not only does sexual sin ruin the holy and honorable living to which the Christian men should aspire, but it also is a sin against one's fellow men—whether they be Christian or not. To have a sexual affair with another man's **wife** or member of his household wrongs that other man. It takes advantage of a trusting relationship. God does not overlook these sins; instead, he **avenges all such sins.** So important was this that Paul and Silas had already **solemnly warned** the new Christians in Thessalonica. While Paul was focusing on the men because of the society he lived in, it is important to note that these principles are just as true for women.

4:7 The Greek word translated **called** means "to call forth" or "to summon." Paul always made it clear that salvation was God's initiative and that people are "called" to be his. "Calling" includes a commitment on the part of believers **to be holy, not to live impure lives.**

4:8 God laid down **these rules**—basically, one rule—sex is for married people (a man and a woman) only. **Anyone who refuses to live** by this simple rule, who treats sexual sin lightly, **is not disobeying human rules** because human rules change (witness the change in "sexual rules" in the American culture over the last 50 years). To go with the flow of the surrounding culture and to disregard God's rules about sexuality are tantamount to **rejecting God.**

Paul would later write to the believers in Corinth (another sexually immoral city, and incidentally, the city where Paul was at the time he wrote the letter to the Thessalonians): "Run away from sexual sin! No other sin so clearly affects the body as this one does. For sexual immorality is a sin against your own body" (1 Corinthians 6:8). Sexual sin is a violation of one's own body. Paul described it as a sin that affects the body like no other, a sin that is against one's own body, affecting not just the flesh (promiscuous sex can lead to disease), but to the whole being and personality. Sexual sin has disastrous effects. What an enticement it can be for all people, and believers are not exempt. Clearly, other sins also affect the body, such as gluttony or drunkenness, but no other sin has the same effect on the memory, personality, or soul of a person as sexual sin. Paul argues that in intercourse, people are united (1 Corinthians 6:17). Their spirits are not involved in quite the same way in other sins. Also, Paul argues that believers' bodies are the temple of God (1 Corinthians 6:19-20). People violate God's purpose for their bodies when they commit sexual sins. Believers need to exercise alertness and awareness to stay away from places where temptation is strong, and they need to use strong, evasive action if they find themselves entrapped.

To reject God in such a way is to despise the wonderful gift of his **Holy Spirit** and to reject Christ's ultimate sacrifice on sinners' behalf. The Thessalonians had received that gift, and they ought to live in thankfulness and obedience. In Galatians 5:22-23, Paul describes the fruit of the Holy Spirit in believers' lives. One of these fruits is self-control—referring to mastery over sinful human desires. When believers surrender to the Holy Spirit, he gives them the strength to follow God's rules.

4:9 Paul switched gears here: from exhorting the Thessalonian believers about sexual purity to exhorting those who needed to work and not depend on others (4:11-12). In between, he commended them that he did not need to exhort them about **Christian love**, for it seemed that they had learned that lesson from **God himself** through the Holy Spirit. The Greek word used here for love, *philadelphia*, is the kind of love that binds people together (John 13:34-35; 1 John 2:7-8). Often used for blood relations in Greek literature, the New Testament writers used *philadelphia* for "faith relations" in the family of God.

This is a "brotherly love" **that should be shown among God's people.** Not only did sexual purity set the believers apart from the culture around them, but so did the love they showed for one another. Indeed, it was a trademark of the first church (Acts 2:43-47; 4:32-35).

4:10 The Thessalonian believers did not need instruction about showing God's love, but Paul urged them forward. Although their love was **already strong,** not only among themselves but also **toward all the Christians in all of Macedonia,** Paul begged the believers to **love them more and more.** There is always more to learn about love, always more depth to be plumbed, always more ways to show it. Paul wanted them to understand that love was not an end in itself, but a continual process.

4:11-12 Another group of believers in the church needed some warning (see also 5:14). Believers are to be responsible in all areas of life. Some of the Thessalonian Christians had adopted a life of idleness, depending on others for handouts (see Ephesians 6:6-7). The reason for their idleness is unknown. However, because a discussion of the Second Coming follows this section, it can be inferred that these people may have decided to sit around and wait for Christ's return. They may have genuinely thought they should spend all their time working to bring others into the Kingdom, but they were being a drain on their fellow believers.

It seems that these people were not quiet about this either, so Paul first exhorted them to focus their **ambition** on leading **a quiet life** and **minding** their **own business,** rather than meddling in others' business (see also 5:14; 2 Thessalonians 3:11). The injunction to working with their **hands** may have been distasteful, for Greeks looked down on manual labor as fit only for slaves. Paul was a tentmaker, however, and used his hard, manual labor as an example to all believers (2:9-11).

The reason for Paul's warning? He wanted the believers to be involved in honest labor so that **people who are not Christians will respect the way** the believers lived. He also did not want any believers to **need to depend on others to meet** their **financial needs.** Again, Paul had been working for these same reasons. Those who work hard to support themselves are a positive witness, both outside and inside the church. (See also Ephesians 4:28.)

1 THESSALONIANS 4:13–5:28

THE HOPE OF THE RESURRECTION / 4:13–5:11

Paul always taught people about the future—that salvation carried a promise of eternal life. He surely told his audiences that the same Jesus Christ who died, arose, and ascended would one day return. This would be his "Second Coming" (2:19). The believers knew that this could occur at any time and that it would be unannounced. The rest of chapter 4 and the first part of chapter 5 seem to be addressing several questions that had come from the church through Timothy regarding the resurrection of believers and the Second Coming.

4:13 A question to Paul from the Thessalonian believers regarded **the Christians who have died.** The believers had been taught that Christ would one day return and take his people to himself— every believer should be ready for that return at any moment. Apparently, in the interim as the believers awaited Christ's return, some of them had died. The Thessalonians were wondering why this had happened before Christ's return, and what would happen to those who had died before he came back. Some may have feared that believers who had died would miss the Kingdom. No doubt, the thought that their loved ones would not be with Christ caused them great sorrow.

This contrasts strongly with Paul's view (1 Corinthians 15:53-55; Philippians 1:21-23). Paul wanted the Thessalonians to understand that death is *not* the end. When Christ returns, all believers—dead and alive—will be reunited, never to suffer or die again. Believers need not **be full of sorrow like people who have no hope.** Paul recognized that the death of loved ones naturally results in grieving; but when Christians grieve for Christians who have died, there is a difference. Their grief is not hopeless. While the pain is real, the fact is that these loved ones will be seen again as the following verses describe.

4:14 Believers can have hope in the resurrection because of what happened to Jesus. Because **Jesus died and was raised to life again,** believers can also trust that those who have died will also be resurrected (see also 1 Corinthians 15:12-20). Then, **when Jesus comes, God will bring back with Jesus all the Christians who have died.** Believers who have died are with the Lord already! They are presently with God and will come with Jesus. They haven't missed out—in fact, they are enjoying God's presence. Second

Corinthians 5:8 and Philippians 1:21-22 teach that believers go to be with the Lord at death.

4:15-16 What did Paul mean when he wrote, **I can tell you this directly from the Lord?** Either this was something that the Lord had revealed directly to Paul, or it was a teaching of Jesus that had been passed along orally by the apostles and other Christians. Nevertheless, there was no disputing what Paul was about to say. He wanted these believers to understand that neither the dead nor the living would be at any disadvantage with regard to Christ's return. All believers will share the blessings of the resurrection. Those who have died are already with Christ and will be with him when he returns (4:14); those **who are still living** when Christ returns **will not rise to meet him ahead of those who are in their graves.** Instead, **all the Christians who have died will rise from their graves** first. Knowing exactly when the dead will be raised, in relation to the other events at the Second Coming, is not as important as knowing why Paul wrote these words. He wrote them to challenge and motivate believers to comfort and encourage one another when loved ones die. This passage can be a great comfort when any believer dies. The same love that unites believers in this life (4:9) will unite them when Christ returns and reigns for eternity.

The Second Coming will occur in God's timing. He alone brings it about. Christ, who is the **Lord himself,** will descend **from heaven,** for that is where he has been since after his resurrection (Acts 1:9-11). Christ's return will be unmistakable. No one will miss it, for he will descend with a **shout,** with the **call of the archangel,** and with the **trumpet call of God.** Whether these are three different ways of referring to one sound, whether they happen simultaneously, or happen in sequence is unknown. But these sounds will herald his return. Paul used distinctive imagery associated with the end times. An *archangel* is a high or holy angel appointed to a special task. Clearly, the angelic hosts will be taking part in this celebration of Christ's return to take his people home (Mark 8:38). A **trumpet** blast will usher in the new heaven and earth (Revelation 11:15). The Jews would understand the significance of this because trumpets were always blown to signal the start of great festivals and other extraordinary events (Numbers 10:10).

4:17 After the dead have risen from their graves, the believers **who are still alive and remain on the earth will be caught up in the clouds to meet the Lord in the air.** A reference to "clouds" in the Bible often symbolizes the presence of God (Exodus 13:21; 14:19; 19:16; 24:15; 40:34-38; Mark 9:7; Acts 1:9). There are differing views about whether this taking of the believers and the Second Coming of Christ occur at the same time, as noted below.

Clearly, all believers—whether they are alive or have died at the time of Christ's return—will be together with one another and with the Lord **forever.** This supernatural event will cause a great reunion among believers who are alive and those who have already died. Both groups will experience Christ's return together. This joyous reunion will go on forever.

This verse provides a clear picture of what is called the "rapture." But Paul does not say exactly when this will happen in relationship to the other great event of the end times: the tribulation. So there are three main views regarding the timing of the rapture with respect to the tribulation:

1. Pre-tribulationists point to the period of tribulation (described in Revelation) that occurs before the Second Coming of Christ and believe that the rapture of the believers will occur before this time of tribulation. They believe, therefore, that believers will be in heaven while the earth goes through a time of great tribulation. This view sees the believers meeting Christ in the clouds, but places his Second Coming as later.
2. Mid-tribulationists say that the rapture will occur at the mid-point of the time period of tribulation. The believers will be on earth for the first half of that time of tribulation but then will be raptured and will escape the last half, which will be a time of intense suffering. This view also sees Christ's Second Coming as a separate and later event.
3. Post-tribulationists believe that the believers will remain on the earth during the time of

tribulation prior to Christ's Second Coming. Then, when Christ returns in the clouds, believers will be caught up to be with him.

While Christians may differ regarding the timing of this rapture, all believe that it will happen and that it will be a joyous reunion of all believers, living and dead. Paul's point was not to give his readers a timeline or a literal description of how all the end-time events would fit together. Instead, he wanted to reassure the Thessalonians that their fellow believers who had died would not miss out on Christ's return and eternal Kingdom.

4:18 The Thessalonians did not need to continue worrying about the spiritual state of those who had died. Paul explained to these believers that being dead or alive at the return of Christ would make no difference, for Christ would bring all his people together to be with him forever. Instead of worrying, they should **comfort and encourage each other with these words.** Even in the face of death, believers know that their Lord is ultimately triumphant.

5:1-2 The phrase **day of the Lord** refers to a future time when God will intervene directly and dramatically in world affairs. Predicted and discussed often in the Old Testament (Isaiah 13:6-12; Joel 2:28-32; Amos 5:18; Zephaniah 1:14-18), the day of the Lord will include both punishment and blessing. Christ will judge sin and set up his eternal Kingdom. Paul had already taught at length about this and explained that it **will come unexpectedly, like a thief in the night** (see also Matthew 24:36, 43-44; 2 Peter 3:10; Revelation 3:3; 16:15).

Some have attempted to pinpoint dates or prove how certain present events fulfill prophecy. Jesus made it clear and Paul reiterated, however, that no one knows when Christ will return. It will be unexpected and on God's timetable. Jesus predicted that, before his return, many believers would be misled by false teachers claiming to have revelations from God (Mark 13:5-6). According to Scripture, the one clear sign of Christ's return will be his unmistakable appearance in the clouds. This will be seen by all people (Mark 13:26; Revelation 1:7). In other words, believers do not have to wonder whether a certain person is the Messiah or whether the times in which they live are the "end times." When Jesus returns, everyone will know beyond a doubt because it will be evident. Beware of groups who claim special knowledge of the last days because no one knows when that time will be.

5:3 The comparison of Christ's coming to a thief (5:1-2) pictures it as sudden and unexpected; the comparison of it to **a woman's birth pains** pictures that it will be unavoidable (see also Mark 13:8). Some who will not be waiting for Christ will think that everything is safe—they will be lulled into a false sense that **everything is peaceful and secure** (see also Jeremiah 6:14; 8:11; Ezekiel 13:10; Micah 3:5). However, they will find themselves facing sudden **disaster.** The Greek word for "destruction" *(olethros)* is also used in 2 Thessalonians 1:9, where it denotes separation from God. When Christ returns, that *will* be the end—there will be no reprieves, no second chances, **no escape.**

5:4-5 The believers in Thessalonica were not **in the dark;** that is, they were not ignorant of what was to occur. God has chosen not to tell his people everything about Christ's return, but believers know all that they need to know. From the moment Christ ascended into heaven, the promise remains that someday, just as he went, he will return (Acts 1:11). For believers, that promise is not scary; instead, it is a promise of hope. Because believers **are all children of light and of the day,** that return will be a time of great joy.

The contrasts of "light" and "darkness," and "day" and "night," are often used in the Bible to describe the difference between good and evil, between God's people and the people of the world. Light represents what is good, pure, true, holy, and reliable. Darkness represents what is sinful and evil. "Children of the light," God's children, have nothing to fear regarding the Second Coming—although they are responsible to be ready.

5:6-7 Usually thieves break into homes at night when everyone is sleeping. Jesus' Second Coming *will* happen, and it will happen with surprise like a thief breaking in, but God's people should **be on guard, not asleep.** The way to be ready for Jesus' return is not in knowing when he will return, for he won't give that information. Instead, readiness lies in being **alert** and **sober.** The children of the light will be awake and ready when the Lord returns. Paul pictures those who constantly expect the Lord to return at any moment. They are not dallying in sin or falling into temptation, or being waylaid by their own doubts. We also must walk close to God in daily fellowship with him so that, at the Second Coming, we will be ready.

This contrasts with the rest of the world, the **others** of the "darkness" and of the "night" who are **asleep** at the Lord's return. The word translated "asleep" is used for moral indifference (see Mark 13:36; Ephesians 5:14). These people aren't waiting for the Lord, aren't caring that he could return, and are even getting **drunk**—a metaphor for their moral indifference toward the holy God. Because unbelievers are people of the "darkness" and of the "night," their lives are focused on their own pleasures and obsessions, and not on alertness and moral readiness for the coming of Christ.

5:8 People who **live in the light** have a whole different reason to be alive. Life is not all about personal pleasure but about loving and serving God and getting to know him better. The reward for being God's children is that when he returns, he will take his people to eternal blessing. This means that in this sinful world, the world of "darkness" and "night," believers have to be different. First of all, they must **think clearly.** Believers need to realize that they are in a battle. Spiritual warfare is very real, and Satan does not easily accept people leaving his kingdom for God's Kingdom. So believers must be armed and ready, like a soldier, **protected by the body armor of faith and love,** and **wearing** a **helmet** of **confidence** in their **salvation** (see also Ephesians 6:11-13).

Believers face a powerful army whose goal is to defeat Christ's church. Those who believe in Christ are assured of victory. They must engage in the struggle until Christ returns, however, because Satan is constantly battling against all who are on the Lord's side. Christians need supernatural power to defeat Satan, and God has provided this by giving his Holy Spirit and his armor for protection. Believers have faith and love to protect their hearts, and confidence to keep their minds focused on the goal—God's eternal Kingdom.

5:9-10 In order to wear "confidence" as a helmet (5:8), believers must know in what (or in whom) they have confidence. God saved his people, so he will **not pour out his anger on** them. God's wrath is very real. Sin will be punished, and those who have refused his offer of forgiveness will indeed face punishment (Revelation 20:11-15). But believers will not face the condemnation that their sins deserve. Instead, they will **live with** God **forever** because they have put their faith in Jesus' sacrifice on the cross for forgiveness of their sins. The confidence rests secure, **whether** believers **are dead or alive** at Christ's return. Salvation is a certainty because the Christ who is coming is the same Christ who died for sinners.

5:11 Despite persecution and their sorrow over fellow believers who had died, the Christians needed to **encourage each other** about the certainty of their future reunion with all believers who had gone on before (4:13-18) and the promise of eternal life through Jesus Christ (5:9-10). They ought also to **build each other up** in the faith. Even as one believer receives encouragement, he or she at another time will be in a position to offer it. The mutual giving and receiving in the body of Christ keep the church strong against the forces that attack it. God's people always need to stand together as they anticipate their Savior's return.

PAUL'S FINAL ADVICE / 5:12-22

Paul wanted to leave some final instructions to all the believers so that they could continue to build up one another (5:11). This section focuses on three parts of life in a local church and how the relationships ought to work—from the pastors and leadership, through the fellowship and responsibilities of the believers, and finally to how they ought to worship. The instructions are as vital to churches today as they were in the first century.

5:12 The **brothers and sisters** in the church needed to show **honor** to those in leadership in order for everything to function smoothly. The word "honor" is also translated "respect." These **leaders in the Lord's work** probably were the elders who held positions of leadership and responsibility. Elders carried great responsibility, and they were expected to be good examples. Because these men **work hard among** the believers, they deserved to be honored. Paul expressed a similar thought in his letter to Timothy (1 Timothy 5:17).

The leadership structure in local churches began very early. As Paul planted a church and then moved on, he needed to leave behind an organized group of believers (Acts 11:30; 14:23; 1 Timothy 4:14; Titus 1:5; James 5:14; 1 Peter 5:1). Paul could not stay in each church, but he knew that these new churches needed strong spiritual leadership. Leaders were chosen to teach sound doctrine, to help believers mature spiritually, and to equip believers to live for Jesus Christ despite opposition. Acts 14:23 describes Paul and Barnabas' return to some of the churches that they had planted. Part of the reason that Paul and Barnabas risked their lives to return to these cities was to organize the churches' leadership.

Timothy may have also reported back to Paul some concern regarding a lack of respect by the Christians for their leaders. Perhaps the leaders had been warning **against all that is wrong,** and in so doing, had been the target of criticism. Paul explained that these men had been put in positions of responsibility for a reason. Therefore, believers should respect and heed their words.

5:13 Leaders are not to be ignored or argued with, they are to be thought of **highly** and given **wholehearted love because of their work.** When believers respect their leaders and join them in their work for God's Kingdom, the church will grow. Of course, it also helps if the leader does not have to spend all his time in dealing with internal conflicts—hence, Paul's reminder that believers should **live peaceably with each other.** All are to work together to build the Kingdom and to serve one another. The best way for this "peace" to occur is for all believers to serve with their God-given gifts, to let others use *their* gifts, and then to respect and love one another for what God is doing through them.

5:14 While the leaders have special responsibility to guide the church, believers are not exempt from their responsibilities to care for one another. Paul singled out three groups in this church and "urged" the believers to look after or deal with them—each in a different way.

First, they are to **warn those who are lazy.** The word "warn" is also in 5:12 and means to firmly admonish. They were to warn the lazy, idle believers. The word translated "lazy" is used only in the letters to the Thessalonians (see also 2 Thessalonians 3:6, 7, 11) and seems to have been a particular concern for this church. The Greek word translated "lazy" (*ataktous*) was used for soldiers who would not stay in the ranks. These people had set themselves outside the prescribed pattern for the church—everyone else was working and serving, but they would not. The problem with idle people is that, because they are not busy enough with valuable activities, they usually stir up trouble of one kind or another. These people need to be warned to get back in line and to use their God-given gifts in service for the Kingdom.

Second, they are to **encourage those who are timid.** The lazy need to be warned, but the **timid** need to be encouraged. The "timid" are the fearful people who lack confidence—perhaps in themselves or even in their faith. They have become discouraged or worried, possibly by persecution or by the deaths of their fellow believers (3:13). These people need loving instruction from their fellow believers to calm their fears and to build their confidence.

Jesus' preeminent lordship. John 5:22-23 says that all should honor the Son just as they honor the Father. Again Jesus' true deity and oneness with the Father are revealed.

2:11 Every tongue will confess the basic truth of Christianity: **Jesus Christ is Lord.** This does not mean that eventually everyone will be saved. Every tongue in heaven, on earth, and under the earth will recognize Jesus as Lord, either because of belief or because of mere acknowledgment of the undisputable fact. No tongue will be silent; no knee will remain unbowed. All of creation will recognize Jesus Christ as Lord.

SHINE BRIGHTLY FOR CHRIST / 2:12-18

Believers ought to follow Christ's example not only to bring unity and peace to the church, but also so that no one in the outside world would be able to find any fault with them. Philippi was a pagan city; Paul wanted these believers to be unified, morally pure, and filled with good works so that they could bring the light of Christ into their dark world. Is your light shining for Christ?

2:12-13 The Philippian church was dear to Paul's heart. He didn't want his absence from them to be a detriment to their spiritual growth. So he requested that they **always** be **careful to follow** his **instructions,** even while he was **away.** They must **put into action God's saving work** by **obeying God with deep reverence and fear.** Paul was calling the entire church to work together to rid themselves of divisions and discord. Although believers are saved once for all when they accept Jesus Christ as Lord, it is in the grind of everyday life that salvation is **put into action.** Paul wanted the Philippians to put their salvation into practice for the health of the church. As they did so, they would not do it on their own. Through his Holy Spirit, **God** would be **working in** them for the tasks he wanted them to do (1 Corinthians 12:4-7). He would give the Philippians **the desire to obey him and the power to do what pleases him** to bring true unity to the church. God works in believers; believers do God's work. Believers are partners with God.

2:14-15 Paul had advice for how they could go about acting out their faith—they should **stay away from complaining and arguing.** Paul returned to the basic problem described in 2:1-4, the arrogance that leads to dissension. **Complaining** translates from a word that describes a bad attitude which expresses itself in constant grumbling. The word for **arguing** has a legal connotation and may refer to the Philippian Christians going to civil courts to settle their differences, an action Paul condemned elsewhere (1 Corinthians 6:1-11).

Complaining and arguing are completely opposite to Christ's attitude (2:5-8), which believers are to emulate. They also give people a bad impression of the church, and no one should be able to **speak a word of blame against** the believers. If all that people know about a church is that its members constantly argue, complain, and gossip, they get a bad impression of Christ and the gospel. Unbelievers then feel justified in criticizing the Christians. Probably more churches have split from causes related to arguing and complaining than from heresy.

Instead, believers' lives ought to be **clean,** meaning beyond reproach, incurring no justifiable criticism. This does not mean sinless perfection; instead, the church was to be beyond the criticism of the unbelieving world. Their lives also ought to be **innocent.** There ought to be nothing within the church that would weaken its strength or contaminate the truth. The church's members then could be **children of God in a dark world full of crooked and perverse people.** Without a doubt, the Philippian believers lived in a generation filled with dishonesty and perversion. While believers are rescued out of the present evil age (Galatians 1:4) and are no longer of the world (John 17:16), they are not taken out of the world (John 17:15). They are "in" the world and have been given a commission to go "into" the world with the Good News (John 17:18). The church of Philippi needed to fulfill its mission in the world, and it could best do so by being clean and innocent children of God right in the middle of the depraved culture. The contrast with their culture would be so stark that the believers would **shine brightly.** They bring the light of truth into the darkness of depravity, as stars light up the darkness of the night.

2:16 The Philippian church should **hold tightly to the word of life** by spreading the truth of the gospel beyond the doors of the church. To do this, they must be grounded in the truth, refusing to compromise. When Paul saw the church remaining

Third, they are to **take tender care of those who are weak.** The word for "take tender care" is *antechesthe* (also translated simply as "help"); it pictures the action of holding on to these people, wrapping arms around them, clinging to them. This is the kind of help suggested for the spiritually "weak," those weak in faith, those in need (such as financial need) or those who might be struggling with the sins associated with paganism that Paul wrote about in 4:3-8. These might be struggling, needy, or immature Christians who need the arms of strong fellow believers to guide them, give them support, and let them know they are not alone. See also Romans 5:6; 14:1; 1 Corinthians 8:9.

Finally, being **patient with everyone** is the glue that holds the relationships together. In any group where a variety of people come together and are expected to be a loving family, godly patience will be required of everyone. The word for "patient" (*makrothumia*) is also translated "long-suffering." This is an attribute of God (Exodus 34:6; Psalm 103:8), a fruit of the Holy Spirit (Galatians 5:22), and a characteristic of love (1 Corinthians 13:4). God is patient with people, and so Christians should be. In addition, God has given his Spirit to help his people be patient with one another.

5:15 To a church under persecution, the command against retaliation is especially poignant. **See that no one pays back evil for evil.** Personal revenge and retaliation are clearly forbidden to those who call themselves followers of Christ (Matthew 5:39, 44; Romans 12:17-21). There would be times where relationships between believers would be strained. They would also need to remember that they should never pay back evil for evil, but **should always try to do good to each other and to everyone else**—thus including those in the church and those outside, even their enemies. That believers should "always try" indicates a lifestyle of kindness that should permeate all their dealings with people.

5:16 Paul counseled this persecuted church to **always be joyful.** Paul had just commanded the believers to love one another, and then to rejoice. True joy transcends the rolling waves of circumstance. Joy comes from a consistent relationship with Jesus Christ. When believers' lives are intertwined with Christ, he will help them to walk through adversity without sinking into debilitating lows and to manage prosperity without moving into deceptive highs. The joy of living with Jesus Christ daily will keep believers always joyful. They can rejoice because of their sure salvation and their future hope. Nothing that happens on this earth can compare with the glory that awaits God's people.

5:17 Paul did not expect believers to spend all their time on their knees or with their eyes closed when he said they should **keep on praying.** In fact, he was quite adamant that everyone had work to do (5:14; 2 Thessalonians 3:6-7, 11). It is possible, however, for believers to have a prayerful attitude at all times. This attitude is built upon acknowledging dependence on God, realizing his presence within, and determining to obey him fully. Then it will be natural to pray frequent, spontaneous, short prayers.

5:18 Evil will happen to believers. When it strikes, they can still be **thankful** for God's presence and for the good he will accomplish through the distress. Usually, God uses difficult times to build people's character and strengthen their faith. It is easy to give thanks for the blessings; it is more difficult to give thanks for the blessings in disguise. By far, the most difficult task is to give thanks **no matter what happens**—even the situations that make no sense or are extremely painful. Yet this difficult task has been assigned to all believers, **for this is God's will for you who belong to Christ Jesus.** Learning to give thanks in everything means learning to trust God completely. When a believer can give thanks so willingly, he or she has trusted that God is completely in control of all situations and is working out his will.

5:19 To "stifle" means to douse a fire, so to **stifle the Holy Spirit** would be forbidding or restraining his work. By warning the believers **not** to stifle the Holy Spirit, Paul may have meant that the believers in Thessalonica should not grieve the Spirit through any of the sins that have been mentioned in this letter—immorality and laziness, for example. But the context suggests (see next verse) that Paul was referring to a situation in the church in which some of the believers had been limiting or forbidding the exercise of certain spiritual gifts, such as prophecy or speaking in tongues. Paul warned that no one should ignore or toss aside the gifts the Holy Spirit gives. The following verses specifically mention prophecy (5:20). Sometimes, the immature use of spiritual gifts causes divisions in a church. Rather than trying to solve the problems, these believers may have been attempting to stifle those gifts. No one should stifle the Holy Spirit's work in anyone's life but encourage the full expression of these gifts to benefit the whole body of Christ.

5:20-21 God appointed certain people as prophets to the church (1 Corinthians 12:10, 28). These people had special gifts in ministering God's messages to his people. At times they would foretell the future (Acts 11:28; 21:9, 11), but more often they would exhort, encourage, and strengthen

God's people (Acts 15:32; 1 Corinthians 14:29).
God spoke through prophets—inspiring them with
specific messages for particular times and places.
This gift provided insight, warning, correction,
and encouragement (see 14:3). The Thessalonians
apparently were scoffing **at prophecies.** These
prophecies would have been heard in the context
of worship, although opinions differ on what these
entailed. The Reformers (Calvin, Luther) believed
that sermons are the exercise of the gift of prophecy. Other scholars say that prophecy refers to
spontaneous, Spirit-inspired messages that are
orally delivered in the congregation for the edification and encouragement of the body of Christ.

The gift of prophecy is highly regarded. It is second only to the highest rank of being an apostle
(1 Corinthians 12:28; Ephesians 4:11) and is a
gift to be aspired to, for it helps edify believers
(1 Corinthians 14:5, 10-12). The words spoken,
therefore, should not be treated contemptuously.
Paul was not advocating blind acceptance of every
word spoken by any self-styled prophet. Instead,
believers were to **test everything** against God's
word in Scripture, discern what was true and what
was false, and then **hold on to what is good.** The

word translated "good" *(kalos)* was sometimes
used to describe what was genuine—as a genuine
coin is opposed to a counterfeit. All believers are
responsible to listen, discern, and learn.

Christians should not believe everything they
hear just because someone says it is a message
inspired by God. There are many ways to **test** teachers to see if their message is truly from the Lord.
One is to check to see if their words match what God
says in the Bible. Other tests include their commitment to the body of believers (1 John 2:19), their
lifestyle (1 John 3:23-24), and the fruit of their ministry (1 John 4:6). The most important test of all is
what they believe about Christ.

5:22 The separation is real and important: believers must "hold on to what is good" (5:21) and at
the same time **keep away from every kind of evil.**
Paul did not mean that believers must literally
withdraw from the world, for to do so would mean
that they could not shed the light of Christ so that
more might come to him. Believers can, however,
make sure that they don't give evil a foothold by
avoiding tempting situations and concentrating
on obeying God. (See also Romans 12:9.)

PAUL'S FINAL GREETINGS / 5:23-28

The conduct Paul has been prescribing is beyond human possibility. People will not naturally
rejoice always, pray continually, and give thanks in every situation (5:16-18), nor can they keep
away from all evil (5:22). Paul did not expect them to do this in their own strength; he prayed
that God would help them.

5:23 Paul described God as **the God of peace.**
Jesus had told his disciples that he would give
them peace (John 14:27; 16:33). The end result
of the Holy Spirit's work in believers' lives is
deep and lasting peace. Unlike worldly peace,
which is usually defined as the absence of conflict, this peace is confident assurance in any
circumstance; with Christ's peace, no believer
needs to fear the present or the future.

Paul prayed that God would work in the
believers' lives to make them **holy.** As God takes
up residence within a believer, he begins the
process of "sanctification"—the change that he
makes in each believer's life. Believers are sanctified (set apart) by the work of Christ. It is initiated by God's Spirit when they believe. It is a
process whereby believers dedicate themselves to
proper living. While "perfection" will not occur
until believers are fully glorified, sanctification is
the process of moving toward that goal, moving
toward Christlikeness. In order to be made holy
in every way, God will need to work in all areas

of a person's life—the **whole spirit and soul
and body.** This expression is Paul's way of saying
that God must be involved in every aspect of a
believer's life. As believers live in God's presence,
he will keep them **blameless** for Christ's return.
Perhaps the Thessalonian believers were wondering, when their fellow believers died before the
Second Coming, if those dead believers would be
able to receive this perfection from Christ. Paul
explained that the supernatural process would
occur for all believers.

5:24 The Thessalonians could count on these
promises because **God is faithful.** God created
the world, and he has faithfully ordered it and
kept it since the creation. Because God is faithful,
believers can count on him to fulfill his promises
to them. If God can oversee the forces of nature,
surely he can see his people through the trials
they face. Trusting in God's faithfulness day by
day gives confidence in his great promises for
the future. What he has promised, **he will do.**

5:25 Paul spent a lot of time in prayer for the believers in the various churches. He mentioned several times his own prayers for the Thessalonians (1:2; 3:10, 12-13; 5:23; 2 Thessalonians 1:11; 3:1). But Paul also asked believers to **pray for** him and his coworkers, as well (see also Ephesians 6:19; Colossians 4:3; 2 Thessalonians 3:1). Every believer, even this gifted apostle, needs the prayers of fellow believers.

5:26 Paul asked that the believers **greet each other in Christian love** to help break down the divisions in this church. He wanted his readers to express their love and unity to one another.

5:27 Paul's wording here is very strong, **I command you in the name of the Lord,** means something like, "I put you on oath before the Lord." Paul did not write merely to the leaders; he had written to everyone, so **all the Christians** needed to hear every word of it. For every Christian to hear this letter, it had to be read in a public meeting. Paul wanted to make sure that everyone had the opportunity to hear his message because he was answering important questions and offering needed encouragement.

5:28 As Paul began this letter (1:1), so he ended it. Paul's final prayer was for **the grace of our Lord Jesus Christ to be with** them. Paul often ended his letters this way, asking his readers to continue to experience God's undeserved kindness and love every day of their lives, and then to pass along that grace to others.

After Paul visited Thessalonica on his second missionary journey, he went on to Berea, Athens, and Corinth (Acts 17–18). From Corinth, Paul wrote his two letters to the Thessalonian church.

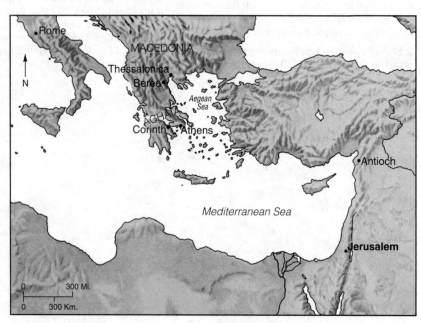

2 THESSALONIANS

INTRODUCTION
Communication can be tricky. What is heard and repeated is not always what was said in the first place.

Evidently, that's what happened in Thessalonica. Paul had written his warm and personal first letter to teach, encourage, and strengthen the believers there. Perhaps the most powerful message of Paul's letter was his teaching about the Second Coming. Paul wanted to comfort those who had lost loved ones and to give all of them hope. Jesus would soon return, and they should be ready.

Many of the Thessalonians, however, had heard the wrong message. Or they may have received false information from outsiders who, because of ignorance or selfish motives, had twisted the truth. Thinking Paul was stating that Jesus would come at any minute, some of them may have stopped working and started watching. The increased persecution of the church made this interpretation of Paul's words more plausible. *Surely this is the Day of the Lord,* many must have thought.

Upon learning of this miscommunication and misunderstanding, Paul wrote quickly, instructing further about the Second Coming and the Day of the Lord.

As you read 2 Thessalonians, think of how the first-century believers in that Greek city must have received Paul's message and how they probably changed their behavior. And consider what you should do to be ready for Christ's return—it's closer now than ever before.

AUTHOR
Paul (Saul of Tarsus): apostle of Christ, missionary, gifted teacher, and founder of the church at Thessalonica.

Just like 1 Thessalonians, the first verse of 2 Thessalonians mentions Paul, Silas, and Timothy as those who were sending this letter. The contents, however, clearly reveal Paul to be the primary author, for he often uses the pronoun "I." Paul's authorship of 2 Thessalonians was widely accepted by the early church.

For more about Paul, see the Author section in the Introduction to the book of Romans. See also the Introduction to the book of 1 Thessalonians.

DATE AND SETTING
Written from Corinth around A.D. 51, a few months after 1 Thessalonians.

Shortly after writing his first letter to the church at Thessalonica, Paul wrote 2 Thessalonians. He wrote this letter from Corinth also. The content of 2 Thessalonians verifies Corinth as the location.

- Paul, Timothy, and Silas were still together (1:1), and Corinth is the only place the three were known to have gathered after the initial evangelism of Thessalonica (see Acts 18:5).
- The condition of the Thessalonian church was much the same: The believers were still being persecuted (compare 1 Thessalonians 1:6 to 2 Thessalonians 1:4). In spite of its troubles, the Thessalonian church was still growing (compare 1 Thessalonians 1:8 to 2 Thessalonians 1:3).

AUDIENCE
The believers in Thessalonica.

Second Thessalonians was written to the same group of people to whom 1 Thessalonians was written: the believers in Thessalonica. Because of the similarities between the two letters, some critical scholars have asserted that each letter was sent to a distinct group in the Thessalonian church: 1 Thessalonians to the Jewish Christians and 2 Thessalonians to the Gentile Christians. This may be a convenient explanation for the similarities between the two letters, but the evidence for this theory is meager. Paul's other letters address Jews and Gentiles together, encouraging them to become one in Christ (see Romans 10:12; Galatians 3:28). It would have been uncharacteristic of Paul to send two separate letters and would merely have promoted more division in the church.

OCCASION AND PURPOSE
To clear up confusion about the Second Coming of Christ.

After sending his first letter to the church in Thessalonica, Paul received additional news about the believers there. They were enduring intense persecution and great hardship, but despite their troubles, they were clinging to the faith. Some, however, were claiming that Jesus had already returned. These believers may have misunderstood Paul's statement that Christ's return would be as unexpected as a thief coming in the middle of the night (1 Thessalonians 5:1-3). Or perhaps they had received another letter, claiming to be from Paul, that simply declared that Christ had already returned (2:2-3). That rumor, along with persecution, was disrupting and weakening the young church. Thinking they were in the final days, some believers were refusing to work (compare 1 Thessalonians 5:14 with 2 Thessalonians 3:11-12).

Paul knew that he had to write a second letter to dispel the rumors and to guide the young church. In summary, this letter reveals the heart of a concerned pastor. Paul didn't want any false teaching to distract his new converts from the Christian faith. They had already suffered too much for Christ to be sidetracked by idle gossip.

MESSAGE
The letter begins with Paul's trademark personal greeting and a statement of thanksgiving for their faith (1:1-3). He mentions their perseverance in spite of their persecution and trials (1:4) and uses this situation to broach the subject of Christ's return. At that time, Christ will vindicate the righteous who endure and will punish the wicked (1:5-12).

Paul then directly answers the misunderstanding concerning the timing of the events of the end times. He tells them not to listen to rumors and reports that the day of the Lord has already begun (2:1-2), because a number of events must occur before Christ returns (2:3-12). Meanwhile, they should stand firm for Christ's truth (2:13-15), receive God's encouragement and hope (2:16-17), pray for strength and for the spread of the Lord's message (3:1-5), and warn those who are unruly, meaning idle (3:6-15). Paul ends with personal greetings and a benediction (3:16-18).

The main themes in the book of 2 Thessalonians include: *Persecution, Christ's Return, Great Rebellion,* and *Persistence.*

Persecution (1:4-12; 3:1-5). Knowing that believers were being persecuted for their faith, Paul encouraged the church to persevere despite their troubles and trials. He affirmed that God would bring victory to his faithful followers and judge those who persecute them.

IMPORTANCE FOR TODAY. Christians are still being persecuted because of their strong faith in Christ. Some of the persecutions are overt and obvious. But many are subtle and secretive. In both cases, believers need to focus on God and his goodness, love, and call to faithfulness. God has promised to reward faith by giving believers his power and helping them bear persecution. Suffering for the faith will strengthen us to serve Christ. We must be faithful to him.

Christ's Return (1:5-7; 2:1-12). Because Paul had written that Christ could return at any moment, some of the Thessalonian believers had stopped working in order to wait for him. Certainly believers should be prepared for the Second Coming. But this preparation includes faithfully fulfilling the work to which God has called them, living upright and moral lives, and using their gifts and talents for God's glory.

IMPORTANCE FOR TODAY. Christ will return and bring total victory to all who trust in him. This truth should give believers hope regardless of their circumstances. It also should motivate believers to make the most of the time they have left on earth, to use their gifts, and to spread the Good News. If we are ready, we need not be concerned about *when* he will return. We should stand firm, keep working, and wait for Christ.

Great Rebellion (2:3-12). Before Christ's return, a great rebellion against God will be led by the man of lawlessness (the Antichrist). God will remove all the restraints on evil before he brings judgment on the rebels. The Antichrist will attempt to deceive many.

IMPORTANCE FOR TODAY. We should not be afraid when we see evil increase. God is in control, no matter how evil the world becomes. God guards us during Satan's attacks. We can have victory over evil by remaining faithful to God.

Persistence (1:4, 11-12; 2:13-17; 3:1-15). Members of the Thessalonian church had quit working and had become disorderly and disobedient. Paul chastised them for their idleness. He called them to show courage and true Christian conduct. He also challenged them to pray for courage and for each other and to stand firm in their faith.

IMPORTANCE FOR TODAY. Believers must never get so tired of doing right that they stop doing it. Instead, we should stand strong in our faith and continue to live the way God wants us to live. We can be persistent by making the most of our time and talent. Our endurance will be rewarded. When do you feel like giving up or giving in? What can you do to ensure your faithfulness to the Lord?

OUTLINE OF 2 THESSALONIANS
  I. The Bright Hope of Christ's Return (1:1–:17)
 II. Living in the Light of Christ's Return (3:1-18)

2 THESSALONIANS 1

GREETINGS FROM PAUL / 1:1-2

Paul wrote this letter from Corinth less than a year after he wrote 1 Thessalonians. He and his companions, Timothy and Silas, had visited Thessalonica on Paul's second missionary journey (Acts 17:1-10). They established the church there, but Paul had to leave suddenly because of persecution. This prompted him to write his first letter (1 Thessalonians), which contains words of comfort and encouragement. Paul then heard how the Thessalonians had responded to this letter. The good news was that they were continuing to grow in their faith. But the bad news was that false teachings about Christ's return were spreading, leading many to quit their jobs and wait for the end of the world. So Paul wrote to the Thessalonians again. While the purpose of Paul's first letter was to comfort the Thessalonians with the assurance of Christ's second coming, the purpose of this second letter was to correct false teaching about the Second Coming.

1:1 This second letter to the church in Thessalonica begins just like 1 Thessalonians. **Paul** was the head of the missionary team that had brought the gospel to that city. **Silas** is called a prophet (Acts 15:32) and was highly regarded in the Jerusalem church. Paul had chosen Silas to accompany him on his second missionary journey (Acts 15:40). Silas is mentioned in the salutation of both letters to the Thessalonians, and he worked with **Timothy** in Corinth (2 Corinthians 1:19). At this point, all three of these men were in Corinth (Acts 18:5).

Thessalonica was the capital and largest city of the Roman province of Macedonia. The most important Roman highway—extending from Rome to the Orient—went through Thessalonica. This highway, along with the city's busy seaport, made Thessalonica one of the wealthiest and most flourishing trade centers in the Roman Empire. Thessalonica was a free city, meaning it was allowed self-rule and was exempted from most of the restrictions placed by Rome on other cities.

Paul had planted **the church** when he and his companions had visited Thessalonica on the second missionary journey (Acts 17:1-10). The Thessalonian believers had strong faith, for despite persecution, they had endured (see 1 Thessalonians 1:7-10).

1:2 Paul often would begin his letters with a greeting of **grace** and **peace.** "Grace" is God's unmerited favor bestowed upon sinful people; "peace" refers to the peace that Christ made between believers and God through his death on the cross. By calling God **our Father,** Paul presented God as the Father of all believers, shown by God's sovereign authority and his loving care for his children. Paul calls Jesus **Lord,** meaning master, one who deserves obedience. The young Thessalonian church experienced God's grace and peace during a time of trial. This strengthened their faith, and made them an example to the rest of the believers in other cities across the empire.

ENCOURAGEMENT DURING PERSECUTION / 1:3-12

A few months earlier, Timothy had returned to check on the Thessalonian believers and had returned to Paul with the good news of their faith (1 Thessalonians 3:5-6). Paul had written 1 Thessalonians to express his great joy as well as to answer some questions. But some time had passed, and Paul had heard about some other problems in Thessalonica—the church was still facing persecution. False teachers were giving wrong information about the Second Coming, and some of the believers had stopped working in order to wait for Christ's return.

1:3 Paul had prayed that the Thessalonians' faith would deepen and that their love would grow and overflow (1 Thessalonians 3:10, 12; 4:10). In the months since he had last written them, Paul could see that their **faith** was **flourishing** and they were **all growing in love for each other.** That was quite a testament to the faith of these believers—especially considering the persecution they continued to endure (1:4; 1 Thessalonians 1:6). No wonder Paul **always** thanked **God** in his prayers for these believers, knowing that such thanksgiving was **right.** Paul was not flattering them; the praise he gave them, both in the last letter (1 Thessalonians 1:4-10) and here, was sincere. God had truly been working in these believers' lives.

1:4 Apparently, it was not Paul's pattern to **proudly tell God's other churches** about one group of believers in order to boast about certain characteristics. In the case of the Thessalonians, however, Paul sang their praises, just as others had already been doing (1 Thessalonians 1:7-10).

The word *hupomone*, translated **endurance,** is the same word used in 1 Thessalonians 1:3. It pictures not passive acceptance in the face of difficulty, but active strength against it, exhibited by **faithfulness.** The Thessalonian believers remained faithful to God even **in all the persecutions and hardships** they were **suffering.** Paul had been persecuted during his first visit to Thessalonica (Acts 17:5-9). No doubt those who had responded to his message and had become Christians were continuing to face persecution.

1:5-6 Persecution and suffering are unavoidable for those who want to follow the Lord (see John 15:20-21). Therefore, the fact that the Thessalonians were being allowed to suffer for their faith, and the fact that in doing so their faith, love, and hope were increasing and strengthening (1:3-4) was evidence that **God** was using **this persecution to show his justice.** Through suffering, God's people are strengthened. In suffering, they can remember that they would be made **worthy of his Kingdom.** Suffering is not a prerequisite to salvation, but suffering and subsequent faithfulness through suffering shows God's work in

believers' lives and thus their worthiness for his Kingdom.

Sufferings also set up the perpetrators for punishment. **In his justice,** God **will punish those who** were persecuting them. God will act with complete justice when he punishes sinners. God will see to it that those who inflicted persecution and suffering will themselves receive much worse.

1:7-8 Not only will God punish the evildoers, but he will also **provide rest** for those who were **being persecuted.** Paul placed himself and his companions along with the Thessalonian believers as people who needed "rest" from God. There are two dimensions of this "rest." Believers can be relieved in knowing that their sufferings are strengthening them, making them ready for Christ's Kingdom (1:5). They can also be relieved to know that all wrongs will be righted when God's final judgment is executed.

So when will this happen? While those enduring suffering would wish for a quick judgment, it may be that the payback does not occur in this life. But this will happen for sure **when the Lord Jesus appears from heaven.** The **flaming fire** is a picture of God's holy presence (Exodus 13:21; Deuteronomy 4:12, 24; Isaiah 66:15; Revelation 1:13-14), and the **mighty angels** are also described in Matthew 25:31; 1 Thessalonians 3:13; Revelation 5:11; 12:7.

When the Lord Jesus returns, he will bring **judgment on those who don't know God and on those who refuse to obey the Good News.** The act of punishment belongs to God alone; he will deliver the vengeance that sinners deserve.

1:9-10 Paul has explained when and who will be punished; this passage explains what that judgment will be. **They will be punished with everlasting destruction, forever separated from the Lord.** The word "punished" pictures what God will do to those who have been rebellious. At Christ's return, there will only be two groups of people. Those who belong to him and those who do not. Jesus told a parable about this; it is recorded in Matthew 25:31-46. There are no gray areas in God's judgment. Those who have not identified with Christ and confessed him as Lord will have no hope, no second chance, no other appeal (see 1 Thessalonians 5:3). The place of eternal destruction means eternal separation from God—being "separated" from his presence. The unbelievers will be banned or excluded from the presence of God, who is the Source of life. It is banishment from God—just what rebels deserve. The believers, persecuted and weak as they may be, however, have the Lord and **his glorious power** on their side. The power of the oppressors is meaningless when compared to the mighty power of God.

When Christ returns, he will **receive glory and praise from his holy people.** The day of grief for the rebellious will be a day of celebration for believers. The Thessalonian believers would **be among those praising him on that day**—as will everyone across the ages who has **believed** the message of salvation in Jesus Christ.

1:11-12 Paul and his coworkers kept on **praying** for the Thessalonian believers, just as Paul prayed for all the churches. Although the promise of future glory is sure, believers still have a battle here on earth and the need for constant prayer from fellow believers. What were Paul and his coworkers praying for? First, that **God** would **make** them **worthy of the life to**

which he called them. To be made "worthy" has the same meaning here as it did in 1:5. Salvation is sure, but the prospect of the glorious future should be an incentive to holy living—and believers will need one another's support and prayers as they seek to live out their faith. The "calling" from God is that his people become like Christ (Romans 8:29). This calling is a gradual, lifelong process that will be completed when we see Christ face to face (1 John 3:2). To be worthy of this calling means to want to do what is right and good.

Second, they were praying that God would **fulfill all** their **good intentions and faithful deeds** so that **everyone will give honor** to Jesus Christ. The ultimate goal of all believers ought to be to glorify Christ through their actions, words, thoughts, and motives. When believers live to honor Christ, Christ is honored in them.

This can happen **because of the undeserved favor of our God and Lord, Jesus Christ.** Believers cannot show Christ's glory or be glorified in him because of anything they can do— it is only because of God's grace. Only by God's grace did Jesus come to die for sinners; only by God's grace can people receive his sacrifice and be saved from their sins.

2 THESSALONIANS 2

EVENTS PRIOR TO THE LORD'S SECOND COMING / 2:1-12

Some of the Thessalonian believers seemed to have accepted some wrong teaching regarding Christ's Second Coming (2:2-3) and what would happen in the world before he returned. Paul had already taught them much when he was with them and had explained more in his first letter (1 Thessalonians 4–5). This letter tells of a time of great rebellion against God led by a man of lawlessness (the Antichrist). During this time God will remove all restraints on evil, and then he will execute his final judgment.

2:1-2 This introduces the main topic of this letter. He had already taught them **about the coming again of** the Lord **and how** all believers **will be gathered together to meet him.** Apparently, Paul had heard further questions from these believers, so he added more details about what would happen at Christ's Second Coming. Also, he knew that persecution was taking its toll on the believers (1 Thessalonians 1:6; 2 Thessalonians 1:4-7). So he wanted to teach them and encourage them.

Verse 2 describes one of the false teachings about Christ's Second Coming. Some were saying **that the day of the Lord has already begun.**

This final event of history has two aspects to it: (1) the last judgment on all evil and sin; (2) the final reward for faithful believers. At that time, God will intervene directly and dramatically in world affairs. Righteousness and truth will prevail, and Christ will judge sin and set up his eternal Kingdom. First, there will be much suffering, for evil will climax as the end draws near.

False teachers were saying that the judgment day had already begun. This caused many believers to wait expectantly for vindication and relief from suffering. These false teachers had claimed to have had **a vision, a revelation, or a letter supposedly** from Paul and his companions apparently stating what the false teachers were teaching. Paul does not identify the source of this false teaching any further, so we do not know.

When Christ didn't come and when suffering continued, the believers were becoming **shaken** and **troubled.** These words picture unsettled minds and a continuing state of anxiety. They certainly wondered if they had somehow missed out or if they were not going to be saved. Paul assured them that they should not be worried by these false teachers and should listen to him, instead. Paul's authority as an apostle and their relationship of trust with him should affirm that any teaching that contradicted what he had given them needed to be questioned. Paul had shown that he would answer the Thessalonians' questions directly himself or send one of his coworkers. At the end of this letter, Paul would sign with his own hand to authenticate this document.

Paul told them plainly that the day of the Lord had not yet come; three other events would have to happen first. (1) The rebellion must occur (2:3); (2) the man of lawlessness must be revealed (2:3); (3) the restraint of lawlessness must be removed (2:7).

2:3 The coming of the day of the Lord will be "like a thief in the night" (1 Thessalonians 5:2); even so, certain events will precede it. The final day of the Lord **will not come until there is a great rebellion against God and the man of lawlessness is revealed.** This "rebellion" will be a massive revolt against God. It may begin among those who believe in God and spread to all people who refuse to accept Christ. Thus, it will include Jews who abandon God and some members of the church whose faith is nominal. While rebellion against God seems widespread even today, as the coming of Christ nears, this apostasy and active opposition against God will intensify.

During the rebellion, a remarkable man will come into public view. He will have considerable power from Satan and will personify evil. Throughout history, certain individuals have epitomized evil and have been hostile to everything Christ stands for (see 1 John 2:18; 4:3; 2 John 7). These "antichrists" have lived in every generation, and others like them will continue to work their evil. Then, just before Christ's Second Coming, "the man of lawlessness," a completely evil man, will arise. He will be Satan's tool, equipped with Satan's power (2:9). This man will oppose all law, both God's moral laws, as well as civil laws. He will promote immorality and anarchy. This "lawless" man will be *the* Antichrist. He will have been in the world, but then he will rise to power and notoriety, shown by the word "revealed." The book of Revelation speaks of a "beast" that

symbolizes the Antichrist (Revelation 13:5-8). The beast symbolizes the Antichrist—not Satan, but someone under Satan's power and control (see also Revelation 16:13 and 19:20 where he is the second member of the false trinity). Satan's evil will culminate in a final Antichrist, a man who will focus all the powers of evil against Jesus Christ and his followers, bringing **destruction.** Yet even this man, for all the power that he will attain, is ultimately doomed to destruction (see Revelation 20:10).

God still reigns and his victory is certain. The evil man will be destroyed, but not before God uses him. During this time of great rebellion, the full extent of wickedness will be demonstrated and rebellion against God will be shown in all its horror and ugliness. Always, through all suffering throughout the ages, God is drawing people to himself, calling them to repent. This will continue during those last days.

2:4-5 This man of lawlessness will attempt, and even will seem to be able to, dethrone God and anything else that is worshiped (idols, nature, self), and then will demand worship and obedience to himself alone. The phrase, **position himself in the temple of God** pictures one who proclaims **that he himself is God.** Many have claimed such allegiance throughout history (Roman rulers, various political leaders) and many have been pointed out by others as being the Antichrist, but this one human, yet to come, will be the final, decisive personification of lawlessness, evil, and rebellion against God.

This description of the man of lawlessness is similar to the description of Antiochus Epiphanes, who was predicted in Daniel 11:36-37. It also refers to the "sacrilegious object" noted in Mark 13:14-19. This refers to the desecration of the Temple by God's enemies through pagan idolatry and sacrifice (see Deuteronomy 29:16-18; 2 Kings 16:3-4; 23:12-14). The first fulfillment of such an abomination occurred in 168 B.C. by Antiochus Epiphanes. He sacrificed a pig to Zeus on the sacred Temple altar. This act incited the Maccabean wars. The second fulfillment occurred when Jesus' prediction of the destruction of the Temple (Mark 13:2) came true. In A.D. 70, the Roman army would destroy Jerusalem and desecrate the Temple. Some scholars say that a third fulfillment is yet to come. This may look far forward to the end times and to the Antichrist. In the end times, the Antichrist will commit the ultimate sacrilege by setting himself up (perhaps having a statue erected) and ordering everyone to worship him. (See also Revelation 13:14-15.)

Apparently, Paul had taught the Thessalonians about the Second Coming of Christ and the end times. Either they had forgotten his teaching, or the false teachers had been confusing them.

2:6-7 In the present world—the world of the Thessalonians and the world today—two simultaneous events are happening. First, **this lawlessness is already at work secretly**, although it may not be clearly seen for what it is. The work that the Antichrist, the man of lawlessness, will do is already going on. "Secret" means something hidden, behind the scenes, but something God will reveal. "Lawlessness" is the hidden, subtle, underlying force from which all sin springs. Second, even though this power is working, so is the one who **is holding him back**. Civilization still has a modicum of decency through law enforcement, education, science, and reason. Although we are horrified by criminal acts, the world has yet to see the real horror of complete lawlessness. This will happen when **the one who is holding it back steps out of the way.**

Who (or what) "holds back" the man of lawlessness? It seems that the Thessalonians knew that answer (**you know**) from Paul's previous teaching. So Paul referred to it here, but did not repeat it. Commentators have considered three possibilities for the identity of this "restrainer": (1) government and law, which help to curb evil; (2) the ministry and activity of the church and the effects of the Good News; (3) the Holy Spirit. The Bible is not clear on the identity of this restrainer, only that he will not restrain forever. Then the man of lawlessness will be revealed and will do his evil work (as described in 2:3-4). Why will God allow this evil man to act with unrestrained wickedness? To show people and nations their own sinfulness and to show them by bitter experience the true alternative to the lordship of Christ. People totally without God can act no better than vicious animals.

2:8 After the one who restrains rampant evil is removed, **then the man of lawlessness will be revealed.** For a period of time, he will have great power and act with notorious evil (as noted in 2:2-4). Just as this man of lawlessness will be revealed in God's timing, however, so he will also be destroyed. There will be an end to this man's evil. Indeed, when **the Lord Jesus** returns, he **will consume** the Antichrist **with the breath of his mouth.** This picture comes from Isaiah 11:4, "He will rule against the wicked and destroy them with the breath of his mouth." No matter how powerful this evil man may become, he is no more than a flame to be blown out by the breath of the Lord.

A further picture is seen in the description that the man of lawlessness will be destroyed **by the splendor of** Christ's **coming.** As a mere breath renders the Antichrist powerless, so the very appearance of Christ on the scene will ruin him.

2:9-10 This verse answers the question that might have been plaguing the Thessalonians, and even modern readers. How will this one man become so powerful? How will he attain such notoriety and loyalty from the masses? The answer is that this man will be Satan's tool. **He will come to do the work of Satan with counterfeit power and signs and miracles.** Jesus had warned that "false messiahs and false prophets will rise up and perform great miraculous signs and wonders so as to deceive, if possible, even God's chosen ones" (Matthew 24:24). If even the numerous antichrists will have extraordinary powers (1 John 2:18), this one, who will be filled with Satan's power, will do signs that are even more extraordinary. But while Jesus and his followers did miracles of compassion for the purpose of bringing glory to God, the Antichrist will do miracles characterized by evil and deceit for the purpose of bringing glory to himself (see Revelation 13:13-14; 16:14; 19:20).

It will be this power that will **fool those who are on their way to destruction**—those who refused **to believe the truth that would save them.** But true Christians will stand firm because they understand what is happening and will not be turned away. The statement that they "refused" the truth shows that, at that point in time, God's offer of salvation will still be available. The evil let loose upon the world will be used by God as a last chance for many. The choice will be crystal clear. Because the Antichrist will have taken over every other religion (2:4), the only two options will be to worship Christ or to worship the Antichrist. The unbelievers in the world will be so enamored of this powerful person that they will choose to follow him—away from God and into eternal death.

2:11-12 Those who make the choice to follow the Antichrist will be confirmed in that choice by God who **will send great deception upon them, and they will believe all these lies.** They will continue to be deceived further and further—beyond simply believing the delusion—actively forwarding its cause. Again, the choice is made clear: over against "the truth" of the gospel (2:10) is "the lie" of the Antichrist. The truth that God is God versus the lie that the Antichrist is God.

That "God sends" this delusion shows his sovereignty in this entire event. At no point will God be out of control, even as Satan unleashes his power through the Antichrist. God's sovereignty is displayed in this way in Revelation 17:17, "For God has put a plan into their minds, a plan that will carry out his purposes. They will mutually agree to give their authority to the scarlet beast, and so the words of God will be fulfilled."

God will use the people's rebellion as a judgment against them. By their own free will they will choose to rebel. As condemnation on their sin, God will harden their hearts in unbelief. The result of the choice for "believing the lie" is that **they will be condemned.** The path toward condemnation is downhill and slippery. It begins

with fascination with evil and leads to an acceptance of the lie and simultaneous rejection of the truth, powerful delusions that lead one deeper into evil so that it is accepted and even enjoyed. At that point, people's hearts are hardened against God and his Word, for they do not feel any need for it.

BELIEVERS SHOULD STAND FIRM / 2:13-17

Having just painted the picture of a world taken over by evil, Paul now exhorts the believers to stand firm in their faith. Every passage in the New Testament about the Lord's return ends with ethical mandates, as found in this section and in chapter 3.

2:13 Once again, Paul and his companions paused to **thank God** for what he had done and was continuing to do through the Thessalonian believers. In contrast to people who will rebel against God and face eternal destruction, those who believe have a glorious future. **God chose the** Thessalonian believers **to be among the first to experience salvation;** they were among the early believers, the first in Thessalonica, and they had been chosen by God for that special privilege. Paul consistently taught that salvation begins and ends with God. The Thessalonian believers had been chosen by God from the beginning. Present and future persecution and suffering should not lead to panic. Instead, believers should stand firm.

2:14 God's "call" came to these Thessalonians through his human emissaries, Paul and his companions. God worked through Paul, Silas, Timothy, and others, who brought the Good News to the Thessalonians so they could **share in the glory** of the **Lord Jesus Christ.** The Thessalonians were facing persecution for their faith; Paul had just finished describing a time on earth of even more intense persecution. There was no doubt

about the outcome. Those who believe would share in Christ's glory when he comes to restore justice on the earth (see 1:5-10).

2:15 Paul knew that the Thessalonians would face pressure from persecutions, false teachers, worldliness, and apathy. They would be tempted to waver from the truth and even to leave the faith. **With all these things in mind,** Paul urged them to **stand firm and keep a strong grip on everything** that Paul and his companions had **taught.** The Thessalonians had received much teaching in person, and they had Paul's letters. They would need to hold on to the truth they had been taught.

2:16-17 Through **his special favor,** God and Christ **gave** the believers **everlasting comfort and good hope.** Christianity is not a faith of questions and worries—not a faith in which believers must wait until the end to see if they will make it. Instead, believers are given hope and encouragement of the certainty of God's promises. It always helps, however, to pray for believers everywhere—especially those facing persecution for their faith—that God would **comfort** them and give them **strength** to continue to do **good.**

2 THESSALONIANS 3

PAUL'S REQUEST FOR PRAYER / 3:1-5

Paul had been writing about the future, describing the coming of the Antichrist and the future days of rebellion and lawlessness. That man of evil has not yet come because he is being held back. Evil is at work in the world, but it is also being held in check. What does that mean for Christians? How are they to live in this present evil world, as they are preparing for the next?

3:1 Paul prayed regularly for the believers in the various churches, and he did not hesitate to ask for

their prayers in return. As he prepared to offer final words of advice, he first asked them to **pray for** him and his coworkers (the Greek word means "keep on praying"). The focus of Paul's desire was **that the Lord's message will spread rapidly and be honored wherever it goes.** The preaching of the Good News would result in honor being given to the Lord because of the marvelous results in the lives of those who believe. The Thessalonians had been an exemplary congregation (1 Thessalonians 1:6-10). Paul wanted them to pray for God's power to intervene in other places so that many would be saved and God would be glorified through it.

3:2 In addition to praying for more converts, Paul asked the believers to also pray that they would **be saved from wicked and evil people.** As the gospel message advances, it always faces severe opposition. The spiritual battle rages intensely for people's souls, and Satan does not easily let go of his own. Thus, the apostles needed prayer. If Paul asked for it, how much more should believers today pray for one another as they seek to share the gospel message—whether across the street or across the world. Paul's enemies were those who did not believe in the gospel message and were actively working against it.

3:3 At the end of his first letter (1 Thessalonians 5:24), Paul reminded the believers of God's faithfulness—he can be depended upon to keep his promises because he is loyal and he is constant. Because of that faithfulness, God would make them **strong** and **guard** them **from the evil one.** As the spiritual battle intensifies, the true enemy of all believers is really only one person—the "evil one," Satan himself. Because the Lord is faithful, he will protect his gospel message, and it will continue to spread across the world and achieve results. Because the Lord is faithful, he will strengthen and protect the believers.

This does not mean that they will never face difficulties; it just means that God is faithful. The result for all believers will be to spend eternity with God. That promise will never change.

Yet even so, prayer is a vital factor behind all of this activity. As the missionaries spread God's message, they understand that spiritual forces were at work—the faithful Lord with them, the evil one against them. They realized that they were not involved in a merely human endeavor. They were on the Lord's battlefields under his command, with his authority, knowing they would win. Yet they needed his guidance and the constant prayers of believers every step of the way.

3:4 Christ is faithful, but his followers must do their part in being obedient. Paul has confidence that the Thessalonian believers were **practicing the things** he had **commanded** them. His confidence rested not in the Thessalonians themselves, but in God who had chosen them. They had more than shown their obedience to the teachings of the apostles, even as they had experienced persecution. Believers at this time did not have the New Testament, so they had to listen carefully to the teachings of the apostles; therefore, Paul spoke of them doing what he and the other apostles "commanded" because their teaching came from God.

3:5 Paul's prayer for these believers was that **the Lord** would **bring** them **into an ever deeper understanding of the love of God and the endurance that comes from Christ.** Wanting the believers to move forward with commitment, Paul asked God to guide the believers as they meditated on God's love for them and on Christ's patient endurance. Such inner determination would enable them to face and overcome their difficulties.

AN EXHORTATION TO PROPER LIVING / 3:6-15
Besides the Second Coming, the topic of laziness among believers takes up the most space in the letter. The fact that Paul had already discussed this in his first letter shows that the problem had not been solved but had continued. This caused Paul great concern, so he gave stern commands.

3:6 Paul had already discussed the issue of idle Christians in the first letter, but apparently the problem had continued (1 Thessalonians 5:14). Perhaps Paul's instruction had not been strong enough, so this passage made it clear that his commands regarding idleness came **with the authority of our Lord Jesus Christ.** The first letter tells Christians to "warn those who are lazy" (5:14)—that is, the believers were to firmly admonish those who were *ataktos*, a word used for soldiers who would

not stay in the ranks. While everyone else was working and serving, they would not. Some were probably using the excuse of waiting for Christ to return. They may have considered working as too menial or as unspiritual, equivalent to laying up treasures on earth rather than in heaven. They may have been creating a problem by expecting wealthier people in the church to support them. But Paul was firm that these believers were not honoring their faith.

Paul's command goes a step further: no longer are believers told to "warn" these lazy people; they are told to **stay away from any Christian who lives in idleness and doesn't follow the tradition of hard work we gave you.** This does not refer to excommunication from the church, but to withdrawing intimate fellowship from them. By refusing to associate with these people, the Christians were rebuking them, hoping to get them to change their conduct. Basically, Paul was saying, "Cut off their support!"

3:7-8 Paul's first letter describes how he and his companions had worked during their stay in Thessalonica. They **were never lazy** and had not taken food **without paying for it.** They did not want to be a **burden** to anyone but wanted to pay their own way. Paul and his companions probably enjoyed hospitality at various times during their ministry; Paul's point was that he did not expect hospitality or impose it on anyone. Trained as a tentmaker (Acts 18:3), Paul had worked at this job, and then took time to preach the gospel, teach, and build up a body of believers in this city. Because the people who had brought the gospel to the Thessalonians had worked to not be a burden on anyone, so should the new believers in the city **follow** that **example.**

3:9 Paul and the other missionaries had **the right** to expect lodging and food in exchange for the message they had brought (Luke 10:7; 1 Corinthians 9:7-14). Though most traveling preachers did this, Paul did not want to be a burden on others. He did not want to appear to be preaching in order to be housed and fed. In some places he did accept such gifts, but in Thessalonica he did not. So strong was his passion for spreading the gospel message that he would not allow anything to hinder its progress. If it seemed that to accept food and lodging would hinder his effectiveness as a minister of the gospel, then he would gladly waive his rights and work to pay his way. In this way, the missionaries had made themselves **an example to follow.** Those who share the gospel message with others must not only speak the message but live it as well; they must be examples worthy of imitation.

3:10 Not only had Paul and Silas been an example of Christian living to the Thessalonians, but they had also explained clearly what was expected. The **rule** regarding laziness had been given right from the start. They had said at that time: **Whoever does not work should not eat.** The saying may have been coined anywhere and may have been a common theme among laborers, as they worked together or as they trained apprentices. Paul took and applied it to the Christian life so as to show

believers that laziness, in any form, is not acceptable. Because Christians are known for their kindness, some might want to take advantage of them. Paul sternly reprimanded such thinking. Those who refused to work should not be given food. If they can earn money for their food, they should do so without depending on others to care for them.

Be careful not to use this verse on those who are willing but unable to work. It is too easy to glibly dismiss the difficult conditions of those with disabilities, lack of job training, or lack of job availability. Paul's harsh words are for people who are unwilling to work when they have both the ability and the opportunity.

3:11-12 Here is the reason for Paul's hard-hitting words on this topic of laziness. Word had reached Paul in Corinth **that some of** the believers in Thessalonica were **idle, refusing to work and wasting time meddling in other people's business.** So Paul was not the only one concerned about this issue; the believers in Thessalonica had felt it so important that they had notified Paul. Perhaps they had taken Paul's advice in the first letter but had seen no results, so they wanted him to deal directly with these people.

It is possible that these idle people were being idle for "spiritual" reasons. Some people in the Thessalonian church may have been saying that people should set aside their responsibilities, quit work, do no future planning, and just wait for the Lord's return. Or they may have thought that labor was beneath them and wanted to spend their time being spiritual. But not being busy only made them busybodies. Their lack of activity was leading them into sin. They had become a burden to the church, which was supporting them; they were wasting time that could have been used for helping others.

These church members may have thought that they were being more spiritual by not working, but Paul sternly commanded them to **settle down and get to work** earning their **own living.** Paul did not mince words with these people. That Paul made these commands **in the name of the Lord Jesus** reveals his understanding of his authority as an apostle—even as a personal representative of the Lord himself.

3:13 To those hard-working believers, those who were not lazy, Paul told them to **never get tired of doing good.** In contrast to the idlers who had persisted in their idleness even since Paul's last letter, these hard-working believers should not let the idlers cause them to become dispirited in their work. Paul knew that the believers could become discouraged when they tried to do right and received no word of thanks or saw no tangible results. But Paul challenged all the believers to keep on doing good and to trust God for the results.

3:14-15 Paul repeated his direction regarding this issue: **Take note of those who refuse to obey** and **stay away from them** (see 3:6). The hope was that the idle people would become **ashamed** of their actions and finally become so hungry (when no one would support and feed them) that they would be forced back to work. Paul was not advising coldness or cruelty, for these people were not **enemies.** They were misguided and mistaken, but they were not to be thrown out of the church. They needed a good dose of tough love—the kind of love that should be shown **to a Christian who needs to be warned.**

PAUL'S FINAL GREETINGS / 3:16-18
Paul knew that the church would need to deal with false teaching regarding the Second Coming (as discussed in chapter 2) and with those members who were not living as they should (as discussed in chapter 3). Paul had issued teachings and commands, but the believers would have to carry them out. In his closing words, Paul prayed for peace for the church so that they could handle these issues and then continue strong in the work of the Kingdom.

3:16 Just as Paul began his letter with "grace and peace" (1:2), so he ended it. Paul referred to **the Lord of peace** often at the end of his letters (see Romans 15:33; 16:20; 2 Corinthians 13:11; Philippians 4:9). The peace God gives does not mean absence of conflict (John 14:27; 16:33). The peace God gives is confident assurance in any circumstance. Not only did the believers have peace, but they also had the Lord himself, for he would **give them his peace no matter what** happened.

3:17 Usually Paul would dictate his letters to a scribe, but often he would end the letter with a note in his own handwriting (see also 1 Corinthians 16:21; Galatians 6:11; Colossians 4:18; Philemon 19). This assured the recipients that false teachers were not writing letters in Paul's name—as was a concern in Thessalonica (see 2:2). It also gave the letters a personal touch.

3:18 Paul often closed his letters with a prayer of grace for the believers. This closing is identical with his first letter (1 Thessalonians 5:28). Paul wanted his readers to continue to experience **the grace of our Lord Jesus Christ.** "Grace" is undeserved favor from God to his people. This grace from God would help believers in their daily walk with him.

1 TIMOTHY

INTRODUCTION

The wise coach gives his junior quarterback valuable game time—the experience will prepare the young athlete for the starting role next fall . . . or sooner. The wise employer watches for promising young employees, then helps them learn new skills and assume greater responsibilities. Wise parents nurture and teach their children, helping them mature and grow into responsible adults. Wise leaders serve as mentors to emerging, potential leaders.

The next generation holds a vital position in every family, institution, movement, or church—for leadership, vision, life . . . for its future. The apostle Paul knew this truth.

Paul began to follow Christ as an adult. Through a dramatic confrontation on the way to capture and imprison the hated believers in Jesus, Paul's life changed dramatically (Acts 9:1-19). Soon he became known as a fearless champion of the Christian cause, a peerless evangelist, and a pioneering missionary. With strong commitment, deep courage, and boundless energy, Paul went to the ends of his world, preaching and teaching the Good News of Christ to all who would listen. Although thousands had responded to the gospel message and churches had been planted and were growing, Paul knew that the future of the Christian movement would depend on new leadership. Given the hostile environment of the Roman world and the advancing age of the apostles, in a short time the first generation of Christian leaders would be gone. Then who would direct, guide, evangelize, and spread the Word? So Paul encouraged younger coworkers like Timothy and Titus to "teach these great truths to trustworthy people who are able to pass them on to others" (2 Timothy 2:2).

AUTHOR

Paul: the great apostle and missionary of the church.

The first line of this letter to Timothy names Paul as the author (1:1). Paul and Timothy probably met on Paul's first missionary journey (Timothy accompanied Paul on his second journey) when Paul preached at Lystra (Acts 14:6-7). Timothy's grandmother and mother had come to faith first and had been a great influence on him (2 Timothy 1:5; 3:14-15). Their faithful witness and instruction in the Scriptures prepared Timothy also to follow Christ. In addition, Timothy must have seen Paul stoned at Lystra for his faith, dragged out of the city and left for dead, and then return to life after the prayers of the believers. All of these factors must have had a profound effect on Timothy, convincing him that Jesus was, in fact, the promised Messiah. Paul calls Timothy his "child" or "son"

(1 Corinthians 4:17; 2 Timothy 2:1), implying a relationship as Timothy's spiritual father.

Beyond leading young Timothy to Christ, Paul became Timothy's mentor, bringing him along as a fellow missionary and appointing him to a leadership position in the church. Ever since meeting in Lystra, Paul and Timothy were close, as friends, brothers in Christ, and partners in the ministry. In fact, Paul's last known message is his second letter to Timothy, in which he asks Timothy to visit him in prison as soon as possible (2 Timothy 4:9). Paul's letters to Timothy stand as a powerful witness to the close relationship these men enjoyed as Paul gave Timothy encouragement, guidance, and strong instruction.

For more about Paul, see the Author section in the Introduction to the book of Romans.

DATE AND SETTING

Written to the churches in Ephesus and the surrounding area approximately A.D. 64 from Rome or Macedonia (possibly Philippi) just prior to Paul's final imprisonment.

The gospel had come to Ephesus through Apollos, an outstanding orator and young believer (Acts 18:24). But when Paul visited the city for the first time (on his third missionary journey), he found many who had an incomplete faith (Acts 19:4). So Paul told the Ephesians about Jesus (Acts 19:5). They responded to his teaching and received the Holy Spirit (Acts 19:6). Paul stayed and ministered in Ephesus for more than two years, first in the synagogue, and then in the lecture hall of Tyrannus (Acts 19:8-10). After a riot ensued, instigated by Demetrius the silversmith, Paul gave final words of encouragement to the believers and left for Macedonia (Acts 19:23–20:1). A few months later, before leaving the area, Paul met with the Ephesian elders at Miletus. During this meeting, Paul warned the Ephesian elders about false teachers who would try to draw believers away from the truth (Acts 20:28-31). After a time of challenge and prayer and an emotional farewell, Paul sailed to Jerusalem (Acts 20:13–21:1). Paul had a very warm and close relationship with the church at Ephesus, and he was concerned for their spiritual well-being.

Although nothing more is said about Ephesus in the book of Acts, Paul probably visited the city after his release from his first Roman imprisonment (see his possible itinerary below). During this visit (with Timothy), he discovered that a number of spiritual problems had arisen during his absence. Paul and Timothy stayed in Ephesus for a while to teach and to straighten things out. When Paul had to leave for Macedonia, he left Timothy there as his representative to lead the church (1:3).

The area surrounding Ephesus probably had a number of young churches, not just one, with each church led by an elder. Thus, Paul did not appoint Timothy as the "elder" of the churches, but rather as his representative, carrying his apostolic authority to instruct the church (2:1-15) and to appoint elders and deacons (3:1-13).

AUDIENCE

Timothy and the church at large.

Timothy was born and reared in Lystra in Lycaonia. Timothy's mother, Eunice, and grandmother Lois were devout Jews who had come to faith in Christ (Acts 16:1; 2 Timothy 1:5), but his father was a Greek. Evidently the father was not a Jewish proselyte or a convert to Christianity, since Timothy had not been circumcised (Acts 16:3). Timothy's mother and grandmother had carefully taught him the Old Testament Scriptures (2 Timothy 3:15), so he was open to the gospel when he heard Paul preach on his first visit to Lystra (Acts 14:6-7).

Because of Timothy's growth in the faith and his spiritual gifts, Paul chose him to become a partner in spreading the gospel on the second missionary journey (Acts 16:1-3). Paul also may have seen Timothy as one who was free from the prejudices of many Jews—Timothy had a mixed family (a Jewish mother and a Greek father). To avoid a problem with the Jews in the area, Paul circumcised Timothy before they left (Acts 16:3). Paul also ordained Timothy at this time (4:14).

Although Paul trusted Timothy completely and expected him to be a strong leader in the church, Paul also was very aware of Timothy's weaknesses. Timothy was very young and, evidently, was shy and hesitant. So Paul warned him against being intimidated by his opponents and their teachings (4:12; 2 Timothy 1:5, 7; 3:10; see also 1 Corinthians 16:10-11). In addition, Timothy may have had stomach problems (5:23).

As requested, Timothy left his family in Lystra to travel with Paul. On that journey Timothy helped establish the churches at Philippi, Thessalonica, and Berea (Acts 16:1–17:14). When Paul left Berea early to go to Athens, he left Timothy and Silas behind. But Paul sent word for them to join him as soon as possible (Acts 17:13-15).

Soon after Timothy arrived at Athens, Paul sent him to Thessalonica to strengthen the faith of the believers there (1 Thessalonians 3:1-2). Later, Timothy rejoined Paul at Corinth and helped establish that church (Acts 18:5). The Bible doesn't say whether Timothy traveled with Paul from Corinth to Ephesus and then to Caesarea, Jerusalem, Antioch, and back to Ephesus (Acts 18:18–19:1). We do read, however, that Timothy worked with Paul at Ephesus (Acts 19:22). Then Paul sent him (and Erastus) to Greece to minister to churches there and to prepare the way for a possible visit by Paul, while Paul stayed at Ephesus (Acts 19:22; 1 Corinthians 4:17; 16:10). Before Paul left Ephesus, however, Timothy rejoined him (Romans 16:21; 2 Corinthians 1:1). Then they traveled together to Macedonia, to Achaia, back to Macedonia, and on to Asia (Acts 20:1-5).

The book of Acts makes no mention of Timothy during the record of Paul's trip to Jerusalem, arrest, two-year imprisonment at Caesarea, and voyage to Rome (Acts 21:1–28:16). We know that either Timothy was with Paul during those years or he rejoined Paul at Rome during the early months of imprisonment, because we read that he was with Paul in Rome (Philippians 1:1; 2:19; Colossians 1:1; Philemon 1).

During Paul's first imprisonment, he planned to send Timothy to Philippi (Philippians 2:19-23). Paul may not have done this, however, because of his early release. After Paul's release from prison, Timothy traveled with Paul to Ephesus, where he was left to care for the church (1:3—see the possible itinerary above). Although Paul asked Timothy to visit him in prison during the second imprisonment, there is no evidence that Timothy made it there before Paul was executed.

Because of the reference in Hebrews to Timothy being out of prison (Hebrews

13:23-24), there is speculation that Timothy had been imprisoned in Rome and then later released. According to tradition, Timothy was martyred during the reign of either Domitian or Nerva.

OCCASION AND PURPOSE

False teachers and potential divisions at Ephesus and a possible delay in Paul's arrival to the area. Paul wanted to encourage and instruct Timothy about the organization of a local church and to help him deal with false doctrines.

Having been released from his first Roman imprisonment and apparently on his way to Asia Minor, Paul traveled to the island of Crete and left Titus there to finish organizing the churches (Titus 1:5). Then Paul went to Ephesus, where he was joined by Timothy, who evidently had returned from Philippi (Philippians 2:19-23). Paul and Timothy discovered that heretical teachers were spreading false teachings, just as Paul had predicted would happen (Acts 20:29-30). These false teachers were preying especially on women, new believers who were enjoying unprecedented freedom in Christ to study the Bible and be involved in worship.

As he left Ephesus, Paul left Timothy behind as his representative to reorganize the church there (1:3). Evidently Paul had planned to see Timothy again, where he could have instructed him in person. But Paul was delayed, so he wrote his instructions in the epistle we know as 1 Timothy (3:14-15).

Although 1 Timothy is addressed to one individual, undoubtedly the contents of the letter were meant for the church at large. The epistle is filled with exhortations for the whole church, not just personal matters. Paul warned about false teachers (1:3-7; 6:3-10), gave instructions for worship (2:1-15) and how to deal with various groups in the church (5:1-21), and explained how to choose elders and deacons (3:1-13). Paul gave special instructions about how women should behave in the church because they were susceptible to the false teachings and because many were flaunting their new Christian freedom (2:9-15).

First Timothy is also a letter of encouragement for a young pastor who must have been intimidated by older and more mature members. Paul told Timothy not to let his age limit his ministry (4:12) and to boldly exercise his gifts (4:14-16).

MESSAGE

Paul's first letter to Timothy affirms their relationship (1:2). Paul begins his fatherly advice, warning Timothy about false teachers (1:3-11) and urging him to hold on to his faith in Christ (1:12-20). Next, Paul considers public worship, emphasizing the importance of prayer (2:1-7) and order in church meetings (2:8-15). This leads to a discussion of the qualifications of church leaders—elders and deacons. Here Paul lists specific criteria for each office (3:1-16).

Paul speaks again about false teachers, telling Timothy how to recognize them and respond to them (4:1-16). Next, he gives practical advice on pastoral care to the young and old (5:1, 2), widows (5:3-16), elders (5:17-25), and slaves (6:1, 2). Paul concludes by exhorting Timothy to guard his motives (6:3-10), to stand firm in his faith (6:11, 12), to live above reproach (6:13-16), and to minister faithfully (6:17-21).

The main themes in the book of 1 Timothy include: *Sound Doctrine, Public Worship, Church Leadership, Caring Church,* and *Personal Discipline.*

Sound Doctrine (1:3-11; 4:1-10; 6:3-5). Paul's first challenge to Timothy and the Ephesian believers was to combat the false teachers who had infiltrated the church. Paul warned Timothy about these heretics three times in this letter. After each warning, Paul exhorted Timothy to cling tightly to the faith, to be strong, and to live rightly (1:18-19; 4:9-16; 6:11-21). The exact nature of the heresy is unclear from the text, but Paul referred to myths and spiritual pedigrees (1:4), a strain of legalism (4:3), unhealthy desire to quibble (6:4), and teaching for personal, financial gain (6:5). Paul urged Timothy to combat the false teachings by confronting the false teachers (4:6; 6:12) and by having nothing to do with them or their ideas (4:7). Paul also urged Timothy to have love (1:5; 6:11), a sincere and strong faith (1:5, 19; 6:12), a clear conscience (1:5, 19), and a godly life (4:7; 6:11). The greatest weapon against heresy is sound doctrine (1:10; 4:16; 6:3)—holding to the truth and living it. Sound doctrine is also high on the list of qualities needed in elders and deacons (3:9).

IMPORTANCE FOR TODAY. The only way to identify what is false is to know the truth. God's truth is contained in his word, the Bible. Thus our theology (that is, our doctrine, what we believe) should be consistent with what the Bible says. Unless we are grounded in the Word, we will be susceptible to any number of false teachings. In addition to being well grounded, we also should avoid anyone who twists the words of the Bible for his or her own purpose. And we should confront and expose false teaching and teachers whenever we find them. How well do you know God's word? Be a student of the Bible, reading, studying, and applying it. And pay careful attention to "sound doctrine" so that you will be able to identify false teaching and stand against it.

Public Worship (2:1-15). Beyond the issue of false teachers, Paul's next area of concern for church life was worship. Paul began by emphasizing the necessity and centrality of prayer. Next, Paul discussed the conduct of women in worship. Evidently the actions of some women had been disruptive. Paul explained that although they were enjoying new freedom in Christ to study the Bible and to worship with men, women should not rush into leadership or flaunt their freedom (2:9-15). In both issues, Paul's focus was unity. The implication is that there were potential or real divisions in the Ephesian church that threatened to disrupt worship.

IMPORTANCE FOR TODAY. People attend worship services for many reasons: some come out of habit; others make it a social occasion; some simply want to be seen; a few are so eager to teach and lead that they eagerly follow false teachers with hollow promises. But any motive that does not flow from sincere devotion to Christ holds potential for trouble in the church. Women and men should worship with humility and submission, praying together for God's direction and for the needs of others. What draws you to worship? How often do you pray with your brothers and sisters in the faith?

Church Leadership (3:1-16). Paul gave specific instructions concerning the qualifications for church leaders so that the church might honor God and operate smoothly. Again, the fact that this section has such prominence in the letter seems to imply that less than qualified men were leading the various congregations (or were aspiring to be leaders). In fact, it is likely that the false teachers were former and current leaders in the church. As Paul's representative and with apostolic authority, Timothy was to make sure that church leaders had spiritual maturity, specific spiritual gifts, sound theology, a solid family life, and a good reputation.

IMPORTANCE FOR TODAY. There is no more important role than church leadership; therefore, those selected to fill leadership positions in local churches must be of the highest caliber, wholly committed to Christ and strong in their faith. If you are a new or young Christian, your first priority should be to develop your Christian character. Don't be anxious to hold a church leadership position. May your motive be to seek God, not to fulfill your own ambition.

Caring Church (5:1-20; 6:1-2, 17-19). Jesus told his disciples that the world would know that they were his followers by their love for each other (John 13:35). The greatest witness the Ephesian believers could make for Christ in their world would be as a caring church. But the command to love must result in specific actions. So Paul outlined for Timothy the way the church should treat older men (5:1), younger men (5:1), older women (5:2), younger women (5:2), widows (5:3-6, 9-16), and church elders (5:17-20), and how slaves should respond to their masters (6:1-2). In addition, Paul encouraged Timothy to challenge rich members to invest their wealth in helping others (6:17-19).

IMPORTANCE FOR TODAY. The church has a responsibility to care for the needs of all its members, especially the sick, the poor, and the widowed. Caring must go beyond good intentions. Caring for the family of believers demonstrates our Christlike attitude and exhibits genuine love to nonbelievers. What plan does your church have to care for members in need? What can you do to help those who are suffering and struggling? Look for ways to put Christ's love into action in your church and community.

Personal Discipline (4:11-16; 5:21-25; 6:6-16, 20-21). Paul knew that it took discipline to be an effective church leader. Timothy, like the elders, had to guard his motives, minister faithfully, and live righteously. Paul told Timothy to do what God has called him to do despite his young age. In fact, Timothy should set an example of spirituality and right living (4:11-12). Paul also told Timothy to diligently exercise his spiritual gifts, preaching, teaching, and leading (4:13-16). As God's man and Paul's representative, Timothy must keep himself pure, avoiding worldly temptations, especially the love of money (5:21-25; 6:6-10). Finally, Paul urged Timothy to be disciplined by keeping his eyes on Christ (6:11-16) and refusing to become sidetracked by endless, empty discussions (6:20-21).

IMPORTANCE FOR TODAY. All church leaders must keep morally and spiritually fit. To stay in good spiritual shape, you must stay focused on Christ and on your calling, discipline yourself to study God's word and to obey it, and put your spiritual abilities to work. What distracts you from serving Christ wholeheartedly? What has God called you to do to serve him? Be an example to others of how a mature Christian should live.

OUTLINE OF 1 TIMOTHY

1 TIMOTHY 1

GREETINGS FROM PAUL / 1:1-2

Paul wrote these instructions to Timothy, a young pastor who was also Paul's associate.
But they were certainly directed to a wider audience. Paul wanted the believers in Ephesus
to comply with his commands through his representative, Timothy. Because Paul addressed
the requirements of various roles within the local church, his directions continue to apply
to church leaders today.

1:1 Apostle comes from the Greek word *apostolos*,
meaning "one who is sent." **Paul** was an apostle
appointed personally by **Christ Jesus** himself. His
commission to this position came directly from
God on the road to Damascus (see 1 Corinthians
9:1; 15:8). The title **apostle** was basically reserved
for certain followers of Christ who had accompanied Jesus and had seen the risen Lord. Paul presented this important credential of apostleship in
most of his letters as a foundation for his instructions. Paul expected to be heard because he represented Jesus Christ.

Paul calls God **our Savior**. Paul used the
phrase "our Savior" six times in the letters to
Timothy and Titus (see 1 Timothy 1:1; 2:3; 4:10;
Titus 1:3; 2:10; 3:4). Paul may have used this
particular Greek word, *soter*, because, at the time,
the cruel emperor Nero applied it to himself.
The apostle would not have hesitated to repudiate
Nero's claim. Paul reminded his readers who the
true Savior was.

Paul calls Christ Jesus **our hope**. Our hope
rests in Jesus Christ. He is the embodiment of our
faith, the basis for our eternal life. When we place
our hope in Christ, we are not pacified with vague
"maybes," rather we are given certainties. We
"hope" for what we already know is ours.

1:2 Paul addressed many of his letters to churches
across the Roman Empire, and these letters were
meant to be read aloud to all the believers. This letter, although **written to Timothy**, was also meant to
be read to the entire congregation in the church at
Ephesus (and beyond) (see 1:3). First Timothy has
been called the first of the "Pastoral" Epistles (1 and
2 Timothy and Titus). All of Paul's letters express
pastoral concerns, but these three relate specifically
to local church issues. Paul and Timothy had developed a special bond, like father and son. Paul probably led Timothy to the Lord, so he was a **true child
in the faith**. For more on Timothy, see the Audience
section in the Introduction.

Paul used **grace** and **peace** as a standard greeting
in all of his letters. However, it is only in his letters to
Timothy that he used **mercy**. "Mercy" carries with it
the Old Testament picture of God's loving-kindness.
God's mercy helps us day by day. Paul knew that
Timothy was facing a difficult situation in Ephesus,
so he added the word **mercy** to reassure Timothy of
God's protection and guidance. By using the phrase,
God our Father and Christ Jesus our Lord, Paul
pointed to Jesus as a full person of the Godhead.
Both God the Father and Christ the Lord are coequal
in providing the resources of grace, mercy, and peace.
Paul recognized the full deity of Jesus.

WARNINGS AGAINST FALSE TEACHINGS / 1:3-11

After communicating volumes with his brief greeting, Paul abruptly turned his attention to
one of the immediate reasons for his letter—Timothy's struggle with false teachers. Paul had
left Timothy in Ephesus as a personal deterrent to those who were promoting their own brands
of religion. To help Timothy, Paul reminded him of the central points in the conflict, then
followed with a personal comparison between himself and the false teachers (1:12-16).

1:3 Paul first visited **Ephesus** on his second missionary journey (Acts 18:19-21). Later, on his third

missionary journey, he stayed there for almost
three years (Acts 19). Ephesus (along with Rome,

Corinth, Antioch, and Alexandria) was a major city in the Roman Empire. Ephesus was a center for the commerce, politics, and religions of Asia Minor, and the location of the temple dedicated to the goddess Artemis. Paul left Timothy in the troubled Ephesian church while he traveled on to Macedonia, and then wrote to his young protégé from there.

Paul gave Timothy a difficult task. It seems that the rather timid disciple may have been reluctant, for Paul gave strong commands and loving encouragement to young Timothy. He was to be undaunted and unintimidated by those teachers (who were probably older men, see 4:12) who were **teaching wrong doctrine;** that is, doctrine other than the teaching of Jesus, the apostles, and the Old Testament. The English word **doctrine** came to mean the central truths, or principles, of a philosophy or religion. Paul used the term in writing to Timothy to refer to the unchanging truths of the gospel. No one was at liberty to change that doctrine.

1:4 What were these **myths and spiritual pedigrees?** There are two possibilities: (1) The church at Ephesus may have been troubled by the same type of heresy that threatened the church at Colosse—the teaching that to be acceptable to God, a person had to discover a certain hidden knowledge and had to worship angels (Colossians 2:8, 18). (2) Thinking that it would aid in their salvation, some Ephesians constructed mythical stories based on Old Testament history or genealogies. Perhaps they placed too much emphasis on Jewish writings such as the Book of Jubilees.

These myths and pedigrees only served to promote **arguments** and lead to discussion about ideas that did not come from Scripture but from the minds of the false teachers. This, in turn, did not **help people live a life of faith in God** because it took valuable time away from teaching the truth of Scripture and spreading the gospel. Therefore, Paul urged Timothy to remain in Ephesus, instead of traveling on with him, in order to stifle the false teachers, who were motivated by their own interests rather than Christ's.

1:5 Paul expanded his **instruction** to Timothy by reminding him and anyone else who would read the letter that the correction of the false teachers would do them good, not harm. The false teachers were motivated by mere curiosity and a desire to gain prestige as intellectuals. In contrast, genuine Christian teachers are **filled with love.** There are three sources of real love:

1. In Matthew 5:8, Jesus said, "God blesses those whose hearts are pure." A **pure heart** is devoted

to God and free from guilt and corruption. We must keep ourselves morally straight. God purifies us, but there is action we must take to keep morally fit. Daily application of God's word has a purifying effect on our heart and mind. It enables us to love freely.
2. In order to love properly, our **conscience** must be **clear.** First, it must be clean from unconfessed sin so that guilt doesn't hinder us. Second, our motives must be free from pride and personal gain. Then we can love openly.
3. When we attempt to love others without **sincere faith** in Christ, our efforts to minister become hollow and self-serving. Sincere faith enables us to love genuinely.

The commands and instructions in this letter to Timothy reveal Paul's desire to maintain the purest truth in all the church's teachings. As a mother nourishes her child with pure foods, so Paul nourished the infant church with only pure teaching—the truth of God's word. He focused on the truth and love of the gospel (see 1 Corinthians 13).

1:6-7 Paul wrote against those who wanted to be **teachers of the law of Moses.** These men taught strange philosophical theories and ideas loosely based on the Pentateuch (the first five books of the Old Testament). These men were either Gentiles who were impressed with Judaism or Jews who did not know much but wanted to gain respect. The false teachers at Ephesus had constructed vast speculative systems, and then they argued about the minor details of their wholly imaginary ideas! They wandered away from the gospel, the truth, and love and slipped into meaningless drivel that helped no one and, in fact, hurt the church.

1:8 The false teachers wanted to become famous as teachers of God's law, but they misunderstood the law's purpose. The law was not meant to give believers a list of commands for every occasion, but to show unbelievers their sin and bring them to God. God's law is also important for believers. To use the law **as God intended** means understanding that God's law gives direction for living a holy life. In Exodus 20, God shows his people the true function and beauty of his laws. The commandments were designed to lead Israel to a life of practical holiness. In these commandments people could see the nature of God and his plan for how they should live. Galatians 2:11-21 shows us that God's law offers direction, not justification. Paul wrote in Romans 7:12, "The law itself is holy," but following the law can never make us acceptable to God.

1:9-11 The law exists **not for people who do what is right,** but for those who continue in their sin.

The list Paul includes follows the order of the Ten Commandments in Exodus 20. The first set of sinners corresponds to the first four commandments (Exodus 20:1-11):

- **the disobedient**—who cannot be taught
- **the rebellious**—who cannot be disciplined
- **the ungodly**—who show no reverence for God
- **the sinful**—who **consider nothing sacred and defile what is holy**

The second set violates the next six commandments (Exodus 20:12-16):

- **those who murder their father or mother**— the ultimate act of dishonoring one's parents
- **those who murder other people**—breaking the command not to murder
- **those who are sexually immoral or homosexual**—dealing with adultery and all sexual sin
- **slave traders**—also translated "kidnappers," picturing the worst form of theft

- **liars and oath breakers**—those who violate the commandment not to bear false witness
- **those who do anything else that contradicts the right teaching**—covers anything that might be missed.

Paul had been **entrusted** with this **Good News** (Acts 9:15-19; 1 Thessalonians 2:4; Titus 1:3). This call became Paul's life mission as he preached the gospel across the Roman Empire, including Ephesus, where this letter was directed (Acts 20:17-27). All who hear, believe, and accept this "right teaching" have also been entrusted with it.

In short, the law is meant to reveal our sin, but using it as guidelines for our response to God leaves us no better off than the false teachers. The law has a descriptive, not a prescriptive, role. It brings us face-to-face with our problem but does not tell us how to solve it. The Good News challenges us to respond in faith to God, who, through Christ, will forgive us our sins.

PAUL'S GRATITUDE FOR GOD'S MERCY / 1:12-17

In the previous paragraph Paul included a hard listing of sinful behaviors. But his reason was not for self-righteousness—pointing out other people's sins to make himself look better. In the face of our tendency to despair when confronted with our own sinfulness, Paul could cheerfully say, "Well, just look at how desperate I was, and what God's mercy has done for me!" Paul was convinced that if God could save him, then God could save anyone.

1:12-13 His catalog of common sins reminded Paul of his own sin (he called himself the "worst" of sinners, 1:15). But instead of allowing that memory to overwhelm him, he overflowed with gratefulness that God had considered him **trustworthy** and had appointed him to **serve** in spreading the Good News of salvation to his fellow Jews and to the Gentiles (see Acts 9:15; 11:25-26; 13:1-3). Paul was certainly **thankful,** for at one time he **used to scoff at the name of Christ.** Paul did not exaggerate his past performance. Scripture reveals Paul as an archenemy of Christians (Acts 8:1, 3; 9:1; 22:4; 26:9, 11; Galatians 1:13), that he **hunted down** God's **people, harming them in every way** he could. Paul persecuted Christians because he sincerely believed that he was serving God by stamping out this distortion of his beloved Jewish faith. Despite all of his knowledge as a learned Pharisee (Acts 23:6), Paul remained in **ignorance** about Jesus' true identity and stubbornly remained in **unbelief,** even after seeing the unwavering faith of Stephen and the other Christians whom he persecuted and perhaps even killed. Paul had the

chance to believe, but missed it. Yet God came to Paul even as he set out to capture more Christians, offering grace, mercy, and a new start.

1:14 Paul had blasphemed Jesus Christ, denied the Christian faith, and hated Christians; but God's grace had overcome it all, filling Paul **completely with faith and the love of Christ Jesus.** God supplied what Paul lacked, and not only supplied it, but gave it to him in exceeding abundance. In order to express the overwhelming sense of God's kindness and grace, Paul coined a compound word, *huperpleonazein,* meaning "to superabound." God's undeserved favor toward us is always greater than any words we may use to describe it.

1:15 This **true saying** is a nonnegotiable truth. We are not asked to consider, but to fully accept. We are invited to submit rather than question. This is truth and **everyone should believe it: Christ Jesus came into the world to save sinners.** Paul summarized and personalized the Good News: Jesus didn't come merely to show us how to live a better life or to challenge us to be better people. He came to offer us salvation that leads to eternal life. No matter how entrenched your sin, Christ can save you. Have you accepted his offer?

Although Paul was a deeply religious Jew, zealous for his faith, he realized that in his ignorance, unbelief, and desire to destroy the Christian faith, he was indeed **the worst** of sinners. We think of Paul as a great hero of the faith, but Paul never saw himself that way because he remembered his life before he met Christ. Paul recognized both that he had been a sinner and that he was now saved by grace. He recognized his past, but did not wallow in it. Humility and gratitude should mark the life of every Christian. Never forget that you too are a sinner saved by grace.

1:16 Jesus came to this zealous persecutor, not striking him with judgment (as some might expect), but offering him **mercy.** Looking back, Paul realized Jesus' **great patience** in dealing with him; and what an example of mercy Paul gave to us! Jesus offers us mercy; we too can come to him, **believe in him,** and receive forgiveness and **eternal life.**

1:17 Reflecting on how good God has been to him, who was a blasphemer and persecutor, caused Paul to praise God. This verse is a typical doxology given by Paul as a natural, emotional response to these reflections about the mercy of God. When Paul realized all that God had done for him, he was left with no other words than **glory and honor to God forever and ever.** God, our **King,** is eternal—that is, he can never cease to exist. He is **unseen**—we cannot see him or touch him; he is Spirit. **He alone is God**—not one of many.

TIMOTHY'S RESPONSIBILITY / 1:18-20
From the high point of praise to God, Paul turned his attention back to Timothy. The young disciple faced a difficult situation in the church at Ephesus, but Paul knew he could handle the challenge. What Timothy needed in the meantime was encouragement and helpful instructions. Like a coach preparing his eager young fighter for the match of his life, Paul put an imaginary arm around Timothy's shoulders and passed on a few last-minute instructions.

1:18 These **instructions** (see 1:3, 5) refer to the job **Timothy** was sent to do in Ephesus—that is, quieting the false teachers. Paul was expressing again his confidence in entrusting Timothy with an important ministry. Further instruction for Timothy's work in the church is given in the remainder of this letter.

Referring to **the prophetic words spoken** about Timothy, Paul made it clear that his choice of Timothy was not made solely on the basis of their friendship or his hunches about Timothy's abilities. Other believers had noted qualities in Timothy that Paul was happy to affirm and to put to work for the gospel. Scholars have suggested two possibilities for these previous prophecies about Timothy: (1) These were Old Testament promises prophesied by the prophets, promises that Timothy claimed. (2) These were prophetic utterances at Timothy's ordination (Acts 14:23; 1 Timothy 4:14). Timothy had been set apart for ministry when elders laid their hands on him (see 4:14). Apparently at Timothy's "commissioning," several believers had prophesied about his gifts and strengths. These words from the Lord must have encouraged Timothy throughout his ministry. We can only guess who gave the prophecies and what they said; in any case, Paul reminded Timothy of these statements to encourage him.

Paul employed a military metaphor to describe Timothy's work in Ephesus; it would indeed be a **fight,** but victory would achieve the good of the believers and the church—it was the worthwhile fight of the faith. We are reminded of Paul's words to Timothy as Paul neared death, "I have fought a good fight" (2 Timothy 4:7). Paul often used military language to refer to our spiritual struggle (see Ephesians 6:11-16; 1 Thessalonians 5:8; 2 Timothy 2:3).

1:19 One's faith and one's morals cannot be separated. To **cling tightly** to the Christian **faith,** and live by it, results in a **clear conscience.** Faith and good conscience are like armor for the Christian. They keep us from giving in to temptation and to debilitating spiritual and moral sidetracks. Rejecting the faith and refusing to listen to one's conscience will end in **shipwrecked faith.** This deliberate action reflects heresy, not just backsliding.

1:20 Apparently these two men had been members of the church (because Paul had put them out of the church). We don't know who **Alexander** was—he may have been an associate of **Hymenaeus,** or the coppersmith mentioned in 2 Timothy 4:14 who hurt Paul. But he was not the Alexander mentioned in the riot at Ephesus (Acts 19:33). Hymenaeus's error is explained in 2 Timothy 2:17-18. He weakened people's faith by teaching that the resurrection of the dead had already occurred.

To be **turned over to Satan** means that Paul removed these men from the fellowship of the church and back into the world—Satan's domain. Paul did this so that they would see their error and repent. The ultimate purpose of this punishment was correction so that they would **learn not to blaspheme God.** (See also 1 Corinthians 5:1-5; 2 Corinthians 2:5-8; 4:4; 2 Thessalonians 3:14-15.) The church today is often lax in disciplining Christians who deliberately sin. Deliberate disobedience

should be responded to quickly and sternly to prevent the entire congregation from being affected. But discipline must be done in a way that tries to bring the offender back to Christ and into the loving embrace of the church. The definition of discipline includes these words: strengthening, purifying, training, correcting, and perfecting. Condemnation, suspicion, withholding of forgiveness, or permanent exile should not be a part of church discipline.

1 TIMOTHY 2

INSTRUCTIONS ABOUT WORSHIP / 2:1-15

The next two chapters cover Paul's thinking on the expected character and behavior of believers when they are functioning as a church. Among the most hotly debated passages written by Paul, this one begins with guidelines for prayer (2:1-8) and moves on to what appear to be rigid restrictions placed on women (2:9-15) within the church. The range of interpretations varies from those who would still forbid women from teaching in the church to those who would write Paul off as presenting views not applicable to today.

If Paul's purpose in writing this letter was to guide Timothy in his confrontations with the false teachers (1:3), then that purpose must be used to understand Paul's instructions. What Paul told Timothy to do in the volatile environment in Ephesus may not be what he would have directed a church to do where peace and harmony prevailed. We must understand the problem that Paul was addressing within Timothy's situation before we conclude what applications might be made to our own. We must remember that Paul shares God's desire for everyone to be saved (2:4). To that end, he wants Christian men to pursue holiness and Christian women to conduct themselves appropriately in the church.

2:1 Paul's **urge** echoed his original mission for Timothy (1:3). False teaching had to be challenged, and right actions needed to be reinforced. Paul placed primary importance on prayer.

The different words used for prayer focus not so much on different types of prayer as on the scope of prayer—that we can come to God with **requests, plead for God's mercy,** and **give thanks.** Although God is all-powerful and all-knowing, he has chosen to let us help him change the world through our prayers. How this works is a mystery to us because of our limited understanding, but it is a reality. This verse highlights the words **for all people.** Readers often miss the inclusiveness of the word and focus instead on the examples that Paul immediately gave. A common application of this verse, therefore, urges prayer for government leaders. Paul's purpose, however, was most likely to broaden the possibilities for prayer rather than narrowing them. Paul's examples

may well have caused Timothy to think of the very persons with whom he was in conflict—the false teachers. Both "kings" and "those in authority" were enemies of the early church. False teachers were people in authority (2:2) who were promoting error and creating controversies in the Ephesian church. Yet Paul urged Timothy to pray for everyone, including his opponents.

In situations of personal conflict, one of the ways to test our objectivity is whether or not we can honestly pray for those with whom we disagree. Jesus was quite clear, "Pray for those who persecute you" (Matthew 5:44).

2:2 Paul's command to **pray for kings** was remarkable considering that Nero, a notoriously cruel ruler, was the current emperor (A.D. 54–68). When Paul wrote this letter, persecution was a growing threat to believers. Later, when Nero needed a scapegoat for the great fire that destroyed much of Rome in A.D. 64, he blamed the Roman Christians so as to take the focus off himself. That triggered severe persecution throughout the Roman Empire. Not only were Christians denied certain privileges in society; some were even publicly butchered, burned, or fed to lions. But believers were taught to support the government and those **in authority,** not rebel against it (Romans 13:1-6; 1 Peter 2:13-25).

Paul did not explain what to pray, but his list in verse 1 was broad enough to include whatever prayer might be appropriate to any situation. He also gave the purpose behind his command to pray. God sets up and removes all rulers; he is ultimately in control (see Psalm 2). Praying for the salvation of the rulers in Rome (and for the return of the noninterfering policy against Christians) would help restore the **peace and quietness** the Christians had enjoyed prior to the persecution (see 1 Peter 2:12; 3:9).

Even in nations where Christians do not face persecution, they still need to be constantly praying for their leaders. Every day decisions are made in the halls of government that shape the policies, the future, even the morality of the nation. Constant prayer can be a mighty weapon against Satan's domination so believers can continue with their work of spreading the gospel **in godliness and dignity.** Godliness means true reverence and religious devotion that leads to exemplary conduct. Dignity means serious purpose, moral earnestness. These descriptive words do not imply private spiritual living. Rather, they convey a public faith consistent with God's purpose to achieve the salvation of persons and bring them "to a knowledge of the truth" (2:4).

2:3-4 It may be difficult to pray for the salvation of civil leaders, but these prayers are **good** and pleasing to **God,** who alone is **Savior.** The immediate context for Timothy included the conflict within the church with the false teachers. But even in this confrontation, the goal was to bring about their salvation. The recent mention of Hymenaeus and Alexander (1:20) illustrates the importance of redemptive discipline. While these men had been "turned over to Satan" (1:20) and were therefore outside the church, the door of repentance still would have been open to them (see, for example, 1 Corinthians 5:3-5 and 2 Corinthians 2:5-11). In the meantime, they were among the subjects for prayer by the gathered church.

The fact that God **wants everyone to be saved and to understand the truth** does not mean that all *will* be saved—the Bible affirms that many people reject Christ (Matthew 25:31-46; John 12:44-50; Hebrews 10:26-29). But God's desire is that all people would be saved, and he has provided in Christ the means to salvation. First Timothy 4:10 shows that the guarantee of salvation applies only to those who receive it. Paul was not teaching about election here; rather, he was showing God's intent that the gospel go to all people.

2:5-6 These verses cite three foundational truths of the gospel:

1. **There is only one God.** Judaism and Christianity shared the common belief that there is only one God (in direct opposition to the Greek and Roman pantheons and to the polytheism of the surrounding nations). The foundation for this teaching is Deuteronomy 6:4-9 (see also 1 Corinthians 8:4).
2. There is also **one Mediator who can reconcile God and people, Christ Jesus.** Jesus said, "I am the way, the truth, and the life. No one can come to the Father except through me" (John 14:6). Muslims also believe that there is only "one God," but they differ in how he makes himself known. For the Muslims, God is Allah, and Muhammad is his prophet. The Jews believe in one God yet still await their Messiah; they believe in Moses as this mediator. Some of the Jews in Ephesus as well as the Gnostics may have regarded angels as mediators. The Romans were praising Caesar as their God. The Christians understand that Christ Jesus is our mediator because he is God.
3. **He gave his life to purchase freedom for everyone.** God is holy, sinless, morally perfect. People are, by nature, sinners. A holy God cannot embrace sinners any more than light can embrace darkness. For hundreds of years, the Jews sacrificed animals to God in order to maintain a right relationship with him. The sacrifices reminded them that sin has consequences and that only spilled blood would be enough to cover the people's sins. Yet, even that wasn't God's complete plan, for **at the proper time,** he sent his Son to become the final sacrifice, to pay for the sins of all people (past, present, and future) with his own blood.

Christians can respect other beliefs and religions, but we must hold firmly to the three beliefs stated above without the slightest change. Although Christianity may appear "narrow" or "intolerant," it is willing to embrace everyone who believes. There is only one God; there is only one Mediator; that Mediator gave himself as a ransom—he paid the price. There is nothing more to do except believe. The gospel invitation to believe is centered in Jesus Christ. Believing in something or someone other than Jesus may be faith; but it is not the Christian faith.

2:7 Paul had been **chosen** as a **preacher.** He was also an **apostle.** He operated with a sense of divine commission. He had been given the special privilege of teaching **the Gentiles about faith and truth.** This was the **absolute truth,** a point made not for Timothy's sake, but for the church in Ephesus.

2:8 Continuing the theme of prayer (begun in 2:1), Paul focused on public worship in the church. Prayer in the congregation should be given by **men** (Greek, *andras*). To **pray with holy hands lifted up to God** may appear somewhat unusual, but it was, in fact, the accepted way of prayer among Jews and the earliest Christians. In Old Testament times, prayers were made with the face pointed toward heaven and palms turned upward with hands outstretched. This conveyed supplication and longing for God's blessing. Quite often, hands were used symbolically to show the humble attitude of the person praying.

But these men who prayed needed **holy hands;** in other words, they had to be "clean" before God. In Timothy's context, the outward forms of prayer needed to be authenticated by the absence of **anger and controversy.** Paul's concern indicates that the spiritual life of the Ephesian church was being undermined by ineffective prayers and divisive teaching. If individuals should be free from anger and quarreling while they prayed, how much more should those who offered prayer on behalf of others!

Paul's desire that men alone should pray seems to contradict 1 Corinthians 11:5, where he stated that women who prayed or prophesied should do so with their heads covered. Most likely this problem of women leading in prayer and teaching applied specifically to the Corinthian and Ephesian situations. In these churches, recently converted and emancipated women tended to interrupt the service with improper questions or remarks. Paul urged them to defer to the men. But he was not generally refusing to let women participate in public prayer (see also the discussion on 2:11).

It should also be noted that this verse does not limit prayer to the clergy or the elders, but encourages prayer from laymen. It wasn't until later in the church that some wrongly restricted prayer to clergymen.

2:9 As the men were to show their right attitudes with "holy hands," so the women in the Ephesian congregation were to show their holy attitudes with a **modest** outward **appearance.** Paul emphasized that their internal character was far more important than their outward adornment. Women's standard for dress was to be characterized by **decent and appropriate clothing.** Paul's appeal here was to good taste and good sense within the culture.

Women believers were to "dress" their behavior in a manner that complemented rather than clashed with their character. Women who worshiped in the Christian church should not be given to ostentation, costly attire, and excessive adornment. Neither was seductive or sexually suggestive clothing appropriate. They were not to detract from the worship by drawing **attention to themselves.** That the Christian women in Ephesus not **fix their hair** or wear **gold or pearls or expensive clothes** meant again that their emphasis should not be how they looked, but on who they were.

To understand these instructions, we must look at them in light of the whole Bible. Jesus set women free. He treated them as human beings. He recognized and responded to their needs as human needs. He taught women and included them as his followers. He proved himself to be their Savior, too. The accepted view of women in the time of Christ was as property rather than persons. Jesus personally shattered that conception. The gospel offered to women the gift of personhood—they were worthy of salvation.

Paul's instructions to the Christian women in Ephesus must be read in both their immediate and larger contexts before applying them. The immediate context was the church in Ephesus, which was suffering from the effect of false teachers who used women as their prime targets (see 2 Timothy 3:6-9). These women were also affected by their personal experiences within Ephesian culture. They would have struggled as much with cultural conditioning as we do.

The larger context includes what Paul taught elsewhere about the role and place of women in the church. One key statement occurs in Paul's letter to the Galatians: "There is no longer . . . male nor female . . . you are one in Christ Jesus" (Galatians 3:28). Note also Peter's speech at Pentecost (Acts 2:17-18). Women were not being singled out, nor should these instructions be binding outside of the church. Modesty and self-restraint are for everyone at all times, but these specific prohibitions applied to the church in Ephesus. Possibly, some Christian women in the Ephesian church were trying to gain respect by looking beautiful rather than by becoming Christlike in character. Some may have thought that they could win unbelieving husbands to Christ through their appearance (see Peter's counsel to such women in 1 Peter 3:1-6). In addition, Paul may have been referring to particular styles in Ephesus that were associated with prostitutes in the local temples. Artemis (also called Diana) was the goddess of Ephesus (see Acts 19:28). Considered the goddess of fertility, she was represented by a carved figure with many breasts.

A large statue of her (the rock for which was said to have come from heaven, Acts 19:35) was in the great temple at Ephesus. That temple was one of the wonders of the ancient world. The festival of Artemis involved wild orgies and carousing. Obviously, Christian women should not look like or even copy the styles of the prostitutes in the temple of Artemis.

While there is nothing wrong with Christian women wanting to look nice, each woman must examine her own motives. Today's world places great emphasis on beauty. Christian women, while they can dress nicely and take care of their appearance, must at the same time not let their appearance become all-encompassing, and they must not enhance their appearance merely for "sex appeal" or attention-getting.

2:10 A carefully groomed and well-decorated exterior is artificial and cold without inner beauty. Scripture does not prohibit a woman from wanting to be attractive. Beauty, however, begins inside a person. A gentle, modest, loving character gives a light to the face that cannot be duplicated by the best cosmetics and jewelry in the world. Christian women are not to try to be unattractive; instead, Paul called them to reject the world's standard for attractiveness. A Christian's adornment comes not from what she puts on, but from what she does for others.

While the church should not regulate what can or cannot be worn inside its doors (indeed many who need to know the Lord might not be able to enter if specific standards had to be met), those who **claim to be devoted to God** ought to dress sensibly and modestly, choosing instead to **make themselves attractive by the good things they do.**

2:11 Many women have read these verses and been distressed. However, to understand these verses, we must understand the situation in which Paul and Timothy worked. In first-century Jewish culture, women were not allowed to study. Jews and Gentiles regarded it disgraceful for women to discuss issues with men in public. The Jews were stricter, not even allowing women to teach the male children past the age of five. In Greek philosophy, Plato granted women equality with men. Aristotle severely limited their activities, and his view was more widely accepted.

When Paul said that women could **learn,** he was affirming their recognition as teachable members of the church. Christian women were given "equal rights" with men when it came to studying the Holy Scriptures. This was an amazing freedom for many of the Jewish and Gentile women who had become Christians.

There were several problems in the Ephesian and Corinthian churches that made teaching in this area difficult. Some women, converted Jews, had grown up in an atmosphere repressive toward women. Suddenly these women experienced their freedom in Christ. Some may have overreacted, flaunting their freedom and disrupting the church service. In addition, some of the women may have been converts from the cult of temple prostitution, so widespread in these major cities. These women were immature in the faith and doctrine of Christianity. They needed to learn, not teach. Against this backdrop, we have the influence of the false teachers who emphasized elitism and special knowledge. A third group would be widows or weak-willed women (identified in 1 Timothy 5:3-16 and 2 Timothy 3:5-9) upon whom the false teachers were preying. These women should not be put up front to pray or teach until their doctrine had been straightened out.

Such women were to learn at home from their fathers or husbands; they were to maintain silence and not disturb the worship services (1 Corinthians 14:35). They were to speak, pray, or prophesy only when it was from the Spirit (1 Corinthians 11:5). Paul's prohibition was not against women in general. In several places Paul wrote about women in the church who were coworkers—helping him (Romans 16:1-3) and contending beside him for the faith (Philippians 4:2-3). Paul said women were coheirs of the image of God in Christ, that they were full members of the body of Christ, and that they fully shared in the responsibilities and gifts of serving.

Women were to learn **quietly and submissively.** The Greek word for "quietly" used here *(hesuchia)* and in verses 2 and 12 means settled, calm, with voluntary restraint. Another Greek word, *sigao,* means "to be silent," which is used in Luke 18:39 and 1 Corinthians 14:34. "Submission" warns against presumptive and inappropriate grasping after authority.

2:12 This statement, **I do not let,** is part of a series of present tense commands in this chapter ("I urge," 2:1; "I want," 2:8 and 2:9). Unfortunately, the translation reads as if Paul wrote, "I never permit a woman to teach." Also, the grammatical order in Greek for this phrase carries less force than the English one ("To teach, a woman I am not allowing") and completes the thought about attentive learning in verse 11. The women in the Ephesian church were allowed to learn, but not to **teach men.** Given the tension between the influx and recognition of women as fellow heirs of Christ within the church on the one hand, and the serious problems being caused by the false teachers on the other, Paul was affirming one right (to learn and **listen quietly**) while withholding another right (to teach) because of the condition of the church at the time. They did not need more teachers; rather, they all needed to return to the foundational truths of the gospel (2:3-7).

Some interpret this passage to mean that women should never teach in the assembled church; however, other passages point out that Paul allowed women to teach. Paul's commended coworker, Priscilla, taught Apollos, the great preacher (Acts 18:24-26). In addition, Paul frequently mentioned other women who held positions of responsibility in the church. Phoebe worked in the church (Romans 16:1). Mary, Tryphena, and Tryphosa were the Lord's workers (Romans 16:6, 12), as were Euodia and Syntyche (Philippians 4:2).

More likely, Paul restrained the Ephesian women from teaching because they didn't yet have enough knowledge or experience. The Ephesian church had a particular problem with false teachers. Both Timothy's presence and Paul's letters were efforts to correct the problem. Evidently, the women were especially susceptible to the false teachings (2 Timothy 3:1-9) because they did not yet have enough biblical knowledge to discern the truth. Paul may have been countering the false teachers' urging that women should claim a place of equality for prominence in the church. Because these women were new converts, they did not yet have the necessary experience, knowledge, or Christian maturity to teach those who already had extensive scriptural education. Paul was telling Timothy not to put anyone (in this case, women) into a position of leadership who was not yet mature in the faith (see 5:22). This deeper principle applies to churches today (3:6).

The expression, **have authority**, found only here in the New Testament, implies a domineering, forceful attitude—an abuse of authority. Of course, no one should exercise abusive authority over anyone. The danger Paul was counteracting included a competitive struggle for power within the church as women took their rightful place. But conversely, Paul nowhere teaches male authority over women expressed in harsh domination.

Paul's instruction to the women of Ephesus displayed his missionary strategy. Because his desire was to reach the people of Ephesus with the gospel, he called for moderation and restraint against the potential misuse of freedom. Both Jews and Greeks in Ephesus would be scandalized by women usurping authority over men. This would have created confusion and resentment among the pagans whom the Ephesian Christians were trying to reach. So Paul was giving a local strategy of restraint, not issuing unchanging rules of organization. Remember that equality of worth between the sexes was a completely foreign concept in both Hebrew and Roman cultures. It was not expected nor was it offered. The equality given by Christ was radical (see Galatians 3:26-28).

2:13 In previous letters Paul had discussed male/female roles in marriage (Ephesians 5:21-33; Colossians 3:18-19). Here he talks about male/female roles within the church. Some scholars see these verses about **Adam** and **Eve** as an illustration of what was happening in the Ephesian church. Just as Eve had been deceived in the Garden of Eden, so the women in the church were being deceived by false teachers. Just as Adam was the first human created by God, so the men in the church in Ephesus should be the first to speak and teach, because they had more training. Eve should have turned to Adam for advice about Satan's words to her because Adam had more experience with God's instructions. It was also necessary to simplify the task of weeding out the false teachers, also men, who were destroying the church from within. This view, then, stresses that Paul's teaching here is not universal; rather, it applies to churches with similar problems.

Other scholars, however, contend that the principles Paul points out are based on God's design for his created order—God established these roles to maintain harmony in both the family and the church (see Genesis 2:18). God assigned roles and responsibilities in order for his created world to function smoothly. Although there must be lines of authority, even in marriage, there should *not* be lines of superiority. God created men and women with unique and complementary characteristics. We must not let the issue of authority and submission become a wedge to destroy what can be excellent working relationships, with men and women using their varied gifts and abilities to accomplish God's work.

2:14 Paul was not excusing **Adam** for his part in the fall (Genesis 3:6-7, 17-19). On the contrary, in his letter to the Romans, Paul placed the primary blame for humanity's sinful nature on Adam (Romans 5:12-21). Eve had not been told directly by God about the trees—Adam had instructed her. In turn, God instructed Adam about the trees before Eve was created. For Eve, the struggle was over whether to submit to Adam's command or to the serpent's words that seemed to offer her knowledge and understanding. But when Adam ate of the fruit, he directly disobeyed God. He was not **deceived**; he sinned outright. By then, however, Eve had already sinned.

This verse should not be taken to prove that women are more gullible than men in general. In Ephesus, due to the persuasiveness of the male false teachers, some women *were* gullible. Paul didn't use this verse to say women were easily deceived, but to point out that Eve should have submitted to Adam in her particular situation.

2:15 The phrase **saved through childbearing** has been understood in several ways:

1. The childbearing mentioned here refers to the birth of Jesus Christ. Women (and men) are saved spiritually because of the most important birth, that of Christ himself. This argument is based on a very obscure reference to Christ and the Incarnation. It would be unlikely for Paul to be so indirect.
2. Man sinned, so men were condemned to painful labor. Woman also sinned, so women were condemned to pain in childbearing. Pain caused a serious complication, but childbearing was not the curse. Both men and women, however, can be saved through trusting Christ and obeying him. Although this is true, it does not seem as forceful in light of the context.
3. From the lessons learned through the trials of childbearing, women can develop qualities that teach them about love, trust, submission, and service. Although this is true, it hardly seems to be the main point.
4. Women who fulfill their God-given roles of childbearing and child rearing are demonstrating true commitment and obedience to Christ. One of the most important roles for a wife and mother is to care for her family. This seems to be the most legitimate interpretation in light of the larger context and also in reference to 5:3-15. The women in Ephesus were abandoning their God-given purpose because of the false

teachers. So Paul was telling them that caring for their families, or remarrying if they were younger widows, was one way for them to remain effective and to live faithful lives of service. By means of bearing children, raising them, and fulfilling their design, women would be saved from the evils of Ephesian society and maintain a pure testimony to the lordship of Christ. Paul placed before the women of Ephesus the goal to **live in faith, love, holiness, and modesty.**

Scholars have written many volumes to present various views of the role of women in worship and leadership. There seems to be enough evidence and divided opinion to conclude that the complete answer cannot be derived from 1 Timothy. Church bodies have to decide the issue for their own congregations. Nonetheless, we would do well to consider the following statements:

- Scripture must be regarded in context. Paul gave other teachings about male/female relationships; all must be considered.
- Paul's clear teachings must be used to clarify what seems less clear.
- Though Scripture is not bound to culture, it is definitely targeted to culture. Paul was focusing on the Ephesians' problem.
- Remember Paul's missionary strategy. His local strategy for Ephesus may not be normative for all time.
- We must be consistent. If we allow women to wear jewelry, but do not permit them to teach, we may be guilty of selectiveness.
- We must not let culture define how the church is run. If culture dictated a militant feminism, we should be against it. But if culture dictated a view of women more subordinated than the Bible suggests, we should oppose that as well.

1 TIMOTHY 3

LEADERS IN THE CHURCH / 3:1-13
The list of qualifications for church office, which is similar to other lists in the Jewish and Greco-Roman world, is not a rigid judgment list for disqualifying certain people. Rather, it serves as a barometer for spiritual maturity. Those who aspire to a church office must realize that living a blameless and pure life requires effort and self-discipline. All believers, even if they never plan to be church leaders, should strive to follow these guidelines because they are consistent with what God says is true and right. The strength to live according to God's will comes from Christ.

3:1 The word **elder** referred to a pastor or anyone who exercised an overseeing position. The New Testament uses several words for church leaders; the most common are apostle, overseer, bishop, elder, and deacon. At first, the office of "apostle" referred only to the Twelve and a select few others, like Paul, but it came to be used in a less technical sense for church representatives (see 2 Corinthians 8:23; Philippians 2:25). Elders were leaders in specific congregations, and the words were used interchangeably in Paul's letters. They were the teachers. Deacons were the administrators in these early churches—handling people, administration, finances, etc.

There apparently was a **saying** regarding church leadership, and Paul cited it here as **true.** It is good to desire to be a spiritual leader. **Desires** means "sets one's heart on something." Leadership is **an honorable responsibility.** Paul stressed its importance. However, as Paul would point out, the standards are high.

3:2 Paul enumerated several qualifications for an **elder.** He must live a life that **cannot be spoken against,** meaning he must have no flaw in his conduct that would be grounds for any kind of accusation. He must be blameless. The term serves as a general opening summary of character. A leader within the church should have a good reputation among believers. Leadership sets the tone. What follows are the building blocks of that reputation.

The qualification, **he must be faithful to his wife,** has lent itself to different interpretations. Some say this shows that he should be married. This view gains strength from the fact that the false teachers forbade marriage (4:3). However, both Paul and Timothy were unmarried. If Paul taught that a leader must be married, he would be unable himself to lead and would be contradicting his instructions in 5:14 and 1 Corinthians 7:25-33. Most likely, the leader, if he is married, must be a one-woman man, standing against the immoral standards present in the pagan culture at Ephesus. The Bible rejects marriage as convenience and demands faithfulness and participation in the one flesh created by husband and wife (see Genesis 2:24; Ephesians 5:22-33).

That he **exhibit self-control** was another way of saying a leader ought to possess sound and balanced judgment, or even common sense. Each of these qualities may be required for leaders, but they ought to be the goal of all believers.

A church leader must **live wisely,** meaning that his life should be marked by moderation, limits, not extreme or excessive, with an absence of extravagance. We might use the term "balanced" to indicate that this leader possesses the appropriate emphasis on each of the priorities in his life.

A good reputation refers to basic social graces—ordinary dignified behavior. The Greek word is derived from *kosmos,* "the world or universe," and pictures a person who lives in harmony with the way God created the world to function.

Hospitality was widely emphasized in Middle Eastern cultures and in the Old Testament (see Exodus 22:21). Believers are commanded to be hospitable (Hebrews 5:10; 13:2; 1 Peter 4:9; 3 John 5), so a leader should also **enjoy having guests in his home.**

Christian leaders must be **able to teach.** One of the most important tasks of any church leader is to teach the Scriptures to those in the congregation. The leader must understand and be able to communicate the profound truths of Scripture, as well as deal with those false teachers who mishandle them.

3:3 An elder must **not be a heavy drinker,** for obvious reasons. Many of these qualities may have characterized the false teachers who caused quarrels in the church (see 6:3-4).

He must not be **violent** or quarrelsome. A violent person is an abusive individual. Abuse may take many forms (verbal, physical, sexual, even spiritual), but it rises from a deep disrespect for others. Mental illness may also be involved. Such a person tends to be defensive, insecure, and insensitive. A person with a history of verbal battles may find it difficult to lead effectively. Such a person should not be selected to lead. In contrast, he **must be gentle** and **peace loving.** Such a person is free from harshness, sternness, or violence.

A Christian leader must **not** be **one who loves money** (see 6:5-10). Leaders must have a proper attitude for handling finances in the church. This affects the ethical use of church funds and the administration of proper programs for raising money. It also implies that making money should not be a prime motive for a candidate seeking a church leadership position. Many would-be leaders combine love of money with a quarrelsome nature and end up quarreling in the church over money matters. Such a person should not be selected to lead.

3:4-5 The qualifications for both elders and deacons hinge on the man's ability to manage his own household (see also 3:12). It is not absolutely required that an elder be married or have children. If he does, however, he must **manage his own family well.** The word **manage** means compassionate governing, leading, and directing (see 1 Thessalonians 5:12; 1 Timothy 5:17), not stern, cruel, tyrannical, and authoritarian dominance. This type of family leadership reflects the parallel between church and home seen in Ephesians 5:28–6:9.

It makes sense that Paul would use this requirement, for no one can run a household effectively without love and firmness, mercy and guidelines. And if parents don't model what they teach, children rarely follow except under pressure. There are two thoughts in this phrase: on one hand, while it is true that children should show **respect** and **obey** their parents, respect and obedience are by-products of responsible leadership in the home. The best way to see a person's ability to handle a large responsibility is to see how he or she performs a small one. The ability to handle his **household** forms a training ground for a man's ability to handle the family of God in the **church**. The same love, compassion, firmness, and mercy are needed for both duties.

3:6 New believers should become secure and strong in the faith before taking leadership roles in the church. Too often, when desperate for workers, the church places a **new Christian** in a position of leadership prematurely. New believers should have a part in God's service, but they should not be put into leadership positions until they are firmly grounded in their faith, with a solid Christian lifestyle and a knowledge of the word of God. Otherwise, the new believer **might be proud of being chosen so soon, and the Devil will use that pride to make him fall.** The reference to the Devil teaches that in the same way Satan fell because of pride, there waits the danger of pride to new believers who are given responsibility before they are ready. New believers who are too quickly promoted can be easy targets for the Devil's powerful temptation: pride. Pride can seduce emotions and cloud our reason. It can make those who are immature susceptible to the influence of unscrupulous people.

3:7 Requiring the leaders to have a good reputation with people **outside the church** (that is, nonbelievers in the community) gave the church at large a good reputation in the community. Church leaders, being the most visible people in the church to the secular world, would do well to maintain the highest of standards and the best reputation. Seeing several church leaders make headlines in recent years for tax evasion, wrongful use of solicited funds, and sexual escapades certainly damages the credibility of the church. Church leaders who follow Paul's advice keep their church from facing unnecessary abuse. Otherwise, the result is to **fall into the Devil's trap and be disgraced** with both the believers and nonbelievers.

This trap may either be the moral failure and resultant judgment that a man chosen as leader will fall into, or it could mean the trap of temptation leading to pride as mentioned in verse 6. When Christian leaders have a bad reputation, it keeps nonbelievers from coming to Christ.

3:8 "Deacon" means "one who serves." This position was possibly begun by the apostles in the Jerusalem church (Acts 6:1-6) to care for the physical needs of the congregation. Deacons were leaders in the church, and their qualifications resemble those of the elders; yet their roles were probably somewhat different as they carried out some of the more practical tasks of running and maintaining a church.

We must remember, however, that Paul was probably describing a role or function more than defining an office or position. The original term still generally applied to a class of slaves. Paul's explanation of these roles within the church emphasized the point that the name or title was to be given to someone who was already living out these character qualities. While Paul did not mention teaching requirements for deacons, their lives would have still been models of Christian discipleship.

Deacons, as recognized leaders in the church, also had a high profile and thus were required to be **respected.** This is not the same term for respectability applied to the elders (3:2). Here the term can mean "serious" or "honorable." Deacons were to take their responsibilities seriously and conscientiously. They should be men of dignity. They also should **have integrity,** referring to honesty without hypocrisy. Sometimes translated, "not double-tongued," this could refer to not gossiping, or to not saying one thing to one person and another to someone else. Like elders, deacons **must not be heavy drinkers** and they **must not be greedy for money.** They must be uninterested in such pursuits.

In some churches today, the office of deacon has lost its importance. New Christians are often asked to serve in this position, but that is not the New Testament pattern. Paul said that potential deacons should be tested before they are asked to serve (3:10).

3:9 Deacons must be men with spiritual depth, **committed to the revealed truths of the Christian faith.** The seven men chosen to help the apostles in the early church were "well-respected and . . . full of the Holy Spirit and wisdom" (Acts 6:3). While Luke never called Stephen and his companions "deacons," they have traditionally been held up as early models of the service orientation of that role. They were men whose outward actions demonstrated that the gospel had taken deep root in their lives.

Deacons must not only know God's truth, they must **live** it, resulting in **a clear conscience** (see note on 1:5). Their lifestyles must be consistent with their beliefs. This must necessarily be true for all Christians, and any man chosen for the office of deacon will have shown these qualities beforehand.

3:10 This refers not to some formal testing, but rather to observation by those who appoint deacons. The candidate will have shown the required moral characteristics and approved doctrine (3:9) consistently in the ordinary activities of church membership. A man who has proven his **character and ability** over time can then serve as a deacon. Testing deacons is needed today. They should not be appointed without consideration of their doctrine and their Christian life.

3:11 In Greek, the same word, *gune,* is used for "woman" and for "wife." So three possible interpretations have been given for the identity of these **wives:**

1. These women were the deacons' wives.
2. These are women in general. However, the context of church leadership speaks against this interpretation.
3. These women are female deacons or "deaconesses," such as Phoebe in Romans 16:1. This interpretation is based on the use of **in the same way** to show the parallel to verse 8.

Whatever the case, Paul expected the behavior of prominent women in the church to be just as responsible and blameless as that of prominent

men. They are to be **respected and must not speak evil of others;** that is, they must not have a problem with gossiping. They should **exercise self-control,** their lives marked by moderation and limits, not extreme or excessive, with an absence of extravagance. Being **faithful in everything they do** is an important requirement for anyone who would fulfill many duties on behalf of the congregation. A helper who constantly forgets to fulfill her duties or only does them halfway is not suitable for service in the church.

Although the women in the church at Ephesus were not (at least in the present circumstances) allowed to teach in the formal sense, they were still expected to model all the character qualities of mature believers.

3:12 A **deacon must be faithful to his wife, and he must manage his children and household well.** This requirement matches the requirement for elders spelled out in verses 2, 4-5, and is included for deacons for the same reasons.

3:13 Deacons are required to have the same high standards as elders for a position that, to many, might seem very unattractive and menial. But God doesn't see it that way. Those who fulfill their servant roles faithfully **will be rewarded with respect from others** who recognize and appreciate their service. They will also **have increased confidence in their faith in Christ Jesus.** The faithful servant is able to speak boldly of the faith and serve confidently, assured that what he or she does is appreciated and valued by the Lord Jesus Christ. Humble service may lack earthly rewards, but heavenly rewards are promised.

THE TRUTHS OF OUR FAITH / 3:14-16

Paul hoped to arrive in Ephesus and see Timothy within a short time of this letter's arrival. In case Paul arrived later than planned, he wrote these instructions to Timothy and the Ephesian church. This letter most likely confirmed instructions about governing the church already given to Timothy by Paul. This letter's arrival, prior to Paul's appearance, would have bolstered Timothy's authority in the church to continue to guide the church according to these instructions and to counteract the false teachers.

3:14-15 Again, in opposition to the false teachers who were full of false beliefs, Paul aimed at truthful behavior within the church. Actions speak louder than words, and in harmony they create an attractive song. Paul also knew that if he got the Ephesian Christians behaving as God wanted them to live, the noise of the false teachers would be drowned out.

Lest there be any doubt, Paul identified **the household of God** as **the church of the living God**

(see also 1 Corinthians 3:16-17; 2 Corinthians 6:16; Ephesians 2:20-22). This "church" does not refer to any particular physical building; rather, it is a collection of all believers in Ephesus and, by extension, across the world. These believers, each serving and worshiping in their individual churches, are the **pillar and support** of God's **truth.** The church is not the source of this truth; rather, it functions as the custodian of and the witness to the truth. Those who believe God's truth have the power to change the world. That truth is outlined in the hymn Paul quoted from in the following verses.

3:16 In this short paragraph, probably an excerpt from an early hymn of the church, Paul affirmed the humanity and divinity of Christ. (For other examples of hymns, see Ephesians 5:19; Colossians 3:6; and Philippians 2:5.) By so doing, Paul revealed the heart of the gospel, **the great mystery of our faith.** Every phrase of the hymn is a "mystery" beyond our comprehension yet available for us to believe. We accept the truth as it has been revealed to us. And the results of our belief are life-changing.

Christ appeared in the flesh. Jesus was a man; his incarnation provides the basis for our being right with God (Philippians 2:7-8 ; see also Romans 1:3).

He was shown to be righteous by the Spirit. Jesus' resurrection showed that the Holy Spirit's power was in him (Acts 2:32-33).

He was seen by angels. Jesus is divine and exalted (Philippians 2:9; see also Colossians 2:15; Hebrews 1:6). Presumably, the entire drama of the Incarnation was a spectacle for the angels. They were witnesses and heralds of his coming. But within this poetic expression, the role of the angels and their exposure to Christ exceeds his time on earth.

He was announced to the nations, pointing to the worldwide proclamation of the gospel (Colossians 1:23).

He was believed on in the world. Christ is not only preached among all nations, but he also is believed on across the world. This points to a continual fulfillment today as Christ is still preached in nations that have not heard of him.

Finally, **he was taken up into heaven.** This refers to the Ascension: "The same one who came down is the one who ascended higher than all the heavens, so that his rule might fill the entire universe" (Ephesians 4:10).

1 TIMOTHY 4:1–5:2

WARNINGS AGAINST FALSE TEACHERS / 4:1-5

Paul's mind turned from the exalted role of the church in the plan of God (3:16) to the obstacles that were preventing the Ephesian believers from being totally effective. Paul warned the church of the tactics and teachings of its enemies. False teachers were (and still can be) a threat to the church. Paul knew that their teachings, if left unchecked, would greatly distort Christian truth. This critical danger would come from within the church.

4:1-2 The false teaching in Ephesus was no surprise; the betrayal of the gospel had been foreseen. Paul's phrase, **the Holy Spirit tells us clearly,** most likely refers to warnings repeatedly given by Jesus and the apostles against the dangers of false teaching. But Paul's direct concern here was not just about the teachers themselves as much as for those who would be deceived by them.

The **last times** began with Christ's resurrection and will continue until his return, when he will set up his Kingdom and judge all humanity. Jesus and the apostles forewarned us that during that interim, including the time period we live in, false teachers will abound—loving money and attention, distorting the truth, dividing believers, and causing many to go astray as they **follow lying spirits and teachings that come from demons** (see Matthew 24:5; Romans 16:18; James 3:15; 2 Peter 2:1; 1 John 3:7-9). These participants in the

church will **turn away from** the faith, even though they may appear to still be faithful believers. **They pretend to be religious, but their consciences are dead.** Paul had no patience for false teaching and no soft words for false teachers. He never said that the false teachers misunderstood the gospel or that they simply taught in error. Rather, they were **hypocrites and liars,** with their teaching coming from Satan himself.

4:3-4 Satan deceives people by offering a clever imitation of the real thing. The false teachers, perhaps under Jewish influence, gave stringent rules forbidding marriage and demanding abstinence from certain foods. Later, these teachings became part of what we know as Gnosticism—a belief that spirit is good, but the physical world is evil. Thus, anything done for the body's pleasure or to fulfill its needs (such as sex or eating) was considered evil. To be "good" and to achieve a higher spiritual state, a person must deny all evil, including natural physical desires. Their demands made the false teachers appear self-disciplined and righteous. But their strict disciplines for the body could not remove sin.

Paul had explained the Christian understanding of marriage in 1 Corinthians 7 and Ephesians 5:21-33. Although Paul advised against marriage in some situations, he always upheld marriage as ordained by God and as an illustration of Christ's relationship to his church. But he denied the false teaching that it was **wrong to be married.** In the same way, a certain amount of abstinence from all food some of the time and from some kinds of food all the time is basic to good health. Abstinence from food for the sake of prayer (fasting) has a history of service in spiritual training. But saying that it is **wrong to eat certain foods** does not make a person better than anyone else or bring

him or her closer to God. Error can be taught under the guise of devotion.

The false teaching was wrong in its conclusions: the physical world is not inherently evil. The physical world that **God created** should be received with **thanksgiving** by those **who know and believe the truth.** All foods are acceptable by those who regard God as their Provider and thank him for them (Romans 14:6; 1 Corinthians 10:30). Because they know the Creator personally, Christians can enjoy his creation all the more, receiving it **gladly, with thankful hearts.**

4:5 As we recognize God's hand in all the pleasures of his creation and as we offer him thanks, we take what is ordinary and make it extraordinary. In short, **it is made holy by the word of God and prayer.** God pronounced his creation good. Therefore, we are in agreement with God's declaration when we see all creation as suitable for special use.

A GOOD SERVANT OF CHRIST JESUS / 4:6–5:2

Here Paul directed some personal instructions for Timothy to take to the Ephesian church. His words establish a pattern of individual disciplines that would be helpful for any person taking on spiritual responsibilities. The aging apostle desired for his disciple both an effective ministry and a healthy personal life.

4:6 A **worthy servant** faithfully teaches the truth to those in his care. If Timothy would faithfully **explain** what Paul has been talking about to others, he would be **fed** in the process. Proper spiritual nourishment promotes spiritual growth. Proper nourishment for Timothy included constant meditation on **the message of faith** (the gospel message) and **true teaching** (Paul's instructions that Timothy was to communicate).

Timothy had been sent into a setting where there were conflicts over eating habits. Minor matters were being inflated into major issues. Paul was echoing the dietary concerns of the false teachers by emphasizing to Timothy that what really mattered was the feeding of the soul.

4:7 Paul emphasized the absurdity of the false teachings by calling them **godless ideas and old wives' tales** (see also 1:3-4). Timothy needed to understand the false teaching in order to fight it effectively with the truth, but then he was to **not waste time** on it. Instead, he should **spend his time and energy in training** himself **for spiritual fitness.** Paul often borrowed athletic words to emphasize the need for spiritual training (see 1 Corinthians 9:24; Galatians 2:2; 5:7; 2 Timothy 4:7). "Training" emphasizes the point that spiritual

development does not happen by chance. An athlete is focused and committed, constantly training, refusing to let up, always striving. Believers must have the same focus and commitment, refusing to be sidetracked by wrong teaching.

4:8-9 **Physical exercise,** while benefiting the body, has no eternal benefit. Being in good physical shape positively affects health and perhaps mental outlook; yet **spiritual exercise** affects everything. It benefits its practitioner **in both this life and the next.** The key issue is how we use our time. Some people spend ten to fifteen hours a week in physical activity, but spend little time in Bible study, prayer, and service. Paul was not urging Timothy toward a life of asceticism or stiff and narrow godliness. His practical instructions (see 4:12-16) were to be carried out in relationship with others. To Paul it was obvious that **this is true, and everyone should accept it.** Believers who do spiritual exercise really do have the best of both worlds—they receive immediate and eternal benefits, and they benefit others as they instruct and model the Christian life.

4:10 Believers **work hard and suffer much** because of eternity. Eternity with God is not just hope for a possible occurrence, it is **hope** set on a certainty because it is hope **in the living God**—not on a philosophy, a human being, a material possession, or a standard of behavior (see Colossians 1:29).

As elsewhere (1:1; 2:3; Titus 1:3; 2:10; 3:4), Paul attached the role of **Savior** to God. God in his fullness—Father, Son, and Holy Spirit—was active in carrying out the plan of salvation. Christ is the Savior **of all people** in the sense that his work on the cross was sufficient to provide salvation for everyone (see 2:6), but it is **particularly for those who believe** because salvation becomes effective only for those who trust him. Universalism is not taught in this passage. The offer of salvation has a universal range but does not impose itself on those unwilling to respond. This argument was aimed at the false teachers who attempted to restrict salvation to an elite few and put many more requirements on it than believing in God.

4:11 Timothy may have been somewhat shy. Paul encouraged Timothy to take charge as he told Timothy to **teach these things and insist that everyone learn them,** probably referring to all the matters in this letter. To people like the false teachers and their disciples, Timothy would have to issue commands. It was also his responsibility to continually train the believers in Ephesus.

4:12 The Greek word *neotes* (translated **young**) could refer to anyone up to the age of forty. By this time, Timothy was probably in his thirties. Although he was not a youth, he may have been considerably younger than some believers in his congregation. After serving under Paul, they may have looked down on this younger man who was put in charge of their church. Timothy could not control anyone's prejudice about his age, but he was not to be intimidated. Instead, he should **be an example to all believers.** He must not give anyone ammunition to use his youthfulness against him. Timothy's character, and not his age, would determine his authority to lead.

Timothy was not left to ponder how Paul expected him to be an example. Rather than offering general motivation to be an example, the old apostle issued a checklist.

- **What you teach**—Our words create impressions that either facilitate or complicate all other communication. Timothy was to teach with gentle authority while avoiding useless or argumentative conversation (see 4:11; 5:1; 6:3-4, 20).
- **The way you live**—Our lifestyle as well as our specific behaviors must be consistent with the gospel. Timothy was to conduct himself as a representative of Jesus Christ even in the details of daily living (see 6:6-10).

- **Love**—When we say the right words and live the right way but lack love, we are demonstrating a legalistic view of God's expectations (see 1 Corinthians 13:1-7). After words and actions have had their say, love makes the message ring true or false.
- **Faith**—Sooner or later, people around us will need to understand what motivates our speech, life, and love. A genuine combination of the above will present to others a way of life filled with hope. Faith finally speaks clearly when speech, life, and love have created a hearing.
- **Purity**—Paul ended this list with a rarely used term for virtue and chastity. As used here, the word implies integrity and consistency and reinforces the entire list. Perhaps Paul even had the idea of transparency in mind. The above qualities were to be developed, not just for public display, but as the uniform texture of Timothy's life.

4:13 Paul hoped to visit Timothy and the believers in Ephesus soon (see also 3:14-15). Besides carefully observing his private life to keep it above reproach, Timothy was also to give attention and preparation to his public ministry in three main areas, which are then described. Timothy was to **focus on reading the Scriptures to the church,** a practice begun in Old Testament times (see Exodus 24:7; Deuteronomy 31:11; Joshua 8:35; 2 Kings 23:2-3; Nehemiah 8:1-18) and continued in the synagogues (Luke 4:16; Acts 15:21; Colossians 4:16; 1 Thessalonians 5:27). He was also to be **encouraging the believers,** through preaching. Timothy was to exhort, that is, to warn, advise, and urge his listeners regarding the words of Scripture, helping them apply those words to their daily lives. **Teaching** refers to training in Christian doctrine. The people needed to know, understand, and constantly be reminded of the great truths of the Christian faith.

4:14 Others should not look down on Timothy (4:12), and neither should he look down on himself. Paul reminded Timothy that he had the necessary requisites to do the difficult work in Ephesus. Among them was a **spiritual gift** from God. Though Paul did not define the gift specifically, he was concerned that Timothy might hesitate or fail to use it. When we see abilities of all kinds (spiritual, relational, technical) as gifts from God, we will be in a better position to see his hand at work through people's efforts.

Timothy's commission as a church leader was **received through the prophecies spoken** to him and **when the elders of the church laid their hands on** him (see also 1:18). Timothy's gift had been publicly recognized. This should help

Timothy's wavering confidence. Timothy could do the task because God had called him to do it, had equipped him to do it, and would be with him through it.

4:15 Paul called Timothy to **give complete attention to** the **matters** about which Paul had been writing, making them his number one priority. As Timothy did so, **progress** would be seen both in his personal life and in the church, and this would end any questioning about Timothy's maturity or credibility.

4:16 In conclusion, Paul advised Timothy to **keep a close watch** on his private life and his public ministry to the church—his **teaching**. His conduct in both areas must be above reproach. If he stayed **true to what is right**, it would benefit him and everyone else. His example would facilitate the salvation of his hearers. Of course, God alone can save, but Paul's words focus on the responsibility of spiritual leaders. By paying attention to his personal spiritual life, Timothy would work out his own salvation (in the sense described in Philippians 2:12), and by paying attention to his teaching, he would help others do the same.

5:1 The wise apostle knew that for this young minister to remain above reproach in dealing with the variety of people in his church, he would have to treat them as family. **Speak harshly** refers to "verbal pounding," or disrespectful treatment. If

correction became necessary, Timothy should not speak harshly; instead, he should appeal to the **older** men with kind exhortation, **respectfully,** as if he were speaking to his **father.** Even correction or rebuke was to be phrased in encouraging terms.

In the same way, Timothy was to speak kindly to **younger men,** as if they were his **brothers.** He was to lead them gently. Without using the specific term, Paul was speaking about submission. Timothy was to practice submissive gentleness in correcting his seniors. He was to do the same in treating his juniors.

5:2 Jesus recognized the personhood of women. They were no longer to be treated as property and, therefore, no longer to be demeaned. Paul affirmed this principle as he explained to Timothy how to treat his sisters in the faith. The most effective method for remaining above reproach would be to treat church members as family members. Thus Timothy should **treat the older women as** if they were his own **mother,** and the **younger women with all purity as** his own **sisters.**

Today, men in the ministry can avoid improper attitudes toward women by following Paul's advice. Men who see women as fellow members in God's family will treat them with all purity—respecting, protecting, and helping them grow spiritually. Purity refers to the same quality that Paul mentioned in 4:12. It covers moral behavior and transparent attitudes without hidden intentions.

1 TIMOTHY 5:3–6:2A

ADVICE ABOUT WIDOWS, ELDERS, AND SLAVES / 5:3–6:2A
Paul thought of Timothy's audience in Ephesus. There, men and women of all ages were under Timothy's care. Paul thought of the groups within the congregation needing special attention. He wanted Timothy to practice good general principles of personal care and also to deal with some specific people-needs. Paul chose the treatment of widows and elders as prime examples. He also had some instructions concerning slaves who were believers.

5:3 Because there were no pensions, no Social Security, no life insurance, and few honorable jobs for women, a **widow** was usually unable to support herself. But the care of widows was apparently becoming a major burden to the congregation in Ephesus and called for clarification as to who was really a widow qualifying for support. Paul advised Timothy to identify those widows who had **no one else to care for** them. The responsibility for caring for the helpless

naturally falls first on their families, the people whose lives are most closely linked with theirs. Paul stressed the importance of families caring for the needs of widows and not leaving it for the church to do, so that the church can care for widows who had no families. A widow who had no children or other family members to support her was doomed to poverty. The church should **care for** such widows, meaning both respectful help and material support.

5:4 A widow who had **children or grandchildren** should be able to look to them for support. Our parents watched over us when we were helpless. We ought to do no less when the roles are reversed. Family members should look after their parents and grandparents. Paul affirmed this as basic common sense understood even by those who were unbelievers (see 5:8). Paul wanted Christian families to be as mutually supporting as possible. He insisted that children and grandchildren take care of the widows in their families, for this would **show godliness at home** and it would please **God very much.** God is pleased when we care for our family members' needs. God underscores the importance of fulfilling these duties by connecting them with the promise of personal benefits in the fifth commandment (Exodus 20:12). Honor certainly involves more than providing care in old age, but the caring treatment of our seniors is part of God's plan.

5:5-6 The **true widow** (see also 5:3) is **alone in this world,** that is, destitute, with no one to turn to for help. However, a Christian widow could turn to the church, setting **her hope in God.** The widows that the church should support are described as women who, since their husbands' deaths, dedicated themselves to God, spending **much time in prayer.** Anna, the prophetess, fit this description (Luke 2:37). This verse sets up a spiritual contrast regarding the lives of two kinds of widows. The "true widow" lives trusting God and ministering to others. She is not wrapped up in self-pity, but finds a place of effective service, beginning with prayer for others. Meanwhile, the other widow is lost to a self-centered lifestyle that Paul described as death.

Unlike their duties to the dedicated widows described in verse 5, the church was *not* to support widows who used their widowhood to live **only for pleasure** or resorted to immoral means of supporting themselves (possibly a reference to prostitution—practically the only "job" a woman could find in New Testament times). A widow who used her life chasing after pleasure was **spiritually dead.** Obviously, such widows should not be supported by the church.

Paul's instructions establish a strong case for wise assistance. The widow's choices define the ministry the church can have in her life. Honoring and assisting a widow who lives for pleasure would enable her to do wrong. But correcting her and offering forgiveness through repentance could still be an effective ministry by the church.

5:7 Repeating his command from 4:11, Paul told Timothy to also **give these instructions** (regarding the church's responsibility to widows, family members' responsibility to widows, and the widows' lifestyle) to the people. If all the instructions would be followed, no one would be **criticized.**

5:8 To default on the basic care and support of a family member is the same as denying the faith, for no one can claim love and allegiance to God and at the same time neglect his or her family (see Matthew 5:46-47). To do so makes people **worse than unbelievers,** for even unbelieving idol-worshipers understood the responsibility of caring for family needs. There are some obligations to those who have given us life that simply must be honored. Our families provide an arena in which we can demonstrate the quality of our love for God. John provided a scathing rebuke to any believer who would dare to claim affection for God but **won't care for their own relatives.** Believers who neglect the most basic human responsibilities have, for all practical purposes, **denied** what they **believe.**

5:9-10 The **list for support** on which widows may be placed may have been a particular group of widows who had taken a pledge committing themselves to work for the church in exchange for financial support. Part of this pledge was a commitment not to remarry so that these women could serve the Lord without distraction (see 5:12). Most importantly, however, the existence of a list indicates that the church identified those in need. The believers combined their resources to meet the needs of a known group.

In order to be included on this list, a widow had to meet three qualifications:

1. She had to be **at least sixty years old.** (Paul's reasons for keeping younger widows off the list for the church's support are explained in verses 11-15.) This was probably not so much a strictly observed age as it was a generally accepted stage beyond which a person's prospects for remarriage were doubtful.
2. She must have been **faithful to her husband.** This qualification is the same as that given for church leaders and deacons (3:2, 12) for the same reason. Obviously a widow who remarried should not be receiving assistance from the church.
3. She **must be well respected by everyone because of the good she has done.** A woman who has raised children (orphans perhaps, or her own but somehow could not care for her now), practiced hospitality, helped those in need, established a good reputation for her kindness, and rendered service to the church would be qualified to be on the list of widows.

5:11-13 These verses appear to be an overly harsh indictment of young widows, however, Paul actually was showing great compassion in this instruction. **Widows** who were **younger** than sixty should not be put on the list of widows (described in 5:9). Most likely, this did not mean that younger widows were refused assistance by the church; rather, younger widows were not to take a pledge of service to the church, which probably included not remarrying. Paul understood that younger women might face normal **physical desires** and might **want to remarry**. While this was perfectly acceptable in most instances, it would be unacceptable if the woman had taken a pledge to the church—then her desires **will overpower** her **devotion to Christ** and she might have to break her vow. Vows of this kind were not required nor demanded, but when made, they were considered as binding as marriage itself. Paul preferred that a young widow not put herself in the position of trying to meet an ideal of chaste widowhood and then wishing she hadn't; instead, she should be free to remarry. In fact, as Paul goes on to point out, a young widow needed to have direction, since merely submitting to her own desires might well lead to a denial of the faith through marriage with an unbeliever or to a lifestyle dishonoring to Christ.

The context of this passage reveals two certain concerns of Paul: (1) Some young widows did not qualify for inclusion among the widows under long-term care by the church (5:9-11), and (2) those young widows not under the care of the church should marry and raise a family in a manner honoring to Christ (5:14). Paul was concerned that these young widows would become victims of undisciplined desires. If they were put on the list and received full support from the church, these younger energetic women, with too much time on their hands, were more susceptible to distractions. Their lack of wisdom that comes with age might lead them to be **lazy**, doing visitation for purposes of **gossiping** and **getting into other people's business**. The picture here describes women busy accomplishing little good and much that is destructive. While this may sound like an extremely negative comment about these women, we ought to note the context and take into account that **anyone** with too much free time can often get into trouble.

5:14 Paul's advice to **younger widows** was to **marry again** (if that became an option), **have children**, and run their **homes**. As any mother knows, that is enough to keep her busy and out of trouble!

Paul had much more in mind here than merely providing a way to keep young widows off the streets. He placed before them a high calling. Note

the two specific roles that he envisioned for these women within marriage. They were to raise children (giving them life and then bearing with them along their road to adulthood). But they were also to take care of their homes. This passage agrees with 2:11-15 in giving women distinct authority within their homes. In Christ, women have worth and worthwhile roles. The immeasurable importance of training the next generation presents a demanding challenge. The outside community would judge Christianity based on how these young widows conducted themselves.

The **enemy** probably refers to Satan and/or those he uses to tear Christians down. Obviously, young women supported by the church who became local busybodies would not give the church a good reputation in the community and nonbelievers would speak **against** the church and Christians. Satan and his followers would give the believers enough trouble without them bringing it on themselves.

5:15 That some of these young widows **have already gone astray and now follow Satan** explains much of the intensity in Paul's expressions throughout this passage. Some women from the church had already broken their commitment to Christ. Though they might still be superficially affiliated with the believers, their lives were representing Satan's power. Turning aside after Satan was probably not total apostasy, but rather the pursuit of a sensually oriented lifestyle leading to idleness, gossip, and at times even false teaching. Their loss bothered Paul. He was determined to help Timothy prevent further losses.

5:16 The role of taking care of her home (5:14) means that women must make sure that any **relatives** who were **widows** must be cared for so as not to **put the responsibility on the church.** In this way, those in need received assistance from their families. Then the church would be freed up to **care for widows who are truly alone.**

This epistle has been attacked frequently as uncharitable toward women. Paul's limitation on the teaching ministry of women recorded in 2:11-15 has often been taken to summarize all that Paul thought and wrote about women in the church. But given the compromised condition of the church in Ephesus, with Timothy and Paul struggling to stem the tide of false teaching, the specific roles, responsibilities, and value given to women are rather remarkable. Male believers were to exemplify the best treatment of women, especially widows. Women themselves were challenged to live full lives, raising children, managing households, caring for others, and being deeply involved in serving ministries. Those who chafe under Paul's seeming failure to give women "up front exposure" ought to remember that Jesus defined that kind of leadership as the most insignificant by Kingdom standards (Luke 22:25-27).

5:17-18 These **elders** carried significant responsibilities in overseeing the congregation. Those who **do their work well should be paid well.** Paul singled out those elders who carried the twin responsibilities of **preaching and teaching** (for related passages, see Matthew 10:5-16; Luke 10:1-12; 1 Corinthians 9:3-14). Preaching and teaching are closely related. Preaching (literally "laboring in the word") involves proclaiming the word of God, explaining its truth, helping learners understand difficult passages, and helping them apply God's word to daily life. Teaching refers more to the extended training of others in Christian doctrine and the gospel message. These roles carried added importance because the New Testament was not yet available in written form. Elders who worked hard for the believers by adding to their responsibilities both preaching and teaching should be paid a stipend. Paul supported his instruction that the elders should be paid by quoting first the Old Testament (Deuteronomy 25:4) and then the words of Jesus himself (Matthew 10:10; Luke 10:7). This double reference shows that both the Old Testament and the Gospels were considered **the Scripture** by Paul.

While seeming odd at first, the reference to the **ox** is very appropriate. Often oxen were used to tread out the grain on a threshing floor. The animal was attached by poles to a large millstone. As it walked around the millstone, its hooves trampled the grain, separating the kernels from the chaff. At the same time, the millstone ground the grain into flour. Muzzling the ox would prevent it from eating while it was working. Paul used this illustration to argue that productive Christian workers should receive financial support. The fact that a person is in Christian ministry doesn't mean that he or she should be poorly paid.

5:19-20 Wherever a group of people work together, conflicts occur. The church and its leaders are not exempt from sin, faults, and mistakes. But criticism may arise for wrong reasons or impure motives—minor imperfections, failure to meet someone's expectations, personality clashes. Thus Paul called upon the Old Testament stipulation that **complaints** should not even be heard **unless there are two or three witnesses to accuse** the person (see Deuteronomy 17:6; 19:15; Matthew 18:16; John 8:17; 2 Corinthians 13:1). But just because there were two or three witnesses

doesn't mean the accused was automatically guilty. A thorough investigation of charges was still required.

If an accusation was confirmed, however, discipline was in order. Then if the church leader persisted in that sin, Timothy was to publicly expose the **sins** and rebuke him. The rebuke must be administered fairly and lovingly for the purpose of restoration, but it should cause all who see it to **have a proper fear of God.** Timothy could not be lax in dealing with elders who persisted in sin. The witness and reputation of the church to the outside world, as well as its own inner purity, depended on fair but consistent discipline.

5:21 As difficult as it might be, Timothy was not to waver on any of these instructions (and perhaps particularly the instructions about rebuking elders when needed). Paul gave Timothy this charge in the sight of **God, Christ Jesus,** and the **holy angels**—all of whom judge sinners (see Matthew 25:31-46; Luke 15:10; 1 Corinthians 4:9; 2 Peter 2:4; Revelation 14:7; 20:1-3). Any needed discipline or rebuke must be administered without regard to Timothy's personal inclinations, as if Timothy were pronouncing judgment before God, Christ, and the angels. For the sake of the church, Timothy needed to **obey these instructions without taking sides or showing special favor to anyone.**

5:22 One way to avoid the sticky problem of disciplining an elder is to be very careful about who is placed in that important position. Timothy should **never be in a hurry about appointing an elder** because he might overlook major problems or sins. Choosing church leaders today is a serious responsibility. They must have the qualities described in 3:1-13 and Titus 1:5-9. Not everyone who wants to be a church leader is ready or capable. Timothy needed to be certain of an applicant's qualifications before asking him to take a leadership position. If Timothy ordained a man who became a liability because of his persistent sinning, and if Timothy allowed that man to remain in the office despite those sins, Timothy would actually **participate in** those **sins** by compromising himself. Instead, he should **keep** himself **pure.**

By staying pure, Timothy would be able to more clearly judge those capable of serving the church as elders. In addition, by dealing immediately with sin among the elders, Timothy would show his convictions, his unwillingness to compromise with sin, which would also help him to remain pure.

5:23 The very mention of **wine** has given rise to questions about why Paul gave this advice to Timothy. Perhaps drinking water of poor quality (water did not come clear and clean from the tap in those days) had led to Timothy's stomach problem and frequent illnesses, so he should stop drinking only **water.** Paul's counsel here was to make use of alcohol for its medicinal value.

Those who come to this text for either open permission to use alcohol or for prohibition against the use of alcohol will be forced to meet on a middle ground. Paul has, in fact, stated a limited application for alcohol. Within this letter, he has already expressed the other extreme by insisting that those in leadership positions not be heavy drinkers (3:3). The distance is great between **a little** wine for the sake of his **stomach** and drunkenness, but some know all too well how quickly that ground can be covered and what destructive results there can be. The validity of the case for either total abstention from or some degree of consumption of alcohol must be constructed from other principles (such as freedom, self-control, moderation, discipline, etc.), and may well have to rely more honestly on personal, situational, and cultural factors.

Whatever the extent of Paul's advice here, it gives us insight into Timothy. Paul's kind words to his dear friend show his concern for Timothy's physical well-being. It also demonstrates his awareness that people in ministry function as whole beings, and that dysfunctions in mental, emotional, spiritual, and physical areas take their toll on effectiveness.

5:24-25 Picking up directly from verse 22, Paul revealed the key difficulty in the task of choosing good leaders in the church. **Some people lead sinful lives,** while others pass by us before their sins become apparent, if they become apparent at all. A person must be known well before deciding whether he is qualified to serve the church in a leadership position. The judgment Paul referred to included both the judgment of God and the judgment required by Timothy in authorizing leaders. Paul was warning Timothy and us about the importance of not judging by immediate appearances. Sometimes problems are easy to see, but others **will not be revealed until later.**

In the same way, some people's **good** deeds may be conspicuous, while others' **good deeds,** done behind the scenes, **won't be known until later.** Many of the leadership qualities that Paul listed in 3:2-7 fit in this category. Some, like hospitality and gentleness, create immediate and visible results, while others, like household management and guilelessness, only become apparent over a period of time.

Both verses 24 and 25 explain why Paul instructed Timothy to choose church leaders carefully. Hasty assessment of men for leadership positions could mean overlooking sins or good qualities; then unqualified men might be chosen and qualified men set aside. The hard fact is that in time, a man's true personality is revealed, for better or for worse. It is far better for the church when leaders are carefully and prayerfully selected.

6:1-2a In the Roman culture of Paul's day, slavery was a deeply rooted institution. It was also widespread, since estimates place the number of slaves at 60 million, or half the population of the empire. Slaves conducted most of the functions of society, from the most menial tasks to work as tutors for children and estate managers. They were used as we use tools, machinery, and technology today. Slavery was economic rather than racially motivated. People usually became slaves as a result of war or poverty.

A great social and legal gulf separated masters and slaves. Both Paul and Peter gave instructions about master/slave relations (see 1 Corinthians 7:20-24; Galatians 3:28; Ephesians 6:5-9; Colossians 3:22-25; Titus 2:9-10; the book of Philemon; 1 Peter 2:13-25). The abolition of slavery was not on the horizon for masters and slaves in the Roman Empire, so instructions about this touchy topic became extremely valuable. While not speaking against the institution of slavery, they gave guidelines for Christian slaves and Christian masters.

Paul wrote specifically to **Christians who are slaves,** explaining that their attitude toward even their unbelieving **masters** should be **full respect.** This appeared to be an obvious instruction if the **master** were a **Christian;** but even so, then the slave should **work all the harder.** Even if the master were an unbeliever, however, the Christian slave should still treat him or her with full respect. By so doing, **the name of God and his teaching will not be shamed.**

Paul's counsel for the master/slave relationship can be applied to the employer/employee relationship today. The attitude and behavior of believers on the job will help or hurt others' openness to the gospel they share. Employees should work hard, showing respect for their employers. In turn, employers should be fair (Ephesians 6:5-9; Colossians 3:22-25). Our work should reflect our faithfulness to and love for Christ. In that way, Christian employees will be a positive witness for Christ to an unbelieving employer.

1 TIMOTHY 6 : 2 B - 2 1

FALSE TEACHING AND TRUE RICHES / 6:2B-10

In this closing section of his instructional letter, Paul returned to discussing how Timothy should handle the false teachers in Ephesus (see 1:3-11). After all, they were one of the causes for this letter. Paul told Timothy to stay away from those who just want to make money from preaching, and from those in the church who stray from the sound teachings of the gospel into controversial arguments.

6:2b-3 Once again Paul repeated the command for Timothy to **teach** the **truths** that Paul was giving **and encourage everyone to obey them.** Paul wanted to make sure Timothy understood that the **false teachers** were denying the truth, **the sound wholesome teaching of the Lord Jesus Christ.** Any teaching different from the Christian doctrine, based upon God's word, was false teaching. Any teaching different from the sound instruction of the gospel of Christ is false teaching. Some commentators believe that at least one of the Gospels (perhaps Luke) may have already been in circulation, allowing believers access to that "wholesome teaching" in written form. In any case, those teachings had been preserved orally and constantly taught to believers.

However, Paul's concern here was not about the form of the instruction, but that the false teachers disagreed with what Jesus Christ had taught and demonstrated. They erred in contradicting and discounting Jesus. False teaching is ungodly teaching; it cannot result in **a godly life.** Our applications of God's word will always depend on how accurately we have understood the teaching of God's word. But these false teachers were not merely mistaken in their doctrine; their evil went deeper. Or rather, it originated in deeper problems. They were not well-intentioned teachers who had made unfortunate mistakes. Their basic motivations were evil.

6:4 Paul revealed the real character of the false teachers behind their veneer of prestige. These are not very flattering words for a group of teachers who apparently thought very highly of themselves! **Conceited** describes the trait of a person having an excessively favorable opinion of his own ability or importance. The false teachers showed all that and more, yet Paul confronted that conceit by explaining that they were actually **ignorant.** The utter falsehood of both the content and the conclusions of their teaching was worthy not of pride, but shame. They

did not agree with the truth, but instead had **an unhealthy desire to quibble over the meaning of words** (1:4, 6) that promoted speculation and led to arguments about ideas that came not from Scripture, but from the minds of the false teachers. The controversial ideas and the disputes about words had a devastating effect in the church. With the believers embroiled in **arguments** over meaningless theories and false doctrine, relationships began to deteriorate. **Jealousy** is followed by **fighting,** meaning competition and/or violent and bitter conflict. **Slander** and **evil suspicions** surely follow. The seeds of false teaching in Ephesus were yielding a harvest of bitterness.

6:5 Here are more characteristics of false teachers: they **always cause trouble** because they all had **corrupt** (debased, depraved, tainted) **minds.** Not only were they ignorant (6:4), but their minds were so corrupt that **the truth** (God's truth) was completely absent. They were motivated by getting **rich.** While Paul instructed the church about the Christian leaders' right to be paid for their services, he made it clear that they should not be greedy (3:3, 8) and should not consider their ministry as a way to get rich. Those who did clearly could not be serving the Lord Christ with pure motives, but instead were serving their selfish desires.

6:6 The false teachers thought religion was a means to get rich; instead, **true religion** is **great wealth** in itself when accompanied by **contentment.** One's religion does not come and go with the uncertainties of material wealth; faith in Christ, with contentment, is the wealth, independent of one's bankbook and possessions. The false teachers had it backward.

True religion (faith in Christ) requires training (4:7) and develops inner spiritual qualities, while at the same time being apparent in the way we relate to others (4:12). It exhibits true character exemplified in the way we serve others. **Contentment** grows from our attitude toward living God's way. To have contentment in Christ requires four decisions about the events and possessions of our life:

1. We must focus on what God has already allowed us to have.
2. We must disregard what we do not have.
3. We must refuse to covet what others may have.
4. We must give thanks to God for each and all of his gifts (4:3-4).

If we fail to make these decisions, our contentment will diminish.

Finally, the **great wealth** that motivated the false teachers was neither lasting nor capable of bringing contentment. Their earthly profits would be left behind. What brings great wealth has to do with eternal values. When material treasures become our focus, we quit contributing to our eternal accounts. Whatever gains we may experience in this life mean nothing if they cause us eternal bankruptcy (see Matthew 6:19-24).

This statement provides the key to spiritual growth and personal fulfillment. We should honor God and center our desires on him, and we should be content with what God is doing in our lives (see Philippians 4:11-13).

6:7 Paul followed up his statement about the true source of contentment by discounting any hope of ultimate contentment based merely on this life. The correct perspective on material possessions—money, houses, clothing, vehicles, jewels, land, etc.—remains eternally the same. They cannot last forever. We can lose, break, or ruin them in this life. **We didn't bring** them with us when we were born, and we **cannot carry anything with us when we die.**

6:8 Human beings have basic needs. Believers and unbelievers alike require **food and clothing** (also implying shelter) for survival. The difference should be that when believers' basic needs are met, they ought to be satisfied and **content,** requiring nothing more. In contrast, unbelievers are driven by society's standards and desires; they cannot be content with only basic needs being met because they must always strive for more.

6:9 After stating the simple plan for living faithfully, Paul challenged the world's view by showing the outcome of trying to gain contentment through the pursuit of wealth. The desire to be rich is, by its very nature, a desire that cannot be satiated. **People who long to be rich** cannot understand contentment because they can never have enough money. The **temptation** of money eventually traps people into doing anything to get money—illegal or immoral—even being willing to hurt others. People's desire for money feeds their greed. Soon their passion plunges **them into ruin and destruction.**

6:10 People often misquote this verse, saying, "money is the root of all evil." But it is the **love of money** that Paul speaks against. Money itself is not evil; in fact, money can do much good for the furthering of God's Kingdom. Money supports missionaries around the globe; money helps organizations fight for Christian causes in government; money supports churches and church leaders; money helps feed the hungry and clothe the poor. Obviously, while God doesn't need money (in fact, all the money in the world belongs to him), he can use money given by generous people to help those in need. These people can give because they control their money. The problem happens when money controls people.

People who love money are controlled by a ruthless, insatiable master, for the love of money can never be satisfied. Loving money **is at the root of all kinds of evil:** marriage problems, illegal acts, blowups in partnerships, envy, immorality, lying, ruthlessness, stealing, and a willingness to even hurt others if it makes money. The worst scenario, of course, is that money would actually lead a person **from the faith.** It's tragic when money replaces God in a person's life. These greedy people found themselves **pierced with many sorrows.** The picture is that they were being impaled by sharp objects that they continued to push against. Instead of God's way, they chose a path that was taking them deeper and deeper into a briar patch of trouble. Instead of the happiness they expected, money brought grief.

It would be a hazardous mistake to conclude that Paul is teaching that we should not be concerned about money. In fact, we should be respectfully asking God for funds with which to carry out our responsibilities and to help others. It is right to ask God for provision for daily life and to do his will (help children through college, pay off the church mortgage, etc.). Paul was concerned about greed more than he was about money.

PAUL'S FINAL INSTRUCTIONS / 6:11-21

In these final verses, Paul included personal words to Timothy, a final doxology to Jesus Christ, and parting words of instruction about those who were being false to the gospel by their lives and teaching.

6:11 In contrast to the "some" of verse 10 who had wandered from the faith in their quest for riches, Paul addressed **Timothy** as a man of God who should **run from all these evil things,** and instead to **follow what is right and good.** This involves wholehearted efforts to grow into the kind of person God has already declared he would be in eternity. To **pursue a godly life** means doing actions in line with God's character. These overlap in meaning—the first emphasizes obedience, while the second emphasizes the God-centered motives for obedience.

Faith and **love** are fundamental to Christianity and basic to Paul's teaching (see 1 Corinthians 13:13). The qualities of faith and love are constantly under improvement by the work of God's Spirit. Our capacity to trust must grow and be renewed, and the development of our love for God and for others involves a lifelong construction project. Believers are to pursue these in the sense that we practice what we already understand, while praying that we might understand and practice more.

Perseverance in persecution and trouble are vital for all believers; Timothy would need an extra dose of perseverance as he led a large congregation through difficult days ahead. Pursuing perseverance would require a willingness to undergo suffering.

Gentleness seems an odd quality for Timothy to pursue; after all, he was already timid and Paul had told him to deal firmly with false teaching. However, gentleness can reveal more power than roughness or harshness. Perhaps by mentioning this Paul was affirming a positive quality that was already a part of Timothy's character. The false teachers could have no power against a righteous, gentle leader with the truth on his side.

6:12 Using the same word he used in 1:18 to describe Timothy's work in Ephesus, Paul described furthering the gospel as a fight—but it is **the good fight for what we believe.** The verb tense in Greek implies that this **fight** is an ongoing, continual process requiring diligence and discipline. Timothy would continue a fight already begun by others. Believers today continue the fight for which Timothy and Paul offered their lives.

Those who fight the good fight of the faith can already **hold tightly** to their prize. **Eternal life** had been **given** to Timothy (as for all believers) at the moment of conversion (see John 5:24; 1 John 3:14; 5:13). When a person confesses faith in Jesus Christ as Savior, eternal life begins. Reflecting the confidence Paul had in the outcome of Timothy's life, Paul reminded him of what he had **confessed so well before many witnesses.** The specific inci-

dent Paul had in mind has been identified as unknown, but the fact of Paul and Timothy's long association would have given the elder any number of occasions to observe the younger's faith in action.

6:13-14 Several times in this letter, Paul has charged, commanded, and urged Timothy toward various actions. Here again, Paul made a **command** to Timothy (see 6:14). Just as Timothy made a good confession before many witnesses, Christ **gave a good testimony before Pontius Pilate.** The good testimony is understanding and telling who Jesus is. Jesus' trial before Pilate is recorded in the Gospels: Matthew 27:11; Mark 15:2; Luke 23:2-3; John 18:36-37. No matter how difficult circumstances might become, Timothy always would have the example of Jesus who remained faithful in the face of death.

Paul urged (6:13) Timothy to obey the **commands with all purity,** referring to Paul's previous instruction to continue in his pursuit of godly character. Then **no one** would be able to **find fault with** him. The commands need only be followed **until our Lord Jesus Christ returns.** At that time, the good fight will be over; the battle will be won.

6:15 The **right time** of the Second Coming is according to God's timetable. Paul's early teachings and writings show that he believed this return would occur very soon. However, at the time of this letter to Timothy, Paul realized that this return might not occur before his death. It would occur in God's own time. As Paul contemplated the glorious display of love and power that will be revealed when Christ returns, he acknowledged God's awesome and transcendent nature.

Paul's doxology may be words from an early Christian hymn or even a Jewish blessing. See Deuteronomy 10:17; Psalm 136:2-3; Revelation 17:14; 19:16 for similar words of praise to God. In any case, Paul's reference to God's plan immediately filled his mind with a word-vision of the one he served with his life. The phrase, **King of kings and Lord of lords,** reveals that there is no other way to ascribe more power and authority than to God alone. Paul used the common titles for human power, but enlarged them by investing in God supreme power over those we consider most powerful. God has no peer.

6:16 Having established some idea of an appropriate title for God, Paul now lists several of the notable characteristics of our divine ruler. God **alone can never die.** He is the only one having immortality in himself. He is not subject to death. Others may be given immortality, but only God has it inherent in his being.

Because he is eternal, he gives us eternal life. The bright glory of God's presence creates a barrier of **light so brilliant that no human can approach him.** Even if the light were removed, God remains invisible, unseen by human eyes (see Exodus 33:17-23; John 1:18). This does not mean God is unknowable, but that his holiness keeps us from seeing him.

God's legitimate power and position require two responses from us: **honor** and submission to his **power.** When we approach God, we must not emphasize our own understanding or self-confidence; instead, we must submit to him and worship his awesome majesty. Any claim to equality with God simply widens the gulf between us. As Paul pointed out to the Romans (Romans 1:21-22), those who treat God lightly will not be able to bear the weight of his judgment.

6:17 After concluding his doxology with a decisive "Amen," Paul returned to the matters at hand. Those most in danger of having an incorrect attitude toward God were the **rich in this world.** In verses 3-10, Paul had instructed those who did not have wealth, but deeply desired it. Here he focused on those who already possessed wealth. Ephesus was a thriving city, and the Ephesian church probably had at least some prosperous members. Perhaps some of the false teachers had already succeeded in amassing a degree of wealth for themselves.

Paul advised Timothy to deal with any potential problems by teaching that having riches carries great responsibility. The wealthy must not be **proud,** nor **trust in their money.** Pride was inappropriate because it indicated that the rich were basing their lives on something **which will soon be gone.** Rather, they should **trust the living God.** He gave them what they have. The rich must be careful to trust only in the living God for their security. The rich need not be ashamed of their riches; those riches are a gift from God, given to be enjoyed. There must always be a balance between avoiding a stale, ascetic life while at the same time keeping oneself from self-indulgence.

6:18 The rich are not to consume their riches on selfish pleasures; rather, they must **use their money to do good.** The general goal to **do good** is broken down into three categories:

1. Being **rich in good works** means practicing "hands-on" giving to others. People are sometimes more effectively helped by personal involvement than by the giving of material objects or money.
2. Giving **generously to those in need** strikes a blow against the self-centeredness of our times.

We learn to do with less so that more may do with some.

3. Being **always ready to share with others** improves our ability to respond quickly and effectively. Experience can help us to always be ready to share.

We can experience a deep fellowship when believers make their resources available to one another. Being rich in good works may not necessarily benefit our financial statement, but in the long run it will be a far more valuable asset in God's eyes.

6:19 Jesus talked about treasure in his Sermon on the Mount (Matthew 6:19-21). The rich must make certain to **store up their treasure** in heaven, investing their riches for eternity. This kind of investment includes tithing and giving offerings in church, but it is much broader. Any unselfish giving to meet the needs of others, especially the poor, creates a deposit in eternity. The person without God who selfishly pursues wealth will lay up a treasure of God's wrath (James 5:1-5).

In so doing, those who give are those who provide a **good foundation for the future** and experience **real life** as it is meant to be. In contrast to those seeking riches and ending in ruin and destruction (6:9), these generous rich people find true life, both on earth and in eternity. Because God is the source of all life (6:13), all those who live his way experience real living!

6:20 One last time, Paul exhorted, encouraged, and urged Timothy to **guard** the teachings and instructions given him. No matter how influential the false teachers would become, Timothy would remain guardian of the truth, teaching it without wavering and without compromise. Paul's ministry on earth would eventually end with his death; Timothy was **entrusted** with the truth of the gospel so that he, in turn, would pass it along to others. A guardian of the truth should not be involved in **godless, foolish discussions** or spend time talking with those who oppose him **with their so-called knowledge,** that is, the false teachers.

6:21 Those who followed the false teachers had **wandered from the faith.** "Wandered" (literally "missed the mark") does not imply a permanent condition, but a dangerous and fruitless one. True believers would not lose their salvation, but if they followed the false teachers, they would waste valuable time in nonsense—time that could have been spent learning about and sharing the Good News.

The closing benediction includes a plural **you,** indicating that Paul expected this letter to be read to the congregation and to other churches. Paul began and ended with **grace**. For him, as it should be for us, grace was never a sociable courtesy but a costly gift from God. Having experienced the grace of God, Paul never tired of praying that others would also experience this grace.

The book of 1 Timothy provides guiding principles for local churches, including rules for public worship and qualifications for overseers (elders, pastors), deacons, and special church workers (widows). Paul told the church leaders to correct incorrect doctrine and to deal lovingly and fairly with all people in the church. The church is not organized simply for the sake of organization, but so that Christ can be honored and glorified. While studying these guidelines, don't lose sight of what is most important in the life of the church— knowing God, working together in harmony, and taking God's Good News to the world.

2 TIMOTHY

INTRODUCTION

What thoughts and feelings must have filled Paul as he sat again in prison, knowing that he soon would face his executioner . . . and then his Lord. Reflecting on his ministry, Paul must have felt joy, remembering his conversion on the road to Damascus, his session with the Jerusalem elders, his trips throughout the world preaching the gospel and planting churches, the explosive spread of Christianity among Gentiles, and his faithful coworkers and close friends: Barnabas, Silas, Priscilla, Aquila, Luke, Peter, James, Mark, Lydia, and so many others. But Paul must have felt a twinge of sadness and regret as he recalled those who had harmed or deserted him or had left the faith: Demas, Alexander, Hymenaeus, and others. Undoubtedly, Paul also experienced moments of intense loneliness. He had been deserted twice—first by those in Asia (1:15), and then by those in Rome at his arrest (4:16). Paul's emotions also must have included concern . . . for young believers, for the churches, and for those he had appointed to carry the ministry forward—young leaders such as Titus, Timothy, and Tychicus.

Paul knew that the new generation of church leaders was ready—trained, experienced, confident, articulate, courageous, and totally committed to Christ. In fact, already they had ministered in very difficult circumstances, confronting false teachers, organizing local churches, evangelizing the lost, and discipling believers. Titus had worked effectively with the infamous Cretans, and Timothy had led and nurtured the church at Ephesus.

As Paul lay in his cell, awaiting martyrdom at the command of the madman Nero, he was not alone with his feelings: visitors had come, Luke was present (4:11), and God was there. And Paul did not spend his final days and hours wallowing in despair—he encouraged and taught others, read (4:13), and wrote.

AUTHOR

Paul, the great apostle and missionary of the church.

Paul's final words were bundled in a letter, to his beloved Timothy, his "true child in the faith" (1 Timothy 1:2). A much more personal and somber letter than the others, 2 Timothy contains no complex refutations of apostasy, detailed instructions for church leaders, profound theological treatises, extensive lessons for young believers, or exhilarating doxologies and benedictions. Instead, in this last letter, brimming with quiet emotion, Paul reflected on his life and encouraged, warned, instructed, and exhorted Timothy. It's as though Paul were saying, "I'm trusting you to carry on, Timothy. Stay faithful, stay strong, watch out, and take care!"

What last words would you write to your loved ones and friends? Paul's words flowed from his life of faith and reflected his deep commitment to his Lord. What could you say or write to encourage someone now?

For more about Paul, see the Author section in the Introduction to the book of Romans. See also the Introduction to the book of 1 Timothy.

DATE AND SETTING
Written about A.D. 66 or 67, from Rome.

Paul had written letters to Timothy (1 Timothy) and Titus in approximately A.D. 64-65, during his time of freedom between Roman imprisonments. Just about two years later, he wrote to Timothy again, but this time from prison. Note that the last three of Paul's thirteen letters were written to men who would lead the church after his death. Paul knew the importance of entrusting the ministry to reliable men and women who would be able to teach others (2:2).

Nero, the fifth Roman emperor, began to reign in A.D. 54, at sixteen years of age. The first few years of his rule were peaceful and gave promise of a bright future. During that time, Paul had appealed to Caesar at his trial in Caesarea (Acts 25:10-11) and thus had been brought to Rome to present his case (A.D. 61). It seems that when Paul eventually went to trial, he was cleared of all charges and freed to resume his ministry. For the next few years, Paul traveled extensively and wrote 1 Timothy and Titus. All this occurred during Nero's reign.

After marrying Poppaea, Nero became brutal and ruthless, killing his own mother, his chief advisers, Seneca and Burrus, and many of the nobility to seize their fortunes. Nero's thirst for publicity pushed him into excessive acts of decadence, including chariot races, combat between gladiators, and the gory spectacle of prisoners thrown to wild beasts. In A.D. 64, fire destroyed a large part of Rome. Suspected of ordering the fire himself (to make room for a new palace), Nero deflected blame by accusing the Christians, a devout religious minority who refused to worship the Emperor. Thus began the terrible persecution of the church, with torture, executions, and Coliseum entertainment. Tacitus wrote:

> Their death was made a matter of sport; they were covered in wild beasts' skins and torn to pieces by dogs; or were fastened to crosses and set on fire in order to serve as torches by night. . . . There arose a feeling of pity because it was felt that they were being sacrificed not for the common good, but to gratify the savagery of one man. (Tacitus, *Annals* 15.44)

During this reign of terror for Christians, Paul was taken prisoner again, apparently at Nicopolis where he had intended to spend the winter (Titus 3:12). Paul was taken to Rome and imprisoned in the Mamertime dungeon, in the center of Rome near the forum.

Paul's first imprisonment (about A.D. 60-62) had been similar to house arrest. He lived in a rented house, in relative comfort but under Roman guard, and was able to welcome numerous visitors (Acts 28:23-30). In contrast, Paul's second Roman prison was dark, damp, dirty, and difficult to find (1:17). In the first, Paul had awaited trial with the privilege of a Roman citizen. In the second, he waited for death as a condemned criminal. Paul still was allowed to write and read, but he was lonely (he wanted to see his friends—4:9-11) and he was cold (he wanted his coat—4:13).

A few months after writing this letter to Timothy, according to tradition, Paul was beheaded on the Ostian Way outside Rome. This occurred shortly before Nero's own death, by suicide, in A.D. 68, just as the Roman senate was declaring Nero "an enemy of the people" because of the atrocities he had committed. Peter also was martyred during Nero's reign.

Timothy probably was still in Ephesus when he received Paul's letter. Paul was lonely and wanted Timothy to come and see him. He sent Tychicus to Ephesus with this letter, with the probable understanding that Tychicus would relieve Timothy of his duties there. Sent as the apostolic representative to that city, Timothy had been charged in Paul's first letter (about A.D. 64) with the responsibility of organizing the churches there and for rooting out the false teachers. While 2 Timothy contains pastoral counsel and instruction for the church, it is essentially a personal letter—Paul revealing his heart and soul to his dear friend.

For more on the church at Ephesus, see the Setting section in the Introduction to the book of 1 Timothy.

AUDIENCE
Timothy and the church at large.

Timothy represented the new generation of leadership for the church. He, Titus, and others were expected to fill the shoes of Paul, Peter, and the other apostles and church leaders. Paul had left Timothy in Ephesus and had given him responsibility for refuting the false teachers and organizing the local congregations. Paul had written Timothy (1 Timothy) with specific instructions for choosing elders and deacons and with a challenge to sound doctrine and personal discipline.

It is not surprising that Paul's final words would be penned to Timothy. Paul was instrumental in Timothy's coming to faith, and he thought of Timothy as a son. They experienced a closeness in friendship and in the body of Christ. Paul knew he could count on his beloved friend and coworker. For more on Timothy, see the Audience section in the Introduction to 1 Timothy.

Through the inspiration of the Holy Spirit, Paul also was writing to the church at large—believers everywhere, then and in the years to come. Because this letter is so specific and personal, its message applies directly to individual Christians, especially church leaders. Much also can be learned from the close relationship enjoyed by Paul and Timothy. Like father and son, siblings, or very close friends, these men had worked together, prayed for each other, and loved one another. In a world hostile to Christ and those who would claim his name, Paul and Timothy had learned the importance of teamwork and of caring for their brothers and sisters in Christ. In fact, in the last few sentences of this letter, Paul referred to at least nine other fellow servants of Christ. If you were writing your last letter, what coworkers in the ministry would you name? Who is your "Timothy"? We must learn to work closely with other believers—the need and our task is too great to try to minister alone.

OCCASION AND PURPOSE
To inspire, challenge, and motivate Timothy to carry on the gospel ministry.

This letter to Timothy is tinged with sadness because Paul realized that soon he would be executed. Reminiscences (1:1-5; 3:10-11), references to death (1:10; 2:11) and suffering (1:12; 2:9; 3:11-12), mention of prison life (1:15-16; 2:9), and hints of impending martyrdom (4:6-8, 18) reveal Paul's realistic understanding of his plight. But this letter is not depressing—Paul filled it with notes of triumph as he wrote of his lifelong commitment to Christ (1:12; 2:11-13; 4:7-8) and as he challenged Timothy to carry on with the work to which they had both been called (1:6-7, 13-14; 2:1-7, 15; 3:14-17; 4:1-2, 5).

Paul had prepared Timothy for this day, and he was sure that his protégé was ready. So he wrote to remind Timothy of his call and the task that lay ahead. Paul also was aware of Timothy's shortcomings; he virtually called Timothy's timidity (1:7) being "ashamed" of Christ and of Paul himself (1:8). Paul was challenging Timothy to get his act together.

Paul was amazing. Although deserted by former friends and facing death, he continued to fight the good fight (4:7) and to challenge and inspire others to greatness. Paul's primary focus was to be faithful to Christ and to his call as a minister of the gospel. Next on Paul's list of priorities, however, stood his deep concern for the church and its new leaders. What holds top billing in your life—personal comfort, financial security, pleasure? As with Paul, if you focus on Christ, you will know how to live . . . and you will know how to die.

MESSAGE

Paul's introduction is tender, and every phrase exudes the love he has for Timothy (1:1-5). He then reminds Timothy of the qualities necessary for a faithful minister of Jesus Christ (1:6–2:13). Timothy should remember his call and use his gifts with boldness (1:6-12), keep to the truth (1:13-18), prepare others to follow him in the ministry (2:1, 2), be disciplined and ready to endure suffering (2:3-7), and keep his eyes and mind focused on Christ (2:8-13). Paul challenges Timothy to hold to sound doctrine, reject error and avoid godless chatter, correctly handle the word of truth (2:14-19), and keep his life pure (2:20-26).

Next, Paul warns Timothy of the opposition that he and other believers would face in the last days from self-centered people who use the church for their own gain and teach false doctrines (3:1-9). Paul tells Timothy to be prepared for these unfaithful people by remembering his example (3:10, 11), understanding the real source of the opposition (3:12, 13), and finding strength and power in the word of God (3:14-17). Then Paul gives Timothy a stirring charge: to preach the word (4:1-4) and to fulfill his ministry until the end (4:5-8).

Paul concludes with personal requests and items of information. In these final words, he reveals his loneliness and his strong love for his brothers and sisters in Christ (4:9-22). The main themes in the book of 2 Timothy include: *Boldness, Faithfulness, Preaching and Teaching,* and *Error.*

Boldness (1:5-12; 4:1-5). Paul knew that Timothy soon would face opposition and persecution and might become disheartened by Paul's imprisonment and death (1:8-9). He also knew that Timothy had the tendency to be timid, so Paul reminded him that God gives a spirit of power, love, and self-discipline, not timidity (1:7). And Paul urged Timothy to carry out his ministry without fear or shame, to utilize boldly the gifts of preaching and teaching that the Holy Spirit had given him.

IMPORTANCE FOR TODAY. We can easily become discouraged when we are persecuted for our faith. And we can be intimidated by the threats of those who oppose us. But the Holy Spirit helps us to be wise and strong, and God honors our confident testimony for him even when we suffer. To get over our fear of what people might say or do to us, we must take our eyes off people and look only to God, remembering that he has promised to be with us through everything (see Romans 8:38-39). In what situations are you afraid to speak up for what you believe? What can you do to strengthen your resolve to live more boldly for Christ?

Faithfulness (1:13-14; 2:1, 3-13; 3:14-15). Because of his difficult situation, Timothy may have been tempted to waver in his faith or even to desert the cause of Christ as others had done (4:10, 16). To resist this temptation, Timothy was to remember Christ's faithfulness in suffering and dying for our sins. In addition, Paul's own example was important, for he had been faithful through countless trials and was still serving Christ, even in prison. Paul urged Timothy to maintain sound doctrine, to be loyal and diligent, and to endure.

IMPORTANCE FOR TODAY. We followers of Christ can count on being opposed and suffering because of what we believe and how we live. People don't like to be reminded that they are sinning and headed for hell. Even in our churches we may face rejection when we stand for the truth. But regardless of the cost, we are to be faithful to Christ and to faithfully proclaim his Word. As we trust Christ, he counts us worthy to suffer, and he will give us the strength we need to be strong and faithful to him. What can you do to prepare for times of discouragement?

Preaching and Teaching (2:2, 22-26; 3:16-17; 4:1-5). Paul had spent most of his life spreading the Good News, winning people to Christ, teaching new Christians, and establishing new churches. Paul had trained Timothy to follow in his footsteps, to preach and teach the gospel. So facing the reality of his own death, Paul passed the leadership torch to Timothy and encouraged him to train others who would be able to carry on after Timothy was gone. Timothy should train these men and women in sound doctrine, in being totally committed to Christ, and in how to teach. In large measure we have heard the gospel and have believed because Paul and Timothy were faithful to teach others how to teach others.

IMPORTANCE FOR TODAY. The two most important tasks of a Christian leader are evangelism (sharing the gospel with others and leading them to Christ) and discipleship (establishing new believers in the faith). A vital part of the discipleship process is preparing people to transmit God's word to others so that they in turn might pass it on. Of course it is not enough just to teach—teaching must be of the highest quality, mining the depths of God's word. Whom are you helping to disciple? What is your church doing to carefully train men and women to teach?

Error (2:14-21; 3:1-13; 4:9-18). Wherever there is truth, lies will arise. Human beings are sinful and will use anything, even religious causes, to meet their self-centered needs. Remember, too, that Satan is constantly twisting the truth and attempting to deceive, so we shouldn't be surprised that false teachers abound. Paul warned Timothy about heretics and spiritual dropouts. Timothy was not to be surprised, discouraged, or defeated by these false teachers and deserters. Instead, he should stay strong in his faith, confront and refute those who would lead the church astray, and continue to boldly preach and teach the truth. And Paul reminded Timothy that God's word, not theories and philosophies, contains God's truth (see 2:15; 3:16-17).

IMPORTANCE FOR TODAY. The Bible warns that in the final days before Christ returns, false teachers will be prevalent. Thus spiritual error and heretics will be increasing through the years. The antidote for false teaching is keeping our eyes on Christ and studying God's word. We must be disciplined and ready to reject heresy. We must know the word of God as our sure defense against error and confusion. How much time each week do you spend in Bible study? What new Christian friend can you help get grounded more firmly in the word?

OUTLINE OF 2 TIMOTHY

  I. Foundations of Christian Service (1:1–2:26)
  II. Difficult Times for Christian Service (3:1–4:22)

2 TIMOTHY 1

GREETINGS FROM PAUL / 1:1-2

As Paul wrote this second letter, the Christian church throughout the empire was facing severe persecution and hardship. Emperor Nero had begun a major persecution in A.D. 64 as part of his plan to pass the blame for the great fire of Rome from himself to the Christians. This persecution spread across the empire and included social ostracism, public torture, and murder.

  Thus, the tone of this letter is somber. Paul, imprisoned for the last time, knew he would soon die. Unlike Paul's first imprisonment in Rome in a house where he continued to teach (Acts 28:16, 23, 30), this time he was probably confined to a cold dungeon, awaiting his death (4:6-8). As Paul awaited execution, he wrote this letter to his dear friend Timothy, a younger man who was like a son to him (1:2). How Timothy must have cherished this last letter from his beloved mentor and friend.

1:1 As at the beginning of 1 Timothy, Paul identifies himself by name and also by his authority. **Paul** was an **apostle,** meaning "one who is **sent.**" Paul was not one of the original twelve disciples (who were called apostles after Jesus' resurrection), yet Jesus appeared to Paul personally and commissioned him to be an apostle (Acts 9:1-6; 26:12-18). Paul did not seek this apostleship; instead, he was chosen by God. Thus, Paul could truthfully say he was an apostle **by God's will.** Obviously, this formal introduction was unneces-

sary for Timothy; however, Paul knew that his letters and teachings ultimately would reach a much larger audience, so he included these credentials in the salutation.

  The phrase, **the life he has promised through faith in Christ Jesus,** provides almost a summary statement of Paul's theology. To have faith in Christ Jesus involves trusting him, identifying with him, seeing ourselves under his protection and authority, and recognizing his presence in us.

1:2 Paul most likely met the young **Timothy** and his mother, Eunice, and grandmother, Lois (1:5), when Paul and Barnabas visited Lystra, a city in the province of Galatia, on the first missionary journey (see Acts 14:8-21). The young disciple traveled the empire with Paul, preaching and teaching the Good News. He became Paul's assistant—traveling with, and sometimes for, the great apostle.

That Paul referred to Timothy as **my dear son** reveals the special relationship that had developed between them, like a father and son. The term of endearment also indicates that this letter will be directed more toward Timothy himself.

Grace and **peace** appear in the greeting of all of Paul's letters. In his letters to Timothy, however, he added **mercy** (see also 1 Timothy 1:2). "Mercy" pictures God's "lovingkindness" so often written about in the Old Testament. God's mercy helps us day by day. Paul loved Timothy dearly, so he added "mercy" to reassure Timothy of God's constant protection and guidance, especially important as Paul faced his own death.

ENCOURAGEMENT TO BE FAITHFUL / 1:3-18

Paul's gentle words provide a clearer picture of Timothy's character. After their years of working companionship, the separated ministries had been difficult for both men. The parting had been painful (1:4). When Paul thought of his young disciple's faithfulness, he was reminded of Lois and Eunice, who had made a contribution to Timothy's faith. With these examples in mind, Paul was encouraged, and he proceeded to offer encouragement to Timothy. He elaborated on their shared role as guardians, heralds, and teachers of the gospel.

1:3 Paul constantly prayed for the churches he founded and visited (see Romans 1:8; Philippians 1:3; Colossians 1:3); and Paul prayed **constantly** for Timothy, his friend, his fellow traveler, his son in the faith, and a strong leader in the Christian church. Although the two men were separated from each other, their prayers provided a source of mutual encouragement. Sitting in a damp Roman prison cell, the great missionary Paul could no longer preach and travel, but he could pray. Paul's dearest friend, Timothy, ministered in Ephesus with believers very dear to him. Paul expressed his thankfulness to God for Timothy and his ministry, praying for him **night and day.** Paul knew he would die soon, but Timothy had been well prepared to carry on strong leadership in the Christian church. Paul would die; Christ's message would not.

Paul's almost parenthetical statement, that he worshiped God **with a clear conscience** mirrors his words in 1 Timothy 1:5 (also Acts 24:16). Most likely, Paul was describing his life of service to God as being wholehearted and without regrets (see Romans 1:9). As Paul looked back over his life (mainly his life since his call to apostleship and ministry), he could confidently say that he had accomplished what God had called him to do.

1:4 We don't know when Paul and Timothy had last parted, but it was probably when Paul was arrested and taken to Rome for his second imprisonment. The **tears** they had shed at parting had revealed the depth of their relationship. Timothy brought Paul great joy. Paul longed to see Timothy again, so twice more in this letter Paul requested that Timothy do his best to come to him soon (see 4:9, 21).

1:5 Timothy's **mother** and **grandmother, Eunice** and **Lois,** were early Christian converts, possibly through Paul's ministry in their home city, Lystra (Acts 16:1). They had communicated their strong Christian faith to Timothy, even though his Greek father (Acts 26:1) was probably not a believer. Paul mentioned that he knew Timothy **sincerely** trusted **the Lord** because Timothy's genuine faith stood in bold contrast to the insincerity of many who had deserted Paul (see 1:15; 2:17-18; 3:1-9, 13; 4:3-4, 10, 14, 16). Paul had no doubts concerning Timothy's faith.

Sincere faith means possessing heartfelt trust, not merely professing religious words. We must have genuine, authentic faith to face our work and challenges. Faith requires us to be steadfast and unwavering when we are under pressure or facing opposition. To trust God each day is a decision we must make, not an emotion that we feel. Is your faith halfhearted? Do you rely on how you feel to determine your faithfulness to God?

1:6 In telling Timothy to **fan into flames the spiritual gift God gave** him, Paul was encouraging him to persevere. At the time of his ordination, Timothy had received a special gift of the Spirit to enable him to serve the church (1 Timothy 4:14). This gift was most likely the gift of ministry, the special grace from God to do Christian service. Verse 7 supports that concept. Paul's words, **when I laid my hands on you,** most likely meant that Timothy's spiritual gift had been given to him, along with a prophecy, when Paul and the elders laid their hands on him and set him apart for ministry.

Rather than asking Timothy to restart a cold fire, Paul was encouraging him to fan a young fire to keep it at full flame. Timothy did not need new revelations or new gifts; he needed only to "fan" the gift of leadership he already had received, as well as to have courage and self-discipline for holding on to the truth in the days to come (see 1:13-14). When Timothy used his gift, the Holy Spirit would go with him and give him power. God never gives us a task to do without empowering us to carry it out.

1:7 Timothy experienced constant opposition to his message and to himself as a leader. His youth (see 1 Timothy 4:12), his association with Paul, and his leadership had come under fire from believers and nonbelievers alike. Perhaps Timothy felt intimidated, angered, even helpless in face of the opposition from the false teachers. Whatever the degree of his difficulties, Paul urged Timothy to boldness by reminding him of his call, his gift, and God's provision (see 1:6). **God has not given** his people **a spirit of fear and timidity;** rather God provides:

- **Power**—We do not need to have naturally powerful personalities. God gives strength of character and confidence that wins us respect when we face opposition as we speak, preach, and live the truth. God supernaturally replaces any timidity on the servant's part with boldness. Such power is difficult to discredit.
- **Love**—Accompanying the power to speak the truth must be love for the listeners, believers and nonbelievers alike. Love separates Christians from the heathen world around them. Indeed, love separated the minister of Christ from the false teachers. Such love is difficult to dismiss.
- **Self-discipline**—This can also be translated "self-control" or "sound mind." In order to lead others, true ministers must control themselves. To put it another way, a good leader must have a cool head. Such control, such "soundness" is difficult to disclaim.

All of these qualities are gifts of the Spirit, not just natural tendencies. They function best in harmony. Under the pressures of leadership, people tend to gravitate toward a desire for power and boldness as the most effective tools for success. But used alone, these qualities are self-defeating. The inclusion of love and self-control clearly indicates that a leader's effectiveness comes from God's Spirit. We may be impressed by a leader who exhibits boldness and power, but without love or self-control, such a leader is little more than a bully.

1:8 In this time of mounting persecution, Timothy may have been struggling with fears as he continued to preach the gospel. His fears would have been based on fact—believers were being arrested and executed. Against such opposition, Paul urged Timothy to **never be ashamed to tell others about the Lord,** and not to be **ashamed** that Paul sat in prison for his testimony. Paul was sure of God's hand in his present situation, and that he was **in prison for Christ.** Paul told Timothy to **be ready to suffer.** Eventually, Timothy would be jailed for preaching the gospel (Hebrews 13:23). But Paul promised Timothy that God would give him reliable **strength** and that he would be able to endure if suffering came. When believers undergo suffering, they need not rely on their own strength for survival and sustenance; instead, God gives power and strength to endure.

1:9 Salvation forms the core of the gospel, the Good News. There would be no gospel without the sacrifice that Jesus Christ made for our sins. **God saved** his people; God **chose** his people **to live a holy life.** God's purpose in salvation was to redeem people for himself—people who lived to glorify him. Holy living seeks God's view instead of the self-centered view. Holiness expects to find God involved in every facet of life. Holiness consistently turns away from self-pleasing answers in order to please God.

God did this not because we deserved it, but because that was his plan long before the world began—to show his love and kindness to us through Christ Jesus. Salvation and holiness rely on the Giver alone, not on the receiver. God's sovereign choice alone, through his planned purpose and his astounding grace, allowed sinners to receive salvation and the right to stand holy before him. Everything fits into the framework of God's sovereignty. We create neither the opportunity nor the possibility of our salvation. God graciously allows us to simply respond to his plan. We are saved only because of Jesus' death on the cross in our place. Only because he took the punishment we deserved does God offer salvation and holiness.

1:10-11 Salvation through Christ was planned by God since eternity; it was made **plain** to people **by the coming of Christ Jesus, our Savior.** This **coming** was in human form—Christ Jesus on earth, in a human body, preaching, teaching, healing, dying, and rising again. His becoming visible and touchable allowed humans access to him in a way that had not been available before the Incarnation.

Through his death and resurrection, Christ **broke the power of death and showed us the way to everlasting life.** He ended death's claim of invincibility and mortally wounded this terrible foe. All human beings still must die, but death is not the end. Believers are given eternal life beginning at the moment of salvation. Believers are immortal—of necessity dying physically, but not forever. They will rise again. This is the mystery our Savior, Jesus Christ, brought to light **through the Good News.** Paul had been commissioned to proclaim this Good News. As **a preacher,** Paul announced or proclaimed the message; as **an apostle,** he acted as one who was sent; as **a teacher,** he imparted knowledge and gave instruction. Timothy obviously already knew this information. It seems that Paul added these words as he marveled at the wonder of his own call to such a tremendous responsibility.

1:12 Because Paul had traveled the empire announcing and teaching the Good News, he was **suffering in prison.** His faithfulness to God's call had led him to suffering as a common criminal. But Paul had no doubts and no apologies. He was **not ashamed,** for he knew he had put his confidence in the right Person and had given his life for the right cause. A lifetime of experience with the Lord—joys, sorrows, pain, frustration, persecution, prayer, ministry, guidance, sustenance—had taught Paul about God in whom he trusted.

The phrase, **he is able to guard what I have entrusted to him,** (literally, "my deposit") has been taken to mean: (1) Paul knew that God would guard the souls of those converted through his preaching; (2) Paul trusted God to guard his own soul until Christ's second coming; or (3) Paul was confident that, though he was in prison and facing death, God would carry out the gospel ministry and guard the teaching through others such as Timothy. The word for "deposit" carries the meaning of placing valuables in the hands of a friend who would keep them safe while you are on a journey. This meaning supports view 3 above, that the deposit was Paul's message and ministry (see 1:14; to 1 Timothy 6:20).

Paul may have expressed his confidence to encourage Timothy, who was undoubtedly discouraged by the problems in Ephesus and fearful of persecution. Even in prison, Paul knew that God was still in control. No matter what setbacks or problems we face, we can trust fully in God. He will fulfill all his promises on **the day of his return.**

1:13 Timothy did not need to wonder about the content of **right teaching**—he could always recall Paul's teaching and read Paul's letters as his

pattern. Like a sure foundation, Paul's pattern would keep Timothy from straying from the truth. Timothy had every resource needed to carry on his ministry, and it boiled down to teaching only the truth, and living **in the faith and love** that he had **in Christ Jesus.** Sound teaching requires both faith in the heart and genuine love for the Lord. Sound teaching also helps people remain true to the tenets of the Christian faith because it refers to orthodox teaching (see 1 Timothy 1:10; 6:3).

1:14 Timothy was to **carefully guard** the truth that had been **entrusted** to him—not by burying it and keeping it hidden, but by entrusting it to faithful men and women, who would teach it to others, who in turn would teach it to others, and on through the centuries. Because men like Timothy guarded the truth as Paul had commanded, two thousand years later we too have the true gospel, the sound doctrine, that we are commanded to entrust to others. Only **with the help of the Holy Spirit** could the truth remain untainted, guarded, and protected as it passed through the centuries.

1:15 Ephesus was the leading city in the **province of Asia,** if not all of Asia Minor. By saying that **all the Christians** had **deserted** him, Paul may have been referring to a general lack of concern or support for him in his difficult time of need. Many had refused to stand up for him or at least stay at his side during his trial. This occurred not accidentally, but apparently on purpose. This caused Paul much pain. The "everyone" was not literal, but was used by Paul as a sweeping generalization. Those who were resisting Timothy were, in the same action, abandoning Paul. The fact that just a few had remained faithful heightened Paul's sense of having been deserted.

Nothing more is known about **Phygelus** and **Hermogenes,** who evidently opposed Paul's ministry and/or his authority; the fact that Paul named them could mean that he least expected their desertion or that he knew they were in Ephesus. They may have held leadership positions. Apparently Timothy knew the situation, for Paul added no further details. In any case, these men serve as a warning that even leaders can fall.

1:16 In contrast to those who deserted him, Paul mentioned **Onesiphorus** as a true and loyal friend. Unashamed of Paul's imprisonment, Onesiphorus refreshed Paul. The stigma attached to Paul's chains and any concern about being identified as a friend of this prisoner did not faze this faithful brother who **visited and encouraged** Paul **in prison.** Paul prayed that God would show **special kindness** to him **and all his family** for his kindness to Paul.

1:17 Onesiphorus lived in Ephesus, but for some reason had been in **Rome** and, while there, had gone out of his way to search for Paul until he had **found** him. The aging apostle saw in Onesiphorus a brother who allowed neither inconvenience nor potential embarrassment to keep him from tracking Paul down. Onesiphorus's visits had refreshed the lonely prisoner.

1:18 Paul prayed that **the Lord** would **show** Onesiphorus **special kindness on the day of**

Christ's return. He was certain that there would be an accounting of each person's life, and that unrewarded service for Christ in this life would be openly proclaimed. Apparently Timothy was familiar with Onesiphorus and his service in **Ephesus.** The service Onesiphorus rendered to Paul in faraway Rome was not isolated; Onesiphorus had a record of service in Ephesus as well. Paul's statement to Timothy gives us a beautiful insight into the character of this otherwise unknown servant of God.

2 TIMOTHY 2

A GOOD SOLDIER OF CHRIST JESUS / 2:1-13

Good parents want their children eventually to leave home and succeed on their own. But after the good-byes and the well-wishes, parents wonder, "Did we teach them well enough to survive?" So parents continue to offer advice. Paul's last letter to Timothy sounds like wise parental counsel. After affirming Timothy for the good character he had already demonstrated (see 1:5), Paul hinted at Timothy's "debt" of faith to his mother and grandmother (see 1:5). Then he expressed his confidence in Timothy as the right choice to carry on the ministry in Ephesus. Like a father discussing his son's future choices, Paul used three vocations to illustrate what it's like to serve God: military service, athletic training, and farming. Each vocation showed Timothy that he, and all Christians, must work hard and trust God for the long-range results.

2:1 Many of Paul's associates had deserted him, but at least one had remained (1:15-16). Paul challenged his **dear son** to be unashamed of the gospel, unashamed of his standing as a leader in the Christian church, unafraid of the false teachers, courageous through hardship and persecution. How? Through the **special favor God** gave him **in Christ Jesus.** How can someone **be strong** with God's favor? The term implies being helped by someone else, in this case God. Paul was telling Timothy to draw strength from God as he focused on the favor that he would receive through his relationship with Christ Jesus. And he should use this strength in God's service.

2:2 Timothy heard Paul preach to many diverse groups of people. The message Paul wanted Timothy to "guard" (1:14) was not a privately shared secret, but the accumulation of public teaching. Here Paul reminded Timothy that his essential role as guardian meant ensuring that **these great truths** were taught to **trustworthy people who are able to pass them on to others.** Timothy was to keep

the process of teaching going. This is a pattern for discipleship. It requires leaders to have a program for developing new leaders who can carry on the ministry. Since Paul, there has been a link from disciple to disciple, from generation to generation. We must keep that link intact. Paul was telling Timothy to pass on what had proven to be true and **confirmed by many reliable witnesses.**

Paul told Timothy to entrust that truth to reliable people who were both loyal to the faith and able to teach. The stress was on **reliability** more than position (see v. 21). Like ripples from a stone thrown into a pool of water, the gospel would spread across the world. When Paul wrote these words to Timothy, he realized that the transmission of the gospel truth to the next generation was passing into the hands of second-generation believers. Up to this point, the Good News was being spread solely by word of mouth and the lives of believers. The Gospels and various letters written by Paul and others may have just begun to be circulated, but they were not gathered into a book called the New Testament until years later. For a while, Timothy had the only copy of 2 Timothy in existence. Part of entrusting the gospel to others was accomplished when painstaking, handwritten copies of the precious letters were made.

If today's church consistently followed Paul's advice, there would be an incredible spread of the gospel as well-taught believers would teach others and commission them, in turn, to teach still others. Disciples need to be equipped to pass on their faith; new believers must be taught to make disciples of others (see Ephesians 4:12-13).

2:3 Paul had given this warning in Lystra, Iconium, and Antioch (Acts 14:22-23). Thus Paul was returning to a theme that he knew would test the mettle of his disciple—suffering. Paul wanted young Timothy to have no illusions: being faithful to the truth, unwilling to twist it for personal gain (unlike many of the false teachers, 1 Timothy 6:3-5), and constantly preaching it even against the persecution that would inevitably lead to suffering. As Paul had suffered, so Timothy would **endure suffering along with** him (he was eventually imprisoned, see Hebrews 13:23).

Paul followed with three examples to illustrate the attitude that Christ's followers must have through suffering (for the same three examples, see 1 Corinthians 9:7, 24). Each example encouraged Timothy in a different aspect of his ministry.

First, Paul wrote of the **soldier.** Paul often used military metaphors (see, for example, Romans 7:23; 2 Corinthians 6:7; 10:3-5; Ephesians 6:10-18; Philippians 2:25; 1 Timothy 1:18; Philemon 2). From the military model, Timothy should learn endurance, purpose, bravery, and obedience. Every soldier expects to lose personal autonomy and to experience adverse conditions; so Timothy should expect both hardship and suffering in his ministry of the gospel.

2:4 Paul instilled a sense of purpose and obedience in Timothy. A good soldier obeys the commanding officer. The soldier's call to service takes precedence over **the affairs of this life,** referring to any business or distraction that gets in the way of the mission. The phrase **tied up** means "entangled, absorbed." While this life's involvements are not wrong in themselves, they become a problem if the Christian gets so entangled in them that his or her ministry suffers. Christian workers, whether pastors or laymen, must watch their outside involvements carefully. Business ventures, serving on committees or boards, volunteer assignments, and/or home projects can eat up valuable time and energy. Paul wanted Timothy to understand that a good minister of the gospel must have a single-minded purpose—to preach the truth and, if necessary, to suffer for it.

Renouncing whatever could entangle him or her leaves the good soldier free to obey without reservations. This in turn satisfies **the one who has enlisted you in his army.** The effectiveness of a military unit depends on its single-minded commitment to follow the leader in the accomplishment of the mission. Christ demands unquestioning loyalty and obedience from his servants.

2:5 Next Paul used the **athlete** as an example. A competitor had to know the rules of his event, train diligently with an understanding of those rules, and finally compete according to the **rules.** Competitors in the Olympic games also had rules regarding their training—they were required to swear that they had trained for at least ten months. Only then could a competitor be qualified to enter an event. Every event was governed by rules and boundaries; an athlete who failed to compete within those boundaries faced **disqualification.** But those who competed fairly were eligible to receive the victor's **prize.**

What were **the Lord's rules** that Paul wanted Timothy to **follow?** We must be careful not to give the impression that Christians are rules-oriented or legalistic. We do, however, live under the rule of Christ. We have become athletes by God's grace through faith in Christ. We have accomplished nothing to merit that status, but Christ freely made us members of his team. We must wholeheartedly enter into training and competition (ministry to the church and the world) representing Jesus Christ in every facet of our lives.

2:6 From **farmers,** Timothy should learn that physical labor produces results. But only **hardworking** farmers will **enjoy the fruit of their labor**—a good crop. The farmer knows that seeds will not plant themselves; the harvest will not walk into the barn. The farmer must go out into the fields to sow the seed, water it, protect it, and finally harvest the crop. The reward will be a share of the crops for the farmer and his family to eat, and the rest to sell.

The soldier, athlete, and farmer all teach us the same lesson—to persevere to the end—while also helping us understand other requirements for Christian service.

- The soldier must trust the commanding officer and desire to please him so that obeying the commander becomes central, even when difficulties are encountered. Pleasing Christ gives strength to endure hardship.
- The athlete accepts the rules of the competition in order to complete the challenge of the game, including its difficulties.
- The farmer works hard at plowing, planting, waiting, weeding, and harvesting, and is entitled to enjoy the results.

• The soldier submits to the officer; the athlete to the code of the competition; the farmer to the laws of nature and agriculture. The believer submits to Jesus Christ. In him we have a gracious commanding officer: one who provides an example and directions for our course, and who rewards the hard and patient work of his servants.

2:7 Either Paul was worried that Timothy was not getting the point, or he was confident that the Lord would give Timothy **understanding** and insight into the wisdom of Paul's words as Timothy reflected on them. Whether what Paul wanted him to **think about** referred to the three illustrations above or to all of Paul's words to Timothy, the point remains that all believers need to rely on God's wisdom as they reflect on Scripture in order to understand how to apply it to their lives.

2:8-9 Paul's response begins with **Jesus Christ.** Paul firmly stated that Jesus is fully man (**a man born into King David's family**) and fully God (**raised from the dead**). These phrases express a central doctrine for all Christians and the core of **the Good News.**

Paul made two emphases about Jesus Christ. First, that Jesus Christ is risen from the dead. Because Christ alone has conquered death, he alone can be our Lord. His resurrection encourages any who suffer that they can be hopeful in him. Second, that Jesus Christ is the royal Messiah, the descendant of David. Christ alone has the messianic qualification, and he alone fulfills the promises of God to David that he would rule forever. So Paul stressed Jesus' humanity, showed how Jesus is connected with the Old Testament promises to David, and encouraged all believers to endure hardship because of what Christ has done for us. Paul was **chained** in prison and was **suffering** because of this message. He was being treated **like a criminal.** Such was the persecution against believers—they were considered criminals by the Roman authorities.

But chains could not stop the **word of God,** for it **cannot be chained.** By **word of God,** Paul meant the gospel truth. Although Paul was sitting in chains, he did not feel ashamed or worthless. He knew that the gospel message, entrusted to Timothy and other faithful people, could not be chained (Philippians 1:12-18; 1 Thessalonians 3:1). Even if the Romans succeeded in imprisoning, even killing, every Christian leader, they could never stop the spread of the Good News. God's word would continue to spread, despite persecution, and change lives everywhere.

2:10 Despite Paul's imprisonment, God's word would continue to work, calling out **to those God has chosen** (those who had not yet trusted in Christ as Savior). Paul could confidently **endure anything** knowing that God remained in control. Sometimes suffering has no other benefit than what others will learn from our experience of pain. A woman endures the pains of childbirth for the sake of her child. We must never think of suffering as some form of work of merit to earn our salvation or to work off our guilt, nor as some form of punishment from God. Although Paul experienced very real pain as he spread the gospel, he focused on the results of his suffering—others were finding salvation in Christ.

Who are "the chosen"? While the concept of "election" has generated fierce doctrinal differences, most of these differences come from theological and philosophical points of view, not the Bible itself. In this context, Paul indicated that the chosen are those to whom will be brought **salvation and eternal glory.** Paul makes no claim to know who they are. Their identification falls under the sovereignty of God. For Paul, God authored salvation and commissioned him to spread the word; God knows who will respond. Paul was so sure of God's purpose that he was willing to suffer to see that salvation realized.

2:11-13 This **true saying** quoted in these verses was probably an early Christian hymn or a quotation used in a Christian ceremony; though it would be equally proper to say that Paul may have provided here, under the inspiration of the Holy Spirit, another one of the early hymns of the church.

The first couplet of this hymn contrasts death and life—the believer's death to sin at the moment of salvation and the new life begun now with Christ in the world and in eternity. Believers have died **with** Christ because they have identified with him as symbolized by the sacrament of baptism. The promise is that their identification with him in death means that he will raise them to **live with him.**

This second couplet contrasts endurance and rewards. Those who live for Christ may face severe **hardship** that must be endured. Christ endured and now reigns (1 Corinthians 15:25); all believers who **endure** to the end shall also **reign with him** (Revelation 3:21; 5:10; 20:4).

The third couplet reveals that commitment to Christ must be total, no turning back; to **deny** results in being denied (see also Matthew 10:32-33). The Greek tense in the phrase "if we deny" is future. These words provided a solemn warning; but to deny Christ was unthinkable to the early Christians, even in the face of mounting persecution. True believers might be faithless and weak at times; they might falter when giving a testimony (see 2:13), but they would never deny their Lord.

The last couplet reveals the depth of the relationship between believers and Christ the Lord; when we fail at times, this does not mean God will reject us forever. These words apply not to faithless unbelievers, but to believers who at times fail the Lord. Humans, by their very nature, are prone to failure; and Christians, though born again, are still human. But even when believers **are unfaithful,** God **remains faithful.** Believers are secure in Christ's promises. This does not give a license for faithlessness; rather, it eases our conscience when we fail, allowing us to come back to the Father and start anew. God does not deny those for whom he died, **for he cannot deny himself.**

AN APPROVED WORKER / 2:14-26

The second half of chapter 2 echoes the first letter to Timothy. Apparently, the task of confronting wrong teaching and continuing the good work of discipling believers was not past the crisis stage. As he had done previously, Paul emphasized to Timothy that his moral and spiritual conduct would provide the greatest confirmation of his teaching. No matter how others may respond to the gospel, Timothy himself must remain a consistent example (1 Timothy 4:12).

2:14 Paul's instruction in the previous verses was meant for all the believers, not just Timothy. These instructions would need to be given often, and Timothy would need to **remind** and **command everyone.** All believers, no matter how many years they have believed, need to be reminded of the basis of their faith and how to relate that faith to circumstances of life.

Paul urged Timothy to remind the believers not to argue over unimportant details (**stop fighting over words**) because **such arguments are useless,** and even harmful. False teachers caused strife and divisions by their meaningless quibbling over unimportant details (see 1 Timothy 6:3-5). Quarreling about words is a major problem today. Churches split over nonessentials. Quarrelsome people nitpick church programs, undermine productivity with criticism, and verbally attack the innocent. When someone shows a pattern of quarrelsomeness, church leaders should visit that person to deal with the issues in private.

The false teachers were promoting myths and pedigrees (1 Timothy 1:4) and quibbled about words and details that focused not on Scripture, but on their own ideas. This took valuable time away from teaching the truth of Scripture and spreading the gospel. The believers who got caught up in these quarrels about words wasted their time, and some even ended up "ruined" rather than being spiritually strengthened.

2:15 The antithesis of the false teachers are ministers who **work hard** for God. **A good worker** who **correctly explains the word of truth** would be the most effective silencer of the false teachers. The Christians would need unity, strength, and the truth of the gospel to survive the persecutions ahead, to impart the truth to future generations. This incredible responsibility means individual teachers, ministers, and leaders must seek not the approval of people, but the approval of God. An unashamed worker can present his or her life and ministry to God, knowing that God will **approve** the quality of work. Approval of one's ministry before God will depend on how well one has proclaimed, explained, and applied the word of truth. We must help the gospel cut a straight path and do nothing to hinder it.

2:16 In important areas of Christian teaching, believers should carefully work through disagreements. But bickering long hours over words and theories that are not central to the Christian faith and life are not more than **godless, foolish discussions** that provoke anger and **lead to more and more ungodliness.** Learning and discussing are not bad unless they keep believers constantly focusing on false doctrine or unhelpful trivialities. Believers must not let anything keep them from their work for and service to God. Paul said that the false teachers who engaged in teaching that is contrary to God's word will advance in ungodliness. The false teachers will progress to even worse forms of disruption and sinfulness (see 3:9).

2:17-18 Paul understood the addictive power of false teaching as people feel the need to be in on these supposedly "intellectual" discussions. Paul compared the spiritual deterioration ("more and more ungodliness," 2:16) caused by this false teaching to **cancer,** a fatal disease. The spread and deadly result of false teaching could not be more aptly described.

Hymenaeus is also mentioned in 1 Timothy 1:20, where he is included with a man named Alexander. Paul had handed these men over to Satan—put them out of the church. Just as cancer must be removed from the body for it to survive, these false teachers were removed from the body of believers so they could cause no more harm. Nothing further is known about **Philetus**. The false teaching of Hymenaeus and Philetus that **the resurrection of the dead** had **already occurred** was undermining some of the believers' faith. These false teachers denied the resurrection of the body. These men in Ephesus grew up under Greek philosophy and a Greek understanding of the world. Greek philosophy viewed the spirit as immortal and the body as evil. Thus, a doctrine that taught the resurrection of the body was especially difficult to believe. So the false teachers tried to combine the doctrine of the resurrection with Greek philosophy in order to make it make sense to them. They taught that when a person became a Christian and was spiritually reborn, that was the only resurrection he or she would ever experience. To them, resurrection was symbolic and spiritual, not real and physical. But this was a **lie**.

2:19 False teaching, for all its enticing qualities, will not last. Although it plagued the first-century church and still has footholds today, it cannot prevail against **God's truth** which **stands like a foundation stone**. Heresies, false teachers, even persecution, cannot destroy the truth taught in God's churches. It stands and will stand until Christ returns.

These next two phrases appear as if they were written on the foundation stone described above (for a similar use of the metaphor, see Romans 4:11; 1 Corinthians 9:2). This **inscription** can be compared to God's seal—a sign of authenticity and approval.

The first statement, **The Lord knows those who are his,** may refer to the words of Moses at the time of Korah's rebellion. Korah and several associates challenged Moses' leadership. Moses replied that the Lord himself would reveal to all who were truly his (Numbers 16:4-5). In a shocking display of power, God vindicated Moses' leadership.

These words should encourage all believers. False teachers may cause problems, but God knows his true followers. The Lord sees all who preach and teach in his name, and he knows those who are his.

This second statement, **Those who claim they belong to the Lord must turn away from all wickedness,** could be from Numbers 16:26 (in the same context as above); however, most commentators prefer to compare it with Isaiah 52:11, citing the use of the same verb in the Greek translation of Isaiah (Septuagint). Those who are the Lord's, those who call on his name, must be responsible to turn away from wickedness.

Both inscriptions together remind the believers of God's sovereign control over his church and the believers' responsibility to turn from evil and maintain pure and holy lives. Timothy did not need to fear for the future of the church, for God was in con-

trol. Timothy's responsibility, and indeed the responsibility of every believer, was to stay free from sin and the contamination spread by the false teachers.

God does his part by helping us discern true from false believers; then we must do our part in turning away from wickedness. We must not only repudiate the false teachers, we must also refuse to take part in their false teaching. We should not attend or sponsor meetings, purchase tapes or books, or support them in any way.

2:20 Paul changed his metaphor from a building to household **utensils**, but continued the same theme. In a large house there are **expensive utensils** made of **gold and silver** that are used only on **special occasions**; other utensils, made of **wood and clay,** are **cheap** and **for everyday use.** Again Paul makes the distinction between commonly useful and uncommonly useful workers of God, pointing out to Timothy that both will be found in the church. It doesn't work to stretch the details of the metaphor too far; Paul's point is that believers should desire to be special "utensils" ready for any special service needed by God.

2:21 Paul may have been emphasizing the individual believer's moral purity in order to fulfill the role God has chosen him or her to play in the household. This most likely refers to personal inward cleansing from involvement in false teachings. People who desire to be used by God must be cleansed from sin and then **keep** themselves **pure** by refraining from contacts and activities that could soil them. This does not require a person's isolation from the world (for sin is all around); it refers more specifically to involvement with those whose goal is to lead people away from the faith. Cleansed people who stay away from corrupting influences can be used **for** God's **purpose** and are then **ready for the Master to use for every good work.** How much more powerful the church of God would be in the world if all believers were "clean utensils" ready for the Master's use!

2:22 Paul knew Timothy very well from their years of travel together, and most likely he knew Timothy's weak spots. Timothy was a young man (1 Timothy 4:12), at least young for the responsibilities he carried, so Paul offered no-nonsense advice. The **youthful lusts** mentioned here are not only sexual, but also the other passions characteristic of the young—impatience, contentiousness, favoritism, egotism, intolerance, etc. (see also 1 Timothy 6:11). As was frequently the case with Paul, when he issued a warning he followed it with an alternative positive strategy. Timothy was to **run from** temptation but **follow anything** that would make him **want to do right,** referring to actions that are morally upright and virtuous. In a word, it expresses a way of life that seeks to model itself after God's directions. Rather than claiming perfection or settling for mediocrity, righteousness requires the pursuit of obedience. Paul also advised Timothy to **pursue faith and love and peace.** Faith and love are fundamental to Christianity and basic to Paul's teaching (see 1 Corinthians 13:13).

In spite of the individual challenge that Paul presented, he was not permitting Timothy to function alone. He was to find strength and encouragement in the **companionship of those who call on the Lord with pure hearts.** There were others for whom he was responsible, but also some who would be peers and share a deep and common desire to be faithful.

2:23 While peace should be the norm among believers, we should not entertain false teachings to keep people happy. Paul's language here does not forbid contact with such people, as is demonstrated by verse 25, where the guidelines for treating opponents imply some level of interaction.

There can be no doubt about the problem caused by the false teachers—Paul repeated it several times in his letters to Timothy and Titus. They got people caught up in **foolish, ignorant arguments that only start fights** and that divided the church (see also 1 Timothy 1:4, 6-7; 4:1, 7; 6:3-5, 20-21; 2 Timothy 2:14, 16-17, 23-24; 4:2-4; Titus 1:9, 13-14; 3:2, 9). Timothy's best approach was to simply not **get involved** with them. To argue would only make Timothy angry and draw him into the very trap being set by the false teachers.

2:24 The Lord's servants are specifically Timothy and those chosen as leaders in the church. The expression alludes almost without doubt to the pictures of the suffering servant of God found in Isaiah (Isaiah 52:13-15; 53:1-12). The Christian who imitates Christ in this way will bear the experience of "wounds" as he or she attempts to relate compassionately to those who may strike out in hurt or anger. Some people like to **quarrel** because they have never been listened to before; when we demonstrate kindness, we may find openness where before there was only a wall of arguments.

As a minister of the gospel, Timothy did not have to quarrel with the false teachers; to quarrel could be seen as a need to come to a compromise. There could be no compromise between the gospel truth and the false teachers. Instead, Timothy should promote unity by being **kind** to everyone. The hard, sharp edge of the truth required the skilled hand of someone who could relate compassionately with others.

Timothy had already met the requirement for a church leader of having the ability to **teach effectively** (see 1 Timothy 3:2). Paul exhorted him to remain confident in his teaching and to continue teaching the truth to those willing to learn. At the same time, he would need to **be patient with difficult people.** The Greek word for "patient" is used only here in the New Testament; it literally means "to face ill treatment without resentment."

2:25 Timothy's goal was to **gently teach** his opponents the correct understanding of the **truth.** Therefore, he needed to maintain contact that would lead to interaction with these people, while at the same time resisting their error. Instead of antagonizing opponents, he should calmly and gently correct their wrong ideas in the hopes that **God** would **change those people's hearts, and they will believe the truth.** Timothy's first desire ought to be to bring them back into the church, not to punish them (see 1 Thessalonians 3:6, 15).

2:26 To **come to their senses** could also be translated "return to soberness." In other words, the false teachers have gotten "drunk," with the result of losing their senses and getting caught in **the Devil's trap.** Satan is at the root of all false teaching and division in the church. He knows the strength of a unified church and fears it. So he creates a "trap"— money, fame, pride of feeling intellectual—to draw people away from the faith and to false teaching. They are then **held captive by him to do whatever he wants.** But there is hope—**escape** is possible.

2 TIMOTHY **3**:1–4:5

THE DANGERS OF THE LAST DAYS / 3:1-9

Paul's suffering left him with few illusions about his future; he would die before Christ returned. As has already been pointed out, this letter has the recurring tone of someone setting his personal matters in order.

Paul began this chapter with remarks about degenerating conditions in society. Both Paul and Timothy had witnessed how bad "the last days" would become. Paul listed a whole catalog of attitudes and behaviors typical of "last days" people. This list also described the false teachers in Ephesus. Paul characterized them as belonging to the perennial crop of "opposition" leaders who create a following for themselves. Timothy was to resist their methods and their underlying purposes.

3:1 This reference to the **last days** reveals Paul's sense of urgency. But warnings about the last days were certainly not unique to Paul. It was a common theme among the leaders of the early church (see Acts 2:17; James 5:3; 2 Peter 3:3; Jude 18). **Very difficult times** means "hard to bear, dangerous, troublesome." Paul's warning deserves our full attention. The "last days" began after Jesus' resurrection, when the Holy Spirit came upon the believers at Pentecost. The last days will continue until Christ's second coming. Paul could speak about the last days as a future event (emphasizing conditions present at the close of the last days), or as a present reality (emphasizing the truth that the state of depravity in the world is always ripe for harvest). This means that *we* are living in the last days. It should not surprise us, then, to see the moral degeneration of society around us. Paul warned us that it would happen, as did Jesus (see Matthew 24).

3:2 When people misdirect their **love**—toward **themselves** and **money**—there can be no love left to direct toward others. Then moral corruption naturally results, as noted in the following characteristics. To be **boastful and proud** pictures a heart full of pride that manifests itself in outward boastfulness. Such characteristics reveal a person's inflated self-importance and necessarily leads them to looking down on others. **Scoffing at God** means speaking disrespectfully of him. Not only are these people guilty of an overinflated sense of their own importance, they also verbally abuse God himself.

The extent of moral degeneration can be seen in the rejection of the most intimate human ties with many blatantly **disobedient to their parents.** This behavior willfully breaks the fifth commandment to honor one's father and mother (see Exodus 20:12). The commandment was given because God understood the importance of strong families. To "honor" parents means speaking well of them and politely to them. It also means acting in a way that shows them courtesy and respect. It means following their teaching and example of putting God first. Parents have a special place in God's sight. Even children who find it difficult to get along with their parents are still commanded to honor

them. When parents are not respected and honored, disobedience naturally results, and the breakdown of the family easily follows. Paul understood that when families fall apart, "very difficult times" (3:1) follow.

People are in a sad state when they are **ungrateful** and cannot appreciate anything. In Romans 1:21, Paul noted that ingratitude was second only to dishonoring God as a just cause for God's judgment on humanity. This leads them to **consider nothing sacred.** People who set aside God in order to live only to please themselves can only go one direction—toward wickedness. They instinctively resist anyone or any ideas that would force them to measure themselves by God's standards.

3:3 People will be **unloving.** The same word is used in only one other place in the New Testament (Romans 1:31), in a passage where Paul listed the characteristics of people who refuse God and follow their own inclinations. Indeed, because these people love only themselves and their money (possessions), as Paul noted in verse 2, they are unloving toward everyone and everything else.

Unforgiving people cannot allow for other people's mistakes or weaknesses. They are unyielding, unrelenting, and often are filled with extreme bitterness and anger over their own hurts. They simply refuse to forgive, even if presented with the opportunity. Eventually, they become unable to forgive, even when they might acknowledge the need to do so.

People who **slander others** are quick to spread falsehoods. Slanderers enjoy spreading gossip and malicious reports about others. Destroying another's good reputation gives them perverse pleasure. Without **self-control,** they cannot restrain their actions, their feelings, or their words.

Cruel people ("brutes") are like untamed animals, or "uncivilized" people. They are insensitive and crude, even savage. People will be so evil that they actually **have no interest in what is good.**

3:4 The next two characteristics begin with the *pro-* prefix in Greek, indicating a disposition toward some behavior or attitude.

To **betray** one's **friends** is to be treacherous. In some cases, betrayal of another might enhance a person's standing or enrich him or her; at other times, the betrayal could be a vengeful act. Combined with slander (3:3), truth goes by the wayside.

Being **reckless** can also be translated "headstrong" and "rash." Such people act foolishly and carelessly, completely unconcerned about the consequences for themselves or others. They are determined to have their own way, regardless of advice to the contrary.

These people are **puffed up with pride,** having an exaggerated opinion of their importance, intelligence, wit, appearance, etc. The idea differs from "lovers of self" in verse 2, for that trait can at least be concealed, while the very nature of pride involves being noticed by others.

The list ends, as it began, with those whose **love** has become so misdirected that they can only think of **pleasure rather than God.** Those who fail to acknowledge God eventually aren't able to love God.

3:5 Often these evil characteristics appear in a context of respectability. Religion is not gone; in fact, these character qualities are frequently exhibited by people known for their "religiousness." However, as Paul wrote, they **act as if they are religious,** using godliness as a cloak of respectability. **But they will reject the power that could make them godly,** denying God's power over their lives. The "act" could include going to church, knowing Christian doctrine, using Christian clichés, and following a community's Christian traditions. Such practices can make a person outwardly look good, but if the inner attitudes of belief, love, and worship are lacking, the public appearance is hollow, meaningless.

Paul warned Timothy not to be deceived by people who only appear to be Christians. It may be difficult to distinguish them from true Christians at first, but their daily behavior will give them away. The characteristics described in 3:2-4 are unmistakable. In fact, the false teachers plaguing the Ephesian church most likely exemplified many of those characteristics that Paul listed above. Paul had already advised Timothy to **stay away from** these troublemakers (2:23)—which probably meant excommunication.

3:6 Because of their cultural background, women in the Ephesian church had no formal religious training. They enjoyed their new freedom to study Christian truths, but their eagerness to learn made them a target for false teachers. At this time in history, there were almost no opportunities for women to be employed. Also, the church at Ephesus had a significantly large group of widows (1 Timothy 5:3-16). Thus, there were many women who may not have been fully occupied during the day. They became targets for the false teachers.

The expression, **work their way into people's homes,** indicates the insidious methods of the false teachers. They targeted **vulnerable women.** Then with all their intellectual-sounding talk, the false teachers captivated these women and won their **confidence.** These women were especially vulnerable because they were **burdened with the guilt of sin** (that is, their consciences were laden with guilt) and **controlled by many desires** (their personal appetites and aspirations, remnants from their pagan days, were so strong as to still cause them problems, probably leading to their overwhelmed consciences!). Their weakness combined with their guilt made them easy targets for the "cures" that the false teachers brought. Paul warned Timothy to watch out for men who would take advantage of these women.

3:7 These women were **forever following new teachings,** making them easy targets for the false teachers. But without basic knowledge of the faith that leads to repentance and forgiveness of their sins, these women would only get confused and never be able to recognize and understand the **truth.** Churches that have little or no biblical and theological content in their teaching program fall right into this error. People who attend this kind of church are easy targets for false teachers. It is possible to be a perpetual student and never graduate to accepting the truth and putting it into practice. But honest seekers and true students look for answers and, when they find them, continue in their study and application of that truth. The accumulation of seminars, classes, Bible studies, and books without specific application in our daily lives can easily become our own version of what Paul was describing here. Remember this as you study God's word. Seek to find God's truth and will for your life.

3:8-9 According to Jewish legend, **Jannes and Jambres** were two of the magicians who counterfeited Moses' miracles before Pharaoh (Exodus 7:11-12). Paul explained that just as **Moses** exposed and defeated them (Exodus 8:18-19), God would overthrow the false teachers who were plaguing the Ephesian church. While the false teachers' threat to the church was very real both across the Roman world and in our world today (hence, Paul's advice about dealing with them in this and many other letters), the threat will never be fatal to the gospel. Just as Jannes and Jambres's fake power was eventually revealed by God's power through Moses (Exodus 8:18-19; 9:11), so **what fools they are** would eventually become clear to **everyone.** Whatever the temporary success of the false teachers, eventually they would be completely humiliated.

Paul did not specify how that would happen. Perhaps it would not be until Christ's return; or perhaps God would ensure that discerning believers will see through the deception; or perhaps God would work behind the scenes in such a way that the false teachers will be unmasked for who they really are.

PAUL'S CHARGE TO TIMOTHY / 3:10–4:5

Paul laced his letters with encouragement, challenges, hopes, and affirmations for Timothy. In this last section before his closing remarks, Paul reflected on the significance of his and Timothy's life together. Paul gave the consistency of his own example and the trustworthiness of Scripture as two dependable guides for Timothy's future. Paul's words and actions created a seamless pattern for the younger man.

3:10 After strongly denouncing the false teachers and their foolishness, Paul turned his attention back to **Timothy,** who could look at Paul as an example of living out the opposite characteristics of those described in verses 2-9. That Timothy "knew" about all the activities and characteristics listed here and in verse 11 does not necessarily mean he was an eyewitness. Some of the persecutions mentioned in verse 11 happened before Paul had met Timothy. But Timothy had heard about some of these situations; however, undoubtedly he knew others from personal experience. Paul's words here are not proud; rather, they are a testimony to the truth of the gospel and God's faithfulness, meant to encourage young Timothy. Paul was also using himself as a model for what Timothy should be doing in his leadership role in Ephesus.

Timothy knew the content of Paul's teaching; it was the truth as opposed to the false teachers' lies, myths, and godless arguments. Timothy had been privileged to hear Paul **teach** many times, to many audiences, on a variety of topics. Paul's teaching would be of no value if it did not impact his life— but it did, as the following characteristics reveal.

Timothy knew **how** Paul lived. This phrase refers to Paul's manner of life, his general behavior. Timothy had lived and traveled with Paul; he had seen Paul happy, sad, angry, and worried; he had watched Paul handle difficult people and problems; he had seen him study and had heard him pray. Paul's way of life should have been a shining example to Timothy.

Timothy knew Paul's **purpose in life,** his central mission, his chief aim. Traveling with the tireless missionary must have quickly convinced Timothy of Paul's single-minded focus on his mission. Paul never took that calling lightly.

Timothy knew Paul's **faith, love,** and **patient endurance.** Paul called on Timothy to exhibit these qualities, for they are basic Christian virtues (1 Timothy 6:11). The word **endurance** can also be translated "steadfastness," referring to a person's ability to remain strong under pressure. Paul expected Timothy to model these same character traits in Ephesus.

3:11 Paul mentioned **persecution and suffering** to contrast his experience with that of the pleasure-seeking false teachers. These persecutions occurred during the first missionary journey. Paul had met Timothy at the beginning of his second missionary journey, but Timothy certainly had heard about these experiences. In 2 Corinthians 11:23-33, Paul had summarized his lifetime of persecutions and sufferings for the sake of the gospel.

In **Antioch** (in Pisidia), the Jews stirred up some people and Paul was driven out (Acts 13:50). In **Iconium,** they were mistreated and stoned (Acts 14:4-6). In **Lystra,** Timothy's hometown, Paul had been stoned, dragged out of the city, and left for dead (Acts 14:19). At times, Paul had been miraculously delivered (as in Philippi, see Acts 16:25-26); at other times, Paul had to suffer through the persecution (as with the stoning in Lystra). To be **delivered** through persecution and suffering does not necessarily mean escaping from it; Paul knew that God would deliver him as often as needed until Paul's work on earth was done. Indeed, Paul suffered in prison and certainly realized that he would be called on to face the ultimate persecution—death. Paul trusted God that his time had come, that his work was completed, and that he would see his Savior face-to-face.

3:12 In this charge, Paul was telling Timothy that people who desire to **live a godly life in Christ Jesus will suffer persecution.** Paul knew that truth from his own experience. Jesus had warned his disciples: "Since they persecuted me, naturally they will persecute you" (John 15:20).

Today, most Christians do not face outright persecution just for being Christians (although being a Christian is still against the law in some places in the world). Those who worship freely and unhindered should be deeply grateful. However, we should not assume that this verse does not apply to us. If we stand up for Christian values, we can expect opposition and hostility from the world. Based upon the testimony of countless believers who have lived before us, we can expect to meet with some form of persecution or resistance if we persist in living in obedience to Christ. Absence of persecution may not mean unfaithfulness, but if our lives as Christians never affect the world, we may have to question the depth of our commitment.

3:13 But even as believers faced persecution, **evil people and imposters will flourish.** These wicked people were progressing toward their wicked goal and dragging others down with them (see 1 Peter 4:2-5).

3:14 Besieged by false teachers and the inevitable pressures of a growing ministry, Timothy might have been tempted at times to abandon his faith or modify his doctrine. Paul counseled Timothy to look to his past and **remain faithful to the things** he had been **taught** about Jesus that he knew were eternally true. The false teachers might constantly move on to new and more exciting concepts and ideas for discussion and argument, but Timothy needed to stand secure on what he had learned and firmly believed. This did not mean that Timothy needed no further study, but that the basics that Timothy had learned from people he trusted would never change.

3:15 Timothy was one of the first second-generation Christians: he had become a Christian, not because an evangelist preached a powerful sermon, but because his mother and grandmother had taught him the Scriptures when he was a small child (1:5). For Timothy, the **holy Scriptures** were primarily the Old Testament—Genesis to Malachi. The sources for Timothy's faith could provide another encouragement to continue in the faith: Paul, his mentor and friend, who provided an unmistakable example of God's faithfulness; the inerrant Scriptures that Timothy had studied and loved since **childhood;** and Timothy's dear mother and grandmother who nurtured and loved him. Scripture, God's word, teaches about salvation; but knowing Scripture alone saves no one (many Jews had known Scripture from childhood, yet had opposed Jesus and the salvation he offered—see 2 Corinthians 3:15-16; Paul himself exemplified that in his early years, Acts 26:9-11). The Scriptures show people their need for **salvation** and show them how to get it—**by trusting in Christ Jesus.**

3:16 Timothy had known the Scriptures from childhood, so he knew that all Scripture was inspired by God. When Paul spoke of **all Scripture,** he was primarily referring to the Old Testament, since it was complete at that time. But the scope of Paul's assertion would include any writing that was considered authoritative enough to be read in church meetings, which by the end of the first century would have included the four Gospels and Paul's writings. According to 2 Peter 3:15-16, Paul's writings were classified as "Scriptures."

The Scriptures, affirmed Paul, were **inspired by God.** A translation closer to the original Greek would be, "All Scripture is God-breathed." This tells us that every word of the Bible was breathed out from God. The words of the Bible came from God and were written by men. The apostle Peter affirmed this when he said that "it was the Holy Spirit who moved the prophets to speak from God" (2 Peter 1:21).

Paul's words here reminded Timothy that because Scripture is inspired and infallible, it is also **useful.** The Bible is not a collection of stories, fables, myths, or merely human ideas about God. It is not a human book. Through the Holy Spirit, God revealed his person and plan to certain believers, who wrote down his message for his people. This process is known as "inspiration." The writers wrote from their own personal, historical, and cultural contexts. Although they used their own minds, talents, language, and style, they wrote what God wanted them to write. Scripture is completely trustworthy because God was in control of its writing. Its words are entirely authoritative for our faith and lives.

Scripture was profitable to every aspect of Timothy's ministry. Scripture:

- can **teach us what is true.** The content and teaching of truth, which must flow from and be consistent with Scripture. By calling the Bible "God-breathed," Paul was identifying its divine source; by making it the source of doctrine, he was reminding Timothy of its authority. Teaching that contradicted biblical doctrine was to be rejected, corrected, or replaced by accurate teaching.
- can **make us realize what is wrong in our lives.** The initial impact of true doctrine involves the confrontation of false teaching and understanding. The offensiveness of some who teach biblical truth may have to be excused, but the offensiveness of biblical truth to error and evil requires no apology.
- **straightens us out** by helping us see our errors. In the area of correction, the Scriptures have two roles: (1) they provide a complete presentation of the teaching, where only part of the truth has been present; and (2) they provide for a right understanding and application where true doctrine may have been taught but has not taken effect.
- **teaches us to do what is right** by showing us how to please and glorify God. The nature of Scripture allows us to teach it confidently to our children and to learn from it ourselves.

The Bible is not purely a record of the past—the history of the Jews and then of the church.

Rather, every story, every prophecy, every teaching, every admonition, and every command points beyond to the author, God, who came to us in Jesus Christ. God confronts us in the pages of his Word—telling us how much he loves us, how we can become his children, and how we should live to please him.

3:17 Scripture's purpose is to prepare and equip believers **for every good thing God wants** them **to do.** Timothy carried a heavy responsibility in Ephesus, but through his faith in and reliance on God's word, he was capable and proficient—able to meet all duties and challenges. Believers should study the Bible so that they will know how to do Christ's work in the world. Knowledge of God's word is not useful unless it strengthens our faith and leads us to do good (Ephesians 2:10).

4:1 Paul had used these words previously (see 1 Timothy 5:21), but this time he included references to judgment and to Christ's return. Perhaps thoughts of judgment could not escape Paul's thoughts as his own death neared. The time when Christ would appear **to set up his Kingdom,** although still future in Paul's thought, was so certain as to be part of this charge and encouragement to Timothy. If we are convinced that Christ's return is inevitable, we too will be powerfully motivated by that fact. Thus Paul **solemnly** urged Timothy with the five specific commands that follow. The aged apostle knew that his death was at hand and that he might not see Timothy again. Therefore these words held heavy importance. Paul wanted Timothy to realize how critical it was for him to obey his words. Timothy would stand before the Lord at the Last Judgment and answer for how he responded to Paul's charge.

4:2 First and foremost, Timothy was to **preach the word of God**—the message of the gospel. The word suggests vigorous proclamation! Paul wanted Timothy to be bold and passionate. It was up to Timothy to preach the gospel so that the Christian faith could spread throughout the world.

Timothy should always **be persistent, whether the time is favorable or not.** Paul, soon to die, may have looked back on his life realizing how short the time had been. Paul urged Timothy to make the most of the time he would be allotted on this earth. Timothy would need to **patiently correct** those who were in error by explaining the truth, helping them to understand and accept it. He should **rebuke** those who were sinning by

explaining their sin and their need for repentance. He should **encourage** those who were growing, for even those growing in the faith need instruction and guidance. Patience should always characterize Timothy's attitude as he dealt with the people in his church; **good teaching** (or doctrine) should be the basis for his words.

4:3-4 When Paul spoke about false teaching, he usually focused on the evil intentions of the false teachers. However, false teachers could not flourish if they had no audience. Here Paul was pointing out the fault on the part of the listeners. They would **no longer listen to right teaching** because it said what they didn't want to hear, convicting them and making demands they didn't want to follow. So these people would turn to others who would tell them what was more palatable. Like the false prophets of Old Testament times, these false teachers would teach what their audience **wanted to hear.** These people would turn away from the truth taught by Timothy, wandering off into the false teachers' **strange myths** (1 Timothy 1:4). What they would hear made sense, seemed true, and made them comfortable. So wandering away from the difficult truth was easy.

4:5 Timothy should **keep a clear mind in every situation** as he interacted with people by not reacting quickly. Keeping his head would make him morally alert to temptation, resistant to pressure, and vigilant. He should not **be afraid of suffering,** for the suffering, hardship, persecution, and struggles would only intensify in the days and months ahead. Many in Timothy's ministry would look to Timothy as their example. Timothy would have to endure for he must continue to **work at bringing others to Christ.** That work was to proclaim the gospel to all people at all times, calling on them to repent and be saved. Whatever the obstacles, opposition of false teachers, problems of church administration, distractions, or discouragements, Timothy was not to allow any of them to keep him from his appointed task. Finally, he must **complete the ministry God** had **given** him. Nothing should deter Timothy from carrying out his duties until the day when his ministry would be completed (that is, at his death).

How can we know when we have fully carried out our ministry? By defining ministry in terms of lifelong goals rather than temporary jobs, positions, and opportunities. Then, when life ends, we will be able to say with Paul, "I have fought a good fight, I have finished the race, I have remained faithful" (4:7).

2 TIMOTHY 4:6-22

PAUL'S FINAL WORDS / 4:6-18

Paul's words about his departure would communicate to Timothy that he would not be able to count on Paul's presence or encouragement much longer. Shared leadership was ending. Timothy must take charge.

4:6 Paul viewed his **life** as an **offering,** poured out before God. He knew that his **death** was near. Paul's commitment was total; thus, sacrificing his life to build others' faith seemed to him a joyous reward.

4:7 Paul's three phrases, in the perfect tense, convey finality. Paul knew this was the end. He had called Timothy to "fight the good fight" (1 Timothy 6:12); his own **fight** was over. The fight had been worthwhile, and he had fought well.

Paul's **race** was **finished,** or at least the end was clearly in sight. It is important to note that Paul made no claim to having won the race; he was content with having finished it. Marathon runners know the exhilaration of finishing the grueling miles of that race—they are thankful just to cross the finish line. Completion is a significant accomplishment, revealing incredible endurance and determination.

I have remained faithful means Paul had guarded and preserved the gospel message. Paul had called Timothy to "guard what God has entrusted to you" (1 Timothy 6:20). Paul had remained faithful to the message that had been entrusted to him; this also had been entrusted to Timothy. Paul had never wavered in his faith and trusted that soon he would experience all the promises on which he had based his life and ministry.

4:8 In Roman athletic games, a laurel wreath was given to the winners. A symbol of triumph and honor, it was the most coveted prize in ancient Rome. This is probably what Paul was referring to when he spoke of a **prize.** Waiting for Paul, laid up for him, was a reward—**the crown of righteousness.** This phrase could be taken to mean that righteousness itself is the reward (as in James 1:12 and Revelation 2:10, where the "crown of life" is the reward of eternal life), or that the crown is the reward for righteousness (see 3:16). In either case, Paul knew that a reward awaited him.

Paul would receive his reward from **the Lord, the righteous Judge.** Soon to be condemned to death for his faith, Paul would ultimately be vindicated by God himself. Paul's reward would be given on **that great day of his return.** This crown of righteousness, this reward, was not for Paul alone. It is promised to **all who eagerly look forward to his glorious return.** What an encouragement to Timothy, to the loyal believers in his church, and to all believers. Whatever we may face—discouragement, persecution, or death—we know our reward is with Christ in eternity.

4:9 Both here and in verse 21, Paul urged Timothy to come **soon,** preferably "before winter." We don't know what season of the year this was written, but this letter would have to be carried from Rome to Ephesus, and Timothy would then have to make the return trip. The whole process would take a few months. Paul knew his execution was imminent, but he had no idea how quickly it would be carried out. The Roman judicial system often had long delays in its processes; more likely, it was Paul's feeling of loneliness and isolation that prompted him to say "come soon." He longed to see Timothy one last time.

4:10 Demas is also mentioned in Colossians 4:14 and Philemon 24. Demas loved **the things of this life** and so had **deserted** Paul. Perhaps he was ashamed of Paul's chains and not willing to face the same fate for the Christian faith. Demas may not have deserted the faith, but he deserted the apostle in his time of need.

Mentioning Demas reminded Paul of more faithful coworkers. Paul did not criticize **Crescens** and **Titus** for leaving; apparently they had been sent to do the Lord's work in **Galatia** and **Dalmatia** (on the eastern shore of the Adriatic Sea). That Titus was dispatched from Rome to Dalmatia suggests that he no longer ministered in Crete (which was the focus of Paul's letter to Titus).

4:11 Demas had deserted; Crescens, Titus, and Tychicus (4:12) had been sent on various missions; only **Luke** the doctor (Colossians 4:14) remained with Paul, possibly to help minister to his physical needs. Luke had accompanied Paul on the second and third missionary journeys, as well as the voyage to Rome (as noted by the "we" sections in Acts 16–28). This traveling companion and historian (author of the Gospel of Luke and the book of Acts) probably had to frequently use his medical expertise as Paul and his companions were injured with whips and stones in their travels. He may have even been Paul's secretary for this epistle, putting 2 Timothy into writing as the aging apostle dictated. In addition, Luke probably cared for Paul's illness, described as a "thorn in the flesh" in 2 Corinthians 12:7-8. Luke had shared Paul's first Roman imprisonment. He is also mentioned in Colossians 4:14 and Philemon 24.

Paul missed his young helpers, Timothy and **Mark.** Timothy was to pick up Mark (apparently Mark was located somewhere along Timothy's route) and bring him along. This statement reveals an incredible change in Mark and in Paul's opinion of him. Mark had left Paul and Barnabas on the first missionary journey, and this had greatly upset Paul (Acts 13:13; 15:36-41). Barnabas had wanted to give Mark another chance, but Paul had flatly refused. This had led to the separation of Paul and Barnabas; Paul took Silas on the second missionary journey; but Barnabas took Mark on to Cyprus, to preach there. Barnabas (known for being an encourager) had apparently had a significant impact on the young Mark, for he later proved to be a worthy minister. At some point, Paul recognized Mark as a good friend and trusted Christian leader (Colossians 4:10; Philemon 24). Mark had also been Peter's assistant (1 Peter 5:13) and composed the Gospel named after him, based on Peter's words.

4:12 Tychicus, a trusted companion (Acts 20:4) and messenger (he delivered the letters of Ephesians and Colossians—see Ephesians 6:21; Colossians 4:7), had already left for **Ephesus.** The phrase here could mean that Tychicus would be delivering this letter to Timothy, being sent also to assume Timothy's role while Timothy traveled to Rome to see Paul. Tychicus was apparently useful for such ministries (see Titus 3:12).

4:13 Because he was a prisoner in a damp and chilly dungeon, Paul asked Timothy to **bring** him his **coat,** a heavy outer garment, circular in shape with a hole in the middle for the head. Paul had left it at the home of a man named **Carpus,** apparently where Paul stayed on one of his visits to **Troas** (but probably not the visit mentioned in Acts 20:6, for that was several years earlier). Troas would also have been right on Timothy's way from Ephesus to Rome, so Timothy could stop and pick it up.

Even more than the coat, Paul wanted his **books** and **papers.** Paul's arrest may have occurred so suddenly that he was not allowed to return home to gather his personal belongings. The books would have included parts of the Old Testament. The papers were very likely parchment or papyrus codices, frequently used in the first century for notebooks, memoranda, or first drafts of literary works. Perhaps these papers were draft copies of some of Paul's epistles.

In our age of disposables we find it difficult to visualize that a person in Paul's day would have just one excellent, durable, and probably valuable coat to use for a lifetime, often passing it on to children or heirs. Items like coats were too important, too difficult to make, to make poorly. Almost anything written was of great value as well. Paul was a scholar and would have gathered for his use a small but effective personal library. When Paul asked for books and papers, he wasn't asking for his whole library, but for a few treasured documents.

4:14-15 Alexander may have been a witness against Paul at his trial, thus doing Paul **much harm.** This may be the Alexander mentioned in 1 Timothy 1:20, although Alexander was a common name. Timothy apparently knew the man and the situation. Timothy should **be careful of,** be on his guard against, and stay away from Alexander. If Timothy were to arrive in Rome after Paul's death, he would be Alexander's next likely target. The message Alexander opposed could mean the gospel message, or Paul's words at his trial, where Alexander may have been a witness against Paul (4:14). In the end, **the Lord will judge him for what he has done.**

4:16 This **first time** Paul **was brought before the judge** was most likely a preliminary hearing at which advocates for the accused were usually heard. The Roman legal system allowed for several steps in the prosecution of an accused criminal. Clearly, the mention of a "first" indicates an expectation of a second defense. Perhaps the inconclusiveness of the first hearing was causing a lengthy delay.

In any case, **no one** had come to speak in Paul's defense or to stand by in his support; everyone had **abandoned** him (compare 1:15). Although sorely disappointed, Paul seemed to understand, for he hoped that this would **not be counted against them** (compare this to Jesus' words from the cross, Luke 23:34). Paul realized the fear the Christians were feeling; it had become extremely dangerous to be identified as a Christian in Rome. Emperor Nero had blamed the Christians for starting a great fire in Rome (A.D. 64). He had decreed that the Christians should be persecuted through torture and death as punishment. Three or four years later, when this letter was written, fear was still very present, causing Paul's fellow believers to be unwilling to defend him before the Roman authorities.

4:17 Although no human being had come to support Paul at his hearing, **the Lord** had **stood with** him. (See Mark 13:9-11 and Matthew 10:17-19, where Jesus promised help to those arrested for preaching the gospel.) Paul had sensed both the presence and the power of Christ giving him **strength**. Christ had helped Paul not just for Paul's benefit alone. He had supplied Paul with spiritual power, wisdom, and preaching skills in order to **preach the Good News in all its fullness for all the Gentiles to hear.** Even at the trial before the Roman authorities who were ready to execute this Christian leader, Paul had proclaimed the gospel! That Paul was **saved from certain death** most likely described his deliverance from extreme danger (see,

for example, Psalm 22:21; Daniel 6:22). Paul knew he wouldn't get out of prison alive, though he was experiencing a temporary reprieve due to a delay in the Roman judicial system.

4:18 Although rescued from certain death at the first hearing (and certainly at many times over the years of his ministry), Paul realized that the end was near. He was prepared to die, confident in God's power and sovereignty. The Lord's deliverance mentioned here would not be physical this time, but spiritual. Here Paul was affirming his belief in eternal life after death. Anyone facing a life and death struggle can be comforted and encouraged knowing that God will bring each believer **safely to his heavenly Kingdom.** Just as Paul praised God in life (see, for example, Galatians 1:5; Ephesians 3:21), he also praised God in the face of death.

PAUL'S FINAL GREETINGS / 4:19-22

As Paul reached the end of his life, he could look back and know he had been faithful to God's call. Now it was time to pass the torch to the next generation, preparing leaders to take his place so that the world would continue to hear the life-changing message of Jesus Christ. Timothy was Paul's living legacy, a product of Paul's faithful teaching, discipleship, and example. Because of Paul's work with many believers, including Timothy, the world is full of believers today who are also carrying on the work.

4:19 Priscilla and Aquila were fellow Christian leaders with whom Paul had lived and worked (see Acts 18:2-3, 18, 26; Romans 16:3; 1 Corinthians 16:19). While in Corinth, Priscilla, Aquila, and Paul had made tents together. Priscilla and Aquila were an itinerant couple who used the freedom and the money provided by their tentmaking skills to carry out a ministry of hospitality and teaching in various places. They had lived in Rome and Corinth. This time they were in Ephesus, undoubtedly helping Timothy with his work.

Onesiphorus had visited and encouraged Paul in jail during this final imprisonment (see discussion 1:16-18). Paul ended the final chapter in his book and in his life by greeting those who were closest to him.

4:20 Erastus was one of Paul's trusted companions and Timothy's close friend (Acts 19:22). Timothy would be interested in his whereabouts. The same would be true of **Trophimus**, another companion and friend of both men (Acts 20:4; 21:29). Perhaps Trophimus was to have accompanied Paul from Asia to Rome on this last visit, but had to be left in **Miletus** because he was **sick.**

Commitment to ministry does not mean immunity to diseases, discouragement, or death. Paul experienced in himself and in his closest associates the realities of serving God in frail human frames under difficult circumstances. Timothy might not have been aware of Trophimus's illness and would have been glad to know the location of this friend from Ephesus.

4:21 Paul certainly wanted to see his friend as soon as possible (4:9). The request that Timothy try to arrive **before winter** probably included that desire—Paul knew that sailing on the Adriatic Sea was shut down for several weeks during winter because of extreme danger. This also gives insight into Paul's desire to have his coat (4:13) before cold weather set in.

Nothing further is known of the four men listed by name. Paul sent greetings from **all the brothers and sisters,** even though most had deserted him at his trial (4:16). Paul's spirit of forgiveness in including greetings from them must not be missed.

4:22 The first sentence was directed personally to Timothy. The second includes the plural **you** and gives a final good-bye to all the believers.

Tradition says that after Paul was released from prison in Rome (before his second and final Roman imprisonment), he and Titus traveled together for a while. They stopped in Crete, and when it was time for Paul to go, he left Titus behind to help the churches there.

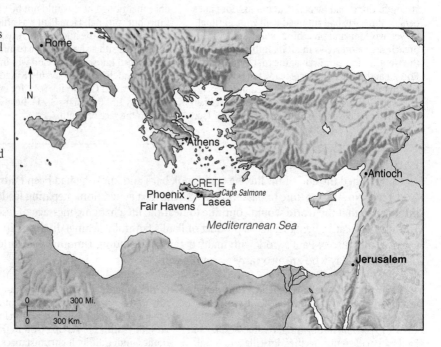

TITUS

INTRODUCTION

Paul is known for his extensive missionary travels, his powerful preaching and teaching, and his courageous witness for Christ. Undoubtedly, most Christians today would characterize him as a hard-line champion of the truth, who rejected compromise and accepted no excuses. Certainly that describes Paul—especially as we read his story in Acts and in his powerful epistles. Speaking to Galatian believers about the false teachers among them, he stated: "If anyone preaches any other gospel than the one you welcomed, let God's curse fall upon that person" (Galatians 1:9). Paul stood strong for the gospel and against all who would twist it or undermine his ministry.

We must also remember, however, that Paul was a loving, compassionate man. He genuinely cared for people and built many solid relationships wherever he traveled. In fact, Paul concluded most of his letters with personal greetings to close friends and fellow ministers (see especially Romans 16:1-16).

The Pastoral Epistles (1 Timothy, 2 Timothy, Titus) testify to Paul's tender and loving nature. Paul considered Timothy and Titus to be his "sons" in the faith, and he treated them as such, leading, mentoring, guiding, and counseling them in their ministry and personal lives.

AUTHOR

Paul, the great apostle and missionary of the church.

As with 1 and 2 Timothy, the very first line in the letter to Titus clearly establishes Paul as author. Although certain scholars in the past several decades have tried to disprove Paul's authorship of this book, the balance of the historical evidence continues to favor Paul. In fact, much of the anti-Paul sentiment seems to be based on the difficulty of placing the writing of the letter to Titus within the narrative in Acts. (See the discussion under "Date" in the introduction to 1 Timothy.) Some critics have also remarked that the writing style and content of Titus differs from Paul's other letters, but these doubts can be easily resolved by recalling the occasion and purpose of the book. The needs and problems of the church in Crete differed greatly from those in Corinth, Ephesus, and Thessalonica. When Paul wrote to Titus (and Timothy), the churches were much more established than when he wrote his earlier letters (see the discussion under "Date" below). In fact, it would be too simplistic to expect the style and content to be the same when the recipients, occasions, and purposes were so different.

Paul addressed this letter, "To Titus, my true child in the faith" (1:4). We don't know the circumstances of Titus's conversion to Christ—the epistles reveal little about his background, and he is not mentioned in Acts—but Titus probably came to faith under Paul's ministry.

DATE AND SETTING
About A.D. 64 or 65, just after 1 Timothy, possibly from Corinth or Nicopolis. Written to Titus who was ministering on the island of Crete.

Students of the book of Acts will wonder when this visit took place, since Acts does not record a visit by Paul to Crete. Most likely, Paul and Titus went to Crete following Paul's release from his first Roman imprisonment (Acts 28:16). Paul traveled and ministered for two or three years before again being imprisoned by Rome and ultimately executed in A.D. 66 or 67.

Crete lies southeast of Greece in the Mediterranean Sea, just south of the Aegean Sea. At 160 miles long and 35 miles wide, Crete is one of the larger islands in the Mediterranean. It is quite mountainous but with very fertile valleys. The highest mountain is Mount Ida, the traditional birthplace of the Greek god Zeus. Crete has an ancient history, having been the center of the great Minoan culture that developed during the Middle and Late Bronze Ages. This Roman province had a hundred cities, many of which were scattered along the coast. These coastal towns were heavily populated and fiercely independent. Cretans had a dubious reputation in the Mediterranean world. Epimenides (600 B.C.) called them "liars, evil beasts, slow bellies" (quoted by Paul in 1:12), and Leonides (488 B.C.) said Cretans were "always brigands and piratical, and unjust."

Crete is not mentioned in Acts as a stop on Paul's missionary journeys; thus scholars surmise that the gospel must have come to that island by way of Jerusalem and Pentecost. Crete had a large Jewish population, so each year many Cretan Jews would travel to Jerusalem for the festival. At the celebration recorded in Acts 2, Cretan Jews witnessed the power of the Holy Spirit (Acts 2:11), heard the gospel in their native language, and responded. When they returned home, they brought the Christian faith with them. The churches on Crete, therefore, were begun in much the same way as those in Rome.

Evidently the character flaws of Cretans in general had been brought into the churches (1:10-16), so Titus had to contend with an unruly and self-centered group of believers. But Paul knew that Christ could change them into people who "do good deeds all the time" (3:8).

You may think that your church is filled with "Cretans." Remember, Christ can transform individual lives and churches.

AUDIENCE
Titus and the church at large.

Little is known about Titus because he is not mentioned by name in Acts. But Titus must have been a remarkable man, because Paul trusted him and assigned him great responsibility. Galatians 2:3 states that Titus was an uncircumcised Gentile, a Greek—most likely he had come to faith in Christ under Paul's ministry. It seems amazing that such a faithful and trusted partner and leader of the church would not appear in Acts, so some scholars surmise that Titus may have been Luke's brother and that Luke omitted his name from the account.

Titus's faith must have been strong, for Paul presented him to church leaders in Jerusalem as a prime example of a Gentile convert worthy of acceptance by the church. Paul related this incident in Galatians 2:1-5. Tension had been building in the church over whether to accept Paul's practice of baptizing Gentiles without insisting that they first become circumcised and submit to Jewish laws and rituals. So Paul traveled to Jerusalem to fight for the truth that salvation is by grace through faith alone. He won this test case—Titus was not compelled to be circumcised. This issue finally was resolved at the Jerusalem council (Acts 15:1-35).

Titus became Paul's key troubleshooter. First, Paul sent him to the church at Corinth, an undisciplined and struggling body of believers in a pagan environment. Titus's first assignment was to resolve the tensions between Paul and the Corinthians (2 Corinthians 7:6-16; 12:18), something that Timothy had been unable to do (1 Corinthians 4:17; 16:10-11; 4:17). Titus was so successful there that Paul sent him back to collect money from the Corinthians for the church in Jerusalem (2 Corinthians 8:6; 16-24). Here, in the letter to Titus, we find that Paul had sent Titus to Crete, an area known for violence and immorality. Titus's task was to "complete our work there" (1:5). Later, we discover that Titus visited Paul in Rome during the second imprisonment and then was sent to Dalmatia (a region on the eastern coast of the Adriatic Sea), another difficult area (2 Timothy 4:10). Paul trusted Titus to be his representative, to resolve conflicts, to collect money, and to organize churches. According to ancient tradition, Titus returned to Crete in old age. He died and was buried there at the age of 94.

Titus kept a low profile—we know much less of him than of Paul and other first-century Christian leaders. And Titus was an unlikely leader—a Greek, not an eyewitness to Christ's life; a Gentile convert, not a Jewish student of the Scriptures. Yet Titus had a profound ministry and impact on church history. God can use a person, regardless of his or her background, nationality, sex, or education, to make a difference in the world. God can use you.

OCCASION AND PURPOSE
To bolster Titus's authority as Paul's apostolic representative in Crete and to give Titus clear instructions about each aspect of his work in the churches there.

It seems that after Paul's release from the Roman prison in about A.D. 62, he traveled with Titus to Crete, where they ministered together. When Paul continued his travels, he left Titus behind as his representative, to help organize and strengthen the churches there (1:5).

Paul wrote this letter at about the same time as his first letter to Timothy. Having placed these two protégés in strategic locations, Paul wanted to encourage them and counsel them about carrying out their responsibilities. Paul knew through reputation (1:12) and firsthand experience (1:5) that the ministry in Crete would be difficult, so he wanted to give Titus information and ammunition for dealing with the problems he would encounter. Paul's location is unknown, but he may have written from Corinth or Nicopolis (on the western coast of Greece), where he had decided to spend the winter (3:12). Evidently when Paul heard that Zenas and Apollos were traveling to Crete (3:13), he decided to send this letter to Titus with them.

The most important task given to Titus was to instruct and organize the churches on the island. Cretans had the earned reputation of being lazy and immoral

(1:12); therefore, sound theology and church discipline were imperative. Already Judaizers were influencing many with their false teachings (1:10-16); these divisive individuals needed to be stopped (3:9-11). And because people seemed to be easily swayed and turned from the truth, each church needed dedicated and spiritual leaders.

Although this letter is addressed to an individual (Titus), Paul also meant for it to be helpful for the churches in Crete.

MESSAGE
Paul begins with a longer than usual greeting and introduction, outlining the leadership progression: Paul's ministry (1:1-3), Titus's responsibilities (1:4-5), and those leaders whom Titus would appoint and train (1:5). Paul then lists pastoral qualifications (1:6-9) and contrasts faithful elders with the false leaders and teachers (1:10-16).

Next, Paul emphasizes the importance of good deeds in the life of the Christian, telling Titus how to relate to the various age groups in the church (2:2-6). He urges Titus to be a good example of a mature believer (2:7-8) and to teach with courage and conviction (2:9-15). He then discusses the general responsibilities of Christians in society: Titus should remind the people of these (3:1-8), and he should avoid divisive arguments (3:9-11). Paul concludes with a few matters of itinerary and personal greetings (3:12-15).

The main themes in the book of Titus include: *Character, Church Relationships, A Good Life,* and *Citizenship.*

Character (1:5-16). Paul had left Titus in Crete to "complete our work there and appoint elders in each town" (1:5). So Paul gave Titus a list of qualities for "elders." These church leaders must be of the highest character, as evidenced by a strong family life (1:6) and a good reputation in the community (1:7-8). They also must be firmly grounded in their faith and able to teach others (1:9). These qualifications were important because of the sinful world surrounding the church (1:12) and because of the potential for heresy and divisions within the church (1:10-11, 13-16). As Paul's representative, with apostolic authority, Titus was to make sure that church leaders exhibited strong moral character and spiritual maturity.

IMPORTANCE FOR TODAY. Churches need leaders who are totally committed to Jesus Christ and who are living the way God wants them to live. It is not enough to be educated, have special abilities and gifts, or to have a loyal following to be Christ's kind of leader. Church leaders must have self-control, spiritual and moral fitness, and Christian character. God wants Christians to aspire to leadership in his church, but they must be the right kind of leaders. Who you are is more important than what you can do.

Church Relationships (2:1-10, 15; 3:9-11). Part of Titus's responsibility during his stay on Crete was to teach believers how they should act in the world and with each other (2:15). Paul encouraged Titus to teach with integrity and seriousness and to set a good example for all the believers, especially the new church leaders (2:7-8). Paul emphasized the importance of right teaching (2:1), and he told Titus to rebuke all who would steer believers astray (3:9-11). Paul explained to Titus how his teaching should relate to the various groups in the church. Older Christians should teach younger men and women and be good examples to them

(2:2-5). Young people should be self-controlled (2:6), and slaves should be trust-worthy (2:10). People of every age and group have a lesson to learn and a role to play in the church, and all should be positive witnesses for Christ in the world (2:2, 8, 10).

IMPORTANCE FOR TODAY. Christians who truly believe "right teaching" (2:1) live out what the Bible teaches in their relationships. A local church is a collection of old, young, male, female, rich, and poor, so a church in which believers love each other and get along will draw people to Christ (2:10). Pride and self-indulgence can divide any church, but the antidote is submission to Christ and to each other, as well as self-control. Treat your relationships with other believers as an outgrowth of your faith and part of your witness to the world.

A Good Life (3:3-8; 12-15). Paul reminded Titus that before trusting Christ they had been disobedient to God and enslaved to sin (3:3), but Christ had trans-formed them (3:4-7). The gospel message is that a person is saved by grace through faith (3:5-7), not by living a good life. But the gospel changes people's lives, so that they eventually perform good deeds (3:8) and become totally devoted to serving others (3:14).

IMPORTANCE FOR TODAY. A good life is a witness to the gospel's power. Chris-tians must have commitment and discipline to serve. When we remember what Christ has done for us, we will be motivated to share his love with others. In what ways are you putting your faith into action by serving others?

Citizenship (2:11–3:2). Paul told Titus to instruct believers that how they live outside the church was very important. Christians must say "yes" to God and "no" to ungodly living in the world (2:12-14). Believers also should be good citizens in society, obeying the government (3:1) and working honestly (3:2).

IMPORTANCE FOR TODAY. How a Christian fulfills his or her duties is a witness to the watching world. A believer's community life should reflect Christ's love as much as his or her church life does. Your neighbors should know that you are a faithful church member and a good citizen.

OUTLINE OF TITUS

TITUS 1

GREETINGS FROM PAUL / 1:1-4

Christian tradition suggests a missionary visit by Paul and Titus shortly after the first trial. Paul planted the church and left Titus to look after the early organizational phase and to oversee the new congregations. Because the gospel had only recently been preached on the island, believers were susceptible to a number of strong influences. So Titus needed to be on guard. Also, the church in Crete needed strong Christian leaders; Titus was responsible to choose and prepare them.

1:1 Paul identified himself by name and by authority. He called himself a **slave** of God—that is, one who was committed to obeying God. (This is the only place where Paul used this particular phrase to describe himself.) Even though Paul was not one of the original twelve disciples (later called apostles), he had been specially called by God as an **apostle** to bring the Good News to the Gentiles (Acts 9:1-16). Paul's twofold reference to himself combines humble obedience with confident authority on his part.

As a servant and apostle, Paul focused his life on two main concerns: **faith** and **truth**. God sent Paul to **bring faith to those God has chosen and to teach them to know the truth.** God's chosen are those who have responded to the gospel. Although we can't totally understand the doctrine of election, it gives us tremendous insight into God's love and wisdom. After responding to faith, God's people then need training in the truth so that they can **live godly lives.**

Paul's view of ministry was always long-term. He was not content to aim at people merely responding to the gospel. His goal was to bring people to spiritual maturity in Christ.

1:2 God's **truth,** taught by Paul to God's chosen, **gives them the confidence of eternal life.** Believers' confidence regarding their eternal future is based on a good foundation, for God himself has **promised** it **before the world began.** The promise did not come at a point when sin entered the world or even at the moment that God sent Christ to deal with the problem of sin; rather, Christ's coming and the promise

of eternal life had been planned by God from the beginning. God has been and always will be in supreme control of the universe, world events, and the future of his people.

Confidence is also based on the fact that God **cannot lie.** Apparently lying was commonplace in Crete (see 1:12). Paul made it clear at the start that God does not lie. Trust in God's character forms the foundation of our faith. Because God *is* truth, he is the source of all truth, and he cannot lie. This puts him in complete contrast to Satan, who is the father of lies (John 8:44). The eternal life that God has promised will be ours because he keeps his promises.

1:3 The promise came before time began. The revealing of that promise, God's **Good News,** the hope of eternal life, came **at the right time.** That is, God sent his Son at the proper time, the time of his own choosing (see Romans 5:6; Galatians 4:4; Ephesians 1:9-12; 1 Timothy 2:6), to bring the word of salvation to light. And Paul, at an opportune time in history, was called by God to **announce** this Good News to **everyone.**

1:4 Titus, a Greek, was one of Paul's most trusted and dependable coworkers. As a **true child,** he may have been one of Paul's converts. Although not mentioned in Acts, other epistles point out that Titus fulfilled several missions on Paul's behalf. Paul repeated his standard greeting (**grace and peace**) with a slight change. The last term repeats the thought of verse 3. Paul used the term **Savior** for both **God the Father** and **Christ Jesus,** thereby revealing his understanding of God's nature and work in salvation (see also 1:3; 2:10, 13; 3:4, 6).

TITUS'S WORK IN CRETE / 1:5-16

Unlike the pressing matter of the false teachers that was on Paul's mind when he wrote to Timothy in Ephesus, Paul's letter to Titus focused on establishing healthy churches on Crete.

In both cases, identifying good leaders was a priority. But in Ephesus leaders were needed to get the church back on track, while on Crete effective leaders were needed to get the church moving in the right direction. Paul wanted Titus to choose the right people to lead the growing church in Crete.

1:5 Crete is a long (150 miles), narrow **island** in the Mediterranean Sea, southeast of Greece. Among its population were many Jews. The earliest converts there were probably Cretan Jews who had been in Jerusalem at Pentecost (Acts 2:11) more than thirty years before Paul wrote this letter. Perhaps there had been some renewed contact with Paul when he was there as a prisoner on his first journey to Rome for trial. Later, he and Titus returned for an evangelistic visit.

Apparently Paul did not stay long in Crete, so he left Titus, his trusted and able fellow worker, to **complete** the **work** of establishing correct teaching and dealing with false teachers, as well as appointing **elders in each town.** Paul had appointed elders in various churches during his journeys (Acts 14:23). On Paul's return from the first missionary journey, he took extra time to revisit every church and establish each church's leadership. He could not stay in each church, but he knew that these new churches needed strong spiritual leaders. The men chosen were to lead the churches by teaching sound doctrine, helping believers mature spiritually, and equipping believers to live for Jesus Christ despite opposition. The following verses give the qualifications for elders.

1:6 Paul briefly described some qualifications that **an elder** should have. Paul had given Timothy a similar set of instructions for choosing leaders in the Ephesian church (see 1 Timothy 3:1-7; 5:22). Notice that most of the qualifications involve character, not knowledge or skill. A person's lifestyle and relationships provide a window into his character. Consider these qualifications as you evaluate people for positions of leadership in your church. It is important to have leaders who can effectively preach God's word; but even more importantly, they must live out God's word and be examples for others to follow.

The first qualification is to **be well thought of for his good life.** An elder must have no conduct that would be grounds for any kind of accusation. He must be above reproach. Again, the point here is not that the leaders cannot be blamed, but rather that when blamed, their life will prove the falsehood of the blame.

He must be faithful to his wife means that a church leader should not be promiscuous but should be faithful in his marriage. This did not prohibit an unmarried person from becoming an elder. That his

children must be believers who are not wild or rebellious would show that the church leader has proven that he can lead his own household. An elder's children should have received spiritual training and should be believers. This will prove that they care about teaching correct doctrine and discipling others. Obviously, those whose children are rebelling, running wild, and refusing to obey would not be fit for the important position of leading God's people. How one's children live attests to how the Christian life is practiced at home.

1:7 An elder must live a blameless life, emphasizing that this quality is essential in any person who is **God's minister.** Church leaders who act unworthily and bring blame and reproach on themselves also damage God's work.

Paul's guidelines take on added significance in the Cretan setting, for Cretans were known as having disreputable character (see 1:12). Sometimes the leadership guidelines from Scripture will harmonize with the prevailing standards for mature leaders in a culture, and, at other times, they will conflict. Apparently, Titus was to be careful with the Cretans.

A pitfall of leadership is becoming **arrogant.** But pride can seduce emotions and cloud reason, making a church leader ineffective. Pride and conceit were the Devil's downfall, and he uses pride to trap others. In addition, a **quick-tempered** person will speak and act without thinking—hurting people and damaging the church's work and reputation.

These last three prohibitions had particular significance for Titus's search for church leaders in first-century Crete. A church leader must not be **a heavy drinker** or **violent** (often the result of being quick-tempered or drunk). Furthermore, the leaders Titus chose should serve out of love, not because they are **greedy for money.**

1:8 After listing characteristics a church leader should *not* have, Paul lists these positive qualities. Hospitality was of primary importance in this culture. Believers were commanded to be hospitable (see 3 John), so their leaders should **enjoy having guests,** revealing devotion and concern for the welfare of others. Paul insisted that the leaders be known for loving **all that is good.** This person displays that goodness in the spiritual realm as he lives **wisely** and is **fair** to others. A believer who is **devout** will most likely also have a **disciplined**

life, picturing a person who, like an athlete, is constantly "in training" in his Christian life and service. (See note on 1 Timothy 3:2 for more on "self-control.")

1:9 The church leader must meet moral and spiritual requirements in his personal life, and be reliable in his understanding and teaching of the **message he was taught.** The last phrase actually occurs first in the Greek for emphasis. The message as it had been taught by the apostles was the **trustworthy** message that church leaders must teach their congregation. They must **be strong and steadfast** so that they can **encourage others with right teaching** and point out the errors of those who **oppose** them.

Pastors must fulfill a positive and a negative function in handling the truth. They must encourage by preaching, supporting, and reinforcing people as they follow the truth. But pastors must also confront and refute false ideas. Confident leaders with backbone, courage, and an irrefutable message would stand in strong contrast with Cretan lifestyles, character traits, and false teachers (described in the following verses).

1:10 The false teachers Paul and Titus faced were **those who insist on circumcision for salvation—** the Judaizers (see also 1:14). These were Jews who taught that the Gentiles had to obey all the Jewish laws, rules, and rituals before they could become Christians. This regulation confused new Christians and caused problems in many churches where Paul had preached the Good News. Paul wrote letters to several churches to help them understand that Gentile believers did not have to become Jews first in order to be Christians—God accepts anyone who comes to him in faith (see Romans 1:17; Galatians 3:2-7). Although the Jerusalem council had dealt with this issue (see Acts 15), devout Jews who refused to believe in Jesus still were trying to cause problems in the Christian churches. The ruling of the Jerusalem council may have been honored by those within the churches, but these outsiders did not recognize the apostles as having any authority.

Here Paul identified three characteristics of this brand of false teachers:

1. They **rebel against right teaching,** flouting the authority of Paul and Titus.
2. They **engage in useless talk,** speaking lots of words and saying nothing.
3. They **deceive people** because they do not have the truth.

1:11 These false teachers **must be silenced;** the Greek word literally means "to muzzle." **Their**

wrong teaching was ruining people's faith—**whole families** had been affected, causing confusion in the church. These teachers taught not the trustworthy message of the gospel (1:9) but their own ideas. Their goal was not to glorify the Lord and build his church but to make **money.** Naturally it was hoped that these people would respond to the truth and be united with the true body of believers.

1:12 Paul quoted a line from a poem by Epimenides, a poet and philosopher who had lived in **Crete** 600 years earlier. Paul called him a **prophet** because other ancient writers (notably Aristotle and Cicero) did so, and because his own countrymen gave him that title. Paul was not saying he was a prophet in the biblical sense. The quotation reveals basic character flaws in the Cretans. They were **liars, cruel animals** (referring to unrestrained brutality and lives out of control), and **lazy gluttons.** The reputation of the Cretans was so bad that the verb form of their name (*kretizo*) was used by the Greeks to indicate lying. Paul applied this familiar phrase to the false teachers.

1:13 The Cretans could hardly argue with one of their own honored prophets, so neither did Paul. Having been in Crete, Paul knew from firsthand experience the type of people with whom Titus was dealing. Paul's recommended remedy was to **rebuke** the wavering believers **sternly,** then, if possible, to restore them to strength **in the faith.**

A forceful, direct response early would prevent utter chaos in the church later. If the first believers were to develop unhealthy spiritual lives, they would carry their "disease" into the ongoing life of the church. Better to deal with the problem right away than to let it build up. But even here, the goal demanded that even the least hopeful candidates for the church be given the opportunity to come to faith.

1:14 Apparently, the false teaching centered on two errors: first, **Jewish myths** (probably some useless speculations on the Old Testament, see also 1 Timothy 1:4). Titus may well have been facing various shades of syncretism, in which diluted Judaism was being blended with various forms of paganism to yield a deadly brand of godless religion. Second, these human **commands** most likely focused on rules and rituals, especially Jewish laws regarding what was clean and unclean (as is evident from Paul's words in verses 15-16).

Titus faced the lethal combination of religion and falsehood. Such mixtures have always presented a challenge to God's people. Today the spirit of our times applauds those who create their own personal religion. Self-made rules and guidelines that come from human teaching and not God should never be the basis for Christian thought.

1:15 Phrases like this one, **everything is pure to those whose hearts are pure,** must be understood in both immediate and wide contexts. Paul was not teaching moral relativism ("As long as I can call myself pure, whatever I choose to do is therefore pure"), but he was speaking against superficial, external legalism. Dietary restrictions or food laws presented a form of religion that people thought provided spiritual substance, but which proved to be empty of real spiritual help. Those who believe sound doctrine and live their faith do not need to worry about rules and rituals regarding what is clean or unclean. No stronger denunciation could be made to these false teachers who taught the need for following rules and rituals in order to be clean and pure. Because of their inner corruption, **nothing is pure**—nothing they do, say, give, or teach could be pure because **their minds and consciences** were **defiled.** Echoing Jesus' teaching in Mark 7:15-19 and Luke 11:39-41, Paul explained that a person who is pure on the inside cannot be corrupted by outside influences; but a person who is corrupt on the inside corrupts everything around him. There can be no purity for such a person.

1:16 The "corrupt and unbelieving" (1:15) false teachers claimed to **know God,** but their actions revealed their true nature. No matter what rules they claimed to follow, they denied God **by the way they** lived. The false teachers professed knowledge of God and, with their Jewish background, may have been well versed in the Old Testament. But they based their faith on works, not on the Lord Jesus Christ, thus they denied the God they claimed to know. Paul employed strong words because the sin of these false teachers deserved strong condemnation. Paul called them **despicable,** revealing his disgust at their sin and hypocrisy; **disobedient,** because they acted against the God they claimed to know; **worthless for doing anything good,** because people who live in rebellion against God cannot do any works that please him.

TITUS 2

PROMOTE RIGHT TEACHING / 2:1-15

In chapter 1, Paul set the primary goal for Titus's ministry in Crete: Titus was to teach all the new converts to become "strong in the faith" (1:13). Paul commented on the primary social relationships that were central to the growth of the church in Crete. He did not try to change the system; instead, he sought to change the persons within the systems. Marriages, homes, slavery, and work are all transformed more profoundly from within than from without. Through Titus, Paul was planting seeds of significant change in every facet of life on Crete. But it all depended on the truth of the gospel message.

2:1 The word **but** contrasts this verse with the previous verses. Whereas the false teachers were deceivers (1:10), Titus was to **promote the kind of living that reflects right teaching.** Knowledge and acceptance of "right teaching" should lead to righteous living. Behavior should match belief; thus, in the following verses, Paul gave Titus examples of the right behavior expected of several types of people in the churches.

2:2 The **older men,** though technically not "elders," were the senior members of the community, and should be examples of maturity. They were the "pool" from which elders were to be appointed. Because they were mature members of the commu-

nity and examples to younger men, Titus should teach the older men to **exercise self-control,** meaning that their lives should show moderation and clearheadedness, with an absence of extravagance. To be **worthy of respect** means that they should be "serious minded." They should act as dignified and honorable adults (see also 2:3, 7). To **live wisely** contrasts with the lifestyle in a heathen atmosphere. They needed to monitor and restrain their passions, anger, and words. **Strong faith** meant that they were to have a healthy and personal faith in God by maintaining the Christian truth. **Love** meant that they should be loving, not bitter; their love was to be personal and outgoing (see John 13:34). **Patience** required endurance and steadfastness.

2:3 Paul's directive for Titus to **teach** women was in itself a startling departure from the way women were usually treated. The inequalities found in society were not to be brought into church relationships. We honor older people when we consider them capable of still being nurtured.

The **older women** must also be taught—their lifestyles should be **appropriate**—dignified, worthy of honor, Christlike. Older Christian women should have a respectful attitude toward all aspects of life and toward people of all ages. They were **not to go around speaking evil of others** (gossips), nor should they be **heavy drinkers**. Instead, these older women **should teach others what is good.** This meant not necessarily public sharing, but sharing their wisdom, knowledge, and faith with their circles of family and friends. No woman should regard her life as less valuable when children have left or after retirement from a career. Nor should they capitulate to despair or loneliness. We need their wisdom, prayers, and examples.

2:4 Specifically, the older women could **train the younger women** in the church by word and by example. Paul wanted the older women to teach "what is good" (2:3), and here he explained that in detail. First, they could encourage the young women in the church to **love their husbands and their children**. This seems obvious, but Paul may have included this because of special problems in Crete, or even because of the influence of the false teachers to disregard these responsibilities (see 1:11).

2:5 As with the older men and women, these younger women needed **to live wisely.** The next word, **pure,** means to control their passions and desires, remaining true to their husbands (perhaps Paul also mentioned this because of a particular problem in Crete). These young wives and mothers should **take care of their homes** (which, as any homemaker knows, can be a challenging and diverse career in itself) and **do good.**

In addition, the young women were to be **submissive to their husbands.** Submission between marriage partners is an often misunderstood concept. This text, for example, cannot be used to promote the general subjugation of all women under all men. For marriage and family relationships to run smoothly, there must be one appointed leader— God has appointed the husband and father to be this leader. The wife should willingly follow her husband's leadership in Christ, acknowledging that this is his responsibility.

Maturity provides the key to understanding submission. The husband must not be a tyrant, faithless, unloving, or impatient, as previously mentioned in verse 2. He should be worthy of respect. Likewise, the woman should not be rebellious, undermining or contradicting the man. Submission means to accept the relationship that God has designed, voluntarily subjecting oneself to God's order and fulfilling the responsibilities that come with it. For more of Paul's advice about marriage, see 1 Corinthians 7:1-40; Ephesians 5:22-33.

Paul's purpose in these instructions, and every believer's purpose in following them, was to glorify God. The believers were being watched; if they lived righteous and blameless lives, they would **not bring shame on the word of God.** For the believers to continue living in sin amounted to denying God's word and God himself, who had saved them from sin and expected them to obey his commands.

2:6 Paul urged Titus to **encourage the young men to live wisely in all they do.** Young men today, as much as in ancient times, may lack this quality. If young men exercise self-restraint, balance, and common sense, they can save themselves much trouble in all areas of life.

2:7-8 Titus, qualifying as a "younger man" himself, was urged to **be an example** for the young men in the churches he led (see also 1 Timothy 4:12). His authoritative words could have no impact if not backed up by a blameless life of **doing good deeds.** Titus's teaching should emphasize wise living while his lifestyle should be an example of that.

From speaking of Titus's actions, Paul turned to Titus's public ministry of **teaching.** His life should **reflect the integrity and seriousness** of what he taught and would contrast him with the false teachers, who taught lies. This quality of **integrity** would come from careful Bible study and prayer. This would be especially important as Titus taught or confronted others about spiritual or moral issues. If he acted impulsively or unreasonably, he would more likely start arguments than convince people of the truth. **Seriousness** indicates teaching with reverence so that Titus's words would be respected and taken seriously. Paul counseled Titus to be above criticism in how he taught. Because of his unique role in Crete, his life must display a remarkable degree of correctness. He would be constantly on display. Titus's every word must be measured so that he would remain above reproach and condemnation. His exemplary life, teaching, and speech would shame those who might want to **argue** with him.

2:9-10 Slavery was common in Paul's day. Millions of slaves occupied the empire, and many of them found their way into the early churches. Slavery was an institution and would not be changed overnight. Thus, Paul did not condemn the institution of slavery in any of his letters. But Paul advised both Christian slaves and masters to be loving and responsible in their conduct (see also Ephesians 6:5-9; Colossians 3:22-25; 1 Timothy 6:1-2; 1 Peter 2:18-25).

Slaves were to **obey their masters** by nature of their position, but the difference Paul hoped to teach them was in their attitude toward their masters and toward the work they performed. They should treat their masters with respect, and they should **do their best to please them.** They no longer served because they had to; they served because they loved the Lord and their masters and because they took pride in their work. That the slaves were not to **talk back** meant that they should not be stubborn, unmanageable, or resistant to authority. That they should not **steal** referred to any type of theft that might be classified as "petty larceny." Slaves might be tempted to take "small" needed items, but Christian slaves must resist that temptation in order to **show themselves to be entirely trustworthy and good.** They would impress their masters and other slaves with the depth of change that God had performed in their lives, making others want to know more about the Christian faith.

2:11 God's salvation was offered to all the different people in the groups he had just identified. **God,** by his **grace,** sent Christ to earth; because of Christ's death on the cross, **salvation** is available to **all people.** The grace of God was **revealed** in Christ, referring to the incarnation. That message of grace arrived in Crete with Paul and Titus. We can hardly imagine the impact! When the gospel light is turned on in a place of darkness, changes are inevitable. Those who respond are transformed; those who resist and reject the message can do so, but they must face the consequences.

2:12-13 All of Paul's instructions in verses 1-10 can be summed up in these two phrases. Believers must **turn from godless living and sinful pleasures.** We live in an **evil world** where many totally reject God's influence in any area of life. Christians must renounce that attitude. Sinful pleasures are desires for the pleasures and activities of this world (1 John 2:16). Believers must replace those desires with positive characteristics: **self-control, right conduct, and devotion to God.** The motivation for righteous living is looking forward to **that wonderful event when the glory of our great God and Savior, Jesus Christ, will be revealed.** We can look forward to Christ's wonderful return with eager expectation and hope. Our hope makes us live each day ready morally and ethically to serve him.

2:14 The "great God and Savior, Jesus Christ," whose return believers await, is the same Jesus Christ who came to earth and died for our sins. Christ's act of sacrifice is summed up in the words **gave his life.** It indicates that he gave himself voluntarily. It was an act of love for us. He wanted to **free us from every kind of sin.** Christ paid the ultimate price. He removed our bondage to sin that made us lawless rebels. Christ has accomplished the work required to **cleanse** those whom he died to save (see 1 John 1:7; Hebrews 9:12-14). This purification is a process, often called "sanctification." We are not only free from the sentence of death for our sin, but we are also purified from sin's influence as we grow in Christ. His redemption took care of the past; his purification makes the present and future an exciting and challenging prospect.

Through his redemption, God made **us his very own people.** The phrase has an important Old Testament background. The basis of the covenant was God's choosing this people and purifying them to be set apart for his special use. As people who are cleansed and restored and who understand the awesome price paid on our behalf, we should thank God. We should also live according to God's will, **totally committed to doing what is right.** Then, when Christ returns, he will find us ready, waiting, and doing good works.

2:15 Paul repeated his command to Titus to be unafraid in his teaching ministry among the believers in Crete. **These things** referred to verses 1-10 above. Titus must **teach** or speak out (as opposed to being silent and thus allowing wrongdoing and sin), **encourage** (exhort, advise, commend, and/or admonish, depending on the need), and do **correcting when necessary** (express disapproval, reprimand if needed). In short, he was to persist by every means at his disposal to communicate to those in Crete what he had learned from Paul. Titus could do this on divine **authority,** for he had been entrusted by God with leadership gifts and with this ministry in Crete.

No doubt, as Titus exercised his God-given authority, some would **ignore or disregard** him, either because he was younger than they were or because they didn't agree with his decisions. Paul had made a similar statement with respect to Timothy's youth in 1 Timothy 4:12. The impact of the phrase communicates the idea that neither Titus nor Timothy should allow anyone else's definition of who they were to affect what they knew themselves to be. Titus should follow God's leading as he completed his mission among the Cretan churches.

TITUS 3

DO WHAT IS GOOD / 3:1-8

Most of chapter 2 covered relationships and responsibilities of believers. In this chapter, Paul discussed Christian behavior in the context of government and society. The quality of our earthly citizenship should reflect the confidence we have in our heavenly citizenship! Because we are citizens of the eternal Kingdom, we can live with hope and serve people in the earthly kingdom.

3:1 In addition to teaching, encouraging, and correcting (2:15), a Christian leader must also **remind** his congregation **to submit to the government and its officers**. As the believers awaited the return of Christ and living eternally with him in his government (2:13), they had to live under worldly authorities. So Paul explained how believers in Crete could best do that—by subjecting themselves to government rulers and authorities and by obeying civil laws. He did not want any trouble with the authorities that would bring the church under suspicion (see also Romans 13:1-7; 1 Peter 2:13-17).

Christians understand obedience to the government in different ways. All Christians agree that we are to live at peace with the state as long as the state allows us to live by our religious convictions. For hundreds of years, however, there have been at least three interpretations of how we are to do this:

1. Some Christians believe that the state is so corrupt that Christians should have as little to do with it as possible. Although they should be good citizens as long as they can do so without compromising their beliefs, they should not work for the government, vote in elections, or serve in the military. Although this fulfills the principle of abstaining from evil, it prevents the Christian from being salt and light in the governmental, political, and military systems.
2. Others believe that God has given the state authority in certain areas and the church authority in others. Christians can be loyal to both and can work for either. They should not, however, confuse the two. In this view, church and state are concerned with two totally different spheres—the spiritual and the physical. Thus they complement each other but do not work together. This view is very legitimate and supports Jesus' teaching to give to Caesar what is Caesar's and to God what is

God's (see Matthew 22:21), but it can lead to isolation from the political world and indifference toward state leaders.
3. Still others believe that Christians have a responsibility to make the state better. They can do this politically, by electing Christian or other high-principled leaders. They can also do this morally, by serving as an influence for good in society. In this view, church and state ideally work together for the good of all. This view is preferred and seems to best portray the New Testament teaching. Nowhere does Jesus call laymen to leave political or social service as a requirement for discipleship. Its inherent danger would be for the Christian to get so involved in worldly affairs that the Christian mission is lost.

Besides being **obedient**, Paul mentioned readiness **to do what is good**—in other words, a willingness to serve. No doubt Christians who obeyed the government gave a good witness for their faith among the authorities; Christians active in community service and/or government had great opportunities to witness for Christ.

3:2 These bridge-building characteristics revealed changed lives and made the gospel message attractive to unbelievers. All Christians should check their conduct against these traits. To **not speak evil of anyone** meant forbidding Christians to spread evil rumors or gossip (see James 3:9). Believers were not to be caught making reports about others that would prove to be untrue. We should be like Christ, who did not retaliate when he was insulted (1 Peter 2:23).

To **avoid quarreling** means to be peaceable. Christians were to be known as peacemakers in their relationships and within the church. There may be disagreements, but the believers should actively avoid, not the disagreement, but quarreling about it. When disagreements degenerate into quarreling, there is little possibility of preserving peace and working toward a solution.

To **be gentle and show true humility** follows Christ's example. Christians should not be agitators but conciliators. Believers could show gentleness and humility to unbelievers in their neighborhoods by offering help without strings attached. When we help unbelievers, we open a door for the gospel.

3:3 The Cretans had a reputation for certain vices (1:12), yet Paul well understood that all believers once were sinners and had lived far from God (see also 1 Corinthians 6:9-11; Ephesians 4:17-24). Paul never forgot the change that God had made in his life, beginning with his experience on the Damascus road (Acts 9:1-22). Paul included himself, Titus, the believers in Crete, and all believers across the world in the list of past rebels.

Foolish is used here as it is in Proverbs for those who arrogantly rebel against God and go their own way. Instead of being submissive, obedient, and ready to do good (3:1), they were **disobedient** toward God because of sin, and **misled** by false teachers so that they **became slaves to many wicked desires and evil pleasures.** Without God, all unbelievers are enslaved to their passions and desires. Left alone, human nature can only go from bad to worse. Instead of avoiding slander and quarrels, being peaceful, considerate, and humble (3:2), their **lives were full of evil and envy.** No matter how much "love" the world tries to create without God, the overriding power of sin produces a greater amount of hatred. Thus there is no hope for sinful humanity apart from the intervention of the holy God, our Creator.

3:4-6 Fortunately for us, God intervened. God's **kindness and love** appeared in the human form of Jesus Christ. By his death, **he saved us** from our deserved punishment for disobeying God. He offered this salvation because of his **mercy** alone, not because we deserved it by doing **good things.** Paul summarized what God does for us when he saves us. God **washed away our sins.** As Paul explains the transaction, when believers receive this washing of rebirth, all sins, not merely some, are washed away. We gain **new life** with all its treasures. The process is complete. We can experience what we have in new ways, but we have received the whole package! We live a "new" life because of **the Holy Spirit** (see Romans 8:9-17) whom he **generously poured out upon us because of what Jesus Christ our Savior did.**

All three persons of the Trinity are mentioned in these verses because all three participate in the work of salvation. Based upon the redemptive work of his Son, the Father forgives and sends the Holy Spirit to wash away our sins and continually renew us.

3:7 From Adam we inherited guilt, a sinful nature (the tendency to sin), and God's punishment. Because Jesus took the punishment we deserved for sin and made us right before God, we can trade punishment for forgiveness. We have been **declared not guilty.** We can trade our sin for Jesus' righteousness. When we do that, **we know that we will inherit eternal life.** Eternal life began the moment we gave our life to Christ, but there is more to come! Our experience now is only a foretaste of what God has guaranteed to us in the future!

3:8 The things Paul wrote were **true** so Titus ought to constantly **insist on them.** The believers must show their beliefs through their conduct. They must **be careful to do good deeds all the time.** Sound doctrine must manifest itself in good works. Such teaching and action profits the believers as well as the unbelievers to whom the church witnesses.

PAUL'S FINAL REMARKS AND GREETINGS / 3:9-15

As Titus proceeded with the task of planting and nurturing the church, Paul reminded him that he would encounter resistance. The aging apostle Paul had summarized the key points of the faith that Titus was to communicate. Titus must lead in such a way so that the truth would not be compromised by arguments, curious teachings, or conflicts over power. Some people in the church would not listen and follow even when they were patiently and repeatedly corrected. These people would lead others astray and cause divisions in the church. Titus was not to tolerate their divisive behavior. He would have to put those people out of the church.

3:9 If sound teaching and good deeds were beneficial (3:8), obviously **foolish discussions** were **useless and a waste of time.** The false teaching in

Crete apparently had Jewish roots and focused on two errors: **spiritual pedigrees** and **quarrels and fights about obedience to Jewish laws**—probably some useless speculations on the Old Testament rules and rituals, especially Jewish laws regarding what was clean and unclean. Similar to the methods used by false teachers in Ephesus and Colosse, these teachers were causing controversies, arguments, and quarrels about their own wholly imaginary ideas. The "spiritual pedigrees" may have included imaginary genealogies of angels. These were needed, so the false teachers said, because believers had to worship angels as well as God.

Paul warned Titus and Timothy to **not get involved in** the false teachers' debates and arguments, to not even bother to answer their pretentious positions. This did not mean that the church leaders should refuse to study, discuss, and examine different interpretations of difficult Bible passages. Paul was warning against petty quarrels, not honest discussion that leads to wisdom. As foolish arguments develop, they should rebuke the false teaching (1:13) and turn the discussion back to a helpful and profitable direction. Meanwhile, the faithful minister should continue to emphasize those truths that God wants taught.

3:10-11 Paul gave a similar warning at the end of Romans 16:17-20 and follows Jesus' pattern in Matthew 18:15-17. Besides avoiding the false teachers' debates, Titus needed to take specific action toward the false teachers themselves, as with anyone who **is causing divisions** among the believers. Even more than their doctrine, their church-wrecking behavior had to be stopped. While false teachers outside the church were to be avoided, a person inside the church must be warned not to cause division or threaten the unity of the church. Paul allowed for two warnings before having **nothing more to do with** the person because they have **turned away from the truth, are sinning, and condemn themselves.** A person's refusal to stop teaching false doctrine and to stop causing division in the church (even after being lovingly admonished) evidenced severe stubbornness.

A local church cannot modify its doctrine for every new idea or accommodate every person's viewpoint. It may be better to risk having a member leave for another church that emphasizes his or her theological "hot button" than to try to be a church that caters to every conceivable theological taste. A church cannot get to the important work of evangelism and service to others if the theological base is shaky or if the church is embroiled in theological controversy.

3:12 Nothing is known about **Artemas. Tychicus** was one of Paul's trusted companions (Acts 20:4) and a messenger (he delivered the letters of Ephe-

sians and Colossians to the churches in those cities—Ephesians 6:21; Colossians 4:7). Paul planned to **send** one of these men to Crete to fill in for Titus so Titus could go to meet Paul. We do not know Paul's location at the writing of this letter to Titus; however, he noted here that he wanted to **winter** in **Nicopolis.** Three places in the Roman Empire were named Nicopolis (literally "city of victory"), so named after some conquest. The city mentioned here probably was on the western coast of Greece. Titus would have to leave soon because sea travel was dangerous in the winter months.

3:13 Nothing is known about **Zenas the lawyer,** except that he would have been an expert in the law—either Hebrew or Roman, depending on his nationality (his name is Greek, so we might assume the latter). **Apollos** was a famous Christian preacher. A native of Alexandria in North Africa, he became a Christian in Ephesus and was trained by Aquila and Priscilla (Acts 18:24-28; 1 Corinthians 1:12). From the context, it appears that Zenas and Apollos were on a preaching mission in Crete. Thus Titus, as leader of the churches in Crete, should be an example to the believers, encouraging hospitality and financial assistance in order that these missionaries would be helped **with their trip** and have **everything they need.** (For more about hospitality and help for traveling preachers in the days of the early church, see 2 and 3 John.)

3:14 Paul repeated his words of verses 1 and 8, again stressing the importance of learning **to do good by helping others.** Speaking to the Cretan believers as **our people,** Paul urged them to focus these good works on providing for **urgent needs.** Taking on normal responsibilities ensured that no one would be **unproductive.** Paul's view of productivity differs radically with today's view. Most people think "productive" means becoming affluent, achieving notoriety, or holding a high position. But Paul emphasized good deeds and fruitful Christian ministry to the needs of others. We must remember that it is the Holy Spirit who makes us fruitful as we use the opportunities given us (Galatians 5:22-23).

3:15 We do not know who was included in the **everybody** who were with Paul; however, such **greetings** occurred in many of his letters with the people listed (see for example, 1 Corinthians 1:19-20; Colossians 4:10-15; 2 Timothy 4:9-12). Paul, in turn, sent greetings to all the faithful believers in Crete.

Paul used a similar closing in both his letters to Timothy, asking that **God's grace be with** them **all.** The inclusion of "all" indicates that this letter was to be read to a wider audience than just Titus.

PHILEMON

INTRODUCTION

Invisible walls divide people into the "ins and outs," the "haves and have nots," and an endless assortment of groups, cliques, and castes. Determined by race, skin color, nationality, money, background, education, status, religion, gender, or ability, individuals are judged, categorized, and put in their place. When those social barriers are crossed, usually it is at a great price.

But Jesus broke the barriers that divide men and women from each other and from God. In a male-dominated society, he spoke freely with women (Matthew 9:18-26; Luke 8:1-3). In the face of holier-than-thou hypocrites, he enjoyed meals with sinners (Matthew 9:10-13). Ignoring years of prejudice and discrimination, he associated with Samaritans (John 4:1-42) and Gentiles (Luke 7:1-10; 8:26-39). And he continually sought to bring outcasts and the powerless into his fold: the crippled and lame (Luke 6:1-11), the desperately ill (Matthew 8:1-4; Luke 17:11-19), the blind (Luke 18:35-42; Mark 8:22-26; John 9:1-7), children (Mark 10:13-16), swindlers and cheaters (Mark 11:13-17; Luke 19:1-10), and the poor (Mark 3:7-12; Luke 21:1-4).

Following in the footsteps of his Lord, Paul became the apostle to the Gentiles as he traveled extensively and shared Christ's message with all types of people. In fact, writing to the Galatians Paul declared: "There is no longer Jew or Gentile, slave or free, male or female. For you are all Christians" (Galatians 3:28).

Perhaps the greatest example of the barrier-shattering power of the gospel is seen here in Philemon, where Paul reunites a rich slave-owner and his runaway slave, now both members of God's family.

As you read this personal letter of reconciliation, consider what divides you from your brothers and sisters in Christ. Ask God to obliterate those walls and bring you together.

AUTHOR

Paul, apostle, pastor, friend.

The very first word of this letter names Paul as the writer. In Colossians, Paul explained that, along with his letter to the believers in Colosse, he would be sending Onesimus (Colossians 4:9). Tychicus would deliver both. This letter to Philemon focuses on this same Onesimus. Clearly, then, Paul wrote both letters at about the same time and sent them together.

For more about Paul, see the Author section in the Introduction to the book of Romans.

DATE AND SETTING
Written from a Roman prison in about A.D. 60 (See the Introduction to Philippians.)

This letter was written at about the same time as Ephesians and Colossians. Paul wrote that he was a prisoner (1:1, 9, 23) and in chains (1:10, 13), so clearly he was in prison. And the reference in Colossians 4:9 implies that he would send this letter to Philemon along with his runaway slave, Onesimus.

AUDIENCE
Philemon and the church at large.

Philemon was a leader in the church at Colosse—the church met at his house (1:2). Evidently Philemon was a wealthy slaveholder who had been converted to Christ under Paul's ministry (1:19). Slaveholders had absolute power over their slaves. Whether or not Philemon was a kind owner, Onesimus had run away and could be beaten, jailed, or even killed for his offense according to Roman law.

People could become slaves by being born to a woman who was a slave, as punishment for a crime, by being kidnapped from another land, and by being conquered by another nation (slave dealers would buy captured prisoners and send them to the slave markets to be sold for a profit). Sometimes, however, parents would sell their children into slavery. And some would voluntarily become slaves in order to pay a debt.

Slavery was taken for granted in the first century—85 to 90 percent of the inhabitants of Italy were slaves. Usually those with financial means would own slaves. Under Roman law, a slave could expect to be set free in seven years. How slave owners treated their slaves could vary greatly, depending on the temperament of the owner and the performance of the slave. Owners could inflict cruel punishments upon slaves, considered as their property, usually by whipping or beating them with a stick. Like thieves, runaway slaves were branded on the forehead. Others were imprisoned. Many slaves died from mistreatment or imprisonment, but it was illegal to take the life of a slave without a court order. Philemon had the power; Onesimus was powerless.

OCCASION AND PURPOSE
Onesimus had come to faith in Christ while in Rome and was returning to Colosse, to his master, Philemon.

Because of his unique imprisonment in a rented house, Paul was able to have a steady stream of visitors and to freely preach and teach the word for two years (Acts 28:17-31). During that time, the young man Onesimus heard the Good News and became a follower of Christ (1:10). Onesimus had stolen money from his master, Philemon, and had fled to Rome. Now, as a new Christian, he was preparing to return to Colosse and to Philemon.

Paul wrote this letter on behalf of Onesimus, urging Philemon to see the young man not as a slave but as a "brother in the Lord" (1:16). Thus Paul hoped that Philemon would welcome him (1:17), forgive him (1:18-19), and perhaps even free him (1:21).

Paul's appeal is based on their common love for Christ (1:9), on their relationship (1:17-19), and on his authority as an apostle (1:8). Philemon's response is unknown, but it would be difficult to imagine him not welcoming Onesimus as his new brother in Christ.

One of the lessons of this short letter is the example of Paul. He wrote as the advocate of Onesimus, trusting him to return, to submit to Philemon, and to live with the consequences of his actions. Paul believes in Onesimus, that he is a true brother in the faith. Paul does more than write and endorse this runaway slave, he also backs up his words with his money—Paul offers to pay for anything Onesimus may have broken or stolen (1:18).

Another lesson concerns the power of the gospel to bring people together. At opposite poles in their society stood Philemon and Onesimus, yet they became unified brothers through their common faith in Christ. God can reconcile people, regardless of their differences or offenses.

With whom do you need to be reconciled? What new Christian needs your affirmation and support?

MESSAGE

Onesimus "belonged" to Philemon, a member of the Colossian church and Paul's friend. But Onesimus, the slave, had stolen from his master and run away. He ran to Rome, where he met Paul and there he responded to the Good News and came to faith in Christ (1:10). So Paul wrote to Philemon and reintroduced Onesimus to him, explaining that he was sending him back, not just as a slave but as a brother (1:11-12, 16). Tactfully, he asked Philemon to accept and forgive his brother (1:10, 14-15, 20). The barriers of the past and the new ones erected by Onesimus's desertion and theft should divide them no longer—they are one in Christ.

The main themes in the book of Philemon include: *Forgiveness, Barriers,* and *Respect.*

Forgiveness (1:17-21). Philemon was Paul's friend, but he also was the legal owner of the slave Onesimus. He could have punished Onesimus severely, as a runaway and as a thief. Paul asked this dear friend not only to withhold punishment, but to forgive Onesimus and to accept him as a new Christian brother, welcoming him into his home as he would welcome Paul (1:17).

IMPORTANCE FOR TODAY. Many factors divide people today, including disagreements, politics, arguments, and personal offenses. Yet Christians are to be unified, demonstrating the love of Christ by their love for each other (John 13:34-35). Thus, Christian relationships must be filled with forgiveness and acceptance. Who has wronged you? With what brother or sister in Christ do you feel estranged, distant, or angry? Who do you need to forgive? Build bridges, not walls.

Barriers (1:10-16). Slavery was widespread in the Roman Empire, but no one is lost to God or beyond his love, not even the poorest slave. Slavery was a thick barrier, but God can break through anything that divides people. And God tells us, as those committed to Christ, to love all kinds of people. Christian love and fellowship should overcome all barriers.

IMPORTANCE FOR TODAY. In Christ, we are one family. No walls of racial, economic, political, or social differences should separate us. Christ wants to work through us to remove barriers between brothers and sisters. What can you do to fellowship with Christians of other races? How can you reach out to those from different cultures and social standing?

Respect (1:4-9, 21-25). Paul was a friend of both Philemon and Onesimus. He had the authority as an apostle to tell Philemon what to do (1:8). Yet Paul chose to appeal to his friend in Christian love rather than to order him what to do. Paul clearly made his desires known, but he treated Philemon with respect, as a peer and fellow believer.

IMPORTANCE FOR TODAY. Tactful persuasion will accomplish much more than strong commands when dealing with people. No one appreciates being bossed around or ordered what to do. Remember to be courteous and to treat people with respect.

OUTLINE OF PHILEMON

I. Paul's Appreciation of Philemon (1:1-7)
II. Paul's Appeal for Onesimus (1:8-25)

PHILEMON 1

GREETINGS FROM PAUL / 1:1-3

Onesimus, a domestic slave, belonged to Philemon, a wealthy man and a member of the church in Colosse. Onesimus had run away from Philemon and made his way to Rome, where he met Paul, who apparently led him to Christ (1:10). Paul convinced Onesimus that running from his problems wouldn't solve them, and he persuaded Onesimus to return to his master. In Colossians 4:9, Paul regarded Onesimus as a trusted associate. Paul wrote this letter to Philemon to ask him to be reconciled to his runaway slave.

1:1 Although neither **Paul** nor **Timothy** had visited the church in Colosse, they had, during their earlier travels, met individual Colossians such as Epaphras, Philemon, Archippus, and Apphia who, after their conversion, had returned with the gospel to their native city. So Philemon was a friend and fellow believer. But this letter does not present doctrine or give commands; instead, it is a request on behalf of another believer. Paul chose to introduce himself in this letter as being **in prison for preaching the Good News about Christ Jesus.** This is the only one of Paul's letters where he used such an introduction.

Timothy visited Paul frequently during his imprisonment (see also Colossians 1:1) and was with Paul in Rome when he wrote this letter. Timothy was not imprisoned with Paul, but he had stayed in Rome to encourage Paul and to help with ministry needs. Although mentioned in the saluta-

tion, Timothy is not considered a coauthor. Paul wrote in the first person throughout this letter (the same is true for the letter to the Philippians).

Philemon was a wealthy Greek landowner living in Colosse. He had been converted under Paul's ministry (1:19), perhaps in Ephesus or some other city where he had met and talked with Paul. During Paul's years of ministry in nearby Ephesus, Philemon had been building up the Colossian church, which would meet in his home (1:2). Thus Paul considered him a **much loved coworker.** Like most wealthy landowners of ancient times, Philemon owned slaves. Onesimus, the subject of this letter, was one of those slaves.

1:2 Apphia probably was Philemon's wife or another close relative who helped manage his household; otherwise, she would not have been greeted with Philemon in a letter concerning a domestic matter. At this time, women handled the day-to-day responsibilities of the slaves. Thus, the final decision about Onesimus would have been as much her choice as Philemon's. Paul greeted Apphia as **our sister,** that is, a sister in the Christian faith. **Archippus** may have been Philemon's son, or perhaps an elder in the Colossian church (at the end of the letter to the Colossians, Paul had given special encouragement to a man named Archippus; see Colossians 4:17). In either case, Paul included him as a recipient of the letter, possibly so that Archippus would read the letter with Philemon and encourage him to take Paul's advice.

The early churches always met in people's homes. Because of sporadic persecutions and the great expense involved, church buildings were not constructed at this time (church buildings were not built until the third century). Many congregations were small enough that the entire church could meet in one home. Because Philemon was one of those who had worked to begin the church at Colosse, it was natural that believers would meet in his **house. The church** could refer to the entire body of believers, although it seems unlikely because Paul had been writing a letter to the entire Colossian church at this same time. It may have been that, as in any large city even today, smaller groups of believers met regularly in various private homes. One group met in Philemon's home; some met in other believers' homes, such as Nympha's. Paul had greeted Nympha and the church in her house in Colossians 4:15. (For references to other house churches, see Romans 16:5 and 1 Corinthians 16:19-20.)

Because of the personal nature of this letter, Paul apparently chose not to include his instructions to Philemon in his general letter to the Colossians. Paul greeted the believers who met in Philemon's home because Paul knew that not only would this group know about the runaway slave, but they would also become Onesimus's "family" upon his return as a new believer. The church would need to understand Paul's request and Philemon's response to it. Then there would be no gossip, and they could immediately and lovingly accept Onesimus into their fellowship.

1:3 Paul used **grace** and **peace** as a standard greeting in all his letters. "Grace" is God's undeserved favor—his loving-kindness shown to sinners whereby he saves them and gives them strength to live for him; "peace" refers to the peace that Christ made between sinners and God through his death on the cross. Peace refers to that inner assurance and tranquility that God places in a person, producing confidence and contentment in Christ. Only God can grant such wonderful gifts.

The phrase **God our Father** focuses on the family relationship among all believers as God's children. In the context of this letter, Paul was emphasizing the family relationship that the master, Philemon, and the slave, Onesimus, had because both were believers. By using the phrase, **Lord Jesus Christ,** Paul was pointing to Jesus as a full person of the Godhead and was recognizing Jesus' full deity. God the Father and Christ the Lord are coequal in providing grace and peace.

PAUL'S THANKSGIVING AND PRAYER / 1:4-7

Most ancient letters included a thanksgiving for the addressee immediately after the salutation. With these words, Paul was expressing his love for Philemon. Paul constantly prayed for churches and for individual believers who had specific needs.

1:4-5 Philemon had been converted under Paul's ministry and then had returned to Colosse. Although Paul had never visited Colosse, he had heard (perhaps from Onesimus or Epaphras) about Philemon's continued **trust in the Lord Jesus** and **love for all of God's people.** Paul was saying that if Philemon truly loved *all* the believers, then he certainly would be willing to include another believer—Onesimus—in that love.

1:6 This verse describes Paul's prayer and introduces the request that Paul will make to Philemon in this letter. The word **you** is singular (as in 1:4)—this was what Paul prayed for Philemon

himself. The Greek word *koinonia* is rendered in these verses as **generous.** *Koinonia* is a difficult word to translate, but it incorporates the true outworking of Christian love in the body of Christ. The word focused on Philemon's relationship with other Christians. Paul prayed that Philemon's faith would show itself in *koinonia* among the believers. Paul prayed that Philemon would **put his generosity to work.** Paul will soon ask Philemon to welcome Onesimus as if he were Paul, and that Philemon should charge any of Onesimus's debts to Paul (1:17-19). This is true *koinonia*, Christians giving to one another and caring for one another because they belong to one another.

1:7 The **love** that Philemon showed to all the believers (1:5) had also given Paul **much joy and comfort.** Philemon probably had acted out his faith among the believers in many ways beyond sharing his home for church meetings. But Paul was concerned less about Philemon's actions than about the spirit in which he was performing them. Paul hoped that Philemon's loving spirit—which had given others joy, encouragement, and refreshment—would also show itself in his dealings with Onesimus.

PAUL'S APPEAL FOR ONESIMUS / 1:8-22

While in prison, Paul had led Onesimus to the Lord. So he asked Philemon to forgive his runaway slave who had become a Christian and, even going beyond forgiveness, to accept Onesimus as a brother. As Christians, we should forgive as we have been forgiven (Matthew 6:12; Ephesians 4:31-32). True forgiveness means that we treat the one we've forgiven as we would want to be treated. Is there someone you say you have forgiven, but who still needs your kindness?

1:8-9 Carrying on the thought from verse 7—the love Philemon had shown to the believer and to Paul ought to be extended to include another. This was indeed **boldly asking a favor**—in the Roman Empire, a master had the right to kill a disobedient slave. In any other situation, Onesimus's action of running away would have signed his death warrant. But Onesimus had met Paul, and Paul knew Philemon, so Paul mediated because of their common brotherhood in Christ.

Paul first described his right to make this appeal to Philemon. Paul was Philemon's **friend** and spiritual father (1:19), but Paul was also an elder and an apostle with authority **in the name of Christ.** Paul was subtly reminding Philemon of his authority. Paul could have demanded how Philemon should act because it was **the right thing to do,** but Paul based his request not on his own authority, but on his friendship with Philemon and Philemon's Christian commitment. Paul wanted Philemon's heartfelt, not grudging, obedience, so he preferred **just to ask** the favor of Philemon.

1:10 In the Greek text, **Onesimus's** name is the last word in this verse, exhibiting Paul's skillful crafting of this letter. After the introduction and sincere compliments to Philemon, he began to state his appeal. He gave Onesimus's name at the last possible moment, not broaching the actual appeal until verse 17. Paul approached Philemon with tact and humility.

Philemon probably had been angered that his slave had disappeared (in Roman times, it was like losing a piece of valuable property). Thus, Paul first explained that his appeal was on behalf of someone who had become his **son** during Paul's imprisonment—that is, someone Paul had led to Christ from prison. Philemon would be dealing with a fellow **believer.**

1:11 Onesimus's name in Greek means "useful." The name was a common name for slaves and is found in many ancient inscriptions. A nameless slave might be given this name with the hope that he would live up to it in serving his master.

Paul used a play on words, saying that Onesimus had formerly had not **been of much use to** Philemon **in the past,** but had become **very useful** both to Paul and, potentially, to Philemon. Under Philemon's service, Onesimus had failed to live up to his name. Paul was confident, however, that this new man with his new life in Christ would live up to his name if Philemon would take him back. In Colossians 4:9, Paul called Onesimus a "faithful and much loved brother." Onesimus had become known for his faithfulness.

1:12-13 Although Paul would have liked to **keep** Onesimus with him, he was sending Onesimus **back** to Philemon along with Paul's **own heart.** Paul asked that Philemon accept Onesimus not only as a forgiven runaway servant, but also as a brother in Christ. This verse suggests that Onesimus himself would deliver this letter to Philemon, so Philemon would need to make his decision as he stood face-to-face with his slave.

Paul was willing to give away his very heart, a part of himself, in order to return Onesimus permanently to Philemon. Onesimus had become part of Paul's ministry team. This was a sacrifice on Paul's part, for Onesimus apparently could have helped Paul on Philemon's behalf. Paul knew that if Philemon were available to be with Paul, he would have helped him in any way he could; therefore, if Paul had kept Onesimus, Philemon would have been helping Paul vicariously. Paul implied that he trusted Onesimus so much that Onesimus's service could be considered in place of Philemon's; therefore, Philemon should be able to trust him as well. Paul, imprisoned **for preaching the Good News,** longed for his friends;

how difficult it was for him to send away this man. Yet Paul knew it was his duty to do so—Roman law demanded that a deserting slave be returned to his legal owner (although Deuteronomy 23:15-16 states the opposite). Because Onesimus belonged to Philemon, Paul chose to send him back.

1:14 Paul would have liked to have kept Onesimus with him (1:13). However, he decided not to try to talk Philemon into allowing Onesimus to return to Rome to serve Paul; Paul might have felt that this was taking undue advantage of his relationship with Philemon. Paul sent Onesimus back to Philemon, preferring that Philemon make the final decision in the matter. The **help** probably did not refer to allowing Onesimus to return to Paul, but that Philemon would pardon his slave from severe punishment since Onesimus had become a new person in Christ. Philemon had to think of Onesimus not as a piece of property, but as a brother in the fellowship.

1:15 Paul considered that all that had happened—Onesimus's desertion and subsequent conversion to Christ—had been part of God's providence. God can overrule and bring good out of human sin and folly. Onesimus had caused trouble and heartache, but he had become a new person, and Philemon would soon **have him back**. The **little while** of Onesimus's absence would be overshadowed by the devotion that would bind him to his master **forever**. They would be together for eternity, but Paul also wanted Philemon to take Onesimus back into his service permanently now.

1:16 For Philemon to accept Onesimus back, he would have to do so with the understanding that Onesimus had a new status—he was a person (that is, not merely a **slave**), and he was also **a beloved brother**. Paul knew how difficult it might be for Philemon to deal with Onesimus as a "brother" after the trouble he had caused. Paul made it clear that he not only trusted Onesimus (1:13) but that he considered Onesimus a brother in Christ. With these words, Paul deftly placed himself, Philemon, and Onesimus all at the same level. While this prisoner, landowner, and slave had very different social positions, they were equals in Christ. While Onesimus had become very dear to Paul, he would **mean much more to** Philemon because Onesimus's former relationship with Philemon had laid the groundwork for a lasting relationship between them.

1:17 In this verse Paul stated his request: **give him the same welcome you would give me.** Like the father of the prodigal son in Jesus' parable (Luke 15:11-32), Philemon should open his arms to welcome Onesimus back to his household and, as a new believer, to the church. God had welcomed Onesimus; so should Philemon. The word **partner** is *koinonon* from the word *koinonia*, translated as generosity. Philemon and Paul shared the *koinonia* described in verse 6. Paul wanted Philemon's attitude toward Onesimus to be based on his attitude toward Paul.

1:18 Onesimus may have confessed some such act to Paul. The only way Onesimus could have financed his flight was to have stolen from his master money or possessions that he could sell. Even if not, he still would be in debt for the work that had not been performed in his absence. This would cause Onesimus to be extremely afraid to return to his master. It was bad enough that he had run away, but if he had also **stolen** money or possessions or had **harmed** his master in any other way, he would be in deep trouble. Thus Paul's letter served as a buffer—giving Onesimus courage to return and giving Philemon the entire picture so that he might deal kindly with his slave.

Any money or possessions that Onesimus had taken certainly were long gone. Onesimus had no means to repay. Paul asked that any money stolen be charged to his own account; in other words, Onesimus no longer would owe Philemon anything, but Paul would. Paul was not suggesting to Philemon that he simply forgive Onesimus's debt; the wrong needed to be righted. Instead, Paul took on that debt on Onesimus's behalf. Onesimus would never know whether the debt was actually demanded and repaid. All he knew was that a debt needed to be paid because of his wrong actions—but that someone else was going to pay it for him. Onesimus got a dose of true Christian love through Paul's action.

1:19 Often, Paul would use a secretary to write his letters as he dictated them (see Romans 16:22). But sometimes at the end of the letters, he would take the pen and write a few words in his **own handwriting** to authenticate the letters (see, for example, Galatians 6:11; Colossians 4:18). For Paul to write the words **I will repay it** emphasized that he was placing himself under legal obligation to do so. Paul was not "just saying" this to placate Philemon; he meant to do so by putting it in writing. If Philemon had demanded repayment, Paul would have had to do it. But it seems that Paul knew his friend well enough to know that he would not demand repayment. While Paul told Philemon to put Onesimus's charge on Paul's "page" in the accounting book, Paul also reminded Philemon that he (Paul) had a huge credit already, in that Philemon owed his **very soul** (his conversion and eternal security) to Paul. Once Onesimus's debt was put on Paul's page, it would be canceled. As Philemon's spiritual father, Paul was hoping that Philemon would feel a debt of gratitude that would cause him to accept Onesimus with a spirit of forgiveness.

1:20 In the matters of ledgers and debts, once Onesimus's debt was repaid, Paul would still have a credit, for who can ever repay someone for bringing him or her to eternal life? Thus Paul asked that the balance be paid in kindness to Onesimus as a **favor** to Paul. Onesimus had been useful to Paul (1:11); Paul hoped that Philemon would find the same. And as Philemon had refreshed the hearts of the saints (1:7), he could hardly do other than refresh Paul's heart as well.

1:21 Paul was not only **confident** that Philemon would welcome Onesimus back, but that Philemon would also do **even more** than Paul asked. This may have been a hint that Philemon would willingly free Onesimus so that he could return to Paul or be freed when Paul got to Colosse. We can be sure that Philemon welcomed Onesimus, but the "even more" is left unknown.

1:22 That Paul would ask Philemon to **keep a guest room ready** in his home indicates that Paul expected to be released (see also Philippians 2:23-24). Some feel that this was Paul's way of reminding Philemon of his apostolic authority. Or it may have been a tongue-in-cheek way of securing a kindly reception for Onesimus because Paul hoped to eventually arrive to check up on what had occurred. It is more likely that Paul was simply hoping to eventually visit these friends who had been praying for him.

His freedom would be secured through these prayers. The words **your** and **you** are plural, focusing on Philemon, Apphia, Archippus, and the church in Philemon's house. Paul had never been to Colosse; the word **return** in Greek simply means "granted" or "given as a gift" (the root of the word is *charis*, "grace"). For Philemon and the church in his home to have their prayers answered with a visit from Paul would indeed be a gift of grace. Paul was released from prison soon after writing this letter, but the Bible doesn't say whether he went to Colosse.

PAUL'S FINAL GREETINGS / 1:23-25

While this is Paul's standard benediction, it certainly had special meaning to Philemon. It would take God's grace working in Philemon to enable him to do something difficult, something unnatural—forgiving, welcoming, and accepting into the fellowship as a brother a slave who had, at least at a previous time, proven himself to be unfaithful and untrustworthy. It would be through God's grace alone that this reconciliation would be possible. Yet the grace was available; Philemon only had to act upon it. If the entire letter was meant to be read to the church that met in Philemon's home, then they too would, by God's grace, also need to welcome and accept Onesimus. God's grace, working in the spirits of believers, makes true fellowship and reconciliation possible within any body of believers.

1:23 The **you** in this verse is singular. These are personal greetings to Philemon. **Epaphras** was well known to the Colossians because he had founded the church there (Colossians 1:7), perhaps while Paul was living in Ephesus (Acts 19:10). Epaphras may have been converted in Ephesus and then had returned to Colosse, his hometown. He was a hero to this church, helping to hold it together in spite of growing persecution and struggles with false doctrine. His report to Paul about the problems in Colosse had prompted Paul to write his letter to the Colossians. Epaphras's greetings to and prayers for the Colossian Christians reveal his deep love for them (Colossians 4:12-13).

It is unclear whether Epaphras was actually in prison with Paul. Paul's words **fellow prisoner in Christ Jesus** may have been a metaphor of warfare or "captivity to Christ." It is more likely that

Epaphras was with Paul voluntarily and would return to Colosse.

1:24 Mark, Aristarchus, Demas, and **Luke** are also mentioned in Colossians 4:10, 14. Mark had accompanied Paul and Barnabas on their first missionary journey (Acts 12:25ff.) and eventually wrote the Gospel of Mark. Luke had accompanied Paul on his third missionary journey and was the writer of the Gospel of Luke and the book of Acts. Demas had been faithful to Paul for a while but then had deserted him (see 2 Timothy 4:10). Paul had sent greetings from these same people in the letter to the Colossians. But in that letter, a man "Jesus who is called Justus" also had sent greetings to Colosse. Much speculation has been done as to why his greetings were not included here, but it may simply have been that he was absent on the day Paul wrote this letter to Philemon.

1:25 The word **your** is plural, indicating that Paul sent this final blessing not to Philemon only, but to the entire church that regularly met in his home (1:2). As Paul had begun his letter with **grace** (1:3), so he ended it with the benediction that the believers would continue to experience God's unmerited favor. The grace of the **Lord Jesus Christ** is with Christians' spirits because the Spirit of Jesus Christ indwells the spirits (the inner selves) of believers (see Romans 8:9-11).

HEBREWS

INTRODUCTION

Faced with the choice of something good or something obviously bad, only a foolish or misguided person would choose "bad." Good should win every time.

At the next level, however, choices become more difficult—deciding between "good" and "better." Again in this case, the logical choice would seem to be "better," but the choice is not as clear-cut as in the former situation: The differences between the two options may seem insignificant, the reasons for choosing what purports to be "better" may be unconvincing, and staying with the familiar "good" may feel comfortable and convenient. Thus, faced with keeping the "good" or moving up to "better," many people stick with what they have, because, after all, it's not "bad."

The next choice is even more difficult—deciding between "better" and "best." Again, the obvious choice should be "best" every time, but many miss what is best and settle, instead, for "better" or simply "good." For them it is better to stay with what they know.

The writer of the letter to the Hebrews had to convince the readers to settle for nothing less than God's **very best** for their lives. Jews were familiar with God's goodness and perfection. After all, they were his chosen people, and through them God had communicated his love and plan for the world. They were the recipients of the covenant, the law, the Tabernacle, and profound religious rituals, and they had been blessed with prophets proclaiming God's messages and priests doing God's work. Judaism was God's way, and it was good.

But Jesus, the Christ, had come, fulfilling the law, making the perfect sacrifice, and initiating the new covenant. Christ was a better prophet, a better priest, and a better sacrifice. In fact, he was the ultimate **"best."** Many Jews had embraced this new way, expressing faith in Christ ("Messiah") as Savior and Lord. Yet the familiar Judaism continued to draw them back. Some returned to the old way, and others attempted to combine the old with the new, forming a hybrid of Judaism and Christianity. And so they were missing God's **best**.

Hebrews is a masterful document written to Jews who were evaluating Jesus or who were struggling with the Christian faith. The message of Hebrews is that Jesus is better, Christianity is superior, and Christ is supreme and completely sufficient for salvation.

As you read Hebrews, catch the profound message of this important book. Judaism may not be calling you back, but many other gods and belief systems clamor for attention and push for allegiance. Regardless of their claims and promises, know that only Jesus is the truth, and only he brings life. Jesus is the **best**, the only way (John 14:6). Don't settle for anything less!

AUTHOR

The authorship of Hebrews has been in doubt since its publication. In fact, none of the early writers who refer to this book mention its author. And no one since early times has been able to identify the author.

Hebrews names no one as author. The inclusion of Hebrews into the New Testament canon came from the Eastern church as early as A.D. 185, mainly because of the traditional belief that Paul had written it. Clement of Alexandria described his teacher's (Pantaenus's) explanation for why Paul did not use his own name in this letter. Pantaenus surmised that Paul refrained from mentioning his name out of reverence to the Lord, who himself had been their Apostle (3:1). Clement accepted this explanation and proposed that the original had been written in Hebrew (Aramaic) and Luke had translated it into Greek. But this is conjecture.

What, then, do we know about the author for certain? From the content of the letter we learn that the author was a teacher and a second-generation Christian (2:3). The writer had thought long and hard about a Christian interpretation of the Old Testament. He or she was probably a Greek-speaking Jew, familiar with the Old Testament Scriptures and with the religious ideas of the Jews. The author claims to share the inheritance of their sacred history, traditions, and institutions (1:1), and writes of them with intimate knowledge and enthusiasm. The author seems to have known the Old Testament only in the Septuagint (ancient Greek translation of the Old Testament), which is followed even where it deviates from the Hebrew. The fact that Hebrews contains teachings that are "Pauline" along with the mention of Timothy in 13:23 seems to suggest that the author knew Paul or associated with those who were close to him. The author used Greek with a purity of style and strong vocabulary, and the style is unlike any other New Testament document. However, the fundamental concepts of Hebrews correspond fully with the writings of Paul and John. Beyond this limited profile, the letter gives few authorship clues.

A number of possible authors who fit the profile have been proposed over the years. **Paul** is one, but while the content of Hebrews does not contradict Paul's writings, the style of Hebrews differs greatly from Paul's letters.

Another suggestion is **Barnabas**, Paul's friend and companion on his first missionary trip (see Acts 9:27; 11:22-26; 12:25; 13:1–14:28; 15:1-41). Barnabas, "Son of Encouragement," was a Levite (Acts 4:36) and thoroughly familiar with the priestly rituals, which form a large portion of this letter. Despite this strong endorsement, however, there is no other evidence or ancient support for Barnabas as author.

Some suggest **Apollos**, the charismatic preacher mentioned from time to time in the New Testament (see Acts 18:24-28; 19:1; 1 Corinthians 1:12; 3:4-6; 4:1, 6; 16:12; Titus 3:13), but we know very little about him. Apollos was a Jew, a native of Alexandria, well educated, and well versed in Scripture. Apollos knew Timothy and had been instructed by Paul, indirectly, through Priscilla and Aquila (Acts 18:25-26). Luther proposed Apollos as the author, and many modern scholars lean in that direction because the epistle displays the kind of allegorical interpretations that were prominent in Alexandria.

Finally, there are many other names that have been proposed. Each one has a bit of support: **Silas,** a member of both Paul's and Peter's circles and possibly the coauthor or secretary for 1 Peter (there are similarities in style between 1 Peter and Hebrews); **Philip** the evangelist (commendation of Paulinism to Jewish Christians in Jerusalem); **Clement of Rome** (nearly identical wording in places between his writings and Hebrews); **Epaphras** (similarities between Colossians and Hebrews); **Priscilla** (the anonymity of the letter—a woman author would have been difficult for the early church to accept); **Priscilla and Aquila** together (the use of the pronoun "we" in many places; for example, 5:11; 6:3, 9, 11-12; 8:1; 9:5; 13:18).

Having no known author is one reason that the early church was slow to include Hebrews as Holy Scripture. In the final analysis, Hebrews's own intrinsic worth won its place in the canon. We can only agree with Origen, who stated in the third century: "But who wrote the epistle, God only knows the truth" (quoted by Eusebius, *Ecclesiastical History* 6.25.14).

DATE AND SETTING
Written in approximately A.D. 60.

Because Clement of Rome used Hebrews, the letter must have been written prior to A.D. 95. An argument from silence is the lack of any reference to the destruction of the Temple in Jerusalem in A.D. 70. Certainly in a book written to Jews, an event of such catastrophic proportions would have been mentioned, especially since it would have strengthened the argument for the superiority of Christ and the new covenant over the Levitical ritual. Thus Hebrews must have been written prior to A.D. 70.

An additional important factor in setting a date for Hebrews is the identification of the persecution referred to in 10:32-34. Three Roman persecutions stand as possibilities: under Claudius in A.D. 49, under Nero beginning in A.D. 64, and under Domitian in the eighties and nineties. Note that the passage says nothing about loss of life. Many believers died under Nero and Domitian, but the persecution suffered by the readers of Hebrews does not seem to have involved martyrdom (12:4). In his persecution, Claudius expelled the Jews from Rome, including Jewish Christians (among whom were Priscilla and Aquila—Acts 18:2). During this expulsion, they would have been publicly mocked, and they would have lost their property. That treatment seems to match the description in chapter 10.

Considering all of the above, Hebrews was probably written in the early fifties or sixties, before the terrible persecution under Nero. This date also seems compatible with the statement that the readers had heard the gospel from those who had heard Jesus (2:3), and that Timothy was still alive (13:23).

AUDIENCE
Hebrew Christians who may have been considering a return to Judaism.

The title "Hebrews" or "To the Hebrews" was not part of the original writing, but appears in some of the earliest copies. Nevertheless, the title is appropriate considering the content, which is narrowly focused on the Old Testament Scriptures and Jewish religious practices. The writer thoroughly discussed the worship in the Tabernacle, the priests and the sacrifices, the covenant, and Jewish heroes including Abraham, Isaac, Jacob, Joseph, Moses, and others. References to "Abraham's descendants" (2:16), the argument that Jesus is superior to Moses (3:1-19), and the emphasis on "rest" (4:1-11) would have appealed to Jews and would have had very little effect on Gentiles.

Traditionally, Hebrews was thought to have been sent to believers in Jerusalem. Jewish Christians there would have been under the greatest pressure to return to their former religion. And they had suffered severe persecution. The problem with this view, however, is that the strong Greek character of the book would not fit as well with Jerusalem readers as it would with those outside Palestine, especially since many of the Greek-speaking Jews had been driven from Jerusalem following the death of Stephen (Acts 8:1-3). Also, remember that the Jerusalem church struggled continually with poverty and would not have been capable of the generosity mentioned in 6:10, 10:34, and 13:16. In addition, Jewish religious life in Jerusalem was dominated by the Temple, to which Hebrews makes no specific reference.

Another possible destination is Alexandria in Egypt. Support for this city comes from apparent signs of an Alexandrian perspective in Hebrews: similarities with the Alexandrian Jewish scholar Philo, the use of the Old Testament, and the dualism between heavenly archetypes and earthly copies. Yet this may mean only that the author was acquainted with Alexandrian thought, not that Alexandria was the destination.

Many other places have been suggested as possible destinations for Hebrews: Colosse, Samaria, Caesarea, Syrian Antioch, Ephesus, Galatia, Cyprus, Corinth, and Berea. None of these has much evidence or support.

A probable destination is Rome. That is where Hebrews was first known and quoted. In a letter written to the Corinthian church on behalf of the Roman church, Clement of Rome revealed his knowledge of this epistle. Certainly the references to persecution fit Roman readers. Also, the greetings from believers in Italy (13:24) points to a Roman connection. Quite possibly the author, writing from another location, knew Italian believers in that city and was sending their greetings back to Rome.

OCCASION AND PURPOSE
To present the sufficiency and superiority of Christ to Hebrew Christians who may have been considering a return to Judaism.

We don't know of a specific occasion for the writing of this important letter, but there is no doubt that believers of all backgrounds were subject to persecution and pressure to renounce their faith. Jewish believers were vulnerable to doubts about Christ and to thinking about turning back to their familiar rituals and old way of thinking. Many had been persecuted severely by their countrymen, branded as heretics, and deserted by their extended family. As they thought back to the past, their Jewish traditions and ceremonies must have seemed wondrously attractive. They were tempted to hold on to the old while, perhaps, secretly professing the new. In this way, they thought, they could have both Judaism and Christianity.

The purpose of the Epistle to the Hebrews, therefore, was to remind and convince readers of the sufficiency and superiority of Christ (9:14), to warn them of the danger of drifting away from Christ (2:3), and to exhort them to faithfulness (3:6).

Although most Western Christians do not face severe persecution from family, friends, and society in general, at times they may look back longingly at their previous life "before Christ." Though not tempted to return to a former religion, they may feel the pull of an old lifestyle, materialism, or the cultural cult of self-worship.

Hebrews speaks to this temptation with the clear message that only Christ brings salvation, only Christ brings forgiveness, only Christ satisfies. And he alone deserves our adoration, worship, and praise.

MESSAGE
The primary message of this book, (as presented from 1:4–10:18) is that Jesus is superior to angels (1:4–2:18), superior to the ancient Jewish leaders (3:1–4:13), and superior to the Jewish priests (4:14–7:28). Christ surpasses Judaism because he has a better covenant (8:1-13), a better sanctuary (9:1-10), and a more sufficient sacrifice for sins (9:11–10:18).

Having established the superiority of Christ, the writer moves on to the practical implications of following Christ. The readers are exhorted to hold on to their new faith, encourage each other, and look forward to Christ's return (10:19-25). They are warned about the consequences of rejecting Christ's sacrifice (10:26-31) and reminded of the rewards for faithfulness (10:32-39). Then the author explains how to live by faith, giving illustrations of the faithful men and women in Israel's history (11:1-40) and giving encouragement and exhortation for daily living (12:1-17). This section ends by comparing the old covenant with the new (12:18-29). The writer concludes with moral exhortations (13:1-17), a request for prayer (13:18, 19), and a benediction and greetings (13:20-25).

The main themes in the book of Hebrews include: *Superiority of Christ, High Priest, Sacrifice, Promise, Maturity, Faith,* and *Endurance.*

Superiority of Christ (1:1-14; 2:5–3:6; 4:14–5:10; 6:13–10:18). Hebrews reveals Jesus' true identity as God in the flesh. Jesus is the ultimate authority. He is greater than any angel or religion. As the divine Son of God, Jesus is superior to any Jewish leader (such as Abraham, Moses, or Joshua). As the perfect man and mediator with God, he is superior to any priest. As one who endured suffering and temptation, but without sin, he knows us thoroughly. Jesus is the complete revelation of God. And he has been exalted to God's right hand (1:3), crowned with glory and honor (2:9).

IMPORTANCE FOR TODAY. In our competitive society, everyone seems obsessed with winning and identifying with the "best." In our pluralistic society, we are aware of a wide range of religions and worldviews. In all of this clutter, however, we must keep our eyes on Christ, remembering that he alone can forgive sins and give eternal life. Jesus has secured your forgiveness and salvation by his death on the cross and by his resurrection. Don't accept any alternative or substitute, no matter how attractive it may seem. Have you understood that Christ is superior in every way?

High Priest (3:1; 4:14–5:10; 6:19–8:6; 9:6–10:22; 13:11-13). In the Old Testament, the high priest represented the Jews before God. He would make blood sacrifices to atone for the people's sins before God. Once a year, on the Day of Atonement, the high priest would enter the Most Holy Place in the Temple to make atonement for the sins of the whole nation. The high priest would approach God only once a year, but Christ is always at God's right hand, interceding for us.

IMPORTANCE FOR TODAY. Jesus Christ is always available to hear us when we pray. He links us with God. In fact, there is no other way to reach the Father except through the Son. Because Jesus lived a sinless life, he was the perfect substitute to die for our sin. And he is the perfect High Priest, having offered himself as the sacrifice. Jesus is our perfect representative with God. Jesus guarantees your access to God the Father. He intercedes for you, so you can come boldly to the Father with your needs. When you sin and are weak, you can come confidently to God for forgiveness and for help. What is keeping you from the Father?

Sacrifice (1:3; 2:9; 7:27; 9:12-14, 24-28; 10:5-22). Old Testament sacrifices had to be perfect: animals without any injuries or blemishes. These animals were killed on the altar, their blood spilled for the sins of the people. Jesus, the divine Son of God and the perfect Son of Man, died on the cross, shedding his blood to secure the forgiveness for all people. Christ's sacrifice was the ultimate fulfillment of all that the Old Testament sacrifices represented.

IMPORTANCE FOR TODAY. Because Christ is the perfect sacrifice for sin, our sins are completely forgiven—past, present, and future. Christ removed sin, which barred us from God's presence and fellowship. We don't automatically receive this forgiveness; we must accept Christ's sacrifice for us. By believing in Christ, you are no longer guilty; you have been cleansed and made whole. His sacrifice cleared the way for you to have eternal life. What can you do to express your gratitude to Christ for his profound love for you and for his work on the cross?

Promise (4:1-11; 6:13-20; 7:18-25; 8:6–9:22; 10:15-16). God made a holy promise, a covenant, with Abraham. In this covenant, God promised to bless Abraham, to make of Abraham's descendants a great nation, and to bless all the world through him. God also promised to be with his people and to give them rest. Although the people often failed to live up to their side of the covenant, God always kept his: through Abraham came the nation of Israel, and eventually Christ. In addition, God brought his people to the Promised Land, and eventually he will bring them to their eternal rest.

IMPORTANCE FOR TODAY. The old covenant made with Abraham was tied to the nation of Israel. God's new covenant, secured through his Son, is available to all who place their trust in Christ. In addition, the new covenant offers total forgiveness and eternal life. Believers can have hope in the future because of what Jesus Christ has done for them. Eventually they will find perfect rest in heaven. Regardless of your circumstances or difficulties, you can have hope in Christ. If you have trusted him for salvation, the covenant promises apply to you.

Maturity (2:11-13; 5:11–6:3). Although God's people are saved from sin and given eternal life when they trust in Christ as Savior, they are given the task of going on and growing in faith. Too often, however, believers remain immature, feeding only on "milk" and not "meat" and arguing over the basics (6:1). Through a living relationship with Christ, however, believers can live blameless lives, be used powerfully by God, and mature in their faith.

IMPORTANCE FOR TODAY. The process of maturing in our faith takes time and discipline. Daily communication with God through prayer and studying his Word produces maturity. When we are mature in our faith, we won't be easily swayed or shaken by temptations or worldly concerns. If you find yourself disputing issues of lifestyle, faith, spiritual gifts, and the end times, you may be spiritually immature. Don't be content to remain a spiritual baby. What can you do to grow in faith?

Faith (11:1-40; 13:1-21). The Bible, from beginning to end, is a book about faith. Many believed God and received multiplied blessings on earth. Others believed God and were persecuted, tortured, and martyred for their faith. God expects his people to come to him in faith and to live by faith, regardless of the circumstances or outcomes. Faith is confident trust in God and his promises. God's greatest promise is that people can be saved from sin and have eternal life through Christ.

IMPORTANCE FOR TODAY. Those who trust in Jesus Christ for salvation, God will transform completely, moving them from guilt to forgiveness, from death to life, and from despair to hope. A life of obedience and trust pleases God. The more you know of God, the more you will trust him. The more you trust, the more you will hope in his promises.

Endurance (2:1-4; 3:1-19; 4:11-16; 6:4-12; 10:19-39; 12:1-29). It wasn't easy to be a Christian in the first century, especially a Jewish Christian. Believers who had come to faith in Christ out of Judaism were ostracized by their families and persecuted by the religious leaders. When the Romans began to persecute Christians, they seized their property, imprisoned and tortured them. These believers felt tremendous pressure to denounce Christianity, to combine Christian teachings with Judaism, or to be secret believers. Hebrews, therefore, warns against apostasy and against slipping back into old habits and beliefs; the message of this book challenges believers to endure to the end.

IMPORTANCE FOR TODAY. Faith enables Christians to face trials. Genuine faith includes the commitment to stay true to God when we are under fire. Endurance builds character and leads to victory. You can have victory in your trials if you keep your focus on Christ and don't give up. What pressures do you feel to return to an old way of life or belief-system? What can you do to keep your eyes on Christ and not on your struggles? Stay true to Christ, and pray for endurance.

OUTLINE OF HEBREWS

I. The Superiority of Christ (1:1–10:18)
   A. Christ is greater than the angels
   B. Christ is greater than Moses
   C. Christ is greater than the Old Testament priesthood
   D. The new covenant is greater than the old
II. The Superiority of Faith (10:19–13:25)

HEBREWS 1

JESUS CHRIST IS GOD'S SON / 1:1-3

Hebrews 1:1–10:18 presents a series of sections showing how Christ is superior to key aspects of Judaism. The new covenant is shown to be far superior to the old. The writer of Hebrews reported that Jesus Christ, the Messiah, initiated a new, long-awaited age. Christ brought spiritual peace and a spiritual Kingdom. Jesus, the Messiah, has already begun his Kingdom on earth in the hearts of his followers. In chapter 1, Christ is presented as the ultimate and superior revelation of God. This can greatly encourage us and help us avoid drifting away from our faith in Christ.

1:1 The writer divides history into two segments or ages: before Christ and after Christ. He calls the time before Christ **long ago.** During that time, God used **prophets** to reveal his message to the people. The original Jewish readers of the book would have remembered that God had spoken **many times and in many ways** to their **ancestors** during Old Testament times. God had spoken to Isaiah in visions (Isaiah 6), to Jacob in a dream (Genesis 28:10-22), and to Abraham and Moses personally (Genesis 18; Exodus 31:18). God had taught Jeremiah through object lessons (Jeremiah 13) and had taught the people through a prophet's marriage (Hosea 1–3). Elsewhere, God had revealed his direction to the people through a pillar of cloud and a pillar of fire (Exodus 13:21) and had guided them in decision making through the Urim and Thummim (see Exodus 28:30; Numbers 27:21).

1:2 The same God who spoke through the prophets had now **spoken through his Son,** through Christ. Jesus completed and fulfilled the message that was originally brought by the prophets and forefathers. The phrase, **God promised everything to the Son as an inheritance,** refers to Jesus as an heir who will take his position as ruler of the new Kingdom. Referring to Christ as the heir gives him the highest honor and position. This passage alludes to the royal Son of Psalm 2:8.

Jesus worked with God to create the world: **through the Son he made the universe and everything in it** (see also John 1:2; 1 Corinthians 8:6; Colossians 1:15-16). Jesus was active at the beginning of time as the agent of creation, and he will act at the end of time as the heir (see Psalm 2:8; Romans 8:17; Galatians 4:7).

1:3 Underneath Jesus' human appearance as a Jewish carpenter-turned-preacher was **God's own**

glory. Jesus does more than merely reflect God, he *is* God. **Everything about** Jesus **represents God exactly.** Therefore, he makes God's essence and nature clear to us (John 1:18). The prophets could only tell God's people what they saw and heard. Jesus was God himself—his message was firsthand.

Christ not only created the universe (1:2), he also **sustains** it. Christ spoke the world into existence (Genesis 1–2), and he supports the world with his omnipotent word (see 11:3). Christ guides the world toward its appointed future—the time when he will receive it as his inheritance (1:2). Because Christ sustains everything, nothing in creation is independent from him. All things are held together in a coherent or logical way, sustained and upheld, prevented from dissolving into chaos. In him alone and **the mighty power of his command,** we find the unifying principle of all life. He is transcendent over all other powers.

He is able to do this because, **after he died** and rose again, he returned to heaven and **sat down** in the place of highest honor. Jesus' death had accomplished what all the animal sacrifices could never do—it cleansed people **from the stain of sin.** This statement reveals the central theme of the letter: Christ's superior sacrifice for sins. No sacrifice for sin could be greater than the sacrifice offered by the Creator—his death on a cross. Jesus cleansed the world from the domination of sin and took the penalty for our individual sins by dying in our place. No other penalty needs to be paid. We can be completely clean because of what Jesus has done.

Now Christ is **in the place of honor at the right hand of the majestic God of heaven.** Quoting from Psalm 110:1, the writer combined two Old Testament thoughts expressing God's greatness and Christ's position. To be seated at the **right hand** of a monarch was to be "second in command"—the literal "right-hand man." This gives a picture of Christ's power and authority over heaven and earth (see also Mark 16:19; Romans 8:34). Psalm 110:1 is a crucial text and provides a guiding force in this book. It is the only place in the Bible where anyone else besides God is described as enthroned in power. This verse became a main text for the early church to be used as an argument for the deity of Christ.

CHRIST IS GREATER THAN THE ANGELS / 1:4-14

Angels are servants of Christ. They play a vital role in today's world as ministering spirits sent to serve those who have accepted God's salvation. God the Father calls Jesus Christ his one and only Son, and he orders angels to worship his Son. If God, who is above all, gives such praise to Jesus Christ, how can we praise him any less?

1:4 The writer here begins a series of arguments proving Jesus' superiority over angels. Angels are spiritual beings created by God and are under his authority (Colossians 1:16). They help carry out God's work on earth by bringing God's messages to people (Luke 1:26; Revelation 14:6-12), protecting God's people (Daniel 6:22; Matthew 18:10), offering encouragement (Genesis 16:7ff.), giving guidance (Exodus 14:19), carrying out punishment (2 Samuel 24:16), patrolling the earth (Zechariah 1:9-14), and fighting the forces of evil (2 Kings 6:16-18; Revelation 20:1-2). Other popular Jewish teachings during New Testament times said that angels brought people's requests to God and interceded for them. Because of all these beliefs about angels, the Jews honored them highly. However, Hebrews emphasizes that Christ and his work far surpass angels and their work. Jesus created the world, sustains the world, reveals God's glory, makes God known, and provides the perfect sacrifice for sins. No angel can accomplish any of these things.

Christ is far greater than the angels because **the name God gave him is far greater than their names.** The "name" he received is contrasted with the angels' names. In that time and culture, names captured the essence of a person (see Genesis 27:36). The "name" Jesus received was "Son." This name identified that his relationship with God, his power to forgive people's sins, and his ability to make God known were far superior to any other created being's.

1:5 Beginning here in 1:5 and continuing through 1:13, the writer strings together seven quotations from the Old Testament. The writer introduces two quotations from the Psalms by saying **God never said to any angel what he said to Jesus.**

The first quote, **"You are my Son. Today I have become your Father,"** comes from a coronation psalm. Psalm 2:7 was also quoted at Jesus' baptism (Mark 1:11) and transfiguration (Mark 9:7), as well as in 2 Peter 1:17. The psalm was originally sung at the crowning of a new king (perhaps originally of David or Solomon). This psalm was used for centuries of Jewish history as a song of worship. Jewish rabbis attached a deeper meaning to the song—one that looked forward to the coming Messiah. Because the Messiah fulfilled the promises of the Old Testament, the writer understands that these Old Testament verses apply to Christ.

God spoke the words, **"I will be his Father, and he will be my Son,"** to David with respect to Solomon (2 Samuel 7:14; 1 Chronicles 17:13). Although Solomon fulfilled these words, Hebrews illustrates that Christ ultimately and completely fulfilled them. In John 7:42, the religious leaders discussed Jesus' authority, and they alluded to this passage in Samuel, which said that the Messiah must come from David's family. The titles of "Father" and "Son" reveal a distinction between these two members of the Godhead. They also reveal the unique relationship of the Son to the Father. No angel can claim such a relationship.

1:6 The writer says that God **presented his honored Son to the world.** In Jewish families the firstborn son held the place of highest privilege and responsibility. As firstborn of creation, Jesus surpasses any created being. Because of this, the writer had no problem ascribing to Christ the words, **"Let all the angels of God worship him."** This is a portion of Deuteronomy 32:43, from the "Hymn of Moses," found in the Septuagint (the ancient Greek version of the Old Testament). It is not found in the Hebrew version or English translations based on the Hebrew. All quotes in Hebrews are from the Septuagint. In the original Old Testament text, "him" refers to the Father. Because only God should be worshiped, this verse is further proof that Jesus has a greater position than the angels—he is God.

1:7 This quote from Psalm 104:4 depicts the angels as **messengers.** Describing angels as **wind** and **flaming fire** continues to show Jesus' superiority by contrasting his everlasting glory with the temporality of the angels. "Wind" and "fire" serve as metaphors to illustrate the angels' status as created beings.

1:8-9 These words celebrate the Son's status. Again, the writer quoted a psalm (45:6-7) that had its origin in the Jewish court. This psalm would be sung at a Jewish king's wedding. In celebrating the high office of king, the people referred to the king as "a god." This title was used out of respect for the king's position as God's representative. The title that the people imperfectly placed on the Jewish king was perfectly true of Christ.

That his **throne endures forever and ever** stresses Jesus' exaltation. His reign is characterized by **righteousness**, as well as **love** for **what is right** and **hate** for **what is wrong**. Only Christ has such perfect love for righteousness and hatred for evil. Christ is superior to any other spiritual being. These qualities allowed Jesus to be **anointed** with **the oil of joy**. The Jews would anoint their kings and their priests with holy oil. This description, therefore, carries a double meaning, revealing that Jesus had been anointed king *and* priest. He was able to be a sacrifice for sins because he was perfect and hated all wickedness. God expressed joy in anointing the perfect king and priest.

1:10-12 These words of Psalm 102:25-27 were originally used of God the Father, but are used here to describe God the Son. Jesus is both the Son and Creator. He is eternal and sovereign and therefore worthy of praise. Hebrews celebrates the perma-nence of Christ by contrasting him with the temporary nature of the world. The world seems permanent to us, but it will one day **wear out like old clothing**. The world, like the clothing, will be rolled up and **fade away**. Christ, however, will be **always the same**. His place is permanent, and he will replace this fading world with a new heaven and new earth (see 12:26-28; Revelation 21).

1:13 Hebrews continues to show how the high position of Christ makes him superior to the angels. This statement (quoted from Psalm 110:1), said that the Messiah will triumph over all his enemies because he is instructed to **sit** at God's **right hand**. This position belongs to Christ and not to any created being. The greatest archangels stand before God (Luke 1:19; Revelation 8:2), but none are allowed to sit, for sitting next to God indicates equality.

God promised to make Jesus' enemies **a footstool for his feet**. This is a picture showing Christ as completely victorious over his enemies. Jesus' honor cannot be superseded, and no angel comes close to this honor.

1:14 Christ possesses the right to sit at God's right hand (1:13), while the angels are his **servants**. The angels are ministering **spirits** who are **sent from God to care for those who will receive salvation**. The angels' purpose is to serve; Christ's purpose is to reign. The fact that angels serve us should encourage us when we feel unloved or forgotten. Because God loves us, he dispatches his angels to help us.

HEBREWS 2

A WARNING AGAINST DRIFTING AWAY / 2:1-4

Highway travelers dislike the sudden appearance of warning signs, but travel could be dangerous without the warnings. The author of Hebrews presents a series of warning signs throughout the book. They aren't flashing lights, but they shout "danger!" If we do not heed the warning, we will not escape. Christ announced salvation, his followers confirmed it, and God testified to it.

2:1 Hebrews was written to encourage Jewish Christians not to turn away from the faith. If these Christians were not careful, pressure from non-believing Jews or other influences could cause them to **drift away** from **the truth**. These words encouraged the readers to **listen very carefully** so as not to lose their bearings. To what were they to listen? The truth of the message of salvation through Jesus Christ alone.

2:2 Verses 2-4 explain why Christians should pay careful attention to their faith. If disregarding Moses' law brought punishment, then disregarding the Good News would bring far greater punishment.

The message God delivered through angels refers to the Old Testament law. The account of angels delivering God's law and putting it into effect was part of Jewish and early-Christian dogma (see Galatians 3:19). Although the book of Exodus does not mention angels, the Jews believed that God worked through angels to give Moses the Ten Commandments (see Acts 7:53). God gave the law to govern the lives of Old Testament believers. Those who believed God and obeyed his instructions received his blessing, while those who rebelled discovered that **people were punished for every violation** and **every act of disobedience** (see Leviticus 26). Throughout the Old Testament, God enforced these laws by blessing people who followed him and condemning people who rejected him.

2:3-4 As Christ surpasses angels, so Christ's message surpasses their message (see 1:1-3). Old Testament believers who followed God received blessings, and those who disobeyed God received punishment. If that was true for the promise brought by angels, then no one who is **indifferent** to the message will **escape** God's punishment.

Three witnesses prove the authenticity of **this great salvation** and why the readers should not be indifferent to it:

1. **The Lord Jesus himself,** not angels or people, **announced** this salvation (see Luke 19:9; John 4:22).
2. **Those who heard him speak,** eyewitnesses to Jesus' ministry, **passed on** Jesus' message. These readers (and apparently the author) had not seen Christ in the flesh. They are like us; we have not seen Jesus personally. We base our belief in Jesus on the eyewitness accounts recorded in the Bible (see John 20:29).
3. **God verified the message by signs and wonders and various miracles and by giving gifts of the Holy Spirit.** These were not given by God to glorify the apostles or to awe the people. Rather, God demonstrated his power through the apostles with these extraordinary events, thereby testifying to the truth of the great salvation that the apostles proclaimed. The **gifts** serve as continuing reminders to believers across the ages that the gospel of salvation is true. It has been announced and confirmed, and many testify to its truth and power even today. To drift away from this truth (2:1) would be both foolish and disastrous.

JESUS, THE MAN / 2:5-18

Jesus came as a human being so that we could see, in human form, what God was like. In turn, Jesus as a human being experienced the same temptations that all people experience, but he did not sin. Then, as a human being, he experienced death. Through his life on earth and sacrifice on the cross, Jesus became a brother to all mankind and a High Priest who suffered on behalf of sinful people. Through his resurrection, he has been exalted to God's right hand. We must live now by his example.

2:5 The phrase **the future world** refers to the future Kingdom that Christ initiated and will fully inherit at his second coming. The future world **will not be controlled by angels,** but by Christ. Angels will continue to serve as God's servants. These words further emphasize the superiority of the Son over the angels (1:13-14).

2:6-8 The writer substantiates the words of 2:5 by here quoting from Psalm 8:3-4, a psalm that tells of human beings' unimportance as well as their greatness. Compared to God's power and the majesty of his creation, people are insignificant. Yet God **crowned** people **with glory and honor** when he created them in his image (Genesis 1:27). God also gave people the responsibility and tremendous **authority over all things** (Genesis 1:28). God intended this key role for people. The phrase, **you made him lower than the angels,** shows human superiority over all other creation, except the angels. Due to their sin, however, people failed

to live up to their potential, correctly fulfill this responsibility, or wisely use their authority. The psalm quoted here originally referred to humanity and its role in creation, and the psalm was regarded as messianic. The author may have been thinking about the double meaning included in the words **son of man,** showing that Jesus fulfilled the role and destiny originally commissioned to people. What humans could not do, Jesus did.

Although God gave humans the authority over **all things** (Genesis 1:28), sin entered the world and inhibited them from fulfilling this command (Genesis 3:17-19). **We have not yet seen all of this happen** because we will not experience perfection in this world. We do not yet see Jesus reigning on earth, but we can picture him in his heavenly glory. He is Lord of all, and one day he will rule on earth as he does now in heaven.

2:9 While we have not seen fulfilled what the psalm writer wrote in Psalm 8, **what we do see**

is Jesus. The words from the psalm previously applied only to humans are here applied to the Messiah. Jesus became human, **made lower than the angels.** He was the only one who lived the human life as intended: sinless and in perfect fellowship with God. Before Christ, the words of Psalm 8 had not been fully realized, but the words were completely fulfilled in Christ. Jesus was not made lower than the angels in his rank or position, but he is described this way because he became part of the physical world; that is, he became human.

Because of Christ's perfect life and sacrifice for sins, he is now **crowned with glory and honor.** Christ was worthy to receive these rewards **because he suffered death for us.** By way of further explanation of this death, the writer elaborated: **By God's grace, Jesus tasted death for everyone in all the world.** Jesus lived and died physically. Jesus died **for everyone in all the world,** but not everyone will be saved. The only way for people to be saved and to receive God's rewards is to "believe on the Lord Jesus" (Acts 16:31).

2:10 Christ, the **perfect leader,** was able to fulfill what no other human was able to fulfill. **Many children** refers back to 2:6-8. Although people were commissioned to rule the earth, their sin kept them from the task. Jesus' sacrifice brings his human brothers and sisters **into glory** that will one day be restored to people in the future Kingdom.

Because God **made everything,** he determines what sacrifice is necessary for sin. He, the Creator of the world, determined what was needed for salvation. **Through the suffering of Jesus** God could bring people **into their salvation.** Jesus did not need to suffer for his own salvation because he was God. His perfect obedience (which led him down the road of suffering) demonstrates that he was the complete sacrifice for us. Through suffering, Jesus completed the work necessary for our salvation.

2:11 Christians are **the ones** Jesus **makes holy.** This action is once and for all. We have been made holy—set apart for God's service. Our sin was poured into Christ at his crucifixion; his righteousness is poured into us at our conversion. This is what Christians mean by Christ's atonement for sin. While God sees us as completely holy through the sacrifice of his Son, we must grow in our holiness as we live for God throughout our lives.

We who have been set apart for God's service, cleansed, and made holy (sanctified) by Jesus now **have the same Father** as he does. Because God has adopted all believers as his children, **Jesus is not ashamed to call** believers **his brothers and sisters.** Those who are not ashamed of Jesus, gladly accept-

ing him as Savior and Lord, will find that Jesus is not ashamed to call them members of his family (Luke 9:26).

2:12 The next two verses give three quotations from the Old Testament to show the relationship between Jesus and believers. Jesus readily identified himself with God's people.

While on the cross, Jesus quoted from the opening words of Psalm 22 (see Matthew 27:46). These words of abandonment at the beginning of this psalm give way to words of praise at the end, quoted here. Jesus' death and humiliation on earth ended in victory, declaring **the wonder of** God's **name** to those who believed, his **brothers and sisters** (2:11). To "declare a name" means to reveal the character of that person. Attributing these words to Jesus from this messianic psalm means that Jesus, through his humanity, revealed God's character. The phrase **among all your people,** quoted here from the Septuagint (the Greek version of the Hebrew Old Testament), has the same Greek word as the New Testament word translated "church."

2:13 These verses, originally recorded in Isaiah 8:17-18, are applied here to Christ, further showing Christ's identification with humanity. Isaiah was persecuted and his message rejected by the people. Isaiah encouraged the people not to listen to false advice, but to God alone. Like Isaiah, Christ put his **trust** in God the Father. Christ readily accepts his relationship with **the children whom God has given** to him. These are his spiritual "children," those who are called his brothers and sisters (2:11), God's people (2:12). Like those faithful to God in Isaiah's day, we should stay true to Christ and ignore the advice that would distract us from following him.

2:14 After building his case that Christ had become a human being, the writer explained why such association and identity were important. Death is the common fear and final experience of all people, and only as a human being, **made of flesh and blood,** could Christ **die** because **only by dying could he break the power of the Devil, who had the power of death.** His death and his return to life showed that death had been defeated (Romans 6:9).

Sin and death are interconnected: Sin results in death. Only by first breaking the power of sin could Christ then break the power of death. He accomplished both through his death and resurrection. In those acts, Christ dealt the final blow to both Satan and death. Although Satan still holds great power over this world, he is mortally wounded. God allows Satan to work, but limits him (see Job 1:12; 2:6;

Ephesians 4:27; 6:11; 1 Timothy 3:7; James 4:7; 1 Peter 5:8-9). Just as salvation is partly realized now and will be fully realized later, in God's Kingdom, so Satan is still at work but will one day be destroyed (Revelation 20:10).

2:15 People have always been **slaves to the fear of dying.** Eventually, however, death strikes everyone. Through Christ, however, we no longer need to fear dying and death. Christ died and rose again and **only in this way could he deliver** humanity. Because Jesus died and arose, we no longer need to be enslaved to the fear of dying. We know that because Jesus rose from the dead, we will also. We will die physically, but we are promised new bodies and a new life in eternity with God. Thus, death becomes the gateway to a new life (1 Corinthians 15:55, 57; 2 Corinthians 5:8).

2:16 Angels were not the objects of God's grace. God sent Jesus to die for people, **the descendants of Abraham,** who were lost in their sin (Romans 5:8). Some believe that this phrase refers only to the Jews, but Jesus had explained that it was through faith in him that people became Abraham's true descendants (John 8:37-39; see also Galatians 3:29). Jesus was born as a Jew, a descendant of Abraham. His death and resurrection offered salvation to all of humanity—both Jews and Gentiles. Abraham's descendants are all who share Abraham's faith. Christ did not become an angel; he became a human in order to help humans.

2:17 Jesus Christ became **like us, his brothers and sisters,** so that he could become **our merciful and faithful High Priest.** In the Old Testament, the high priest was the mediator between God and the people. But Jesus' death and resurrection inaugurated a new covenant. Under the old covenant, the high priests had to go before God once a year; Jesus' death accomplished forgiveness once and for all for those who believe in him. Christ performed perfectly and completely the duties of a high priest. Thus the writer calls him our High Priest, our representative before God.

Jesus became like us **in every respect** except for the sinful nature—Jesus never shared in that part of humanity (4:15; 7:26). Only in this way could he **offer a sacrifice that would take away the sins of the people.** That sacrifice was his life. A holy God cannot overlook sin; thus, the sinfulness of humanity had to be punished. In the Old Testament, God required his people to sacrifice animals ("perfect" animals, healthy and whole) to atone for their sins. At the right time, God dealt once and for all with sin and its ultimate consequence—death and eternal separation from God. Instead of sending all humanity to eternal punishment, God took the punishment himself (Romans 8:3). Sin had to be punished, but Jesus shed his blood—gave his life—to take away our sins so that we wouldn't have to experience spiritual death. His sacrifice transforms our lives and hearts and makes us clean on the inside.

2:18 Jesus came to earth as a human being; therefore, he understands our weaknesses and shows mercy to us. Because he was fully human, Jesus **himself has gone through suffering and temptation.** This suffering refers not only to the Cross, but also to the temptations Jesus experienced throughout his life—from Satan's temptations in the wilderness to the drops of blood he shed in prayer before his crucifixion. Having undergone all the tests and temptations of human life, Jesus **is able to help us when we are being tempted.**

HEBREWS 3

CHRIST IS GREATER THAN MOSES / 3:1-19

Moses has always been highly revered by Jewish people, by the Christian church, and even in Hollywood movies. But Jesus should receive much more honor and glory than Moses. "The Lawgiver," Moses, served God faithfully. But Christ was much more than a servant—he was God's Son. He was put in complete charge of God's house, the church. As Christians, we are part of God's house, and Christ is in charge of us. We must recognize him as our highest authority.

3:1 Chapter 2 tells that we are brothers and sisters along with Christ. We **belong to God,** meaning we are set apart by Jesus for service to God. Because of this relationship, we **are bound for heaven** (2:10).

In 2:1, the writer warned Christians not to "drift away" from their faith. This verse gives a command that will help believers keep from drifting: **Think about this Jesus.** This command comes from a strong Greek verb meaning "to give thoughtful and diligent reflection. Hebrews calls Jesus **God's Messenger and High Priest.** Jesus was sent as God's representative. God sent Jesus to earth as a Messenger; Jesus returned to heaven as our High Priest (a role introduced in 2:17-18). He came delivering God's message to people; he returned bringing people back to God. Jesus now serves as the mediator between people and God (a theme developed in 8:6; 9:15; 12:24). These words would have been especially meaningful to Jewish Christians.

3:2 Few people in Scripture had these three roles: prophet, priest, and leader. Moses was one such man, honored by the Jews. Moses **served faithfully and was entrusted with God's entire house** (see also Numbers 12:7). Moses' life and writings attest to his faithfulness. To the Jewish people, Moses was a great hero; he had led their ancestors, the Israelites, from Egyptian bondage to the border of the Promised Land. He was the prophet through whom God had given the law, and he had written the first five books of the Old Testament. **God's entire house** most likely refers to God's chosen people, among whom Moses exercised his ministry. Moses had served God faithfully, and the writer of Hebrews honored Moses by comparing him to Jesus, who **was faithful to God, who appointed him.** Moses led the people of Israel out of Egyptian bondage; Christ leads us out of bondage to sin. Both were faithful to the work God gave them to do.

3:3 Moses was a human servant; Jesus is worthy of greater honor as the central figure of faith because Jesus is God himself. Although Moses faithfully served in God's house (among God's people) and deserved credit for his work, Jesus **deserves far more glory** because he created that house and possesses the glory of God himself (1:3). Moses worked within the house, but Christ oversees the house.

The Jewish Christians respected Moses as one of God's greatest messengers. In order to show that Christ was superior to the old covenant, the writer both compared and contrasted Jesus and Moses. Because of Moses' faithfulness, he is worthy of great honor. But Jesus is worthy of greater honor. Even the great leader Moses is nowhere near being Christ's equal. Through Moses, lawgiver and leader, God gave the old covenant. But it was merely a shadow of what was coming (10:1). Moses was an intermediary, the people's leader and intercessor (see Exodus 32:11; Numbers 14:13); he could not save the people's souls. Jesus

enacted the new covenant, whereby salvation could be offered to all who believe.

3:4 If the builder deserves more praise than the house (3:3), how much more does God deserve praise, for he **made everything**—referring not just to the Jewish nation or to the Christian church, but to all of creation. The switch from calling Jesus the builder (3:3) to calling God the builder affirms Christ's deity. These first readers, who were considering abandoning Christianity and returning to their Jewish roots and Jewish laws, were in danger of praising the "house" more than the builder. Such action would effectively turn them away from the one who is God, Jesus Christ.

3:5-6 This repeats the thought from 3:2—that **Moses was certainly faithful in God's house,** but he was merely **a servant.** Moses' **work was an illustration of the truths God would reveal later.** Moses wrote the first five books of the Old Testament, recording Israel's history. But that history was not complete; Moses' words point forward to what was to come—fulfillment through God's Son.

Christ, **the faithful Son,** is superior to Moses as a son is superior to a servant. While both had been appointed (3:2), and while both were faithful, Moses was a servant while Christ is **in charge of the entire household,** referring to the church, the believers. Those who are part of God's **household** became so through faith in Christ. Christ makes our salvation secure, but that salvation comes with a solemn responsibility to **keep up our courage and remain confident in our hope in Christ.** Those who profess Christ ought to demonstrate true faith. God had required faithfulness from the great leader Moses and even from the Son himself. All of God's people, his household, the brothers and sisters of Christ, must remain faithful. Christ lives in believers; he will help us remain courageous and hopeful to the end. We are not saved by being steadfast and firm in our faith, but our courage and hope do reveal that our faith is real. Without this enduring faithfulness, we could easily be blown away by the winds of temptation, false teaching, or persecution.

3:7-9 God, through the **Holy Spirit,** is the true author of the Old Testament (see also 10:15). The Holy Spirit inspired the prophets and forefathers (1:1). The Holy Spirit used the quote from Psalm 95 (described in the following paragraphs) to speak to the Hebrew believers of the first century, and it applies to believers today as well.

The quotation comes from a psalm of worship used as an opening to synagogue worship on Friday evening and Sabbath morning. The first part of the psalm calls God's people to worship him. The second part of this psalm (the part that is quoted here) warns the people that worshipers can only worship God if they are not rebelling against him.

The Hebrew readers knew the story well. The generation who left Egypt had witnessed astounding miracles, yet they had lost faith in God. They were poised to enter the Promised Land, but they became afraid of the spies' report of walled cities and giant men. At that point, **they rebelled,** hardening their hearts, refusing to trust that God would help them take the land he had promised them (Numbers 13:26–14:38). Their unbelief kept them from receiving the rewards and blessings God had for them. Although God had miraculously rescued them from Egypt and had demonstrated his power and care over his people, the people disobeyed God. Not only at that point, but throughout the **forty years** of wandering in the **wilderness,** the people constantly **tested God's patience.** He continued to do miracles on their behalf; they continued to harden their hearts against him.

The original readers of this letter were on the verge of abandoning Christ and returning to Judaism. This passage reminded them of the consequences of hardening their hearts against God by using the example of their ancestors. Hopefully, these Christians would learn from their ancestors' mistakes. Believers are warned, **today you must listen, don't harden your hearts.** Hard hearts can be the result of disobedience, rebellion, lack of trust, neglect of worship, refusal to submit, and ungratefulness for what God has done for us.

3:10-11 Rebellion makes God **angry** as expressed in these words from Psalm 95. God does not look away from sin; he acts against it and punishes it. God grew angry because the people's **hearts always** turned **away from** him. The people continually turned away from God in their actions, attitudes, thoughts, and beliefs. If the hearts of the people had honored God, they would have trusted God and entered the Promised Land. But their rebellion led to punishment. The Israelites lost their chance to enter the Promised Land when God said, **"They will never enter my place of rest."** God's **rest** has several meanings in Scripture: (1) the seventh day of Creation and the weekly Sabbath commemorating it (Genesis 2:2; Hebrews 4:4-9); (2) the promised land of Canaan (Deuteronomy 12:8-12; Psalm 95); (3) peace with God now because of our relationship with Christ through faith (Matthew 12:28; Hebrews 4:1, 3, 8-11); and (4) our future eternal life with Christ (Hebrews 4:8-11). All of these meanings were probably familiar to the Jewish Christian readers of this book.

3:12 The lesson from Israel's experience applies to all believers. The readers had not yet revolted against Christ or drifted away from him, but they were in danger of emulating Israel's rebellion. The Israelites, who, with their own eyes, had seen great miracles from God's hand, had fallen away from God. Christians must **be careful** not to fall into the same snare. No Christian is immune from turning away from or rejecting God. Sometimes people gradually drift (as in 2:1-4); sometimes they rebel. We believers should carefully watch our Christian lives.

An **evil and unbelieving** heart leads to dire consequences; it causes a person to turn **away from the living God.** As illustrated by the Israelites, hard hearts can cause rebellion. Turning away from Christianity implies more than turning away from a system of beliefs or a set of doctrines; it means turning away from God.

3:13 A safeguard against believers turning away from God is for them to **warn each other every day.** Believers should continually remind each other to turn away from sin and to stay focused on Christ. People cannot live as Christians in a vacuum. Christians need each other so that they don't become **deceived by sin and hardened against God.** We protect against sin's deceitfulness by checking (1) our private intentions and desires against those of a group of trusted Christian friends, and (2) our group's intentions and desires against the teachings of the word of God.

3:14 Faith is a journey. Believers must be **faithful to the end, trusting God just as firmly as when we first believed.** As time goes by, we must not let doubts or fears draw us away. The writer was concerned that the faith of some of these Hebrew Christians was faltering. He urged them to hold on so that they would, in the end, **share in all that belongs to Christ.** Jewish readers of Hebrews would understand this picture of faith because it was the actual experience of the generation that had fled Egypt in the Exodus. Through unfaithfulness and rebellion, the Israelites had lost God's blessings. The writer turns to this theme in the following verses.

3:15 By repeating a quote used in 3:7, the writer continues to remind the people not to **harden** their **hearts.** The Israelites, **when they rebelled** in the wilderness, did not trust God, nor were they faithful to the end. Christians must be. The repeated (from 3:13) word **today** shows the urgency of this message. Today we can act; we don't know what will happen tomorrow. (For more on hard hearts, see the commentary on 3:7-9.)

3:16-17 The writer's illustration points out that a good beginning does not guarantee a victorious end. If people could rebel against God even after they had actually **heard his voice,** the danger for falling away is real for any Christian. The Israelites saw the plagues God sent on Egypt before **Moses** led the people **out,** yet they **rebelled against God.** The rebellious Israelites failed to enter the Promised Land because they did not believe in God's protection (see Numbers 13–14). So God sent them into **the wilderness** to wander **for forty years.** Those who rebelled **fell** (died) **in the wilderness** without ever experiencing the Promised Land. Open defiance of God leads to catastrophic results, barring entrance to God's rest. We must not take God's wrath lightly.

3:18-19 The rebellious generation of Israelites could not **enter his place of rest** (the Promised Land) **because of their unbelief.** But this "unbelief" was more than just a mental process; their

unbelief caused them to disobey. There is a strong connection between unbelief (the underlying attitude) and disobedience (the resulting action). Both their actions and their beliefs condemned them.

The nation had been rescued from Egypt, had seen God's salvation, and had been given the hope of a new land. Yet they had **disobeyed.** Christians have been rescued from sin, have seen God's salvation, and have been given the hope of eternal life. For those who reject Christ, the penalty is greater than it was for the Israelites. The penalty is God's rejection. Just as Christ was greater than Moses, so those rejecting Christ will receive greater punishment than those who rejected Moses.

HEBREWS 4:1-13

PROMISED REST FOR GOD'S PEOPLE / 4:1-13

The end of chapter 3 explains that the Israelites who rebelled against God never entered "his rest" (referring to the Promised Land in 3:18-19). Having shown that Jesus is superior to the great leader Moses, the author turned to another great Israelite leader, Joshua. God's servant Joshua led Israel into the Promised Land, yet he did not provide God's true "rest" (see 4:8). One greater than Joshua accomplished that.

4:1 While the next generation of Israelites (after those who sinned and died in the wilderness) *did* enter and possess the land, this was still only a shadow of the final "rest" that was to come. The Jewish people refused God's plan and rejected their Savior; thus, the **promise of entering his place of rest still stands**—God has made this rest available to Christians. Since God had barred the rebellious Israelites from his "rest," the promise stands for those who remain obedient to him. The promise has not been fulfilled, but neither has it been revoked. But Christians must learn from the tragic mistake of the Israelites. The writer of Hebrews warned readers how serious it would be to turn away from Christ by saying **we ought to tremble with fear that some of you might fail to get there.** Just as God rejected the rebellious Israelites on the basis of their unbelief (3:19), so he will reject those who turn away from Christ, refuse to believe him, or refuse to follow him.

4:2 The Old Testament Jews received God's message in the great deliverance from Egypt and the covenant given to Moses at Mount Sinai. These New

Testament believers received **this Good News** of God's **place of rest** in the person of Jesus Christ, his death on the cross, and his resurrection. Jews from both the Old Testament era and the New Testament era had received communication from God. But for many, the message **did them no good.** Why not? **They didn't believe what God told them.** Not only must God's message be heard, it must also be combined with faith before it will be effective.

4:3 The point has already been made that the Old Testament Jews had failed to enter God's "rest" (see commentary on 3:10-11, 18-19), yet this promise of rest still stands (4:1). **Only** those **who believe can enter** God's **place of rest.** Believing in Jesus may seem easy, almost effortless, just a nod, a quick prayer, or a walk forward at a church service. While making a profession of faith in Christ is simple, truly believing in Jesus leads to a life of commitment and discipleship that will put the believer at odds with the greedy, self-centered, cruel, and power-grabbing world. People who believe in Jesus find that each day requires a full effort. Those who believe in this way enter God's place of rest.

For those who fail to believe, there is a stern warning (see also 3:11, 18-19; 4:5). Because the Israelites lacked the faith to receive God's rest when he offered it, God, in his **anger**, vowed that they would **never enter** it. God's anger is not spiteful or reactionary. Rather, his anger emerges from the perfection of his character. Since God is perfect, he becomes angry at sin. The Israelites' unbelief caused them to forfeit God's promised rest, **even though his place of rest has been ready since he made the world.** Everything God will do had already been planned and foreseen. The point is that God's rest has been available to his people since the dawn of time. The "rest" offered in the Promised Land merely pictured the true and final rest in heaven for those who believe.

4:4 Genesis 2:2 records that **on the seventh day** after creating the universe, **God rested**, not because he was tired, but to indicate the completion of creation. The world was perfect, and God was satisfied with it, so he rested. This does not mean that God became idle; Jesus taught that God still works (John 5:17). God's rest is both present peace with God and future eternal joy when creation will be renewed, every mark of sin removed, and the world made perfect again. Those who believe will join God in his rest and one day be restored to a perfect condition. Our rest in Christ begins when we trust him to complete his good and perfect work in us.

4:5-6 But to those who don't believe, the author repeats his warning from **the other passage,** taken from Psalm 95 (see also commentary on 3:10-11, 18-19; 4:3). God's people who had seen great miracles in the exodus from Egypt never entered God's rest. Having great leaders like Moses, Joshua, and Caleb did not cover for the people's unbelief and rebellion. Not only did the people's sin keep them from possessing the land, it kept them from close fellowship with God. We must be careful that we don't believe we are Christians just because we belong to a good church or have a good Christian family. The Israelites, God's chosen people, **failed to enter because they disobeyed God.** But that doesn't mean God's place of rest no longer exists. It is still **there for people to enter.**

4:7-8 Humanity did not lose its chance for salvation with Israel's failure, but the writer again warned his readers not to **harden** their hearts (see commentary on 3:7-9).

The phrase, **God set another time,** means that the time of rest will come, indeed it has come, for the time is **today.** At the time of the writing of Psalm 95, partially quoted in this verse, no one had entered God's complete rest. Many Jewish people may have believed that they had already received God's rest by inhabiting **the land of Canaan.** But the writer argues

that it cannot be so. **Joshua** and the Israelites did settle Canaan and did achieve periods of peace and prosperity. Yet, if this had been God's promised rest, **God would not have spoken later about another day of rest.** In other words, there would have been no need for this renewal of the promise recorded here from the psalm written by **David.** If God only intended an earthly kingdom, God would not have promised "another day." Therefore the rest was not in the land, but in God's eternal Kingdom.

4:9 The word **so** indicates that the following is a logical conclusion from what has preceded. The words **special rest** are one word in the Greek, occurring only here in the entire Greek Bible. The kind of rest the author described is different from what the Israelites expected. This rest refers to what God did when he completed creation (see commentary on 4:4, 10). This rest is **still waiting.** It has not been fulfilled, as the author has explained above.

Why would this **special rest** have been so important to the readers of this book? The readers, Jewish Christians, had two important reasons to look forward to rest. (1) Jewish history was filled with wanderings and political turmoil. To finally rest in the full and realized promises of God would be great comfort. (2) Christians in the first century often faced deprivation and hardships, the animosity of Satan's agents, and the carrying of one's "cross"—identifying with Jesus. Those who turned from the Jewish faith to Christianity often incurred the wrath of other Jews (facing excommunication) and of their families (being disowned). To enter God's promised rest was a great promise—struggle will be done and pain will be over.

Yet this rest remains only **for the people of God.** Although the Jewish people who were originally offered the rest had refused it, God's plan could not be thwarted; God offered it to others—both Jews and Gentiles who believe in Jesus Christ as Savior. (This teaching is similar to Jesus' parable of the great banquet recorded in Luke 14:15-24.)

4:10 The author has shown that the rest remains for the people of God—the Christians (4:6, 9). That rest remains and people **will find rest from their labors.** Does this "rest from labors" begin now, or do believers have to wait for heaven? Some suggest that it begins after death, citing Revelation 14:13. Most likely, however, believers do experience God's rest in this present life, but will receive it completely and fully after death when they arrive in heaven. The "labors" from which believers can rest do not mean inactivity. After all, believers have much work to do in this world in order to advance God's Kingdom. "Labors," therefore, may refer to ceasing from trying to work for salvation. Many of these Jewish readers had been brought up under the Pharisees' system of strict laws and rule keeping. These Jewish Christians could rest from those labors, resting instead on what Christ had done. The promised rest for believers is the same as God's rest, and just as certain; it will be **just as God rested after creating the world** (see 4:4).

4:11 This statement is an intentional paradox: **let us do our best to enter that place of rest.** We need to strive to obtain what is ours by promise but not yet ours by experience. The children of Israel had been promised the good land, but it wasn't theirs until they possessed it. All believers must diligently work out their faith, seeking to obey Jesus day by day, drawing closer to God through experiences in life (Philippians 2:12). There is no time while living on earth at which a Christian "arrives" at spirituality. Each day God's people are making a choice either to grow closer to him or to drift away.

Nevertheless, the message here is a warning to people who would be lazy in their spiritual life. Laziness can cause a person to fall into disobedience, and **anyone who disobeys God . . . will fall.** Today's pressures make it easy to ignore or forget the lessons of the past. But the author cautions readers to remember the lessons the Israelites learned about God so they will avoid repeating the Israelites' errors.

4:12-13 God will discern whether or not we make every effort (4:11) and whether or not we have truly come to faith in Christ; **nothing in all creation can hide from him.** We may fool ourselves or other Christians with our spiritual lives, but we cannot deceive God. He knows who we really are because **the word of God is full of living power.** The word of God cannot be taken for granted or disobeyed. The Israelites who rebelled learned the hard way

that when God speaks, they must listen. Going against God means facing judgment and death.

The word of God is living, life-changing, and dynamic as it works in us. The demands of the word of God require decisions. We not only listen to it, we let it shape our lives. Because the word of God is **living,** it applied to these first-century Jewish Christians, and it applies as well as to Christians today. Most books may appear to be dusty artifacts just sitting on a shelf, but the word of God collected in Scripture vibrates with life.

The word of God penetrates through our outer facade and reveals what lies deep inside. The metaphor of **the sharpest knife** pictures the word of God **cutting deep into our innermost thoughts and desires,** revealing **what we really are** on the inside. Nothing can be hidden from God; neither can we hide from ourselves if we sincerely study the word of God. It reaches deep past our outer life as a knife passes through skin.

Two thoughts are presented by the phrase, **everything is naked and exposed before his eyes.** (1) We cannot give excuses, justifications, or reasons—everything is seen for exactly what it is. No one can deceive God. (2) We are exposed, powerless, and defenseless before God. The word refers to the paralyzing grip of a wrestler in a choke hold.

The word of God penetrates like a sword, exposing us to God himself **to whom we must explain all that we have done.** All people must give an account to God, but without trappings and rationalizations. These words give warning that believers must be careful not to drift away, but to obey God wholeheartedly. God is the final Judge. This verse paves the way for the following section describing Jesus Christ as our High Priest. With our lives laid bare before God, we would be hopelessly lost without Christ. Because he took our judgment and serves as our advocate with God, we can rest secure with God.

HEBREWS 4:14–5:10

CHRIST IS OUR HIGH PRIEST / 4:14–5:10
These verses logically follow from 2:17–3:1. The intervening section explains how Jesus is greater than Moses and Joshua, two of Israel's greatest leaders. Jesus is greater than the law Moses gave; he gives a rest greater than Joshua gave in conquering the Promised Land. The writer moved on to show how Jesus is also greater than anyone in the Jewish priesthood, another important part of the Jewish heritage. Our merciful and faithful High Priest, Jesus, became like us in order to die for us, offering the once-and-for-all sacrifice for sin.

4:14 To the Jewish Christian readers, the high priest had been their highest religious authority. The priesthood began with Aaron, Moses' brother (Exodus 28:41). Only the high priest could intercede with God for the sins of the nation (Leviticus 16). But Jesus is a **great High Priest,** better than all the high priests of Israel. Here is why:

- The high priests were humans who could offer sacrifices but could do nothing to take away sin. Jesus gave his life and died as the final sacrifice for sin.
- The high priest could enter the Most Holy Place only once a year to atone for the sins of the nation. Jesus **has gone to heaven** and has unrestricted access to God the Father.
- The high priests were human and sinful themselves. Jesus intercedes between God and people as the sinless **Son of God,** human yet divine.
- The high priests were the highest religious authorities for the Jews. Jesus has more authority than the Jewish high priests because he is both God and man.
- People could not approach God except through a high priest. When Jesus died, the veil that separated the Most Holy Place in the Temple was torn in two, indicating that Jesus' death had opened the way for sinful people to reach a holy God.

Because of all that Christ has done and is doing for us, **let us cling to him and never stop trusting him.** Allow Jesus to be your High Priest; only he can protect you from inevitable judgment (described in 4:12-13). Christ is a faithful High Priest who represents all who trust in him.

4:15 Because Jesus, our **High Priest,** was made like us, he experienced life completely. He grew tired, became hungry, and faced normal human limitations. Thus Jesus **understands our weaknesses.** Not only that, but he also **faced all of the same temptations we do, yet he did not sin.** Jesus, in his humanity, felt the struggle and reality of temptation. Matthew 4:1-11 describes a specific series of temptations from the Devil, but Jesus probably faced temptation throughout his entire earthly life, just as we do (see 1 John 2:16).

4:16 Through his death on the cross, our great High Priest, Jesus, opened access to God. Now people can approach God directly because of Jesus' sacrifice for sins. Because Jesus gave his life to do this for us, **let us come boldly to the throne of our gracious God.** This verse is an open invitation to regard God as a great ally and true friend. Yes, God occupies a throne, a seat of power and authority, but it is a throne of a gracious God. "Grace" means undeserved favor. Our ability to approach God does not come from any merit of our own but depends entirely on him. He is our Father, who loves us as his children. At God's throne, we will not receive anger or be ignored; instead, **we will receive his mercy, and we will find grace to help us when we need it.** God listens to our needs. No request is insignificant, and no problem is too small. God promises to help us at just the right time—his time. This doesn't mean that God promises to solve every need the moment we come to him. Nor does it mean that God will erase the natural consequences of any sin that was committed. It does mean, however, that God listens, cares, and will answer in his perfect way, in his perfect timing.

5:1 The Hebrew readers would have known that **a high priest is a man chosen to represent other human beings in their dealings with God.** A high priest had two primary jobs: representing God to the people by teaching the word of God, and representing the people to God in making atonement for their sins (Leviticus 1–4; 16). The high priest served as the "boss" over all the other priests, so he was in charge of presenting the people's **gifts to God and** offering **their sacrifices for sins.** Every sin required a penalty and a sacrifice in order for the worshiper to receive forgiveness. No person could offer a sacrifice without the aid of a priest as a mediator. The idea of mediator is central to the Bible. Humans subject to sin and by nature inclined to sin need mediation in order for them to establish any relationship with a holy God.

5:2 The Jewish high priest was only a **human, subject to the same weaknesses** as other people. This verse pictures a high priest who, fully alert to his own sinfulness and mortality, empathizes and deals **gently with the people** he represents, even **though they are ignorant and wayward.** The priest's knowledge of the people is intense, personal, and empathetic.

5:3 Of all people, the high priest should understand how humbling a job he had—and how vital a role he played. Without his mediation, the people would perish. He had to **offer sacrifices, both for their sins and for his own sins.** The high priest, while holding an honorable and prestigious position as mediator between God and the people, was not absolved from penalty for his own sin. Neither was he in a special category of human beings or exempt from the law himself.

5:4 The position of high priest carried special **honor,** and **no one** could **become a high priest** just because he wanted to. The high priest had **to**

be called by God for this work, just as Aaron was (Exodus 28:1-3). Aaron, brother to Moses, served as the first high priest of Israel. Leviticus 8 and 9 describe the ordination ceremony for Aaron and his sons. Their "holiness" came from God alone, not from the priestly role.

5:5 As the Old Testament high priests did not take upon themselves the honor but were honored by God's selection, **Christ did not exalt himself to become High Priest.** Christ also was **chosen by God,** as demonstrated by the quotation from Psalm 2:7, **"You are my Son. Today I have become your Father."** Christ became the High Priest and perfectly fulfilled the requirements.

5:6 Although Christ fulfilled the above requirements for becoming the perfect High Priest, he did not have one significant requirement: he was not born into the tribe of Levi and had not descended from Aaron. Jesus was of the tribe of Judah (see Genesis 49:10; Matthew 2:6; Revelation 5:5). Only Levites could be priests, and only descendants of Aaron could be high priests in the Jewish system. The book of Hebrews, however, tells how Christ's priesthood was greater than the Aaronic priesthood by quoting Psalm 110:4: **"You are a priest forever in the line of Melchizedek."** These words, coming from the inspired psalmist David predicted that the Messiah would come from a line of priests not traced back to Aaron. This theme is discussed extensively in chapter 7. The priests in the line of Aaron were not priests forever. Jesus, however, is **a priest forever.** In addition, Aaron's descendants were priests but not kings. Israel's kings could not serve the functions of the priests (those who tried faced dire consequences, such as Saul in 1 Samuel 13:8-14 and Uzziah in 1 Chronicles 26:16-21).

5:7 High priests had to be human (and thus able to sympathize with those they represented), and they had to be called by God. Christ fulfilled both of these requirements (4:15; 5:5-6). Jesus' humanity allowed him to sympathize with us. To show this, the writer reminded the readers of how, **while Jesus was here on earth,** he agonized as he prepared to face death (Luke 22:41-44). Although Jesus cried out to God, asking to be delivered, he was prepared to suffer humiliation, separation from his Father, and death in order to do God's will. He **offered prayers and pleadings, with a loud cry and tears.** He knew he had been sent to die, but in his humanity, he faced great fear and sorrow over what he knew would happen. In his humanity, he did not want to die, but he submitted himself to the Father's will **and God heard his prayers.** Jesus suffered extreme agony and death in submission to God. But his prayer was answered in

that he was saved from the power of death. He overcame death through his resurrection.

5:8 In the kingdoms of any ancient regime, no prince suffers; the crown prince especially is pampered and prepared for kingship. But Jesus, **even though** he **was God's Son . . . learned obedience from the things he suffered.** The bewildering lesson of this verse is that God himself, born of human parentage, actually learned something in the suffering he underwent. Was the all-knowing God in need of learning? Jesus learned about the human condition. That knowledge brought more empathy than intelligence, more personal identification than measurable data.

Like Jesus, believers often learn obedience through their suffering (see 12:2-11). This example from Christ encouraged the readers to remain firm and not drift away from the faith in times of suffering. Just as Christ was perfected through his suffering, so Christians will be, too.

5:9 The author of our salvation was **qualified as a perfect High Priest** through suffering. The word "perfect" does not refer to Jesus' sinless state; Jesus was already perfect before he faced suffering. His perfection was put to the test and came out with flying colors. Because humans experience suffering and death, Christ became fully human and experienced these parts of humanity as well. By sharing our experience of suffering, Christ shared our human experience completely. Because Christ lived, died, and rose again, he became **the source of eternal salvation for all those who obey him.** These last words warned those who would turn away from Christ and turn back to an inferior system. Salvation comes only to those who obey as Christ obeyed—with complete submission to God and his will, even in the face of suffering.

5:10 Going back to the theme in 5:6, Jesus was **designated . . . to be a High Priest in the line of Melchizedek.** All priests in Aaron's family line needed mediation for their own sins. All human priests died and were succeeded by others. But Jesus was fundamentally different. Jesus did not need mediation for personal moral flaws. Jesus died, but rose again to die no more. No one succeeded Jesus; he is a priest forever. He is both human and divine, made perfect through suffering, able to understand our weaknesses. That's quite unlike the Aaronic priesthood, so the writer compares Christ's priesthood with "the line of Melchizedek."

The theme of Melchizedek is postponed until chapter 7 so that the writer can give a parenthetical remark addressing the spiritual state of the readers.

HEBREWS 5:11–6:20

A CALL TO SPIRITUAL GROWTH / 5:11–6:12

The writer will further explore Christ's priesthood (chapter 7), but here pauses the argument to give readers a wake-up call. The concepts that follow in this letter will be understood by growing Christians, not stagnant ones. Christians must not be casual about the word of God; people must listen attentively. Hebrews continually challenges Christians to persevere in their faith.

5:11 Regarding Christ's role as High Priest, there is **much more** that the writer **would like to say.** Instead of working hard in their faith, these Christians were choosing the easier road. The writer illustrates this by saying, **you don't seem to listen, so it's hard to make you understand.** Apparently the writer was personally acquainted with many Jewish believers who fit this description or had heard about their unwillingness to apply some of these important concepts about their faith.

5:12 Apparently, these people had been **Christians** for **a long time;** so long, that they **ought** to have been **teaching others.** However, they had been lazy in their faith and needed **someone to teach** them again **the basic things** in the Scriptures. No wonder they were in danger of drifting (2:1)! Rather than explore and deepen their knowledge of Christ, rather than trying to please God with their actions, they considered abandoning Christ when they faced opposition. **Basic things** refers to the simple message of the gospel and the basic beliefs of the faith. Instead of teaching them to others, these believers needed to be taught all over again. They were like **babies,** still drinking **milk** instead of growing up into eating **solid food**—the more difficult teachings of God's word, such as the significance of Christ's position as High Priest (which the writer had just begun to discuss and will continue to discuss in chapter 7).

5:13 These immature Christians were **living on milk,** that is, they had not grown in their faith. They remained inexperienced and unskilled in applying their knowledge to their lives and **doing what is right.** They had received enough instruction, but they were still acting like infants.

5:14 This verse contrasts the spiritual babies (5:13) with the spiritually **mature.** These mature believers are called thus because they **have trained themselves to recognize the difference between right and wrong and then do what is right.** Spiritually

mature Christians constantly examine themselves, turn away from sin, and learn what actions, thoughts, and attitudes will please God.

6:1-3 Just after admonishing readers for baby-food spirituality, the writer indicated that "real food" would be coming. The writer would not give in to their immaturity and provide them with only milk, because rehashing the basic doctrines would not help them resist the temptation to drift away from Christ. They must gain a deeper understanding, moving beyond **the basics of Christianity.**

Of course, believers don't "leave" these teachings as if they didn't need them anymore; the elementary teachings are essential for all believers to understand. The elementary teachings about Christ include **the importance of turning away from evil deeds and placing our faith in God.** Other basic instruction included **baptisms, the laying on of hands, the resurrection of the dead, and eternal judgment.** These Christians needed to move beyond these basics of their faith to an understanding of Christ as the perfect High Priest and the fulfillment of all the Old Testament prophecies. Rather than arguing about the respective merits of Judaism and Christianity, they needed to seek deeper understanding of God by studying the more difficult concepts in his Word.

6:4-6 Let us first consider the subject of these verses. The writer described certain people with four phrases: (1) **once enlightened,** (2) **experienced the good things of heaven,** (3) **shared in the Holy Spirit,** and (4) **tasted the goodness of the word of God and the power of the age to come.** The writer was saying that **it is impossible** for such people, if they fall away, to be restored to repentance. There are four main interpretations of this passage.

1. One interpretation states that this passage means Christians can lose their salvation. However, this is dismissed by other portions of Scripture (see John 10:27-29; Romans 8:38-39).

2. Some interpret this passage as hypothetical: "if it were possible." But if this passage were only hypothetical, then the warning would be unnecessary.

3. Another interpretation is that the writer may have intended to illustrate someone who seemed to be a Christian but really never was a true follower of Christ. All of the descriptive phrases could describe someone who is not really in the faith. This interpretation is acceptable when considered in the greater context. Hebrews 3:16-19 reviews how each Jew living in the wilderness had seen God's great power, had eaten manna, had accompanied God, and had looked like one of God's people, yet never entered the Promised Land. The writer did not want the Christians to fall into the same category and experience the same fate.

4. Another reasonable interpretation arises by linking this portion of Scripture with 10:25-31 (another severe warning). The writer of Hebrews was warning against a specific kind of apostasy: forsaking Jesus as the perfect sacrifice for sins and returning to animal sacrifices as a means of atoning for sins. Thus, the severe warning is for those Jewish Christians who had originally accepted Christ's redemption through his shed blood and then reverted to offering up the blood of bulls and goats as a means of cleansing their sins.

In the first century, a pagan who investigated Christianity and then went back to paganism would make a clean break with the church. But for Jewish Christians who decided to return to Judaism, the break was less obvious. Their lifestyle remained relatively unchanged. But by deliberately turning away from Christ, they were cutting themselves off from God's forgiveness.

It is **impossible** for people who have professed to be Christians and have experienced all of the beautiful gifts described in these verses, and then turn away from Christ to be restored. Why? **Because they are nailing the Son of God to the cross again by rejecting him.** These people have shown contempt for Christ through their deliberate actions. It would be like personally crucifying Christ again. Many have argued whether someone who turns away from Christ can be restored to Christ. Some point to this passage to prove that a backslider cannot be restored. But "backsliders" are not the subject here. This passage refers to people who walk with Christ for a while and then deliberately turn around and walk the other direction, rejecting Christ. These people can never be restored because they will not *want* to be restored. They

have chosen to harden their hearts against Christ. It is not impossible for God to forgive them; rather, it is impossible for them to be forgiven because they won't repent of their sins.

To the Hebrew Christians, these verses revealed the danger of returning to Judaism and thus committing apostasy. Those who reject Christ will not be saved. Christ died once for all who believe. He will not be crucified again.

6:7-8 In these verses, a farming illustration further describes the argument of 6:4-6. Someone who abandons Christ can be compared to a field that **bears thistles and thorns.** Such land refuses to yield a good crop no matter what attention it gets; **it is useless.** So with those who do not persevere to the end (6:11); their punishment is real and guaranteed—**the farmer will condemn that field and burn it.** (See also Matthew 3:10; John 15:1-6.)

However, believers who stay close to God, seeking to grow closer to him, can be described as those who bear **a good crop** and receive **the blessing of God.** Just as both fields receive **rain,** so both groups receive God's concern and care. Only one group is genuine, however.

6:9 After arguing that it is possible for non-Christians to seem like true Christians, the writer continues that **we really don't believe that it applies to you.** The stern warnings are now balanced with an encouraging note. The writer assures readers that the dire warnings of tragedy and spiritual loss are, thankfully, not going to be enacted against the Hebrew believers. Confidence in the Farmer and a positive survey of the soil overcome the writer's earlier worry about the appearance of weeds (in this case, the Christians who felt like retreating into prior religious ritual). But these Christians must make headway in their Christian faith. They cannot be lazy, but now must move on. The phrase, **you are meant for better things, things that come with salvation,** refers to the new covenant as compared to the old. The **better things** are in the new covenant through Jesus Christ. There would be no reason to return to the "old things" of Judaism that could not bring salvation.

6:10 While believers do not need to work for salvation, salvation ought to change their lives so that they naturally want to serve God, do good works, and advance his Kingdom. Although a believer may not presently be receiving rewards and acclaim, God knows the efforts of love and ministry: **He will not forget** a believer's hard work for him. One example of this hard work was these believers' **caring for other Christians.** As discussed elsewhere in the New Testament, what believers do for others is done for God (Matthew 25:35; Romans 12:6-18; 1 John 4:19-21). Good works do not guarantee salvation, but salvation changes the lives of God's people, leading them to perform good works.

6:11 The service of **loving others** mentioned in 6:10 should be continued **as long as life lasts.** It pleases God when his people serve him. Believers have work to do in the world and should continue showing that diligence to grow and serve. Why? **To make certain that what** is hoped for **will come true.** In other words, we serve, not in order to get to heaven (as in some religions of the world), but because we are assured of the full realization of what we hope for and because we love the one who gave us that assurance. Our conviction must produce actions that show our true colors. We don't serve merely for the fun of it or for humani-

tarian principles, but because our hope is in our future life with Christ.

6:12 The opposite of being diligent is to **become spiritually dull and indifferent** (see 5:11). Believers are to be diligently growing and serving, not sitting back making everyone else do the work. To keep from becoming inactive or indifferent, believers would do well to **follow the example of those who are going to inherit God's promises because of their faith and patience.** The writer anticipates the example of many Old Testament followers of God (who are discussed later in chapter 11; see also 13:7). Their example should be actively imitated, not merely learned and acknowledged. Imitating these people's examples of faith in God will help Christians of all times keep from drifting away from Christ (2:1-4) or becoming hard-hearted (3:7–4:13).

GOD'S PROMISES BRING HOPE / 6:13-20
After encouraging the readers to imitate other faithful people, the writer offered an example from the Old Testament whose example would be worth imitating: Abraham. The readers could trust in God's promises because Abraham did, and he was rewarded.

6:13-14 For these Jewish Christian readers, a well-known example of one who will "inherit God's promises" because of "faith and patience" (6:12) was **Abraham.** God had made a **promise to** Abraham, recorded in Genesis 22:17, **"I will multiply your descendants into countless millions."** It was not really necessary for God to **swear** that he would keep his promise, because God cannot lie or break his word. However, God made the promise, swearing by the greatest standard and with the highest accountability possible—**he took an oath in his own name.** Abraham could not have received greater assurance.

6:15 The author's antidote for apostasy is waiting patiently. **Abraham waited patiently,** and that patience was rewarded. Abraham's patient wait lasted for twenty-five years—from the time God had promised him a son (Genesis 17:16) to Isaac's birth (Genesis 21:1-3). Because our trials and temptations are often so intense, they seem to last for an eternity. Both the Bible and the testimony of mature Christians encourage us to wait for God to act in his timing, even when our needs seem too great to wait any longer. God's promises always come true—we can count on him.

6:16 This description of taking **an oath** has carried over the centuries so that today we understand the concept completely. Even in modern wedding cere-

monies, the oaths (vows) that the man and woman make to each other are witnessed by other people, who are then obliged to hold the two people accountable for their promises. But even more than that, the oath is made before God—**someone greater** holds people to their vows. It follows, then, that **without any question that oath is binding.** We call on greater authority because we know that difficulty in keeping promises may wear at our resources and efforts.

6:17 Humans often need promises sealed with oaths, so God did this for us because he wanted us to **be perfectly sure that he would never change his mind.** Abraham did not see his millions of descendants while he was alive, but he did have one son—the beginning of that fulfillment. Abraham not only had countless descendants in the Jewish nation, but his descendants came to include all people of faith (Galatians 3:7-9). The fulfillment of God's promise to Abraham should convince believers that all of God's promises to them will also be fulfilled.

6:18 God confirmed his **promise** with an **oath** (6:17), and **these two things are unchangeable because it is impossible for God to lie.** God provides us security because of his own character. Patience is our part whereby we **hold on to his promise with confidence.**

The phrase, **we who have fled to him for refuge,** pictures a person who fled to one of the cities of refuge that provided protection for someone who accidentally killed another (Numbers 35). Christians also have fled for safety to the place of security and protection from the punishment against them. Christ provides the safest place, the hope we count on, the encouragement we need. We must "hold on to his promise," grasping it, refusing to let go no matter what might happen around us. For more on this promise, see commentary on 6:11-12.

6:19-20 This confidence (referred to in 6:11-12, 18) is like a strong and trustworthy anchor for our souls, secure and immovable. Not only does this confidence in God's promises hold us secure, but it leads us through the curtain of heaven into God's inner sanctuary. The **inner sanctuary** refers to the Most Holy Place in the Jewish Temple. A curtain hung across the entrance to this room prevented anyone from entering or even getting a fleeting glimpse of the interior of the Most Holy Place where God resided among his people (see also 9:1-8). The high priest could enter there only once a year (on the Day

of Atonement) to stand before God's presence and atone for the sins of the entire nation (see 5:1-3). But Jesus has already gone in there for us, opening the way into God's presence by his death on the cross. His death tore the curtain in two (Mark 15:38), allowing believers to come directly into God's presence. What only the high priest could do before, Christ did and allows us to do as well. In this way, Christ's high-priestly work was different from any other priest. Other priests took people's sacrifices and represented them in the presence of God. Now, through Christ, we can approach the throne with confidence (10:19). Repeating the theme touched on in 5:5-10, the writer again describes Jesus as our eternal High Priest in the line of Melchizedek. An explanation of this comparison follows in chapter 7.

Note Jesus' crucial role in communicating and securing God's eternal promises for us. The promises, an expression of God's holy character, are eternally valid. Jesus activates the promises, eliminating, as it were, the impediment (sin) that renders the promises ineffective. By God's promises and Jesus' intercession, believers are incorporated into the family of God.

HEBREWS 7

MELCHIZEDEK IS COMPARED TO ABRAHAM / 7:1-14

After the warnings given in 5:11–6:12, chapter 7 picks up the theme of 5:10, which says that Christ was designated High Priest in the order of Melchizedek. Jesus is superior in rank and authority to Melchizedek and any other religious authority. In this discussion, the author shows that the Levitical priesthood, very familiar to Jewish readers, has been replaced by a new order of priests who were foreshadowed and characterized by Melchizedek.

7:1-2 The description of **Melchizedek** comes from Genesis 14:18-20. He seems to have been an extraordinary man who served his people in both the offices of **king** and **priest. Salem** may later have become the city of Jerusalem. The appellation **God Most High** means that Melchizedek worshiped the one true God.

This passage refers to the time **when Abraham was returning home after winning a great battle against many kings.** Four kings in Abraham's region had united and had conquered Sodom and other neighboring cities (Genesis 14:1-11). Abraham's nephew Lot and his family lived in Sodom. When Abraham heard that Lot and his family had been captured, Abraham mobilized 318 men for

battle. With a surprise attack, Abraham and his tiny band of men liberated Lot and the others who had been captured (Genesis 14:12-16).

After defeating the four kings, Abraham became the greatest power in the land, and **Melchizedek met him and blessed him.** Then Abraham **took a tenth of all he had won in the battle and gave it to Melchizedek** because Melchizedek was a priest of God Most High. By giving the tithe to Melchizedek, Abraham was giving the gift to God's representative. Although these two men were strangers to each other, they shared a most important characteristic: Both worshiped and served the one God who made heaven and earth. This was a great moment of triumph for Abraham. He had just defeated an army and had freed a large group of captives. If he had any doubt in his mind about who had gained the victory, Melchizedek set the record straight (Genesis 14:20). Abraham recognized that he and this man worshiped the same God.

The original readers of Hebrews would have known that Melchizedek was greater than Abraham because he was able to receive tithes and give a blessing (see 7:7). This argument may not carry the same logical forcefulness for readers today as it did then, but these early Jewish believers understood the argument.

One of the reasons why Melchizedek is so significant is that **his name means "king of justice"** (the suffix of his name, "chizedek," means justice.) He is also the **"king of peace" because** *Salem* **means "peace."** ("Salem" can be translated peace.) In Melchizedek's name and position, justice and peace come together. Therefore, Melchizedek represents the same character traits as the Messiah, Jesus, who revealed God's justice and peace.

Who was Melchizedek? Through the years, many have believed that he was Christ himself appearing in human form to Abraham—technically called a "Christophany" (an appearance of Christ in the Old Testament). This seems unlikely because Melchizedek is said to resemble Christ (7:3). Ancient Jewish interpretation said he was an angelic being, but there is no evidence in Genesis, Psalm 110:4, or Hebrews to support this theory. The best interpretation is that Melchizedek was a non-Jewish, historical priest-king who lived in ancient times and was a symbol and type of Christ.

7:3 To bolster the argument, the author of Hebrews used what is not said in Genesis 14 as much or more as what is said. The Bible does not provide a genealogy for Melchizedek nor a record of his death. While the Bible does not supply details of Melchizedek's life, most likely Melchizedek was a human king and priest who really did have parents, and thus was born and eventually died. Jewish theology and typology, however, is built only on what the Bible text says. Because in the Bible text **there is no record of his father or mother or any of his ancestors,** it is as though he didn't have any. Because the text records **no beginning or end to his life,** it is as though Melchizedek never was born or died. The contrast is being made between Melchizedek and Aaron's priestly line, which depended entirely on genealogy. Priests in Aaron's family succeeded upon the death of the prior priest, making the date of death extremely important. None of the apparatus of the Aaronic priesthood (Exodus 39) applied to Melchizedek, except God's

appointment. In this way, Melchizedek foreshadows Jesus, God's special emissary.

With no record of beginning or end, Melchizedek **remains a priest forever, resembling the Son of God** (see also Psalm 110:4). Hebrews doesn't say that Jesus resembled Melchizedek, but that Melchizedek resembled Jesus. Melchizedek was a real man, a servant of God, whose history is recorded in the book of Genesis in such a way as to make him resemble the one who would come and fulfill completely the offices of priest and king, and who would truly be **a priest forever.**

7:4 As great as Abraham was, Hebrews says that Abraham **recognized how great Melchizedek was by giving him a tenth** of the spoils of the battle. The argument follows a simple logic here. The strength of the argument hinges entirely on this premise: Greater beings receive donations from lesser beings, a very persuasive argument to the original readers. Since Melchizedek received a tithe from Abraham, Melchizedek was greater than Abraham (see 7:7). Because Melchizedek was greater, the author will argue that the priesthood that comes from Melchizedek must be greater than the priesthood that comes from Abraham, who is the "patriarch" of the entire Jewish nation. In the same way, Jesus is in a class altogether different from the prophets, angels, priests, and patriarchs.

7:5-6 The major premise of 7:4 is further explained by the Jewish law. In the Old Testament, as God began teaching the Israelites his laws, he also was teaching his people how to worship him. To help in this, he needed ministers to oversee the operations of the Tabernacle and to help the people maintain their relationship with God. The **descendants of Levi** were set apart, dedicated to serving God. Their jobs meant that they did not have the time to maintain land, so when the tribes were allotted land in the book of Joshua, the Levites were given none. Instead, God arranged for the other tribes to meet the Levites' needs through donations—thus **the law of Moses** commanded the Levites **to collect a tithe from the people.** This was for their support—they were collecting from fellow Jews, **their own relatives.** The gifts came from their "equals."

Now Melchizedek **was not even related to Levi,** yet he **collected a tenth from Abraham.** To comprehend this argument, we need to understand that Abraham represents his entire nation. Israel's first high priest, Aaron, descended from Levi (the tribe of priests), and Levi descended from Abraham. Therefore, if Abraham recognized Melchizedek as his superior, then Melchizedek is also superior to all of Abraham's descendants, including the line of priests. This makes Melchizedek's priesthood greater than the Jewish priesthood. Melchizedek was not related to Levi, and neither was Jesus, who was born into the tribe of Judah.

The priests and Levites owed their position to their birth; they owed their receiving of tithes to provisions in God's law. Melchizedek, however, stands in history as a solitary figure. He was given the tithe, not because of provision in the law, but because Abraham recognized his greatness. Melchizedek, in turn, acknowledged his superior position as he **placed a blessing upon Abraham.**

7:7 For the original readers, this logic secured the conclusion. Melchizedek, as a priest of God Most High, had **the power to bless.** Therefore, Melchizedek must be superior to Abraham, who was **blessed.** A blessing was a significant ritual passed along from fathers to sons, as well as from prominent to less prominent people. Thus it follows that the one who has the power to bless is obviously greater than the one being blessed.

7:8-10 The strength of the argument continues with assumptions that are not as persuasive today as they were in the first century.

First, Melchizedek is compared to Levitical priests, who would receive the tithes, but eventually they would die. Because Scripture does not record Melchizedek's death, it is as if he **lives on** (see 7:3). Because Melchizedek is not recorded to have died, his priesthood extends forever, in contrast to the Levites, who died and passed on their service to their sons. This is how Melchizedek resembled Christ, who really does live and serve forever. What the author asserts about Melchizedek "from the record," Jesus fulfills in person and power. Having died on the cross and risen again, Jesus lives never to die.

Second, Melchizedek is compared to Levitical priests, who paid a tithe to him through their ancestor Abraham. The Levites are represented by their ancestor Abraham: For although Levi wasn't born yet, the seed from which he came was in Abraham's loins when Melchizedek collected the tithe from him. When Abraham gave Melchizedek one-tenth of his booty, the unborn Levites also participated in the action. In this way, Melchizedek would also be greater than the Levites and the Levitical priests. This principle of corporate solidarity was very popular in Eastern and Middle Eastern customs and is often seen in the Old Testament when blessings and punishments are given to sons' sons. Abraham was a great man, and his descendants served as acceptable priests. But Melchizedek was greater and therefore his priesthood was better.

7:11 In 7:11-19, the writer seeks to show how the Levitical priesthood and the ritual system of sacrifice were insufficient to save people. Thus, that system was merely a preparation, a picture, of what would come and fulfill it. If the Levitical priesthood had been sufficient, the author asks, **why did God need to send a different priest?** The Levitical priesthood could not allow people to approach God because the animal sacrifices alone really could do nothing to remove sin. Thus **God's purposes** could not be achieved through the Old Testament priesthood because all along it had been meant as a shadow of what was to come. When this better way would come, the old way would become obsolete (see Hebrews 8:7ff.). A new way would mean a new law and a new system (7:12). God could not simply provide another human priest; instead, he provided something new.

7:12 Provisions for the Levitical priesthood were given in the law—including their duties, ordination, clothing, etc. But the law could not foresee a change in the priesthood, such as a new priest arising from the tribe of Judah (as did Jesus Christ, 7:13). Therefore, **when the priesthood is changed, the law must also be changed to permit it.**

Few things were as stable as the Old Testament law. Kings came and went; high priests died and made way for new high priests. But the law never changed. The Old Testament law is not God's final word, however; it was, in fact, preparatory. Christ himself became the final word. The law was not changed, but rather was fulfilled, rendering the ceremonial parts of the law (such as the system for animal sacrifice) out of date. The ceremonial laws have been superseded by Christ himself, who was the final and sufficient sacrifice.

Christ was not just another priest in the old system; rather, the entire system was changed with Christ as the High Priest in the new system. For readers who were close to lapsing into Judaism, these words would remind them that their old Jewish ways had been fulfilled and replaced by Christ.

7:13-14 By law, only Levites could serve as priests (see commentary on 7:5-6). **The one we are talking about,** Jesus, **belongs to a different tribe—** he **came from the tribe of Judah.** (Luke 2:4; 3:31, 33). Judah, one of the twelve tribes of Israel, was the largest tribe (Numbers 1:20-46), and it was the tribe from which most of Israel's kings had come (see Genesis 49:8-12). Later, Judah was one of the few tribes to return to God after a century of captivity under a hostile foreign power. Also, Judah was prophesied as the tribe through which the Messiah would come (Micah 5:2).

This is only one example, but an undisputed one, that the Old Testament ceremonial law cannot bring salvation. The descendants of Levi were made to be the priests, but God proclaimed that the Messiah would come through the tribe of Judah. This is further proof that the Levitical priesthood was temporary. The better High Priest was coming.

CHRIST IS LIKE MELCHIZEDEK / 7:15-28

Centuries after Melchizedek, the psalmist predicted that the Messiah would be a priest in the order of Melchizedek (Psalm 110:4). More than one thousand years later, the author of Hebrews quoted the psalmist. Melchizedek was not the final priest. Neither was Aaron. Christ became the perfect, final priest. He is the one who allows us to follow him as he enters God's presence.

7:15-17 Old Testament priests were vital to the spiritual life of Israel, but they were imperfect and temporary. Only one priest could fulfill God's plan. The writer explained about this **different priest who has now come.** He is **like Melchizedek** and has a priesthood **in the line of Melchizedek**—as described in 7:1-10. By being in the line of Melchizedek, Jesus Christ was both priest and king. He did not become a priest by **belonging to the tribe of Levi.** As Melchizedek was a Gentile priest, so Jesus did not fit the pattern. As described in 7:13-14, Jesus was not born into the tribe of Levi, but the tribe of Judah. Instead, he became a priest **by the power of a life that cannot be destroyed.** Because there is no record in Scripture of Melchizedek's death, it is as if he never died. So with Jesus—death could not master him. He died, but he rose never to die again. As a result, he will never cease his priestly ministry. Jesus fulfills the qualification of being **a priest forever.** The one who never dies has become the final High Priest, and his sacrifice has forever settled the breach that human sin created between almighty God and sinful humanity. Christ is immortal, fulfilling the prophecy of Psalm 110:4. The old priesthood was incomplete and is now abolished.

7:18-19 The law had limitations. If the law had been the perfect path to God, all the people would have been able to enter God's Most Holy Place. As it was, only the high priest could enter God's presence—and only once a year. Even then, the sacrifices could not completely atone for sin. But God had already planned for a better way: **the old requirement about the priesthood was set aside because it was weak and useless.** There was nothing inherently wrong with the system, for God himself had created it. Rather, it was meant to foreshadow what God would do through his Son.

In addition, **the law made nothing perfect.** This does not mean, however, that the law was purposeless. The law taught the consequences of sin (see Romans 3:20; 5:20) and pointed people to Christ

(see Galatians 3:24-25). But law-keeping cannot save anyone. If the old system couldn't accomplish anything for sinful people, what could they do? The first-century readers needed to realize that **a better hope** had been made available—one that allowed them to **draw near to God.**

7:20-22 God did not have to take **an oath** because he cannot lie. Yet by taking an oath he added emphasis that what he said would definitely be so (see also 3:11; 4:3; 6:17). In the normal matter of the Levitical priesthood, men were appointed based on the law. But this was not so with Jesus. God ordained Jesus' priesthood with an oath when he said, **"The Lord has taken an oath and will not break his vow: 'You are a priest forever'"** (quoted from Psalm 110:4). No similar, explicit oath is mentioned in the establishment of Aaron's priesthood (Exodus 28). The matter of God making an oath, in addition to the power of his word, underscores the argument that Jesus is truly superior in every way—the only Savior.

This "oath" emphasizes that Jesus **guarantees the effectiveness of this better covenant.** The name "Jesus" emphasizes this point. The writer was not talking about Melchizedek or any earthly high priest, but about the Son of God, who is now seated at the right hand of God. Therefore, he is the "guarantee" from God to us. Jesus guarantees God's forgiveness of us, and he guarantees our acceptability with God. Because Jesus lives **forever,** the better covenant is permanent.

7:23-24 The historian Josephus estimated that eighty-three high priests served Israel from the first high priest, Aaron, to the fall of the second Temple in A.D. 70. Each served in his job, and each eventually died. But **Jesus remains a priest forever.** Again the writer contrasted the many people with the perfect One (see also 1:1-3). Every high priest would hand off his job to his successor. Not Christ; **his priesthood will never**

end. Only Jesus is qualified to become a permanent priest for the entire human race.

7:25 Two themes portray Jesus' ministry for the community of believers. First, Jesus **is able, once and forever, to save everyone who comes to God through him.** No one can add to what Jesus did to save us; our past, present, and future sins are all forgiven. In addition, Jesus is with the Father as a guarantee that our sins are forgiven and that we have access to God.

Second, **he lives forever to plead with God on** believers' **behalf.** As our High Priest, Christ is our advocate, the mediator between us and God. His purpose is to intercede for those who follow God. He looks after our interests, presenting our requests to the Father. Christ makes perpetual intercession for us before God. Christ's continuous presence in heaven as the Priest-King assures us that our sins have been paid for and forgiven.

7:26 Concluding the thought begun in 7:23-25, the writer explained again that the Old Testament system has been superseded by a full and final sacrifice. Jesus **is the kind of high priest we need** because he is:

- **holy,** meaning that Jesus knew no sin. Jesus perfectly fulfilled all that God is and all that God required in a high priest who would bring salvation to sinful people (see 4:15).
- **blameless,** meaning he is without evil and is completely innocent. During his earthly life, even as he faced temptation, he remained completely obedient to God and completely without sin (see James 1:27).
- **unstained by sin,** that is, he remains undefiled even as he deals with sinful people in a defiled world (see 1 Peter 1:4).
- **set apart from sinners** because Jesus' sinless life separates him from sinful creation. Yet it was only through his separation by his sinlessness that he could act on our behalf.

- **given the highest place of honor in heaven.** He is greater than any other high priest because he represents people in the very throne room of God.

7:27 The final argument for Jesus' superiority shows the contrast between the essential nature of the priests and Jesus. The priests under the old covenant were merely sinful human beings; thus, they had to make a sacrifice **for their own sins first** before they could offer the sacrifices **for the sins of the people.** And this had to be done **every day** because no sacrifice could permanently remove the stain of sin.

Jesus, however, was completely sinless, never needing to offer a sacrifice for himself, nor did he need to repeat his sacrifice. **When he sacrificed himself** for sins, his perfect sacrifice obliterated the penalty of sins **once for all,** bringing the sacrificial system to an end. He forgave sins—past, present, and future. The Jews did not need to go back to the old system because Christ, the perfect sacrifice, had completed the work of redemption. You don't have to look for another way to have your sins forgiven—Christ was the final sacrifice for you.

7:28 The **high priests under the law of Moses** were not perfect; they were **limited by human weakness.** They could not bring sinners into the perfect presence of God. But God designed another way that he secured with **an oath** (see 7:21). This "oath" was fulfilled and the new priesthood came **after the law** because the law had been surpassed by the appointment of **his Son,** who **has been made perfect forever.**

As we better understand the Jewish sacrificial system, we see that Jesus' death served as the perfect atonement for our sins. His death brings us eternal life. How callous, how cold, how stubborn it would be to refuse God's greatest gift. The original readers would be foolish to abandon Christianity and revert to a system that was now obsolete.

HEBREWS 8

CHRIST IS OUR HIGH PRIEST / 8:1-13

Chapter 7 explained that Jesus is a greater priest than any priest who had descended from Israel's first high priest, Aaron. The writer now summarizes his message; what he has been saying is that Christ is superior to everything in the Jewish priesthood. Whatever the Jewish believers had previously trusted for salvation was merely a shadow of reality, not the reality itself. That shadow is now utterly replaced by the reality of Christ as High Priest.

8:1 Jesus is **our High Priest,** who is seated **in the place of highest honor in heaven, at God's right hand.** This portrayal of Christ is a key argument for the deity of Christ in Hebrews. This place at God's right hand belonged to Christ because he was more than just a high priest; he is God's Son. **Heaven** refers to the heavenly sanctuary (see 8:2), the dwelling place of God, the ultimate and eternal destination for all who believe (4:1; 6:19-20; 11:10; 12:22), and therefore an even greater reality than what we see. This present world is merely a representation or shadow of what will come (see 8:5). Because of this, Christ's ministry will be greater than the priests who served in the earthly Tabernacle or Temple, as we see in the following verse.

8:2 Verse 1 describes Christ's exaltation at God's right hand; verse 2 describes his service. Christ, the exalted one, is a servant who **ministers in the sacred tent** in heaven. Jesus serves by taking his rightful place as our Savior and Mediator. His place in heaven secures our place there. Christ returned to the presence of God in heaven, **the true place of worship that was built by the Lord and not by human hands.** God allows us to enter that same throne room and bring our worship and requests to him. This "true" place of worship does not imply that the Tabernacle and Temple on earth were false but that they were imperfect shadows of the true and perfect place of worship (8:5). Before Christ, the high priest could only enter a special place, the Most Holy Place, to come into the presence of God. Today, through prayer, we can enter the throne room of heaven, and we will one day eternally live in that presence. By extension, then, the "old" way through the Jewish priesthood no longer exists; it is replaced by Jesus Christ, the way, the truth, and the life (John 14:6).

8:3 The high priest's work was **to offer gifts and sacrifices.** Priests had been appointed to offer sacrifices to atone for sin, so Christ, as **our High Priest,** must also **make an offering.** He offered his own life to God in our place—the perfect gift that could never be surpassed. "He sacrificed himself on the cross" (7:27). Christ's sacrifice is all-sufficient; that is, all sins are covered in his once-for-all offering to God. Therefore, his role as priest, his sacrifice, and his service to God all surpass the plan under the old covenant.

8:4 Under the old Jewish system, priests were chosen only from the tribe of Levi, and sacrifices were offered daily on the altar for forgiveness of sins. This system would not have allowed Jesus to **be a priest,** for according to the law, a priest had to come from the tribe of Levi, not Judah (see 7:12-14). The use of the present tense in **there**

already are priests indicates that this book was written before A.D. 70, when the Temple in Jerusalem was destroyed, ending the sacrifices. But Jesus' perfect sacrifice had already ended the need for priests and sacrifices. Christ was appointed High Priest of a new and better system that allows God's people to enter directly into God's presence.

8:5 The priests who offered sacrifices served **in a place of worship that is only a copy, a shadow of the real one in heaven.** This continues to show the insignificance of the Jewish priests' earthly service. Certainly it was important work, but their service was only an illustration of what was coming.

God gave Moses the pattern for the **Tabernacle,** and Moses was warned to follow it carefully, having been warned to **make everything according to the design** God had shown him (see Exodus 25:40). This earthly sanctuary was meant to reflect, however imperfectly, the heavenly Tabernacle. The book of Hebrews does not try to describe heaven; instead, it shows how Christ serves in a better, more personal way than any other priest could. Because the Temple at Jerusalem had not yet been destroyed, using the worship system there as an example would have had a great impact on this original audience. Their Temple, and all they knew about the original Tabernacle constructed by Moses, had been an imperfect picture intended to give the people an appreciation of the heavenly reality that would one day be theirs.

8:6 Although the priests descended from Aaron possessed a job of high honor and dignity, the ministry Jesus has received **is far superior to the ministry of those who serve under the old laws.** Jesus' ministry and the new covenant are superior for several reasons:

- they completely fulfill and replace the priests' ministry and the old covenant;
- they last for eternity, because Jesus is High Priest forever;
- they require no further sacrifices;
- they accomplish what all the other sacrifices could not do—truly atone for sin;
- they provide sinful humanity the opportunity to have a personal relationship with God (see 8:10-11).

This **better covenant is based on better promises** that the writer will discuss in greater detail in 8:10-12.

8:7 The **need for a second covenant** implies that the first covenant was faulty. Does this mean that God ordered Moses and Aaron to begin a way of worship that was mistaken or poorly contracted? No, but the old covenant was in every way preparatory for and pointing to the dynamic of the new covenant (see 7:11-19; also Romans 3–4; 9–11). The old covenant was replaced because it was not eternal, not sufficient to completely deal with sin, and could not provide sinful humanity with a relationship with God. In its time, however, the old covenant was necessary. But it needed to be replaced by a better covenant, as was prophesied by Jeremiah and quoted in the following verses.

8:8 Since the people continually broke God's covenant, God **found fault with the old** covenant. A part of the covenant involved keeping God's laws; however, the Israelites chose to disobey (see Jeremiah 7:23-24). When they failed to keep the requirements imposed on them, they broke the covenant. God, however, promised **a new covenant** that would not be filled with laws about sacrifices and other external responsibilities. Rather, it would bring about spiritual reconciliation by producing change in people's inner beings.

Verses 8-12 quote Jeremiah 31:31-34, which is the longest Old Testament quotation in the New Testament. Jeremiah prophesied about a future time when a better covenant would be established, because the first covenant, given to Moses at Mount Sinai, was imperfect and provisional. The Israelites could not maintain faithfulness to it because their hearts had not been truly changed. This change of heart required Jesus' full sacrifice to remove sin and the Holy Spirit's permanent indwelling. When we turn our lives over to Christ, the Holy Spirit instills in us a desire to obey God.

8:9 The old covenant was broken, not once, but many times. The Jewish readers' **ancestors** had been miraculously freed from slavery in Egypt. In the wilderness, they had received God's laws and had made a covenant of obedience. However, they **did not remain faithful,** and by that disobedience, they voided their part of the agreement. Grieved and offended by the willful disobedience of his chosen people, God **turned** his **back on them.** This means that they faced the consequences of sin instead of receiving the blessings of obedience. While God may have allowed such consequences, he never abandoned his people. Instead, he promised something better for all who would remain faithful.

8:10-12 Under God's new covenant, God's law is inside us. It is no longer an external set of rules and principles. The Holy Spirit reminds us of Christ's words, activates our consciences, influences our motives and desires, and makes us want to obey. Now we desire to do God's will with all our heart and mind.

This new covenant has four provisions:

1. The new covenant provides inward change: **"I will put my laws in their minds . . . I will write them on their hearts."** This means having a new "heart," and with it a new sense of intimacy with God where he is known as Father and where Christians are known as children of God and heirs. This new heart will bring the people's relationship with God to a personal level (not just through intermediaries). Having these laws written on our hearts means that we will want to **obey** God.

2. The new covenant provides intimacy with God: **"I will be their God, and they will be my people."** This reveals a positive, close relationship between God and his people. In the first covenant, people continually failed to live up to this relationship. In the new covenant, this relationship is secured through Jesus Christ. Although the promise was always there, it now has a newer and richer meaning because of the provision of Christ.

3. The new covenant provides knowledge of God: **"Everyone, from the least to the greatest, will already know me."** The new covenant brings a new relationship between people and God, making each believer a priest (1 Peter 2:5, 9). Every believer has access to God through prayer. Every believer can understand God's saving promises as revealed in the Bible because he or she has God as a living presence in his or her heart. Of course, there will still be the need for teachers, but every believer will be able to know God—not just priests or a select few.

4. The new covenant provides complete forgiveness from sins: **"I will forgive their wrongdoings, and I will never again remember their sins."** People of the old covenant had forgiveness of sins (see Exodus 34:6-8; Micah 7:18-20), but they had experienced an incomplete, unlasting forgiveness as demonstrated by the incessant need to make sacrifices for sins. In the new covenant, sin and its effect of separating people from God are eliminated. God wipes out memory of sin and renders sin as if it had never occurred. Sin's impact is completely overcome, making it possible for believers to receive the promised blessing. There is no longer any barrier to our relationship with God.

All four of these characteristics bring about a true righteousness that could not be known under the old covenant.

8:13 Introducing **a new covenant** means that God **has made the first one obsolete.** The old one was fulfilled by Christ and completed by him; therefore, it was no longer needed. Old systems, old sacrifices, and the old priesthood now have no value in securing God's approval. "Hang on to the old covenant if you will," warns Hebrews, "but you're hanging on to a shadow, a bubble ready to burst, a moment passing into history. The old covenant has served its purpose and will soon be just a memory. You can't live in the past, so your real choice is clear: accept the new covenant or none at all."

God does not change his mind. He did not send his Son to repeal, abolish, or annul what he had told his people previously. Instead, the Father sent his Son as the fulfillment of the old covenant. Jesus' coming had been part of God's plan from Creation (see Genesis 3:15). The disciples did not thoroughly understand how Jesus fulfilled the Scriptures until after his death and resurrection (Luke 24:25-27).

HEBREWS 9

OLD RULES ABOUT WORSHIP / 9:1-10

The end of chapter 8 explains that the old (or first) covenant was made obsolete by the new covenant. This chapter discusses that old covenant. As the Israelites had learned God's laws and how to worship him, God had given them instructions for building a place of worship (8:5; see Exodus 25:40). Called the Tabernacle, this portable building traveled with the Hebrews as they traveled to the Promised Land. It became the place where God lived among them.

9:1 The original readers of Hebrews would have known all about the **regulations for worship** that were required by the **first covenant**. The first covenant also had made provision and instructions for **a sacred tent here on earth** (first the Tabernacle, later the Temple).

9:2 The **tent** (or Tabernacle) that God's people used for worship was constructed while the Israelites were en route to the Promised Land. It was a portable structure that could be taken apart and carried when the people moved from place to place. God's instructions for building the Tabernacle are in Exodus 25–31.

The tent had **two rooms**: an inner room (called the Most Holy Place) and an outer room. A priest on duty would enter the **first room,** called **the Holy Place,** each day to commune with God and to tend to the other elements located in this room. The **lampstand,** the menorah, was a seven-branched candlestick standing in the south side of the room (Exodus 25:31-40; 37:17-24). Its candles burned day and night and provided light for the priests as they carried out their duties. The light also symbolized God's presence. The Menorah still remains as a major symbol of the Jewish faith.

The **table** was made of wood and overlaid with pure gold (Exodus 25:23-30; 37:10-16). On this table sat the **loaves of holy bread.** Once a week on the Sabbath, a priest would enter the Holy Place and set twelve freshly baked loaves of bread

on a small table. This bread symbolized God's presence among his people as well as his loving care in meeting their physical needs. The bread was to be eaten only by the priests on duty.

9:3-4 Beyond the first room, the Holy Place, **there was a curtain** (described in Exodus 26:31-33). This curtain prevented anyone from entering or even getting a glimpse of the interior of **the second room called the Most Holy Place,** symbolizing that sinful people could not approach the holy God. The curtain formed the separation between the holy God and sinful people (see 6:19). The original readers would have known of the magnificent curtain in Herod's Temple. It was made of blue, purple, and scarlet woven linen. Figures of the cherubim were embroidered on it. The Most Holy Place was where God himself dwelt. Only the high priest could enter the Most Holy Place, and then, only once a year (on the Day of Atonement) to make atonement for the sins of the whole nation.

The elements in the Most Holy Place included a **gold incense altar,** placed just outside the curtain, for it was used daily (see Exodus 30:6-8; 37:25-28; 40:5). The high priest burned incense on the altar twice daily. The **Ark of the Covenant** was **a wooden chest,** the most holy piece of furniture in the Tabernacle. The wood was acacia wood **covered with gold on all sides** (Exodus 25:10-22; 37:1-9). The Ark symbolized God's covenant with his people. On the annual Day of Atonement, the high priest would enter the Most Holy Place to sprinkle blood on the top of the Ark (called the atonement cover) to atone for the sins of the entire nation.

The Ark of the Covenant itself contained certain holy objects. First described in Exodus 16:32-35, the **gold jar containing some manna** symbolized God's care in providing food for his people in the wilderness. It may have been lost when the Philistines captured the Ark and held it for a time (see 1 Samuel 4–6). **Aaron's staff that sprouted leaves** is first described in Numbers 17:1-11. This staff showed that Aaron's descendants had indeed been chosen by God to care for the priesthood. It certified their authority as priests. This staff was also probably lost during the Philistine control of the Ark (see 1 Samuel 4–6). Also included were **the stone tablets of the covenant with the Ten Commandments written on them.** These two stone tablets were put in the Ark at Mount Sinai. When the Ark was placed in Solomon's Temple, only the tablets of the Ten Commandments were still inside (1 Kings 8:9).

9:5 Next the author described the **glorious cherubim** that decorated the top of the Ark of the Covenant (Exodus 25:18-22). Cherubim are mighty angels. One of the functions of the cherubim was to serve as guardians. These angels guarded the entrances to both the tree of life (Genesis 3:24) and the Most Holy Place (Exodus 26:31-33). The living creatures carrying God's throne in Ezekiel 1 may have been cherubim. With their wings **stretched out over the Ark's cover,** also called **the place of atonement,** these two gold statues were believed to support God's invisible presence. The glory of God's presence hovered over the Ark of the Covenant (see Exodus 40:34-36; Leviticus 16:2).

The **place of atonement** was also called atonement cover or the mercy seat. This place was significant because it was where sin was taken away. The blood from the sacrifice given on the Day of Atonement was sprinkled by the high priest on this cover (Leviticus 16:15-17) and the people experienced God's forgiveness.

The original readers would have been very well acquainted with the apparatus of the Tabernacle. The intention was not to give a commentary on these things; so the writer explained, **we cannot explain all of these things now.**

9:6 Having reminded the people of the basic arrangement of the holy rooms in the Tabernacle, the writer gets to the reason for this discussion. The priests would serve **regularly** in the **first room**—daily offering incense (see Exodus 30:7), setting out the holy loaves on the Sabbath (Leviticus 24:8-9), and trimming the wicks on the candles in order to keep them burning (Exodus 27:20-21).

9:7 In addition to these regular services, **the high priest goes into the Most Holy Place,** but **only once a year** on the Day of Atonement. This day was strictly observed (see Leviticus 23:26-32), and no one was permitted to enter the Most Holy Place on any other day. On this day, the **blood** sprinkled on the place of atonement on the Ark of the Covenant symbolized atonement for the sins of the nation (Leviticus 16:15-30). As part of the yearly ritual, the priest would enter the Most Holy Place with the blood of a bull. This blood would serve to **cover his own sins.** Then the priest would leave the room and return with the blood of a goat. This blood would cover **the sins the people** had **committed in ignorance.** The blood that the priest brought into the Most Holy Place would be sprinkled on the altar of incense and on the front of the place of atonement. (In the day of the original readers, the Ark of the Covenant was missing, so the priest would simply sprinkle the blood into the Most Holy Place.)

9:8 The ceremony carried out on the Day of Atonement revealed that people had no direct approach to God. Ordinary people could never enter God's presence and had to depend on the high priest. A heavy curtain blocked **the Most Holy Place;** thus, this place **was not open to the people.** The way had not yet been revealed—Christ would do that. **As long as the first room** as well as **the entire system were still in use,** people would be unable to approach God directly.

The **Holy Spirit revealed** that the sacrifice system was ineffective for bringing unhindered fellowship with God, and that one day, people would experience a new kind of relationship with God that would effectively remove sin. The old covenant pointed to what Christ would do in the new covenant.

9:9 This older way was simply **an illustration pointing to the present time.** Under the old covenant, the people did not have direct access to God. But under the new covenant made available through Christ, God's people can have access to God and be free from guilt. This guilt was never fully relieved in the old covenant, **for the gifts and sacrifices that the priests offer are not able to cleanse the consciences of the people who bring them.** These sacrifices symbolized atonement for sin and provided a way for the people to continue to worship God, but the sacrifices could not change the people's hearts and lives.

9:10 The writer continues to show why the old system of sacrifice through the priests was inadequate. The people had to keep the Old Testament dietary laws and ceremonial cleansing laws until

Christ came with God's new and better way. The **food, drink,** and **ritual washing** laws (Leviticus 10:8-9; 11; 15:4-27; Numbers 19:7-13) dealt only with **external regulations** that were required under the old covenant.

God replaced this **old system** in order to correct its **limitations.** This order began with the new covenant in Christ when God's laws were written on people's hearts (see commentary on 8:10-12). Perhaps some of the original readers had been considering reverting back to certain ceremonial rules. The book of Hebrews points out that these rules are no longer necessary or spiritually beneficial.

CHRIST IS THE PERFECT SACRIFICE / 9:11-28

Under the first covenant, sins were covered temporarily by the blood of bulls and goats. Under the second covenant, the blood of the supreme sacrifice, Jesus Christ, covered all believers' sins. Under the first covenant, the blood had to be shed and offered to God again and again. Under the new covenant, Jesus' blood was shed once for all. Under the old covenant, the priest physically sprinkled blood on the ceremonially unclean. Under the new covenant, we who believe in Christ are covered by his blood, which was shed two thousand years ago.

9:11 Although the people worshiped under the old covenant for nearly fifteen hundred years, God provided a new way that arrived because **Christ has now become the High Priest.** Christ fulfilled perfectly and completely all that had been illustrated in the old covenant (described in 9:1-10). Christ came as a priest of the new covenant, called **the good things that have come.**

As a high priest, Christ also served in the Tabernacle, but his ministry was in **that great, perfect sanctuary in heaven, not made by human hands and not part of this created world.** Christ's ministry on our behalf was in God's presence, a place where the blood of goats and bulls would have no effect. This point again reveals Christ's superiority.

9:12 This imagery comes from the Day of Atonement rituals described earlier. Just as a priest would enter the earthly Most Holy Place, Christ **took blood into that Most Holy Place** in heaven. But he took **not the blood of goats and calves,** but **his own blood.** With that blood, he **secured our salvation forever.** The real work was done on the cross.

Believers are forgiven on the basis of the shedding of Jesus' blood—he died as the perfect and final sacrifice. (See also Romans 5:9; Ephesians 1:7; 2:13; Colossians 1:20; 1 Peter 1:18-19.) Christ's sacrifice was so perfect and effective that it never needs to be repeated.

9:13 Christ's sacrifice was superior to any of the sacrifices offered under the old covenant. **Under the old system,** the priests offered **goats and bulls** as sacrifices (see commentary on 9:7). The **ashes of a young cow** refer to a ceremony described in Numbers 19:1-10. This ceremony was performed when someone was made unclean and needed to be purified. This ceremony served to purify an unclean person; thus, it **could cleanse people's bodies from ritual defilement.** A ritually defiled person could not participate in Jewish ceremonies until he or she was cleansed (see also Mark 7:15-23; Acts 10:15; 21:28). But the offering only provided ceremonial purity on a temporary basis.

9:14 If the old way of ceremonial cleansings allowed people to be made clean (as described in 9:13), **just think how much more the blood of Christ will purify our hearts.** Christ's sacrifice did more than **purify** ceremonially, which is all the ashes could do, it cleansed **hearts.** When the people sacrificed animals, God considered the people's faith and obedience, cleansed the people from sin, and made them "ceremonially" clean and acceptable according to Old Testament law. But Christ's sacrifice transforms our lives and hearts and makes us clean on the inside. His sacrifice is infinitely more effective than animal sacrifices.

Christ's blood cleansed his followers **from deeds that lead to death.** Before people follow Christ, they are filled with sinful thoughts, actions, and behavior. These deeds defile people, placing them in need of atonement (see 6:1). It could be that the original readers were tempted to revert to sacrifices because of guilty feelings over their sins. It could be that they had difficulty trusting in Christ's forgiveness and felt the urge to do something themselves. In a similar way, Christians today often try to appease their consciences by doing good deeds, giving money, living up to leaders' expectations, or taking on extra responsibilities. For the original readers and for us, the message is clear. Our consciences can be clean on account of what Christ has done.

The purpose of all the cleansing was to allow the people to **worship the living God.** Now that sins are forgiven, we can worship truly and freely. We are not limited to external actions; we can worship in spirit. Our worship does not need to be mediated through a priest; we can worship God on our own with unlimited access to him.

9:15 Because Christ offered himself to God (9:14), **he is the one who mediates the new covenant.** As our High Priest, Christ acts as the mediator, or advocate, between us and God. He intercedes for all who believe, looking after their interests and presenting their requests to God.

Because Christ serves as our Mediator, **all who are invited can receive the eternal inheritance God has promised them.** The phrase, **all who are invited,** refers to all who believe in Jesus Christ and accept his sacrifice on their behalf. That they are "invited" points to God's initiative in giving salvation. The **inheritance** is the final end of the new covenant—believers one day living in heaven with God. This inheritance will last forever.

Christ's sacrificial death saves not only those who died after Christ, but it also saves those who died **under that first covenant.** People in Old Testament times were saved through Christ's sacrifice, although that sacrifice had not yet happened. Those who offered unblemished animal sacrifices were anticipating Christ's coming and his death for sin. There was no point in returning to the sacrificial system after Christ had come and had become the final, perfect sacrifice.

9:16-17 These two verses introduce a parenthetical thought that shows when the new covenant was actually initiated. Through a play on words, the author speaks of someone who **leaves a will.** The word for "will" is the same word elsewhere used as "covenant." The new covenant was inherited by God's people at the **death** of Christ. In essence, he left the new covenant in his will. When he died, it was received by God's people. When Jesus died, the will was enacted and the promised inheritance (salvation and eternal life) was received. His death also provided the blood needed to put the covenant into effect.

9:18 To understand the reason why **blood was required under the first covenant,** we need to understand the Bible's view of sin and forgiveness. God is the sovereign judge of the universe. He is also absolutely holy. As the holy judge of all, he condemns sin and judges it worthy of death. In Old Testament times, God accepted the death of an animal as a substitute for the sinner. The animal's shed blood was **proof** that one life had been given for another. So on the one hand, blood symbol-

ized the death of the animal, but it also symbolized the life that was spared as a result. (See also 9:22.)

9:19 This passage describes the covenant sacrifice of Sinai (Exodus 24:3-8). **After Moses had given the people all of God's laws,** he sealed the covenant with blood. The blood that sealed the covenant, **the blood of calves and goats,** was mixed **with water** to symbolize cleansing. **Scarlet wool** was tied onto the **branches of hyssop bushes** and was used to sprinkle the blood on **the book of God's laws and all the people.** In the ceremony described here, Moses would sprinkle half the blood from the sacrificed animals on the altar to show that the sinner could once again approach God because something had died in his or her place. Moses then would sprinkle the other half of the blood on the people to show that the penalty for their sin had been paid and they could be reunited with God. Through this symbolic act, God's promises to Israel were reaffirmed and lessons were taught about Christ's future sacrificial death.

9:20-21 In the same way that Moses **sprinkled blood on the sacred tent and on everything used for worship,** so Christ shed his blood in order to confirm **the covenant.** As the old covenant was sealed with blood, so was the new covenant. This quote has been adapted from the Septuagint (the Greek version of the Old Testament) of Exodus 24:8.

9:22 Blood from a sacrifice symbolized cleansing and forgiveness, thus **nearly everything was purified by sprinkling with blood.** In fact, **without the shedding of blood, there is no forgiveness of sins.** Why does forgiveness require the shedding of blood? This is no arbitrary decree on the part of a bloodthirsty God, as some have suggested. There is no greater symbol of life than blood because blood keeps us alive. Jesus shed his blood—gave his life—for our sins so that we wouldn't have to experience spiritual death, eternal separation from God. Jesus is the source of life, not death. He gave his own life to pay the penalty for us so that we might live.

9:23 The **earthly tent and everything in it** were, in a way that we don't fully understand, **copies of things in heaven,** illustrating God's heavenly originals, which are far better than the earthly copies. Just as the copies had to be purified, so **the real things in heaven had to be purified with far better sacrifices than the blood of animals.** This purification of the heavenly things can best be understood as referring to Christ's spiritual work for us. Of course, the "better sacrifices" were, in fact, only one sacrifice. The real spiritual work of forgiveness continues in the presence of God as he forgives us because of Christ's death in our place. Why did the heavenly Tabernacle need to be purified? Heaven and God's presence are already holy, so this probably refers to the cleansed people of God, who can now stand in God's presence.

9:24 The priests worked in a symbolic, man-made **earthly place of worship.** Christ, however, **entered into heaven itself to appear now before God.** Among references to priests, Tabernacles, sacrifices, and other ideas unfamiliar to us, we come to this description of Christ as our **Advocate,** appearing in God's presence on our behalf. No intermediary priests or saints are necessary. Christ is our perfect representative. He is on our side at God's side. He is there now, always available.

9:25 Unlike the priests, Christ did not **offer himself again and again, like an earthly high priest** who had to go into **the Most Holy Place** and offer **the blood of an animal year after year.** Christ's sacrifice invalidated any other sacrifice.

9:26 If Christ's sacrifice had followed the pattern of the old covenant, **he would have had to die again and again.** Christ's sacrifice, however, initiated a new covenant and was the perfect sacrifice. As a result, **he came once for all time** and, by doing so,

has removed **the power of sin forever.** Sin is more than just covered; it is obliterated. It is forgiven and forgotten.

9:27-28 Each person lives on earth and then **dies only once. After that,** says the writer, **comes judgment.** All people will stand before God. Those who follow Christ have hope. Christians know that just as death and judgment are certain, so is their hope (9:28). All people die physically, but **Christ died only once as a sacrifice to take away the sins of many people** so that we would not have to die spiritually. Christ's sacrifice was the turning point in history. The word **once** indicates the completeness and finality of Jesus' sacrifice. **Many people** refers to everyone—all humanity (see 2:9).

Jesus went into heaven and likewise **will come again.** Because his death took care of sin completely and finally, he will **not need to deal with our sins again.** That work was finished. Instead, at his second coming, he will **bring salvation to all those who are eagerly waiting for him.** When he returns, he will proclaim the full benefits of salvation. **Those who are eagerly waiting for him** conveys a warning, reminding the readers to remain faithful to Christ during their time of testing and persecution on earth.

HEBREWS 10

CHRIST'S SACRIFICE ONCE FOR ALL / 10:1-18

Until Christ, animal sacrifices took place "year after year" on the Day of Atonement, reminding the people of their guilt. In the new covenant between God and his people, God promises that he will remember our sins no more because of Christ's one-time sacrifice.

10:1-2 The old system in the law of Moses simply offered a **shadow** of what was coming. The **reality of the good things** are the new covenant described in 8:10-12, including direct access to God. Because the law was not the final plan, it was **never able to provide perfect cleansing** from sin. If sacrifices could have made people perfect, they would not have been **repeated again and again, year after year.** Instead, they **would have stopped,** the worshipers **would have been purified,** and guilt feelings **would have disappeared.** But the endless nature of the sacrifices proved their inability to purify worshipers, remove their guilt, and provide closeness with God. Only Christ's sacrifice can purify people

once for all time (see 9:12). Only Christ's sacrifice can remove the guilt from sin and offer clean consciences (see 9:14).

10:3-4 The daily and yearly repetition of the sacrifices **reminded** the people **of their sins,** and taught them that **it is not possible for the blood of bulls and goats to take away sins.** Animal sacrifices provided only a temporary way to deal with sin until Jesus would come to deal with sin permanently.

10:5-7 Although sacrifices were necessary to pay the price of sin, this quotation reveals that God never took pleasure in sacrifices—**you did not want animal sacrifices and grain offerings.** In many places in the Bible, God revealed that he didn't want the sacrifices of a person whose heart was not right. God wanted his people to obey him. The sacrifices were necessary, however, because the people did not live up to the regulations that God had given them.

Applying to Christ the words of Psalm 40:6-8, Christ came to offer his **body** on the cross for us as a sacrifice that is completely acceptable to God. God's new and living way for us to please him comes not by keeping laws or even by abstaining from sin, but by turning to him in faith for forgiveness and then following him in loving obedience. This was what set Christ's sacrifice apart. He followed God's **will**, obeyed him, and offered the perfect sacrifice of perfect obedience.

The entire Old Testament (**the Scriptures**) had **written about** Christ and his coming. The law and the sacrificial system was a shadow of what was to come. Christ fulfilled the law as well as the prophecies that announced the coming of the new covenant.

10:8-9 These two verses repeat the ideas from 10:5-7, reinforcing the contrast between the old way and the new. God **did not want** the sacrifices **required by the law of Moses.** God had never planned for the old system to be the final system. Instead, he provided a new way, a new covenant through Christ, who obeyed God and willingly gave up his life as a perfect sacrifice. Christ **cancels the first covenant in order to establish the second.** Setting aside the first system in order to establish a far better one meant doing away with the system of sacrifices contained in the ceremonial law. (It didn't mean eliminating God's "moral" law, contained in the Ten Commandments.) The ceremonial law prepared people for Christ. With his coming, that system was no longer needed.

10:10 For the seventh time in less than two chapters, the phrase **once for all** is used to underscore the finality of Christ's sacrifice.

God wants his people **to be made holy.** The God of Israel and of the Christian church is holy—he sets the standard for morality. Holiness means being totally devoted or dedicated to God, set aside for his special use, and set apart from sin and its influence. Holiness comes from a sincere desire to obey God and from wholehearted devotion to him. God's qualities make us different. A follower of Christ becomes "holy" (sanctified) **by the sacrifice of the body of Jesus Christ.** We cannot become holy on our own, but God gives us his Holy Spirit to help us obey him and to give us power to overcome sin.

10:11-12 Here again is the point of 10:1 that the priests had to offer sacrifices **day after day.** These sacrifices could **never take away sins.** By contrast, **our High Priest offered himself to God as one sacrifice for sins, good for all time.** The sacrificial system couldn't completely remove sin; Christ's sacrifice did so. Christ now sits **at God's right hand** (see commentary on 1:3, 13; 8:1). He is able to sit because his sacrifice was completely sufficient to take care of sin.

10:13-14 Since that time, Christ **waits until his enemies are humbled** (see also 1:13; Psalm 110:1). Christ paid the penalty for our sins, and by **one offering he perfected forever all those whom he is making holy.** Believers are **perfected forever** because they are new creations whom God sees as holy. Verse 14 contrasts believers (who are being made holy) with people who refuse to believe—the "enemies" mentioned in verse 13.

Although we are made holy when we accept Christ as Savior, God is also continually **making us holy.** In Christ, we are free from the penalty of sin (judgment) and the power of sin (compulsion to sin, death). But while still alive on earth, we are not free from the presence of sin (temptations) and the possibility of sin (failures). We are saved by God's grace, but we still need to grow. We can encourage this growth process by deliberately applying Scripture to all areas of our lives, by accepting the discipline and guidance Christ provides, and by giving God control of our desires and goals.

10:15-17 Again Hebrews states that **the Holy Spirit** is the author of the Old Testament (see also 3:7; 9:8). Quoting again from Jeremiah 31:33-34 (as in 8:10-12), Hebrews makes the connection between Christ's sacrifice and the new covenant. Here again we see a close connection between the forgiveness of sins and the ability to know God. The new covenant and new sacrifice brought forgiveness in a better way than the Levitical system could provide. With sins forgiven, Christians can now enter the real presence of God. The guilt that remained under the old covenant has been permanently removed.

10:18 Christ forgives completely, so there is no need to confess past sins repeatedly. As believers, we can be confident that the sins we confess and renounce are forgiven and forgotten. Because **sins have been forgiven, there is no need to offer any more sacrifices.** God requires no more sacrifices to make people acceptable to him because Christ's once-for-all sacrifice makes people acceptable.

gospel and yet reject Christ, the consequences are severe. For those who learn the truth and then **deliberately continue sinning, there is no other sacrifice that will cover these sins.** When people deliberately reject Christ's offer of salvation, they reject God's most precious gift. They have rejected the only sacrifice that could have saved them.

This warning was given to Jewish Christians who were tempted to reject Christ for Judaism. It applies, however, to anyone who turns away from Christ to another religion or, having understood Christ's atoning work, deliberately turns away from it (Mark 3:28-30). Under the old covenant, the Jews had this threat of punishment if they rejected God's way (see also Numbers 15:30-31). There is no other acceptable sacrifice for sin than the death of Christ on the cross. If, after understanding the gospel message, someone deliberately rejects the sacrifice of Christ, that person cannot be saved because God has not provided any other name under heaven for salvation (see Acts 4:12).

10:27 For those who have rejected Christ, the only future they can **look forward to is God's judgment,** namely **the raging fire that will consume his enemies.** The book of Hebrews is filled with the message of the hope that Christians have. They can look forward to their guaranteed salvation. Those who do not follow Christ, however, also have a guarantee. They will face God's wrath as experienced in the "raging fire" of hell. God promises eternal punishment for those who reject him (see Isaiah 26:11; Revelation 20:11-15).

10:28 Under the old covenant, anyone who **refused to obey the law of Moses** was punished by **death.** All it took was **the testimony of two or three witnesses.** This meant the person had rejected the authority of the Mosaic law; this was as serious as the sin of idolatry. There were sacrifices available for sins that were unintentional, but if someone willfully rejected God's covenant and followed after another god, there was no **mercy** and no sacrifice (Deuteronomy 17:2-7). If God required physical death for breaking the old covenant, the new covenant's punishment would be much greater (10:29).

10:29 Those who reject Christ and deliberately continue to sin (10:26) will receive a terrible punishment, worse than those who refused to follow the old covenant. Those who treated the old covenant in this way received physical death (10:28). Those who treat the new covenant (and Christ) with contempt, however, will receive something far worse than physical death. Because the blessings under the new covenant are greater, there awaits even greater **punishment** for those who

scorn it. The book of Hebrews issues a strong warning and gives three specific indictments against these people.

1. They have **trampled on the Son of God.** To refuse to accept the sacrifice of his life on our behalf is to show contempt and disdain for Christ. The word for "trample underfoot" is vivid and conveys strong antagonism.

2. They have **treated the blood of the covenant as if it were common and unholy** (or "defiled"). The **blood of the covenant** refers to Christ's blood and thus to his death. The importance of the blood has been established in previous verses (7:22; 9:15-18; 10:12-18). Since blood ratified the covenant, to reject the consecrated blood of Christ was the ultimate rejection.

3. They have **insulted and enraged the Holy Spirit who brings God's mercy to his people.** The sacrifice of Christ is tied with the Holy Spirit; therefore, to scorn Christ's sacrifice is to insult and enrage the Holy Spirit (see 9:14). This is equivalent to blasphemy against the Holy Spirit (see Matthew 12:31-32).

10:30-31 The terrible punishment (10:29) will come from the hands of God. Two lines quoted from Moses' farewell song in Deuteronomy 32 emphasize this truth. In this song, Moses warned the people against apostasy and unbelief. God's judgment will come and will be severe: **"I will take vengeance. I will repay."** God, the Sovereign of the universe, has the right to punish those who disobey him. God's holiness and perfect justice demand that he punish those who sin. Only God is allowed to avenge, for he alone is perfect, and he has been wronged by those who reject him. To those who heard the gospel and then treated it with contempt, God says, **"The Lord will judge."** They will be judged because they have rejected God's mercy.

These quotations show that **it is a terrible thing to fall into the hands of the living God.** God's power is awesome, and his punishment terrible. These words give us a glimpse into the awesome holiness of God. He is sovereign; his power is unlimited; he will do as he promises. Those who reject the covenant will be punished. For them, falling into God's hands will be a dreadful experience. They will have no more excuses. They will discover that they were wrong, but it will be too late.

10:32-34 After a harsh warning, the readers are encouraged that their past actions demonstrate their genuine faith. Remembering their past faithfulness should encourage them to persevere in their faith. Like many Christians, these people had a deep love **when they first learned about Christ.** The memory of that closeness and their deep desire to serve him would encourage them during difficult days.

During those **early days,** these believers had remained faithful **even though it meant terrible suffering.** They had been **exposed to public ridicule and beaten.** During those difficult times of persecution, they had encouraged each other, helping each other remain firm by helping fellow believers **who were suffering the same things.** Apparently the recipients of this letter had risked their own reputation and public standing as they **suffered along with those who were thrown into jail.**

In addition, when their goods were **taken from** them, they **accepted it with joy.** The text does not say whether this action was from the local government or from angry neighbors. Either way, the writer points to the good attitude that the people maintained. At that time, they were able to endure because they **knew better things** were **waiting for** them **in eternity.** The word "better" means superior in quality and reality. The believers trusted in God's promises of future tremendous rewards.

10:35-36 These hardships would not cease for the believers, so they would need to continue to have **patient endurance.** The writer implores, **Do not throw away this confident trust in the Lord;** that is, do not abandon your faith in times of persecution, but show by your endurance that your faith is genuine and sincere, and that you will **continue to do God's will.** Such faith means resting in what Christ has done in the past, but it also means trusting him for what he will do in the present and in the future (see Romans 8:12-25; Galatians 3:10-13). Doing so will bring **great reward**—joy today and heavenly possessions in the future—the greatest of which is eternal life.

10:37-38 One of the promises that believers will receive (10:36) is the return of the Christ. Through this quote of Habakkuk 2:3-4, readers are reminded that the day is drawing near (see also 10:25). This second coming of Christ and all the blessings that come with him outweigh any discomfort faced by believers in this life. Those who remain faithful to God are the **righteous** who **will live by faith.** These people will persevere to the end. However, those who turn **away** forfeit the heavenly blessing because they prove that they do not belong to God's household. People who defect from the Christian faith when persecution comes will be forfeiting the ultimate goal of salvation—living forever with Christ.

When the prophet Habakkuk penned these prophetic words, evil and injustice seemed to have the upper hand in Israel. Like Habakkuk, Christians often feel angry and discouraged as they see what goes on in the world. Habakkuk complained vigorously to God about the situation. God's answer to Habakkuk is the same answer he would give us: "Be patient! I will work out my plans in my perfect timing." **The Coming One** (Christ) **will come and not delay.**

10:39 The writer knew that these readers were **not like those who turn their backs on God and seal their fate.** Such people are hard-hearted and stubborn, rejecting Christ as Savior (10:29). Instead, the readers had **faith that assures** their **salvation.** This vote of confidence readies the believers to learn from the examples of faith and perseverance that will be cited in the next chapter. Living by faith is far better than merely fulfilling rituals and rules. The examples of faith in chapter 11 can challenge us to grow in faith and to live in obedience to God each day.

HEBREWS 11

GREAT EXAMPLES OF FAITH / 11:1-40

Chapter 11 serves as a parenthesis; 12:1 resumes the theme of the last part of chapter 10. The words of 10:39 regarding those who believe lead to the description of the faith that causes Christians to hold on and not lose hope in the face of persecution and trials.

11:1 In this wonderful and well-known chapter, **faith** is explained as **the confident assurance that what we hope for is going to happen.** Faith starts with believing in God's character, that he is who he says he is. Faith culminates with believing in God's promises, that he will do what he says

he will do. We often think of the word **hope** in terms of uncertain desire—"I hope it doesn't rain on Saturday." For believers, however, "hope" is a desire based on assurance, and the assurance is based on God's character.

Faith is **the evidence of things we cannot yet**

see, meaning we have complete confidence that God will fulfill his promises, even though we don't yet see any evidence. These include eternal life, future rewards, heaven, and so forth. Faith regards these to be as real as what can be perceived with the senses. This conviction about God's unseen promises allows Christians to persevere in their faith regardless of persecution, opposition, and temptation.

11:2 People with **faith** please God very much. But faith is not something we must do in order to earn salvation. If that were true, then faith would be just one more deed, and human deeds can never save us (Galatians 2:16). Instead, faith is a gift God gives us because he is saving us (Ephesians 2:8).

Even in **days of old** (Old Testament times), grace, not deeds, was the basis of salvation. This is why the book of Hebrews says, "It is not possible for the blood of bulls and goats to take away sins" (10:4). God intended for his people to look beyond the animal sacrifices to him, but too often they instead put their confidence in fulfilling the requirements of the law. When Jesus triumphed over death, he canceled the charges against believers and opened the way to the Father (Colossians 2:12-15). Because God is merciful, he gives us faith. It would be tragic to turn faith into a deed and try to develop it on our own!

When believers have faith, that is, when they have confidence in God, they receive God's **approval**. The rest of the chapter presents examples of men and women who received God's approval because of their faith.

11:3 Here is an illustration of faith. Faith allows us to **understand that the entire universe was formed at God's command.** God created the world from nothing by his creative word alone. Believing this fact requires spiritual perception— that we receive only by faith. This passage reminds us that all of creation was new, not made from preexistent materials. The visible world **did not come from anything that can be seen.** God called the universe into existence out of nothing; he declared that it was to be, and it was (see Genesis 1). We understand this by faith, not because we saw it happen but because we understand from what we read in Scripture and from our relationship with the loving Father that the world was created with a purpose and that we are part of that purpose.

The Jewish believers reading this letter were in danger of returning to Judaism. Many may have desired to turn back because the "visual" nature of the rituals and sacrifices made their faith seem more real. Christianity, however, was based on so many invisible realities that many Jewish Christians may have begun to doubt its reality. Hebrews shows that Christianity's "unseen truths" are more real and more certain than what can be seen.

11:4 Cain and **Abel** were Adam and Eve's first two sons (see Genesis 4:2-5). Cain, a farmer, brought an offering to God from the ground. Abel, a shepherd, brought firstborn sheep. Abel's sacrifice (an animal substitute) was **a more acceptable offering** and **God accepted** it. Therefore, Abel was commended as **a righteous man** (see Matthew 23:35). Because of Abel's **faith,** he **still speaks** by his example.

11:5 Enoch is the next example of faith (see Genesis 5:20-24). Enoch was **approved as pleasing to God,** and as a result, **was taken up to heaven without dying.** This passage states that **God took him** away from earthly life to heavenly life. Enoch is one of two Old Testament characters who never died (the other being Elijah, 2 Kings 2:11-12). God chose to take Enoch without dying because Enoch lived **by faith.** He was a righteous man who was commended as one who pleased God.

11:6 God gave his approval to these Old Testament people because of their faith (11:2). In fact, **it is impossible to please God without faith.** This would have functioned as a warning to those Hebrew Christians whose faith was wavering. No one (not Abel, Enoch, or anyone else) can please God without faith. It is an absolute requirement. All the rituals mean nothing without faith.

To **come to** God has two presuppositions here: (1) The person **must believe that there is a God** and then (2) believe that God **rewards those who sincerely seek him.** Believing that God exists is only the beginning; even the demons believe in God's existence (James 2:19-20). God will not settle for mere acknowledgment of his existence. He wants a personal, dynamic relationship with you that will transform your life.

11:7 Old Testament examples of faith continue with **Noah** who, by faith, believed God's warnings of **something that had never happened before** (Genesis 6–9). Noah had **faith,** and so **built an ark.** Noah's faith **condemned the rest of the world** because it illustrated what the people lacked. Those without faith faced God's judgment; those with faith were saved. Noah is the first person in the Bible to be called "righteous"— **made right in God's sight** (see Genesis 6:9). To say that Noah was righteous and blameless does not mean that he never sinned. Rather, it means that he wholeheartedly loved and obeyed God. For a lifetime, Noah walked step-by-step in faith as a living example to his generation and future generations (see also Matthew 24:37-39; Luke 17:26-27; 1 Peter 3:20; 2 Peter 2:5). The early believers could learn this lesson from Noah: requiring no physical evidence of what was coming, he simply trusted God and obeyed.

11:8 Abraham is the next Old Testament example of faith. Genesis records his faith in Genesis 15:6, and Hebrews has already mentioned his faith in 6:13-15. Two other notable New Testament passages speak of Abraham: Paul used Abraham as an example of justification by faith (Romans 4); James used Abraham as an example of faith that results in works (James 2:20-24). Hebrews explains that **it was by faith that Abraham obeyed**, and it describes three actions resulting from Abraham's faith: (1) he moved to a new home (11:8); (2) he became a father in his old age (11:11); (3) he was willing to obey God's command to sacrifice his only son (11:17). Abraham demonstrated his faith through his actions. His faith made him right with God.

Abraham's faith is first seen in his obedience to **leave home** and **go to another land that God would give him as his inheritance.** Abraham left on the basis of God's promise, **without knowing where he was going** (see Genesis 12:1-9). Abraham trusted in God's promises of even greater blessings in the future. Abraham's life was filled with faith.

Believers can take heart from Abraham's example of faith. God may ask us to give up secure, familiar surroundings in order to carry out his will; he may ask us to do some difficult tasks. But we can be sure that the outcome always will be for our best, drawing us closer to him.

11:9 Abraham lived by faith throughout the rest of his life, continuing to trust God as he lived in the land God promised him. This land was to be his "as his inheritance" (11:8), yet Abraham never possessed the land. Instead, he lived in "his" land **like a foreigner, living in a tent.** He didn't build cities and take over the land, and neither did his son and grandson, **Isaac and Jacob.** That job would be left to their descendants, hundreds of years later. But Abraham believed God's promise that eventually the whole country would belong to him and his descendants (Acts 7:5). Yet even all that time, they understood that the land was not their final destination. Their real home was in heaven. Isaac and Jacob, **to whom God gave the same promise,** also remembered that promise and lived by faith.

11:10 Abraham lived by faith (11:9) because he was **confidently looking forward to a city . . . designed and built by God.** The verb "looking forward" connotes intensely looking forward to and waiting for that city. This was not an earthly city, but **a city with eternal foundations.** This contrasts with the tents in which Abraham lived. This city, though as yet unseen, stretches to eternity; thus, it is permanent and secure. Having God as builder means that everything will be perfect. As Abraham was confident, so can we be.

11:11 It took **faith** for both **Abraham** and **Sarah** to trust in God's divine intervention in their physical bodies that were both **too old** to produce children. In addition, Sarah was **barren** (unable to have children) in her childbearing years. God promised Abraham a son, but Sarah at first doubted that she could become pregnant in her old age. Abraham was one hundred and Sarah was ninety when Isaac was conceived (Genesis 17:1, 15-16; 21:1-7). But **Abraham believed that God would keep his promise.** The faithfulness of God picks up the theme from 10:23.

Promises from God (no matter how unlikely or even impossible they may seem as we look around at our circumstances) can be trusted because we can trust God's character. God cannot lie, and he will not make a promise that he does not intend to keep.

11:12 Abraham and Sarah became parents because of their faith. It didn't matter to them that they seemed to be **too old to have any children.** Because they believed God, he rewarded their faith with a child whose descendants became **a nation with so many people that, like the stars of the sky and the sand on the seashore, there is no way to count them.** This had been part of God's covenant with Abraham (Genesis 22:17 ; see also Genesis 12:2; 15:5). The contrast is being made between Abraham (**one man**) and his countless descendants (the Jews, and eventually all Christians), all because of that one man's faith. God had indeed been faithful to his promise.

11:13 All these faithful ones so far described **died without receiving what God had promised them**—the promise of the new, eternal city (see 11:10). But these heroes saw and welcomed the promise even though it was, as it were, **from a distance.** These people of faith died without receiving all that God had promised, but they never lost their vision of heaven (11:16). Their future hope was not for this earth. Thus **they agreed that they were no more than foreigners and nomads here on earth.** Their "agreement" was not passive receptivity, but an active declaration and pronouncement because of their faith in God.

11:14-16 The world to come will be better than this present world. These people were **foreigners and nomads,** but they were not seeking to return to their old homeland on earth. Instead, they **were looking for a better place, a heavenly homeland, the country of their own** that they saw in the distance (11:13). As they served God and walked with him in this land, they knew that this world was not their home, and they looked forward to that **better place.** Because of these people's faith, **God is not ashamed to be called their God** (see also Exodus 3:6), and **he has prepared a heavenly city for them** (see John 14:2ff).

11:17-18 Abraham trusted God's promises so much that when God commanded him to offer Isaac (his only son) **as a sacrifice,** Abraham obeyed. Abraham passed that test because he was willing to do as God asked. When God promised that many **descendants** would be born through Isaac, Abraham believed. But at God's command, Abraham brought Isaac to the altar, tied him up, placed him on the altar, and was about to sacrifice him, but God intervened at the last minute, sparing Isaac (Genesis 22:1-19). Although he didn't understand God's command, his obedience was prompt and complete.

11:19 Abraham had believed God's promise to bring a great nation out of Isaac; so **Abraham assumed that if Isaac died, God was able to bring him back to life again.** Abraham even had told his servant that the boy would come back alive (see Genesis 22:5). As a result of Abraham's faith, he figuratively received **his son back from the dead.** When Isaac was on the altar, he was as good as dead, but God spared him and restored him to Abraham.

11:20 Other patriarchs are discussed in 11:20-22. **It was by faith that Isaac blessed his two sons, Jacob and Esau.** God chose the younger son, Jacob, to continue the fulfillment of his promise to Abraham (see Genesis 25–36 for the story of Esau; Jacob's story continues to the end of Genesis). The ancient story of deception, greed, birthright, and blessing is of no concern here. Verses 20-21 focus on the "blessing" conferred by aged fathers on their sons. Because of deception, Isaac blessed Jacob (the younger son) instead of Esau, but this would have occurred anyway, for that was God's plan. Esau also received a blessing. The point is that Isaac **had confidence in what God was going to do in the future.**

11:21 Isaac had blessed Jacob and Esau; Jacob's sons had become the fathers of Israel's twelve tribes. Jacob, when he was **old and dying,** believed the promise to Abraham and **blessed** all of his sons, but

also two of his grandsons—**each of Joseph's sons** (Genesis 48:1-22). As noted in Isaac's case, Jacob blessed "out of order"; that is, he blessed the younger son over the older, **by faith,** realizing that it was God's plan. This blessing was directed by God.

11:22 Joseph, one of Jacob's sons, was sold into slavery by his jealous brothers (Genesis 37). Eventually, Joseph was sold again—this time to an official of the pharaoh of Egypt. Because of Joseph's faithfulness to God, he was promoted to a top-ranking position in Egypt. Although Joseph could have used that position to build a personal empire, he remembered God's promise to Abraham. After he had been reconciled to his brothers, Joseph brought his family to be near him. Joseph believed God's promise that **the people of Israel** would leave **Egypt** and return to Canaan. **He was so sure of it that he commanded them to carry his bones with them when they left,** so that he could be buried in the Promised Land (Genesis 50:24-25; Exodus 13:19; Joshua 24:32). Like Isaac, Joseph gave these instructions **when he was about to die.** Even on his deathbed, Joseph persevered in his faith, looking forward to the promises God had made.

11:23 Moses' parents are listed among these great people of faith. Through their faith they recognized that God's hand was on Moses and that he was **an unusual child** (see Exodus 2; 12; 14). Moses' parents disobeyed the king by faith, not being **afraid of what the king might do** to them if he discovered that they had been hiding their child for **three months.** Pharaoh had commanded that all male children born to the Hebrew slaves were to be killed. God used these parents' courageous act to place their son, the Hebrew of his choice, in the house of Pharaoh.

11:24-25 Moses' great faith was also revealed through his difficult decision. Through God's providence, Moses was raised by **Pharaoh's daughter** as a member of Pharaoh's own household (Exodus 1–2)! Although Moses had been given a great Egyptian education, wealth, and status, he rejected this heritage and **chose to share the oppression of God's people instead of enjoying the fleeting pleasures of sin.** Moses knew he could not participate in a comfortable and easy life while his fellow Hebrews were enslaved. Because of his faith, Moses knew that earthly comfort was not the ultimate purpose of his life.

11:26-27 Moses' great secret was that he looked ahead to the fulfillment of God's promises. Moses illustrates that **faith** requires individuals to put their own desires aside for the sake of Christ. He was motivated by **looking ahead to the great reward**

that God would give him. Since this reward would come from his Lord, Moses was willing to **suffer for the sake of the Messiah.** Although Moses did not personally know Jesus Christ, Moses suffered for the sake of doing God's will and for the sake of proclaiming God's way of redemption to the Hebrews; thus, this passage speaks of Moses' suffering for the sake of the Messiah. Because God's history of salvation and redemption continued until Christ, Moses' suffering is linked to the cause of Christ. Rather than make Egypt and this world his home, Moses **left the land of Egypt** and **kept right on going because he kept his eyes on the one who is invisible.** By faith, he was certain of what he could not see (11:1).

11:28 Moses' faith encouraged him to be God's spokesman to the Hebrews. Through this **faith, Moses commanded the people of Israel to keep the Passover.** This incident occurred as the last of a series of plagues that devastated Egypt. The Hebrews followed God's instructions, given through Moses, **to sprinkle blood on the doorposts so that the angel of death would not kill their firstborn sons.** The "blood" was from a lamb slain as part of the Passover meal. That night the firstborn son of every family who did not have blood on the doorposts was killed. The lamb had to be killed in order to get the blood that would protect them. (This foreshadowed the blood of Christ, the Lamb of God, who gave his blood for the sins of all people.)

11:29 **The people of Israel** leaving Egypt provide the next example of faith. **It was by faith** that they **went right through the Red Sea as though they were on dry ground.** The sight of the Red Sea parting and the requirement to walk into the seabed between walls of water must have been terrifying. But through Moses' leadership and their own faith, the people of Israel walked ahead and were delivered from Egypt.

As the people of Israel took the path through the Red Sea, the **Egyptians** followed, but not in faith. As a result, **all** the soldiers in the army **drowned** (see Exodus 14:5-31). This example of the Egyptians would be a warning to those who considered drifting from Christ. God severely punishes those who do not live by faith in him. Those who walk in faith, even into "seas" of difficulty or fear, will find their faith rewarded.

11:30 The wilderness wandering of the Israelites is skipped because it did not demonstrate the faith of the Israelites. In fact, Hebrews 3–4 points out that the people did not exercise faith during this time and therefore received God's punishment.

After the wandering, however, the people

exercised **faith** and obeyed God when they **marched around Jericho seven days, and the walls came crashing down.** The command to march around the city for seven days must have seemed ridiculous (see Joshua 6), but the people believed God and followed his instructions. Their faith encouraged them to obey God. When they obeyed God, they won their first victory.

11:31 When Joshua planned the conquest of Jericho, he sent **spies** to investigate the fortifications of the city. The spies met **Rahab,** who hid them. Rahab is an odd entry in this "hall of faith" because she was a Gentile and a **prostitute** (read the story in Joshua 2 and 6). But she demonstrated her faith in God by welcoming the spies and by trusting God to spare her and her family when the city was destroyed (Joshua 2:9, 11). Rahab's faith was rewarded: she and her family were saved. Even more important, she became an ancestor of Jesus. We read her name in Matthew 1:5—she was the mother of Boaz. Rahab's faith, despite her past sins, is contrasted with those who refused to turn to God and obey him.

11:32-35 The roll call of heroes continues. The Old Testament records the lives of many people who experienced great victories; a few are selected for mention here. None of these people were perfect; in fact, many of their sins are recorded in the Old Testament. But these were among those who believed in God:

- **Gideon,** one of Israel's judges, was known for conquering the Midianite army with only three hundred men who were armed with trumpets and jars (Judges 6:11–8:35).
- **Barak** served with Deborah (another judge of Israel) in conquering the army of General Sisera from Hazor (Judges 4:4-23).
- **Samson,** another judge, was a mighty warrior against God's enemies, the Philistines (Judges 13–16).
- **Jephthah,** still another judge, delivered Israel from the Ammonites (Judges 11:1-33).
- **David,** the beloved king of Israel and a great warrior, brought peace to Israel, defeating all of his enemies.
- **Samuel,** the last judge of Israel, was a very wise leader. He also was a prophet. Samuel, along with **all the prophets,** served God selflessly as they conveyed God's words to an often rebellious people.

These people demonstrated that faith will accomplish much:

- They **overthrew kingdoms.** Throughout their years in the Promised Land, the Israelites had great leaders who brought victory against their enemies. People such as Joshua, all of the judges, and King David were great warriors.

- They **ruled with justice.** Many of the judges, as well as leaders such as Nehemiah, administered justice to the people.
- They **received what God had promised.** Some people actually did see the fulfillment of some of God's promises, such as possession of the Promised Land.
- They **shut the mouths of lions.** Daniel was saved from the mouths of lions (Daniel 6). This statement could also refer to Samson (Judges 14:6) or to David (1 Samuel 17:34-35).
- They **quenched the flames.** Shadrach, Meshach, and Abednego were kept from harm in the furious flames of a fiery furnace (Daniel 3).
- They **escaped death by the edge of the sword.** Elijah (1 Kings 19:2-8) and Jeremiah (Jeremiah 36:19, 26) had this experience.
- Their **weakness was turned to strength.** Hezekiah was one who regained strength after sickness (2 Kings 20).
- They **became strong in battle and put whole armies to flight.** This refers to Joshua, many of Israel's judges, King Saul, and King David.
- Some even **received their loved ones back again from death.** The widow from Zarephath received her son back from the dead because of Elijah (1 Kings 17:17-24), and so did the Shunammite woman, through Elisha (2 Kings 4:8-37).

We, too, can experience victory through faith in Christ. We may have experiences similar to those of the Old Testament saints; more likely, however, our victories will be directly related to the role God wants us to play. Your life may not include the kinds of dramatic events recorded here, but it surely includes moments where faith is tested. Give testimony to those moments, publicly and honestly, and thereby encourage the faith of others.

While the above examples mention great victory—there is a victory that may not seem so. Other believers **were tortured, preferring to die rather than turn from God.** These faithful people experienced the blessings and endured persecution because they **placed their hope in the resurrection.** These people lived by faith because they knew that gaining the world and achieving this world's success was not their objective. They waited for a better life that would begin after death. This promise of a better life encouraged them during persecution and other difficulties.

11:36-38 These descriptions could apply to many people who lived by faith—including some who were part of the community of the original readers of this epistle. Many Christians were persecuted and punished for their faith. They were:

- **mocked**—like Elisha (2 Kings 2:23-25), Nehemiah (Nehemiah 2:19; 4:1), and Jeremiah (Jeremiah 18:12).
- **cut open with whips**—like Jeremiah (Jeremiah 37:15).
- **chained in dungeons**—like Joseph (Genesis 40:15), Samson (Judges 16:21), Micaiah (1 Kings 22:26-27), Hanani (1 Chronicles 16:10), and Jeremiah (Jeremiah 37:16; 38:6).
- killed **by stoning**—like Zechariah (1 Chronicles 24:20-21); according to Jerome, Jeremiah was stoned at the hands of Jewish Egyptians because he denounced their idolatry.
- killed by being **sawed in half**—like Isaiah, presumably. Although we do not know for sure, tradition (from the apocryphal book, The Ascension of Isaiah, chapters 1-5) says that the prophet Isaiah was sawed in half at the command of King Manasseh because Isaiah had predicted the destruction of the temple. Isaiah had at first escaped and hid in the trunk of a tree while in the hill country. Manassah supposedly had the tree sawed in half with Isaiah in it.
- **killed with the sword**—although some prophets did escape death by the sword, others did not (see 1 Kings 19:10).

Many of God's followers who lived before Christ and many who have lived after Christ have been persecuted. Their clothing was the **skins of sheep and goats.** Many faced being **hungry, oppressed, and mistreated.** Some had to wander and hide in the wilderness. Despite their difficult lot, the writer of Hebrews claims that **they were too good for this world.** These people were great men and women of faith.

11:39 All of the above people mentioned by name and those alluded to **received God's approval because of their faith.** These people looked forward to a better day and salvation, but **none of them received all that God had promised.** Of course, they saw some of God's promises fulfilled, but not the promises that referred to the new covenant and the promised eternal Kingdom. These people did not live to see the Kingdom arrive, but their future citizenship was secure there. Thus, they were able to endure suffering.

Hebrews 11 has been called faith's "hall of fame." No doubt the author surprised his readers by this conclusion: these mighty Jewish heroes did not receive God's full reward because they died before Christ came. In God's plan, they and the Christian believers (who were also enduring much testing) would be rewarded together.

11:40 The **far better things** that God has **in mind** refers to the new covenant. The forefathers did not receive this; rather, it is experienced by those who live after the death and resurrection of Christ, for he is the one who introduced the new covenant and the new promises (see commentary on 1:2).

There is a solidarity among believers (see 12:23). Old and New Testament believers will receive **the prize** together. Not only are we one in the body of Christ with all those alive, but we are also one with all those who ever lived. One day all believers will share in the promised blessing with Christ. We will then be complete and perfect in him.

HEBREWS 12

GOD'S DISCIPLINE PROVES HIS LOVE / 12:1-13

The book of Hebrews has, up until 10:19, described the superiority of Jesus Christ and of the new covenant. Hebrews 10:19 through 13:20 describes the church's responsibility in light of Christ's superiority. In chapter 11, faithful people from Jewish history are held up as examples of patient perseverance as they awaited the promises of God.

Chapter 12 contains clues regarding the situation of the believers to whom this letter was written. They have been encouraged not to drift away (2:1), but in this chapter we perceive a community weary of persecution, struggling to stay strong in an increasingly hostile environment, but weakening perhaps to the point of giving up and turning away from their faith.

12:1 The faithful believers throughout the centuries (chapter 11) now stand as **a huge crowd of witnesses to the life of faith.** They do not "witness" as if they were merely spectators, looking down from heaven and watching believers' lives; instead, they witness through the historical record of their faithfulness that constantly encourages those who follow them. These great believers' lives, examples, and faithfulness in God, without seeing his promises, speak to all believers of the rewards of staying in "the race." This metaphor is of a marathon, a test of stamina and commitment, an apt description of the lives of these suffering believers.

The first step of preparation to run the race requires that the racers **strip off every weight** that might slow them down. Christians must be "spiritually trim" and able to run the race unencumbered (see 1 Corinthians 9:25; 2 Timothy 2:3-4). Many "weights" may not be necessarily sinful acts, but could be things that hold us back, such as use of time, some forms of entertainment, or certain relationships. But it is **especially** important to strip off **the sin that so easily hinders our progress.** Sins such as greed, pride, arrogance, lust, gossip, dishonesty, and stealing can cause believers to drift off spiritual course. Then they must **run with endurance the race that God has set before** them. They do not select the course; God marks it out.

12:2 Jesus, our example, perfectly finished his race. Because he stands at the finished line, Christians should keep their **eyes on** him, looking away from other distractions or options. It is upon him that **our faith depends from start to finish.** Jesus is the first who obeyed God perfectly and thus began the new covenant (see also 2:10). He set the course of faith, ran the race first (6:20), and now waits for us to join him at the end, encouraging us all the way. He is also the one who brings us to our intended goal because he was made the perfect High Priest through suffering and obedience (see 2:10, 5:8). He **was willing to die a shameful death on the cross.** Yet Jesus endured all this suffering on account of **the joy he knew would be his afterward.** He kept his eyes focused on the goal of his appointed course, the accomplishment of his priestly work, and his seat **beside God's throne in heaven.** Knowing that a great reward was coming for God's people gave Jesus great joy. He did not look at his earthly discomforts, but he kept his eyes on the spiritual, invisible realities. Like Christ, we should persevere in times of suffering, looking to Christ as our model and concentrating on our heavenly destination.

12:3 When these believers were tempted to focus on their trials, even to the point of considering renouncing their faith, Hebrews encouraged them to **think about all he endured when sinful people did such terrible things to him.** Christ was ridiculed, whipped, beaten, spit upon, and crucified. Even so, he did not give in to fatigue, discouragement, or despair.

By focusing on Christ and what he did on our behalf, we won't **become weary and give up.** Trials can cause us to become discouraged and even to despair. Facing hardship and discouragement, we must not lose sight of the big picture. We are not alone; Jesus stands with us. Many have endured far more difficult circumstances than we have experienced. Suffering trains us for Christian maturity, developing our patience and making our final victory sweet.

12:4 Here we find a clue about the present situation of the readers in that the writer mentions their **struggle against sin.** This "struggle" refers not to personal struggles against temptation, but rather to their struggle against sinful people. Just as Christ struggled against sinful people (12:3), so Christians struggle against opposition from hostile nonbelievers and sometimes even from fellow believers. During their struggle, the Jewish Christians had **not yet given** their **lives.** These readers were facing difficult times of persecution, but none of them had yet died for their faith. As difficult as these times were, they did not compare with the difficulties that Christ faced.

12:5-6 Difficult times may come as a result of God's discipline. In fact, discipline is so important that the writer explains it as the normal experience of believers. The believers should have remembered the words of Proverbs 3:11-12, which say, **My child, don't ignore it when the Lord disciplines you, and don't be discouraged when he corrects you. For the Lord disciplines those he loves, and he punishes those he accepts as his children.** He cares about us enough to help us mature. Like a loving father, he wants us to stay away from what would hurt us and to move along the path toward maturity. Sometimes that involves discipline.

12:7-8 Because God promises to discipline his children, believers must **endure this divine discipline.** The only other choice would be to refuse to endure it, to pout, to grow depressed, or to give up completely. How much better to remember that, when

God disciplines you, he **is treating you as his own children.** Christians will experience God's discipline. Those who are not disciplined are **illegitimate and are not really his children after all.** Under Roman law, illegitimate children also did not receive any inheritance or recognition that came with being a genuine child. When we experience God's discipline, we can be encouraged that we really are God's children.

12:9 The analogy between human fathers and the heavenly Father figures often in Jesus' teachings (see Matthew 7:9-11; 21:28-31; Luke 15:11-32). Here **earthly fathers** are compared to **our heavenly Father.** Verses 7-8 describe the value of discipline and assert that all of God's children will endure discipline; verses 9-10 teach the parallel between God's discipline and earthly parental discipline. All people (or at least the vast majority) had human fathers **who disciplined** them. Rarely did that discipline occur out of cruelty; instead, loving fathers would discipline with the children's best interests in mind. As a result, they have our **respect.**

If we respected the discipline of our earthly parents, **should we not all the more cheerfully submit to the discipline of** our Father in heaven? Submission to God's discipline means not trying to wriggle out of it by making excuses or hardening our hearts; instead, it means allowing the discipline to drive us to our knees before God so that he can teach us the lessons he has for us. When we have this attitude toward God's discipline, we will **live forever**—referring to our ability to truly enjoy this life and to look forward to eternity with God.

12:10 Earthly fathers are imperfect. Sometimes they discipline when they shouldn't or in the wrong way, and sometimes they fail to discipline when they should. But most of them did **the best they knew how** for the **few years** during which they had responsibility for us. Their effort reminds us of the perfection of God's discipline—it is **always right and good for us** (Romans 8:28-29; 1 Corinthians 10:13).

God's discipline also means that **we will share in his holiness.** Discipline may not be enjoyed, but it brings great reward. Sharing in holiness refers to our growth. God's discipline helps Christians become more and more like Christ, mature and complete (see Matthew 5:48; 1 John 3:2).

12:11 While **no discipline is enjoyable while it is happening,** Christians can respond to it by remembering the end result of the discipline. Certainly discipline is **painful;** if it weren't, it would have little effect in combating sin or changing us from within. The result of discipline, however, makes the pain worthwhile: **a quiet harvest of**

right living. When discipline cleans up sin in our lives, it moves us on the pathway toward righteousness and holiness. The promised peace refers both to an inward tranquility and contentment (Philippians 4:11-12; James 1:4) in any circumstance (Philippians 4:6-7).

12:12-13 This passage vividly pictures God as a challenging coach who pushes us to our limits, encouraging us beyond what we think we can attain. **Tired hands** want to stop working. The Christians were at the point of sheer exhaustion; morale was low. Rather than concede defeat, Christians must **take a new grip** to make the effort and always be ready to endure. Discipline or persecution should not cause Christians to fear; instead, difficult times should encourage them to endure. Rather than dropping in defeat, Christians should **stand firm**—even when knees are weak and **legs** are **shaky**—in their confident expectation of Christ's return (see 10:37).

Most "paths" encountered in nature wind and dip along with the terrain. A **straight path,** however, has most likely been constructed by someone who took the effort to move the rocks, level out the holes, and even clear away little pebbles that would be hard on one's feet. This picture of making a straight path ties in with the "righteousness" (12:11) that results in the life of a person who has faced discipline and has worked to remove any stumbling blocks that would impede progress. Hard work obviously helps, but it has another benefit for those who follow behind. Some who follow may indeed be **weak and lame.** We can help them not to **stumble and fall** by encouraging them and working hard to remove the obstacles that may be in the path.

As said throughout this epistle, Christians have the responsibility to encourage one another and to help those who are weak. If the original readers were contemplating a return to Jewish practices, their example would prove discouraging to new Christians. Instead of running in a straight, clear path, they would be adding hindrances and obstacles to the already difficult trip. Believers must not live with only survival in mind—others will follow their example.

A CALL TO LISTEN TO GOD / 12:14-29

Believers have been encouraged to endure suffering as part of God's plan for them and to continue to walk with God in holiness and righteousness. They must also carry certain attitudes and responsibilities to people in this world—both fellow believers as well as nonbelievers (some of whom may even be their persecutors).

12:14 First, believers must **try to live in peace with everyone.** Believers are to have as peaceful relations as possible with their unbelieving neighbors and associates, as well as harmonious relationships within the church. Certainly they should not be the cause of dissension. Christian fellowship should be characterized by peace and building up one another (see 1 Thessalonians 5:11).

In addition to seeking peace, believers must also **seek to live a clean and holy life** (see also 12:10). "Holiness" means devoted or consecrated to God's service. In a practical way, our holiness means honoring God in how we treat others—friends, neighbors, spouse, children, even enemies—and in how we run our businesses, finances, etc. Holiness causes the behavior, thoughts, and attitudes of Christians to be different from unbelievers. Our holiness, provided for us by the death and resurrection of Christ, will allow us to **see the Lord** as he really is, when we go to be with him forever.

12:15 As believers deal with interpersonal relationships in the local church, they should **look after each other.** By doing so, **none . . . will miss out** on the special favor of God. The words "special favor" are also translated "grace," here referring to all the benefits that God has bestowed on his children. Believers should encourage each other to appropriate these blessings, for these will help them stand firm. Too often believers "miss out" because they are not aware of God's promises, teachings, or guidance.

The allusion to the **bitter root of unbelief** comes from the language of Deuteronomy 29:18-19. Moses cautioned that the day the Hebrews chose to turn from God, a root would be planted that would produce **poison.** If such a person assumes to have God's blessing and then proceeds to disobey, this plants an evil seed that begins to grow out of control, eventually yielding a crop of sorrow and pain. But believers can **watch out** that this doesn't happen. Christians should not allow people who undermine faith to remain in the church. Their influence may not be noticeable at first, but it will come (see also 2 Peter 2).

12:16-17 Though there is no mention of Esau's immorality in the Old Testament, certain Jews regarded his marriages to Hittite women as being **immoral** (Genesis 26:34-35; 28:49). Sexual immorality has no place among Christians and should not be tolerated in the church. God forbids sexual sin because he knows its power to destroy us physically and spiritually. No one should underestimate the power of sexual immorality. God wants to protect his people from damaging themselves and others.

Believers are also commanded to see that no one is **godless like Esau.** Esau did not follow the examples of those who kept their eyes focused on heavenly rewards (see chapter 11). Rather than take interest in his birthright, which had great spiritual value, he **traded his birthright as the oldest son for a single meal** (see Genesis 25). A birthright was a special honor given to the first-born son. By trading his birthright, Esau showed complete disregard for the spiritual blessings that would have come his way if he had kept it. Because of this attitude, **when he wanted his father's blessing, he was rejected . . . it was too late.** Esau's sin was impulsiveness and complete disregard for his spiritual heritage. Just as Esau had little regard for spiritual matters, the church should be on the lookout for people who join the church but have no real concern for spiritual matters.

Those who reject God's way will not be given a second chance when it comes time for others to inherit his spiritual blessing. No amount of pleading before God's throne will change his mind about the fate of those who rejected him while alive on earth.

12:18-21 This again contrasts the old and new covenants by contrasting the earthly Mount Sinai (12:18-21) and the heavenly Mount Zion (12:22-24).

The scene described in this passage comes from Exodus 19. As the Israelites were camped at the foot of **Mount Sinai,** God was preparing the nation for receiving his Ten Commandments. God commanded that no one, not even an animal, should touch the mountain under penalty of death (Exodus 19:12-13). The **fire, darkness, gloom, and whirlwind** describe the awesome scene on the mountain, for God himself descended there to speak with Moses (Exodus 19:18-21). A blazing fire engulfed the top half of the mountain; this illustrated the Lord's presence. The loud **trumpet blast** came from the mountain and caused the people to tremble (Exodus 19:16, 19). They **begged God to stop speaking** (Exodus 20:18-19). The fear caused the people to beg that Moses be the lone mediator. They thought they would die if God were to speak directly to them (see Deuteronomy 5:25-27).

The old covenant, with its display of God's awesome power, still was not superior to what God had planned in the new covenant. The old covenant caused only fear from the people; they begged that they would not have to approach God themselves. God, in turn, did not allow them to approach him. God has offered something new (12:22). Returning to this old way would be foolish.

12:22 Instead of coming to a threatening mountain of fear and death, **you have come to Mount Zion.** Mount Zion represents a new community and a new relationship with God, **the city of the living God, the heavenly Jerusalem** (described in Revelation 3:12; 21:2). Here believers live with God and can worship him without reserve. In this city, **thousands of angels in joyful assembly** continually worship God. The new Jerusalem is the future dwelling of the people of God. All Christians will have a new citizenship in God's future Kingdom. Everything will be new, pure, and secure.

12:23 Christians do not enter a covenant in which someone like Moses must go up the mountain to meet with God. Rather, we **have come to the assembly of God's firstborn children.** The **assembly** means the church or congregation, referring to the gathering of believers who have been called out by God for the special purpose of loving, obeying, and worshiping him. We are no longer separated from the angels, but join them in praising God. All believers are God's **firstborn,** for all are promised his inheritance (Ephesians 1:11).

As his children, our **names are written in heaven,** presumably in the Book of Life (Luke 10:20; Philippians 4:3; Revelation 3:5; 13:8; 17:8; 20:12, 15; 21:27). Christians are heavenly citizens, officially registered and recorded. Although Christians worship God in spirit now, one day they will take up residence in heaven and worship him face-to-face.

We do not need an intermediary; we **have come to God himself.** We have free access to God (4:16; 6:19-20; 7:25; 10:19-21). Because our names are written, we have no fear of this God **who is the judge of all people.** Although Christians will be judged (9:27), we do not need to fear it because Christ has taken our punishment. The judgment believers face will be for receiving rewards based on what we have done in our lives.

We can look forward to a glorious eternity, for we are promised that when we die, we will **come to the spirits of the redeemed in heaven who have now been made perfect. Spirits** refers to spiritual beings of people (see 12:9) but not angels, for believers have **been made perfect** by the Savior's death (12:2). This is the day we anticipate, when all believers will have been made complete and will have reached their fulfillment. At death, Christians reach the finish line of their race. At the end is not fear but joy, justice, God's favor, and eternal life in God's heavenly city.

12:24 Believers have also **come to Jesus, the one who mediates the new covenant between God and people.** The only access to God is through Jesus Christ, who is "the way" (John 14:6). This new covenant far surpasses the old covenant; no person who understood the new covenant could ever intelligently choose to revert to the old way. We come **to the sprinkled blood** because through it alone can we receive God's gracious forgiveness.

In contrast with Christ's redeeming blood, **the blood of Abel** is pictured as **crying out for vengeance.** Abel is referred to here because his sacrifice is the first one mentioned in the Bible and because it provided the impetus for the sacrifice system in the old covenant. Abel's blood cried out for vengeance; Christ's blood speaks a "better word," calling all people to repentance. Christ's death brought peace and hope. Christ's blood brought the end of the old covenant and sealed the new one.

12:25 If people refuse to follow God's new covenant, they reject his plan. But more than the plan, they reject God himself. To do so is final and tragic, so the writer again warns his readers: **See to it that you obey God, the one who is speaking to you.** This continues to reflect the awesome picture of Mount Sinai mentioned in 12:18-21. At that time, **the people of Israel** who **refused to listen to Moses did not escape** God's punishment. If they did not escape, and Moses was merely an **earthly messenger,** then **how terrible** is the **danger** of eternal punishment to those who **reject the One who speaks from heaven.**

12:26 When God gave the first covenant, **his voice shook the earth** (Exodus 19:18). Psalm 68:8 also describes an earthquake accompanying God's revelation at Mount Sinai. God promises that he will **once again . . . shake not only the earth but the heavens also** (quoting from Haggai 2:6). At the end of the world, God will shake the earth again. This shaking stands for another major cataclysm in the earth to go along with God's revelation to all the nations. This divine judgment will terrify those who have refused to listen to him and who face his judgment. But to

those who follow God and are members of the new covenant, this will be a moment of glorious expectation, as we wait for our King to return and set up his eternal Kingdom.

12:27 When God shakes the world again, he will do it for a final time. One day, God will shake this world, and it will come apart completely (Mark 13:31; 2 Peter 3:7). At that time, **things on earth** will be destroyed—the earth, the universe, animals, people, and everything else that can be seen. Only what belongs to God's Kingdom will be unshakable. These will **be left,** for they belong to the heavenly city.

Eventually the world will crumble, and only God's Kingdom will last. Those who follow Christ are part of this unshakable Kingdom, and they will withstand the shaking, sifting, and burning. When we feel unsure about the future, we can take confidence from these verses. No matter what happens here, our future is built on a solid foundation that cannot be destroyed. Don't put your confidence in what will be destroyed; instead, build your life on Christ and his unshakable Kingdom. (See Matthew 7:24-27 for the importance of building on a solid foundation.)

12:28 Because this world will one day disappear, faith concentrates on the heavenly promises. The future, unseen world is actually more real than this present one. This one can be shaken and destroyed, but believers **are receiving a kingdom that cannot be destroyed.** Christians receive it by God's grace, not through their own effort or by any means other than God's kindness. Because we have this kind of kingdom, we should **be thankful** and worship God **with holy fear and awe.** When we truly worship God, we do it all the time—not just in a Sunday morning worship service that has a few hymns, an offering, a sermon, and a time of prayer. True worship includes every action of every day. By obeying God, our lives become living sacrifices of worship (see Romans 12:1-2).

12:29 God is worthy of our thanks and worship because he **is a consuming fire.** This description may be taken from Deuteronomy 4:24. God reigns over and will destroy everything that is temporary. Everything that is imperfect and bound by time will end. Only the new covenant and those who are part of it will survive. There could hardly be a more startling conclusion to this letter for these Jewish Christian readers who were considering turning away from the faith. Failure to listen to God, refusing to accept all that he has done, will bring catastrophe.

HEBREWS 13

CONCLUDING WORDS / 13:1-25

After giving commands to pursue peace and holiness (12:14-29), the book of Hebrews presents three commands that deal with the social life of a Christian (13:1-3). This final chapter presents a series of exhortations regarding believers' social, private, and religious lives. The readers are encouraged to make a final break with Judaism. The changeless Christ remains both our great High Priest and the perfect sacrifice. All people need the salvation available only through the Lord Jesus.

13:1 The first command is: **continue to love each other with true Christian love.** The early Christians faced persecution and hatred from the world; hopefully, within the church and in the fellowship of believers, they should be able to find love and encouragement. The church ought to be a haven for believers. The command for believers to love one another was not new (see Leviticus 19:18; John 13:34-35). Believers are to love one another based on Jesus' sacrificial love for them. Such love brings people to Christ and will keep believers strong and united in a world hostile to God. Jesus was a living example of God's love, and we are to be living examples of Jesus' love (see also Romans 12:10; 1 Thessalonians 4:9; 1 Peter 1:22; 2 Peter 1:7).

13:2 The second command is to **show hospitality to strangers.** This kind of hospitality was important because inns of that day were expensive, as well as being centers for pagan practices and criminal activities. This hospitality also helped spread the gospel because traveling missionaries would be able to go to more places and minister to more people if they did not have to stay in inns. These "strangers" to be entertained, however, were *not* to be people who worked against God's Kingdom; that is, believers were not to welcome false teachers into their homes (2 John 10-11; 3 John 5-9).

A further encouragement to this kind of hospitality comes from the biblical record that, through their hospitality, some have **entertained angels without realizing it.** This happened to Abraham (Genesis 18:1-14) and Lot (Genesis 19:1-3). That hospitality was given to and received by angels shows the importance of the hospitality Christians ought to give one another. It is better to offer hospitality generously than to miss the chance to entertain angels.

13:3 The third command focuses on **those in prison.** This instruction was already alluded to in 10:32-34. Believers are to have empathy for prisoners, especially for (but not limited to) Christians imprisoned for their faith. Jesus said that his followers would represent him as they visited people in prison (Matthew 25:36). Others who were **mistreated**—beaten, robbed, assaulted, humiliated—also needed to be remembered. Believers must **suffer with them** and **share** their **sorrow** (see also 1 Corinthians 12:26; 2 Timothy 1:16).

13:4 In addition to commands for the social life of Christians (13:1-3), Hebrews also includes commands for private lives. Believers had a responsibility to **give honor to marriage, and remain faithful to one another in marriage.** This would include promises to love continually, to remain faithful in thought, attitude, and action, and to support and provide for each other.

Hebrews presents two specific ways to "remain faithful." Believers can stay away from **immoral** behavior and **adultery.** Immorality and adultery have split marriages for thousands of years. God's commands against such actions (given for people's own good) have been in place for just as long (see Exodus 20:14, 17; Job 24:15-24; Proverbs 5:15-23). Christians, however, are to maintain high standards (Matthew 5:27-28). Hebrews makes the point that even if no consequences are seen right away, promiscuous people will incur God's wrath—**God will surely judge** them.

13:5 Another command for the believers' private lives concerned material needs: **Stay away from the love of money.** This was also commanded by Jesus (Matthew 6:24; Luke 16:13) and Paul (1 Timothy 3:3; 6:10). Materialistic cravings and greed are a great evil because they show dependence on money rather than on Christ. Materialism is the antithesis of chapters 11–12, where a life pursuing heavenly rather than earthly rewards is extolled. Materialism also demonstrates that someone cares more about items they can see than about spiritual promises that they cannot presently see.

The antidote to greed is contentment, so the writer says, **be satisfied with what you have.** Again, this teaching was given by Jesus (Matthew 6:31-34) and Paul (Philippians 4:11; 1 Timothy 6:6). Our contentment should be in what Christ gives, not in what we can achieve for ourselves. Money cannot save a soul from God's punishment. Money cannot even bring contentment. Where money fails, God does not. **For God has said,** "I will never fail you. I will never forsake you." When faith reminds us that God is in control, we remember that we have all we need.

13:6 Money cannot give security (13:5); only God can truly help us. While we are not guaranteed to have earthly possessions, we are guaranteed that God is our helper. He watches over his people and gives them what they need. Every believer, along with the psalmist (see Psalm 118:6), **can say with confidence** that **the Lord is my helper.** It must have been wonderful for these Jewish believers to realize that, when they became believers, the promises in the psalms could still be used as songs of praise!

When we are confident that God is our helper, we need **not be afraid.** If the king of the universe is on our side, **what can mere mortals do?** Granted, humans can take our possessions, mistreat us, throw us into prison, or even kill us. Humans cannot hurt our souls or affect our salvation (Matthew 10:28). With God as our helper, we truly have nothing to fear!

13:7 Next follows instructions about the religious life of his readers (see also 13:17, 24). Their religious **leaders** had provided examples for others to follow. The leaders referred to here were most likely the founding Christians, the elders of the group **who first taught** them **the word of God.** Although these leaders had died, their influence remained, as evidenced by the existence of the communities of believers. These leaders had copied Christ's example and the example of the great crowd of witnesses (12:1-2). Because they had trusted the Lord and done good, their lives were worth imitating.

13:8 Though times and leaders change, Jesus Christ does not. **Jesus Christ is the same** all the time. He served faithfully **yesterday** (dying on the cross to make atonement for our sins; see 2:17-18). He serves faithfully **today** (interceding for us at the right hand of God; see 4:14-16; 7:25). He will

remain faithful **forever.** Because of what he has done in the past and what he does in the present, he is sufficient for any need any believer will ever have. (See also 1:12.)

Human leaders have much to teach us, and we can learn much from emulating them (13:7), but we must keep our eyes on Christ, our ultimate leader. Unlike any human leaders, he will never change. Christ has been and will be the same forever. In a changing world we can trust our unchanging Lord.

13:9 Since Christ never changes, neither can the new covenant that he initiated. Be careful **not to be attracted by strange, new ideas** (see 1 Timothy 4:16; 6:3; Titus 1:9). In order to do that, believers must be familiar with the correct teachings. Christians today have an advantage of having the entire Bible and Bible study tools. When we hear an interesting new doctrine, we should be sure to study it ourselves and become certain it is true.

Many "strange ideas" arose during the days of the early church. One of these concerned **ceremonial rules about food.** Apparently some false teachers had been teaching these Jewish converts that they still needed to keep the Old Testament ceremonial laws and rituals (such as not eating certain foods). But these laws were useless for conquering a person's evil thoughts and desires (Colossians 2:23). The believers' **spiritual strength** (referring to their inner selves) **comes from God's special favor,** not by the foods they did or did not eat. Laws could influence conduct, but they could not change the heart. The ceremonial foods might fulfill a ritual, but they **don't help those who follow them.** Lasting changes in conduct begin when the Holy Spirit lives in each person. Since God's approval is secured by grace, it was valueless to keep these ceremonial laws.

13:10-12 Returning to similar arguments used throughout the book, Hebrews again compares Christ and the new covenant with the old covenant. Here are further analogies between the Day of Atonement ceremony and Christ's once-for-all sacrifice on the cross (for more on the Day of Atonement, see commentary on chapters 9–10). We read how **the high priest brought the blood of animals into the Holy Place as a sacrifice for sin** (see 9:7). The new detail included here reminds the readers that **the bodies of the animals were burned outside the camp.** The priests could eat the meat of the sacrifices that were offered on a daily basis, but not on the Day of Atonement; on that day, the remainders of the slain animals were burned outside the camp.

In a similar way, **Jesus suffered and died**

outside the city gates (see Matthew 21:39; 27:31-33; John 19:20); this refers to Jesus' crucifixion, which occurred outside the city walls. However, Christ's sacrifice could **make his people holy by shedding his own blood.** Christ's sacrifice was final, once and for all. Those who still were holding on to the old covenant and its trappings (sacrifices, ceremonial foods) have no right to participate in the new covenant that Christ sealed with his death. People cannot partake of both covenants. This was an important point for the Hebrew Christians, who were considering practicing Jewish ceremonial laws in addition to their faith in Christ. To revert to Jewish practices in order to gain God's approval, these people would lose their right to participate in the new covenant.

13:13 When Christians suffer persecution, they join Christ in his suffering. When Christians suffer for the cause of Christ they **go out to him outside the camp and bear the disgrace he bore.** The original readers might experience disgrace because they seemed to be abandoning their Jewish roots, but they could not cling to their roots and still worship at the cross of Christ. The ridicule and persecution came from Jews who didn't believe in Jesus the Messiah. Most of the book of Hebrews explains how Christ is greater than the sacrificial system. Here is the practical implication of this lengthy argument: It may be necessary to leave the "camp" and suffer with Christ. They needed to move outside the safe confinement of their past, their traditions, and their ceremonies to live for Christ.

13:14 The reason given for joining the suffering of Christ is that **this world is not our home.** This is more than a passing point; it provides a key New Testament theme on our true citizenship (Philippians 3:19-21; 1 Peter 1:17; 2:11). We should not be so attached to our worldly possessions that we forget to obey Christ. Life on earth is temporary. It would not be appropriate for Christians to grow too comfortable here. Jobs, money, homes, and hobbies should not become the most important parts of their lives.

Instead, Christians should be like the heroes of faith discussed in chapter 11 and spend their lives **looking forward to our city in heaven, which is yet to come.** We should not be content or attached to this world, because all that we are and have here is temporary. Rather, we should eagerly expect the coming Kingdom. Only our relationship with God and our service to him will last. We shouldn't store our treasures here; we should store them in heaven (Matthew 6:19-21).

13:15 The need for blood sacrifices ended with Jesus' death on the cross. But Christians do have a sacrifice that they can bring **continually**—called here a **sacrifice of praise.** God wants us to offer ourselves, not animals, as living sacrifices—daily laying aside our own desires so that we can follow him. We do this out of gratitude that our sins have been forgiven. We do this **with Jesus' help** because he alone makes our sacrifices acceptable. By continually offering this sacrifice of praise, we proclaim **the glory of his name** and thereby show that we are loyal to him (see also Romans 12:1-2). Since these Jewish Christians, because of their belief in Jesus as the Messiah, no longer worshiped with other Jews, they could consider praise and acts of service their sacrifices. These were sacrifices that they could offer continually, anywhere, anytime.

13:16 Another "sacrifice" that pleases God focuses on service to others. Acts of kindness and sharing our resources are **very pleasing to God,** even when they go unnoticed. In times of persecution especially, Christians depend on one another (see 10:24; 13:20). Doing **good** and a willingness **to share with those in need** strikes a blow at the self-centeredness of our times. Believers experience fellowship with other believers when they make their resources available to those in need.

13:17 Members in the church have the responsibility to **obey** their **spiritual leaders.** While 13:7 referred to past leaders who had died, this verse refers to the present leaders in the various congregations. Wise and God-honoring leaders watch over the church and have the best in mind for their followers. These leaders are concerned for the deepest needs of those in their fellowship. These leaders also take on great responsibility to **watch over** the **souls** of those in their congregations. **They are accountable to God.** Because of this grave responsibility, cooperative followers can greatly ease the burden of leadership. Too many believers create problems and tension for their leaders through endless complaints and interpersonal conflicts. How welcome would cheerfulness, helpfulness, and loyalty be to your leaders!

13:18-19 Apparently the writer of this letter, like his readers, had come face-to-face with persecution. The writer says he and his companions had done nothing wrong—**our conscience is clear**—but requests prayers in order to continue **to live honorably.** Because of this purity before God and purity of motivation, the writer could freely request prayer from fellow believers. In fact, he depended on it. This offers a clue that the writer of Hebrews may have been a former leader of the church who was traveling in another area. This leader requested prayer to **come back** to the readers soon. We do not know what prevented the writer from returning, but it was apparently significant. Whatever the problem was, the writer depended on the support of this church by asking for their prayers.

13:20-21 This doxology describes God as **the God of peace.** This characteristic of God may have been included to promote harmony and to heal the disunity among the readers. Perhaps the writer wanted to encourage those whose faith was wavering due to persecution or to stress the peace between people and God that Jesus established through the Cross (such peace should carry over among God's people).

God **brought again from the dead our Lord Jesus.** That fact proves that Jesus was an effective sacrifice and High Priest and is superior to anyone or anything in the old covenant. In fact, without the Resurrection, there would be no new covenant. The resurrection of Jesus from the dead is the central fact of Christian history. Called here, **the great Shepherd of the sheep,** Christ had laid down his life for the sheep (John 10:11). The new and **everlasting covenant** had been **signed with his blood.**

This closing prayer contains two requests: first, that God would **equip** the believers **with all** they would **need for doing his will** (for more on good works, see 10:24 and 13:16); second, that God would **produce in** them **all that is pleasing to him.** They had begun to do works that accompanied their salvation (6:9-10), but now they needed to mature in this area. So the writer prays for God to perfect them.

These verses (which borrow in part from Isaiah 63:10-14 and Zechariah 11:4 in the Septuagint) include two significant results of Christ's death and resurrection: (1) God works in us to make us the kind of people who will please him; and (2) God equips us to do the kind of work that will please him. Let God change you from within and then use you to help others.

13:22 This letter includes its share of commands, appeals, rebukes, and warnings. Readers are encouraged to take it all seriously, but in the right spirit, realizing that the writer loves them and has only their best in mind. The letter has encouraged the readers to understand Christ's role as priest and understand that the new covenant is superior to the old covenant. These important words could make the difference between their holding on to

Christ or turning away—the difference, literally, between eternal life and eternal death. So the writer urged his readers to **please listen carefully.**

13:23 Other than this statement, the New Testament does not record Timothy's imprisonment. He may have been imprisoned in Rome or Ephesus. This is probably the same **Timothy** who was the disciple of Paul, and to whom Paul wrote two letters that now appear in the New Testament. (For more about Timothy, see the Introduction to Paul's letter to 1 Timothy.)

Timothy traveled the Empire with Paul, serving as his assistant and sometimes as his emissary. Timothy's name is included as cosender on many of Paul's letters to the churches. Timothy became an important leader in the early church, continuing the ministry of the word after Paul's death. Apparently he, too, was put **in jail** at one point but was released. The writer knew Timothy, and if Timothy arrived in time, the writer would **bring him** to see the readers.

13:24-25 Most New Testament letters end with greetings from the writer to others in the church and from the Christians in one locality to the Christians receiving the letter. So this letter offers greetings from the writer to the **leaders and to the other believers.** At the time of this letter, most churches still met in people's homes. These house churches, situated in different localities, needed to be encouraged about their unity with all other believers. The call to greet all the leaders and all of God's people underscored the importance of unity. The writer, in turn, sent **greetings** from **the Christians from Italy.**

A final benediction ends the letter: **May God's grace be with you all.** Concluding with "grace" is an appropriate ending for this letter. God's approval could not be won through ceremonies or through following the old covenant. Rather, God's grace comes through the new covenant.

Hebrews is a call to Christian maturity. It was addressed to first-century Jewish Christians, but it applies to Christians of any age or background. Christian maturity includes making Christ the beginning and the end of our faith. To grow in maturity, we must center our lives on him, not depending on religious ritual, not falling back into sin, not trusting in ourselves, and not letting anything come between us and Christ. Christ is sufficient and superior.

JAMES

INTRODUCTION

The letter from James reads like a Monday morning office memo. From the beginning, he expects his readers to put their faith into action. His challenges are not dated. James addresses practical issues that are as current as this morning's newspaper. The faith that Christians claim must be demonstrated in all the situations and circumstances of life—at work, at home, in the neighborhood, in church. Trials and hardships are not to be seen as hindrances to faith, but as opportunities to exercise healthy faith. Knowing God's word is not enough. That knowledge must be applied to our everyday lives. Real faith is the application of God's truth to ourselves.

AUTHOR

James, son of Joseph and half-brother of Jesus, also known as "James the Just."

What would it have been like to have Jesus in the family? Would Mary and Joseph wonder about their parental responsibilities? Would younger brothers and sisters be jealous, resentful, or awestruck? Would these children have seen anything special about their eldest sibling? Because there is so little information in Scripture about Jesus' early years, we can only speculate about what it would be like to have Jesus as a son or as an older brother. But such was the experience of James, the author of this book that bears his name.

We know very little about the relationship between James and Jesus. We do know, however, that the townsfolk who saw Jesus as a boy and young man rejected his claim to be the Messiah and were amazed at his wisdom and miraculous powers (Matthew 13:53-58). Evidently, Jesus had kept a low profile in Nazareth. These skeptical neighbors included James in their description of Jesus' family: "'He's just a carpenter's son, and we know Mary, his mother, and his brothers—James, Joseph, Simon, and Judas. All his sisters live right here among us. What makes him so great?'" (Matthew 13:55-56; see also Mark 6:1-6).

At one point in Jesus' ministry, his "family" tried to stop him and "take him home" (Mark 3:21); presumably James was one of the family members who claimed that Jesus was "out of his mind."

Certainly Mary and Joseph knew who Jesus was. After all, they had heard the angels predict his miraculous conception (Matthew 1:18-25; Luke 1:38-56), and they had been present at his birth (Luke 2:1-7). In fact, "Mary quietly treasured these things in her heart" (Luke 2:19). They also had seen the boy Jesus grow and mature, with profound wisdom beyond his years (Luke 2:40, 49-52). Surely Mary and Joseph would have explained Jesus' true identity to the rest of the family. But James and the others (including Jude, the author of the book of Jude) remained unconvinced. John explains, "For even his brothers didn't believe in him" (John 7:5).

Yet, just a few years after that incident, James became the leader of the church in Jerusalem (Acts 12:17). We don't know how James attained that important position, though Clement of Alexandria wrote that he was chosen for the office by Peter and John; but clearly he was the leader. In fact, when controversy over Gentile believers threatened to divide the church, Barnabas and Paul met with the elders and apostles in Jerusalem and submitted to their authority with James as the moderator, spokesman, and announcer of the final decision (Acts 15:1-21).

Later, just before Paul's arrest, Paul brought money that he had collected for the church in Jerusalem on his third missionary journey to James and the rest of the elders and "gave a detailed account of the things God had accomplished among the Gentiles through his ministry" (Acts 21:19).

That this James is the James mentioned earlier as Jesus' brother is confirmed by Paul in Galatians 1:18-19: "It was not until three years later that I finally went to Jerusalem for a visit with Peter and stayed there with him for fifteen days. And the only other apostle I met at that time was James, our Lord's brother." Later Paul adds, "In fact, James, Peter, and John, who were known as pillars of the church, recognized the gift God had given me, and they accepted Barnabas and me as their coworkers. They encouraged us to keep preaching to the Gentiles, while they continued their work with the Jews" (Galatians 2:9).

What changed James from a skeptical younger brother to a committed follower of Jesus and outspoken leader of the church? He saw his brother alive—he saw the risen Christ!

Writing to the Corinthians, Paul lists the eyewitnesses to the Resurrection: "I passed on to you what was most important and what had also been passed on to me—that Christ died for our sins, just as the Scriptures said. He was buried, and he was raised from the dead on the third day, as the Scriptures said. He was seen by Peter and then by the twelve apostles. After that, he was seen by more than five hundred of his followers at one time, most of whom are still alive, though some have died by now. Then he was seen by James and later by all the apostles. Last of all, I saw him, too, long after the others, as though I had been born at the wrong time" (1 Corinthians 15:3-8). Jesus appeared personally to his brother James. Imagine that reunion! Then, after the Ascension, we find James with the apostles, Mary, and others, praying continually (Acts 1:12-14) and waiting for the Holy Spirit as Jesus had told them to do (Acts 1:4-5).

This is James who describes himself as "a slave of God and of the Lord Jesus Christ" (1:1) and as a believer "in our glorious Lord Jesus Christ" (2:1). He is a man whose life was changed by Christ: a sibling turned servant; an antagonist turned apologist; a passive observer turned passionate follower.

What a wonderful opportunity we have, to read and study this book authored by God and written by one who had intimate contact with Jesus, who was an eyewitness to the ministry of Jesus and the beginnings of the church as recorded in the Gospels and in Acts.

It should be noted that other men named James are mentioned in the New Testament, and each one, at various times, has been proposed as a possible author of this book. These men include:

A CALL TO PERSEVERE / 10:19-39

The first section, 1:1–10:18, developed the superiority of Christ. The second section, 10:19–13:25, develops the church's responsibility to live in faith. The author applies the doctrines that have been discussed up to this point.

10:19-20 Through his death on our behalf, believers **can boldly enter heaven's Most Holy Place because of the blood of Jesus.** Believers have access to the heavenly sanctuary; that is, they have free access to God. Christ now sits at God's right hand as our High Priest in this heavenly sanctuary (see 6:19-20; 8:1-2; 9:11-12, 24). The **blood** refers to Jesus giving his life for us (see 9:12, 14; 10:19, 29; 12:24; 13:12, 20). This encouragement for boldness is remarkable because, under the old covenant, the **Most Holy Place** was sealed from view by **the sacred curtain.** But Jesus' death in his human body **opened up** access to God. When Jesus died on the cross, the curtain in the Temple (which had replaced the Tabernacle) tore from top to bottom (Mark 15:38), thereby unveiling the glorious reality that believers now have free access to God. **By means of his death,** Jesus opened **the new, life-giving way.** He truly was "the way" itself (John 14:6).

10:21-22 What Christ has done for Christians is the focus of the next three exhortations—the first dealing with their faith in God (10:21-22), the second dealing with their hope in their salvation (10:23), and the third dealing with their love for each other (10:24-25).

Because of believers' relationship with this **great High Priest,** they can **go right into the presence of God.** The author encourages readers to come into God's presence with these characteristics:

True hearts. We come not halfheartedly or with improper motives or pretense, but with pure, undivided, and sincere worship.

Fully trusting him. Christians can approach God boldly, free from guilt because of the work of Jesus Christ. We can go to God without doubting, trusting that he will hear and answer us.

Evil consciences . . . sprinkled with Christ's blood to make us clean. This is sacrificial language. Under the new covenant, hearts and consciences are cleansed (see 9:14). This differed from the old covenant in that it completely cleansed the conscience, not partially or temporarily.

Our bodies . . . washed with pure water. The imagery of an external action actually pictures an inward cleansing. Just as baptism is an outward sign that represents the purification

that Christ does inside us, so this washing speaks of an internal cleansing from sin. Once cleansed, Christians can approach God.

10:23 The readers were encouraged to **hold tightly to the hope,** referring both to what they believe about God and what they say to others. When they were converted and baptized, early Christians confessed what they believed about Christ. Here they were told to hold on to what they had previously claimed **without wavering.** Christians had good reason to hold on to their confession: **God can be trusted to keep his promise.** God made the promise; because God is faithful, we know that what he promised will come to pass.

10:24-25 This word **encourage** means to "stimulate strongly," "arouse," or "incite to riot." Christians need to spur or stimulate each other in two areas: (1) **Love**—not an emotion but a choice to act regardless of our feelings. We are to act lovingly toward other believers. (2) **Good deeds**—works done for the good of others.

Believers also must **not neglect meeting together.** Some Christians (then as well as today) were not going to the church meetings. For whatever reason, these believers were trying to survive on their own. To withdraw from corporate strength is to invite disaster, like a soldier in battle who lags behind the rest of his platoon and becomes an easy target.

Finally, believers must **encourage and warn each other.** These words reveal that Christians are responsible for each other. Christians cannot be concerned just for their own spiritual well-being; they must also encourage others to keep fervent in their love and active in their service to God. This encouragement should happen **especially now that the day of his coming back again is drawing near.** This "day" (Christ's return) is guaranteed; Christ will return. Through the centuries, many Christians have been discouraged because they believed that Christ should have already returned. But Christ has not forgotten, and he has not changed his plans. Christians must live as if the Lord will come back at any moment. Christ must not find us lax in our devotion and preparation.

10:26 This is the second great warning against apostasy (see the first one in 6:4-6). For those who **have received a full knowledge of the truth** of the

- James, the son of Zebedee and brother of John (see Mark 1:19). This James belonged to the inner circle of disciples (with John and Peter). Certainly he would have had the prominence to be a biblical author. But he was executed by Herod in A.D. 44 (Acts 12:2), too early for the writing of this book.
- James, the son of Alphaeus. This James was also one of the original twelve disciples. He is listed as an apostle (for example, Matthew 10:2-3) and quite possibly is "James the younger" (Mark 15:40).
- James, the father of Judas, one of the twelve, not Judas Iscariot (Luke 6:16).

So little is known about these last two men (and any other unmentioned individuals named James) that they are not taken as serious candidates. The book begins with the straightforward statement, "James, a slave of God and of the Lord Jesus Christ" (1:1). The author assumes that his readers (called "Jewish Christians scattered among the nations") would know his identity. This James, the author, must have been someone well-known, with stature and authority in the early church. James, the brother of Jesus and the leader of the Jerusalem church, is the obvious choice. This is also the traditional view (since early in the third century) and the belief of most biblical scholars today.

According to Josephus, a first-century Jewish historian, James was condemned to death by the Jewish Sanhedrin in A.D. 62—just after the death of the Roman governor Festus (see Acts 24:27–26:32) and just before the arrival of his successor Albinus.

DATE

James wrote this book about A.D. 47–49.

There are several reasons for believing that the book of James was written early in the life of the church.

- With James the brother of Christ as the author, the book would have had to be written before A.D. 62, the year of James's martyrdom according to Josephus.
- The book does not mention the Jewish/Gentile controversy of the fifties and sixties. Remember, James was the moderator of the Council of Jerusalem, convened to consider this issue (Acts 15). This council is thought to have been held around A.D. 50. Paul spent much time discussing the problem of the Judaizers in his letters.
- This letter has no mention of the apostle Paul or allusions to his writings. It is probable, therefore, that it was written before Paul's rise to great prominence in the church.
- James does not discuss false teachings, another later issue in the church and a prominent theme in the writings of Paul, Peter, Jude, and John.

The book of James was written after the death of Stephen (A.D. 35), the persecution that caused many of the Jerusalem believers to flee for their lives, the conversion of Paul (A.D. 35), and the death of James the apostle (A.D. 44).

It was written before the Council of Jerusalem (A.D. 50), Paul's second and third missionary journeys (A.D. 50–52, 53–57), Paul's final imprisonment and martyrdom (c. A.D. 67), and the destruction of Jerusalem by Titus (A.D. 70).

Some have argued for a late date by another author because of the excellent

Greek used in the book. James's natural language would have been Aramaic, and he probably would not have been fluent in good Hellenistic Greek. It is possible, however, that James, like Paul (see Colossians 4:18) used a "secretary" to translate his words into Greek, the language of world trade and the appropriate choice to reach those scattered among the nations.

James wrote to Jewish Christians in the first century. He also wrote to us, today, who are also "scattered among the nations." Although separated by nearly twenty centuries, the needs are much the same, and James's message still needs to be heard and applied.

SETTING

Place James probably wrote this letter from Jerusalem, where he lived. Jerusalem was the holy city of the Jews, the focus of the nation's political and religious life. In Jerusalem, Israel's greatest kings had reigned and prophets had ministered. And the temple was there. No matter how far they had been scattered, Jews all over the world looked to Jerusalem as their home and a symbol of God's presence among them. A reading of the last chapters of the Gospels and the first half of Acts provides an eyewitness view of the historical context of this book.

Religion When Jesus walked the streets of this great city, he encountered Pharisees, priests, scribes, and other religious zealots committed to the purity of Judaism. Eventually these religious leaders plotted Jesus' death (see Luke 22:1-6), hoping to stop the spread of what they considered to be heresy. However, after the Resurrection and the coming of the Holy Spirit, the church was born—the disciples preached without fear, and thousands responded to the gospel message (see Acts 2:1-47; 6:7). The religious leaders reacted by working still harder to eliminate the church and obliterate any trace of Jesus' followers (see Acts 6:8–8:3; 9:1-2). Yet the Jerusalem church flourished through this persecution, with James as one of the leaders. Wonderfully, many Jewish religious leaders came to faith in Christ. The Jerusalem church included former priests and Pharisees.

In Jerusalem, the first great crisis of the church was successfully resolved through a church council (Acts 15); yet a few years later, in this same city, the apostle Paul was mobbed in the temple and arrested (Acts 21–22).

James wrote from a city in religious turmoil, with opposition from Sadducees, legalistic Pharisees, and a vengeful high priest. Christians were a persecuted minority.

Politics During these times, Judea was under Roman domination. Herod the Great had been appointed king of the Jews by Augustus in 40 B.C., and he had chosen Jerusalem as his place of residence and reign. All the Roman governors ruled with power and intimidation, but they would often try to keep the peace by appeasing the religious leaders. Herod the Great even had constructed a magnificent temple. And Jesus was crucified when Pilate bowed to political pressure (Matthew 27:15-26). But most Jews chafed under Roman rule and longed for the freedom and glory of the past. Uprisings and insurrections were common, and the land of Palestine continued to be an irritant to the Romans. Eventually Emperor Titus destroyed the city and the temple in A.D. 70.

James wrote from a city in political turmoil, in a land where the people lived under foreign rule, in occupied territory. Christians had to accept their lot and live quiet testimonies within a hostile atmosphere.

Economics In general, the Jews of Jerusalem were poor, although many of the landowners and religious leaders had wealth. In addition, tax collectors like Matthew (Matthew 9:9) and Zacchaeus (Luke 19:1-10) made financial gains by allying themselves with the Romans and exploiting their countrymen. Eventually, however, Jerusalem became desperately poor because of Roman greed and a terrible famine (Acts 11:28-30).

James wrote from a city with an unstable economy and from a people with very few material resources. The Christians in Jerusalem were poor. Because of the conditions in Jerusalem, the Jewish believers were tempted to compromise their values and beliefs in order to escape persecution or to improve their economic situation. Certainly it would have been tempting to be secret believers, blending in with society and not causing problems. Or they might have been tempted to turn away from Christ altogether, giving in to the religious, political, and economic pressures.

Christians today face similar temptations. Although they may not be ruled by a foreign nation, believers are in a distinct minority in the world. Christ's teachings and commands continue to clash with society's values. And many Christians are persecuted socially, economically, and religiously because of their beliefs. Even in "Christian" countries, followers of Christ can feel alienated and ostracized. In an attempt to cope with the surrounding pressures, believers must resist the temptation to become secret Christians and silent witnesses.

AUDIENCE

"To Jewish Christians scattered among the nations" (1:1).

Christianity is Jewish. That may seem like a contradiction, but it's true. Mary, the mother of our Lord, was Jewish, as was Joseph. So Jesus was reared in a Jewish home. And in his public ministry, Jesus came first to the Jews, God's chosen nation, calling them to repentance and faith. All of the original twelve disciples were Jews. Christianity began in the temple and synagogue, as seeking Jews found the Messiah.

Quite naturally, therefore, Jerusalem was the birthplace of the church. That's where Jesus was crucified, and where he arose and later ascended. In Jerusalem the Holy Spirit filled the early band of believers. And that's where the apostles ministered. The Jerusalem church experienced explosive growth, with thousands responding to the gospel (Acts 2:41; 4:4; 5:14; 6:1, 7). Believers met in the temple courts and in homes (Acts 5:42), worshiping, eating, learning, and serving together.

Jesus had told his followers to spread the faith *beyond* Jerusalem, to "Judea, in Samaria, and to the ends of the earth" (Acts 1:8). In the Olivet discourse Jesus predicted terrible persecution and the eventual destruction of Jerusalem (Luke 21:5-24)—Jesus knew that his followers would be scattered. The persecution began soon after Jesus' ascension. Whether or not these early Christians were ready, many of them were forced to spread throughout the Roman Empire (Acts 8:1). They traveled to Samaria, and "as far as Phoenicia, Cyprus, and Antioch of Syria" (Acts 11:19).

The scattered believers "went everywhere preaching the Good News about Jesus" (Acts 8:4), and thus added many new converts to the faith. This created a need for follow-up, spiritual instruction, and encouragement for the new converts. For example, the apostles in Jerusalem sent Peter and John to Samaria to check out Philip's ministry (Acts 8:14), and they sent Barnabas to Antioch when they heard of Greeks being converted there (Acts 11:19-22).

Of course, followers of Jesus, the Messiah, were already living in many foreign lands, having come to faith at Pentecost. Held fifty days after Passover, Pentecost (also called the Feast of Weeks) was a festival of thanksgiving for the harvested crops. Each year, Jews from many nations would gather in Jerusalem for this celebration. According to Acts 2:9-11, "Parthians, Medes, Elamites, people from Mesopotamia, Judea, Cappadocia, Pontus, the province of Asia, Phrygia, Pamphylia, Egypt, and the areas of Libya toward Cyrene, visitors from Rome (both Jews and converts to Judaism), Cretans, and Arabians" heard the Spirit-filled message in their native languages. They also heard Peter's powerful sermon (Acts 2:14-41), and many came to faith in Christ. Returning to their homes, these new converts became an international evangelistic team. In fact, it is likely that the church at Rome was established by those who had heard about Jesus and had believed in him in Jerusalem, at Pentecost.

James, as the leader of the Jerusalem Christian community and as shepherd to a scattered flock, wrote to this large group of Jewish believers in Christ who were living far beyond the walls of Jerusalem. Thus he addressed his letter, "To Jewish Christians scattered among the nations" (1:1). Because this letter was written early in the life of the church (before Paul's missionary journeys), nearly all of the believers would have been Jewish, but it is a book for all Christians, both Jewish and Gentile believers.

James knew what these young believers would be facing as they attempted to live for Christ, far away from the apostles and elders. There would be trials and persecutions, similar to what had driven many of them from their homes. There would be suffering. There would be temptations. There would be pressures. James was concerned that his Christian brothers and sisters should persevere.

James also knew that it is easy to slip back into old habits or spiritual neutrality when one has moved away and is surrounded by those who believe differently. And so he challenged his readers to move beyond mere words into action—to live out their faith.

James was also concerned about the body, the fellowship, and the church. And so he warned of discrimination and divisions and urged believers to guard their speech, to seek divine wisdom, to be humble, and to pray for each other.

The first-century readers of this letter would have appreciated James's direct and practical approach. He got right to the point with Spirit-led answers that they needed.

MESSAGE
James begins his letter by outlining some general characteristics of the Christian life (1:1-27). Next, he exhorts Christians to act justly in society (2:1-13). He follows this practical advice with a theological discourse on the relationship between

faith and action (2:14-26). Then James shows the importance of controlling one's speech (3:1-12). In 3:13-18, James distinguishes two kinds of wisdom—earthly and heavenly. Then he encourages his readers to turn from evil desires and obey God (4:1-12). James reproves those who trust in their own plans and possessions (4:13–5:6). Finally, he exhorts his readers to be patient with each other (5:7-11), to be straightforward in their promises (5:12), to pray for each other (5:13-18), and to help each other remain faithful to God (5:19-20).

The main themes in the book of James include: *Living Faith, Trials, Law of Love, Wise Speech,* and *Wealth.*

Living Faith (1:19–2:26). This is the most familiar theme of the book and the most controversial. In fact, many have believed that what James wrote about "faith and works" contradicts the teachings of Paul. At times, it sounds as though James wrote that we are justified (made righteous in God's sight) by what we do ("deeds" or "works"), where Paul wrote that we are justified by faith alone, not by works.

But there is really no contradiction. Here's why:

First, both James and Paul used the same working definition of "saving faith"—total trust in Jesus Christ. Consider these examples from James: "when your faith is tested, your endurance has a chance to grow" (1:3); "their prayer offered in faith will heal the sick" (5:15). The word "faith" clearly refers to heartfelt and sincere trust.

Paul explained saving faith similarly when he wrote: "What is important is faith expressing itself in love" (Galatians 5:6); "Abraham never wavered in believing God's promise. In fact, his faith grew stronger, and in this he brought glory to God. He was absolutely convinced that God was able to do anything he promised. And because of Abraham's faith, God declared him to be righteous" (Romans 4:20-22). Notice the phrases "never wavered," "absolutely convinced," and "expressing itself in love." To Paul, saving faith was not mere intellectual assent to the facts of the gospel—it was deep and sincere trust in Christ.

Second, both James and Paul were writing to correct misunderstandings of the relationship between faith and works in the process of justification. But they were correcting different problems.

James wrote to correct "easy-believe-ism," the kind of superficial belief in Christ that is mere intellectual assent—the attitude that turns faith into cold orthodoxy, with the person merely believing the right facts about God and Jesus. James explained it this way: "Do you still think it's enough just to believe that there is one God? Well, even the demons believe this, and they tremble in terror!" (2:19). Obviously, demons aren't Christians, and yet in one respect they are "believers." Their kind of belief is far from the faith that saves.

The Jerusalem church had experienced tremendous growth. With this growth there undoubtedly were many "hangers on," spiritual groupies, people who wanted to be part of the Christian crowd but had no depth to their faith. Ananias and Sapphira seem to fit into that category. Their phony profession and dramatic deaths rocked the young church (see Acts 5:1-11). Later in the New Testament, we hear of others who left churches when the going got tough: "These people left our churches because they never really belonged with us; otherwise they would have stayed with us. When they left us, it proved that they do not belong with us" (1 John 2:19).

To deal with this problem head-on, under the inspiration of the Holy Spirit, James pronounced that superficial faith, just believing the facts about Christ, is not enough. True faith involves wholehearted and genuine trust in Jesus Christ and will be evidenced by a changed life. In other words, true faith will produce good works.

Paul's statements, however, were meant to counter a Jewish emphasis on obeying the law (especially the ceremonial law as given in the Pentateuch). Many Jews who had come to faith in Christ felt obligated to observe Jewish laws and customs—some going so far as to insist that all new believers, even Gentiles, should keep Jewish laws, especially circumcision. Paul's strong teaching was that the purpose of the law was to prepare the way for the Messiah (making people aware of their sinfulness and providing a picture of God's perfect sacrifice for sin)—thus the law was fulfilled in Christ. Believers, therefore, were under no obligation to obey Jewish laws. Paul made it clear that salvation is **by grace through faith,** not by slavish obedience to the laws (see Galatians 3:1-6). In fact, it was just this issue that brought Paul to the church council of Jerusalem. There, after Paul presented his case, James spoke for the elders and declared that the Gentile believers were not obligated to keep the Jewish ceremonial laws (see Acts 15:12-29).

In all of this, Paul's main point was that a person could never be good enough to "earn" his or her salvation. And because everyone has sinned, all people fall into this lost category—all fall short. "We are made right in God's sight when we trust in Jesus Christ to take away our sins. And we all can be saved in this same way, no matter who we are or what we have done. For all have sinned; all fall short of God's glorious standard. Yet now God in his gracious kindness declares us not guilty. He has done this through Christ Jesus, who has freed us by taking away our sins" (Romans 3:22-24). Interestingly, James also underlined the universality of sin and the need for salvation when he wrote: "And the person who keeps all of the laws except one is as guilty as the person who has broken all of God's laws" (2:10).

In summary, James was speaking of good deeds *after* conversion, as evidence of faith and a right relationship with God—true faith produces good works. Paul was speaking of good deeds *before* conversion—they can never earn or produce a right relationship with God—obedience follows profession.

IMPORTANCE FOR TODAY. The problem faced by James in the first century is one that is prevalent today. Churches are filled with people who claim to be followers of Christ. Unfortunately, however, the claims of many of those professed followers are hollow because their faith is shallow—their lives belie their profession by specific non-Christian actions and attitudes or by what they fail to do. The application of this theme in the book of James is clear: the church must continually call people to genuine faith in Christ—faith that results in changed lives. And individual Christians should evaluate their level of obedience to their Master and recommit to doing the good works that result from being saved.

How deep is your faith? Do you merely know a lot about God, or do you really know him? Do you have a superficial faith, or do you have a deep trust?

Trials (1:2-18; 5:7-11). The early church was born at a time of severe trials—

remember, James was writing to believers who had been scattered throughout the world by persecution. So it should come as no surprise to find that one of the major themes in this book is how to react to trials and testing.

Many of these trials came from the outside. Zealous Jews, like Saul of Tarsus before his conversion, imprisoned and killed followers of Christ (Acts 6:8–7:60). Public acknowledgment of Christ as Savior and Lord did not lead to popularity, power, and prestige. James also knew of the struggles that would occur on the inside. A trial can test believers' faith, causing doubts and discouragement and making them susceptible to a variety of temptations. And Satan tries to use tough times to divide the church. So James challenged his young flock to recognize the sources of their problems—their sin nature and the evil one (1:13-16), to keep focused on God and his goodness (1:17-18), and to resist Satan's subtle attacks (4:7).

IMPORTANCE FOR TODAY. The way of the cross is not the way of the world— our values, priorities, and lifestyle can be very threatening to those who don't know the Savior. Every day, Christians face scores of decisions that could result in being "persecuted" for their faith. In addition, adversity is a part of life, a result of being mortal and human. We live in a fallen world; and people, all people, get sick, struggle through life, and eventually die. God doesn't promise to spare us from those trials and give us perpetual health, wealth, and good feelings. But he does promise to be with us in everything we face (see John 16:31-33; Romans 8:35-39).

So today, James would urge us, like his first-century readers, to see our trials as tests of faith that can help us grow and mature (1:3-4, 12). He would also tell us, however, to distinguish between external trials and internal temptations, which are rooted in the sinful nature (1:13-15). These self-centered desires must be resisted, and we should focus on God and his love and truth and not on ourselves (1:16-18).

How are you responding to the trials in your life? Are you giving in or keeping the faith? Are you allowing tough times to separate you from other Christians or pull you together?

Law of Love (1:27; 2:8-17; 3:17-18; 4:11-12; 5:19-20). For James, the law of love included looking after "orphans and widows" (1:27), not showing favoritism (2:8-9), being merciful (2:12-13), clothing the naked and feeding the hungry (2:14-17), being a peacemaker (3:17-18), not speaking evil of another (4:11-12), and praying for each other (5:13-16). In fact, keeping the royal law is a powerful demonstration of our faith in Christ, as we discussed earlier under "living faith."

IMPORTANCE FOR TODAY. Our world is filled with those who need compassion, mercy, and love translated into food, shelter, medical care, counsel, and friendship. God's message to the church, and thus to us, through James is to obey the law of love. This means supporting Christian welfare and mission agencies and individuals with our prayers and money. It also means being sensitive to the needs in our neighborhoods and looking for ways that we can become involved personally. "If you really keep the royal law found in Scripture, 'Love your neighbor as yourself,' you are doing right" (2:8).

Are you obeying the law of love? Are you holding tightly to your money, or are you giving to those in need? Are you focused on your own comfort, or are you sacrificing to help others?

Wise Speech (1:19, 26; 3:1-18; 4:11-16; 5:9, 12). At the time James wrote this book, it seems as though many wanted to be teachers in the church, even though they weren't qualified. It is in this context and to those who presumed to be teachers that James wrote his words about the tongue and godly wisdom. James began by warning aspiring teachers that they would be judged very strictly (3:1-2). He then discussed the issue of speech. Of all people, teachers should watch what they say, since most of what they teach directly impacts others.

Next, James discussed "wisdom." Although this may seem to be an abrupt change of thought and a new topic, there is a definite connection between "wisdom," "speech," and teachers. The key to controlling the tongue is to rely on God's wisdom and insight, and not be led by "envy and selfish ambition" (3:13-17). In fact, the ability of a person to control his or her tongue tells much about that person's relationship with God. Teachers are known as "wise" people; after all, they have the answers, and they tell us what to do and teach us how to think. But true wisdom comes from God and will show up in a person's life (3:13), not just in his or her words.

James's readers learned that they would have to be wise and then use their tongues wisely if they ever wanted to become teachers.

IMPORTANCE FOR TODAY. Today, almost any believer can have a teaching role in the church as pastor, elder, Sunday school teacher, youth sponsor, small group leader, counselor, or Bible study teacher. And even if they don't have a recognized teaching position in the church, mature Christians should teach and encourage new believers in the faith. To these teachers in our churches, James would say, "What is the source of your teaching? Where is the wisdom? Watch what you say and make sure it is from God."

Beyond the issue of teachers and teaching, there is a strong application to all believers to guard our mouths. It is easy to be critical of others, to get in the last word, to complain, to brag of our accomplishments, or just to talk to hear ourselves. But those words come directly from "envy and selfish ambition" (3:14). And nothing hurts churches or relationships more quickly than careless or harmful talk.

How is your speech? Are you quick to defend yourself and to get in an authoritative word, or are you a good listener? Do you voice your grievances and blast your opponents, or do you try to speak constructively? Are you quick to pass on the morsel of gossip, or do you remain silent and think the best of others?

Wealth (1:9-12; 2:1-7; 5:1-6). It is not surprising that there are significant references in James's epistle to wealth, especially the relationship between the poor and the rich, because the church in Jerusalem was poor. In fact, this church eventually became so impoverished, especially after a devastating famine, that Paul collected money for them on his third missionary journey (see Acts 11:28-30; 24:17; Romans 15:25-26; 1 Corinthians 16:1-4; 2 Corinthians 8:1–9:5).

A factor that contributed to their poverty was the emphasis on caring for the needy and feeding the hungry in the church. In Acts we read about the concern for widows and the "daily distribution of food" (Acts 6:1-4). Providing food for so many must have been a drain on their personal financial resources. In addition, there were conflicts between the rich and the poor. In the text we read that the rich were exploiting the poor and taking them to court (2:6-7). As in most cultures, society was stratified according to wealth with many becoming rich at the expense of the poor (5:4-6).

It is easy to imagine the mixed feelings of poor Christians: from a human standpoint they envied the rich and wanted to curry their favor with the hope of moving out of poverty, or they may have been filled with anger and desired revenge. Yet as followers of Christ, they were to love their neighbors (2:8).

James's message was direct and clear to both the poor and the rich. To the poor, he gave words of hope, and to the rich, words of warning. First, the poor should realize that they had a "high position" even though they were at the bottom in society (1:9). Second, they should not fawn over wealthy people who came to the church meetings. Wealth was not a mark of spirituality (in fact, the opposite was usually the case), and showing favoritism is a sin (2:1-9). Third, the poor should remember that what really counts is being rich in God's sight (1:12).

James warned the rich that their powerful and comfortable position was temporary (1:10-11). He told rich oppressors that they would be punished for hoarding wealth, cheating workers, and wiping out their opposition (5:1-6). The rich would be condemned not for having wealth, but for what they did to become wealthy and how they used their riches.

IMPORTANCE FOR TODAY. Although much has changed since the first century, society is still stratified, with the wealthy and powerful featured as heroes and role models. Many of the rich use their money to get their way and to oppress the poor. And whatever the source of the wealth, very little is given to help the needy—rather it is hoarded for "the last days," for one's retirement funds or estate (5:3).

James's message hits home. People are foolish (both Christians and non-Christians) to spend their lives on money. Chasing wealth is a futile pursuit because in God's eyes money is worth so little in comparison with what is important and valuable in life—seeking his Kingdom and righteousness (Matthew 6:33). The main trap of accumulating wealth is that it can give a false sense of security; that is, we can begin to trust in money instead of God.

What role does money play in your life? Are you obsessed with gaining wealth, or do you see money as a resource to be used for good? Do you spend, spend, spend on yourself, or are you a good steward of the time, money, and other resources entrusted to you? Do you work to be popular with the rich and influential, or do you associate with the poor, regardless of what others may say or think?

OUTLINE OF JAMES
I. Genuine Religion (1:1-27)
II. Genuine Faith (2:1–3:12)
III. Genuine Wisdom (3:13–5:20)

JAMES 1

GREETINGS / 1:1

How often do we open a letter without checking to see who sent it? Ancient letter writers signed their names right at the beginning, so readers immediately knew the source. Modern readers of the New Testament, however, frequently skip over the address. It strikes us as unimportant. Our oversight is a mistake. The first verses of New Testament books often tell us the writer's identity and how the writers perceived their roles. In James's case, these helpful insights prepare us for the entire letter. We treat letters with more respect when we understand who sent them and why.

1:1 James is only mentioned by name a few times elsewhere in the New Testament (Matthew 13:53-55; Acts 1:12-14; 15:12-21; 1 Corinthians 15:3-8; Galatians 1:19; 2:7-9). As the leader of the Jerusalem church, however, he was known on a first-name basis by the rapidly expanding Christian world. By simply using his first name, James manages to convey both humility and authority as he signs his letter. He could have identified himself as "brother of Jesus," or "leader of the Jerusalem church," but the only addition to his name is the title of **slave of God.** The Greek word *doulos* (slave, servant) refers to a position of complete obedience, utter humility, and unshakable loyalty. Many of the first followers of Christ were, in fact, slaves. But among Christians, the idea of being a slave of Christ became not a position of humiliation, but a place of honor. There can be no greater tribute to a believer than to be known as God's obedient, humble, and loyal servant. The three names, **Lord Jesus Christ,** refer to the unique character of Jesus. He is the heavenly,

exalted **Lord** who will one day return in glory to this world. He is **Jesus,** God come to earth as a human being. He is **Christ,** the anointed one who fulfilled God's purposes by dying for us.

The **Jewish Christians scattered among the nations** referred to Jewish believers who had left Palestine by force or by choice. The deportation of Jews to foreign lands had been practiced since the days of the Assyrians over six hundred years before Christ. But many Jews had also emigrated to other lands in the quest for wealth and opportunity. This network of Jewish communities scattered throughout the Roman Empire became the stepping stones for the spread of the gospel. The book of Acts describes the missionary pattern of Paul and others. In almost every town they visited, the presence of a Jewish synagogue gave them an open forum from which to communicate the Good News. What history records as the splintering of the nation of Israel was used by God to facilitate the spread of his Word.

ENDURING TRIALS AND TEMPTATIONS / 1:2-18

James wrote to believers facing difficult times. Their troubles ranged from personal trials to disabling doubts; from persecution for following Christ to the lure of respectability in their community and the dangers of spiritual pride. James wrote to encourage his brothers and sisters in their faith.

James's approach illustrates the variety of forms that encouragement can take. At times, James confronts. In other places, he gently encourages. He uses hyperbole (extreme illustration) in a way that reminds us of his half brother, Jesus. Sparks and forest fires, rudders and large ships create mental pictures like Jesus created with his needles and camels. James begins his letter looking directly at trials and daring to spur his fellow believers with a challenge: "Meet the very worst that life presents you with joy."

1:2 How can a person consider **trouble** as **an opportunity for joy?** This is a remarkable command—we are to choose to be joyful in situations where joy would naturally be our last response. When certain circumstances make us angry and we want to blame the Lord, James directs us to the healthier alternative—joy. Those who trust in God ought to exhibit a dramatically different, positive response to the difficult events of life.

Our attitude is to be one of genuine rejoicing. This is not joyful anticipation *for* trials. Instead, it is joy *during* trials. The joy is based on confidence in the outcome of the trial. It is the startling realization that trials represent the possibility of growth. In contrast, most people are happy when they escape trials. But James encourages us to have pure joy in the very face of trials. James is not encouraging believers to pretend to be happy. Rejoicing goes beyond happiness. Happiness centers on earthly circumstances and how well things are going here. Joy centers on God and his presence in our experience.

The word **whenever** doesn't allow much room for doubt. We are urged to be joyful not *if* we face trouble, but *whenever.* Trials, problems, situations can be joy robbers if we lack the proper attitude. Where does this trouble come from? The troubles and trials we face can be hardships from without or temptations from within. A trouble may be a hard situation that tests a person's faith such as persecution, a difficult moral choice, or a tragedy. Life's trail is marked with such trials. Enduring one trial is not enough. God's purpose in allowing this process is to develop complete maturity in us.

Considering your troubles to be joy comes from seeing life with God's perspective in mind. We may not be able to understand the specific reasons for God's allowing certain experiences to crush us or wear us down, but we can be confident that his plan is for our good. What may look hopeless or impossible to us never looks that way to God!

1:3 Although we tend to think of testing as a way to prove what we don't know or don't have, being **tested** ought to be seen as a positive opportunity to prove what we have learned. This testing of our faith is a test that has a positive purpose. In this case, the troubles do not determine whether or not believers have faith; rather, the troubles strengthen believers by adding endurance to the faith that is already present. **Endurance** is faith stretched out; it involves trusting God for a long duration. James is not questioning the faith of his readers—he assumes that they trust in Christ. He is not convincing people to believe; he is encouraging believers to remain faithful to the end. James knows that their faith is real, but it lacks maturity.

We cannot really know our own depth until we see how we react under pressure. Precious diamonds begin as coal, subjected to intense pressure over a period of time. Without pressure, coal remains coal. The testing of your faith is the combined pressure that life brings to bear on you. Endurance, like a precious gem, is the intended outcome of this testing. Endurance is not a passive submission to circumstances—it is a strong and active response to the difficult events of life, standing on your feet as you face the storms. It is not simply the attitude of withstanding trials, but the ability to turn them into glory, to overcome them.

1:4 It is not our nature to endure. When it comes to trials, we would rather escape, explain, or exit the difficulty. In fact, we will tend to do almost anything to avoid enduring a trial. Faithful **endurance,** however, generates whole people, recognized as **strong in character,** or mature. We will be seasoned, experienced, well-developed, fit for the tasks God sent us into the world to do. This strength is a quality developed by how much we have learned from the trials we have experienced. We are also **ready for anything** because we have been fully trained. The weaknesses and imperfections are being removed from our character; we are gaining victory over old sins; we are demonstrating a sense of competence about life. This completeness relates to the breadth of our experience.

1:5 If James 1:2-4 describes the benefits of responding correctly to trials, this verse draws attention to our hopelessness without God's assistance. We need a certain kind of **wisdom** in order to let our troubles be an opportunity for joy. That wisdom, says James, comes from **God.**

The wisdom that we need has three distinct characteristics: (1) **It is practical**—The wisdom from God relates to life even during the most trying times. It is not a wisdom isolated from suffering and trials. This wisdom is the tool by which trials are overcome. An intelligent person may have profound ideas, but a wise person puts profound ideas into action. (2) **It is divine**—God's wisdom goes beyond common sense. Common sense does not lead us to choose joy in the middle of trials. This wisdom begins with respect for God, leads to living by God's direction, and results in the ability to tell right from wrong. (3) **It is Christlike**—Asking for wisdom is ultimately asking to be like Christ. The Bible identifies Christ as the "wisdom of God" (1 Corinthians 1:24; 2:1-7).

Recognizing our lack of wisdom might cause us to despair, but God wants us to **ask him.** How do we know that God has answered our request for wisdom? When troubles come we will find ourselves responding with an attitude of joy. We will realize that joy is not our own doing, but is a gift.

Note that what God promises is to supply the wisdom for what must be done. Decisions still will have to be made, and actions will have to be taken. The wisdom is guidance for **what God wants** us **to do,** not his removal of our participation. We must remember that God's promises do not submit to our plans. This verse is not permitting us to ask God for wisdom to bring about our will. Instead, we should humbly ask him for wisdom to remain in his will.

1:6 The one condition for receiving this gift of God is faith—being **sure that** we **really expect** God **to answer.** God will generously give wisdom, but we will not receive it if we do not have confidence that God will answer the request. That lack of confidence reveals a **doubtful mind.** "Doubt" means "a divided mind." Doubting here has nothing to do with doubting whether God can do something; rather, it describes a people "divided" between being self-centered and being God-centered. This is the reason why James adds the idea of the **wave,** because it really means to be **driven and tossed** between self and God. The behavior of sea waves is unsettled, going back and forth, driven **by the wind,** like the doubter's mind. Such a person wavers between choices and may, in the end, make no decision at all. Circumstances become the decision makers in that person's life. When God's promises and commands are given equal authority with our feelings and desires and the world's ideas, the result is an unsettled sea of indecision and chaos.

1:7 The person who asks trustingly does not determine how God will answer, but he or she can be confident in knowing that God will answer. The person who asks doubtfully **should not expect to receive anything from the Lord** because the request was not genuine. When it seems as if God hasn't answered our prayers, we need to begin the search for a solution by asking ourselves whether we were trusting when we prayed. If our loyalties are straightened out, God's answers to prayer are restored to us.

1:8 To **waver back and forth** is to be double-minded. These people may "trust" God and claim to be believers, and yet be filled with doubt, keeping other options open in case God does not prove to be dependable. Wavering people are walking contradictions. Such instability is revealed not only in their prayers, but in all they do. When indecisiveness marks a relationship with God, that instability will affect all of life.

1:9 Next James turns his attention to potential differences among Christians—notably between rich and poor. Although they share a common bond in Christ, they will face different trials as their faith is tested. James returns to this theme throughout his letter.

Some of the believers were **poor,** low on the socioeconomic scale. The Greek word here means "insignificant in the world's eyes, lowly, relatively poor and powerless, lacking in material possessions." They receive the subtle honor of being mentioned first. These scattered Jewish Christians, especially those in Palestine and Syria, would have been in such circumstances. They would have been ostracized by the Jews and often were disowned by their families. This was also a time of famine, and Christians may have suffered severely (Acts 11:28-29).

Contrary to the world's opinion of the poor, James says that **God has honored them.** Their high position is a present reality for these believers. It is their rich heritage as children of God who live in anticipation of participating in Christ's eternal Kingdom (2:5). They may be facing trials and persecution now, but they can be glad that God has honored them as his very own children.

Whatever our social or economic situation, James challenges us to see beyond it to our eternal advantages. What we can have in Jesus Christ outweighs anything in this life. Knowing him gives us our high position, where we find our true dignity.

1:10 As the gospel spread around the Mediterranean world, some who believed would have been **rich** Jews. Some, like Lydia in Philippi (Acts 16:11-15), were Gentiles, and wealthy. To such people, James gives a special challenge. He reminds them not to measure their worth by their riches nor to depend on their possessions for security and joy because earthly treasures will **fade away like a flower in the field.** Christians, rich and poor alike, were being persecuted for their faith. Wealth was not always an effective protection against mob violence (see Acts 17:1-9). As they were being persecuted, the rich looked very much like the poor, and certainly they were on the same level. This identification with poor believers could be part of the "humbling" that James is pointing out. That **God has humbled them** also means to be brought lower in Christ. That is, the rich are great in this world but are made equal to the poor in God's world.

Wealth and the abilities that lead to wealth can create a barrier between us and God. If we are rich, or even if we live what we modestly call a "comfortable" lifestyle, James reminds us that our only lasting security is in a relationship with Christ. We must not trust what money and power seem to guarantee; instead, we must humbly trust in God and his eternal riches.

1:11 James describes a common occurrence in the Middle East. Morning is often welcomed by colorful desert flowers, bursting from the cool night. Their death is sudden as **the hot sun rises.** This withering and fading of wealthy people is as sudden as the death of the wild flowers. Death always intrudes. Life is uncertain. Disaster is possible at any moment.

The poor should be glad that riches mean nothing to God; otherwise poor people would be considered unworthy. The rich should be glad that wealth means nothing to God, because wealth is easily lost. We find true wealth by developing our spiritual lives, not financial assets. James begins his letter by making sure that believers, both poor and rich, see themselves in the same light before God (see Galatians 3:28; Colossians 3:11). James calls his readers to find hope in God's eternal promises.

1:12 The Bible deepens the meaning of how **God blesses the people** to include a deep joy that comes from receiving God's favor. As athletes persevere in training in order to improve their abilities and endurance for competition, so Christians persevere in spiritual training as they **patiently endure testing** that will bring maturity and completeness. Today's trials will seem like training when we face tomorrow's challenges. The way to get into God's winner's circle is to love him and stay faithful even under pressure.

There is a finish line. There are successes along the way—spiritual progress has its mile markers. But the trials of this life are contained in this life. Someday the test will be over. The first chapter of James teaches us that God's long-term goal for us is maturity and completeness, but his eternal goal for us is **the crown of life,** a rich expression of hope. The believer who patiently endures by trusting God will have a life that, though not full of glory and honor, is still truly abundant, joyful, and victorious. Standing the tests of life gives believers even now a taste of eternity. Looking forward to that wonderful reward, and to the one who will present it to us, can be a source of strength and encouragement in times of trial (see also 1 Corinthians 9:24-27; 2 Timothy 4:7-8). Christians can consider themselves truly blessed, no matter what their outward circumstances, because they have been **promised** the crown of life.

1:13 We must have a correct view of God in order to persevere during times of trial. Specifically, we need to understand God's view of our temptations. Trials and temptations always present us with choices. God wants us to make good choices, not evil ones. Hardships can produce spiritual maturity and lead to eternal benefits if endured in faith. But tests can also be failed. We can give in

to temptation. And when we fail, we often use all kinds of excuses and reasons for our actions. The most dangerous of these is to say, **"God is tempting me."** It is crucial for us to remember that God tests people for good; he does not tempt people for evil. Even during temptation we can see God's sovereignty in permitting Satan to tempt us in order to refine our faith and help us grow in our dependence on Christ. Instead of persevering (1:12), we may give in or give up in the face of trial. We might even rationalize that God is at fault for sending such a trying experience, and thus blame God for our failure. From the beginning it has been a natural human response to make excuses and blame others for sin (see Genesis 3:12-13). A person who makes excuses is trying to shift blame to something or someone else. A Christian, on the other hand, accepts responsibility for his or her wrongs, confesses them, and asks God for forgiveness. Because **God is never tempted to do wrong,** he cannot be the author of temptation. James is arguing against the pagan view of the gods where good and evil coexisted. God does not wish evil on people; he does not cause evil; he does not try to trip people up— **he never tempts anyone.**

At this point, the question may be rightly asked: "If God really loves us, why doesn't he protect us from temptation?" A God who kept us from temptation would be a God unwilling to allow us to grow. In order for a test to be an effective tool for growth, it must be capable of being failed. God actually proves his love by protecting us *in* temptation instead of protecting us *from* temptation (1 Corinthians 10:13).

1:14 Some believers thought that since God allowed trials, he must also be the source of temptation. These people could excuse their sin by saying that God was at fault. James corrects this. Temptations come from within, **from the lure of our own evil desires.** James highlights individual responsibility for sin. Desires can be either fed or starved. If the desire itself is evil, we must deny its wish. It is up to us, with God's help. If we encourage our desires, they will soon become actions. The blame for sin is ours alone. The kind of desire James is describing here is desire out of control. It is selfish and seductive.

Does James take Satan off the hook by placing responsibility for temptation on our desires? No, he does not. We may be led by our desires, but it is the Devil behind the impulse when we are going in an evil direction. Temptation comes from evil desires within us, not from God. We can both build and bait our own trap. It begins with an evil thought and becomes sin when we dwell on the thought and allow it to become an action. Like a snowball rolling downhill, sin grows more destructive the more we let it have its way. The best time to stop a temptation is before it is too great or moving too fast to control. (See Matthew 4:1-11; 1 Corinthians 10:13; and 2 Timothy 2:22 for more about escaping temptation.)

1:15 James traces the result of temptation when a person yields to it. Note that the first two steps in the process (**evil desires lead to evil actions**) emphasize the internal nature of sin. When we yield to temptation, our sin sets deadly events into motion—**evil actions lead to death.** There is more to stopping sin than just stopping sinning. Damage has been done. Deciding to "sin no more" may take care of the future, but it does not heal the past. That healing must come through repentance and forgiveness. Sometimes restitution must be made. As serious as the remedy sounds, we can be deeply grateful that there is a remedy at all.

1:16 The danger behind James's warning to us not to be **misled** is the temptation to believe that God does not care, or won't help us, or may even be working against us. The picture is not pretty. If we come to believe we are alone, we have been misled. If we distrust God, we have been misled. And if we dare to accuse God of being the tempter, we have been thoroughly misled.

1:17 So how can we keep from falling into temptation? The way is found in a close relationship with God and the application of his word to daily life. This pattern will lead us to see clearly that every good and perfect gift is from above. In contrast to the view that God sends evil, James points out here that **whatever is good and perfect comes to us from God above.** We can be assured that God always wills the best for us— not good things today and bad things tomorrow. God's character is always trustworthy and reliable—**he never changes or casts shifting shadows** (Malachi 3:6). Nothing can block God's goodness from reaching us. He is undaunted by our inconsistencies and unfaithfulness.

1:18 A shining example of the good things God gives ("whatever is good and perfect") is spiritual birth! We are saved because God **chose to make us his own children.** Our spiritual birth is not by accident or because God had to. The new birth is a gift to all believers (see John 3:3-8; Romans 12:2; Ephesians 1:5; Titus 3:5; 1 Peter 1:3, 23; 1 John 3:9). The **true word** is the gospel, the Good News of salvation (Ephesians 1:13; Colossians 1:5; 2 Timothy 2:15). We hear about the gift of birth through the reading and preaching of the gospel, and we respond to it.

LISTENING AND DOING / 1:19-27

James has spoken of the new birth; he now explains that this new birth should reveal itself in the way we act. He has also connected the new birth with its source, God's word. The ongoing importance of that word will be the subject of the next paragraph. The word that brings us life also guides us in living the life it has brought to us. From the grand scope of God's eternal plan and the unique place of believers in creation, James turns to the painful and practical essentials of living as God's "own children."

1:19 The expression **be quick to listen** is a beautiful way of capturing the idea of active listening. We are not simply to refrain from speaking; we are to be ready and willing to listen. This "quick" listening is obviously to be done with discernment. We are to check what we hear with God's word. If we don't listen both carefully and quickly, we are liable to be led into all kinds of false teaching and error.

Quick to listen and **slow to speak** should be taken together as sides of the same coin. Slowness in speaking means speaking with humility and patience, not with hasty words or nonstop gabbing. Constant talking keeps a person from being able to hear. Wisdom is not always having something to say; it involves listening carefully, considering prayerfully, and speaking quietly. When we talk too much and listen too little, we communicate to others that we think our ideas are much more important than theirs. James wisely advises us to reverse this process. We need to put a mental stopwatch on our conversations and keep track of how much we talk and how much we listen. When people talk to us, do they feel that their viewpoints and ideas have value?

We should also be **slow to get angry.** Anger closes our minds to God's truth (see an example in 2 Kings 5:11; see also Proverbs 10:19; 13:3; 17:28; 29:20). It is anger that erupts when our egos are bruised. It is just the kind of anger that rises from too much fast talking and not enough quick listening.

When injustice and sin occur, we *should* become angry because others are being hurt. But we should not become angry when we fail to win an argument, or when we feel offended or neglected. Selfish anger never helps anybody (see Ecclesiastes 7:9; Matthew 5:21-26; Ephesians 4:26).

1:20 Anger that results in thoughtless, uncontrolled temper and leads to rash, hurtful words **can never make things right in God's sight.** Our anger toward others does not create within us a life that can withstand God's scrutiny. Why not? Because expressed anger tends to be uncontrollable. Anger is inconsistent with Jesus' command to love our enemies (Matthew 5:43-48) and not hate our brothers (Matthew 5:21-26). Anger usurps God's role as judge. In fact, we can be sure our anger is wrong when it keeps us from living as God wants us to live.

1:21 Get rid of all the filth and evil in your lives. According to the Greek, this is a once-for-all action. Why should we do this? Progress in our spiritual lives cannot occur unless we see sin for what it is, quit justifying it, and decide to reject it. James's word picture here has us getting rid of our evil habits and actions like stripping off dirty clothes. After we "get rid," then we need to **humbly accept the message of God,** seeking to live by it because it has been **planted in** our **hearts** and becomes part of our being. God teaches us from the depths of our souls, from the teaching of the Spirit, and by the teaching of Spirit-led people. The soil in which the word is planted must be hospitable in order for it to grow. To make our soil hospitable, we must give up any impurities in our lives. God's word becomes a permanent part of us, guiding us through each day. The implanted word **is strong enough to save** our **souls.** When we absorb the characteristics taught in the word, these are expressed in living. Trials and temptations cannot defeat us if we are applying God's truth to our lives.

1:22 Simply reading, even studying, God's word does not profit us if we do not **obey** what it says. We **listen** to God's **message** not just to know it, but also to do it. We would be **fooling** ourselves to congratulate ourselves about knowledge of Scripture if that's all there is to it. Worthwhile knowledge is a prelude to action; God's word can only grow in the soil of obedience. In order for a lesson to make a difference in a student's life, it must enter the heart and mind, affecting his or her life. It is important to hear God's word, but it is much more important to obey it. We can measure the effectiveness of our Bible study time by the effect it has on our behavior and attitudes. Do we put into action what we have studied?

1:23-24 Some people take a casual look at God's word without letting it affect their lives, like the person who looks so quickly into **a mirror** that flaws go undetected and nothing is changed. They listen

but don't act. The other approach is the intent look, the deep and continued study of God's word that allows a person to see flaws and change his or her life in line with God's standards.

The kind of "mirror" that God's word provides is unique. It shows us our inner nature in the same way that a regular mirror shows our exterior features. Both mirrors reflect what is there. When God's word points out something in us that needs correction, we had better listen and act.

1:25 People who look **steadily** study with serious attention and then make God's law their chosen lifestyle. They study with rapt attention not only once, but continuously; as a result, they remember God's word and **do what it says.** This **law** is **perfect;** it cannot be improved.

This **law sets** people **free** because it is only in obeying God's law that true freedom can be found (compare John 8:31-32). As Christians, we are saved by God's grace, and salvation frees us from sin's control. As believers we are free to live as God created us to live. Of course, this does not mean that we are free to do as we please (1 Peter 2:16)— we are now free to obey God.

God will bless these people who look steadily at God's word, do what it says, don't forget what they have heard, and obey it.

1:26 God's perfect law should be put into practice in our speech. Here James introduces two major themes that he will discuss at length later: the use of the tongue (3:1-12) and the treatment of the unfortunate (throughout the letter).

Knowing how to speak well—as a great teacher would—is not nearly as important as having control of our speech: knowing what to say and where and when to say it. **If you claim to be religious but don't control your tongue, you are just fooling yourself.** The way that others will know whether or not our faith is real is by what we choose to talk about and the way we speak. James will discuss this more in chapter 3.

It is self-deception to have religious practices that do not lead to an ethical lifestyle. Even our outward religious practices are worthless without obedience. And we cannot be obedient if we cannot control our mouths. James does not specify how the tongue offends, but we can imagine a series of ways that our tongues dishonor God—gossip, angry outbursts, harsh criticism, complaining, judging. Our verbal actions speak louder than our religious rituals. Pretending to be religious and convincing ourselves that we are is not only deceptive to others, it is also a deadly self-deception. Conversion is meaningless unless it leads to a changed life. A changed life goes nowhere unless it serves others.

1:27 From a religion easily capable of rationalizing any behavior, James now turns to a relationship where God is allowed to direct the terms of behavior—**pure and lasting religion.** James explains religion in terms of practical service and personal purity. Rituals done with reverence are not wrong; but if a person still refuses to obey God in daily life, his "religion" is not accepted by God.

Pure and lasting religion is not perfect observance of rules and observances; instead, it is a spirit that pervades our hearts and lives (Leviticus 19:18; Isaiah 1:16-17). Like Jesus, James explains religion in terms of a vital inner faith that acts itself out in daily life. Our conduct must be in keeping with our faith (1 Corinthians 5:8). **Orphans and widows** are often mentioned in the concerns of the early church because these were the most obviously "poor" in first-century Israel. The widows, because they had no access to inheritances in Jewish circles, were very much on the outskirts of society. This is why Paul had to develop an entire order concerning widows in his own churches, as in 1 Timothy 5. The widows could not get jobs, and their inheritances went to their oldest sons. It was expected that the widows would be taken care of by their own families, and so the Jews left them with very little economic support. Unless a family member was willing to care for them, they were reduced to begging, selling themselves as slaves, or starving. By caring for these powerless people, the

church put God's word into practice. When we give with no hope of receiving in return, we show what it means to serve others.

Even today, the presence of widows and orphans in our communities and cities makes this directive of James very contemporary. To this group we can also add those who have become de facto widows and orphans through the death of families in divorce. These people have complicated lives. The needs always threaten to overwhelm our human resources. Looking after hurting people is stressful work. Yet we are called to be involved.

In addition, those with pure and lasting religion will **refuse to let the world corrupt them.** To keep ourselves from being corrupted by the world, we need to commit ourselves to Christ's ethical and moral system, not the world's. We are not to adapt to the world's value system based on money, power, and pleasure. True faith means nothing if we are contaminated with such values. James was simply echoing the words of Jesus in what has been called his "high priestly" prayer (John 17), where Jesus emphasized sending his disciples *into* the world but expecting them not to be *of* the world. As we make ourselves available to serve Christ in the world, we must keep putting ourselves under the protection of this prayer. The prayer makes two important points: (1) we remain in the world because that is where Christ wants us; and (2) we will have God's protection.

JAMES 2

DO NOT FAVOR THE RICH / 2:1-13

James 1:19-27 encourages us to put our beliefs into practice. In 2:1-13, James gives a practical lesson: we are not to show favoritism. Such discrimination violates God's truth. James takes it for granted that the believers in the church will welcome strangers. But he is urging them to be alert about the *way* that they welcome strangers into the church. He does not want the warmth or honor of the welcome to be determined by the status or apparent wealth of the visitor. It is showing favoritism based on social standing that James specifically condemns. He makes it a cause for questioning the reality of a person's faith.

2:1 The **brothers and sisters** were members of the church and his family in the Christian faith. The family relationship he is describing is limited to those who **have faith in our glorious Lord Jesus Christ.** Because of their shared position as believers, James's readers were to follow the instructions he was about to give them.

The believers receiving this letter were already guilty of showing **favor to some people more than others.** The believers apparently were judging people based only on externals—physical appearance, status, wealth, power; as a result, they were pandering to and being unduly influenced by people who represented these positions of prestige.

James's command remains important for churches today. Often we treat a well-dressed, impressive-looking person better than someone who looks poor. We do this because we would rather identify with successful people than with apparent failures. The irony, as James reminds us, is that the supposed winners may have gained their impressive lifestyle at our expense. Our churches should show no partiality with regard to people's outward appearance, wealth, or power. The law of love must rule all our attitudes toward others. Too often preferential treatment is given to the rich or powerful when offices for the church need to be filled. Too often, a church brushes aside the suggestions of its more humble or poorer members in favor of the ideas of the wealthy. Such discrimination has no place in our churches.

2:2-3 James launches into a vivid hypothetical case study. Two men were entering the church **meeting.** We can assume that these men were both visiting, since they are described only by appearance. One man was rich, as noted by his **fancy clothes and expensive jewelry.** The other was **poor and dressed in shabby clothes.** In this scenario, the rich man is given **special attention and a good seat.** The believers were impressed by him. He became the object of special service and deference. The poor man, however, gets standing room only, or a seat **on the floor.** He is given neither dignity or comfort. James speaks out against this. It is our relationship with Christ that gives us dignity, not our profession or possessions. When we gather for worship, we ought to be conscious that even if we are familiar with everyone in the room, Christ is present. If there are two or three of us gathered in his name, he is there (Matthew 18:20). Before we worship, we ought to recognize Christ's presence. Can we not assume that he follows his own advice? When Jesus meets with us, does he assume a place of honor or jostle for our attention? Or should we imagine that Jesus takes the place of deepest humility among us and waits to be recognized as Lord? When we neglect or ignore the poor or powerless, we also ignore Christ.

2:4 Such **discrimination** shows that the believers are being **guided by wrong motives.** James condemned their behavior because Christ had made them all one (Galatians 3:28). Why is it wrong to judge a person by his or her economic status? Wealth may indicate intelligence, wise decisions, and hard work. On the other hand, it may mean only that a person had the good fortune of being born into a wealthy family. Or it can even be a sign of greed, dishonesty, and selfishness. When we honor someone just because he or she dresses well, we make appearance more important than character.

Another false assumption that sometimes influ-ences our treatment of the rich is our misunder-standing of God's relationship to wealth. It is deceptively easy to believe riches are a sign of God's blessing and approval. But God does not promise us earthly rewards or riches; in fact, Christ calls us to be ready to suffer for him and give up everything in order to hold on to eternal life (Mat-thew 6:19-21; 19:28-30; Luke 12:14-34; 1 Timothy 6:17-19). We will have untold riches in eternity if we are faithful in our present life (Luke 6:35; John 12:23-25; Galatians 6:7-10; Titus 3:4-8).

2:5 Jesus' first followers were common people. God chose **the poor in this world to be rich in faith.** Christianity has a special message for the poor. In a social system that gave the poor very little, Jesus' message to them was certainly good news. The poor people may not have mattered in that society, but they mattered very much to God. The poor **will inherit the kingdom God promised to those who love him.** The poverty of poor believers is only poverty in the eyes of the world, but they are rich in faith and will inherit the Kingdom. The rich are not excluded from the Kingdom; just as the poor are not "chosen" due to any merit of poverty. However, great riches can stand in the way of a person recognizing his or her need for God (Mark 10:23; Luke 12:34). The poor, on the other hand, have nothing about which they can boast before God (1 Corinthians 1:29). To continue to show favoritism to those who are only rich by the world's standards is not only wrong, but shortsighted.

Rich or poor, believers must obey God and love him. This could be called the heart of James's mes-sage. If we really love God, both our faith in him and our obedience to him will be right. We will not belittle anyone with whom we share a com-mon inheritance.

2:6-7 These believers **insult the poor** because they were not treating them as God treats them. James showed how evil their actions were by making three observations. First, it is the rich who **oppress** others. In this society, the rich oppressed the poor. In James's original case study (2:2-4), both the rich person and the poor person are probably visitors to the church who are unbelievers. At best they are people whose faith is not yet known. So how wrong it is to fawn over this rich person who may not be a believer, and ignore the poor person, who might be a believer.

Second, the rich typically showed no mercy or concern for the poor. They would take the poor **into court,** most likely for not repaying a debt. Wealthy moneylenders often took advantage of the poor. A creditor, if he met a debtor on the street, could literally grab him and drag him into court.

But economic persecution was not the only oppression these believers faced from the wealthy; James's third observation focuses on religious persecution. These rich people are **the ones who slander Jesus Christ** either by speaking evil of him or by insulting Christians. James pointed out the irony that Christians would show favoritism to those who were known to slander Christ!

2:8 Love is the source from which our attitudes toward others should flow. This **royal command** is a law from the King of kings (see Matthew 22:37-40). This law is God's will for his followers: **"Love your neighbor as yourself."** In the Old Testament (Leviticus 19:18; Proverbs 14:21), one's neighbor would be a fellow Israelite; but Jesus' application included everyone with whom we might come into contact. James was calling his readers to obey the royal law of love that would forbid them to discriminate against anyone who entered their fellowship. We are to show favor to everyone, whether the person is rich or poor. We are to be kind, overlooking other superficial trappings.

2:9 Giving **special attention to the rich** is not a minor transgression or an unfortunate oversight; according to James it is **sin,** and those engaged in this action are **guilty of breaking that law** noted in 2:8. Discrimination against anyone on the basis of dress, race, social class, wealth, sex, etc., is a clear violation of the royal law of love. We must treat all people as we would want to be treated. Our attitudes and actions toward others should be guided by love.

2:10 Why is a person who commits **one** sin **as guilty as the person who has broken all of God's laws?** James's point here is that no matter what commandment someone breaks, that person is guilty of an offense against God. He or she has violated the will of God. We cannot excuse the sin of favoritism by pointing to the rest of the good we do. Sin is not simply balanced against good—it must be confessed and forgiven. If we've broken just one law, we are sinners. We can't decide to keep part of God's law and ignore the rest. If we have broken it at all, we need Christ's payment for our sin.

2:11 The law is a unit, and to break one law is to become guilty of the entire law. Jewish theologians of the day would have disagreed with

James, saying some laws were "light" and some "heavy," meaning that breaking some was not as serious as breaking others. It might seem that stumbling on the act of showing favoritism is breaking one of those "least commandments," not nearly as bad as **adultery** or **murder.** But God's law was not written with "heavy" and "light" commands so that obedience to some outweighed obedience to others. Believers are called to consistent obedience.

2:12 Obedience must also be a lifestyle, a habit. **Whenever you speak** and **whatever you do** covers all human behavior (see also Acts 1:1; 7:22; 1 John 3:18). The believers would be **judged** on the basis of their obedience to God's will as expressed in his law. Although God has accepted those who believe in him, we are still called upon to obey him. But his law is not a burden; instead, it sets us **free** because we are obeying out of joy. We are grateful that God has given us freedom from sin's penalty and the Spirit to empower us to do his will.

2:13 Mercy is precisely what the believers were *not* showing when they insulted poor people. If they continued to discriminate, they would be in danger of facing their own judgment without mercy. This is an excellent statement of New Testament ethics: What we do to others we actually do to God, and he returns it upon our heads. We stand before God in need of his mercy. We can't earn forgiveness by forgiving others. But when we withhold forgiveness from others after having received it ourselves, we show that we don't understand or appreciate God's mercy toward us.

Not showing mercy places us only under the judgment of God, but showing mercy places us under God's mercy as well as his judgment. We will always deserve God's judgment because we can never adequately obey God's royal law. But our merciful actions are evidence of our relationship with Christ. And it is that relationship that vindicates us. We stand before God, from whom we know we deserve judgment and upon whom we are depending for mercy. Because of God's character, his **mercy . . . will win out over his judgment against** us. The world is looking for evidence that God is merciful. Being people who have experienced mercy and who express mercy will catch their attention.

FAITH RESULTS IN GOOD WORKS / 2:14-26
The remainder of chapter 2 is often cited to show that the teachings of James and Paul were completely contradictory.

James: "Faith is dead without good deeds" (2:26).
Paul: "We are made right with God through faith and not by obeying the law" (Romans 3:28).

However, careful reading and understanding of both Paul and James will show that instead of contradicting, their writings really complement each other.

First, consider the writers' viewpoints in light of the situations they were addressing in their letters. They were confronting different issues. Paul was responding to the Judaizers, who said works—such as circumcision and observing Jewish ceremonial laws—were necessary for salvation. James was responding to those who believed that mere intellectual agreement was enough to obtain salvation.

Second, there is a difference in the time frame in the believer's life as they make their statements. Paul began at the very beginning—at conversion. No one can ever **earn** God's forgiveness and salvation. We can only accept it. James spoke to the professing believer, one who has already accepted that forgiveness and salvation, explaining that the person must live a new life. No one can be saved by works; no one can be saved without producing works. We are not saved *by* good works, but *for* good works. James's point was not that works must be added to faith, but that genuine faith includes works.

2:14 This person who claims to **have faith** obviously thinks that his belief alone, without any good **actions** (deeds done in obedience to God), is satisfactory in God's sight. However, faith not accompanied by deeds has no saving value. Anyone can say he has faith, but if his lifestyle remains selfish and worldly, then what good is that faith? It is merely faith that believes *about* Jesus, not faith that believes *in* him. **That kind of faith can't save anyone.** Instead, the faith that saves is faith that proves itself in the actions it produces.

Two images help us remember the importance of genuine faith:

1. On one side are people who project confidence in their standing before God and yet show no evidence that their faith affects any of their actions. They may even take pride in the fact that they can believe what they want and that no one has the right to challenge their faith. After all, "only God really knows for sure," they may say.

2. On the other side are people whose lives demonstrate such a frantic flurry of activity that they literally have no time to think or talk about their faith. Those people, whose lives at first exhibit the marks of someone who believes, turn out to have real doubts. They doubt God's acceptance and feel compelled to work very hard in hopes of gaining that acceptance. But trying hard to build merit with God becomes a substitute for faith.

James helps us see that genuine faith will always combine deep trust in God and consistent action in the world. It is not the one who claims to have faith, but the one who actually has faith who is saved.

Someone may ask, "But what if genuine belief never really gets a chance to demonstrate itself in action?" One instance of genuine faith given little time is the case of the thief on the cross who believed in Jesus (Luke 23:32-43). In sight of death, this man acknowledged Jesus as the Christ. Did even this man's short-lived, genuine faith lead to real action? Certainly it did! The dying thief said a few words of profound eloquence: "Jesus, remember me when you come into your Kingdom" (Luke 23:42). The thief could not possibly have known how many times his simple trusting witness during his final agony would give hope to others who felt they were beyond God's help.

Most of us have a great deal more time than the thief on the cross. Do our lives count for as much? Do we declare our faith and then demonstrate its vitality throughout our life?

2:15 James gives an example of a hypothetical person who may have been someone in the church fellowship—**a brother or sister**—who was in real need. To be without **food or clothing** is to be in a desperate yet all-too-common situation. There is hardly a church today within whose walls there are not persons who live without adequate food and shelter.

2:16 Something could be done for this needy person. There would be plenty of clothes and food in the fellowship to care for this person, but the person was sent away empty-handed, with a prayer over his head, but no clothing on his back or food in his stomach.

Too often, we in the church offer mere words—prayers, advice, encouragement—when we are being called upon to act. The need is obvious, and the resources are not lacking, yet the help is not given. **"What good does that do?"** James asks. Faith that does not result in actions is no more effective than a pious wish for the poor person to be warmed and fed. Words without action accomplish nothing.

2:17 A conviction or intellectual belief that refuses to obey the commands of Christ is unprofitable—it is dead. **Good deeds** are the fruit of living **faith.** If there are no positive actions, then the professed faith **is no faith at all—it is dead and useless.** The right actions prove our faith to be real faith. Believing involves faith keeping company with action. If those around us note our actions, they should be led to know the faith that motivates them. If others hear us speak of faith, they must also see us act out that faith.

2:18 This **someone** considers **faith** and **good deeds** to be separate and alternate expressions of Christianity. "You do your deeds, I'll have my faith, and we'll be religious in our own ways." But the two cannot be separated without ceasing to be alive. Faith lives in the action it generates; actions require faith to gain a particular meaning.

James responded with a challenge: **"I can't see your faith if you don't have good deeds, but I will show you my faith through my good deeds."** Faith cannot be demonstrated apart from action. Faith is within us; it can only be seen by the actions it produces through us. Anyone can profess faith, but only action shows its genuineness.

2:19 The acceptance of a creed (even a true one) is not enough to save anyone. The **demons** have complete and thorough conviction that **there is one God,** but they are terrified by that truth. They believe in God only to hate and resist him in every way they can. Their "faith" even moves them to a negative reaction, while the faith of some of James's readers isn't real enough to give them a shiver. The demons **tremble in terror** and demonstrate that their "faith" is real, though misdirected.

2:20 James addresses his hypothetical person who held the above views, calling that person a **fool.** The foolish person is literally a "hollow man." If the faith around which we build our lives turns out to be empty, we are truly hollow people. **When will you ever learn that faith that does not result in good deeds is useless?** There are times when we need more teaching or understanding in order to respond to God's direction. But most often we

know what needs to be done, yet are unwilling to act. When it comes to putting into practice what we know, is it our habit to obey God?

2:21 From his own case studies, James now turns to historical figures from the Old Testament that he expects will confirm what he has been teaching about the importance of active faith. **Abraham** was one of the Old Testament figures most revered by the Jews (see Genesis 11:27–25:11 for Abraham's biography). Abraham's remarkable obedience in being willing to sacrifice his son at God's command was evidence of the works for which Abraham **was declared right with God.**

What was Abraham doing **when he offered his son Isaac on the altar?** He was trusting God. The lesson we can draw from Abraham's life is not a comparison between his sacrifices and ours. We can expect that in one way or another, our faith will have to grow from internal trust to external action. Eventually, like Abraham, we too will have to answer the question, "Do I really trust God?"

2:22 Abraham had great faith in God (Genesis 15:6), but James points out that Abraham's faith was much more than just belief in the one God—the fruit of Abraham's great faith was in his deeds: **His faith was made complete by what he did—by his actions.** His faith produced his actions, and his actions completed his faith, meaning they "perfected" or "matured" it. Mature and complete believers are produced through perseverance in trials; mature and complete faith is produced through works of obedience to God. Faith and works should not be confused with each other, but neither can they be separated from each other.

2:23 Abraham believed God, so God gave Abraham the status of a right relationship with him—and this happened *before* Abraham's noted works (such as his willingness to sacrifice Isaac), and even before Abraham was circumcised (see Paul's words in Romans 4:1-17). The **Scriptures** to which James is referring is Genesis 15:6, **"Abraham believed God, so God declared him to be righteous."** James showed that Abraham's righteousness was the basis and reason for all those actions. Because of Abraham's great faith and obedience, he held the privileged status of being **called "the friend of God"** (see also 1 Chronicles 20:7; Isaiah 41:8). Acting out our trust in God will lead to friendship with him, as it did in Abraham's case.

2:24 We are made right with God by what we do, not by faith alone. Many have said that this statement contradicts Paul's position, who wrote: "We are made right with God through faith and not by obeying the law" (Romans 3:28). Indeed, if both

James and Paul used the term "made right" (justified) in the same way, this verse would contradict Paul's teaching about justification by faith alone. But for James, being "made right" refers to God's final verdict over our entire Christian lives, whereby we are declared righteous for having lived a life that was faithful to the end. For Paul, being "made right" is the initial granting of righteousness upon a person's acceptance of Christ. For James, "works" **(what we do)** are the natural products of true faith; for Paul, "works" ("obeying the law") are what people were trying to do in order to be saved. For James, faith alone is the shallow belief in an idea; no commitment or life change is involved. For Paul, faith is saving faith—the belief that brings about an intimate union with Christ and results in salvation and obedience.

Paul made clear that a person enters into God's Kingdom only by faith; James made clear that God requires good deeds from those who are *in* the Kingdom.

A person receives salvation by faith alone, not by doing works of obedience; but a saved person does works of obedience because of that faith. For people who rely on their religious "busyness" for their salvation or merit before God, Paul's words are critical—those works alone can do nothing to save them. For people who rely on their intellectual assent of a belief, with only a verbal commitment, James's words are critical—their belief alone can do nothing to save them.

Two brief questions that help us monitor our spiritual health are: Who am I trusting? and Why am I working? If we are trusting anyone (including ourselves) other than Christ as the source and provider of our justification, we are lost. If we are acting for any reason other than in obedience and thanksgiving to Christ for what he has done for us, we are lost. We only truly find our salvation in Christ. Out of our trust in him will flow action.

2:25 In the same way, even **Rahab the prostitute was made right with God by her actions.** God's final judgment on a person's life considers the righteousness that person shows through works. But why would James bring up Rahab? After speaking of the great faith of Abraham, the father of Israel, James cited the example of Rahab, a pagan woman with a bad reputation (see Joshua 2:1-24; 6:22-25). But these two people, as opposite as they were, cemented James's argument—both people were **made right with God** on the basis of their **actions** that resulted from their faith. The contrast is not between faith and works, but between genuine faith and false faith.

2:26 Faith and **good deeds** are as important to each other as **body** and **spirit.** Good deeds are not added to faith; instead, the right kind of faith is faith that "works," that results in good deeds. Otherwise, Christianity is nothing more than an idea.

No one is moved to action without faith; no one's faith is real unless it moves him or her to action. The action is obedience to God. This draws us back to James's words in the first part of this chapter concerning care for others. The believer must do what God calls him to do—serve his brothers and sisters in Christ, refuse to discriminate among them, and help them out with good deeds.

Understanding how faith and deeds work together still doesn't mean that our lives will be different. James is about to continue with a series of life situations that we all encounter. It is in these everyday events that we demonstrate our faith to be alive or dead. From time to time, we need to take our own spiritual pulse by matching our lives with God's word. But we also need to have people around us, the body of Christ, whom we can ask, "How do you see me putting my faith in Christ into action?"

JAMES 3

CONTROLLING THE TONGUE / 3:1-12

In the early church, teachers were very important. Both the survival and spiritual depth of believers depended on them. In the church at Antioch, they were ranked in status with the prophets who sent out Paul and Barnabas (Acts 13:1). Teachers were the point of contact for all new believers because converts needed instruction in the facts of the gospel, and teachers would build them up in the faith. The problem, however, was that some teachers had the ability to communicate but were driven by very worldly motivations. They would take leading positions in a church, form cliques, and use their teaching positions to criticize others. In this way, they could maintain their position and importance.

In this chapter, James's immediate concern is with the speech of false teachers who are ruining believers with their uncontrolled tongues. From that immediate concern he launches into the wider area of the use of speech among believers.

3:1 James taught that people should not rush to **become teachers in the church.** Many of his status-conscious readers would have desired the reputable position of teachers in the community. Coming hard on the heels of chapter 2, one of the most honorable "works" that would immediately come to the Jewish mind would be the position of teaching. James has in mind a greater emphasis on spiritual growth and self-control before someone assumed the role of a teacher. Teachers **will be judged by God with greater strictness.** Teaching authority carries with it greater responsibility. As works reveal the depths of a person's faith, so words show the depth of a person's maturity. The teacher is held to greater accountability because of his or her key teaching role (Luke 12:42-48).

3:2 We all make many mistakes or slip up when we are off guard. We all stumble, but our most frequent failures occur when we are speaking. Because we are prone to make mistakes in our speech, we need to be even more careful to let God control what we say. He is capable of guiding our motivation, our thoughts, our very choice of words, and even the impact our communication has on others.

Many people may think that it is impossible to **control their tongues,** but most people haven't even begun to try. The ability to control the tongue is the mark of true maturity for the Christian (see 1:19, "be slow to speak"). When Jesus confronted the religious leaders about their accusations against him, he said that out of the abundance of the heart the mouth speaks—showing that what is inside of a person affects what they do with their speech (Matthew 12:33-37). He also said that we must give account for every careless word we utter (Matthew 12:36). People who can control their tongues will be able to **control themselves in every other way.** The wisdom and love from God and the self-restraint given by the Holy Spirit will help us exercise this control. (See Proverbs 15:1-4 for more on how a mature person controls his or her tongue.)

3:3-5 Bit . . . Rudder . . . Tongue . . . Spark. What do these things have in common? They are all small but very effective controllers—they each direct something much larger than themselves. James is building a case for the damaging power of our words. We see this evidenced in history when dictators such as Adolf Hitler, the Ayatol-

lah Khomeini, Joseph Stalin, and Saddam Hussein used their words to mobilize people to destroy others. We see it evidenced in church splits and in the ruining of a pastor's reputation. And we see how verbal abuse in the home can destroy the very personhood and character of spouses and children.

Satan uses the tongue to divide people and pit them against one another. Idle words are damaging because they quickly spread destruction. We dare not be careless with our words, thinking that we can apologize later, because even when we do, the damage remains. A few words spoken in anger can destroy a relationship that took years to build. Remember that words are like fire; they can neither control nor reverse the damage they do.

3:6 The **tongue** is **full of wickedness** because of the damage it can cause in the world and bring to the rest of the Christian community. The uncontrolled tongue can turn one's life **into a blazing flame of destruction.** This means that the tongue can destroy all the good that we've built up over a lifetime. While we have ministered for years and years and seen abundant fruit, if we fail to control the tongue, we can undo all the good we have built up in our years of ministry. Our speech has a power that few other capabilities possess, for our tongue can be **set on fire by hell itself.** Flames of hate, prejudice, slander, jealousy, and envy seem to come from the very lake of fire where Satan will be punished (see Revelation 20:10, 14-15 for more on the lake of fire).

3:7-8 Although **people can tame all kinds of animals . . . no one can tame the tongue.** Why? Because **it is an uncontrollable evil, full of deadly poison.** The tongue is always capable of evil; it remains untamed throughout life. With our tongues we can lash out and destroy. By recognizing the tongue's deadly capacity, we can take the first steps to keep it under control.

No person can tame the tongue, but Christ can. To do it, he goes straight for the heart (Mark 7:14-15; Psalm 51:10) and the mind (Romans 12:1-2). We should not try to control our tongues with our own strength; we should rely on the Holy Spirit. He will give us increasing power to monitor and control what we say. For when we feel offended or unjustly criticized, the Spirit will remind us of God's love and keep us from reacting. The Holy Spirit will heal the hurt and keep us from lashing out. We can make sure we are in the Spirit's control by incorporating Scripture into our lives and by asking the Spirit to direct our thoughts and actions each day.

3:9-10 How strange that the tongue is able to speak **praises** to **our Lord and Father** at one time, and then it **breaks out into curses against** other people. We should have the same attitude of respect for fellow human beings as we have for God, because they are created in his image. Yet we have this horrible, double-sided tongue, so that **blessing and cursing come pouring out of the same mouth.**

Some people think that the only restraint against foul talk, calling people names, and bad language is social disapproval. But God's word condemns it. James says that the reason we should not curse people is because they have been made in God's likeness. We should not use any word or name that reduces them to anything less than their full stature as God's created beings.

3:11-12 A spring cannot have **both fresh** and **bitter water.** Although different kinds of water won't bubble from the same opening, Christians' speech can be very inconsistent. One time we may speak in a way that honors God and another time in a way that gives Satan power to operate. We can choose how we will respond. If we do not, we give Satan an opening to control us. We should produce the kind of fruit that we've been created and regenerated to produce—the fruit of righteousness (see James 3:18)—just as you would expect to **pick olives** from an olive tree. Only a renewed heart can produce pure speech. If the source of our thoughts and actions is the love of God in our lives, then we will not be able to generate the kind of negative speech that James warns us against.

WISDOM FROM HEAVEN / 3:13-18

James lays down a challenge before the church for those who claimed to have true wisdom: they need to observe the true wisdom that comes from heaven. The church James wrote to was a church under pressure. When under pressure, a church can split into factions. There was no formal clergy or ordination process, so self-styled teachers could emerge, claiming to have wisdom. As each teacher promoted his brand of wisdom and gained a following, the community of believers was divided. In the New Testament church there were many problems with factions or a "party spirit" (see Acts 6; 1 Corinthians 1; see also Philippians 1:17; 2:3).

Jesus taught that we would know true teachers from false ones by how they lived (Matthew 7:15-23). Good teachers will exemplify good life-disciplines. Their activities, actions, and accomplishments will reveal the true heart of their Christian faith. In this section, good deeds are contrasted with bitterness, and humility is contrasted with selfish ambition.

3:13 The truly **wise** person demonstrates his or her understanding of Christ by the way he or she lives. Our works show where our hearts are invested (Matthew 6:19-21, 33). Do our attitudes and motives match our actions? While we may not claim to be wise, we can aim at living in wise ways—**a life of steady goodness.** The guidance given to us in God's word is dependable wisdom. But as we seek to do good deeds, we must watch out for pride. Pride is having an attitude of self-importance about the talents and abilities that God has given us and using them to set ourselves up as superior or to be divisive in our relationships with others. Wisdom, then, involves both actions and attitudes in living. A wise life will display not only goodness, but also humility.

3:14 Being **bitterly jealous** is misguided zeal that results in contentiousness. It is anger at the accomplishments of others. Whenever we find fault with a leader, we must ask ourselves what is motivating us to feel strongly about that person's failure. Do we actually share the same weakness? Do we imagine ourselves doing better in that role? Or are we, in fact, simply envious of the abilities or success God has allowed him or her to have? A positive answer to any of these ought to make us very careful in how we express our criticisms.

Here and in Philippians 2:3, **selfish ambition** refers to leaders in the church who are developing a "party spirit." This produces factions who are for or against the pastor or certain programs, who take sides on issues not necessarily central to the Christian faith. Selfish ambition is the desire to live for one's self and no one or nothing else, only for what a person can get out of it. In an attempt to persuade others, the person may lose his sense of reason and become fanatical. Having confidence in only his knowledge, he arrogantly lords it over others. Such a person should not **brag about being wise** for **that is the worst kind of lie.**

3:15 The source and standards of this kind of wisdom are from the world and not God. Its teachers are self-centered and shallow. This wisdom doesn't come from faith—it is **earthly** and **unspiritual.** "Unspiritual" could refer to the natural man. The term for unspiritual is used in the New Testament for the person who does not have God's Spirit (3:15), or does not accept the guidance that comes from the Spirit of God (1 Corinthians 2:14). This person teaches only the wisdom of this life, based on human feelings and human reasoning alone. The real source of these thoughts is **the Devil** whose purposes are always destructive; they can produce a climate in the church, at home, and at work that damages relationships. Think of how quickly our words, language, and tone of voice can create a destructive climate.

3:16-17 People filled with **jealousy and selfish ambition** think they must be first in everything. They cannot stand to see anyone else in the limelight, or have anyone else cast a shadow on what they do. This leads to desires and strategies for revenge that can lead to disaster. By contrast, the following seven characteristics of heavenly wisdom are strung together like pearls. They are what wisdom is and produces.

The wisdom that comes from heaven is . . . pure. To be fruitful for God, we must have moral and spiritual integrity. **It is also peace loving.** This is peace that goes beyond inner peace; it is opposed to strife. It is peace between people, and between people and God. It must be peace that affects the community. Christians must not only prefer peace, but they should also seek to spread it.

It is **gentle at all times.** This is the opposite of self-seeking. It does not demand its own right. To be gentle is to make allowances for others, to temper justice with mercy. It is the kind of treatment that we would like to receive from others.

This wisdom is also **willing to yield to others.** Heavenly wisdom is reasonable, flexible—willing to listen and to change. Just as good soldiers willingly follow orders from their superiors, people with heavenly wisdom willingly follow God's orders and respond to his correction.

This wisdom is also **full of mercy and good deeds.** God's wisdom is full of God's gracious forgiveness. And his love leads to practical action, helping and serving others. We should be willing to forgive even when the problems we are facing are someone else's fault.

God's wisdom **shows no partiality,** meaning single-minded and free from prejudice toward people and without double-mindedness toward God (1:5-8). Finally, it is **always sincere,** meaning "unhypocritical." God's wisdom makes people genuine.

3:18 Peacemakers are able to **plant seeds of peace and reap a harvest of goodness.** This section gives three suggestions for controlling the tongue:

1. Seek God's wisdom.
2. Admit jealousy and arrogance without trying to cover them up.
3. Create a climate of peace wherever God leads you.

In Matthew 5:9, Jesus promises that the peacemakers will be blessed. Their reward will be to see right relationships between God and people. (For more on sowing wisdom and truth and reaping righteousness see Psalm 1:3; Proverbs 11:30; Galatians 6:7-10; Philippians 1:11.)

JAMES 4

SUBMIT YOURSELVES TO GOD / 4:1-12

At the end of chapter 3, James explains that false wisdom leads to disorder and every kind of evil (3:16), and that true wisdom has wonderful results (3:17-18). From this poetic description of wisdom expressed in general terms, James returns to practical application. His readers need to know what wisdom is, but they need even more to live wisely. Chapter 4 begins with a challenge to change their current behavior. His questions take on the firmness and commitment of a person who understands that unchallenged evil will not go away. James wants his brothers and sisters to resist not only the practices of evil wisdom, but also the source from which this wisdom springs. His plan requires a declaration of allegiance to God and open rebellion from the Devil's ranks.

We need to feel the impact of these same truths as James describes situations that are only too true in churches today. The quarrels and fights that James observed still characterize the life of the body of Christ and seriously hamper the effective communication of the gospel. Outsiders who look to the church as a place of solace and salvation often find it is full of strife. We desperately need God's wisdom in our churches.

4:1 The word **quarrels** refers to fighting without weapons, as in personal conflicts. These conflicts have nothing to do with quarrels with the pagan world; these are quarrels within the church, among believers. James is describing a condition where a group has come to a state of war, with open skirmishes breaking out among people. Sides have been chosen, positions have been dug in. In cases like this, believers have ceased being peacemakers (3:18); instead, they live in open antagonism toward one another. The word **fights** refers to battles with weapons, an armed conflict. It was used figuratively to indicate the struggle between powers, both earthly and spiritual.

Obviously, disagreements will occur in every church. But when they happen, are we wise enough to understand why? Do we know their source? When handled correctly, with godly wisdom, they can lead to growth. Sadly, however, some churches become permanent battlegrounds. New believers find themselves in a cross fire of arguments, resentments, and power struggles that may carry a veneer of spiritual truth, but are more often simply personal conflicts between people. In the process, innocent bystanders are sometimes deeply wounded. Many of us know people who have been alienated from the church because of a conflict that had nothing to do with the gospel.

Fights and quarrels are being caused, not by some external source, but by the people's **evil desires.** When everyone seeks his or her own pleasure, only strife, hatred, and division can result. **At war within** suggests a raging battle fought between the desire to do good and the desire to do evil.

4:2 The craving described here becomes so strong that the people **scheme and kill to get it.** The word **kill** can be taken as a hyperbole for bitter hatred. Instead of rethinking their desires, the people being described by James resort to jealousy, fights, quarrels, and worse. Yet, for all their anxious self-seeking and antagonism in getting what they want, they still **can't possess it.**

Why? We learned (from getting our first tricycle or doll to driving our first new car) that fulfilled desires don't satisfy at the level they advertise.

Sometimes we actually do get just what we wanted, only to discover that we still do not have what we really **needed**—the deep contentment that only comes when we are right with God. Trusted alone, our desires will only lead us to the things of this earth and not to the things of God.

In summary, James's message is: **The reason you don't have what you want is that you don't ask God for it.** In other words, "You don't have what you desire because you don't desire God."

4:3 Almost as bad as not asking is asking wrongly. If we misunderstand the correct use of prayer, we might not pray at all, or we might attempt to manipulate God. Later, James makes it clear that, when we pray, we must humble ourselves before God (4:7). Otherwise we will not be answered. People should not be surprised when their prayers go unanswered because often **their whole motive is wrong.** They were going to spend what they received on their pleasures (the same word as "desires" in 4:1). The people's desires were so strong that they were fighting, quarreling, and then using prayer to get what they wanted. Their motives were not to help others, but to satisfy themselves.

4:4 The shocking word **adulterers** graphically describes the spiritual unfaithfulness of the people and intends to jar them into facing their true spiritual condition. These believers were trying to love God *and* have an affair with the world. The fact that God would express in the strongest terms possible the importance of faithfulness ought to unsettle us. Biblical standards of personal, marital, and spiritual behavior are under a constant attack of erosion. We are bombarded with the message to compromise.

From the world's point of view, we should be flexible, tolerant of sin, and accommodating. But it won't work, because **friendship with this world makes** a person **an enemy of God.** For believers, the world and God are two distinct objects of affection, but they are direct opposites. The **world** is the system of evil under Satan's control, all that is opposed to God. To be friendly with the world, then, is to adopt its values and desires (see also Romans 8:7-8; 2 Timothy 4:10; 1 John 2:15-17). These believers may indeed love God, but they are also infatuated with the benefits of this world's system. They worship God, but they want the influence, living standards, financial security, and perhaps some of the freedom the world offers. These pursuits will only undermine the generosity, caring, and sharing that should characterize Christians.

What then is a believer's proper relationship to the world? Some have used biblical statements like this one from James as a basis for a radical withdrawal from the "world." But withdrawal is not the answer. Although it is true that we are called to be in the world but not to belong to this world (John 17:14), we should love the people in this world enough to give them the gospel. To do so, we need to befriend them without befriending the things of this world that are opposed to God (see 1 John 3:15-17).

4:5 James 4:6 (the next verse) is a quotation from the Old Testament—namely, Proverbs 3:34. However, this expression is not a direct quotation of any verse in the Old Testament. James is following an approach used elsewhere in the New Testament of summarizing Old Testament teaching rather than quoting directly. The Greek text of the phrase, **the Holy Spirit, whom God has placed within us, jealously longs for us to be faithful,** offers several alternative renderings, so the context must help us determine what the writer meant. Either James was saying that God, who caused his Spirit to dwell in the believers, is jealous for their friendship, or he was saying that the spirit that God put in man is one prone to jealousy—and therefore must be kept in check. The point of the statement is to affirm the believers' friendship with God over against the world.

We may say that we will befriend both God and the world, but in practice, we can only choose one way. The more we give ourselves to the world, the stronger will be our allegiance to the world. The more we give ourselves to God, the stronger will be our bond with him. "Wherever your treasure is, there your heart and thoughts will also be" (Matthew 6:21), said Jesus.

To those who make the wise choice, facing what may seem like a hopeless battle, James adds a wonderful word of hope.

4:6 We will need to rely on God's **strength to stand against such evil desires.** That strength is available. Quoting from Proverbs 3:34, James offers hope to those who desire friendship with God. **God sets himself against the proud** because pride makes us self-centered and leads us to conclude that we deserve all we can see, touch, or imagine. It creates greedy appetites for far more than we need. Pride can subtly cause us to no longer see our sins or our need for forgiveness. But humility opens the way for God's grace to flow into our lives; thus, **God shows favor to the humble.** Humility is not weakness; instead, it is the only place that believers gain courage to face all their temptations and sins with God's strength. As God gives us more grace, we realize that this world's seductive attractions are only cheap substitutes for what God has to offer. It is our choice—we can humble ourselves and receive God's grace, or we can continue in our pride and self-sufficiency and experience his anger.

How do we, so prone to pride at the very moments when we think we might be approaching humility, discover true humility? How do we become the kind of humble people who find the overflowing grace that God promises? Having revealed our need, James now points clearly to the way.

4:7 We **humble** ourselves **before God** by recognizing both his friendship and his authority. We enter a relationship with God, not as equals, but as trusting servants. Although he is not specifically defining the term, James is describing the life of faith. True faith responds to God actively rather than passively. Although God initiates and facilitates all that occurs between us and him, our involvement is never entirely excluded. Personal humility before God is part of living faith.

Satan knows that as long as he can stimulate human pride, he can delay God's plan, even if only temporarily. But as powerful as Satan is, his only power over believers is in his powerful temptations. We can **resist the Devil, and he will flee from** us. Conversely, a lack of resistance will practically guarantee ongoing harassment by Satan (see also Ephesians 6:10-18 and 1 Peter 5:6-9).

Once we have identified the Devil as our enemy, we need to understand who he is and how he operates in order to effectively resist him. The Devil's primary purpose is to separate man from God. Destined for destruction, he wants to take as much of creation with him as he possibly can. Among the reasons we so desperately need God's grace is that we are locked in mortal combat with a superior enemy. We need God's help to resist Satan's separating schemes and instead draw near to God.

The commands that follow, and indeed the rest of this letter, are footnotes on the above two statements. Both humility before God and resistance of the Devil are required.

4:8 The idea of humility before God now includes the added benefit of God's immediate response. We can **draw close to God, and God will draw close to** us. The command to **wash your hands** means to purify our actions and change our external behavior. The way we live matters to God. As we draw near to God, we will become aware of habits and actions in our lives that are not pleasing to him. Washing our hands pictures the removal of these things from the way we live. We must distance ourselves from the sins that God points out.

Similarly, the command to **purify your hearts** calls for purity of thoughts and motives—changes on the inside. The people could not remain **hypocrites,** trying to love both God and the world. Purity of heart, then, implies single-mindedness.

4:9 As God draws near to us, we ought to sense our unworthiness. After all, we are being allowed to approach the holy, perfect God.

James has described a long spiritual process in the last eight verses. He began by describing people in conflict with each other and within themselves. Then he described the source of those conflicts as inappropriate desires motivated in large part by trying to stay close to the world and to God. Unmasking of such a life and calling believers to humility may not be a welcome message. Surrender may not come easily. Long-held desires may respond with defiance. Repentance may have to include remembering how far we have broken from God's way before we have turned back.

These different terms, **sorrow, deep grief, sadness,** and **gloom,** capture the struggle of a soul drawing near to God. There is a dying which takes place. This is a call to deep and heartfelt repentance. The people's **laughter** (scornful laughter that refused to take sin seriously) and their **joy** in the world's pleasures need to be completely changed—to mourning over their sins (see also Luke 6:25). Until this happens, there is no room for the laughter of real freedom and the joy of the Lord. The Christian life involves joy—but when we realize our sins, we must be mournful so that we can repent. Only after mourning can we move on to joy in the grace God gives us.

4:10 To **bow down before the Lord** and to **admit** our **dependence on him** means recognizing that our worth comes from God alone. It is recognizing our desperate need for his help and submitting to his will for our lives. Although we do not deserve God's favor, he reaches out to us in love and gives us warmth and dignity, despite our human shortcomings. When we do so, the promise is sure: **he will lift** us **up and give** us **honor.** One of the most touching biblical illustrations of this truth is found

in Jesus' parable of the forgiving father (see Luke 15:11-32). The son took his inheritance and set out to be the world's best friend. It was not until he found himself bankrupt in every way that he repented. He returned home, grieving. The son confessed to his father that he was unworthy to be called a son. But the father lifted him up and welcomed him back into the family. The act of returning required submission. The wayward son's words of repentance required humility. The end result was great joy. Humility before God will be followed by his lifting us up.

4:11 With an abrupt shift from describing an appropriate attitude toward God, James turns to the proper relations between believers. We love God by being humble before him; we love our neighbor by refusing to **speak evil.** To **speak evil** can take many forms. We may speak the truth about a person and still be unkind, or we may spread gossip that others have no business knowing. We may be questioning someone's authority or nullifying their good work by backbiting. Obviously, this hurts the harmony among believers (see also Romans 1:29-30; 2 Corinthians 12:20; 1 Peter 2:1). The tense in the Greek reveals that James is forbidding a practice that is already in progress. The people were in the habit of criticizing one another.

This verse includes the sixth and seventh times in his letter that James has mentioned **God's law** (see 1:25; 2:8-10, 12). It is the royal law—the law that frees or convicts, the law that must be kept. Here the law is under attack. The specific problem being confronted violates the ninth commandment: "Do not testify falsely against your neighbor" (Exodus 20:16). It also violates the more fundamental law of Christ, "Love your neighbor as yourself" (Matthew 22:39; see also Leviticus 19:18). Jesus called this the second greatest commandment (Mark 12:31). If a believer speaks against another believer, he is **criticizing and condemning** the law because he is not showing love and is not treating others as he would like to be treated. His disobedience shows disregard for the law, for he is passing judgment on its validity. By doing so, he is putting himself above God. When we judge one another in this slanderous way, we are clearly failing to submit to God.

4:12 God alone is both the source and enforcer of the law. We who are accountable to God's law cannot place ourselves in God's place. God rewards those who obey the law and destroys those who disobey (see Deuteronomy 32:39; 1 Samuel 2:6; Psalm 68:20; 75:6-7; Matthew 10:28). James also takes away any rights we might claim for criticizing our neighbors. Behind the critical spirit is an attitude that usurps God's authority and is full of pride. There should be no critical, harsh faultfinding in the body of Christ. The principle in this verse does not prohibit the proper action of a church against a member who is acting in flagrant disobedience to God (1 Corinthians 5–6). Rather, James is concerned with the critical speech that condemns or judges others' actions and their standing with God. He is confronting individuals

who might be tempted to set themselves up as personal watchdogs on other believers.

We might think that just criticizing a church member or spreading a little interesting gossip is not that serious—especially when compared to other sins. But the Bible sees it as a sin of utmost seriousness because it breaks the law of love and it tries to usurp God's authority. As we saw in chapter 3, the tongue is a tool of deadly sin. We dare not minimize its danger.

TRUST GOD IN MAKING PLANS / 4:13-17

James maintains the passion of the last section in this new one. The progression has moved from humbling ourselves and our relationships to God, to our future and the need to entrust it to God.

This section includes three essential facts of life that make for good planning:

1. God is in control (4:15)
2. Life is a daily gift (4:15)
3. All our going and doing must be carried out with the first two points in mind.

This section is not an argument against making careful plans; rather, it is a caution to submit to God, even in our planning.

4:13 The **you people** is most likely businesspeople. Addressing this letter to scattered people presumes, at least in part, people moving to establish new lives in distant places. But its lessons apply to any situation that requires planning.

Planning is not evil—in fact, businesspeople are wise to plan ahead. The problem that James addresses, however, is that God is not included in those plans. The merchants plan with arrogance, thinking they can go wherever they like and stay for as long as they like. Their way of planning, doing business, and using money may be honest, but it is really no different than the planning of any pagan businessperson. These Christian business people ought to know better.

4:14 There is a problem with these well-made plans—no one can **know what will happen tomorrow,** to say nothing of a year in the future (see Proverbs 27:1; Luke 12:16-21). These people were planning as if their future was guaranteed. James is not suggesting that they make no plans because of possible disaster, but to be realistic about the future as they trust God to guide them. Because the future is uncertain, it is even more important that we completely depend on God. Our lives are uncertain, **like the morning fog** that covers the countryside in the morning and then is burned away by the sun. Life is short no matter how long we live. We shouldn't be deceived into

thinking we have plenty of time left to live for Christ, to enjoy our loved ones, or to do what we know we should. Today is the day to live for God! Then, no matter when our lives end, we will have fulfilled God's plans for us.

4:15 Believers cannot live independently of God; therefore, our plans cannot ignore him. We must make sure those plans include the clause, **if the Lord wants us to.** We are to plan, but we are to recognize God's higher will and divine sovereignty. This means far more than simply saying, "If God wills," whenever we speak about future plans, for that too can become meaningless. It means planning *with* God as we make our plans. Our plans should be evaluated by God's standards and goals, and they should be prayed over with time spent listening for God's advice. Such planning pleases God.

4:16 These businesspeople, instead of focusing on God's will in their plans, were arrogantly boasting as though they could control their own destiny. Such **boasting is evil** because it takes no thought of God.

4:17 This verse sums up all of chapters 1–4 and the entire ethical problem in the whole book of James. He may be telling these merchants that they know what they should do—that is, honor God in their business practices. If they ignore that, they sin. In a broader sense, James adds these words as an admonition for all his readers to do what he has written: **it is sin to know what you ought to do and then not do it.** They have been told, so they have no excuse.

We tend to limit sins to specific acts—*doing* wrong. But James tells us that sin is also *not* doing what is right. (These two kinds of sin are sometimes called sins of commission and sins of omission.) It is a sin to lie; it can also be a sin to know the truth and not tell it. It is a sin to speak evil of someone; it is also a sin to avoid that person when you know he needs your friendship. We should be willing to help others as the Holy Spirit guides us. If God has directed you to do a kind act, to render a service to others, or to restore a relationship—do it. You will experience a renewed and refreshed vitality to your Christian faith.

JAMES 5

WARNING TO THE RICH / 5:1-6

Chapter 1 included the challenge to see that humble circumstances have distinct spiritual benefits (see 1:9-11) as opposed to riches, which require humility. In chapter 2, James warned about the destructiveness of preferential treatment based on wealth. At the end of chapter 4, James warned against being seduced by the world. He begins chapter 5 by warning wealthy non-Christians of their hopeless end and the worthlessness of their riches. Their wealth will not save them from God's judgment. This should comfort the believers, knowing that any wrongs against them will be avenged. It should also be a clear warning that they shouldn't make riches the focus of their desires because, ultimately, riches amount to nothing.

5:1 These **rich people** are probably not believers, but rich nonbelievers (perhaps the same people referred to in 2:6). Very likely the wealthy landowners are the objects of James's scathing rebuke. These rich people have lavish surroundings, plenty of food, plenty of money. But there are **terrible troubles ahead of** them—not earthly suffering, but eternal suffering—and they should be wailing in sorrow for what they will lose then. The words **weep and groan** were often used in the Old Testament by the prophets to describe the reaction of the wicked when the Day of the Lord (the day of God's judgment) arrives (see Isaiah 13:6; 15:3; Amos 8:3). Jesus said that those who would be excluded from God's Kingdom would be weeping and gnashing their teeth (Matthew 8:12; 22:13; 24:51; 25:30).

5:2 The instability of wealth is the clearest warning of the coming "troubles" of the rich. Goods that are **rotting** and clothing that turns to **rags** indicate the impermanence of life. Their money, security, lavishness, and self-indulgence are as good as rotted because they can do nothing for them in eternity.

5:3 Precious metals have been hoarded away, unused. When it is kept from being used to help others, wealth becomes **worthless.** James warns us that even what seems most indestructible (**gold and silver**) is doomed if it is not put to good use. The uselessness of hoarded gold and silver will **eat away** at them **in hell.** It will reveal the greed, selfishness, and wickedness of the rich. They failed to do good with what they had, and that was sin (4:17).

Few people in the Western world can read this passage with understanding and not be at least singed by its truth. We have probably added a new dimension to the problem in that we have not hoarded in order to preserve for later; rather, we have hoarded in order to waste. Believers today find themselves participating in society's tendency to consume as much as possible without regard to the conditions elsewhere in the world, or even what we will leave to our children and grandchildren. Will not our **treasure stand as evidence against** us **on the day of judgment?**

5:4 These **field workers** worked for rich people during the day and would be paid at the end of the day. They were poor peasants. Most likely they had been forced off their own land by foreclosures, and then they hired themselves out to the wealthy holder of a huge estate. They lived on the verge of starvation—today's wages bought tomorrow's food. If a worker did not receive his pay, his whole family went hungry. If the owner refused to pay, there was little or nothing the worker could do. The money that should have gone to the workers is also evidence against these rich people. The cries of the withheld **wages** and **of the reapers have reached the ears of the Lord Almighty.** The only resource the poor had was to call out to God.

If we are facing oppression, faith requires that we remember God is our strength and our defender. Temporary circumstances do not change the fact of God's sovereignty. God will protect us from spiritual evil in this life and give us the joys we desire in the next. He will insure that justice will be done, and he will judge the oppressors.

5:5 The lifestyles of the rich and famous may make interesting media fodder, but they are noxious to God. These rich, who have taken the land from the poor and then refused to pay their deserved wages, have shown gross lack of concern and selfishness. To this they have added an attitude of wastefulness and self-indulgence that God detests.

A life of **luxury** and **satisfying every whim** is essentially worthless. Money will mean nothing when Christ returns, so we should spend our time accumulating treasures that will be worthwhile in God's eternal Kingdom. Money itself is not the problem: Christian leaders need money to live and support their families; missionaries need money to help them spread the gospel; churches need money

to do their work effectively. It is the **love** of money that leads to evil (1 Timothy 6:10) and causes some to oppress others to get more. This is a warning to all Christians who are tempted to adopt worldly standards rather than God's standards (Romans 12:1-2) and an encouragement to all those who are oppressed by the rich.

For these rich people, their treasure is worldly wealth. They have enjoyed life, feasting as they would on the day when an animal is slaughtered. Ironically, James says that **they** are like fattened animals **ready for the slaughter** when the day of God's judgment arrives (see Jeremiah 12:1-3).

5:6 The condemning and killing of **good people** probably was both active and passive. Inconvenient people may indeed have been murdered; but more likely, the poor people who could not pay their debts were thrown in prison or forced to sell all their possessions. With no means of support and no opportunity even to work off their debts, these poor people and their families often died of starvation. God also considered this murder. Either way, in the unjust system, it was legal. The poor **had no power to defend themselves.** Their only recourse against the evil rich was to cry out to God.

The conditions that James is describing may seem hopeless. Many of the rich will not repent. Believers can live with hope, however, because Christ is coming back. He will bring judgment and justice. It is to Christ's return that James now turns.

PATIENCE IN SUFFERING / 5:7-12

The believers, most of whom were poor, were frequently exploited by the rich and were persecuted because of their faith. This external pressure led to problems in the church as their frustration reached the boiling point. James encouraged the believers to be patient until the Lord's return. But the patience he describes is not passive. It is a patience that involves action. In this section, James illustrates some helpful sources for personal application. After speaking of the need for patience, he proceeds to reveal a number of different lessons that reinforce and apply his theme. The principle of patience will not mean much unless we can apply it to our lives. By looking at life through James's eyes, we discover there are many ways God gives us guidance and encouragement.

5:7 The believers are to **be patient** even in the midst of injustice. The believers need to endure, trust in God through their trials, and refuse to try to get even for wrongs committed against them (see also 1:2, 12; Psalm 37). But patience does not mean inaction. There was work to be done— serving God, caring for one another, and proclaiming the Good News. There is an end point, a time when patience will no longer be needed—**the**

Lord's return. At that time, everything will be made right. The early church lived in constant expectation of Christ's return, and so should we. Because we don't know when Christ will return to bring justice and remove oppression, we must wait with patience (see 2 Peter 3:8-10).

As an example of patience, James talks about the farmer who must **patiently wait for the precious harvest to ripen.** Patience must be exercised and developed between the rains. Even nonfarmers have plenty of opportunities to develop patience. The waiting for the arrival of a baby, starting a new job, finishing school, waiting for a loved one's visit, slowly improving health during a prolonged illness—all these situations try our patience. We will exercise patience as we concentrate on the end result of our waiting. God's way is seldom the quick way, but it is always the complete way.

5:8 Instead of being like the rich people of verse 5 who have "fattened" their hearts on the wealth of this world, believers are to allow the assurance of Christ's return to help them **be patient** and **take courage.** Whatever the circumstances, James encourages us to be rock solid in our faith and to have a faith-inspired joy that permeates every part of life (see 1:2-4). Like the farmer, we invest a long time in our future hope. The farmer is at the mercy of the weather—it is outside his control. But we do know that **the coming of the Lord is near.**

5:9 These believers, facing persecution from the outside and problems on the inside, may naturally find themselves grumbling and criticizing one another. James doesn't want them to be filled with resentment and bitterness toward each other—that would only destroy the unity they so desperately need. Refusing to **grumble about each other** is part of what it means to be patient (5:7). Grumbling against one another indicates a careless attitude of speech. Because of the dangers created by our speech (see James 3:1-12), we cannot afford to be lax in the way we speak to and about each other.

James has already mentioned the **great Judge** (4:12). This Judge is not far away, but **standing at the door.** James is warning believers not to be in the middle of judging, quarreling, criticizing, or gossiping when the one they should be serving returns. Knowledge of Christ's presence is not only comforting; it can also be convicting—especially when we begin behaving as if he were far away.

5:10 Jewish Christians knew the stories of **the prophets,** many of whom suffered greatly or were killed for proclaiming God's message (for example, see Elijah in 1 Kings 19:1ff; Jeremiah in Jeremiah 38; Amos in Amos 7). James is reminding his readers that even those who spoke **in the name of the Lord** had to have **patience in suffering.** Part of his point is that God does not preserve *from* suffering those he has called; rather, he preserves them *in* suffering. They are an example to all believers because of their obedience and faithfulness despite the hardships they endured.

5:11 Here James is leading his readers to apply the lessons from Old Testament lives. For instance, **Job**

may offer us a fascinating look at ancient history and an interesting biography, but Job's best work is as a teacher: one who has suffered and can help us cope with suffering. His life is an example we need to follow. Job may have complained, but he did not stop trusting or obeying God (see Job 1:21; 2:10; 16:19-21; 19:25-27). And the Lord did deliver and restore him (see Job 42:12). The believers, after all the suffering they had endured thus far, were encouraged not to give up—God would deliver and reward them.

We can see clearly from Job's life that perseverance is not the result of understanding. Job never received an explanation from God for his suffering. This is partly because pain is often a part of life that must be endured beyond explanations. There are many things we can understand, but not everything. God's purpose is not that we just develop a mind full of explanations and answers; his purpose is to bring us to a place where we trust him. God does not enjoy watching his people suffer. He allows them to face such pain because a greater good will be produced. In the meantime, James encourages his readers to trust in God, wait patiently, persevere, and remember God's **tenderness and mercy.**

5:12 James is referring to Jesus' words in Matthew 5:34-37. Taking oaths was a common practice, and James wanted it discontinued among the believers. People made disrespectful or arrogant verbal guarantees that they themselves could reverse by legal technicalities. Like boldfaced warranties with lots of fine print, these oaths were intended to create an impression of truth—but those who uttered them did not really expect to be held to them. Christians should **never** need to **take an oath** in order to guarantee the truth of what they say. Our honesty should be unquestionable. Believers should not need oaths, for their speech should always be truthful. There should be no reason for them to have to strengthen a statement with an oath. God will judge our words.

Should we take oaths in court? The oaths forbidden here are those used in casual conversation, not formal oaths taken in a court of law. Legal oaths are intended to bind those who make them. Perjury is a serious offense. Most scholars conclude that James does not require us to refuse to take oaths in court.

A person with a reputation for exaggeration or lying often can't get anyone to believe him on his word alone. For example, this person might say, "I promise!" or "I swear!" Christians should never become like that. Always be honest so that others will believe your **simple yes or no.** By avoiding lies, half-truths, and omissions of the truth, you will become known as a trustworthy person.

FAITHFUL PRAYER / 5:13-18

James closes his letter as he began it, with a call to prayer. James uses his closing words to describe effective prayer. He details prayer in several forms (praise, intercession, confession) and connects prayer with several other important spiritual disciplines (healing, confession, anointing, correction, praise, and mutual forgiveness). If we can say that James's letter summarizes the work of faith, his conclusion focuses on faith's finest work—believers effective in prayer.

5:13 There are many responses to **suffering.** Some of us worry; some of us vow revenge against those who have caused the suffering; some of us let anger burn inside us. Some grumble. But James says the correct response to suffering is to **keep on praying about it** (see also Psalm 30; 50:15; 91:15). This is not necessarily a prayer for deliverance from the trouble, but for the patience and strength to endure it.

If we are fortunate enough to be happy, we should thank God by singing **praises to the Lord** (see also 1 Corinthians 14:15; Ephesians 5:19; Colossians 3:16). Because our praise is directed to God, singing is actually another form of prayer.

5:14 One characteristic of the early church was its concern over and care for the **sick.** Here James encourages the sick to **call for the elders of the church** for counseling and prayer. The elders were spiritually mature people responsible for overseeing local churches (see 1 Peter 5:1-4). The elders would **pray over** the sick person, calling upon the Lord for healing. Then they would anoint him **with oil in the name of the Lord.** As the elders prayed they were to voice clearly that the power for healing resided in the name of Jesus. Anointing was often used by the early church in their prayers for healing. In Scripture, oil was both a medicine (see the parable of the Good Samaritan in Luke 10:30-37) and a symbol of the Spirit of God (as used in anointing kings; see 1 Samuel 16:1-13). Thus the oil may have been a sign of the power of prayer, and it may have symbolized the setting apart of the sick person for God's special attention.

5:15 The prayer must be from the heart, sincere, with trust in and obedience to God behind it, and with no doubting, as in 1:5-8. The **faith** is the role of the elders who are praying, not the sick person's (nothing is said about his or her faith). It is possible that the sick person's faith is exercised in calling the elders. Also, if there is need for confession, the elders will be able to minister to the individual. The process insures dependence of believers on each other.

Not the elders or the oil, but the **Lord** himself does the healing. Does this mean that every prayer for healing guarantees that God will make the sick person well? It must be emphasized here that the prayer offered is a prayer offered in faith—not only the faith that believes God can heal, but also the faith that expresses absolute confidence in God's will. A true prayer of faith will acknowledge God's sovereignty in his answer to that prayer. It is not always God's will to heal those who are ill (see 2 Corinthians 12:7-9). A prayer for healing must be qualified with a recognition that God's will is supreme.

Sin may or may not be the cause of the illness, but an opportunity for confession is given, and the elders are there to receive it. No demand of confession is given, but the opportunity is given that **anyone who has committed sins will be forgiven.** This condition is important because all too often we are prone to assume that sin is the cause of someone's suffering. The Bible teaches that sin can cause sickness (see Mark 2:1-12; 1 Corinthians 5:5; 11:27-30), but it also notes clearly that this is not always the case (see John 9:2-3).

5:16 It is not God's plan that his people be alone. Members of Christ's body should be able to count on others for support and prayer, especially when they are sick or suffering. The elders should be on call to respond to the illness of any member, and the church should stay alert to pray for the healing of any who are sick. But we are often not only guilty of hesitating to lean on each other in our sicknesses and weaknesses. We are even more liable not to **confess** our **sins to each other.**

The recent emphasis on small groups within churches has risen largely from a need to recapture some of these basic features of life in the body of Christ that have been neglected. When Christians are really working to "share each other's troubles and problems," the world does take note, and we come closer to fulfilling "the law of Christ" (see Galatians 6:2). Loving your neighbor as yourself does include, above all else, praying for him or her.

The **earnest prayer of a righteous person has great power and wonderful results** because the person who is praying is righteous. The person is not sinless, but he or she has confessed known sins to God and is completely committed to him and trying to do his will. Again, we can say that the righteous people get what they want in prayer because they want what God wants.

The Christian's most powerful resource is communication with God through prayer. It is the instrument of healing and forgiveness and is a mighty weapon for spiritual warfare. The results are often greater than we thought were possible. Some people see prayer as a last resort, to be tried when all else fails. Our priorities are the reverse of God's. Prayer should come first. God is pleased to use our prayers to accomplish his purposes and he delights in answering our needs, but he is never bound by our prayers. God's power is infinitely greater than ours, so it only makes sense to rely on it—especially because God encourages us to do so.

5:17-18 Prayer is indeed powerful—remember **Elijah?** The story is found in 1 Kings 17:1–18:46. Elijah had great power in prayer. A drought came

as a sign to evil King Ahab of Israel that the idol Baal did not have power over the rain, God did. And when Elijah **prayed earnestly that no rain would fall, none fell for the next three and a half years.** Then he prayed for rain, **and down it poured.**

James uses Old Testament people to illustrate each of his major themes:

- The nature of faith is found in the lives of Abraham and Rahab (2:21-25).
- Perseverance is exemplified by Job (5:11).
- Effective prayer is exemplified by Elijah (5:17-18).

These lives are important to us. They are examples to be followed. When we choose all our models from contemporary people, we may eventually be disappointed by their failures. Other generations of believers cannot let us down. They made their mistakes, persevered, and are now testimonies that life can be lived for God.

RESTORE WANDERING BELIEVERS / 5:19-20

Behind this question about the identity of the wanderer is a pastoral concern. In practice, it makes no difference whether the wanderer was actually a believer or not—we are commanded to attempt to turn the person back to the faith (see Ezekiel 3:18-21; 33:9; 1 Timothy 4:16). If the wanderer should die while wandering, the pastor or group is left to wonder about the eternal state of that person. Families sometimes agonize over the fate of a loved one who has wandered away from the faith. Frankly, we cannot know. To determine what was really occurring within that person we would have to be God. If we have done what we could to reach out to wanderers while they were still living, we must then turn their eternal destiny over to God. James urges Christians to help backsliders return to God. By taking the initiative, praying for the person, and acting in love, we can meet the person where he or she is and encourage his or her return to God.

5:19 Anyone among you refers to a believer who has fallen away from the faith by becoming involved with idolatry or heresy. No one in the group is immune from wandering. The **anyone** could be us. To "wander" means a serious departure from the faith—otherwise known as "apostasy." **Truth,** as used here, does not refer to peripheral doctrinal concerns, but to the central truth of the Christian faith—namely, that Jesus is the Son of God, the Lord and Savior who died for our sins and rose again from the dead. Choices and actions that lead us toward denying the lordship of the living Christ carry us away from the truth.

When someone **wanders away,** the church or Christian community ought to try to bring him **back again,** not for judgment, but for repentance and restoration. When a believer is aware of

another believer's wandering, that knowledge carries with it responsibility for action. All these images portray a community where people care deeply for each other, and wanderers are not allowed to slip through the cracks unnoticed. Are we willing to try to bring back someone who has wandered, or do we simply wring our hands while the person goes off into darkness?

5:20 The error of the wandering **sinner** is so serious as to lead to death—spiritual, eternal **death**—if he or she is not brought back (see 1 Corinthians 11:30; 1 John 5:16). But when the believer repents and returns to God, God will forgive, cover over, and forget that person's sins (see Psalm 32:1; 1 Peter 4:8).

The context is somewhat unclear about the

identity of the wanderer. Is it a person who is a believer wandering away, or is it a person in the group who has not truly believed and is wandering away? Christians disagree over whether or not it is possible for people to lose their salvation, but all agree that those who move away from their faith or who are not genuine in their profession are in serious trouble and need to repent. The point of this verse is clear, though: we are to bring the wanderer back—not debate whether or not the person would be lost if we didn't.

What began with a challenge to endure hardship with joy now closes with an appeal to watch out for each other. Believers are to pursue their faith, together. It is God who saves and keeps, but he allows us to be involved in one another's Christian life.

It is an unforgettable sight to witness the Christian welcome of someone who has strayed and returned, watching God's forgiveness work through the body of Christ as believers accept the person who is repenting. From the view of eternity, it must really be like a cover being pulled over **many sins.**

The letter of James is Christianity with its sleeves rolled up. It is the working person's practical guide to living the Christian faith. It spells out what it means to follow Jesus day by day. James emphasizes faith in action. Theories are for theologians, but James is interested in life! Right living is the evidence and result of faith. The church must serve with compassion, speak lovingly and truthfully, live in obedience to God's commands, and love one another. The body of believers ought to be an example of heaven's principles applied on earth, drawing people to Christ through love for God and one another. If we truly believe God's word, we will **live it** day by day. God's word is not merely something we read or think about, but something we do.

1 PETER

INTRODUCTION

Remember when the opposition began? At first, they were subtle—junior high friends decided that going to church was "stupid." In the later teen years, you found that your Christian lifestyle contrasted sharply with that of most of your peers, and often they would make fun of your purity and stand for Christ. As you grew in age and experience, you discovered that the attacks increased, especially when you spoke up against wrongdoing, took time to help those in need, and shared your faith. Your strong witness by life and word cost you friends and threatened your job.

Regardless of your personal persecution, you probably have not come close to what first-century believers experienced. A quick perusal of Acts will reveal stonings, beatings, imprisonments, murderous plots, and executions—all for spreading the truth about Christ. Some of the most severe of the persecutions came at the hands of Nero. This Roman emperor became obsessed with eliminating Christians and their faith. The Roman historian Tacitus said, "Besides being put to death, [Christians] were made to serve as objects of amusement; they were clad in the hides of beasts and torn to death by dogs; others were crucified, others set on fire to serve to illuminate the night when daylight failed" (*Annals* 15.44). The price for following Christ was high.

First Peter was written to persecuted Christians, to those living in Rome and throughout the Roman province of Asia. This letter encourages believers to remain strong; it explains how to live during difficult times; it offers hope to all who suffer for the faith. First Peter speaks to believers in all ages—those in the first century and in our century. God tells us how to respond to our tough times, especially when we are persecuted for what we believe. Read 1 Peter and discover courage, strength, and hope.

AUTHOR

Peter: apostle of Christ, one of the original twelve disciples, outspoken leader, and courageous preacher.

We first meet Peter when his brother, Andrew, brings him to Jesus (John 1:40-42). The sons of John (John 1:42; 21:15-17) and probably from Bethsaida in Galilee (John 1:44), Peter and his brother were fishermen on the Sea of Galilee (Matthew 4:18; Mark 1:16) and partners of James and John (Luke 5:10). Peter and Andrew first followed John the Baptist. When John pointed out Jesus as the "Lamb of God" (John 1:29), Andrew accepted his teacher's testimony and immediately left to get his brother, Simon, to introduce him to the Messiah. Jesus addressed

Peter addressed his letter to the churches located throughout Bithynia, Pontus, Asia, Galatia, and Cappadocia. Paul had evangelized many of these areas; other areas had churches that were begun by the Jews who were in Jerusalem on the day of Pentecost, heard Peter's

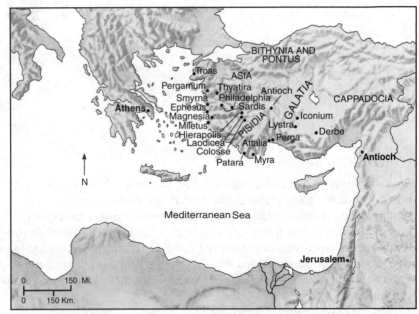

powerful sermon, became Christians, and returned home with the gospel (see Acts 2:9-11).

Andrew's brother as "Simon " and then changed his name to "Peter," meaning "rock" or "stone" (John 1:42).

This initial encounter seems to have had little effect on Peter because he returned to Capernaum to continue his vocation as a fisherman, perhaps awaiting further instructions. Subsequently, Jesus twice called Peter to follow him. The call first occurred on the Sea of Galilee, where the four business partners were fishing together. They left their nets to "fish for people" (Matthew 4:18-22). The second, confirming call occurred when Jesus selected the Twelve (Mark 3:13-19).

Almost immediately, Peter assumed the unofficial role of leader of the disciples. He regularly served as their spokesman and is named first in all the lists (see, for example, Matthew 14:28; 15:15; 18:21; 26:35, 40; Mark 8:29; 9:5; 10:28; John 6:68). More than likely, Peter's leadership arose from his character and personality. Totally devoted to his Lord, Peter enthusiastically spoke out and took the lead.

Belonging to the inner circle of disciples and being a powerful force in the early church, Peter is mentioned in the New Testament more often than all of the other eleven put together. Peter was present when Jesus raised Jairus's daughter from the dead. He also was privileged to be one of just four to hear Jesus' discourse on the fall of Jerusalem and the end of the world (Mark 13:3ff). He and only two others (James and John) were at the Transfiguration (Matthew 17:1) and were very close to Jesus in Gethsemane (Mark 14:33). Peter and one other disciple (John) were sent to prepare for the Last Supper (Luke 22:8). Peter also was present when Christ gave the great commission (Matthew 28:16-20) and when he ascended into heaven (Luke 24:44-53).

Although Jesus had renamed him "rock," at first Peter was anything but rock solid. Impulsive, he often spoke without thinking (see, for example, his rebuke of Christ in Matthew 16:22 and his comments after the Transfiguration in Matthew 17:4), and he jumped to defend Jesus with a sword (John 18:10). Despite his best intentions, Peter tended to respond quite poorly under pressure, falling asleep in the garden during Jesus' most difficult hour (Matthew 26:40-41) and vehemently denying the Lord when accused of being his follower (Matthew 26:69-74).

Peter's life provides strong testimony to the reality of the Resurrection and the power of the Holy Spirit. Consider the great contrast between his earlier pattern as leader of the disciples and his later actions as leader of the early church. Peter preached boldly and powerfully, at Pentecost (Acts 2) and beyond. Jailed and then warned by the Jewish religious leaders not to preach about Jesus, Peter did so anyway (Acts 4:13-20). Later, Peter was jailed again, this time by civil authorities. Herod already had executed James, and Peter would be next. But God miraculously released Peter, who continued to minister in Jesus' name (Acts 12:1-19).

Other significant events in the life and ministry of Peter include: leading the disciples through the process of choosing a successor to Judas Iscariot (Acts 1:15-26), condemning Ananias and Sapphira for lying to the Holy Spirit (Acts 5:1-11), denouncing Simon the Sorcerer (Acts 8:18-23), healing Aeneas and restoring Tabitha to life (Acts 9:34-40), baptizing the first Gentile Christians (Cornelius and his household, Acts 10), and participating significantly in the Council at Jerusalem (Acts 15:1-11).

At first, Peter ministered exclusively among the Jews (Acts 1:1–5:41). But that began to change when persecution against Christians intensified in Jerusalem. At this time, many Christians scattered throughout Judea and Samaria, but they preached the gospel as they went, and many Samaritans responded (Acts 8:4-8). Soon thereafter, Peter and John were sent to verify that, in fact, the conversions were real (Acts 8:14-25), and Peter's ministry began to expand. Not long afterward, on a journey throughout the country, teaching believers, healing the sick, and telling the Good News about God's salvation, Peter received a vision from God (Acts 9:32–10:16). Through this vision, Peter realized that Gentiles were no longer to be considered "unclean" and should be told about Christ. Thus, when invited by Roman servants to come to the home of Cornelius, the centurion, Peter agreed and traveled to Caesarea. There, in the home of this Roman soldier, Peter preached and then witnessed the power of God transform these uncircumcised Gentiles (Acts 10:22-48). Later, when Peter explained his actions, the apostles and others praised God (Acts 11:18). Peter learned from personal experience that God's message was for all the world. Later, Peter seems to have become an intermediary between the two main factions of the early church: Jewish Christianity, centered in Jerusalem, and the ministry to the Gentiles, championed by Paul (see Acts 15:6-11).

As described above, after the Ascension, Peter's early ministry was focused in Jerusalem. But then he seems to have traveled beyond, perhaps even to Pontus, Galatia, Cappadocia, Asia, and Bithynia (1:1), the areas mentioned as destinations for this epistle. Eventually, Peter traveled to Rome, where he ministered among the beleaguered believers. This must have occurred after Paul's first imprisonment (A.D. 59–62), for Paul's prison epistles make no mention of Peter. This letter probably was written around A.D. 64, just before the terrible persecution of Christians by Emperor Nero (A.D. 65–67). Strong tradition holds that Peter was executed in

Rome by Nero in A.D. 67, crucified upside down, feeling that he was unworthy
to die as Jesus had. Jesus' words to Peter in John 21:18-19 seem to imply a death
by crucifixion, but no historical proof has been found to confirm this tradition.

By God's mercy, Peter became a fearless and outspoken servant of his risen
Lord, eventually dying for his faith. God changed this man, and he can change
you, too, into a rock-solid witness for Christ!

That Peter wrote this book bearing his name is attested to by its content.
Reminiscences of personal acquaintance with Christ fill this letter (for example,
compare 5:5 with John 13:3-5). The content of this epistle also seems to parallel
Peter's speeches recorded in Acts. Compare, for example, 1:17 with Acts 10:34;
1:21 with Acts 2:32-36 and Acts 10:40; and 2:7-8 with Acts 4:10-11.

DATE AND SETTING
Written from Rome in about A.D. 64.

According to the unanimous testimony of the early church, Peter ministered in
Rome until his martyrdom. Peter wrote this letter from Rome, around A.D. 64, just
before the intense persecution of the church under Nero. Rome was the capital
city of the vast and mighty Roman Empire, which stretched from Britain to Arabia.
With a population of approximately one million, Rome was the diplomatic and
trade center of the world and the largest city.

At first, Christianity was tolerated in Rome as a sect of Judaism. But in the last
few years of Emperor Nero's reign (he ruled from A.D. 54 until his death in 68), he
authorized capturing, torturing, and killing Christians. In A.D. 64, a large part of
Rome was destroyed by fire, probably started at Nero's order. The emperor publicly
accused the Christians in the city, giving him an excuse for terrible atrocities,
including throwing believers to wild dogs in the Colosseum, as a spectator sport.
During these terrible persecutions, believers were forced to choose between the
emperor and Christ; those who chose Christ often died for their faith. Both Paul
and Peter are believed to have been victims of Nero's reign of terror.

Certainly Peter would have seen the mounting persecution, leading him, under
the inspiration of the Holy Spirit, to warn believers of "many trials" (1:6), beatings
"for doing right" (2:20), suffering "for doing what is right" (3:14, 17), participating "with Christ in his suffering" (4:13), and suffering "according to God's will"
(4:19). With all these warnings, Peter includes words of encouragement and hope
(1:7-9; 4:12-19; 5:10-11) and instructions for how to live (1:13-21; 2:1-3, 11-25;
3:1-17; 4:1-11; 5:1-9).

AUDIENCE
Christians scattered throughout Asia Minor.

The opening sentence of 1 Peter identifies the audience as "God's chosen
people who are living as foreigners" in other lands. This phrase and the numerous
Old Testament quotes have led many to believe that Peter was writing to Jewish
Christians. This probably is not the case, however. Most likely, Peter was writing
to Christians of all nationalities.

Pontus, Galatia, Cappadocia, Asia, and Bithynia (1:1) refer to formerly independent territories in northern Asia Minor (modern Turkey). Since 130 B.C., all of
these territories had been under Roman control. The population was a mix of

many races and cultures, including the native peoples, cultured Greeks, Orientals, and Jews. At the end of the first century A.D., the total population of these five huge provinces was approximately 8.5 million, one million of whom were Jews and eighty thousand, Christians. Luke explains in Acts that Paul did not minister in these northern provinces on any of his missionary journeys. On one occasion, he was forbidden by the Holy Spirit to travel there and directed, instead, to Troas and then to Macedonia (Acts 16:6-12). How this area was evangelized is unknown; perhaps it was through Peter, who may have traveled there with his wife (see 1 Corinthians 9:5) after the Council of Jerusalem (Acts 15:1-29), or perhaps through the scattering of the believers.

OCCASION AND PURPOSE
To offer encouragement and hope to Christians scattered throughout northern Asia Minor.

Peter had suffered much for preaching the gospel of Christ (see Acts 5:17-42; 8:1; 12:1-19)—he was no stranger to persecution. Nor were the Jewish believers who had been ostracized by their unbelieving families and hounded by the Council. But this was a new experience for the Gentile Christians. Christianity was beginning to be considered a separate religion and not simply a Jewish sect. Thus Christians were no longer protected and were being persecuted by the state. This letter implies that these persecutions were just beginning on the local level. As a small minority, believers certainly must have felt like "foreigners" (1:1). Writing from Rome, Peter could see the change in Nero. Surely he could sense the growing threat and would know that more severe persecutions by the state would follow shortly. Peter wrote to encourage and comfort his beloved brothers and sisters and to prepare them for the persecution that was sure to come.

Peter's letter overflows with feelings of triumph in adversity, looking forward to God's glorious future. Even as they were suffering, believers could have the confident assurance of God's work in their lives and of their ultimate salvation.

Peter provides a powerful example of an encourager. He was not writing from a secure location, removed from the hardships of Roman life. Peter lived at the center of the persecution; yet, as he had for decades, he continued to preach courageously about his risen Lord until he, too, became a victim of Nero's murderous schemes. Despite personal hardships, Peter, like Paul, wrote to encourage others, to build them up in their faith, and to give them direction and guidance. In your struggles, do you look inward or outward? Do you tend to feel sorry for yourself or to encourage others?

MESSAGE
Peter begins by thanking God for salvation (1:2-6). He explains to his readers that trials will refine their faith (1:7-9). They should believe in spite of their circumstances; for many in past ages believed in God's plan of salvation, even the prophets of old who wrote about it but didn't understand it. But now salvation has been revealed in Christ (1:10-13). In response to such a great salvation, Peter commands them to live holy lives (1:14-16), to reverently fear and trust God (1:17-21), to be honest and loving (2:1-3), and to become like Christ (2:1-3).

Jesus Christ, as "the living cornerstone" upon whom the church is to be built

(2:4, 6), is also the stone that was rejected, causing those who are disobedient to stumble and fall (2:7-8). But the church, built upon this stone, is to be God's holy priesthood (2:9-10).

Next, Peter explains how believers should live during difficult times (2:11–4:11). Christians should be above reproach (2:12-17), imitating Christ in all their social roles—masters and servants, husbands and wives, church members and neighbors (2:18–3:17). Christ should be our model for obedience to God in the midst of great suffering (3:18–4:11). Peter then outlines the right attitude to have about persecution: Expect it (4:12), be thankful for the privilege of suffering for Christ (4:13-18), and trust God for deliverance (4:19). Next, Peter gives some special instructions: Elders should care for God's flock (5:1-4), younger men should be submissive to those who are older (5:5-6), and everyone should trust God and resist Satan (5:7-11). Peter concludes by introducing Silas and by sending personal greetings, possibly from the church in Rome, and from Mark (5:12-14).

The main themes in the book of 1 Peter include: *Salvation, Persecution, Christian Living, God's Family, Family Life,* and *Judgment.*

Salvation (1:1-5, 10-12, 18-20; 2:4, 6, 21-25; 3:18-22; 5:4). Salvation is a gracious gift from God. We are God's "elect" (1:1); that is, he **chose** us out of his love for us, sending Jesus to die in our place, to pay the penalty for our sin. (Seven times in five chapters, 1 Peter refers to believers being "elect" or "chosen.") The Holy Spirit cleanses us from sin when we believe (1:2; 2:23-24; 3:18). Eternal life belongs to those who trust in Christ. God has promised it, so we can count on it (1:3-5; 5:4).

Peter reminded his readers of the reality of their relationship with Christ. He explained that their salvation was based, not on feelings or circumstances, but on the truth, goodness, and sovereignty of God. They were chosen by God and saved by grace. That truth is the basis of hope.

IMPORTANCE FOR TODAY. No matter what we are going through—pain, persecution, loneliness—we can be confident in our relationship with God if we put our faith in Christ. Our safety, security, and identity rest in him. And think of it: If we experience joy in our relationship with Christ now, how much greater our joy will be when he returns and we see him face-to-face! God has a wonderful future for us; God has chosen us and we belong to him. Such a hope should motivate us to serve Christ with great commitment.

Persecution (1:6-9; 2:19-21; 3:14-17; 4:12-19; 5:10). The recipients of this letter were suffering because of their commitment to Christ. Peter realized this and knew that the persecutions would increase dramatically in the next few years, during Nero's reign. So Peter wrote to offer faithful believers comfort and hope.

Christians should expect to be ridiculed and rejected for their faith; after all, Christ's values and virtues contrast greatly with those of the world. Persecution should make believers stronger, however, because it can refine their faith. God's message through Peter is that followers of Christ can face suffering victoriously, as the Lord did, if they rely on him.

IMPORTANCE FOR TODAY. Christians still suffer for what they believe. In some countries, Christians are punished or even killed for their faith. In other countries, they face ridicule and rejection at school, at work, in the neighborhood, and even at home. We should expect persecution, but we don't have to be terrified by it. We know that God is with us in our suffering, giving us courage, comfort, and peace and strengthening our faith. We also know that one day we will live eternally with Christ. These truths should give us the confidence, patience, and hope to stand firm, even when persecuted.

Christian Living (1:13-25; 2:1-5, 9-21; 3:8-16; 4:1-11, 19; 5:1-12). As a distinct minority in a non-Christian world, Peter urged believers to be holy (1:15-16). This meant keeping their focus on Christ, obeying him, and living as citizens of God's "holy nation" (2:9). It would involve submitting to authorities (2:13), respecting others (2:17), doing good (3:9-13; 4:19), sharing the Good News (3:15), keeping a clear conscience (3:16), being disciplined (4:7; 5:8), and being humble (5:1-6).

IMPORTANCE FOR TODAY. We also live in a non-Christian society, one that is filled with pressures and temptations that threaten to conform us to the world's values and lifestyles. Instead of giving in, we should be "holy," standing out from the crowd because of our love, humility, and discipline—all evidence of our strong commitment to Christ. And we should "always be ready to explain" our faith (3:15), pointing family, friends, coworkers, and neighbors to Christ.

God's Family (1:14, 22; 2:4-10; 3:8; 5:12-14). Believers are privileged to belong to God's family, a community with Christ as the founder and foundation. Everyone in this community is related—all brothers and sisters, loved equally by God. The recipients of this letter were far from Peter, but they were his brothers and sisters in Christ. Although Peter was an apostle and a revered teacher and leader in the church, he was also their brother, a fellow member of God's royal family.

IMPORTANCE FOR TODAY. Because Christ is the foundation of our family, we must be devoted, loyal, and faithful to him. By obeying our Lord, we show that we are his children. We may be "foreigners" in this world (1:1), but we are God's "very own possession" (2:9). This means that regardless of the rejection we feel in society, we can feel accepted and loved by our spiritual family. It also means that we should live differently from those who don't know the Lord and make a difference for Christ in the world.

Family Life (3:1-7). Peter encouraged the wives of unbelievers to submit to their husbands' authority as a means of winning them to Christ. He also urged all family members to treat each other with respect, displaying sympathy, love, compassion, and humility.

IMPORTANCE FOR TODAY. The family is under attack today, by Satan and by a society that values living for oneself and for the moment. So families are falling apart, with soaring divorce rates and mothers and fathers deserting their spouses and children. Christians should model what the family can and should be. We must treat our family members lovingly, especially those who don't know the Lord. Although it isn't easy, willing service is the best way to influence loved ones. To gain the strength we need for self-discipline and submission, we should pray for God's help.

Judgment (1:17; 3:18-22; 4:7, 17-18; 5:4). God will judge with perfect justice. Everyone who has ever lived will face God, who will punish evildoers and those who have persecuted God's people. Those who have placed their trust in Christ and who love God will be rewarded with life forever in God's presence.

IMPORTANCE FOR TODAY. Every person is accountable to God for what he or she has done with Christ and for how he or she has lived. Thus we must leave judgment of others to him. This means not hating or even resenting those who persecute us. Instead, we should pray for them, that they may come to know the Savior too. We also should realize that we will be held responsible for how we live each day. This truth should motivate us to obey God and do what is right.

OUTLINE OF 1 PETER
   I. God's Great Blessings to His People (1:1–2:10)
  II. The Conduct of God's People in the Midst of Suffering (2:11–4:19)
 III. The Shepherding of God's People in the Midst of Suffering (5:1-14)

1 PETER **1**:1 – 2:3

GREETINGS FROM PETER / 1:1-2
The apostle Peter wrote this letter to encourage believers who would likely face trials and persecution under Emperor Nero. During most of the first century, Christians were not hunted down and killed throughout the Roman Empire. They could, however, expect social and economic persecution from three main sources: the Romans, the Jews, and their own families. All Christians would very likely be misunderstood; some would be harassed; a few would be tortured and even put to death. Peter may have been writing especially for new Christians and those planning to be baptized. He wanted to warn them about what lay ahead—they needed his encouraging words to help them face opposition.

1:1 In the style of ancient letters, **Peter** began by identifying himself. He was an **apostle,** the title Jesus had given to the twelve disciples (Luke 6:13). The title **apostle** designated one who had authority to set up and supervise churches and discipline them if necessary. Even more than a title of authority, "apostle" means one sent on a mission, like an envoy or ambassador. As an apostle **of Jesus Christ,** Peter wrote with authority because, like the Old Testament prophets, he wrote God's very words. The recipients of this letter (including us) should remember Peter's connection with Jesus, his powerful ministry, and his authority to speak. (For more information about Peter, see the Author section in the Introduction to 1 Peter.)

The recipients of this letter were **God's chosen people,** that is, both Jewish and Gentile Christians. Although God initiated our calling, based totally on his wisdom, we who are called still must respond and choose to follow him. All believers have been called and chosen by God.

When people accept Jesus Christ as Savior and Lord, God transfers their citizenship from the world to heaven (Philippians 3:20). Thus, while they live on this earth, they are like **foreigners** in this world. The world becomes a "foreign land" to believers because their real home is heaven and they are only on earth temporarily.

The church began in Jerusalem, but before long it had spread across the Roman Empire and beyond. Peter wrote this letter to both Jewish and Gentile believers in churches scattered throughout various Roman provinces. Most likely, Peter planned for the letter to be circulated from one church to the next throughout each area. He may have separated the names of each province to indicate the circular route that the bearer of this letter would travel.

1:2 This verse mentions all three members of the Trinity—**God the Father,** God the Son (**Jesus Christ**), and God the Holy **Spirit.** All members of the Trinity work to bring about our salvation and provide a threefold assurance to believers. Although Christians are "foreigners" in this world (1:1), they take comfort in the fact that God **chose** them **long ago.**

God's "choosing" of believers has generated fierce doctrinal differences among Christians; most of these differences come from theological and philosophical points of view about what the Bible means. God alone originates and accomplishes our salvation because of his grace. We do nothing to earn it. Being "chosen" does not remove the necessity for people to choose to follow him. The fact that God knows all events and decisions beforehand, even ordains them beforehand, does not mean that he forces the actions of his creatures, leaving them no choice. God took the initiative

and chose people before they had done anything to deserve it. He had intimate knowledge of these future believers; he knew who would believe, and he knew them personally. These chosen ones were known by God the Father as a father knows his children, except that God knew about them from eternity past. God is not trapped in time—what he knows is from eternity past into eternity future.

God makes his choice effective by the presence of the Holy Spirit in those who believe, resulting in obedience. Only the Spirit can draw people to a saving relationship with God. The Spirit comes to the chosen people to make them **holy,** meaning that God sees his children as holy because they have been **cleaned by** his Son's shed **blood.** But believers also are becoming holy as they learn to live for God. This is called "sanctification"—the process of Christian growth through which the Holy Spirit makes us like Christ. The obvious result is that the believers **obeyed.** The constant cleansing from sin available to us because of Christ's sacrifice enables us to obey God faithfully.

God's special favor refers to his grace—given to undeserving people. **Peace** refers to the peace that Christ made between sinners and God through his Son's death on the cross. Peter wanted these believers, scattered as they were across the empire's provinces, to be united in their experience of God's favor and peace in their daily lives.

THE HOPE OF ETERNAL LIFE / 1:3-12

Even as these believers faced persecution, they could remember God's grace and continue to live as God desired. Not all believers are persecuted for their faith, but everyone faces times of stress, discouragement, or despair. This section introduces the blessings of salvation (1:3-12). Peter's words echo through the centuries, reminding us of God's grace and sovereignty over all of life, encouraging us to glorify and live for him.

1:3 Peter launched into praise of God the Father, who had chosen and cleansed the believers (1:2). **All honor** goes to **God.** The Old Testament believers praised God, but the New Testament believers praised him with an entirely new name, one never used in the Old Testament: **Father of our Lord Jesus Christ.** God is "Father," the first person of the Trinity. He did not exist before the Son, for the Son has always existed (John 1:1-3; 17:5, 24). God the Father sent the Son, and the Son responded in full obedience.

We find God's **mercy** always at the center of any discussion of salvation. Only God's mercy would allow him to have compassion for sinful and rebellious people. Salvation is **given** to us because of God's **boundless mercy** alone. That salvation is called **the privilege of being born**

again. Jesus used this concept of new birth when he told Nicodemus that he had to be "born again" in order to see God's Kingdom (see John 3). In the new birth, we become dead to sin and alive to God with a fresh beginning. People can do no more to accomplish their "new birth" than they could do to accomplish their own natural birth. In his introductory comments, Peter thanked God for the new spiritual lives of the believers to whom he was writing.

Believers are born again not for this world, in which they are no more than foreigners, but for **a wonderful expectation** of life to come. That expectation is based on the conviction that God will keep his promises to raise us **because Jesus Christ rose again from the dead.** By rising from the dead, Christ made the necessary power available for our resurrection (1 Corinthians 15:22). Christ's resurrection makes us certain that we too will be raised from the dead. Believers are "born again" from their sinful state into the life of grace, which, in the end, will become a life of glory. We shouldn't be discouraged by earthly trials, for we have the Resurrection to be our backup.

1:4 The word translated **inheritance** is also used in the Old Testament to describe the inheritance to which the Jews had looked forward in the Promised Land of Canaan (Numbers 32:19; Deuteronomy 2:12; 19:8-10). Christians look forward to another **inheritance**—eternal life with God. Jesus Christ is God's only Son; thus he is sole heir (Mark 12:7). However, as children of God, believers also become heirs with Christ (Romans 8:17) of this **priceless** inheritance.

Peter used three Greek words, each beginning with the same letter and ending with the same syllable in Greek, to describe this inheritance *(aphthartos, amiantos, amarantos)*. This inheritance is **pure**—it won't lose its glory or freshness. It is **undefiled**—it will never become unfit for us or polluted by sin. It is **beyond the reach of change and decay**—meaning it will never pass away, disappear, or come to ruin as the result of hostile forces. These words contrast this inheritance with all earthly, human possessions. Nothing in the natural order—catastrophe, sin, age, evil—can affect it. God has made it indestructible, existing for all eternity.

Believers have noncancelable and nontransferable reservations in heaven. The inheritance is **kept in heaven** for us. The word **kept** is in the perfect tense in Greek, expressing a past activity with results that continue in the present; God has been keeping and still keeps the inheritance there—prepared, reserved, certain, and waiting. No matter what harm might come to believers on earth, the inheritance awaits, for it is kept safe with God.

1:5 In these words, Peter answered concerns that might have arisen in the minds of persecuted believers: Will we be able to endure and remain faithful to Christ if persecution becomes more intense? What good is an inheritance kept in heaven if we are not kept safe?

Peter explained that, in spite of persecution and even violent death, **God, in his mighty power, will protect** them. The word translated **protect** is a military term used to refer to a garrison within a city (see also 2 Thessalonians 3:3; Jude 1:24). It's an inner area of protection. No matter how the world persecuted or killed believers' bodies, God was guarding their souls. Peter gave a double-

locked security for believers. First, the inheritance is protected (1:4); second, the believers are protected to receive that inheritance because they were **trusting him.**

Believers have already received salvation through their acceptance of Jesus Christ as Savior, but the fullness of that salvation, its complete rewards and blessings, will be **revealed on the last day**—that is, the judgment day of Christ (see Romans 14:10; Revelation 20:11-15). What has started will be fully disclosed when he returns.

1:6 Because of the promises of the inheritance, believers can **be truly glad**—referring to deep, spiritual joy (see Luke 1:46-47; Acts 16:34; 1 Peter 4:13). This type of rejoicing remains, unhindered and unchanged by what happens in this present life. Believers would have **to endure many trials.** When Peter wrote of **trials,** he meant the response of an unbelieving world to people of faith. Christians became the target of persecution for four main reasons: (1) They refused to worship the emperor as a god and thus were viewed as atheists and traitors. (2) They refused to worship at pagan temples, so business for these moneymaking enterprises dropped wherever Christianity took hold. (3) They didn't support the Roman ideals of self, power, and conquest, and the Romans scorned the Christian ideal of self-sacrificing service. (4) They exposed and rejected the horrible immorality of pagan culture.

Grief and suffering do not happen without cause or reason. While it may never be clear to us, God must be trusted to carry out his purposes, even in times of trial. All believers face such trials when they let their lights shine into the darkness. We must accept trials as part of the refining process that burns away impurities and prepares us to meet Christ. Trials teach us patience (Romans 5:3-4; James 1:2-3) and help us grow to be the people God wants. In comparison to the **wonderful joy ahead,** the trials last only **for a while.** Because of this they could rejoice, even as they suffered grief.

1:7 While God may have different purposes in the trials that face his people, one overriding result of all **trials** is clear: they **test** people's **faith,** showing that it is **strong and pure.** To God, believers' faith is **more precious than mere gold,** the most valuable and durable substance of the time.

Genuine faith is indestructible for all eternity. However, it may take the **fire** of trials, struggles, and persecutions to purify it, removing impurities and defects. God values a fire-tested (or "stress-tested") faith. Through trials, God burns away our self-reliance and self-serving attitudes, so that our genuineness reflects his glory and brings praise to him.

How do trials prove the strength and purity of one's faith? A person living a comfortable life may find it very easy to be a believer. But to keep one's faith in the face of ridicule, slander, persecution, or even death proves the true value of that faith. Such faith results in **praise and glory and honor** bestowed upon the believers by God himself when Jesus Christ returns (**is revealed**) to judge the world and take believers home.

1:8 Peter had known Jesus Christ personally—talked with him, walked with him, questioned him, professed faith in him. Yet Peter understood that most of the believers to whom he wrote had not known Jesus in the flesh. He commended their **love** for **him even though** they had **never seen him** (see also John 20:29). And even though they could not **see him,** they put their **trust** in **him.** To **trust** him means "to put one's confidence in," "to depend upon."

We, like Peter's audience, have not ever seen Christ in the flesh, but one day our faith will be rewarded when Christ returns to take us home. On that day and for eternity, we shall see him face-to-face (Revelation 22:3-5). Until then, we live by faith, with hope and joy. This ought to give us **glorious, inexpressible joy.**

1:9 Believers express joy (1:8) because of their belief in and love for Jesus Christ. The **reward for trusting Christ will be the salvation of** their **souls.** Believers receive salvation when they accept Jesus Christ as Savior, yet salvation will not be complete until Jesus Christ returns and makes everything new. In the meantime, we continue growing in the Christian life and experiencing more and more of the blessings of salvation. As we continue to believe and rejoice, we also continue to grow toward maturity in Christ and to our promised salvation.

1:10-11 This salvation, now so clear to those who believe, had been a mystery to the Old Testament **prophets** who wrote about it through the inspiration of **the Spirit of Christ,** but **wanted to know more about** it. The prophets were amazed by the prophecies God gave them. **They had many questions,** and they wondered what was meant by **Christ's suffering.** Peter was saying, "How can you be discouraged? Don't you realize that you have seen the fulfillment of all the prophets' yearning?" Jesus once said to his listeners, "Many prophets and godly people have longed to see and hear what you have seen and heard, but they could not" (Matthew 13:17 ; see also Luke 10:23-24). The believers of Peter's day (as well as believers today) had the privilege of understanding the prophets' writings better than the prophets themselves had understood them. All of those prophets' predictions regarding the life, death, and resurrection of Jesus Christ had been completely fulfilled. Other prophecies concerning the end times are being or are yet to be fulfilled.

1:12 The Spirit revealed to the prophets that the prophecies would **not happen during their life-time.** The prophets had the great honor of having Christ's Spirit speak through them, but the privileges of our understanding are even greater and should move us to an even deeper commitment to Christ.

All the experiences regarding the coming salvation that the prophets had so wanted to see and hear have now **been announced by those who preached** the **Good News.** As the **Spirit** inspired the prophets, so he inspired the apostles and missionaries in the first century. This **is all so wonderful that even the angels** are watching these events unfold. Angels are spiritual beings created by God who help carry out his work on earth. Just as the prophets could not understand or experience the coming salvation and grace because it would occur after their lifetimes, neither can the angels understand or experience it because they are spiritual beings who do not need the blood of Christ to save them.

The word translated "watching" means to peek into a situation as an outsider. The angels watch (and often are sent to minister to) believers as they struggle and face ridicule or persecution. The angels know that God's people are recipients of God's grace and blessings and that one day they will be highly honored in the coming Kingdom.

A CALL TO HOLY LIVING / 1:13–2:3

Peter gave a bold challenge. The next section details the ethical responsibilities of those who have experienced the blessings of salvation described in 1:3-12. The promises God makes to believers and the hope we have should motivate us to holy living. This means being mentally alert, morally disciplined, and spiritually focused. This is hard work. Are you ready to meet Christ?

1:13 Because the prophets had foretold the great privileges of the gospel and, with even the angels, long to understand them better, believers should show the same kind of earnest and alert concern regarding the way they live.

To **think clearly** refers to spiritual and mental attitudes. To lead holy lives in an evil world, the believers would need a new mind-set. They also needed to monitor and restrain their sexual and material desires, anger, and words. **Exercise self-control** is also translated "discipline yourselves." Peter wanted the believers to remember that as they lived in the world, they needed to keep full possession of their minds and bodies so as not to be enticed away from God.

Peter has described true faith in 1:1-13, and in 1:14 he begins a series of moral commands that stretch throughout the rest of his letter. In a few words, Peter explained how believers can reflect God's character and priorities and follow God's commands. As they **look forward to the special blessings that will come,** they will be encouraged to change their mind-sets to be in line with God's plans for them, to change their lifestyles to glorify God, and to persevere during difficulties and persecutions.

1:14 All believers are God's children. As such, we are to **obey God.** Believers ought not live in the same manner that they lived before they were saved. At that time, they **didn't know any better,** but now they should not **slip back into** their **old ways of doing evil.** The evil desires still exist, but believers have a new goal for their lives. They must break with the past and depend on the power of the Holy Spirit to help them overcome evil desires and obey God.

1:15 God's holiness means that he is completely separated from sin and evil. Holiness pervades his character—he **is holy.** He is the opposite of anything profane. Believers must **be holy in every-thing** they do—that is, totally devoted or dedicated to God, set aside for his special use and set apart from sin and its influence. Our holy God expects us to imitate him by following his high moral standards.

Believers should be set apart and different because of God's qualities in their lives. Our focus and priorities must be his. We have already been declared holy because of our faith in Christ, but we must work out that divine family likeness in our day-by-day walk, behavior, and conduct. We cannot become holy on our own, but God gives us his Holy Spirit to help us. We will not achieve perfect holiness in this life; Peter's words mean that all parts of our lives and character should be

in the process of becoming conformed, both inwardly and outwardly, to God's holy standards.

1:16 To confirm his words in 1:15, Peter quoted the Old Testament Scriptures, which would be familiar to the Jewish Christians in his audience, **"You must be holy because I am holy."** These words are from Leviticus 11:44-45; 19:2; 20:7. Originally this command applied to the Jews, God's chosen nation, but Peter applied them to the Christians, God's chosen people from all nations.

1:17 God was their loving **Father to whom** they could **pray,** yet he was also a strong disciplinarian and the impartial Judge of the entire universe. This judging could refer to God's future judgment of believers when they will be rewarded for how they have lived, but the present tense of the verb **judges** makes more sense if it is applied to God's present judgment and discipline on believers during their lives on earth.

When God judges, he **has no favorites.** Just as these believers constantly called on God for help because they knew he loved them, they should also be careful how they lived: **Live in reverent fear of him during your time as foreigners here on earth.** Reverent fear is not the fear of a slave for a ruthless master, but the healthy and fervent respect of a believer for the all-powerful God. Because God is the Judge of all the earth, believers dare not ignore him or treat him casually. We should not assume that our privileged status as God's children gives us freedom to do whatever we want. A good parent administers discipline without favoritism. We should not be spoiled children, but grateful children who love to show respect for our heavenly Father.

1:18-19 The word **ransom** was used when someone paid money to buy back a slave's freedom. In Old Testament times, a person's debts could result in that person's being sold as a slave. The next of kin could **ransom** the slave (buy his or her freedom), a transaction involving money or valuables of some kind. However, silver and gold can do nothing to change anyone's spiritual condition. No amount of money can buy our salvation. It has to be done God's way, not with money, but **with the precious lifeblood of Christ, the sinless, spotless Lamb of God.** That **God paid a ransom to save** us means that he paid the price to set sinners free from slavery to sin. Christ paid the debt we owed for violating the righteous demands of the law. Christ purchased our freedom, and it cost him his own life. Only the sacrificial death of Christ on the cross was effective atonement for our sins. The Old Testament saints sacrificed lambs in order to atone for their sins, but New Testament believers have had their sins covered by the blood of the sinless Savior.

1:20 Christ's sacrifice for the world's sins was not an afterthought, not something God decided to do when the world spun out of control. This plan was set in motion by the all-knowing, eternal God **long before the world began.** In eternity past, God chose his people (1:2) and planned that Christ would redeem them. Christ has always existed with God (John 1:1), but had been **sent to the earth for all to see.** The redemption God accomplished for believers through Christ—not understood even by the prophets who wrote about them (1:10-11)—should cause us to be even more concerned to live according to his high moral standards. Peter's words, **he did this for you,** provided an intensely personal note, encouraging his readers that Christ's coming and the entire plan of salvation are for individual believers, loved and chosen by God.

1:21 It is **through Christ** that believers **have come to trust in God.** The fact that God **raised Christ from the dead and gave him great glory** is the foundation for our **faith and hope** for two reasons: (1) through Christ's resurrection and glorification, God openly declares that he has accepted Christ as our righteous substitute, thereby giving us access to God; (2) through Christ's resurrection and glorification, believers can receive power from the Holy Spirit (John 16:5-15). The power that resurrected and glorified Christ is the same power that enables us to believe. Because Christ ransomed us, we must no longer fear God and face his judgment; instead, we set our faith and hope **confidently in God,** trusting in the one who planned our salvation from eternity past. As God raised Christ from the dead, we believe and expect that he will also raise us.

1:22 This is one of the strongest statements on brotherly love in the New Testament, for it virtually makes brotherly love the goal of our conversion. Peter expected that growth in purity and holiness would result in deeper love among Christians—not merely outward appearance or profession, but **sincere love** for Christian **brothers and sisters.** Despite our differences and disagreements, we can have sincere love for one another, and as we grow in holiness, we can learn to **love each other intensely** because of the Holy Spirit within us.

Such love is not possible in the world at large, for it doesn't understand the love that results when people are **cleansed from** their **sins** and have **accepted the truth of the Good News.** This experience brings together even very different believers on the common ground of forgiveness in Christ and requires them to love one another as Christ loved them (John 13:34-35).

1:23 Peter gave another reason to love others: Believers have a common ground in Christ. We have all **been born again;** we are sinners saved by grace. Our **new life did not come from** our **earthly parents;** that life will one day **end in death.** Our **new life will last forever** because it was given to us by **the eternal, living word of God.** God's word lives and endures forever, because God who gave it lives and endures from eternity past to eternity future. The powerful, **living** word of God himself, recorded in Scripture, brings new life to believers; the **eternal** word of God himself assures the permanence of that new life. It is only through hearing and/or reading these words that people can find eternal life, for the Scriptures tell the gospel message and make the way of salvation clear to those who seek it.

1:24-25 Quoting **the prophet,** Isaiah 40:6-8, Peter reminded believers that everything in this life—possessions, accomplishments, people—will eventually fade away and disappear. As the **grass** and **wildflowers** bloom for a season then wither and fall, so all of this life is transitory in nature; it will pass away. Only **the word of the Lord will last forever.** Peter's readers would face suffering and persecution, but that would be only temporary. The word of the Lord was **the Good News that** had been **preached** to them. That Good News is good for eternity.

2:1 As noted in 1:22, believers need to get rid of any attitude or hindrance that could threaten this love for brothers and sisters in Christ. **Get rid of** is also translated "put away" or "put off." The same phrase is used in other New Testament passages, always indicating removing one's former life of sin as one would take off a garment (see also Romans 13:12; Ephesians 4:22, 25; Colossians 3:8; James 1:21). The Greek tense indicates that this is a decisive act. Peter addressed this command to rid oneself of sin only to born-again Christians (1:23) who, having a new God-given nature within them, have the ability to break with their past life of sin. While we cannot become completely sin-free in this life, no matter how hard we try to put aside sin, we are commanded to get rid of sin in order to become more like Christ.

Peter listed several types of sin to remove from our lives. The sins Peter listed here fight against love and cause dissension among believers. The first two sins mentioned refer to general categories. The last three sins refer to the specific acts that flow out of them.

- **Malicious behavior** means doing evil despite the good that has been received; the desire to harm other people. Malice may be hidden behind good actions.

- **Deceit** means deliberately tricking or misleading by lying (see also 3:10).
- **Hypocrisy** means that people say one thing but do another; playacting; presenting good motives that mask selfish desire.
- **Jealousy** means desiring something possessed by someone else. This causes discontent and resentment as believers make unhealthy comparisons to one another. It also makes them unable to be thankful for the good that comes to others.
- **Backstabbing** means destroying another's good reputation by lies, gossip, rumor-spreading, etc. Malice often manifests itself through back-stabbing (slander).

2:2 As newborn babies crave milk, so born-again believers should **crave** (long for) **pure spiritual milk** that will nourish them and help them grow to maturity. This points to the word of God, which provides spiritual life to those who partake of it. Like milk, the essential nourishment for babies, God's word sustains life and gives growth. The purity of God's word means that there is no imperfection, no flaws, no dilutions, and that it will not deceive or lead people astray. (Note that "milk" is used in a positive context. This verse should not be compared to 1 Corinthians 3:2 and Hebrews 5:12-13, where the writers employed a similar metaphor but used milk—in contrast to meat—as depicting the diet of immature believers.)

By using the term **baby**, Peter was not implying

that his readers were young believers; indeed, some of them had been Christians for as many as thirty years. Instead, he may have been picking up the reference to being "born again" in 1:23. Peter was saying that believers should always crave more and more of God's word in the same way that **a baby cries for milk.** Then, by taking that nourishment, believers **can grow into the fullness of** their **salvation.** Salvation is an ongoing experience from the time of the new birth until the time Christ returns. At that time, salvation will be completed (1:5). In the meantime, as we live on this earth, we must constantly partake of God's word so that we can "grow up" in our salvation. We must not remain spiritual babies, but become mature in Christ (2 Peter 3:18).

2:3 Peter picked up the beautiful invitation in Psalm 34:8 and placed it in the past tense for these believers: "Taste and see that the Lord is good" (see also Jeremiah 15:16). The believers had already taken that first step in following God by accepting his salvation, and had been given **a taste of the Lord's kindness.** As they lived out their Christian lives, growing to maturity in the faith, they were tasting more and more of the Lord's goodness. That should only serve to whet their appetites. The more we taste God's goodness, the more tasteless other worldly options will become. We must not fill our lives with cheap substitutes so that we lose our craving for the truth contained in God's word.

1 PETER 2:4-25

LIVING STONES FOR GOD'S HOUSE / 2:4-12
In describing the church as God's spiritual house, Peter drew on Old Testament texts that would be familiar to his Jewish Christian readers: Psalm 118:22; Isaiah 8:14; 28:16. They would have understood the living stones to be Israel; then Peter used the image of the "cornerstone" for Christ. Again Peter was demonstrating that Christ did not cancel the Jewish heritage but had fulfilled it. Peter encouraged his readers by emphasizing their true identity and unity in Christ. We too should strive to be usable, obedient elements in God's work.

2:4 Using a new metaphor here, Peter employed Old Testament imagery to describe believers' relationship with God. Believers can constantly **come to** (or approach) **Christ.** The words "come to" do not refer to initial salvation, but to constantly drawing near and coming into Christ's presence. In the Old Testament, only the priests had that

privilege; under the new covenant, all believers can enter into God's presence at any time, with any need.

Peter described Christ as **a living cornerstone;** the "stone" imagery is taken from Psalm 118:22 and other Old Testament passages quoted in the following verses. Jesus had applied these words to himself when he spoke of being rejected by his own people (Matthew 21:42; Mark 12:10-11; Luke 20:17). Peter had quoted this verse in his speech on the day of Pentecost (Acts 4:11-12). Peter added the adjective "living." Christ lives and imparts life to those who believe in him. Also from Psalm 118:22 is the fact that Christ was **rejected by the people.** Although rejected by many, Christ is now the "cornerstone" of the church, the most important part. He is **precious to God who chose him.** Although chosen and precious to God, Christ had to suffer greatly in order to accomplish God's will—it was his "precious blood" (1:19) that redeemed us. Therefore, believers are also very precious to God. Peter encouraged these persecuted believers by telling them that they, like Christ, had been chosen by God.

2:5 Peter carried the imagery further, describing believers also as **living stones** because they are made alive by Christ, the living cornerstone. If these "stones" are "living," then what activities should they be doing? First of all, they should welcome being built into God's **spiritual temple.** Because God is spirit (John 4:24), he lives in a spiritual house among his people, no longer in any particular physical building.

Believers not only are the stones that make up God's spiritual house, but they also serve there as **holy priests, who offer the spiritual sacrifices.** This is a twofold metaphor. We are both the temple (see 1 Corinthians 6:19) and the priests who serve in it. Just as priests served in the temple, so believers are to be priests. Peter used words from Exodus 19:6, where God promised Israel that they would be "a kingdom of priests" and a "holy nation" if they remained obedient to God. God's people, all who believe in Jesus Christ, have become this holy priesthood. The Old Testament priests entered God's presence at specific times and only after carefully following ritual cleansing instructions; God's people can enter God's presence at any time, for they have been cleansed by the Holy Spirit (Hebrews 4:16).

The Old Testament priests offered animal sacrifices in the Temple; God's people offer sacrifices too, but these are "spiritual sacrifices" (see Romans 12:1; Ephesians 5:2; Philippians 4:18; Hebrews 13:15-16). We see from Scripture that every part of our lives—our jobs, activities, recreation, attitudes, giving, outlook, goals—should be given as a spiritual sacrifice to God. When we learn to please God and follow his directions and guidance, all we do delights him. These sacrifices are "spiritual" because we can only give ourselves to God with the Holy Spirit's help. Just as the aroma of the Old Testament sacrifices pleased God, so our service can be a sweet aroma to God, continually giving him delight.

2:6 To support his words in 2:4-5, Peter quoted from **the Scriptures,** citing several Old Testament passages. First, in Isaiah 28:16, God promised to establish a **cornerstone,** the first stone laid in a building, making the foundation stable and the walls plumb and square. That this stone would be laid in **Jerusalem** meant not only that Christ had lived in and around Jerusalem, but also that this new building (the Christian church and the new covenant) with Christ as the cornerstone would actually replace the old building (the Jerusalem Temple and the old covenant).

This cornerstone is a person, and **anyone who believes in him will never be disappointed** (see also Romans 9:33; 10:11). Christians will sometimes face disappointment in this life, but their trust in God is never misplaced. God will not let them down. These words greatly comforted believers facing persecution. As a building rests on its cornerstone, so believers rest on Christ. We can safely put our confidence in Christ because he will certainly give to us the eternal life he promises.

2:7 To you who believe addressed the Christians to whom Peter wrote as well as Christians today. Jesus Christ is indeed **precious,** meaning highly valued or esteemed. Not only is Christ precious to the Father (2:4), he is also precious to those who follow him.

While this is true, most scholars take issue with this translation of the Greek text, saying that this is an unlikely rendering of the Greek. They prefer that this phrase be translated, "Therefore the honor [or preciousness] is to you, the believers" or "This honor belongs to you who believe." This would follow from Peter's words in 2:6. It also contrasts the preciousness of believers, and the honor they will receive, with the dishonor and shame facing those who reject Christ. While believers receive preciousness and honor from God, unbelievers face a different result. They do not regard the Stone as precious and chosen; instead, they **reject** him. Jesus referred to these words when he spoke of being rejected by his own people (Matthew 21:42; Mark 12:10-11; Luke 20:17). In Matthew 21:42 and Acts 4:11, the **builders** were the Jewish religious leaders. Peter used "builders" to refer to all people across the ages who toss Christ aside like an unwanted stone, choosing to build the foundations of their lives on something else. However, they were mistaken to reject him because God took the rejected stone and made it **the cornerstone** of the church.

2:8 Quoting once again from the prophet Isaiah (Isaiah 8:14), Peter further explained that not only were the builders who rejected the stone humiliated that it later became the cornerstone, they also had stumbled and fallen over this stone. The word "stumbled" can mean tripping and falling, or it can mean taking offense at or rejecting something or someone. Peter explained that **they stumble because they do not listen to God's word or obey it**—this disobedience refers not to slipups by one who tries to obey; rather it means outright rejection of the Word and the Messiah that the Word promised, and a rebellious stance toward God. Some stumble over Christ because they reject him or refuse to believe that he is who he claims to be. They have stumbled over the one person who could save them, and they have fallen into God's hands for judgment.

Their stumbling and disobedience were **planned by God**. What does that mean? Some scholars take 1 Thessalonians 5:9 and Romans 9:22-23 to prove double predestination. This means that some are predestined to belief unto salvation, and others are predestined to disbelief unto damnation. It would be more natural here to take Peter's point to be that God has predestined punishment for those who disbelieve, so that only the consequence of disbelief is ordained. The fact of predestination does not imply that all our choices are predetermined. Because God is not limited by time as we are, he "sees" past, present, and future at the same time. Parents sometimes "know" how their children will behave before the fact. We don't conclude from these parents' foreknowledge that they made their children act that way. God's foreknowledge, insofar as we can understand it, means that God knows who will accept the offer of salvation and who will reject it.

To explain foreknowledge and predestination in any way that implies that every action and choice we make has been not only preknown, but even predetermined, seems to contradict those Scriptures that declare that our choices are real, that they matter, and that there are consequences to the choices we make. Those who choose to disobey will stumble and fall.

2:9 This verse contrasts the privilege and destiny of believers with that of unbelievers (described in 2:8). Believers are **a chosen people**, a distinct group from the rest of the world, unified by the Holy Spirit. Just as the nation of Israel had been God's chosen people, Christians have become God's people, not by physical birth into a certain race but by spiritual rebirth into God's family through Jesus Christ.

Believers also are **a kingdom of priests, God's**

holy nation (Exodus 19:6). Being part of a "priesthood" is a high honor for believers. Christians speak of "the priesthood of all believers." In Old Testament times, people did not approach God directly. Instead, a priest would act as an intermediary between God and sinful human beings. With Christ's victory on the cross, that pattern changed. Now believers can come directly into God's presence without fear (Hebrews 4:16). Also, they have been given the responsibility of bringing others to him (2 Corinthians 5:18-21). United with Christ as members of his body, believers join in his priestly work of reconciling God and people. "Holy nation" refers to Christians as a people who are distinct from all the others because of their devotion to God.

Believers are God's **very own possession**. Similar language is found in Exodus 19:5 and Malachi 3:17. God's people are those who are faithful to him; thus this refers to Christians.

God's special people are to **show others the goodness of God, for he called you out of the darkness into his wonderful light.** Christians were redeemed with a special purpose—to glorify and praise the one who has called them out of the darkness of sin and of their hostile surroundings into the light of eternal life.

2:10 This verse is an adaptation of Hosea 1:9-10 and 2:23. Hosea, God's prophet, was describing God's rejection of Israel, followed by future restoration. Paul used these same verses from Hosea and applied them to the Gentile believers (Romans 9:25-26). Peter applied these verses to the New Testament church as a whole.

Just as Israel had been, at one time, rejected by God without any hope of forgiveness for their sins, so Christians had been, at one time, rejected by God without any hope of mercy. But believers are now **the people of God** because they have been chosen by him (2:9) and **have received his mercy.** "Mercy" means God's compassionate treatment of us even though we deserve the full measure of his justice. God had no obligation to gather a people together to whom he would show mercy; not one of us deserves his slightest concern. God drawing a people unto himself and lavishing mercy on them gives overwhelming evidence of his great love. This mercy ought to affect the way every believer lives, as Peter will point out in the following verses.

2:11 Peter warned the believers to remember their status as **foreigners and aliens** in the world. These words are also used together in Genesis 23:4 and Psalm 39:12. The world is not the Christian's true home; our real home is with Christ. We are passing through this world on the way to our home in heaven's glory; therefore, we ought to remain as untouched as possible by this world's rampant sin, keeping **away from evil desires.** Because we will not escape our sinful surroundings until Christ returns, and because we still have a sinful nature that wants us to act on its desires, we will not be able to remain completely free of sin and its effects. But we can keep away by controlling the desires right from the start.

Why must believers keep away from sinful desires? Because those desires **fight against** our **very souls.** Once we become believers, a battle has begun, for Satan is the enemy of Christ and his followers. The word "souls" refers to the inner, spiritual part of a person (see also 1:22). Desires come from deep within us; often our sinful desires never actually become sinful actions. Peter wrote that while believers know that their lives and actions must be changed by Christ, they also must have their inner lives transformed. Sinful desires may seem much less evil than sinful actions, but Peter explained that they too can hurt us as they war against our souls. Entertaining evil desires, even if those desires are never acted upon, takes our focus off of Christ and turns our hearts from

heavenly to earthly desires. All evil actions begin with a single thought; therefore, Peter advised believers to kill sin right at its root.

2:12 This thought follows from 2:11 without a break in the Greek text—the believers were to have their inner selves under control so that their outer lives would be honoring to God. Believers are called to honor God by living honorably and morally upright in and in spite of an unholy world so that **unbelieving neighbors** will glorify God. Peter's advice sounds like Jesus' advice recorded in Matthew 5:16. If believers' actions are **honorable,** even hostile people might end up praising God. Peter's readers were scattered among unbelieving Gentiles who were inclined to believe and spread vicious lies about Christians, accusing them of wrongdoing, blaming them without cause. Attractive, gracious, and upright behavior on the part of Christians could show these rumors to be false and could even win some of the unsaved critics to the Lord's side. Peter urged the believers not to be surprised when persecution and false accusations arose, and to live above reproach so that the accusations would have to be dropped.

RESPECTING PEOPLE IN AUTHORITY / 2:13-17

At this point in Peter's letter, the focus changes from theological to practical. Up to this point, Peter had explained that the believers were to live holy lives, revealing their status as God's chosen people. In this section, Peter offered practical advice for holy living in an unholy and often hostile world. As believers who have received God's mercy (2:10), we ought to live worthy of our calling. This begins the next major section of 1 Peter (2:11–3:12). It centers on the Christians' relationships to non-Christians. Because we are the community of God (2:4-10), we must live like it.

2:13-14 Peter commanded believers to **accept all authority,** meaning to submit (see 2:18–3:1). God is honored when we accept and respect those in authority over us. We do this **for the Lord's sake,** so that he is glorified by our orderly submission.

In telling his readers to accept the authority of **the king,** Peter was speaking of Emperor Nero, a notoriously cruel tyrant who ruled from A.D. 54–68. The emperor was the supreme ruler over all Roman provinces—including the areas to which Peter addressed this letter. The emperor Nero was considered the supreme authority by his subjects, even worshiped by them. The Christians should never worship the emperor, but they should obey his laws because he was an authority put in place by God (Romans 13:1-2). But Peter was not telling believers to compromise their Holy Spirit-directed consciences. Remember, Peter had told the high

priest years before, "We must obey God rather than human authority" (Acts 5:29). At other times, God had approved disobedience to human authorities (see, for example, Exodus 1:17; Daniel 3:13-18; 6:10-24; Acts 4:18-20; Hebrews 11:23). In those cases, the government had called upon God's people to sin against God and God's people had to submit to the higher power—God himself. But in most aspects of daily life, it was desirable for Christians to live according to the law of their land, whether or not they agreed with the policies. Christians were not to rebel against Rome— Roman law was the only restraint against lawlessness. In addition, it wouldn't take much for an imperial edict to fall on a group who had become known for causing unrest within the empire. The Christians' quiet submission might allow them to continue to spread the gospel freely. If they were to be persecuted, it should be for obeying God, and not for breaking moral or civil laws. Peter himself would later be put to death for his faith during Emperor Nero's intense persecution of Christians.

The king (or emperor), with supreme authority, would delegate responsibility to representatives in the territories under the empire's control. These **officials** would carry out the emperor's commands, enforce the laws, and keep the peace in the provinces. They had been **appointed** to **punish all who do wrong and to honor those who do right.** While no government carries out these functions perfectly, most attempt to do so in order to maintain peace and safety for their citizens.

Today, one-third of all Christians live in freedom while the other two-thirds live under repressive governments. Scripture does not recommend one form of government over another. Rather, it simply asks Christians to accept the government under whose authority they find themselves and to cooperate with the rulers as far as the Holy Spirit-directed conscience will allow. Believers must do this "for the Lord's sake"—so that his Good News and his people will be respected.

2:15 Peter exhorted the believers to live **good lives** so that **those who make foolish accusations** against the believers would be silenced. The word **silence** is more literally "to muzzle"—in other words, to shut them up. This repeats the idea of 2:12. These unbelievers should finally have to admit that they could hold nothing against Christians except their faith.

2:16 Here Peter was outlining a paradox of the Christian life. Christians are **free** yet they are **slaves.** They can live as free people but must use their freedom to glorify God. We glorify God when we serve him faithfully. Believers are not free to do whatever they want or to use their freedom as **an excuse to do evil.** We cannot use freedom and forgiveness as a cloaking device for self-indulgence, adultery, or poor spending habits. Christ is our leader, and serving him provides our limits.

2:17 These four short sentences summarize how believers can live peacefully in the world. First, **show respect for everyone.** The word "respect" means to honor, value, or esteem. Believers should be especially conscious that God made all people in his image, whether or not they believe in Christ.

While believers are to "respect" everyone, they have an extra obligation to their **Christian brothers and sisters.** They are called to **love** them. The word for "love" is *agapao*, referring to volitional, self-sacrificial love. The believers of Peter's day needed to stand together as a unified force against coming persecution. They needed to maintain the bond of love.

To **fear God** means to show deep respect, reverence, and awe. While believers are to respect and love God as well, they are also to fear him. Proper fear leads to obedience. They should **show respect for the king,** but they should "fear" God. When we honor the king, we should give the government its rights, what it owns, what it controls; but we may not give to the government those rights that belong to God alone.

SLAVES / 2:18-25

Believers who were servants were not set free from serving their masters, but they were set free from slavery to sin. While their masters might not be Christians, that did not allow the servants to be disrespectful or lazy. They needed to remember that their ultimate Master was God himself (Colossians 3:23-24). These people were not permanent slaves, but neither were they merely servants. Their positions were semipermanent. They did not have legal or economic freedom but often were paid for their services and could eventually hope to purchase their freedom. For more on slaves, see 1 Corinthians 7:21; Ephesians 6:5-8; 1 Timothy 6:1-2; Titus 2:9-10.

2:18 Peter had already commanded believers to accept authority (2:13). Here he specifically addressed Christians who were **slaves** in pagan homes. The Greek word means a household servant. Peter called these servants to **accept the authority of** their **masters,** meaning that they should cooperate, be loyal, and willingly obey.

Like Paul, Peter neither condemned nor condoned slavery. To attempt to rebel against the system would only bring the wrath of the powerful Roman Empire and would hurt the cause of the gospel. So the apostles suggested that the believers should live within the system, hoping to transform it by first transforming lives through salvation in Jesus Christ. Thus Peter commanded that the believing slaves simply serve well and show respect, not just to Christian masters or to those who were **kind and reasonable,** but also to masters who were **harsh.** It would take God's grace for Christian slaves to loyally and obediently serve such a master. Peter encouraged loyalty and perseverance even in the face of unjust treatment.

2:19 Many of the readers of this letter, slaves who had become Christians, would have known all too well what it meant to **patiently endure unfair treatment.** It would please God if these believers trusted him as they endured "pain" (referring to mental, not physical, anguish) caused by unjust suffering. Being patient **for the sake of** their **conscience** means that when they suffered, they were remembering God's care and love for them even as they suffered. They focused on the fact that they were suffering injustice as Christ had suffered injustice, and they knew that one day God would right all wrongs. This gave them the proper attitude, enabled them to persevere, and kept their practice from being mere passive acceptance.

2:20 While bearing the pain of unjust suffering is commendable before God, there is no special commendation for patiently bearing punishment that is deserved. The word for **beaten** means to strike with one's fist (see also Mark 14:65). Christian slaves who patiently endured suffering when they had done nothing to deserve it would please God. However, if they suffered for **doing wrong,** then they would **get no credit.**

2:21 Why have believers been **called** (see also 1:15; 2:9) to **suffering?** Because such suffering was endured by **Christ.** Jesus had told Peter and the other disciples at the Last Supper: "A servant is not greater than the master. Since they persecuted me, naturally they will persecute you" (John 15:20). When we patiently suffer injustice, we are following our supreme **example** in Christ.

That the believers were to **follow in his steps** means to follow in Jesus' complete peace and trust in God. Christ has given believers an example of how they are to face injustice and persecution. Peter set up Christ as the model for the believers to follow; his example would have greatly comforted these believers, who soon would be persecuted for their faith. They should face injustice from harsh masters or from other authorities with supreme dignity, trusting God's control.

2:22 Peter quoted from Isaiah 53:9, Isaiah's prophecy about the suffering of the coming Messiah. Christ's suffering was completely unjust because he **never sinned** or **deceived anyone;**

there was no good reason for his being condemned to death (even Pilate saw that—see John 19:4). From personal experience Peter knew that Jesus was perfect. He had lived and traveled with Jesus for three years. Intimate relationships often reveal the worst in people, but Peter had seen the truth of the prophet's words. Christ was completely sinless in his life and in his words.

2:23 This is another allusion to Isaiah 53, this time verse 7: "He was oppressed and treated harshly, yet he never said a word. He was led as a lamb to the slaughter. And as a sheep is silent before the shearers, he did not open his mouth." Jesus **did not retaliate** nor did he **threaten.** How tempting it must have been to expose the liars at his trial, to come down from the cross in a great display of power, or to blast his enemies with God's wrath. **He left his case in the hands of God, who always judges fairly.** Jesus suffered patiently because he knew that God would have the final say. Jesus regarded God as sovereign, so he put the outcome of his life in God's hands. Believers can entrust themselves and their suffering into God's hands. Knowing that God will ultimately right all wrongs is a great comfort to believers who are suffering, and it helps them respond correctly in their sufferings.

2:24 This phrase also comes from Isaiah 53: **He personally carried away our sins** (from 53:12); **you have been healed by his wounds** (from 53:5). Only Christ himself, the sinless Son of God, could bear our sins **on the cross.** Christ took the death penalty for sin, dying in our place, so that we would not have to suffer the punishment that we deserve. In a transaction we cannot comprehend, God placed the sins of the world on Jesus Christ, **so we can be dead to sin and live for what is right.** Because all our wrongdoing is forgiven, we are reconciled to God. All who believe in Jesus Christ as Savior can have this new life and live in union with him. Our evil desires, our bondage to sin, and our love of sin died with Christ on the cross. This is called substitutionary atonement. Jesus died as our substitute; his wounds have healed ours.

2:25 This verse also echoes Isaiah: **Once you were wandering like lost sheep** (from 53:6). Sheep need the constant protection of a shepherd or they will wander away, following their noses and sometimes getting into great danger. People can be like that, wandering through life in whatever direction circumstances might take them. But that was in the past; **now you have turned to your Shepherd, the Guardian of your souls.** At conversion, each believer returns from going his or her own way (the way of sin). Peter described God as a "Shepherd" who tirelessly looks after the sheep, guiding and protecting them (see Psalm 23:1-4; Ezekiel 34:11-16; Luke 15:5-7; John 10:11-16). Whatever trials and difficulties they might face, the Shepherd would always be by their side, and the Guardian of their souls would protect and seal them for eternity.

1 PETER 3

WIVES / 3:1-6

In 2:11-25, Peter had explained that the believers needed to act in an exemplary manner before the unbelieving world. He told them to be subject to authority (2:13) and then described two areas of that authority: citizens to the government (2:13-17) and slaves to masters (2:18-20). In these verses he added wives to husbands (3:1-7). Anarchy results if there is no authority. As Christians, we should not rebel against authority, but work within the system and serve God.

3:1-2 The phrase **in the same way** (or "likewise," *homoios*) most likely referred to 2:13, "Accept all authority." The word *homoios* has a slightly different slant than the word *kathos*, another word that is translated "in the same way." If Peter had used the word *kathos*, he would have meant that wives should serve their husbands in the same way that slaves serve their masters. However, the word *homoios* focuses the comparison in other areas. While wives are to serve their husbands "in the same way" as slaves serve their masters, Peter was not saying that wives were slaves. Instead, the wives' service should have positive motives ("for the Lord's sake," 2:13) and should be consistent no matter what the attitude of the one in authority ("even if they are harsh," 2:18). Christian wives were to accept the authority of their husbands in obedience to Christ to keep harmony in the family and to encourage unbelieving husbands to believe.

Submission of the wife to the husband is an often misunderstood concept, although it is taught in several places in the New Testament (see, for example, Ephesians 5:24; Colossians 3:18; 1 Peter 3:1, 5). It may be the least popular Christian teaching in society. These texts do not teach the general subjugation of all women under all men. The principle of submission does not require a woman to become a doormat. When a Christian wife interacted with an unbelieving husband, she needed to be submissive according to cultural norms in order to save her marriage and sometimes even her life. But she ought not participate in her husband's pagan religion or submit to actions that dishonored God. However, when both wife and husband were Christians, the woman should respect the God-given authority of her husband,

while the husband exercised his authority in a loving and gentle manner. For marriage and family relationships to run smoothly, there must be one appointed leader—and God has appointed the husband and father. The wife should willingly follow her husband's leadership in Christ, acknowledging that this is his responsibility. Submission does not mean blind obedience, nor does it mean inferiority. A wife who accepts her husband's authority is accepting the relationship that God has designed and giving her husband leadership and responsibility.

In the first century, when a man became a Christian, he usually would bring his whole family into the church with him (see, for example, the story of the conversion of the Philippian jailer, Acts 16:29-34). By contrast, a woman who became a Christian usually came into the church alone. Under Roman law, the husband and father had absolute authority over all members of his household, including his wife. A wife who demanded her rights as a free woman in Christ could endanger her marriage and her life if her husband disapproved. Instead, she should live her new faith through **pure, godly behavior.** Peter reassured Christian women who were married to unbelievers that they need not preach to their husbands; their husbands would see **their godly lives.** At the very least, the men would then allow these wives to continue practicing their faith. At best, their husbands would become Christians too.

3:3-4 As today, society's focus was on **outward beauty.** Such beauty was achieved in **fancy hairstyles, expensive jewelry,** and **beautiful clothes.** But Peter contrasted putting beautiful "things" on the outside to make oneself beautiful, versus revealing the natural inner beauty that a Christian woman should have because of Christ (see 3:4).

This passage is teaching that women should not count on their beauty coming from outward adornments, not that women can't braid their hair or wear gold jewelry or nice clothes. (Paul wrote almost the exact words to the women in the Ephesian church; see 1 Timothy 2:9-10.) Christian women should not be obsessed by fashion or overly concerned with their outward appearance. On the other hand, neither should they be so unconcerned that they do not bother to care for themselves. Beauty and adornments have their place, but they must be kept in proper perspective. Christian women should let their **beauty** come **from within, the unfading beauty of a gentle and quiet spirit.** Their beauty should come from their personality, and the attitudes, thoughts, and motivations that are revealed in words and actions. For believers, this inner self has been transformed by the Holy Spirit. To be "gentle" means showing humility, consideration of others, not insisting on one's own rights, not being pushy or overly assertive (see also Galatians 5:23). To be "quiet" refers to the same attitude as that described by "gentle," also focusing on not causing dissensions with inappropriate words or gossip.

3:5-6 The holy women of the past were both holy and **beautiful,** not because they lived perfect lives and had perfect looks, but because they **trusted God.** Another ancient writer understood this: "Charm is deceptive, and beauty does not last; but a woman who fears the Lord will be greatly praised" (Proverbs 31:30). These women trusted in God and knew how to submit to the authority God had established, by accepting **the authority of their husbands** (as described in 3:1-2 above).

Peter used one woman in particular as an example: **Sarah, who obeyed her husband, Abraham, when she called him her master.** Peter commended her attitude of obedience, hanging his argument on Sarah's use of "master." Sarah's submission certainly wasn't slavish. She insisted that Hagar and Ishmael (Abraham's other wife and first son) be sent away. Abraham didn't like it, but went along with her request. Apparently God approved of Sarah's request as supported by his answer to Abraham, "Do just as Sarah says" (Genesis 21:10, 12).

Why did Peter use Sarah as an example? Sarah was considered the mother of God's people (as Abraham was the father, according to God's covenant promises, Genesis 12:1-3). Not only was Sarah an example to be followed because of her faithfulness to God and to her husband (she did submit to Abraham to have the child), but also because she was the mother of all believers—under the old covenant, the mother of the Jewish nation; under the new covenant, the mother of all who believe (see Galatians 4:22-26). Peter saw Christian women as true **daughters** of Sarah, and thus true daughters of God. So they should **do what is right without fear of what your husbands might do.** A Christian woman's faith in God would help her not to be afraid. In context, this could refer to them not fearing the physical harm that might come to them from their husbands, not fearing the result of submitting to their husbands, or not fearing what might happen if they had to disobey their husbands because their husbands asked them to do wrong or evil acts. It could also refer to the theme of persecution throughout this letter, recommending that these women not be afraid of anything that might come upon them or their families. But in this context, their fear and hope in God (3:5) allowed them both to reverence (3:2) and not fear (3:6) their husbands.

HUSBANDS / 3:7

In 3:1-6, Peter taught Christian women to submit to the husband's authority, but the Christian husband must use his authority with consideration and respect for his wife. He must not be a tyrant, faithless, unloving, or impatient. Likewise, the wife should not be rebellious, subversive, or contradicting.

3:7 Just as the wives were to accept authority, so the husbands **in the same way** were to **give honor to their wives.** That a husband should **treat** his wife **with understanding** implies more than just a kind attitude; it goes deeper, implying that his consideration of his wife is based on his knowledge of her needs, desires, gifts, and abilities. A husband who acts on his knowledge of his wife will greatly enrich her life, as well as his own. This is the explicit message of Paul in Ephesians 5:25-27.

While the wife **may be weaker** than the husband, she is his **equal partner.** In this context, being weaker refers to physical weakness, not to moral, spiritual, or intellectual inferiority. Peter used the term not to diminish women, but to build a case for respecting them. The men were not to bully their wives physically or sexually. Women had less authority in the marriage, so the husbands were encouraged to use their authority with respect for their wives. Their authority did not excuse abuse of power. While the woman may be "weaker," she is also a "partner," implying a side-by-side relationship of working together. A man who respects his wife will protect, honor, and help her. He will stay with her. He will respect her opinions, listen to her advice, be considerate of her needs, and relate to her both privately and publicly with love, courtesy, insight, and tact.

Some women have chafed under the biblical assertion that they are "weaker" and that they are to submit to their husbands. But these women need to remember that they are equal with men in God's eyes. Even though God gave husbands authority in the marriage and family, wives are equal to their husbands in spiritual privileges and eternal relationships. Both men and women who are believers are partners **in God's gift of new life**—eternal life. If husbands are not considerate and respectful to their wives, their prayers will **not be heard.** If men use their position to mistreat their wives, their relationship with God will suffer. A man should not expect to have a vital ministry in life or prayer if he is mistreating his wife in any way.

ALL CHRISTIANS / 3:8-12
Peter knew that the believers would soon face persecution. He reminded these believers that they would need unity, and love and support from one another. Peter also assured the believers that no matter what sufferings they might have to face, God would vindicate them and punish their enemies. Rather than fear our enemies, we are to quietly trust in God as the Lord of all.

3:8 In saying **finally,** Peter was summing up a series of exhortations concerning submission. Peter listed five building blocks for unity as Christians lived in their pagan culture. These blocks will build relationships among any group of believers.

1. **Be of one mind** refers to working together for the common goal of spreading the gospel, having common attitudes and ideas. Just as different notes form chords to make beautiful harmonies, so different people can live and work together for God.
2. Be **full of sympathy** means being willing to share in others' needs and being responsive to their feelings, having sensitivity and compassion toward others.
3. **Loving one another** means loving fellow Christians (brothers and sisters in Christ). The Greek word is *philadelphos*, referring not only to family love, but to the special love that should draw all Christians together.
4. To have **tender hearts** means to be conscious of others' needs but includes a drive to alleviate the need in some way. Believers ought to be deeply touched and moved by the hurts, pain, needs, and joys of fellow believers and then act to help them. They should be affectionate and sensitive, quick to give emotional support.
5. To have **humble minds** means having an honest estimate of oneself before God. Humility does not negate one's own worth or abilities, nor does it inflate them. Instead, a humble Christian

can honestly view his or her characteristics and abilities with thankfulness to God. Humble people can encourage one another and rejoice in each other's successes.

3:9 After describing how Christians should act toward one another, Peter described how they should act toward those in the pagan culture—a culture that would soon (if it hadn't already) become very hostile toward them. While it would be most natural to **repay evil for evil** and to **retaliate,** Jesus had taught and exemplified otherwise (Matthew 5:39, 44). Believers were not to retaliate, but were to **pay them back with a blessing.** Believers' speech should always be characterized by blessings, never curses, but "blessing" refers to more than words of kindness. The spiritual sense of the word refers to believers offering the gospel to those who persecute them. This is what **God wants** them **to do** and he would **bless** them for it. Believers still may be persecuted, but they can depend on God's blessings, whether physical or spiritual.

3:10 Verses 10-12 are a quotation of Psalm 34:12-16. (Peter also quoted from this Psalm in 2:3.) The theme of Psalm 34 is that God hears and helps those who are afflicted or in trouble—a perfect psalm considering the theme of this letter.

The phrase, **if you want a happy life and good days,** may refer to people who trust God and who are (or want to be) enjoying their earthly lives no matter what the outward circumstances. These people have found contentment in God and can live "good days" no matter how bad their situations might become. The answer is found in living righteously, as suggested by both the psalmist and the apostle.

In order to do so, watch what you say. People who desire life and good days keep their tongues **from speaking evil** and their lips from **telling lies.** The word **evil** could refer to any type of speech that is displeasing to God; **lies** means to deliberately trick or mislead.

3:11 People's words are connected to their actions. When believers **turn away from evil,** their God-honoring speech is then accompanied doing **good.** To live **in peace** means more than simply the absence of conflict. Effective peacemakers must **work hard** at peace. They build good relationships, knowing that peace is a by-product of commitment. They anticipate problems and deal with them before they occur. When conflicts arise, peacemakers bring them into the open and deal with them before they grow unmanageable.

3:12 God will **watch over those who do right.** Nothing happens to God's people that he has not allowed for some purpose. Whatever happens, God's people know that his promises of blessing—whether in this life or in the life to come—are certain.

Not only are the Lord's eyes open and watching, but **his ears are open to their prayers.** He listens when his people call to him. He knows all their needs. He hears their prayers in suffering. These words would have been a great comfort to these suffering Christians. Not only were they seen, heard, and ultimately protected, but those who hurt them would be judged. Believers are not to retaliate; instead, they must trust that God will avenge the wrongs his people have suffered.

SUFFERING FOR DOING GOOD / 3:13-22

Up to this point in the letter, the theme of the persecution facing these young churches has been in the background. At this point, however, it becomes a prominent theme in this letter. After describing the attitudes and actions that should characterize God's people (3:8-12), Peter began to explain how the believers should live in an evil world in the face of persecution.

3:13-14 Common sense tells people that if they **do good,** they will be protected from punishment or **harm.** It is usually much wiser for believers to do what is good and to follow the authorities and laws so that they won't be persecuted unnecessarily. Peter was not indicating that if the believers behaved well, they would escape persecution and ill treatment. In fact, they might **suffer for doing what is right.** Persecution comes for a variety of reasons. Even though it may not seem like it from a worldly point of view, these believers who suffered for doing what was right, would be rewarded. If the believers were living righteously and continued to be persecuted, no one would be able to harm them spiritually or change God's promises to them. Alluding to Isaiah 8:12-13, Peter counseled the believers to not **be afraid** of persecution or **worry** about it. Evil people's threats were empty because they could not harm the eternal souls of God's people.

3:15 Instead of being afraid of people, believers are to focus on Christ himself. By acknowledging Christ as **Lord** and Savior, they would recognize his holiness and be able to rest in him. There would be no room in their hearts for fear. Instead, they can **always be ready to explain** the reason for their **Christian hope.** While Peter may have been thinking about believers speaking in a court, he seems also to have had in mind the everyday informal inquiries that might be directed at the believers—from either hostile or friendly neighbors.

Unbelievers can see that Christians have something different; only "hope" gives us strength and joy in hardships and persecutions. Unbelievers will ask about it; believers must be ready to tell them. All Christians must be ready and able to give a reasonable defense of their faith. They need not be apologists or theologians, but every Christian ought to be able to clearly explain his or her own reasons for being a Christian.

3:16 Believers must not be obnoxious, but share their faith **in a gentle and respectful way.** To **keep** one's **conscience clear** refers to one's personal integrity before God alone, as he or she lives consistently with their knowledge of God. Unbelievers also have consciences that ought to guard their morality and actions (Romans 2:14-15), but a Christian's conscience has been transformed by God. The Holy Spirit helps each believer know and understand God's will, and sensitizes his or her conscience to God's desires. All believers should keep clear consciences. To do that, believers can avoid willful disobedience. If we do disobey, we should stay in constant communication with God, repenting and asking forgiveness. Each time we deliberately ignore our conscience, we harden our heart. Over a period of time our capacity to tell right from wrong will diminish. As we walk with God, he will speak to us through our conscience, letting us know the difference between right and wrong.

Just by being Christians, these believers could find themselves facing persecution; they ought not supply their enemies with ammunition by also breaking laws or acting and speaking in an evil way. If the Christians' lives were above reproach, unbelievers would end up **ashamed** when they **speak evil against** them. They would realize that they had done nothing more than slander someone's **good life**.

3:17-18 Peter referred to the advice he had given servants in 2:19-20, suggesting that if Christians were to **suffer**, it should never be for **doing wrong**. If they had to suffer at all, they should suffer only for **doing good**. Their example is Christ. He **never sinned**, yet he **suffered, died**. Christ's suffering resulted in his death for **sins**. Although he seemed to have been defeated, he **was raised to life in the Spirit**. Christ's death was **once for all time**. His sacrifice was sufficient. No one else will have to die for people's sins; Christ will not have to die again.

3:19-20 The word **so** forms a break in thought here and refers back to "in the Spirit" in the previous verse. The meaning of **preached to the spirits in prison** is not completely clear, mainly because the word translated "spirits" *(pneumata)* can be used to refer to human spirits, angels, or demons (the singular *pneuma* is also used to refer to God's Holy Spirit). The passage further indicates that these "spirits in prison" are **those who disobeyed long ago when God waited patiently while Noah was building his boat. Only eight people were saved from drowning in that terrible flood.** This passage has been tackled by many scholars over the years and given a variety of interpretations. Three main questions arise: (1) Who were the "spirits" to whom Christ made his proclamation? (2) When did Christ make this proclamation? (3) What was the content of this proclamation? Following are the main interpretations of Peter's words:

1. Some explain that between Christ's crucifixion and resurrection, he went to the realm of the dead, to hell or hades. There he preached to "the spirits in prison"—meaning either all the people who lived before him who had died and gone to hell, or the fallen angels who had sinned by marrying human women before the Flood (a view highly dependent on apocryphal literature).

The content of Christ's proclamation may have been to offer the sinful people a second chance at salvation (this is most unlikely because nowhere in Scripture does God offer a "second chance"), or to tell the sinful people and/or fallen angels that their condemnation was final and eternal. Still others say that Christ was preaching to all those who had repented before they died in the Flood. They had been "in prison" awaiting their release by Christ into heaven. They say that Christ, between his death and resurrection, announced salvation to God's faithful followers who had been waiting for their salvation during the whole Old Testament era.

2. During Noah's building of the ark (120 years), Christ's "spirit" was in Noah preaching to all the unbelieving people. First Peter 1:11 refers to the "Spirit of Christ" residing in the Old Testament prophets. This view takes Christ's reference to Noah literally and holds that the "spirits" were humans (rather than angels or demons). Christ spoke through Noah to the people for 120 years as Noah was building the ark (Genesis 6:3). During that time, God was waiting patiently for any to repent of their sins. But none did. These unbelievers on earth were the "spirits in prison" who were imprisoned by their sin, or they were the souls of the evil human race of that day that are now "in prison," hades (they died long ago in the Flood), awaiting God's final judgment at the end of the age. Those who consider this to be the correct meaning of Peter's words consider that Noah and his family were a righteous minority among a huge majority of evil people. Just as Noah faced unjust persecution, so Peter's readers were also facing unjust persecution. Just as Noah had no converts, they might not either. Just as Noah knew that judgment would come soon, so Peter's readers knew that God would soon judge the world. Ultimately, as Noah and his family were saved from the floodwaters, so those who believe will be saved from eternal death.

3. Between Christ's death and resurrection, or after Christ's ascension, he preached the triumph of his resurrection to the fallen angels. It is likely that Christ was simply making the announcement of his finished work on the cross and, by so doing, declaring his victory. The "prison" was an abyss near heaven, a kind of "storage place" for the evil angels. His declaration confirmed the testimonies of Enoch and Noah. By doing this, it confirmed the condemnation of those who had refused to believe, while assuring the salvation of Noah and believers. The spirits are fallen angels typified by those who instigated gross immorality in the days of Noah (Genesis

6:2). Many scholars favor this view because 2 Peter 2:4-5 and Jude 6 link the angels that sinned with the judgment of the Flood by God in the days of Noah. According to these verses in 2 Peter, these angels of God were cast into hell, literally Tartarus, a place of confinement prior to their judgment. Tartarus, therefore, is the prison mentioned here. Sometime after Christ was resurrected, he made a proclamation to these fallen angels. (See discussion of Tartarus in 2 Peter 2:4.)

Therefore, to answer the three key questions noted above: the fallen angels were the spirits; the time of the proclamation is not known for certain, but either it was between Jesus' death and resurrection or at the time of his ascension; the content of Christ's message was to proclaim his victory to the fallen angels. The passage shows that Christ's glorious reign extends over all the evil authorities and fallen angels that had wreaked havoc on the earth in Noah's day and were still doing so in Peter's time. Yet Peter offered his readers a vision: while the forces of evil could not yet be completely silenced (in fact, they actively continued to work against believers), the believers could rest assured that Christ had already won the battle.

3:21 Speaking of the water of the Flood led Peter to explain that Noah being saved from drowning **is a picture of baptism.** When dealing with symbols in the Bible, we must always ask, What is being symbolized? It was neither the ark nor the water that "saved" Noah, but the power of God conveyed in a promise. The Greek word for "picture" refers to a person, event, object, or act that anticipates or foreshadows a more perfect fulfillment of the essential idea. So the floodwaters convey some meaning and point toward baptism.

The Flood came as a judgment upon evil people, but for Noah it brought deliverance from their mockery and sin, ushering him into a new life. In baptism, believers identify with Jesus Christ, who separates us from the lost and gives us new life. Baptism is a sign of the new covenant, identifying the person baptized with the people of God, the Christian community. It is not the ceremony, the water, nor the **removal of dirt** from the **body** (referring not to physical cleansing but to a spiritual cleansing) that saves. The water of baptism does not "wash away sin" literally. Instead, baptism is the outward symbol of the inner transformation that happens in the hearts of those who believe (Romans 6:3-5; Galatians 3:27; Colossians 2:12). Baptism does not save anyone, but the belief it represents results in salvation. Its efficacy comes from **the power of Jesus Christ's resurrection.**

Baptism is also **an appeal to God from a clean conscience.** The Holy Spirit convicts the person's mind and heart of sin, calling for a response or pledge of faith. This pledge is confirmed outwardly and tangibly in baptism. This pledge toward God implies that baptism conveys believers' desire to please God and therefore ask God for help to live out the reality of that inner transformation in their daily lives through repentance and forgiveness.

3:22 Peter now entered into an exaltation of Christ and his victory over all opposition, whether attacks of Satan or the cruel treatment of the government. Peter himself had been an eyewitness. He saw Jesus' ascension (Acts 1:9). Jesus had **gone to heaven,** a place beyond the clouds, beyond our human sight. There Jesus **is seated in the place of honor next to God.** Christ has royal power and dignity as a result of his resurrection (Matthew 22:44; Mark 12:36; Acts 2:34; Romans 8:34; Colossians 3:1; Hebrews 1:13). Thus, **angels and authorities and powers** are **bowing before him.** In this context, these words refer to all spiritual beings in the universe, both good and evil. Everything in earth and heaven is already subject to Christ. One day in the future, when he comes to judge, his power and authority will be made known to everyone.

1 PETER 4

LIVING FOR GOD / 4:1-11

Peter wrote a great deal about the way believers' lives should differ from the ordinary pattern of the world. The use of their God-given abilities is one of those ways. God has given every person special skills or abilities. Each time these skills are used to serve others, God is glorified. How can you use your gifts and abilities to serve others and glorify God?

4:1 In 3:17-18, Peter explained that Christ had suffered and died for sins, once for all, and that believers should be ready to suffer. In 3:17, he explained that if they had to suffer, it should be for doing good, not for doing evil, in order to be a good witness to unbelievers. Here the point is slightly different. Believers ought to be ready to suffer as Christ suffered—not simply to be a good witness to others, but in order to stay away from sin.

The phrase **arm yourselves** is a military metaphor. With what were they to arm themselves? **The same attitude** that Christ had toward suffering. This does not mean that believers should actively seek martyrdom. Nonetheless, they should arm themselves for death if necessary. If believers suffer, it ought to be for living the Christian faith; they ought to suffer courageously, knowing that God will ultimately be victorious. Those who are armed with this intention have an unswerving resolve to do God's will in every situation; those so armed will be able to stand strong in the face of any persecution. They can persevere because of their personal relationship with Jesus Christ (see John 15:20-21).

Having died in Christ, Christians are one with him and are legally free from the penalty of sin. They are in union with Christ, so they regard themselves as dead to sin. Believers are no longer bound by sin's penalty; they must strive, in practice, to be free from its power. Suffering can be helpful in that area. Just as Christ's sufferings led to death and resurrection, so our suffering can help us **stop sinning** and enter more fully into a new life of service to God.

Christ's suffering made him victorious over Satan; believers' suffering, if they follow Christ's example, can strengthen their faith and solidify their obedient lifestyle. Believers ought to "arm" themselves with a resolve to be like Christ when they face suffering.

4:2 When believers have so armed themselves (4:1), their strengthened faith and resolve to obey will cause them to **be anxious to do the will of God.** This describes the difference between believers' lives without Christ and their new lives with him. Before conversion, they lived only to satisfy their **evil desires;** after conversion, they are concerned with living by God's will, not their own.

4:3 Peter urged the believers to no longer live as they had **in the past.** His list of evil activities resembles Paul's in Romans 13:13. These are examples of what does not please God: actions, activities, and attitudes that belong to the darkness. These have no place in believers' lives.

- **Immorality** is open and excessive indulgence in sexual sins.
- **Lust** is sinful human desire.
- **Feasting and drunkenness** refers to excessive eating and use of wine and strong drink.
- **Wild parties** (orgies) were often filled with sexual promiscuity. These were often associated with festivals of some pagan gods.
- **Worship of idols** refers to idolatrous acts. Peter culminated his list with these words, indicating that many of the above acts were associated with the worship of pagan gods.

4:4 When a person becomes a Christian, sometimes his or her lifestyle changes drastically. This was especially true for first-century believers who had come out of the morally corrupt pagan world. Many of Peter's readers were Jewish Christians, but, as 4:3 indicates, many also had come from a pagan background. Former Jews would have at least led a morally upright life, while former pagans had been involved in the activities that Peter had just listed (4:3). Christians no longer desire to **join** their pagan friends **in the wicked things they do.** These friends had sought pleasure by denying themselves nothing. Together, they did it all. When the Christians stopped, their friends not only **are very surprised,** but they also **say evil things.** This describes the reaction of people who love darkness when they become confronted by the light. A believer's refusal to participate in an activity is a silent condemnation of that activity. Unbelievers then react with hostility, often because they want to justify their actions or silence their own consciences.

4:5-6 Unbelievers who live immorally (4:3) and who say evil things about Christians (4:4) will one day **have to face God.** This gives believers great relief and confidence—they will receive justice. **God will judge everyone, both the living and the dead.** And judgment may come at any moment. **That is why the Good News was preached even to those who have died.** These words have caused debate among scholars, resulting in four main views:

1. Some tie this verse back to 3:18-20 and Christ's proclamation of salvation to the unbelievers who lived before he came. But an understanding of a "second chance" after death in this verse argues against everything else in Scripture, and would be unhelpful to Peter's readers who were being encouraged to persevere in suffering.
2. Others look back also to 3:18-20, but say that Christ was preaching salvation to those Old Testament people who had believed in God in the time before Christ preached on earth, offering them the gift he brought—eternal life.

3. Still others say that this verse refers to the gospel proclaimed by the apostles to those on the earth who were physically alive but spiritually dead.

4. Most likely, however, Peter was referring to those dead at that time of his writing who had heard and accepted the gospel. Many people in the early church had concerns about life after death. In Thessalonica, Christians worried that loved ones who died before Christ's return might never see Christ (1 Thessalonians 4:13-18). They wondered if those who died would be able to experience the promised eternal life. Peter explained that these believers, **although their bodies were punished with death**—that is, they died physically as everyone dies physically—will still one day **live in the spirit as God does.**

Peter's readers needed to be reminded that the dead (both the faithful and their oppressors) would be raised from the dead—the faithful to eternal reward, the unfaithful to eternal punishment. God's judgment will be perfectly fair, Peter pointed out, because even those dead from ages past had heard the gospel. The Good News was first announced when Jesus Christ preached on the earth, but it has been operating since before the creation of the world (Ephesians 1:4), and it eternally affects all people, the dead as well as the living.

4:7 This verse gives us the vertical component (how we relate to God) to help us overcome the pressure to sin. Verses 8 and 9 give the horizontal component (how we relate to other people). The fact that God is "ready to judge" (4:5) means that **the end of the world is coming soon.** These early Christians who faced persecution took great comfort in the fact that their suffering would one day end and that the evil ways of the wicked would be judged. The Lord is ready and waiting, desiring that the gospel should be preached to all the nations before he returns. Peter, like the other apostles, was always aware that Christ could return at any moment (see Romans 13:11-12; 1 Corinthians 7:29; 1 Thessalonians 4:13–5:3; 1 John 2:18). Likewise, believers today must always remember that Christ can come at any time.

The shortness of time remaining should motivate believers to **be earnest and disciplined in** their **prayers.** The meaning for today calls for self-discipline when we pray. Rather than merely a quick blessing on our food or a three-minute devotional, we should reserve extended times for sober, direct communication with God. Lack of prayer will render us unprepared for the end times:

4:8 Mutual **love**, support, and encouragement would also be a great defense. No Christian is an island; no one is alone. When believers experience deep love from the fellowship, they have the human network of support that can help them through any crisis. The same thought as **love covers a multitude of sins** is found in Proverbs 10:12: "Hatred stirs up quarrels, but love covers all offenses." Peter may have been quoting from this or from a proverb of his day that was based loosely on this verse. This does not mean that love ignores, overlooks, or tries to hide sin. Instead, Peter probably was thinking back to his words in 4:1-2 that the believers should live the rest of their lives according to God's will and not human desires. As believers, they should stop sinning. The "covering of sins," then, is the ability that believers have to forgive one another because Christ has forgiven them. Love works as a shock absorber, cushioning and smoothing out the bumps and irritations caused by fellow believers.

4:9 To **cheerfully share** one's **home** is different from social entertaining. Entertaining focuses on the host—the home must be spotless; the food must be well prepared and abundant; the host must appear relaxed and good-natured. Sharing the home, in contrast, focuses on the guests. Their needs—whether for a place to stay, nourishing food, a listening ear, or acceptance—are the primary concern. This can happen in a messy home. It can happen around a dinner table where the main dish is canned soup. Believers should not hesitate to share with **those who need a meal or a place to stay** just because they are too busy or not wealthy enough to entertain. Hospitality is a strong expression of love, which Peter already commanded the believers to show (4:8).

4:10 Each person has received one or more **spiritual gifts** from **God**—a talent or ability empowered by the Holy Spirit and able to be used in the ministry of the church. Spiritual gifts help God's people to serve and love one another (4:8) and continue the work of spreading the gospel. Some of this **great variety** of gifts are listed in Romans 12:6-8; 1 Corinthians 12:4-11, 27-31; and Ephesians 4:11-12—these lists are different and are by no means exhaustive. When believers humbly recognize their partnership in the body of Christ, their gifts can be used effectively.

When believers use their gifts in humble service to others, **God's generosity can flow through** them. The gifts God gives believers are as varied and many-faceted as are the believers themselves. As God's grace varies in its dealings with people, so God's gifts (given because of his grace) are varied in their administration of his grace as Christ's body on earth. To **manage them well** means not to hide the gifts, but to use them as they were meant to be used—serving and building up the body of Christ.

4:11 Peter encouraged the believers to use their gifts (4:10). Men and women with gifts that required being **a speaker** must be responsible with what they said, speaking **as though God himself were speaking through** them. Likewise, those gifted with abilities that centered on helping others also have a responsibility—to serve not in their own strength but **with all the strength**

and energy that God supplies. If believers serve in their own strength alone or in order to look good to others, they will begin to find serving a wearisome task. But to serve with God's strength is to be able to go above and beyond, and to do so for one purpose: **God will be given glory in everything through Jesus Christ.** When believers use their gifts as God directs (to help others and build up the church), others will see Jesus Christ in them and will glorify him for the help they have received.

SUFFERING FOR BEING A CHRISTIAN / 4:12-19

The early Christians must have wondered why they were targeted with such abuse and hatred when they were living peacefully and striving to do God's will. However, Jesus himself suffered, and he warned his followers that they too would face suffering. Peter offered this warning to his readers as well.

4:12-13 Christians ought not **be surprised** at the **fiery trials** they were **going through.** Like Christ, Christians should expect to face persecution. These were not **something strange**—persecution had followed the gospel from the time of Jesus' crucifixion. Believers should expect persecution and suffering because they are part of God's plan to perfect Christians. Even Christ was not spared from persecution (Romans 8:32). Instead of being bewildered by trials, Peter exhorted the believers to **be very glad** because when they suffered for their faith in Christ, they were becoming **partners with Christ in his suffering.** If we suffer, it shows our identification with Christ and it shows that our faith is genuine. Since Christ was persecuted, we also will be persecuted and, thereby, participate in his suffering. If we persevere, we will enjoy our future inheritance with him. Servants who know the suffering of Christ will **have the wonderful joy of sharing his glory.**

This does not mean that all suffering is the result of good Christian conduct. Sometimes a person will grumble, "He's just picking on me because I'm a Christian," when it's obvious to everyone else that the person's own unpleasant behavior is the cause of his or her problems. It may take careful thought or wise counsel to determine the real cause of our suffering. We can be assured, however, that whenever we suffer because of our loyalty to Christ, he will be with us all the way.

4:14 Peter offered a specific example of the type of suffering the believers might face. To be **insulted** means to face verbal abuse, to be reviled, ridiculed, or slandered. Not only will suffering believers find great joy when Christ returns (4:13), but **the glori-**

ous Spirit of God (that is, the Holy Spirit) would **come upon** them. Christ will send his Spirit to strengthen those who are persecuted for their faith.

4:15 Peter has made the point that not all suffering results in blessing (2:20). If believers must suffer, it must be because of their faith, for that alone results in blessing. They ought not be counted among those who murder, steal, do evil, or meddle in other people's matters. Such people deserve the punishment and suffering they receive, and there is no blessing in such suffering.

4:16 Peter reminded his readers that it was **no shame to suffer for being a Christian.** While believers ought not seek out suffering, neither should they try to avoid it. Instead, Peter admonished them to keep on doing what was right regardless of the suffering it might bring. In that suffering they could **praise God for the privilege of being called by his wonderful name.** As bearers of Christ's name, Christians are his representatives on this earth; therefore, in everything they do, including what might seem like shameful suffering, they can glorify God.

4:17 This **time for judgment** refers both to final judgment and also to God's refining discipline (Hebrews 12:7). In 1 Peter 1:17, Peter warned that God judges all people according to their deeds. He also disciplines and judges his **own children** in order to refine them, as Peter has explained in 1:6-7. This judgment purifies and strengthens believers, readying them for God's Kingdom. But for **those who have never believed God's Good News,** the judgment will be a **terrible fate.**

4:18 Reinforcing his rhetorical question in 4:17, Peter continued by quoting from Proverbs 11:31. If the **righteous** (believers) experience difficulty in their refining process, how much more horrible will be the great disaster experienced for eternity by **the godless and sinners** who chose to reject Christ.

The phrase **barely saved** means "with difficulty." Peter was not introducing uncertainty to the believers' salvation. Instead, he was talking about the difficult road believers must travel. It is not easy to be a Christian; we must count the cost.

4:19 With the word **so,** Peter drew a conclusion to his words in the previous verses. Peter consistently encouraged his readers that their suffering was all under God's control. If they suffered for the faith, they were **suffering according to God's will.** Their suffering was not because God had lost control; rather, all that happens to believers is according to his will. While it is difficult to accept that one's suffering is part of God's plan, we can find comfort in understanding that, as part of God's will, suffering has a reason, a goal, and an end. For believers, suffering is a purifying process to draw us closer to God.

Thus, in times of suffering, believers must **trust** themselves **to the God who made** them. The word "trust" means to give over to someone for safekeeping. Jesus used the word on the cross (Luke 23:46). This also follows Christ's example (2:23). If the believers trusted themselves to the one who created them, they would have nothing to fear.

Even in suffering, as Peter had admonished throughout his letter, the Christians must **keep on doing what is right.** Peter often recommended doing good works as a response to being persecuted (see 2:12, 15, 20; 3:1-2, 13, 17). Paul also recommended this response (Romans 12:14-18; Titus 3:1, 14). If the believers would "do good" even in the face of injustice, they would reveal that they truly had entrusted themselves to God, that they were suffering for their faith alone, which is commendable before God (2:20), and that their attitude toward suffering might draw others to faith as well (2:12).

God created the world, and he has faithfully ordered it and kept it since the creation. Because we know that God is faithful, we know that he will **never fail** us. If God can oversee the forces of nature, surely he can see us through the trials we face. We must never doubt his loving concern for us or his ability to rescue us.

1 PETER 5

ADVICE FOR ELDERS AND YOUNG MEN / 5:1-11

Peter wrote this letter just before Emperor Nero began cruelly persecuting Christians in Rome and throughout the empire. About thirty years earlier, Peter, fearing for his life, had three times denied even knowing Jesus (John 18:15-27). Since then, having learned how to stand firm in an evil world, Peter encouraged other Christians, who were facing pressure to deny their faith. Peter believed and lived what he wrote in this letter—later he was executed by the Romans for believing in and preaching Christ. In this section, Peter addressed three groups: elders, younger men, and the church as a whole. Those who stand for Christ will be persecuted because the world is ruled by Christ's greatest enemy. But just as the small group of early believers stood against persecution, so we must be willing to stand for our faith with the patience, endurance, and courage that Peter exhibited.

5:1 This continues the thought in 4:12-19. Since God's judgment will "begin first among God's own children" (4:17), then the **elders** of those congregations carry great responsibility. Elders were the appointed leaders in the churches (see Acts 14:23; 20:17; 1 Timothy 5:17, 19; Titus 1:5-6) and were to lead the churches by teaching sound doctrine, helping believers mature spiritually, and equipping believers to live for Jesus Christ despite opposition. Elders carried great responsibility, and they were expected to be good examples.

Peter appealed as a **fellow elder,** thereby identifying with the other church leaders, although he had authority as one of the apostles. Peter had been **a witness to the sufferings of Christ.** Actually he did not witness Jesus' crucifixion because he had denied and deserted Jesus; the word "witness" in this verse does not mean "eyewitness." Neither he nor all these elders had been eyewitnesses; however, they had all been called to "witness" (testify or bring news about) Christ's sufferings to those under their charge. As witnesses, they could also share in those sufferings, personally "witnessing" those sufferings in their own lives.

But they share in even more, for Peter, along with the other elders, as well as all believers, will **share** Christ's **glory** and **honor when he returns.** Peter and the believers shared in Christ's glory at present, and they would also share that glory when it would be revealed at the last day (the Second Coming).

5:2-3 Peter's command that the elders **care for the flock of God** echoed Jesus' words to Peter himself, "Take care of my sheep" (John 21:16). The same Greek word is used in both places, meaning "to shepherd," "to tend," or "to take care of," "to pastor." The "flock" is the believers; elders had charge over individual churches and thus over a certain part of God's "flock." Elders were to be like shepherds who lead, guide, and protect the sheep under their care. Believers would need good leaders as they faced persecution.

This passage describes three possible problems that elders might face and how they should respond:

Wrong motivation. **Watch over it willingly, not grudgingly.** Elders should serve out of love for God. Peter called upon them to make God's will their own, eagerly seeking to please God in it. Pastors and elders should serve willingly in churches today. Too often a slate of elders becomes hard to fill because of unwillingness by people in the congregation to serve.

Wrong goals. **Not for what you will get out of it, but because you are eager to serve God.** In many of the churches, elders were paid for their services; however, that remuneration alone probably would not make an elder rich. This temptation to be greedy probably arose because the church's finances (the money collected for the poor, etc.) usually were entrusted to the elder or overseer. The opportunity to abuse the trust was very real. Thus, both Peter and Paul explained that elders were to be paid adequately and were to be trustworthy with money (see 1 Timothy 3:8; 5:17-18; Titus 1:7, 11). Instead of money, elders were to focus on serving. The word for "eager" is very strong in the Greek, expressing great zeal and enthusiasm. Today pastors receive pay for serving, but pastors can fall prey to the greedy desire for money. Not

having money can lead to as much preoccupation with funds as having a lot of money.

Wrong methods. **Don't lord it over the people assigned to your care, but lead them by your good example.** Elders lead by example, not force. "Lording it over" means "forcefully domineering or subduing." Elders also must fight the temptation to abuse their authority and hurt the church under their care. The formula Jesus used was always that those who led were to be the best servants (Mark 10:42-45). The leaders were to be examples of humility and servanthood. Leaders must not bully or steamroll people.

5:4 Elders were to be shepherds of God's flock, but they were answerable to the **head Shepherd** (also called "the good shepherd" in John 10:11, 14 and "great Shepherd" in Hebrews 13:20). The word **comes** refers to Christ's second coming, when he will return to judge all people. At that time, the elders (along with all believers) will receive a **reward, a never-ending share in** Christ's **glory and honor.** This is a proper motivation for service in the face of suffering and temptation. All believers will be declared winners and will receive a wonderful, everlasting reward. This could be their source of strength and encouragement in times of trial.

5:5 As Peter had presented the best plan for household relationships, so here he described the best plan for church relationships. The **younger men** should **accept the authority of the elders,** meaning to submit to their decisions and to treat them respectfully (unless, of course, they lead people into sin). Finally, **all** the believers had a responsibility in the congregation: they should **serve each other in humility.** Humility means being able to put others' needs and desires ahead of one's own (see Philippians 2:3-4). Young people should follow the leadership of the older people (especially those who have been put in authority over them as elders). The elders, in turn, should lead by example. All should actively serve one another. No doubt Peter remembered how Christ served his disciples with humility as he washed their feet (see John 13:1-17).

Peter quoted from Proverbs 3:34 to make his point. The believers must deal with one another in humility because **"God sets himself against the proud, but he shows favor to the humble"** (see also James 4:6). Not only does pride keep people from listening to or following God, it also can keep older people from trying to understand young people and young people from listening to those who are older.

5:6 Because God sets himself against the proud
and shows favor to the humble (5:5), Peter
admonished the believers to **humble** themselves.
This would be an act of the will; humility does not
come naturally. But when the believers humbled
themselves **under the mighty power of God,** they
were actually submitting to his care and protection.
They must humble themselves even in the face of
persecution because God would **honor** them.
Being "honored" refers to a reversal of past misfor-
tunes and troubles, triumph over their oppressors,
and participation in Christ's glory. The honoring
may be in this life or in the next. In any case it will
be **in his good time;** that is, in God's perfect time.
Most likely, Peter was thinking of that last day,
when the head Shepherd would appear (5:4) and
all those who have faithfully followed would be
exalted and given eternal glory.

5:7 This verse explains what it means for believers
to humble themselves (5:6). It is not negative
and reactive; believers are not abandoned to the
arbitrary will of God. Rather, it is positive and
active: **Give all your worries and cares to God,
for he cares about what happens to you.** Peter
explained that the believers who continued to
carry their worries, anxieties, stresses, and daily
struggles by themselves showed that they had not
trusted God fully. It takes humility, however, to
turn everything (literally, "throw your anxieties")
over to God and trust that he cares. God is not
indifferent; he knows what he's doing in our
lives. Sometimes we think that struggles caused
by our own sin and foolishness are not God's
concern. But when we turn to God in repentance,
he will bear the weight even of those struggles.
Letting God have your anxieties calls for action,
not passivity. Don't submit to circumstances, but
to the Lord who controls circumstances. Peter
wanted the believers facing persecution and suffering to remember to give their troubles to God
and that he cared.

5:8 At the same time that believers can cast all their
cares on God, they must still **be careful** and **watch
out.** As soldiers wait and watch, so believers must
be constantly alert for the enemy. All of the persecution facing believers ultimately comes down to
one source: **the Devil, your great enemy.** The
Devil has other names—Satan, Accuser, Beelzebub—but he is the source of all evil in the world.
He hates God and is God's archenemy; thus he
also hates God's people and is their enemy as well.
While Satan has no power against God, he does
what he can to harm God's people. Peter described
him as prowling **around like a roaring lion, looking for some victim to devour.** Lions attack sick,

young, or straggling animals; they choose victims
who are alone or not alert. Lions prowl quietly,
watching and waiting, suddenly pouncing when
their victims least suspect it.

Peter warned believers to be alert for Satan,
especially in times of suffering and persecution, for
he walks up and down the earth (Job 1:7) seeking
whom he or his demons can attack and defeat.
(For more on demons, see Mark 1:23-26 and Ephesians 6:12.) When believers feel alone, weak, helpless, and cut off from other believers, they can
become so focused on their troubles that they forget to watch for danger. In those times, believers
are especially vulnerable to Satan's attacks, which
come in various forms, often at a person's weakest
spot—temptation, fear, loneliness, worry, depression, persecution. Therefore, Peter and Paul urged
the believers to always be alert for Satan's tricks.

5:9 James wrote that if the believers resisted the
Devil, he would flee from them (James 4:7). Once
we have identified the Devil as our enemy, we
need to understand who he is and how he operates
in order to effectively **take a firm stand against
him.** Satan is the leader of angelic beings who
revolted against God and were banished from
heaven. His primary purpose now is to separate
people from God. Destined for destruction, Satan
wants to take as much of creation with him as he
possibly can. We desperately need God's grace
because we are locked in mortal combat with a
superior enemy; we need God's help to resist this
enemy, Satan. The best way for believers to take
a firm stand is to **be strong in** their **faith.** This
means trusting in Christ, who has already defeated
Satan and will ultimately destroy him. Paul
described the "armor" that believers must wear
in Ephesians 6:10-18.

These believers were encouraged also to remember that they were not alone in their suffering.
Other **Christians** scattered **all over the world** were
suffering for the faith; this fact should give them
strength. All of this, of course, was under God's
control and was accomplishing his purposes.

5:10-11 When we are suffering, we often feel as
though our pain will never end. Peter gave these
faithful Christians the wider perspective. In comparison with eternity, their suffering would last
only **a little while.** This repeats what Peter said in
1:6. Some of Peter's readers would be strengthened
and delivered in their own lifetimes. Others would
be released from their suffering through death.
After that time of suffering, God promises to
restore (set right what has gone wrong, put in
order, complete), **support** (by admonition and
guidance), **strengthen** (give courage no matter

what happens), and **place** them **on a firm foundation** (build on a "rock," therefore being unmovable). While their suffering will be only for a little while, their **glory** in **Christ** will be **eternal.** In life or in death, God's purposes will be accomplished and his promises to believers will be fulfilled because believers have been **called** into God's eternal glory. God called—this was his initiative. He will do as he promised because **all power is his forever and ever.**

PETER'S FINAL GREETINGS / 5:12-14

Many of the letters in our Bible close with the writer's personal greetings to friends and colleagues in the letter's destination. In this case, Peter's letter would be carried along to various churches, so Peter greeted no one in particular, but rather sent greetings from those with him in Rome. No doubt the letters of Peter, Paul, James, John, and Jude offered great comfort to the Christians scattered across the world. Believers realized a unity in Christ, a bond of love, and a common future together that could help them survive whatever the world might bring. The worldwide Christian family is a continual blessing to believers who find they have Christ in common, even if they live in different cultures.

5:12 Silas apparently served as the secretary to Peter, writing this letter as Peter dictated it. He may then have carried this letter to the churches of Asia Minor. More likely, he took it to the first church, from which it was sent along by messengers from one church to another, perhaps along the route implied in 1:1.

Silas was **a faithful brother** to Peter and to other church leaders as well. Silas was one of the men chosen to deliver the letter from the Jerusalem Council to the church in Antioch (Acts 15:22). He accompanied Paul on his second missionary journey (Acts 15:40–18:11), was mentioned by Paul in the salutation of his letters to the Thessalonians (1 Thessalonians 1:1; 2 Thessalonians 1:1), and ministered with Timothy in Corinth (2 Corinthians 1:19).

Peter described the reason for his brief letter— to **encourage** believers and to **assure** them **that the grace of God** would be **with** them, no matter what might happen. Grace would help them stand fast, and by standing fast, they would receive the reward of that grace—glory with Christ.

5:13 Peter was in **Rome** when he wrote this letter and was sending **greetings** from the church there. **Mark,** also called John Mark, was known to many of this letter's readers because he had traveled widely (Acts 12:25–13:13; 15:36-41) and was recognized as a leader in the church (Colossians 4:10; Philemon 24). Mark was probably with the disciples at the time of Jesus' arrest (Mark 14:51-52). Mark knew Peter well, and Peter looked on him as a **son,** a close associate in Christ's service. Tradition holds that Peter was Mark's main source of information when Mark wrote his Gospel. Paul had mentioned that Mark was with him at an earlier time in Rome (Colossians 4:10), so it is likely that he returned there at one time and was with Peter at the writing of this letter.

5:14 Peter wanted his readers to express their **Christian love** to one another, for they would need each other for strength in the days ahead. (Compare Paul's closing words in Romans 16:16; 1 Corinthians 16:20; 2 Corinthians 13:12; 1 Thessalonians 5:26.)

Thus, Peter ended as he began, with peace (1:2). Peter's final words, **peace be to all,** underscore what was most needed by the Christians: peace in the middle of turmoil. They could not count on worldly peace, for it was not to be. Instead, they would find peace within, by resting in God's grace. Only those **who are in Christ** can have such peace.

2 PETER

INTRODUCTION

Who taught you how to read? ride a bike? shoot a basketball? solve algebraic equations? repair an appliance? prepare a meal? understand the political process? draw closer to God?

Whether parents, coaches, professors, pastors, or friends, we hold our teachers in high regard. They have opened our eyes, provided counsel, broadened our horizons, solved mysteries, and filled our minds. We have benefited greatly from their wisdom and expertise. That's what makes **false** teachers so dangerous. Misusing their privileged position and betraying trust, for the sake of pride, reward, or ambition, they prey on the unsuspecting and lead many astray.

Knowing this powerful influence of teachers, the apostles and other church leaders continually warned against those who would twist the truth and lead believers astray. That was the purpose of 2 Peter. Written to strengthen the church to resist the internal challenge to their faith, this brief letter warns of false teachers who deny Christ and scoffers who mock his return. Believers are to beware and to keep their focus on Christ.

Our world is filled with cult leaders, religious scams, and others who would lead people astray. Estimates of the number of cults worldwide run as high as ten thousand. Some of these cults and many false teachers have infiltrated the church. Read 2 Peter and determine to grow in your faith and to reject every type of false teaching.

AUTHOR

Peter: apostle of Christ, one of the original twelve disciples, outspoken leader, and courageous preacher.

Second Peter has less external, historical evidence for its genuineness than any other New Testament book. That is because it is so short, contains very little new information, and is not addressed to a specific individual or church. But the writer identifies himself as Simon Peter and alludes, accurately, to events in Peter's life. These include the Transfiguration (1:16-18) and Jesus' prediction of Peter's death (1:12-14; see also John 21:18). Because the letter claims to have been written by the apostle and has been accepted by most of the church for many centuries as being the inspired Word of God and thus belonging in the canon of Scripture, we affirm that Peter is the author.

For more about Peter, see the Author section in the Introduction to the book of 1 Peter.

DATE AND SETTING
Written from Rome in about A.D. 67.

As was mentioned in the Introduction to 1 Peter, the traditional view is that
Peter was executed by crucifixion in Rome by Nero in A.D. 67. Thus this letter
would have been written just before his death.

At age sixteen, in A.D. 54, Nero became the fifth Roman emperor. At first, his
reign was peaceful, giving promise of a bright future. At this time, Paul had
appealed to Caesar in the trial in Caesarea (Acts 25:10-11) and, consequently,
had been brought to Rome to present his case (A.D. 61). We presume that Paul
eventually went to trial and was cleared of all charges, for he was freed to resume
his ministry. He used his new freedom to travel extensively. During this time
(A.D. 62–67) Peter likely came to Rome and wrote 1 Peter (approximately A.D. 64).
There is no evidence that Peter and Paul were in Rome together except during the
time just before both were executed.

After he married Poppaea, Emperor Nero became brutal and ruthless, killing
his own mother, his chief advisers Seneca and Burrus, and many of the nobility,
in order to seize their fortunes. The downward spiral continued, fueled by Nero's
lust for attention and excitement. He sponsored wild chariot races, combat
between gladiators, and the gory spectacle of prisoners torn apart by wild dogs.
Seeing Nero's insane path and sensing the increased persecution of the church,
Peter wrote his first epistle to warn believers and to encourage them to be strong
and to have hope during their suffering.

In A.D. 64, fire destroyed a large part of Rome. Nero is thought to have ordered
the fire himself to make room for a new palace. Deflecting blame from himself, he
accused the Christians. This devout religious group made a convenient scapegoat
because they were a small minority and because they were popularly thought to
engage in many wicked practices, including their refusal to worship the emperor.
Thus began the pursuit, capture, and imprisonment of believers, leading to torture
and execution. In A.D. 67, Peter wrote his final words in 2 Peter, urging believers
to reject false teachers and to hold fast to the truth. With death in sight, Peter
reminded his readers of their great heritage and urged them to look forward to
the day of the Lord. Soon thereafter, Peter fell victim to Nero's thirst for blood.

Eventually, during this time of intense persecution, Paul was arrested again and
returned to Rome. In this prison experience, he was isolated and lonely, awaiting
execution (2 Timothy 4:9-18). Paul was martyred in the spring of A.D. 68, just
before Nero's death.

AUDIENCE
The church at large.

Peter hints at his intended audience in 3:1: "This is my second letter to you,
dear friends, and in both of them I have tried to stimulate your wholesome thinking and refresh your memory." It seems, therefore, that the "chosen people who
are living as foreigners" in various places (1 Peter 1:1) also received this letter.
However, a comparison of the opening of the first letter with the second seems
to indicate that Peter was addressing a much wider group of believers. Though
not specified, the intended recipients of this letter were Christians who had been
taught the basics of the faith (1:12-13, 16).

OCCASION AND PURPOSE

To warn Christians about false teachers and to urge them to grow in their faith and in their knowledge of Christ.

Peter knew that he was about to die at the order of Nero and at the hands of a Roman executioner (1:13-15), so he wrote to remind believers to be strong in their faith after his departure (1:3-11, 19-21; 3:1-7).

Peter also had heard of "false teachers" who were twisting the truth, teaching for their own financial gain, and leading believers astray. Evidently, these teachers were elevating themselves and their own ideas and interpretations ("clever lies" 2:3) above Christ (2:1). So Peter wrote to warn believers of these greedy men, exposing their heresies and predicting their punishment (2:1-22). Jude also warns of this heresy. (For more, see the Introduction to the book of Jude.)

This false teaching seems to be the idea that through knowledge a person can find his or her identity and relationship with God. Thus, the false teachers were claiming to have special wisdom and insight—the inside track to finding God. This was an early version of Gnosticism, a heresy that would hit the church full force in the second century. Full-blown Gnosticism emphasized that special knowledge provides the way to spirituality. This knowledge was attained through astrology and magic and was available only to those who had been initiated into the Gnostic system. Another Gnostic belief, that all matter is inherently evil and only the spiritual and nonmaterial is of itself good, led to the idea that God could not have created the world and would have no contact with it. Therefore they taught that God, in Christ, never could have become a human person. If matter is evil, how could God ever be united with a human body? Thus they denied either the humanity or the complete deity of Christ (in their view, he couldn't have been both).

Peter concludes this brief letter by reminding his readers of the sure second coming of their Lord and urging them, in light of Christ's return, to guard their faith and to be ready (3:3-18).

MESSAGE

After a brief greeting (1:1), Peter gives the antidote for stagnancy and shortsightedness in the Christian life (1:2-11). Then he explains that his days are numbered (1:12-15) and that the believers should listen to his messages and the words of Scripture (1:16-21).

Next, Peter gives a blunt warning about false teachers (2:1-22). They will become prevalent in the last days (2:1-2), they will do or say anything for money (2:3), they will spurn the things of God (2:2, 10-11), they will do whatever they feel like doing (2:12-17), they will be proud and boastful (2:18-19), and they will be judged and punished by God (2:3-10, 20-22).

Peter concludes his brief letter by explaining why he has written it (3:1-18): to remind them of the words of the prophets and apostles that predicted the coming of false teachers, to give the reasons for the delay in Christ's return (3:1-13), and to encourage them to beware of heresies and to grow in their faith (3:14-18).

The main themes in the book of 2 Peter include: *Diligence, False Teachers,* and *Christ's Return.*

Diligence (1:5-11, 19-21; 3:14-18). With his last words to the faithful followers of Christ, Peter urges them to continue to grow in their goodness, knowledge, self-control, perseverance, godliness, kindness, and love (1:5-7). Real faith is demonstrated by faithful behavior. Peter knew that believers who are diligent in Christian growth won't backslide or be deceived by false teachers.

IMPORTANCE FOR TODAY. Just as babies and children need to grow and mature physically and mentally, so too Christians need to grow spiritually. Our growth began, by faith, at our spiritual birth. The spiritual maturation process continues by faith and culminates in love for others. To keep growing, we need to know God, stay close to him, and remember what we have learned from him. And we must faithfully obey him. How's your spiritual maturity? Are you growing in your faith?

False Teachers (2:1-22; 3:3-5, 17). Peter warned believers to beware of false teachers. These men were proud of their position, promoted sexual sin, and advised against keeping the Ten Commandments. Peter countered these teachers by exposing their lies (2:1-3, 10-11, 14, 18-19; 3:3, 16), predicting their eventual punishment (2:1, 3-10, 12-22; 3:16), and emphasizing the Spirit-inspired Scriptures as the ultimate authority (1:16-21; 3:2, 15-16).

IMPORTANCE FOR TODAY. Today, false teachers wrench Bible verses out of context, entice believers down doctrinal tangents, build large followings for their own power and profit, and exploit the gullible and weak. Christians need discernment in order to discover false teachers and courage to resist and refute their lies. God will give us what we need if we read, study, and apply his Word, the Bible. To reject error, we need to know the truth. How well grounded are you in the basic doctrines of the Christian faith? How well do you know your Bible?

Christ's Return (3:3-14). The day of the Lord will come. That's when Christ suddenly will return, to rescue his own from this evil world, to punish the ungodly—those who refuse to believe in Christ—and to create a new heaven and earth where believers will live forever. "Scoffers" mock the second coming of Christ (3:3-4), but God's people know that it is sure. No one knows when Christ will return; but when it happens, everyone will know. Christians take hope in this promise.

IMPORTANCE FOR TODAY. The cure for complacency, lawlessness, and heresy is found in the confident assurance that Christ will return. He has not come yet because God is still giving unbelievers time to repent of their sins and to turn to him. To be ready for Christ's return, Christians must stay strong in their faith, trusting God and resisting the pressures and temptations of the world. What should you do to be ready for Christ's return? What can you say to those who don't believe in the Second Coming because it hasn't happened yet?

OUTLINE OF 2 PETER

2 PETER 1

GREETINGS FROM PETER / 1:1-2

First Peter was written just before the time that the Roman emperor Nero began to persecute Christians. Second Peter was written two or three years later (between A.D. 66 and 68), after persecution had intensified. First Peter was a letter of encouragement to the Christians who were suffering, but 1 Peter focuses on the church's internal problems, especially on the false teachers who were causing people to doubt their faith and turn away from Christianity. Second Peter combats the heresies by denouncing the evil motives of the false teachers and reaffirming Christianity's truths: the authority of Scripture, the primacy of faith, and the certainty of Christ's return.

1:1 In contrast to 1 Peter 1:1, this letter begins with the name **Simon Peter.** The different form of the name may merely have to do with different writers who recorded Peter's words as he wrote the letter. Peter had been one of Jesus' twelve disciples and one of the three (with James and John) to whom Jesus had given special training. He often acted as spokesman for the disciples, sometimes being rebuked for not thinking before he spoke. The story of Peter's denial of Jesus and later restoration by him were well known to the early church. (For more about Peter, see the Author section in the Introduction to 1 and 1 Peter.)

Peter identified himself first as a **slave,** meaning one who is subject to the will and wholly at the disposal of his master. Peter used the term to express his absolute devotion and subjection to Jesus Christ. The title **apostle** designated his apostolic position as leader and one of the twelve original disciples (see Matthew 10:2; John 20:21-23). It also designated authority to set up and supervise churches and discipline them if necessary. Even more than a title of authority, "apostle" means one sent on a mission, like an envoy or an ambassador. Peter and the other apostles (including Paul, see Romans 1:1) had been chosen, called, and given the authority and responsibility to evangelize the world.

Peter wrote to believers **who share the same precious faith** he and the other apostles had; **faith given** to them **by Jesus Christ,** the **God and Savior.** Peter reassured these believers that their faith was equal to the faith of the apostles; it was just as precious and just as sure, for it was faith in God and in Jesus Christ who, by his death, made people **right with God.**

1:2 The first part of Peter's greeting here is identical to 1 Peter 1:2. He wished them God's **special favor,** unmerited by people but freely given by God, and **peace,** referring to the peace that Christ made between sinners and God. The persecuted and suffering believers may have been feeling very little favor and an absence of peace. But Peter reassured them that both favor and peace could be theirs.

Peter was concerned that the believers' faith remain sound and steadfast. Only by getting to **know Jesus better and better** could they remain faithful in the face of false teaching (a theme in this letter). But knowledge must not remain static; that is, believers must not have knowledge for the sake of knowledge. Their knowledge must lead to changed behavior (or "godliness"), as is explained in the next verse.

GROWING IN THE KNOWLEDGE OF GOD / 1:3-11

Salvation does not depend on positive character qualities and good works; rather, it produces those qualities and works. A person who claims to be saved while remaining unchanged does not understand faith or what God has done for him or her. Faith in and knowledge of the Lord Jesus Christ that leads to growth in these qualities causes believers to make a difference in their world and persevere to the end.

1:3 Jesus' **divine power,** or the divine power that Jesus Christ shares with God, is the power well-known to believers, for it raised Christ from the dead. The word **us** refers to all believers—Peter, the other apostles, and all readers of this letter. Christ's power manifests itself in the lives of Christians, for that power gives believers **everything we need for living a godly life.** The power to grow doesn't come from within us, but from God. Because we don't have the resources to live as he requires, God gives us everything we need for godly living (to keep us from sin and to help us live for him). "Godly" means moral uprightness and honoring of God.

The phrase, **he has called us to receive his own glory and goodness,** explains what attracts people to Jesus in the first place. Jesus' glory (the impact of who he is, his splendor) and his goodness (also translated "moral excellence") draw sinful, seeking people to him. When they come to Christ, they have access to the knowledge they need in order to live for him. "Called" means that believers are chosen (see 1 Peter 1:2, 15; 2:9, 21; 3:9; 5:10 for more on "chosen"). They are called to salvation and to live for God.

1:4 Through Jesus' divine **power,** Christ also has **given us all of his rich and wonderful promises.** What are these promises? When Christ came, he made promises of the new messianic age. Peter referred to Christ's second coming (1:16; 3:4, 9-10, 12), the new heavens and earth (3:13), and the believers' welcome into Christ's Kingdom.

Christ will help his people **escape the decadence all around** them **caused by evil desires.** Many first-century false teachers emphasized a secret "knowledge" of God; such people were called Gnostics (from the Greek word for "knowledge"). Gnosticism undermined Christianity in several basic ways: (1) it insisted that important secret knowledge was hidden from most believers; (2) it taught that the body was evil; (3) it contended that Christ only seemed to be human but was not. While these false teachers spoke about secret knowledge, Peter wrote of "knowing" Jesus Christ. Pagan philosophers puzzled over "godliness" and "goodness," deciding that these were impossible; Peter used those words to explain that the one true God's divine power imparts godliness and goodness to those who believe in him. Philosophers also discussed at length how people could escape "decadence" in the world and instead **share** in the **divine** (divinity belonging to the spiritual world rather than the physical world). They concluded that people had to try to get away from the material world into the spiritual realm by keeping strict laws or refusing any type of pleasure. Peter

used their language to explain that all their conclusions were incorrect; people escape decadence and share in the divine nature as God's gift through Christ's death and resurrection.

1:5 Because of God's great gift, their promised destiny, believers must **make every effort to apply the benefits of these promises to** their lives by working toward a standard of high moral living. While Christ gives the power and the divine nature, believers must make use of that power by making every effort to set aside their sinful desires and actively seek the qualities Peter described below (in addition to others, such as the fruit of the Spirit outlined in Galatians 5:22-23). As Christians make every effort, they will continue to become more and more like Christ.

Believers are to use God's power and every ounce of determination to **produce** the eight characteristics mentioned.

Faith is, of course, the first characteristic, for without it, Christians are no different from the pagans in the world around them. The faith Peter referred to is faith in Christ, faith that brings them into the family of God. While people might have some of the following characteristics by nature, those are worthless in eternity without being grounded in faith.

But Christians were not to stop at faith alone. Peter knew, like James, that faith without works is dead. The believers had work to do. Their faith was to **produce a life of moral excellence.** The word is also translated "virtue." The Greek word is used only here, in 1:3 above, and in Philippians 4:8. In all cases, it signifies high moral standards that surpass those of pagans. While uncommon in the New Testament, this word was familiar to Greek moral philosophy. While the Greek philosophers discussed such excellence at length, Peter once again explained that true goodness could be found only in relationship with Christ. To their faith, believers were to add lifestyles that mirrored Christ's (1:3). Their motive for such high standards? The shining moral quality of Christ's life compels us to be our very best.

That life of moral excellence should lead **to knowing God better.** Knowledge was a word common in the Greek lists of virtues. Thus Peter included it here with a specifically Christian focus. "Knowledge" as used here refers not to the knowledge of God that leads to salvation; rather, here *gnosis* is that knowledge that leads to wisdom and discernment that enables believers to live godly lives (see Ephesians 5:17; Philippians 1:9; Hebrews 5:14).

1:6 Knowing God leads to self-control, a word used only here and in Acts 24:25 and Galatians

5:23 (as one of the fruits of the Spirit). Self-control refers to mastery over sinful human desires in every aspect of life. This was another highly prized virtue for the Greeks. Their focus, of course, was entirely on self-effort, but the problem was that self-effort always fails in the long run because it may control the body but does not affect inward desires. We know from Romans 8:13 and Galatians 5:22-23 that Christians have the Holy Spirit's help to gain self-control.

The quality of self-control must then lead to **patient endurance,** the ability to steadfastly endure suffering or evil without giving up one's faith. Endurance is not a stoic indifference to whatever fate allows; rather, it springs from faith in God's goodness and control over all that happens in believers' lives.

Such endurance **leads to godliness.** This is another word that is unusual to the New Testament, but common to Greek ethics lists of that day. Paul emphasized godliness in the Pastoral Epistles as being the virtue that should characterize the life and conduct of the believers (see 1 Timothy 6:6, 11; 2 Timothy 3:5; Titus 1:1; 2:12). Godliness was the primary word for "religion" and referred to a person's correct attitudes toward God and people, usually referring to performing obligatory duties. Here in 1 Peter the word describes an awareness of God in all of life—a lifestyle that exemplifies Christ and is empowered by him (the same word is used in 1:3). Christians must have a right relationship with God and right relationships with fellow believers. The false teachers claimed such "godliness," but were sadly lacking in reverence toward God and in good attitudes toward others.

1:7 If godliness includes right attitudes toward others, then godliness should lead to **love for other Christians.** In non-Christian circles, this word referred to affection between family members. Peter extended its meaning in this letter to include the family of believers. It is an especially intense love (see 1 Peter 1:22; Hebrews 10:24) that considers others as brothers and sisters.

Showing love for other believers should translate into **genuine love for everyone.** While Christians must exhibit love for other believers, their love must also go deeper than mere affection. That affection should grow into the kind of love that always puts others first, seeking their highest good. The Greek word *agape* refers to self-sacrificial love. It is the kind of love God demonstrated in saving us. Such love among believers allows for weaknesses and imperfections, deals with problems, affirms others, and has a strong commitment and loyalty. Such a bond will hold the believers together no matter what persecutions and suffering they may face.

1:8 The eight qualities mentioned above ought to be part of every believer's life, but they are not static. Believers don't merely "have" these qualities; instead, they **grow** in these qualities by practicing them in the rough-and-tumble of daily life. As these characteristics increase, they help believers **become productive and useful in** their **knowledge of** the **Lord Jesus Christ.** Our faith must go beyond what we believe; it must become a dynamic part of all we do, resulting in good fruit and spiritual maturity.

1:9 In contrast to believers who are increasing in the positive qualities Peter mentioned above, believers who **fail to develop these virtues,** who are not growing in these qualities, **are blind or, at least, very shortsighted.** Peter had harsh words for believers who refused to grow. The word for shortsighted can mean "to blink" or "to shut the eyes." Peter may also have meant that these believers were intentionally closing their eyes to Christ's light, thus causing spiritual blindness. That they have **forgotten that God has cleansed them from their old life of sin** pictures those who deliberately put out of their mind all that Christ had done in erasing the sins they committed before they were saved. A believer who is "forgetful" of this and refuses to grow becomes unfruitful for God.

1:10 Believers must **work hard to prove that** they really are among those God has called and chosen.** The believers must determine to live for God no matter how difficult it might become and to grow in the virtues mentioned above. Their status as called and chosen was not in doubt because it was of God's initiative. The believers' behavior, however, would "prove" that call by their good qualities and good works. They were "proving" their call and election, not for God, but for themselves.

The believers to whom Peter wrote were in danger of turning to the doctrine of false teachers who were teaching that immoral living incurred no judgment. These false teachers said that once people were "saved," they could live any way they pleased. Peter countered this teaching, explaining that Christians must match their calling and election with holy living. If they did this, they would **never stumble or fall away** (see Colossians 1:22-23; 2 Timothy 2:12-13). The word "stumble" means more than merely to "trip." It means to come to grief or ruin, referring to the day of judgment, when sin takes the unbeliever and rebel into eternal damnation.

1:11 Those who live fruitful and productive lives for God, who do not disastrously stumble along the path to **the eternal Kingdom** (heaven) will find the gates **open wide.** All believers will experience a wonderful welcome into their true home, the eternal Kingdom of the Lord and Savior. Those who have been called and chosen, but have been unfruitful and have stumbled much along the way, will still reach the Kingdom and receive their salvation, but it will be, as Paul wrote in 1 Corinthians 3:15, "escaping through a wall of flames." Whether this welcome will be any different is unknown, but Peter encouraged his readers to stay true to the faith to ensure a rich welcome. Looking toward our future eternal life provides the motivation for right living now. We must be centered on heaven's priorities, not those of this world. We can face hardships and still be faithful to God because we know the bright future he has for us. How wonderful it is to contemplate that God wants, expects, and waits for us.

PAYING ATTENTION TO SCRIPTURE / 1:12-21

The times were difficult—persecution was increasing from without; false teachers were spewing evil doctrine from within. Peter encouraged the believers to continue to stand firm on the basics of their faith, to continue to remind themselves of these truths (even though they knew them already), and to reestablish themselves in the truth they had been taught.

1:12 Because of the glories awaiting the believers, Peter intended to **keep on reminding** them not to allow their salvation to become a license for immoral living, nor to rest content in the knowledge of the gospel without obeying it and applying it to their lives. He knew these believers were **standing firm in the truth**. Standing firm in the truth is a source of spiritual strength.

1:13-15 Peter would **keep on reminding** the believers and try to **make these things clear to** them so they would **remember them long after** he was gone. The phrase **as long as I live** emphasizes the transitory nature of this life on earth. Peter reminds us that the eternal realm matters, not the temporal. Peter knew that he would **soon die**. Many years before, Christ had prepared Peter for the kind of death Peter would face, although the only timing Peter knew was that he would be "old" (see John 21:18-19). At the writing of this letter, Peter knew that his death was at hand. Scholars have discussed whether Peter had received some kind of revelation so that he knew his death was coming, or whether Peter simply thought he would die because of the intense persecution in Rome and his being a prominent Christian figure in the church. In any case, Peter was martyred for the faith in about A.D. 68. According to some traditions, he was crucified upside down, at his own request, because he did not feel worthy to die in the same manner as his Master.

1:16 Peter explained that he and the other apostles (**we**), the original carriers of the gospel message, had not been **making up clever stories** when they spoke of the **power of our Lord Jesus Christ and his coming again**. Most likely, Peter was defending the gospel against accusations from false teachers that the Incarnation, Resurrec-

tion, and Second Coming were myths (see 3:4; 2 Timothy 2:17-18).

Peter had **seen his majestic splendor with his own eyes**. Peter was referring to the Transfiguration, where Jesus' divine identity had been revealed to Peter and two other disciples, James and John (see Matthew 17:1-8; Mark 9:2-8; Luke 9:28-36). At the Transfiguration, the three disciples received a foretaste of what Christ would be like in glory and what eternity with him would be like. This was grounded in experience and fact, without embellishment or speculation. The believers must always remember that the truth they received was truth indeed, passed on by those who had lived with and learned from Jesus. Peter emphasized his authority as an eyewitness as well as the God-inspired authority of Scripture to prepare the way for his harsh words against the false teachers. If these wicked men were contradicting the apostles and the Bible, their message could not be from God. Peter's affirmation that they **were not making up clever stories** denies the charge from some liberal scholars that the Gospels are merely myth. Peter and the apostles staked their lives on the truth of those narratives.

1:17 Peter wrote what only an eyewitness to this event could have written. At the Transfiguration, Jesus had **received honor and glory from God the Father**. The Transfiguration was a brief glimpse of Jesus' true glory. This was God's divine affirmation of everything Jesus had done and was about to do. The Transfiguration assured the disciples that their commitment was well placed and their eternity was secure. Jesus was truly the Messiah, the divine Son of God. On earth, Jesus appeared as a man, a poor carpenter from Nazareth turned itinerant preacher. But at the Transfiguration, Jesus' true identity was revealed with the glorious radiance that he had before coming to earth (John 17:5; Philippians 2:6) and that he will have when he returns in glory to establish his Kingdom (Revelation 1:14-15).

During the Transfiguration, a cloud appeared and enveloped the group on the mountain (Jesus, Elijah, Moses, Peter, James, and John). **God's glorious, majestic voice called down from heaven** and singled out Jesus from Moses and Elijah as the long-awaited Messiah who possessed divine authority. As he had done at Jesus' baptism (Mark 1:11), God gave verbal approval of his Son. The voice spoke to the three disciples, saying, **"This is my beloved Son; I am fully pleased with him."**

1:18 Not only had the three disciples (**we ourselves** refers to Peter, James, and John) seen Christ's honor and glory, but they also had **heard** about it as well—from God himself! Peter's testimony counters the heresy of the false teachers. They pointed to esoteric knowledge as the basis of salvation and holiness. Peter pointed to a heavenly origin of the voice, not earthly knowledge. The Transfiguration obviously had had a profound impact on Peter. As he prepared for his death, his last words of assurance to future believers focused on the reliability of the gospel. Peter knew that his eternal glory was sure, for he had seen it with his own eyes. Thus, he could assure all believers that they too would one day share in this glory.

1:19 As Peter reflected on the assurances of the Second Coming—what he and the other apostles had seen, heard, and experienced—he was reminded of another assurance (**we** here could still refer to the apostles, or more likely Peter may have meant that all believers in general also have this assurance). He added the prophets to the mixture of evidence, showing the error of the false teachers. What God had said on the mountain should give the believers **even greater confidence in the message proclaimed by the prophets.** These words could mean that the Transfiguration verified and validated all that the prophets had foreseen—God would come to earth as a human; Jesus Christ was that person, human but glorious, who would save people from their sins. More likely, these words could mean that if the people were having trouble believing Peter, then they could go back to the Old Testament Scriptures; there they would find the same truth.

They should also **pay close attention to** the Scriptures as one would pay attention to **a light shining in a dark place.** The Old Testament Scriptures verify the gospel, making even more certain its truth. The believers were encouraged to continue in this manner **until the day Christ appears and his brilliant light shines in** their **hearts.** Until the day comes when Christ returns to dispel all darkness, believers have Scripture as a light and the Holy Spirit to illuminate Scripture for us and guide us as we seek the truth. But when Christ is completely revealed, Scripture will no longer be needed.

1:20-21 Peter wrote here of revelation, the source of all Scripture. One's belief about revelation is foundational for faith. Christians must be able to rest on the infallibility of Scripture, or their faith is of no value. Hence Peter's words, **above all, you must understand that no prophecy in Scripture ever came from the prophets themselves.** Perhaps the false teachers were denying Scripture by denying its divine origin, saying that the words were merely the writers' interpretations, not God's words. Scripture (specifically the Old Testament prophecies) did not originate with any man nor was it interpreted by the prophets themselves as they delivered the message. Peter reaffirmed the divine origin of Old Testament prophecy, that **the Holy Spirit moved the prophets to speak from God.** Scripture did not come from the creative work of the prophets' own invention or interpretation. The same God who spoke to the disciples at the Transfiguration had spoken to the prophets, guiding them in their writings. God inspired the writers, so their message is authentic and reliable. God used the talents, education, and cultural background of each writer (they were not taking dictation); and God cooperated with the writers in such a way to ensure that the message he intended was faithfully communicated through the words they wrote. Through the Holy Spirit, God revealed his person and plan to certain believers, who wrote down his message for his people. The process of "inspiration" makes Scripture completely trustworthy because God was in control of its writing. The Bible's words are entirely accurate and authoritative for our faith and for our lives. Through knowledge of the Scriptures, believers would be able to recognize and stand firm against false teaching; through the knowledge of the Scriptures, believers would have all the tools and guidance they would need to live for God.

2 PETER 2

FALSE TEACHERS / 2:1-22

This chapter includes severe warnings against the false teachers who had infiltrated the church and threatened to turn young believers away from the truth. (It contains parallels to Jude 4-16. See the Introduction to 1 Peter for explanation.) Peter spared no words against these false teachers, explaining their evil characteristics and motives, the danger of their teaching, and the certainty of their fate. Believers today would do well to heed Peter's warnings against false teachers; the danger is great.

2:1 The end of chapter 1 leads into the topic of his letter. Peter had explained that God had worked through humans to give his words to people (1:21). At the same time, however, evil was at work. The true prophets spoke and wrote God's words, but **there were also false prophets in Israel.** In Old Testament times, false prophets contradicted the true prophets (see, for example, Deuteronomy 13:1-5; 1 Kings 18:19; 22:6ff.; Jeremiah 23:16-40; 28:1-17), telling people only what they wanted to hear. These "false prophets" did not speak God's words, and they brought messages to make the people and the kings feel good. Scripture explains that these false prophets would face God's judgment (Deuteronomy 18:20-22).

Coming from within the churches, the **false teachers** worked to **teach their destructive heresies about God.** How can we distinguish **destructive heresies** from "differences of opinion"? The term "heresy" applies to cardinal doctrines whose misinterpretation would be destructive to Christianity. "Differences of opinion" apply to issues that will never be fully solved. We've known the cardinal doctrines for fifteen hundred years (such as the deity of Christ, the Trinity, substitutionary atonement) while we will always "agree to disagree" on the others (Calvinism vs. Arminianism, infant baptism, roles of women in the church, etc.). These were destructive heresies because the teachers wanted to **turn** the believers **against their Master who bought them** through his shed blood on the cross. A teaching is destructive if it teaches anything but the truth about Jesus. Any deviation from the truth is no longer the truth. The word for "turn against" means to contradict, reject, or disavow. Thus, these heresies could have taken the form of (1) denying Christ's second coming, or (2) denying Christ's lordship by disobeying his teaching and practicing immorality. Some false

teachers were belittling the significance of Jesus' life, death, and resurrection. Some claimed that Jesus could not be God. Others claimed that he could not have been a real human being. These teachers often allowed and even encouraged all kinds of wrong and immoral acts, especially sexual sin (see 2:10, 14).

Peter revealed the seriousness of denying Christ, for turning away from him would bring **a swift and terrible end.** This would not happen immediately—for many false teachers worked and prospered. When that certain destruction came, however, it would be swift and final.

The question arises, How could these false teachers, who had been believers and whom the Lord had "bought," end up in eternal destruction? There are five main views about this question:

1. These false teachers had been believers, but had lost their salvation. The problem with this view is that it contradicts other Scriptures that say a person cannot lose his or her salvation (see John 3:16; 5:24; 10:28-29; Romans 8:28-39).
2. These false teachers had joined the Christian community and seemed to be part of it, but they later denounced Christ and tried to convince others to do the same.
3. These false teachers were "bought" in the sense of "created," but not "saved." The problem here is that a different word would have been used if Peter had meant this.
4. These false teachers only said that they were saved, "bought" by Christ's blood. But they were lying. Possibly, but who can know?
5. These false teachers had been "bought" by the blood of Christ, as Christ's blood is sufficient to save everyone who ever lived if everyone chose to believe. However, the false teachers never accepted Christ as their Savior and thus were

never saved in the first place. Potentially Christ died for everyone, but only those who believe and follow will be saved.

Of the five views, the second and fifth are the most plausible.

2:2 Despite the certainty of their destruction, the false teachers, unfortunately, will be successful in two areas. First, **many will follow their evil teaching and shameful immorality.** Such practices were common in pagan societies and often were part of pagan religions. Popularity was certainly not the right criterion for the truth. Second, **Christ and his true way will be slandered.** They would discredit the Christian gospel taught by Jesus Christ, who is the Way, the Truth, and the Life (see John 14:6; see also Psalm 119:30). In his first letter, Peter had explained at length the importance of Christians living blamelessly before the unbelieving world (1 Peter 2:11-12; 3:13-15). Those who followed the false teachers into shameful living would malign the gospel before the world.

2:3 Peter spared no words in his condemnation of the false teachers. He exposed their prime motivation—**greed.** Only **money,** not truth, mattered to them (see also 1 Peter 5:2). Students ought to pay their teachers, but these false teachers were attempting to make more money by making up **clever lies**—distorting the truth and saying what people wanted to hear. The teaching that people can live as they please without fear of punishment would be very popular!

Their **destruction** may not arrive immediately, but when it comes, it will be swift and certain. The teachers may seem to get away with their exploitation for a while, but **God** had **condemned them long ago.** In 3:9, Peter explained to the believers that God's promises were sure, no matter how long they had to wait for them. Perhaps the false teachers said that because God's promises had not come about, they were nothing more than untrue stories "made up" by the disciples. Peter took their argument and explained that no matter how long it might take and no matter how successful the false teachers might seem to be, their condemnation and destruction were sure.

2:4 If some people still did not believe in future judgment and punishment, Peter gave examples of how God had judged evil in the past. He pointed out that **God did not spare even the angels when they sinned.** This could be a reference to the angels who rebelled along with Satan (Ezekiel 28:15) or to the sin of the angels described in Genesis 6:1-4 (see also Jude 1:6 and Revelation 12:7). More likely, it is the incident recorded in Genesis 6,

because the following verses relate to incidents also taken from that portion of Genesis—the Flood and the judgment of Sodom and Gomorrah. If God did not even spare his angels, neither will he spare the false teachers.

The angels who sinned were thrown **into hell.** That phrase in Greek is one word (used only here in the New Testament), literally meaning "to cast into Tartarus." In Greek mythology, Tartarus, located in the lowest part of the underworld, was the place of punishment of rebellious gods and the departed spirits of very evil people. These angels were imprisoned in this hell, **in gloomy caves and darkness.** This might also be the place of punishment set aside in the heavenly realm (1 Peter 3:19-20). The place of confinement cannot be identified, but it is totally in God's control. These sinful angels will wait in hell, a place of punishment, **until the judgment day,** referring to their final doom (Matthew 25:41). False teachers will face the same judgment as the rebellious angels.

2:5 Another example of God's certain judgment of evil is the **vast flood** that **destroyed the whole world of ungodly people.** Peter referred to the Flood three times in his two letters (see 1 Peter 3:20; 1 Peter 2:5; 3:6). God **did not spare the ancient world**—for the great sinfulness of all mankind led him to destroy the entire rebellious civilization. Yet even as God was destroying all the sinful people in Noah's day, he powerfully protected **Noah and his family of seven** (Genesis 8:16). **Noah** had **warned the world of God's righteous judgment,** but no one believed him. God's punishment is not arbitrary. Those who deserve punishment will receive his punishment; those who trust in him will receive his grace. Peter's readers should understand the comparison—those who choose the wrong path face eternal consequences.

2:6 A third example of God's certain punishment of evil is **the cities of Sodom and Gomorrah.** Genesis 18–19 describes the sinfulness of these cities and Abraham's effort to keep them from being destroyed. When not even ten righteous people could be found in the cities, God destroyed them by burning them to **heaps of ashes and swept them off the face of the earth** (Genesis 19:24-25). The cities do not even exist today. Archaeologists believe they may have been buried by the waters of the Dead Sea.

Peter explained that the horror of these cities' ending is **an example of what will happen to ungodly people.** Great will be the suffering of the ungodly; their ending will result in punishment, gloom, and banishment from the presence of God.

In our day, God's punishment on the unrighteous seems less of a preaching and teaching priority. Do we, like the false teachers, think we have outgrown this clear doctrine of Scripture? We have a lot of emphasis on tolerance of others and the self-help benefits of the Bible, but we must not dilute God's clear words of warning. To turn away from God is to turn to ruin. From such ruin, there will be no escape. Don't neglect teaching about God's judgment.

2:7-8 Just as Noah had been protected from the Flood that destroyed the earth, so **Lot,** Abraham's nephew, had been rescued from Sodom and Gomorrah's destruction. Lot had chosen to settle near **Sodom** (Genesis 13:12-13), but **was distressed by the wickedness he saw and heard day after day.** Lot lived in Sodom and apparently was a man of some importance there, for when the angels went to take Lot from the city, they found him sitting in the gateway of the city, where city officials met.

Peter described Lot as **a righteous man** who was horrified by the evil in the city. Angel visitors rescued Lot and his family by taking them away from the city before it was destroyed. The Genesis account does not make Lot appear to have been very "righteous" at all. But for all his flaws, Lot stood out as a righteous man in an extremely evil society. When God chose to bring swift and complete judgment on the evil of these cities, he also graciously saved his own.

Just as God rescued Lot from Sodom, so he is able to rescue us from the temptations and trials we face in a wicked world. Lot was not sinless, but he put his trust in God and was spared when Sodom was destroyed. God will punish those who cause the temptations and trials, so we need never worry about justice being done.

2:9 These words were comforting to Peter's readers and continue to be comforting to believers today. **The Lord knows how to rescue godly people from their trials.** Noah and Lot had stood the "trial," staying true to God alone while surrounded by sin and hatred. The early Christians also lived in a hostile environment, often facing persecution. If they could stand firm, they would be rescued.

The examples cited above also show that God knows how to punish **the wicked right up until the day of judgment.** Peter's wording refers back to 2:4, which speaks of the rebellious angels being "kept" until the "judgment." Scholars have debated the meaning of this verse. Peter may have meant that the unrighteous (his focus was still the false teachers and their followers, 2:3) were

under punishment in this life, will be punished after death, and will face destruction at that final day of judgment (2:3; Revelation 20:11-15). Others have taken Peter's words to mean that sinners who have died are presently suffering as they await the final judgment. Finally, others place the words in the future tense—that the unrighteous are being kept now for a future judgment. The last interpretation seems most likely because Peter points to final deliverance for the righteous at the Lord's return, so the false teachers' destiny is set for them at the great judgment (Revelation 20:11-15).

2:10 The certainty of the punishment described in the previous verses is for all evil people, but **he is especially hard on those who follow their own evil, lustful desires and who despise authority.** This wording refers to sexual promiscuity, immorality, and even perverted sexual practices. "Authority" could refer to church leaders, angelic powers (as in the remainder of this verse, below), or to the false teachers' denial of Christ. Most likely, the authority despised by the false teachers referred to all three; they didn't want anyone over them. The false teachers lived as they pleased and laughed at the prospect of a Second Coming and judgment by God. Peter wanted to make it clear that people would not get away with such sin.

With pride and arrogance, they dared **even to scoff at the glorious ones.** (A similar passage is in Jude 1:8-10.) Scholars have considered these "glorious ones" to be church leaders, angels, or fallen angels. The most widely held opinion is that these "glorious ones" are the fallen angels—the guilty celestial beings who deserve condemnation—thus, they are the fallen angels also mentioned in 2:4. The false teachers "slandered" the spiritual realities they did not understand (2:12), perhaps by taking Satan's power lightly and doubting the existence of supernatural evil powers. They lived immoral lives and, when rebuked for doing so and thus following Satan, they would simply laugh at the idea of Satan at all.

2:11 Peter pointed out the false teachers' audacity in scoffing at the glorious ones (2:10) by explaining that even the good **angels** in heaven, though far **greater in power and strength** than evil angels, **never speak out disrespectfully against the glorious ones.** While not even the angels would accuse Satan on their own authority, the false teachers arrogantly did so, revealing their ignorance of God *and* of Satan. Their complete irreverence in the form of immoral living (thus mocking God's laws) and slander of the evil angels (thus flaunting their self-attested authority) would result in severe punishment.

2:12 The **false teachers** arrogantly rebelled against God and spoke as though Satan's influence meant nothing (see 2:11), laughing at **powers** they knew **little about.** All their supposed knowledge was worthless; they really understood nothing. Without mincing words, Peter further described these false teachers as **unthinking animals, creatures of instinct.** Like beasts, the false teachers would be **destroyed.**

2:13 These teachers had been so obvious in their sinfulness that it was shameful that any of the believers should follow them. While the false teachers tried to pass themselves off as superior teachers with great knowledge, they indulged **in evil pleasures in broad daylight.** Such acts would be done under cover of darkness. These men were so arrogant, however, that they did not even attempt to cover up their behavior, making them no longer fit to be with the Christians. Thus the false teachers were **a disgrace and a stain** among them, ruining the Christians' gatherings by their very presence. The **feast** may refer to part of the celebration of the Lord's Supper. In one of the greatest of hypocritical acts, they attended the sacred feasts designed to promote love and unity among believers, while at the same time they reveled in **deceitfulness.** These men were guilty of more than false teaching and promoting evil pleasures; they were guilty of leading others away from the truth. **Destruction** would be **their reward.**

2:14 Peter had no soft words for these false teachers, no excuses for their behavior. Their sinful words and actions came from deep within; their thoughts and motives were evil.

- **They commit adultery with their eyes** means that they could not look on women without lusting for them. They were turning church meetings into opportunities for sexual encounters.
- Their **lust** was **never satisfied** because they were bound in sin, acting like brute beasts that follow instinct without any rational faculties (2:12). These men were in bondage to sin and to the power of Satan (2:10).
- They made a **game of luring unstable people into sin** means that, like a fisherman baiting fish, the false teachers waited out their catch. They didn't waste time with the strong believers, but sought out those who were not firmly grounded in the faith, or had doubts, or were "outside" the fellowship for one reason or another. Pretending patience and interest, they could entice these people away from the faith and into their dangerous "net."
- **They train themselves to be greedy** means that

the false teachers had exercised themselves (the Greek word for "trained" is the word from which we derive "gymnasium") in being greedy and in getting what they coveted. These men were really good at being greedy because, no matter how much they got, they always wanted more.

These teachers who were leading Christians away from the faith were filled with pride, immorality, sensuality, greed, lust, blasphemy, slander, and self-will. No wonder Peter called these men **doomed and cursed.** This was a common Hebrew phrase to describe those who would face certain destruction from the hand of God.

2:15-16 Peter once again looked to the Old Testament for an illustration to apply to these false teachers. They followed in the steps of another man who had led many astray. Numbers 22–24 tells the story of **Balaam** who was hired by a pagan king to curse Israel. He did what God told him to do for a time, but eventually his evil motives and desire for **money** won out (Numbers 25:1-3; 31:16). The false teachers were not interested in serving God; instead, they were using religion for financial gain and personal advancement (see also Jude 1:11 and commentary there).

Balaam claimed to do only what God told him, but the money was a strong temptation. Balaam probably thought that he could figure out a way to obey God, yet get the money anyway. On his way to see King Balak, three times Balaam's **donkey** saw the angel of the Lord standing in their path, ready to kill Balaam. Each time, the donkey stopped and refused to go forward. Each time, Balaam beat the donkey. Finally, the donkey **rebuked him with a human voice.** Balaam obeyed God and refused to curse the Israelites. Like Balaam, the false teachers' attitudes were akin to madness. Balaam at least listened to the donkey. The false teachers listened to no one. Like Balaam, the false teachers expected to get away with their sin, but they would receive their reward.

2:17 The false teachers' messages ended only in disappointment. Like a **dried-up spring** or **clouds blown away,** their messages were **promising much but delivering nothing.** Their fate had already been sealed in **blackest darkness.** The word **darkness** stood for the final fate of all wicked people. The false teachers would be forever cast from God's light into the darkness of hell itself.

2:18 The false teachers drew attention to themselves by their **foolish boasting.** They spoke often and loudly, but their words were ultimately **empty.** They had no substance, no truth. Instead, they lured **back**

into sin those who had **just escaped from such wicked living.** By using **lustful desire as their bait,** the false teachers were able to draw new Christians away from the gospel truth. A salvation that is future only, that allows people to indulge every sinful desire and passion here on earth without punishment, can be enticing. Who would believe such a message? Not the strong followers of Christ, so the false teachers focused on new converts not yet firmly rooted in the faith or free of pagan associations and habits. To these young believers, the empty, boastful words sounded convincing.

2:19 The **freedom** the false teachers promised was freedom to live as one pleased. However, such freedom was empty, for the false teachers were not free. Instead, they were **slaves to sin and corruption.** They began to taste the freedom found in Christ, but they perverted it by resisting the rules of love their new Master gave. They tossed these aside, in the name of freedom, only to find themselves enslaved once again. Why? Because **you are a slave to whatever controls you.** Many believe that freedom means doing anything they want. But no one is ever completely free in that sense. The freedom Christ brings is freedom from sin, not freedom to do whatever we want. Too often freedom from rules, structure, or obedience leads to an addiction or preoccupation with the new pleasures freedom offers. But these actions can quickly enslave a person.

If people refuse to follow God, their only option is to follow their own sinful desires and become enslaved to what their bodies want. Only Christ can promise and deliver true freedom, for only those who submit their lives to Christ are set free from slavery to sin.

2:20-21 The false teachers had identified themselves as believers. But to **then get tangled up with sin and become its slave again** only made them **worse off than before.** The false teachers had learned about Christ and how to be saved, but

then had rejected the truth, the only way out of sin, the only way of salvation. Like a person sinking in quicksand who refuses to grab the rope thrown to him or her, the one who turns away from Christ casts aside his or her only means of escape.

Indeed, Peter went even further: **It would be better if they had never known the right way to live than to know it and then reject the holy commandments.** Peter offered a comparison, not an option, between the two. He said ignorance is better than apostasy because the one who persists in self-delusion in fact refuses God's help and forgiveness. In the case of the false teachers, they not only violated it, but taught others to do so, giving them an even greater responsibility (see Jesus' words in Mark 9:42). A child who disobeys his parents out of ignorance of the rules is better off than a child who deliberately and willfully disobeys.

In the early church, apostasy was considered an especially horrible sin; to be baptized and then to turn from the faith amounted to committing the unforgivable sin, for it meant turning one's back on God, never to return. Thus Peter wrote these stunning words that they would have been better off never having known God's truth than deliberately blaspheming his grace, love, and forgiveness by rejecting them.

2:22 Those who knew the truth and turned away from it (2:20-21) were among the lowest of the low. To Jews, no creatures were lower than dogs and pigs. The first proverb is taken from Proverbs 26:11; the second probably was a well-known saying in the first century. The meaning of both proverbs is the same: those who return to evil after being cleansed are no better than a **dog** that throws up and **returns to its vomit,** or a **pig** that is **washed** and then **returns to the mud.** Those who make an outward profession of religion without out a Spirit-controlled inner transformation will soon return to their old way of life.

2 PETER 3

THE DAY OF THE LORD IS COMING / 3:1-16

The previous chapter focused on denouncing the false teachers. This chapter returns to the faithful believers, offering them love and encouragement to remember God's words to them (3:1-2), to remember God's timing is different from their expectation so that they could counter the scoffers (3:8), to be faithful (3:14), and to stay away from false teaching (3:17).

3:1 Peter's purpose was to remind the believers that their lives ought to be characterized by **wholesome thinking** (meaning sincerity or purity of understanding). Plato had used this phrase to refer to pure reason uncontaminated by the senses. The thinking and intentions of God's people must be able to stand up under scrutiny and not be led astray by immoral desires (Philippians 4:8-9).

3:2 The way to maintain "wholesome thinking" (3:1) is to **remember and understand** Scripture. **The holy prophets** had written about the coming of the Messiah, and what he would command through his **apostles.** Most likely this refers to the law as upheld by Jesus in the Sermon on the Mount and propagated by the apostles (see 2:21).

The Holy Spirit unified the prophets and apostles in an unchanging message of hope and truth. The prophets had written of the Messiah, who would come to bring judgment and restore the Kingdom; those words had come to pass. The apostles had spoken and written that Jesus the Messiah would return to bring judgment. Thus believers should live expectantly, knowing that those words will also come to pass.

3:3 We, along with the first-century believers, ought to be prepared for anything because we have been warned what to watch for and how to live. Peter wrote that **in the last days there will be scoffers.** The "last days" began with Christ's resurrection and will continue until his return, when he will set up his Kingdom and judge all humanity. Jesus and the apostles warned that during that interim, including the time period we live in, scoffers **will laugh at the truth** (see 1 Timothy 4:1-2; 2 Timothy 3:1-9). Once again, Peter was referring to false teachers who deny Jesus Christ and thereby deny his second coming (3:4). These false teachers will laugh at the truth of God's word and instead **do every evil thing they desire.** Peter called the believers to remember the Scriptures and to live to please God; but the false teachers will scoff at the Scriptures and will live to please themselves and their sinful desires. Ironically, the very presence of these men who scoffed at prophecy was itself fulfillment of prophecy.

3:4 The false teachers' scoffing focused on Christ's second coming. Jesus had **promised** that he would **come back** (Mark 13:24-27), but many years had passed and nothing had happened. The scoffers based their argument on the fact that **everything has remained exactly the same since the world was first created.**

Many first-century Christians believed that Jesus would come in their lifetime. When Christians began to die without experiencing the Lord's return, some began to doubt. These were prime targets for the false teachers, who pointed out that perhaps it was all a lie and Christ was never going to return. The false teachers argued that ever since creation, the world has continued in a natural order, a system of cause-and-effect. They did not believe that God would intervene or allow anything out of the ordinary (such as miracles) to occur. Therefore, they scoffed at teachings about a Second Coming and the end of the world.

3:5-6 What these scoffers were forgetting in their argument (that the world had remained unchanged since creation) was that **God made the heavens.** The Creation disproves their "all things continue" argument because the creation of the earth was an imposed change on the formless void (Genesis 1:1-2). The very reason the world was continuing on in a stable, predictable pattern was because God, in his grace, had created it that way. However, this stability should not be taken for granted. The false teachers **deliberately forgot** that God also had destroyed the evil world **with a mighty flood.**

3:7 As God destroyed the earth before, he **has also commanded that the heavens and the earth will be consumed by fire on the day of judgment.** In Noah's day the earth was judged by water; at the Second Coming it will be judged by fire (see Isaiah 66:15-16; Malachi 4:1; Revelation 19:20; 20:10-15). Judgment has already been decided. **Ungodly people will perish;** it is only a matter of God's timing. Scholars have debated whether Peter was referring to a literal fiery destruction of the entire universe with new heavens and earth to follow, or to "fire of judgment." Second Peter is the only New Testament book that says the world will actually be destroyed by fire (3:10-11). The passages cited above refer primarily to the fire of God's judgment. If taken that way, the fire purifies the earth, burns up the Lord's enemies and the futile works of humanity, and makes the earth new for Christ's eternal reign. Peter's point was that destruction would come, and the godless (those who have not believed) will not escape.

3:8 Peter had made his point that Christ would certainly return and bring judgment, but the question still remained, "Why was the Lord delaying so long?" Peter offered two reasons in 3:8-9. First of all, the Lord does not count time as people do. He is above and outside of the sphere of time. God sees all of eternity past and eternity future. Indeed, to him **a day is like a thousand years** and **a thousand years is like a day** (Psalm 90:4). God may have seemed slow to these believers as they faced persecution every day and longed to be delivered. But God is not slow; he simply doesn't operate according to our timetable.

3:9 The second reason for the Lord **being slow about his promise to return** was his patience. He **does not want anyone to perish, so he is giving more time for everyone to repent.** He wants as many people as will to come to faith in him. God is not "slow" at all; rather, according to his timetable, he is being exceedingly patient, giving people time to turn to him. Love is the reason that he delays the destruction of the world.

Some have attempted to make this verse mean that ultimately everyone will be saved. But nowhere does Scripture teach universal salvation. This verse means that God, in his great compassion, does not desire that anyone should "perish" (referring to eternal destruction). He wants every person to turn to him and trust him. God is loving, but he also executes perfect justice. His perfect love causes him to be merciful to those who recognize their sin and turn back to him, but he cannot ignore those who willfully sin. Wicked people die both physically and spiritually. God takes no joy in their deaths; he would prefer that they turn to him and have eternal life. However, the promise of judgment and destruction show that God knows that many will not choose to follow him.

3:10 The day of the Lord is the day of Christ's return and of God's judgment on the earth. Peter repeated a warning used by Jesus Christ, that this day **will come as unexpectedly as a thief** (see also Matthew 24:42-44). Christ's second coming will be swift, sudden, unexpected, and terrible for those who do not believe in him. The day of the Lord will be a time of judgment and destruction. Again quoting words that he had heard Jesus say, Peter described the coming end (see Matthew 24:29; Luke 21:25). Peter described three aspects of the conflagration:

1. **The heavens will pass away with a terrible noise** describes the end of the earth's atmosphere and the sky above.
2. **Everything in them will disappear in fire** could mean that the celestial bodies will also be destroyed (the sun, moon, stars, and planets).
3. **The earth and everything on it will be exposed to judgment** is an extremely difficult phrase, which has given rise to numerous textual variants in various manuscripts. Some of the readings speak of the earth disappearing, others of it being burned up, and others of it being "exposed" so that all the works that people counted on in this earth in place of God will be revealed for their futility, and then they will all be annihilated. (See also Hebrews 1:10-12.)

When will these events occur? Some have placed them between the events of Revelation 20 (the thousand-year reign of Christ, Satan's doom, the final judgment) and Revelation 21 (new heaven and new earth, the descent of the new Jerusalem).

Peter explained that this earth will not last forever. As God intervened in the past to judge the earth by water, so one day he will intervene again. But in that day, the judgment will be by fire, and everything will be destroyed. Those who presume to take God's delay of this judgment to mean that they can do as they please will find themselves surprised upon his return. And when the destruction occurs, there will be no second chances and no escape for those who have chosen to disobey the Creator. However, in the following verses, Peter turned his attention to the believers, writing to them about how they should live in light of the coming judgment.

3:11-12 Peter's description of the coming destruction of the earth ought to cause Christians to carefully examine their lives so that they are **holy** and **godly.** Such lives would be in direct contrast to the unholy living and godlessness found in the world. Such lives, lived through faith in Jesus Christ, will continue on after the coming destruction. Because of that knowledge, the Christians need not fear **that day;** they could instead actually **look forward** to it.

Peter wrote that the believers can also actually **hurry it along** by continuing to live holy (dedicated to God and separated from evil) and godly (characterized by personal piety and worship) lives, praying (Matthew 6:10), and telling people about the gospel (Matthew 24:14). Christians are not called to sit and wait for the inevitable end; instead, our mission during our time on earth is to live for God and to tell the world the gospel message. Jesus had explained that, before his return, "the Good News must first be preached to every nation" (Mark 13:10).

As noted above, at the end **God will set the heavens on fire and the elements will melt away in the flames** (3:10). These will happen as a direct result of the coming of the day of God. The earth's destruction will not be the result of any natural winding-down of the universe, but the result of God's sovereign will, occurring according to his plan.

3:13 Believers look forward to the end of the earth only because it means the fulfillment of another of God's promises—his creation of **the new heavens and new earth.** God's purpose for people is not destruction but re-creation; not annihilation, but renewal. God will purify the heavens and earth with fire; then he will create them anew. All believers can joyously look forward to the restoration of God's good world (Romans 8:21). In a beautiful description of the new heavens and earth, believers are assured that it will be **a world where everyone is right with God** because God himself will live among his people (see Revelation 21:1-4, 22-27).

3:14 Because believers can trust God's promise to bring them into a new earth, and because they **are waiting for these things to happen,** they ought to live **a pure and blameless life.** To say it another way, only this powerful hope could entice us to live righteously. God's Kingdom will be characterized by peace with God; therefore, believers ought to practice **peace with God** now, in preparation for living in the Kingdom. We should not become lazy and complacent just because Christ has not yet returned. Instead, we should live in eager expectation of his coming. What would you like to be doing when Christ returns? That is how you should be living each day.

3:15-16 As the believers waited, perhaps impatiently, for the Lord's return, Peter reminded them that **the Lord is waiting so that people have time to be saved.** God's patience means salvation for many more who will have the chance to respond to the gospel message.

When reading the various letters of the New Testament, it is interesting to study the interrelationships among the writers. Peter was one of Jesus' twelve disciples. He later became the undisputed leader of the church in Jerusalem. **Paul** came along later, after he was converted on the Damascus road by a vision of Jesus Christ (Acts 9). Paul was also considered an apostle. Peter and Paul had

great respect for each other as they worked in the ministries to which God had called them.

By the time of Peter's writing, Paul's letters already had a widespread reputation. Peter backed up his words with the believers' apparent knowledge that Paul had also written to them about this very topic. Peter recognized the value of Paul's letters in the growth of the church, for he described Paul as writing them **with the wisdom God gave him.** The teachings of the apostles were never distorted by the person or area of ministry. Whether the letter came from Paul or Peter, the message could be depended on to be the same, for it had come from God himself. Notice that Peter wrote of Paul's letters as if they were on a level with **other parts of Scripture.** Already the early church was considering Paul's letters to be inspired by God. Both Peter and Paul were aware that they were speaking God's word along with the Old Testament prophets (see 1 Thessalonians 2:13). In the early days of the church, the letters from the apostles were read to the believers and often passed along to other churches. Sometimes the letters were copied and then passed on. The believers regarded these writings to be as authoritative as the Old Testament Scriptures.

Some readers may have been put off by some of Paul's comments that were **hard to understand.** But the cure is not to listen to those who would twist the truth, but instead to continue to increase in the knowledge of Jesus. The better we know Jesus, the less attractive false teaching will be. The false teachers twisted all of Scripture to mean whatever they wanted. However, this would result in **disaster.**

PETER'S FINAL WORDS / 3:17-18
No matter where we are in our spiritual journey, no matter how mature we are, the sinful world always will challenge our faith. We still have much room for growth. If every day we find some way to draw closer to Christ, we will be prepared to stand for truth in any and all circumstances.

3:17 Peter wanted his readers to be warned **ahead of time** about the danger of false teachers, explaining the false teachers' tactics and future destruction. Being forewarned, the believers would **not be carried away by the errors** of the false teachers. To "be carried away" means to be led astray into error. The word pictures a person following along behind a crowd. The implication is that keeping company with false teachers or those who follow them will inevitably cause the believer to also be led astray and **lose** his **secure footing.**

3:18 Peter concluded this brief letter as he had begun, by urging his readers to **grow** (the verb is a present imperative, meaning "continue growing")

in the special favor and knowledge of the **Lord and Savior Jesus Christ**—to get to know Christ better and better.

Believers "grow in favor" as they understand that they are living by God's grace alone—so everything they do is a result of that grace. Believers "grow in knowledge" as they search and study the Scriptures, pray, listen to sound teachers, and apply that knowledge to their daily lives. If they do these, they will not need to fear being influenced by false teachers. Christ is Lord, divine and omnipotent; he is Savior, the one who accomplished humanity's salvation. To him be **all glory and honor** in this age and in the new eternal age to come. **Amen,** so be it.

1 JOHN

INTRODUCTION

With a flick of the wall switch, the light chases away shadows, reassuring the child that her monsters were only imaginary. Another switch turns on a powerful battery-powered beam and keeps the hiker on the trail after dark. Other lights warn, guide, illuminate, regulate, and decorate. Light—pure and bright—cuts through darkness, exposing reality and demanding attention. Those who walk in light see clearly and know where to go. But those who walk in darkness grope, stumble, and turn the wrong way.

In his Gospel, John proclaimed that Jesus, the "light of the world," had come to illuminate truth and to lead men and women to God (John 1:4-9; 8:12). Here in this first letter, John urged all to forsake darkness and live in the light (1 John 1:5-7).

Do you yearn for direction in life? Follow the light.

Do you doubt and wonder what's real? Turn on his light.

Do you stumble and fall? Walk in the light.

Read 1 John and know that your Light has come. Let it shine!

AUTHOR

The apostle John.

The similarities between the Gospel of John and these letters identified as 1, 2, and 3 John are so remarkable that it would be difficult to argue that these writings were done by two different people. The syntax, the vocabulary, and the thematic developments are so strikingly similar that even the inexperienced reader can tell that the letters were penned by the writer of the Gospel. Therefore, once the writer of John's Gospel is identified, we can automatically identify the writer of the letters.

The author's proclamation as an eyewitness is just as pronounced in the first letter as it is in the Gospel. In 1 John, the author claimed to be among those who heard, saw, and even touched the eternal Word made flesh (1:1-5). In other words, John lived and traveled with the man Jesus. As such, his testimony is firsthand; he was an eyewitness of the greatest person to enter human history. Surely no human knew Jesus better than John.

At the beginning of 2 and 3 John, this author identified himself as "the Elder." This title probably pointed to John's position at that time as the oldest living apostle and chief leader among the churches in the Roman province of Asia (otherwise known as Asia Minor). This is made clear in 1 John by the way he addressed the believers as his "dear children" (2:1, 18, 28; 3:7; 5:21).

For more about John, see the Author section in the Introduction to the Gospel of John.

DATE AND SETTING

Written in about A.D. 90 from Ephesus.

John and the other apostles were probably forced to leave Jerusalem by A.D. 70, if not earlier, due to mounting persecution. It is possible that John gathered with some of the Samaritan converts (see John 4:1-42; Acts 8:9-17) and some of John the Baptist's followers in Palestine, where they continued to preach the word. Sometime thereafter (but probably no earlier than A.D. 70), they migrated to the Roman province of Asia and began a successful ministry among the Gentiles.

John wrote a Gospel for these Gentile believers somewhere around A.D. 80–85. Sometime thereafter, some of the members of the community left to form a rival group. John, therefore, wrote a letter (1 John) in order to deal with the crisis by encouraging the believers to remain in Christ and in the fellowship and by denouncing those who had left. First John was probably written around A.D. 85–90. Second John must have been written in the same time period because it dealt with the same issue, warning the believers not to receive the traveling teachers who were spreading the false teachings of those who had left the church. Third John has the same characteristics; John cautioned Gaius about Diotrephes, who had evidently been affected by the secessionists and had a negative attitude about John and his coworkers.

Although there are no references in the Gospel or the three letters concerning where they were written, according to the earliest traditions of the church, John wrote all four books from Ephesus.

AUDIENCE

The church in Ephesus and believers in nearby churches.

In recent years various scholars have tried to identify the original Johannine community—the group of believers for whom John wrote his Gospel and letters. That there was a special community of believers seems evident from the way John speaks to them and of them in his three letters. The apostle John and the believers knew each other well, and the believers accepted the teachings of the apostle as "the truth." John encouraged them to stay in fellowship with him (and the other apostles); if they did so, they would enjoy true fellowship with the Father and the Son (see 1:1-4).

In the Gospel, this link between the believers, John, and Jesus is also made evident. Throughout the Gospel, John reveals that he had a special relationship with Jesus. Just as the Son was the one qualified to explain the Father to humankind because of his special relationship with the Father (John 1:18), so too John, who reclined on Jesus' chest, was qualified to explain Jesus' message to his readers because of his relationship with Jesus. Because of his relationship to Jesus, John's testimony to his community could be trusted.

A careful study of the letters seems to indicate that the readers were close to John—close enough to be considered his family. They depended on him for his eyewitness account about Jesus and for his insights about his personal relationship with Jesus. John's readers were believers of all ages who needed to be affirmed as a community in love, life, and truth.

OCCASION AND PURPOSE
To reassure Christians in their faith and to counter false teachings.

If it is true that John wrote these letters to certain local churches in Asia—especially to those around Ephesus—one of the reasons that prompted his first epistle was that a heretical faction had developed within the church, a faction that promoted heretical teachings concerning the person of Christ. Scholars have identified this heresy as Docetism generally and pointed specifically to Cerinthus as the perpetrator of the specific brand of Docetism.

The Docetists denied that Jesus had actually become flesh and blood; they denied that God had come in a human body (see 4:1-3). According to Irenaeus, Cerinthus "represented Jesus as having not been born of a virgin, but as being the son of Joseph and Mary according to the ordinary course of human genera-tion, while he nevertheless was more righteous, prudent, and wise than other men. Moreover, after his baptism, Christ descended upon him in the form of a dove from the Supreme Ruler, and that then he proclaimed the unknown Father, and performed miracles. But at last Christ departed from Jesus, and that then Jesus suffered and rose again, while Christ remained impassable, inasmuch as he was a spiritual being" (*Against Heresies*, 3.4). John refuted the Cerinthian heresy in 5:5-8 (see the comments at that point in the commentary).

The heretical faction within the church (or churches) that John was addressing eventually left the fellowship. In so doing, they exposed the reality that they did not genuinely belong to God's family (2:18-19). But their false teachings still lingered in the minds of the faithful. So John wrote to clear the air of all the falsehoods and bring the believers back to the pure beginning of the gospel and to the basics of the Christian life. John urged his readers

- to have fellowship with God in the light
- to confess their sins
- to love God
- to love their fellow Christians
- to abide in Christ
- to purify themselves from worldly lusts
- to know God personally and experientially
- to appreciate the gift of eternal life
- to follow the Spirit of truth (and the anointing) in discerning false teachings
- to esteem Jesus Christ as the true God

Above all these items, John stressed how necessary it was for the early believers to maintain a proper relationship with those who had been with Jesus. In the prologue (1:1-4) to 1 John, he invites all the believers to participate in the one apostolic fellowship. Fellowship is a two-way, simultaneous experience: both with fellow believers and with God. This is to safeguard against pseudo-spirituality and extreme individualism. Throughout this first letter, John seems to have been addressing his comments to those who were claiming to have a relationship with God, yet had left the fellowship of believers and did not love the brothers and sisters in Christ.

Today, those who claim to follow Christ need a fresh dose of the message of 1 John, examining themselves in light of these basics of the Christian faith.

MESSAGE

John opens this letter by giving his credentials as an eyewitness of the Incarnation and by stating his reason for writing (1:1-4). He then presents God as "light," symbolizing absolute purity and holiness (1:5-7), and he explains how believers can walk in the light and have fellowship with God (1:8-10). If they do sin, Christ is their defender (2:1-2). John urges them to obey Christ fully and to love all the members of God's family (2:3-17). He warns his readers of "antichrists" and the Antichrist who will try to lead them away from the truth (2:18-29).

In the next section, John presents God as "love"—giving, dying, forgiving, and blessing (3:1–4:21). God *is* love, and because God loves us, he calls us his children and makes us like Christ (3:1-2). This truth should motivate us to live close to him (3:3-6). We can be sure of our family relationship with God when our life is filled with good works and love for others (3:7-24). Again, John warns of false teachers who twist the truth. We should reject these false teachers (4:1-6) as we continue to live in God's love (4:7-21).

In the last section, John presents God as "life" (5:1-21). God's life is in his Son. To have his Son is to have eternal life.

The main themes in the book of 1 John include: *Sin, Love, Family of God, Truth and Error,* and *Assurance.*

Sin (1:5-10; 2:1-2, 12-17; 3:4-9; 5:16-21). Even Christians sin. Sin requires God's forgiveness, and Christ's death provides it. Determining to live according to God's standards in the Bible shows that believers' lives are being transformed. Throughout this epistle, John calls into question all professed spirituality (for example, see 1:6, 8; 2:4, 6, 9). Talk is cheap; reality must be tested by one's relationship with the members of the church community. John urged the believers to know the truth and to live in it.

IMPORTANCE FOR TODAY. We cannot deny our sin nature, maintain that we are above sinning, or minimize the consequences of sin in our relationship with God. We must resist the attraction of sin, yet we must confess when we do sin. Be honest with yourself and with God. Admit your sin to him and live in the freedom of his forgiveness.

Love (2:7-11; 3:10-11, 14-16, 23; 4:7-21; 5:1-3). In John's letters, all talk of one's living in God must be tested by how one lives with his or her companions in Christ. This leads to one of the primary themes in these letters: love for God must be exhibited in love for others. If we could ask John what is the one message he wanted us to get from these letters, he would probably say, "Love each other." This command did not originate from John; it came straight from the lips of Jesus (see John 13:34; 15:17). John repeated this command often (1 John 2:7; 3:11; 2 John 5-6), basing it on the premise that since "God is love," then all who claim to know God must exhibit that nature in their relationship with others. Jesus commands his followers to love others as he did. This love is evidence that they are truly saved. God is the creator of love; he cares that his children love each other.

IMPORTANCE FOR TODAY. It is easy to talk about love and how much we love people, but love means putting others first. Love is action—showing others that we care—not just words. To show love, we must give sacrificially of our time and money to meet the needs of others. Look for tangible ways to express God's love to others, especially fellow believers. Instead of buying the latest fashions, buy meals or clothes for poor families; instead of pushing for recognition, encourage others and give them the credit; instead of remembering with resentment a past hurt, forgive and let it go. Love others for Christ.

Family of God (1:1-4; 2:18-21, 24-25, 28-29; 3:1-3, 10-20; 4:20-21). The one, unique fellowship between the Father and the Son began in eternity, was manifest in time through the incarnation of the Son, was introduced to the apostles, and then through the apostles was extended to each and every believer. Those who entered this fellowship by believing in Christ became members of God's family—the Christian community, a community that was held together by their common experience of the Trinity and by their acknowledgment of the truth as defined by the apostles. God's life in his children enables them to love their fellow family members.

IMPORTANCE FOR TODAY. How people treat others shows who their Father is. God's children love others, especially those in the family of faith. Some think they can live for God on their own; but God created us for fellowship. He wants us to love and care for our brothers and sisters in Christ. Live as a faithful member of God's family, becoming involved in a local church and reaching out in love to your brothers and sisters.

Truth and Error (2:4-6, 18-23, 26-27; 3:7-9; 4:1-6). False teachers were as present in the young church as false prophets had been in Old Testament Israel. John wanted believers to know the truth so they would be able to distinguish it from error. The word "antichrist" occurs only four times, all in John's epistles (1 John 2:18, 22; 4:3; 2 John 7). First John 2:18 refers also to "many antichrists." John assumed that his Christian readers knew about the Antichrist and had been taught to expect his coming (2:18-27). The presence of many antichrists, in fact, indicated that the end times had arrived. But John warned that a final Antichrist would yet make an appearance. He, like the others, would deny that Jesus is the Christ. According to 1 John, anyone who denies that Jesus is the Christ, that he is the unique Son of God, or that he has come in the flesh is the "Antichrist." The biblical term, however, principally refers to a particular person in whom that denial reaches its consummate expression and who will play a key role in the final stage of history.

IMPORTANCE FOR TODAY. God is truth and light, so the more we get to know him, the better we can keep focused on the truth. Many people today claim to have "a message from God"—the truth. The key question to ask of each teacher and any teaching, however, is, "Does it really agree with the biblical teaching that Jesus Christ, God's Son, actually became man with a human body?" True teachers affirm God's word and teach that Jesus was fully God and fully man. Don't be led astray by any teaching that denies Christ's deity or humanity. Check the message; test the claims.

Assurance (2:3-6; 3:19-24; 5:1-15, 19-20). Several times in this letter, John assures readers that they can "know" or "be sure." They can know that they "belong to him" (2:3), that they are "living in the truth" (3:19), that God lives in them (3:24), and that God hears their prayers (5:15). God is in control of heaven and earth. Because his Word is true, believers can have assurance of eternal life and victory over sin. By faith, they can be certain of their eternal destiny with him.

IMPORTANCE FOR TODAY. Assurance of our relationship with God is a promise, but it is also a way of life. We build our confidence by trusting in God's word and in Christ's provision for our sin. Competing teachers can cause confusion, and tough times can bring doubts. Regardless of what is happening around us or to us, however, we can be assured of God's presence and love and of our eternal destination. If you have trusted in Christ as your Savior, you *have* eternal life. God lives in you, and you are on your way to experience heaven. Live with the assured confidence of the reality of God.

OUTLINE OF 1 JOHN
  I. God Is Light (1:1–2:29)
  II. God Is Love (3:1–4:21)
  III. God Is Life (5:1-21)

1 JOHN **1**:1–2:6

INTRODUCTION / 1:1-4
John's first letter opens as does his Gospel—with a prologue. When John began his Gospel, he recalled how he (and the other disciples, for whom he was a spokesman) had beheld the Son's glory, the glory as of a unique Son from the Father (John 1:14). Then John described Jesus as the one who was both God and the Son of God living near the heart of the Father (John 1:18). In both the Gospel and the letter, John revealed that he (with the apostles) had heard, seen, and even touched God in his bodily expression in Jesus Christ. The apostles realized that the Word of Life, who had been in face-to-face fellowship with the Father for all eternity, had entered into time to relate to them in a human body. They shared the Good News so that, across the world and down through the ages, we might also experience this fellowship.

1:1 This letter is attributed to John, one of Jesus' original twelve disciples. Along with Peter and James, he had a special relationship with Jesus. This letter was written between A.D. 85 and 90 from Ephesus, before John's exile to the island of Patmos (see Revelation 1:9). Jerusalem had been destroyed in A.D. 70, and Christians had been scattered throughout the empire.

Unlike the style of most letters at this time, this letter does not give the name of its writer at the beginning. Both 2 and 3 John begin with "the Elder" and follow with the name of the addressee. This letter, however, includes no author's name, except the understanding that this is an elder of the church writing to his "dear children" (2:1). (The Author section in the Introduction offers more

information about this letter's authorship.) This unaddressed, unsigned letter was probably more of a written sermon or treatise sent to several of the churches in and around Ephesus that were under John's care. As the oldest living apostle, John was the "elder statesman" of Christianity; he had watched the church deal with conflict from within and persecution from without. Plentiful false teachers were accelerating the downward slide of many away from the Christian faith. John wrote this letter to put believers back on track.

God (**the one who existed from the beginning**) came into the world as a human in the person of Jesus Christ. John and the other apostles (**we**) had **heard, seen,** and **touched him.** When the Son entered into time, his fellowship with the Father also entered into time. Thus, to have heard Jesus was to have heard the Father speaking in the Son (John 14:10, 24), to have seen Jesus was to have seen the Father (John 14:8-10), and to have known Jesus was to have known him who was one with the Father (John 10:30, 38).

John called Jesus **the Word of life.** In his Gospel, John had written, "In the beginning the Word already existed. He was with God, and he was God" (John 1:1). As the "Word," the Son of God fully conveys and communicates God. John's use of **the Word** is a good title for the Son who both created the universe with God and then came to earth to be the perfect expression of God to humanity. Jesus, the Word, reveals God's mind to human beings. Not only is Jesus Christ "the Word," he is the Word **of life**—of spiritual life. People may be physically alive but spiritually dead. Jesus, however, as the express image of God himself, gives both spiritual life and eternal life to all who believe in him (1:2).

1:2 Divine, eternal life resided in Christ, so John described Jesus as **this one who is life from God** and repeated the fact that **we have seen him.** He, the other disciples, and thousands of other people had indeed "seen" Jesus. Jesus was more than just a human being. John's work during the many years since Jesus' ascension had been to **testify and announce** to everyone that Jesus **is the one who is eternal life.** Because Christ *is* eternal life, those who trust in him also have eternal life.

In Greek, the phrase, **he was with the Father,** suggests that the Word was face-to-face with the Father. This common Greek expression indicated a personal relationship. By using this expression, John was saying that the Word (the Son) and God (the Father) enjoyed an intimate, personal relationship from the beginning. In Jesus' intercessory prayer, recorded in John 17, he revealed that the Father had loved him before the foundation of the world (John 17:24). The words **then he was shown to us** refer to the revelation of the Son of God in human form (see John 10:30; 14:7-10).

1:3 The plural pronoun **we,** used throughout the prologue, refers, at times, to John and the other apostles (for whom John was acting as spokesman) and also to John and any other believers who had seen Jesus Christ in bodily form. These people had **actually seen and heard** Jesus Christ; they told about it **so that** others **may have fellowship with** them, referring to the life (spiritual and eternal) that all Christians share in a living relationship or partnership. When the disciples were regenerated by the Holy Spirit, they actually entered into fellowship **with the Father and with his Son, Jesus Christ.** Having been brought into this living union, the apostles became the new initiators—introducing this fellowship to others and encouraging them to enter into fellowship with them.

As an eyewitness to Jesus' ministry, John was qualified to teach the truth about him. The readers of this letter had not seen and heard Jesus themselves, but they could trust that what John wrote was accurate. Believers today are like those second- and third-generation Christians. Though they have not personally seen, heard, or touched Jesus, they have the New Testament record of his eyewitnesses, and they can trust that these eyewitnesses spoke the truth about him.

1:4 Just as the proclamation of the Good News was for others to join the fellowship (1:3), so John was **writing these things** to encourage the readers' participation in both the fellowship and the **joy** that he (John) and the other believers were experiencing. Proclamation produces fellowship; fellowship produces joy. John's joy would be **complete** if his readers remained in the fellowship and did not wander off into false teaching. John, caretaker of the churches and "spiritual father" to many of the believers in and around Ephesus, would only be able to experience "complete joy" if his "children" were experiencing the blessings of fellowship with one another and with God.

In Galatians 5:22, joy is a fruit or by-product of the Holy Spirit's work in believers' lives. Joy also comes as the result of harmonious relationships among believers (Acts 13:52; Philippians 2:2).

LIVING IN THE LIGHT / 1:5–2:6

When Jesus was on earth, his divine life illuminated the inner lives of his followers. Everywhere he was present, he gave light. This light penetrated people—exposing their sin and revealing divine truth. No one could come into contact with Jesus without being enlightened.

1:5 John's message emphasized that **God is light.** Light enables people to do their work. It produces growth in crops; it reveals beauty and provides

safety. Light represents what is good, pure, true, holy, and reliable. Light reveals; light shines. God is so completely "light" that **there is no darkness** in him at all. "Darkness" represents what is sinful and evil. God is untainted by any evil or sin. Thus, "God is light" means that God is perfectly holy and true and that he alone can guide people out of the darkness of sin.

1:6 While "light" has many connotations, this reference points specifically to God's purity. Therefore, those who claim to **have fellowship with God** are living in God's light, trying to live holy and pure lives for him. To claim to belong to God but then to **go on living in spiritual darkness** is hypocritical. In fact, John says that people are **lying.** Christ will expose and judge such deceit.

Here John was confronting the first of three claims (see also 1:8 and 1:10) of the false teachers: that people can have fellowship with God and still walk in sin. False teachers who thought that the physical body was evil or worthless taught one of two approaches to behavior: either they insisted on denying bodily desires through rigid discipline, or they approved of gratifying every physical lust because the body was going to be destroyed anyway. Here John was stating that no one can claim to be a Christian and still live in evil and immorality.

1:7 Those who claim to follow the Son must be **living in the light of God's presence.** They must be illumined by the truth of God's character. To "live in the light" requires constant contact with God and no tolerance for dishonesty, hypocrisy, or sin. **Living in the light** comes from continuous effort to take on Christ's qualities. This involves complete transformation from within.

Living in the light leads to **fellowship with each other.** This fellowship among believers results from each believer's having fellowship with God. True spirituality manifests itself in community fellowship. One cannot say that he or she communes with God and then refuse to commune with God's people. Such was the case with some of the false teachers of John's day, and this situation exists among false cults today. Often their followers and leaders claim to have special relationships with God, but they don't affiliate with other believers. They stay isolated and withdraw from everyone else. John's point is that the natural result of living in the light (in fellowship with God) should be joyful relationships with other Christians.

Another result of living in the light is that **the blood of Jesus, his Son, cleanses us from every sin.** John emphasized that the death of Christ saves people, not the false teachers' knowledge. The verb **cleanses** also means "purifies." Sin is not only forgiven, it is erased. How does Jesus' blood do that? In Old Testament times, believers would symboli-

cally transfer their sins to an animal, which they then would sacrifice (see a description of this ceremony in Leviticus 4). The animal died in their place to pay for their sin and to allow them to continue living in God's favor. God graciously forgave them because of their faith in him and because they obeyed his commandments concerning the sacrifice. Those sacrifices anticipated the day when Christ would completely remove sin. Real cleansing from sin came with Jesus, the "Lamb of God who takes away the sin of the world" (John 1:29).

Those who "live in the light," the true believers, will still find themselves at times in sin. Christians will not be made completely perfect until Jesus returns and brings them into his Kingdom. When they do sin, however, God has already made provision to deal with those sins through the blood of his Son. That provision allows God's people to continue to walk in the light—dealing with sin through confession and receiving his forgiveness so that fellowship with God and with others can remain unhindered.

1:8 John attacked the second claim of the false teachers (see also 1:6 and 1:10): that people could **have no sin.** The false teachers refused to take sin seriously. In saying that they had no sin, they may have been saying that they did not need Jesus' death on the cross. They may have considered that Jesus' death abolished all sin, including the ability to sin. Or, they may have been teaching the false notion that the spirit and body are completely separate and that whatever a person does in the body does not affect the spirit.

John explained that those who believe the possibility of human sinlessness are **fooling** themselves and **refusing to accept the truth** as expressed in God's word. The truth of God's word does not change: people are sinful. Though Jesus condemned sin once for all, Christians still sin.

1:9 Being God's people does not mean denying sin (1:8), but confessing it. Because all people are sinners, Jesus had to die. Because sin is not completely eradicated from the lives of those who believe in Jesus, God graciously gave his followers provision for the problem of sin. John explained it here in a nutshell: **If we confess . . . he is faithful and just to forgive.**

To **confess** our sins means to agree with God that an act or thought was wrong, to acknowledge this to God, to seek forgiveness, and to make a commitment to not let it happen again. Confession of sins is necessary for maintaining continual fellowship with God, which in turn will enable people to have good fellowship with members of the church community.

Confession is supposed to free people to enjoy fellowship with Christ. But some Christians do not understand how it works. They feel so guilty that they confess the same sins over and over; then they wonder if they might have forgotten something. Other Christians believe that God forgives them when they confess, but if they died with unconfessed sins, they would be forever lost. These Christians do not understand that God **wants** to forgive people. He allowed his beloved Son to die just so he could offer them pardon. When people come to Christ, he forgives all the sins they have committed or will ever commit. They don't need to confess the sins of the past all over again, and they don't need to fear that God will reject them if they don't keep their slate perfectly clean. Of course, believers should continue to confess their sins, but not because failure to do so will make them lose their salvation. Believers' relationship with Christ is secure. Instead, they should confess so that they can enjoy maximum fellowship and joy with him.

That God is **faithful** means he is dependable and keeps his promises. God promises forgiveness, even in the Old Testament (Jeremiah 31:34; Micah 7:19-20). God wants to forgive his people; he wants to maintain close fellowship with them. But this can only happen when the way to him is cleared of sin's debris—and that can only happen through confession.

That God is **just** means that he could not overlook people's sin. He could not decide to let people get away with sin or to make the penalty less severe. "The wages of sin is death" (Romans 6:23). Sacrifices had been offered for sin, and blood had been spilt from the beginning. This could not change because God does not change. Justice would have to be done in order to decisively deal with sin. But instead of making people pay for their sins, God took the punishment upon himself through his Son. In this way, justice was done, and the way was paved for God **to forgive us and to cleanse us from every wrong.** Those who confess their sins to God can trust in his forgiveness because they can trust in his character.

1:10 The false teachers not only denied that sin breaks people's fellowship with God (1:6) and that they had a sinful nature (1:8), but some even had the audacity to make a third claim—that they had **not sinned.** These false teachers thought that their superior knowledge had placed them out of the realm of sin, rendering them incapable of sinning. This claim went beyond telling a lie (1:6) or merely fooling themselves (1:8); this claim was **calling God a liar.** God says that all have sinned—otherwise he would not have needed to send his Son. To claim sinlessness treats the Cross with con-

tempt and Christ's suffering as worthless. To do this, said John, shows that God's **word has no place in our hearts.**

John wanted his readers to understand that people who make such a denial of sinful acts do not have the Word of God permeating and changing their lives because the Word of God clearly states throughout that all people sin and all need a Savior (1 Kings 8:46; Psalm 14:3; Isaiah 53:6; 64:6; Romans 3:23; 6:23). People cannot be forgiven if they do not recognize their sin.

2:1 The first step for living in the light (1:5, 7) is to confess sin (1:9). The second step is to forsake all sin (2:1). John emphasized human sinfulness in chapter 1 in order to make his readers despise their sin and try to stay free from it. **So that you will not sin** means that you will try to stay free from sin by avoiding it, refusing it, but then also confessing it when it does happen. Christians will sin because they have not yet been made perfect. John fully understood this. He did not want his readers to take the inevitability of sinning as an excuse to sin. The tension between the phrases "so that you will not sin" and **if you do sin** forms a balance between a too harsh or too lenient view of sin. "Believers have no business sinning," says John, "but when they do sin . . . God has provided a way for them to be cleansed."

When believers sin and then come to the Father for forgiveness, **there is someone to plead for** them **before the Father.** This "one" is **Jesus Christ, the one who pleases God completely.** Christ's righteousness contrasts with humanity's sinfulness. Not only is Jesus the Judge's Son, but he also has already paid the penalty. Because Jesus Christ fulfilled the law and paid sin's penalty for all who believe, he can plead for them on the basis of justice as well as mercy. Believers cannot be punished because someone else has already taken the punishment for them.

2:2 When Jesus Christ speaks to the Father in people's defense (2:1), he doesn't falsely claim that they are innocent. Instead, he maintains that they are guilty of sin but then points out that he has already paid the penalty. Because Jesus Christ **is the sacrifice for our sins** (see also 4:10), he can stand before God as the believers' mediator. His death satisfied the wrath of God against sin and paid the death penalty for it. He took away **not only** the **sins** of John and his fellow believers, but also **the sins of all the world.**

Christ's atoning sacrifice is sufficient for the sins of every person in the world. While Christ's death is sufficient for every sin of every person who ever lived or ever will live, it becomes effectual only for those who confess their sin, accept the sacrifice, and embrace Christ as Lord and Savior. John was not teaching universal salvation—that everyone was saved by Christ whether he or she believed or not. We know this from John's statements in 2:19-23; obviously the antichrists had not found forgiveness and acceptance in Christ.

2:3-4 Up to this point in the letter, John has been warning against the false teachers and those who left the church to follow them. The people who remained in the church, John's readers, may have been wondering, **"How can we be sure that we belong to him?"** In other words, "How can we know that we're Christians?" This passage gives two ways to know: if you do what Christ says and live as Christ wants.

People can know that they belong to Jesus Christ if they are **obeying his commandments.** This letter lists several proofs for how people can know Christ and belong to him. Obedience provides one clear indication. This does not mean that believers must follow a list of rules without one slip, nor does it mean that people must demonstrate obedience before they can come to know God. Instead, obedience comes as the natural out-working of a person's faith and love for the Lord. True believers wholeheartedly accept and submit to God's will as he has revealed it in his Word. If a person claims to **belong to God, but doesn't obey God's commandments,** he or she **is a liar.** Since anyone can claim to know Christ, you can check his or her authenticity by seeing whether or not he or she obeys God's word.

2:5-6 Obedience is linked not merely with knowing God but with loving him. **Those who obey God's word really do love him.** By this obedience and love, believers can **know** that they **live in him.** Jesus portrayed in human terms absolute obedience to the Father. Anyone who wonders how to obey God can look at Jesus. Those who truly desire to **live in God should live their lives as Christ did.** To "live as Christ did" doesn't mean choosing twelve disciples, performing great miracles, and being crucified. People cannot merely copy Christ's life. Much of what Jesus did had to do with his identity as God's Son and his special role in dying for sin. Anyone's claim to live in Christ must be backed up by following his example of complete obedience to God and loving service to people.

1 JOHN 2:7-29

A NEW COMMANDMENT / 2:7-29

Genuine believers not only commit themselves to obeying God (2:3), but they also have deep and sincere love for fellow believers. The Christian principle of love is "new" because believers' ability to love one another is motivated by their love for Christ, who first loved them.

2:7 The commandment **to love one another** is both old and new. For the Jews, the command to love others was as old as the Pentateuch (Leviticus 19:18), and as new as Jesus' words (John 13:34). Thus, John knew that he was **not writing a new commandment** because **it is an old one you have always had.** However, Jesus called the commandment "new" because he interpreted it in a radically new way. The newness of Jesus' command focused on the practice of love.

2:8 Yet this commandment to love **is also new,** because the new commandment to love departs from the old characteristics of the law with its emphasis on outward conformity to certain regulations.

The commandment to love one another **is true** in Christ and is true among the believers. The command to love first reached its truest and fullest expression in the life of the Lord Jesus Christ. He demonstrated true love by coming into the world and giving his life for all who believe. Thus the command should also be true in you— that is, in all who claim to follow Christ.

Although **the true light is already shining** and the darkness has not passed away completely, **the darkness is disappearing** slowly but surely. Thanks to the victory of Christ, the outcome of the conflict between light and darkness is a foregone conclusion. The conflict continues, however. But like the first rays of sun at dawn slowly but steadily piercing the darkness, so the **true light** experienced and shared by Christians is growing.

2:9 These next few verses highlight the absolute contrast drawn between light and darkness, love and hate, God and the world. The two contrasts cannot coexist. This verse teaches that a person who claims to be **in the light** (1:7) should then, by extension, also be filled with love (2:7-8). If that person makes this claim **but hates a Christian brother or sister,** then the claim to be in the light is false. That person **is still in darkness.** Living in love is living in the light, since the gospel both illuminates people's minds and warms their hearts to love (see 4:20). Love should be the unifying force and the identifying mark of the Christian community. Love is the key to walking in the light, because believers cannot grow spiritually while they hate others.

2:10-11 As the opposite to 2:9, verse 10 explains that actions reveal faith: **anyone who loves other Christians is walking in the light.** There is nothing in such a person to make him or her, or **anyone** else, **stumble.** In contrast, people who claim to be Christians yet hate **a Christian brother or sister** are not grounded in the truth, as seen by their actions. They **are walking in darkness.** In the context of this letter, those who hated other Christians probably referred to the false teachers and their followers who had left the fellowship of the church and thereby had rejected John and the other true Christians. They claimed to love God, but they hated other children of God. "Believers" who hate are in darkness and not light, in sin and not in fellowship with God. They are **lost, having been blinded by the darkness** (see also 2 Peter 1:9). To hate, then, is to choose the darkness and to shut oneself off from the light. To hate is to separate oneself from the presence of God and from the fellowship of other believers.

2:12 The next three verses contain two sets of triplets that describe John's readers as children (2:12), mature ones (2:13), and young (2:13). The term **dear children** refers not to age, but was a term of endearment that John used for all those to whom he was writing. Christ used the same words when speaking to his disciples (John 13:33). Many had come to Jesus through John's ministry, so he called them his own "children." These true followers had in common the fact that their **sins** were **forgiven because of Jesus.** They had accepted the fact of their sinfulness, had confessed their sins, and had been forgiven because of Jesus' death on the cross.

2:13 Described as **mature** in their faith, these believers **know Christ, the one who is from the beginning.** They have longtime experience with their faith and have knowledge befitting their maturity. Described as **young** people, the term

pictures action: **you have won your battle with Satan.** Christians must understand that they are in a war zone and that they are constantly at battle with the forces of Satan. In conquering the false teachers, they had defeated Satan (see 1 Timothy 4:1-2; 2 Timothy 2:24-26 for Paul's view on how Satan enters into false teaching). The use of the past tense, "have won," shows a battle won, although the war will not end until Jesus Christ returns. Because Christ has already defeated Satan, all Christians can go into the battle knowing that they are on the winning side (see Romans 8:31-39; Ephesians 6:10-18; Colossians 2:15).

2:14 This verse repeats the message of 2:13 to fathers and then amplifies the message to young people. The overlap of the advice can be seen here where John wrote to **you, children, because you have known the Father.** The phrase refers to experiential knowledge. All Christians ought to have personal knowledge of God the Father through Jesus Christ his Son; otherwise, they cannot be believers. The **mature** believers **know Christ, the one who is from the beginning.** They have grasped that Christ is eternal, thus are not swayed by the false teachers. To the **young** people, John wrote that they **are strong with God's word living in** them, and he repeated that they **have won** their **battle with Satan.** This strength is not the natural physical vigor of young people but the power of God's Word in them through the Holy Spirit.

2:15 Believers must love God (2:5) and love their brothers and sisters in Christ (2:10), but they must **stop loving this evil world and all that it offers.** John was writing to those in the church who had remained true to their faith. They had withstood false teaching and had remained unified together with other believers. But John warned against a secret spiritual danger that could still threaten them. The "world," as used here, refers to the realm of Satan's influence, the system made up of those who hate God and his will. Believers should love the people of the world enough to share God's message with them, but they should not love the morally corrupt system in place in the world. Satan controls this evil world. His world opposes God and his followers and tempts those followers away from God and into sin (see James 4:4).

John wanted to show his readers that to attempt to love both God and the world would be as impossible as trying to combine light and darkness (1:5). Therefore, **when you love the world, you show that you do not have the love of the Father in you.** These words do not mean that believers are to remove themselves from all contact with the sinful world (that would be virtually impossible), nor are they to stoically refrain from anything pleasurable. They do mean that when contact with the sinful world and its worldly pleasures specifically disagrees with God's word, then Christians are to turn away from "the world" in order to obey God.

2:16 John warned his readers against loving the world and all that it offers (2:15) because what **the world offers** is **not from the Father.** Jesus made clear this tension when he said, The "world" here, as in 2:15, is the present evil system that is ruled by Satan and opposed to God. This "world" has rebelled and fallen into sin. Nothing in this world system loves the Father or finds its source in him.

John placed what **the world offers** into three basic categories. These three categories are subjective, for they speak of attitudes of the heart. Believers may look perfectly clean and serene on the outside but harbor any or all of these attitudes inside. John feared that this might happen, so he was warning the believers to restrain such desires.

- **The lust for physical pleasure.** Jesus spoke of how adultery begins not with the act, but with the desire (Matthew 5:28). These words picture any kind of desire but especially the craze for sex. No doubt the people of ancient Ephesus understood this—the pagan religions of their city glorified sex. The world today has many similarities. Sex in all of its immoral and grotesque forms is splashed throughout movies, television, magazines, and computer screens. This appeals to the sinful nature. While this category seems to refer mostly to sexual lust, it could include any sort of selfish or greedy cravings simply to satisfy one's physical desires in rebellion against God.

- **The lust for everything we see.** Sins of craving and accumulating possessions (bowing to the god of materialism) could be placed in this category. While sex may also be included here, people's "eyes" can lust after many things. Believers must not become obsessed with what they see.

- **Pride in our possessions.** This refers to both the inward attitude and the outward boasting because of an obsession with one's status or possessions.

All three categories show selfishness and greed. Yet these sins, so subtle as to begin almost unnoticed within the heart, become the temptations that lead to the sin's outworkings in people's lives.

2:17 The people who live in rebellion to God with their transient, unfulfilling desires (2:16) are focusing on a world that is already **fading away.** The workaholic will die unfulfilled. The greedy politi

cian will die in despair. The pleasure-mad partygoers will find their lives ruined by drugs or alcohol. Indulgence never satisfies; it only whets the appetite for more. Christians, however, understand that the world will not last forever and that no one lives on this planet forever. Because they are believers who **do the will of God,** however, they **will live forever.** To turn away from the sinful world and hold on to God means to hold on to the eternal. Those who trust in God have already begun a life everlasting.

2:18 The term **last hour** is used only here in the New Testament. It refers to the "last days" or the "end times"—the time between Christ's first and second comings (see Joel 2:28; Micah 4:1). The first-century readers of 1 Peter lived in the "last days," and so do believers today. The word **last** also gives a sense of urgency. Christ will return soon.

You have heard (referring to the teachings from the apostles) **that the Antichrist is coming.** (Paul wrote about this in 2 Thessalonians 2:3-10.) John mentioned this not so that believers would try to identify the person, but so that they might be ready for anything that would threaten their faith.

Besides, as John went on, already such persons who could fit that description have come on the scene—**already many such antichrists have appeared.** From the earliest days of the church in and around Ephesus, false teachers had been a problem. When Paul bid his final farewell to the elders of the Ephesian church, he warned, "I know full well that false teachers, like vicious wolves, will come in among you" (Acts 20:29). These are merely precursors to the one Antichrist. Throughout history there have been individuals who epitomized evil and who were hostile to everything for which Christ stands. These antichrists have lived in every generation and will continue to work their evil. There are many cult leaders today who, through their teachings, draw people away from true faith. Then just before Christ's second coming, a completely evil man will arise. He will be Satan's tool, equipped with Satan's power (2 Thessalonians 2:9). This man will be *the* Antichrist. These other "antichrists" are the false teachers who deny (1) that Jesus is the Christ (2:22), (2) that Jesus is God's Son (2:23), and (3) that Jesus was God incarnate in human form (4:2; 2 John 1:7). They are liars and deceivers. Jesus warned about them in Matthew 24:24.

During this "last hour," these antichrists—these false teachers who pretend to be Christians and who lure weak members away from Christ—will continue to be active, just as they were in John's day. Believers must be grounded in God's word. They must teach the truth clearly and carefully to the peripheral, weak members among them in the church so that they won't fall prey to these teachers.

2:19 These false teachers, these antichrists, were not total strangers to the churches; they had been part of the church community, in fellowship with John and the other believers. Then **these people left the churches** and evidently became promoters of false teachings about Jesus (see 4:1; 2 John 7). When their teachings were not accepted by the Christians or by those in leadership, they left. John explained that **they never really belonged** among the Christians in the first place. When the false teachers left, they **proved** that they were never true believers. If they had been true believers, John stated, **they would have stayed.**

All who attend church may not be true believers. The true believers may not now be able to discern the false believers, but they may in time. It may happen when some leave the churches and the teachings of Christ, proving that they never belonged. Or it may not happen until the Day of Judgment when Christ will separate his true followers from those who never belonged.

2:20 John faced the false believers head-on by telling the true believers that **the Holy Spirit has come upon** them and they **know the truth.** The Holy Spirit has been given to believers by the Father and the Son and promised by Jesus (John 14:16-17; 15:26 16:13). When a person becomes a Christian, he or she receives the Holy Spirit (2 Corinthians 1:21-22). John compared the believers with the ones who had left the fellowship and thus proved that they never belonged there. They did not receive Jesus Christ as Savior, so they did not receive the Holy Spirit. They did not know the truth, even though they may have claimed special wisdom and insight. Christians can withstand false teachers' attacks by relying on the Holy Spirit's help (see 2:27).

2:21 Those with the Holy Spirit (2:20) not only know the truth about the Father and the Son but can also detect **the difference between truth and falsehood.** John wrote, not giving them further teaching; the false teachers were attempting to do that. Instead, he was reaffirming the truth that had already been taught to them and that they had believed.

2:22 The great truth is that Jesus is the Christ, the Son of God, who came in the flesh to die for sin. To deny this amounts to blatant heresy—John battled this as the central focus of the false teaching. A man named Cerinthus, an avowed enemy of the apostle John, said that **Jesus is not the Christ.** He spoke of "Jesus" and "the Christ" as two separate beings who were united only from the time of Jesus' baptism to the time of his crucifixion. Cerinthus taught that "the Christ" left Jesus at the Crucifixion. In other words, Jesus was no more than a mere man who, for a time, had been given divine power. Anyone who would teach this heresy, said John, **is the great liar. Such people are antichrists, for they have denied the Father and the Son.** They are believing a lie, and lies are from Satan (John 8:42-44).

2:23 Apparently, the antichrists in John's day were claiming faith in God while denying and opposing the Son. To do so, John firmly stated, is impossible. Because Jesus is God's Son and the Messiah, **anyone who denies the Son doesn't have the Father either.** Many cultists today call themselves Christians, but they deny the deity of Jesus Christ. Some churches, such as the Unitarian church, deny the unique status of Christ as the Son of God.

John reiterated that no one can claim to have special knowledge of God while denying Jesus Christ's deity and humanity. In both his Gospel and his letters, John made it very clear that the Father can be known only through the Son (John 3:11; 5:37; 6:46; 8:16, 29, 38; 16:32). Three times Jesus announced that he and the Father were one (John 10:30, 38; 14:9-10; 17:21). Denying Jesus means denying God, then the converse is also true: **anyone who confesses the Son has the Father also.** The disciples, however, found it difficult to conceptualize the Father about whom Jesus so often talked. During his last discourse with his disciples, Jesus again spoke of the Father. Exasperated, Philip blurted out, "Lord, show us the Father and we will be satisfied" (John 14:8). Jesus told Philip, "Anyone who has seen me has seen the Father!" The Son was and has always been the image of the invisible God (2 Corinthians 4:4; Colossians 1:15; Hebrews 1:3).

2:24-25 Many of these Christians had heard the gospel message from John himself. They knew that Christ was God's Son, that he had died for their sins, that he had been raised to give them new life, and that he would return and establish his Kingdom in its fullness. But their fellowship was being infiltrated by teachers who were denying these basic doctrines of the Christian faith, and some of the believers were in danger of succumbing to false arguments. John encouraged them to **remain faithful to what** they had **been taught from the beginning**—to hold on to the Christian truth that had changed their lives. If the believers resisted the lies of the antichrists, they would **continue to live in fellowship with the Son and with the Father.** By clinging to the truth about God the Father and

Christ his Son, believers can be sure they will never be separated from fellowship with God. That fellowship will literally continue forever, for Jesus **promised** that his followers would be given **eternal life.** John recorded many of these promises in his Gospel (John 3:14-15, 36; 6:40, 47, 57; 17:2-3). The believers understood the character of the one who made these promises and could trust that he would fulfill them.

2:26 As in 2:12-14 and 2:21, John took pains to clarify his purpose in writing and to affirm the practical import of his teachings. The false teachers were trying to lead people into error, away from the basic gospel that had been taught in the beginning. John wrote as he did because the Christians needed to **be aware of those who want to lead them astray.** To move away from the basic teachings into various sidelines that contradict those basics is to be "led astray" into heresy. These false teachers not only left the faith and the fellowship, but they wanted to lead others astray as well.

2:27 The true believers had **received the Holy Spirit** and he lived **within** them. This means that believers can place their total trust in him, rely on him for guidance and strength, and live as he directs. It implies a personal, life-giving relationship. The same idea is in John 15:5, in Jesus' words about his being the vine and his followers the branches (see also 1 Peter 3:24; 4:15).

You don't need anyone to teach you means that Christians can tell the lying antichrists, "We do not need another teacher because the Holy Spirit, the Spirit of truth, teaches us, so we will **continue in what he has taught** us, and **continue to live in Christ.**" This does not mean that Christians should turn away from the counsel of faithful ministers and attempt to make it on their own—in

fact, that often will lead them astray. Instead, it means that Christians can discern truth and reject falsehood. The better believers know the truth, the more easily they will be able to identify a lie.

The fact that the Spirit **teaches all things** refers to the basic gospel truths essential for salvation. This does not mean that all believers will know and understand everything, nor does it mean that the Spirit will add new revelation to what has already been taught. Instead, through the Spirit, believers know enough to keep them from throwing away their faith in Christ and believing the lies of the false teachers.

2:28 John was so anxious for the believers' spiritual lives that he said over and over that they should **continue to live in fellowship with Christ.** Although believers already have fellowship with Christ through his indwelling Spirit, a time is coming when they will see him face-to-face in all his glory (3:2). Those who have continued in him will **be full of courage and not shrink back from him in shame** when **he returns** at his second coming. Persevering in their relationship with Christ ensures that believers will remain in the true faith. Continuing in the faith keeps them truly ready for Christ's return.

2:29 Believers know that **God is always right.** If a person's actions demonstrate his or her allegiance, then **all who do what is right are his children.** People do not become children of God by doing right; instead, doing right is a sign that people have already become God's children. Because true faith always results in good deeds, those who claim to have faith *and* who consistently do right are true believers. Good deeds cannot produce salvation (see Ephesians 2:8-9), but they are necessary proof that true faith is actually present (James 2:14-17).

1 JOHN 3

LIVING AS CHILDREN OF GOD / 3:1-10

Verse 1 tells Christians who they are—members of God's family—his children. Verse 2 tells them who they are becoming—reflections of God. The rest of the chapter tells what believers have as they grow to resemble God: (1) victory over sin (3:4-9); (2) love for others (3:10-18); and (3) confidence before God (3:19-24).

3:1 John's statement at the end of chapter 2 that believers are God's children caused him to marvel at **how very much** God **loves us** that he would

allow **us to be called his children.** Great as he is, God has brought believers into the loving, intimate relationship of children with their Father. John was emphasizing the assurance believers can have that they **really are** God's children.

But being God's children separates them from the world. The world does not desire to know God, and it even refused to recognize Christ as God's Son (John 1:10; 15:18-19), so believers can hardly expect the **world** to **understand** their special relationship with God as his children.

3:2 Not sometime in the future, not when Christ returns, but **already** believers are **God's children.** Yet God's people have a future, as John further explained that **we can't even imagine what we will be like when Christ returns.** Christians have been born into God's family, and they presently enjoy God's kindness and blessings through Christ. But in the future they will also fully share in his glory. Believers don't yet know the specifics, but they **do know that when he comes** they **will be like him.** This hints of what this future glory will be like. Christ will be revealed and his people will be like him, for they **will see him as he really is.** The Greek word for "see" involves more than a merely physiological occurrence; it means "perceiving," "recognizing," even "appreciating." In order for people to truly know each other—to see each other as they really are—they have to share similar experiences. Therefore, in order to see Jesus as he really is, Christians must experience the power of his resurrection and the fellowship of his sufferings. This was Paul's aspiration (see Philippians 3:7-14); it was also John's, as expressed in the following verse.

3:3 Because Jesus Christ lived without sin (he was **pure**), believers **will keep themselves pure.** To be pure means to be morally and ethically free from the corruption of sin. This is an ongoing cleansing process, beginning at rebirth and continuing until the day Jesus returns. The more pure his people become, the clearer will be their view of Jesus, who is pure through and through. God also purifies Christians, but they must take steps to remain morally fit (see 1 Timothy 5:22; James 4:8; 1 Peter 1:22).

3:4 After defining purity, John next defined sin, presenting negatively the same truth he just expressed positively in 3:1-3. Since being born of God demands self-purification, then a life of sin, or a continual lack of purity, demonstrates that one cannot really be God's child. Sin cannot coexist with the new nature derived from the new birth. **Sin is opposed to the law of God.** Those who keep on sinning are active rebels against God.

There is a difference between committing a sin and continuing to sin. Even the most faithful believers sometimes commit sins, but they do not cherish a particular sin and choose to commit it. A believer who commits a sin repents, confesses, and finds forgiveness. Those who continue to sin, by contrast, will not repent of what they are doing. Thus, they never confess and never receive forgiveness. They live in opposition to God, no matter what religious claims they make.

3:5 Besides the fact that sin is rebellion against God, another reason that Christians should not sin is because **Jesus came to take away** their **sins.** In other words, to know of such a sacrifice and then to keep on sinning depreciates that sacrifice. The reason Jesus came to earth was to take away people's sins. This could only happen because **there is no sin in him,** so he could provide a suitable sacrifice. Under the Old Testament sacrifice system, Jews offered a lamb without blemish as a sacrifice for sin. Jesus is "the Lamb of God who takes away the sin of the world" (John 1:29). Because Jesus lived a perfect life and sacrificed himself for sin, people can be completely forgiven (2:2). Only he could bridge the gap between the sinless God and sinful people. Jesus died on the cross in our place, taking all our wrongdoing upon himself, saving us from the ultimate consequences of our sin—eternal judgment. Because Jesus still lives and still has no sin in him, it follows that he is totally opposed to sin. It also follows, then, that those who claim to be his people must be totally opposed to sin.

3:6 Those who **continue to live in** Christ **won't sin.** The Greek word behind "continue to live" is the same verb John used in his Gospel about the branches continuing to live in the vine (John 15:1-8). As a branch lives in the vine, it draws its life from the vine. As believers live in Christ, they are free from the power of sin. Living in sin and living in God are mutually exclusive, like darkness and light.

John was confronting various types of false teachers. Some taught that they were sinless, actually unable to sin. They claimed superiority over everyone else. These teachings are refuted in 1:8-10. To this group, John explained that while Christians should indeed be "sinless," it was not the kind of sinlessness that the false teachers claimed to have. Experience bears out the fact that sin is still very much in every believer's life (see 1:7; 2:1). Yet believers can stop living a life of sin through sensitivity to sin when it occurs, sincere repentance from sin, and acceptance of forgiveness from the one who already took the punishment.

Some claimed to have a special relationship with God despite their sinful conduct. They assumed that their behavior did not matter to God. These teachings are refuted in 1:5-7 and 2:1-6. To this second group of false teachers, John explained that sin was indeed very important to God. In fact, to keep sinning proves that they did not "live in God" at all: **those who keep on sinning have never known him or understood who he is.** Christians seek to remain "sinless" in God's eyes by continually confessing sin to God and repenting of it. But they do not **keep on sinning,** meaning that they do not impose upon God's forgiveness by taking it for granted in order to keep on living as they please. When they repent of sin, they truly desire to remain free of that sin.

3:7 Apparently, the false teachers who were denying the doctrine of Christ (2:22) were also claiming that they knew God, yet they were living unrighteous lives (see 1:6). John warned his **dear children** not to **let anyone deceive** them **about this: When people do what is right, it is because they are righteous, even as Christ is righteous.** Believers' righteousness is given to them by Christ and naturally leads to doing righteous acts. In the same way, a tree that bears good fruit is a good tree. The fruit doesn't make the tree good; it shows that it is good.

3:8 Satan is the founder of lawless rebellion against God. Therefore, **when people keep on sinning, it shows they belong to the Devil.** The Devil **has been sinning since the beginning**— even before the creation of the world. Since then, as the prince of this world, he has been both sinning and causing people to sin. The false teachers who spoke lies and sinned without remorse showed that they belonged to the Devil himself (see 2:22). Those who followed these teachers were aligning themselves with the Devil and thus fighting against Christ.

There is a cure for sin, however, because **the Son of God came to destroy these works of the Devil.** The Greek word behind "destroy" does not mean

to annihilate; rather, it means "to break down" (see Ephesians 2:14), "to undo," "to render ineffective." Though it would have made more sense, humanly speaking, for Christ to have obliterated Satan, he didn't. Instead, Christ came to undo Satan's work and thereby free people from sin and all its awful consequences. John was therefore arguing that Christians cannot be involved in what Christ came to destroy.

3:9 At first glance, these words appear to completely contradict what John said earlier: "If we say we have no sin, we are only fooling ourselves" (1:8). This passage states that **those who have been born into God's family do not sin . . . they can't keep on sinning, because they have been born of God.** So, do Christians sin or don't they?

Experience tells every Christian that sin still has its hold. For true believers, however, deep inside their spirits, they aspire not to sin. This aspiration comes from the life of God within them. When they were "born again," a new life was born inside (2 Corinthians 5:17). Christians have this new life—**God's life is in them.** They desire not to sin, and they fully renounce sin because sin is entirely incompatible with their new life. Although, at times, they may give in to sin, they are continually fighting against it. Sin is still active, but it no longer has complete control over them. The Holy Spirit works, through the Word of God, to set his people apart from sin—to make them holy and pure, as Christ is (3:3). (See also 5:18.)

3:10 John spoke in absolutes; he offered no middle ground: a person belongs either to God or to the Devil. The conclusion of the matter is that believers **can tell who are children of God and who are children of the Devil.** The way to tell the "pretenders" is to see whether they **obey God's commands** (see also 2:3-5) and whether they **love other Christians** (see also 2:7-11).

LOVE ONE ANOTHER / 3:11-24

God's children must be loving, yet many fail to love. So often today there is deep dislike among Christians. Churches struggle with issues that divide the members. All churches need to work on love and harmony. Jesus wanted his followers to be unified as a powerful witness to the reality of God's love. Believers must help to unify their churches. They can pray for other Christians, avoid gossip, build others up, work together in humility, give their time and money, exalt Christ, and refuse to get involved in divisive matters.

3:11 This comes not as a command, as in the old system of the law, but as an announcement of something good. The **message** announced from God requires believers to **love** their brothers and sisters in

God's family. The **beginning** refers to the time Jesus first told his disciples to love one another (see John 13:34-35; 15:17) and to the time John's audience first became believers (see also commentary on 2:7).

3:12 Cain and Abel were Adam and Eve's first two sons. Abel offered a sacrifice that pleased God, while Cain's sacrifice was unacceptable (Genesis 4:1-16; Hebrews 11:4). Cain brought grain and fruits for his offering, while Abel brought an animal from his flock. Abel's sacrifice (an animal substitute) was more acceptable to God, both because it was a blood sacrifice and, most important, because of Abel's attitude when he offered it. After Cain's sacrifice was rejected, God gave him the chance to right his wrong and try again. God even encouraged him to do so. But Cain refused, and his jealous anger drove him to murder. **And why did he kill his brother? Because Cain had been doing what was evil, and his brother had been doing what was right.** John's point was not that Cain murdered and became a child of the Devil; rather, because Cain **belonged to the evil one,** his anger and jealousy drove him to murder (see also John 8:44). John wanted his readers to understand the terrible results of refusing to love one another (3:11). Lack of love can lead to anger, jealousy, hatred— and, finally, even to murder.

3:13 After telling the disciples to love one another, John added, **don't be surprised . . . if the world hates you** (see also John 15:18-19). The world is hostile to God (2:15). Jesus wants his followers to be distinctive; he sets them apart from the world. Their very separation, however, arouses unbelievers' animosity. When people become Christians, sometimes their lives change drastically. This was especially true for first-century believers who had come out of the morally corrupt pagan world— John's readers lived in Ephesus. Former pagans would have been involved in many evil activities. After becoming believers, however, they no longer wanted to be involved in such things. As Cain did with Abel, unbelievers reacted in hostility, often because they wanted to justify their own actions or silence their consciences. When a person stands aside from certain activities, it makes the others think—and often they don't like that.

3:14 The world may hate Christians, but Christians must express love for one another. Love for fellow believers proves that a believer has **passed from** the realm of **death** to the sphere of **eternal life** (see John 5:24). Their love does not earn them eternal life; instead, their love is evidence that they already have eternal life (see also 2:10). Christians must ask whether they have this love; if they do, then they can be sure that they have eternal life and that this will be publicly revealed when Christ comes.

By contrast, **a person who has no love is still dead.** This is the condition of all people by nature.

A person who does not have love shows that he or she has not **passed from death to eternal life.**

3:15 If a heart is empty of love, hate fills in the void (3:14). If a person hates someone, it is like wishing that the other were dead, and the Lord sees the inner desire as equal to the outward act that would result from it (see Matthew 5:21-22). Therefore, **anyone who hates another Christian is really a murderer at heart.**

3:16 To understand real love, believers need only to look at their Lord for the example. They can **know what real love is because Christ gave up his life** for all people. Christ's example shows believers that real love involves self-sacrifice, which, as 3:17-19 points out, must result in self-sacrificial actions.

Because Christ is the example, believers **ought to give up their lives for their Christian brothers and sisters.** They do this by becoming truly concerned about the needs of their Christian brothers and sisters and by unselfishly giving time, effort, prayer, and possessions to supply those needs. Such an attitude would result in actually dying for a brother or sister if this were ever necessary. Believers' own lives should not be more precious to them than God's own Son was to him.

3:17-18 These verses give an example of how believers can lay down their lives for others—to help those in need with their worldly goods. Seldom will believers be called upon to experience martyrdom for another. However, every day they will face needy people whom they ought to be willing to help if they have the resources to do so; most people have more than they need. This parallels James's teaching (James 2:14-17): Believers should be willing to help a **brother or sister in need.** Talk is cheap, so **just saying we love each other** is not enough. Faith not accompanied by love for others is worthless. Love should be shown by **actions.**

3:19-20 As Christians proceed in their lives with Christ, it will happen that their **hearts** will **condemn** them. Whatever the source—an overactive conscience, the realization that they don't love others enough, or even Satan's false accusations— they will feel the accusation. Whenever this happens, they can look at how they are living out their faith by their **actions** and thus can **know** that they are **living in the truth.** In this context, the basis for their assurance is the good works that they do. Believers can **be confident** in God's presence by reminding themselves that God's love has been active in their lives as they have helped others.

The ambiguity of the statement **for God is greater than our hearts** has prompted two interpretations.

Some see it as consoling believers whose hearts (or consciences) condemn them of sin in general. They can hold on to the sign of sonship—God's love. Others think that the phrase intensifies John's warning. The condemning voice of conscience merely echoes the judgment of God, who knows each life. Thus, believers cannot gloss over or excuse their sins as insignificant. In both cases, by claiming God's forgiveness through Christ, believers can come confidently to God, recognizing that his grace and mercy are greater than their guilt. Because God **knows everything,** Christians can trust that he thoroughly understands and will forgive their sins and help them grow in the areas where they need it most.

Then what should believers do with the gnawing accusations of their consciences? They should not ignore them or rationalize their behavior, but they should set their hearts on God's love. When they feel guilty, they should remind themselves that God knows their motives as well as their actions. His voice of assurance is stronger than the accusing voice of conscience. God will not condemn his children, for whom his Son died (Romans 8:1; Hebrews 9:14-15).

3:21-22 John's readers knew Christ's commands and could test themselves by them. If their **conscience is clear,** they **can come to God** without fear and **with bold confidence.** When believers approach God, they can trust that they **will receive whatever** they **request because** they **obey him and do the things that please him.** This statement follows what Jesus said in his final discourse to his disciples, as recorded in John 15:7: "But if you stay joined to me and my words remain in you, you may ask any request you like, and it will be granted." When a believer is remaining in Christ and Christ's words are remaining in the believer, his or her prayers will be answered. This does not

mean that all requests are granted; the context of John 15 suggests that the prayers should pertain to fruit bearing and glorifying the Father. The same holds true for John's statement, **we will receive whatever we request.** Believers' requests will be honored by God when they are focused on accomplishing God's will.

3:23 John has been expressing exactly what Jesus had said. This had also been **his commandment—** which is one commandment expressed in two parts. There are not two separate commands, but one, since faith and love cannot be separated. Believers must **believe in the name of his Son, Jesus Christ** and **love one another.** They cannot love one another without having faith in Christ or truly believe in him without having love for other believers.

3:24 God and the believers live in one another. The presence of the Spirit in each believer's life makes this possible. The Christian lives in the Spirit, and the Spirit lives in the Christian. The best analogy is a human being's relationship to air. People must live "in" the air so that the air can come into them.

The indwelling Spirit provides believers with the presence of the indwelling Christ. That the **Holy Spirit lives in** people means that Christ lives in them (see Romans 8:9-11). When Christ gave his Spirit to live in Christians, he gave himself to live in them (see John 14:16-20; 1 Corinthians 15:45; 2 Corinthians 3:17-18).

The mutual relationship—believers living in Christ as he lives in them—shows itself in Christians who keep these three essential commands: (1) believe in Christ, (2) love the brothers and sisters, and (3) live morally upright lives. The Spirit's presence is not only spiritual and mystical, but it is also practical. Believers' conduct verifies his presence.

1 JOHN 4

DISCERNING FALSE PROPHETS / 4:1-6

Those who have the Holy Spirit within (3:24) have the ability to discern the truth from error because the anointing of the Spirit teaches them about these things. The doctrinal test is outlined in this paragraph. Those who have the Spirit of God confess that Jesus, God's Son, has come in bodily form. In other words, they acknowledge the full reality of the Incarnation. False prophets who deny these basic truths are antichrists. In analyzing the wide spectrum of teachers and books on spirituality available today, the test should be: What do they teach about the person of Jesus Christ?

4:1 The **test** believers are to use is given in 4:2-3. The responsibility for testing the spirits rests not merely on scholars or church leaders but on every Christian. **Do not believe everyone who claims to speak by the Spirit** means that the believers should not believe everything they hear just because someone says it is a message from God. They should test the message to see if it is truly from the Lord. One way is to check to see if it matches God's word, the Bible. Other tests include the teachers' commitment to the body of believers (2:19), their lifestyles (3:23-24), and the fruit of their ministries (4:6). The most important test of all, however, is what they believe about Christ (4:2). Do they teach that Jesus is fully God and fully man? The first-century world was filled with **many false prophets** who were claiming to speak for God. The believers needed to apply these tests in order to discern truth from error.

The term "false prophets" is another name for the many antichrists (see 2:18-19). Whereas a true prophet is one who receives direct revelation from God, a false prophet only claims to have received direct revelation from God, but has not. The test is similar to that administered to false prophets in Deuteronomy 13:1-5; 18:15-22.

4:2 To know that a prophet has **the Spirit of God,** that is, if his message is truth from God, we must discover if he **acknowledges that Jesus Christ became a human being.** A true teacher of God believes that Jesus of Nazareth as revealed in the Gospels is the Messiah of God, God's only and unique incarnation of himself. A true teacher must also teach that Jesus became a man with a human body. God the Son is forever fully God and fully man, though in immortal, incorruptible flesh. A teacher who denies Jesus' full and true humanity proves that he is not from God.

4:3 The false prophets claimed to speak by the Spirit's inspiration. In this context, refusing to **acknowledge Jesus** means denying Jesus' true person as both God and man. Those who do that are **not from God.** Therefore, there is only one other source: the spirit operating in the false prophets is **the spirit of the Antichrist** (2:18), the spirit of deception (4:6). Pronouncements about false teachers, false messiahs, and the coming of the Antichrist should not have been news to Christians, for they had heard that these people were coming. Jesus had warned the disciples (Matthew 24:15, 24-26); the apostles, in turn, had warned the believers about false teaching (see 2 Thessalonians 2:3-12; 2 Peter 3:3-7).

The spirit of the Antichrist **is already here** refers to the hostile attitude of those who were denying

that Christ had already been present. John does not seem to have been saying that the final Antichrist had come (see 2:18). As Paul wrote in 2 Thessalonians 2:7-8, the man of lawlessness has not yet been revealed, but his spirit is at work.

4:4 In contrast to those who are against God, John reassured his readers that they **belong to God.** Though these believers may have been feeling weak and confused, they had remained true to the faith and so had **already won** their **fight with these false prophets.** They had not been won over to the false point of view, nor had they abandoned the church. Christians don't have to overpower false teachers to conquer them; rather, they can overcome false teachers and their teachings by recognizing them and then refusing to follow them. These believers had already done this; they had not succumbed to the false teachers. They had done this by the power of God's Spirit within them, **because the Spirit who lives in you is greater than the spirit who lives in the world** (referring to the Devil who inspires false prophets in their work of deception, see also 1 Timothy 4:1).

Some Christians want to do this spiritual battle as individuals. They take the word **you** as "the Spirit who lives in **me.**" But the pronoun is plural, thus referring to the community of believers. Believers do have personal assurance of the Holy Spirit's presence within. But they must not attempt to do battle against Satan alone. They need others for prayer, resources, advice, guidance, protection, healing, and more.

4:5 These people are the false prophets who **belong to this world** and not to God. In John's Gospel and letters, the term **world** describes the world system of beliefs and the community of those who stand in opposition to God (see 4:3). The false teachers, being a part of the world system, **speak from the world's viewpoint** and so find acceptance by the world that **listens to them.** False teachers are popular with the world because, like the false prophets of the Old Testament, they tell people what they want to hear. John warned that Christians who faithfully teach God's word will not win popularity contests in the world. People don't want to hear their sins denounced; they don't want to listen to demands that they change their behavior. A false teacher will be well received by non-Christians.

4:6 The **we** primarily refers to the apostles, who were the first true teachers of Christ, followed by many others who taught the truth of the gospel. The world gladly accepts and listens to false teachers, but the apostles found another audience— **those who know God** or were open to knowing

God. The world, or those who **do not belong to God,** rejected the apostles' message.

This provides another way to determine who has **the Spirit of truth or the spirit of deception.** According to the Gospel of John (John 14:17, 26; 15:26; 16:13-15), the **Spirit of truth** is the Holy Spirit, who proceeds from God and teaches the truth about Christ (see also 1 Peter 2:20, 27). All who are indwelt by the Spirit of truth and anointed by the Spirit can know the truth; God did not reserve that truth for only a special few. **The spirit of deception** comes from Satan, the "father of lies" (John 8:44), and leads people into error. Believers can distinguish between these "spirits" by the character and message of the one speaking.

LOVING ONE ANOTHER / 4:7-21

This epistle continues with love as a major theme: Love among Christians demonstrates love *for* God and love *from* God, for God is love. That love was demonstrated unmistakably by Jesus. The response of the children of God, then, should be to love one another, to the end that God's love may be perfected (reach its designated goal) in them. In this paragraph, being born of God, loving God, and knowing God are inextricably intertwined.

4:7-8 John repeated his call to Christians to **continue to love one another** (see also 3:10-18, 23). God is the source of all love; therefore, **love comes from God.** Jesus Christ, sent from God the Father, embodied love and demonstrated that love in his life on earth. Such love does not come naturally for humans. We are not born with it, neither can we learn it. Believers receive God's love only through the Holy Spirit.

The phrase **anyone who loves is born of God** does not trivialize the relationship with God as given to anyone who simply knows how to "love." Only those who have experienced the new birth are able to have the love described here. Those who have received this gift are endowed with the nature of God and thereby become partakers of the divine love. Love for fellow Christians provides proof of spiritual birth and relationship with God.

In addition, John says, anyone who loves **knows God.** This speaks of an ongoing knowledge—"getting to know" God—a continual, growing, spiritual knowledge based on actual experience of God in believers' lives. It follows, then, that a person **who does not love** other Christians has never known God. The Greek verb for "know" is in the aorist tense, thereby indicating that this person not only doesn't know God now but has never known him.

The statement **God is love** ought not be turned around to say "Love is God" or watered down to "God is loving," as if this were just one of God's attributes. Rather, love is God's very essence. It is not one of God's many activities; instead, all of his activities are imbued with love. When he disciplines or teaches, for example, he does so with love. And conversely, because he loves, he disciplines and teaches. Because he is love, he can do nothing without love.

4:9 Believers must not only say that they love, love must be shown by their actions. This also follows God's example, for he **showed how much he loved us by sending his only Son** to die for us. Those who believe can have **eternal life through him.** Jesus is God's only Son. All believers are sons and daughters of God, but only Jesus has this special unique relationship (see John 1:18; 3:16). The great proof of God's love, as well as the motive for our love, is that he sent his only Son, who is life, so that we could live through him.

4:10 Of all the different kinds of love, God's love—*agape* love—is the truest. Greek has four words to depict four different kinds of love: (1) *eros* for sexual passion, (2) *storge* for family devotion, (3) *philos* for friendship, and (4) *agape* for loving-kindness. The fourth word was used exclusively by John to characterize God's love. It speaks of compassion, regard, kindness, and unselfishness. This kind of love motivated God to send his Son to the world to die for undeserving sinners—that kind of love is real love.

Not that we loved God, but that he loved us. The love relationship was initiated by God; people had nothing to do with it. How could we? All people were totally dead to God—dead in trespasses and sins (see Ephesians 2:1). He loved us even though we were totally unworthy of his love. He loved us so much that he **sent his Son as a sacrifice to take away our sins.** By removing sin, God removed the barrier between him and his people (Romans 5:1-2; Ephesians 2:18) so that he could live within his people and they could live within him.

4:11 God's supreme love is the motive of believers' love for **each other.** Because believers are born of God, they should resemble their Father, who is love. As they grow in appreciation of God's love for them, their love for him and for other Christians will grow as well. The way God loves people—sacrificially, unselfishly, completely—provides the example for how believers should love each other.

4:12 No one has ever seen God reiterates what John wrote in the prologue to his Gospel (John 1:18), which recalls what God said to Moses in Exodus 33:20. Moses wanted to see God's glory, but he was not allowed to because, as God explained, no human can see God and live.

If no one has ever seen God, then how can people ever know him? Because of Christ's sacrifice, the Holy Spirit could enter believers' lives. Through the Holy Spirit, **God lives in** Christians. God can be "seen" through believers as they **love each other.** With the Holy Spirit within each believer's life, Christians can love one another (see 4:16). Their love reveals that God himself is present and that they are partaking of the divine nature (see 2 Peter 1:3-8). Believers' love for God grows stronger when they see its results in their loving actions toward each other. As their love develops toward maturity and completeness, **his love is brought to full expression through** his people. When believers love one another, the invisible God reveals himself to others through them, and his love is made complete.

4:13 After Jesus' resurrection, believers could **live in him,** that is, in God, because **God has given us his Spirit.** According to John 14:16-20, the disciples would begin to experience what it meant to live in God and have God live in them once Christ sent them the Holy Spirit. Thereafter, they would know that the Son is in the Father, they are in the Son, and the Son is in them (John 14:20). When people become Christians, they receive the Holy Spirit. God's presence in their lives is **proof** that they really belong to him.

4:14 In addition to the gift of the Holy Spirit to believers, another way believers can trust in this relationship with God is that the message came from those who had **seen with** their **own eyes and now testify that the Father sent his Son to be the Savior of the world.** We refers to the apostles and other eyewitnesses of Christ's life on earth (see 1:1-3). They were appointed by Christ to testify to others about their firsthand, eyewitness experiences (1:3). Therefore, Christians have two proofs of God's love for them: (1) the indwelling presence of God's Spirit and (2) the eyewitness testimonies of the apostles and those who knew Jesus.

4:15 When people **proclaim that Jesus is the Son of God,** they are declaring their belief that Jesus is

God's one and only Son who came to earth as a human being, died on a cross, rose again, and returned to heaven. They also believe that his death on the cross won forgiveness for sin. Jesus Christ is not a mere human being, nor is he one among many deities. People who believe this about Jesus **have God living in them, and they live in God.** This mutual indwelling, experienced by the Father and Son (John 10:38; 14:10; 17:21), is a special privilege for believers (see John 14:20; 15:5; 17:21-24).

4:16 This time **we** refers to John and his readers, rather than just the apostles. These believers **know** (by experience) **how much God loves** them, and they **have put** their **trust in him.** Note the intimate connection of knowledge and faith. Believers know that God loves them—he shows his love in many ways (4:10). As they trust in this love and live in it day by day, they come to understand that **God is love, and all who live in love live in God, and God lives in them.** It is one thing to know and believe in God's love; it is quite another to actually appropriate God's love into a person's life so that the person "lives in love." As noted in 4:8, because God is love, his people ought to be experiencing his transcendent and glorious love on a daily basis because he "lives" in them.

4:17 Because of this mutual indwelling—God abiding in believers and they abiding in him—the believers' **love grows more perfect.** The word **perfect** does not mean "flawless," but "mature." This perfection happens as each believer's relationship with God, who *is* love, grows. His perfect love becomes free to work completely in and through them.

This perfect, mature love produces believers who **will not be afraid on the day of judgment.** On that day, God will require all people to account for their lives. Those who have followed him will live with him forever. Yet God's people don't have to wait until that day to find out if they "made it." They have that confidence now.

The sentence, **we are like Christ here in this world,** seems perplexing because it seems to mean that Christians are now completely like Christ, when experience says that they have a long way to go. So the statement must have something to do with believers' standing or position before God. Because of Jesus' death on the cross, God transfers Jesus' righteousness to believers (an act called justification, Romans 3:22-26), thereby enabling them to stand before God with confidence.

4:18 Because believers are becoming like God (4:17), they certainly need not **fear** his **judgment.**

To be fearful is to lack confidence; to lack confidence is to show that God's **love has not been perfected** in that person. Believers ought not be afraid of the future, eternity, or God's judgment, because of God's love. They know that he loves them perfectly (Romans 8:38-39). They can resolve any fears first by focusing on God's immeasurable love and then by allowing him to love others through them. God's love will quiet fears and give confidence.

4:19 Believers' **love,** whether for God or for others, is based on God's love for them. God's love is the source, the initiator. People cannot love this way on their own; it happens **as a result of his loving** people **first** (see 4:9-10). God's love is far above all human love. Because believers abide in God and thus abide in love (4:16), God's love fills them and overflows from them. Such "otherworldly" love then becomes the characteristic of God's people. They can love as he loves. Such love overflows to others who experience God's love as well.

4:20-21 John, again, was probably quoting the spiritual elitists who boasted often of their relationship with God. This boast, **I love God,** can be tested by the person's love for the community of God. If that person **hates another Christian,** their love for God should be questioned. Such was the case with Diotrephes, who refused to have fellowship with John and his coworkers (see 3 John 9-10). In fact, John says that such a **person is a liar.** John explains, very logically, that **if we don't love people we can see, how can we love God, whom we have not seen?** If a believer does not love his or her Christian brothers and sisters, who are God's visible representatives, how can that person possibly love the invisible God? It is easy to claim to love God when that love doesn't cost anything more than weekly attendance at religious services. But the real test of a person's love for God is how that person treats the people right in front of him or her—family members and fellow believers. People cannot truly love God while neglecting to love their **Christian brothers and sisters** as well.

1 JOHN 5

FAITH IN THE SON OF GOD / 5:1-12

To discern whether a person is a true Christian, one needs to look at what that person truly believes about Jesus Christ. The true believer "believes that Jesus is the Christ." The continuing activity of believing proves that a person is a child of God.

5:1 Belief that **Jesus is the Christ** proves that a person **is a child of God.** Those who believe this, then, love **the Father,** and by extension, love **his children.** Christians are a part of God's family, with fellow believers as brothers and sisters. God determines who the other family members are. Believers are simply called to accept and love them because they love God.

5:2 Just as believers' love for their brothers and sisters is the sign and test of their love for God, so their love for God (tested by obedience, 5:3) is the only basis of their love for Christian brothers and sisters. John was not contradicting what he had written in 4:20-21; rather, he was insisting that love for God and love for fellow believers cannot be separated.

5:3 Love for God and love for others (5:2) do not exist alone in a believer; they must be accompanied by obedience: **loving God means keeping**

his **commandments.** This echoes what Jesus said to his disciples, as recorded in the Gospel of John (John 14:15, 21, 23-24, 31; 15:10). Jesus had one commandment for them: Love one another (John 13:34; 15:17). This one command is not **difficult;** in fact, it should delight the believer to love God through his or her obedience (Matthew 11:28-30).

5:4-5 **Every child of God** has the power that **defeats this evil world** (see 5:5; also John 16:33). Here and in 5:5, the word connotes military conquest. Faith, **trusting Christ,** provides the power source and the means to participate in the **victory** Christ won for them through his sacrifice and resurrection (see John 16:33). The collective power, given by God to believers, can overcome this opposition. **The ones who believe that Jesus is the Son of God** are the only ones who will **win this battle against the world** so permeated with false, anti-Christian teachings. By holding fast to their faith in Jesus as God's Son, Christians will not be lured away to false teachings.

5:6 At his **baptism** and at his death, Jesus' identity as **God's Son** was clearly revealed (see John 1:29-34; 19:28-37). When John commented about **water** and **blood**, he was refuting the claims of Cerinthus that Jesus was "the Christ" only between his baptism and his death—that is, he was merely human until he was baptized, at which time "the Christ" then descended upon him but later left him before his death on the cross. But if Jesus died only as a man, he could not have taken upon himself the sins of the world, and Christianity would be an empty religion. Only an act of God could take away the punishment that sin deserves. The Holy Spirit **gives us the testimony that this is true.** The Spirit's primary role continues to be to reveal Christ to the believers and to affirm Christ's message.

5:7-8 These verses have to do with the three critical phases in Jesus' life where he was manifested as God incarnate, the Son of God in human form. This was made evident at his baptism (the **water**), his death (the **blood**), and his resurrection (the **Spirit**). At his baptism, Jesus was declared to be God's beloved Son (see Matthew 3:16-17). At his bloody crucifixion, Jesus was recognized by others as God's Son (see Mark 15:39). In his resurrection, Jesus was designated the Son of God in power (Romans 1:3-4). **These three witnesses agree** in one aspect: each event demonstrated that the man Jesus was the divine Son of God.

5:9 According to the Jewish law, the testimony of one person is not a valid witness. Truth or validity has to be established by two or three witnesses (Deuteronomy 17:6; 19:15). **Since** people **believe human testimony** when validated by two or three witnesses, John explained that **surely** they could **believe the testimony that comes from God.** The Gospels twice record God's clear declaration that Jesus is God's Son—at Jesus' baptism (Matthew 3:16-17) and at his transfiguration (Matthew 17:5). John said that if they believe testimony

from people, then they can surely rely on the three-fold witness of God (5:8). The three witnesses, described in 5:8, agree because God himself is behind them. All three form a single "testimony from God" that Jesus is the Christ.

5:10 When people **believe in the Son of God,** they know that everything the apostles taught about him is true. They know without any doubt because the Spirit who regenerated them gives them an inner witness to that reality (see Romans 8:16; Galatians 4:6). God's Spirit, alive in their spirit, witnesses to the fact that everything Jesus said and did was true. In fact, that is the primary function of the Spirit—to testify and reveal Jesus to every believer (see John 14:26; 15:26; 16:7-13).

Those who don't believe the testimony that God has given concerning his Son (5:7-9) should realize that by rejecting what God has so plainly said, they are **calling God a liar.** John was blasting the false teachers who claimed to know God but did not believe what God himself had said concerning his Son. This was logically impossible and amounted to calling God a liar.

5:11 This is what God has testified and what the false teachers refused to believe: God **has given us eternal life, and this life is in his Son.** The divine, eternal life resides in Christ, who makes it available to all who believe in him. That Jesus is indeed God's Son has been established by testimony from God himself (5:7-9). Believers have eternal life in relationship to and in union with Jesus Christ, who is himself "life" (John 1:4; 14:6), and they have eternal life because of him (2 Timothy 1:10).

5:12 Human beings do not have life in themselves; they receive life from God. Through faith, believers have Christ within, **so whoever has God's Son has life**—eternal life—now. They possess a new nature and enjoy fellowship with God. Believers can be certain that they have eternal life. Because they have received life through the Son, they can be assured of having everlasting life in the future. For those who do not believe, however, the opposite is also true: **whoever does not have his Son does not have life.**

CONCLUSION / 5:13-21

The final nine verses of 1 Peter comprise its epilogue. The epilogue has two functions: to summarize the main body of the letter and to prompt readers to apply what they have read. John provided several specific ways in which the community of believers could act on what he had written.

5:13 Only those who **believe in** the deity of **the Son of God** can absorb what John has written in

this letter and apply it. Above all else, John wanted his readers to have no more doubts about their faith, but instead to **know** they **have eternal life.** The letter, written to believers who had been unsettled in their faith by false teachers, encouraged them to continue in the faith and affirmed their possession of eternal life. John wanted his readers to know—to be sure—that they had eternal life. They could base their certainty on God's promise that he has given them eternal life through his Son.

5:14-15 Believers also **can be confident** that God **will listen** to their prayers. Confidence means boldness or freedom to speak to Christ (see Hebrews 4:16). They will be answered **whenever they ask him for anything in line with his will** (see also John 14:13-14; 15:16; 16:21-24).

So how can believers pray that way? How do they know what is God's will? This happens as a part of their growth in their relationship with Jesus Christ. When people choose to place their will in line with God's will, the Holy Spirit in them will teach them to understand God's will more completely. The Holy Spirit reveals God's will as it is taught in the Bible. The Holy Spirit, in turn, helps them to pray in line with God's will (see Romans 8:26-27). Jesus himself was a model of this: he taught his followers to pray for God's will to be accomplished on earth (Matthew 6:10), and he chose God's will over his own in accepting the bitter cup—death on the cross (Matthew 26:39-42).

In communicating with God, therefore, believers do not demand what they want or think they need; rather, they discuss with God what *he* wants for them. When believers align their prayers to God's will, **he is listening when** they **make** their **requests.** And since they know that he hears their prayers, they can be certain that he will give them a definite answer. Praying in line with God's will is the key to getting **what** they **ask for.** They should not think that they can obtain anything they want in order to benefit themselves. Prayer in line with God's will is prayer for the benefit of God's Kingdom, as the next verses illustrate.

5:16-17 This example describes the kind of petition that God will answer. Because the believers have been called to love one another, it follows, then, that they ought to care enough to intercede with God in prayer if they **see any Christian sinning in a way that does not lead to death.** Intercessory prayer forms a vital part of the fellowship of the church (see John 20:23). The faithful prayers of believers in the church can help restore the wayward or backslidden Christian. Their prayers can affect the conviction of the Holy Spirit in the person's life, as well as restore such ones to a wholesome Christian life.

The question then arises: what is the difference between sin that doesn't lead to death and **sin that leads to death?** John's readers apparently understood the difference, since John did not elaborate further. Three theories have been given for how to interpret these words:

A specific sin. In Moses' law, some sins were punishable by death; others required a sacrifice for repentance and restoration (Leviticus 20; Numbers 18:22). This verse, then, could apply to a specific sin punishable by death. This interpretation leads to a differentiation, taught in the Roman Catholic church, between mortal sins (the seven sins leading to death) and venial sins (sins that are pardonable). The New Testament records instances of sins that caused the deaths of church members committing them (see, for example, Acts 5:1-11; 1 Corinthians 5:5; 11:30; 1 Timothy 1:20; James 5:15; Revelation 2:23). But John did not refer to physical death as much as to sin that leads to spiritual death.

Apostasy. Some have interpreted these words to indicate Christians who have rejected Christ and turned away from the faith. Their sin of apostasy will lead to their spiritual ruin (see discussion on 2:24). There are two versions of this argument. Some believe that Christians can turn away from the faith and that this is a prayer for them as they are starting to wander before they backslide too far. Others see this as a hypothetical situation. Believers ought to pray for people to be faithful so they will not be tempted to turn away. However, in response to both of these cases, John did not state that this person who was sinning is or ever was a believer.

Heretical denial of the faith. Because John was writing against false teachers who denied Jesus' deity and acted immorally, the "sin that leads to death" most likely refers to the attitude of continued rebellion against God and the unrepentant spirit that would never receive salvation. By rejecting the only way of salvation, the false teachers and their followers were putting themselves out of reach of prayer.

While **every wrong is sin,** that is, all unrighteousness is sin—including the sin committed by believers (1:7, 9; 3:4)—**not all sin leads to death.** The sin that ends in death includes both the **act** of deliberately denying that Jesus is the Christ, the Son of God, and the **state** of spiritual death that deliberately rejects Christ, destroying faith and love. John did not forbid prayer for the one who rejects Christ, but neither did he encourage it.

5:18 Believers, those who are **part of God's family, do not make a practice of sinning** because **God's Son holds them securely.** Christians commit sins, of course, but they ask God to forgive them, and then they continue serving him. God has freed believers from their slavery to **the evil one,** and he keeps them safe from Satan's continued attacks. The rest of the world does not have the Christian's freedom to obey God. Unless unbelievers come to Christ in faith, they have no choice but to obey Satan. There is no middle ground; either people belong to God and obey him, or they live under Satan's control.

5:19 Believers can **know** their position with God and in eternity. They know they **are children of God,** and because of that, they have been freed from Satan's power. While the rest of **the world** is under the power and control of the evil one, Christians stand apart, separate from the world (non-Christian society) and from Satan, united together with God. Even those the world considers wise, great, and respectable are under Satan's domain (see 2:15-17; 3:1, 13; 4:3-5; 5:4-5).

5:20 Again, John reminded the believers of what they "know" to be true: they **know that the Son of God has come.** The false teachers had done their best to set Christ aside, to make him unimportant, and to have so-called "knowledge of God" without him. But John has been explaining throughout this letter that this is impossible. Jesus Christ is central to true Christian faith. Jesus came to earth, returned to heaven, and now is present through his Holy Spirit. The Son's purpose in coming to earth was to reveal God the Father and to enable the believers to know him experientially (see John 17:3). The Holy Spirit **has given** believers **understanding so that** they **can know the true God.** Just as the Holy Spirit teaches believers about Christ and points to him, so the Son teaches about and points to the Father.

To be **in God** is to be **in his Son, Jesus Christ,** for when believers are united to the Son, they are also united to the Father (see John 17:21-24). **He is the only true God** refers to Christ. The Father is the source of eternal life and Jesus Christ reveals that life (John 1:4; 14:6), so also **he is eternal life.** Only through his death and resurrection was eternal life made available to humanity.

5:21 The letter closes with a final affectionate caution. Given the context of this letter, **anything that might take God's place,** probably refers to false teachings that present false images of Jesus Christ. God's place can be taken by substitutes for the true faith, anything that robs Christ of his full deity and humanity, any human idea that claims to be more authoritative than the Bible, any loyalty that replaces God at the center of our lives. John was bluntly saying that to follow the false teachers would amount to turning away from God. The results would be the same.

In this letter, John presented a clear picture of Christ. What Christians think about Jesus Christ is central to their teaching, preaching, and living. Jesus is the God-man, fully God and fully human at the same time. He came to earth to die in the place of sinners, for their sins. Through faith in him, believers are given eternal life and the power to do his will. Every person must decide the answer to the most important question—who is Jesus Christ?

2 JOHN

INTRODUCTION

Truth is hard to find. Consider contemporary advertisements—we are barraged by spectacular claims, implicit and explicit, for a multitude of products. Consumers wonder where to spend their money. And listen to the political rhetoric in an election year—filled with promises, charges, and countercharges. Citizens hardly know which way to vote. Joining these voices are the proponents of a wide variety of philosophies and ideologies, all alleging truth.

First-century believers heard a similar cacophony, with false teachers preaching a false gospel and threatening to turn many away from the truth. So under the inspiration of the Holy Spirit, John quickly wrote this strong letter, urging readers to focus on Christ, truly the Truth.

As you read 2 John, recommit to being a person of the Truth.

AUTHOR

The apostle John.

First, 2, and 3 John were written by the same author, for their tone, style, and thematic development are extremely similar. The grammar, style, and vocabulary of 2 John compare very closely to 1 John. In fact, eight of the thirteen verses of the second letter are almost identical to verses in 1 John.

Second and 3 John have been placed among the General Epistles by virtue of their association with 1 John, but they are not General Epistles. Second John was addressed to an individual or a specific local church, and 3 John was addressed to a specific individual, Gaius.

For more about John, see the Author section in the Introduction to the Gospel of John.

DATE AND SETTING

Written in approximately A.D. 90 from Ephesus.

Second John was written in a setting similar to that of 1 John. This church was being harassed by the heresies that were attacked in 1 John. The heresies were denounced, and the church was warned not to entertain the messengers of the heresy. This epistle was probably sent to one of the churches in a cluster of churches in Asia Minor that were the recipients of John's apostolic ministry (see following comments under "Audience").

The information concerning date of writing is inadequate to make any decision. The similarity to 1 John strongly suggests a similar era.

AUDIENCE
The "chosen lady and to her children" (1:1).

Some commentators think this was a specific woman (with her children). Other commentators believe that John was using this address as a surrogate for a particular local church (as perhaps Peter also did in 1 Peter 5:13). The nature of the epistle points to a corporate personality—the local church—rather than a private individual (see comments on 1:5-6, 8, 10, 12).

OCCASION AND PURPOSE
To emphasize the basics of following Christ—truth and love—and to warn against false teachers.

The purpose of the letter is twofold. In the first place, the recipient was urged to live in the truth and to continue practicing Christian love. The second, and more compelling, reason was the warning against the deceivers who refused to acknowledge Christ and persuaded others to do the same. Love indeed has its limits when it comes to showing hospitality to those who refuse to acknowledge Christ as God's Son come to earth in a human body. The deceivers were probably the same heretics identified in the first letter.

MESSAGE
The apostle John had seen Truth and Love firsthand—he had been with Jesus. So affected was this disciple that all of his writings, from the Gospel to the book of Revelation, are filled with this theme: Truth and love are vital to the Christian and are inseparable in the Christian life. Second John, his brief letter to a dear friend, is no different. John says to live in the truth and obey God (1:4), watch out for deceivers (1:7), and love God and each other (1:6). John's second letter can be called a miniversion of 1 John. All the same major themes appear in 2 John that one reads in 1 John. In both letters, John wanted his readers to (1) live in the truth, (2) love one another, (3) be on guard against false teachers and adhere to the apostolic teachings—especially about Jesus, God's Son come in the flesh—in the face of Gnostic infiltration into the church.

The main themes in the book of 2 John include: *Truth, Love,* and *False Teachers.*

Truth (1:1-5). Following God's word, the Bible, is essential to Christian living because God is truth. Jesus said, "I am the way, the truth, and the life. No one can come to the Father except through me" (John 14:6). Christ's true followers consistently obey his truth.

IMPORTANCE FOR TODAY. To resist false teaching, we must focus on the truth—God's holy Word and his Son, our Savior. To be loyal to Christ's teaching, we must seek to know the Bible, but we must never twist its message to meet our own needs or for our own purposes, nor should we encourage those who misuse it. Keep focused on Christ. Stand for the truth.

Love (1:3-6). Christ commanded that his followers love one another (John 15:12-13). By loving each other they would be following his example; thus the world would know they were his disciples. Love is the most basic ingredient of true Christianity.

IMPORTANCE FOR TODAY. To obey Christ fully, we must believe his command to love others. Helping, giving, and meeting needs put love into practice. Be committed to love, for Christ's sake.

False Teachers (1:7-11). Believers must be wary of religious leaders who are not true to Christ's teachings. These false teachers and preachers must not be given a platform to spread their false teachings.

IMPORTANCE FOR TODAY. We must check any spiritual leader (pastor, elder, teacher, etc.) against God's word. And we must reject and resist all who make Christ any less than fully God and fully man. Don't encourage those who are opposed to Christ. Don't associate with false teachers. Be aware of what is being taught in your church.

OUTLINE OF 2 JOHN

I. Watch Out for False Teachers (1:1-11)
II. John's Final Words (1:12-13)

2 JOHN 1

GREETINGS / 1:1-3

In the first four verses of this short letter, the word "truth" appears five times. False teachings were beginning to infiltrate the church; this prompted John to counter these falsehoods with strong admonitions to the believers about knowing and living in the truth concerning Jesus Christ. In his letter called 1 John, John explained clearly to the believers how they could know that they were grounded in the truth and how they could discern whether teachers were true or false.

The obvious follow-up, then, was the question of how the believers should act toward the false teachers who had been causing so much trouble in their churches (the issue John addressed in 1 John). Both 2 and 3 John focus on "truth" and on refusing to give a hearing, hospitality, or any sort of encouragement to those who do not teach the truth.

1:1 In this informal letter, **John** did not stand on his authority as an apostle but spoke of himself as an **Elder**—one who watched over the believers with loving concern for their spiritual well-being. John had been one of Jesus' twelve disciples. He wrote the Gospel of John, three letters, and the book of Revelation. He may have been the only remaining living member of the twelve disciples. The word **Elder** also refers to John's age; he must have been an old man when he wrote this epistle. Obviously his readers recognized the author from this title alone. For more about John, see the Author section in the Introduction to the Gospel of John.

Most translators do not identify the recipient of this letter as an individual because the letter does not speak of the **chosen lady** with any particular details (in contrast to 3 John, which speaks specifically of Gaius, Diotrephes, and Demetrius). Most likely, therefore, **the chosen lady** refers to a local church. Verses 6, 12, and 13 also point to a corporate recipient (see comments there).

As a local church, the **children** are the members of the church. At this time, most churches were smaller groups of people that met in homes. Sometimes several house churches would meet in the city at the same time (see Philemon 1:2). John dearly loved these believers. In 1 John, he revealed his love by calling them his "dear children" (1 John 2:1, 12, 18, 28; 3:7, 18; 4:4; 5:21). The corporate love of all believers for one another comes through in John's words **whom I love in the truth, as does everyone else who knows God's truth.** John spoke of this corporate love also in his first letter (1 John 2:9-11; 3:10-20; 4:7-21; 5:1). Believers love one another, not because of common attraction or total compatibility, but because of the common truth they believe and share. Truth functions as the bond of believers' fellowship, but it also keeps out false teachers.

1:2 The truth that lives in us and will be in our hearts forever personifies "truth." God gave the truth to people in Jesus Christ, the full expression and embodiment of truth (John 14:6; Ephesians 4:21). Thus, truth dwells in believers because Christ dwells in them as the Spirit of truth (John 14:15-17; 16:13). "Truth" therefore includes, but means more than, correct precepts or a set of orthodox teachings—truth centers in Jesus Christ. The truth is the reality of Jesus Christ, as opposed to the lies of the false teachers (see

1 John 2:21-23). People may choose to deny the truth and leave the fellowship, but that doesn't change the truth. Because Christ is eternal, truth is also eternal, not subject to change. Because Christ lives in believers, both he and his truth will be with them forever.

1:3 The words **grace** and **peace** were standard greetings in many letters of the day. **Grace** means God's undeserved favor shown to sinners whereby he saves them and gives them strength to live for him. John added the word **mercy** to his greeting. God reveals his **mercy** by forgiving and freeing people from sin, resulting in peace between them and God. **Peace** refers to the peace that Christ made between sinners and God through his death on the cross. Peace also refers to that inner assurance and tranquility that God places in the heart, producing confidence and contentment in Christ. Grace, mercy, and peace keep on coming like a spring-fed well that never runs dry.

The title **God our Father** points to the unique relationship Christians have with God. He is a father to them; they are his children. **Jesus Christ is his Son,** showing the unique relationship between God and Jesus. While all believers can call God their Father, only Jesus is the unique Son of God who is one with God himself.

Truth and love form a bridge into the remainder of the letter. John speaks more directly about truth in verses 2 and 4 and about love in verse 5. Truth and love always go hand in hand.

LIVE IN THE TRUTH / 1:4-11

Christianity had spread to many cities in the world. Sometimes there were several house churches in a city. True teachers and false teachers were proliferating. Because there were many false teachings about Jesus Christ in the days of the early church, the apostles had to describe which teachings about Jesus were true and which were false. Believers who adhered to the apostolic teachings—both in doctrine and in practice—were living in the truth.

1:4 John had only met **some** of the believers in the church and was glad to **find them living in the truth.** John was probably speaking of those he met at some place other than the local church itself. His joy at meeting them and then discovering that they were living in the truth prompted him to write this epistle. In identifying only "some" of the children, he was not necessarily excluding the others. Rather, he was speaking only of those he met. In both cases, the apostle rejoiced in the believers who had not allowed the false teachers to lead them away from the truth.

Living in the truth refers to the Christians conducting their lives as they had been **commanded**

by the Father. The commandment to live in the truth came from the Father through the Son to the disciples (see John 15:15), who passed it on to the believers (Matthew 28:19-20). As John had explained in another letter, "And this is his commandment: We must believe in the name of his Son, Jesus Christ, and love one another, just as he commanded us" (1 John 3:23). To live in the truth, therefore, involves believing in Jesus Christ as God's Son (faith) and loving others (action).

1:5 John urged the church to **love one another.** This was **not a new commandment;** the believers had heard this **from the beginning.** The Christians had been taught this commandment from the time they first heard the gospel preached (see John 13:35; 1 John 2:7; 3:11). The statement that Christians should love one another is a recurrent New Testament theme. Yet love for one's neighbor is an old command, first appearing in the third book of Moses (Leviticus 19:18). Believers can show love in many ways: by avoiding prejudice and discrimination, by accepting people, by listening, helping, giving, serving, and by refusing to judge. Knowing God's command is not enough. Those who claim to love God and believe in his Son must put their faith into practice by loving. (See also Matthew 22:37-39 and 1 John 2:7-10.)

1:6 Lest anyone wonder what John meant by the word "love," he explained it here. Love does not focus on emotions or feelings; instead, **love means doing what God has commanded.** Love is expressed by obedience; obedience fulfills the command to love. The one command to **love one another** sums up all of God's commands, and obedience to God's commands is the sure test of love. John made the same proclamation in his first letter (see 1 John 3:11, 16-19).

Four times in verses 4-6 appears a form of the word "command." Yet the commands are obeyed through love. John wanted his readers to know that he spoke as an Elder, as an apostle, and as a loving father to his children—with authority from God himself. The false teachers had no such authority, and their lifestyles did not exemplify love.

1:7 Here is the warning of this letter: Beware of the **many deceivers** (that is, the false teachers) who **do not believe that Jesus Christ came to earth in a real body.** John's first letter mentioned this heresy (see 1 John 4:2-3). Jesus had warned his disciples that false teachers would arise and lead many astray (Matthew 7:15; 24:11, 24). Jesus' words had come true, for many of these false teachers had **gone out into the world.** One group in particular, called the Docetists, denied Jesus' humanity and instead promoted the falsehood that he only *seemed* to have a human body. Believers, however, must hold on to what they believed—that Jesus is truly the Son of God who came to earth as a human. He is both fully human and fully God.

Every false teacher is against Christ—he or she is **a deceiver and an antichrist** (see 1 John 2:18-19; 4:3). These deceivers foreshadow the one final Antichrist who will embody all the deception of earlier anti-Christian systems and teachers. Many false teachers taught that the spirit is good and matter is evil; therefore, they reasoned that Jesus could not have been both God and man. In strong

terms, John warned against this kind of teaching, and he warned Christians not to be deceived (1:8-9) and not to give encouragement or hospitality to the deceivers (1:10-11; see 1 John 2:26).

Many false teachers still promote an unbiblical understanding of Jesus. These teachers are dangerous because they distort the truth and undermine the foundations of the Christian faith. They use the right words, but they change the meanings. The way your teachers live shows a lot about what they believe about Christ. For more on testing teachers, see 1 John 4:1.

1:8 John was warning believers to **watch out** and not be deceived. Jesus warned his disciples that many would come with lies and would try to deceive the believers (Matthew 24:4-5, 24). John did not want these believers to follow the lies of the false teachers and thus **lose the prize** that the apostles (**we**) had worked to bring them—the gospel truth and the **full reward** for their loyal service. All who value the truth and persistently hold to it will win their full reward. Those who live for themselves and justify their self-centeredness by teaching false doctrines will lose that reward (see Matthew 7:21-23).

1:9 This verse explains the "loss" referred to in verse 8. John did not want the believers to lose what had been brought to them—**the teaching of Christ.** This may refer to teaching about Christ (that he is the Son of God, see 1:7) or to Christ's teachings about loving others (such as recorded in 1:6 above and in John 15:12-17). John may have had both in mind because both are fundamental to the Christian faith. To **wander beyond** these teachings literally means "leading forward" ("to go before" or "to run ahead"). This may be a sarcastic remark about the way in which the false teachers proudly claimed to be offering "advanced" teaching, but they had gone beyond the boundaries of true Christian belief and, in the process, had lost God himself. To turn away from the truth of Christ is to **not have fellowship with God.** In contrast, believers who **continue in the teaching of Christ** will find unbroken **fellowship with both the Father and the Son.** John had written previously, "Anyone who confesses the Son has the Father also" (1 John 2:23). To have Christ is to have God, for they are one (see John 1:18; 14:7, 9).

1:10-11 In the early days of the church, believers met in homes (see Romans 16:5; Colossians 4:15). The only way to deal with a teacher who arrives and **does not teach the truth about Christ** is to refuse to welcome him or **encourage him in any way.** If he was not teaching the truth, the believers must not even give him a hearing. In John's historical context, the command, **don't invite him into**

your house, probably referred to a house meeting of the church, which would have been visited by various teachers traveling from local church to local church.

Listening to the false teachers, said John, would make a believer **a partner in his evil work.** Encouraging or helping false teachers, even if only to attempt to show "Christian kindness," identified believers with, and tacitly gave approval of, the false teachers. Believers cannot have a partnership both with God's children and also with antichrists who are God's enemies.

It may seem rude to turn people away, but how much better it is to be faithful to God than merely be courteous to people! John was not teaching that the church should not welcome unbelievers or even those who have been led astray by false teachers. He was teaching, however, that the door must be closed to those teachers who are dedicated to opposing the true teachings of God and who come to the church in order to "bring" their message. There is a difference between hospitality to strangers whom believers can win for Christ, and hospitality to those who are focused on winning believers away from Christ. Christians must trust God and discern the difference.

JOHN'S FINAL WORDS / 1:12-13
The letter closes with a promise of further communication in person, so as to give each other complete joy.

1:12 John's desire to **talk** with the believers—rather than write more—accounts for the brevity of the letter. John hoped to visit these believers personally and discuss the truths of the gospel more fully. As the apostle, Elder, and father in the faith, he desired to come to them as a true teacher. As he and the believers fellowshiped together, their **joy** would **be complete.** John also made that statement in his other letters (1 John 1:4; 3 John 1:13-14). John's joy was made full by his fellowship with other believers.

1:13 Since the **sister, chosen by God** is not named, John was probably referring to the sister church where he was staying while he wrote this letter.

The children, then, referred to the church members. Believers in all churches all over the world have a common faith in Jesus Christ. Because of this, they share one another's joys and sorrows. While the believers in these churches may not have known one another, they sent **greetings** to these fellow Christians.

False teaching is serious business, and Christians dare not overlook it. It is so serious that John wrote this letter to warn against it. There are so many false teachings in the world that believers might be tempted to take many of them lightly. Instead, they should realize the dangers false teachings pose and actively refuse to give heresies any foothold in their lives or in their churches.

3 JOHN

INTRODUCTION

- Loyal . . . kind . . . friendly . . . reliable . . .
- Cynical . . . cheap . . . irresponsible . . . bitter . . .

Descriptive and definitive words come to mind when specific names are spoken.
A certain man is described as generous, another as stingy. One woman is pictured
as outgoing, another as reserved. People are known for their actions; over time,
they build reputations, and adjectives accumulate on their personal resumes.

For example, little is known about Gaius or Demetrius, except that both men
were generous and faithful. And Diotrephes barely makes a ripple in history,
except that he is described as self-centered and mean-spirited.

Third John may be short, but it speaks much about the value of a good reputation. As you read this letter from the beloved apostle John, consider how you
might be described and determine to be known as one who follows close to Christ.

AUTHOR
The apostle John.

For information about John, see the Author section in the Introduction to the
Gospel of John.

DATE AND SETTING
Written in about A.D. 90 from Ephesus.

Third John was also written in a similar setting to 1 and 2 John. There is insufficient information to establish date or additional setting. The familiar terminology
and writing style tie it closely to the other two letters.

AUDIENCE
Gaius, a prominent Christian in one of the churches known to John.

Third John was written to Gaius. Although the New Testament mentions several
men with the name Gaius (Acts 19:29; 20:4; Romans 16:23; 1 Corinthians 1:14), it
would be difficult to say that any one of these was the same as the Gaius in 3 John.
At any rate, Gaius was commended for his Christian walk and hospitality and so
was Demetrius, both of whom stand in sharp contrast to Diotrephes, "who loves
to be the leader" (1:9).

OCCASION AND PURPOSE
To commend a faithful believer, Gaius.

The problem faced in this situation was a certain Diotrephes, who was repudiating the authority of "the Elder" (John) and trying to frustrate his leadership. The letter is addressed to Gaius, who was still loyal to the elder. John commended Gaius and asked him to provide for the genuine missionaries who would be passing through.

MESSAGE

This is a personal letter from John to Gaius. For Gaius, hospitality was a habit, and his reputation for friendship and generosity, especially to traveling teachers and missionaries (1:5), had spread. To affirm and thank Gaius for his Christian lifestyle, and to encourage him in his faith, John wrote this personal note.

John's format for this letter centers around three men: Gaius, the example of one who follows Christ and loves others (1:1-8); Diotrephes, the self-proclaimed church leader who does not reflect God's values (1:9-11); and Demetrius, who also follows the truth (1:12). John encourages Gaius to practice hospitality, continue to walk in the truth, and do what is right.

The main themes in the book of 3 John include: *Hospitality, Pride,* and *Faithfulness.*

Hospitality (1:5-10). This letter encourages those who were kind to others, welcoming traveling Christian workers into their homes.

IMPORTANCE FOR TODAY. Faithful Christian teachers and missionaries need the support of the Christians among whom they minister. This loving support helps them financially and encourages them in the work to which God has called them. Extend hospitality to others whenever you can. This will make you a partner in their ministry.

Pride (1:9-11). Diotrephes is described as one "who loves to be the leader" (1:9). Self-centered and prideful, he not only refused to offer hospitality, but he also set himself up as a church boss, trying to undermine John and his authority. Pride disqualified Diotrephes from being a real leader in the church.

IMPORTANCE FOR TODAY. Self-centeredness continues to divide churches. All believers, especially Christian leaders, must avoid pride and its deleterious effects. Humbly use your gifts to serve God, not yourself. And be careful not to misuse your position of leadership.

Faithfulness (1:1-5, 12). Gaius and Demetrius were commended for their faithfulness to Christ and for their faithful work in the church. John held them up as examples of faithful, selfless servants.

IMPORTANCE FOR TODAY. Christian workers who serve faithfully should be acknowledged and encouraged so that they won't grow weary of serving. Look for ways to encourage faithful Christians. And determine to be one who is known as a faithful servant of Jesus Christ.

OUTLINE OF 3 JOHN

I. God's Children Live by the Standards of the Gospel (1:1-12)
II. John's Final Words (1:13-15)

3 JOHN 1

GREETINGS / 1:1-4

The main body of this letter has two purposes. The first paragraph (1:5-8) commends Gaius for his hospitality to the itinerant missionaries who are traveling and preaching the gospel message. The missionaries have spoken well of Gaius's love for the church.

The second paragraph (1:9-12) warns against the insubordination of a certain man named Diotrephes. His love of power and authority has led him not only to defy John's authority but also to convince others to follow his defiance or be excommunicated. He has refused to entertain the genuine itinerant preachers. Gaius is warned not to be influenced by Diotrephes's example.

1:1 The author of the second epistle identified himself in the same way. **John the Elder** was one of Jesus' original twelve disciples. In addition to this letter, he wrote two other letters, the Gospel of John, and the book of Revelation. For more about John, see the Author section in the Introduction to the Gospel of John. As in the previous letters, John did not focus on his apostolic authority but spoke of himself as an **Elder** who watched over the believers with loving concern. The word "elder" refers also to John's age; he must have been an old man when he wrote this epistle.

Gaius was a common name in the Roman Empire. Men named Gaius appear in the pages of the New Testament (Acts 19:29; 20:4; Romans 16:23; 1 Corinthians 1:14), but it is unclear if any of them are the same "Gaius" to whom John wrote this letter. John considered Gaius a **dear friend** (see 1:2, 5, 11). Perhaps Gaius had shared his home and hospitality with John at some time during John's travels. If so, John would have appreciated his actions because traveling preachers depended on hospitality to survive (see Matthew 10:11-16). The tenor of this letter indicates that Gaius occupied a position of leadership and responsibility in a local church. Gaius may have owed his conversion to John (see 1:4).

1:2 John was concerned for Gaius's physical (**body**) and spiritual (**soul**) well-being. While this was a conventional expression used in ancient letter writing, John's sincerity was revealed in his love for Gaius. John also may have been pointing out that concern for physical and spiritual go together. This was the opposite of the popular heresy that taught the separation of spirit and matter and that despised the physical life.

1:3 These **brothers** (fellow believers) were either emissaries sent by John to check on the situation in various churches under John's purview, or they were traveling teachers—the kind who promoted apostolic truth, as opposed to those who spread falsehoods. They reported back to John and told him about Gaius's **faithfulness** and that he was **living in the truth.** This truth was Gaius's loyalty to Christ and to the gospel; it marked his character and life.

1:4 John's **children** were his spiritual children, the members of the Christian communities he served. John wrote of his "children" because he was the spiritual father of many, probably including Gaius. John's joy came from hearing that the believers under his care were not straying from the gospel message but were living **in the truth** (see also 2 John 1:4). To **live in the truth** means living out the truth by expressing it in one's behavior. Gaius was doing this, and John had **no greater joy** than to see it happen in the life of one of his spiritual children. Apparently others in the church were doing the same as well.

CARING FOR THE LORD'S WORKERS / 1:5-12

Traveling teachers were probably sent from various churches to proclaim and teach the gospel. Because false teachers were infiltrating the churches, strong believers who taught the truth were very important. These traveling prophets, evangelists, and teachers were helped on their way by people like Gaius who housed and fed them. Finding good accommodations was very difficult for travelers who had no friends in the area. Inns were not very good places to stay. Hospitality from the believers was vital to the spread of the gospel. As noted in 2 John, however, the believers were *not* to show such hospitality to false teachers.

1:5 Gaius had been willing to open his home and **take care of the traveling teachers** who were **passing through.** He lovingly cared for these men who served the Lord, even when they were **strangers** to him. These teachers were partners in the truth (1:8) and deserved to be helped. John called this **a good work.**

Hospitality is a lost art in many churches today. Christians would do well to invite more people for meals—fellow church members, young people, traveling missionaries, visitors, and the needy. This is an active and much-appreciated way to show Christian love.

1:6-7 The traveling Christian workers whom Gaius had helped had mentioned his **friendship and loving deeds** in **the church** where John was present. Gaius's selfless kindness was held up as an example for others. John affirmed Gaius in his willingness to **send** the teachers **on their way in a manner that pleases God,** meaning that he helped them according to the custom of the times, which included providing rest, encouragement, and needed supplies as they continued their travels.

The reason these teachers deserved help from believers was that **they are traveling for the Lord.** These were not merely Christian tourists; these people were traveling with a purpose—to preach the gospel of Jesus Christ. That they would **accept nothing from those who are not Christians** means that they did not ask for support from nonbelievers because they didn't want anyone questioning their motives for preaching.

1:8 When Christians **support** someone who is spreading the gospel, they are in a very real way **partners with them for the truth.** This is the other side of the principle in 2 John 1:10. Not everyone should go to the mission field; those who work for Christ at home are vital to the ministries of those who go and who need support. Believers can support missionaries by praying for them and by giving them money, hospitality, and time.

1:9 The **brief letter** referred to here was probably neither 1 or 2 John, but another letter that no longer exists. Apparently, John had previously **sent a letter to the church** (of which Gaius was a member), encouraging them to welcome and help the traveling teachers whom John was sending their

way, and perhaps to give support to help them along their journey. But a man named **Diotrephes** had refused to **acknowledge** the apostle's **authority.** Diotrephes, **who loves to be the leader,** apparently refused to support these traveling preachers, thus snubbing John in the process. Diotrephes had an important position in the church but was blinded with pride and self-importance. He ignored the letter, perhaps even destroying it. This necessitated John's writing this letter to Gaius so his words would be heard.

1:10 John would deal with Diotrephes personally if he were able to go to Gaius's church. This verse explains some of what Diotrephes was **doing.** He apparently wanted to control the church. John denounced four errors of Diotrephes. First, he did not acknowledge the authority of other spiritual leaders (1:9). Second, he was saying **wicked things** about those leaders. The Greek word literally means "to talk nonsense." Third, he refused **to welcome the traveling teachers.** He regularly refused to give hospitality to the brothers sent from John. Fourth, he was putting **out of the church** those who disagreed with him.

Diotrephes was trying to dominate the church and lord it over all the members—telling them who to receive and who not to receive. Gaius had apparently not listened to Diotrephes but had continued to be hospitable. For this, John commended him. Not only was Gaius doing what was right, he was doing it in the face of persecution from those in his own church.

Sins such as pride, jealousy, and slander are still present in the church; thus when a leader makes a habit of encouraging sin and discouraging right actions, he or she must be stopped. If no one speaks up, great harm can come to the church. John was prepared to publicly expose Diotrephes before the whole church.

1:11 John encouraged Gaius to not be influenced by Diotrephes's **bad example,** but to instead **follow only what is good**—that is, to continue showing support and hospitality. Human beings are imitators by nature, but they must choose whom they will imitate. John encouraged Gaius to continue to follow what is good, for **those who do good prove that they are God's children.** To give in to Diotrephes would be giving in to evil, and

those who do evil prove that they do not know God. True Christians are known by their actions. John wrote at length in his first letter about how believers must show love for one another. Those who do not love do not know God, for God is love (1 John 4:8, 16).

1:12 John here mentioned a man named **Demetrius** in a way that made him a complete opposite to Diotrephes. Nothing is known about Demetrius except that he may have carried this letter from John to Gaius. The book of Acts mentions an Ephesian silversmith named Demetrius who opposed Paul (Acts 19:24), but this is probably another man. When Demetrius arrived, Gaius certainly opened his home to him.

Everyone was speaking **highly of Demetrius, even truth itself.** The goodness of Demetrius's life was evident when it was compared to the gospel standard of truth, which involves real acts of love and hospitality. In addition to the testimony of everyone who knew Demetrius, and of the truth itself, John and his coworkers also gave him their commendations.

JOHN'S FINAL WORDS / 1:13-15

The letter closes with a promise of further, personal communication, followed by some greetings.

1:13-15 John had **much to tell** his readers, and modern readers wish that he had written more. But since John was anxious to deal with the situation in person, he limited his written words. He hoped to see them soon and **talk face to face.** John said much the same thing at the end of his other short letter (2 John 1:12).

May God's peace be with you forms a standard closing. Gaius would need the peace that Jesus gives in the days ahead (John 20:19-26), especially as he continued to refuse to acknowledge Diotrephes's leadership. The **friends** sending **their greetings** were other believers. John also asked Gaius to give his **personal greetings** to each of the **friends** there. John was thinking of them as individuals he knew and loved, not merely as a group. This statement shows that John knew many individuals in that particular Christian community.

JUDE

INTRODUCTION

Half-truths, statements taken out of context, misleading descriptions, words changed in meaning, and outright fabrications are designed to deceive, to hide the truth. Liars have many motives: to make a sale, to win an election, to hide wrong-doing, to enhance an image, to beat a rival, to cheat someone, to gain the favor of a coach, teacher, friend, parent, employer, or spouse. Whatever the reason, the real character of the liar is exposed when the truth is revealed.

In the early years of the church, liars arose—truth-twisters who deliberately rejected God's word and the lordship of Christ and designed, instead, their own theology. The motive for these men was to gain power and money. Responding to this threat to the church, the apostles and other church leaders published warnings, urging Christians to be alert, to know the truth, and to reject the liars and their lies. That's what motivated Jude to pen his short letter.

As you read Jude, think about the possible false teachers in your world and determine to "defend the truth" (1:3).

AUTHOR

Jude: son of Joseph, brother of James, and half-brother of Jesus.

Immediately the writer of this short letter identifies himself as "Jude, a slave of Jesus Christ and a brother of James" (1:1), so the question is which James and which Jude (a form of the Hebrew name Judah—Greek "Judas"—a common Jewish name). The most widely accepted answer is that Jude and James are the sons of Joseph mentioned in Matthew 13:55 and Mark 6:3 and, thus, the half-brothers of Jesus. Eventually, James had become the head of the church in Jerusalem (see Acts 12:17; 15:13-21; Galatians 1:18-19; 2:11-13). He also wrote the Bible book bearing his name (in about A.D. 47–49). The renown of James would explain why Jude described himself as "a brother of James" (1:1). This is an unusual description since at this time a person usually would describe himself as someone's son rather than as someone's brother.

Like James, Jude did not believe in Jesus at first. In fact, they had rejected him (Mark 3:21) and had ridiculed him (John 7:1-5). After Christ's resurrection, however, Jesus "was seen by James" (1 Corinthians 15:7). Evidently, this is what convinced James that Jesus was, in fact, the Messiah, the Savior, God in the flesh. Perhaps Jude was with James at the time, or perhaps James led his brother to the Lord. Whatever the case, both men became vocal witnesses for Christ and leaders in the young church. Note also that both men begin their books by describing themselves not as equals or family but as slaves of Jesus Christ (James 1:1; Jude 1:1).

Little else is known of Jude. He, along with Mary and his other brothers, were in the upper room just before Pentecost (Acts 1:14), and he traveled with his wife as he performed missionary work (1 Corinthians 9:5).

DATE AND SETTING
Perhaps written from Palestine in about A.D. 65.

Jude's location and the date of his writing are unknown. As James' brother and active in the Jerusalem church, the most likely place would seem to be Palestine. But Paul implies that Jude and his wife may have served as traveling missionaries (1 Corinthians 9:5). If this is true, Jude could have been almost anywhere in the Roman Empire when he wrote this letter.

The similarity between Jude and 2 Peter indicates that they probably were written at about the same time, since they both addressed the same issue faced by the church, a pre-Gnostic heresy. Also, because neither 2 Peter nor Jude refers to the destruction of the Jerusalem Temple, both letters probably were written before A.D. 70.

AUDIENCE
Jewish Christians scattered throughout the world.

Little is known for sure about the intended readers of this letter except that it is addressed, "to all who are called to live in the love of God the Father and the care of Jesus Christ" (1:1). This description sounds as though Jude was writing to all believers and not a specific church or segment of the church. His appeal to Old Testament personalities and stories (for example, the Exodus, the destruction of Sodom and Gomorrah, Moses, Cain, Balaam, Korah's rebellion, and Enoch) seems to indicate that his intended audience had a strong Jewish heritage. As a Jewish believer himself, Jude's tendency would have been to minister among Hebrew Christians, like his brother James, who specifically addressed his letter "to Jewish Christians" (James 1:1).

Some think that Jude was writing to the same audience for whom 2 Peter was intended, because of the heresy addressed by both letters. But there is no evidence for this. Evidently, these false teachers were becoming a problem for most of the churches. Paul addressed a similar problem in his letter to the Colossians.

It is likely, therefore, that Jude wrote this letter to Jewish Christians to whom he had ministered, in Palestine and elsewhere.

OCCASION AND PURPOSE
To warn believers about false teachers and their heresy.

Jude wrote that at first he had intended to write about defending the faith (1:3); however, the Holy Spirit compelled him to warn his fellow believers about the false teachers who had infiltrated their churches (1:4). These false teachers were ignoring the teachings of the apostles (1:17), ridiculing theology (1:10, 18), and twisting the message of God's grace in order to excuse their sexual immorality. Jude urged his readers to build themselves up in their understanding of God and his Word (1:20), pray (1:20), reject all false teaching (1:23), and focus on Christ (1:24-25).

MESSAGE

God's word and the gift of eternal life have infinite value and have been entrusted to Christ's faithful followers. There are many people who live in opposition to God and his followers. They twist God's truth, seeking to deceive and destroy the unwary. But God's truth must go forth, carried and defended by those who have committed their lives to God's Son. It is an important task, an awesome responsibility, and a profound privilege to have this commission. This was Jude's message to Christians everywhere. Opposition would come and godless teachers would arise, but Christians should "defend the truth" (1:3) by rejecting all falsehood and immorality (1:4-19), remembering God's mighty acts of rescue and punishment (1:5-11, 14-16) and the warnings of the apostles (1:17-19). His readers are to build up their own faith through prayer (1:20), keeping close to Christ (1:21), helping others (1:22-23), and hating sin (1:23). Then Jude concludes with a glorious benediction of praise to God (1:24-25).

The main themes in the book of Jude include: *False Teachers* and *Apostasy.*

False Teachers (1:4, 8, 10-19). Jude warned against false teachers and leaders who reject the lordship of Christ, undermine the faith of others, and lead people astray. He pointed out that these men had already infiltrated the church, making them even more dangerous. He also explained that these leaders and any who follow them will be severely punished by God.

IMPORTANCE FOR TODAY. We must stoutly defend Christian truth, avoiding all compromise of the basics of the faith and rejecting all who would twist Scripture to fit their own immoral agenda. Make sure that you avoid leaders and teachers (even in the church) who change the Bible to suit their own purposes. Genuine servants of God will faithfully portray Christ in their words and conduct. Watch out for anyone who tries to make Jesus anything less than the King of kings and Lord of lords and who tries to make the Bible anything less than the inspired Word of God.

Apostasy (1:4-9, 10-11, 14-19, 22-25). Jude also warned against apostasy—turning away from Christ—presenting examples from the Old Testament of those who turned away and were punished. We must remember that God punishes all who rebel against him. We must be careful not to drift away from a firm commitment to Christ.

IMPORTANCE FOR TODAY. People who do not seek to know the truth in God's word are susceptible to apostasy. Become a student of the Scriptures and keep your focus on Christ. Guard against any false teachings that would distract you or pull you away from God's truth.

OUTLINE OF JUDE

I. The Danger of False Teachers (1:1-16)

II. The Duty to Fight for God's Truth (1:17-25)

JUDE 1

GREETINGS FROM JUDE / 1:1-2

Jude's letter focuses on "apostasy"—when people turn away from God's truth and embrace false teachings. Jude reminded his readers of God's judgment on those who had left the faith in the past. This letter warns against false teachers—in this case, probably those who were promoting an early form of Gnosticism. Gnostics opposed two of the basic tenets of Christianity—the incarnation of Christ and the call to Christian ethics. Jude wrote to combat these false teachings and to encourage true doctrine and right conduct.

1:1 Jude was a common Jewish name. Scholars have various opinions about Jude's identity. (For a discussion of this, see the Author section in the Introduction to this book.) The overwhelming majority consider him to be a half brother of Jesus (Matthew 13:55; Mark 6:3). In his introduction, Jude identified himself as **a brother of James**. This James was not one of the apostles named James, but another of Jesus' half brothers (he is referred to in Galatians 1:19). Apparently, Jude held some authority (as revealed in this letter). He most likely traveled as a missionary (see 1 Corinthians 9:5) and naturally would have wanted to write a letter to his converts whose faith was being threatened by false teaching.

Oddly enough, Jude did not refer to himself as a brother of Jesus Christ. It would seem that this would have carried even more authority. Like James (see James 1:1), Jude simply identified himself as **a slave of Jesus Christ**. As believers, they focused on their spiritual relationship with their Lord and considered themselves privileged to be called his slaves.

Jude did not specify any destination for his letter. Instead, he addressed it to **all who are called to live in the love of God the Father and the care of Jesus Christ**. Being "called" also is referred to as "elected," "chosen," or "predestined." God's Spirit calls people out of darkness into the light of Christ, convinces them of their sinfulness, shows them what Christ can do for them, and then helps them to accept Christ. God's **love** prompted his call; his

love will continue now and forever. God's love never changes. The believers across the ancient world, often facing persecution, could count on the fact that they were and always would be enfolded by God's love. In addition, believers are kept in Jesus care and will receive the certain rewards of Christ's promised blessing. At Christ's second coming, believers will be ready to receive their full salvation and to live eternally with him.

1:2 Mercy carries with it the Old Testament picture of God's loving-kindness or compassion. God's mercy helps believers day by day. Jude knew that the believers were facing difficult situations in the world—a society focused on selfish pleasure, ready to persecute believers at any provocation, with false teachers looking to tear the churches apart. Mercy helps believers in their times of need (Hebrews 4:16).

Peace refers to the peace that Christ made between us and God through his death on the cross. Only God can give true and lasting peace (John 14:27). The believers needed an abundance of inner peace and quiet confidence as they faced the turmoil in their world and as they stood up to the false teachers.

Love comes from God, for God himself is love (1 John 4:7-8). Believers who are grounded in God's love can resist the lies of the false teachers and remain solid in their stand against persecution and temptation. God will generously grant their requests and meet their needs.

THE DANGER OF FALSE TEACHERS / 1:3-16

Jude called the believers to action, to defend the faith, calling for hard work, diligent study, willingness to stand against society's desire to water down the gospel, speaking up for the truth and bearing the burden of interpreting the timeless truth to a changing society. The believers could not (and would never be able to) sit back and idly enjoy the mercy, peace, and love of their faith (1:2). Rather, their Christian faith must be defended against the onslaught of false teaching.

1:3 Although Jude's brief letter does not mention his intended readers, it addresses specific concerns about false teaching that was threatening the churches. Yet that was not Jude's original intention, as stated in verse 3, **planning to write about the salvation we all share.** However, an urgent concern caused him to **write about something else**—namely, false teaching. In this letter he wanted to urge the believers to **defend the truth of the Good News.** Jude probably intended that this letter to be circulated. Thus, he specified no particular church or area.

The Greek word translated **defend** occurs only here in the New Testament. Often it is used in secular literature to describe the intense struggle in an athletic contest. **The truth** refers to the entire body of beliefs taught by the apostles and held by the Christians (see Acts 2:42). This truth is **unchanging, once for all time** given to God's **holy people.** All Christians had been entrusted with the faith— to keep it pure and to teach it to others. Therefore, all Christians should stand ready to defend the faith as they would defend any prized possession.

1:4 Jude's compulsion to write this letter came because of **some godless people** (false teachers) who had **wormed their way in among** the believers; that is, they had entered the church. These may have been traveling teachers who had come and had established themselves in communities and churches with the sole aim of perverting the Christian gospel. (For example, in Galatians 2:4, Paul talked about the Judaizers who had infiltrated Christian groups.) These false teachers did not belong in the church and were no better than intruders among the believers.

Their teaching was dangerous because they were **saying that God's forgiveness allows us to live immoral lives.** The true gospel teaches that people are freed from sin by believing in Jesus Christ as Savior and Lord. This happens by God's forgiveness alone. However, the purpose of this forgiveness is to move people to holy living and service to God. The false teachers twisted God's grace, saying that forgiveness from sin means that people can live any way they please, fulfilling their sinful pleasures without inhibition. In their arrogance, these false teachers claimed that their privileged status within God's grace put them above moral law. Even today, some Christians minimize sin, believing that how they live has little to do with their faith. But what a person truly believes will be revealed by how he or she acts. Those who truly have faith will show it by their deep respect for God and their sincere desire to live according to the principles in his Word. Twisting God's grace to allow for flagrant sexual sin is a horrible perversion of the gospel. For doing this, the false teachers and their followers would pay dearly. In fact, their **fate was determined long ago.** This refers to previously written condemnation of anyone who is a false teacher or false prophet. God's true prophets had warned against false prophets (see, for example, Isaiah 44:25; Jeremiah 50:36). Jesus had warned his disciples that false teachers would come (Matthew 7:15; 24:11, 24; Luke 6:26). The apostles often denounced false teachers in their letters (see 2 Corinthians 11:5; Galatians 1:6-9; Philippians 3:2; Colossians 2:8, 16-19; 1 Timothy 1:3; 6:3; 2 Timothy 3:6; 2 Peter 2; 1 John 4:1). These false teachers would eventually receive their just reward.

There could be no other fate except condemnation, for these teachers had **turned against** the **only Master and Lord, Jesus Christ.** With their flagrant sexual sinning in the name of God's grace, these false teachers were denying Christ as their Master and Lord, replacing him with themselves and their appetites. While claiming to know God, their actions denied him (see Titus 1:16). They taught lies, and in so doing they denied the basics of the Christian faith (1 John 2:22). Such a denial also ends in judgment and destruction (see Matthew 10:33).

So how are believers today to discern false teaching? Heresies can be discovered through asking probing questions. We can guard against heresies by asking these questions about any religious group:

1. Does it stress man-made rules and taboos rather than God's grace?
2. Does it foster a critical spirit toward others, or does it exercise discipline discreetly and lovingly?
3. Does it stress formulas, secret knowledge, or special visions more than the Word of God?
4. Does it elevate self-righteousness, honoring those who keep the rules, rather than elevating Christ?
5. Does it neglect Christ's universal church, claiming to be an elite group?
6. Does it teach humiliation of the body as a means to spiritual growth rather than focusing on the growth of the whole person?

7. Does it disregard the family rather than holding it in high regard as the Bible does?

1:5 To prove that the determined fate (1:4) was certain to come upon the false teachers and all unbelievers, Jude wanted to **remind** the believers of three examples of God's punishment of sin and rebellion in the past (1:5-7). Such judgment also awaited the sin and rebellion of the false teachers.

First, Jude reminded his readers about God's people, Israel, who, although **the whole nation was rescued** out of slavery in **Egypt,** not everyone entered the Promised Land. The entire nation had received God's deliverance, seeing his incredible miracles in accomplishing their exodus. But when they arrived at the entrance to the Promised Land, many rebelled against God, refusing to believe that he could or would protect them. Their unbelief resulted in destruction. From the original group, only Caleb and Joshua (and their families) were allowed to enter Canaan because God **destroyed every one of those who did not remain faithful** (see Hebrews 3:16-19).

Jude used Israel's experience on the threshold of the Promised Land to explain that even some among God's people can turn away. The false teachers had come from the ranks of the believers. While not truly followers of Christ, they were saying and doing many of the right things, even as they were teaching their wrong doctrines. They understood that they could find deliverance from bondage to sin (like bondage to Egypt), yet they were choosing sin over salvation. The obvious result, Jude wrote, would be that they, like the disobedient Israelites, would be destroyed.

1:6 This second example of God's punishment of disobedience describes certain **angels,** not those who live in heaven and glorify God, but those **who did not stay within the limits of authority God gave them but left the place where they belonged.** Once pure, holy, and living in God's presence, they gave in to pride and joined Satan to rebel against God. They left their positions of authority and their dwelling with God, resulting in eventual doom. Peter explained that God "did not spare even the angels when they sinned" (2 Peter 2:4). Scholars differ as to which rebellion Jude referred. This could refer either to the angels who rebelled with Satan (Ezekiel 28:15), or more likely to the sin of the "sons of God" described in Genesis 6:1-4 (an interpretation given in the book of Enoch in the Apocrypha, when angels came to earth and took women as sexual partners; see also Revelation 12:7). Though not in the Bible, Jewish theology at this time held that some fallen angels (demons) were held in chains and some were free

to roam this world to oppress people. For more on the book of Enoch, see verse 14. Jude's readers apparently understood his meaning, as well as the implication that if God did not spare his angels, neither would he spare the false teachers. Pride and lust had led to civil war and to the angels' fall. The false teachers' pride and lust would lead to judgment and destruction.

As for these disobedient angels, **God has kept them chained in prisons of darkness, waiting for the day of judgment.** These angels were imprisoned in Tartarus (see comments on 1 Peter 3:19-20; 2 Peter 2:4). Some scholars describe the "chains" as metaphors for the confinement of "darkness"; others take them to be literal chains in a dark pit somewhere in this earthly sphere. Most likely this place of punishment is in a heavenly realm that is set aside for punishment (see comments on 1 Peter 3:19). These sinful angels will be "kept" in a place of punishment until the great day of judgment, when they will face their final doom (Matthew 25:41).

1:7 Finally, as a third example of God's judgment of disobedience, Jude pointed out that **Sodom and Gomorrah and their neighboring towns were destroyed by fire.** The inhabitants were so full of sin that God wiped the cities off the face of the earth. The people were following their own sinful natures, indulging in **sexual immorality** and pursuing **sexual perversion.** God "rained down fire and burning sulfur" (Genesis 19:24) as punishment. So complete was God's judgment and destruction that the cities no longer exist today. Archaeologists believe they may be under the waters of the Dead Sea.

The destruction of these cities served as **a warning of the eternal fire that will punish all who are evil.** The fire that rained on the evil cities pictures the fire that awaits unrepentant sinners. Many people don't want to believe that God will punish people with "eternal fire" for rejecting him. But this is clearly taught in Scripture. Sinners who don't seek forgiveness from God will face eternal darkness. Jude warned all who rebel against, ignore, or reject God.

1:8 The **false teachers** used **dreams** and visions for sources of their **authority.** Drawing from his three analogies above, Jude indicted the false teachers in three areas:

1. They **live immoral lives.** Like the citizens of Sodom and Gomorrah, they follow wherever their sinful desires lead them, even into homosexuality. These people taught that Christian freedom placed believers above moral rules. No one living in such a way should

attempt to speak for God. By doing so, these false teachers brought great judgment on themselves.

2. They **defy authority.** This "authority" could refer to church leaders, angelic powers (as below), or the Lord himself. Most likely, the false teachers rejected the authority of all of these. They lived to please themselves and dismissed the prospect of a Second Coming and judgment by God.

3. They would **scoff at the power of the glorious ones.** In light of the comparable verse in 2 Peter 2:11, the celestial beings mentioned here most likely are the fallen angels—the guilty celestial beings who deserve condemnation. The false teachers "slandered" the spiritual realities they did not understand, perhaps by taking Satan's power too lightly. Thus, the statement in verse 9 that the archangel Michael did not dare to slander Satan himself shows the arrogance of these false teachers.

Jude was emphasizing that the false teachers were immoral, insubordinate, and irreverent. Jude hardly needed to say more. The believers had no reason for listening to or following such people.

1:9 Michael is **one of the mightiest of the angels,** sometimes called an archangel, reflecting the ranking of angels that was part of Jewish tradition. In Daniel 10:13, 21 and 12:1, Michael is also referred to as a mighty angel. This incident is not recorded in Scripture. The Bible merely states that Moses died and no one knows where his grave is (Deuteronomy 34:5-6). The background for this dispute over Moses' body can be found in an ancient book titled, "The Assumption of Moses." The story, obviously known to the early believers, explains that Michael had been sent to bury Moses' body. According to "The Assumption of Moses," when Michael prepared to do his task, he began **arguing with Satan about Moses' body.** Satan is a fallen angel. He is real, not symbolic, and is constantly fighting against those who follow and obey God. The story explains that Satan said Moses' body rightfully belonged to him because Moses had committed murder (see Exodus 2:12). While Michael had every reason to expose Satan's lies, he **did not dare accuse Satan of blasphemy.** Michael, instead of using his own authority, left the matter in his Master's hands, saying simply, **"The Lord rebuke you."** He did not rely on his own power and authority.

Jude wanted the believers to understand that if even the mightiest angels are careful about how they address other powers, even evil ones, how much more should mere people watch their words

when speaking of celestial powers, good or evil. If even a powerful angel of God did not dare to speak a judgment on God's behalf, then neither should the false teachers claim to speak for God when they knew nothing about him.

1:10 In contrast to Michael's refusal to slander even Satan himself (1:9), the false teachers scoffed at celestial power (1:8) and mocked and cursed **the things they do not understand.** Many of these false teachers claimed to possess a superior, secret knowledge that gave them authority. They considered themselves to be the only ones to truly "understand" God. Yet by their slander, they revealed not superior knowledge, but profound ignorance. In fact, for all their pride, they were no better than **animals.** They could really do no more than **whatever their instincts tell them**—that is, how to fulfill their sexual desires. While claiming superior knowledge and status, these false teachers had only the most basic knowledge—how to fulfill their lust. They had no understanding beyond that of the animals; their status was not above the rest of humanity, but was, in reality, below it.

Their refusal to heed God's voice left them enslaved to sin and their sinful passions. The only things these men truly understood were the passions and lusts that enslaved them. Even though they claimed to be able to indulge themselves without retribution, eventually they would **bring about their own destruction.**

1:11 Jude reminded his readers of three classic examples of men who had lived as they pleased and had been punished for doing so. These stories illustrate attitudes that are typical of false teachers—pride, selfishness, jealousy, greed, lust for power, and disregard of God's will.

Cain murdered his brother out of vengeful jealousy (Genesis 4:1-16). There are various interpretations of Cain's **example**—that he **killed his brother.** Jude may have been referring to Cain's desire to devise another way of worship rather than the way God intended (Hebrews 11:4), to Cain's intense envy of his brother, or to Cain's selfish, evil heart that led him to murder (1 John 3:12). Just as Cain murdered his brother, so the false teachers "murder" people's souls. Just as Cain did not care about his brother, murdering him out of envy, so the false teachers did not care about their followers, willingly leading them along the pathway to destruction. Like Cain, the false teachers were defying God's authority and acting out of sinful passion.

Balaam prophesied out of greed, not out of obedience to God's command (Numbers

22–24; see also 2 Peter 2:15-16). The false teachers were following in the steps of Balaam, a man who had led many astray. A pagan king had hired Balaam, a prophet, to curse Israel. At first, Balaam obeyed God; eventually, however, his evil motives and desire for money won out. Like Balaam, the false teachers were not interested in serving God; they **will do anything for money**, using religion only for financial gain and personal advancement.

Korah rebelled against God's divinely appointed leaders, wanting the power for himself (Numbers 16:1-35). By leading a revolt against God's divinely appointed leaders, Korah was actually revolting against God. The punishment was literally earthshaking when the earth split apart and swallowed those who rebelled with their households and possessions. Like Korah, the false teachers had revolted against the divinely appointed leadership of the apostles and church leaders, setting themselves up in opposition.

Through these three Old Testament pictures, Jude painted these false teachers. They were without love (like Cain), greedy for money (like Balaam), and insubordinate to God-appointed authorities (like Korah). God's punishment on them is certain.

1:12-13 When the Lord's Supper was celebrated in the early church, believers would eat a full meal before sharing the bread and wine of communion. The meal was called a **fellowship** meal (or love feast); it was designed to be a sacred time of fellowship to prepare one's heart for the Lord's Supper. However, the false teachers were joining these meals and ruining the Christians' gatherings by their very presence. The false teachers were like **dangerous reefs** along a shoreline, ready to **shipwreck** the believers. Jude spared no words in describing the danger of these false teachers' involvement with the believers. In the worst sort of hypocrisy, these intruders who had stolen in among the believers (1:4) were participating in the love feast while at the same time living and speaking in opposition to Christ.

They were **shameless** in their selfishness. They cared nothing for the believers, their celebration, or the God the believers worshiped. Instead of looking after others' needs, the false teachers' only concern was their own needs.

In four vivid word pictures taken from nature, Jude further described the false teachers. First, **they are like clouds blowing over dry land without giving rain**—all show but no substance. Like waterless clouds, they were **promising** rain but

floated on by, **producing nothing.** While they might claim superior knowledge, the false teachers had nothing of substance to assuage anyone's spiritual thirst.

Second, the false teachers **are like trees without fruit at harvesttime.** A fruitless tree in autumn may refer to a sterile tree, which was as good as dead because it produced no fruit. A tree **pulled out by the roots** was completely **dead.** Jude compared the false teachers to trees promising fruit but giving none. They were "once dead" because they had never taken root (they were never believers), and they had never borne spiritual fruit in their lives. They were **doubly dead** because just as fruitless trees are uprooted and burned, so the false teachers would face eternal punishment.

Third, the false teachers **are like wild waves of the sea, churning up the dirty foam of their shameful deeds.** Like the wild waves that make lots of noise as they restlessly thrash about, the false teachers restlessly and loudly were spewing their teaching. Jude used the image recorded in Isaiah 57:20. As debris and filth caught in the foam are cast up on the shore, so the false teachers' shameful actions would be cast up for all to see.

Fourth, the false teachers were **wandering stars, heading for everlasting gloom and darkness.** For centuries, the fixed stars in the heavens have guided seafarers and navigators in travels around the earth. But wandering (or shooting) stars offer no guidance and no light. They appear bright for a few moments but shoot across the sky and disappear into darkness. The false teachers were as useless as wandering stars because they offered no direction and no light. Their teachings might seem "bright" for a while, but these teachers would find that their eternal judgment and punishment are certain; they have reservations that cannot be changed or canceled.

1:14-15 We know a little about **Enoch** from the Old Testament (Genesis 5:21-24). He was in the lineage of Jesus Christ (Luke 3:37). The apocryphal book called Enoch describes Enoch as living **seven generations after Adam.** He was the seventh in order because Adam was counted as the "first" in the Jewish way of recording generations. During the period between the writing of the Old and New Testaments, Enoch had become a popular figure in Jewish writing. He was thought to be a figure of the Messiah and was considered to have had expert knowledge about the heavens (see Hebrews 11:5).

Jude was quoting from a prophecy in the book of Enoch (1 Enoch 1:9), written in the time between the Testaments (second century B.C.) and familiar to the early Christians. While this book did not become a part of the canon of Scripture,

Jude considered this prophecy to be correct and authoritative, and he quoted words that were familiar to his readers and affirmed by other Scriptures. This prophecy clinched Jude's argument of future judgment. Enoch had prophesied that the Lord would return in great glory, bringing with him **thousands of his holy ones.** Scripture also describes Jesus returning to earth with many angels ("holy ones")—see Deuteronomy 33:2; Daniel 7:10; Zechariah 14:5; Matthew 16:27; 24:30-31; 25:31; Hebrews 12:22.

Jude continued to quote from Enoch's prophecy, saying that the Lord would return to earth and bring the people of the world to judgment, and convict the ungodly of all the evil things they have done in rebellion and of all the insults that godless sinners have spoken against him. These false teachers' character, actions, and words will result in a guilty conviction on the day when the Lord returns.

1:16 Jude explained four areas of evil things done in rebellion (1:15). First, as **grumblers and complainers** they constantly found fault in everyone and everything, except in themselves. When people stray from God, they may become habitual complainers, unable to see God or good in anything (see Exodus 16–17; Numbers 14–17; 1 Corinthians 10:10).

Second, they did **whatever evil they** felt like doing. This has already been made clear by Jude's words in 1:4, 8, 10-13, 15. Without regard for God's laws or even for basic morality, these men shamelessly indulged their lusts, acting on their passions and desires. Their only god was self, and they worshiped that god wholeheartedly.

Third, they were **loudmouthed braggarts.** This means they were boastful men, swollen with pride. They had denied Christ and spoken against him (1:15); these bombastic words might have been their erroneous doctrines spoken loudly with the hopes of impressing others and making a name for themselves.

Fourth, these false teachers would **flatter others to get favors in return.** Flattery is phony, and the false teachers used it as a cover-up for their real intentions. Instead of loving people, they used them, using flattery if necessary to get what they wanted.

Jude could hardly have said worse about anyone. Sparing no words for these false teachers, he laid their attitudes, words, and actions out for all to see. He meant for the Christians to take this irrefutable evidence and decide for themselves about these men.

A CALL TO REMAIN FAITHFUL / 1:17-23
The audience to whom Jude wrote was vulnerable to heresies and to temptations toward immoral living. Jude encouraged the believers to remain firm in their faith and trust in God's promises for their future. This was vital because they were living during a time of increased disloyalty to the faith. We too are living in the last days, much closer to the end than were the original readers of this letter. We, too, are vulnerable to doctrinal error. We too are tempted to give in to sin. Although there is much false teaching around us, we need not be afraid or give up in despair—God can keep us from falling, and he guarantees that if we remain faithful, he will bring us into his presence and give us everlasting joy.

1:17-18 In addition to examples from the Old Testament of God's punishment of sin (1:5-7) and citations from prophecy about the Second Coming (1:14-15), Jude appealed to the believers to **remember what the apostles** had said regarding false teachers. The words of the apostles were already being considered authoritative and on the level with Scripture. The words quoted here, **"in the last times there would be scoffers whose purpose in life is to enjoy themselves in every evil way imaginable,"** parallel 2 Peter 3:3. The "last times" began with Christ's resurrection and will continue until his return, when he will set up his Kingdom and judge all humanity. Jesus and the apostles forewarned all believers that during that

interim, including the time period in which we live, "scoffers" will come. To "scoff" means to show contempt for something by one's actions and language, to mock. These false teachers scoffed at the truth and taught their own lies. They despised all morality and religion. Jesus had warned against the deception of false teachers (Mark 13:21-23), as had Paul (Acts 20:28-31; 2 Thessalonians 2:1-12; 1 Timothy 4:1; 2 Timothy 3:1-5), Peter (2 Peter 2:1–3:7), and John (1 John 2:22; 4:1-3; 2 John). Because Jesus and the apostles had warned against false teachers, the church must also be prepared.

1:19 These false teachers should have been easy to spot. They were not godly ministers; rather, they lived **by natural instinct**—living to please themselves and their sinful desires. They did **not have God's Spirit living in them.** They set themselves above all other Christians because of their imagined superior knowledge and understanding of their "freedom" in Christ. Those allegedly enlightened enough to join them regarded themselves as distinct and superior from others in the church. Thus, Jude condemned these false teachers for **creating divisions.**

Ironically, the very presence of these false teachers who scoffed at the apostles' teachings and at the prophecies of the Second Coming was a fulfillment of prophecy. The apostles had indicated that these false teachers would be abundant in "the last days" (see 1 Timothy 4:1-2; 1 John 2:18-26). Their presence only further assured the believers that Christ would soon return.

1:20 The believers could stand against the false teachers if they followed Jude's advice in four areas. First, they must **build** on the firm **foundation** of their **faith**, standing strong and unified (see also 1 Corinthians 3:9-17; Ephesians 2:20-22). They could do this by staying close to other believers and by continuing in worship, including taking the Lord's Supper.

Second, Jude encouraged the believers to **continue to pray** in the power and strength of the **Holy Spirit.** The Holy Spirit prays on behalf of believers (Romans 8:26-27; Galatians 4:6; Ephesians 6:18), opens their minds to Jesus (John 14:26), and teaches believers more about their Lord (John 15:26). Prayer is the lifeline that connects all Christians to their Savior. Believers must never stop praying.

1:21 Third, believers should **live in such a way that God's love** could **bless** them. This means that the believers must stay close to God and his people, not listening to false teachers who would try to pull them away (John 15:9-10). Obedience is the key. The false teachers had flouted obedience and thus had stepped out of God's love.

Fourth, the believers should patiently **wait for the eternal life** promised by the **Lord Jesus Christ.** The promises will come true. Christ will return and bring his people into eternal glory with him. While believers have already received his **mercy,** they must wait for the consummation of that mercy when their salvation will be made complete

(2 Peter 3:11-12, 14). Believers wait in confident expectation. God's promises are not "ifs" but "whens." They must know, beyond any doubt, that their Savior will soon return for them.

1:22-23 Although the false teachers were hopelessly entrenched in their sin and Satan's grip, the believers had a responsibility to those who had fallen prey to false teaching.

The first group consists of those believers who have listened to the false teachers and have begun to doubt God's truth. They still have reservations, so they have not yet joined the false teachers. These people are not to be ridiculed; rather, they are to be shown mercy and carefully drawn back into the church by providing them with the true teaching of the gospel. Believers who are well taught in the faith can **show mercy to those whose faith is wavering** by quietly and calmly talking with them, explaining the false teachers' error, and reminding them of the truth they had originally received.

The second group has gone beyond doubting. Agreeing with the false teachers, they are on the road to destruction. They need someone to literally step in their path and **rescue** them **from the flames of judgment.** The "flames" refer to the eternal punishment awaiting the false teachers (1:4). If we saw someone about to be burned by fire, we would quickly grab that person and pull him or her out of harm's way. That's the attitude the true believers are to have toward those sliding toward false teaching. We need to grab them and pull them away before it is too late. We need ministers and teachers who know how to refute false teaching and defend Christianity so that they can rescue the misinformed.

The third group refers to those already in the false teachers' camps—those who have already joined them. These people also need **mercy,** but believers must **be careful** so as not to be **contaminated by their sins.** While believers might try to rescue those deceived people, they must do so without allowing themselves to become contaminated by the false teaching. This will be a difficult task, one to be undertaken with healthy fear and respect for the spiritual warfare when God's power meets head-on with Satan's power. Believers have God on their side, but they must remember not to attempt anything in their own power lest they too fall prey to the false teachers' lies.

A PRAYER OF PRAISE / 1:24-25
As the letter began, so it ended—with assurance. In this great doxology, Jude stressed the mighty power of God to keep us securely in him.

1:24 God **is able to keep** believers from falling prey to false teachers. Although false teachers were widespread and dangerous, although it would be dangerous to attempt to rescue slipping fellow Christians, the believers should not retreat or be afraid. Instead, they should trust God and remain rooted and grounded in him. God can be trusted to **bring** all believers **into his glorious presence.** We should praise him for this great promise. The believers could trust that God would do as he promised and one day bring them to himself. But that will not be a day of punishment (as it will be for the false teachers). Rather, it will be a day of joy, for God will present his people **innocent of sin and with great joy.** When Christ appears, and we are given our new bodies, we will be like him (1 John 3:2). Coming into Christ's presence will be a time of "great joy" for God and for all believers.

1:25 Contemplating the great joy awaiting all believers and the fulfillment of God's promises of eternal glory, Jude praised God with a beautiful doxology. Jude had originally intended to write about the salvation all believers shared (1:3); he got his chance here. This one final verse captures the focus and goal of believers' salvation and faith. Christianity is not a series of made-up ideas or free-floating thoughts; it is faith in a person—not just any person, but **God** who became **our Savior, through Jesus Christ.** To this God alone the believers should ascribe

- **glory**—God's powerful radiance, his greatness, his complete moral superiority and splendor
- **majesty**—God's transcendent greatness
- **power**—God's self-contained might, his control over the world
- **authority**—God's sovereignty over all physical and moral laws in the entire universe

These qualities reside in God alone. Jesus Christ is **our Lord,** meaning that he too has all glory, majesty, power, and authority as God himself. This was true before the ages began, and it is true in the present day. And it will continue to be true **forevermore.**

REVELATION

INTRODUCTION

Hollywood studios produce spectacular displays for movie-theater entertainment. With computer-generated images and other high-tech tricks, movies present special effects that seem almost beyond comprehension. Aliens and dinosaurs come to life; explorers travel faster than light; animals and trees dance, sing, and talk. Viewers marvel at the show, then return to reality as the credits roll.

That's great entertainment. But we know it's not real. Now flip to the back of your Bible, to the last book—Revelation. As you read, you soon will become immersed in a fantastic display of sights, sounds, colors, and images. If you feel overwhelmed and amazed, think of what the original witness to these events, John, must have felt as vision after vision assaulted his senses. No adjectives can adequately describe *this* multimedia show. Trumpets, thrones, lightening, thunder, lampstands, awful creatures, millions of majestic angels, a mighty chorus, fiery horses, plagues, terrible bowls . . . one scene follows another, moving steadily and decisively toward the ultimate finale.

This is a story of martyrs and battles, of demons and angels, of things to come. Revelation reveals God and his plan for the future. And it's true.

AUTHOR

John the apostle, son of Zebedee and Salome, and younger brother of James.

In a book filled with obscure images and vague allusions, one thing comes through loud and clear: the name of the author. At the very beginning, Revelation identifies its source: "This is a revelation from Jesus Christ . . . sent to God's servant John" (1:1). The statement asserts that Jesus Christ himself gave this revelation to a man named John.

The early church fathers—including Justin Martyr, Irenaeus, and Hippolytus—uniformly identified this John as the apostle of the same name, the one who abandoned his father's fishing nets to follow Jesus (Matthew 4:21-22). It is clear from the Gospels that the apostle John was very close to Jesus. Jesus singled out Peter, James, and John to accompany him to Jairus's home to witness the resurrection of Jairus's daughter (Mark 5:37-43). Then, on two separate occasions, Jesus asked the three men to go away with him to a secluded place to spend time in prayer. At the first of these occasions, John witnessed the dazzling transfiguration of Jesus as he was joined by two heavenly guests, Moses and Elijah (Luke 9:28-31). The second occasion came during that agonizing night Jesus spent in the Garden of Gethsemane before his arrest (Matthew 26:36-38). John also helped make preparations for the Last Supper (Luke 22:8). What a great privilege to have been such a close confidant of the Lord Jesus himself!

Apparently, John's proximity to the Master made him quite bold. He didn't shrink from asking Jesus if he could sit in a place of honor in the coming Kingdom (Mark 10:35-37). John even offered to call down fire from heaven to wipe out a Samaritan village that had rejected Jesus (Luke 9:54-55). In each case, Jesus reined in the misplaced enthusiasm of this "Son of Thunder" (see Mark 3:17). Yet John's clear loyalty to his Lord and Savior should be admired. His love for Jesus motivated him to stay close in the darkest hour. On the day of Jesus' crucifixion, John stood at the foot of the cross, where Jesus entrusted him with the care of Jesus' earthly mother (John 19:26-27). No wonder John humbly described himself as the disciple Jesus loved (John 13:23; 19:26; 20:2; 21:20-24).

It is certainly understandable, therefore, that Jesus would appear to this beloved apostle at a later date, to entrust him with a very special message for the church (Revelation 1:9-19). So, near the end of his life, John received a vision from Christ, which he recorded for the benefit of the seven churches in Asia and for Christians everywhere, throughout history.

Although much evidence affirms the apostle John as Revelation's author, a few scholars aren't convinced. Dionysius, a fourth-century bishop of Alexandria, was the first known doubter of this apostle's authorship of Revelation. Dionysius pointed out the following:

- Revelation has a completely different structure than John's other writings—including the Gospel of John, 1 John, 2 John, and 3 John.
  - None of John's writings allude to Revelation.
  - The rough and inaccurate Greek of Revelation sharply contrasts with the polished and faultless Greek of John's Gospel and letters.
- Dionysius cautiously suggested that a prophet named John, who lived in Ephesus in the first century, had written this book.
- The differences in Greek style between Revelation and John's writings are real but can be easily explained. The primary difference comes from the fact that John was writing apocalyptic literature—that is, he was recording the images he saw while he was seeing them. This style of writing, if left uncorrected, would account for its poor grammar and awkward syntax. The subject matter of Revelation also accounts for the difference in style. John's other writings are instructional or historical, while Revelation is the record of an extraordinary vision—a vision that couldn't be expressed with the precise syntax of the Greek language.

Although Bible scholars cannot assert with certainty that the "John" of Revelation is the apostle John, no other viable alternative has been offered. The evidence for Dionysius's "John of Ephesus" is slim. Thus, we have no substantial reasons to doubt that the apostle John was the one who witnessed the remarkable visions recorded in this book, appropriately titled "Revelation."

For more on John the apostle, see the Author section in the Introduction to the Gospel of John.

DATE AND SETTING
Written around A.D. 90–95 from the island of Patmos.

Readers don't have to guess or research where Revelation was written. The text clearly names the location as the island of Patmos: "I am John, your brother. In Jesus we are partners in suffering and in the Kingdom and in patient endurance. I was exiled to the island of Patmos for preaching the word of God and speaking about Jesus" (1:9). Patmos, with its rugged volcanic hills, lies about fifty-five kilometers off the southwest coast of Asia Minor and is only twelve kilometers long and seven kilometers wide.

John had been sent to that barren and rocky island off the coast of present-day Turkey because he had fearlessly proclaimed the gospel. John had been banished to Patmos as the Roman authorities continued moving against the church. Threatened by John's powerful ministry, they viewed John as a dangerous leader of the Christian sect. During this exile, while John was separated from his Christian brothers and sisters, the risen Jesus appeared to him in a spectacular vision.

Although the place of John's vision is identified in the text, the exact time is not. Most of the evidence seems to point to Emperor Domitian's reign, around A.D. 90–95. The early church father Irenaeus made this case. Modern scholars agree with Irenaeus, believing that after writing Revelation, John was released from Patmos, whereupon he returned to Ephesus, where he had been ministering before his exile. Then, several years later, around A.D. 100, John died. This progression of events fits well with the evidence in Revelation itself. The writer described himself as a brother and companion of the believers in Ephesus and nearby cities (1:9-11)—an appropriate statement for a leader of the Ephesian church.

The letters to the seven churches in Asia Minor in 2–3 speak of a spiritual decline—something that certainly could have occurred during the forty or so years after their foundings. The church of Laodicea is described as rich in 3:17. Since the city was completely destroyed by an earthquake in A.D. 60–61, it would have been difficult to say this of Laodicea much before A.D. 90.

Some believe that Revelation was written during Nero's reign, between the years A.D. 54 and 68, the time of Nero's greatest persecution of the Christians. The best argument for this date is that the apostle John may have written the description of the New Jerusalem (21:1-27) before the destruction of the old city in A.D. 70. Another explanation for an early date is that the number 666 works as a possible cryptic reference to Nero. When the words "Nero Caesar" are transcribed into Hebrew, the numeric value of the Hebrew letters can be calculated as 666. Another argument is that the persecution that Nero instigated against Christians could be coincidental with the persecution in the book of Revelation.

In the last analysis, however, the evidence seems to support the early church tradition that the apostle John wrote Revelation on the island of Patmos around A.D. 90–95.

AUDIENCE
The churches in Ephesus, Smyrna, Pergamum, Thyatira, Sardis, Philadelphia, and Laodicea and believers everywhere.

Although Revelation touches on all of human history, it is specifically addressed to seven churches located in what today is southwestern Turkey. Reliable historical sources from the second century A.D. describe the apostle John as ministering in Ephesus around A.D. 70–100, so he would have been intimately familiar with the strengths and weaknesses of the churches he was addressing.

Before John worked in Ephesus, Paul had labored there. Paul had founded the Ephesian church on his second missionary journey. At that time Paul had been on his way to Jerusalem, so he had left mature Christians—Aquila and Priscilla—to carry on the work (Acts 18:19-21, 24-26). On his third missionary journey, Paul stayed in Ephesus for three full years, making it a center for evangelistic activity for the present-day region of Turkey. The city was ideally suited for this strategic purpose because it was located at the intersection of two major overland routes: the coastal road running north to Troas and the western road that headed toward Laodicea. In addition, Ephesus sat on the Cayster River and, therefore, had easy access to the shipping traffic in the Aegean Sea. Because of this central and strategic location, Ephesus had become a commercial and cultural hub of the region. Another attraction in Ephesus was a great temple to Artemis, the fertility goddess. Visitors flocked to this temple every year (Acts 19:23-27). Paul envisioned Ephesus as the center of Christianity, rather than paganism, in the region.

In the lecture hall of Tyrannus, Paul organized an evangelism school to train teachers and preachers in the gospel message (Acts 19:9-10). For three years Paul stayed in Ephesus. (The "two years" of Acts 19:10 only account for part of Paul's stay there.) Most likely, during this time all the churches addressed in Revelation were founded. These churches—Ephesus, Smyrna, Pergamum, Thyatira, Sardis, Philadelphia, and Laodicea—were located on a circular postal route in southwestern Asia Minor (present-day Turkey).

PURPOSE
To reveal the full identity of Christ and to give warning and hope to believers.

Because of the description in Revelation of Christian martyrs and a beast who demands worship (13:1-8), many readers of Revelation have assumed that the cities to which the apostle John wrote were being severely persecuted. Indeed, these communities were experiencing some persecution. John himself had been exiled to Patmos for preaching the gospel (1:9), and Antipas in Pergamum had been put to death for his adherence to Christ (2:13). Nero was the first Roman emperor to persecute Christians. Yet his persecution of Christians was local and not Empire-wide. Nero blamed the Christians in Rome for the devastating fire that had destroyed much of the city.

It wasn't until the reign of Domitian (A.D. 81–96) that refusing to worship the Roman emperor became a punishable offense throughout the Empire. Before that time, emperor worship had been spreading throughout the Roman Empire but hadn't been enforced. But even with the decree that all should worship him as "God and Lord," there isn't much evidence from Domitian's reign of widespread persecution of Christians. Most of the persecution of Christians in the first century consisted of local challenges to specific groups of believers. Out of the seven churches addressed in Revelation, John encouraged only three (Smyrna, Pergamum, and Philadelphia) to endure suffering and persecution.

This book seems to be more concerned about false teaching, sexual immorality, divisions within congregations, lack of love for God and others, and complacency toward the things of God. The greatest threat to these churches was internal, not external—the spread of false teaching and spiritual compromise (2:14-16, 20-22;

3:4, 15-17). So Revelation wasn't necessarily addressed to a persecuted minority. Instead, it was a wake-up call to a complacent, compromising church.

Revelation highlights the unseen realities that these congregations were ignoring. Vivid and terrifying visions illustrate a furious battle between good and evil—a battle of which the eventual outcome has been already determined. Ultimately, God will win! The only question was whether the members of these churches would be on God's side or on Satan's side. The answer to this question was a matter of life and death.

Understanding Apocalyptic Literature. To understand Revelation, we must recognize that John, the author, wrote in a specific genre—apocalyptic literature. From 200 B.C. to A.D. 100, certain groups of Jews and Christians used this writing style to describe the end of the world and God's judgment. Apocalyptic literature uses fantastic imagery to remind readers of the invisible, supernatural battle occurring behind the events of human history. Within the Bible, in addition to Revelation, the clearest examples of apocalyptic literature are Daniel 10–12 and Mark 13. Outside of Scripture, there are *The Assumption of Moses, The Apocalypses of Ezra, The Shepherd of Hermas,* and *Baruch.* Non-canonical apocalypses usually name no author but are written as though prominent Old Testament figures, such as Moses or Ezra, were seeing the future. There are three key characteristics of apocalyptic literature.

1. All apocalyptic literature claims to be a revelation from God. The Greek word for "apocalypse" *(apokalupsis)* actually means "revelation." Thus, in the book of Revelation, God gives a glimpse into the future. Revelation consists of four visions, each introduced by an invitation to see what the future holds (1:11; 4:1; 17:1; 21:9). In these visions world history is portrayed as a great war between God and Satan. In the end God defeats Satan and emerges as the winner of this great struggle. As you read Revelation, keep in mind the big picture—the cosmic warfare between good and evil.
2. Apocalypses are symbolic. Mysterious imagery, numerology, cosmic journeys, supernatural beings, and strange beasts fill the pages of apocalyptic works. This type of literature attempts to describe invisible, supernatural events in human terms. By their very nature, these images go beyond what is known, as apocalyptic writers point to supernatural realities through striking symbols. At this point it is important to note that in order to understand the symbols in Revelation, we must consider their meaning to the **first-century** readers and not impose contemporary events and people on the text. Apocalyptic writers never intended for the symbols to be interpreted as literal photographs of the future. Instead, they wanted their graphic and disturbing images to symbolize events, beings, or traits in the supernatural realm. For example, 1:16 describes Christ as having a sharp, double-edged sword in his mouth. By comparing this image to Hebrews 4:12-13 (which describes the Word of God as a double-edged sword that penetrates the soul and judges every thought), it becomes clear that this sword is a symbol for Christ's words. Christ's words are so full of truth that they can cleanly separate good from evil, truth from falsehood. Christ with his words of truth will be the ultimate Judge of all people.
3. Apocalyptic literature highlights God's supernatural intervention in history—the times when God decisively acts in ways that transcend natural laws.

Revelation doesn't try to encourage people to discover God's workings within the natural laws that people take for granted. Instead, the visions in this book picture God acting purposefully to end the way things have always been. Revelation describes God defeating evil in this world once and for all and establishing peace and justice forever. In the end God will interrupt the natural world so dramatically that the earth and sky will flee from his presence (20:11). God will replace the old world with a radically new one (21:1). On the new earth, for example, neither sun nor moon will be needed (21:23).

Though most of this book is apocalyptic, not all of it is. Revelation also contains straightforward prophecy (1:3; 22:7, 10, 18-19) and seven letters of admonition from Jesus Christ (1:4–3:22). As prophecy, it focuses on believers' responsibilities in this world and their relationships to an eternal future spent with God. As an epistle to seven churches, it gives advice and encouragement to believers in seven separate churches. This is the only book in the Bible that promises a blessing to those who listen to its words and do what it says (1:3).

Revelation is a hybrid of apocalypse and prophecy written within the framework of an ancient Greek letter. The purpose of this letter was to inspire believers to overcome all obstacles by steadfastly holding on to their faith (2:7, 17, 25-26; 3:5, 11-12, 21). Despite the many strange images and mysterious symbols, the central message of Revelation is clear: God controls all of history, and Christ will return to earth to judge it and to reward those who have joined his side in the fight against evil and who have remained faithful to him (22:7, 12-13, 20).

Interpreting Revelation. Revelation is a book of symbols. Every symbol in this book was understandable by people in the first century. This was a first-century book, written to the believers of the first-century church; yet it also has significance for Christians two thousand years later. The questions to ask when reading the book are, What was God saying to John's original readers? What would they have understood from John's words? Why did God use a particular symbol to get across his message?

Revelation is a book about the future and about the present. It offers future hope to all believers, especially those who have suffered for their faith, by proclaiming Christ's total triumph over evil and the reality of eternal life with him. It also gives present guidance as it teaches us about Jesus Christ and how we should live for him now. Through graphic pictures, we learn that Jesus Christ is coming again, that evil will be judged, and that the dead will be raised to judgment, resulting in eternal life or eternal destruction.

Revelation is one of the most mysterious books of the Bible. For centuries people have debated various aspects of the book—for example, the timing of the rapture of the church, the nature of the millennial reign of Christ, and the timing of Christ's return (before, in the middle of, or after the Great Tribulation). And debates have raged over the identity of the Beast, the number 666, and the Great Prostitute. Unfortunately, these debates have fueled such great controversy that Christians have been divided, and churches have even split over these issues.

Every Christian who approaches this book must realize that if these questions have been debated over centuries, then God probably made them not clear on purpose. Churches and seminaries have made their interpretations of these debated issues part of their doctrinal statements. But they must understand that other Christians who disagree with their positions are doing only that—disagreeing. The positions regarding postmillennialism versus premillennialism do not make a difference as to whether one is a believer or not. The cardinal doctrine is whether a person believes that Christ, the Savior and King, will indeed one day return for his people and whether one has trusted in him as personal Savior. From there, the timing of Christ's return or when the church will be raptured are merely issues for discussion—not fundamental doctrines that affect a person's salvation.

Believers should study Revelation carefully, always realizing that whatever position they eventually take will meet with disagreement from other sincere Christians. Believers must have respect for those who, on the basis of the biblical evidence and their own studies, accept a different position. We must recognize and condemn heresy, teaching that directly contradicts Scripture, such as someone giving a date for Christ's return when Christ has clearly said no one can know the date. But when Scripture is not clear on certain issues, and especially when those issues have been debated throughout church history without agreement, then believers should lovingly accept people who disagree.

Historically, Christians have taken four main approaches to interpret Revelation.

1. One approach is to understand the book as describing the events immediately preceding and following Christ's second coming. Christians who interpret Revelation this way are called "futurists." These believers insist that the judgments of the seals, trumpets, and bowls (see 5:1–16:21) are future events that will occur at the end of history.

    Typically, futurists insist that the key to interpreting Revelation can be found in the description of the sealed scroll, which only the Lamb, Jesus, is worthy to open (5:1-14). Each time the Lamb opens one of the scroll's seven seals, the earth experiences a cataclysmic event. Thus, futurists believe that the descriptions of famine, war, and devastation in the central chapters of Revelation depict the final days of human history. According to this view, the Beast of Revelation 13 is the Antichrist, who will appear in the end times to deceive people.

2. Many of the Reformers—Luther, Calvin, and others—interpreted Revelation much differently. They understood this mysterious book as a prophetic survey of church history. Joachim of Fiore (1135–1202) was the first person to interpret Revelation this way; he considered that the book prophesies the events of Western history from the early church until his own time. In this approach, called the "historicist" view, each one of the seven churches in Revelation 2–3 represents a certain stage of church history, from the early church to the church of the Middle Ages to, perhaps, even the modern-day church. According to this view, therefore, the Beast of Revelation would represent a specific person or institution in history. The historicist view doesn't enjoy much favor today because there hasn't been any agreement on the specific historical events that Revelation describes.

3. Other scholars believe that Revelation simply describes events confined to the apostle John's day. This is called the "preterist" view ("preterist" means "past action"). According to this perspective, for example, the Beast in Revelation 13

represents the Roman Empire because Revelation's original readers would have readily identified the Roman Empire as the primary opponent of the church.

4. Another group of interpreters understands Revelation as being primarily "symbolic." They believe that through symbols Revelation presents timeless truths that were relevant to the original readers and are relevant to readers today. According to the symbolic view, Revelation essentially describes a battle between good and evil that occurs throughout world history. Proponents of the symbolic perspective assert that Revelation's fundamental message can be understood by everyone—a person born in the Roman Empire in the first century, someone living in New Zealand in the nineteenth century, or someone living in America today. An extreme symbolic approach would spiritualize the entire book, asserting that Revelation predicts no specific historical events. The Beast, according to the symbolic view, would represent the power of all those who oppose Christ and who have opposed him throughout all of world history.

Whenever you hear someone talking about his or her view of Revelation, remember these four basic interpretative approaches. Some preachers and Bible teachers use more than one.

This commentary often presents several interpretations of a specific passage. Yet the basic approach of this commentary is to treat Revelation as a prophetic book, as the book itself claims to be (1:3; 22:7-21). Thus, this commentary will attempt to show how Revelation unveils the future and the end of human history. This commentary, however, will also describe what Revelation would have meant to its original readers in ancient Asia Minor.

In the final analysis, the central idea, on which all four basic interpretations agree, is that Christ will return some time in the future. This return will be a welcome sight to his people, for at that time Christ will defeat evil, judge evildoers, and reward the righteous. As you read Revelation, look beyond the symbols and interpretations to your sovereign God and to your Savior, Jesus Christ. And take hope—his victory is sure!

A QUICK JOURNEY THROUGH REVELATION

Revelation is a complex book that has baffled interpreters for centuries. We can avoid a great deal of confusion by understanding the literary structure of this book. This approach will allow us to understand the individual scenes within the overall structure of Revelation and keep us from getting unnecessarily bogged down in the details of each vision. John gives hints throughout the book to indicate a change of scene, a change of subject, or a flashback to an earlier scene.

John begins by relating the circumstances that led to the writing of this book (1:1-20), then relates special messages given him by Jesus for the seven churches of Asia Minor (2:1–3:22).

Suddenly caught up into heaven, John sees a vision of God Almighty on his throne. All of Christ's followers and the heavenly angels are worshiping God (4:1-11). John watches as God gives a scroll with seven seals to the worthy Lamb, Jesus Christ (5:1-14). The Lamb begins to open the seals one by one. As each seal is opened, a new vision appears.

As the first four seals are opened, riders appear on horses of various colors; war, famine, disease, and death are in their paths (6:1-8). As the fifth seal is opened, John sees those in heaven who have been martyred for their faith in Christ (6:9-11).

A set of contrasting images appears at the opening of the sixth seal. On one side, there is a huge earthquake, stars fall from the sky, and the sky rolls up like a scroll (6:12-17). On the other side, multitudes are before the great throne, worshiping and praising God and the Lamb (7:1-17).

Next, the seventh seal is opened (8:1-5), unveiling a series of God's judgments announced by seven angels with seven trumpets. The first four angels bring hail, fire, a burning mountain, and a falling star, and the sun and the moon are darkened (8:6-13). The fifth trumpet announces the coming of locusts with the power to sting (9:1-12). The sixth trumpet heralds the coming of an army of warriors on horses (9:13-21). In 10:1-11, John is given a little scroll to eat. Following this, John is commanded to measure the temple of God (11:1-2). He sees two witnesses, who proclaim God's judgment on the earth for three and a half years (11:3-14).

Finally, the seventh trumpet sounds, calling the rival forces of good and evil to a decisive battle. On one side is Satan and his forces; on the other side stands Jesus Christ with his forces (11:15–14:5). During this battle God reveals the absolute futility of Satan, who knows his time is short (12:12) and who, though he desires power and wants to rule, can only parody God and Christ. For example, the fatal wound that heals (13:3, 12) is an imitation of the Resurrection, and the mark of the Beast (13:16-18) imitates God's seal (7:3-4). In the midst of this call to battle, John sees three angels announcing the final judgment (14:6-13). Two angels begin to reap this harvest of judgment on the earth (14:14-20). Following on the heels of these two angels are seven more angels, who pour out God's judgment on the earth from seven bowls (15:1–16:21). One of these seven angels reveals to John a vision of a great prostitute called Babylon riding a scarlet beast (17:1-18). After the defeat of Babylon (18:1-24), a great multitude in heaven shouts praise to God for his mighty victory (19:1-10).

The last three and a half chapters of Revelation catalogue the events that complete Christ's victory over the enemy: the judgment of the rebellious nations, the Beast, and the false prophet (19:11-21); Satan's one-thousand-year imprisonment (20:1-10); the final judgment (20:11-15); and the creation of a new earth and a new Jerusalem (21:1–22:6). An angel then gives concluding instructions concerning the visions John has seen and what to do once he has written them all down (22:7-11).

Revelation concludes with the promise of Christ's return, an offer to drink of the water of life that flows through the great street of the new Jerusalem, and a warning to those who read the book (22:12-21). John finishes by praying, "Amen. Come, Lord Jesus" (22:20).

This book, and thus the whole Bible, ends with a message of warning and hope for men and women of every generation. Christ is victorious, and all evil has been conquered. As you read Revelation, marvel at God's grace in the salvation of the saints and his power over the evil forces of Satan, and take hope in the reality of his ultimate victory.

MESSAGE
The main themes of the book of Revelation are: *God's Sovereignty, Christ's Return, God's Faithful People, Judgment,* and *Hope.*

God's sovereignty (5:1-14; 11:15-18; 20:1–22:21). The sovereignty of God is a foundational theological truth. It asserts that God totally controls what happens in the world, the universe, and human life. Nothing occurs outside of God's direct or permissive will. Although this truth permeates all of Scripture, it is most clear in Revelation, where the culmination of history, the final judgment of all people, and the vindication of the righteous are vividly pictured. God is sovereign, greater than any power in the universe. God is incomparable, far above and beyond any religion, government, or leader, including Satan. God controls history for the purpose of uniting true believers in loving fellowship with him.

IMPORTANCE FOR TODAY. Assaulted with negative news from across the world and in our own communities, we can feel powerless and hopeless. Often it seems as though the forces of evil control life and will triumph. Revelation teaches the opposite. Though Satan's power may temporarily increase, we must not be led astray. God is all-powerful. He is in control and will bring his true family safely into eternal life. Because God cares for us, we can trust him with every aspect of our lives.

Christ's return (19:11-16; 20:4-6; 21:1-7; 22:6-21). When Christ came to earth as a man, he came as a perfect "Lamb," without blemish or spot, fulfilling God's requirement of a perfect sacrifice for sin. When Christ returns, he will come as the triumphant "Lion," the rightful ruler and conqueror. Christ will defeat Satan, settle accounts with all those who have rejected him, and usher his faithful followers into eternity. Because finite humans are limited by time and space, it can seem as though Christ will never return—twenty centuries have passed since his first coming. Yet to God those years are but a flicker as his plan unfolds in his eternal present. The clear message of Revelation is that Christ's coming is sure—he *will* return. And he could come at any moment. What a triumphant and glorious day that will be!

IMPORTANCE FOR TODAY. For centuries struggling and suffering Christians have been given hope and strength to endure by having the knowledge that their Savior could return at any time. We know that God's timing is perfect. Thus, Christ will return at just the right moment (Ephesians 1:10). At that time, he will come as King and Judge. Since no one knows when Christ will appear (Matthew 24:36), we must always be ready. This means keeping our faith strong and living as God wants us to live.

God's faithful people (14:1-5; 20:4-6; 21:3-4). Soon after Revelation was written, the church came under tremendous pressure from without and from within. Believers were pressured by the government, with threats of violent persecution, to renounce their faith in Christ and to worship the emperor. At the same time, a number of heresies threatened to negatively influence believers and divide the church. John wrote to encourage believers to resist the demands to worship the Roman emperor and to be devoted only to Christ. Revelation identifies the faithful people and explains how they should live until Christ returns.

IMPORTANCE FOR TODAY. Christians today still face pressures to compromise or reject their faith. In many countries persecution is as violent as it was in ancient Rome. In more affluent and civilized areas, believers face more subtle pressure to worship "Caesar." And heresies have never been in short supply. God's message in Revelation is clear: stay focused on Christ and his Word; stay faithful and true to your calling. Regardless of the sources and strength of pressure and persecution, we must be faithful. Victory is sure for those who resist temptation and who make loyalty to Christ their top priority.

Judgment (6:10-17; 11:15-19; 15:1–16:21; 18:1–20:15; 22:10-15). As first-century believers looked at their world, they must have wondered at the seeming triumph of evil. The church was being persecuted, the government was corrupt, and pagan morality was the norm. Revelation clearly shows that God is just; eventually all evildoers will be punished. One day God's anger toward sin will be fully and completely unleashed. At that time Satan will be defeated with all of his agents, and false religion will be destroyed. God will reward the faithful with eternal life, and all who refuse to believe in him will face eternal punishment.

IMPORTANCE FOR TODAY. Because human nature is still sinful and because Satan still lives and works in the world, evil and injustice are prevalent. Living as a distinct minority in faith and morality, Christians can become discouraged and feel defeated. But the strong message of Revelation is that evil and injustice will not prevail forever; God's final judgment will put an end to them. We can take hope in this sure promise from God. But we also should spread this truth to others: no one who rejects Christ will escape God's punishment.

Hope (1:3, 7-8; 2:7, 11, 17, 26-29; 3:8-13, 20-22; 4:1-11; 7:9-17; 14:13; 19:1-10; 20:4-6; 21:1–22:7, 22:17-21). Surrounded by enemies, overwhelmed by pain and grief, or confronted by seemingly insurmountable obstacles, a person can lose hope. The first-century believers must have struggled with maintaining a hopeful perspective during those dark days of persecution and depravation. In contrast, Revelation presents the promise that one day God will create a new heaven and a new earth. All believers will live with him forever in perfect peace and security. Regardless of their present troubles, believers can look ahead with hope, trusting in their loving God.

IMPORTANCE FOR TODAY. Today people still struggle with discouragement, doubt, and defeat. Depression has become epidemic as men and women feel that they are trapped in hopeless circumstances. Even Christians can lose hope in the midst of trials. But the message of Revelation still rings hope through the night. We know that what God has promised will come true. And each day the Lord's appearing is one day closer. When we have confidence in this truth and in our ultimate destination, we can follow Christ with unwavering dedication, no matter what we must face.

OUTLINE OF REVELATION

I. Letters to the Churches (1:1–3:22)
II. Message for the Church (4:1–22:21)
   A. Worshiping God in heaven
   B. Opening the seven seals
   C. Sounding the seven trumpets
   D. Observing the great conflict
   E. Pouring out the seven plagues
   F. Seizing the final victory
   G. Making all things new

REVELATION 1

PROLOGUE / 1:1-3

The book of Revelation unveils Christ's full identity and God's plan for the end of the world, and it focuses on Jesus Christ, his second coming, his victory over evil, and the establishment of his Kingdom. As you read and study Revelation, don't focus so much on the timetable of the events or the details of John's imagery that you miss the main message—the infinite love, power, and justice of the Lord Jesus Christ.

1:1 The word **revelation** is the Greek word *apokalupsis*, from which the word "apocalypse" is derived. A "revelation" exposes what was formerly hidden or secret. The revelation recorded in this book will give believers information that had been formerly veiled but would now be disclosed.

Readers need to understand some characteristics of apocalyptic literature in the Bible. The Bible's apocalyptic sections are revelations from God. Revelation is God's giving his people a peek into the future. Apocalyptic literature emphasizes God's supernatural acts. Revelation highlights God's power by focusing on the end times, when God will interrupt human history and defeat evil once and for all. Apocalyptic literature is symbolic. It attempts to describe supernatural actions with graphic symbols of real events, things, or traits. For example, Christ is described in Revelation 5:6 as having "seven horns and seven eyes." The number seven represents perfection. A horn symbolizes power. So "seven horns" speak of Jesus' extraordinary power, and "seven eyes" speak of his ability to see all things.

This book is the revelation **from Jesus Christ. God** gave the revelation of his plan to Jesus Christ (see also John 1:18; 5:19-23; 12:49; 17:8). Jesus Christ, in turn, sent his **angel,** who revealed it to **John** (see also 22:16). The angel will explain various scenes to John, acting as a guide. John, **God's servant,** then passed the message along to the churches—**God's other servants.** The phrase, **the events that will happen soon,** means imminence. Today's readers know that nearly two thousand years have passed since the time this was proclaimed. We must remember that God is timeless (2 Peter 3:8). In God's eyes the future is just around the corner, even though it may seem far away to us. No one knows when these events will happen, so believers should live at all times as though Christ will come in the next moment.

According to tradition, John, the author, was the only one of Jesus' original twelve disciples who was still alive at this time (that is, if the date of A.D. 90–95 is accepted; see the Introduction). John wrote the Gospel of John and the letters of 1, 2, and 3 John.

Jesus gave his message to John in a vision, allowing him to see and record certain future events so that they could be an encouragement to all believers. The vision includes many signs and symbols that convey the essence of what is to happen. What John saw, in most cases, was indescribable, so he used illustrations to show what it was like. Readers of this symbolic language don't have to understand every detail—John himself didn't. Instead, we must realize that John's imagery reveals that Christ is indeed the glorious and victorious Lord of all. Some of Revelation's original readers were being severely persecuted because of their faith. The awesome and sometimes frightening pictures of Jesus' ultimate victory over evil were intended to encourage them to persevere.

For information on the four main ways to interpret Revelation, see the Introduction, "Understanding Apocalyptic Literature."

1:2 John saw the vision and then **faithfully reported the word of God and the testimony of Jesus Christ.** Revelation, according to John, is God's word—not simply John's narration of what he saw. It is an eternal message. The words of this book describe the promises and actions of God that have come true through Jesus. Revelation, as difficult as it may be to understand, should not be neglected. It should be read and studied, for it is the word of God and the testimony of Christ to all believers, from the first century to today.

1:3 This promise that **God blesses** the reader and listeners sets John's writing apart from other Jewish apocalyptic literature and points out that these words were inspired by God. This is the first of seven beatitudes in Revelation (see also 14:13; 16:15; 19:9; 20:6; 22:7, 14).

Who is blessed? **The one who reads this prophecy to the church.** The public reading of Scripture was common in Jewish heritage (see, for example, Nehemiah 8:2-3; Luke 4:16; Acts 13:15). Christians also read Scripture aloud in public because copies of the Gospels and the letters of the apostles were not available to every believer. In addition to the reader, God **blesses all who listen to it and obey what it says.** "Listen" and "obey" are important terms and major themes of the book. The blessed ones are those who come to church to listen to God's word and then obey it so that it changes their lives (Ephesians 4:13).

Revelation is a book of "prophecy" that is both prediction (foretelling future events) and proclamation (preaching about who God is and what he will do). Prophecy is more than telling the future. Behind the predictions are important principles about God's character and promises. These words will bless the hearers because through them they can get to know God better and be able to trust him more completely.

JOHN'S GREETING TO THE SEVEN CHURCHES / 1:4-8

John began to address the recipients of this letter, a letter that would be sent along the roads through the various cities with the churches to whom John was writing. After this brief greeting comes a doxology of praise to God.

1:4-5a Jesus told **John** to write to **the seven churches** that knew and trusted John and had read his earlier letters (see 1:9, 11). These were literal churches in literal cities. The letter was addressed so that it could be read and passed on in a systematic fashion, following the main Roman road clockwise around **the province of Asia** (now called Turkey).

These were not the only churches in Asia at the time. For example, Troas (Acts 20:5ff), Colosse (Colossians 1:2), and Hierapolis (Colossians 4:13) also had churches. Why did the Lord direct John to write to these seven in particular? It is possible that the number seven, as with the other sevens in the book, signifies completeness. While the seven churches were actual churches, they also represented all churches throughout the ages.

The Trinity—the Father (**the one who is, who always was, and who is still to come**), the Holy Spirit (**the sevenfold Spirit**), and the Son (**Jesus Christ**)—is the source of all truth (John 14:6-17; 1 John 2:27; Revelation 19:11).

All of time is encompassed in the "Father"— he is, was, and will be. This title is used only in Revelation (see also 11:17; 16:5). God is eternally present and therefore able to help his people in any age, in any situation. The "sevenfold Spirit" has been identified by some to mean the seven angelic beings or messengers for the churches (see a further discussion at 1:20). Others have interpreted this to refer to those angels that accompany Christ at his return (Luke 9:26; 1 Timothy 5:21). But the reference to the Trinity here gives more weight to the interpretation that the sevenfold Spirit is the Holy Spirit.

Jesus is seen in all his sovereignty. He is the **faithful witness** of the truth from God, who sent him to earth to die for sins. He died and was **the first to rise from the dead** never to die again (see also Colossians 1:18). He is also portrayed as **the commander of all the rulers of the world**—an all-powerful King, victorious in battle, glorious in peace. When he returns, he will be recognized for who he really is. Then, "at the name of Jesus every knee will bow, in heaven and on earth and under the earth, and every tongue will confess that Jesus Christ is Lord, to the glory of God the Father" (Philippians 2:10-11).

1:5b-6 This doxology concludes the prologue to this book. John was writing to believers experiencing persecution; yet he assured them that Jesus not only continuously cared for and loved them but also had set them free, no matter how they might feel. Jesus had set them free from their sins **by shedding his blood,** that is, through his death on the cross. Through that blood, he had made his people **his kingdom and his priests who serve before God his Father.** Israel had been called to be "a kingdom of priests " (Exodus 19:6). This saying describes Christians as the continuation of the Old Testament people of God—his kingdom and priests (see also Hebrews 13:15; 1 Peter 2:5, 9). Together, believers make up a Kingdom of which Christ is their King; individually they are priests because each has direct access to God because of the sacrifice of Christ on the cross. Their whole purpose, of course, is to serve God.

1:7 The book of Revelation describes that day when he will return to earth. That Jesus will come **with the clouds of heaven** summarizes the message of Revelation. Jesus' second coming will be visible and victorious. **Everyone will see him**

arrive (Mark 13:26), and they will know it is Jesus. When Christ returns, he will conquer evil and will judge all people according to their deeds (Revelation 20:11-15). **Even those who pierced him** will see him, probably referring to the Jews who were responsible for his death (see Acts 2:22-23; 3:14-15). John saw Jesus' death with his own eyes, and he never forgot the horror of it (see John 19:34-35). However, all people across the ages who have rejected Christ have themselves "pierced" him with their indifference to his sacrifice on their behalf. **All the nations of the earth**—both Jews and Gentiles—**will weep because of him.** They will mourn because they know they will be facing God and his judgment and will be destroyed.

1:8 Alpha and **Omega** are the first and last letters of the Greek alphabet. The Lord God is the beginning and the end. God the Father is the eternal Lord and Ruler of the past, present, and future (see also 4:8; Isaiah 44:6; 48:12-15). God is sovereign over history and is in control of everything. **The one who is, who always was, and who is still to come** is also described in 1:4. The phrase **the Almighty One** comes out of the Old Testament and conveys military imagery, referring to God as a mighty warrior. The military imagery helped the people in the churches to whom this book was written understand that they had the ultimate Warrior fighting on their side. God rules over all.

VISION OF THE SON OF MAN / 1:9-20

John again gave his name as the author of the letter and described his whereabouts and why he was there. Next he explained his commissioning to write this letter to the churches. Then he described his vision of the exalted Christ, leaving no mistake as to Christ's true identity. The vision has much in common with Isaiah 6 and Ezekiel 1.

1:9 Although **John** was an apostle and an elder of the church, he described himself as their **brother** in Christ because he and the persecuted believers were **partners in suffering** as persecution against believers began to escalate at the end of the century. They were partners in God's coming **Kingdom** because they were already its citizens. And they were partners in **patient endurance** as they awaited the arrival of God's coming Kingdom.

John had paid for his faithfulness of **preaching the word of God and speaking about Jesus** by being **exiled to the island of Patmos,** a small rocky island about ten miles long and six miles wide in the Aegean Sea, about fifty miles offshore from the city of Ephesus on the Asia Minor seacoast (see map). The Romans used Patmos for banishing political prisoners. Although John was away from the churches and unable to travel, his exile did not stop what God would do through John, nor did it stop God's message from getting to his churches.

1:10-11 On **the Lord's Day** (Sunday), John **was worshiping in the Spirit,** which refers to a visionary experience given to John by the Holy Spirit. In this vision John heard **a voice that sounded like a trumpet blast.** The trumpet heralds the return of Christ (1 Corinthians 15; 1 Thessalonians 4). The voice commanded John to **write down** what he would see in the visions. John's record then became this book, which he would **send** to the **seven churches.** The contents of specific messages to these churches are in chapters 2 and 3.

1:12-14 The **seven gold lampstands** are the seven churches in Asia to whom this letter is addressed (Revelation 1:11, 20). (See also Zechariah 4:1-10 for his vision of seven lamps.) Jesus, **the Son of Man,** stands among them. No matter what the churches face, Jesus is in control and protects them with his all-encompassing love and reassuring power. The **long robe** pictures Jesus as a leader. The **gold sash across his chest** reveals him as the high priest who goes into God's presence to obtain forgiveness of sin for those who have believed in him. In the first century, wearing a sash, especially across the chest, indicated leadership and authority. Hebrews 2:17 identifies Jesus as the final high priest. His snowy **white hair** indicates his wisdom and divine nature (see also Daniel 7:9). His blazing **eyes** symbolize judgment of all evil (see Daniel 10:6) and deep insight, not only over the churches and the believers but over the entire course of history (see also 2:18; 19:12).

1:15 The **feet** like **bronze** picture an exalted person with great power (also from Daniel). Bronze usually symbolized the might of Rome—bronze shields and breastplates were used by the Roman army. Again, this is a picture of an all-powerful Victor (see also Ezekiel 1:13, 27; 8:2; and Daniel 10:6). The **voice** like **mighty ocean waves** (see also 19:6) evokes the image of a huge waterfall roaring over a high cliff. Thus, the voice is powerful and awesome. When this man speaks with authority, nothing else can be heard.

1:16 In his **right hand,** Christ holds **seven stars,** explained in 1:20 as "the angels of the seven churches" to whom this letter is addressed (1:11). That Christ is holding the stars implies his protection of these churches as he walks among them.

There are two swords in Revelation. Chapter 19 has the "great sword." The sword here is the **sharp two-edged sword.** This type of sword, invented by the Romans, represents invincible might. The double-edged sword was light and sharp on both edges. These swords gave such a great advantage in hand-to-hand combat that the Roman army was called "the short swords." It made them virtually invincible. This sword is coming **from** Jesus' **mouth,** symbolizing the power and force of his message. Jesus' words of judgment are as sharp as swords; he is completely invincible.

This shining **brilliance** of **his face** probably describes Christ's entire being. The same sort of picture is described in the Transfiguration, an event that John himself had witnessed (10:1; Matthew 17:2).

1:17-18 John's response to the awesome sight of the glorious Son of Man was to fall **at his feet as dead.** Most likely this was not a trance; rather, it was in response to having seen a spectacular vision. The message given by this glorious figure—Christ—is the same one that had been given to the women at the tomb (Matthew 28:5): **"Don't be afraid!"** For those who believe, there is no need to fear. This Christ is **the First and the Last**—essentially the same as the Alpha and the Omega (see also Isaiah 44:6). Christ is **the living one**—not a dead idol but alive and always with his people, every moment, in control of all things. He is the same one who was resurrected. He **died;** that is, he experienced physical death on the cross. But now he is **alive forever and ever.** Because Jesus rose from the dead, he can promise the same for his people.

Jesus holds **the keys of death and the grave,** which give him complete control over that

domain. Christ alone has absolute authority over people's lives and deaths. He alone can free people from the ultimate enemy, death. Believers need not fear death because Christ holds the keys (see Luke 16:23).

1:19 The command to **write down** what John had seen is repeated (see also 1:11). The phrase **what you have seen** is a general statement referring to **both the things that are now happening and the things that will happen later.** The vision that will unfold in the following chapters will include present and future events intertwined—events that both are and will be. Every future revelation has relevance for the present—the churches to whom this letter was written. The revelation also applies to churches and believers even today, two thousand years later.

1:20 Christ explains that **the seven stars are the angels of the seven churches.** But just who are the "angels of the seven churches"? Because the Greek word *angeloi* can mean angels or messengers, some believe that they are angels designated to guard the churches; others believe that they are elders or pastors of the churches. The case for angels as the correct interpretation comes from the fact that every other use of "angels" in Revelation refers to heavenly beings. However, because the seven letters in Revelation 2–3 contain reprimands against the messengers, and angels are not ever considered to be heads of churches, it is doubtful that these angels are heavenly messengers. If these are earthly leaders or messengers, they are accountable to God for the churches they represent.

The **seven gold lampstands** among which Christ had been standing (1:13) represent **the seven churches** to whom this letter would be circulated (1:11). The churches may have been facing difficulties and persecution, but they must never forget that Christ was standing among them, totally in control.

REVELATION 2

THE MESSAGE TO THE CHURCH IN EPHESUS / 2:1-7

The first letter is addressed to the church in Ephesus—the crossroads of civilization—considered to be a city of great political importance. Aquila, Priscilla, and Paul had planted the church in Ephesus (see Acts 19); Timothy had ministered there (1 Timothy 1:3); John, the writer of this letter, was closely associated with the church. The carrier of this letter to the churches would have landed at the port of Ephesus and begun his journey by visiting the church there.

The basic problem with the church in Ephesus is that even though church members had stood fast against evil and false teaching, they had left their love—their basic love for Christ and for one another.

2:1 **Ephesus** was a center of land and sea trade, for three major land-trade routes converged in the city, and a large port sat on its coast on the Aegean Sea. Along with Alexandria in Egypt and Antioch in Syria, Ephesus was one of the three most influential cities in the eastern part of the Roman Empire. Paul had ministered in Ephesus for three years and had warned the Ephesian believers that false teachers would come and try to draw people away from the faith (see Acts 20:29-31). False teachers did indeed cause problems in the Ephesian church, but the church resisted them, as we can see from Paul's letters to Timothy, who stayed in Ephesus when Paul left for Macedonia. John spent much of his ministry in this city and knew that these believers had resisted false teaching (2:2).

Although John was writing, the words are clearly from Christ, **the one who holds the seven stars in his right hand** and **walks among the seven gold lampstands** (1:13, 16). Christ controls the churches. Christ is described differently in every letter, mainly because each description is tied to the problems of the specific church. Ephesus, the mother church of all the other churches, was filled with pride. That Christ held these churches in his hand shows that he was in control over the churches. Ephesus had become a large, proud church, and Christ's message would remind them that he alone is the head of the body of believers.

2:2-3 Christ commended the church at Ephesus for **hard work**, **patient endurance**, intolerance of **evil people**, examining the **claims** of false apostles, and how they **patiently suffered**. All of these characteristics show a church busy with good works and suffering willingly for the cause of Christ. The Ephesian believers knew evil when they saw it and did not tolerate it. False teachers had been a problem in the Ephesian church, just as the apostle Paul had anticipated (Acts 20:29-30). The message to the church in Ephesus shows that false teachers had indeed come in among the believers, but Christ commended them for discovering and weeding out the **liars**.

2:4 Despite the commendations, Christ had something against this church—they **did not love** Christ **or each other as** much as they had **at first**. The Ephesians, though commended for their zeal in protecting the faith, had fallen into caring more about orthodoxy than love.

Every church should have pure faith and root out heresy. But these good efforts should spring from their love for Jesus Christ and for other believers. Both Jesus and John stressed love for one another as an authentic proof of the gospel (John 13:34; 1 John 3:18-19). In the battle to maintain sound teaching and moral and doctrinal purity, it is possible to lose a charitable spirit.

2:5 Paul had once commended the church at Ephesus for its love for God and for others (Ephesians 1:15). But the church had **fallen** away from that **first love**. Jesus called this church back to love. They needed to **turn back** to Christ and **work** as they **did at first**—love as they had originally loved, with enthusiasm and devotion.

If they refused to repent, however, Christ said that he would come and **remove** the church's **lampstand from its place**, meaning the church would cease to be a church. Just as the seven-branched candlestick in the Temple gave light for the priests to see, the churches were to give light to their surrounding communities. But Jesus warned them that their lights could go out. In fact, Jesus himself would extinguish any light that did not fulfill its purpose. The church had to repent of its sins.

2:6 Christ added a further commendation to this church in Ephesus—he credited them for hating **the deeds of the immoral Nicolaitans**, which Christ also hated. The Nicolaitans were believers who had compromised their faith in order to enjoy some of the sinful practices of Ephesian society, including idolatry and sexual immorality. The Nicolaitans had amalgamated some Greek, some Christian, and some Jewish practices to form a sort of civil religion. It may have been that they were willing to worship in the imperial cult, worshiping the emperor, justifying it as a civil duty. They were probably advocates of freedom and compromise, but the Ephesian church had taken a strong stand against these heretics.

2:7 Each of the seven letters ends with the exhortation, **Anyone who is willing to hear should listen to the Spirit and understand what the Spirit is saying to the churches**. The words of the Spirit are the words of Christ. Note that all the letters were to be read to all the churches. Those who "hear" what is read should then "listen to the Spirit" in order to understand what the Spirit is saying and to know what should be done. Those who listen and do what the Spirit leads them to do will be **victorious**. These who are victorious will remain faithful to Christ no matter what the cost.

Those victorious ones will **eat from the tree of life in the paradise of God**. The Garden of Eden contained the tree of life and the tree of the knowledge of good and evil (see Genesis 2:9). Eating from the tree of life brought eternal life with God;

eating from the tree of knowledge brought the ability to discern good and evil and, therefore, to choose evil. When Adam and Eve ate from the tree of knowledge, they disobeyed God's command. So they were excluded from Eden and barred from eating from the tree of life. Eventually, evil will be destroyed, and believers will be brought into a restored paradise. In the new earth, everyone will eat from the tree of life and will live forever (22:2, 19). Eating from the tree of life pictures the gift of eternal life. In paradise God will restore the perfect fellowship that existed in the Garden of Eden before sin entered and ruined the relationship between people and God.

THE MESSAGE TO THE CHURCH IN SMYRNA / 2:8-11

The port city of Smyrna lay thirty-five miles up the coast, north of Ephesus. It also had an excellent harbor on the Aegean Sea and rivaled Ephesus in the export business. This is the only one of the seven cities that is still in existence; its modern name is Izmir. The church in Smyrna was one of the two churches that received no rebukes from Christ.

2:8 Smyrna, like Ephesus, was a proud and beautiful city. Smyrna also had earned the right to be self-governing. It had a large library, stadium, and the largest public theater in Asia. The city had become a center for the cult of emperor worship. Smyrna received permission (over several other cities who requested) to build a temple to the emperor Tiberius in 23 B.C.. Under the emperor Domitian (who ruled from A.D. 81 to 96), emperor worship was required for all Roman citizens. Those who refused could receive the death penalty. Once a year, all citizens were required to burn incense on an altar to Caesar, after which they would receive a certificate proving that they had done their civil duty. While this was more an act of political loyalty than a religious act, the citizen had to say, while burning the incense, "Caesar is lord." Many Christians considered this act blasphemous and refused to do it.

In addition to being a center for the imperial cult, Smyrna also had a large Jewish population that actively opposed the Christians. Thus, the church in this city struggled against two hostile forces: a Gentile population that was loyal to Rome and supported emperor worship and a large Jewish population strongly opposed to Christianity. Persecution and suffering were inevitable in that kind of environment.

The description of Christ given to this small church on the verge of being snuffed out by persecution is that Christ is **the First and the Last, who died and is alive** (see 1:17-18). Although this church was almost dead due to persecution, Christ was reminding them that he was sovereign and eternal. No matter what they faced, Christ already knew about it; as the "First and the Last," nothing could take him by surprise. Christ identified himself as the one who died and came back to life again. Even if believers have to suffer to the point of death, Christ, the one who "came to life again," would raise them to eternal life with him.

2:9 The church in Smyrna was **suffering** because of persecution, and believers faced **poverty** even in this wealthy city. This probably refers to material poverty because Christ immediately assured them that despite their poverty, they were **rich**—referring to their heavenly riches (see James 2:5). These Christians' poverty may have come from sanctions against them as part of the persecution they faced.

Much of the persecution seems to have been coming from the **Jews** who, as noted above, were actively opposing Christianity. They may have claimed to have descended from Abraham, but true Jews (God's people) are those who have accepted Jesus as Messiah and Savior (Galatians 3:29). Because these Jews had rejected the Messiah, they were, in reality, no more than **a synagogue of Satan** (John 8:31-47). These Jews were serving Satan's purposes, not God's, when they gathered to worship, because they hated and persecuted the true people of God, the Christians.

2:10 Christ told the believers in Smyrna, who had already been facing persecution and suffering, that they ought not to be afraid of what they were **about to suffer.** More was coming, yet they should remember that although the Jews and Roman authorities were carrying out the persecution, behind any actions against them was **the Devil** himself. Satan would cause some of the believers to be thrown **into prison** and even be killed. The persecution would continue for **ten days**—probably symbolizing that although persecution would be intense, it would be relatively short and have a definite beginning and end. God was in complete control. The church was challenged to **remain faithful** to Christ even when **facing death** and they would receive **the crown of life.** Smyrna was famous for its athletic games. Each champion would receive a crown, a victory wreath. In ancient Rome this was the most sought-after prize. To have gained this wreath meant that one had done special acts for Rome and would be considered a patron of the Empire. This can be compared to being knighted in England. In contrast, those who have suffered for their faith will receive "the crown of life" in God's Kingdom.

2:11 Whoever is victorious—that is, whoever stands strong for the faith despite persecution and suffering—**will not be hurt by the second death.**

The Greek negative is emphatic—they will not in any way be hurt. Believers and unbelievers alike experience physical death. The first death for those in Smyrna might well be martyrdom. But even then they would be victorious because they would not face the second death. All people will be resurrected, but believers will be resurrected to eternal life with God, while unbelievers will be resurrected to be punished with a second death—eternal separation from God (see also 20:14; 21:8, 27; 22:15).

THE MESSAGE TO THE CHURCH IN PERGAMUM / 2:12-17

After leaving Smyrna, a letter carrier traveled along the coast of the Aegean Sea for about forty miles. Then the road turned northeast along the Caicus River. About ten miles inland stood the impressive city of Pergamum, built on a hill one thousand feet above the surrounding countryside, creating a natural fortress. Rivaling Ephesus as the leading city in the region, Pergamum had become the capital of the province of Asia and the center of Asian culture. It was proud of its links with Rome.

The problem in Pergamum was leniency toward those in the church who were compromising their faith with the idol worship and sexual immorality of pagan worship. Compromise can be good and is often needed, but the church must never compromise the basic tenets of the Christian faith.

2:12 Pergamum, a sophisticated city and center of Greek culture and education, boasted a 200,000-volume library that was second only to the famous library in Alexandria in Egypt. According to legend, when Pergamum tried to lure away from Alexandria one of its librarians, the king in Alexandria stopped exporting papyrus to Pergamum. This embargo resulted in Pergamum's development of what became known as parchment, a writing material made from animal skins. Pergamum was the center of four of the most important gods of the day—Zeus, Athene, Dionysus, and Asclepius. The city's chief god was Asclepius, whose symbol was a serpent and who was considered the god of healing. People came to Pergamum from all over the world to seek healing from this god.

The city was also a center for the imperial cult. While Smyrna had built temples to the emperor, Pergamum was the first city to receive permission to build a temple dedicated to a governing emperor, Augustus, whose temple was built in 29 B.C.

The proconsul of Pergamum had been granted the rare power known as "the right of the sword," meaning that he could perform executions. To the church in this city, Christ described himself as **the one who has a sharp two-edged sword** (1:16). Just as the sword was a symbol of Rome's authority and judgment, Jesus' sharp, double-edged sword represents God's ultimate authority and judgment. Only Christ has ultimate power over life and death.

2:13 As the center for four idolatrous cults, Pergamum was called the city of the **great throne of Satan.** Idolatry is satanic. Surrounded by the worship of idols and of the Roman emperor as god, the church at Pergamum refused to renounce its faith. The believers **refused to deny** Christ, even after Satan's worshipers had killed one of their members. It was not easy to be a Christian in Pergamum.

2:14-15 Despite commending believers for holding fast to the faith (2:13), Christ had **a few complaints** against this church in Pergamum. Apparently, some in the church were tolerating those who were teaching or practicing what Christ opposed. Christ described the church as tolerating some believers who were **like Balaam, who showed Balak how to trip up the people of Israel.** Balaam had done that, in a roundabout way, by influencing some in Israel **to worship idols by eating food offered to idols and by committing sexual sin.**

The complete story of Balak and Balaam is recorded in Numbers 22–25. In brief, Balak was a king who feared the large number of Israelites traveling through his country, so he hired Balaam, a sorcerer, and told him to pronounce a curse on them. Balaam had refused at first, but an offer of money had changed his mind. Numbers 25:1-3 describes the Israelite men getting involved with pagan women and then worshiping the gods of

Moab. While these verses do not mention Balaam, Numbers 31:16 explains that Balaam knew he could undermine Israel's worship and power by sending the Moabite women to entice the men of Israel. Balaam's influence caused great disaster for Israel, and he has earned the station as one who led people astray (see 2 Peter 2:15; Jude 1:11).

The church in Pergamum had stood strong against persecution, but what Satan could not accomplish from without he was trying to do from within—through Balaam-like deceit. Christ rebuked the church for tolerating those who, like Balaam, were undermining people's faith. Apparently some in the church were corrupting others in their attempt to justify idol worship—perhaps by joining in with civic ceremonies where idols were worshiped. Eating food offered to idols probably refers to these people's taking part in pagan feasts. Sexual sin may also be understood as being part of certain pagan festivities.

The church also had *some* **Nicolaitans among them—people who follow the same teaching and commit the same sins** as those who were like Balaam. These two groups were essentially the same in their practices. The Nicolaitans are described in 2:6 as those whose actions Christ hates. The believers in Ephesus had recognized the error of these people, but apparently the believers in Pergamum were being deceived by it. The Nicolaitans were Christians who had compromised their faith in order to enjoy the sinful pleasures of their society. But such compromise could only dilute their faith; thus, Christ said it could not be tolerated.

2:16 The church should get rid of those who were attempting to compromise where there could be no compromise. A church who tolerates such people will find that Christ will come **suddenly and fight against them with the sword of** his **mouth.** This sword represents God's judgment against rebellious nations (19:15, 21) and all forms of sin. If the church did not repent of its sin and deal with the compromisers, then God would come and do it—and that would be disastrous.

2:17 This closing calls upon readers to **listen to the Spirit and understand.** Those who are **victorious** (faithful against compromise) will be given a reward that here includes three symbols: hidden manna, a white stone, and a new name.

Being able to **eat of the manna that has been hidden away in heaven** suggests spiritual nourishment that faithful believers will receive for keeping their churches doctrinally pure. On the journey toward the promised land, God provided manna from heaven to the Israelites for their physical nourishment (Exodus 16:13-18). The hidden manna symbolizes the promises and blessings that will come with the arrival of the Messiah. Jesus, the bread of life (John 6:51), provides spiritual nourishment that satisfies our deepest hunger. Those who were refusing to revel in the pagan feasts of Pergamum were promised the manna that would satisfy hunger and bring blessing.

It is unclear what the **white stone** represents or what the **new name** on each stone will be. Because these stones seem to relate to the hidden manna, they may be symbols of the believer's eternal nourishment, or eternal life. Small stones served many purposes in ancient times. Some were given to the poor to help them obtain food, like food stamps. Some were used as invitations to a banquet. The invited person would bring along the stone in order to be admitted. Each stone would have an invited person's name on it. For those who refused to go to the pagan banquets, a place was reserved at the Messiah's banquet in heaven. The stones may be significant because each will bear the new name of every person who truly believes in Christ. Alternately, the new name may be Christ's name as it will be fully revealed (19:12). Or perhaps, because a person's name represented his or her character, it may be that the new name signifies the believer's transformed life and character because of Christ's saving work. The new name may be the evidence that a person has been accepted by God and declared worthy to receive eternal life. In any case, we know that God will give believers new names and new hearts.

THE MESSAGE TO THE CHURCH IN THYATIRA / 2:18-29

A letter carrier, upon leaving Pergamum, would travel southeast about forty miles, over a range of small hills, and finally into the fertile plain of Lycus. There he would find Thyatira, a city known for its manufacturing. The problem in Thyatira was a woman, called Jezebel, who was teaching compromise with the pagan world. Christ condemned such teaching. There can be no compromise with evil. Believers must be discerning in order to see evil for what it is.

2:18 Thyatira was a working person's town, a center for manufacturing. The city was filled with many trade guilds for commerce such as cloth making, dyeing, leatherworking, bronzeworking, and pottery making. Lydia, Paul's first convert in Philippi, was a merchant from Thyatira (Acts 16:14). The city was not important as a center for any temples to particular gods, although Apollo was worshiped as a guardian of the city. This was combined with the required worship of the emperor, considered an incarnation of Apollo and thus a son of Zeus himself. Besides Apollo, each guild appears to have had its own patron deity with its own festivals.

Christ's description of himself as the speaker to this church is that he is **the Son of God.** This sets him against Apollo and the emperor, who were said to be sons of the chief god, Zeus. This title is used nowhere else in Revelation. This Son of God has **eyes like flames of fire** and **feet like polished bronze** (see 1:14-15; see also Daniel 10:6). The blazing eyes indicate the penetrating power of his vision; the feet of bronze indicate strength for executing judgment.

2:19 The believers in Thyatira were commended for their good deeds. Christ sees all good deeds. He knew of the believers' **love** for one another (love that the Ephesian church had lost—2:4-5), their **faith**, their **service**, and their **patient endurance.** Christ was pleased to see their **constant improvement in all these things.**

2:20 Thyatira had the opposite problem that Ephesus had. Whereas the Ephesian church had been good at dealing with false teachers but had lacked love, the church in Thyatira had lots of love but had become tolerant of false teachers. And, as was happening in Pergamum, the church in Thyatira was tolerating false teaching that was attempting to compromise with the pagan society.

In this case, the problem was **Jezebel, who calls herself a prophet,** a woman from among the believers, who claimed to have the gift of prophecy. She may indeed have had unusual gifts, but she was using her influence to teach positions that were contrary to God's word, misleading the believers. Like Balaam, she was leading the people into **worship** of **idols** and **sexual sin** (2:14-15), probably by teaching that immorality was not a serious matter for believers. Her name may have been Jezebel, or John may have used the name Jezebel to symbolize the kind of evil she was promoting. Jezebel, a pagan Philistine queen of Israel, was considered the most evil woman who ever lived. She had led Israel's king, Ahab, into Baal worship and eventually had spread that idolatry throughout all of Israel (see 1 Kings 16:31-33; 19:1-2; 21:1-15; 2 Kings 9:7-10, 30-37). "Jezebel" was being tolerated in the Thyatiran church—perhaps her manner was so manipulative and persuasive that many did not notice, or perhaps no one realized the severe danger into which she was placing the entire church.

Most of the people in the city were tradesmen, so they belonged to various guilds. These guilds (such as potters, tentmakers, etc.) each had an area in the city and a guild hall, which functioned as a center for the guild's religious and civic activities. Usually the guild would hold a banquet at the hall once a week, and these banquets would often be centered on idolatry—featuring meat sacrificed to idols and, most likely, some form of sexual license as part of the revelry. Jezebel was probably encouraging the believers, mostly tradespeople themselves, to continue to take part in their guilds' activities as their civic duty. A refusal to join the guilds and take part in their activities would mean certain economic hardship. Jezebel suggested a way of compromise. Christ was pleased neither with this woman's teaching nor with the fact that the church tolerated her.

2:21-22 God in his mercy had given Jezebel **time to repent** of her wicked ways, **but she would not turn away from her immorality.** Consequently, God was going to punish her with sickness and suffering. The reference to those who **commit adultery with her** may refer to both involvement in sexual immorality and in idolatry by way of her teaching. Those involved would also be punished **unless** they turned **away from all their evil deeds.**

2:23 The phrase **I will strike her children dead** most likely refers to Jezebel's followers, her spiritual "children," those whom she had convinced to compromise with the pagan world. God wanted the church to deal with Jezebel. This judgment would be an example so that **all the churches** would know that God can see **the thoughts and intentions of every person.** No matter how a person appears on the outside, God alone knows what is going on in that person's heart. No one can hide from Christ; he knows what is in every person's heart and mind. Those who work against Christ will be found out and will receive **whatever** they **deserve.**

2:24-25 Many in the church in Thyatira had **not followed** Jezebel and had seen through her deception. After the church would repent and get rid of Jezebel and her **false teaching,** Christ would not place any other responsibilities on them other than simply to **hold tightly** to what they had until his return. All they needed was their pure faith, not the **depths of Satan** that Jezebel had been teaching.

This teaching of **deeper truths** probably involved so-called secret insights that were guaranteed to promote deeper spiritual life. Jezebel may have considered her insights to be deeper knowledge of God, but Christ explained that these "truths" were really the teachings of Satan. Christ condemned her teaching.

2:26-27 Christ says that those who **are victorious** (over Jezebel, etc.) and **who obey to the very end** will rule over Christ's enemies and reign with him as he judges evil. The promised **authority over all the nations** fulfills Psalm 2, a messianic psalm describing how God will hand the nations of the world over to Christ (Psalm 2:8-9). Christ applies this psalm to the readers by showing that the future reign of the Messiah will be shared with those who remain faithful (see 1:6; 3:21; 20:6; 1 Corinthians 6:2).

The **iron rod** and smashed **clay pots** symbolize total judgment (see Isaiah 30:12-14; Jeremiah 19:11). This warning was being given to the cults. Believers dare not take a light view of heresy, because heresy will destroy people for eternity. Those who stay true, however, will rule with Christ. This promise must have been a great encouragement to the believers in Thyatira who were facing difficulties because of their faith in Christ.

2:28 Those who are victorious in Thyatira were promised the **same authority** that Christ had received from the Father; they would also receive **the morning star.** Christ is called the morning star in 2:28; 22:16; and 2 Peter 1:19. A morning star appears just before dawn, when the night is coldest and darkest. When the world is at its bleakest point, Christ will burst onto the scene, exposing evil with his light of truth and bringing his promised reward. The morning star may also picture the authority given to the saints because of their faithfulness (see Numbers 24:17).

2:29 The conclusion that marks each of these messages to the churches implores everyone to **listen** and **understand what the Spirit is saying to the churches.** All these letters would be read to all the churches. The message included in each letter was for more than just the church to whom it had been written. The others churches should listen and hear, as should churches of the present day. We, too, are called to listen and understand what the Spirit is saying to us.

REVELATION 3

THE MESSAGE TO THE CHURCH IN SARDIS / 3:1-6

The letter carrier continued south from Thyatira for about thirty miles to reach the city of Sardis. The problem in this church was not heresy but spiritual death. Despite its reputation for being active, Sardis was infested with sin. The church's deeds were evil, and its clothes were soiled. The Spirit had no words of commendation for this church that looked so good on the outside but was so corrupt on the inside.

3:1 The wealthy city of **Sardis** had been one of the most powerful cities in the ancient world due to heavy trade among the Aegean islands. Gold and silver coins were first minted at Sardis. The city also claimed to have discovered the art of dyeing wool. Sardis was also known for its impressive necropolis, or cemetery, with hundreds of burial mounds. Sardis had declined, however, by the time of the Roman Empire. Sardis had requested the honor of building a temple to Caesar, but they were refused, and the honor went to Smyrna instead. The wealth of the city eventually led to moral decadence. The city had become lethargic, its past splendor a decaying memory.

Christ had no words of commendation for this church. It seems to have been untroubled by heresy from within or persecution from without. Yet this church had compromised with its pagan surroundings.

Christ described himself as **the one who has the sevenfold Spirit of God and the seven stars** (see 1:4, 16). The "sevenfold Spirit of God" is another name for the Holy Spirit. The seven stars are the messengers, or leaders, of the churches (see 2:1). Knowing this church's deeds, Christ had no good words to say. The believers may have had a **reputation for being alive, but** they were **dead.** Like the city itself, the church in Sardis may have been trying to live on past glory. They had compromised with the surrounding society to the point that they had become lethargic. They were as good as asleep, so Jesus told them to wake up and repent.

3:2 The following verses record five commands focusing on watchfulness. The city had been sacked twice because the watchmen on the walls had not seen the enemies scaling the cliffs. Thinking that they were impregnable on the mountaintop led to a deadly complacence. What had happened to the city was happening to the church, and it needed to **wake up**. The situation was not completely hopeless—if they caught themselves in time, they could **strengthen what little remains** even though it, too, was **at the point of death**.

Christ knew all their deeds, and condemned them as **far from right in the sight of God**. The church may have looked impressive from the outside, but there was no spiritual motivation or power behind its deeds. In letters to the other churches, Christ commended deeds of love, faithfulness, obedience, and perseverance. Sardis, however, had none of these qualities.

3:3 Christ commanded the church at Sardis to obey the Christian truth they had **believed at first** about Christ. They needed to return to the apostolic teaching that had changed their lives and once again make it their central focus. These believers had slipped away from that teaching into compromise with the world. If they refused, Christ would come **unexpected as a thief**, as unexpected as the soldiers who had climbed the walls to capture the city. The soldiers had brought destruction; Christ would bring punishment, giving them what they deserved. In this context, the phrase refers not to the Second Coming (1 Thessalonians 5:2; 2 Peter 3:10) but to judgment.

3:4-5 Not every believer in Sardis was being condemned for complacency and compromise with the world. Christ pointed out that **some** had **not soiled their garments with evil deeds**. These believers were being faithful. It must have been encouraging to those few who had been attempting to live for Christ in this dead church that Christ was commending them as worthy of his name. Christ promises a threefold reward for these faithful few.

To be **clothed in white** means to be set apart for God, cleansed from sin, and made morally and spiritually pure. Revelation mentions white robes several times. (3:18; 4:4; 6:11; 7:9, 13; 19:14). The white of these garments symbolizes the purity that comes when one has been "washed" in Christ's blood. Only those who have allowed Christ to cleanse them from their sins and clothe them in white will be able to reign with him (2:27).

The **Book of Life** refers to the heavenly registry of those who have accepted salvation in Christ. This expression appears elsewhere in the Bible. The picture of God's "book" first appears in Exodus 32:32-33. Also, the psalmist had cried out against his enemies, "Erase their names from the Book of Life; don't let them be counted among the righteous" (Psalm 69:28). Daniel had prophesied, "At that time every one of your people whose name is written in the book will be rescued"(Daniel 12:1). This "book" symbolizes God's knowledge of who belongs to him. At that time cities had registry books, so having one's name removed meant losing citizenship. A city would also erase a person's name from the registry when he or she died. For the citizens of heaven, however, death is not a cause for one's name to be removed; instead, it is the way of entrance.

Some have suggested that Christ's statement that he will "never erase" certain names leaves open the possibility that he might erase some name, and may imply that people can lose their salvation. In other words, can a name be written in the book and then later erased? It would be shaky to base one's theology of salvation on this symbol, so it is best to take Christ's statement at face value. Those who remain faithful to him are promised future honor and eternal life—they are guaranteed citizenship in heaven.

Christ **will announce** to the hosts of heaven that the believers belong to him. Christ had stated, "If anyone acknowledges me publicly here on earth, I will openly acknowledge that person before my Father in heaven"(Matthew 10:32). Believers can have no greater reward than to stand in heaven with Christ and have him announce, **"They are mine."**

3:6 Again Christ emphasizes the importance for the readers of Revelation to **listen** and **understand**. The message in this letter is also for you.

THE MESSAGE TO THE CHURCH IN PHILADELPHIA / 3:7-13

About twenty-five miles southeast of Sardis on a high plateau sat the city of Philadelphia. The city was also about one hundred miles due east of Smyrna (another city on the letter carrier's route). Christ had no words of rebuke for this church. Though small and struggling, the church in Philadelphia had stayed true to Christ, and he told them simply to hold on to what they had.

3:7 Philadelphia had been founded by the citizens of Pergamum in a frontier area as a gateway to the central plateau of Asia Minor. In Philadelphia merged trade routes leading to Mysia, Lydia, and Phrygia. Rome's imperial postal route also went through Philadelphia, earning the city the name Gateway to the East. Plains to the north were suitable for growing grapes, so Philadelphia's economy was based on agriculture and industry. The earthquake of A.D.17 that had destroyed Sardis had also been particularly devastating to Philadelphia because the city was near a fault line, and it had suffered many aftershocks. This kept the people worried, causing most of them to live outside the city limits.

Philadelphia was a small church in a difficult area with no prestige and no wealth, discouraged because it hadn't grown. But Christ had no words of rebuke for this small, seemingly insignificant church, and he described himself to the church in Philadelphia as **the one who is holy and true.** This title was a familiar title for God (see Isaiah 40:25; Habakkuk 3:3; Mark 1:24; John 6:69).

For Christ to hold **the key of David** means that he has the authority to open the door to his future Kingdom. This alludes to an event recorded in Isaiah 22:15-25 when the official position of secretary of state in Judah was taken from Shebna and given to Eliakim. God through Isaiah said to Eliakim: "I will give him the key to the house of David—the highest position in the royal court. He will open doors, and no one will be able to shut them; he will close doors, and no one will be able to open them" (Isaiah 22:22). Christ holds absolute power and authority over entrance into his future Kingdom. After the door is opened, **no one can shut** it—salvation is assured. Once it is shut, **no one can open** it—judgment is certain.

3:8 The church may have been small (**you have little strength**) and may have had little impact upon the city, but it had **obeyed** and had not denied God. They had been faithful in a difficult area. The phrase, **I have opened a door for you that no one can shut,** may mean that the church had a prime location for missionary activity—they had an open door that no one could shut. The meaning, however, may refer to the Jewish believers who had been excommunicated from the synagogue for their faith in Christ (see 3:9). While the door to the synagogue may have been closed to them, Christ had opened the door to eternal life. No one could keep them out if they trusted in Christ.

3:9 Apparently there was significant conflict between the Christians and the Jews in Philadelphia. As in the letter to the church in Smyrna (2:9),

Christ referred to those who called themselves Jews but who were really **liars** and **those who belong to Satan.** These people, descended from Abraham and Jews by birth, vehemently opposed and persecuted the Christians for their belief that Jesus was the Messiah. Because of their opposition, Christ considered them as belonging to Satan. True Jews (God's people) have accepted Jesus as Messiah and Savior (see Romans 2:28-29; Galatians 3:29; 6:16). These Jews who had rejected the Messiah truly belonged to Satan, not to God. They had shut the Christians out of their synagogues, but Christ says that he **will force** these people to **come and bow down at** the feet of his faithful people. Then **they will acknowledge** that the Christians are indeed the ones whom Christ loves. At Christ's return, true believers will be vindicated.

3:10 The believers had endured patiently, as Christ had commanded, so Christ promised to **protect** them **from the great time of testing that will come upon the whole world to test those who belong to this world.** Some believe that this protection from "the great time of testing" means there will be a future time of great tribulation from which true believers will be spared. This is a key verse for those who subscribe to the pre-Tribulation-Rapture theory—that believers will be kept from this time of testing because they will not be on the earth then, having been taken to heaven in what is called the "Rapture" (based on 1 Corinthians 15:51-53; 1 Thessalonians 4:15-17). Others believe that the verse refers to times of great distress in general, the church's suffering through the ages. Others interpret the protection to mean that the church will go through the time of tribulation and that God will keep them strong during it, providing spiritual protection from the forces of evil (7:3). The verb "protect" is the same Greek verb in the Lord's prayer ("Deliver us from the evil one," Matthew 6:13). As Jesus said before his death, "I'm not asking you to take them out of the world, but to keep them safe from the evil one" (John 17:15).

This "great time of testing" is also described as the Great Tribulation or Day of the Lord, mentioned also in Daniel 12:2; Mark 13:19; and 2 Thessalonians 2:1-12. All the judgments recorded in the remainder of the book of Revelation take place during this time of tribulation. While believers may have to face difficulty and suffering, they will certainly be protected from God's wrath and judgment.

3:11 For the churches in Ephesus (2:5), Pergamum (2:16), and Sardis (3:3), Christ's **coming** would be a time for them to fear if they did not repent, for he would come as their judge. To the church in

Philadelphia, however, Christ's words **I am coming quickly** would not be threatening. Rather, they would be a promise to the believers of his imminent return. The word "quickly" should be taken as "soon" or "without warning" (see 1:1, 3). In the meantime, they should **hold on to what they have,** referring to obedience and refusal to deny Christ (3:8). Their reward would be a **crown**—referring to the wreath awarded to winners of athletic contests (see 1 Corinthians 9:25; 2 Timothy 4:8). Philadelphia was known for its games and festivals, so the picture of the eternal crown awaiting believers was especially meaningful (see also 2:10).

3:12 The believers **who are victorious** and remain faithful to the end receive the promise to **become pillars in the Temple of God.** The word "pillars" symbolizes permanence and stability. Philadelphia was constantly threatened by earthquakes. Often experiencing tremors, the people would evacuate the city and stay in temporary dwellings in the rural areas. Sometimes the pillars would be the

only part of a building left standing after an earthquake. This permanence is further stressed in the next phrase, **they will never have to leave it.**

Christ also gives these victorious believers three further promises. He will **write God's name on them, they will be citizens in the new Jerusalem,** and **they will have** Christ's **new name inscribed upon them.** This "new name" of Christ has not been revealed, but those who are victorious and persevere will have this new name inscribed upon them. For more on the new Jerusalem, see 21:2.

This threefold promise pictures believers belonging to God, having citizenship in heaven, and having a special relationship with Christ. The new Jerusalem is the future dwelling of the people of God (21:2). They will be citizens in God's future Kingdom. Everything will be new, pure, and secure.

3:13 This closing is the same as for the letters to the other churches: all should **listen to the Spirit and understand** what is being said.

THE MESSAGE TO THE CHURCH IN LAODICEA / 3:14-22

At the end of the route was Laodicea, about forty-five miles southeast of Philadelphia. The problem in this church was self-sufficiency, which caused believers to forget their need of pure love and faith in the Savior.

3:14 Laodicea was the wealthiest of the seven cities. The city was known for its banks, its manufacture of a rare black wool, and a medical school that produced eye salve. Laodicea lay at the juncture of two major trade routes between Rome and the Orient. The main road from Ephesus on the coast into Asia ran through Laodicea, as did the route from the capital of the province in Pergamum to the Mediterranean coast. The city had a poor water supply. A six-mile long aqueduct brought water to the city from the south, so by the time it reached the city, the water was lukewarm. The city was a center for the imperial cult as well as for the worship of Asclepius (god of healing) and Zeus (chief of the gods). The city also had a fairly large Jewish population.

The church may have been founded by Epaphras (see Colossians 4:12). It is not known whether Paul ever visited the city, although he did write them a letter, and the letter to the Colossians was read by the Laodicians (Colossians 4:16).

To this church, Christ is described as **the Amen—the faithful and true witness.** The word "amen" signals an acknowledgment of something true and binding. Christ was true and faithful, but

the Laodiceans were not. They were rich and powerful, but they were not "faithful and true."

3:15-16 This allusion to the Laodicean water supply is a fitting metaphor for the activities of this church. Laodicea had always had a problem with its water supply. The city of Hierapolis, to the northwest, was famous for its hot mineral springs. An aqueduct had been built to bring water to the city from the hot springs. But by the time the water reached the city, it was neither hot nor refreshingly cool—only lukewarm and filled with minerals (impure), so it tasted terrible. According to Christ, these believers were **neither hot nor cold;** instead, they were merely **lukewarm,** as bland as the tepid water that came into the city.

Many have thought that this cold and hot refers to spirituality—and that Christ would rather have "cold" people (without faith at all, or without any sort of growth) than "lukewarm" believers (who believe some). They take the word "cold" to be negative and "hot" to be positive, with "lukewarm" in between. Instead, both "cold" and "hot" should be taken as positive. Christ wished that the church had cold, refreshing purity or hot, therapeutic value, but it had neither.

3:17 Laodicea was a wealthy city, and apparently the church was also a wealthy church. It is unclear whether the Laodiceans were claiming spiritual or material wealth. They may have been materially rich and assuming that riches were a sign of God's blessing on them. With their wealth came an attitude of self-sufficiency—feeling that they did not **need a thing.** They were materially secure and felt spiritually safe—with no need for further growth. Unfortunately, that attitude made them blind to their own true condition—**wretched, miserable, poor, blind, and naked.** Contrast this with the church in Smyrna; they were poor, but Christ called them rich (2:9). The Laodicean believers may have been wealthy, but spiritually they were impoverished. While the city prided itself on extreme financial wealth, a productive textile industry, and the special healing eye salve, the church's true spiritual condition left it poor, naked, and blind (see 3:18).

3:18 Laodicea was known for its great wealth, but Christ told the Laodiceans to **buy** their **gold** from him; then they would have real spiritual treasures (see 1 Timothy 6). They had fool's gold in their bank accounts, gold from this world with no spiritual or eternal value. Only with Christ's gold would they **be rich.**

The city was proud of its cloth and dyeing industries. They had developed a black wool that had become famous all over the Roman Empire and was bringing huge prices. Although they had wealth in their clothing, they were naked before God. They were self-centered. But Christ told them to purchase **white garments** (his righteousness) from him so they would **not be shamed by** their **nakedness.** Laodicea prided itself on a precious eye salve that healed many eye problems, but its people were spiritually blind. Christ told them to get **ointment** from him to heal their **eyes** so they could **see** the truth (John 9:39). Christ was showing the Laodiceans that true value is not in material possessions but in a right relationship with God. Their possessions and achievements were valueless compared with the everlasting future of Christ's Kingdom.

3:19 There was a second chance for this church; Christ offered them the opportunity to repent. His correction and discipline would come because of his **love** for the church (Proverbs 3:12). Christ will **spit out** those who disobey (3:16), but he will discipline those he loves. Because of such mercy, believers should willingly repent, realizing their need for Christ in every part of their lives and ministry. Then they will be effective for him.

3:20 The Laodicean church was complacent and rich. They felt self-satisfied, but they didn't have Christ's presence among them. Christ knocked at the **door** of their hearts, but they were so busy enjoying worldly pleasures that they didn't notice him trying to enter. The pleasures of this world— money, security, material possessions—can be dangerous because their temporary satisfaction can make people—even believers—indifferent to God's offer of lasting satisfaction.

Many have taken this verse as a help in evangelism, picturing Christ wanting to enter an individual's heart. The context is actually Christ speaking to an entire church. The people in the church in Laodicea needed to accept Christ for the first time, for some of them had never made that commitment. Others needed to return to wholehearted faith in him. Christ is knocking on their door, desiring that the Laodicean church remember its need for him and open the door. He would **come in** and **share a meal** with the believers, picturing table fellowship. In Oriental fashion, this "eating" referred to the main meal of the day in which intimate friends would share together. Such a meal portrays the kind of fellowship that will exist in the coming Kingdom of the Messiah (19:9; Isaiah 25:6-8; Luke 22:30). The church needed to repent of its self-sufficiency and compromise and return to Christ.

3:21 This promise that **everyone who is victorious** will **sit** with Christ on his **throne** refers to the heavenly Kingdom (see also 1:6, 9; 2:26-27). Believers' reign with Christ is mentioned in several places in Scripture (see, for example, Matthew 19:28; Luke 22:28-30; Romans 8:17; 2 Timothy 2:12). This promise is certain because Christ won that right for believers through his own victory on the cross. **Victorious** over sin and death when he rose again, he **sat with** his **Father on his throne** (see Mark 16:19).

3:22 At the end of each message to these churches, believers were urged to **listen** and take to heart what had been written to them. Although a different message was addressed to each church, all the messages contain warnings and principles for everyone. Which letter speaks most directly to your church? Which has the greatest bearing on your own spiritual condition at this time? How will you respond?

REVELATION 4

WORSHIPING GOD IN HEAVEN / 4:1-11

The book now shifts from the seven churches in Asia to the future of the worldwide church. John saw the course of coming events similar to the way Daniel and Ezekiel had seen them. Many of these passages contain clear spiritual teachings, but others seem beyond our ability to understand. The clear teaching of this book is that God will defeat all evil in the end. Meanwhile, we must live in obedience to Jesus Christ, the coming Conqueror and Judge.

Revelation 4–5 provide glimpses into Christ's glory. Chapter 4 is John's vision into the throne room of heaven. God is on the throne, orchestrating all the events that John recorded. The world is under his control, and he will carry out his plans as Christ initiates the final battle with the forces of evil.

4:1 After writing the letters to the seven churches, John **looked** and **saw a door standing open in heaven** (see also Ezekiel 1:1). It is God who opens the door, so this is God revealing these visions to John and to us. This first **voice** that sounded like a **trumpet** was the voice of Christ (see 1:10-11). The voice spoke again and told John to **"come up here."** From there, Christ would show John **what must happen**—that is, after the time of the letters to the churches in chapters 2 and 3. These would be visions of the end of the world and the beginning of Christ's Kingdom.

Some who subscribe to the pre-Tribulation theory see a veiled reference to the rapture of the church in the words of Christ to "come up." But the text indicates that John alone was commanded to be transported in the Spirit to heaven. The Rapture is not mentioned specifically in the book of Revelation. For more on the Rapture, see 1 Thessalonians 4:13-17.

4:2-3 Four times in the book of Revelation, John wrote that he was in the Spirit (1:10; 4:2; 17:3; 21:10). This expression means that the Holy Spirit was giving him a vision—showing him situations and events that he could not have seen with mere human eyesight. All true prophecy comes from God through the Holy Spirit (1:10; 2 Peter 1:20-21).

John **saw a throne in heaven and someone sitting on it** (compare with 1 Kings 22:19; Isaiah 6:1; Ezekiel 1:1). The throne of God is mentioned forty times in the book of Revelation. The throne symbolizes God's absolute authority. For the first-century readers, the most powerful throne in the world would have been Caesar's throne. Caesar sat on the most glorious throne in the world and had

control of one-half of the gross national product of the Roman Empire. His glory and wealth, however, were nothing compared to God's. God's throne **was as brilliant as gemstones. Jasper and carnelian** were semiprecious stones. Caesar's pomp and splendor were nothing compared to the **glow of an emerald** that **circled** God's throne **like a rainbow.** The stones symbolize great wealth—God owns all the riches of the entire world. These gemstones were the most pure elements known at that time—and God transcends even these. John did not describe this person on the throne, other than to mention the brilliant light around him. God alone is sovereign; Caesar is not a god. Only God is God.

4:4 Surrounding God's throne were twenty-four thrones with **twenty-four elders** sitting on them. John did not identify these twenty-four elders. Evidently, the worship they were providing was more significant than who they were. Scholars have proposed several possibilities for the identity of these twenty-four elders:

- Because there were twelve tribes of Israel in the Old Testament and twelve apostles in the New Testament, the twenty-four elders (twelve plus twelve) in this vision represent all the redeemed of God for all time (both before and after Christ's death and resurrection). They symbolize all those—both Jews and Gentiles—who are now part of God's family. The twenty-four elders show us that *all* the redeemed of the Lord are worshiping him.
- The twenty-four elders are the heavenly counterpart of the twenty-four priestly ranks who served the Temple (1 Chronicles 23:6; 24:7-18).

• Most likely, the elders are an angelic group providing this worship, and the reference to twenty-four remains speculative. Their continuous praise supports this view, and the fact that they serve with, but are distinguished from, the four living creatures (4:11; 5:9-10; 11:17-18; 19:4). The twenty-four elders are beings who live in heaven and worship God at his throne (see also 14:3). Though they are crowned and dressed in white, they clearly do not represent the church. These leaders sing of human believers, not about themselves (5:9). In view of their actions, such as worshiping and offering bowls of incense, they seem to be a special order of angels.

4:5 In Revelation, **lightning** and **thunder** are associated with significant events in heaven. Lightning and thunder had filled the sky at Mount Sinai when God had given the people his laws (Exodus 19:16). The Old Testament often uses such imagery to reflect God's power and majesty (see Psalm 77:18). In Revelation, thunder and lightning always form part of the scene in God's throne room and highlight a significant coming event—for example, they mark the seventh seal (8:5), the seventh trumpet (11:19), and the seventh bowl (16:18).

The **seven lampstands** represent the Holy Spirit (see also comments on 1:4 and Ezekiel 1:13; Zechariah 4:2-6). **The seven spirits of God** is another name for the Holy Spirit.

4:6 Glass was very rare in New Testament times, and crystal-clear glass was virtually impossible to find. The **sea of glass** serves as the magnificent floor of God's throne room and highlights both the magnificence and holiness of God. It is probably not a literal "sea"; rather, it is a metaphor for the scene. No earthly ruler can compare with the awesomeness of God. See also Job 37:18 and Ezekiel 1:22.

The **four living beings** are angelic beings of high order, serving as part of the worship and government in heaven (see Isaiah 6:1-4; Ezekiel 1:5-25). Isaiah 6:2 refers to these beings as "seraphim." The seraphim surround God's throne, lead others in worship, and proclaim God's holiness. The **eyes** picture knowledge and alertness. They see and scrutinize everything. These are powerful figures, as noted by the wings (4:8). These four living beings also appear throughout Revelation (see also 5:6, 8, 14; 6:1; 7:11; 14:3; 15:7; 19:4).

4:7 The Old Testament prophet Ezekiel saw four similar beings in one of his visions (Ezekiel 1:5-10; 10:14). In his vision, however, each had four faces. In John's vision, each has only one face. In Ezekiel's vision, God called Ezekiel to be a prophet. God showed Ezekiel that the coming destruction of Jerusalem was punishment for Judah's sins. Ezekiel prophesied during the time when the Babylonians sacked Jerusalem. In John's vision, the living beings will show to John the final destruction of the world as punishment for sin. The appearance of these creatures symbolizes the highest expression of God's attributes. The animal-like appearances of these four creatures include majesty and power (the **lion**), faithfulness (the **ox**), intelligence (the **human**), and sovereignty (the **eagle**).

4:8 A further description of these four **living beings** indicates that each had **six wings,** indicating power and swiftness (see Isaiah 6:2). The **eyes** all around are mentioned again (4:6) and indicate complete knowledge—that is, they could perceive and understand everything that was happening. Their continuous praises to God reveal constant worship.

The four living beings sing about God's holiness. The repetition three times of the word **holy** means ultimate holiness (see also Isaiah 6:3). **Lord God Almighty** pictures the ultimate, divine Warrior (see commentary on 1:8). Churches of all ages facing persecution gain great comfort knowing that no matter what happens on earth, God is almighty. Those who are victorious will one day join in praise with the angels. The phrase **who always was, who is, and who is still to come** describes God's transcendence over time—he is eternal (see also commentary on 1:4).

4:9-10a The actions of these living beings picture complete worship and submission to God. **The one who lives forever and ever** emphasizes God's eternality (see 5:14; 10:6; 15:7). God is far more worthy of worship than any person because he lives forever (see Psalms 45:6; 102:27). His **throne** symbolizes his power and authority (see also 4:2-3). As the **living beings** praise God, the **twenty-four elders fall down and worship.** That they "fall down" refers to lying prostrate in a position of submission and adoration. Their worship means giving God all **glory and honor and thanks.**

4:10b-11 These verses are the second hymn sung in Revelation (see 4:8), a hymn of praise to God for his work in creation. The point of this chapter is summed up in this verse: All creatures in heaven and earth will praise and honor God because he is the Creator and Sustainer of **everything.** No king or emperor can make such a claim. No Roman emperor could ever be acknowledged for creating heaven and earth. This role belongs to God alone (14:7; 21:5; Romans 8:18-25).

The phrase **you are worthy** was used to herald the entrance of an emperor when he came in his triumphal procession. Later, the emperor Domitian added the phrase "our Lord and God" as a reference to himself, thereby promoting the cult of emperor worship. Christians, however, are to acknowledge only one Lord and God.

Earthly honor and power is to be laid before the throne, just as the living beings **lay their crowns before the throne.** This demonstrates that all authority and honor belong to God. He delegates his authority to others, but it belongs to him.

REVELATION 5

THE LAMB OPENS THE SCROLL / 5:1-14

Revelation 5 continues the glimpse into heaven begun in chapter 4. The scene in Revelation 5 shows that only the Lamb, Jesus Christ, is worthy to open the scroll, which reveals the events of future history. Jesus, not Satan, holds the future. Jesus Christ is in control; he alone is worthy to set into motion the events of the last days of history. Verses 9, 12, and 13 contain three hymns. The first two worship the Lamb; the third one worships God and the Lamb.

5:1 The phrase **the one who was sitting on the throne** refers to 4:2-3, where John had been taken to the throne room of heaven. This one on the throne is God himself. In his **right hand** God is holding **a scroll.** In John's day some books were written on scrolls—pieces of papyrus or vellum up to thirty feet long, rolled up and sealed with clay or wax. Other books were written in codex form— much like our modern book. The **seven seals** indicate the importance of the scroll's contents, and they guaranteed the secrecy of the document. The book had writing on both sides. John does not tell us the exact contents of the book, but it seems that, from what follows in chapters 5–8, it is none other than the content of the rest of the book of Revelation. As each seal is broken, another part of the book is revealed. The final seal, the seventh one, opens the way to the seven trumpets, and so on through the rest of Revelation.

5:2-3 As God was holding the scroll, **a strong angel** asked, **"Who is worthy to break the seals on this scroll and unroll it?"** The identity of this angel is unknown. The question, **shouted with a loud voice,** went out across all of creation to find someone worthy to bring history to its appointed end. But **no one in heaven or on earth or under the earth** could be found who had the authority and purity to **open the scroll and read it.** This emphasizes the sovereignty and centrality of Christ. He alone was able to open the scroll.

5:4-5 John **wept** that **no one could be found who was worthy to open the scroll and read it.** John wept because he knew that the unopened scroll would mean that the closing scene of history could

not begin; thus, evil would continue unabated on the earth, and there would be no future for God's people. But one of the **elders** (4:4, 10) told John not to weep any longer, because someone was worthy to open the scroll—**the Lion of the tribe of Judah.** This phrase comes from the prophecy that Jacob gave to his son Judah in Genesis 49:9-10. This is considered to be a prophecy of the Messiah, born in the line of Judah, who would be the only one whom all nations would one day obey. From Judah's line had been born King David, hence the phrase, **heir to David's throne,** which alludes to Isaiah 11:1-5. Christ, the Messiah, is the fulfillment of God's promise that a descendant of David would rule forever (2 Samuel 7:16; see also Romans 15:12).

The Messiah, Jesus Christ, has conquered. Christ proved himself worthy by living a perfect life of obedience to God, dying on the cross to pay the penalty for the sins of the world, and rising from the dead to demonstrate his power and authority over evil and death. Only Christ conquered sin, death, hell, and Satan himself, so only he can open the scroll and break its seven seals, setting in motion the forces that will bring about the final destruction of all evil.

5:6 One of the elders called John to look at the Lion (5:5), but when John looked, he saw a **Lamb.** Christ the Lamb was the perfect sacrifice for the sins of all mankind; therefore, only he can save his people from the terrible events that will be revealed by the scroll. This is a beautiful picture: the Lion of the tribe of Judah became a slain Lamb, who is here seen as a conquering Lamb at the center of the throne of God.

This Lamb is different from a dead Passover lamb,

however. This Lamb is standing upright, conquering and triumphant, like a strong ram. This Lamb has **seven horns and seven eyes,** symbolizing perfect (the number seven) power and wisdom. The horns symbolize strength and power (see 1 Kings 22:11; Zechariah 1:18). Although Christ is a sacrificial lamb, he is not weak. The eyes are further described as **the seven spirits of God that are sent out into every part of the earth,** most likely referring to the Holy Spirit (see 1:4; Zechariah 4:2-10; John 14:26; 15:26; 16:7-15).

5:7-8 Christ **stepped forward and took the scroll** from his Father, who was seated **on the throne.** Christ was worthy to take the scroll because of his sacrifice on the cross, by which salvation was won for all who believe. In this vision the time had come for God to unleash the final acts of history before setting up his Kingdom. Christ would open the scroll and begin the process that would bring about the end of this fallen world.

As Christ took the scroll, **the four living beings and the twenty-four elders fell down before the Lamb.** This pictures all of the heavenly beings worshiping the Son, just as they had done for the one on the throne (4:10), thereby acknowledging Christ's deity. The **harp** that each held would be used as music for the "new song" they would sing (5:9; see also Psalm 33:2-3). The **gold bowls filled with incense** are described as **the prayers of God's people** (see Psalm 141:2). These prayers from the believers on earth were for God to bring his justice to the earth, as later chapters will describe (see 6:10; 8:3-4). The administration of God's righteous justice will mean deliverance for God's faithful people and punishment on those who have rejected God and persecuted his people.

5:9-10 The remainder of this chapter contains three hymns of praise. This first **new song** was sung by the twenty-four elders and the four living creatures (**they** refers to 5:7-8). In 5:11-12, the singing group will grow to include countless angels. Finally, in 5:13, "every creature in heaven and on earth and under the earth" begins to sing. This is a celebration of salvation. Jesus' worthiness comes from his self-

sacrifice. Because he is **worthy,** he is able to **take the scroll and break its seals and open it.**

The song of the twenty-four elders and the four living creatures praises Christ's work. (See Psalm 96 for a similar song.) The fact that the Lamb was **killed** refers to Christ's death on the cross as recorded in the Gospels. Through his **blood** shed on the cross, he **ransomed** his people. A "ransom" was the price paid to release a slave from bondage. Through his death Jesus would redeem his people from the bondage of sin and death. The disciples thought that as long as Jesus was alive, he could save them. But Jesus revealed that only his death would save them and all those who trust in him.

God has ransomed people **from every tribe, language, people, and nation.** God's message of salvation and eternal life is not limited to a specific culture, race, or country. Anyone who comes to God in repentance and faith is accepted by him and will be part of his Kingdom. We must not allow prejudice or bias to keep us from sharing Christ with others. Christ welcomes all people into his Kingdom.

5:11-12 The worship that had begun with the four living beings and twenty-four elders here spreads to all of heaven with all of the angels. In 5:13-14, all creation will join in the praise. The phrase **thousands and millions** pictures a countless number of angels—the entire angelic host. Daniel saw a similar vision (Daniel 7:10). The angels sang a hymn of praise. This sevenfold praise may have been a chant that was antiphonal to the elders' hymn of 5:9-10. Each word describes a quality of God that was bestowed upon Christ, making him worthy.

5:13-14 Finally, the choir grew to **every creature in heaven and on earth and under the earth and in the sea.** They sang both to the **one sitting on the throne** as well as **to the Lamb**—both God and his Son. In response to the song of creation, the **four living beings said, "Amen!"** in agreement. The **twenty-four elders** responded by falling and worshiping the one on the throne (God) and the Lamb (Christ). Everything created, both in heaven and in earth, will one day worship God and his Son (Philippians 2:10-11).

REVELATION 6

THE LAMB BREAKS THE FIRST SIX SEALS / 6:1-17

This is the first of three seven-part judgments. In chapter 5, a scroll with seven seals had been handed to Christ, who is the only one worthy to break the seals and open the scroll, setting into motion the events of the end of the world (5:1-5). In chapter 6, the scroll is opened as each seal is broken. This scroll is not completely opened until the seventh seal is broken (8:1). The contents of the scroll reveal mankind's depravity and portray God's authority over the events of human history.

Each of the judgments (seals, trumpets, bowls) includes seven parts. The first four judgments involve natural disasters on the earth; the last three are cosmic disasters. There are three views about how to understand this series of judgments—seals, trumpets, bowls:

Recapitulation View. According to this view, the three sets of judgments repeat each other (are cyclical); they present three ways of viewing the same judgments. Because the trumpets and the bowls have the same order, many have concluded that the three sets are repetitive. In addition, in all three sets, the first four of the seven judgments are very similar, as are the last three of each set of seven. Exact repetition, however, occurs only in the trumpets and bowls.

Consecutive View. This view holds that judgments will follow in the order described in Revelation: first the seals, then the trumpets, then the bowls—in other words, Revelation is describing twenty-one separate events. Thus, chapters 6–16 in Revelation would be chronological.

Progressive Intensification View. The key to this view is understanding the results of the judgments. The seals destroy one-fourth of the earth; the trumpets destroy one-third; the bowls affect everything. The picture seems to be one of progressive intensity, with each of these sets of judgments ending in the same place—that is, the end of history.

These views are helpful as you consider and study the book of Revelation. While many will feel very strongly about one view or another, only God knows the truth. He left much of Revelation unclear to his people for a reason, perhaps so we'll study it and be watchful and morally alert. One truth is sure: as God prepares to end history and usher in his Kingdom, he will bring judgments.

The horses represent God's judgment of people's sin and rebellion. God is directing human history—even using his enemies to accomplish his purposes. The four horses provide a foretaste of the final judgments yet to come. Some view this chapter as a parallel to Jesus' words about the end times (see Matthew 24:4-8; Mark 13:5-13; Luke 21:8-19). The imagery of colored horses and riders comes from Zechariah 1:8-17; 6:1-8. In Zechariah, the colors of the horses have no special significance; in Revelation, the colors of the horses do have symbolic meaning, as described below. In Zechariah, the horses and riders went out to patrol the earth; in Revelation, they are sent out to bring disaster.

6:1-2 The Lamb, Christ, **broke** open the **first** seal and with that came the first of four riders on horseback. **One of the four living beings** called loudly, **"Come!"** probably beckoning the rider on the horse. A **white horse** with a rider holding **a bow** had a **crown** placed on his head and he **rode out to win many battles.**

This is the only rider who didn't bring catastrophe (the others initiated warfare, famine, and death); this rider went out to **gain the victory.** There is much debate over who or what this horseman represents. Some have suggested that this rider symbolizes the proclamation of the Good News of Christ. They see the white horse as being

"good" and therefore the rider on a good mission. Others believe that the rider on the white horse is Christ himself, for Christ later appears on a white horse (19:11). Jesus is closely associated with the color white in Revelation (see 1:14; 6:11; 14:14).

The fact that this white horse and its rider precede three other horsemen who wreak havoc on the earth, however, suggests that the white horseman might represent the lust for conquest. When mankind is bent on conquest, the result is warfare, famine, and death. The color white could correspond, then, to conquest. Most likely, the rider on the white horse represents sinful mankind's desire for conquest; when this occurs, many suffer.

6:3-4 At the breaking of the **second seal,** a rider on a **red** horse appeared. He was **given a mighty sword** and was sent out **to remove peace from the earth.** The picture here is of warfare. Throughout history, conquest has led to warfare and civil war. The rider on the white horse went out to "win many battles," and in his wake came warfare. The color of this horse, red, symbolizes great blood-shed upon the earth.

6:5-6 Christ **broke the third seal** and a **black horse** arrived. This **rider was holding a pair of scales** for weighing food. The words of the four living beings regarding the amount of food for **a day's pay** pictures wartime inflation. First-century readers would have interpreted this amount as twelve to fifteen times what they were used to paying. What a person would earn in a day would buy only enough food to feed that person, no one else, not even his or her family. This then would lead to widespread famine, another devastating result of warfare. Following on the heels of the red horse of warfare, therefore, comes a black horse, which represents the sorrow and desolation of warfare that leaves people without money or food. The phrase, **"Don't waste the olive oil and wine,"** could be a warning to conserve two staples.

6:7-8 The **Lamb broke the fourth seal,** and the **fourth living being** called a rider on a **pale green** horse. The rider's name was **Death.** Following close behind was **the Grave.** The drive for conquest (white horse), had led to warfare and bloodshed (red horse), which had brought famine and pestilence (black horse), resulting in death and the grave (pale green horse). The color indicates the color of **a corpse.** The four riders were given power over **one-fourth of the earth** to kill people **with the sword and famine and disease and wild animals.** Death by wild beasts would be expected when millions of people have died through war, famine, and plague. The number of one-fourth of the earth, working from present-day numbers, would mean over a billion people would die in this first wave of judgment were it to happen today. Nothing that cataclysmic has occurred in all of history.

6:9 After the four horses have ridden off, **the Lamb broke the fifth seal.** It reveals an **altar** in heaven, under which are **the souls of all who had been martyred** for faithfully proclaiming **the word of God.** They had been killed for standing up for Christ and for his word (see also 13:15; 18:24; 20:4). The altar represents the altar of sacrifice in the Temple, where animals would be sacrificed to atone for sins. Instead of the animals' blood at the base of the altar, John saw the souls of martyrs who had died for preaching the gospel. The word

for "souls" *(psyche)* refers to the persons or to their lives. These martyrs were told that still more would lose their lives for believing in Christ (6:11). In the face of warfare, famine, persecution, and death, Christians need to stand firmly for what they believe. Only those who endure to the end will be rewarded by God (14:12; Mark 13:13).

6:10-11 The souls of the martyrs beneath the altar were calling out for vengeance for their deaths, asking God **how long** it would be before he would judge the earth and avenge their blood. This is an imprecatory prayer—a prayer for vengeance against God's enemies. Just as David had written psalms that called for vengeance against his enemies (for example, Psalms 35; 94:3), so these martyrs asked for vengeance and vindication against **the people who belong to this world** (see also 3:10; 8:13; 11:10; 13:8, 12; 17:2, 8). These words may sound harsh when used in prayer, but the martyrs were calling for God's justice, and they were leaving the vengeance to God. God promises to help the persecuted and to bring judgment on unrepentant sinners.

The martyrs were told to **rest a little longer until the full number of the servants of Jesus had been martyred.** God is not waiting until a certain number are killed; rather, he is waiting for the appointed time to arrive. He promises, however, that those who suffer and die for their faith will not be forgotten. In fact, they will be rewarded and honored by God. Today, oppressed people may wish for justice immediately, as these martyrs did, but they must be patient. God works according to his own timetable, and he promises to act. No suffering for the sake of God's Kingdom, however, is wasted. God will vindicate his people, but he will do it in his time, not ours.

The **white robe** that each martyr was wearing, as throughout the book of Revelation, symbolizes purity (see also 3:4; 7:11). White robes were worn for special ceremonies in Greek cities.

6:12-14 The **sixth seal** changed the scene back to the physical world. The first five judgments had been directed toward specific areas, but this judgment was over the whole world. The entire population would be afraid when the earth itself trembled. With the opening of the sixth seal, **there was a great earthquake,** followed by other cosmic disturbances. To properly understand these events, we must go beyond the literal meaning. These word pictures were common to many of John's readers and stood for the coming "day of the Lord" or "day of judgment." The earthquake in Scripture always pictures God's presence (see Exodus 19:18; Isaiah 2:19-21; Haggai 2:6). The color of the **sun**

is that of **cloth** worn in times of mourning. The
moon will appear **red** due to whatever in the
atmosphere caused the sun to be darkened. The
stars falling to earth could refer to a terrifying
meteor shower with meteors striking the earth
(see also Joel 2:30-31; Mark 13:21-25). The disap-
pearance of **mountains** and **islands** will probably
result from the great earthquake (see Hebrews
12:26-27).

Finally, the sky will roll up **like a scroll** (see
also Isaiah 34:4). Those who interpret this book
as chronological will consider this to be the end
of the first round of judgments. Those who picture
the book as cyclical, or as showing varying intensity with all the judgments ending at the return of
Christ, see the rolling up of the sky as the time

when Christ opens heaven and returns to earth
(19:11).

6:15-17 As the earthquake moved the mountains
and the sky was filled with terrifying signs, everyone
on the earth, from the rich and powerful to the citizens, to the slaves, all hid from God. They recognized that the end of the world had come and they
hoped to **hide from the face of the one who sits
on the throne and from the wrath of the Lamb.**
The people were so terrified of the one seated on the
throne that they would prefer that an avalanche fall
on them rather than have to face God. The evil people on the earth dread God more than they dread
death. They do not realize that even death cannot
help them to escape their judgment by God.

REVELATION 7

GOD'S PEOPLE WILL BE PRESERVED / 7:1-8

The sixth seal had been opened, and the people of the earth had tried to hide from God, asking
who would be able to survive God's judgment (6:17). Just when destruction seemed sure, four
angels held back the four winds of judgment until God's people were sealed as his own. This
sealing occurred in this interlude between the sixth and seventh seals. An interlude also comes
between the sixth and seventh trumpets (10:1–11:13) but not between the sixth and seventh
bowls (16:12-21). The faithful believers would be kept safe. This chapter contains two pictures:
first, the sealing of the 144,000; second, the great multitude worshiping before God's throne.

7:1 John saw **four angels** who were **standing at
the four corners of the earth** (referring to the
whole earth, the four points of the compass). The
sudden silence and the angels **holding back the
four winds from blowing upon the earth** picture
God's protection from harm; they contrast the
peace and security of the believers with the terror
of those hiding in the rocks (6:16). The winds
described here picture harmful winds as agents
of God bringing destruction (see Daniel 7:2).
The four angels hold back the winds so that **not
a leaf rustled in the trees, and the sea became
as smooth as glass.** This scene contrasts with the
earthquakes and meteor showers that had just
occurred (6:12-13).

7:2-3 Another angel came from the **east** who had
the seal of the living God. In ancient days, a king
would push his signet ring into wax on a scroll or
document as a seal to mark his ownership and to
protect its contents. God places his own seal on his

followers, identifying them as his own and guaranteeing his protection over their souls. Here, God's
seal was placed **on the foreheads of his servants.**
This seal would be counterfeited by Satan in 13:16
(a seal known as "the mark of the beast"). These
two marks would separate the people into two distinct categories—those owned by God and those
owned by Satan. Ezekiel 9:4-7 records God sending
a divine messenger through Jerusalem to mark the
foreheads of those who still worshiped the one
true God. Here, the seal that the angel put on the
believers' foreheads was the name of the Lamb and
his Father's name (see 14:1).

Pretribulationists believe that Christians will
have been raptured—removed from this world
to meet the Lord in the air—just before the tribulation begins. They believe that this seal means that
many others will become believers during the
time of tribulation—these new believers will
receive this seal. According to this verse, the only
believers who will suffer through this terrible evil

and persecution will be those who become Christians during the tribulation, perhaps because they had witnessed the rapture of true believers. Both those who think that the Christians will be raptured before the tribulation, as well as those who think they will remain on earth throughout, agree that the seal put on believers' foreheads will protect them (see 3:10).

7:4-8 The number of those who were **sealed** is **144,000.** This does not mean that only 144,000 people alive on the earth at that time will be saved. Most likely, it is a symbolic number: 12 x 12 x 1,000, symbolizing completeness. A similar multiple appears in 21:16, when John was measuring the new Jerusalem (see also 14:1).

Some believe that **the tribes of Israel** refers specifically to Jews—that there will be a great revival among the Jews and that many will be saved. Some say that there will be exactly 144,000 Jews saved—perhaps to be evangelists for the rest of the great multitude (7:9). This list differs slightly from the lists of the twelve tribes that occur in various places in the Old Testament. Some reasons for the differences could be: (1) Judah is mentioned first because Judah is both the tribe of David and of Jesus the Messiah (Genesis 49:8-12; Matthew 1:1). (2) Levi had no tribal allotment because of the Levites' work for God in the Temple (Deuteronomy 18:1), but here the tribe is given a place as a reward for faithfulness. (3) Dan is not mentioned because it was known for rebellion and idolatry—traits unacceptable for God's followers (Genesis 49:17). (4) The two tribes representing Joseph (usually called Ephraim and Manasseh, after Joseph's sons) are here called Joseph and Manasseh because of Ephraim's rebellion. See Genesis 49 for the story of the beginning of these twelve tribes.

Most likely, however, this listing of the twelve tribes is symbolic of all of God's true followers—the "true Israel," which is the church (Romans 2:29; 9:6; Galatians 3:29; 6:16; 1 Peter 2:9). All of God's followers will be brought safely to him; not one will be overlooked or forgotten. When persecution begins, the faithful will have already been sealed (marked by God), and they will remain true to him until the end.

PRAISE FROM THE GREAT MULTITUDE / 7:9-17
This "vast crowd" is the redeemed multitude, the great international family of God, offering praise to him. These are the ones who have been protected, redeemed, and purified.

7:9-10 In 7:4, John had heard the number of those sealed; here, he **saw a vast crowd, too great to count.** This fulfilled God's promise to Abraham that he would have descendants too numerous to count (Genesis 15:5; 32:12; Romans 9:6-8; Galatians 3:29).

Who is this great multitude? In 7:14, they are described as those who have come "out of the great tribulation." Some interpreters identify them as the martyrs described in 6:9, but they may also be the same group as the 144,000 just mentioned (7:4-8), for that may be a symbolic number indicating all believers who had been sealed. In other words, John may have seen the final state of the believers who survive the tribulation. This interpretation seems to be supported by 7:15-17, where the believers are described as serving God day and night—thereby picturing eternity. This scene provides great comfort to all believers facing persecution. Those who will face the great tribulation have a guaranteed future with God.

The angels, elders, and living beings of chapters 4 and 5 were joined by a huge crowd of people. No distinctions of race, ethnic background, or gender exist in this worshiping community. These were the redeemed people—those who had accepted Christ's sacrifice on their behalf and had experienced God's forgiveness. They sing about **salvation.** These were **clothed in white,** symbolizing their purity because of the salvation they had received (3:4-5; 4:4; 19:14). The martyrs in 6:11 had been given white robes—thus, some think this crowd that has come through the tribulation is those who have been martyred for their faith. They were holding **palm branches in their hands,** symbolizing the joy of this occasion, as they stood before God and the Lamb (see also John 12:13).

7:11-12 The **angels,** the **elders,** and **the four living beings** had stood before the throne in John's earlier vision. For more information about the elders, see the commentary on 4:4. For more information on the four living beings, see the commentary on 4:6-7.

After the redeemed sang their song (7:9-10), these worshiped God and sang to him seven words of praise because of the salvation he had given to all the redeemed. Jesus said, "There is joy in the presence of God's angels when even one sinner repents" (Luke 15:10). Imagine the great joy of the angels in heaven when they stand with this count-less crowd of believers who had repented of sin and accepted the salvation of the Lamb.

7:13-14 One of the twenty-four elders turned to John and anticipated his question regarding the identity of this great crowd in white robes, **"Where do they come from?"** These people have come **out of the great tribulation.** They have persevered, standing true for Christ. Some may have been martyred, but probably not all of them. They have been redeemed, for they have **washed their robes in the blood of the Lamb and made them white.** It is difficult to imagine how blood could make any cloth white, but the blood of Jesus Christ is the world's greatest purifier because it removes the stain of sin (Hebrews 9:14). White symbolizes sinless perfection or holiness, which can be given to people only by the death of the sinless Lamb of God on their behalf. This is a picture of how believers are saved through faith (see Isaiah 1:18; Romans 3:21-26).

For explanation on the various views of the great tribulation, see commentary on 7:2-3 above.

7:15-17 According to 7:1-8, the believers receive a seal to protect them through a time of great tribu-lation and suffering; in 7:9-17, John receives a glimpse into the future—the believers finally with God in heaven. All who have been faithful through the ages were singing before God's throne. Their tribulations and sorrows were over: no more tears for sin, for all sins were forgiven; no more tears for suffering, for all suffering was over; no more tears for death, for all believers had been resurrected to die no more.

The phrase **day and night** means continuous, unceasing service to God—that "service" refers to worship and praise (22:3-5) The **Temple** is not limited to some particular building in heaven, nor is it a reference to the Temple in Jerusalem; instead, all of heaven is God's sanctuary. God will satisfy every need. That **they will never again be hungry or thirsty,** and **fully protected from the scorching noontime heat** echoes Isaiah's proph-ecy (see Isaiah 49:10). God's care extends to every part of life—he **will wipe away all their tears.** These are the blessings that God will provide to his people.

REVELATION 8

THE LAMB BREAKS THE SEVENTH SEAL / 8:1-5
Chapter 7 was an interlude. At the end of chapter 6, the sixth seal had been opened (6:12). Here at the beginning of chapter 8, the Lamb opens the seventh and last seal.

8:1-2 The Lamb broke the seventh seal, which was the last on the scroll (5:1). When the seal was opened, **there was silence throughout heaven for about half an hour** (see Habakkuk 2:20; Zechariah 2:13). This is the silence of breathless expectancy, as all of heaven waited for the hand of God to move. When the seventh seal was opened, the seven trumpet judgments were revealed. In the same way, the seventh trumpet will announce the seven bowl judgments in 11:15 and 16:1-21.

Seven angels were given **seven trumpets.** The trumpet judgments, like the seal judgments, are only partial. God's final and complete judgment had not yet come. The Lamb had opened the seven seals to set in motion events of judgment, but angels had been given the power to execute the trumpet and bowl judgments.

Throughout the Old Testament, trumpets had a variety of meanings and purposes. Moses was

instructed to make two silver trumpets that would call the people together, move the tribes forward on their journey, sound an alarm, or signify the feast days (Numbers 10:3, 5-6, 9-10). The trumpets herald the arrival of the day of God's wrath.

Apparently, the events of 8:3-5 occur immedi-ately following this time of silence.

8:3-4 Then John saw **another angel,** not one of the seven, who had **a gold incense burner** and came to the **altar** (also mentioned in 6:9). The angel was given **a great quantity of incense,** which was used **to mix with the prayers of God's people.** The angel acted in the role of a priest, presenting the prayers of the saints to God. The incense symbolized the offered prayers, and the angel was merely the agent. **The smoke of the incense, mixed with the prayers of the saints, ascended up to God** (see Exodus 30:7-9). These prayers are most likely prayers for justice and deliverance, as described in 6:10. God brings judgment in response to the prayers of his people. One of the reasons for the trumpet judgments is God's answer to the prayers of the saints.

8:5 Then the angel filled the incense burner with fire from the altar and threw it upon the earth. Ezekiel described a similar scene (Ezekiel 10:2-7), thereby picturing judgment on the city of Jerusalem as God's glory departed. The fire from the altar being thrown to the earth symbolizes the prayers of the saints on earth being answered. God was about to act on their behalf. The **thunder, lightning,** and **earthquake** are the beginning of his answer to their prayers. These indicate that God is about to take action and answer (Exodus 19:16-19).

THE FIRST FOUR TRUMPETS / 8:6-13

The seven trumpet judgments call forth a series of God's plagues on his enemies. These judgments affected every part of the world. Unlike the bowl judgments described in chapter 16, the first six trumpets were targeted on just a third of the cosmos and were intended to produce repentance (9:20-21).

The trumpet and the bowl judgments symbolically reenacted the plagues of Egypt recorded in Exodus 7–12. The plagues had two purposes:

- They were directed against the gods of Egypt. Every plague was directed at a force that the Egyptians thought was on their side because they worshiped that force. For example, the Egyptians worshiped the sun, so God sent a plague of darkness (Exodus 10:21-29); they worshiped the Nile River, so God sent a plague to turn the sacred river to blood (7:14-24). The first purpose of the plagues against Egypt was to prove the powerlessness of the Egyptian gods.
- The plagues were oriented to the cycle of nature. The Egyptians worshiped many gods representing the various forces of nature so that nature would feed and take care of them. The second purpose of the plagues was to show the Egyptians that God controlled nature and that Egypt's gods controlled nothing. In the trumpet and bowl judgments, the world that these people are worshiping will turn against them. Through these judgments, God will once again bring punishment upon those who oppress his people, just as he did in Egypt.

The plagues showed the helplessness of the people of Egypt, who worshiped false gods. In the same way, through these trumpet and bowl judgments, God will show the people of this world their helplessness and hopelessness without him.

8:6 Returning to the action of 8:2, the **seven angels** who had been given **the seven trumpets** got ready to **blow their mighty blasts.** The picture is of these mighty angels raising the trumpets to their lips and then awaiting the signal to blow at the appropriate time. The trumpet blasts have three purposes: (1) to warn that judgment is certain, (2) to call the forces of good and evil to battle, and (3) to announce the return of the King, the Messiah.

8:7 At the beginning of chapter 7, an angel had called for the angels holding back the four winds to not hurt "the land or the sea or the trees" until God's servants had been sealed (7:1-3). But after they had been sealed, God's fury was unleashed upon the earth.

The first angel blew his trumpet, and hail and **fire mixed with blood were thrown down upon the earth.** This compares to the seventh plague on Egypt when hailstorms killed anything that was outside (people and animals) and destroyed much vegetation (Exodus 9:13-35). Some have suggested that this could refer to volcanic activity; others say that this is a violent storm, with the fire representing lightning and the blood referring to the color of the sky. (see also Ezekiel 38:22; Joel 2:31; Luke 21:25-26).

The result is that **one-third of the earth was set on fire,** along with **one-third of the trees** and **all the grass.** Since only one-third of the earth was destroyed by these trumpet judgments, this was only a partial judgment from God. His full wrath was yet to be unleashed. The purpose of this judgment was to warn people to repent.

8:8-9 When the **second angel blew his trumpet,** one-third of the sea was destroyed. The **great mountain of fire was thrown into the sea,** causing the disruption. Some suggest that this refers to a falling meteor or asteroid that, upon impact in the sea, disrupts the ecology of the sea and creates a tidal wave. The water is described as becoming **blood,** with the result that **one-third of all things living in the sea died.** This compares to the first plague when the Nile River was turned to blood (Exodus 7:14-24). This plague on the sea somehow also affected **one-third of all the ships on the sea** because they were **destroyed.** Perhaps this occurred from a tidal wave caused by the "great mountain of fire" that had been thrown into the sea.

For an economy centered around the sea for its trade and food, as was Rome's, this would be especially terrifying. Because travel by land was slow, Rome depended on the sea for most of its transport of goods. The key cities in the Roman Empire were the ports on the Mediterranean Sea. Rome's navy insured the safety of travel on the Mediterranean. But they could do nothing against God's judgment.

8:10-11 When **the third angel blew his trumpet,** the results affected all the inland waters—**one-third of the rivers** and **the springs of water.** This occurred when **a great flaming star fell out of the sky.** This may be a comet. It is named **Bitterness,** picturing the bitterness of sorrow and death. This reversed the miracle that God had performed for his people in the wilderness at Marah—turning the bitter water sweet so that it would be drinkable (Exodus 15:22-25). Here, sweet water was turned **bitter,** making it undrinkable and causing many people to die.

This also compares to the first plague against Egypt when the water was turned to blood and made undrinkable (Exodus 7:24). This judgment affects one-third of all the fresh water on the earth—horrible, but still not total and final judgment.

8:12 The **fourth angel blew his trumpet** and the celestial bodies were affected. The picture is of the **sun** and **stars** losing some of their light, but more than that, **one-third of the day was dark** and **one-third of the night** with no moonlight. This compares to the ninth plague of darkness that descended upon Egypt (Exodus 10:21-29). During a portion of the day and a portion of the night, there was absolute darkness on the earth. (See also Isaiah 13:10; Joel 2:2; Amos 5:18; Mark 13:24.) The darkness of the fourth trumpet judgment set the stage for the last three trumpets that would bring demonic activity on the earth.

8:13 This verse provides a transition from the four trumpet blasts that caused havoc on nature to the three coming blasts that would let loose demonic forces to attack people on the earth.

Habakkuk used the image of eagles to symbolize swiftness and destruction (see Habakkuk 1:8). The picture is of a strong, powerful bird, here called an **eagle** (also a carrion bird), flying over all the earth, warning of the terrors yet to come. While the first four trumpet judgments were horrible, the eagle is saying that worse was yet to come. There is one **"terror"** for each remaining trumpet blast.

While both believers and unbelievers experience the terrors described in 8:7-12, **all who belong to this world** refers to the unbelievers who will meet spiritual harm through the next three trumpet judgments. God has guaranteed believers protection from spiritual harm (7:2-3; 9:4).

REVELATION **9**

THE FIFTH TRUMPET BRINGS THE FIRST TERROR / 9:1-12
Revelation 9 records the fifth and sixth trumpet judgments—the first two "terrors" (8:13). The first four trumpet judgments had brought disaster upon nature; with the fifth and sixth, demons were sent to attack the people of the earth and torment them. Ironically, the demonic forces destroyed their own worshipers. They were sent against those who did not have the seal of God and had, therefore, chosen to side with Satan (9:4).

9:1-2 The first "terror" occurred when **the fifth angel blew his trumpet.** John saw **a star that had fallen to earth from the sky.** There is much debate as to the identity of this star, whether the "star" is Satan, a fallen angel, Christ, or a good angel. Some scholars point to 9:11 and identify this angel with the "angel from the bottomless pit," thus, a demon (see also 12:4, 9; Isaiah 14:12; Luke 10:18). If the star is a demon, he loosed evil forces upon the inhabitants of the earth. The evil forces, however, were only allowed to harm those who belonged to them, not the sealed believers (9:4). Most likely, this "star" is a good angel, because he **was given the key to the shaft of the bottomless pit,** and that key, normally, would be held by Christ (1:18), and because in 20:1 an angel came down from heaven with this key. If it is a good angel, then he was simply obeying God's directions to let loose calamity upon the earth. Most importantly, this angel is under God's control and authority.

The bottomless pit, is the eternal destination of the wicked and the abode of the demonic forces (see Luke 8:31; 2 Peter 2:4; Jude 1:6; also referred to in 9:11; 11:7; 17:8; 20:1-3). It is full of smoke and fire, for when it was opened, **smoke poured out as though from a huge furnace.** There is so much smoke upon the opening of this pit that **the sunlight and air were darkened.**

9:3-6 Out of the billowing **smoke** come **locusts.** God had also sent a plague of locusts on Egypt (Exodus 10:1-20). This locust plague, however, fulfilled the words of the prophet Joel, who described a locust plague as a foreshadowing God's coming judgment (Joel 1:6–2:11). In the Old Testament, locusts symbolized destruction because they destroyed all vegetation (Deuteronomy 28:42; 1 Kings 8:37; Psalm 78:46). In what is called a plague, millions of locusts (grasshoppers) travel in a column many feet deep and miles in length. So many destroy everything in an area—grass, trees, and crops. This locust infestation spells destruction on agricultural societies. In the 1950s, locusts devoured several hundred thousand square miles of vegetation in the Middle East.

Here, however, these locusts were **told not to hurt the grass or plants or trees.** This is a very different kind of "locust" plague, for they looked like horses (9:7; Joel 2:4) and they were **given power to sting like scorpions.** These "locusts" were terrifying. In fact, they were demons—evil spirits ruled by Satan who tempt people to sin. They did not attack vegetation but, instead, attacked **all the people who did not have the seal of God on their foreheads** (7:3). This invasion of demons tortured people who did not believe in God. Believers, however, were pro-

tected from this (3:10; 7:3-4). The demons were not allowed to **kill** people but to cause **agony like the pain of scorpion stings.** These would be so painful that **people will seek death,** but would be unable to do so. God would not allow them to escape punishment by dying—instead, they would have to suffer. The demons could only torment people for **five months**—the lifespan of a locust, as well as the length of the harvesttime on earth during which locusts plagues could come. The limitations placed on the demons show that they are under God's authority.

9:7-10 This description is very similar to what locusts actually look like upon close observation (see Joel 2:4), but these locusts are exaggerated and much bigger than life—supernatural locusts. That they **had human faces** probably indicates that these were not mere insects but were intelligent beings. These locusts were not just out for food but were sent to make war against their own followers. **Their teeth were like the teeth of a lion** is also a description found in Joel's prophecy (Joel 1:6). These locusts had **armor made of iron,** making them invincible. No one would be able to fight against them. Their wings had the roaring. sound of **an army of chariots rushing into battle.** This was the most fearsome sound of warfare in the ancient world. No one could stand against war chariots (see also Joel 2:5).

9:11 This army of locusts had **a king.** He was **the angel from the bottomless pit.** Most likely, this was not the same angel who unlocked the pit in 9:1 but a different angel, an emissary of Satan (see commentary on 9:1).

This angel's name is given in both Hebrew (**Abaddon**) and in **Greek (Apollyon),** both meaning "Exterminator" or "Destroyer." The Greek name may relate to the god Apollo, who was believed to be the leader of all the gods and was adopted as the patron god of the emperor. One of the symbols of Apollo was a locust. Roman emperors, such as Domitian, liked to portray themselves as the incarnate Apollo. Ironically, John may have linked this leader from hell (the locust king) with the emperor. Most likely, this is a powerful demon, similar to a commander in the hierarchy of demons, but not Satan himself.

9:12 In the Old Testament, the word **terror** always refers to coming judgment. Though carried out by demonic powers, these events are actually divine judgments. Satan is at the mercy of God's power. At this point, **two more terrors are coming.**

THE SIXTH TRUMPET BRINGS THE SECOND TERROR / 9:13-21

The sixth angel will set into motion the sixth trumpet judgment and the second "terror" that must be sent on the earth. According to 6:9, the altar was where the souls of all who had been martyred were waiting for God's punishment to be executed on their enemies. Their prayers called for vengeance, and God was releasing it in these "terrors" (8:13).

9:13-16 When **the sixth angel blew his trumpet,** a voice came **from the four horns of the gold altar.** It is unknown whether this was the voice of God or of another angel. The "horns" refer to the altar in the Temple and its four projections, one at each corner (see Exodus 27:2).

This angel would **release the four angels who are bound at the great Euphrates River.** The word "angels" here means fallen angels or demons, for in Scripture, God's angels are never bound. These four unidentified demons would be exceedingly evil and destructive. They were held back by God and would be released at a specific time, doing only what God allowed them to do. They **had been prepared** for this very moment.

The four "angels" (demons) command **an army of 200 million mounted troops,** sent out to **kill one-third of all the people on the earth.** This affects only those who did not have the seal of God on their foreheads (9:4, 20). As with the torture inflicted during the sixth trumpet, these demons were attacking their own followers.

This could correspond to the plague in Egypt of the death of the firstborn sons. In that final plague, the angel of death came and killed the firstborn sons of the Egyptian families but passed over the homes of the Israelites (Exodus 11). Many men died in Egypt that night, but that will not compare to the terror that will come upon the earth when these demonic mounted troops arrive. In 6:7-8, one-fourth of mankind had been killed; here, one-third more was killed. Thus, over one-half of the people in the world would have been killed by God's great judgments. Even more would have been killed if God had not set limits on the destruction.

In John's day, two hundred million mounted troops in an army was inconceivable. In the censuses taken in the Roman Empire, the number of people in the entire Empire totaled around two hundred million. So for the people of that day, that meant one demonic horseman for every person in the Empire. At the height of World War II, all soldiers on both sides numbered about seventy million. The math itself should have shocked the people into realizing that this is more than a natural disaster. But so hardened are the surviving two-thirds of earth's inhabitants that they remained unrepentant (9:21).

9:17-19 John saw this army of two hundred million as **horses** and **riders** with brightly colored **armor.** They were released to kill with **three plagues.** This sort of destruction had fallen on the evil cities of Sodom and Gomorrah (see Genesis 19:24). **Sulfur,** or brimstone, was found near regions with volcanic activity and, in the Bible, it represents the wrath of God (see 14:10; Isaiah 30:33; 34:9). Many interpreters see modern canons or tanks in this picture. John reminds us that these figures were **in my vision** and, most likely, are symbolic representations of demonic hordes, not descriptions of actual human armies. The figure of the horse is more like the description of the Leviathan in Job 41:19-21.

The entire picture in this vision is horrifying. There is much symbolism in these descriptions. The main point to remember is that God released these demonic hordes to kill their own followers. This should warn those who refuse to repent.

9:20-21 This outpouring of judgment upon the earth was a final attempt by God to bring people to repentance. They had a chance to **turn from their evil deeds** but, unfortunately, they did not. They saw what was occurring but **still refused** to turn to God, desiring instead to continue to **worship demons and idols.**

Idolatry is demonic; it is worship of Satan (1 Corinthians 10:20). Demons hate the very people who worship them, torturing and killing them, yet people still prefer those demons over God. They **did not repent** and turn to God. For example, in the occult today, people worship demons. Their practices include sacrifices of babies, murder, mutilation, and sacrifices of animals. These people are worshiping very destructive powers. With the popularity of the occult in books and movies, the church must strongly teach about the destructive and hateful power of demons.

This is why there has to be eternal punishment. God does everything he can do to draw people to himself, but these people want to continue in their idol worship and live out what that worship leads to—**murders, witchcraft, immorality,** and **thefts.** They have chosen their side and so must remain there. God does not want anyone to perish (2 Peter 3:9); however, when God's call is consistently rejected, then judgment must fall.

REVELATION 10

THE ANGEL AND THE SMALL SCROLL / 10:1-11

Chapter 10 introduces an interlude between the sixth and seventh trumpets, much as chapter 7 was an interlude between the sixth and seventh seals. This interlude extends from 10:1–11:14. No corresponding interlude exists between the sixth and seventh bowl judgments, for at that time, the end will have come and there will be no time for further warning.

As noted earlier, the Scripture does not state whether these events follow in sequence, are cyclical, or are merely intensifying with each set of seven judgments. God has chosen not to explain these visions totally. This book reveals God's judgment upon evil and his bringing of his own to be with him forever. When and how that all happens is for us to discuss and study in order to be morally and spiritually prepared. Believers should not allow their different beliefs regarding the end times to distract them from the hope in Christ's return.

10:1 John then saw **another mighty angel coming down from heaven.** Some have suggested that this angel was actually Christ because of the divine imagery surrounding this angel's appearance. While this description sounds much like the description of Christ in 1:13-16, most likely, it is not Christ, for he is never called an "angel" anywhere else in Revelation. Also, he would not speak with an oath, as described in 10:6. Others suggest that this is the same angel as described in Daniel 12:7. This angel is a very powerful, high-ranking angel who has come down from heaven to announce the final judgments on the earth. The **cloud** usually described the presence of God in the Old Testament (Exodus 13:21; 40:34; 1 Chronicles 5:13-14). The **rainbow** had been a promise to Noah that God would not destroy the earth again with a flood (Genesis 9:8-17). The angel's face **shone like the sun,** much like the face of Christ at the Transfiguration (Matthew 17:2). The feet **like pillars of fire** could recall the pillar of fire in the wilderness (Exodus 14:20).

10:2 This powerful archangel was carrying **a small scroll** that **he had unrolled.** Two scrolls appear in Revelation. The first contains a revelation of judgments against evil and was unrolled by the Lamb (chapters 5 and 6). The contents of the second little scroll are not indicated, but it also may contain a revelation of judgment.

So large and powerful was the angel that he **stood with his right foot on the sea and his left foot on the land.** Many of John's readers may have immediately pictured the Colossus of Rhodes, a statue built in Rhodes, an island between Crete and Turkey. The magnificent statue of Apollo, the sun god, was one of the seven wonders of the ancient world. It stood about 105 feet high—one foot was on the island and the other foot was on the mainland. It was the greatest statue ever built in the ancient world. Ships would sail in the waterway between the statue's legs. It was destroyed by an earthquake in 227 B.C.

This angel standing on the sea and on the land indicates that his words would affect all creation, not just a limited part, as did the seal and trumpet judgments. The seventh trumpet (11:15) would usher in the seven bowl judgments, which would bring an end to the present world. When this universal judgment comes, God's truth would prevail.

10:3-4 The **shout** of this mighty angel sounded to John **like the roar of a lion.** When the angel spoke, **the seven thunders answered.** This is a picture of the awesome sight of God on Mount Sinai (Exodus 19:19). This thunderous reply was spoken by God and must have been understandable, for John began to write down what was said. He was stopped from doing so, however, by another **voice** that told him to **keep** these words **secret** (see also Daniel 12:4).

10:5-7 The angel **lifted his right hand to heaven** (see also Daniel 12:7) and **swore an oath in the name of the one who lives forever and ever—** referring to God (1:4). This description highlights the truth that God is eternal and controls all of time—what a comfort for persecuted believers. The oath declares that **God will wait no longer.** With the sounding of the seventh trumpet, God would bring about the end of history—**God's mysterious plan will be fulfilled.** "Mystery" is a key word in the New Testament. The word is almost synonymous with the word "revelation." In the Bible, the word "mystery" refers to a divine secret. All of time has been pointing forward to this moment. All prophecy will be fulfilled—everything will occur just as God had announced **to his servants the prophets.** From the very beginning, God had promised that, despite the peoples' sin, he would one day defeat evil. From the moment Adam sinned, all of history has been pointing toward this blowing of the final trumpet.

The time of final judgment has come. God would stop giving warnings and offers of repentance. All restraint would be removed, and the Antichrist would be revealed (2 Thessalonians 2:3). The forces of God and Satan would meet in final confrontation, as foretold by Daniel (Daniel 12:1).

10:8-9 **The voice from heaven** told John to go to the magnificent angel and **take the unrolled scroll.** So John obeyed. When he took it, the angel told him to **eat** the scroll.

Some think that this scroll is the word of God, but that is probably too general. More likely, the scroll represents the revelations of God as given to John in this book. Like the prophet Ezekiel, John would eat this scroll that would **taste like honey** (see also Psalm 119:103; Jeremiah 15:16) but would make his **stomach sour** (Ezekiel 2:9–3:3). This could mean that the scroll was full of words of comfort, as well as gloom. Through the command to eat this scroll, God was confirming John's prophetic role, as he did with Ezekiel. Receiving the word of God can be a pleasant experience, but it often results in the unpleasant task of speaking judgment on evil. Believers know that victory is sure, but they are pained by the difficulties they must endure and by many people's stubborn refusal to repent.

10:10-11 John **took** and **ate** the little scroll, and it did just as the angel had said—tasted **sweet** but made his stomach **sour.** Then the angel gave John another command, **"You must prophesy again about many peoples, nations, languages, and kings"** (see also 7:9). John would prophesy about a world that had turned from God. There would be no distinctions among people—the message would be for all. The only distinction left would be those who had the mark of the beast and those who had been sealed by God. The following chapters contain these prophecies.

REVELATION 11

THE TWO WITNESSES / 11:1-14

This section contains many elements that have stimulated much discussion among interpreters. There is no authoritative way to determine if the statements should be taken literally, or if they figuratively represent forces at work in the future. If they refer to literal events, we will not know until they happen. If they are figurative, we must have some idea to what the figures correspond. Two prophets, or witnesses, arrived and gave messages from God. The beast entered the vision and began his evil attacks.

11:1 In 10:8-10, John had become a participant in his vision—taking the little scroll from the angel and eating it. In this chapter, John again was participating, for he was **given a measuring stick** and told to **go and measure the Temple of God and the altar, and count the number of worshipers.** Prophets often were asked to perform symbolic actions in order to dramatize their message to the people (see, for example, Isaiah 20:2-4; Ezekiel 4). John's action recorded here is much like Ezekiel's in Ezekiel 40–42.

There are two main interpretations of the Temple that John was told to measure. (1) The Temple, the altar, and the worshipers are literal and focus on the Jews and their place in these final days. (2) The Temple, altar, and the worshipers are symbolic and refer to the "true Israel," the church, consisting of all believers in Christ.

Those who believe that this is a reference to the Jews have two slightly different views. Some understand the Temple to be a real, physical rebuilt Jewish Temple in Jerusalem. This view envisions the Antichrist permitting the rebuilding of the Temple in Jerusalem and the restoration of Jewish worship. After three and a half years, however, the Antichrist will break his treaty with the Jews and destroy the city. Then Christ will return to deliver the Jewish people. Others who also consider this section to refer to the Jews believe that the Temple and the city of Jerusalem are not to be taken literally. Instead, they say, John was predicting the eventual salvation of the Jewish people (see also Romans 11:26). The Temple, altar, and worshipers represent the believing Jews, while the outer courtyard represents the unbelieving Jews.

The second way of interpreting this passage is that it refers not just to the Jews but to all believers. In this view, the Temple is a symbol of the church (all true believers—whether Jews or Gentiles).

Some who believe that the believers have already been raptured (taken to heaven) by this time will say that this action is primarily focused on the Jews, as a way to draw them to Christ before the end. Those who believe that the Christians are still on the earth understand this to refer to God's protection of his people, similar to his sealing them in 7:3 (see also 1 Corinthians 3:16-17; 2 Corinthians 6:16; Ephesians 2:19-22; Revelation 2:4-10).

John measured the Temple and the altar and then counted the worshipers, showing that God was building walls of protection around his people to spare them from spiritual harm, although they could face physical harm (see 13:7). John was told not to measure "the outer courtyard" for that area had been "turned over to the nations" (11:2); however, the Temple would be a place of safety reserved for all those who had remained faithful to God. Similarly, an angel would measure the new Jerusalem in 21:15-17. The measurements symbolically show the perfection of this new home for God's people. Its inhabitants are protected from all evil.

Ezekiel had been told to describe the Temple in his vision to the people in Israel "so they will be ashamed of all their sins" (Ezekiel 43:10). The basic law of the Temple is "holiness" (Ezekiel 43:12), and the description was meant to contrast God's holiness against idol worship. John's measuring of the Temple differentiates God's people from those who worshiped the beast.

We simply do not know if this scene is in heaven or on earth, so we must ask what God, through his Spirit, wishes us to grasp from John's actions. Most likely, this Temple refers to all believers. As Peter wrote, "And now God is building you, as living stones, into his spiritual Temple" (1 Peter 2:5). While there may be a special role for faithful Jews in the future, we simply do not know what it will be. The measuring most likely means that God will protect his people (see 11:19).

11:2 The **outer courtyard** of the Temple that had been standing in Jerusalem was also called the Court of the Gentiles. It was set aside as a place of worship for Gentiles who had converted to Judaism and the worship of the one true God. In this case, as the area where John did no measurements, the outer courtyard represents those who would not be spiritually protected from the punishments to come.

This courtyard had been **turned over to the nations** who **will trample the holy city for 42 months.** This statement could refer to Jesus' words about a time of great apostasy (Mark 13) and the coming of the Antichrist, who will rule over the nations, trample the holy city, and set himself up as god (see also 2 Thessalonians 2:3-4). During this time, many will turn to the worship of evil. God's true and faithful people, however, will be protected from spiritual harm (see 3:10). The entire city, including the Temple, will be trampled, so God's people will face persecution and death, but they will come safely to heaven.

The outer courtyard had been turned over "to the nations." The word "nations" has also been translated "Gentiles." The Greek word, *ethne,* is used several times in Revelation and never means "Gentiles" as opposed to Jews. Instead, it stands for peoples of the earth—groups of people such as believers (2:26; 21:24, 26) or those in rebellion against God (11:18; 14:8; 19:15). In this case, the "nations" are those in rebellion against God. They "trample the holy city," causing spiritual apostasy and physical suffering.

Some literally interpret the "holy city" as Jerusalem (see Nehemiah 11:1; Isaiah 48:2; 52:1; Daniel 9:24; Matthew 27:53 where Jerusalem is referred to as "the holy city.") and believe that one day the Jews' Temple will be rebuilt in the "holy city," Jerusalem. Others see the "holy city" as a symbolic reference to the Jews. If these references to the Temple, courtyard, and holy city refer just to Jews, then this would be the only place in Revelation where it occurs. Thus, this has caused many to interpret this as another reference to believers, with the holy city as the church. The Antichrist's forces would attack and persecute the Christians. But God placed a time limit on this persecution; it would last only for 42 months.

The expression "42 months" occurs only here and in 13:5, although its equivalent can be found in other places. In 11:3 and 12:6, it is "1,260 days" (42 months x 30 days for each month). In 12:14, it is "time, times, and half a time" (a year, two years, and half a year), equaling three and a half years. This "three and a half years" is half of seven years, an important length of time in Daniel's prophecy.

In his vision, Daniel saw a king who "will defy the Most High and wear down the holy people of the Most High . . . they will be placed under his control for a time, times, and half a time" (Daniel 7:25). This king would make a seven-year treaty, "but after half this time, he will put an end to the sacrifices and offerings. Then as a climax to all his terrible deeds, he will set up a sacrilegious object that causes desecration" (Daniel 9:27). Finally, at the end of his prophecy, Daniel asked when the vision would be accomplished. The answer: "It will go on for a time, times, and half a time. When the shattering of the holy people has finally come to an end, all these things will have happened" (Daniel 12:7). And the angel added, "From the time the daily sacrifice is taken away and the sacrilegious object that causes desecration is set up to be worshiped, there will be 1,290 days" (Daniel 12:11).

In Daniel, the trampling and the setting up of a "sacrilegious object" in the Temple has been interpreted as (1) the desecration of the Temple by Antiochus IV Epiphanes in 168-167 B.C. (see Daniel 11:31); (2) the destruction of the Temple by the Roman general Titus in A.D. 70 when one million Jews were killed; or (3) the future reign of the Antichrist (see Matthew 24:15; Revelation 13:5-7). As with so much of Bible prophecy, Daniel may have been seeing all those events rolled into one. Jesus, when speaking of the future, had said, "The time will come when you see what Daniel the prophet spoke about: the sacrilegious object that causes desecration standing in the holy place. . . . That will be a time of greater horror than anything the world has ever seen or will ever see again. In fact, unless that time of calamity is shortened, the entire human race will be destroyed. But it will be shortened for the sake of God's chosen ones. Jerusalem will be conquered and trampled down by the Gentiles until the age of the Gentiles comes to an end" (Matthew 24:15, 21-22; Luke 21:24).

Daniel's prediction had come true when Antiochus Epiphanes had sacrificed a pig to Zeus on the sacred Temple altar. Jesus' words also were remembered when General Titus placed an idol on the site of the burned Temple after destroying Jerusalem. Yet both Daniel and Jesus were describing more than current events; they were also foreseeing the end times. The Antichrist will also become like a god and will be worshiped by the peoples of the earth (Revelation 13). There will not be the danger of the "entire human race" being destroyed, as Jesus had said, until the events recorded here in Revelation occur.

In Revelation, the three and a half years are equivalent to the length of time the holy city will trampled (11:2), the two witnesses prophesy (11:3), the woman is protected from the Dragon (12:6, 14), and the Antichrist (the "beast") reigns (13:5-7). That these time periods are the same length may or may not mean that they will occur at the same time. They all may be simultaneous. Another explanation is that the first three and a half years of that seven-year period involve the preaching of the two witnesses and the protection of the woman in the wilderness (a symbol explained in chapter 12), while the second three and a half years is the time of the Antichrist's (the "beast") reign and the trampling of the holy city.

Another question involves whether these are actual calendar years or symbolic lengths of time. The answer is unknown, although John used numbers as symbolic in other places in Revelation (see 2:10; 4:4; 7:4). The numbers here could be symbolic but still describe distinct periods of time. In Revelation, however, the number seven symbolizes perfection and completeness, so it is possible that the seven years simply refers to the completion of time, God's perfect timing. The main point is that God has set time limits and is in complete control of all of the events that will occur at the end of history. His plan will be completed; the plans of evil will be thwarted.

11:3 Despite the fact that the holy city will be trampled and God's people will suffer under the Antichrist, God **will give power to two witnesses.** During this time of tribulation, the merciful God will still offer people a chance to hear and respond to the truth.

There are two views about the identity of the two witnesses. The first view is that these witnesses are two men sent to prophesy to the Jews. In this regard, various names of Old Testament saints have been suggested (Enoch and Elijah, because both had been taken to heaven without dying; or Moses and Elijah, because both did similar miracles). Moses and Elijah also appeared with Christ at his transfiguration (see Matthew 17:1-7). Jewish tradition anticipates that Moses and Elijah will return before the end (see Deuteronomy 18:15-18; Malachi 4:5-6). The other view is that the two witnesses symbolize the witnessing church.

These two witnesses are described as **clothed in sackcloth,** the ancient garb of the prophets of God (Isaiah 20:2; Daniel 9:3; Zechariah 13:4). Wearing sackcloth was a sign of mourning (Isaiah 37:1-2; Jeremiah 4:8; 6:26; Jonah 3:5-8). These prophets were in mourning for what was happening to God's people and the evil that runs rampant in the world. These witnesses **will prophesy during those**

1,260 days, that is, during the same time period of 42 months (42 x 30 days per month) that the holy city is being trampled (11:2).

11:4 John described these **two prophets** as **two olive trees.** This picture is in Zechariah 4:14. Zechariah saw a vision of a lampstand and two olive trees. In the context of Zechariah, these two anointed ones may have referred to Joshua and Zerubbabel who had the special task of completing the rebuilding of God's Temple in Jerusalem after its destruction by the Babylonians (Zechariah 4:6-10; 8:11-14). Zechariah's vision had been given to encourage and strengthen Joshua and Zerubbabel in their difficult task, for the people who were rebuilding the Temple had been facing much opposition. Surely it must have encouraged them to hear from God's prophet that God was on their side. Like Joshua and Zechariah, the two witnesses stood before the Lord, doing his work despite great opposition.

John also described the two witnesses as **two lampstands.** There is much debate about what the "lampstands" symbolize. Many think they symbolize the church because the churches to whom John wrote are called "lampstands" (1:12-13, 20). The two witnesses may symbolize Jews and Christians joined in the church, or they could be the martyrs (two churches were especially being persecuted as reported in the letters in chapters 2 and 3—the churches at Smyrna and Philadelphia).

Oil and light often symbolize spiritual revival, and the two witnesses will speak God's message and spark a revival among the people on the earth. Some take this to mean that there will be a great harvest among the Jews who will become believers through the testimony of these two prophets. In any case, the power and authority of the prophets (or the church as a whole) to witness comes from God alone—not by might or by power, but by his Spirit (Zechariah 4:6).

11:5 These two witnesses, here called **prophets,** were divinely protected so that they could give the testimony that God had called them to give. **If anyone tries to harm them, fire flashes from their mouths and consumes their enemies.** Their ability to do this was a judgment from God against those who would stop them from delivering their message. Note, Elijah had called down fire from heaven (1 Kings 18:36-38; 2 Kings 1:10-14). It is unknown what aspects of this description are literal and which are symbolic. But the point is that no one will be able to stop these two prophets until God's appointed time (see 11:7).

11:6 Like Elijah, these prophets **have power to shut the skies so that no rain will fall.** Elijah had done the same, as recorded in 1 Kings 17:1, 7.

These prophets would stop the rain from falling **for as long as they prophesy**—meaning 1,260 days (11:3) or three and a half years, the same amount of time that Elijah had kept the rain from falling (James 5:17; also Luke 4:25).

Like Moses, these prophets also **have the power to turn the rivers and oceans into blood, and to send every kind of plague upon the earth as often as they wish** (Exodus 7-11). With the devastation already caused by the seals and the trumpets, the additional horror of a drought and no drinkable water would bring great suffering to those left on the earth. Through these difficulties, God would call people to turn to him. This would be their last and only hope. They must believe the message of these prophets from God.

11:7 At the end of the 1,260 days (three and a half years), the two witnesses would **complete their testimony.** God had given them that amount of time to preach the message of salvation, but then God would remove their supernatural protection and powers and would allow **the beast that comes up out of the bottomless pit** to **conquer** and **kill them.**

Who is this "beast"? In Revelation, the word "beast" refers to the Antichrist. This is the first of 36 references to this person in this book. He is also mentioned in other places in the Bible. Daniel described the beast as a "little horn," who would speak arrogantly (Daniel 7:8-27). The Antichrist would blasphemously set himself against God by persecuting believers and defiling the Lord's holy place (Daniel 9:27; 11:20-39). Jesus also predicted a sacrilegious figure who would terrorize God's people (Mark 13:14, 20). Paul wrote of a man of lawlessness who would seek to dethrone God and use Satan's power to deceive people (2 Thessalonians 2:3-4, 9-10). John is the only biblical writer to use the term "Antichrist," described as an opponent of Christ (1 John 2:18, 22; 4:3; 2 John 7).

This vision presents a figure who fulfills these earlier prophecies. Abruptly introduced here, more details are given in coming chapters. This man of evil, known as the beast, would be dedicated to opposing God. Using Satan's power (12:9), the beast would gain control over the world, force people to worship him, establish the wicked kingdom of Babylon, and persecute those who refuse to worship him (13:16-17).

Some individuals in history stand out as so evil that people of their time have considered them to be the Antichrist of Scripture—people like Caligula, Nero, Stalin, and Hitler. The Bible teaches, however, that *many* antichrists will appear, but one will stand out (1 John 2:18). People who have been completely "against Christ" have done their evil in this world, but one will come who will be even more wicked and powerful. He will be *the* Antichrist, the beast, as first mentioned here in 11:7. This beast will come out of a great rebellion against God and then will be revealed (2 Thessalonians 2:3, 7). While postmillennialists typically interpret these passages as having already been fulfilled, most other Christians believe that these prophecies refer to a figure in the future, *the* Antichrist, who will arise at the very end of history to oppose God.

The beast would attack and kill the two witnesses. Up to this point, the witnesses had been supernaturally protected from harm for 1,260 days. But then God would allow them to be killed by the Antichrist. Just as the "little horn" was "waging war against the holy people and was defeating them" (Daniel 7:21), so the Antichrist would kill God's representatives. Whether these two witnesses are two literal individuals or represent groups of people, the Antichrist would be allowed to attack, overpower, and kill them.

11:8 After the beast would kill them, he would refuse even to give them a burial, preferring to desecrate their bodies by allowing them to **lie in the main street of Jerusalem.** In the eastern world, to be deprived of burial is an act of great indignity.

John wrote that the city is **called "Sodom" and "Egypt,"** but more exactly, it would be the place **where their Lord was crucified.** Some commentators believe that the city where the witnesses will be killed is Jerusalem, figuratively called Sodom and Egypt because of the sin and idolatry there. Sodom represents the epitome of sexual sin and idolatry; Egypt represents the height of persecution and hatred of God's people. Both Sodom and Egypt had been destroyed by God's power (Genesis 19:24-25; Exodus 12:31-33; 14:27-28). If this is literally the city of Jerusalem, this once great city and capital of Israel would become enemy territory, a place of immorality and persecution of God's people.

11:9-10 The bodies of the two witnesses would not be buried but left in the street (11:8) **for three and a half days.** That time period corresponds to the three and a half years of their ministry (1,260 days; 11:3). For the mid-Tribulation position, these three and a half days are the Great Tribulation. Refusing to **bury** the bodies was the greatest dishonor that could be given. In fact, the people are so happy about the deaths of these men that they **give presents to each other to celebrate** the deaths of the prophets **who had tormented them.** The words of these prophets had pricked people's consciences, and they did not want to hear the message. The

ability of the prophets to inflict physical affliction in the form of drought, plagues, and spoiled water supply (11:6) had also been a torment to the people who had blamed the prophets for those troubles. The world today rejoices when God's spokesmen for truth and morality are silenced or suffer setbacks.

11:11-12 Because God always controls events and timing, these two witnesses remained dead for only **three and a half days** (see 11:9). Their bodies had been left out for all to see, but suddenly, **the spirit of life from God entered them, and they stood up.** Later, the Antichrist would copy this resurrection (13:3).

Obviously, the merriment surrounding their death stopped, and **terror struck all who were staring at them.** Next, a voice from heaven said, **"Come up here!"** Then the two witnesses **rose to heaven in a cloud.**

Mid-tribulationists base much of their view on these verses. They believe that the church will be raptured after three and a half years of the tribulation, at the sounding of the seventh trumpet (which occurs in 11:15; see also 1 Corinthians 15:52). According to this view, the church will face persecution for the first three and a half years of the seven-year tribulation period (Daniel 7:25; 9:27). In the second half of the tribulation, the Antichrist and those who chose to follow him will be the target of God's wrath. Mid-tribulationists also believe that the book of Revelation is chronological, so that this rapture will occur halfway through the years of tribulation. Mid-tribulationists see the two witnesses as representing the believers being raptured at the mid-point of the tribulation, calling the two witnesses to "come up." That they go up to heaven in a cloud compares to 1 Thessalonians 4:16-17.

Those who believe that the book of Revelation is cyclical (that is, the visions are repetitions of one another, intensifying as they go) may see this as the rapture of the church. They would say, however, that the rapture will occur at the end of the tribulation rather than in the middle, for this event occurs just before the last trumpet.

The two witnesses ascend to heaven in full view of their enemies who had been gleeful over their deaths. The main point is that God alone possesses authority over life and death and that only those who believe in him will be taken to be with him forever.

11:13 As part of the vindication of his two witnesses, God sent a **terrible earthquake** immediately after the ascension of the two witnesses— an earthquake that **destroyed a tenth of the**

city. Ezekiel had prophesied of an earthquake that would precede the end of history (Ezekiel 38:19-20). Zechariah also had seen the Mount of Olives split in two (Zechariah 14:3-5).

In this earthquake, **seven thousand people** were killed. The survivors were **terrified,** but they **gave glory to the God of heaven** (see 14:6-7). It is possible that these survivors were converted by the miraculous acts they had just seen, or that this glory they gave to God was no more than forced homage. That is, they may have recognized that

God is all-powerful but may not have repented of their sins.

11:14 The flying eagle had warned of three "terrors" (8:13). The first terror was recorded in 9:1-12; the **second terror** in 9:13-21 and 11:1-13. The **third terror is coming quickly.** Most likely, 11:18 hints at a third terror that will include the battle of Armageddon—the final battle between God and Satan. This will begin when the angel sounds the seventh trumpet.

THE SEVENTH TRUMPET BRINGS THE THIRD TERROR / 11:15-19

The first six trumpets had been blown in 8:6–9:21, then there was an interlude, just as there had been an interlude between the sixth and seventh seals (see 6:1–8:5). In addition, the fifth trumpet had brought in what was considered the first of three "terrors" (see 8:13), the sixth trumpet ushered in the second terror, and the seventh trumpet would bring the third terror.

11:15 The seventh angel blew his trumpet, in essence announcing the arrival of the King. There was now no turning back. The coming judgments were no longer partial but complete in their destruction. God unleashed his full wrath on the evil world that refused to turn to him (9:20-21). When his wrath would begin, there would be no escape.

The song of triumph by the heavenly hosts introduces the great themes of the following chapters. The end times had begun. When Christ first came, he brought in the Kingdom, yet his fulfilled Kingdom was still to come. The Kingdom is with God's people spiritually but has not been fulfilled historically. This verse refers to that final consummation. This is a worship pageant, portraying in heaven what will be unfolded on earth.

11:16-17 The **twenty-four elders** are mentioned again as **sitting on their thrones before God** and then falling on their faces in worship. These elders **give thanks** to God. This is much like the song they had sung in 4:8 and 4:11. There, however, they had referred to God as "the one who always was, who is, and who is still to come." Here, God **is** and **was,** but no longer "is to come" because he had come and fulfilled history. He had taken his **great power,** meaning he had unleashed his power against evil, and had **begun to reign.** (For more information on these elders, see commentary at 4:4 and 7:11.)

11:18 The **nations** of the world **were angry,** but Christ's **wrath** would subdue them; he would **destroy all who have caused destruction on the earth** (see also Psalm 2:1-2, 4-5). Not only did Christ bring wrath, he also brought judgment and rewards. The judgment is described in chapter 20.

No one will escape judgment, for Christ will even **judge the dead.** All believers (God's **servants**—the **prophets** and the **holy people**) will be rewarded according to their deeds. Throughout Revelation, the prophets are held in high esteem, separate from the rest of the believers, although joined with them as those who reverence God (see also 16:6; 18:20, 24; 22:6, 9). Unbelievers will be brought from the grave to face judgment and punishment for their sins. For more on judgment and rewards, see commentary in chapter 20.

11:19 Most likely, this was not a physical **Temple** sitting in the clouds, for the point is made later that there would be no Temple in the new Jerusalem (21:22). John had already seen God's throne and the altar in **heaven** (4:2; 6:9; 8:3). What John was seeing is the place where God dwells and the **Ark of his covenant,** which had always symbolized God's presence and faithfulness among his people. God's promises would be fulfilled and his purposes completed.

In this vision of God's open Temple, John saw heavenly worship before God himself. There would be no sin to act as a barrier between God and his people. In addition, the Ark of his covenant symbolized God's presence with his people. That John saw the Ark also assured the readers of God's presence and protection in their coming trials.

The flashes of **lightning, thunder, hailstorm,** and **earthquake** indicate God's signature on these events. These events occur here, at the sounding of the seventh trumpet, and they also occurred at the opening of the seventh seal (8:5). This will occur again at the pouring out of the seventh bowl (16:18-21).

REVELATION 12:1-17

THE WOMAN AND THE DRAGON / 12:1-17

The seventh trumpet (11:15) ushers in the bowl judgments (15:1–16:21), but in the intervening chapters (12–14), an interlude, John saw several signs regarding the cosmic warfare in Revelation—the conflict between God and Satan. He saw the source of all sin, evil, persecution, and suffering on the earth, and he understood why the great battle between the forces of God and Satan must soon take place. In these chapters the nature of evil is exposed, and Satan is revealed in all his wickedness.

In 12:1-6, the reader is given a description of the scene; the rest of the chapter (12:7-17) amplifies various parts of that basic scene. The picture of warfare between good and evil—between God and Satan—is found in 12:1-6. The next three sections—12:7-12; 12:13-17; and chapter 13—expand the story of 12:1-6. Much like a symphony where the first movement sets the theme and the rest of the movements supply variations on the theme, so the first six verses set the theme and the next three "movements" supply the variations. The scenes focus on three characters—the dragon, the woman, and the child. The first scene records the birth of the child (12:1-6), the second highlights the expulsion of the dragon from heaven (12:7-12), and the third shows the dragon attacking the woman and her children (12:13-17). Not many of these details can be traced to specific people or events but are used to depict God's victory over evil and our need to trust in him.

12:1 The **woman** here represents much more than a woman. Pictured as a superhuman figure, she was **clothed with the sun** and had **the moon under her feet.** She was also wearing a victor's crown, **a crown of twelve stars.**

In the Old Testament, the nation of Israel is pictured as the wife of God (Isaiah 54:5-6; Jeremiah 3:6-8; 31:32; Ezekiel 16:32; Hosea 2:16). This woman represents the faithful people in Israel who had been waiting for the Messiah who would be born from among them (Isaiah 9:6-7; Micah 5:2). They had recognized and had accepted the Messiah when he had come. Later in the chapter, this woman will represent all believers—Jews and Gentiles.

12:2 God had set apart the Jews for himself (Romans 9:4-5), and that nation had given birth to the Messiah, who would "rule all nations with an iron rod" (12:5; see also Psalm 2:9). In this part of the vision, John saw that this woman, Israel, **was pregnant** and awaiting **delivery** of the Messiah (see also Isaiah 26:17-18; 54:1; 66:7-12; Hosea 13:13; Micah 4:9-10; 5:2-3; Matthew 24:8). When Mary gave birth to a tiny baby in Bethlehem, the entire universe took notice, for this event held cosmic significance.

This picture also symbolizes the nation of Israel agonizing for centuries as it awaited the coming Messiah, the deliverer, who would destroy evil and usher in God's eternal Kingdom.

12:3 John saw **a large red dragon,** who was Satan (12:9). Satan was originally created for God's glory. But Satan arrogantly rebelled against God because he desired to be like God instead of giving glory to God (1 Timothy 3:6; Jude 6). After Adam and Eve's sin in the Garden of Eden, God had promised to destroy Satan and his demons and reestablish his own Kingdom. Speaking to the serpent, God had said, "You and the woman will be enemies, and your offspring and her offspring will be enemies. He will crush your head, and you will strike his heel" (Genesis 3:15). The offspring who ultimately crushes Satan's head is God's promised Savior, Jesus Christ. Jesus demonstrated his power over Satan through his miracles and exorcisms (Matthew 12:28-29). Hearing of his disciples' success on their first mission to spread his word, Jesus had said, "I saw Satan falling from heaven as a flash of lightning. And I have given you authority over all the power of the enemy" (Luke 10:18-19). Jesus' sacrificial death on the cross and his resurrection sealed his victory over Satan (Colossians 2:15; see also John 12:31; 16:11).

Although a great battle had been won, the war was not over. Since Eden, Satan has been the avowed enemy of God and his people, as pictured in John's vision. In the end, Satan will fight against God's people and will wage a final war against God. At that time, Satan will be decisively defeated.

This dragon is pictured as having **seven heads and ten horns, with seven crowns on his heads.** These are not supernatural, heavenly crowns, as the crown of twelve stars on the woman's head (12:1); instead, these heads and crowns symbolize nations over which Satan has control. Throughout Revelation, the number seven signifies completeness, so the seven heads and seven crowns could picture the totality of Satan's control over the earth. The dragon has authority only in this world. The "ten horns" allude to Daniel 7:7 and 24. The ten horns, or ten kings, are also mentioned in Revelation 17:12. The huge statue in Nebuchadnezzar's vision also had ten toes (Daniel 2:41-42). It is unclear whether these ten kings will be actual kings and nations or even the exact number ten, but Revelation 17:12-14 says they will make war against Christ. As the King of kings, Christ will conquer them.

12:4 This verse describes the fall of Satan (see details on 12:7-9). John saw a vision of the dragon standing **before the woman** waiting to **devour the baby.** This reminds us of the slaughter of the young boys in Bethlehem by Herod (Matthew 2:16). Herod was Satan's emissary, used by Satan to attempt to kill the child Jesus.

12:5 The woman **gave birth to a boy.** This boy child is Jesus, born to a devout Jew named Mary (Luke 1:26-33), born to the entire nation of Israel. But this boy would not be killed by Satan, for he would be born **to rule all nations with an iron rod** (see Psalm 2:6-9). As a shepherd defends his flock, so Christ will defend his church against those who attempt to destroy it. The iron rod pictures Jesus as the ultimate warrior. His life on earth is not pictured in this story, for John immediately saw the child **snatched away from the dragon** and **caught up to God and to his throne.** Jesus came to earth, accomplished his work, and then returned to heaven. This is the Ascension (Acts 1:9). Satan may have fought Jesus, but nothing stopped him from doing what he had been sent to earth to do.

12:6 The **wilderness** represents a place of spiritual refuge and protection from Satan, probably not meant to be literal because this chapter is mostly symbolic. In this place **prepared** by God, he cared for her **for 1,260 days**—the same number noted for the trampling of the holy city (11:2), the minis-

try of the two witnesses (11:3), and the rule of the beast (13:5). God would care for his people during the entire time when evil would be in control in the world. In the wilderness, God's people would be hounded by the people on the earth (those who would follow the beast), but God would watch over them. Many would be martyred, but God would care for them. The word translated **care** is literally "nourish." The woman will be provided with food miraculously, just as Elijah was cared for in the wilderness by God (1 Kings 17:2-4). God also provided manna in the wilderness for his people (Exodus 16:4).

Some think that this woman pictures the Jewish believers only. Others suggest that she symbolizes all believers, the true Israel. Depending on one's view of when the believers will be taken to heaven (before, in the middle of, or after this time of Great Tribulation), these symbols may be identified in different ways. Because God has chosen not to make it clear, it is best to simply understand that God is promising spiritual protection for his people who are still on the earth during this difficult time.

12:7-9 This is the first expansion on the pictures described in 12:1-6. What John saw next fills in for the readers more detail of what was described in 12:4 regarding Satan's expulsion from heaven.

Satan's expulsion from heaven began as a **war in heaven** between **Michael and the angels** of God and **the dragon** (Satan) **and his angels.** Michael is a high-ranking angel (called an archangel). Throughout Jewish literature, Michael is named as the one who comes to the aid of God's people. He was seen as one of their protectors (see also Daniel 10:13, 21; 12:1; Jude 1:9). Notice that the battle here was not between God and Satan or between Christ and Satan but between Michael and Satan. Warfare raged, and **the dragon lost the battle.** As a result, Satan and his minions were **forced out of heaven.** Having lost their place, they are already vanquished foes. Satan was **thrown down to the earth,** and he went about his work of **deceiving the whole world**—his final revolt before his destruction (20:10).

Here, the great dragon is identified as **the ancient serpent called the Devil, or Satan.** The Devil is not a symbol or legend; he is very real. The Devil, God's enemy, constantly tries to hinder God's work, but he is limited by God's power and can do only what he is permitted to do (Job 1:6–2:6). The name Satan means "accuser" (12:10). He actively looks for people to accuse and attack (1 Peter 5:8-9). Satan likes to pursue believers who are vulnerable in their faith, who are spiritually weak, or who are isolated from other believers (1 Peter 5:8).

Some consider this verse to describe warfare in the ancient past, but others think that Satan's fall to earth took place at Jesus' resurrection or ascension and that the 1,260 days (12:6) are a symbolic way of referring to the time between Christ's first and second comings. Still others say that Satan's defeat will occur in the middle of a literal seven-year Tribulation period, following the rapture of the church and preceding the second coming of Christ and the beginning of Christ's one-thousand-year reign. Regardless of the interpretation, God's clear teaching is that Christ is victorious—Satan has already been defeated because of Christ's death on the cross (12:10-12). Even though God permits the Devil to do his work in this world, God is still in control. And Jesus has complete power over Satan; he defeated Satan when he died and rose again. One day Satan will be bound forever, never again to do his evil work (20:10).

Satan fell to the earth with "all his angels"— referring to demons. This world is their prison, where, as the enemies of God, they work against God's people. Satan is not omnipresent—he cannot be everywhere at once, so his demons work for him. Demons are fallen angels, sinful spiritual beings who have Satan as their leader (Matthew 25:41; Luke 11:15). Revelation highlights three evil powers who will oppose God's people during the end times: Satan, pictured as a dragon (Revelation 12:9); the beast, better known as the Antichrist (13:1-10); and the false prophet (13:11; 16:13). Demons serve as agents of this evil trinity. They seduce people, will establish the notorious kingdom of Babylon, and will lead a worldwide offensive against God's people (16:1-14).

12:10-12 Verses 10-12 comprise a hymn of praise to God for the defeat of Satan when he was thrown out of heaven. Despite Satan's power on this earth, he is and always will be a vanquished foe. A voice proclaims the victory of God's Kingdom and Christ's authority: **Salvation** means deliverance—not just spiritual salvation from sin, but freedom from the clutches of Satan. This had occurred because of God's power (strength exerted for believers) and Kingdom (his rule in believers' lives), and because of the authority of his Son. Both the Father and the Son have given this deliverance.

There is a promise that Satan is ultimately and forever defeated **because of the blood of the Lamb and because of their testimony.** The critical blow to Satan had come when the Lamb, Jesus Christ, had shed his blood for sinful humanity. The victory had been won by sacrifice—Christ's death to pay the penalty for sin. Those who accept this sacrifice become victors along with the Lamb. They confirm their loyalty to the Lamb through

their testimony—some even to the point of death. The martyrs who were **not afraid to die** revealed their ultimate victory in that final act of faith. When a believer dies, Satan may think he has gained a victory. In reality, however, he has lost. In fact, he loses every time a believer dies. The victory of the saints is the heart of Revelation. In each of the letters to the seven churches (chapters 2–3), Christ had promised that those who are victorious will receive great reward.

Those in heaven will **rejoice.** But those left on earth will face **terror.** The reason? **The Devil has come down to you in great anger, and he knows that he has little time.** Knowing that his doom is sealed and that he will ultimately be defeated, Satan, in great anger, lashes out, attempting to take as many people with him as he can, as well as causing suffering and pain to those who are on God's side. Although the Devil is very powerful, as can be seen by the condition of our world, he is always under God's control. That is, he can only do what God permits him to do. One of the reasons God allows Satan to work evil and bring temptation is so that the false believers will be weeded out from Christ's true believers. Knowing that the last great confrontation with Jesus was near, Satan was desperately trying to recruit as great an enemy force as possible for this final battle.

12:13 Verses 7-12 describe the war in heaven and expand on verse 4; verses 13-17 describe the war on earth, expanding on verse 6. **The dragon realized that he had been thrown down to the earth** and was angry. He had lost the war in heaven (12:8), lost access to God and, thus, no longer was allowed to accuse the believers (12:10-11). He could not attack the child because the child had been taken up to heaven (12:5), and knew that his time was short (12:12). In his attempt to bring as many people with him, and in his anger at God's people, the dragon **pursued the woman who had given birth to the child.** The word "pursued" is the same word translated "persecute." Satan is stalking and killing God's people, hoping to do as much damage as possible. The woman symbolizes God's people. It is unclear if this refers to the Jews or to all believers. But those on earth at this time who believe in Jesus will be hounded by Satan. His anger at Christ will be redirected at Christ's people.

12:14 This verse repeats 12:6. The text says that the woman **was given two wings like those of a great eagle,** picturing divine protection and deliverance (see also Exodus 19:4; Deuteronomy 32:10-11; Psalm 91:4; Isaiah 40:31). Eagles were the largest birds known in Palestine. These great wings **allowed her to fly to a place prepared for**

her in the wilderness, a place of safety, **where she would be cared for and protected.** God had prepared this safe place, as noted in 12:6.

The 1,260 days mentioned in 12:6 correspond to the **time, times, and half a time** mentioned here. "Time" means one year; "times" means two years; and "half a time" means half a year. This equals three and a half years, or 42 months (see 11:2), or 1,260 days (42 months x 30 days per month). Thus, the woman would be protected during the time of persecution. This could refer to the time period of the trampling of the holy city (11:2) or to the time when the Antichrist reigns (13:5), or to both, depending on how these time periods fall. The point is that God has prepared a place of spiritual protection for his people during the time when Satan will rampage across the earth. Many will die, but that will be their greatest victory over Satan. The time of that rampage has an end because God will bring an end to Satan and all evil.

12:15-16 The dragon spewed water **from its mouth,** hoping to **drown the woman. A flood** is a common Old Testament picture of overwhelming evil (see Psalms 18:4; 32:6; 69:1-2; 124:2-5; Nahum 1:8). This is a flood of lies and deceit in an attempt to drown the woman in sin. This could refer to the river of lies that will threaten Christians in the last days (see 13:14; Matthew 24:24; 2 Thessalonians 2:9-11).

Next, John saw that **the earth helped her by opening its mouth and swallowing the river** so that the flood could not hurt the woman. God used the earth to protect his people. God delivered Israel from Pharaoh by parting the Red Sea; once again, God supernaturally intervenes on behalf of his people (see Exodus 14:21-22; see also Isaiah 26:20; 42:15; 43:2; 50:2).

12:17 If the woman represents faithful Jews, then the phrase, **the rest of her children,** could refer to all believers—the entire church—**all who keep God's commandments and confess that they belong to Jesus.** If the woman represents all believers (both Jew and Gentile), then "the rest of her children" could refer to all who come to Christ through the testimony of God's people or to those specifically chosen for martyrdom. Because Satan could not bring down the group (the Jewish believers or the church at large), he waged war against individuals. "The rest of her children" could also refer to all of God's people after the first child, Jesus. All believers are considered to be Jesus' family (Romans 8:29; Hebrews 2:11).

REVELATION 12:18–13:18

THE BEAST OUT OF THE SEA / 12:18–13:10
Chapter 13 introduces Satan's (the dragon's) two evil accomplices: (1) the beast out of the sea (the Antichrist, 13:1-10) and (2) the beast out of the earth (the false prophet, 13:11-18). Together, the three evil beings form an unholy trinity in direct opposition to the Holy Trinity of God the Father, God the Son, and God the Holy Spirit.

12:18 The beast was foreshadowed in 11:7 as the one who would attack the two witnesses. He was described there as the beast from the bottomless pit. At this point, John would see the beast arrive. The dragon (the subject of chapter 12) was **waiting on the shore of the sea,** ready to call out one who would help him pursue God's people.

13:1 The **beast** rose **up out of the sea** to do the dragon's (Satan's) bidding. John described the beast as horrible to look at, for **it had seven heads and ten horns, with ten crowns on its horns.** Much like the description of the dragon in 12:3, this could simply be a picture of the dragon's authority over the beast. It may also be that the ten horns represent national leaders who followed the beast; their crowns symbolized their authority, but they actually belonged to the beast—who belonged to Satan. Initially, this beast was identified with Rome because the Roman Empire, in its early days, encouraged an evil lifestyle, persecuted believers, and opposed God and his followers. But the beast also symbolizes the Antichrist—not Satan, but someone under Satan's power and control who would be able to draw the whole world to himself.

On each head the beast had **names that blasphemed God.** Some have suggested that these refer to the divine names that had been given to various Roman emperors. Whether referring to the Roman emperors or not, these blasphemous names signified the beast's challenge of God's sovereignty and his setting himself up as god.

13:2 This Antichrist seems like a combination of the four beasts that Daniel had seen centuries earlier in a vision (Daniel 7:4-8), combining the characteristics of a **leopard,** a **bear,** and a **lion.** In Daniel's vision, the lion with eagle's wings represented Babylon with her swift conquests (statues of winged lions have been recovered from Babylon's ruins). The bear that ravaged the lion was Medo-Persia. The three ribs in its mouth represented the conquests of three major enemies. The leopard was Greece, its wings picturing the swiftness of Alexander the Great's campaign as he conquered much of the civilized world in four years (334-330 B.C.). The leopard's four heads were the four divisions of the Greek Empire after Alexander's death. The fourth beast pointed to both Rome and the end times. Many Bible scholars believe that the ten horns on the fourth beast correspond to the ten kings who will reign shortly before God sets up his everlasting Kingdom (see also Revelation 13:1). These ten kings had still not come to power at the time of John's vision recorded in the book of Revelation (17:12). The little horn is a future human ruler or the antichrist (see also 2 Thessalonians 2:3-4). God was illustrating the final end of all worldly kingdoms in contrast to his eternal Kingdom.

In combining these four beasts, John's vision reveals the epitome of evil power. The **dragon** (Satan) gave the beast (the Antichrist) **his own power and throne and great authority.** Those same words are used in the hymns in Revelation sung to God. So Satan attempted to again make a false copy, by giving his beast his power, throne, and authority. As the dragon (12:17) was in opposition to God, so the beast from the sea was against Christ and may be seen as Satan's false messiah. The Antichrist will appropriate the powers of government and religion in himself. As a political figure, the Antichrist will become so powerful that opposing him will be futile. All nations on earth will serve him. Opposition against the Antichrist's rule will be brutally suppressed. Only those who are branded with the beast's mark, showing their loyalty to him, will be able to participate in the world's economy.

13:3 Using spectacular miracles, the Antichrist persuaded the world to accept his false teachings. The beast seduced the world by imitating Christ's resurrection when he recovered from a **fatal wound.** People will follow him because they will be awed by his power and miracles. Paul had written, "This evil man will come to do the work of Satan with counterfeit power and signs and miracles. He will use every kind of wicked deception to fool those who are on their way to destruction because they refuse to believe the truth that would save them" (2 Thessalonians 2:9-10).

13:4 The ultimate goal of the dragon was, of course, to draw people away from Christ and to himself. He wanted people's worship. Thus, the people who were astounded by the beast **worshiped the dragon for giving the beast such power,** in addition to worshiping **the beast.** Worshiping anything other than Christ *is* worshiping Satan. The people **explained, "Who is able to fight against** the beast?" Some scholars think the beast will actually bring world peace so that no one can fight against him. But that peace will be based on domination and without real substance; thus, it will be shallow and short-lived.

13:5-6 The Antichrist **was allowed to speak great blasphemies against God,** exalting himself as God. This compares to the "little horn" that Daniel had seen, "The little horn had . . . a mouth that was boasting arrogantly" (Daniel 7:8). He blasphemed God by placing himself in God's position. The Antichrist slandered God's **name and all who live in heaven, who are his temple** (God's people). Such pride and blasphemy are the heart of this world. The Antichrist will be the archenemy of all who side with Christ.

Whether one subscribes to the pre-Tribulation or post-Tribulation theory, the text is clear that there will be believers on earth during the Tribulation. Those who believe that the Christians will have been taken before this time think that the believers on earth will be those who will become Christians during this time of tribulation. Those who believe the church will not be taken until after the Tribulation would assert that all believers on the earth at this time will face this persecution.

The Antichrist will unite all nations and all religions under his authority. Even so, the power given to the beast will be limited by God. He will allow the beast to exercise authority only for a short time—**forty-two months.** This is the same time period as noted in 11:2 for the trampling of the holy city, in 11:3 for the ministry of the two witnesses (stated as 1,260 days), and in 12:6 and 12:14 for the protection of the woman (God's people). (For more information on that time period, see commentary on 11:2.) Even while the beast is in power, God is still in control (11:15; 12:10-12).

13:7-8 The Antichrist was responsible for unleashing the Tribulation, the most intense period of persecution God's people would ever experience (Mark 13:14, 20). The beast would be **allowed** (by God) **to wage war against God's holy people and to overcome them** (see also 12:17; Daniel 7:21). The phrase, "wage war" does not refer to a military campaign (at least not yet), but to harassing God's people. The Antichrist would "overcome" believers, but he could only do so physically, as part of this world. In reality, those who died for the faith are the ultimate overcomers, for they have participated in Christ's death (12:11). The Antichrist could not harm God's holy people spiritually. The Antichrist would establish worldwide dominance—given by God—**to rule over every tribe and people and language and nation.** He would demand to be worshiped as God (13:8). And many *will* worship him. But only those **whose names were not written in the Book of Life.** As noted in 3:5, the Book of Life is a register in heaven of those who have trusted in Christ for their salvation (see also 17:8; 20:12, 15; 21:27). Only the people whose names are written in this register will be accepted into heaven. Despite the horrors of this time of tribulation, not one believer will be lost,

for their names are in the book. Two types of people exist—those whose names are in the book and those whose names are not in the book.

The Book of Life **belongs to the Lamb who was killed before the world was made.** This refers to God's plan from eternity past to have his Son redeem mankind from sin.

13:9-10 This phrase, **anyone who is willing to hear should listen and understand,** also appears at the end of all the letters to the seven churches. It warns readers that they had better listen.

These verses come from Jeremiah 15:2. Here they describe how believers should act during this time of tribulation by the beast (see 14:12). They understand that God is in control. He already has it all in his plan—some **who are destined for prison will be arrested and taken away.** Some who are **destined for death will be killed.** Their job, at this point, would be to show **endurance and faith.** God has the battle under control; this time of persecution would only draw closer the time of Christ's glorious return. See 1 Peter 2:19-24 for more on suffering patiently.

THE BEAST OUT OF THE EARTH / 13:11-18

The first beast had come out of the sea (13:1), but this second beast came out of the earth. Later identified as the false prophet (16:13; 19:20; 20:10), he was a counterfeit of the Holy Spirit. This beast completed the unholy trinity with the dragon (Satan) and the beast from the sea (the Antichrist). The false prophet would be in charge of the worldwide worship of the first beast.

13:11 There is a further imitation of Christ, the Lamb of God, in that the false prophet has **two horns like those of a lamb** (5:6). Perhaps his very similarity to Christ will be part of his deceptiveness. He may appear good, helpful, and caring—an "angel of light" (2 Corinthians 11:14). The **beast** looked like a lamb but **spoke** like **a dragon.** The source of his words was Satan himself—the dragon.

As with their interpretation of the first beast, scholars are divided about the beast from the earth. The different thoughts are that the second beast represents either (1) a movement or power, or (2) an individual who, at the end times, will arise along with the Antichrist to take control of the world. Those who believe that this beast represents a movement or power point to the first beast as representing the worldwide anti-God system, with the second beast representing false teachers who cause people to stray.

13:12 The first beast's authority came from Satan; the second beast **exercised all the authority of the first beast.** This second beast's job was to make all

the earth and those who belong to this world to worship the first beast.** The false prophet was in position when the Antichrist was killed and came back to life. Then the false prophet made everyone worship the Antichrist.

13:13-15 The second beast was also empowered to do **astounding miracles, such as making fire flash down from heaven.** Again, in copycat style, this was the same miracle that the two witnesses for God could perform (11:5), which is a reference to a miracle of Elijah recorded in 1 Kings 18:36-38. Ironically, Elijah had performed that miracle so that God could show who was a true prophet and who was not. Christ had warned, "False messiahs and false prophets will rise up and perform miraculous signs and wonders so as to deceive, if possible, even God's chosen ones" (Mark 13:22). This miracle and others **deceived all the people who belong to this world.**

As with all worship that is not of the one true God, this worship of the beast is idolatry. The false prophet **ordered the people of the world to make** a great statue of the first beast. This brings to mind the great statue that Nebuchadnezzar, king of Babylon, had built to himself and then had required everyone to worship (Daniel 3:1-11).

The false prophet **was permitted** (by God) **to give life to this statue so that it could speak.** The statue seemed to live and supposedly spoke to its worshipers. This, again, convinced many on this earth. The God of the Christians seemed to be mysteriously silent and invisible, but this god could be seen and he spoke audibly. No wonder many followed. And no wonder the believers needed to be warned so that they would not be swayed from the truth.

The heart of the false prophet's power is in the next words, **anyone refusing to worship** the statue **must die.** Christianity had become a capital offense—for only those who followed Christ were unwilling to worship the beast's image. This was universal persecution.

13:16-17 The false prophet went further in the worship of the beast by requiring **everyone,** no matter their age or social status, **to be given a mark on the right hand or on the forehead.** The mark is described as **the name of the beast or the number representing his name** (13:18). This mark of the beast was designed to mock the seal that God had already placed on his followers (7:2-3). Just as God had marked his people to save them, so Satan's beast marked his people to save them from the persecution that he would inflict upon God's followers. Identifying this particular mark is not as important as identifying the purpose of the mark. Those who accepted it showed their allegiance to Satan, their willingness to operate within the economic system he promoted, and their rebellion against God. To refuse the mark

meant to commit oneself entirely to God, preferring death to compromising one's faith in Christ.

People will have to worship the beast in order to receive the mark and to be able to **buy or sell anything.** Clearly those who refuse the mark (the Christians) will be set up for economic ruin, homelessness, and hunger. In the end times, no one will be able to buy or sell anything without the mark of the beast.

13:18 The meaning of this number has been discussed more than that of any other part of the book of Revelation. The three sixes have been said to represent many things including the unholy trinity of Satan, the first beast, and the false prophet (16:13).

Wisdom is needed to understand this. Throughout church history, people have assigned numerical values to the letters of names to try to identify the beast. The first readers of this book probably applied the number to the Emperor Nero, a man symbolizing all the evils of the Roman Empire. (The Greek letters of Nero's name represent numbers that total **666.**) The number continues to be linked with various world leaders, institutions, and types of economic transactions.

Because the book of Revelation is filled with symbolism, this number probably is also symbolic. The number seven is used in the book as a symbol of God's perfection. Conversely, the number six symbolizes human imperfection. So 666, then, symbolizes **the number of a man**—all human beings and their continued imperfection. Three sixes together—666—implies a trinity of imperfection—a parody of the number seven. The number symbolizes the worldwide dominion and complete evil of this unholy trinity designed to undo Christ's work and overthrow him.

REVELATION 14

THE LAMB AND THE 144,000 / 14:1-5

Chapter 13 describes the onslaught of evil that will occur when Satan and his helpers control the world. Chapter 14 gives a glimpse into eternity to show believers what awaits them if they endure. Their suffering will not be meaningless; it will only be a prelude into eternity with God. This chapter explains what will happen to those who refuse to receive the mark of the beast, and what will happen eventually to the beast and his servants.

14:1 The battle was still occurring on the earth—believers were being persecuted and killed for their faith, unable to buy or sell

anything because they had refused to worship the beast (13:15-17). To encourage John, God revealed what would await believers in heaven, reminding him that believers have been sealed by God.

The **Lamb** is Jesus the Messiah, and **Mount Zion** is probably the heavenly Jerusalem. This scene contrasts with the dragon standing on the edge of the sea and the evil world empire (13:1). "Mount Zion," here, may refer to the earthly location where Christ will begin his millennial reign, or it may refer to the church, the heavenly Mount Zion (Hebrews 12:22). Chapter 21 will describe that new city—the New Jerusalem. This scene pictures the ultimate victory of Christ and his followers. The battle may be raging on earth, but the war has already been won.

Standing with the Lamb are **144,000 who had his name and his Father's name written on their foreheads.** This contrasts with the reference in 13:16 to the unbelievers on earth who had received the mark of the beast on their foreheads.

This group of 144,000 represents the same spiritual reality as the group of 144,000 in 7:4, the number symbolizing completeness (see commentary on 7:4). The 144,000 mentioned in 7:4 had been sealed against the difficulties to come on earth. That is, all those who have been or will be saved are protected spiritually and sealed for heaven. In this passage, all those who had been sealed and promised heaven were standing with Christ. In other words, no believers will be lost, forgotten, or misplaced. Everyone who has been sealed with God's seal will one day be with Christ. All believers throughout history will be with Christ. The promise is certain. The number will be complete.

14:2 John heard **a sound from heaven.** He described it as **the roaring of a great waterfall or the rolling of mighty thunder.** Many different voices had spoken to John in his vision. Thus far, he has described them as sounding like "thunder" or a "waterfall." Here he also described the sound as **many harpists playing together.** This scene of great rejoicing in heaven includes victorious singing and instrumental music. This was not an angelic choir singing, but the 144,000 who had been redeemed (14:3).

14:3 The 144,000 who had been sealed by God and brought to their reward in heaven **sang a**

wonderful **new song in front of the throne of God and before the four living beings and the twenty-four elders** (see commentary on 4:4 and 4:6). The angel choir had sung a "new song" in 5:9, but the new song mentioned here could only be sung by the people who had been **redeemed from the earth**—purchased by the blood of the Lamb (see also 7:14; 12:11; 19:13). The angels, creatures, and elders could not sing it, for they had not experienced redemption from sin so they could not **learn the song.** The redeemed sang a glorious song of praise to the Lamb, who was standing with them, and the hosts of heaven were the audience. Only because of his sacrifice were they able to be in heaven.

14:4-5 They refers to the 144,000, the true believers whose robes had been washed and made white in Christ's blood (7:14) through his death. They are described as **spiritually undefiled, pure as virgins,** meaning that they had not been involved with the pagan world system. In the Old Testament, idolatry was often portrayed as spiritual adultery (Jeremiah 3:6; Hosea 2:5). These believers were spiritually pure; they had remained faithful to Christ. They are pictured as the pure bride of Christ (see also 21:9).

They were **following the Lamb wherever he goes,** indicating that they had followed him exclusively—referring to following Christ's instructions and his example. They **have been purchased from among people** means that Christ had bought them with his blood (5:9; 7:14; 12:11; 19:13). The price of people's sin was paid on the cross—a free gift. But only those who accept that gift are saved. The phrase, **a special offering to God and to the Lamb** refers to the act of dedicating the first part of the harvest as holy to God (Exodus 23:19; see also James 1:18). These believers had been dedicated solely and completely to God. They belonged to no one else—and never would.

No falsehood was found in these believers' mouths—**they are blameless.** These believers, bought by Christ's blood and redeemed, had also been made perfect in the presence of the Lamb. In contrast to the evil world that loves "to live a lie" (22:15), these people were blameless because of their faith in Christ.

THE THREE ANGELS / 14:6-13

In this section, three angels contrast the destiny of believers with that of unbelievers. This is a transition between the picture of the coming triumph of God's people and the pouring out of the seven bowl judgments upon the earth. God will judge evil.

14:6-7 Another angel flew and announced a message to the people of the earth (as did the eagle in 8:13). This angel was **carrying the everlasting Good News to preach to the people who belong to this world.** The angel's message called people to **fear God** and give glory to him because **the time has come when he will sit as judge.** Even in these final moments of judgment, God gave the people the opportunity to repent.

The message is proclaimed to everyone—**every nation, tribe, language, and people;** therefore, no one can have the excuse that they did not know the gospel message. As Paul said in Romans, "They have no excuse whatsoever for not knowing God" (Romans 1:20). This is a key theme of Revelation—whenever there has been a time of judgment, there has been a preceding time of warning, when people are given the opportunity to repent. However, those who refuse want nothing to do with God; their punishment is justified.

14:8 A second **angel followed** the first angel, **shouting** that **Babylon is fallen** (see also Isaiah 21:9; Jeremiah 51:8). In the Old Testament, Babylon was the name of both an evil city and an immoral empire—a world center for idol worship. Outside that city, Nebuchadnezzar had built a great statue to himself and had required everyone to worship it (Daniel 3:1-6; compare Revelation 13:14-15). King Nebuchadnezzar had reached the apex of power and pride, only to find himself judged by God (Daniel 4:28-33). The Babylonians had ransacked Jerusalem and had taken many of the people of Judah into captivity (see 2 Kings 24 and 1 Chronicles 36). Just as Babylon had been Judah's worst enemy, the Roman Empire was the worst enemy of the early Christians. John, who probably did not dare speak openly against Rome, was applying the name "Babylon" to this enemy of God's people (Rome)—and, by extension, to all of God's enemies of all times. "Babylon" is the name given to the civilization that was seduced by the beast (see also 17:1-9). This world system is filled with idolatry, corruption, and sexual sin (18:2-3, 7), a wellspring of ungodly religion, government, and economics.

The angel's words here are a prediction: the actual fall of the city would not occur until the judgment of the last bowl (16:19). God would judge this evil power **because she seduced the nations of the world and made them drink the wine of her passionate immorality** (see also 17:2). This draws from the prophecy of Jeremiah (Jeremiah 51:7). This pictures the godlessness and sinfulness of those who have been lured away from God into a world system that fulfills their lusts and passions but ultimately destroys them. Ultimately, God will destroy this evil and judge the people.

14:9-11 A **third** angel **followed** the first two, **shouting** a warning to **anyone who worships the beast and his statue** (13:14), or **accepts his mark on the forehead or the hand,** so that they can continue to function in the world (13:16-18).

In chapter 13, the believers were told how difficult it would be for them if they refused the mark of the beast. In these verses, an angel explained to the nonbelievers what would happen to them if they *do* receive the mark of the beast. Their eventual judgment would be much worse and the consequences eternal. While those who belong to God would suffer and be killed, they would have a glorious eternity awaiting them (14:1-5). Those who worship the beast and accept his mark, however, would be choosing to operate according to the Antichrist's world economic system and would ultimately face God's judgment. To get what the world values, these people would have turned away from God and violated Christian principles.

Thus, they must **drink the wine of God's wrath.** The Old Testament often pictures God's anger as being in a cup, ready to be poured out (see Job 21:20; Psalm 75:8; Isaiah 51:17; Jeremiah 25:15-38). This cup of wrath is **undiluted.** God's wrath will be in its strongest form. The full extent of his anger, undiluted by mercy and grace, would soon be poured out on those who had adamantly refused to turn from sin and receive his salvation.

Their future torment will be **with fire and burning sulfur**—a picture taken from the destruction of Sodom and Gomorrah (Genesis 19:24). Fire and sulfur are used as instruments of torture in 19:20; 20:10; and 21:8. The actual picture may be symbolic, but there is no doubt as to the horror and finality of this judgment, for **the smoke of their torment rises forever and ever.** In contrast to the redeemed who could "rest from all their toils and trials" (14:13), the unbelievers would have **no relief day or night** from their torment. Having chosen the side of the **beast,** they would suffer for it. Jesus described eternal punishment as "unquenchable fires" (Mark 9:44). For more on eternal punishment, see commentary at 20:10.

14:12 A similar statement is in 13:10 regarding the difficulties that believers will face under the Antichrist. This verse follows the promise of God's punishment for the wicked as an encouragement to **God's holy people to endure persecution patiently and remain firm to the end.** This news about God's ultimate triumph should encourage God's people to remain faithful through every trial and persecution, even death. The result of refusing to worship the Antichrist will be temporal; but the result of turning from Christ will be eternal.

14:13 The angels had spoken, and John heard another **voice from heaven.** This time John was commanded to **write this down,** emphasizing its importance to the readers. The voice pronounced the second of seven beatitudes in Revelation: **Blessed are those who die in the Lord from now on.** (The first beatitude is in 1:3.) Believers would face persecution and death at the hands of the Antichrist and his worldwide power and influence. The phrase "from now on" doesn't mean that some martyrs for the faith would not be blessed; in fact, those already dead are waiting for the final vindication (6:9-11).

Those who die in the Lord **are blessed indeed, for they will rest from all their toils and trials.**

The torment of unbelievers will leave them with "no relief day or night" (14:11), but the believers who go to be with Christ will have "rest." This "rest" does not mean that heaven will be one big easy chair. The "toils" and "trials" refer to the difficulties of remaining steadfast in the faith in the evil world. Their "rest" is the cessation of persecution. In addition, **their good deeds follow them.** The unbelievers may have done some "good deeds" during their time on earth, but those deeds will not save them. In the end, those good deeds will be destroyed. But God remembers believers' good deeds; indeed, they are the basis for the rewards he will give (1 Corinthians 3:13-15; Ephesians 6:8).

THE HARVEST OF THE EARTH / 14:14-20

The final verses of this chapter give two visions of final judgment. Verses 14-16 describe the harvest of the earth compared to a grain harvest. Verses 17-20 picture the horror of this final judgment of God upon sin.

14:14 John sees **the Son of Man,** Christ. In the vision, Christ may be waiting for the angelic messenger to announce the time of the harvest, just as other angels have announced the judgments. He wore **a gold crown on his head** and had **a sharp sickle in his hand**—waiting for the announcement that the harvest of the earth was to begin.

14:15-16 An angel came from the Temple—referring to the presence of God—bringing with him the command to **use the sickle.** The phrase **the crop is ripe on the earth** takes the Old Testament picture of divine judgment as a "harvest" (see Jeremiah 51:33; Hosea 6:11; Joel 3:13). One of Jesus' parables also describes the end times as a harvest, "Let both grow together until the harvest. Then I will tell the harvesters to sort out the weeds and burn them and to put the wheat in the barn" (Matthew 13:30).

Without any further detail, **the one sitting on the cloud swung his sickle over the earth, and the whole earth was harvested.** There is some debate about who was being harvested—God's people or the sinners. Some scholars have suggested that 14:14-16 pictures the harvesting of God's people, while 14:17-18 pictures the harvest of sinners. Most likely, however, as Jesus' parable seems to indicate, 14:14-16 indicates the harvest of all people. This is a general picture of the final judgment, with the elect being taken to heaven and the unbelievers being sent to eternal punishment, as recorded in the following verses.

14:17-18 Another angel arrived **from the Temple in heaven,** also from the presence of God (14:15).

This angel **also had a sharp sickle.** This is probably a third picture of the same reality of coming judgment. First was the cup of unmixed wine to be poured out (14:10), second was the grain harvest (14:15-16), and third was the grape harvest (14:17-20). This third image stresses the violent nature of this final judgment. The Old Testament also pictures divine judgment as a grape harvest (see Isaiah 63:1-6; Lamentations 1:15; Joel 3:13). Revelation 19:15 describes the return of the victorious Christ, "He trod the winepress of the fierce wrath of almighty God").

The angel **who has power to destroy the world with fire** could refer to the angel who had authority over the fire on the altar (8:3-5). The altar is connected both with the souls of the martyrs (6:9) and the prayers of the saints (8:3), both of which play a part in bringing about this final drama of ultimate judgment.

The angel with the sickle is told to **gather the clusters of grapes from the vines of the earth, for they are fully ripe for judgment.** While the previous picture of the harvest in 14:14-16 may have pictured both the bringing of the righteous to heaven and the destruction of the wicked, this picture is only of the judgment of the wicked. The clusters of grapes probably have no special symbolism other than indicating that the time for harvest had come. They were "ripe for judgment," which means there would be no more waiting.

14:19-20 Obeying the command (14:18), the angel **swung his sickle** across the earth and **loaded the grapes** (picturing the unbelievers who will receive punishment) **into the great winepress of God's wrath.** A "winepress" was a large vat or trough where grapes would be collected and then smashed. The juice would flow out of a duct that led into a large holding vat. The unbelievers are collected and **trodden in the winepress outside the city,** possibly referring to Jerusalem. Since Jesus was crucified outside the walls of Jerusalem, this

great scene of judgment is pictured there (see also Joel 3:12-14; Zechariah 14:1-4; John 19:20; Hebrews 13:12).

The grisly detail of the blood flowing out pictures the ultimate horror of this judgment. The distance of **180 miles** is approximately the north-south length of Palestine. The hyperbole is meant to show the total and complete destruction of the wicked.

REVELATION 15:1-4

THE SONG OF MOSES AND OF THE LAMB / 15:1-4

John was describing not two separate songs but one song celebrating deliverance and victory. They had been delivered from the power of the Antichrist, but they were in heaven because they had been delivered from sin through the death of the Lamb. Each line comes from a phrase in the Psalms or Prophets.

15:1 This next event that John **saw in heaven** was **seven angels** who **were holding the seven last plagues.** These plagues were in golden bowls, given to these angels by one of the four living creatures (15:6-7). The seven last plagues are also called the seven bowl judgments. They actually begin in the next chapter. These plagues would end the reign of terror by the Antichrist, the reign of Satan, and evil itself, bringing **God's wrath to completion.**

15:2 John saw **what seemed to be a crystal sea mixed with fire.** This is similar to the "sea of glass" described in 4:6, located before the throne of God. Here it was mixed with fire to represent wrath and judgment. Those who stood beside it had been **victorious over the beast** (the Antichrist, 13:1ff), **and his statue** (13:14), **and the number representing his name** (13:18). They had refused to receive the mark of the beast, had refused to worship his image, and thus had faced persecution, difficulty, and perhaps even martyrdom. This is the complete group of

all believers (see also 14:1-5). They were **holding harps,** preparing for a song of worship and praise (see also 5:8).

15:3-4 The **song of Moses** had celebrated Israel's deliverance from Egypt and the defeat of the Egyptian army at the Red Sea (Exodus 15). The song would be sung in the afternoon service each Sabbath as a reminder to the Jews of God's deliverance and sovereignty. The **song of the Lamb** here celebrated the ultimate deliverance of God's people from the power of Satan.

The song glorifies God and his ultimate victory over all the world. That **all nations will come and worship** him does not mean that eventually everyone will be saved. The thought is very much like that recorded in Philippians 2:10, "every knee will bow"; it means that whether in grateful worship or defeated submission, eventually all nations will give the honor to Christ that is his due (see commentary at 14:6-7).

REVELATION 15:5-16:21

THE SEVEN BOWLS OF THE SEVEN PLAGUES / 15:5-16:21

Seven angels were given seven bowls from which they would pour out the seven "bowl judgments," the last plagues to be visited upon the earth. Unlike the previous plagues from the seals, which had destroyed one-fourth of the earth (chapters 6-8), and the trumpets, which had destroyed another third of the earth (chapters 8–11), these plagues were directed only against the Antichrist's followers but affected the entire earth. These judgments were complete and final, culminating in the abolition of all evil and the end of the world. These would bring about the end of the Antichrist's reign.

15:5-6 The **Temple in heaven, God's Tabernacle** is a Greek translation for the Hebrew "Tent of Meeting" (see Numbers 17:7; 18:2). The imagery recalls the Exodus in the wilderness when the Ark of his covenant (the symbol of God's presence among his people) resided in the Tabernacle. The Tabernacle was a portable place of worship that the Israelites would carry with them as they journeyed through the wilderness. Later, when they settled in the Promised Land, a permanent structure was built—the Temple. Both words, Tabernacle and Temple, refer to the place of God's residence among his people.

John again saw this "tabernacle" **thrown wide open** (see also 11:19). The **seven angels** who come out were **clothed in spotless white linen with gold belts across their chests** (see also Daniel 10:5). Their garments, reminiscent of the high priest's clothing (and of Christ's—1:13), show that they were free from corruption, immorality, and injustice. They had come out from God's presence to do God's bidding. These angels would be in charge of the **seven plagues**—that is, the **bowls** with the plagues—just as seven angels had blown the seven trumpets (8:6).

15:7-8 In what appears to be a solemn ceremony, **one of the four living beings** (see commentary at 4:6) **handed each of the seven angels a gold bowl filled with the terrible wrath of God.** When these bowls would be poured out, there would be no escape, and the judgment would be complete. The **smoke** that filled the Temple is the manifestation of **God's glory and power** (see also Exodus 19:18; 40:34-35; 1 Kings 8:10-11; Isaiah 6:4).

God's glory filled the Temple, appearing like smoke, and God set in motion the final phase of judgment. The fact that **no one** would be able to **enter the Temple until the seven angels had completed pouring out the seven plagues** indicates that the time for intercession had passed. No one could come before God to stay his hand. It seems that even the time of worship and praise was suspended as God brought about this final act of history. It is as if heaven was waiting.

16:1 A mighty voice shouted **from the Temple.** Isaiah had heard a similar voice, "What is that terrible noise from the Temple? It is the voice of the Lord taking vengeance against his enemies" (Isaiah 66:6). This was probably the voice of God com-

manding the angels, **"Go your ways and empty out the seven bowls of God's wrath on the earth."**

16:2 The outpouring of these bowls occurred in rapid succession, one right after the other, but the effects of each seem to have lingered. For example, the **malignant sores** that people get here still affect them during the fifth plague (16:10-11), along with the sunburns they received during the fourth plague.

When the **first angel** poured out his bowl, everyone **broke out** in horrible sores. This compares with another of the plagues on Egypt—the plague of boils (Exodus 9:10-11). These sores affected **everyone who had the mark of the beast** (13:16) **and who worshiped his statue** (13:14-15). God's wrath was only upon the unbelievers.

Those who subscribe to the pre-Tribulation theory assert that because the believers have already been raptured, those who become believers after the rapture will still be on the earth but will be protected from these plagues. Those who subscribe to the mid-Tribulation theory say that just before these universal plagues hit, the believers are raptured so that the only people left on the earth at this point will be unbelievers. Those who subscribe to the post-Tribulation theory say that the believers are still on the earth going through this difficulty. But even as these plagues hit, the believers will be protected by the seal of Christ they have received (7:3) and the promise of protection (3:10).

16:3 The **second angel poured out his bowl.** This time the sea **became like the blood of a corpse,** killing everything in it. During the second trumpet, a third of the water of the sea had become blood, killing a third of the sea creatures (8:8-9). This time, the entire sea turned to blood (see also Exodus 7:20-21).

16:4 The **third angel poured out his bowl** of God's wrath, and this time **the rivers and springs—the** inland waters—also turned to **blood.** During the third trumpet judgment, one-third of the rivers and springs were turned bitter so that they were undrinkable (8:10-11). In this bowl judgment, all the inland waters were affected, leaving people with nothing to drink. Water, a basic necessity for human life, was gone.

16:5-6 The horror of the plague of blood upon all water led to a pause in heaven, during which time

the angel who had authority over all water
explained the logic and justice of the plague.
Ironically, those who had shed believers' blood
were left with blood to drink. They are punished
with the methods of their own crimes. The **holy
people** and the **prophets** had been killed, their
blood **poured out on the earth**. So the **just reward**
for the murderers was to give them **blood to
drink**. God's judgment reflects his righteous and
just nature.

16:7 This second **voice** confirmed what the angel
had said (16:5). The personification of the **altar**
acclaiming God shows that everyone and everything
will praise God, acknowledging his righteousness
and perfect justice. The "altar" could refer to the
souls under the altar—the martyrs—who had been
waiting for this day to arrive (6:9-11).

16:8-9 After a brief interlude, **the fourth angel
poured out his bowl on the sun**. This intensified
the sun's heat so that it scorched people **with its
fire**. The fourth trumpet had caused the sun and
the moon to stop giving light for portions of
the day (8:12). This fourth bowl was much more
serious. This is a picture of a solar explosion that
reaches out and scorches the earth with fire. Fire
is a common theme for judgment in the Bible
(see, for example, Deuteronomy 28:22; Luke
16:24; 1 Corinthians 3:13; 2 Peter 3:7).

The people on earth were **burned by this blast
of heat**. They knew that these judgments had come
from God, and they **cursed** him for sending them.
But still they refused to recognize God's authority
and repent of their sins. The contrast with those
protected is unmistakable: "These are the ones
coming out of the great tribulation. . . . they will
be fully protected from the scorching noontime
heat" (7:14, 16).

The reason for the phrase **they did not repent** is
to show the complete depravity of the people left
on the earth. They had totally and irrevocably
rejected God. They cursed (literally, blasphemed)
his name. They had taken on the character of the
beast (13:6) and had committed the unforgivable
sin by rejecting God with absolute finality.

16:10-11 The fifth, sixth, and seventh bowls deal
with Armageddon. The **fifth angel poured out his
bowl on the throne of the beast**. This bowl was
directed on the controller of the inhabitants of the
earth—the beast, the Antichrist, who had been
placed into power by Satan (see chapter 13). His
"throne" was merely an imitation of God's great
throne in heaven (4:2-11).

When the fifth bowl was poured out, the
Antichrist's **kingdom was plunged into darkness**.
This was not like the partial darkness that had

occurred during the fourth trumpet (8:12). This
was total and complete darkness—like the plague
visited upon Egypt (Exodus 10:23). Some take this
"darkness" to refer to the total depravity and evil
that comes from the leadership of the Antichrist.
Others see it as a scientific phenomenon that after
the flaring up of the sun (as described in the fourth
bowl), the sun virtually burns itself out and is
dark. Whether physical or merely spiritual, this
"darkness" caused great **anguish** among the people
of the earth; they were in abject fear of this total
physical and / or spiritual darkness. They were also
still suffering **pains and sores**—probably from the
boils in the first bowl (16:2) and the burns of the
fourth bowl (16:8).

But the same phrase is repeated from 16:9: **they
cursed the God of heaven** and they **refused to
repent**. These people knew that God exists (none
of them were atheists), but they decided that they
hated him.

16:12 When the **sixth angel poured out his bowl,
the great Euphrates River** was **dried up**. In comparison, the sixth trumpet also mentions the
Euphrates River and describes an invading army
of demons (9:14-21). The Euphrates River was a
natural protective boundary between the Roman
Empire and the empires to the east. If the Euphrates River dried up, nothing could hold back invading armies. The **kings from the east** have been
identified in many ways. In 16:14, the kings from
the east are joined by "the rulers of the world,"
drawn together to the battlefield, a coalition that
would bring its armies to the final battle against
God Almighty and his hosts.

16:13-14 These **three evil spirits** confirm that
these kings were the combined forces of evil coming to the final battle. One evil spirit came from
the mouth of the dragon (12:3-9), a second out
of the mouth of **the beast** (13:1-10), and the third
out of the mouth of **the false prophet** (13:11-18).
The evil trinity spawned three evil spirits **that
looked like frogs**. Frogs were unclean animals in
Jewish kosher law (Leviticus 11:10-11, 41). These
were the **miracle-working demons**.

Demons are fallen angels who had joined Satan
in his rebellion against God and now are evil spirits under Satan's control (possibly described in
12:7-9). During these last days, the demons will be
set loose to perform their destruction, ironically,
on those who have rejected Christ and are on the
side of Satan (see also commentary on 9:3). The
demonic forces will come together to this final battle. These evil spirits will cause **all the rulers of the
world to gather for battle against the Lord**. The
imagery of the demons coming out of the mouths

of the three evil rulers signifies the verbal enticements and propaganda that will draw many people
to their evil cause.

In this vision, the battle is now set for **that great
judgment day of God Almighty**—God already
knows that the demons are coming, and this is part
of the plan. The final outcome has already been
decided. Throughout the Bible, the phrase "day of
the Lord" is used in two different ways: (1) it can
mean the end times (beginning with Christ's birth
and continuing into the present); (2) it can mean the
final judgment day at the end of time. In Scripture,
the phrase is always used in connection with an
extraordinary happening, whether a present event
(such as a locust plague in Joel 1:15), a near future
event, or the final period of history when God will
defeat all the forces of evil. The final day of the Lord
is pictured as a time when God will intervene directly
and dramatically in world affairs. Predicted and discussed often in the Old Testament (Isaiah 13:6-12;
Ezekiel 38–39; Joel 2:11, 28-32; 3:2; Zephaniah
1:14-18; 14:1-21), the day of the Lord will include
both punishment and blessing. God will triumph
completely. Christ will judge sin and set up his eternal Kingdom. The day of the final battle pictured in
this text will be the time when the entire system of
human opposition to God will be destroyed.

16:15 This is the third of seven beatitudes in Revelation—**blessed are all who are watching for me**
(see also 1:3; 14:13). This is a warning to the Christian, spoken by the Lord. Jesus **will come as unexpectedly as a thief** (see also Matthew 24:42-44;
Luke 12:39-40; 1 Thessalonians 5:2, 4; 2 Peter 3:10).
The teaching of the unexpectedness of Christ's
return occurs throughout the New Testament.
Believers who are still on the earth must be on their
guard, watching, morally and spiritually prepared,
with **their robes ready.** The word "robes" refers to
purification attained by the cleansing of Christ's
blood (7:9-14). Christ had also given this warning
to the churches at Sardis (3:2-4) and Laodicea
(3:18). The warning is that believers should not be
swayed by the miraculous signs performed by the
demons of the evil trinity. They must persevere,
remain true to the faith, and wait with readiness.
That way they **will not need to walk naked and
ashamed.** Just as the robes refer to purity through
Christ's blood, to be "naked" means having one's
sinfulness exposed for all to see. This, of course,
would lead to shame. For more on being rightfully
clothed, see Colossians 3:12-17.

16:16 The evil spirits (16:13) **gathered all the rulers
and their armies** (the kings of the east in 16:12, and
the kings of the whole world in 16:14) **to a place
called** *Armageddon* **in Hebrew.** Some archaeologists

have located this battlefield near the city of Megiddo
(southeast of the modern port of Haifa), which
guarded a large plain in northern Israel. This is a
strategic location near a prominent international
highway leading north from Egypt through Israel,
along the coast, and on to Babylon. Megiddo overlooks the entire plain southward toward Galilee
and westward toward the mountains of Gilboa.
Over 200 battles have been fought in this area (see,
for example, Judges 5:19; 2 Kings 9:27). While this
may be the location of the battle, the actual meaning of Armageddon is unknown. The word *har* in
Hebrew means "mountain," but there is no mountain in the area of Megiddo. "Mountain" may have
been used to describe God's presence—for he often
would meet with people on mountains (Exodus
19:3, 11-23; 24:12; 1 Kings 19:11; Ezekiel 40:2;
Matthew 17:1). The Aramaic meaning of the word
"Armageddon" is "mount of the assembly"; thus,
this may refer to the assembly of the kings who
come to fight. John's unusual use of the explanation
"in Hebrew" to a group of readers who for the most
part probably did not know Hebrew probably alerts
them to the symbolic nature of what he was writing
(see also 9:11).

Although the actual location is uncertain, we *are*
told what will happen. This will truly be a "world
war," except that the entire world will be on the
same side. They will assemble to fight together
against God. The armies of the east will march to
Armageddon by crossing the dried-up Euphrates
River (16:12). But the Lord will appear, and the
earth will shake.

Some Christians believe that the battle of Armageddon will be a spiritual rather than a physical
conflict. Others believe that the battle is being
fought now.

Dispensational premillennialists believe that
the battle of Armageddon begins when the king of
the north and the king of the south converge on
Israel to attack the Antichrist and his troops. After
these armies are defeated, the kings of the east
invade Israel (16:16). Then Christ will intervene
and demonstrate his power by destroying all
remaining foes (19:19-21).

Amillennialists and **historic premillennialists**
believe that evil and destruction will increase in
the last days. Christians will be present on earth
during this period of Tribulation. Both amillennialists and historic premillennialists believe that
the vision of Armageddon in Revelation figuratively portrays the final rebellion against God. As
a result, they pay more attention to Christ's second
coming than to the battle itself.

Postmillennialists believe that evangelists and
Christians who try to spread God's word will always

face obstacles. Postmillennialists don't believe that wickedness and persecution will significantly increase as the world draws to a close. Instead, because they think the church is gradually transforming society, they believe that Armageddon is a picture of Christ's victory over evil forces throughout church history. God's word will triumph over all opposition and establish the millennial Kingdom.

While interpretations differ, all believers agree that Jesus has already defeated both Satan and death (1:18; Matthew 12:25-29). At some point, Christ will decisively demonstrate his power over Satan and his evil forces.

16:17-18 This verse echoes 11:15-19, where we saw the seventh trumpet sounding, followed by voices in heaven shouting that Christ's Kingdom had come (11:15). Then there was lightning, thunder, a hailstorm, and an earthquake (11:19; see also 4:5; 8:5). Here, when **the seventh angel poured out his bowl**, he did so **into the air**, which was followed by **a mighty shout** that **came from the throne of the Temple**. It announced that **it is finished**. This also was followed by **thunder, lightning**, and **an earthquake** (the hailstorm is described in 16:21). The earthquake would be **greater than ever before in human history.**

History was finished; the end had come— proleptically speaking. With the bowl, God's wrath was completed. The reason for the creation of mankind was coming to fruition.

16:19-20 In Revelation, the phrase **the great city of Babylon** refers both to an evil city and an immoral empire, a world center for idol worship. Just as Babylon had been an enemy of the Jews (by conquering Jerusalem and taking many of the people into captivity, 2 Kings 25), so Rome was the enemy of the Christians. The name Babylon, the "great city," is used to describe the focal point of anti-Christian activity. John's readers would immediately have identified this great city as Rome, and they would have been correct. Yet they did not know, nor did John, that many years would pass before this event occurred, nor did they know that

both Babylon and Rome were models of the future and the ultimate collapse of the entire world system that would reject God. The great city's division into **three pieces** symbolizes its complete destruction. This foreshadows what John would describe in more detail in chapters 17 and 18.

Not only that, but also **cities around the world fell into heaps of rubble.** So great is this earthquake that every city in the world will be destroyed—New York, Chicago, Mexico City, Hong Kong, Paris, London, Tokyo, Sydney—all will be flattened by this worldwide earthquake. This will indeed be an earthquake "greater than ever before in human history" (16:18) for places that had never had earthquakes will be destroyed.

In 14:8, an angel had described the fall of Babylon, and in 14:9, another angel spoke of the Beast's followers drinking the undiluted wine of God's wrath. This is a further description of God giving the city **the cup that was filled with the wine of his fierce wrath.** Babylon had seduced the nations (see 17:2) and so deserved punishment.

The earthquake will be so severe that **every island** will disappear. The earth will have such an upheaval that it will flatten the **mountains** so that they cannot even be found (see also 6:12-14). Other earthquakes have occurred in Revelation, but this will be the last and worst.

16:21 Along with the lightning, the thunder, and the earthquake, there was a **hailstorm** so severe that huge **hailstones** fell from heaven onto the people on earth. The Old Testament records God using hail to punish Israel's enemies (Joshua 10:11), and Ezekiel described a hailstorm (Ezekiel 38:18-22). Even golf-ball sized hail will cause severe damage. Imagine the horrible destruction and death caused by these seventy-five-pound hailstones. The cities had already been destroyed by the earthquake, but anything left standing was smashed by the hail. But still, the people on earth **cursed God.** After each of these three final plagues, the inhabitants of the earth continued to blaspheme God (16:9, 11, 21).

REVELATION 17

THE GREAT PROSTITUTE / 17:1-18

The destruction of Babylon mentioned in 16:17-21 is now described in greater detail (see the commentary at 16:19-20). Verses 1-6 describe John's vision of the prostitute and the scarlet beast; the remainder of the chapter describes the interpretation of the symbols.

17:1-2 One of the angels **who had poured out** the bowls **came** to John **and spoke** to him. The angel wanted to show John what those seven bowls had been directed against. The angel would show John **the judgment that is going to come on the great prostitute.** The "great prostitute" is also called "Babylon" in 17:5 and "the great city that rules over the kings of the earth" in 17:18. To the early Christians, this great prostitute represented the early Roman Empire with its many gods and the blood of Christian martyrs on its hands.

Rome was the capital city of the vast and mighty Roman Empire, an empire that stretched from Britain to Arabia. In John's day, Rome was the largest city in the world, with a population of approximately one million. But for all its power, it was exceedingly immoral. Christians ran afoul of Roman society and values and thus found themselves severely persecuted. With Rome's backdrop of paganism and persecution, it is no wonder that Rome was seen as the epitome of evil. Like Babylon, Rome became a symbol of paganism and opposition to Christianity.

But the prostitute represents far more than just the Roman Empire. This "great prostitute," Babylon, symbolizes any economic, political, or military system that is hostile to God (see 17:5) and an eventual worldwide system that will encompass more evil than has been seen thus far in the world. Babylon had been a huge empire in its day; Rome was even larger as the Caesars took over many countries and gained their allegiance. In the end, the Antichrist will set up a final worldwide empire that will encompass all the nations and will be immoral and completely anti-God. At this time will occur the great apostasy—many will turn away from God, leave the churches, and follow the beast. The prostitute **sits on many waters,** described in 17:15 as "masses of people of every nation and language." The great prostitute, therefore, represents all the forces in the end who will come together to oppose God.

The great prostitute, rather than being described as any particular city of any particular time period, exists where there is satanic deception and resistance to God. This was true in many ancient kingdoms, such as Babylon, Egypt, Tyre, Nineveh, and Rome. The "prostitute" represents the seductiveness of any governmental system that uses immoral means to gain its own pleasure, prosperity, and advantage. This worldwide kingdom of the beast will draw in all **the rulers of the world.** The immorality and drunkenness describe the actions of people who have completely turned away from the true God and have been lured into evil and idolatry.

17:3 John was taken **in spirit into the wilderness** where he would see this great prostitute. Four times in Revelation, John is described as being "in the spirit" or carried away in the spirit (1:10; 4:2; 17:3; 21:10). This means that the Holy Spirit transformed and elevated John's mind and spirit so that he could see prophetic visions. These could have been in the form of a trance or an ecstatic experience.

John saw **a woman sitting on a scarlet beast.** This woman is, of course, the great prostitute described in 17:1. Most likely, this "scarlet beast" is Satan, for he is described in 12:3 as a "large red dragon," but this beast is also identified as the beast out of the sea (13:1). All three have the same source—and all are described as having **seven heads and ten horns** (as noted in 12:3; 13:1). These heads and horns are further described by John in verses 9-18.

The beast from the sea is further described as having names on each head that blasphemed God. This scarlet beast also was **written all over with blasphemies against God.** This beast—the Antichrist controlled by Satan—is the supreme enemy of the church and God's people. The woman represents the world system of evil; the beast represents the power supporting that world system. The blasphemous names are probably the names the beast takes upon himself in calling himself God.

17:4 This **woman,** the great prostitute, was dressed in **purple and scarlet clothing,** signifying royalty and luxury. The purple and scarlet dyes were extremely expensive in the first century; no common person ever wore purple or scarlet. She was also wearing **beautiful jewelry made of gold and precious gems and pearls,** signifying wealth and materialism.

The woman was holding **a gold goblet full of obscenities and the impurities of her immorality.** In a sense, that was her inner person—she was extremely immoral. She was a prostitute—beautifully clothed but obscene and impure. Her veneer could not hide what was in her goblet.

17:5 The further description of the woman on the beast focuses on the **mysterious name** that **was written on her forehead.** The "mysterious name" shows that the true source and nature of evil is being revealed. The title **Babylon the Great** describes an entire world system that will be the culmination of all evil, leading people away from God (see commentary on 17:1-2). This woman is a picture of Babylon, which had taken God's people into captivity; she also is a picture of Rome with its luxury and decadence. But she is far more than just one particular city or empire in history.

She is actually the "mother" of them all. She is the source of all evil, the source of all rebellion against God throughout history, of which various nations have taken part. She is **the Mother of All Prostitutes and Obscenities in the World.** For all her great finery (17:4), she is no more than a prostitute rebelling against God.

17:6 The woman riding the beast **was drunk,** certainly a pastime in the city of Rome and in the cult worship. However, this woman was drunk **with the blood of God's holy people.** She had gorged herself with this drink—meaning that she lived to hurt and to slaughter the people of God. This was her reason for being. This world power had the authority of the beast "to wage war against God's holy people and to overcome them" (13:7). The woman had become intoxicated with the slaughter of God's followers. John's reaction at the sight was total amazement. The woman and beast present a horrifying picture of the true nature of evil.

17:7-8 The **angel** asked why John was **so amazed.** This is the true nature of evil, so perhaps believers should not be surprised at its sheer ugliness. The angel said that he would explain to John **the mystery of this woman and of the beast.** The remainder of this chapter interprets the beast; chapter 18 explains more about the prostitute.

The beast, as noted in 17:3, signifies the Antichrist and his power source, Satan. In a parody of the description of Christ (4:8), Satan is referred to as one who had exercised his power (**was alive**), was bound when Christ died on the cross (**isn't now**), and then will have a time at the end of history during which to exercise great authority on the earth and to go into battle with God at Armageddon (**will soon come**) before he is finally destroyed. This also could describe the beast in 13:3 who had recovered form a fatal wound. The beast was alive, then dead, and then came back to life. The beast's resurrection symbolizes the persistence of evil. His source is **the bottomless pit**—the abode of the demonic forces, the eternal destination of the wicked, the place of the beast's final **eternal destruction** (see 9:1, 11; 11:7; 20:1-3; Luke 8:31; 2 Peter 2:4; Jude 1:6).

This resurgence of evil power will convince many to join forces with the beast. They will be so astonished by his resurrection (a copy of Christ's true resurrection) that they will follow him. These people, **whose names were not written in the Book of Life,** received the beast's mark (13:16).

17:9-10 Many scholars think that, in this explanation, the angel was referring to Rome, the city famous for its **seven hills.** Rome symbolized all evil in the world—any person, religion, group,

government, or structure that opposed Christ. John was writing during a time of persecution of believers, with Rome at the focal point. His original readers may have immediately associated the "seven hills" with Rome. Certainly, Rome portrays the power and corruption that those final evil days will encompass. In addition, because the hills **also represent seven kings,** some have linked the seven kings with seven of Rome's emperors counting from Tiberius to Domitian (however, three emperors are omitted from their list). All of those attempts are problematic, for there are arbitrary omissions that must be made in order to make them fit with the formula given: **five kings have already fallen, the sixth now reigns, and the seventh is yet to come, but his reign will be brief.**

Others connect the seven kings to seven world kingdoms. The first five would be Egypt, Assyria, Babylon, Persia, and Greece (they had already fallen), the one that *is* would be Rome (present tense for John's day), and the one yet to come would be the final kingdom of the Antichrist (although this theory has its problems at 17:11). While this fits fairly well, it again depends on arbitrary omissions in order to make the numbers work.

It is also possible that the number seven is used here as it is everywhere else in Revelation as symbolic of completeness (seven seals, seven trumpets, seven bowls). The seven heads could indicate complete blasphemy, with the seven kings referring to the complete number of kings who will rule until the end, with the end coming when the complete number has been reached (similar to the complete number of the martyrs in 6:11). The question then arises why John included the numeric formula. Some scholars point to an ancient seal showing the seven-headed monster of chaos being killed. In the seal, four of the heads are dead, but the creature is still living with three active heads. But it obviously faces imminent death. John could be describing the evil as being progressively destroyed. The battle has been fought and won in the past; the battle is presently being fought; and the battle will continue to be fought until the beast is completely defeated. John's numeric formula also could simply mean that he is declaring the imminent end of history. Time is passing (five sevenths have passed) and has a definite end point which is all in God's plan.

Whatever the interpretation, Rome was indeed a preview of that final thrust of evil and hatred of all who love God. While God has chosen to keep this vague, believers ought to be careful about attempting to decipher what God has chosen not to make clear. It is far more important to realize that, even as the power of evil gains control of the whole world, God is in charge.

17:11 The seven heads are seven hills, which are interpreted as seven kings, but here an **eighth king** is introduced, who **was alive and then died.** This eighth king is **the scarlet beast** himself—identified elsewhere as Satan or the Antichrist (see commentary at 17:3). As the seventh seal leads into the first trumpet, and the seventh trumpet into the first bowl, so the seven kings lead into the final king who actually embodies all of them. This eighth king, then, *is* the Antichrist himself. He is not simply another evil ruler; he is evil itself. He will become a human being—a leader, a king. But again, God's sovereignty shows itself—the Antichrist **will go to his doom.**

17:12 With this verse, John returned to the future in his vision, describing the Antichrist and what would occur during his rule. The **ten horns** are **ten kings** who will be the Antichrist's minions and will rule under him (see also Daniel 7:7, 24). The ten horns represent kings of nations yet to arise. Some have suggested that these ten kings **who have not yet risen to power** are ten future kings who will reign over the world under the Antichrist or even the ten nations of the European Common Market. The number ten may be literal, or, more likely, it symbolizes the totality of the powers on earth that will serve the Antichrist and war against Christ. Rome will be followed by other powers. Rome is a good example of how the Antichrist's system will work, demanding complete allegiance, and ruling by raw power, oppression, and slavery. Whoever the ten kings are, they will give their power to the Antichrist and will make war against the Lamb. Their authority will have been given by Satan and simply allowed by God. But their authority will only last **one brief moment.** The beast was given authority for forty-two months (13:5), but these kings will have only a moment, highlighting the brevity of their time of power.

John's readers would have understood the authority given to these kings by the beast as similar to the authority the emperors gave to local governors or kings. When Rome conquered a country, the empire allowed local kings, such as Herod the Great in Palestine, to continue to rule as long as they gave allegiance to the Empire.

17:13-14 These "ten kings" (which may be an actual or symbolic number) will **give their power and authority to** the beast. These human kings will allow themselves to be completely possessed by Satan (or his demons). The beast will have one job for these kings—to **wage war against the Lamb.**

The outcome, however, is guaranteed: **the Lamb will defeat them.** The outcome of the war has

already been determined. Even as Satan will seem to gain the upper hand in the final days, the end is already known. Christ will win because **he is Lord over all lords and King over all kings** (see 19:16; Deuteronomy 10:17; Daniel 2:47). He is above all the kings of the earth; he is the final authority.

17:15 The **angel** continued his description of the vision that John was seeing (17:7). The **prostitute** is described as sitting "on many waters" (17:1). The great prostitute is called "Babylon" (17:5) and the imagery of the waters comes from Jeremiah's prophecy to Babylon, whose water source was the Euphrates River, "You are a city rich with water, a great center of commerce, but your end has come" (Jeremiah 51:13). Although Babylon and Rome are in view, again this great prostitute represents a far-reaching, anti-God power that will encompass the world. The angel explained that the waters **represent masses of people of every nation and language.** The Antichrist will influence (or even possess) the leaders across the world, but his influence will extend to all people. The "masses" also will be overtaken by the great prostitute and will be enamored by her. In doing so, they will become hostile to God. The leaders and the people will be joined in their adoration of the Antichrist.

17:16 This verse describes the nature and outcome of evil. In a dramatic turn of events, the **beast** on whom the prostitute rides will turn on her and destroy her. In fact, the beast has hated the prostitute all along. This is how evil operates. Destructive by its very nature, it turns on itself. The beast and the ten kings (Satan and the leaders) will end up destroying what they have made. The very evil of the culture they have created will leave it in shambles. They will bring that culture *to* ruin. Despite the great beauty and luxury of the prostitute's clothing and jewels (17:4), the beast will **strip her naked.** She will be completely destroyed—her flesh eaten and her remains burned. The horror of her demise parallels the penalty in the Old Testament for prostitution (Leviticus 21:9), the end of the wicked queen Jezebel (2 Kings 9:30-37), and the fate of the allegorical Oholibah, who represented the apostate Israelites in Ezekiel's prophecy (Ezekiel 23:11-35).

17:17 In an ironic twist, John wrote that **God has put into the minds** of the ten kings **a plan that will carry out his purposes.** (17:13). God will bring about the destruction of the great prostitute (17:16) by allowing the evil to run its course. Even as Satan overruns the world and finally destroys his own kingdom and followers, God still rules. All of these events will be completely under God's control. His words **will be fulfilled.** God's plans will happen just as he says. God even uses people opposed to him as tools to carry out his will.

17:18 The angel explains John's vision further, describing the **woman** (the "great prostitute" in 17:1, 3) as **the great city that rules over the kings of the earth.** As noted in the commentary on 17:1, John's original readers would have identified this immediately with Rome—the capital of an empire that had spread across much of the known world,

a city filled with immorality and idolatry and famous for its active persecution of Christians. The vision surely represents that, but it also means far more. Like Rome, and Babylon before her, this "woman" is the worldwide system of power and influence that will be completely rebellious against God and subservient to the Antichrist. Babylon and Rome were forerunners of what will be far bigger and more horrible than anything John or his readers could have imagined.

REVELATION 18

THE FALL OF BABYLON / 18:1-24

Chapter 17 describes the "great prostitute," called "Babylon the Great," (17:5) and why she would need to be destroyed (17:1). This section describes that destruction—how it occurred and its effect upon the inhabitants of the world. First, an angel proclaimed judgment on the great city (18:1-8). The rulers of the world lament the destruction of the city (18:9-10), as do the merchants who have become rich through trade (18:11-16), the ship owners, and the captains of the merchant ships (18:18-20).

18:1 John saw **another angel** who had **great authority.** This angel was so glorious that **the earth grew bright with his splendor**—he was like the sun, reflecting the glory of God himself from whose presence the angel had come. This angel would be bringing the final message of destruction upon the evil world system of the Antichrist.

18:2 As described in the commentary in 17:1, the name **Babylon** was immediately assumed by John's readers to be Rome. While they would have been correct, the symbol goes far beyond Rome to a world-encompassing system of religion and economics that will be under the control of the Antichrist and completely against God and his people.

The glorious angel shouted that the **great city is fallen.** The **hideout of demons and evil spirits** is literally a prison or watchtower, like a haunt, from which the evil beings watch over the desolate ruins. This is an image of desperate desolation. **Buzzards** are carrion birds found in desolate places. The Old Testament records many prophecies against the ancient city of Babylon, which are appropriate parallels to the total destruction described by John for this metaphorical "Babylon" to come (see Isaiah 13:19-22; 21:2, 9; 47:8-11; Jeremiah 50:13, 39). The angel announced that the formerly great, luxurious city had become a total

wasteland, filled with everything evil and unclean. It is a haunt of evil spirits.

18:3 The reason that Babylon fell is described here—**all the nations have drunk the wine of her passionate immorality** (see also 17:2). Babylon personifies everything that is evil—sexual immorality, idolatry, greed, and oppression. The people of the world have turned completely away from God and have enjoyed the seductiveness of what she was offering through her immorality and idolatry. The Old Testament uses adultery to describe spiritual apostasy (see, for example, Jeremiah 3:2; Hosea 4:10). In the last days, apostasy will reach a pinnacle in the worship of the beast (13:15).

The rulers of the world have committed adultery with her, meaning that they have committed shameful sins—giving up what is most important for what is gratifying. This "adultery" probably refers to both sinful alliances and the total abandoning of God's morality. Also, **the merchants throughout the world have grown rich as a result of her luxurious living.** They were seduced by the great riches that could be gained by their relationship with her. Isaiah 47:8 describes the great luxury of Babylon and God's judgment of it. Their luxury led to pride and self-sufficiency. Part of this adultery was in taking the mark of the beast because these merchants could not buy or sell without it (13:17).

18:4-5 Jeremiah had prophesied regarding the ancient city of Babylon, "Flee from Babylon! Save yourselves! Don't get trapped in her punishment! It is the Lord's time for vengeance; he will fully repay her" (Jeremiah 51:6). So **another voice** warned about this future evil system and called to God's people not to **take part in her sins.** Just as God had brought vengeance upon the ancient city because of her cruelty to others, so God **is ready to judge** the crimes of all nations who have fought God and persecuted his people—resulting in sins that **are piled as high as heaven.** God remembers, and he will punish. As an answer to all the questions of why wicked people prosper, God points out here that he knows it all and will punish it all.

God's people are called to separate themselves—to "come away"—from evil for two reasons: (1) not to share in society's sins, and (2) not to eventually share in that society's punishment by God. Believers must always be aware that they must not compromise with a godless society. To compromise will mean facing punishment. Although "come out" can refer to a physical separation from the places of evil, it always refers to a spiritual, mental, and emotional separation from the sins that plague the current society. The church must always stand firm on the foundations of the faith, never swaying at the whims of society.

18:6-7 The people of Babylon had lived in luxury and pleasure. The city had boasted of being a **queen** who **will not experience sorrow.** Isaiah had prophesied of Babylon, "You are a pleasure-crazy kingdom, living at ease and feeling secure, bragging as if you were the greatest in the world! You say, 'I'm self-sufficient and not accountable to anyone! I will never be a widow or lose my children'" (Isaiah 47:8).

Rome also had great luxury and pride, as have other powerful kingdoms. In the end, this great kingdom would receive what it had meted out. The Roman law, *lex talionis*, was that a person's punishment should match his or her crime. During this judgment, however, the angel asked God to **give her a double penalty for all her evil deeds.**

Jeremiah had written of ancient Babylon, "May Babylon be repaid for all the violence she did to us. May the people of Babylonia be paid in full for all the blood they have spilled" (Jeremiah 51:34-35).

18:8 For all of Babylon's self-sufficiency, pride, and power (18:6), the ugliness of her evil will eventually overtake her. The most beautiful, pow-erful, and evil city in the world will not be able to stand when the holy God intervenes and allows the evil to run its course to destruction. **In a single day** (possibly figurative, but signifying a very short time), she will face **death, mourning, and famine**—all that she had been able to avoid thus far through her wealth and power.

In the end, the city will be **consumed by fire,** unable to escape the destruction, unable to stop the raging fire as it sweeps and destroys. Jeremiah had prophesied of ancient Babylon, "The wide walls of Babylon will be leveled to the ground, and her high gates will be burned. The builders from many lands have worked in vain, for their work will be destroyed by fire!" (Jeremiah 51:58).

18:9-10 Those who control various parts of the economic system will mourn at Babylon's fall. Verses 9-20 are a funeral dirge for the fall of Babylon, sung by three different groups: the rulers of the world (18:9-10), the merchants (18:11-16), and the ship owners (18:17-20). These have all grown rich because of the evil economy represented by Babylon. The fall of the evil world system will affect all who enjoyed and depended on it. No one will remain unaffected by Babylon's fall.

First, **the rulers** who had given their power to the beast had committed **immoral acts** with her. As a reward for their subservience, these kings **enjoyed her great luxury.** But when the city is destroyed, they will be **terrified by her great torment** and will **stand at a distance.** Most likely, the destruction is so great that they don't want to be caught up in it. They do not attempt to rescue the city because they realize it is futile. These rulers will be terrified because, without Babylon, they will be nothing. They are terrified for Babylon, but more important, they are terrified for themselves.

18:11-13 The next group to join the funeral dirge are the **merchants** (18:11-16). These people **weep and mourn** because **there is no one left to buy their goods.** The collapse of the economy will mean the end of their trade and income.

This list of various merchandise illustrates the extreme materialism of this society. Few of these goods are necessities—most are luxuries, including precious metals, jewels, and cloth, aromatic perfumes, and foods. Even people had become no more than commodities—**human lives** were the **slaves** who would have been sold to Babylon.

Rome was a city of great luxury and extravagance. The Roman emperors were known for their sumptuous lifestyles, clothing, and banquets. This list of exotic commodities describes the breadth of the trade that usually would come into the port of Rome. Much of the list is identical to the types of trade mentioned in Ezekiel 27:12-22, describing a former maritime trade power, the city of Tyre. Rome's luxury and extravagance led to decadence that eventually destroyed her. In the end, Tyre also had been destroyed, "The merchants of the nations shake their heads at the sight of you, for you have come to a horrible end and will be no more" (Ezekiel 27:36).

18:14 The **fancy things** refer to all the exotic imports that would come into cities like Tyre and Rome. People love these things, but when Babylon is destroyed, all will be **gone forever.** The luxury and splendor of this world will not last.

18:15-17a Like the kings of the world (18:9-10), **the merchants** will also be **terrified** at the torment of the great city. They too will **weep and cry.** The description of the **beautiful** city matches the description of the great prostitute in 17:4. These merchants will be terrified at the swiftness and totality of the great city's destruction. With the economy collapsed, there will no longer be a market for the exotic and pricey goods that the merchants had traded and from which they had grown wealthy.

18:17b-19 The third group to join the funeral dirge will be the **shipowners and captains of the merchant ships and their crews**—all who earn their living from the sea. The vast amount of trade was carried on, at least partially, by ships arriving from far distant lands. As the merchants had become rich on the commodities, those who ran the ships had become rich delivering them. With the fall of the great city, their services will no longer be required. There will be no one to buy and nothing to trade. As the city goes up in smoke, **they will throw dust on their heads to show their great sorrow.** Ezekiel had written of Tyre, "All the oarsmen abandon their ships; the sailors and helmsmen come to stand on the shore. They weep bitterly as they throw dust on their heads and roll in ashes" (Ezekiel 27:29-30). In one moment, everything they know goes up in smoke.

18:20 In contrast to the weeping and mourning of the people at the fall of Babylon, the heavens will rejoice. The call to rejoice is extended to the **holy people of God and apostles and prophets**—the people who have been persecuted and killed because they refused to join Babylon's system and worship the beast (17:6). Babylon's fall will be God's judgment on behalf of his people.

18:21 This **boulder as large as a great millstone** would be a stone about fifteen to twenty feet wide, a foot thick, and weighing thousands of pounds—heavier than any human being could even move. But **a mighty angel** picked it up and **threw it into the ocean.** As a huge boulder, hurtled through the air, sinks to the bottom of the sea, so would Babylon **disappear forever.**

Jeremiah had given a similar prophecy to the city of Babylon (Jeremiah 51:60-64). Babylon, Rome, and the future focal point of the Antichrist's reign will have great glory and power and then will disappear like a rock beneath the waves. All that the people had lived for—their great luxuries and power—will become a millstone around their necks and will drag them to the bottom of the sea.

18:22-23 The mighty city, thrown like a boulder into the sea, will be destroyed and silenced. This city had been filled with **music.** There had been busy industry in its humming economy. The **milling of grain** had provided plenty of food. People had enjoyed life, and there had been wedding celebrations. But when it all collapses, all that will be no more. There will be complete darkness, **without a single lamp.** This will be total and utter destruction.

Why will this happen? **Because her merchants, who were the greatest in the world, deceived the nations with her sorceries.** The word "sorceries" probably does not refer to black magic, although that was certainly practiced in the Roman Empire and will certainly be a part of any worship of Satan. Instead, it pictures the "spell" under which Rome, and this flourishing economy, puts its people. They are so enamored by the greatness of their culture that they believe it will last forever. They willingly worship the beast in order to partake in what they perceive as the peace and joy that they think the beast has brought (13:14-17).

18:24 This is the great sin of Babylon, of Rome, and of the Antichrist's kingdom. The inhabitants of the world enjoy the great prosperity that the beast's economy brings them. However, in the **streets** of that great city, **the blood of the prophets was spilled. Babylon was the one who slaughtered God's people all over the world.** Certainly this was true of Rome, for being a Christian in the Roman Empire was tantamount to treason. The emperors considered themselves to be gods, and, of all their peoples, it was the Christians who refused to worship them. Persecution under the emperors Nero and Domitian reached the heights of horror.

REVELATION 19

SONGS OF VICTORY IN HEAVEN / 19:1-10

These first five verses of chapter 19 describe the end of the destruction of Babylon the Great (chapters 17–18). In contrast to the funeral dirges of the kings, merchants, and seamen (18:9-19), the crowd in heaven sings a great song of praise. This vast crowd in heaven begins praising God for his victory (19:1-3). Then the twenty-four elders join the chorus (19:4). Finally, the great choir of heaven once again praises God—the wedding of the Lamb has come (19:6-8). In Matthew 25:1-13, Christ had compared the coming of his Kingdom to a wedding for which his people must be prepared.

19:1-3 This is the only place in the New Testament where the word **hallelujah** is found, and it occurs in verses 1, 3, 4, and 6. The word is derived from a combination of two Hebrew words, *halal* and *Jah*, meaning "Praise Yahweh" or "Praise God." The word can be found in the Old Testament, especially in Psalms 113–118, known as the Hallelujah psalms.

The song in Revelation praises God for his **just and true** judgments (see also 15:3; 16:5, 7). He is praised for avenging the murders of his people. The punishment of the evil adversaries of God and his people is cause for praise in heaven. God **has punished the great prostitute who corrupted the earth with her immorality, and he has avenged the murder of his servants.** The identity of this "great prostitute" is explained in the commentary on 17:1. Her corruption of the earth is described in chapters 17–18. The beast and his kingdom will be judged for deceiving the nations and for killing God's servants. The "great prostitute," the evil city, has been destroyed and **the smoke from that city ascends forever and forever** (see also 9:2; 14:11; 18:9, 18). Babylon's destruction will be final. She will never rise again.

19:4 The identity of the **twenty-four elders** and the **four living beings** is explained in 4:4 and 4:6. These joined with the vast crowd (19:1) in praise to **God, who was sitting on the throne. They fell down** in worship, indicating a position of total humility and subservience to God (see also 4:10; 5:14; 7:11; 11:16). They cried out **Amen,** affirming what God had done.

19:5 The closing of this song of praise was given by **a voice** located near **the throne.** This was not God's voice, because the words "praise our God" would not have come from God. The voice came from one of the heavenly beings and called upon **all** of God's **servants, from the least to the greatest, all who fear him,** to praise him. "Fear" refers to reverence for God. These are all of God's redeemed people called to join in praise to the God who had saved them from the end brought by Satan and evil—the burning fires of Babylon.

19:6-8 The multitude was singing, rejoicing, exulting, and giving glory to God in a time of celebration like nothing ever seen before, for it will celebrate **the wedding feast of the Lamb,** referring to Christ. This next great vision, the bride getting ready for her wedding, contrasts with the "great prostitute" of 17:1. **His bride has prepared herself**—the bride is the new Jerusalem (21:2, 9-10), the church, the believers, those redeemed by Christ's blood. This is the culmination of human history—the judgment of the wicked and the wedding of the Lamb and his bride, the church.

In the Old Testament, the figure of a wedding banquet, with the bride as God's people Israel, pictured God's eternal love and protection over them (Isaiah 24:6-8; 54:5-7; 61:10; 62:5; Hosea 2:19). In some of his parables about the Kingdom of God, Jesus used the imagery of a wedding banquet (Matthew 22:2-14; 25:1-13; Luke 14:15-24). John the Baptist spoke of Jesus as the bridegroom (John 3:29), and Jesus described himself that way (Matthew 9:15; Luke 5:34-35). Other New Testament writers described God's people—all believers, both Jews and Gentiles—as Christ's bride (2 Corinthians 11:2; Ephesians 5:23-32).

The bride's clothing stands in sharp contrast to the gaudy clothing of the great prostitute (17:4). The bride was **permitted to wear the finest white linen.** In John's day, linen was expensive—only the very wealthy wore clothing made with linen. Here the bride of Christ, the believers, were wearing the finest, explained as representing **the good deeds done by the people of God** (see also 3:4-5, 18; 4:4; 6:11; 7:9, 14; 15:6; 19:14). These "righteous acts" were not religious deeds done by believers so that they could be saved; instead, the acts reflected the fact that the saints had been saved in order to do good works (Ephesians 2:10).

The bride wore this clothing that had been purchased for her by the blood of Christ; she made herself "ready" through her faithfulness to Christ until the day of the "wedding," when she would be joined with him.

19:9 This verse includes the fourth of seven beatitudes in Revelation (see also 1:3; 14:13; 16:15; 20:6; 22:7; 22:14). Each beatitude describes the "blessedness" of those who have remained faithful to Christ. In this case, the believers were "blessed" because they had been **invited to the wedding feast of the Lamb.** At this banquet will be all those who have trusted Christ for salvation; they will come from every nation. Jesus had stated, "I tell you this, that many Gentiles will come from all over the world and sit down with Abraham, Isaac, and Jacob at the feast in the Kingdom of Heaven" (Matthew 8:11).

In the parable of the wedding feast (Matthew 22), Jesus described a king who prepared a great banquet and, while many guests had been invited, at the time of the banquet they all refused to come. They had taken on other commitments that they decided were more important. So the king filled his banquet hall with others who *did* come when invited. The point is that God has invited people to join him at this great feast. Blessed are those who have accepted the invitation to the marriage supper.

As an assurance to the readers of the absolute truth of the wedding banquet of Christ in which they would take part, the angel told John, **"These are true words that come from God."** God's true words stand forever.

19:10 Whether John had mistaken this heavenly being for Christ, or whether he was simply overcome with the emotion of the promise he had just foreseen, John **fell down** at the angel's **feet to worship him.** But the angel stopped him, **"No, don't worship me."** The Bible forbids worship of angels, for, as the angel said, **"I am a servant of God, just like you and the other believers who testify of their faith in Jesus."** The powerful angelic beings thus far described in Revelation—despite their amazing strength and glory—were simply faithful servants of God, as are all believers who tell about their faith in Jesus.

These servants of Christ had testified of their faith in Jesus, and the angel said that **the essence of prophecy is to give a clear witness for Jesus.** "Clear witness" also means "testimony" (1:9; 6:9; 12:11, 17; 17:6; 20:4). All believers are, in a sense, prophets because they testify of their faith. For many of the believers mentioned here, it had meant testifying to their own deaths. The word "prophecy" means more than seeing and foretelling the future, although in some cases that is true (especially in the Old Testament prophets and in John's case here). The main purpose of prophecy is to communicate God's message.

THE RIDER ON THE WHITE HORSE / 19:11-21

The vision shifts again. Heaven opened and Jesus appeared, this time not as a Lamb but as a warrior on a white horse (symbolizing victory). Jesus had come first as a Lamb to be a sacrifice for sin, but he will return as a Conqueror and King to execute judgment (2 Thessalonians 1:7-10). Jesus' first coming brought forgiveness; his second will bring judgment. The battle lines had been drawn between God and evil, and the world was waiting for the King to ride onto the field.

19:11-12 This verse describes the second coming of Christ—the moment God's people had been waiting for (see Mark 14:62; Luke 24:30). Christ's return will be unmistakable. **Heaven** will be **opened,** as Christ, on **a white horse,** makes his entrance. The white horse symbolizes victory. (Some think this is the same rider as mentioned in 6:2, who was also on a white horse. They suggest that the rider symbolized Christ and the spread of the Good News across the world. See commentary at 6:2 for more information.)

This rider is **named Faithful and True,** who **judges fairly and then goes to war.** The order of words indicates that the warfare is a result of God's judgment on the inhabitants of the earth who have completely rejected him. Although Jesus is called "Faithful and True," "Word of God" (19:13), and "King of kings and Lord of lords" (19:16), these verses imply that no name can do him justice. He is greater than any description or expression the human mind can devise.

His eyes were bright like flames of fire (see

also 1:14; 2:18). Christ's **many crowns** symbolize his ultimate authority. He has **a name written on him, and only he knew what it meant.** Although many possibilities have been proposed, most likely this is a name that the believers were not meant to know, at least not yet.

19:13 The believers who had come out of the Great Tribulation had "washed their robes in the blood of the Lamb and made them white" (7:14). Christ himself, when he rides to the earth on the white horse, will be **clothed with a robe dipped in blood.** Some suggest that this is the blood of the martyrs; some think it is the blood of Christ's enemies (referring to a similar passage in Isaiah 63:1-6); others think that this is the Lamb's own blood which, ultimately, brings about this final day of victory. Another name is given for Christ, **the Word of God.** Jesus is the final word of God, the voice of God himself, the revealer of God.

19:14 Accompanying Christ are **the armies of heaven,** referring to all believers who have been taken to heaven (in the Rapture, which will have occurred at some point prior to this although believers are divided as to when this will happen). Here the believers will be returning to earth with Christ as part of his vast army. They will be **dressed in pure white linen,** as noted also in 19:8. Some suggest that this army will be angels because Christ had spoken of returning with his angels (Matthew 24:30-31). Most likely, however, this army will be believers because 17:14 says that the victory will come through the Lamb "and his people."

The believers will come with Christ **on white horses.** They will not come to fight, however, for there will not need to be a battle. Christ will conquer with his potent word (19:15).

19:15 Christ is described as having a **sharp sword** coming from his mouth. This is also seen in 1:16 and 2:12. The word for "sword" used here, however, is not the small two-edged sword but a mighty sword that is four or five feet long. This was the sword used by cavalry soldiers. Christ's words of judgment are as sharp as swords. With that sword, he **struck down the nations.** Isaiah had prophesied of Christ, "He will rule against the wicked and destroy them with the breath of his mouth" (Isaiah 11:4).

The picture of Christ ruling **with an iron rod** (or scepter) describes him beating down the nations (see also 2:27). This is not a king's scepter that is merely symbolic of power; instead, it is a club with which he will destroy them. The psalmist had written of the Messiah, "You will break [the nations] with an iron rod and smash them like clay pots" (Psalm 2:9).

Lastly, Christ is pictured as treading **the winepress of the fierce wrath of almighty God.** The winepress image appeared in 14:19-20; it describes God's great wrath against those who had rejected him. Here, God's fierce anger is directed at all of sin personified. At this point, God will totally destroy sin and evil. A winepress is a large vat where grapes are collected and then crushed. It is often used in the Bible to symbolize judgment (Isaiah 63:3-6; Lamentations 1:15; Joel 3:12-13).

19:16 Most of the world will be worshiping the beast, the Antichrist, whom they believe has all power and authority. Then suddenly out of heaven Christ and his army will appear. **On his robe and thigh** (easily seen, for he is on a horse) **was written this title: King of kings and Lord of lords.** This title indicates God's sovereignty. It is used elsewhere in Scripture, always indicating God's absolute sovereignty over all other kings and lords (see 17:14; Deuteronomy 10:17; Daniel 2:47; 1 Timothy 6:15).

19:17-18 John saw another **angel;** this one described as **standing in the sun** and calling out **to the vultures**—birds of carrion. This will be the most gruesome single act of carnage ever in the history of mankind; the entire army will come to do battle and, with the word of Christ, they will be totally annihilated. Their **flesh** will be left for the birds to eat, for there will be no one left to bury the dead. A previous description of this battle included how "the blood flowed from the winepress in a stream about 180 miles long and as high as a horse's bridle" (14:20). This **great banquet** is a grim contrast to the wedding feast of the Lamb (19:9). Both will be provided by God—but one will be a celebration, the other will be devastation.

The angel called the birds together before the battle. Again, the picture is clear of the certainty of the final outcome. Ezekiel had written God's words to him in a prophecy of this final battle, **"And now, son of man, call all the birds and wild animals," says the Sovereign Lord. "Say to them, 'Gather together for my great sacrificial feast. Come from far and near to the mountains of Israel, and there eat the flesh and drink the blood. . . . Feast at my banquet table—feast on horses, riders, and valiant warriors'"** (Ezekiel 39:17, 20).

19:19 This **beast** is the same one that had risen out of the sea (chapter 13; see commentary there). The **kings of the earth** refer to the "ten horns" that John had seen on the beast (see 13:1), and, most likely, their number symbolizes all the kings of the earth who pledge allegiance to the Antichrist. At the pouring out of the sixth bowl of God's wrath, "miracle-working demons caused all the rulers of the world to gather for battle against the Lord . . . to a place called *Armageddon*" (16:14-16). Chapter 16 gave a preview of what was to come and how; chapter 19 describes the event itself. Here, verse 19 tells of the assembly for the battle of Armageddon. (For further information on this battle and the various viewpoints regarding it, see commentary at 16:16.)

The beast and the kings of the earth and their armies gathered **to fight against the one sitting on the horse** (Christ) **and his army** (the redeemed). The battle lines had been drawn, and the greatest confrontation in the history of the world was about to begin.

19:20 The two armies sat facing each other—the beast and all the kings of the earth versus the rider on the white horse and his redeemed people. Suddenly, the battle was over. There was no fight, for, in a second, the end had come. There was no need for a battle because the victory had been won centuries earlier when the rider on the white horse, Christ, had died on a cross. At that time, Satan had been defeated; here at Armageddon, he is finally stripped of all his power. Satan's **beast** (the Antichrist, described in 13:1-10) **was captured,** along with his **false prophet** who had **deceived all**

who had **accepted the mark of the beast.** This is described in 13:11-18.

The beast and the false prophet were captured and **thrown alive into the lake of fire that burns with sulfur.** This is the final destination of all evil. At this point, however, only these two evil beings received this punishment. This lake is different from the bottomless pit referred to in 9:1; it is mentioned in 14:10-11 and 19:3. There are several statements concerning both spiritual powers and people being thrown into the lake of fire. Here, the Antichrist and the false prophet were thrown into the fiery lake. Next, their leader, Satan himself, will be thrown into that lake (20:10), and finally death and the grave (20:14). Afterward, everyone whose name is not recorded in the Book of Life will be thrown into the lake of fire (20:15).

19:21 With the two leaders captured (the Beast and the false prophet), the army was left to be destroyed. Christ, with **the sharp sword** of his **mouth** (19:15), kills the entire army of rebellious kings and soldiers in one fell swoop. His sword of judgment falls and destroys everything. The **vultures,** who had been called ahead of time by the angel (19:17-18), **gorged themselves on the dead bodies.** With no one left on the planet to bury these dead, they were abandoned to the carrion birds to devour.

REVELATION 20

THE THOUSAND YEARS / 20:1-6

Chapter 20 has probably engendered more argument, discussion, and books than any other section of Revelation. Much of how a person understands this chapter will depend on the approach taken in the other sections of the book. There are three main views of the Millennium that differ over: (1) whether the millennial reign of Christ is an earthly historical reign of peace or a spiritual reign in the hearts of God's people; (2) whether this millennial reign is a literal one thousand years or another length of time.

Whether the one thousand years is a literal or figurative number, most likely, the Millennium will occur in history; it will probably be an earthly reign of Christ that follows his second coming.

20:1 The end of chapter 19 describes the Beast, the false prophet, and all their followers thrown into the lake of fire. This vision at the beginning of chapter 20 describes Christ's dealings with Satan. An **angel** came from **heaven with the key to the bottomless pit and a heavy chain in his hand.** In 9:1-12, an angel had arrived with the key to the bottomless pit and had released the

locusts as part of the fifth trumpet judgment. This may be the same angel.

20:2-3 Several names are used here for the same being—the **dragon,** the **old serpent,** the **Devil,** and **Satan** (see also 12:9 for another list of these names). The angel **seized** Satan, **bound him,** and **threw him into the bottomless pit,** locking the door. Satan was put away and could not get out until God would decide to let him out. God's sovereignty is emphasized again.

This describes a different situation than that in 12:7-13. Chapter 12 describes Satan's fall from heaven and his freedom to roam the earth (12:17). Chapter 20 describes Satan being removed from the earth for a time in order that he **could not deceive the nations anymore.** God did not bind the dragon as punishment—that would occur later (20:10)—but to stop him from deceiving the nations. But who are "the nations"? It appears that, at the battle of Armageddon (16:14-16; 19:19), only the beast, the false prophets, the kings of the nations, and their armies were destroyed. The battle at Armageddon did not kill the entire population of the earth. Therefore, some unbelievers would still be alive (the believers would be with Christ, for they had been part of his army, 19:14). Satan will be bound for a **thousand years.** Whether symbolic or literal, this time period of Satan's imprisonment matches the time period of Christ's reign (20:4-6).

Those who propose that this Millennium time period is not limited to a thousand years (the amillennialists) and believe that it is the time between the first and second comings of Christ interpret this binding as referring to Satan being kept from working in the lives of believers and from stopping the gospel's advance. Others explain, however, that the word "nations" is always used in Revelation to describe unbelievers. It seems clear, therefore, that Satan will be bound and locked away from deceiving the unbelievers (still alive after Armageddon), while Christ rules during this period. The words describing how Satan is locked and sealed away indicate that his activity on earth will be completely stopped for this period of time. During this time, the unbelievers will experience true justice and God's perfect rule over the earth.

Why is there a millennium? Why doesn't God go straight from Armageddon to eternity? Why this interim and then another final battle—Gog and Magog? We don't know, but it appears that unbelievers on earth are given the opportunity to experience what the rule of God is like. However, as shown in the following verses, even though unbelievers will experience the reign of Christ, they will continue to rebel against God even without Satan's deceptive influence. And the moment that Satan is let out of the prison, these people will flock after Satan and go to war against Christ. This will prove their absolute depravity, their true allegiance, and the necessity of the final punishment in the lake of fire.

20:4-6 Satan has been bound and thrown into the bottomless pit so that for a thousand years he will not be able to deceive the nations. Here Revelation describes who will take part in that thousand-year reign of Christ, free from the influence of evil.

First, John saw **thrones.** The **people sitting on the thrones had been given the authority to judge.** Who are those sitting on the thrones? The Scripture does not identify them specifically. Many interpreters believe that these are those who had been martyred for their faith, but the problem with this theory is that the martyrs are not mentioned until the last part of the verse. Some suggest that this is only the twenty-four elders (4:4) or that this forms an angelic court of some kind. In Matthew 19:28, the apostles are promised that they will judge from twelve thrones. First Corinthians 6:2-3 says that the saints will judge the world. What we can determine is that this is a court in heaven composed of those whom God wants to assist in judgment (see also Daniel 7:26).

Next, he saw **the souls of those who had been beheaded for their testimony about Jesus, for proclaiming the word of God.** Then a problem arises with the translation. Between the sentence describing the martyrs and the sentence that says they **had not worshiped the beast or his statue, nor accepted his mark,** the Greek includes the words "and who," which can be taken as a further description of the martyrs, or as a description of an entirely different group. If the latter is the case, John saw the martyrs, whom he had described in 6:9-11, as well as others who were martyred during the Great Tribulation. Then he saw a separate group who had not worshiped the beast.

If "those who had not worshiped the beast" is merely a further description of the martyrs, then it appears that only the martyrs **came to life again, and they reigned with Christ for a thousand years**—a reward for their ultimate faithfulness to Christ by giving up their lives. This **first resurrection** could be a resurrection only of the martyrs. If so, then the rest of the believers along with the unbelievers are described as **the rest of the dead** who do **not come back to life until the thousand years** are over. At this point, God will separate the unbelievers from the believers, sending the former to the lake of fire and granting the latter eternal life. However, some commentators think that all believers partake of the "first resurrection" because all believers have been freed from the **second death**—that is, the lake of fire. The phrase "come back to life" refers to a physical resurrection of their bodies. These believers will have new bodies, as described in 1 Corinthians 15:51-53.

Those who do not believe in a literal thousand-year reign of Christ say that this first resurrection is spiritual (in believers' hearts at salvation), and that the Millennium is their spiritual reign with Christ on earth between his first and second comings. During this time, believers are priests of God because Christ reigns in their hearts. In this view, the second resurrection is the bodily resurrection of all people for judgment. Others believe that the first resurrection

occurs after Satan is set aside. It is a physical resurrection of believers who then reign with Christ on the earth for a literal 1,000 years. The second resurrection will occur at the end of this Millennium when God will judge unbelievers who have died.

These believers are "blessed," the fifth of seven beatitudes in Revelation (1:3; 14:13; 16:15; 19:9; 22:7, 14).

THE DEFEAT OF SATAN / 20:7-10

At Armageddon, the beast and the false prophet had been thrown into the lake of fire. Then Satan was locked away for a thousand years. Upon his release, he immediately goes on the offensive against Christ and his people. But his end will be like his followers—he too will be cast into the lake of fire.

20:7-8 Satan had been locked up for a thousand years so that he could no longer deceive the nations (20:2-3). But at the end of that thousand years, **Satan will be let out of his prison** (this is planned by God, see 2:3). Immediately, Satan will **deceive the nations from every corner of the earth.** The unbelievers still on the earth after the battle of Armageddon will have lived through the thousand-year reign of Christ, but as soon as Satan is set free, they will be deceived and ready **for battle.** This reaction demonstrates that Satan will not repent. It also shows that people rebel against God no matter how long or how many chances they are given to repent. The source of rebellion against God comes not from the environment or even from Satan himself but from within the human heart.

The names **Gog and Magog** symbolize all the nations of the earth that join together to battle God. Noah's son, Japheth, had a son named Magog (Genesis 10:2). Ezekiel presented Gog, of the land of Magog, as a leader of forces against Israel (Ezekiel 38–39). This comparison is used in Revelation, as is so much other Old Testament prophecy, because of the similarity of evil forces battling against God's people and God's cataclysmic victory. Whether symbolic or literal, Gog represents the aggregate military might of all the forces opposed to God. Many say that the battle Ezekiel described will occur at the end of human history, but there are many differences between the events described in Ezekiel and the final battle of Revelation 20. Regardless of when this battle will occur, the message is clear: God will deliver his people. No enemy will be able to stand against his mighty power.

20:9 This vast army of people, led by Satan himself, **went up on the broad plain of the earth**

and surrounded God's people and the beloved city. The unbelievers attacked the believers. "Beloved city" probably refers to Jerusalem, but it may be a way of describing God's people. These people will be surrounded by this great evil army.

Before a battle can even ensue, however, **fire from heaven came down on the attacking armies and consumed them** (see also Ezekiel 38:22; 39:6). God totally destroyed this entire army. All of Satan's followers were destroyed in an instant.

20:10 The **Devil,** Satan, the one who had been let free and had **betrayed** all the nations, received his just punishment. He was **thrown into the lake of fire that burns with sulfur, joining the beast and the false prophet** (19:20). The evil trinity was gone forever (for more on the beast and the false prophet, see chapter 13). Satan's power is not eternal—he will meet his doom. He began his evil work in mankind at the beginning (Genesis 3:1-6) and continues it today, but he will be destroyed and never a threat to anyone again (for more information on the lake of burning sulfur, see commentary at 19:3 and 19:20). Those in that place will face torment **day and night forever and ever.**

The description of the torment in this lake of burning sulfur has caused a debate regarding the true nature of this place. Some believe in a doctrine of "annihilationism"—meaning that after death, the wicked are utterly obliterated and consumed through God's judgment. Their "torment" is knowing that they will never come to life again. This view is based on the fact that much of the biblical imagery of hell—a consuming fire, destruction, and perishing—may imply eternal death. Another view is that this lake of burning sulfur (and its implication of the fires of hell) may be symbolic of a certain kind of horror that will be appropriate punishment. The exact nature of this lake of fire is unknown, but certainly it is not a place one would desire to go. (For more information on the lake of fire, see commentary at 14:9-11.)

THE FINAL JUDGMENT / 20:11-15

At the judgment, the books will be opened. These books contain the recorded deeds of everyone, good or evil. Everyone's life will be reviewed and evaluated. No one is saved by deeds, but deeds are seen as clear evidence of a person's actual relationship with God. Jesus will look at how we have handled gifts, opportunities, and responsibilities. God's gracious gift of salvation does not free us from the requirement of faithful obedience and service. Each of us must serve Christ in the best way we know and live each day knowing the books will be opened.

20:11 Next, John saw **a great white throne** with someone **sitting on it.** He did not identify the one on the throne. Throughout Revelation, it is God who is pictured as sitting on a throne (see, for example, 4:2; 7:10; 19:4). Daniel had a similar vision (Daniel 7:9-10). Some suggest that the one sitting on the great white throne is Jesus, citing several verses (Matthew 25:31; John 5:22; 2 Corinthians 5:10). Most likely, the little verse that solves the mystery is found in Jesus' statement, "The Father and I are one" (John 10:20); thus, the one throne is occupied by the Father and the Son as one.

With the appearance of this one on the throne, **the earth and sky fled from his presence, but they found no place to hide.** This poetic imagery could describe the dissolution of everything material and corrupt in the presence of God as Judge; it could also depict the end of the old earth and old heavens—in preparation for the creation of the new (21:1). (See also Isaiah 51:6; Matthew 24:35; 2 Peter 3:10-12.)

20:12-13 The dead, both great and small probably refers to all people—believers and nonbelievers. No one will escape God's scrutiny. Why they are called "the dead" is uncertain. Some suggest that this is only the judgment of unbelievers because they would be the ones still dead who would take part in the second resurrection (20:5). However, it most likely stands for everyone, for God "will judge everyone, both the living and the dead" (1 Peter 4:5). Christ described the judgment of all people (Matthew 25:31-33, 46).

This is the great and final judgment, the place where the **books** will be **opened,** including **the Book of Life.** As noted in 3:5, this is the heavenly registry of those who have accepted Christ's gift of salvation. All people will be **judged according to the things written in the books, according to what they had done.** The idea of judgment by works is a theme throughout the Old and New Testaments (Psalm 62:12; Jeremiah 17:10; Daniel 7:10; Romans 2:6; 14:10-12; 1 Corinthians 3:12-15; 2 Corinthians 5:10; 1 Peter 1:17). No one will be forgotten at this final gathering.

Believers will be judged—not to see if they merit eternal life, for their names will already be in the Book of Life. This will be a judgment for rewards. Believers' works cannot save them, but their deeds are important to God. The deeds with which believers build their lives *do* matter (1 Corinthians 3:11-15). Unbelievers also will be judged according to their works, but, of course, no works, no matter how good, will be able to save them.

20:14-15 And death and the grave were thrown into the lake of fire. This is the second death— the lake of fire. And anyone whose name was not found in the Book of Life was thrown into the lake of fire. God's judgment is complete. As Paul said, "The last enemy to be destroyed is death" (1 Corinthians 15:26). Isaiah had foreseen this day: "He will swallow up death forever" Isaiah 25:8). The lake of fire is the ultimate destination of everything wicked—Satan, the beast, the false prophet, the demons, death, Hades, and anyone whose name was not written in the book of life. This is the second death. They died the first time physically; this time their death was spiritual. The lake of fire was prepared by God for the Devil and his angels (Matthew 25:41). Those who refuse to believe in Christ will share the Devil's judgment.(For more on the "lake of fire" see commentary at 19:3; 19:20; 20:10.)

REVELATION **21**:1–22:6

THE NEW JERUSALEM / 21:1–22:6

John watched as this gigantic city descended to the new earth created by God. The city was a 1,400-mile square with 200-foot high walls. Made of pure gold, it was decorated with all kinds of beautiful gems. Its gates opened in every direction, as evidence of the church's success in proclaiming Christ to every nation (5:9; 21:13). At the very center of this city was God, the enthroned Lamb. The light from his throne illumined the entire city. From his throne, a crystal-clear river of life was flowing. At the river's bank, the tree of life was flourishing, producing twelve different kinds of fruit for the healing of the nations. "Nothing evil will be allowed to enter" (21:27), for this is where God will reign!

21:1 John sees **a new heaven and a new earth, for the old heaven and the old earth had disappeared.** The earth and sky had fled from God's presence (see 20:11), and this new heaven and earth had taken their place. When sin entered the human race, it and all creation were corrupted (Romans 8:20-22). All of this "newness" is not merely physical but also spiritual and moral. Everything will be "new" because "God is now among his people" (21:3).

That **the sea was also gone** could refer to evil being gone, for the sea was associated with evil (the beast had come out of the sea, 13:1). This could mean that there will be no oceans in the new earth. It probably means, however, that all evil will be forever banished (21:4).

The Old Testament prophets had predicted that God would create a brand-new earth and heaven. Isaiah described this (Isaiah 65:17-19) as had Peter (2 Peter 3:12-13).

21:2 In addition to a new heaven and a new earth is a new city. **The holy city, the new Jerusalem** descends out of heaven **from God.** The "new Jerusalem" is where God lives among his people. At the end of time, God will come down to his new heaven and new earth to be with his renewed people. The church in Philadelphia was promised "all who are victorious . . . will be citizens in the city of my God—the new Jerusalem that comes down from heaven from my God" (3:12).

That this city is called "the new Jerusalem" indicates a relationship to the "old Jerusalem," the capital of Israel. As the old creation had been corrupted by sin, so the old Jerusalem had been the city where prophets were killed and where Christ himself was crucified. Jesus had lamented over the city (Matthew 23:37). Yet throughout the Old Testament are rich promises for the future restoration of Israel—God's people. This new Jerusalem will be God's dwelling place among his people (see commentary at 21:3).

God's people, all believers, will live in this magnificent city, described as a **beautiful bride prepared for her husband**—pure and radiant, ready to join the one she loves (see also 21:9). In 19:7-9, God's people, the church, are described as a bride making herself ready for the marriage feast (see commentary there); here, the new Jerusalem is also described as a bride. Whether Jerusalem is an actual city, or symbolic of the community of God's people, is unknown. But we are certain that there will be relationships in the new Jerusalem—first between God and his people, and second among God's people.

21:3 A **loud shout from the throne** (not from God, but probably an angel near the throne) announced the words all of creation had been waiting to hear: **"Look, the home of God is now among his people! . . . God himself will be with them."** What had been foreshadowed in God's presence in the Tabernacle (Exodus 40:34-35), in the Temple (1 Kings 8:10-11), and in the bodily presence of God himself in Jesus (John 1:14) will become a reality in the new Jerusalem. As God had walked with Adam and Eve in the Garden (Genesis 3:8), so **he will live with** his people. This desire to be in the presence of God should be our strongest desire here on earth and the focus of all our worship.

21:4 The utter joy of living in God's presence is indescribable; Revelation explains what will *not* be there. **There will be no more death or sorrow or**

crying or pain. All that has caused sadness and suffering will be taken away. All sin that has been the source of sorrow will be gone. Isaiah had seen a future day of no more sorrow and sighing (Isaiah 35:10). There can be no evil in God's glorious presence; therefore, **the old world and its evils are gone forever.** The "old world" where Satan ran free and sin ran rampant will be replaced by God's world.

21:5 This time, God himself, **the one sitting on the throne,** spoke (see also 1:8). His words describe the reality of what was happening: **"Look, I am making all things new!"** God is the Creator. The Bible begins with the majestic story of God creating the universe, and it concludes with his creating a new heaven and a new earth. This is a tremendous hope and encouragement for believers. God told John to **write this** so that believers across the generations, awaiting this glorious future, can be encouraged to know that these words are **trustworthy and true.** Because God has spoken, believers can know of the absolute certainty that these events will one day occur. God's word never changes.

21:6 Just as God finished the work of creation (Genesis 2:1-3) and Jesus finished the work of redemption (John 19:30), so they will finish the entire plan of salvation by inviting the redeemed into a new creation and proclaim, **"It is finished!"**

God said, **"I am the Alpha and the Omega— the Beginning and the End."** This repeats 1:8 (see also 1:17; 2:8), where Christ had said this to John. *Alpha* and *Omega* are the first and last letters of the Greek alphabet. God is sovereign over history and in control of everything.

God promised that he would **give the springs of the water of life without charge** to **all who are thirsty.** This water is also described in 22:1, and it symbolizes eternal life. Jesus had told the Samaritan woman about this water (John 4:13-14), as well as all who would believe in him (John 7:37-38). Water pictures the reward of those who have been "victorious" (21:7). They will no longer have any needs, for their needs will be completely met by God throughout all eternity.

21:7-8 Verses 7 and 8 form an interlude; they are directed to the readers who must make a choice whether they will be part of the **victorious** ones who **will inherit all these blessings** (21:7) or the **cowards who turn away from** God and face **their doom** (21:8). Because they stubbornly refused to drink from the water of life and receive salvation in Christ, their doom will be **the second death**—the lake of fire. The "first death" is physical death. But all the dead will be raised to be judged, and those

who are sent away to punishment will face the "second death," which is spiritual.

John described the beast's followers. This list is not meant to be exhaustive, but is representative of all sin and rebellion against God. Those who refuse to believe, no matter how good or moral they are, will join those whose sins are more blatant, as recorded in this list. All unbelievers will face the same punishment. This is a warning to those who may be Christians in name only to be certain of their salvation. Which will they choose? The water of life, or the fire of the second death? Those who can endure the testing of evil and remain faithful will be rewarded by God.

21:9 The remainder of the chapter is a stunning description of the new city of God. The vision is symbolic and shows that the believers' new home with God will defy description. They will not be disappointed by it in any way. **One of the seven angels** told John that he would show him the **bride, the wife of the Lamb**—referring to the church (the believers, 19:7-8) and the new Jerusalem (21:2) all rolled into one in this awesome vision. (For more on the imagery of the bride as the wife of the Lamb, see commentary at 19:7-8 and 21:2.) In contrast to the great prostitute, who symbolizes the evil system and the people who rebelled against God, the bride represents those who remained faithful to Christ and now are prepared to join him.

21:10-11 John was again in spirit—this time carried away to a great, high mountain. From that vantage point, the angel showed John the holy city, Jerusalem, descending out of heaven from God.

This is a further description of what John had written in 21:2—this time describing the city itself. Verses 10-14 describe the beauty of this city: These descriptions are not meant to be taken literally, but the fact that this is a symbolic vision does not diminish the glory of what John was attempting to describe. Often John drew upon Old Testament imagery (as from Ezekiel's prophecies) in his attempt to describe the indescribable. As with the imagery of the bride, this city pictures the future, glorious dwelling place of the believers. John has already described eternal life in the new heaven and new earth (21:3-6); here he described heaven's physical characteristics—absolute and incomparable beauty.

This city had no lights in it; instead, it radiated with **the glory of God.** John did not have electric or neon lights as a reference point, so he used the picture of a clear jewel, perhaps cut with many facets, radiating and reflecting light. **Jasper** had been used earlier in describing the appearance of God himself (4:3) and is used again in 21:11, 18-19.

21:12-13 Next, John described the **walls** of the city. In John's day, most cities had walls around them, so in this part of the vision John described what would be the ideal city to his audience. There were **twelve gates,** three on each side of the city. **The names of the twelve tribes of Israel were written on the gates.** Ezekiel had seen a similar vision (see Ezekiel 48:30-34). Each gate was guarded by an angel, once again describing for John's audience the ideal city with high walls (and watchmen at every gate).

21:14 The great, high wall of the city **had twelve foundation stones.** Ancient city walls would have huge stones as their foundations. This city had only twelve foundation stones—these were indeed huge stones. While the gates had the names of the twelve tribes, these stones had the **names of the twelve apostles of the Lamb.** Jesus told the apostles that they would rule the twelve tribes (Matthew 19:28; Luke 22:30). The term "twelve apostles" could refer to the original twelve disciples, but other believers had been called "apostles" (such as Paul and Barnabas). It is more important to understand the symbolism that the church rests on the work of the apostles—the first followers of Jesus. Paul had written, "We are [God's] house, built on the foundation of the apostles and the prophets. And the cornerstone is Christ Jesus himself. We who believe are carefully joined together, becoming a holy temple for the Lord" (Ephesians 2:20-21).

21:15-17 The angel had **a gold measuring stick to measure the city, its gates, and its wall.** The city's measurements are symbolic of a place that will hold all God's people. These measurements are all multiples of 12, the number for God's people: there were 12 tribes in Israel and 12 apostles who started the church. In Greek, the measurements are 144 (12 x 12) cubits **(216 feet)** thick; there are 12 layers in the walls, and 12 gates in the city; and the height, length, and breadth are all the same: 12,000 stadia **(1,400 miles).** The new Jerusalem is a perfect **cube,** the same shape as the Most Holy Place in the Temple (1 Kings 6:20). This act of measuring shows its completeness as noted in 11:1 and in Ezekiel 40–41.

21:18 That **the wall was made of jasper** and that God himself is described as appearing like jasper (4:3) indicates that everything in the city would radiate the presence of God. This holy city, in the shape of a perfect cube, is reminiscent of the Most Holy Place in the Tabernacle and in the Temple. In Solomon's Temple, the Most Holy Place was splendid, with its interior overlaid with pure gold (1 Kings 6:21-22). So this entire city is **pure gold,**

as clear as glass. Its clearness indicates its lack of impurity; nothing will impede its ability to transmit God's glory.

21:19-20 The **foundation stones** of the wall were **inlaid with twelve gems.** The significance of each stone has been debated. Some have suggested that this imagery comes from the breastplate of the high priest, which had twelve precious stones on it (Exodus 28:17-20), even though the identifications of the stones are different. This is the most likely source of the imagery, indicating that what had once been the high priest's privilege alone had become part of the very foundation of the city of God, made available to all people. The high priest would enter the Most Holy Place (again, this is the same shape as the city—a cube) only once each year on the Day of Atonement to make a sacrifice for the sins of the entire nation. The Most Holy Place was the place of God's presence. In the new Jerusalem, all of God's people will constantly be in his presence. Nothing will ever again separate them from him.

The names of the various stones indicate jewels of various colors—all of them rare and beautiful. The picture John gives of this city indicates beauty beyond description.

21:21 Each of the **twelve gates** (21:11) was made **from a single pearl.** Pearls were very valuable in ancient times (see Matthew 13:45-46), so a pearl large enough to make a gate for this great city would be beyond imagining. In addition, **the main street was pure gold, as clear as glass,** just like the rest of the city (21:18). Again the emphasis is on its purity and transparency in order to radiate the glory of God.

21:22 This beautiful city, like any other city in the ancient world, would be expected to have a temple—a central place of worship. Many ancient cities would have several temples for the various gods the people worshiped. The focal point of worship in Jerusalem was God's Temple. That Temple, the center of God's presence among his people, was the primary place of worship. In the new Jerusalem, however, **no temple could be seen** because God's presence would be everywhere. He would be worshiped throughout the city. **The Lord God Almighty and the Lamb are its temple.** Their presence would be enough.

21:23 God had remade the heavens (21:1). Perhaps, when he did so, he didn't re-create a sun or a moon. The new city **has no need of sun or moon** for the radiance of God's glory **is its light.** Isaiah had also foreseen this (Isaiah 60:19-21). John, in his Gospel, had recorded Jesus' statement, "I am the light of the world" (John 8:12).

21:24-25 Elsewhere in Revelation, the word **nations** referred to the nations of the earth that joined the Antichrist (see 11:2, 18; 18:3, 23; 19:15). Here, however, the term refers to God's people. This shows the culmination of the conversion offered to all nations (5:9; 11:18; 14:6-7). This does not mean universal salvation, as some have suggested, but that God has chosen from every tribe, nation, people, and language who will come to be part of his great city. The city will be lit by the glory of God and the Lamb (21:23), and the people **will walk in its light.** All people on earth, even the **rulers of the world** who experienced power and glory in this world, will simply **bring their glory** to God's throne, casting down their crowns before him. Their splendor will be nothing compared to what they will experience in eternity.

The city's gates will **never close.** This does not imply that outside of the new Jerusalem, unsaved people are still roaming around. Instead, this pictures a city with open gates on a new earth where believers will dwell throughout. Ancient cities shut their gates at night for security purposes. However, since **there is no night,** and since all evil will have been eradicated, these gates will stay open constantly. Revelation seems to picture great activity coming and going from the city.

21:26-27 In contrast to the worldly nations' trade with evil Babylon (chapter 18), the nations (again describing God's people) **will bring their glory and honor into the city.** John again made the point that **nothing evil will be allowed to enter.** This does not indicate that evil would still be present in some realm outside the great city. All evil will be gone. Instead, in 20:7-8, John was warning his contemporary readers that they would not be in this glorious place unless their names **are written in the Lamb's Book of Life.** (For more on the Book of Life, see 3:5 and 20:12-15.)

22:1-2 This section describes what could be called the "new Eden." What the first Garden of Eden was supposed to be is fulfilled here. What Adam and Eve would have had if they had not fallen is what is given to God's people. Adam and Eve lost Paradise; here, God has remade it.

The angel showed John a pure river with the water of life, clear as crystal, flowing from the throne of God and of the Lamb, coursing down the center of the main street. The water of life is a symbol of eternal life. Jesus used this same image with the Samaritan woman (John 4:7-14). It pictures fullness of life with God and the eternal blessings that come when people believe in him and allow him to satisfy their spiritual thirst (see 22:17). The Garden of Eden also had a river run-ning through it that watered it (2:10). In both the Old and New Testaments, water pictures salvation and the refreshment of the Holy Spirit. Ezekiel's vision also had a river with trees growing along it (Ezekiel 47:1-12). God in Christ, who is the water of life (John 7:37-38), is the source of this constant stream of blessing and refreshment for his people. This river flows down the middle of the main street of the city and is accessible to everyone.

This **tree of life** can be compared to the tree of life in the Garden of Eden (Genesis 2:9; see also Ezekiel 47:12.) After Adam and Eve sinned, they were forbidden to eat from the tree of life. But because of the forgiveness of sin through the blood of Jesus, there will be no evil or sin in the new Jerusalem. Believers will be able to eat freely from the tree of life when sin's control is destroyed and eternity with God is secure. This tree (one tree or many trees) grows **on each side of the river** and bears **twelve crops of fruit,** with a new crop **every month.** Adam and Eve had been cut off from the tree of life because of their sin (Genesis 3:22-24); now the tree has fruit available for everyone— fresh fruit, not just once a year with a dry time in between, but new fruit every month.

In addition to the fruit, **the leaves** of the tree **were used for medicine to heal the nations.** Why would the nations need to be healed if all evil has been eliminated? John was alluding to Ezekiel 47:12, where water flowing from the temple produced trees with healing leaves. He was not implying that there would be illness in the new earth; he was emphasizing that the water of life would produce health and strength wherever it would go. God's people in his Kingdom will have no physical or spiritual needs. All the hurts of the nations will have been healed.

22:3-4 The phrase **no longer will anything be cursed** could mean that nothing accursed will be in God's presence. This would fulfill Zechariah 14:11. More likely, this refers to God lifting the curse that had been placed in Eden (Genesis 3:17-18). The phrase **the throne of God and of the Lamb** indicates the oneness of God and the Lamb, as well as God's presence right among his people and they will **see his face.** The face of God had not been seen by anyone since Adam and Eve sinned. Even Moses, the great lawgiver who went up on the mountain to meet with God, had only been able to see God from the back (Exodus 33:20). Here in heaven, however, God's people will see him face-to-face (1 John 3:2). To be able to see God's face suggests intimate personal relationship.

In addition, God's people will have **his name** written **on their foreheads.** This points out God's ownership. God's people had been "sealed" (7:3), and this seal previously had been described as being in the form of the Father's name (14:1). The point is that this is the same group—God will bring his own safely to his eternal Kingdom.

22:5 The point that **there will be no night** was noted in 21:25. This indicates that there will be no more evil, no more darkness, and no more time (for God had created day and night, along with the sun and the moon, to mark the passage of time—Genesis 1:14-15). The people in the city will not need **lamps or sun—for the Lord God will shine on them,** as was also noted in 21:23 (see commentary there).

The result of the entire book of Revelation is in

this verse: God's people, those who have been redeemed by the blood of Jesus, **will reign forever and ever** (see also Daniel 7:18, 28). Eternal life is ours now and forever.

22:6 John referred to **the angel** (as opposed to "an" angel), so this is probably the same angel who had shown him the heavenly city (21:9; 22:1). The revelation closes with an angel explaining that what John has written is **trustworthy and true.** Throughout the ages, God had been telling his prophets **what the future holds,** and he did so again in this prophecy to John. Revelation describes **what will happen soon** (see also 1:1). The word "soon" means imminent—and implies certainty.

REVELATION 22 :7-21

JESUS IS COMING / 22:7-21
These verses form the epilogue to this book. An angel expressed the authenticity of the prophecy, and at the very end, Jesus warned that the end would indeed come soon.

22:7 From Jesus himself come the words of assurance: **"Look, I am coming soon!"** The word "soon" *(taxu)* means that his coming will be quick and without delay. It may not be "soon" according to human timing (after all, John wrote this two thousand years ago), but it is certain to occur; it is imminent. Jesus clearly told his followers, "So be prepared, because you don't know what day your Lord is coming. You also must be ready all the time. For the Son of Man will come when least expected" (Matthew 24:42, 44).

Then follows the sixth of seven beatitudes in the book: **"Blessed are those who obey the prophecy written in this scroll."** (The other beatitudes are found in 1:3; 14:13; 16:15; 19:9; 20:6; 22:14; see the chart at 14:13.) Like the beatitude at 1:3, the one listed here promises a blessing to those who obey God by heeding the warnings of this prophecy.

22:8-9 Next, **John** signed his name, so to speak, as the one who **saw and heard all these things.** John did not imagine what he had written; he had actually seen and heard everything he had recorded. He understood that he had been given an awesome privilege. Once again overwhelmed, John wrote that he **fell down to worship the angel** who had given him the inspired glimpse of the future. But again (as at 19:10), the angel prohibited John's

worship, telling him to worship God. God alone is worthy of worship and adoration. He is above all creation, even the angels.

22:10 The angel told John what to do after his vision had ended. Instead of sealing up what he had written, as Daniel had been commanded to do (Daniel 12:4-12), John was told, **"Do not seal up the prophetic words you have written, for the time is near."** John's prophecy was to be left open so that all could read and understand. This message was needed immediately by the churches of John's day, as well as believers across the years until Christ's return. Daniel's message had been sealed because it was not a message for Daniel's time. But the book of Revelation was a message for John's time and is relevant today. As Christ's return approaches, there is an increased polarization between God's followers and Satan's followers. We must read the book of Revelation, hear its message, and be prepared for Christ's certain return.

22:11 The angel was not recommending evil living in this verse. Instead, this note follows on the heels of the angel's words that "the time is near" (22:10). Indeed, it may be so near that there would be no time for people to alter their lifestyles. The angel is showing how our choices lead to consequences. Like a train running down a track, the consequences will ultimately come for the choices we make. God is always calling people to repent, but when Christ returns, the opportunity will have passed. This is a call to the readers to make up their minds now and live for God. People will reap the consequences for the kinds of lives they have led; those who have done **wrong** and who have been **vile** will face that in eternity, and those who have done **good** and have been **holy** will be rewarded accordingly, as noted in 22:12.

22:12-13 Christ here spoke, reiterating that he would be **coming soon** (22:7). He would bring a **reward** that would be given to his people, according to their **deeds.** (For more on these rewards, see commentary at 20:12-13.) Our reward will be a place in God's Kingdom (see Matthew 25:34-40; Mark 9:47; 10:29-30), not on the basis of merit (good deeds) but because of God's gracious promise to people of faith (Luke 12:31-32). The believer's true reward is God's presence and power through the Holy Spirit. Later, in eternity, believers will be rewarded for their faith and service. No act of mercy will be forgotten; no true believer will be abandoned. (For more on rewards, see Matthew 16:27; 19:27-30; Luke 6:23, 35; 1 Corinthians 3:8, 13-15; 9:25; James 1:12.)

Although all God's people will be saved and will enjoy the reward of eternity with him, a number of rewards seem to be given to individuals, according to what they have done. God will look at each individual's heart; thus, it may be that a quiet saint praying daily beside her bed will receive even greater reward than a flamboyant, well-known preacher. It may be that the woman who used her gifts to the fullest extent will be rewarded more greatly than the one who believed but was too afraid to reach her potential. God will not bestow his rewards in ways that we humans might. Each believer's job is to serve God to his or her fullest potential with a heart that is right with him.

Next, Christ repeated the words he had spoken at the beginning of the Revelation: **"I am the Alpha and the Omega, the First and the Last, the Beginning and the End"** (see 1:8, 17 and commentary there). The Creator began and will end time itself.

22:14 This verse includes the seventh and final beatitude in Revelation (the others were in 1:3; 14:13; 16:15; 19:9; 20:6; 22:7; see the chart at 14:13): **Blessed are those who wash their robes.** This picture symbolizes those who seek to purify themselves from a sinful way of life. These people had been dirty with sin, but Christ had cleansed them through his death on the cross. They had accepted his salvation by "washing their robes." The verb in

7:14 was aorist, indicating an action in a specific time in the past. Here, the verb is present tense, indicating continuous action. This verse is a call to the believers to strive daily to remain faithful and ready for Christ's return. They do not need to be saved over and over; but they should continue to "wash their robes" and so remain clean and ready.

Those who do so **can enter through the gates of the city and eat the fruit from the tree of life.** Entering the city indicates joining the redeemed people in eternity (the "city" is described in 21:10-27). In Eden, Adam and Eve had been barred from any access to the tree of life because of their sin (Genesis 3:22-24). In the new earth, God's people will eat from the tree of life because their sins have been removed by Christ's death and resurrection. Those who eat the fruit of this tree will live forever.

22:15 Verse 14 describes those who will live in the Kingdom of God for eternity; those who cannot be there are described in this verse. This is not meant to be an exhaustive list of sins, nor does it indicate that, somehow, sinners will surround the holy city. Instead, as in 21:8, this symbol pictures that those who have washed their robes and have been cleansed of sin will be in the city, but these others will not be in the city; instead, they will be in the lake of fire, as described in 20:15 and 21:8. They are characterized as **dogs**—a term used in Scripture for something impure or unclean. The emphasis is that nothing evil and no sinner will be in God's presence to corrupt or harm any of the faithful.

22:16 Jesus again spoke (as he had previously, 22:12-13), describing himself as the ultimate fulfillment of everything that had been promised. Christ had sent his angel to show John all that would come to pass (see 1:1), so that the message could be given to **the churches** (all churches, but especially those mentioned in chapters 2–3 who would receive this letter).

Jesus is both David's source and the heir to his throne. As the Creator of all, he existed long before **David.** As a human, however, Jesus was one of David's direct descendants (see Isaiah 11:1-5; Matthew 1:1-17). As the Messiah, he is the **bright morning star,** the light of salvation to all (see 2:28; 2 Peter 1:19). In Numbers 24:17, Balaam declared, "I see him, but not in the present time. I perceive him, but far in the distant future. A star will rise from Jacob; a scepter will emerge from Israel." The "star" may have referred both to King David and David's greater descendant, Jesus Christ. As the morning star is the first star to be seen in the darkness before the dawn, so Christ, the morning star, promises that the night of tribulation will soon be over and the new Kingdom is about to dawn.

22:17 Both the Holy **Spirit** and the **bride,** the church, extend the invitation to all the world to come to Jesus and experience the joys of salvation in Christ. Everyone who hears the message is invited to **come.** Everyone who is **thirsty** is invited to come and **drink the water of life without charge.** This evil world is desperately thirsty for living water, and many are dying of thirst. But it's still not too late. One day it will be too late, as Revelation has clearly shown, but the invitation is still being offered.

22:18-19 This warning is given to anyone who might purposefully distort the message in this book. Moses gave a similar warning (Deuteronomy 4:1-4). People must handle the Bible with care and great respect, so that its message is not distorted. No human explanation or interpretation of God's word should be elevated to the same authority as the text itself.

This warning is given to everyone who hears the prophetic words of this book—not just future scribes who might recopy the text, but everyone who even hears the revelation must be careful not to add or remove anything. To do so carries a severe warning that God will remove that person's share in the tree of life and in the holy city that are described in this book. Many have taken this verse to refer to the Bible in its entirety, but it is actually focused on this book of Revelation. Yet all of God's word should be handled with such care. It is a serious matter to tamper with God's word, carrying a punishment with eternal consequences.

22:20-21 Jesus testified to the truth of this entire revelation to John in 22:7, 12, 16; then he added one final message, **"Yes, I am coming soon!"** No one knows the day or the hour, but Jesus is coming soon and unexpectedly. This is good news to those who trust him, but a terrible message for those who have rejected him and stand under judgment. Soon means at any moment, and his people must be ready for him, always prepared for his return.

John ended by saying, **Amen,** let it be so. With him, God's people across the world say, **Come, Lord Jesus!** Then John pronounced a benediction on those who had read or listened to the words of this book: **The grace of the Lord Jesus be with you all.** People need that grace in order to become God's children; God's children need that grace daily as they seek to be overcomers for him. In the end, his grace, and nothing else, brings his people to be with him forever.

HARMONY OF THE GOSPELS

250 EVENTS IN THE LIFE OF CHRIST

All four books in the Bible that tell the story of Jesus Christ—Matthew, Mark, Luke, and John—stand alone, emphasizing a unique aspect of Jesus' life. But when these are blended into one complete account, or harmonized, we gain new insights about the life of Christ.

This harmony combines the four Gospels into a single chronological account of Christ's life on earth. It includes every chapter and verse of each Gospel, leaving nothing out.

The harmony is divided into 250 events. The title of each event is identical to the title found in the corresponding Gospel. Parallel passages found in more than one Gospel have identical titles, helping you to identify them quickly.

Each of the 250 events in the harmony is numbered. The number of the event corresponds to the number next to the title in the Bible text. When reading one of the Gospel accounts, you will notice, at times, that some numbers are missing or out of sequence. The easiest way to locate these events is to refer to the harmony.

In addition, if you are looking for a particular event in the life of Christ, the harmony can help you locate it more rapidly than paging through all four Gospels. Each of the 250 events has a distinctive title keyed to the main emphasis of the passage to help you locate and remember the events.

This harmony will help you to better visualize the travels of Jesus, study the four Gospels comparatively, and appreciate the unity of their message.

I. BIRTH AND PREPARATION OF JESUS CHRIST

	Matthew	Mark	Luke	John
1. Luke's purpose in writing			1:1-4	
2. God became a human				1:1-18
3. The record of Jesus' ancestors	1:1-17		3:23-38	
4. An angel promises the birth of John to Zechariah			1:5-25	
5. An angel promises the birth of Jesus to Mary			1:26-38	
6. Mary visits Elizabeth			1:39-56	
7. John the Baptist is born			1:57-80	
8. An angel appears to Joseph	1:18-25			
9. Jesus is born in Bethlehem			2:1-7	
10. Shepherds visit Jesus			2:8-20	
11. Mary and Joseph bring Jesus to the Temple			2:21-40	
12. Visitors arrive from eastern lands	2:1-12			

	Matthew	Mark	Luke	John
13. The escape to Egypt	2:13-18			
14. The return to Nazareth	2:19-23			
15. Jesus speaks with the religious teachers			2:41-52	
16. John the Baptist prepares the way for Jesus	3:1-12	1:1-8	3:1-18	
17. The baptism of Jesus	3:13-17	1:9-11	3:21-22	
18. Satan tempts Jesus in the wilderness	4:1-11	1:12-13	4:1-13	
19. John the Baptist declares his mission				1:19-28
20. John the Baptist proclaims Jesus as the Messiah			1:29-34	
21. The first disciples follow Jesus				1:35-51
22. Jesus turns water into wine				2:1-12

II. MESSAGE AND MINISTRY OF JESUS CHRIST

	Matthew	Mark	Luke	John
23. Jesus clears the Temple	2:13-25			
24. Nicodemus visits Jesus at night				3:1-21
25. John the Baptist tells more about Jesus				3:22-36
26. Herod puts John in prison			3:19-20	
27. Jesus talks to a woman at the well				4:1-26
28. Jesus tells about the spiritual harvest				4:27-38
29. Many Samaritans believe in Jesus				4:39-42
30. Jesus preaches in Galilee	14:12-17	1:14-15	4:14-15	4:43-45
31. Jesus heals a government official's son				4:46-54
32. Jesus is rejected at Nazareth			4:16-30	
33. Four fishermen follow Jesus	4:18-22	1:16-20		
34. Jesus teaches with great authority		1:21-28	4:31-37	
35. Jesus heals Peter's mother-in-law and many others	8:14-17	1:29-34	4:38-41	
36. Jesus preaches throughout Galilee	4:23-25	1:35-39	4:42-44	
37. Jesus provides a miraculous catch of fish			5:1-11	
38. Jesus heals a man with leprosy	8:1-4	1:40-45	5:12-16	
39. Jesus heals a paralyzed man	9:1-8	2:1-12	5:17-26	
40. Jesus eats with sinners at Matthew's house	9:9-13	2:13-17	5:27-32	
41. Religious leaders ask Jesus about fasting	9:14-17	2:18-22	5:33-39	
42. Jesus heals a lame man by a pool				5:1-15
43. Jesus claims to be the Son of God				5:16-30
44. Jesus supports his claim				5:31-47
45. The disciples pick wheat on the Sabbath	12:1-8	2:23-28	6:1-5	
46. Jesus heals a man's hand on the Sabbath	12:9-14	3:1-6	6:6-11	
47. Large crowds follow Jesus	12:15-21	3:7-12		
48. Jesus chooses the twelve disciples		3:13-19	6:12-16	
49. Jesus gives the Beatitudes	5:1-12		6:17-26	
50. Jesus teaches about salt and light	5:13-16			
51. Jesus teaches about the law	5:17-20			

	Matthew	Mark	Luke	John
52. Jesus teaches about anger	5:21-26			
53. Jesus teaches about lust	5:27-30			
54. Jesus teaches about divorce	5:31-32			
55. Jesus teaches about vows	5:33-37			
56. Jesus teaches about revenge	5:38-42			
57. Jesus teaches about loving enemies	5:43-48		6:27-36	
58. Jesus teaches about giving to the needy	6:1-4			
59. Jesus teaches about prayer	6:5-15			
60. Jesus teaches about fasting	6:16-18			
61. Jesus teaches about money	6:19-24			
62. Jesus teaches about worry	6:25-34			
63. Jesus teaches about judging others	7:1-6	6:37-42		
64. Jesus teaches about asking, looking, knocking	7:7-12			
65. Jesus teaches about the way to heaven	7:13-14			
66. Jesus teaches about fruit in people's lives	7:15-20		6:43-45	
67. Jesus teaches about building on a solid foundation	7:21-29		6:46-49	
68. A Roman officer demonstrates faith	8:5-13		7:1-10	
69. Jesus raises a widow's son from the dead			7:11-17	
70. Jesus eases John's doubt	11:1-19		7:18-35	
71. Jesus promises rest for the soul	11:20-30			
72. A sinful woman anoints Jesus' feet			7:36-50	
73. Women accompany Jesus and the disciples			8:1-3	
74. Religious leaders accuse Jesus of getting his power from Satan	12:22-37	3:20-30		
75. Religious leaders ask Jesus for a miracle	12:38-45			
76. Jesus describes his true family	12:46-50	3:31-35	8:19-21	
77. Jesus tells the parable of the four soils	13:1-9	4:1-9	8:4-8	
78. Jesus explains the parable of the four soils	13:10-23	4:10-25	8:9-18	
79. Jesus tells the parable of the growing seed		4:26-29		
80. Jesus tells the parable of the weeds	13:24-30			
81. Jesus tells the parable of the mustard seed	13:31-32	4:30-34		
82. Jesus tells the parable of the yeast	13:33-35			
83. Jesus explains the parable of the weeds	13:36-43			
84. Jesus tells the parable of hidden treasure	13:44			
85. Jesus tells the parable of the pearl merchant	13:45-46			
86. Jesus tells the parable of the fishing net	13:47-52			
87. Jesus calms the storm	8:23-27	4:35-41	8:22-25	
88. Jesus sends demons into a herd of pigs	8:28-34	5:1-20	8:26-39	
89. Jesus heals a bleeding woman and restores a girl to life	9:18-26	5:21-43	8:40-56	
90. Jesus heals the blind and mute	9:27-34			
91. The people of Nazareth refuse to believe		6:1-6	13:53-58	
92. Jesus urges the disciples to pray for workers			9:35-38	
93. Jesus sends out the twelve disciples	10:1-15	6:7-13	9:1-6	

	Matthew	Mark	Luke	John
94. Jesus prepares the disciples for persecution	10:16-42			
95. Herod kills John the Baptist	14:1-12	6:14-29	9:7-9	
96. Jesus feeds 5,000	14:13-21	6:30-44	9:10-17	6:1-15
97. Jesus walks on water	14:22-33	6:45-52		6:16-21
98. Jesus heals all who touch him	14:34-36	6:53-56		
99. Jesus is the true bread from heaven				6:22-40
100. The people disagree that Jesus is from heaven				6:41-59
101. Many disciples desert Jesus				6:60-71
102. Jesus teaches about inner purity	15:1-20	7:1-23		
103. Jesus sends a demon out of a girl	15:21-28	7:24-30		
104. Jesus heals many people	15:29-31	7:31-37		
105. Jesus feeds 4,000	15:32-39	8:1-10		
106. Leaders demand a miraculous sign	16:1-4	8:11-13		
107. Jesus warns against wrong teaching	16:5-12	8:14-21		
108. Jesus restores sight to a blind man		8:22-26		
109. Peter says Jesus is the Messiah	16:13-20	8:27-30	9:18-20	
110. Jesus predicts his death the first time	16:21-28	8:31–9:1	9:21-27	
111. Jesus is transfigured on the mountain	17:1-13	9:2-13	9:28-36	
112. Jesus heals a demon-possessed boy	17:14-21	9:14-29	9:37-43	
113. Jesus predicts his death the second time	17:22-23	9:30-32	9:44-45	
114. Peter finds the coin in the fish's mouth	17:24-27			
115. The disciples argue about who would be the greatest	18:1-6	9:33-37	9:46-48	
116. The disciples forbid another to use Jesus' name		9:38-41	9:49-50	
117. Jesus warns against temptation	18:7-9	9:42-50		
118. Jesus warns against looking down on others	18:10-14			
119. Jesus teaches how to treat a believer who sins	18:15-20			
120. Jesus tells the parable of the unforgiving debtor	18:21-35			
121. Jesus' brothers ridicule him				7:1-9
122. Jesus teaches about the cost of following him	8:18-22		9:51-62	
123. Jesus teaches openly at the Temple				7:10-31
124. Religious leaders attempt to arrest Jesus				7:32-52
125. Jesus forgives an adulterous woman				7:53–8:11
126. Jesus is the light of the world				8:12-20
127. Jesus warns of coming judgment				8:21-30
128. Jesus speaks about God's true children				8:32-47
129. Jesus states he is eternal				8:48-59
130. Jesus sends out 72 messengers			10:1-16	
131. The 72 messengers return			10:17-24	
132. Jesus tells the parable of the Good Samaritan			10:25-37	
133. Jesus visits Mary and Martha			10:38-42	
134. Jesus teaches his disciples about prayer			11:1-13	

	Matthew	Mark	Luke	John
135. Jesus answers hostile accusations			11:14-28	
136. Jesus warns against unbelief			11:29-32	
137. Jesus teaches about the light within			11:33-36	
138. Jesus criticizes the religious leaders			11:37-54	
139. Jesus speaks against hypocrisy			12:1-12	
140. Jesus tells the parable of the rich fool			12:13-21	
141. Jesus warns about worry			12:22-34	
142. Jesus warns about preparing for his coming			12:35-48	
143. Jesus warns about coming division			12:49-53	
144. Jesus warns about the future crisis			12:54-59	
145. Jesus calls the people to repent			13:1-9	
146. Jesus heals the crippled woman			13:10-17	
147. Jesus teaches about the Kingdom of God			13:18-21	
148. Jesus heals the man who was born blind				9:1-12
149. Religious leaders question the blind man				9:13-34
150. Jesus teaches about spiritual blindness				9:35-41
151. Jesus is the good shepherd				10:1-21
152. Religious leaders surround Jesus at the Temple				10:22-42
153. Jesus teaches about entering the Kingdom			13:22-30	
154. Jesus grieves over Jerusalem			13:31-35	
155. Jesus heals a man with swollen limbs			14:1-6	
156. Jesus teaches about seeking honor			14:7-14	
157. Jesus tells the parable of the great festival			14:15-24	
158. Jesus teaches about the cost of being a disciple			14:25-35	
159. Jesus tells the parable of the lost sheep			15:1-7	
160. Jesus tells the parable of the lost coin			15:8-10	
161. Jesus tells the parable of the lost son			15:11-32	
162. Jesus tells the parable of the shrewd manager			16:1-18	
163. Jesus tells about the rich man and the beggar			16:19-31	
164. Jesus tells about forgiveness and faith			17:1-10	
165. Lazarus becomes ill and dies				11:1-16
166. Jesus comforts Mary and Martha				11:17-37
167. Jesus raises Lazarus from the dead				11:38-44
168. Religious leaders plot to kill Jesus				11:45-57
169. Jesus heals ten men with leprosy			17:11-19	
170. Jesus teaches about the coming of the Kingdom of God			17:20-37	
171. Jesus tells the parable of the persistent widow			18:1-8	
172. Jesus tells the parable of two men who prayed			18:9-14	
173. Jesus teaches about marriage and divorce	19:1-12	10:1-12		
174. Jesus blesses the children	19:13-15	10:13-16	18:15-17	
175. Jesus speaks to the rich young man	19:16-30	10:17-31	18:18-30	
176. Jesus tells the parable of the vineyard workers	20:1-16			
177. Jesus predicts his death the third time	20:17-19	10:32-34	18:31-34	

	Matthew	Mark	Luke	John
178. Jesus teaches about serving others	20:20-28	10:35-45		
179. Jesus heals a blind beggar	20:29-34	10:46-52	18:35-43	
180. Jesus brings salvation to Zacchaeus's home			19:1-10	
181. Jesus tells the parable of the king's ten servants			19:11-27	
182. A woman anoints Jesus with perfume	26:6-13	14:3-9		12:1-11
183. Jesus rides into Jerusalem on a young donkey	21:1-11	11:1-11	19:28-44	12:12-19
184. Jesus clears the Temple again	21:12-17	11:12-19	19:45-48	
185. Jesus explains why he must die				12:20-36
186. Most of the people do not believe in Jesus				12:37-43
187. Jesus summarizes his message				12:44-50
188. Jesus says the disciples can pray for anything	21:18-22	11:20-26		
189. Religious leaders challenge Jesus' authority	21:23-27	11:27-33	20:1-8	
190. Jesus tells the parable of the two sons	21:28-32			
191. Jesus tells the parable of the evil farmers	21:33-46	12:1-12	20:9-19	
192. Jesus tells the parable of the wedding dinner	22:1-14			
193. Religious leaders question Jesus about paying taxes	22:15-22	12:13-17	20:20-26	
194. Religious leaders question Jesus about the Resurrection	22:23-33	12:18-27	20:27-40	
195. Religious leaders question Jesus about the greatest commandment	22:34-40	12:28-34		
196. Religious leaders cannot answer Jesus' question	22:41-46	12:35-37	20:41-44	
197. Jesus warns against the religious leaders	23:1-12	12:38-40	20:45-57	
198. Jesus condemns the religious leaders	23:13-36			
199. Jesus grieves over Jerusalem again	23:37-39			
200. A poor widow gives all she has		12:41-44	21:1-4	
201. Jesus tells about the future	24:1-25	13:1-23	21:5-24	
202. Jesus tells about his return	24:26-35	13:24-31	21:25-33	
203. Jesus tells about remaining watchful	24:36-51	13:32-37	21:34-38	
204. Jesus tells the parable of the ten bridesmaids	25:1-13			
205. Jesus tells the parable of the loaned money	25:14-30			
206. Jesus tells about the final judgment	25:31-46			

III. DEATH AND RESURRECTION OF JESUS CHRIST

207. Religious leaders plot to kill Jesus	26:1-5	14:1-2	22:1-2	
208. Judas agrees to betray Jesus	26:14-16	14:10-11	22:3-6	
209. Disciples prepare for the Passover	26:17-19	14:12-16	22:7-13	

	Matthew	Mark	Luke	John
210. Jesus washes the disciples' feet				13:1-20
211. Jesus and the disciples share the Last Supper	26:20-30	14:17-26	22:14-30	13:21-30
212. Jesus predicts Peter's denial			22:31-38	13:31-38
213. Jesus is the way to the Father				14:1-14
214. Jesus promises the Holy Spirit				14:15-31
215. Jesus teaches about the vine and the branches				15:1-17
216. Jesus warns about the world's hatred				15:18–16:4
217. Jesus teaches about the Holy Spirit				16:5-15
218. Jesus teaches about using his name in prayer				16:16-33
219. Jesus prays for himself				17:1-5
220. Jesus prays for his disciples				17:6-19
221. Jesus prays for future believers				17:20-26
222. Jesus again predicts Peter's denial	26:31-35	14:27-31		
223. Jesus agonizes in the garden	26:36-46	14:32-42	22:39-46	
224. Jesus is betrayed and arrested	26:47-56	14:43-52	22:47-53	18:1-11
225. Annas questions Jesus				18:12-24
226. Caiaphas questions Jesus	26:57-68	14:53-65		
227. Peter denies knowing Jesus	26:69-75	14:66-72	22:54-65	18:25-27
228. The council of religious leaders condemns Jesus	27:1-2	15:1	22:66-71	
229. Judas hangs himself	27:3-10			
230. Jesus' trial before Pilate	27:11-14	15:2-5	23:1-5	18:28-37
231. Jesus stands trial before Herod			23:6-12	
232. Pilate hands Jesus over to be crucified	27:15-26	15:6-15	23:13-25	18:38–19:16
233. Roman soldiers mock Jesus	27:27-31	15:16-20		
234. Jesus is led away to be crucified	27:32-34	15:21-24	23:26-31	19:17
235. Jesus is placed on the cross	27:35-44	15:25-32	23:32-43	19:18-27
236. Jesus dies on the cross	27:45-56	15:33-41	23:44-49	19:28-37
237. Jesus is laid in the tomb	27:57-61	15:42-47	23:50-56	19:38-42
238. Guards are posted at the tomb	27:62-66			
239. Jesus rises from the dead	28:1-7	16:1-8	24:1-12	20:1-10
240. Jesus appears to Mary Magdalene		16:9-11		20:11-18
241. Jesus appears to the women	28:8-10			
242. Religious leaders bribe the guards	28:11-15			
243. Jesus appears to two believers traveling on the road		16:12-13	24:13-34	
244. Jesus appears to his disciples			24:35-43	20:19-23
245. Jesus appears to Thomas		16:14		20:24-31
246. Jesus appears to seven disciples				21:15-25
247. Jesus challenges Peter				21:15-25
248. Jesus gives the great commission	28:16-20	16:15-18		
249. Jesus appears to the disciples in Jerusalem			24:44-49	
250. Jesus ascends into heaven		16:19-20	24:50-53	

BIBLIOGRAPHY

Adamson, James B. *The Epistle of James*. The New International Commentary on the New Testament. Grand Rapids: Eerdmans, 1976.

Adels, Jill Haak. *The Wisdom of the Saints*. New York: Oxford University Press, 1987.

Aune, David E. *Revelation 1–5*. Word Biblical Commentary Series. Dallas: Word, 1997.

_____. *Revelation 6–16*. Word Biblical Commentary Series. Nashville: Thomas Nelson, 1998.

_____. *Revelation 17–22*. Word Biblical Commentary Series. Nashville: Thomas Nelson, 1998.

Barclay, William, trans. *The Gospel of John*. Vols. 1 and 2. Philadelphia: The Westminster Press, 1975.

_____. *The Letter to the Romans*. Philadelphia: The Westminster Press, 1975.

_____. *The Letters of James and Peter*. Philadelphia: The Westminster Press, 1961.

_____. *The Letters to Timothy, Titus, and Philemon*. Philadelphia: The Westminster Press, 1975.

Barker, Glenn W. "1, 2, 3 John." In *The Expositor's Bible Commentary*. Vol. 12. Edited by Frank E. Gaebelein. Grand Rapids: Zondervan, 1981.

Barrett, C. K. *Commentary of the Epistle to the Romans*. New York: Harper and Row, 1957.

_____. *The First Epistle to the Corinthians*. New York: Harper & Row, 1968.

_____. *The Gospel According to St. John*. Philadelphia: The Westminster Press, 1978.

_____. *The Second Epistle to the Corinthians*. Black's New Testament Commentary. Peabody, Mass.: Hendrickson Publishers, 1973.

Barth, Marcus. *Ephesians: Introduction, Translation, and Commentary on Chapters 1–3. The Anchor Bible*. Garden City, N.Y.: Doubleday & Company, Inc., 1974.

_____. *Ephesians: Introduction, Translation, and Commentary on Chapters 4–6. The Anchor Bible*. Garden City, N.Y.: Doubleday & Company, Inc., 1974.

Bauckham, Richard J. *Jude, 2 Peter*. Word Biblical Commentary Series. Waco, Tex.: Word, 1983.

Bauer, Walter, William F. Arndt, Wilbur F. Gingrich, and Frederick Danker. *A Greek-English Lexicon of the New Testament and Other Early Christian Literature*. Chicago: University of Chicago Press, 1979.

Beasley-Murray, George R. *John*. Word Biblical Commentary. Waco, Tex.: Word, 1987.

Beers, V. Gilbert. *The Victor Handbook of Bible Knowledge*. Wheaton, Ill.: Victor Books, 1981.

Belleville, Linda L. *Second Corinthians*. The IVP New Testament Commentary Series. Downers Grove, Ill.: InterVarsity Press, 1996.

Blanchard, John. *Gathered Gold*. Hertfordshire, England: Evangelical Press, 1984.

_____. *More Gathered Gold*. Hertfordshire, England: Evangelical Press, 1986.

Blum, Edwin A. "1 and 2 Peter, Jude." In *The Expositor's Bible Commentary*. Vol. 12. Edited by Frank E. Gaebelein. Grand Rapids: Zondervan, 1981.

Bock, Darrell L. *Luke*. The IVP New Testament Commentary Series. Downers Grove, Ill.: InterVarsity Press, 1994.

_____. *Luke*. Vol. 1. Baker Exegetical Commentary on the New Testament. Grand Rapids: Baker Books, 1994.

_____. *Luke*. Vol. 2. Baker Exegetical Commentary on the New Testament. Grand Rapids: Baker Books, 1996.

Boice, James Montgomery. "Galatians." In *The Expositor's Bible Commentary*. Vol. 10. Edited by Frank E. Gaebelein. Grand Rapids: Zondervan, 1976.

Bowman, John W. *The Letter of James*. The Layman's Bible Commentary Series. Atlanta: John Knox Press, 1962.

Brown, Raymond E. *The Community of the Beloved Disciples*. New York: Paulist Press, 1979.

_____. *The Gospel According to John*. The Anchor Bible Commentary. New York: Doubleday, 1966.

Bruce, F. F. *The Acts of the Apostles*. 3d ed. Grand Rapids: Eerdmans, 1990.

_____. *The Book of Acts*. Grand Rapids: Eerdmans, 1976.

_____. *Commentary on Galatians*. Grand Rapids: Eerdmans, 1982.

_____. *The Epistle of Paul to the Romans*. New Testament Commentaries. Grand Rapids: Eerdmans, 1985.

_____. *The Epistle to the Hebrews*. New International Commentary on the New Testament. Grand Rapids: Eerdmans, 1964.

_____. *The Epistles of John: Introduction, Exposition, and Notes*. Grand Rapids: Eerdmans, 1970.

_____. *The Epistles to the Colossians, to Philemon, and to the Ephesians*. New International Commentary on the New Testament. Grand Rapids: Eerdmans, 1984.

_____. *The Gospel of John*. Grand Rapids: Eerdmans, 1983.

_____. *Philippians*. New International Biblical Commentary Series. Peabody, Mass.: Hendrickson Publishers, 1989.

_____. *1 and 2 Thessalonians*. Word Biblical Commentary Series. Waco, Tex.: Word, 1982.

Burdick, Donald W. "James." In *The Expositor's Bible Commentary.* Vol. 12. Edited by Frank E. Gaebelein. Grand Rapids: Zondervan, 1981.

Burton, Ernest DeWitt. *A Critical and Exegetical Commentary on the Epistle to the Galatians.* The International Critical Commentary. Edinburgh, Scotland: T. & T. Clark, 1921.

Calvin, John. *Acts.* Crossway Classic Commentaries. Edited by Alister McGrath and J. I. Packer. Wheaton, Ill.: Crossway Books, 1995.

————. *Commentary on the Epistle of Paul the Apostle to the Romans.* Reprint, Grand Rapids: Eerdmans, 1947.

Carson, D. A. *The Gospel According to John.* Grand Rapids: Eerdmans, 1991.

Christensen, Chuck, and Winnie Christensen. *God in Action: Mark's View of Jesus.* Wheaton, Ill.: Harold Shaw Publishers, 1972.

Clowney, Edmund P. *The Message of 1 Peter: The Way of the Cross.* Downers Grove, Ill.: InterVarsity Press, 1988.

Cole, R. Alan. *Galatians.* Tyndale New Testament Commentaries. Grand Rapids: Eerdmans, 1988.

————. *The Gospel According to St. Mark: An Introduction and Commentary.* Tyndale New Testament Commentaries. Grand Rapids: Eerdmans, 1988.

Comfort, Philip W. *I Am the Way: A Spiritual Journey through the Gospel of John.* Grand Rapids: Baker, 1994.

Culpepper, R. Allen. *The Johannine School.* Missoula, Mont.: Scholars Press, 1975.

Davids, Peter H. *James.* New International Biblical Commentary Series. Peabody, Mass.: Hendrickson Publishers, 1989.

De Dietrich, Suzanne. *Matthew.* The Layman's Bible Commentary Series. Atlanta: John Knox Press, 1982.

Donfried, K. P., ed. *The Romans Debate.* Peabody, Mass.: Hendrickson Publishers, 1991.

Douglas, J. D., ed. *The New Greek-English Interlinear New Testament.* Translated by Robert K. Brown and Philip W. Comfort. Wheaton, Ill.: Tyndale House Publishers, 1990.

Douglas, J. D., and Philip W. Comfort, eds. *New Commentary on the Whole Bible: New Testament.* Wheaton, Ill.: Tyndale House Publishers, 1990.

Dunn, James D. G. *Romans 1–8.* Word Biblical Commentary Series. Dallas: Word, 1988.

Earle, Ralph. "1 Timothy." In *The Expositor's Bible Commentary.* Vol. 11. Edited by Frank E. Gaebelein. Grand Rapids: Zondervan, 1978.

————. "2 Timothy." In *The Expositor's Bible Commentary.* Vol. 11. Edited by Frank E. Gaebelein. Grand Rapids: Zondervan, 1978.

Edwards, James R. *Romans.* New International Biblical Commentary Series. Peabody, Mass.: Hendrickson Publishers, 1992.

English, Donald. "The Message of Mark, The Mystery of Faith." In *The Bible Speaks Today.* Edited by John R. W. Stott. Downers Grove, Ill.: InterVarsity Press, 1992.

Erickson, Millard J. *Christian Theology.* Grand Rapids: Baker Book House, 1985.

Evans, Craig A. *Luke.* New International Biblical Commentary Series. Edited by W. Ward Gasque. Peabody, Mass.: Hendrickson Publishers, 1990.

Fee, Gordon D. *The First Epistle to the Corinthians.* Grand Rapids: Eerdmans, 1987.

————. *God's Empowering Presence: The Holy Spirit in the Letters of Paul.* Peabody, Mass.: Hendrickson Publishers, 1994.

————. *1 and 2 Timothy, Titus.* New International Biblical Commentary Series. Peabody, Mass.: Hendrickson Publishers, 1988.

Ferguson, S. B., D. F. Wright, and J. I. Packer, eds. *New Dictionary of Theology.* Downers Grove, Ill.: InterVarsity Press, 1988.

Filson, Floyd V. *The Gospel According to John.* The Layman's Bible Commentary Series. Edited by Balmer H. Kelly. Atlanta: John Knox Press, 1963.

Foreman, Kenneth J. *Romans, 1 Corinthians, 2 Corinthians.* The Layman's Bible Commentary Series. Atlanta: John Knox Press, 1961.

Foulkes, Francis. *The Letter of Paul to the Ephesians.* Tyndale New Testament Commentaries. Grand Rapids: Eerdmans, 1988.

France, R. T. *The Gospel According to Matthew: An Introduction and Commentary.* Tyndale New Testament Commentaries. Grand Rapids: Eerdmans, 1985.

Gaebelein, Frank E., ed. *The Expositor's Bible Commentary.* Vol. 8. Grand Rapids: Zondervan, 1984.

Green, Joel B., and Scot McKnight, eds. *Dictionary of Jesus and the Gospels.* Downers Grove, Ill.: InterVarsity Press, 1992.

Green, Michael. *The Second General Epistle of Peter and the General Epistle of Jude.* Tyndale New Testament Commentaries. Grand Rapids: Eerdmans, 1988.

Grudem, Wayne. *First Peter.* Tyndale New Testament Commentaries. Grand Rapids: Eerdmans, 1988.

Guelich, Robert A. *Mark 1–8:26.* Word Biblical Commentary Series. Waco, Tex.: Word, 1989.

Guthrie, Donald. *Hebrews.* Tyndale New Testament Commentaries. Grand Rapids: Eerdmans, 1988.

————. *New Testament Introduction: Hebrews to Revelation.* Downers Grove, Ill.: InterVarsity Press, 1962.

————. *The Pastoral Epistles.* Rev. ed. Tyndale New Testament Commentaries. Grand Rapids: Eerdmans, 1990.

Gutzke, Manford George. *Plain Talk on John.* Grand Rapids: Zondervan, 1968.

Hagner, Donald A. *Hebrews.* New International Biblical Commentary Series. Peabody, Mass.: Hendrickson Publishers, 1990.

————. *Matthew 1–13.* Word Biblical Commentary Series. Dallas: Word, 1993.

————. *Matthew 14-28.* Word Biblical Commentary Series. Dallas: Word, 1995.

Harris, Murray. "2 Corinthians." In *The Expositor's Bible Commentary.* Vol. 10. Edited by Frank E. Gaebelein. Grand Rapids: Zondervan, 1976.

Harrison, Everett. *Acts: The Expanding Church.* Chicago: Moody Press, 1975.

————. "Romans." In *The Expositor's Bible Commentary.* Vol. 10. Edited by Frank E. Gaebelein. Grand Rapids: Zondervan, 1976.

Hawthorne, Gerald F. *Philippians.* Word Biblical Commentary Series. Waco, Tex.: Word. 1983.

Hawthorne, Gerald F., Ralph Martin, and Daniel Reid, eds. *Dictionary of Paul and His Letters.* Downers Grove, Ill.: InterVarsity Press, 1993.

Hiebert, D. Edmond. "Titus." In *The Expositor's Bible Commentary.* Vol. 11. Edited by Frank E. Gaebelein. Grand Rapids: Zondervan, 1978.

Hughes, Philip E. *Paul's Second Epistle to the Corinthians.* Grand Rapids: Eerdmans, 1962.

Hughes, R. Kent. *James: Faith That Works.* Wheaton, Ill.: Crossway Books, 1991.

_____. *Romans: Righteousness from Heaven.* Wheaton, Ill.: Crossway Books, 1991.

Hughes, Robert B., and J. Carl Laney. *New Bible Companion.* Wheaton, Ill.: Tyndale House Publishers, 1990.

Hunter, Archibald M. *Galatians, Ephesians, Philippians, Colossians.* The Layman's Bible Commentary Series. Atlanta: John Knox Press, 1982.

Hurtado, Larry W. *Mark.* New International Biblical Commentary Series: New Testament. Peabody, Mass.: Hendrickson Publishers, 1989.

Jackman, David. *The Message of John's Letters.* Downers Grove, Ill.: InterVarsity Press, 1988.

Jensen, Irving L. *1 and 2 Timothy and Titus: A Self-Study Guide.* Chicago: Moody Press, 1973.

Johnson, Alan F. *Romans: The Freedom Letter.* Vols. 1 and 2. Everyman's Bible Commentary Series. Chicago: Moody Press, 1985.

_____. "Revelation." In *The Expositor's Bible Commentary.* Vol. 12. Edited by Frank E. Gaebelein. Grand Rapids: Zondervan, 1996.

Kelley, J. N. D. *A Commentary on the Epistles of Peter and of Jude.* Black's New Testament Commentary. London: Adam and Charles Black, 1977.

_____. *A Commentary on the Pastoral Epistles.* Peabody, Mass.: Hendrickson Publishers, 1960.

Kent, Homer A., Jr. *Light in the Darkness.* Grand Rapids: Baker Book House, 1974.

_____. "Philippians." In *The Expositor's Bible Commentary.* Vol. 11. Edited by Frank E. Gaebelein. Grand Rapids: Zondervan, 1978.

_____. *The Pastoral Epistles.* Chicago: Moody Press, 1986.

Knight, George W. III. *The Pastoral Epistles.* New International Greek Testament Commentary Series. Grand Rapids: Eerdmans, 1992.

Kruse, Colin. *Second Corinthians.* Tyndale New Testament Commentaries. Grand Rapids: Eerdmans, 1987.

Lane, William. *The Gospel According to Mark.* Grand Rapids: Eerdmans, 1979.

_____. *Hebrews 1–8.* Word Biblical Commentary Series. Waco, Tex.: Word, 1991.

_____. *Hebrews 9–13.* Word Biblical Commentary Series. Waco, Tex.: Word, 1991.

Lea, Thomas D., and Hayne P. Griffin Jr. *1, 2 Timothy, Titus.* The New American Commentary. Nashville: Broadman, 1992.

Liefield, Walter. "Luke." In *The Expositor's Bible Commentary.* Vol. 8. Edited by Frank Gaebelein. Grand Rapids: Zondervan, 1984.

Lightfoot, J. B. *The Epistle of St. Paul to the Galatians.* Grand Rapids: Zondervan, 1980.

Longenecker, Richard. "Acts." In *The Expositor's Bible Commentary.* Vol. 9. Edited by Frank E. Gaebelein. Grand Rapids: Zondervan, 1981.

_____. *Galatians.* Word Biblical Commentary Series. Dallas: Word, 1990.

Love, Julian Price. *1 John, 2 John, 3 John, Jude, Revelation.* The Layman's Bible Commentary. Atlanta: John Knox Press, 1960.

Luther, Martin. *Commentary on the Epistle to the Romans.* Grand Rapids: Kregel Publications, 1954.

_____. *A Commentary on St. Paul's Epistle to the Galatians.* London: James Clarke & Co. Ltd., 1953.

Mare, W. Harold. "1 Corinthians." In *The Expositor's Bible Commentary.* Vol. 10. Edited by Frank E. Gaebelein. Grand Rapids: Zondervan, 1976.

Marshall, I. Howard. *Acts.* Tyndale New Testament Commentaries. Grand Rapids: Eerdmans, 1986.

_____. *The Epistles of John.* Grand Rapids: Eerdmans, 1978.

_____. *1 Peter.* Downers Grove, Ill.: InterVarsity Press, 1991.

Martin, Ralph P. *Colossians and Philemon.* Greenwood, S.C.: The Attic Press, Inc., 1974.

_____. *James.* Word Biblical Commentary Series. Waco, Tex.: Word, 1988.

_____. *Philippians.* Tyndale New Testament Commentaries. Grand Rapids: Eerdmans, 1987.

_____. *Second Corinthians.* Word Biblical Commentary Series. Waco, Tex.: Word, 1986.

Martin, Ralph P., and Peter H. Davids, eds. *Dictionary of the Later New Testament and Its Developments.* Downers Grove, Ill.: InterVarsity Press, 1997.

Metzger, Bruce. *A Textual Commentary on the Greek New Testament.* New York: United Bible Societies, 1971.

Meyer, F. B. *Devotional Commentary.* Wheaton, Ill.: Tyndale House Publishers, 1989.

Michaels, J. Ramsey. *John.* New International Biblical Commentary Series. Peabody, Mass.: Hendrickson Publishers, 1989.

_____. *1 Peter.* Word Biblical Commentary Series. Dallas: Word, 1988.

Miller, Donald G. *Luke.* The Layman's Bible Commentary Series. Atlanta: John Knox Press, 1959.

Moo, Douglas. *James.* Rev. ed. Tyndale New Testament Commentaries. Grand Rapids: Eerdmans, 1988.

_____. *Romans 1–8.* Wycliffe Exegetical Commentary Series. Chicago: Moody Press, 1991.

Morgan, G. Campbell. *The Gospel According to Mark.* New York: Fleming H. Revell Co., 1927.

Morris, Leon. *The First and Second Epistles to the Thessalonians.* New International Commentary on the New Testament. Grand Rapids: Eerdmans, 1991.

_____. *First Corinthians.* Tyndale New Testament Commentaries. Grand Rapids: Eerdmans, 1988.

_____. *The Gospel According to John.* New International Commentary on the New Testament. Grand Rapids: Eerdmans, 1971.

_____. *The Gospel According to Matthew.* Grand Rapids: Eerdmans, 1992.

_____. "Hebrews." In *The Expositor's Bible Commentary.* Vol. 12. Edited by Frank E. Gaebelein. Grand Rapids: Zondervan, 1981.

_____. *Luke*. Tyndale New Testament Commentaries. Grand Rapids: Eerdmans, 1988.

_____. *Revelation*. Tyndale New Testament Commentaries. Grand Rapids: Eerdmans, 1987.

_____. *1 and 2 Thessalonians*. Tyndale New Testament Commentaries. Grand Rapids: Eerdmans, 1984.

Mounce, Robert H. *Matthew*. New International Biblical Commentary Series. Edited by W. Ward Gasque. Peabody, Mass.: Hendrickson Publishers, 1991.

_____. *The Book of Revelation*. New International Commentary on the New Testament. Grand Rapids: Eerdmans, 1977.

Newman, Barclay, and Eugene Nida. *A Translator's Handbook on the Gospel of John*. New York: United Bible Societies, 1980.

Nicoll, W. Robertson, ed. *The Expositor's Greek New Testament*. Vol. 1. Grand Rapids: Eerdmans, 1961.

Nolland, John. *Luke 1–9:20*. Word Biblical Commentary Series. Dallas: Word, 1989.

_____. *Luke 9:21–18:34*. Word Biblical Commentary Series. Dallas: Word, 1993.

_____. *Luke 18:35–24:53*. Word Biblical Commentary Series. Dallas: Word, 1993.

O'Brien, Peter T. *Colossians, Philemon*. Word Biblical Commentary Series. Waco, Tex.: Word, 1982.

Ogilvie, Lloyd J., ed. *The Communicator's Commentary: Matthew*. Dallas: Word, 1982.

Osborne, June, and Chris Sugden. *Luke*. Bible Study Commentary. Fort Washington, Pa.: Christian Literature Crusade, 1987.

Patzia, Arthur G. *Ephesians, Colossians, Philemon*. New International Biblical Commentary Series. Peabody, Mass.: Hendrickson Publishers, 1990.

Polhill, John B. *Acts*. New American Commentary. Vol. 26. Nashville: Broadman, 1992.

Robertson, A. T. *Word Pictures in the Greek New Testament*. Nashville: Broadman, 1932.

Rolston, Holmes. *1 Thessalonians, 2 Thessalonians, 1 Timothy, 2 Timothy, Titus, Philemon*. The Layman's Bible Commentary. Atlanta: John Knox Press, 1961.

Rupprecht, Arthur A. "Philemon." In *The Expositor's Bible Commentary*. Vol. 11. Edited by Frank E. Gaebelein. Grand Rapids: Zondervan, 1978.

Ryrie, Charles. *The Acts of the Apostles*. Chicago: Moody Press, 1961.

Sanday, William, and Arthur C. Headlam. *A Critical and Exegetical Commentary on the Epistle to the Romans*. Edinburgh: T. & T. Clark, 1964.

Schnackenburg, Rudolph. *The Gospel According to St. John*. Translated by Kevin Smyth. New York: Crossroad Publishing Company, 1982.

Smalley, Stephen S. *1, 2, 3 John*. Word Biblical Commentary Series. Dallas: Word, 1984.

Stott, John R. W. *The Gospel and the End of Time*. Downers Grove, Ill.: InterVarsity Press, 1991.

_____. *The Letters of John*. Tyndale New Testament Commentaries. Grand Rapids: Eerdmans, 1988.

_____. *The Message of 2 Timothy*. Downers Grove, Ill.: InterVarsity Press, 1973.

_____. *Only One Way: The Message of Galatians*. Downers Grove, Ill.: InterVarsity Press, 1968.

Tasker, R. V. G. *The General Epistle of James*. Tyndale New Testament Commentaries. London: Tyndale Press, 1956.

_____. *The Gospel According to St. John: An Introduction and Commentary*. Tyndale New Testament Commentaries. Grand Rapids: Eerdmans, 1988.

Tenney, Merrill C. *Galatians: The Charter of Christian Liberty*. Grand Rapids: Eerdmans, 1957.

_____. "The Gospel of John." In *The Expositor's Bible Commentary*. Vol. 9. Edited by Frank E. Gaebelein. Grand Rapids: Zondervan, 1981.

_____. *New Testament Survey*. Grand Rapids: Eerdmans, 1976.

Thomas, Robert L. "1 and 2 Thessalonians." In *The Expositor's Bible Commentary*. Vol. 11. Edited by Frank E. Gaebelein. Grand Rapids: Zondervan, 1978.

Turner, George Allen. *The New and Living Way*. Minneapolis: Bethany Fellowship, 1975.

Vaughn, Curtis. "Colossians." In *The Expositor's Bible Commentary*. Vol. 11. Edited by Frank E. Gaebelein. Grand Rapids: Zondervan, 1978.

Vine, W. E. *The Epistles of John*. Grand Rapids: Zondervan, 1970.

_____. *Expository Dictionary of New Testament Words*. Old Tappan, N.J.: Fleming H. Revell, 1966.

Wall, Robert W. *Colossians and Philemon*. The IVP New Testament Commentary Series. Downers Grove, Ill.: InterVarsity Press, 1993.

Walvoord, John F., and Roy B. Zuck, eds. *Bible Knowledge Commentary: New Testament*. Wheaton, Ill.: Victor Books, 1983.

Ward, Ronald A. *Commentary on 1 and 2 Timothy and Titus*. Dallas: Word, 1974.

Westcott, B.F. *The Epistles of St. John: The Greek Text with Notes and Essays*. London: MacMillan, 1883.

_____. *Gospel According to St. John*. 1881. Reprint, Grand Rapids: Zondervan, 1973.

Westcott, B. F., and F. J. A. Hort. *Introduction to the New Testament in the Original Greek*, with "Notes on Select Readings." New York: Harper and Brothers, 1882.

Wood, A. Skevington. "Ephesians." In *The Expositor's Bible Commentary*. Vol. 11. Edited by Frank E. Gaebelein. Grand Rapids: Zondervan, 1978.

Wright, N. T. *Colossians and Philemon*. Tyndale New Testament Commentaries. Grand Rapids: Eerdmans, 1988.

Wuest, Kenneth S. *Mark in the Greek New Testament for the English Reader*. Grand Rapids: Eerdmans, 1965.

_____. *Wuest's Word Studies: Romans*. Grand Rapids: Eerdmans, 1955.

Yarbrough, Robert W. *John*. Chicago: Moody Press, 1991.